The TIME ALMANAC 2000

BORGNA BRUNNER

EDITOR

...nior Vice President
...abeth Buckley Kubik

Senior Contributing Editors
Otto T. Johnson, Beth Rowen

Database/Production Manager
Susan Hyde

Contributing Editors *Christine Frantz
(Sports), Javier Mateu (Countries),
Arthur Reed (Current Events),
Tasha M. Vincent (Business)*

Production Editor *Christine Frantz*

Proofreading and Fact-checking
*Katie Blatt, Laura Lutz King,
Diane Larson, Elaine Rho, Dan Shafto*

Editorial Assistants *Kate Pritchard,
Renée Scott, Zoe Segal-Reichlin,
Kate Wrigley*

Graphics *Barbara Pennucci*

Technical Support *Karl DeBisschop*

In this millennial edition, the editors would like to give special thanks to Jim Murphy of Mail-Well Graphics for his many years of expertly shepherding the almanac through the printing process.

Contributing Editor *Kelly Knauer*

Design *Anthony Kosner*

Pictures *Patricia Cadley*

President *Stuart Hotchkiss*

Director *David Arfine*

Product Manager *Kenneth Maehlum*

Retail Manager *Thomas Mifsud*

Editorial Operations Manager
John Calvano

Book Production Manager
Jessica McGrath

Assistant Book Production Managers
Jonathan Polsky, Kristen Lizzi

The TIME Almanac welcomes comments and suggestions from readers. Though the editors carefully consider each suggestion, because of the volume of correspondence we receive we cannot respond personally to each writer. The *TIME Almanac* does not rule on bets or wagers.

Editorial Office
Information Please
20 Park Plaza
Boston, MA 02116
Email: ipa@infoplease.com

Customer Service
Attention: TIME Almanac
PO Box 11016
Des Moines, IA 50336-1016

ISBN: 1-883013-65-8 Paperback
ISBN: 1-883013-67-4 Hardcover
ISSN: 0073-7860

If you would like to order copies of the hardcover almanac, please call us at 1-800-327-6388 (Monday through Friday, 7:00 a.m.–8:00 p.m. or Saturday, 7:00 a.m.–6:00 p.m. Central Time).

Printed in the United States of America.
WP Pa BP Hbd 10 9 8 7 6 5 4 3 2 1

Keyword Index

Section Index

Page numbers followed by "n" indicate information in footnotes.

THE TIME ALMANAC 2000

The millennium is the comet that crosses the calendar every thousand years. It throws off metaphysical sparks. It promises a new age, or an apocalypse. It is a magic trick that time performs, extracting a millisecond from its eternal flatness and then, poised on that transitional instant, projecting a sort of hologram that teems with the summarized life of the thousand years just passed and with visions of the thousand now to come.

An Appointment with the Future

The millennium represents the ritual death and rebirth of history, one thousand-year epoch yielding to another

By LANCE MORROW TIME

The approaching millennium year 2000 is counted from the birth of Jesus Christ in Bethlehem of Judea, in the year (so the Bible says) when Caesar Augustus decreed that a census of the world be taken. A millennial year has thus occurred only once before: fifty generations ago, in the year 1000, on what was a very different, more primitive planet Earth. So this one has a strange, cosmic prestige, a quality of the almost unprecedented. The world approaches it in states of giddiness, expectation and, consciously or unconsciously, a certain anxiety. The millennium looms as civilization's most spectacular birthday, but, as it approaches, the occasion also sends out nagging threats of comeuppance.

Arbitrary Advent

The millennial date is an arbitrary mark on the calendar, decreed around the year 525 by the calculations of an obscure monk. The celebrated 2000, a triple tumbling of naughts, gets some of its status from humanity's fascination with zeroes—the so-called tyranny of tens that makes a neat, right-angle architecture of accumulating years, time sawed into stackable solidities, like children's blocks. And it is true, of course, that the moment may signify little to non-Christians.

Nonetheless, the millennium is freighted with immense historical symbolism and psychological power. It does not depend on objective calculation, but entirely on what people bring to it—their hopes, their anxieties, the metaphysical focus of their attention. The millennium is essentially an event of the imagination.

Thousand-year blocks of time enforce a chastening standard of weight and scale. The millennium has a gravitational pull that draws in the largest meanings, if only because its frame of reference is so enormous. The millennial drama represents nothing less than the ritual death and rebirth of history, one thousand-year epoch yielding to another. Such imponderable masses of time overwhelm and humble the individual life span, reducing human tragedies and accomplishments to windblown powder.

Launching Pad for the Future

The year 2000 has long been a fixed point in the distance, a temporal horizon line. In recent years the young have begun to calculate how old they will be at the turn of the millennium. Older people have wondered if they would live to see it. The millennium has also served as a projected launch platform for humankind's most ambitious, far-reaching projects. The year 2000 would be the Year One of a better age, the decisive border at which the Future would start. Now that the destination of 2000 is approaching with a kind of dopplered urgency, people are bound to wonder what the future will look like after that. What will be the new frontier beyond 2000?

The passage into a new millennium will occur this time in the global electronic village. It will be the first (obviously, given the state of technology in the year 1000) to be observed simultaneously worldwide, with one rotation of the planet. Almost every human intelligence will be focused for an instant in a solidarity of collective wonder and vulnerability—Mystery in the Age of Information.

The millennium is almost by definition a moment of extreme possibilities, arousing fantasies that veer wildly between earthly paradise and annihilation. "The human mind abhors a vacuum," says Michael Barkun, a political scientist at the University of Syracuse. "Where certainties are absent, we make do with probabilities, and where probabilities are beyond our power to calculate, we seek refuge from insupportable ignorance in a future of our own imagining."

Apocalypse Now

Dark meanings still reverberate like distant thunder from the last millennial passage. There was no widespread panic at the approach of the year 1000, as some writers have claimed, but an inescapable note of Armageddon was in the air. Men pondered over the text of the last days in the book of *Revelation:* "And I saw a new heaven and a new earth: for the first heaven and the first earth were passed away; and there was no more sea" (*Revelation 21:1*).

In the year 1000, the Four Horsemen of the Apocalypse—War, Plague, Famine, and Death—were riding unimpeded. To be sure, the apocalyptic Four have a sort of chronic credibility: They have

been prominent in every century. The world would be paradise indeed if they visited only at each turning of a thousand years. But in the centuries since the first millennium, zealous, punitive preachers have endlessly invoked the Four, backing up their threats of doom with *Revelation.*

Millennial expectations at the beginning of this century brightened, however, and for a while shone with optimism and self-confidence. The 1939 World's Fair (just before Hitler marched into Poland) was organized around the sleek theme, "Building the World of Tomorrow." In 1965 (just before the Vietnam War began in earnest), the American Academy of Arts and Sciences brought together its "Commission on the Year 2000." The chairman, sociologist Daniel Bell, declared, "The problem of the future consists in defining one's priorities and making the necessary commitments." In other words, as Barkun observes, "We get the future we are prepared for."

20th-Century Doomsday Books

But in the past quarter-century millennial visions have grown darker, lurid as a Brueghel. The best-selling nonfiction book of the 1970s in America was Christian author Hal Lindsey's jeremiad, *The Late Great Planet Earth.* Among many other things, Lindsey predicted that the Soviet Union would invade Israel and that, after millions of the righteous were gathered up in the eschatological event known as the "rapture," Jesus would descend from the heavens to preside over the real New World Order. In his 1974 book *Armageddon, Oil and the Middle East Crisis,* John F. Walvoord projected his vision: "Destruction on a formerly incomprehensible scale is clearly predicted for the end time in the book of

The Future: A TIME/CNN Poll

IN WHICH VARIOUS INTRIGUING QUESTIONS ARE POSED TO THE GREAT AMERICAN PUBLIC

Do you think the world will be in better shape at the end of the 21st century than it is today?		**If you had to predict, which of the following do you think are likely to occur in the 21st century?**	**Which of each pair has had the most impact on the course of history in the past thousand years?**
Better	41%	Scientists will find a cure for AIDS — 75%	Printing press — 47%
Worse	32%		Television — 51%
About the same	15%	Scientists will find a cure for cancer — 80%	Christopher Columbus — 65%
		Scientists will find a cure for the common cold — 39%	Neil Armstrong — 33%
Compared with the 20th century, do you think the 21st century will have more:		The average American will live to be 100 — 57%	Thomas Edison — 55%
Wars	32%		Albert Einstein — 41%
Environmental disasters	59%	A woman will be president of the U.S. — 76%	Beethoven — 58%
Poverty	61%		The Beatles — 39%
Disease	53%	A black will be president of the U.S. — 76%	American Revolution — 46%
Hope for the future	62%		World War II — 50%
		Automobiles will no longer run on gasoline — 75%	Electricity — 79%
Will religion play a greater role in the lives of people in this country after the year 2000?		Computers will be as smart as humans and have personalities like humans — 44%	Automobile — 17%
Greater	55%		Abraham Lincoln — 59%
Lesser	37%	Humans will make regular trips to other planets — 43%	Martin Luther King, Jr. — 36%
		Beings who live on other planets will come in contact with us — 32%	Gunpowder — 41%
Will the Second Coming of Jesus Christ occur sometime during the next thousand years?			Nuclear weapons — 56%
Yes	53%		From a telephone poll of 800 adult Americans for TIME/CNN by Yankelovich Inc. Sampling error ± 3.5%.
No	31%		

Revelation and may be the result of nuclear war." Evangelist Pat Robertson has said that in the millennial age the saved will be empowered to control geologic faults spiritually and thereby prevent earthquakes.

Where science and technology once seemed to offer a redemptive promise, they have grown more problematic. As the second millennium approaches, they often appear to be agents of either nuclear destruction, computer dominance, or materialistic over-consumption and earth poisoning. Many of these fears converged in the uproar over the Y2K phenomenon. This simple error in computer coding offered latter-day Luddites a convenient receptacle for their fear of all things technological, and as Y2K fairs, newsletters, and Web sites multiplied, it became clear that many people would welcome a digital apocalypse. The naively shining Cities of Tomorrow have deteriorated into a vision of *Blade Runner,* wherein a sinister polyglot brainlessness reigns, a sort of neofeudal brutality in the air.

Armageddon

The pressures of such anxieties have encouraged in some quarters an ethic of millenarian asceticism, a New Age impulse to withdraw from the older promises of the consumer society and its plenitude. Barkun predicts that the approaching millennium will bring an increasingly skeptical attitude toward gratuitous technology and a renewed attraction to life in small, self-sufficient rural communities. People will tend to cultivate spiritual and aesthetic values in opposition to material gratification. And the emotional view of the future will swing sharply back and forth, from exultant hope to bitter despair. The millennium will be the best of times. Or else it will be the worst of times. An

age of unprecedented wonders will begin. Or else all the planetary debts will come simultaneously and cataclysmically due. Either/Or.

The early 1990s brought the disintegration of the Soviet Union and—briefly—an end to the world's nuclear nightmares. But still it seemed that the slower-working apocalypses of vanishing ozone and overpopulation and world hunger and AIDS were menacingly clustered around the end of the millennium. Perhaps the world's imagination needs an agenda of dooms, if only to make it focus upon its New Millennium resolutions. So all Four Horsemen seem to be up and riding again, joined by the digital Fifth.

What astonishments will arrive after 2000? We like to say that time will tell. But time is elastic and mysterious and, in its wild, undifferentiated state, uninhabitable by humans. Life needs its days and nights, its waking and sleeping, its seasons, its routines, its appointment books. People organize their lives by drawing lines, segmenting time, measuring their progress—clocking themselves. Time is the organizing principle of conscious human effort. It may be difficult to understand sometimes, but it is what we have, all we have, the medium in which we swim.

In that lies the meaning of the millennium. Delineated time is history's narrative framework—the way to make sense out of beginnings, middles, and ends. Everyone is born, and dies, in the middle of history's larger story. The millennium is a chance (the rarest) to see, or to imagine that we see, the greater human story, filed in the file drawer with a click of completeness. Envisioning the end of one era and the beginning of another somehow infuses life with narrative meaning. And surviving the millennial passage, for those who do, may even have about it a wistful savor of the afterlife.   ☐

Millennial Questions
When Does the Next Millennium Officially Begin?

Although January 1, 2000, has a millennial ring to it, the new age actually begins on a less resounding date: January 1, 2001. Common sense might suggest that the year 2000 is the dawning of the third millennium, but it is in fact the waning of the second.

The first millennium began in C.E. 1. There is no year zero in our calendar: the sequence of years passes directly from 1 B.C.E. to C.E. 1. Adding a thousand years to the year 1 equals the year 1001, marking the start of the second millennium. Add another thousand to reach the beginning of the third millennium: January 1, 2001.

There is no doubt that both New Year's Eves 2000 and 2001 will spark huge celebrations—one because it is the true millennial milestone, and the other because there is nothing quite like the numerical elegance of January 1, 2000. Popular opinion, however, overwhelmingly favors the 2000 celebration: all the Times Square hotels are booked for December 31, 1999, and the

Jan. 1, 2000, of the Gregorian calendar translates into:	
Calendar	Year
Julian	1999
Hebrew	5760
Islamic	1420
Indian(Saka)	1921
Chinese	4698
(year of the dragon)	

various millennium tours arranging for you to celebrate on top of Mount Kilimanjaro or at the base of the pyramids are scheduled for the end of 1999, not 2000.

Bear in mind, however, that both 2000 and 2001 are years based on a fundamental calendrical flaw. The 6th-century monk Dionysius Exiguus (also called Dennis the Short) recast the calendar so that years would be counted from the birth of Christ (*anno Domini* [A.D.]; in the year of the Lord) instead of the beginning of the reign of the Roman emperor Diocletian (anno Diocletiani). A.D. 532—formerly *anno Diocletiani* 248—became the first year counted according to the Christian era. Dionysius, however, miscalculated the birth of Christ, which is believed by many scholars to have been 4 B.C. Had the years been recalibrated accordingly, the millennium would have occurred on Jan. 1, 1997. In other words, why squabble about the millennium—we've already missed it!

Where Will the Sun First Rise on January 1, 2000?

Just exactly where the dawn of the new age will take place has become an international argument, with several places claiming to be the first to greet the millennium. Below are several of the more credible candidates.

Caroline Island, Kiribati: Caroline Island, one of the 33 South Pacific coral atolls that make up the nation of Kiribati, will be the first land to see the dawn as it crosses the International Date Line, signifying the changeover from December 31, 1999, to January 1, 2000. Kiribati owes this distinction to a relatively recent change in its timekeeping. Consisting of three island groups—the Gilbert, Phoenix, and Line Islands—Kiribati straddles the International Date Line. To the west of the International Date Line lie the Gilberts, to the east stretch the Phoenix and Line Islands. This once meant that it could be Monday in the Gilberts but Sunday in the Phoenix Islands—not an easy way to run a country. So in 1993 Kiribati decided to consolidate all three island groups under a single time zone, and the nation selected the Gilbert Islands, west of the Date Line, as the standard (the capital, Tarawa, is located in the Gilberts).

In 1996 Kiribati's time change suddenly caught the attention of its neighbors, as various South Pacific islands began making preparations for a big bash on New Year's Eve 2000. At issue were tourist dollars—revelers would no doubt flock to the place where the New Year's bells would toll first. Kiribati, it seemed, had scooped its island neighbors on the first dawn: its easternmost point, Caroline Island, is the first place the Sun crosses the International Date Line, since the demarcation line had been moved to accommodate Kiribati's time change—even though its longitude is 150°15′ west, almost 30 degrees from the 180° meridian.[1] Tonga had considered itself the first country that would greet the New Year—and the king of Tonga is reportedly not pleased. The Chatham Islands, part of New Zealand, had also counted on being first. Kiribati, however, will see the first rays of the year 2000 a full 80 minutes before Tonga and 22 minutes before the Chathams. Just to make sure there was no longer room for argument, Caroline renamed itself Millennium Island.

Gisborne, New Zealand: This town on the East Cape of New Zealand's North Island has also claimed to be the right place at the right time for New Year's Eve 2000. In strictly geographic terms, Gisborne has a point. At 178°35′ east longitude, it is less than two degrees from the International Date Line, but since the Date Line bends east and west rather than sticking to the 180° meridian, Gisborne has to forfeit its position to the various countries who have tailored the time zones to conform to their political borders. Gisborne still claims some distinction in spite of the Kiribati affair—according to the London *Times*, it is the first place west of the Date Line with good bars.

Balleny Islands, Antarctica: If the first sunrise is taken to mean the first piece of land to see the dawn in the year 2000, the answer would be the uninhabited islands of Balleny, Antarctica. On January 1, 2000, the Sun will rise over the island at 13:41 UT, whereas Caroline Island, Kiribati, will not see its rays until 15:43 UT. Because of the short rotation of Earth at the poles, the Sun is below the horizon for less than one hour per day in January. But it sure is an inhospitable place for a New Year's celebration.

Greenwich, England: If time rather than the sunrise is the determining factor, then Greenwich, England, where each day begins at the prime meridian at 00:00 UT, will mark the official start of the year 2000.

---

1. The International Date Line, which generally follows the 180° meridian, diverges east or west in certain locations to ensure that most of a country's territory is grouped in the same time zone. In the case of Kiribati, the Date Line loops to 150°15′ west longitude to encompass the Phoenix and Line Islands.

Y2K Panic: What Do We Really Have to Fear?

Not a day goes by without some news about the turn of the century and its effects on computers. Those systems designed without the capacity to handle four-digit years will be mighty confused come January 1, 2000, and may think it's January 1, 1900. Now that computer chips are embedded in everything from global positioning satellites to toasters, there are lots of computers to check up on. But which systems are actually in danger of failing, and with what probable results?

The Good News

Fears about **travel**, particularly within the U.S., seem to be largely overblown. There is no evidence that computer chips inside your car or truck will fail as a result of the change, because the items they control are not date-dependent. Amtrak and commuter railroads claim to be ready, and air travel should not be a problem, either. The Federal Avia-

tion Administration has already reached 100% Y2K compliance for its computers, including those used for air traffic control, going through heavy testing without a hitch. Most of the top foreign travel destinations have also reported that they are taking steps to ensure Y2K compliance for air traffic control systems, airlines, and airports.

Banks have also led the way in preparing their systems for the year 2000. Consolidation in the financial sector means that the number of firms that need to address the problem is relatively small, and many are based in the U.S. The bottom line: there should be no reason to worry about bank accounts or mutual funds held by large firms. Even ATM withdrawals and the direct deposit of checks have passed Y2K testing.

The food industry reports that the Y2K transition should have little impact on the **food supply,** and while it is always a good idea to store some food in

TIME/CNN Poll

■ **How concerned are you about the Y2K bug problem?**

Somewhat/very concerned . . . . `59%`
Not very/not at all concerned . . . . `39%`

■ **Might you take any of these actions to protect yourself from possible problems associated with the Y2K bug?**

Take extra cash out of bank account . . . . `47%`
Stockpile water and food . . . . `33%`
Not fly on an airplane . . . . `26%`
Keep family members at home . . . . `26%`
Stockpile fuel for car or house . . . . `23%`
Arm yourself with a shotgun . . . . `13%`
Move to a rural area . . . . `12%`

■ **Are the following likely to happen when the year 2000 begins?**

	Very/somewhat likely
Equipment with computers will fail	`59%`
Banking system will be disrupted	`53%`
Riots or other social unrest will occur	`38%`
The world as we know it will end	`9%`

case of emergency, there should be no need for frenzied, Y2K-induced shopping sprees. **Phones** will also work. The Federal Communications Commission has determined that the large firms, which serve the vast majority of Americans, will suffer few if any ill effects.

Industry and government officials predict that the possibility of **fuel shortages** or massive **power outages** across the nation are very slim. While minor local outages cannot be ruled out, the electric power industry as a whole has taken aggressive measures for Y2K compliance.

We Have Nothing to Fear But . . .

The most significant problems posed by the millennium bug may result from panic. People who fear that they will be unable to buy food, fuel, or other commodities may hoard supplies before the end of the year. Though there might not otherwise be any problem with supply chains, the removal of large quantities of goods from stores by panicked people may create shortages.

What's the Problem?

The Y2K problem is this. Many of the world's computers and microchip circuitry, the ones that run everything from cash machines and VCRs to interstate electric-power grids and intercontinental ballistic missiles, contain a programming oversight that makes them incapable of reading the date 2000. To represent years, computers generally use just the last two digits. When 1999—that's 99 in computer language—rolls over at midnight to 00, computers that have not had the glitch repaired will conclude that the date is 1900. That can lead to a surprising range of malfunctions, and not just in such obviously date-sensitive tasks as billing. There is no clear agreement, even among sober experts, of how bad the Y2K computer problem will be. The most likely problems involve temporary glitches, especially overseas, in billing and invoice systems, that could cause some disruptions in business and government. The Internal Revenue Service, you will be relieved to know, promises to be prepared. (So it's true what they say about death and taxes.)

Similarly, logical and reasoned actions taken by individuals can incite panic when expanded to a large scale. Imagine if, purely as a precaution, everyone liquidates 20% of his or her stock holdings and withdraws an extra $500 or $1,000 from the bank on New Year's Eve. With everyone trying to sell stocks, even just a portion of their holdings, the market will drop precipitously, encouraging still more people to sell, and probably in greater quantities. If ATMs run short of cash, word may spread that there is no money, which again would cause panic. The Treasury Department is preparing to avert just such a crisis by having $50 billion in extra cash to be ready to meet any increase in demand.

The level of dependency on computers that we've reached as a nation makes it unlikely that we'll survive the Y2K transition without seeing any problems. But any technical complications stemming from the turn of the century are more likely to be on the local scale. And of course you may experience frustrating glitches with your PC. But isn't that always a risk?

Y2K Resource Guide

President's Council on Year 2000 Conversion
www.y2k.gov 1-888-USA-4Y2K (1-888-872-4925)

U.S. Government's Chief Information Officers (CIO) Council Committee on Year 2000
www.itpolicy.gsa.gov/mks/yr2000/cioy2k.htm

U.S. General Services Administration Y2K checklist:
www.itpolicy.gsa.gov/mks/yr2000/y2kflier.htm

Consumer Information Center "Year 2000 and You"
www.pueblo.gsa.gov/cic_text/misc/y2k/y2k.htm

Federal Deposit Insurance Corporation
www.fdic.gov/about/y2k/brochure

Office of the Comptroller of the Currency
www.occ.treas.gov/y2k/default.htm 1-800-613-6743

U.S. Small Business Administration Help for the Year 2000 www.sba.gov/y2k 1-800-U-ASK-SBA (1-800-827-5722)

Y2K Community Conversations
www.y2k.gov/community/usmap.html#table

U.S. Dept. of Transportation International Civil Aviation Y2K Information Review
www.y2ktransport.dot.gov/fly2k/International.asp

U.S. Dept. of Agriculture "Questions and Answers: Food Supply and Year 2000"
www.usda.gov/aphis/FSWG/q

Federal Emergency Management Agency "Y2K Bulletin: Preparedness Guide"
www.fema.gov/y2k/bltn00.htm. Call (1-800-480-2520)

Millennium Milestones

Reducing the millennium to a laundry list of highlights cannot pretend to be a definitive or accurate exercise, but if ever there was a time for such a foolhardy and brash undertaking, this would be it. Note that only events judged to have *world* significance are included. For a less whirlwind glance at the last thousand years, see pages 123–152 of the Headline History section.

1066—Norman Conquest of Britain
1095—Pope Urban II calls for Crusades
1100s—Angkor Wat is built
1206—Genghis Khan begins creation of largest land empire in history
1215—Magna Carta signed
1260—Chartres Cathedral consecrated
1271—Marco Polo begins travels to Asia
1273—Thomas Aquinas's *Summa theologica*
1300s—Renaissance begins in Italy
1347—Bubonic plague spreads in Europe
c.1387—Chaucer's *Canterbury Tales*
1399—Tamerlane begins last great conquest
1438—Incan Empire formed in Peru
1455—Gutenberg's movable-type printing press produces the Bible
1492—Columbus reaches the New World
1509—Michelangelo begins painting Sistine Chapel
1513—Machiavelli's *The Prince*
1517—Martin Luther initiates Reformation
1519—Aztec Empire at height as Spanish arrive
1520—Suleiman I "the Magnificent" presides over the Ottoman Empire's greatest period
1522—Magellan's expedition circumnavigates the globe
1543—Copernicus postulates a heliocentric universe
1582—Pope Gregory XII reforms calendar
1603—Shakespeare's *Hamlet*
1605—Cervantes's *Don Quixote,* first modern novel
1609—Galileo makes first astronomical observations with a telescope
1643—Taj Mahal completed
1664—Newton's theory of universal gravitation
1667—Milton's *Paradise Lost*
1684—Leibniz's calculus published
1769—Watt patents first practical steam engine
1721—Bach completes the Brandenburg Concertos
1760—Industrial Revolution begins in England
1764—Mozart (aged eight) writes first symphony
1776—U.S. Declaration of Independence; Adam Smith's *Wealth of Nations*
1787—U.S. Constitution signed
1789—French Revolution begins
1792—Wollstonecraft's *Vindication of the Rights of Woman*
1796—Jenner discovers smallpox vaccine
1808—Beethoven's *Fifth Symphony*
1815—Battle of Waterloo crushes Napoleon
1819—Bolívar defeats Spanish forces at Boyacá
1826—Niepce takes first photograph
1833—Slavery abolished in British Empire
1842—Long uses first anesthetic (ether)
1859—Darwin's *On the Origin of Species;* Lenoir builds first practical internal-combustion engine

1862—Pasteur's experiments lead to germ theory; Salon des Refusés introduces impressionism
1867—Japan ends 675-year shogun rule
1876—Bell patents the telephone
1879—Edison invents electric light
1880s—Europe colonizes African continent
1885—World's first skyscraper built in Chicago
1893—New Zealand becomes first country in the world to grant women the vote
1895—Lumiére brothers introduce motion pictures; Marconi sends first radio signals
1897—Herzl launches Zionist movement
1900—Freud's *Interpretation of Dreams*
1903—Wright brothers fly first motorized airplane
1905—Einstein announces theory of relativity
1907—Picasso's *Les Demoiselles d'Avignon* introduces cubism
1911—Rutherford discovers structure of atom
1913—Ford develops first moving assembly line
1914—World War I begins
1916—Sanger founds international birth control movement
1917—Lenin leads the Bolshevik Revolution
1918—Global "Spanish flu" epidemic
1922—Joyce's *Ulysses* published
1927—Farnsworth demonstrates working model of a television; Lemaitre proposes big bang theory
1928—Fleming discovers penicillin
1929—Hubble proposes theory of expanding universe; U.S. stock market crash precipitates global depression
1939—Hitler invades Poland; World War II begins
1942—Nazi leaders at Wannsee Conference coordinate "final solution to the Jewish question"
1945—Atomic bombs are dropped on Hiroshima and Nagasaki; first electronic computer, ENIAC, is built
1946—First meeting of U.N. General Assembly; Churchill's "Iron Curtain" speech marks beginning of Cold War
1947—Gandhi's civil disobedience movement leads to an independent India
1949—Communist victory in China under Mao Zedong
1950s—Abstract expressionism introduced
1953—Watson, Crick, and Franklin discover DNA's structure
1954—*Brown v. Board of Education* begins unraveling of U.S. racial segregation
1957—Russia launches first satellite, *Sputnik I*
1959—Leakeys uncover hominid fossils
1969—Armstrong and Aldrin walk on the Moon; Internet (ARPA) goes online
1980—Smallpox eradicated
1981—Scientists identify AIDS
1989—Fall of Communism in Eastern Europe
1991—Breakup of Soviet Union; apartheid ends in South Africa

The News of 1999: Nation

Acquittal on High Crimes

A Senate trial in the first two months of 1999 followed President Clinton's impeachment in Dec. 1998. On Feb. 12, the Senate acquitted the President on both counts of impeachment after failing to achieve a simple majority, much less the two-thirds majority needed for conviction. On the charge of grand jury perjury, the vote was 55–45 with 10 Republicans voting for acquittal along with all 45 Democrats. The vote on obstruction of justice was 50–50, with 5 Republicans crossing party lines to vote for acquittal.

Social Security versus Tax Cuts

In the aftermath of impeachment, angry Republicans in Congress intensified their anti-Clinton acrimony at the expense of legislation. Rabid partisanship and distrust characterized both sides of the debate on what to do with a surprising $14 billion in budget surplus projections. The President, riding high on glowing reports that the 1996 welfare overhaul had been a success, pushed for further social reform—specifically, revisions to the Social Security, education, and health care systems. Republicans countered with calls for drastic tax cuts during the federal budget negotiations for 2000, despite the fact that polls have repeatedly shown that Americans prefer increased social spending over tax breaks.

Jury Still Out on Gun Control

Despite the encouraging FBI report that the murder rate continues to plummet—it is now at its lowest level since 1967—a spate of isolated killing sprees in 1999 traumatized the nation and revived the gun control debate. On April 20, Eric Harris, 18, and Dylan Klebold, 17, killed 12 fellow students, themselves, and a teacher at Columbine High School in Littleton, Colo. A series of appalling killings followed throughout the summer and fall, including one at a community center and another at a church. *(See also pp. 44–47, 873.)*

Public soul searching struggled to explain these senseless acts, focusing in particular on the school shootings, all of which had been committed by white, suburban teenage boys. Media violence, lack of parental supervision, and adolescent alienation were prevalent explanations, with the more conservative elements of society attributing the trend to evil and godlessness. Senate leader Trent Lott claimed that "when we stopped having prayer in schools, things started going to pot." While conservatives argued that gun control was not the solution—guns don't kill people, it's people who kill people, the argument goes—liberals countered that if there was less access to guns, people would be killing people much less frequently.

The Senate, in response to the public outcry after the Columbine shootings, passed a bill that called for mandatory background checks on buyers at gun shows. But as public outrage faded, the powerful gun lobby again stepped up the pressure on Congress. House Republicans sponsored a pale imitation of the Senate bill, which Democrats angrily rejected.

Where politicians have failed, however, the courts have been more effective. A recent lawsuit found that gun manufacturers "substantially and disproportionately" increased production of guns that appeal to criminals, and another lawsuit determined that manufacturers deliberately oversupply states that have weak gun laws, fully aware that the extra guns will make their way onto the black market. Reflecting the tactic used against the tobacco industry, gun control advocates have begun using the courts as an effective David to topple the Goliaths of the gun industry. Colt, for example, found itself slapped with 28 lawsuits, and announced in October that it would essentially cease selling handguns to civilians.

White House Wannabes Start Early

Iowa's January 2000 caucuses were expected to signal the real starting line of the next presidential race, but political pundits declared that the race had in fact begun in earnest with Iowa's August 15 Republican straw poll—a full 14 months before election day. Stressing "compassionate conservatism," George W. Bush quickly emerged as the Republican frontrunner, amassing an astounding $50 million by the end of September—more money than any candidate in history. Weighed down by the Clinton albatross and a top-heavy campaign organization, Vice President Al Gore, heir apparent to the Democratic ticket, found unexpected competition from maverick Bill Bradley, former Senator of New Jersey. The absence of dynamic issues in such prosperous times and the ennui from premature media saturation led to a frivolous, celebrity-laden side show featuring the likes of Warren Beatty and Donald Trump.

Superpower Takes a Back Seat

The four days of air strikes against Iraq in Dec. 1998, an international P.R. disaster for the U.S. and Britain, were followed by a low-profile war of attrition, in which hundreds of almost daily bombings have been directed against Iraqi targets within the no-fly zones. Although the air strikes continued throughout the year, the press all but ignored them, particularly during the Kosovo crisis. In that latter conflict, the U.S. and Britain took the lead in NATO's war on Belgrade, a war the American public cautiously embraced. Since the grisly deaths of American soldiers in Somalia in 1993, the public has lowered its threshold for sacrifice on foreign soil.

In its role as the world's only superpower, however, the U.S. lost considerable credibility in 1999: not only did its enormous U.N. debt remain in arrears, but the Senate summarily rejected ratification of the Comprehensive Test Ban Treaty in October. Deeply disappointed, Clinton contended that without U.S. participation, the treaty lost all clout as a nuclear safeguard, a frightening thought given the recent nuclear pugilism of Pakistan, India, and North Korea. □

The News of 1999: World

NATO Rallies for Kosovo

Years of unrest in Yugoslavia's province of Kosovo erupted into war in the spring of 1999. Formerly an autonomous province in Tito's Yugoslavia, Kosovo was stripped of self-rule in 1989 by President Slobodan Milosevic. A Serbian ultra-nationalist, Milosevic began systematically repressing Yugoslavia's non-Serbs, including the 90% of Kosovo's population that is Muslim and ethnic Albanian. As one after another of the Balkan states broke free from Yugoslavia and Serbian hegemony, the secessionist longings of Kosovo, the poorest of the Balkans, were largely discounted by the international community. In 1996 the Kosovo Liberation Army, a militant secessionist movement, began attacking Serbian authorities in Kosovo; by March 1998, the Yugoslavian army and Serbian militias had brutally clamped down on the region, massacring civilians as well as KLA guerrillas, and deporting hundreds of thousands of ethnic Albanians. After months of fruitless diplomacy by the West, NATO began Operation Allied Force on March 24, 1999, launching air strikes against Belgrade that continued for 78 consecutive days.

Weeks of daily bombings destroyed significant Serbian military targets, yet Milosevic showed no signs of relenting—in fact, he stepped up efforts to empty the province of its ethnic Albanians. Not only did it seem that NATO's actions exacerbated the violence in Kosovo, but its reluctance to send in ground troops to support the air war struck many as naive and shortsighted—while NATO fought in the air, the annihilation of Kosovars and the region was proceeding on the ground. NATO countries, however, feared that the inevitable casualties of a ground war in a remote corner of the Balkans would dampen the resolve of public opinion. Aided at the end by a strong KLA offensive and Belgrade's apprehension of a future ground war, NATO's hesitation over deploying ground troops ultimately paid off. Milosevic finally agreed to sign a UN-approved peace agreement on June 9.

Since then a five-nation peace-keeping force has occupied the territory, and a staggering 860,000 refugees have begun returning to the ruins of Kosovo. The political status of Kosovo remains uncertain, as does the status of Milosevic, who, after turning his beleaguered country into a pariah state, remains in power while an unpromising lot of fractious opposition leaders fight among themselves.

Although the initial reason for NATO's involvement in Kosovo was the prevention of a wider Balkan war, once the extent of Serbian atrocities became known, NATO's stated purpose became the prevention of a human rights calamity—making Kosovo one of the rare recent conflicts in which humanitarian concerns have superseded realpolitik.

Russian Roulette

Russian President Boris Yeltsin's increasingly erratic behavior led to his appointment of three different prime ministers in 1999. After sacking Yevgeny Primakov in May and Sergei Stepashin in August, Yeltsin settled on Vladimir Putin, whom he installed as a strongman to crush the resurgence of guerrilla warfare by Islamic militants in Chechnya. Just three years after the bloody 1994–96 Chechen-Russian war ended in devastation and stalemate, the fighting started again, erupting first in Chechnya's neighbor Dagestan in August. After several terrorist bombings in Moscow and other cities in September, Russia again turned its ire on Chechnya, launching air strikes and following with ground troops.

Kashmiri Shell Game

The disputed region of Kashmir has been at the root of chronic antagonism between Pakistan and India, and their enmity has grown potentially more dangerous now that both have demonstrated nuclear weapon capabilities. Insurgent forces—which Pakistan claims are autonomous Kashmiri "freedom fighters"—made incursions into Indian-controlled Kashmiri territory in May 1999. According to New Delhi, these troops were in fact Pakistani army regulars and Muslim mercenaries, a view shared by most of the world. India fought back with air strikes and ground troops, and by August Pakistan retreated.

The Pakistani military, deeply unhappy with Prime Minister Nawaz Sharif's handling of the Kashmir crisis as well as other issues, deposed him on Oct. 12, and Gen. Pervez Musharraf took control. The Pakistani public, accustomed to military rule for 25 of the nation's 52-year history, generally viewed the coup as a positive step, and hoped it would bring a badly needed economic upswing.

Nightmare in East Timor

A Portuguese colony for 400 years until abruptly abandoned in 1975, East Timor was seized within a year by Indonesia. The Indonesian occupation led to widespread repression and the deaths of an estimated 200,000 Timorese, earning Indonesia a global reputation for human rights abuses.

In February 1999, former Indonesian president Suharto's successor, B. J. Habibie, unexpectedly announced his willingness to hold a referendum on East Timorese independence, reversing 25 years of Indonesian intransigence. As the referendum on self-rule drew closer, fighting between separatist guerrillas and pro-Indonesian paramilitary forces in East Timor intensified. The U.N.-sponsored referendum had to be rescheduled twice because of violence. On Aug. 30, 1999, 78.5% of the population voted to secede from Indonesia. In the days following the referendum, pro-Indonesian militias and Indonesian soldiers retaliated by razing towns, slaughtering civilians, and forcing a third of the population out of the province.

Despite repeated assurances that Indonesia would restore order, Habibie and the powerful head of the military, Gen. Wiranto, were either unwilling or unable to stop the bloodbath. The rampage was primarily carried out by paramilitary forces who had been trained and armed by the military and then allowed to run amok (a word that is in fact derived from Indonesian). The U.N.'s lack of foresight exacerbated the violence: after encouraging the populace to exercise their rights by participating in a free and democratic election, the U.N. failed to make provisions for protecting them from the inevitably brutal aftermath. Only after enormous international pressure did Indonesia finally allow a hastily assembled peacekeeping force into East Timor on Sept. 12.

Led by Australia, the international force followed the precedent set in Kosovo: it intervened in the plight of a backwater region for no larger motive than humanitarian and democratic ideals. Australia in particular had much to lose by going against its Indonesian neighbor. The stance of the 1999 peacekeepers was a far cry from 1976, when the U.S. and other nations stood by while East Timor was invaded by Indonesia, an important Western ally and trading partner.

Israeli and Irish Peace Talks

The embryonic Northern Irish coalition government was stillborn the day it was to convene, July 16, 1999. The impasse was the result of Sinn Fein's insistence that the I.R.A. would only begin giving up its illegal weapons after the formation of the new government, while Unionists demanded disarmament first. Subsequent talks on the agreement, which would have ended three decades of direct rule from London, have gone nowhere, despite the last-ditch intervention of former Sen. George Mitchell, who helped engineer the 1998 landmark Good Friday Agreement.

The stalemated Middle East peace talks that faltered under Israeli prime minister Benjamin Netanyahu revived with the election of the Labour Party's Ehud Barak, who managed to forge a broad, stable coalition government. At his inauguration (July 6, 1999) Prime Minister Barak announced that "nothing is more important in my view than . . . putting an end to the 100-year conflict in the Middle East." By this he meant not only peace with the Palestinians, but with Syria as well. Barak also promised to end the low-grade war that has barraged Southern Lebanon since 1985, which has been fueled by Syrian-backed Hezbollah guerrillas. No thaw in Syrian-Israeli relations is thus far discernible, but Israel has moved ahead with the 1998 Wye Accord, ceding additional territory to the Palestinians.   □

What Happened in 1999: Month by Month

Highlights of key events of the year, organized month by month, in three categories for easy reference. For the year's major Supreme Court decisions, *see* pp. 99–100. Countries of the World covers specific international events, country by country. *See also* People in the News and 1999 Deaths for more current events coverage.

January 1999

WORLD

Iraqi Appeal Splits Arab Nations (Jan. 5): Saddam Hussein more isolated after calling for revolt against leaders who failed to support him in U.S. attacks in Dec.

U.S. and Iraqi Planes Clash (Jan. 5): Jet fighters battle for first time in six years over Iraqi no-fly zone.

Massacre in Eastern Congo Reported (Jan. 5): About 500 said to have been slain during previous week by soldiers aligned with Tutsi rebels. **(Jan. 6):** Rebel leaders admit soldiers had killed about 400 Hutu militiamen, but deny they had massacred 500 civilians.

Brazil Devalues Currency Eight Percent (Jan. 13): Action follows decline in stock market and resignation of central bank president.

Serbs Attack Albanian Rebels (Jan. 15): At least fifteen separatists killed and two peace workers wounded. British monitor and his translator are first international observers to be wounded in Kosovo conflict.

Mutilated Bodies of Ethnic Albanians Found (Jan. 16): International monitors shocked by discovery of 45 disfigured corpses in worst killing incident of nearly year-old conflict. Many shot at close range.

Independence a Possibility for East Timor (Jan. 28): Indonesian officials at U.N.-sponsored talks say for first time that independence may be option if autonomy proposals fall through.

NATO Authorizes Kosovo Air Attack (Jan. 30): Threatens military action if Serbia does not agree to begin talks with ethnic Albanian leaders.

NATION

More Spacecraft Join Mission to Mars (Jan. 3): Robot lander and two piggybacked microprobes launched on second stage of NASA's project to probe soil of planet for water in form of ice crystals.

U.S. Plans to Ease Restrictions on Cuba (Jan. 4): New policy would let millions more dollars flow to Cubans and allow more direct flights, mail service, and trade.

Elizabeth Dole Looks to 2000 Election (Jan. 4): Resignation as head of the American Red Cross seen as a move for presidential race. Dole, a Cabinet member for Reagan and Bush, is married to 1996 G.O.P. presidential candidate Bob Dole.

Hastert Elected Speaker of the House (Jan. 6): In opening day for 106th Congress, Dennis Hastert (R-Ill.) is chosen to replace Newt Gingrich.

Senate Opens Impeachment Trial (Jan. 7): Chief Justice William H. Rehnquist swears in senators to "do impartial justice" in deciding whether to remove President Clinton from office for perjury and obstruction of justice.

Clinton Settles Paula Jones's Lawsuit (Jan. 12): Pays $850,000 to end legal action by former Arkansas employee who accused him of sexual misconduct.

U.S. Seeks Revision of Missile-Defense Pact (Jan. 20): Clinton administration asks Russia to renegotiate 1972 Anti-Ballistic Missile Treaty to allow limited national system of missile defenses.

BUSINESS/SCIENCE/SOCIETY

Agreement Saves Basketball Season (Jan. 6): Players and owners of National Basketball Association end 191-day tie-up and settle on abbreviated season.

Scandals Over Olympic Games Erupt (Jan. 8): Two Salt Lake City organizers of 2002 games resign as bribery charges emerge. **(Jan. 24):** President of International Olympic Committee expels six members for taking improper benefits in Salt Lake City scandal over bidding.

Michael Jordan Retires from Bulls (Jan. 13): Fans wish basketball legend well as he ends career that lasted 13 seasons and brought Chicago six NBA titles.

Female Genital Mutilation Banned in Senegal (Jan. 14): Parliament eradicates traditional practice that is painful, damaging, and sometimes lethal. About one-fifth of girls in Senegal had experienced circumcision.

Hand Transplant Performed in U.S. (Jan. 24): Doctors in Louisville, Ky., replace left hand of N.J. man with one from a recently dead donor. It is first such procedure performed in U.S.

Hundreds Killed in Colombian Earthquake (Jan. 25): Nearly 1,000 dead and 4,000 injured in the city of Armenia. Quake is Colombia's worst in more than a century.

HIV Virus Traced to Chimpanzee Subspecies (Jan. 31): International team of scientists hopes discovery may help improve AIDS therapies and lead to vaccine.

February 1999

WORLD

U.S. Expands Air Strikes on Iraq (Feb. 2): Pilots hit wide range of military targets under broadened rules for attacks over northern and southern no-fly zones.

King Hussein of Jordan Dies at 63 (Feb. 7): Ruler of Hashemite Kingdom since 1952 succumbs to cancer soon after being flown home from U.S. clinic. His eldest son is crowned as King Abdullah II.

Germany Approves Fund for Nazi Victims (Feb. 9): Agrees to compensation, financed by industrial and banking leaders, to block lawsuits in U.S. against companies that used forced and slave labor in World War I.

Northern Ireland Restructured (Feb. 16): Assembly votes for political changes that give Roman Catholic minority more power and call for end to sectarian violence.

Leaders of India and Pakistan Meet (Feb. 20): Prime Minister Atal Behari Vajpayee of India travels to Pakistan for cordial meeting with Pakistan's Nawaz Sharif. **(Feb. 21):** Leaders pledge to strive for peace following discussions on nuclear weapons and disputed Kashmir territory.

Kurdish Leader Charged with Treason (Feb. 23): Abdullah Ocalan arraigned in Turkey, where he faces death penalty. Turkish authorities accuse him of causing thousands of deaths in Kurdish uprisings. Protests spread across Europe after Ocalan's capture in Kenya.

Serb Forces Mass on Kosovo Border (Feb. 26): Pentagon fears move threatens to undermine any progress in ending strife between Serbs and ethnic Albanians.

Nigeria Elects President (Feb. 28): Gen. Olusegun Obasanjo, former military ruler, wins in first presidential election in 16 years. Promises to follow the "path of democracy" as president.

NATION

Anti-Abortion Group Penalized (Feb. 2): U.S. jury in Ore. rules against organization that displayed "wanted" posters listing names of abortion providers on Web site. $107 million payment will go to Planned Parenthood and group of doctors.

Racial Tension in Washington (Feb. 3): Mayor asks white aide who resigned after using the word "niggardly" in conversation with black colleague to return to post. The word, which is not a racial epithet, means "miserly."

Senate Acquits President Clinton (Feb. 12): Verdict follows five-week impeachment trial on charges brought by House. In vote of 55–45, Senate rejects perjury charge in connection with President's affair with White House intern. A 50–50 split blocks obstruction of justice charge, with several Republicans breaking ranks to vote for acquittal. No Democrats vote to convict. Trial is second in 210-year history of the U.S.

President Says He's "Profoundly Sorry" (Feb. 12): After acquittal by Senate, Clinton asserts verdict signals "time of reconciliation and renewal."

Republicans Move to Reshape Image (Feb. 15): Hold town meeting in Mich. as first in series following unpopular impeachment trial. Party, receiving warm response, hopes to bolster support for broad tax reductions.

U.S. Trade Deficit Reported at Record High (Feb. 19): Commerce Dept. reports level rose 53 percent in 1998 to a record of $168.8 billion. Global financial troubles caused first decline in U.S. exports in over a decade.

BUSINESS/SCIENCE/SOCIETY

N.Y.C. Police Kill Unarmed Man (Feb. 4): Four undercover officers seeking rape suspect shoot at Ahmed Diallo, 22, 41 times when he reaches into his pocket while being questioned. The immigrant street merchant, originally from Guinea, had no criminal record.

Gates Foundations Get $3.3 Billion (Feb. 5): Microsoft chairman William H. Gates and wife Melinda bolster assets of two philanthropic institutions.

Mike Tyson Sentenced in Assault Case (Feb. 5): Former heavyweight champion sentenced in Md. court to year in jail for attack on two men after minor traffic accident.

Pilots' Strike Cripples American Airlines (Feb. 8): More than 300 weekend flights canceled as scores of pilots call in sick. **(Feb. 17):** Ten-day strike comes to an end. American claims it lost $100 million in revenue and canceled more than 7,000 flights during sick-out.

Smoker Wins $51.5 Million Verdict (Feb. 9): Calif. jury awards largest judgment ever reached in a smoking-related case. Woman said her inoperable lung cancer was caused by decades of smoking cigarettes, primarily the Philip Morris Marlboro brand.

Gun Makers Found Liable in Shootings (Feb. 11): Federal jury in Brooklyn rules nine of 25 named in suit were collectively at fault because marketing and distribution practices facilitate illegal gun trafficking.

Oregon Reports 15 Deaths Under Suicide Law (Feb. 17): Terminally ill persons took lethal medication in 1998 under world's only program for legally sanctioned assisted suicide.

Scientists Slow Speed of Light (Feb. 17): Danish researchers find way to slow rate to 38 miles per hour, from ordinary 186,171 miles per second.

Texan Convicted in Dragging Death (Feb. 23): Jury in Jasper, Tex., finds John William King, 24, white supremacist, guilty of murdering James Byrd, Jr., 49, the black man he and two friends tied to their pickup truck. **(Feb. 25):** Jury, after brief deliberation, decides on death sentence.

Avalanches Sweep Through Alps (Feb. 21–28): Many dead and missing in series of avalanches in Swiss and Austrian Alpine region. More than 70 have died in Europe due to avalanches this winter.

Baptist Leader Convicted of Theft (Feb. 27): Rev. Henry J. Lyons, president of largest black religious organization, found guilty in Fla. court of racketeering and stealing millions from church arson recovery fund.

March 1999

WORLD

U.S. Heats Up Trade Battle with Europe (March 3): Imposes 100% tariff on luxury products and threatens to ban supersonic Concorde from landing in U.S.

Eastern European Nations Join NATO (March 12): Three former Soviet Bloc countries, Czech Republic, Poland, and Hungary, restore important European ties.

U.S. and North Korea Agree on Inspection (March 16): Pact reached after months of negotiations will allow

U.S. access to huge underground site of suspected atomic weapons undertaking. North Korea to receive food aid in return.

NATO Launches Attack on Serbia (March 24): Cruise missiles and bombs pound Kosovo, Belgrade, and other targets. Barrage intended to punish Yugoslav leader Slobodan Milosevic and Serbian military for yearlong assault against ethnic Albanian separatists.

Pinochet Arrest Upheld in London (March 24): Law Lords rule that former Chilean dictator must remain in England and face possible extradition to Spain on charges including murder, kidnapping, and torture.

U.S. Plane Goes Down in Yugoslavia (March 27): Pilot of F-117 stealth fighter rescued six hours later. Aircraft is first Allied loss in Balkan conflict.

Thousands of Ethnic Albanians Flee Kosovo (March 30): Villages in Northwest empty as residents threatened with death join 60,000 refugees forced to flee another area a day earlier.

Three G.I.s Captured by Serbs (March 31): Reported missing during patrol of Macedonia's border with Yugoslavia. The three had reported they were surrounded and under fire.

NATION

Marine Pilot Acquitted in Deaths (March 4): Military court clears Capt. Richard J. Ashby of murder charges after plane severed ski gondola cables, killing 20 at Italian resort. Italian officials and public react with fury.

U.S. Reports Theft of Nuclear Secrets by China (March 5): Says China used data stolen from American government laboratories to miniaturize its bombs. **(March 8):** Taiwan-born computer expert Wen Ho Lee discharged from Los Alamos, N.M., laboratory for security breaches after F.B.I. names him prime suspect. Lee denies wrongdoing.

Senate Approves Missile Defense System (March 17): Votes, 97–3, for the prompt building of a network to intercept missiles fired by rogue nations such as North Korea and Iran. **(March 18):** House, 371–105, votes to support principle of national missile defense system.

Congress Votes for Republican Budget (March 25): House and Senate approve big tax cut and head toward showdown with White House over spending priorities.

BUSINESS/SCIENCE/SOCIETY

Sport Utility Vehicles Criticized (March 1): Federal study finds them unusually harmful to cars they collide with, causing about 2,000 deaths in 1996.

Key N.C.A.A. Rule Discarded (March 8): U.S. judge finds test score requirement set by National Collegiate Athletic Association to put black student–athletes at unfair disadvantage.

Medical Benefits Seen in Marijuana (March 17): Government study confirms active ingredients appear to help treat pain and other symptoms related to AIDS.

Verdict Favors Tobacco Companies (March 18): Federal jury in Ohio rules that they do not have to repay dozens of union health and benefit plans for costs of treating illnesses related to smoking.

First Nonstop Balloon Trip around World (March 20): Bertrand Piccard (Switzerland) and Brian Jones (U.K.) land *Breitling Orbiter 3* after passing finish line over Mauritania, to end 20-day voyage.

Rudder Flaw Found in Boeing 737s (March 23): U.S. report says airliner is subject to rare malfunctions that have caused two crashes and several close calls.

39 Die in Alps Tunnel Fire (March 24): French and Italian officials report fire in Mont Blanc tunnel started in heavy truck and quickly spread to some 30 other vehicles.

Dr. Kevorkian Convicted of Second-Degree Murder (March 26): Michigan jury finds physician guilty of giving fatal injection to man with terminal illness. Action had been broadcast on TV's *60 Minutes.*

Bodies of Yosemite Tourists Identified (March 27): Carole Sund, daughter Julie Sund, and friend Silvina Pelosso had been missing since Feb. 15. Remains found in charred rental car near national park.

Computer Virus Snarls Internet (March 27): Worldwide affliction, nicknamed "Melissa," forces several large corporations to shut down email servers.

Record Award in Smoking Lawsuit (March 30): Ore. jury rules Philip Morris must pay $81 million to family of man who smoked Marlboro cigarettes for forty years before dying of lung cancer.

April 1999

WORLD

NATO to Help Kosovo Refugees (April 3): Announces it will coordinate airlift to take in supplies and remove almost 100,000 Kosovars to U.S. and Europe.

Two Libyan Suspects Face Trial (April 5): Arrive in Netherlands to be tried on charges of planting bomb that blew up Pan Am Flight 103 over Scotland in 1988. The explosion killed 270 people, including 189 Americans.

U.S.–China Trade Talks a Failure (April 8): President Clinton and Prime Minister Zhu Rongji fail to reach agreement in Washington meeting. In news conference, Zhu denies China has stolen U.S. atomic secrets. **(April 9):** Officials of both nations move to protect environment and increase airline traffic between U.S. and China.

Civilians Killed by Allied Warplane (April 14): Unknown number killed in southern Kosovo. Serbs say several groups of ethnic Albanian refugees were bombed and more than 70 were killed. **(April 15):** In Brussels, NATO officials admit that an Allied plane had mistakenly bombed a civilian vehicle while trying to stop Serb forces from attacking Albanians.

Pakistan Tests Ballistic Missile (April 14): Fires new and improved version of weapon three days after India launched missile able to carry nuclear warhead.

Ex-Prime Minister Sentenced in Pakistan (April 15): Benazir Bhutto must serve five years in prison for having taken kickbacks while in office in mid-1990s. She had been removed as prime minister twice on corruption charges.

Algerians Protest Election Result (April 16): Police break up street demonstrations after candidate supported by army, Abdelaziz Bouteflika, is declared winner of presidential contest. Angry voters claim election was rigged.

Government of India Collapses (April 17): Hindu nationalist-led regime loses, 269–270, in closest parliamentary defeat in India's 51 years of independence. Elections to be held within six months. No strong alternative Cabinet prepared to take over.

Two Allies Press U.S. on Ground Forces (April 21): Britain and France call for serious consideration of sending troops to Kosovo without peace settlement.

NATION

Marine Sentenced in Ski Accident (April 2): Military jury orders discharge from Corps for navigator of jet that severed ski lift cable in Italy, killing 20. Capt. Joseph P. Schweitzer was charged with obstructing justice by destroying videotape of incident.

U.S. Judge Finds Clinton in Contempt (April 12): Court in Ark. rules President willfully provided false testimony about relationship with Monica S. Lewinsky in sexual misconduct action brought by Paula Corbin Jones. Judge, Susan Webber Wright, is a former law student of Clinton.

Ken Starr Calls for End to Independent Counsel Law (April 13): Tells Senate he thinks nation would be better off without statute under which he operated while investigating Clinton's activities.

U.S. Says China Stole Atom Warhead Design (April 20): New report concludes that China obtained information concerning U.S.'s most advanced nuclear weapon from government laboratory.

U.S. to Retain Smallpox Virus Sample (April 22): Clinton decision to keep stock faces fierce opposition from scientists and scores of nations that recommended in 1996 that remaining viruses be destroyed.

BUSINESS / SCIENCE / SOCIETY

Suspect in Email Virus Arrested (April 2): N.J. programmer David L. Smith accused of writing and sending "Melissa" virus that infected more than 100,000 computers worldwide a week earlier.

Matthew Shepard Killer Sentenced (April 5): Russell A. Henderson, 21, draws two consecutive life sentences after pleading guilty in Wyo. court to kidnapping and killing homosexual college student.

U.S. Jury Acquits Susan McDougal (April 12): Ark. panel clears her of obstructing justice by refusing to testify before a grand jury about President and Mrs. Clinton's financial dealings. Jury deadlocked on two criminal contempt charges.

Dr. Kevorkian Sentenced in Killing (April 13): Mich. metes 10-to-25 year prison term to physician for administering lethal injection in assisted suicide broadcast on TV's *60 Minutes*.

School Massacre in Colorado (April 20): Students Eric Harris, 18, and Dylan Klebold, 17, storm Columbine High School in Littleton with guns and explosives. They kill twelve other students and a teacher, then themselves. Nation alarmed over spread of school violence. **(April 22):** Investigators report finding large homemade bomb in school kitchen and speculate that the killers planned to destroy the school.

May 1999

WORLD

Three American G.I. Prisoners Freed (May 2): Milosevic releases men following appeal from Rev. Jesse Jackson. Soldiers in good health despite 31 days of confinement in Yugoslav cells.

Bombing Attacks Put London on Alert (May 1): Third bombing in three weeks leaves total of at least four dead and more than 100 wounded. Attacks target ethnic minorities and gays. **(May 2):** Engineer, 22, charged with murder in three bombings.

NATO Bombs Hit Chinese Embassy (May 7): Three journalists killed and many other people injured in accidental attack on building in Belgrade. NATO officials blame faulty intelligence. China calls U.N. emergency meeting.

A Pope's First Visit to Orthodox Country (May 7): John Paul II arrives in Romania. **(May 8):** Pope and Patriarch Teoctist of Romanian Orthodox Church join in asking immediate end to fighting in Kosovo.

Protests Erupt in Chinese Cities (May 9 et seq.): Thousands march in angry demonstration against bombing of Belgrade embassy. Mobs hurl objects at U.S. embassy in Beijing, where ambassador James Sasser is trapped for more than 48 hours. Chinese government supports protests. **(May 14):** Clinton expresses condolences to China over embassy bombing.

NATO Admits Casualties in Bombing of Village (May 15): Acknowledges that at least 80 civilians may have been killed in attack on military command post near southern Kosovo village of Korisa.

Impeachment Move Blocked in Russia (May 15): Parliament fails to impeach President Yeltsin on five charges, including one that he waged an illegal war against Chechnya in 1995 and 1996. Yeltsin remains object of attacks by both friends and enemies.

Sonia Gandhi Steps Down (May 17): Resigns as president of India's Congress Party after colleagues say she should not be prime minister because she was born in Italy. She is the widow of former prime minister Rajiv Gandhi. **(May 25):** After outpouring of support from party, Gandhi triumphantly withdraws resignation.

Labor Party Wins in Israeli Election (May 17): Ehud Barak, party leader, elected as Prime Minister. Voters reject leader of three years, Benjamin Netanyahu.

New Russian Prime Minister Confirmed (May 19): Parliament approves appointment of Sergei V. Stepashin, a Yeltsin loyalist and former national police head.

Indian Jets Strike Kashmir Guerrillas (May 26): India claims that hundreds of guerrillas in the disputed territory are Islamic militants backed by Pakistan.

Hague Tribunal Indicts Milosevic (May 27): Issues arrest warrants charging Yugoslav President and four other senior officers with crimes against humanity in Kosovo. Charges include murder, forced deportation, and persecution of ethnic Albanians.

NATION

Marine Pilot Punished for Obstructing Justice (May 10): Capt. Richard Ashby, 32, sentenced to six months in prison and dismissal from Corps for helping destroy videotape of ski gondola accident. He had been acquitted of manslaughter charges in March.

China Campaign Aid Reported (May 11): Former Democratic fund-raiser Johnny Chung, who had admitted fraud, tells House panel high Chinese intelligence official in 1996 promised him $300,000 for Presidential election campaign.

Treasury Secretary Announces Resignation (May 12): Robert E. Rubin, chief architect of Clinton economic policy during period of prosperity, will step down. President plans to nominate as successor Lawrence H. Summers, Deputy Secretary of the Treasury.

Crime in U.S. Falls for Seventh Consecutive Year (May 16): F.B.I. reports violent and property crimes each dropped 7 percent in 1998, largest annual drop since beginning of downward trend in 1992.

Senate, 73–25, Votes for Gun Control Measures (May 20): Approves juvenile-crime bill including requirements for safety locks and background checks on purchasers of firearms at gun shows. Vice President Gore breaks deadlock on key amendment.

BUSINESS / SCIENCE / SOCIETY

Lost Space Capsule Found in Ocean (May 2): *Mercury* discovered off Fla. shore after 38 years. Carried Gus Grissom on America's second manned space flight.

Okla. and Kans. Hit by Devastating Tornadoes (May 3): 41 killed in Okla., 5 in Kans. as twisters destroy more than 1,500 buildings and injure over 500 other people. One tornado reported to be a mile wide at times.

Citadel Graduates First Woman (May 8): Nancy Mace, 21, survives harsh experience at S.C. military college.

Talk Show Penalized (May 8): Mich. jury orders *The Jenny Jones Show* to pay $25 million to family of a murdered gay man who appeared on show. Victim, Scott Amedure, was killed in March 1995 by one-time friend Jonathan T. Schmitz, to whom Amedure revealed his secret crush on national TV.

Student Wounds Six at Conyers, Ga. School (May 20): Alleged gunman T. J. Solomon, 15, wounds fellow students at Heritage High. Tearfully surrenders to assistant principal. **(May 21):** Boy reported to have taken the two guns he used after breaking into stepfather's gun cabinet.

Clinton Friend Pleads Guilty in U.S. Court (May 21): Yah Lin Trie, Democratic fund-raiser, admits to felony of causing false statements to be made to Federal Election Commission.

Policeman Pleads Guilty in N.Y.C. Torture Case (May 25): Officer Justin Volpe, 27, admits to brutally beating Haitian immigrant Abner Louima and sodomizing him with a wooden stick in Brooklyn police station in 1997. Four other white officers face trial in racially charged case.

June 1999

WORLD

European Union Plans Military Role (June 3): Will create command headquarters and forces of its own for peacekeeping and peacemaking missions.

African National Congress Wins Election (June 3): Gains second term in landslide victory. Thabo Mbeki, replacing retiring president Nelson Mandela, is expected to control more than two-thirds of Parliament.

Hong Kong Remembers Tiananmen Square (June 4): More than 70,000 gather for peaceful demonstration to mark massacre in Beijing ten years previously. It is only such observance to be held on Chinese soil.

Algerian Rebel Group Ends Struggle (June 6): Islamic Salvation Army abandons armed activities after 21–month cease-fire. Government grants amnesty to members.

Serbs Agree to Leave Kosovo (June 9): Accept accord allowing military force under NATO command to occupy Kosovo. NATO officials reach tentative agreement with Liberation Army leaders for gradual disbanding of K.L.A. **(June 10):** NATO suspends bombing of Yugoslavia after 78th day, as Serbian troops begin to withdraw. **(June 11):** Allies taken by surprise as Russia, unhappy with its uncertain role in the peace plan, sends peacekeeping troops to Kosovo border. **(June 18):** After tense negotiations, U.S. and Russia sign agreement allowing Russian troops to integrate into NATO peace force.

U.S. and Russia Agree to Cut Arms Threat (June 16): Pact extends, by seven years, programs to reduce threat from nuclear, biological, chemical, and other weapons of mass destruction.

Antipoverty Loan for China Approved (June 24): World Bank overrules U.S. and backs $160 million for resettlement of 58,000 farmers in ethnically Tibetan area. Payment will be delayed until independent board reviews impact.

Turkish Court Dooms Kurdish Rebel Leader (June 29): Sentences Abdullah Ocalan to death for 15–year armed campaign against Turkish oppression. Worldwide reaction is quiet compared to massive protests that erupted after Ocalan's capture in Feb.

Coalition Government Formed in Israel (June 30): Prime Minister-elect Ehud Barak ends six-week process in deal with ultra-Orthodox Shas Party. New government to be composed of seven parties with widely differing views.

NATION

Senate Votes $265 Billion for Pentagon (June 8): Passes appropriations bill 93–4. It includes pay increase for military personnel and prohibits spending money on reconstruction of Serbia so long as President Slobodan Milosevic is in power.

Clinton Denounces Racial Profiling (June 9): Orders Federal law-enforcement agencies to collect data on race and ethnicity of people they question, search, or arrest, to determine role of skin color.

House Defeats Gun Control Bill (June 18): In 280–147 vote, rejects firearms restrictions that are weaker than legislation approved by Senate. Liberals, moderates, and conservatives join to block measure after bitter debate over causes of violence among American children.

Senate Approves Payment to U.N. (June 22): Votes 98–1 to authorize more than $800 million in back dues but reduces future U.S. contributions. Bill moves next to House.

Clinton Proposes Medicare Shake-Up (June 29): Calls for structural changes to meet new needs. Plan adds coverage of prescription drugs and would keep Medicare solvent 12 years longer than currently expected, until 2027.

Independent Counsel Law Dies (June 30): Decisions on ethics investigations of high officials left to Attorney General, who will decide when to appoint special counsels.

BUSINESS/SCIENCE/SOCIETY

Death Toll 12 in Alpine Tunnel Fire (June 2): Salvage workers recover bodies from tangled wreckage of multi-vehicle collision in Salzburg, Austria, tunnel.

U.S. and Canada Agree on Salmon Quotas (June 3): Seek to end long dispute. Comprehensive plan for thousands of miles along Pacific coast will include a conservation fund to help protect fish.

Two New Elements Added to Periodic Table (June 7): Scientists at Lawrence Berkeley National Laboratory in Calif. announce creation of elements with atomic numbers 118 and 116 in April by using cyclotron accelerator to hurl Krypton atoms at a lead target.

Theaters to Require Photo IDs (June 8): Heeding the President, movie houses across country agree to require teenagers to show identification before entering R-rated films without an adult. Move is an effort to curb youth violence that may be influenced by entertainment industry.

Prince Edward Ties the Knot (June 19): Marries Sophie Rhys-Jones in relatively low-key ceremony at Windsor Castle.

A.M.A. Approves Union for Doctors (June 23): American Medical Association delegates vote to form organization to achieve equality with powerful managed-care health-maintenance groups.

July 1999

WORLD

Women's Groups Challenge Vatican (July 1): Worldwide organizations at U.N. conference attack Vatican efforts to block plan to limit population growth through family planning and abortion.

Israeli Prime Minister Takes Office (July 6): Ehud Barak pledges top aim will be to seek "true, lasting peace" with Arabs. **(July 7):** Announces plans for conferences about Syria and Palestinian territory with Arab leaders and President Clinton.

European Union Shakes Up Leadership (July 9): Nineteen new members appointed to Executive Commission in "new era of change" after resignation of entire previous commission in March amid accusations of corruption and mismanagement.

Protests Spread Throughout Iran (July 12): Students demonstrate in 18 cities and towns as pro-democracy movement spreads. Security police and vigilantes seek to crush crowds outside Teheran University. **(July 17):** Student leaders announce temporary ban on protests, but press government for major changes.

Taiwanese Leader Challenges "One China" Policy (July 11): Beijing angered as Lee Teng-hui says China and Taiwan should interact on state-to-state level.

Serbs Blamed for 10,000 Kosovo Deaths (July 17): Reports indicate even more may have been killed in three-month push to drive Albanians from Kosovo.

Israel to Bolster Jet Fighter Fleet (July 18): Plans to add at least 50 more F–16s, making its fleet the largest outside of the U.S.

King Hassan II of Morocco Dies at 70 (July 23): Monarch for 38 years served as intermediary in peace efforts between Egypt and Israel.

NATION

House Votes Congressional Pay Increase (July 15): Approves, 275–147, $4,600 raise in January and doubling of next President's salary to $400,000.

Senate Votes G.O.P Health Care Plan (July 15): By 53–47, approves proposal to regulate managed-care providers. Rejects Democratic move to expand patients' ability to sue those companies.

Pentagon Misuse of Funds Charged (July 21): Report by House panel says hundreds of millions of dollars were spent on projects that Congress had never approved, including secret Air Force program.

House G.O.P. Passes Large Tax Cut (July 22): Vote of 223–208 approves $792 billion reduction over next decade.

Linda Tripp Indicted Over Tapes (July 30): Maryland jury charges illegal taping of Monica Lewinsky calls.

BUSINESS/SCIENCE/SOCIETY

H.M.O.s Plan to Cut Expenses (July 1): Will increase Medicare premiums or trim benefits for most elderly subscribers because they consider Federal payments they receive to be inadequate.

Dr. J Father of Tennis Star (July 2): As rising tennis star Alexandra Stevenson, 18, tries to dodge questions about identity of her father, basketball legend Julius Erving steps up and reveals long-kept secret.

White Supremacist Goes on Shooting Spree (July 2–5): In series of seven drive-by shootings targeting blacks, Jews, and Asians, Benjamin N. Smith kills two and wounds eight in Midwest. **(July 5):** Smith shoots and kills self in Ill. police chase.

Vaccine Fights Brain Disease in Mice (July 7): Scientists find it effective in preventing and reversing a primary abnormality associated with Alzheimer's disease. Effect on humans still unproven.

U.S. Women Win Soccer Championship (July 10): Americans capture second World Cup after close match against China. Scoreless game goes into double overtime before ending 5–4 on penalty kicks.

Murder Charges Filed in Valujet Crash (July 13): Florida blames aviation maintenance company, a company officer, and two mechanics for fire that caused deaths of 110 aboard DC-10 in 1996 Everglades crash.

Suspect Surrenders in Serial Killings (July 13): Mexican fugitive Rafael Reséndez-Ramirez suspected in eight killings. Said to have hopped freight trains to avoid capture.

John F. Kennedy Jr. Lost at Sea (July 16): Plane he was piloting disappears near Martha's Vineyard, off Mass. coast, with wife, Carolyn Bessette Kennedy, and her sister Lauren G. Bessette. Disappearance of Kennedy, aged 38, arouses national and worldwide mourning. **(July 17):** Debris from crashed plane recovered. **(July 21):** Bodies of three victims found trapped in plane's wreckage. Crash is later attributed to pilot error.

Woman Heads Space Shuttle Crew (July 16): Col. Eileen M. Collins arrives at Cape Canaveral as first woman to lead a space mission. Others join her for shuttle *Columbia*'s mission to launch X-ray telescope.

Two Markets Plan Public Role (July 23): New York Stock Exchange and Nasdaq move to convert from non-profit institutions to for-profit corporations.

Suspect Confesses to Four Yosemite Killings (July 26): Cary Stayner, 37, admits to beheading 26-year-old park ranger Joie Ruth Armstrong on July 21 and killing three female tourists in Feb. Says he was instructed by "voices in his head."

Drought Plagues Eastern States (July 27 et seq.): Lack of rain causes worst drought on record for four northeastern states and causes heavy crop damage to several other states.

Gunman Kills Nine in Atlanta (July 29): Day-trader Mark Barton, 44, opens fire in two brokerage firms. He wounds 13 others before being chased by police to a service station and shooting himself.

August 1999

WORLD

Yeltsin Ousts Prime Minister (Aug. 9): Replaces Sergei Stepashin with Vladimir Putin in fourth government shake-up in 17 months.

China Rejects Visit by Pope (Aug. 9): Turns down efforts by Vatican. Beijing reported to base decision on papal ties with Taiwan and not with mainland.

Indians Shoot Down Unarmed Pakistani Plane (Aug. 10): All 16 aboard plane killed by fighter craft near disputed border. Both India and Pakistan claim jet was over their territory. Tensions increase between the rival nuclear powers.

Yugoslav Cabinet Reshuffled (Aug. 12): Prime Minister Momir Bilatovic acts in face of antigovernment demonstrations. Brings in strongly nationalist Serbs.

Uganda and Rwanda Reach Accord (Aug. 17): Leaders agree on immediate cease-fire to end three days of fighting between their troops in Congo. The usually friendly nations support rival rebel factions against Congolese president Laurent Kabila.

Thousands Perish in Turkish Earthquake (Aug. 17): Magnitude 7.4 quake in northwest region kills more than 15,600 and leaves 600,000 homeless. Damages estimated at $6.5 billion. **(Aug. 18):** More than 1,000 relief workers from nineteen countries join search for victims.

Russian Money Laundering Charged (Aug. 18): Law enforcement officials say billions of dollars have been channeled through Bank of New York in the last year in what is believed to be a major operation by organized crime figures in Russia.

North Korean Famine Reported Eased (Aug. 19): U.N. report says international food aid has helped nation emerge from prolonged severe period. Experts say years of hunger have cost millions of lives.

Thousands Exhort Milosevic to Quit (Aug. 19): Tens of thousands rally outside Belgrade Federal Parliament to demand resignation. Opposition leaders divided.

Russia Regains Dagestan Territory (Aug. 25): Federal troops raise Russian flag over Dagestan mountain villages seized three weeks previously by Islamic militants from secessionist republic of Chechnya.

East Timor Votes for Independence (Aug. 31): Hundreds of thousands of voters reject autonomy, choosing to break away from Indonesia, which had been in control in 1975. U.N. helps monitor elections.

NATION

F.C.C. Relaxes TV Station Ownership Rules (Aug. 5): For first time, allows single company or network to own two broadcasting stations in nation's largest cities.

Senate Confirms U.N. Appointment (Aug. 5): After 14 months, approves Richard C. Holbrooke to be chief American delegate. After months of opposition by Republican leaders, the final obstacle, Sen. Charles Grassley (R-Iowa) relents.

Pentagon Revises Policy on Homosexuals (Aug. 13): Requires troops to receive more training to prevent harassment of homosexuals.

F.B.I. Reveals New Details on Waco Standoff (Aug. 25): Admits to possibility that pyrotechnic tear-gas canisters were used against Branch Davidian sect on last day of 1993 stand-off in Texas. More than 80 people were killed when compound caught fire. Source of fire remains a mystery, as F.B.I. denies the devices were responsible. **(Aug. 26):** Attorney General calls for new investigation of case.

BUSINESS/SCIENCE/SOCIETY

Train Crash in India Kills Hundreds (Aug. 2): Cars crushed in head-on collision, killing more than 250.

$16 Million Paid for Assassination Film (Aug. 3): Arbitrators rule U.S. must reimburse heirs of Abraham Zapruder for record of Kennedy shooting.

Parents Cautioned on Children's TV (Aug. 5): American Academy of Pediatrics warns that television viewing can affect mental, social, and physical health of children.

$23 Million Verdict in Diet Pill Case (Aug. 5): Texas jury awards sum to woman who said she suffered heart damage after using fen-phen. Verdict is first in thousands of cases pending across country.

Gunman Opens Fire in L.A. (Aug. 10): White supremacist Buford Furrow, Jr., 37, wounds five at North Valley Jewish Community Center. Upon fleeing, he shoots and kills a Filipino-American postal worker. **(Aug. 11):** Furrow surrenders in Las Vegas, admitting to murder.

Tornado Damages Salt Lake City (Aug. 11): Rare twister kills one and injures more than 70 in Utah capital. Mayor estimates $150 million in property damage.

Evolution Rejected in Kansas (Aug. 14): State Board of Education votes to delete virtually any mention of theory from state's science curriculum.

Decline in AIDS Deaths Slows (Aug. 26): Health experts report in new study that drop in AIDS death rate from 1997 to 1998 was 20%, half that of the previous year's decline. Number of new HIV infections in 1998 continues to hold steady from previous several years, at roughly 40,000.

Liquid Discovered in Object From Space (Aug. 26): NASA scientists find water trapped in four-and-a-half billion year old meteorite that landed in Tex. in 1998.

Last Full Crew Leaves Russian Space Station (Aug. 28): Two Russians and a French cosmonaut climb into escape capsule for descent to Earth from 13-year-old *Mir*. Lack of funding makes it likely spacecraft will be programmed to burn up and land in ocean.

DDT Defended as Malaria Weapon (Aug. 28): Public health officials say pesticide, facing increasing bans, is necessary to stop worldwide spread of disease.

AT&T Lowers Long-Distance Rates (Aug. 30): Follows two rivals, MCI Worldcom and Sprint. Moves benefit consumers but threaten phone companies' profits.

September 1999

WORLD

NATO and U.N. Agree on K.L.A. Role (Sept. 2): Part of Kosovo Liberation Army will be allowed to survive as lightly armed civilian emergency force.

Middle East Peace Accord Announced (Sept. 4): Barak and Arafat plan to finalize borders between Israel and Palestinians by Feb. 15, 2000. Accord includes land-for-security agreement outlined in Wye Accord in fall of 1998. Brokered in presence of U.S. Secretary of State Madeleine Albright.

Militia Attacks East Timor Citizens (Sept. 6): Backed by Indonesian military in burning homes, killing residents, and forcing thousands to flee to hills.

Israel Bans Force in Interrogations (Sept. 6): Supreme Court outlaws security forces' routine use of coercive measures, denounced by critics as torture.

Yeltsin Denies Corruption Charges (Sept. 8): Russian president assures Clinton that accusations against him and his family are politically motivated.

Explosions Kill Hundreds in Russia (Sept. 16): Fifth bombing in less than three weeks kills 18 in southern city, with more than 200 wounded. Almost 200 have died in series of explosions; authorities blame Islamic militants.

Clinton Sends Troops to East Timor (Sept. 16): Force of 200 will be responsible for intelligence, logistics, communication, and transport. **(Sept. 20):** U.N. force arrives and meets no resistance. Indonesian President had conceded that his forces had been unable to control violence in territory.

Army to Investigate Korean War Massacre (Sept. 29): Opens new probe following Associated Press report that U.S. troops killed hundreds of civilians under South Korean bridge in 1950. Veterans' accounts of incident are conflicting.

Japan Experiences Its Worst Nuclear Accident (Sept. 30): 69 people exposed to high levels of radiation after workers accidentally trigger chain reaction at fuel plant. More than 160 nearby residents forced to evacuate homes.

NATION

Clintons Choose Post-White House Dwelling (Sept. 2): Sign contract to buy $1.7 million 11-room Dutch colonial home in Westchester County, N.Y., suburb. Location suggests run for U.S. Senate by first lady is likely.

Clinton Announces Gun Buyback Plan (Sept. 9): Seeks $15 million to purchase firearms from gun owners as move to fight gun violence.

House Votes Limit on Class-Action Suits (Sept. 23): Approves strict curbs on actions against tobacco companies, gun makers, and many other businesses.

BUSINESS/SCIENCE/SOCIETY

American Youth Convicted in Israel (Sept. 2): Tel Aviv judges find teenager, Samuel Sheinbein, guilty in Maryland slaying. He had fled to Israel to avoid prosecution. Plea agreement evaluated.

Media Cleared in Diana's Death (Sept. 3): French judge dismisses all charges in investigation of photographers' role in Paris crash that killed Princess.

Embezzlement Suspect Caught in Germany (Sept. 4): Four-month manhunt ends when F.B.I. tracks down 44-year-old money manager Martin Frankel. He is accused of embezzling more than $200 million.

Record Media Merger Planned (Sept. 7): Viacom Inc. announces it will acquire CBS corporation for $37.3 billion, creating second largest media company.

End to School Busing Where It Began (Sept. 10): Judges order Charlotte, N.C., to halt program, ruling that forced integration was no longer necessary. System had pioneered in practice 30 years previously.

Gunman Goes on Rampage in Texas Church (Sept. 15): Larry Gene Ashbrook, 47, opens fire on teenagers at Baptist service in Fort Worth. Assailant kills seven before shooting self as police officers arrive.

Hurricane Batters East Coast (Sept. 17 et seq.): Winds and flooding from storm Floyd cause wide havoc from Fla. to New England. Nine believed to have been killed. Three days after hurricane strikes N.C., almost two-thirds of state remains paralyzed.

Earthquake Rocks Taiwan (Sept. 21): Buildings toppled, trapping hundreds. **(Sept. 22):** Death toll more than 1,700. Rescuers work night and day to reach thousands under debris.

Mars-Orbiting Craft Destroyed (Sept. 23): $125 million robotic vehicle reported missing just before scheduled mission. Was first craft ever dispatched to check weather on planet. **(Sept. 30):** Embarrassed NASA says mistake caused by navigators who assumed figures provided by contractor were in metric units, when in fact they were English measurements.

October 1999

WORLD

Commuter Trains Collide in London (Oct. 5): Worst British train crash in quarter century claims up to 40 lives. Accident blamed on poorly visible signal that had been missed by drivers eight times in the past four years.

Russian Planes Attack Chechen Village (Oct. 7): Elistanzhi bombed then invaded by tanks. Continues two months of fighting as Russia tries to control Islamic militants.

Vajpayee Victorious in Indian Election (Oct. 7): Prime Minister keeps post and his 22-party National Democratic Alliance wins majority of Parliamentary seats. Leader's popularity based partly on support of nuclear development and tough stance in struggle with Pakistan over Kashmir.

British Magistrate OKs Pinochet Extradition (Oct. 8): A year after former Chilean dictator's arrest in London, Spain's request for his extradition on charges of torture continues to move through British legal system. **(Oct. 14):** Chile asks Britain to allow Pinochet's return home on grounds of his poor health.

U.N. Worker Killed in Yugoslavia (Oct. 11): Bulgarian man beaten and shot by ethnic Albanians after speaking Serbian. **(Oct. 12):** Two U.N. employees and seven other people killed in Burundi after humanitarian convoy is seized by rebels. **(Oct. 13):** During tough week for U.N., six employees and their interpreter are taken hostage by gunmen in Georgia. $300,000 ransom demanded.

World's Six Billionth Inhabitant Born (Oct. 11): U.N. chooses baby boy in Sarajevo to represent population landmark.

Government Ousted in Pakistan (Oct. 12): Surprise military coup raises concern over future of new nuclear power. **(Oct. 15):** Despite international urging toward democracy, coup leader Gen. Pervaiz Musharraf assumes power, suspending constitution and dissolving parliament.

NATION

U.S. Conducts Missile Defense System Test (Oct. 2): Receives international criticism after successful test of missile interceptor over Pacific. Argues Asia and Mideast nuclear development have created need for limited nuclear defense programs.

UPS Announces End to Gun Deliveries (Oct. 7): United Parcel Service will no longer ship handguns by ground service. Claims shipments can be too easily stolen.

Clinton Proposes Conservation Plan (Oct. 13): Ambitious initiative calls for preservation of over 40 million acres of roadless forest.

Al Gore Wins Support from Labor Union (Oct. 13): AFL-CIO officially endorses vice president in his run for the White House. Boost comes as opponent Bill Bradley makes gains in polls.

Grand Jury Closes Ramsey Investigation (Oct. 13): Lack of evidence prevents indictments before deadline in closely followed mystery. Many believe John and Patsy Ramsey to be responsible for the 1996 murder of their six-year-old daughter, JonBenet, in Boulder, Colo.

Nuclear Test-Ban Treaty Fails (Oct. 13): In blow to President, Senate rejects treaty, 51–48. The 1996 agreement, which cannot enter into effect until all 44

nuclear-capable nations have ratified it, has only been accepted by 26. U.S. receives harsh criticism from world leaders, including allies.

Ailing Doctor Airlifted from Antarctica (Oct. 16): Dr. Jerri Nielsen, 47, of Ohio, had been treating herself with chemotherapy after finding a lump in her breast five months earlier. Sub-zero temperatures had delayed her rescue until the end of the polar winter.

BUSINESS/SCIENCE/SOCIETY

Controversial Art Exhibit Opens in Brooklyn (Oct. 2): Hundreds protest British exhibit featuring dissected animals and a portrait of the Virgin Mary utilizing elephant dung. Mayor Rudolph Giuliani sparks First Amendment debate in vowing to cut city's funding to museum.

Storms Devastate Mexico (Oct. 4 et seq.): More than a week of torrential rains results in country's worst disaster in a decade. At least 342 confirmed dead in floods and mudslides.

MCI Probable Buyer for Sprint (Oct. 4): $100 billion merger will be largest in U.S. if approved.

Female Editor to Head AMA Journal (Oct. 8): Dr. Catherine De Angelis is first woman to hold post for American Medical Association.

Record-Setting Webcast Targets Poverty (Oct. 9): Concert broadcast on Internet features series of performances in London, Geneva, and New York. U.N.-sponsored event to raise money and awareness for poor. Nearly 2.4 million viewers visit Web site, setting record for most hits.

Philip Morris Admits Harm in Smoking (Oct. 13): Nation's largest tobacco company finally acknowledges cigarette link to cancer and other diseases. Web site announcement is seen as public image strategy.

1999 Nobel Prize Winners

Peace: Doctors Without Borders, a French-based global organization. Since 1971 it has provided emergency medical assistance to populations plagued by violence and brutality in more than 80 countries. Said the Nobel Committee, "Each fearless and self-sacrificing helper shows each victim a human face, stands for respect for that person's dignity and is a source of hope for peace and reconciliation."

Literature: Günter Grass (Germany), "whose frolicsome black village fables portray the forgotten face of history." Grass, whose novel *The Tin Drum* (1961) brought him world renown, writes fiercely and eloquently about the anguish of war and reunification in his native Germany.

Physics: Gerardus 't Hooft (Netherlands) and Martinus J. G. Veltman (Netherlands). According to the Academy, the two researchers have "placed particle physics theory on a firmer mathematical foundation." The researchers' theory links electromagnetic and "weak" interactions—the process which produces nearly all of the sun's energy.

Chemistry: Ahmed H. Zewail (Egypt and U.S.) who has created the world's fastest camera, which captures atoms in motion much as a slow-motion replay captures a sporting event. The academy stated that his contributions "have brought about a revolution in chemistry and adjacent sciences."

Medicine: Dr. Günter Blobel (Germany and U.S.), who was honored by the Academy "for the discovery that proteins have intrinsic signals that govern their transport and localization in the cell."

Economics: Robert A. Mundel (U.S.), a Columbia University economist, for his work on monetary dynamics and optimum currency areas. The Academy stated Mundel "has established the foundation for the theory that dominates practical policy considerations of monetary and fiscal policy in open economies."

The One Hundred Sixth Congress
Composition of the 105th and 106th Congresses

106th Congress	Rep.	Dem.	Ind.	Male	Female	105th Congress	Rep.	Dem.	Ind.	Male	Female
Senate	54	45	1	91	9	Senate	55	45	—	91	9
House	222	211	1	376	58	House	228	206	1	380	55

The Senate

In the following list, the senior senator is listed first. Dates in left column indicate term in office; birthdates are given in parentheses after name and party affiliation. All terms are for six years and expire in January. Mailing address: The Senate, Washington, D.C. 20515. NOTE: As of July 31, 1999.

Alabama
1987–2005 Richard Shelby (R) (1934)
1997–2003 Jeff Sessions (R) (1946)
Alaska
1969–2003 Ted Stevens (R) (1923)
1981–2005 Frank H. Murkowski (R) (1933)
Arizona
1987–2005 John McCain (R) (1936)
1995–2001 Jon Kyl (R) (1942)
Arkansas
1997–2003 Tim Hutchinson (R) (1949)
1999–2005 Blanche Lincoln (D) (1960)
California
1993–2001 Dianne Feinstein (D) (1933)
1993–2005 Barbara Boxer (D) (1940)
Colorado
1993–2005 Ben Nighthorse Campbell (R) (1933)
1997–2003 Wayne Allard (R) (1943)
Connecticut
1981–2005 Christopher J. Dodd (D) (1944)
1989–2001 Joseph I. Lieberman (D) (1942)
Delaware
1971–2001 William V. Roth, Jr. (R) (1921)
1973–2003 Joseph R. Biden, Jr. (D) (1942)
Florida
1987–2005 Bob Graham (D) (1936)
1989–2001 Connie Mack (R) (1940)
Georgia
1993–2005 Paul Douglas Coverdell (R) (1939)
1997–2003 Max Cleland (D) (1942)
Hawaii
1963–2005 Daniel K. Inouye (D) (1924)
1990–2001 Daniel K. Akaka (D) (1924)
Idaho
1991–2003 Larry E. Craig (R) (1945)
1999–2005 Mike Crapo (R) (1951)
Illinois
1997–2003 Richard J. Durbin (D) (1944)
1999–2005 Peter G. Fitzgerald (R) (1960)
Indiana
1977–2001 Richard G. Lugar (R) (1932)
1999–2005 Evan Bayh (D) (1955)
Iowa
1981–2005 Chuck E. Grassley (R) (1933)
1985–2003 Tom Harkin (D) (1939)
Kansas
1997–2005 Sam Brownback (R) (1956)
1997–2003 Pat Roberts (R) (1936)
Kentucky
1985–2003 Mitch McConnell (R) (1942)
1999–2005 Jim Bunning (R) (1931)
Louisiana
1987–2005 John B. Breaux (D) (1944)
1997–2003 Mary L. Landrieu (D) (1955)
Maine
1995–2001 Olympia J. Snowe (R) (1947)
1997–2003 Susan M. Collins (R) (1952)

Maryland
1977–2001 Paul Sarbanes (D) (1933)
1987–2005 Barbara A. Mikulski (D) (1936)
Massachusetts
1963–2001 Edward M. Kennedy (D) (1932)
1985–2003 John F. Kerry (D) (1943)
Michigan
1979–2003 Carl Levin (D) (1934)
1995–2001 Spencer Abraham (R) (1952)
Minnesota
1991–2003 Paul Wellstone (D) (1944)
1995–2001 Rod Grams (R) (1948)
Mississippi
1979–2003 Thad Cochran (R) (1937)
1989–2001 Trent Lott (R) (1941)
Missouri
1987–2005 Christopher S. "Kit" Bond (R) (1939)
1995–2001 John Ashcroft (R) (1942)
Montana
1978–2003 Max Baucus (D) (1941)
1989–2001 Conrad Burns (R) (1935)
Nebraska
1989–2001 Robert Kerrey (D) (1943)
1997–2003 Charles Hagel (R) (1946)
Nevada
1987–2005 Harry Reid (D) (1939)
1989–2001 Richard Bryan (D) (1937)
New Hampshire
1991–2003 Bob Smith (I) (1941)
1993–2005 Judd Gregg (R) (1947)
New Jersey
1983–2001 Frank R. Lautenberg (D) (1924)
1997–2003 Robert Torricelli (D) (1951)
New Mexico
1973–2003 Pete V. Domenici (R) (1932)
1983–2001 Jeff Bingaman (D) (1943)
New York
1977–2001 Daniel P. Moynihan (D) (1927)
1999–2005 Charles E. Schumer (D) (1950)
North Carolina
1973–2003 Jesse Helms (R) (1921)
1999–2005 John Edwards (D) (1953)
North Dakota
1987–2001 Kent Conrad (D) (1948)
1993–2005 Byron L. Dorgan (D) (1942)
Ohio
1995–2001 Mike DeWine (R) (1947)
1999–2005 George Voinovich (R) (1936)
Oklahoma
1989–2005 Don Nickles (R) (1948)
1994–2003 James M. Inhofe (R) (1934)
Oregon
1996–2005 Ron Wyden (D) (1949)
1997–2003 Gordon Smith (R) (1952)
Pennsylvania
1981–2005 Arlen Specter (R) (1930)
1995–2001 Rick Santorum (R) (1958)

Rhode Island
1976–2001 John H. Chafee (R) (1922)
1997–2003 Jack Reed (D) (1949)
South Carolina
1957–2003 Strom Thurmond (R) (1902)
1966–2005 Ernest Hollings (D) (1922)
South Dakota
1987–2005 Thomas A. Daschle (D) (1947)
1997–2003 Tim Johnson (D) (1946)
Tennessee
1995–2003 Fred Thompson (R) (1942)
1995–2001 William Frist (R) (1952)
Texas
1985–2003 Phil Gramm (R) (1942)
1995–2001 Kay Bailey Hutchison (R) (1943)
Utah
1977–2001 Orrin G. Hatch (R) (1934)
1993–2005 Robert F. Bennett (R) (1933)

Vermont
1975–2005 Patrick Leahy (D) (1940)
1989–2001 James M. Jeffords (R) (1934)
Virginia
1979–2003 John Warner (R) (1927)
1989–2001 Charles Robb (D) (1939)
Washington
1989–2001 Slade Gorton (R) (1928)
1993–2005 Patty Murray (D) (1950)
West Virginia
1959–2001 Robert C. Byrd (D) (1917)
1985–2003 John D. "Jay" Rockefeller IV (D) (1937)
Wisconsin
1989–2001 Herbert Kohl (D) (1935)
1993–2005 Russ Feingold (D) (1953)
Wyoming
1995–2001 Craig Thomas (R) (1933)
1997–2003 Michael B. Enzi (R) (1944)

The House of Representatives

In the following lists, the numeral indicates the Congressional District represented; AL is for representatives At Large. All terms expire January 2001. Mailing address: House of Representatives, Washington, D.C. 20515. NOTE: As of July 31, 1999.

Alabama
1. Sonny Callahan (R)
2. Terry Everett (R)
3. Bob Riley (R)
4. Robert Aderholt (R)
5. Robert E. "Bud" Cramer, Jr. (D)
6. Spencer Bachus (R)
7. Earl F. Hilliard (D)

Alaska
AL Don Young (R)

Arizona
1. Matt Salmon (R)
2. Ed Pastor (D)
3. Bob Stump (R)
4. John B. Shadegg (R)
5. Jim Kolbe (R)
6. J. D. Hayworth (R)

Arkansas
1. Marion Berry (D)
2. Vic Snyder (D)
3. Asa Hutchinson (R)
4. Jay Dickey (R)

California
1. Mike Thompson (D)
2. Wally Herger (R)
3. Doug Ose (R)
4. John T. Doolittle (R)
5. Robert T. Matsui (D)
6. Lynn C. Woolsey (D)
7. George Miller (D)
8. Nancy Pelosi (D)
9. Barbara Lee (D)
10. Ellen O. Tauscher (D)
11. Richard W. Pombo (R)
12. Tom Lantos (D)
13. Fortney Pete Stark (D)
14. Anna G. Eshoo (D)
15. Tom Campbell (R)
16. Zoe Lofgren (D)
17. Sam Farr (D)
18. Gary A. Condit (D)
19. George Radanovich (R)
20. Calvin M. Dooley (D)
21. William M. Thomas (R)
22. Lois Capps (D)
23. Elton Gallegly (R)
24. Brad Sherman (D)
25. Howard P. "Buck" McKeon (R)

26. Howard L. Berman (D)
27. James E. Rogan (R)
28. David Dreier (R)
29. Henry A. Waxman (D)
30. Xavier Becerra (D)
31. Matthew G. Martinez (D)
32. Julian C. Dixon (D)
33. Lucille Roybal-Allard (D)
34. Grace F. Napolitano (D)
35. Maxine Waters (D)
36. Steven T. Kuykendall (R)
37. Juanita Millender-McDonald (D)
38. Steve Horn (R)
39. Edward R. Royce (R)
40. Jerry Lewis (R)
41. Gary G. Miller (R)
42. (vacant)
43. Ken Calvert (R)
44. Mary Bono (R)
45. Dana Rohrabacher (R)
46. Loretta Sanchez (D)
47. Christopher Cox (R)
48. Ron Packard (R)
49. Brian P. Bilbray (R)
50. Bob Filner (D)
51. Randy "Duke" Cunningham (R)
52. Duncan Hunter (R)

Colorado
1. Diana DeGette (D)
2. Mark Udall (D)
3. Scott McInnis (R)
4. Bob Schaffer (R)
5. Joel Hefley (R)
6. Thomas G. Tancredo (R)

Connecticut
1. John B. Larson (D)
2. Sam Gejdenson (D)
3. Rosa L. DeLauro (D)
4. Christopher Shays (R)
5. James H. Maloney (D)
6. Nancy L. Johnson (R)

Delaware
AL Michael N. Castle (R)

Florida
1. Joe Scarborough (R)
2. Allen Boyd (D)
3. Corrine Brown (D)
4. Tillie K. Fowler (R)
5. Karen L. Thurman (D)

6. Cliff Stearns (R)
7. John L. Mica (R)
8. Bill McCollum (R)
9. Michael Bilirakis (R)
10. C. W. Bill Young (R)
11. Jim Davis (D)
12. Charles T. Canady (R)
13. Dan Miller (R)
14. Porter J. Goss (R)
15. Dave Weldon (R)
16. Mark Foley (R)
17. Carrie P. Meek (D)
18. Ileana Ros-Lehtinen (R)
19. Robert Wexler (D)
20. Peter Deutsch (D)
21. Lincoln Diaz-Balart (R)
22. E. Clay Shaw, Jr. (R)
23. Alcee L. Hastings (D)

Georgia
1. Jack Kingston (R)
2. Sanford Dixon Bishop, Jr. (D)
3. Mac Collins (R)
4. Cynthia A. McKinney (D)
5. John Lewis (D)
6. Johnny Isakson (R)
7. Bob Barr (R)
8. Saxby Chambliss (R)
9. Nathan Deal (R)
10. Charlie Norwood (R)
11. John Linder (R)

Hawaii
1. Neil Abercrombie (D)
2. Patsy T. Mink (D)

Idaho
1. Helen Chenoweth (R)
2. Michael K. Simpson (R)

Illinois
1. Bobby L. Rush (D)
2. Jesse L. Jackson, Jr. (D)
3. William O. Lipinski (D)
4. Luis V. Gutierrez (D)
5. Rod R. Blagojevich (D)
6. Henry J. Hyde (R)
7. Danny K. Davis (D)
8. Philip M. Crane (R)
9. Janice D. Schakowsky (D)
10. John Edward Porter (R)
11. Jerry Weller (R)
12. Jerry F. Costello (D)

13. Judy Biggert (R)
14. J. Dennis Hastert (R)
15. Thomas W. Ewing (R)
16. Donald A. Manzullo (R)
17. Lane Evans (D)
18. Ray LaHood (R)
19. David D. Phelps (D)
20. John Shimkus (R)

Indiana

1. Peter J. Visclosky (D)
2. David M. McIntosh (R)
3. Tim Roemer (D)
4. Mark E. Souder (R)
5. Stephen E. Buyer (R)
6. Dan Burton (R)
7. Edward A. Pease (R)
8. John N. Hostettler (R)
9. Baron P. Hill (D)
10. Julia Carson (D)

Iowa

1. James A. Leach (R)
2. Jim Nussle (R)
3. Leonard L. Boswell (D)
4. Greg Ganske (R)
5. Tom Latham (R)

Kansas

1. Jerry Moran (R)
2. Jim Ryun (R)
3. Dennis Moore (D)
4. Todd Tiahrt (R)

Kentucky

1. Ed Whitfield (R)
2. Ron Lewis (R)
3. Anne M. Northup (R)
4. Ken Lucas (D)
5. Harold Rogers (R)
6. Ernie Fletcher (R)

Louisiana

1. David Vitter (R)
2. William J. Jefferson (D)
3. W. J. "Billy" Tauzin (R)
4. Jim McCrery (R)
5. John Cooksey (R)
6. Richard Baker (R)
7. Christopher John (D)

Maine

1. Thomas H. Allen (D)
2. John E. Baldacci (D)

Maryland

1. Wayne T. Gilchrest (R)
2. Robert L. Ehrlich, Jr. (R)
3. Benjamin L. Cardin (D)
4. Albert Russell Wynn (D)
5. Steny H. Hoyer (D)
6. Roscoe G. Bartlett (R)
7. Elijah E. Cummings (D)
8. Constance A. Morella (R)

Massachusetts

1. John W. Olver (D)
2. Richard E. Neal (D)
3. James P. McGovern (D)
4. Barney Frank (D)
5. Martin T. Meehan (D)
6. John F. Tierney (D)
7. Edward J. Markey (D)
8. Michael E. Capuano (D)
9. John Joseph Moakley (D)
10. William D. Delahunt (D)

Michigan

1. Bart Stupak (D)
2. Peter Hoekstra (R)
3. Vernon J. Ehlers (R)
4. Dave Camp (R)
5. James A. Barcia (D)

6. Fred Upton (R)
7. Nick Smith (R)
8. Debbie Stabenow (D)
9. Dale E. Kildee (D)
10. David E. Bonior (D)
11. Joe Knollenberg (R)
12. Sander M. Levin (D)
13. Lynn Rivers (D)
14. John Conyers, Jr. (D)
15. Carolyn C. Kilpatrick (D)
16. John D. Dingell (D)

Minnesota

1. Gil Gutknecht (R)
2. David Minge (D)
3. Jim Ramstad (R)
4. Bruce F. Vento (D)
5. Martin Olav Sabo (D)
6. Bill Luther (D)
7. Collin C. Peterson (D)
8. James L. Oberstar (D)

Mississippi

1. Roger F. Wicker (R)
2. Bennie G. Thompson (D)
3. Charles W. "Chip" Pickering, Jr. (R)
4. Ronnie Shows (D)
5. Gene Taylor (D)

Missouri

1. William "Bill" Clay (D)
2. James M. Talent (R)
3. Richard A. Gephardt (D)
4. Ike Skelton (D)
5. Karen McCarthy (D)
6. Pat Danner (D)
7. Roy Blunt (R)
8. Jo Ann Emerson (R)
9. Kenny Hulshof (R)

Montana

AL Rick Hill (R)

Nebraska

1. Doug Bereuter (R)
2. Lee Terry (R)
3. Bill Barrett (R)

Nevada

1. Shelley Berkley (D)
2. Jim Gibbons (R)

New Hampshire

1. John E. Sununu (R)
2. Charles F. Bass (R)

New Jersey

1. Robert E. Andrews (D)
2. Frank A. LoBiondo (R)
3. Jim Saxton (R)
4. Christopher H. Smith (R)
5. Marge Roukema (R)
6. Frank Pallone, Jr. (D)
7. Bob Franks (R)
8. Bill Pascrell, Jr. (D)
9. Steven R. Rothman (D)
10. Donald M. Payne (D)
11. Rodney P. Frelinghuysen (R)
12. Rush D. Holt (D)
13. Robert Menendez (D)

New Mexico

1. Heather Wilson (R)
2. Joe Skeen (R)
3. Tom Udall (D)

New York

1. Michael P. Forbes (R)
2. Rick Lazio (R)
3. Peter T. King (R)
4. Carolyn McCarthy (D)
5. Gary L. Ackerman (D)
6. Gregory W. Meeks (D)

7. Joseph Crowley (D)
8. Jerrold Nadler (D)
9. Anthony D. Weiner (D)
10. Edolphus Towns (D)
11. Major R. Owens (D)
12. Nydia M. Velázquez (D)
13. Vito Fossella (R)
14. Carolyn B. Maloney (D)
15. Charles B. Rangel (D)
16. José E. Serrano (D)
17. Eliot L. Engel (D)
18. Nita M. Lowey (D)
19. Sue W. Kelly (R)
20. Benjamin A. Gilman (R)
21. Michael R. McNulty (D)
22. John E. Sweeney (R)
23. Sherwood L. Boehlert (R)
24. John M. McHugh (R)
25. James T. Walsh (R)
26. Maurice D. Hinchey (D)
27. Thomas M. Reynolds (R)
28. Louise McIntosh Slaughter (D)
29. John J. LaFalce (D)
30. Jack Quinn (R)
31. Amo Houghton (R)

North Carolina

1. Eva M. Clayton (D)
2. Bob Etheridge (D)
3. Walter B. Jones (R)
4. David E. Price (D)
5. Richard Burr (R)
6. Howard Coble (R)
7. Mike McIntyre (D)
8. Robin Hayes (R)
9. Sue Wilkins Myrick (R)
10. Cass Ballenger (R)
11. Charles H. Taylor (R)
12. Melvin L. Watt (D)

North Dakota

AL Earl Pomeroy (D)

Ohio

1. Steve Chabot (R)
2. Rob Portman (R)
3. Tony P. Hall (D)
4. Michael G. Oxley (R)
5. Paul E. Gillmor (R)
6. Ted Strickland (D)
7. David L. Hobson (R)
8. John A. Boehner (R)
9. Marcy Kaptur (D)
10. Dennis J. Kucinich (D)
11. Stephanie Tubbs Jones (D)
12. John R. Kasich (R)
13. Sherrod Brown (D)
14. Thomas C. Sawyer (D)
15. Deborah Pryce (R)
16. Ralph Regula (R)
17. James A. Traficant, Jr. (D)
18. Robert W. Ney (R)
19. Steven C. LaTourette (R)

Oklahoma

1. Steve Largent (R)
2. Tom A. Coburn (R)
3. Wes Watkins (R)
4. J. C. Watts, Jr. (R)
5. Ernest J. Istook, Jr. (R)
6. Frank D. Lucas (R)

Oregon

1. David Wu (D)
2. Greg Walden (R)
3. Earl Blumenauer (D)
4. Peter A. DeFazio (D)
5. Darlene Hooley (D)

Pennsylvania

1. Robert A. Brady (D)
2. Chaka Fattah (D)

3. Robert A. Borski (D)
4. Ron Klink (D)
5. John E. Peterson (R)
6. Tim Holden (D)
7. Curt Weldon (R)
8. James C. Greenwood (R)
9. Bud Shuster (R)
10. Don Sherwood (R)
11. Paul E. Kanjorski (D)
12. John P. Murtha (D)
13. Joseph M. Hoeffel (D)
14. William J. Coyne (D)
15. Patrick J. Toomey (R)
16. Joseph R. Pitts (R)
17. George W. Gekas (R)
18. Michael F. Doyle (D)
19. William F. Goodling (R)
20. Frank Mascara (D)
21. Phil English (R)

Rhode Island
1. Patrick J. Kennedy (D)
2. Robert A. Weygand (D)

South Carolina
1. Marshall "Mark" Sanford (R)
2. Floyd Spence (R)
3. Lindsey O. Graham (R)
4. Jim DeMint (R)
5. John M. Spratt, Jr. (D)
6. James E. Clyburn (D)

South Dakota
AL John R. Thune (R)

Tennessee
1. William L. Jenkins (R)
2. John J. Duncan, Jr. (R)
3. Zach Wamp (R)
4. Van Hilleary (R)
5. Bob Clement (D)
6. Bart Gordon (D)

7. Ed Bryant (R)
8. John S. Tanner (D)
9. Harold E. Ford, Jr. (D)

Texas
1. Max Sandlin (D)
2. Jim Turner (D)
3. Sam Johnson (R)
4. Ralph M. Hall (D)
5. Pete Sessions (R)
6. Joe Barton (R)
7. Bill Archer (R)
8. Kevin Brady (R)
9. Nick Lampson (D)
10. Lloyd Doggett (D)
11. Chet Edwards (D)
12. Kay Granger (R)
13. Mac Thornberry (R)
14. Ron Paul (R)
15. Rubén Hinojosa (D)
16. Silvestre Reyes (D)
17. Charles W. Stenholm (D)
18. Sheila Jackson-Lee (D)
19. Larry Combest (R)
20. Charles A. Gonzalez (D)
21. Lamar S. Smith (R)
22. Tom DeLay (R)
23. Henry Bonilla (R)
24. Martin Frost (D)
25. Ken Bentsen (D)
26. Richard K. Armey (R)
27. Solomon P. Ortiz (D)
28. Ciro D. Rodriguez (D)
29. Gene Green (D)
30. Eddie Bernice Johnson (D)

Utah
1. James V. Hansen (R)
2. Merrill Cook (R)
3. Chris Cannon (R)

Vermont
AL Bernie Sanders (I)

Virginia
1. Herbert H. "Herb" Bateman (R)
2. Owen B. Pickett (D)
3. Robert C. Scott (D)
4. Norman Sisisky (D)
5. Virgil H. Goode, Jr. (D)
6. Bob Goodlatte (R)
7. Tom Bliley, Jr. (R)
8. James P. Moran (D)
9. Rick Boucher (D)
10. Frank R. Wolf (R)
11. Thomas M. Davis (R)

Washington
1. Jay Inslee (D)
2. Jack Metcalf (R)
3. Brian Baird (D)
4. Doc Hastings (R)
5. George R. Nethercutt, Jr. (R)
6. Norman D. Dicks (D)
7. Jim McDermott (D)
8. Jennifer Dunn (R)
9. Adam Smith (D)

West Virginia
1. Alan B. Mollohan (D)
2. Robert E. Wise, Jr. (D)
3. Nick Joe Rahall II (D)

Wisconsin
1. Paul Ryan (R)
2. Tammy Baldwin (D)
3. Ron Kind (D)
4. Gerald D. Kleczka (D)
5. Thomas M. Barrett (D)
6. Thomas E. Petri (R)
7. David R. Obey (D)
8. Mark Green (R)
9. F. James Sensenbrenner, Jr. (R)

Wyoming
AL Barbara Cubin (R)

The Governors of the Fifty States

State	Governor	Current term[1]	State	Governor	Current term[1]
Ala.	Don Siegelman (D)	1999–2003	Mont.	Marc Racicot (R)	1997–2001
Alaska	Tony Knowles (D)	1998–2002[2]	Nebr.	Mike Johanns (R)	1999–2003
Ariz.	Jane Dee Hull (R)	1999–2003	Nev.	Kenny Guinn (R)	1999–2003
Ark.	Mike Huckabee (R)	1999–2003	N.H.	Jeanne Shaheen (D)	1999–2001
Calif.	Gray Davis (D)	1999–2003	N.J.	Christine Todd Whitman (R)	1998–2002
Colo.	Bill Owens (R)	1999–2003	N.M.	Gary E. Johnson (R)	1999–2003
Conn.	John G. Rowland (R)	1999–2003	N.Y.	George E. Pataki (R)	1999–2003
Del.	Thomas R. Carper (D)	1997–2001	N.C.	James B. Hunt, Jr. (D)	1997–2001
Fla.	Jeb Bush (R)	1999–2003	N.D.	Edward T. Schafer (R)	1997–2001
Ga.	Roy E. Barnes (D)	1999–2003	Ohio	Bob Taft (R)	1999–2003
Hawaii	Benjamin J. Cayetano (D)	1998–2002[2]	Okla.	Frank Keating (R)	1999–2003
Idaho	Dirk Kempthorne (R)	1999–2003	Ore.	John Kitzhaber (D)	1999–2003
Ill.	George H. Ryan (R)	1999–2003	Pa.	Tom Ridge (R)	1999–2003
Ind.	Frank O'Bannon (D)	1997–2001	R.I.	Lincoln C. Almond (R)	1999–2003
Iowa	Tom Vilsack (D)	1999–2003	S.C.	Jim Hodges (D)	1999–2003
Kans.	Bill Graves (R)	1999–2003	S.D.	William J. Janklow (R)	1999–2003
Ky.	Paul E. Patton (D)	1995–1999[2]	Tenn.	Don Sundquist (R)	1999–2003
La.	Mike Foster (R)	1996–2000	Tex.	George W. Bush (R)	1999–2003
Maine	Angus S. King, Jr. (I)	1999–2003	Utah	Michael O. Leavitt (R)	1997–2001
Md.	Parris N. Glendening (D)	1999–2003	Vt.	Howard Dean (D)	1999–2001
Mass.	Argeo Paul Cellucci (R)	1999–2003	Va.	James S. Gilmore (R)	1998–2002
Mich.	John Engler (R)	1999–2003	Wash.	Gary Locke (D)	1997–2001
Minn.	Jesse Ventura (RF)[3]	1999–2003	W. Va.	Cecil H. Underwood (R)	1997–2001
Miss.	Kirk Fordice (R)	1996–2000	Wis.	Tommy G. Thompson (R)	1999–2003
Mo.	Mel Carnahan (D)	1997–2001	Wyo.	Jim Geringer (R)	1999–2003

1. Except where indicated, all terms begin and end in January. 2. Term begins and ends in December. 3. Reform Party.
NOTE: As of July 31, 1999.

Senate and House Standing Committees, 106th Congress

Committees of the Senate

Aging (20 members)
Chairman: Charles E. Grassley (Iowa)
Ranking Dem.: John B. Breaux (La.)

Agriculture, Nutrition, and Forestry (18 members)
Chairman: Richard G. Lugar (Ind.)
Ranking Dem.: Tom Harkin (Iowa)

Appropriations (28 members)
Chairman: Ted Stevens (Alaska)
Ranking Dem.: Robert C. Byrd (W.Va.)

Armed Services (20 members)
Chairman: John Warner (Va.)
Ranking Dem.: Carl Levin (Mich.)

Banking, Housing, and Urban Affairs (20 members)
Chairman: Phil Gramm (Tex.)
Ranking Dem.: Paul S. Sarbanes (Md.)

Budget (22 members)
Chairman: Pete V. Domenici (N.M.)
Ranking Dem.: Frank R. Lautenberg (N.J.)

Commerce, Science, and Transportation (20 members)
Chairman: John McCain (Ariz.)
Ranking Dem.: Ernest F. Hollings (S.C.)

Energy and Natural Resources (20 members)
Chairman: Frank H. Murkowski (Alaska)
Ranking Dem.: Jeff Bingaman (N.M.)

Environment and Public Works (18 members)
Chairman: John H. Chafee (R.I.)
Ranking Dem.: Max Baucus (Mont.)

Ethics (6 members)
Chairman: Robert C. Smith (N.H)
Ranking Dem.: Harry Reid (Nev.)

Finance (20 members)
Chairman: William V. Roth, Jr. (Del.)
Ranking Dem.: Daniel Patrick Moynihan (N.Y.)

Foreign Relations (18 members)
Chairman: Jesse Helms (N.C.)
Ranking Dem.: Joseph R. Biden Jr. (Del.)

Governmental Affairs (16 members)
Chairman: Fred Thompson (Tenn.)
Ranking Dem.: Joseph Liebermann (Conn.)

Health, Education, Labor, and Pensions (18 members)
Chairman: James M. Jeffords (Vt.)
Ranking Dem.: Edward M. Kennedy (Mass.)

Indian Affairs (14 members)
Chairman: Ben Nighthorse Campbell (Colo.)
Ranking Dem.: Daniel K. Inouye (Hawaii)

Intelligence (17 members)
Chairman: Richard C. Shelby (Ala.)
Ranking Dem.: Robert Kerrey (Neb.)

Judiciary (18 members)
Chairman: Orrin G. Hatch (Utah)
Ranking Dem.: Patrick J. Leahy (Vt.)

Rules and Administration (16 members)
Chairman: Mitch McConnell (Ky.)
Ranking Dem.: Christopher Dodd (Conn.)

Small Business (18 members)
Chairman: Christopher S. Bond (Mo.)
Ranking Dem.: John Kerry (Mass.)

Veterans' Affairs (12 members)
Chairman: Arlen Specter (Pa.)
Ranking Dem: John D. Rockefeller IV (W.Va.)

Year 2000 Technology Problem (9 members)
Chairman: Robert F. Bennett (Utah)
Ranking Dem: Christopher J. Dodd (Conn.)

Committees of the House

Agriculture (51 members)
Chairman: Larry Combest (Tex.)
Ranking Dem.: Charles W. Stenholm (Tex.)

Appropriations (61 members)
Chairman: C. W. Bill Young (Fla.)
Ranking Dem.: David R. Obey (Wis.)

Armed Services (60 members)
Chairman: Floyd D. Spence (S.C.)
Ranking Dem.: Ike Skelton (Mo.)

Banking and Financial Services (60 members)
Chairman: Jim Leach (Iowa)
Ranking Dem.: John J. LaFalce (N.Y.)

Budget (43 members)
Chairman: John R. Kasich (Ohio)
Ranking Dem.: John M. Spratt Jr. (S.C.)

Commerce (53 members)
Chairman: Thomas J. Bliley, Jr. (Va.)
Ranking Dem.: John D. Dingell (Mich.)

Education and the Workforce (49 members)
Chairman: Bill Goodling (Pa.)
Ranking Dem.: William L. Clay (Mo.)

Government Reform (44 members)
Chairman: Dan Burton (Ind.)
Ranking Dem.: Henry A. Waxman (Calif.)

House Administration (9 members)
Chairman: William M. Thomas (Calif.)
Ranking Dem.: Steny H. Hoyer (Md.)

International Relations (49 members)
Chairman: Benjamin A. Gilman (N.Y.)
Ranking Dem.: Sam Gejdenson (Conn.)

Judiciary (37 members)
Chairman: Henry J. Hyde (Ill.)
Ranking Dem.: John Conyers, Jr. (Mich.)

Resources (52 members)
Chairman: Don Young (Alaska)
Ranking Dem.: George Miller (Calif.)

Rules (13 members)
Chairman: David Dreier (Calif.)
Ranking Dem.: Joe Moakley (Mass.)

Science (48 members)
Chairman: F. James Sensenbrenner, Jr. (Wis.)
Ranking Dem.: Ralph M. Hall (Tex.)

Small Business (36 members)
Chairman: James M. Talent (Mo.)
Ranking Dem.: Nydia M. Velázquez (N.Y.)

Standards of Official Conduct (10 members)
Chairman: Lamar S. Smith (Tex.)
Ranking Dem.: Howard L. Berman (Calif.)

Transportation and Infrastructure (75 members)
Chairman: Bud Shuster (Pa.)
Ranking Dem.: James L. Oberstar (Minn.)

Veterans' Affairs (31 members)
Chairman: Bob Stump (Ariz.)
Ranking Dem.: Lane Evans (Ill.)

Ways and Means (39 members)
Chairman: Bill Archer (Texas)
Ranking Dem.: Charles B. Rangel (N.Y.)

Speakers of the House of Representatives

Dates served	Congress	Name and state	Dates served	Congress	Name and state
1789–1791	1	Frederick A. C. Muhlenberg (Pa.)	1869–1875	41–43	James G. Blaine (Maine)
1791–1793	2	Jonathan Trumbull (Conn.)	1875–1876	44	Michael C. Kerr (Ind.)[6]
1793–1795	3	Frederick A. C. Muhlenberg (Pa.)	1876–1881	44–46	Samuel J. Randall (Pa.)
1795–1799	4–5	Jonathan Dayton (N.J.)[1]	1881–1883	47	J. Warren Keifer (Ohio)
1799–1801	6	Theodore Sedgwick (Mass.)	1883–1889	48–50	John G. Carlisle (Ky.)
1801–1807	7–9	Nathaniel Macon (N.C.)	1889–1891	51	Thomas B. Reed (Maine)
1807–1811	10–11	Joseph B. Varnum (Mass.)	1891–1895	52–53	Charles F. Crisp (Ga.)
1811–1814	12–13	Henry Clay (Ky.)[2]	1895–1899	54–55	Thomas B. Reed (Maine)
1814–1815	13	Langdon Cheves (S.C.)	1899–1903	56–57	David B. Henderson (Iowa)
1815–1820	14–16	Henry Clay (Ky.)[3]	1903–1911	58–61	Joseph G. Cannon (Ill.)
1820–1821	16	John W. Taylor (N.Y.)	1911–1919	62–65	Champ Clark (Mo.)
1821–1823	17	Philip P. Barbour (Va.)	1919–1925	66–68	Frederick H. Gillett (Mass.)
1823–1825	18	Henry Clay (Ky.)	1925–1931	69–71	Nicholas Longworth (Ohio)
1825–1827	19	John W. Taylor (N.Y.)	1931–1933	72	John N. Garner (Tex.)
1827–1834	20–23	Andrew Stevenson (Va.)[4]	1933–1934	73	Henry T. Rainey (Ill.)[7]
1834–1835	23	John Bell (Tenn.)	1935–1936	74	Joseph W. Byrns (Tenn.)[8]
1835–1839	24–25	James K. Polk (Tenn.)	1936–1940	74–76	William B. Bankhead (Ala.)[9]
1839–1841	26	Robert M. T. Hunter (Va.)	1940–1947	76–79	Sam Rayburn (Tex.)
1841–1843	27	John White (Ky.)	1947–1949	80	Joseph W. Martin, Jr. (Mass.)
1843–1845	28	John W. Jones (Va.)	1949–1953	81–82	Sam Rayburn (Tex.)
1845–1847	29	John W. Davis (Ind.)	1953–1955	83	Joseph W. Martin, Jr. (Mass.)
1847–1849	30	Robert C. Winthrop (Mass.)	1955–1961	84–87	Sam Rayburn (Tex.)[10]
1849–1851	31	Howell Cobb (Ga.)	1963–1971	87–91	John W. McCormack (Mass.)[11]
1851–1855	32–33	Linn Boyd (Ky.)	1971–1977	92–94	Carl Albert (Okla.)[12]
1855–1857	34	Nathaniel P. Banks (Mass.)	1977–1987	95–99	Thomas P. O'Neill, Jr. (Mass.)[13]
1857–1859	35	James L. Orr (S.C.)	1987–1989	100–101	James C. Wright, Jr. (Tex.)[14]
1859–1861	36	Wm. Pennington (N.J.)	1989–1995	101–103	Thomas S. Foley (Wash.)
1861–1863	37	Galusha A. Grow (Pa.)	1995–1999	104–105	Newt Gingrich (Ga.)[15]
1863–1869	38–40	Schuyler Colfax (Ind.)	1999–	106–	Dennis Hastert (Ill.)
1869–1869	40	Theodore M. Pomeroy (N.Y.)[5]			

1. George Dent (Md.) was elected Speaker pro tempore for April 20 and May 28, 1798. 2. Resigned during second session of 13th Congress. 3. Resigned between first and second sessions of 16th Congress. 4. Resigned during first session of 23rd Congress. 5. Elected Speaker and served the day of adjournment. 6. Died between first and second sessions of 44th Congress. During first session, there were two Speakers pro tempore: Samuel S. Cox (N.Y.), appointed for Feb. 17, May 12, and June 19, 1876, and Milton Sayler (Ohio), appointed for June 4, 1876. 7. Died in 1934 after adjournment of second session of 73rd Congress. 8. Died during second session of 74th Congress. 9. Died during third session of 76th Congress. 10. Died between first and second sessions of 87th Congress. 11. Not a candidate in 1970 election. 12. Not a candidate in 1976 election. 13. Not a candidate in 1986 election. 14. Resigned during first session of 101st Congress. 15. Resigned Jan. 3, 1999, three days before the first session of the 106th Congress. *Source: Congressional Directory.*

Floor Leaders of the Senate

Democratic	Republican
Gilbert M. Hitchcock, Neb. (Min. 1919–20)	Charles Curtis, Kan. (Maj. 1925–29)
Oscar W. Underwood, Ala. (Min. 1920–23)	James E. Watson, Ind. (Maj. 1929–33)
Joseph T. Robinson, Ark. (Min. 1923–33, Maj. 1933–37)	Charles L. McNary, Ore. (Min. 1933–44)
Alben W. Barkley, Ky. (Maj. 1937–46, Min. 1947–48)	Wallace H. White, Jr., Maine (Min. 1944–47, Maj. 1947–48)
Scott W. Lucas, Ill. (Maj. 1949–50)	Kenneth S. Wherry, Neb. (Min. 1949–51)
Ernest W. McFarland, Ariz. (Maj. 1951–52)	Styles Bridges, N.H. (Min. 1951–52)
Lyndon B. Johnson, Tex. (Min. 1953–54, Maj. 1955–60)	Robert A. Taft, Ohio (Maj. 1953)
Mike Mansfield, Mont. (Maj. 1961–77)	William F. Knowland, Calif. (Maj. 1953–54, Min. 1955–58)
Robert C. Byrd, W. Va. (Maj. 1977–81, Min. 1981–86, Maj. 1987–88)	Everett M. Dirksen, Ill. (Min. 1959–69)
George John Mitchell, Maine (Maj. 1989–1994)	Hugh Scott, Pa. (Min. 1969–1977)
Thomas A. Daschle, S.D. (Min. 1995–)	Howard H. Baker, Jr., Tenn. (Min. 1977–81, Maj. 1981–84)
	Robert J. Dole, Kan. (Maj. 1985–86, Min. 1987–94, Maj. 1995–96)
	Trent Lott, Miss. (Maj. 1996–)

NOTE: Min. = Minority Leader; Maj. = Majority Leader. *Source:* United States Senate, Secretary for the Majority.

How a President Is Nominated and Elected

The Conventions

The National Conventions of both major parties are held during the summer of a presidential-election year. Earlier, each party selects delegates by primaries, conventions, committees, etc.

At each convention, a temporary chairman is chosen. After a credentials committee seats the delegates, a permanent chairman is elected. The convention then votes on a platform, drawn up by the platform committee.

By the third or fourth day, presidential nominations begin. The chairman calls the roll of states alphabetically. A state may place a candidate in nomination or yield to another state.

Voting, again alphabetically by roll call of states, begins after all nominations have been made and seconded. A simple majority is required in each party, although this may require many ballots.

Finally, the vice-presidential candidate is selected. Although there is no law saying that the candidates *must* come from different states, it is, practically, necessary for this to be the case. Otherwise, according to the Constitution (*see* the 12th Amendment), electors from that state could vote for only one of the candidates and would have to cast their other vote for some person of another state. This could result in a presidential candidate's receiving a majority electoral vote and his or her running mate's failing to do so.

The Electoral College

The next step in the process is the nomination of electors in each state, according to its laws. These electors must not be Federal office holders. In the November election, the voters cast their votes for electors, not for president. In some states, the ballots include only the names of the presidential and vice-presidential candidates; in others, they include only names of the electors. Nowadays, it is rare for electors to be split between parties. The last such occurrence was in North Carolina in 1968[1]; the last before that, in Tennessee in 1948. On three occasions (1824, 1876, and 1888), the presidential candidate with the largest popular vote failed to obtain an electoral-vote majority.

Each state has as many electors as it has Senators and Representatives. For the 1992 election, the total electors were 538, based on 100 Senators and 435 Representatives, plus 3 electoral votes from the District of Columbia as a result of the 23rd Amendment to the Constitution.

On the first Monday after the second Wednesday in December, the electors cast their votes in their respective state capitols. Constitutionally they may vote for someone other than the party candidate but usually they do not since they are pledged to one party and its candidate on the ballot. Should the presidential or vice-presidential candidate die between the November election and the December meetings, the electors pledged to vote for him or her could vote for whomever they pleased. However, it seems certain that the national committee would attempt to get an agreement among the state party leaders for a replacement candidate.

The votes of the electors, certified by the states, are sent to Congress, where the president of the Senate opens the certificates and has them counted in the presence of both houses on January 6. The new president is inaugurated at noon on January 20.

Should no candidate receive a majority of the electoral vote for president, the House of Representatives chooses a president from among the three highest candidates, voting, not as individuals, but as states, with a majority (now 26) needed to elect. Should no vice-presidential candidate obtain the majority, the Senate, voting as individuals, chooses from the highest two.

1. In 1956, one of Alabama's 11 electoral votes was cast for Walter B. Jones. In 1960, six of Alabama's 11 electoral votes and one of Oklahoma's eight electoral votes were cast for Harry Flood Byrd. (Byrd also received all eight of Mississippi's electoral votes.)

Electoral College List of States and Votes, 1996 Presidential Election

(total electoral votes: 538; majority needed to elect: 270)

State	Votes	State	Votes	State	Votes
Alabama	9	Kentucky	8	North Dakota	3
Alaska	3	Louisiana	9	Ohio	21
Arizona	8	Maine	4	Oklahoma	8
Arkansas	6	Maryland	10	Oregon	7
California	54	Massachusetts	12	Pennsylvania	23
Colorado	8	Michigan	18	Rhode Island	4
Connecticut	8	Minnesota	10	South Carolina	8
Delaware	3	Mississippi	7	South Dakota	3
District of Columbia	3	Missouri	11	Tennessee	11
Florida	25	Montana	3	Texas	32
Georgia	13	Nebraska	5	Utah	5
Hawaii	4	Nevada	4	Vermont	3
Idaho	4	New Hampshire	4	Virginia	13
Illinois	22	New Jersey	15	Washington	11
Indiana	12	New Mexico	5	West Virginia	5
Iowa	7	New York	33	Wisconsin	11
Kansas	6	North Carolina	14	Wyoming	3

Presidential Election of 1996, Electoral and Popular Vote Summary

Principal Candidates for President and Vice President:
Democratic—William J. Clinton; Albert A. Gore, Jr.
Republican—Robert J. Dole; Jack F. Kemp
Independent—H. Ross Perot; Pat Choate

	William J. Clinton		Robert J. Dole		H. Ross Perot		Electoral votes		
	Popular vote	%	Popular vote	%	Popular vote	%	D	R	I
Alabama	662,165	43%	769,044	50%	92,149	6%	0	9	0
Alaska	80,380	33	122,746	51	26,333	11	0	3	0
Arizona	653,288	46	622,073	44	112,072	8	8	0	0
Arkansas	475,171	54	325,416	37	69,884	8	6	0	0
California	5,119,835	51	3,828,380	38	697,847	7	54	0	0
Colorado	671,152	44	691,848	46	99,629	7	0	8	0
Connecticut	735,740	52	483,109	35	139,523	10	8	0	0
Delaware	140,355	52	99,062	37	28,719	11	3	0	0
D.C.	158,220	85	17,339	9	3,611	2	3	0	0
Florida	2,546,870	48	2,244,536	42	483,870	9	25	0	0
Georgia	1,053,849	46	1,080,843	47	146,337	6	0	13	0
Hawaii	205,012	57	113,943	32	27,358	7	4	0	0
Idaho	165,443	34	256,595	52	62,518	13	0	4	0
Illinois	2,341,744	54	1,587,021	37	346,408	8	22	0	0
Indiana	887,424	42	1,006,693	47	224,299	10	0	12	0
Iowa	620,258	50	492,644	40	105,159	8	7	0	0
Kansas	387,659	36	583,245	54	92,639	9	0	6	0
Kentucky	636,614	46	623,283	45	120,396	9	8	0	0
Louisiana	927,837	52	712,586	40	123,293	7	9	0	0
Maine	312,788	52	186,378	31	85,970	14	4	0	0
Maryland	966,207	54	681,530	38	115,812	6	10	0	0
Massachusetts	1,571,763	61	718,107	28	227,217	9	12	0	0
Michigan	1,989,653	52	1,481,212	38	336,670	9	18	0	0
Minnesota	1,120,438	51	766,476	35	257,704	12	10	0	0
Mississippi	394,022	44	439,838	49	52,222	6	0	7	0
Missouri	1,025,935	47	890,016	41	217,188	10	11	0	0
Montana	167,922	41	179,652	44	55,229	13	0	3	0
Nebraska	236,761	35	363,467	54	71,278	10	0	5	0
Nevada	203,974	44	199,244	43	43,986	9	4	0	0
New Hampshire	246,214	49	196,532	39	48,390	10	4	0	0
New Jersey	1,652,329	54	1,103,078	36	262,134	8	15	0	0
New Mexico	273,495	49	232,751	42	32,257	6	5	0	0
New York	3,756,177	59	1,933,492	31	503,458	8	33	0	0
North Carolina	1,107,849	44	1,225,938	49	168,059	7	0	14	0
North Dakota	106,905	40	125,050	47	32,515	12	0	3	0
Ohio	2,148,222	47	1,859,883	40	483,207	11	21	0	0
Oklahoma	488,105	40	582,315	48	130,788	11	0	8	0
Oregon	649,641	47	538,152	39	121,221	9	7	0	0
Pennsylvania	2,215,819	49	1,801,169	40	430,984	10	23	0	0
Rhode Island	233,050	60	104,683	27	43,723	11	4	0	0
South Carolina	506,283	44	573,458	50	64,386	5	0	8	0
South Dakota	139,333	43	150,543	46	31,250	10	0	3	0
Tennessee	909,146	48	863,530	46	105,918	5	11	0	0
Texas	2,459,683	44	2,736,167	49	378,537	7	0	32	0
Utah	221,633	33	361,911	54	66,461	10	0	5	0
Vermont	137,894	53	80,352	31	31,024	12	3	0	0
Virginia	1,091,060	45	1,138,350	47	159,861	7	0	13	0
Washington	1,123,323	50	840,712	37	201,003	9	11	0	0
West Virginia	327,812	51	233,946	37	71,639	11	5	0	0
Wisconsin	1,071,971	49	845,029	39	227,339	10	11	0	0
Wyoming	77,934	37	105,388	50	25,928	12	0	3	0
Total	**47,402,357**	**49%**	**39,198,755**	**41%**	**8,085,402**	**8%**	**379**	**159**	**0**

NOTE: Total electoral votes = 538. Total electoral votes needed to win = 270. *Source:* Federal Election Commission.

National Political Conventions Since 1856

Opening date	Party	Where held	Opening date	Party	Where held
June 17, 1856	Republican	Philadelphia	June 14, 1932	Republican	Chicago
June 2, 1856	Democratic	Cincinnati	June 27, 1932	Democratic	Chicago
May 16, 1860	Republican	Chicago	June 9, 1936	Republican	Cleveland
April 23, 1860	Democratic	Charleston and Baltimore	June 23, 1936	Democratic	Philadelphia
June 7, 1864	Republican[1]	Baltimore	June 24, 1940	Republican	Philadelphia
Aug. 29, 1864	Democratic	Chicago	July 15, 1940	Democratic	Chicago
May 20, 1868	Republican	Chicago	June 26, 1944	Republican	Chicago
July 4, 1868	Democratic	New York City	July 19, 1944	Democratic	Chicago
June 5, 1872	Republican	Philadelphia	June 21, 1948	Republican	Philadelphia
June 9, 1872	Democratic	Baltimore	July 12, 1948	Democratic	Philadelphia
June 14, 1876	Republican	Cincinnati	July 17, 1948	(3)	Birmingham
June 28, 1876	Democratic	St. Louis	July 22, 1948	Progressive	Philadelphia
June 2, 1880	Republican	Chicago	July 7, 1952	Republican	Chicago
June 23, 1880	Democratic	Cincinnati	July 21, 1952	Democratic	Chicago
June 3, 1884	Republican	Chicago	Aug. 20, 1956	Republican	San Francisco
July 11, 1884	Democratic	Chicago	Aug. 13, 1956	Democratic	Chicago
June 19, 1888	Republican	Chicago	July 25, 1960	Republican	Chicago
June 6, 1888	Democratic	St. Louis	July 11, 1960	Democratic	Los Angeles
June 7, 1892	Republican	Minneapolis	July 13, 1964	Republican	San Francisco
June 21, 1892	Democratic	Chicago	Aug. 24, 1964	Democratic	Atlantic City
June 16, 1896	Republican	St. Louis	Aug. 5, 1968	Republican	Miami Beach
July 7, 1896	Democratic	Chicago	Aug. 26, 1968	Democratic	Chicago
June 19, 1900	Republican	Philadelphia	July 10, 1972	Democratic	Miami Beach
July 4, 1900	Democratic	Kansas City	Aug. 21, 1972	Republican	Miami Beach
June 21, 1904	Republican	Chicago	July 12, 1976	Democratic	New York City
July 6, 1904	Democratic	St. Louis	Aug. 16, 1976	Republican	Kansas City, Mo.
June 16, 1908	Republican	Chicago	Aug. 11, 1980	Democratic	New York City
July 7, 1908	Democratic	Denver	July 14, 1980	Republican	Detroit
June 18, 1912	Republican	Chicago	Aug. 20, 1984	Republican	Dallas
June 25, 1912	Democratic	Baltimore	July 16, 1984	Democratic	San Francisco
June 7, 1916	Republican	Chicago	July 18, 1988	Democratic	Atlanta
June 14, 1916	Democratic	St. Louis	Aug. 15, 1988	Republican	New Orleans
June 8, 1920	Republican	Chicago	July 13, 1992	Democratic	New York City
June 28, 1920	Democratic	San Francisco	Aug. 17, 1992	Republican	Houston
June 10, 1924	Republican	Cleveland	Aug. 10, 1996	Republican	San Diego
June 24, 1924[2]	Democratic	New York City	Aug. 26, 1996	Democratic	Chicago
June 12, 1928	Republican	Kansas City	July 29, 2000	Republican	Philadelphia
June 26, 1928	Democratic	Houston	Aug. 14, 2000	Democratic	Los Angeles

1. The Convention adopted name Union party to attract War Democrats and others favoring prosecution of war. 2. In session until July 10, 1924. 3. States' Rights delegates from 13 southern states.

National Committee Chairs Since 1944

Chairman and (state)	Term	Chairman and (state)	Term
Republican		**Democratic**	
Herbert Brownell, Jr. (N.Y.)	1944–1946	Robert E. Hannegan (Mo.)	1944–1947
Carroll Reece (Tenn.)	1946–1948	J. Howard McGrath (R.I.)	1947–1949
Hugh D. Scott, Jr. (Pa.)	1948–1949	William M. Boyle, Jr. (Mo.)	1949–1951
Guy G. Gabrielson (N.J.)	1949–1952	Frank E. McKinney (Ind.)	1951–1952
Arthur E. Summerfield (Mich.)	1952–1953	Stephen A. Mitchell (Ill.)	1952–1954
Wesley Roberts (Kan.)	1953	Paul M. Butler (Ind.)	1955–1960
Leonard W. Hall (N.Y.)	1953–1957	Henry M. Jackson (Wash.)	1960–1961
Meade Alcorn (Conn.)	1957–1959	John M. Bailey (Conn.)	1961–1968
Thruston B. Morton (Ky.)	1959–1961	Lawrence F. O'Brien (Mass.)	1968–1969
William E. Miller (N.Y.)	1961–1964	Fred R. Harris (Okla.)	1969–1970
Dean Burch (Ariz.)	1964–1965	Lawrence F. O'Brien (Mass.)	1970–1972
Ray C. Bliss (Ohio)	1965–1969	Jean Westwood (Utah)	1972
Rogers C. B. Morton (Md.)	1969–1971	Robert S. Strauss (Tex.)	1972–1977
Robert Dole (Kan.)	1971–1973	Kenneth M. Curtis (Me.)	1977
George H. Bush (Tex.)	1973–1974	John C. White (Tex.)	1977–1981
Mary Louise Smith (Iowa)	1974–1977	Charles T. Manatt (Calif.)	1981–1985
William E. Brock III (Tenn.)	1977–1981	Paul G. Kirk, Jr. (Mass.)	1985–1989
Richard Richards (Utah)	1981–1983	Ronald H. Brown (D.C.)	1989–1993
Frank J. Fahrenkopf, Jr. (Nevada)	1983–1989	David Wilhelm (Ill.)	1993–1994
Lee Atwater (S.C.)	1989–1991	Christopher J. Dodd (Conn.)	1995–1996
Clayton K. Yeutter (Neb.)	1991–1992	Steven Grossman (Mass.)	1996–1997
Richard Bond (N.Y.)	1992–1993	Joe Andrew (Ind.)	1999–
Haley Barbour (Miss.)	1993–1997		
Jim Nicholson (Colo.)	1997–		

Republican National Committee: 310 First St., S.E., Washington, D. C. 20003. *Democratic National Committee:* 430 South Capitol St., S.E., Washington, D.C. 20003.

Presidential Elections, 1789–1996

For the original method of electing the president and the vice president (elections of 1789, 1792, 1796, and 1800), *see* Article II, Section 1, of the Constitution. The election of 1804 was the first one in which the electors voted for president and vice president on separate ballots. (See Amendment XII to the Constitution.)

Year	Presidential candidate	Party	Electoral votes	Year	Presidential candidate	Party	Electoral votes
1789[1]	George Washington	(no party)	69	1796	John Adams	Federalist	71
	John Adams	(no party)	34		Thomas Jefferson	Dem.-Rep.	68
	Scattering	(no party)	35		Thomas Pinckney	Federalist	59
	Votes not cast		8		Aaron Burr	Dem.-Rep.	30
					Scattering		48
1792	George Washington	Federalist	132				
	John Adams	Federalist	77	1800[2]	Thomas Jefferson	Dem.-Rep.	73
	George Clinton	Anti-Federalist	50		Aaron Burr	Dem.-Rep.	73
	Thomas Jefferson	Anti-Federalist	4		John Adams	Federalist	65
	Aaron Burr	Anti-Federalist	1		Charles C. Pinckney	Federalist	64
	Votes not cast		6		John Jay	Federalist	1

Year	Presidential candidate	Party	Electoral votes	Vice-presidential candidate	Party	Electoral votes
1804	Thomas Jefferson	Dem.-Rep.	162	George Clinton	Dem.-Rep.	162
	Charles C. Pinckney	Federalist	14	Rufus King	Federalist	14
1808	James Madison	Dem.-Rep.	122	George Clinton	Dem.-Rep.	113
	Charles C. Pinckney	Federalist	47	Rufus King	Federalist	47
	George Clinton	Dem.-Rep.	6	John Langdon	Ind. (no party)	9
	Votes not cast		1	James Madison	Dem.-Rep.	3
				James Monroe	Dem.-Rep.	3
				Votes not cast		1
1812	James Madison	Dem.-Rep.	128	Elbridge Gerry	Dem.-Rep.	131
	De Witt Clinton	Federalist	89	Jared Ingersoll	Federalist	86
	Votes not cast		1	Votes not cast		1
1816	James Monroe	Dem.-Rep.	183	Daniel D. Tompkins	Dem.-Rep.	183
	Rufus King	Federalist	34	John E. Howard	Federalist	22
	Votes not cast		4	James Ross	Ind. (no party)	5
				John Marshall	Federalist	4
				Robert G. Harper	Ind. (no party)	3
				Votes not cast		4
1820	James Monroe	Dem-Rep	231	Daniel D. Tompkins	Dem.-Rep.	218
	John Quincy Adams	Ind. (no party)	1	Richard Stockton	Ind. (no party)	8
	Votes not cast		3	Daniel Rodney	Ind. (no party)	4
				Richard Rush	Ind. (no party)	1
				Robert G. Harper	Ind. (no party)	1
				Votes not cast		3
1824[3]	John Quincy Adams	(no party)	84	John C. Calhoun	(no party)	182
	Andrew Jackson	(no party)	99	Nathan Sanford	(no party)	30
	William H. Crawford	(no party)	41	Nathaniel Macon	(no party)	24
	Henry Clay	(no party)	37	Andrew Jackson	(no party)	13
				Martin Van Buren	(no party)	9
				Henry Clay	(no party)	2
				Votes not cast		1
1828	Andrew Jackson	Democratic	178	John C. Calhoun	Democratic	171
	John Quincy Adams	Natl. Rep.	83	Richard Rush	Natl. Rep.	83
				William Smith	Democratic	7
1832	Andrew Jackson	Democratic	219	Martin Van Buren	Democratic	189
	Henry Clay	Natl. Rep.	49	John Sergeant	Natl. Rep.	49
	John Floyd	Ind. (no party)	11	Henry Lee	Ind. (no party)	11
	William Wirt	Antimasonic[4]	7	Amos Ellmaker	Antimasonic	7
	Votes not cast		2	William Wilkins	Ind. (no party)	30
				Votes not cast		2
1836	Martin Van Buren	Democratic	170	Richard M. Johnson[5]	Democratic	147
	William H. Harrison	Whig	73	Francis Granger	Whig	77
	Hugh L. White	Whig	26	John Tyler	Whig	47
	Daniel Webster	Whig	14	William Smith	Ind. (no party)	23
	W. P. Mangum	Ind. (no party)	11			

Year	Presidential candidate	Party	Electoral votes	Vice-presidential candidate	Party	Electoral votes
1840	William H. Harrison[6]	Whig	234	John Tyler	Whig	234
	Martin Van Buren	Democratic	60	Richard M. Johnson	Democratic	48
				L. W. Tazewell	Ind. (no party)	11
				James K. Polk	Democratic	1
1844	James K. Polk	Democratic	170	George M. Dallas	Democratic	170
	Henry Clay	Whig	105	Theo. Frelinghuysen	Whig	105
1848	Zachary Taylor[7]	Whig	163	Millard Fillmore	Whig	163
	Lewis Cass	Democratic	127	William O. Butler	Democratic	127
1852	Franklin Pierce	Democratic	254	William R. King	Democratic	254
	Winfield Scott	Whig	42	William A. Graham	Whig	42
1856	James Buchanan	Democratic	174	John C. Breckinridge	Democratic	174
	John C. Fremont	Republican	114	William L. Dayton	Republican	114
	Millard Fillmore	American[8]	8	A. J. Donelson	American[8]	8
1860	Abraham Lincoln	Republican	180	Hannibal Hamlin	Republican	180
	John C. Breckinridge	Democratic	72	Joseph Lane	Democratic	72
	John Bell	Const. Union	39	Edward Everett	Const. Union	39
	Stephen A. Douglas	Democratic	12	H. V. Johnson	Democratic	12
1864	Abraham Lincoln[9]	Union[10]	212	Andrew Johnson	Union[15]	212
	George B. McClellan	Democratic	21	G. H. Pendleton	Democratic	21
1868	Ulysses S. Grant	Republican	214	Schuyler Colfax	Republican	214
	Horatio Seymour	Democratic	80	Francis P. Blair, Jr.	Democratic	80
	Votes not counted[11]		23	Votes not counted[11]		23

NOTE: Due to the communications constrictions of the time and the lack of formal political party organizations, the framers of the Constitution specified that the president and vice president be chosen based upon the votes cast by members of an electoral college rather than by a direct popular vote. Eventually, states began to change the method by which electors cast their votes. Today, all but two states, Maine and Nebraska, have a winner-take-all system in which a popular vote decides which candidates will be given all of a given state's electoral votes. The number of popular votes won by each presidential candidate are listed here for elections beginning in 1872.

Year	Presidential candidate	Party	Electoral votes	Popular votes	Vice-presidential candidate and party
1872	Ulysses S. Grant	Republican	286	3,597,132	Henry Wilson—R
	Horace Greeley	Dem., Liberal Rep.	(12)	2,834,125	B. Gratz Brown—D, LR—(47)
	Thomas A. Hendricks	Democratic	42		Scattering—(19)
	B. Gratz Brown	Dem., Liberal Rep.	18		Votes not counted—(14)
	Charles J. Jenkins	Democratic	2		
	David Davis	Democratic	1		
	Votes not counted		17		
1876[13]	Rutherford B. Hayes	Republican	185	4,033,768	William A. Wheeler—R
	Samuel J. Tilden	Democratic	184	4,285,992	Thomas A. Hendricks—D
	Peter Cooper	Greenback	0	81,737	Samuel F. Cary—G
1880	James A. Garfield[14]	Republican	214	4,449,053	Chester A. Arthur—R
	Winfield S. Hancock	Democratic	155	4,442,035	William H. English—D
	James B. Weaver	Greenback	0	308,578	B. J. Chambers—G
1884	Grover Cleveland	Democratic	219	4,911,017	Thomas A. Hendricks—D
	James G. Blaine	Republican	182	4,848,334	John A. Logan—R
	Benjamin F. Butler	Greenback	0	175,370	A. M. West—G
	John P. St. John	Prohibition	0	150,369	William Daniel—P
1888	Benjamin Harrison	Republican	233	5,440,216	Levi P. Morton—R
	Grover Cleveland	Democratic	168	5,538,233	A. G. Thurman—D
	Clinton B. Fisk	Prohibition	0	249,506	John A. Brooks—P
	Alson J. Streeter	Union Labor	0	146,935	Charles E. Cunningham—UL
1892	Grover Cleveland	Democratic	277	5,556,918	Adlai E. Stevenson—D
	Benjamin Harrison	Republican	145	5,176,108	Whitelaw Reid—R
	James B. Weaver	People's[15]	22	1,041,028	James G. Field—Peo
	John Bidwell	Prohibition	0	264,133	James B. Cranfill—P
1896	William McKinley	Republican	271	7,035,638	Garret A. Hobart—R
	William J. Bryan	Dem., People's[15]	176	6,467,946	Arthur Sewall—D—(149) Thomas E. Watson—Peo—(27)
	John M. Palmer	Natl. Dem.	0	133,148	Simon B. Buckner—ND
	Joshua Levering	Prohibition	0	132,007	Hale Johnson—P

Year	Presidential candidate	Party	Electoral votes	Popular votes	Vice-presidential candidate and party
1900	William McKinley[16]	Republican	292	7,219,530	Theodore Roosevelt—R
	William J. Bryan	Dem., People's[15]	155	6,358,071	Adlai E. Stevenson—D, Peo
	Eugene V. Debs	Social Democratic	0	94,768	Job Harriman—SD
1904	Theodore Roosevelt	Republican	336	7,628,834	Charles W. Fairbanks—R
	Alton B. Parker	Democratic	140	5,084,491	Henry G. Davis—D
	Eugene V. Debs	Socialist	0	402,400	Benjamin Hanford—S
1908	William H. Taft	Republican	321	7,679,006	James S. Sherman—R
	William J. Bryan	Democratic	162	6,409,106	John W. Kern—D
	Eugene V. Debs	Socialist	0	402,820	Benjamin Hanford—S
1912	Woodrow Wilson	Democratic	435	6,286,214	Thomas R. Marshall—D
	Theodore Roosevelt	Progressive	88	4,126,020	Hiram Johnson—Prog
	William H. Taft	Republican	8	3,483,922	Nicholas M. Butler—R[17]
	Eugene V. Debs	Socialist	0	897,011	Emil Seidel—S
1916	Woodrow Wilson	Democratic	277	9,129,606	Thomas R. Marshall—D
	Charles E. Hughes	Republican	254	8,538,221	Charles W. Fairbanks—R
	A. L. Benson	Socialist	0	585,113	G. R. Kirkpatrick—S
1920	Warren G. Harding[18]	Republican	404	16,152,200	Calvin Coolidge—R
	James M. Cox	Democratic	127	9,147,353	Franklin D. Roosevelt—D
	Eugene V. Debs	Socialist	0	917,799	Seymour Stedman—S
1924	Calvin Coolidge	Republican	382	15,725,016	Charles G. Dawes—R
	John W. Davis	Democratic	136	8,385,586	Charles W. Bryan—D
	Robert M. LaFollette	Progressive, Socialist	13	4,822,856	Burton K. Wheeler—Prog, S
1928	Herbert Hoover	Republican	444	21,392,190	Charles Curtis—R
	Alfred E. Smith	Democratic	87	15,016,443	Joseph T. Robinson—D
	Norman Thomas	Socialist	0	267,420	James H. Maurer—S
1932	Franklin D. Roosevelt	Democratic	472	22,821,857	John N. Garner—D
	Herbert Hoover	Republican	59	15,761,841	Charles Curtis—R
	Norman Thomas	Socialist	0	884,781	James H. Maurer—S
1936	Franklin D. Roosevelt	Democratic	523	27,751,597	John N. Garner—D
	Alfred M. Landon	Republican	8	16,679,583	Frank Knox—R
	Norman Thomas	Socialist	0	187,720	George Nelson—S
1940	Franklin D. Roosevelt	Democratic	449	27,244,160	Henry A. Wallace—D
	Wendell L. Willkie	Republican	82	22,305,198	Charles L. McNary—R
	Norman Thomas	Socialist	0	99,557	Maynard C. Krueger—S
1944	Franklin D. Roosevelt[19]	Democratic	432	25,602,504	Harry S. Truman—D
	Thomas E. Dewey	Republican	99	22,006,285	John W. Bricker—R
	Norman Thomas	Socialist	0	80,518	Darlington Hoopes—S
1948	Harry S. Truman	Democratic	303	24,179,345	Alben W. Barkley—D
	Thomas E. Dewey	Republican	189	21,991,291	Earl Warren—R
	J. Strom Thurmond	States' Rights Dem.	39	1,176,125	Fielding L. Wright—SR
	Henry A. Wallace	Progressive	0	1,157,326	Glen Taylor—Prog
	Norman Thomas	Socialist	0	139,572	Tucker P. Smith—S
1952	Dwight D. Eisenhower	Republican	442	33,936,234	Richard M. Nixon—R
	Adlai E. Stevenson	Democratic	89	27,314,992	John J. Sparkman—D
1956	Dwight D. Eisenhower	Republican	457	35,590,472	Richard M. Nixon—R
	Adlai E. Stevenson	Democratic	73[20]	26,022,752	Estes Kefauver—D
1960	John F. Kennedy[21]	Democratic	303	34,226,731	Lyndon B. Johnson—D
	Richard M. Nixon	Republican	219[22]	34,108,157	Henry Cabot Lodge—R
1964	Lyndon B. Johnson	Democratic	486	43,129,484	Hubert H. Humphrey—D
	Barry M. Goldwater	Republican	52	27,178,188	William E. Miller—R
1968	Richard M. Nixon	Republican	301	31,785,480	Spiro T. Agnew—R
	Hubert H. Humphrey	Democratic	191	31,275,166	Edmund S. Muskie—D
	George C. Wallace	American Independent	46	9,906,473	Curtis F. LeMay—AI
1972	Richard M. Nixon[23]	Republican	520[24]	47,169,911	Spiro T. Agnew—R
	George McGovern	Democratic	17	29,170,383	Sargent Shriver—D
	John G. Schmitz	American	0	1,099,482	Thomas J. Anderson—A
1976	Jimmy Carter	Democratic	297	40,830,763	Walter F. Mondale—D
	Gerald R. Ford	Republican	240[25]	39,147,973	Robert J. Dole—R
	Eugene J. McCarthy	Independent	0	756,631	None

Year	Presidential candidate	Party	Electoral votes	Popular votes	Vice-presidential candidate and party
1980	Ronald Reagan	Republican	489	43,899,248	George Bush—R
	Jimmy Carter	Democratic	49	36,481,435	Walter F. Mondale—D
	John B. Anderson	Independent	0	5,719,437	Patrick J. Lucey—I
1984	Ronald Reagan	Republican	525	54,455,075	George Bush—R
	Walter F. Mondale	Democratic	13	37,577,185	Geraldine A. Ferraro—D
1988	George H. Bush	Republican	426	48,886,097	J. Danforth Quayle—R
	Michael S. Dukakis	Democratic	111[26]	41,809,074	Lloyd Bentsen—D
1992	William J. Clinton	Democratic	370	44,909,889	Albert A. Gore, Jr.—D
	George H. Bush	Republican	168	39,104,545	J. Danforth Quayle—R
	H. Ross Perot	Independent	0	19,742,267	James B. Stockdale—I
1996	William J. Clinton	Democratic	379	47,402,357	Albert A. Gore, Jr.—D
	Robert J. Dole	Republican	159	39,198,755	Jack F. Kemp—R
	H. Ross Perot	Independent	0	8,085,402	Pat Choate—I

1. Only 10 states participated in the election. The New York legislature chose no electors, and North Carolina and Rhode Island had not yet ratified the Constitution. 2. As Jefferson and Burr were tied, the House of Representatives chose the president. In a vote by states, 10 votes were cast for Jefferson, 4 for Burr; 2 votes were not cast. 3. As no candidate had an electoral-vote majority, the House of Representatives chose the president from the first three. In a vote by states, 13 votes were cast for Adams, 7 for Jackson, and 4 for Crawford. 4. The Antimasonic Party on Sept. 26, 1831, was the first party to hold a nominating convention to choose candidates for president and vice president. 5. As Johnson did not have an electoral-vote majority, the Senate chose him 33–14 over Granger, the others being legally out of the race. 6. Harrison died April 4, 1841, and Tyler succeeded him April 6. 7. Taylor died July 9, 1850, and Fillmore succeeded him July 10. 8. Also known as the Know-Nothing Party. 9. Lincoln died April 15, 1865, and Johnson succeeded him the same day. 10. Name adopted by the Republican National Convention of 1864. Johnson was a War Democrat. 11. 23 Southern electoral votes were excluded. 12. See Election of 1872 in Unusual Voting Results. 13. See Election of 1876 in Unusual Voting Results. 14. Garfield died Sept. 19, 1881, and Arthur succeeded him Sept. 20. 15. Members of People's Party were called Populists. 16. McKinley died Sept. 14, 1901, and Roosevelt succeeded him the same day. 17. James S. Sherman, Republican candidate for vice president, died Oct. 30, 1912, and the Republican electoral votes were cast for Butler. 18. Harding died Aug. 2, 1923, and Coolidge succeeded him Aug. 3. 19. Roosevelt died April 12, 1945, and Truman succeeded him the same day. 20. One electoral vote from Alabama was cast for Walter B. Jones. 21. Kennedy died Nov. 22, 1963, and Johnson succeeded him the same day. 22. Sen. Harry F. Byrd received 15 electoral votes. 23. Nixon resigned Aug. 9, 1974, and Gerald R. Ford succeeded him the same day. 24. One electoral vote from Virginia was cast for John Hospers, Libertarian Party. 25. One electoral vote from Washington was cast for Ronald Reagan. 26. One electoral vote from West Virginia was cast for Lloyd Bentsen.

Composition of Congress, by Political Party, 1971–1999

			House			Senate		
Year	President and party	Congress	Majority party	Minority party	Other	Majority party	Minority party	Other
1971[1]	Nixon (R)	92nd	D-254	R-180	—	D-54	R-44	2
1973[1,2]	Nixon (R)	93rd	D-239	R-192	1	D-56	R-42	2
1975[3]	Ford (R)	94th	D-291	R-144	—	D-60	R-37	2
1977[4]	Carter (D)	95th	D-292	R-143	—	D-61	R-38	1
1979[4]	Carter (D)	96th	D-276	R-157	—	D-58	R-41	1
1981[4]	Reagan (R)	97th	D-243	R-192	—	R-53	D-46	1
1983	Reagan (R)	98th	D-269	R-165	—	R-54	D-46	—
1985	Reagan (R)	99th	D-252	R-182	—	R-53	D-47	—
1987	Reagan (R)	100th	D-258	R-177	—	D-55	R-45	—
1989	Bush (R)	101st	D-259	R-174	—	D-55	R-45	—
1991[5]	Bush (R)	102nd	D-267	R-167	1	D-56	R-44	—
1993[5]	Clinton (D)	103rd	D-258	R-176	1	D-57	R-43	—
1995[5]	Clinton (D)	104th	R-230	D-204	1	R-52	D-48	—
1997[5]	Clinton (D)	105th	R-228	D-206	1	R-55	D-45	—
1999[5]	Clinton (D)	106th	R-223	D-211	1	R-55	D-45	—

NOTES: — Represents zero. D = Democrat, R = Republican. Data for beginning of first session of each Congress (as of January 3), except as noted. Excludes vacancies at beginning of session. 1. Senate had one Independent and one Conservative-Republican. 2. House had one Independent-Democrat. 3. Senate had one Independent, one Conservative-Republican, and one undecided (New Hampshire). 4. Senate had one Independent. 5. House had one Independent-Socialist. Source: U.S. Congress, Joint Committee on Printing, Congressional Directory.

Facts About Elections

Candidate with highest popular vote: Reagan (1984), 54,455,075.

Candidate with highest electoral vote: Reagan (1984), 525.

Candidate carrying most states: Nixon (1972) and Reagan (1984), 49.

Candidate running most times: Norman Thomas, six (1928, 1932, 1936, 1940, 1944, 1948).

Candidate elected, defeated, then reelected: Cleveland (1884, 1888, 1892).

Residency Requirements for Voting

The Supreme Court decision of March 21, 1972, declared lengthy requirements for voting in state and local elections unconstitutional and suggested that 30 days was an ample period. Most of the states have changed or eliminated their durational residency requirements to comply with the ruling, as shown.

State	Residency requirement
Alabama	No durational residency requirement. 10-day registration requirement. In-person registration by 5 p.m., eleven days before election date.
Alaska	30-day residency requirement. If otherwise qualified but has not been a resident of the election district for at least 30 days preceding the date of a presidential election, is entitled to register and vote for presidential and vice-presidential candidates.
Arizona	30-day residency requirement. Residency in the state 29 days preceding the election.
Arkansas	No durational residency requirement.
California	Must be a registered voter 29 days before an election; 20-day residency requirement.
Colorado	Residency requirement of 25 days immediately preceding the election.
Connecticut	No durational residency requirement. Registration deadline 14th day before election; registration and party enrollment deadline by 12 noon the day before primary.
Delaware	No durational residency requirement. Must reside in Delaware and register by the last day that the books are open for registration.
District of Columbia	No durational residency requirement. Registration stops 30 days before any election. Voters must inform Board of Elections of change of address within 30 days of moving.
Florida	No durational residency requirement. 29-day registration requirement before national election; 29-day registration requirement before first and second state primary.
Georgia	No durational residency requirement. 30-day registration requirement.
Hawaii	No durational residency requirement. 30-day registration requirement.
Idaho	30-day residency requirement. May register 25 days prior to any election with County Clerk. If eligible to vote, an individual may register in person at the polling place on election day at the resident precinct and complete a registration card, make an oath, and provide proof of residence.
Illinois	30-day residency requirement.
Indiana	30-day residency requirement.
Iowa	No durational residency requirement. 10-day registration requirement. In-person registration by 5 p.m., eleven days before election date.
Kansas	14-day residency requirement.
Kentucky	28-day residency requirement.
Louisiana	No durational residency requirement. Register 24 days prior to any election.
Maine	No durational residency requirement.
Maryland	No durational residency requirement.
Massachusetts	No durational residency requirement. No residency required to register to vote.
Michigan	30-day residency requirement.
Minnesota	Permits registration and voting on election day with approved ID; 20-day residency requirement.
Mississippi	30-day residency requirement. 30 days registration required; 60 days if registration is by mail.
Missouri	No durational residency requirement. Must be registered by the fourth Wednesday prior to election.
Montana	30-day residency requirement.
Nebraska	No durational residency requirement. Registration deadline is second Friday prior to election.
Nevada	30-day residency requirement.
New Hampshire	No durational residency requirement. Registration deadline is 10 days prior to election. Same-day registrations for federal and state elections.
New Jersey	30-day residency requirement.
New Mexico	No durational residency requirement. Must register 28 days before election.
New York	30-day residency requirement.
North Carolina	30-day residency requirement.
North Dakota	30-day residency requirement.
Ohio	30-day residency requirement.
Oklahoma	No durational residency requirement.
Oregon	Must register by close of business day of registering agencies (which varies), 21st day before the election.
Pennsylvania	30-day residency requirement. 30-day registration requirement.
Rhode Island	30-day residency requirement.
South Carolina	No durational residency requirement. Registration certificate not valid for 30 days, but if you move within the state you can vote in old precinct during the 30 days.
South Dakota	No durational residency requirement. 15-day registration requirement.
Tennessee	30-day residency requirement. 30-day registration requirement.
Texas	No durational residency requirement. 30-day registration requirement.
Utah	30-day residency requirement.
Vermont	10–12 day residency requirement. Administrative cut-off date for processing applications is second Saturday before the election, by 12 noon.
Virginia	No durational residency requirement.
Washington	30-day residency requirement. 30-day registration requirement.
West Virginia	No durational residency requirement. 30-day registration requirement.
Wisconsin	10-day residency requirement.
Wyoming	No durational residency requirement. 30-day registration requirement.

Source: Questionnaires to the states.

Plurality and Majority

In order to win a plurality, a candidate must receive a greater number of votes than anyone running against him. If he receives 50 votes, for example, and two other candidates receive 49 and 2, he will have a plurality of one vote over his closest opponent.

However, a candidate does not have a majority unless he receives more than 50% of the total votes cast. In the example above, the candidate does not have a majority, because his 50 votes are less than 50% of the 101 votes cast.

Unusual Voting Results

Election of 1872

The presidential and vice-presidential candidates of the Liberal Republicans and the northern Democrats in 1872 were Horace Greeley and B. Gratz Brown. Greeley died Nov. 29, 1872, before his 66 electors voted. In the electoral balloting for president, 63 of Greeley's votes were scattered among four other men, including Brown.

Election of 1876

In the election of 1876 Samuel J. Tilden, the Democratic candidate, received a popular majority but lacked one undisputed electoral vote to carry a clear majority of the electoral college. The crux of the problem was in the 22 electoral votes which were in dispute because Florida, Louisiana, South Carolina, and Oregon each sent in two sets of election returns.

In the three southern states, Republican election boards threw out enough Democratic votes to certify the Republican candidate, Hayes. In Oregon, the Democratic governor disqualified a Republican elector, replacing him with a Democrat. Since the Senate was Republican and the House of Representatives Democratic, it seemed useless to refer the disputed returns to the two houses for solution. Instead Congress appointed an Electoral Commission with five representatives each from the Senate, the House, and the Supreme Court. All but one Justice was named, giving the Commission seven Republican and seven Democratic members. The naming of the fifth Justice was left to the other four. He was a Republican who first favored Tilden but, under pressure from his party, switched to Hayes, ensuring his election by the Commission voting 8 to 7 on party lines.

Minority Presidents

Fourteen candidates (three of them twice) have become president of the United States with a popular vote less than 50% of the total cast. It should be noted, however, that in elections before 1872, presidential electors were not chosen by popular vote in all states. Adams's election in 1824 was by the House of Representatives, which chose him over Jackson, who had a plurality of both electoral and popular votes, but not a majority in the electoral college.

The "minority" presidents are listed below.

Votes Received by Minority Presidents

Year	President	Electoral percent	Popular percent	Year	President	Electoral percent	Popular percent
1824	John Q. Adams	31.8%	29.8%	1892	Grover Cleveland (D)	62.4%	46.0%
1844	James K. Polk (D)	61.8	49.3	1912	Woodrow Wilson (D)	81.9	41.8
1848	Zachary Taylor (W)	56.2	47.3	1916	Woodrow Wilson (D)	52.1	49.3
1856	James Buchanan (D)	58.7	45.3	1948	Harry S. Truman (D)	57.1	49.5
1860	Abraham Lincoln (R)	59.4	39.9	1960	John F. Kennedy (D)	56.4	49.7
1876	Rutherford B. Hayes (R)	50.1	47.9	1968	Richard M. Nixon (R)	56.1	43.4
1880	James A. Garfield (R)	57.9	48.3	1992	William J. Clinton (D)	68.8	43.0
1884	Grover Cleveland (D)	54.6	48.8	1996	William J. Clinton (D)	70.4	49.0
1888	Benjamin Harrison (R)	58.1	47.8				

National Voter Turnout in Federal Elections: 1960–1996

Year	Voting-age population	Voter registration	Voter turnout	Turnout of voting-age population (percent)
1998	200,929,000	141,850,558	73,117,022	36.4%
1996	196,511,000	146,211,960	96,456,345	49.1
1994	193,650,000	130,292,822	75,105,860	38.8
1992	189,529,000	133,821,178	104,405,155	55.1
1990	185,812,000	121,105,630	67,859,189	36.5
1988	182,778,000	126,379,628	91,594,693	50.1
1986	178,566,000	118,399,984	64,991,128	36.4
1984	174,466,000	124,150,614	92,652,680	53.1
1982	169,938,000	110,671,225	67,615,576	39.8
1980	164,597,000	113,043,734	86,515,221	52.6
1978	158,373,000	103,291,265	58,917,938	37.2
1976	152,309,190	105,037,986	81,555,789	53.6
1974	146,336,000	96,199,020[1]	55,943,834	38.2

Year	Voting-age population	Voter registration	Voter turnout	Turnout of voting-age population (percent)
1972	140,776,000	97,328,541	77,718,554	55.2%
1970	124,498,000	82,496,747[2]	58,014,338	46.6
1968	120,328,186	81,658,180	73,211,875	60.8
1966	116,132,000	76,288,283[3]	56,188,046	48.4
1964	114,090,000	73,715,818	70,644,592	61.9
1962	112,423,000	65,393,751[4]	53,141,227	47.3
1960	109,159,000	64,833,096[5]	68,838,204	63.1

1. Registrations from Iowa not included. 2. Registrations from Iowa and Mo. not included. 3. Registrations from Iowa, Kans., Miss., Mo., Nebr., and Wyo. not included. D.C. did not have independent status. 4. Registrations from Ala., Alaska, D.C., Iowa, Kans., Ky., Miss., Mo., Nebr., N.C., N.D., Okla., S.D., Wis., and Wyo. not included. 5. Registrations from Ala., Alaska, D.C., Iowa, Kans., Ky., Miss., Mo., Nebr., N.M., N.C., N.D., Okla., S.D., Wis., and Wyo. not included. *Source:* Federal Election Commission. Data drawn from Congressional Research Service reports, Election Data Services Inc., and State Election Offices.

The Declaration of Independence

On April 12, 1776, the legislature of North Carolina authorized its delegates to the Continental Congress to join with others in a declaration of separation from Great Britain; the first colony to instruct its delegates to take the actual initiative was Virginia on May 15. On June 7, 1776, Richard Henry Lee of Virginia offered a resolution to the Congress to the effect "that these United Colonies are, and of right ought to be, free and independent States. . . ." A committee consisting of Thomas Jefferson, John Adams, Benjamin Franklin, Robert R. Livingston, and Roger Sherman was organized to "prepare a declaration to the effect of the said first resolution." The Declaration of Independence was adopted on July 4, 1776. Most delegates signed the Declaration August 2, but George Wythe (Va.) signed August 27; Richard Henry Lee (Va.), Elbridge Gerry (Mass.), and Oliver Wolcott (Conn.) in September; Matthew Thornton (N.H.), not a delegate until September, in November; and Thomas McKean (Del.), although present on July 4, not until 1781 by special permission, having served in the army in the interim.

In Congress, July 4, 1776
The unanimous Declaration of the thirteen United States of America

When in the Course of human events it becomes necessary for one people to dissolve the political bands which have connected them with another, and to assume among the powers of the earth, the separate and equal station to which the Laws of Nature and of Nature's God entitle them, a decent respect to the opinions of mankind requires that they should declare the causes which impel them to the separation.

We hold these truths to be self-evident, that all men are created equal, that they are endowed by their Creator with certain unalienable Rights, that among these are Life, Liberty and the pursuit of Happiness.—That to secure these rights, Governments are instituted among Men, deriving their just powers from the consent of the governed.—That whenever any Form of Government becomes destructive of these ends, it is the Right of the People to alter or to abolish it, and to institute new Government, laying its foundation on such principles and organizing its powers in such form, as to them shall seem most likely to effect their Safety and Happiness. Prudence, indeed, will dictate that Governments long established should not be changed for light and transient causes; and accordingly all experience hath shewn that mankind are more disposed to suffer, while evils are sufferable, than to right themselves by abolishing the forms to which they are accustomed. But when a long train of abuses and usurpations, pursuing invariably the same Object evinces a design to reduce them under absolute Despotism, it is their right, it is their duty, to throw off such Government, and to provide new Guards for their future security.—Such has been the patient sufferance of these Colonies; and such is now the necessity which constrains them to alter their former Systems of Government. The history of the present King of Great Britain is a history of

repeated injuries and usurpations, all having in direct object the establishment of an absolute Tyranny over these States. To prove this, let Facts be submitted to a candid world.

He has refused his Assent to Laws, the most wholesome and necessary for the public good.

He has forbidden his Governors to pass Laws of immediate and pressing importance, unless suspended in their operation till his Assent should be obtained; and when so suspended, he has utterly neglected to attend to them.

He has refused to pass other Laws for the accommodation of large districts of people, unless those people would relinquish the right of Representation in the Legislature, a right inestimable to them and formidable to tyrants only.

He has called together legislative bodies at places unusual, uncomfortable, and distant from the depository of their Public Records, for the sole purpose of fatiguing them into compliance with his measures.

He has dissolved Representative Houses repeatedly, for opposing with manly firmness his invasions on the rights of the people.

He has refused for a long time, after such dissolutions, to cause others to be elected; whereby the Legislative Powers, incapable of Annihilation, have returned to the People at large for their exercise; the State remaining in the mean time exposed to all the dangers of invasion from without, and convulsions within.

He has endeavoured to prevent the population of these States; for that purpose obstructing the Laws for Naturalization of Foreigners; refusing to pass others to encourage their migrations hither, and raising the conditions of new Appropriations of Lands.

He has obstructed the Administration of Justice, by refusing his Assent to Laws for establishing Judiciary Powers.

He has made Judges dependent on his Will alone, for the tenure of their offices, and the amount and payment of their salaries.

He has erected a multitude of New Offices, and sent hither swarms of Officers to harass our people, and eat out their substance.

He has kept among us, in times of peace, Standing Armies without the Consent of our legislatures.

He has affected to render the Military independent of and superior to the Civil Power.

He has combined with others to subject us to a jurisdiction foreign to our constitution, and unacknowledged by our laws; giving his Assent to their Acts of pretended Legislation:

For quartering large bodies of armed troops among us:

For protecting them, by a mock Trial, from punishment for any Murders which they should commit on the Inhabitants of these States:

For cutting off our Trade with all parts of the world:

For imposing Taxes on us without our Consent:

For depriving us in many cases, of the benefits of Trial by Jury:

For transporting us beyond Seas to be tried for pretended offences:

For abolishing the free System of English Laws in a neighbouring Province, establishing therein an Arbitrary government, and enlarging its Boundaries so as to render it at once an example and fit instrument for introducing the same absolute rule into these Colonies:

For taking away our Charters, abolishing our most valuable Laws and altering fundamentally the Forms of our Governments:

For suspending our own Legislatures, and declaring themselves invested with power to legislate for us in all cases whatsoever.

He has abdicated Government here, by declaring us out of his Protection and waging War against us.

He has plundered our seas, ravaged our Coasts, burnt our towns, and destroyed the lives of our people.

He is at this time transporting large Armies of foreign Mercenaries to compleat the works of death, desolation, and tyranny, already begun with circumstances of Cruelty & Perfidy scarcely paralleled in the most barbarous ages, and totally unworthy the Head of a civilized nation.

He has constrained our fellow Citizens taken Captive on the high Seas to bear Arms against their Country, to become the executioners of their friends and Brethren, or to fall themselves by their Hands.

He has excited domestic insurrections amongst us, and has endeavoured to bring on the inhabitants of our frontiers, the merciless Indian Savages, whose known rule of warfare, is an undistinguished destruction of all ages, sexes and conditions.

In every stage of these Oppressions We have Petitioned for Redress in the most humble terms: Our repeated Petitions have been answered only by repeated injury, A Prince, whose character is thus marked by every act which may define a Tyrant, is unfit to be the ruler of a free people.

Nor have We been wanting in attentions to our British brethren. We have warned them from time to time of attempts by their legislature to extend an unwarrantable jurisdiction over us. We have reminded them of the circumstances of our emigration and settlement here. We have appealed to their native justice and magnanimity, and we have conjured them by the ties of our common kindred to disavow these usurpations, which would inevitably interrupt our connections and correspondence. They too have been deaf to the voice of justice and of consanguinity. We must, therefore, acquiesce in the necessity, which denounces our Separation, and hold them, as we hold the rest of mankind, Enemies in War, in Peace Friends.

We, therefore, the Representatives of the United States of America, in General Congress, Assembled, appealing to the Supreme Judge of the world for the rectitude of our intentions, do, in the Name, and by Authority of the good People of these Colonies, solemnly publish and declare, That these United Colonies are, and of Right ought to be Free and Independent States; that they are Absolved from all Allegiance to the British Crown, and that all political connection between them and the State of Great Britain, is and ought to be totally dissolved; and that as Free and Independent States, they have full Power to levy War, conclude Peace, contract Alliances, establish Commerce, and to do all other Acts and Things which Independent States may of right do.—And for the support of this Declaration, with a firm reliance on the protection of Divine Providence, we mutually pledge to each other our Lives, our Fortunes and our sacred Honor.

—John Hancock

New Hampshire
Josiah Bartlett
Wm. Whipple
Matthew Thornton

Rhode Island
Step. Hopkins
William Ellery

Connecticut
Roger Sherman
Sam'el Huntington
Wm. Williams
Oliver Wolcott

New York
Wm. Floyd
Phil. Livingston
Frans. Lewis
Lewis Morris

New Jersey
Richd. Stockton
Jno. Witherspoon
Fras. Hopkinson
John Hart
Abra. Clark

Pennsylvania
Robt. Morris
Benjamin Rush
Benj. Franklin
John Morton
Geo. Clymer
Jas. Smith
Geo. Taylor
James Wilson
Geo. Ross

Massachusetts-Bay
Saml. Adams

John Adams
Robt. Treat Paine
Elbridge Gerry

Delaware
Caesar Rodney
Geo. Read
Tho. M'Kean

Maryland
Samuel Chase
Wm. Paca
Thos. Stone
Charles Carroll of Carrollton

Virginia
George Wythe
Richard Henry Lee
Th. Jefferson

Benj. Harrison
Ths. Nelson, Jr.
Francis Lightfoot Lee
Carter Braxton

North Carolina
Wm. Hooper
Joseph Hewes
John Penn

South Carolina
Edward Rutledge
Thos. Heyward, Junr.
Thomas Lynch, Junr.
Arthur Middleton

Georgia
Button Gwinnett
Lyman Hall
Geo. Walton

Constitution of the United States of America

(Historical text has been edited to conform to contemporary American usage. The bracketed words are designations for your convenience; they are not part of the Constitution.)

The oldest federal constitution in existence was framed by a convention of delegates from twelve of the thirteen original states in Philadelphia in May, 1787, Rhode Island failing to send a delegate. George Washington presided over the session, which lasted until September 17, 1787. The draft (originally a preamble and seven Articles) was submitted to all thirteen states and was to become effective when ratified by nine states. It went into effect on the first Wednesday in March, 1789, having been ratified by New Hampshire, the ninth state to approve, on June 21, 1788. The states ratified the Constitution in the following order:

Delaware	December 7, 1787	South Carolina	May 23, 1788
Pennsylvania	December 12, 1787	New Hampshire	June 21, 1788
New Jersey	December 18, 1787	Virginia	June 25, 1788
Georgia	January 2, 1788	New York	July 26, 1788
Connecticut	January 9, 1788	North Carolina	November 21, 1789
Massachusetts	February 6, 1788	Rhode Island	May 29, 1790
Maryland	April 28, 1788		

[Preamble]

We the people of the United States, in order to form a more perfect Union, establish justice, insure domestic tranquility, provide for the common defence, promote the general welfare, and secure the blessings of liberty to ourselves and our posterity, do ordain and establish this Constitution for the United States of America.

Article I

Section 1

[Legislative powers vested in Congress.] All legislative powers herein granted shall be vested in a Congress of the United States, which shall consist of a Senate and House of Representatives.

Section 2

[Composition of the House of Representatives.—1.] The House of Representatives shall be composed of members chosen every second year by the people of the several States, and the electors in each State shall have the qualifications requisite for electors of the most numerous branch of the State Legislature.

[Qualifications of Representatives.—2.] No Person shall be a Representative who shall not have attained to the age of twenty-five years, and been seven years a citizen of the United States, and who shall not, when elected, be an inhabitant of that State in which he shall be chosen.

[Apportionment of Representatives and direct taxes—census.[1]—3.] (Representatives and direct taxes shall be apportioned among the several States which may be included within this Union, according to their respective numbers, which shall be determined by adding to the whole number of free persons, including those bound to service for a term of years, and excluding Indians not taxed, three fifths of all other persons.) The actual enumeration shall be made within three years after the first meeting of the Congress of the United States, and within every subsequent term of ten years, in such manner as they shall by law direct. The number of Representatives shall not exceed one for every thirty thousand, but each State shall have at least one Representa-

tive; and until such enumeration shall be made, the State of New Hampshire shall be entitled to choose three, Massachusetts eight, Rhode-Island and Providence Plantations one, Connecticut five, New York six, New Jersey four, Pennsylvania eight, Delaware one, Maryland six, Virginia ten, North Carolina five, South Carolina five, and Georgia three.

[Filling of vacancies in representation.—4.] When vacancies happen in the representation from any State, the Executive Authority thereof shall issue writs of election to fill such vacancies.

[Selection of officers; power of impeachment.—5.] The House of Representatives shall choose their Speaker and other officers; and shall have the sole power of impeachment.

Section 3[2]

[The Senate.—1.] The Senate of the United States shall be composed of two Senators from each State, chosen by the Legislature thereof, for six years; and each Senator shall have one vote.

[Classification of Senators; filling of vacancies.—2.] Immediately after they shall be assembled in consequence of the first election, they shall be divided as equally as may be into three classes. The seats of the Senators of the first class shall be vacated at the expiration of the second year, of the second class at the expiration of the fourth year, and of the third class at the expiration of the sixth year, so that one-third may be chosen every second year; and if vacancies happen by resignation, or otherwise, during the recess of the Legislature of any State, the Executive thereof may make temporary appointments (until the next meeting of the Legislature, which shall then fill such vacancies).

[Qualification of Senators.—3.] No person shall be a Senator who shall not have attained to the age of thirty years, and been nine years a citizen of the United States, and who shall not, when elected, be an inhabitant of that State for which he shall be chosen.

[Vice President to be President of Senate.—4.] The Vice President of the United States shall be President of the Senate, but shall have no vote, unless they be equally divided.

[Selection of Senate officers; President pro tempore.—5.] The Senate shall choose their other

---

1. The clause included in parentheses is amended by the 14th Amendment, Section 2. 2. The first paragraph of this section and the part of the second paragraph included in parentheses are amended by the 17th Amendment.

officers, and also a President pro tempore, in the absence of the Vice President, or when he shall exercise the office of President of the United States.

[Senate to try impeachments.—6.] The Senate shall have the sole power to try all impeachments. When sitting for that purpose, they shall be on oath or affirmation. When the President of the United States is tried, the Chief Justice shall preside: and no person shall be convicted without the concurrence of two thirds of the members present.

[Judgment in cases of Impeachment.—7.] Judgment in cases of impeachment shall not extend further than to removal from office, and disqualification to hold and enjoy any office of honor, trust, or profit under the United States: but the party convicted shall nevertheless be liable and subject to indictment, trial, judgment and punishment, according to Law.

Section 4

[Control of congressional elections.—1.] The times, places, and manner of holding elections for Senators and Representatives, shall be prescribed in each State by the Legislature thereof; but the Congress may at any time by law make or alter such regulations, except as to the places of choosing Senators.

[Time for assembling of Congress³—2.] The Congress shall assemble at least once in every year, and such meeting shall be on the first Monday in December, unless they shall by law appoint a different day.

Section 5

[Each house to be the judge of the election and qualifications of its members; regulations as to quorum.—1.] Each House shall be the judge of the elections, returns, and qualifications of its own members, and a majority of each shall constitute a quorum to do business; but a smaller number may adjourn from day to day, and may be authorized to compel the attendance of absent members, in such manner, and under such penalties as each House may provide.

[Each house to determine its own rules.—2.] Each House may determine the rules of its proceedings, punish its members for disorderly behavior, and, with the concurrence of two thirds, expel a member.

[Journals and yeas and nays.—3.] Each House shall keep a journal of its proceedings, and from time to time publish the same, excepting such parts as may in their judgment require secrecy; and the yeas and nays of the members of either House on any question shall, at the desire of one fifth of those present, be entered on the journal.

[Adjournment.—4.] Neither House, during the session of Congress, shall, without the consent of the other, adjourn for more than three days, nor to any other place than that in which the two Houses shall be sitting.

Section 6

[Compensation and privileges of members of Congress.—1.] The Senators and Representatives shall receive a compensation for their services, to be ascertained by law, and paid out of the Treasury of the United States. They shall in all cases, except treason, felony, and breach of the peace, be privileged from arrest during their attendance at the session of their respective Houses, and in going to and returning from the same; and for any speech or debate in either House, they shall not be questioned in any other place.

[Incompatible offices; exclusions.—2.] No Senator or Representative shall, during the time for which he was elected, be appointed to any civil office under the authority of the United States, which shall have been created, or the emoluments whereof shall have been increased during such time; and no person holding any office under the United States shall be a member of either House during his continuance in office.

Section 7

[Revenue bills to originate in House.—1.] All bills for raising revenue shall originate in the House of Representatives; but the Senate may propose or concur with amendments as on other bills.

[Manner of passing bills; veto power of President.—2.] Every bill which shall have passed the House of Representatives and the Senate, shall, before it becomes a law, be presented to the President of the United States; if he approve he shall sign it, but if not he shall return it, with his objections to that House in which it shall have originated, who shall enter the objections at large on their journal, and proceed to reconsider it. If after such reconsideration two thirds of that House shall agree to pass the bill, it shall be sent, together with the objections, to the other House, by which it shall likewise be reconsidered, and if approved by two thirds of that House, it shall become a law. But in all such cases the votes of both Houses shall be determined by yeas and nays, and the names of the persons voting for and against the bill shall be entered on the journal of each house, respectively. If any bill shall not be returned by the President within ten days (Sundays excepted) after it shall have been presented to him, the same shall be a law, in like manner as if he had signed it, unless the Congress by their adjournment prevent its return, in which case it shall not be a law.

[Concurrent orders or resolutions, to be passed by President.—3.] Every order, resolution, or vote to which the concurrence of the Senate and House of Representatives may be necessary (except on a question of adjournment) shall be presented to the President of the United States; and before the same shall take effect, shall be approved by him, or being disapproved by him, shall be repassed by two thirds of the Senate and House of Representatives, according to the rules and limitations prescribed in the case of a bill.

Section 8

[General powers of Congress.⁴]

[Taxes, duties, imposts, and excises.—1.] The Congress shall have power to lay and collect taxes, duties, imposts and excises, to pay the debts and provide for the common defense and general welfare of the United States; but all duties, imposts and excises shall be uniform throughout the United States;

---

3. Amended by the 20th Amendment, Section 2. 4. By the 16th Amendment, Congress is given the power to lay and collect taxes on income.

[Borrowing of money.—2.] To borrow money on the credit of the United States;

[Regulation of commerce.—3.] To regulate commerce with foreign nations, and among the several States, and with the Indian tribes;

[Naturalization and bankruptcy.—4.] To establish a uniform rule of naturalization, and uniform laws on the subject of bankruptcies throughout the United States;

[Money, weights and measures.—5.] To coin money, regulate the value thereof, and of foreign coin, and fix the standard of weights and measures;

[Counterfeiting.—6.] To provide for the punishment of counterfeiting the securities and current coin of the United States;

[Post offices.—7.] To establish post offices and post roads;

[Patents and copyrights.—8.] To promote the progress of science and useful arts, by securing for limited times to authors and inventors the exclusive right to their respective writings and discoveries;

[Inferior courts.—9.] To constitute tribunals inferior to the Supreme Court;

[Piracies and felonies.—10.] To define and punish piracies and felonies committed on the high seas, and offences against the law of nations;

[War; marque and reprisal.—11.] To declare war, grant letters of marque and reprisal, and make rules concerning captures on land and water;

[Armies.—12.] To raise and support armies, but no appropriation of money to that use shall be for a longer term than two years;

[Navy.—13.] To provide and maintain a navy;

[Land and naval forces.—14.] To make rules for the government and regulation of the land and naval forces;

[Calling out militia.—15.] To provide for calling forth the militia to execute the laws of the Union, suppress insurrections, and repel invasions;

[Organizing, arming, and disciplining militia. —16.] To provide for organizing, arming, and disciplining, the militia, and for governing such part of them as may be employed in the service of the United States, reserving to the States, respectively, the appointment of the officers, and the authority of training the militia according to the discipline prescribed by Congress;

[Exclusive legislation over District of Columbia.—17.] To exercise exclusive legislation in all cases whatsoever, over such district (not exceeding ten miles square) as may, by cession of particular States, and the acceptance of Congress, become the seat of the Government of the United States, and to exercise like authority over all places purchased by the consent of the Legislature of the State in which the same shall be, for the erection of forts, magazines, arsenals, dock-yards, and other needful buildings;—And

[To enact laws necessary to enforce Constitution.—18.] To make all laws which shall be necessary and proper for carrying into execution the foregoing powers, and all other powers vested by this Constitution in the Government of the United States, or in any department or officer thereof.

Section 9

[Migration or importation of certain persons not to be prohibited before 1808.—1.] The migration or importation of such persons as any of the States now existing shall think proper to admit, shall not be prohibited by the Congress prior to the year one thousand eight hundred and eight, but a tax or duty may be imposed on such importation, not exceeding ten dollars for each person.

[Writ of habeas corpus not to be suspended; exception.—2.] The privilege of the writ of habeas corpus shall not be suspended, unless when in cases of rebellion or invasion the public safety may require it.

[Bills of attainder and ex post facto laws prohibited.—3.] No bill of attainder or ex post facto law shall be passed.

[Capitation and other direct taxes.—4.] No capitation, or other direct, tax shall be laid, unless in proportion to the census or enumeration herein before directed to be taken.[5]

[Exports not to be taxed.—5.] No tax or duty shall be laid on articles exported from any State.

[No preference to be given to ports of any States; interstate shipping.—6.] No preference shall be given by any regulation of commerce or revenue to the ports of one State over those of another: nor shall vessels bound to, or from, one State, be obliged to enter, clear, or pay duties in another.

[Money, how drawn from treasury; financial statements to be published.—7.] No money shall be drawn from the Treasury, but in consequence of appropriations made by law; and a regular statement and account of the receipts and expenditures of all public money shall be published from time to time.

[Titles of nobility not to be granted; acceptance by government officers of favors from foreign powers.—8.] No title of nobility shall be granted by the United States: and no person holding any office of profit or trust under them, shall, without the consent of the Congress, accept of any present, emolument, office, or title, of any kind whatever, from any king, prince, or foreign state.

Section 10

[Limitations of the powers of the several States.—1.] No State shall enter into any treaty, alliance, or confederation; grant letters of marque and reprisal; coin money; emit bills of credit; make any thing but gold and silver coin a tender in payment of debts; pass any bill of attainder, ex post facto law, or law impairing the obligation of contracts, or grant any title of nobility.

[State imposts and duties.—2.] No State shall, without the consent of the Congress, lay any imposts or duties on imports or exports, except what may be absolutely necessary for executing its inspection laws; and the net produce of all duties and imposts, laid by any State on imports or exports, shall be for the use of the Treasury of the United States; and all such laws shall be subject to the revision and control of the Congress.

[Further restrictions on powers of States.—3.] No State shall, without the consent of Congress, lay any duty of tonnage, keep troops, or ships of war in time of peace, enter into any agreement or compact

---

5. *See* the 16th Amendment.

with another state, or with a foreign power, or engage in war, unless actually invaded, or in such imminent danger as will not admit of delay.

Article II

Section 1

[The President; the executive power.—1.] The executive power shall be vested in a President of the United States of America. He shall hold his office during the term of four years, and, together with the Vice President, chosen for the same term, be elected, as follows

[Appointment and qualifications of presidential electors.—2.] Each State shall appoint, in such manner as the Legislature thereof may direct, a number of electors, equal to the whole number of Senators and Representatives to which the State may be entitled in the Congress: but no Senator or Representative, or person holding an office of trust or profit under the United States, shall be appointed an elector.

[Original method of electing the President and Vice President.[6]] (The electors shall meet in their respective States, and vote by ballot for two persons, of whom one at least shall not be an inhabitant of the same State with themselves. And they shall make a list of all the persons voted for, and of the number of votes for each; which list they shall sign and certify, and transmit sealed to the seat of the Government of the United States, directed to the President of the Senate. The President of the Senate shall, in the presence of the Senate and House of Representatives, open all the certificates, and the votes shall then be counted. The person having the greatest number of votes shall be the President, if such number be a majority of the whole number of electors appointed; and if there be more than one who have such majority, and have an equal number of votes, then the House of Representatives shall immediately choose by ballot one of them for President; and if no person have a majority, then from the five highest on the list the said House shall in like manner choose the President. But in choosing the President, the votes shall be taken by States, the representation from each State having one vote; A quorum for this purpose shall consist of a member or members from two thirds of the States, and a majority of all the states shall be necessary to a choice. In every case, after the choice of the President, the person having the greatest number of votes of the electors shall be the Vice President. But if there should remain two or more who have equal votes, the Senate should choose from them by ballot the Vice President.)

[Congress may determine time of choosing electors and day for casting their votes.—3.] The Congress may determine the time of choosing the electors, and the day on which they shall give their votes; which day shall be the same throughout the United States.

[Qualifications for the office of President.[7]—4.] No person except a natural born citizen, or a citizen of the United States, at the time of the adoption of this Constitution, shall be eligible to the office of President; neither shall any person be eligible to that office who shall not have attained to the age of thirty-five years, and been fourteen years a resident within the United States.

[Filling vacancy in the office of President.[8]—5.] In case of the removal of the President from office, or of his death, resignation, or inability to discharge the powers and duties of the said office, the same shall devolve on the Vice President, and the Congress may by law provide for the case of removal, death, resignation or inability, both of the President and Vice President, declaring what officer shall then act as President, and such officer shall act accordingly, until the disability be removed, or a President shall be elected.

[Compensation of the President.—6.] The President shall, at stated times, receive for his services, a compensation, which shall neither be increased nor diminished during the period for which he shall have been elected, and he shall not receive within that period any other emolument from the United States, or any of them.

[Oath to be taken by the President.—7.] Before he enter on the execution of his office, he shall take the following oath or affirmation:—"I do solemnly swear (or affirm) that I will faithfully execute the office of President of the United States, and will to the best of my ability, preserve, protect, and defend the Constitution of the United States."

Section 2

[The President to be commander in chief of army and navy and head of executive departments; may grant reprieves and pardons.—1.] The President shall be Commander in Chief of the Army and Navy of the United States, and of the militia of the several States, when called into the actual service of the United States; he may require the opinion, in writing, of the principal officer in each of the executive departments, upon any subject relating to the duties of their respective offices, and he shall have power to grant reprieves and pardons for offences against the United States, except in cases of impeachment.

[President may, with concurrence of Senate, make treaties, appoint ambassadors, etc.; appointment of inferior officers, authority of Congress over.—2.] He shall have power, by and with the advice and consent of the Senate, to make treaties, provided two thirds of the Senators present concur; and he shall nominate, and by and with the advice and consent of the Senate, shall appoint ambassadors, other public ministers and consuls, judges of the Supreme Court, and all other officers of the United States, whose appointments are not herein otherwise provided for, and which shall be established by law: but the Congress may by law vest the appointment of such inferior officers, as they think proper, in the President alone, in the courts of law, or in the heads of departments.

[President may fill vacancies in office during recess of Senate.—3.] The President shall have power to fill up all vacancies that may happen during the recess of the Senate, by granting commissions which shall expire at the end of their session.

---

6. This clause has been superseded by the 12th Amendment. 7. For qualifications of the Vice President, *see* the 12th Amendment. 8. Amended by the 20th Amendment, Sections 3 and 4.

Section 3

[**President to give advice to Congress; may convene or adjourn it on certain occasions; to receive ambassadors, etc.; have laws executed and commission all officers.**] He shall from time to time give to the Congress information of the state of the Union, and recommend to their consideration such measures as he shall judge necessary and expedient; he may, on extraordinary occasions, convene both Houses, or either of them, and in case of disagreement between them, with respect to the time of adjournment, he may adjourn them to such time as he shall think proper; he shall receive ambassadors and other public ministers: he shall take care that the laws be faithfully executed, and shall commission all the officers of the United States.

Section 4

[**All civil officers removable by impeachment.**] The President, Vice President, and all civil officers of the United States shall be removed from office on impeachment for, and conviction of, treason, bribery, or other high crimes and misdemeanors.

Article III

Section 1

[**Judicial powers; how vested; term of office and compensation of judges.**] The judicial Power of the United States, shall be vested in one Supreme Court, and in such inferior courts as the Congress may from time to time ordain and establish. The judges, both of the supreme and inferior courts, shall hold their offices during good behavior, and shall, at stated times, receive for their services, a compensation, which shall not be diminished during their continuance in office.

Section 2

[**Jurisdiction of Federal courts[9]—1.**] The judicial power shall extend to all cases, in law and equity, arising under this Constitution, the laws of the United States, and treaties made, or which shall be made, under their authority; to all cases affecting ambassadors, other public ministers and consuls; to all cases of admiralty and maritime jurisdiction; to controversies to which the United States, shall be a party; to controversies between two or more States; between a State and citizens of another State; between citizens of different States; between citizens of the same State claiming lands under grants of different states, and between a State, or the citizens thereof, and foreign states, citizens, or subjects.

[**Original and appellate jurisdiction of Supreme Court.—2.**] In all cases affecting ambassadors, other public ministers and consuls, and those in which a State shall be party, the Supreme Court shall have original jurisdiction. In all the other cases before mentioned, the Supreme Court shall have appellate jurisdiction, both as to law and fact, with such exceptions, and under such regulations, as the Congress shall make.

[**Trial of all crimes, except impeachment, to be by jury.—3.**] The trial of all crimes, except in cases of impeachment, shall be by jury; and such trial shall be held in the State where the said crimes shall have been committed; but when not committed within any State, the trial shall be at such place or places as the Congress may by law have directed.

Section 3

[**Treason defined; conviction of.—1.**] Treason against the United States, shall consist only in levying war against them, or, in adhering to their enemies, giving them aid and comfort. No person shall be convicted of treason unless on the testimony of two witnesses to the same overt act, or on confession in open court.

[**Congress to declare punishment for treason; proviso.—2.**] The Congress shall have power to declare the punishment of treason, but no attainder of treason shall work corruption of blood, or forfeiture except during the life of the person attained.

Article IV

Section 1

[**Each State to give full faith and credit to the public acts and records of other States.**] Full faith and credit shall be given in each State to the public acts, records, and judicial proceedings of every other State. And the Congress may by general laws prescribe the manner in which such acts, records, and proceedings shall be proved, and the effect thereof.

Section 2

[**Privileges of citizens.—1.**] The citizens of each State shall be entitled to all privileges and immunities of citizens in the several States.

[**Extradition between the several States.—2.**] A person charged in any State with treason, felony, or other crime, who shall flee from justice, and be found in another State, shall on demand of the Executive authority of the State from which he fled, be delivered up, to be removed to the State having jurisdiction of the crime.

[**Persons held to labor or service in one State, fleeing to another, to be returned.—3.**] No person held to service or labor in one State, under the laws thereof, escaping into another, shall, in consequence of any law or regulation therein, be discharged from such service or labor, but shall be delivered up on claim of the party to whom such service or labor may be due.

Section 3

[**New States.—1.**] New States may be admitted by the Congress into this Union; but no new State shall be formed or erected within the jurisdiction of any other State; nor any State be formed by the junction of two or more States, or parts of States, without the consent of the Legislatures of the States concerned as well as of the Congress.

[**Regulations concerning territory.—2.**] The Congress shall have power to dispose of and make all needful rules and regulations respecting the territory or other property belonging to the United States; and nothing in this Constitution shall be so construed as to prejudice any claims of the United States, or of any particular State.

Section 4

[**Republican form of government and protection guaranteed the several States.**] The United States shall guarantee to every State in this Union a Republican form of government, and shall protect each of

---

9. This section is abridged by the 11th Amendment.

them against invasion; and on application of the Legislature, or of the Executive (when the Legislature cannot be convened) against domestic violence.

Article V

[**Ways in which the Constitution can be amended.**] The Congress, whenever two thirds of both Houses shall deem it necessary, shall propose amendments to this Constitution, or, on the application of the Legislatures of two thirds of the several States shall call a convention for proposing amendments, which, in either case, shall be valid to all intents and purposes, as part of this Constitution, when ratified by the Legislatures of three fourths of the several States, or by conventions in three fourths thereof, as the one or the other mode of ratification may be proposed by the Congress; provided that no amendment which may be made prior to the year one thousand eight hundred and eight shall in any manner affect the first and fourth clauses in the ninth Section of the first Article; and that no State, without its consent, shall be deprived of its equal suffrage in the Senate.

Article VI

[**Debts contracted under the confederation secured.—1.**] All debts contracted and engagements entered into, before the adoption of this Constitution, shall be as valid against the United States under this Constitution, as under the Confederation.

[**Constitution, laws, and treaties of the United States to be supreme.—2.**] This Constitution, and the laws of the United States which shall be made in pursuance thereof; and all treaties made, or which shall be made, under the authority of the United States, shall be the supreme law of the land; and the judges in every State shall be bound thereby, any thing in the Constitution or laws of any State to the contrary notwithstanding.

[**Who shall take constitutional oath; no religious test as to official qualification.—3.**] The Senators and Representatives before mentioned, and the members of the several State Legislatures, and all executive and judicial officers, both of the United States and of the several States, shall be bound by oath or affirmation, to support this Constitution; but no religious test shall ever be required as a qualification to any office or public trust under the United States.

Article VII

[**Constitution to be considered adopted when ratified by nine States.**] The ratification of the conventions of nine States shall be sufficient for the establishment of this Constitution between the States so ratifying the same.

Done in convention by the unanimous consent of the States present the seventeenth day of September in the year of our Lord one thousand seven hundred and eighty seven and of the independence of the United States of America the Twelfth. In witness whereof we have hereunto subscribed our names.

George Washington
President and Deputy from Virginia

New Hampshire	David Brearley	John Dickinson	**South Carolina**
John Langdon	Jona. Dayton	Richard Bassett	J. Rutledge
Nicholas Gilman		Jaco. Broom	Charles Cotesworth
Massachusetts	**Pennsylvania**	**Maryland**	Pinckney
Nathaniel Gorham	B. Franklin	James McHenry	Charles Pinckney
Rufus King	Thomas Mifflin	Dan. of St. Thos. Jenifer	Pierce Butler
Connecticut	Robt. Morris	Danl. Carroll	**Georgia**
Wm. Saml. Johnson	Geo. Clymer	**Virginia**	William Few
Roger Sherman	Thos. FitzSimons	John Blair	Abr. Baldwin
New York	Jared Ingersoll	James Madison, Jr.	Attest: William Jackson,
Alexander Hamilton	James Wilson		Secretary
	Gouv. Morris	**North Carolina**	
New Jersey	**Delaware**	Wm. Blount	
Wil. Livingston	Geo. Read	Richd Dobbs Spaight	
Wm. Paterson	Gunning Bedford Jun.	Hu. Williamson	

Amendments to the Constitution of the United States

(Amendments I to X inclusive, popularly known as the Bill of Rights, were proposed and sent to the states by the first session of the First Congress. They were ratified Dec. 15, 1791.)

Amendment I

[**Freedom of religion, speech, of the press, and right of petition.**] Congress shall make no law respecting an establishment of religion, or prohibiting the free exercise thereof; or abridging the freedom of speech, or of the press; or the right of the people peaceably to assemble, and to petition the Government for a redress of grievances.

Amendment II

[**Right of people to bear arms not to be infringed.**] A well regulated militia, being necessary to the security of a free State, the right of the people to keep and bear arms, shall not be infringed.

Amendment III

[Quartering of troops.] No soldier shall, in time of peace be quartered in any house, without the consent of the owner, nor in time of war, but in a manner to be prescribed by law.

Amendment IV

[Persons and houses to be secure from unreasonable searches and seizures.] The right of the people to be secure in their persons, houses, papers, and effects, against unreasonable searches and seizures, shall not be violated, and no warrants shall issue, but upon probable cause, supported by oath or affirmation, and particularly describing the place to be searched, and the persons or things to be seized.

Amendment V

[Trials for crimes; just compensation for private property taken for public use.] No person shall be held to answer for a capital, or otherwise infamous crime, unless on a presentment or indictment of a Grand Jury, except in cases arising in the land or naval forces, or in the militia, when in actual service in time of war or public danger; nor shall any person be subject for the same offence to be twice put in jeopardy of life or limb; nor shall be compelled in any criminal case to be a witness, against himself, nor be deprived of life, liberty, or property, without due process of law; nor shall private property be taken for public use, without just compensation.

Amendment VI

[Civil rights in trials for crimes enumerated.] In all criminal prosecutions, the accused shall enjoy the right to a speedy and public trial, by an impartial jury of the State and district wherein the crime shall have been committed, which district shall have been previously ascertained by law, and to be informed of the nature and cause of the accusation; to be confronted with the witnesses against him; to have compulsory process for obtaining witnesses in his favor, and to have the assistance of counsel for his defense.

Amendment VII

[Civil rights in civil suits.] In suits at common law, where the value in controversy shall exceed twenty dollars, the right of trial by jury shall be preserved, and no fact tried by a jury, shall be otherwise re-examined in any court of the United States, than according to the rules of the common law.

Amendment VIII

[Excessive bail, fines, and punishments prohibited.] Excessive bail shall not be required, nor excessive fines imposed, nor cruel and unusual punishments inflicted.

Amendment IX

[Reserved rights of people.] The enumeration in the Constitution, of certain rights, shall not be construed to deny or disparage others retained by the people.

Amendment X

[Powers not delegated, reserved to states and people respectively.] The powers not delegated to the United States by the Constitution, nor prohibited by it to the States, are reserved to the States, respectively, or to the people.

Amendment XI

(The proposed amendment was sent to the states Mar. 5, 1794, by the Third Congress. It was ratified Feb. 7, 1795.)

[Judicial power of United States not to extend to suits against a State.] The judicial power of the United States shall not be construed to extend to any suit in law or equity, commenced or prosecuted against one of the United States by citizens of another State, or by citizens or subjects of any foreign state.

Amendment XII

(The proposed amendment was sent to the states Dec. 12, 1803, by the Eighth Congress. It was ratified July 27, 1804.)

[Present mode of electing President and Vice-President by electors.[1]]

The electors shall meet in their respective states, and vote by ballot for President and Vice President, one of whom, at least, shall not be an inhabitant of the same state with themselves; they shall name in their ballots the person voted for as President, and in distinct ballots the person voted for as Vice President, and they shall make distinct lists of all persons voted for as President, and of all persons voted for as Vice President, and of the number of votes for each, which lists they shall sign and certify, and transmit sealed to the seat of the government of the United States, directed to the President of the Senate; the President of the Senate shall, in the presence of the Senate and House of Representatives, open all the certificates and the votes shall then be counted; the person having the greatest number of votes for President, shall be the President, if such number be a majority of the whole number of electors appointed; and if no person have such majority, then from the persons having the highest numbers not exceeding three on the list of those voted for as President, the House of Representatives shall choose immediately, by ballot, the President. But in choosing the President, the votes shall be taken by states, the representation from each State having one vote; a quorum for this purpose shall consist of a member or members from two thirds of the states, and a majority of all the states shall be necessary to a choice. And if the House of Representatives shall not choose a President whenever the right of choice shall devolve upon them, before the fourth day of March next following, then the Vice President shall act as President, as in the case of the death or other constitutional disability of the President. The person having the greatest number of votes as Vice President, shall be the Vice President, if such number be a majority of the whole number of electors appointed, and if no person have a majority, then from the two highest numbers on the list, the Senate shall choose the Vice President; a quorum for the purpose shall consist of two thirds of the whole

---

1. Amended by the 20th Amendment, Sections 3 and 4.

number of Senators, and a majority of the whole number shall be necessary to a choice. But no person constitutionally ineligible to the office of President shall be eligible to that of Vice President of the United States.

Amendment XIII

(The proposed amendment was sent to the states Feb. 1, 1865, by the Thirty-eighth Congress. It was ratified Dec. 6, 1865.)

Section 1

[Slavery prohibited.] Neither slavery nor involuntary servitude, except as a punishment for crime whereof the party shall have been duly convicted, shall exist within the United States, or any place subject to their jurisdiction.

Section 2

[Congress given power to enforce this article.] Congress shall have power to enforce this article by appropriate legislation.

Amendment XIV

(The proposed amendment was sent to the states June 16, 1866, by the Thirty-ninth Congress. It was ratified July 9, 1868.)

Section 1

[Citizenship defined; privileges of citizens.] All persons born or naturalized in the United States, and subject to the jurisdiction thereof, are citizens of the United States and of the State wherein they reside. No State shall make or enforce any law which shall abridge the privileges or immunities of citizens of the United States; nor shall any State deprive any person of life, liberty, or property, without due process of law; nor deny to any person within its jurisdiction the equal protection of the laws.

Section 2

[Apportionment of Representatives.] Representatives shall be apportioned among the several States according to their respective numbers, counting the whole number of persons in each State, excluding Indians not taxed. But when the right to vote at any election for the choice of electors for President and Vice President of the United States, Representatives in Congress, the executive and judicial officers of a State, or the members of the Legislature thereof, is denied to any of the male inhabitants of such State, being twenty-one years of age, and citizens of the United States, or in any way abridged, except for participation in rebellion, or other crime, the basis of representation therein shall be reduced in the proportion which the number of such male citizens shall bear to the whole number of male citizens twenty-one years of age in such State.

Section 3

[Disqualification for office; removal of disability.] No person shall be a Senator or Representative in Congress, or elector of President and Vice President, or hold any office, civil or military, under the United States, or under any State, who, having previously taken an oath, as a member of Congress, or as an officer of the United States, or as a member of any State Legislature, or as an executive or judicial officer of any State, to support the Constitution of the United States, shall have engaged in insurrection or rebellion against the same, or given aid or comfort to the enemies thereof. But Congress may, by a vote of two thirds of each House, remove such disability.

Section 4

[Public debt not to be questioned; payment of debts and claims incurred in aid of rebellion forbidden.] The validity of the public debt of the United States, authorized by law, including debts incurred for payment of pensions and bounties for services in suppressing insurrection or rebellion, shall not be questioned. But neither the United States nor any State shall assume or pay any debt or obligation incurred in aid of insurrection or rebellion against the United States, or any claim for the loss or emancipation of any slave; but all such debts, obligations, and claims shall be held illegal and void.

Section 5

[Congress given power to enforce this article.] The Congress shall have power to enforce, by appropriate legislation, the provisions of this article.

Amendment XV

(The proposed amendment was sent to the states Feb. 27, 1869, by the Fortieth Congress. It was ratified Feb. 3, 1870.)

Section 1

[Right of certain citizens to vote established.] The right of citizens of the United States to vote shall not be denied or abridged by the United States or by any State on account of race, color, or previous condition of servitude.

Section 2

[Congress given power to enforce this article.] The Congress shall have power to enforce this article by appropriate legislation.

Amendment XVI

(The proposed amendment was sent to the states July 12, 1909, by the Sixty-first Congress. It was ratified Feb. 3, 1913.)
[Taxes on income; Congress given power to lay and collect.] The Congress shall have power to lay and collect taxes on incomes, from whatever source derived, without apportionment among the several States, and without regard to any census or enumeration.

Amendment XVII

(The proposed amendment was sent to the states May 16, 1912, by the Sixty-second Congress. It was ratified April 8, 1913.)
[Election of United States Senators; filling of vacancies; qualifications of electors.] The Senate of the United States shall be composed of two Senators from each State, elected by the people thereof, for six years; and each Senator shall have one vote. The electors in each State shall have the qualifications requisite for electors of the most numerous branch of the State Legislatures.

When vacancies happen in the representation of any State in the Senate, the executive authority of such State shall issue writs of election to fill such vacancies: Provided, that the legislature of any State may empower the executive thereof to make temporary appointment until the people fill the vacancies by election as the legislature may direct.

This amendment shall not be so construed as to affect the election or term of any Senator chosen before it becomes valid as part of the Constitution.

Amendment XVIII[2]

(The proposed amendment was sent to the states Dec. 18, 1917, by the Sixty-fifth Congress. It was ratified by three quarters of the states by Jan. 16, 1919, and became effective Jan. 16, 1920.)

Section 1

[Manufacture, sale, or transportation of intoxicating liquors, for beverage purposes, prohibited.] After one year from the ratification of this article the manufacture, sale, or transportation of intoxicating liquors within, the importation thereof into, or the exportation thereof from the United States and all territory subject to the jurisdiction thereof for beverage purposes is hereby prohibited.

Section 2

[Congress and the several States given concurrent power to pass appropriate legislation to enforce this article.] The Congress and the several States shall have concurrent power to enforce this article by appropriate legislation.

Section 3

[Provisions of article to become operative, when adopted by three fourths of the States.] This article shall be inoperative unless it shall have been ratified as an amendment to the Constitution by the legislatures of the several States, as provided in the Constitution, within seven years from the date of the submission hereof to the States by Congress.

Amendment XIX

(The proposed amendment was sent to the states June 4, 1919, by the Sixty-sixth Congress. It was ratified Aug. 18, 1920.)

[The right of citizens to vote shall not be denied because of sex.] The right of citizens of the United States to vote shall not be denied or abridged by the United States or by any State on account of sex.

[Congress given power to enforce this article.] Congress shall have power to enforce this article by appropriate legislation.

Amendment XX

(The proposed amendment, sometimes called the "Lame Duck Amendment," was sent to the states Mar. 3, 1932, by the Seventy-second Congress. It was ratified Jan. 23, 1933; but, in accordance with Section 5, Sections 1 and 2 did not go into effect until Oct. 15, 1933.)

Section 1

[Terms of President, Vice President, Senators, and Representatives.] The terms of the President and Vice President shall end at noon on the twentieth day of January, and the terms of Senators and Representatives at noon on the third day of January, of the years in which such terms would have ended if this article had not been ratified; and the terms of their successors shall then begin.

Section 2

[Time of assembling Congress.] The Congress shall assemble at least once in every year, and such meeting shall begin at noon on the third day of January, unless they shall by law appoint a different day.

Section 3

[Filling vacancy in office of President.] If, at the time fixed for the beginning of the term of the President, the President-elect shall have died, the Vice President-elect shall become President. If a President shall not have been chosen before the time fixed for the beginning of his term, or if the President-elect shall have failed to qualify, then the Vice President shall have qualified; and the Congress may by law provide for the case wherein neither a President-elect nor a Vice President-elect shall have qualified, declaring who shall then act as President, or the manner in which one who is to act shall be selected, and such person shall act accordingly until a President or Vice President shall have qualified.

Section 4

[Power of Congress in Presidential succession.] The Congress may by law provide for the case of the death of any of the persons from whom the House of Representatives may choose a President whenever the right of choice shall have devolved upon them, and for the case of the death of any of the persons from whom the Senate may choose a Vice President whenever the right of choice shall have devolved upon them.

Section 5

[Time of taking effect.] Sections 1 and 2 shall take effect on the 15th day of October following the ratification of this article.

Section 6

[Ratification.] This article shall be inoperative unless it shall have been ratified as an amendment to the Constitution by the legislatures of three fourths of the several States within seven years from the date of its submission.

Amendment XXI

(The proposed amendment was sent to the states Feb. 20, 1933, by the Seventy-second Congress. It was ratified Dec. 5, 1933.)

Section 1

[Repeal of Prohibition Amendment.] The eighteenth article of amendment to the Constitution of the United States is hereby repealed.

Section 2

[Transportation of intoxicating liquors.] The transportation or importation into any State, territory, or possession of the United States for delivery or use therein of intoxicating liquors, in violation of the laws thereof, is hereby prohibited.

Section 3

[Ratification.] This article shall be inoperative unless it shall have been ratified as an amendment to the Constitution by convention in the several States, as provided in the Constitution, within seven years from the date of the submission thereof to the States by the Congress.

Amendment XXII

(The proposed amendment was sent to the states Mar. 21, 1947, by the Eightieth Congress. It was ratified Feb. 27, 1951.)

---

2. Repealed by the 21st Amendment.

Section 1
[**Limit to number of terms a President may serve.**] No person shall be elected to the office of the President more than twice, and no person who has held the office of President, or acted as President, for more than two years of a term to which some other person was elected President shall be elected to the office of the President more than once. But this article shall not apply to any person holding the office of President when this article was proposed by the Congress, and shall not prevent any person who may be holding the office of President, or acting as President, during the term within which this article becomes operative from holding the office of President or acting as President during the remainder of such term.

Section 2
[**Ratification.**] This article shall be inoperative unless it shall have been ratified as an amendment to the Constitution by the legislatures of three fourths of the several States within seven years from the date of its submission to the States by the Congress.

Amendment XXIII
(The proposed amendment was sent to the states June 16, 1960, by the Eighty-sixth Congress. It was ratified March 29, 1961.)

Section 1
[**Electors for the District of Columbia.**] The District constituting the seat of Government of the United States shall appoint in such manner as the Congress may direct: A number of electors of President and Vice President equal to the whole number of Senators and Representatives in Congress to which the District would be entitled if it were a State, but in no event more than the least populous State; they shall be in addition to those appointed by the States, but they shall be considered, for the purposes of the election of President and Vice President, to be electors appointed by a State; and they shall meet in the District and perform such duties as provided by the twelfth article of amendment.

Section 2
[**Congress given power to enforce this article.**] The Congress shall have the power to enforce this article by appropriate legislation.

Amendment XXIV
(The proposed amendment was sent to the states Aug. 27, 1962, by the Eighty-seventh Congress. It was ratified Jan. 23, 1964.)

Section 1
[**Payment of poll tax or other taxes not to be prerequisite for voting in federal elections.**] The right of citizens of the United States to vote in any primary or other election for President or Vice President, for electors for President or Vice President, or for Senator or Representative in Congress, shall not be denied or abridged by the United States or any State by reasons of failure to pay any poll tax or other tax.

Section 2
[**Congress given power to enforce this article.**] The Congress shall have the power to enforce this article by appropriate legislation.

Amendment XXV
(The proposed amendment was sent to the states July 6, 1965, by the Eighty-ninth Congress. It was ratified Feb. 10, 1967.)

Section 1
[**Succession of Vice President to Presidency.**] In case of the removal of the President from office or of his death or resignation, the Vice President shall become President.

Section 2
[**Vacancy in office of Vice President.**] Whenever there is a vacancy in the office of the Vice President, the President shall nominate a Vice President who shall take office upon confirmation by a majority vote of both Houses of Congress.

Section 3
[**Vice President as Acting President.**] Whenever the President transmits to the President pro tempore of the Senate and the Speaker of the House of Representatives his written declaration that he is unable to discharge the powers and duties of his office, and until he transmits to them a written declaration to the contrary, such powers and duties shall be discharged by the Vice President as Acting President.

Section 4
[**Vice President as Acting President.**] Whenever the Vice President and a majority of either the principal officers of the executive departments or of such other body as Congress may by law provide, transmit to the President pro tempore of the Senate and the Speaker of the House of Representatives their written declaration that the President is unable to discharge the powers and duties of his office, the Vice President shall immediately assume the powers and duties of the office as Acting President.

Thereafter, when the President transmits to the President pro tempore of the Senate and the Speaker of the House of Representatives his written declaration that no inability exists, he shall resume the powers and duties of his office unless the Vice President and a majority of either the principal officers of the executive department or of such other body as Congress may by law provide, transmit within four days to the President pro tempore of the Senate and the Speaker of the House of Representatives their written declaration that the President is unable to discharge the powers and duties of his office. Thereupon Congress shall decide the issue, assembling within forty-eight hours for that purpose if not in session. If the Congress, within twenty-one days after receipt of the latter written declaration, or, if Congress is not in session, within twenty-one days after Congress is required to assemble, determines by two thirds vote of both Houses that the President is unable to discharge the powers and duties of his office, the Vice President shall continue to discharge the same as Acting President; otherwise, the President shall resume the powers and duties of his office.

Amendment XXVI
(The proposed amendment was sent to the states Mar. 23, 1971, by the Ninety-second Congress. It was ratified July 1, 1971.)

Section 1
[**Voting for 18-year-olds.**] The right of citizens of the United States, who are 18 years of age or older,

to vote shall not be denied or abridged by the United States or by any state on account of age.

Section 2
[Congress given power to enforce this article.] The Congress shall have power to enforce this article by appropriate legislation.

Amendment XXVII
(Ratified May 7, 1992.)
[Congressional raises.] No law, varying the compensation for the services of the Senators and Representatives, shall take effect, until an election of Representatives shall have intervened.

Order of Presidential Succession

1. The Vice President
2. Speaker of the House
3. President pro tempore of the Senate
4. Secretary of State
5. Secretary of the Treasury
6. Secretary of Defense
7. Attorney General
8. Secretary of the Interior
9. Secretary of Agriculture
10. Secretary of Commerce
11. Secretary of Labor
12. Secretary of Health and Human Services
13. Secretary of Housing and Urban Development
14. Secretary of Transportation
15. Secretary of Energy
16. Secretary of Education
17. Secretary of Veterans Affairs

NOTE: An official cannot succeed to the Presidency unless that person meets the Constitutional requirements.

History of the Flag

Source: Encyclopaedia Britannica.

The first official American flag, the Continental or Grand Union flag, was displayed on Prospect Hill, Jan. 1, 1776, in the American lines besieging Boston. It had 13 alternate red and white stripes, with the British Union Jack in the upper left corner.

On June 14, 1777, the Continental Congress adopted the design for a new flag, which actually was the Continental flag with the red cross of St. George and the white cross of St. Andrew replaced on the blue field by 13 stars, one for each state. No rule was made as to the arrangement of the stars, and while they were usually shown in a circle, there were various other designs. It is uncertain when the new flag was first flown, but its first official announcement is believed to have been on Sept. 3, 1777.

The first public assertion that Betsy Ross made the first Stars and Stripes appeared in a paper read before the Historical Society of Pennsylvania on March 14, 1870, by William J. Canby, a grandson. However, Mr. Canby on later investigation found no official documents of any action by Congress on the flag before June 14, 1777. Betsy Ross's own story, according to her daughter, was that Washington, Robert Morris, and George Ross, as representatives of Congress, visited her in Philadelphia in June 1776, showing her a rough draft of the flag and asking her if she could make one. However, the only actual record of the manufacture of flags by Betsy Ross is a voucher in Harrisburg, Pa., for 14 pounds and some shillings for flags for the Pennsylvania navy.

On Jan. 13, 1794, Congress voted to add two stars and two stripes to the flag in recognition of the admission of Vermont and Kentucky to the Union. By 1818, there were 20 states in the Union, and as it was obvious that the flag would soon become unwieldy, Congress voted April 18 to return to the original 13 stripes and to indicate the admission of a new state simply by the addition of a star the following July 4. The 49th star, for Alaska, was added July 4, 1959; and the 50th star, for Hawaii, was added July 4, 1960.

The first Confederate flag, adopted in 1861 by the Confederate convention in Montgomery, Ala., was called the Stars and Bars; but because of its similarity in colors to the American flag, there was much confusion in the Battle of Bull Run. To remedy this situation, Gen. G. T. Beauregard suggested a battle flag, which was used by the Southern armies throughout the war. The flag consisted of a red field on which was placed a blue cross of St. Andrew separated from the field by a white fillet and adorned with 13 white stars for the Confederate states.[1] In May 1863, at Richmond, an official flag was adopted by the Confederate Congress. This flag was white and twice as long as wide; the union, two-thirds the width of the flag, contained the battle flag designed for Gen. Beauregard. A broad transverse stripe of red was added Feb. 4, 1865, so that the flag might not be mistaken for a signal of truce.

1. 11 states formally seceded, and unofficial groups in Kentucky and Missouri adopted ordinances of secession. On this basis, these two states were admitted to the Confederacy, although the official state governments remained in the Union.

The Pledge of Allegiance to the Flag[1]

I pledge allegiance to the Flag of the United States of America, and to the Republic for which it stands, one Nation under God,[2] indivisible, with liberty and justice for all.

1. The original pledge was published in the Sept. 8, 1892, issue of *The Youth's Companion* in Boston. For years, the authorship was in dispute between James B. Upham and Francis Bellamy of the magazine's staff. In 1939, after a study of the controversy, the United States Flag Association decided that authorship be credited to Bellamy.
2. The phrase "under God" was added to the pledge on June 14, 1954.

The Statue of Liberty

The Statue of Liberty ("Liberty Enlightening the World") is a 225-ton, steel-reinforced copper female figure, 152 ft. in height, facing the ocean from Liberty Island[1] in New York Harbor. The right hand holds aloft a torch, and the left hand carries a tablet upon which is inscribed: "July IV MDCCLXXVI."

The statue was designed by Frédéric Auguste Bartholdi of Alsace as a gift to the United States from the people of France to memorialize the alliance of the two countries in the American Revolution and their abiding friendship. The French people contributed the $250,000 cost.

The 150-foot pedestal was designed by Richard M. Hunt and built by Gen. Charles P. Stone, both Americans. It contains steel underpinnings designed by Alexander Eiffel of France to support the statue. The $270,000 cost was borne by popular subscription in this country. President Grover Cleveland accepted the statue for the United States on Oct. 28, 1886.

On Sept. 26, 1972, President Richard M. Nixon dedicated the American Museum of Immigration, housed in structural additions to the base of the statue. In 1984 scaffolding went up for a major restoration and the torch was extinguished on July 4. It was relit with much ceremony July 4, 1986 to mark its centennial.

On a tablet inside the pedestal is engraved the following sonnet, written by Emma Lazarus (1849–1887):

The New Colossus
Not like the brazen giant of Greek fame.
With conquering limbs astride from land to land;
Here at our sea-washed, sunset gates shall stand
A mighty woman with a torch, whose flame
Is the imprisoned lightning, and her name
Mother of Exiles. From her beacon-hand
Glows world-wide welcome; her mild eyes
    command
The air-bridged harbor that twin cities frame.
"Keep, ancient lands, your storied pomp!" cries she
With silent lips. "Give me your tired, your poor,
Your huddled masses yearning to breathe free,
The wretched refuse of your teeming shore.
Send these, the homeless, tempest-tost to me,
I lift my lamp beside the golden door!"

1. Called Bedloe's Island prior to 1956.

The Mayflower Compact

On Sept. 6, 1620, the *Mayflower,* a sailing vessel of about 180 tons, started her memorable voyage from Plymouth, England, with about 100[1] pilgrims aboard, bound for Virginia to establish a private permanent colony in North America. Arriving at what is now Provincetown, Mass., on Nov. 11 (Nov. 21, new-style calendar), 41 of the passengers signed the famous "Mayflower Compact" as the boat lay at anchor in that Cape Cod harbor. A small detail of the pilgrims, led by William Bradford, assigned to select a place for permanent settlement, landed at what is now Plymouth, Mass., on Dec. 21 (n.s.).

The text of the compact follows:

In the name of God, Amen. We, whose names are underwritten, the Loyal Subjects of our dread Sovereign Lord, King *James,* by the Grace of God, of *Great Britain, France* and *Ireland,* King, *Defender of the Faith,* &c.

Having undertaken for the Glory of God, and Advancement of the Christian Faith, and the Honour of our King and Country, a voyage to plant the first colony in the northern Parts of Virginia; do by these Presents, solemnly and mutually in the Presence of God and one of another, covenant and combine ourselves together into a civil Body Politick, for our better Ordering and Preservation, and Furtherance of the Ends aforesaid; And by Virtue hereof to enact, constitute, and frame, such just and equal Laws, Ordinances, Acts, Constitutions and Offices, from time to time, as shall be thought most meet and convenient for the General good of the Colony; unto which we promise all due Submission and Obedience.

In Witness whereof we have hereunto subscribed our names at *Cape Cod* the eleventh of *November,* in the Reign of our Sovereign Lord, King *James* of *England, France* and *Ireland,* the eighteenth, and of *Scotland* the fifty-fourth. *Anno Domini,* 1620

John Carver	William Mullins	John Billington	Peter Brown
Digery Priest	Thomas English	Thomas Tinker	John Turner
William Brewster	John Howland	Samuel Fuller	Edward Tilly
Edmund Margesson	Stephen Hopkins	Richard Clark	John Craxton
John Alden	Edward Winslow	John Allerton	Thomas Rogers
George Soule	Gilbert Winslow	Richard Warren	John Goodman
James Chilton	Miles Standish	Edward Liester	Edward Fuller
Francis Cooke	Richard Bitteridge	William Bradford	Richard Gardiner
Moses Fletcher	Francis Eaton	Thomas Williams	William White
John Ridgate	John Tilly	Isaac Allerton	Edward Doten
Christopher Martin			

1. Historians differ as to whether 100, 101, or 102 passengers were aboard.

The Star-Spangled Banner

Francis Scott Key, 1814

O say, can you see, by the dawn's early light,
What so proudly we hail'd at the twilight's last gleaming?
Whose broad stripes and bright stars, thro' the perilous fight,
O'er the ramparts we watch'd, were so gallantly streaming?
And the rockets' red glare, the bombs bursting in air,
Gave proof thro' the night that our flag was still there.
O say, does that star-spangled banner yet wave
O'er the land of the free and the home of the brave?

On the shore dimly seen thro' the mists of the deep,
Where the foe's haughty host in dread silence reposes,
What is that which the breeze, o'er the towering steep,
As it fitfully blows, half conceals, half discloses?
Now it catches the gleam of the morning's first beam,
In full glory reflected, now shines on the stream:
'Tis the star-spangled banner: O, long may it wave
O'er the land of the free and the home of the brave!

And where is that band who so vauntingly swore
That the havoc of war and the battle's confusion,
A home and a country should leave us no more?
Their blood has wash'd out their foul footsteps' pollution.
No refuge could save the hireling and slave
From the terror of flight or the gloom of the grave:
And the star-spangled banner in triumph doth wave
O'er the land of the free and the home of the brave.

O thus be it ever when free-men shall stand
Between their lov'd home and the war's desolation;
Blest with vict'ry and peace, may the heav'n-rescued land
Praise the Pow'r that hath made and preserv'd us a nation!
Then conquer we must, when our cause it is just,
And this be our motto: "In God is our trust!"
And the star-spangled banner in triumph shall wave
O'er the land of the free and the home of the brave!

On Sept. 13, 1814, Francis Scott Key visited the British fleet in Chesapeake Bay to secure the release of Dr. William Beanes, who had been captured after the burning of Washington, D.C. The release was secured, but Key was detained on ship overnight during the shelling of Fort McHenry, one of the forts defending Baltimore. In the morning, he was so delighted to see the American flag still flying over the fort that he began a poem to commemorate the occasion. First published under the title "Defense of Fort M'Henry," and later as "The Star-Spangled Banner," the poem soon attained wide popularity as sung to the tune "To Anacreon in Heaven." The origin of this tune is obscure, but it may have been written by John Stafford Smith, a British composer born in 1750. "The Star-Spangled Banner" was officially made the National Anthem by Congress in 1931, although it already had been adopted as such by the Army and the Navy.

Territorial Expansion

Accession	Date	Area[1]	Accession	Date	Area[1]
United States	—	3,536,278	Other territory	—	4,664
Territory in 1790	—	891,364	Philippines	1898	115,600[2]
Louisiana Purchase	1803	831,321	Puerto Rico	1899	3,426
Florida	1819	69,866	Guam	1899	209
Texas	1845	384,958	American Samoa	1900	77
Oregon	1846	283,439	Canal Zone[3]	1904	553
Mexican Cession	1848	530,706	Virgin Islands of U.S.	1917	134
Gadsden Purchase	1853	29,640	Trust Territory of Pacific Islands	1947	177[4]
Alaska	1867	591,004	All other	—	14
Hawaii	1898	6,471	**Total, 1990**	—	**3,787,319**

1. Total land and water area in square miles. 2. Became independent in 1946. 3. Reverted to Panama. 4. Land area only; Palau only Trust Territory remaining. *Source:* U.S. Bureau of the Census, Web: www.census.gov.

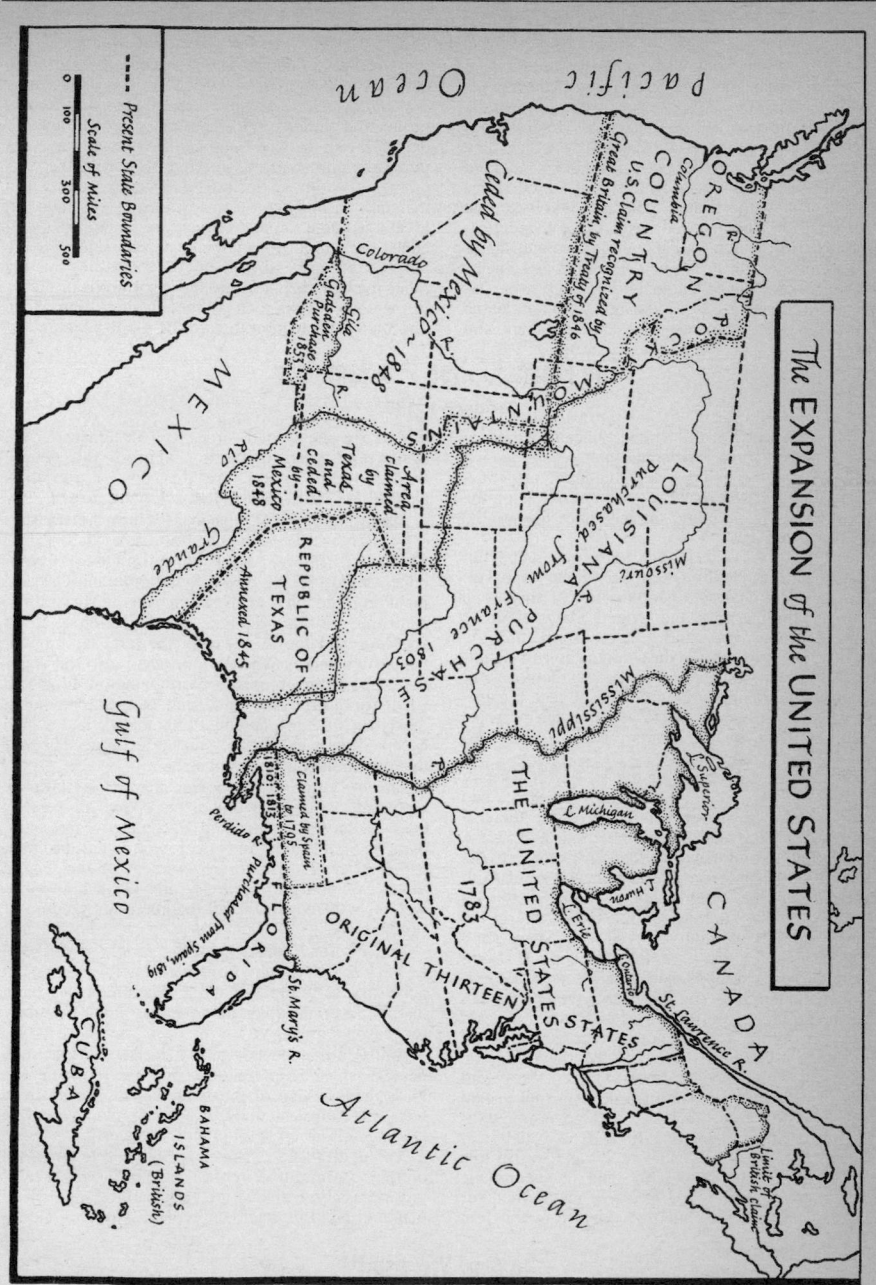

The EXPANSION of the UNITED STATES

The Monroe Doctrine

The Monroe Doctrine was announced in President James Monroe's message to Congress, during his second term on Dec. 2, 1823, in part as follows:

"In the discussions to which this interest has given rise, and in the arrangements by which they may terminate, the occasion has been deemed proper for asserting as a principle in which rights and interests of the United States are involved, that the American continents, by the free and independent condition which they have assumed and maintain, are henceforth not to be considered as subjects for future colonization by any European power. . . . We owe it, therefore, to candor and to the amicable relations existing between the United States and those powers to declare that we should consider any attempt on their part to extend their system to any portion of this hemisphere as dangerous to our peace and safety. With the existing colonies or dependencies of any European power we have not interfered and shall not interfere. But with the governments who have declared their independence and maintain it, and whose independence we have, on great consideration and on just principles, acknowledged, we could not view any interposition for the purpose of oppressing them or controlling in any other manner their destiny by any European power in any other light than as the manifestation of an unfriendly disposition toward the United States."

The Emancipation Proclamation

January 1, 1863

By the president of the United States of America: A Proclamation.

Whereas on the 22d day of September, A.D. 1862, a proclamation was issued by the president of the United States, containing, among other things, the following, to wit:

"That on the 1st day of January, A.D. 1863, all persons held as slaves within any State or designated part of a State the people whereof shall then be in rebellion against the United States shall be then, thenceforward, and forever free; and the executive government of the United States, including the military and naval authority thereof, will recognize and maintain the freedom of such persons and will do not act or acts to repress such persons, or any of them, in any efforts they may make for their actual freedom."

"That the executive will on the 1st day of January aforesaid, by proclamation, designate the States and parts of States, if any, in which the people thereof, respectively, shall then be in rebellion against the United States; and the fact that any State or the people thereof shall on that day be in good faith represented in the Congress of the United States by members chosen thereto at elections wherein a majority of the qualified voters of such States shall have participated shall, in the absence of strong countervailing testimony, be deemed conclusive evidence that such State and the people thereof are not then in rebellion against the United States."

Now, therefore, I, Abraham Lincoln, president of the United States, by virtue of the power in me vested as Commander-in-Chief of the Army and Navy of the United States in time of actual armed rebellion against the authority and government of the United States, and as a fit and necessary war measure for suppressing said rebellion, do, on this 1st day of January, A.D. 1863, and in accordance with my purpose so to do, publicly proclaimed for the full period of one hundred days from the first day above mentioned, order and designate as the States and parts of States wherein the people thereof, respectively, are this day in rebellion against the United States the following, to wit:

Arkansas, Texas, Louisiana (except the parishes of St. Bernard, Plaquemines, Jefferson, St. John, St. Charles, St. James, Ascension, Assumption, Terrebonne, Lafourche, St. Mary, St. Martin, and Orleans, including the city of New Orleans), Mississippi, Alabama, Florida, Georgia, South Carolina, North Carolina, and Virginia (except the forty-eight counties designated as West Virginia, and also the counties of Berkeley, Accomac, Northhampton, Elizabeth City, York, Princess Anne, and Norfolk, including the cities of Norfolk and Portsmouth), and which excepted parts are for the present left precisely as if this proclamation were not issued.

And by virtue of the power and for the purpose aforesaid, I do order and declare that all persons held as slaves within said designated States and parts of States are, and henceforward shall be, free; and that the Executive Government of the United States, including the military and naval authorities thereof, will recognize and maintain the freedom of said persons.

And I hereby enjoin upon the people so declared to be free to abstain from all violence, unless in necessary self-defense; and I recommend to them that, in all cases when allowed, they labor faithfully for reasonable wages.

And I further declare and make known that such persons of suitable condition will be received into the armed service of the United States to garrison forts, positions, stations, and other places, and to man vessels of all sorts in said service.

And upon this act, sincerely believed to be an act of justice, warranted by the Constitution upon military necessity, I invoke the considerate judgment of mankind and the gracious favor of Almighty God.

"In God We Trust"

"In God We Trust" first appeared on U.S. coins after April 22, 1864, when Congress passed an act authorizing the coinage of a 2-cent piece bearing this motto. Thereafter, Congress extended its use to other coins. On July 30, 1956, it became the national motto.

The Confederate States of America

State	Seceded from Union	Readmitted to Union[1]	State	Seceded from Union	Readmitted to Union[1]
1. South Carolina	Dec. 20, 1860	July 9, 1868	7. Texas	March 2, 1861	March 30, 1870
2. Mississippi	Jan. 9, 1861	Feb. 23, 1870	8. Virginia	April 17, 1861	Jan. 26, 1870
3. Florida	Jan. 10, 1861	June 25, 1868	9. Arkansas	May 6, 1861	June 22, 1868
4. Alabama	Jan. 11, 1861	July 13, 1868	10. North Carolina	May 20, 1861	July 4, 1868
5. Georgia	Jan. 19, 1861	July 15, 1870[2]	11. Tennessee	June 8, 1861	July 24, 1866
6. Louisiana	Jan. 26, 1861	July 9, 1868			

NOTE: Four other slave states—Delaware, Kentucky, Maryland, and Missouri—remained in the Union. 1. Date of readmission to representation in U.S. House of Representatives. 2. Second readmission date. First date was July 21, 1868, but the representatives were unseated March 5, 1869.

Lincoln's Gettysburg Address

The Battle of Gettysburg, one of the most noted battles of the Civil War, was fought on July 1–3, 1863. On Nov. 19, 1863, the field was dedicated as a national cemetery by President Lincoln in a two-minute speech that was to become immortal. At the time of its delivery the speech was relegated to the inside pages of the papers, while a two-hour address by Edward Everett, the leading orator of the time, caught the headlines.

The following is the text of the address revised by President Lincoln from his own notes:

Fourscore and seven years ago our fathers brought forth on this continent a new nation conceived in liberty and dedicated to the proposition that all men are created equal. Now we are engaged in a great civil war testing whether that nation, or any nation so conceived and so dedicated, can long endure. We are met on a great battlefield of that war. We have come to dedicate a portion of that field as a final resting-place for those who here gave their lives that that nation might live. It is altogether fitting and proper that we should do this. But, in a larger sense, we cannot dedicate, we cannot consecrate, we cannot hallow this ground. The brave men, living and dead, who struggled here have consecrated it far above our poor power to add or detract. The world will little note nor long remember what we say here, but it can never forget what they did here. It is for us the living rather to be dedicated here to the unfinished work which they who fought here have thus far so nobly advanced. It is rather for us to be here dedicated to the great task remaining before us—that from these honored dead we take increased devotion to that cause for which they gave the last full measure of devotion—that we here highly resolve that these dead shall not have died in vain, that this nation under God shall have a new birth of freedom, and that government of the people, by the people, for the people shall not perish from the earth.

The Early Congresses

At the urging of Massachusetts and Virginia, the First Continental Congress met in Philadelphia on Sept. 5, 1774, and was attended by representatives of all the colonies except Georgia. Patrick Henry of Virginia declared: "The distinctions between Pennsylvanians, New Yorkers, and New Englanders are no more. I am not a Virginian but an American." This Congress, which adjourned Oct. 26, 1774, passed intercolonial resolutions calling for extensive boycott by the colonies against British trade.

The following year, most of the delegates from the colonies were chosen by popular election to attend the Second Continental Congress, which assembled in Philadelphia on May 10. As war had already begun between the colonies and England, the chief problems before the Congress were the procuring of military supplies, the establishment of an army and proper defenses, the issuing of continental bills of credit, etc. On June 15, 1775, George Washington was elected to command the Continental army. Congress adjourned Dec. 12, 1776.

Other Continental Congresses were held in Baltimore (1776–1777), Philadelphia (1777), Lancaster, Pa. (1777), York, Pa. (1777–1778), and Philadelphia (1778–1781).

In 1781, the Articles of Confederation, although establishing a league of the thirteen states rather than a strong central government, provided for the continuance of Congress. Known thereafter as the Congress of the Confederation, it held sessions in Philadelphia (1781–1783), Princeton, N.J. (1783), Annapolis, Md. (1783–1784), and Trenton, N.J. (1784). Five sessions were held in New York City between the years 1785 and 1789.

The Congress of the United States, established by the ratification of the Constitution, held its first meeting on March 4, 1789, in New York City. Several sessions of Congress were held in Philadelphia, and the first meeting in Washington, D.C., was on Nov. 17, 1800.

Presidents of the Continental Congresses

Name	Elected	Birth and death dates	Name	Elected	Birth and death dates
Peyton Randolph, Va.	9/5/1774	c.1721–1775	John Hanson, Md.	11/5/1781	1715–1783
Henry Middleton, S.C.	10/22/1774	1717–1784	Elias Boudinot, N.J.	11/4/1782	1740–1821
Peyton Randolph, Va.	5/10/1775	c.1721–1775	Thomas Mifflin, Pa.	11/3/1783	1744–1800
John Hancock, Mass.	5/24/1775	1737–1793	Richard Henry Lee, Va.	11/30/1784	1732–1794
Henry Laurens, S.C.	11/1/1777	1724–1792	John Hancock, Mass.[1]	11/23/1785	1737–1793
John Jay, N.Y.	12/10/1778	1745–1829	Nathaniel Gorham, Mass.	6/6/1786	1738–1796
Samuel Huntington, Conn.	9/28/1779	1731–1796	Arthur St. Clair, Pa.	2/2/1787	1734–1818
Thomas McKean, Del.	7/10/1781	1734–1817	Cyrus Griffin, Va.	1/22/1788	1748–1810

1. Resigned May 29, 1786, never having served, because of continued illness.

The Great Seal of the U.S.

On July 4, 1776, the Continental Congress appointed a committee consisting of Benjamin Franklin, John Adams, and Thomas Jefferson "to bring in a device for a seal of the United States of America." After many delays, a verbal description of a design by William Barton was finally approved by Congress on June 20, 1782. The seal shows an American bald eagle with a ribbon in its mouth bearing the device *E pluribus unum* (One out of many). In its talons are the arrows of war and an olive branch of peace. On the reverse side it shows an unfinished pyramid with an eye (the eye of Providence) above it. Although this description was adopted in 1782, the first drawing was not made until four years later, and no die has ever been cut.

Assassinations and Attempts in U.S. Since 1865

Lincoln, Abraham (President of U.S.): Shot April 14, 1865, in Washington, D.C., by John Wilkes Booth; died April 15.

Seward, William H. (Secretary of State): Escaped assassination (though injured) April 14, 1865, in Washington, D.C., by Lewis Powell (or Paine), accomplice of John Wilkes Booth.

Garfield, James A. (President of U.S.): Shot July 2, 1881, in Washington, D.C., by Charles J. Guiteau; died Sept. 19.

McKinley, William (President of U.S.): Shot Sept. 6, 1901, in Buffalo by Leon Czolgosz; died Sept. 14.

Roosevelt, Theodore (ex-President of U.S.): Escaped assassination (though shot) Oct. 14, 1912, in Milwaukee while campaigning for President.

Cermak, Anton J. (Mayor of Chicago): Shot Feb. 15, 1933, in Miami by Giuseppe Zangara, who attempted to assassinate Franklin D. Roosevelt; Cermak died March 6.

Roosevelt, Franklin D. (President-elect of U.S.): Escaped assassination unhurt Feb. 15, 1933, in Miami.

Long, Huey P. (U.S. Senator from Louisiana): Shot Sept. 8, 1935, in Baton Rouge by Dr. Carl A. Weiss; died Sept. 10.

Truman, Harry S. (President of U.S.): Escaped assassination unhurt Nov. 1, 1950, in Washington, D.C., as 2 Puerto Rican nationalists attempted to shoot their way into Blair House.

Kennedy, John F. (President of U.S.): Shot Nov. 22, 1963, in Dallas, Tex., allegedly by Lee Harvey Oswald; died same day. Injured was Gov. John B. Connally of Texas. Oswald was shot and killed two days later by Jack Ruby.

King, Martin Luther, Jr. (civil rights leader): Shot April 4, 1968, in Memphis by James Earl Ray; died same day.

Malcolm X, also known as El-Hajj Malik El-Shabazz (black activist): Shot and killed in a New York City auditorium; his killer(s) were never positively identified.

Kennedy, Robert F. (U.S. Senator from New York): Shot June 5, 1968, in Los Angeles by Sirhan Bishara Sirhan; died June 6.

Wallace, George C. (Governor of Alabama): Shot and critically wounded in assassination attempt May 15, 1972, at Laurel, Md., by Arthur Herman Bremer. Wallace paralyzed from waist down.

Ford, Gerald R. (President of U.S.): Escaped assassination attempt Sept. 5, 1975, in Sacramento, Calif., by Lynette Alice (Squeaky) Fromme, who pointed but did not fire .45-caliber pistol. Escaped assassination attempt in San Francisco, Calif., Sept. 22, 1975, by Sara Jane Moore, who fired one shot from a .38-caliber pistol that was deflected.

Jordan, Vernon E., Jr. (civil rights leader): Shot and critically wounded in assassination attempt May 29, 1980, in Fort Wayne, Ind.

Reagan, Ronald (President of U.S.): Shot in left lung in Washington by John W. Hinckley, Jr., on March 30, 1981; three others also wounded.

"High Crimes and Misdemeanors:" A Short History of Impeachment

The Mechanics of Impeachment

The right to impeach public officials is secured by the U.S. Constitution in Article I, Sections 2 and 3, which discuss the procedure, and in Article II, Section 4, which indicates the grounds for impeachment: "the President, Vice President, and all civil officers of the United States shall be removed from office on impeachment for, and conviction of, treason, bribery, or other high crimes and misdemeanors."

Removing an official from office requires two steps: (1) a formal accusation, or impeachment, by the House of Representatives, and (2) a trial and conviction by the Senate. Impeachment requires a majority vote of the House; conviction is more difficult, requiring a two-thirds vote by the Senate. The vice president presides over the Senate proceedings in the case of all officials except the president, whose trial is presided over by the Chief Justice of the Supreme Court. This is because the vice president can hardly be considered a disinterested party—if his or her boss is forced out of office he or she is next in line for the top job!

What are "High Crimes and Misdemeanors"?

Bribery, perjury, and treason are among the least ambiguous reasons meriting impeachment, but the ocean of wrongdoing encompassed by the Constitution's stipulation of "high crimes and misdemeanors" is vast. Abuse of power and serious misconduct in office fit this category, but one act that is definitely not grounds for impeachment is partisan discord. Several impeachment cases have confused political animosity with genuine crimes. Since Congress, the vortex of partisanship, is responsible for indicting, trying, and convicting public officials, it is necessary for the legislative branch to temporarily cast aside its factional nature and adopt a judicial role.

The Infamous Sixteen

Since 1797 the House of Representatives has impeached sixteen federal officials. These include two presidents, a cabinet member, a senator, a justice of the Supreme Court, and eleven federal judges. Of those, the Senate has convicted and removed seven, all of them judges. Not included in this list are the office holders who have resigned rather than face impeachment, most notably, President Richard M. Nixon.

The Small Fry

The first official impeached in this country was Senator William Blount of Tennessee for a plot to help the British seize Louisiana and Florida from Spain in 1797. The Senate dismissed the charges on Jan. 14, 1799, determining that it had no jurisdiction over its own members. The Senate and the House do, however, have the right to discipline their members, and the Senate expelled Blount the day after his impeachment.

Judge John Pickering of New Hampshire was the first impeached official actually convicted. He was found guilty of drunkenness and unlawful rulings, on March 12, 1804, and was believed to have been insane.

Associate Justice Samuel Chase, a strong Federalist, was impeached but acquitted of judicial bias against anti-Federalists. The acquittal on March 1, 1805, established that political differences were not grounds for impeachment.

Other officials impeached were implicated in bribery, cheating on income tax, perjury, and treason.

The Big Fish

Two U.S. presidents have been impeached: Andrew Johnson, the seventeenth chief executive, and William J. Clinton, the forty-second.

Johnson, a Southern Democrat who became president after Lincoln's assassination, supported a mild policy of Reconstruction after the Civil War. The Radical Republicans in Congress were furious at his leniency toward ex-Confederates and obvious lack of concern for ex-slaves, demonstrated by his veto of civil rights bills and opposition to the Fourteenth Amendment. To protect Radical Republicans in Johnson's administration and diminish the strength of the president, Congress passed the Tenure of Office Act in 1867, which prohibited the president from dismissing office holders without the Senate's approval. A defiant Johnson tested the constitutionality of the Act by attempting to oust Secretary of War Edwin M. Stanton. His violation of the Act became the basis for impeachment in 1868. But the Senate was one vote short of the two-thirds majority needed to convict, and Johnson was acquitted May 26, 1868.

Senator Charles Sumner, witness to the proceedings, defined them as "political in character." Historians today generally agree with his assessment and consider the grounds for Johnson's impeachment flimsy—the Tenure of Office Act was partially repealed in 1887, and then declared unconstitutional in 1926.

Bill Clinton was ultimately dragged down—though not defeated—by the "character issues" brought into question even before his election. An investigation into some suspect real estate dealings in which Clinton was involved prior to his presidency failed to turn up any implicating evidence. However, Independent Counsel Kenneth Starr managed to unravel a tangled web of alleged sexual advances and affairs in Clinton's past. The trail led to former White House intern Monica S. Lewinsky. After months of denials, including in a videotaped legal testimony, Clinton admitted in August of 1998 that he had had a sexual relationship with the young woman during the time of her internship.

The infamous "Starr Report" outlining the findings of the Independent Counsel's investigation was delivered to the House of Representatives on Sept. 9, 1998 and subsequently made available to the public. Many felt the report, filled with lurid details of Clinton's sexual encounters with Lewinsky, to be a political attack against the President rather than a legal justification for his impeachment. Of the 11 possible grounds for impeachment cited by Starr, four were eventually approved by the House Judiciary Committee: grand jury perjury, civil suit perjury, obstruction of justice, and abuse of power.

On December 19, following much debate over the constitutionality of the proceedings and whether or not Clinton could be punished by censure rather than impeachment, the House of Representatives held its historic vote. Clinton was impeached on two counts, grand jury perjury (228–206) and obstruction of justice (221–212), with the votes split along party lines. The Senate Republicans, however, were unable to gather enough support to achieve the two-thirds majority required for his conviction. On Feb. 12, 1999, the Senate acquitted President Clinton on both counts. The perjury charge failed by a vote of 55–45, with 10 Republicans voting against impeachment along with all 45 Democrats. The obstruction of justice vote was 50–50, with 5 Republicans breaking ranks to vote against impeachment. (*See also* William Jefferson Clinton, pp. 117–118)

The One That Got Away

Of thirty-five attempts at impeachment, only nine have come to trial. Because it cripples Congress with a lengthy trial, impeachment is infrequent.

Many officials, seeing the writing on the wall, resign rather than face the ignominy of a public trial.

The most famous of these cases is of course that of President Richard Nixon, a Republican. After five men hired by Nixon's reelection committee were caught burglarizing Democratic party headquarters at the Watergate Complex on June 17, 1972, President Nixon's subsequent behavior—his cover-up of the burglary and refusal to turn over evidence—led the House Judiciary Committee to issue three articles of impeachment on July 30, 1974. The document also indicted Nixon for illegal wire tapping, misuse of the CIA, perjury, bribery, obstruction of justice, and other abuses of executive power. "In all of this," the Articles of Impeachment summarize, "Richard M. Nixon has acted in a manner contrary to his trust as president and subversive of constitutional government, to the great prejudice of the cause of law and justice, and to the manifest injury of the people of the United States." Impeachment appeared inevitable, and Nixon resigned on Aug. 9, 1974.

Impeachments of Federal Officials

Source: Congressional Directory.

The procedure for the impeachment of Federal officials is detailed in Article I, Section 3, of the Constitution. The Senate has sat as a court of impeachment in the following cases:

William Blount, Senator from Tennessee; charges dismissed for want of jurisdiction, Jan. 14, 1799.

John Pickering, Judge of the U.S. District Court for New Hampshire; removed from office March 12, 1804.

Samuel Chase, Associate Justice of the Supreme Court; acquitted March 1, 1805.

James H. Peck, Judge of the U.S. District Court for Missouri; acquitted Jan. 31, 1831.

West H. Humphreys, Judge of the U.S. District Court for the middle, eastern, and western districts of Tennessee; removed from office June 26, 1862.

Andrew Johnson, President of the United States; acquitted May 26, 1868.

William W. Belknap, Secretary of War; acquitted Aug. 1, 1876.

Charles Swayne, Judge of the U.S. District Court for the northern district of Florida; acquitted Feb. 27, 1905.

Robert W. Archbald, Associate Judge, U.S. Commerce Court; removed Jan. 13, 1913.

George W. English, Judge of the U.S. District Court for eastern district of Illinois; resigned Nov. 4, 1926; proceedings dismissed.

Harold Louderback, Judge of the U.S. District Court for the northern district of California; acquitted May 24, 1933.

Halsted L. Ritter, Judge of the U.S. District Court for the southern district of Florida; removed from office April 17, 1936.

Harry E. Claiborne, Judge of the U.S. District Court for the district of Nevada; removed from office Oct. 9, 1986.

Alcee L. Hastings, Judge of the U.S. District Court for the southern district of Florida; removed from office Oct. 20, 1988.

Walter L. Nixon, Judge of the U.S. District Court for Mississippi; removed from office Nov. 3, 1989.

William J. Clinton, President of the United States; acquitted Feb. 12, 1999.

How a Bill Becomes a Law

When a Senator or a Representative introduces a bill, he sends it to the clerk of his house, who gives it a number and title. This is the *first reading,* and the bill is referred to the proper committee.

The committee may decide the bill is unwise or unnecessary and *table* it, thus killing it at once. Or it may decide the bill is worthwhile and hold hearings to listen to facts and opinions presented by experts and other interested persons. After members of the committee have debated the bill and perhaps offered amendments, a vote is taken; and if the vote is favorable, the bill is sent back to the floor of the house.

The clerk reads the bill sentence by sentence to the house, and this is known as the *second reading.* Members may then debate the bill and offer amendments. In the House of Representatives, the time for debate is limited by a *cloture rule,* but there is no such restriction in the Senate for cloture, where 60 votes are required. This makes possible a *filibuster,* in which one or more opponents hold the floor to defeat the bill.

The *third reading* is by title only, and the bill is put to a vote, which may be by voice or roll call, depending on the circumstances and parliamentary rules. Members who must be absent at the time but who wish to record their vote may be paired if each negative vote has a balancing affirmative one.

The bill then goes to the other house of Congress, where it may be defeated, or passed with or without amendments. If the bill is defeated, it dies. If it is passed with amendments, a joint Congressional committee must be appointed by both houses to iron out the differences.

After its final passage by both houses, the bill is sent to the president. If he approves, he signs it, and the bill becomes a law. However, if he disapproves, he *vetoes* the bill by refusing to sign it and sending it back to the house of origin with his reasons for the veto. The objections are read and debated, and a roll-call vote is taken. If the bill receives less than a two-thirds vote, it is defeated and goes no further. But if it receives a two-thirds vote or greater, it is sent to the other house for a vote. If that house also passes it by a two-thirds vote, the president's veto is *overridden,* and the bill becomes a law.

Should the president desire neither to sign nor to veto the bill, he may retain it for ten days, Sundays excepted, after which time it automatically becomes a law without signature. However, if Congress has adjourned within those ten days, the bill is automatically killed, that process of indirect rejection being known as a *pocket veto.*

The White House

Source: Department of the Interior, U.S. National Park Service.

The White House, the official residence of the president, is at 1600 Pennsylvania Avenue in Washington, D.C. 20500. The site, covering about 18 acres, was selected by President Washington and Pierre Charles L'Enfant, and the architect was James Hoban. The design appears to have been influenced by Leinster House, Dublin, and James Gibb's *Book of Architecture.* The cornerstone was laid Oct. 13, 1792, and the first residents were President John Adams and First Lady Abigail Adams in November 1800. The building was burned by the British in 1814 during the War of 1812.

From December 1948 to March 1952, the interior of the White House was rebuilt, and the outer walls were strengthened.

The rooms for public functions are on the first floor; the second and third floors are used as the residence of the president and first family. The most celebrated public room is the East Room, where formal receptions take place. Other public rooms are the Red Room, the Green Room, and the Blue Room. The State Dining Room is used for formal dinners. There are 132 rooms.

U.S. Capitol

When the French architect and engineer Maj. Pierre L'Enfant first began to lay out the plans for a new Federal city (now Washington, D.C.), he noted that Jenkins' Hill, overlooking the area, seemed to be "a pedestal waiting for a monument." It was here that the U.S. Capitol would be built. The basic structure as we know it today evolved over a period of more than 150 years. In 1792 a competition was held for the design of a capitol building. Dr. William Thornton, a physician and amateur architect, submitted the winning plan, a simple, low-lying structure of classical proportions with a shallow dome. Later, internal modifications were made by Benjamin Henry Latrobe. After the building was burned by the British in 1814, Latrobe and architect Charles Bulfinch were responsible for its reconstruction. Finally, under Thomas Walter, who was Architect of the Capitol from 1851 to 1865, the House and Senate wings and the imposing cast iron dome topped with the Statue of Freedom were added, and the Capitol assumed the form we see today. It was in the old Senate chamber that Daniel Webster cried out, "Liberty and Union, now and forever, one and inseparable!" In Statuary Hall, which used to be the old House chamber, a small disk on the floor marks the spot where John Quincy Adams was fatally stricken after more than 50 years of service to his country. A whisper from one side of this room can be heard across the vast space of the hall. Visitors can see the original Supreme Court chamber a floor below the Rotunda.

In addition to its historical association, the Capitol Building is also a vast artistic treasure house. The works of such famous artists as Gilbert Stuart, Rembrandt Peale, and John Trumbull are displayed on the walls. The Great Rotunda, with its 180-foot- (54.9-m-) high dome, is decorated with a massive fresco by Constantino Brumidi, which extends some 300 feet (90 m) in circumference. Throughout the building are many paintings of events in U.S. history and sculptures of outstanding Americans. The Capitol itself is situated on a 68-acre (27.5-ha) park designed by the 19th-century landscape architect Frederick Law Olmsted. There are free guided tours of the Capitol, which include admission to the House and Senate galleries. Those who wish to visit the visitors' gallery in either wing without taking the tour may obtain passes from their Senators or Representatives. Visitors may ride on the monorail subway that joins the House and Senate wings of the Capitol with the Congressional office buildings.

Washington Monument

Construction of this magnificent Washington, D.C., monument, which draws some two million visitors a year, took nearly a century of planning, building, and controversy. Provision for a large equestrian statue of George Washington was made in the original city plan, but the project was soon dropped. After Washington's death it was taken up again, and a number of false starts and changes of design were made. Finally, in 1848, work was begun on the monument that stands today. The design, by architect Robert Mills, then featured an ornate base. In 1854, however, political squabbling and a lack of money brought construction to a halt. Work was resumed in 1880, and the monument was completed in 1884 and opened to the public in 1888. The tapered shaft, faced with white marble and rising from walls 15 feet thick (4.6 m) at the base was modeled after the obelisks of ancient Egypt. The monument, one of the tallest masonry constructions in the world, stands just over 555 feet (169 m). Memorial stones from the 50 States, foreign countries, and organizations line the interior walls. The top, reached only by elevator, commands a panoramic view of the city.

The Liberty Bell

The Liberty Bell was cast in England in 1752 for the Pennsylvania Statehouse (now named Independence Hall) in Philadelphia. It was recast in Philadelphia in 1753. It is inscribed with the words, "Proclaim liberty throughout all the land unto all the inhabitants thereof" (Lev. 25:10). The bell was rung on July 8, 1776, for the first public reading of the Declaration of Independence. Hidden in Allentown during the British occupation of Philadelphia, it was replaced in Independence Hall in 1778. The bell cracked on July 8, 1835, while tolling the death of Chief Justice John Marshall. In 1976 the Liberty Bell was moved to a special exhibition building near Independence Hall.

Arlington National Cemetery

Arlington National Cemetery occupies 612 acres in Virginia on the Potomac River, directly opposite Washington. This land was part of the estate of John Parke Custis, Martha Washington's son. His son, George Washington Parke Custis, built the mansion which later became the home of Robert E. Lee. In 1864, Arlington became a military cemetery. More than 240,000 service members and their dependents are buried there. Expansion of the cemetery began in 1966, using a 180-acre tract of land directly east of the present site.

In 1921, an Unknown American Soldier of World War I was buried in the cemetery; the monument at the Tomb of the Unknown Soldier was opened to the public without ceremony in 1932. Two additional Unknowns, one from World War II and one from the Korean War, were buried May 30, 1958.

The Unknown Serviceman of Vietnam was buried on May 28, 1984. In June 1998 his body was disinterred and recent DNA-testing technology was used to identify him as First Lt. Michael Blassie, an Air Force pilot from St. Louis. It is possible that technology will prevent there from ever being another "unknown" buried in the tomb.

The inscription carved on the Tomb of the Unknowns reads:

HERE RESTS IN
HONORED GLORY
AN AMERICAN
SOLDIER
KNOWN BUT TO GOD

Firsts in America

This selection is based on our editorial judgment. Other sources may list different firsts.

Admiral in U.S. Navy: David Glasgow Farragut, 1866.

Airmail route, first transcontinental: Between New York City and San Francisco, 1920.

Assembly, representative: House of Burgesses, founded in Virginia, 1619.

Bank established: Bank of North America, Philadelphia, 1781.

Birth in America to English parents: Virginia Dare, born Roanoke Island, N.C., 1587.

Black newspaper: *Freedom's Journal,* 1827, edited by John B. Russworm.

Black U.S. diplomat: Ebenezer D. Bassett, 1869, minister-resident to Haiti.

Black elected governor of a state: L. Douglas Wilder, Virginia, 1990.

Black elected to U.S. Senate: Hiram Revels, 1870, Mississippi.

Black elected to U.S. House of Representatives: Jefferson Long, Georgia, 1870.

Black associate justice of U.S. Supreme Court: Thurgood Marshall, Oct. 2, 1967.

Black U.S. cabinet minister: Robert C. Weaver, 1966, Secretary of the Department of Housing and Urban Development.

Botanic garden: Established by John Bartram in Philadelphia, 1728, and is still in existence in its original location.

Cartoon, colored: "The Yellow Kid," by Richard Outcault, in *New York World,* 1895.

College: Harvard, founded 1636.

College to establish coeducation: Oberlin College (Ohio), 1833.

Electrocution of a criminal: William Kemmler in Auburn Prison, Auburn, N.Y., Aug. 6, 1890.

Five and Dime Store: Founded by Frank Woolworth, Utica, N.Y., 1879 (moved to Lancaster, Pa., same year).

Fraternity, Greek-letter: Phi Beta Kappa; founded Dec. 5, 1776, at College of William and Mary.

Gay and lesbian civil rights advocacy organization: National Gay and Lesbian Task Force, founded in New York City, 1973.

Gay Power: Rioting following police raid on N.Y.C. gay bar, the Stonewall Inn, mobilizes gay community and leads to birth of gay liberation movement, June 27, 1969.

Homosexual, acknowledged, elected to high local office: Harvey Milk, 1977, San Francisco Board of Supervisors.

Law to be declared unconstitutional by U.S. Supreme Court: Judiciary Act of 1789. Case: *Marbury v. Madison,* 1803.

Library, circulating: Philadelphia, 1731.

Newspaper, illustrated daily: *New York Daily Graphic,* 1873.

Newspaper published daily: *Pennsylvania Packet and General Advertiser,* Philadelphia, Sept. 1784.

Newspaper published over a continuous period: *The Boston News-Letter,* April 1704.

Newsreel: Pathé Frères of Paris, in 1910, circulated a weekly issue of their *Pathé Journal.*

Oil well, commercial: Titusville, Pa., 1859.

Panel quiz show on radio: *Information Please,* May 17, 1938.

Postage stamps issued: 1847.

Public School: Boston Latin School, Boston, 1635.

Radio station licensed: KDKA, Pittsburgh, Pa., Oct. 27, 1920.

Railroad, transcontinental: Central Pacific and Union Pacific railroads, joined at Promontory, Utah, May 10, 1869.

Savings bank: The Provident Institute for Savings, Boston, 1816.

Science museum: Founded by Charleston (S.C.) Library Society, 1773.

Skyscraper: Home Insurance Co., Chicago, 1885 (10 floors, 2 added later).

Slaves brought into America: At Jamestown, Va., 1619, from a Dutch ship.

Sorority: Kappa Alpha Theta, at De Pauw University, 1870.

State to abolish capital punishment: Michigan, 1847.

State to enter Union after original 13: Vermont, 1791.

Steam-heated building: Eastern Hotel, Boston, 1845.

Steam railroad (carried passengers and freight): Baltimore & Ohio, 1830.

Strike on record by union: Journeymen Printers, New York City, 1776.

Subway: Opened in Boston, 1897.

"Tabloid" picture newspaper: *The Illustrated Daily News* (now *The Daily News*), New York City, 1919.

Vaudeville theater: Gaiety Museum, Boston, 1883.

Woman astronaut appointed shuttle commander: Lt. Col. Eileen Collins, *Columbia,* launched July 1999.

Woman astronaut to ride in space: Dr. Sally K. Ride, 1983.

Woman astronaut to walk in space: Dr. Kathryn D. Sullivan, 1984.

Woman cabinet member: Frances Perkins, Secretary of Labor, 1933.

Woman candidate for President: Victoria Claflin Woodhull, nominated by National Woman's Suffrage Assn. on ticket of Nation Radical Reformers, 1872.

Woman candidate for Vice President: Geraldine A. Ferraro, nominated on a major party ticket, Democratic Party, 1984.

Woman doctor of medicine: Elizabeth Blackwell; M.D. from Geneva Medical College of Western New York, 1849.

Woman elected governor of a state: Nellie Tayloe Ross, Wyoming, 1925.

Woman elected to U.S. Senate: Hattie Caraway, Arkansas; elected Nov. 1932.

Woman member of U.S. House of Representatives: Jeannette Rankin (Mont.); elected Nov. 1916.

Woman member of U.S. Senate: Rebecca Latimer Felton (Ga.); appointed Oct. 3, 1922.

Woman member of U.S. Supreme Court: Sandra Day O'Connor; appointed July 1981.

Woman Secretary of State: Madeleine Albright, appointed Dec. 1996.

Woman suffrage granted: Wyoming Territory, 1869.

Written constitution: *Fundamental Orders of Connecticut,* 1639.

Figures and Legends in American Folklore

Appleseed, Johnny (John Chapman, 1774–1847): Massachusetts-born nurseryman; reputed to have spread seeds and seedlings out of which grew the apple orchards of the Midwest.

Billy the Kid (William H. Bonney, 1859–1881): Desperado who killed his first man before he reached his teens; after short life of crime in Wild West was gunned down by Sheriff Pat Garrett; symbol of lawless West.

Boone, Daniel (1734–1820): Frontiersman and Indian fighter, about whom legends of early America have been built; figured in Byron's *Don Juan.*

Buffalo Bill (William F. Cody, 1846–1917): Buffalo hunter and Indian scout; many of the legends about him stem from his own Wild West show, which he operated in late 19th century.

Bunyan, Paul: Mythical lumberjack; subject of tall tales throughout timber country (that he dug Grand Canyon, for example).

Crockett, Davy (1786–1836): Frontiersman, Congressman, and defender of the Alamo, his backwoods humor and larger-than-life adventures made him synonymous with the Wild West.

James, Jesse (1847–1882): Bank and train robber; often portrayed as the American Robin Hood.

Jones, Casey (John Luther Jones, 1863–1900): Example of heroic locomotive engineer given to feats of prowess; died in wreck when his Illinois Central "Cannonball" express hit a freight train at Vaughan, Miss.

Ross, Betsy (1752–1836): Member of Philadelphia flag-making family; reported to have designed and sewn first American flag. (Report is without confirmation.)

Uncle Sam: Personification of U.S. and its people; origin uncertain; may be based on inspector of government supplies in Revolutionary War and War of 1812.

States by Order of Entry into Union

State	Entered Union	Year settled	Repre-sentatives in Congress[1]	State	Entered Union	Year settled	Repre-sentatives in Congress[1]
1. Delaware	Dec. 7, 1787	1638	1	26. Michigan	Jan. 26, 1837	1668	16
2. Pennsylvania	Dec. 12, 1787	1682	21	27. Florida	Mar. 3, 1845	1565	23
3. New Jersey	Dec. 18, 1787	1660	13	28. Texas	Dec. 29, 1845	1682	30
4. Georgia	Jan. 2, 1788	1733	11	29. Iowa	Dec. 28, 1846	1788	5
5. Connecticut	Jan. 9, 1788	1634	6	30. Wisconsin	May 29, 1848	1766	9
6. Massachusetts	Feb. 6, 1788	1620	10	31. California	Sept. 9, 1850	1769	52
7. Maryland	Apr. 28, 1788	1634	8	32. Minnesota	May 11, 1858	1805	8
8. South Carolina	May 23, 1788	1670	6	33. Oregon	Feb. 14, 1859	1811	5
9. New Hampshire	June 21, 1788	1623	2	34. Kansas	Jan. 29, 1861	1727	4
10. Virginia	June 25, 1788	1607	11	35. West Virginia	June 20, 1863	1727	3
11. New York	July 26, 1788	1614	31	36. Nevada	Oct. 31, 1864	1849	2
12. North Carolina	Nov. 21, 1789	1660	12	37. Nebraska	Mar. 1, 1867	1823	3
13. Rhode Island	May 29, 1790	1636	2	38. Colorado	Aug. 1, 1876	1858	6
14. Vermont	Mar. 4, 1791	1724	1	39. North Dakota	Nov. 2, 1889	1812	1
15. Kentucky	June 1, 1792	1774	6	40. South Dakota	Nov. 2, 1889	1859	1
16. Tennessee	June 1, 1796	1769	9	41. Montana	Nov. 8, 1889	1809	1
17. Ohio	Mar. 1, 1803	1788	19	42. Washington	Nov. 11, 1889	1811	9
18. Louisiana	Apr. 30, 1812	1699	7	43. Idaho	July 3, 1890	1842	2
19. Indiana	Dec. 11, 1816	1733	10	44. Wyoming	July 10, 1890	1834	1
20. Mississippi	Dec. 10, 1817	1699	5	45. Utah	Jan. 4, 1896	1847	3
21. Illinois	Dec. 3, 1818	1720	20	46. Oklahoma	Nov. 16, 1907	1889	6
22. Alabama	Dec. 14, 1819	1702	7	47. New Mexico	Jan. 6, 1912	1610	3
23. Maine	Mar. 15, 1820	1624	2	48. Arizona	Feb. 14, 1912	1776	6
24. Missouri	Aug. 10, 1821	1735	9	49. Alaska	Jan. 3, 1959	1784	1
25. Arkansas	June 15, 1836	1686	4	50. Hawaii	Aug. 21, 1959	1820	2

1. Does not include Senators. *Source:* Compiled from various sources by the editors.

Presidential Libraries

The presidential library system is made up of ten presidential libraries and one presidential project. These are not traditional libraries, but rather repositories for preserving and making available the papers, records, and other historical materials of the presidents since Herbert Hoover. The presidential library system formally began in 1939, when President Franklin Roosevelt donated his personal and presidential papers to the federal government. Roosevelt believed that presidential papers are an important part of the national heritage and should be accessible to the public.

Hoover Library

Herbert Hoover National Historic Site
211 Parkside Drive
P.O. Box 488
West Branch, IA 52358-0488
http://hoover.nara.gov

Roosevelt Library

511 Albany Post Road
Hyde Park, NY 12538-1999
http://www.academic.marist.edu/fdr

Truman Library

500 West U.S. Highway 24
Independence, MO 64050-1798
http://www.trumanlibrary.org

Eisenhower Library

200 SE 4th Street
Abilene, KS 67410-2900
http://www.eisenhower.utexas.edu

Kennedy Library

Columbia Point
Boston, MA 02125-3398
http://www.cs.umb.edu/jfklibrary/

Johnson Library

2313 Red River Street
Austin, TX 78705-5702
http://www.lbjlib.utexas.edu

The Nixon Project[1]

National Archives at College Park
8601 Adelphi Road
College Park, MD 20740-6001
http://metalab.unc.edu/lia/president/nixon.html

Ford Library

1000 Beal Avenue
Ann Arbor, MI 48109-2114
http://www.ford.utexas.edu

Carter Library

1 Copenhill Avenue, NE
Atlanta, GA 30307-1406
http://carterlibrary.galileo.peachnet.edu

Reagan Library

40 Presidential Drive
Simi Valley, CA 93065-0666
http://www.reagan.utexas.edu

Bush Library

701 University Drive East, Suite 300
College Station, TX 77840-9554
http://csdl.tamu.edu/bushlib

1. The Nixon Project is not affiliated with the Richard Nixon Library and Birthplace in Yorba Linda, Calif., a private institution that was established by Nixon in 1990. *Source:* National Archives and Records Administration; Web: www.nara.gov/nara/president.

Presidents

	Name and (party)[1]	Term	State of birth	Born	Died	Religion	Age at inaug.	Age at death
1.	Washington (F)[2]	1789–1797	Va.	2/22/1732	12/14/1799	Episcopalian	57	67
2.	J. Adams (F)	1797–1801	Mass.	10/30/1735	7/4/1826	Unitarian	61	90
3.	Jefferson (DR)	1801–1809	Va.	4/13/1743	7/4/1826	Deist	57	83
4.	Madison (DR)	1809–1817	Va.	3/16/1751	6/28/1836	Episcopalian	57	85
5.	Monroe (DR)	1817–1825	Va.	4/28/1758	7/4/1831	Episcopalian	58	73
6.	J. Q. Adams (DR)	1825–1829	Mass.	7/11/1767	2/23/1848	Unitarian	57	80
7.	Jackson (D)	1829–1837	S.C.	3/15/1767	6/8/1845	Presbyterian	61	78
8.	Van Buren (D)	1837–1841	N.Y.	12/5/1782	7/24/1862	Reformed Dutch	54	79
9.	W. H. Harrison (W)[3]	1841	Va.	2/9/1773	4/4/1841	Episcopalian	68	68
10.	Tyler (W)	1841–1845	Va.	3/29/1790	1/18/1862	Episcopalian	51	71
11.	Polk (D)	1845–1849	N.C.	11/2/1795	6/15/1849	Methodist	49	53
12.	Taylor (W)[3]	1849–1850	Va.	11/24/1784	7/9/1850	Episcopalian	64	65
13.	Fillmore (W)	1850–1853	N.Y.	1/7/1800	3/8/1874	Unitarian	50	74
14.	Pierce (D)	1853–1857	N.H.	11/23/1804	10/8/1869	Episcopalian	48	64
15.	Buchanan (D)	1857–1861	Pa.	4/23/1791	6/1/1868	Presbyterian	65	77
16.	Lincoln (R)[4]	1861–1865	Ky.	2/12/1809	4/15/1865	Liberal	52	56
17.	A. Johnson (U)[5]	1865–1869	N.C.	12/29/1808	7/31/1875	[6]	56	66
18.	Grant (R)	1869–1877	Ohio	4/27/1822	7/23/1885	Methodist	46	63
19.	Hayes (R)	1877–1881	Ohio	10/4/1822	1/17/1893	Methodist	54	70
20.	Garfield (R)[4]	1881	Ohio	11/19/1831	9/19/1881	Disciples of Christ	49	49
21.	Arthur (R)	1881–1885	Vt.	10/5/1830	11/18/1886	Episcopalian	50	56
22.	Cleveland (D)	1885–1889	N.J.	3/18/1837	6/24/1908	Presbyterian	47	71
23.	B. Harrison (R)	1889–1893	Ohio	8/20/1833	3/13/1901	Presbyterian	55	67
24.	Cleveland (D)[7]	1893–1897	—	—	—	—	55	—
25.	McKinley (R)[4]	1897–1901	Ohio	1/29/1843	9/14/1901	Methodist	54	58
26.	T. Roosevelt (R)	1901–1909	N.Y.	10/27/1858	1/6/1919	Reformed Dutch	42	60
27.	Taft (R)	1909–1913	Ohio	9/15/1857	3/8/1930	Unitarian	51	72
28.	Wilson (D)	1913–1921	Va.	12/28/1856	2/3/1924	Presbyterian	56	67
29.	Harding (R)[3]	1921–1923	Ohio	11/2/1865	8/2/1923	Baptist	55	57
30.	Coolidge (R)	1923–1929	Vt.	7/4/1872	1/5/1933	Congregationalist	51	60
31.	Hoover (R)	1929–1933	Iowa	8/10/1874	10/20/1964	Quaker	54	90
32.	F. D. Roosevelt (D)[3]	1933–1945	N.Y.	1/30/1882	4/12/1945	Episcopalian	51	63
33.	Truman (D)	1945–1953	Mo.	5/8/1884	12/26/1972	Baptist	60	88
34.	Eisenhower (R)	1953–1961	Tex.	10/14/1890	3/28/1969	Presbyterian	62	78
35.	Kennedy (D)[4]	1961–1963	Mass.	5/29/1917	11/22/1963	Roman Catholic	43	46
36.	L. B. Johnson (D)	1963–1969	Tex.	8/27/1908	1/22/1973	Disciples of Christ	55	64
37.	Nixon (R)[8]	1969–1974	Calif.	1/9/1913	4/22/1994	Quaker	56	81
38.	Ford (R)	1974–1977	Neb.	7/14/1913	—	Episcopalian	61	—
39.	Carter (D)	1977–1981	Ga.	10/1/1924	—	Southern Baptist	52	—
40.	Reagan (R)	1981–1989	Ill.	2/6/1911	—	Disciples of Christ	69	—
41.	Bush (R)	1989–1993	Mass.	6/12/1924	—	Episcopalian	64	—
42.	Clinton (D)	1993–	Ark.	8/19/1946	—	Baptist	46	—

1. F—Federalist; DR—Democratic-Republican; D—Democratic; W—Whig; R—Republican; U—Union. 2. No party for first election. The party system in the U.S. made its appearance during Washington's first term. 3. Died in office. 4. Assassinated in office. 5. The Republican National Convention of 1864 adopted the name Union Party. It renominated Lincoln for president; for vice president it nominated Johnson, a War Democrat. Although frequently listed as a Republican vice president and president, Johnson undoubtedly considered himself strictly a member of the Union Party. When that party broke apart after 1868, he returned to the Democratic Party. 6. Johnson was not a professed church member; however, he admired the Baptist principles of church government. 7. Second nonconsecutive term. 8. Resigned Aug. 9, 1974.

Vice Presidents

	Name and (party)[1]	Term	State of birth	Birth and death dates	President served under
1.	John Adams (F)[2]	1789–1797	Massachusetts	1735–1826	Washington
2.	Thomas Jefferson (DR)	1797–1801	Virginia	1743–1826	J. Adams
3.	Aaron Burr (DR)	1801–1805	New Jersey	1756–1836	Jefferson
4.	George Clinton (DR)[3]	1805–1812	New York	1739–1812	Jefferson and Madison
5.	Elbridge Gerry (DR)[3]	1813–1814	Massachusetts	1744–1814	Madison
6.	Daniel D. Tompkins (DR)	1817–1825	New York	1774–1825	Monroe
7.	John C. Calhoun[4]	1825–1832	South Carolina	1782–1850	J. Q. Adams and Jackson
8.	Martin Van Buren (D)	1833–1837	New York	1782–1862	Jackson
9.	Richard M. Johnson (D)	1837–1841	Kentucky	1780–1850	Van Buren
10.	John Tyler (W)[5]	1841	Virginia	1790–1862	W. H. Harrison
11.	George M. Dallas (D)	1845–1849	Pennsylvania	1792–1864	Polk
12.	Millard Fillmore (W)[5]	1849–1850	New York	1800–1874	Taylor

	Name and (party)[1]	Term	State of birth	Birth and death dates	President served under
13.	William R. King (D)[3]	1853	North Carolina	1786–1853	Pierce
14.	John C. Breckinridge (D)	1857–1861	Kentucky	1821–1875	Buchanan
15.	Hannibal Hamlin (R)	1861–1865	Maine	1809–1891	Lincoln
16.	Andrew Johnson (U)[5]	1865	North Carolina	1808–1875	Lincoln
17.	Schuyler Colfax (R)	1869–1873	New York	1823–1885	Grant
18.	Henry Wilson (R)[3]	1873–1875	New Hampshire	1812–1875	Grant
19.	William A. Wheeler (R)	1877–1881	New York	1819–1887	Hayes
20.	Chester A. Arthur (R)[5]	1881	Vermont	1830–1886	Garfield
21.	Thomas A. Hendricks (D)[3]	1885	Ohio	1819–1885	Cleveland
22.	Levi P. Morton (R)	1889–1893	Vermont	1824–1920	B. Harrison
23.	Adlai E. Stevenson (D)	1893–1897	Kentucky	1835–1914	Cleveland
24.	Garrett A. Hobart (R)[3]	1897–1899	New Jersey	1844–1899	McKinley
25.	Theodore Roosevelt (R)[5]	1901	New York	1858–1919	McKinley
26.	Charles W. Fairbanks (R)	1905–1909	Ohio	1852–1918	T. Roosevelt
27.	James S. Sherman (R)[3]	1909–1912	New York	1855–1912	Taft
28.	Thomas R. Marshall (D)	1913–1921	Indiana	1854–1925	Wilson
29.	Calvin Coolidge (R)[5]	1921–1923	Vermont	1872–1933	Harding
30.	Charles G. Dawes (R)	1925–1929	Ohio	1865–1951	Coolidge
31.	Charles Curtis (R)	1929–1933	Kansas	1860–1936	Hoover
32.	John N. Garner (D)	1933–1941	Texas	1868–1967	F. D. Roosevelt
33.	Henry A. Wallace (D)	1941–1945	Iowa	1888–1965	F. D. Roosevelt
34.	Harry S. Truman (D)[5]	1945	Missouri	1884–1972	F. D. Roosevelt
35.	Alben W. Barkley (D)	1949–1953	Kentucky	1877–1956	Truman
36.	Richard M. Nixon (R)	1953-1961	California	1913–1994	Eisenhower
37.	Lyndon B. Johnson (D)[5]	1961–1963	Texas	1908–1973	Kennedy
38.	Hubert H. Humphrey (D)	1965–1969	South Dakota	1911–1978	L. B. Johnson
39.	Spiro T. Agnew (R)[6]	1969–1973	Maryland	1918–1996	Nixon
40.	Gerald R. Ford (R)[7]	1973–1974	Nebraska	1913–	Nixon
41.	Nelson A. Rockefeller (R)[8]	1974–1977	Maine	1908–1979	Ford
42.	Walter F. Mondale (D)	1977–1981	Minnesota	1928–	Carter
43.	George Bush (R)	1981–1989	Massachusetts	1924–	Reagan
44.	J. Danforth Quayle (R)	1989–1993	Indiana	1947–	Bush
45.	Albert A. Gore, Jr. (D)	1993–	Washington, D.C.	1948—	Clinton

1. F—Federalist; DR—Democratic-Republican; D—Democratic; W—Whig; R—Republican; U—Union. 2. No party for first election. The party system in the U.S. made its appearance during Washington's first term as president. 3. Died in office. 4. Democratic-Republican with J. Q. Adams; Democratic with Jackson. Calhoun resigned in 1832 to become a U.S. Senator. 5. Succeeded to presidency on death of president. 6. Resigned Oct. 10, 1973, after pleading no contest to Federal income tax evasion charges. 7. Nominated by Nixon on Oct. 12, 1973, under provisions of 25th Amendment. Confirmed by Congress on Dec. 6, 1973, and was sworn in same day. He became president Aug. 9, 1974, upon Nixon's resignation. 8. Nominated by Ford Aug. 20, 1974; confirmed by Congress on Dec. 19, 1974, and was sworn in same day.

Burial Places of the Presidents

President	Burial place	President	Burial place
Washington	Mt. Vernon, Va.	Hayes	Fremont, Ohio
J. Adams	Quincy, Mass.	Garfield	Cleveland, Ohio
Jefferson	Charlottesville, Va.	Arthur	Albany, N.Y.
Madison	Montpelier Station, Va.	Cleveland	Princeton, N.J.
Monroe	Richmond, Va.	B. Harrison	Indianapolis
J. Q. Adams	Quincy, Mass.	McKinley	Canton, Ohio
Jackson	The Hermitage, nr. Nashville, Tenn.	T. Roosevelt	Oyster Bay, N.Y.
		Taft	Arlington National Cemetery
Van Buren	Kinderhook, N.Y.	Wilson	Washington National Cathedral
W. H. Harrison	North Bend, Ohio	Harding	Marion, Ohio
Tyler	Richmond, Va.	Coolidge	Plymouth, Vt.
Polk	Nashville, Tenn.	Hoover	West Branch, Iowa
Taylor	Louisville, Ky.	F. D. Roosevelt	Hyde Park, N.Y.
Fillmore	Buffalo, N.Y.	Truman	Independence, Mo.
Pierce	Concord, N.H.	Eisenhower	Abilene, Kan.
Buchanan	Lancaster, Pa.	Kennedy	Arlington National Cemetery
Lincoln	Springfield, Ill.	L. B. Johnson	Stonewall, Tex.
A. Johnson	Greeneville, Tenn.	Nixon	Yorba Linda, Calif.
Grant	New York City		

Wives and Children of the Presidents

President	Wife's name	Year and place of wife's birth	Married	Wife died	Children[1] Sons	Daughters
Washington	Martha Dandridge Custis	1732, Va.	1759	1802	—	—
John Adams	Abigail Smith	1744, Mass.	1764	1818	3	2
Jefferson [2]	Martha Wayles Skelton	1748, Va.	1772	1782	1	5
Madison	Dorothy "Dolley" Payne Todd	1768, N.C.	1794	1849	—	—
Monroe	Elizabeth "Eliza" Kortright	1768, N.Y.	1786	1830	—	2
J. Q. Adams	Louisa Catherine Johnson	1775, England	1797	1852	3	1
Jackson	Rachel Donelson Robards	1767, Va.	1791	1828	—	—
Van Buren	Hannah Hoes	1788, N.Y.	1807	1819	4	—
W. H. Harrison	Anna Symmes	1775, N.J.	1795	1864	6	4
Tyler	Letitia Christian	1790, Va.	1813	1842	3	4
	Julia Gardiner	1820, N.Y.	1844	1889	5	2
Polk	Sarah Childress	1803, Tenn.	1824	1891	—	—
Taylor	Margaret Smith	1788, Md.	1810	1852	1	5
Fillmore	Abigail Powers	1798, N.Y.	1826	1853	1	1
	Caroline Carmichael McIntosh	1813, N.J.	1858	1881	—	—
Pierce	Jane Means Appleton	1806, N.H.	1834	1863	3	—
Buchanan	(Unmarried)	—	—	—	—	—
Lincoln	Mary Todd	1818, Ky.	1842	1882	4	—
A. Johnson	Eliza McCardle	1810, Tenn.	1827	1876	3	2
Grant	Julia Dent	1826, Mo.	1848	1902	3	1
Hayes	Lucy Ware Webb	1831, Ohio	1852	1889	7	1
Garfield	Lucretia Rudolph	1832, Ohio	1858	1918	5	2
Arthur	Ellen Lewis Herndon	1837, Va.	1859	1880	2	1
Cleveland	Frances Folsom	1864, N.Y.	1886	1947	2	3
B. Harrison	Caroline Lavinia Scott	1832, Ohio	1853	1892	1	1
	Mary Scott Lord Dimmick	1858, Pa.	1896	1948	—	1
McKinley	Ida Saxton	1847, Ohio	1871	1907	—	2
T. Roosevelt	Alice Hathaway Lee	1861, Mass.	1880	1884	—	1
	Edith Kermit Carow	1861, Conn.	1886	1948	4	1
Taft	Helen Herron	1861, Ohio	1886	1943	2	1
Wilson	Ellen Louise Axson	1860, Ga.	1885	1914	—	3
	Edith Bolling Galt	1872, Va.	1915	1961	—	—
Harding	Florence Kling DeWolfe	1860, Ohio	1891	1924	—	—
Coolidge	Grace Anna Goodhue	1879, Vt.	1905	1957	2	—
Hoover	Lou Henry	1875, Iowa	1899	1944	2	—
F. D. Roosevelt	(Anna) Eleanor Roosevelt	1884, N.Y.	1905	1962	5	1
Truman	Bess Wallace	1885, Mo.	1919	1982	—	1
Eisenhower	Mamie Geneva Doud	1896, Iowa	1916	1979	2	—
Kennedy	Jacqueline Lee Bouvier	1929, N.Y.	1953	1994	2	1
L. B. Johnson	Claudia Alta "Lady Bird" Taylor	1912, Tex.	1934	—	—	2
Nixon	Thelma Catherine "Pat" Ryan	1912, Nev.	1940	1993	—	2
Ford	Elizabeth "Betty" Bloomer Warren	1918, Ill.	1948	—	3	1
Carter	Rosalynn Smith	1928, Ga.	1946	—	3	1
Reagan	Jane Wyman	1914, Mo.	1940[3]	—	1[4]	1
	Nancy Davis	1921 (?)[5], N.Y.	1952	—	1	1
Bush	Barbara Pierce	1925, N.Y.	1945	—	4	2
Clinton	Hillary Rodham	1946, Ill.	1975	—	—	1

1. Includes children who died in infancy. 2. Number of children listed here reflects only children Jefferson had with Martha Wayles Skelton. Scientists and historians are debating DNA evidence suggesting Jefferson fathered at least one child with slave Sally Hemings. 3. Divorced in 1948. 4. Adopted. 5. Birthday officially given as 1923 but her high school and college records show 1921 for year of birth.

Government Officials

Cabinet Members With Dates of Appointment

Although the Constitution made no provision for a president's advisory group, the heads of the three executive departments (State, Treasury, and War) and the Attorney General were organized by Washington into such a group; and by about 1793, the name "Cabinet" was applied to it. With the exception of the Attorney General up to 1870 and the Postmaster General from 1829 to 1872, Cabinet members have been heads of executive departments.

Cabinet members are appointed by the president, subject to the confirmation of the Senate; and as their terms are not fixed, they may be replaced at any time by the president. At a change in Administration, it is customary for Cabinet members to tender their resignations, but they remain in office until successors are appointed.

The table of Cabinet members lists only those members who actually served after being duly commissioned.

The dates shown are those of appointment. "Cont." indicates that the term continued from the previous Administration for a substantial amount of time.

With the creation of the Department of Transportation in 1966, the Cabinet consisted of 12 members. This figure was reduced to 11 when the Post Office Department became an independent agency in 1970 but, with the establishment in 1977 of a Department of Energy, became 12 again. Creation of the Department of Education in 1980 raised the number to 13. Creation of the Department of Veterans' Affairs in 1989 raised the number to 14.

Washington

Secretary of State	Thomas Jefferson, 1789
	Edmund Randolph, 1794
	Timothy Pickering, 1795
Secretary of the Treasury	Alexander Hamilton, 1789
	Oliver Wolcott, Jr., 1795
Secretary of War	Henry Knox, 1789
	Timothy Pickering, 1795
	James McHenry, 1796
Attorney General	Edmund Randolph, 1789
	William Bradford, 1794
	Charles Lee, 1795

J. Adams

Secretary of State	Timothy Pickering (Cont.)
	John Marshall, 1800
Secretary of the Treasury	Oliver Wolcott, Jr. (Cont.)
	Samuel Dexter, 1801
Secretary of War	James McHenry (Cont.)
	Samuel Dexter, 1800
Attorney General	Charles Lee (Cont.)
Secretary of the Navy	Benjamin Stoddert, 1798

Jefferson

Secretary of State	James Madison, 1801
Secretary of the Treasury	Samuel Dexter (Cont.)
	Albert Gallatin, 1801
Secretary of War	Henry Dearborn, 1801
Attorney General	Levi Lincoln, 1801
	Robert Smith, 1805
	John Breckinridge, 1805
	Caesar A. Rodney, 1807
Secretary of the Navy	Benjamin Stoddert (Cont.)
	Robert Smith, 1801

Madison

Secretary of State	Robert Smith, 1809
	James Monroe, 1811
Secretary of the Treasury	Albert Gallatin (Cont.)
	George W. Campbell, 1814
	Alexander J. Dallas, 1814
	William H. Crawford, 1816
Secretary of War	William Eustis, 1809
	John Armstrong, 1813
	James Monroe, 1814
	William H. Crawford, 1815
Attorney General	Caesar A. Rodney (Cont.)
	William Pinckney, 1811
	Richard Rush, 1814
Secretary of the Navy	Paul Hamilton, 1809
	William Jones, 1813
	B. W. Crowninshield, 1814

Monroe

Secretary of State	John Quincy Adams, 1817
Secretary of the Treasury	William H. Crawford (Cont.)
Secretary of War	John C. Calhoun, 1817
Attorney General	Richard Rush (Cont.)
	William Wirt, 1817
Secretary of the Navy	B. W. Crowninshield (Cont.)
	Smith Thompson, 1818
	Samuel L. Southard, 1823

J. Q. Adams

Secretary of State	Henry Clay, 1825
Secretary of the Treasury	Richard Rush, 1825
Secretary of War	James Barbour, 1825
	Peter B. Porter, 1828
Attorney General	William Wirt (Cont.)
Secretary of the Navy	Samuel L. Southard (Cont.)

Jackson

Secretary of State	Martin Van Buren, 1829
	Edward Livingston, 1831
	Louis McLane, 1833
	John Forsyth, 1834
Secretary of the Treasury	Samuel D. Ingham, 1829
	Louis McLane, 1831
	William J. Duane, 1833
	Roger B. Taney[1], 1833
	Levi Woodbury, 1834
Secretary of War	John H. Eaton, 1829
	Lewis Cass, 1831
Attorney General	John M. Berrien, 1829
	Roger B. Taney, 1831
	Benjamin F. Butler, 1833
Postmaster General[2]	William T. Barry, 1829
	Amos Kendall, 1835
Secretary of the Navy	John Branch, 1829
	Levi Woodbury, 1831
	Mahlon Dickerson, 1834

1. Not confirmed by the Senate. 2. The Postmaster General did not become a Cabinet member until 1829. Earlier Postmasters General were: Samuel Osgood (1789), Timothy Pickering (1791), Joseph Habersham (1795), Gideon Granger (1801), Return J. Meigs, Jr. (1814), and John McLean (1823).

Van Buren

Secretary of State	John Forsyth (Cont.)
Secretary of the Treasury	Levi Woodbury (Cont.)
Secretary of War	Joel R. Poinsett, 1837
Attorney General	Benjamin F. Butler (Cont.)
	Felix Grundy, 1838
	Henry D. Gilpin, 1840
Postmaster General	Amos Kendall (Cont.)
	John M. Niles, 1840
Secretary of the Navy	Mahlon Dickerson (Cont.)
	James K. Paulding, 1838

W. H. Harrison

Secretary of State	Daniel Webster, 1841
Secretary of the Treasury	Thomas Ewing, 1841
Secretary of War	John Bell, 1841
Attorney General	John J. Crittenden, 1841
Postmaster General	Francis Granger, 1841
Secretary of the Navy	George E. Badger, 1841

Tyler

Secretary of State	Daniel Webster (Cont.)
	Abel P. Upshur, 1843
	John C. Calhoun, 1844
Secretary of the Treasury	Thomas Ewing (Cont.)
	Walter Forward, 1841
	John C. Spencer[1], 1843
	George M. Bibb, 1844

Secretary of War	John Bell (Cont.)
	John C. Spencer, 1841
	James M. Porter[1], 1843
	William Wilkins, 1844
Attorney General	John J. Crittenden (Cont.)
	Hugh S. Legaré, 1841
	John Nelson, 1843
Postmaster General	Francis Granger (Cont.)
	Charles A. Wickliffe, 1841
Secretary of the Navy	George E. Badger (Cont.)
	Abel P. Upshur, 1841
	David Henshaw[1], 1843
	Thomas W. Gilmer, 1844
	John Y. Mason, 1844

1. Not confirmed by the Senate.

Polk

Secretary of State	James Buchanan, 1845
Secretary of the Treasury	Robert J. Walker, 1845
Secretary of War	William L. Marcy, 1845
Attorney General	John Y. Mason, 1845
	Nathan Clifford, 1846
	Isaac Toucey, 1848
Postmaster General	Cave Johnson, 1845
Secretary of the Navy	George Bancroft, 1845
	John Y. Mason, 1846

Taylor

Secretary of State	John M. Clayton, 1849
Secretary of the Treasury	William M. Meredith, 1849
Secretary of War	George W. Crawford, 1849
Attorney General	Reverdy Johnson, 1849
Postmaster General	Jacob Collamer, 1849
Secretary of the Navy	William B. Preston, 1849
Secretary of the Interior	Thomas Ewing, 1849

Fillmore

Secretary of State	Daniel Webster, 1850
	Edward Everett, 1852
Secretary of the Treasury	Thomas Corwin, 1850
Secretary of War	Charles M. Conrad, 1850
Attorney General	John J. Crittenden, 1850
Postmaster General	Nathan K. Hall, 1850
	Samuel D. Hubbard, 1852
Secretary of the Navy	William A. Graham, 1850
	John P. Kennedy, 1852
Secretary of the Interior	Thos. M. T. McKennan, 1850
	Alex. H. H. Stuart, 1850

Pierce

Secretary of State	William L. Marcy, 1853
Secretary of the Treasury	James Guthrie, 1853
Secretary of War	Jefferson Davis, 1853
Attorney General	Caleb Cushing, 1853
Postmaster General	James Campbell, 1853
Secretary of the Navy	James C. Dobbin, 1853
Secretary of the Interior	Robert McClelland, 1853

Buchanan

Secretary of State	Lewis Cass, 1857
	Jeremiah S. Black, 1860
Secretary of the Treasury	Howell Cobb, 1857
	Philip F. Thomas, 1860
	John A. Dix, 1861
Secretary of War	John B. Floyd, 1857
	Joseph Holt, 1861
Attorney General	Jeremiah S. Black, 1857
	Edwin M. Stanton, 1860
Postmaster General	Aaron V. Brown, 1857
	Joseph Holt, 1859
	Horatio King, 1861
Secretary of the Navy	Isaac Toucey, 1857
Secretary of the Interior	Jacob Thompson, 1857

Lincoln

Secretary of State	William H. Seward, 1861
Secretary of the Treasury	Salmon P. Chase, 1861
	William P. Fessenden, 1864
	Hugh McCulloch, 1865
Secretary of War	Simon Cameron, 1861
	Edwin M. Stanton, 1862
Attorney General	Edward Bates, 1861
	James Speed, 1864
Postmaster General	Montgomery Blair, 1861
	William Dennison, 1864
Secretary of the Navy	Gideon Welles, 1861
Secretary of the Interior	Caleb B. Smith, 1861
	John P. Usher, 1863

A. Johnson

Secretary of State	William H. Seward (Cont.)
Secretary of the Treasury	Hugh McCulloch (Cont.)
Secretary of War	Edwin M. Stanton (Cont.)
	John M. Schofield, 1868
Attorney General	James Speed (Cont.)
	Henry Stanbery, 1866
	William M. Evarts, 1868
Postmaster General	William Dennison (Cont.)
	Alexander W. Randall, 1866
Secretary of the Navy	Gideon Welles (Cont.)
Secretary of the Interior	John P. Usher (Cont.)
	James Harlan, 1865
	Orville H. Browning, 1866

Grant

Secretary of State	Elihu B. Washburne, 1869
	Hamilton Fish, 1869
	George S. Boutwell, 1869
	William A. Richardson, 1873
	Benjamin H. Bristow, 1874
	Lot M. Morrill, 1876
Secretary of War	John A. Rawlins, 1869
	William W. Belknap, 1869
	Alphonso Taft, 1876
	James D. Cameron, 1876
Attorney General	Ebenezer R. Hoar, 1869
	Amos T. Akerman, 1870
	George H. Williams, 1871
	Edwards Pierrepont, 1875
	Alphonso Taft, 1876
Postmaster General	John A. J. Creswell, 1869
	Marshall Jewell, 1874
	James N. Tyner, 1876
Secretary of the Navy	Adolph E. Borie, 1869
	George M. Robeson, 1869
Secretary of the Interior	Jacob D. Cox, 1869
	Columbus Delano, 1870
	Zachariah Chandler, 1875

Hayes

Secretary of State	William M. Evarts, 1877
Secretary of the Treasury	John Sherman, 1877
Secretary of War	George W. McCrary, 1877
	Alexander Ramsey, 1879
Attorney General	Charles Devens, 1877
Postmaster General	David M. Key, 1877
	Horace Maynard, 1880
	Richard W. Thompson, 1877
	Nathan Goff, Jr., 1881
Secretary of the Interior	Carl Schurz, 1877

Garfield

Secretary of State	James G. Blaine, 1881
Secretary of the Treasury	William Windom, 1881
Secretary of War	Robert T. Lincoln, 1881
Attorney General	Wayne MacVeagh, 1881
Postmaster General	Thomas L. James, 1881
Secretary of the Navy	William H. Hunt, 1881
Secretary of the Interior	Samuel J. Kirkwood, 1881

Arthur

Secretary of State	James G. Blaine (Cont.)
	F. T. Frelinghuysen, 1881
Secretary of the Treasury	William Windom (Cont.)
	Charles J. Folger, 1881
	Walter Q. Gresham, 1884
	Hugh McCulloch, 1884
Secretary of War	Robert T. Lincoln (Cont.)
Attorney General	Wayne MacVeagh (Cont.)
	Benjamin H. Brewster, 1881
Postmaster General	Thomas L. James (Cont.)
	Timothy O. Howe, 1881
	Walter Q. Gresham, 1883
	Frank Hatton, 1884
Secretary of the Navy	William H. Hunt (Cont.)
	William E. Chandler, 1882
Secretary of the Interior	Samuel J. Kirkwood (Cont.)
	Henry M. Teller, 1882

Cleveland

Secretary of State	Thomas F. Bayard, 1885
Secretary of the Treasury	Daniel Manning, 1885
	Charles S. Fairchild, 1887
Secretary of War	William C. Endicott, 1885
Attorney General	Augustus H. Garland, 1885
Postmaster General	William F. Vilas, 1885
	Don M. Dickinson, 1888
Secretary of the Navy	William C. Whitney, 1885
Secretary of the Interior	Lucius Q. C. Lamar, 1885
	William F. Vilas, 1888
Secretary of Agriculture	Norman J. Colman, 1889

B. Harrison

Secretary of State	James G. Blaine, 1889
	John W. Foster, 1892
Secretary of the Treasury	William Windom, 1889
	Charles Foster, 1891
Secretary of War	Redfield Proctor, 1889
	Stephen B. Elkins, 1891
Attorney General	William H. H. Miller, 1889
Postmaster General	John Wanamaker, 1889
Secretary of the Navy	Benjamin F. Tracy, 1889
Secretary of the Interior	John W. Noble, 1889
Secretary of Agriculture	Jeremiah M. Rusk, 1889

Cleveland

Secretary of State	Walter Q. Gresham, 1893
	Richard Olney, 1895
Secretary of the Treasury	John G. Carlisle, 1893
Secretary of War	Daniel S. Lamont, 1893
Attorney General	Richard Olney, 1893
	Judson Harmon, 1895
Postmaster General	Wilson S. Bissell, 1893
	William L. Wilson, 1895
Secretary of the Navy	Hilary A. Herbert, 1893
Secretary of the Interior	Hoke Smith, 1893
	David R. Francis, 1896
Secretary of Agriculture	Julius Sterling Morton, 1893

McKinley

Secretary of State	John Sherman, 1897
	William R. Day, 1898
	John Hay, 1898
Secretary of the Treasury	Lyman J. Gage, 1897
Secretary of War	Russell A. Alger, 1897
	Elihu Root, 1899
Attorney General	Joseph McKenna, 1897
	John W. Griggs, 1898
	Philander C. Knox, 1901
Postmaster General	James A. Gary, 1897
	Charles E. Smith, 1898
Secretary of the Navy	John D. Long, 1897
Secretary of the Interior	Cornelius N. Bliss, 1897
	Ethan A. Hitchcock, 1898
Secretary of Agriculture	James Wilson, 1897

T. Roosevelt

Secretary of State	John Hay (Cont.)
	Elihu Root, 1905
	Robert Bacon, 1909
Secretary of the Treasury	Lyman J. Gage (Cont.)
	Leslie M. Shaw, 1902
	George B. Cortelyou, 1907
Secretary of War	Elihu Root (Cont.)
	William H. Taft, 1904
	Luke E. Wright, 1908
Attorney General	Philander C. Knox (Cont.)
	William H. Moody, 1904
	Charles J. Bonaparte, 1906
Postmaster General	Charles E. Smith (Cont.)
	Henry C. Payne, 1902
	Robert J. Wynne, 1904
	George B. Cortelyou, 1905
	George von L. Meyer, 1907
Secretary of the Navy	John D. Long (Cont.)
	William H. Moody, 1902
	Paul Morton, 1904
	Charles J. Bonaparte, 1905
	Victor H. Metcalf, 1906
	Truman H. Newberry, 1908
Secretary of the Interior	Ethan A. Hitchcock (Cont.)
	James R. Garfield, 1907
Secretary of Agriculture	James Wilson (Cont.)
Secretary of Commerce and Labor	George B. Cortelyou, 1903
	Victor H. Metcalf, 1904
	Oscar S. Straus, 1906

Taft

Secretary of State	Philander C. Knox, 1909
Secretary of the Treasury	Franklin MacVeagh, 1909
Secretary of War	Jacob M. Dickinson, 1909
	Henry L. Stimson, 1911
Attorney General	George W. Wickersham, 1909
Postmaster General	Frank H. Hitchcock, 1909
Secretary of the Navy	George von L. Meyer, 1909
Secretary of the Interior	Richard A. Ballinger, 1909
	Walter L. Fisher, 1911
Secretary of Agriculture	James Wilson (Cont.)
Secretary of Commerce and Labor	Charles Nagel, 1909

Wilson

Secretary of State	William J. Bryan, 1913
	Robert Lansing, 1915
	Bainbridge Colby, 1920
Secretary of the Treasury	William G. McAdoo, 1913
	Carter Glass, 1918
	David F. Houston, 1920
Secretary of War	Lindley M. Garrison, 1913
	Newton D. Baker, 1916
Attorney General	James C. McReynolds, 1913
	Thomas W. Gregory, 1914
	A. Mitchell Palmer, 1919
Postmaster General	Albert S. Burleson, 1913
Secretary of the Navy	Josephus Daniels, 1913
Secretary of the Interior	Franklin K. Lane, 1913
	John B. Payne, 1920
Secretary of Agriculture	David F. Houston, 1913
	Edwin T. Meredith, 1920
Secretary of Commerce	William C. Redfield, 1913
	Joshua W. Alexander, 1919
Secretary of Labor	William B. Wilson, 1913

Harding

Secretary of State	Charles E. Hughes, 1921
Secretary of the Treasury	Andrew W. Mellon, 1921
Secretary of War	John W. Weeks, 1921
Attorney General	Harry M. Daugherty, 1921
Postmaster General	Will H. Hays, 1921
	Hubert Work, 1922
	Harry S. New, 1923

Secretary of the Navy	Edwin Denby, 1921
Secretary of the Interior	Albert B. Fall, 1921
	Hubert Work, 1923
Secretary of Agriculture	Henry C. Wallace, 1921
Secretary of Commerce	Herbert Hoover, 1921
Secretary of Labor	James J. Davis, 1921

Coolidge

Secretary of State	Charles E. Hughes (Cont.)
	Frank B. Kellogg, 1925
Secretary of the Treasury	Andrew W. Mellon (Cont.)
Secretary of War	John W. Weeks (Cont.)
	Dwight F. Davis, 1925
Attorney General	Harry M. Daughtery (Cont.)
	Harlan F. Stone, 1924
	John G. Sargent, 1925
Postmaster General	Harry S. New (Cont.)
Secretary of the Navy	Edwin Denby (Cont.)
	Curtis D. Wilbur, 1924
Secretary of the Interior	Hubert Work (Cont.)
	Roy O. West, 1928
Secretary of Agriculture	Henry C. Wallace (Cont.)
	Howard M. Gore, 1924
	William M. Jardine, 1925
Secretary of Commerce	Herbert Hoover (Cont.)
	William F. Whiting, 1928
Secretary of Labor	James J. Davis (Cont.)

Hoover

Secretary of State	Frank B. Kellogg (Cont.)
	Henry L. Stimson, 1929
Secretary of the Treasury	Andrew W. Mellon (Cont.)
	Ogden L. Mills, 1932
Secretary of War	James W. Good, 1929
	Patrick J. Hurley, 1929
Attorney General	William D. Mitchell, 1929
Postmaster General	Walter F. Brown, 1929
Secretary of the Navy	Charles F. Adams, 1929
Secretary of the Interior	Ray Lyman Wilbur, 1929
Secretary of Agriculture	Arthur M. Hyde, 1929
Secretary of Commerce	Robert P. Lamont, 1929
	Roy D. Chapin, 1932
Secretary of Labor	James J. Davis (Cont.)
	William N. Doak, 1930

F. D. Roosevelt

Secretary of State	Cordell Hull, 1933
	E. R. Stettinius, Jr., 1944
Secretary of the Treasury	William H. Woodin, 1933
	Henry Morgenthau, Jr., 1934
Secretary of War	George H. Dern, 1933
	Harry H. Woodring, 1936
	Henry L. Stimson, 1940
Attorney General	Homer S. Cummings, 1933
	Frank Murphy, 1939
	Robert H. Jackson, 1940
	Francis Biddle, 1941
Postmaster General	James A. Farley, 1933
	Frank C. Walker, 1940
Secretary of the Navy	Claude A. Swanson, 1933
	Charles Edison, 1940
	Frank Knox, 1940
	James Forrestal, 1944
Secretary of the Interior	Harold L. Ickes, 1933
Secretary of Agriculture	Henry A. Wallace, 1933
	Claude R. Wickard, 1940
Secretary of Commerce	Daniel C. Roper, 1933
	Harry L. Hopkins, 1938
	Jesse H. Jones, 1940
	Henry A. Wallace, 1945
Secretary of Labor	Frances Perkins, 1933

Truman

Secretary of State	E. R. Stettinius, Jr. (Cont.)
	James F. Byrnes, 1945
	George C. Marshall, 1947
	Dean Acheson, 1949
Secretary of the Treasury	Henry Morgenthau, Jr. (Cont.)
	Frederick M. Vinson, 1945
	John W. Snyder, 1946
Secretary of Defense	James Forrestal, 1947
	Louis A. Johnson, 1949
	George C. Marshall, 1950
	Robert A. Lovett, 1951
Attorney General	Francis Biddle (Cont.)
	Tom C. Clark, 1945
	J. Howard McGrath, 1949
	James P. McGranery, 1952
Postmaster General	Frank C. Walker (Cont.)
	Robert E. Hannegan, 1945
	Jesse M. Donaldson, 1947
Secretary of the Interior	Harold L. Ickes (Cont.)
	Julius A. Krug, 1946
	Oscar L. Chapman, 1949
Secretary of Agriculture	Claude R. Wickard (Cont.)
	Clinton P. Anderson, 1945
	Charles F. Brannan, 1948
Secretary of Commerce	Henry A. Wallace (Cont.)
	W. Averell Harriman, 1946
	Charles Sawyer, 1948
Secretary of Labor	Frances Perkins (Cont.)
	Lewis B. Schwellenbach, 1945
	Maurice J. Tobin, 1948
Secretary of War[1]	Henry L. Stimson (Cont.)
	Robert P. Patterson, 1945
	Kenneth C. Royall, 1947
Secretary of the Navy[1]	James Forrestal (Cont.)

1. On July 26, 1947, the Departments of War and of the Navy were incorporated into the Department of Defense.

Eisenhower

Secretary of State	John Foster Dulles, 1953
	Christian A. Herter, 1959
Secretary of the Treasury	George M. Humphrey, 1953
	Robert B. Anderson, 1957
Secretary of Defense	Charles E. Wilson, 1953
	Neil H. McElroy, 1957
	Thomas S. Gates, Jr., 1959
Attorney General	Herbert Brownell, Jr., 1953
	William P. Rogers, 1958
Postmaster General	Arthur E. Summerfield, 1953
Secretary of the Interior	Douglas McKay, 1953
	Frederick A. Seaton, 1956
Secretary of Agriculture	Ezra Taft Benson, 1953
Secretary of Commerce	Sinclair Weeks, 1953
	Lewis L. Strauss[1], 1958
	Frederick H. Mueller, 1959
Secretary of Labor	Martin P. Durkin, 1953
	James P. Mitchell, 1953
Secretary of Health, Education, and Welfare	Oveta Culp Hobby, 1953
	Marion B. Folsom, 1955
	Arthur S. Flemming, 1958

1. Not confirmed by the Senate.

Kennedy

Secretary of State	Dean Rusk, 1961
Secretary of the Treasury	C. Douglas Dillon, 1961
Secretary of Defense	Robert S. McNamara, 1961
Attorney General	Robert F. Kennedy, 1961
Postmaster General	J. Edward Day, 1961
	John A. Gronouski, 1963
Secretary of the Interior	Stewart L. Udall, 1961
Secretary of Agriculture	Orville L. Freeman, 1961
Secretary of Commerce	Luther H. Hodges, 1961
Secretary of Labor	Arthur J. Goldberg, 1961
	W. Willard Wirtz, 1962

Secretary of Health, Education, and Welfare	Abraham A. Ribicoff, 1961
	Anthony J. Celebrezze, 1962

L. B. Johnson

Secretary of State	Dean Rusk (Cont.)
Secretary of the Treasury	C. Douglas Dillon (Cont.)
	Henry H. Fowler, 1965
	Joseph W. Barr[1], 1968
Secretary of Defense	Robert S. McNamara (Cont.)
	Clark M. Clifford, 1968
Attorney General	Robert F. Kennedy (Cont.)
	N. de B. Katzenbach, 1965
	Ramsey Clark, 1967
Postmaster General	John A. Gronouski (Cont.)
	Lawrence F. O'Brien, 1965
	W. Marvin Watson, 1968
Secretary of the Interior	Stewart L. Udall (Cont.)
Secretary of Agriculture	Orville L. Freeman (Cont.)
Secretary of Commerce	Luther H. Hodges (Cont.)
	John T. Connor, 1964
	A. B. Trowbridge, 1967
	C. R. Smith, 1968
Secretary of Labor	W. Willard Wirtz (Cont.)
Secretary of Health, Education, and Welfare	Anthony J. Celebrezze (Cont.)
	John W. Gardner, 1965
	Wilbur J. Cohen, 1968
Secretary of Housing and Urban Development	Robert C. Weaver, 1966
	Robert C. Wood[1], 1969
Secretary of Transportation	Alan S. Boyd, 1966

1. Recess appointment.

Nixon

Secretary of State	William P. Rogers, 1969
	Henry A. Kissinger, 1973
Secretary of the Treasury	David M. Kennedy, 1969
	John B. Connally, 1971
	George P. Shultz, 1972
	William E. Simon, 1974
Secretary of Defense	Melvin R. Laird, 1969
	Elliot L. Richardson, 1973
	James R. Schlesinger, 1973
Attorney General	John N. Mitchell, 1969
	Richard G. Kleindienst, 1972
	Elliot L. Richardson, 1973
	William B. Saxbe, 1974
Postmaster General[1]	William M. Blount, 1969
Secretary of the Interior	Walter J. Hickel, 1969
	Rogers C. B. Morton, 1971
Secretary of Agriculture	Clifford M. Hardin, 1969
	Earl L. Butz, 1971
Secretary of Commerce	Maurice H. Stans, 1969
	Peter G. Peterson, 1972
	Frederick B. Dent, 1973
Secretary of Labor	George P. Shultz, 1969
	James D. Hodgson, 1970
	Peter J. Brennan, 1973
Secretary of Health, Education, and Welfare	Robert H. Finch, 1969
	Elliot L. Richardson, 1970
	Caspar W. Weinberger, 1973
Secretary of Housing and Urban Development	George Romney, 1969
	James T. Lynn, 1973
Secretary of Transportation	John A. Volpe, 1969
	Claude S. Brinegar, 1973

1. The Postmaster General is no longer a Cabinet member.

Ford

Secretary of State	Henry A. Kissinger (Cont.)
Secretary of the Treasury	William E. Simon (Cont.)
Secretary of Defense	James R. Schlesinger (Cont.)
	Donald H. Rumsfeld, 1975
Attorney General	William B. Saxbe (Cont.)
	Edward H. Levi, 1975
Secretary of the Interior	Rogers C. B. Morton (Cont.)
	Stanley K. Hathaway, 1975
	Thomas S. Kleppe, 1975

Secretary of Agriculture	Earl L. Butz (Cont.)
	John Knebel, 1976
Secretary of Commerce	Frederick B. Dent (Cont.)
	Rogers C. B. Morton, 1975
	Elliot L. Richardson, 1976
Secretary of Labor	Peter J. Brennan (Cont.)
	John T. Dunlop, 1975
	William J. Usery, Jr., 1976
Secretary of Health, Education, and Welfare	Caspar W. Weinberger (Cont.)
	F. David Mathews, 1975
Secretary of Housing and Urban Development	James T. Lynn (Cont.)
	Carla A. Hills, 1975
Secretary of Transportation	Claude S. Brinegar (Cont.)
	William T. Coleman, Jr., 1975

Carter

Secretary of State	Cyrus R. Vance, 1977
	Edmund S. Muskie, 1980
Secretary of the Treasury	W. Michael Blumenthal, 1977
	G. William Miller, 1979
Secretary of Defense	Harold Brown, 1977
Attorney General	Griffin B. Bell, 1977
	Benjamin R. Civiletti, 1979
Secretary of the Interior	Cecil D. Andrus, 1977
Secretary of Agriculture	Bob S. Bergland, 1977
Secretary of Commerce	Juanita M. Kreps, 1977
	Philip M. Klutznick, 1979
Secretary of Labor	F. Ray Marshall, 1977
Secretary of Health and Human Services[1]	Joseph A. Califano, Jr., 1977
	Patricia Roberts Harris, 1979
Secretary of Housing and Urban Development	Patricia Roberts Harris, 1977
	Moon Landrieu, 1979
Secretary of Transportation	Brock Adams, 1977
	Neil E. Goldschmidt, 1979
Secretary of Energy	James R. Schlesinger, 1977
	Charles W. Duncan, Jr., 1979
Secretary of Education	Shirley Mount Hufstedler, 1979

1. Known as Department of Health, Education, and Welfare until May 1980.

Reagan

Secretary of State	Alexander M. Haig, Jr., 1981
	George P. Shultz, 1982
Secretary of the Treasury	Donald T. Regan, 1981
	James A. Baker 3rd, 1985
	Nicholas F. Brady, 1988
Secretary of Defense	Caspar W. Weinberger, 1981
	Frank C. Carlucci, 1987
Attorney General	William French Smith, 1981
	Edwin Meese 3rd, 1985
	Richard L. Thornburgh, 1988
Secretary of the Interior	James G. Watt, 1981
	William P. Clark, 1983
	Donald P. Hodel, 1985
Secretary of Agriculture	John R. Block, 1981
	Richard E. Lyng, 1986
Secretary of Commerce	Malcolm Baldrige, 1981
	C. William Verity, Jr., 1987
Secretary of Labor	Raymond J. Donovan, 1981
	William E. Brock, 1985
	Ann Dore McLaughlin, 1987
Secretary of Health and Human Services	Richard S. Schweiker, 1981
	Margaret M. Heckler, 1983
	Otis R. Bowen, 1985
Secretary of Housing and Urban Development	Samuel R. Pierce, Jr., 1981
Secretary of Transportation	Andrew L. Lewis, Jr., 1981
	Elizabeth H. Dole, 1983
	James H. Burnley 4th, 1987
Secretary of Energy	James B. Edwards, 1981
	Donald P. Hodel, 1983
	John S. Herrington, 1985
Secretary of Education	T. H. Bell, 1981
	William J. Bennett, 1985
	Lauro F. Cavazos, 1988

Bush

Secretary of State	James A. Baker 3d, 1989
	Lawrence S. Eagleburger, 1992
Secretary of the Treasury	Nicholas F. Brady (Cont.)
Secretary of Defense	Richard Cheney, 1989
Attorney General	Richard L. Thornburgh (Cont.)
	William P. Barr, 1992
Secretary of the Interior	Manuel Lujan Jr., 1989
Secretary of Agriculture	Clayton K. Yeutter, 1989
	Edward Madigan, 1991
Secretary of Commerce	Robert A. Mosbacher Sr., 1989
	Barbara H. Franklin, 1992
Secretary of Labor	Elizabeth H. Dole, 1989
	Lynn Martin, 1991
Secretary of Health and Human Services	Louis W. Sullivan, 1989
Secretary of Housing and Urban Development	Jack F. Kemp, 1989
Secretary of Transportation	Samuel K. Skinner, 1989
	Andrew Card, 1992
Secretary of Energy	James D. Watkins, 1989
Secretary of Education	Lauro F. Cavazos (Cont.)
	Lamar Alexander, 1991
Secretary of Veterans' Affairs	Edward J. Derwinski, 1989

Clinton

Secretary of State	Warren M. Christopher, 1993
	Madeleine Albright, 1996
Secretary of the Treasury	Lloyd Bentsen, 1993
	Robert E. Rubin, 1995–1999
	Lawrence H. Summers, 1999
Secretary of Defense	Les Aspin, 1993
	William J. Perry, 1994
	William S. Cohen, 1997
Attorney General	Janet Reno, 1993
Secretary of the Interior	Bruce Babbitt, 1993
Secretary of Agriculture	Mike Espy, 1993
	Dan Glickman, 1995
Secretary of Commerce	Ronald H. Brown, 1993
	Mickey Kantor, 1996
	William M. Daley, 1997
Secretary of Labor	Robert B. Reich, 1993
	Alexis Herman, 1997
Secretary of Health and Human Services	Donna E. Shalala, 1993
Secretary of Housing and Urban Development	Henry G. Cisneros, 1993
	Andrew M. Cuomo, 1997
Secretary of Transportation	Federico F. Pena, 1993
	Rodney Slater, 1997
Secretary of Energy	Hazel R. O'Leary, 1993
	Frederico F. Pena, 1997
	Bill Richardson, 1998
Secretary of Education	Richard W. Riley, 1993
Secretary of Veterans' Affairs	Jesse Brown, 1993
	Togo D. West, Jr., 1998

Members of the Supreme Court of the United States

Mailing address for the Supreme Court: U.S. Supreme Court Building, 1 First Street NE, Washington, D.C. 20543.

Name, state	Service Term	Yrs	Birth Place	Date	Died	Religion
Chief Justices						
John Jay, N.Y.	1789–1795	5	N.Y.	1745	1829	Episcopal
John Rutledge, S.C.	1795	0	S.C.	1739	1800	Church of England
Oliver Ellsworth, Conn.	1796–1800	4	Conn.	1745	1807	Congregational
John Marshall, Va.	1801–1835	34	Va.	1755	1835	Episcopal
Roger B. Taney, Md.	1836–1864	28	Md.	1777	1864	Roman Catholic
Salmon P. Chase, Ohio	1864–1873	8	N.H.	1808	1873	Episcopal
Morrison R. Waite, Ohio	1874–1888	14	Conn.	1816	1888	Episcopal
Melville W. Fuller, Ill.	1888–1910	21	Maine	1833	1910	Episcopal
Edward D. White, La.	1910–1921	10	La.	1845	1921	Roman Catholic
William H. Taft, Conn.	1921–1930	8	Ohio	1857	1930	Unitarian
Charles E. Hughes, N.Y.	1930–1941	11	N.Y.	1862	1948	Baptist
Harlan F. Stone, N.Y.	1941–1946	4	N.H.	1872	1946	Episcopal
Frederick M. Vinson, Ky.	1946–1953	7	Ky.	1890	1953	Methodist
Earl Warren, Calif.	1953–1969	15	Calif.	1891	1974	Protestant
Warren E. Burger, Va.	1969–1986	17	Minn.	1907	1995	Presbyterian
William H. Rehnquist, Ariz.	1986–	—	Wis.	1924	—	Lutheran
Associate Justices						
James Wilson, Pa.	1789–1798	8	Scotland	1742	1798	Episcopal
John Rutledge, S.C.	1790–1791	1	S.C.	1739	1800	Church of England
William Cushing, Mass.	1790–1810	20	Mass.	1732	1810	Unitarian
John Blair, Va.	1790–1796	5	Va.	1732	1800	Presbyterian
James Iredell, N.C.	1790–1799	9	England	1751	1799	Episcopal
Thomas Johnson, Md.	1792–1793	0	Md.	1732	1819	Episcopal
William Paterson, N.J.	1793–1806	13	Ireland	1745	1806	Protestant
Samuel Chase, Md.	1796–1811	15	Md.	1741	1811	Episcopal
Bushrod Washington, Va.	1799–1829	30	Va.	1762	1829	Episcopal
Alfred Moore, N.C.	1800–1804	3	N.C.	1755	1810	Episcopal
William Johnson, S.C.	1804–1834	30	S.C.	1771	1834	Presbyterian
Brockholst Livingston, N.Y.	1807–1823	16	N.Y.	1757	1823	Presbyterian
Thomas Todd, Ky.	1807–1826	18	Va.	1765	1826	Presbyterian
Gabriel Duval, Md.	1811–1835	23	Md.	1752	1844	French Protestant

Name, state	Service Term	Yrs	Birth Place	Date	Died	Religion
Joseph Story, Mass.	1812–1845	33	Mass.	1779	1845	Unitarian
Smith Thompson, N.Y.	1823–1843	20	N.Y.	1768	1843	Presbyterian
Robert Trimble, Ky.	1826–1828	2	Va.	1777	1828	Protestant
John McLean, Ohio	1830–1861	31	N.J.	1785	1861	Methodist-Epis.
Henry Baldwin, Pa.	1830–1844	14	Conn.	1780	1844	Trinity Church
James M. Wayne, Ga.	1835–1867	32	Ga.	1790	1867	Protestant
Philip P. Barbour, Va.	1836–1841	4	Va.	1783	1841	Episcopal
John Catron, Tenn.	1837–1865	28	Pa.	1786	1865	Presbyterian
John McKinley, Ala.	1837–1852	14	Va.	1780	1852	Protestant
Peter V. Daniel, Va.	1841–1860	18	Va.	1784	1860	Episcopal
Samuel Nelson, N.Y.	1845–1872	27	N.Y.	1792	1873	Protestant
Levi Woodbury, N.H.	1845–1851	5	N.H.	1789	1851	Protestant
Robert C. Grier, Pa.	1846–1870	23	Pa.	1794	1870	Presbyterian
Benjamin R. Curtis, Mass.	1851–1857	5	Mass.	1809	1874	(2)
John A. Campbell, Ala.	1853–1861	8	Ga.	1811	1889	Episcopal
Nathan Clifford, Maine	1858–1881	23	N.H.	1803	1881	(1)
Noah H. Swayne, Ohio	1862–1881	18	Va.	1804	1884	Quaker
Samuel F. Miller, Iowa	1862–1890	28	Ky.	1816	1890	Unitarian
David Davis, Ill.	1862–1877	14	Md.	1815	1886	(4)
Stephen J. Field, Calif.	1863–1897	34	Conn.	1816	1899	Episcopal
William Strong, Pa.	1870–1880	10	Conn.	1808	1895	Presbyterian
Joseph P. Bradley, N.J.	1870–1892	21	N.Y.	1813	1892	Presbyterian
Ward Hunt, N.Y.	1872–1882	9	N.Y.	1810	1886	Episcopal
John M. Harlan, Ky.	1877–1911	33	Ky.	1833	1911	Presbyterian
William B. Woods, Ga.	1880–1887	6	Ohio	1824	1887	Protestant
Stanley Matthews, Ohio	1881–1889	7	Ohio	1824	1889	Presbyterian
Horace Gray, Mass.	1882–1902	20	Mass.	1828	1902	(3)
Samuel Blatchford, N.Y.	1882–1893	11	N.Y.	1820	1893	Presbyterian
Lucius Q. C. Lamar, Miss.	1888–1893	5	Ga.	1825	1893	Methodist
David J. Brewer, Kan.	1889–1910	20	Asia Minor	1837	1910	Protestant
Henry B. Brown, Mich.	1890–1906	15	Mass.	1836	1913	Protestant
George Shiras, Jr., Pa.	1892–1903	10	Pa.	1832	1924	Presbyterian
Howell E. Jackson, Tenn.	1893–1895	2	Tenn.	1832	1895	Baptist
Edward D. White, La.*	1894–1910	16	La.	1845	1921	Roman Catholic
Rufus W. Peckham, N.Y.	1895–1909	13	N.Y.	1838	1909	Episcopal
Joseph McKenna, Calif.	1898–1925	26	Pa.	1843	1926	Roman Catholic
Oliver W. Holmes, Mass.	1902–1932	29	Mass.	1841	1935	Unitarian
William R. Day, Ohio	1903–1922	19	Ohio	1849	1923	Protestant
William H. Moody, Mass.	1906–1910	3	Mass.	1853	1917	Episcopal
Horace H. Lurton, Tenn.	1909–1914	4	Ky.	1844	1914	Episcopal
Charles E. Hughes, N.Y.*	1910–1916	5	N.Y.	1862	1948	Baptist
Willis Van Devanter, Wyo.	1910–1937	26	Ind.	1859	1941	Episcopal
Joseph R. Lamar, Ga.	1910–1916	4	Ga.	1857	1916	Ch. of Disciples
Mahlon Pitney, N.J.	1912–1922	10	N.J.	1858	1924	Presbyterian
James C. McReynolds, Tenn.	1914–1941	26	Ky.	1862	1946	Disciples of Christ
Louis D. Brandeis, Mass.	1916–1939	22	Ky.	1856	1941	Jewish
John H. Clarke, Ohio	1916–1922	5	Ohio	1857	1945	Protestant
George Sutherland, Utah	1922–1938	15	England	1862	1942	Episcopal
Pierce Butler, Minn.	1923–1939	16	Minn.	1866	1939	Roman Catholic
Edward T. Sanford, Tenn.	1923–1930	7	Tenn.	1865	1930	Episcopal
Harlan F. Stone, N.Y.*	1925–1941	16	N.H.	1872	1946	Episcopal
Owen J. Roberts, Pa.	1930–1945	15	Pa.	1875	1955	Episcopal
Benjamin N. Cardozo, N.Y.	1932–1938	6	N.Y.	1870	1938	Jewish
Hugo L. Black, Ala.	1937–1971	34	Ala.	1886	1971	Baptist
Stanley F. Reed, Ky.	1938–1957	19	Ky.	1884	1980	Protestant
Felix Frankfurter, Mass.	1939–1962	23	Austria	1882	1965	Jewish
William O. Douglas, Conn.	1939–1975	36	Minn.	1898	1980	Presbyterian
Frank Murphy, Mich.	1940–1949	9	Mich.	1890	1949	Roman Catholic
James F. Byrnes, S.C.	1941–1942	1	S.C.	1879	1972	Episcopal
Robert H. Jackson, Pa.	1941–1954	13	N.Y.	1892	1954	Episcopal
Wiley B. Rutledge, Iowa	1943–1949	6	Ky.	1894	1949	Unitarian
Harold H. Burton, Ohio	1945–1958	13	Mass.	1888	1964	Unitarian
Tom C. Clark, Tex.	1949–1967	17	Tex.	1899	1977	Presbyterian
Sherman Minton, Ind.	1949–1956	7	Ind.	1890	1965	Roman Catholic
John M. Harlan, N.Y.	1955–1971	16	Ill.	1899	1971	Presbyterian
William J. Brennan, Jr., N.J.	1956–1990	33	N.J.	1906	1997	Roman Catholic
Charles E. Whittaker, Mo.	1957–1962	5	Kan.	1901	1973	Methodist
Potter Stewart, Ohio	1958–1981	23	Mich.	1915	1985	Episcopal

| Name, state | Service | | Birth | | Died | Religion |
	Term	Yrs	Place	Date		
Byron R. White, Colo.	1962–1993	31	Colo.	1917	—	Episcopal
Arthur J. Goldberg, Ill.	1962–1965	2	Ill.	1908	1990	Jewish
Abe Fortas, Tenn.	1965–1969	3	Tenn.	1910	1982	Jewish
Thurgood Marshall, N.Y.	1967–1991	24	Md.	1908	1993	Episcopal
Harry A. Blackmun, Minn.	1970–1994	24	Ill.	1908	1999	Methodist
Lewis F. Powell, Jr., Va.	1972–1987	15	Va.	1907	1998	Presbyterian
William H. Rehnquist, Ariz.*	1972–1986	14	Wis.	1924	—	Lutheran
John Paul Stevens, Ill.	1975–	—	Ill.	1920	—	Protestant
Sandra Day O'Connor, Ariz.	1981–	—	Tex.	1930	—	Episcopal
Antonin Scalia, D.C.	1986–	—	N.J.	1936	—	Roman Catholic
Anthony M. Kennedy, Calif.	1988–	—	Calif.	1936	—	Roman Catholic
David H. Souter, N.H.	1990–	—	Mass.	1939	—	Episcopal
Clarence Thomas, D.C.	1991–	—	Ga.	1948	—	Roman Catholic
Ruth Bader Ginsburg, D.C.	1993–	—	N.Y.	1933	—	Jewish
Stephen G. Breyer, Mass.	1994–	—	Calif.	1938	—	n.a.

NOTE: n.a. = not available. *Served as both Chief Justice and Associate Justice. 1. Congregational; later Unitarian. 2. Unitarian; then Episcopal. 3. Unitarian or Congregational. 4. Not a member of any church.

Milestone Cases in Supreme Court History

1803 *Marbury v. Madison* was the first instance in which a law passed by Congress was declared unconstitutional. The decision greatly expanded the power of the Court by establishing its right to overturn acts of Congress, a power not explicitly granted by the Constitution.

1819 *McCulloch v. Maryland* upheld the right of Congress to create a Bank of the United States, ruling that it was a power implied but not enumerated by the Constitution. The case is significant because it advanced the doctrine of implied powers, or a loose construction of the Constitution. The Court, Chief Justice John Marshall wrote, would sanction laws reflecting "the letter and spirit" of the Constitution.

1857 *Dred Scott v. Sanford* was a highly controversial case that intensified the national debate over slavery. The case involved Dred Scott, a slave, who was taken from a slave state to a free territory. Scott filed a lawsuit claiming that because he had lived on free soil he was entitled to his freedom. Chief Justice Roger B. Taney disagreed, ruling that blacks were not citizens and therefore could not sue in Federal Court. Taney further inflamed anti-slavery forces by declaring that Congress had no right to ban slavery from U.S. territories.

1896 *Plessy v. Fergusson* was the infamous case that asserted that "equal but separate accommodations" for blacks on railroad cars did not violate the "equal protection under the laws" clause of the 14th Amendment. By defending the constitutionality of racial segregation, the Court paved the way for the repressive Jim Crow laws of the south. The lone dissenter on the Court, Justice John Marshall Harlan, protested, "The thin disguise of 'equal' accommodations . . . will not mislead anyone."

1954 *Brown v. Board of Education of Topeka* invalidated racial segregation in schools, and led to the unraveling of de jure segregation in all areas of public life. In the unanimous decision spearheaded by Chief Justice Earl Warren, the Court invalidated the Plessy ruling, declaring "in the field of public education, the doctrine of 'separate but equal' has no place," and contending that "separate educational facilities are inherently unequal." Future Supreme Court Justice Thurgood Marshall was one of the NAACP lawyers who successfully argued the case.

1973 *Roe v. Wade* legalized abortion and is at the center of the current controversy between "Pro-Life" and "Pro-Choice" advocates. The Court ruled that a woman has the right to an abortion without interference from the government in the first trimester of pregnancy, contending that it is part of her "right to privacy." The Court maintained that right to privacy is not absolute, however, and granted states the right to intervene in the second and third trimesters of pregnancy.

Notable Decisions of the U.S. Supreme Court, 1998–1999 Term

Administration Appeals Rejected (Nov. 9, 1998): Justices bar two Clinton moves to block grand jury testimony by Secret Service agents and President's lawyer in investigation of Monica Lewinsky affair.

Campaign Finance Appeals Rejected (Nov. 16, 1998): Supreme Court justices reject moves by Ohio and Arkansas questioning limits on political spending and contributions.

Police Search Powers Limited (Dec. 8, 1998): Justices rule unanimously that issuing a speeding ticket does not automatically give police right to search car.

Census Count by Sampling Rejected (Jan. 25, 1999): Justices rule, 5–4, that traditional head count must be used in 2000. Justices reject Administration's plan for statistical sampling to prevent wide undercounting.

Timothy McVeigh's Appeal Rejected (March 8, 1999): Justices refuse to hear appeal by man sentenced to death for Oklahoma City bombing in 1995 that killed 168.

Court Restricts Immigrants' Rights (May 3, 1999): Rules unanimously that foreigners who have committed serious crimes in home countries are ineligible for refugee status despite risk of persecution if deported.

Racially Drawn Districts Approved (May 17, 1999): Justices rule unanimously that even deliberate concentration of black voters is permissible as long as state's motive is potentially political, not racial.

Welfare Restrictions Overruled (May 17, 1999): Court, 7–2, decides state programs may not restrict new residents to benefits due them in home states.

Ruling on Sexual Harassment in School (May 24, 1999): In 5–4 decision, Justices find that school districts can be liable under Federal law for offenses by students.

Access to Federal Courts Limited (June 7, 1999): Justices' 6–3 decision rules that state prisoners who have not first appealed to state's highest court cannot appeal to Federal level.

Disability Legal Coverage Restricted (June 22, 1999): By 7–2 votes in three bias cases, Court rules that persons whose condition can be corrected by wearing glasses or taking their medications do not fall under protection of Americans With Disabilities Act of 1990.

Death Sentence Upheld in Test Case (June 21, 1999): Justices divide, 5–4, in first such case under expanded federal death-penalty law. Reject argument that jury had not received sufficient information before sentencing retired Army Ranger in killing of enlisted woman in Tex. in 1995.

Witness Deal-Making Retained (June 21, 1999): Court, without comment, rejects lower court's decision that offering leniency for testimony amounts to bribery.

Executive Departments and Agencies

Source: United States Government Manual, 1997–1998.

Unless otherwise indicated, addresses shown are in Washington, D.C.

White House Offices and Agencies

Office of Administration
Old Executive Office Bldg., 725 Seventeenth Street, N.W. (20503)
  Established: Dec. 12, 1977
  Director: Ada L. Posey
Office of National Drug Control Policy
Executive Office of the President (20503)
  Established: Jan. 29, 1989
  Director: Barry R. McCaffrey
Council of Economic Advisers (CEA)
Room 314, Old Executive Office Bldg. (20501)
  Members: 3
  Established: Feb. 20, 1946
  Chair: Janet L. Yellen
Council on Environmental Quality
Room 360, Old Executive Office Bldg. (20501)
  Established: 1969
  Chair: Kathleen A. McGinty
Office of Management and Budget
Executive Office Bldg. (20503)
  Established: July 1, 1939
  Director: Jacob J. Lew
Office of Science and Technology Policy
Old Executive Office Building (20502)
  Established: May 11, 1976
  Director: Neal F. Lane
National Security Council (NSC)
Old Executive Office Bldg. (20506)
  Members: 4
  Established: July 26, 1947
  Chair: The President
  National Security Adviser: Samuel R. (Sandy) Berger
  Other members: Vice President; Secretary of State; Secretary of Defense
Office of the United States Trade Representative
600 17th St., N.W. (20508)
  Established: Jan. 15, 1963
  Trade Representative: Charlene Barshefsky

Executive Departments

Department of Agriculture
14th & Independence Ave., S.W. (20250).
  Established: May 15, 1862. Administered by Commissioner of Agriculture until 1889, when it was made executive department.
  Secretary: Dan Glickman
  Deputy Secretary: Richard Rominger
Department of Commerce
14th St. between Constitution Ave. & Constitution Ave., N.W. (20230)
  Established: Department of Commerce and Labor was created Feb. 14, 1903. On March 4, 1913, all labor activities were transferred out of Department of Commerce and Labor and it was renamed Department of Commerce.
  Secretary: William M. Daley
Department of Defense
Office of the Secretary, The Pentagon (20301-1155)
  Established: July 26, 1947, as National Military Establishment; name changed to Department of Defense on Aug. 10, 1949. Subordinate to Secretary of Defense are Secretaries of Army, Navy, Air Force.
  Secretary: William S. Cohen
  Deputy Secretary: John Hamre
  Secretary of Army: Louis Caldera
  Secretary of Navy: John H. Dalton
  Secretary of Air Force: F. Whitten Peters (acting)
  Commandant of Marine Corps: Gen. Charles C. Krulak
  Joint Chiefs of Staff: Gen. Harry Sheltoni, Chairman; Gen. Joseph W. Ralston, Vice Chairman; Gen. Dennis J. Reimer, Army; Adm. Jay L. Johnson, Navy; Gen. Michael E. Ryan, Air Force; Gen. Charles C. Krulak, Marine Corps.
Department of Education
600 Independence Ave., S.W. (20202)
  Established: Oct. 17, 1979
  Secretary: Richard Riley
  Deputy Secretary: Marshall Smith (acting)
Department of Energy
1000 Independence Ave., S.W. (20585)
  Established: Oct. 1, 1977
  Secretary: Bill Richardson
  Deputy Secretary: T. J. Glauthier
Department of Health and Human Services
200 Independence Ave., S.W. (20201)
  Established: Department of Health, Education, and Welfare was created April 11, 1953, replacing Federal Security Agency created in 1939. On Oct. 17, 1979, the Department of Education became a separate department.
  Secretary: Donna Shalala
  Surgeon General: David Satcher
Department of Housing and Urban Development
451 7th St., S.W. (20410)
  Established: Nov. 9, 1965, replacing Housing and Home Finance Agency created in 1947
  Secretary: Andrew M. Cuomo
  Deputy Secretary: Saul Ramirez, Jr.
Department of the Interior
1849 C St. (20240)
  Established: March 3, 1849
  Secretary: Bruce Babbitt
  Deputy Secretary: David Hayes (acting)
Department of Justice
10th St. and Constitution Ave., N.W. (20530)
  Established: Office of Attorney General was created Sept. 24, 1789. Although one of the original Cabinet members, the Attorney General was not an executive department head until June 22, 1870, when the Department of Justice was established.

Attorney General: Janet Reno
Deputy Attorney General: Eric H. Holder, Jr.
Solicitor General: Seth P. Waxman
Director of FBI: Louis J. Freeh
Department of Labor
200 Constitution Ave., N.W. (20210)
   Established: Bureau of Labor was created in 1884 under Department of the Interior; later became independent department without executive rank. Returned to bureau status in Department of Commerce and Labor, but on March 4, 1913, became independent executive department under its present name.
   Secretary: Alexis M. Herman
   Deputy Secretary: Edward Montgomery (acting)
Department of State
2201 C St., N.W. (20520)
   Established: 1781 as Department of Foreign Affairs; reconstituted, 1789, following adoption of Constitution; name changed to Department of State Sept. 15, 1789.
   Secretary: Madeleine Albright
   U.N. Ambassador: Richard Holbrooke
Department of Transportation
400 7th St., S.W. (20590)
   Established: Oct. 15, 1966, as result of Department of Transportation Act, which became effective April 1, 1967.
   Secretary: Rodney E. Slater
   Deputy Secretary: Mortimer L. Downey
Department of the Treasury
1500 Pennsylvania Ave., N.W. (20220)
   Established: Sept. 2, 1789
   Secretary: Lawrence H. Summers
   Deputy Secretary: Stuart E. Eizenstat
   Treasurer of the U.S.: Mary Ellen Withrow
Department of Veterans' Affairs
810 Vermont Avenue, N.W. (20420)
   Established: March 15, 1989, replacing Veterans Administration created in 1930
   Secretary: Togo D. West, Jr.
   Deputy Secretary: Hershel Gober

Major Independent Agencies

U.S. Arms Control and Disarmament Agency
320 21st St., N.W., (20451)
   Established: Sept. 26, 1961
   Director: John Holum
Central Intelligence Agency (CIA)
Washington, D.C. (20505)
   Established: 1947
   Director of Central Intelligence: George J. Tenet
U.S. Commission on Civil Rights
624 9th St. (20425)
   Established: 1957
   Chair: Mary Frances Berry
Consumer Product Safety Commission
East West Towers, 4330 East West Highway, Bethesda, Md. (20814)
   Established: Oct. 27, 1972
   Chairperson: Ann Brown
Corporation for National Service
1201 New York Ave., N.W. (20525)
   Established: Sept. 1993
   CEO: Harris Wofford
Environmental Protection Agency (EPA)
401 M St., S.W. (20460)
   Established: Dec. 2, 1970
   Administrator: Carol M. Browner
Equal Employment Opportunity Commission (EEOC)
1801 L St. (20507)
   Members: 5
   Established: July 2, 1965
   Chair: Ida L. Castro
Farm Credit Administration (FCA)
1501 Farm Credit Dr., McLean, Va. (22102)
   Members: 13

   Established: March 27, 1933
   Chair: Marsha P. Martin
Federal Deposit Insurance Corporation (FDIC)
550 17th St., N.W. (20429)
   Established: June 16, 1933
   Chair: Donna Tanoue
Federal Election Commission (FEC)
999 E St., N.W. (20463)
   Members: 6
   Established: 1975
   Chair: Scott E. Thomas
Federal Maritime Commission
800 North Capitol St., N.W. (20573–0001)
   Members: 5
   Established: Aug. 12, 1961
   Chair: Harold J. Creel, Jr.
Federal Mediation and Conciliation Service (FMCS)
2100 K St., N.W. (20427)
   Established: 1947
   Director: C. Richard Barnes (acting)
Federal Reserve System (FRS), Board of Governors of
20th St. & Constitution Ave., N.W. (20551)
   Members: 7
   Established: Dec. 23, 1913
   Chair: Alan Greenspan
Federal Trade Commission (FTC)
Pennsylvania Ave. at 6th St., N.W. (20580)
   Members: 5
   Established: Sept. 26, 1914
   Chair: Robert Pitofsky
General Services Administration (GSA)
General Services Building, 18th and F Sts., N.W. (20405)
   Established: July 1, 1949
   Administrator: David J. Barram
U.S. Information Agency
301 Fourth St., S.W. (20547)
   Established: Aug. 1, 1953. Reorganized April 1, 1978.
   Director: Penn Kemble (acting)
National Aeronautics and Space Administration (NASA)
300 E St., S.W. (20546)
   Established: 1958
   Administrator: Daniel S. Goldin
National Foundation on the Arts and the Humanities
1100 Pennsylvania Ave., N.W., (20506)
   Established: 1965
   Chairs: National Endowment for the Arts, Chair, William Ivey; National Endowment for the Humanities, Chair, William R. Ferris
National Labor Relations Board (NLRB)
1099 14th St., N.W. (20570)
   Members: 5
   Established: July 5, 1935
   Chair: John C. Truesdale
National Mediation Board
Suite 250 East, 1301 K St., N.W. (20572)
   Established: June 21, 1934
   Chair: Magdalena G. Jacobsen
National Science Foundation (NSF)
4201 Wilson Blvd., Arlington, Va. (22230)
   Established: 1950
   Director: Rita R. Colwell
National Transportation Safety Board
490 L'Enfant Plaza, S.W. (20594)
   Members: 5
   Established: April 1, 1967, as an independent agency supported by the Dept. of Transportation. Ties with Dept. of Transportation officially ended in 1975.
   Chair: James Hall
Nuclear Regulatory Commission (NRC)
One White Flint North, 11555 Rockville Pike, Rockville, Md. (20852)
   Members: 5
   Established: Jan. 19, 1975
   Chair: Shirley Jackson

Office of Personnel Management (OPM)
1900 E St., N.W. (20415)
  Established: Jan. 1, 1979
  Director: Janice R. Lachance
U.S. Postal Service
475 L'Enfant Plaza West, S.W. (20260-0010)
  Established: In 1775 with the appointment of Benjamin Franklin as the first Postmaster General under the Continental Congress. In 1970 became independent agency headed by 11-member board of governors.
  Postmaster General: William J. Henderson
  Deputy Postmaster General: Michael S. Coughlin
Securities and Exchange Commission (SEC)
450 5th St., N.W. (20549)
  Members: 5
  Established: July 2, 1934
  Chair: Arthur Levitt
Selective Service System (SSS)
1515 Wilson Blvd., Arlington, Va. 22209-2425
  Established: Sept. 16, 1940
  Director: Gil Coronado
Small Business Administration (SBA)
409 3rd St., S.W. (20416)
  Established: July 30, 1953
  Administrator: Aida Alvarez
U.S. International Trade Commission
500 E St., S.W. (20436)
  Members: 6
  Established: Sept. 8, 1916
  Chair: Lynn Bragg
Tennessee Valley Authority (TVA)
400 West Summit Hill Drive, Knoxville, Tenn. (37902). Washington office: One Massachusetts Ave., N.W. (20444-0001).
  Members of Board of Directors: 3
  Established: May 18, 1933
  Chairman: Craven H. Crowell, Jr.

Other Independent Agencies

Administrative Conference of the United States—2120 L St., N.W., Ste. 500 (20037)
American Battle Monuments Commission—Pulaski Bldg., 20 Massachusetts Ave., N.W., Room 5127 (20314)
Appalachian Regional Commission—1666 Connecticut Ave., N.W., Room 601 (20235)
Commission of Fine Arts—441 F St., N.W., Ste. 312 (20001)
Commodity Futures Trading Commission—1155 21st St., N.W. (20581)
Export-Import Bank of the United States—811 Vermont Ave., N.W. (20571)

Federal Emergency Management Agency—500 C St., S.W. (20472)
Federal Housing Finance Board—1777 F St., N.W. (20006)
Federal Labor Relations Authority—607 14th St., N.W. (20424-0001)
Inter-American Foundation—901 N. Stuart St., 10th Floor, Arlington, Va. (22203)
National Commission on Libraries and Information Science—1110 Vermont Ave., N.W., Ste. 820 (20005-3552)
National Credit Union Administration—1775 Duke St., Alexandria, Va. (22314–3428)
Occupational Safety and Health Review Commission—1120 20th St., N.W. (20036–3419)
Panama Canal Commission—1825 I St., N.W., Suite 1050 (20006-5402)
Peace Corps—1111 20th St., N.W. (20526)
Pension Benefit Guaranty Corporation—1200 K St., N.W. (20005-4026)
Postal Rate Commission—1333 H St., N.W., Ste. 300 (20268–0001)
President's Committee on Employment of People With Disabilities—1331 F St., N.W., Ste. 300 (20004)
President's Council on Physical Fitness and Sports—701 Pennsylvania Ave., N.W., Suite 250 (20004)
U.S. Railroad Retirement Board (RRB)—844 N. Rush St., Ninth Floor, Chicago, Ill. (60611-2092); Office of Legislative Affairs: 1310 G St., N.W, Suite 500 (20005–3004).
U.S. Parole Commission—Dept. of Justice, 5550 Friendship Blvd., Ste. 420, Chevy Chase, Md. (20815)

Legislative Department

Architect of the Capitol—U.S. Capitol Building (20515)
General Accounting Office (GAO)—441 G St., N.W. (20548)
Government Printing Office (GPO)—732 North Capitol St., N.W. (20401)
Library of Congress—101 Independence Ave., S.E. (20540)
United States Botanic Garden—Office of Executive Director, 245 First St., S.W. (20024)

Quasi-Official Agencies

American National Red Cross—430 Seventeenth St., N.W. (20006)
Legal Services Corporation—750 First St., N.E. (20002-4250)
National Academy of Sciences, National Academy of Engineering, National Research Council, Institute of Medicine—2101 Constitution Ave., N.W. (20418)
National Railroad Passenger Corporation (Amtrak)—60 Massachusetts Ave., N.E. (20002)
Smithsonian Institution—1000 Jefferson Dr., S.W. (20560)

Biographies of the Presidents

GEORGE WASHINGTON was born on Feb. 22, 1732 (Feb. 11, 1731/2, old style) in Westmoreland County, Va. While in his teens, he trained as a surveyor, and at the age of 20 he was appointed adjutant in the Va. militia. For the next three years, he fought in the wars against the French and Indians, serving as Gen. Edward Braddock's aide in the disastrous campaign against Ft. Duquesne. In 1759, he resigned from the militia, married Martha Dandridge Custis, a widow with children, and settled down as a gentleman farmer at Mount Vernon, Va.

As a militiaman, Washington had been exposed to the arrogance of the British officers, and his experience as a planter with British commercial restrictions increased his anti-British sentiment. He opposed the Stamp Act of 1765 and after 1770 became increasingly prominent in organizing resis-

tance. A delegate to the Continental Congress, Washington was selected as commander in chief of the Continental Army and took command at Cambridge, Mass., on July 3, 1775.

Inadequately supported and sometimes covertly sabotaged by the Congress, in charge of troops who were inexperienced, badly equipped, and impatient of discipline, Washington conducted the war on the policy of avoiding major engagements with the British and wearing them down by harassing tactics. His able generalship, along with the French alliance and the growing weariness within Britain, brought the war to a conclusion with the surrender of Cornwallis at Yorktown, Va., on Oct. 19, 1781.

The chaotic years under the Articles of Confederation led Washington to return to public life in the hope of promoting the formation of a strong central government. He presided over the Constitutional Convention and yielded to the universal demand that he serve as first president. He was inaugurated on April 30, 1789, in New York, the first national capital. In office, he sought to unite the nation and establish the authority of the new government at home and abroad. Greatly distressed by the emergence of the Hamilton-Jefferson rivalry, Washington worked to maintain neutrality but actually sympathized more with Hamilton. Following his unanimous re-election in 1792, his second term was dominated by the Federalists. His Farewell Address on Sept. 17, 1796 (published but never delivered) rebuked party spirit and warned against "permanent alliances" with foreign powers.

He died at Mount Vernon on Dec. 14, 1799.

JOHN ADAMS born on Oct. 30 (Oct. 19, old style), 1735, at Braintree (now Quincy), Mass. A Harvard graduate, he considered teaching and the ministry but finally turned to law and was admitted to the bar in 1758. Six years later, he married Abigail Smith. He opposed the Stamp Act, served as lawyer for patriots indicted by the British, and by the time of the Continental Congresses, was in the vanguard of the movement for independence. In 1778, he went to France as commissioner. Subsequently he helped negotiate the peace treaty with Britain, and in 1785 became envoy to London. Resigning in 1788, he was elected vice president under Washington and was re-elected in 1792.

Though a Federalist, Adams did not get along with Hamilton, who sought to prevent his election to the presidency in 1796 and thereafter intrigued against his administration. In 1798, Adams's independent policy averted a war with France but completed the break with Hamilton and the right-wing Federalists; at the same time, the enactment of the Alien and Sedition Acts, directed against foreigners and against critics of the government, exasperated the Jeffersonian opposition. The split between Adams and Hamilton resulted in Jefferson's becoming the next president. Adams retired to his home in Quincy. He and Jefferson died on the same day, July 4, 1826, the 50th anniversary of the adoption of the Declaration of Independence.

His *Defence of the Constitutions of Government of the United States* (1787) contains original and striking, if conservative, political ideas.

THOMAS JEFFERSON was born on April 13 (April 2, old style), 1743, at Shadwell in Goochland (now Albemarle) County, Va. A William and Mary graduate, he studied law, but from the start showed an interest in science and philosophy. His literary skill and political clarity brought him to the forefront of the revolutionary movement in Virginia. As delegate to the Continental Congress, he drafted the Declaration of Independence. In 1776, he entered the Virginia House of Delegates and initiated a comprehensive reform program for the abolition of feudal survivals in land tenure and the separation of church and state.

In 1779, he became governor, but constitutional limitations on his power, combined with his own lack of executive energy, caused an unsatisfactory administration, culminating in Jefferson's virtual abdication when the British invaded Virginia in

1781. He retired to his beautiful home at Monticello, Va., to his family. His wife, Martha Wayles Skelton, whom he married in 1772, died in 1782.

Jefferson's *Notes on Virginia* (1784–85) illustrate his many-faceted interests, his limitless intellectual curiosity, his deep faith in agrarian democracy. Sent to Congress in 1783, he helped lay down the decimal system and drafted basic reports on the organization of the western lands. In 1785 he was appointed minister to France, where the Anglo-Saxon liberalism he had drawn from John Locke, the British philosopher, was stimulated by contact with the thought that would soon ferment in the French Revolution. In 1789, Washington appointed him Secretary of State. While favoring the Constitution and a strengthened central government, Jefferson came to believe that Hamilton contemplated the establishment of a monarchy. Growing differences resulted in Jefferson's resignation on Dec. 31, 1793.

Elected vice president in 1796, Jefferson continued to serve as spiritual leader of the opposition to Federalism, particularly to the repressive Alien and Sedition Acts. He was elected president in 1801 by the House of Representatives as a result of Hamilton's decision to throw the Federalist votes to him rather than to Aaron Burr, who had tied him in electoral votes. He was the first president to be inaugurated in Washington, which he had helped to design.

The purchase of Louisiana from France in 1803, though in violation of Jefferson's earlier constitutional scruples, was the most notable act of his administration. Re-elected in 1804, with the Federalist Charles C. Pinckney opposing him, Jefferson tried desperately to keep the United States out of the Napoleonic Wars in Europe, employing to this end the unpopular embargo policy.

After his retirement to Monticello in 1809, he developed his interest in education, founding the University of Virginia and watching its development with never-flagging interest. He died at Monticello on July 4, 1826. Jefferson had an enormous variety of interests and skills, ranging from education and science to architecture and music.

JAMES MADISON was born in Port Conway, Va., on March 16, 1751 (March 5, 1750/1, old style). A Princeton graduate, he joined the struggle for independence on his return to Virginia in 1771. In the 1770s and 1780s he was active in state politics, where he championed the Jefferson reform program, and in the Continental Congress. Madison was influential in the Constitutional Convention as leader of the group favoring a strong central government and as recorder of the debates; and he subsequently wrote, in collaboration with Alexander Hamilton and John Jay, the *Federalist* papers to aid the campaign for the adoption of the Constitution.

Serving in the new Congress, Madison soon emerged as the leader in the House of the men who opposed Hamilton's financial program and his pro-British leanings in foreign policy. Retiring from Congress in 1797, he continued to be active in Virginia and drafted the Virginia Resolution protesting the Alien and Sedition Acts. His intimacy with Jefferson made him the natural choice for Secretary of State in 1801.

In 1809, Madison succeeded Jefferson as president, defeating Charles C. Pinckney. His wife, Dolley Payne Todd, whom he married in 1794, brought a new social sparkle to the executive mansion. In the meantime, increasing tension with Britain culminated in the War of 1812—a war for which the United States was unprepared and for which Madison lacked the executive talent to clear out incompetence and mobilize the nation's energies. Madison was re-elected in 1812, running against the Federalist De Witt Clinton. In 1814, the British actually captured Washington and forced Madison to flee to Virginia.

Madison's domestic program capitulated to the Hamiltonian policies that he had resisted 20 years before and he now signed bills to establish a United States Bank and a higher tariff.

After his presidency, he remained in retirement in Virginia until his death on June 28, 1836.

JAMES MONROE was born on April 28, 1758, in Westmoreland County, Va. A William and Mary graduate, he served in the army during the first years of the Revolution and was wounded at Trenton. He then entered Virginia politics and later national politics under the sponsorship of Jefferson. In 1786, he married Elizabeth (Eliza) Kortright.

Fearing centralization, Monroe opposed the adoption of the Constitution and, as senator from Virginia, was highly critical of the Hamiltonian program. In 1794, he was appointed minister to France, where his ardent sympathies with the Revolution exceeded the wishes of the State Department. His troubled diplomatic career ended with his recall in 1796. From 1799 to 1802, he was governor of Virginia. In 1803, Jefferson sent him to France to help negotiate the Louisiana Purchase and for the next few years he was active in various negotiations on the Continent.

In 1808, Monroe flirted with the radical wing of the Republican Party, which opposed Madison's candidacy; but the presidential boom came to naught and, after a brief term as governor of Virginia in 1811, Monroe accepted Madison's offer to become Secretary of State. During the War of 1812, he vainly sought a field command and instead served as Secretary of War from September 1814 to March 1815.

Elected president in 1816 over the Federalist Rufus King, and re-elected without opposition in 1820, Monroe, the last of the Virginia dynasty, pursued the course of systematic tranquilization that won for his administrations the name "the era of good feeling." He continued Madison's surrender to the Hamiltonian domestic program, signed the Missouri Compromise, acquired Florida, and with the able assistance of his Secretary of State, John Quincy Adams, promulgated the Monroe Doctrine in 1823, declaring against foreign colonization or intervention in the Americas. He died in New York City on July 4, 1831, the third president to die on the anniversary of Independence.

JOHN QUINCY ADAMS was born on July 11, 1767, at Braintree (now Quincy), Mass., the son of John Adams, the second president. He spent his early years in Europe with his father, graduated from Harvard, and entered law practice. His anti-Paine newspaper articles won him political attention. In 1794, he became minister to the Netherlands, the first of several diplomatic posts that

occupied him until his return to Boston in 1801. In 1797, he married Louisa Catherine Johnson.

In 1803, Adams was elected to the Senate, nominally as a Federalist, but his repeated displays of independence on such issues as the Louisiana Purchase and the embargo caused his party to demand his resignation and ostracize him socially. In 1809, Madison rewarded him for his support of Jefferson by appointing him minister to St. Petersburg. He helped negotiate the Treaty of Ghent in 1814, and in 1815 became minister to London. In 1817 Monroe appointed him Secretary of State where he served with great distinction, gaining Florida from Spain without hostilities and playing an equal part with Monroe in formulating the Monroe Doctrine.

When no presidential candidate received a majority of electoral votes in 1824, Adams, with the support of Henry Clay, was elected by the House in 1825 over Andrew Jackson, who had the original plurality. Adams had ambitious plans of government activity to foster internal improvements and promote the arts and sciences, but congressional obstructionism, combined with his own unwillingness or inability to play the role of a politician, resulted in little being accomplished. After being defeated for re-election by Jackson in 1828, he successfully ran for the House of Representatives in 1830. There, though nominally a Whig, he pursued as ever an independent course. He led the fight to force Congress to receive antislavery petitions and fathered the Smithsonian Institution.

Adams had a stroke while on the floor of the House, and died two days later on Feb. 23, 1848. His long and detailed *Diary* gives a unique picture of the personalities and politics of the times.

ANDREW JACKSON was born on March 15, 1767, in what is now generally agreed to be Waxhaw, S.C. After a turbulent boyhood as an orphan and a British prisoner, he moved west to Tennessee, where he soon qualified for law practice but found time for such frontier pleasures as horse racing, cockfighting, and dueling. His marriage to Rachel Donelson Robards in 1791 was complicated by subsequent legal uncertainties about the status of her divorce. During the 1790s, Jackson served in the Tennessee Constitutional Convention, the United States House of Representatives and Senate, and on the Tennessee Supreme Court.

After some years as a country gentleman, living at the Hermitage near Nashville, Jackson in 1812 was given command of Tennessee troops sent against the Creeks. He defeated the Indians at Horseshoe Bend in 1814; subsequently he became a major general and won the Battle of New Orleans over veteran British troops, though after the treaty of peace had been signed at Ghent. In 1818, Jackson invaded Florida, captured Pensacola, and hanged two Englishmen named Arbuthnot and Ambrister, creating an international incident. A presidential boom began for him in 1821, and to foster it, he returned to the Senate (1823–25). Though he won a plurality of electoral votes in 1824, he lost in the House when Clay threw his strength to Adams. Four years later, he easily defeated Adams.

As president, Jackson greatly expanded the power and prestige of the presidential office and carried through an unprecedented program of domestic reform, vetoing the bill to extend the United States

Bank, moving toward a hard-money currency policy, and checking the program of federal internal improvements. He also vindicated federal authority against South Carolina with its doctrine of nullification and against France on the question of debts. The support given his policies by the workingmen of the East as well as by the farmers of the East, West, and South resulted in his triumphant re-election in 1832 over Clay.

After watching the inauguration of his handpicked successor, Martin Van Buren, Jackson retired to the Hermitage, where he maintained a lively interest in national affairs until his death on June 8, 1845.

MARTIN VAN BUREN was born on Dec. 5, 1782, at Kinderhook, N.Y. After graduating from the village school, he became a law clerk, entered practice in 1803, and soon became active in state politics as state senator and attorney general. In 1820, he was elected to the United States Senate. He threw the support of his efficient political organization, known as the Albany Regency, to William H. Crawford in 1824 and to Jackson in 1828. After leading the opposition to Adams's administration in the Senate, he served briefly as governor of New York (1828–1829) and resigned to become Jackson's Secretary of State. He was soon on close personal terms with Jackson and played an important part in the Jacksonian program.

In 1832, Van Buren became vice president; in 1836, president. The Panic of 1837 overshadowed his term. He attributed it to the overexpansion of the credit and favored the establishment of an independent treasury as repository for the federal funds. In 1840, he established a 10-hour day on public works. Defeated by Harrison in 1840, he was the leading contender for the Democratic nomination in 1844 until he publicly opposed immediate annexation of Texas, and was subsequently beaten by the Southern delegations at the Baltimore convention. This incident increased his growing misgivings about the slave power.

After working behind the scenes among the antislavery Democrats, Van Buren joined in the movement that led to the Free-Soil Party and became its candidate for president in 1848. He subsequently returned to the Democratic Party while continuing to object to its pro-Southern policy. He died in Kinderhook on July 24, 1862. His *Autobiography* throws valuable sidelights on the political history of the times.

His wife, Hannah Hoes, whom he married in 1807, died in 1819.

WILLIAM HENRY HARRISON was born in Charles City County, Va., on Feb. 9, 1773. Joining the army in 1791, he was active in Indian fighting in the Northwest, became secretary of the Northwest Territory in 1798 and governor of Indiana in 1800. He married Anna Symmes in 1795. Growing discontent over white encroachments on Indian lands led to the formation of an Indian alliance under Tecumseh to resist further aggressions. In 1811, Harrison won a nominal victory over the Indians at Tippecanoe and in 1813 a more decisive one at the Battle of the Thames, where Tecumseh was killed.

After resigning from the army in 1814, Harrison had an obscure career in politics and diplomacy,

ending up 20 years later as a county recorder in Ohio. Nominated for president in 1835 as a military hero whom the conservative politicians hoped to be able to control, he ran surprisingly well against Van Buren in 1836. Four years later, he defeated Van Buren but caught pneumonia and died in Washington on April 4, 1841, a month after his inauguration. Harrison was the first president to die in office.

JOHN TYLER was born in Charles City County, Va., on March 29, 1790. A William and Mary graduate, he entered law practice and politics, serving in the House of Representatives (1817–21), as governor of Virginia (1825–27), and as senator (1827–36). A strict constructionist, he supported Crawford in 1824 and Jackson in 1828, but broke with Jackson over his United States Bank policy and became a member of the Southern state-rights group that cooperated with the Whigs. In 1836, he resigned from the Senate rather than follow instructions from the Virginia legislature to vote for a resolution expunging censure of Jackson from the Senate record.

Elected vice president on the Whig ticket in 1840, Tyler succeeded to the presidency on Harrison's death. His strict-constructionist views soon caused a split with the Henry Clay wing of the Whig party and a stalemate on domestic questions. Tyler's more considerable achievements were his support of the Webster-Ashburton Treaty with Britain and his success in bringing about the annexation of Texas.

After his presidency he lived in retirement in Virginia until the outbreak of the Civil War, when he emerged briefly as chairman of a peace convention and then as delegate to the provisional Congress of the Confederacy. He died on Jan. 18, 1862. He married Letitia Christian in 1813 and, two years after her death in 1842, Julia Gardiner.

JAMES KNOX POLK was born in Mecklenburg County, N.C., on Nov. 2, 1795. A graduate of the University of North Carolina, he moved west to Tennessee, was admitted to the bar, and soon became prominent in state politics. In 1825, he was elected to the House of Representatives, where he opposed Adams and, after 1829, became Jackson's floor leader in the fight against the Bank. In 1835, he became Speaker of the House. Four years later, he was elected governor of Tennessee, but was beaten in tries for re-election in 1841 and 1843.

The supporters of Van Buren for the Democratic nomination in 1844 counted on Polk as his running mate, but when Van Buren's stand on Texas alienated Southern support, the convention swung to Polk on the ninth ballot. He was elected over Henry Clay, the Whig candidate. Rapidly disillusioning those who thought that he would not run his own administration, Polk proceeded steadily and precisely to achieve four major objectives—the acquisition of California, the settlement of the Oregon question, the reduction of the tariff, and the establishment of the independent treasury. He also enlarged the Monroe Doctrine to exclude all non-American intervention in American affairs, whether forcible or not, and he forced Mexico into a war that he waged to a successful conclusion.

His wife, Sarah Childress, whom he married in 1824, was a woman of charm and ability. Polk died in Nashville, Tenn., on June 15, 1849.

ZACHARY TAYLOR was born at Montebello, Orange County, Va., on Nov. 24, 1784. Embarking on a military career in 1808, Taylor fought in the War of 1812, the Black Hawk War, and the Seminole War, meanwhile holding garrison jobs on the frontier or desk jobs in Washington. A brigadier general as a result of his victory over the Seminoles at Lake Okeechobee (1837), Taylor held a succession of Southwestern commands and in 1846 established a base on the Rio Grande, where his forces engaged in hostilities that precipitated the war with Mexico. He captured Monterrey in September 1846 and, disregarding Polk's orders to stay on the defensive, defeated Santa Anna at Buena Vista in February 1847, ending the war in the northern provinces.

Though Taylor had never cast a vote for president, his party affiliations were Whiggish and his availability was increased by his difficulties with Polk. He was elected president over the Democrat Lewis Cass. During the revival of the slavery controversy, which was to result in the Compromise of 1850, Taylor began to take an increasingly firm stand against appeasing the South; but he died in Washington on July 9, 1850, during the fight over the Compromise. He married Margaret Mackall Smith in 1810. His bluff and simple soldierly qualities won him the name Old Rough and Ready.

MILLARD FILLMORE was born at Locke, Cayuga County, N.Y., on Jan. 7, 1800. A lawyer, he entered politics with the Anti-Masonic Party under the sponsorship of Thurlow Weed, editor and party boss, and subsequently followed Weed into the Whig Party. He served in the House of Representatives (1833–35 and 1837–43) and played a leading role in writing the tariff of 1842. Defeated for governor of New York in 1844, he became State comptroller in 1848, was put on the Whig ticket with Taylor as a concession to the Clay wing of the party, and became president upon Taylor's death in 1850.

As president, Fillmore broke with Weed and William H. Seward and associated himself with the pro-Southern Whigs, supporting the Compromise of 1850. Defeated for the Whig nomination in 1852, he ran for president in 1856 as candidate of the American, or Know-Nothing, Party, which sought to unite the country against foreigners in the alleged hope of diverting it from the explosive slavery issue. Fillmore opposed Lincoln during the Civil War. He died in Buffalo on March 8, 1874.

He was married in 1826 to Abigail Powers, who died in 1853, and in 1858 to Caroline Carmichael McIntosh.

FRANKLIN PIERCE was born at Hillsboro, N.H., on Nov. 23, 1804. A Bowdoin graduate, lawyer, and Jacksonian Democrat, he won rapid political advancement in the party, in part because of the prestige of his father, Gov. Benjamin Pierce. By 1831 he was Speaker of the New Hampshire House of Representatives; from 1833 to 1837, he served in the federal House and from 1837 to 1842 in the Senate. His wife, Jane Means Appleton, whom he married in 1834, disliked Washington and the somewhat dissipated life led by Pierce; in 1842 Pierce resigned from the Senate and began a successful law practice in Concord, N.H. During the Mexican War, he was a brigadier general.

Thereafter Pierce continued to oppose antislavery tendencies within the Democratic Party. As a result, he was the Southern choice to break the deadlock at the Democratic convention of 1852 and was nominated on the 49th ballot. In the election, Pierce overwhelmed Gen. Winfield Scott, the Whig candidate.

As president, Pierce followed a course of appeasing the South at home and of playing with schemes of territorial expansion abroad. The failure of his foreign and domestic policies prevented his renomination. He died in Concord on Oct. 8, 1869, in relative obscurity.

JAMES BUCHANAN was born near Mercersburg, Pa., on April 23, 1791. A Dickinson graduate and a lawyer, he entered Pennsylvania politics as a Federalist. With the disappearance of the Federalist Party, he became a Jacksonian Democrat. He served with ability in the House (1821–31), as minister to St. Petersburg (1832–33), and in the Senate (1834–45), and in 1845 became Polk's Secretary of State. In 1853, Pierce appointed Buchanan minister to Britain, where he participated with other American diplomats in Europe in drafting the expansionist Ostend Manifesto.

He was elected president in 1856, defeating John C. Frémont, the Republican candidate, and former President Millard Fillmore of the American Party. The growing crisis over slavery presented Buchanan with problems he lacked the will to tackle. His appeasement of the South alienated the Stephen Douglas wing of the Democratic Party without reducing Southern militancy on slavery issues. While denying the right of secession, Buchanan also denied that the federal government could do anything about it. He supported the administration during the Civil War and died in Lancaster, Pa., on June 1, 1868.

The only president to remain a bachelor throughout his term, Buchanan used his charming niece, Harriet Lane, as White House hostess.

ABRAHAM LINCOLN was born in Hardin (now Larue) County, Ky., on Feb. 12, 1809. His family moved to Indiana and then to Illinois, and Lincoln gained what education he could along the way. While reading law, he worked in a store, managed a mill, surveyed, and split rails. In 1834, he went to the Illinois legislature as a Whig and became the party's floor leader. For the next 20 years he practiced law in Springfield, except for a single term (1847–49) in Congress, where he denounced the Mexican War. In 1855, he was a candidate for senator and the next year he joined the new Republican Party.

A leading but unsuccessful candidate for the vice-presidential nomination with Frémont, Lincoln gained national attention in 1858 when, as Republican candidate for senator from Illinois, he engaged in a series of debates with Stephen A. Douglas, the Democratic candidate. He lost the election, but continued to prepare the way for the 1860 Republican convention and was rewarded with the presidential nomination on the third ballot. He won the election over three opponents.

From the start, Lincoln made clear that, unlike Buchanan, he believed the national government had the power to crush the rebellion. Not an abolitionist, he held the slavery issue subordinate to that of preserving the Union, but soon perceived that the war could not be brought to a successful conclusion without freeing the slaves. His administration was hampered by the incompetence of many Union generals, the inexperience of the troops, and the harassing political tactics both of the Republican Radicals, who favored a hard policy toward the South, and the Democratic Copperheads, who desired a negotiated peace. The Gettysburg Address of Nov. 19, 1863, marks the high point in the record of American eloquence. Lincoln's long search for a winning combination finally brought Generals Ulysses S. Grant and William T. Sherman to the top; and their series of victories in 1864 dispelled the mutterings from both Radicals and Peace Democrats that at one time seemed to threaten Lincoln's re-election. He was re-elected in 1864, defeating Gen. George B. McClellan, the Democratic candidate. His inaugural address urged leniency toward the South: "With malice toward none, with charity for all . . . let us strive on to finish the work we are in; to bind up the nation's wounds . . ." This policy aroused growing opposition on the part of the Republican Radicals, but before the matter could be put to the test, Lincoln was shot by the actor John Wilkes Booth at Ford's Theater, Washington, on April 14, 1865. He died the next morning.

Lincoln's marriage to Mary Todd in 1842 was often unhappy and turbulent, in part because of his wife's pronounced instability.

ANDREW JOHNSON was born at Raleigh, N.C., on Dec. 29, 1808. Self-educated, he became a tailor in Greeneville, Tenn., but soon went into politics, where he rose steadily. He served in the House of Representatives (1843–54), as governor of Tennessee (1853–57), and as a senator (1857–62). Politically he was a Jacksonian Democrat and his specialty was the fight for a more equitable land policy. Alone among the Southern Senators, he stood by the Union during the Civil War. In 1862, he became war governor of Tennessee and carried out a thankless and difficult job with great courage. Johnson became Lincoln's running mate in 1864 as a result of an attempt to give the ticket a nonpartisan and nonsectional character. Succeeding to the presidency on Lincoln's death, Johnson sought to carry out Lincoln's policy, but without his political skill. The result was a hopeless conflict with the Radical Republicans who dominated Congress, passed measures over Johnson's vetoes, and attempted to limit the power of the executive concerning appointments and removals. The conflict culminated with Johnson's impeachment for attempting to remove his disloyal Secretary of War in defiance of the Tenure of Office Act which required senatorial concurrence for such dismissals. The opposition failed by one vote to get the two thirds necessary for conviction.

After his presidency, Johnson maintained an interest in politics and in 1875 was again elected to the Senate. He died near Carter Station, Tenn., on July 31, 1875. He married Eliza McCardle in 1827.

ULYSSES SIMPSON GRANT was born (as Hiram Ulysses Grant) at Point Pleasant, Ohio, on April 27, 1822. He graduated from West Point in 1843 and served without particular distinction in the Mexican War. In 1848 he married Julia Dent. He resigned from the army in 1854, after warnings from his commanding officer about his drinking habits,

and for the next six years held a wide variety of jobs in the Middle West. With the outbreak of the Civil War, he sought a command and soon, to his surprise, was made a brigadier general. His continuing successes in the western theaters, culminating in the capture of Vicksburg, Miss., in 1863, brought him national fame and soon the command of all the Union armies. Grant's dogged, implacable policy of concentrating on dividing and destroying the Confederate armies brought the war to an end in 1865. The next year, he was made full general.

In 1868, as Republican candidate for president, Grant was elected over the Democrat, Horatio Seymour. From the start, Grant showed his unfitness for the office. His Cabinet was weak, his domestic policy was confused, and many of his intimate associates were corrupt. The notable achievement in foreign affairs was the settlement of controversies with Great Britain in the Treaty of London (1871), negotiated by his able Secretary of State, Hamilton Fish.

Running for re-election in 1872, he defeated Horace Greeley, the Democratic and Liberal Republican candidate. The Panic of 1873 graft scandals close to the presidency created difficulties for his second term.

After retiring from office, Grant toured Europe for two years and returned in time to accede to a third-term boom, but was beaten in the convention of 1880. Illness and bad business judgment darkened his last years, but he worked steadily at the *Personal Memoirs*, which were to be successful when published after his death at Mount McGregor, near Saratoga, N.Y., on July 23, 1885.

RUTHERFORD BIRCHARD HAYES was born in Delaware, Ohio, on Oct. 4, 1822. A graduate of Kenyon College and the Harvard Law School, he practiced law in Lower Sandusky (now Fremont) and then in Cincinnati. In 1852 he married Lucy Webb. A Whig, he joined the Republican party in 1855. During the Civil War he rose to major general. He served in the House of Representatives from 1865 to 1867 and then confirmed a reputation for honesty and efficiency in two terms as Governor of Ohio (1868–72). His election to a third term in 1875 made him the logical candidate for those Republicans who wished to stop James G. Blaine in 1876, and he was nominated.

The result of the election was in doubt for some time and hinged upon disputed returns from South Carolina, Louisiana, Florida, and Oregon. Samuel J. Tilden, the Democrat, had the larger popular vote but was adjudged by the strictly partisan decisions of the Electoral Commission to have one fewer electoral vote, 185 to 184. The national acceptance of this result was due in part to the general understanding that Hayes would pursue a conciliatory policy toward the South. He withdrew the troops from the South, took a conservative position on financial and labor issues, and urged civil service reform.

Hayes served only one term by his own wish and spent the rest of his life in various humanitarian endeavors. He died in Fremont on Jan. 17, 1893.

JAMES ABRAM GARFIELD, the last president to be born in a log cabin, was born in Cuyahoga County, Ohio, on Nov. 19, 1831. A Williams graduate, he taught school for a time and entered Republican politics in Ohio. In 1858, he married Lucretia

Rudolph. During the Civil War, he had a promising career, rising to major general of volunteers; but he resigned in 1863, having been elected to the House of Representatives, where he served until 1880. His oratorical and parliamentary abilities soon made him the leading Republican in the House, though his record was marred by his unorthodox acceptance of a fee in the DeGolyer paving contract case and by suspicions of his complicity in the Crédit Mobilier scandal.

In 1880, Garfield was elected to the Senate, but instead became the presidential candidate on the 36th ballot as a result of a deadlock in the Republican convention. In the election, he defeated Gen. Winfield Scott Hancock, the Democratic candidate. Garfield's administration was barely under way when he was shot by Charles J. Guiteau, a disappointed office seeker, in Washington on July 2, 1881. He died in Elberton, N.J., on Sept. 19.

CHESTER ALAN ARTHUR was born at Fairfield, Vt., on Oct. 5, 1830. A graduate of Union College, he became a successful New York lawyer. In 1859, he married Ellen Herndon. During the Civil War, he held administrative jobs in the Republican state administration and in 1871 was appointed collector of the Port of New York by Grant. This post gave him control over considerable patronage. Though not personally corrupt, Arthur managed his power in the interests of the New York machine so openly that President Hayes in 1877 called for an investigation and the next year Arthur was suspended.

In 1880 Arthur was nominated for vice president in the hope of conciliating the followers of Grant and the powerful New York machine. As president upon Garfield's death, Arthur, stepping out of his familiar role as spoilsman, backed civil service reform, reorganized the Cabinet, and prosecuted political associates accused of post office graft. Losing machine support and failing to gain the reformers, he was not nominated for a full term in 1884. He died in New York City on Nov. 18, 1886.

(STEPHEN) GROVER CLEVELAND was born at Caldwell, N.J., on March 18, 1837. He was admitted to the bar in Buffalo, N.Y., in 1859 and lived there as a lawyer, with occasional incursions into Democratic politics, for more than 20 years. He did not participate in the Civil War. As mayor of Buffalo in 1881, he carried through a reform program so ably that the Democrats ran him successfully for governor in 1882. In 1884 he won the Democratic nomination for president. The campaign contrasted Cleveland's spotless public career with the uncertain record of James G. Blaine, the Republican candidate, and Cleveland received enough Mugwump (independent Republican) support to win.

As president, Cleveland pushed civil service reform, opposed the pension grab and attacked the high tariff rates. While in the White House, he married Frances Folsom in 1886. Renominated in 1888, Cleveland was defeated by Benjamin Harrison, polling more popular but fewer electoral votes. In 1892, he was elected over Harrison. When the Panic of 1893 burst upon the country, Cleveland's attempts to solve it by sound-money measures alienated the free-silver wing of the party, while his tariff policy alienated the protectionists. In 1894, he sent troops to break the Pullman strike. In foreign affairs, his firmness caused Great Britain to back down in the Venezuela border dispute.

In his last years Cleveland was an active and much-respected public figure. He died in Princeton, N.J., on June 24, 1908.

BENJAMIN HARRISON was born in North Bend, Ohio, on Aug. 20, 1833, the grandson of William Henry Harrison, the ninth president. A graduate of Miami University in Ohio, he took up the law in Indiana and became active in Republican politics. In 1853, he married Caroline Lavinia Scott. During the Civil War, he rose to brigadier general. A sound-money Republican, he was elected senator from Indiana in 1880. In 1888, he received the Republican nomination for president on the eighth ballot. Though behind on the popular vote, he won over Grover Cleveland in the electoral college by 233 to 168.

As president, Harrison failed to please either the bosses or the reform element in the party. In foreign affairs he backed Secretary of State Blaine, whose policy foreshadowed later American imperialism. Harrison was renominated in 1892 but lost to Cleveland. His wife died in the White House in 1892 and Harrison married her niece, Mary Scott (Lord) Dimmick, in 1896. After his presidency, he resumed law practice. He died in Indianapolis on March 13, 1901.

WILLIAM MCKINLEY was born in Niles, Ohio, on Jan. 29, 1843. He taught school, then served in the Civil War, rising from the ranks to become a major. Subsequently he opened a law office in Canton, Ohio, and in 1871 married Ida Saxton. Elected to Congress in 1876, he served there until 1891, except for 1883–85. His faithful advocacy of business interests culminated in the passage of the highly protective McKinley Tariff of 1890. With the support of Mark Hanna, a shrewd Cleveland businessman interested in safeguarding tariff protection, McKinley became governor of Ohio in 1892 and Republican presidential candidate in 1896. The business community, alarmed by the progressivism of William Jennings Bryan, the Democratic candidate, spent considerable money to assure McKinley's victory.

The chief event of McKinley's administration was the war with Spain, which resulted in the United States' acquisition of the Philippines and other islands. With imperialism an issue, McKinley defeated Bryan again in 1900. On Sept. 6, 1901, he was shot at Buffalo, N.Y., by Leon F. Czolgosz, an anarchist, and he died there eight days later.

THEODORE ROOSEVELT was born in New York City on Oct. 27, 1858. A Harvard graduate, he was early interested in ranching, in politics, and in writing picturesque historical narratives. He was a Republican member of the New York Assembly in 1882–84, an unsuccessful candidate for mayor of New York in 1886, a U.S. Civil Service Commissioner under Benjamin Harrison, Police Commissioner of New York City in 1895, and Assistant Secretary of the Navy under McKinley in 1897. He resigned in 1898 to help organize a volunteer regiment, the Rough Riders, and take a more direct part in the war with Spain. He was elected governor of New York in 1898 and vice president in 1900, in spite of lack of enthusiasm on the part of the bosses.

Assuming the presidency of the assassinated McKinley in 1901, Roosevelt embarked on a wide-ranging program of government reform and conservation of natural resources. He ordered antitrust suits against several large corporations, threatened to intervene in the anthracite coal strike of 1902, which prompted the operators to accept arbitration, and, in general, championed the rights of the "little man" and fought the "malefactors of great wealth." He was also responsible for such progressive legislation as the Elkins Act of 1901, which outlawed freight rebates by railroads; the bill establishing the Department of Commerce and Labor; the Hepburn Act, which gave the I.C.C. greater control over the railroads; the Meat Inspection Act; and the Pure Food and Drug Act.

In foreign affairs, Roosevelt pursued a strong policy, permitting the instigation of a revolt in Panama to dispose of Colombian objections to the Panama Canal and helping to maintain the balance of power in the East by bringing the Russo-Japanese War to an end, for which he won the Nobel Peace Prize, the first American to achieve a Nobel prize in any category. In 1904, he decisively defeated Alton B. Parker, his conservative Democratic opponent.

Roosevelt's increasing coldness toward his successor, William Howard Taft, led him to overlook his earlier disclaimer of third-term ambitions and to re-enter politics. Defeated by the machine in the Republican convention of 1912, he organized the Progressive Party (Bull Moose) and polled more votes than Taft, though the split brought about the election of Woodrow Wilson. From 1915 on, Roosevelt strongly favored intervention in the European war. He became deeply embittered at Wilson's refusal to allow him to raise a volunteer division. He died in Oyster Bay, N.Y., on Jan. 6, 1919. He was married twice: in 1880 to Alice Hathaway Lee, who died in 1884, and in 1886 to Edith Kermit Carow.

WILLIAM HOWARD TAFT was born in Cincinnati on Sept. 15, 1857. A Yale graduate, he entered Ohio Republican politics in the 1880s. In 1886 he married Helen Herron. From 1887 to 1890, he served on the Ohio Superior Court; 1890–92, as solicitor general of the United States; 1892–1900, on the federal circuit court. In 1900 McKinley appointed him president of the Philippine Commission and in 1901 governor general. Taft had great success in pacifying the Filipinos, solving the problem of the church lands, improving economic conditions, and establishing limited self-government. His period as Secretary of War (1904–08) further demonstrated his capacity as administrator and conciliator, and he was Roosevelt's hand-picked successor in 1908. In the election, he polled 321 electoral votes to 162 for William Jennings Bryan, who was running for the presidency for the third time.

Though he carried on many of Roosevelt's policies, Taft got into increasing trouble with the progressive wing of the party and displayed mounting irritability and indecision. After his defeat in 1912, he became professor of constitutional law at Yale. In 1921 he was appointed Chief Justice of the United States Supreme Court. He died in Washington, D.C., on March 8, 1930.

(THOMAS) WOODROW WILSON was born in Staunton, Va., on Dec. 28, 1856. A Princeton graduate, he turned from law practice to post-graduate work in political science at Johns Hopkins University, receiving his Ph.D. in 1886. He taught at Bryn Mawr, Wesleyan, and Princeton, and in 1902 was made president of Princeton. After an unsuccessful attempt to democratize the social life of the university, he welcomed an invitation in 1910 to be the Democratic gubernatorial candidate in New Jersey, and was elected. His success in fighting the machine and putting through a reform program attracted national attention.

In 1912, at the Democratic convention in Baltimore, Wilson won the nomination on the 46th ballot and went on to defeat Roosevelt and Taft in the election. Wilson proceeded under the standard of the New Freedom to enact a program of domestic reform, including the Federal Reserve Act, the Clayton Antitrust Act, the establishment of the Federal Trade Commission, and other measures designed to restore competition in the face of the great monopolies. In foreign affairs, while privately sympathetic with the Allies, he strove to maintain neutrality in the European war and warned both sides against encroachments on American interests.

Re-elected in 1916 as a peace candidate, he tried to mediate between the warring nations; but when the Germans resumed unrestricted submarine warfare in 1917, Wilson brought the United States into what he now believed was a war to make the world safe for democracy. He supplied the classic formulations of Allied war aims and the armistice of Nov. 11, 1918 was negotiated on the basis of Wilson's Fourteen Points. In 1919 he strove at Versailles to lay the foundations for enduring peace. He accepted the imperfections of the Versailles Treaty in the expectation that they could be remedied by action within the League of Nations. He probably could have secured ratification of the treaty by the Senate if he had adopted a more conciliatory attitude toward the mild reservationists; but his insistence on all or nothing eventually caused the diehard isolationists and diehard Wilsonites to unite in rejecting a compromise.

In September 1919 Wilson suffered a paralytic stroke that limited his activity. After leaving the presidency he lived on in retirement in Washington, dying on Feb. 3, 1924. He was married twice—in 1885 to Ellen Louise Axson, who died in 1914, and in 1915 to Edith Bolling Galt.

WARREN GAMALIEL HARDING was born in Morrow County, Ohio, on Nov. 2, 1865. After attending Ohio Central College, Harding became interested in journalism and in 1884 bought the *Marion* (Ohio) *Star*. In 1891 he married a wealthy widow, Florence Kling De Wolfe. As his paper prospered, he entered Republican politics, serving as state senator (1899–1903) and as lieutenant governor (1904–06). In 1910, he was defeated for governor, but in 1914 was elected to the Senate. His reputation as an orator made him the keynoter at the 1916 Republican convention.

When the 1920 convention was deadlocked between Leonard Wood and Frank O. Lowden, Harding became the dark-horse nominee on his solemn affirmation that there was no reason in his past that he should not be. Straddling the League question,

Harding was easily elected over James M. Cox, his Democratic opponent. His Cabinet contained some able men, but also some manifestly unfit for public office. Harding's own intimates were mediocre when they were not corrupt. The impending disclosure of the Teapot Dome scandal in the Interior Department and illegal practices in the Justice Department and Veterans' Bureau, as well as political setbacks, profoundly worried him. On his return from Alaska in 1923, he died unexpectedly in San Francisco on Aug. 2.

(JOHN) CALVIN COOLIDGE

(JOHN) CALVIN COOLIDGE was born in Plymouth, Vt., on July 4, 1872. An Amherst graduate, he went into law practice at Northampton, Mass., in 1897. He married Grace Anna Goodhue in 1905. He entered Republican state politics, becoming successively mayor of Northampton, state senator, lieutenant governor and, in 1919, governor. His use of the state militia to end the Boston police strike in 1919 won him a somewhat undeserved reputation for decisive action and brought him the Republican vice-presidential nomination in 1920. After Harding's death Coolidge handled the Washington scandals with care and finally managed to save the Republican Party from public blame for the widespread corruption.

In 1924, Coolidge was elected without difficulty, defeating the Democrat, John W. Davis, and Robert M. La Follette running on the Progressive ticket. His second term, like his first, was characterized by a general satisfaction with the existing economic order. He stated that he did not choose to run in 1928.

After his presidency, Coolidge lived quietly in Northampton, writing an unilluminating autobiography and conducting a syndicated column. He died there on Jan. 5, 1933.

HERBERT CLARK HOOVER

HERBERT CLARK HOOVER was born at West Branch, Iowa, on Aug. 10, 1874, the first president to be born west of the Mississippi. A Stanford graduate, he worked from 1895 to 1913 as a mining engineer and consultant throughout the world. In 1899, he married Lou Henry. During World War I, he served with distinction as chairman of the American Relief Committee in London, as chairman of the Commission for Relief in Belgium, and as U.S. Food Administrator. His political affiliations were still too indeterminate for him to be mentioned as a possibility for either the Republican or Democratic nomination in 1920, but after the election he served Harding and Coolidge as Secretary of Commerce.

In the election of 1928, Hoover overwhelmed Gov. Alfred E. Smith of New York, the Democratic candidate and the first Roman Catholic to run for the presidency. He soon faced the worst depression in the nation's history, but his attacks upon it were hampered by his devotion to the theory that the forces that brought the crisis would soon bring the revival and then by his belief that there were too many areas in which the federal government had no power to act. In a succession of vetoes, he struck down measures proposing a national employment system or national relief, he reduced income tax rates, and only at the end of his term did he yield to popular pressure and set up agencies such as the Reconstruction Finance Corporation to make emergency loans to assist business.

After his 1932 defeat, Hoover returned to private business. In 1946, President Truman charged him with various world food missions; and from 1947 to 1949 and 1953 to 1955, he was head of the Commission on Organization of the Executive Branch of the Government. He died in New York City on Oct. 20, 1964.

FRANKLIN DELANO ROOSEVELT

FRANKLIN DELANO ROOSEVELT was born in Hyde Park, N.Y., on Jan. 30, 1882. A Harvard graduate, he attended Columbia Law School and was admitted to the New York bar. In 1910, he was elected to the New York State Senate as a Democrat. Reelected in 1912, he was appointed Assistant Secretary of the Navy by Woodrow Wilson the next year. In 1920, his radiant personality and his war service resulted in his nomination for vice president as James M. Cox's running mate. After his defeat, he returned to law practice in New York. In August 1921, Roosevelt was stricken with infantile paralysis while on vacation at Campobello, New Brunswick. After a long and gallant fight, he recovered partial use of his legs. In 1924 and 1928, he led the fight at the Democratic national conventions for the nomination of Gov. Alfred E. Smith of New York, and in 1928 Roosevelt was himself induced to run for governor of New York. He was elected, and was reelected in 1930.

In 1932, Roosevelt received the Democratic nomination for president and immediately launched a campaign that brought new spirit to a weary and discouraged nation. He defeated Hoover by a wide margin. His first term was characterized by an unfolding of the New Deal program, with greater benefits for labor, the farmers, and the unemployed, and the progressive estrangement of most of the business community.

At an early stage, Roosevelt became aware of the menace to world peace posed by totalitarian fascism, and from 1937 on he tried to focus public attention on the trend of events in Europe and Asia. As a result, he was widely denounced as a warmonger. He was re-elected in 1936 over Gov. Alfred M. Landon of Kansas by the overwhelming electoral margin of 523 to 8, and the gathering international crisis prompted him to run for an unprecedented third term in 1940. He defeated Wendell L. Willkie.

Roosevelt's program to bring maximum aid to Britain and, after June 1941, to Russia was opposed, until the Japanese attack on Pearl Harbor restored national unity. During the war, Roosevelt shelved the New Deal in the interests of conciliating the business community, both in order to get full production during the war and to prepare the way for a united acceptance of the peace settlements after the war. A series of conferences with Winston Churchill and Joseph Stalin laid down the bases for the postwar world. In 1944 he was elected to a fourth term, running against Gov. Thomas E. Dewey of New York.

On April 12, 1945, Roosevelt died of a cerebral hemorrhage at Warm Springs, Ga., shortly after his return from the Yalta Conference. His wife, (Anna) Eleanor Roosevelt, whom he married in 1905, was a woman of great ability who made significant contributions to her husband's policies.

HARRY S. TRUMAN was born on a farm near Lamar, Mo., on May 8, 1884. During World War I, he served in France as a captain with the 129th Field Artillery. He married Bess Wallace in 1919. After engaging briefly and unsuccessfully in the haberdashery business in Kansas City, Mo., Truman entered local politics. Under the sponsorship of Thomas Pendergast, Democratic boss of Missouri, he held a number of local offices, preserving his personal honesty in the midst of a notoriously corrupt political machine. In 1934, he was elected to the Senate and was re-elected in 1940. During his first term he was a loyal but quiet supporter of the New Deal, but in his second term, an appointment as head of a Senate committee to investigate war production brought out his special qualities of honesty, common sense, and hard work, and he won widespread respect.

Elected vice president in 1944, Truman became president upon Roosevelt's sudden death in April 1945 and was immediately faced with the problems of winding down the war against the Axis and preparing the nation for postwar adjustment.

The years 1947–48 were distinguished by civil-rights proposals, the Truman Doctrine to contain the spread of Communism, and the Marshall Plan to aid in the economic reconstruction of war-ravaged nations. Truman's general record, highlighted by a vigorous Fair Deal campaign, brought about his unexpected election in 1948 over the heavily favored Thomas E. Dewey.

Truman's second term was primarily concerned with the Cold War with the Soviet Union, the implementing of the North Atlantic Pact, the United Nations police action in Korea, and the vast rearmament program with its accompanying problems of economic stabilization.

On March 29, 1952, Truman announced that he would not run again for the presidency. After leaving the White House, he returned to his home in Independence, Mo., to write his memoirs. He further busied himself with the Harry S. Truman Library there. He died in Kansas City, Mo., on Dec. 26, 1972.

DWIGHT DAVID EISENHOWER was born in Denison, Tex., on Oct. 14, 1890. His ancestors lived in Germany and emigrated to America, settling in Pennsylvania, early in the 18th century. His father, David, had a general store in Hope, Kans., which failed. After a brief time in Texas, the family moved to Abilene, Kan.

After graduating from Abilene High School in 1909, Eisenhower did odd jobs for almost two years. He won an appointment to the Naval Academy at Annapolis, but was too old for admittance. Then he received an appointment in 1910 to West Point, from which he graduated as a second lieutenant in 1915.

He did not see service in World War I, having been stationed at Fort Sam Houston, Tex. There he met Mamie Geneva Doud, whom he married in Denver on July 1, 1916, and by whom he had two sons: Doud Dwight (died in infancy) and John Sheldon Doud.

Eisenhower served in the Philippines from 1935 to 1939 with Gen. Douglas MacArthur. Afterward, Gen. George C. Marshall, the Army Chief of Staff, brought him into the War Department's General Staff and in 1942 placed him in command of the invasion of North Africa. In 1944, he was made Supreme Allied Commander for the invasion of Europe.

After the war, Eisenhower served as Army Chief of Staff from November 1945 until February 1948, when he was appointed president of Columbia University.

In December 1950, President Truman recalled Eisenhower to active duty to command the North Atlantic Treaty Organization forces in Europe. He held his post until the end of May 1952.

At the Republican convention of 1952 in Chicago, Eisenhower won the presidential nomination on the first ballot in a close race with Senator Robert A. Taft of Ohio. In the election, he defeated Gov. Adlai E. Stevenson of Illinois.

Through two terms, Eisenhower hewed to moderate domestic policies. He sought peace through Free World strength in an era of new nationalisms, nuclear missiles, and space exploration. He fostered alliances pledging the United States to resist "Red" aggression in Europe, Asia, and Latin America. The Eisenhower Doctrine of 1957 extended commitments to the Middle East.

At home, the popular president lacked Republican Congressional majorities after 1954, but he was re-elected in 1956 by 457 electoral votes to 73 for Stevenson.

While retaining most Fair Deal programs, he stressed "fiscal responsibility" in domestic affairs. A moderate in civil rights, he sent troops to Little Rock, Ark., to enforce court-ordered school integration.

With his wartime rank restored by Congress, Eisenhower returned to private life and the role of elder statesman, with his vigor hardly impaired by a heart attack, an ileitis operation, and a mild stroke suffered while in office. He died in Washington, D.C., on March 28, 1969.

JOHN FITZGERALD KENNEDY was born in Brookline, Mass., on May 29, 1917. His father, Joseph P. Kennedy, was Ambassador to Great Britain from 1937 to 1940.

Kennedy was graduated from Harvard University in 1940 and joined the Navy the next year. He became skipper of a PT boat that was sunk in the Pacific by a Japanese destroyer. Although given up for lost, he swam to a safe island, towing an injured enlisted man.

After recovering from a war-aggravated spinal injury, Kennedy entered politics in 1946 and was elected to Congress. In 1952, he ran against Senator Henry Cabot Lodge, Jr., of Massachusetts, and won.

Kennedy was married on Sept. 12, 1953, to Jacqueline Lee Bouvier, by whom he had three children: Caroline, John Fitzgerald, Jr. (died in a 1999 plane crash), and Patrick Bouvier (died in infancy).

In 1957 Kennedy won the Pulitzer Prize for a book he had written earlier, *Profiles in Courage*.

After strenuous primary battles, Kennedy won the Democratic presidential nomination on the first ballot at the 1960 Los Angeles convention. With a plurality of only 118,574 votes, he carried the election over Vice President Richard M. Nixon and became the first Roman Catholic president.

Kennedy brought to the White House the dynamic idea of a "New Frontier" approach in dealing with problems at home, abroad, and in the dimensions of space. Out of his leadership in his first few months in office came the 10-year Alliance for Progress to aid Latin America, the Peace Corps, and accelerated programs that brought the first Americans into orbit in the race in space.

Failure of the U.S.-supported Cuban invasion in April 1961 led to the entrenchment of the Communist-backed Castro regime, only 90 miles from United States soil. When it became known that Soviet offensive missiles were being installed in Cuba in 1962, Kennedy ordered a naval "quarantine" of the island and moved troops into position to eliminate this threat to U.S. security. The world seemed on the brink of a nuclear war until Soviet Premier Khrushchev ordered the removal of the missiles.

A sudden "thaw," or the appearance of one, in the cold war came with the agreement with the Soviet Union on a limited test-ban treaty signed in Moscow on Aug. 6, 1963.

In his domestic policies, Kennedy's proposals for medical care for the aged and aid to education were defeated, but on minimum wage, trade legislation, and other measures he won important victories.

Widespread racial disorders and demonstrations led to Kennedy's proposing sweeping civil rights legislation. As his third year in office drew to a close, he also recommended an $11-billion tax cut to bolster the economy. Both measures were pending in Congress when Kennedy, looking forward to a second term, journeyed to Texas for a series of speeches.

While riding in an automobile procession in Dallas on Nov. 22, 1963, he was shot to death by an assassin firing from an upper floor of a building. The alleged assassin, Lee Harvey Oswald, was killed two days later in the Dallas city jail by Jack Ruby, owner of a strip-tease place.

At 46 years of age, Kennedy became the fourth president to be assassinated and the eighth to die in office.

LYNDON BAINES JOHNSON was born in

Stonewall, Tex., on Aug. 27, 1908. On both sides of his family he had a political heritage mingled with a Baptist background of preachers and teachers. Both his father and his paternal grandfather served in the Texas House of Representatives.

After his graduation from Southwest Texas State Teachers College, Johnson taught school for two years. He went to Washington in 1932 as secretary to Rep. Richard M. Kleberg. During this time, he married Claudia Alta Taylor, known as "Lady Bird." They had two children: Lynda Bird and Luci Baines.

In 1935, Johnson became Texas administrator for the National Youth Administration. Two years later, he was elected to Congress as an all-out supporter of Franklin D. Roosevelt, and served until 1949. He was the first member of Congress to enlist in the armed forces after the attack on Pearl Harbor. He served in the Navy in the Pacific and won a Silver Star.

Johnson was elected to the Senate in 1948 after he had captured the Democratic nomination by only 87 votes. He was 40 years old. He became the Senate Democratic leader in 1953. A heart attack in 1955 threatened to end his political career, but he recovered fully and resumed his duties.

At the height of his power as Senate leader, Johnson sought the Democratic nomination for president in 1960. When he lost to John F. Kennedy, he surprised even some of his closest associates by accepting second place on the ticket.

Johnson was riding in another car in the motorcade when Kennedy was assassinated in Dallas on Nov. 22, 1963. He took the oath of office in the presidential jet on the Dallas airfield.

With Johnson's insistent backing, Congress finally adopted a far-reaching civil-rights bill, a voting-rights bill, a Medicare program for the aged, and measures to improve education and conservation. Congress also began what Johnson described as "an all-out war" on poverty.

Amassing a record-breaking majority of nearly 16 million votes, Johnson was elected president in his own right in 1964, defeating Senator Barry Goldwater of Arizona.

The double tragedy of a war in Southeast Asia and urban riots at home marked Johnson's last two years in office. Faced with disunity in the nation and challenges within his own party, Johnson surprised the country on March 31, 1968, with the announcement that he would not be a candidate for re-election. He died of a heart attack suffered at his LBJ Ranch on Jan. 22, 1973.

RICHARD MILHOUS NIXON was born in Yorba

Linda, Calif., on Jan. 9, 1913, to Midwestern-bred parents, Francis A. and Hannah Milhous Nixon, who raised their five sons as Quakers.

Nixon was a high school debater and was undergraduate president at Whittier College in California, where he was graduated in 1934. As a scholarship student at Duke University Law School in North Carolina, he graduated third in his class in 1937.

After five years as a lawyer, Nixon joined the Navy in August 1942. He was an air transport officer in the South Pacific and a legal officer stateside before his discharge in 1946 as a lieutenant commander.

Running for Congress in California as a Republican in 1946, Nixon defeated Rep. Jerry Voorhis. As a member of the House Un-American Activities Committee, he made a name as an investigator of Alger Hiss, a former high State Department official, who was later jailed for perjury. In 1950, Nixon defeated Rep. Helen Gahagan Douglas, a Democrat, for the Senate. He was criticized for portraying her as a Communist dupe.

Nixon's anti-Communism ideals, his Western roots, and his youth figured into his selection in 1952 to run for vice president on the ticket headed by Dwight D. Eisenhower. Demands for Nixon's withdrawal followed disclosure that California businessmen had paid some of his Senate office expenses. His televised rebuttal, known as "the Checkers speech" (named for a cocker spaniel given to the Nixons), brought him support from the public and from Eisenhower. The ticket won easily in 1952 and again in 1956.

Eisenhower gave Nixon substantive assignments, including missions to 56 countries. In Moscow in 1959, Nixon won acclaim for his defense of U.S. interests in an impromptu "kitchen debate" with Soviet Premier Nikita S. Khrushchev.

Nixon lost the 1960 race for the presidency to John F. Kennedy.

In 1962, Nixon failed in a bid for California's governorship and seemed to be finished as a national candidate. He became a Wall Street lawyer, but kept his old party ties and developed new ones through constant travels to speak for Republicans.

Nixon won the 1968 Republican presidential nomination after a shrewd primary campaign, then made Gov. Spiro T. Agnew of Maryland his surprise choice for vice president. In the election, they edged out the Democratic ticket headed by Vice President Hubert H. Humphrey by 510,314 votes out of 73,212,065 cast.

Committed to winding down the U.S. role in the Vietnamese War, Nixon pursued "Vietnamization"—training and equipping South Vietnamese to do their own fighting. American ground combat forces in Vietnam fell steadily from 540,000 when Nixon took office to none in 1973 when the military draft was ended. But there was heavy continuing use of U.S. air power.

Nixon improved relations with Moscow and reopened the long-closed door to mainland China with a good-will trip there in February 1972. In May of that year, he visited Moscow and signed agreements on arms limitation and trade expansion and approved plans for a joint U.S.–Soviet space mission in 1975.

Inflation was a campaign issue for Nixon, but he failed to master it as president. On Aug. 15, 1971, with unemployment edging up, Nixon abruptly announced a new economic policy: a 90-day wage-price freeze, stimulative tax cuts, a temporary 10% tariff, and spending cuts. A second phase, imposing guidelines on wage, price, and rent boosts, was announced October 7.

The economy responded in time for the 1972 campaign, in which Nixon played up his foreign-policy achievements. Played down was the burglary on June 17, 1972, of Democratic national headquarters in the Watergate apartment complex in Washington. The Nixon–Agnew re-election campaign cost a record $60 million and swamped the Democratic ticket headed by Senator George McGovern of South Dakota with a plurality of 17,999,528 out of 77,718,554 votes. Only Massachusetts, with 14 electoral votes, and the District of Columbia, with 3, went for McGovern.

In January 1973, hints of a cover-up emerged at the trial of six men found guilty of the Watergate burglary. With a Senate investigation under way, Nixon announced on April 30 the resignations of his top aides, H. R. Haldeman and John D. Ehrlichman, and the dismissal of White House counsel John Dean III. Dean was the star witness at televised Senate hearings that exposed both a White House cover-up of Watergate and massive illegalities in Republican fund-raising in 1972.

The hearings also disclosed that Nixon had routinely tape-recorded his office meetings and telephone conversations.

On Oct. 10, 1973, Agnew resigned as vice president, then pleaded no-contest to a negotiated federal charge of evading income taxes on alleged bribes. Two days later, Nixon nominated the House minority leader, Rep. Gerald R. Ford of Michigan, as the new vice president. Congress confirmed Ford on Dec. 6, 1973.

In June 1974, Nixon visited Israel and four Arab nations. Then he met in Moscow with Soviet leader Leonid I. Brezhnev and reached preliminary nuclear arms limitation agreements.

But, in the month after his return, Watergate ended the Nixon regime. On July 24 the Supreme Court ordered Nixon to surrender subpoenaed tapes. On July 30, the Judiciary Committee referred three impeachment articles to the full membership. On August 5, Nixon bowed to the Supreme Court and released tapes showing he halted an FBI probe of the Watergate burglary six days after it occurred. It was in effect an admission of obstruction of justice, and impeachment appeared inevitable.

Nixon resigned on Aug. 9, 1974, the first president ever to do so. A month later, President Ford issued an unconditional pardon for any offenses Nixon might have committed as president, thus forestalling possible prosecution.

In 1940, Nixon married Thelma Catherine (Pat) Ryan. They had two daughters, Patricia (Tricia) and Julie, who married Dwight David Eisenhower II, grandson of the former president.

He died on April 22, 1994, in New York City of a massive stroke.

GERALD RUDOLPH FORD was born Leslie King Jr. in Omaha, Neb., on July 14, 1913, the only child of Leslie and Dorothy Gardner King. His parents were divorced in 1915. His mother moved to Grand Rapids, Mich., and married Gerald R. Ford. The boy was renamed for his stepfather.

Ford captained his high school football team in Grand Rapids, and a football scholarship took him to the University of Michigan, where he starred as varsity center before his graduation in 1935. A job as assistant football coach at Yale gave him an opportunity to attend Yale Law School, from which he graduated in the top third of his class in 1941.

He returned to Grand Rapids to practice law, but entered the Navy in April 1942. He saw wartime service in the Pacific on the light aircraft carrier *Monterey* and was a lieutenant commander when he returned to Grand Rapids early in 1946 to resume law practice and dabble in politics.

Ford was elected to Congress in 1948 for the first of his 13 terms in the House. He was soon assigned to the influential Appropriations Committee and rose to become the ranking Republican on the subcommittee on Defense Department appropriations.

As a legislator, Ford described himself as "a moderate on domestic issues, a conservative in fiscal affairs, and a dyed-in-the-wool internationalist." He carried the ball for Pentagon appropriations, was a hawk on the war in Vietnam, and kept a low profile on civil-rights issues.

Ford was also dependable and hard-working and popular with his colleagues. In 1963, he was elected chairman of the House Republican Conference. He served in 1963-1964 as a member of the Warren Commission, which investigated the assassination of John F. Kennedy. A revolt by dissatisfied younger Republicans in 1965 made him minority leader.

Ford shelved his hopes for the speakership on Oct. 12, 1973, when Nixon nominated him to fill the vice presidency left vacant by Agnew's resignation under fire. It was the first use of the procedures for filling vacancies in the vice presidency laid down in the 25th Amendment to the Constitution, which Ford had helped enact.

Congress confirmed Ford as vice president on Dec. 6, 1973. Once in office, he said he did not believe Nixon had been involved in the Watergate scandals, but criticized his stubborn court battle against releasing tape recordings of Watergate-related conversations for use as evidence.

The scandals led to Nixon's unprecedented resignation on Aug. 9, 1974, and Ford was sworn in immediately as the 38th president, the first to enter the White House without winning a national election.

Ford assured the nation when he took office that "our long national nightmare is over" and pledged "openness and candor" in all his actions. He won a warm response from the Democratic 93rd Congress when he said he wanted "a good marriage" rather than a honeymoon with his former colleagues. In December 1974 Congressional majorities backed his choice of former New York Gov. Nelson A. Rockefeller as his successor in the again-vacant vice presidency.

The cordiality was chilled by Ford's announcement on Sept. 8, 1974, that he had granted an unconditional pardon to Nixon for any crimes he might have committed as president. Although no formal charges were pending, Ford said he feared "ugly passions" would be aroused if Nixon were brought to trial. The pardon was widely criticized.

To fight inflation, the new president first proposed fiscal restraints and spending curbs and a 5% tax surcharge that got nowhere in the Senate and House. Congress again rebuffed Ford in the spring of 1975 when he appealed for emergency military aid to help the governments of South Vietnam and Cambodia resist massive Communist offensives.

In November 1974, Ford visited Japan, South Korea, and the Soviet Union, where he and Soviet leader Leonid I. Brezhnev conferred in Vladivostok and reached a tentative agreement to limit the number of strategic offensive nuclear weapons. It was Ford's first meeting as president with Brezhnev, who planned a return visit to Washington in the fall of 1975.

Politically, Ford's fortunes improved steadily in the first half of 1975. Badly divided Democrats in Congress were unable to muster votes to override his vetoes of spending bills that exceeded his budget. He faced some right-wing opposition in his own party, but moved to pre-empt it with an early announcement—on July 8, 1975—of his intention to be a candidate in 1976.

Early state primaries in 1976 suggested an easy victory for Ford despite Ronald Reagan's bitter attacks on administration foreign policy and defense programs. But later Reagan primary successes threatened the President's lead. At the Kansas City convention, Ford was nominated by the narrow margin of 1,187 to 1,070. But Reagan had moved the party to the right, and Ford himself was regarded as a caretaker president lacking in strength and vision. He was defeated in November by Jimmy Carter.

In 1948, Ford married Elizabeth Anne (Betty) Bloomer. They had four children, Michael Gerald, John Gardner, Steven Meigs, and Susan Elizabeth.

JAMES EARL CARTER, JR., was born in the tiny village of Plains, Ga., Oct. 1, 1924, and grew up on the family farm at nearby Archery. Both parents were fifth-generation Georgians. His father, James Earl Carter, was known as a segregationist, but treated his black and white workers equally. Carter's mother, Lillian Gordy, was a matriarchal presence in home and community and opposed the then-prevailing code of racial inequality. The future president was baptized in 1935 in the conservative Southern Baptist Church and spoke often of being a "born again" Christian, although committed to the separation of church and state.

Carter married Rosalynn Smith, a neighbor, in 1946. Their first child, John William, was born a year later in Portsmouth, Va. Their other children are James Earl III, born in Honolulu in 1950; Donnel Jeffrey, born in New London, Conn., in 1952; and Amy Lynn, born in Plains in 1967.

In 1946 Carter was graduated from the U.S. Naval Academy at Annapolis and served in the nuclear-submarine program under Adm. Hyman G. Rickover. In 1954, after his father's death, he resigned from the Navy to take over the family's flourishing warehouse and cotton gin, with several thousand acres for growing seed peanuts.

Carter was elected to the Georgia Senate in 1962. In 1966 he lost the race for Governor, but was elected in 1970. His term brought a state government reorganization, sharply reduced agencies, increased economy and efficiency, and new social programs, all with no general tax increase. In 1972 the peanut farmer–politician set his sights on the presidency and in 1974 built a base for himself as he criss-crossed the country as chairman of the Democratic Campaign Committee, appealing for revival and reform. In 1975 his image as a typical Southern white was erased when he won support of most of the old Southern civil-rights coalition after endorsement by Rep. Andrew Young, black Democrat from Atlanta, who had been the closest aide to the Rev. Martin Luther King, Jr. At Carter's 1971 inauguration as Governor he had called for an end to all forms of racial discrimination.

In the 1976 spring primaries, he won 19 out of 31 with a broad appeal to conservatives and liberals, black and white, poor and well-to-do. Throughout his campaigning Carter set forth his policies in his soft Southern voice, and with his electric-blue stare faced down skeptics who joked about "Jimmy Who?" His toothy smile became his trademark. He was nominated on the first roll-call vote of the 1976 Bicentennial Democratic National Convention in New York, and defeated Gerald R. Ford in November. Likewise, in 1980 he was renominated on the first ballot after vanquishing Senator Edward M. Kennedy of Massachusetts in the primaries. At the convention he defeated the Kennedy forces in their attempt to block a party rule that bound a large majority of pledged delegates to vote for Carter. In the election campaign, Carter attacked his rivals, Ronald Reagan and John B. Anderson, independent, with the warning that a Reagan Republican victory would heighten the risk of war and impede civil rights and economic opportunity. In November Carter lost to Reagan, who won 489 Electoral College votes and 51% of the popular tally, to 49 electoral votes and 41% for Carter.

In his one term, Carter fought hard for his programs against resistance from an independent-minded Democratic Congress that frustrated many pet projects although it overrode only two vetoes. Many of his difficulties were traced to his aides' brusqueness in dealing with Capitol Hill and insensitivity to Congressional feelings and tradition. Observers generally viewed public dissatisfaction with the "stagflation" economy as a principal factor in his defeat. Others included his jittery performance in the debate Oct. 28 with Reagan, staff problems, friction with Congress, long gasoline lines, and the months-long Iranian crisis, including the abortive

sally in April 1980 to free the hostages. Yet, assessments of his record noted many positive elements. There was, for one thing, peace throughout his term, with no American combat deaths and with a brake on the advocates of force. Regarded as perhaps his greatest personal achievements were the Camp David accords between Israel and Egypt and the resulting treaty—the first between Israel and an Arab neighbor. The treaty with China and the Panama Canal treaties were also major achievements. Carter worked for nuclear-arms control. His concern for international human rights was credited with saving lives and reducing torture, and he supported the British policy that ended internecine warfare in Rhodesia, now Zimbabwe. Domestically, his environmental record was a major accomplishment. His judicial appointments won acclaim; the Southerner who had forsworn racism made 265 choices for the Federal bench that included minority members and women. He also ended the U.S. practice of holding petroleum prices far below world levels with price decontrols.
—Arthur P. Reed, Jr.

RONALD WILSON REAGAN rode to the presidency in 1980 on a tide of resurgent right-wing sentiment among an electorate battered by winds of unwanted change, longing for a distant, simpler era.

He left office in January 1989 with two-thirds of the American people approving his performance during his two terms. It was the highest rating for any retiring president since World War II. In his farewell speech, Reagan exhorted the nation to cling to the revival of patriotism that he had fostered. And he spoke proudly of the economic recovery during his Administrations, although regretting the huge budget deficit, for which, in part, many blamed his policies.

Reagan had retained the public's affection as he applied his political magic to policy goals. His place in history will rest, perhaps, on the short- and intermediate-range missile treaty consummated on a cordial visit to the Soviet Union that he had once reviled as an "evil empire." Its provisions, including a ground-breaking agreement on verification inspection, were formulated in four days of summit talks in Moscow in May 1988 with the Soviet leader, Mikhail S. Gorbachev.

Reagan can point to numerous domestic achievements as well: sharp cuts in income tax rates, sweeping tax reform, creating economic growth without inflation, and reducing the unemployment rate, among others. He failed, however, to win the "Reagan Revolution" on such issues as abortion and school prayer, and he seemed aloof from "sleazy" conduct by some top officials.

In his final months Reagan campaigned aggressively to win election as president for his two-term vice president, George Bush.

Reagan's popularity with the public dipped sharply in 1986 when the Iran-Contra scandal broke, shortly after the Democrats gained control of the Senate. Observers agreed that Reagan's presidency had been weakened, if temporarily, by the two unrelated events. Then the weeks-long Congressional hearings in the summer of 1987 heard an array of Administration officials, present and former, tell their tales of a White House riven by deceit and undercover maneuvering. Yet no breath of illegality touched the President's personal reputation; on Aug.

12, 1987, he told the nation that he had not known of questionable activities but agreed that he was "ultimately accountable."

Ronald Reagan, actor turned politician, New Dealer turned conservative, came to films and politics from a thoroughly Middle-American background—middle class, Middle West, and small town. He was born in Tampico, Ill., Feb. 6, 1911, the second son of John Edward Reagan and Nelle Wilson Reagan, and the family later moved to Dixon, Ill. The father, of Irish descent, was a shop clerk and merchant with Democratic sympathies. It was an impoverished family; young Ronald sold homemade popcorn at high school games and worked as a lifeguard to earn money for his college tuition. When the father got a New Deal WPA job, the future president became an ardent Roosevelt Democrat.

Reagan won a B.A. degree in 1932 from Eureka (Ill.) College, where a photographic memory aided in his studies and in debating and college theatricals. In a Depression year, he was making $100 a week as a sports announcer for radio station WHO in Des Moines, Iowa, from 1932 to 1937. His career as a film and TV actor stretched from 1937 to 1966, and his salary climbed to $3,500 a week. As a World War II captain in Army film studios, Reagan recoiled from what he saw as the laziness of Civil Service workers, and moved to the Right. As president of the Screen Actors Guild, he resisted what he considered a Communist plot to subvert the film industry. With advancing age, Reagan left leading-man roles and became a television spokesman for the General Electric Company.

With oratorical skill his trademark, Reagan became an active Republican. At the behest of a small group of conservative Southern California businessmen, he ran for governor with a pledge to cut spending, and was elected by almost a million votes over the political veteran, Democratic Gov. Edmund G. Brown, father of later governor Jerry Brown.

In the 1980 election battle against Jimmy Carter, Reagan broadened his appeal by espousing moderate policies, gaining much of his support from disaffected Democrats and blue-collar workers. The incoming Administration immediately set out to "turn the government around" with a new economic program. Over strenuous Congressional opposition, Reagan triumphed on his "supply side" theory to stimulate production and control inflation through tax cuts and sharp reductions in government spending.

The president won high acclaim for his nomination of Sandra Day O'Connor as the first woman on the Supreme Court. His later nominations met increasing opposition but did much to tilt the Court's orientation to the Right.

In 1982, the President's popularity had slipped as the economy declined into the worst recession in 40 years, with persistent high unemployment and interest rates. Initial support for "supply side" economics faded but the President won crucial battles in Congress.

Internationally, Reagan confronted numerous critical problems in his first term. The successful invasion of Grenada accomplished much diplomatically. But the intervention in Lebanon and the withdrawal of Marines after a disastrous terrorist attack were regarded as military failures.

The popular president won reelection in the 1984 landslide, with the economy improving and inflation under control. Domestically, a tax reform bill that Reagan backed became law. But the constantly growing budget deficit remained a constant irritant, with the President and Congress persistently at odds over priorities in spending for defense and domestic programs. His foreign policy met stiffening opposition, with Congress increasingly reluctant to increase spending for the Nicaraguan "Contras" and the Pentagon and to expand the development of the MX missile. But even severe critics praised Reagan's restrained but decisive handling of the crisis following the hijacking of an American plane in Beirut by Muslim extremists. The attack on Libya in April 1986 galvanized the nation, although it drew scathing disapproval from the NATO alliance.

Barely three months into his first term, Reagan was the target of an assassin's bullet; his courageous comeback won public admiration.

Reagan is devoted to his wife, Nancy, whom he married after his divorce from the screen actress Jane Wyman. The children from his first marriage are Maureen, his daughter by Wyman, and Michael, an adopted son. He had two children by Nancy: Patricia and Ron. Reagan continues to struggle with Alzheimer's disease, which he developed in the years following his presidency.
—*Arthur P. Reed, Jr.*

GEORGE HERBERT WALKER BUSH was born
June 12, 1924, in Milton, Mass., to Prescott and Dorothy Bush. The family later moved to Connecticut. The youth studied at the elite Phillips Academy in Andover, Mass.

The future president joined the Navy after war broke out and at 18 became the Navy's youngest commissioned pilot, serving from 1942 to 1945. The man later derided by some as a "wimp" fought the Japanese on 58 missions and was shot down once. He won the Distinguished Flying Cross.

After the war, Bush earned an economics degree and a Phi Beta Kappa key in two and a half years at Yale University. While there he captained the baseball team and was initiated into "Skull and Bones," the prestigious Yale secret society.

In 1945 Bush married Barbara Pierce of Rye, N.Y., daughter of a magazine publisher. With his bride, Bush moved to Texas instead of entering his father's investment banking business. There he founded his oil company and by 1980 reported an estimated wealth of $1.4 million.

Throughout his whole career, Bush had the backing of an established family, headed by his father, the autocratic and wealthy Prescott Bush, who was elected to the Senate from Connecticut in 1952. And his family helped the young patrician become established in his early business ventures, a rich uncle raising most of the capital required for founding the oil company.

In the 1960s, Bush won two contests for a Texas Republican seat in the House of Representatives, but lost two bids for a Senate seat and one for the presidency. After Bush's second race for the Senate, President Nixon appointed him U.S. delegate to the United Nations with the rank of Ambassador and he later became Republican National Chairman. He headed the United States liaison office in Beijing before becoming Director of Central Intelligence.

In 1980 Bush became Reagan's running mate despite earlier criticism of Reagan "voodoo economics" and by the 1984 election had won acclaim for devotion to Reagan's conservative agenda despite his own reputation as somewhat more liberally inclined. Nevertheless, die-hard right-wingers could find satisfaction in Bush's war record and his government service, particularly with the C.I.A. Throughout he remained influential in White House decisions, particularly in foreign affairs.

In the 1988 campaign, Bush's choice of Senator Dan Quayle of Indiana for vice president surprised his friends and provoked criticism and ridicule that continued even after the Administration was established in office. Nonetheless Bush strongly defended his choice.

George Herbert Walker Bush became president on January 20, 1989, with his theme harmony and conciliation after the often-turbulent Reagan years. With his calm and unassuming manner, he emerged from his subordinate vice-presidential role with an air of quiet authority. His Inaugural address emphasized "A new breeze is blowing, and the old bipartisanship must be made new again."

In his first months, the President, the nation's 41st, established himself as his own man and all but erased memories of what many had regarded as his fiercely abrasive presidential election campaign of 1988 and questionable tactics against his Democratic opponent. People liked his easy style and readiness to compromise even as he remained a staunch conservative, although that readiness had disconcerted some conservatives.

Bush's early Cabinet choices reflected a pragmatic desire for an efficient, nonideological government. And with his usual cautious instinct, in 1990 he nominated to the Supreme Court the scholarly David H. Souter, with broadly conservative views. Souter was confirmed without a bruising battle.

In his first year, Bush, a World War II hero, had won plaudits at home and abroad for his confident, competent conduct at the NATO 40th anniversary summit meeting in Brussels, the Paris economic conference, on his tour of Eastern Europe, and at the Malta conference with Gorbachev. Grave challenges in that year were the Lebanese hostage crisis and the ongoing war against drug trafficking.

Domestically, Bush had to cope with such issues as the *Exxon Valdez* oil spill in Alaska and the dispute over flag-burning restrictions, which was resolved, if only for a time, in mid-1990.

But in his second year, 1990, the President confronted a mounting array of problems, the most critical being on the domestic side. Chief among them were the staggering and mushrooming budget deficit and the savings and loan crisis. Other vexing issues were the question of cutting defense expenditures with consequent economic dislocation, the war on drugs, and environmental matters.

At home, the President's popularity dipped sharply from its near-record public approval following the invasion of Panama in late 1989. This plunge followed Bush's recantation of his campaign "no new taxes" pledge as he sat down with Congressional leaders to tame the budget deficit and deal with a faltering economy.

In 1991, the 67-year-old president emerged as the leader of an international coalition of Western democracies, Japan, and even some Arab states that freed invaded Kuwait and vanquished, at least for a time, Iraq's President Saddam Hussein and his armies.

A nation grateful at feeling the end of the "Vietnam syndrome" gave the President an overall rating of 89 percent in a Gallup poll in March after the end of the war. The approval rate fell as the year went on, but a solid majority continued to approve the President's performance, although with growing concern about the faltering economy and other domestic problems. And there were nagging doubts about the Persian Gulf war, Its motives and conduct, and about the ensuing refugee crisis.

A major Bush accomplishment in 1991 was the Strategic Arms Reduction Treaty (Start), signed in July with Soviet president Mikhail S. Gorbachev at their fourth summit conference, marking the end of the long weapons buildup. Succeeding events in the Soviet Union and the apparent disintegration of the Communist empire could only enhance his status.

The year also saw the President undergoing treatment for Graves' disease, a thyroid disorder, from which he suffered serious side effects.

In the 1992 presidential election, Bush was defeated by Gov. Bill Clinton of Arkansas.

The Bushes have lived in 17 cities and more than a score of homes and have traveled in as many countries. In her husband's frequent absences during the early years, Mrs. Bush was often matriarch of a family of four boys (George, Jeb, Neil, and Marvin) and a girl (Dorothy).

After the Clinton inauguration in January, the Bushes returned to Houston, Texas.
—*Arthur P. Reed, Jr.*

WILLIAM JEFFERSON CLINTON was born William Jefferson Blythe III in Hope, Ark., on Aug. 19, 1946. He was named for his father, who was killed in an automobile accident before Clinton's birth. Virginia Kelley, his mother, eventually married Roger Clinton, a car dealer, whose surname the future president later adopted.

In high school in Hot Springs, Ark., Clinton considered becoming a doctor, but politics beckoned after a meeting with President John F. Kennedy in Washington, D.C., on a Boys' Nation trip. He earned a B.S. in international affairs in 1968 at Georgetown University, having spent his junior year working for Arkansas Senator J. William Fulbright. He was a Rhodes scholar at Oxford between 1968 and 1970. He then attended Yale Law School, where he met his future wife, Hillary Rodham, a Wellesley graduate. The couple has one child, Chelsea.

Clinton taught at the University of Arkansas (1974–1976), was elected state attorney general (1976), and in 1979 became the nation's youngest governor. But he was defeated for reelection by voters irate at a rise in the state's automobile license fees. In 1982 he was elected again. This time he reined in liberal tendencies to accommodate the conservative bent of the voters.

Clinton became the 42nd U.S. president following a turbulent political campaign. He overcame vigorous personal attacks on his character and on his actions during the Vietnam War, which he actively opposed. The "character issue" stemmed from allegations of infidelity, which Clinton refuted in a television interview in which he and Hillary avowed their relationship was solid. Throughout his term in office, Clinton was dogged by allegations relating to the Whitewater real estate deal in which he and Hillary were involved prior to the 1992 election. Though the Clintons were never accused of any wrongdoing, partners in the venture were convicted of fraud and conspiracy in a trial in 1996.

The problems faced by the new president were as daunting as they were varied. In January 1993 he became embroiled with the military leadership over his campaign pledge to allow homosexuals to serve openly in the armed services. He ultimately agreed to a compromise, dubbed the "don't ask, don't tell" policy. His first year also saw Clinton wrangling with Congress over the Federal budget and economic policy.

In his second year, Clinton faced persistent troubles on the domestic front, with acrimonious battles raging over health care, welfare reform, and crime prevention. A health care reform package crafted by his wife failed to gain sufficient support. Clinton had to reduce his objective from massive overhaul to incremental reform.

Clinton won major victories with the passage of the North American Free Trade Agreement (NAFTA), which took effect Jan. 1, 1994, and the Global Agreement on Tariffs and Trade (GATT), which led to the establishment in 1995 of the World Trade Organization (WTO). Congress also approved a deficit reduction bill, rules allowing abortion counseling in federally funded clinics, a waiting period for handgun purchases (the Brady Bill), and a national service program.

Foreign affairs, once a weak point for a man elected on a domestic economic agenda, became a proving ground for Clinton. He improved his international image when the Israel–Jordan peace agreement was signed at the White House in the summer of 1994 by Israeli prime minister Yitzhak Rabin and Jordan's King Hussein. In the fall of that year, the administration succeeded in restoring Haiti's ousted president, Jean-Bertrand Aristide, to power. Clinton scored again by bolstering Russian president Boris Yeltsin's popularity with promises of economic aid.

The problems in Eastern Europe were Clinton's next big challenge. Though he wanted desperately to end the brutal ethnic cleansing in Bosnia, he did not want to commit American ground troops to do so. A peace accord involving American peacekeeping troops was ultimately signed in Dayton, Ohio, in November 1995.

The 1994 elections resulted in a Republican-controlled Congress, and 1995 was largely a tug-of-war between the White House and Capitol Hill over budget-balancing and other key points of the G.O.P.'s "Contract with America," crafted by Speaker of the House Newt Gingrich.

In 1996, anticipating the fall election, Clinton moved to the political center by approving several major and widely popular legislative measures. Included was a welfare-reform bill that reversed several decades of federal policy.

Foreign affairs plagued Clinton's presidency in 1996. In Russia, Clinton's support for Yeltsin drew criticism as the war for Chechen independence erupted. In the Middle East, Israeli-Palestinian disputes continued and Iraq invaded Kurdish territory. Clinton responded to the Iraqi aggression by ordering missile attacks on Iraqi planes and ground forces.

A soaring economy facilitated an agreement on balanced-budget legislation in 1997. Political harmony, however, did not extend far, as the character issues that had dogged Clinton for years soon began to emerge once again. A series of investigations was begun to determine whether Clinton and Vice President Gore had participated in questionable fund-raising practices in their 1996 campaign.

Clinton was again able to strengthen his place on the world stage in 1998. In April, former Senate majority leader George Mitchell, Clinton's hand-picked envoy, helped broker a historic peace agreement aimed at ending decades of fighting between Protestants and Catholics in Northern Ireland. In May-June Clinton made a controversial diplomatic visit to China. Despite pre-trip criticism, Clinton was generally praised for making advancements in U.S. relations with the most populous country in the world while taking a clear stance against Chinese human rights practices.

As his tenure wore on, Clinton came under increasing pressure from Kenneth Starr, the independent counsel who in 1994 took over the investigation of the Clintons' involvement in the Whitewater land deal. Over time, Starr's brief was expanded to include other matters, such as the death of White House lawyer Vincent Foster, the handling of firings in the White House travel office, and shocking allegations of sexual misconduct by Clinton.

The President seemed to win a point in April 1998 when a federal judge in Arkansas threw out a long-pending sexual harassment suit brought by Paula Corbin Jones, a former Arkansas state employee. But Starr had already begun investigating the possibility that Clinton had perjured himself in his testimony in the Jones case over an alleged affair with a young White House intern, Monica S. Lewinsky. A few months earlier, Clinton had adamantly denied ever having engaged in sexual relations with Lewinsky, or of asking anyone to lie to cover up the affair.

Despite the explosive charges, Clinton's overall popularity among Americans remained high. The country seemed willing to ignore his weaknesses in character, much as they did in the 1992 elections, as long as the economy was good, his policies were popular, and the United States remained strong abroad. On Aug. 17, 1998, Clinton made history by becoming the first U.S. president to testify in front of a grand jury, in an investigation of his own possibly criminal conduct. In an address to the nation that evening, he now admitted to having had an "inappropriate" relationship with Lewinsky, but reaffirmed that he did not ask anyone to lie about or cover up the affair.

By August, the Lewinsky scandal so dominated Clinton's agenda that when he responded to the bombing of two American embassies in Africa by sending U.S. cruise missiles to strike alleged terrorist sites in Sudan and Afghanistan, many questioned whether the strike was a ploy to draw attention away from his domestic plight.

On Sept. 9, Starr—a conservative Republican whose investigation was seen by Clinton supporters as a politically inspired vendetta—delivered his report to the House of Representatives. While the report outlined 11 possible grounds for impeachment, none stemmed from the initial subjects of the investigation, including the Whitewater real estate deal. The real focus of the accusations seemed to be

Clinton's moral conduct, and the "Starr Report" graphically detailed his sexual affair.

Despite the American population's general disapproval of a trial (which was reflected in poll after poll), Congress moved forward in its highly partisan and acrimonious impeachment proceedings. In December the House Judiciary Committee approved four articles of impeachment: for grand jury perjury, civil suit perjury, obstruction of justice, and abuse of power. Republicans rejected Democrats' call to censure Clinton for "reprehensible conduct" rather than continue with impeachment, and on Dec. 19, Clinton became the second president in American history to be impeached. Two of the four articles of impeachment passed (Article I, grand jury perjury, and Article III, obstruction of justice), the votes drawn along party lines. After a Senate trial in Jan.–Feb. 1999, Clinton was acquitted on both counts. On the charge of perjury, the vote was 55–45 with 10 Republicans voting for acquittal along with all 45 Democrats. On the charge of obstruction of justice, the vote was 50–50, with 5 Republicans joining Democrats in voting for acquittal.

While the impeachment trial overshadowed all other activity in Washington for a good portion of 1998, Clinton was forced to respond to continued problems with Iraq at the end of the year. In December, Saddam Hussein blocked a weapons inspection by the United Nations. The U.N. responded with airstrikes that would continue on a nearly-daily basis for the next three months, and then off and on through the spring and summer, as Iraq taunted the U.S. and its allies further by shooting at jets patrolling the no-fly zones set up after the Persian Gulf war.

In the spring of 1999, the Middle East took a back seat to disturbing developments in the Balkans. Reports of continued ethnic cleansing in the Serbian province of Kosovo were growing. Clinton and his British counterpart, Tony Blair, helped lead the push for NATO intervention, which resulted in a 78-day bombing campaign against Serbia that began in March. Political arguing over whether to send in NATO ground troops began to heat up, with Clinton receiving some sharp criticism for holding back on their deployment. Clinton was ultimately justified, however, as Serbian President Slobodan Milosevic finally agreed to a peace treaty, signed June 9.

Following the Kosovo conflict Clinton faced the challenge of smoothing over important international relationships. Russia, a traditional ally of Serbia, had opposed NATO airstrikes from the start. The fragile relationship between the U.S. and China was also shaken up on May 7, when NATO accidentally bombed the Chinese embassy in Belgrade, killing three journalists.

The summer of 1999 found Washington debating what to do with a surprisingly large budget surplus. The President, riding high on reports that the 1996 welfare overhaul was achieving great success, pushed for further social reform—specifically, revisions in the Social Security and health care systems. Republicans countered with calls for drastic tax cuts.

The President also prepared for the 2000 elections, in which his support would be called upon not only by presidential hopeful Al Gore, but by Clinton's wife as well. By fall 1999, after several months of rumored consideration, the First Lady appeared likely to make a run for the U.S. Senate in New York.

In any broad overview of history, arbitrary compartmentalization of facts is self-defeating (and makes locating interrelated people, places, and things that much harder). Therefore, Headline History is designed as a "timeline"—a chronology that highlights both the march of time and interesting, sometimes surprising, juxtapositions. *See also* related sections of the almanac, particularly Inventions and Discoveries, U.S. Government and History, and Countries of the World.

B.C.E.

Before the Common Era (B.C.E.) or Before Christ (B.C.)

4.5 billion B.C.E. Planet Earth formed.

3 billion B.C.E. First signs of primeval life (bacteria and blue-green algae) appear in oceans.

600 million B.C.E. Earliest date to which fossils can be traced.

4.4 million B.C.E. Earliest known hominid fossils (*Australopithecus ramidis*) found in Aramis, Ethiopia, 1994.

4.2 million B.C.E. *Australopithecus anamensis* found in Lake Turkana, Kenya, 1995.

3.2 million B.C.E. *Australopithecus afarenis* (nicknamed "Lucy") found in Ethiopia, 1974.

2.5 million B.C.E. *Homo habilis* ("Handy Man"), first brain expansion and first chipped stones.

1.8 million B.C.E. *Homo erectus* ("Upright Man"). Brain size twice that of Australopithecine species.

1.7 million B.C.E. *Homo erectus* leaves Africa.

100,000 B.C.E. First modern *Homo sapiens* in South Africa.

70,000 B.C.E. Neanderthal man (use of fire and advanced tools).

35,000 B.C.E. Neanderthal man replaced by later groups of *Homo sapiens* (i.e. Cro-Magnon man, etc.).

18,000 B.C.E. Cro-Magnons replaced by later cultures.

15,000 B.C.E. Migrations across Bering Straits into the Americas.

10,000 B.C.E. Semi-permanent agricultural settlements in Old World.

10,000–4,000 B.C.E. Development of settlements into cities and development of skills such as the wheel, pottery and improved methods of cultivation in Mesopotamia and elsewhere.

4500–3000 B.C.E. Sumerians in the Tigris and Euphrates valleys develop a city-state civilization; first phonetic writing (c. 3500 B.C.E.). Egyptian agriculture develops. Western Europe is neolithic, without metals or written records. Earliest recorded date in Egyptian calendar (4241 B.C.E.). First year of Jewish calendar (3760 B.C.E.). Copper used by Egyptians and Sumerians.

3000–2000 B.C.E. Pharaonic rule begins in Egypt. King Khufu (Cheops), 4th dynasty (2700–2675 B.C.E.), completes construction of the Great Pyramid at Giza (c. 2680 B.C.E.). The Great Sphinx of Giza (c. 2540 B.C.E.) is built by King Khafre. Earliest Egyptian mummies. Papyrus. Phoenician settlements on coast of what is now Syria and Lebanon. Semitic tribes settle in Assyria. Sargon, first Akkadian king, builds Mesopotamian empire. The Gilgamesh epic (c. 3000 B.C.E.). Abraham leaves Ur (c. 2000 B.C.E.). Systematic astronomy in Egypt, Babylon, India, China.

3000–1500 B.C.E. The most ancient civilization on the Indian subcontinent, the sophisticated and extensive Indus Valley civilization, flourishes in what is today Pakistan. In Britain, Stonehenge erected according to some unknown astronomical rationale. Its three main phases of construction are thought to span c. 3000–1500 B.C.E.

2000–1500 B.C.E. Hyksos invaders drive Egyptians from Lower Egypt (17th century B.C.E.). Amosis I frees Egypt from Hyksos (c. 1600 B.C.E.). Assyrians rise to power—cities of Ashur and Nineveh. Twenty-four-character alphabet in Egypt. Israelites enslaved in Egypt. Cuneiform inscriptions used by Hittites. Peak of Minoan culture on Isle of Crete—earliest form of written Greek. Hammurabi, king of Babylon, develops oldest existing code of laws (18th century B.C.E.).

Ra, Egyptian Sun God (3000–2000 B.C.E.)

The Great Pyramid at Giza (c. 2680 B.C.E.)

Stonehenge (c. 3000–1500 B.C.E.)

**Pythagoras
(c. 582–c. 507 B.C.E.)**

**Buddha
(c. 563–c. 483 B.C.E.)**

1500–1000 B.C.E. Ikhnaton develops monotheistic religion in Egypt (c. 1375 B.C.E.). His successor, Tutankhamen, returns to earlier gods. Moses leads Israelites out of Egypt into Canaan—Ten Commandments. Greeks destroy Troy (c. 1193 B.C.E.). End of Greek civilization in Mycenae with invasion of Dorians. Chinese civilization develops under Shang Dynasty. Olmec civilization in Mexico—stone monuments; picture writing.

1000–900 B.C.E. Solomon succeeds King David, builds Jerusalem temple. After Solomon's death, kingdom divided into Israel and Judah. Hebrew elders begin to write Old Testament books of Bible. Phoenicians colonize Spain with settlement at Cadiz.

900–800 B.C.E. Phoenicians establish Carthage (c. 810 B.C.E.). The *Iliad* and the *Odyssey,* perhaps composed by Greek poet Homer.

800–700 B.C.E. Prophets Amos, Hosea, Isaiah. First recorded Olympic games (776 B.C.E.). Legendary founding of Rome by Romulus (753 B.C.E.). Assyrian king Sargon II conquers Hittites, Chaldeans, Samaria (end of Kingdom of Israel). Earliest written music. Chariots introduced into Italy by Etruscans.

700–600 B.C.E. End of Assyrian Empire (616 B.C.E.)—Nineveh destroyed by Chaldeans (Neo-Babylonians) and Medes (612 B.C.E.). Founding of Byzantium by Greeks (c. 660 B.C.E.). Building of the Acropolis in Athens. Solon, Greek lawgiver (640-560 B.C.E.). Sappho of Lesbos, Greek poet (fl. 610–c. 580 B.C.E.). Lao-tse, Chinese philosopher and founder of Taoism (born c. 604 B.C.E.).

600–500 B.C.E. Babylonian King Nebuchadnezzar builds empire, destroys Jerusalem (586 B.C.E.). Babylonian Captivity of the Jews (starting 587 B.C.E.). Hanging Gardens of Babylon. Cyrus the Great of Persia creates great empire, conquers Babylon (539 B.C.E.), frees the Jews. Athenian democracy develops. Aeschylus, Greek dramatist (525-465 B.C.E.). Pythagoras, Greek philosopher and mathematician (c. 582– c. 507 B.C.E.). Confucius (551-479 B.C.E.) develops ethical and social philosophy in China. The *Analects* or Lun-yü ("collected sayings") are compiled by the second generation of Confucian disciples. Buddha (c. 563-c. 483 B.C.E.) founds Buddhism in India.

SOME ANCIENT CIVILIZATIONS

Name	Approximate dates	Location	Major cities
Akkadian	2350-2230 B.C.E.	Mesopotamia, parts of Syria, Asia Minor, Iran	Akkad, Ur, Erich
Assyrian	1800-889 B.C.E.	Mesopotamia, Syria	Assur, Nineveh, Calah
Babylonian	1728-1686 B.C.E. (old) 625-539 B.C.E. (new)	Mesopotamia, Syria, Palestine	Babylon
Cimmerian	750-500 B.C.E.	Caucasus, northern Asia Minor	—
Egyptian	2850-715 B.C.E.	Nile valley	Thebes, Memphis, Tanis
Etruscan	900-396 B.C.E.	Northern Italy	—
Greek	900-200 B.C.E.	Greece	Athens, Sparta, Thebes, Mycenae, Corinth
Hittite	1640-1200 B.C.E.	Asia Minor, Syria	Hattusas, Nesa
Indus Valley	3000-1500 B.C.E.	Pakistan, Northwestern India	—
Lydian	700-547 B.C.E.	Western Asia Minor	Sardis, Miletus
Mede	835-550 B.C.E.	Iran	Media
Minoan	3000-1100 B.C.E.	Crete	Knossos
Persian	559-330 B.C.E.	Iran, Asia Minor, Syria	Persepolis, Pasargadae
Phoenician	1100-332 B.C.E.	Palestine (colonies: Gibraltar, Carthage, Sardinia)	Tyre, Sidon, Byblos
Phrygian	1000-547 B.C.E.	Central Asia Minor	Gordion
Roman	500 B.C.E.-C.E. 300	Italy, Mediterranean region, Asia Minor, western Europe	Rome, Byzantium
Scythian	800-300 B.C.E.	Caucasus	—
Sumerian	3200-2360 B.C.E.	Mesopotamia	Ur, Nippur

500–400 B.C.E. Greeks defeat Persians: battles of Marathon (490 B.C.E.), Thermopylae (480 B.C.E.), Salamis (480 B.C.E.). Peloponnesian Wars between Athens and Sparta (431-404 B.C.E.)—Sparta victorious. Pericles comes to power in Athens (462 B.C.E.). Flowering of Greek culture during the Age of Pericles (450-400 B.C.E.). The Parthenon is built in Athens as a temple of the goddess Athena (447–432 B.C.E.). Ictinus and Callicrates are the architects and Phidias is responsible for the sculpture. Sophocles, Greek dramatist (496-c.406 B.C.E.). Hippocrates, Greek "Father of Medicine" (born 460 B.C.E.). Xerxes I, king of Persia (rules 485-465 B.C.E.).

Confucius (551–479 B.C.E.)

400–300 B.C.E. Pentateuch—first five books of the Old Testament evolve in final form. Philip of Macedon, who believed himself to be a descendant of the Greek people, assassinated (336 B.C.E.) after subduing the Greek city-states; succeeded by son, Alexander the Great (356-323 B.C.E.), who destroys Thebes (335 B.C.E.), conquers Tyre and Jerusalem (332 B.C.E.), occupies Babylon (330 B.C.E.), invades India, and dies in Babylon. His empire is divided among his generals; one of them, Seleucis I, establishes Middle East empire with capitals at Antioch (Syria) and Seleucia (in Iraq). Trial and execution of Greek philosopher Socrates (399 B.C.E.). Dialogues recorded by his student, Plato (c. 427–348 or 347 B.C.E.). Euclid's work on geometry (323 B.C.E.). Aristotle, Greek philosopher (384-322 B.C.E.). Demosthenes, Greek orator (384-322 B.C.E.). Praxiteles, Greek sculptor (400-330 B.C.E.).

300–251 B.C.E. First Punic War (264-241 B.C.E.): Rome defeats the Carthaginians and begins its domination of the Mediterranean. Temple of the Sun at Teotihuacan, Mexico (c. 300 B.C.E.). Invention of Mayan calendar in Yucatán—more exact than older calendars. First Roman gladiatorial games (264 B.C.E.). Archimedes, Greek mathematician (287-212 B.C.E.).

Parthenon (447–432 B.C.E.)

250–201 B.C.E. Second Punic War (219-201 B.C.E.): Hannibal, Carthaginian general (246-142 B.C.E.), crosses the Alps (218 B.C.E.), reaches gates of Rome (211 B.C.E.), retreats, and is defeated by Scipio Africanus at Zama (202 B.C.E.). Great Wall of China built (c. 215 B.C.E.).

200-151 B.C.E. Romans defeat Seleucid King Antiochus III at Thermopylae (191 B.C.E.)—beginning of Roman world domination. Maccabean revolt against Seleucids (167 B.C.E.).

150–101 B.C.E. Third Punic War (149-146 B.C.E.): Rome destroys Carthage, killing 450,000 and enslaving the remaining 50,000 inhabitants. Roman armies conquer Macedonia, Greece, Anatolia, Balearic Islands, and southern France. Venus de Milo (c. 140 B.C.E.). Cicero, Roman orator (106-43 B.C.E.).

Plato (c. 427–348 or 347 B.C.E.)

100–51 B.C.E. Julius Caesar (100-44 B.C.E.) invades Britain (55 B.C.E.) and conquers Gaul (France) (c. 50 B.C.E.). Spartacus leads slave revolt against Rome (71 B.C.E.). Romans conquer Seleucid empire. Roman general Pompey conquers Jerusalem (63 B.C.E.). Cleopatra on Egyptian throne (51-31 B.C.E.). Chinese develop use of paper (c. 100 B.C.E.). Virgil, Roman poet (70-19 B.C.E.). Horace, Roman poet (65-8 B.C.E.).

50–1 B.C.E. Caesar crosses Rubicon to fight Pompey (50 B.C.E.). Herod makes Roman governor of Judea (47 B.C.E.). Caesar murdered (44 B.C.E.). Caesar's nephew, Octavian, defeats Mark Antony and Cleopatra at Battle of Actium (31 B.C.E.), and establishes Roman empire as Emperor Augustus—rules 27 B.C.E.-C.E. 14. Pantheon built for the first time under Agrippa, 27 B.C.E. Ovid, Roman poet (43 B.C.E.-C.E. 18).

C.E.

The Common Era (C.E.) or Christian Era (A.D.)

1–49 Birth of Jesus Christ (variously given from 4 B.C.E. to C.E. 7). After Augustus, Tiberius becomes emperor (dies, 37), succeeded by Caligula (assassinated, 41), who is followed by Claudius. Crucifixion of Jesus (probably 30). Han dynasty in China founded by Emperor Kuang Wu Ti. Buddhism introduced to China.

50–99 Claudius poisoned (54), succeeded by Nero (commits suicide, 68). Missionary journeys of Paul the Apostle (34-60). Jews revolt against Rome; Jerusalem destroyed (70). Roman persecutions of Christians begin (64). Colosseum built in Rome (71-80). Trajan (rules 98-116); Roman empire extends to Mesopotamia, Arabia, Balkans. First Gospels of St. Mark, St. John, St. Matthew.

Roman Aqueduct Montpellier, France

Mayan Pyramid at Chichén Itzá

Celtic Cross

Japanese Pagoda

Viking Ship (c. 900)

100–149 Hadrian rules Rome (117-138); codifies Roman law, rebuilds Pantheon, establishes postal system, builds wall between England and Scotland. Jews revolt under Bar Kokhba (122-135); final *Diaspora* (dispersion) of Jews begins.

150–199 Marcus Aurelius rules Rome (161-180). Oldest Mayan temples in Central America (c. 200).

200–249 Goths invade Asia Minor (c. 220). Roman persecutions of Christians increase. Persian (Sassanid) empire re-established. End of Chinese Han dynasty.

250–299 Increasing invasions of the Roman empire by Franks and Goths. Buddhism spreads in China. Classic period of Mayan civilization (250–900); develop hieroglyphic writing, advances in art, architecture, science.

300–349 Constantine the Great (rules 312-337) reunites eastern and western Roman empires, with new capital (Constantinople) on site of Byzantium (330); issues Edict of Milan legalizing Christianity (313); becomes a Christian on his deathbed (337). Council of Nicaea (325) defines orthodox Christian doctrine. First Gupta dynasty in India (c. 320).

350–399 Huns (Mongols) invade Europe (c. 360). Theodosius the Great (rules 392-395)—last emperor of a united Roman empire. Roman empire permanently divided in 395: western empire ruled from Rome; eastern empire ruled from Constantinople.

400–449 Western Roman empire disintegrates under weak emperors. Alaric, king of the Visigoths, sacks Rome (410). Attila, Hun chieftain, attacks Roman provinces (433). St. Patrick returns to Ireland (432) and brings Christianity to the island. St. Augustine's *City of God* (411).

450–499 Vandals destroy Rome (455). Western Roman empire ends as Odoacer, German chieftain, overthrows last Roman emperor, Romulus Augustulus, and becomes king of Italy (476). Ostrogothic kingdom of Italy established by Theodoric the Great (493). Clovis, ruler of the Franks, is converted to Christianity (496). First schism between western and eastern churches (484).

500–549 Eastern and western churches reconciled (519). Justinian I, the Great (483-565), becomes Byzantine emperor (527), issues his first code of civil laws (529), conquers North Africa, Italy, and part of Spain. Plague spreads through Europe (542 *et seq.*). Arthur, semi-legendary king of the Britons (killed, c. 537). Boëthius, Roman scholar (executed, 524).

550–599 Beginnings of European silk industry after Justinian's missionaries smuggle silkworms out of China (553). Mohammed, founder of Islam (570-632). Buddhism in Japan (c. 560). St. Augustine of Canterbury brings Christianity to Britain (597). After killing about half the population, plague in Europe subsides (594).

600–649 Mohammed flees from Mecca to Medina (the *Hegira*); first year of the Muslim calendar (622). Muslim empire grows (634). Arabs conquer Jerusalem (637), destroy Alexandrian library (641), conquer Persians (641). Fatima, Mohammed's daughter (606-632).

650–699 Arabs attack North Africa (670), destroy Carthage (697). Venerable Bede, English monk (672-735).

700–749 Arab empire extends from Lisbon to China (by 716). Charles Martel, Frankish leader, defeats Arabs at Tours/Poitiers, halting Arab advance in Europe (732). Charlemagne (742-814). Introduction of pagodas in Japan from China.

750–799 Charlemagne becomes king of the Franks (771). Caliph Harun al-Rashid rules Arab empire (786-809): the "golden age" of Arab culture. Vikings begin attacks on Britain (790), land in Ireland (795). City of Machu Picchu flourishes in Peru.

800–849 Charlemagne crowned first Holy Roman Emperor in Rome (800). Charlemagne dies (814), succeeded by his son, Louis the Pious, who divides France among his sons (817). Arabs conquer Crete, Sicily, and Sardinia (826-827).

850–899 Norsemen attack as far south as the Mediterranean but are thwarted (859), discover Iceland (861). Alfred the Great becomes king of Britain (871), defeats Danish invaders (878). Russian nation founded by Vikings under Prince Rurik, establishing capital at Novgorod (855-879).

900–949 Beginning of Mayan Post-Classical period (900–1519). Vikings discover Greenland (c. 900). Arab Spain under Abd ar-Rahman III becomes center of learning (912-961). Otto I becomes King of Germany (936).

950–999 Mieczyslaw I becomes first ruler of Poland (960). Eric the Red establishes first Viking colony in Greenland (982). Hugh Capet elected King of France in 987; Capetian dynasty to rule until 1328. Musical notation systematized (c.

990). Vikings and Danes attack Britain (988-999). Otto I crowned Holy Roman Emperor by Pope John XII (962).

1000–1099 (C.E.)

c. 1000–1300 Classic Pueblo period of Anasazi culture; cliff dwellings.

c.1000 Hungary and Scandinavia converted to Christianity. Viking raider Leif Ericson discovers North America, calls it Vinland. *Beowulf,* Old English epic.

c. 1008 Murasaki Shikibu finishes *The Tale of Genji,* the world's first novel.

1009 Muslims destroy Holy Sepulchre in Jerusalem.

1013 Danes control England. Canute takes throne (1016), conquers Norway (1028), dies (1035); kingdom divided among his sons: Harold Harefoot (England), Sweyn (Norway), Hardecanute (Denmark).

1040 Macbeth murders Duncan, king of Scotland.

1053 Robert Guiscard, Norman invader, establishes kingdom in Italy, conquers Sicily (1072).

1054 Final separation between Eastern (Orthodox) and Western (Roman) churches.

1055 Seljuk Turks, Asian nomads, move west, capture Baghdad, Armenia (1064), Syria, and Palestine (1075).

1066 William of Normandy invades England, defeats last Saxon king, Harold II, at Battle of Hastings, crowned William I of England ("the Conqueror").

1068 Construction on the Cathedral in Pisa, Italy, begins.

1073 Emergence of strong papacy when Gregory VII is elected. Conflict with English and French kings and German emperors will continue throughout medieval period.

1095 At Council of Clermont, Pope Urban II calls for a holy war to wrest control of Jerusalem from Muslims, which launches the First Crusade (1096), one of at least 8 European military campaigns between 1095 and 1291 to regain the Holy Land.

1100–1199 (C.E.)

1100–1300 Construction of Cathedral at Chartres, France.

1144 Second Crusade begins.

c. 1150 Angkor Wat is completed.

1150–67 Universities of Paris and Oxford founded in France and England.

1162 Thomas á Becket named Archbishop of Canterbury, murdered by Henry II's men (1170). Troubadours (wandering minstrels) glorify romantic concepts of feudalism.

1169 Ibn-Rushd begins translating Aristotle's works.

1189 Richard I ("the Lionhearted") succeeds Henry II in England, killed in France (1199), succeeded by King John. Third Crusade.

1200–1299 (C.E.)

1200–1204 Fourth Crusade.

1211 Genghis Khan invades China, captures Peking (1214), conquers Persia (1218), invades Russia (1223), dies (1227).

1212 Children's Crusade.

1215 King John forced by barons to sign Magna Carta at Runneymede, limiting royal power.

1217 Fifth Crusade.

1228 Sixth Crusade.

**Mesa Verde
Cliff Dwellings
(c. 1000–1300)**

**Cathedral and Tower
at Pisa**

Chartres Cathedral

**King John
(1167–1216)**

THE CRUSADES (1096–1291)

In 1095 at Council of Clermont, Pope Urban II calls for war to rescue Holy Land from Muslim infidels. The *First Crusade* (1096) is assembled in response to Emperor Alexius I. The Christians capture Antioch (1098) and Jerusalem (1099). They establish the Crusader States, ruled by Europeans. It is the only successful crusade. The *Second Crusade* begins after the Seljuk Turks recapture Edessa, one of the Crusader States, in 1144. It is led by King Louis VIII of France and Holy Roman Emperor Conrad III. Crusaders perish in Asia Minor (1147).

Saladin controls Egypt (1171), unites Islam in Holy War *(Jihad)* against Christians, recaptures Jerusalem (1187). *Third Crusade* (1189) under kings of France, England, and Germany fails to reduce Saladin's power. *Fourth Crusade* (1200-1204)—French knights sack Greek Christian Constantinople, establish Latin empire in Byzantium. Greeks re-establish Orthodox faith (1262).

Children's Crusade (1212)—Only 1 of 30,000 French children and about 200 of 20,000 German children survive to return home. Other Crusades—*Fifth,* against Egypt (1217), *Sixth* (1228), *Seventh* (1248), *Eighth* (1270). Mamelukes conquer Acre; end of the Crusades (1291).

**Thomas Aquinas
(1225–74)**

**The Duomo in
Florence**

**Joan of Arc
(1412–1431)**

**Michelangelo's David
(1504)**

**Balboa
(1475–1517)**

1231   The Inquisition begins as Pope Gregory IX assigns Dominicans responsibility for combating heresy. Torture used (1252). Ferdinand and Isabella establish Spanish Inquisition (1478). Tourquemada, Grand Inquisitor, forces conversion or expulsion of Spanish Jews (1492). Forced
conversion of Moors (1499). Inquisition in Portugal (1531). First Protestants burned at the stake in Spain (1543). Spanish Inquisition abolished
(1834).

1241   Mongols defeat Germans in Silesia, invade Poland and Hungary, withdraw from Europe after Ughetai, Mongol leader, dies.

1248   Seventh Crusade.

1251   Kublai Khan governs China, becomes ruler of Mongols (1259), establishes Yuan dynasty in China (1280), invades Burma (1287), dies (1294).

1270   Eighth Crusade.

1271   Marco Polo of Venice travels to China, in court of Kublai Khan (1275-
1292), returns to Genoa (1295) and writes *Travels.*

1273   Thomas Aquinas stops work on *Summa Theologica,* the basis of all
Catholic theological teaching; never completes it.

1295   English King Edward I summons the Model Parliament.

1300–1399 (c.e.)

1312–37   Mali Empire reaches its height in Africa under King Mansa Musa.

c.1325   The beginning of the Renaissance in Italy: writers Dante, Petrarch,
Boccaccio; painter Giotto. Development of *Noh* drama in Japan. Aztecs
establish Tenochtitlán on site of modern Mexico City. Peak of Muslim
culture in Spain. Small cannon in use.

1337–1453   Hundred Years' War—English and French kings fight for control
of France.

1347–1351   At least 25 million people die in Europe's "Black Death" (bubonic
plague).

1368   Ming Dynasty begins in China.

1376–82   John Wycliffe, pre-Reformation religious reformer, and followers
translate Latin Bible into English.

1378   The Great Schism (to 1417)—rival popes in Rome and Avignon, France,
fight for control of Roman Catholic Church.

c.1387   Chaucer's *Canterbury Tales.*

1400–1499 (c.e.)

1407   Casa di San Giorgio, one of the first public banks, founded in Genoa.

1415   Henry V defeats French at Agincourt. Jan Hus, Bohemian preacher and
follower of Wycliffe, burned at stake in Constance as heretic.

1418–60   Portugal's Prince Henry the Navigator sponsors exploration of Africa's coast.

1420   Brunelleschi begins work on the Duomo in Florence.

1428   Joan of Arc leads French against English, captured by Burgundians
(1430) and turned over to the English, burned at the stake as a witch
after ecclesiastical trial (1431).

1438   Incas rule in Peru.

1450   Florence becomes center of Renaissance arts and learning under the
Medicis.

1453   Turks conquer Constantinople, end of the Byzantine empire, beginning
of the Ottoman empire.

1455   The Wars of the Roses, civil wars between rival noble factions, begin in
England (to 1485). Having invented printing with movable type at
Mainz, Germany, Johann Gutenberg completes first Bible.

1462   Ivan the Great rules Russia until 1505 as first czar; ends payment of tribute to Mongols.

1492   Moors conquered in Spain by troops of Ferdinand and Isabella. Columbus becomes first European to encounter Caribbean islands, returns to
Spain (1493). Second voyage to Dominica, Jamaica, Puerto Rico (1493-
1496). Third voyage to Orinoco (1498). Fourth voyage to Honduras and
Panama (1502–1504).

1497   Vasco da Gama sails around Africa and discovers sea route to India
(1498). Establishes Portuguese colony in India (1502). John Cabot,
employed by England, reaches and explores Canadian coast. Michelangelo's *Bacchus* sculpture.

1500–1599 (c.e.)

1501   First black slaves in America brought to Spanish colony of Santo Domingo.

c.1503   Leonardo da Vinci paints the *Mona Lisa.* Michelangelo sculpts the
David (1504).

1506 St. Peter's Church started in Rome; designed and decorated by such artists and architects as Bramante, Michelangelo, da Vinci, Raphael, and Bernini before its completion in 1626.

1509 Henry VIII ascends English throne. Michelangelo paints the ceiling of the Sistine Chapel.

1513 Balboa becomes the first European to encounter the Pacific Ocean.

1517 Turks conquer Egypt, control Arabia. Martin Luther posts his 95 theses denouncing church abuses on church door in Wittenberg—start of the Reformation in Germany.

1519 Ulrich Zwingli begins Reformation in Switzerland. Hernando Cortes conquers Mexico for Spain. Charles I of Spain is chosen Holy Roman Emperor Charles V. Portuguese explorer Ferdinand Magellan sets out to circumnavigate the globe.

Martin Luther
(1483–1546)

1520 Luther excommunicated by Pope Leo X. Suleiman I ("the Magnificent") becomes Sultan of Turkey, invades Hungary (1521), Rhodes (1522), attacks Austria (1529), annexes Hungary (1541), Tripoli (1551), makes peace with Persia (1553), destroys Spanish fleet (1560), dies (1566). Magellan reaches the Pacific, is killed by Philippine natives (1521). One of his ships under Juan Sebastián del Cano continues around the world, reaches Spain (1522).

1524 Verrazano, sailing under the French flag, explores the New England coast and New York Bay.

1527 Troops of the Holy Roman Empire attack Rome, imprison Pope Clement VII—the end of the Italian Renaissance. Castiglione writes *The Courtier*. The Medici family expelled from Florence.

Henry VIII
(1491–1547)

1532 Pizarro marches from Panama to Peru, kills the Inca chieftain, Atahualpa, of Peru (1533). Machiavelli's *Prince* published posthumously.

1535 Reformation begins as Henry VIII makes himself head of English Church after being excommunicated by Pope. Sir Thomas More executed as traitor for refusal to acknowledge king's religious authority. Jacques Cartier sails up the St. Lawrence River, basis of French claims to Canada.

1536 Henry VIII executes second wife, Anne Boleyn. John Calvin establishes Reformed and Presbyterian form of Protestantism in Switzerland, writes *Institutes of the Christian Religion*. Danish and Norwegian Reformations. Michelangelo's *Last Judgment*.

1541 John Knox leads Reformation in Scotland, establishes Presbyterian church there (1560).

Queen Elizabeth I
(1533–1603)

1543 Publication of *On the Revolution of Heavenly Bodies* by Polish scholar Nicolaus Copernicus—giving his theory that the earth revolves around the sun.

1545 Council of Trent to meet intermittently until 1563 to define Catholic dogma and doctrine, reiterate papal authority.

1547 Ivan IV ("the Terrible") crowned as Czar of Russia, begins conquest of Astrakhan and Kazan (1552), battles nobles (boyars) for power (1564), kills his son (1580), dies, and is succeeded by his weak and feeble-minded son, Fydor I.

1553 Roman Catholicism restored in England by Queen Mary I.

1556 Akbar the Great becomes Mogul emperor of India, conquers Afghanistan (1581), continues wars of conquest (until 1605).

1558 Queen Elizabeth I ascends the throne (rules to 1603). Restores Protestantism, establishes state Church of England (Anglicanism). Renaissance will reach height in England—Shakespeare, Marlowe, Spenser.

William Shakespeare
(1564–1616)

1561 Persecution of Huguenots in France stopped by Edict of Orleans. French religious wars begin again with massacre of Huguenots at Vassy. St. Bartholomew's Day Massacre—thousands of Huguenots murdered (1572). Amnesty granted (1573). Persecution continues periodically until Edict of Nantes (1598) gives Huguenots religious freedom (until 1685).

1568 Protestant Netherlands revolts against Catholic Spain; independence will be acknowledged by Spain in 1648. High point of Dutch Renaissance—painters Rubens, Van Dyck, Hals, and Rembrandt.

1570 Japan permits visits of foreign ships. Queen Elizabeth I excommunicated by Pope. Turks attack Cyprus and war on Venice. Turkish fleet defeated at Battle of Lepanto by Spanish and Italian fleets (1571). Peace of Constantinople (1572) ends Turkish attacks on Europe.

Rembrandt van Rijn
(1606–1669)

1580 Francis Drake returns to England after circumnavigating the globe; knighted by Queen Elizabeth I (1581). Montaigne's *Essays* published.

1582 Pope Gregory XIII implements the Gregorian calendar.

**Marie de Medici
(1573–1642)**

**Galileo
(1564–1642)**

**Pocahontas
(c. 1595–1617)**

Taj Mahal

**John Milton
(1608–1674)**

1583 William of Orange rules The Netherlands; assassinated on orders of Philip II of Spain (1584).

1587 Mary, Queen of Scots, executed for treason by order of Queen Elizabeth I. Monteverdi's *First Book of Madrigals.*

1588 Defeat of the Spanish Armada by English. Henry, King of Navarre and Protestant leader, recognized as Henry IV, first Bourbon king of France. Converts to Roman Catholicism in 1593 in attempt to end religious wars.

1590 Henry IV enters Paris, wars on Spain (1595), marries Marie de Medici (1600), assassinated (1610). Spenser's *The Faerie Queen.* El Greco's *St. Jerome.* Galileo's experiments with falling objects.

1598 Boris Godunov becomes Russian Czar. Tycho Brahe describes his astronomical experiments.

1600–1699 (C.E.)

1600 Giordano Bruno burned as a heretic. English East India Company established.

1603 Ieyasu rules Japan, moves capital to Edo (Tokyo). Shakespeare's *Hamlet.*

1605 Cervantes's *Don Quixote de la Mancha,* the first modern novel.

1607 Jamestown, Virginia, established—first permanent English colony on American mainland. Pocahontas, daughter of Chief Powhatan, saves life of John Smith.

1609 Samuel de Champlain establishes French colony of Quebec. The *Relation,* the first newspaper, debuts in Germany.

1610 Galileo sees the moons of Jupiter through his telescope.

1611 Gustavus Adolphus elected King of Sweden. King James Version of the Bible published in England. Rubens paints his *Descent from the Cross.*

1614 John Napier discovers logarithms.

1618 Start of the Thirty Years' War—Protestants revolt against Catholic oppression; Denmark, Sweden, and France will invade Germany in later phases of war. Kepler proposes last of 3 laws of planetary motion.

1619 A Dutch ship brings the first African slaves to British North America.

1620 Pilgrims, after three-month voyage in *Mayflower,* land at Plymouth Rock. Francis Bacon's *Novum Organum.*

1623 New Netherland founded by Dutch West India Company.

1630 Massachusetts Bay Colony.

1632 Maryland founded by Lord Baltimore.

1633 Inquisition forces Galileo to recant his belief in Copernican theory.

1642 English Civil War. Cavaliers, supporters of Charles I, against Roundheads, parliamentary forces. Oliver Cromwell defeats Royalists (1646). Parliament demands reforms. Charles I offers concessions, brought to trial (1648), beheaded (1649). Cromwell becomes Lord Protector (1653). Rembrandt paints his *Night Watch.*

1643 Taj Mahal completed.

1644 End of Ming Dynasty in China—Manchus come to power. Descartes's *Principles of Philosophy.*

1648 End of the Thirty Years' War. German population about half of what it was in 1618 because of war and pestilence.

1658 Cromwell dies; son Richard resigns and Puritan government collapses.

1660 English Parliament calls for the restoration of the monarchy; invites Charles II to return from France.

1661 Charles II is crowned King of England. Louis XIV begins personal rule as absolute monarch; starts to build Versailles.

1664 British take New Amsterdam from the Dutch. English limit "Nonconformity" with re-established Anglican Church. Isaac Newton's experiments with gravity.

1665 Great Plague in London kills 75,000.

1666 Great Fire of London. Molière's *Misanthrope.*

1667 Milton's *Paradise Lost,* widely considered the greatest epic poem in English.

1682 Pennsylvania founded by William Penn.

1683 War of European powers against the Turks (to 1699). Vienna withstands three-month Turkish siege; high point of Turkish advance in Europe.

1685 James II succeeds Charles II in England, calls for freedom of conscience (1687). Protestants fear restoration of Catholicism and demand "Glorious Revolution." William of Orange invited to England and James II escapes to France (1688). William III and his wife, Mary, crowned. In France, Edict of Nantes of 1598, granting freedom of worship to Huguenots, is revoked by Louis XIV; thousands of Protestants flee.

1689 Peter the Great becomes Czar of Russia—attempts to westernize nation and build Russia as a military power. Defeats Charles XII of Sweden at Poltava (1709). Beginning of the French and Indian Wars (to 1763), campaigns in America linked to a series of wars between France and England for domination of Europe.

1690 William III of England defeats former King James II and Irish rebels at Battle of the Boyne in Ireland. John Locke's *Human Understanding.*

1700–1799 (C.E.)

1701 War of the Spanish Succession begins—the last of Louis XIV's wars for domination of the continent. The Peace of Utrecht (1714) will end the conflict and mark the rise of the British Empire. Called Queen Anne's War in America, it ends with the British taking New Foundland, Acadia, and Hudson's Bay Territory from France, and Gibraltar and Minorca from Spain.

Sir Isaac Newton
(1642–1727)

1704 Deerfield (Mass.) Massacre of English colonists by French and Indians. Bach's first cantata. Jonathan Swift's *Tale of a Tub. Boston News Letter*—first newspaper in America.

1707 United Kingdom of Great Britain formed—England, Wales, and Scotland joined by parliamentary Act of Union.

1729 Bach's *St. Matthew Passion.* Isaac Newton's *Principia* translated from Latin into English.

1732 Benjamin Franklin begins publishing *Poor Richard's Almanack.* James Oglethorpe and others found Georgia.

Frederick the Great
(1712–1786)

1735 John Peter Zenger, New York editor, acquitted of libel in New York, establishing press freedom.

1740 Capt. Vitus Bering, Dane employed by Russia, discovers Alaska. Frederick II "the Great" crowned King of Prussia.

1746 British defeat Scots under Stuart Pretender Prince Charles at Culloden Moor. Last battle fought on British soil.

1751 Publication of the *Encyclopédie* begins in France, the "bible" of the Enlightenment.

1755 Samuel Johnson's *Dictionary* first published. Great earthquake in Lisbon, Portugal—over 60,000 die. U.S. postal service established.

1756 Seven Years' War (French and Indian Wars in America) (to 1763), in which Britain and Prussia defeat France, Spain, Austria, and Russia. France loses North American colonies; Spain cedes Florida to Britain in exchange for Cuba. In India, over 100 British prisoners die in "Black Hole of Calcutta."

Samuel Johnson
(1709–1784)

1757 Beginning of British Empire in India as Robert Clive, British commander, defeats Nawab of Bengal at Plassey.

1759 British capture Quebec from French. Voltaire's *Candide.* Haydn's *Symphony No. 1.*

1762 Catherine II ("the Great") becomes Czarina of Russia. J. J. Rousseau's *Social Contract.* Mozart tours Europe as six-year-old prodigy.

1765 James Watt invents the steam engine. Britain imposes the Stamp Act on the American colonists.

THE REVOLUTIONARY WAR

Conflicts increase between colonists and Britain on western frontier because of royal edict limiting western expansion (1763) and regulation of colonial trade and increased taxation of colonies (Writs of Assistance allow search for illegal shipments, 1761; Sugar Act, 1764; Currency Act, 1764; Stamp Act, 1765; Quartering Act, 1765; Duty Act, 1767. Boston Massacre (1770). Lord North attempts conciliation (1770). Boston Tea Party (1773), followed by punitive measures passed by Parliament—the "Intolerable Acts."

First Continental Congress (1774) sends "Declaration of Rights and Grievances" to King George III, urges colonies to form Continental Association. Paul Revere's ride and Lexington and Concord battle between Massachusetts Minutemen and British (1775).

Second Continental Congress (1775), while sending "olive branch" to the king, begins to raise army, appoints Washington commander-in-chief, and seeks alliance with France. Some colonial legislatures urge their delegates to vote for independence. Declaration of Independence **(July 4, 1776)**.

Major Battles of the Revolutionary War: *Long Island:* Howe defeats Putnam's division of Washington's Army in Brooklyn Heights, but Americans escape across East River (1776). *Trenton and Princeton:* Washington defeats Hessians at Trenton, British at Princeton. Winters at Morristown (1776-77). Howe winters in Philadelphia; Washington at Valley Forge (1777-78). Burgoyne surrenders British army to General Gates at *Saratoga* (1777).

France recognizes American independence (1778). The War moves south: Savannah captured by British (1778); Charleston occupied (1780); Americans fight successful guerrilla actions under Marion, Pickens, and Sumter. In the West, George Rogers Clark attacks Forts Kaskaskia and Vincennes (1778-1779), defeating British in the region. Cornwallis surrenders at *Yorktown,* Virginia **(Oct. 19, 1781).** By 1782, Britain is eager for peace because of conflicts with European nations. *Peace of Paris* (1783): Britain recognizes American independence.

Benjamin Franklin
(1706–1790)

George Washington
(1732–1799)

Alexander Hamilton
(1755–1804)

Ludwig van Beethoven
(1770–1827)

1769   Sir William Arkwright patents a spinning machine—an early step in the Industrial Revolution.

1770   The Boston Massacre.

1772   Joseph Priestley and Daniel Rutherford independently discover nitrogen. Partition of Poland—in 1772, 1793, and 1795, Austria, Prussia, and Russia divide land and people of Poland, end its independence.

1773   The Boston Tea Party.

1774   First Continental Congress drafts "Declaration of Rights and Grievances."

1775   The American Revolution begins with battle of Lexington and Concord. Second Continental Congress. Priestley discovers hydrochloric and sulfuric acids.

1776   Declaration of Independence. Gen. Washington crosses the Delaware Christmas night. Adam Smith's *Wealth of Nations*. Edward Gibbon's *Decline and Fall of the Roman Empire*. Thomas Paine's *Common Sense*. Fragonard's *Washerwoman*. Mozart's *Haffner Serenade*.

1778   Capt. James Cook discovers Hawaii. Franz Mesmer uses hypnotism.

1781   Immanuel Kant's *Critique of Pure Reason*. Herschel discovers Uranus.

1783   Revolutionary War ends with Treaty of Paris. William Blake's poems. Beethoven's first printed works.

1784   Crimea annexed by Russia. John Wesley's *Deed of Declaration*, the basic work of Methodism.

1785   Russians settle Aleutian Islands.

1787   The Constitution of the United States signed. Lavoisier's work on chemical nomenclature. Mozart's *Don Giovanni*.

1788   French *Parlement* presents grievances to Louis XVI who agrees to convening of Estates-General in 1789—not called since 1613. Goethe's *Egmont*. Laplace's *Laws of the Planetary System*.

1789   French Revolution begins with the storming of the Bastille. In U.S., George Washington elected President with all 69 votes of the Electoral College, takes oath of office in New York City. Vice President: John Adams. Secretary of State: Thomas Jefferson. Secretary of Treasury: Alexander Hamilton.

1790   H.M.S. *Bounty* mutineers settle on Pitcairn Island. Aloisio Galvani experiments on electrical stimulation of the muscles. Philadelphia temporary capital of U.S. as Congress votes to establish new capital on Potomac. U.S. population about 3,929,000, including 698,000 slaves. Lavoisier formulates *Table of 31 chemical elements*.

1791   U.S. Bill of Rights ratified. Boswell's *Life of Johnson*.

1793   Louis XVI and Marie Antoinette executed. Reign of Terror begins in France. Eli Whitney invents the cotton gin, spurring the growth of the cotton industry and helping to institutionalize slavery in the U.S. South.

1794   Kosciusko's uprising in Poland quelled by the Russians. In U.S., Whiskey Rebellion in Pennsylvania as farmers object to liquor taxes. Reign of Terror ends with execution of Robespierre.

1796   Napoleon Bonaparte, French general, defeats Austrians. In the U.S., Washington's Farewell Address (**Sept. 17**); John Adams elected President; Thomas Jefferson, vice president. Edward Jenner introduces smallpox vaccination.

1798   Napoleon extends French conquests to Rome and Egypt. U.S. Navy Department established.

FRENCH REVOLUTION (1789–1799)

Revolution begins when Third Estate (Commons) delegates swear not to disband until France has a constitution. Paris mob storms Bastille, symbol of royal power (**July 14, 1789**). National Assembly votes for Constitution, Declaration of the Rights of Man, a limited monarchy, and other reforms (1789-90). Legislative Assembly elected, Revolutionary Commune formed, and French Republic proclaimed (1792). War of the First Coalition—Austria, Prussia, Britain, Netherlands, and Spain fight to restore French nobility (1792-97).

Start of series of wars between France and European powers that will last, almost without interruption, for 23 years. Louis XVI and Marie Antoinette executed. Committee of Public Safety begins Reign of Terror as political control measure. Interfactional rivalry leads to mass killings. Danton and Robespierre executed. Third French Constitution sets up Directory government (1795). Napoleon abolishes the Directory, establishes the Consulate, becomes the First Consul of France (1799).

1799 Rosetta Stone discovered in Egypt. Napoleon leads coup that overthrows Directory, establishes the Consulate, becomes First Consul—one of three who rule France together.

1800–1899 (c.e.)

1800 Napoleon conquers Italy, firmly establishes himself as First Consul in France. In the U.S., federal government moves to Washington. Robert Owen's social reforms in England. William Herschel discovers infrared rays. Alessandro Volta produces electricity.

1801 Austria makes temporary peace with France. United Kingdom of Great Britain and Ireland established with one monarch and one parliament; Catholics excluded from voting.

Napoleon Bonaparte
(1769–1821)

1803 U.S. negotiates Louisiana Purchase from France: for $15 million, U.S. doubles its domain, increasing its territory by 827,000 sq. mi. (2,144,500 sq km), from Mississippi River to Rockies and from Gulf of Mexico to British North America.

1804 Haiti declares independence from France; first black nation to gain freedom from European colonial rule. Napoleon transforms the Consulate of France into an empire, proclaims himself emperor of France, systematizes French law under *Code Napoleon*. In the U.S., Alexander Hamilton is mortally wounded in duel with Aaron Burr. Lewis and Clark expedition begins exploration of what is now northwestern U.S.

1805 Lord Nelson defeats the French-Spanish fleets in the Battle of Trafalgar. Napoleon victorious over Austrian and Russian forces at the Battle of Austerlitz.

Edgar Allan Poe
(1809–1849)

1807 Robert Fulton makes first successful steamboat trip on *Clermont* between New York City and Albany.

1808 French armies occupy Rome and Spain, extending Napoleon's empire. Britain begins aiding Spanish guerrillas against Napoleon in Peninsular War. In the U.S., Congress bars importation of slaves. Beethoven's *Fifth* and *Sixth Symphonies* performed.

1812 Napoleon's Grand Army invades Russia in June. Forced to retreat in winter, most of Napoleon's 600,000 men are lost. In the U.S., war with Britain declared over freedom of the seas for U.S. vessels (War of 1812). U.S.S. *Constitution* sinks British frigate.

Richard Wagner
(1813–1883)

1814 French defeated by allies (Britain, Austria, Russia, Prussia, Sweden, and Portugal) in War of Liberation. Napoleon exiled to Elba, off Italian coast. Bourbon King Louis XVIII takes French throne. George Stephenson builds first practical steam locomotive.

1815 Napoleon returns: "Hundred Days" begin. Napoleon defeated by Wellington at Waterloo, banished again to St. Helena in South Atlantic. Congress of Vienna: victorious allies change the map of Europe. War of 1812 ends with treaty of Ghent.

1819 Simón Bolívar liberates New Granada (now Colombia, Venezuela, and Ecuador) as Spain loses hold on South American countries; named President of Colombia.

1820 Missouri Compromise—Missouri admitted as slave state but slavery barred in rest of Louisiana Purchase north of 36°30′ N.

Harriet Beecher
Stowe
(1811–1896)

1821 Guatemala, Panama, and Santo Domingo proclaim independence from Spain.

1822 Greeks proclaim a republic and independence from Turkey. Turks invade Greece. Russia declares war on Turkey (1828). Greece also aided by France and Britain. War ends and Turks recognize Greek independence (1829). Brazil becomes independent of Portugal. Schubert's *Eighth Symphony* ("The Unfinished").

1823 U.S. Monroe Doctrine warns European nations not to interfere in Western Hemisphere.

1824 Mexico becomes a republic, three years after declaring independence from Spain. Bolívar liberates Peru, becomes its president. Beethoven's *Ninth Symphony.*

Walt Whitman
(1819–1892)

1825 First passenger-carrying railroad in England.

1826 Joseph-Nicéphore Niepce takes the world's first photograph.

WAR OF 1812

British interference with American trade, impressment of American seamen, and "War Hawks" drive for western expansion lead to war. American attacks on Canada foiled; U.S. Commodore Perry wins battle of Lake Erie (1813). British capture and burn Washington (1814) but fail to take Fort McHenry at Baltimore. Andrew Jackson repulses assault on New Orleans after treaty of Ghent ends war (1815). War settles little but strengthens U.S. as independent nation.

**Dred Scott
(1795?–1858)**

**Charles Darwin
(1809–1882)**

**Frederick Douglass
(1817–1895)**

**Harriet Tubman
(c. 1820–1913)**

**Chief Joseph
(c. 1840–1904)**

1830 French invade Algeria. Louis Philippe becomes "Citizen King" as revolution forces Charles X to abdicate. Mormon church formed in U.S. by Joseph Smith.

1831 Polish revolt against Russia fails. Belgium separates from the Netherlands. In U.S., Nat Turner leads unsuccessful slave rebellion.

1833 Slavery abolished in British Empire.

1834 Charles Babbage invents "analytical engine," precursor of computer. McCormick patents reaper.

1836 Boer farmers start "Great Trek"—Natal, Transvaal, and Orange Free State founded in South Africa. Mexican army besieges Texans in Alamo. Entire garrison, including Davy Crockett and Jim Bowie, wiped out. Texans gain independence from Mexico after winning Battle of San Jacinto. Dickens's *Pickwick Papers.*

1837 Victoria becomes Queen of Great Britain. Mob kills Elijah P. Lovejoy, Illinois abolitionist publisher.

1839 First Opium War (to 1842) between Britain and China, over importation of drug into China.

1840 Lower and Upper Canada united.

1841 U.S. President Harrison dies (**April 4**) one month after inauguration; John Tyler becomes first vice president to succeed to Presidency.

1843 Wagner's opera *The Flying Dutchman.*

1844 Democratic convention calls for annexation of Texas and acquisition of Oregon ("Fifty-four-forty-or-fight"). Five Chinese ports opened to U.S. ships. Samuel F. B. Morse patents telegraph.

1845 Congress adopts joint resolution for annexation of Texas. Edgar Allan Poe publishes *The Raven and Other Poems.*

1846 U.S. declares war on Mexico. California and New Mexico annexed by U.S. Brigham Young leads Mormons to Great Salt Lake. W. T. Morton uses ether as anesthetic. Sewing machine patented by Elias Howe. Frederick Douglass launches abolitionist newspaper *The North Star.* Failure of potato crop causes famine in Ireland.

1848 Revolt in Paris: Louis Philippe abdicates; Louis Napoleon elected President of French Republic. Revolutions in Vienna, Venice, Berlin, Milan, Rome, and Warsaw. Put down by royal troops in 1848-49. U.S.-Mexico War ends; Mexico cedes claims to Texas, California, Arizona, New Mexico, Utah, Nevada. U.S. treaty with Britain sets Oregon Territory boundary at 49th parallel. Karl Marx and Friedrich Engels's *Communist Manifesto.* Harriet Tubman escapes from slavery and joins the Underground Railroad. Women's Rights Convention in Seneca Falls, N.Y.

1849 California gold rush begins.

1850 Henry Clay opens great debate on slavery, warns South against secession.

1851 Herman Melville's *Moby-Dick.*

1852 South African Republic established. Louis Napoleon proclaims himself Napoleon III ("Second Empire"). Harriet Beecher Stowe's *Uncle Tom's Cabin.*

1853 Crimean War begins as Turkey declares war on Russia. Commodore Perry reaches Tokyo.

1854 Britain and France join Turkey in war on Russia. In U.S., Kansas-Nebraska Act permits local option on slavery; rioting and bloodshed. Japanese allow American trade. Antislavery men in Michigan form Republican Party. Tennyson's *Charge of the Light Brigade.* Thoreau's *Walden.*

1855 Armed clashes in Kansas between pro- and anti-slavery forces. Florence Nightingale nurses wounded in Crimea. Walt Whitman's *Leaves of Grass.*

1856 Flaubert's *Madame Bovary.*

1857 Supreme Court, in Dred Scott decision, rules that a slave is not a citizen. Financial crisis in Europe and U.S. Great Mutiny (Sepoy Rebellion) begins in India. India placed under crown rule as a result.

1858 Pro-slavery constitution rejected in Kansas. Abraham Lincoln makes strong antislavery speech in Springfield, Ill.: "...this Government cannot endure permanently half slave and half free." Lincoln-Douglas debates. First trans-Atlantic telegraph cable completed by Cyrus W. Field.

1859 John Brown raids Harpers Ferry; is captured and hanged. Work begins on Suez Canal. Unification of Italy starts under leadership of Count Cavour, Sardinian premier. Joined by France in war against Austria. Edward Fitzgerald's translation of *The Rubaiyat of Omar Khayyam.* Charles Darwin's *Origin of Species.* J. S. Mill's *On Liberty.*

1860 South Carolina secedes from the Union.

1861 U.S. Civil War begins as attempts at compromise fail. Mississippi, Florida, Alabama, Georgia, Louisiana, and Texas secede; with South Carolina, they form the Confederate States of America, with Jefferson Davis as president. Virginia, Arkansas, Tennessee, North Carolina secede and join Confederacy. First Battle of Bull Run (Manassas).Congress creates Colorado, Dakota, and Nevada territories; adopts income tax; Lincoln inaugurated. Serfs emancipated in Russia. Pasteur's theory of germs. Independent Kingdom of Italy proclaimed under Sardinian King Victor Emmanuel II.

1862 Several major Civil War battles: Battle of Shiloh, Second Battle of Bull Run (Manassas), Battle of Antietam.

1863 French capture Mexico City; proclaim Archduke Maximilian of Austria emperor. Battle of Gettysburg.

1864 Gen. Sherman's Atlanta campaign and "march to the sea."

1865 Gen. Lee surrenders to Grant at Appomattox; the Civil War is over. Lincoln fatally shot at Ford's Theater by John Wilkes Booth. Vice President Johnson sworn as successor. Booth caught and dies of gunshot wounds; four conspirators are hanged. Joseph Lister begins antiseptic surgery. Gregor Mendel's *Law of Heredity.* Lewis Carroll's *Alice's Adventures in Wonderland.*

1866 Alfred Nobel invents dynamite (patented in Britain, 1867). Seven Weeks' War: Austria defeated by Prussia and Italy.

1867 Austria-Hungary Dual Monarchy established. French leave Mexico; Maximilian executed. Dominion of Canada established. U.S. buys Alaska from Russia for $7,200,000. South African diamond field discovered. Volume I of Marx's *Das Kapital.* Strauss's *Blue Danube.*

1868 Revolution in Spain; Queen Isabella deposed, flees to France. In U.S., Fourteenth Amendment giving civil rights to blacks is ratified. Georgia under military government after legislature expels blacks.

1869 First U.S. transcontinental rail route completed. James Fisk and Jay Gould's attempt to control gold market causes Black Friday panic. Suez Canal opens. Mendeleev's periodic table of elements.

1870 Franco-Prussian War (to 1871): Napoleon III capitulates at Sedan. Revolt in Paris; Third Republic proclaimed.

1871 France surrenders Alsace-Lorraine to Germany; war ends. German Empire proclaimed with Prussian King as Kaiser Wilhelm I. Fighting with Apaches begins in American West. Boss Tweed corruption exposed in New York. The Chicago Fire, with 250 deaths and $196-million damage. Stanley meets Livingston in Africa.

1872 Congress gives amnesty to most Confederates. Jules Verne's *Around the World in 80 Days.*

Abraham Lincoln
(1809–1865)

Robert E. Lee
(1807–1870)

William Tecumseh
Sherman
(1820–1891)

THE CIVIL WAR

Apart from the matter of slavery, the Civil War arose out of both the economic and political rivalry between an agrarian South and an industrial North and the issue of the right of states to secede from the Union.

1861 After South Carolina secedes **(Dec. 20, 1860)**, Mississippi, Florida, Alabama, Georgia, Louisiana, and Texas follow, forming the Confederate States of America, with Jefferson Davis as president **(Jan.-March)**. War begins as Confederates fire on Fort Sumter **(April 12)**. Lincoln calls for 75,000 volunteers. Southern ports blockaded by superior Union naval forces. Virginia, Arkansas, Tennessee, and North Carolina secede to complete 11-state Confederacy. Union army advancing on Richmond repulsed at first Battle of Bull Run (Manassas) **(July)**.

1862 Edwin M. Stanton named Secretary of War **(Jan.)**. Grant wins first important Union victory in West, at Fort Donelson; Nashville falls **(Feb.)**. Ironclads, Union's *Monitor* and Confederate's *Virginia (Merrimac)* duel at Hampton Roads **(March)**. New Orleans falls to Union fleet under Farragut; city occupied **(April)**. Grant's army escapes defeat at Shiloh. Memphis falls as Union gunboats control upper Mississippi **(June)**. Confederate General Robert E. Lee victorious at second Battle of Bull Run (Manassas) **(Aug.)**. Union army under McClellan halts Lee's attack on Washington in the Battle of Antietam **(Sept.)**. Lincoln removes McClellan for lack of aggressiveness. Burnside's drive on Richmond fails at Fredericksburg **(Dec.)**. Union forces under Rosecrans chase Bragg through Tennessee; battle of Murfreesboro **(Oct.-Jan. 1863)**.

1863 Lee defeats Hooker at Chancellorsville; "Stonewall" Jackson, Confederate general, dies **(May)**. Confederate invasion of Pennsylvania stopped at Gettysburg by George Meade—Lee loses 20,000 men—the greatest battle of the War **(July)**. It and the Union victory at Vicksburg mark the war's turning point. Union general George H. Thomas, the "Rock of Chickamauga," holds Bragg's forces on Georgia-Tennessee border **(Sept.)**. Sherman, Hooker, and Thomas drive Bragg back to Georgia. Tennessee restored to the Union **(Nov.)**.

1864 Ulysses S. Grant named commander-in-chief of Union forces **(March)**. In the Wilderness campaign, Grant forces Lee's Army of Northern Virginia back toward Richmond **(May-June)**. Sherman's Atlanta campaign and "march to the sea" **(May-Sept.)**. Farragut's victory at Mobile Bay **(Aug.)**. Hood's Confederate army defeated at Nashville. Sherman takes Savannah **(Dec.)**.

1865 Sheridan defeats Confederates at Five Forks; Confederates evacuate Richmond **(April)**. On April 9, Lee surrenders to Grant at Appomattox.

**Johannes Brahms
(1833–1897)**

**Samuel Clemens
(Mark Twain)
(1835–1910)**

Statue of Liberty

**Marie Curie
(1867–1934)**

1873   Economic crisis in Europe. U.S. establishes gold standard.

1875   First Kentucky Derby.

1876   Sioux kill Gen. George A. Custer and 264 troopers at Little Big Horn River. Alexander Graham Bell patents the telephone.

1877   After Presidential election of 1876, Electoral Commission gives disputed Electoral College votes to Rutherford B. Hayes despite Tilden's popular majority. Russo-Turkish war (ends in 1878 with power of Turkey in Europe broken). Reconstruction ends in the American South. Thomas Edison patents phonograph. The Nez Perce leader Chief Joseph is forced to surrender. Tchaikovsky's *Swan Lake.*

1878   Congress of Berlin revises Treaty of San Stefano, ending Russo-Turkish War; makes extensive redivision of southeastern Europe. First commercial telephone exchange opened in New Haven, Conn.

1880   U.S.-China treaty allows U.S. to restrict immigration of Chinese labor.

1881   President Garfield fatally shot by assassin; Vice President Arthur succeeds him. Charles J. Guiteau convicted and executed (1882).

1882   Terrorism in Ireland after land evictions. Britain invades and conquers Egypt. Germany, Austria, and Italy form Triple Alliance. In U.S., Congress adopts Chinese Exclusion Act. Rockefeller's Standard Oil Trust is first industrial monopoly. In Berlin, Robert Koch announces discovery of tuberculosis germ.

1883   Congress creates Civil Service Commission. Brooklyn Bridge and Metropolitan Opera House completed.

1885   British Gen. Charles G. "Chinese" Gordon killed at Khartoum in Egyptian Sudan.

1886   Bombing at Haymarket Square, Chicago, kills seven policemen and injures many others. Eight alleged anarchists accused—three imprisoned, one commits suicide, four hanged. (In 1893, Illinois Governor Altgeld, critical of trial, pardons three survivors.) Statue of Liberty dedicated. Geronimo, Apache Indian chief, surrenders.

1887   Queen Victoria's Golden Jubilee. Sir Arthur Conan Doyle's first Sherlock Holmes story, *A Study in Scarlet.*

1888   Historic March blizzard in Northeast U.S.—many perish, property damage exceeds $25 million. George Eastman's box camera (the Kodak). J. B. Dunlop invents pneumatic tire. Jack the Ripper murders in London.

1889   Second (Socialist) International founded in Paris. Indian Territory in Oklahoma opened to settlement. Thousands die in Johnstown, Pa. flood. Eiffel Tower built for the Paris exposition. Mark Twain's *A Connecticut Yankee in King Arthur's Court.*

1890   Congress votes to pass Sherman Antitrust Act. Sioux Chief Sitting Bull arrested and killed by police on Pine Ridge reservation; two weeks later, U.S. troops kill over 200 Sioux at Battle of Wounded Knee.

1892   Battle between steel strikers and Pinkerton guards at Homestead, Pa.; union defeated after militia intervenes. Silver mine strikers in Idaho fight non-union workers; U.S. troops dispatched. Diesel engine patented.

1894   Sino-Japanese War begins (ends in 1895 with China's defeat). In France, Capt. Alfred Dreyfus convicted on false treason charge (pardoned in 1906). In U.S., Jacob S. Coxey of Ohio leads "Coxey's Army" of unemployed on Washington. Eugene V. Debs calls general strike of rail workers to support Pullman Company strikers; strike broken, Debs jailed for six months. Thomas A. Edison's kinetoscope given first public showing in New York City.

1895   X-rays discovered by German physicist Wilhelm Roentgen. Auguste and Louis Lumière premiere motion pictures at a café in Paris.

SPANISH-AMERICAN WAR (1898–1899)

War fires stoked by "jingo journalism" as American people support Cuban rebels against Spain. American business sees economic gain in Cuban trade and resources and American power zones in Latin America. Outstanding events: Submarine mine sinks U.S. battleship *Maine* in Havana Harbor **(Feb. 15)**; 260 killed; responsibility never fixed. Congress declares independence of Cuba **(Apr. 19).** Spain declares war on U.S. **(Apr. 24);** Congress **(Apr. 25)** formally declares nation has been at war with Spain since **Apr. 21.** Commodore George Dewey wins seven-hour battle of Manila Bay **(May 1).** Spanish fleet destroyed off Santiago, Cuba **(July 3);** city surrenders **(July 17).** Treaty of Paris (ratified by Senate 1899) ends war. U.S. given Guam and Puerto Rico and agrees to pay Spain $20 million for Philippines. Cuba independent of Spain; under U.S. military control for three years until **May 20, 1902.** Yellow fever is eradicated and political reforms achieved.

1896 Supreme Court's *Plessy v. Ferguson* decision—"separate but equal" doctrine. Alfred Nobel's will establishes prizes for peace, science, and literature. Marconi receives first wireless patent in Britain. William Jennings Bryan delivers "Cross of Gold" speech at Democratic Convention in Chicago. First modern Olympic games held in Athens, Greece.

1898 Chinese "Boxers," anti-foreign organization, established. They stage uprisings against Europeans in 1900; U.S. and other Western troops relieve Peking legations. U.S. Battleship *Maine* is sunk in Havana Harbor. Spanish-American War begins. U.S. destroys Spanish fleet near Santiago, Cuba. Pierre and Marie Curie discover radium and polonium.

1899 Boer War (or South African War): conflict between British and Boers (descendants of Dutch settlers of South Africa). Causes rooted in long-standing territorial disputes and in friction over political rights for English and other "uitlanders" following 1886 discovery of vast gold deposits in Transvaal. (British victorious as war ends in 1902.) Casualties: 5,774 British dead, about 4,000 Boers. Union of South Africa established in 1908 as confederation of colonies; becomes British dominion in 1910.

Sigmund Freud
(1856–1939)

1900–1999 (C.E.)

1900 Hurricane ravages Galveston, Tex.; 6,000 drown. Fauvist movement in painting begins, led by Henri Matisse. Sigmund Freud's *The Interpretation of Dreams*. Carrie Chapman Catt succeeds Susan B. Anthony as president of National Woman Suffrage Association.

1901 Queen Victoria dies, and is succeeded by her son, Edward VII. As President McKinley begins second term, he is shot fatally by anarchist Leon Czolgosz. Theodore Roosevelt sworn in as successor.

1902 Enrico Caruso's first gramophone recording. Aswan Dam completed.

1903 Wright brothers, Orville and Wilbur, fly first powered, controlled, heavier-than-air plane at Kitty Hawk, N.C. Henry Ford organizes Ford Motor Company. The Boston Red Sox win the first World Series against the Pittsburgh Pirates. Du Bois publishes *The Souls of Black Folk.*

Carrie Chapman Catt
(1859–1947)

1904 Russo-Japanese War begins—competition for Korea and Manchuria. *Entente Cordiale:* Britain and France settle their international differences. General theory of radioactivity by Rutherford and Soddy. New York City subway opens.

1905 In Russo-Japanese War, Port Arthur surrenders to Japanese; Russia suffers other defeats. President Roosevelt mediates Treaty of Portsmouth, N.H., which recognizes Japan's control of Korea and restores southern Manchuria to China. The Russian Revolution of 1905 begins on "Bloody Sunday" when troops fire onto a defenseless group of demonstrators in St. Petersburg. Strikes and riots follow. Sailors on battleship *Potemkin* mutiny; reforms, including first Duma (parliament), established by Czar Nicholas II's "October Manifesto." Albert Einstein's special theory of relativity and other key theories in physics. Franz Lehar's *Merry Widow.*

Albert Einstein
(1879–1955)

1906 San Francisco earthquake and three-day fire; more than 500 dead. Roald Amundsen, Norwegian explorer, fixes magnetic North Pole.

1907 Second Hague Peace Conference, of 46 nations, adopts 10 conventions on rules of war. Financial panic of 1907 in U.S. Mahler begins work on "Song of the Earth." Oklahoma becomes 46th state.

1908 Earthquake kills 150,000 in southern Italy and Sicily. U.S. Supreme Court, in Danbury Hatters' case, outlaws secondary union boycotts. Model T produced by Ford Motor Company.

Vladimir Lenin
(1870–1924)

1909 North Pole reportedly reached by American explorers Robert E. Peary and Matthew Henson. The National Association for the Advancement of Colored People is founded in New York by prominent black and white intellectuals and led by W. E. B. Du Bois.

1910 Boy Scouts of America incorporated. Angel Island, in San Francisco Bay, becomes immigration center for Asians entering U.S.

1911 First use of aircraft as offensive weapon in Turkish-Italian War. Italy defeats Turks and annexes Tripoli and Libya. Chinese Republic proclaimed after revolution overthrows Manchu dynasty. Sun Yat-sen named president. Mexican Revolution: Porfirio Diaz, president since 1877, replaced by Francisco Madero. Triangle Shirtwaist Company fire in New York; 146 killed. Amundsen reaches South Pole. Richard Strauss's *Der Rosenkavalier.* Irving Berlin's *Alexander's Ragtime Band.*

Robert Peary
(1856–1920)

**W. E. B. Du Bois
(1868–1963)**

**Woodrow Wilson
(1856–1924)**

**Bessie Smith
(1894–1937)**

1912 Balkan Wars (1912–13) resulting from territorial disputes: Turkey defeated by alliance of Bulgaria, Serbia, Greece, and Montenegro; London peace treaty (1913) partitions most of European Turkey among the victors. In second war (1913), Bulgaria attacks Serbia and Greece and is defeated after Romania intervenes and Turks recapture Adrianople. *Titanic* sinks on maiden voyage; over 1,500 drown. New Mexico and Arizona admitted as states.

1913 Suffragettes demonstrate in London. Garment workers strike in New York and Boston; win pay raise and shorter hours. 16th Amendment (income tax) and 17th (popular election of U.S. senators) adopted. Bill creating U.S. Federal Reserve System becomes law. Stravinsky's *The Rite of Spring*. Woodrow Wilson becomes 28th U.S. President. Armory Show introduces modern art to U.S.; Duchamp's *Nude Descending a Staircase* shocks public.

1914 World War I begins: Austrian Archduke Francis Ferdinand and wife Sophie are assassinated; Austria declares war on Serbia, Germany on Russia and France, Britain on Germany. Panama Canal officially opened. Congress sets up Federal Trade Commission, passes Clayton Antitrust Act. U.S. Marines occupy Veracruz, Mexico, intervening in civil war to protect American interests.

1915 *Lusitania* sunk by German submarine. Second Battle of Ypres. U.S. banks lend $500 million to France and Britain. Genocide of estimated 600,000 to 1 million Armenians by Turkish soldiers. D. W. Griffith's film *Birth of a Nation*. Albert Einstein's *General Theory of Relativity*.

1916 Congress expands armed forces. Battle of Verdun. Battle of the Somme. Tom Mooney arrested for San Francisco bombing (pardoned in 1939). Pershing fails in raid into Mexico in quest of rebel Pancho Villa. U.S. buys Virgin Islands from Denmark for $25 million. President Wilson re-elected with "he kept us out of war" slogan. "Black Tom" explosion at munitions dock in Jersey City, N.J., $40,000,000 damages; traced to German saboteurs. Margaret Sanger opens first birth control clinic. Easter Rebellion in Ireland put down by British troops. Jeannette Rankin becomes first woman elected to Congress.

1917 First U.S. combat troops in France as U.S. declares war on Germany **(April 6).** Third Battle of Ypres. Russian Revolution of 1917—climax of long unrest under czars. February Revolution—Nicholas II forced to abdicate, liberal government created. Kerensky becomes prime minister and forms provisional government **(July).** In October Revolution, Bolsheviks seize power in armed coup d'état led by Lenin and Trotsky. Kerensky flees. Balfour Declaration promises Jewish homeland in Palestine. U.S. declares war on Austria-Hungary **(Dec. 7).** Armistice between

---

WORLD WAR I (1914–1918)

Imperial, territorial, and economic rivalries led to the "Great War" between the Central Powers (Austria-Hungary, Germany, Bulgaria, and Turkey) and the Allies (U.S., Britain, France, Russia, Belgium, Serbia, Greece, Romania, Montenegro, Portugal, Italy, Japan). About 10 million combatants killed, 20 million wounded.

1914 Austrian Archduke Francis Ferdinand and wife assassinated in Sarajevo by Serbian nationalist, Gavrilo Princip **(June 28).** Austria declares war on Serbia **(July 28).** Germany declares war on Russia **(Aug. 1),** on France **(Aug. 3),** invades Belgium **(Aug. 4).** Britain declares war on Germany **(Aug. 4).** Germans defeat Russians in Battle of Tannenberg on Eastern Front **(Aug.).** First Battle of the Marne **(Sept.).** German drive stopped 25 miles from Paris. By end of year, war on the Western Front is "positional" in the trenches.

1915 German submarine blockade of Great Britain begins **(Feb.).** Dardanelles Campaign—British land in Turkey **(April),** withdraw from Gallipoli **(Dec. to Jan. 1916).** Germans use gas at second Battle of Ypres **(April–May).** *Lusitania* sunk by German submarine—1,198 lost, including 128 Americans **(May 7).** On Eastern Front, German and Austrian "great offensive" conquers all of Poland and Lithuania; Russians lose 1 million men (by **Sept. 6)** "Great Fall Offensive" by Allies results in little change from 1914 **(Sept.–Oct.).** Britain and France declare war on Bulgaria **(Oct. 14).**

1916 Battle of Verdun—Germans and French each lose about 350,000 men **(Feb.).** Extended submarine

warfare begins **(March).** British-German sea battle of Jutland **(May);** British lose more ships, but German fleet never ventures forth again. On Eastern Front, the Brusilov offensive demoralizes Russians, costs them 1 million men **(June–Sept.).** Battle of the Somme—British lose over 400,000; French, 200,000; Germans, about 450,000; all with no strategic results **(July–Nov.).** Romania declares war on Austria-Hungary **(Aug. 27).** Bucharest captured **(Dec.).**

1917 U.S. declares war on Germany **(April 6).** Submarine warfare at peak **(April).** On Italian Front, Battle of Caporetto—Italians retreat, losing 600,000 prisoners and deserters **(Oct.-Dec.).** On Western Front, Battles of Arras, Champagne, Ypres (third battle), etc. First large British tank attack **(Nov.).** U.S. declares war on Austria-Hungary **(Dec. 7).** Armistice between new Russian Bolshevik government and Germans **(Dec. 15).**

1918 Great offensive by Germans **(March-June).** Americans' first important battle role at Château-Thierry—as they and French stop German advance **(June).** Second Battle of the Marne **(July-Aug.)**—start of Allied offensive at Amiens, St. Mihiel, etc. Battles of the Argonne and Ypres panic German leadership **(Sept.-Oct.).** British offensive in Palestine **(Sept.).** Germans ask for armistice **(Oct. 4).** British armistice with Turkey **(Oct.).** German Kaiser abdicates **(Nov.).** Hostilities cease on Western Front **(Nov. 11).**

new Russian Bolshevik government and Germans **(Dec. 15)**. Sigmund Freud's *Introduction to Psychoanalysis.*

1918 Russian revolutionaries execute the former czar and his family. Russian Civil War between Reds (Bolsheviks) and Whites (anti-Bolsheviks); Reds win in 1920. Allied troops (U.S., British, French) intervene **(March);** leave in 1919. Second Battle of the Marne **(July-Aug.)** German Kaiser abdicates **(Nov.)**; hostilities cease on the Western Front. Japanese hold Vladivostok until 1922. World-wide influenza epidemic strikes; by 1920, nearly 20 million are dead. In U.S. alone, 500,000 perish.

1919 Third International (Comintern) establishes Soviet control over international Communist movements. Paris peace conference. Versailles Treaty, incorporating Woodrow Wilson's draft Covenant of League of Nations, signed by Allies and Germany; rejected by U.S. Senate. Congress formally ends war in 1921. 18th (Prohibition) Amendment adopted. Alcock and Brown make first trans-Atlantic non-stop flight. Mahatma Gandhi initiates satyagraha ("truth force") campaigns, beginning his nonviolent resistance movement against British rule in India.

Mahatma Gandhi
(1869–1948)

1920 League of Nations holds first meeting at Geneva, Switzerland. U.S. Dept. of Justice "red hunt" nets thousands of radicals; aliens deported. Women's suffrage (19th) amendment ratified. Treaty of Sèvres dissolves Ottoman Empire. First Agatha Christie mystery. Sinclair Lewis's *Main Street.*

1921 Reparations Commission fixes German liability at 132 billion gold marks. German inflation begins. Major treaties signed at Washington Disarmament Conference limit naval tonnage and pledge to respect territorial integrity of China. In U.S., Nicola Sacco and Bartolomeo Vanzetti, Italian-born anarchists, convicted of armed robbery murder; case stirs world-wide protests; they are executed in 1927.

William Butler Yeats
(1865–1939)

1922 Mussolini marches on Rome; forms Fascist government. Irish Free State, a self-governing dominion of British Empire, officially proclaimed. Kemal Atatürk, founder of modern Turkey, overthrows last sultan.

1923 Adolf Hitler's "Beer Hall Putsch" in Munich fails; in 1924 he is sentenced to five years in prison where he writes *Mein Kampf;* released after eight months. Occupation of Ruhr by French and Belgian troops to enforce reparations payments. Widespread **Ku Klux Klan** violence in U.S. Earthquake destroys third of Tokyo. George Gershwin's *Rhapsody in Blue.* Bessie Smith, known as "the Empress of the Blues," makes her first record. Irish poet William Butler Yeats wins Nobel Prize in Literature.

Robert Frost
(1874–1963)

1924 Death of Lenin; Stalin wins power struggle, rules as Soviet dictator until death in 1953. Italian Fascists murder Socialist leader Giacomo Matteotti. Interior Secretary Albert B. Fall and oilmen Harry Sinclair and Edward L. Doheny are charged with conspiracy and bribery in the Teapot Dome scandal, involving fraudulent leases of naval oil reserves. In 1931, Fall is sentenced to year in prison; Doheny and Sinclair acquitted of bribery. Nathan Leopold and Richard Loeb convicted in "thrill killing" of Bobby Franks in Chicago; defended by Clarence Darrow; sentenced to life imprisonment. (Loeb killed by fellow convict in 1936; Leopold paroled in 1958, dies in 1971.) Robert Frost wins first of four Pulitzers.

Pablo Picasso
(1881–1973)

1925 Nellie Tayloe Ross elected governor of Wyoming; first woman governor elected in U.S. Locarno conferences seek to secure European peace by mutual guarantees. John T. Scopes convicted and fined for teaching evolution in a public school in Tennessee "Monkey Trial"; sentence set aside. John Logie Baird, Scottish inventor, transmits human features by television. Adolf Hitler publishes Volume I of *Mein Kampf.*

1926 General strike in Britain brings nation's activities to standstill. U.S. marines dispatched to Nicaragua during revolt; they remain until 1933. Gertrude Ederle of U.S. is first woman to swim English Channel. Ernest Hemingway's *The Sun Also Rises.*

1927 German economy collapses. Socialists riot in Vienna; general strike follows acquittal of Nazis for political murder. Trotsky expelled from Russian Communist Party. Charles A. Lindbergh flies first successful solo non-stop flight from New York to Paris. Ruth Snyder and Judd Gray convicted of murder of Albert Snyder; they are executed at Sing Sing prison in 1928. Babe Ruth hits 60 home runs in the season; record stands for next 34 years. *The Jazz Singer,* with Al Jolson, first part-talking motion picture.

Babe Ruth
(George Herman Ruth)
(1895–1948)

Benito Mussolini
(1883–1945)

Joseph Stalin
(1879–1953)

Adolf Hitler
(1889–1945)

1928 Kellogg-Briand Pact, outlawing war, signed in Paris by 65 nations. Alexander Fleming discovers penicillin. Richard E. Byrd starts expedition to Antarctic; returns in 1930. Anthropologist Margaret Mead publishes *Coming of Age in Samoa. Oxford English Dictionary* published after 44 years of research.

1929 Trotsky expelled from U.S.S.R. Lateran Treaty establishes independent Vatican City. In U.S., stock market prices collapse, with U.S. securities losing $26 billion—first phase of Depression and world economic crisis. St. Valentine's Day gangland massacre in Chicago.

1930 Britain, U.S., Japan, France, and Italy sign naval disarmament treaty. Nazis gain in German elections. Cyclotron developed by Ernest O. Lawrence, U.S. physicist. Pluto discovered by astronomers.

1931 Spain becomes a republic with overthrow of King Alfonso XIII. German industrialists finance 800,000-strong Nazi party. British parliament enacts statute of Westminster, legalizing dominion equality with Britain. Mukden Incident begins Japanese occupation of Manchuria. In U.S., Hoover proposes one-year moratorium of war debts. Harold C. Urey discovers heavy hydrogen. Gangster Al Capone sentenced to 11 years in prison for tax evasion (freed in 1939; dies in 1947). Notorious Scottsboro trial begins, exposing depth of Southern racism. "The Star Spangled Banner" officially becomes national anthem.

1932 Nazis lead in German elections with 230 Reichstag seats. Famine in U.S.S.R. In U.S., Congress sets up Reconstruction Finance Corporation to stimulate economy. Veterans march on Washington—most leave after Senate rejects payment of cash bonuses; others removed by troops under Douglas MacArthur. U.S. protests Japanese aggression in Manchuria. Amelia Earhart is first woman to fly Atlantic solo. Charles A. Lindbergh's baby son kidnapped, killed. (Bruno Richard Hauptmann arrested in 1934, convicted in 1935, executed in 1936.)

1933 Hitler appointed German chancellor, gets dictatorial powers. Reichstag fire in Berlin; Nazi terror begins. Germany and Japan withdraw from League of Nations. Giuseppe Zangara executed for attempted assassination of President-elect Roosevelt in which Chicago Mayor Cermak is fatally shot. Roosevelt inaugurated ("the only thing we have to fear is fear itself"); launches New Deal. Prohibition repealed. U.S.S.R. recognized by U.S.

1934 Chancellor Dollfuss of Austria assassinated by Nazis. Hitler becomes Führer. U.S.S.R. admitted to League of Nations. Dionne sisters, first quintuplets to survive beyond infancy, born in Canada. Mao Zedong begins the Long March north with 100,000 soldiers.

1935 Saar incorporated into Germany after plebiscite. Nazis repudiate Versailles Treaty, introduce compulsory military service. Mussolini invades Ethiopia; League of Nations invokes sanctions. Roosevelt opens second

---

THE HOLOCAUST (1933–1945)

"Holocaust" is the term describing the Nazi annihilation of about 6 million Jews (two thirds of the pre-World War II European Jewish population), including 4,500,000 from Russia, Poland, and the Baltic; 750,000 from Hungary and Romania; 290,000 from Germany and Austria; 105,000 from The Netherlands; 90,000 from France; 54,000 from Greece.

The Holocaust was unique in its being *genocide*—the systematic destruction of a people solely because of religion, race, ethnicity, nationality, or sexual preference—on an unmatched scale. Along with the Jews, another 9 to 10 million people—Gypsies, Slavs (Poles, Ukrainians, and Belarussians), homosexuals, and the disabled—were exterminated.

1933 Hitler named German Chancellor **(Jan.).** Dachau, first concentration camp, established **(March).** Boycotts against Jews begin **(April).**

1935 Anti-Semitic Nuremberg Laws passed by Reichstag; Jews lose citizenship and civil rights **(Sept.).**

1937 Buchenwald concentration camp opens **(July).**

1938 Extension of anti-Semitic laws to Austria after annexation **(March).** *Kristallnacht* (Night of Broken Glass)—anti-Semitic riots and destruction of Jewish institutions in Germany and Austria **(Nov. 9).** 26,000 Jews sent to concentration camps; Jewish children expelled from schools **(Nov. 9-10).** Expropriation of

Jewish property and businesses **(Dec.).**

1940 As war continues, Einsatzgruppen (mobile killing squads) follow German army into conquered lands, rounding up and massacring Jews and other "undesirables."

1941 Goering instructs Heydrich to carry out the "final solution to the Jewish question" **(July 31).** Deportation of German Jews begins; massacres of Jews in Odessa and Kiev **(Nov.);** and in Riga and Vilna **(Dec.).**

1942 Mass killings using Zyklon-B begin at Auschwitz-Birkenau **(Jan.).** Nazi leaders attend Wannsee Conference to coordinate the "final solution" **(Jan. 20).** 100,000 Jews from Warsaw Ghetto deported to Treblinka death camp **(July).**

1943 Warsaw Ghetto uprisings **(Jan. and April);** Ghetto exterminated **(May).**

1944 476,000 Hungarian Jews sent to Auschwitz **(May-June).** D-day **(June 6).** Soviet Army liberates Maidanek death camp **(July).** Nazis try to hide evidence of death camps **(Nov.).**

1945 As Allies advance, Nazis force concentration camp inmates on death marches. Americans liberate Buchenwald and British liberate Bergen-Belsen camps **(April).** Nuremberg War Crimes Trial **(Nov. 1945 to Oct. 1946).**

phase of New Deal in U.S., calling for social security, better housing, equitable taxation, and farm assistance. Huey Long assassinated in Louisiana.

1936 Germans occupy Rhineland. Italy annexes Ethiopia. Rome-Berlin Axis proclaimed (Japan to join in 1940). Trotsky exiled to Mexico. King George V dies; succeeded by son, Edward VIII, who soon abdicates to marry an American-born divorcée, and is succeeded by brother, George VI. Spanish civil war begins. Hundreds of Americans join the "Lincoln Brigades." (Franco's fascist forces defeat Loyalist forces by 1939, when Madrid falls.) War between China and Japan begins, to continue through World War II. Japan and Germany sign anti-Comintern pact; joined by Italy in 1937.

1937 Hitler repudiates war guilt clause of Versailles Treaty; continues to build German power. Italy withdraws from League of Nations. U.S. gunboat *Panay* sunk by Japanese in Yangtze River. Japan invades China, conquers most of coastal area. Amelia Earhart lost somewhere in Pacific on round-the-world flight. Picasso's *Guernica* mural.

1938 Hitler marches into Austria; political and geographical union of Germany and Austria proclaimed. Munich Pact—Britain, France, and Italy agree to let Germany partition Czechoslovakia. Douglas "Wrong-Way" Corrigan flies from New York to Dublin. Fair Labor Standards Act establishes minimum wage. Orson Welles's radio broadcast *War of the Worlds.*

1939 Germany invades Poland; occupies Bohemia and Moravia; renounces pact with England and concludes 10-year non-aggression pact with U.S.S.R. Russo-Finnish War begins; Finns to lose one-tenth of territory in 1940 peace treaty. World War II begins. In U.S., Roosevelt submits $1,319-million defense budget, proclaims U.S. neutrality, and declares limited emergency. Einstein writes FDR about feasibility of atomic

Dorothea Lange's photo "Migrant Mother" (1936) documented the Great Depression (1929–1940)

Amelia Earhart (1897–1937)

WORLD WAR II (1939–1945)

Axis powers (Germany, Italy, Japan, Hungary, Romania, Bulgaria) *vs.* Allies (Britain, France, U.S.S.R., Australia, Belgium, Brazil, Canada, China, Denmark, Greece, Netherlands, New Zealand, Norway, Poland, South Africa, Yugoslavia).

1939 Germany invades Poland and annexes Danzig; Britain and France give Hitler ultimatum **(Sept. 1)**, declare war **(Sept. 3)**. Disabled German pocket battleship *Admiral Graf Spee* blown up off Montevideo, Uruguay, on Hitler's orders **(Dec. 17)**. Limited activity ("Sitzkrieg") on Western Front.

1940 Nazis invade Netherlands, Belgium, and Luxembourg **(May 10)**. Chamberlain resigns as Britain's prime minister; Churchill takes over **(May 10)**. Germans cross French frontier **(May 12)** using air/tank/infantry "Blitzkrieg" tactics. Dunkerque evacuation—about 335,000 out of 400,000 Allied soldiers rescued from Belgium by British civilian and naval craft **(May 26–June 3)**. Italy declares war on France and Britain; invades France **(June 10)**. Germans enter Paris; city undefended **(June 14)**. France and Germany sign armistice at Compiègne **(June 22)**. Nazis bomb Coventry, England **(Nov. 14)**.

1941 Germans launch attacks in Balkans. Yugoslavia surrenders—General Mihajlovic continues guerrilla warfare; Tito leads left-wing guerrillas **(April 17)**. Nazi tanks enter Athens; remnants of British Army quit Greece **(April 27)**. Hitler attacks Russia **(June 22)**. Atlantic Charter—FDR and Churchill agree on war aims **(Aug. 14)**. Japanese attacks on Pearl Harbor, Philippines, Guam force U.S. into war; U.S. Pacific fleet crippled **(Dec. 7)**. U.S. and Britain declare war on Japan. Germany and Italy declare war on U.S.; Congress declares war on those countries **(Dec. 11)**.

1942 British surrender Singapore to Japanese **(Feb. 15)**. Roosevelt orders Japanese and Japanese Americans in western U.S. to be exiled to "relocation centers," many for the remainder of the war **(Feb. 19)**. U.S. forces on Bataan peninsula in Philippines surrender **(April 9)**. U.S. and Filipino troops on Corregidor island in Manila Bay surrender to Japanese **(May 6)**. Village of Lidice in Czechoslovakia razed by Nazis

(June 10). U.S. and Britain land in French North Africa **(Nov. 8)**.

1943 Casablanca Conference—Churchill and FDR agree on unconditional surrender goal **(Jan. 14-24)**. German 6th Army surrenders at Stalingrad—turning point of war in Russia **(Feb. 1-2)**. Remnants of Nazis trapped on Cape Bon, ending war in Africa **(May 12)**. Mussolini deposed; Badoglio named premier **(July 25)**. Allied troops land on Italian mainland after conquest of Sicily **(Sept. 3)**. Italy surrenders **(Sept. 8)**. Nazis seize Rome **(Sept. 10)**. Cairo Conference: FDR, Churchill, Chiang Kai-shek pledge defeat of Japan, free Korea **(Nov. 22-26)**. Teheran Conference: FDR, Churchill, Stalin agree on invasion plans **(Nov. 28-Dec. 1)**.

1944 U.S. and British troops land at Anzio on west Italian coast and hold beachhead **(Jan. 22)**. U.S. and British troops enter Rome **(June 4)**. D-Day—Allies launch Normandy invasion **(June 6)**. Hitler wounded in bomb plot **(July 20)**. Paris liberated **(Aug. 25)**. Athens freed by Allies **(Oct. 13)**. Americans invade Philippines **(Oct. 20)**. Germans launch counteroffensive in Belgium—Battle of the Bulge **(Dec. 16)**.

1945 Yalta Agreement signed by FDR, Churchill, Stalin—establishes basis for occupation of Germany, returns to Soviet Union lands taken by Germany and Japan; U.S.S.R. agrees to friendship pact with China **(Feb. 11)**. Mussolini killed at Lake Como **(April 28)**. Admiral Doenitz takes command in Germany; suicide of Hitler announced **(May 1)**. Berlin falls **(May 2)**. Germany signs unconditional surrender terms at Rheims **(May 7)**. Allies declare V-E Day **(May 8)**. Potsdam Conference—Truman, Churchill, Atlee (after **July 28**), Stalin establish council of foreign ministers to prepare peace treaties; plan German postwar government and reparations **(July 17-Aug. 2)**. A-bomb dropped on Hiroshima by U.S. **(Aug. 6)**. U.S.S.R. declares war on Japan **(Aug. 8)**. Nagasaki hit by A-bomb **(Aug. 9)**. Japan agrees to surrender **(Aug. 14)**. V-J Day—Japanese sign surrender terms aboard battleship *Missouri* **(Sept. 2)**.

**Franklin Delano
Roosevelt
(1882–1945)**

**Winston Churchill
(1874–1965)**

**Harry S. Truman
(1884–1972)**

Atomic Bomb

**Anne Frank
(1929–1945)**

bomb. New York World's Fair opens. DAR refuses to allow Marian Anderson to perform. *Gone with the Wind* premieres.

1940 Hitler invades Denmark, the Netherlands, Belgium, France, and Luxembourg. Churchill becomes Britain's Prime Minister. Trotsky assassinated in Mexico. Estonia, Latvia, and Lithuania annexed by U.S.S.R. U.S. trades 50 destroyers for leases on British bases in Western Hemisphere. Selective Service Act signed. The first official network television broadcast is put out by NBC.

1941 Germany attacks the Balkans and Russia. Japanese surprise attack on U.S. fleet at Pearl Harbor brings U.S. into World War II; U.S. and Britain declare war on Japan. Manhattan Project (atomic bomb research) begins. Roosevelt enunciates "four freedoms," signs Lend-Lease Act, declares national emergency, promises aid to U.S.S.R. Orson Welles's *Citizen Kane.*

1942 Nazi leaders attend Wannsee Conference to coordinate the "final solution to the Jewish question," the systematic genocide of Jews known as the Holocaust. Declaration of United Nations signed in Washington. Women's military services established. Enrico Fermi achieves nuclear chain reaction. More than 120,000 Japanese and persons of Japanese ancestry living in western U.S. moved to "relocation centers," some for the duration of the war (Executive Order 9066). Coconut Grove nightclub fire in Boston kills 491.

1943 Churchill and Roosevelt hold Casablanca Conference. Mussolini deposed. President freezes prices, salaries, and wages to prevent inflation. Income tax withholding introduced.

1944 Allies invade Normandy on D-Day **(June 6)**. G.I. Bill of Rights enacted. Bretton Woods Conference creates International Monetary Fund and World Bank. Dumbarton Oaks Conference—U.S., British Commonwealth, and U.S.S.R. propose establishment of United Nations. Battle of the Bulge **(Dec. 16)**. Gunnar Myrdal's *An American Dilemma.*

1945 Yalta Conference (Roosevelt, Churchill, Stalin) plans final defeat of Germany **(Feb.)**. Hitler commits suicide; Germany surrenders **(May 7)**; **May 8** is declared V-E Day. San Francisco Conference establishes U.N. **(April–June)**. FDR dies **(April 12)**. Potsdam Conference (Truman, Churchill, Stalin) establishes basis of German reconstruction **(July–Aug.)**. U.S. drops atomic bombs on Japanese cities of Hiroshima **(Aug. 6)** and Nagasaki **(Aug. 8)**. Japan signs official surrender on V-J Day **(Sept. 2)**.

1946 First meeting of U.N. General Assembly opens in London **(Jan. 10)**. League of Nations dissolved **(April)**. Italy abolishes monarchy **(June)**. Verdict in Nuremberg war trial: 12 Nazi leaders (including 1 tried in absentia) sentenced to hang; 7 imprisoned; 3 acquitted **(Oct. 1)**. Goering commits suicide a few hours before 10 other Nazis are executed **(Oct. 15)**. Winston Churchill's "Iron Curtain" speech warns of Soviet expansion. Juan Perón becomes president of Argentina. Benjamin Spock's childcare classic published.

1947 Britain nationalizes coal mines **(Jan. 1)**. Peace treaties for Italy, Romania, Bulgaria, Hungary, Finland signed in Paris **(Feb. 10)**. Soviet Union rejects U.S. plan for U.N. atomic-energy control **(March 4)**. Truman Doctrine proposed—the first significant U.S. attempt to "contain" communist expansion **(March 12)**. Marshall Plan for European recovery proposed—a coordinated program to help European nations recover from ravages of war **(June)**. (By 1951, this "European Recovery Program" had cost $11 billion.) India and Pakistan gain independence from Britain **(Aug. 15)**. U.S. Air Force pilot Chuck Yeager becomes first person to break the sound barrier **(Oct. 14)**. Jackie Robinson joins the Brooklyn Dodgers. Anne Frank's *The Diary of a Young Girl* published.

1948 Gandhi assassinated in New Delhi by Hindu fanatic **(Jan. 30)**. Communists seize power in Czechoslovakia **(Feb. 23-25)**. Burma and Ceylon granted independence by Britain. Organization of American States (OAS) Charter signed at Bogotá, Colombia **(April 30)**. Nation of Israel proclaimed; British end Mandate at midnight; Arab armies attack **(May 14)**. Berlin airlift begins **(June 21)**; ends **May 12, 1949**. Stalin and Tito break **(June 28)**. Independent Republic of Korea is proclaimed, following election supervised by U.N. **(Aug. 15)**. Verdict in Japanese war trial: 18 imprisoned **(Nov. 12)**; Tojo and six others hanged **(Dec. 23)**. United States of Indonesia established as Dutch and Indonesians settle conflict **(Dec. 27)**. Alger Hiss, former U.S. State Department official, indicted on perjury charges after denying passing secret documents to communist spy ring; convicted in second trial (1950) and sentenced to five-year prison term. Truman ends racial segregation in military. Alfred Kinsey publishes *Sexual Behavior in the American Male*. Tennessee Williams's *A Streetcar Named Desire* wins Pulitzer.

1949 Cease-fire in Palestine **(Jan. 7)**. Truman proposes Point Four Program to help world's less developed areas **(Jan. 20)**. Israel signs armistice with Egypt **(Feb. 24)**. Start of North Atlantic Treaty Organization (NATO)—treaty signed by 12 nations **(April 4)**. German Federal Republic (West Germany) established **(Sept. 21)**. Truman discloses Soviet Union has set off atomic explosion **(Sept. 23)**. Communist People's Republic of China formally proclaimed by Chairman Mao Zedong **(Oct. 1)**. South Africa institutionalizes apartheid.

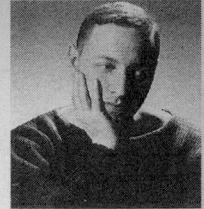

Tennessee Williams (1911–1983)

1950 Brink's robbery in Boston; almost $3 million stolen **(Jan. 17)**. Truman orders development of hydrogen bomb **(Jan. 31)**. Korean War begins when North Korean Communist forces invade South Korea. Assassination attempt on President Truman by Puerto Rican nationalists **(Nov. 1)**. McCarthyism begins.

1951 Six nations agree to Schuman Plan to pool European coal and steel **(March 19)**—in effect Feb. 10, 1953. Julius and Ethel Rosenberg sentenced to death for passing atomic secrets to Russians **(March)**. Japanese peace treaty signed in San Francisco by 49 nations **(Sept. 8)**. Color television introduced in U.S. Libya gains independence.

1952 George VI dies; his daughter becomes Elizabeth II **(Feb. 6)**. NATO conference approves European army **(Feb.)**. AEC announces "satisfactory" experiments in hydrogen-weapons research; eyewitnesses tell of blasts near Enewetak **(Nov.)**. Ralph Ellison's *The Invisible Man*.

Woody Guthrie (1912–1967)

1953 Gen. Dwight D. Eisenhower inaugurated President of United States **(Jan. 20)**. Stalin dies **(March 5)**. Malenkov becomes Soviet Premier; Beria, Minister of Interior; Molotov, Foreign Minister **(March 6)**. Dag Hammarskjöld begins term as U.N. Secretary-General **(April 10)**. James Watson and Francis Crick publish their discovery of the molecular model of DNA **(April-May)**. Edmund Hillary of New Zealand and Tenzing Norgay of Nepal reach top of Mt. Everest **(May 29)**. East Berliners rise against Communist rule; quelled by tanks **(June 17)**. Egypt becomes republic ruled by military junta **(June 18)**. Julius and Ethel Rosenberg executed in Sing Sing prison **(June 19)**. Korean armistice signed **(July 27)**. Moscow announces explosion of hydrogen bomb **(Aug. 20)**. Tito becomes president of Yugoslavia. Ernest Hemingway wins Pulitzer for *The Old Man and the Sea*.

Dwight D. Eisenhower (1890–1969)

1954 First atomic submarine *Nautilus* launched **(Jan. 21)**. Five U.S. Congressmen shot on floor of House as Puerto Rican nationalists fire from spectators' gallery; all five recover **(March 1)**. *Army v. McCarthy* inquiry—Senate subcommittee report blames both sides **(Apr. 22-June 17)**. Dien Bien Phu, French military outpost in Vietnam, falls to Vietminh army **(May 7)**. U.S. Supreme Court (in *Brown v. Board of Education of Topeka*) unanimously bans racial segregation in public schools **(May 17)**. Eisenhower launches world atomic pool without Soviet Union **(Sept. 6)**. Eight-nation Southeast Asia defense treaty (SEATO) signed at Manila **(Sept. 8)**. West Germany is granted sovereignty, admitted to NATO and Western European Union **(Oct. 23)**. Dr. Jonas Salk starts inoculating children against polio. Algerian War of Independence against France begins **(Nov.)**; France struggles to maintain colonial rule until 1962 when it agrees to Algeria's independence. William Faulkner's *A Fable* wins Pulitzer.

1955 Nikolai A. Bulganin becomes Soviet Premier, replacing Malenkov **(Feb. 8)**. Churchill resigns; Anthony Eden succeeds him **(April 6)**. Federal Republic of West Germany becomes a sovereign state **(May 5)**. Warsaw

---

KOREAN WAR (1950–1953)

1950 North Korean Communist forces invade South Korea **(June 25)**. U.N. calls for cease-fire and asks U.N. members to assist South Korea **(June 27)**. Truman orders U.S. forces into Korea **(June 27)**. North Koreans capture Seoul **(June 28)**. Gen. Douglas MacArthur designated commander of unified U.N. forces **(July 8)**. Pusan Beachhead—U.N. forces counterattack and capture Seoul **(Aug.-Sept.)**, capture Pyongyang, North Korean capital **(Oct.)**. Chinese Communists enter war **(Oct. 26)**, force U.N. retreat toward 39th parallel **(Dec.)**.

1951 Gen. Matthew B. Ridgeway replaces MacArthur after he threatens Chinese with massive retaliation **(April 11)**. Armistice negotiations **(July)** continue with interruptions until **June 1953**.

1953 Armistice signed **(July 27)**. Chinese troops withdraw from North Korea **(Oct. 26, 1958)**, but over 200 violations of armistice noted to **1959**.

**Fidel Castro
(1926–)**

**John H. Glenn, Jr.
(1921–)**

**Martin Luther King, Jr.
(1929–1968)**

Pact, east European mutual defense agreement, signed **(May 14)**. Argentina ousts Perón **(Sept. 19)**. President Eisenhower suffers coronary thrombosis in Denver **(Sept. 24)**. Rosa Parks refuses to sit at the back of the bus. Martin Luther King, Jr., leads black boycott of Montgomery, Ala., bus system **(Dec. 1)**; desegregated service begins **Dec. 21, 1956.** AFL and CIO become one organization—AFL-CIO **(Dec. 5)**. Tennessee Williams's *Cat on a Hot Tin Roof* wins Pulitzer.

1956 Nikita Khrushchev, First Secretary of U.S.S.R. Communist Party, denounces Stalin's excesses **(Feb. 24)**. First aerial H-bomb tested over Namu islet, Bikini Atoll—10 million tons TNT equivalent **(May 21)**. Workers' uprising against Communist rule in Poznan, Poland, is crushed **(June 28-30)**. Egypt takes control of Suez Canal **(July 26)**. Israel launches attack on Egypt's Sinai peninsula and drives toward Suez Canal **(Oct. 29)**. British and French invade Egypt at Port Said **(Nov. 5)**. Cease-fire forced by U.S. pressure stops British, French, and Israeli advance **(Nov. 6)**. Revolt starts in Hungary—Soviet troops and tanks crush anti-Communist rebellion **(Nov.)**. Morocco gains independence. Ingmar Bergman's *The Seventh Seal*. Woody Guthrie composes "This Land is Your Land." Allen Ginsburg's *Howl*.

1957 Eisenhower Doctrine calls for aid to Mideast countries which resist armed aggression from Communist-controlled nations **(Jan. 5)**. The "Little Rock Nine" integrate Arkansas high school. Eisenhower sends troops to quell mob and protect school integration **(Sept. 24)**. Russians launch *Sputnik I,* first earth-orbiting satellite—the Space Age begins **(Oct. 4)**.

1958 European Economic Community (Common Market) becomes effective **(Jan. 1)**. Army's Jupiter-C rocket fires first U.S. earth satellite, *Explorer I,* into orbit **(Jan. 31)**. Egypt and Syria merge into United Arab Republic **(Feb. 1)**. Khrushchev becomes Premier of Soviet Union as Bulganin resigns **(Mar. 27)**. Gen. Charles de Gaulle becomes French premier **(June 1)**, remaining in power until 1969. Eisenhower orders U.S. Marines into Lebanon at request of President Chamoun, who fears overthrow **(July 15)**. New French constitution adopted **(Sept. 28)**, de Gaulle elected president of 5th Republic **(Dec. 21)**.

1959 Cuban President Batista resigns and flees—Castro takes over **(Jan. 1)**. Tibet's Dalai Lama escapes to India **(Mar. 31)**. St. Lawrence Seaway opens, allowing ocean ships to reach Midwest **(April 25)**. Alaska and Hawaii become states.

1960 American U-2 spy plane, piloted by Francis Gary Powers, shot down over Russia **(May 1)**. Khrushchev kills Paris summit conference because of U-2 **(May 16)**. Top Nazi murderer of Jews, Adolf Eichmann, captured by Israelis in Argentina **(May 23)**—executed in Israel in 1962. Powers sentenced to prison for 10 years **(Aug. 19)**—freed in **February 1962** in exchange for Soviet spy. Communist China and Soviet Union split in conflict over Communist ideology. Senegal, Ghana, Nigeria, Madagascar, and Zaire (Belgian Congo) gain independence. Cuba begins confiscation of $770 million of U.S. property **(Aug. 7)**. There are 900 U.S. military advisers in South Vietnam.

1961 U.S. breaks diplomatic relations with Cuba **(Jan. 3)**. Robert Frost recites "The Gift Outright" at John F. Kennedy's inauguration as President of U.S. **(Jan. 20)**. Moscow announces putting first man in orbit around earth, Maj. Yuri A. Gagarin **(April 12)**. Cuba invaded at Bay of Pigs by an estimated 1,200 anti-Castro exiles aided by U.S.; invasion crushed **(April 17)**. First U.S. spaceman, Navy Cmdr. Alan B. Shepard, Jr., rockets 116.5 miles up in 302-mile trip **(May 5)**. Virgil Grissom becomes second American astronaut, making 118-mile-high, 303-mile-long rocket flight over Atlantic **(July 21)**. Gherman Stepanovich Titov is launched in Soviet spaceship *Vostok II:* makes 17 1/2 orbits in 25 hours, covering 434,960 miles before landing safely **(Aug. 6)**. East Germans erect Berlin Wall between East and West Berlin to halt flood of refugees **(Aug. 13)**. U.S.S.R. fires 50-megaton hydrogen bomb, biggest explosion in history **(Oct. 29)**. There are 2,000 U.S. military advisers in South Vietnam.

1962 Lt. Col. John H. Glenn, Jr., is first American to orbit Earth—three times in 4 hr 55 min **(Feb. 20)**. France transfers sovereignty to new republic of Algeria **(July 3)**. Cuban missile crisis—U.S.S.R. to build missile bases in Cuba; Kennedy orders Cuban blockade, lifts blockade after Russians back down **(Aug.-Nov.)**. James H. Meredith, escorted by federal marshals, registers at University of Mississippi **(Oct. 1)**. Pope John

XXIII opens Second Vatican Council (**Oct. 11**)—Council holds four sessions, finally closing **Dec. 8, 1965.** Cuba releases 1,113 prisoners of 1961 invasion attempt (**Dec. 24**). Burundi, Jamaica, Western Samoa, Uganda, and Trinidad and Tobago become independent. William Faulkner wins Pulitzer for *The Reivers.* Rachel Carson's *Silent Spring.*

1963 France and West Germany sign treaty of cooperation ending four centuries of conflict (**Jan. 22**). Michael E. De Bakey implants artificial heart in human for first time at Houston hospital; plastic device functions and patient lives for four days (**April 21**). Pope John XXIII dies (**June 3**)—succeeded **June 21** by Cardinal Montini, who becomes Paul VI. U.S. Supreme Court rules no locality may require recitation of Lord's Prayer or Bible verses in public schools (**June 17**). U.K.'s Profumo scandal (**June**). Civil rights rally held by 200,000 blacks and whites in Washington, D.C.; Martin Luther King delivers "I have a dream" speech (**Aug. 28**). Washington-to-Moscow "hot line" communications link opens, designed to reduce risk of accidental war (**Aug. 30**). President Kennedy shot and killed by sniper in Dallas, Tex. Lyndon B. Johnson becomes President same day (**Nov. 22**). Lee Harvey Oswald, accused assassin of President Kennedy, is shot and killed by Jack Ruby, Dallas nightclub owner (**Nov. 24**). Kenya achieves independence. Betty Friedan publishes *The Feminine Mystique.* There are 15,000 U.S. military advisers in South Vietnam.

1964 U.S. Supreme Court rules that Congressional districts should be roughly equal in population (**Feb. 17**). Jack Ruby convicted of murder in slaying of Lee Harvey Oswald; sentenced to death by Dallas jury (**March 14**)—conviction reversed **Oct. 5, 1966;** Ruby dies **Jan. 3, 1967,** before second trial can be held. Three civil rights workers—Schwerner, Goodman, and Cheney—murdered in Mississippi (**June**). Twenty-one arrests result

John F. Kennedy
(1917–1963)

VIETNAM WAR (1950–1975)

U.S., South Vietnam, and Allies versus North Vietnam and National Liberation Front (Viet Cong).

1950 President Truman sends 35-man military advisory group to aid French fighting to maintain colonial power in Vietnam.

1954 After defeat of French at Dien Bien Phu, Geneva Agreements (**July**) provide for withdrawal of French and Vietminh to either side of demarcation zone (DMZ) pending reunification elections, which are never held. Presidents Eisenhower and Kennedy (from 1954 onward) send civilian advisers and, later, military personnel to train South Vietnamese.

1960 Communists form National Liberation Front in South.

1960–1963 U.S. military advisers in South Vietnam rise from 900 to 15,000.

1963 Ngo Dinh Diem, South Vietnam's premier, slain in coup (**Nov. 1**).

1964 North Vietnamese torpedo boats reportedly attack U.S. destroyers in Gulf of Tonkin (**Aug. 2**). President Johnson orders retaliatory air strikes. Congress approves Gulf of Tonkin resolution (**Aug. 7**) authorizing President to take "all necessary measures" to win in Vietnam, allowing for the war's expansion.

1965 U.S. planes begin combat missions over South Vietnam. In **June,** 23,000 American advisers committed to combat. By end of year over 184,000 U.S. troops in area.

1966 B-52s bomb DMZ, reportedly used by North Vietnam for entry into South (**July 31**).

1967 South Vietnam National Assembly approves election of Nguyen Van Thieu as President (**Oct. 21**).

1968 U.S. has almost 525,000 men in Vietnam. In Tet offensive (**Jan.-Feb.**), Viet Cong guerrillas attack Saigon, Hue, and some provincial capitals. In My Lai massacre, American soldiers kill 300 Vietnamese villagers (**March 16**). President Johnson orders halt to U.S. bombardment of North Vietnam (**Oct. 31**). Saigon and N.L.F. join U.S. and North Vietnam in Paris peace talks.

1969 President Nixon announces Vietnam peace offer (**May 14**)—begins troop withdrawals (**June**). Viet Cong forms Provisional Revolutionary Government. U.S. Senate calls for curb on commitments (**June 25**). Ho Chi Minh, 79, North Vietnam president, dies (**Sept. 3**); collective leadership chosen. Some 6,000 U.S. troops pulled back from Thailand and 1,000 marines from Vietnam (announced **Sept. 30**). Massive demonstrations in U.S. protest or support war policies (**Oct. 15**).

1970 U.S. troops invade Cambodia in order to destroy North Vietnamese sanctuaries (**May 1**).

1971 Congress bars use of combat troops, but not air power, in Laos and Cambodia (**Jan. 1**). South Vietnamese troops, with U.S. air cover, fail in Laos thrust. Many American ground forces withdrawn from Vietnam combat. *New York Times* publishes Pentagon papers, classified material on expansion of war (**June**).

1972 Nixon responds to North Vietnamese drive across DMZ by ordering mining of North Vietnam ports and heavy bombing of Hanoi-Haiphong area (**April 1**). Nixon orders "Christmas bombing" of North to get North Vietnamese back to conference table (**Dec.**).

1973 President orders halt to offensive operations in North Vietnam (**Jan. 15**). Representatives of North and South Vietnam, U.S., and N.L.F. sign peace pacts in Paris, ending longest war in U.S. history (**Jan. 27**). Last American troops departed in their entirety (**March 29**).

1974 Both sides accuse each other of frequent violations of cease-fire agreement.

1975 Full-scale warfare resumes. South Vietnam Premier Nguyen Van Thieu resigns (**April 21**). South Vietnamese government surrenders to North Vietnam; U.S. Marine Embassy guards and U.S. civilians and dependents evacuated (**April 30**). More than 140,000 Vietnamese refugees leave by air and sea, many to settle in U.S. Provisional Revolutionary Government takes control (**June 6**).

1976 Election of National Assembly paves way for reunification of North and South.

The Beatles

**Malcolm X
(1925–1965)**

**Thurgood Marshall
(1908–1993)**

**Lyndon B. Johnson
(1908–1973)**

**Richard Nixon
(1913–1994)**

in trial and conviction of seven by federal jury. Nelson Mandela sentenced to life imprisonment (**June 11**). Congress approves Gulf of Tonkin resolution (**Aug. 7**). President's Commission on the Assassination of President Kennedy issues Warren Report concluding that Lee Harvey Oswald acted alone. The Beatles appear on *The Ed Sullivan Show*.

1965 Rev. Dr. Martin Luther King, Jr., and more than 2,600 other blacks arrested in Selma, Ala., during three-day demonstrations against voter-registration rules (**Feb. 1**). Malcolm X, black-nationalist leader, shot to death at Harlem rally in New York City (**Feb. 21**). U.S. Marines land in Dominican Republic as fighting persists between rebels and Dominican army (**April 28**). Medicare, senior citizens' government medical assistance program, begins (**July 1**). Blacks riot for six days in Watts section of Los Angeles: 34 dead, over 1,000 injured, nearly 4,000 arrested, fire damage put at $175 million (**Aug. 11-16**). Power failure in Ontario plant blacks out parts of eight northeastern states of U.S. and two provinces of southeastern Canada (**Nov. 9**). Ralph Nader's *Unsafe at Any Speed*.

1966 Black teenagers riot in Watts, Los Angeles; two men killed and at least 25 injured (**March 15**). Supreme Court decides *Miranda v. Arizona*.

1967 Three Apollo astronauts—Col. Virgil I. Grissom, Col. Edward White II, and Lt. Cmdr. Roger B. Chaffee—killed in spacecraft fire during simulated launch (**Jan. 27**). Biafra secedes from Nigeria (**May**). Israeli and Arab forces battle; six-day war ends with Israel occupying Sinai Peninsula, Golan Heights, Gaza Strip, and east bank of Suez Canal (**June 5**). Red China announces explosion of its first hydrogen bomb (**June 17**). Racial violence in Detroit; 7,000 National Guardsmen aid police after night of rioting. Similar outbreaks occur in New York City's Spanish Harlem, Rochester, N.Y., Birmingham, Ala., and New Britain, Conn. (**July 23**). Thurgood Marshall sworn in as first black U.S. Supreme Court justice (**Oct. 2**). Dr. Christiaan N. Barnard and team of South African surgeons perform world's first successful human heart transplant (**Dec. 3**)—patient dies 18 days later.

1968 North Korea seizes U.S. Navy ship *Pueblo;* holds 83 on board as spies (**Jan. 23**). Tet offensive, turning point in Vietnam war (**Jan.-Feb.**). My Lai massacre (**March 16**). President Johnson announces he will not seek or accept presidential renomination (**March 31**). Martin Luther King, Jr., civil rights leader, is slain in Memphis (**April 4**)—James Earl Ray, indicted in murder, captured in London on **June 8**. In 1969 Ray pleads guilty and is sentenced to 99 years. Sen. Robert F. Kennedy is shot and critically wounded in Los Angeles hotel after winning California primary (**June 5**)—dies **June 6**. Sirhan B. Sirhan convicted 1969. Czechoslovakia is invaded by Russians and Warsaw Pact forces to crush liberal regime (**Aug. 20**).

1969 Richard M. Nixon is inaugurated 37th President of the U.S. (**Jan. 20**). Stonewall riot in New York City marks beginning of gay rights movement (**June 28**). Apollo 11 astronauts—Neil A. Armstrong, Edwin E. Aldrin, Jr., and Michael Collins—take man's first walk on moon (**July 20**). Sen. Edward M. Kennedy pleads guilty to leaving scene of fatal accident at Chappaquiddick, Mass. (**July 18**) in which Mary Jo Kopechne was drowned—gets two-month suspended sentence (**July 25**). Woodstock Festival (**Aug.**). *Sesame Street* debuts.

1970 Biafra surrenders after 32-month fight for independence from Nigeria (**Jan. 12**). Rhodesia severs last tie with British Crown and declares itself a racially segregated republic (**March 1**). U.S. troops invade Cambodia (**May 1**). Four students at Kent State University in Ohio slain by National Guardsmen at demonstration protesting incursion into Cambodia (**May 4**). Senate repeals Gulf of Tonkin resolution (**June 24**).

1971 Supreme Court rules unanimously that busing of students may be ordered to achieve racial desegregation (**April 20**). Anti-war militants attempt to disrupt government business in Washington (**May 3**)—police and military units arrest as many as 12,000; most are later released. *Pentagon Papers* published (**June**). Twenty-sixth Amendment to U.S. Constitution lowers voting age to 18. U.N. seats Communist China and expels Nationalist China (**Oct. 25**).

1972 President Nixon makes unprecedented eight-day visit to Communist China and meets with Mao Zedong **(Feb.)**. Britain takes over direct rule of Northern Ireland in bid for peace **(March 24)**. Gov. George C. Wallace of Alabama is shot by Arthur H. Bremer at Laurel, Md., political rally **(May 15)**. Five men are apprehended by police in attempt to bug Democratic National Committee headquarters in Washington, D.C.'s Watergate complex—start of the Watergate scandal **(June 17)**. Supreme Court rules that death penalty is unconstitutional **(June 29)**. Eleven Israeli athletes at Olympic Games in Munich are killed after eight members of an Arab terrorist group invade Olympic Village; five guerrillas and one policeman are also killed **(Sept. 5)**. "Christmas bombing" of North Vietnam **(Dec.)**.

Mao Zedong
(1893–1976)

1973 Great Britain, Ireland, and Denmark enter European Economic Community **(Jan. 1)**. Vietnam War ends with signing of peace pacts **(Jan. 27)**. Nixon, on national TV, accepts responsibility, but not blame, for Watergate; accepts resignations of advisers H. R. Haldeman and John D. Ehrlichman, fires John W. Dean III as counsel **(April 30)**. Greek military junta abolishes monarchy and proclaims republic **(June 1)**. U.S. bombing of Cambodia ends, marking official halt to 12 years of combat activity in Southeast Asia **(Aug. 15)**. Chile's Marxist president, Salvadore Allende, is overthrown **(Sept. 11)**. Fourth and biggest Arab-Israeli conflict begins as Egyptian and Syrian forces attack Israel as Jews mark Yom Kippur, holiest day in their calendar **(Oct. 6)**. Spiro T. Agnew resigns as Vice President and then, in federal court in Baltimore, pleads no contest to charges of evasion of income taxes on $29,500 he received in 1967, while Governor of Maryland. He is fined $10,000 and put on three years' probation **(Oct. 10)**. In the "Saturday Night Massacre," Nixon fires special Watergate prosecutor Archibald Cox and Deputy Attorney General William D. Ruckelshaus; Attorney General Elliot L. Richardson resigns **(Oct. 20)**. Egypt and Israel sign U.S.-sponsored cease-fire accord **(Nov. 11)**. Supreme Court rules on *Roe v. Wade*. Duke Ellington's autobiography, *Music is My Mistress,* is published.

Duke Ellington
(1899–1974)

1974 Patricia Hearst, 19-year-old daughter of publisher Randolph Hearst, kidnapped by Symbionese Liberation Army **(Feb. 5)**. House Judiciary Committee adopts three articles of impeachment charging President Nixon with obstruction of justice, failure to uphold laws, and refusal to produce material subpoenaed by the committee **(July 30)**. Richard M. Nixon announces he will resign the next day, the first President to do so **(Aug. 8)**. Vice President Gerald R. Ford of Michigan is sworn in as 38th President of the U.S. **(Aug. 9)**. Ford grants "full, free, and absolute pardon" to ex-President Nixon **(Sept. 8)**.

Gerald R. Ford
(1913–)

1975 John N. Mitchell, H. R. Haldeman, John D. Ehrlichman found guilty of Watergate cover-up **(Jan. 1)**; sentenced to 30 months to 8 years in jail **(Feb. 21)**. Pol Pot and Khmer Rouge take over Cambodia **(April)**. American merchant ship *Mayaguez,* seized by Cambodian forces, is rescued in operation by U.S. Navy and Marines, 38 of whom are killed **(May 15)**. *Apollo* and *Soyuz* spacecraft take off for U.S.-Soviet link-up in space **(July 15)**. President Ford escapes assassination attempt in Sacramento, Calif. **(Sept. 5)**. President Ford escapes second assassination attempt in 17 days **(Sept. 22)**.

Jimmy Carter
(1924–)

1976 Supreme Court rules that blacks and other minorities are entitled to retroactive job seniority **(March 24)**. Ford signs Federal Election Campaign Act **(May 11)**. Supreme Court rules that death penalty is not inherently cruel or unusual and is a constitutionally acceptable form of punishment **(July 3)**. Nation celebrates Bicentennial **(July 4)**. Israeli airborne commandos attack Uganda's Entebbe Airport and free 103 hostages held by pro-Palestinian hijackers of Air France plane; one Israeli and several Ugandan soldiers killed in raid **(July 4)**. Mysterious disease that eventually claims 29 lives strikes American Legion convention in Philadelphia **(Aug. 4)**. Jimmy Carter elected U.S. President **(Nov. 2)**.

1977 First woman Episcopal priest ordained **(Jan. 1)**. Scientists identify previously unknown bacterium as cause of mysterious "legionnaire's disease" **(Jan. 18)**. Carter pardons Vietnam draft evaders **(Jan. 21)**. Scientists report using bacteria in lab to make insulin **(May 23)**. Supreme Court rules that states are not required to spend Medicaid funds on elective abortions **(June 20)**. Deng Xiaoping, purged Chinese leader, restored to power as "Gang of Four" is expelled from Communist Party **(July 22)**. South African activist Stephen Biko dies in police custody

**Pope John Paul II
(1920–)**

**Anwar Sadat
(1918–1981)**

**Ayatollah Ruhollah
Khomeini
(1900–1989)**

**Ronald Reagan
(1911–)**

**Sandra Day O'Connor
(1930–)**

(Sept. 12). Nuclear-proliferation pact, curbing spread of nuclear weapons, signed by 15 countries, including U.S. and U.S.S.R. **(Sept. 21)**.

1978 President chooses Federal Appeals Court Judge William H. Webster as F.B.I. Director **(Jan. 19)**. Rhodesia's Prime Minister Ian D. Smith and three black leaders agree on transfer to black majority rule **(Feb. 15)**. U.S. Senate approves Panama Canal neutrality treaty **(March 16)**; votes treaty to turn canal over to Panama by year 2000 **(April 18)**. Former Italian Premier Aldo Moro kidnapped by left wing terrorists, who kill five bodyguards **(March 16)**; he is found slain **(May 9)**. Californians in referendum approve Proposition 13 for nearly 60% slash in property tax revenues **(June 6)**. Supreme Court, in Bakke case, bars quota systems in college admissions but affirms constitutionality of programs giving advantage to minorities **(June 28)**. Pope Paul VI, dead at 80, mourned **(Aug. 6)**; new Pope, John Paul I, 65, dies unexpectedly after 34 days in office **(Sept. 28)**; succeeded by Karol Cardinal Wojtyla of Poland as John Paul II **(Oct. 16)**. "Framework for Peace" in Middle East signed by Egypt's President Anwar Sadat and Israeli Premier Menachem Begin after 13-day conference at Camp David led by President Carter **(Sept. 17)**. Jim Jones's followers commit mass suicide in Jonestown, Guyana **(Nov. 18)**.

1979 Oil spills pollute ocean waters in Atlantic and Gulf of Mexico **(Jan. 1, June 8, July 21)**. Ohio agrees to pay $675,000 to families of dead and injured in Kent State University shootings **(Jan. 4)**. Vietnam and Vietnam-backed Cambodian insurgents announce fall of Phnom Penh, Cambodian capital, and collapse of Pol Pot regime **(Jan. 7)**. Shah leaves Iran after year of turmoil **(Jan. 16)**; revolutionary forces under Muslim leader, Ayatollah Ruhollah Khomeini, take over **(Feb. 1** *et seq.***)**. Conservatives win British election; Margaret Thatcher new Prime Minister **(March 28)**. Nuclear power plant accident at Three Mile Island, Pa., releases radiation **(March 28)**. Carter and Brezhnev sign SALT II agreement **(June 14)**. Nicaraguan President Gen. Anastasio Somoza Debayle resigns and flees to Miami **(July 17)**; Sandinistas form government **(July 19)**. Earl Mountbatten of Burma, 79, British World War II hero, and three others killed by blast on fishing boat off Irish coast **(Aug. 27)**; two I.R.A. members accused **(Aug. 30)**. Iranian militants seize U.S. Embassy in Teheran and hold hostages **(Nov. 4)**. Soviet invasion of Afghanistan stirs world protests **(Dec. 27)**.

1980 Six U.S. Embassy aides escape from Iran with Canadian help **(Jan. 29)**. F.B.I.'s undercover operation "Abscam" (for Arab scam) implicates public officials **(Feb. 2)**. U.S. breaks diplomatic ties with Iran **(April 7)**. Eight U.S. servicemen are killed and five are injured as helicopter and cargo plane collide in abortive desert raid to rescue American hostages in Teheran **(April 25)**. Supreme Court upholds limits on federal aid for abortions **(June 30)**. Shah of Iran dies at 60 **(July 27)**. Anastasio Somoza Debayle, ousted Nicaragua ruler, and two aides assassinated in Asunción, Paraguay capital **(Sept. 17)**. Iraq troops hold 90 square miles of Iran after invasion; 8-year Iran-Iraq war begins **(Sept. 19)**. Ronald Reagan elected President in Republican sweep **(Nov. 4)**. Three U.S. nuns and lay worker found shot in El Salvador **(Dec. 4)**. John Lennon of the Beatles shot dead in New York City **(Dec. 8)**.

1981 Ronald Reagan takes oath as 40th President **(Jan. 20)**. U.S.-Iran agreement frees 52 hostages held in Teheran since 1979 **(Jan. 20)**; hostages welcomed back in U.S. **(Jan. 25)**. President Reagan wounded by gunman, with press secretary and two law-enforcement officers **(March 30)**. Pope John Paul II wounded by gunman **(May 14)**. Supreme Court rules, 4-4, that former President Nixon and three top aides may be required to pay monetary damages for unconstitutional wiretap of home telephone of former national security aide **(June 22)**. Reagan nominates Judge Sandra Day O'Connor, 51, of Arizona, as first woman on Supreme Court **(July 7)**. More than 110 die in collapse of aerial walkways in lobby of Hyatt Regency Hotel in Kansas City; 188 injured **(July 18)**. Air controllers strike, disrupting flights **(Aug. 3)**; government dismisses strikers **(Aug. 11)**. AIDS is first identified.

1982 British overcome Argentina in Falklands war **(April 2-June 15)**. Israel invades Lebanon in attack on P.L.O. **(June 4)**. John W. Hinckley, Jr. found not guilty because of insanity in shooting of President Reagan **(June 21)**. Alexander M. Haig, Jr., resigns as Secretary of State **(June**

25). Equal Rights Amendment fails ratification (**June 30**). Princess Grace, 52, dies of injuries when car plunges off mountain road; daughter Stephanie, 17, suffers serious injuries (**Sept. 14**). Lebanese Christian Phalangists kill hundreds of people in two Palestinian refugee camps in West Beirut (**Sept. 15**). Leonid Brezhnev, Soviet leader, dies at 75 (**Nov. 10**). Yuri V. Andropov, 68, chosen as successor (**Nov. 15**). Permanent artificial heart implanted in human for first time in Dr. Barney B. Clark, 61, at University of Utah Medical Center in Salt Lake City (**Dec. 2**).

1983 Pope John Paul II signs new Roman Catholic code incorporating changes brought about by Second Vatican Council (**Jan. 25**). Second space shuttle, *Challenger,* makes successful maiden voyage, which includes the first U.S. space walk in nine years (**April 4**). U.S. Supreme Court declares many local abortion restrictions unconstitutional (**June 15**). Sally K. Ride, 32, first U.S. woman astronaut in space as a crew member aboard space shuttle *Challenger* (**June 18**). U.S. admits shielding former Nazi Gestapo chief Klaus Barbie, 69, the "butcher of Lyon," wanted in France for war crimes (**Aug. 15**). Benigno S. Aquino, Jr., 50, political rival of Philippines President Marcos, slain in Manila (**Aug. 21**). South Korean Boeing 747 jetliner bound for Seoul apparently strays into Soviet airspace and is shot down by a Soviet SU-15 fighter after it had tracked the airliner for two hours; all 269 aboard are killed, including 61 Americans (**Aug. 30**). Terrorist explosion kills 237 U.S. Marines in Beirut (**Oct. 23**). U.S. and Caribbean allies invade Grenada (**Oct. 25**).

1984 Bell System broken up (**Jan. 1**). France gets first deliveries of Soviet natural gas (**Jan. 1**). Syria frees captured U.S. Navy pilot, Lieut. Robert C. Goodman, Jr. (**Jan. 3**). U.S. and Vatican exchange diplomats after 116-year hiatus (**Jan. 10**). Reagan orders U.S. Marines withdrawn from Beirut international peacekeeping force (**Feb. 7**). Yuri V. Andropov dies at 69; Konstantin U. Chernenko, 72, named Soviet Union leader (**Feb. 9**). Italy and Vatican agree to end Roman Catholicism as state religion (**Feb. 18**). Reagan ends U.S. role in Beirut by relieving Sixth Fleet from peacekeeping force (**March 30**). Congress rebukes President Reagan on use of federal funds for mining Nicaraguan harbors (**April 10**). Soviet Union withdraws from summer Olympic games in U.S., and other bloc nations follow (**May 7** *et seq.*). José Napoleón Duarte, moderate, elected president of El Salvador (**May 11**). Three hundred slain as Indian Army occupies Sikh Golden Temple in Amritsar (**June 6**). Thirty-ninth Democratic National Convention, in San Francisco, nominates Walter F. Mondale and Geraldine A. Ferraro (**July 16-19**). Thirty-third Republican National Convention, at Dallas, renominates President Reagan and Vice President Bush (**Aug. 20-25**). Brian Mulroney and Conservative party win Canadian election in landslide (**Sept. 4**). Indian Prime Minister Indira Gandhi assassinated by two Sikh bodyguards; 1,000 killed in anti-Sikh riots; son Rajiv succeeds her (**Oct. 31**). President Reagan re-elected in landslide with 59% of vote (**Nov. 7**). Toxic gas leaks from Union Carbide plant in Bhopal, India, killing 2,000 and injuring 150,000 (**Dec. 3**).

1985 Ronald Reagan, 73, takes oath for second term as 40th President (**Jan. 20**). General Westmoreland settles libel action against CBS (**Feb. 18**). Prime Minister Margaret Thatcher addresses Congress, endorsing Reagan's policies (**Feb. 20**). U.S.S.R. leader Chernenko dies at 73 and is replaced by Mikhail Gorbachev, 54 (**March 11**). Two Shi'ite Muslim gunmen capture TWA airliner with 133 aboard, 104 of them Americans (**June 14**); 39 remaining hostages freed in Beirut (**June 30**). Supreme Court, 5-4, bars public school teachers from parochial schools (**July 1**). Arthur James Walker, 50, retired naval officer, convicted by federal judge of participating in Soviet spy ring operated by his brother, John Walker (**Aug. 9**). P.L.O. terrorists hijack *Achille Lauro,* Italian cruise ship, with 80 passengers, plus crew (**Oct. 7**); American, Leon Klinghoffer, killed (**Oct. 8**); Italian government toppled by political crisis over hijacking (**Oct. 16**). John A. Walker and son, Michael I. Walker, 22, sentenced in Navy espionage case (**Oct. 28**). Reagan and Gorbachev meet at summit (**Nov. 19**); agree to step up arms control talks and renew cultural contacts (**Nov. 21**). Terrorists seize Egyptian Boeing 737 airliner after takeoff from Athens (**Nov. 23**); 59 dead as Egyptian forces storm plane on Malta (**Nov. 24**). U.S. budget-balancing bill enacted (**Dec. 12**).

Indira Gandhi
(1917–1984)

Corazon Aquino
(1933–)

Mikhail S. Gorbachev
(1931–)

Margaret Thatcher
(1925–)

Sally K. Ride
(1951–)

William Rehnquist
(1924–)

George Bush
(1924–)

Benazir Bhutto
(1953–)

1986 Spain and Portugal join European Economic Community (**Jan. 1**). President freezes Libyan assets in U.S. (**Jan. 8**). Supreme Court bars racial bias in trial jury selection (**Jan. 14**). *Voyager 2* spacecraft reports secrets of Uranus (**Jan. 26**). Space shuttle *Challenger* explodes after launch at Cape Canaveral, Fla., killing all seven aboard (**Jan. 28**). Haiti President Jean-Claude Duvalier flees to France (**Feb. 7**). President Marcos flees Philippines after ruling 20 years, as newly elected Corazon Aquino succeeds him (**Feb. 26**). Prime Minister Olaf Palme of Sweden shot dead (**Feb. 28**). Austrian President Kurt Waldheim's service as Nazi army officer revealed (**March 3**). Union Carbide agrees to settlement with victims of Bhopal gas leak in India (**March 22**). Halley's comet yields information on return visit (**April 10**). U.S. planes attack Libyan "terrorist centers" (**April 14**). Desmond Tutu elected Archbishop in South Africa (**April 14**). Major nuclear accident at Soviet Union's Chernobyl power station alarms world (**April 26** *et seq.*). Ex-Navy analyst, Jonathan Jay Pollard, 31, guilty as spy for Israel (**June 4**). Supreme Court reaffirms abortion rights (**June 11**). World Court rules U.S. broke international law in mining Nicaraguan waters (**June 27**). Supreme Court voids automatic provisions of budget-balancing law (**July 7**). Jerry A. Whitworth, ex-Navy radioman, convicted as spy (**July 24**); he is also part of Walker family spy ring. Muslim captors release Rev. Lawrence Martin Jenco (**July 26**). Senate Judiciary Committee approves William H. Rehnquist as Chief Justice of U.S. (**Aug. 14**). House votes arms appropriations bill rejecting Administration's "star wars" policy (**Aug. 15**). Three Lutheran church groups in U.S. set to merge (**Aug. 29**). Congress overrides Reagan veto of stiff sanctions against South Africa (**Sept. 29** and **Oct. 2**). Congress approves immigration bill barring hiring of illegal aliens, with amnesty provision (**Oct. 17**). Reagan signs $11.7-billion budget reduction measure (**Oct. 21**). He approves sweeping revision of U.S. tax code (**Oct. 22**). Democrats triumph in elections, gaining eight seats to win Senate majority (**Nov. 4**). Secret initiative to send arms to Iran revealed (**Nov. 6** *et seq.*); Reagan denies exchanging arms for hostages and halts arms sales (**Nov. 19**); diversion of funds from arms sales to Nicaraguan Contras revealed (**Nov. 25**).

1987 William Buckley, U.S. hostage in Lebanon, reported slain (**Jan. 20**). Supreme Court rules Rotary Clubs must admit women (**May 4**). Iraqi missiles kill 37 in attack on U.S. frigate *Stark* in Persian Gulf (**May 17**); Iraqi president apologizes (**May 18**). Prime Minister Thatcher wins rare third term in Britain (**June 11**). Supreme Court Justice Lewis F. Powell, Jr., retires (**June 26**). Klaus Barbie, 73, Gestapo wartime chief in Lyon, sentenced to life by French court for war crimes (**July 4**). Oliver North, Jr., tells Congressional inquiry higher officials approved his secret Iran-Contra operations (**July 7-10**). Admiral John M. Poindexter, former National Security Adviser, testifies he authorized use of Iran arms sale profits to aid Contras (**July 15-22**). George P. Shultz testifies he was deceived repeatedly on Iran-Contra affair (**July 23-24**). Defense Secretary Caspar W. Weinberger tells inquiry of official deception and intrigue (**July 31, Aug. 3**). Reagan says Iran arms-Contra policy went astray and accepts responsibility (**Aug. 12**). Severe earthquake strikes Los Angeles, leaving 100 injured and six dead (**Oct. 1**). Senate, 58-42, rejects Robert H. Bork as Supreme Court Justice (**Oct. 23**).

1988 U.S. and Canada reach free trade agreement (**Jan. 2**). Robert C. McFarlane, former National Security Adviser, pleads guilty in Iran-Contra case (**March 11**). U.S. Navy ship shoots down Iranian airliner in Persian Gulf, mistaking it for jet fighter; 290 killed (**July 3**). Terrorists kill nine tourists on Aegean cruise (**July 11**). Democratic convention nominates Gov. Michael Dukakis of Massachusetts for President and Texas Senator Lloyd Bentsen for Vice President (**July 17** *et seq.*). Republicans nominate George Bush for President and Indiana Senator Dan Quayle for Vice President (**Aug. 15** *et seq.*). Plane blast kills Pakistani President Mohammad Zia ul-Haq (**Aug. 17**). Republicans sweep 40 states in election. Bush beats Dukakis (**Nov. 8**). Benazir Bhutto, first Islamic woman prime minister, chosen to lead Pakistan (**Dec. 1**). Pan-Am 747 explodes from terrorist bomb and crashes in Lockerbie, Scotland, killing all 259 aboard and 11 on ground (**Dec. 21**).

1989   U.S. planes shoot down two Libyan fighters over international waters in Mediterranean (**Jan. 4**). Emperor Hirohito of Japan dead at 87 (**Jan. 7**). George Herbert Walker Bush inaugurated as 41st U.S. President (**Jan. 20**). Iran's Ayatollah Khomeini declares author Salman Rushdie's book *The Satanic Verses* offensive and sentences him to death (**Feb. 14**). Ruptured tanker *Exxon Valdez* sends 11 million gallons of crude oil into Alaska's Prince William Sound (**March 24**). Tens of thousands of Chinese students take over Beijing's Tiananmen Square in rally for democracy (**April 19** *et seq.*). U.S. jury convicts Oliver North in Iran-Contra affair (**May 4**). More than one million in Beijing demonstrate for democracy; chaos spreads across nation (**mid-May** *et seq.*). Mikhail S. Gorbachev named Soviet President (**May 25**). Thousands killed in Tiananmen Square as Chinese leaders take hard line toward demonstrators (**June 4** *et seq.*). Army Gen. Colin R. Powell is first black Chairman of Joint Chiefs of Staff (**Aug. 9**). P. W. Botha quits as South Africa's President (**Aug. 14**). *Voyager 2* spacecraft speeds by Neptune after making startling discoveries about the planet and its moons (**Aug. 29**). Deng Xiaoping resigns from China's leadership (**Nov. 9**). After 28 years, Berlin Wall is open to West (**Nov. 11**). Czech Parliament ends Communists' dominant role (**Nov. 30**). Romanian uprising overthrows Communist government (**Dec. 15** *et seq.*); President Ceausescu and wife executed (**Dec. 25**). U.S. troops invade Panama, seeking capture of Gen. Manuel Noriega (**Dec. 20**); resistance to U.S. collapses (**Dec. 24**). Dalai Lama wins Nobel Peace Prize.

François Mitterrand
(1916–1996)

General Colin Powell
(1937–)

1990   Gen. Manuel Noriega surrenders in Panama (**Jan. 3**). Yugoslav Communists end 45-year monopoly of power (**Jan. 22**). Soviet Communists relinquish sole power (**Feb. 7**). South Africa frees Nelson Mandela, imprisoned 27 1/2 years (**Feb. 11**). Violeta Barrios de Chamorro inaugurated as Nicaraguan President. Hubble Space Telescope launched (**April 25**). U.S.-Soviet summit reaches accord on armaments (**June 1**). Supreme Court upsets law banning flag burning (**June 11**). Western Alliance ends Cold War and proposes joint action with Soviet Union and Eastern Europe (**July 6**). U.S. Appeals Court overturns Oliver North's Iran-Contra conviction (**July 20**). Iraqi troops invade Kuwait and seize petroleum reserves, setting off Persian Gulf War (**Aug. 2** *et seq.*). East and West Germany reunited (**Oct. 3**). Republicans set back in midterm elections (**Nov. 8**). Gorbachev assumes emergency powers (**Nov. 17**). Leaders of 34 nations in Europe and North America proclaim a united Europe (**Nov. 21**). Margaret Thatcher resigns as British Prime Minister (**Nov. 22**); John Major succeeds her (**Nov. 28**).

Saddam Hussein
(1937–)

THE PERSIAN GULF WAR (Aug. 2, 1990–April 6, 1991)

1990 Iraq invades its tiny neighbor, Kuwait, after talks break down over oil production and debt repayment. Iraqi Pres. Saddam Hussein later annexes Kuwait and declares it a 19th province of Iraq (**Aug. 2**). President Bush believes that Iraq intends to invade Saudi Arabia and take control of the region's oil supplies. He begins organizing a multi-national coalition to seek Kuwait's freedom and restoration of its legitimate government. The U.N. Security Council authorizes economic sanctions against Iraq. Pres. Bush orders U.S. troops to protect Saudi Arabia at the Saudis' request and "Operation Desert Shield" begins (**Aug. 6**). 230,000 American troops arrive in Saudi Arabia to take defensive action, but when Iraq continues a huge military buildup in Kuwait, the President orders an additional 200,000 troops deployed to prepare for a possible offensive action by the U.S.-led coalition forces. He subsequently obtains a U.N. Security Council resolution setting a **Jan. 15, 1991** deadline for Iraq to withdraw unconditionally from Kuwait (**Nov. 8**).

1991 Pres. Bush wins Congressional approval for his position with the most devastating air assault in history

against military targets in Iraq and Kuwait (**Jan. 16**). He rejects a Soviet-Iraq peace plan for a gradual withdrawal that does not comply with all the U.N. resolutions and gives Iraq an ultimatum to withdraw from Kuwait by noon **Feb. 23** (**Feb. 22**). The President orders the ground war to begin (**Feb. 24**). In a brilliant and lightning-fast campaign, U.S. and coalition forces smash through Iraq's defenses and defeat Saddam Hussein's troops in only four days of combat. Allies enter Kuwait City (**Feb. 26**). Iraqi army sets fire to over 500 of Kuwait's oil wells as final act of destruction to Kuwait's infrastructure. Pres. Bush orders a unilateral cease-fire 100 hours after the ground offensive started (**Feb. 27**). Allied and Iraqi military leaders meet on battlefield to discuss terms for a formal cease-fire to end the Gulf War. Iraq agrees to abide by all of the U.N. resolutions (**Mar. 3**). The first Allied prisoners of war are released (**Mar. 4**). Official cease-fire accepted and signed (**April 6**). 532,000 U.S. forces served in Operation Desert Storm. There were a total of 148 U.S. battle deaths during the Gulf War, 145 nonbattle deaths, and 467 wounded in action.

Hubble Space Telescope

**Lech Walesa
(1943–)**

**Toni Morrison
(1931–)**

Lech Walesa wins Poland's runoff Presidential election **(Dec. 9)**. Haiti elects leftist priest as President in first democratic election **(Dec. 17)**.

1991 U.S. and Allies at war with Iraq **(Jan. 15)**. Warsaw Pact dissolves military alliance **(Feb. 25)**. Cease-fire ends Persian Gulf War; U.N. forces are victorious **(April 3)**. Europeans end sanctions on South Africa **(April 15)**. Supreme Court limits death row appeals **(April 16)**. Winnie Mandela sentenced in kidnapping **(May 13)**. William H. Webster retires as Director of CIA; Robert H. Gates succeeds him **(May 14)**. France agrees to sign 1968 treaty banning spread of atomic weapons **(June 3)**. Communist Government of Albania resigns **(June 4)**. Jiang Qing, widow of Mao, commits suicide **(June 4)**. South African Parliament repeals apartheid laws **(June 5)**. Warsaw Pact dissolved **(July 1)**. Boris N. Yeltsin inaugurated as first freely elected president of Russian Republic **(July 10)**. Bush-Gorbachev summit negotiates strategic arms reduction treaty **(July 31)**. China accepts nuclear nonproliferation treaty **(Aug. 10)**. Lithuania, Estonia, and Latvia win independence **(Aug. 25)**; Bush recognizes them **(Sept. 2)**. Haitian troops seize president in uprising **(Sept. 30)**. U.S. suspends assistance to Haiti **(Oct. 1)**. Professor Anita Hill accuses Judge Clarence Thomas of sexual harassment **(Oct. 6)**; Senate, 52-48, confirms Thomas for Supreme Court after stormy hearings **(Oct. 15)**. Israel and Soviet Union resume relations after 24 years **(Oct. 18)**. U.S. indicts two Libyans in 1988 bombing of Pan Am Flight 103 over Lockerbie, Scotland **(Nov. 15)**. Anglican envoy Terry Waite and U.S. Prof. Thomas M. Sutherland freed by Lebanese **(Nov. 18)**. Last three U.S. hostages freed in Lebanon **(Dec. 2-4)**. Soviet Union breaks up after President Gorbachev's resignation; constituent republics form Commonwealth of Independent States **(Dec. 25)**.

1992 A text-based Web browser is made available to the public **(Jan.)**; within a few years, millions of people become regular users of the World Wide Web. Yugoslav Federation broken up **(Jan. 15)**. Bush and Yeltsin proclaim formal end to Cold War **(Feb. 1)**. U.S. lifts trade sanctions against China **(Feb. 21)**. U.S. recognizes three former Yugoslav republics **(April 7)**. Gen. Noriega, former Panama leader, convicted in U.S. court **(April 9)**. Four officers acquitted in Los Angeles beating of Rodney King; violence erupts in Los Angeles **(April 29** *et seq.***)**. Caspar W. Weinberger indicted in Iran-Contra affair **(June 16)**. Last Western hostages freed in Lebanon **(June 17)**. Supreme Court reaffirms right to abortion **(June 29)**. Democrats nominate Bill Clinton and Al Gore **(July 1)**. Gen. Noriega sentenced to 40 years on drug charges **(July 10)**. Court clears *Exxon Valdez* skipper **(July 10)**. Israeli Parliament approves Yitzhak Rabin's coalition government, dominated by Labor Party **(July 13)**. Four police officers indicted in Rodney King beating **(Aug. 5)**. North American trade compact announced **(Aug. 12)**. Republicans renominate Bush and Quayle **(Aug. 20)**. U.N. expels Serbian-dominated Yugoslavia **(Sept. 22)**. Senate ratifies second Strategic Arms Limitation Treaty **(Oct. 1)**. Top Japanese leader, Shin Kanemaru, resigns in scandal **(Oct. 14)**. Bill Clinton elected President, Al Gore Vice President; Democrats keep control of Congress **(Nov. 3)**. Russian Parliament approves START treaty **(Nov. 4)**. U.S. forces leave Philippines, ending nearly a century of American military presence **(Nov. 24)**. Czechoslovak Parliament approves separation into two nations **(Nov. 25)**. U.N. approves U.S.-led force to guard food for Somalia **(Dec. 3)**. Prince and Princess of Wales agree to separate **(Dec. 9)**. Bush pardons former Reagan Administration officials involved in Iran-Contra affair **(Dec. 24)**.

1993 Vaclav Havel elected as Czech President **(Jan. 26)**. Clinton agrees to compromise on military's ban on homosexuals **(Jan. 29)**. U.S. begins airlift of supplies to besieged Bosnia towns **(Feb. 28)**. Federal agents besiege Texas Branch Davidian religious cult after six are killed in raid **(March 1** *et seq.***)**. Five arrested, sixth sought in bombing of World Trade Center in New York **(March 29)**. Two police officers convicted in Los Angeles on civil rights charges in Rodney King beating **(April 17)**; sentenced **Aug. 4**. Fire kills 72 as cult standoff in Texas ends with federal assault **(April 19)**. President of Sri Lanka assassinated **(May 1)**. British Commons approves European unity pact **(May 20)**. Twenty-two U.N. troops killed in Somalia **(June 5)**. Ruth Bader Ginsburg appointed to

Supreme Court (**June 14**). Iraq accepts U.N. weapons monitoring (**July 19**). Vincent W. Foster, Jr., senior White House lawyer, commits suicide (**July 22**). Midwest flood damage expected to exceed $10 billion (**July 24**). Israeli-Palestinian accord reached (**Aug. 28**). U.S. agents blamed in Waco, Tex., siege (**Oct. 1**). Yeltsin's forces crush revolt in Russian Parliament (**Oct. 4** *et seq.*). China breaks nuclear test moratorium (**Oct. 5**). Canada's opposition Liberal Party regains power in landslide (**Oct. 25**). Europe's Maastricht Treaty takes effect, creating European Union (**Nov. 1**). Jean Chretien sworn in as Canada's 20th Prime Minister (**Nov. 4**). House of Representatives approves North American Free Trade Agreement (**Nov. 17**); Senate follows (**Nov. 21**). South Africa adopts majority rule constitution (**Nov. 18**). Clinton signs Brady bill regulating firearms purchases (**Nov. 30**). Toni Morrison wins Nobel prize for literature.

**Nelson Mandela
(1918–)**

1994 Serbs' heavy weapons pound Sarajevo (**Jan. 5-6**). Olympic figure skater Nancy Kerrigan attacked (**Jan. 6**); three arrested in attack (**Jan. 13**). Major earthquake jolts Los Angeles; 51 dead (**Jan. 17** *et seq.*). Clinton ends trade embargo on Vietnam (**Feb. 9**). Aldrich Ames, high C.I.A. official, charged with spying for Soviets (**Feb. 22**). Four convicted in World Trade Center bombing (**March 4**). Mexican Presidential candidate assassinated (**March 23**). Thousands dead in Rwanda massacre (**April 6**). South Africa holds first interracial national election (**April 29**); Nelson Mandela elected President. Israel and Palestinians sign accord (**May 4**). Clinton accused of sexual harassment while Governor of Arkansas (**May 6**). Congress votes protection for women's health clinics (**May 12**). Jacqueline Kennedy Onassis dies of cancer (**May 20**). O. J. Simpson arrested in killings of wife, Nicole Brown Simpson, and friend, Ronald Goldman (**June 18**). Supreme Court approves limit on abortion protests (**June 30**). Senate confirms Stephen G. Breyer for Supreme Court (**July 29**). Women's health clinic doctor shot dead outside Florida clinic (**July 29**); U.S. indicts accused killer (**Aug. 12**). Major league baseball players strike (**Aug. 13**). "Carlos the Jackal," international terrorist, captured (**Aug. 15**). I.R.A. declares cease-fire in Northern Ireland (**Aug. 31**). Small plane crashes against White House (**Sept. 12**). Baseball owners end season and cancel World Series (**Sept. 14**). Powerful earthquake strikes Japan (**Oct. 4**). Aristide returns to joyous Haiti (**Oct. 4**). U.S. sends forces to Persian Gulf (**Oct. 7**). Ulster Protestants declare cease-fire (**Oct. 13**). Israel and Jordan sign peace treaty (**Oct. 17**). Reagan, 83, reveals Alzheimer's disease (**Nov. 6**). G.O.P. wins control of House and Senate (**Nov. 8**). Aristide forms Haitian Government with Prime Minister and full Cabinet (**Nov. 9**). Clinton orders Bosnian arms embargo ended (**Nov. 10**). Killer of women's health doctor sentenced twice (**Dec. 2**). Newt Gingrich named House Speaker (**Dec. 5**). Bentsen resigns as Treasury Secretary (**Dec. 6**). Russians attack secessionist Republic of Chechnya (**Dec. 11** *et seq.*). John Salvi kills two at Massachusetts Planned Parenthood clinic (**Dec. 30**).

**Jean-Bertrand Aristide
(1953–)**

**Dalai Lama
(1935–)**

1995 Republicans take control of Congress (**Jan. 4**). More than 5,000 dead in Japanese earthquake (**Jan. 17** *et seq.*). Criminal trial of O. J. Simpson opens in California (**Jan. 24**). U.S. rescues Mexico's economy with $20-billion aid program (**Feb. 21**). Senate rejects balanced-budget amendment (**March 2**). Russian space station greets first Americans (**March 14**). Nerve gas attack in Tokyo subway kills eight and injures thousands. The Aum Shinrikyo ("Supreme Truth") cult is to blame (**March 20**). Major League Baseball strike ends (**April 2**). Appeals court upholds woman's plea to enter Citadel military academy (**April 13**). U.N. Council votes easier sanctions for Iraq (**April 14**). Scores killed as terrorist's car bomb blows up block-long Oklahoma City federal building (**April 19**); Timothy McVeigh, 27, Army veteran, arrested as suspect (**April 21**); authorities seek second suspect, link right-wing paramilitary groups to bombing (**April 22**). Death toll 2,000 in Rwanda massacre (**April 22**). Fighting escalates in Bosnia and Croatia (**May 1**). U.S. shuttle docks with Russian space station (**June 27**). F.B.I. suspends four in Idaho siege inquiry (**Aug. 11**). France explodes nuclear device in Pacific; wide protests ensue (**Sept. 5**). Senator Bob Packwood of Oregon resigns under pressure for sexual and official misconduct (**Sept. 6**). Israelis and Palestinians agree on transferring West Bank to Arabs (**Sept. 24**). Los Angeles jury finds O. J. Simpson not guilty of murder charges (**Oct. 3**). Pope John Paul II visits U.S. on whirlwind tour (**Oct. 4-8**). Warring parties agree on cease-fire in Bosnia (**Oct. 5**). Million Man March draws

**Yitzhak Rabin
(1922–1995)**

Seamus Heaney
(1939–)

Ella Fitzgerald
(1918–1996)

Madeleine Albright
(1937–)

Kofi Annan
(1938–)

hundreds of thousands of black men to capital (**Oct. 16**). Quebec narrowly rejects independence from Canada (**Oct. 30**). Israel Prime Minister Yitzhak Rabin slain by Jewish extremist at peace rally (**Nov. 4**). U.S. servicemen admit rape of Japanese schoolgirl in Okinawa (**Nov. 7**). Nigeria hangs writer Ken Saro-Wiwa and eight other minority rights advocates (**Nov. 10**). Irish voters approve end to constitutional ban on divorce (**Nov. 24**). Combatants sign Bosnia peace treaty (**Dec. 14**). House move stalls Congress-White House negotiations to avert government shutdown (**Dec. 20**). Seamus Heaney wins Nobel prize for literature.

1996 U.S. budget crisis in fourth month (**Jan 3**). Global warming climbs to record (**Jan. 3**). Clinton approves resumption of many government operations (**Jan. 6**). Chechens capture 2,000 Russians (**Jan. 9**). Senate ratifies major arms reduction treaty (**Jan. 26**). France announces end to nuclear tests (**Jan. 29**). At least 73 dead in Sri Lankan suicide bombing (**Feb. 1**). Suicide bombers kill 59 in Israel (**March 4**). Bob Dole sweeps Republican primaries (**March 5**). Britain alarmed by deadly cow disease (**March 20** *et seq.*). U.N. tribunal charges war crimes by Bosnian Muslims and Croats (**March 22**). Commerce Secretary Ronald H. Brown, 54, killed in plane crash (**April 3**). F.B.I. arrests suspected Unabomber (**April 3**). Clinton signs line-item veto bill (**April 9**). President blocks ban on late-term abortions (**April 10**). Nations pledge $1.23 billion in aid to rebuild Bosnia (**April 22**). South Africa gets new constitution (**May 8**). Valujet crashes in Everglades; all 110 aboard killed (**May 11**). Chechnya peace treaty signed (**May 27**). Israel elects Benjamin Netanyahu as prime minister (**May 31**). China agrees to world ban on atomic testing (**June 6**). Leaders in Balkans sign accord on arms limits (**June 14**). Jazz great Ella Fitzgerald dies (**June 15**). Truck bomb kills 19 at U.S. base in Saudi Arabia (**June 25**). Boris Yeltsin is reelected in Russian election (**July 3**). Prince Charles and Princess Diana agree on divorce (**July 12**). 747 airliner crashes in Atlantic off Long Island; all 230 aboard perish (**July 17**). Bomb mars Summer Olympic games in Atlanta (**July 25**). Clinton signs bill to raise minimum wage (**Aug. 2**). Congress passes welfare reform bill (**Aug. 2**); approved by Clinton (**Aug. 22**). Republican convention opens in San Diego (**Aug. 12**); Bob Dole and Jack Kemp nominated (**Aug. 14**). Democrats convene in Chicago (**Aug. 26**). Iraqis strike at Kurdish enclave (**Aug. 31**); after warning, U.S. attacks Iraq's southern air defenses (**Sept. 2–3**); Iraq halts attacks on U.S. planes enforcing flight exclusion zones in north and south (**Sept. 13**). Virginia Military Institute agrees to admit women (**Sept. 21**). Violence flares in Jerusalem over Israel opening tourist tunnel (**Sept. 24**). Taliban Muslim fundamentalists capture Afghan capital (**Sept. 27**). Ethnic violence breaks out in Zairian refugee camps (**Oct. 13**); thousands of refugees from Rwanda and Burundi abandon camps (**Oct. 21**). Clinton-Gore ticket wins national election; Republicans retain control of Congress (**Nov. 5**). Bomb kills 13 in Russian cemetery (**Nov. 10**). Mid-air collision in India kills 342 (**Nov. 12**). Clinton approves Canadian plan for U.N.-backed relief mission for 1.2 million Hutu refugees starving in eastern Zaire (**Nov. 13**). Texaco settles racial bias suit (**Nov. 15**). Hundreds of thousands of Hutu refugees return to Rwanda (**Nov. 15–18**). Clinton appoints Madeleine Albright as first female U.S. secretary of state (**Dec. 5**). Kofi Annan named U.N. Secretary-General (**Dec. 13**). F.B.I. agent charged with spying for Moscow (**Dec. 18**). Thousands march in Belgrade in continuing protest against president's annulment of election results (**Dec. 26**).

1997 Two Hutu sentenced to death in Rwandan genocide (**Jan. 3**). Floods cause wide damage in U.S. West (**Jan. 5**). Newt Gingrich re-elected as House Speaker (**Jan. 7**). Hebron agreement signed; Israel gives up large part of West Bank city of Hebron (**Jan. 16**). U.S. shuttle joins Russian space station (**Jan. 17**). Gingrich found guilty of ethics violations (**Jan. 17**). President Clinton starts second term (**Jan. 20**). U.S., U.K., and France agree to freeze Nazis' gold loot (**Feb. 3**). O. J. Simpson found liable in civil suit (**Feb. 5**). Deng Xiaoping, Chinese leader, dead at 92 (**Feb. 19**). Israeli government approves establishment of Jewish settlement in East Jerusalem, a setback in Middle East peace process (**Feb. 26**). Tornadoes wreak havoc in Arkansas, Ohio, and Kentucky (**March 3**). Senate dooms balanced-budget amendment (**March 4**). State of anarchy in Albania when third of population loses savings because of pyramid schemes (**March 13**). Hale-Bopp Comet is the closest it will be to

Earth until 4397 (**March 22**). Heaven's Gate cult members commit mass suicide in California (**March 27**). U.S. Appeals Court upholds California ban on affirmative action (**April 8**). U.S. judge upholds California marijuana law (**April 11**). Tiger Woods breaks multiple records in Masters golf tournament (**April 13**). Fire kills 300 pilgrims outside Mecca (**April 15**). Senate, 74–26, approves chemical-weapons treaty (**April 24**). Thousands flee North Dakota flood (**April 27**). U.N. tribunal convicts Bosnian Serb for killings and tortures (**May 7**). Sergeant Major of the Army, Gene C. McKinney, charged in sex cases (**May 7**). Russian President Yeltsin signs Chechnya peace treaty (**May 12**). U.S.-Russian spaceship linkup in orbit ends (**May 21**). U.S. jobless rate for May reported 4.8 percent, lowest since 1973 (**June 6**). European Union bolsters currency merger (**June 16**). Historic tobacco settlement proposed (**June 20**). Congress votes major tax cuts (**June 26**). Hong Kong returns to Chinese rule (**June 30**). U.S. spacecraft begins exploration of Mars (**July 4**). Andrew Cunanan murders fashion designer Gianni Versace at end of a killing spree (**July 15**). Khmer Rouge hold trial of longtime leader Pol Pot (**July 25**). White House and G.O.P. agree on measure to balance budget (**July 28**). U.S. spacecraft transmits thousands of pictures from Mars (**Aug. 8**). Clinton exercises new line-item veto (**Aug. 11**). Timothy J. McVeigh sentenced to death for Oklahoma City bombing (**Aug. 14**). Princess Diana, 36, killed with two others in Paris car crash (**Aug. 31**). Three Islamic suicide bombers kill four persons in Jerusalem (**Sept. 4**). Mother Teresa dead at 87 (**Sept. 5**). Worldwide public mourning marks Princess Diana's funeral (**Sept. 6**). Swiss plan first payment to Holocaust victims (**Sept. 17**). U.S. space shuttle docks with Russian *Mir,* bringing new astronaut (**Sept. 27**). Militant Taliban leaders seize Kabul (**Sept. 27**). Israeli Prime Minister Netanyahu center of controversy over failed attempt to assassinate militant Islamic leader (**Oct. 6**). Iraq expels all U.S. members of U.N. arms-inspection team (**Oct. 29**). G.O.P. victorious in off-year elections (**Nov. 4**). Pakistani convicted in 1993 C.I.A. killings (**Nov. 10**). Two convicted in New York Trade Center bombing (**Nov. 12**). Egyptian Islamic militants kill 62 at Luxor tourist site (**Nov. 17**). F.B.I. ends 16-month investigation of crash of Flight 800 off Long Island; denies sabotage (**Nov. 18**). Attorney General exonerates Clinton and Gore on fund-raising calls (**Dec. 2**). European Union plans to admit six nations (**Dec. 13**). Gunmen kill 45 in raid on Indian village in Mexico (**Dec. 22**). U.S. company launches first commercial spy satellite (**Dec. 24**). Paris court convicts "Carlos the Jackal" of murder (**Dec. 24**).

1998 Unabomber, Theodore Kaczynski, pleads guilty (**Jan. 8**). Floods and freezing rain cripple Northeast (**Jan. 9**). Ramzi Ahmed Yousef sentenced to life for 1993 World Trade Center bombing (**Jan. 9**). Iraq blocks U.N. weapons inspection (**Jan. 13**). Drastic economic reforms agreed on for Indonesia (**Jan. 15**). Pope John Paul II visits Cuba for five days (**Jan. 21–25**). President accused in White House sex scandal; denies allegations of affair with White House intern, Monica Lewinsky (**Jan. 21** *et seq.*). President outlines first balanced budget in 30 years (**Feb. 3**). U.S. plane cuts ski cable in Italy and sends car plunging; 20 killed (**Feb. 3**). Thousands dead in Afghanistan quake (**Feb. 4** *et seq.*). U.S. court rules line-item veto unconstitutional (**Feb. 12**). Republican filibuster blocks campaign-spending reform (**Feb. 26**). Serbs battle ethnic Albanians in Kosovo (**March 5** *et seq.*). U.S. drops condemnation of China's human rights record (**March 13**). Sergeant Major Gene C. McKinney acquitted on sex charges (**March 13**). Vatican regrets inaction in Holocaust (**March 16**). Presbyterians keep ban on gay clergy (**March 18**). Hindu nationalist Vajpayee becomes India's prime minister (**March 19**). Clinton acclaimed on visit to Africa (**March 23** *et seq.*). F.D.A. approves Viagra, male impotence drug (**March 27**). House defeats election reform bill (**March 30**). Federal judge in Arkansas throws out Paula Jones case (**April 1**). Landmark peace settlement, the Good Friday Accord, reached in Northern Ireland (**April 10**). U.S. trade deficit biggest in decade (**April 17**). Irish Parliament backs peace agreement (**April 22**). Russian Parliament approves prime minister appointee, Sergei Kiriyenko (**April 24**). Europeans agree on single currency, the euro (**May 3**). Unabomber sentenced to four life terms (**May 4**). India conducts three atomic tests despite worldwide disapproval (**May 11, 13**). Indonesian dictator Suharto steps down after 32 years in power (**May 21**). Pakistan stages five nuclear tests in response to India's (**May 29, 30**). Serbs renew attack

Hale-Bopp Comet

Mother Teresa
(1910–1997)

Princess Diana
(1961–1997)

Mars Sojourner Rover

Euro 100

**William J. Clinton
(1946–)**

**Boris Yeltsin
(1931–)**

on Kosovo rebels **(June 1)**. Life sentence meted out to Terry Nichols, convicted in Oklahoma City bombing fatal to 168 **(June 4)**. Nigerian dictator Sani Abacha dies **(June 8)**. Chinese use of U.S. satellites reported **(June 12)**. President Clinton visits China **(June 25 et seq.)**. Congress votes to overhaul I.R.S. **(July 9)**. Japanese voters oust ruling party **(July 12)**. Independent counsel Kenneth Starr subpoenas Clinton to testify in Grand Jury investigation of reported White House sex scandal **(July 25)**. Iraq ends cooperation with U.N. arms inspectors **(Aug. 5)**. Monica Lewinsky testifies before Grand Jury about affair with Clinton **(Aug. 6)**. U.S. embassies in Kenya and Tanzania bombed **(Aug. 7)**. Clinton testifies on closed-circuit before Grand Jury; admits to affair with White House intern in televised address to nation **(Aug. 17)**. Russia fights to avert financial collapse **(Aug. 17)**. U.S. cruise missiles hit suspected terrorist bases in Sudan and Afghanistan **(Aug. 20)**. North Korea fires missile across Japan **(Aug. 31)**. U.N. tribunal convicts Rwandan in genocide; first such verdict ever **(Sept. 2)**. Swissair jet crashes; kills 229 **(Sept. 2)**. Starr Report by independent counsel outlines case for impeachment proceedings against President **(Sept. 11)**. Senate sustains veto of bill to outlaw late-term abortions **(Sept. 18)**. Iran lifts death threat against Salman Rushdie **(Sept. 24)**. German Chancellor Helmut Kohl defeated by Gerhard Schröder **(Sept. 27)**. U.S. budget surplus largest in three decades. House Judiciary Committee votes to investigate possible impeachment of President **(Oct. 5)**. China signs international accord to improve human rights **(Oct. 5)**. Matthew Shepard, gay Wyoming student, fatally beaten in hate crime; two arrested **(Oct. 6 et seq.)**. NATO, on verge of air strikes, reaches settlement with Milosevic on Kosovo **(Oct. 12)**. Former Chilean dictator Pinochet arrested in London **(Oct. 16)**. Wye Mills Agreement between Netanyahu and Arafat moves Middle East peace talks forward **(Oct. 23)**. More than 10,000 die in Central American hurricane **(Nov. 1)**. Democrats unexpectedly gain five House seats in national election; Republicans keep control of House and Senate **(Nov. 3)**. Astronaut John Glenn returns to Earth after encore space mission **(Nov. 7)**. House Speaker Gingrich to step down **(Nov. 9)**. House panel drafts impeachment charges; votes along party lines to approve four articles **(Dec. 11–12)**. Osama bin Laden, Islamic extremist, reported to plot terrorist attacks on U.S. targets in Persian Gulf **(Dec. 15)**. U.S. and other aid nations agree to press for deep govermental and economic reforms in Bosnia **(Dec. 15)**. Clinton orders air strikes on Iraq **(Dec. 16–19)**. House impeaches President Clinton along party lines on two charges, perjury and obstruction of justice. Senators divide on plan for trial or censure **(Dec. 19)**.

PICTURE CREDITS

The editors wish to thank the following organizations and individuals who have contributed illustrations to Headline History.

Agence France Press/Archive Photos: **Mao Zedong;** AIP Niels Bohr Library: **Marie Curie, Albert Einstein;** AMW Pressedienst/Archive Photos: **Nelson Mandela;** Archive Photos: **Richard Wagner, William Butler Yeats, Pablo Picasso, Anne Frank, Woody Guthrie, Robert Frost, William Faulkner, The Beatles, Mahatma Gandhi, Duke Ellington, Tennessee Williams, Toni Morrison, Seamus Heaney, Ella Fitzgerald, Lech Walesa, Princess Diana, Pope John Paul, Mother Teresa, Yitzhak Rabin, Malcolm X, William Rehnquist, Anwar Sadat;** Linda J. Barnes: **the Duomo in Florence;** British Information Services: **Margaret Thatcher;** Consolidated News/Archive Photos: **Jean-Bertrand Aristide;** Tina Diodati: **Aqueduct, Parthenon;** Embassy of the Philippines: **Corazon Aquino;** The French Consulate, Boston: **François Mitterrand;** Gerald R. Ford Library: **Gerald Ford;** Peter F. Harrington: **Stonehenge;** Erik Hjortshoj: **Pagoda;** Imapress/Archive Photos: **Boris Yeltsin;** INA/Reuters/Archive Photos: **Saddam Hussein;** John Fitzgerald Kennedy Library, Boston: **John F. Kennedy;** Priscilla Lee: **Dalai Lama;** Leo Baeck Inst./Archive Photos: **Sigmund Freud;** Jimmy Carter Library: **Jimmy Carter;** The Library of Congress Picture Collection: **Pocahontas, Taj Mahal, Edgar Allan Poe, Harriet Tubman, Walt Whitman, Dred Scott, Samuel Clemens (Mark Twain), Henri Matisse, W. E. B. Du Bois, Woodrow Wilson, Bessie Smith, Dorothea Lange photo, Amelia Earhart, Harry S. Truman, John H. Glenn, Jr., Richard Nixon, Lyndon B. Johnson;** Pete Maio: **Mesa Verde;** Muzammil Paha/Reuters/Archive Photos: **Benazir Bhutto;** National Archives and Records Admin.: **Frederick Douglass, Harriet Beecher Stowe, Abraham Lincoln, Robert E. Lee, William Tecumseh Sherman, Chief Joseph, Benito Mussolini, Franklin Delano Roosevelt, Adolf Hitler, Winston Churchill, Atomic Bomb, Dwight D. Eisenhower, Rev. Martin Luther King, Jr.;** NASA: **Hubble Space Telescope;** NASA/JPL/Caltech: **Mars Sojourner Rover;** Novosti Photos: **Vladimir Lenin, Mikhail S. Gorbachev;** Elaine Ouellette: **Pantheon in Rome;** The Permanent Mission of India to the U.N.: **Indira Gandhi;** Permanent Mission of Islamic Republic of Iran to the U.N.: **Ayatollah Ruhollah Khomeini;** Renée Scott: **Celtic Cross, Mayan Pyramid;** The Republican National Committee: **Ronald Reagan, George Bush;** Kim Storm: **Egyptian Pyramid;** United Nations: **Fidel Castro, Kofi Annan;** U.S. Army Photos: **Joseph Stalin, Yalta Conference, General Colin Powell;** U.S. State Department: **Madeleine Albright;** U.S. Supreme Court: **Thurgood Marshall, Sandra Day O'Connor;** Tasha Vincent: **Cathedral and Tower at Pisa, Chartres Cathedral, Michelangelo's David, Statue of Liberty;** The White House: **William J. Clinton.**

A Profile of the World

Source: The World Factbook, 1998.

Geography

Total area: 510,072 million sq km (196.93 million sq mi.). **Land area:** 148.94 million sq km (57.50 sq mi.). **Water area:** 361,132 million sq km (139.43 sq mi.). **Comparative area:** Land area about 15 times the size of the United States. **Note:** 70.8% of the world is water, 29.2% is land.

Land boundaries: The land boundaries in the world total 251,480.24 km (157,175.15 mi.) (not counting shared boundaries twice).

Maritime claims: *Contiguous zone:* 24 nm (nautical miles) claimed by most but can vary. *Continental shelf:* 200-m (656 ft.) depth claimed by most or to the depth of exploration, others claim 200 nm or to the edge of the continental margin. *Exclusive fishing zone:* 200 nm claimed by most but can vary. *Exclusive economic zone:* 200 nm claimed by most but can vary. *Territorial sea:* 12 nm claimed by most but can vary.

Climate: Two large areas of polar climates are separated by two rather narrow temperate zones from a wide equatorial band of tropical to subtropical climates.

Terrain: Highest elevation is Mt. Everest at 8,848 meters (29,028 ft.) and lowest land depression is the Dead Sea at –400 meters (–1,312 ft.) below sea level. The greatest ocean depth is the Mariana Trench at 10,924 meters in the Pacific Ocean.

Land use: *Arable land:* 10%. *Permanent crops:* 1%. *Meadows and pastures:* 26%. *Forests and woodlands:* 32%. *Other:* 31% (1993 est.).

People

Population: 6,007,486,448 (Aug. 23, 1999, est. from U.S. Census Bureau)
Growth rate: 1.3% (1998 est.)
Birth rate: 22 births/1,000 population (1998 est.)
Death rate: 9 deaths/1,000 live births (1998 est.)
Sex ratio (at birth): 1.06 male(s)/female (1998 est.)

Infant mortality rate: 58 deaths/1,000 live births (1998 est.)
Life expectancy at birth: *Total population:* 63 years. *Male:* 61 years. *Female:* 65 years (1998 est.)
Total fertility rate: 2.9 children born/woman (1998 est.)
Literacy: Age 15 and over can read and write (1999 est.— U.N. figs.) *Combined:* 79.4%. *Male:* 85.2%. *Female:* 73.6%.

Government and Economy

Political divisions: 266 sovereign nations, dependent areas, other, and miscellaneous entries
GDP: GWP (gross world product)—purchasing power parity—$38 trillion (1997 est.)
GDP—real growth rate: 4% (1997 est.)
GDP—per capita: $6,500 (1997 est.)
Inflation rate (consumer price index): *All countries:* 25% *Developed countries:* 2%–4% typically (1997 est.). *Developing countries:* 10%–60% typically (1997 est.). **Note:** *National inflation rates vary widely. individual cases, from stable prices in Japan to hyperinflation in a number of developing countries.*
Labor force: 2.24 billion (1992)
Unemployment rate: 30% combined unemployment and underemployment in many nonindustrialized countries; developed countries, typically 5%–12% unemployment (1997 est.)
Exports: $5 trillion (f.o.b. 1997 est.)
Imports: $5.1 trillion (c.i.f., 1997 est.)
External debt: $2 trillion for less developed countries (1997 est.)
Industrial production growth rate: 5% (1997 est.)
Industries: Industry worldwide is dominated by the onrush of technology, especially in computers, robotics, telecommunications, and medicines and medical equipment; most of these advances take place in Organization for Economic Cooperation and Development (OECD) nations.

Most and Least Livable Countries: The Human Development Index, 1999

The Human Development Index (HDI), published annually by the UN, ranks nations according to their citizens' quality of life rather than strictly by a nation's traditional economic figures. The criteria for calculating rankings are the combination of the following: life expectancy, adult literacy, school enrollment, and per capita GDP. The index ranks a total of 174 countries; below are the 30 highest and lowest rated countries.

Most Livable Countries, 1999		Least Livable Countries, 1999	
1. Canada	16. Austria	1. Sierra Leone	16. Malawi
2. Norway	17. Luxembourg	2. Niger	17. Uganda
3. United States	18. New Zealand	3. Ethiopia	18. Djibouti
4. Japan	19. Italy	4. Burkina Faso	19. Tanzania
5. Belgium	20. Ireland	5. Burundi	20. Benin
6. Sweden	21. Spain	6. Mozambique	21. Côte d'Ivoire
7. Australia	22. Singapore	7. Guinea-Bissau	22. Senegal
8. Netherlands	23. Israel	8. Eritrea	23. Haiti
9. Iceland	24. Hong Kong, China	9. Mali	24. Zambia
10. United Kingdom	25. Brunei Darussalam	10. Central African Republic	25. Bangladesh
11. France	26. Cyprus	11. Rwanda	26. Mauritania
12. Switzerland	27. Greece	12. Gambia	27. Yemen
13. Finland	28. Portugal	13. Chad	28. Madagascar
14. Germany	29. Barbados	14. Guinea	29. Nigeria
15. Denmark	30. Korea, Rep. of	15. Angola	30. Bhutan

Source: Human Development Report, 1999, United Nations.

Country Statistics at a Glance

Country rankings of the type presented below cannot pretend to be definitive; instead they aspire only to provide the reader with a general approximation of the high and low ends on a particular scale. Country data vary enormously depending on the sources, and the absence of reliable data on some countries requires their omission, which further skews the results.

LARGEST COUNTRIES[1] (in sq mi.): 1999

(1)	Russia	6,592,800
(2)	Canada	3,851,809
(3)	China	3,691,521
(4)	United States	3,536,341
(5)	Brazil	3,286,470
(6)	Australia	2,966,150
(7)	India	1,229,737
(8)	Argentina	1,072,067
(9)	Kazakhstan	1,049,000
(10)	Sudan	967,491

SMALLEST COUNTRIES[1] (in sq mi.): 1999

(1)	Vatican City	0.17
(2)	Monaco	0.73
(3)	Nauru	8.2
(4)	Tuvalu	10.0
(5)	San Marino	23.6
(6)	Liechtenstein	61.0
(7)	Marshall Islands	70.0
(8)	St. Kitts & Nevis	100.0
(9)	Maldives	115.0
(10)	Malta	122.0

HIGHEST POPULATION DENSITY[2] (per sq mi.): 1999

(1)	Monaco	44,040
(2)	Singapore	14,315
(3)	Malta	3,128
(4)	Maldives	2,621
(5)	Bahrain	2,611
(6)	Bangladesh	2,286
(7)	Taiwan	1,591
(8)	Barbados	1,561
(9)	Mauritius	1,502
(10)	Nauru	1,293

HIGHEST GDP PER CAPITA[3] (PPP in US dollars): 1997

(1)	Luxembourg[4]	$33,700
(2)	United States	30,200
(3)	Norway	27,400
(4)	Monaco	25,000
(5)	Japan	24,500
(6)	United Arab Emirates	24,000
(7)	Switzerland	23,800
(8)	Belgium	23,200
	Denmark	23,200
(10)	Liechtenstein	23,000

LOWEST GDP PER CAPITA[3] (PPP in US dollars): 1997

(1)	Congo, Democratic Republic of the	$400
(2)	Rwanda	440
(3)	Ethiopia	530
(4)	Sierra Leone	540
(5)	Chad	600
	Eritrea	600
	Mali	600
	Somalia	600
(9)	Burundi	660
(10)	Niger	670

LOWEST POPULATION DENSITY[2] (per sq mi.): 1999

(1)	Greenland	0.1
(2)	Western Sahara	1.5
(3)	Mongolia	4.0
(4)	Namibia	5.0
(5)	Australia	6.0
	Botswana	6.0
	Mauritania	6.0
(8)	Iceland	7.0
	Libya	7.0
	Suriname	7.0

HIGHEST INFLATION[3]: 1997

(1)	Turkmenistan	992.0%
(2)	Bulgaria	579.0
(3)	Afghanistan	240.0
(4)	Romania	151.0
(5)	Turkey	99.0
(6)	Angola	92.0
(7)	Malawi[4]	83.4
(8)	Belarus	65.0
	Guinea-Bissau	65.0
(10)	São Tomé and Príncipe	60.0

LOWEST INFLATION[3]: 1997

(1)	Nauru[5]	−3.6%
(2)	St. Lucia	−2.3
(3)	Bahrain	−2.0
(4)	Kiribati	−0.6
(5)	Seychelles[4]	−0.3
(6)	Switzerland	−0.1
(7)	Saudi Arabia	0.0
(8)	Ethiopia	0.0
(9)	Argentina	0.3
(10)	Bahamas	0.4

HIGHEST INFANT MORTALITY RATE[2]: 1998 (deaths per 1,000 births)

(1)	Afghanistan	140.55
(2)	Western Sahara	136.67
(3)	Malawi	132.14
(4)	Angola	129.19
(5)	Guinea	126.32
(6)	Sierra Leone	126.23
(7)	Somalia	125.77
(8)	Ethiopia	124.57
(9)	Mali	119.44
(10)	Mozambique	117.56

HIGHEST LIFE EXPECTANCY[2] (in years): 1998

(1)	Andorra	83.46
(2)	San Marino	81.47
(3)	Australia	80.14
(4)	Japan	80.11
(5)	Canada	79.37
(6)	Sweden	79.29
(7)	Switzerland	78.99
(8)	Iceland	78.96
(9)	Singapore	78.84
(10)	France	78.63

LOWEST LIFE EXPECTANCY[2] (in years): 1998

(1)	Malawi	36.30
(2)	Zambia	36.96
(3)	Swaziland	38.11
(4)	Zimbabwe	38.86
(5)	Botswana	39.89
(6)	Ethiopia	40.46
(7)	Namibia	41.26
(8)	Rwanda	41.31
(9)	Niger	41.96
(10)	Uganda	43.06

LOWEST INFANT MORTALITY RATE[2]: 1998 (deaths per 1,000 births)

(1)	Finland	3.80
(2)	Singapore	3.84
(3)	Sweden	3.91
(4)	Japan	4.07
(5)	Andorra	4.08
(6)	Switzerland	4.87
(7)	Norway	4.96
(8)	Luxembourg	4.99
(9)	Austria	5.10
(10)	Australia	5.11
	Denmark	5.11
	Netherlands	5.11

Sources: 1. Information Please Data Base. 2. U.S. Census Bureau, International Data Base. 3. *The World Factbook, 1998.* 4. Figure is for 1995. 5. Figure is for 1993. Note: Only countries for which statistics were available in sources 1, 2, or 3 figure in these lists.

World's 50 Most Populous Cities

Rank	City and country	Population[1]	Rank	City and country	Population[1]
1.	Seoul, South Korea	10,231,217	26.	Wuhan, China	4,040,113
2.	São Paulo, Brazil	10,017,821	27.	Guangzhou, China	3,935,193
3.	Bombay (Mumbai), India	9,925,891	28.	Madras, India	3,841,396
4.	Jakarta, Indonesia	9,112,652	29.	Baghdad, Iraq	3,841,268
5.	Moscow, Russia	8,368,449	30.	Pusan, South Korea	3,814,325
6.	Istanbul, Turkey	8,274,921	31.	Singapore	3,737,000
7.	Mexico City, Mexico	8,235,744	32.	Sydney, Australia	3,713,500
8.	Shanghai, China	8,214,384	33.	Caracas, Venezuela	3,672,779
9.	Tokyo, Japan	7,967,614	34.	Los Angeles, U.S.	3,553,638
10.	New York City, U.S.	7,380,906	35.	Berlin, Germany	3,458,763
11.	Beijing, China	7,362,426	36.	Alexandria, Egypt	3,380,000
12.	Delhi, India	7,206,704	37.	Yokohama, Japan	3,319,815
13.	London, U.K.	7,074,265	38.	Melbourne, Australia	3,189,200
14.	Cairo, Egypt	6,800,000	39.	Chongqing, China	3,127,178
15.	Teheran, Iran	6,750,043	40.	Hyderabad, India	3,058,093
16.	Hong Kong, China	6,502,000	41.	Ho Chi Minh City, Vietnam	3,015,743
17.	Bangkok, Thailand	5,882,000	42.	Haerbin, China	2,990,921
18.	Tianjin, China	5,855,044	43.	Buenos Aires, Argentina	2,965,403
19.	Lima, Peru	5,681,941	44.	Chengdu, China	2,954,872
20.	Rio de Janeiro, Brazil	5,606,497	45.	Ahmedabad, India	2,954,526
21.	Santafé de Bogotá, Colombia	4,945,448	46.	Ankara, Turkey	2,937,524
22.	Shenyang, China	4,669,737	47.	Xian, China	2,872,539
23.	Santiago, Chile	4,640,635	48.	Madrid, Spain	2,866,850
24.	Calcutta, India	4,399,819	49.	Pyongyang, North Korea	2,741,260
25.	St. Petersburg, Russia	4,232,105	50.	Chicago, U.S.	2,721,547

NOTE: Figures are for latest available years. 1. Population figures are for the city proper, which may include some rural areas. *Source: 1997 Demographic Yearbook,* United Nations.

World's 30 Most Populous Countries: 1999 and 2025

	1999			2025 (projected)	
Rank	Country	Population	Rank	Country	Population
1.	China	1,246,871,951	1.	India	1,415,273,665
2.	India	1,000,848,550	2.	China	1,407,739,146
3.	United States	272,639,608	3.	United States	335,359,714
4.	Indonesia	216,108,345	4.	Indonesia	287,985,072
5.	Brazil	171,853,126	5.	Pakistan	211,675,333
6.	Russia	146,393,569	6.	Brazil	209,586,835
7.	Pakistan	138,123,359	7.	Nigeria	203,423,396
8.	Bangladesh	127,117,967	8.	Bangladesh	179,129,264
9.	Japan	126,182,077	9.	Mexico	141,592,523
10.	Nigeria	113,828,587	10.	Russia	138,841,556
11.	Mexico	100,294,036	11.	Philippines	120,519,345
12.	Germany	82,087,361	12.	Japan	119,864,560
13.	Philippines	79,345,812	13.	Congo (Kinshasa)	105,737,162
14.	Vietnam	77,311,210	14.	Vietnam	103,908,883
15.	Egypt	67,273,906	15.	Ethiopia	98,762,736
16.	Turkey	65,599,206	16.	Egypt	97,431,183
17.	Iran	65,179,752	17.	Iran	90,889,233
18.	Thailand	60,609,046	18.	Turkey	89,736,104
19.	Ethiopia	59,680,383	19.	Germany	75,372,295
20.	United Kingdom	59,113,439	20.	Thailand	70,315,728
21.	France	58,978,172	21.	Burma	68,106,967
22.	Italy	56,735,130	22.	United Kingdom	59,984,961
23.	Congo (Kinshasa)	50,481,305	23.	Colombia	58,287,171
24.	Ukraine	49,811,174	24.	France	57,806,479
25.	Burma	48,081,302	25.	Tanzania	50,660,932
26.	South Korea	46,884,800	26.	Italy	50,351,674
27.	South Africa	43,426,386	27.	Uganda	49,181,434
28.	Colombia	39,309,422	28.	Argentina	48,351,219
29.	Spain	39,167,744	29.	Afghanistan	48,044,542
30.	Poland	38,608,929	30.	Algeria	46,675,820

Source: U.S. Department of Commerce, U.S. Census Bureau, International Data Base.

Six Billion of Us

According to the U.S. Census Bureau, the world population reached 6 billion on July 19, 1999, at about 12:24:02 AM GMT (July 18 at 8:24:02 PM EDT). The Census figure is an estimate and not meant to be an exact accounting of every birth and death throughout the world. Differing estimates exist. The United Nations celebrated the "Day of 6 Billion" three months later, on October 12, 1999.

World Population Milestones
- 1 billion in 1804
- 2 billion in 1927 (123 years later)
- 3 billion in 1960 (33 years later)
- 4 billion in 1974 (14 years later)
- 5 billion in 1987 (13 years later)
- 6 billion in 1999 (12 years later)

Source: United Nations Population Division.

Area and Population of Countries
Mid-1999 Estimates

Country	Area (in sq km)	Population	Country	Area (in sq km)	Population
Afghanistan	647,500	25,824,882	Equatorial Guinea	28,050	465,746
Albania	28,750	3,364,571	Eritrea	121,320	3,984,723
Algeria	2,381,740	31,133,486	Estonia	45,226	1,408,523
Andorra	450	65,939	Ethiopia	1,127,127	59,680,383
Angola	1,246,700	11,177,537	Fiji	18,270	812,918
Antigua and Barbuda	440	64,246	Finland	337,030	5,158,372
Argentina	2,766,890	36,737,664	France	547,030	58,978,172
Armenia	29,800	3,409,234	Gabon	267,670	1,225,853
Australia	7,686,850	18,783,551	The Gambia	11,300	1,336,320
Austria	83,858	8,139,299	Georgia	69,700	5,066,499
Azerbaijan	86,600	7,908,224	Germany	356,910	82,087,361
The Bahamas	13,940	283,705	Ghana	238,540	18,887,626
Bahrain	620	629,090	Greece	131,940	10,707,135
Bangladesh	144,000	127,117,967	Grenada	340	97,008
Barbados	430	259,191	Guatemala	108,890	12,335,580
Belarus	207,600	10,401,784	Guinea	245,860	7,538,953
Belgium	30,510	10,182,034	Guinea-Bissau	36,120	1,234,555
Belize	22,960	235,789	Guyana	214,970	705,156
Benin	112,620	6,305,567	Haiti	27,750	6,884,264
Bhutan	47,000	1,951,965	Honduras	112,090	5,997,327
Bolivia	1,098,580	7,982,850	Hungary	93,030	10,186,372
Bosnia and Herzegovina	51,233	3,482,495	Iceland	103,000	272,512
Botswana	600,370	1,464,167	India	3,287,590	1,000,848,550
Brazil	8,511,965	171,853,126	Indonesia	1,919,440	216,108,345
Brunei	5,770	322,982	Iran	1,648,000	65,179,752
Bulgaria	110,910	8,194,772	Iraq	437,072	22,427,150
Burkina Faso	274,200	11,575,898	Ireland	70,280	3,632,944
Burma (Myanmar)	678,500	48,081,302	Israel	20,770	5,749,760
Burundi	27,830	5,735,937	Italy	301,230	56,735,130
Cambodia	181,040	11,626,520	Jamaica	10,990	2,652,443
Cameroon	475,440	15,456,092	Japan	377,835	126,182,077
Canada	9,976,140	31,006,347	Jordan	89,213	4,561,147
Cape Verde	4,030	405,748	Kazakhstan	2,717,300	16,824,825
Central African Republic	622,980	3,444,951	Kenya	582,650	28,808,658
Chad	1,284,000	7,557,436	Kiribati	717	85,501
Chile	756,950	14,973,843	North Korea	120,540	21,386,109
China, People's Republic of	9,596,960	1,246,871,951	South Korea	98,480	46,884,800
Colombia	1,138,910	39,309,422	Kuwait	17,820	1,991,115
Comoros	2,170	562,723	Kyrgyzstan	198,500	4,546,055
Republic of Congo	342,000	2,716,814	Laos	236,800	5,407,453
Democratic Republic of the Congo (formerly Zaire)	2,345,410	50,481,305	Latvia	64,100	2,353,874
			Lebanon	10,400	3,562,699
Costa Rica	51,100	3,674,490	Lesotho	30,350	2,128,950
Côte d'Ivoire	322,460	15,818,068	Liberia	111,370	2,923,725
Croatia	56,538	3,676,865	Libya	1,759,540	4,992,838
Cuba	110,860	11,096,395	Liechtenstein	160	32,057
Cyprus	9,250	754,064	Lithuania	65,200	3,584,966
Czech Republic	78,703	10,280,513	Luxembourg	2,586	429,080
Denmark	43,094	5,356,845	Macedonia	25,333	2,022,604
Djibouti	22,000	447,439	Madagascar	587,040	14,873,387
Dominica	750	64,881	Malawi	118,480	10,000,416
Dominican Republic	48,730	8,129,734	Malaysia	329,750	21,376,066
Ecuador	283,560	12,562,496	Maldives	300	300,220
Egypt	1,001,450	67,273,906	Mali	1,240,000	10,429,124
El Salvador	21,040	5,839,079	Malta	320	381,603

Country	Area (in sq km)	Population	Country	Area (in sq km)	Population
Marshall Islands	181.3	65,507	Seychelles	455	79,164
Mauritania	1,030,700	2,581,738	Sierra Leone	71,740	5,296,651
Mauritius	1,860	1,182,212	Singapore	647.5	3,531,600
Mexico	1,972,550	100,294,036	Slovakia	48,845	5,396,193
Micronesia	702	131,500	Slovenia	20,256	1,970,570
Moldova	33,700	4,460,838	Solomon Islands	28,450	455,429
Monaco	1.95	32,149	Somalia	637,660	7,140,643
Mongolia	1,565,000	2,617,379	South Africa	1,219,912	43,426,386
Morocco	446,550	29,661,636	Spain	504,750	39,167,744
Mozambique	801,590	19,124,335	Sri Lanka	65,610	19,144,875
Namibia	825,418	1,648,270	Sudan	2,505,810	34,475,690
Nauru	21	10,605	Suriname	163,270	431,156
Nepal	140,800	24,302,653	Swaziland	17,360	985,335
Netherlands	41,526	15,807,641	Sweden	449,964	8,911,296
New Zealand	268,680	3,662,265	Switzerland	41,290	7,275,467
Nicaragua	129,494	4,717,132	Syria	185,180	17,213,871
Niger	1,267,000	9,962,242	Taiwan	35,980	22,113,250
Nigeria	923,770	113,828,587	Tajikistan	143,100	6,102,854
Norway	324,220	4,438,547	Tanzania	945,090	31,270,820
Oman	212,460	2,446,645	Thailand	514,000	60,609,046
Pakistan	803,940	138,123,359	Togo	56,790	5,081,413
Palau	458	18,467	Tonga	748	109,082
Panama	78,200	2,778.526	Trinidad and Tobago	5,130	1,102,096
Papua New Guinea	461,690	4,705,126	Tunisia	163,610	9,513,603
Paraguay	406,750	5,434,095	Turkey	780,580	65,599,206
Peru	1,285,220	26,624,582	Turkmenistan	488,100	4,366,383
Philippines	300,000	79,345,812	Tuvalu	26	10,588
Poland	312,683	38,608,929	Uganda	236,040	22,804,973
Portugal	92,391	9,918,040	Ukraine	603,700	49,811,174
Qatar	11,437	723,542	United Arab Emirates	82,880	2,344,402
Romania	237,500	22,334,312	United Kingdom	244,820	59,113,439
Russia	17,075,200	146,393,569	United States	9,629,091	272,639,608
Rwanda	26,340	8,154,933	Uruguay	176,220	3,308,523
Saint Kitts and Nevis	269	42,838	Uzbekistan	447,400	24,102,473
Saint Lucia	620	154,020	Vanuatu	14,760	189,036
Saint Vincent and Grenadines	340	120,519	Vatican City	.44	850
Samoa	2,860	229,979	Venezuela	912,050	23,203,466
San Marino	60	25,061	Vietnam	329,560	77,311,210
São Tomé and Príncipe	960	154,878	Western Sahara	266,000	239,333
Saudi Arabia	1,960,582	21,504,613	Yemen	527,970	16,942,230
Senegal	196,190	10,051,930	Zambia	752,610	9,663,535
Serbia and Montenegro	102,350	11,206,847	Zimbabwe	390,580	11,163,160

Source: U.S. Census Bureau, International Data Base and *The World Factbook, 1998.*

Kingdoms and Monarchs of the World

Country	Monarch	Type of monarchy	Country	Monarch	Type of monarchy
Bahrain	Sheikh Hamad ibn 'Isa Al Khalifah	Traditional	Monaco	Prince Rainier III	Constitutional principality
Belgium	King Albert II	Constitutional	Morocco	King Muhammad VI	Constitutional
Bhutan	King Jigme Singye Wangchuk	Constitutional	Nepal	King Birendra Bir Bikram Shah Deva	Constitutional
Brunei	Sultan Haji Hassanal Bolkiah	Constitutional	The Netherlands	Queen Beatrix	Constitutional
Cambodia	King Norodom Sihanouk	Constitutional	Norway	King Harald V	Constitutional
Denmark	Queen Margrethe II	Constitutional	Oman	Sultan Qabus ibn Sa'id	Absolute
Japan	Emperor Akihito	Constitutional	Qatar	Emir Sheikh Hamad ibn Khalifah Al Thani	Traditional
Jordan	King Abdullah II	Constitutional			
Kuwait	Sheik Jaber al-Ahmad al-Sabah	Constitutional	Saudi Arabia	King Fahd bin 'Abdulaziz	Absolute
			Spain	King Juan Carlos I	Parliamentary
Lesotho	King Letsie III	Constitutional	Swaziland	King Mswati III	Near-absolute
Liechtenstein	Prince Hans Adam II	Constitutional	Sweden	King Carl XVI Gustaf	Constitutional
Luxembourg	Grand Duke Jean	Constitutional	Thailand	King Bhumibol Adulyadej	Constitutional
Malaysia	Salehuddin Abdul Aziz Shah	Constitutional	Tonga	King Taufa'ahau Tupou IV	Constitutional
			United Kingdom	Elizabeth II	Constitutional[1]

1. Also parliamentary democracy.

Territories, Colonies, and Dependencies

Source: The World Factbook, 1998.

The following is a list of dependencies—territories under the jurisdiction of another country.

Under Australian Jurisdiction (6)
Ashmore and Cartier Islands
Christmas Island
Cocos (Keeling) Islands
Coral Sea Islands
Heard Island and McDonald Islands
Norfolk Island

Under Danish Jurisdiction (2)
Faeroe Islands
Greenland

Under Dutch Jurisdiction (2)
Aruba
Netherlands Antilles

Under French Jurisdiction (16)
Bassas da India
Clipperton Island
Europa Island
French Guiana
French Polynesia
French Southern and Antarctic Lands
Glorioso Islands
Guadeloupe
Juan de Nova Island
Martinique
Mayotte
New Caledonia
Reunion
Saint Pierre and Miquelon
Tromelin Island
Wallis and Futuna

Under New Zealand Jurisdiction (3)
Cook Islands
Niue
Tokelau

Under Norwegian Jurisdiction (3)
Bouvet Island
Jan Mayen
Svalbard

Under Portuguese Jurisdiction until Dec. 20, 1999 (1)
Macau
A Chinese territory under Portuguese administration, Macau will be returned to Chinese administration on December 20, 1999.

Under UK Jurisdiction (15)
Anguilla
Bermuda
British Indian Ocean Territory
British Virgin Islands
Cayman Islands
Falkland Islands
Gibraltar
Guernsey
Jersey
Isle of Man
Montserrat
Pitcairn Islands
Saint Helena
South Georgia and the South Sandwich Islands
Turks and Caicos Islands

Under U.S. Jurisdiction (14)
American Samoa
Baker Island
Guam
Howland Island
Jarvis Island
Johnston Atoll
Kingman Reef
Midway Islands
Navassa Island
Northern Mariana Islands
Palmyra Atoll
Puerto Rico
Virgin Islands
Wake Island

Disputed Territories (6): Antarctica, Gaza Strip, Paracel Islands, Spratly Islands, West Bank, Western Sahara

Infant Mortality Rates and Life Expectancy at Birth, by Sex, for Selected Countries, 1999

Country	Infant deaths per 1,000 live births	Life expectancy at birth (years)	Country	Infant deaths per 1,000 live births	Life expectancy at birth (years)
North America			Netherlands	5.11	78.15
Canada	5.47	79.37	Norway	4.96	78.36
Mexico	24.62	72.00	Poland	12.76	73.06
United States	6.33	76.23	Portugal	6.73	75.88
Central and South America			Russia	23.00	65.12
Brazil	35.37	64.06	Slovakia	9.48	73.46
Chile	10.02	75.46	Spain	6.41	77.71
Costa Rica	12.89	76.04	Sweden	3.91	79.29
Ecuador	30.69	72.16	Switzerland	4.87	78.99
Guatemala	46.15	66.45	United Kingdom	5.78	77.37
Panama	23.35	74.66	**Asia**		
Peru	38.97	70.38	Bangladesh	69.68	60.60
Trinidad and Tobago	18.56	70.66	China	43.31	69.92
Uruguay	13.49	75.83	India	60.81	63.40
Venezuela	26.51	72.95	Iran	29.73	69.76
Europe			Israel	7.78	78.61
Albania	42.90	69.00	Japan	4.07	80.11
Austria	5.10	77.48	Pakistan	91.86	59.38
Belgium	6.17	77.53	South Korea	7.57	74.30
Cyprus	7.68	77.10	Sri Lanka	16.12	72.67
Czech Republic	6.67	74.35	Syria	36.42	68.09
Denmark	5.11	76.51	**Africa**		
Finland	3.80	77.32	Egypt	67.46	62.39
France	5.62	78.63	Kenya	59.07	47.02
Germany	5.14	77.17	South Africa	51.99	54.76
Greece	7.13	78.43	**Oceania**		
Hungary	9.46	71.18	Australia	5.11	80.14
Ireland	5.94	76.39	New Zealand	6.22	77.82
Italy	6.30	78.51			

Source: U.S. Census Bureau, International Data Base.

Prevalence of Contraceptive Use in Selected Countries[1]

Country	Year of data	No method	Any method	Pill	IUD	Condom	Sterilization Male	Sterilization Female	Other modern	Tradi-tional
Australia	1986	23.9%	76.1%	24.0%	4.9%	4.4%	10.4%	27.7%	0.8%	3.9%
Bangladesh	1993–1994	55.4	44.6	17.4	2.2	3.0	1.1	8.1	4.5	8.4
Brazil	1996	23.3	76.7	20.7	1.1	4.4	2.6	40.1	1.3	6.4
Canada	1984	26.9	73.1	11.0	5.8	7.9	12.9	30.6	1.5	3.6
China	1992	23.1	76.9	2.7	30.3	2.0	8.8	32.1	n.a.	1.0
Colombia	1995	27.8	72.2	12.9	11.1	4.3	0.7	25.7	4.6	12.9
Costa Rica	1993	25.0	75.0	18.0	9.0	16.0	1.0	20.0	1.0	10.0
Denmark	1988	22.0	78.0	26.0	11.0	22.0	5.0	5.0	3.0	7.0
Egypt	1995	52.1	47.9	10.4	30.0	1.4	n.a.	1.1	2.5	2.4
El Salvador	1993	46.7	53.3	8.7	2.1	2.1	n.a.	31.5	4.0	5.0
Ethiopia	1990	95.7	4.3	1.9	0.3	0.1	(2)	0.2	(2)	1.7
France	1994	24.9	75.1	36.9	19.6	5.2	0.3	4.6	1.1	7.5
India	1992–1993	59.3	40.7	1.2	1.9	2.4	3.5	27.4	(2)	4.3
Indonesia	1994	45.3	54.7	17.1	10.3	0.9	0.7	3.1	20.1	2.7
Iran	1992	35.0	65.0	23.0	7.0	6.0	1.0	8.0	(2)	20.0
Jamaica	1993	38.0	62.0	21.5	1.0	16.9	n.a.	12.5	6.5	3.6
Japan	1992	36.0	64.0	n.a.	n.a.	n.a.	n.a.	n.a.	n.a.	n.a.
Jordan	1990	65.1	34.9	4.6	15.3	0.8	(2)	5.6	0.6	8.0
Kenya	1993	67.0	33.0	9.6	4.3	0.9	n.a.	5.6	7.2	5.4
Mexico	1987	47.3	52.7	9.7	10.2	1.9	0.8	18.6	3.4	8.1
New Zealand	1976	30.5	69.5	28.6	4.4	8.0	9.1	11.4	n.a.	9.8
Nigeria	1990	94.0	6.0	1.2	0.8	0.4	n.a.	0.3	0.8	2.5
Pakistan	1990–1991	88.2	11.8	0.7	1.3	2.7	(2)	3.5	0.8	2.8
Peru	1996	35.8	64.2	6.2	12.0	4.4	0.2	9.5	9.0	22.9
Romania	1993	42.7	57.3	3.2	4.3	4.0	n.a.	1.4	1.0	43.4
Russia	1994	33.2	66.8	4.0	33.1	n.a.	n.a.	n.a.	11.5	18.2
South Africa	1988	50.3	49.7	13.2	5.3	0.7	1.4	8.0	19.8	1.2
South Korea	1991	21.0	79.0	3.0	9.0	10.0	12.0	35.0	(2)	10.0
Switzerland	1994–1995	18.1	81.9	34.1	6.0	14.2	8.3	13.7	1.2	4.4
Thailand	1987	34.5	65.5	18.6	6.9	1.1	5.7	22.8	8.5	1.9
Turkey	1993	37.4	62.6	4.9	18.8	6.6	0.0	2.9	1.3	28.1
United Kingdom	1989	28.0	72.0	25.0	6.0	16.0	12.0	11.0	1.0	7.0
United States	1990	29.3	70.7	14.5	1.0	7.9	13.6	23.7	4.6	3.3
Uzbekistan	1996	44.4	55.6	1.7	45.8	1.7	n.a.	n.a.	2.1	4.3
Venezuela	1977	39.7	60.3	18.8	10.5	5.9	0.1	9.4	5.0	10.7

1. Data refer to currently married women, 15–49. 2. Less than 0.5 percent. n.a. = not available. *Source: World Population Profile: 1998,* U.S. Census Bureau.

Legal Abortions in Selected Countries, 1985–1996

Country	1985	1989	1990	1991	1992	1993	1994	1995	1996
Bulgaria	132,041	132,021	144,644	—	132,891	107,416	97,567	97,023	—
Canada	60,956	70,705	71,092	70,277	70,408	72,434	71,630	70,549	—
Cuba	138,671	151,146	147,530	124,059	—	86,906	89,421	83,963	—
Denmark	19,919	21,456	20,589	19,729	18,833	18,607	17,598	17,720	—
Finland	13,832	12,658	12,232	11,747	11,071	10,342	10,013	9,884	10,437
France	173,335	161,646	161,129	162,902	158,940	157,886	—	—	—
Germany[1]	—	149,196	145,267	124,377	118,609	111,236	103,586	97,937	—
Greece	180	2,292	1,216	11,109	11,977	12,289	—	—	—
Hungary	81,970	90,508	90,394	89,931	87,065	75,258	74,491	76,957	76,600
Iceland	705	670	714	658	743	827	775	807	858
India	583,704	582,161	596,345	581,215	—	—	—	—	—
Israel	18,406	15,216	15,509	15,767	18,444	17,164	16,903	—	—
Italy	210,192	166,290	161,285	157,262	150,271	145,229	135,956	134,137	—
Japan	550,127	466,876	456,797	436,299	413,032	386,807	364,350	343,024	338,867
Netherlands	17,300	17,996	18,384	19,568	19,422	19,804	20,811	20,932	22,441
New Zealand	7,130	10,200	11,173	11,594	11,460	—	—	—	—
Norway	14,599	16,208	15,551	15,528	15,164	14,909	—	13,672	—
Poland	135,564	80,127	59,417	30,878	11,640	1,208	874	559	491
Russia	—	4,427,713	4,103,425	3,608,412	3,436,695	3,243,957	2,481,493	2,766,362	—
Singapore	23,512	20,619	18,654	17,798	17,073	16,476	15,690	14,504	14,362
Sweden	30,838	37,920	37,489	35,788	34,849	34,169	32,293	—	32,117
United Kingdom	180,983	180,622	184,092	178,416	171,260	173,686	169,964	167,297	—
United States	1,588,600	1,396,658	1,429,577	1,388,937	1,359,145	—	—	1,210,883	—

1. Figures for Germany represent those available after the unification of the Federal Republic of Germany and the German Democratic Republic in October 1990. NOTE: Data latest available. *Source:* United Nations, *Demographic Yearbook, 1997.*

Crude Marriage Rates for Selected Countries
(per 1,000 population)

Country	1998	1997	1990	Country	1998	1997	1990	Country	1998	1997	1990
Australia	—	5.8	6.9	Hungary	4.5	4.6	6.4	Portugal	6.7	6.5	7.3
Austria	4.8	5.1	5.8	Ireland	—	4.3	5.0	Romania	6.4	6.5	8.3
Belgium	4.4	4.7	6.6	Israel	—	5.6	7.0	Russia	5.8	6.3	8.9
Bulgaria	4.3	4.1	6.7	Italy	—	4.8	5.4	Sweden	3.5	3.7	4.7
Czech Republic[1]	5.4	5.6	8.4	Japan	6.3	6.2	5.8	Switzerland	—	5.3	6.9
Denmark	6.5	6.4	6.1	Luxembourg	—	4.8	6.2	United Kingdom	—	—	6.8
Finland	4.5	4.6	4.8	Netherlands	—	5.5	6.4	United States	—	8.9	9.8
France	4.8	4.8	5.1	New Zealand	—	5.3	7.0	Yugoslavia[3]	5.0	5.3	6.2
Germany[2]	5.1	5.2	6.5	Norway	—	—	5.2				
Greece	5.5	5.7	5.8	Poland	5.4	5.3	6.7				

1. Data prior to 1993 pertain to the former Czechoslovakia. 2. All data pertaining to Germany prior to 1990 are for West Germany. 3. Beginning January 1992, data refer to the Federal Republic of Yugoslavia. Prior to that date, data refer to the Socialist Federal Republic of Yugoslavia. *Source:* United Nations, *Monthly Bulletin of Statistics, May 1999.*

Percentage of Divorces in Selected Countries

Country	Divorces (as % of marriages) 1996	Country	Divorces (as % of marriages) 1996	Country	Divorces (as % of marriages) 1996	Country	Divorces (as % of marriages) 1996
Belarus	68%	United States	49	Denmark	35	Spain	17
Russian Federation	65	Hungary	46	Slovakia	34	Azerbaijan	15
Sweden	64	Canada	45	Bulgaria	28	Croatia	15
Latvia	63	Norway	43	Israel	26	Cyprus	13
Ukraine	63	France	43	Slovenia	26	Tajikistan	13
Czech Republic	61	Germany	41	Kyrgyzstan	25	Georgia	12
Belgium	56	Netherlands	41	Romania	24	Italy	12
Finland	56	Switzerland	40	Portugal	21	Uzbekistan	12
Lithuania	55	Iceland	39	Poland	19	Albania	7
United Kingdom	53	Kazakhstan	39	Armenia	18	Turkey	6
Moldova	52	Luxembourg	39	Greece	18	Macedonia	5
		Austria	38	Turkmenistan	18		

Communications in Selected Countries

Country	Main telephone lines per 1,000 people 1996	Televisions per 1,000 people 1996	Personal computers per 1,000 people 1996	Internet hosts per 1,000 people 1998	Number of daily newspapers 1996
Argentina	174	345[1]	34.1	1.75	181
Australia	519	666	311.3	42.70	65
Bulgaria	313	361	29.8[1]	0.81	17
Chile	156	277	45.1	2.07	52
China	45	252	3.0	0.00	39
Colombia	118	185	23.3	0.52	37
Egypt	50	126[1]	5.8	0.05	17
France	564	598[1]	150.7	7.87	117
Greece	509	442[1]	35.3	3.89	156
India	15	64	1.5	0.01	—
Indonesia	21	232	4.8	0.10	69
Israel	441	300[1]	116.3	14.20	34
Japan	489	700	128.0	11.00	122
Mexico	95	193[1]	29.0	0.92	295
Norway	555	569	284.5	71.80	83
Russian Federation	175	386	23.7	1.05	285
Saudi Arabia	106	263[1]	37.2	0.01	13
South Africa	100	123	37.7	3.82	17
Switzerland	640	493	408.5	27.90	88
Thailand	70	167	16.7	0.03	30
Turkey	224	309	13.8	0.54	57
Uganda	2	26	0.5	0.01	2
United Kingdom	528	612[1]	192.6	23.30	99
United States	640	806[1]	362.4	88.90	1,520
Vietnam	16	180	3.3	—	10
Zimbabwe	15	29[1]	6.7	0.07	2

1. Data refer to 1995. *Source: Human Development Report, 1999,* United Nations.

Gross Domestic Product Per Capita, 1997

More Than $15,000
Andorra
Aruba
Australia
Austria
Bahamas, The
Belgium
Bermuda
Brunei
Canada
Cayman Islands
Denmark
Faroe Islands
Finland
France
Germany
Gibraltar
Greenland
Guam
Hong Kong
Iceland
Ireland
Israel
Italy
Japan
Kuwait
Liechtenstein
Luxembourg
Macau
Monaco
Netherlands
New Zealand
Norway
Portugal
Qatar
San Marino
Singapore
Spain
Sweden
Switzerland
United Arab Emirates
United Kingdom
United States

$10,001 to $15,000
Bahrain
Barbados
British Virgin Islands
Chile
Cyprus
Czech Republic
Greece
Guam
Malaysia
Malta
Man, Isle of
Mauritius
Netherlands Antilles

Northern Mariana Islands
Saudi Arabia
St. Pierre and Miquelon
South Korea
Taiwan
Trinidad and Tobago
Virgin Islands (U.S.)

$3,001 to $10,000
Algeria
Anguilla
Antigua and Barbuda
Argentina
Belarus
Botswana
Brazil
Bulgaria
Colombia
Cook Islands
Costa Rica
Croatia
Dominican Republic
Ecuador
Egypt
Estonia
Fiji
French Guiana
French Polynesia
Gabon
Grenada
Guadeloupe
Guatemala
Hungary
Indonesia
Iran
Jamaica
Jordan
Latvia
Lebanon
Libya
Lithuania
Martinique
Mexico
Montserrat
Morocco
Namibia
Nauru
New Caledonia
Oman
Palau
Panama
Paraguay
Peru
Philippines
Poland
Puerto Rico
Reunion
Romania

Russia
St. Kitts and Nevis
St. Lucia
Seychelles
Slovakia
Slovenia
South Africa
Sri Lanka
Suriname
Swaziland
Syria
Thailand
Tunisia
Turkey
Turks and Caicos Islands
Uruguay
Venezuela

$1,000 to $3,000
Albania
American Samoa
Armenia
Azerbaijan
Bangladesh
Belize
Benin
Bolivia
Bosnia and Herzegovina
Burma
Cameroon
Cape Verde
Congo, Republic of
Côte d'Ivoire
Cuba
Djibouti
Dominica
El Salvador
Equatorial Guinea
Gaza Strip
Georgia
Ghana
Guinea
Guyana
Haiti
Honduras
India
Iraq
Kazakhstan
Kenya
Kyrgyzstan
Laos
Lesotho
Maldives
Marshall Islands
Mauritania
Micronesia
Moldova
Mongolia

Nepal
Nicaragua
Nigeria
Nive
Pakistan
Papua New Guinea
St. Vincent and Grenadines
Samoa
Senegal
Serbia and Montenegro
Solomon Islands
Togo
Tonga
Turkmenistan
Uganda
Ukraine
Uzbekistan
Vanuatu
Vietnam
Wallis and Futuna Islands
West Bank
Yemen
Zimbabwe

Less than $1,000
Afghanistan
Angola
Bhutan
Burkina Faso
Burundi
Cambodia
Central African Republic
Chad
Comoros
Congo, Dem. Republic of
Eritrea
Ethiopia
Gambia, The
Guinea-Bissau
Kiribati
Liberia
Macedonia
Madagascar
Malawi
Mali
Mayotte
Mozambique
Niger
North Korea
Rwanda
São Tomé and Príncipe
Sierra Leone
Somalia
Sudan
Tajikistan
Tanzania
Tokelau
Tuvalu
Zambia

Source: CIA Handbook of International Economic Statistics.

Corruption Survey Labels Denmark the World's Least Corrupt

According to the 1998 annual survey by Transparency International, a Berlin-based organization that ranks countries according to their governments' propensity to accept bribes, Denmark is the least corrupt country in the world. Next on the list of most honest countries are Finland, Sweden, New Zealand, Iceland, Canada, Singapore, the Netherlands, Norway, and Switzerland. The United States ranked 17th. Cameroon was ranked the most corrupt country, followed by Paraguay, Honduras, Tanzania, Nigeria, Indonesia, Colombia, Venezuela, Ecuador, and Russia.

Euro Conversion Rates

On Jan. 1, 1999, eleven European countries began using the euro electronically, as a denomination for debt issues and bank accounts. The actual notes and coins will not enter circulation until Jan. 2002, completely replacing local currencies by July 1, 2002. The conversion rates for the participating currencies were fixed as follows.

13.76	Austrian schillings		0.79	Irish punts
40.34	Belgian francs		1,936.27	Italian lire
2.20	Dutch guilders		40.34	Luxembourg francs
5.95	Finnish markkas		200.48	Portuguese escudos
6.56	French francs		166.39	Spanish pesetas
1.96	German marks			

Selected Foreign Currencies

Country	Currency	Country	Currency	Country	Currency
Afghanistan	Afghani	Haiti	Gourde	Oman	Rials Omani
Albania	Lek	Honduras	Lempira	Pakistan	Rupee
Algeria	Algerian Dinar	Hungary	Forint	Panama	Balboa
Antigua and Barbuda	E. Caribbean Dollar[1]	Iceland	Krona	Papua New Guinea	Kina
		India	Rupee		
Argentina	Peso	Indonesia	Rupiah	Paraguay	Guarani
Armenia	Dram	Iran	Rial	Philippines	Peso
Aruba	Aruban Florin	Iraq	Dinar	Poland	Zloty
Australia	Australian Dollar	Ireland[2]	Irish Pound	Portugal[2]	Escudo
Austria[2]	Schilling	Israel	New Shekel	Qatar	Riyal
Bahamas, The	Bahamanian Dollar	Italy[2]	Lira	Russia	Ruble
		Jamaica	Jamaica Dollar	Rwanda	Rwanda Franc
Bangladesh	Taka	Japan	Yen	Saudi Arabia	Riyal
Barbados	Barbados Dollar	Jordan	Dinar	Seychelles	Rupee
Belgium[2]	Franc	Kazakhstan	Tenge	Sierra Leone	Leone
Belize	Belize Dollar	Kenya	Kenya Shilling	Singapore	Singapore Dollar
Benin	Cfa Franc[3]	Korea, South	Won	Slovakia	Koruna
Bhutan	Ngultrum	Kuwait	Dinar	Slovenia	Tolar
Botswana	Pula	Kyrgyzstan	Soms	Solomon Islands	Solomon Isl. Dollar
Brazil	Real	Laos	Kip		
Bulgaria	Lev	Latvia	Lats	South Africa	Rand
Burma	Kyat	Lebanon	Lebanese Pound	Spain[2]	Peseta
Cambodia	Riels	Lesotho	Loti	Sri Lanka	Rupee
Canada	Canadian Dollar	Liberia	Liberian Dollar	Suriname	Guilder
Cape Verde	Escudo	Libya	Libyan Dinar	Swaziland	Langeni
Chile	Peso	Lithuania	Litas	Sweden	Krona
China	Yuan	Luxembourg[2]	Franc	Switzerland	Swiss Franc
Comoros	Comorian Franc	Macedonia	Denar	Syria	Syrian Pound
Costa Rica	Colon	Madagascar	Malagasy Franc	Tanzania	Tanzania Shilling
Croatia	Kuna	Malaysia	Ringgit	Thailand	Baht
Cyprus	Cyprus Pound	Maldives	Rufiyaa	Tonga	Pa'Anga
Czech Republic	Koruna	Malta	Maltese Liri	Trinidad and Tobago	Tt Dollar
Denmark	Krone	Mauritania	Ouguiyas		
Djibouti	Djibouti Franc	Mauritius	Rupee	Tunisia	Dinar
Dominican Republic	Peso	Mexico	New Peso	Turkey	Lira
		Moldova	Leu	Uganda	Uganda Shilling
Ecuador	Sucre	Mongolia	Tugrik	Ukraine	Hryvnia
Egypt	Egyptian Pound	Morocco	Dirham	United Arab Emirates	Dirham
El Salvador	Colon	Mozambique	Metical		
Estonia	Kroon	Namibia	Namibia Dollar	United Kingdom	Pound Sterling
Ethiopia	Birr	Nepal	Rupee	Uruguay	Peso
Fiji	Fiji Dollar	Netherlands[2]	Guilder	Vanuatu	Vatu
Finland[2]	Markka	Netherlands Antilles	Guilder	Venezuela	Venezuela
France[2]	Franc			Yemen	Rial
Germany[2]	Deutsche Mark	New Zealand	New Zealand Dollar	Zambia	Kwacha
Greece	Drachma			Zimbabwe	Zimbabwe Dollar
Guatemala	Quetzal	Nicaragua	Cordoba		
Guyana	Guyana Dollar	Norway	Krone		

1. The E. Caribbean dollar is also the currency used in Dominica, Grenada, Saint Kitts and Nevis, Saint Lucia, and Saint Vincent and the Grenadines. 2. As of 1/1/99, country also began using the euro. 3. The Cfa franc (Communaute Financiere Africaine) is also the currency used in Burkina Faso, Cameroon, Central African Republic, Chad, Rep. of Congo, Côte d'Ivoire, Equatorial Guinea, Gabon, Mali, Niger, Senegal, and Togo. *Source: Statistical Abstract of the United States, 1998.*

The Death Penalty Worldwide

**Death Penalty
Outlawed**
Andorra
Angola
Australia
Austria
Azerbaijan
Belgium
Bulgaria
Oambodia
Canada
Cape Verde
Colombia
Costa Rica
Croatia
Czech Republic
Denmark
Dominican Republic
Ecuador
Estonia
Finland
France
Georgia
Germany
Greece
Guinea-Bissau
Haiti
Honduras
Hungary
Iceland
Ireland
Italy
Kiribati
Liechtenstein
Lithuania
Luxembourg
Macedonia (former Yugoslav Republic)
Marshall Islands
Maurltlus
Micronesia (Federated States)
Moldova
Monaco
Mozambique
Namibia
Nepal
Netherlands
New Zealand
Nicaragua
Norway
Palau
Panama
Paraguay

Poland
Portugal
Romania
San Marino
São Tomé and Príncipe
Slovakia
Slovenia
Solomon Islands
South Africa
Spain
Sweden
Switzerland
Tuvalu
Uruguay
Vanuatu
Vatican City State
Venezuela

**Death Penalty
Permitted in
Exceptional Cases[1]**
Argentina
Bolivia
Bosnia-Herzegovina
Brazil
Cook Islands
Cyprus
El Salvador
Fiji
Israel
Malta
Mexico
Peru
Seychelles
United Kingdom

**De Facto Ban
on Death Penalty[2]**
Albania
Bermuda
Bhutan
Brunei Darussalam
Central African Republic
Congo (Republic)
Côte d'Ivoire
Djibouti
Gambia
Grenada
Madagascar
Maldives
Mali
Nauru

Niger
Papua New Guinea
Senegal
Sri Lanka
Suriname
Togo
Tonga
Western Samoa

**Death Penalty
Permitted**
Afghanistan
Algeria
Antigua and Barbuda
Armenia
Bahamas
Bahrain
Bangladesh
Barbados
Belarus
Belize
Benin
Botswana
Burkina Faso
Burundi
Cameroon
Chad
Chile
China (People's Republic)
Comoros
Congo (Democratic Republic)
Cuba
Dominica
Egypt
Equatorial Guinea
Eritrea
Ethiopia
Gabon
Ghana
Guatemala
Guinea
Guyana
India
Indonesia
Iran
Iraq
Jamaica
Japan
Jordan
Kazakhstan
Kenya
Korea, North

Korea, South
Kuwait
Kyrgyzstan
Laos
Latvia
Lebanon
Lesotho
Liberia
Libya
Malawi
Malaysia
Mauritania
Mongolia
Morocco
Myanmar
Nigeria
Oman
Pakistan
Palestinian Authority
Philippines
Qatar
Russian Federation
Rwanda
St. Kitts and Nevis
St. Lucia
St. Vincent and the Grenadines
Saudi Arabia
Sierra Leone
Singapore
Somalia
Sudan
Swaziland
Syria
Taiwan (Republic of China)
Tajikistan
Tanzania
Thailand
Trinidad and Tobago
Tunisia
Turkey
Turkmenistan
Uganda
Ukraine
United Arab Emirates
United States of America
Uzbekistan
Vietnam
Yemen
Yugoslavia (Federal Republic)
Zambia
Zimbabwe

NOTE: There were 1,625 executions in 1998. Of those, 80% were in China (1,067), Congo (100), the United States (68), and Iran (66).1. Exceptional crimes include some committed under military law or crimes commited in wartime. 2. Death penalty is sanctioned by law but has not been the practice for 10 or more years. *Source:* Amnesty International, Feb. 1999.

Countries with Nuclear Weapons Capability

Acknowledged Nuclear Weapons Capability:

Britain	France	Pakistan	United States
China	India	Russia	

Unacknowledged Nuclear Weapons Capability:
Israel

Seeking Nuclear Weapons Capability:

Iran	Iraq

Abandoned Nuclear Weapons Development:

North Korea—An accord was reached with the North Korean government in 1994 to freeze and dismantle nuclear weapons development.

South Africa—Constructed but then voluntarily dismantled 6 uranium bombs.

Belarus, Kazakhstan, Ukraine—When Soviet Union broke up, these former states possessed nuclear warheads that they have since given up.

Source: U.S. State Department, *Time Magazine.*

World Military Expenditures

The total military spending of all countries in the world fell in 1995 for the eighth consecutive year to $864 billion, 34% below the all-time peak of $1.36 trillion in 1987. Military spending by the United States in 1995 was $278 billion—by far the largest percentage of the world's share—32%. The United States spent 3.7 times that of second-ranked Russia. China, ranked third (though roughly estimated), increased its spending by $5 billion, while Japan (fourth-ranked) declined.

Top 15 Countries with Highest Military Expenditures

Rank	Country	In millions of dollars	Rank	Country	In millions of dollars	Rank	Country	In millions of dollars
1.	United States	$277,800	6.	Germany	$41,160	11.	China–Taiwan	$13,140
2.	Russia	76,000	7.	United Kingdom	33,400	12.	Brazil	10,900
3.	China–Mainland	63,510	8.	Italy	19,380	13.	Canada	9,077
4.	Japan	50,240	9.	Saudi Arabia	17,210	14.	Israel	8,734
5.	France	47,770	10.	Korea, South	14,410	15.	Spain	8,652

Source: U.S. Arms Control and Disarmament Agency, *World Military Expenditures and Arms Transfers, 1995.*

Military Expenditures Ranked by Percentage of Country's Gross National Product, 1995

Rank	Country	Percentage	Rank	Country	Percentage	Rank	Country	Percentage
1.	Bosnia and Herzegovina	n.a.	45.	Lebanon	3.7%	90.	South Africa	2.2%
2.	Korea, North	28.6%	46.	Korea, South	3.4	91.	Ethiopia	2.2
3.	Oman	16.7	47.	Macedonia	3.3	92.	Nicaragua	2.2
4.	Serbia and Montenegro	n.a.	48.	Mauritania	3.2	93.	Moldova	2.1
			49.	Algeria	3.2	94.	Namibia	2.1
5.	Yemen	n.a.	50.	France	3.1	95.	Netherlands	2.0
6.	Saudi Arabia	13.5	51.	Cambodia	3.1	96.	Finland	2.0
7.	Kuwait	11.6	52.	Chad	3.0	97.	Tunisia	2.0
8.	Iraq	n.a.	53.	Angola	3.0	98.	Cameroon	n.a.
9.	Russia	11.4	54.	Malaysia	3.0	99.	Lesotho	1.9
10.	Croatia	10.5	55.	United Kingdom	3.0	100.	Germany	1.9
11.	Israel	9.6	56.	Liberia	n.a.	101.	Denmark	1.8
12.	Jordan	7.7	57.	Slovakia	3.0	102.	Tanzania	1.8
13.	Syria	7.2	58.	Suriname	3.0	103.	Indonesia	1.8
14.	Pakistan	6.1	59.	Burkina Faso	2.9	104.	Italy	1.8
15.	Sierra Leone	6.1	60.	Haiti	2.9	105.	Mali	1.8
16.	Sudan	n.a.	61.	Congo	2.9	106.	Fiji	1.7
17.	Libya	6.0	62.	Ukraine	2.9	107.	Peru	1.7
18.	Brunei	6.0	63.	Bulgaria	2.8	108.	Bangladesh	1.7
19.	Cyprus	5.8	64.	Guinea-Bissau	2.8	109.	Argentina	1.7
20.	Egypt	5.7	65.	Zambia	2.8	110.	Trinidad & Tobago	1.7
21.	Greece	5.5	66.	Azerbaijan	2.8			
22.	Mozambique	5.4	67.	Sweden	2.8	111.	Turkmenistan	1.7
23.	Bahrain	5.4	68.	Norway	2.7	112.	Canada	1.7
24.	Botswana	5.3	69.	Iran	2.6	113.	Brazil	1.7
25.	Rwanda	5.2	70.	Swaziland	2.6	114.	Belgium	1.6
26.	China-Taiwan	5.0	71.	Colombia	2.6	115.	Senegal	1.6
27.	United Arab Emirates	4.8	72.	Portugal	2.6	116.	Equatorial Guinea	1.6
			73.	Gabon	2.6			
28.	Singapore	4.7	74.	Vietnam	2.5	117.	Belize	1.6
29.	Gambia, The	4.6	75.	Romania	2.5	118.	Malawi	1.6
30.	Sri Lanka	4.6	76.	Central African Republic	n.a.	119.	Switzerland	1.6
31.	Djibouti	4.4				120.	Spain	1.6
32.	Qatar	4.4	77.	Thailand	2.5	121.	Cuba	1.5
33.	Burundi	4.4	78.	Australia	2.5	122.	Slovenia	1.5
34.	Morocco	4.3	79.	Georgia	2.4	123.	Philippines	1.5
35.	Laos	4.1	80.	India	2.4	124.	Hungary	1.5
36.	Zimbabwe	4.0	81.	Uruguay	2.4	125.	Guinea	1.5
37.	Turkey	4.0	82.	Mongolia	2.4	126.	Papua New Guinea	1.4
38.	Burma	3.9	83.	Czech Republic	2.3			
39.	United States	3.8	84.	Poland	2.3	127.	Ghana	1.4
40.	Uzbekistan	3.8	85.	Uganda	2.3	128.	Honduras	1.4
41.	Chile	3.8	86.	China-Mainland	2.3	129.	Paraguay	1.4
42.	Tajikistan	3.7	87.	Kenya	2.3	130.	Panama	1.4
43.	Afghanistan	n.a.	88.	Togo	2.3	131.	Dominican Republic	1.3
44.	Ecuador	3.7	89.	Bolivia	2.3	132.	Guatemala	1.3

Rank	Country	Percentage	Rank	Country	Percentage	Rank	Country	Percentage
133.	New Zealand	1.3%	145.	Kyrgyzstan	n.a.	157.	Nigeria	n.a.
134.	Ireland	1.3	146.	Mexico	1.0%	158.	São Tomé &	n.a.
135.	Guyana	1.3	147.	Japan	1.0		Príncipe	
136.	Benin	1.2	148.	Nepal	.9	159.	Luxembourg	.7%
137.	Niger	1.1	149.	Kazakhstan	.9	160.	Costa Rica	.6
138.	Venezuela	1.1	150.	Armenia	.9	161.	Lithuania	.5
139.	Malta	1.1	151.	Madagascar	.9	162.	Bhutan	n.a.
140.	Albania	1.1	152.	Austria	.9	163.	Mauritius	.3
141.	Ivory Coast	1.1	153.	Latvia	.9	164.	Zaire	.3
142.	Estonia	1.1	154.	Jamaica	.8	165.	Somalia	n.a.
143.	El Salvador	1.1	155.	Barbados	.8	166.	Iceland	0
144.	Cape Verde	1.0	156.	Belarus	.8	167.	Eritrea	—

Source: U.S. Arms Control and Disarmament Agency, *World Military Expenditures and Arms Transfers, 1995.*

Worldwide Armed Conflicts

(1990–1996)

An armed conflict is defined as "major" when at least 1,000 battle-related deaths have occurred since the beginning of the conflict. Major armed conflicts are divided into two categories: war (more than 1,000 battle-related deaths during the year in question) and intermediate (less than 1,000 battle-related deaths in a given year). All regions of the world have witnessed at least one major armed conflict during the 1990s.

	1990	1991	1992	1993	1994	1995	1996
Europe / Total	1	2	4	6	5	3	2
War	0	1	2	4	1	2	1
Intermediate	1	1	2	2	4	1	1
Middle East / Total	5	7	5	6	6	6	6
War	1	3	1	1	2	1	1
Intermediate	4	4	4	4	4	5	5
Asia / Total	15	12	13	11	11	12	11
War	6	7	7	4	2	2	2
Intermediate	2	2	0	3	5	4	3
Africa / Total	11	11	7	7	7	6	6
War	9	9	7	4	2	2	3
Intermediate	2	2	0	3	5	4	3
Americas / Total	4	4	3	3	3	3	3
War	3	1	3	2	0	0	0
Intermediate	1	3	0	1	3	3	3

Source: International Federation of Red Cross and Red Crescent Societies and the Department of Peace and Conflict Research, Uppsala University, Sweden. Reprinted with permission.

Worldwide Refugees, 1997

Group or Country of Origin	Number	Group or Country of Origin	Number	Group or Country of Origin	Number
Palestinians	3,743,000*	Burma	215,000*	Iran	35,000
Afghanistan	2,622,000*	Armenia	188,000*	Tajikistan	32,000*
Bosnia and Herzegovina	557,000*	Congo/Zaire	132,000	Guatemala	30,000
Iraq	526,000*	China (Tibet)	128,000	Nicaragua	19,000
Somalia	486,000*	Bhutan	113,000*	Mali	16,000
Liberia	475,000*	Sri Lanka	100,000*	Laos	14,000
Sudan	353,000	Western Sahara	86,000*	India	13,000*
Croatia	335,000*	Cambodia	77,000	Chad	12,000
Eritrea	323,000*	Mauritania	55,000	Ghana	12,000
Sierra Leone	297,100*	Ethiopia	48,000*	Georgia	11,000
Vietnam	281,000	Uzbekistan	46,000	Turkey	11,000
Burundi	248,000*	Rwanda	43,000	Niger	10,000*
Angola	223,000*	Bangladesh	40,000	Uganda	10,000
Azerbaijan	218,000*	Congo (Brazzaville)	40,000		

* Sources vary widely in number reported. *Source:* U.S. Committee for Refugees. Reprinted with permission.

State-Sponsored Terrorism

The U.S. State Department has labeled the following countries state sponsors of international terrorism: Cuba, Iran, Iraq, Libya, North Korea, Sudan, and Syria.

Major sources: Questionnaires to the individual countries; C.I.A. *World Factbook 1999;* Center for International Research, Bureau of the Census; *The Columbia Encyclopedia; The World Book Encyclopedia; Encyclopedia Britannica;* and various newspapers. (information as of Sept. 23, 1999)

Definitions: Gross domestic product (GDP): The value of all goods and services produced domestically; Purchasing power parity (PPP): The PPP method involves the use of standardized international dollar price weights, which are applied to the GDP produced in a given economy. The data derived from the PPP method provide a better comparison of economic well-being between countries than conversions at official currency exchange rates. Literacy rates and population figures are supplied by the U.S. Census Bureau.

Afghanistan

ISLAMIC EMIRATE OF AFGHANISTAN

National name: Dowlat-e Eslami-ye Afghanestan
Head of State: Mullah Mohammad Omar (1996)
Area: 250,000 sq. mi. (647,500 sq. km)
Population (1999 est.): 25,824,882 (average annual rate of natural increase: 2.49%); birth rate: 41.9/1000; infant mortality rate: 140.6/1000; density per sq. mi.: 103
Capital: Kabul. **Largest cities (1993 est.):** Kabul, 1,424,400; Kandahar, 225,500; Herat, 177,300; Mazare-Sharif, 131,000. **Monetary unit:** Afghani.
Languages: Pushtu, Dari Persian, other Turkic and minor languages. **Ethnicity/race:** Pashtun 38%, Tajik 25%, Uzbek 6%, Hazara 19%, minor ethnic groups (Chahar Aimaks, Turkmen, Baloch, and others).
Religion: Islam (Sunni, 84%; Shi'ite, 15%); other 1%).
Literacy rate: 29%
Economic summary: GDP/PPP (1997 est.): $19.3 billion; $800 per capita. **Real growth rate:** n.a. **Inflation:** 240% (1996 est.). **Arable land:** 12%. **Products:** wheat, fruit, nuts, karakul pelts, wool, mutton. **Labor force:** 7.1 million; labor force in industry, 10.2%; agriculture and animal husbandry, 67.8%; commerce, 5%; construction, 6.3%; services and other, 10.7%. **Unemployment:** 8% (1995 est.). **Industry:** textiles, soap, furniture, shoes, fertilizer, cement, handwoven carpets, natural gas, oil, coal, copper. **Natural resources:** natural gas, petroleum, coal, copper, talc, barites, sulfur, lead, zinc, iron ore, salt, precious and semi-precious stones.
Exports: $80 million (1996 est.): fruits and nuts, handwoven carpets, wool, cotton, hides and pelts, precious and semi-precious gems. **Imports:** $150 million (1996 est.): food and petroleum products, most consumer goods. **Major trading partners:** F.S.U., Pakistan, Iran, Japan, Singapore, India, U.K., Belgium, Luxembourg, Czechoslovakia, South Korea, Germany.

Geography Afghanistan, approximately the size of Texas, is bordered on the north by Turkmenistan, Uzbekistan, and Tajikistan, on the extreme northeast by China, on the east and south by Pakistan, and by Iran in the west. The country is split east to west by the Hindu Kush mountain range, rising in the east to heights of 24,000 feet (7,315 m). With the exception of the southwest, most of the country is covered by high snow-capped mountains and is traversed by deep valleys.

Government On Sept. 27, 1996, the ruling members of the Afghan government were displaced by members of the Islamic Taliban movement, who have declared themselves the legitimate government of Afghanistan. The U.N. has deferred a decision on the question of legitimacy. Mullah Mohammad Omar, known as the Emir al-Momineen (Leader of the Faithful) has served as the de facto leader since the Taliban came to power in 1996.

History Darius I and Alexander the Great were the first to use Afghanistan as the gateway to India. Islamic conquerors arrived in the 7th century, and Genghis Khan and Tamerlane followed in the 13th and 14th centuries.

In the 19th century, Afghanistan became a battleground in the rivalry of imperial Britain and Czarist Russia for control of Central Asia. Three Anglo-Afghan Wars (1839–42, 1878–80, and 1919) ended inconclusively. In 1893 Britain established an unofficial border, the Durand Line, separating Afghanistan from British India, and London granted full independence in 1919. Emir Amanullah founded an Afghan monarchy in 1926.

During the cold war, King Mohammed Zahir Shah developed close ties with the Soviet Union, accepting extensive economic assistance from Moscow. He was overthrown in 1973 by his cousin Mohammed Daoud, who was himself ousted in a 1978 coup by Noor Taraki. Taraki and his successor, Babrak Karmal, attempted to create a Marxist state. However, the new leadership was criticized by armed insurgents who bitterly opposed communism and hoped to create an Islamic state in Afghanistan. Fearing his government was on the verge of collapse, Karmal called for Soviet troops. Moscow responded with a full-scale invasion of the country in Dec. 1979.

The Soviets were met with fierce resistance from groups already energized by opposition to the Karmal government. The guerrilla forces, calling themselves *mujahedeen*, pledged a jihad, or holy war, to expel the invaders. Initially armed with outdated weapons, the mujahedeen became a focus of U.S. cold war strategy against the Soviet Union, and with Pakistan's help, Washington began funneling sophisticated arms to the resistance. Moscow's troops were soon bogged down in a no-win conflict with determined Afghan fighters. In April 1988 the U.S.S.R., U.S., Afghanistan, and Pakistan signed accords calling for an end to outside aid to the warring factions. In return, a Soviet withdrawal took place in Feb. 1989, but the pro-Soviet government of President Najibullah was left in the capital, Kabul.

By mid-April 1992 Najibullah was ousted as Islamic rebels advanced on the capital. Almost immediately, the various rebel groups began fighting one another for control. Amid the chaos of competing factions, a group calling itself the Taliban—consisting of Islamic students—seized control of Kabul in Sept. 1996. It imposed harsh fundamentalist laws, including stoning for adultery and severing hands for theft. Women were prohibited from work and school, and were required to cover themselves in public from head to toe—including their entire face. By fall 1998 the Taliban controlled about 90% of the country, with the remainder in the hands of an opposition alliance headed by former president Burhanuddin Rabbani, whose government is still recognized by the United Nations. In May 1998, U.N.-sponsored peace talks among the warring factions broke down and fighting in the mountainous north of the country resumed.

On Aug. 20, 1998, U.S. cruise missiles struck a terrorism training complex in Afghanistan believed to have been financed by Osama bin Laden, a wealthy Islamic radical sheltered by the Taliban. The U.S. asked for the deportation of bin Laden, whom they believed was involved in the bombing of the U.S. embassies in Kenya and Tanzania on Aug. 7, 1998.

In 1999, the Taliban concentrated on defeating the forces of Ahmed Shah Masood, their last significant hurdle in gaining complete control of Afghanistan. The Taliban's scorched-earth tactics and human rights abuses have further isolated it from the international community. Only three governments—Pakistan, Saudi Arabia, and the U.A.R.—recognize the Taliban as Afghanistan's legitimate government.

Albania

THE REPUBLIC OF ALBANIA

National name: Republika E Shqiperise
President: Rexhep Mejdani (1997)
Prime Minister: Pandeli Majko (1998)
Area: 11,100 sq. mi. (28,750 sq. km)
Population (1999 est.): 3,364,571 (average annual rate of natural increase: 1.34%); birth rate: 20.7/1000; infant mortality rate: 42.9/1000; density per sq. mi.: 303
Capital and largest city (1991 est.): Tiranë, 300,000.
Monetary unit: Lek. **Languages:** Albanian, Greek.
Ethnicity/race: Albanian 95%, Greeks 3%, other 2%: Vlachs, Gypsies, Serbs, and Bulgarians (1989 est.)..
Religions (1980): Muslim, 70%; Albanian Orthodox, 20%; Roman Catholic, 10%. **Literacy rate:** 72%
Economic summary: GDP/PPP (1997 est.): $4.5 billion; $1,2370 per capita. **Real growth rate:** –8%. **Inflation:** 40%. **Unemployment:** 14%. **Arable land:** 21%. **Agriculture:** wide range of temperate-zone crops and livestock. **Labor force:** (1994 est.) 1.692 million; by occupation: agriculture, 49.5%; private sector, 22.2%; state sector, 28.3%. **Industry:** food processing, textiles and clothing, lumber, oil, cement, chemicals, mining, basic metals, hydropower. **Natural resources:** petroleum, natural gas, coal, chromium, copper, timber, nickel. **Exports:** $228 million (f.o.b., 1996): asphalt, metals and metallic ores, electricity, crude oil, vegetables, fruits, and tobacco. **Imports:** $879 million (f.o.b., 1996): machinery, consumer goods, grains.
Major trading partners: Italy, Greece, Germany, Belgium, U.S., Bulgaria, Turkey, Macedonia.

Geography Albania is situated on the eastern shore of the Adriatic Sea, with Montenegro and Serbia to the north, Macedonia to the east, and Greece to the south. Slightly larger than Maryland, Albania may be divided into two major regions: a mountainous highland region (north, east, and south) constituting 70% of the land area, and a western coastal lowland region that contains nearly all of the country's agricultural lands and is the most densely populated part of Albania.

Government Emerging democracy.

History A part of Illyria in ancient times, and later of the Roman Empire, Albania was ruled by the Byzantine Empire from C.E. 535 to 1204. An alli-

ance (1444–66) of Albanian chiefs failed to halt the advance of the Ottoman Turks, and the country remained under at least nominal Turkish rule for more than four centuries, until it proclaimed its independence on Nov. 28, 1912.

Largely agricultural, Albania is one of the poorest countries in Europe. A battlefield in World War I, after the war it became a republic in which a conservative Muslim landlord, Ahmed Zogu, proclaimed himself president in 1925, and king (Zog I) in 1928. He ruled until Italy annexed Albania in 1939. Communist guerrillas under Enver Hoxha seized power in 1944, near the end of World War II. Hoxha was a devotee of Stalin, emulating the Soviet leader's repressive tactics, imprisoning or executing landowners and others who did not conform to the socialist ideal. Hoxha eventually broke with Soviet communism in 1961 because of differences with Khrushchev, and then aligned himself with Chinese communism, which he also abandoned in 1978 after the death of Mao. From then on Albania went its own way to forge its individual version of the socialist state, and became one of the most isolated countries in the world. Hoxha was succeeded by Ramiz Alia in 1982.

The elections in March 1991 gave the Communists a decisive majority. But a general strike and street demonstrations soon forced the all-Communist cabinet to resign. In June 1991 the Communist Party of Labor renamed itself the Socialist Party and renounced its past ideology. The opposition Democratic Party won a landslide victory in the 1992 elections. But Albania's experiment with democratic reform and a free-market economy went disastrously awry in March 1997, when large numbers of its citizens invested in shady, get-rich-quick pyramid schemes. When five of these schemes collapsed in the beginning of the year, robbing Albanians of an estimated $1.2 billion in savings, their rage turned against the government, which appeared to have sanctioned the nationwide swindle. Rioting broke out, the country's fragile infrastructure collapsed, and gangsters and rebels overran the country, resulting in more than 1,500 deaths. A multinational protection force eventually restored order and set up the elections that formally ousted President Sali Berisha.

In spring 1999, Albania was heavily involved in the affairs of its fellow ethnic Albanians to the north, in Kosovo. Albania served as an outpost for NATO troops, and took in approximately 440,000 Kosovar refugees, about half the total number of ethnic Albanians who were driven from their homes in Kosovo.

Algeria

DEMOCRATIC AND POPULAR REPUBLIC OF ALGERIA

National name: Al Jumhuriyah al Jaza'iriyah ad Dimuqratiyah ash Shabiyah
President: Abdel-Aziz Bouteflika (1999)
Prime Minister: Ismail Hamdani (1998)
Area: 919,595 sq. mi. (2,381,740 sq. km)
Population (1999 est.): 31,133,486 (average annual rate of natural increase: 2.15%); birth rate: 27.0/1000; infant mortality rate: 43.8/1000; density per sq. mi.: 34
Capital: Algiers. **Largest cities (1987):** Algiers, 1,507,241; Oran, 628,558; Constantine, 440,842; Annaba, 305,526. **Monetary unit:** Dinar. **Languages:**

Arabic (official), French, Berber dialects. **Ethnicity/race:** Arab-Berber 99%, European less than 1%. **Religion:** 99% Islam (Sunni). **Literacy rate:** 57%. **Economic summary: GDP/PPP** (1997 est.): $120.4 billion; $4,000 per capita. **Real growth rate:** 2.5%. **Inflation:** 7%. **Unemployment:** 28%. **Arable land:** 3%. **Agriculture:** wheat, barley, oats, wine, citrus fruits, olives, livestock. **Labor force:** 7.8 million (1996 est.); by occupation: government, 29.5%; agriculture, 22%; construction and public works, 16.2%; industry, 13.6%; commerce and services, 13.5%; transportation and communication, 5.2% (1989). **Industry:** petroleum, natural gas, light industries, mining, electrical, petrochemical, food processing. **Natural resources:** petroleum, natural gas, iron ore, phosphates, uranium, lead, zinc. **Exports:** $13.1 billion (f.o.b., 1997 est.): petroleum and natural gas, 97%. **Imports:** $10 billion (f.o.b., 1997 est.): capital goods, food and beverages, consumer goods. **Major trading partners:** Italy, U.S., France, Spain, Germany.

Geography Nearly four times the size of Texas, Algeria is bordered on the west by Morocco and Western Sahara and on the east by Tunisia and Libya. To the south are Mauritania, Mali, and Niger. The Saharan region, which is 85% of the country, is almost completely uninhabited. The highest point is Mount Tahat in the Sahara, which rises 9,850 feet (3,000 m).

Government Parliamentary republic.

History Excavations in Algeria have indicated that *Homo erectus* resided there between 500,000 and 700,000 years ago. Phoenician traders settled on the coast in the 1st millennium B.C.E. As ancient Numidia, Algeria became a Roman colony, part of what was called Mauretania Caesariensis, at the close of the Punic Wars (145 B.C.E.). Conquered by the Vandals about C.E. 440, it fell from a high state of civilization to virtual barbarism, from which it partly recovered after an invasion by Arabs about 650. Christian during its Roman period, the indigenous Berbers were then Islamized. Falling under control of the Ottoman Empire by 1536, Algiers served for three centuries as the headquarters of the Barbary pirates. Ostensibly to rid the region of the pirates, the French occupied Algeria in 1830 and made it a part of France in 1848.

Algerian independence movements led to the uprisings of 1954–55, which developed into full-scale war. In 1962, French president Charles de Gaulle began the peace negotiations, and on July 5, 1962, Algeria was proclaimed independent. In Oct. 1963, Ahmed Ben Bella was elected president, and the country became socialist. He began to nationalize foreign holdings and aroused opposition. He was overthrown in a military coup on June 19, 1965, by Col. Houari Boumediène, who suspended the constitution and sought to restore financial stability.

In Dec. 1991 in the first parliamentary elections ever held in Algeria, the fundamentalist Islamic Salvation Front (Front Islamique du Salut; FIS) won the largest number of votes. To thwart the electoral results, the army cancelled the general election, which plunged the country into a bloody civil war. An estimated 100,000 people have been massacred by Islamic terrorists since war began in Jan. 1992.

The undeclared civil war escalated in 1997–98 in its brutality and senselessness. Islamic extremists, who had originally focused their attacks on government officials and then shifted to intellectuals and journalists, abandoned political motivations entirely and targeted defenseless villagers. The mass slaughters were as savage as they were random, and the government was markedly ineffectual in stemming the violence. There is some evidence that the army in fact looked the other way while its civilians were slaughtered. Algeria refused international mediation, and kept the outside world largely in the dark about the war within its borders.

After President Zeroual announced his desire to retire early, elections were held in April 1999. Six of the seven candidates withdrew at the last minute in protest of election fraud. The lone remaining candidate, Abdel-Aziz Bouteflika, won 73.8% of the vote. Bouteflika is attempting to implement a plan of national reconciliation that includes an amnesty for Islamic militants not convicted of murder or rape. The Sept. 1999 referendum on his peace plan passed with 98% of the vote.

Andorra

PRINCIPALITY OF ANDORRA

National name: Valls d'Andorra
Head of Government: Marc Forné Molné (1994)
Area: 175 sq. mi. (450 sq. km)
Population (1999 est.): 65,939 (average annual growth rate: 0.48%); birth rate: 10.3/1000; infant mortality rate: 4.1/1000; density per sq. mi.: 377
Capital and largest city (1993 est.): Andorra la Vella, 22,390. **Monetary units:** French franc and Spanish peseta. **Languages:** Catalán (official), French, Spanish. **Ethnicity/race:** Spanish 61%, Andorran 30%, French 6%, other 3%. **Religion:** Roman Catholic. **Literacy rate:** 100%
Economic summary: GDP/PPP (1995 est.): $1.2 billion; $18,000 per capita. **Real growth rate:** n.a. **Inflation:** n.a. **Unemployment:** 0%. **Arable land:** 2%. **Agriculture:** tobacco, rye, wheat, barley, oats, vegetables, sheep raising. **Labor force:** n.a. **Industry:** tourism, sheep, timber, tobacco, banking. **Natural resources:** water power, mineral water, timber, iron ore, lead. **Exports:** $47 million (f.o.b., 1995): electricity, tobacco products, furniture. **Imports:** $1 billion (1995): consumer goods, food. **Major trading partners:** France, Spain, U.S.

Geography Andorra is nestled high in the Pyrenees Mountains on the French-Spanish border.

Government A parliamentary co-principality composed of the bishop of Urgel (Spain) and the president of France.

History An autonomous and semi-independent co-principality, Andorra has been under the joint suzerainty of the French state and the Spanish bishops of Urgel since 1278. In the late 20th century, Andorra became a popular tourist destination and an important international retail center because of its opportunities for various winter sports, low taxes, and lack of customs duties. In 1990 Andorra approved a customs union treaty with the EU permitting free movement of industrial goods between the two, but Andorra would apply the EU's external tariffs to third countries. This treaty went into effect on July 1, 1991. Andorra became a member of the U.N. in 1993 and a member of the Council of Europe in 1994.

Angola

REPUBLIC OF ANGOLA

President: José Eduardo dos Santos (1979)
Area: 481,350 sq. mi. (1,246,700 sq. km)
Population (1999 est.): 11,177,537 (average annual rate of natural increase: 2.68%); birth rate: 43.1/1000; infant mortality rate: 129.2/1000; density per sq. mi.: 23
Capital and largest city (1993): Luanda, 2,000,000.
Other large cities (1993 est.): Huambo, 400,000; Lubango, 105,000. **Monetary unit:** Kwanza.
Languages: Bantu, Portuguese (official). **Ethnicity/ race:** Ovimbundu 37%, Kimbundu 25%, Bakongo 13%, mestico (mixed European and Native African) 2%, European 1%, other 22%. **Religions:** Roman Catholic, 47%; Protestant, 38%; Indigenous, 15%.
Literacy rate: 42%
Economic summary: GDP/PPP (1996 est.): $8.32 billion; $800 per capita. **Real growth rate:** 9%. **Inflation:** 92% (mid-1997 est.). **Unemployment:** extensive. **Arable land:** 2%. **Agriculture:** bananas, sugarcane, coffee, sisal, corn, cotton, manioc (tapioca), tobacco, vegetables, plantains, livestock, forest products, fish. **Labor force:** 2.783 million; by occupation: agriculture, 85%; industry, 15% (1985 est.). **Industry:** petroleum, diamonds, iron ore, phosphates, feldspar, bauxite, uranium, gold, cement, basic metal products, fish processing, food processing, brewing, tobacco products, sugar. **Natural resources:** petroleum, diamonds, iron ore, phosphates, copper, feldspar, gold, bauxite, uranium. **Exports:** $4 billion (f.o.b., 1996 est.): crude oil, diamonds, refined petroleum products, gas, coffee, sisal, fish, timber, cotton. **Imports:** $1.7 billion (f.o.b., 1995 est.): machinery and electrical equipment, vehicles and spare parts, medicines, food, textiles and clothing, substantial military supplies. **Major trading partners:** U.S., EU, Brazil.

Geography Angola, more than three times the size of California, extends for more than 1,000 miles (1,609 km) along the South Atlantic in southwestern Africa. The Democratic Republic of the Congo and the Republic of Congo are to the north and east, Zambia is to the east, and Namibia is to the south. A plateau averaging 6,000 feet (1,829 m) above sea level rises abruptly from the coastal lowlands. Nearly all the land is desert or savanna, with hardwood forests in the northeast.

Government Angola underwent a transition from a one-party socialist state to a nominally multiparty democracy in 1992.

History The original inhabitants of Angola are thought to have been Khoisan speakers. After C.E. 1000, large numbers of Bantu speakers migrated to the region and became the dominant group. Angola derives its name from the Bantu kingdom of Ndongo, whose name for its king is *ngola*.

Explored by the Portuguese navigator Diego Cao in 1482, Angola became a link in trade with India and Southeast Asia. Later it was a major source of slaves for Portugal's New World colony of Brazil. Development of the interior began after the Berlin Conference in 1885 fixed the colony's borders, and British and Portuguese investment fostered mining, railways, and agriculture.

Following World War II, independence movements began but were sternly suppressed by Portuguese military force. The major nationalist organizations were the Popular Movement for the Liberation of Angola (MPLA), a Marxist party, National Front for the Liberation of Angola (FNLA), and the National Union for the Total Independence of Angola (UNITA). After 14 years of war, Portugal finally granted independence to Angola in 1975. The MPLA, which had led the independence movement, has controlled the government ever since. But after its long war for independence, the new country has yet to experience an extended period of peace. UNITA disputed the MPLA's ascendancy, and civil war broke out almost immediately. With the Soviet Union and Cuba supporting the Marxist MPLA, and the United States and South Africa supporting the anti-communist UNITA, the country became a cold war battleground.

With the waning of the cold war and the withdrawal of Cuban troops in 1989, the MPLA began to make the transition to a multiparty democracy. Despite shifting ideologies, the civil war continued for more than 30 years, with UNITA's charismatic rebel leader, Jonas Savimbi, armed and sustained by his control of approximately 80% of the country's diamond trade. Free elections took place in 1992, with incumbent president José Eduardo dos Santos and the MPLA winning the U.N.-certified election over Savimbi and UNITA. Savimbi then withdrew, charging election fraud, and the civil war resumed.

In 1997 Angola played a crucial role in the civil wars of both the Republic of Congo and the Democratic Republic of the Congo. By aiding in the overthrow of these countries' leaders, Pascal Lissouba and Mobutu Sese Seko, the Angolan government was also able to destroy the UNITA strongholds within the borders of these countries. Angola again came to the aid of the Democratic Republic of the Congo's new leader, Laurent Kabila, in 1998, helping to fight the rebellion against his shaky year-old administration.

Four years of relative peace took place between 1994 and 1998 when the United Nations, at a cost of $1.6 billion, oversaw the 1994 Lusaka peace accord. In 1997 it was agreed that a coalition government with UNITA would be implemented. But Savimbi violated the accord repeatedly by refusing to give up his strongholds, failing to demobilize his army, and retaking territory. As a result, the government suspended coalition rule in Sept. 1998, and the country again plunged into civil war, which analysts say neither side has the military power to win.

Since Jan. 1999, UNITA has gained the upper hand in the fighting, taking control of 70% of the country in just six months. The U.N. has pulled out of the country, sharply criticizing both sides for making peace untenable. Massive starvation has engulfed Angola's civilians, who have been attacked by both government soldiers and the rebels. Both sides also continue to plant land mines, making Angola one of the most heavily mined countries in the world.

Antigua and Barbuda

Sovereign: Queen Elizabeth II (1952)
Governor-General: James Beethoven Carlisle (1993)
Prime Minister: Lester Bryant Bird (1994)
Land area: 171 sq. mi. (440 sq. km)
Population (1999 est.): 64,246 (average annual growth rate: 1.05%); birth rate: 16.2/1000; infant mortality rate: 20.7/1000; density per sq. mi.: 376
Capital and largest city (1991): St. John's, 21,514; Codrington (capital of Barbuda), est. pop. 1,000.

Monetary unit: East Caribbean dollar. **Language:** English. **Ethnicity/race:** black, British, Portuguese, Lebanese, Syrian. **Religions:** Anglican and Roman Catholic. **Literacy rate:** 90%

Economic summary: GDP/PPP (1997 est.): $470 million; per capita $7,400. **Real growth rate:** 3.3%. **Inflation:** 2.5% (1996). **Unemployment:** (1995 est.) 5%–10%. **Arable land:** 18%. **Agriculture:** cotton, fruits, vegetables, bananas, coconuts, cucumbers, mangoes, sugarcane, livestock. **Labor force:** 30,000; by occupation: industry, 7%; commerce and services, 82%; agriculture, 11%. **Industry:** tourism, construction, light manufacturing (clothing, alcohol, household appliances). **Exports:** $45 million (f.o.b., 1996 est.): petroleum products, manufactures, food and live animals, machinery and transport equipment. **Imports:** $350.8 million (f.o.b., 1996 est.): food and live animals, machinery and transport equipment, manufactures, chemicals, oil. **Major trading partners:** Organization of Eastern Caribbean States, Barbados, Guyana, Trinidad and Tobago, U.S., U.K., Canada.

Member of Commonwealth of Nations

Geography Antigua, the larger of the two main islands located 295 miles (420 km) south-southeast of San Juan, P.R., is low-lying except for a range of hills in the south that rise to their highest point at Boggy Peak (1,330 ft.; 405 m). Well-wooded Antigua is 108 sq. miles (280 sq. km); the island dependencies of Redonda (an uninhabited rocky islet) and Barbuda (a coral island formerly known as Dulcina) are 0.5 sq. miles (1.30 sq. km) and 62 sq. miles (161 sq. km), respectively.

Government Parliamentary democracy.

History Antigua was explored by Christopher Columbus in 1493 and named for the Church of Santa Maria de la Antigua in Seville. Antigua was colonized by Britain in 1632; Barbuda was first colonized in 1678. The country joined the West Indies Federation in 1958. With the breakup of the federation, it became one of the West Indies Associated States in 1967, self-governing its internal affairs. Full independence was granted Nov. 1, 1981.

The Bird family has controlled the islands since Vere C. Bird founded the Antigua Labor Party in the mid-1940s. Bird, the former prime minister, and his sons, one of whom is the current prime minister, have a history of corruption that includes money laundering, arms sales, drug trafficking, and extortion. In recent years the Russian Mafia has gained a foothold on the island. The U.K. and the U.S. have increased their pressure on Antigua to halt its illegal activities—the U.S. State Department bluntly called the island "one of the most attractive centers for money launderers."

Argentina

ARGENTINE REPUBLIC

National name: República Argentina.
President: Carlos S. Menem (1989)
Area: 1,072,067 sq. mi. (2,766,890 sq. km)
Population (1999 est.): 36,737,664 (average annual rate of natural increase: 1.23%); birth rate: 19.9/1000; infant mortality rate: 18.4/1000; density per sq. mi.: 34
Capital and largest city (1999 est.): Buenos Aires: city proper 3,000,000; metro. area 12,000,000. **Other large cities (1999 est.):** Córdoba, 1,200,000; Rosario, 950,000; Mar del Plata, 900,000; Mendoza, 400,000.
Monetary unit: Peso. **Languages:** Spanish, English, Italian, German, French. **Ethnicity/race:** European

97% (mostly of Spanish and Italian descent), 3% other (mostly Indian or mestizo). **Religions:** Roman Catholic 92%, Protestant 2%, Jewish 2%, other 4%. **Literacy rate:** 96.2% (1990)

Economic summary: GDP/PPP (1997 est.): $348.2 billion; $9,700 per capita. **Real growth rate:** 8.4%. **Inflation:** 0.3%. **Unemployment:** 15% (Aug. 1999). **Arable land:** 9%. **Agriculture:** wheat, corn, sorghum, soybeans, sugar beets, livestock. **Labor force:** (1995 est.) 14.5 million; industry: 31%, agriculture, 12%, services, 57% (1985 est.). **Industry:** food processing, motor vehicles, consumer durables, textiles, chemicals and petrochemicals, printing, metallurgy, steel. **Natural resources:** fertile plains of pampas, lead, zinc, tin, copper, iron ore, manganese, petroleum, uranium. **Exports:** $25.4 billion (f.o.b., 1997): meat, wheat, corn, oilseed, manufactures, fuels. **Imports:** $30.3 billion (c.i.f., 1997): machinery and equipment, chemicals, metals, transport equipment, agricultural products. **Major trading partners:** Brazil, U.S., Chile, Netherlands, Italy, Germany, France.

Geography Second in South America only to Brazil in size and population, Argentina is a plain, rising from the Atlantic to the Chilean border and the towering Andes peaks. Aconcagua (23,034 ft.; 7,021 m) is the highest peak in the world outside Asia. Argentina is also bordered by Bolivia and Paraguay on the north, and by Uruguay and Brazil on the east. The northern area is the swampy and partly wooded Gran Chaco, bordering on Bolivia and Paraguay. South of that are the rolling, fertile Pampas, which are rich in agriculture and sheep- and cattle-grazing and support most of the population. Next southward is Patagonia, a region of cool, arid steppes with some wooded and fertile sections.

Government Republic.

History First explored in 1516 by Juan Díaz de Solís, Argentina developed slowly under Spanish colonial rule. Buenos Aires was settled in 1580; the cattle industry was thriving as early as 1600. Invading British forces were expelled in 1806–07, and after Napoléon conquered Spain (1808), the Argentinians set up their own government in 1810. On July 9, 1816, independence was formally declared.

As it had in World War I, Argentina proclaimed neutrality at the outbreak of World War II, but in the closing phase declared war on the Axis powers on March 27, 1945. Juan D. Perón, an army colonel, emerged as the strongman of the postwar era, winning the presidential elections of 1946 and 1951. Perón's political strength was reinforced by his second wife—Eva Duarte de Perón (Evita)—and her popularity with the working classes. Although she never held a government post, Evita acted as de facto minister of health and labor, establishing a national charitable organization, and awarding generous wage increases to the unions, who responded with political support for Perón. Opposition to Perón's increasing authoritarianism led to a coup by the armed forces, which sent Perón into exile in 1955, three years after Evita's death. Argentina entered a long period of military dictatorships with brief intervals of constitutional government.

The former dictator returned to power in 1973 and his third wife, Isabel Martínez de Perón, was elected vice president. After Perón's death in 1974, she became the hemisphere's first woman chief of state, but was deposed in 1976 by a military junta.

On April 2, 1982, Lt. Gen. Leopoldo Galtieri, commander of the army and the new president, landed thousands of troops on the Falkland Islands and reclaimed *Las Malvinas*, their Spanish name, as national territory. By May 21, more than 5,000 British marines and paratroopers landed and regained control of the islands. Galtieri resigned three days after the surrender of the island garrison on June 14. Maj. Gen. Reynaldo Bignone succeeded him.

In the presidential election of Oct. 1983, Raúl Alfonsín, leader of the middle-class Radical Civic Union, handed the Peronist Party its first defeat since its founding. However, the twin economic problems of growing unemployment and quadruple-digit inflation led to a Peronist victory in the elections of May 1989. Inflation of food prices provoked riots that induced Alfonsín to step down in June 1989, six months early, in favor of the new Peronist president, Carlos Menem. A group of army leaders and their followers attempted an uprising on Dec. 3, 1990. Most commanders, however, stood by the legitimate government, and the insurrection was suppressed in less than 24 hours.

In 1991, President Menem hammered out a vast deregulation of the economy designed to reverse decades of state intervention and protectionism. In Sept. 1995, Argentina and the U.K. signed an agreement to promote oil and gas exploration in the Southwest Atlantic, defusing a potentially difficult issue and opening the way to further cooperation between the two nations. The president and his ruling Peronist Party saw their popularity dramatically fall in 1997 as the result of increasing social disturbances, a scandal over presidential links to an alleged mobster, and a high unemployment rate. Menem had the constitution changed in 1994 to allow him to serve for a second term; in 1998 he planned to change it again to allow for a third term but abandoned the idea after threats of civil disobedience.

Throughout the 1990s, the Argentine government continued to demonstrate economic credibility through further economic adjustment and conclusion of a new arrangement with the International Monetary Fund at the end of 1997. Beginning in Sept. 1998, however, Argentina faced its worst recession in a decade, and the ever-rising unemployment rate hit 15% in Aug. 1999. The economic woes of its trading partner Brazil have exacerbated Argentina's problems. Brazil, which traditionally bought almost one-third of Argentina's exports, bought 30% less in 1999. Unrest in the provinces—where unemployment is legion—led to riots in late summer.

Armenia

President: Robert Kocharian (1998)
Prime Minister: Vazgen Sarkisyan (1999)
Area: 11,500 sq. mi. (29,800 sq. km)
Population (1999 est.): 3,409,234 (average annual rate of increase: 0.45%) (Armenian, 93%; others, Kurds, Ukrainians, and Russians); birth rate: 13.5/1000; infant mortality rate: 41.1/1000, density per sq. mi.: 296
Capital and largest city (1998 est.): Yerevan, 1,226,000; other large cities (1998 est.): Gyumri (Leninakan), 121,000; Vanadzor, 74,000; Abovian, 54,000. **Monetary unit:** Dram. **Language:** Armenian.
Ethnicity/race: Armenian 93%, Azeri 3%, Russian 2%, other (mostly Yezidi Kurds) 2% (1989) Note: as of the end of 1993, virtually all Azeris had emigrated from Armenia.. **Religion:** Armenian Orthodox, 94%.
Literacy rate: 100% (1970)
Economic summary: GDP/PPP (1997 est.): $9.5 billion; $2,750 per capita. **Real growth rate:** 2.7%. **Inflation:**

13.2%. **Unemployment:** 10.6% officially unemployed, with large numbers underemployed (June 1997). **Arable land:** 17%. **Agriculture:** fruit, vegetables, vineyards, livestock. **Labor force:** (1997) 1.6 million; manufacturing, mining, and construction 25%, agriculture 38%, services 37%. **Industry:** much of industry is shut down; metal-cutting machine tools, forging-pressing machines, electric motors, tires, knitted wear, hosiery, shoes, silk fabric, washing machines, chemicals, trucks, watches, instruments, microelectronics. **Exports:** $290 million (f.o.b., 1996): gold and jewelry, aluminum, transport equipment, electrical equipment, scrap metal. **Imports:** $727 million (c.i.f., 1996): grain, other foods, fuel, other energy. **Major trading partners:** Iran, Russia, Turkmenistan, Georgia, U.S., EU.

Geography Armenia is located in the southern Caucasus and is the smallest of the former Soviet republics. It is bounded by Georgia on the north, Azerbaijan on the east, Iran on the south, and Turkey on the west. Contemporary Armenia is a fraction the size of ancient Armenia. A land of rugged mountains and extinct volcanoes, its highest point is Mount Aragats, 13,435 ft. (4,095 m).

Government Republic.

History One of the world's oldest civilizations, Armenia once included Mount Ararat, which biblical tradition identifies as the mountain that Noah's ark rested on after the flood. It was the first country in the world to officially embrace Christianity as its religion (c. 300).

In the 6th century B.C.E., Armenians settled in the kingdom of Urartu (the Assyrian name for Ararat), which was in decline. Under Tigrane the Great (fl. 95–55 B.C.E.) the Armenian empire reached its height and became one of the most powerful in Asia, stretching from the Caspian to the Mediterranean Seas. Throughout most of its long history, however, Armenia has been invaded by a succession of empires. Under constant threat of domination by foreign forces, Armenians became both cosmopolitan as well as fierce protectors of their culture and tradition.

Over the centuries Armenia was conquered by Greeks, Romans, Persians, Byzantines, Mongols, Arabs, Ottoman Turks, and Russians. From the 16th century through World War I major portions of Armenia were controlled by their most brutal invader, the Ottoman Turks, under whom they experienced discrimination, religious persecution, heavy taxation, and armed attacks. In response to Armenian nationalist stirrings, the Turks massacred thousands of Armenians in 1894 and 1896. The most horrific massacre took place in April 1915 during World War I, when the Turks ordered the deportation of the Armenian population to the deserts of Syria and Mesopotamia. According to the majority of historians, between 600,000 and 1.5 million Armenians were murdered or died of starvation. The Armenian massacre is considered the first genocide in the 20th century. Turkey denies that a genocide took place, and claims that a much smaller number died in a civil war.

After the Turkish defeat in World War I, the independent Republic of Armenia was established on May 28, 1918, but survived only until Nov. 29, 1920, when it was annexed by the Soviet Army. On March 12, 1922, the Soviets joined Georgia, Armenia, and Azerbaijan to form the Transcaucasian Soviet Socialist Republic, which became part of the

U.S.S.R. In 1936, after a reorganization, Armenia became a separate constituent republic of the U.S.S.R. Since 1988, Armenia has been involved in a territorial dispute with Azerbaijan over the enclave of Nagorno-Karabakh, to which both lay claim. Also in 1988, a devastating earthquake killed thousands and wreaked economic havoc.

Armenia declared its independence from the collapsing Soviet Union on Sept. 23, 1991. In the years that followed, Armenia successfully fought Azerbaijan for control of Nagorno-Karabakh. The majority population of the enclave are Armenian Christians who want to secede from Azerbaijan and join Armenia. A cease-fire agreement was reached between the two countries in 1994, but the fate of Nagorno-Karabakh remains unresolved. Azerbaijan has offered broad autonomy to the enclave in exchange for the withdrawal of Armenian troops from Azeri lands. But the enclave wants either full independence or annexation to Armenia.

An Armenian diaspora has existed throughout the nation's history, and Armenian emigration has been particularly heavy since independence from the Soviet Union. An estimated 60% of the total eight million Armenians worldwide live outside the country, with one million each in the U.S. and Russia. Significant Armenian communities are located in Georgia, France, Iran, Lebanon, Syria, Argentina, and Canada.

Australia

COMMONWEALTH OF AUSTRALIA

Sovereign: Queen Elizabeth II (1952)
Governor-General: Sir William Deane (1996)
Prime Minister: John Howard (1996)
Area: 2,966,150 sq. mi. (7,686,850 sq. km)
Population (1999 est.): 18,783,551 (average annual rate of natural increase: 0.63%); birth rate: 13.2/1000; infant mortality rate: 5.1/1000; density per sq. mi.: 6
Capital (1996 est.): Canberra, 307,700. **Largest cities (1993 est.):** Sydney, 3,713,500; Melbourne, 3,189,200; Brisbane, 1,520,600; Perth, 1,295,100; Adelaide, 1,079,200; . **Monetary unit:** Australian dollar.
Language: English. **Ethnicity/race:** Caucasian 95%, Asian 4%, aboriginal (353,000) and other 1%.
Religions: Anglican 26.1%, Roman Catholic 26.0%, other Christian 24.3%. **Literacy rate:** 100%
Economic summary: GDP/PPP (1997 est.): $394 billion. $21,400 per capita. **Real growth rate:** 3.3%. **Inflation:** 1%. **Unemployment:** 8.4% (1997). **Arable land:** 6%. **Agriculture:** wheat, barley, sugarcane, fruits, cattle, sheep, poultry. **Labor force:** 9.2 million (Dec. 1997) services, 73%; industry, 22%; agriculture, 5%. **Natural resources:** bauxite, coal, iron ore, copper, tin, silver, uranium, nickel, tungsten, mineral sands, lead, zinc, diamonds, natural gas, petroleum. **Exports:** $68 billion (f.o.b, 1997 est.): coal, gold, meat, wool, alumina, iron ore, wheat, machinery and transport equipment. **Imports:** $67 billion (f.o.b, 1997 est.): machinery and transport equipment, computers and office machines, crude oil and petroleum products. **Major trading partners:** Japan, Association of Southeast Asian Nations, South Korea, U.S., New Zealand, U.K., Taiwan, Hong Kong, China. **Member of Commonwealth of Nations**

Geography The continent of Australia, with the island state of Tasmania, is approximately equal in area to the United States (excluding Alaska and Hawaii). Mountain ranges run from north to south along the east coast, reaching their highest point in Mount Kosciusko (7,308 ft.; 2,228 m). The western half of the continent is occupied by a desert plateau that rises into barren, rolling hills near the west coast. It includes the Great Victoria Desert to the south and the Great Sandy Desert to the north. The Great Barrier Reef, extending about 1,245 miles (2,000 km), lies along the northeast coast. The island of Tasmania (26,178 sq. mi.; 67,800 sq. km) is off the southeastern coast.

Government Democracy. Symbolic executive power is vested in the British monarch, who is represented throughout Australia by the governor-general.

History The first inhabitants of Australia were the Aborigines, who migrated there at least 40,000 years ago from Southeast Asia. There may have been between a half million to a full million Aborigines at the time of European settlement; today there are about 350,000.

Dutch, Portuguese, and Spanish ships sighted Australia in the 17th century; the Dutch landed at the Gulf of Carpentaria in 1606. In 1616 the territory became known as New Holland. The British arrived in 1688, but it was not until Captain James Cook's voyage in 1770 that Great Britain claimed possession of the vast island, calling it New South Wales. A British penal colony was set up at Port Jackson (what is now Sydney) in 1788, and about 161,000 transported English convicts were settled there until the system was suspended in 1839.

Free settlers established six colonies: New South Wales (1786), Tasmania (then Van Diemen's Land) (1825), Western Australia (1829), South Australia (1834), Victoria (1851), and Queensland (1859). Various gold rushes attracted settlers, as did the mining of other minerals. Sheep farming and grain soon became important economic enterprises. The six colonies became states and in 1901 federated into the Commonwealth of Australia with a constitution that incorporated British parliamentary and U.S. federal traditions. Australia became known for its liberal legislation: free compulsory education, protected trade unionism with industrial conciliation and arbitration, the secret ballot, women's suffrage, maternity allowances, and sickness and old-age pensions.

Australia fought alongside Britain in World War I, notably with the Australia and New Zealand Army Corps (ANZAC) in the Dardanelles campaign (1915). Participation in World War II brought Australia closer to the United States. Parliamentary power in the second half of the 20th century shifted between three political parties: the Australian Labour Party, the Liberal Party, and the National Party. Australia relaxed its discriminatory immigration laws in the 1960s and 1970s, which favored Northern Europeans. Thereafter, about 40% of its immigrants came from Asia, diversifying a population that was predominantly of English and Irish heritage.

In March 1996 the opposition Liberal Party National Party coalition easily won the national elections, removing the Labour Party after 13 years in power. Pressure from the new, conservative One Nation Party threatened to reduce the gains made by Aborigines and to limit immigration. An Aboriginal movement had grown in the 1960s that gained full citizenship and improved education for the country's poorest socioeconomic group.

In Sept. 1999, Australia led the international peace keeping force sent to restore order in East Timor, Indonesia. Pro-Indonesian militias had begun massacring civilians following a U.N.-sponsored referendum that overwhelmingly called for East Timor's independence.

Australian External Territories

Norfolk Island (13 sq. mi.; 36.3 sq. km) was placed under Australian administration in 1914. Population 2,285 (1996 census). A former penal colony, Norfolk Island became home to the entire population of Pitcairn Island in 1856. The 194 residents of tiny Pitcairn—all of whom were the descendants of the mutineers from the HMS *Bounty* and their Tahitian wives—embarked on the 3,700-mile journey to Norfolk because of overpopulation. Many Norfolk residents can trace their genealogy directly to the adventurers from *Bounty*.

The Ashmore and Cartier Islands (0.8 sq. mi.), situated in the Indian Ocean off the northwest coast of Australia, came under Australian administration in 1934.

The Australian Antarctic Territory (2,360,000 sq. mi.; 6,112,400 sq. km) is made up of all the islands and territories, other than Adélie Land, situated south of lat. 60°S and lying between long. 160° to 45°E. It came under Australian administration in 1936.

Heard Island and the McDonald Islands (158 sq. mi.; 409.2 sq. km), lying in the sub-Antarctic, were placed under Australian administration in 1947. The islands are uninhabited.

Christmas Island (52 sq. mi.; 134.7 sq. km) is situated in the Indian Ocean. It came under Australian administration in 1958. Most of the island's residents had been phosphate miners until the 1990s, when the Australian-based Casinos Austria International Ltd. built a $45 million casino on Christmas Island. As a result, the population has more than doubled, to 2,195 (July 1998 est.).

Coral Sea Islands (400,000 sq. mi.; 1,036,000 sq. km, but only a few sq. mi. of land) became a territory of Australia in 1969. There is no permanent population on the islands.

Cocos (Keeling) Islands are made up of a group of 27 small coral islands in two separate atolls in the Indian Ocean, 1,721 miles (2,768 km) northwest of Perth. West Island is the largest, about 6.2 miles (10 km) long. The islands became an Australian territory in 1955. In April 1984 the residents voted to merge with Australia. The population of the Cocos is 604 (July 1995).

Austria

REPUBLIC OF AUSTRIA

National name: Republik Österreich
President: Thomas Klestil (1992)
Chancellor: Viktor Klima (1997)
Area: 32,375 sq. mi. (83,850 sq. km)
Population (1999 est.): 8,139,299 (average annual rate of natural increase: −0.04%); birth rate 9.6/1000; infant mortality rate: 5.1/1000; density per sq. mi.: 251
Capital and largest city (1991 est.): Vienna, 1,600,000.
Other large cities (1995 est.): Graz, 237,150; Linz, 203,000; Salzburg, 144,000; Innsbruck, 118,000.

Monetary units: Schilling and euro. **Languages:** German 98% (small Slovene, Croatian, and Hungarian-speaking minorities). **Religions:** Roman Catholic 85%, Protestant 6%, other 9%. **Ethnicity/ race:** German 99.4%, Croatian 0.3%, Slovene 0.2%. **Literacy rate:** 99%
Economic summary: GDP/PPP (1997 est.): $174.1 billion; $21,400 per capita. **Real growth rate:** 2.1%. **Inflation:** 1.3%. **Unemployment:** 7.1% (Jan. 1998). **Arable land:** 17%. **Agriculture:** grains, potatoes, sugar beets, wine, fruit, dairy products, cattle, pigs, poultry, sawn wood. **Labor force:** (1996), 3.646 million; services 66.1%, industry and crafts 29.6%, agriculture and forestry 1.3%. **Industries:** food, iron and steel, machines, textiles, chemicals, electrical, paper and pulp, tourism, mining, motor vehicles. **Natural resources:** iron ore, oil, timber, magnesite, lead, coal, lignite, copper, hydropower. **Exports:** $57.8 billion (1996): machinery and equipment, iron and steel, lumber, textiles, paper products, chemicals. **Imports:** $67.3 billion (1996): petroleum, foodstuffs, machinery and equipment, vehicles, chemicals, textiles and clothing, pharmaceuticals. **Major trading partners:** EU (mostly Germany and Italy), Eastern Europe, Japan, U.S.

Geography Slightly smaller than Maine, Austria includes much of the mountainous territory of the eastern Alps (about 75% of the area). The country contains many snowfields, glaciers, and snowcapped peaks, the highest being the Grossglockner (12,530 ft.; 3,819 m). The Danube is the principal river. Forests and woodlands cover about 40% of the land.

Government Federal republic.

History Settled in prehistoric times, the central European land that is now Austria was overrun in pre-Roman times by various tribes, including the Celts. After the fall of the Roman Empire, of which Austria was part, the area was invaded by Bavarians and Slavic Avars. Charlemagne conquered the area in C.E. 788 and encouraged colonization and Christianity. In 1252, Ottokar, king of Bohemia, gained possession, only to lose the territories to Rudolf of Hapsburg in 1278. Thereafter, until World War I, Austria's history was largely that of its ruling house, the Hapsburgs. Austria emerged from the Congress of Vienna in 1815 as the continent's dominant power. The *Ausgleich* of 1867 provided for a dual sovereignty, the empire of Austria and the kingdom of Hungary, under Franz Joseph I, who ruled until his death on Nov. 21, 1916. The Austrian-Hungarian minority rule of this immensely diverse empire became increasingly difficult in an age of emerging nationalist movements. When Archduke Francis Ferdinand was assassinated by a Serbian nationalist in Sarajevo in 1914, World War I, as well as the destruction of the Austro-Hungarian Empire, began.

During World War I, Austria-Hungary was one of the Central powers with Germany, Bulgaria, and Turkey, and the conflict left the country in political chaos and economic ruin. Austria, shorn of Hungary, was proclaimed a republic in 1918, and the monarchy was dissolved in 1919. A parliamentary democracy was set up by the constitution of Nov. 10, 1920. To check the power of Nazis advocating union with Germany, Chancellor Engelbert Dolfuss in 1933 established a dictatorship, but was assassinated by the Nazis on July 25, 1934. Kurt von Schuschnigg, his successor, struggled to keep Austria independent, but on March 12, 1938, German troops occupied the country, and Hitler proclaimed its *Anschluss* (union) with Germany, annexing it to the Third Reich.

After World War II, the U.S. and Britain declared the Austrians a "liberated" people. But the Russians prolonged the occupation. Finally Austria concluded a state treaty with the U.S.S.R. and the other occupying powers and regained its independence on May 15, 1955. The second Austrian republic, established Dec. 19, 1945, on the basis of the 1920 constitution (amended in 1929), was declared by the federal Parliament to be permanently neutral.

On June 8, 1986, former U.N. Secretary-General Kurt Waldheim was elected to the ceremonial office of president in a campaign marked by controversy over his alleged links to Nazi war crimes in Yugoslavia (he was replaced by diplomat Thomas Klestil in 1992). On Jan. 1, 1995, Austria became a member of the European Union. Despite the membership, it retained its strict constitutional neutrality and forbade the stationing of foreign troops on its soil.

In 1998, Austria discussed the return of hundreds of art objects now owned by Austria that had been confiscated by the Nazi regime from their former, primarily Jewish, owners. Deadly avalanches struck several Austrian villages in Feb. 1999, the worst avalanches in the Alps since 1970. In Aug. 1999, Austrian police arrested Gen. Momir Talic, the highest-ranking Bosnian Serb military official, wanted by the U.N. on war crimes charges.

Azerbaijan

REPUBLIC OF AZERBAIJAN

President: Heydar Aliyev (1993)
Prime Minister: Artur Rasizade (1996)
Area: 33,400 sq. mi. (86,600 sq. km)
Population (1999 est.): 7,908,224 (average annual rate of natural increase: 1.21%). Birth rate: 21.6/1000; infant mortality rate: 82.5/1000; density per sq. mi.: 237
Capital and largest city (1991): Baku, 1,713,300, a port on the Caspian Sea. Other large cities: Ganja (1989), 278,000; Sumgait, 231,000. **Monetary unit:** Manat.
Languages: Azerbaijani Turkic, 82%; Russian, 7%; Armenian, 2%. **Ethnicity/race:** Azeri 90%, Dagestani 3.2%, Russian 2.5%, Armenian 2.3%, other 2% (1995 est.). Note: almost all Armenians live in the separatist Nagorno-Karabakh region. **Religions:** Muslim, 87%; Russian Orthodox, 5.6%; Armenian Orthodox, 2%.
Economic summary: GDP/PPP (1997 est.): $11.9 billion; $1,460 per capita. **Real growth rate:** 5.8%. **Inflation:** 3.7%. **Unemployment:** 20% (1996 est.). **Arable land:** 18%. **Agriculture:** cotton, grain, rice, grapes, fruit, vegetables, tea, tobacco, cattle, pigs, sheep, goats. **Labor force:** 2.789 million (1990); agriculture and forestry, 32%; industry and construction, 26%; other, 42%. **Industry:** petroleum and natural gas, petroleum products, oilfield equipment, steel, iron ore, cement, chemicals, petrochemicals, textiles. **Exports:** $1.3 billion (f.o.b., 1996 est.): oil and gas, chemicals, oilfield equipment, textiles, cotton. **Imports:** $900 million (c.i.f., 1996): machinery and parts, consumer durables, foodstuffs, textiles. **Major trading partners:** C.I.S., European countries, Turkey.

Geography Azerbaijan is located on the western shore of the Caspian Sea at the southeastern extremity of the Caucasus. The region is a mountainous country. About 7% of it is arable land. The Kura River Valley is the area's major agricultural zone.

Government Constitutional republic.

History Azerbaijan was known in ancient times as Albania. The area was the site of many conflicts involving Arabs, Kazars, and Turks. After the 11th century, the territory became dominated by Turks and eventually a stronghold of the Shi'ite Muslim religion and Islamic culture. The territory of Soviet Azerbaijan was acquired by Russia from Persia through the Treaty of Gulistan in 1813 and the Treaty of Turkamanchai in 1828.

After the Bolshevik Revolution, Azerbaijan declared its independence from Russia in May 1918. The republic was reconquered by the Red Army in 1920, and was annexed into the Transcaucasian Soviet Socialist Republic in 1922. It was later reestablished as a separate Soviet Republic on Dec. 5, 1936. Azerbaijan declared independence from the collapsing Soviet Union on Aug. 30, 1991.

Since 1983, Azerbaijan and Armenia have been feuding over the enclave of Nagorno-Karabakh. The majority of the enclave's inhabitants are Armenian Christians agitating to secede from the predominantly Muslim Azerbaijan and join with Armenia. War broke out in 1988 when Nagorno-Karabakh tried to break away and annex itself to Armenia, and since then Armenia has controlled Nagorno-Karabakh. A cease-fire agreement was reached between the two countries in 1994, with Armenia retaining its hold over the disputed enclave. Azerbaijan has offered broad autonomy to the enclave in exchange for the withdrawal of Armenian troops from Azeri lands, but the enclave wants either full independence or annexation to Armenia. In July and Aug. 1999 the presidents of Azerbaijan and Armenia met to negotiate a settlement on the disputed enclave, but none of the results of the ongoing discussions have been announced.

The country's economic troubles are expected to be transformed through Western investment in Azerbaijan's oil resources, an untapped reserve whose estimated worth is trillions of dollars. Since 1994, the Azerbaijan state oil company (SOCAR) has signed several billion-dollar agreements with international oil companies. A total of 15 production-sharing agreements have been signed; only one, run by BP-led Azerbaijan International Operating Company (AIOC) is thus far producing crude oil. Azerbaijan's pro-Western stance and its careful economic management have made it the most attractive of the oil-rich Caspian countries for foreign investment. In the four years since its independence, the country has undergone rapid privatization and the IMF has given it high marks as one of the most successful economic overhauls ever.

But difficult negotiations over the route of the pipeline have stalled Azerbaijan's potential oil boom. Routes from Russia, Turkey, Georgia, and Iran have been proposed, and U.S., Russian, British, Iranian, and Chinese contenders in the "pipeline war" are all vying for dominance. In the volatile Caucasus region the options are complex, since all the proposed routes must pass through an unstable field of political, ethnic, religious, and environmental land mines.

Bahamas

COMMONWEALTH OF THE BAHAMAS

Sovereign: Queen Elizabeth II (1952)
Governor-General: Sir Orville Alton Turnquest (1995)
Prime Minister: Hubert Ingraham (1992)
Area: 5,380 sq. mi. (13,940 sq. km)
Population (1999 est.): 283,705 (average annual rate of natural increase: 1.52%); birth rate: 20.6/1000; infant mortality rate: 18.4/1000; density per sq. mi.: 53
Capital and largest city (1991 census): Nassau, 171,542. **Monetary unit:** Bahamian dollar. **Language:** English. **Ethnicity/race:** black 85%, white 15%. **Religions:** Baptist, 29%; Anglican, 23%; Roman Catholic, 22%, others. **Literacy rate:** 95%
Economic summary: GDP/PPP (1997 est.): $5.36 billion; $19,400 per capita. **Real growth rate:** 3.5%. **Inflation:** 0.4% (1997). **Unemployment:** 10% (1997 est.). **Labor force:** 146,600 (1996); government, 30%; tourism, 40%; business services, 10%; agriculture, 5% (1995 est.). **Agriculture:** citrus, vegetables, poultry. **Industries:** tourism, banking, cement, oil refining and transshipment, salt production, rum, aragonite, pharmaceuticals, spiral-welded steel pipe. **Natural resources:** salt, aragonite, timber. **Exports:** $201.7 million (f.o.b., 1996): pharmaceuticals, cement, rum, crawfish, refined petroleum products. **Imports:** $1.26 billion (c.i.f., 1996): foodstuffs, manufactured goods, crude oil, vehicles, electronics. **Major trading partners:** U.S., Spain, U.K., Norway, France, Italy, Finland, Iran, Denmark. **Member of Commonwealth of Nations**

Geography The Bahamas are an archipelago of about 700 islands and 2,400 uninhabited islets and cays lying 50 miles off the east coast of Florida. They extend for about 760 miles (1,223 km). Only about 30 of the islands and cays are inhabited; the most important is New Providence (80 sq. mi.; 207 sq. km), on which Nassau is situated. Other islands include Grand Bahama, Abaco, Eleuthera, Andros, Cat Island, and San Salvador (or Watling's Island). All the islands of the archipelago are composed of coraline limestone, mostly lie only a few feet above sea level, and are generally flat.

Government Commonwealth.

History The Arawak Indians were the first inhabitants of the Bahamas. Columbus' first encounter with the New World on Oct. 12, 1492, was the Bahamian island of San Salvador. The British first built settlements on the islands in the 17th century. In the early 18th century, the Bahamas were a favorite pirate haunt.

The Bahamas were a crown colony from 1717 until they were granted internal self-government in 1964. The islands moved toward greater autonomy in 1968 after the overwhelming victory in general elections of the Progressive Liberal Party, led by Prime Minister Lynden O. Pindling, over the predominately white United Bahamians Party. With its new mandate from the 85% black population, Pindling's government negotiated a new constitution with Britain under which the colony became the Commonwealth of the Bahama Islands in 1969. On July 10, 1973, the Bahamas became an independent nation.

Hubert A. Ingraham, of the Free National Movement Party, was sworn in as prime minister on Aug. 20, 1992, ending 25 years of rule by the Progressive Liberal Party. In Sept. 1999, Hurricane Floyd caused severe damage throughout the archipelago.

Bahrain

STATE OF BAHRAIN

Emir: Sheik Hamad bin Isa al-Khalifa (1999)
Prime Minister: Sheik Khalifah ibn Sulman al-Khalifa (1970)
Area: 240 sq. mi. (620 sq. km)
Population (1999 est.): 629,090 (average annual rate of natural increase: 1.86%); birth rate: 21.9/1000; infant mortality rate: 14.8/1000; density per sq. mi.: 2,621
Capital (1992 est.): Al-Manámah, 140,401. **Monetary unit:** Bahrain dinar. **Languages:** Arabic (official), English, Farsi, Urdu. **Ethnicity/race:** Bahraini 63%, Asian 13%, other Arab 10%, Iranian 8%, other 6%. **Religion:** Islam. **Literacy rate:** 77%
Economic summary: GDP/PPP (1997 est.): $8.2 billion, $13,700 per capita. **Real growth rate:** 2.7%. **Inflation:** –2%. **Unemployment:** 15% (1996 est.). **Labor force:** 140,000; industry, commerce, and service 78%, government 21%, agriculture 1% (1994). **Arable land:** 1%. **Agriculture:** fruit, vegetables, poultry, dairy products, shrimp, fish. **Industry:** petroleum processing and refining, aluminum smelting, offshore banking, ship repairing; tourism. **Natural resources:** oil, natural gas, fish. **Exports:** $4.6 billion (f.o.b., 1996): petroleum and petroleum products 61%, aluminum 7%. **Imports:** $3.7 billion (f.o.b., 1996): nonoil 63%, crude oil 37%. **Major trading partners:** India, Japan, Saudi Arabia, U.S., U.A.E., U.K., Switzerland.

Geography Bahrain is an archipelago in the Persian Gulf off the coast of Saudi Arabia. The islands for the most part are level expanses of sand and rock. A causeway connects Bahrain to Saudi Arabia.

Government Traditional monarchy.

History Known in ancient times as Dilmun, Bahrain was an important center of trade by the 3rd millennium B.C.E. The islands were ruled by the Persians in the 4th century C.E., and then by Arabs until 1541, when the Portuguese invaded them. Persia again claimed Bahrain in 1602. In 1783 Ahmad ibn al-Khalifah took over, and the al-Khalifahs remain the ruling family today. Bahrain became a British protectorate in 1820. It did not gain full independence until Aug. 14, 1971.

Although oil was discovered in Bahrain in the 1930s, it was relatively little compared to other Gulf states, and the wells are expected to be the first in the region to dry up. Sheik Isa ibn-Sulman al-Khalifa, who became emir in 1961, was determined to diversify his country's economy, and set about establishing Bahrain as a major financial center. The country provides its people with free medical care, education, and old-age pensions.

Conflicts between the Shi'ites and Sunnis are a continuing problem in Bahrain. The Sunni minority, to which the ruling al-Khalifa family belongs, controls nearly all the power and wealth in the country. Shi'ite Muslims have continued to agitate for more representation in government, and minor violent clashes, including several bombings, have led to about two dozen deaths since 1994.

Bahrain has been an important Western ally, serving as a Western air base during the Persian Gulf War in 1991, and continuing to serve as the base of the United States' Fifth Fleet, which patrols the Gulf. After ruling for four decades, Sheik Isa ibn-Sulman al-Khalifah died on March 6, 1999. He was succeeded by his son, Sheik Hamad bin Isa al-Khalifa, who is said to share his father's pro-Western policies.

Bangladesh

PEOPLE'S REPUBLIC OF BANGLADESH

President: Shahabuddin Ahmed (1996)
Prime Minister: Sheik Hasina Wazed (1996)
Area: 55,598 sq. mi. (144,000 sq. km)
Population (1999 est.): 127,117,967 (average annual rate of natural increase: 1.67%); birth rate: 25.2/1000; infant mortality rate: 69.7/1000; density per sq. mi.: 2,286
Capital and largest city : Dhaka: city proper (1991 census) 3,839,000; metro. area (1996 est.) 8,500,000. **Other large cities (est. mid-1994):** Chittagong, 3,000,000; Khulna, 2,000,000. **Monetary unit:** Taka. **Principal languages:** Bangla (official), English. **Ethnicity/race:** Bengali 98%, Biharis 250,000, tribals less than 1 million. **Religions:** Muslim 83%, Hindu 16%, Buddhist, Christian, other. **Literacy rate:** 35%
Economic summary: GDP/PPP (1997 est.): $167 billion; $1,330 per capita. **Real growth rate:** 5.5%. **Inflation:** 2.5% (1996). **Unemployment:** 35.2% (1996). **Arable land:** 73%. **Agriculture:** rice, jute, tea, wheat, sugarcane, potatoes, beef, milk, poultry. **Labor force:** 56 million; agriculture 63%, services 25%, industry and mining 10% (1996). **Industry:** jute manufacturing, cotton textiles, food processing, steel, fertilizer. **Natural resources:** natural gas, arable land, timber. **Exports:** $3.9 billion (1996): garments, jute and jute goods, leather, frozen fish, seafood. **Imports:** $6.9 billion (1996): capital goods, textiles, food, petroleum products. **Major trading partners:** Western Europe, U.S., Hong Kong, Japan, India, China, Singapore. **Member of Commonwealth of Nations**

Geography Bangladesh, on the northern coast of the Bay of Bengal, is surrounded by India, with a small common border with Burma in the southeast. It is approximately the size of Wisconsin. The country is low-lying riverine land traversed by the many branches and tributaries of the Ganges and Brahmaputra Rivers. Elevations average less than 600 feet (183 m) above sea level. Tropical monsoons and frequent floods and cyclones inflict heavy damage in the delta region.

Government Republic within the British Commonwealth.

History What is now called Bangladesh is part of the historic region of Bengal, the northeastern portion of the Indian subcontinent. The earliest reference to the region was to a kingdom called Vanga, or Banga (c.1000 B.C.E.). Buddhists ruled for centuries, but by the 10th century Bengal was primarily Hindu. In 1576, Bengal became part of the Mogul Empire, and the majority of East Bengalis converted to Islam. Bengal was ruled by British India from 1757 until Britain withdrew in 1947, and Pakistan was founded out of the two predominantly Muslim regions of the Indian subcontinent. West Pakistan and East Pakistan were united by religion (Islam), but their peoples were separated by culture, physical features, and 1,000 miles of Indian territory. Bangladesh consists primarily of East Bengal (West Bengal is part of India and its people are primarily Hindu) plus the Sylhet district of the Indian state of Assam. For almost 25 years after independence from Britain, its history was part of Pakistan's (*see* Pakistan).

Tension between East and West Pakistan developed from the outset because of their vast geographic, economic, and cultural differences. East Pakistan's Awami League, a political party founded by the Bengali nationalist Sheik Mujibur Rahman in 1949, sought independence from West Pakistan. Although 56% of the population resided in East Pakistan, the West held the lion's share of political and economic power. In 1970 East Pakistanis secured a majority of the seats in the National Assembly. President Yahya Khan postponed the opening of the National Assembly in an attempt to circumvent East Pakistan's demand for greater autonomy. As a consequence East Pakistan seceded, and the independent state of Bangladesh, or Bengali nation, was proclaimed on March 26, 1971. Civil war broke out, and with the help of Indian troops in the last few weeks of the war, East Pakistan defeated West Pakistan on Dec. 16, 1971. An estimated one million Bengalis were killed in the fighting or later slaughtered. Ten million more took refuge in India. In Feb. 1974, Pakistan agreed to recognize the independent state of Bangladesh.

Founding president Sheikh Mujibur was assassinated in 1975, as was the next president, Zia ur-Rahman. On March 24, 1982, Gen. Hossain Mohammad Ershad, army chief of staff, took control in a bloodless coup but was forced to resign on Dec. 6, 1990, amid violent protests and numerous allegations of corruption. A succession of prime ministers governed in the 1990s, including Khaleda Zia, wife of the assassinated president Zia ur-Rahman, and the current prime minister and leader of the liberal Awami League, Hasina Wazed, the daughter of Sheik Mujibur. Disastrous floods in 1998 stranded nearly eight million people and damaged crops and structures.

Bangladesh is facing a catastrophic public health crisis today. Dangerous levels of arsenic have been found in groundwater, the result of a safe-water program sponsored by UNICEF, the government, and other aid organizations 25 years ago. To save people from drinking contaminated river and pond water, between 3 and 4 million wells were built throughout the country. In the past few years, however, it was discovered that arsenic naturally occurring in the ground has seeped into the water, causing slow poisoning over many years. The World Bank has estimated that as many as 18 million people may be affected.

Barbados

Sovereign: Queen Elizabeth II (1952)
Governor-General: Sir Clifford Husbands (June 1996)
Prime Minister: Owen Arthur (1994)
Area: 166 sq. mi. (430 sq. km)
Population (1999 est.): 259,191; (growth rate: 0.63%); birth rate: 14.5/1000; infant mortality rate: 16.7/1000; density per sq. mi.: 1,561
Capital and largest city (1990): Bridgetown, 6,700. **Monetary unit:** Barbados dollar. **Language:** English. **Ethnicity/race:** African 80%, European 4%, other 16%. **Religions:** Anglican, 40%; Methodist, 7%; Pentecostal, 8%; Roman Catholic, 4%. **Literacy rate:** 99%
Economic summary: GDP/PPP (1997 est.): $2.8 billion; $10,900 per capita. **Real growth rate:** 3%. **Inflation:** 2.4% (1996). **Unemployment:** 16.2% (1996). **Arable land:** 37%. **Agriculture:** sugarcane, vegetables, cotton. **Industry:** tourism, sugar, light manufacturing, component assembly for export. **Labor force:** (1996), 68,900; services 75%, industry 15%, agriculture 10%

(1996 est.). **Exports:** $235 million (f.o.b., 1995): sugar and molasses, rum, other foods and beverages, chemicals, electrical components, clothing. **Imports:** $763 million (c.i.f., 1995): consumer goods, machinery, foodstuffs, construction materials, chemicals, fuel, electrical components. **Major trading partners:** U.S., U.K., Trinidad and Tobago, Windward Islands, Japan. **Member of Commonwealth of Nations**

Geography An island in the Atlantic about 300 miles (483 km) north of Venezuela, Barbados is only 21 miles long (34 km) and 14 miles across (23 km) at its widest point. It is circled by fine beaches and narrow coastal plains. The highest point is Mount Hillaby (1,105 ft.; 337 m) in the north central area.

Government Parliamentary democracy.

History Barbados is thought to have been originally inhabited by Arawak Indians. By the time Europeans explored the island, however, it was uninhabited.

Barbados was settled by the British in 1627. Slaves were brought in from Africa to work sugar plantations, and from the time of its settlement, the population was about 90% black. Slavery was abolished in the British Empire in 1834, and in 1838 slaves on the island gained their freedom.

Barbados became a crown colony in 1885 and was a member of the Federation of the West Indies from 1958 to 1962. Britain granted the colony independence on Nov. 30, 1966, and it became a parliamentary democracy within the Commonwealth.

Since independence, Barbados has been politically stable. However, local anger over rulings by the final appeals court, appointed by Queen Elizabeth, led to the creation in 1997 of a constitutional commission to consider abandoning all ties to Great Britain. President Arthur, who has seen Barbados's unemployment fall from 22% to 11%, was reelected in 1999 by a landslide.

Belarus

REPUBLIC OF BELARUS

President: Alyaksandr Lukashenka (1994)
Prime Minister: Syarhei Linh (1996)
Area: 80,200 sq. mi. (207,600 sq. km)
Population (1999 est.): 10,401,784 (average annual rate of natural increase: –0.40%) (in 1989: Belarussian, 77.9%; Russian, 13.2%; Polish, 4.1%; Ukrainian, 2.9%; Jewish, 1.1%); birth rate: 9.7/1000; infant mortality rate: 14.4/1000; density per sq. mi.: 130
Capital (1992 est.): Mensk (Minsk), 1,666,000. **Other large cities (1992 est.):** Gomel, 517,300; Vitebsk, 373,000; Mogilyov, 364,000; Grodno, 291,800; Brest, 284,000; Bobruysk, 224,000. **Monetary unit:** Belarussian ruble. **Language:** Belarussian (White Russian). **Ethnicity/race:** Belarussian 77.9%, Russian 13.2%, Polish 4.1%, Ukrainian 2.9%, other 1.9%. **Religion:** Orthodoxy is predominant. **Literacy rate:** 100%
Economic summary: GDP/PPP (1997 est.): $50.4 billion; $4,800 per capita. **Real growth rate:** 8.5%. **Inflation:** 65%. **Unemployment:** 3.3% (July 1997). **Arable land:** 29%. **Agriculture:** grain, potatoes, vegetables, meat, milk. **Labor force:** 4.3 million; industry and construction, 40%; agriculture and forestry, 19%; services, 41%. **Industry:** tractors, metal-cutting machine tools, off-highway dump trucks, wheel-type earthmovers for construction and mining, eight-wheel-drive high-flotation trucks, equipment for animal husbandry and livestock feeding, motorcycles, television sets, chemical fibers, fertilizer, linen fabric, wool fabric, radios, refrigerators, other consumer goods. **Exports:** $5.4 billion (f.o.b., 1996): machinery and transport equipment, chemicals, foodstuffs. **Imports:** $6.7 billion (c.i.f., 1996): fuel, natural gas, industrial raw materials, textiles, sugar. **Major trading partners:** Russia, Ukraine, Poland, Germany.

Geography Much of Belarus (formerly the Belarussian Soviet Socialist Republic of the U.S.S.R., and then Byelorussia) is a hilly lowland with forests, swamps, and numerous rivers and lakes. There are wide rivers emptying into the Baltic and Black Seas. Its forests cover over one-third of the land and its peat marshes are a valuable natural resource. The largest lake is Narach, 31 sq. mi. (79.6 sq. km).

Government Republic.

History In the 5th century, Belarus (also known as White Russia) was colonized by east Slavic tribes. Kiev dominated it from the 9th to 12th centuries. After the destruction of Kiev by the Mongols in the 13th century, the territory was conquered by the dukes of Lithuania, although it retained an amount of autonomy. Belarus became part of the Grand Duchy of Lithuania, which merged with Poland in 1569. Following the partitions of Poland in 1772, 1793, and 1795, in which Poland was divided among Russia, Prussia, and Austria, Belarus became part of the Russian empire.

Following World War I, Belarus proclaimed itself a republic, only to find itself occupied by the Red Army soon after its March 1918 announcement. The Polish-Soviet War of 1918–21 was fought to decide the fate of Belarus. West Belarus was ceded to Poland; the larger eastern part formed the Belorussian S.S.R., and was then joined to the U.S.S.R. in 1922. In 1939, the Soviet Union took back West Belarus from Poland under the secret protocol of the Nazi-Soviet Nonaggression Pact and incorporated it into the Belarussian Soviet Socialist Republic. Occupied by the Nazis in World War II, Belarus was one of the most devastated battlefields.

Belarus declared its sovereignty in July 1990 and its independence in Aug. 1991. The Chernobyl nuclear power plant in Ukraine exploded in 1986, and 70% of its radioactivity fell on Belarus. Cancer and other illnesses have multiplied as a result.

The Belarus president, Nikolai Dementei, a communist hard-liner, was forced to resign under pressure following the Aug. 1991 attempted coup, and Stanislav S. Shushkevich, first deputy chairman of the Parliament, assumed leadership of the country. Belarus became a cofounder of the Commonwealth of Independent States (C.I.S.) in Dec. 1991. In Jan. 1994, the country's Parliament ousted its reform-minded leader in protest against his support for market economics. In March 1994, Parliament adopted a new constitution, creating a presidency, and reconstructed the 260-seat Parliament.

With much fanfare, Belarus and Russia signed a treaty in April 1997 aimed at significantly increasing cooperation between the two states, stopping just short of union. In 1999, there was discussion of a pan-Slav union, uniting the rump Yugoslavia under Milosevic, with Russia and Belarus. This also came to nothing.

The Russian financial crisis that began in fall 1998 severely affected Belarus's Soviet-style planned economy. Belarus is almost completely dependent on Russia, which buys 70% of its exports.

Critics continue to denounce the increasingly oppressive political atmosphere and human rights violations in Belarus under the Soviet-style authoritarianism of President Alyaksandr Lukashenko. In 1999, the year President Lukashenko was to step down, he held what international opinion widely believed to have been a rigged national referendum, which changed the constitution and allowed him to cancel the elections and remain president. As he explained the constitutional changes, "I have not yet done everything, and that is why I will be in power for a long time," he said.

Belgium

KINGDOM OF BELGIUM

National name: Royaume de Belgique—Koningrijk van België
Sovereign: King Albert II (1993)
Prime Minister: Guy Verhofstadt (1999)
Area: 11,781 sq. mi. (30,510 sq. km)
Population (1999 est.): 10,182,034 (average annual rate of natural increase: –0.05%); birth rate: 10.0/1000; infant mortality rate: 6.2/1000; density per sq. mi.: 883
Capital and largest city (1994): Brussels, 949,070 (metro area). **Other large cities (1994):** Antwerp, 476,044; Ghent, 229,900; Liège, 207,496; Charleroi, 206,898; Bruges, 116,724. **Monetary units:** Belgian franc and euro. **Languages:** Flemish, 57%; French, 32%; bilingual (Brussels), 10%; German, 0.7%. **Ethnicity/race:** Fleming 55%, Walloon 33%, mixed or other 12%. **Religion:** Roman Catholic, 75%. **Literacy rate:** 99%
Economic summary: GDP/PPP (1997 est.): $236.3 billion; $23,200 per capita. **Real growth rate:** 2.3%. **Inflation:** 1.7%. **Unemployment:** 12.75% (1997). **Arable land:** 24%. **Agriculture:** sugar beets, fresh vegetables, fruits, grain, tobacco, beef, veal, pork, milk. **Labor force:** 4.283 million (1997); services, 69.7%; industry, 27.7%; agriculture, 2.6% (1992). **Industry:** engineering and metal products, motor vehicle assembly, processed food and beverages, chemicals, basic metals, textiles, glass, petroleum, coal. **Exports:** $172 billion (f.o.b., 1997): iron and steel, transportation equipment, tractors, diamonds, petroleum products. **Imports:** $158.5 billion (c.i.f., 1997): fuels, grains, chemicals, foodstuffs. **Major trading partners:** EU, U.S., former Communist countries.

Geography Located in western Europe, Belgium has about 40 miles of seacoast on the North Sea, at the Strait of Dover, and is approximately the size of Maryland. The Meuse and the Schelde, Belgium's principal rivers, are important commercial arteries.

Government Parliamentary democracy under a constitutional monarch.

Under the 1994 constitution, autonomy was granted to the Walloon region (Wallonia), the Flemish region (Flanders), and the bilingual Brussels-Capital region; autonomy was also guaranteed for the Flemish-, French-, and German-speaking "communities." The central government retains responsibility for foreign policy, defense, taxation, and social security; the regional governments are responsible for transport, the environment, and trade promotion; the "community" governments oversee cultural and personal matters, including education.

History Belgium occupied part of the Roman province of Belgica, named after the Belgae, a people of ancient Gaul. The area was conquered by Julius Caesar in 57–50 B.C.E., then was overrun by the Franks in the 5th century. It was part of Charlemagne's empire in the 8th century, then in the next century was absorbed into Lotharingia and later into the duchy of Lower Lorraine. In the 12th century it was partitioned into the duchies of Brabant and Luxembourg, the bishopric of Liège, and the domain of the count of Hainaut, which included Flanders. In the 16th century, Belgium, with most of the area of the low countries, passed to the duchy of Burgundy and was inherited by Charles V, who incorporated it into his Holy Roman Empire. Then, in 1555, the low countries were united with Spain. By the Treaty of Utrecht in 1713, the country's sovereignty passed to Austria. During the wars that followed the French Revolution, Belgium was occupied and later annexed to France. But with the downfall of Napoléon, the Congress of Vienna in 1815 gave the country to the Netherlands. The Belgians revolted in 1830 and declared their independence.

Germany's invasion of Belgium in 1914 set off World War I. The Treaty of Versailles (1919) gave the areas of Eupen, Malmédy, and Moresnet to Belgium. Leopold III succeeded Albert, king during World War I, in 1934. In World War II, Belgium was overwhelmed by Nazi Germany, and Leopold III was held prisoner. When he attempted to return in 1950, socialists and liberals revolted. He abdicated July 16, 1951, and his son, Baudouin, became king. Because of growing opposition to Belgian rule in its African colonies, Belgium granted independence to Congo (now Democratic Republic of the Congo) in 1960 and to Ruanda-Urundi (now the nations of Rwanda and Burundi) in 1962.

Divisions between Flemings and Walloons grew, and linguistic regionalization increased, culminating in the revised constitution of 1994, which granted more autonomy to Belgium's three regions and language "communities."

Contributing to the growing secessionist movement has been the Belgian government's legion incompetence and corruption. In 1991, a deputy prime minister was murdered in a contract killing that remained unsolved. In 1998, Belgian statesman and former NATO secretary-general Willy Claes was convicted of bribery. International relations fared no better. Belgian peacekeeping troops abandoned Rwanda, a former colony, at the height of the 1994 genocide against the Tutsis. The discovery of a child sex and murder ring in 1996 led to further national outrage that was compounded by disclosures that official negligence and corruption had resulted in even more children's deaths. As the scandal continued into 1997, it fueled pressure for reform of the political, judicial, and police systems.

It was evident that little had changed, however, when Belgium stumbled into its next crisis in spring 1999. Dioxin, a cancer-causing chemical, was leaked into batches of chicken feed, contaminating the country's poultry and dairy products. Government ministers admitted to keeping the public in the dark for months after they realized the public health danger. As a consequence, voters gave conservatives dominance in Parliament for the first time in more than a century, and Prime Minister Jean-Luc Dehaene resigned on June 14.

Belize

Sovereign: Queen Elizabeth II (1952)
Governor-General: Colville Young (1993)
Prime Minister: Said Musa (1998)
Area: 8,867 sq. mi. (22,960 sq. km)
Population (1999 est.): 235,789 (average annual rate of natural increase: 2.48%); birth rate: 30.2/1000; infant mortality rate: 31.6/1000.; density per sq. mi.: 27
Capital (1997 est.): Belmopan, 5,845. **Largest city (1997 est.):** Belize City, 52,500. **Monetary unit:** Belize dollar. **Languages:** English (official), Creole, Spanish, Garifuna, Mayan. **Ethnicity/race:** mestizo 44%, Creole 30%, Maya 11%, Garifuna 7%, other 8%. **Religions:** Roman Catholic, 62%; Protestant, 30%. **Literacy rate:** 91%
Economic summary: GDP/PPP (1997 est.): $680 million; $3,000 per capita. **Real growth rate:** 2.9%. **Inflation:** 1%. **Unemployment:** 13%. **Arable land:** 2%. **Agriculture:** bananas, coca, citrus, sugarcane, lumber, fish, cultured shrimp. **Labor force:** 71,000; agriculture, 30%; services, 16%; government, 15.4%; commerce, 11.2%; manufacturing, 10.3%. **Industry:** garment production, food processing, tourism, construction. **Natural resources:** arable land potential, timber, fish. **Exports:** $166 million (f.o.b., 1996): sugar, citrus fruits, bananas, clothing, fish products, molasses, wood. **Imports:** $262 million (c.i.f., 1996): machinery and transportation equipment, food, manufactured goods, fuels, chemicals, pharmaceuticals. **Major trading partners:** U.S., U.K., other EU, Canada, Mexico. **Member of Commonwealth of Nations**

Geography Belize is situated on the Caribbean Sea south of Mexico and east and north of Guatemala in Central America. In area, it is about the size of New Hampshire. Most of the country is heavily forested with various hardwoods. Mangrove swamps and cays along the coast give way to hills and mountains in the interior. The highest point is Victoria Peak, 3,681 feet (1,122 m).

Government Parliamentary democracy within the British Commonwealth.

History The Mayan civilization spread into the area of Belize between 1500 B.C.E. and C.E. 300 and flourished until about C.E. 1200. Several major archeological sites—notably Caracol, Lamanai, Lubaantun, Altun Ha, and Xunantunich—reflect the advanced civilization and much denser population of that period. European contact began in 1502 when Columbus sailed along the coast. The first recorded European settlement was begun by shipwrecked English seamen in 1638. Over the next 150 years, more English settlements were established. This period was also marked by piracy, indiscriminate logging, and sporadic attacks by Indians and neighboring Spanish settlements. Great Britain first sent an official representative to the area in the late 18th century, but Belize was not formally termed the Colony of British Honduras until 1840. It became a crown colony in 1862. Subsequently, several constitutional changes were enacted to expand representative government. Full internal self-government under a ministerial system was granted in Jan. 1964.

Guatemala had long made claims on Honduran territory. Although the dispute between Guatemala and Great Britain remained unresolved, Belize became independent on Sept. 21, 1981, after having been self-governing since 1964. Guatemala recognized Belize's sovereignty in Sept. 1991 and abandoned its territorial claim, although unease remains.

Belize traditionally maintains a deep interest in the environment and sustainable development and its efforts to increase eco-tourism have been somewhat successful. In 1998, Prime Minister Said Musa launched an ambitious plan to encourage economic growth while furthering social-sector development.

Benin

REPUBLIC OF BENIN

National name: Republique du Benin
President: Mathieu Kerekou (1996)
Area: 43,483 sq. mi. (112,620 sq. km)
Population (1999 est.): 6,305,567 (average annual rate of natural increase: 3.30%); birth rate: 45.4/1000; infant mortality rate: 97.8/1000; density per sq. mi.: 145
Capital and largest city (1996): Porto-Novo (official), 177,660; Cotonou (de facto capital) 33,212. **Other large city (1992):** Djougou, 132,192. **Monetary unit:** Franc CFA. **Ethnic groups:** Fons and Adjas, Baribas, Yorubas, Mahls. **Languages:** French, African languages. **Ethnicity/race:** African 99% (42 ethnic groups, most important being Fon, Adja, Yoruba, Bariba), Europeans 5,500. **Religions:** indigenous, 70%; Christian, 15%; Islam, 15%. **Literacy rate:** 23%
Economic summary: GDP/PPP (1997 est.): $11.3 billion; $1,900 per capita. **Real growth rate:** 5.8%. **Inflation:** 3.5%. **Unemployment:** n.a. **Arable land:** 13%. **Agriculture:** corn, sorghum, cassava (tapioca), yams, beans, rice, cotton, palm oil, peanuts, poultry, livestock. **Labor force:** n.a. **Industry:** textiles, cigarettes, beverages, food, construction materials, petroleum. **Natural resources:** some offshore oil, limestone, marble, timber. **Exports:** $192 million (f.o.b., 1995): cotton, crude oil, palm products, cocoa. **Imports:** $693 million (c.i.f., 1995): foodstuffs, beverages, tobacco, petroleum products, intermediate goods, capital goods, light consumer goods. **Major trading partners:** Brazil, Portugal, Morocco, Libya, France, Thailand, China, Hong Kong.

Geography This West African nation on the Gulf of Guinea, between Togo on the west and Nigeria on the east, is about the size of Tennessee. It is bounded also by Burkina Faso and Niger on the north. The land consists of a narrow coastal strip that rises to a swampy, forested plateau and then to highlands in the north. A hot and humid climate blankets the entire country.

Government Republic under a multiparty democratic rule.

History The Abomey kingdom of the Dahomey, or Fon, peoples was established in 1625. A rich cultural life flourished, and Benin's wooden masks, bronze statues, tapestries, and pottery are world renowned. One of the smallest and most densely populated states in Africa, Benin was annexed by the French in 1893 and incorporated into French West Africa in 1904. It became an autonomous republic within the French Community in 1958, and on Aug. 1, 1960, Dahomey was granted its independence within the community.

Gen. Christophe Soglo deposed the first president, Hubert Maga, in an army coup in 1963. He dismissed the civilian government in 1965, proclaiming himself chief of state. A group of young army officers seized power in Dec. 1967, deposing Soglo. In Dec. 1969,

Benin had its fifth coup of the decade, with the army again taking power. In May 1970, a three-man presidential commission with a six-year term was created to take over the government. In May 1972, yet another army coup ousted the triumvirate and installed Lt. Col. Mathieu Kerekou as president. Between 1974 and 1989 Dahomey embraced socialism, and changed its name to the People's Republic of Benin. The name *Benin* commemorates an African kingdom that flourished from the 15th to the 17th century in what is now southwestern Nigeria. In 1990 Benin abandoned Marxist ideology, began moving toward multiparty democracy, and changed its name again, to the Republic of Benin.

Since 1990 the government has embarked on a vast privatization drive. The sale of SONICOG (a producer of butter, soap, and edible oils) in 1997 was contingent on the retention of the entire labor force. Presidential elections in March 1996 resulted in a victory for former president and Marxist military ruler Kerekou, with 52.49% of the vote, over the incumbent Soglo. Prime Minister Adrien Houngbedji resigned from President Kerekou's cabinet in 1998, and the president, after reshuffling his cabinet, announced that there would no longer be a prime minister position in the government.

Bhutan

KINGDOM OF BHUTAN

National name: Druk-yul
Ruler: King Jigme Singye Wangchuck (1972)
Area: 18,000 sq. mi. (47,000 sq. km)
Population (1999 est.): 1,951,965 (average annual rate of natural increase: 2.25%); birth rate: 36.8/1000; infant mortality rate: 109.3/1000; density per sq. mi.: 108
Capital and largest city (1993): Thimphu (official), 30,340. **Monetary unit:** Ngultrum. **Language:** Dzongkha (official). **Ethnicity/race:** Bhote 50%, ethnic Nepali 35%, indigenous or migrant tribes 15%. **Religions:** Buddhist, 75%; Hindu, 25%. **Literacy rate:** n.a.
Economic summary: GDP/PPP (1995 est.): $1.3 billion; $730 per capita. **Real growth rate:** 6.9% (1995 est.). **Inflation:** 7% (FY 96/97 est.). **Unemployment:** n.a. **Arable land:** 2%. **Labor force:** n.a.; agriculture: 93%; services: 5%; industry and commerce: 2%. **Agriculture:** rice, corn, root crops, citrus, food grains; dairy products, eggs. **Industry:** cement, wood products, processed fruits, alcoholic beverages, calcium carbide. **Natural resources:** timber, hydropower, gypsum, calcium carbide. **Exports:** $77.4 million (f.o.b., 1996 est.): cardamom, gypsum, timber, handicrafts, cement, fruit, electricity (to India), precious stones, spices. **Imports:** $104.1 million (c.i.f., 1996 est.): fuel and lubricants, grain, machinery and parts, vehicles, fabrics, rice. **Major trading partners:** India, Bangladesh, Japan, U.K., Germany, U.S.

Geography Mountainous Bhutan, half the size of Indiana, is situated on the southeast slope of the Himalayas, bordered on the north and east by Tibet and on the south and west and east by India. The landscape consists of a succession of lofty and rugged mountains running generally from north to south and separated by deep valleys. In the north, towering peaks reach a height of 24,000 feet (7,315 m).

Government In the 1990s, the king gradually gave up absolute rule, transforming his kingdom into a constitutional monarchy.

History Although archeological exploration of Bhutan has been limited, evidence of civilization in the region dates back to at least 2000 B.C.E. Aboriginal Bhutanese, known as Monpa, are believed to have migrated from Tibet. The traditional name of the country since the 17th century has been Drukyul, Land of the Drokpa (Dragon People), a reference to the dominant branch of Tibetan Buddhism that is still practiced in the Himalayan kingdom.

British troops invaded the region in 1865, and negotiated an agreement under which Britain agreed to pay an annual allowance to the Bhutanese monarchy on condition of good behavior. A treaty between India and the seat of government, Thimphu, in 1949 increased this subsidy and placed Bhutan's foreign affairs under Indian control. Until the 1960s Bhutan was largely isolated from the rest of the world, and its people carried on a tranquil, traditional way of life of farming and trading that had remained intact for centuries. After China invaded Tibet, however, Bhutan strengthened its ties and contact with India in an effort to avoid Tibet's fate. New roads and other connections to India began to end its isolation. In the 1960s Bhutan also undertook social modernization, abolishing slavery and the caste system, emancipating women, and enacting land reform. In 1985, Bhutan made its first diplomatic links with non-Asian countries.

A pro-democracy campaign emerged in 1991 that the government claimed was composed largely of Nepali immigrants. As a result of the campaign, some 100,000 Nepali civil servants were either evicted or encouraged to emigrate. Most of them crossed the border back into Nepal, where they were housed in U.N.-administered refugee camps. The mass exodus prompted the International Red Cross to investigate charges of human rights violations in 1993. By 1995, discussions with Nepal over the problem had born little fruit, with Thimphu insisting that the refugees had left of their own free will or were Nepali nationals wanting to immigrate to Bhutan.

In 1998, King Jigme Singye Wangchuck voluntarily curtailed his powerful monarchy by yielding to the formerly rubber-stamp legislature, giving it the right to remove him from leadership and appoint his cabinet. The move was the largest step to date in a gradual program to dilute the monarchy after nearly a century of absolute rule. Income tax was introduced, with tax forms due for the first time in Feb. 2000.

Bolivia

REPUBLIC OF BOLIVIA

National name: República de Bolivia
President: Hugo Banzer Suárez (1997)
Area: 424,162 sq. mi. (1,098,580 sq. km)
Population (1999 est.): 7,982,850 (average annual rate of natural increase: 2.11%); birth rate: 30.7/1,000; infant mortality rate: 62.0/1000; density per sq. mi.: 19
Historic and judicial capital (1997 est.): Sucre, 131,800
Administrative capital and largest city (1997 est.): La Paz, 713,400. **Other large cities (1997 est.):** Santa Cruz, 697,000; Cochabamba, 407,800; El Alto, 405,500; Oruro, 184,000. **Monetary unit:** Boliviano. **Languages:** Spanish (official), Quechua, Aymara, Guarani. **Ethnicity/race:** Quechua 30%, Aymara 25%, mestizo (mixed European and Indian ancestry) 25%–30%, European 5%–15%. **Religion:** Roman Catholic, 85%. **Literacy rate:** 82%

Economic summary: GDP/PPP (1997 est.): $23.1 billion; $3,000 per capita. **Real growth rate:** 4.4%. **Inflation:** 7% (1997). **Unemployment:** 10%. **Arable land:** 2%. **Agriculture:** coffee, coca, cotton, corn, sugarcane, rice, potatoes, timber. **Industry:** mining, smelting, petroleum, food and beverages, tobacco, handicrafts, clothing. **Labor force:** 2.5 million; agriculture: n.a.; services and utilities: n.a.; manufacturing, mining, and construction: n.a. **Natural resources:** tin, natural gas, petroleum, zinc, tungsten, antimony, silver, iron, lead, gold, timber. **Exports:** $1.4 billion (f.o.b., 1997): metals, natural gas, soybeans, jewelry, wood. **Imports:** $1.7 billion (c.i.f., 1997): capital goods, chemicals, petroleum, food (1993 est.). **Major trading partners:** U.S., U.K., Colombia, Peru, Argentina, Japan, Brazil, Chile.

Geography Landlocked Bolivia is equal in size to California and Texas combined. Brazil forms its eastern border; its other neighbors are Peru and Chile on the west and Argentina and Paraguay on the south. The western part, enclosed by two chains of the Andes, is a great plateau—the Altiplano, with an average altitude of 12,000 ft. (3,658 m). Almost half the population lives on the plateau, which contains Oruro, Potosí, and La Paz. At an altitude of 11,910 feet (3,630 m), La Paz is the highest administrative capital city in the world. The Oriente, a lowland region ranging from rain forests to grasslands, comprises the northern and eastern two-thirds of the country. Lake Titicaca, at an altitude of 12,507 ft. (3,812 m), is the highest commercially navigable body of water in the world.

Government Republic.

History Famous since Spanish colonial days for its mineral wealth, modern Bolivia was once a part of the ancient Incan empire. After the Spaniards defeated the Incas in the 16th century, Bolivia's predominantly Indian population was reduced to slavery. The remoteness of the Andes helped protect the Bolivian Indians from the European diseases that decimated other South American Indians. But the existence of a large indigenous group forced to live under the thumb of their colonizers created a stratified society of haves and have-nots that continues to this day.

By the end of the 17th century the mineral wealth had begun to dry up. The country won its independence in 1825 and was named after Simón Bolívar, the famous liberator. Hampered by internal strife, Bolivia lost great slices of territory to three neighboring nations. Several thousand square miles and its outlet to the Pacific were taken by Chile after the War of the Pacific (1879–84). In 1903, a piece of Bolivia's Acre province, rich in rubber, was ceded to Brazil. And in 1938, after losing the Chaco War of 1932–35 to Paraguay, Bolivia gave up its claim to nearly 100,000 square miles of the Gran Chaco. Political instability ensued.

In 1965, a guerrilla movement mounted from Cuba and headed by Maj. Ernesto (Ché) Guevara began a revolutionary war. With the aid of U.S. military advisers, the Bolivian army smashed the guerrilla movement, capturing and killing Guevara on Oct. 8, 1967. Faltering steps toward restoration of civilian government were halted abruptly on July 17, 1980, when Gen. Luis Garcia Meza Tejada seized power. A series of military leaders followed before the military returned the government to civilian rule in 1982, when Hernán Siles Zuazo became president. Under Siles's left-of-center government, the country was regularly shut down by work stoppages, and the bulk of Bolivia's natural resources—natural gas, gold, lithium, potassium, and tungsten—were either sold on the black market or left in the ground. The country also had the lowest per capita income in South America, and inflation approached 3000%. In 1985, Siles decided he was unable to carry on and quit a year early.

Since 1985, Bolivia has implemented economic changes that have been phenomenally successful. Still at the bottom of the South American economic ladder, its economy has steadily improved over the past fifteen years. Political stability has helped. The standard joke about Bolivia's instability was to compare it to a long-playing record: "33 revolutions a minute."

In June 1993 Gonzalo Sánchez de Lozada was elected president, running on a platform calling for free-market policies and privatization. Former general Hugo Bánzer was elected president for the second time in Aug. 1997. Bánzer pledged to wipe out illicit coca production and drug trafficking in Bolivia by the end of his term in 2002. He has also initiated a rural literacy campaign, and is implementing a plan for the poor to acquire loans.

Bosnia and Herzegovina
THE FEDERATION OF BOSNIA AND HERZEGOVINA

President: Ante Jelavic (Bosnian Croat) (1999)
Co-Prime Ministers: Alija Izetbegovic (Bosnian Muslim, and chairman) and Zivko Radisic (Bosnian Serb)
Area: 19,741 sq. mi. (51,233 sq. km)
Population (1999 est.): 3,482,495 (all data dealing with population is subject to considerable error because of the dislocations caused by military action and ethnic cleansing); (average annual rate of natural increase: –0.15%); Birth rate: 9.4/1000; infant mortality rate: 24.5/1000; density per sq. mi.: 176
Capital and largest city (1994 est.): Sarajevo, 300,000 (unofficial). . **Other large cities (1991, prewar est.):** Banja Luka, 195,139; Mostar, 126,067 . **Monetary unit:** Dinar. **Language:** The language that used to be known as Serbo-Croatian but is now known as Serbian, Croatian, or Bosnian, depending on the speaker's ethnic and political affiliation. It is written in Latin and Cyrillic.. **Ethnicity/race:** Serb 40%, Muslim 38%, Croat 22% (1998 est.). **Religions:** Slavic Muslim, 44%; Orthodox, 31%; Catholic, 15%; Protestant, 4%, other, 6%.
Economic summary: GDP/PPP (1997 est.): $4.41 billion, **Real growth rate:** 35%, **Inflation:** n.a. **Unemployment:** 40%–50% (1996 est.) **Labor force:** 1,026,254. **Industry:** steel, coal, iron ore, lead, zinc, manganese, bauxite, vehicle assembly, textiles, tobacco products, wooden furniture, tank and aircraft assembly, domestic appliances, oil refining; much of capacity damaged or shut down (1995). **Agriculture:** wheat, corn, fruits, vegetables, livestock. **Exports:** $152 million (1995 est.). **Imports:** $1.1 billion (1995 est.). **Major trading partners:** n.a.

Geography Bosnia and Herzegovina make up a triangular-shaped republic, about half the size of Kentucky, on the Balkan peninsula. The Bosnian region in the north is mountainous and covered with thick forests. The Herzegovina region in the south is largely a rugged and flat farmland. It has a narrow coastline without natural harbors stretching 13 miles (20 km) along the Adriatic Sea.

Government Emerging democratic republic. Following the postwar general elections in 1996, a three-person multiethnic rotating presidency was formed.

History The general region that is now called Bosnia and Herzegovina was called Illyricum in ancient times. The Romans conquered the area in the 2nd and 1st centuries B.C.E. and folded it into the Roman province of Dalmatia. In the 4th and 5th centuries C.E. the Goths overran this portion of the declining Roman Empire and occupied the area until the 6th century, when the Byzantine empire claimed it. Slavs began settling in the region during the 7th century C.E., and Bosnia was alternately ruled by Serbs and Croats under the overall rule of Byzantium. Later Bosnia came under Hungarian rule in the middle of the 12th century, after which it emerged as an independent country for the first time. Medieval Bosnia reached the height of its power and prestige during the 14th century, when it controlled many of the surrounding territories including Herzegovina. During this period, religious strife arose among Roman Catholics, Orthodox, and Muslims, weakening the country. In 1463, Ottoman Turks conquered the nation, and much of the population gradually converted to Islam.

Neighboring Serbia and Montenegro fought against the Ottoman Empire in 1876, and were aided by the Russians, their fellow Slavs. At the Congress of Berlin in 1878 following the end of the Russo-Turkish War (1877–78), Austria-Hungary was given a mandate to occupy and govern Bosnia and Herzegovina, in an effort by Europe to ensure that Russia did not dominate the Balkans. Although the provinces were still officially part of the Ottoman Empire, they were annexed by the Austro-Hungarian Empire on Oct. 7, 1908. As a result, relations with Serbia, which had claims on Bosnia and Herzegovina, became embittered. The hostility between the two countries climaxed in the assassination of Austrian Archduke Franz Ferdinand in Sarajevo on June 28, 1914, by a Serbian nationalist. This event precipitated the start of World War I (1914–18). Bosnia and Herzegovina were annexed to Serbia as part of the newly formed Kingdom of Serbs, Croats, and Slovenes on Oct. 26, 1918. The name was later changed to Yugoslavia in 1929.

When Germany invaded Yugoslavia in 1941, Bosnia and Herzegovina were made part of Nazi-controlled Croatia. During the German and Italian occupation, Bosnian and Herzegovinian resistance fighters fought a fierce guerrilla war against the Ustachi, the Croatian Fascist troops. At the end of World War II, Bosnia and Herzegovina were reunited into a single state as one of the six republics of the newly reestablished Communist Yugoslavia, under Marshall Tito. His authoritarian control kept the ethnic enmities of his patchwork nation in check. Tito died in 1980, and with growing economic dissatisfaction and the fall of the iron curtain over the next decade, Yugoslavia began to splinter.

In Dec. 1991, Bosnia and Herzegovina declared independence from Yugoslavia and asked for recognition by the European Union (EU). In a March 1992 referendum, Bosnian voters chose independence, and President Izetbegovic declared the nation an independent state. Unlike the other former Yugoslav states, which were generally composed of a dominant ethnic group, Bosnia was an ethnic tangle of Muslims (44%), Serbs (31%), and Croats (17%), and this mix contributed to the duration and savagery of its fight for independence.

Both the Croatian and Serbian presidents had planned to partition Bosnia between themselves. Attempting to carve out their own enclaves, the Serbian minority, with the help of the Serbian Yugoslav army, took the offensive and laid siege, particularly on Sarajevo, and began its ruthless campaigns of ethnic cleansing, which involved the expulsion or massacre of Muslims. Croats also began carving out their own communities. By the end of Aug. 1992, rebel Bosnian Serbs had conquered over 60% of Bosnia. The war did not begin to wane until NATO stepped in, bombing Serb positions in Bosnia in Aug. and Sept. 1995. This was followed by a joint offensive by Bosnian Muslim and Croatian forces that took back a significant amount of critical Bosnian territory.

U.S.-sponsored peace talks in Dayton, Ohio, led to an agreement in 1995 that called for a Muslim-Croat federation and a Serb entity within the larger federation of Bosnia. Sixty thousand NATO troops were to supervise its implementation. Fighting abated and orderly elections were held in Sept. 1996. President Alija Izetbegovic, a Bosnian Muslim, or Bosniac, won the majority of votes to become the leader of the three-member presidency, each representing one of the three ethnic groups.

But this alliance of unreconstructed enemies had little success in creating a working government or keeping violent clashes in check. The terms of the Dec. 1995 Dayton Peace Accord were largely ignored by Bosnian Serbs, with its former president, arch-nationalist Radovan Karadzic, still in de facto control of the Serbian enclave. Many indicted war criminals, including Karadzic, remain at large. Despite NATO's pledge in Oct. 1997 to remain in Bosnia beyond the 1998 mandate, the peacekeeping force remained mired in chronic ambivalence, unable to decide whether to jump into the fray or remain passive, hoping its presence was enough to spawn peace.

The crucial priorities facing postwar Bosnian leaders were rebuilding the economy, resettling the estimated one million refugees still displaced, and establishing a working government. Progress on these goals has been minimal, and a massive corruption scandal uncovered in 1999 severely tested the good will of the international community. Millions of dollars from international aid projects earmarked for reconstruction and humanitarian purposes had been pilfered by Bosnian officials, according to an American-led international antifraud unit. The country had received $5.1 billion in aid since 1995 by a hopeful international community supporting the dream that the quagmire of the Balkans could be surmounted.

Botswana

REPUBLIC OF BOTSWANA

President: Festus Mogae (1998)
Area: 231,800 sq. mi. (600,370 sq. km)
Population (1999 est.): 1,464,167 (average annual rate of natural increase: 1.05%); birth rate: 31.5/1000; infant mortality rate: 59.1/1000; density per sq. mi.: 6
Capital and largest city (1992 est.): Gaborone, 138,000. **Monetary unit:** Pula. **Languages:** English,

Setswana. **Ethnicity/race:** Batswana 95%, Kalanga, Basarwa, and Kgalagadi 4%, white 1%. **Religions:** indigenous beliefs, 50%; Christian, 50%. **Literacy rate:** 74%

Economic summary: GDP/PPP (1997 est.): $5 billion, $3,300 per capita. **Real growth rate:** 6%. **Inflation:** 10% (1996 est.). **Unemployment:** 20%–40% (1997 est.). **Arable land:** 1%. **Agriculture:** sorghum, maize, millet, pulses, groundnuts (peanuts), beans, cowpeas, sunflower seed, livestock. **Labor force:** (1995), 235,000 formal sector employees; 100,000 public sector; 135,000 private sector including 14,300 who are employed in various mines in South Africa; most others engaged in cattle raising and subsistence agriculture (1995 est.). **Industry:** diamonds, copper, nickel, coal, salt, soda ash, potash, livestock processing. **Natural resources:** diamonds, copper, nickel, salt, soda ash, potash, coal, iron ore, silver. **Exports:** $2.31 billion (f.o.b., 1996 est.): diamonds, 71%; copper and nickel, 5%; meat, 3%. **Imports:** $1.6 billion (c.i.f., 1996 est.): foodstuffs, vehicles and transport equipment, textiles, petroleum products. **Major trading partners:** Europe, Southern African Customs Union (SACU), Zimbabwe. **Member of Commonwealth of Nations**

Geography Twice the size of Arizona, Botswana is in south-central Africa, bounded by Namibia, Zambia, Zimbabwe, and South Africa. Most of the country is near-desert, with the Kalahari occupying the western part of the country. The eastern part is hilly, with salt lakes in the north.

Government Parliamentary democracy.

History The earliest inhabitants of the region were the San, who were followed by the Tswana. About half the country today is ethnic Tswana. The term for the country's people, *Batswana,* refers to national rather than ethnic origin.

Encroachment by the Zulu in the 1820s and by Boers from Transvaal in the 1870s and 1880s threatened the peace of the region. In 1885 Britain established the area as a protectorate, then known as Bechuanaland. In 1961, Britain granted a constitution to the country. Self-government began in 1965, and on Sept. 30, 1966, the country became independent. Botswana is Africa's oldest democracy.

The new country maintained good relations with its white-ruled neighbors, but gradually changed its policies, harboring rebel groups from South Rhodesia as well as some from South Africa.

Although Botswana is rich in diamonds, it has high unemployment and stratified socioeconomic classes. In 1999 it suffered its first budget deficit in 16 years because of a slump in the international diamond market. Yet it remains one of the wealthiest as well as most stable countries on the continent.

After 17 years in power, 72-year-old President Ketumile Masire retired in 1997, and Festus Mogae, an Oxford-educated economist, became the new president.

Brazil
FEDERATIVE REPUBLIC OF BRAZIL

National name: República Federativa do Brasil
President: Fernando Henrique Cardoso (1995)
Area: 3,286,470 sq. mi. (8,511,965 sq. km)
Population (1999 est.): 171,853,126 (average annual rate of natural increase: 1.16%); birth rate: 20.4/1000; infant mortality rate: 35.4/1000; density per sq. mi.: 52
Capital (1997 est.): Brasilia, 1,800,000. **Largest cities:**
São Paulo: city proper (1995 est.) 10,017,821; metro. area (1996 est.) 16,792,000; Rio de Janeiro: city proper (1995 est.) 5,606,497; metro area (1996 est.) 10,264,000; Porto Alegre, 3,000,000; Recife, 2,900,999; Salvador, 2,600,000; Belo Horizonte, 2,600,000. **Monetary unit:** Real. **Language:** Portuguese. **Ethnicity/race:** white (includes Portuguese, German, Italian, Spanish, Polish) 55%, mixed white and African 38%, African 6%, other (includes Japanese, Arab, Amerindian) 1%. **Religion:** Roman Catholic, 90% (nominal). **Literacy rate:** 81%

Economic summary: GDP/PPP (1997 est.): $1.04 trillion; $6,300 per capita. **Real growth rate:** 3%. **Inflation:** 4.8% (1997). **Unemployment:** 7%. **Arable land:** 5%. **Agriculture:** coffee, soybeans, wheat, rice, corn, sugarcane, cocoa, citrus, beef. **Labor force:** (1989 est.), 57 million; services, 42%; agriculture, 31%; industry, 27%. **Industry:** textiles, shoes, chemicals, cement, lumber, iron ore, tin, steel, aircraft, motor vehicles and parts, other machinery and equipment. **Natural resources:** bauxite, gold, iron ore, manganese, nickel, phosphates, platinum, tin, uranium, petroleum, hydropower, timber. **Exports:** $53 billion (f.o.b., 1997): iron ore, soybean bran, orange juice, footwear, coffee, motor vehicle parts. **Imports:** $61.4 billion (f.o.b., 1997): crude oil, capital goods, chemical products, foodstuffs, coal. **Major trading partners:** EU, Latin America, U.S., Argentina, Japan.

Geography Brazil covers nearly half of South America and is the continent's largest nation. It extends 2,965 miles (4,772 km) north-south, 2,691 miles (4,331 km) east-west, and borders every nation on the continent except Chile and Ecuador. Brazil may be divided into the Brazilian Highlands, or plateau, in the south and the Amazon River Basin in the north. More than a third of Brazil is drained by the Amazon and its more than 200 tributaries. The Amazon is navigable for ocean steamers to Iquitos, Peru, 2,300 miles (3,700 km) upstream. Southern Brazil is drained by the Plata system—the Paraguay, Uruguay, and Paraná Rivers. The most important stream entirely within Brazil is the São Francisco, navigable for 1,000 miles (1,903 km), but broken near its mouth by the 275-foot (84 m) Paulo Afonso Falls.

Government Federal republic.

History Brazil is the only Latin American nation that derives its language and culture from Portugal. The native inhabitants mostly consisted of the nomadic Tupí-Guaraní Indians. Adm. Pedro Alvares Cabral claimed the territory for Portugal in 1500. The early explorers brought back a wood that produced a red dye, *pau-brasil,* from which the land received its name. Portugal began colonization in 1532 and made the area a royal colony in 1549.

During the Napoleonic Wars, King João VI, fearing the advancing French armies, fled the country in 1808 and set up his court in Rio de Janeiro. João was drawn home in 1820 by a revolution, leaving his son as regent. When Portugal sought to reduce Brazil again to colonial status, the prince declared Brazil's independence on Sept. 7, 1822, and became Pedro I, emperor of Brazil. Harassed by his Parliament, Pedro I abdicated in 1831 in favor of his five-year-old son, who became emperor in 1840 (Pedro II). The son was a popular monarch, but discontent built up and, in 1889, following a military revolt, he had to abdicate. Although a republic was proclaimed, Brazil was ruled by military dictatorships until a revolt permitted a gradual return to stability under civilian presidents.

President Wenceslau Braz cooperated with the Allies and declared war on Germany during World War I. In World War II, Brazil again cooperated with the Allies, welcoming Allied air bases, patrolling the South Atlantic, and joining the invasion of Italy after declaring war on the Axis powers.

In the last of a long series of military coups, Gen. João Baptista de Oliveira Figueiredo became president in 1979 and pledged a return to democracy in 1985. The election of Tancredo Neves on Jan. 15, 1985, the first civilian president since 1964, brought a nationwide wave of optimism, but when Neves died on April 21, Vice President Sarney became president. Sarney was widely distrusted because he had previously been a member of the military regime's political party. Collor de Mello won the election of late 1989, pledging to lower the chronic hyperinflation by following the path of free-market economics. When Collor faced impeachment by Congress because of a corruption scandal in Dec. 1992 and resigned, Vice President Itamar Franco assumed the presidency.

A former finance minister, Fernando Cardoso won the presidency in the Oct. 1994 election with 54% of the vote. Cardoso has engineered the disposal of inefficient government-owned monopolies in the telecommunication, electrical power, port, mining, railway, and banking industries. In his short time in office Cardoso's economic acumen has made a measurable dent in Brazil's poverty level.

In Jan. 1999, the Asian economic crisis spread to Brazil. Rather than prop up the currency through financial markets, Brazil opted to let the currency float, which sent the real plummeting—at one time as much as 40%. Cardoso has been highly praised by the international community for quickly turning around his country's economic crisis. He has shown strong political courage in forcing belt tightening measures on the economy, causing short-term misery and discontent in an effort to reap long-term stability and growth.

Brunei Darussalam

STATE OF BRUNEI DARUSSALAM

Sultan: Haji Hassanal Bolkiah (1967)
Area: 2,226 sq. mi. (5,770 sq. km)
Population (1999 est.): 322,982 (annual rate of natural increase: 1.95%); birth rate: 24.7/1000; infant mortality rate: 22.8/1000; density per sq. mi.: 145
Capital and largest city (1991 est.): Bandar Seri Begawan, 52,300. **Other large cities:** Seria 23,511, Kuala Belait 19,335. **Monetary unit:** Brunei dollar.
Languages: Malay (official), Chinese, English.
Ethnicity/race: Malay 64%, Chinese 20%, other 16%.
Religions: Islam (official religion), 67%; Buddhist, 12%; Christian, 9%; indigenous beliefs and other, 12%. **Literacy rate:** 80%
Economic summary: GDP/PPP (1997 est.): $5.4 billion; $18,000 per capita. **Real growth rate:** 3.5%. **Inflation:** 2% (1997 est.). **Unemployment:** 4.8% (1994 est.). **Arable land:** 1%. **Agriculture:** rice, cassava (tapioca), bananas, water buffalo. **Labor force:** 144,000 (includes foreign workers and military personnel) (1995 est.); government, 48%; production of oil, natural gas, services, and construction, 42%; agriculture, forestry, and fishing, 4%; other, 6% (1986 est.). **Industry:** petroleum, petroleum refining, liquefied natural gas, construction. **Natural resources:**

petroleum, natural gas, timber. **Exports:** $2.62 billion (f.o.b., 1996 est.): crude oil, liquefied natural gas, petroleum products. **Imports:** $2.65 billion (c.i.f., 1996 est.): machinery and transport equipment, manufactured goods, food, chemicals. **Major trading partners:** Association of Southeast Asian Nations (ASEAN), Japan, South Korea, U.K., Taiwan, Singapore, U.S., Malaysia

Geography   About the size of Delaware, Brunei is an independent sultanate on the northwest coast of the island of Borneo in the South China Sea, wedged between the Malaysian states of Sabah and Sarawak. Three-quarters of the thinly populated country is covered with tropical rain forest; there are rich oil and gas deposits.

Government   Constitutional sultanate.

History   Brunei (pronounced broon-eye) was trading with China during the 6th century C.E., and, through allegiance to the Javanese Majapahit kingdom (13th to 15th century), it came under Hindu influence. In the early 15th century, with the decline of the Majapahit kingdom and widespread conversion to Islam, Brunei became an independent sultanate. Brunei was a powerful state from the 16th to the 19th century, ruling over the northern part of Borneo and adjacent island chains. But it fell into decay and lost Sarawak in 1841, became a British protectorate in 1888 and a British dependency in 1905. Japan occupied Brunei during World War II; it was liberated by Australia in 1945.

The sultan regained control over internal affairs in 1959, but Britain retained responsibility for the state's defense and foreign affairs until 1984, when the sultanate became fully independent. Sultan Bolkiah was crowned in 1968 at the age of 22, succeeding his father, Sir Omar Ali Saifuddin, who had abdicated. During his reign, exploitation of the rich Seria oilfield had made the sultanate wealthy. Brunei has one of the highest per capita incomes in Asia, and the sultan is believed to be the richest man in the world after Microsoft's Bill Gates. In recent years, a sex scandal involving the royal family has rocked the nation and the sultan has had to punish his wayward younger brother, Prince Jefri, for squandering billions of dollars. In Aug. 1998, Oxford-educated Prince Al-Muhtadee Billah was inaugurated as heir to the 500-year-old monarchy.

Bulgaria

REPUBLIC OF BULGARIA

National name: Narodna Republika Bulgariya
President: Petur Stoyanov (1997)
Prime Minister: Ivan Kostov (1997)
Area: 42,823 sq. mi. (110,910 sq. km)
Population (1999 est.): 8,194,772 (average annual rate of natural increase: −0.45%); birth rate: 8.7/1000; infant mortality rate: 12.4/1000; density per sq. mi.: 191
Capital and largest city (1994 est.): Sofia, 1,113,674. **Largest cities (1994 est.):** Plovdiv, 345,205; Varna, 307,200; Burgas, 198,439; Ruse, 170,209. **Monetary unit:** Lev. **Language:** Bulgarian. **Ethnicity/race:** Bulgarian 85.3%, Turk 8.5%, Gypsy 2.6%, Macedonian 2.5%, Armenian 0.3%, Russian 0.2%, other 0.6%. **Religions:** Bulgarian Orthodox 85%, Muslim 13%, Jewish 0.8%, Roman Catholic 0.5%, Uniate Catholic 0.2%, Protestant, Gregorian-Armenian, and other 0.5%. **Literacy rate:** 98%
Economic summary: GDP/PPP (1997 est.): $35.6

billion, $4,100 per capita. **Real growth rate:** –7.4%. **Inflation:** 579%. **Unemployment:** 14%. **Arable land:** 37%. **Agriculture:** grain, oilseed, vegetables, fruits, tobacco, livestock. **Labor force:** 3.57 million (1996 est.); industry, 41%; agriculture, 18%; other, 41% (1992). **Industry:** machine building and metal working, food processing, chemicals, textiles, construction materials, ferrous and nonferrous metals. **Exports:** $4.9 billion (f.o.b., 1997): machinery and equipment, agriculture and food, textiles and apparel, metals, minerals, and fuels, chemicals and plastics. **Imports:** $4.5 billlion (c.i.f., 1997 est.): fuels, minerals, and raw materials, machinery and equipment, textiles and apparel, agricultural products, metals and ores, chemicals and plastics. **Major trading partners:** Organization for Economic Development (OECD), CIS, Central and Eastern Europe, Arab countries

Geography Two mountain ranges and two great valleys mark the topography of Bulgaria, a country the size of Tennessee and situated on the Black Sea. The Balkan Mountains cross the center of the country, rising to a height of 6,888 feet (2,100 m). The Rhodope, Rila, and Pirin Mountains are to the west and south. The Maritsa is Bulgaria's principal river, and the Danube also flows through the country, forming most of the northern boundary with Romania.

Government Democratic republic.

History The Thracians lived in what is now known as Bulgaria from about 3500 B.C.E.; they were incorporated into the Roman Empire by the first century C.E. At the decline of the empire, the Goths, Huns, Bulgars, and Avars invaded. The Bulgars, who crossed the Danube from the north in C.E. 679, took control of the region. Although the country bears the name of the Bulgars, the Bulgar language and culture died out, replaced by a Slavic language, writing, and religion. In 865, Boris I adopted Orthodox Christianity. The Bulgars twice conquered most of the Balkan peninsula between 893 and 1280. But in 1396 they were invaded by the Ottoman Empire, which made Bulgaria a Turkish province until 1878. Ottoman rule was harsh and inescapable, given Bulgaria's proximity to its oppressor. In 1878, Russia forced Turkey to give Bulgaria its independence after the Russo-Turkish War (1877–78), but the European powers, fearing Russia's and Bulgaria's dominance in the Balkans, intervened at the Congress of Berlin (1878), limited Bulgaria's territory, and fashioned it into a small principality ruled by the nephew of the Russian czar, Alexander of Battenburg.

Alexander was succeeded in 1887 by Prince Ferdinand of Saxe-Coburg-Gotha, who declared a kingdom independent of Russia on Oct. 5, 1908. In the First Balkan War (1912–13), Bulgaria and the other members of the Balkan League fought against Turkey to regain Balkan territory. Angered by the small portion of Macedonia it received after the battle—it considered Macedonia an integral part of Bulgaria—the country instigated the Second Balkan War (June–Aug. 1913) against Turkey as well as its former allies. Bulgaria lost the war and all the territory it had gained in the First Balkan War. Bulgaria joined Germany in World War I in the hope of again gaining Macedonia. After this second failure, Ferdinand abdicated in favor of his son in 1918. Boris III squandered Bulgaria's resources and assumed dictatorial powers in 1934–35. Bulgaria fought on the side of the Nazis in World War II, but after Russia declared war on Bulgaria on Sept. 5, 1944, Bulgaria switched sides. Three days later, on Sept. 9, 1944, a communist coalition took control of the country and set up a government under Kimon Georgiev.

A Soviet-style People's Republic was established in 1947 and Bulgaria acquired the reputation of being the most slavishly loyal to Moscow of all the East European communist countries. The general secretary of the Bulgarian Communist Party, Todor Zhikov, resigned in 1989 after 35 years in power. His successor, Peter Mladenov, purged the Politburo, ended the communist monopoly on power, and held free elections in May 1990 that led to a surprising victory for the communists, renamed the Bulgarian Socialist Party (BSP). Mladenov was forced to resign in July 1990. In Oct. 1991, the Union of Democratic Forces won, forming Bulgaria's first noncommunist government since 1946. Power has shifted back and forth between the pro-Western Union of Democratic Forces (UDF) and the BSP during the 1990s. The economy continued to deteriorate amid growing concern over the spread of organized crime. The new UDF government, elected in 1997, pledged to work toward qualifying for membership in the EU and NATO. During the Kosovo crisis, NATO asked Bulgaria to refuse to allow Russian aircraft to fly through its airspace. NATO, however, in an unexplained blunder, bombed a house near the Bulgarian capital of Sofia instead of a Serbian target.

Burkina Faso

National name: Burkina Faso
President: Blaise Compaore (1991)
Prime Minister: Kadre Desire Ouedraogo (1996)
Area: 105,870 sq. mi. (274,200 sq. km)
Population (1999 est.): 11,575,898 (average annual rate of natural increase: 2.83%); birth rate: 44.8/1000; infant mortality rate: 107.2/1000; density per sq. mi.: 109
Capital and largest city (1994 est.): Ouagadougou, 500,000. **Monetary unit:** Franc CFA. **Languages:** French, tribal languages. **Ethnicity/race:** Mossi (about 24%), Gurunsi, Senufo, Lobi, Bobo, Mande, Fulani. **Religions:** Muslim, 50%; Christian (mainly Roman Catholic), 10%; indigenous beliefs, 40%. **Literacy rate:** 18%
Economic summary: GDP/PPP (1997 est.): $10.3 billion; $950 per capita. **Real growth rate:** 6%. **Inflation:** 3% (1996 est.). **Unemployment:** n.a. **Arable land:** 13%. **Agriculture:** peanuts, shea nuts, sesame, cotton, sorghum, millet, corn, rice, livestock. **Labor force:** n.a.; in agriculture, 80%; industry, 15%; commerce, services, and government, 5%. **Industry:** cotton lint, beverages, agricultural processing, soap, cigarettes, textiles, gold. **Natural resources:** manganese, limestone, marble, gold, antimony, copper, nickel, bauxite, lead, phosphates, zinc, silver. **Exports:** $298 million (f.o.b., 1995 est.): cotton, animal products, gold. **Imports:** $500 million (f.o.b., 1995 est.): machinery, food products, petroleum. **Major trading partners:** Côte d'Ivoire, France, Italy, Mali, Togo, Nigeria.

Geography Slightly larger than Colorado, Burkina Faso, formerly known as Upper Volta, is a landlocked country in West Africa. Its neighbors are Côte d'Ivoire, Mali, Niger, Benin, Togo, and Ghana. The country consists of extensive plains, low hills, high savannas, and a desert area in the north.

Government Military rule since independence.

History Burkina Faso was originally inhabited by the Bobo, Lobi, and Gurunsi peoples, with the Mossi and Gurma peoples immigrating to the region in the 14th century. The lands of the Mossi empire became a French protectorate in 1897, and by 1903 France had subjugated the other ethnic groups. Called Upper Volta by the French, it became a separate colony in 1919, was partitioned among Niger, the Sudan, and Côte d'Ivoire in 1932, and was reconstituted in 1947. An autonomous republic within the French Community, Upper Volta became independent on Aug. 5, 1960.

President Maurice Yameogo was deposed on Jan. 3, 1966, by a military coup led by Col. Sangoulé Lamizana, who dissolved the National Assembly and suspended the constitution. Constitutional rule returned in 1978 with the election of an Assembly and a presidential vote in June in which Gen. Lamizana won by a narrow margin over three other candidates.

On Nov. 25, 1980, a bloodless coup took place that put Gen. Lamizana under house arrest. Col. Sayé Zerbo took charge as the president of the Military Committee of Reform for National Progress. Maj. Jean-Baptiste Ouedraogo toppled Zerbo in another coup on Nov. 7, 1982. Captain Thomas Sankara, in turn, deposed Ouedraogo a year later. His government changed the country's name on Aug. 3, 1984, to Burkina Faso ("the land of upright men") to sever ties with its colonial past. In Feb. 1996 a little-known economist, Kadre Desire Ouedraogo, became prime minister.

Burma (Myanmar)

UNION OF BURMA OR UNION OF MYANMAR

National name: Pyidaungsu Myanmar Naingngandau
Head of State (Chairman): Senior Gen. Than Shwe (1992)
Area: 265,039 sq. mi. (678,500 sq. km)
Population (1999 est.): 48,081,302 (average annual rate of natural increase: 1.61%); birth rate: 28.5/1000; infant mortality rate: 76.3/1000; density per sq. mi.: 184
Capital: Rangoon (Yangon). **Largest cities (est. 1983):** Rangoon (Yangon), 2,458,712; Mandalay, 532,895.
Monetary unit: Kyat. **Languages:** Burmese, minority languages. **Ethnicity/race:** Burman 68%, Shan 9%, Karen 7%, Rakhine 4%, Chinese 3%, Mon 2%, Indian 2%, other 5%. **Religions:** Buddhist 89.5%, Christian 4.9%, Muslim 3.8%, Hindu 0.05%, Animist 1.3%.
Literacy rate: 81%
Economic summary: GDP/PPP (1997 est.): $55.7 billion; $1,190 per capita. **Real growth rate:** 6%. **Inflation:** 30%–40%. **Arable land:** 15%. **Agriculture:** paddy rice, corn, oilseed, sugarcane, pulses, hardwood. **Unemployment:** n.a. **Labor force:** (FY 95/96 est.), 18.8 million; agriculture, 65.2%; industry, 14.3%; trade, 10.1%; government, 6.3%; other, 4.1% (FY 88/89 est.). **Industry:** agricultural processing, textiles and footwear, wood and wood products, copper, tin, tungsten, iron, construction materials, pharmaceuticals, fertilizer. **Natural resources:** petroleum, timber, tin, antimony, zinc, copper, tungsten, lead, coal, marble, limestone, precious stones, natural gas. **Exports** (1996): $693 million: pulses, beans, teak, rice, rubber, hardwood. **Imports** (1996): $1.4 billion: machinery, transport equipment, construction materials, food products, consumer goods. **Major trading partners:** Singapore, China, Indonesia, India, Thailand, Japan, Malaysia.

Geography Slightly smaller than Texas, Burma occupies the northwest portion of the Indochinese peninsula. India lies to the northwest and China to the northeast. Bangladesh, Laos, and Thailand are also neighbors. The Bay of Bengal touches the southwestern coast. The fertile delta of the Irrawaddy in the south contains a network of intercommunicating canals and nine principal river mouths.

Government Military regime. In 1989, the military government changed the name of Burma to Myanmar. The U.S. State Department does not recognize the name Myanmar or the military regime that represents it.

History The ethnic origins of modern Burma (also known as Myanmar) are a mixture of Indo-Aryans, who began pushing into the area around 700 B.C.E., and the Mongolian invaders under Kublai Khan who penetrated the region in the 13th century. Anawrahta (1044–77) was the first great unifier of Burma.

In 1612 the British East India Company sent agents to Burma, but the Burmese doggedly resisted efforts of British, Dutch, and Portuguese traders to establish posts on the Bay of Bengal. Through the Anglo-Burmese War in 1824–26 and two subsequent wars, the British East India Company expanded to the whole of Burma by 1886. Burma was annexed to India, then became a separate colony in 1937.

During World War II, Burma was a key battleground; the 800-mile Burma Road was the Allies' vital supply line to China. The Japanese invaded the country in Dec. 1941, and by May 1942 had occupied most of it, cutting off the Burma Road. After one of the most difficult campaigns of the war, Allied forces liberated most of Burma prior to the Japanese surrender in Aug. 1945.

Burma became independent on Jan. 4, 1948. In 1951 and 1952, the socialists achieved power. In 1968, after the government had made headway against communist and separatist rebels, the military regime adopted a policy of strict nonalignment and set out to follow "the Burmese Way" to socialism. But the insurgents continued to be active.

The civilian government was overthrown in Sept. 1988 by a military junta led by Gen. Saw Maung, an associate of U Ne Win. Virtually the entire country protested the takeover, but demonstrations were brutally quashed. When the new government held elections in May 1990, the opposition National League for Democracy won in a landslide. But the military, or SLORC (State Law and Order Restoration Council), refused to recognize the election results. The leader of the opposition, Aung San Suu Kyi, was awarded the Nobel Peace Prize in 1991, which focused world attention on SLORC's repressive policies. Daughter of the assassinated general Aung San, who was revered as the father of Burmese independence, Suu Kyi remained under house arrest from 1989 until July 10, 1995. A new constitution was drafted in 1994 that called for an elected executive branch but appeared designed specifically to forbid Suu Kyi from becoming president. Suu Kyi continued to protest against the government, but almost every move she made was answered with a counterblow from SLORC.

Although the ruling junta has maintained a tight grip on Burma since 1988, it has not been able to subdue an insurgency in the country's south that has gone on for decades. The ethnic Karen movement has sought an independent homeland along Burma's southern border with Thailand. The economy has been in a state of collapse except for the junta-controlled heroin trade, the universities remained closed, and the AIDS epidemic, unrecognized by the junta, has gripped the country.

In April 1997 the U.S. government imposed sanctions intended to prevent U.S. private investment in Burma. In 1998, Suu Kyi's party set a deadline of Aug. 21 for the convening of the 1990 Parliament, which was never allowed to meet after its election. Suu Kyi also challenged the unofficial ban on her leaving the capital, a move that brought retaliation against many of her supporters. In the boldest protests since 1998, opposition politicians, headed by Suu Kyi, declared in Sept. 1998 that they would act as the country's Parliament and announced that the ruling junta was illegitimate. Thereafter, the government detained hundreds of opposition members and staged several huge demonstrations in which participants called for the deportation of Suu Kyi.

Burundi

REPUBLIC OF BURUNDI

National name: Republika Y'Uburundi
President: Pierre Buyoya (1996)
Prime Minister: Pascal Firmin Ndmira (1996)
Area: 10,747 sq. mi. (27,830 sq. km)
Population (1999 est.): 5,735,937 (average annual rate of natural increase: 2.40%); birth rate: 41.3/1000; infant mortality rate: 99.4/1000; density per sq. mi.: 534
Capital and largest city (1994 est.): Bujumbura, 300,000. **Other large city (est. 1982):** Gitega, 101,827. **Monetary unit:** Burundi franc. **Languages:** Kirundi and French (official), Swahili. **Ethnicity/race:** Hutu (Bantu) 85%, Tutsi (Hamitic) 14%, Twa (Pygmy) 1%. **Religions:** Roman Catholic, 62%; Protestant, 5%; indigenous, 32%. **Literacy rate:** 41%
Economic summary: GDP/PPP (1997 est.): $4 billion; $660 per capita. **Real growth rate:** 4.4%. **Inflation:** 26% (1996 est.). **Arable land:** 44%. **Agriculture:** coffee, cotton, tea, corn, sorghum, sweet potatoes, bananas, manioc (tapioca), meat, milk, hides. **Labor force:** 1.9 million; agriculture 93%, government 4%, industry and commerce 1.5%; services 1.5% (1983 est.). **Industry:** blankets, shoes, soap, assembly of imported components, public works construction, food processing. **Natural resources:** nickel, uranium, rare earth oxides, peat, cobalt, copper, unexploited platinum, vanadium. **Exports:** $40 million (f.o.b., 1996): coffee, tea, cotton, hides. **Imports:** $127 million (c.i.f., 1996): capital goods, petroleum products, foodstuffs, consumer goods. **Major trading partners:** EU, U.S., Asia.

Geography Wedged between Tanzania, the Democratic Republic of the Congo, and Rwanda in east-central Africa, Burundi occupies a high plateau divided by several deep valleys. It is equal in size to Maryland.

Government Republic.

History The Hutu people migrated to Burundi some time before the 11th century; the Tutsi people followed approximately 300 or 400 years later. Although the Tutsi have always been in the minority, they have historically held most of the political and economic power in the country.

Burundi was once part of German East Africa. Belgium won a League of Nations mandate in 1923,

and subsequently Burundi, with Rwanda, was transferred to the status of a United Nations trust territory. In 1962, Burundi gained independence and became a kingdom under Mwami Mwambutsa IV, a Tutsi. A Hutu rebellion took place in 1965, leading to brutal Tutsi retaliations. Mwambutsa was deposed by his son, Ntaré V, in 1966. Ntaré in turn was overthrown the same year in a military coup by Premier Michel Micombero, also a Tutsi. In 1970–71, a civil war erupted, leaving more than 100,000 Hutu dead.

On Nov. 1, 1976, Lt. Col. Jean-Baptiste Bagaza led a coup and assumed the presidency. He suspended the constitution and announced that a 30-member Supreme Revolutionary Council would be the governing body. In Sept. 1987 Bagaza was overthrown by Maj. Pierre Buyoya, who became president. Ethnic hatred again flared in Aug. 1988, and about 20,000 Hutu were slaughtered. Buyoya, however, began reforms to heal the country's ethnic rift. The Burundi Democracy Front's candidate, Melchior Ndadaye, won the country's first democratic presidential elections, held on June 2, 1993. Ndadaye, the first Hutu to assume power in Burundi, was killed within months during a coup. The second Hutu president, Cyprien Ntaryamira, was killed on April 6, 1994, when a plane carrying him and the Rwandan president was shot down. As a result, Hutu youth gangs began massacring Tutsi; the Tutsi-controlled army retaliated by killing Hutus.

The frequency of ethnic clashes increased, developing into a low-intensity civil war. A six-nation regional proposal to send troops into Burundi to maintain peace and order was devised in July 1996. Distrustful of the scheme, the Tutsi-dominated army led a coup deposing the Hutu president and installed Major Pierre Buyoya that month. More than 200,000 people have been killed since the conflict began, and both the Tutsi-dominated army and the Hutu rebel forces are responsible for the continuing slaughter.

Cambodia

King: Norodom Sihanouk (1991)
Prime Minister: Hun Sen (1993)
Area: 69,884 sq. mi. (181,040 sq. km)
Population (1999 est.): 11,626,520 (average annual rate of natural increase: 2.49%); birth rate: 41.1/1000; infant mortality rate: 105.1/1000; density per sq. mi.: 166
Capital and largest city (1991 est.): Phnom Penh, 900,000. **Monetary unit:** Riel. **Ethnic groups:** Khmer, 90%; Chinese, 5%; other minorities 5%. **Languages:** Khmer (official), French, English. **Ethnicity/race:** Khmer 90%, Vietnamese 5%, Chinese 1%, other 4%. **Religions:** 95% Theravada Buddhist, 5% others. **Literacy rate:** 69%
Economic summary: GDP/PPP (1997 est.): $7.7 billion; $715 per capita. **Real growth rate:** 1.5%. **Inflation:** 9.5%. **Arable land:** 13%. **Agriculture:** rice, rubber, corn, vegetables. **Labor force:** 2.5–3.0 million; 80% in agriculture. **Unemployment:** n.a. **Industry:** rice milling, fishing, wood and wood products, rubber, cement, gem mining, textiles. **Natural resources:** timber, gemstones, iron ore, manganese, phosphate, hydropower potential. **Exports:** $615 million (1996 est.): timber, garments, rubber, soybeans, sesame. **Imports:** $1 billion (1996 est.): cigarettes, construction materials, petroleum products, machinery, motor vehicles. **Major trading partners:** Singapore, Japan, Thailand, Hong Kong, Indonesia, Malaysia, U.S., Vietnam, Australia.

Geography Situated on the Indochinese peninsula, Cambodia is bordered by Thailand and Laos on the north and Vietnam on the east and south. The Gulf of Siam is off the western coast. The country, the size of Missouri, consists chiefly of a large alluvial plain ringed by mountains and on the east by the Mekong River. The plain is centered on Lake Tonle Sap, which is a natural storage basin of the Mekong.

Government Constitutional monarchy.

History The area that is present-day Cambodia came under Khmer rule about C.E. 600, when the region was at the center of a vast empire that stretched over most of Southeast Asia. Under the Khmers, who were Hindus, a magnificent temple complex was constructed at Angkor. Buddhism was introduced in the 12th century during the rule of Jayavaram VII. However, the kingdom, then known as Kambuja, fell into decline after Jayavaram's reign and was nearly annihilated by Thai and Vietnamese invaders. Its power steadily diminished until 1863, when France colonized the region, joining Cambodia, Laos, and Vietnam into a single protectorate known as French Indochina.

The French quickly usurped all but ceremonial powers from the monarch, Norodom. When he died in 1904, the French passed over his sons and handed the throne to his brother, Sisowath. Sisowath and his son ruled until 1941, when Norodom Sihanouk was elevated to power. Sihanouk's coronation, along with the Japanese occupation during the war, worked to reinforce a sentiment among Cambodians that the region should be free from outside control. After World War II, Cambodians sought independence, but France was reluctant to part with its colony. Cambodia was granted independence within the French Union in 1949. But the French-Indochinese War provided an opportunity for Sihanouk to gain full military control of the country. He abdicated in 1955 in favor of his parents, remaining head of the government, and when his father died in 1960, became chief of state without returning to the throne. In 1963, he sought a guarantee of Cambodia's neutrality from all parties to the Vietnam War.

However, North Vietnamese and Vietcong troops had begun using eastern Cambodia as a safe haven from which to launch attacks into South Vietnam, making it increasingly difficult to stay out of the war. An indigenous Communist guerrilla movement known as the Khmer Rouge also began to put pressure on the government in Phnom Penh. On March 18, 1970, while Sihanouk was abroad, anti-Vietnamese riots broke out and Sihanouk was overthrown by Gen. Lon Nol. The Vietnam peace agreement of 1973 stipulated withdrawal of foreign forces from Cambodia, but fighting continued between Hanoi-backed insurgents and U.S.-supplied government troops.

Combat climaxed in April 1975 when the Lon Nol regime was overthrown by Pol Pot, leader of the Khmer Rouge forces. The four years of nightmarish Khmer Rouge rule led to the state-sponsored extermination of citizens by its own government. Between 1 million and 2 million people were massacred on the "killing fields" of Cambodia or worked to death through forced labor. Pol Pot's radical vision of transforming the country into a Marxist agrarian society led to the virtual extermination of the country's professional and technical class.

Pol Pot was ousted by Vietnamese forces on Jan. 8, 1979, and a new pro-Hanoi government led by Heng Samrin was installed. Pol Pot and 35,000 Khmer Rouge fighters fled into the hills of western Cambodia, where they were joined by forces loyal to the ousted Sihanouk in a guerrilla movement aimed at overthrowing the Heng Samrin government. The Vietnamese plan originally called for a withdrawal by early 1990 and a negotiated political settlement. The talks became protracted, however, and a U.N. agreement was not signed until 1992, when Sihanouk was appointed leader of an interim Supreme National Council to run the country until elections could be held in 1993.

Free elections in May 1993 saw the defeat of Heng Samrin's successor, Hun Sen, who refused to accept the outcome of the vote and insisted instead on a power-sharing agreement. Under the arrangement, Hun Sen and Sihanouk's son, Prince Norodom Ranariddh, would act as co–prime ministers.

The Khmer Rouge stronghold in the western jungles splintered in 1997, with factions either battling each other or defecting. Ranariddh and Hun Sen both courted Khmer Rouge factions in an effort to shore up their power. In early July, Hun Sen took advantage of the charged political atmosphere to depose Ranariddh, officially the first prime minister and the country's only popularly elected leader. Hun Sen later launched a brutal purge, executing more than 40 political opponents. Skirmishes between Ranariddh's forces and Hun Sen's troops continued through the fall. Meanwhile, King Norodom Sihanouk, a beloved but ineffectual figurehead, was unable to broker peace between Hun Sen and his son, Prince Ranariddh.

Shortly after the July coup, the Khmer Rouge organized a show trial of their notorious leader, Pol Pot, in an apparent bid to distance themselves from the bloody history of his regime. Visibly enfeebled from reported bouts with malaria, Pol Pot had not been seen by the West in more than two decades. He was sentenced to house arrest for his crimes against humanity. On April 15, 1998, Pol Pot died and his body was quickly cremated by former Khmer Rouge comrades.

In the July 1998 election, Hun Sen was victorious over opposition leaders Sam Rainsy and Prince Ranariddh, but the opposition parties accused him of voter fraud. Rainsy organized protests that turned into violent riots. Although Hun Sen's CCP Party won the most seats, it needed a coalition with Ranariddh's FUNCINPEC Party to reach the two-thirds majority needed to form a government. After months in limbo, a coalition government was formed in Nov. 1998, with Hun Sen as sole prime minister and Ranariddh accepting the lesser role of president of the National Assembly. With the election resolved, Cambodia was able to regain its U.N. seat, lost nearly a year earlier following Hun Sen's coup.

In 1999, the government and U.N. officials held negotiations regarding a war crimes tribunal for senior Khmer Rouge officials. Although the U.N. is willing to allow the trial to take place in Cambodia with Cambodian participation, it is skeptical about the fairness of such a trial, given Cambodia's corrupt judicial system and demonstrated incompetence. This year Cambodia arrested the last Khmer Rouge guerrilla at large, Ta Mok, as well as Duch, who ran the notorious Tuol Sleng prison. Numerous other members of the Khmer Rouge live openly in Cambodia.

Cameroon

REPUBLIC OF CAMEROON

National name: République du Cameroun
President: Paul Biya (1988)
Prime Minister: Peter Musonge Mafani (1996)
Area: 183,569 sq. mi. (475,440 sq. km)
Population (1999 est.): 15,456,092 (average annual rate of natural increase: 2.79%); birth rate: 41.8/1000; infant mortality rate: 75.7/1000; density per sq. mi.: 84
Capital: Yaoundé. **Largest cities (1991 est.):** Douala, 908,000; Yaoundé, 730,000. **Monetary unit:** Franc CFA. **Languages:** French and English (both official); 24 major African language groups. **Ethnicity/race:** Cameroon Highlanders 31%, Equatorial Bantu 19%, Kirdi 11%, Fulani 10%, Northwestern Bantu 8%, Eastern Nigritic 7%, other African 13%, non-African less than 1%. **Religions:** 51% indigenous beliefs, 33% Christian, 16% Muslim. **Literacy rate:** 54%
Economic summary: GDP/PPP (1997 est.): $30.9 billion; $2,100 per capita. **Real growth rate:** 5%. **Inflation:** 3%. **Unemployment:** n.a. **Arable land:** 13%. **Agriculture:** coffee, cocoa, cotton, rubber, bananas, oilseed, grains, root starches, livestock, timber. **Labor force:** n.a. **Industry:** petroleum production and refining, food processing, light consumer goods, textiles, lumber. **Natural resources:** petroleum, bauxite, iron ore, timber, hydropower potential. **Exports:** $1.9 billion (f.o.b., 1996): crude oil and petroleum products, lumber, cocoa beans, aluminum, coffee, cotton. **Imports:** $1.5 billion (f.o.b., 1996): machines and electrical equipment, food, consumer goods, transport equipment, petroleum products. **Major trading partners:** EU, African countries, Korea, Taiwan, China, U.S.

Geography Cameroon is a Central African nation on the Gulf of Guinea, bordered by Nigeria, Chad, the Central African Republic, the Republic of Congo, Equatorial Guinea, and Gabon. It is nearly twice the size of Oregon. Mount Cameroon (13,350 ft.; 4,069 m), near the coast, is the highest elevation in the country. The main rivers are the Benue, Nyong, and Sanaga.

Government After a 1972 plebiscite, a unitary nation was formed out of East and West Cameroon to replace the former federal republic.

History Bantu speakers were among the first groups to settle Cameroon, followed by the Muslim Fulani in the 18th and 19th centuries. The land escaped colonial rule until 1884, when treaties with tribal chiefs brought the area under German domination. After World War I, the League of Nations gave the French a mandate over 80% of the area, and the British 20% adjacent to Nigeria. After World War II, when the country came under a U.N. trusteeship in 1946, self-government was granted, and the Cameroon People's Union emerged as the dominant party by campaigning for reunification of French and British Cameroon and for independence. Accused of being under Communist control, the party waged a campaign of revolutionary terror from 1955 to 1958, when it was crushed. In British

Cameroon, unification was also promoted by the leading party, the Kamerun National Democratic Party, led by John Foncha.

France set up Cameroon as an autonomous state in 1957, and the next year its legislative assembly voted for independence by 1960. In 1959 a fully autonomous government of Cameroon was formed under Ahmadou Ahidjo. Cameroon became an independent republic on Jan. 1, 1960. In 1961 the southern part of the British territory joined the new Federal Republic of Cameroon and the northern section voted for unification with Nigeria. The president of Cameroon since independence, Ahmadou Ahidjo, was replaced in 1982 by the prime minister, Paul Biya. Both administrations were characterized by authoritarian rule. Calls for reform led to constitutional amendments in 1993 providing for a democratic form of government. In 1998, the watchdog organization, Transparency International, ranked Cameroon the most corrupt country in the world.

Canada

Sovereign: Queen Elizabeth II (1952)
Governor-General: Roméo LeBlanc (1995)
Prime Minister: Jean Chrétien (1993)
Area: 3,851,809 sq. mi. (9,976,140 sq. km)
Population (1999 est.): 31,006,347. Average annual rate of natural increase: 0.46%; birth rate: 11.9/1000; infant mortality rate: 5.5/1000; density per sq. mi.: 8
Capital: Ottawa, Ontario. **Largest cities (1996 census; metropolitan areas):** Toronto, 4,263,757; Montreal, 3,326,510; Vancouver, 1,831,665; Ottawa/Hull, 1,010,498; Edmonton, 862,597; Calgary, 821,628; Quebec, 671,889; Winnipeg, 667,209; Hamilton, 624,360; London, 398,616. **Monetary unit:** Canadian dollar. **Languages:** English, French (both official). **Ethnicity/race:** British Isles origin 40%, French origin 27%, other European 20%, indigenous Indian and Inuit 1.5%, other, mostly Asian 11.5%. **Religions:** 46% Roman Catholic, 16% United Church, 10% Anglican. **Literacy rate:** 99%
Economic summary: GDP/PPP (1997 est.): $658 billion; $21,700 per capita. **Real growth rate:** 3.5%. **Inflation:** 1.8% (1997). **Unemployment:** 8.6% (Dec. 1997). **Arable land:** 5%. **Agriculture:** wheat, barley, oilseed, tobacco, fruits, vegetables, dairy products, forest products, fish. **Labor force:** 15.3 million; services 75%, manufacturing 16%, agriculture 3%, construction 5%, other 1% (1997). **Industry:** processed and unprocessed minerals, food products, wood and paper products, transportation equipment, chemicals, fish products, petroleum and natural gas. **Exports:** $208.6 billion (f.o.b., 1997): newsprint, wood pulp, timber, crude petroleum, machinery, natural gas, aluminum, motor vehicles and parts, telecommunications equipment. **Imports:** $194.4 billion (c.i.f., 1997): crude oil, chemicals, motor vehicles and parts, durable consumer goods, computers, telecommunications equipment and parts. **Major trading partners:** U.S., Japan, U.K., Germany, South Korea, The Netherlands, China, France, Mexico, Taiwan.

Geography Covering most of the northern part of the North American continent and with an area larger than that of the United States, Canada has an extremely varied topography. In the east the mountainous maritime provinces have an irregular coastline on the Gulf of St. Lawrence and the Atlantic. The St. Lawrence plain, covering most of southern Quebec and Ontario, and the interior continental plain, covering southern Manitoba and

Saskatchewan and most of Alberta, are the principal cultivable areas. They are separated by a forested plateau rising from Lakes Superior and Huron.

Westward toward the Pacific, most of British Columbia, Yukon, and part of western Alberta are covered by parallel mountain ranges, including the Rockies. The Pacific border of the coast range is ragged with fjords and channels. The highest point in Canada is Mount Logan (19,850 ft.; 6,050 m), which is in the Yukon. The two principal river systems are the Mackenzie and the St. Lawrence. The St. Lawrence, with its tributaries, is navigable for over 1,900 miles (3,058 km).

Government Canada is a federation of 10 provinces (Alberta, British Columbia, Manitoba, New Brunswick, Newfoundland, Nova Scotia, Ontario, Prince Edward Island, Quebec, and Saskatchewan) and three territories (Northwest Territories, Yukon, and as of April 1, 1999, Nunavut), most of whose powers were spelled out in the British North America Act of 1867. With the passing of the Constitutional Act of 1982, the act and the constitutional amending power were transferred from the British Parliament to Canada so that the Canadian constitution is now entirely in the hands of Canadians.

While the governor-general is officially the representative of Queen Elizabeth II, in reality the governor-general acts only upon the advice of the Canadian prime minister.

History The first inhabitants of Canada were native Indian peoples, primarily the Inuit (Eskimo). The Norse explorer Leif Eriksson probably reached the shores of Canada (Labrador or Nova Scotia) in c.e. 1000, but the history of the white man in the country actually began in 1497, when John Cabot, an Italian in the service of Henry VII of England, reached Newfoundland or Nova Scotia. Canada was taken for France in 1534 by Jacques Cartier. The actual settlement of New France, as it was then called, began in 1604 at Port Royal in what is now Nova Scotia; in 1608, Quebec was founded. France's colonization efforts were not very successful, but French explorers by the end of the 17th century had penetrated beyond the Great Lakes to the western prairies and south along the Mississippi to the Gulf of Mexico. Meanwhile, the English Hudson's Bay Company had been established in 1670. Because of the valuable fisheries and fur trade, a

Population by Provinces and Territories

Province	1997	1998
	(in thousands)	
Alberta	2,847.0	2,914.5
British Columbia	3,933.3	4,008.9
Manitoba	1,145.2	1,138.6
New Brunswick	762.0	752.9
Newfoundland	563.6	543.8
Nova Scotia	947.9	934.2
Ontario	11,407.7	11,413.6
Prince Edward Island	137.2	136.5
Quebec	7,419.9	7,334.5
Saskatchewan	1,023.5	1,024.2
Northwest Territories	67.5	67.3
Yukon Territory	31.6	31.7
Nunavut	—	25.0

Source: Statistics Canada.

conflict developed between the French and English; in 1713, Newfoundland, Hudson Bay, and Nova Scotia (Acadia) were lost to England. During the Seven Years' War (1756–63), England extended its conquest, and the British Maj. Gen. James Wolfe won his famous victory over Gen. Louis Montcalm outside Quebec on Sept. 13, 1759. The Treaty of Paris in 1763 gave England control.

At that time the population of Canada was almost entirely French, but in the next few decades, thousands of British colonists emigrated to Canada from the British Isles and from the American colonies. In 1849, the right of Canada to self-government was recognized. By the British North America Act of 1867, the dominion of Canada was created through the confederation of Upper and Lower Canada, Nova Scotia, and New Brunswick. Prince Edward Island joined the dominion in 1873. In 1869, Canada purchased from the Hudson's Bay Company the vast middle west (Rupert's Land) from which the provinces of Manitoba (1870), Alberta (1905), and Saskatchewan (1905) were later formed. In 1871, British Columbia joined the dominion. The country was linked from coast to coast in 1885 by the Canadian Pacific Railway.

During the formative years between 1866 and 1896, the Conservative Party, led by Sir John A. Macdonald, governed the country, except during the years 1873–78. In 1896, the Liberal Party took over and, under Sir Wilfrid Laurier, an eminent French Canadian, ruled until 1911. By the Statute of Westminster in 1931 the British dominions, including Canada, were formally declared to be partner nations with Britain, "equal in status, in no way subordinate to each other," and bound together only by allegiance to a common Crown.

Newfoundland became Canada's 10th province on March 31, 1949, following a plebiscite. Canada also includes three territories—the Yukon Territory, the Northwest Territories, and the newest territory, Nunavut. This area includes all of the Arctic north of the mainland, Norway having recognized Canadian sovereignty over the Svendrup Islands in the Arctic in 1931.

The Liberal Party, led by William Lyon Mackenzie King, dominated Canadian politics from 1921 until 1957, when it was succeeded by the Progressive Conservatives. The Liberals, under the leadership of Lester B. Pearson, returned to power in 1963. Pearson remained prime minister until 1968, when he retired and was replaced by a former law professor, Pierre Elliott Trudeau. Trudeau maintained Canada's defensive alliance with the United States, but began moving toward a more independent policy in world affairs. Trudeau's election was considered in part a response to the most serious problem confronting the country, the division between French- and English-speaking Canadians, which had led to a separatist movement in the predominantly French province of Quebec. In 1974, the provincial government voted to make French the official language of Quebec. In Dec. 1979, the Quebec law making French the exclusive official language of the province was voided by the Canadian Supreme Court. Resolving a dispute that had occupied Trudeau since the beginning of his tenure, Queen Elizabeth II, in Ottawa on April 17, 1982, signed the Constitution Act, cutting the last legal tie between Canada and Britain. The constitution

Canadian Governors-General and Prime Ministers since 1867

Term of Office	Governor-General	Term	Prime Minister	Party
1867–1868	Viscount Monck[1]	1867–1873	Sir John A. Macdonald	Conservative
1869–1872	Baron Lisgar	1873–1878	Alexander Mackenzie	Liberal
1872–1878	Earl of Dufferin	1878–1891	Sir John A. Macdonald	Conservative
1878–1883	Marquess of Lorne	1891–1892	Sir John J. C. Abbott	Conservative
1883–1888	Marquess of Lansdowne	1892–1894	Sir John S. D. Thompson	Conservative
1888–1893	Baron Stanley of Preston	1894–1896	Sir Mackenzie Bowell	Conservative
1893–1898	Earl of Aberdeen	1896	Sir Charles Tupper	Conservative
1898–1904	Earl of Minto	1896–1911	Sir Wilfrid Laurier	Liberal
1904–1911	Earl Grey	1911–1917	Sir Robert L. Borden	Conservative
1911–1916	Duke of Connaught	1917–1920	Sir Robert L. Borden	Unionist
1916–1921	Duke of Devonshire	1920–1921	Arthur Meighen	Unionist
1921–1926	Baron Byng of Vimy	1921–1926	W. L. Mackenzie King	Liberal
1926–1931	Viscount Willingdon	1926	Arthur Meighen	Conservative
1931–1935	Earl of Bessborough	1926–1930	W. L. Mackenzie King	Liberal
1935–1940	Baron Tweedsmuir	1930–1935	Richard B. Bennett	Conservative
1940–1946	Earl of Athlone	1935–1948	W. L. Mackenzie King	Liberal
1946–1952	Viscount Alexander	1948–1957	Louis S. St. Laurent	Liberal
1952–1959	Vincent Massey	1957–1963	John G. Diefenbaker	Conservative
1959–1967	George P. Vanier	1963–1968	Lester B. Pearson	Liberal
1967–1973	Roland Michener	1968–1979	Pierre Elliott Trudeau	Liberal
1974–1979	Jules Léger	1979–1980	Charles Joseph Clark	Conservative
1979–1984	Edward R. Schreyer	1980–1984	Pierre Elliott Trudeau	Liberal
1984–1990	Jeanne Sauvé	1984–1984	John Turner	Liberal
1990–1995	Raymond John Hnatyshyn	1984–1993	Brian Mulroney	Conservative
1995–	Roméo LeBlanc	1993–1993	Kim Campbell	Conservative
		1993–	Jean Chrétien	Liberal

1. Became governor-general of British North America in 1861.

retains Queen Elizabeth as queen of Canada and keeps Canada's membership in the Commonwealth.

In the national election on Sept. 4, 1984, the Progressive Conservative Party scored an overwhelming victory, fundamentally changing the country's political landscape. The Conservatives, led by Brian Mulroney, a 45-year-old corporate lawyer, won the highest political majority in Canadian history. The dominant foreign issue was a free-trade pact with the U.S., a treaty bitterly opposed by the Liberal and New Democratic Parties. The conflict led to elections in Nov. 1988 that solidly reelected Mulroney and gave him a mandate to proceed with the agreement.

The issue of separatist sentiments in French-speaking Quebec flared up again in 1990 with the failure of the Meech Lake Accord. The accord was designed to ease the Quebecers' fear of losing their identity within the English-speaking majority by giving Quebec constitutional status as a "distinct society." In an attempt to keep Canada united, the three major political parties came to an agreement in Feb. 1992 on constitutional reforms. Voters in the Northwest Territories authorized the division of their region in two, creating a homeland for Canadian Eskimos, the Inuits, which in April 1999 became the territory of Nunavut. Also in 1992, Canada announced its decision to withdraw its combat units from NATO command. The economy continued to be mired in a long recession that many blamed on the free-trade agreement. A national referendum was held in Oct. 1992 on the proposal to change the constitution to ensure greater representation in Parliament for the more populous regions and thereby the French-speaking Quebecers. The referendum, however was defeated.

Brian Mulroney's popularity continued to slump in 1992 and early 1993, leading to his decision to retire prior to the required November election. The governing Progressive Conservative Party chose Defense Minister Kim Campbell as its leader in June, making her the first female prime minister in Canadian history.

The national election in Oct. 1993 resulted in the reemergence of the Liberal Party and the installation of Jean Chrétien as prime minister. The Quebec referendum on secession in Oct. 1995 yielded a narrow rejection of the proposal. But the separatists vowed to try again. Early parliamentary elections in June 1997 gave a reduced majority to the ruling Liberals. The Reform Party, based largely in the West, replaced the Bloc Quebecois as the official opposition.

On April 1, 1999, the Northwest Territories were officially divided to create a new territory in the east that would be governed by Canada's Inuits, who make up 85% of the area's population. Composed of 770,000 square miles of mostly snow and ice reaching well to the north of the Arctic Circle, the 25,000 residents of Nunavut will be governed from the new capital, Iqaluit.

Cape Verde

REPUBLIC OF CAPE VERDE

National name: República de Cabo Verde
President: Antonio Mascarenhas Monteiro (1991)
Prime Minister: Carlos Wahnon Veiga (1991)
Area: 1,557 sq. mi. (4,030 sq. km)
Population: (1999 est.): 405,748 (average annual rate of natural increase: 2.67%); birth rate: 33.5/1000; infant mortality rate: 45.5/1000; density per sq. mi.: 261
Capital (1990): Praia, 61,797. **Other large city (est. 1982):** Mindelo, 50,000. **Monetary unit:** Cape Verdean escudo. **Languages:** Portuguese, Criuolo. **Ethnicity/race:** Creole (mulatto) 71%, African 28%, European 1%. **Religion:** Roman Catholic fused with indigenous beliefs. **Literacy rate:** 67%
Economic summary: GDP/PPP (1997 est.): $538 million; $1,3700 per capita. **Real growth rate:** 4.5%.

Inflation: 6.2% (1996). **Unemployment:** n.a. **Arable land:** 11%. **Agriculture:** bananas, corn, beans, sweet potatoes, sugarcane, coffee, peanuts, fish. **Labor force:** n.a. **Industry:** food and beverages, fish processing, shoes and garments, salt mining, ship repair. **Natural resources:** salt, basalt rock, pozzuolana (volcanic ash used to produce hydraulic cement), limestone, kaolin, fish. **Exports:** $12.8 million (f.o.b., 1996 est.): shoes, garments, fish, bananas, hides. **Imports:** $237 million (f.o.b., 1996 est.): foodstuffs, consumer goods, industrial products, transport equipment, fuels. **Major trading partners:** Portugal, Spain, France, U.K., The Netherlands, U.S.

Geography Cape Verde, only slightly larger than Rhode Island, is an archipelago in the Atlantic 385 miles (500 km) west of Senegal.

The islands are divided into two groups: Barlavento in the north, composed of Santo Antão (291 sq. mi.; 754 sq. km), Boa Vista (240 sq. mi.; 622 sq. km), São Nicolau (132 sq. mi.; 342 sq. km), São Vicente (88 sq. mi.; 246 sq. km), Sal (83 sq. mi.; 298 sq. km), and Santa Luzia (13 sq. mi.; 34 sq. km); and Sotavento in the south, consisting of São Tiago (383 sq. mi.; 992 sq. km), Fogo (184 sq. mi.; 477 sq. km), Maio (103 sq. mi.; 267 sq. km), and Brava (25 sq. mi.; 65 sq. km). The islands are mostly mountainous, with the land deeply scarred by erosion. There is an active volcano on Fogo.

Government Republic.

History Uninhabited upon their discovery in 1456, the Cape Verde islands became part of the Portuguese empire in 1495. A majority of their modern inhabitants are of mixed Portuguese and African ancestry.

Positioned on the great trade routes between Africa, Europe, and the New World, the islands became a prosperous center for the slave trade, but suffered economic decline after the slave trade was abolished in 1876. In the 20th century Cape Verde has served as a shipping port.

In 1951 Cape Verde's status changed from a Portuguese colony to an overseas province, and in 1961 the inhabitants became full Portuguese citizens. An independence movement led by the African Party for the Independence of Guinea-Bissau (another former Portuguese colony) and Cape Verde (PAIGC) was founded in 1956, and on July 5, 1975, the islands became independent.

Elections on Jan. 13, 1991, resulted in the ruling African Party for the Independence of Cape Verde losing its majority in the 79-seat Parliament. The big winner was the Movement for Democracy, whose candidate, Antonio Monteiro, won the subsequent presidential election on Feb. 17. These were the first free elections since independence in 1975. In the presidential ballot of Feb. 1996, Monteiro handily won reelection.

Central African Republic

National name: République Centrafricaine
Head of Government: Gen. André Kolingba (1986)
President: Ange-Félix Patassé (1993)
Prime Minister: Anicet Georges Dologuele (1999)
Area: 241,313 sq. mi. (622,980 sq. km)
Population (1999 est.): 3,444,951 (average annual rate of natural increase: 2.18%); birth rate: 38.3/1000; infant mortality rate: 103.4/1000; density per sq. mi.: 14
Capital and largest city (1990 est.): Bangui, 706,000.

Monetary unit: Franc CFA. **Languages:** French (official), Sangho, Arabic, Hansa, Swahili. **Ethnicity/race:** Baya 34%, Banda 27%, Sara 10%, Mandjia 21%, Mboum 4%, M'Baka 4%, Europeans 6,500 (including 3,600 French). **Religions:** 24% indigenous beliefs, 50% Protestant and Roman Catholic with animist influence, 15% Muslim, 11% other. **Literacy rate:** 38%

Economic summary: GDP/PPP (1997 est.): $3.3 billion; $1,000 per capita. **Real growth rate:** n.a.. **Inflation:** 4% (1996 est.). **Unemployment:** 6% (1993). **Arable land:** 3%. **Agriculture:** cotton, coffee, tobacco, manioc (tapioca), yams, millet, corn, bananas, timber. **Labor force:** n.a. **Industry:** diamond mining, sawmills, breweries, textiles, footwear, assembly of bicycles and motorcycles. **Natural resources:** diamonds, uranium, timber, gold, oil. **Exports:** $171 million (f.o.b., 1995): diamonds, timber, cotton, coffee, tobacco. **Imports:** $174 million (f.o.b., 1995): food, textiles, petroleum products, machinery, electrical equipment, motor vehicles, chemicals, pharmaceuticals, consumer goods, industrial products. **Major trading partners:** France, Belgium-Luxembourg, Italy, Japan, U.S., Spain, Iran, Democratic Republic of the Congo, Republic of the Congo, EU, Algeria, Cameroon, Namibia.

Geography Situated about 500 miles (805 km) north of the equator, the Central African Republic is a landlocked nation bordered by Cameroon, Chad, the Sudan, the Democratic Republic of the Congo, and the Republic of Congo.

Twice the size of New Mexico, it is covered by tropical forests in the south and semidesert land in the east. The Ubangi and the Shari are the largest of many rivers.

Government Multiparty republic since 1991.

History From the 16th to 19th centuries, the people of this region were ravaged by slave traders. The Banda, Baya, Ngbandi, and Azande make up the largest ethnic groups.

The French occupied the region in 1894. As the colony of Ubangi-Shari, what is now the Central African Republic was united with Chad in 1905. In 1910 it was joined with Gabon and the Middle Congo to become French Equatorial Africa. After World War II a rebellion in 1946 forced the French to grant self-government. In 1958 the territory voted to become an autonomous republic within the French Community, and on Aug. 13, 1960, President David Dacko proclaimed the republic's independence from France. Dacko moved the country into Beijing's orbit, but was overthrown in a coup on Dec. 31, 1965, by Col. Jean-Bédel Bokassa, army chief of staff.

On Dec. 4, 1976, the Central African Republic became the Central African Empire. Marshal Jean-Bédel Bokassa, who had ruled the republic since he took power in 1965, was declared Emperor Bokassa I. Brutality and excess characterized his regime. He was overthrown in a coup on Sept. 20, 1979. Former president David Dacko returned to power and changed the country's name back to the Central African Republic. An army coup on Sept. 1, 1981, deposed President Dacko again.

In 1991, President Kolingba, under pressure, announced a move toward multiparty democracy. Elections in Aug. 1993 saw the defeat of Kolingba and the victory of Prime Minister Patassé as president. A military revolt was crushed with the aid of French soldiers in Jan. 1997. At the end of 1999 the country will hold presidential elections, its second election since multiparty politics were reinstituted.

Chad

REPUBLIC OF CHAD

National name: République du Tchad
President: Lieut. Gen. Idriss Deby (1990)
Prime Minister: Nassour Guelengdoussia Ouaido (1997)
Area: 495,752 sq. mi. (1,284,000 sq. km)
Population (1999 est.): 7,557,436 (average annual rate of natural increase, 2.65%); birth rate: 43.1/1000; infant mortality rate: 115.3/1000; density per sq. mi.: 15
Capital and largest city (1993): N'Djamena, 529,555.
Monetary unit: Franc CFA. **Languages:** French and Arabic (official), more than 100 tribal languages.
Ethnicity/race: North and center: Muslims (Arabs, Toubou, Hadjerai, Fulbe, Kotoko, Kanembou, Baguirmi, Boulala, Zaghawa, and Maba); South: non-Muslims (Sara [the largest ethnic group, 25% of the population], Ngambaye, Mbaye, Goulaye, Moundang, Moussei, Massa). **Religions:** Islam, 44%; Christian, 33%; traditional, 23%. **Literacy rate:** 30%
Economic summary: GDP/PPP (1997 est.): $4.3 billion; $600 per capita. **Real growth rate:** 5.5%. **Inflation:** 15% (1997 est.). **Unemployment rate:** n.a. **Arable land:** 3%. **Agriculture:** cotton, sorghum, millet, peanuts, rice, potatoes, manioc (tapioca), cattle, sheep, goats, camels. **Labor force:** n.a.; in agriculture, 85%. **Industries:** cotton textiles, meat packing, beer brewing, natron (sodium carbonate), soap, cigarettes, construction materials. **Natural resources:** petroleum, uranium, natron, kaolin, fish. **Exports:** $259 million (f.o.b., 1996 est.): cotton, cattle, textiles. **Imports:** $301 million (f.o.b., 1996 est.): machinery and transportation equipment, industrial goods, petroleum products, foodstuffs; textiles. **Major trading partners:** Portugal, Germany, South Africa, France, Cameroon, Nigeria, U.S.

Geography A landlocked country in north-central Africa, Chad is about 85% the size of Alaska. Its neighbors are Niger, Libya, the Sudan, the Central African Republic, Cameroon, and Nigeria. Lake Chad, from which the country gets its name, lies on the western border with Niger and Nigeria. In the north is a desert that runs into the Sahara.

Government Republic.

History The area around Lake Chad has been inhabited since at least 500 B.C.E. In the 8th century C.E. Berbers began migrating to the area. Islam arrived in 1085, and by the 16th century a trio of rival kingdoms flourished: the Kanem-Bornu, the Baguirmi, and Ouaddaï. In 1883–93, all three kingdoms came under the rule of the Sudanese conqueror Rabih al-Zubayr. In 1900, Rabih was overthrown by the French, who absorbed these kingdoms into the colony of French Equatorial Africa, as part of Ubangi-Shari, in 1910.

France began the country's development after 1920, when it became a separate colony. In 1946, French Equatorial Africa was admitted to the French Union, and in 1958 the Chad territory became an autonomous republic within the French Union. An independence movement led by the first premier and president, François (later Ngarta) Tombalbaye, achieved complete independence on Aug. 11, 1960. Tombalbaye was killed in the 1975 coup and succeeded by Gen. Félix Malloum, who faced a Libyan-financed civil war throughout his tenure in office. In 1977 Libya seized a strip of Chadian land and launched an invasion two years later.

Nine rival groups meeting in Lagos, Nigeria, in March 1979 agreed to form a provisional government headed by Goukouni Oueddei, a former rebel leader. Fighting broke out again in Chad in March 1980, when Defense Minister Hissen Habré challenged Goukouni and seized the capital. Libyan president Muammar al-Qaddafi in Jan. 1981 proposed a merger of Chad with Libya. The Libyan proposal was rejected and Libyan troops withdrew from Chad that year, but in 1983 they poured back into the northern part of the country in support of Goukouni. France, in turn, sent troops into southern Chad in support of Habré. Government troops then launched an offensive in early 1987 that drove the Libyans out of most of the country.

After the overthrow of Habré's government, Idriss Deby, a former defense minister and head of a rebel group (Patriotic Salvation Movement), declared himself president, dissolved the legislature (elected the previous July), and suspended the constitution. In 1998 Chad joined the war taking place in the Democratic Republic of the Congo on the side of President Laurent Kabila, who has been fighting against Congolese rebels for two years.

Chile

REPUBLIC OF CHILE

National name: República de Chile
President: Eduardo Frei Ruiz-Tagle (1994)
Area: 292,132 sq. mi. (756,950 sq. km)
Population (1999 est.): 14,973,843 (average annual rate of natural increase: 1.23%); birth rate: 17.8/1000; infant mortality rate: 10.0/1000; density per sq. mi.: 51
Capital and largest city (1996 est.): Santiago, 4,601,434. **Other large cities (1996 est.):** Concepción, 356,371; Viña del Mar, 326,448; Valparaíso, 282,850; Talcahuano, 265,060; Temuco, 246,304. **Monetary unit:** Peso. **Language:** Spanish. **Ethnicity/race:** European and European-Indian 95%, Indian 3%, other 2%. **Religions:** Roman Catholic, 89%; Protestant, 11%; small Jewish and Muslim populations. **Literacy rate:** 95%
Economic summary: GDP/PPP (1997 est.): $168.5 billion; $11,600 per capita. **Real growth rate:** 7.1%. **Inflation:** 6% (1997). **Unemployment:** 6.1% (1997). **Arable land:** 5%. **Agriculture:** wheat, corn, grapes, beans, sugar beets, potatoes, fruit, beef, poultry, wool, timber, fish. **Labor force:** 5.7 million (1997 est.); services 38.3%, industry and commerce 33.8%, agriculture, forestry, and fishing 19.2%, mining 2.3%, construction 6.4% (1990). **Industry:** copper, other minerals, foodstuffs, fish processing, iron and steel, wood and wood products, transport equipment, cement, textiles. **Natural resources:** copper, timber, iron ore, nitrates, precious metals, molybdenum. **Exports:** $16.9 billion (f.o.b., 1997): copper, other metals and minerals, wood products, fish and fishmeal, fruits. **Imports:** $18.2 billion (f.o.b., 1997): capital goods, spare parts, raw materials, petroleum, foodstuffs (1994). **Major trading partners:** EU, U.S., Asia, Latin America.

Geography Situated south of Peru and west of Bolivia and Argentina, Chile fills a narrow 1,800-mile (2,897 km) strip between the Andes and the Pacific. Its area is nearly twice that of Montana. One-third of Chile is covered by the towering ranges of the Andes. In the north is the driest place on Earth, the Atacama Desert, and in the center is a 700-mile-long (1,127 km) thickly populated valley with most of Chile's arable land. At the southern tip of Chile's mainland is Punta Arenas, the southernmost city in the world, and beyond that lies the Strait of Magellan and Tierra del Fuego, an island divided between Chile and Argentina. The southernmost point of South America is Cape Horn, a 1,390-foot (424-m) rock on Horn Island in the Wollaston group, which belongs to Chile. Chile also claims sovereignty over 482,628 sq. mi. (1,250,000 sq. km) of Antarctic territory, the Juan Fernández Islands, about 400 miles (644 km) west of the mainland, and Easter Island, about 2,000 miles (3,219 km) west.

Government Republic.

History Chile was originally under the control of the Incas in the north and the nomadic Araucanos in the south. In 1541, a Spaniard, Pedro de Valdivia, founded Santiago. Chile won its independence from Spain in 1818 under Bernardo O'Higgins and an Argentinian, José de San Martin. O'Higgins, dictator until 1823, laid the foundations of the modern state with a two-party system and a centralized government.

The dictator from 1830 to 1837, Diego Portales, fought a war with Peru in 1836–39 that expanded Chilean territory. Chile fought the War of the Pacific with Peru and Bolivia from 1879 to 1883, winning Antofagasta, Bolivia's only outlet to the sea, and extensive areas from Peru. A revolt in 1890 led by Pedro Montt overthrew, in 1891, José Balmaceda and established a parliamentary dictatorship that existed until a new constitution was adopted in 1925. Industrialization began before World War I and led to the formation of Marxist groups. Juan Antonio Ríos, president during World War II, was originally pro-Nazi but in 1944 led his country into the war on the side of the Allies.

A small abortive army uprising in 1969 raised the fear of military intervention in preventing a Marxist, Salvador Allende Gossens, from taking office after his election to the presidency on Sept. 4, 1970. Dr. Allende was the first president in a non-Communist country freely elected on a Marxist-Leninist program. Allende quickly established relations with Cuba and the People's Republic of China and nationalized several American companies. Allende's overthrow and death in an army assault on the presidential palace in Sept. 1973 ended a 46-year era of constitutional government in Chile.

The takeover was led by a four-man junta headed by Army Chief of Staff Augusto Pinochet Ugarte, who assumed the office of president. Committed to "exterminat[ing] Marxism," the junta embarked on a right-wing dictatorship. It suspended Parliament, banned political activity, and broke relations with Cuba. In 1977, Pinochet, in a speech marking his fourth year in power, promised elections by 1985 if conditions warranted. Earlier, he had abolished DINA, the secret police, and decreed an amnesty for political prisoners. Pinochet was inaugurated on March 11, 1981, for an eight-year term as president, at the end of which, according to the constitution adopted six months earlier, the junta would nominate a civilian as successor. He stepped down in Jan. 1990 in favor of Patricio Aylwin, who was elected in Dec. 1989 as the head of a 17-party coalition. The election of Dec. 1993 saw the reemergence of a member of the Frei family, with Eduardo Frei Ruiz-

Tagle, the candidate of a center-left coalition, winning the presidency. His father had been president from 1964 to 1970.

In March 1998, Gen. Augusto Pinochet Ugarte retired as army commander in chief. By Oct., the government of Spain was trying to extradite Pinochet from England, where he was undergoing medical treatment, to try him for the genocide, torture, and kidnapping of thousands of people, including Spanish nationals, during his 17-year dictatorship. While his supporters argued that Pinochet had diplomatic immunity, opinion polls suggested that two-thirds of Chileans considered him guilty and that most wanted him tried in Chile. Pinochet remained in custody in England while fighting the Spanish extradition order.

China

PEOPLE'S REPUBLIC OF CHINA

National name: Zhonghua Renmin Gongheguo
President: Jiang Zemin (1993)
Premier: Zhu Rongji (1998)
Area: 3,691,521 sq. mi. (9,596,960 sq. km)[1]
Population (1999 est.): 1,246,871,951 (average rate of natural increase: 0.81%); birth rate: 15.1/1000; infant mortality rate: 43.3/1000; density per sq. mi.: 338. China has 56 ethnic groups. In 1991, the Han people accounted for 92% of the population
Capital: Beijing. **Largest cities :** Shanghai: city proper (1990) 8,214,384, metro area (1996 est.) 13,659,000; Beijing (Peking): city proper (1990) 7,362,426; metro. area (1996 est.) 11,414,000; Tianjin (Tientsin): city proper (1990) 5,855,044; metro. area. (1995 est.) 10,687,000. 1990 figs.: Shenyang (Mukden), 4,669,737; Wuhan, 4,040,113; Guangzhou, 3,935,193; Chungking (Chongqing) 3,127,178; Haerbin, 2,990,921; Chengdu, 2,954,872; Xian, 2,872,539. .
Monetary unit: Yuan. **Languages:** Chinese, Mandarin, also local dialects. **Ethnicity:** Han Chinese 91.9%, Zhuang, Uygur, Hui, Yi, Tibetan, Miao, Manchu, Mongol, Buyi, Korean, and other nationalities 8.1%. **Religions:** Officially atheist but traditional religion contains elements of Confucianism, Taoism, Buddhism. **Literacy rate:** 84%
Economic summary: GDP/PPP (1997 est.): $4.25 trillion (may be overstated by as much as 25%); $3,460 per capita. **Real growth rate:** 8.8%. **Inflation:** 2.8%. **Unemployment:** in urban areas, officially 4%. **Arable land:** 10%. **Agriculture:** rice, wheat, potatoes, sorghum, peanuts, tea, millet, barley, cotton, other fibers, oilseed, pork and other livestock products, fish. **Labor force:** 623.9 million; agriculture and forestry, 53%; industry and commerce, 26%; construction and mining, 7%. social services, 4%; other, 10% (1995). **Industry:** iron and steel, coal, machine building, armaments, textiles and apparel, petroleum, cement, chemical fertilizers, footwear, toys, food processing, autos, consumer electronics, telecommunications. **Natural resources:** coal, iron ore, petroleum, mercury, tin, tungsten, antimony, manganese, molybdenum, vanadium, magnetite, aluminum, lead, zinc, uranium, hydropower potential. **Exports:** $182.7 billion (f.o.b., 1997): electrical machinery, clothing, footwear, toys, mineral fuels, leather, plastics, fabrics. **Imports:** $142.4 billion (c.i.f., 1997): mechanical appliances, electrical machinery, mineral fuels, plastics, iron and steel, fabrics, cotton and yarn. **Major trading partners:** Hong Kong, U.S., Japan, South Korea, Germany, The Netherlands, Taiwan, Singapore.

1. Including Manchuria and Tibet.

Geography China is slightly larger in area than the U.S. The greater part of the country is mountainous. Its principal ranges are the Tien Shan, the Kunlun chain, and the Trans-Himalaya. In the southwest is Tibet, which China annexed in 1950. The Gobi Desert lies to the north. China proper consists of three great river systems: the Yellow River (Huang Ho), 2,109 miles (5,464 km) long; the Chang Jiang (Yangtze Kiang), the third-longest river in the world at 2,432 miles (6,300 km); and the Zhujiang (Si Kiang), 848 miles (2,197 km) long.

Government Communist state.

History The earliest recorded human settlements in what is today called China were discovered in the Huang Ho basin and date from about 5000 B.C.E. During the Shang Dynasty (1500–1000 B.C.E.), the precursor of modern China's ideographic writing system developed, allowing the emerging feudal states of the era to achieve an advanced stage of civilization, rivaling in sophistication anything found at the time in Europe, the Middle East, or the Americas. It was following this initial flourishing of civilization, in a period known as the Chou Dynasty (1122–249 B.C.E.), that Lao-tse, Confucius, Mo Ti, and Mencius contributed the foundation of Chinese philosophical thought.

The feudal states, often at war with one another, were first united under Emperor Ch'in Shih Huang Ti, during whose reign (246–210 B.C.E.) work was begun on the Great Wall of China, a monumental bulwark against invasion from the West. Although the Great Wall symbolized China's desire to protect itself from the outside world, under the Han Dynasty (206 B.C.E.–C.E. 220), the civilization opened extensive commercial trading with the West.

In the T'ang Dynasty (618–907), often called the golden age of Chinese history, painting, sculpture, and poetry flourished, and woodblock printing, which enabled the mass production of books, made its earliest known appearance. The Mings, last of the native rulers (1368–1644), overthrew the Mongol, or Yuan, Dynasty (1271–1368) established by Kublai Khan. The Mings in turn were overthrown in 1644 by invaders from the north, the Manchus.

China remained largely isolated from the rest of the world's civilizations, closely restricting foreign activities. By the end of the 18th century only Canton (location of modern-day Hong Kong) and the Portuguese port of Macao were open to European merchants. But with the first Anglo-Chinese War in 1839–42, a long period of instability and concessions to Western colonial powers began. Following the war, several ports were opened up for trading, and Hong Kong was ceded to Britain. Treaties signed after further hostilities (1856–60) weakened Chinese sovereignty and gave foreigners immunity from Chinese jurisdiction. European powers took advantage of the disastrous Sino-Japanese War of 1894–95 to gain further trading concessions from China. Peking's response, the Boxer Rebellion (1900), was suppressed by an international force.

The death of Empress Dowager Tzu Hsi in 1908 and the accession of the infant emperor Hsüan T'ung (Pu-Yi) were followed by a nationwide rebellion led by Dr. Sun Yat-sen, who overthrew the Manchus and became the first president of the Provisional Chinese Republic in 1911. Dr. Sun resigned in favor of Yuan Shih-k'ai, who suppressed the Republicans in a bid to consolidate his power. Yuan's death in June 1916 was followed by years of civil war between rival militarists and Dr. Sun's Republicans. Nationalist forces, led by General Chiang Kai-shek and with the advice of Communist experts, soon occupied most of China, setting up a Kuomintang regime in 1928. Internal strife continued, however, and Chiang eventually broke with the Communists.

On Sept. 18, 1931, Japan launched an invasion of Manchuria, capturing the province. Tokyo set up a puppet state dubbed Manchukuo and installed the last Manchu emperor, Henry Pu-Yi (Hsüan T'ung), as its nominal leader. Japanese troops moved to seize China's northern provinces in July 1937, but were resisted by Chiang, who had been able to use the Japanese invasion to unite most of China behind him. Within two years, however, Japan had seized most of the nation's eastern ports and railways. The Kuomintang government retreated first to Hankow and then to Chungking, while the Japanese set up a puppet government at Nanking, headed by Wang Jingwei.

Japan's surrender in 1945 touched off civil war between the Kuomintang forces under Chiang and Communists led by Mao Zedong, who had been battling since the 1930s for control of China. Despite U.S. aid, the Kuomintang were overcome by the Soviet-supported Communists, and Chiang and his followers were forced to flee the mainland, establishing a government-in-exile on the island of Formosa (Taiwan). The Mao regime proclaimed the People's Republic of China on Oct. 1, 1949, with Beijing as the new capital and Zhou Enlai as premier.

After the Korean War began in June 1950, China led the Communist bloc in supporting North Korea, and on Nov. 26, 1950, the Mao regime sent troops to assist the North in its efforts to capture the South.

In an attempt to restructure China's primarily agrarian economy, Mao undertook the "Great Leap Forward" campaign in 1958, a disastrous program that aimed to combine the establishment of rural communes with a crash program of village industrialization. The Great Leap forced the abandonment of farming activities, leading to widespread famine in which more than 20 million people died of malnutrition.

In 1959, a failed uprising against China's invasion and occupation of Tibet forced Tibetan Buddhism's spiritual leader, the Dalai Lama, and 100,000 of his followers to flee to India. The invasion of Tibet, as well as border disputes between China and India—with whom Moscow had warm relations—and a perceived rivalry for the leadership of the world Communist movement caused a serious souring of relations between China and the U.S.S.R., former allies.

The failure of the Great Leap Forward touched off a power struggle within the Chinese Communist Party between Mao and his supporters, and a reformist faction, including future premier Deng Xiaoping. Mao moved to Shanghai, and from that base he and his supporters waged what they called the Cultural Revolution. Beginning in the spring of 1966, Mao ordered the closing of schools and the formation of ideologically pure Red Guard units, dominated by youths and students. The Red Guards campaigned against "old ideas, old culture, old habits, and old customs." Millions died as a series of violent purges were carried out. By early 1967, the Cultural Revolution had succeeded in bolstering Mao's position as China's paramount leader.

Anxious to exploit the Sino-Soviet rift, the Nixon administration made a dramatic announcement in July 1971 that National Security Adviser Henry Kissinger had secretly visited Beijing and reached an agreement whereby Nixon would visit China. The movement toward reconciliation, which signaled the end of the U.S. containment policy toward China, provided momentum for China's admission to the U.N. Despite U.S. opposition to expelling Taiwan (Nationalist China), the world body overwhelmingly voted to oust Taiwan in favor of Beijing's Communist government.

President Nixon went to Beijing for a week early in 1972, meeting Mao as well as Zhou. The summit ended with a historic communiqué on Feb. 28, in which both nations promised to work toward improved relations. Full diplomatic relations were barred by China as long as the U.S. continued to recognize the legitimacy of Nationalist China.

Following Zhou's death on Jan. 8, 1976, his successor, Vice Premier Deng Xiaoping, was supplanted within a month by Hua Guofeng, former minister of public security. Hua became permanent premier in April. In Oct. he was named successor to Mao as chairman of the Communist Party. But Mao's death on Sept. 10 unleashed the bitter intraparty rivalries that had been suppressed since the Cultural Revolution. Old opponents of Mao launched a campaign against his widow, Jiang Qing, and three of her "radical" colleagues. The so-called Gang of Four was denounced for having undermined the party, the government, and the economy. They were tried and convicted in 1981. Meanwhile, in 1977 Deng Xiaoping was reinstated as deputy premier, chief of staff of the army, and member of the Central Committee of the Politburo.

Beijing and Washington announced full diplomatic relations on Jan. 1, 1979, and the Carter administration abrogated the Taiwan defense treaty. Deputy Premier Deng sealed the agreement with a visit to the U.S. that coincided with the opening of embassies in both capitals on March 1. On Deng's return from the U.S., Chinese troops invaded and briefly occupied an area along Vietnam's northern border. The action was seen as a response to Vietnam's invasion of Cambodia and ouster of the Khmer Rouge government, which China had supported.

In 1981, Deng protégé Hu Yaobang replaced Hua Guofeng as party chairman. Deng became chairman of the committee's military commission, giving him control over the army. The body's 215 members concluded the session with a statement holding Mao Zedong responsible for the "grave blunder" of the Cultural Revolution.

Under Deng Xiaoping's leadership, meanwhile, China's Communist ideology went through a massive reinterpretation, and sweeping economic changes were set in motion in the early 1980s. The Chinese scrapped the personality cult that idolized Mao Zedong, muted Mao's old call for class struggle and exportation of the Communist revolution, and imported Western technology and management techniques to replace the Marxist tenets that had slowed modernization. Deng concluded an agreement for the return of Hong Kong following the expiration of Britain's 99-year lease on the territory on July 1, 1997.

The removal of Hu Yaobang as party chairman in Jan. 1987 signaled a hard-line resurgence within the party. Hu—who had become a hero to many reform-minded Chinese—was replaced by former premier Zhao Ziyang. With the death of Hu in April 1989, the ideological struggle spilled into the streets of the capital, as student demonstrators occupied Beijing's Tiananmen Square in May, calling for democratic reforms. Less than a month later, the demonstrations were crushed in a bloody crackdown as troops and tanks moved into the square and fired on protesters, killing several hundred.

In annual sessions of the rubber-stamp National People's Congress in 1992 and 1993, the government called for accelerating the drive for economic reform, but the sessions were widely seen as an effort to maintain China's moves toward a market economy while retaining political authoritarianism. At the session in 1993, Communist Party leader Jiang Zemin was elected president, while hard-liner Li Peng was reelected to another five-year term as prime minister. Since 1993, the Chinese economy has continued to grow rapidly. In Nov. the Central Committee adopted a resolution envisaging the conversion of state-owned enterprises into joint-stock companies, and the creation of a central bank and modern tax system.

Deng Xiaoping's death in Feb. 1997 left a younger generation in charge of managing the enormous country. Hong Kong's reversion to Chinese rule on July 1 was watched with studied concern by the international community for signs of future developments within other parts of China. In 1998, Prime Minister Zhu Rongji introduced a sweeping program to privatize state-run businesses and further liberalize the nation's economy, a move lauded by Western economists.

Chinese-U.S. relations in May 1999 were severely strained when Congress accused China of stealing U.S. nuclear secrets over the past two decades. Relations eroded even further, when a month later, the U.S. mistakenly bombed the Chinese embassy in Belgrade during Operation Allied Force, killing three Chinese journalists and wounding 20 others. The accidental nature of the bombing struck the Chinese government as highly implausible.

In July 1999 Taiwan's prime minister Lee Teng-hui infuriated China by announcing he was abandoning the longstanding "One China" policy, a tacit declaration of Taiwan's independence. China, which considers Taiwan a renegade province that will eventually be united with the mainland, has announced it will use force should Taiwan continue issuing incendiary statements. In Aug. 1999, China rounded up thousands of members of the Falun Gong sect, a highly popular religious movement that combines elements of Buddhism, Taoism, and martial arts. China, which has now outlawed the sect, was thought to consider the apolitical spiritual group threatening because its numbers exceeded the membership of the Chinese Communist Party.

Hong Kong

Status: Special Administrative Region of the People's Republic of China
Chief Executive: Tung Chee Hwa (1997)
Area: 416 sq. mi. (1,077 sq. km)
Population (1999 est.): 6,847,125 (average annual rate of natural increase: 0.69%); birth rate: 12.9/1000; infant

mortality rate: 5.2/1000; density per sq. mi.: 16,459
Capital (1996 est.): Victoria (Hong Kong Island),
6,311,000. **Monetary unit:** Hong Kong dollar. **Literacy
rate:** 81%
Economic summary: GDP/PPP (1997 est.): $175.2
billion; $26,800 per capita. **Real growth rate:** 5.5%.
Inflation: 5.1%. **Unemployment:** 3.1% (Jan.–March
1999). **Arable land:** 6%. **Agriculture:** fresh
vegetables, poultry. **Labor force:** 3.183 million (1997);
wholesale, retail, hotels, restaurants, 32.4%; social
services, 9.9%; manufacturing, 9.9%, financing,
insurance, real estate, 13.0%; transport and
communications, 5.7%; construction, 2.6%; other,
26.5% (June 1997). **Industry:** textiles, clothing,
tourism, electronics, plastics, toys, watches, clocks.
Exports: $180.7 billion (including reexports; f.o.b.,
1996): clothing, textiles, yarn and fabric, footwear,
electrical appliances, watches and clocks, toys.
Imports: $198.6 billion (c.i.f., 1996): foodstuffs,
transport equipment, raw materials, semimanufactures,
petroleum. **Major trading partners:** China, U.S.,
Japan, Germany, U.K., Taiwan, Singapore.

The territory of Hong Kong consists of the island
of Hong Kong (32 sq. mi.; 83 sq. km), Stonecutters'
Island, Kowloon Peninsula, and the New Territories
on the adjoining mainland. The island of Hong
Kong, located at the mouth of the Pearl River about
90 miles (145 km) southeast of Canton, was ceded
to Britain in 1841. Stonecutters' Island and
Kowloon were annexed in 1860, and the New Territories, which are mainly agricultural lands, were
leased from China in 1898 for 99 years. Hong Kong
was attacked by Japanese troops on Dec. 7, 1941,
and surrendered the following Christmas. It
remained under Japanese occupation until Aug.
1945.

After two years of painstaking negotiation,
authorities of Britain and the People's Republic of
China agreed in 1984 that Hong Kong would return
to Chinese sovereignty on July 1, 1997, when Britain's lease on the New Territories expired. They also
agreed that the vibrant capitalist enclave on China's
coast would retain its status as a free port, with its
laws remaining unchanged for 50 years.

The chief executive under the new government,
Tung Chee Hwa, formulated a policy agenda based
upon the concept of "one country, two systems,"
thus preserving Hong Kong's economic freedom.
Hong Kong will continue to have its own finances
and issue its own travel documents, and Beijing will
not levy taxes. In early 1998, Hong Kong fell into a
deep recession, with unprecedented unemployment
and sharply falling prices, but by spring 1999 the
financial center's economy began to rebound.

Colombia

REPUBLIC OF COLOMBIA

National name: República de Colombia
President: Andrés Pastrana Arango (1998)
Area: 439,735 sq. mi. (1,138,910 sq. km)
Population (1999 est.): 39,309,422 (average annual rate
of natural increase, 1.89%); birth rate: 24.5/1000; infant
mortality rate: 24.3/1000; density per sq. mi.: 89
Capital and largest city (1993): Santafé de Bogotá
4,945,448. **Largest cities (1995 est.):** Cali, 1,718,871;
Medellín, 1,621,356; Barranquilla, 1,064,255;
Cartagena, 745,689. **Monetary unit:** Peso.
Language: Spanish. **Ethnicity/race:** mestizo 58%,
white 20%, mulatto 14%, black 4%, mixed black-Indian
3%, Indian 1%. **Religion:** 95% Roman Catholic.
Literacy rate: 87%

Economic summary: GDP/PPP (1997 est.): $231.1
billion; $6,200 per capita. **Real growth rate:** 3.1%.
Inflation: 17.7%. **Unemployment:** 12.2%. **Arable
land:** 4%. **Agriculture:** coffee, cut flowers, bananas,
rice, tobacco, corn, sugarcane, cocoa beans, oilseed,
vegetables, forest products, shrimp farming. **Labor
force:** 16.8 million (1997 est.); services, 46% ;
agriculture, 30%; industry, 24% (1990). **Industry:**
textiles, food processing, oil, clothing and footwear,
beverages, chemicals, cement, gold, coal, emeralds.
Natural resources: petroleum, natural gas, coal, iron
ore, nickel, gold, copper, emeralds. **Exports:** $11.4
billion (f.o.b., 1997 est.): petroleum, coffee, coal,
bananas, fresh cut flowers. **Imports:** $13.5 billion
(c.i.f., 1997 est.): industrial equipment, transportation
equipment, consumer goods, chemicals, paper
products. **Major trading partners:** U.S., EC, Brazil,
Venezuela, Japan.

Geography Colombia, in the northwestern part of
South America, is the only country on that continent
that borders both the Atlantic and Pacific Oceans. It
is nearly equal in size to the combined areas of
California and Texas. Colombia is bordered by
Panama on the northwest, on the east by Venezuela
and Brazil, and on the southwest by Peru and Ecuador. Through the western half of the country, three
Andean ranges run north and south, merging into
one at the Ecuadorean border. The eastern half is a
low, jungle-covered plain, drained by spurs of the
Amazon and Orinoco Rivers, inhabited mostly by
isolated, tropical-forest Indian tribes. The fertile plateau and valley of the eastern range are the most
densely populated parts of the country.

Government Republic.

History Little is known about the various Indian
tribes who inhabited Colombia before the Spanish
arrived. In 1510 Spaniards founded Darien, the first
permanent European settlement on the American
mainland. In 1538 they established the colony of
New Granada, the area's name until 1861.

After a 14-year struggle, in which Simón Bolívar's Venezuelan troops won the battle of Boyacá in
Colombia on Aug. 7, 1819, independence was
attained in 1824. Bolívar united Colombia, Venezuela, Panama, and Ecuador in the Republic of Greater
Colombia (1819–30), but lost Venezuela and Ecuador to separatists. Two political parties dominated
the region: the Conservatives believed in a strong
central government and a powerful church; the Liberals believed in a decentralized government, strong
regional power, and a less influential role for the
church. Bolívar was himself a Conservative, while
his vice president, Francisco de Paula Santander,
was the founder of the Liberal Party.

Santander served as president between 1832 and
1836, a period of relative stability, but by 1840 civil
war erupted. Other periods of Liberal dominance
(1849–57 and 1861–80), which sought to disestab-
lish the Roman Catholic Church, were marked by
insurrection. Nine different governments followed,
each rewriting the constitution. In 1861, the country
was called the United States of New Granada, in
1863 it became the United States of Colombia, and
in 1885, it became the Republic of Colombia. In
1899 a brutal civil war broke out, the War of a
Thousand Days, that lasted until 1902. The following year, Colombia lost its claims to Panama
because it refused to ratify the lease to the U.S. of

the Canal Zone. Panama declared its independence in 1903 and went ahead with the creation of the U.S. deal.

The Conservatives held power until 1930, when revolutionary pressure put the Liberals back in power. The Liberal administrations of Enrique Olaya Herrera and Alfonso López (1930–38) were marked by social reforms that failed to solve the country's problems, and in 1946, insurrection and banditry broke out, claiming hundreds of thousands of lives by 1958. Laureano Gómez (1950–53); the army chief of staff, Gen. Gustavo Rojas Pinilla (1953–56); and a military junta (1956–57) sought to curb disorder by repression.

The Liberals won a solid majority in 1982, but a party split enabled Belisario Betancur Cuartas, the Conservative candidate, to win the presidency on May 31. After his inauguration, he ended the state of siege that had existed almost continuously for 34 years. In an official war against drug trafficking, Colombia became a public battleground with bombs, killings, and kidnappings. In 1989 a leading presidential candidate, Luis Carlos Galán, was murdered. In an effort to quell the terror, President Gaviria proposed lenient punishment in exchange for surrender by the leading drug dealers. In addition, in 1991 the constitutional convention voted to ban extradition. In July 1992 Pablo Escobar of the Medellín drug cartel escaped from prison in an operation that left six dead. He died the next year, but the Medellín drug cartel continues to operate.

In the country's closest presidential contest in 24 years, Ernesto Samper, the candidate of the Liberal Party, won 50% of the vote in June 1994. Amid allegations of having accepted campaign contributions from drug traffickers, Samper in May 1996 ordered emergency security measures in southern Colombia to fight leftist rebels, but the House of Representatives absolved him of the charges by a 111–43 vote. In 1997 a constitutional amendment that allowed for nonretroactive extradition was passed. Civil unrest, intermittent guerrilla clashes, and drug wars continued through 1999.

Comoros

UNION OF COMOROS ISLANDS

President: Col. Azaly Assoumani (1999)
Area: 690 sq. mi. (2,170 sq. km)
Population (1999 est.): 562,723 (average annual rate of natural increase: 3.11%); birth rate: 40.3/1000; infant mortality rate: 81.6/1000; density per sq. mi.: 816
Capital and largest city (1990 est.): Moroni (on Grande Comoro), 23,432. **Monetary unit:** Franc CFA.
Languages: Shaafi Islam (Swahili dialect), Malagasu, French, Arabic. **Ethnicity/race:** Antalote, Cafre, Makoa, Oimatsaha, Sakalava. **Religions:** Sunni Muslim, 86%; Roman Catholic, 14%. **Literacy rate:** 48%
Economic summary: GDP/PPP (1997 est.): $400 million; $685 per capita. **Real growth rate:** 3.5%. **Inflation:** 3.5% (1996 est.). **Unemployment:** 20% (1996 est.). **Arable land:** 35%. **Agriculture:** vanilla, cloves, perfume essences, copra, coconuts, bananas, cassava (tapioca). **Labor force:** 144,500 (1996 est.); 80% agriculture, 3% government. **Industries:** tourism, perfume distillation, textiles, furniture, jewelry, construction materials, soft drinks. **Exports:** $11.4 million (f.o.b., 1996 est.): vanilla, ylang-ylang, cloves, perfume oil, copra. **Imports:** $70 million (f.o.b., 1996 est.): rice and other foodstuffs, consumer goods,

petroleum products, cement, transport equipment. **Major trading partners:** France, Germany, U.S., South Africa, Kenya, Singapore.

Geography The Comoros Islands—Grande Comoro (Ngazidja), Anjouan, Mohéli, and Mayotte (which is not part of the country and retains ties to France)—are an archipelago of volcanic origin in the Indian Ocean, 190 miles off the coast of Mozambique.

Government Islamic republic run by a military junta.

History Comoros had been visited by travelers from Africa, Madagascar, Indonesia, and Arabia before the first Europeans encountered the islands. Arabic influence has been the strongest.

Under French rule since 1886, the Comoros declared themselves independent on July 6, 1975. However, Mayotte, with a Christian majority, voted against joining the other, mainly Islamic, islands, in the move to independence. It remains a French overseas territory.

A month after independence, Justice Minister Ali Soilih staged a coup with the help of a group of white mercenaries known as Les Affreux (The Terrible Ones), overthrowing the new nation's first president, Ahmed Abdallah. He was himself overthrown on May 13, 1978. In 1989 another coup took place.

A slump in world prices during the 1990s for Comoros's main exports, vanilla and ylang-ylang, exacerbated the country's poverty—the annual per capita income is less than $700.

The island of Anjouan declared independence on Aug. 3, 1997, after months of protests and clashes with security forces. The secessionists wanted a return to French rule, contending that independence from France has brought economic disaster and political chaos. Mohéli, the smallest island, also seceded. But France refused to support the secession of either island.

In Sept. 1997, President Mohamed Taki's forces attempted to retake Anjouan, but failed. Taki then declared a state of emergency. Peace talks in spring 1999 ended inconclusively when all other Anjouan representatives failed to sign a peace agreement that the other two islands had agreed to. Anti-Anjouan riots took place on Grande Comoros, and on April 30, 1999, Col. Azaly Assoumani led a coup, overthrowing interim president Tadjidine. He promised interim military rule would end in a year. This was the first of Comoros's four coups to be carried out by the Comorian army itself rather than mercenaries. The other three were led by the notorious French mercenary leader, "Colonel" Bob Denard. The island of Anjouan continued to fight against the government on Grande Comoro throughout 1999.

Congo

REPUBLIC OF CONGO

National name: République Populaire du Congo
President: Denis Sassou-Nguesso (1997)
Area: 132,046 sq. mi. (342,000 sq. km)
Population (1999 est.): 2,716,814 (average annual rate of natural increase: 2.16%); birth rate: 38.0/1000; infant mortality rate: 100.6/1000; density per sq. mi.: 21
Capital and largest city (1992 est.): Brazzaville, 937,580. **Other large city (1992 est.):** Pointe-Noire,

576,206. **Monetary unit:** Franc CFA. **Languages:** French, Lingala, Kikongo, others. **Ethnicity/race:** south: Kongo 48%; north: Sangha 20%, M'Bochi 12%; center: Teke 17%, Europeans 8,500 (mostly French). **Religions:** 50% Christian, 48% animist, 2% Muslim. **Literacy rate:** 57%
Economic summary: GDP/PPP (1996 est.): $5.25 billion; $2,000 per capita. **Real growth rate:** 4%. **Inflation:** 3% (1996 est.). **Unemployment rate:** n.a. **Arable land:** 0%. **Agriculture:** cassava (tapioca), sugar, rice, corn, peanuts, vegetables, coffee, cocoa, forest products. **Labor force:** n.a. **Industry:** petroleum extraction, cement kilning, lumbering, brewing, sugar milling, palm oil, soap, cigarette making. **Natural resources:** petroleum, timber, potash, lead, zinc, uranium, copper, phosphates, natural gas. **Exports:** $1.2 billion (f.o.b., 1995): crude oil, lumber, plywood, sugar, cocoa, coffee, diamonds. **Imports:** $670 million (c.i.f., 1995): intermediate manufactures, capital equipment, construction materials, foodstuffs, petroleum products. **Major trading partners:** Belgium-Luxembourg, Taiwan, U.S., Italy, France, The Netherlands, Italy.

Geography The Congo is situated in west-central Africa astride the equator. It borders Gabon, Cameroon, the Central African Republic, the Democratic Republic of the Congo, and the Angola exclave of Cabinda, with a short stretch of coast on the South Atlantic. Its area is nearly three times that of Pennsylvania. Most of the inland is tropical rain forest, drained by tributaries of the Congo River, which flows south along the eastern border with the Democratic Republic of the Congo to Stanley Pool. The narrow coastal plain rises to highlands separated from the inland plateaus by the 200-mile-wide Niari River valley, which gives passage to the coast.

Government Republic.

History In precolonial times, the region now called the Republic of Congo was dominated by three kingdoms: Kongo (originating about c.e. 1000), the Loango (flourishing in the 17th century), and Tio. After the Portuguese located the Congo River in 1482, commerce was carried on with the tribes, especially the slave trade.

The Frenchman Pierre Savorgnan de Brazza signed a treaty with Makoko, ruler of the Bateke people, in 1880, thus establishing French control. It was first called French Congo, and after 1905 Middle Congo. With Gabon and Ubangi-Shari, it became the colony of French Equatorial Africa in 1910. Abuse of laborers led to public outcry against the French colonialists as well as rebellions among the Congolese, but the exploitation of the native workers continued until 1930. During World War II the colony joined Chad in supporting the Free French cause against the Vichy government. The Congo proclaimed its independence without leaving the French Community in 1960, calling itself the Republic of Congo.

Congo's second president, Alphonse Massemba-Débat, instituted a Marxist-Leninist government. In 1968, Maj. Marien Ngouabi overthrew him but kept Congo on a socialist course. He was sworn in for a second five-year term in 1975. A four-man commando squad assassinated Ngouabi on March 18, 1977. Col. Joachim Yhombi-Opango, army chief of staff, assumed the presidency on April 4. Yhombi-Opango resigned on Feb. 4, 1979, and was replaced by Col. Denis Sassou-Nguesso.

In July 1990 the leaders of the ruling party voted to end the one-party system. A national political conference, hailed as a model for sub-Saharan Africa, renounced Marxism in 1991, and scheduled the country's first free elections for 1992. The national conference ending in June 1991 rewrote the constitution.

Political and ethnic tensions intensified in 1993 after legislative elections in May and runoffs in June. The opposition's rejection of the results developed into violence. A peace agreement was achieved between the government and the opposition in Aug. 1994. A four-month civil war (June 5–Oct. 15, 1997) devastated Brazzaville, the capital. Buttressed by military aid from Angola, former Marxist dictator Denis Sassou-Nguesso overthrew President Pascal Lissouba, the country's first democratically elected president.

In 1999, the country laid off 34,000 civil servants and expected to lay off 10,000 more in a cost-cutting measure recommended by the country's donors, the World Bank and the International Monetary Fund.

Congo, Democratic Republic of the

DEMOCRATIC REPUBLIC OF THE CONGO
President: Laurent Kabila (1997)
Area: 905,365 sq. mi. (2,345,410 sq. km)
Population (1999 est.): 50,481,305 (average annual rate of natural increase: 3.14%); birth rate: 46.4/1000; infant mortality rate: 99.5/1000; density per sq. mi.: 56
Capital and largest city (1994 est.): Kinshasa, 4,655,313. **Other large cities:** Lubumbashi, 851,381; Mbuji-Mayi, 806,475; Kisangani, 417,517; Kolwezi, 417,810. **Monetary unit:** Zaire. **Languages:** French (official), English, Bantu dialects, mainly Swahili, Lingala, Ishiluba, and Kikongo. **Ethnicity/race:** over 200 African ethnic groups, the majority are Bantu; the four largest tribes—Mongo, Luba, Kongo (all Bantu), and the Mangbetu-Azande (Hamitic)—make up about 45% of the population. **Religions:** Roman Catholic 50%, Protestant 20%, Kimbanguist 10%, Islam 10%; syncretic and traditional, 10%. **Literacy rate:** 72%
Economic summary: GDP/PPP (1996 est.): $18 billion; $400 per capita. **Real growth rate:** 1.5%. **Inflation:** n.a. **Unemployment:** n.a. **Arable land:** 3%. **Agriculture:** coffee, sugar, palm oil, rubber, tea, quinine, cassava (tapioca), bananas, root crops, corn, fruits, wood products. **Labor force:** 14.51 million (1993 est.); agriculture 65%, industry 16%, services 19% (1991 est.). **Industry:** mining, mineral processing, consumer products, cement, diamonds. **Natural resources:** copper, cobalt, cadmium, petroleum, industrial and gem diamonds, gold, silver, zinc, managenese, tin, germanium, uranium, radium, bauxite, iron ore, coal, hydropower potential, timber. **Exports:** $1.9 billion (f.o.b., 1996 est.): diamonds, copper, coffee, cobalt, crude oil. **Imports:** $1.1 billion (f.o.b., 1996 est.): consumer goods, foodstuffs, mining and other machinery, transport equipment, and fuels. **Major trading partners:** Belgium, U.S., France, Germany, Italy, U.K., Japan, South Africa.

Geography Congo, in west-central Africa, is bordered by the Congo Republic, the Central African Republic, the Sudan, Uganda, Rwanda, Burundi, Tanzania, Zambia, Angola, and the Atlantic Ocean. It is one-quarter the size of the U.S. The principal rivers are the Ubangi and Bomu in the north and the Congo in the west, which flows into the Atlantic.

The entire length of Lake Tanganyika lies along the eastern border with Tanzania and Burundi.

Government Dictatorship.

History Formerly the Belgian Congo, this territory was inhabited by ancient Negrito peoples (Pygmies), who were pushed into the mountains by Bantu and Nilotic invaders. The American correspondent Henry M. Stanley navigated the Congo River in 1877 and opened the interior to exploration. Commissioned by King Leopold II of the Belgians, Stanley made treaties with native chiefs that enabled the king to obtain personal title to the territory at the Berlin Conference of 1885.

Criticism of forced labor under royal exploitation prompted Belgium to take over administration of the Congo, which remained a colony until agitation for independence forced Brussels to grant freedom on June 30, 1960. The Katanga Province seceded from the new republic on July 11, and another mining province, South Kasai, followed. Belgium sent paratroopers to quell the civil war, and with President Joseph Kasavubu and Premier Patrice Lumumba of the national government in conflict, the United Nations flew in a peacekeeping force.

Kasavubu staged an army coup in 1960 and handed Lumumba over to the Katangan forces. A U.N. investigating commission found that Lumumba had been killed by a Belgian mercenary in the presence of Tshombe. Dag Hammarskjold, U.N. secretary-general, died in a plane crash en route to a peace conference with Tshombe on Sept. 17, 1961.

U.N. Secretary-General U Thant submitted a national reconciliation plan in 1962 that Tshombe rejected. Tshombe's troops fired on the U.N. force in Dec., and in the ensuing conflict Tshombe capitulated on Jan. 14, 1963. The peacekeeping force withdrew, and, in a complete about-face, Kasavubu named Tshombe premier in order to fight a spreading rebellion. Tshombe used foreign mercenaries, and with the help of Belgian paratroops airlifted by U.S. planes, defeated the most serious opposition, a Communist-backed regime in the northeast.

Kasavubu abruptly dismissed Tshombe in 1965 and was himself ousted by Gen. Joseph-Desiré Mobutu, army chief of staff. The new president nationalized the Union Minière, the Belgian copper mining enterprise that had been a dominant force in the Congo since colonial days. The plane carrying the exiled Tshombe was hijacked in 1967 and he was held prisoner in Algeria until his death from a heart attack was announced on June 29, 1969.

Mobutu eliminated opposition to win the election in 1970. In 1975, he nationalized much of the economy, barred religious instruction in schools, and decreed the adoption of African names. On March 8, 1977, invaders from Angola calling themselves the Congolese National Liberation Front pushed into Shaba and threatened the important mining center of Kolwezi. France and Belgium responded to Mobutu's pleas for help with weapons, but the U.S. gave only nonmilitary supplies. In April, France flew 1,500 Moroccan troops to Shaba to defeat the invaders, who were, Mobutu charged, Soviet-inspired and Cuban-led. U.S. intelligence sources, however, confirmed Soviet and Cuban denials of any participation and identified the rebels as former Katanga gendarmes who had fled to Angola after their 1963 defeat.

In April 1990 Mobutu announced he intended to introduce multiparty democracy, but that elections in Jan. 1991 would reduce the number of political parties to two besides his own. Opposition leaders denounced the scheme as giving Mobutu's party an unfair advantage.

In early 1993 Mobutu rejected Western demands that he yield power and announced plans to regroup his one-party Parliament, dismissing the main opposition leader, Prime Minister Tshisekedi. In Jan. 1994 Mobutu dissolved Parliament and dismissed his prime minister, which led to a general strike in the capital.

Mobutu Sese Seko was overthrown in May 1997, ending one of the world's most corrupt and megalomaniacal regimes. The last of the CIA-nurtured cold war despots, Mobutu deftly courted France and the U.S., which used Zaire as a launching pad for covert operations against bordering countries, particularly Marxist Angola. Mobutu's disastrous policies drove his country to economic collapse while he siphoned off millions of dollars for himself.

Laurent Kabila and his long-standing but little-known guerrilla movement launched a seven-month campaign that ousted Mobutu. The country was renamed the Democratic Republic of the Congo, its name before Mobutu changed it to Zaire in 1971. Mobutu's downfall began in Oct. 1996, when he planned to banish the Zairian Tutsis who had lived for centuries in eastern Zaire. Neighboring Rwanda's Tutsi-led government came to their aid, as did other rebel groups, one of which was led by Kabila. After conquering eastern Zaire, Kabila earned the support of a host of Mobutu's enemies, including Uganda, Burundi, Tanzania, Zambia, Zimbabwe, and Angola. His troops swept through the country, encountering little resistance. Mobutu fled in exile to Morocco on May 16, where he died of cancer in Sept.

Elation over Mobutu's downfall faded as Kabila's own autocratic style emerged and he seemed devoid of a clear plan for reconstructing the country. He stymied U.N. human rights investigations into the alleged massacres of Hutu refugees and continued to depend on foreign troops for border skirmishes rather than establish a strong national army. Many Congolese dismissed him as a puppet ruler who allowed his country to be overrun by outsiders, particularly the Rwandans. At the same time he has alienated many of his former supporters, including Rwanda and Uganda.

In Aug. 1998, Congolese rebel forces, led by ethnic Tutsis in eastern Congo, who are backed by Rwanda and Uganda, began attacking Kabila's forces. The rebels gained control of a large portion of the country until Angolan, Namibian, and Zimbabwean troops came to Kabila's aid and pushed the rebels back. In July 1999, a cease-fire agreement was signed by all six of the countries involved, and after much wrangling, the rival rebel forces also signed the agreement. The accord stipulates an immediate cease-fire, the withdrawal of foreign troops, the establishment of international observers, and national meetings between Kabila, the rebels, and opposition leaders—a plan that seems highly optimistic given the chaotic muddle of the conflict and the multitude of factions involved.

Costa Rica

REPUBLIC OF COSTA RICA

National name: República de Costa Rica
President: Miguel Angel Rodríguez (1998)
Area: 19,652 sq. mi. (51,100 sq. km)
Population (1999 est.): 3,674,490 (average annual rate of natural increase: 1.83%); birth rate: 22.5/1000; infant mortality rate: 12.9/1000; density per sq. mi.: 187
Capital and largest city (1994 est.): San José, 315,909. **Monetary unit:** Colón. **Language:** Spanish. **Ethnicity/race:** white (including mestizo) 96%, black 2%, Indian 1%, Chinese 1%. **Religion:** 95% Roman Catholic. **Literacy rate:** 93%
Economic summary: GDP/PPP (1997 est.): $19.6 billion; $5,500 per capita. **Real growth rate:** 3%. **Inflation:** 11.2%. **Unemployment:** 5.7%. **Arable land:** 6%. **Agriculture:** coffee, bananas, sugar, corn, rice, beans, potatoes, beef, timber. **Labor force:** 868,300; industry and commerce, 35.1%; government and services, 33%; agriculture, 27%; other, 4.9% (1985 est.). **Industry:** food processing, textiles and clothing, construction materials, fertilizer, plastic products. **Natural resource:** hydropower potential. **Exports:** $2.9 billion (f.o.b., 1996): coffee, bananas, textiles, sugar. **Imports:** $3.4 billion (c.i.f., 1996): raw materials, consumer goods, capital equipment, petroleum. **Major trading partners:** U.S., Germany, Italy, Guatemala, El Salvador, The Netherlands, U.K., France, Japan, Mexico, Venezuela.

Geography This Central American country lies between Nicaragua to the north and Panama to the south. Its area slightly exceeds that of Vermont and New Hampshire combined. It has a narrow Pacific coastal region. Cocos Island (10 sq. mi.; 26 sq. km), about 300 miles (483 km) off the Pacific Coast, is under Costa Rican sovereignty.

Government Democratic republic.

History Costa Rica was inhabited by 25,000 Indians when Columbus explored it in 1502. Few of the Indians survived the Spanish conquest, which began in 1563. The region grew slowly and was administered as a Spanish province. Costa Rica achieved independence in 1821 but was absorbed for two years by Agustín de Iturbide in his Mexican empire. It became a republic in 1848. Except for the military dictatorship of Tomás Guardia from 1870 to 1882, Costa Rica has enjoyed one of the most democratic governments in Latin America.

Rodrigo Carazo Odio became president in 1978. His tenure was marked by a disastrous decline in the economy. Oscar Arias Sanchez, who became president in 1986, prevented the neighboring Nicaraguan Contra rebels from using Costa Rican territory as a safe haven, and played a central role in negotiating settlements in both the Nicaraguan and the Salvadoran civil wars. He was awarded the Nobel Peace Prize in 1987.

José Maria Figueres Olsen of the National Liberation Party became president in 1994. He favored greater government intervention in the economy and other measures that the International Monetary Fund was unhappy about. As a result, the World Bank withheld $100 million of financing. In 1998, Miguel Angel Rodríguez of the Social Christian Unity Party became president. A border dispute with Nicaragua has threatened Costa Rica's tourism industry in the ecologically rich San Juan River area. Talks between the two nations regarding the border issue began in mid-1999.

Côte d'Ivoire

REPUBLIC OF CÔTE D'IVOIRE

National name: République de la Côte d'Ivoire
President: Henri Konan Bédié (1993)
Prime Minister: Daniel Kablan Duncan (1993)
Area: 124,502 sq. mi. (322,460 sq. km)
Population (1999 est.): 15,818,068 (average annual rate of natural increase: 2.56%); birth rate: 41.8/1000; infant mortality rate: 94.2/1000; density per sq. mi.: 127
Capital (1988): Yamoussoukro (official); Abidjan (administrative) (since March 1983), 106,786. **Largest city (est. 1988):** Abidjan, 2,797,000. **Monetary unit:** Franc CFA. **Languages:** French and African languages (Diaula esp.). **Ethnicity/race:** Baoule 23%, Bete 18%, Senoufou 15%, Malinke 11%, Agni, foreign Africans (mostly Burkinabe and Malians, about 3 million). **Religions:** 60% indigenous, 23% Islam, 17% Christian. **Literacy rate:** 54%
Economic summary: GDP/PPP (1997 est.): $25.8 billion; $1,700 per capita. **Real growth rate:** 6.5%. **Inflation:** 3.4%. **Unemployment:** n.a. **Arable land:** 8%. **Agriculture:** coffee, cocoa beans, bananas, palm kernels, corn, rice, manioc (tapioca), sweet potatoes, sugar, cotton, rubber, timber. **Labor force:** n.a. **Industry:** foodstuffs, beverages, wood products, oil refining, automobile assembly, textiles, fertilizer, construction materials, electricity. **Natural resources:** petroleum, diamonds, manganese, iron ore, cobalt, bauxite, copper. **Exports:** $4.2 billion (f.o.b., 1996): cocoa, coffee, tropical woods, petroleum, cotton, bananas, pineapples, palm oil, cotton, fish. **Imports:** $3.2 billion (f.o.b., 1996): food, consumer goods, capital goods, fuel, transport equipment. **Major trading partners:** France, Germany, Italy, The Netherlands, Burkina Faso, Mali, U.S., U.K., Nigeria, Ghana.

Geography Côte d'Ivoire (also known as the Ivory Coast), in western Africa on the Gulf of Guinea is a little larger than New Mexico. Its neighbors are Liberia, Guinea, Mali, Burkina Faso, and Ghana. The country consists of a coastal strip in the south, dense forests in the interior, and savannas in the north.

Government Presidential/parliamentary democracy. The government is headed by a president who is elected every five years by popular vote, together with a National Assembly of 175 members.

History Côte d'Ivoire was originally made up of numerous isolated settlements; today it represents more than sixty distinct tribes, including the Beti, Senufo, Baule, Anyi, Malinke, Dan, and Lobi. Côte d'Ivoire attracted both French and Portuguese merchants in the 15th century who were in search of ivory and slaves. French traders set up establishments early in the 19th century, and in 1842, the French obtained territorial concessions from local tribes, gradually extending their influence along the coast and inland. The area was organized as a territory in 1893, became an autonomous republic in the French Union after World War II, and achieved independence on Aug. 7, 1960. The Côte d'Ivoire formed a customs union in 1959 with Dahomey (Benin), Niger, and Burkina Faso. The nation's economy is one of the most developed in sub-Saharan Africa. It is the world's largest exporter of cocoa and one of the largest exporters of coffee.

From independence until his death in 1993, Felix Houphouët-Boigny served as president. Massive protests by students, farmers, and professionals forced the president to legalize opposition parties and hold the first contested presidential election in Oct. 1990, which Houphouët-Boigny won with 81% of the vote. Beginning in Sept. 1998, thousands of demonstrators protested a constitutional revision that granted President Henri Konan Bédié greatly enhanced powers. Bédié has also promoted the concept of *ivoirité*, which, roughly translated, means "pure Ivoirian pride." He has done so to disqualify his chief political rival, Alassane D. Ouattara, from elections—Ouattara was born in Burkina Faso, not Côte d'Ivoire. Although its defenders describe ivoirité as a term of positive national pride, it has led to a dangerous xenophobia, with numerous ethnic Malians and Burkinans being driven out of the country in 1999.

Croatia

REPUBLIC OF CROATIA

President: Franjo Tudjman (1990)
Prime Minister: Zlatko Matesa (1995)
Area: 21,829 sq. mi. (56,538 sq. km)
Population (1999 est.): 4,676,865 (average annual rate of natural increase: −0.08%), Birth rate: 10.3/1000; infant mortality rate: 7.8/1000; density per sq. mi.: 214
Capital (1991): Zagreb, 930,753. **Other large cities (1991):** Split, 189,444; Rijeka, 167,757; Osijek, 129,792. **Monetary unit:** Kuna (May 1994).
Language: Croatian. **Ethnicity/race:** Croat 78%, Serb 12%, Muslim 0.9%, Hungarian 0.5%, Slovenian 0.5%, others 8.1% (1991). **Literacy rate:** 97%. **Religions:** Catholic 76.5%, Orthodox 11.1%, Slavic Muslim 1.2%, Protestant 0.4%, others 10.8%
Economic summary: GDP/PPP (1997 est.): $22.7 billion; $4,500 per capita. **Real growth rate:** 4.4%. **Inflation:** 3.7%. **Unemployment:** 15.9% (year end 1997). **Industry:** chemicals and plastics, machine tools, fabricated metals, electronics, pig iron and rolled-steel products, aluminum, paper, wood products, construction materials, textiles, shipbuilding, petroleum and petroleum refining, food and beverages, tourism. **Agriculture:** wheat, corn, sugar beets, sunflower seed, alfalfa, clover, olives, citrus, grapes, vegetables, livestock breeding, dairy farming. **Exports:** $4.3 billion (f.o.b., 1997): machinery and transport equipment, miscellaneous manufactures, chemicals, food and live animals, raw materials, fuels and lubricants, and beverages and tobacco. **Imports:** $9.1 billion (c.i.f., 1997): machinery and transport equipment, fuels and lubricants, food and live animals, chemicals, miscellaneous manufactured articles, raw materials, beverages and tobacco. **Major trading partners:** Germany, Italy, Slovenia.

Geography Croatia is a former Yugoslav republic on the Adriatic Sea; it is about the size of West Virginia. Part of Croatia is a barren, rocky region lying in the Dinaric Alps. The Zagorje region north of the capital, Zagreb, is a land of rolling hills, and the fertile agricultural region of the Pannonian Plain is bordered by the Drava, Danube, and Sava Rivers in the east. Over one-third of Croatia is forested.

Government Parliamentary democracy.

History The original home of the Slavic Croats was in an area that was part of the Republic of Ukraine. During the 6th century C.E., other tribes arrived in the region, which was then part of the Roman province of Pannonia. The Croats converted to Christianity between the 7th and 9th century and adopted the Roman alphabet under the suzerainty of Charlemagne. In C.E. 925, the Croats defeated Byzantine and Frankish invaders and established their own independent kingdom, which reached its peak during the 11th century. A civil war ensued in 1089, which later led to the country being conquered by the Hungarians in 1091. The signing of the *Pacta Conventa* by Croatian tribal chiefs and the Hungarian king in 1102 united the two nations politically under the Hungarian monarch, but Croatia retained its autonomy.

When the Hungarians were defeated by the Turks in 1526, most of Croatia fell under Ottoman rule until the end of the 17th century. It maintained its Catholicism (the religion of about 80% of the country) during the centuries of Muslim rule, and its religion has always been one of Croatia's defining characteristics, distinguishing it from the other Balkan states. The rest of Croatia elected Ferdinand of Austria as its king and became associated with the Hapsburgs of Austria. After the establishment of the Austro-Hungarian kingdom in 1867, Croatia and Slovenia became part of Hungary until the collapse of Austria-Hungary in 1918 following its defeat in World War I. On Oct. 29, 1918, Croatia proclaimed its independence and joined in union with Montenegro, Serbia, and Slovenia to form the Kingdom of Serbs, Croats, and Slovenes. The name was changed to Yugoslavia in 1929.

When Germany invaded Yugoslavia in 1941, Croatia became a Nazi puppet state. Croatian Fascists, the Ustachi, slaughtered countless Serbs and Jews during the war. After Germany was defeated in 1945, Croatia was made into a republic of the newly reestablished Communist nation of Yugoslavia. In June 1991, the Croatian Parliament passed a declaration of independence from Yugoslavia. A six-month civil war followed with the Serbian-dominated Yugoslavian army. The war claimed thousands of lives and wrought mass destruction.

A U.N. cease-fire was arranged on Jan. 2, 1992. The Security Council in Feb. approved sending a 14,000-member peacekeeping force to monitor the cease-fire and protect the minority Serbs in Croatia. In a 1993 referendum the Serb-occupied portion of Croatia (Krajina) resoundingly voted for integration with Serbs in Bosnia and Serbia proper. Although the Zagreb government and representatives of Krajina signed a cease-fire in March 1994, further negotiations broke down. In a lightning-quick operation, the Croatian army retook western Slavonia in May 1995. Similarly, in Aug. the central Croatian region of Krajina, held by Serbs, was returned to Zagreb's control.

Announcing on television in 1999 that "national issues are more important than democracy," President Tudjman continued to alienate Croatians with his authoritarian rule, out-of-touch nationalism, and disastrous handling of the war-shattered economy.

Cuba

REPUBLIC OF CUBA

National name: República de Cuba
President: Fidel Castro (1976)
Area: 42,843 sq. mi. (110,860 sq. km)
Population (1999 est.): 11,096,395 (average annual rate of natural increase: 0.55%); birth rate: 12.9/1000; infant mortality rate: 7.8/1000; density per sq. mi.: 259
Capital and largest city (1994 est.): Havana, 2,241,000. **Other large cities (1994 est.):** Santiago de Cuba, 440,084; Camagüey, 293,961; Holguin, 242,085; Guantánamo, 207,796; Santa Clara, 205,400. **Monetary unit:** Peso. **Language:** Spanish. **Ethnicity/race:** mulatto 51%, white 37%, black 11%,

Chinese 1%. **Religion:** at least 85% nominally Roman Catholic before Castro assumed power. **Literacy rate:** 94%

Economic summary: GDP/PPP (1997 est.): $16.9 billion; $1,540 per capita. **Real growth rate:** 2.5%, **Inflation:** n.a. **Unemployment:** 8% (1996 est.). **Arable land:** 24%. **Agriculture:** sugarcane, tobacco, citrus, coffee, rice, potatoes and other tubers, beans, livestock. **Labor force:** (1996 est.), 4.5 million; services and government, 30%; industry, 22%; agriculture, 20%; commerce, 11%, construction, 10%; transportation and communications, 7%. **Industry:** sugar, petroleum, food, tobacco, textiles, chemicals, paper and wood products, metals, cement, fertilizers, consumer goods, agricultural machinery. **Natural resources:** cobalt, nickel, iron ore, copper, manganese, salt, timber, silica, petroleum. **Exports:** $1.9 billion (f.o.b., 1997 est.): sugar, nickel, tobacco, shellfish, medical products, citrus, coffee. **Imports:** $3.2 billion (c.i.f., 1997 est.): petroleum, food, machinery, chemicals. **Trading partners:** Russia, The Netherlands, Canada, Spain, Mexico.

Geography The largest island of the West Indies group (equal in area to Pennsylvania), Cuba is also the westernmost—just west of Hispaniola (Haiti and the Dominican Republic), and 90 miles (145 km) south of Key West, Florida, at the entrance to the Gulf of Mexico. The island is mountainous in the southeast and south-central area (Sierra Maestra). It is flat or rolling elsewhere. Cuba also includes numerous smaller islands, islets, and cays.

Government Communist state.

History Arawak (or Taino) Indians inhabiting Cuba when Columbus landed on the island in 1492 died off from diseases brought by sailors and settlers. By 1511, Spaniards under Diego Velásquez were founding settlements that served as bases for Spanish exploration. Cuba also became an assembly point for treasure looted by the conquistadores, attracting French and English pirates.

Black slaves and free laborers were imported to work sugar and tobacco plantations, and waves of chiefly Spanish immigrants maintained a European character in the island's culture. Early slave rebellions and conflicts between colonials and Spanish rulers laid the foundation for an independence movement that turned into open warfare from 1867 to 1878. Slavery was abolished in 1886. In 1895, the poet José Marti led the struggle that finally ended Spanish rule, thanks largely to U.S. intervention in 1898 after the sinking of the battleship *Maine* in Havana harbor.

A treaty in 1899 made Cuba an independent republic under U.S. protection. The U.S. occupation, which ended in 1902, suppressed yellow fever and brought large American investments. From 1906 to 1909, Washington invoked the Platt Amendment to the treaty, which gave the U.S. the right to intervene in order to suppress any revolt. U.S. troops came back in 1912 and again in 1917 to restore order. The Platt Amendment was abrogated in 1934.

Fulgencio Batista, an army sergeant, led a revolt in 1933 that overthrew the regime of President Gerado Machado. Batista's Cuba was a police state. Corrupt officials used intimidation and took payoffs from American gamblers who operated casinos, demanded bribes from Cubans for various public services, and enriched themselves with raids on the public treasury.

Fidel Castro Ruz, a tall, bearded attorney in his thirties who had been in exile in Mexico, landed in Cuba on Christmas Day 1956 with a band of 12 fellow revolutionaries, evaded Batista's soldiers, and set up headquarters in the jungled hills of the Sierra Maestra range. By 1958 his force had grown to about 2,000 guerrillas, for the most part young and middle-class. Castro's brother Raul, and Ernesto (Ché) Guevara, an Argentine physician, were his top lieutenants. Businessmen and landowners who opposed the Batista regime gave financial support to the rebels. The United States, meanwhile, cut off arms shipments to Batista's army. The beginning of the end for Batista came when the rebels routed 3,000 government troops and captured Santa Clara, capital of Las Villas province 150 miles from Havana, and a trainload of Batista reinforcements refused to get out of their railroad cars. On New Year's Day 1959, Batista flew to exile in the Dominican Republic and Castro took over the government. Crowds cheered the revolutionaries on their seven-day march to the capital.

The United States initially welcomed what looked like the prospect for a democratic Cuba, but a rude awakening came within a few months when Castro established military tribunals for political opponents, jailed hundreds, and began to veer leftward. Castro disavowed Cuba's 1952 military pact with the U.S. He confiscated U.S. investments in banks and industries and seized large U.S. landholdings, turning them first into collective farms and then into Soviet-type state farms. The United States broke relations with Cuba on Jan. 3, 1961. Castro forged an alliance with the Soviet Union.

From the ranks of the Cuban exiles who had fled to the U.S., the Central Intelligence Agency recruited and trained an expeditionary force, numbering less than 2,000 men, to invade Cuba, with the expectation that the invasion would spark an uprising of the Cuban populace against Castro. Planned under the Eisenhower administration, President John F. Kennedy gave the go-ahead for the invasion in early 1961, but rejected a CIA proposal for U.S. planes to provide air support. The landing at the Bay of Pigs on April 17, 1961, was a fiasco. Not only did the invaders fail to receive any support from the populace, but Castro's tanks and artillery made short work of the small force.

A Soviet attempt to change the global power balance by installing medium-range missiles in Cuba—capable of striking targets in the United States with nuclear warheads—provoked a crisis between the superpowers in 1962 that had the potential of touching off World War III. Denouncing the Soviets for "deliberate deception," President Kennedy on Oct. 22 announced that the U.S. Navy would enforce a "quarantine" of shipping to Cuba and search Soviet-bloc ships to prevent the missiles themselves from reaching the island. After six days of tough public statements on both sides and secret diplomacy, Soviet premier Nikita Khrushchev on Oct. 28 ordered the missile sites dismantled and shipped back to the Soviet Union, in return for a U.S. pledge not to attack Cuba.

A Soviet satellite in the 1960s and 1970s, Cuba helped spread the Communist revolution in the Western hemisphere. The U.S. established limited diplomatic ties with Cuba on Sept. 1, 1977. Emigration increased dramatically after April 1, 1980, when Castro, irritated by the granting of asylum to would-be refugees by the Peruvian embassy in Havana, removed guards and allowed 10,000 Cubans to swarm into the embassy grounds.

As an airlift began taking the refugees to Costa Rica, Castro opened the port of Mariel to a "freedom flotilla" of ships and yachts from the United States, many of them owned or chartered by Cuban-Americans to bring out relatives. It wasn't until after the refugees had reached the United States that it was discovered that the regime had opened prisons and mental hospitals to permit criminals, homosexuals, and others unwanted by the Cuban government to join the refugees.

For most of President Ronald Reagan's first term, U.S.-Cuban relations were frozen. But late in 1984, an agreement was reached between the two countries. Cuba would take back more than 2,700 Cubans who had come to the United States in the Mariel exodus but were not eligible to stay in the country under U.S. immigration law because of criminal or psychiatric disqualification. Castro canceled the agreement when the U.S. began the Radio Marti broadcasts in May 1985 to bring a non-Communist viewpoint to the Cuban people.

With the collapse of communism in eastern Europe, Cuba's foreign trade plummeted as did aid from Russia, producing the worst economic crisis in the island's history. The government moved slightly toward a mixed economy in 1993 by permitting limited private enterprise in a number of trades and services and allowing Cubans to possess convertible currencies. In March 1996, the U.S. passed the Helms-Burton Act, which further extended the U.S. trade embargo on Cuba by penalizing non-U.S. companies doing business with Cuba. Reaction to the measure was widespread international condemnation that included the U.S.'s North American neighbors, Canada, Mexico, and the Caribbean nations. Christmas was declared an official holiday in Cuba in 1997, for the first time since the revolution, in preparation for Pope John Paul II's historic visit to Cuba in Jan. 1998. By Castro's allowing the pope's visit, he raised hopes that the gesture signaled a new openness, easing of restrictions, and increased religious freedom for Cubans.

In mid-1999, the U.S. sent negotiators to Havana to begin talks on better communication between the U.S. and Cuba regarding drug shipments in the Caribbean, despite protests from some Cuban-Americans. The U.S. government stated that the action was not part of an effort to normalize relations with Cuba.

Cyprus

REPUBLIC OF CYPRUS

National name: Kypriaki Dimokratia—Kibris Cumhuriyeti
President: Glafcos Klerides (1993)
Area: 3,572 sq. mi (9,250 sq. km)
Population (1998 est.): 754,064; (average annual rate of natural increase: 0.62%; birth rate: 13.6/1000; infant mortality rate: 7.7/1000; density per sq. mi.: 211
Capital and largest city (1993): Lefkosia (Nicosia) (in government-controlled area), 186,400. **Monetary unit:** Cyprus pound. **Languages:** Greek, Turkish (official), English is widely spoken. **Ethnicity/race:** total: Greek 78% (99.5% of the Greeks live in the Greek area, 0.5% live in the Turkish area), Turkish 18% (1.3% live in the Greek area, 98.7% live in the Turkish area),

other 4%. **Religions (1993 est.):** Greek Orthodox, 78%; Sunni Muslim, 18%; Maronite, Armenian, Apostolic, Latin and others, 4%. **Literacy rate:** 94%
Economic summary (Greek area): GDP/PPP (1997 est.): $9.75 billion; $15,000 per capita. **Real growth rate:** 2.5%. **Inflation:** 3.5%. **Unemployment:** 3.3%. **Arable land:** 12%. **Agriculture:** potatoes, citrus, vegetables, barley, grapes, olives. **Labor force:** 299,700; services, 62%; industry, 25%; agriculture, 13%. **Industry:** food, beverages, textiles, chemicals, metal products, tourism, wood products. **Natural resources:** copper, pyrites, asbestos, gypsum, timber, salt, marble, clay earth pigment. **Exports:** $1.3 billion (f.o.b., 1996): citrus, potatoes, grapes, wine, cement, clothing, shoes. **Imports:** $3.6 billion (f.o.b., 1996): consumer goods, petroleum and lubricants, food and feed grains, machinery. **Major trading partners:** Russia, Bulgaria, U.K., U.S., Italy, Germany, Greece.

Economic summary (Turkish area): GDP/PPP (1997 est.): $1.44 billion; $8,000 per capita. **Real growth rate:** 1.7%. **Inflation:** 87.5%. **Unemployment:** 6.4% (1996). **Labor force:** 76,500 (1996); services, 66%; industry, 11%; agriculture, 23% (1995). **Exports:** $70.5 million (f.o.b., 1996): citrus, potatoes, textiles. **Imports:** $318.4 million (f.o.b., 1996): food, minerals, chemicals, machinery. **Major trading partners:** Turkey, U.K., other EU. **Member of Commonwealth of Nations**

Geography The third-largest island in the Mediterranean (one and one-half times the size of Delaware), Cyprus lies off the southern coast of Turkey and the western shore of Syria. The highest peak is Mount Olympus at 6,406 feet (1,953 m).

Government Republic. Mediation efforts by the U.N. seek to achieve reunification of the island under one federated system of government.

History Cyprus was the site of early Phoenician and Greek colonies. For centuries its rule passed through many hands. It fell to the Turks in 1571, and a large Turkish colony settled on the island.

In World War I, at the outbreak of hostilities with Turkey, Britain annexed the island. It was declared a crown colony in 1925. For centuries the Greek population, regarding Greece as its mother country, has sought self-determination and reunion with Greece (*enosis*). The resulting quarrel with Turkey threatened NATO. Cyprus became an independent nation on Aug. 16, 1960, with Britain, Greece, and Turkey as guarantor powers.

Archbishop Makarios, president since 1959, was overthrown on July 15, 1974, by a military coup led by the Cypriot National Guard. The new regime named Nikos Giorgiades Sampson as president and Bishop Gennadios as head of the Cypriot Church to replace Makarios. Diplomacy failed to resolve the crisis. Turkey invaded Cyprus by sea and air on July 20, 1974, asserting its right to protect the Turkish Cypriote minority. Geneva talks involving Greece, Turkey, Britain, and the two Cypriote factions failed in mid-Aug., and the Turks subsequently gained control of 40% of the island. Some 180,000 Greek Cypriots were uprooted by the Turkish troops. Greece made no armed response to the superior Turkish force, but bitterly suspended military participation in the NATO alliance. The tension continued after Makarios returned to become president on Dec. 7, 1974. He offered self-government to the Turkish minority, but rejected any solution "involving transfer of populations and amounting to partition of Cyprus."

Turkish Cypriots proclaimed a separate state under Rauf Denktas in the northern part of the island on Nov. 15, 1983, naming it the "Turkish Republic of Northern Cyprus." The U.N. Security Council, in its Resolution 541 of Nov. 18, 1983, declared this action legally invalid and called for withdrawal. No country except Turkey has recognized this illegal entity.

In 1988, George Vassiliou, a conservative and critic of U.N. proposals to reunify Cyprus, became president. The purchase of missiles capable of reaching the Turkish coast evoked threats of retaliation from Turkey in 1997, and Cyprus's plans to deploy more missiles in Aug. 1999 again raised Turkey's ire.

Czech Republic

President: Vaclav Havel (1993)
Prime Minister: Milos Zeman (1998)
Area: 30,464 sq. mi. (78,703 sq. km)
Population (1999 est.): 10,280,513 (average annual rate of natural increase: –0.10%); birth rate: 9.8/1000; infant mortality rate: 6.7/1000; density per sq. mi.: 337
Capital and largest city (Jan. 1, 1994): Prague, 1,215,771. **Other large cities:** Brno, 389,727; Ostrava, 326,396; Plzen, 172,402; Olomouc, 106,003.
Monetary unit: Koruna. **Languages:** Czech; Slovak minority. **Ethnicity/race:** Czech 94.4%, Slovak 3%, Polish 0.6%, German 0.5%, Roma (Gypsy) 0.3%, Hungarian 0.2%, other 1%. **Religions:** atheist 39.8%, Roman Catholic 39.2%, Protestant 4.6%, Orthodox 3%, other 13.4%. **Literacy rate:** 99%
Economic summary: GDP: (1997 est.): $111.9 billion; $10,800 per capita. **Real growth rate:** 0.7%. **Inflation:** 10% (1997). **Unemployment:** 5% (1997 est.). **Natural resources:** hard coal, soft coal, kaolin, clay, graphite. **Industry:** fuels, ferrous metallurgy, machinery and equipment, coal, motor vehicles, glass, armaments. **Agriculture:** grains, potatoes, sugar beets, hops, fruit, pigs, cattle, poultry, forest products. **Labor force:** (1997), 5.124 million; industry, 33.1%; agriculture, 6.9%; construction, 9.1%; services 43.7%; transport and communications, 7.2% (1994). **Exports:** $21.7 billion (f.o.b., 1996): machinery and equipment, manufactured goods, raw materials and fuel, food. **Imports:** $27.7 billion (f.o.b., 1996): machinery and equipment, manufactured goods, raw materials and fuels, food. **Major trading partners:** EU, CEFTA, Slovakia, European Free Trade Association (EFTA).

Geography The Czech Republic's central European landscape is dominated by the Bohemian Massif, which rises to heights of 3,000 feet (900 m) above sea level. This ring of mountains encircles a large elevated basin, the Bohemian Plateau. The principal rivers are the Elbe and the Vltava.

Government Parliamentary democracy.

History Probably about the 5th century C.E., Slavic tribes from the Vistula basin settled in the region of the traditional Czech lands of Bohemia, Moravia, and Silesia. The Czechs founded the kingdom of Bohemia, the Premyslide dynasty, which ruled Bohemia and Moravia from the 10th to the 16th century. One of the Bohemian kings, Charles IV, holy Roman emperor, made Prague an imperial capital and a center of Latin scholarship. The Hussite movement founded by Jan Hus (1369?–1415) linked the Slavs to the Reformation and revived Czech nationalism, previously under German domination. A Hapsburg, Ferdinand I, ascended the

throne in 1526. The Czechs rebelled in 1618, precipitating the Thirty Years' War (1618–48). Defeated in 1620, they were ruled for the next 300 years as part of the Austrian empire. Full independence from the Hapsburgs was not achieved until the end of World War I, following the collapse of the Austrian-Hungarian Empire.

A union of the Czech lands and Slovakia was proclaimed in Prague on Nov. 14, 1918, and the Czech nation became one of the two component parts of the newly formed Czechoslovakian state. In March 1939, German troops occupied Czechoslovakia, and Czech Bohemia and Moravia became German protectorates for the duration of World War II. The former government returned in April 1945 when the war ended and the country's pre-1938 boundaries were restored. When elections were held in 1946, Communists became the dominant political party and gained control of the Czechoslovakian government in 1948. Thereafter, the former democracy was turned into a Soviet-style state.

Nearly 42 years of Communist rule ended when Vaclav Havel, a highly respected writer and dissident, was elected president of Czechoslovakia in 1989. The return of democratic political reform saw a strong Slovak nationalist movement emerge by the end of 1991, which sought independence for Slovakia. When the general elections of June 1992 failed to resolve the continuing coexistence of the two republics within the federation, Czech and Slovak political leaders agreed to separate their states into two fully independent nations. On Jan. 1, 1993 the Czechoslovakian federation was dissolved and two separate independent countries were established— the Czech Republic and Slovakia.

In March 1999, the Czech Republic joined NATO. The country's next goal in international relations is to gain entrance into the European Union.

Denmark

KINGDOM OF DENMARK
National name: Kongeriget Danmark
Sovereign: Queen Margrethe II (1972)
Prime Minister: Poul Nyrup Rasmussen (1993)
Area: 16,833 sq. mi. (43,094 sq. km)[1]
Population (1999 est.): 5,356,845 (average annual rate of natural increase: .06%); birth rate: 11.6/1000; infant mortality rate: 5.1/1000; density per sq. mi.: 322
Capital and largest city (1992): Copenhagen, 1,339,395. **Other large cities (1992):** Århus, 204,139; Odense, 140,886; Ålborg, 114,970. **Monetary unit:** Krone. **Languages:** Danish, Faeroese, Greenlandic (an Inuit dialect), small German-speaking minority. **Ethnicity/race:** Scandinavian, Eskimo, Faeroese, German. **Religions:** Evangelical Lutheran 91%, other Protestant and Roman Catholic 2%, other 7%. **Literacy rate:** 99%
Economic summary: GDP/PPP (1997 est.): $122.5 billion; $23,200 per capita. **Real growth rate:** 3%. **Inflation:** 2.2%. **Unemployment:** 7.9%. **Arable land:** 60%. **Agriculture:** grain, potatoes, rape, sugar beets, meat, dairy products, fish. **Labor force:** 2,895,950; private services, 40%; government services, 30%; manufacturing and mining, 19%; construction, 6%; agriculture, forestry, fishing, 5% (1995). **Industry:** food processing, machinery and equipment, textiles and clothing, chemical products, electronics, construction, furniture, wood products, shipbuilding. **Natural resources:** petroleum, natural gas, fish, salt, limestone, stone, gravel and sand. **Exports:** $48.8

billion (f.o.b., 1996): machinery and instruments, meat and meat products, fuels, dairy products, ships, fish, chemicals. **Imports:** $43.2 billion (c.i.f., 1996); machinery and equipment, petroleum, chemicals, grain and foodstuffs, textiles, paper. **Major trading partners:** Germany, Sweden, U.K., Norway, France, The Netherlands, U.S., Japan, FSU.

1. Excluding Faeroe Islands and Greenland.

Geography Smallest of the Scandinavian countries (half the size of Maine), Denmark occupies the Jutland peninsula, a lowland area. The country also consists of several islands in the Baltic Sea; the two largest are Sjælland, the site of Copenhagen, and Fyn.

Government Constitutional monarchy.

History From 10,000 to 1500 B.C.E., the population of present-day Denmark evolved from a society of hunters and fishers into an agricultural one. Called Jutland by the end of the 8th century, its mariners belonged to the Vikings, or Norsemen, who raided western Europe and the British Isles from the 9th to 11th century.

The country was Christianized by Saint Ansgar and Harald Blaatand (Bluetooth)—the first Christian king—in the 10th century. Harald's son, Sweyn, conquered England in 1013. His son, Canute the Great, who reigned from 1014 to 1035, united Denmark, England, and Norway under his rule; the southern tip of Sweden was part of Denmark until the 17th century. On Canute's death, civil war tore apart the country until Waldemar I (1157–82) reestablished Danish hegemony over the north.

In 1282, the nobles won the Great Charter, and Eric V was forced to share power with Parliament and a Council of Nobles. Waldemar IV (1340–75) restored Danish power, checked only by the Hanseatic League of north German cities allied with ports from Holland to Poland. His daughter, Margrethe, in 1397 Denmark, Norway, and Sweden united under her rule. But Sweden later achieved autonomy and in 1523, under Gustavus I, independence.

Denmark supported Napoléon, for which it was punished at the Congress of Vienna in 1815 by the loss of Norway to Sweden.

In 1864, the Prussians, under Bismarck, and the Austrians made war on Denmark as an initial step in the unification of Germany. Denmark was neutral in World War I.

In 1940, Denmark was invaded by the Nazis. King Christian X reluctantly cautioned his fellow Danes to accept the occupation, but there was widespread resistance against the Nazis. Denmark was the only occupied country in World War II to save all its Jews from extermination, by smuggling them out of the country.

Beginning in 1944, Denmark's relationship with its territories changed substantially. In that year, Iceland declared its independence from Denmark, ending a union that had existed since 1380. In 1948, the Faeroe Islands, which had also belonged to Denmark since 1380, were granted home rule, and in 1953, Greenland officially became a territory of Denmark.

A referendum on the Maastricht Accord, which paved the way for greater EU economic integration, passed in May 1993. Denmark has been a member of the EC (now the EU) since 1973.

Outlying Territories of Denmark

Faeroe Islands

Status: Autonomous part of Denmark
Chief of State: Queen Margrethe II (1972)
High Commissioner: Vibeke Larsen (1995)
Prime Minister: Anfinn Kallsberg (1998)
Area: 540 sq. mi. (1,399 sq. km)
Population (1999 est.): 41,059 (average annual growth rate: 0.35%); birth rate: 12.5/1000; infant mortality rate: 10.3/1000; density per sq. mi.: 76
Capital and largest city (1993 est.): Tórshavn, 16,100.
Monetary unit: Faeroese krone. **Languages:** Faeroese, Danish (both official). **Ethnicity/race:** Scandinavian. **Literacy rate:** 99%

This group of 18 islands, of which 17 are inhabited, are located in the North Atlantic about 200 miles (322 km) northwest of the Shetland Islands. They were settled by the Vikings, the ancestors of the modern-day Faeroese, in the 8th century. The Faeroese language is derived from Old Norse. The islands joined Denmark in 1386 and have been part of the Danish kingdom ever since. The Faeroes have had home rule, under Danish authority, since 1948.

Greenland

Status: Autonomous part of Denmark
Chief of State: Queen Margrethe II (1972)
High Commissioner: Gunnar Martens (1995)
Premier: Jonathan Motzfeldt (1997)
Area: 840,000 sq. mi. (incl. 708,069 sq. mi. covered by icecap) (2,175,600 sq. km)
Population (1999 est.): 59,827 (growth rate: 0.84%); birth rate: 15.2/1000; infant mortality rate: 20.1/1000; density per sq. mi.: 0.1.
Capital and largest city (1995 est.): Godthaab, 12,723.
Monetary unit: Krone. **Ethnicity/race:** Greenlander 87% (Eskimos and Greenland-born whites), Danish and other 13%. **Literacy rate:** 99%

The Inuit are believed to have crossed from North America to northwest Greenland, the world's largest island, between 4000 B.C.E. and C.E. 1000. Greenland was colonized in C.E. 985–86 by Eric the Red. The Norse settlements declined in the 14th century, however, mainly as a result of a cooling in Greenland's climate, and in the 15th century they became extinct. In 1721, Greenland was recolonized by the Royal Greenland Trading Company of Denmark.

Greenland was under U.S. protection during World War II, but maintained Danish sovereignty. A definitive agreement for the joint defense of Greenland within the framework of NATO was signed in 1951. A large U.S. air base at Thule in the far north was completed in 1953.

Under 1953 amendments to the Danish constitution, Greenland became part of Denmark, with two representatives in the Danish Folketing. On May 1, 1979, Greenland gained home rule, with its own local Parliament (Landsting). In Feb. 1982, Greenlanders voted to withdraw from the European Union, which they had joined as part of Denmark in 1973.

Djibouti

REPUBLIC OF DJIBOUTI

National name: Jumhouriyya Djibouti
President: Ismail Omar Guelleh (1999)
Prime Minister: Barkat Gourad Hamadou (1978)
Area: 8,878 sq. mi. (22,000 sq. km)
Population (1999 est.): 447,439 (average annual rate of natural increase: 2.68%); birth rate: 41.2/1000; infant

mortality rate: 100.2/1000; density per sq. mi.: 50
Capital (1992 est.): Djibouti, 395,000. **Monetary unit:**
Djibouti franc. **Languages:** Arabic, French, Afar,
Somali. **Ethnicity/race:** Somali 60%, Afar 35%,
French, Arab, Ethiopian, and Italian 5%. **Religions:**
Muslim, 94%; Christian, 6%. **Literacy rate:** 48%
Economic summary: GDP/PPP (1997 est.): $520
million; $1,200 per capita. **Real growth rate:** 0.5%.
Inflation: 3%. **Unemployment:** 40%–50% (1996 est.).
Arable land: n.a.. **Agriculture:** fruits, vegetables,
goats, sheep, camels. **Labor force:** 282,000;
agriculture, 75%; industry, 11%; services, 14% (1991
est.). **Industry:** limited to a few small-scale
enterprises, such as dairy products and mineral-water
bottling. **Natural resources:** geothermal areas.
Exports: $39.6 million (f.o.b., 1996 est.): hides and
skins, coffee (in transit). **Imports:** $200.5 million
(f.o.b., 1996 est.): foods, beverages, transport
equipment, chemicals, petroleum products. **Major
trading partners:** Ethiopia, Somalia, Yemen, Saudi
Arabia, France, Italy, Thailand.

Geography Djibouti lies in northeastern Africa on
the Gulf of Aden at the southern entrance to the Red
Sea. It borders on Ethiopia, Eritrea, and Somalia.
The country, the size of Massachusetts, is mainly a
stony desert, with scattered plateaus and highlands.

Government Republic with a unicameral legislature.

History Ablé immigrants from Arabia migrated to
what is now Djibouti in about the 3rd century B.C.E.
Their descendants are the Afars, one of the two
main ethnic groups that make up Djibouti today.
Somali Issas arrived thereafter. Islam came to the
region in C.E. 825.

Djibouti was acquired by France between 1843
and 1886 by treaties with the Somali sultans. Small,
arid, and sparsely populated, it is important chiefly
because of the capital city's port, the terminal of the
Djibouti–Addis Ababa railway that carries 60% of
Ethiopia's foreign trade. Originally known as
French Somaliland, the colony voted in 1958 and
1967 to remain under French rule. It was renamed
the Territory of the Afars and Issas in 1967 and took
the name of its capital city on attaining independence. On June 27, 1977, France transferred sovereignty to the new nation of Djibouti. On Sept. 4,
1992, voters approved in referendum a new multiparty constitution. In 1991 conflict between the
Afars and the Issa-dominated government erupted
and the continued warfare has ravaged the country.

Dominica

COMMONWEALTH OF DOMINICA

President: Vernon Shaw (1998)
Prime Minister: Edison James (1995)
Area: 290 sq. mi. (750 sq. km)
Population: (1999 est.): 64,881 (average annual rate
of natural increase 1.06%); birth rate: 16.9/1000; infant
mortality rate: 8.8/1000; density per sq. mi.: 224
Capital and largest city (1991): Roseau, 15,853.
Monetary unit: East Caribbean dollar. **Languages:**
English and French patois. **Ethnicity/race:** black,
Carib Indians. **Religions:** Roman Catholic, 77%;
Protestant, 15%. **Literacy rate:** 94%
Economic summary: GDP/PPP (1996 est.): $208
million; $2,500 per capita. **Real growth rate:** 3.7%.
Inflation: 1.7%. **Unemployment:** 15% (1992 est.).
Arable land: 9%. **Agriculture:** bananas, citrus,
mangoes, root crops, coconuts, forestry and fisheries

potential. **Labor force:** 25,000; agriculture, 40%;
industry and commerce. 32%; services, 28% (1984).
Industry: soap, coconut oil, tourism, copra, furniture,
cement blocks, shoes. **Exports:** $51.8 million (f.o.b.,
1996): bananas, soap, bay oil, vegetables, grapefruit,
oranges. **Imports:** $98.1 million (f.o.b., 1996):
manufactured goods, machinery and equipment, food,
chemicals. **Major trading partners:** U.K., U.S., The
Netherlands, Canada. **Member of Commonwealth of
Nations**

Geography Dominica is a mountainous island of
volcanic origin of the Lesser Antilles in the Caribbean south of Guadeloupe and north of Martinique.

Government Republic.

History Explored by Columbus in 1493, Dominica
was claimed by Britain and France until 1763, when
it was formally ceded to Britain. Dominica, along
with other Windward Isles, became a self-governing
member of the West Indies Associated States in free
association with Britain in 1967.

Dissatisfaction over the slow pace of reconstruction after Hurricane David devastated the island in
Sept. 1979 brought a landslide victory for the Freedom Party in July 1980. The vote gave the prime
ministership to Mary Eugenia Charles, a strong
advocate of free enterprise. The Freedom Party won
again in 1985 and 1990, and the government pursued a policy of divesting itself of state enterprises.
The opposition United Workers' Party captured the
general election of June 1995. In 1997 Dominica
became the first Caribbean country to participate in
the work of Green Globe, aiming to make Dominica
a model eco-tourism destination.

Dominican Republic

National name: República Dominicana
President: Leonel Fernández Reyna (1996)
Area: 18,704 sq. mi. (48,730 sq. km)
Population (1999 est.): 8,129,734 (average annual rate
of natural increase: 2.03%); birth rate: 26.0/1000; infant
mortality rate: 42.5/1000; density per sq. mi.: 435
Capital and largest city (1993): Santo Domingo,
2,100,000. **Other large city (1993):** Santiago de los
Caballeros, 690,000. **Monetary unit:** Peso.
Languages: Spanish, English widely spoken.
Ethnicity/race: white 16%, black 11%, mixed 73%.
Religion: 90% Roman Catholic. **Literacy rate:** 84%
Economic summary: GDP/PPP (1997 est.): $38.3
billion; $4,700 per capita. **Real growth rate:** 7%.
Inflation: 10.9%. **Unemployment:** 30% (1996 est.).
Arable land: 21%. **Agriculture:** sugarcane, coffee,
cotton, cocoa, tobacco, rice, beans, potatoes, corn,
bananas, cattle, pigs, dairy products, meat, eggs.
Labor force: (1991 est.), 2.3–2.6 million; agriculture,
50%; services and government, 32%; industry, 18%.
Industry: tourism, sugar processing, ferronickel and
gold mining, textiles, cement, tobacco. **Natural
resources:** nickel, bauxite, gold, silver. **Exports:** $815
million (f.o.b., 1996): ferronickel, sugar, gold, coffee,
cocoa. **Imports:** $3.7 billion (f.o.b., 1996): foodstuffs,
petroleum, cotton and fabrics, chemicals and
pharmaceuticals. **Major trading partners:** U.S., EU,
Canada, Japan, Puerto Rico, Venezuela, The
Netherlands Antilles, Mexico.

Geography The Dominican Republic in the West
Indies occupies the eastern two-thirds of the island
of Hispaniola, which it shares with Haiti. Its area
equals that of Vermont and New Hampshire combined. Duarte Peak, at 10,417 feet (3,175 m), is the
highest point in the West Indies.

Government Republic.

History The Dominican Republic was explored by Columbus on his first voyage in 1492. He named it La Española, and his son, Diego, was its first viceroy. The capital, Santo Domingo, founded in 1496, is the oldest European settlement in the Western Hemisphere.

Spain ceded the colony to France in 1795, and Haitian blacks under Toussaint L'Ouverture conquered it in 1801. In 1808 the people revolted and captured Santo Domingo the next year, setting up the first republic. Spain regained title to the colony in 1814. In 1821 Spanish rule was overthrown, but in 1822 the colony was again reconquered by the Haitians. In 1844 the Haitians were thrown out, and the Dominican Republic was established, headed by Pedro Santana. Uprisings and Haitian attacks led Santana to make the country a province of Spain from 1861 to 1865.

President Buenaventura Báez, faced with an economy in shambles, attempted to have the country annexed to the U.S. in 1870, but the U.S. Senate refused to ratify a treaty of annexation. Disorder continued until the dictatorship of Ulíses Heureaux; in 1916, when chaos broke out again, the U.S. sent in a contingent of marines, who remained until 1934.

A sergeant in the Dominican army trained by the marines, Rafaél Leonides Trujillo Molina, overthrew Horacio Vásquez in 1930 and established a dictatorship that lasted until his assassination 31 years later.

Leftists rebelled on April 24, 1965, and U.S. president Lyndon Johnson sent in marines and troops. After a cease-fire on May 6, a compromise installed Hector Garcia-Godoy as provisional president. Joaquin Balaguer won in free elections in 1966 against Bosch, and a peacekeeping force of 9,000 U.S. troops and 2,000 from other countries withdrew. Balaguer restored political and economic stability.

In 1978, the army suspended the counting of ballots when Balaguer trailed in a fourth-term bid. After a warning from president Jimmy Carter, however, Balaguer accepted the victory of Antonio Guzmán of the opposition Dominican Revolutionary Party. Salvador Jorge Blanco of the Dominican Revolutionary Party was elected president on May 16, 1982, defeating Balaguer and Bosch. Balaguer was again elected president in May 1986 and remained in office for the next ten years.

In 1996, U.S.-raised Leonel Fernandez secured more than 51% of the vote through an alliance with Balaguer. The first item on the president's agenda was the partial sale of a number of state-owned enterprises. As of 1997, investors are allowed to own a maximum of 50% of the stock in the companies.

Increased employment of Haitian sugarcane cutters led to a wave of anti-Haitian feeling. More than 15,000 Haitians were deported in 1996 and 1997 before the two countries reached an agreement to halt large-scale repatriations and respect human rights. Fernandez has been praised for changing his country's decades-long isolationist stance and for improving diplomatic relations with other Caribbean countries, but he has been criticized for doing little to reform corruption and alleviate the poverty that affects 60% of the population.

Ecuador

REPUBLIC OF ECUADOR

National name: República del Ecuador
President: Jamil Mahuad (1998)
Area: 106,822 sq. mi (283,560 sq. km)
Population (1999 est.): 12,562,496 (average annual rate of natural increase: 1.72%); birth rate: 22.3/1000; infant mortality rate: 30.7/1000; density per sq. mi.: 118
Capital (1998 est.): Quito, 1,500,000. **Other large cities (1998 est.):** Guayaquil, 2,000,000; Cuenca, 200,000.
Monetary unit: Sucre. **Languages:** Spanish (by 90% of population), Quéchua. **Ethnicity/race:** mestizo (mixed Indian and Spanish) 55%, Indian 25%, Spanish 10%, black 10%. **Religion:** Roman Catholic, 95%.
Literacy rate: 90%
Economic summary: GDP/PPP (1997 est.): $53.4 billion; $4,400 per capita. **Real growth rate:** 3.4%. **Inflation:** 43% (1998). **Unemployment:** 6.9% (Aug. 1997 est.). **Arable land:** 6%. **Agriculture:** bananas, coffee, cocoa, rice, potatoes, manioc, plantains, sugarcane, cattle, sheep, pigs, beef, pork, dairy products, balsa wood, fish, shrimp. **Labor force:** 4.2 million; agriculture, 29%; manufacturing, 18%; services, 38% (1990). **Industry:** petroleum, food processing, textiles, metalwork, paper products, wood products, chemicals, plastics, fishing, lumber. **Exports:** $3.4 billion (f.o.b., 1997): petroleum, bananas, shrimp, cut flowers, fish. **Imports:** $2.9 billion (c.i.f., 1997): transport equipment, consumer goods, vehicles, machinery, chemicals. **Major trading partners:** U.S., Latin America, EU, Asia.

Geography Ecuador, about equal in area to Nevada, is in the northwest part of South America fronting on the Pacific. To the north is Colombia and to the east and south is Peru. Two high and parallel ranges of the Andes, traversing the country from north to south, are topped by tall volcanic peaks. The highest is Chimborazo at 20,577 feet (6,272 m). The Galápagos Islands (or Colón Archipelago; 3,029 sq. mi.; 7,845 sq. km), in the Pacific Ocean about 600 miles (966 km) west of the South American mainland, became part of Ecuador in 1832.

Government Republic.

History The tribes in the northern highlands of Ecuador formed the Kingdom of Quito around C.E. 1000. It was absorbed, by conquest and marriage, into the Inca empire. Spanish conquistador Francisco Pizarro conquered the land in 1532, and through the 17th century a thriving colony was built by exploitation of the Indians. The first revolt against Spain occurred in 1809. Ecuador then joined Venezuela, Colombia, and Panama in a confederacy known as Greater Colombia.

On the collapse of this union in 1830, Ecuador became independent. Revolts and dictatorships followed; it had 48 presidents during the first 131 years of the republic. Conservatives ruled until the revolution of 1895 ushered in nearly a half century of Radical Liberal rule, during which the church was disestablished and freedom of worship, speech, and press was introduced. Although it was under military rule in the 1970s, the country did not experience the violence and repression characteristic of other Latin American military regimes. Its last twenty years of democracy, however, have been largely ineffectual because of a weak executive branch and a strong, fractious Congress. In 1997, former president Abdala Bucaram was removed from office for mental instability.

Peru invaded Ecuador in 1941 and was able to seize a large tract of Ecuadorian territory in the disputed Amazonian area; the volatile situation flared up into war again in 1981 and 1995. In May 1999, the presidents of Ecuador and Peru signed a treaty ending a nearly 60-year border dispute involving the stretch of Amazon jungle.

In 1998, Ecuador experienced one of its worst economic crises. El Nino had inflicted about $3 billion in damages, the price of its principal export, oil, plunged, and its inflation rate, 43%, was the highest in Latin America. In 1999, the government was near bankruptcy and the currency lost 40% of its value against the dollar. The president's economic austerity plan was protested with massive strikes in March.

Egypt

ARAB REPUBLIC OF EGYPT

President: Hosni Mubarak (1981)
Prime Minister: Kamal Ganzouri (1996)
Area: 386,900 sq. mi. (1,001,450 sq. km)
Population (1999 est.): 67,273,906 (average annual rate of natural increase: 1.85%); birth rate: 26.8/1000; infant mortality rate: 67.5/1000; density per sq. mi.: 174
Capital and largest city: Cairo: city proper (1992 est.) 6,800,000; metro. area (1996 est.) 9,900,000. **Other large cities (1992 est.):** Alexandria, 3,380,000; Giza, 2,144,000; Shubra el Khema, 834,000; El Mahalla el Kubra, 408,000. **Monetary unit:** Egyptian pound.
Language: Arabic. **Ethnicity/race:** Eastern Hamitic stock (Egyptians, Bedouins, and Berbers) 99%, Greek, Nubian, Armenian, other European (primarily Italian and French) 1%. **Religions:** Islam, 94%; Christian (mostly Coptic), 6%. **Literacy rate:** 48%
Economic summary: GDP/PPP (1997 est.): $267.1 billion; $4,400 per capita. **Real growth rate:** 5.2%. **Inflation:** 4.9% (1997). **Unemployment:** 9.4% (1997 est.). **Arable land:** 2%. **Agriculture:** cotton, rice, corn, wheat, beans, fruits, vegetables, cattle, water buffalo, sheep, goats, fish. **Labor force:** 17.4 million (1996 est.); agriculture, 40%; services, including government, 38%; industry, 22% (1990 est.). **Industry:** textiles, food processing, tourism, chemicals, petroleum, construction, cement, metals. **Natural resources:** petroleum, natural gas, iron ore, phosphates, manganese, limestone, gypsum, talc, asbestos, lead, zinc. **Exports:** $5.1 billion (f.o.b., FY 96/97 est.): crude oil and petroleum products, cotton yarn, raw cotton, textiles, metal products, chemicals. **Imports:** $15.5 billion (c.i.f., FY 96/97 est.): machinery and equipment, foods, fertilizers, wood products, durable consumer goods, capital goods. **Major trading partners:** EU, U.S., Japan.

Geography Egypt, at the northeast corner of Africa on the Mediterranean Sea, is bordered on the west by Libya, on the south by the Sudan, and on the east by the Red Sea and Israel. It is nearly one and one-half times the size of Texas. Egypt is divided into two unequal, extremely arid regions by the landscape's dominant feature, the northward-flowing Nile River. The Nile starts 100 miles (161 km) south of the Mediterranean and fans out to a sea front of 155 miles between the cities of Alexandria and Port Said.

Government Republic.

History Egyptian history dates back to about 4000 B.C.E., when the kingdoms of upper and lower Egypt, already highly sophisticated, were united.

Egypt's "Golden Age" coincided with the 18th and 19th dynasties (16th to 13th century B.C.E.), during which the empire was established. Persia conquered Egypt in 525 B.C.E., Alexander the Great subdued it in 332 B.C.E., and then the dynasty of the Ptolemies ruled the land until 30 B.C.E., when Cleopatra, last of the line, committed suicide and Egypt became a Roman, then Byzantine, province. Arab caliphs ruled Egypt from 641 until 1517, when the Turks took it for their Ottoman Empire.

Napóleon's armies occupied the country from 1798 to 1801. In 1805, Mohammed Ali, leader of a band of Albanian soldiers, became pasha of Egypt. After completion of the Suez Canal in 1869, the French and British took increasing interest in Egypt. British troops occupied Egypt in 1882, and British resident agents became its actual administrators, though it remained under nominal Turkish sovereignty. In 1914, this fiction was ended, and Egypt became a protectorate of Britain.

Egyptian nationalism forced Britain to declare Egypt an independent, sovereign state on Feb. 28, 1922, although the British reserved rights for the protection of the Suez Canal and the defense of Egypt. In 1936, by an Anglo-Egyptian treaty of alliance, all British troops and officials were to be withdrawn, except from the Suez Canal Zone. When World War II started, Egypt remained neutral. British imperial troops finally ended the Nazi threat to Suez in 1942 in the battle of El Alamein, west of Alexandria. In 1951, Egypt abrogated the 1936 treaty and the 1899 Anglo-Egyptian condominium of the Sudan. Rioting and attacks on British troops in the Suez Canal Zone followed, reaching a climax in Jan. 1952. The army, led by Gen. Mohammed Naguib, seized power on July 23, 1952. Three days later, King Farouk abdicated in favor of his infant son. The monarchy was abolished and a republic proclaimed on June 18, 1953, with Naguib holding the posts of provisional president and premier. He relinquished the latter in 1954 to Gamal Abdel Nasser, leader of the ruling military junta, who was confirmed as president in a referendum on June 23, 1956.

Nasser's policies embroiled his country in continual conflict. In 1956, the U.S. and Britain withdrew their pledges of financial aid for the building of the Aswan High Dam. In response, Nasser nationalized the Suez Canal and expelled British oil and embassy officials. Israel, barred from the canal and exasperated by terrorist raids, invaded the Gaza Strip and the Sinai Peninsula. Britain and France, after demanding Egyptian evacuation of the canal zone, attacked Egypt on Oct. 31, 1956. Worldwide pressure forced Britain, France, and Israel to halt the hostilities. A U.N. emergency force occupied the canal zone, and all troops were evacuated in the spring of 1957.

On June 5, 1967, Israel invaded the Sinai Peninsula, the East Bank of the Jordan River, and the zone around the Gulf of Aqaba. A U.N. ceasefire on June 10 saved the Arabs from complete rout. Nasser declared the 1967 cease-fire void along the canal in April 1969 and began a war of attrition. The U.S. peace plan of June 19, 1970, resulted in Egypt's agreement to reinstate the cease-fire for at least three months, (from Aug.) and to accept Israel's existence within "recognized and secure" frontiers that might emerge from U.N.-mediated talks. In return, Israel accepted the principle of withdrawing from occupied territories. On Sept. 28, 1970, Nasser died of a heart attack. Anwar el-Sadat, an associate of Nasser and a former newspaper editor, became the next president.

In July 1972, Sadat ordered the expulsion of Soviet "advisers and experts" from Egypt because the Russians had not provided the sophisticated weapons he felt were needed to retake territory lost to Israel in 1967. The fourth Arab-Israeli War broke out on Oct. 6, 1973 during the Jewish holiday of Yom Kippur. Egypt swept deep into the Sinai, while Syria strove to throw Israel off the Golan Heights. A U.N.-sponsored truce was accepted on Oct. 22. In Jan. 1974, both sides agreed to a settlement negotiated by U.S. Secretary of State Henry A. Kissinger that gave Egypt a narrow strip along the entire Sinai bank of the Suez Canal. In June, President Nixon made the first visit by a U.S. president to Egypt and full diplomatic relations were established. The Suez Canal was cleared and reopened on June 5, 1975.

In the most audacious act of his career, Sadat flew to Jerusalem at the invitation of Prime Minister Menachem Begin and pleaded before Israel's Knesset on Nov. 20, 1977, for a permanent peace settlement. The Arab world reacted with fury—only Morocco, Tunisia, Sudan, and Oman approved. Egypt and Israel signed a formal peace treaty on March 26, 1979. The pact ended 30 years of war and established diplomatic and commercial relations.

Egyptian and Israeli officials met in the Sinai desert on April 26, 1979, to implement the peace treaty calling for the phased withdrawal of occupation forces from the peninsula. By mid-1980, two-thirds of the Sinai was transferred, but progress was not matched elsewhere—the negotiation of Arab autonomy in the Gaza Strip and the West Bank remained stymied. Sadat halted further talks in Aug. 1980 because of continued Israeli settlement of the West Bank. On Oct. 6, 1981, Sadat was assassinated by extremist Muslim soldiers at a parade in Cairo. Vice President Hosni Mubarak, a former air force chief of staff, succeeded him. Israel completed the return of the Sinai to Egyptian control on April 25, 1982. Israel's invasion of Lebanon in June brought a marked cooling in Egyptian-Israeli relations, but not a disavowal of the peace treaty.

While President Mubarak's stand during the Persian Gulf War won wide praise in the West, domestically this position proved far less popular. A presidential referendum in Oct. 1993 supported Mubarak's bid for a third term, although only a third of the population registered to vote. The government has concentrated much of its time and attention in recent years combating Islamic extremism, particularly attacks against Copts (Egyptian Christians). In 1999, Egypt was the first country Ehud Barak visited in his capacity as the new prime minister of Israel, signifying Egypt's crucial role in Middle East relations.

El Salvador

REPUBLIC OF EL SALVADOR

National name: República de El Salvador
President: Francisco Guillermo Flores Pérez (1999)
Area: 8,260 sq. mi. (21,040 sq. km)
Population (1999 est.): 5,839,079 (average annual rate of natural increase: 2%); birth rate: 26.2/1000; infant mortality rate: 28.4/1000; density per sq. mi.: 707

Capital and largest city (1993 est.): San Salvador, 972,810. **Other large cities (1993 est.):** Santa Ana, 208,322; San Miguel, 161,156; Zacatecoluca, 81,035. **Monetary unit:** Colón. **Language:** Spanish. **Ethnicity/race:** mestizo 94%, Indian 5%, white 1%. **Religion:** Roman Catholic. **Literacy rate:** 73%
Economic summary: GDP/PPP (1997 est.): $17.8 billion; $3,000 per capita. **Real growth rate:** 4%. **Inflation:** 2%. **Unemployment:** 7.7%. **Arable land:** 27%. **Agriculture:** coffee, sugarcane, corn, rice, beans, oilseed, cotton, sorghum, beef, dairy products, shrimp. **Labor force:** 2.26 million (1997 est.); agriculture, 40%; commerce, 16%; manufacturing, 15%; government, 13%; financial services, 9%; transportation, 6%; other, 1%. **Industry:** food processing, beverages, petroleum, chemicals, fertilizer, textiles, furniture, light metals. **Natural resources:** hydropower, geothermal power, petroleum. **Exports:** $1.96 billion (f.o.b., 1997 est.): coffee, sugar, shrimp, textiles. **Imports:** $3.5 billion (c.i.f., 1997 est.): raw materials, consumer goods, capital goods, fuels. **Major trading partners:** U.S., Guatemala, Germany, Costa Rica, Honduras, Mexico, Panama, Venezuela, Japan.

Geography   Situated on the Pacific coast of Central America, El Salvador has Guatemala to the west and Honduras to the north and east. It is the smallest of the Central American countries, its area equal to that of Massachusetts, and the only one without an Atlantic coastline. Most of the country is on a fertile volcanic plateau about 2,000 feet (607 m) high.

Government   Republic.

History   The Pipil Indians, descendants of the Aztecs, were the first inhabitants of El Salvador. They were thought to have migrated to the region in the 11th century. The first Europeans to arrive were the Spanish in 1524. A year later, Pedro de Alvarado, a lieutenant of Corté's, conquered El Salvador.

El Salvador, with the other countries of Central America, declared its independence from Spain on Sept. 15, 1821, and was part of a federation of Central American states until that union was dissolved in 1838. For decades after its independence, El Salvador experienced numerous revolutions and wars against other Central American republics. From 1931 to 1979 El Salvador was ruled by a series of military dictatorships.

In the 1970s discontent with societal inequalities, a poor economy, and the repressive measures of dictatorship led to civil war between the government, the right-wing ARENA party, and leftist anti-government guerrilla units, whose leading group was the Farabundo Martí National Liberation Front (FMLN). The U.S., extending its cold-war policy to Central America, intervened on the side of the military, despite its scores of human rights violations. The presidency of José Napoleón Duarte, a moderate civilian, from 1984–89, offered an alternative to the stark political extremes of right and left, but Duarte was unable to end the war and was not reelected. In 1989, Alfredo Cristiani of ARENA was elected.

On Jan. 16, 1992, the government signed a peace treaty with the guerrilla forces, formally ending the 12-year civil war that had claimed the lives of 75,000. Since then, El Salvador's presidents have been members of the ARENA party, including the current president, Francisco Flores, who took office in 1999.

Equatorial Guinea

REPUBLIC OF EQUATORIAL GUINEA
National name: Républica de Guinea Ecuatorial
President: Col. Teodoro Obiang Nguema Mbasogo (1979)
Prime Minister: Angel Serafin Seriche Dougan (1996)
Area: 10,830 sq. mi. (28,050 sq. km)
Population (1999 est.): 465,746 (average annual rate of natural increase: 2.55%); birth rate: 38.5/1000; infant mortality rate: 91.2/1000; density per sq. mi.: 43
Capital and largest city (1983): Malabo, 30,418.
Monetary unit: CFA Franc. **Languages:** Spanish (official), French (2nd official) pidgin English, Fang, Bubi, Creole. **Ethnicity/race:** Bioko (primarily Bubi, some Fernandinos), Rio Muni (primarily Fang), Europeans less than 1,000, mostly Spanish. **Religions:** Roman Catholic, Protestant, traditional. **Literacy rate:** 50%
Economic summary: GDP/PPP (1997 est.): $660 million; $1,500 per capita. **Real growth rate:** n.a. **Inflation:** 6% (1996 est.). **Unemployment:** n.a. **Arable land:** 5%. **Agriculture:** coffee, cocoa, rice, yams, cassava (tapioca), bananas, palm oil nuts, manioc, livestock, timber. **Labor force:** n.a. **Industries:** fishing, sawmilling. **Natural resources:** timber, petroleum, small unexploited deposits of gold, manganese, uranium. **Exports:** $197 million (f.o.b., 1996 est.): petroleum, timber, cocoa. **Imports:** $248 million (c.i.f., 1996 est.): petroleum, food, beverages, clothing, machinery. **Major trading partners:** U.S., Japan, Spain, China, Nigeria, Cameroon, France.

Geography Equatorial Guinea, formerly Spanish Guinea, consists of Rio Muni (10,045 sq. mi.; 26,117 sq. km), on the western coast of Africa, and several islands in the Gulf of Guinea, the largest of which is Bioko (formerly Fernando Po) (785 sq. mi.; 2,033 sq. km). The other islands are Annobón, Corisco, Elobey Grande, and Elobey Chico. The total area is twice that of Connecticut.

Government President with a 17-member Supreme Military Council since a 1979 coup.

History The mainland was originally inhabited by Pygmies. The Fang and Bubi migrated there in the 17th century and to the main island of Fernando Po (now called Bioko) in the 19th century. In the 18th century, the Portuguese ceded land to the Spanish that included Equatorial Guinea. From 1827 to 1844, Britain administered Fernando Po, but it was then reclaimed by Spain. Río Muni, the mainland, was not occupied by the Spanish until 1926. Spanish Guinea, as it was then called, gained independence from Spain on Oct. 12, 1968. It is Africa's only Spanish-speaking country.

From the outset, President Francisco Macías Nguema, considered the father of independence, began a brutal reign, destroying the economy of the fledgling country and abusing human rights. Calling himself the "Unique Miracle," Nguema is considered one of the worst despots in African history. In 1971, the U.S. State Department reported that his regime was "characterized by abandonment of all government functions except internal security, which was accomplished by terror; this led to the death or exile of up to one-third of the population."

On Aug. 3, 1979, Nguema was overthrown and executed by his nephew, Lieut. Col. Teodoro Obiang Nguema Mbasogo. Obiang has been gradually modernizing the country, but has retained many of his uncle's dictatorial practices, including the amassing of personal wealth by siphoning it from the public coffers. A recent petroleum bonanza promises to boost the country's standard of living, but the president's family is believed to control the industry.

Eritrea

President: Isaias Afwerki (1993)
Area: 45,754 sq. mi. (121,320 sq. km)
Population (1999 est.): 3,984,723 (of which 0.5 million are refugees awaiting repatriation). Average annual rate of natural increase: 3.02%; birth rate: 42.6/1000; infant mortality rate: 76.8/1000; density per sq. mi.: 87
Capital and largest city (1993): Asmara, 400,000. Other major cities: the ports of Massawa and Assab.
Monetary unit: Birr. **Languages:** Afar, Bilen, Kunama, Nara, Arabic, Tobedawi, Saho, Tigre, Tigrinya.
Ethnicity/race: ethnic Tigrinya 50%, Tigre and Kunama 40%, Afar 4%, Saho (Red Sea coast dwellers) 3%. **Religions:** Islam and Eritrean Orthodox Christianity. **Literacy rate:** 20%
Economic summary: GDP/PPP (1996 est.): $2.2 billion; $600 per capita. **Real growth rate:** 6.8%. **Inflation:** 4% (1997 est.). **Unemployment:** n.a. **Labor force:** n.a. **Industries:** food processing, beverages, clothing, textiles. **Agriculture:** sorghum, lentils, vegetables, maize, cotton, tobacco, coffee, sisal, livestock, fish. **Natural resources:** gold, potash, zinc, copper, salt, probably oil and natural gas, fish. **Exports:** $71 million (1996 est.): livestock, sorghum, textiles, food, small manufactures. **Imports:** $499 million (1996 est.): processed foods, machinery, petroleum products.
Major trading partners: Ethiopia, Sudan, Saudi Arabia, U.S., Italy, Yemen, United Arab Emirates.

Geography Eritrea was formerly the northernmost province of Ethiopia and is about the size of Indiana. Much of the country is mountainous. Its narrow Red Sea coastal plain is one of the hottest and driest places in Africa. The cooler central highlands have fertile valleys that support agriculture. Eritrea is bordered by the Sudan on the north and west, the Red Sea on the north and east, and Ethiopia and Djibouti on the south.

Government A transitional government committed to a democratic system.

History Eritrea was part of the first Ethiopian kingdom of Askum until its decline in the 8th century C.E. It came under the control of the Ottoman Empire in the 16th century, and later of the Egyptians. The Italians captured the coastal areas in 1885, and the Treaty of Uccialli (May 2, 1889) gave Italy sovereignty over part of Eritrea. The Italians named their colony after the Roman name for the Red Sea—Mare Erythraeum—and ruled it up until World War II. The British captured Eritrea in 1941 and later administered it as a U.N. Trust Territory until it became federated with Ethiopia on Sept. 15, 1952. It was made an Ethiopian province on Nov. 14, 1962. A civil war broke out against the Ethiopian government led by rebel groups who opposed the union and wanted independence for Eritrea. The bitter conflict raged on for 17 years against the hardline Communist regime of the Ethiopian dictator, Mengistu Haile Mariam, until he was overthrown in May 1991.

The Eritrean People's Liberation Front (EPLF) took control of Eritrea and shared power in a multiparty government in Addis Ababa with the Ethiopian People's Revolutionary Democratic Front

(EPRDF). They agreed to hold a referendum on Eritrean independence within two years and on April 23–25, 1993, Eritrean voters almost unanimously opted for an independent republic. Ethiopia recognized Eritrea's sovereignty on May 3, 1993, and sought a new era of cooperation between the two countries.

While relations with Ethiopia remained good in 1995, those with the Sudan deteriorated. In Nov. 1996 Eritrea accused the Sudan of plotting to assassinate the president. The mission was thwarted by a Sudanese antigovernment group. Sudan denied the charge, although Eritrea provided specific names and dates of those allegedly involved.

Since Eritrea's independence, Eritrea and Ethiopia had disagreed about the exact demarcation of their borders, and in May 1998 border clashes broke out between them. After an eight-month lull that both sides used to reinforce their 600-mile common border, civil war broke out again in earnest. Both impoverished countries have spent millions of dollars on warplanes and weapons, tens of thousands of soldiers have died, and refugees are legion. The war also spilled over into Somalia, currently a stateless country, because one of its warlords has allied himself with Eritrea. In Sept. 1999 peace talks were underway, but broke down when Ethiopia refused to go along with the terms.

Estonia

REPUBLIC OF ESTONIA

National name: Eesti
President: Lennart Meri (1992)
Prime Minister: Mart Laar (1999)
Area: 17,666 sq. mi. (45,226 sq. km)
Population (1999 est.): 1,408,523 (average annual rate of natural increase: –0.52%); birth rate: 9.1/1000; infant mortality rate: 13.8/1000; density per sq. mi.: 77
Capital and largest city (1992 est.): Tallinn, 471,608. Other large city (1992 est.): Tartu, 113,400. **Monetary unit:** Kroon. **Languages:** Estonian (official), Russian, Finnish, English. **Ethnicity/race:** Estonian 61.5%, Russian 30.3%, Ukrainian 3.2%, Belorussian 1.8%, Finn 1.1%, other 2.1% (1989). **Religions:** Lutheran, 78%; Orthodox, 19%. **Literacy:** 100%
Economic summary: GDP/PPP (1997 est.): $9.34 billion; $6,450 per capita. **Real growth rate:** 10%. **Inflation:** 11.2%. **Unemployment:** 3.6%. **Labor force** (1996 est.): 785,000; industry and construction, 42%; agriculture and forestry, 20%; other, 38% (1990). **Industries:** shale oil, shipbuilding, phosphates, electric motors, excavators, cement, furniture, clothing, textiles, paper, shoes, apparel. **Natural resources:** oil shale (kukersite), peat, phosphorite, amber, cambrian blue clay. **Agriculture:** potatoes, fruits, vegetables, livestock and dairy products, fish. **Exports:** $2 billion (f.o.b., 1996): textiles 16%, food products 16%, machinery and equipment 16%, metals 9% (1995). **Imports:** $3.2 billion (c.i.f., 1996): machinery and equipment 29%, foodstuffs 14%, minerals 13%, textiles 13%, metals 12% (1995). **Major trading partners:** Finland, Russia, Sweden, Germany, Latvia.

Geography Estonia is mainly a lowland country that borders on the Baltic Sea. It has numerous lakes and forests and many rivers, most draining northward into the Gulf of Finland or eastward into Lake Peipus. Lake Peipus is Estonia's largest lake and is important to the fishing and shipping industries.

Government Parliamentary democracy.

History Born out of World War I, this small Baltic state enjoyed a mere two short decades of independence before it was absorbed again by its powerful neighbor, the Soviet Union. Estonians were able to resist assaults by Vikings, Danes, Swedes and Russians before the 13th century. In 1346 the Danes, who possessed northern Estonia, sold the land to the Teutonic Knights of Germany, who already possessed Livonia (southern Estonia and Latvia). The Teutonic Knights reduced the Estonians to serfdom. In 1526, the Swedes took over, and the power of the German (Balt) landowning class was reduced. But after 1721, when Russia succeeded Sweden as the ruling power under the Peace of Nystad, the Estonians were subject to a double bondage—the Balts and the czarist officials. The oppression lasted until the closing months of World War I, when Estonia finally achieved independence after a victorious war (1918–20). Shortly after the start of World War II, the nation was occupied by Russian troops and incorporated as the 16th republic of the U.S.S.R. in 1940. Germany occupied the nation from 1941 to 1944, when it was retaken by the Soviets.

Estonia declared independence from the Soviet Union in March 1990. Soviet resistance ensued, but by 1991, after recognition by European and other countries, the Soviet Union recognized Estonian nationhood on Sept. 6, 1991. U.N. membership followed on Sept. 17, 1991. The newly independent nation embraced free-market reforms. Fueled by foreign investments, economic advances continued unabated in 1997. This prompted the European Commission (EC) to recommend that Estonia begin accession talks for membership in the European Union.

At the end of 1998, Estonia relaxed the strict citizenship requirements that kept the country's 1.5 million Russian speakers—about one-third of the population—from gaining citizenship. In an attempt to foster Estonian language and culture after 50 years of Soviet domination, Estonia instituted policies of reverse discrimination, denying citizenship to those who could not speak Estonian. Estonia's reforms have granted citizenship to children born in Estonia of Russian-speaking parents, a change that has eased the way for Estonia's entry into the European Union.

Ethiopia

FEDERAL DEMOCRATIC REPUBLIC OF ETHIOPIA

President: Negasso Gidada (1995)
Prime Minister: Meles Zenawi (1995)
Area: 446,952 sq. mi. (1,127,127 sq. km)
Population (1999 est.): 59,680,383 (average annual rate of natural increase: 2.29%); birth rate: 44.3/1000; infant mortality rate: 124.6/1000; density per sq. mi.: 134
Capital and largest city (1993 est.): Addis Ababa, 2,200,186. **Monetary unit:** Birr. **Languages:** Amharic (official), English, Orominga, Tigrigna, over 70 languages spoken. **Ethnicity/race:** Oromo 40%, Amhara and Tigrean 32%, Sidamo 9%, Shankella 6%, Somali 6%, Afar 4%, Gurage 2%, other 1%. **Religions:** Ethiopian Orthodox, 35%–40%; Islam, 40%–45%; animist, 15%–20%; other, 5%. **Literacy rate:** 28%
Economic summary: GDP/PPP (1997 est.): $29 billion; $530 per capita. **Real growth rate:** 5%. **Inflation:** (1996 est.): 0%. **Unemployment:** n.a. **Arable land:** 12%. **Agriculture:** cereals, pulses, coffee, oilseed, sugarcane, potatoes, other vegetables, hides, cattle, sheep, goats. **Industry:** food processing, beverages, textiles, chemicals, metals processing, cement. **Natural**

resources: small reserves of gold, platinum, copper, potash, natural gas. **Labor force:** n.a.; agriculture and animal husbandry, 80%; government and services, 12%; industry and construction, 8% (1985). **Exports:** $418 million (f.o.b., 1996): coffee, leather products, gold. **Imports:** $1.23 billion (f.o.b., 1996 est.): food and live animals, petroleum and petroleum products, chemicals, machinery, motor vehicles and aircraft. **Major trading partners:** Germany, Japan, Djibouti, Saudi Arabia, Italy, U.S.

Geography Ethiopia is in east-central Africa, bordered on the west by the Sudan, the east by Somalia and Djibouti, the south by Kenya, and the northeast by Eritrea. It is nearly three times the size of California. Over its main plateau land, Ethiopia has several high mountains, the highest of which is Ras Dashan at 15,158 feet (4,620 m). The Blue Nile, or Abbai, rises in the northwest and flows in a great semicircle east, south, and northwest before entering the Sudan. Its chief reservoir, Lake Tana, lies in the northwestern part of the plateau.

Government Federal republic.

History Archeologists have found the oldest known human ancestors in Ethiopia, including *Ardipithecus ramidus* (c. 4.4 million years old) and *Australopithecus afarensis* (c. 3.2 million years old). Originally called Abyssinia, Ethiopia is sub-Saharan Africa's oldest state, and its Solomonic dynasty claims descent from King Menelik I, traditionally believed to have been the son of the queen of Sheba and King Solomon. The current nation is a consolidation of smaller kingdoms that owed feudal allegiance to the Ethiopian emperor.

Hamitic peoples migrated to Ethiopia from Asia Minor in prehistoric times. Semitic traders from Arabia penetrated the region in the 7th century B.C.E. Its Red Sea ports were important to the Roman and Byzantine Empires. Coptic Christianity was brought to the region in C.E. 341, and a variant of it became Ethiopia's state religion. Ancient Ethiopia reached its peak in the 5th century, then was isolated by the rise of Islam and weakened by feudal wars.

Modern Ethiopia emerged under Emperor Menelik II, who established its independence by routing an Italian invasion in 1896. He expanded Ethiopia by conquest. Disorders that followed Menelik's death brought his daughter to the throne in 1917, with his cousin, Tafari Makonnen, as regent and heir apparent. When the empress died in 1930, Tafari was crowned Emperor Haile Selassie I.

Haile Selassie, called the "Lion of Judah," outlawed slavery and tried to centralize his scattered realm, in which 70 languages were spoken. In 1931, he created a constitution, revised in 1955, that called for a Parliament with an appointed senate and an elected chamber of deputies, and a system of courts. But basic power remained with the emperor.

Fascist Italy invaded Ethiopia on Oct. 3, 1935, forcing Haile Selassie into exile in May 1936. Ethiopia was annexed to Eritrea, then an Italian colony, and to Italian Somaliland, forming Italian East Africa. In 1941, British troops routed the Italians, and Haile Selassie returned to Addis Ababa. In 1952, Eritrea was incorporated into Ethiopia.

On Sept. 12, 1974, Haile Selassie was deposed, the constitution suspended, and Ethiopia proclaimed a socialist state under a collective military dictatorship called the Provisional Military Administrative

Council (PMAC), also known as the Derg. U.S. aid stopped, and Cuban and Soviet aid began. Lt. Col. Mengistu Haile Mariam became head of state in 1977. During this period Ethiopia fought against Eritrean secessionists as well as Somali rebels, and the government fought against its own people in a campaign called the "red terror." Mengistu remained leader until 1991, when his greatest supporter, the Soviet Union, dismantled itself.

A group called the Ethiopian People's Revolutionary Democratic Front seized the capital in 1991, and in May a separatist guerrilla organization, the Eritrean People's Liberation Front, took control of the province of Eritrea. The two groups agreed that Eritrea would have an internationally supervised referendum on independence. This election took place in April 1993 with almost unanimous support for Eritrean independence. Ethiopia accepted and recognized Eritrea as an independent state within a few days. Sixty-eight leaders of the former military government were put on trial in April 1996 on charges that included genocide and crimes against humanity.

Since Eritrea's independence, Eritrea and Ethiopia had disagreed about the exact demarcation of their borders, and in May 1998 Eritrea initiated border clashes that developed into a full-scale war that left tens of thousands dead and further destroyed both countries' ailing economies. The war has spilled over into Somalia, currently a stateless country, because one of its warlords had allied himself with Eritrea. In Aug. 1999, the countries began peace negotiations, which quickly broke down and were replaced by continued fighting.

Fiji

REPUBLIC OF FIJI

President: Ratu Sir Kamisese Mara (1994)
Prime Minister: Mahendra Chaudhry (1999)
Area: 7,078 sq. mi. (18,270 sq. km)
Population (1999 est.): 812,918 (average annual rate of natural increase: 1.66%); birth rate: 22.8/1000; infant mortality rate: 16.3/1000; density per sq. mi.: 115
Capital (1990 est.): Suva (on Viti Levu), 200,000.
Monetary unit: Fiji dollar. **Languages:** Fijian, Hindustani, English (official). **Ethnicity/race:** Fijian 49%, Indian 46%, European, other Pacific Islanders, overseas Chinese, and other 5%. **Religions:** Christian, 52%; Hindu, 38%; Islam, 8%; other, 2%. **Literacy rate:** 79%
Economic summary: GDP/PPP (1996 est.): $5.1 billion; $6,500 per capita. **Real growth rate:** 3% **Inflation:** 3% (1997 est.). **Unemployment:** 6%. **Arable land:** 10%. **Agriculture:** sugarcane, coconuts, cassava (tapioca), rice, sweet potatoes, bananas, cattle, pigs, horses, goats, fish. **Labor force:** 235,000; subsistence agriculture, 67%; wage earners, 18%; salary earners, 15% (1987). **Industry:** sugar, tourism, copra, gold, silver, clothing, lumber, small cottage industries. **Natural resources:** timber, fish, gold, copper, offshore oil potential. **Exports:** $639 million (f.o.b., 1996): sugar, clothing, gold, processed fish, lumber. **Imports:** $947 million (c.i.f., 1996): machinery and transport equipment, petroleum products, food, consumer goods, chemicals. **Major trading partners:** EU, Australia, other Pacific island countries, Japan, New Zealand, U.S.

Geography Fiji consists of 332 islands in the southwestern Pacific Ocean about 1,960 miles (3,152 km) from Sydney, Australia. About 110 of these islands are inhabited. The two largest are Viti Levu (4,109 sq. mi.; 10,642 sq. km) and Vanua

Levu (2,242 sq. mi.; 5,807 sq. km). The island of Rotuma (18 sq. mi.; 47 sq. km), about 400 miles (644 km) to the north, is a province of Fiji. The largest islands in the group are mountainous and volcanic, with the tallest peak being Mount Victoria (4,341 ft.; 1,323 m) on Viti Levu.

Government Republic.

History Fiji, which had been inhabited since the second millennium B.C.E., was explored by the Dutch and the British in the 17th and 18th centuries. In 1874, an offer of cession by the Fijian chiefs was accepted, and Fiji was proclaimed a possession and dependency of the British Crown. In the 1880s large-scale cultivation of sugarcane began. During World War II, the archipelago was an important air and naval station on the route from the U.S. and Hawaii to Australia and New Zealand.

Fiji became independent on Oct. 10, 1970. The next year it joined the five-island South Pacific Forum, which intends to become a permanent regional group to promote collective diplomacy of the newly independent nations. In Oct. 1987, Brig. Gen. Sitiveni Rabuka, staged a coup, declared Fiji a republic, and removed it from the British Commonwealth. The military coup caused an exodus of thousands of Fijians of Indian origin who suffered ethnic discrimination at the hands of the government.

In July 1997, the Parliament unanimously approved a new constitution for Fiji. The new constitution, which took effect in July 1998, provided for a multiracial cabinet and raised the prospect of a coalition government. The previous constitution, from 1990, guaranteed the political dominance to ethnic Fijians over ethnic Indians. Following the approval of the new constitution, Fiji was readmitted to the Commonwealth of Nations.

Finland

REPUBLIC OF FINLAND

National name: Suomen Tasavalta—Republiken Finland
President: Martti Ahtisaari (1994)
Prime Minister: Paavo Lipponen (1995)
Area: 130,558 sq. mi. (337,030 sq. km)
Population (1999 est.): 5,158,372 (average annual rate of natural increase: 0.11%); birth rate: 10.8/1000; infant mortality rate: 3.8/1000; density per sq. mi.: 40
Capital and largest city (1995 est.): Helsinki, 515,765. **Other large cities (1995 est.):** Espoo, 186,507; Tampere, 179,251; Vantaa, 164,376; Turku, 162,370.
Monetary units: Markka and euro. **Languages:** Finnish, Swedish (both official); small Sami- (Lapp) and Russian-speaking minorities. **Ethnicity/race:** Finn 93%, Swede 6%, Sami (Lapp) 0.11%, Romany (Gypsy) 0.12%, Tatar 0.02%. **Religions:** Evangelical Lutheran, 90%; Greek Orthodox, 1.2%; none, 9%; other, 1%. **Literacy rate:** 100%
Economic summary: GDP/PPP (1997 est.): $102.1 billion; $20,000 per capita. **Real growth rate:** 4.6%. **Inflation:** 1.2%. **Unemployment:** 14.6%. **Arable land:** 8%. **Agriculture:** cereals, sugar beets, potatoes, dairy cattle, fish. **Labor force:** 2.533 million; public services, 30.4%; industry, 20.9%; commerce, 15%; finance, insurance, and business services, 10.2%; agriculture and forestry, 8.6%; transport and communications,

7.7%; construction, 7.2%. **Industries:** metal products, shipbuilding, pulp and paper, copper refining, foodstuffs, chemicals, textiles, clothing. **Natural resources:** timber, copper, zinc, iron ore, silver. **Exports:** $38.4 billion (f.o.b., 1996): paper and pulp, machinery, chemicals, metals, timber. **Imports:** $29.3 billion (c.i.f., 1996): foodstuffs, petroleum and petroleum products, chemicals, transport equipment, iron and steel, machinery, textile yarn and fabrics, fodder grains. **Major trading partners:** EU (Germany, U.K.), Sweden, U.S., Japan, Russia.

Geography Finland is three times the size of Ohio. It is heavily forested and contains thousands of lakes, numerous rivers, and extensive areas of marshland. Except for a small highland region in the extreme northwest, the country is a lowland less than 600 feet (180 m) above sea level. Off the southwest coast are the Swedish-populated Åland Islands (581 sq. mi.; 1,505 sq. km), which have had an autonomous status since 1921.

Government Republic.

History The first inhabitants of Finland were the Sami (Lapp) people. When Finnish speakers migrated to Finland in the first millennium B.C.E., the Sami were forced to move northward to the arctic regions, with which they are traditionally associated. The Finns' repeated raids on the Scandinavian coast impelled Eric IX, the Swedish king, to conquer the country in 1157. It was made a part of the Swedish kingdom and converted to Christianity.

By 1809 the whole of Finland was conquered by Alexander I of Russia, who set up Finland as a grand duchy. The period of Russification (1809–1914) sapped Finnish political power and made Russian the country's official language. When Russia became engulfed by the March Revolution of 1917, Finland seized the opportunity to declare independence on July 20, 1917.

The U.S.S.R. attacked Finland on Nov. 30, 1939, after Finland refused to give into Soviet territorial demands. The Finns staged a strong defense for three months before capitulating. They were forced to cede the Soviets 16,000 square miles (41,440 sq. km) to the U.S.S.R. Under German pressure, the Finns joined the Nazis against Russia in 1941, but were defeated again and ceded the Petsamo area to the U.S.S.R. In 1948, a treaty of friendship and mutual assistance was signed by the two nations. Finland continued to pursue a foreign policy of nonalignment throughout the cold war era.

Running on a platform to revitalize the economy, Ahtisaari, a Social Democrat, won the country's first direct presidential election in a runoff in Feb. 1994. Previously, presidents had been chosen by electors. Finland became a member of the European Union in Jan. 1995, but made it clear it would not become a full member of the western European Union. Showing concern over NATO expansion eastward, Russian president Yeltsin in March 1997 iterated his view that Finnish membership in the military alliance was unacceptable, due to Finland's policy of non-alignment. On Jan. 1, 1999, Finland, along with ten other European countries, adopted the euro as its currency.

France

FRENCH REPUBLIC

National name: République Française
President: Jacques Chirac (1995)
Prime Minister: Lionel Jospin (1997)
Area: 211,208 sq. mi. (547,030 sq. km)
Population (1999 est.): 58,978,172 (average annual rate of natural increase: 0.46%); birth rate: 11.38/1000; infant mortality rate: 5.6/1000; density per sq. mi.: 279
Capital and largest city: Paris. **Other large cities:** Paris: city proper (1991 census) 2,156,766; metro. area (1995 est.) 9,469,000; Marseille, 801,000; Lyon, 415,000; Toulouse, 359,000; Nice, 342,000; Strasbourg, 252,000; Nantes, 245,000; Bordeaux, 201,000. **Monetary units:** French Franc and euro.
Languages: French, declining regional dialects (Provençal, Breton, Alsatian, Corsican). **Ethnicity/race:** Celtic and Latin with Teutonic, Slavic, North African, Southeast Asian, and Basque minorities.
Religions: Roman Catholic, 81%; Protestant, 1.7%; Muslim, 6.9%; Jewish, 1.3%. **Literacy rate:** 99%
Economic summary: GDP/PPP (1997 est.): $1.32 trillion; $22,700 per capita. **Real growth rate:** 2.3%. **Inflation:** 2% (1996). **Unemployment:** 12.4% (1997). **Arable land:** 33%. **Agriculture:** wheat, cereals, sugar beets, potatoes, wine grapes, beef, dairy products, fish. **Labor force:** 25.5 million, services, 69%; industry, 26%; agriculture, 5% (1995). **Industries:** steel, machinery, chemicals, automobiles, metallurgy, aircraft, electronics, mining, textiles, food processing, tourism. **Natural resources:** coal, iron ore, bauxite, fish, timber, zinc, potash. **Exports:** $275 billion (f.o.b., 1997 est.): machinery and transportation equipment, chemicals, foodstuffs, agricultural products, iron and steel products, textiles and clothing. **Imports:** $256 billion (f.o.b., 1997 est.): crude oil, machinery and equipment, agricultural products, chemicals, iron and steel products. **Major trading partners:** Germany, Italy, U.K., Spain, Belgium-Luxembourg, U.S., The Netherlands, Japan, Russia, China.

Geography France is about 80% the size of Texas. In the Alps near the Italian and Swiss borders is western Europe's highest point—Mont Blanc (15,781 ft.; 4,810 m). The forest-covered Vosges Mountains are in the northeast, and the Pyrénées are along the Spanish border. Except for extreme northern France, the country may be described as four river basins and a plateau. Three of the streams flow west—the Seine into the English Channel, the Loire into the Atlantic, and the Garonne into the Bay of Biscay. The Rhône flows south into the Mediterranean. For about 100 miles (161 km), the Rhine is France's eastern border. In the Mediterranean, about 115 miles (185 km) east-southeast of Nice, is the island of Corsica (3,367 sq. mi.; 8,721 sq. km).

Government Fifth republic.

History Archeological excavations indicate that France has been continuously settled since Paleolithic times. The Celts, who were later called *Gauls* by the Romans, migrated from the Rhine valley into what is now France. In about 600 B.C.E. Greeks and Phoenicians established settlements along the Mediterranean, most notably at Marseille. Julius Caesar conquered part of Gaul in 57–52 B.C.E., and it remained Roman until Franks invaded in the 5th century.
The Treaty of Verdun (C.E. 843) divided the territories corresponding roughly to France, Germany, and Italy among the three grandsons of Charle-

magne. Charles the Bald inherited *Francia Occidentalis,* which became an increasingly feudalized kingdom. By C.E. 987, the crown passed to Hugh Capet, a princeling who controlled only the Ile-de-France, the region surrounding Paris. For 350 years, an unbroken Capetian line added to its domain and consolidated royal authority until the accession in 1328 of Philip VI, first of the Valois line. France was then the most powerful nation in Europe, with a population of 15 million.
The missing pieces in Philip Valois's domain were the French provinces still held by the Plantagenet kings of England, who also claimed the French crown. Beginning in 1338, the Hundred Years' War eventually settled the contest. After France's victory in the final battle, Castillon (1453), the Valois were the ruling family, and the English had no French possessions left except Calais. Once Burgundy and Brittany were added, the Valois's holdings resembled modern France. Protestantism spread throughout France in the 16th century and led to civil wars. Henry IV, of the Bourbon dynasty, issued the Edict of Nantes (1598), granting religious tolerance to the Huguenots (French Protestants). Absolute monarchy reached its apogee in the reign of Louis XIV (1643–1715), the Sun King, whose brilliant court was the center of the Western world.
After a series of costly foreign wars that weakened the government, the French Revolution plunged France into a bloodbath beginning in 1789 with the establishment of the First Republic and ending with a new authoritarianism under Napoléon Bonaparte, who had successfully defended the infant republic from foreign attack and then made himself first consul in 1799 and emperor in 1804. The Congress of Vienna (1815) sought to restore the pre-Napoléonic order in the person of Louis XVIII, but industrialization and the middle class, both fostered under Napoléon, built pressure for change, and a revolution in 1848 drove Louis Philippe, last of the Bourbons, into exile. Prince Louis Napoléon, a nephew of Napoléon I's, declared the Second Empire in 1852 and took the throne as Napoléon III. His opposition to the rising power of Prussia ignited the Franco-Prussian War (1870–71), ending in his defeat, his abdication, and the creation of the Third Republic.
A new France emerged from World War I as the continent's dominant power. But four years of hostile occupation had reduced northeast France to ruins. Beginning in 1919, French foreign policy aimed at keeping Germany weak through a system of alliances, but it failed to halt the rise of Adolf Hitler and the Nazi war machine. On May 10, 1940, Nazi troops attacked, and, as they approached Paris, Italy joined with Germany. The Germans marched into an undefended Paris and Marshal Henri Philippe Pétain signed an armistice on June 22. France was split into an occupied north and an unoccupied south, Vichy France, the latter becoming a totalitarian German puppet state with Pétain as its chief. Allied armies liberated France in Aug. 1944, and a provisional government in Paris headed by Gen. Charles de Gaulle was established. The Fourth Republic was born on Dec. 24, 1946. The empire became the French Union; the National Assembly was strengthened and the presidency weakened; and France joined NATO. A war against Communist insurgents in French Indochina, now Vietnam, was

Rulers of France

Name	Born	Ruled[1]	Name	Born	Ruled[1]
Carolingian Dynasty			Louis XV the Well-Beloved	1710	1715–1774
Pepin the Short	c. 714	751–768	Louis XVI	1754	1774–1792[13]
Charlemagne[2]	742	768–814	Louis XVII (Louis Charles de	1785	1793–1795
Louis I the Pious[3]	778	814–840	France)[14]		
Charles I the Bald[4]	823	840–877	**First Republic**		
Louis II the Stammerer	846	877–879	National Convention	—	1792–1795
Louis III[5]	c. 863	879–882	Directory (Directoire)	—	1795–1799
Carloman[5]	?	879–884	**Consulate**		
Charles II the Fat[6]	839	884–887[7]	Napoléon Bonaparte[15]	1769	1799–1804
Eudes (Odo), count of Paris	?	888–898	**First Empire**		
Charles III the Simple[8]	879	893–923[9]	Napoléon I	1769	1804–1815[16]
Robert I[10]	c. 865	922–923	**Restoration of House of Bourbon**		
Rudolf (Raoul), duke of Burgundy	?	923–936	Louis XVIII le Désiré	1755	1814–1824
Louis IV d'Outremer	c. 921	936–954	Charles X	1757	1824–1830[17]
Lothair	941	954–986	**Bourbon-Orleans Line**		
Louis V the Sluggard	c. 967	986–987	Louis Philippe ("Citizen King")	1773	1830–1848[18]
Capetian Dynasty			**Second Republic**		
Hugh Capet	c. 940	987–996	Louis Napoléon[19]	1808	1848–1852
Robert II the Pious[11]	c. 970	996–1031	**Second Empire**		
Henry I	1008	1031–1060	Napoléon III (Louis Napoléon)	1808	1852–1870[20]
Philip I	1052	1060–1108	**Third Republic (Presidents)**		
Louis VI the Fat	1081	1108–1137	Louis Adolphe Thiers	1797	1871–1873
Louis VII the Young	c.1121	1137–1180	Marie E. P. M. de MacMahon	1808	1873–1879
Philip II (Philip Augustus)	1165	1180–1223	François P. J. Grévy	1807	1879–1887
Louis VIII the Lion	1187	1223–1226	Sadi Carnot	1837	1887–1894
Louis IX (St. Louis)	1214	1226–1270	Jean Casimir-Périer	1847	1894–1895
Philip III the Bold	1245	1270–1285	François Félix Faure	1841	1895–1899
Philip IV the Fair	1268	1285–1314	Émile Loubet	1838	1899–1906
Louis X the Quarreler	1289	1314–1316	Clement Armand Fallières	1841	1906–1913
John I[12]	1316	1316	Raymond Poincaré	1860	1913–1920
Philip V the Tall	1294	1316–1322	Paul E. L. Deschanel	1856	1920–1920
Charles IV the Fair	1294	1322–1328	Alexandre Millerand	1859	1920–1924
House of Valois			Gaston Doumergue	1863	1924–1931
Philip VI	1293	1328–1350	Paul Doumer	1857	1931–1932
John II the Good	1319	1350–1364	Albert Lebrun	1871	1932–1940
Charles V the Wise	1337	1364–1380	**Vichy Government (Chief of State)**		
Charles VI the Well-Beloved	1368	1380–1422	Henri Philippe Pétain	1856	1940–1944
Charles VII	1403	1422–1461	**Provisional Government (Presidents)**		
Louis XI	1423	1461–1483	Charles de Gaulle	1890	1944–1946
Charles VIII	1470	1483–1498	Félix Gouin	1884	1946–1946
Louis XII the Father of the People	1462	1498–1515	Georges Bidault	1899	1946–1947
Francis I	1494	1515–1547	**Fourth Republic (Presidents)**		
Henry II	1519	1547–1559	Vincent Auriol	1884	1947–1954
Francis II	1544	1559–1560	René Coty	1882	1954–1959
Charles IX	1550	1560–1574	**Fifth Republic (Presidents)**		
Henry III	1551	1574–1589	Charles de Gaulle	1890	1959–1969
House of Bourbon			Georges Pompidou	1911	1969–1974
Henry IV of Navarre	1553	1589–1610	Valéry Giscard d'Estaing	1926	1974–1981
Louis XIII	1601	1610–1643	François Mitterrand	1916	1981–1995
Louis XIV the Great	1638	1643–1715	Jacques Chirac	1932	1995–

1. For kings and emperors through the Second Empire, year of end of rule is also that of death, unless otherwise indicated. 2. Crowned Emperor of the West in 800. His brother, Carloman, ruled as king of the Eastern Franks from 768 until his death in 771. 3. Holy Roman Emperor, 814–840. 4. Holy Roman Emperor, 875–877 as Charles II. 5. Ruled jointly, 879–882. 6. Holy Roman Emperor, 881–887, as Charles III. 7. Died 888. 8. King, 893–898, in opposition to Eudes. 9. Died 929. 10. Not counted in regular line of kings of France by some authorities. Elected by nobles but killed in Battle of Soissons. 11. Sometimes called Robert I. 12. Posthumous son of Louis X; lived for only five days. 13. Executed 1793. 14. Titular king only. 15. As first consul, Napoléon held the power of government. In 1804, he became emperor. 16. Abdicated first time, June 1814. Reentered Paris, March 1815, after escape from Elba; Louis XVIII fled to Ghent. Abdicated second time, June 1815. He named as his successor his son, Napoléon II, who was not acceptable to the Allies. He died 1821. 17. Died 1836. 18. Died 1850. 19. President; became emperor in 1852. 20. Died 1873.

abandoned after the defeat of French forces at Dien Bien Phu in 1954. A new rebellion in Algeria threatened a military coup, and on June 1, 1958, the assembly invited de Gaulle to return as premier with extraordinary powers. He drafted a new constitution for a Fifth Republic, adopted on Sept. 28, which

strengthened the presidency and reduced legislative power. He was elected president on Dec. 21, 1958.

France next turned its attention to decolonization in Africa; the French protectorates of Morocco and Tunisia had received independence in 1956. French West Africa was partitioned and the new nations were granted independence in 1960. Algeria, after a long civil war, finally became independent in 1962. Relations with most of the former colonies remained amicable. De Gaulle took France out of the NATO military command in 1967 and expelled all foreign-controlled troops from the country. De Gaulle's government was weakened by massive protests in May 1968 when student rallies became violent and millions of factory workers engaged in wildcat strikes across France. After normalcy was reestablished by 1969, de Gaulle's successor, Georges Pompidou, modified Gaullist policies to include a classical laissez-faire attitude toward domestic economic affairs. The conservative, pro-business climate contributed to the election of Valéry Giscard d'Estaing as president in 1974.

Socialist François Mitterrand attained a stunning victory in the May 10, 1981, presidential election. The victors immediately moved to carry out campaign pledges to nationalize major industries, halt nuclear testing, suspend nuclear power plant construction, and impose new taxes on the rich. The Socialists' policies during Mitterrand's first two years created a 12% inflation rate, a huge trade deficit, and devaluations of the franc. In March 1986, a center-right coalition led by Jacques Chirac won a slim majority in legislative elections. Chirac became prime minister, initiating a period of "cohabitation" between him and the Socialist president, Mitterrand. Mitterrand's decisive reelection in 1988 led to Chirac, being replaced as premier by Michel Rocard, a Socialist. Relations, however, cooled with Rocard, and in May 1991 he was replaced with Edith Cresson, France's first female prime minister and, like Mitterrand, a Socialist. But Cresson's unpopularity forced Mitterrand to replace Cresson with a more well-liked Socialist, Pierre Bérégovoy, who eventually was embroiled in a scandal and committed suicide. Mitterrand did succeed in helping draft the Maastricht Treaty and, after winning a slim victory in a referendum, confirming close economic and security ties between France and the European Union (EU).

On his third try Chirac won the presidency in May 1995, campaigning vigorously on a platform to reduce unemployment. He moved quickly to cement ties with Germany and the rest of the EU. Elections for the National Assembly in 1997 gave the Socialist coalition a majority. Shortly after becoming president, Chirac resumed France's nuclear testing in the South Pacific, despite widespread international protests as well as rioting in the countries affected by it. Socialist leader Lionel Jospin became prime minister in 1997. On Jan. 1, 1999, France adopted the euro as its currency. In the spring of 1999, the country took part in the NATO airstrikes in Kosovo, despite some internal opposition.

Overseas Departments

Overseas Departments elect representatives to the National Assembly, and the same administrative organization as that of continental France applies to them.

French Guiana (including Inini)
Status: Overseas Department
Prefect: Dominique Vian (1997)
Area: 32,253 sq. mi. (83,534 sq. km)
Population (1999 est.): 167,982; growth rate: 1.88%; birth rate 23.3/1000; infant mortality rate 12.9/1000; density per sq. mi.: 5
Capital and largest city (1995 est.): Cayenne, 41,659. **Monetary unit:** Franc. **Language:** French. **Ethnicity/race:** black or mulatto 66%, white 12%, East Indian, Chinese, Amerindian 12%, other 10%. **Religion:** Roman Catholic. **Literacy rate:** 80%
Economic summary: GDP/PPP (1993 est.): $800 million; $6,000 per capita. **Inflation:** (1992) 2.5%. **Unemployment:** 24.1% (1993 est.). **Arable land:** 0%. **Agriculture:** rice, corn, bananas, sugar cane. **Labor force** (1993): 46,300; services, government and commerce, 60.6%; industry, 21.2%; agriculture, 18.2% (1980). **Industry:** timber, rum, rosewood essence, gold mining, processed shrimp. **Natural resources:** bauxite, timber, cinnabar, kaolin. **Exports:** $80 million (f.o.b., 1994): shrimp, timber, rum, rosewood essence, clothing. **Imports:** $605 million (c.i.f., 1994): food (grains, processed meat), machinery and transport equipment, fuels and chemicals. **Major trading partners:** France, EU, Germany, Belgium, Luxembourg, U.S.

French Guiana, lying north of Brazil and east of Suriname on the northeast coast of South America, was variously settled by the Spanish, Dutch, and French. The Treaty of Breda awarded France the territory in 1667. The French used it as a penal colony between 1852 and 1939, which included the infamous Devil's Island. In 1958 it became an Overseas Department of the French Republic, which sends two elected representatives to France's National Assembly and one to the Senate. Since then, many indigenous French Guianians have called for increased autonomy, although only around 5% favor independence from France, partly due to the vast subsidies from the French government. The European Space Center at Kourou has brought a corner of French Guiana into the modern world and attracted a sizable expatriate workforce.

Guadeloupe
Status: Overseas Department
Prefect: Jean Fedini (1997)
Area: 327 sq. mi. (1,848 sq. km)
Population (1999 est.): 420,943 (average annual growth rate: 1.07%); birth rate: 16.3/1000; infant mortality rate: 8.5/1000; density per sq. mi.: 1,287
Capital (1990): Basse-Terre, 14,000. **Largest city (1990):** Pointe-à-Pitre, over 26,029. **Monetary unit:** Franc. **Languages:** French, Creole patois. **Ethnicity/race:** black or mulatto 90%, white 5%, East Indian, Lebanese, Chinese less than 5%. **Religion:** Roman Catholic. **Literacy rate:** 91%
Economic summary: GDP/PPP (1995 est.): $3.7 billion; $9,200 per capita. **Real growth rate:** n.a. **Inflation:** (1990), 3.7%. **Unemployment:** (1995), 31.3%. **Arable land:** 14%. **Agriculture:** bananas, sugarcane, tropical fruits and vegetables, cattle, pigs, goats. **Labor force:** (1993), 128,000; agriculture, 15%; industry, 20%; services, 65%. **Industry:** construction, cement, rum, sugar, tourism. **Exports:** $145 million (f.o.b., 1994): bananas, sugar, rum. **Imports:** $1.6 billion (c.i.f., 1994): foodstuffs, fuels, vehicles, clothing and other consumer goods, construction materials. **Major trading partners:** France, Martinique, EU, U.S., Japan.

Guadeloupe, in the West Indies about 300 miles (483 km) southeast of Puerto Rico, was explored by Columbus in 1493. It consists of the twin islands of Basse-Terre and Grande-Terre and five dependencies—Marie-Galante, Les Saintes, La Désirade, St. Barthélemy, and the northern three-fifths of St. Martin. The volcano Soufrière (4,813 ft.;

1,467 m), also called La Grande Soufrière, is the highest point on Guadeloupe. Violent activity in 1976 and 1977 caused thousands to flee their homes. French colonization began in 1635, and in 1674 Guadeloupe became part of the domain of France. In 1958, Guadeloupe voted in favor of the new constitution of the French Fifth Republic and remained an Overseas Department of the French Republic. It is represented in the French National Assembly by four deputies and in the French Senate by two senators.

Martinique

Status: Overseas Department
Prefect: Jean-François Cordet
Area: 436 sq. mi. (1,128 sq. km)
Population (1999 est.): 411,539 (average annual growth rate: 1.04%); birth rate: 16.3/1000; infant mortality rate: 6.8/1000; density per sq. mi.: 944
Capital and largest city (1990): Fort-de-France, 100,072. Other cities (1990): Le Lamentin, 30,026; Schoelcher, 19,683; Sainte-Marie, 19,683. **Monetary unit:** Franc. **Languages:** French, Creole patois. **Ethnicity/race:** African and African-white-Indian mixture 90%, white 5%, East Indian, Lebanese, Chinese less than 5%. **Religion:** Roman Catholic. **Literacy rate:** 100%
Economic summary: GDP/PPP (1995 est.): $3.95 billion, $10,000 per capita. **Inflation:** (1990), 3.9%. **Unemployment:** (1994), 23.5%. **Real growth rate:** n.a. **Arable land:** 8%. **Agriculture:** pineapples, avocados, bananas, flowers, vegetables, sugarcane for rum. **Labor force:** 160,000; agriculture 10%, industry 17%, services 73% (1992). **Industry:** construction, rum, cement, oil refining, sugar, tourism. **Natural resources:** coastal scenery and beaches, cultivable land. **Exports:** $220 million (f.o.b., 1994): refined petroleum products, bananas, rum, pineapples. **Imports:** $1.6 billion (c.i.f., 1994): petroleum products, crude oil, foodstuffs, construction materials, vehicles, clothing and other consumer goods. **Major trading partners:** France, Guadeloupe, French Guiana, U.K., Italy, Germany, Japan, U.S.

Martinique, a mountainous island lying in the Lesser Antilles about 300 miles (483 km) northeast of Venezuela, was probably explored by Columbus in 1502 and was taken for France in 1635. Martinique became a domain of the French crown in 1674. In 1958, Martinique voted in favor of the new constitution of the French Fifth Republic and remained an Overseas Department of the French Republic, sending four deputies to the French National Assembly and two senators to the French Senate. Martinique's young people continue to emigrate heavily, mostly to France.

Réunion

Status: Overseas Department
Prefect: Robert Pommies (1996)
Area: 970 sq. mi. (2,512 sq. km)
Population (1999 est.): 717,723 (average annual growth rate: 1.75%); birth rate: 22.2/1000; infant mortality rate: 6.9/1000; density per sq. mi.: 740
Capital and largest city (1993): Saint-Denis, 121,999. Other cities (est. 1993): Saint-Paul, 71,667; Saint-Pierre, 58,846; Le Tampon, 47,598. **Monetary unit:** Franc. **Languages:** French, Creole. **Ethnicity/race:** French, African, Malagasy, Chinese, Pakistani, Indian. **Religion:** Roman Catholic, 70%
Economic summary: GDP/PPP (1996 est.): $3 billion, $4,300 per capita. **Real growth rate:** 4%. **Inflation:** n.a. **Unemployment:** (1994), 35%. **Arable land:** 17%.

Agriculture: sugarcane, vanilla, tobacco, tropical fruits, vegetables, corn. **Labor force:** 242,169 (1993); agriculture, 8%; industry, 19%; services, 73% (1990). **Industries:** sugar, rum, cigarettes, handicraft Items, flower oil extraction. **Natural resources:** fish, arable land. **Exports:** $171.776 million (f.o.b., 1994): sugar, rum and molasses, perfume essences, lobster. **Imports:** $2.354 billion (c.i.f., 1994): manufactured goods, food, tobacco, beverages, machinery and transportation equipment, raw materials, petroleum products. **Major trading partners:** France, Mauritius, Bahrain, South Africa, Italy, Madagascar.

Of volcanic origin, Réunion consists mostly of rugged mountains in an advanced state of dissection by short torrential rivers. It is located about 450 miles (724 km) east of Madagascar, in the Indian Ocean. First explored by Portuguese navigators in the 16th century, the island of Réunion, then uninhabited, was taken as a French possession in 1642. African slaves were imported first to work coffee and then sugar plantations; with the abolition of slavery in 1848, indentured laborers from Indochina, India, and East Africa were brought in. In 1958, Réunion approved the constitution of the Fifth French Republic and remained an Overseas Department of the French Republic. Réunion elects five deputies to the French National Assembly and three to the Senate. The island is administered by an appointed prefect and a general council composed of 44 elected members.

Overseas Territories

Overseas Territories are comparable to Departments, except that their administrative organization includes a locally elected government.

French Polynesia

Status: Overseas Territory
High Commissioner: Jean Aribaud (1999)
Area: 1,609 sq. mi. (4,167 sq. km)
Population (1999 est.): 242,073 (average annual growth rate: 1.7%); birth rate: 22.1/1000; infant mortality rate: 13.6/1000; density per sq. mi.: 150
Capital (1988): Papeete (on Tahiti), 23,555. **Monetary unit:** Pacific financial community franc. **Language:** French. **Ethnicity/race:** Polynesian 78%, Chinese 12%, local French 6%, metropolitan French 4%. **Religions:** Protestant, 55%; Roman Catholic, 30%; Other, 16%. **Literacy rate:** 98%
Economic summary: GDP/PPP (1995 est.): $1.76 billion, $8,000 per capita. **Real growth rate:** n.a. **Inflation:** (1994) 1.5%. **Labor force:** (1988) 118,744; agriculture 13%, industry 19%, services 68% (1992 est.). **Unemployment:** (1992 est.) 15%. **Principal agricultural products:** coconuts, vanilla, vegetables, fruits, poultry, beef, dairy products. **Industries:** tourism, pearls, agricultural processing, handicrafts. **Exports:** $245 million (f.o.b., 1994): cultured pearls, coconut products, mother-of-pearl, vanilla, shark meat. **Imports:** $967 million (c.i.f., 1994): fuels, foodstuffs, equipment. **Major trading partners:** France, U.S.

The term French Polynesia is applied to the scattered French possessions in the South Pacific—Mangareva (Gambier), Makatea, the Marquesas Islands, Rapa, Rurutu, Rimatara, the Society Islands, the Tuamotu Archipelago, Tubuai, Raivavae, and the island of Clipperton—which were organized into a single colony in 1903. There are 120 islands, of which 25 are uninhabited.

The president of the Territorial Government is assisted by a Council of Government and a popularly elected Territorial Assembly. The principal and most populous island—Tahiti, in the Society group—was claimed as French in 1768. In 1958, French Polynesia voted in favor of the new constitution of the French Fifth Republic and remained an Overseas Territory of the French Republic. The indigenous people are mostly Maoris.

The Pacific Nuclear Test Center on the atoll of Mururoa, 744 miles (1,200 km) from Tahiti, was completed in 1966. In 1975 worldwide opposition forced the French to move the testing underground on Fangataufa. To compensate the residents for the nuclear weapons tests in 1995–96, France offered a 10-year $194-million annual compensation package. An independence movement continues to flourish in French Polynesia.

New Caledonia and Dependencies

Status: Overseas Territory
High Commissioner: Thierry Lataste (1998)
Area: 7,374 sq. mi. (19,103 sq. km)
Population (1999 est.): 197,361 (average annual growth rate: 1.59%); birth rate: 20.7/1000; infant mortality rate: 12.2/1000; density per sq. mi.: 27
Capital (1989): Nouméa, 65,110. **Monetary unit:** Pacific financial community franc. **Languages:** French, Melanesian and Polynesian dialects. **Ethnicity/race:** Kanak (Melanesian) 42.5%, European 37.1%, Wallisian 8.4%, Polynesian 3.8%, Indonesian 3.6%, Vietnamese 1.6%, other 3%. **Religions:** Roman Catholic, 60%; Protestant, 30%. **Literacy rate:** 91%
Economic summary: GDP/PPP (1995 est.): $1.5 billion, $8,000 per capita; **Real growth rate:** n.a. **Inflation:** (1996 est.) 1.7%. **Unemployment:** (1994) 15%. **Agriculture:** vegetables, beef, other livestock products. **Industry:** nickel mining and smelting. **Natural resources:** nickel, chrome, iron, cobalt, manganese, silver, gold, lead, copper. **Labor force:** 70,044 (1988): agriculture, 32%; industry, 20%; services, 40%; mining, 8% (1992). **Exports:** $500 million (f.o.b., 1996): ferronickels, nickel ore. **Imports:** $930 million (c.i.f., 1996): foods, transport equipment, machinery and electrical equipment, fuels, minerals. **Major trading partners:** Japan, France, U.S., Australia, Taiwan, Singapore, New Zealand.

New Caledonia (6,466 sq. mi.; 16,747 sq. km), about 1,070 miles (1,722 km) northeast of Sydney, Australia, was explored by Capt. James Cook in 1774 and annexed by France in 1853. The government also administers the Isle of Pines, the Loyalty Islands (Uvéa, Lifu, and Maré), the Belep Islands, the Huon Island group, and Chesterfield Islands. The native people are Melanesians called the Kanak. In 1984, the French National Assembly passed a law that granted internal autonomy to New Caledonia. In 1998 the Noumea Accords postponed discussions about independence for the territory until at least 2013.

Southern and Antarctic Lands

Status: Overseas Territory
Administrator: Brigitte Girardin (1998)
Area: 3,004 sq. mi. (7,781 sq. km, excluding Adélie Land)
Capital: Port-au-Français
This territory is uninhabited except for the personnel of scientific bases. It consists of Adélie Land (166,752 sq. mi.; 431,888 sq. km) on the Antarctic mainland (which the U.S. does not recognize) and the following islands in the southern Indian Ocean:

the Kerguelen and Crozet archipelagos and the islands of Saint-Paul and New Amsterdam.

Wallis and Futuna Islands

Status: Overseas Territory
Administrator: Christian Dors (1998)
Area: 106 sq. mi. (274 sq. km)
Population (1999 est.): 15,129; growth rate 1.77%; birth rate 22.3/1000; infant mortality rate 20.9/1000; density per sq. mi.: 143
Capital (1983): Mata-Utu. **Languages:** French, Wallisian. **Ethnicity/race:** Polynesian. **Religion:** Roman Catholic. **Literacy rate:** 50%
Economic summary: GDP/PPP (1995 est.): $28.7 million, $2,000 per capita. **Industries:** copra, handicrafts, fishing, lumber. **Agriculture:** breadfruit, yams, taro, bananas, pigs, goats. **Exports:** $370,000 (f.o.b., 1995 est.): copra, handicrafts. **Imports:** $13.5 million (c.i.f., 1995 est.): foodstuffs, manufactured goods, transport equipment, fuel, clothing.

The two island groups in the South Pacific between Fiji and Samoa were settled by French missionaries at the beginning of the 19th century. A protectorate was established in the 1880s. There is a French-appointed high administrator, a 20-member Territorial Assembly, and a deputy and a senator to the French national Parliament. The three traditional Polynesian kings also help decide internal policy matters. Following a referendum by the Polynesian inhabitants, the status was changed to that of an Overseas Territory in 1961.

Territorial Collectivities

The Territorial Collectivity status was created in 1976 for Mayotte; it was conceived as being midway between an Overseas Territory and an Overseas Department. A Territorial Collectivity is represented in the French National Assembly by a deputy and in the French Senate by a senator. The head of government, the prefect, is appointed by the French government.

Saint Pierre and Miquelon

Status: Territorial Collectivity
Prefect: Rémi Thuaue (1998)
Area: 93 sq. mi. (242 sq. km)
Population (1999 est.): 6,966; growth rate 0.69%; birth rate 12.3/1000; infant mortality rate 8.1/1000; density per sq. mi.: 75
Capital (1990): Saint Pierre, 5,683. **Ethnicity/race:** Basques and Bretons (French fishermen). **Literacy rate:** 99%
Economic summary: GDP/PPP (1996 est.): $74 million, $11,000 per capita. **Unemployment:** 11%. **Industries:** fish processing and supply base for fishing fleets, tourism. **Labor force:** 2,971 (1995). **Exports:** $5 million (f.o.b., 1995): fish and fish products, fox and mink pelts. **Imports:** $70.2 million (c.i.f., 1995): meat, clothing, fuel, electrical equipment, machinery, building materials. **Major trading partners:** U.S., France, U.K., Canada, Portugal, The Netherlands.

The sole remnant of the French colonial empire in North America, these islands were first occupied by the French in 1604. Their only importance arises from proximity to the Grand Banks, located 10 miles south of Newfoundland, making them the center of the French Atlantic cod fisheries. On July 19, 1976, the islands became an Overseas Department of the French Republic. In May 1985, the archipelago was given a new status with a new name,

Territorial Collectivity, because the former departmental arrangement conflicted with the tariff structure of the European Economic Community (now European Union), to which France belongs.

Mayotte

Status: Territorial Collectivity
Prefect: Philippe Boisadam (1995)
Area: 146 sq. mi. (378 sq. km)
Population (1999 est.): 149,336; average annual rate of natural increase 3.72%; birth rate 46.1/1000; infant mortality rate 69.1/1000; density per sq. mi.: 1,023
Capital and largest city (1991): Mamoudzou (Dzaoudzi), 20,450
Economic summary: GDP/PPP (1997 est.): $63 million, $600 per capita. **Real growth rate:** n.a. **Inflation rate:** n.a. **Unemployment:** 38% (1991 est.). **Industries:** lobster and shrimp industry. **Agriculture:** vanilla, ylang-ylang, coffee, copra. **Labor force:** n.a. **Natural resources:** negl. **Exports:** $3.64 million (f.o.b., 1996): ylang-ylang (perfume essence), vanilla, copra. **Imports:** $131.5 million (f.o.b., 1996): building materials, machinery and transportation equipment, metals, chemicals, rice, clothing, flour. **Major trading partners:** France, Comoros, Réunion, Africa, Southeast Asia.

France gained colonial control over Mayotte in 1843. It is the most populous of the four Comoros Islands in the Indian Ocean off Mozambique in Africa. Mayotte chose to remain a French dependency rather than join the other Comoran islands in declaring independence in 1975. Comoros laid claim to Mayotte shortly after independence and continues to do so.

Gabon

GABONESE REPUBLIC

National name: République Gabonaise
President: Omar Bongo (1967)
Premier: Jean-François Ntoutoume (1999)
Area: 103,346 sq. mi. (267,670 sq. km)
Population (1999 est.): 1,225,853 (average annual rate of natural increase: 1.48%); birth rate: 27.9/1000; infant mortality rate: 83.1/1000; density per sq. mi.: 12
Capital and largest city (1994): Libreville, 419,596. Other cities (1994): Port-Gentil, 80,000; Franceville, 42,000. **Monetary unit:** Franc CFA. **Language:** French (official). **Ethnicity/race:** (1993) Bantu tribes, including six major tribal groupings: Fang 25%, Punu 23%, Nzeiby 13%, Mbede (Obamba/Bateke) 9%, Kota 7%, and Myene 5%; Pygmies 0.7%, naturalized population 0.3%, foreigners 15%. **Religions:** Catholic 75%, Protestant 20%, Animist 4%. **Literacy rate:** 61%. **Economic summary: GDP/PPP** (1996 est.): $6 billion; $5,000 per capita. **Real growth rate:** 3%. **Inflation:** 6.2%. **Unemployment:** 10%–14% (1993 est.). **Arable land:** 1%. **Agriculture:** cocoa, coffee, sugar, palm oil, rubber, okoume (a tropical softwood), cattle, fishing. **Labor force:** n.a.; agriculture, 65%; industry and commerce, services. **Industry:** food and beverage, textile, lumbering and plywood, cement, petroleum extraction and refining, manganese, uranium, gold mining, chemicals, ship repair. **Natural resources:** petroleum, manganese, uranium, gold, timber, iron ore. **Exports:** $3.1 billion (f.o.b., 1996 est.): crude oil, timber, manganese, uranium. **Imports:** $969 million (f.o.b., 1996 est.): machinery and equipment, foodstuffs, chemicals, petroleum products, construction materials. **Major trading partners:** U.S., France, Japan, China, Spain, Germany, Côte d'Ivoire, The Netherlands. **Member of French Community**

Geography This West African country with the Atlantic as its western border is also bounded by Equatorial Guinea, Cameroon, and the Congo. Its area is slightly less than Colorado's. Most of the country is covered by a dense tropical forest.

Government Republic.

History The earliest humans in Gabon were believed to be the Babinga, or Pygmies, dating back to 7000 B.C.E., who were later followed by Bantu groups from southern and eastern Africa. Now there are many tribal groups in the country, the largest being the Fang peoples, who constitute 25% of the population.

Gabon was first explored by the Portuguese navigator Diego Cam in the 15th century. In 1472 the Portuguese explorers encountered the mouth of the Como River, and named it "Rio de Gabao," river of Gabon, which later became the name of the country. The Dutch began arriving in 1593, and the French in 1630. In 1839, the French founded their first settlement on the left bank of the Gabon estuary and gradually occupied the hinterland during the second half of the 19th century. It was organized as a French territory in 1888 and became an autonomous republic within the French Union after World War II, and an independent republic on Aug. 17, 1960.

After his conversion to Islam in 1973, President Bongo changed his given name, Albert Bernard, to Omar. He has been reelected every five years since 1967. Strikes and riots led to a transitional constitution in May 1990 legalizing political parties and calling for free elections. In its first multiparty election in Dec. 1993, the incumbent president received just over 51% of the vote, while the opposition candidate refused to accept defeat; he alleged fraud and tried to establish a rival government.

In Dec. 1998, President Bongo, who has ruled the country for 31 years, was elected for an additional seven. Gabon lacks roads, schools, and adequate health care, yet the oil-rich country has lined the pockets of its ruler, who, according to the French weekly *L'Autre Afrique*, is said to own more real estate in Paris than any other foreign leader. Despite his reputation for corruption and authoritarianism, however, Bongo has a strong national following.

Gambia, The

REPUBLIC OF THE GAMBIA

President: Colonel Yahya A. J. J. Jammeh (1997)
Area: 4,093 sq. mi. (11,300 sq. km)
Population (1999 est.): 1,336,320 (average annual rate of natural increase: 3.02%); birth rate: 42.8/1000; infant mortality rate: 75.3/1000; density per sq. mi.: 326
Capital (1986): Banjul, 44,188. **Monetary unit:** Dalasi. **Languages:** Native tongues, English (official). **Ethnicity/race:** African 99% (Mandinka 42%, Fula 18%, Wolof 16%, Jola 10%, Serahuli 9%, other 4%), non-Gambian 1%. **Religions:** Islam, 90%; Christian, 9%; traditional, 1%. **Literacy rate:** 27%. **Economic summary: GDP/PPP** (1997 est.): $1.23 billion; $1,000 per capita. **Real growth rate:** 2.1%. **Inflation:** 2.2%. **Unemployment:** n.a. **Arable land:** 18%. **Agriculture:** peanuts, millet, sorghum, rice, corn, cassava (tapioca), palm kernels, cattle, sheep, goats, forest and fishing resources not fully exploited. **Labor force:** n.a.; agriculture, 75.0%; industry, commerce and services, 18.9%; government, 6.1%. **Industry:** processing peanuts, fish, and hides;

tourism, beverages, agricultural machinery assembly, woodworking, metalworking, clothing. **Natural resources:** fish. **Exports:** $160 million (f.o.b., 1995): peanuts and peanut products, 70%; fish, cotton lint, palm kernels. **Imports:** $140 million (c.i.f., 1995): foodstuffs, manufactures, raw materials, fuel, machinery and transport equipment. **Major trading partners:** Japan, Senegal, Hong Kong, France, Switzerland, U.K., Indonesia, China, Côte d'Ivoire, Germany. **Member of Commonwealth of Nations**

Geography Situated on the Atlantic coast in westernmost Africa and surrounded on three sides by Senegal, Gambia is twice the size of Delaware. The Gambia River flows for 200 miles (322 km) through Gambia on its way to the Atlantic. The country, the smallest on the continent, averages only 20 miles (32 km) in width.

Government Republic.

History Since the 13th century, the Wolof, Malinke, and Fulani peoples settled in what is now The Gambia. The Portuguese were the first European explorers, encountering the Gambia River in 1455, and in 1681 the French founded an enclave at Albredabut. During the 17th century, Gambia was settled by various companies of English merchants. Slavery was the chief source of revenue before it was abolished in 1807. Gambia became a crown colony in 1843 and an independent nation within the Commonwealth of Nations on Feb. 18, 1965. Full independence was approved in a 1970 referendum, and on April 24 of that year Gambia proclaimed itself a republic.

Elections of April 29, 1992, returned President Jawara for a fifth term. His People's Progressive Party won 25 of the 36 seats in the House of Representatives. A military coup led by Capt. Yahya Jammeh deposed the president in July 1994, suspended the constitution, and banned political parties. Jammeh promised new elections, which were held in Sept. 1996, and he won 55% of the vote against his nearest rival, Ousseynou Darboe. In April 1997 he completed the promised return to civilian rule. Censorship of the press and a ban on some opposition parties, however, continue to mar the country's transition to democracy.

Georgia

GEORGIA

National Name: Sakartvelo
President: Eduard Shevardnadze (1992)
Secretary of State: Vazha Lordkipanidze (1999)
Area: 26,900 sq. mi. (69,700 sq. km)
Population (1999 est.): 5,066,499; average annual rate of natural increase: −0.27%; birth rate: 11.6/1000; infant mortality rate: 52.0/1000; density per sq. mi.: 188
Capital and largest city (1991): Tbilisi, 1,279,000. Other cities (1989): Kutaisi, 235,000; Batoumi, 136,000; and Sokhumi, 121,000. **Monetary unit:** Lari.
Languages: Georgian (official), 71%; Russian, 9%; Armenian, 7%; Azerbaijani, 6%. **Ethnicity/race:** Georgian 70.1%, Armenian 8.1%, Russian 6.3%, Azeri 5.7%, Ossetian 3%, Abkhaz 1.8%, other 5%.
Religions: Georgian Orthodox, 65%; Russian Orthodox, 10%; Armenian Orthodox, 8%; Muslim, 11%
Economic summary: GDP/PPP (1997 est.): $8.1 billion; $1,570 per capita. **Real growth rate:** 11.8%.
Inflation: 7.1%. **Unemployment:** 16% (1996 est.).
Labor force: 2.2 million (1996): industry and construction, 31%; agriculture and forestry, 25%; other,

44% (1990). **Industry:** steel, aircraft, machine tools, foundry equipment, electric locomotives, tower cranes, electric welding equipment, machinery for food preparation and meat packing, electric motors, process control equipment, trucks, tractors, textiles, shoes, chemicals, wood products, wine. **Agriculture:** citrus, grapes, tea, vegetables, potatoes, livestock. **Exports:** $400 million (f.o.b., 1996 est.): citrus fruits, tea, wine, other agricultural products, diverse types of machinery, ferrous and nonferrous metals, textiles, chemicals, fuel reexports. **Imports:** $733 million (c.i.f., 1996 est.): fuel, grain and other foods, machinery and parts, transport equipment. **Major trading partners:** Russia, Turkey, Armenia, Azerbaijan, Bulgaria.

Geography Georgia is bordered by the Black Sea in the west, by Turkey and Armenia in the south, by Azerbaijan in the east, and by Russia in the north. The republic also includes the Abkhaz and Adzhar autonomous republics and the Yugo-Ossetian Autonomous Oblast. Mount Elbrus (Lalbuzi in Georgian) at 18,841 feet is the highest peak in Europe.

Government Republic.

History Georgia became a kingdom about 4 B.C.E. and Christianity was introduced in C.E. 337. During the reign of Queen Tamara (1184–1213), its territory included the whole of Transcaucasia. During the 13th century, Tamerlane and the Mongols decimated its population. From the 16th century on, the country was the scene of a struggle between Persia and Turkey. In the 18th century it became a vassal to Russia in exchange for protection from the Turks and Persians.

Georgia joined Azerbaijan and Armenia in 1917 to establish the anti-Bolshevik Transcaucasian Federation, and upon its dissolution, proclaimed its independence in 1918. In 1922, Georgia, Armenia, and Azerbaijan were annexed by the U.S.S.R. and formed the Transcaucasian Soviet Socialist Republic. In 1936, it became a separate Soviet republic. Under Soviet rule Georgia was transformed from an agrarian country to a largely industrial, urban society.

Georgia proclaimed its independence from the U.S.S.R. on April 6, 1991. In Jan. 1992, its leader Zviad Gamsakhurdia was sacked, and later accused of dictatorial policies, the jailing of opposition leaders, human rights abuses, and clamping down on the media. A ruling military council was established by the opposition until a civilian authority could be restored. In 1992–93, the government engaged in armed conflict with separatists in the breakaway province of Abkhazia. In 1994, Russia and Georgia signed a cooperation treaty that authorized Russia to keep three military bases in Georgia and allowed Russians to train and equip the Georgian army. In 1996, Georgia and its breakaway region of South Ossetia agreed to a cessation of hostilities in their six-year conflict. With little progress in resolving the Abkhazia situation, however, Parliament in April 1997 voted overwhelmingly to threaten Russia with loss of its military bases should it fail to extend Russian military control over the separatist region. In 1998 the U.S. and Britain began an operation to remove nuclear material from Georgia, dangerous remains from its Soviet years.

Germany

FEDERAL REPUBLIC OF GERMANY

National name: Bundesrepublik Deutschland
President: Johannes Rau (1999)
Chancellor: Gerhard Schröder (1998)
Area: 137,826 sq. mi. (356,910 sq. km)
Population (1999 est.): 82,087,361 (average annual growth rate: –0.21%); birth rate: 8.7/1000; infant mortality rate: 5.1/1000; density per sq. mi.: 596
Capital and largest city (1995 est.): Berlin (capital since Oct. 3, 1990), 3,471,418. **Other large cities (1997):** Hamburg, 1,703,800; Munich, 1,251,100; Cologne, 963,300; Frankfurt, 656,200; Essen, 619,600; Dortmund, 601,500; Stuttgart, 592,000; Düsseldorf, 573,100; Bremen, 551,000; Hanover, 526,400; Duisberg, 536,500. **Monetary units:** Deutsche Mark and euro. **Language:** German. **Ethnicity/race:** German 91.5%, Turkish 2.4%, Italians 0.7%, Greeks 0.4%, Poles 0.4%, Other 4.6%. **Religions:** Protestant 38%, Roman Catholic 34%, Muslim 1.7%, Unaffiliated or other 26.3%. **Literacy rate:** 99%
Economic summary GDP/PPP (1997 est.): $1.74 trillion; $20,800 per capita. **Real growth rate:** 2.4%. **Inflation:** (1997) 1.8%. **Unemployment:** 12%. **Labor force:** 38.7 million; industry, 41%; agriculture; 3%; services, 56% (!995). **Exports:** $521.1 billion (f.o.b., 1996): manufactures 88.2% (including machines and machine tools, chemicals, motor vehicles, iron and steel products), agricultural products 5.0%, raw materials 2.3%, fuels 1.0%, other 3.5% (1995). **Imports:** $455.7 billion (f.o.b., 1996): manufactures 74.2%, agricultural products 9.9%, fuels 6.4%, raw materials 5.9%, other 3.6% (1995). **Industry:** western: among the world's largest producers of iron, steel, coal, cement, chemicals, machinery, vehicles, machine tools, electronics, food and beverages; eastern: metal fabrication, chemicals, brown coal, shipbuilding, machine building, food and beverages, textiles, petroleum refining. **Agriculture:** western: potatoes, wheat, barley, sugar beets, fruit, cabbage, cattle, pigs, poultry; eastern: wheat, rye, barley, potatoes, sugar beets, fruit, pork, beef, chicken, milk, hides. **Natural resources:** iron ore, coal, potash, timber, lignite, uranium, copper, natural gas, salt, nickel. **Major trading partners:** EU (France, U.K., The Netherlands, Italy, Belgium-Luxembourg), eastern Europe, other west European countries, U.S., Japan, NICs, China, OPEC, other.

Geography   Located in central Europe, Germany is made up of the North German Plain, the Central German Uplands (Mittelgebirge), and the Southern German Highlands. The Bavarian plateau in the southwest averages 1,600 feet (488 m) above sea level, but it reaches 9,721 feet (2,962 m) in the Zugspitze Mountains, the highest point in the country. Germany's major rivers are the Danube, the Elbe, the Oder, the Weser, and the Rhine. Germany is about the size of Montana.

Government   Parliamentary democracy.

History   The Celts are believed to have been the first inhabitants of Germany. They were followed by German tribes at the end of the 2nd century B.C.E. German invasions destroyed the declining Roman Empire in the 4th and 5th centuries C.E. One of the tribes, the Franks, attained supremacy in western Europe under Charlemagne, who was crowned Holy Roman Emperor in C.E. 800. By the Treaty of Verdun (843), Charlemagne's lands east of the Rhine were ceded to the German Prince Louis. Additional territory acquired by the Treaty of Mersen (870) gave Germany approximately the area it maintained throughout the Middle Ages. For several centuries after Otto the Great was crowned king in 936, German rulers were also usually heads of the Holy Roman Empire.

By the 14th century, the Holy Roman Empire was little more than a loose federation of the German princes who elected the Holy Roman Emperor. In 1438, Albert of Hapsburg became emperor, and for the next several centuries the Hapsburg line ruled the Holy Roman Empire until its decline in 1806. Relations between state and church were changed by the Reformation, which began with Martin Luther's 95 theses, and came to a head in 1547, when Charles V scattered the forces of the Protestant League at Mühlberg. Freedom of worship was guaranteed by the Peace of Augsburg (1555), but the Counter Reformation took place later, and a dispute over the succession to the Bohemian throne brought on the Thirty Years' War (1618–48), which devastated Germany and left the empire divided into hundreds of small principalities virtually independent of the emperor.

Meanwhile, Prussia was developing into a state of considerable strength. Frederick the Great (1740–86) reorganized the Prussian army and defeated Maria Theresa of Austria in a struggle over Silesia. After the defeat of Napoléon at Waterloo (1815), the struggle between Austria and Prussia for supremacy in Germany continued, reaching its climax in the defeat of Austria in the Seven Weeks' War (1866) and the formation of the Prussian-dominated North German Confederation (1867). The architect of this new German unity was Otto von Bismarck, a conservative, monarchist, and militaristic Prussian prime minister. He unified all of Germany in a series of three wars against Denmark (1864), Austria (1866), and France (1870–71). On Jan. 18, 1871, King Wilhelm I of Prussia was proclaimed German emperor in the Hall of Mirrors at Versailles. The North German Confederation, created in 1867, was abolished, and the Second German Reich, consisting of the North and South German states, was born. With a powerful army, an efficient bureaucracy, and a loyal bourgeoisie, Chancellor Bismarck consolidated a powerful centralized state.

Wilhelm II dismissed Bismarck in 1890 and embarked upon a "New Course," stressing an intensified colonialism and a powerful navy. His chaotic foreign policy culminated in the diplomatic isolation of Germany and the disastrous defeat in World War I (1914–18). The Second German Empire collapsed following the defeat of the German armies in 1918, the naval mutiny at Kiel, and the flight of the kaiser to The Netherlands. The Social Democrats, led by Friedrich Ebert and Philipp Scheidemann, crushed the Communists and established a moderate state, known as the Weimar Republic, with Ebert as president. President Ebert died on Feb. 28, 1925, and on April 26, Field Marshal Paul von Hindenburg was elected president. The mass of Germans regarded the Weimar Republic as a child of defeat, imposed upon a Germany whose legitimate aspirations to world leadership had been thwarted by a world conspiracy. Added to this were a crippling currency debacle, a tremendous burden of reparations, and acute economic distress.

Adolf Hitler, an Austrian war veteran and a fanatical nationalist, fanned discontent by promising a Greater Germany, abrogation of the Treaty of Versailles, restoration of Germany's lost colonies, and the destruction of the Jews, whom he scapegoated as the reason for Germany's downfall and depressed economy. When the Social Democrats and the Communists refused to combine against the Nazi threat, President von Hindenburg made Hitler the chancellor on Jan. 30, 1933. With the death of von Hindenburg on Aug. 2, 1934, Hitler repudiated the Treaty of Versailles and began full-scale rearmament. In 1935 he withdrew Germany from the League of Nations, and the next year he reoccupied the Rhineland and signed the anti-Comintern pact with Japan, at the same time strengthening relations with Italy. Austria was annexed in March 1938. By the Munich agreement in Sept. 1938, he gained the Czech Sudetenland, and in violation of this agreement he completed the dismemberment of Czechoslovakia in March 1939. His invasion of Poland on Sept. 1, 1939, precipitated World War II.

Hitler established death camps to carry out "the final solution to the Jewish question." By the end of the war, Hitler's Holocaust had killed 6 million Jews, as well as Gypsies, homosexuals, Communists, the handicapped, and others not fitting the Aryan ideal. After some dazzling initial successes in 1939–42, Germany surrendered unconditionally to Allied and Soviet military commanders on May 8, 1945. On June 5 the four-nation Allied Control Council became the the de facto government of Germany.

(For details of World War II and of the Holocaust, see Headline History, World War II.)

At the Berlin (or Potsdam) Conference (July 17–Aug. 2, 1945) President Truman, Premier Stalin, and Prime Minister Clement Attlee of Britain set forth the guiding principles of the Allied Control Council: Germany's complete disarmament and demilitarization, destruction of its war potential, rigid control of industry, and decentralization of the political and economic structure. Pending final determination of territorial questions at a peace conference, the three victors agreed to the ultimate transfer of the city of Königsberg (now Kaliningrad) and its adjacent area to the U.S.S.R. and to the administration by Poland of former German territories lying generally east of the Oder-Neisse Line. For purposes of control, Germany was divided into four national occupation zones.

The Western powers were unable to agree with the U.S.S.R. on any fundamental issues. Work of the Allied Control Council was hamstrung by repeated Soviet vetoes; and finally, on March 20, 1948, Russia walked out of the council. Meanwhile, the U.S. and Britain had taken steps to merge their zones economically (Bizone); and on May 31, 1948, the U.S., Britain, France, and the Benelux countries agreed to set up a German state comprising the three Western Zones. The U.S.S.R. reacted by clamping a blockade on all ground communications between the Western Zones and West Berlin, an enclave in the Soviet Zone. The Western Allies countered by organizing a gigantic airlift to fly supplies into the beleaguered city, assigning 60,000 men to it. The U.S.S.R. was finally forced to lift the blockade on May 12, 1949.

The Federal Republic of Germany was proclaimed on May 23, 1949, with its capital at Bonn. In free elections, West German voters gave a majority in the Constituent Assembly to the Christian Democrats, with the Social Democrats largely making up the opposition. Konrad Adenauer became chancellor, and Theodor Heuss of the Free Democrats was elected first president.

The East German states adopted a more centralized constitution for the Democratic Republic of Germany, put into effect on Oct. 7, 1949. The U.S.S.R. thereupon dissolved its occupation zone but Soviet troops remained. The Western Allies declared that the East German Republic was a Soviet creation undertaken without self-determination and refused to recognize it. Soviet forces created a state controlled by the secret police with a single party, the Socialist Unity (Communist) Party.

Agreements in Paris in 1954 giving the Federal Republic full independence and complete sovereignty came into force on May 5, 1955. Under the agreement, West Germany and Italy became members of the Brussels treaty organization created in 1948 and renamed the Western European Union. West Germany also became a member of NATO. In 1955 the U.S.S.R. recognized the Federal Republic. The Saar territory, under an agreement between France and West Germany, held a plebiscite and despite economic links to France, elected to rejoin West Germany on Jan. 1, 1957.

The division between West Germany and East Germany was intensified when the Communists erected the Berlin Wall in 1961. In 1968, the East German Communist leader, Walter Ulbricht, imposed restrictions on West German movements into West Berlin. The Soviet-bloc invasion of Czechoslovakia in Aug. 1968 added to the tension. West Germany in 1970 signed a treaty with Poland, renouncing force and setting Poland's western border as the Oder-Neisse Line. It subsequently resumed formal relations with Czechoslovakia in a pact that "voided" the Munich treaty that gave Nazi Germany the Sudetenland. By 1973, normal relations were established between East and West Germany and the two states entered the United Nations.

Willy Brandt, winner of a Nobel Peace Prize for his foreign policies, was forced to resign in 1974 when an East German spy was discovered to be one of his top staff members. Succeeding him was a moderate Social Democrat, Helmut Schmidt. Schmidt staunchly backed U.S. military strategy in Europe, staking his political fate on the strategy of placing U.S. nuclear missiles in Germany unless the Soviet Union reduced its arsenal of intermediate missiles. The chancellor also strongly opposed nuclear freeze proposals.

Helmut Kohl of the Christian Democrat Party became chancellor in 1982. An economic upswing in 1986 led to Kohl's reelection. The fall of the Communist government in East Germany left only Soviet objections to German reunification to be dealt with. This was resolved in July 1990. On Oct. 3, 1989, the German Democratic Republic acceded to the Federal Republic and Germany became a united and sovereign state for the first time since 1945.

Following unification, the Federal Republic became the second-largest country in Europe after the Soviet Union. A reunited Berlin serves as the official capital, although the government would continue to have administrative functions in Bonn during the 12-year transition period. The issue of the cost of reunification and the modernization of the former East Germany were serious considerations facing the reunified nation. Germany ratified the Maastricht Treaty in Oct. 1993, being the last of the 12 EU members to do so. Voters in the relatively new state of Brandenburg in the east rejected in May 1996 a proposal to merge with Berlin, dramatizing a lingering psychological division between eastern and western Germany.

Owing to a budget deficit that threatened the country's eligibility for introducing the future common European currency, the government in June 1997 proposed to revalue its foreign exchange holdings. Germany's other main challenge was to render Germany competitively attractive as an industrial location by radically reducing taxes so as to attract investment capital, foreign and domestic, within the EU, and thus lower the high rate of unemployment.

In its most important election in decades, on Sept. 27, 1998, Germans chose Social Democrat Gerhard Schröder as chancellor over Christian Democrat incumbent Helmut Kohl, ending a 16-year-long rule that oversaw the reunification of Germany and symbolized the end of the cold war in Europe. A centrist in the style of Clinton and Blair, Schröder campaigned for "the new middle" and promised to rectify Germany's high unemployment rate of 10.6%.

Tension between the old-style left-wing and the more pro-business pragmatists within Schröder's government came to a head with the abrupt resignation of Finance Minister Oskar Lafontaine in March 1999, who was also chairman of the ruling Social Democratic Party. Lafontaine's plans to raise taxes on industry and raise German wages—already nearly the highest in the world—went against the more centrist policies of Schröder. Hans Eichel is chosen to become the next finance minister. Germany had one of the slowest rates of economic growth in western Europe—on par with Italy—and the most that was expected in 1999 was mild improvement. But in June Schröder presented an ambitious reform package that cuts billions from the federal budget and offers lower corporate taxes. In Sept. 1999, the German Parliament returned to its historic seat in Berlin.

Germany joined the other NATO allies in the military conflict in Kosovo in 1999. Before the Kosovo crisis, Germans had not participated in an armed conflict since World War II. It agreed to take 40,000 Kosovar refugees, the most of any NATO country.

Ghana

REPUBLIC OF GHANA

President: Jerry John Rawlings (1981)
Area: 92,100 sq. mi. (238,540 sq. km)
Population (1999 est.): 18,887,626 (average annual rate of natural increase: 2.14%); birth rate: 31.8/1000; infant mortality rate: 76.2/1000; density per sq. mi.: 205
Capital: Accra. **Largest cities (est. 1988):** Accra, 949,100; Kumasi, 385,200; Tamale, 151,100.
Monetary unit: Cedi. **Languages:** English (official), Native tongues (Brong Ahafo, Twi, Fanti, Ga, Ewe, Dagbani). **Ethnicity/race:** black African 99.8% (major tribes: Akan 44%, Moshi-Dagomba 16%, Ewe 13%,

Ga 8%), European and other 0.2%. **Religions:** indigenous beliefs, 38%; Islam, 30%; Christian, 24%. **Literacy rate:** 60%
Economic summary: GDP/PPP (1997 est.): $36.2 billion; $2,000 per capita. **Real growth rate:** 3%. **Inflation:** 27.7%. **Unemployment:** 20%. **Arable land:** 12%. **Agriculture:** cocoa, rice, coffee, cassava (tapioca), peanuts, corn, shea nuts, bananas, timber. **Labor force:** n.a.; agriculture and fishing, 61%; industry, 10%; services, 29% (1996 est.). **Industry:** mining, lumbering, light manufacturing, aluminum smelting, food processing. **Natural resources:** gold, timber, industrial diamonds, bauxite, manganese, fish, rubber. **Exports:** $1.57 billion (f.o.b., 1996 est.): gold, cocoa, timber, tuna, bauxite, aluminum, manganese ore, diamonds. **Imports:** $1.84 billion (c.i.f., 1995): capital equipment, petroleum, consumer goods, foods, intermediate goods. **Major trading partners:** U.K., Germany, U.S., The Netherlands, Japan, Nigeria. **Member of Commonwealth of Nations**

Geography A West African country bordering on the Gulf of Guinea, Ghana is bounded by Côte d'Ivoire to the west, Burkina Faso to the north, Togo to the east, and the Atlantic Ocean to the south. It compares in size to Oregon, and its largest river is the Volta.

Government Republic.

History Several major civilizations flourished in the general region of what is now Ghana. The ancient empire of Ghana (located 500 miles northwest of the contemporary state) reigned until the 13th century. The Akan peoples established the next major civilization, beginning in the 13th century, and then the Ashanti empire flourished in the 18th and 19th centuries.

Called the Gold Coast, the area was first seen by Portuguese traders in 1470. They were followed by the English (1553), the Dutch (1595), and the Swedes (1640). British rule over the Gold Coast began in 1820, but it was not until after quelling the severe resistance of the Ashanti in 1901 that it was firmly established. British Togoland, formerly a colony of Germany, was incorporated into Ghana by referendum in 1956. Created as an independent country on March 6, 1957, Ghana, as the result of a plebiscite, became a republic on July 1, 1960.

Premier Kwame Nkrumah attempted to take leadership of the Pan-African Movement, holding the All-African People's Congress in his capital, Accra, in 1958 and organizing the Union of African States with Guinea and Mali in 1961. But he oriented his country toward the Soviet Union and China and built an autocratic rule over all aspects of Ghanaian life. In Feb. 1966, while Nkrumah was visiting Beijing and Hanoi, he was deposed by a military coup led by Gen. Emmanuel K. Kotoka.

A series of military coups followed and on June 4, 1979, Flight Lieutenant Jerry Rawlings overthrew Lt. Gen. Frederick Akuffo's military rule. Rawlings permitted the election of a civilian president to go ahead as scheduled the following month, and Hilla Limann, candidate of the People's National Party, took office. Charging the civilian government with corruption and repression, Rawlings staged another coup on Dec. 31, 1981. As chairman of the Provisional National Defense Council, Rawlings instituted an austerity program and reduced budget deficits. In the elections of late 1992 Rawlings won a majority of the votes for president.

Despite consistent economic growth, almost daily demonstrations occurred largely in protest against the introduction of a 17.5% value-added tax in March 1995. In June it was removed, and the finance minister resigned in July. Elections in Dec. 1996 saw the reelection of Rawlings as president with 57% of the vote. His party also secured 133 of the 200 seats in Parliament. The opposition New Patriotic Party won 60 seats.

Greece

HELLENIC REPUBLIC

National name: Elliniki Dimokratia
President: Kostis Stephanopoulos (1995)
Prime Minister: Kostas Simitis (1996)
Area: 50,961 sq. mi. (131,940 sq. km)
Population (1999 est.): 10,707,135 (average annual rate of natural increase: 0.01%); birth rate: 9.5/1000; infant mortality rate: 7.1/1000; density per sq. mi.: 210
Capital: Athens. **Largest cities (1991 est.):** Athens, 3,000,000; Thessaloníki, 720,000; Piraeus, 170,000; Patras, 155,000. **Monetary unit:** Drachma.
Language: Greek. **Ethnicity/race:** Greek 98%, other 2% note: the Greek government states there are no ethnic divisions in Greece. **Religions:** Greek Orthodox, 98%; Muslim, 1.3%; Other, 0.7%. **Literacy rate:** 93%
Economic summary: GDP/PPP (1997 est.): $137.4 billion; $13,000 per capita. **Real growth rate:** 3.7%. **Inflation:** 6%. **Unemployment:** 10%. **Arable land:** 19%. **Agriculture:** wheat, corn, barley, sugar beets, olives, tomatoes, wine, tobacco, potatoes, meat, dairy products. **Labor force:** 4.21 million; services, 52%; agriculture, 23%; industry, 25% (1995). **Industry:** tourism, food and tobacco processing, textiles, chemicals, metal products, mining, petroleum. **Natural resources:** bauxite, lignite, magnesite, petroleum, marble. **Exports:** $9.8 billion (f.o.b., 1997 est.): manufactured goods, foodstuffs, fuels. **Imports:** $27 billion (c.i.f., 1997 est.): manufactured goods, foodstuffs, fuels. **Major trading partners:** EU (Germany, Italy, France, U.K.), U.S.

Geography Located in southern Europe, Greece forms an irregular-shaped peninsula in the Mediterranean with two additional large peninsulas projecting from it: the Chalcidice and the Peloponnese. The Greek Islands are generally subdivided into two groups, according to location: the Ionian Islands (including Corfu, Cephalonia, and Leucas) west of the mainland and the Aegean Islands (including Euboea, Samos, Chios, Lesbos, and Crete) to the east and south. North-central Greece, Epirus, and western Macedonia all are mountainous. The main chain of the Pindus Mountains extends from northwestern Greece to the Peloponnese. Mount Olympus, rising to 9,570 feet (2,909 m), is the highest point in the country.

Government Ceremonial executive power is held by the president; the prime minister heads the government and is responsible to a 300-member unicameral Parliament.

History Indo-European peoples, including the Mycenaeans, began entering Greece about 2000 B.C.E. and set up sophisticated civilizations. About 1200 B.C.E. the Dorians, another Indo-European people, invaded Greece, and a dark age followed, known mostly through the Homeric epics. At the end of this time, classical Greece began to emerge (c. 750 B.C.E.) as a loose composite of city-states

with a heavy involvement in maritime trade and a devotion to art, literature, politics, and philosophy. Greece reached the peak of its glory in the 5th century B.C.E., but the Peloponnesian War (431–404 B.C.E.) weakened the nation and it was conquered by Philip II and his son Alexander the Great of Macedonia, who considered themselves Greek. By the middle of the 2nd century B.C.E., Greece had declined to the status of a Roman province. It remained within the eastern Roman Empire until Constantinople fell to the Crusaders in 1204. In 1453, the Turks took Constantinople and by 1460, Greece was a Turkish province with its Orthodox Church intact. The insurrection made famous by the poet Lord Byron broke out in 1821, and in 1827 Greece won independence with sovereignty guaranteed by Britain, France, and Russia.

The protecting powers chose Prince Otto of Bavaria as the first king of modern Greece in 1832 to reign over an area only slightly larger than the Peloponnese peninsula. Chiefly under the next king, George I, chosen by the protecting powers in 1863, Greece acquired much of its present territory. During his 57-year reign, a period in which he encouraged parliamentary democracy, Thessaly, Epirus, Macedonia, Crete, and most of the Aegean islands were added from the disintegrating Turkish empire. Unfavorable economic conditions forced about one-sixth of the entire Greek population to emigrate (mostly to the U.S.) in the late 19th and early 20th centuries. An unsuccessful war against Turkey after World War I brought down the monarchy, to be replaced by a republic in 1923.

Two military dictatorships and a financial crisis brought George II back from exile, but only until 1941, when Italian and German invaders defeated tough Greek resistance. After British and Greek troops liberated the country in Oct. 1944, Communist guerrillas staged a long military campaign against the government. The Greek government received U.S. aid under the Truman Doctrine, the predecessor of the Marshall Plan, and eliminated the Communist guerilla threat. A military junta seized power in April 1967, sending young King Constantine II into exile. Col. George Papadopoulos, as prime minister, converted the government to republican form in 1973 and as president, ended martial law. He was moving to restore democracy when he was ousted in Nov. of that year by the military. The regime of the "colonels," which had tortured its opponents and scoffed at human rights, collapsed in 1974, after having bungled an attempt to seize Cyprus. A referendum in Dec. 1974, five months after the demise of the military dictatorship, ended the Greek monarchy and established a republic. Former premier Karamanlis returned from exile to become premier of Greece's first civilian government since 1967. Greece has continued to be ruled by freely elected civilian governments ever since and on Jan. 1, 1981, Greece became the 10th member of the European Union.

Greece continued to experience tensions with Turkey over a disputed unpopulated 10-acre island and over Cyprus, which is divided into Greek and Turkish sectors. Turkey's severe earthquake in Aug. 1999, however, moved Greece to provide humanitarian assistance, and brought about a slight thaw in relations.

The Greeks were the most vocal dissenters within the NATO alliance regarding the 1999 intervention in Kosovo. They were both wary of the economic and political instability that would accompany a large influx of refugees and reluctant to ignore an Eastern Orthodox religious history shared with the Serbs. Still, the Greeks agreed to take in 5,000 refugees.

Grenada

STATE OF GRENADA

Sovereign: Queen Elizabeth II (1952)
Governor-General: Daniel Williams (1996)
Prime Minister: Keith C. Mitchell (1995)
Area: 133 sq. mi. (340 sq. km)
Population (1999 est.): 97,008 (average annual growth rate 2.25%); birth rate: 27.6/1000; infant mortality rate: 11.1/1000; density per sq. mi.: 729
Capital and largest city (1991): St. George's, 4,439.
Monetary unit: East Caribbean dollar. **Ethnic groups (1991):** black African descent 85%, mixed 11%, white, other 0.3%. **Language:** English. **Ethnicity/race:** black African. **Religions:** Roman Catholic, 64%; Anglican, 21%. **Literacy rate:** 98%
Economic summary: GDP/PPP (1996 est.): $300 million; $3,200 per capita. **Real growth rate:** 3.1%. **Inflation:** 3.2%. **Unemployment:** 20% (Oct. 1996). **Arable land:** 15%. **Agriculture:** bananas, cocoa, nutmeg, mace, citrus, avocados, root crops, sugarcane, corn, vegetables. **Labor force:** 36,000; services, 31%; agriculture, 24%; construction, 8%; manufacturing, 5%; other, 32% (1985). **Industry:** food and beverages, textiles, light assembly operations, tourism, construction. **Natural resources:** timber, tropical fruit, deepwater harbors. **Exports:** $24 million (f.o.b., 1996 est.): bananas, cocoa, nutmeg, fruit and vegetables, clothing, mace. **Imports:** $128 million (f.o.b., 1996 est.): food, manufactured goods, machinery, chemicals, fuel. **Major trading partners:** U.K., U.S., The Netherlands, Japan. **Member of Commonwealth of Nations**

Geography Grenada (the first "a" is a long vowel) is the most southerly of the Windward Islands, about 100 miles (161 km) from the Venezuelan coast. It is a volcanic island traversed by a mountain range, the highest peak of which is Mount St. Catherine (2,756 ft.; 840 m).

Government Parliamentary democracy. A governor-general represents the sovereign, Elizabeth II.

History The Arawak Indians were the first to inhabit Grenada, but they were all eventually massacred by the belligerent Carib Indians. When Columbus arrived on the island in 1498 he encountered the Caribs, who in fact continued to rule over the island for another 150 years. The French gained control of the island in 1672 and held on to it until 1762, when British forces invaded. The black slaves, who had been shipped to the island to work on the plantations, were granted freedom in 1833. After more than 200 years of British rule, most recently as part of the West Indies Associated States, Grenada became independent on Feb. 7, 1974, with Eric M. Gairy as prime minister.

In 1979 the Marxist New Jewel Movement staged a coup, and its leader, Maurice Bishop, became prime minister. Bishop, a protégé of Cuba's President Castro, was killed in a military coup on Oct. 19, 1983.

In an effort to establish order on the island and eliminate the Cuban military presence, U.S. president Ronald Reagan ordered an invasion of Grenada on Oct. 25 involving over 1,900 U.S. troops and a small military force from Barbados, Dominica, Jamaica, St. Lucia, and St. Vincent. The troops met strong resistance from Cuban military personnel on the island but soon occupied it. After a gradual withdrawal of peacekeeping forces, a centrist coalition led by Herbert A. Blaize, a 66-year-old lawyer, won a parliamentary majority in 1984. Parliamentary elections in June 1995 gave the opposition New National Party a majority of seats and allowed its leader, Dr. Keith C. Mitchell, to form a new government. Mitchell flew to Cuba in April 1997 to meet with Castro and signed an economic cooperation agreement. In 1998 Castro made his first official state visit to the island. In 1999, Prime Minister Mitchell became one of only two prime ministers in Grenada's history to be reelected.

Guatemala

REPUBLIC OF GUATEMALA

National name: República de Guatemala
President: Alvaro Arzú Irigoyen (1996)
Area: 42,042 sq. mi. (108,890 sq. km)
Population (1999 est.): 12,335,580 (average annual rate of natural increase: 2.88%); birth rate: 35.6/1000; infant mortality rate: 46.2/1000; density per sq. mi.: 293
Capital and largest city (1994 est.): Guatemala City, 1,150,452. **Other large cities (1994 est.):** Mixco, 413,002; Villa Nueva, 154,508. **Monetary unit:** Quetzal. **Languages:** Spanish, Indian languages. **Ethnicity/race:** Mestizo—mixed Amerindian-Spanish ancestry (in local Spanish called Ladino) 56%, Amerindian or predominantly Amerindian 44%. **Religions:** Roman Catholic, Protestant, Mayan. **Literacy rate:** 55%
Economic summary: GDP/PPP (1997 est.): $45.8 billion; $4,000 per capita. **Real growth rate:** 4.1%. **Inflation:** 9%. **Unemployment:** 5.2%. **Arable land:** 12%. **Agriculture:** sugarcane, corn, bananas, coffee, beans, cardamom, cattle, sheep, pigs, chickens. **Labor force:** 3.32 million (1997 est.); agriculture. 58%; services, 14%; manufacturing, 14%; commerce, 7%; construction, 4%; transport, 2.6%; utilities, 0.3%; mining, 0.1% (1995). **Industry:** sugar, textiles and clothing, furniture, chemicals, petroleum, metals, rubber, tourism. **Natural resources:** petroleum, nickel, rare woods, fish, chicle. **Exports:** $2.9 billion (f.o.b., 1997 est.): coffee, sugar, bananas, cardamom, petroleum. **Imports:** $3.3 billion (c.i.f., 1997 est.): fuel and petroleum products, machinery, grain, fertilizers, motor vehicles. **Major trading partners:** U.S., El Salvador, Honduras, Costa Rica, Germany, Mexico, Venezuela, Japan, Germany.

Geography The northernmost of the Central American nations, Guatemala is the size of Tennessee. Its neighbors are Mexico on the north and west, and Belize, Honduras, and El Salvador on the east. The country consists of three main regions—the cool highlands with the heaviest population, the tropical area along the Pacific and Caribbean coasts, and the tropical jungle in the northern lowlands (known as the Petén). The principal mountain range rises to the highest elevation in Central America and contains many volcanic peaks. Volcanic eruptions are frequent.

Government Republic.

History Once the site of the impressive ancient Mayan civilization, Guatemala was conquered by Spanish conquistador Pedro de Alvarado in 1524 and set itself up as a republic in 1839 after the United Provinces of Central America collapsed. From 1898 to 1920, the dictator Manuel Estrada Cabrera ran the country and welcomed U.S. investment, and from 1931 to 1944, Gen. Jorge Ubico Castaneda served as strongman.

After Ubico's overthrow in 1944, liberaldemocratic coalitions led by Juan José Arévalo (1945–51) and Jacobo Arbenz Guzmán (1951–54) instituted sweeping social and political reforms that strengthened the peasantry and urban workers at the expense of the military and big landowners like the United Fruit Company. With covert U.S. backing, a revolt was led by Col. Carlos Castillo Armas, and Arbenz took refuge in Mexico.

A 36-year civil war followed between a succession of right-wing governments led by the military and leftist rebels. The administration of Gen. Romeo Lucas Garcia was charged by Amnesty International with responsibility for at least 5,000 political murders in a reign of brutality and corruption that brought a cutoff of U.S. military aid in 1978.

More military leaders followed until civilian Marco Vinicio Cerezo Arévalo took office in 1986. He was followed by Jorge Serrano Elías in 1991. In 1993, Serrano moved to dissolve Congress and the Supreme Court and suspend constitutional rights, but the military deposed Serrano and allowed the inauguration of de Leon Carpio, the former attorney general of human rights. A peace agreement was signed in Dec. 1996 ending the longest civil war in Latin American history. By the time the war had run its course, an estimated 150,000 died and 50,000 were missing. In June 1997, the new president Álvaro Arzú Irigoyen and the guerrilla movement leader Ricardo Ramirez were awarded the UNESCO Houphouet-Bolgny Peace Prize.

In an effort toward national reconciliation, a Guatemalan truth commission issued a report on Feb. 25, 1999, detailing the numerous human rights abuses committed during the war. The report charged that the army was responsible for 93% of the atrocities and that the rebels (the Guatemalan National Revolutionary Unit) were responsible for 3%. As a consequence, the former guerrillas apologized for their crimes, and President Clinton apologized for U.S. support of the right-wing military governments. The army, however, has not acknowledged its guilt.

In June 1999, Cuba's state-owned airline began direct flights to Guatemala. Guatemala had reestablished diplomatic relations with Cuba in Jan. 1998, 37 years after the country's conservative government broke off ties with Castro's government.

Guinea

REPUBLIC OF GUINEA

National name: République de Guinée
President: Lansana Conté (1984)
Premier: Lamine Sidime (1999)
Area: 94,925 sq. mi. (245,860 sq. km)
Population (1999 est.): 7,538,953 (average annual rate of natural increase: 2.33%); birth rate: 40.6/1000; infant mortality rate: 126.3/1000; density per sq. mi.: 79
Capital and largest city (1995 est.): Conakry, 1,508,000. **Monetary unit:** Guinean franc.

Languages: French (official), native tongues (Malinké, Susu, Fulani). **Ethnicity/race:** Peuhl 40%, Malinke 30%, Soussou 20%, smaller tribes 10%. **Religions:** Islam, 85%; 7% indigenous, 8% Christian. **Literacy rate:** 24% in French; 48% in local languages
Economic summary: GDP/PPP (1997 est.): $8.3 billion; $1,100 per capita. **Real growth rate:** 4.8%. **Inflation:** 3.5% (1996 est.). **Arable land:** 2%. **Agriculture:** rice, coffee, pineapples, palm kernels, cassava (tapioca), bananas, sweet potatoes, cattle, sheep, goats, timber. **Unemployment rate:** n.a. **Labor force:** 2.4 million (1983); agriculture, 80%; industry and commerce, 11%; services, 5.4%; civil service, 3.6%. **Industry:** bauxite, gold, diamonds, alumina refining, light manufacturing and agricultural processing industries. **Natural resources:** bauxite, iron ore, diamonds, gold, uranium, hydropower, fish. **Exports:** $748 million (1995 est.): bauxite, alumina, diamonds, gold, coffee, fish, agricultural products. **Imports:** $809 million (1995 est.): petroleum products, metals, machinery, transport equipment, textiles, grain and other foodstuffs. **Major trading partners:** U.S., Belgium-Luxembourg, Ireland, Spain, France, Côte d'Ivoire, Hong Kong.

Geography Guinea, in West Africa on the Atlantic, is also bordered by Guinea-Bissau, Senegal, Mali, Côte d'Ivoire, Liberia, and Sierra Leone. Slightly smaller than Oregon, the country consists of a coastal plain, a mountainous region, a savanna interior, and a forest area in the Guinea Highlands. The highest peak is Mount Nimba at 5,748 ft. (1,752 m).

Government Republic.

History Beginning in C.E. 900, the Soussou migrated from the north and began settling in the area that is now Guinea. The Soussou civilization reached its height in the 13th century. Today the Soussou make up about 20% of Guinea's population. From the 16th to the 19th century, the Fulani empire dominated the region. In 1849, the French claimed it as a protectorate. First called Rivières du Sud, the protectorate was rechristened French Guinea, and finally, in 1895, it became part of French West Africa.

Guinea achieved independence on Oct. 2, 1958, and became an independent state with Sékou Touré as president. Under Touré, the country became the first avowedly Marxist state in Africa. Diplomatic relations with France were suspended in 1965, with the Soviet Union replacing France as the country's chief source of economic and technical assistance.

Prosperity came in 1960 after the start of exploitation of bauxite deposits. Touré was reelected to a seven-year term in 1974 and again in 1981. Touré died after 26 years as president in March 1984. A week later, a military regime headed by Col. Lansana Conté took power. Conté became president and his coconspirator in the coup, Col. Diara Traoré, became prime minister, but Conté later demoted Traoré to education minister. Traoré tried to seize power on July 4, 1985, while Conté was out of the country, but his attempted coup was crushed by troops loyal to Conté.

In 1989, President Conté announced that Guinea would move to a multiparty democracy. A new constitution approved in a nationwide referendum in Dec. 1990 provided for the establishment of a directly elected multiparty Parliament (five-year terms) and a popularly elected president for a maximum of two five-year terms, and a judiciary independent of either the presidency or the legislature. A transitional Committee for National Recovery (CTRN) replaced the military committee to guide implementation of the new constitution.

In 1991 voters approved a new constitution that would lead the country to democracy. Under mounting popular pressure Conté, declared in April 1992 that constitutional rule would begin. In Dec. 1993 elections the president's Unity and Progress Party took almost 51% of the vote cast. In Feb. 1996 rebellious soldiers demanding pay in arrears besieged the presidential palace. Loyal troops repulsed the attacks.

Guinea has had ongoing difficulties with its neighbor Liberia, which was embroiled in a long civil war during the 1990s. The fighting in Liberia spilled over the border into Guinea on several occasions, and border skirmishes continued after the civil war subsided. Guinea had taken sides against rebel leader Charles Taylor in Liberia's civil war and was part of the Nigerian-led ECOMOG forces that intervened in the crisis. As a consequence, President Conté's relations with Taylor remained sour after Taylor became Liberia's president in 1997. In Sept. 1999, Guinea accused Liberia of massacring villagers in a border town. An accord was signed in Nigeria later that month, which promised better relations between the nations, as well as with war-torn Sierra Leone, which shares a border with both countries.

Guinea-Bissau

REPUBLIC OF GUINEA-BISSAU
National name: Républica da Guiné-Bissau
President: Malam Bacai Sanhá (Interim) (1999)
Prime Minister: Francisco José Fadul (1998)
Area: 13,948 sq. mi. (36,120 sq. km)
Population (1999 est.): 1,234,555 (average annual rate of natural increase: 2.31%); birth rate: 38.2/1000; infant mortality rate: 109.5/1000; density per sq. mi.: 89
Capital and largest city (1991 est.): Bissau, 200,000.
Monetary unit: Guinea-Bissau peso. **Languages:** Portuguese Criolo, African languages. **Ethnicity/race:** African 99% (Balanta 30%, Fula 20%, Manjaca 14%, Mandinga 13%, Papel 7%), European and mulatto less than 1%. **Religions:** traditional, 65%; Islam, 30%; Christian, 5%. **Literacy rate:** 37% (1991 est.)
Economic summary: GDP/PPP (1997 est.): $1.15 billion; $975 per capita. **Real growth rate:** 5%. **Inflation:** 65% (1996). **Unemployment:** n.a. **Labor force:** 480,000 **Arable land:** 11%. **Agriculture:** rice, corn, beans, cassava (tapioca), cashew nuts, peanuts, palm kernels, cotton, fishing and forest potential not fully exploited. **Industry:** agricultural products processing, beer, soft drinks. **Natural resources:** fish, timber, phosphates, bauxite, unexploited deposits of petroleum. **Exports:** $25.8 million (f.o.b., 1996 est.): cashews, fish, peanuts, palm kernels, sawn lumber. **Imports:** $63 million (c.i.f., 1996 est.): foodstuffs, transport equipment, petroleum products, machinery and equipment. **Major trading partners:** Spain, India, Thailand, Italy, Portugal, Japan, Côte d'Ivoire.

Geography A neighbor of Senegal and Guinea in West Africa, on the Atlantic coast, Guinea-Bissau is about half the size of South Carolina. The country is a low-lying coastal region of swamps, rain forests, and mangrove-covered wetlands, with about 25 islands off the coast. The Bijagos archipelago extends 30 miles (48 km) out to sea.

Government Republic.

History The land now known as Guinea-Bissau was once the kingdom of Gabú, which was part of the larger Mali empire. After 1546 Gabú became more autonomous, and at least portions of the kingdom existed until 1867. The first European to encounter Guinea-Bissau was the Portuguese explorer Nuño Tristão in 1446; colonists in the Cape Verde Islands obtained trading rights in the territory, and it became a center of the Portuguese slave trade. In 1879 the connection with the islands was broken.

The African Party for the Independence of Guinea-Bissau and Cape Verde (another Portuguese colony) was founded in 1956 and guerrilla warfare by nationalists grew increasingly effective. By 1974 the rebels controlled most of the countryside, where they formed a government that was soon recognized by scores of countries. The military coup in Portugal in April 1974 brightened the prospects for freedom, and in Aug. the Lisbon government signed an agreement granting independence to the province. The new republic took the name Guinea-Bissau.

In Nov. 1980, Prémier João Bernardo Vieira headed a military coup that deposed Luis Cabral, president since 1974. In his 19 years of rule, Vieira was criticized for crony capitalism and corruption and for failing to alleviate the poverty of Guinea-Bissau, one of the world's poorest countries. Vieira also brought in troops from Senegal and the Republic of Guinea to help fight against an insurgency movement, a highly unpopular move. The rebels managed to gain control of most of the country and part of the capital in 1998 before a Nov. peace deal halted the fighting. But in May 1999, after the presidential guard refused to disarm, the rebels deposed Vieira.

Guyana

COOPERATIVE REPUBLIC OF GUYANA
President: Bharrat Jagdeo (1999)
Prime Minister: Samuel Hinds (1997)
Area: 83,000 sq. mi. (214,970 sq. km)
Population (1999 est.): 705,156 (average annual rate of natural increase: 0.92%); birth rate: 18.2/1000; infant mortality rate: 48.6/1000; density per sq. mi.: 8
Capital and largest city (1992 est.): Georgetown, 248,500. **Monetary unit:** Guyana dollar. **Languages:** English (official), Amerindian dialects. **Ethnicity/race:** East Indian 51%, black and mixed 43%, Amerindian 4%, European and Chinese 2%. **Religions:** Hindu, 34%; Protestant, 18%; Islam, 9%; Roman Catholic, 18%; Anglican, 16%. **Literacy rate:** 96%
Economic summary GDP/PPP: (1996 est.), $1.8 billion; $2,500 per capita. **Real growth rate:** 5%. **Inflation:** (1997 est.) 4.5%. **Unemployment:** (1992 est.), 12%. **Labor force:** n.a. **Arable land:** 2%. **Agriculture:** sugar, rice, wheat, vegetable oils, beef, pork, poultry, dairy products, development potential for fishing and forestry. **Labor force:** n.a. **Industry:** bauxite, sugar, rice milling, timber, fishing (shrimp), textiles, gold mining. **Natural resources:** bauxite, gold, diamonds, hardwood timber, shrimp, fish. **Exports:** $546 million (f.o.b., 1996): sugar, gold, bauxite/alumina, rice, shrimp, molasses. **Imports:** $589 million (c.i.f., 1996 est.): manufactures, machinery, petroleum, food. **Major trading partners:** Canada, U.S., U.K., Trinidad and Tobago, Netherlands Antilles. **Member of Commonwealth of Nations**

Geography Guyana is the size of Idaho and is situated on the northern coast of South America east of Venezuela, west of Suriname, and north of Brazil. The country consists of a low coastal area and the Guyana Highlands, a tropical forest zone covering more than 80% of the country, in the south. There is an extensive north-south network of rivers.

Government Republic.

History The Dutch, English, and French established colonies in what is now known as Guyana, but by the early 17th century the majority of the settlements were Dutch. During the Napoleonic wars Britain took over the Dutch colonies of Berbice, Demerara, and Essequibo, which became British Guiana in 1831.

Slavery was outlawed in 1834, and the great need for plantation workers led to a large wave of immigration, primarily of East Indians. Today, about half of the population is of East Indian descent and about 43% are of African descent.

British Guiana was made a crown colony in 1928, and in 1953 it was granted home rule. In 1950, Forbes Burnham and Cheddi Jagan, the former black and the latter East Indian, created the colony's first political party, which was dedicated to gaining the colony's independence. The two leaders split in 1955, creating separate parties. The leftist Jagan and the more moderate Burnham were to dominate Guyanan politics for decades to come. On May 26, 1966, the country gained independence, and resumed its traditional name, Guyana.

Burnham and his People's National Congress ruled Guyana for 21 years, until Burnham's death in 1985. In 1992, Jagan's People's Progressive Party won a majority in the general election. Jagan, who had served as prime minister in the 1960s while Guyana was still a colony, became president. Upon President Jagan's death in March 1997, Prime Minister Samuel Hinds assumed the presidency. Nine days later the American-born Janet Jagan, the late president's widow, became prime minister, then executive president. President Jagan decided to resign in Aug. 1999, and Finance Minister Bharrat Jagdeo assumed the presidency for the rest of her term.

In April 1999, more than 10,000 civil service workers went on strike, saying they needed pay hikes to counter rising prices. The eight-week strike ended in June, but the aftereffects would be felt for much longer since the strike crippled the postal service and hospitals and hindered domestic and international trade.

Haiti

REPUBLIC OF HAITI

National name: République d'Haïti
President: René García Préval (1996)
Prime Minister: Jacques-Edouard Alexis (1999)
Area: 10,714 sq. mi. (27,750 sq. km)
Population (1999 est.): 6,884,264 (average annual rate of natural increase: 1.86%); birth rate: 32.6/1000; infant mortality rate: 97.6/1000; density per sq. mi.: 643
Capital and largest city (1993 est.): Port-au-Prince, 1.5 million. **Monetary unit:** Gourde. **Languages:** Creole, French. **Ethnicity/race:** black 95%, mulatto and European 5%. **Religions:** Roman Catholic, 80%; Protestant, 16%; Vaudou, 95%. **Literacy rate:** 53%
Economic summary: GDP/PPP (1997 est.): $7.1 billion; $1,070 per capita. **Real growth rate:** 1.1%. **Inflation:** 17%. **Unemployment:** 60% (1996 est.). **Arable land:** 20%. **Agriculture:** coffee, mangoes, sugarcane, rice, corn, sorghum, wood. **Labor force:** 3.6 million (1995); agriculture, 66%; services, 25%; industry, 9%. **Industry:** sugar refining, flour milling, textiles, cement, tourism, light assembly industries based on imported parts. **Natural resources:** none. **Exports:** $90 million (f.o.b., 1996): light manufactures, coffee, other agriculture. **Imports:** $665 million (f.o.b., 1996): machines and manufactures, food and beverages, petroleum products, chemicals, fats and oils. **Major trading partners:** U.S., EU.

Geography Haiti, in the West Indies, occupies the western third of the island of Hispaniola, which it shares with the Dominican Republic. About the size of Maryland, Haiti is two-thirds mountainous, with the rest of the country marked by great valleys, extensive plateaus, and small plains.

Government Republic.

History Visited by Columbus on Dec. 6, 1492, Haiti's native Arawaks fell victim to Spanish rule. In 1697 Haiti became a French possession known as Saint-Dominique. An insurrection among a slave population of 480,000 in 1791 ended with a declaration of independence by Pierre-Dominique Toussaint l'Ouverture in 1801. Napoléon Bonaparte suppressed the independence movement, but it eventually triumphed in 1804 under Jean-Jacques Dessalines, who gave the new nation the Arawak name Haiti.

Its prosperity was hampered by internal strife as well as disputes with neighboring Santo Domingo during a succession of 19th-century dictatorships; a bankrupt Haiti accepted a U.S. customs receivership from 1905 to 1941. Occupation by U.S. Marines from 1915 to 1934 brought a measure of stability and a population growth that made Haiti the most densely populated nation in the hemisphere.

In 1949, after four years of democratic rule by President Dumarsais Estimé, dictatorship returned under Gen. Paul Magloire, who was succeeded by François Duvalier, nicknamed "Papa Doc," in 1957. Duvalier established a dictatorship based on secret police, known as the "Tontons Macoutes," who gunned down opponents of the regime. Duvalier's son, Jean-Claude, or "Baby Doc," succeeded his father in 1971 as ruler of the poorest nation in the Western Hemisphere. His infamous dictatorship, marked by pervasive corruption and repression, rivaled that of his father's. Duvalier fled the country in 1986 amid strong protests and the country remained under military rule.

Jean-Bertrand Aristide, a Roman Catholic priest, was sworn in as president on Feb. 7, 1991—the country's first democratically elected chief executive. President Aristide was replaced by a de facto regime in Oct. 1991 following a military coup on Sept. 30, 1991. He was reinstated in Oct. 1993 by a U.S.-led multinational force appointed by U.N. Resolution 940. A U.S. peace mission in Sept. 1994 reached a compromise with the military leaders, avoiding a U.S. invasion. Acting as peacekeepers, 20,000 U.S. troops landed in Haiti, allowing Aristide to return in mid-Oct. Freely elected president René Préval was inaugurated in Feb. 1996. American troops were gradually reduced to 500, most of whom helped to repair Haiti's collapsed infrastructure. Despite free elections, the country's economic and political situation continued to deteriorate. In early June 1997 Prime Minister Rosny Smarth announced his resignation, and in Feb. 1999 President Préval dissolved Parliament and ruled by decree after the Parliament would not approve any of his candidates for prime minister. He then appointed Jacques-Edouard Alexis to the position. Elections were announced for Nov. or Dec. 1999. By the end of 1999, the remaining American troops are expected to leave Haiti, despite the fragility of this nascent democracy.

Honduras

REPUBLIC OF HONDURAS

National name: República de Honduras
President: Carlos Roberto Flores Facusse (1998)
Area: 43,872 sq. mi. (112,090 sq. km)
Population (1999 est.): 5,997,327 (average annual rate of natural increase: 2.38%); birth rate: 31.0/1000; infant mortality rate: 40.8/1000; density per sq. mi.: 137
Capital and largest city (1995): Tegucigalpa, 1,500,000.
Monetary unit: Lempira. **Languages:** Spanish (official), English widely spoken in business. **Ethnicity/race:** mestizo (mixed Indian and European) 90%, Indian 7%, black 2%, white 1%. **Religions:** Roman Catholic, 94%, Protestant minority. **Literacy rate:** 73%
Economic summary: GDP/PPP (1997 est.): $12.7 billion; $2,200 per capita. **Real growth rate:** 4.5%. **Inflation:** 15%. **Unemployment:** 6.3%; underemployed, 30% (1997). **Arable land:** 15%. **Agriculture:** bananas, coffee, citrus, beef, timber, shrimp. **Labor force:** 1.3 million (1997 est.); agriculture, 62%; services, 20%; manufacturing, 9%; construction, 3%; other, 6% (1985). **Industry:** sugar, coffee, textiles, clothing, wood products. **Natural resources:** timber, gold, silver, copper, lead, zinc, iron ore, antimony, coal, fish. **Exports:** $1.3 billion (f.o.b., 1996): bananas, coffee, shrimp, lobster, minerals, meat, lumber. **Imports:** $1.8 billion (c.i.f., 1996): machinery and transport equipment, industrial raw materials, chemical products, manufactured goods, fuel and oil, foodstuffs. **Major trading partners:** U.S., Germany, Belgium, Japan, Spain, Guatemala, Mexico, El Salvador.

Geography Honduras, in the north-central part of Central America, has a 400-mile (644-km) Caribbean coastline and a 40-mile (64-km) Pacific frontage. Its neighbors are Guatemala to the west, El Salvador to the south, and Nicaragua to the east. The second-largest country in Central America, Honduras is slightly larger than Tennessee. Generally mountainous, the country is marked by fertile plateaus, river valleys, and narrow coastal plains.

Government Republic.

History Honduras was part of the Mayan civilization during the first millennium, and its cultural vortex was Copàn. Columbus explored the country on his last voyage in 1502. Honduras, with four other countries of Central America, declared its independence from Spain in 1821 and was part of a federation of Central American states until 1838. In that year it seceded from the federation and became a completely independent country. Political unrest rocked the country in the early 20th century, including an occupation by U.S. Marines, until it was quelled by the dictatorship of General Tiburcio Carias Andino in 1932.

In July 1969, El Salvador invaded Honduras after Honduran landowners had deported several thou-

sand Salvadorans. By threatening economic sanctions and military intervention, the OAS induced El Salvador to withdraw. Although parliamentary democracy returned with the election of Roberto Suazo Córdova as president in 1982 after a decade of military rule, Honduras faced severe economic problems and tensions along its border with Nicaragua. "Contra" rebels, waging a guerrilla war against the Sandinista regime in Nicaragua, used Honduras as a training and staging area. At the same time, the United States used Honduras as a site for military exercises and built bases to train both Honduran and Salvadoran troops.

The lack of a final resolution of a maritime border dispute with Nicaragua led to incidents in 1997 in which Nicaraguan and Honduran gunboats exchanged fire in the disputed waters. In Nov. 1997 Carlos Flores Facussé of the Liberal Party was elected president. Honduras suffers from rapid population growth, high unemployment, inflation, a lack of basic services, and economic dependence on coffee and bananas, which are subject to sharp price fluctuations. But upon taking office on Jan. 27, 1998, Flores inaugurated programs of reform and modernization of the Honduran government and economy, with emphasis on helping Honduras's poorest citizens while maintaining the country's fiscal health and improving international competitiveness.

In Oct. 1998, Hurricane Mitch caused devastating destruction in Honduras. More than 13,000 Hondurans were killed by the hurricane, 2 million were left homeless, and damages to housing and infrastructure alone exceeded $5 billion.

Hungary

REPUBLIC OF HUNGARY

National name: Magyar Köztársaság
President: Árpád Göncz (1990)
Premier: Viktor Orbán (1998)
Area: 35,919 sq. mi. (93,030 sq. km)
Population (1999 est.): 10,186,372 (average annual rate of natural increase: –0.25%); birth rate: 10.8/1000; infant mortality rate: 9.5/1000; density per sq. mi.: 284
Capital and largest city (1995 est.): Budapest, 2,008,546. **Other large cities (1995 est.):** Debrecen, 210,000; Miskolc, 182,000; Szeged, 169,000; Pécs, 163,000. **Monetary unit:** Forint. **Languages:** Magyar (Hungarian), 98.2%; Other, 1.8%. **Ethnicity/race:** Hungarian 89.9%, Gypsy 4%, German 2.6%, Serb 2%, Slovak 0.8%, Romanian 0.7%. **Religions:** Roman Catholic, 67.5%; Protestant, 25%; atheist and others, 7.5%. **Literacy rate:** 98%
Economic summary: GDP/PPP (1997 est.): $73.2 billion; $7,400 per capita. **Real growth rate:** 4.4%. **Inflation:** 18%. **Unemployment:** 9%. **Arable land:** 51%. **Agriculture:** wheat, corn, sunflower seed, potatoes, sugar beets, pigs, cattle, poultry, dairy products. **Labor force:** (1996 est.), 4.5 million; services 65%, industry 26.7%, agriculture 8.3%. **Industry:** mining, metallurgy, construction materials, processed foods, textiles, chemicals, motor vehicles. **Natural resources:** bauxite, coal, natural gas, fertile soils. **Exports:** $16 billion (f.o.b., 1996): machinery and equipment, other manufactures, agriculture and food products, raw materials, fuels and electricity. **Imports:** $18.6 billion (f.o.b., 1996): machinery and equipment, other manufactures, fuels and electricity, agricultural and food products, raw materials. **Major trading partners:** EU (Germany, Australia, Italy), Former Soviet Union (F.S.U.).

Geography This central European country is the size of Indiana. Most of Hungary is a fertile, rolling plain lying east of the Danube River, and drained by the Danube and Tisza Rivers. In the extreme northwest is the Little Hungarian Plain. South of that area is Lake Balaton (250 sq. mi.; 648 sq. km).

Government Republic.

History By 14 B.C.E., western Hungary was part of the Roman Empire's provinces of Pannonia and Dacia. The area east of the Danube was never a part of the Roman Empire and was largely occupied by various Germanic and Asiatic peoples. In C.E. 896 all of Hungary was invaded by the Magyars, who founded a kingdom. Christianity was accepted during the reign of Stephen I (Saint Stephen), 977–1038. A devastating invasion by the Mongols killed half of Hungary's population in 1241. The peak of Hungary's great period of medieval power came during the reign of Louis I the Great (1342–82), whose dominions touched the Baltic, Black, and Mediterranean Seas. War with the Turks broke out in 1389, and for more than 100 years the Turks advanced through the Balkans. When the Turks smashed a Hungarian army in 1526, western and northern Hungary accepted Hapsburg rule to escape Turkish occupation. Transylvania became independent under Hungarian princes. Intermittent war with the Turks was waged until a peace treaty was signed in 1699.

After the suppression of the 1848 revolt against Hapsburg rule, led by Louis Kossuth, the dual monarchy of Austria-Hungary was set up in 1867. The dual monarchy was defeated with the other Central Powers in World War I. After a short-lived republic in 1918, the chaotic Communist rule of 1919 under Béla Kun ended with the Romanians occupying Budapest on Aug. 4, 1919. When the Romanians left, Adm. Nicholas Horthy entered the capital with a national army. The Treaty of Trianon of June 4, 1920, cost Hungary 68% of its land and 58% of its population. Meanwhile, the National Assembly had restored the legal continuity of the old monarchy and, on March 1, 1920, Horthy was elected regent. Following the German invasion of Russia on June 22, 1941, Hungary joined the attack against the Soviet Union, but the war was not popular and Hungarian troops were almost entirely withdrawn from the eastern front by May 1943. German occupation troops set up a puppet government after Horthy's appeal for an armistice with advancing Soviet troops on Oct. 15, 1944, had resulted in his overthrow. The German regime soon fled the capital, however, and on Dec. 23 a provisional government was formed in Soviet-occupied eastern Hungary. On Jan. 20, 1945, the government signed an armistice in Moscow. Early the next year, the National Assembly approved a constitutional law abolishing the thousand-year-old monarchy and establishing a republic.

By the Treaty of Paris (1947), Hungary had to give up all territory it had acquired since 1937 and to pay $300 million reparations to the U.S.S.R., Czechoslovakia, and Yugoslavia. In 1948 the Communist Party, with the support of Soviet troops, seized control. Hungary was proclaimed a People's Republic and one-party state in 1949. Industry was nationalized, the land collectivized into state farms, and the opposition terrorized by the secret police.

The terror, modeled after that of the U.S.S.R., reached its height with the trial and life imprisonment of József Cardinal Mindszenty, the leader of Hungary's Roman Catholics, in 1948. On Oct. 23, 1956, an anti-Communist revolution broke out in Budapest. To cope with it, the Communists set up a coalition government and called former premier Imre Nagy back to head the government. But he and most of his ministers were swept by the logic of events into the anti-Communist opposition, and he declared Hungary a neutral power, withdrawing from the Warsaw Treaty and appealing to the United Nations for help. One of his ministers, János Kádár, established a counterregime and asked the U.S.S.R. to send in military power. Soviet troops and tanks suppressed the revolution in bloody fighting after 190,000 people had fled the country. Under Kádár (1956–88), Communist Hungary henceforth maintained more liberal policies in the economic and cultural spheres, and Hungary became the most liberal of the Soviet-bloc nations of eastern Europe. Continuing his program of national reconciliation, Kádár emptied prisons, reformed the secret police, and eased travel restrictions.

Hungary's Communists abandoned their monopoly on power in 1989 voluntarily and the constitution was amended in Oct. 1989 to allow a multiparty state. The last Soviet troops left Hungary in June 1991, thereby ending almost 47 years of military presence. The transition to a market economy proved difficult. Hungary strengthened its ties with Poland and Czechoslovakia but grew concerned about the fate of ethnic Hungarians in neighboring countries. Hungary normalized relations with the Catholic Church in 1997 by signing an agreement concerning restitution or compensation for property seized during the Communist era.

In April 1999, Hungary became part of NATO, along with the Czech Republic and Poland. Only weeks after officially joining NATO, the country was called upon to stand up to its former ally, Russia, by blocking a shipment of Russian fuel and food destined for Yugoslavia during the Kosovo crisis.

Iceland

REPUBLIC OF ICELAND

National name: Lydveldid Island
President: Ólafur Ragnar Grímsson (1996)
Prime Minister: David Oddsson (1991)
Area: 39,709 sq. mi. (103,000 sq. km)[1]
Population (1999 est.): 272,512 (average annual rate of natural increase: 0.79%); birth rate: 14.9/1000; infant mortality rate: 5.2/1000; density per sq. mi.: 7
Capital and largest city (1994 est.): Reykjavik, 103,036. **Monetary unit:** Icelandic króna. **Language:** Icelandic. **Ethnicity/race:** homogeneous mixture of descendants of Norwegians and Celts. **Religions:** Church of Iceland (Evangelical Lutheran) 96%, other Protestant and Roman Catholic 3%, none 1%..
Literacy rate: 100%
Economic summary: GDP/PPP (1997 est.): $5.71 billion; $21,000 per capita. **Real growth rate:** 4.9%. **Inflation:** 2.3% (1996). **Unemployment:** 3.8% (1997 est.). **Arable land:** 0%. **Agriculture:** potatoes, turnips, cattle, sheep, fish. **Labor force:** 131,000; manufacturing 12.9%, fishing and fish processing 11.8%, construction 10.7%, other services 59.5%, agriculture 5.1% (1996 est.). **Industries:** fish processing, aluminum smelting, ferrosilicon production, geothermal power, tourism. **Natural resources:** fish,

hydropower, geothermal power, diatomite. **Exports:** $1.8 billion (f.o.b., 1996): fish and fish products, animal products, aluminum, ferrosilicon, diatomite. **Imports:** $2 billion (f.o.b., 1996): machinery and transportation equipment, petroleum products, foodstuffs, textiles. **Major trading partners:** U.K., Germany, U.S., Japan, Denmark, France, Norway, Sweden.

1. Including some offshore islands.

Geography Iceland, an island about the size of Kentucky, lies in the north Atlantic Ocean east of Greenland and just touches the Arctic Circle. It is one of the most volcanic regions in the world. The island is dotted with small freshwater lakes, and there are many natural phenomena, including hot springs, geysers, sulfur beds, canyons, waterfalls, and swift rivers. More than 13% of the area is covered by snowfields and glaciers, and most of the people live in the 7% of the island that is made up of fertile coastland. The Gulf stream keeps Iceland's climate milder than one would expect from an island near the Arctic Circle.

Government Constitutional republic.

History The earliest inhabitants of Iceland were Irish hermits, who left the island upon the arrival of the pagan Norse people in the late 9th century C.E. A constitution drawn up c. 930 created a form of democracy and provided for an *Althing*, the world's oldest practicing legislative assembly. The island's early history was preserved in the Icelandic sagas of the 13th century.

In 1262–64, Iceland came under Norwegian rule and passed to ultimate Danish control through the unification of the kingdoms of Norway, Sweden, and Denmark (the Kalmar Union) in 1397.

In 1874, Icelanders obtained their own constitution, and in 1918, Denmark recognized Iceland, via the Act of Union, as a separate state with unlimited sovereignty. It remained, however, nominally under the Danish monarchy.

During the German occupation of Denmark during World War II, British, then American, troops occupied Iceland and used it for a strategic air base. While officially neutral, Iceland cooperated with the Allies throughout the conflict. On June 17, 1944, after a popular referendum, the Althing proclaimed Iceland an independent republic.

The country joined the North Atlantic Treaty Organization in 1949, and subsequently received an American air force base in 1951. In 1970, it was admitted to the European Free Trade Association. Iceland unilaterally extended its territorial fishing limit from 3 to 200 nautical miles in 1972, precipitating a dispute with the U.K. known as the "cod wars," which ended in 1976, when the U.K. recognized the new limits. In 1980, the Icelanders elected a woman to the office of the presidency, the first elected female chief of state (i.e., president as distinct from prime minister) in the world.

After the recession of the early 1990s, Iceland began strengthening its economy. Government projections in mid-1997 showed that the country would have a large budget surplus for the year owing to fiscal management and a healthy economy. The government hoped to cut public spending further and boost the surplus.

India

REPUBLIC OF INDIA

National name: Bharat
President: K. R. Narayanan (1997)
Prime Minister: Atal Bihari Vajpayee (1998)
Area: 1,229,737 sq. mi. (3,287,590 sq. km)
Population (1999 est.): 1,000,848,550 (average annual rate of natural increase: 1.69%); birth rate: 25.4/1000; infant mortality rate: 60.8/1000; density per sq. mi.: 814
Capital (1991): New Delhi, 294,149. **Largest cities:** Bombay (Mumbai): city proper (1991 census) 9,925,891; metro. area (1996 est.) 15,725,000; Delhi: city proper (1991 census) 7,206,704; metro. area (1996 est.) 10,298,000; Calcutta: city proper (1991 census) 4,339,819; metro. area (1996 est.) 12,118,000; Madras (Chennai), 3,841,396; Hyderabad, 2,964,638; Ahmedabad, 2,876,710; Bangalore, 2,660,088; Kanpur, 1,874,409. **Monetary unit:** Rupee. **Principal languages:** Hindi (official), English (official), Bengali, Gujarati, Kashmiri, Malayalam, Marathi, Oriya, Punjabi, Tamil, Telugu, Urdu, Kannada, Assamese, Sanskrit, Sindhi (all recognized by the constitution). Dialects, 1,652. **Ethnicity/race:** Indo-Aryan 72%, Dravidian 25%, Mongoloid and other 3%. **Religions:** Hindu, 82.6%; Islam, 11.3%; Christian, 2.4%; Sikh, 2%; Buddhists, 0.71%; Jains, 0.48%. **Literacy rate:** 52%
Economic summary: GDP/PPP (1997 est.): $1.534 trillion; $1,600 per capita. **Real growth rate:** 5%. **Inflation:** 7%. **Unemployment:** n.a. **Arable land:** 56%. **Agriculture:** rice, wheat, oilseed, cotton, jute, tea, sugarcane, potatoes, cattle, water buffalo, sheep, goats, poultry, fish. **Labor force:** (1997 est.), 390 million; agriculture 67%, services 18%, industry 15% (1995 est.). **Industry:** textiles, chemicals, food processing, steel, transportation equipment, cement, mining, petroleum, machinery. **Natural resources:** coal, iron ore, manganese, mica, bauxite, titanium ore, chromite, natural gas, diamonds, petroleum, limestone. **Exports:** $33.9 billion (f.o.b., 1997): gems and jewelry, clothing, engineering goods, chemicals, leather manufactures, cotton yarn and fabric. **Imports:** $39.7 billion (c.i.f., 1997): crude oil and petroleum products, machinery, gems, fertilizer, chemicals. **Major trading partners:** U.S., Hong Kong, U.K., Germany, Belgium, Kuwait, Saudi Arabia, Japan. **Member of Commonwealth of Nations**

Geography One-third the area of the United States, the Republic of India occupies most of the subcontinent of India in south Asia. It borders on China in the northeast. Other neighbors are Pakistan on the west, Nepal and Bhutan on the north, and Burma and Bangladesh on the east.

The country can be divided into three distinct geographic regions: the Himalayan region in the north, which contains some of the highest mountains in the world, the Gangetic Plain, and the plateau region in the south and central part. Its three great river systems have extensive deltas and all rising in the Himalayas: the Ganges, 1,540 miles (2,478 km), the Indus, and the Brahmaputra.

India includes several groups of islands—the Laccadives (14 islands) in the Arabian Sea and the Andamans (204 islands) and the Nicobars (19 islands) in the Bay of Bengal.

Government Federal republic.

History One of the earliest civilizations, the Indus Valley civilization, flourished on the Indian subcontinent from c. 2600 B.C.E. to c. 2000 B.C.E. The Aryans who invaded India c. 1500 B.C.E. from the northwest found a land that was already home to an advanced civilization. They introduced Sanskrit and the Vedic religion, a forerunner of Hinduism, to the area. Buddhism was founded in the 6th century B.C.E. and spread throughout northern India, most notably by one of the great ancient kings of the Mauryan dynasty, Asoka (c. 269–232 B.C.E.), who also unified most of the Indian subcontinent for the first time.

In 1526, Muslim invaders founded the great Mogul empire, centered on Delhi, which lasted, at least in name, until 1857. Akbar the Great (1542–1605) strengthened and consolidated this empire. The long reign of his great-grandson, Aurangzeb (1618–1707), represents both the greatest extent of the Mogul empire and the beginning of its decay.

Vasco da Gama, the Portuguese explorer, visited India first in 1498, and for the next 100 years the Portuguese had a virtual monopoly on trade with the subcontinent. Meanwhile, the English founded the East India Company, which set up its first factory at Surat in 1612 and began expanding its influence, fighting the Indian rulers and the French, Dutch, and Portuguese traders simultaneously.

Bombay, taken from the Portuguese, became the seat of English rule in 1687. The defeat of French and Mogul armies by Lord Clive in 1757 laid the foundation of the British Empire in India. The East India Company continued to suppress native uprisings and extend British rule until 1858, when the administration of India was formally transferred to the British Crown following the Sepoy Mutiny of native troops in 1857–58.

After World War I, in which the Indian states sent more than 6 million troops to fight beside the Allies, Indian nationalist unrest rose to new heights under the leadership of a Hindu lawyer, Mohandas K. Gandhi, called Mahatma Gandhi. His philosophy of civil disobedience called for nonviolent noncooperation against British authority. He soon became the leading spirit of the Indian National Congress Party, which was the spearhead of revolt. In 1919 the British gave added responsibility to Indian officials, and in 1935 India was given a federal form of government and a measure of self-rule.

In 1942, with the Japanese pressing hard on the eastern borders of India, the British War Cabinet tried and failed to reach a political settlement with nationalist leaders. The Congress Party took the position that the British must quit India. In 1942, fearing mass civil disobedience, the government of India carried out widespread arrests of Congress leaders, including Gandhi.

Gandhi was released in 1944 and negotiations for a settlement were resumed. Finally, in Aug. 1947, India gained full independence. The victory was soured, however, by the partitioning of the predominantly Muslim regions of the north into the separate nation of Pakistan. The Muslim League, led by Mohammed Ali Jinnah, demanded a separate nation for the Muslim minority to prevent Hindu political and social domination. Indian Hindus, however, had hoped for a unified rather than balkanized Indian subcontinent. Lord Mountbatten as viceroy partitioned India along religious lines and split the provinces of Bengal and the Punjab, which both nations claimed. The partition of Pakistan and India led to the largest migration in human history, with 17 million people fleeing across the borders in both directions to escape the bloody riots occurring among sectarian groups. Armed conflict also broke out over rival claims to the princely states of Jammu and Kashmir.

Jawaharlal Nehru, nationalist leader and head of the Congress Party, was made prime minister. In 1949 a constitution, along the lines of the U.S. Constitution, was approved making India a sovereign republic. Under a federal structure the states were organized on linguistic lines. The dominance of the Congress Party contributed to stability. In 1956 the republic absorbed the former French settlements. Five years later, the republic forcibly annexed the Portuguese enclaves of Goa, Damao, and Diu.

Nehru died in 1964. His successor, Lal Bahadur Shastri, died on Jan. 10, 1966. Nehru's daughter, Indira Gandhi, became prime minister, and she continued his policy of nonalignment.

In 1971 the Pakistani army moved in to quash the independence movement in East Pakistan that was supported by India, and some 10 million Bengali refugees poured across the border into India, creating social, economic, and health problems. After numerous border incidents, India invaded East Pakistan and in two weeks forced the surrender of the Pakistani army. East Pakistan was established as an independent state and renamed Bangladesh.

In the summer of 1975, the world's largest democracy veered suddenly toward authoritarianism when a judge in Allahabad, Mrs. Gandhi's home constituency, found Gandhi's landslide victory in the 1971 elections invalid because civil servants had illegally aided her campaign. Amid demands for her resignation, Mrs. Gandhi decreed a state of emergency on June 26 and ordered mass arrests of her critics, including all opposition party leaders except the Communists.

Despite strong opposition to her repressive measures, particularly resentment against compulsory birth control programs, Mrs. Gandhi in 1977 announced parliamentary elections for March. At the same time, she freed most political prisoners. The landslide victory of Morarji R. Desai unseated Mrs. Gandhi, but she staged a spectacular comeback in the elections of Jan. 1980.

In 1984, she ordered the Indian army to root out a band of Sikh holy men and gunmen who were using the most sacred shrine of the Sikh religion, the Golden Temple in Amritsar, as a base for terrorist raids in a violent campaign for greater political autonomy in the strategic Punjab border state. The perceived sacrilege to the Golden Temple kindled outrage among many of India's 14 million Sikhs and brought a spasm of mutinies and desertions by Sikh officers and soldiers in the army.

On Oct. 31, 1984, Mrs. Gandhi was assassinated by two men identified by police as Sikh members of her bodyguard. The ruling Congress Party chose her older son, Rajiv Gandhi, to succeed her as prime minister for four years. While running for reelection, former prime minister Rajiv Gandhi was assassinated on May 22, 1991, by Tamil militants who objected to India's mediation of the civil war in Sri Lanka. Final phases of the election were postponed for a month. When they were resumed, the Congress Party and its allies won 236 seats in the lower house, 20 short of a majority. P. V. Narasimha Rao was chosen to form a new government.

The ruling Congress Party lost the parliamentary elections of May 1996, and its waning has resulted in a period of political instability. The Hindu nationalist

Bharatiya Janata Party's leader, Atal Bihari Vajpayee, became prime minister in May 1996, but his government lasted only 13 days. H. D. Deve Gowda of the United Front coalition became the next prime minister. Losing the support of the Congress Party, Prime Minister Deve Gowda lost a confidence vote in April 1997. Foreign Minister Inder Gujral was sworn in later that month, only to be replaced by Atal Vajpayee in March 1998, his second time as prime minister (his first term lasting less than two weeks). Vajpayee is the first Hindu nationalist to become prime minister, and the chauvinistic ideology of his party has made a number of Muslims and moderate Hindus uneasy.

In May 1998 India set off five nuclear tests, surprising the international community, which widely condemned India's pro-nuclear stance. Despite international urgings for restraint, Pakistan responded by conducting several nuclear tests of its own two weeks later. India has resisted signing the Comprehensive Test Ban Treaty for nuclear weapons and has been slapped with sanctions by the U.S. and other countries. Less than a year later, in April 1999, both India and Pakistan tested nuclear-capable ballistic missiles. On April 17, Prime Minister Atal Bihari Vajpayee's government lost a confidence vote, leaving India's government in disarray.

India and Pakistan have held various talks about the disputed territory of Kashmir, which is the issue at the base of their chronic antagonism as well as their recent displays of nuclear strength. India controls two-thirds of this Himalayan region, which is the only Indian state that is predominantly Muslim.

The Indian Air Force launched air strikes on May 26, 1999, and later sent in ground troops against Islamic guerrilla forces in Kashmir. India blamed Pakistan for orchestrating the attacks by sending soldiers and mercenaries across the so-called Line of Control that divides Kashmir between India and Pakistan. Pakistan countered that the guerrillas are independent Kashmiri freedom fighters struggling for India's ouster from the region. Most international sources agreed with India's assumption that Pakistan was arming the soldiers. In Aug. Pakistan was forced to withdraw.

Native States Most of the 560-odd native states and subdivisions of pre-1947 India acceded to the new nation, and the central government pursued a vigorous policy of integration. This took three forms: merger into adjacent provinces, conversion into centrally administered areas, and grouping into unions of states. Finally, under a controversial reorganization plan effective on Nov. 1, 1956, the unions of states were abolished and merged into adjacent states, and India became a union of 15 states and 8 centrally administered areas. A 16th state was added in 1962, and in 1966, the Punjab was partitioned into two states. Today India consists of 25 states and 7 Union Territories.

In April 1975, the Indian Parliament voted to make the 300-year-old kingdom of Sikkim a full-fledged Indian state, and the annexation took effect on May 16. Situated in the Himalayas, Sikkim was a virtual dependency of Tibet until the early 19th century. Under an 1890 treaty between China and Great Britain, it became a British protectorate, and was made an Indian protectorate after Britain quit the subcontinent.

Indonesia

REPUBLIC OF INDONESIA

National name: Republik Indonesia
President: Bacharuddin Jusuf Habibie (1998)
Area: 735,268 sq. mi. (1,919,440 sq. km)[1]
Population (1999 est.): 216,108,345 (average annual rate of natural increase: 1.46%); birth rate: 22.8/1000; infant mortality rate: 57.3/1000; density per sq. mi.: 294
Capital and largest city: Jakarta: city proper (1995 est.) 9,160,500; metro. area (1995 est.) 11,500,000. **Other large cities (1995 est.):** Surabaya, 2,701,300; Bandung, 2,368,200; Medan, 1,909,700; Semarang, 1,366,500. **Monetary unit:** Rupiah. **Languages:** Bahasa Indonesia (official), Dutch, English, and more than 583 languages and dialects. **Ethnicity/race:** Javanese 45%, Sundanese 14%, Madurese 7.5%, coastal Malays 7.5%, other 26%. **Religions:** Islam, 87%; Christian, 9%; Hindu, 2%; other, 2%. **Literacy rate:** 84%
Economic summary: GDP/PPP (1997 est.): $960 billion; $4,600 per capita. **Real growth rate:** 4%. **Inflation:** 50% (1998 est.). **Unemployment:** (1998 est.) 15%, underemployment 50%. **Arable land:** 10%. **Agriculture:** rice, cassava (tapioca), peanuts, rubber, cocoa, coffee, palm oil, copra, other tropical products, poultry, beef, pork, eggs. **Labor force:** 67 million; agriculture 44%, manufacturing 13%, construction 5%, transport and communications 4%, other 34% (1995 est.). **Industry:** petroleum and natural gas, textiles, mining, cement, chemical fertilizers, plywood, food, rubber, tourism. **Natural resources:** petroleum, tin, natural gas, nickel, timber, bauxite, copper, fertile soils, coal, gold, silver. **Exports:** $53.4 billion (f.o.b., 1997): textiles/garments, wood products, electronics, footwear. **Imports:** $41.6 billion (f.o.b., 1997): manufactures, raw materials, foodstuffs, fuels. **Major trading partners:** Japan, U.S., Singapore, South Korea, Taiwan, China, Hong Kong, Germany, Australia.

1. Includes West Irian (former Netherlands New Guinea), renamed Irian Jaya in March 1973 (159,355 sq. mi.; 421,981 sq. km), and former Portuguese Timor (5,763 sq. mi.; 14,874 sq. km), annexed in 1976.

Geography Indonesia is an archipelago in Southeast Asia consisting of 17,000 islands (6,000 inhabited) and straddles the equator. The largest islands are Sumatra, Java (the most populous), Bali, Kalimantan (Indonesia's part of Borneo), Sulawesi (Celebes), the Nusa Tenggara islands, the Maluku Islands, and Irian Jaya (western part of New Guinea). Its neighbor to the north is Malaysia and to the east is Papua New Guinea.

Indonesia, part of the "ring of fire," has the largest number of active volcanoes in the world. Earthquakes are frequent. The "Wallace Line," a zoological demarcation between Asian and Australian flora and fauna, divides Indonesia.

Government Republic.

History The 17,000 islands that make up Indonesia were home to a diversity of cultures and indigenous beliefs when the islands came under the influence of Hindu priests and traders in the first and second centuries C.E. Muslim invasions began in the 13th century, and most of the archipelago had converted to Islam by the 15th. Portuguese traders arrived early in the next century but were ousted by the Dutch around 1595. The Dutch United East India Company established posts on the island of Java, in an effort to control the spice trade.

After Napoléon subjugated The Netherlands in 1811, the British seized the islands but returned them to the Dutch in 1816. In 1922 Indonesia was made an integral part of the Dutch kingdom. During World War II, Japan seized the islands. Tokyo was primarily interested in Indonesia's oil, which was vital to the war effort, and tolerated fledgling nationalists such as Sukarno and Mohammed Hatta. After Japan's surrender, Sukarno and Hatta proclaimed Indonesian independence on Aug. 17, 1945. Allied troops, mostly British Indian forces, fought nationalist militia to reassert the prewar status quo until the arrival of Dutch troops.

In Nov. 1946, a draft agreement on forming a Netherlands-Indonesian Union was reached, but differences in interpretation resulted in more fighting between Dutch and nationalist forces. Following a bitter war for independence, leaders on both sides agreed to terms of a union on Nov. 2, 1949. The transfer of sovereignty took place at Amsterdam on Dec. 27, 1949. In Feb. of 1956 Indonesia abrogated the union, and began seizing Dutch property in the islands.

In 1963, Netherlands New Guinea (the Dutch portion of the island of New Guinea) was transferred to Indonesia and renamed West Irian, which became Irian Jaya in 1973. Hatta and Sukarno, the cofathers of Indonesian independence, split over Sukarno's concept of "guided democracy," and under Sukarno's rule the Indonesian Communist Party (PKI) steadily increased its influence.

Three years later, Sukarno was named president for life. Sukarno enjoyed mass support for his policies, but a growing power struggle between the military and the PKI loomed over his government. After an attempted military coup was put down by army chief of staff General Suharto and officers loyal to him, Suharto's forces killed hundreds of thousands of suspected Communists in a massive purge aimed at undermining Sukarno's rule.

Suharto took over the reins of government and gradually eased Sukarno out of office, completing his consolidation of power in 1967. Under Suharto the military assumed an overarching role in national affairs, and relations with the West were enhanced. Indonesia's economy improved dramatically and national elections were permitted, although the opposition was so tightly controlled as to virtually choke off dissent.

In 1975, Indonesia invaded the former Portuguese half of the island of Timor and seized the territory in 1976. A separatist movement developed at once. Unlike the rest of Indonesia, which had been a Dutch colony, East Timor was governed by the Portuguese for 400 years, and although 90% of Indonesians are Muslim, the East Timor are primarily Catholic. More than 200,000 Timorese are reported to have died from famine, disease, and fighting since the annexation. East Timor has received international attention for human rights abuses, and in 1996 two East Timorese resistance activists, Bishop Carlos Filipe Ximenes Belo and José Ramos-Horta, received the Nobel Peace Prize.

In the summer of 1997, Indonesia suffered a major economic setback along with most other Asian economies. Banks failed and the value of Indonesia's currency, the rupiah, plummeted. Antigovernment demonstrations took to the streets and riots broke out, directed mainly at the country's prosperous ethnic Chinese. As the economic crisis deepened, student demonstrators occupied the national Parliament, demanding Suharto's ouster. On May 21, 1998,

Suharto stepped down, ending 32 years of rule and handing over power to Vice President B. J. Habibie. The Asian economic crisis hit Indonesia the hardest, and in 1998 one in five jobs were lost. Student unrest continued after Suharto's downfall, although the students' agenda for reform was vague.

June 7, 1999, marked Indonesia's first free parliamentary election since 1955. The ruling Golkar Party took a backseat to the Indonesian Democracy Party-Struggle (PDI-P), led by Megawati Sukarnoputri, the daughter of Sukarno, Indonesia's first president. She had been the head of the PDI in 1994 until Suharto had her removed. Presidential elections are expected in Nov. 1999.

Aceh, Ambon (in the Moluccas), Borneo, and Irian Jaya saw rioting and violence in 1999. But nowhere was the violence more brutal and unjust than in East Timor. Habibie at first showed a softening of Indonesia's position on East Timor, unexpectedly announcing in Feb. 1999 that he was willing to hold a referendum on East Timorese independence. Despite the good news, the sudden Indonesian about-face was accompanied by heightened fighting between separatist guerrillas and pro-Indonesian paramilitary forces, who were armed by the Indonesian military. Twice rescheduled because of violence, a U.N.-organized referendum took place on Aug. 30, 1999, with 79% of the population voting to secede from Indonesia. In the days following the election, pro-Indonesian militias and Indonesian soldiers massacred civilians and forced a third of the population out of the region. Despite repeated assurances that order would be restored to the region, Habibie and the head of the military, Gen. Wiranto, were either unwilling or unable to stop the violent rampage. After enormous international pressure, Indonesia finally agreed to allow U.N. forces into East Timor on Sept. 12. Led by Australia, an international peacekeeping force began restoring order to the ravaged region.

Iran

ISLAMIC REPUBLIC OF IRAN

Chief of State: Ayatollah Khamenei (1989)
President: Mohammad Khatami (1997)
Area: 636,293 sq. mi. (1,648,000 sq. km)
Population (1999 est.): 65,179,752 (average annual rate of natural increase: 1.53%); birth rate: 20.7/1000; infant mortality rate: 29.7/1000; density per sq. mi.: 102
Capital: Teheran. **Largest cities (1994 est.):** Teheran, 6,750,043; Mashad, 1,964,489; Isfahan, 1,220,595; Tabriz, 1,166,203. **Monetary unit:** Rial. **Languages:** Farsi (Persian), Azari, Kurdish, Arabic. **Ethnicity/race:** Persian 51%, Azerbaijani 24%, Gilaki and Mazandarani 8%, Kurd 7%, Arab 3%, Lur 2%, Baloch 2%, Turkmen 2%, other 1%. **Religions:** Shi'ite Muslim, 95%; Sunni Muslim, 4%. **Literacy rate:** 54% (1996)
Economic summary: GDP/PPP (1997 est.): $371.2 billion; $5,500 per capita. **Real growth rate:** 3.2%. **Inflation:** 23% (1996). **Unemployment:** over 30% (1/98 est.). **Arable land:** 10%. **Agriculture:** wheat, rice, other grains, sugar beets, fruits, nuts, cotton, dairy products, wool, caviar. **Labor force:** 15.4 million; agriculture, 33%; manufacturing, 21% (1988 est.). **Industry:** petroleum, petrochemicals, textiles, cement and other construction materials, food processing, metal fabricating, armaments. **Natural resources:** petroleum, natural gas, coal, chromium, copper, iron ore, lead, manganese, zinc, sulfur. **Exports:** $19 billion (f.o.b., 1997 est.): petroleum, carpets, fruits, nuts,

hides, iron, steel. **Imports:** $15.6 billion (f.o.b., 1997 est.): machinery, military supplies, metalworks, foodstuffs, pharmaceuticals, technical services, refined oil products. **Major trading partners:** Japan, U.S., U.K., Germany, South Korea, U.A.E., Italy, Belgium.

Geography　Iran, a Middle Eastern country south of the Caspian Sea and north of the Persian Gulf, is three times the size of Arizona. It shares borders with Iraq, Turkey, Azerbaijan, Turkmenistan, Armenia, Afghanistan, and Pakistan.

In general, the country is a plateau averaging 4,000 feet (1,219 m) in elevation. There are also maritime lowlands along the Persian Gulf and the Caspian Sea. The Elburz Mountains in the north rise to 18,603 feet (5,670 m) at Mount Damavend. From northwest to southeast, the country is crossed by a desert 800 miles (1,287 km) long.

Government　Iran has been an Islamic theocracy since the Pahlavi monarchy regime was overthrown on Feb. 11, 1979.

History　The region now called Iran was occupied by the Medes and the Persians in the 1500s B.C.E., until the Persian king Cyrus the Great overthrew the Medes and became ruler of the Achaemenid (Persian) Empire, which reached from the Indus to the Nile at its zenith in 525 B.C.E. Persia fell to Alexander in 331–330 B.C.E., and a succession of other rulers: the Seleucids (312–302 B.C.E.), the Greek-speaking Parthians (247 B.C.E.–C.E. 226), the Sasanians, and the Arab Muslims (in 641). By the mid-800s Persia had become an international scientific and cultural center. In the 12th century it was invaded by the Mongols. The Safavid dynasty (1501–1722), under whom the dominant religion became Shi'ite Islam, followed, and was then replaced by the Qajar Dynasty (1794–1925).

During the Qajar dynasty, the Russians and the British fought for economic control of the area, and during World War I Iran's neutrality did not stop it from becoming a battlefield for Russian and British troops. A coup in 1921 brought Reza Kahn to power. In 1925 he became shah and changed his name to Reza Shah Pahlavi. He subsequently did much to modernize the country and abolished all foreign extraterritorial rights.

The country's pro-Axis allegiance in World War II led to Anglo-Russian occupation of Iran in 1941 and deposition of the shah in favor of his son, Mohammed Reza Pahlavi. Pahlavi's Westernization programs alienated the clergy, and his authoritarian rule led to massive demonstrations during the 1970s, to which the shah responded with the imposition of martial law in Sept. 1978. The shah and his family fled Iran on Jan. 16, 1979, and the exiled cleric Ayatollah Ruhollah Khomeini returned to establish an Islamic theocracy. Khomeini proceeded with his plans for revitalizing Islamic traditions. He urged women to return to the veil, banned alcohol, Western music, and mixed bathing, shut down the media, closed universities, and eliminated political parties. Revolutionary militants invaded the U.S. embassy in Teheran on Nov. 4, 1979, seized staff members as hostages, and precipitated an international crisis. Khomeini refused all appeals, even a unanimous vote by the U.N. Security Council demanding immediate release of the hostages. Iranian hostility toward Washington was reinforced by the Carter administration's economic boycott and deportation order against Iranian students in the U.S., the break in diplomatic relations, and ultimately an aborted U.S. raid in April aimed at rescuing the hostages.

As the first anniversary of the embassy seizure neared, Khomeini and his followers insisted on their original conditions: guarantee by the U.S. not to interfere in Iran's affairs, cancellation of U.S. damage claims against Iran, release of $8 billion in frozen Iranian assets, an apology, and the return of the assets held by the former imperial family. These conditions were largely met and the 52 American hostages were released on Jan. 20, 1980, ending 444 days in captivity.

The sporadic war with Iraq regained momentum in 1982, as Iran launched an offensive in March and regained much of the border area occupied by Iraq in late 1980. The stalemated war with Iraq dragged on well into 1988. Although Iraq expressed its willingness to cease fighting, Iran stated that it would not stop the war until Iraq agreed to pay for war damages, and to punish the Iraqi government leaders involved in the conflict. On July 20, 1988, Khomeini, after a series of Iranian military reverses, agreed to cease-fire negotiations with Iraq. A cease-fire went into effect on Aug. 20, 1988. Khomeini died in June 1989 and Ayotollah Khamenei succeeded him as the supreme leader.

By early 1991 the Islamic revolution appeared to have lost much of its militancy. Attempting to revive a stagnant economy, President Rafsanjani took measures to decentralize the command system and introduce free-market mechanisms.

Mohammad Khatami, a little-known moderate cleric, former newspaperman, and national librarian, won the presidential election with 70% of the vote on May 23, 1997, a stunning victory over the conservative ruling elite. Khatami has supported greater social and political freedoms, and has made overtures for friendlier relations with the West.

His steps at liberalizing the strict clerical rule governing the country has put him at odds with the supreme leader, Ayatollah Khamenei. In 1998, Tehran mayor Gholam-Hossein Karbaschi, a strong supporter of Khatami's liberalization process, was sentenced to prison for embezzlement. Many saw this as a politically motivated attack aimed at Khatami.

In Sept. 1998 Iran deployed thousands of troops on its border with Afghanistan after the Taliban admitted killing eight Iranian diplomats and a journalist. Iran, mainly Shi'ite, supports the rebels fighting against the extremist Sunni Taliban.

In July 1999, pro-democracy students held a demonstration to protest the closure of a reformist newspaper. Once security forces entered the fray, however, the demonstration turned into six days of rioting, leading to the arrest of more than 1,000 students.

While students and other liberals have been pressuring President Khatami to implement greater freedoms, Iran's military, the Revolutionary Guard, has warned him of their growing impatience with his reformist measures. Khatami has struggled to keep to a middle course, and has characterized Iran as passing through a difficult transitional period that has necessarily provoked tension between hardliners and liberals. His goal is to ensure that Iran eventually emerges as a nation of "lasting pluralism and Islamic democracy."

Iraq

REPUBLIC OF IRAQ

National name: Jumhouriyat Al Iraq
President: Saddam Hussein (1979)
Area: 167,920 sq. mi. (437,072 sq. km)
Population (1999 est.): 22,427,150 (average annual rate of natural increase: 3.19%); birth rate: 38.4/1000; infant mortality rate: 62.4/1000; density per sq. mi.: 134
Capital: Baghdad. **Largest cities (est. 1987):** Baghdad, 3,841,136; Mosul, 664,221; Irbil, 485,968; Karkuk (Kirkuk), 418,624; Basra, 406,296. **Monetary unit:** Iraqi dinar. **Languages:** Arabic (official) and Kurdish. **Ethnicity/race:** Arab 75%–80%, Kurdish 15%–20%, Turkoman, Assyrian or other 5%. **Religions:** Muslim 97% (Shi'ite 60%–65%, Sunni 32%–37%), Christian or other 3%. **Literacy rate:** 60%
Economic summary: GDP/PPP (1997 est.): $42.8 billion, $2,000 per capita. **Real growth rate:** 0%. **Inflation:** n.a. **Unemployment:** n.a. **Arable land:** 12%. **Agriculture:** wheat, barley, rice, vegetables, dates, other fruit, cotton, cattle, sheep. **Labor force:** 4.4 million (1989); services, 48%; agriculture, 30%; industry, 22%. **Industry:** petroleum, chemicals, textiles, construction materials, food processing. **Exports:** n.a.; crude oil. **Imports:** n.a.; manufactures, food. **Major trading partners:** Jordan, Turkey, France, Vietnam, Australia.

Geography Iraq, a triangle of mountains, desert, and fertile river valley, is bounded on the east by Iran, on the north by Turkey, on the west by Syria and Jordan, and on the south by Saudi Arabia and Kuwait. It is twice the size of Idaho. The country has arid desert land west of the Euphrates, a broad central valley between the Euphrates and Tigris, and mountains in the northeast.

Government One-party republic.

History From earliest times Iraq was known as Mesopotamia—the land between the rivers—for it embraces a large part of the alluvial plains of the Tigris and Euphrates Rivers.

An advanced civilization existed by 4000 B.C.E. Sometime after 2000 B.C.E. the land became the center of the ancient Babylonian and Assyrian Empires. Mesopotamia was conquered by Cyrus the Great of Persia in 538 B.C.E., and by Alexander in 331 B.C.E. After an Arab conquest in C.E. 637–40, Baghdad became capital of the ruling caliphate. The country was cruelly pillaged by the Mongols in 1258, and during the 16th, 17th, and 18th centuries was the object of repeated Turkish-Persian competition.

Nominal Turkish suzerainty imposed in 1638 was replaced by direct Turkish rule in 1831. In World War I, Britain occupied most of Mesopotamia and was given a mandate over the area in 1920. The British renamed the area Iraq and recognized it as a kingdom in 1922. In 1932 the monarchy achieved full independence. Britain again occupied Iraq during World War II because of its pro-Axis stance in the initial years of the war.

Iraq became a charter member of the Arab League in 1945, and Iraqi troops took part in the Arab invasion of Palestine in 1948.

King Faisal II, born on May 2, 1935, succeeded his father, Ghazi I, who was killed in an automobile accident on April 4, 1939. Faisal and his uncle, Crown Prince Abdul-Illah, were assassinated in July 1958 in a swift revolutionary coup that ended the monarchy and brought to power a military junta headed by Abdul Karem Kassim. Kassim reversed the monar-

chy's pro-Western policies, attempted to rectify the economic disparities between rich and poor, and began to form alliances with Communist countries.

Kassim was overthrown and killed in a coup staged on March 8, 1963, by the Ba'ath Socialist Party. Abdel Salam Arif, a leader in the 1958 coup, staged another coup in Nov. 1963, driving the Ba'ath members of the revolutionary council from power. He adopted a new constitution in 1964. In 1966, he, two cabinet members, and other supporters died in a helicopter crash. His brother, Gen. Abdel Rahman Arif, assumed the presidency, crushed the opposition, and won an indefinite extension of his term in 1967.

His regime was ousted in July 1968 by a junta led by Maj. Gen. Ahmed Hassan al-Bakr of the Ba'ath Party. Bakr and his second-in-command, Saddam Hussein, imposed authoritarian rule in an effort to end the decades of political instability that followed World War II.

One of the world's leading producers of oil, Iraq's oil revenues were used to develop one of the strongest military forces in the region. On July 16, 1979, President Bakr was succeeded by Saddam Hussein, whose regime eventually developed an international reputation for repression, human rights abuses, and terrorism.

A long-standing territorial dispute over control of the Shatt-al-Arab waterway between Iraq and Iran broke into full-scale war on Sept. 20, 1980. Iraqi planes attacked Iranian airfields and the Abadan refinery, and Iraqi ground forces moved into Iran. Despite the smaller size of its armed forces, Iraq took and held the initiative by seizing Abadan and Khurramshahr together with substantial Iranian territory by Dec., and beating back Iranian counterattacks in Jan.

In 1982, the Iraqis fell back to their own country and dug themselves in behind sandbagged defensive fortifications. From the beginning of the war in Sept. 1980 to Sept. 1984, foreign military analysts estimated that more than 150,000 Iraqis had been killed. The Iraqis clearly wanted to end the war, but the Iranians refused. In Feb. 1986, Iranian forces gained on two fronts; but Iraq retook most of the lost ground in 1988 and a cease-fire took effect that Aug.

In July 1990, President Hussein claimed that Kuwait was flooding world markets with oil and forcing down prices. A mediation attempt by Arab leaders failed, and on Aug. 2, 1990, over this and territorial claims, Iraqi troops invaded Kuwait and set up a puppet government. On Jan. 18, 1991, U.N. forces, under the leadership of U.S. General Norman Schwarzkopf, launched Operation Desert Storm, liberating Kuwait in less than a week.

Despite rebellions by both Shi'ites and Kurds following Iraq's crushing defeat in the Gulf War, Saddam Hussein maintained his draconian grip on Iraq. The U.N. Security Council has barred Iraq from selling oil except in exchange for food and medicine. Despite the debilitating effects of U.N. sanctions, Hussein continued to defy the terms of the cease-fire agreement, waging a propaganda campaign that blamed the U.S. for the starvation and poverty suffered by the Iraqi people rather than his own refusal to meet the terms required to remove sanctions. Several minor military skirmishes between Iraqi and U.S. forces have resulted.

On Nov. 13, 1997, Iraq expelled the American members of the U.N. inspection team mandated to ascertain that Iraq has destroyed all its nuclear, chemical, biological, and ballistic arms. Under the 1991 cease-fire resolution, the U.N. would not lift sanctions until Iraq fully complied. The standoff stretched on over months and as tensions rose, the U.S. began a military buildup in the Gulf. In Feb. 1998 U.N. secretary-general Kofi Annan brokered a peaceful solution to the stand-off. Over the next months Baghdad continued to impede the U.N. inspection team, demanding that sanctions be lifted. Finally, in Aug. 1998 Hussein put a complete halt to the inspections. This time, the U.S. opted for diplomatic arm-twisting rather than military threats, and in Sept. the U.N. Security Council voted unanimously that the lifting of sanctions would not be discussed until cooperation with U.N. arms inspectors resumed

On Oct. 31 the United States and Britain threatened Iraq with the possibility of a military strike if it did not begin cooperating. On Nov. 14 Iraq agreed to unconditional cooperation with the U.N. inspectors, and the United States and Britain called off planned military action. But on Dec. 15, chief U.N. weapons inspector Richard Butler reported that Iraq had not lived up to its promise. The following day the United States and Britain began four days of air strikes, which ended on Dec. 19, the day before the Islamic holy month of Ramadan began. The attacks focused on command centers, missile factories, and airfields—targets that the Pentagon believed would damage Iraq's weapons stores.

Since then, the U.S. and Britain have waged a war of attrition against Iraq, conducting almost daily bombings of Iraqi targets within the no-fly zones that were established after the 1991 Gulf War. Although the international community had largely condemned the four days of bombing in Dec., it has remained almost indifferent to the hundreds of air strikes that have been launched since then. The press virtually ignored the bombings, particularly during the Kosovo crisis.

The aim of the British and American military appeared to be to continue the sustained, low-level warfare in an effort to erode Iraqi military strength and, if fortunate, drive Hussein from power. The U.N. remains divided on how to handle the humanitarian situation in Iraq and on the issue of U.N. arms inspections.

Ireland

National name: Ireland, or Eire in the Irish language
President: Mary McAleese (1997)
Taoiseach (Prime Minister): Bertie Ahern (1997)
Area: 27,136 sq. mi. (70,280 sq. km)
Population (1999 est.): 3,632,944 (average annual rate of natural increase: 0.52%); birth rate: 13.6/1000; infant mortality rate: 5.9/1000; density per sq. mi.: 134
Capital: Dublin. **Largest cities (1991):** Dublin, 1,056,666; Cork, 293,254; Galway, 131,503; Limerick, 112,975. **Monetary units:** Irish pound (punt) and euro. **Languages:** English, Irish Gaelic. **Ethnicity/race:** Celtic, English. **Religions:** Roman Catholic 93%, Anglican 3%, none 1%, unknown 2%, other 1%. **Literacy rate:** 98%
Economic summary: GDP/PPP (1997 est.): $59.9 billion; $18,600 per capita. **Real growth rate:** 6%. **Inflation:** 1.6%. **Unemployment:** 11.8%. **Arable land:** 13%. **Agriculture:** turnips, barley, potatoes, sugar

beets, wheat, meat and dairy products. **Labor force:** (1997 est.), 1.52 million; services, 62.1% manufacturing and construction, 27%; agriculture, forestry, and fishing, 10%; utilities, 0.9%. **Industries:** food products, brewing, textiles, clothing, chemicals, pharmaceuticals, machinery, transportation equipment, glass and crystal. **Natural resources:** zinc, lead, natural gas, barite, copper, gypsum, limestone, dolomite, peat, silver. **Exports:** $54.8 billion (f.o.b., 1997): chemicals, data processing equipment, industrial machinery, live animals, animal products. **Imports:** $44.9 billion (c.i.f., 1997): food, animal feed, data processing equipment, petroleum and petroleum products, machinery, textiles, clothing. **Major trading partners:** EU (U.K., Germany, France), U.S.

Geography Ireland is situated in the Atlantic Ocean and separated from Great Britain by the Irish Sea. Half the size of Arkansas, it occupies the entire island except for the six counties that make up Northern Ireland. Ireland resembles a basin—a central plain rimmed with mountains, except in the Dublin region. The mountains are low, with the highest peak, Carrantuohill in County Kerry, rising to 3,415 feet (1,041 m). The principal river is the Shannon, which begins in the north-central area, flows south and southwest for about 240 miles (386 km), and empties into the Atlantic.

Government Republic.

History In the Stone and Bronze Ages, Ireland was inhabited by Picts in the north and a people called the Erainn in the south, the same stock, apparently, as in all the isles before the Anglo-Saxon invasion of Britain. About the 4th century B.C.E., tall, red-haired Celts arrived from Gaul or Galicia. They subdued and assimilated the inhabitants and established a Gaelic civilization. By the beginning of the Christian Era, Ireland was divided into five kingdoms—Ulster, Connacht, Leinster, Meath, and Munster. Saint Patrick introduced Christianity in C.E. 432 and the country developed into a center of Gaelic and Latin learning. Irish monasteries, the equivalent of universities, attracted intellectuals as well as the pious and sent out missionaries to many parts of Europe and, some believe, to North America.

Norse depredations along the coasts, starting in 795, ended in 1014 with Norse defeat at the Battle of Clontarf by forces under Brian Boru. In the 12th century, the pope gave all of Ireland to the English Crown as a papal fief. In 1171, Henry II of England was acknowledged "Lord of Ireland," but local sectional rule continued for centuries, and English control over the whole island was not reasonably absolute until the 17th century. In the Battle of the Boyne (1690), the Catholic King James II and his French supporters were defeated by the Protestant King William III (of Orange).

By the Act of Union (1801), England and Ireland became the "United Kingdom of Great Britain and Ireland." A steady decline in the Irish economy followed in the next decades. The population had reached 8.25 million when the great potato famine of 1846–48 took many lives and drove more than 2 million people to immigrate to North America.

In the meantime, anti-British agitation continued along with demands for Irish home rule. The advent of World War I delayed the institution of home rule and resulted in the Easter Rebellion in Dublin (April 24–29, 1916), in which Irish nationalists unsuccessfully attempted to throw off British rule. Guerrilla warfare against British forces followed proclamation of a republic by the rebels in 1919. The Irish Free State was established as a dominion on Dec. 6, 1922, with the six northern counties remaining as part of the United Kingdom. The constitution of 1937 changed the nation's name to Éire. Ireland was neutral in World War II.

In 1948, Eamon de Valera, American-born leader of the Sinn Fein, who had won the establishment of the Free State in 1921 in negotiations with Britain's David Lloyd George, was defeated by John A. Costello, who demanded final independence from Britain. The Republic of Ireland was proclaimed on April 18, 1949. It withdrew from the Commonwealth, but in 1955 Ireland entered the United Nations. Throughout the 1960s, two antagonistic currents dominated Irish politics. One sought to bind the wounds of the rebellion and civil war. The other was the effort of the outlawed Irish Republican Army to bring Northern Ireland into the republic.

Under the First Programme for Economic Expansion (1958–63), economic protection was dismantled and foreign investment encouraged. This prosperity brought profound social and cultural changes to what had been one of the poorest and least technologically advanced countries in Europe. Ireland joined the European Economic Community (now the EU) in 1973. In the 1990 presidential election, Mary Robinson was elected the republic's first woman president. The election of a candidate with socialist and feminist sympathies was regarded as a watershed in Irish political life, reflecting the changes taking place in Irish society. Irish voters approved the Maastricht Treaty, which paved the way for the establishment of the EU, by a large majority in a referendum held in 1992. In 1993, the Irish and British governments signed a joint peace initiative (the Downing Street Declaration), in which they pledged to seek mutually agreeable political structures in Northern Ireland and between the two islands. A referendum on allowing divorce under certain conditions—hitherto constitutionally forbidden—was held in Nov. 1995 and narrowly passed.

In 1998 hope for a solution to the troubles in Northern Ireland seemed palpable. A landmark settlement, the Good Friday Accord of April 10, 1998, came after 22 months of intensive negotiations that involved eight of the ten Northern Irish political parties. Chaired by former U.S. senator George Mitchell, the talks were advanced by a high-profile set of mediators, including British prime minister Tony Blair, Irish prime minister Bertie Ahern, and President Bill Clinton. The accord called for Protestants to share political power with the minority Catholics, and gave the Republic of Ireland a voice in Northern Irish affairs. The resounding commitment to the settlement was demonstrated in a dual referendum on May 22: the North approved the accord by a vote of 71% to 29%, and in the Irish Republic 94% favored it. Although the process of forming the new coalition government proceeded over the course of the year, it came crashing down in July 1999, the very month the nascent government was to assemble for the first time. The sticking point was the timetable for the I.R.A.'s disarmament: Sinn Fein insisted the I.R.A. would begin giving up its illegal weapons after the new government formed; Unionists demanded disarmament first.

Israel

STATE OF ISRAEL

National name: Medinat Yisra'el
President: Ezer Weizman (1993)
Prime Minister: Ehud Barak (1999)
Area: 8,020 sq. mi. (20,770 sq. km)
Population (1999 est.): 5,749,760[1] (average annual rate of natural increase: 1.37%); birth rate: 19.8/1000; infant mortality rate: 7.8/1000; density per sq. mi.: 717
Capital and largest city (1993 est.): Jerusalem[2], 550,500. **Other large cities (1993 est.):** Tel Aviv, 355,900; Haifa, 250,000. **Monetary unit:** Shekel.
Languages: Hebrew, Arabic, English. **Ethnicity/race:** Jewish 82% (Israel-born 50%, Europe/Americas/Oceania-born 20%, Africa-born 7%, Asia-born 5%), non-Jewish 18% (mostly Arab) (1993 est.). **Religions:** Judaism, 82%; Islam, 14%; Christian, 2%; others, 2%. **Literacy rate:** 92%
Economic summary: GDP/PPP (1997 est.): $96.7 billion; $17,500 per capita. **Real growth rate:** 1.9%. **Inflation:** 9%. **Unemployment:** 7.7%. **Arable land:** 17%. **Agriculture:** citrus and other fruits, vegetables, cotton, beef, poultry, dairy products. **Labor force:** (1997), 2.3 million; public services, 31.3%; manufacturing, 20.2%; finance and business, 13.1%; commerce, 12.8%; construction, 7.5%; personal and other services, 6.4%; transport, storage, and communications, 6.2%; agriculture, forestry, and fishing, 2.6%. **Industry:** food processing, diamond cutting and polishing, textiles and apparel, chemicals, metal products, military equipment, transport equipment, electrical equipment, potash mining, high-technology electronics, tourism. **Natural resources:** copper, phosphates, bromide, potash, clay, sand, sulfur, asphalt, manganese, small amounts of natural gas and crude oil. **Exports:** $20.7 billion (f.o.b., 1997): machinery and equipment, cut diamonds, chemicals, textiles and apparel, agricultural products, metals. **Imports:** $28.6 billion (c.i.f., 1997): military equipment, investment goods, rough diamonds, oil, consumer goods. **Major trading partners:** EU, U.S., Japan.

1. Includes West Bank, Gaza Strip, East Jerusalem. 2. Not recognized by U.S., which recognizes Tel Aviv.

Geography Israel, slightly larger than Massachusetts, lies at the eastern end of the Mediterranean Sea. It is bordered by Egypt on the west, Syria and Jordan on the east, and Lebanon on the north. Northern Israel is largely a plateau traversed from north to south by mountains and broken by great depressions, also running from north to south.

The maritime plain of Israel is remarkably fertile. The southern Negev region, which comprises almost half the total area, is largely a wide desert steppe area. Parts of it have been irrigated and cultivated. The Jordan, the only important river, flows from the north through Lake Hule (Waters of Merom) and Lake Kinneret (Sea of Galilee or Sea of Tiberias), finally entering the Dead Sea, 1,312 feet (400 m) below sea level. This "sea," which is actually a salt lake (394 sq. mi.; 1,020 sq. km), has no outlet, its water balance being maintained by evaporation.

Government Republic.

History Palestine, considered a holy land by Jews, Muslims, and Christians, and homeland of the modern state of Israel, was known as Canaan to the ancient Hebrews. Palestine's name derives from the Philistines, a people who occupied the southern coastal part of the country in the 12th century B.C.E.

A Hebrew kingdom established in 1000 B.C.E. was later split into the kingdoms of Judah and Israel; they were subsequently invaded by Assyrians, Babylonians, Egyptians, Persians, Romans, and Alexander the Great of Macedonia. By C.E. 135, few Jews were left in Palestine; most lived in the scattered and tenacious communities of the Diaspora. Palestine became a center of Christian pilgrimage after the emperor Constantine converted to that faith. The Arabs took Palestine from the Byzantine empire in C.E. 634–40. Interrupted only by Christian Crusaders, Muslims ruled Palestine until the 20th century (Turkish rule from 1516). During World War I, British forces defeated the Turks in Palestine and governed the area under a League of Nations mandate from 1923.

As part of the 19th-century Zionist movement, Jews had begun settling in Palestine as early as 1820. This effort to establish a Jewish homeland had received British approval in the Balfour Declaration of 1917. During the 1930s, Jews persecuted by the Hitler regime poured into Palestine. The postwar acknowledgment of the Holocaust—Hitler's genocide of 6 million Jews—increased international interest in and sympathy for the cause of Zionism. However, Arabs in Palestine and surrounding countries bitterly opposed prewar and postwar proposals to partition Palestine into Arab and Jewish sectors. The British mandate to govern Palestine ended after the war, and in 1947 the U.N. voted to partition Palestine. When the British officially withdrew on May 14, 1948, the Jewish National Council proclaimed the State of Israel

U.S. recognition came within hours. The next day, Arab forces from Egypt, Jordan, Syria, Lebanon, and Iraq invaded the new nation. By the cease-fire on Jan. 7, 1949, Israel had increased its original territory by 50%, taking western Galilee, a broad corridor through central Palestine to Jerusalem, and part of modern Jerusalem. Chaim Weizmann and David Ben-Gurion became Israel's first president and prime minister. The new government was admitted to the U.N. on May 11, 1949.

The next clash with Arab neighbors came when Egypt nationalized the Suez Canal in 1956 and barred Israeli shipping. Coordinating with an Anglo-French force, Israeli troops seized the Gaza Strip and drove through the Sinai to the east bank of the Suez Canal, but withdrew under U.S. and U.N. pressure. In the Six-Day War of 1967, Israel made simultaneous air attacks against Syrian, Jordanian, and Egyptian air bases, totally defeating the Arabs. Expanding its territory by 200%, Israel at the cease-fire held the Golan Heights, the West Bank of the Jordan River, Jerusalem's Old City, and all of the Sinai and the east bank of the Suez Canal.

In the face of Israeli reluctance even to discuss the return of occupied territories, the fourth Arab-Israeli War erupted on Oct. 6, 1973, with a surprise Egyptian and Syrian assault on the Jewish high holy day of Yom Kippur. Initial Arab gains were reversed when a cease-fire took effect two weeks later, but Israel suffered heavy losses.

A dramatic breakthrough in the tortuous history of Mideast peace efforts occurred on Nov. 9, 1977, when Egypt's president Anwar Sadat declared his willingness to go anywhere to talk peace. Prime Minister Menachem Begin on Nov. 15 extended an invitation to the Egyptian leader to address the Knesset. Sadat's arrival in Israel four days later raised worldwide hopes, but a peace agreement between Egypt and Israel was long in coming. On March 14, 1979, the Knesset approved a final peace treaty, and 12 days later Begin and Sadat signed the document, together with President Jimmy Carter, in a White House ceremony. Israel began its withdrawal from the Sinai, which it had annexed from Egypt, on May 25, and the two countries opened their border on May 29.

Although Israel withdrew its last settlers from the Sinai in April 1982, the fragile Mideast peace was shattered on June 9 by a massive Israeli assault on southern Lebanon, where the Palestinian Liberation Organization was entrenched. The PLO had long plagued Israelis with terrorist actions. Israel destroyed PLO strongholds in Tyre and Sidon and reached the suburbs of Beirut on June 10. A U.S.-mediated accord between Lebanon and Israel, signed on May 17, 1983, provided for Israeli withdrawal from Lebanon. Israel eventually withdrew its troops from the Beirut area, but kept them in southern Lebanon, where occasional skirmishes would continue. Lebanon, under pressure from Syria, canceled the accord in March 1984.

A continual source of tension has been the relationship between the Jews and the Palestinians living within Israeli territories. Most Arabs fled the region when the state of Israel was declared, but those who remain now make up almost one-fifth of the population of Israel. They are about two-thirds Muslim, as well as Christian and Druze. Palestinians living on the West Bank and the Gaza Strip fomented the riots begun in 1987, known as the *Intifadeh*. Violence heightened as Israeli police cracked down and Palestinians retaliated. Continuing Jewish settlement of lands designated for Palestinians has added to the unrest.

In 1989 the leader of the PLO, Yasir Arafat, reversed decades of PLO polemic by acknowledging Israel's right to exist. He stated his willingness to enter negotiations to create a Palestinian political entity that would coexist with the Israeli state.

In 1991 Israel was struck by Iraqi missiles during the Persian Gulf War. The Israelis did not retaliate in order to preserve the international coalition against Iraq. In 1992 Yitzhak Rabin became prime minister. He halted the disputed Israeli settlement of the occupied territories. Highly secretive talks in Norway resulted in an agreement between the PLO and the Israeli government (the Oslo agreement, 1993). The accord stipulated a five-year plan in which Palestinians of the West Bank and the Gaza Strip would gradually become self-governing. In 1994 Israel signed a peace treaty with Jordan. Israel has no formal peace with Syria or Lebanon.

On Nov. 4, 1995, Prime Minister Rabin was slain by a Jewish extremist, jeopardizing the tenuous progress toward peace. Shimon Peres succeeded him until May 1996 elections for the Knesset gave Israel a new hard-line prime minister, Benjamin Netanyahu, by a razor-thin margin. Netanyahu reversed or stymied much of the Oslo agreement, contending that it offered too many concessions too fast and jeopardized Israelis' safety. Elections for seats on the Palestinian Council and for its president took place in Jan. 1996. Yasir Arafat obtained an easy victory as president.

Israeli-Palestinian peace negotiations in 1997 were repeatedly undermined by both sides. Although the Hebron accord was signed in Jan., calling for the withdrawal of Israeli troops from the city, the construction of new Jewish settlements on the West Bank in March profoundly upset progress toward peace. Some Jews cited the influx of immigration from Russia (since the collapse of the Soviet Union, more than 700,000 Russian Jews arrived in Israel) as necessitating the additional settlements. Others believe that Netanyahu wishes to curb Palestinian expectations raised by the Oslo agreement.

Terrorism erupted again in 1997 when radical Hamas suicide bombers claimed the lives of more than 20 Israeli civilians. Netanyahu, accusing Palestinian Authority president Arafat of lax security, retaliated with draconian sanctions against Palestinians working in Israel, including the withholding of millions of dollars in tax revenue, a blatant violation of the Oslo agreements. Netanyahu persisted in authorizing right-wing Israelis to build new settlements in mostly Arab East Jerusalem. Arafat, meanwhile, seemed unwilling or unable to curb the violence of extremist Arabs.

An Oct. 1998 summit at Wye Mills, Md., generated the first real progress in the stymied Middle East peace talks in 19 months, with Israeli prime minister Benjamin Netanyahu and Palestinian president Yasir Arafat settling several important interim issues called for by the 1993 Oslo Peace Accords. The Palestinians agreed to remove language from their founding charter that called for the dismantling of the Jewish state; Israelis agreed to cede an additional 13% of the West Bank.

Although Israel did complete the first of three withdrawals from the West Bank on Nov. 20, released 250 Palestinian prisoners, and authorized the opening of the Gaza airport, the peace accord began unraveling almost immediately. Disagreement over the Israeli release of Palestinian prisoners led to violence in the West Bank and Gaza, for which each side blamed the other. To buttress the flagging accord, President Clinton visited the Gaza Strip on Dec. 15, becoming the first American president to set foot on Palestinian-occupied land. The visit coincided with the vote of the Palestine National Council to formally eliminate language from the organization's charter that calls for the destruction of Israel.

Netanyahu found himself attacked from both sides of the political spectrum—the left accused him of intentionally thwarting the peace process and the right accused him of betrayal, having elected him in the belief that he would never give up Israeli territory. In mid-Dec. Parliament voted to dissolve Netanyahu's government and hold elections in the spring, putting the peace negotiations on hold.

By the end of April 1999, Israel had made 41 air raids on Hezbollah guerrillas in Lebanon. The guerrillas were fighting against Israeli troops and their allies, the South Lebanon Army militia, who have occupied a security zone set up in 1985 to guard Israel's borders. Public pressure in Israel to withdraw the troops has grown, and the issue dominated the Israeli election campaign in spring 1999. Ehud Barak of the Labour Party won the election with 55.9% of the vote, against 43.9% for incumbent Benjamin Netanyahu of Likud. Yasir Arafat originally planned to declare Palestinian statehood on May 4, but postponed that decision until an undefined time after the election, so as not to provoke Israeli hard-liners and lessen the chance of resuming the peace talks.

Barak created a broad coalition government and on his inauguration (July 6, 1999) announced that "nothing is more important in my view than ... putting an end to the 100-year conflict in the Middle East." By this he meant not only pursuing peace with the Palestinians, but establishing relations with Syria and ending the low-grade war in Southern Lebanon with the Syrian-backed Hezbollah guerrillas. In Sept. 1999, Barak and Arafat signed a modified version of the previously agreed-upon Wye Accord. Israel released some Palestinian prisoners and has promised to cede more occupied territory.

Italy

ITALIAN REPUBLIC

Italian name: Repubblica Italiana
President: Carlo Azeglio Ciampi (1999)
Prime Minister: Massimo D'Alema (1998)
Area: 116,500 sq. mi. (301,230 sq. km)
Population (1999 est.): 56,735,130 (average annual rate of natural increase: –0.1%); birth rate: 9.3/1000; infant mortality rate: 6.3/1000; density per sq. mi.: 487
Capital and largest city (1994 est.): Rome, 2,693,383. **Other large cities:** Milan, 1,561,438; Naples, 1,204,149; Turin, 952,736; Genoa, 706,754; Palermo, 694,749; Florence, 460,924; Bologna, 394,969; Catania, 372,212; Bari, 355,352; Venice, 306,439.
Monetary units: Lira and euro. **Languages:** Italian; small German-, French-, and Slovene-speaking minorities. **Ethnicity/race:** Italian (includes small clusters of German-, French-, and Slovene-Italians in the north and Albanian-Italians and Greek-Italians in the south), Sicilians, Sardinians. **Religions:** Roman Catholic 98%, other 2%. **Literacy rate:** 97%
Economic summary: GDP/PPP (1997 est.): $1.24 trillion, $21,500 per capita. **Real growth rate:** 1.5%. **Inflation:** 1.9%. **Unemployment:** 12.2%. **Arable land:** 31%. **Agriculture:** fruits, vegetables, grapes, potatoes, sugar beets, soybeans, grain, olives, meat and dairy products, fish. **Labor force:** 22.851 million; services, 61%; industry, 32%; agriculture, 7% (1996). **Industry:** tourism, machinery, iron and steel, chemicals, food processing, textiles, motor vehicles, clothing, footwear, ceramics. **Natural resources:** mercury, potash, marble, sulfur, dwindling natural gas and crude oil reserves, fish, coal. **Exports:** $250.8 billion (f.o.b., 1996): metals, textiles and clothing, production machinery, motor vehicles, transportation equipment, chemicals. **Imports:** $190 billion (c.i.f., 1996): industrial machinery, chemicals, transport equipment, petroleum, metals, food, agricultural products. **Major trading partners:** EU, U.S., OPEC.

Geography Italy, slightly larger than Arizona, is a long peninsula shaped like a boot bounded on the west by the Tyrrhenian Sea and on the east by the Adriatic. Approximately 600 of Italy's 708 miles (1,139 km) of length are in the long peninsula that projects into the Mediterranean from the fertile basin of the Po River. The Apennine Mountains, branching off from the Alps between Nice and Genoa, form the peninsula's backbone, and rise to a maximum height of 9,560 feet (2,912 m) at the Gran Sasso d'Italia (Corno). The Alps form Italy's northern boundary.

Italy has many northern lakes, lying below the snow-covered peaks of the Alps. The largest are

Garda (143 sq. mi.; 370 sq. km), Maggiore (83 sq. mi.; 215 sq. km), and Como (55 sq. mi.; 142 sq. km). The Po, the principal river, flows from the Alps on Italy's western border and crosses the Lombard plain to the Adriatic Sea.

Several islands form part of Italy. Sicily (9,926 sq. mi.; 25,708 sq. km) lies off the toe of the boot, across the Strait of Messina, with a steep and rock-bound northern coast and gentler slopes to the sea in the west and south. Mount Etna, an active volcano, rises to 10,741 feet (3,274 m), and most of Sicily is more than 500 feet (3,274 m) in elevation. Sixty-two miles (100 km) southwest of Sicily lies Pantelleria (45 sq. mi.; 117 sq. km), and south of that are Lampedusa and Linosa. Sardinia (9,301 sq. mi.; 24,090 sq. km), which is just south of Corsica and about 125 miles (200 km) west of the mainland, is mountainous, stony, and unproductive.

Government Republic.

History The migrations of Indo-European peoples into Italy probably began about 2000 B.C.E. and continued down to 1000 B.C.E. From about the 9th century B.C.E. until it was overthrown by the Romans in the 3rd century B.C.E., the Etruscan civilization dominated the area. By 264 B.C.E. all Italy south of Cisalpine Gaul was under the leadership of Rome. For the next seven centuries, until the barbarian invasions destroyed the western Roman Empire in the 4th and 5th centuries C.E., the history of Italy was largely the history of Rome. From C.E. 800 on, the Holy Roman Emperors, Roman Catholic popes, Normans, and Saracens all vied for control over various segments of the Italian peninsula. Numerous city-states, such as Venice and Genoa, whose political and commercial rivalries were intense, and many small principalities flourished in the late Middle Ages. Although Italy remained politically fragmented for centuries, it became the cultural center of the Western world from the 13th to the 16th century.

In 1713, after the War of the Spanish Succession, Milan, Naples, and Sardinia were handed over to the Hapsburgs of Austria, which lost some of its Italian territories in 1735. After 1800, Italy was unified by Napoléon, who crowned himself king of Italy in 1805; but with the Congress of Vienna in 1815, Austria once again became the dominant power in a disunited Italy. Austrian armies crushed Italian uprisings in 1820–21 and 1831. In the 1830s Giuseppe Mazzini, brilliant liberal nationalist, organized the Risorgimento (Resurrection), which laid the foundation for Italian unity. Disappointed Italian patriots looked to the House of Savoy for leadership. Count Camille di Cavour (1810–61), premier of Sardinia in 1852 and the architect of a united Italy, joined England and France in the Crimean War (1853–56), and in 1859, helped France in a war against Austria, thereby obtaining Lombardy. By plebiscite in 1860, Modena, Parma, Tuscany, and the Romagna voted to join Sardinia. In 1860, Giuseppe Garibaldi conquered Sicily and Naples and turned them over to Sardinia. Victor Emmanuel II, king of Sardinia, was proclaimed king of Italy in 1861. The annexation of Venetia in 1866 and of papal Rome in 1870 marked the complete unification of peninsular Italy into one nation under a constitutional monarchy.

Italy declared its neutrality upon the outbreak of World War I on the ground that Germany had embarked upon an offensive war. In 1915, Italy entered the war on the side of the Allies but obtained less territory than it expected in the postwar settlement. Benito ("Il Duce") Mussolini, a former socialist, organized discontented Italians in 1919 into the Fascist Party to "rescue Italy from Bolshevism." He led his Black Shirts in a march on Rome and, on Oct. 28, 1922, became premier. He transformed Italy into a dictatorship, embarking on an expansionist foreign policy with the invasion and annexation of Ethiopia in 1935 and allying himself with Adolf Hitler in the Rome-Berlin Axis in 1936. When the Allies invaded Italy in 1943, Mussolini's dictatorship collapsed; he was executed by Partisans on April 28, 1945, at Dongo on Lake Como. Following the armistice with the Allies (Sept. 3, 1943), Italy joined the war against Germany as a cobelligerent. A June 1946 plebiscite rejected monarchy and a republic was proclaimed. The peace treaty of Sept. 15, 1947, required Italian renunciation of all claims in Ethiopia and Greece and the cession of the Dodecanese to Greece and of five small Alpine areas to France. The Trieste area west of the new Yugoslav territory was made a free territory (until 1954, when the city and a 90-square-mile zone were transferred to Italy and the rest to Yugoslavia).

Italy became an integral member of NATO and the European Economic Community (later the EU) as it successfully rebuilt its postwar economy. A prolonged outbreak of terrorist activities by the left-wing Red Brigades threatened domestic stability in the 1970s, but by the early 1980s the terrorist groups had been suppressed. Scandal brought the long reign of the Christian Democrats to an end when Italy's 40th premier since World War II, Arnaldo Forlani, was forced to resign in the wake of disclosure that many high-ranking Christian Democrats and civil servants belonged to a secret Masonic lodge known as "P-2." During 1993, the nation was riveted by a political scandal of a seemingly ever-growing size involving the Mafia and many government leaders. In a referendum, voters approved changing the proportional system of representation in the Senate for one utilizing majority voting. This series of scandals led to the collapse of the post–World War II party system and new parties filled the political vacuum. In 1996, Italians elected a government dominated by a center-left coalition for the first time since the proclamation of the Italian Republic. In 1997, Italian forces assumed leadership of a military mission to protect international aid reaching strife-torn Albania. The Communists, Italy's single largest party, refused to support the operation but refrained from withdrawing support from the government.

Italy adopted the euro as its currency in Jan. 1999. Treasury secretary Carlo Ciampi, who is credited with the economic reforms that permitted Italy to enter the European Monetary Union, was elected president in May 1999. Italy joined its NATO partners in the Kosovo crisis. Aviano Air Base in northern Italy was a crucial base for launching air strikes into Kosovo and Yugoslavia.

Jamaica

Sovereign: Queen Elizabeth II (1952)
Governor-General: Howard F. H. Cooke (1991)
Prime Minister: Percival J. Patterson (1992)
Area: 4,411 sq. mi. (10,990 sq. km)
Population (1999 est.): 2,652,443 (average annual rate of natural increase: 1.48%); birth rate: 20.2/1000; infant mortality rate: 13.9/1000; density per sq. mi.: 601
Capital and largest city (1991 est.): Kingston, 104,000.
Monetary unit: Jamaican dollar. **Languages:** English, Jamaican Creole. **Ethnicity/race:** African 76.3%, Afro-European 15.1%, East Indian and Afro-East Indian 3%, white 3.2%, Chinese and Afro-Chinese 1.2%, other 1.2%. **Religions:** Protestant, 55.9%; Roman Catholic, 5%; other, 39.1%. **Literacy rate:** 98%
Economic summary: GDP/PPP (1996 est.): $9.5 billion; $3,660 per capita. **Real growth rate:** –1.4%. **Inflation:** 17%. **Unemployment:** 16%. **Arable land:** 14%. **Agriculture:** sugarcane, bananas, coffee, citrus, potatoes, vegetables, poultry, goats, milk. **Labor force:** 1.14 million (1996); services, 41%; agriculture, 22.5%; industry, 19% (1989). **Industry:** tourism, bauxite, textiles, food processing, light manufactures. **Natural resources:** bauxite, gypsum, limestone. **Exports:** $1.4 billion (f.o.b., 1996): alumina, bauxite, sugar, bananas, rum. **Imports:** $2.9 billion (f.o.b., 1996 est.): machinery and transport equipment, construction materials, fuel, food, chemicals. **Major trading partners:** U.S., U.K., Canada, The Netherlands, Norway, Trinidad and Tobago, Japan. **Member of Commonwealth of Nations**

Geography Jamaica is an island in the West Indies, 90 miles (145 km) south of Cuba and 100 miles (161 km) west of Haiti. It is a little smaller than Connecticut. The island is made up of coastal lowlands, a limestone plateau, and the Blue Mountains, a group of volcanic hills, in the east. Blue Mountain (7,402 ft.; 2,256 m) is the tallest peak.

Government Parliamentary democracy.

History Jamaica was inhabited by Arawak Indians when Columbus explored it in 1494 and named it St. Iago. It remained under Spanish rule until 1655, when it became a British possession. The island prospered from wealth brought by buccaneers to their base, Port Royal, the capital, until the city disappeared into the sea in 1692 after an earthquake. The Arawaks died off from disease and exploitation, and slaves, mostly black, were imported to work sugar plantations. During the 17th and 18th centuries the British were consistently harassed and attacked by the Maroons, armed and organized freed slaves who operated from rural Jamaica. Abolition of the slave trade (1807), emancipation of the slaves (1833), and a gradual drop in sugar prices led to depressed economic conditions that resulted in an uprising in 1865. The following year Jamaica's status was changed to that of a crown colony, and conditions improved considerably. Introduction of banana cultivation made the island less dependent on the sugar crop for its well-being.

On May 5, 1953, Jamaica attained internal autonomy, and in 1958 it led in organizing the West Indies federation. This effort at Caribbean unification failed. A nationalist labor leader, Sir Alexander Bustamente, led a campaign for withdrawal from the federation. As the result of a popular referendum in 1961, Jamaica became independent on Aug. 6, 1962.

Michael Manley, of the People's National Party, became prime minister in 1972 and initiated a socialist program.

The Labour Party defeated Manley's People's National Party in 1980 and its capitalist-oriented leader, Edward P. G. Seaga, became prime minister. He instituted measures to encourage private investment. Like other Caribbean countries, Jamaica was hard-hit by the 1981–82 recession. By 1984, austerity measures that Seaga instituted in the hope of bringing the economy back into balance included elimination of government subsidies. Devaluation of the Jamaican dollar made Jamaican products more competitive on the world market and Jamaica achieved record growth in tourism and agriculture. While manufacturing also grew, the cost of many foods went up 50% to 75% and thousands of Jamaicans fell deeper into poverty.

In 1989, Manley swept back into power with a clear-cut victory. He indicated that he would pursue more centrist policies than he did in his previous administration. Manley stepped down in 1992 for reasons of health, and was replaced by P. J. Patterson. In May 1997 the government signed a "Shiprider Agreement" allowing U.S. authorities, in an effort to curb drug trafficking, to enter Jamaican waters and search vessels with the Jamaican government's permission.

A 31% increase in gasoline taxes on April 16, 1999, prompted three days of heavy rioting. As a result, the prime minister reduced the increase by half and looked for other ways of handling the country's $37 million shortfall.

Japan

National name: Nippon
Emperor: Akihito (1989)
Prime Minister: Keizo Obuchi (1998)
Area: 145,874 sq. mi. (377,835 sq. km)
Population (1999 est.): 126,182,077 (average annual rate of natural increase: 0.24%); birth rate: 10.5/1000; infant mortality rate: 4.1/1000; density per sq. mi.: 865
Capital and largest city: Tokyo: city proper (1995 census) 7,967,614; metro. area (1996 est.) 27,242,000. **Other large cities:** Osaka: city proper (1995 census) 2,602,352; metro area (1996 est.) 10,618,000; Yokohama, 3,307,136; Nagoya, 2,162,000; Sapporo, 1,719,000; Kobe, 1,501,000; Kyoto, 1,456,000; Fukuoka, 1,263,000; Kawasaki, 1,196,000; Hiroshima, 1,099,000. **Monetary unit:** Yen. **Language:** Japanese. **Ethnicity/race:** Japanese 99.4%, other 0.6% (mostly Korean). **Religions:** Shintoist, 111.8 million; Buddhist, 93.1 million; Christian, 1.4 million; other, 11.4 million. **Literacy rate:** 99%
Economic summary: GDP/PPP (1997 est.): $3.08 trillion; $24,500 per capita. **Real growth rate:** 0.9%. **Inflation:** 1.7%. **Unemployment:** 3.4%. **Arable land:** 11%. **Agriculture:** rice, sugar beets, vegetables, fruit, pork, poultry, dairy products, eggs, fish. **Labor force:** (March 1997): 67.23 million; trade and services, 50%; manufacturing, mining, and construction, 33%; utilities and communication, 7%; agriculture, forestry, and fishing, 6%; government, 3% (1994). **Industry:** steel, nonferrous metallurgy, heavy electrical equipment, construction and mining equipment, motor vehicles and parts, electronic and telecommunication equipment, machine tools, automated production systems, locomotives and railroad rolling stock, ships, chemicals, textiles, processed foods. **Natural resources:** negligible mineral resources, fish.

Exports: $421 billion (f.o.b., 1997): machinery, motor vehicles, consumer electronics. **Imports:** $339 billion (c.i.f., 1997): manufactures, foodstuffs and raw materials, fossil fuels. **Major trading partners:** U.S., Southeast Asia, EU, China.

Geography An archipelago extending in an arc more than 1,744 miles (2,790 km) from northeast to southwest in the Pacific, Japan is separated from the east coast of Asia by the Sea of Japan. It is approximately the size of Montana.

Japan's four main islands are Honshu, Hokkaido, Kyushu, and Shikoku. The Ryukyu chain to the southwest was U.S.-occupied from 1945 to 1972, when it reverted to Japanese control, and the Kurils to the northeast are Russian-occupied. The surface of the main islands consists largely of mountains separated by narrow valleys.

Located within a geologically active region, Japan sustains approximately 1,000 earthquakes per year, though most are minor. Offshore earthquakes can produce tsunamis, massive ocean waves that can wreak destruction along the Pacific shore. Several of Japan's mountains are active volcanoes.

Government Constitutional monarchy.

History Legend attributes creation of Japan to the sun goddess, from whom the emperors were descended. The first of them was Jimmu, supposed to have ascended the throne in 660 B.C.E., a tradition that constituted official doctrine until 1945.

Recorded Japanese history begins in approximately C.E. 400, when the Yamato clan, eventually based in Kyoto, managed to exact a loose control of the other family groups of central and western Japan. Contact with Korea introduced Buddhism to Japan at about this time. Through the 700s Japan was much influenced by China, and the Yamato clan set up an imperial court similar to that of China. In the ensuing centuries, the authority of the imperial court was undermined as powerful gentry families vied for control.

At the same time, warrior clans were rising to prominence as a distinct class known as samurai. In 1192 the Minamoto clan set up a military government under their leader, Yoritomo. He was designated shogun (military dictator). For the following 700 years, shoguns from a succession of clans ruled in Japan, while the imperial court existed in relative obscurity.

First contact with the West came in about 1542, when a Portuguese ship off course arrived in Japanese waters. Portuguese traders, Jesuit missionaries, and Spanish, Dutch, and English traders followed. Suspicious of Christianity and of Portuguese support of a local Japanese revolt, the shoguns of the Tokugawa period (1603–1867) prohibited all trade with foreign countries; only a Dutch trading post at Nagasaki was permitted. Western attempts to renew trading relations failed until 1853, when Commodore Matthew Perry sailed an American fleet into Tokyo Bay. Trade with the West was forced upon Japan under terms less than favorable to the Japanese. Strife caused by these actions brought down the feudal world of the shoguns. In 1868 the emperor Meiji came to the throne, and the shogun system was abolished.

Japan quickly made the transition from a medieval to a modern power. An imperial army was established with conscription, and parliamentary

government was formed in 1889. The Japanese began to take steps to extend their empire. After a brief war with China in 1894–95, Japan acquired Formosa (Taiwan), the Pescadores Islands, and part of southern Manchuria. China also recognized the independence of Korea (Chosen), which Japan later annexed (1910).

In 1904–05, Japan defeated Russia in the Russo-Japanese War, gaining the territory of southern Sakhalin (Karafuto) and Russia's port and rail rights in Manchuria. In World War I Japan seized Germany's Pacific islands and leased areas in China. The Treaty of Versailles then awarded it a mandate over the islands.

At the Washington Conference of 1921–22, Japan agreed to respect Chinese national integrity, but in 1931 invaded Manchuria. The following year, Japan set up this area as a puppet state, "Manchukuo," under Emperor Henry Pu-Yi, the last of China's Manchu Dynasty. On Nov. 25, 1936, Japan joined the Axis. The invasion of China came the next year followed by the Pearl Harbor attack on the U.S. on Dec. 7, 1941. Japan won its first military engagements during the war, extending its power over a vast area of the Pacific. Yet after 1942 the Japanese were forced to retreat, island by island, to their own country. The dropping of atomic bombs on the cities of Hiroshima and Nagasaki in 1945 by the United States finally brought the government to admit defeat. Japan surrendered formally on Sept. 2, 1945, aboard the battleship *Missouri* in Tokyo Bay. Southern Sakhalin and the Kuril Islands reverted to the U.S.S.R., and Formosa (Taiwan) and Manchuria to China. The Pacific islands remained under U.S. occupation.

Gen. Douglas MacArthur was appointed supreme commander of the U.S. occupation of postwar Japan (1945–52). In 1947 a new constitution took effect. The emperor became largely a symbolic head of state. The U.S. and Japan signed a security treaty in 1951, allowing for U.S. troops to be stationed in Japan. In 1952 Japan regained full sovereignty, and in 1972 the U.S. returned to Japan the Ryuku Islands, including Okinawa.

Japan's postwar economic recovery was nothing short of remarkable. New technologies and manufacturing were undertaken with great success. A shrewd trade policy gave Japan larger shares in many Western markets, an imbalance that caused some tensions with the U.S. The close involvement of Japanese government in the country's banking and industry produced accusations of protectionism. Yet economic growth continued through the 1970s and 1980s, eventually making Japan the world's second-largest economy (after the U.S.).

Japan has also been criticized for hesitation to take an active role in world affairs. Its failure to join the international coalition in the Persian Gulf War in 1991 was a case in point. Japanese prime minister Toshiki Kaifu pledged to provide $9 billion to the U.S. to help defray the expense of the latter's operations in the Persian Gulf. The government attempted to push legislation that would have permitted Japan to send a military contingent to the Gulf in noncombat roles. This was defeated amid public outcry against it.

During the 1990s, Japan has suffered an economic downturn marked by scandals involving government officials, bankers, and leaders of industry. Banks have closed under the weight of bad loans, unemployment has risen, real estate values have dropped, and many businesses have failed. Japan, the world's second-largest economy behind the United States, succumbed to the Asian economic crisis in 1998, experiencing its worst recession since World War II. These setbacks led to the resignation of Prime Minister Ryutaro Hashimoto in July 1998. He was replaced by Keizo Obuchi. In 1999 Japan seemed to make slight progress in an economic recovery. The International Monetary Fund reported in Sept. 1999 that "several signals point to a limited recovery of the Japanese economy."

Jordan

THE HASHEMITE KINGDOM OF JORDAN

National name: Al Mamlaka al Urduniya al Hashemiyah
Ruler: King Abdullah II (1999)
Prime Minister: Abdul Rauf al-Rawabdeh (1999)
Area: 34,573 sq. mi (89,213 sq. km) excludes West Bank
Population (1999 est.): 4,561,147 (average annual rate of natural increase: 3.05%); birth rate: 34.3/1000; infant mortality rate: 32.7/1000; density per sq. mi.: 132
Capital and largest city (1994 est.): Amman, 963,490.
Largest cities (1994 est.): Zarka, 420,900 (1990); Irbid, 208,201; As-Salt, 187,014. **Monetary unit:** Jordanian dinar. **Languages:** Arabic (official), English. **Ethnicity/race:** Arab 98%; Circassian 1%, Armenian 1%. **Religions:** Islam, 92%; Christian, 6%; Other, 2%. **Literacy rate:** 80%
Economic summary: GDP/PPP (1997 est.): $20.7 billion; $4,800 per capita. **Real growth rate:** 5.3%. **Inflation:** 3%. **Unemployment:** 15% (official rate, actual rate: 20%–25%) (1997 est.). **Arable land:** 4%. **Agriculture:** wheat, barley, citrus, tomatoes, melons, olives, sheep, goats, poultry. **Labor force:** (1997 est.), 1.6 million: industry, 11.4%; commerce, restaurants, and hotels, 10.5%; construction, 10%; transport and communications, 8.7%; agriculture, 7.4%; other services, 52% (1992). **Industries:** phosphate mining, petroleum refining, cement, potash, light manufacturing. **Natural resources:** phosphates, potash, shale oil. **Exports:** $1.53 billion (f.o.b., 1997): phosphates, fertilizers, manufactures, potash, agricultural products. **Imports:** $3.7 billion (c.i.f., 1997): crude oil, machinery, transport equipment, food, live animals, manufactured goods. **Major trading partners:** Iraq, India, Saudi Arabia, EU, Indonesia, U.A.E., U.S., Japan, Turkey.

Geography The Middle East kingdom of Jordan is bordered on the west by Israel and the Dead Sea, on the north by Syria, on the east by Iraq, and on the south Saudi Arabia. It is comparable in size to Indiana. Arid hills and mountains make up most of the country. The southern section of the Jordan River flows through the country.

Government Constitutional hereditary monarchy.

History In biblical times, the country that is now Jordan contained the lands of Edom, Moab, Ammon, and Bashan. Together with other Middle Eastern territories, Jordan passed in turn to the Assyrians, the Babylonians, the Persians, and, about 330 B.C.E., the Seleucids. Conflict between the Seleucids and the Ptolemies enabled the Arabic-speaking Nabataeans to create a kingdom in southeastern Jordan. In C.E. 106 it became part of the Roman province of Arabia and in 633–36 was conquered by the Arabs. In the 16th century, Jordan submitted to Ottoman Turkish rule and was administered from Damascus. Taken from the Turks by the British in World War I, Jordan (formerly known as Transjordan) was separated from the Palestine mandate in 1920, and in 1921, placed under the rule of Abdullah ibn Hussein.

In 1923, Britain recognized Jordan's independence, subject to the mandate. In 1946, grateful for Jordan's loyalty in World War II, Britain abolished the mandate. That part of Palestine occupied by Jordanian troops was formally incorporated by action of the Jordanian Parliament in 1950. King Abdullah was assassinated in 1951. His son Talal was deposed as mentally ill the next year. Talal's son Hussein, born on Nov. 14, 1935, succeeded him.

From the beginning of his reign, Hussein had to steer a careful course between his powerful neighbor to the west, Israel, and rising Arab nationalism, frequently a direct threat to his throne. Riots erupted when he joined the Central Treaty Organization (the Baghdad Pact) in 1955, and he incurred further unpopularity when Britain, France, and Israel attacked the Suez Canal in 1956, forcing him to place his army under nominal command of the United Arab Republic of Egypt and Syria. The 1961 breakup of the UAR eased Arab national pressure on Hussein, who was the first to recognize Syria after it reclaimed its independence. Jordan was swept into the 1967 Arab-Israeli War, however, and lost the old city of Jerusalem and all of its territory west of the Jordan river, the West Bank. Embittered Palestinian guerrilla forces virtually took over sections of Jordan in the aftermath of defeat, and open warfare broke out between the Palestinians and government forces in 1970.

Despite intervention of Syrian tanks, Hussein's Bedouin army defeated the Palestinians. The Jordanians drove out the Syrians and 12,000 Iraqi troops who had been in the country since the 1967 war. Ignoring protests from other Arab states, Hussein, by mid-1971, crushed Palestinian strength in Jordan and shifted the problem to Lebanon, where many of the guerrillas had fled. As Egypt and Israel neared final agreement on a peace treaty early in 1979, Hussein met with Yasir Arafat, the PLO leader, on March 17 and issued a joint statement of opposition. Although the U.S. pressed Jordan to break Arab ranks on the issue, Hussein elected to side with the great majority, cutting ties with Cairo and joining the boycott against Egypt.

Jordan's stance during the Persian Gulf War strained relations with the U.S. and led to the termination of U.S. aid. The signing of a national charter by King Hussein and leaders of the main political groups in June 1991 meant political parties were permitted in exchange for acceptance of the constitution and the monarchy. King Hussein's decision to join the Middle East peace talks in mid-1991 helped restore his country's relations with the U.S.

In July 1994 King Hussein and the Israeli prime minister signed a declaration ending the state of belligerency between the two countries. A peace between the two countries was signed on Oct. 26, 1994, although a clause in it calling the king "custodian" of Islamic holy shrines in Jerusalem angered the PLO. In the wake of the agreement Jordan's relations with the U.S. and with the moderate Arab states, including Saudi Arabia, warmed. In 1997, Jordan began negotiating with the United

States about membership in the World Trade Organization, determined to attract foreign investment. On Feb. 7, 1999, King Hussein died of cancer after 46 years on the throne, sending the Middle East and much of the world into mourning for the influential Middle East statesman. Just weeks earlier, on Jan. 26, King Hussein unexpectedly deposed his brother, Prince Hassan, who had been heir apparent for 34 years, and named his eldest son, Abdullah, 37, as the new crown prince. King Abdullah II, a popular military leader with little political experience, was crowned on Feb. 7.

Kazakhstan

REPUBLIC OF KAZAKHSTAN

President: Nursultan A. Nazarbayev (1990)
Prime Minister: Nurlan Balgimbayev (1997)
Area: 1,049,000 sq. mi. (2,717,300 sq. km)
Population (1999 est.): 16,824,825; average annual rate of natural increase: 0.68%; birth rate: 17.2/1000; infant mortality rate, 58.8/1000; density per sq. mi.: 16
Capital (1995 est.): Astana, 280,200 (capital since 1997) . **Largest cities (1991):** Almaty (former capital), 1,200,000; Karaganda, 608,600; Shymkent, 438,000; Ust-Kamenogorsk, 332,900; Taraz, 312,300; Aqmola, 287,000; Aqtöbe, 266,600. **Monetary unit:** Tenge.
Languages: Kazak (Qazaq), official language spoken by over 40% of population; Russian, official language spoken by two-thirds of population and used in everyday business. **Ethnicity/race:** Kazak (Qazaq) 46%, Russian 34.7%, Ukrainian 4.9%, German 3.1%, Uzbek 2.3%, Tatar 1.9%, other 7.1% (1996).
Religions: Muslim, 47%; Russian Orthodox 44%, Protestant 2%, other 7%. **Literacy rate:** 98%
Economic summary: GDP/PPP (1997 est.): $50 billion; $3,000 per capita. **Real growth rate:** 2.1%. **Inflation:** 12%. **Unemployment:** 2.6% (official figure, but large numbers of underemployed) (Dec. 1996 est.). **Labor force:** 6.9 million; industry 27%; agriculture and forestry, 23%; other, 50% (1996). **Industries:** oil, coal, iron ore, manganese, chromite, lead, zinc, copper, titanium, bauxite, gold, silver, phosphates, sulfur, iron and steel, nonferrous metal, tractors and other agricultural machinery, electric motors, construction materials. **Agriculture:** grain, mostly spring wheat, cotton, wool, meat. **Exports:** $5.6 (1996): oil, ferrous and nonferrous metals, chemicals, grain, wool, meat, coal. **Imports:** $6 billion (1996): machinery and parts, industrial materials, oil and gas. **Trading partners:** Russia, Ukraine, Uzbekistan, The Netherlands, China, Turkey, Germany.

Geography Kazakhstan lies in the north of the central Asian republics and is bounded by Russia in the north, China in the east, the Kyrgyzstan and Uzbekistan in the south, and the Caspian Sea and part of Turkmenistan in the west. It has almost 15,000 miles (24,000 km) of coastline on the Caspian Sea. Kazakhstan is slightly more than twice the size of Texas. The territory is mostly steppe land with hilly plains and plateaus.

Government Republic.

History The indigenous Kazakhs were a nomadic Turkic people who belonged to several divisions of Kazakh hordes. They grouped together in settlements and lived in dome-shaped tents made of felt called "yurts." Their tribes migrated seasonally to find pastures for their herds of sheep, horses, and goats. Although they had chiefs, the Kazakhs were rarely united as a single nation under one great leader. Their tribes fell under Mongol rule in the 13th century and they were dominated by Tartar khanates until the area was conquered by Russia in the 18th century.

The area became part of the Kirgiz Autonomous Republic formed by the Soviet authorities in 1920, and in 1925 this entity's name was changed to the Kazakh Autonomous Soviet Socialist Republic (Kazakh A.S.S.R.). After 1927, the Soviet government began forcing the nomadic Kazakhs to settle on collective and state farms, and the Soviets continued the czarist policy of encouraging large numbers of Russians and other Slavs to settle in the region.

Owing to the region's intensive agricultural development and its use as a testing ground for nuclear weapons by the Soviet government, serious environmental problems developed by the late 20th century. Along with the other central Asian republics, Kazakhstan obtained its independence from the collapsing Soviet Union in 1991. Kazakhstan proclaimed its membership in the Commonwealth of Independent States on Dec. 21, 1991, along with ten other former Soviet republics. In 1993, the country overwhelmingly approved the Nuclear Non-Proliferation Treaty. In 1994, the Kazakh government resolved to transfer the national capital from Almaty to Aqmola by 2000. The president restructured and consolidated many operations of the government in 1997, eliminating a third of the government ministries and agencies.

In Jan. 1999, Nursultan Nazarbayev was sworn into office for another seven years, although the election was widely criticized because an opposition leader was disqualified from running on a technicality. Despite his authoritarianism, Nazarbayev, who has ruled Kazakhstan since 1989 when it was still part of the Soviet Union, is a widely popular leader. Kazakhstan has the potential for becoming one of central Asia's richest countries because of its huge mineral resources and its liberalized economy, which encourages Western investment.

Kenya

REPUBLIC OF KENYA

National name: Jamhuri ya Kenya
President: Daniel arap Moi (1978)
Area: 224,960 sq. mi. (582,650 sq. km)
Population (1999 est.): 28,808,658 (average annual rate of natural increase: 1.62%); birth rate: 30.8/1000; infant mortality rate: 59.1/1000; density per sq. mi.: 128
Capital and largest city (1991 est.): Nairobi, 2,000,000. **Other large city:** Mombasa, 600,000. **Monetary unit:** Kenyan shilling. **Languages:** English (official), Swahili (national), and several other languages spoken by 25 ethnic groups. **Ethnicity/race:** Kikuyu 22%, Luhya 14%, Luo 13%, Kalenjin 12%, Kamba 11%, Kisii 6%, Meru 6%, Asian, European, and Arab 1%, other 15%. **Religions:** Protestant, 40%; Roman Catholic, 36%; traditional, 6%; Islam, 16%, others, 2%. **Literacy rate:** 69%
Economic summary: GDP/PPP (1997 est.): $45.3 billion; $1,600 per capita. **Real growth rate:** 2.9% **Inflation:** 8.8% (1996). **Unemployment:** 35% urban (1994 est.). **Arable land:** 7%. **Agriculture:** coffee, tea, corn, wheat, sugarcane, fruit, vegetables, dairy products, beef, pork, poultry, eggs. **Labor force:** 8.78 million; agriculture, 75%–80%; nonagriculture, 20%–25% (1993 est.). **Industry:** small-scale consumer goods (plastic, furniture, batteries, textiles, soap, cigarettes, flour), processing agricultural products, oil refining, cement, tourism.

Natural resources: gold, limestone, soda ash, salt barytes, rubies, fluorspar, garnets, wildlife. **Exports:** $2.1 billion (f.o.b., 1996): tea, coffee, petroleum products. **Imports:** $2.9 billion (f.o.b., 1996): machinery and transportation equipment, consumer goods, petroleum products. **Major trading partners:** Uganda, U.K., Tanzania, Germany, The Netherlands, U.S., U.A.E., Japan. **Member of Commonwealth of Nations**

Geography Kenya lies across the equator in east-central Africa on the coast of the Indian Ocean. It is twice the size of Nevada. Kenya borders Somalia to the east, Ethiopia to the north, Tanzania to the south, Uganda to the west, and Sudan to the northwest. In the north, the land is arid; the southwestern corner is in the fertile Lake Victoria Basin; and a length of the eastern depression of Great Rift Valley separates western highlands from those that rise from the lowland coastal strip. Large game reserves have been developed.

Government Republic.

History Paleontologists believe people may first have inhabited Kenya about 2 million years ago. In the 700s Arab seafarers established settlements along the coast, and the Portuguese took control of the area in the early 1500s. More than 40 ethnic groups reside in Kenya. Its largest group, the Kikuyu, migrated to the region at the beginning of the 18th century.

The land became a British protectorate in 1890 and a crown colony in 1920, when it went by the name British East Africa. Nationalist stirrings began in 1940s, and in 1952 the Mau Mau movement, made up of Kikuyu militants, rebelled against the government. The fighting lasted until 1956.

On Dec. 12, 1963, Kenya became fully independent. Jomo Kenyatta, a nationalist leader during the independence struggle who had been jailed by the British, became its first president. From 1964 to 1992 the country was ruled as a one-party state by the Kenya African National Union (KANU), first under Kenyatta and then under Daniel arap Moi. Demonstrations and riots pressured Moi to allow for multiparty elections in 1992.

The economy has not flourished under Daniel arap Moi's rule. In the 1990s Kenya's infrastructure began disintegrating and official graft was rampant, contributing to the withdrawal of much foreign aid. In early 1995 President Moi moved against the opposition, and ordered the arrest of anyone who insulted him. In June the renowned paleontologist Richard Leakey registered a new political party in protest of the government's policies.

A series of disasters plagued Kenya in 1997 and 1998: severe flooding destroyed roads, bridges, and crops; epidemics of malaria and cholera overwhelmed the ineffectual health care system; and ethnic clashes erupted between the Kikuyu and Kalenjin ethnic groups in the Rift Valley.

On Aug. 7, 1998, the U.S. embassy in Nairobi was bombed by terrorists, killing 243 and injuring more than 1,000. The embassy in neighboring Tanzania was bombed the same day, killing 10.

In a surprising decision, President Moi appointed his critic and political opponent Richard Leakey as cabinet secretary and head of the civil service. Some believe the president is not serious about reform but wishes to give the appearance of cleaning up Kenya's corrupt bureaucracy, hence the high profile appointment of Leakey. This third-generation white Kenyan, son of paleontologists Louis and Mary Leakey, was highly effective as head of the Kenya Wildlife Service, and is expected to introduce a greater amount of efficiency and fairness into the Kenyan government.

Kiribati
REPUBLIC OF KIRIBATI

President: Teburoro Tito (1994)
Area: 280 sq. mi. (717 sq. km)
Population (1999 est.): 85,501 (average annual growth rate: 1.86%); birth rate: 26.1/1000; infant mortality rate: 48.2/1000; density per sq. mi.: 305
Capital (1990): Tarawa, 25,154. **Monetary unit:** Australian dollar. **Languages:** English (official), I-Kiribati (Gilbertese). **Ethnicity/race:** Micronesian. **Religions:** Roman Catholic, 52.6%; Protestant, 40.9%. **Literacy rate:** 90%
Economic summary: GDP/PPP (1996 est.): $62 million; $800 per capita. **Real growth rate:** 1.9% **Inflation:** –0.6% **Unemployment:** 2%, underemployment, 70% (1992 est.). **Arable land:** n.a. **Agriculture:** copra, taro, breadfruit, sweet potatoes, vegetables, fish. **Labor force:** 7,870 economically active, not including subsistence farmers (1985 est.). **Industry:** fishing, handicrafts. **Exports:** $6.7 million (f.o.b., 1996 est.): copra, seaweed, fish. **Imports:** $37.4 million (c.i.f., 1996 est.): foodstuffs, machinery and equipment, miscellaneous manufactured goods, fuel. **Major trading partners:** U.S., Australia, New Zealand, Fiji, Japan. **Member of Commonwealth of Nations**

Geography Kiribati, formerly the Gilbert Islands, consists of three widely separated main groups of southwest Pacific islands, the Gilberts on the equator, the Phoenix Islands to the east, and the Line Islands farther east. Ocean Island, producer of phosphates until it was mined out in 1981, is also included in the 2 million square miles of ocean. Most of the islands of Kiribati are low-lying coral atolls built on a submerged volcanic chain and encircled by reefs.

Government Republic.

History Kiribati was first settled by early Austronesian-speaking peoples long before the 1st century C.E.. Fijians and Tongans arrived about the 14th century and subsequently merged with the older groups to form the traditional I-Kiribati Micronesian society and culture. The islands were first sighted by British and American ships in the late 18th and early 19th centuries and the first British settlers arrived in 1837. A British protectorate since 1892, the Gilbert and Ellice Islands became a crown colony in 1915–16. Kiritimati (Christmas) Atoll became a part of the colony in 1919, the Phoenix Islands in 1937.

Tarawa and others of the Gilbert group were occupied by Japan during World War II. Tarawa was the site of one of the bloodiest battles in U.S. Marine Corps history when Marines landed in Nov. 1943 to dislodge the Japanese defenders. The Gilbert Islands and Ellice Islands (now Tuvalu) were separated in 1975 and granted internal self-government by Britain. Kiribati became independent on July 12, 1979.

Kiribati's 1995 act of moving the international date line far to the east, so that it encompassed Kiribati's Line Islands group, courted controversy. The move, which fulfilled one of President Tito's campaign promises, was intended to enable Kiribati to become the first country to reach midnight on Dec. 31, 1999 and welcome the new millennium—an event of significance for tourism. In 1999, Kiribati was accepted for membership in the U.N., though it has not yet formally joined the organization.

Korea, North

DEMOCRATIC PEOPLE'S REPUBLIC OF KOREA

National name: Choson Minjujuui Inmin Konghwaguk
Head of State: Kim Jong Il (1994)
Premier: Hong Song Nam (1997)
Area: 46,768 sq. mi. (120,540 sq. km)
Population (1999 est.): 21,386,109 (average annual rate of natural increase: 1.45%); birth rate: 21.4/1000; infant mortality rate: 25.5/1000; density per sq. mi.: 457
Capital and largest city (1993): Pyongyang,2,741,260.
Monetary unit: Won. **Language:** Korean. **Ethnicity/race:** racially homogeneous. **Religions:** Buddhism and Confucianism, religious activities almost nonexistent. **Literacy rate:** 100%
Economic summary: GDP/PPP (1997 est.): $21.8 billion; $900 per capita. **Real growth rate:** –3.7%. **Inflation:** n.a. **Unemployment:** n.a. **Arable land:** 14%. **Agriculture:** rice, corn, potatoes, soybeans, pulses, cattle, pigs, pork, eggs. **Labor force:** 9.615 million; agricultural, 36%; nonagricultural, 64%. **Industry:** military products, machine building, electric power, chemicals, mining (coal, iron ore, magnesite, graphite, copper, zinc, lead, precious metals), metallurgy, textiles, food processing. **Natural resources:** coal, lead, tungsten, zinc, graphite, magnesite, iron ore, copper, gold, pyrites, salt, fluorspar, hydropower. **Exports:** $912 million (f.o.b., 1996 est.): minerals, metallurgical products, agricultural and fishery products, manufactures (including armaments). **Imports:** $1.95 billion (c.i.f., 1996 est.): petroleum, grain, coking coal, machinery and equipment, consumer goods. **Major trading partners:** China, Japan, South Korea, Germany, Hong Kong, Russia, Singapore.

Geography Korea is a 600-mile (966 km) peninsula jutting out from Manchuria and China (and a small portion of the U.S.S.R.) into the Sea of Japan and the Yellow Sea off eastern Asia. North Korea occupies an area slightly smaller than Pennsylvania north of the 38th parallel.

The country is almost completely covered by a series of north-south mountain ranges separated by narrow valleys. The Yalu River forms part of the northern border with Manchuria.

Government Communist dictatorship.

History The ancient history of the Korean peninsula can be traced to the Neolithic Age, when Turkic-Manchurian-Mongol peoples migrated into the region from China. The first agriculturally based settlements appeared around 6000 B.C.E. Some of the larger communities of this era were established along the Han-gang River near modern-day Seoul, others near Pyongyang and Pusan. According to ancient lore, Korea's earliest civilization, known as Choson, was founded in 2333 B.C.E. by Tan-gun.

In the 17th century, Korea became a vassal state of China and was cut off from outside contact until the Sino-Japanese War of 1894–95. Following Japan's victory, Korea was granted independence. By 1910 Korea had been annexed by Japan, which

developed the country but never won over the Korean nationalists who continued to agitate for independence.

After Japan's surrender at the conclusion of World War II, the Korean peninsula was partitioned into two occupation zones, divided at the 38th parallel. The U.S.S.R. controlled the north, with the U.S. taking charge of the south. In 1948, the division was made permanent with the establishment of the separate regimes of North and South Korea. The Democratic People's Republic of Korea (North Korea) was established on May 1, 1948, with Kim Il Sung as president.

Hoping to unify the Koreas under a single Communist government, the North launched a surprise invasion of South Korea on June 25, 1950. In the following days, the U.N. Security Council condemned the attack and demanded an immediate withdrawal.

President Harry S. Truman ordered U.S. air and naval units into action to enforce the U.N. order. The British government followed suit, and soon a U.N. multinational command was set up to aid the South Koreans.

The North Korean invaders swiftly seized Seoul and surrounded the allied forces in the peninsula's southeast corner near Pusan. In a desperate bid to reverse the military situation, U.N. Commander Gen. Douglas MacArthur ordered an amphibious landing at Inchon on Sept. 15 and routed the North Korean army. MacArthur's forces pushed north across the 38th parallel, approaching the Yalu River.

Prompted by this successful counteroffensive, Communist China entered the war, forcing the U.N. troops into a headlong retreat. Seoul was lost again, then regained; ultimately the war stabilized near the 38th parallel but dragged on for two years while negotiations took place. An armistice was agreed to on July 27, 1953.

By early 1994 tensions had mounted over international inspection of North Korea's nuclear sites. Kim Il Sung's death on July 8, 1994 introduced a period of uncertainty, as his son, Kim Jong-Il assumed the leadership mantle. Negotiations over the country's suspected atomic weapons dragged on, but an agreement was reached in June 1995 which included a provision for providing the North with a South Korean nuclear reactor.

The nuclear crises that characterized the mid-1990s were overshadowed when famine struck the nation's 24 million inhabitants. Two years of floods were followed by severe droughts in 1997 and 1998, causing devastating crop failures. Although international relief programs saved many people, the situation was still considered serious in 1998, with aid agencies warning that North Korea's nationalized food distribution program had virtually shut down, forcing many people to rely on bark and wild plants to sustain themselves. The severity of the famine continued in 1999. Because of lack of fuel and machinery parts, and weather conditions that have encouraged parasites, only 10% of North Korea's rice fields have been worked. Despite the staggering food crisis, hermetic North Korea remains one of the world's few remaining hard-line Communist regimes.

In Sept. 1998 North Korea launched a test missile over Japan, claiming it was simply a scientific satellite. This launch alarmed Japan and much of the rest of the world about North Korea's intentions regarding reentry into the nuclear arms race. In 1999, North Korea agreed to allow the United States to conduct ongoing inspections of a suspected nuclear development site, Kumchangri, which North Korea admits has been devised for "a sensitive military purpose." In exchange, the U.S. would increase food aid and initiate a program for bringing potato production to the country.

Antagonism between North and South Korea erupted into open aggression twice in six months: in Dec. 1998, South Korea discovered a North Korean spy submarine deep in its waters and sank it; in June 1999, South Korea hit one North Korean torpedo boat and sank another after the North Korean vessels transgressed into South Korean waters in the Yellow Sea. In late summer, there were signs that North Korea might test a new version of the long-range rocket it launched over Japan a year earlier.

In the fall of 1999, North Korea's four years of severe famine, considered to have been one of the worst in the 20th century, had begun to wane. Experts have estimated that from 1995 through 1998, 2 million to 3 million people died of hunger.

Korea, South

REPUBLIC OF KOREA

National name: Taehan Min'guk
President: Kim Dae Jung (1998)
Prime Minister: Kim Jong Pil (1998)
Area: 38,031 sq. mi. (98,480 sq. km)
Population (1999 est.): 46,884,800 (average annual rate of natural increase: 1.03%); birth rate: 16.0/1000; infant mortality rate: 7.6/1000; density per sq. mi.: 1,233
Capital and largest city: Seoul: city proper (1995 est.) 10,231,217; metro. area (1996 est.) 11,768,000. **Other large cities:** Pusan, 3,814,235; Taegu, 2,449,000; Inchon, 2,308,000. **Monetary unit:** Won. **Language:** Korean. **Ethnicity/race:** homogeneous (except for about 20,000 Chinese). **Religions (est. mid-1996):** Christian, 48.2%; Buddhist, 48.8%; Confucianist, 0.8%; Chondogyo (religion of the Heavenly Way), 0.2%; Other, 2%. **Literacy rate:** 98%
Economic summary: GDP/PPP (1997 est.): $631.2 billion; $13,700 per capita. **Real growth rate:** 6%. **Inflation:** 5% (1996). **Unemployment:** 2% (1996). **Arable land:** 19%. **Agriculture:** rice, root crops, barley, vegetables, fruit, cattle, pigs, chickens, milk, eggs, fish. **Labor force:** (1991), 20 million; services and other, 52%; mining and manufacturing, 27%; agriculture, fishing, forestry, 21%. **Industries:** electronics, automobile production, chemicals, shipbuilding, steel, textiles, clothing, footwear, food processing. **Natural resources:** coal, tungsten, graphite, molybdenum, lead, hydropower. **Exports:** $129.8 billion (f.o.b., 1996): electronic and electrical equipment, machinery, steel, automobiles, ships, textiles, clothing, footwear, fish. **Imports:** $150.2 billion (c.i.f., 1996): machinery, electronics and electronic equipment, oil, steel, transport equipment, textiles, organic chemicals, grains. **Major trading partners:** U.S., EU, Japan.

Geography Slightly larger than Indiana, South Korea lies below the 38th parallel on the Korean peninsula, bordering the East Sea and the Yellow Sea. It is mountainous in the east; in the west and south are many harbors on the mainland and offshore islands.

Government Republic.

History South Korea came into being after World War II, the result of a 1945 agreement reached by the Allies at the Potsdam Conference, making the 38th parallel the boundary between a northern zone of the Korean peninsula to be occupied by the U.S.S.R. and southern zone to be controlled by U.S. forces. (For details, see Korea, North.)

Elections were held in the U.S. zone in 1948 for a national assembly, which adopted a republican constitution and elected Syngman Rhee as the nation's president. The new republic was proclaimed on Aug. 15 and was recognized as the legal government of Korea by the U.N. on Dec. 12, 1948.

On June 25, 1950, North Korean Communist forces launched a massive surprise attack on South Korea, quickly overrunning the capital, Seoul. U.S. armed intervention was ordered on June 27 by President Harry S. Truman, and on the same day the U.N. invoked military sanctions against North Korea. Gen. Douglas MacArthur was named commander of the U.N. forces. U.S. and South Korean troops fought a heroic holding action, but by the first week of Aug. were forced back to a 4,000-square-mile beachhead in southeast Korea. There they stood off superior North Korean forces until Sept. 15, when a major U.N. amphibious assault was launched deep behind Communist lines at Inchon, the port of Seoul.

By Sept. 30, U.N. forces were in complete control of South Korea. They then crossed the 38th parallel and pursued retreating Communist forces into North Korea. In late October, as U.N. forces neared the Sino-Korean border, several hundred thousand Chinese Communist troops entered the conflict, pushing MacArthur's forces back to the border between North and South Korea. By the time truce talks began on July 10, 1951, U.N. forces had crossed over the parallel again and were driving back into North Korea. Cease-fire negotiations dragged on for two years before an armistice was finally signed at Panmunjom on July 27, 1953, leaving a devastated Korea in need of large-scale rehabilitation. No official peace treaty has ever been signed between the former combatants.

Rhee, after 12 years in office, was forced to resign in 1960 amid rising discontent with his autocratic leadership. Po Sun Yun was elected to succeed him, but political instability continued. In 1961, Gen. Park Chung Hee seized power and subsequently began a program of economic reforms designed to stimulate the nation's economy. The U.S. stepped up military aid, strengthening South Korea's armed forces to 600,000 men. Park's assassination on Oct. 26, 1979, by Kim Jae Kyu, head of the Korean Central Intelligence Agency, brought a liberalizing trend as new president Choi Kyu Hah freed imprisoned dissidents.

The release of opposition leader Kim Dae Jung in Feb. 1980 sparked antigovernment demonstrations that turned into riots, which were brutally suppressed by authorities. Kim, the most visible leader of the opposition, was imprisoned again. Choi resigned on Aug. 16. Chun Doo Hwan, head of a military Special Committee for National Security Measures, was the sole candidate as the electoral college confirmed him as president on Aug. 27. In 1986–87, South Korea's opposition demanded the president be selected by direct popular vote. After weeks of protest and rioting, Chun agreed to the demand. A split in the opposition led to Roh Tae Woo's election on Dec. 16, 1987.

In Aug. of 1996 Roh was convicted on bribery charges and Chun was convicted for bribery as well as his role in the 1979 coup and the 1980 crackdown on rioters. In 1997, an accumulation of corrupt business practices and bad loans led to a series of bankruptcies and a massive devaluation of South Korea's currency. The political instability that followed helped former dissident Kim Dae Jung become the first South Korean president ever to be elected from the political opposition.

In 1998 the Asian economic crisis bottomed out in South Korea, and it began rebounding in 1999—the only sizable Asian economy to do so.

Antagonism between North and South Korea recently erupted into open aggression twice in six months: in Dec. 1998, South Korea discovered a North Korean spy submarine deep in its waters and sank it; in June 1999, South Korea hit one North Korean torpedo boat and sank another after the North Korean vessels trespassed into South Korean waters in the Yellow Sea.

Kuwait

STATE OF KUWAIT

National name: Dawlat al Kuwayt
Emir: Sheik Jaber al-Ahmad al-Sabah (1977)
Prime Minister: Sheik Saad al-Abdullah Al-Sabah (1978)
Area: 6,880 sq. mi. (17,820 sq. km)
Population (1999 est.): 1,991,115 (average annual rate of natural increase: 1.81%); birth rate: 20.5/1000; infant mortality rate: 10.3/1000; density per sq. mi.: 289
Capital (1990 est.): Kuwait, 151,060. **Other large city (1993 est.):** as-Salimiyah, 116,104. **Monetary unit:** Kuwaiti dinar. **Languages:** Arabic and English.
Ethnicity/race: Kuwaiti 45%, other Arab 35%, South Asian 9%, Iranian 4%, other 7%. **Religions:** Islam 85% (Shi'ite 30%, Sunni 45%, other 10%); Christian, Hindu, Parsi, and other 15%. **Literacy rate:** 73%
Economic summary: GDP/PPP (1997 est.): $46.3 billion; $22,300 per capita. **Real growth rate:** 1%. **Inflation:** 3.2% (1996). **Unemployment:** 1.8% (official 1996 est.). **Labor force:** 1.1 million (1996 est.): government and social services, 50%; services, 40%; industry and agriculture, 10%. **Industries:** petroleum, petrochemicals, desalination, food processing, construction materials, salt, construction. **Natural resources:** petroleum, fish, shrimp, natural gas. **Exports:** $14.7 billion (f.o.b., 1996): oil and refined products, fertilizers. **Imports:** $7.7 billion (f.o.b., 1996): food, construction materials, vehicles and parts, clothing. **Major trading partners:** Japan, U.S., The Netherlands, Singapore, U.K., Germany, Italy.

Geography Kuwait is situated northeast of Saudi Arabia at the northern end of the Persian Gulf, south of Iraq. It is slightly larger than Hawaii. The low-lying desert land is mainly sandy and barren.

Government Kuwait is a constitutional monarchy, governed by the al-Sabah family.

History Kuwait is believed to have been part of an early civilization in the 3rd millennium B.C.E. and to have traded with Mesopotamian cities. Archeological and historical traces disappeared around the first millennium B.C.E. At the beginning of the 18th century C.E., the 'Anizah tribe of central Arabia founded Kuwait City, which became an autonomous sheikdom by 1756. 'Abd Rahim of the Al Sabah became

the first sheik, and his descendants continue to rule Kuwait today. In the late 18th and early 19th century the sheikdom belonged to the fringes of the Ottoman Empire. Kuwait obtained British protection in 1897 when the sheik feared that the Turks would expand their hold over the area. In 1961, Britain ended the protectorate, giving Kuwait independence, but agreed to give military aid on request. Iraq immediately threatened to occupy the area, and the British sent troops to defend Kuwait. Soon afterward the Arab League sent in troops, replacing the British. Iraq's claim was dropped when the Arab League recognized Kuwait's independence on July 20, 1961. Kuwait typically followed a neutral and mediatory policy among Arab states.

Oil was discovered there in the 1930s, and Kuwait proved to have 20% of the world's known oil resources. Since 1946 it has been the world's second-largest oil exporter. The sheik, who receives half the profits, devotes most of them to the education, welfare, and modernization of his kingdom. In 1966, Sheik Sabah designated a relative, Jaber al-Ahmad al-Sabah, as his successor. By 1968, the sheikdom had established a model welfare state, and it sought to establish dominance among the sheikdoms and emirates of the Persian Gulf.

In July 1990, Iraqi president Hussein blamed Kuwait for falling oil prices. After a failed Arab mediation attempt to solve the dispute peacefully, Iraq invaded Kuwait on Aug. 2, 1990, set up a pro-Iraqi provisional government, and drained Kuwait of its economic resources. A coalition of Arab and Western military forces drove Iraqi troops from Kuwait in a mere four days, from Feb. 23–27, ending the Persian Gulf War. The emir returned to his country from Saudi Arabia in mid-March. Martial law, in effect since the end of the Gulf War, ended in late June. The U.S. sent 2,400 troops to the country in August 1992 as part of a training exercise but this was widely interpreted as a show of strength to Saddam Hussein.

The general election of Oct. 1992 was a success for supporters of a return to Islamic law. A political independent was named speaker of the Parliament, and the opposition held 31 of the 50 seats. Iraqi "training" maneuvers near the Kuwaiti border in Oct. 1994 renewed fears of aggression in the country. A Kuwaiti appeal brought the quick deployment of U.S. and British troops and equipment. In 1999, Kuwait gave women the right to vote and run for Parliament, the only country on the conservative Arabian peninsula to do so besides Qatar, which gave women the vote in the same year.

Kyrgyzstan

THE KYRGYZ REPUBLIC

President: Askar Akaev (1990)
Prime Minister: Amangeldy Muraliyev (1999)
Area: 76,000 sq. mi. (198,500 sq. km)
Population (1999 est.): 4,546,055; (Kyrgyz, 52%; Russian, 21%; Uzbek, 13%, other, 14%); average annual rate of natural increase: 1.31%; birth rate: 21.8/1000; infant mortality rate: 75.9/1000; density per sq. mi.: 60
Capital and largest city (1994): Bishkek (formerly Frunze), 631,000. **Other large city (1994):** Osh 213,000. **Monetary unit:** Som. **Languages:** Kyrgyz (official); Russian is de facto second language of communication. **Ethnicity/race:** Kirghiz 52.4%, Russian 18%, Uzbek 12.9%, Ukrainian 2.5%, German

2.4%, other 11.8%. **Religions:** Muslim 75%, Russian Orthodox 20%, other 5%. **Literacy rate:** 100% **Economic summary: GDP/PPP** (1997 est.): $9.7 billion, $2,100 per capita. **Real growth rate:** 10%. **Inflation:** 15%. **Unemployment:** 8% (Dec. 1996 est.). **Natural resources:** abundant hydroelectric potential; significant deposits of gold and rare earth metals; locally exploitable coal, oil, and natural gas; other deposits of nepheline, mercury, bismuth, lead, and zinc. **Industries:** small machinery, textiles, food processing, cement, shoes, sawn logs, refrigerators, furniture, electric motors, gold, rare earth metals. **Agriculture:** wool, tobacco, cotton, potatoes, vegetables, grapes, fruits and berries; sheep, goats, cattle. **Labor force:** 1.7 million; agriculture and forestry, 40%; industry and construction, 19%; other, 41% (1995 est.). **Exports:** $506 million (1996): cotton, wool, meat, tobacco; gold, mercury, uranium, hydropower; machinery; shoes. **Imports:** $890 million (1996): grain, lumber, industrial products, ferrous metals, fuel, machinery, textiles, footwear. **Trading partners:** China, U.K., former Soviet Union, Turkey, Cuba, U.S., Germany.

Geography Kyrgyzstan (formerly Kirghizia) is a rugged country with the Tien Shan mountain range covering approximately 95% of the whole territory. The mountaintops are covered with perennial snow and glaciers. Kyrgyzstan borders Kazakhstan on the north and northwest, Uzbekistan in the southwest, Tajikistan in the south, and China in the southeast. The republic is the same size in area as the state of Nebraska.

Government Constitutional republic.

History The native Kyrgyz are a Turkic people who in ancient times first settled in the Tien Shan mountains. They were traditionally pastoral nomads. There was extensive Russian colonization in the 1900s and Russian settlers were given much of the best agricultural land. This led to an unsuccessful and disastrous revolt by the Kyrgyz people in 1916. Kyrgyzstan became part of the Soviet Federated Socialist Republic in 1924, and was made an autonomous republic in 1926. It became a constituent republic of the U.S.S.R. in 1936. The Soviets forced the Kyrgyz to abandon their nomadic culture and brought modern farming and industrial production techniques into their society. It has greatly changed their traditional way of life.

Kyrgyzstan proclaimed its independence from the Soviet Union on Aug. 31, 1991. On Dec. 21, 1991, Kyrgyzstan joined the Commonwealth of Independent States. The country joined the U.N. and the IMF in 1992 and adopted a shock-therapy economic program. Voters endorsed market reforms in a referendum held in Jan. 1994, and in 1996, referendum voters overwhelmingly endorsed proposed constitutional changes that enhanced the power of the president. Representatives of the country along with those of Russia, China, Kazakhstan, and Tajikistan signed a non-aggression agreement in April 1996. In March 1997, Russian border control was extended until the end of the year as authorities in Kyrgyzstan grew increasingly concerned about the growth of the illegal narcotics trade in the country.

In 1999, several groups of radical Islamic gunmen, believed to be from Uzbekistan or Tajikistan, have led raids and kidnappings from camps in Kyrgyzstan's mountains.

Laos
LAO PEOPLE'S DEMOCRATIC REPUBLIC

President: Khamtai Siphandon (1998) **Prime Minister:** Sisavat Keobounphan (1998) **Area:** 91,429 sq. mi. (236,800 sq. km) **Population (1999 est.):** 5,407,453 (average annual rate of natural increase: 2.74%); birth rate: 39.9/1000; infant mortality rate: 89.3/1000; density per sq. mi.: 59 **Capital and largest city (1990):** Vientiane, 442,000. **Monetary unit:** Kip. **Languages:** Lao (official), French, English. **Ethnicity/race:** Lao Loum (lowland) 68%, Lao Theung (upland) 22%, Lao Soung (highland) including the Hmong ("Meo") and the Yao (Mien) 9%, ethnic Vietnamese/Chinese 1%. **Religions:** Buddhist, 85%; animist and other, 15%. **Literacy rate:** 45% **Economic summary: GDP/PPP** (1997 est.): $5.9 billion; $1,150 per capita. **Real growth rate:** 1.5%. **Inflation:** 16%. **Unemployment:** (1995 est.): 1.7% overall, 4.5% in urban areas. **Arable land:** 3%. **Agriculture:** sweet potatoes, vegetables, corn, coffee, sugarcane, cotton; water buffalo, pigs, cattle, poultry; tobacco. **Labor force:** 1–1.5 million; agriculture, 80% (1997 est.). **Industry:** tin and gypsum mining, timber, electric power, agricultural processing, construction, garments. **Natural resources:** timber, hydropower, gypsum, tin, gold, gemstones. **Exports:** $313.1 million (f.o.b., 1996): wood products, garments, electricity, coffee, tin. **Imports:** $678 million (c.i.f., 1996): machinery and equipment, vehicles, fuel. **Major trading partners:** Vietnam, Thailand, Germany, France, Japan, China, Singapore.

Geography A landlocked nation in Southeast Asia occupying the northwestern portion of the Indochinese peninsula, Laos is surrounded by China, Vietnam, Cambodia, Thailand, and Burma. It is twice the size of Pennsylvania.

Laos is a mountainous country, especially in the north, where peaks rise above 9,000 feet (2,800 m). Dense forests cover the northern and eastern areas. The Mekong River, which forms the boundary with Burma and Thailand, flows entirely through the country for 932 miles (1,500 km) of its course.

Government Communist state.

History The Lao people migrated into Laos from southern China from the 8th century c.e. onward. In the 14th century the first Laotian state was founded, the Lan Xang kingdom, which ruled Laos until it split into three separate kingdoms in 1713. During the 18th century the three kingdoms came under Siamese (Thai) rule, and in 1893 became a French protectorate. Its territory was incorporated into the union of Indochina. A strong nationalist movement developed during World War II, but France reestablished control in 1946 and made the king of Luang Prabang constitutional monarch of all Laos. France granted semiautonomy in 1949 and then, spurred by the Viet Minh rebellion in Vietnam, full independence within the French Union in 1950.

In 1951, Prince Souphanouvong organized the Pathet Lao, a Communist independence movement, in North Vietnam. Viet Minh and Pathet Lao forces invaded central Laos, and civil war resulted. By the Geneva agreements of 1954 and an armistice of 1955, two northern provinces were given to the Pathet Lao; the rest went to the royal regime. Full sovereignty was given to the kingdom by the Paris agreements of Dec. 29, 1954. In 1957, Prince Souvanna Phouma, the royal premier, and the Pathet Lao leader, Prince Souphanouvong, the premier's half-brother, agreed to reestablishment of a unified government, with Pathet Lao participation and integration of Pathet Lao forces into the royal army. The agreement broke down in 1959, and armed conflict began anew.

In 1960, the struggle became three-way as Gen. Phoumi Nosavan, controlling the bulk of the royal army, set up in the south a pro-Western revolutionary government headed by Prince Boun Gum. General Phoumi took Vientiane in December, driving Souvanna Phouma into exile in Cambodia. The Soviet bloc supported Souvanna Phouma. In 1961, a ceasefire was arranged and the three princes agreed to a coalition government headed by Souvanna Phouma.

But North Vietnam, the U.S. (in the form of Central Intelligence Agency personnel), and China remained active in Laos after the settlement. North Vietnam used a supply line (Ho Chi Minh Trail) running down the mountain valleys of eastern Laos into Cambodia and South Vietnam, particularly after the U.S.–South Vietnamese incursion into Cambodia in 1970 stopped supplies via Cambodian seaports.

An agreement reached in 1973 revived coalition government. The Communist Pathet Lao seized complete power in 1975, installing Souphanouvong as president and Kaysone Phomvihane as premier. Since then other parties and political groups have been moribund and most of their leaders have fled the country. The monarchy was abolished on Dec. 2, 1975, when the Pathet Lao ousted a coalition government and King Sisavang Vatthana abdicated.

The Supreme People's Assembly in August 1991 adopted a new constitution that dropped all references to socialism but retained the one-party state. In addition to implementing market-oriented policies, the country has passed laws governing property, inheritance, and contracts.

During 1995 the country began making more diplomatic overtures toward its neighbors. Economic agreements were reached with Burma, and Laos's border disputes with Thailand in the 1980s gave way to warmer relations. The U.S. announced a lifting of its ban on aid to the nation.

By most international estimates, Laos is one of the ten poorest countries in the world. The subsistence farmers who make up more than 80% of the population have been plagued with bad agricultural conditions—alternately flood or drought—since 1993.

Latvia

THE REPUBLIC OF LATVIA

National name: Latvija
President: Vaira Vike-Freiberga (1999)
Prime Minister: Andris Skele (1999)
Area: 25,400 sq. mi. (64,100 sq. km)
Population (1999 est.): 2,353,874; average annual rate of natural increase: –0.77%; birth rate: 8.1/1000; infant mortality rate: 17.2/1000; density per sq. mi.: 93
Capital and largest city (1993 est.): Riga, 874,000. **Other large cities:** Daugavpils, 125,000; Liepaja, 108,000. **Monetary unit:** Lats. **Language:** Latvian. **Ethnicity/race:** Latvian 51.8%, Russian 33.8%, Belarussian 4.5%, Ukrainian 3.4%, Polish 2.3%, other 4.2%. **Religions:** Lutheran, Catholic, and Baptist. **Literacy:** 100%
Economic summary: GDP/PPP (1997 est.): $10.4 billion; $4,260 per capita. **Real growth rate:** 6%. **Inflation:** 7.4%. **Unemployment:** 7% (1996). **Labor force:** 1.4 million (1997): industry 41%, agriculture and forestry 16%, services 43% (1990). **Industries:** buses, vans, street and railroad cars, synthetic fibers,

agricultural machinery, fertilizers, washing machines, radios, electronics, pharmaceuticals, processed foods, textiles; dependent on imports for energy, raw materials, and intermediate products. **Agriculture:** grain, sugar beets, potatoes, vegetables; meat, milk, eggs; fish. **Natural resources:** amber, peat, limestone, dolomite. **Exports:** $1.4 billion (f.o.b., 1996): wood and wood products, textiles, foodstuffs. **Imports:** $2.3 billion (c.i.f., 1996): fuels, machinery and equipment, chemicals. **Major trading partners:** Russia, other C.I.S., Germany, Sweden, U.K., Finland.

Geography Latvia borders Estonia on the north, Lithuania in the south, the Baltic Sea with the Gulf of Riga in the west, Russia in the east, and Belarus in the southeast. Latvia is largely a fertile lowland with numerous lakes and hills to the east.

Government Parliamentary democracy.

History Baltic tribespeople settled along the Baltic Sea, and lacking a centralized government, fell prey to more powerful peoples. In the 13th century they were overcome by the Livonian Brothers of the Sword, a German order of knights whose mission was to conquer and Christianize the Baltic region. The land became part of the state of Livonia until 1561. Germans made up the ruling class of Livonia and Baltic tribes made up the peasantry, and German became the official language of the region.

Poland conquered the territory in 1562, until Sweden took over the land in 1629, and ruled over it until 1721. Then the land passed to Russia. From that time until 1918, the Latvians remained Russian subjects, although they preserved their language, customs, and folklore.

The Russian Revolution of 1917 gave them their opportunity for freedom, and the Latvian republic was proclaimed on Nov. 18, 1918. The republic lasted little more than 20 years. Plagued by political instability, Latvia essentially became a dictatorship under President Karlis Ulmanis. It was occupied by Russian troops in 1939 and incorporated into the Soviet Union in 1940. Latvia allied itself with Germany in World War II, and German armies occupied the nation from 1941 to 1943–44. Of the 70,000 Jews living in Latvia during the war, 95% were massacred. In 1944, Russia again took control of Latvia.

Latvia was one of the most economically well-off and industrialized parts of the Soviet Union. When a coup against Soviet president Mikhail Gorbachev failed in 1991, the Baltic nations saw an opportunity to free themselves from Soviet domination and, following the actions of Lithuania and Estonia, Latvia declared its independence on Aug. 21, 1991. European and most other nations quickly recognized their independence, and on Sept. 2, 1991, President Bush announced full diplomatic recognition for Latvia, Estonia, and Lithuania. The Soviet Union recognized Latvia's independence on Sept. 6, and U.N. membership followed on Sept. 17, 1991.

Because Latvians' ethnic identity had been quashed throughout its history by foreign rulers, the new Latvian republic set up strict citizenship laws, limiting citizenship to ethnic Latvians and to those who had lived in the region before Soviet rule in 1940. This denied about 452,000 of the country's 740,000 ethnic Russians of citizenship.

Latvia's bid to join the European Union was not accepted in talks that began in 1997. In addition to improving its administrative systems, Latvia was told that it had to speed up naturalization of minorities, in particular its large number of Russians. In 1998, a referendum passed easing the citizenship rules, although it was still necessary to be competent in the Latvian language, which many believe is unreasonable to expect of older or poorly educated ethnic Russians. Latvia's admission to the EU and NATO was still under consideration in 1999.

Lebanon

REPUBLIC OF LEBANON

National name: Al-Joumhouriya al-Lubnaniya
President: Émile Lahoud (1998)
Premier: Selim al-Hoss (1998)
Area: 4,015 sq. mi. (10,400 sq. km)
Population (1999 est.): 3,562,699 (average annual rate of natural increase: 1.61%); birth rate: 22.5/1000; infant mortality rate: 30.5/1000; density per sq. mi.: 887
Capital and largest city (1991 est.): Beirut, 1,100,000.
Other large cities: Tripoli, 240,000; Sidon, 100,000.
Monetary unit: Lebanese pound. **Languages:** Arabic (official), French, English. **Ethnicity/race:** Arab 95%, Armenian 4%, other 1%. **Religions:** Islam, 60%; Christian, 40% (17 recognized sects); Judaism negl. (1 sect). **Literacy rate:** 80%
Economic summary: GDP/PPP (1997 est.): $15.2 billion; $4,400 per capita. **Real growth rate:** 4%. **Inflation:** 9%. **Unemployment:** 18%. **Arable land:** 21%. **Agriculture:** citrus, vegetables, potatoes, olives, tobacco, hemp (hashish); sheep, goats. **Labor force:** 1 million plus as many as 1 million foreign workers (1996 est.); services, 62%; industry, 31%; agriculture, 7% (1997 est.). **Industry:** banking; food processing; jewelry; cement; textiles; mineral and chemical products; wood and furniture products; oil refining; metal fabricating. **Exports:** $1.018 billion (f.o.b., 1996): paper and paper products, food stuffs, textiles and textile products, jewelry, metals and metal products, electrical equipment and products, chemical products, transport vehicles. **Imports:** $7.559 billion (c.i.f., 1996): machinery and transport equipment, foodstuffs, consumer goods, chemicals, textiles, metals, fuels. **Major trading partners:** U.A.E., Saudi Arabia, Kuwait, Syria, Jordan, France, Italy, U.S., Germany, U.K., Japan.

Geography Lebanon lies at the eastern end of the Mediterranean Sea north of Israel and west of Syria. It is four-fifths the size of Connecticut.

The Lebanon Mountains, which parallel the coast on the west, cover most of the country, while on the eastern border is the Anti-Lebanon range. Between the two lies the Bekaa Valley, the principal agricultural area.

Government Republic.

History After World War I, France was given a League of Nations mandate over Lebanon and its neighbor Syria, which together had previously been a single political unit in the Ottoman Empire. France divided them in 1920 into separate colonial administrations, drawing a border that separated predominantly Muslim Syria from the kaleidoscope of religious communities in Lebanon where Maronite Christians were then dominant. After 20 years of the French mandate regime, Lebanon's independence was proclaimed on Nov. 26, 1941, but full independence came in stages. Under an agreement between representatives of Lebanon and the French National Committee of Liberation, most of the powers exercised by France were transferred to the Lebanese government on Jan. 1, 1944. The evacuation of French troops was completed in 1946.

According to the National Pact, different religious communities are represented in the government by having a Maronite Christian president, a Sunni Muslim prime minister, and a Shi'ite National Assembly speaker. The arrangement worked for two decades. Civil war broke out in 1958, with Muslim factions led by Kamal Jumblat and Saeb Salam rising in insurrection against the Lebanese government headed by President Camille Chamoun, a Maronite Christian favoring close ties to the West. At Chamoun's request, President Eisenhower on July 15 sent U.S. troops to reestablish the government's authority.

Clan warfare between various religious factions in Lebanon goes back centuries. The hodgepodge includes Maronite Christians, who since independence have dominated the government; Sunni Muslims, who have prospered in business and shared political power; the Druze, who hold a faith incorporating aspects of Islam and Gnosticism; and Shi'ite Muslims.

A new—and bloodier—Lebanese civil war that broke out in 1975 resulted in the addition of still another ingredient in the brew—the Syrians. In the fighting between Lebanese factions, 40,000 Lebanese were estimated to have been killed and 100,000 wounded between March 1975 and Nov. 1976. At that point, a Syrian-dominated Arab Deterrent Force intervened and brought large-scale fighting to a halt.

Palestinian guerrillas staging raids on Israel from Lebanese territory drew punitive Israeli raids on Lebanon, and two large-scale Israeli invasions. The Israelis withdrew in June after the U.N. Security Council created a 6,000-man peacekeeping force for the area, called UNIFIL. As they departed, the Israelis turned their strong points over to a Christian militia that they had organized, instead of to the U.N. force.

The second Israeli invasion came on June 6, 1982, and this time it was total. It was in response to an assassination attempt by Palestinian terrorists on the Israeli ambassador in London. As a stronghold of the PLO, Lebanon became the Israelis' target. Israel's government had complained that Lebanon had countenanced the presence of these militant Palestinians.

A U.S. envoy negotiated the dispersal of most of the PLO to other Arab nations and Israel pulled back some of its forces. The violence seemed to have come to an end when, on Sept. 14, Bashir Gemayel, the 34-year-old president-elect, was killed by a bomb that destroyed the headquarters of his Christian Phalangist Party.

The day after Gemayel's assassination, Israeli troops moved into West Beirut in force. On Sept. 17 it was revealed that Christian militiamen had massacred hundreds of Palestinians in two refugee camps, but Israel denied responsibility. On Sept. 20, Amin Gemayel, older brother of Bashir Gemayel, was elected president by the Parliament.

The massacre in the refugee camps prompted the return of a multinational peacekeeping force composed of U.S. Marines and British, French, and Italian soldiers. Their mandate was to support the central Lebanese government, but they soon found themselves drawn into the struggle for power between different Lebanese factions. During their stay in Lebanon, 260 U.S. Marines and about 60

French soldiers were killed, most of them in suicide bombings of the Marine and French army compounds on Oct. 23, 1983. The multinational force left in the spring of 1984.

In July 1986, Syrian observers took position in Beirut to monitor a peacekeeping agreement. The agreement broke down and fighting between Shi'ite and Druze militia in West Beirut became so intense that Syrian troops moved in force in Feb. 1987, suppressing militia resistance.

In early 1991 the Lebanese government, backed by Syria, attempted to regain control over the south and disband all private militias, thereby ending the 16-year civil war. These conflicts destroyed much of the infrastructure and industry of Lebanon.

In the general elections of Aug. 1992 most Christians abstained from voting, demanding that Syrian forces first leave the country. The new legislature consisted of mostly pro-Syrian members. The largest Christian party was further weakened when in Jan. 1993 it appeared to split into two factions.

In June 1999, Israel bombed Southern Lebanon, its most severe attack on Lebanon since 1996. The attack took place just before Israeli prime minister Netanyahu left office. The new Israeli prime minister, Ehud Barak, brought new hope for the withdrawal of Israeli troops from southern Lebanon, and an end to the low-grade war that has taken place since 1985 between Israeli troops and Hezbollah guerrillas. Barak has promised to withdraw troops within a year and to make peace with Syria, which controls the guerrillas.

Lesotho

KINGDOM OF LESOTHO

Sovereign: King Letsie III (1990)
Prime Minister: Pakalitha Mosisili (1998)
Area: 11,720 sq. mi. (30,350 sq. km)
Population (1999 est.): 2,128,950 (average annual rate of natural increase: 1.8%); birth rate: 31.3/1000; infant mortality rate: 77.6/1000; density per sq. mi.: 182
Capital and largest city (1992): Maseru (1992), 170,000. **Monetary unit:** Loti. **Languages:** English and Sesotho (official); also Zulu and Xhosa. **Ethnicity/race:** Sotho 99.7%, Europeans 1,600, Asians 800. **Religions:** Christian, 80%; indigenous beliefs; Muslim; and Bahai. **Literacy rate:** 56% (1989)
Economic summary: GDP/PPP (1997 est.): $5.1 billion; $2,500 per capita. **Real growth rate:** 9%. **Inflation:** 8.7% (1996 est.). **Unemployment:** substantial unemployment and underemployment effecting more than half of the labor force (1996 est.). **Arable land:** 11%. **Agriculture:** corn, wheat, pulses, sorghum, barley; livestock. **Labor force:** 689,000; subsistence agriculture, 86%. **Natural resources:** water, agricultural and grazing land, some diamonds and other minerals. **Industries:** food, beverages, textiles, handicrafts; construction; tourism. **Exports:** $218 million (f.o.b., 1996 est.): clothing, wool, footwear, road vehicles, mohair. **Imports:** $1.1 billion (c.i.f., 1996 est.): corn, clothing, building materials, vehicles, machinery, medicines, petroleum products. **Major trading partners:** South African Customs Union, North America, Asia, EU. **Member of Commonwealth of Nations**

Geography Mountainous Lesotho, the size of Maryland, is surrounded by the Republic of South Africa in the east-central part of that country except for short borders on the east and south with two discontinuous units of the Republic of Transkei. The

Drakensberg Mountains in the east are Lesotho's principal chain. Elsewhere the region consists of rocky tableland.

Government Constitutional monarchy.

History Lesotho (formerly Basutoland) was constituted a native state under British protection by a treaty signed with the native chief Moshesh in 1843. It was annexed to Cape Colony in 1871, but in 1884 it was restored to direct control by the Crown. The colony of Basutoland became the independent nation of Lesotho on Oct. 4, 1966, with King Moshoeshoe II as sovereign.

In the 1970 elections, Ntsu Mokhehle, head of the Basutoland Congress Party, claimed a victory, but Prime Minister Leabua Jonathan declared a state of emergency, suspended the constitution, and arrested Mokhehle. King Moshoeshoe returned after a compromise with Jonathan in which the new constitution would name him head of state but forbid his participation in politics.

After the king refused to approve the replacements in Feb. 1990 of individuals dismissed by Justin Metsino Lekhanya, the chairman of the Military Council, the latter stripped the king of his executive power. Then in early March Lekhanya sent the king into exile. In November the king was dethroned, and his son was sworn in as King Letsie III.

Lekhanya was himself forced to resign in April 1991 and Col. Ramaema became the new chairman in May. In Jan. 1995 the crown reverted to the father of Letsie III, Moshoeshoe II. Letsie again became crown prince. In 1996, however, King Moshoeshoe died in an automobile accident and Letsie again assumed the throne.

In fall 1998, hundreds of demonstrators protested for weeks in front of the king's palace, claiming voting fraud in the May elections that put Prime Minister Pakalitha Mosisili in power. They demanded that the government step down and hold new elections. Troops from South African and Botswanan entered the country to stop the riots and put down an army mutiny.

Liberia

REPUBLIC OF LIBERIA

President: Charles Taylor (1997)
Area: 43,000 sq. mi. (111,370 sq. km)
Population (1999 est.): 2,923,725 (average annual rate of natural increase: 3.05%); birth rate: 41.5/1000; infant mortality rate: 100.6/1000; density per sq. mi.: 68
Capital and largest city (1993 est.): Monrovia, 1,000,000. **Monetary unit:** Liberian dollar.
Languages: English (official) and tribal dialects. **Ethnicity/race:** indigenous African tribes 95% (including Kpelle, Bassa, Gio, Kru, Grebo, Mano, Krahn, Gola, Gbandi, Loma, Kissi, Vai, and Bella), Americo-Liberians 5% (descendants of former slaves). **Religions:** traditional, 70%; Christian, 10%; Islam, 20%. **Literacy rate:** 40%
Economic summary: GDP/PPP (1997 est.): $2.6 billion; $1,000 per capita. **Real growth rate:** n.a. **Inflation:** n.a. **Unemployment:** n.a. **Arable land:** 1%. **Agriculture:** rubber, coffee, cocoa, rice, cassava (tapioca), palm oil, sugarcane, bananas; sheep, goats; timber. **Labor force:** agriculture, 70%. **Industry:** rubber processing, food processing, construction materials, furniture, palm oil processing, iron ore, diamonds. **Natural resources:** iron ore, timber, diamonds, gold. **Exports:** $667 million (f.o.b., 1995

est.): diamonds, iron ore, rubber, timber, coffee.
Imports: $5.8 billion (f.o.b., 1995 est.) mineral fuels,
chemicals, machinery, transportation equipment,
manufactured goods; rice and other foodstuffs. **Major
trading partners:** U.S., EU, The Netherlands,
Singapore, Japan, China, South Korea, ECOWAS.

Geography Lying on the Atlantic in the southern
part of West Africa, Liberia is bordered by Sierra
Leone, Guinea, and Côte d'Ivoire. It is comparable
in size to Tennessee.

Most of the country is a plateau covered by dense
tropical forests, which thrive under an annual rainfall of about 160 inches a year.

Government Republic.

History Africa's first republic, Liberia was
founded in 1822 as a result of the efforts of the
American Colonization Society to settle freed
American slaves in West Africa. The society contended that the immigration of blacks to Africa was
an answer to the problem of slavery as well as to
what they felt was the incompatibility of the races.
Over the course of forty years, about 12,000 slaves
were voluntarily relocated. Originally called Monrovia, the colony became the Free and Independent
Republic of Liberia in 1847.

The English-speaking Americo-Liberians, descendants of former American slaves, make up only 5%
of the population, but have historically dominated
the intellectual and ruling class. Liberia's indigenous population is primarily composed of Mande,
Kwa, and Mel peoples.

The government of Africa's first republic was
modeled after that of the United States, and Joseph
Jenkins Roberts of Virginia was elected the first
president. Ironically, Liberia's constitution denied
indigenous Liberians equal rights with the lighter-
skinned American emigrants and their descendants.

After 1920, considerable progress was made
toward opening up the interior, a process that was
spurred in 1951 by the establishment of a 43-mile
(69-km) railroad to the Bomi Hills from Monrovia.
In July 1971, while serving his sixth term as president, William V. S. Tubman died following surgery
and was succeeded by his long-time associate, Vice
President William R. Tolbert, Jr.

Tolbert was ousted in a military coup carried out
April 12, 1980, by Master Sgt. Samuel K. Doe, who
was backed by the U.S. government. A rebellion led
by Charles Taylor, a former Doe aide, started in Dec.
1989 and, with the help of Côte d'Ivoire and Burkina
Faso, took control of Liberia's key population and
economic centers by mid-July 1990. His three
attempts to take the capital failed, however, and the
bloody civil war continued. By mid-April 1996 factional fighting by the country's warlords had destroyed
any last vestige of normality and civil society.

In what was considered by international observers
a free election, Charles Taylor won 75.3% of the
presidential vote in July 1997. Since then, however,
Taylor's government has focused more on armed
security rather than reconstructing of the country
after its seven-year civil war. While Taylor attempts
to fashion himself as a democratic political leader,
his behavior remains that of a militia rebel.

Taylor has supplied neighboring rebels in Sierra
Leone with troops and weapons in an effort to
topple Sierra Leone's democratically elected president, Ahmed Tejan Kabbah.

Libya

SOCIALIST PEOPLE'S LIBYAN ARAB JAMAHIRIYA

National name: Socialist People's Libyan Arab
Jamahiriya
Head of State: Col. Muammar al-Qaddafi (1969)
Secretary of the General People's Committee:
Muhammad Ahmad al-Mangoush (1997)
Area: 679,536 sq. mi. (1,759,540 sq. km)
Population (1999 est.): 4,992,838; (average annual rate
of natural increase: 2.4); birth rate: 27.3/1000; infant
mortality rate: 28.2/1000; density per sq. mi.: 7
Capital: Tripoli. **Largest cities (est. 1988):** Tripoli,
591,062; Benghazi, 446,250. **Monetary unit:** Libyan
dinar. **Languages:** Arabic, Italian and English widely
understood in major cities. **Ethnicity/race:** Berber and
Arab 97%, Greeks, Maltese, Italians, Egyptians,
Pakistanis, Turks, Indians, Tunisians. **Religion:** Islam.
Literacy rate: 64%
Economic summary: GDP/PPP (1997 est.): $38 billion;
$6,700 per capita. **Real growth rate:** 0.5%. **Inflation:**
30%. **Unemployment:** 25%. **Arable land:** 1%.
Agriculture: wheat, barley, olives, dates, citrus,
vegetables, peanuts; meat, eggs. **Labor force:** 1
million; industry 31%, services 27%, government 24%,
agriculture 18% (July 1998 est.). **Industries:**
petroleum, food processing, textiles, handicrafts,
cement. **Natural resources:** petroleum, natural gas,
gypsum. **Exports:** $9 billion (f.o.b., 1995): crude oil,
refined petroleum products, natural gas. **Imports:** $6.2
billion (f.o.b., 1995): machinery, transport equipment,
food, manufactured goods. **Major trading partners:**
Italy, Germany, Spain, France, Turkey, Greece, Egypt,
U.K., Tunisia, eastern Europe.

Geography Libya stretches along the northeastern
coast of Africa between Tunisia and Algeria on the
west and Egypt on the east; to the south are the
Sudan, Chad, and Niger. It is one-sixth larger than
Alaska. A greater part of the country lies within the
Sahara. Along the Mediterranean coast and farther
inland is arable plateau land.

Government Military dictatorship.

History The first inhabitants of Libya were Berber
tribes. In the 7th century B.C.E., Phoenicians colonized the eastern section of Libya, called Tripolitania, and Greeks colonized the western portion,
called Cyrenaica. Tripolitania was for a time under
Carthaginian control. It became part of the Roman
empire from 46 B.C.E. to C.E. 436, after which it was
sacked by the Vandals. Cyrenaica belonged to the
Roman empire from the 1st century B.C.E. until its
decline, after which it was invaded by Arab forces
in C.E. 642. Beginning in the 16th century, both Tripolitania and Cyrenaica nominally became part of
the Ottoman Empire.

Tripolitania was one of the outposts for the Barbary pirates who raided Mediterranean merchant
ships or required them to pay tribute. In 1801 the
pasha of Tripoli raised the price of tribute, which led
to the Tripolitan war with the United States. When
the peace treaty was signed on June 4, 1805, U.S.
ships no longer had to pay tribute to Tripoli.

Following the outbreak of hostilities between
Italy and Turkey in 1911, Italian troops occupied
Tripoli. Italian sovereignty was recognized in 1912.
Libyans continued to fight the Italians until 1914, by
which time Italy controlled most of the land. Italy
formally united Tripolitania and Cyrenaica in 1934
as the colony of Libya.

Libya was the scene of much desert fighting during
World War II. After the fall of Tripoli on Jan. 23,

1943, it came under Allied administration. In 1949, the U.N. voted that Libya should become independent, and in 1951 it became the United Kingdom of Libya. Oil was discovered in the impoverished country in 1958, and eventually transformed its economy.

On Sept. 1, 1969, 27-year-old Colonel Muammar al-Qaddafi deposed the king and revolutionized the country, making it a pro-Arabic, anti-Western, Islamic republic with socialist leanings. It was also rabidly anti-Israeli. A notorious firebrand, Qaddafi aligned himself with dictators, such as Uganda's Idi Amin, and fostered anti-Western terrorism.

On Aug. 19, 1981, two U.S. Navy F-14s shot down two Soviet-made SU-22s of the Libyan air force that had attacked them in air space above the Gulf of Sidra. On March 24, 1986, U.S. and Libyan forces skirmished in the Gulf of Sidra, and two Libyan patrol boats were sunk. Qaddafi's troops also supported rebels in Chad but suffered major military reverses in 1987. A two-year-old U.S. covert policy to destabilize the Libyan government ended in failure in Dec. 1990.

On Dec. 21, 1988, a Boeing 747 exploded in flight over Lockerbie, Scotland, the result of a terrorist bomb, killing all 259 people aboard and 11 on the ground. Two Libyan intelligence agents were indicted, but Qaddafi refused to hand them over, leading to U.N.-approved trade and air traffic embargoes in 1992. On April 5, 1999, after years of negotiations, Libya surrendered the two men. The suspects, Abdel Basset Ali al-Megrahi and Lamen Khalifa Fhimah, will be tried in The Netherlands, though it will be considered Scottish soil for the duration of the trial. As a result of Libya's cooperation, the United Nations lifted sanctions against Libya, which had severely affected the Libyan economy. European companies almost immediately began to court the oil-rich nation once again.

Liechtenstein

PRINCIPALITY OF LIECHTENSTEIN

Ruler: Prince Hans Adam II (1989)
Prime Minister: Mario Frick (1993)
Area: 61 sq. mi. (160 sq. km)
Population (1999 est.): 32,057 (average annual growth rate: 0.49%); birth rate: 12.2/1000; infant mortality rate: 5.2/1000; density per sq. mi.: 526
Capital and largest city (1994): Vaduz, 5,067.
Monetary unit: Swiss franc. **Languages:** German (official), Alemmanic dialect. **Ethnicity/race:** Alemannic 87.5%; Italian, Turkish, and other 12.5% . **Religions:** Roman Catholic 80%, Protestant 6.9%, unknown 5.6%, other 7.5%. **Literacy rate:** 100%
Economic summary: GDP/PPP (1996 est.): $713 million; $23,000 per capita. **Real growth rate:** n.a. **Inflation:** 0.5% (1997 est.). **Unemployment:** 1.6% (1997). **Arable land:** 25%. **Agriculture:** wheat, barley, maize, potatoes; livestock, dairy products. **Labor force:** 22,891 (including 13,847 foreigners); industry, trade, and building 46%, services 52%, agriculture, fishing, forestry, and horticulture 2% (1996 est.). **Industry:** electronics, metal manufacturing, textiles, ceramics, pharmaceuticals, food products, precision instruments, tourism. **Natural resource:** hydroelectric potential. **Exports:** $2.47 billion (1996): small specialty machinery, dental products, stamps, hardware, pottery. **Imports:** $917.3 million (1996): machinery, metal goods, textiles, foodstuffs, motor vehicles. **Major trading partners:** Switzerland, EU and EFTA countries

Geography Tiny Liechtenstein, not quite as large as Washington, D.C., lies on the east bank of the Rhine River south of Lake Constance between Austria and Switzerland. It consists of low valley land and Alpine peaks. Falknis (8,401 ft.; 2,561 m) and Naafkopf (8,432 ft.; 2,570 m) are the tallest.

Government Constitutional monarchy.

History The Liechtensteiners are descended from the Alemanni tribe that came into the region after c.e. 500. Founded in 1719, Liechtenstein was a member of the German Confederation from 1815 to 1866, when it became an independent principality. It abolished its army in 1868 and has managed to stay neutral and undamaged in all European wars since then. Liechtenstein still claims 1,600 sq. km of Czech territory (the royal family's ancestral home) confiscated in 1918; the Czech Republic insists that restitution does not go back before Feb. 1948, when the Communists seized power. In a referendum on July 1, 1984, male voters granted women the right to vote in national (but not local) elections—a victory for Prince Hans Adam. A treaty negotiated between EFTA and the European Union linking the two as the European Economic Area was ratified in a Dec. 1993 vote, but Switzerland rejected it. After renegotiation the treaty was again subjected to a referendum in April 1995 and approved. Liechtenstein won a special concession limiting immigration.

Lithuania

REPUBLIC OF LITHUANIA

National name: Lietuva
President: Valdas Adamkus (1998)
Prime Minister: Rolandas Paksas (1999)
Area: 25,212 sq. mi. (65,200 sq. km)
Population (1998 est.): 3,600,158; (average annual rate of natural increase: –0.45%); birth rate: 10.5/1000; infant mortality rate: 14.7/1000; density per sq. mi: 142
Capital and largest city (1993 est.): Vilnius, 590,100. **Other large cities:** Kaunas, 429,000; Klaipéda, 206,400. **Monetary unit:** Litas. **Languages:** Lithuanian (official), Polish, Russian. **Ethnicity/race:** Lithuanian 80.1%, Russian 8.6%, Polish 7.7%, Belarussian 1.5%, other 2.1%. **Religions:** Catholic, 85%; others include Lutheran, Russian Orthodox, Protestant, evangelical Christian Baptist, Islam, Judaism. **Literacy:** 98%
Economic summary: GDP/PPP (1997 est.): $15.4 billion; $4,230 per capita. **Real growth rate:** 6% (1997 est.). **Inflation:** 8.6% (1997 est.). **Unemployment rate:** 6.7% (Jan. 1998). **Labor force:** 1.8 million; industry and construction, 42%; agriculture and forestry, 20%; other 38% (1997). **Natural resources:** peat. **Industry:** metal-cutting machine tools, electric motors, television sets, refrigerators and freezers, petroleum refining, shipbuilding, furniture making, textiles, food processing, fertilizers, agricultural machinery, optical equipment, electronic components, computers, amber. **Agriculture:** grain, potatoes, sugar beets, vegetables, meat, milk, eggs, fish, flax fiber. **Exports:** $3.3 billion (1996): agricultural products, mineral products, textiles, machinery, live animals. **Imports:** $4.4 billion (1996): mineral production, machinery, transport equipment, chemicals, textiles, foodstuff. **Major trading partners:** Russia, Germany, Belarus, Latvia, Ukraine, Poland, Italy, Denmark.

Geography Lithuania is situated on the eastern shore of the Baltic Sea and borders Latvia on the north, Belarus on the east and south, Poland and the

Kaliningrad region of Russia on the southwest. It is a country of gently rolling hills, many forests, rivers and streams, and lakes. Its principal natural resource is agricultural land.

Government Parliamentary democracy.

History The Liths, or Lithuanians, united in the 12th century under the rule of Mindaugas, who became king in 1251. Through marriage, one of the later Lithuanian rulers became the king of Poland (Ladislaus II) in 1386, uniting the countries. In 1410, the Poles and Lithuanians defeated the powerful Teutonic Knights at Tannenberg. From the 14th to the 16th century, Poland and Lithuania made up one of medieval Europe's largest empires, stretching from the Black Sea almost to Moscow. The two countries formed a confederation for almost 200 years, and in 1569 they formally united. Russia, Prussia, and Austria partitioned Poland in 1772, 1792, and 1795. As a consequence, Lithuania came under Russian rule after the last partition. Russia attempted to emerse Lithuania in Russian culture and language, but anti-Russian sentiment continued to grow. Following World War I and the collapse of Russia, Lithuania declared independence (1918), under German protection.

The republic was then annexed by the Soviet Union in 1940. From June 1941 to 1944 it was occupied by German troops, with whom Lithuania served in World War II. Some 240,000 Jews were massacred in Lithuania during the Nazi years. In 1944 Russian again annexed Lithuania.

The Lithuanian independence movement reemerged in 1988. In 1990, Vytautas Landsbergis, the non-Communist head of the largest Lithuanian popular movement (Sajudis), was elected president. On the same day, the Supreme Council rejected Soviet rule and declared the restoration of Lithuania's independence, the first Baltic republic to take this action. Confrontation with the Soviet Union ensued along with economic sanctions, but they were lifted after both sides agreed to a face-saving compromise. Lithuania's independence was quickly recognized by major European and other nations, including the United States. The Soviet Union finally recognized the independence of the Baltic states on Sept. 6. U.N. admittance followed on Sept. 17, 1991. Successful implementation of structural and legislative reforms in Lithuania attracted greater foreign direct investments by the mid-1990s.

Luxembourg

GRAND DUCHY OF LUXEMBOURG

National name: Grand-Duché de Luxembourg
Ruler: Grand Duke Jean (1964)
Premier: Jean-Claude Juncker (1995)
Area: 999 sq. mi. (2,586 sq. km)
Population (1999 est.): 429,080 (average annual rate of natural increase: 1.02%); birth rate: 10.4/1000; infant mortality rate: 5.0/1000; density per sq. mi.: 430
Capital and largest city (1991): Luxembourg, 75,622.
  Monetary units: Luxembourg franc and euro.
  Languages: Luxermbourgish, French, German.
  Ethnicity/race: Celtic base (with French and German blend), Portuguese, Italian, and European (guest and worker residents). **Religions:** Roman Catholic 97%, Protestant and Jewish 3%. **Literacy rate:** 100%
Economic summary: GDP/PPP (1997 est.): $13.48 billion; $33,700 per capita. **Real growth rate:** 3.6%.

Inflation: 2.3% (1995). **Unemployment:** 3.5% (1997). **Arable land:** 24%. **Agriculture:** barley, oats, potatoes, wheat, fruit, wine grapes, livestock products. **Labor force:** 213,100; one-third are foreign workers; trade, restaurants, hotels, 20%; mining, quarrying, manufacturing, 16%; other market services, 18%; community, social, personal services, 14%; construction, 11%; finance, insurance, real estate, business services, 9%; transport, storage, communications, 8%; agriculture, hunting, forestry, fishing, 1%; electricity, water, gas, 1% (1995 est.). **Industry:** banking, iron and steel, food processing, chemicals, metal products, engineering, tires, glass, aluminum. **Natural resources:** Iron ore (no longer exploited). **Exports:** $7.1 billion (f.o.b., 1996): finished steel products, chemicals, rubber products, glass, aluminum, other industrial products. **Imports:** $9.4 million (c.i.f., 1996): minerals, metals, foodstuffs, quality consumer goods. **Major trading partners:** Germany, France, Belgium, U.K., The Netherlands.

Geography Luxembourg is about half the size of Delaware. The Ardennes Mountains extend from Belgium into the northern section of Luxembourg. The rolling plateau of the fertile Bon Pays is in the south.

Government Constitutional monarchy.

History Luxembourg, once part of Charlemagne's empire, became an independent state in C.E. 963, when Siegfried, count of Ardennes, became sovereign of Lucilinburhuc ("Little Fortress"). In 1060, Conrad, a descendant of Siegfried, took the title count of Luxembourg. From the 15th to the 18th century, Spain, France, and Austria held it in turn. The Congress of Vienna in 1815 made it a Grand Duchy and gave it to William I, king of The Netherlands. In 1839 the Treaty of London ceded the western part of Luxembourg to Belgium. The eastern part, continuing in personal union with the Netherlands and a member of the German Confederation, became autonomous in 1848 and a neutral territory by decision of the London Conference of 1867, governed by its grand duke. Germany occupied the duchy in World Wars I and II. Allied troops liberated the enclave in 1944.

Luxembourg joined NATO in 1949, the Benelux Economic Union (with Belgium and The Netherlands) in 1948, and the European Economic Community (later the EU) in 1957. In 1961, Prince Jean, son and heir of Grand Duchess Charlotte, was made head of state, acting for his mother. She abdicated in 1964, and Prince Jean became grand duke. Grand Duchess Charlotte died in 1985. Luxembourg's Parliament approved the "Maastricht Accord," paving the way for the economic unity of the EU in July 1992.

Macedonia

REPUBLIC OF MACEDONIA[1]

National Name: Republica Makedonija
President: Kiro Gligorov (1991)
Prime Minister: Ljupco Georgievski (1998)
Area: 9,928 sq. mi. (25,333 sq. km)
Population (1999 est.): 2,022,604 (average annual rate of natural increase: 0.72%); birth rate: 15.2/1000; infant mortality rate: 18.7/1000; density per sq. mi.: 204
Capital and largest city (1994 est.): Skopje, 444,229.
  Other large cities: Bitola, 84,002; Prelep, 70,152; Kumanovo, 68,148. **Monetary unit:** Denar.
  Languages: Macedonian, which uses the Cyrillic alphabet, 70%; Albanian, 21%; Turkish, 3%; other, 6%.
  Ethnicity/race: Macedonian 65%, Albanian 22%,

Turkish 4%, Serb 2%, Rom (Gypsy) 3%, other 4%.
Religions (1994): Eastern Orthodox, 67%; Muslim, 30%
Economic summary: GDP/PPP (1997 est.): $2 billion; $960 per capita. **Real growth rate:** 1.5%. **Inflation:** 3.5%. **Unemployment:** 30%. **Labor force:** 591,773 (June 1994); manufacturing and mining, 40% (1992). **Industry:** coal, metallic chromium, lead, zinc, ferronickel, textiles, wood products, tobacco. **Agriculture:** rice, tobacco, wheat, corn, millet, cotton, sesame, mulberry leaves, citrus, vegetables, beef, pork, poultry, mutton. **Exports:** $1.2 billion (f.o.b., 1996): manufactured goods, machinery and transport equipment, food, beverage, tobacco. **Imports:** $1.6 billion (c.i.f., 1996): fuels, chemicals, machinery and equipment. **Major trading partners:** Germany, Italy, Austria, Bulgaria, other former Yugoslav republics, Greece.

1. The U.N. recognized the Republic of Macedonia on April 8, 1993, under the temporary name the Former Yugoslav Republic of Macedonia. The U.S. recognized Macedonia as a state in Feb. 1994.

Geography Macedonia is a landlocked state in the heart of the Balkans and is slightly smaller than the state of Vermont. It is a mountainous country with small basins of agricultural land linked by rivers. The three major rivers are the Aliakmon, the Vardar, and the Strymon. The Vardar is the largest and most important river.

Government Republic.

History The Republic of Macedonia occupies the western half of the ancient Kingdom of Macedonia. Historic Macedonia was defeated by Rome and became a Roman province in 148 B.C.E. After the Roman Empire was divided in C.E. 395, Macedonia was intermittently ruled by the Byzantine Empire until Turkey took possession of the land in 1389. The Ottoman Turks dominated Macedonia for the next five centuries, up until 1913. During the 19th and 20th centuries, there was a constant struggle by the Balkan powers to possess Macedonia for its economic and strategic military corridors. The Treaty of San Stefano in 1878 ending the Russo-Turkish War gave the largest part of Macedonia to Bulgaria. Bulgaria lost much of its Macedonian territory when it was defeated by the Greeks and Serbs in the Second Balkan War of 1913. Most of Macedonia went to Serbia and the remainder was divided among Greece and Bulgaria.

In 1914, Serbia, which included Macedonia, joined in union with Croatia, Slovenia, and Montenegro to form the kingdom of Serbs, Croats, and Slovenes, which was renamed Yugoslavia in 1929. Bulgaria joined the Axis powers in World War II and occupied parts of Yugoslavia including Macedonia in 1941. During the occupation of their country, Macedonian resistance fighters fought a guerrilla war against the invading troops. The Yugoslavian republic was reestablished after the defeat of Germany in 1945, and in 1946, the government removed Macedonia from Serbian control and made it an autonomous Yugoslavian republic. Later, when President Tito recognized the Macedonian people as a separate nation, the Macedonians strove to develop their own culture and language separate from Bulgaria and Serbia.

In Jan. 1992, Macedonia declared its independence from Yugoslavia and asked for recognition from the European Union nations. In Dec. 1993, six European nations recognized Macedonia; it was later recognized by the U.N. and the U.S. In Oct. 1995, Greece lifted its trade embargo as a result of an agreement recognizing Macedonia's right to its national title. Also in 1995, Macedonia was admitted into the Council of Europe. The Macedonian government, in 1997, urged NATO to extend its peacekeeping role in the Balkans beyond its mid-1998 mandate, saying NATO troops provided a stabilizing role. Ethnic tensions between ethnic Albanians and ethnic Macedonians continue to rise. In 1999, as a result of the Kosovo crisis, Macedonia accepted 140,000 refugees from the war.

Madagascar

REPUBLIC OF MADAGASCAR

National name: Repoblikan'i Madagasikara
President and Head of State: Didier Ratsiraka (1997)
Prime Minister: Tantely Andrianarivo (1998)
Area: 226,660 sq. mi. (587,040 sq. km)
Population (1999 est.): 14,873,387 (average annual rate of natural increase: 2.80%); birth rate: 41.5/1000; infant mortality rate: 89.1/1000; density per sq. mi.: 66
Capital and largest city (1993 est.): Antananarivo, 1,000,000. **Monetary unit:** Malagasy franc.
Languages: Malagasy, French. **Ethnicity/race:** Malayo-Indonesian (Merina and related Betsileo), Cotiers (mixed African, Malayo-Indonesian, and Arab ancestry—Betsimisaraka, Tsimihety, Antaisaka, Sakalava), French, Indian, Creole, Comoran.
Religions: traditional, 52%; Christian, 41%; Islam, 7%. **Literacy rate:** 80%
Economic summary: GDP/PPP (1997 est.): $10.3 billion; $730 per capita. **Real growth rate:** 3%. **Inflation:** 19.8% (1996). **Unemployment:** n.a. **Arable land:** 4%. **Agriculture:** coffee, vanilla, sugarcane, cloves, cocoa, rice, cassava (tapioca), beans, bananas, peanuts, livestock products. **Labor force:** 4.9 million in subsistence agriculture (96% of total labor force not receiving money wages). **Industry:** meat processing, soap, breweries, tanneries, sugar, textiles, glassware, cement, automobile assembly plant, paper, petroleum, tourism. **Natural resources:** graphite, chromite, coal, bauxite, salt, quartz, tar sands, semiprecious stones, mica, fish. **Exports:** $493 million (f.o.b., 1996 est.): coffee, cloves, vanilla, shellfish, sugar, petroleum products. **Imports:** $612 million (f.o.b., 1996 est.): intermediate manufactures, capital goods, consumer goods, food, petroleum. **Major trading partners:** France, U.S., Japan, Italy, Hong Kong, Singapore.

Geography Madagascar lies in the Indian Ocean off the southeast coast of Africa opposite Mozambique. The world's fourth-largest island, it is twice the size of Arizona. The country's low-lying coastal area gives way to a central plateau. The once densely wooded interior has largely been cut down.

Government Multiparty republic.

History The Malagasy are of mixed Malayo-Indonesian and African-Arab ancestry. Indonesians are believed to have migrated about C.E. 700. King Andrianampoinimerina (1787–1810) ruled the major kingdom on the island, and his son, Radama I (1810–28) unified much of the island. The French made the island a protectorate in 1885, and then in 1894–95 ended the monarchy, exiling Queen Rànavàlona III to Algiers. A colonial administration was set up, to which the Comoro Islands were attached in 1908, and other territories later. In World

War II, the British occupied Madagascar, which retained ties to Vichy France.

An autonomous republic within the French Community since 1958, Madagascar became an independent member of the community in 1960. In May 1973, an army coup led by Maj. Gen. Gabriel Ramanantsoa ousted Philibert Tsiranana, president since 1959. Comdr. Didier Ratsiraka, named president on June 15, 1975, announced that he would follow a socialist course and, after nationalizing banks and insurance companies, declared all mineral resources nationalized. Repression and censorship characterized his regime. Ratsiraka was reelected in 1989 in a suspicious election that led to riots as well as the formation of a multiparty system in 1990. In 1991 Ratsiraka agreed to share power with democratically minded opposition leader, Albert Zafy, who then overwhelmingly won the presidential elections in Feb. 1993. But Zafy was impeached by Parliament for abusing his constitutional powers during an economic crisis and lost the 1996 presidential election to Ratsiraka, who became president in Feb. 1997.

Malawi

REPUBLIC OF MALAWI

President: Bakili Muluzi (1994)
Area: 45,747 sq. mi. (118,480 sq. km)
Population (1999 est.): 10,000,416 (average annual rate of natural increase: 1.57%); birth rate: 39.5/1000; infant mortality rate: 132.1/1000; density per sq. mi.: 219
Capital (1993 est.): Lilongwe, 260,000. **Largest city (1993 est.):** Blantyre, 399,000. **Monetary unit:** Kwacha. **Languages:** English and Chichewa (National). **Ethnicity/race:** Chewa, Nyanja, Tumbuko, Yao, Lomwe, Sena, Tonga, Ngoni, Ngonde, Asian, European. **Religions:** Christian, 75%; Islam, 20%. **Literacy rate:** 49%
Economic summary: GDP/PPP (1997 est.): $8.6 billion; $900 per capita. **Real growth rate:** 6%. **Inflation:** 83.4% (1995). **Unemployment:** n.a. **Arable land:** 18%. **Agriculture:** tobacco, sugarcane, cotton, tea, corn, potatoes, cassava (tapioca), sorghum, pulses, cattle, goats. **Labor force:** 3.5 million; agriculture, 86%; wage earners, 14%. **Industry:** tea, tobacco, sugar, sawmill products, cement, consumer goods. **Natural resources:** limestone, uranium, coal, bauxite. **Exports:** $405 million (f.o.b., 1995): tobacco, sugar, tea, coffee, peanuts, wood products. **Imports:** $475 million (f.o.b., 1995): food, petroleum products, semimanufactures, consumer goods, transportation equipment. **Major trading partners:** U.K., U.S., Japan, Germany, South Africa, Zimbabwe. **Member of Commonwealth of Nations**

Geography Malawi is a landlocked country the size of Pennsylvania in southeastern Africa, surrounded by Mozambique, Zambia, and Tanzania. Lake Malawi, formerly Lake Nyasa, occupies most of the country's eastern border. The north-south Rift Valley is flanked by mountain ranges and high plateau areas.

Government Multiparty democracy.

History Early human inhabitants of what is now Malawi date to 8000–2000 B.C.E. Bantu-speaking peoples migrated there between the 1st and 4th centuries C.E. A large slave trade took place in the 18th and 19th centuries, and brought Islam to the region. At the same time, missionaries introduced Christian-

ity. Several major kingdoms were established in the precolonial period: the Maravi in 1480, the Ngonde in 1600, and in the Chikulamayembe in the 18th century.

The first European to make extensive explorations in the area was David Livingstone in the 1850s and 1860s. In 1884, Cecil Rhodes's British South African Company received a charter to develop the country. The company came into conflict with the Arab slavers in 1887–89. Britain annexed what was then called the Nyasaland territory in 1891 and made it a protectorate in 1892. Sir Harry Johnstone, the first high commissioner, used Royal Navy gunboats to wipe out the slavers.

Between 1951 and 1953 Britain combined Nyasaland with the colonies of Northern and Southern Rhodesia to form a federation, a move protested by black Africans who were wary of alignment with the ultra conservative white-minority rule in South Rhodesia. On July 6, 1964, Nyasaland became the independent nation of Malawi. Two years later, it became a republic within the Commonwealth of Nations. Dr. Hastings K. Banda, Malawi's first prime minister, became its first president. In 1971 he became president for life, further consolidating his authoritarian rule. In addition to allowing former colonialists to retain considerable power in the country, he maintained warm relations with the white-minority government of South Africa. These policies drew heavy criticism from Malawian citizens and other African nations. In 1992 Banda faced violent protests.

Bakili Muluzi won the country's first free election in May 1994, ending Banda's 30-year rule. He was sworn in a few days later and quickly released the remaining political prisoners. Budget trimming was the order of the day in 1995, which received commendation from the International Monetary Fund. In the 1999 presidential elections, incumbent Bakili Muluzi of the United Democratic Front (UDF) won 52.2% of the vote.

Malaysia

Paramount Ruler: His Majesty Tuanku Salehuddin Abdul Aziz Shah ibni al-Marhum Hisamuddin Alam Shah (1999)
Prime Minister: Mahathir bin Mohamad (1981)
Area: 128,328 sq. mi. (339,750 sq. km)
Population (1999 est.): 21,376,066 (average annual rate of natural increase: 2.08%); birth rate: 26.1/1000; infant mortality rate: 21.7/1000; density per sq. mi.: 167
Capital and largest city (1991 est.): Kuala Lumpur, 1,145,000. **Largest cities (1991 est.):** Georgetown (Pinang), 220,000; Ipoh, 382,600. **Monetary unit:** Ringgit. **Languages:** Malay (official), Chinese, Tamil, English. **Ethnicity/race:** Malay and other indigenous 59%, Chinese 32%, Indian 9%. **Ethnic divisions:** 59% Malay and other indigenous; 32% Chinese; 9% Indian. **Religions:** Malays (all Muslims), Chinese (predominantly Buddhists), Indians (predominantly Hindus). **Literacy rate:** 78%
Economic summary: GDP/PPP (1997 est.): $227 billion; $11,100 per capita. **Real growth rate:** 7.4%. **Inflation:** 36% (1996). **Unemployment:** 2.6%. **Arable land:** 3%. **Agriculture:** Peninsular Malaysia—natural rubber, palm oil, rice; Sabah—subsistence crops, rubber, timber, coconut, rice; Sarawak—rubber, pepper, timber. **Labor force:** (1996 est.), 8.398 million; manufacturing, 25%; agriculture, forestry, and fisheries, 21%; local trade and tourism, 17%; services, 12%; government 11%; construction, 8%. **Industry:** Peninsular Malaysia—rubber and oil palm processing

and manufacturing, light manufacturing industry, electronics, tin mining and smelting, logging and processing timber; Sabah—logging, petroleum production; Sarawak—agriculture processing, petroleum production and refining, logging. **Natural resources:** tin, petroleum, timber, copper, iron ore, natural gas, bauxite. **Exports:** $78.2 billion (1996): electronic equipment, petroleum and petroleum products, palm oil, wood and wood products, rubber textiles. **Imports:** $78.4 billion (1996): machinery and equipment, chemicals, food. **Major trading partners:** U.S., Singapore, Japan, Hong Kong, U.K., Thailand, Germany, Taiwan, South Korea. **Member of Commonwealth of Nations**

Geography Malaysia is on the Malay Peninsula in southeast Asia. The nation also includes Sabah and Sarawak on the island of Borneo to the east. Its area slightly exceeds that of New Mexico.

Most of Malaysia is covered by forest, with a mountain range running the length of the peninsula. Extensive forests provide ebony, sandalwood, teak, and other woods.

Government Constitutional monarchy.

History The ancestors of the people that now inhabit the Malaysian peninsula first migrated to the area between 2500 and 1500 B.C.E. Those living in the coastal regions had early contact with Chinese and Indians; seafaring traders from India brought with them Hinduism, which was blended with the local animist beliefs. As Muslims conquered India, they spread the religion of Islam to Malaysia. In the 15th century C.E., Islam acquired a firm hold on the region when the Hindu ruler of the powerful city-state of Malacca, Parameswara Dewa Shah, was overthrown by his Muslim half-brother, Mudzaffar Shah.

British and Dutch interest in the region grew in the 1800s, with the British East India Company establishing a trading settlement on the island of Singapore. Trade soared, with Singapore's population growing from only 5,000 in 1820 to nearly 100,000 in just 50 years. In the 1880s, Britain formally established protectorates in Malaysia. At about the same time, rubber trees were introduced from Brazil. With the mass production of automobiles, rubber became a valuable export, and laborers were brought in from India to work the rubber plantations.

Following the Japanese occupation of Malaysia during World War II, a growing nationalist movement prompted the British to establish the semi-autonomous Federation of Malaya in 1948. But Communist guerrillas took to the jungles to begin a war of national liberation against the British, who declared a state of emergency to quell the insurgency, which lasted until 1960.

The independent state of Malaysia came into existence on Sept. 16, 1963, as a federation of Malaya, Singapore, Sabah (North Borneo), and Sarawak. In 1965, Singapore withdrew from the federation to become a separate nation. Since 1966, the 11 states of former Malaya have been known as West Malaysia, and Sabah and Sarawak have been known as East Malaysia.

By the late 1960s Malaysia was torn by communal rioting directed against Chinese and Indians, who controlled a disproportionate share of the country's wealth. Beginning in 1968, the government moved to achieve greater economic balance through a national economic policy.

Malaysia was significantly affected in 1978 by the "boat people" fleeing Vietnam. Because the refugees were mostly ethnic Chinese, the government was apprehensive about any increase in a minority that previously had been the source of internal conflict in the country. In April 1988, it announced that within the year it would cease accepting refugees.

In the 1980s, Dr. Mohamed Mahathir succeeded Datuk Hussein as prime minister. Mahathir instituted economic reforms that would transform Malaysia into one of the so-called Asian Tigers. Throughout the 1990s, Mahathir embarked on a massive project to build a new capital from scratch in an attempt to bypass congested Kuala Lumpur.

Beginning in 1997 and continuing through the next year, Malaysia suffered from the Asian currency crisis, with the Malaysian ringgit plummeting. Mahathir blamed market speculators for the crisis, and many of his ambitious building projects had to be placed on hold as a result of the economic downturn.

In Sept. 1998 Prime Minister Mahathir bin Mohamad sacked his heir apparent, Anwar Ibrahim, from his posts as deputy prime minister and finance minister, after a disagreement over how to deal with the country's economic problems. In defiance, Anwar launched a reform movement attacking the government. The prime minister then jailed Anwar, who was beaten and charged with trumped-up corruption and sex crimes. In April 1999, after the longest trial in Malaysian history, Ibrahim was sentenced to an unexpectedly severe six-year jail sentence. Protests followed in Malaysia and international condemnation was swift. Another trial followed, this time for sodomy, and from the various rulings of the Malaysian courts, it became clear that the judicial system was in the hands of the government. In Sept. 1999 Anwar was rushed to the hospital because of arsenic poisoning from food served to him in jail.

Instead of following the economic prescriptions of the International Monetary Fund and World Bank, the prime minister went his own way, opting for fixed exchange rates and capital controls. In late 1999, Malyasia was on the road to economic recovery and it appeared Mahathir's measures were working.

Maldives

REPUBLIC OF MALDIVES

President: Maumoon Abdul Gayoom (1978)
Area: 115 sq. mi. (300 sq. km)
Population (1999 est.): 300,220 (average annual rate of natural increase: 3.37%); birth rate: 39.3/1000; infant mortality rate: 38.1/1000; density per sq. mi.: 2,611
Capital and largest city (1995 census): Malé, 62,973.
Monetary unit: Maldivian Rufiyaa. **Languages:** Dhivehi (official); Arabic, Hindi, and English are also spoken. **Ethnicity/race:** Sinhalese, Dravidian, Arab, African. **Religion:** Islam (Sunni Muslim). **Literacy rate:** 91%
Economic summary: GDP/PPP: (1997 est.): $500 million; $1,800 per capita. **Real growth rate:** 6.2%. **Inflation:** 6.3%. **Unemployment:** negl. **Arable land:** 10%. **Agriculture:** coconuts, corn, sweet potatoes, fishing. **Labor force:** 56,435 (1990 est.); fishing industry and agriculture, 25%; services, 21%; manufacturing and construction, 21%; trade, restaurants, and hotels, 16%; transportation and communication, 10%; other, 7%. **Industry:** fish, processed coconut, handicraft. **Natural resource:** fish. **Exports:** $59 million (f.o.b., 1996): fish, clothing. **Imports:** $302 million (f.o.b., 1996): intermediate and

capital goods, consumer goods, petroleum products.
Major trading partners: Thailand, U.S., Singapore, U.K., Germany, India, Sri Lanka, Japan.

Geography The Republic of Maldives is a group of atolls in the Indian Ocean about 417 miles (671 km) southwest of Sri Lanka. Its 1,190 coral islets stretch over an area of 35,200 square miles (90,000 sq. km). With concerns over global warming and the shrinking of the polar ice caps, Maldives feels directly threatened, as none of its islands rises more than six feet above sea level.

Government Republic.

History The Maldives (formerly called the Maldive Islands) were first settled in the 5th century B.C.E. by Buddhist seafarers from India and Sri Lanka. According to tradition, Islam was adopted in C.E. 1153. Originally the islands were under the suzerainty of Ceylon (now Sri Lanka). They came under British protection in 1887 and were a dependency of the then-colony of Ceylon until 1948. The independence agreement with Britain was signed July 26, 1965. For centuries a sultanate, the islands adopted a republican form of government in 1952, but the sultanate was restored in 1954. In 1968, however, as the result of a referendum, a republic was again established in the recently independent country. Ibrahim Nasir, president since 1968, was removed from office by the Majlis in Nov. 1978 and replaced by Maumoon Abdul Gayoom. President Gayoom was elected to a fourth five-year term in Oct. 1993. Ever concerned with the possibility of rising sea levels, the Maldives, one of the world's poorest nations, has constructed, with Japanese aid, a line of concrete breakwaters along the capital's southern coast.

Mali

REPUBLIC OF MALI

National name: République de Mali
President of the Republic: Alpha Oumar Konaré (1992)
Prime Minister: Ibrahima Boubacar Keita (1994)
Area: 478,819 sq. mi. (1,240,000 sq. km)
Population (1999 est.): 10,429,124 (average annual rate of natural increase: 3.09%); birth rate: 49.5/1000; infant mortality rate: 119.4/1000; density per sq. mi.: 22
Capital and largest city (1992 est.): Bamako, 746,000.
Monetary unit: Franc CFA. **Languages:** French (official); African languages. **Ethnicity/race:** Mande 50% (Bambara, Malinke, Sarakole), Peul 17%, Voltaic 12%, Songhai 6%, Tuareg and Moor 10%, other 5%.
Religions: Islam, 90%; traditional, 9%; Christian, 1%.
Literacy rate: 32%
Economic summary: GDP/PPP (1997 est.): $6 billion; $600 per capita. **Real growth rate:** 6%. **Inflation:** 3% (1997 est.). **Unemployment:** n.a. **Arable land:** 2%.
Agriculture: millet, corn, rice, cotton, peanuts, vegetables, cattle, sheep, goats. **Labor force:** n.a.; agriculture, 80%; services, 19%; industry and commerce, 1% (1981). **Industry:** minor local consumer goods production and food processing, construction, phosphate and gold mining. **Natural resources:** gold, phosphates, kaolin, salt, limestone, uranium, bauxite, iron ore, manganese, tin, and copper deposits are known but not exploited. **Exports:** $473 million (f.o.b., 1996 est.): cotton, livestock, gold. **Imports:** $797 million (f.o.b., 1996 est.): machinery and equipment, foodstuffs, construction materials, petroleum, textiles.
Major trading partners: western Europe.

Geography Most of Mali, in West Africa, lies in the Sahara. A landlocked country four-fifths the size of Alaska, it is bordered by Guinea, Senegal, Mauritania, Algeria, Niger, Burkina Faso, and the Côte d'Ivoire. The only fertile area is in the south, where the Niger and Senegal Rivers provide irrigation.

Government Republic.

History Caravan routes have passed through Mali since C.E. 300. The Malinke empire ruled regions of Mali from the 12th to 16th centuries, and the Songhai empire reigned over the Timbuktu-Gao region in the 15th century. Morocco conquered Timbuktu in 1591, and ruled over it for two centuries. Subjugated by France by the end of the 19th century, the land became a colony in 1904 (named French Sudan in 1920) and in 1946 became part of the French Union. On June 20, 1960, it became independent and, under the name of Sudanese Republic, was federated with the Republic of Senegal in the Mali federation. However, Senegal seceded from the Federation on Aug. 20, 1960, and the Sudanese Republic then changed its name to the Republic of Mali on Sept. 22.

In the 1960s, Mali concentrated on economic development, continuing to accept aid from both Soviet bloc and Western nations, as well as international agencies. In the late 1960s, it began retreating from close ties with China. But a purge of conservative opponents brought greater power to President Modibo Keita, and in 1968 the influence of the Chinese and their Malian sympathizers increased. The army overthrew the government on Nov. 19, 1968, and until 1991, Mali was under a military dictatorship. Mali and Burkina Faso fought a brief border war from Dec. 25th to 29th, 1985. Mali's second multiparty national elections took place in May 1997, with President Konaré winning reelection.

Malta

MALTA

President: Guido de Marco (1999)
Prime Minister: Eddie Fenech Adami (1998)
Area: 122 sq. mi. (320 sq. km)
Population (1999 est.): 381,603 (average annual rate of natural increase: 0.37%); birth rate: 11.0/1000; infant mortality rate: 7.4/1000; density per sq. mi.: 3,128
Capital (1992 est.): Valletta, 9,183. **Largest city (est. 1990):** Sliema, 13,541. **Monetary unit:** Maltese lira.
Languages: Maltese and English (both official).
Ethnicity/race: Maltese (descendants of ancient Carthaginians and Phoenicians, with strong elements of Italian and other Mediterranean stock), Spanish, English, Arab. **Religion:** Roman Catholic, 98%.
Literacy rate: 88%
Economic summary: GDP/PPP (1997 est.): $4.9 billion; $12,900 per capita. **Real growth rate:** 2.8%.
Inflation: 2.3% (1997). **Unemployment:** 3.7% (Sept. 1996). **Arable land:** 38%. **Agriculture:** potatoes, cauliflower, grapes, wheat, barley, tomatoes, citrus, cut flowers, green peppers, pork, milk, poultry, eggs.
Labor force: 148,085 (Sept. 1996); public services, 34%; other services, 32%; manufacturing and construction, 22%, agriculture, 2%. **Industries:** tourism, electronics, shipbuilding and repair, construction, food and beverages, textiles, footwear, clothing, tobacco. **Natural resources:** limestone, salt.
Exports: $1.7 billion (f.o.b., 1996): machinery and transport equipment, clothing and footwear, printed matter. **Imports:** $2.8 billion (c.i.f., 1996): food, petroleum, machinery and semimanufactured goods.
Major trading partners: Germany, Italy, U.K., U.S.
Member of Commonwealth of Nations

Geography The five Maltese islands—Malta, Gozo, Comino, Comminotto, and Filflawith—have a combined land area smaller than Philadelphia. Malta is located in the Mediterranean Sea, about 60 miles (97 km) south of the southeastern tip of Sicily.

History The strategic importance of Malta was recognized by the Phoenicians, who occupied it, as did, in turn, the Greeks, Carthaginians, and Romans. The apostle Paul was shipwrecked there in C.E. 60. With the division of the Roman Empire in C.E. 395, Malta was assigned to the eastern portion dominated by Constantinople. Between 870 and 1090, it came under Arab rule. In 1091 the Norman noble Roger I, then ruler of Sicily, came to Malta with a small retinue and defeated the Arabs. The Knights of St. John (Malta), who obtained the three habitable Maltese islands of Malta, Gozo, and Comino from Charles V in 1530, reached their highest fame when they withstood an attack by superior Turkish forces in 1565. Napoléon seized Malta in 1798, but the French forces were ousted by British troops the next year, and British rule was confirmed by the Treaty of Paris in 1814.

Malta was heavily attacked by German and Italian aircraft during World War II, but was never invaded by the Axis powers. Malta became an independent nation on Sept. 21, 1964, and a republic on Dec. 13, 1974, but remained in the British Commonwealth. In 1979, when its alliance with Great Britain ended, Malta sought to guarantee its neutrality through agreements with other countries. Although Malta applied for membership in the European Union, when the Labour Party won the election in Oct. 1996, it froze Malta's EU application and withdrew from the NATO Partnership for Peace program in an effort to maintain its neutrality. When the Nationalist Party won the Sept. 1998 elections, however, it revived the EU accession bid.

Marshall Islands

REPUBLIC OF THE MARSHALL ISLANDS

President: Imata Kabua (1997)
Total land area: 70 sq. mi (181.3 sq. km), includes the atolls of Bikini, Eniwetok, and Kwajalein
Population (1999 est.): 65,507; average annual rate of natural increase 3.86%; birth rate 45.3/1000; infant mortality rate 43.4/1000; density per sq. mi.: 936
Capital and largest city (1990 est.): Majuro, 20,000.
Languages. Both Marshallese and English are official languages. Marshallese is a language in the Malayo-Polynesian family. **Ethnicity/race:** Micronesian. **Religions:** predominantly Christian, mostly Protestant. **Literacy rate:** 91%
Economic summary: GDP/PPP (1996 est.): $98 million; per capita, $1,680. **Real growth rate:** 2%. **Inflation:** 4% (1996 est.). **Unemployment:** 16% (1991 est.).
Agriculture: coconuts, cacao, taro, breadfruit, fruits, pigs, chickens. **Labor force:** (1986), 4,800.
Industries: copra, fish, tourism, craft items from shell, wood, and pearls, offshore banking (embryonic). **Natural resources:** phosphate deposits, marine products, deep seabed minerals. **Exports:** $17.5 million (f.o.b., 1996 est.): coconut oil, fish, trochus shells. **Imports:** $71.8 million (c.i.f., 1996 est.): foodstuffs, machinery and equipment, beverages and tobacco, fuels. **Major trading partners:** U.S., Japan, Australia, New Zealand.

Geography The Marshall Islands, east of the Carolines, are divided into two chains: the western, or Ralik, group, including the atolls Jaluit, Kwaja-

lein, Wotho, Bikini, and Eniwetok; and the eastern, or Ratak, group, including the atolls Mili, Majuro, Maloelap, Wotje, and Likiep. The islands are of the coral-reef type and rise only a few feet above sea level. The Marshall Islands comprise an area slightly larger than Washington, D.C.

Government Constitutional government in free association with the U.S.

History Micronesian peoples were the first inhabitants of the archipelago. The islands were explored by the Spanish in the 16th century and were named for a British captain in 1788. Germany unsuccessfully attempted to colonize the islands in 1885. Japan claimed them in 1914, but after several battles during World War II, the U.S. seized them from the Japanese. In 1947, the U.N. made the island group, along with the Mariana and Caroline archipelagos, a U.S. trust territory.

U.S. nuclear testing took place between 1946–58 on the islands of Bikini and Enewetak. The people of Bikini were removed to another island, and a total of 23 U.S. atomic and hydrogen bomb tests were conducted. Despite clean-up attempts, the islands remain uninhabited today because of nuclear contamination. The U.S. paid the islands $183.7 million in damages in 1983.

The United States and the Marshall Islands signed a Compact of Free Association in 1986, which meant the islands became self-governing but would receive U.S. military and economic aid. The Marshall Islands were admitted to the U.N. on Sept. 17, 1991.

In 1997, President Kabua deferred plans for a feasibility study of a controversial proposal to develop Bikini as a commercial nuclear-waste dump for radioactive material produced by Asian power plants. The Compact of Free Association with the U.S. and the associated economic aid are scheduled to expire in 2001. In 1999 the U.S. approved a one-time $3.8-million payment to the relocated people of Bikini atoll.

Mauritania

ISLAMIC REPUBLIC OF MAURITANIA

National name: République Islamique de Mauritanie
President: Col. Maaouye Ould Sidi Ahmed Taya (1984)
Prime Minister: Cheikh El Afia Ould Mohamed Khouna (1996)
Area: 397,953 sq. mi. (1,030,700 sq. km)
Population (1999 est.): 2,581,738 (average annual rate of natural increase: 2.99%); birth rate: 44.1/1000; infant mortality rate: 76.5/1000; density per sq. mi.: 6
Capital and largest city (1992 est.): Nouakchott, 480,000. **Monetary unit:** Ouguyia. **Languages:** Arabic (official) and French. **Ethnicity/race:** mixed Maur/black 40%, Maur 30%, black 30%. **Religion:** Islam. **Literacy rate:** 34%
Economic summary: GDP/PPP (1996 est.): $4.1 billion; $1,750 per capita. **Real growth rate:** 6% (1996 est.). **Inflation:** 4.7% (1996). **Unemployment:** (1995 est.), 23%. **Arable land:** 0%. **Agriculture:** dates, millet, sorghum, root crops, cattle, sheep, fish products. **Labor force:** 465,000 (1981 est.); 45,000 wage earners; agriculture, 47%; services, 29%; industry and commerce, 14%; government, 10%. **Industry:** fish processing, mining of iron ore and gypsum. **Natural resources:** copper, iron ore, gypsum, fish, phosphate. **Exports:** $494 million (f.o.b., 1996): fish and fish products, iron ore, gold. **Imports:** $457 million (c.i.f.,

1996): foodstuffs, consumer goods, petroleum products, capital goods. **Major trading partners:** Japan, Algeria, China, Spain, Italy, France, U.S.

Geography Mauritania, three times the size of Arizona, is situated in northwest Africa with about 350 miles (592 km) of coastline on the Atlantic Ocean. It is bordered by Morocco on the north, Algeria and Mali on the east, and Senegal on the south. The country is mostly desert, with the exception of the fertile Senegal River valley in the south and grazing land in the north.

Government Military government. The legal system is based on Islam.

History Mauritania was first inhabited by blacks and Berbers, and it became a center for the Berber Almoravid movement, which sought to spread Islam through western Africa. It was first explored by the Portuguese in the 15th century, but by the 19th century the French gained control. They organized the area into a territory in 1904, and made it part of French West Africa.

Mauritania became an independent nation on Nov. 28, 1960, and was admitted to the United Nations in 1961 over the strenuous opposition of Morocco, which claimed the territory. With Moors, Arabs, Berbers, and blacks frequently in conflict, the government in the late 1960s sought to make Arab culture dominant to unify the country.

Mauritania acquired administrative control of the southern part of the former Spanish Sahara when the colonial administration withdrew in 1975, under an agreement with Morocco and Spain. Increased military spending and rising casualties in Western Sahara helped bring down the civilian government of Ould Daddah in 1978. A succession of military rulers followed.

In 1989 Mauritania fought a border war with Senegal. Although the country voted in the U.N. to support the embargo against Iraq, the government actually leaned the other way.

Although slavery was officially outlawed in 1980, it is believed that approximately 100,000 blacks are still enslaved.

Mauritius

President: Cassam Uteem (1992)
Prime Minister: Navin Ramgoolam (1995)
Area: 787 sq. mi. (1,860 sq. km)
Population (1999 est.): 1,182,212 (average annual rate of natural increase: 1.18%); birth rate: 18.5/1000; infant mortality rate: 16.2/1000; density per sq. mi.: 1,502
Capital and largest city (1993 est.): Port Louis, 134,516. **Monetary unit:** Mauritian rupee.
Languages: English (official), French, Creole, Hindi, Urdu, Hakka, Bojpoori. **Ethnicity/race:** Indo-Mauritian 68%, Creole 27%, Sino-Mauritian 3%, Franco-Mauritian 2%. **Religions:** Hindu, 52%, Christian, 28.3%; Islam, 16.6%; other, 3.1%. **Literacy rate:** 81%
Economic summary: GDP/PPP (1996 est.): $11.7 billion; $10,300 per capita. **Real growth rate:** 5.4%. **Inflation:** 6.5% (1996). **Unemployment:** 1.8% (1995). **Arable land:** 49%. **Agriculture:** sugarcane, tea, corn, potatoes, bananas, pulses, cattle, goats, fish. **Labor force:** 514,000 (1995); construction and industry, 36%; services, 24%; agriculture and fishing, 14%; trade, restaurants, hotels, 16%; transportation and communication, 7%; finance, 3%. **Natural resources:** arable land, fish. **Exports:** $1.6 billion (f.o.b.), 1996

est.): sugar, clothing and textiles. **Imports:** $2.2 billion (c.i.f., 1996 est.): foodstuffs, manufactured goods, capital equipment, petroleum products, chemicals. **Major trading partners:** France, Germany, Italy, India, Hong Kong, U.S. **Member of Commonwealth of Nations**

Geography Mauritius is a mountainous island in the Indian Ocean east of Madagascar.

Government Republic within the British Commonwealth.

History After a brief Dutch settlement, French immigrants who came in 1715 named the island Île de France and established the first road and harbor infrastructure, as well as the sugar industry, under the leadership of Gov. Mahe de Labourdonnais. Blacks from Africa and Madagascar came as slaves to work in the cane fields. In 1810, the British captured the island and in 1814, by the Treaty of Paris, it was ceded to Great Britain along with its dependencies.

Indian immigration, which followed the abolition of slavery in 1835, rapidly changed the fabric of Mauritian society, and the country flourished with the increased cultivation of sugarcane. The opening of the Suez Canal in 1869 heralded the decline of Mauritius as a port-of-call for ships rounding the southern tip of Africa, bound for South and East Asia. The economic instability of the price of sugar, the main crop, in the first half of the 20th century brought civil unrest, then economic, administrative, and political reforms. Mauritius became independent on March 12, 1968.

The effects of Cyclone Claudette in 1979, and of falling world sugar prices in the early 1980s, led the government to initiate a vigorous program of agricultural diversification and to develop the processing of imported goods for the export market. The country formally broke ties with the British Crown in March 1992, becoming a republic within the Commonwealth.

Mexico

UNITED MEXICAN STATES

Official name: Estados Unidos Mexicanos
President: Ernesto Zedillo (1994)
Area: 761,600 sq. mi. (1,972,550 sq. km)
Population (1999 est.): 100,294,036 (average annual rate of natural increase: 2.02%); birth rate: 25/1000; infant mortality rate: 24.6/1000; density per sq. mi.: 132
Capital and largest city (1995): Mexico City: city proper (1990 census) 8,235,744; metro. area (1996 est.) 16,908,000. **Other large cities (1995):** Guadalajara, 2,178,000; Monterrey, 1,702,000; Ecatepec, 1,456,438 (part of Mexico City metropolitan area); Nezahualcóyotl, 1,259,543; Puebla, 1,222,177.
Monetary unit: Peso. **Languages:** Spanish, Indian languages. **Ethnicity/race:** mestizo (Indian-Spanish) 60%, Amerindian or predominantly Amerindian 30%, Caucasian or predominantly Caucasian 9%, other 1%.
Religions: nominally Roman Catholic, 97%; Protestant, 3%. **Literacy rate:** 87%
Economic summary: GDP/PPP (1997 est.): $694.3 billion; $7,700 per capita. **Real growth rate:** 7.3%. **Inflation:** 15.7%. **Unemployment:** 3.7% urban, plus considerable underemployment. **Arable land:** 12%. **Agriculture:** corn, wheat, soybeans, rice, beans, cotton, coffee, fruit, tomatoes, beef, poultry, dairy products, wood products. **Labor force:** (1994), 36.6 million (1996); services, 28.8%; agriculture, forestry,

hunting, and fishing, 21.8%; commerce, 17.1%; manufacturing, 16.1%; construction, 5.2%; public administration and national defense, 4.4%; transportation and communications, 4.1%. **Industries:** food and beverages, tobacco, chemicals, iron and steel, petroleum, mining, textiles, clothing, motor vehicles, consumer durables, tourism. **Natural resources:** petroleum, silver, copper, gold, lead, zinc, natural gas, timber. **Exports:** $110.4 billion (f.o.b., 1997 est.): crude oil, oil products, coffee, silver, engines, motor vehicles, cotton, consumer electronics. **Imports:** $109.8 billion (f.o.b., 1997 est.): metal-working machines, steel mill products, agricultural machinery, electrical equipment, car parts for assembly, repair parts for motor vehicles, aircraft, and aircraft parts. **Major trading partners:** U.S., Japan, Germany, Canada, South Korea, Italy, France.

Geography Mexico is bordered by the United States to the north, Belize and Guatemala to the southeast; Mexico is about one-fifth the size of the United States. Baja California in the west is an 800-mile (1,287-km) peninsula and forms the Gulf of California. In the east are the Gulf of Mexico and the Bay of Campeche, which is formed by Mexico's other peninsula, the Yucatán. The center of Mexico is a great, high plateau, open to the north, with mountain chains on the east and west and with ocean-front lowlands lying outside of them.

Government Federal republic.

History At least three great civilizations—the Mayas, the Olmecs, and later the Toltecs—preceded the wealthy Aztec empire, conquered in 1519–21 by the Spanish under Hernando Cortés. Spain ruled Mexico as part of the viceroyalty of New Spain for the next 300 years until Sept. 16, 1810, when the Mexicans first revolted. They continued the struggle and finally won independence in 1821.

From 1821 to 1877, there were two emperors, several dictators, and enough presidents and provisional executives to make a new government on the average of every nine months. Mexico lost Texas (1836), and after defeat in the war with the U.S. (1846–48) it lost the area made up of the present states of California, Nevada, and Utah, most of Arizona and New Mexico, and parts of Wyoming and Colorado under the Treaty of Guadalupe Hidalgo. In 1855, the Indian patriot Benito Juárez began a series of liberal reforms, including the disestablishment of the Catholic Church, which had acquired vast property. A subsequent civil war was interrupted by the French invasion of Mexico (1861), the crowning of Maximilian of Austria as emperor (1864), and then his overthrow and execution by forces under Juárez, who again became president in 1867.

The years after the fall of the Dictator Porfirio Diaz (1877–80 and 1884–1911) were marked by bloody political-military strife and trouble with the U.S., culminating in the punitive U.S. expedition into northern Mexico (1916–17) in unsuccessful pursuit of the revolutionary Pancho Villa. Since a brief period of civil war in 1920, Mexico has enjoyed a period of gradual agricultural, political, and social reforms. The Partido Nacional Revolucionario (PNR; National Revolutionary Party), dominated by revolutionary and reformist politicians from northern Mexico, was established in 1929; it continued to control Mexico throughout the 20th century and was renamed the Partido Revolucionario Institucional (PRI; Institutional Revolutionary Party) in 1946. Relations with the U.S. were again disturbed in 1938 when all foreign oil wells were expropriated, but an agreement on compensation was finally reached in 1941.

Following World War II, the government placed heavy emphasis on economic growth. During the mid-1970s, under the leadership of President José López Portillo, Mexico emerged as one of the world's major petroleum-producing countries. By the end of Portillo's term, however, Mexico had accumulated a huge external debt because of the government's unrestrained borrowing on the strength of its petroleum revenues. The collapse of oil prices in 1986 cut into Mexico's export earnings and worsened the situation.

In Jan. 1994, Mexico joined Canada and the United States in the North American Free Trade Agreement (NAFTA), which will phase out all tariffs over a 15-year period, and in Jan. 1996, became a founding member of the World Trade Organization (WTO).

In 1994, the leading presidential candidate was shot and killed in Tijuana. The campaign manager was then selected to be the party's presidential candidate. Zedillo won the election by more than 20% and the PRI party retained its majority in both legislative houses. In Feb. 1995, agreement was reached with the U.S. to prevent the collapse of Mexico's private banks. The strict provisions, however, gave the U.S. virtual veto power over key elements in Mexico's economic policy.

Elections in July 1997 brought a stunning upset for the long ruling PRI, which lost control of the lower legislative house and the mayoralty of Mexico City, in what observers called the freest election in the country's history.

In May 1999, the PRI broke with its tradition of the president handpicking his successor by instituting an open primary candidate selection process. The next presidential elections are scheduled for 2000.

Micronesia

FEDERATED STATES OF MICRONESIA

President: Leo A. Falcam (1999)
Total area: 271 sq. mi (702 sq. km). Land area, same (includes islands of Pohnpei, Yap, Chuuk, and Kosrae)
Population (1999 est.): 131,500 (average annual rate of natural increase: 2.13%); birth rate: 27.3/1000; infant mortality rate: 34/1000; density per sq. mi.: 485
Capital: Palikir. **Languages:** English is the official and common language; major indigenous languages are Chukese, Pohnpeian, Yapase, and Kosrean.
Ethnicity/race: nine ethnic Micronesian and Polynesian groups. **Literacy rate:** 85%
Economic summary: GDP/PPP: (1996 est.), $220 million; $1,760 per capita. **Real growth rate:** 1%. **Inflation:** 4%. **Unemployment:** 27% (1989). **Agriculture:** black pepper, tropical fruits and vegetables, coconuts, cassava (tapioca), sweet potatoes, pigs, chickens. **Labor force:** n.a.; two-thirds are government employees. **Industries:** tourism, construction, fish processing, craft items from shell, wood and pearls. **Natural resources:** forests, marine products, deep-seabed minerals. **Exports:** $73 million (f.o.b., 1996 est.): fish, garments, bananas, black pepper. **Imports:** $168 million (c.i.f., 1996 est.): food, manufactured goods, machinery and equipment, beverages. **Major trading partners:** Japan, U.S., Guam, Australia.

Geography The Federated States of Micronesia is composed of the island states of Yap, Chuuk (Truk), Pohnpei (Ponape), and Kosrae, all in the Caroline Islands. The islands vary geologically from high mountainous islands to low, coral atolls, with volcanic outcroppings on Pohnpei, Kosrae, and Chuuk. They are located 3,200 miles (5,150 km) west-southwest of Hawaii, in the north Pacific Ocean.

Government Constitutional government in free association with the United States since Nov. 1986.

History The islands, inhabited by Micronesian and Polynesian peoples, were colonized by Spain in the 17th century. Germany purchased them from Spain in 1898. They were occupied by the Japanese in 1914, but American forces seized them from the Japanese during World War II. On April 2, 1947, the United Nations Security Council created the Trust Territory of the Pacific Islands. The trust placed the Northern Mariana, Caroline, and Marshall Islands under the administration of the United States.

The Micronesian Federation became self-governing in 1979. In 1983, the F.M.A. voted to accept a Compact of Free Association with the U.S., and in Nov. 1986, the U.S. government declared the Trust Territory agreements no longer in effect—thereby granting the Federated States of Micronesia full independence.

The F.M.A. was admitted to the United Nations on Sept. 17, 1991. In July 1993, the country became a member of the International Monetary Fund. Micronesia, as well as many other South Pacific countries, is alarmed by the affect continued global warming will have on their islands—the consequent rise in the level of the oceans threatens low-lying islands with flooding and eventually, with submergence.

Moldova

REPUBLIC OF MOLDOVA

President: Petru Lucinschi (1997)
Prime Minister: Ion Sturza (1999)
Area: 13,000 sq. mi. (33,700 sq. km)
Population (1999 est.): 4,460,838 (average annual rate of natural increase: 0.19%); birth rate: 14.4/1000; infant mortality rate: 43.5/1000, density per sq. mi.: 343
Capital and largest city (1991): Chisinau, 676,700. **Other large cities (1991 est.):** Tiraspol, 186,000; Beltsy, 165,000; Bendery (Tighina), 141,500.
Monetary unit: Moldovan Lem. **Languages:** Moldovan (official; virtually the same as Romanian), Russian, Gagauz (a Turkish dialect). **Religions (1991):** Eastern Orthodox 98.5%, Jewish 1.5%, Baptist (only about 1,000 members). **Ethnicity/race:** Moldavian/Romanian 64.5%, Ukrainian 13.8%, Russian 13%, Gagauz 3.5%, Jewish 1.5%, Bulgarian 2%, other 1.7% (1989 figures)
Economic summary: GDP/PPP (1997 est.): $10.8 billion; $2,400 per capita. **Real growth rate:** -2%. **Inflation:** 11.2%. **Unemployment:** 1.4% (includes only officially registered unemployed; large numbers of underemployed workers). **Arable land:** 53%. **Agriculture:** vegetables, fruits, wine, grain, sugar beets, sunflower seed, tobacco, meat, milk. **Labor force:** 2.42 million (1995); agriculture, 46.1%; industry, 13.9%; other, 40% (1996). **Industries:** food processing, agricultural machinery, foundry equipment, refrigerators and freezers, washing machines, hosiery, sugar, vegetable oil, shoes, textiles. **Natural resources:** lignite, phosphorites, gypsum. **Exports:**

$816 million (1997): foodstuffs, wine, tobacco, textiles and footwear, machinery. **Imports:** $1.16 billion (1997): oil, gas, coal, steel, machinery, foodstuffs, automobiles and other consumer durables. **Major trading partners:** Russia, Kazakhstan, Ukraine, Uzbekistan, Romania, Germany.

Geography Moldova (formerly Moldavia) is a landlocked republic of hilly plains lying west of the Carpathian Mountains between the Prut and Dneister (Dnestr) Rivers. The country is sandwiched between Romania and Ukraine. The area is a very fertile region with rich black soil (chernozem) covering three-quarters of the territory.

Government Democratic republic.

History Most of what is now Moldova was the independent principality of Moldavia in the 14th century. In the 16th century it came under Ottoman Turkish rule. Russia acquired Moldavian territory in 1791, and again in 1812 (the Treaty of Bucharest) when Turkey gave up the province of Bessarabia[1] to Russia. Turkey held the rest of Moldavia but it was passed to Romania in 1918. Russia did not recognize the cession of this territory.

In 1924, the U.S.S.R. established Moldavia as an Autonomous Soviet Socialist Republic. As a result of the Nazi-Soviet Nonaggression Pact of 1939, Romania was forced to cede all of Bessarabia to the Soviet Union in 1940. The Soviets merged the Moldavia A.S.S.R. with the Romanian-speaking districts of Bessarabia to form the Moldavian Soviet Socialist Republic. During World War II, Romania joined Germany in the attack on the Soviet Union and reconquered Bessarabia. But Soviet troops retook the territory in 1944 and reestablished the Moldavian S.S.R.

For many years, Romania and the U.S.S.R. disputed each other's territorial claims over Bessarabia. Following the aborted coup against Soviet president Mikhail Gorbachev, Moldavia proclaimed its independence in Sept. 1991, and changed its name to the Romanian spelling, Moldova.

Conflict between ethnic Romanians and the Russian-Ukrainian majority in Trans-Dniester erupted upon independence. Trans-Dniester separatists (primarily ethnic Russians and Ukrainians) fought for independence from Moldova, and in the early 1990s the Russian army offered the separatists military aid and occupied the region. In the south, another breakaway republic attempted to secede—Gagauzia—which is composed mostly of Turkic Christians.

In Aug. 1994, Moldova adopted a new constitution which emphasized the country's independent identity from Romania, which had always considered it Romanian in essence.

By 1995, the dispute with Gagauzia had dissolved, and in May 1997, Moldova and Trans-Dniester signed a document in Moscow agreeing to the integrity of the country and calling for the removal of Russian troops upon the conclusion of a definite peace settlement. The Russian financial crisis in fall 1998 was expected to severely affect Moldova, which relies on Russia for 60% of its foreign trade.

1. The area between the Prut and Dniester Rivers.

Monaco

PRINCIPALITY OF MONACO

National name: Principauté de Monaco
Ruler: Prince Rainier III (1949)
Minister of State: Michel Lévêque (1997)
Area: 0.73 sq. mi. (465 acres) (1.95 sq. km)
Population (1999 est.): 32,149 (average annual growth rate: –0.11%); birth rate 10.7/1000; infant mortality rate: 6.5/1000; density per sq. mi.: 44,040
Capital and largest city (1995 est.): Monaco, 30,400.
Monetary unit: French franc. **Languages:** French (official), English, Italian, Monégasque. **Ethnicity/race:** French 47%, Monegasque 16%, Italian 16%, other 21%. **Religion:** Roman Catholic, 95%. **Literacy rate:** 99%
Economic summary: GDP/PPP (1996 est.): $800 million; $25,000 per capita. **Real growth rate:** n.a. **Inflation rate:** n.a. **Unemployment:** 3.1% (1994). **Agriculture:** none. **Labor force:** 30,540 (1 Jan. 1994). **Natural resources:** none. **Exports:** n.a. **Imports:** n.a. Full customs integration with France, which collects and rebates Monacan trade duties; also participates in EU.

Geography Monaco is a tiny, hilly wedge driven into the French Mediterranean coast; it is nine miles east of Nice, France.

Government Constitutional monarchy.

History The Phoenicians, and after them the Greeks, had a temple on the Monacan headland honoring Hercules. From *Monoikos*, the Greek surname for this mythological strong man, the principality took its name. After being independent for 800 years, Monaco was annexed to France in 1793 and was placed under Sardinia's protection in 1815. By the Franco-Monegasque treaty of 1861, Monaco went under French guardianship but continued to be independent. A treaty made with France in 1918 contained a clause providing that, in the event that the male Grimaldi dynasty should die out, Monaco would become an autonomous state under French protection.

Monaco has a tourist business that runs as high as 1.5 million visitors a year and is famous for its beaches and casinos. It had gaming tables as early as 1856. Five years later, a 50-year concession to operate the games was granted to François Blanc, of Bad Homburg. This concession passed into the hands of a private company in 1898.

Prince Rainier III, born on May 31, 1923, succeeded his grandfather, Louis II, on the latter's death, May 9, 1949. Rainier was married, in 1956, to U.S. actress Grace Kelly and they subsequently had three children. Their son, Prince Albert Louis Pierre (b. 1958) is heir to the throne. Immensely popular, Princess Grace died on Sept. 14, 1982, of injuries received in a car accident near Monte Carlo. She was 52.

Monaco's practice of providing a tax shelter for French businessmen resulted in a 1962 dispute between the countries. A compromise was reached by which French citizens with less than five years residence in Monaco were taxed at French rates, and taxes were imposed on Monegasque companies doing more than 25% of their business outside the principality. In 1967, Rainier took control of the Société des Bains de Mer, operator of the famous Monte Carlo gambling casino, in a program to increase hotel and convention space. The country was admitted to the U.N. in May 1993, making it the smallest country represented there. The country celebrated the 700th anniversary of the Grimaldi reign during 1997.

Mongolia

MONGOLIA

President: Ntsaagiyn Bagabandi (1997)
Prime Minister: Rinchinnyamiyn Amarjargal (1999)
Area: 604,250 sq. mi. (1,565,000 sq. km)
Population (1999 est.): 2,617,379 (average annual rate of natural increase: 1.45%); birth rate: 22.5/1000; infant mortality rate: 64.6/1000; density per sq. mi.: 4
Capital and largest city (1993 est.): Ulan Bator, 619,000.
Monetary unit: Tugrik. **Languages:** Mongolian, 90%; also Turkic, Russian, and Chinese. **Ethnicity/race:** Mongol 90%, Kazak 4%, Chinese 2%, Russian 2%, other 2%. **Religions:** predominantly Tibetan Buddhist; Islam about 4%. **Literacy rate:** 97% (est.)
Economic summary: GDP/PPP (1997 est.): $5.6 billion; $2,200 per capita. **Real growth rate:** 3.3%. **Inflation:** 17.5%. **Unemployment:** 15% (1997 est.). **Labor force:** 1.115 million (mid-1993 est.); primarily herding/agricultural. **Arable land:** 1%. **Agriculture:** wheat, barley, potatoes, forage crops, sheep, goats, cattle, camels, horses. **Industries:** copper, construction materials, mining (particularly coal), food and beverage, processing of animal products. **Natural resources:** oil, coal, copper, molybdenum, tungsten, phosphates, tin, nickel, zinc, wolfram, fluorspar, gold. **Exports:** $418 million (f.o.b., 1997 est.): copper, cashmere, livestock, animal products, wool, hides, fluorspar, other nonferrous metals. **Imports:** $443.4 million (f.o.b., 1997 est.): fuels, food products, industrial consumer goods, chemicals, building materials, machinery and equipment, sugar, tea. **Major trading partners:** Russia, China, Japan, Austria

Geography Mongolia lies in central Asia between Siberia on the north and China on the south. It is slightly larger than Alaska.

The productive regions of Mongolia—a tableland ranging from 3,000 to 5,000 feet (914 to 1,524 m) in elevation—are in the north, which is well drained by numerous rivers, including the Hovd, Onon, Selenga, and Tula. Much of the Gobi Desert falls within Mongolia.

Government Independent sovereign republic now in transition from Communism.

History Nomadic tribes that periodically plundered agriculturally based China from the west are recorded in Chinese history dating back more than 2,000 years. It was to protect China from these marauding peoples that the Great Wall was constructed around 200 B.C.E. The name *Mongol* comes from a small tribe whose leader, Ghengis Khan, began a conquest that would eventually encompass an enormous empire stretching from Asia to Europe, as far west as the Black Sea and as far south as India and the Himalayas. However, by the 14th century, the kingdom was in serious decline, with invasions from a resurgent China and internecine warfare.

The State of Mongolia was formerly known as Outer Mongolia. It contains the original homeland of the historic Mongols, whose power reached its zenith during the 13th century under Kublai Khan. The area accepted Manchu rule in 1689, but after the Chinese Revolution of 1911 and the fall of the Manchus in 1912, the northern Mongol princes expelled the Chinese officials and declared independence under the Khutukhtu, or "Living Buddha."

In 1921 Soviet troops entered the country, and facilitated the establishment of a republic by Mongolian revolutionaries in 1924. China also made a claim to the region, but was too weak to assert it. Under the 1945 Chinese-Russian Treaty, China agreed to give up Outer Mongolia, which, after a plebiscite, became a nominally independent country.

Allied with the U.S.S.R. in its dispute with China, Mongolia began mobilizing troops along its borders in 1968 when the two powers became involved in border clashes on the Kazakh-Sinkiang frontier to the west and at the Amur and Ussuri Rivers. A 20-year treaty of friendship and cooperation, signed in 1966, entitled Mongolia to call upon the U.S.S.R. for military aid in the event of invasion.

In 1989, the Mongolian democratic revolution began, led by Sanjaasurengiyn Zorig. Free elections held in Aug. 1990 produced a multiparty government, though it was still largely Communist. As a result, Mongolia has moved only gradually toward a market economy. With the collapse of the U.S.S.R., however, Mongolia was deprived of Soviet aid. Many of the country's factories were forced to shut down, and unemployment rose to 30%. Primarily in reaction to the economic turmoil, the Communist Mongolian People's Revolutionary Party (MPRP) won a significant majority in parliamentary elections in 1992. In 1996, however, the Democratic Alliance, an electoral coalition, defeated the MPRP, breaking with Communist rule for the first time since 1921. But in 1997, a former Communist and chairman of the People's Revolutionary Party, Ntsaagiyn Bagabandi, was elected president, further strengthening the hand of the antireformers.

Disagreement within Mongolia's ruling coalition over the pace and direction of market reforms in April 1998 caused a shake-up that thrust Tsakhiagiyn Elbegdorj, a proreform politician, into the prime minister's position. But parliamentary crosspurposes led to his resignation, and a succession of prime ministers followed.

Morocco

KINGDOM OF MOROCCO

National name: al-Mamlaka al-Maghrebia
Ruler: King Muhammad VI (1999)
Prime Minister: Abderrahmane El Youssoufi (1998)
Area: 172,413 sq. mi. (446,550 sq. km)
Population (1999 est.): 29,661,636 (average annual rate of natural increase: 1.97%); birth rate: 25.8/1000; infant mortality rate: 51.0/1000; density per sq. mi.: 172
Capital (1993 est.): Rabat, 1,220,000. **Largest cities:** Casablanca, 2,943,000; Marrakech, 602,000; Fez, 564,000; Salé, 521,000. **Monetary unit:** Dirham.
Languages: Arabic, French, Berber dialects, Spanish.
Ethnicity/race: Arab-Berber 99.1%, other 0.7%, Jewish 0.2%. **Religions:** Islam, 98.7%, Christian, 1.1%; Jewish, 0.2%. **Literacy rate:** 50%
Economic summary: GDP/PPP (1997 est.): $107 billion; $3,500 per capita. **Real growth rate:** -2.2%. **Inflation:** 3%. **Unemployment:** 16% (1997 est.). **Arable land:** 21%. **Agriculture:** barley, wheat, citrus, wine, vegetables, olives, livestock. **Labor force:** 7.4 million; agriculture, 50%; services, 26%; industry, 15%; other 9% (1985). **Industry:** phosphate rock mining and processing, food processing, leather goods, textiles, construction, tourism. **Natural resources:** phosphates, iron ore, zinc, fish, salt, lead, manganese. **Exports:** $6.9 billion (f.o.b., 1996): food and beverages, semiprocessed goods, consumer goods, phosphates. **Imports:** $9.7 billion (c.i.f., 1996): semiprocessed goods, capital goods, food and beverages, fuel and lubricants, raw materials, consumer goods. **Major trading partners:** EU, U.S., Libya, Japan, India, Saudi Arabia, Brazil.

Geography Morocco, about one-tenth larger than California, lies across the Strait of Gibraltar on the Mediterranean and looks out on the Atlantic from the northwest shoulder of Africa. Algeria is to the east and Mauritania to the south. On the Atlantic coast there is a fertile plain. The Mediterranean coast is mountainous. The Atlas Mountains, running northeastward from the south to the Algerian frontier, average 11,000 feet (3,353 m) in elevation.

Government Constitutional monarchy.

History Morocco has been the home of the Berbers since the second millennium B.C.E. In C.E. 46, Morocco was annexed by Rome as part of the province of Mauritania until the Vandals overran this portion of the declining empire in the 5th century. The Arabs invaded circa 685, bringing Islam. The Berbers joined them in invading Spain in C.E. 711, but then revolted against them, resenting their secondary status. In 1086, Berbers took control of large areas of Moorish Spain until they were expelled in the 13th century.

The land was rarely unified, and was usually ruled by small tribal states. Conflicts between Berbers and Arabs were chronic. Portugal and Spain began invading Morocco, which helped to unify the land in defense. In 1660 Morocco came under the control of the Alawite dynasty. It is a sherif dynasty—descended from the prophet Muhammad—and rules Morocco to this day.

During the 17th and 18th centuries Morocco was one of the Barbary states, the headquarters of pirates who pillaged Mediterranean traders. European powers became interested in colonizing the country beginning in 1840, and there were frequent clashes with the French and Spanish. Finally, in 1904, France and Spain concluded a secret agreement that divided Morocco into zones of French and Spanish influence, with France controlling almost all of Morocco and Spain controlling the small southwestern portion, which became known as Spanish Sahara. Morocco became an even greater object of European rivalry by the turn of the century, leading almost to a European war in 1905 when Germany attempted to gain a foothold in the mineral-rich country. By terms of the Algeciras Conference (1906), the sultan of Morocco maintained control of his lands and France's privileges were curtailed. The conference was an telling indication of what was to come in World War I, with Germany and Austria-Hungary lining up on one side of the territorial dispute, and France, Britain, and the United States on the other.

In 1912, the sultan of Morocco, Moulay Abd al-Hafid, permitted French protectorate status. Nationalism began to grow during World War II. Sultan Mohammed V was deposed by the French in 1953 and replaced by his uncle, but nationalist agitation forced his return in 1955. On his death on Feb. 26, 1961, his son, Hassan, became king. France and Spain recognized the independence and sovereignty of Morocco in 1956. Sultan Sidi Muhammad formed a constitutional government, and in 1961 Moulay Hassan succeeded his father as Hassan II. in the 1990s King Hassan promulgated "Hassanian democracy," which allowed for significant political freedom while at the same time retaining ultimate power for the monarch.

Maintaining excellent relations with the West, King Hassan became the second Arab leader to meet with an Israeli leader when, on July 21, 1986, Prime Minister Shimon Peres came to Morocco. Morocco was also the first Arab state to condemn the 1990 Iraqi invasion of Kuwait. In Aug. 1999, King Hassan II died after 38 years on the throne and his son, Prince Sidi Muhammad, was crowned King Muhammad VI.

Morocco's occupation of Western Sahara has been criticized by the international community. In the 1970s, tens of thousands of Moroccans crossed the border into Spanish Sahara to back their government's contention that the northern part of the territory was historically part of Morocco. Spain, which had controlled the territory since 1912, withdrew in 1976, creating a power vacuum that was filled by Morocco in the north and Mauritania in the south. When Mauritania withdrew in Aug. 1979, Morocco overran the remainder of the territory. A rebel group, the Polisario Front, has fought against Morocco since 1976 for the independence of Western Sahara on behalf of the indigenous Saharawis. In 1981, King Hassan agreed to a cease-fire with a referendum under international supervision to decide the fate of the Sahara territory, but the dispute remains unresolved.

Mozambique

REPUBLIC OF MOZAMBIQUE

National name: República de Moçambique
President: Joaquim Chissanó (1986)
Prime Minister: Pascoal Mocumbi (1994)
Area: 303,073 sq. mi. (801,590 sq. km)
Population (1999 est.): 19,124,335 (average annual rate of natural increase: 2.54%); birth rate: 42.8/1000; infant mortality rate: 117.6/1000; density per sq. mi.: 63
Capital and largest city (1996 est.): Maputo, 1,095,300. **Monetary unit:** Metical. **Languages:** Portuguese (official), Bantu languages. **Ethnicity/race:** indigenous tribal groups 99.6% (Shangaan, Chokwe, Manyika, Sena, Makua, and others), Europeans 0.06%, Euro-Africans 0.2%, Indians 0.08%. **Religions:** traditional, 60%; Christian, 30%; Islam, 10%. **Literacy rate:** 33%
Economic summary: GDP/PPP (1997 est.): $14.6 billion; $800 per capita. **Real growth rate:** 8%. **Inflation:** 5.8%. **Unemployment:** n.a. **Arable land:** 4%. **Agriculture:** cotton, cashew nuts, sugarcane, tea, cassava (tapioca), corn, rice, tropical fruits, beef, poultry. **Labor force:** n.a.; agriculture, 80% (1993). **Industry:** food, beverages, chemicals (fertilizer, soap, paints), petroleum products, textiles, cement, glass, asbestos, tobacco. **Natural resources:** coal, titanium, natural gas. **Exports:** $226 million (f.o.b., 1996 est.): cashews, cotton, sugar, shrimp, copra, citrus. **Imports:** $802 million (c.i.f., 1996 est.) food, clothing, farm equipment, petroleum. **Major trading partners:** Spain, South Africa, Portugal, U.S., France, Japan.

Geography Mozambique stretches for 1,535 miles (2,470 km) along Africa's southeast coast. It is nearly twice the size of California. Tanzania is to the north; Malawi, Zambia, and Zimbabwe to the west; and South Africa and Swaziland to the south.

The country is generally a low-lying plateau broken up by 25 sizable rivers that flow into the Indian

Ocean. The largest is the Zambezi, which provides access to central Africa. The principal ports are Maputo, Beira, and Nacala.

Government Multiparty republic.

History Bantu-speakers migrated to Mozambique in the first millennium, and Arab and Swahili traders settled the region thereafter. It was explored by Vasco da Gama in 1498, and first colonized by Portugal in 1505. By 1510, the Portuguese had control of all the former Arab sultanates on the east African coast. Mozambique was administered as part of Goa, in India, until 1752, when it received its own captain-general. Portuguese colonial rule was repressive.

Guerrilla activity began in 1963 and became so effective by 1973 that Portugal was forced to dispatch 40,000 troops to fight the rebels. A cease-fire was signed in Sept. 1974, and after having been under Portuguese colonial rule for 470 years, Mozambique became independent on June 25, 1975. The first president, Samora Moises Machel, had been the head of the National Front for the Liberation of Mozambique (FRELIMO) in its 10-year guerrilla war for independence. He died in a plane crash on Oct. 19, 1986, and was succeeded by his foreign minister, Joaquim Chissano.

On Jan. 25, 1985, after a decade of independence, the government was locked in a five-year-old paralyzing war with antigovernment guerrillas, known as the MNR, backed by the white minority government in South Africa. The guerrilla movement weakened President Chissano's attempts to institute socialism, which he then decided to abandon in 1989. A new constitution was drafted calling for three branches of government and granting civil liberties. A cease-fire agreement was signed in Oct. 1992 between the government and the MNR to end 16 years of civil war.

In April 1994 the president announced that a multiparty general election would be held in late October. The incumbent won. In Nov. 1995 the country was the first non-former-British colony to become a member of the British Commonwealth. The president's disciplined economic plan has been extremely successful, winning the country foreign confidence and aid.

Myanmar

SEE BURMA.

Namibia

REPUBLIC OF NAMIBIA

President: Sam Nujoma (1990)
Prime Minister: Hage Geingob (1990)
Status: Independent Country
Area: 318,261 sq. mi. (825,418 sq. km)
Population (1999 est.): 1,648,270 (average annual growth rate: 1.57%); birth rate: 35.6/1000; infant mortality rate: 65.9/1000; density per sq. mi.: 5
Capital and largest city (1992 est.): Windhoek, 161,000
Summer capital (est. 1980): Swakopmund, 17,500.
Monetary unit: Namibian dollars. **Languages:** Afrikaans, German, English (official), several indigenous. **Ethnicity/race:** black 86%, white 6.6%, mixed 7.4%. Note: about 50% of the population belong to the Ovambo tribe and 9% to the Kavangos tribe;

other ethnic groups are: Herero 7%, Damara 7%, Nama 5%, Caprivian 4%, Bushmen 3%, Baster 2%, Tswana 0.5%. **Religion:** Predominantly Christian. **Literacy rate:** 38%
Economic summary: GDP/PPP (1996 est.): $6.2 billion; $3,700 per capita. **Real growth rate:** 3%. **Inflation:** 8%. **Unemployment:** 30%–40% including underemployment (1997). **Arable land:** 1%. **Agriculture:** corn, millet, sorghum, livestock. **Labor force:** 500,000; agriculture, 49%; industry and commerce, 25%; services, 5%; government, 18%; mining, 3% (1994 est.). **Products:** canned meat, dairy products, tanned leather, textiles, clothing. **Natural resources:** diamonds, copper, uranium, gold, lead, tin, lithium, cadmium, zinc, salt, vanadium, natural gas, fish, suspected deposits of oil, natural gas, coal, iron ore. **Exports:** $1.45 billion (f.o.b., 1996 est.): diamonds, copper, lead, zinc, beef cattle, karakul pelts, marble, semi-precious stones, uranium, beef, gold. **Imports:** $1.55 billion (f.o.b., 1996 est.): construction materials, fertilizer, grain, foodstuffs, petroleum products and fuel. **Major trading partners:** Australia, U.K., South Africa, France, Germany, Switzerland, U.S., Japan.

Geography Namibia, bounded on the north by Angola and Zambia and on the east by Botswana and South Africa in the south. It is for the most part a portion of the high plateau of southern Africa with a general elevation of from 3,000 to 4,000 feet.

Government Republic.

History The San peoples may have inhabited what is now Namibia more than 2000 years ago. The Bantu-speaking Herero migrated there in the 1600s. The Ovambo, the largest ethnic group today, migrated there in the 1800s.

In the late 15th century, the Portuguese explorer Bartolomeu Dias became the first European to visit Namibia. Formerly called South-West Africa, the territory became a German colony in 1884. In 1908 German troops massacred the majority of the Herero population. The land was taken by South African forces in 1915, becoming a South African mandate by the terms of the Treaty of Versailles in 1920.

South Africa's application for incorporation of the territory was rejected by the U.N. General Assembly in 1946 and South Africa was invited to prepare a trusteeship agreement instead. By a law passed in 1949, however, the territory was brought into much closer association with South Africa—including representation in its Parliament.

In 1968, the U.N. called for South Africa's withdrawal from the territory, which was given the name *Namibia*. When South Africa refused, the UN Security Council and the International Court of Justice condemned it. Under a 1974 Security Council resolution, South Africa was required to begin the transfer of power to the Namibians by May 30, 1975, or face U.N. action. Prime Minister Balthazar J. Vorster rejected U.N. supervision, claiming that his government was prepared to negotiate Namibian independence, but not with the South-West African People's Organization (SWAPO), the principal black separatist group. Meanwhile, the all-white legislature of South-West Africa eased several laws on apartheid in public places.

Despite international opposition, the Turnhalle Conference in Windhoek drafted a constitution to organize an interim government based on racial divisions, a proposal overwhelmingly endorsed by white voters in the territory in 1977. At the urging of ambassadors of the five Western members of the Security Council, South Africa on June 11 announced rejection of the Turnhalle constitution and acceptance of the Western proposal to include the South-West African People's Organization in negotiations.

As policemen wielding riot sticks charged demonstrators in a black South-West Africa township, South Africa handed over limited powers to a new, multiracial administration in the former German colony on June 17, 1985. Installation of the new government ended South Africa's direct rule, but South Africa retained an effective veto over the new government's decisions along with responsibility for the territory's defense and foreign policy.

An agreement between South Africa, Angola, and Cuba arranged for elections for a constituent assembly in Nov. 1989 to establish a new government. SWAPO won 57% of the vote, a majority but not enough to dictate a constitution unilaterally. In Feb. 1990, SWAPO leader Sam Nujoma was elected president and took office when Namibia became independent on March 21, 1990.

In Sept. 1999, fighting took place between Namibian troops and separatists from the Caprivi Strip, a narrow corridor jutting out of Namibia that provides the country with access to the Zambezi River.

Nauru
REPUBLIC OF NAURU

President: Rene Harris (1999)
Area: 8.2 sq. mi. (21 sq. km)
Population (1999 est.): 10,605; average annual growth rate: 1.29%; birth rate 18/1000; infant mortality rate 40.6/1000; density per sq. mi.: 1,293
Capital (1983): Yaren, 559. **Monetary unit:** Australian dollar. **Languages:** Nauruan and English. **Ethnicity/race:** Nauruan 58%, other Pacific Islander 26%, Chinese 8%, European 8%. **Religions:** Protestant, 58%; Roman Catholic, 24%; Confucian and Taoist, 8%. **Literacy rate:** 99%
Economic summary: GDP/PPP (1993 est.): $100 million; $10,000 per capita. **Real growth rate:** n.a. **Inflation:** –3.6%, (1993). **Unemployment:** 0%. **Agriculture:** coconuts predominate. **Labor force:** employed in mining phosphates, public administration, education, and transportation. **Industry:** phosphate mining, financial services, coconut products. **Natural resources:** phosphates. **Exports:** $25.3 million (f.o.b., 1991): phosphates. **Imports:** $21.1 million (c.i.f., 1991): food, fuel, manufactures, building materials, machinery. **Major trading partners:** Australia, New Zealand, U.K., Japan. **Special relationship within the Commonwealth of Nations**

Geography Nauru (pronounced NAH-oo-roo) is an island in the Pacific just south of the equator, about 2,500 miles (4,023 km) southwest of Honolulu.

Government Republic.

History In 1798, a British navigator became the first European to visit the island. Germany annexed it in 1888, and by the turn of the century, phosphate, a lucrative fertilizer, began to be mined. The island was placed under joint Australian, New Zealand, and British mandate after World War I. The Japanese occupied the island during World War II, and forced 1,200 Nauruans—roughly two-thirds of the population—to relocate. In 1947, it became a U.N. trusteeship administered by Australia. By 1967, the phosphate mining industry finally came under control of the islanders, and on Jan. 31, 1968, Nauru became one of the world's smallest independent republics.

Devastated by almost a century of phosphate strip mining by foreign companies, Nauru appealed to the International Court of Justice. In 1993, Australia offered Nauru an out-of-court settlement for damages, agreeing to pay $2.5 million Australian dollars for 20 years. New Zealand and the U.K. additionally agreed to pay a one-time settlement of $12 million each. Declining phosphate prices, the high cost of maintaining an international airline, and investments that did not perform well combined to make the economy flounder in the late 1990s. In 1999, Nauru gained membership in the United Nations.

Nepal

KINGDOM OF NEPAL

Ruler: King Birendra Bir Bikram Shah Deva (1972)
Prime Minister: Krishna Prasad Bhattarai (1999)
Area: 54,463 sq. mi. (140,800 sq. km)
Population (1999 est.): 24,302,653 (average annual rate of natural growth: 2.51%); birth rate: 35.3/1000; infant mortality rate: 73.6/1000; density per sq. mi.: 446
Capital and largest city (1993): Kathmandu, 535,000. **Other large cities:** Lalitpur, 190,000; Biratnagar, 132,000. **Monetary unit:** Nepalese rupee.
Languages: Nepali (official), Newari, Bhutia, Maithali.
Ethnicity/race: Newars, Indians, Tibetans, Gurungs, Magars, Tamangs, Bhotias, Rais, Limbus, Sherpas.
Religions: Hindu, 90%; Buddhist, 5%; Islam, 3%.
Literacy rate: 26%
Economic summary: GDP/PPP (1997 est.): $31.1 billion; $1,370 per capita. **Real growth rate:** 4.2%. **Inflation:** 7.5%. **Unemployment:** n.a.; substantial underemployment (1996). **Arable land:** 17%. **Agriculture:** rice, corn, wheat, sugarcane, root crops, milk, water buffalo meat. **Labor force:** (1996 est.) 10 million; agriculture, 81%; services, 16%; industry, 3% (note: severe lack of skilled labor). **Industries:** tourism, carpet, textile, small rice, jute, sugar, and oilseed mills, cigarette, cement and brick production. **Natural resources:** quartz, water, timber, hydropower potential, scenic beauty, small deposits of lignite, copper, cobalt, iron ore. **Exports:** $419 million (f.o.b., 1997 est., but does not include unrecorded border trade with India): clothing, carpets, leather goods, jute goods, grain. **Imports:** $1.6 billion (c.i.f., 1997 est.): petroleum products, fertilizer, machinery. **Major trading partners:** India, U.S., Germany, Singapore, U.K., Japan.

Geography A landlocked country the size of Arkansas, lying between India and the Tibetan Autonomous Region of China, Nepal contains Mount Everest (29,108 ft.; 8,872 m), the tallest mountain in the world. Along its southern border, Nepal has a strip of level land that is partly forested, partly cultivated. North of this is the slope of the main section of the Himalayan range, including Everest and many other peaks higher than 8,000 m.

Government In Nov. 1990, King Birendra promulgated a new constitution and introduced a multiparty democracy in Nepal.

History The first civilizations in Nepal, which flourished around the 6th century B.C.E., were confined to the fertile Kathmandu Valley where the present-day capital of the same name is located today. It was in this region that Prince Siddhartha Gautama was born circa 563 B.C.E. Gautama achieved enlightenment as Buddha, and spawned Buddhist belief.

Nepali rulers' early patronage of Buddhism largely gave way to Hinduism, reflecting the increased influence of India, around the 12th century C.E. Though the successive dynasties of the Gopalas, the Kiratis, and the Licchavis expanded their rule, it was not until the reign of the Malla kings from C.E. 1200–1769 that Nepal assumed the approximate dimensions of the modern state.

The kingdom of Nepal was unified in 1768 by King Prithvi Narayan Shah, who had fled India following the Moghul conquests of the subcontinent. Under Shah and his successors Nepal's borders expanded as far west as Kashmir and as far east as Sikkim (now part of India). A commercial treaty was signed with Britain in 1792, and again in 1816 after more than a year of hostilities with the British East India Company.

In 1923, Britain recognized the absolute independence of Nepal. Between 1846 and 1951, the country was ruled by the Rana family, which always held the office of prime minister. In 1951, however, the king took over all power and proclaimed a constitutional monarchy. Mahendra Bir Bikram Shah became king in 1955. After Mahendra died of a heart attack in 1972, Prince Birendra, at 26, succeeded to the throne.

In 1990, a pro-democracy movement forced King Birendra to lift the ban on political parties and appoint an opposition leader to head an interim government as prime minister. The first free election in three decades provided a victory for the liberal Nepali Congress Party in 1991, although the Communists made a strong showing. A small Maoist guerrilla movement has been operating in the countryside since 1996.

In its ten years of democracy, Nepal has been led by seven different prime ministers, as one government after another failed. Parliament has been characterized by fragile alliances and mercurial coalitions. As a Nepali economist put it, "Democracy has more or less meant multiparty chaos. Coalitions of odd bedfellows with no ideological compatibility have been running things." In addition, corruption among MPs has been legion. Government officials belong to what has been called the "Pajero culture," a reference to the expensive Japanese cars, on which the king's courtiers and MPs do not pay the heavy import taxes that ordinary Nepalese are subject to. Because Parliament has been in constant flux, many MPs have lined their pockets as quickly as possible, knowing they may be out of a job at any moment. Voter accountability is nil.

In 1999, the political scene changed when Nepalis gave the majority of the seats in Parliament to the Nepali Congress Party, thereby giving one party enough security to attempt to effectively govern. Krishna Prasad Bhattarai, a famous Nepali freedom fighter who was imprisoned for 14 years by the king's government, became the prime minister, announcing, "Democracy has a solid future in Nepal. Don't you think it's about time?"

The Netherlands

KINGDOM OF THE NETHERLANDS

National name: Koninkrijk der Nederlanden
Sovereign: Queen Beatrix (1980)
Premier: Wim Kok (1994)
Area: 16,221 sq. mi. (41,526 sq. km)
Population (1999 est.): 15,807,641 (average annual rate of natural increase: 0.27%; birth rate: 11.4/1000; infant mortality rate: 5.1/1000; density per sq. mi.: 986
Capital and largest city (1994 est.): Amsterdam, 724,096. **Other large cities (1994 est.):** Rotterdam, 598,521; The Hague (seat of government), 445,279; Utrecht, 234,106; Eindhoven, 196,130. **Monetary units:** Guilder and euro. **Language:** Dutch. **Ethnicity/race:** Dutch 96%, Moroccans, Turks, and other 4% (1988). **Religions:** Roman Catholic 34%, Protestant 25%, Muslim 3%, other 2%, unaffiliated 36%. **Literacy rate:** 99%
Economic summary: GDP/PPP (1997 est.): $343.9 billion; $22,000 per capita. **Real growth rate:** 3.25%. **Inflation:** 2%. **Unemployment:** 6.9% (1997). **Arable land:** 27%. **Agriculture:** grains, potatoes, sugar beets, fruits, vegetables, livestock. **Labor force:** 6.6 million (1997); services, 75%; manufacturing and construction, 23%; agriculture, 2% (1996). **Industries:** agroindustries, metal and engineering products, electrical machinery and equipment, chemicals, petroleum, fishing, construction, microelectronics. **Natural resources:** natural gas, petroleum, fertile soil. **Exports:** $203.1 billion (f.o.b., 1997): manufactures and machinery, chemicals, processed food and tobacco, agricultural products. **Imports:** $1.791 trillion (c.i.f., 1997): raw materials and semifinished products, consumer goods, transportation equipment, food products, crude oil. **Major trading partners:** EU (Germany, Belgium-Luxembourg, U.K.), central and eastern Europe, U.S.

Geography The Netherlands, on the coast of the North Sea, is twice the size of New Jersey. Part of the great plain of north and west Europe, The Netherlands has maximum dimensions of 190 by 160 miles (360 by 257 km) and is low and flat except in Limburg in the southeast, where some hills rise to 300 feet (92 m). About half the country's area is below sea level, making the famous Dutch dikes a requisite to the use of much land. Reclamation of land from the sea through dikes has continued through recent times. All drainage reaches the North Sea, and the principal rivers—Rhine, Maas (Meuse), and Schelde—have their sources outside the country.

Government Constitutional monarchy.

History Julius Caesar found the low-lying Netherlands inhabited by Germanic tribes—the Nervii, Frisii, and Batavi. The Batavi on the Roman frontier did not submit to Rome's rule until 13 B.C.E., and then only as allies.

The Franks controlled the region from the 4th to the 8th century, and it became part of Charlemagne's empire in the 8th and 9th centuries C.E.. The area later passed into the hands of Burgundy and the Austrian Hapsburgs, and finally in the 16th century came under Spanish rule.

When Philip II of Spain suppressed political liberties and the growing Protestant movement in The Netherlands, a revolt led by William of Orange broke out in 1568. Under the Union of Utrecht (1579), the seven northern provinces became the United Provinces of The Netherlands. War between the United Provinces and Spain continued into the 17th century, but in 1648 Spain finally recognized Dutch independence.

The Dutch East India Company was established in 1602, and by the end of the 17th century Holland was one of the great sea and colonial powers of Europe.

The nation's independence was not completely established until after the Thirty Years' War (1618–48), when the country's rise as a commercial and maritime power began. In 1688, the English Parliament invited William of Orange, stadtholder, and his wife, Mary Stuart, to rule England as William III and Mary II. William then used the combined resources of England and The Netherlands to wage war on Louis XIV's France. In 1814, all the provinces of Holland and Belgium were merged into one kingdom, but in 1830 the southern provinces broke away to form the kingdom of Belgium. A liberal constitution was adopted by The Netherlands in 1848. The country remained neutral during World War I.

In spite of its neutrality in World War II, The Netherlands was invaded by the Nazis in May 1940, and the Dutch East Indies were later taken by the Japanese. The nation was liberated in May 1945. In 1948, after a reign of 50 years, Queen Wilhelmina abdicated and was succeeded by her daughter Juliana.

In 1949, after a four-year war, The Netherlands granted independence to the Dutch East Indies, which became the Republic of Indonesia. The Netherlands also joined NATO that year. The Netherlands joined the European Economic Community (later, the EU) in 1958. In 1999, it adopted the single European currency, the euro.

In 1963, it turned over the western half of New Guinea to Indonesia, ending 300 years of Dutch presence in Asia. Attainment of independence by Suriname on Nov. 25, 1975, left The Netherlands Antilles and Aruba as the country's only overseas territories.

Although prostitution is legal, the government moved in July 1997 to permit the operation of brothels as a means of regulating the former. Only those with a valid resident's permit would be permitted to be employed in the brothels. In 1999, The Netherlands again defied convention by preparing to legalize euthanasia.

The Sovereign, Queen Beatrix Wilhelmina Armgard, born on Jan. 31, 1938, assumed the throne in 1980. In 1967, Beatrix gave birth to a son, Willem-Alexander Claus George Ferdinand, the first male heir to the throne since 1884.

Netherlands Autonomous Countries

Netherlands Antilles
Status: Part of the Kingdom of The Netherlands
Governor: J. M. Saleh (1990)
Premier: Susanne Camelia-Römer (1998)
Area: 313 sq. mi. (800 sq. km)
Population (1999 est.): 207,827 (average annual growth rate: 1.05%); birth rate: 17.1/1000; infant mortality rate: 12.6/1000; density per sq. mi.: 664. **Ethnicity/race:** mixed African 85%, Carib Indian, European, Latin, Asian
Capital and largest city (1993 est.): Willemstad, 197,019. **Literacy rate:** 94%

Economic summary: GDP/PPP (1997 est.): $2.4 billion; $11,500 per capita. **Real growth rate:** –1.3%. **Inflation:** 3.6%. **Unemployment:** 12.8% (1993). **Arable land:** 10%. **Agriculture:** aloes, sorghum, peanuts, vegetables, tropical fruit. **Labor force:** 89,000; government, 65%; industry and commerce, 28% (1983). **Industry:** tourism (Curaçao, Saint-Martin, and Bonaire), petroleum refining (Curaçao), petroleum transshipment facilities (Curaçao and Bonaire), light manufacturing (Curaçao). **Natural resources:** phosphates (Curaçao only), salt (Bonaire only). **Exports:** n.a.; petroleum products. **Imports:** $1.4 billion (f.o.b., 1996 est.): crude petroleum, food, manufactures. **Major trading partners:** U.S., Brazil, Colombia, Venezuela, The Netherlands, Japan.

The Netherlands Antilles are composed of two groups of Caribbean islands 500 miles (805 km) apart: Curaçao (173 sq. mi.; 448 sq. km) and Bonaire (95 sq. mi.; 246 sq. km) are located about 40 miles (64 km) off the Venezuelan coast.

Originally inhabited by Arawak Indians, these two islands as well as Aruba were claimed by Spain in 1527, and then by the Dutch in 1643. The Dutch Lesser Antilles to the north—Sint Eustatius, the southern part of Saint Martin (Dutch: Sint Maarten), and Saba—make up the remainder of the island federation. First inhabited by the Carib Indians, Saint Martin was explored by Columbus in 1493. In 1845 the six islands (then including Aruba) officially formed The Netherlands Antilles. In 1994 the islands voted to preserve their federation with The Netherlands.

Aruba

Status: Part of the Kingdom of The Netherlands
Governor: Olindo Koolman (1992)
Prime Minister: Henny Eman (1994)
Area: 75 sq. mi. (193 sq. km)
Population (1999 est.): 68,675; growth rate 0.68%; birth rate: 13.3/1000; infant mortality rate: 7.8/1000; density per sq. mi.: 916
Capital and largest city (1991 est.): Oranjestad, 20,050. **Ethnicity/race:** mixed European/Caribbean Indian 80%. **Literacy rate:** 95%
Economic summary: GDP/PPP (1996 est.): $1.4 billion; $21,000 per capita. **Real growth rate:** 5%. **Inflation:** 3.5% (1996). **Unemployment:** 0.5% (1994). Little agriculture. **Industry:** tourism, light manufacturing (tobacco, beverages, consumer goods). **Exports:** $1.3 billion (f.o.b., 1995, including oil reexports): mostly petroleum products. **Imports:** $1.8 billion (f.o.b., 1995): food, consumer goods, manufactures. **Major trading partners:** U.S., EU.

Aruba, an island slightly larger than Washington D.C., lies 18 miles (28.9 km) off the coast of Venezuela in the southern Caribbean.

The Arawak Indians were the first inhabitants of Aruba. Spain explored the island in 1499, and more than a century later The Netherlands (1636) claimed the island. After a brief rule by the British, the Dutch again took control of the island in 1816, and it officially became part of The Netherlands Antilles in 1846.

On Jan. 1, 1986, Aruba seceded from the federation, but decided in 1994 to indefinitely postpone the transition to full independence. The Netherlands controls Aruba's defense and foreign affairs, but all internal affairs are handled by an island government directing its own civil service, judiciary, revenue, and currency.

New Zealand

Sovereign: Queen Elizabeth II (1952)
Governor-General: Sir Michael Hardie Boys (1996)
Prime Minister: Jenny Shipley (1997)
Area: 103,884 sq. mi. (268,680 sq. km) (excluding dependencies)
Population (1999 est.): 3,662,265 (average annual growth rate: 0.69%); birth rate: 14.4/1000; infant mortality rate: 6.2/1000; density per sq. mi.: 35
Capital: Wellington. **Largest cities (est. 1995):** Auckland, 952,600; Wellington, 331,100; Christchurch, 324,400. **Monetary unit:** New Zealand dollar.
Languages: English, Maori. **Ethnicity/race:** European 88%, Maori 8.9%, Pacific Islander 2.9%, other 0.2%.
Religions: Christian, 81%; none or unspecified, 18%; Hindu, Confucian, and other, 1%. **Literacy rate:** 99%
Economic summary: GDP/PPP (1997 est.): $63.4 billion; $17,700 per capita. **Real growth rate:** 2.5%. **Inflation:** 2%. **Unemployment:** 5.9% (Dec. 1996). **Arable land:** 9%. **Agriculture:** wheat, barley, potatoes, pulses, fruits, vegetables, wool, meat, dairy products, fish. **Labor force:** 1,634,500 (Sept. 1995); services, 64.6%; industry, 25%; agriculture, 10.4% (1994). **Industries:** food processing, wood and paper products, textiles, machinery, transportation equipment, banking and insurance, tourism, mining. **Natural resources:** natural gas, iron ore, sand, coal, timber, hydropower, gold, limestone. **Exports:** $18.5 billion (1997): wool, lamb, mutton, beef, fish, cheese, chemicals, forestry products, fruits and vegetables, manufactures, dairy products, wood. **Imports:** $19.2 billion (1997): machinery and equipment, vehicles and aircraft, petroleum, consumer goods, plastics. **Major trading partners:** Japan, Australia, U.K., U.S.
Member of Commonwealth of Nations

Geography New Zealand, about 1,250 miles (2,012 km) southeast of Australia, consists of two main islands and a number of smaller, outlying islands so scattered that they range from the tropical to the antarctic. The country is the size of Colorado. New Zealand's two main components are North Island and South Island, separated by Cook Strait, which varies from 16 to 190 miles (26 to 396 km) in width. North Island (44,281 sq. mi.; 115,777 sq. km) is 515 miles (829 km) long and volcanic in its south-central part. This area contains many hot springs and beautiful geysers. South Island (58,093 sq. mi.; 151,215 sq. km) has the Southern Alps along its west coast, with Mount Cook (12,283.3 ft.; 3,754 m) the highest point. The largest of the outlying islands are the Auckland Islands (234 sq. mi.; 606 sq. km), Campbell Island (44 sq. mi.; 114 sq. km), the Antipodes Islands (24 sq. mi.; 62 sq. km), and the Kermadec Islands (13 sq. mi.; 34 sq. km).

Government Parliamentary democracy.

History Maoris were the first inhabitants of New Zealand, arriving on the islands in about C.E. 1000. Maori oral history maintains the Maoris came to the island in seven canoes from other parts of Polynesia. In 1642 New Zealand was explored by Abel Tasman, a Dutch navigator. British captain James Cook made three voyages to the islands, beginning in 1769. Britain formally annexed the islands in 1840.

The Treaty of Waitangi (Feb. 6, 1840) between the British and several Maori tribes promised to protect Maori land if the Maoris recognized British rule. Encroachment upon the land by European settlers was relentless, however, and skirmishes between the two groups intensified.

From the outset, the country has been in the forefront in instituting social welfare legislation. New Zealand was the world's first country to give women the right to vote (1893). It adopted old age pensions (1898); a national child welfare program (1907); social security for the aged, widows, and orphans, along with family benefit payments; minimum wages; a 40-hour work week and unemployment and health insurance (1938); and socialized medicine (1941).

New Zealand fought with the Allies in both world wars as well as in Korea. In 1999, it became part of the U.N. peacekeeping force sent to East Timor to restore order after the bloody rampage of pro-Indonesian militias, who took revenge on the province for voting for independence from Indonesia.

Cook Islands and Overseas Territories

The Cook Islands (93 sq. mi.; 241 sq. km) were placed under New Zealand administration in 1901. They achieved self-governing status in association with New Zealand in 1965. **Population (1999 est.):** 20,200; growth rate 1.72%; birth rate: 22.4/1000; infant mortality rate: 24.7/1000; density per square mile: 217. The seat of government is on Rarotonga Island. **Economic summary: GDP/PPP** (1993 est.): $57 million; $3,000 per capita. **Exports:** $3.9 million (f.o.b., 1993): citrus juice, clothing, canned fruit, and pineapple juice. **Imports:** $67 million (c.i.f., 1993): foodstuffs, textiles, fuels, timber. Nearly all of the trade is with New Zealand; some with Japan, Australia, and U.S.

Niue (100 sq. mi.; 259 sq. km) was formerly administered as part of the Cook Islands. It was placed under separate New Zealand administration in 1901 and achieved self-governing status in association with New Zealand in 1974. The capital is Alofi. **Population (1998 est.):** 1,837; growth rate –3.65%. **Economic summary: GDP/PPP** (1993 est.): $2.4 million; per capita, $1,200. **Exports:** $117,500 (f.o.b., 1989): canned coconut cream, copra, honey, passion fruit products, pawpaw, root crops, limes, footballs, stamps, handicrafts. **Imports:** $4.1 million (c.i.f., 1989): food, live animals, manufactured goods, machinery, fuels, chemicals, lubricants, drugs. **Major trading partners:** New Zealand, Fiji, Japan.

The Ross Dependency (160,000 sq. mi.; 414,400 sq. km), an Antarctic region, was placed under New Zealand administration in 1923.

Tokelau (4 sq. mi.; 10 sq. km) was formerly administered as part of the Gilbert and Ellice Islands colony. It was placed under New Zealand administration in 1925. Its population is about 1,443 (July 1998 est.).

Nicaragua

REPUBLIC OF NICARAGUA

National name: República de Nicaragua
President: Arnoldo Alemán (1997)
Area: 50,180 sq. mi. (129,494 sq. km)
Population (1999 est.): 4,717,132 (average annual rate of natural increase: 2.94%); birth rate: 35.0/1000; infant mortality rate: 40.5/1000; density per sq. mi.: 94
Capital and largest city (1992 est.): Managua, 974,000. **Monetary unit:** Cordoba. **Language:** Spanish. **Ethnicity/race:** mestizo (mixed Amerindian

and white) 69%, white 17%, black 9%, Indian 5%.
Religions: Roman Catholic, 95%; Protestant, 5%.
Literacy rate: 57%
Economic summary: GDP/PPP (1997 est.): $9.3 billion; $2,100 per capita. **Real growth rate:** 6%. **Inflation:** 11.6% (1996). **Unemployment:** 16%; underemployment, 36%. **Arable land:** 9%. **Agriculture:** coffee, bananas, sugarcane, cotton, rice, corn, cassava (tapioca), citrus, beans, beef, veal, pork, poultry, dairy products. **Labor force:** 1.5 million; services, 54%; agriculture, 31%; industry, 15% (1995 est.). **Industries:** food processing, chemicals, metal products, textiles, clothing, petroleum refining and distribution, beverages, footwear. **Natural resources:** gold, silver, copper, tungsten, lead, zinc, timber, fish. **Exports:** $635 million (f.o.b., 1996): coffee, seafood, bananas, sugar, meat, gold. **Imports:** $1.1 billion (c.i.f., 1996): consumer goods, machinery and equipment, petroleum products. **Major trading partners:** U.S., Central America, Germany, Canada, Venezuela, Japan.

Geography Largest but most sparsely populated of the Central American nations, Nicaragua borders on Honduras to the north and Costa Rica to the south. It is slightly larger than New York State. Nicaragua is mountainous in the west, with fertile valleys. A plateau slopes eastward toward the Caribbean. Two big lakes—Nicaragua, about 100 miles long (161 km), and Managua, about 38 miles long (61 km)—are connected by the Tipitapa River. The Pacific coast is volcanic and very fertile. The Caribbean coast, swampy and indented, is aptly called the "Mosquito Coast."

Government Republic.

History Nicaragua, which derives its name from the chief of the area's leading Indian tribe during the Spanish Conquest, was first settled by the Spanish in 1522. The country achieved independence from Spain in 1838. For the next century, Nicaragua's politics were dominated by the competition for power between the Liberals, who were centered in the city of León, and the Conservatives, centered in Granada.

To back up its support of the new Conservative government in 1909, the U.S. sent a small detachment of Marines to Nicaragua and kept them there from 1912 to 1925. The Bryan-Chamorro Treaty of 1916 (terminated in 1970) gave the U.S. an option on a canal route through Nicaragua, and naval bases. Disorder after the 1924 elections brought in the U.S. Marines again. A guerrilla leader, Gen. César Augusto Sandino, began fighting the occupation force in 1927. He fought the U.S. troops until their withdrawal in 1933.

Gen. Anastasio Somoza García emerged, after ordering the assassination of Sandino, and ruled as dictator from 1936 until his assassination in 1956. He was succeeded by his son Luis, who alternated with trusted family friends in the presidency until his death in 1967. Another son, Maj. Gen. Anastasio Somoza Debayle, became president in 1967. The Somozas ruled Nicaragua with an iron fist, making Nicaragua less dependent on banana income, exiling political foes, and amassing a great family fortune.

Sandinista guerrillas, leftists who took their name from Gen. Sandino, launched an offensive in May 1979. After seven weeks of fighting, Somoza fled the country on July 17, 1979. The Sandinistas assumed power on July 19, promising to maintain a mixed economy, a nonaligned foreign policy, and a pluralist political system. On Jan. 23, 1981, the Reagan administration suspended U.S. aid, charging that Nicaragua, with the aid of Cuba and the Soviet Union, was supplying arms to rebels in El Salvador. The Sandinistas denied the charges. Later that year, Nicaraguan guerrillas known as "Contras," began a war to overthrow the Sandinistas. The elections were finally held on Nov. 4, 1984, with Daniel Ortega, the Sandinista junta coordinator, winning the presidency. The war intensified in 1986–87, with the resupplied Contras establishing themselves inside the country. Negotiations sponsored by the Contadora (neutral Latin American) nations foundered, but a peace plan sponsored by Arias, the Costa Rican president, led to a treaty that was signed by the Central American leaders in Aug. 1987.

Violetta Barrios de Chamorro, owner of the opposition paper *La Prensa,* led a broad anti-Sandinista coalition to victory in the presidential and legislative elections of 1990, ending 11 years of Sandinista rule. After a year in office, however, President Chamorro found herself besieged. Business groups were dissatisfied with the pace of reforms; Sandinistas, upset with what they regarded as the dismantling of their earlier achievements, threatened to take up arms again. In Feb. 1991 the president brought the military under her direct command. By early 1993 relations between the president and the coalition that backed her had soured over charges of corruption and the continuing influence of the Sandinistas on the government and the army. Former Managua mayor and Conservative candidate Arnoldo Aleman won the 1996 election. His closest rival was former president and Sandinista Daniel Ortega.

In 1998, Hurricane Mitch devastated Nicaragua, killing more than 9,000 people, leaving 2 million people homeless, and causing $10 billion in damages. Many Nicaraguans fled to the U.S., which had extended an immigration amnesty program, lasting until July 1999, to Nicaraguans.

Niger

REPUBLIC OF NIGER

National name: République du Niger
Head, National Reconciliation Council: Daouda Malam Wanke (1999)
Prime Minister: Ibrahim Hassane Mayaki (1997)
Area: 489,206 sq. mi. (1,267,000 sq. km)
Population (1999 est.): 9,962,242 (average annual rate of natural increase: 2.95%); birth rate: 52.3/1000; infant mortality rate: 112.8/1000; density per sq. mi.: 20
Capital and largest city (1988): Niamey, 398,265.
Other large cities: Zinder, 120,900; Maradi, 112,970.
Monetary unit: Franc CFA. **Ethnicity/race:** Hausa 56%, Djerma 22%, Fula 8.5%, Tuareg 8%, Beri Beri (Kanouri) 4.3%, Arab, Toubou, and Gourmantche 1.2%, about 4,000 French expatriates. **Languages:** French (official); Hausa; Songhai; Arabic. **Religions:** Islam, 80%; Animist and Christian, 20%. **Literacy rate:** 28%
Economic summary: GDP/PPP (1997 est.): $6.3 billion; $670 per capita. **Real growth rate:** 4.5%. **Inflation:** 5.3% (1996). **Unemployment rate:** n.a. **Arable land:** 3%. **Agriculture:** cowpeas, cotton, peanuts, millet, sorghum, cassava (tapioca); rice, cattle, sheep, goats, camels, donkeys, horses, poultry. **Labor force:** 70,000; agriculture, 90%; industry and commerce, 6%; government, 4%. **Industry:** cement, brick, textiles, food processing, chemicals, slaughterhouses, uranium mining. **Natural resources:** uranium, coal, iron ore,

tin, phosphates, gold, petroleum. **Exports:** $188 million (f.o.b., 1996): uranium ore, oil, cowpeas, livestock products, onions. **Imports:** $374 million (c.i.f., 1996): consumer goods, primary materials, machinery, vehicles and parts, petroleum, cereals. **Major trading partners:** France, Nigeria, Burkina Faso, Côte d'Ivoire, Japan, China, Belgium-Luxembourg.

Geography Niger, in West Africa's Sahara region, is four-fifths the size of Alaska. It is surrounded by Mali, Algeria, Libya, Chad, Nigeria, Benin, and Burkina Faso. The Niger River in the southwest flows through the country's only fertile area. Elsewhere the land is semiarid.

Government Military rule.

History The nomadic Tuaregs were the first inhabitants in the Sahara region. The Hausa (14th century), the Zerma (17th century), the Gobir (18th century), and Fulani also established themselves in the region now called Niger.

Niger was incorporated into French West Africa in 1896. There were frequent rebellions, but when order was restored in 1922, the French made the area a colony. In 1958, the voters approved the French constitution and voted to make the territory an autonomous republic within the French community. The republic adopted a constitution in 1959 but the next year withdrew from the community, proclaiming its independence.

During the 1970s the country's economy flourished from uranium production, but when uranium prices fell in the 1980s, its brief period of prosperity ended. The 1974 army coup ousted President Hamani Diori, who had held office since 1960. An estimated 2 million people were starving in Niger, but 200,000 tons of imported food, half U.S.-supplied, substantially ended famine conditions by the year's end. The new president, Lt. Col. Seyni Kountché, chief of staff of the army, installed a 12-man military government. A predominantly civilian government was formed by Kountché in 1976.

In 1993 the country's first multiparty election resulted in the presidency of Ousmane Mahamane, who was then deposed in a Jan. 1996 coup. The constitution was suspended and the president arrested. In July the military leader of the coup, Ibrahim Baré Maïnassara, was declared president in a rigged election.

A cease-fire between the government and Tuareg rebels (Revolutionary Armed Forces of the Sahara) went into effect in 1995, and in June 1997, the Democratic Renewal Front, a hold-out Tuareg rebel group, also agreed to sign a peace accord. The nomadic Tuaregs, of Berber and Arab descent, have a fiercely insular culture and share little affinity with the black African majority of Niger. The impoverished Tuaregs have received little of the economic aid they were promised, which is not surprising given Niger's political instability and desperate poverty.

President Ibrahim Baré Maïnassara, considered a corrupt and ineffectual leader, was assassinated in April 1999 by his own guards. Ever since he had overthrown Niger's only democratically elected president, political unrest had dogged his presidency. The prime minister was retained, and the National Reconciliation Council, responsible for the coup, promised that elections would follow in nine months.

Nigeria

FEDERAL REPUBLIC OF NIGERIA

President: Olusegun Obasanjo (1999)
Area: 356,700 sq. mi. (923,770 sq. km)
Population (1999 est.): 113,828,587; average annual rate of natural increase: 2.89%; birth rate: 41.8/1000; infant mortality rate: 69.5/1000; density per sq. mi.: 319
Capital (1995 est.): Abuja, 339,000. **Largest cities:** Lagos: city proper (1996 est.) 1,518,000; metro. area (1996 est.) 10,878, 000. **Other large cities:** Ibadan, 1,365,000; Ogbomosho, 711,900; Kano, 657,300.
Monetary unit: Naira. **Languages:** English (official), Hausa, Yoruba, Ibo, and more than 200 others.
Ethnicity/race: Hausa, Fulani, Yoruba, Ibo, Kanuri, Ibibio, Tiv, Ijaw. **Religions:** Islam, 50%; Christian, 40%; indigenous, 10%. **Literacy rate:** 51%
Economic summary: GDP/PPP (1996 est.): $132.7 billion; $1,300 per capita. **Real growth rate:** 3.3%. **Inflation:** 12% (1997 est.). **Unemployment:** 28% (1992 est.). **Arable land:** 33%. **Agriculture:** cocoa, peanuts, palm oil, corn, rice, sorghum, millet, cassava (tapioca), yams, rubber, cattle, sheep, goats, pigs, fishing and forest resources extensively exploited. **Labor force:** 42.844 million; agriculture, 54%; government, 15%; industry, commerce and services, 19%. **Industries:** crude oil, coal, tin, columbite, palm oil, peanuts, cotton, rubber, wood, hides and skins, textiles, cement and other construction materials, food products, footwear, chemicals, fertilizer, printing, ceramics, steel. **Natural resources:** petroleum, tin, columbite, iron ore, coal, limestone, lead, zinc, natural gas. **Exports:** $15 billion (f.o.b., 1996): petroleum and petroleum products, cocoa, rubber. **Imports:** $8 billion (c.i.f., 1996): machinery, chemicals, transportation equipment, manufactured goods, food and animals. **Major trading partners:** EU, U.S., Japan. **Member of Commonwealth of Nations**

Geography Nigeria, one-third larger than Texas and the largest country in Africa, is situated on the Gulf of Guinea in West Africa. Its neighbors are Benin, Niger, Cameroon, and Chad. The lower course of the Niger River flows south through the western part of the country into the Gulf of Guinea. Swamps and mangrove forests border the southern coast; inland are hardwood forests.

Government Multiparty government.

History The first inhabitants of what is now Nigeria were thought to have been the Nok people (500 B.C.E.–circa C.E. 200). The Kanuri, Hausa, and Fulani peoples subsequently migrated there. Islam was introduced in the 13th century, and the empire of Kanem controlled the area from the end of the 11th century to the 14th.

The Fulani empire ruled the region from the beginning of the 19th century until the British annexed Lagos in 1851 and seized control of the rest of the region by 1886. It formally became the Colony and Protectorate of Nigeria in 1914. During World War I, native troops of the West African frontier force joined with French forces to defeat the German garrison in the Cameroons.

On Oct. 1, 1960, Nigeria gained independence, becoming a member of the Commonwealth of Nations and joining the United Nations. Organized as a loose federation of self-governing states, the independent nation faced an overwhelming task of unifying a country with 250 ethnic and linguistic groups.

Rioting broke out in 1966, and military leaders, primarily of Ibo ethnicity, seized control. In July, a second military coup put Col. Yakubu Gowon in power, a choice unacceptable to the Ibos. Also in that year, the Muslim Hausas in the north massacred the predominantly Christian Ibos in the east, many of whom had been driven from the north. Thousands of Ibos took refuge in the eastern region, which declared its independence as the Republic of Biafra on May 30, 1967. Civil war broke out. In Jan. 1970, after 31 months of civil war, Biafra surrendered to the federal government.

Gowon's nine-year rule was ended in 1975 by a bloodless coup that made Army Brigadier Muritala Rufai Mohammed the new chief of state. The return of civilian leadership was established with the election of Alhaji Shehu Shagari as president in 1979. An oil boom in the 1970s buoyed the economy and by the 1980s Nigeria was considered an exemplar of African democracy and economic well-being.

The military again seized power in 1984, only to be followed by another military coup the following year. Maj. Gen. Ibrahim Babangida announced that the country would be returned to civilian rule, but after the presidential election of June 12, 1993, he voided the results. Nevertheless, Babangida resigned as president in Aug. In Nov. the military, headed by defense minister Sani Abacha, seized power again.

Corruption and notorious governmental inefficiency as well as a harshly repressive military regime characterized Abacha's reign over this oil-rich country. A U.N. fact-finding mission in 1996 reported that Nigeria's "problems of human rights are terrible and the political problems are terrifying." During the 1970s Nigeria had the 33rd highest per-capita income in the world, but by 1997 it had dropped to the 13th poorest.

Nigeria has established itself as West Africa's superpower through its military interventions in the civil wars of Liberia and Sierra Leone. Although Nigeria was unsuccessful in its attempt to defeat Charles Taylor's invasion of Liberia, in Sierra Leone Nigerian troops played a major role in overthrowing the military junta in 1998 and restoring its democratically elected president to power. In Sept. 1999, however, its troops, called ECOMOG, pulled out of Sierra Leone, leaving its fragile president to forge peace with the rebels. Nigeria's costly war efforts have been unpopular with its own people, who feel Nigeria's dire economic situation is being unnecessarily drained.

Under military rule for all but ten years since independence from Britain, the military has reneged on its promises to give up power eight times. Despite international pressure to institute democratic rule, the notoriously authoritarian Gen. Sani Abacha, whose formidable security forces kept a tight reign over the country, refused to loosen his absolute grip on political and military power. Abacha's repressive rule turned Nigeria into an international pariah. The hanging of writer Ken Saro-Wiwa in 1995 because he protested against the government was condemned around the world.

Abacha died of a heart attack on June 8, 1998, and was succeeded by another military ruler, Gen. Abdulsalam Abubakar, who also pledged to step aside for an elected leader by May 1999. Abubakar's freeing of political prisoners and other gestures of easing the military's iron-clad rule have shown some signs of hope for Nigeria. However, the sudden and some believe suspicious death of opposition leader Mashood Abiola, who had been imprisoned by the military ever since he legally won the 1993 presidential election, was a crushing blow to democratic proponents. In Feb. 1999 free presidential elections led to an overwhelming victory for General Olusegu Obasanjo, a former member of the military elite who was imprisoned for three years for criticizing the military rule, and released just eight months before his election.

Norway

KINGDOM OF NORWAY

National name: Kongeriket Norge
Sovereign: King Harald V (1991)
Prime Minister: Kjell Magne Bondevik (1997)
Area: 125,049 sq. mi. (324,220 sq. km)
Population (1999 est.): 4,438,547 (average annual growth rate: 0.24%); birth rate: 12.5/1000; infant mortality rate: 5.0/1000; density per sq. mi.: 35
Capital and largest city (1995): Oslo, 483,401. **Other large cities:** Bergen, 221,717; Trondheim, 142,927; Stavanger, 103,496. **Monetary unit:** Krone.
Languages: Two official forms of Norwegian: Bokmål and Nynorsk. **Ethnicity/race:** Germanic (Nordic, Alpine, Baltic), Lapps (Sami). **Religions:** Evangelical Lutheran 87.8% (state church), other Protestant and Roman Catholic 3.8%, none 3.2%, unknown 5.2%.
Literacy rate: 99%
Economic summary: GDP/PPP (1997 est.): $120.5 billion; $27,400 per capita. **Real growth rate:** 3.5%. **Inflation:** 2%. **Unemployment:** 2.6%. **Arable land:** 3%. **Agriculture:** oats, other grains, beef, milk, livestock output exceeds value crops, fish. **Labor force:** 2.13 million; services, 71%; industry, 23%; agriculture, forestry and fishing, 6% (1993). **Industry:** petroleum and gas, food processing, shipbuilding, pulp and paper products, metals, chemicals, timber, mining, textiles, fishing. **Natural resources:** petroleum, copper, natural gas, pyrites, nickel, iron ore, zinc, lead, fish, timber, hydropower. **Exports:** $49.3 billion (f.o.b., 1996): petroleum and petroleum products, metals and products, foodstuffs, chemicals and raw materials, natural gas, ships. **Imports:** $35.1 billion (c.i.f., 1996): machinery and equipment and manufactured consumer goods, chemicals and other industrial inputs, foodstuffs. **Major trading partners:** EU (U.K., Germany, Denmark, The Netherlands, France, Sweden), U.S., Japan.

Geography Norway is situated in the western part of the Scandinavian peninsula. It extends about 1,100 miles (1,770 km) from the North Sea along the Norwegian Sea to more than 300 miles (483 km) above the Arctic Circle, the farthest north of any European country. It is slightly larger than New Mexico. Nearly 70% of Norway is uninhabitable and covered by mountains, glaciers, moors, and rivers. The hundreds of deep fjords that cut into the coastline give Norway an overall oceanfront of more than 12,000 miles (19,312 km). Galdhø Peak, at 8,100 feet (2,469 m), is Norway's highest point and the Glåma (Glomma) is the principal river, at 372 miles (598 km) long.

Government Constitutional monarchy.

History Norwegians, like the Danes and Swedes, are of Teutonic origin. The Norsemen, also known as Vikings, ravaged the coasts of northwestern Europe from the 8th to the 11th century and were ruled by local chieftains. Olaf II Haraldsson became the first effective king of all Norway in 1015 and began converting the Norwegians to Christianity. After 1442, Norway was ruled by Danish kings until 1814, when it was united with Sweden—although retaining a degree of independence and receiving a new constitution—in an uneasy partnership. In 1905, the Norwegian Parliament arranged a peaceful separation and invited a Danish prince to the Norwegian throne—King Haakon VII. A treaty with Sweden provided that all disputes be settled by arbitration and that no fortifications be erected on the common frontier.

When World War I broke out, Norway joined with Sweden and Denmark in a decision to remain neutral and to cooperate in the joint interest of the three countries. In World War II, Norway was invaded by the Germans on April 9, 1940. It resisted for two months before the Nazis took complete control. King Haakon and his government fled to London, where they established a government-in-exile. Maj. Vidkun Quisling, who served as Norway's premier during the war, was the most notorious of the Nazi collaborators. The word for traitor, *quisling*, bears his name. He was executed by the Norwegians on Oct. 24, 1945.

Despite severe losses in the war, Norway recovered quickly as its economy expanded. The country led the world in social experimentation. It entered the North Atlantic Treaty Organization in 1949. In the late 20th century, the Labor Party and the Conservative Party seesawed for control, each sometimes having to lead minority governments. An important debate has been over Norway's membership in the European Union. In an advisory referendum held in Nov. 1994, voters rejected seeking membership for their nation in the EU. The country became the second-largest net oil exporter after Saudi Arabia in 1995. Norway continued to experience rapid economic growth in the late 1990s.

Dependencies of Norway

Svalbard (24,208 sq. mi.; 62,700 sq. km), in the Arctic Ocean about 360 miles north of Norway, consists of the Spitsbergen group and several smaller islands, including Bear Island, Hope Island, King Charles Land, and White Island (or Gillis Land). The capital is Longyearbyen. It came under Norwegian administration in 1925. Population 2,594 (July 1998 est.); growth rate: −3.55%. 62% of the population is Russian and Ukrainian; 38% are Norwegian. Coal mining is major economic activity. There is also some trapping of seal, polar bear, fox, and walrus. **Bouvet Island** (23 sq. mi.; 60 sq. km), an island nature reserve in the South Atlantic about 1,600 miles south-southwest of the Cape of Good Hope, came under Norwegian administration in 1928. It is uninhabited.

Jan Mayen Island (147 sq. mi.; 380 sq. km), in the Arctic Ocean between Norway and Greenland, came under Norwegian administration in 1929. There are no permanent inhabitants, just workers at the navigation base and weather/radio station. **Peter I Island** (96 sq. mi.; 249 sq. km), lying off Antarctica in the Bellinghausen Sea, came under Norwegian administration in 1931. **Queen Maud Land,** a section of Antarctica, came under Norwegian administration in 1939.

Oman

SULTANATE OF OMAN

National name: Saltonat Uman
Sultan: Qabus ibn Sa'id (1970)
Area: 82,030 sq. mi. (212,460 sq. km)[1]
Population (1999 est.): 2,446,645 (average annual rate of natural increase: 3.37%); birth rate: 38.0/1000; infant mortality rate: 24.7/1000; density per sq. mi.: 30
Capital and largest city (1991 est.): Muscat, 350,000. **Monetary unit:** Omani rial. **Languages:** Arabic (official); also English and Indian languages. **Ethnicity/race:** Arab, Baluchi, South Asian (Indian, Pakistani, Sri Lankan, Bangladeshi), African. **Religion:** Islam, 95%. **Literacy rate:** 65.8%
Economic summary: GDP/PPP (1997 est.): $17.2 billion; $8,000 per capita. **Real growth rate:** 3.5%. **Inflation:** 1% (1996). **Unemployment:** n.a. **Agriculture:** dates, limes, bananas, alfalfa, vegetables, camels, cattle, fish. **Labor force:** 780,500; agriculture, 37% (1993 est.). **Industry:** crude oil production and refining, natural gas production, construction, cement, copper. **Natural resources:** petroleum, copper, asbestos, some marble, limestone, chromium, gypsum, natural gas. **Exports:** $7.6 billion (f.o.b., 1997 est.): petroleum, reexports: fish, processed copper, textiles. **Imports:** $4.8 billion (f.o.b., 1997 est.): machinery, transport equipment, manufactured goods, food, livestock, lubricants. **Major trading partners:** Japan, South Korea, China, Thailand, U.S., U.A.E., U.K., France.

1. Excluding the Kuria Muria Islands.

Geography Oman is a 1,000-mile-long (1,700-km) coastal plain at the southeastern tip of the Arabian peninsula lying on the Arabian Sea and the Gulf of Oman. The interior is a plateau. The country is the size of Kansas.

Government Absolute monarchy.

History Arabs migrated to Oman from the 9th century B.C.E. onward, and conversion to Islam occurred in the 7th century C.E. Muscat, the capital of the geographical area known as Oman, was occupied by the Portuguese from 1508 to 1648. Then it fell to Ottoman Turks, but in 1741 Ahmad ibn Sa'id forced them out. The descendants of Sultan Ahmad rule Oman today.

He expanded his empire to East Africa, and for a time the Omani capital was in Zanzibar. After 1861, however, Zanzibar fell from Omani control.

The sultans and imams of Oman clashed continuosly throughout the 20th century until 1959, when the last Ibadi imam was evicted from the country. In a palace coup on July 23, 1970, the sultan, Sa'id bin Taimur, who had ruled since 1932, was overthrown by his son, who promised to establish a modern government and use newfound oil wealth to aid the people of this very isolated state. Oman joined the Arab League and the United Nations in 1971.

A long border dispute with Yemen ended in late Oct. 1992 when the sultan signed an agreement with the Yemeni president. In 1997, Oman and Yemen signed maps defining the border between the two countries. Sultan Qabus in June 1997 granted women the right to be elected to the country's consultative body, the Shura Council.

Pakistan

ISLAMIC REPUBLIC OF PAKISTAN

President: Mohammad Rafiq Tarar (1998)
Prime Minister: Nawaz Sharif (1997)
Area: 310,400 sq. mi. (803,940 sq. km)[1]
Population (1999 est.): 138,123,359 (average annual growth rate: 2.31%); birth rate: 33.5/1000; infant mortality rate: 91.9/1000; density per sq. mi.: 445
Capital (1981 census): Islamabad, 201,000. **Largest cities:** Karachi: city proper (1981 census) 5,208,132; metro. area (1996 est.) 10,119,000; Lahore, 2,952,700; Faisalabad, (Lyallpur) 1,920,000; Rawalpindi, 920,000; Hyderabad, 795,000. **Monetary unit:** Pakistan rupee. **Principal languages:** Punjabi 48%, Sindhi 12%, Siraiki (a Punjabi variant) 10%, Pashtu 8%, Urdu (official) 8%, Balochi 3%, Hindko 2%, Brahui 1%, English, Burushaski, and others. **Ethnicity/race:** Punjabi, Sindhi, Pashtun (Pathan), Baloch, Muhajir (immigrants from India and their descendants). **Religions:** Islam, 97%; Hindu, Christian, Buddhist, Parsi. **Literacy rate:** 35%
Economic summary GNP/PPP: (1997 est.): $344 billion; $2,600 per capita. **Real growth rate:** 3.1%. **Inflation:** 11.8% (FY96/97). **Unemployment:** n.a. **Arable land:** 27%. **Agriculture:** cotton, wheat, rice, sugarcane, fruits, vegetables, milk, beef, mutton, eggs. **Labor force:** 37.8 million (1998); agriculture, 47%; mining and manufacturing, 17%; services, 17%; other, 19%. **Industry:** textiles, food processing, beverages, construction materials, clothing, paper products, shrimp. **Natural resources:** land, extensive natural gas reserves, limited petroleum, poor quality coal, iron ore, copper, salt, limestone. **Exports:** $8.2 billion (FY96/97): cotton, rice, textiles, clothing, leather, carpets. **Imports:** $11.4 billion (FY96/97): petroleum, petroleum products, machinery, transportation equipment, vegetable oils, animal fats, chemicals. **Major trading partners:** EU, Hong Kong, U.S., Japan.

1. Excluding Kashmir and Jammu.

Geography Pakistan is situated in the western part of the Indian subcontinent, with Afghanistan and Iran on the west, India on the east, and the Arabian Sea on the south. The name "Pakistan" is derived from the Urdu words "Pak" (meaning pure) and "stan" (meaning country). It is nearly twice the size of California.

The northern and western highlands of Pakistan contain the towering Karakoram and Pamir mountain ranges, which include some of the world's highest peaks: K2 (28,250 ft. [8,611 m]) and Nanga Parbat (26,660 ft. [8,126 m]). The Baluchistan Plateau lies to the west, and the Thar Desert and an expanse of alluvial plains, the Punjab and Sind, lie to the east. The 1,000-mile-long (1,609 km) Indus River and its tributaries flow through the country from the Kashmir region to the Arabian Sea.

Government Federal republic.

History Pakistan was one of the two original successor states to British India, which was partitioned along religious lines in 1947. For almost 25 years following independence, it consisted of two separate regions, East and West Pakistan, but now is made up only of the western sector. Both India and Pakistan have laid claim to the Kashmir region, and this territorial dispute led to war in 1949, again in 1965 and 1971, and remains unresolved.

What is now Pakistan was in prehistoric times the Indus Valley civilization (c. 2500–1700 B.C.E.). A series of invaders—Aryans, Persians, Greeks, Arabs,

Turks, and others—controlled the region for the next several thousand years. Islam, the dominant religion, was introduced in c.e. 711. In 1526, the land became part of the Mogul Empire, which ruled most of the Indian subcontinent from the 16th to the mid-18th century. By 1857 the British became the dominant power in the region. With Hindus holding most of the economic, social, and political advantages, the Muslim minority's dissatisfaction grew, leading to the formation of the nationalist Muslim League in 1906 by Mohammed Ali Jinnah (1876–1949). The league supported Britain in the Second World War while the Hindu nationalist leaders, Nehru and Gandhi, refused. In return for the league's support of Britain, Jinnah expected British backing for Muslim autonomy. Britain agreed to the formation of Pakistan as a separate dominion within the Commonwealth in Aug. 1947, a bitter disappointment to India's dream of a unified subcontinent. Jinnah became governor-general. The partition of Pakistan and India along religious lines resulted in the largest migration in human history, with 17 million people fleeing across the borders in both directions to escape the sectarian violence accompanying the partition.

Pakistan became a republic on March 3, 1956, with Major General Iskander Mirza becoming the first president. Military rule prevailed for the next two decades. Tensions between East and West Pakistan existed from the outset. Separated by more than a thousand miles, the two regions shared few cultural and social traditions other than religion. To the growing resentment of East Pakistan, the West monopolized the country's political and economic power. In 1970, East Pakistan's Awami League, led by the Bengali leader Sheik Mujibur Rahman, secured a majority of the seats in the National Assembly. President Yahya Khan postponed the opening of the National Assembly to skirt East Pakistan's demand for greater autonomy, provoking civil war. The independent state of Bangladesh, or Bengali nation, was proclaimed on March 26, 1971. Indian troops entered the war in its last weeks fighting on the side of the new state. Pakistan was defeated on Dec. 16, 1971, and President Yahya Khan stepped down. Zulfikar Ali Bhutto took over Pakistan and accepted Bangladesh as an independent entity. In 1976 formal relations between India and Pakistan resumed.

Pakistan's first elections under civilian rule took place in March 1977, and the overwhelming victory of Bhutto's Pakistan People's Party (PPP) was denounced as fraudulent. A rising tide of violent protest and political deadlock led to a military takeover on July 5 by Gen. Mohammed Zia ul-Haq. Bhutto was tried and convicted for the 1974 murder of a political opponent, and despite worldwide protests was executed on April 4, 1979, touching off riots by his supporters. Zia declared himself president on Sept. 16, 1978, and ruled by martial law until Dec. 30, 1985. A measure of representative government was restored with the election of a new National Assembly in Feb. 1985, although leaders of opposition parties were banned from the election. On Aug. 19, 1988, President Zia was killed in a mid-air explosion of a Pakistani Air Force plane. Elections at the end of 1988 brought longtime Zia opponent Benazir Bhutto, daughter of Zulfikar Bhutto, into office as prime minister.

In the 1990s, Pakistan saw a shaky succession of governments. Benazir Bhutto was prime minister twice and dismissed each time by the president for incompetence or corruption. Nawaz Sharif's government is now in power for the third time. In April 1997 Parliament amended the constitution to prevent a president from dismissing a government.

India's detonation of five nuclear tests in May 1998 near Pakistan's borders further deteriorated relations between the two countries, and in an act of nuclear brinksmanship, Pakistan evened the score by conducting nuclear tests of its own on May 28th and May 30th. In the fall of 1998, Pakistan indicated a willingness to sign a nuclear test-ban treaty to rid itself of Western sanctions, which had been imposed since the nuclear testing. Pakistan began talks about the disputed territory of Kashmir, a major factor in its antagonistic relationship with India—Pakistan controls one-third of Kashmir, which is a predominantly Muslim territory. Both India and Pakistan continued their tit-for-tat military testing by launching nuclear-capable ballistic missiles in April 1999. The next month, fighting broke out in Kashmir when Pakistani fighters crossed over the so-called Line of Control that divides Pakistani and Indian Kashmir. The Indian Air Force launched air strikes on May 26, 1999 and later sent in ground troops. India blamed Pakistan for orchestrating the attacks; Pakistan countered that the guerrillas are Kashmiri freedom fighters struggling for India's ouster from the region. Most sources believe that soldiers are a mix of Pakistani army regulars and armed militants. In July, Pakistani forces withdrew.

Palau

REPUBLIC OF PALAU

President: Kuniwo Nakamura (1993)
Total area: 177 sq. mi. (458 sq. km)
Population (1999 est.): 18,467 (average rate of natural increase: 1.38%); birth rate: 21.6/1000; infant mortality rate: 18.5/1000; density per sq. mi.: 104
Capital and largest city (1995): Koror, 12,299.
Monetary unit: U.S. dollar used. **Languages:** Palauan is the official language, though English is commonplace. **Ethnicity/race:** Palauans are a composite of Polynesian, Malayan, and Melanesian races. **Religions:** Christian. About one-third of the islanders observe Modekngei religion, indigenous to Palau. **Literacy rate:** 86%
Economic summary: GDP/PPP: (1997 est.): $160 million (note: GDP numbers reflect U.S. spending), $8,800 per capita. **Real growth rate:** 10%. **Inflation rate:** n.a. **Unemployment:** 7%. **Agriculture:** coconuts, copra, cassava (tapioca), sweet potatoes. **Labor force:** n.a. **Industry:** tourism, craft items (from shell, wood, pearls), some commercial fishing and agriculture. **Natural resources:** forests, minerals (especially gold), marine products, deep-seabed minerals. **Exports:** $14.3 million (f.o.b., 1996); trochus (a shellfish), tuna, copra, handicrafts. **Imports:** $72.4 million (f.o.b., 1996). **Major trading partners:** U.S., Japan.

Geography The Palau island chain consists of about 200 islands located in the western Pacific Ocean 528 mi. (650 km) southeast of the Philippines. The islands vary geologically from the high mountainous largest island, Babelthuap, to low, coral islands usually fringed by large barrier reefs.

Government Republic.

History The Palau islands' position on the western threshold of Oceania and their proximity to Southeast Asia have led to the population being a mixture of Malay, Melanesian, Filipino, and Polynesian ancestry. Visited by the Spanish navigator Ruy López de Villalobos in 1543, the islands remained under nominal Spanish ownership for more than 300 years before Spain sold them to Germany in 1899. Japan occupied Palau during World War I and received a mandate over them from the League of Nations in 1920. They remained in Japanese control and served as an important naval base until the U.S. seized them during World War II. After the war they became a U.N. trusteeship (1947), administered by the U.S. Palau signed a compact of free association with the U.S. in 1992, requiring the U.S. to provide economic aid in exchange for the right to build and maintain U.S. military facilities in Palau. Palau became a sovereign state in 1994.

Palestinian State (proposed)

WEST BANK AND GAZA STRIP

President: Yasir Arafat (1996)
Area: West Bank: 2,263 sq. mi. (5,860 sq. km); Gaza Strip: 139 sq. mi. (360 sq. km)
Population (July 1998 est.): West Bank: 1,555,919, in addition: 155,000 Israeli settlers in West Bank, 164,000 in East Jerusalem), Gaza Strip: 1,054,173 (in addition: 6,000 Israeli settlers in the Gaza Strip [Aug. 1996 est.]) (average annual rate of natural increase: West Bank: 3.7%, Gaza Strip: 6.4%); birth rate: West Bank: 36.7/1000, Gaza Strip: 49.1/1000; infant mortality rate: West Bank: 26.4/1,000, Gaza Strip: 24.5/1000; density per sq. mi.: West Bank: 828.5, Gaza Strip: 7,627
Capital: Undetermined. **Largest cities (1996 est.):** Hebron, 294,116; Nablus, 217,935. **Monetary units:** New Israeli shekels, Jordanian dinars, U.S. dollars.
Languages: Arabic, Hebrew, English, French.
Ethnicity/race: West Bank: Palestinian Arab and other 83%, Jewish 17%; Gaza Strip: Palestinian Arab and other 99.4%, Jewish 0.6%. **Religions:** West Bank: Muslim 75%, Jewish 17%, Christian and other 8%; Gaza Strip: Muslim 98.7%, Christian 0.7%, Jewish 0.6%
Economic summary: GDP/PPP (1996 est.): West Bank: $2.8 billion; $1,600 per capita. Gaza Strip: $1 billion; $1,100. **Real growth rate (both):** –6.9%. **Inflation (both):** 8.4%. **Unemployment (both):** 28% (1997 est.) **Arable land:** West Bank: 27%; Gaza Strip: 24%. **Agriculture (both):** olives, citrus and other fruits, vegetables, beef, dairy products: **Labor force:** n.a.; West Bank: agriculture 33%, industry 13%, services 54%; Gaza Strip: services 66%, industry 21%, agriculture 13%. **Industry (both):** cement, textiles, soap, olive-wood carvings, mother-of-pearl souvenirs. **Natural resources (both):** negl. **Exports (both):** $630 million (f.o.b., 1997 est.): olives, fruit, vegetables, limestone. **Imports (both):** $1.7 billion (c.i.f., 1997 est.): food, consumer goods, construction materials. **Major trading partners (both):** Jordan, Israel, Egypt.

Geography The West Bank is mostly composed of limestone hills (conventionally called the Samarian Hills north of Jerusalem and the Judaean Hills south of Jerusalem) having an average height of 2,300 to 3,000 feet (700 to 900 m). The Gaza Strip is located between Israel and Egypt on the Mediterranean coast. It is a flat to rolling sand- and dune-covered coastal plain.

Government The Palestinian Authority (PA), with Arafat its elected leader, took control of the newly non-Israeli-occupied areas, assuming all governmental duties in 1994. Permanent peace talks and implementation of Palestinian self-rule in the West Bank and Gaza Strip are still ongoing.

History The history of the proposed modern Palestinian state, which is expected to be formed from the territories of the West Bank and Gaza Strip, began with the British Mandate of Palestine. From Sept. 29, 1923, until May 14, 1948, Britain controlled the region, but by 1947 Britain appealed to the U.N. to solve the complex problem of competing Palestinian and Jewish claims to the land. In Aug. 1947, the U.N. proposed dividing Palestine into a Jewish state, an Arab state, and a small international zone. Arabs rejected the idea. As soon as Britain pulled out of Palestine in 1948, neighboring Arab nations invaded, intent on crushing the newly declared State of Israel. Israel emerged victorious, affirming its sovereignty. The remaining areas of Palestine were divided by Transjordan (now Jordan), which annexed the West Bank, and Egypt, which gained control of the Gaza Strip.

Through a series of political and social policies, Jordan sought to consolidate its control over the political future of Palestinians and to become their speaker. Jordan even extended citizenship to Palestinians in 1949—Palestinians constituted about two-thirds of the country's population. In the Gaza Strip, administered by Egypt from 1948–67, poverty and unemployment were high and most Palestinians lived in refugee camps.

In the Arab-Israeli war of 1967, Israel, over a period of six days, defeated the military forces of Egypt, Syria, and Jordan and annexed the territories of East Jerusalem, the Golan Heights, the West Bank, the Gaza Strip, and all of the Sinai peninsula by defeating the military forces of Egypt, Syria, and Jordan. The Palestine Liberation Organization (PLO), formed in 1964, was a terrorist organization bent on Israel's annihilation. Palestinian rioting, demonstrations, and terrorist acts against Israelis became chronic. In 1974, PLO leader Yasir Arafat addressed the U.N. general assembly, the first stateless government to do so. Violence again escalated in 1987 during the *intifada* ("shaking off"), a new era in Palestinian mass mobilization. In 1988, Arafat proclaimed the independence of the Palestinian State (including the West Bank and Gaza Strip), as a government-in-exile, and publicly eschewed terrorism.

In 1993, highly secretive talks in Norway between the PLO and the Israeli government resulted in the Oslo agreement. The accord stipulated a five-year plan in which Palestinians of the West Bank and the Gaza Strip would gradually become self-governing. On Sept. 13, 1993, Arafat and Israeli prime minister Yitzak Rabin signed the historic "Declaration of Principles." As part of the agreement, Israel pulled out of the Gaza Strip and Jericho in the West Bank in 1994. The Palestinian Authority (PA), with Arafat its elected leader, took control of the newly non-Israeli-occupied areas, assuming all governmental duties. Permanent peace talks and implementation of Palestinian self-rule in the West Bank and Gaza

Strip are still ongoing, after six years. The election in 1999 of Israeli prime minister Ehud Barak was viewed by moderate Palestinians as a positive step toward resolving the remaining differences between Israel and the PA.

Panama

REPUBLIC OF PANAMA

National name: República de Panamá
President: Mireya Moscoso (1999)
Area: 29,761 sq. mi. (78,200 sq. km)
Population (1999 est.): 2,778,526 (average annual rate of natural increase: 1.66%); birth rate: 21.7/1000; infant mortality rate: 23.4/1000; density per sq. mi.: 93
Capital and largest city (1993 est.): Panama City, 450,668. **Other large cities:** San Miguelito, 293,564; Colón, 137,825. **Monetary unit:** Balboa. **Languages:** Spanish (official); many bilingual in English. **Ethnicity/race:** mestizo (mixed Indian and European ancestry) 70%, West Indian 14%, white 10%, Indian 6%.
Religions: Roman Catholic, over 93%; Protestant, 6%. **Literacy rate:** 89%
Economic summary: GDP/PPP (1997 est.): $18 billion; $6,700 per capita. **Real growth rate:** 3.6%. **Inflation:** 1.2%. **Unemployment:** 13.1%. **Arable land:** 7%. **Agriculture:** bananas, corn, sugarcane, rice, coffee, vegetables, livestock, fishing. **Labor force:** 1.044 million (1997 est.); government and community services, 31.8%; agriculture, hunting, fishing, 26.8%; commerce, restaurants, hotels, 16.4%; manufacturing and mining, 9.4%; construction, 3.2%; transportation and communications, 6.2%; finance, insurance, and real estate, 4.3%. **Industry:** construction, petroleum refining, brewing, cement and other construction materials, sugar milling. **Natural resources:** copper, mahogany forests, shrimp. **Exports:** $592 million (f.o.b., 1997 est.): bananas, sugar, shrimp, coffee, clothing. **Imports:** $2.95 billion (c.i.f., 1997 est.): capital goods, crude oil, foodstuffs, consumer goods, chemicals. **Major trading partners:** U.S., EU, Central America and Caribbean, Japan.

Geography The southernmost of the Central American nations, Panama is south of Costa Rica and north of Colombia. The Panama Canal bisects the isthmus at its narrowest and lowest point, allowing passage from the Caribbean Sea to the Pacific Ocean. Panama is slightly smaller than South Carolina. It is marked by a chain of mountains in the west, moderate hills in the interior, and a low range on the east coast. There are extensive forests in the fertile Caribbean area.

Government Republic.

History Explored by Columbus in 1502 on his fourth voyage and explored by Balboa in 1513, Panama was the principal shipment point for supplies to and from South and Central America in colonial days. In 1821, when Central America revolted against Spain, Panama joined Colombia, which had already declared its independence. For the next 82 years, Panama attempted unsuccessfully to break away from Colombia. Between 1850 and 1900 Panama had 40 administrations, 50 riots, 5 attempted secessions, and 13 U.S. interventions. After U.S. proposals for canal rights over the narrow isthmus had been rejected by Colombia, Panama proclaimed its independence from Colombia with U.S. backing in 1903.

For canal rights in perpetuity, the U.S. paid Panama $10 million and agreed to pay $250,000 each year, which was increased to $430,000 in 1933. It was further increased under a revised treaty signed in 1955. In exchange, the U.S. got the Canal Zone—a 10-mile-wide strip across the isthmus—and a considerable degree of influence in Panama's affairs.

Panama and the U.S. agreed in 1974 to negotiate the eventual reversion of the canal to Panama, despite strongly expressed opposition in the U.S. Congress. The texts of two treaties—one governing the transfer of the canal and the other guaranteeing its neutrality after transfer—were signed by President Omar Torrijos Herara and President Carter in Washington on Sept. 7.

The treaties provided for gradual transfer of the operations of the canal to Panamanians, the phasing out of U.S. military bases, and reversion of lands and waters used in the management of the canal. Similarly, Panama was to assume jurisdiction over the zone by degrees. A second pact promised an open and neutral canal in peace and war for all nations. The transfer was to be completed by Dec. 31, 1999. A Panamanian referendum approved the treaties in Oct., but further changes were insisted upon by the U.S. Senate. The principal change specified that although only Panama would maintain forces in its territory after Dec. 31, 1999, the U.S. would have the right to use military force to keep the canal operating if it should become obstructed. The U.S. Senate approved the treaties in March–April 1978.

Nicolas Ardito Barletta, Panama's first directly elected president in 16 years, was inaugurated on Oct. 11, 1984, for a five-year term. He was a puppet of behind-the-scenes strongman Gen. Manuel Noriega and was replaced by vice president Eric Arturo Delvalle, another Noriega supporter, a year later. In 1988, Noriega was indicted in the U.S. for drug trafficking, but when Delvalle attempted to fire him, he forced the National Assembly to replace Delvalle with Manuel Solis Palma. In Dec. 1989, the assembly named Noriega the "maximum leader" and declared the U.S. and Panama to be in a state of war. In Dec. 1989, 24,000 U.S. troops seized control of Panama City in an attempt to capture Noriega after a U.S. soldier was killed in Panama. On Jan. 3, 1990, Noriega surrendered himself to U.S. custody and was transported to Miami to stand trial for drug trafficking (he was subsequently convicted). Guillermo Endara, who probably would have won the election suppressed by Noriega, was installed as president.

Ernesto Pérez Balladares of the Democratic Revolutionary Party, whose campaign invoked memories of the party's founder, Omar Torrijos, won the May 1994 elections. In June 1997, a new law created an autonomous Canal Authority to administer the Panama Canal after the U.S. relinquishes its last controls over the waterway. By mid-1999, the U.S.'s troop withdrawal was well under way, paving the way for complete Panamanian control of the Canal Zone.

Panama Canal. First conceived by the Spaniards in 1524, when King Charles V of Spain ordered a survey of a waterway across the isthmus, a construction concession was granted by the Colombian government in 1878 to St. Lucien N. B. Wyse, representing a French company. Two years later, the French Canal Company, inspired by Ferdinand de Lesseps, began construction of what was to have been a sea-level canal. The effort ended in bankruptcy nine years later and the United States ultimately paid the French $40 million for their rights and assets. The U.S. project, built on territory controlled by the United States, and calling for the creation of an interior lake connected to both oceans by locks, began in 1904 and was completed in 1914.

Papua New Guinea

Sovereign: Queen Elizabeth II (1952)
Governor General: Silas Atopare (1997)
Prime Minister: Mekere Morauta (1999)
Area: 178,704 sq. mi. (461,690 sq. km)
Population (1999 est.): 4,705,126 (average annual rate of natural increase: 2.26%); birth rate: 32.0/1000; infant mortality rate: 55.6/1000; density per sq. mi.: 26
Capital and largest city (1994 est.): Port Moresby, 250,000. **Monetary unit:** Kina. **Languages:** English, Tok Pisin (a Melanesian Creole English), Hiri Motu, and 717 distinct native languages. **Ethnicity/race:** Papuan, Melanesian, Negrito, Micronesian, Polynesian. **Religions:** over half are Christian, remainder indigenous. **Literacy rate:** 50%
Economic summary: GDP/PPP (1996 est.): $11.6 billion; $2,650 per capita. **Real growth rate:** 2.3%. **Inflation:** 11.6%. **Unemployment:** n.a. **Agriculture:** coffee, cocoa, coconuts, palm kernels, tea, rubber, sweet potatoes, fruit, vegetables, poultry, pork. **Labor force:** 1.941 million; agriculture, 64% (1993 est.). **Industry:** copra crushing, palm oil processing, plywood production, wood chip production, mining of gold, silver, and copper, crude oil production, construction, tourism. **Natural resources:** copper, gold, silver, timber, natural gas, oil, fisheries. **Exports:** $2.5 billion (f.o.b., 1996): gold, copper ore, oil, logs, coffee, palm oil, cocoa, lobster. **Imports:** $1.7 billion (c.i.f., 1996): machinery and transport equipment, manufactured goods, food, fuels, chemicals. **Major trading partners:** Australia, U.K., Japan, Singapore, U.S., South Korea, Germany. **Member of Commonwealth of Nations**

Geography Papua New Guinea occupies the eastern half of the island of New Guinea, just north of Australia, and many outlying islands. The Indonesian province of Irian Jaya is to the west. To the north and east are the islands of Manus, New Britain, New Ireland, and Bougainville, all part of Papua New Guinea. About one-tenth larger than California, its mountainous interior has only recently been explored. Two major rivers, the Sepik and the Fly, are navigable for shallow-draft vessels.

Government Parliamentary democracy.

History The first inhabitants of the island New Guinea were Papuan, Melanesian, and Negrito tribes, who altogether spoke more than 700 distinct languages. The eastern half of New Guinea was first explored by Spanish and Portuguese explorers in the 16th century. In 1828, the Dutch formally took possession of the western half of the island (now the province of Irian Jaya, Indonesia). In 1885, Germany formally annexed the northern coast and Britain took similar action in the south. In 1906, Britain transferred its rights to British New Guinea to a newly independent Australia, and the name of the territory was changed to the Territory of Papua. Australian troops invaded German New Guinea (called Kaiser-Wilhelmsland) in World War I and gained control of the territory under a League of Nations mandate. New Guinea and some of Papua were invaded by Japanese forces in 1942. After

being liberated by the Australians in 1945, it became a United Nations trusteeship, administered by Australia. The territories were combined and called the Territory of Papua and New Guinea.

Australia granted limited home rule in 1951. Autonomy in internal affairs came nine years later, and in Sept. 1995, Papua New Guinea achieved complete independence from Britain in Sept. 1975, becoming, at that time, a full member of the Commonwealth.

A violent nine-year secessionist movement took place on the island of Bougainville. In 1989, guerrillas of the Bougainville Revolutionary Army (BRA) shut down the island's Australian-owned copper mine, a major source of revenue for the country. The rebels believed that Bougainville deserved a greater share of the earnings for its copper. In 1990, the BRA declared Bougainville's independence, whereupon the government blockaded the island until Jan. 1991, when a peace treaty was signed. In 1997, Papua New Guinea's government hired South African mercenary soldiers to fight on Bougainville in order to end the long-running crisis, but this action led to massive demonstrations and the mercenary contract was rescinded. In April 1998, a cease-fire was declared.

On July 17, 1998, an earthquake-triggered tsunami (tidal wave) off the northern coast of Papua New Guinea killed at least 1,500 people and left thousands more injured and homeless.

In July 1999 Prime Minister Bill Skate resigned after he caused diplomatic trouble by recognizing Taiwan as a separate political entity from mainland China. Mekere Morauta became prime minister on July 1999.

Paraguay

REPUBLIC OF PARAGUAY

National name: República del Paraguay
President: Luis Ángel González Macchi (1999)
Area: 157,047 sq. mi. (406,750 sq. km)
Population (1999 est.): 5,434,095 (average annual rate of natural increase: 2.66%); birth rate: 31.9/1000; infant mortality rate: 36.4/1000; density per sq. mi.: 35
Capital and largest city (1992): Asunción, 502,426. **Other large cities (1992):** Ciudad del Este, 133,893; San Lorenzo, 133,311. **Monetary unit:** Guaraní. **Languages:** Spanish (official), Guaraní. **Ethnicity/race:** mestizo (mixed Spanish and Indian) 95%, whites plus Amerindians 5%. **Religion:** Roman Catholic, 90%. **Literacy rate:** 90%
Economic summary: GDP/PPP (1997 est.): $21.9 billion; $3,900 per capita. **Real growth rate:** 2.6%. **Inflation:** 6.2% (1997). **Unemployment:** 8.2% (urban 1996 est.). **Arable land:** 6%. **Agriculture:** cotton, sugarcane, soybeans, corn, wheat, tobacco, cassava (tapioca), fruits, vegetables, beef, pork, eggs, milk, timber. **Labor force:** (1995 est.), 1.8 million; agriculture, 45%. **Industry:** meat packing, oilseed crushing, milling, brewing, textiles, other light consumer goods, cement, construction. **Natural resources:** iron ore, timber, manganese, limestone, hydropower. **Exports:** $1.1 billion (f.o.b., 1997 est.): cotton, soybeans, meat products, timber, coffee, tung oil, vegetable oils. **Imports:** $2.5 billion (c.i.f., 1996 est.): capital goods, consumer goods, foodstuffs, raw materials, fuels. **Major trading partners:** Brazil, The Netherlands, Argentina, U.S., Uruguay, Chile, Hong Kong.

Geography California-size Paraguay is surrounded by Brazil, Bolivia, and Argentina in south-central South America. Eastern Paraguay, between the Paraná and Paraguay Rivers, is upland country with the thickest population settled on the grassy slope that inclines toward the Paraguay River. The greater part of the Chaco region to the west is covered with marshes, lagoons, dense forests, and jungles.

Government Republic.

History Indians speaking Guaraní—the most common language in Paraguay today, after Spanish—were the country's first inhabitants. In 1526 and again in 1529, Sebastian Cabot explored Paraguay when he sailed up the Paraná and Paraguay Rivers. From 1608 until their expulsion from the Spanish dominions in 1767, the Jesuits maintained an extensive establishment in the south and east of Paraguay. In 1811, Paraguay revolted against Spanish rule and became a nominal republic under two consuls.

Paraguay was governed by three dictators during the first 60 years of independence. The third, Francisco López, waged war against Brazil and Argentina in 1865–70, a conflict in which the male population was almost wiped out. A new constitution in 1870, designed to prevent dictatorships and internal strife, failed to do so, and not until 1912 did a period of comparative economic and political stability begin. The Chaco War (1932–35) with Bolivia won Paraguay more western territory.

After World War II, politics became particularly unstable. Alfredo Stroessner ruled as dictator from 1954 until 1989, during which he was responsible for the torture and murder of thousands of political opponents. Although the Stroessner regime was criticized by the U.S. during the Carter administration for violating human rights, Paraguay did not suffer cuts in U.S. military aid—the U.S.'s conditional support of Stroessner's dictatorship was part of its cold war policy in South America to stamp out communism. Only five officials in Paraguay have been convicted for torture and killing during Stroessner's regime, and Stroessner himself lives in asylum in neighboring Brazil.

Stroessner was overthrown by an army leader, Gen. Andres Rodriguez, in 1989. Rodriguez won in Paraguay's first multi-candidate election in decades. Paraguay's new constitution went into effect in 1992. In 1993, Juan Carlos Wasmosy, a wealthy businessman and the candidate of the governing Colorado Party, won a five-year term in freely held elections. In June 1997, a banking crisis struck Paraguay, involving the president, his entire government, and the central bank president. Raúl Cubas Grau was elected president in May 1998.

Vice President Luis María Argaña was assassinated in March 1999. On March 28 President Cubas was forced out of office because of his alleged involvement in the assassination—the vice president had been critical of the president's refusal to jail his mentor, Gen. Lino Oviedo, who was convicted of leading a failed 1996 coup against President Wasmosy.

The new president, Luis Ángel González Macchi, has begun to substantially overhaul the government, and for the first time since Stroessner was overthrown in 1989, political and economic power was no longer entirely within the hands of the corrupt and military-backed Colorado Party. The U.S. has accused the Colorado Party of smuggling, money laundering, trafficking Bolivian cocaine, and supporting international terrorist organizations.

Peru

REPUBLIC OF PERU

National name: República del Perú
President: Alberto Fujimori (1990)
Prime Minister: Víctor Joy Way (1999)
Area: 496,222 sq. mi. (1,285,220 sq. km)
Population (1999 est.): 26,624,582 (average annual rate of natural increase: 2.04%); birth rate: 26.1/1000; infant mortality rate: 39.0/1000; density per sq. mi.: 54
Capital and largest city : Lima: city proper (1993 est.) 5,681,941; metro. area (1995 est.) 7,452,000. **Other large cities:** Arequipa, 939,800; Callao, 648,000; Trujillo, 1,287,000; Chiclayo, 951,000. **Monetary unit:** Nuevo Sol (1991). **Languages:** Spanish, Quéchua, Aymara, and other native languages. **Ethnicity/race:** Indian 45%, mestizo (mixed Indian and European ancestry) 37%, white 15%, black, Japanese, Chinese, and other 3%. **Religion:** Roman Catholic. **Literacy rate:** 85%
Economic summary: GDP/PPP (1997 est.): $110.2 billion; $4,420 per capita. **Real growth rate:** 7.3%. **Inflation:** 6.7% (1997). **Unemployment:** 8.2%, extensive underemployment (1996). **Arable land:** 3%. **Agriculture:** coffee, cotton, sugarcane, rice, wheat, potatoes, plantains, coca, poultry, red meats, dairy products, wool, fish. **Labor force:** 7.6 million (1996 est.); agriculture, mining and quarrying, manufacturing, construction, transport, services. **Industries:** mining of metals, petroleum, fishing, textiles, clothing, food processing, cement, auto assembly, steel, shipbuilding, metal fabrication. **Natural resources:** copper, silver, gold, petroleum, timber, fish, iron ore, coal, phosphate, potash. **Exports:** $5.9 billion (f.o.b., 1996): copper, zinc, fishmeal, crude petroleum and byproducts, lead, refined silver, coffee, cotton. **Imports:** $9.2 billion (f.o.b., 1996): machinery, transport equipment, foodstuffs, petroleum, iron and steel, chemicals, pharmaceuticals. **Major trading partners:** U.S., Japan, U.K., China, Germany, Colombia, Chile, Venezuela.

Geography Peru, in western South America, extends for nearly 1,500 miles (2,414 km) along the Pacific Ocean. Colombia and Ecuador are to the north, Brazil and Bolivia to the east, and Chile to the south. Five-sixths the size of Alaska, Peru is divided by the Andes Mountains into three sharply differentiated zones. To the west is the coastline, much of it arid, extending 50 to 100 miles (80 to 160 km) inland. The mountain area, with peaks over 20,000 feet (6,096 m), lofty plateaus, and deep valleys, lies centrally. Beyond the mountains to the east is the heavily forested slope leading to the Amazonian plains.

Government Republic.

History Peru was once part of the great Incan empire and later the major vice-royalty of Spanish South America. It was conquered in 1531–33 by Francisco Pizarro. On July 28, 1821, Peru proclaimed its independence, but the Spanish were not finally defeated until 1824. For a hundred years thereafter, revolutions were frequent; a new war was fought with Spain in 1864–66, and unsuccessful war was fought with Chile from 1879 to 1883 (the War of the Pacific).

Peru emerged from 20 years of dictatorship in 1945 with the inauguration of President José Luis Bustamante y Rivero after the first free election in many decades. But he served for only three years and was succeeded in turn by Gen. Manual A. Odria, Manuel Prado y Ugarteche, and Fernando Belaúnde Terry. On Oct. 3, 1968, Belaúnde was overthrown by Gen. Juan Velasco Alvarado. Velasco nationalized the nation's second-biggest bank and turned two large newspapers over to Marxists in 1970, but he also allowed a new agreement with a copper-mining consortium of four American firms. In 1975, Velasco was replaced in a bloodless coup by his premier, Gen. Francisco Morales Bermudez, who promised to restore civilian government. In elections held on May 18, 1980, Belaúnde Terry, the last previous civilian president and the candidate of the conservative parties that have traditionally ruled Peru, was elected president again.

Peru's fragile democracy survived this period of stress. In 1985, Belaúnde Terry was the first elected president to turn over power to a constitutionally elected successor since 1945. Alberto Fujimori won the 1990 elections. Citing continuing terrorism, drug trafficking, and corruption, Fujimori in April 1992 dissolved Congress, suspended the constitution, and imposed censorship. A new constitution was approved in 1993. In Jan. 1995 fighting flared once again along part of the disputed border with Ecuador, as it had in 1941 and 1981. In April, President Fujimori was reelected, and his party (Change 90–New Majority) obtained a majority in the legislature.

In Dec. 1996, Tupac Amaru rebels seized control of the diplomatic compound of the Japanese ambassador's residence in Lima, holding 72 hostages. The standoff continued until April when government forces successfully stormed the residence, freeing the hostages. In the months that followed Fujimori came under fire for his increasingly authoritarian style. In 1997, the disastrous effects of El Niño caused the failure of the fish harvest and a severe drought in Peru.

In May 1999, the presidents of Ecuador and Peru signed a treaty ending the nearly 60-year border dispute involving a stretch of Amazon jungle. The two countries have fought three wars and numerous smaller skirmishes over the border.

The Philippines

REPUBLIC OF THE PHILIPPINES

National name: Republika ng Pilipinas
President: Joseph Estrada (1998)
Area: 115,830 sq. mi. (300,000 sq. km)
Population (1999 est.): 79,345,812 (average annual rate of natural increase: 2.14%; birth rate: 27.9/1000; infant mortality rate: 33.9/1000; density per sq. mi.: 685
Capital and largest city : Manila: city proper (1995 est.) 1,654,761; metro. area (1995 est.) 9,280,000. **Other large cities:** Quezon City, 1,669,776; Cebu, 610,415.
Monetary unit: Peso. **Languages:** Filipino (based on Tagalog), English; regional languages: Tagalog, Ilocano, Cebuano, others. **Ethnicity/race:** Christian Malay 91.5%, Muslim Malay 4%, Chinese 1.5%, other 3%. **Religions:** Roman Catholic, 84%; Protestant, 10%; Islam, 5%; Buddhist and other, 3%. **Literacy rate:** 94%
Economic summary: GDP/PPP (1997 est.): $244 billion; $3,200 per capita. **Real growth rate:** 5.1%. **Inflation:** 5.1% (1997). **Unemployment:** 8.7% (1997). **Arable land:** 19%. **Agriculture:** rice, coconuts, corn, sugarcane, bananas, pineapples, mangoes, pork, eggs, beef, fish. **Labor force:** 29.13 million; agriculture, 43.4%; services, 22.6%; government services, 17.9%; industry and commerce, 16.1% (1995). **Industries:** textiles, pharmaceuticals, chemicals, food processing, wood products, electronics assembly, petroleum refining, fishing.

Natural resources: timber, petroleum, nickel, cobalt, silver, gold, salt, copper. **Exports:** $25 billion (f.o.b., 1997 est.): electronics and telecommunications, machinery and transport, garments, other. **Imports:** $34 billion (f.o.b., 1997 est.): raw materials and intermediate goods, capital goods, consumer goods, fuels. **Major trading partners:** U.S., Japan, EU, A.S.E.A.N., Hong Kong, Taiwan, Saudi Arabia.

Geography The Philippine Islands are an archipelago of over 7,000 islands lying about 500 miles (805 km) off the southeast coast of Asia. The overall land area is comparable to that of Arizona. Only about 7% of the islands are larger than one square mile, and only one-third have names. The largest are Luzon in the north (40,420 sq. mi.; 104,687 sq. km), Mindanao in the south (36,537 sq. mi.; 94,631 sq. km), and Samar (5,124 sq. mi.; 13,271 sq. km). The islands are of volcanic origin, with the larger ones crossed by mountain ranges. The highest peak is Mount Apo (9,690 ft.; 2,954 m) on Mindanao.

Government Republic.

History Ferdinand Magellan, the Portuguese navigator in the service of Spain, explored the Philippines in 1521. Twenty-one years later, a Spanish exploration party named the group of islands in honor of Prince Philip, who was later to become Philip II of Spain. Spain retained possession of the islands for the next 350 years.

The Philippines were ceded to the U.S. in 1899 by the Treaty of Paris after the Spanish-American War. Meanwhile, the Filipinos, led by Emilio Aguinaldo, had declared their independence. They initiated guerrilla warfare against U.S. troops that persisted until the capture of Aguinaldo in 1901. By 1902, peace was established except among the Islamic Moros on the southern island of Mindanao.

The first U.S. civilian governor-general was William Howard Taft (1901–04). The Jones Law (1916) provided for the establishment of a Philippine Legislature composed of an elective Senate and House of Representatives. The Tydings-McDuffie Act (1934) provided for a transitional period until 1946, at which time the Philippines would become completely independent. Under a constitution approved by the people of the Philippines in 1935, the Commonwealth of the Philippines came into being with Manuel Quezon y Molina as president.

On Dec. 8, 1941, the islands were invaded by Japanese troops. Following the fall of Gen. Douglas MacArthur's forces at Bataan and Corregidor, Quezon established a government-in-exile that he headed until his death in 1944. He was succeeded by Vice President Sergio Osmeña. U.S. forces under MacArthur reinvaded the Philippines in Oct. 1944 and, after the liberation of Manila in Feb. 1945, Osmeña reestablished the government.

The Philippines achieved full independence on July 4, 1946. Manual A. Roxas y Acuña was elected its first president, succeeded by Elpidio Quirino (1948–53), Ramón Magsaysay (1953–57). Carlos P. García (1957–61), Diosdado Macapagal (1961–65), and Ferdinand E. Marcos (1965–86).

Under Marcos, civil unrest broke out in opposition to the leader's despotic rule. Martial law was declared on Sept. 21, 1972, and Marcos proclaimed a new constitution that ensconced himself as president. Martial law was officially lifted on Jan. 17, 1981, but Marcos and his wife Imelda retained broad powers.

Despite warnings that his life would be endangered, opposition leader Benigno S. Aquino returned to the Philippines from self-exile on Aug. 21, 1983. He was shot to death as he was being escorted from his plane by military police at Manila International Airport. There was widespread suspicion that Marcos had ordered Aquino's assassination. The event became a watershed in modern Filipino political history, acting as a catalyst for opposition groups and the "People Power" movement, led by the late leader's widow, Corazon Aquino.

In an attempt to resecure American support, Marcos set presidential elections for Feb. 7, 1986. With the support of the Catholic Church, Corazon Aquino declared her candidacy. Marcos was declared the official winner, but independent observers reported widespread election fraud and vote-rigging. Anti-Marcos protests exploded in the capital Manila, Defense Minister Juan Enrile and Lt. Gen. Fidel Ramos defected to the opposition, and Marcos lost virtually all support; he was forced to flee into exile and entered the U.S. on Feb. 25, 1986.

The Aquino government survived coup attempts by Marcos supporters and other right-wing elements, including one in Nov. by Enrile. Legislative elections on May 11, 1987, gave pro-Aquino candidates a large majority. Negotiations on renewal of leases for U.S. military bases threatened to sour relations between the two countries. Volcanic eruptions from Mount Pinatubo, however, severely damaged Clark Air Base, and in July 1991 the U.S. decided simply to abandon it.

In elections in May 1992, Gen. Fidel Ramos, who had the support of outgoing Aquino, won the presidency in a seven-way race. In Sept. of that year, the U.S. Navy turned over the Subic Bay naval base to the Philippines, ending a long-standing U.S. military presence. Meanwhile, the separatist Moro National Liberation Front was fighting a protracted war for an Islamic homeland on Mindanao, the southernmost of the two main islands. In 1996, the group agreed to a government plan designed to grant it a greater degree of political autonomy. An administrative body, headed by the former rebel chief, was established to oversee development on the southern islands. Although frequent and violent clashes continue between the army and another rebel group, the Moro Islamic Liberation Front, separate peace talks were ongoing in 1998.

Even as the Philippines experienced a somewhat lower rate of growth than many of its Asian neighbors throughout the 1990s, it was also spared the brunt of the region's financial crisis following a wave of currency devaluations sparked in July 1997. In May 1998, 61-year-old former action film star Joseph Estrada was elected president of the Philippines, succeeding Fidel Ramos, who declined to contest elections.

Poland

REPUBLIC OF POLAND

National name: Rzeczpospolita Polska
President: Aleksander Kwasniewski (1995)
Prime Minister: Jerzy Buzek (1997)
Area: 120,727 sq. mi. (312,683 sq. km)
Population (1999 est.): 38,608,929 (average annual rate of natural increase: 0.09%); birth rate: 10.6/1000; infant mortality rate: 12.8/1000; density per sq. mi.: 320
Capital and largest city (1994 est.): Warsaw,

1,642,700. **Other large cities:** Lodz, 833,700; Krakow, 745,100; Wroclaw, 642,300; Poznan, 582,800; Gdansk, 463,100; Szczecin, 417,700. **Monetary unit:** Zloty. **Language:** Polish. **Ethnicity/race:** Polish 97.6%, German 1.3%, Ukrainian 0.6%, Belarussian 0.5% (1990 est.). **Religions:** Roman Catholic, 95% (about 75% practicing); Russian Orthodox, Protestant, and other, 5%. **Literacy rate:** 98%
Economic summary: GDP/PPP (1997 est.): $280.7 billion; $7,250 per capita. **Real growth rate:** 6.9%. **Inflation:** 15%. **Unemployment:** 12% (1997). **Arable land:** 47%. **Agriculture:** potatoes, milk, cheese, fruits, vegetables, wheat, poultry and eggs, pork, beef. **Labor force:** 17.7 million (1997 est.); industry and construction, 29.9%; agriculture, 26%; services, 44.1% (1996). **Industries:** machine building, iron and steel, coal mining, chemicals, shipbuilding, food processing, glass, beverages, textiles. **Natural resources:** coal, sulfur, copper, natural gas, silver, lead, salt. **Exports:** $26.4 billion (f.o.b., 1997 est.): intermediate goods, machinery and transport equipment, consumer goods, foodstuffs, fuels. **Imports:** $44.5 billion (f.o.b., 1997 est.): machinery and transport equipment, intermediate goods, chemicals, consumer goods, food, fuels. **Major trading partners:** Germany, Russia, France, Italy, U.S., The Netherlands, U.K.

Geography Poland, a country the size of New Mexico, is in north-central Europe. Most of the country is a plain with no natural boundaries except the Carpathian Mountains in the south and the Oder and Neisse Rivers in the west. Other major rivers, which are important to commerce, are the Vistula, Warta, and Bug.

Government Democratic state.

History Great (north) Poland was founded in C.E. 966 by Mieszko I, who belonged to the Piast dynasty. The tribes of southern Poland then united to form Little Poland. In C.E. 1047 both Great Poland and Little Poland united under the rule of Casimir I the Restorer. Poland merged with Lithuania by royal marriage in 1386. The Polish-Lithuanian state reached the peak of its power between the 14th and 16th century, scoring military successes against the (Germanic) Knights of the Teutonic Order, the Russians, and the Ottoman Turks.

Lack of a strong monarchy enabled Russia, Prussia, and Austria to carry out a first partition of the country in 1772, a second in 1792, and a third in 1795. For more than a century thereafter, there was no Polish state, just Austrian, Prussian, and Russian sectors, but the Poles never ceased their efforts to regain their independence. The Polish people revolted against Russian, Prussian, and Austrian dominance throughout the 19th century. Poland was formally reconstituted in Nov. 1918, with Marshal Josef Pilsudski as chief of state. In 1919, Ignace Paderewski, the famous pianist and patriot, became the first premier. In 1926, Pilsudski seized complete power in a coup and ruled dictatorially until his death on May 12, 1935.

Despite a 10-year nonaggression pact signed in 1934, Hitler attacked Poland on Sept. 1, 1939. Soviet troops invaded from the east on Sept. 17, and on Sept. 28 a German-Soviet agreement divided Poland between the U.S.S.R. and Germany. Wladyslaw Raczkiewicz formed a government-in-exile in France, which moved to London after France's defeat in 1940. All of Poland was occupied by Germany after the Nazi attack on the U.S.S.R. in June

1941. Nazi Germany's occupation policy in Poland was designed to eradicate Polish culture through mass executions and to exterminate the country's large Jewish minority.

The Polish government-in-exile was replaced with the Communist-dominated Polish Committee of National Liberation by the Soviet Union in 1944. Moving to Lublin after that city's liberation, it proclaimed itself the Provisional Government of Poland. Some former members of the Polish government in London joined with the Lublin government to form the Polish Government of National Unity, which Britain and the U.S. recognized. On Aug. 2, 1945, in Berlin, President Harry S. Truman, Joseph Stalin, and Prime Minister Clement Attlee of Britain established a new de facto western frontier for Poland along the Oder and Neisse Rivers. (The border was finally agreed to by West Germany in a nonaggression pact signed on Dec. 7, 1970.) On Aug. 16, 1945, the U.S.S.R. and Poland signed a treaty delimiting the Soviet-Polish frontier. Under these agreements, Poland was shifted westward. In the east it lost 69,860 square miles (180,934 sq. km); in the west it gained (subject to final peace-conference approval) 38,986 square miles (100,973 sq. km).

A new constitution in 1952 made Poland a "people's democracy" of the Soviet type. In 1955, Poland became a member of the Warsaw Treaty Organization, and its foreign policy became identical to that of the U.S.S.R. The government undertook persecution of the Roman Catholic Church as a remaining source of opposition. Wladyslaw Gomulka was elected leader of the United Workers (Communist) Party in 1956. He denounced the Stalinist terror, ousted many Stalinists, and improved relations with the church. Most collective farms were dissolved, and the press became freer. A strike that began in shipyards and spread to other industries in August 1980 produced a stunning victory for workers when the economically hard-pressed government accepted for the first time in a Marxist state the right of workers to organize in independent unions.

Led by Solidarity, a free union founded by Lech Walesa, workers launched a drive for liberty and improved conditions. A national strike for a five-day work week in Jan. 1981 led to the dismissal of Premier Pinkowski and the naming of the fourth premier in less than a year, Gen. Wojciech Jaruzelski. Martial law was declared on Dec. 13, when Walesa and other Solidarity leaders were arrested. It formally ended in 1984 but the government retained emergency powers. Increasing opposition to the government because of the failing economy led to a new wave of strikes in 1988. Unable to totally quell the dissent, the government relegalized Solidarity and allowed it to compete in elections.

Solidarity members won a stunning victory in 1989, taking almost all the seats in the Senate and all of the 169 seats they were allowed to contest in the Sejm. This gave them substantial influence in the new government. Taduesz Mazowiecki was appointed prime minister. Solidarity leader Lech Walesa won the presidential election of 1990 with 74% of the vote. In 1991, the first fully free parliamentary election since World War II resulted in representation for 29 political parties. In the second democratic parliamentary election of Sept. 1993, voters returned power to ex-Communists and their allies. In 1995, Aleksander Kwasniewski, leader of the successor to the Communist Party, won the presidency over Walesa, despite strong support for Walesa from the church. In 1997, the Solidarity Electoral Action (AWS), a loose coalition of some 30 right-wing groups dominated by the Solidarity trade union, handily defeated the former Communists. Also in 1997, the Polish Parliament voted to abolish the death penalty. The pope visited Poland in 1999, which some believe may be his last visit to his homeland. In 1999, Poland became part of NATO, along with the Czech Republic and Hungary.

Portugal

REPUBLIC OF PORTUGAL

National name: República Portuguesa
President: Jorge Sampaio (1996)
Prime Minister: Antonio Guterres (1995)
Area: 36,090 sq. mi. (92,391 sq. km)
Population (1999 est.): 9,918,040 (average annual rate of natural increase: 0.02%); birth rate: 10.5/1000; infant mortality rate: 6.7/1000; density per sq, ml.: 279
Capital and largest city (1991): Lisbon, 677,790. **Other large city (1991):** Oporto, 350,000. **Monetary units:** Escudo and euro. **Language:** Portuguese. **Ethnicity/ race:** Homogeneous Mediterranean stock in mainland, Azores, Madeira Islands; citizens of black African descent who immigrated to mainland during decolonization number less than 100,000. **Religions:** Roman Catholic 97%, 1% Protestant, 2% other. **Literacy rate:** 85%
Economic summary: GDP/PPP (1997 est.): $149.5 billion; $15,200 per capita. **Real growth rate:** 3.3%. **Inflation:** 2.3%. **Unemployment:** 7%. **Arable land:** 26%. **Agriculture:** grain, potatoes, olives, grapes, sheep, cattle, goats, poultry, meat, dairy products. **Labor force:** (1996 est.), 4.53 million; services, 56%; manufacturing, 23%; agriculture, forestry, fisheries, 11%; construction, 8%; utilities, 1%; mining, 1% (1995). **Industries:** textiles and footwear, wood pulp, paper and cork, metalworking, oil refining, chemicals, fish canning, wine, tourism. **Natural resources:** fish, forests (cork), tungsten, iron ore, uranium ore, marble. **Exports:** $23.8 billion (f.o.b., 1996): clothing and footwear, machinery, cork and paper products, hides. **Imports:** $33.9 billion (c.i.f., 1996): machinery and transport equipment, agricultural products, chemicals, petroleum, textiles. **Major trading partners:** EU, U.S.

Geography Portugal occupies the western part of the Iberian Peninsula and is slightly smaller than Indiana. The country is crossed by three large rivers that rise in Spain, flow into the Atlantic, and divide the country into three geographic areas. The Minho River, part of the northern boundary, cuts through a mountainous area that extends south to the vicinity of the Douro River. South of the Douro, the mountains slope to the plains around the Tejo River. The remaining division is the southern one of Alentejo. The Azores stretch over 340 miles (547 km) in the Atlantic, and consist of nine islands with a total area of 902 square miles (2,335 sq. km). Madeira, consisting of two inhabited islands, Madeira and Porto Santo, and two groups of uninhabited islands, lie in the Atlantic about 535 miles (861 km) southwest of Lisbon.

Government Republic.

History An early Celtic tribe, the Lusitanians, are believed to have been the first inhabitants of Portugal. The Roman Empire conquered the region in about 140 B.C.E. Toward the end of the Roman Empire, the Visigoths had invaded the entire Iberian peninsula.

In the middle of the 12th century, Portugal was a part of Moorish Spain until it won its independence. King John I (1385–1433) unified his country at the expense of the Castilians and the Moors of Morocco. The expansion of Portugal was brilliantly coordinated by John's son, Prince Henry the Navigator. In 1488, Bartolomeu Dias reached the Cape of Good Hope, proving that Asia was accessible by sea. In 1498, Vasco da Gama reached the west coast of India. By the middle of the 16th century, the Portuguese Empire extended to West and East Africa, Brazil, Persia, Indochina, and Malaya.

In 1581, Philip II of Spain invaded Portugal and held it for 60 years, precipitating a catastrophic decline in Portuguese commerce. Courageous and shrewd explorers, the Portuguese proved to be inefficient and corrupt colonizers. By the time the Portuguese monarchy was restored in 1640, Dutch, English, and French competitors began to seize the lion's share of the world's colonies and commerce. Portugal retained Angola and Mozambique in Africa, and Brazil (until 1822).

The corrupt King Carlos, who ascended the throne in 1889, made Joao Franco the premier with dictatorial power in 1906. In 1908, Carlos and his heir were shot dead on the streets of Lisbon. The new king, Manoel II, was driven from the throne in the revolution of 1910 and Portugal became a French-style republic. Traditionally friendly to Britain, Portugal fought in World War I on the Allied side in Africa as well as on the Western Front. Weak postwar governments and a revolution in 1926 brought Antonio Oliveira Salazar to power. As minister of finance (1928–40) and premier (1932–68), Salazar ruled Portugal as a virtual dictator. He kept Portugal neutral in World War II but gave the Allies naval and air bases after 1943. Portugal joined NATO as a founding member in 1949 but did not gain admission to the United Nations until 1955.

Portugal's foreign and colonial policies met with increasing difficulty both at home and abroad beginning in the 1950s—the bloodiest and most protracted wars against colonialism in Africa were fought against the Portuguese. Portugal lost the tiny remnants of its Indian empire—Goa, Daman, and Diu—to Indian military occupation in 1961, the year an insurrection broke out in Angola. For the next 13 years, Salazar, who died in 1970, and his successor, Marcello Caetano, fought independence movements amid growing world criticism. Leftists in the armed forces, weary of a losing battle, launched a successful revolution on April 25, 1974. After the 1974 revolution, the new military junta gave up its territories, beginning with Portuguese Guinea in Sept. 1974, which became the Republic of Guinea-Bissau. The decolonization of the Cape Verde Islands and Mozambique was effected in July 1975. Angola achieved independence later that same year, thus ending a colonial involvement in that continent that had begun in 1415. Full-scale, internationalized civil war, however, followed Portugal's departure from Angola, and Indonesia forcibly annexed independent East Timor. Also in that year, the government nationalized banking, transport, heavy industries, and the media. Portugal continued to experience social, economic, and political upheavals for the next decade.

Portugal was admitted to the European Economic Community (now European Union) on Jan. 1, 1986,

and on Feb. 16, Mario Soares became the country's first civilian president in 60 years. Aníbal Cavaço Silva, an advocate of free-market economics and the Social Democratic candidate, was elected as prime minister in 1985, signaling a more politically stable era. General elections in Oct. 1995 went to the Socialist Party, which fell just short of an absolute majority in the assembly. Lisbon mayor Jorge Sampaio, a socialist, won the race for president in Jan. 1996. Portugal's socialist government continued to take advantage of rosy economic conditions in 1997, and in 1999 it became a founding member of the European Economic and Monetary Union (EMU). After Portugal's former territory, East Timor, was plunged into violence when its people voted to separate from Indonesia in Aug. 1999, Portugal was in the forefront of urging the U.N. to send in an armed, international peacekeeping force to protect the East Timorese from pro-Indonesian militia groups.

Portuguese Overseas Territory

Macau

Status: Territory
Governor: Vasco Rocha Vieira (1991)
Area: 6 sq. mi. (15.5 sq. km)
Population (1999 est.): 437,312 (average annual growth rate: 0.90%); birth rate: 12.5/1000; infant mortality rate: 4.2/1000; density per sq. mi.: 72,885
Capital (1991): Macau, 326,460. **Monetary unit:** Patacá. **Languages:** Portuguese and Chinese (Cantonese) are both official languages. **Ethnicity/race:** Chinese 95%, Portuguese 3%, other 2%. **Religions:** Buddhist 45%, Roman Catholic 7%, Protestant 1%, none 45.8%, other 1.2%. **Literacy rate:** 90% (1981)
Economic summary: GDP/PPP (1997 est.): $7.8 billion; $15,600 per capita. **Real growth rate:** –0.3%. **Inflation:** 3.9%. **Unemployment:** 3.6% (1995). **Agriculture:** rice, vegetables. **Labor force:** (1995) 271,228; industry, 28%; restaurants and hotels, 28%; other services, 44%. **Industry:** clothing, textiles, toys, electronics, footwear, tourism. **Exports:** $1.99 billion (f.o.b., 1996 est.): textiles, clothing, toys, electronics, cement. **Imports:** $1.99 billion (c.i.f., 1996 est.): raw materials, foodstuffs, capital goods, fuels, lubricants. **Major trading partners:** Hong Kong, China, U.S., EU, Japan.

Macau comprises the peninsula of Macau and the two small islands of Taipa and Colôane on the South China coast, about 35 miles (53 km) from Hong Kong. Established by the Portuguese in 1557, it is the oldest European outpost in China, but Portugal's sovereign rights to the port were not recognized by China until 1887. The port has been eclipsed in importance by Hong Kong, but it is still a busy distribution center and also has an important fishing industry. Chinese culture predominates, overlaid by a veneer of Portuguese architecture and customs. In 1987, Portugal and China reached an agreement to return Macau to Chinese rule on Dec. 20, 1999. They agreed upon provisions to insure the autonomy of Macau, including its right to elect local leaders, the right of its residents to travel freely, and the right to maintain its way of life for 50 years after the start of Chinese rule.

Qatar

STATE OF QATAR

Emir: Sheikh Hamad bin Khalifa al-Thani (1995)
Prime Minister: Abdullah bin Khalifa al-Thani (1996)
Area: 4,468 sq. mi. (11,439 sq. km)
Population (1999 est.): 723,542 (average annual rate of natural increase: 1.32%; birth rate: 16.8/1000; infant mortality rate: 17.3/1000; density per sq. mi.: 181
Capital (1990 est.): Doha, 300,000. **Monetary unit:** Qatari riyal. **Languages:** Arabic; English is also widely spoken. **Ethnicity/race:** Arab 40%, Pakistani 18%, Indian 18%, Iranian 10%, other 14%. **Religion:** Islam, 95%. **Literacy rate:** 76%
Economic summary: GDP/PPP (1997 est.): $11.2 billion; $16,700 per capita. **Real growth rate:** 10%. **Inflation:** 2.5% (1996). **Unemployment:** n.a. **Agriculture:** fruits, vegetables, poultry, dairy products, beef, fish. **Labor force:** 233,000 (1993 est.) 83% of the population is nonnational. **Industries:** crude oil production and refining, fertilizers, petrochemicals, steel reinforcing bars, cement. **Natural resources:** petroleum, natural gas, fish. **Exports:** $5.8 billion (f.o.b., 1997 est.): petroleum products, steel, fertilizers. **Imports:** $5 billion (f.o.b., 1997 est.): machinery and equipment, consumer goods, food, chemicals. **Major trading partners:** Japan, Singapore, South Korea, Australia, U.A.E., Italy, U.K., France, Germany.

Geography Qatar occupies a small peninsula that extends into the Persian Gulf from the east side of the Arabian Peninsula. Saudi Arabia is to the west and the United Arab Emirates to the south. The country is mainly barren.

Government Traditional monarchy.

History Qatar was once controlled by the sheikhs of Bahrain, but in 1867 war broke out between the people and their absentee rulers. To keep the peace in the Gulf, the British installed Muhammad ibn Thani Al Thani, head of a leading Qatari family, as the region's ruler. In 1893, the Ottoman Turks made incursions into Qatar, but the emir successfully deflected them. In 1916, the emir agreed to allow Qatar to become a British protectorate.

Oil was discovered in the 1940s, bringing wealth to the country in the 1950s and 1960s. About 85% of Qatar's income from exports comes from oil. Its people have one of the highest per capita incomes in the world. In 1971, Qatar was to join the other emirates of the Trucial Coast to become part of the United Arab Emirates. But both Qatar and Bahrain decided against the merger and instead became independent nations.

Qatar permitted the international forces to use Qatar as a base during the 1991 Persian Gulf War. A border dispute erupted with Saudi Arabia that was settled in Dec. 1992. A territorial dispute with Bahrain over the Hawar Islands remains unresolved, however. In 1994, Qatar signed a defense pact with the U.S., becoming the third Gulf state to do so.

In June 1995 Crown Prince Hamad bin Khalifa al-Thani deposed his father, primarily because the king was out-of-step with the country's economic reforms. Much of the power had already been in the crown prince's hands. The new emir has lifted press censorship and instituted other liberal reforms, including the first democratic election in its history. Although the 1999 election—for the 29-member municipal council—was a minor election, it involved major political change: women were permitted to vote in the election as well as run for office.

Romania

REPUBLIC OF ROMANIA

President: Emil Constantinescu (1996)
Prime Minister: Radu Vasile (1998)
Area: 91,700 sq. mi. (237,500 sq. km)
Population (1999 est.): 22,334,312 (average annual rate of natural increase: –0.15%); birth rate: 10.1/1000; infant mortality rate: 18.1/1000; density per sq. mi.: 244
Capital and largest city (1992): Bucharest, 2,351,000. **Largest cities (1992):** Constanta, 350,476; Iasi, 342,994; Timisoara, 334,278; Cluj-Napoca, 328,008; Galati, 325,788; Brasov, 323,835. **Monetary unit:** Leu. **Languages:** Romanian (official); Hungarian- and German-speaking minorities. **Ethnicity/race:** Romanian 89.1%, Hungarian 8.9%, German 0.4%, Ukrainian, Serb, Croat, Russian, Turk, and Gypsy 1.6%. **Religions:** Romanian Orthodox 70%, Roman Catholic 6% (of which 3% are Uniate), Protestant 6%, unaffiliated 18%. **Literacy rate:** 96%
Economic summary: GDP/PPP (1997 est.): $114.2 billion; $5,300 per capita. **Real growth rate:** –6.6%. **Inflation:** 151%. **Unemployment:** 8.8%. **Arable land:** 41%. **Agriculture:** corn, wheat, sugar beets, sunflower seed, potatoes, grapes, milk, eggs, meat. **Labor force:** 10.1 million (1996 est.): industry, 28.6%, agriculture, 34.4%, trade, 10.4%, construction, 5.1%, other, 21.5% (1995). **Industries:** mining, timber, construction materials, metallurgy, chemicals, machine building, food processing, petroleum production and refining. **Natural resources:** petroleum (reserves declining), timber, natural gas, coal, iron ore, salt. **Exports:** $8.4 billion (f.o.b., 1997 est.): textiles and footwear, metals and metal products, mineral products, chemicals, other. **Imports:** $10.4 billion (f.o.b., 1997 est.): fuels and minerals, machinery and transport equipment, food and agricultural goods, chemicals, other. **Major trading partners:** Germany, Italy, France, Turkey, The Netherlands, China, Russia, U.S., Egypt.

Geography Romania is in southeastern Europe, and is slightly smaller than Oregon. The Carpathian Mountains divide Romania's upper half from north to south and connect near the center of the country with the Transylvanian Alps, running east and west. North and west of these ranges lies the Transylvanian plateau, and to the south and east are the plains of Moldavia and Walachia. In its last 190 miles (306 km), the Danube River flows through Romania only. It enters the Black Sea in northern Dobruja, just south of the border with the Ukraine.

Government Republic.

History Most of Romania was the Roman province of Dacia from about c.e. 100 to 271. From the 3rd to the 12th century, wave after wave of barbarian conquerors overran the native Daco-Roman population. Subjection to the first Bulgarian empire (8th–10th century) brought Eastern Orthodox Christianity to the Romanians. In the 11th century, Transylvania was absorbed into the Hungarian empire. By the 16th century, the main Romanian principalities of Moldavia and Walachia had become satellites within the Ottoman Empire, although they retained much independence. After the Russo-Turkish War of 1828–29, they became Russian protectorates. The nation became a kingdom in 1881 after the Congress of Berlin.

At the start of World War I, Romania proclaimed its neutrality, but later joined the Allied side and in 1916 declared war on the Central Powers. The armistice of Nov. 11, 1918, gave Romania vast territories from Russia and the Austro-Hungarian Empire, doubling its size. The areas acquired included Bessarabia, Transylvania, and Bukovina. The Banat, a Hungarian area, was divided with Yugoslavia. King Carol II was crowned in 1930 and transformed the throne into a royal dictatorship. In 1938, he abolished the democratic constitution of 1923. In 1940, the country was reorganized along Fascist lines, and the Fascist Iron Guard became the nucleus of the new totalitarian party. On June 27, the Soviet Union occupied Bessarabia and northern Bukovina. King Carol II dissolved Parliament, granted the new premier, Ion Antonescu, full power, abdicated his throne, and went into exile.

Romania subsequently signed the Axis Pact on Nov. 23, 1940, and the following June joined in Germany's attack on the Soviet Union, reoccupying Bessarabia. About 270,000 Jews were massacred in Fascist Romania. Following the invasion of Romania by the Red Army in Aug. 1944, King Michael led a coup that ousted the Antonescu government. An armistice with the Soviet Union was signed in Moscow on Sept. 12, 1944. A Communist-dominated government bloc won elections in 1946, Michael abdicated on Dec. 30, 1947, and in 1955 Romania joined the Warsaw Treaty Organization and the United Nations.

Nikolae Ceausescu, famous for his secret police's brutality, ruled from 1965 to 1989, when he was overthrown by a coup rising from opposition to his repressive domestic policies. Ceausescu instituted a rigorous austerity program in the 1980s to pay for the huge foreign debt that Romania had accumulated in the 1970s; as a result, the Romanians saw their standard of living plummet. An army-assisted rebellion in Dec. 1989 led to Ceausescu's overthrow, trial, and execution. The May 1990 elections were won by the National Salvation Front, whose formerly Communist leaders called for a gradual and controlled transition to a free-market economy in Romania.

The country applied for membership in the EU in June 1995 and much legislation that year was crafted in hopes of meeting that objective. Nevertheless, the reform process proceeded slowly. Growing dissatisfaction with the government's inefficiencies and economic policies led to a wave of protests by workers, students, and others that peaked in 1997, and again in 1999, when coal miners striked.

Russia

RUSSIAN FEDERATION

President: Boris N. Yeltsin (1991)
Prime Minister: Vladimir Putin (1999)
Area: 6,592,800 sq. mi. (17,075,200 sq. km)
Population (1999 est.): 146,393,569 (average annual rate of natural increase: −0.53%); birth rate: 9.6/1000; infant mortality rate: 23.0/1000; density per sq. mi.: 22
Capital and largest city: Moscow: city proper (1995 est.) 8,368,449; metro. area (1995 est.) 8,598,896.
Other large cities: St. Petersburg, 4,232,105; Novosibirsk, 1,418,200; Samara, 1,222,500; Chelyabinsk, 1,124,500; Yekaterinburg, 1,347,000; Nizhny Novgorod, 1,424,600; Kazau, 1,092,300; Perm, 1,086,100; Ufa, 1,091,800; Volgograd, 1,000,400.
Monetary unit: Ruble. **Religions:** Russian Orthodox, Muslim, others. **Ethnicity/race:** Russian 81.5%, Tatar 3.8%, Ukrainian 3%, Chuvash 1.2%, Bashkir 0.9%, Byelorussian 0.8%, Moldavian 0.7%, other 8.1%.
Languages: Russian, others. **Literacy rate:** 98%
Economic summary: GDP/PPP (1997 est.): $692

billion; $4,700 per capita (1997 est.). **Real growth rate:** 0.4%. **Inflation:** 11% (1997). **Unemployment:** 9%, considerable underemployment. **Agriculture:** grain, sugar beets, sunflower seed, vegetables, fruits, meat, milk. **Labor force:** (1997), 66 million.
Industries: mining and extractive industries producing coal, oil, gas, chemicals, and metals, machine building, shipbuilding, road and rail transportation equipment, communications equipment, agricultural machinery, tractors, construction equipment, electric power generating and transmitting equipment, medical and scientific instruments, consumer durables, textiles, foodstuffs, handicrafts. **Natural resources:** oil, natural gas, coal, strategic minerals, timber. **Exports:** $86.7 billion (1997): petroleum and petroleum products, natural gas, wood and wood products, metals, chemicals, wide variety of civilian and military manufactures. **Imports:** $66.9 billion (1997): machinery and equipment, consumer goods, medicines, meat, grain, sugar, semifinished metal products. **Major trading partners:** Europe, North America, Japan, Third World countries.

Geography The Russian Federation is the largest republic of the Commonwealth of Independent States. It occupies an area about one and four-fifths of the size of the United States and occupies most of eastern Europe and north Asia. Russia stretches from the Baltic Sea in the west to the Pacific Ocean in the east and from the Arctic Ocean in the north to the Black Sea and the Caucasus, the Altai, and Sayan Mountains, and the Amur and Ussuri Rivers in the south. It is bordered by Norway and Finland in the northwest, Estonia, Latvia, Belarus, and Ukraine in the west, Georgia and Azerbaijan in the southwest, and Kazakhstan, Mongolia, and China along the southern border. The federation is composed of 21 republics.

Government Constitutional republic.

History Tradition says the Viking Rurik came to Russia in C.E. 862 and founded the first Russian dynasty in Novgorod. The various tribes were united by the spread of Christianity in the 10th and 11th centuries; Vladimir "the Saint" was converted in 988. During the 11th century, the grand dukes of Kiev held such centralizing power as existed. In 1240, Kiev was destroyed by the Mongols, and the Russian territory was split into numerous smaller dukedoms. Early dukes of Moscow extended their dominion over other Russian cities through their office of tribute collector for the Mongols and because of Moscow's role as an administrative and trade center.

In the late 15th century, Duke Ivan III acquired Novgorod and Tver and threw off the Mongol yoke. Ivan IV, the Terrible (1533–84), first Muscovite czar, is considered to have founded the Russian state. He crushed the power of rival princes and boyars (great landowners), but Russia remained largely medieval until the reign of Peter the Great (1689–1725), grandson of the first Romanov czar, Michael (1613–45). Peter made extensive reforms aimed at Westernization and, through his defeat of Charles XII of Sweden at the Battle of Poltava in 1709, he extended Russia's boundaries to the west. Catherine the Great (1762–96) continued Peter's Westernization program and also expanded Russian territory, acquiring the Crimea, Ukraine, and part of Poland. During the reign of Alexander I (1801–25), Napoléon's attempt to subdue Russia was defeated (1812–13), and new territory was gained, including

Finland (1809) and Bessarabia (1812). Alexander originated the Holy Alliance, which for a time crushed Europe's rising liberal movement.

Alexander II (1855–81) pushed Russia's borders to the Pacific and into central Asia. Serfdom was abolished in 1861, but heavy restrictions were imposed on the emancipated class. Revolutionary strikes, following Russia's defeat in the war with Japan, forced Nicholas II (1894–1917) to grant a representative national body (Duma), elected by narrowly limited suffrage. It met for the first time in 1906, little influencing Nicholas in his reactionary course.

World War I demonstrated czarist corruption and inefficiency and only patriotism held the poorly equipped army together for a time. Disorders broke out in Petrograd (renamed Leningrad and now St. Petersburg) in March 1917, and defection of the Petrograd garrison launched the revolution. Nicholas II was forced to abdicate on March 15, 1917, and he and his family were killed by revolutionists on July 16, 1918. A provisional government under the successive premierships of Prince Lvov and a moderate, Alexander Kerensky, lost ground to the radical, or Bolshevik, wing of the Socialist Democratic Labor Party. On Nov. 7, 1917, the Bolshevik Revolution, engineered by N. Lenin[1] and Leon Trotsky, overthrew the Kerensky government and authority was vested in a Council of People's Commissars, with Lenin as premier.

The humiliating Treaty of Brest-Litovsk (March 3, 1918) concluded the war with Germany, but civil war and foreign intervention delayed Communist control of all Russia until 1920. A brief war with Poland in 1920 resulted in Russian defeat.

Emergence of the U.S.S.R.

The Union of Soviet Socialist Republics was established as a federation on Dec. 30, 1922. The death of Lenin on Jan. 21, 1924, precipitated an intraparty struggle between Joseph Stalin, general secretary of the party, and Trotsky, who favored swifter socialization at home and fomentation of revolution abroad. Trotsky was dismissed as commissar of war in 1925 and banished from the Soviet Union in 1929. He was murdered in Mexico City on Aug. 21, 1940, by a political agent. Stalin further consolidated his power by a series of purges in the late 1930s, liquidating prominent party leaders and military officers. Stalin assumed the premiership on May 6, 1941.

Soviet foreign policy, at first friendly toward Germany and antagonistic toward Britain and France and then, after Hitler's rise to power in 1933, becoming anti-Fascist and pro-League of Nations, took an abrupt turn on Aug. 24, 1939, with the signing of a nonaggression pact with Nazi Germany. The next month, Moscow joined in the German attack on Poland, seizing territory later incorporated into the Ukrainian and Belarussian S.S.R.'s. The Russo-Finnish War (1939–40) added territory to the Karelian S.S.R. set up on March 31, 1940; the annexation of Bessarabia and Bukovina from Romania became part of the new Moldavian S.S.R. on Aug. 2, 1940; and the annexation of the Baltic republics of Estonia, Latvia, and Lithuania in June 1940 created the 14th, 15th, and 16th Soviet republics. The illegal annexation of the Baltic republics

1. N. Lenin was the pseudonym taken by Vladimir Ilich Ulyanov. It is sometimes given as Nikolai Lenin or V. Lenin.

was never acknowledged by the U.S. for the 51 years leading up to Soviet recognition of Estonia, Latvia, and Lithuania's independence on Sept. 6, 1991. The Soviet-German collaboration ended abruptly with a lightning attack by Hitler on June 22, 1941, which seized 500,000 square miles of Russian territory before Soviet defenses, aided by U.S. and British arms, could halt it. The Soviet resurgence at Stalingrad from Nov. 1942 to Feb. 1943 marked the turning point in a long battle, ending in the final offensive of Jan. 1945. Then, after denouncing a 1941 nonaggression pact with Japan in April 1945, when Allied forces were nearing victory in the Pacific, the Soviet Union declared war on Japan on Aug. 8, 1945, and quickly occupied Manchuria, Karafuto, and the Kuril Islands.

The U.S.S.R. built a cordon of Communist states running from Poland in the north to Albania and Bulgaria in the south, including East Germany, Czechoslovakia, Hungary, and Romania, which composed the territories the Soviet troops occupied at the war's end. With its eastern front solidified, the Soviet Union launched a political offensive against the non-Communist West, moving first to block the Western access to Berlin. The Western powers countered with an airlift, completed unification of West Germany, and organized the defense of western Europe in the North Atlantic Treaty Organization (NATO). Stalin died on March 6, 1953, and was succeeded the next day by G. M. Malenkov as premier.

The new power in the Kremlin was Nikita S. Khrushchev, first secretary of the party. Khrushchev formalized the eastern European system into a Council for Mutual Economic Assistance (Comecon) and a Warsaw Pact Treaty Organization as a counterweight to NATO. The Soviet Union exploded a hydrogen bomb in 1953, developed an intercontinental ballistic missile by 1957, sent the first satellite into space (Sputnik I) in 1957, and put Yuri Gagarin in the first orbital flight around Earth in 1961. Khrushchev's downfall stemmed from his decision to place Soviet nuclear missiles in Cuba and then, when challenged by the U.S., backing down and removing the weapons. He was also blamed for the ideological break with China after 1963. Khrushchev was forced into retirement on Oct. 15, 1964, and was replaced by Leonid I. Brezhnev as first secretary of the party and Aleksei N. Kosygin as premier.

U.S. president Jimmy Carter and Brezhnev signed the SALT II treaty in Vienna on June 18, 1979, setting ceilings on each nation's arsenal of intercontinental ballistic missiles. The U.S. Senate refused to ratify the treaty because of the invasion of Afghanistan by Soviet troops on Dec. 27, 1979. On Nov. 10, 1982, Soviet radio and television announced the death of Leonid Brezhnev. Yuri V. Andropov, who had formerly headed the K.G.B., became his successor, but died less than two years later, in Feb. 1984. Konstantin U. Chernenko, a 72-year-old party stalwart who had been close to Brezhnev, succeeded him.

In the months following Chernenko's assumption of power, the Kremlin took on a hostile mood toward the West of a kind rarely seen since the height of the cold war 30 years before. Led by Moscow, all the Soviet bloc countries except Romania boycotted the 1984 Summer Olympic Games in Los Angeles—tit-for-tat for the U.S.-led boycott of the

Rulers of Russia since 1533

Name	Born	Ruled [1]	Name	Born	Ruled [1]
Ivan IV the Terrible	1530	1533–1584	Nicholas I	1796	1825–1855
Theodore I	1557	1584–1598	Alexander II	1818	1855–1881
Boris Godunov	c.1551	1598–1605	Alexander III	1845	1881–1894
Theodore II	1589	1605–1605	Nicholas II	1868	1894–1917[7]
Demetrius I[2]	?	1605–1606	**PROVISIONAL GOVERNMENT (PREMIERS)**		
Basil IV Shuiski	?	1606–1610[3]	Prince Georgi Lvov	1861	1917–1917
"Time of Troubles"	—	1610–1613	Alexander Kerensky	1881	1917–1917
Michael Romanov	1596	1613–1645	**POLITICAL LEADERS OF U.S.S.R.**		
Alexis I	1629	1645–1676	Vladimir Ilyich Lenin	1870	1917–1924
Theodore III	1656	1676–1682	Aleksei Rykov	1881	1924–1930
Ivan V[4]	1666	1682–1689[5]	Vyacheslav Molotov	1890	1930–1941
Peter I the Great[4]	1672	1682–1725	Joseph Stalin[8]	1879	1941–1953
Catherine I	c.1684	1725–1727	Georgi M. Malenkov	1902	1953–1955
Peter II	1715	1727–1730	Nikolai A. Bulganin	1895	1955–1958
Anna	1693	1730–1740	Nikita S. Khrushchev	1894	1958–1964
Ivan VI	1740	1740–1741[6]	Leonid I. Brezhnev	1906	1964–1982
Elizabeth	1709	1741–1762	Yuri V. Andropov	1914	1982–1984
Peter III	1728	1762–1762	Konstantin U. Chernenko	1912	1984–1985
Catherine II the Great	1729	1762–1796	Mikhail S. Gorbachev	1931	1985–1991
Paul I	1754	1796–1801	**PRESIDENT OF RUSSIA**		
Alexander I	1777	1801–1825	Boris Yeltsin	1931	1991–

1. For czars through Nicholas II, year of end of rule is also that of death, unless otherwise indicated. 2. Also known as Pseudo-Demetrius. 3. Died 1612. 4. Ruled jointly until 1689, when Ivan was deposed. 5. Died 1696. 6. Died 1764. 7. Killed 1918. 8. General secretary of Communist Party, 1924–53.

1980 Moscow Games, in the view of most observers. After 13 months in office, Chernenko died on March 10, 1985. He had been ill much of the time and left only a minor imprint on Soviet history. Chosen to succeed him as Soviet leader was Mikhail S. Gorbachev, who led the Soviet Union in its long-awaited shift to a new generation of leadership. Unlike his immediate predecessors, Gorbachev did not also assume the title of president but wielded power from the post of party general secretary.

The Soviet Union took much criticism in early 1986 over the April 24 meltdown at the Chernobyl nuclear plant and its reluctance to give out any information on the accident.

In June 1987, Gorbachev obtained the support of the Central Committee for proposals that would loosen some government controls over the economy and in June 1988, an unusually open party conference approved several resolutions reforming the Soviet system. These included a shift of some power from the party to local soviets, and a ten-year limit on the terms of elected government and party officials. Gorbachev was elected president in 1989. The elections to the Congress were the first competitive elections in the Soviet Union since 1917. Dissident candidates won a surprisingly large minority although pro-government deputies maintained a strong lock on the Supreme Soviet.

Dissolution of the U.S.S.R. The possible beginning of the fragmentation of the Communist Party took place when Boris Yeltsin, leader of the Russian S.S.R. who urged faster reform, left the Communist Party along with other radicals. In March 1991, the Soviet people were asked to vote on a referendum on national unity engineered by Gorbachev. The resultant victory for the federal government was tempered by the separate approval in Russia for the creation of a popularly elected presidency of the Russian republics. The bitter election contest for the Russian presidency, principally between Yeltsin and a Communist loyalist, resulted in a major victory for

Yeltsin. He took the oath of office for the new position on July 10, 1991.

Reversing his relative hard-line position, Gorbachev together with leaders of nine Soviet republics signed an accord called the Union Treaty, which was meant to preserve the unity of the nation. In exchange the federal government would have turned over control of industrial and natural resources to the individual republics. An attempted coup d'état took place on Aug. 19, 1991, orchestrated by a group of eight senior officials calling itself the State Committee on the State of Emergency. Boris Yeltsin, barricaded in the Russian Parliament building, defiantly called for a general strike. The next day huge crowds demonstrated in Leningrad, and Yeltsin supporters fortified barricades surrounding the Parliament building. On Aug. 21 the coup committee disbanded, and at least some of its members attempted to flee Moscow. The Soviet Parliament formally reinstated Gorbachev as president. Two days later he resigned from his position as general-secretary of the Communist Party and recommended that its Central Committee be disbanded. On Aug. 29 the Parliament approved the suspension of all Communist Party activities pending an investigation of its role in the failed coup. At the time of the attempted coup, the republic's president, Boris Yeltsin, was the most popular political figure in the former Soviet Union. A leading reformer, he became the first directly elected leader in Russian history and received 60% of the vote for president of the Russian Republic.

Yeltsin championed the cause for national reconstruction and the adoption of a Union Treaty with the other republics to create a free-market economic association. On Dec. 12, 1991, the Russian Parliament ratified Yeltsin's plea to establish a new commonwealth of independent nations open to all former members of the Soviet Union. The new union was created with the governments of Ukraine and Belarus who along with Russia were the three original cofounders of the Soviet Union in 1922. After the end of the Soviet Union, Russia and ten other Soviet republics joined in a Commonwealth of Independent States on Dec. 21, 1991.

At the start of 1992, Russia embarked on a series of dramatic economic reforms, including the freeing of prices on most goods, which led to an immediate downturn. A national referendum on confidence in Yeltsin and his economic program took place in April 1993. To the surprise of many, the president and his shock-therapy program won by a resounding margin. In Sept., Yeltsin dissolved the legislative bodies left over from the Soviet era. The impasse between the executive and the legislature resulted in an armed conflict on Oct. 3. Yeltsin prevailed largely through the support of the military and other forces.

The southern republic Chechnya's president accelerated his region's drive for independence in 1994. In Dec., Russian troops closed the borders and sought to squelch the independence drive. The Russian military forces met firm and costly resistance. Shortly before the scheduled presidential election of June 1996, a cease-fire was arranged in Chechnya. Yeltsin started the year with slim chances for reelection. But bolstered by favorable media attention, fear of a Communist resurgence, and vigorous campaigning, he won the second round of voting in July against a Communist opponent. In May 1997, the two-year war formally ended with the signing of a peace treaty that adroitly avoided the issue of Chechen independence.

Yeltsin bounded back into the political fray in March 1997 after eight months' absence caused by sickness. His first action was to reshuffle the cabinet to include new ministers with strong reform credentials. The "young reformers" announced plans to overhaul taxation, housing, and welfare; restore central control over headstrong regional leaders; and curb the power of Russia's monopolies (natural gas, electricity, and railways). These plans for reform, however, went awry.

In March 1998 Yeltsin dismissed his entire government and replaced Prime Minister Viktor Chernomyrdin with the young and little known fuel and energy minister Sergei Kiriyenko. On Aug. 28, 1998, amid the Russian stock market's free fall, the Russian government halted trading of the ruble on international currency markets. This financial crisis led to a long-term economic downturn and to political upheaval. President Boris Yeltsin then sacked Prime Minister Kiriyenko and reappointed Chernomyrdin. The Duma rejected Chernomyrdin, and on Sept. 11 elected foreign minister Yevgeny Primakov as prime minister. The repercussions of Russia's financial emergency were felt throughout the Commonwealth of Independent States.

Impatient with Yeltsin's chronic illnesses and increasingly erratic behavior, the Duma attempted to impeach him in May 1999 on five charges: provoking the 1991 fall of the Soviet Union, using force to dissolve the Parliament in 1993, starting the ill-conceived 1994–96 war in Chechnya, ruining the nation's military, and impoverishing the Russian people through ruinous economic policies—the charge regarding Chechnya was considered the only one with a chance of approval. But the impeachment motion was quickly quashed and soon Yeltsin was on the ascendancy again. In keeping with his capri-cious style, Yeltsin dismissed Prime Minister Yevgeny Primakov and replaced him with Interior Minister Sergei Stepashin. Just three months later, however, Yeltsin ousted Stepashin and replaced him with Vladimir Putin on Aug. 9, 1999, announcing that in addition to serving as prime minister, the former KGB agent was his choice as a successor in the 2000 presidential election.

During the Kosovo crisis, Russia sided with its Slavic allies, the Serbs. Regularly calling for a halt to NATO bombing, Yeltsin seemed almost more upset about his marginal role in the conflict than the fact that Serbia was under attack. Russia regularly claimed to be able to finesse a peace deal with the Serbs, yet little diplomatic progress emerged from their efforts. When NATO peacekeeping troops moved into Kosovo, Russia insisted that it take part, yet refused to take orders from NATO.

Militant rebels in Dagestan, a Russian republic next to Chechnya, announced a jihad against Russia in Aug. 1999, and in an effort to create an Islamic state in Dagestan, began fighting against Russian troops. Despite Russian assumptions that the rebellion would be quickly crushed, fighting continued in Sept.

Rwanda

RWANDESE REPUBLIC

National name: Repubulika y'u Rwanda
President: Pasteur Bizimungu (1994)
Prime Minister: Pierre-Célestin Rwigema (1995)
Area: 10,169 sq. mi. (26,340 sq. km)
Population (1999 est.): 8,154,933 (average annual rate of natural increase: 1.94%); birth rate: 39.0/1000; infant mortality rate: 112.9/1000; density per sq. mi.: 802
Capital and largest city (1991): Kigali, 232,733.
Monetary unit: Rwanda franc. **Languages:** Kinyarwanda, French, Swahili, English. **Ethnicity/race:** Hutu 80%, Tutsi 19%, Twa (Pygmoid) 1%. **Religions:** Roman Catholic, 56%; Protestant, 18%; Islam, 1%; Animist, 25%. **Literacy rate:** 50%
Economic summary: GDP/PPP (1996 est.): $3 billion; $440 per capita. **Real growth rate:** 13.3.%. **Inflation:** 7.4% (1996 est.). **Unemployment:** n.a. **Arable land:** 35%. **Agriculture:** coffee, tea, pyrethrum (insecticide made from chrysanthemums), bananas, beans, sorghum, potatoes, livestock. **Labor force:** 3.6 million; agriculture, 93%; government and services, 5%; industry and commerce, 2%. **Industries:** mining of cassiterite (tin ore) and wolframite (tungsten ore), tin, cement, processing of agricultural products, small-scale beverage production, soap, furniture, shoes, plastic goods, textiles, cigarettes. **Natural resources:** gold, cassiterite (tin ore), wolframite (tungsten ore), natural gas, hydropower. **Exports:** $62.3 million (f.o.b., 1996 est.): coffee, tea, cassiteritie, wolframite, pyrethrum. **Imports:** $202.4 million (f.o.b., 1996 est.): foodstuffs, machines and equipment, capital goods, steel, petroleum products, cement and construction material. **Major trading partners:** Brazil, EU, Kenya, U.S., Tanzania.

Geography Rwanda, in east-central Africa, is surrounded by Congo, Uganda, Tanzania, and Burundi. It is slightly smaller than Maryland. Steep mountains and deep valleys cover most of the country. Lake Kivu in the northwest, at an altitude of 4,829 feet (1,472 m) is the highest lake in Africa. Extending north of it are the Virunga Mountains, which include the volcano Karisimbi (14,187 ft.; 4,324 m), Rwanda's highest point.

Government Republic.

History The original inhabitants of Rwanda were the Twa, a Pygmy people who now make up only 1% of the population. It is not certain when the Hutu migrated to the region, except that they were well established by the time the Tutsi arrived in the 14th century. The military skills of the Tutsi led to their dominance over the Hutu, a dominance that remained unchanged over centuries, despite their minority status.

Rwanda, which became a part of German East Africa in 1890, was first visited by European explorers in 1854. During World War I, it was occupied in 1916 by Belgian troops. After the war, it became a Belgian League of Nations mandate, along with Burundi, under the name of Ruanda-Urundi. The mandate was made a U.N. trust territory in 1946. Until the Belgian Congo achieved independence in 1960, Ruanda-Urundi was administered as part of that colony. Belgium at first maintained Tutsi dominance but eventually encouraged power sharing between Hutu and Tutsi. Ethnic tensions led to civil war, forcing many Tutsi into exile. When Rwanda became the independent nation of Rwanda on July 1, 1962, it was under Hutu rule.

In Oct. 1990 rebel Tutsi (RPF) in exile in Uganda invaded. Peace accords were signed in Aug. 1993, calling for a coalition government. After the downing of an aircraft in April 1994 carrying the presidents of Rwanda and Burundi, both of whom died in the crash, deep-seated ethnic hatred erupted and Hutus slaughtered an estimated 800,000 Tutsi civilians. It is believed that the plane was shot down by Hutu extremists who rejected the Hutu-Tutsi power-sharing plan proposed by President Juvénal Habyarimana, a Hutu moderate. Although the genocidal slaughter seemed a spontaneous eruption of hatred, it has in fact been shown to have been carefully orchestrated. In response, Tutsi rebels swept across the country in a 14-week civil war, routing the largely Hutu government. In the immediate aftermath an estimated 1.7 million Hutu fled across the border into neighboring Zaire (now the Democratic Republic of the Congo), creating an international humanitarian problem.

Amid the legitimate refugees were Hutu militiamen who began waging guerrilla warfare from Zaire. The Hutu guerrillas in Zaire, as well as Zaire's threat to exile their own ethnic Tutsi, led to Rwanda's support of rebel forces bent on overthrowing Mobutu Sese Seko's Zaire. But Rwanda's support for the new regime of Laurent Kabila in the Democratic Republic of the Congo soon turned to disenchantment. The new government was not able to prevent the raids from Hutu guerrillas that continued to traumatize the country and destabilize the region. In Aug. 1998, a little more than a year after Kabila took over, a rebellion began against his reign. Despite their denials, it is believed to have been instigated by Rwanda and Uganda.

Refugee problems, continued massacres, and the scars of genocide continued to haunt the national psyche. In Sept. 1998, a U.N. tribunal sentenced Jean Kambanda, a former prime minister of Rwanda, to life in prison for his part in the 1994 genocide. He became the first person in history to be convicted for the crime of genocide, first defined in the 1948 Genocide Convention after World War II.

St. Kitts and Nevis

FEDERATION OF ST. KITTS AND NEVIS

Sovereign: Queen Elizabeth II (1952)
Governor General: Sir Cuthbert Sebastian (1996)
Prime Minister: Denzil Douglas (1995)
Area: St. Kitts 65 sq. mi. (169 sq. km); Nevis 35 sq. mi. (100 sq. km)
Population (1999 est.): 42,838 (average annual rate of natural increase: 1.45%); birth rate: 22.6/1000; infant mortality rate: 17.4/1000; density per sq. mi.: 428
Capital: Basseterre (on St. Kitts), 19,000. **Largest town on Nevis:** Charlestown, 1,771. **Monetary unit:** East Caribbean dollar. **Ethnicity/race:** black African. **Literacy rate:** 98%
Economic summary: GDP/PPP (1996 est.): $235 million; $5,700 per capita. **Real growth rate:** 5.8%. **Inflation:** 3.1% (1996). **Unemployment:** 4.3% (May 1995). **Arable land:** 22%. **Agriculture:** sugarcane, vegetables, bananas, rice, yams. **Labor force:** 18,172 (June 1995); services, 69%; manufacturing, 31%. **Industry:** tourism, sugar processing, salt, cotton, clothing, copra, footwear, beverages. **Exports:** $39.1 million (f.o.b., 1996 est.): machinery, food, electronics, beverages, and tobacco. **Imports:** $131.5 million (f.o.b., 1996 est.): machinery, manufactures, food, fuels. **Major trading partners:** U.S., U.K., Japan, Trinidad and Tobago, Japan, Canada.

Geography St. Kitts and Nevis are related physiographically by a volcanic mountain chain that dominates the central core of both islands. St. Kitts is roughly oval in shape except for a long, narrow peninsula to the southeast. St. Kitts' highest point is Mount Liamuiga (3,792 feet [1,156 m]), which has a lake in its forested crater. The Narrows, a 2-mile-(3-kilometer-) wide channel, separates the two islands. The circularly shaped Nevis is surrounded by coral reefs and the island is almost entirely a single mountain, Nevis Peak (3,232 feet [985 m]).

Government Constitutional monarchy.

History When Christopher Columbus explored the islands in 1493, they were inhabited by the Carib people. St. Kitts, formerly St. Christopher, was settled by the British in 1623; Nevis in 1628. The French settled on St. Kitts in 1627, and an Anglo-French rivalry lasted for more than 100 years. After a decisive British victory over the French at Brimstone Hill in 1782, the islands came under permanent British control. The islands, including nearby Anguilla, were united in 1882. They joined the West Indies federation in 1958 and remained in that association until its dissolution in 1962. St. Kitts-Nevis-Anguilla became an associated state of the United Kingdom in 1967. Anguilla seceded in 1980, and St. Kitts and Nevis became independent on Sept. 19, 1983.

A drop in world sugar prices hurt the nation's economy through the mid-1980s, and the government sought to reduce the islands' dependence on sugar production and to diversify the economy. In 1990, the premier of Nevis announced that he intended to seek an end to the federation with St. Kitts by 1992, but a local election in June 1992 put the idea on hold. In Aug. 1998, 62% of Nevis voters favored a referendum permitting Nevis to secede, but the vote fell short of the two-thirds majority required.

St. Lucia

Sovereign: Queen Elizabeth II (1952)
Governor-General: H. E. William George Mallet (1996)
Prime Minister: Pearlette Louisy (1997)
Area: 238 sq. mi. (620 sq. km)
Population (1999 est.): 154,020 (average annual rate of natural increase: 1.61%); birth rate: 21.6/1000; infant mortality rate: 16.6/1000; density per sq. mi.: 647
Capital and largest city (1992 est.): Castries, 13,600.
Monetary unit: East Caribbean dollar. **Languages:** English and patois. **Ethnicity/race:** African descent 90.3%, mixed 5.5%, East Indian 3.2%, white 0.8%.
Religions: Roman Catholic, 90%; Protestant, 7%; Anglican, 3%. **Literacy rate:** 67%
Economic summary: GDP/PPP (1996 est.): $600 million; $3,800 per capita. **Real growth rate:** 0.8%.
Inflation: −2.3%. **Unemployment:** (1996 est.), 15%.
Labor force: 43,800; agriculture, 43.4%; services, 38.9%; industry and commerce, 17.7% (1983 est.).
Arable land: 8%. **Agriculture:** bananas, coconuts, cocoa, citrus fruit, vegetables, root crops. **Industry:** clothing, assembled electronics, beverages, corrugated cardbord boxes, tourism, coconut processing, lime processing. **Exports:** $79.5 million (f.o.b., 1996 est.): bananas, cocoa, clothing, vegetables, fruits, coconut oil. **Imports:** $270.6 million (f.o.b., 1996 est.): foodstuffs, machinery and equipment, chemicals, fuels, manufactured goods.
Major trading partners: U.K., U.S., Caribbean countries, Japan, Canada. **Member of Commonwealth of Nations**

Geography One of the Windward Islands of the eastern Caribbean, St. Lucia lies just south of Martinique. It is of volcanic origin. A chain of wooded mountains runs from north to south, and from them flow many streams into fertile valleys.

Government Parliamentary democracy. A governor-general represents the sovereign, Queen Elizabeth II.

History The first inhabitants of St. Lucia were the Arawak Indians, who were forced off the island by the Caribs. Explored by Spain and then France, St. Lucia became a British territory in 1814 and one of the Windward Islands in 1871. With other Windward Islands, St. Lucia was granted home rule in 1967 as one of the West Indies Associated States. On Feb. 22, 1979, St. Lucia achieved full independence in ceremonies boycotted by the opposition St. Lucia Labour Party, which had advocated a referendum before cutting ties with Britain. The United Workers Party (UWP), then in power, called for new elections and was defeated by the St. Lucia Labour Party (SLP). The UWP was returned to power in the elections of 1982, 1987, and 1992.

Parliamentary elections in May 1997 gave the opposition St. Lucia Labour Party 16 of the 17 seats. The SLP had stressed economic issues and corruption, but the United Workers Party denied the corruption charges.

St. Vincent and The Grenadines

Sovereign: Queen Elizabeth II (1952)
Governor-General: Sir Charles Antrobus (1996)
Prime Minister: Sir James Fitz-Allen Mitchell (1984)
Area: 150 sq. mi. (340 sq. km)
Population (1999 est.): 120,519 (average annual rate of natural increase: 1.31%); birth rate: 18.3/1000; infant mortality rate: 15.2/1000; density per sq. mi.: 803
Capital and largest city (1992 est.): Kingstown, 15,466.
Monetary unit: East Caribbean dollar. **Languages:** English (official), French patois. **Ethnicity/race:** African descent, white, East Indian, Carib Indian.
Religions: Anglican, 47%; Methodist, 28%; Roman Catholic, 13%. **Literacy rate:** 96%
Economic summary: GDP/PPP (1996 est.): $259 million; $2,200 per capita. **Real growth rate:** 1%.
Inflation: 3.6%. **Unemployment:** 35%–40% (1994 est.). **Arable land:** 10%; **Agriculture:** bananas, coconuts, sweet potatoes, spices, cattle, sheep, pigs, goats, fish. **Labor force:** 67,000 (1984 est.); in agriculture 26%, industry 17%, services 57% (1980 est.). **Industry:** food processing, cement, furniture, clothing, starch. **Exports:** $46 million (f.o.b., 1996): bananas, arrowroot, eddos and dasheen (taro), tennis racquets. **Imports:** $127 million (f.o.b., 1996): foodstuffs, machinery and equipment, chemicals, fuels, minerals, fertilizers. **Major trading partners:** U.K., U.S., Caribbean nations. **Member of Commonwealth of Nations**

Geography St. Vincent, chief island of the chain, is 18 miles (29 km) long and 11 miles (18 km) wide, and is located 100 miles (161 km) west of Barbados. The island is mountainous and well forested. St. Vincent is dominated by the volcano Mount Soufrière, which rises to 4,048 feet (1,234 m). The Grenadines, a chain of nearly 600 islets with a total area of only 17 square miles (27 sq. km), extend for 60 miles (96 km) between St. Vincent and Grenada. The main islands in the Grenadines are Bequia, Balliceau, Canouan, Mayreau, Mustique, Isle D'Quatre, Petit Saint Vincent, and Union Island.

Government Constitutional monarchy.

History The Carib Indians were the first inhabitants of St. Vincent before the Europeans arrived and the island still contains a sizable number of Carib artifacts. Explored by Columbus in 1498, and alternately claimed by Britain and France, St. Vincent became a British colony by the Treaty of Paris in 1763. In 1773, the island was divided between the Caribs and the British, but conflicts between the groups persisted. In 1796, the Caribs revolted and were subdued. Thereafter the British deported most of them to islands in the Gulf of Honduras. Sugarcane cultivation brought thousands of African slaves and, later, Portuguese and East Indian laborers.

The islands won home rule in 1969 as part of the West Indies Associated States, after being part of the federation of the West Indies from 1958 until its dissolution in 1962. They achieved full independence Oct. 26, 1979. Prime Minister Milton Cato's government quelled a brief rebellion on Dec. 8, 1979, attributed to economic problems following the eruption of La Soufrière in April 1979 (which had caused the evacuation of the northern two-thirds of the island). The eruption, followed by Hurricane Allen in 1980, seriously damaged the nation's economy, particularly the important banana crop, in the 1980s. But by the 1990s the economy had begun to rebound and the small tourism industry began to grow. In 1996, St. Vincent and the Grenadines signed agreements with the U.S. that allowed U.S. Coast Guard personnel to pursue suspected drug smugglers into their territorial waters and provided for extradition of criminals. In 1997, the country's permanent representative to the Organization of American States assumed the chairmanship of that body's Permanent Council.

Samoa

INDEPENDENT STATE OF SAMOA

Head of State: Malietoa Tanumafili II (1962)
Prime Minister: Tuilaepa Sailele Malielegaoi (1998)
Area: 1,093 sq. mi. (2,860 sq. km)
Population (1999 est.): 229,979 (average annual growth rate: 2.34%); birth rate: 28.8/1000; infant mortality rate: 30.5/1000; density per sq. mi.: 210
Capital and largest city (1991): Apia, 32,859.
Monetary unit: Tala. **Languages:** Samoan and English. **Ethnicity/race:** Samoan 92.6%, Euronesians 7% (persons of European and Polynesian blood), Europeans 0.4%. **Religions:** Christian, 99.7%.
Literacy rate: 98.3%
Economic summary: GDP: (1996 est.): $450 million; $2,100 per capita. **Real growth rate:** 5.9%. **Inflation:** 7.5% (1996 est.). **Arable land:** 19%. **Agriculture:** coconuts, bananas, taro, yams. **Labor force:** 82,500 (1991 est.); 65% employed in agriculture, 30% in services, 5% in industry. (1995 est.). **Industry:** timber, tourism, processed food, fish. **Natural resource:** timber.
Exports: $10 million (f.o.b., 1996): copra, fish, beer, coconut oil and cream. **Imports:** $100 million (c.i.f., 1996): food, manufactured goods, machinery. **Major trading partners:** New Zealand, EU, Australia, American Samoa, U.S., Fiji, Japan. **Member of Commonwealth of Nations.**

Geography Samoa, formerly Western Samoa, is in the South Pacific Ocean about 2,200 miles (3,540 km) south of Hawaii. The larger islands in the Samoan chain, Upolu and Savai'i, are mountainous and of volcanic origin. There is little level land except in the coastal areas, where most cultivation takes place.

Government Constitutional monarchy.

History Polynesians, possibly from Tonga, first settled in the Samoan islands about 1000 B.C.E. Samoa was explored by Dutch and French traders in the 18th century. Toward the end of the 19th century, conflicting interests of the U.S., Britain, and Germany resulted in an 1899 treaty that recognized the paramount interests of the United States in those islands west of 171° W (American Samoa) and Germany's interests in the other islands (Western Samoa).

New Zealand seized Western Samoa from Germany in 1914, and in 1946 it became a U.N. trust territory administered by New Zealand.

A resistance movement to New Zealand rule, known as the *Mau* movement ("strongly held view"), helped to edge the islands toward independence on Jan. 1, 1962. A constitutional monarchy, Samoa has a legislative assembly whose members are from the *matai*, or titled class.

Barraged regularly by cyclones that have wreaked havoc on the country's primarily agrarian economy, Samoa has begun stepping up its tourism industry—not such a difficult undertaking in this archetypical South Pacific paradise.

A referendum in 1990 gave most women the right to vote for the first time. In 1997, a new constitutional amendment changed the country's name to Samoa.

San Marino

MOST SERENE REPUBLIC OF SAN MARINO

National name: Repubblica di San Marino
Captains Regent: Antonello Baciocchi and Rosa Zafferani (1999)
Area: 23.4 sq. mi. (60 sq. km)
Population (1999 est.): 25,061 (average annual growth rate 0.22%); birth rate: 10.4/1000; infant mortality rate: 5.4/1000; density per sq. mi.: 1,062
Capital and largest city (1992 est.): San Marino, 2,397.
Monetary unit: Italian lira. **Language:** Italian.
Ethnicity/race: Sammarinese, Italian. **Religion:** Roman Catholic. **Literacy rate:** 96%
Economic summary: GDP/PPP (1997 est.): $500 million; $20,000 per capita. **Real growth rate:** 4.8%. **Inflation:** 5.3% (1995). **Unemployment:** 3.6% (April 1996). **Arable land:** 17%. **Agriculture:** wheat and other grains, grapes, olives, cheese, cattle, horses, pigs, meat, hides. **Labor force:** 15,600 (1995); services, 55%; industry, 43%; agriculture, 2% (1993). The tourist sector contributed over 50% of GDP.
Industry: tourism, textiles, electronics, ceramics, cement, wine, and olive oil. **Exports:** (trade data are included with the statistics for Italy) building stone, lime, chestnuts, wheat, hides, baked goods. **Imports:** (trade data are included with the statistics for Italy) manufactured consumer goods, food. Major trading partner: Italy.

Geography One-tenth the size of New York City, San Marino is surrounded by Italy. It is situated in the Apennines, a little inland from the Adriatic Sea near Rimini.

Government Republic.

History According to tradition, San Marino was founded about C.E. 350 and had the good luck for centuries to stay out of the many wars and feuds on the Italian peninsula. It is the oldest republic in the world. San Marino has survived, completely intact, attacks by other self-governing Italian city-states, the Napoleonic Wars, the unification of Italy, and two world wars. Those born in San Marino remain citizens and can vote no matter where they live. Throughout the 1990s San Marino has taken a more active role in international diplomacy, establishing strong diplomatic and economic ties to a host of other countries.

São Tomé and Príncipe

DEMOCRATIC REPUBLIC OF SÃO TOMÉ AND PRÍNCIPE

President: Miguel Trovoada (1991)
Prime Minister: Guilherme Posser da Costa (1999)
Area: 370 sq. mi. (960 sq. km)
Population (1999 est.): 154,878 (average annual growth rate: 3.52%); birth rate: 43.3/1000; infant mortality rate: 52.9/1000; density per sq. mi.: 419
Capital and largest city (1990 est.): São Tomé, 43,420.
Monetary unit: Dobra. **Language:** Portuguese.
Ethnicity/race: mestico, angolares (descendants of Angolan slaves), forros (descendants of freed slaves), servicais (contract laborers from Angola, Mozambique, and Cape Verde), tongas (children of servicais born on the islands), Europeans (primarily Portuguese).
Religions: Roman Catholic, Evangelical Protestant, Seventh-Day Adventist. **Literacy rate:** 57%
Economic summary: GDP/PPP (1996 est.): $154 million; $1,000 per capita. **Real growth rate:** 1.5%.
Inflation: 60% (1996 est.). **Unemployment:** 28% (1996 est.). **Arable land:** 2%. **Agriculture:** cocoa, copra, coconuts, palm kernels, cinnamon, pepper,

papaya, beans, poultry, fish, coffee, bananas. **Labor force:** Most engaged in subsistence agriculture and fishing. Shortages of skilled workers. **Industry:** shirts, soap, beer, processed fish, light construction, textiles, lumber. **Exports:** $4.9 million (f.o.b., 1996 est.): cocoa, coffee, copra, palm oil. **Imports:** $19.6 million (c.i.f., 1996 est.): textiles, machinery, electrical equipment, petroleum products, food products. **Major trading partners:** Netherlands, Portugal, Germany, China, Angola.

Geography The tiny volcanic islands of São Tomé and Príncipe lie in the Gulf of Guinea about 150 miles (240 km) off West Africa. São Tomé (about 330 sq. mi.; 859 sq. km) is covered by a dense mountainous jungle, out of which have been carved large plantations. Príncipe (about 40 sq. mi.; 142 sq. km) consists of jagged mountains. Other islands in the republic are Pedras Tinhosas and Rolas. About 95% of the population lives on São Tomé.

Government Republic.

History São Tomé and Príncipe, believed to have been originally uninhabited, were explored by Portuguese navigators in 1471 and settled by the end of the century. Intensive cultivation by slave labor made the islands a major producer of sugar during the 17th century but output declined until the introduction of coffee and cacao in the 19th century brought new prosperity. The island of São Tomé was the world's largest producer of cacao in 1908 and the crop is still the most important. Working conditions for laborers, however, were horrendous, and in 1909 British and German chocolate manufacturers boycotted São Tomé cocoa in protest. An exile liberation movement was formed in 1953 after Portuguese landowners quelled labor riots by killing several hundred African workers.

The Portuguese revolution of 1974 brought the end of the overseas empire and the new Lisbon government transferred power to the liberation movement on July 12, 1975. A former prime minister and dissident, Miguel Trovoada, was elected president in March 1991 after the withdrawal of the two other candidates. In April 1995 Príncipe became autonomous. In Aug. a bloodless military coup was reversed through Angolan mediation. In Dec. an agreement was struck on forming a coalition government. President Trovoada won reelection in July 1996 against challenger and former president Pinto da Costa. Protests erupted in April 1997 when the government, in response to its inability to pay for imported oil, raised gasoline prices 140% in order to stem demand.

Saudi Arabia

KINGDOM OF SAUDI ARABIA

National name: Al-Mamlaka al-'Arabiya as-Sa'udiya
King and Prime Minister: King Fahd bin 'Abdulaziz (1982)
Area: 865,000 sq. mi. (1,960,582 sq. km)
Population (1999 est.): 21,504,613 (average annual rate of natural increase: 3.25%); birth rate: 37.4/1000; infant mortality rate: 38.8/1000; density per sq. mi.: 25
Capital: Riyadh. **Largest cities (1993):** Riyadh, 3,000,000; Jeddah, 2,500,000; Makkah (Mecca) (1994 est.), 550,000. **Monetary unit:** Riyal. **Languages:** Arabic, English widely spoken. **Ethnicity/race:** Arab 90%, Afro-Asian 10%. **Religion:** Islam, 100%.
Literacy rate: 62%

Economic summary: GDP/PPP (1997 est.): $206.5 billion; $10,300 per capita. **Real growth rate:** 4%. **Inflation:** 0%. **Unemployment:** n.a. **Arable land:** 2%. **Agriculture:** dates, grains, livestock, wheat, fish, flowers. **Labor force:** 7 million; government, 40%; industry and oil, 25%; services, 30%; agriculture, 5%. **Industry:** construction, cement, plastic products, steel, packaged goods. **Natural resources:** oil, natural gas, iron ore. **Exports:** $56.7 billion (f.o.b., 1996): petroleum and petroleum products 90%. **Imports:** $25.4 billion (f.o.b., 1996): machinery and equipment, foodstuffs, chemicals, motor vehicles, textiles. **Major trading partners:** U.S., Germany, U.K. and other Western European countries, South Korea, Taiwan, Japan, Singapore.

Geography Saudi Arabia occupies most of the Arabian Peninsula, with the Red Sea and the Gulf of Aqaba to the west, the Arabian Gulf to the east. Neighboring countries are Jordan, Iraq, Kuwait, Qatar, the United Arab Emirates, the Sultanate of Oman, Yemen, and Bahrain, connected to the Saudi mainland by a causeway. Saudi Arabia contains the world's largest continuous sand desert, the Rub Al-Khali, or Empty Quarter. Its oil region lies primarily in the eastern province along the Arabian Gulf.

Government Saudi Arabia was an absolute monarchy until 1992, at which time the Sa'ud royal family introduced the country's first constitution. The legal system is based on the Sharia (Islamic law).

History Saudi Arabia is not only the homeland of the Arab peoples—it is thought that the first Arabs originated on the Arabian penninsula—but the homeland of Islam, the world's second largest religion. Muhammad founded Islam there and it is the location of the two holy pilgrimage cities of Mecca and Medina. The Islamic calendar begins in 622, the year of the hegira, or Muhammad's flight from Mecca. A succession of invaders attempted to control the peninsula, but by 1517 the Ottoman Empire dominated, and in the middle of the 18th century, it was divided into separate principalities. In 1745 Muhammad ibn 'Abd al-Wahhab began calling for the purification and reform of Islam, and the Wahhabi movement swept across Arabia. By 1811, Wahhabi leaders had waged a jihad—a holy war—against other forms of Islam on the peninsula, and succeeded in uniting much of it. By 1818, however, the Wahhabis had been driven out of power again by the Ottomans and their Egyptian allies.

The kingdom of Saudi Arabia is almost entirely the creation of King Ibn Saud (1882–1953). A descendant of Wahhabi leaders, he seized Riyadh in 1901 and set himself up as leader of the Arab nationalist movement. By 1906 he had established Wahhabi dominance in Nejd and conquered Hejaz in 1924–25. Hejaz and Nejd were merged to form the kingdom of Saudi Arabia in 1932, which was an absolute monarchy ruled by *sharia,* Islamic law. A year later the region of Asir was incorporated into the kingdom.

Oil was discovered in 1936, and commercial production began during World War II. Its wealth allowed the country to provide free health care and education while not collecting any taxes from its people. Saudi Arabia was neutral until nearly the end of the war, but it was permitted to be a charter member of the United Nations. The country joined the Arab League in 1945 and took part in the 1948–49 war against Israel. Saudi Arabia still does not recognize the state of Israel. On Ibn Saud's death in 1953, his eldest son, Saud, began an 11-year reign marked by an increasing hostility toward the radical Arabism of Egypt's Gamal Abdel Nasser. In 1964, the ailing Saud was deposed and replaced by the premier, Crown Prince Faisal, who gave vocal support but no military help to Egypt in the 1967 Arab-Israeli War.

Faisal's assassination by a deranged kinsman in 1975 shook the Middle East, but failed to alter his kingdom's course. His successor was his brother, Prince Khalid. Khalid gave influential support to Egypt during negotiations on Israeli withdrawal from the Sinai Desert. King Khalid died of a heart attack in 1982, and was succeeded by his half-brother, Prince Fahd bin 'Abdulaziz, who had exercised the real power throughout Khalid's reign. King Fahd, a pro-Western modernist, chose his 58-year-old half-brother, Abdullah, as Crown Prince.

Saudi Arabia and the smaller, oil-rich Arab states on the Persian Gulf, fearful that they might become Ayatollah Ruhollah Khomeini's next targets if Iran conquered Iraq, made large financial contributions to the Iraqi war effort during the 1980s. At the same time, cheating by other members of the Organization of Petroleum Exporting Countries (OPEC), competition from nonmember oil producers, and conservation efforts by consuming nations combined to drive down the world price of oil. Saudi Arabia has one-third of all known oil reserves, but falling demand and rising production outside OPEC combined to reduce its oil revenues from $120 billion in 1980 to less than $25 billion in 1985, threatening the country with domestic unrest and undermining its influence in the Gulf area.

At the start of 1996, King Fahd passed authority to Crown Prince Abdullah, saying he needed rest. Although not an abdication, it was unclear how long the king would be absent. In 1998 the country's oil income fell by 40% because of a worldwide decline in prices, and entered its first recession in 6 years.

Senegal

REPUBLIC OF SENEGAL

National name: République du Sénégal
President: Abdou Diouf (1981)
Prime Minister: Mamadou Lamine Loum (1998)
Area: 75,954 sq. mi. (196,190 sq. km)
Population (1999 est.): 10,051,930 (average annual rate of natural increase: 3.32%); birth rate: 43.9/1000; infant mortality rate: 59.8/1000; density per sq. mi.: 132
Capital and largest city (1994 est.): Dakar, 1,729,823. **Monetary unit:** Franc CFA. **Ethnicity/race:** Wolof 36%, Fulani 17%, Serer 17%, Toucouleur 9%, Diola 9%, Mandingo 9%, European and Lebanese 1%, other 2%. **Languages:** French (official); Wolof, Serer, other ethnic dialects. **Religions:** Islam, 92%; indigenous, 6%; Christian, 2%. **Literacy rate:** 38%
Economic summary: GDP/PPP (1997 est.): $15.6 billion; $1,850 per capita. **Real growth rate:** 4.7%. **Inflation:** 2.5% (1997). **Unemployment:** n.a.; urban youth, 40%. **Arable land:** 12%. **Agriculture:** peanuts, millet, corn, rice, sorghum, cotton, tomatoes, green vegetables, cattle, poultry, pigs, fish. **Labor force:** 2.509 million; 77% subsistence-level agriculture workers; less than 1% wage earners (private sector, 40%; government and parapublic, 60%). **Industry:** agricultural and fish processing, phosphate mining,

fertilizer production, petroleum refining, construction materials. **Natural resources:** fish, phosphate, iron ore. **Exports:** $986 million (f.o.b., 1996): fish, ground nuts (peanuts), petroleum products, phosphates, cotton. **Imports:** $1.4 billion (f.o.b., 1996): foods and beverages, consumer goods, capital goods, petroleum products. **Major trading partners:** U.S., Western European countries, African neighbors, Japan, China, India.

Geography The capital of Senegal, Dakar, is the westernmost point in Africa. The country, slightly smaller than South Dakota, surrounds Gambia on three sides and is bordered on the north by Mauritania, on the east by Mali, and on the south by Guinea and Guinea-Bissau.

Senegal is mainly a low-lying country, with a semidesert area in the north and northeast and forests in the southwest. The largest rivers include the Senegal in the north and the Casamance in the south tropical climate region.

Government Parliamentary democracy with socialist leanings.

History The Toucouleur people, among the early inhabitants of Senegal, converted to Islam in the 11th century, although their religious beliefs retained strong elements of animism. The Portuguese had some stations on the banks of the Senegal River in the 15th century, and the first French settlement was made at Saint-Louis in 1659. Gorée Island became a major center for the Atlantic slave trade through the 1700s, and millions of Africans were shipped from there to the New World. The British took parts of Senegal at various times, but the French gained possession in 1840 and made it part of French West Africa in 1895. In 1946, together with other parts of French West Africa, Senegal became an overseas territory of France. On June 20, 1960, it became an independent republic federated with Mali.

In 1973, Senegal joined with six other states to create the West African Economic Community. In elections of Feb. 21, 1993, President Diouf was reelected. In June 1997 the government announced its intended sale of 49% of the state-owned, highly profitable electric company SENELEC to a private firm. The government would retain the majority share. Clashes in the Casamance region between separatists and government troops took place throughout 1997.

Serbia and Montenegro

FEDERAL REPUBLIC OF YUGOSLAVIA

National name: Srbija-Crna Gora
President: Slobodan Milosevic (1997)
Prime Minister: Momir Bulatovic (1998)
Area: 39,449 sq. mi. (102,350 sq. km)
Population (1999 est.): 11,206,847 (Montenegro: 680,369, Serbia: 10,526,478) (average annual rate of natural increase: Montenegro: 0.07%, Serbia: –0.02%); birth rate: Montenegro: 13.55/1000, Serbia: 12.6/1000; infant mortality rate: Montenegro: 11.2/1000, Serbia: 17.1/1000; density per sq. mi.: 284
Capital and largest city (1994 est.): Belgrade, 1,168,454. **Other large cities:** Novi Sad, 179,626; Nis, 175,391; Pristina, 155,499. **Monetary unit:** Yugoslav new dinar. **Languages:** Serbo-Croatian 95%, Albanian 5%. **Ethnicity/race:** Serbs 63%, Albanians 14%, Montenegrins 6%, Hungarians 4%,

other 13%. **Religions:** Orthodox 65%, Muslim 19%, Roman Catholic 4%, Protestant 1%, other 11%.
Literacy rate: 90.5%
Economic summary:GDP/PPP (1997 est.): $24.3 billion; per capita $2,280; **Growth rate:** 7%. **Inflation:** 7%. **Unemployment:** more than 35% (1995 est.). **Arable land:** n.a. **Labor force:** 2.178 million; industry, 41%; services, 35%; trade and tourism, 12%; transportation and communication, 7%; agriculture, 5% (1994). **Industry:** machine building (incl. aircraft, trucks, automobiles), mining (coal, bauxite, iron ore, limestone), nonferrous metallurgy, consumer goods, electronics, chemicals, petroleum products, pharmaceuticals. **Exports:** $2.8 billion (1996 est.): manufactured goods, food and live animals, raw materials. **Imports:** $6.2 billion (1996 est.): machinery and transport equipment, fuels and lubricants, other manufacturers, chemicals, raw materials, food, and animals. **Major trading partners:** former Soviet republics, Russia, EU, Eastern European countries.

Geography Serbia and Montenegro are about the size of the state of Kentucky and largely mountainous. The northeastern section of Serbia is part of the rich, fertile Danubian Plain drained by the Danube, Tisa, Sava, and Morava River systems. Montenegro is a jumbled mass of mountains, containing also some grassy slopes and fertile river valleys.

Government The current federation is the third state to call itself by the name Yugoslavia, officially referring to itself as the Federal Republic of Yugoslavia. The United States, however, does not recognize it by that name because the U.S. does not consider the Serbian and Montenegrin federation the successor state of Yugoslavia. Serbia and Montenegro are a federal republic.

History Yugoslavia was formed on Dec. 4, 1918, from the patchwork of Balkan states and territories. World War I began there with the assassination of Archduke Franz Ferdinand of Austria at Sarajevo on June 28, 1914. The new kingdom of Serbs, Croats, and Slovenes included the former kingdoms of Serbia and Montenegro; Bosnia-Herzegovina, previously administered jointly by Austria and Hungary; Croatia-Slavonia, a semiautonomous region of Hungary; and Dalmatia, formerly administered by Austria. King Peter I of Serbia became the first monarch; his son, Alexander I, succeeded him on Aug. 16, 1921. Croatian demands for a federal state forced Alexander to assume dictatorial powers in 1929 and to change the country's name to Yugoslavia. Serbian dominance continued despite his efforts, amid the resentment of other regions. A Macedonian associated with Croatian dissidents assassinated Alexander in Marseilles, France, on Oct. 9, 1934, and his cousin, Prince Paul, became regent for the king's son, Prince Peter.

Paul's pro-Axis policy brought Yugoslavia to sign the Axis Pact on March 25, 1941, and opponents overthrew the government two days later. On April 6 the Nazis occupied the country, and the young king and his government fled. Two guerrilla armies—the Chetniks under Draza Mihajlovic supporting the monarchy, and the Partisans under Tito (Josip Broz) leaning toward the U.S.S.R.—fought the Nazis for the duration of the war. In 1943, Tito established an Executive National Committee of Liberation to function as a provisional government. Tito won the election held in the fall of 1945, as monarchists boycotted the vote. A new Assembly

abolished the monarchy and proclaimed the Federal People's Republic of Yugoslavia, with Tito as prime minister. Tito ruthlessly eliminated the opposition and broke with the Soviet bloc in 1948. Yugoslavia followed a middle road, combining orthodox Communist control of politics and general overall economic policy with a varying degree of freedom in the arts, travel, and individual enterprise. Tito became president in 1953 and president-for-life under a revised constitution adopted in 1963.

After Tito's death on May 4, 1980, a rotating presidency designed to avoid internal dissension was put into effect immediately, and the feared clash of Yugoslavia's multiple nationalities and regions appeared to have been averted. In May 1991 Croatian voters supported a referendum calling for their republic to become an independent nation. A similar referendum passed in Dec. in Slovenia. In June the respective Parliaments in both republics passed declarations of independence. Ethnic violence flared almost immediately. The largely Serbian-led Yugoslav military pounded breakaway Bosnia and Herzegovina, leading the U.N. Security Council in May 1992 to impose economic sanctions on the Belgrade government.

Despite rampant inflation reaching approximately 3000% per month in Dec. 1993, the Serbian government of Slobodan Milosevic maintained its effective control over the rump Yugoslavia. Trade sanctions were lifted in Dec. 1995 following the signing of the Dayton Accords. In June 1996, the U.N. Security Council lifted its heavy weapons embargo. Large groups of demonstrators in 1996–97 engaged in several months of daily protests after Slobodan Milosevic refused to recognize opposition victories in local elections and in elections in Montenegro. Constitutionally barred from another term as president of Serbia, Milosevic became president of the Federal Republic of Yugoslavia (Serbia and Montenegro) in July 1997.

The situation in Serbia's provinces of Montenegro and Kosovo grew divisive in 1997 and 1998. In May 1998, Montenegro elected the reform-minded Milo Djukanovic as president. Not only is he an outspoken critic of Yugoslav president Slobodan Milosevic but he has openly contemplated secession.

Since Feb. 1998 the Yugoslav army and Serbian police have fought against the separatist Kosovo Liberation Army, but their scorched-earth tactics were concentrated on ethnic Albanian civilians—Muslims who make up 90% of Kosovo's population. More than 900 Kosovars were killed in the fighting, and the hundreds of thousands forced to flee their homes were without adequate food and shelter. Although Serbs make up only 10% of Kosovo's population, the region figures strongly in Serbian nationalist mythology.

NATO was reluctant to intervene because Kosovo—unlike Bosnia in 1992—was legally a province of Yugoslavia. The proof of civilian massacres finally gave NATO the impetus to intervene for the first time ever in the dealings of a sovereign nation with its own people. In an Oct. 12, 1998, truce brokered by American diplomat Richard Holbrooke, and under the threat of a military air strike—for which there was little enthusiasm among several NATO countries—Pres. Slobodan Milosevic agreed to the withdrawal of military forces. Fighting continued, however, and neither side accepted Washington's proposal for the province—Kosovars demanded full independence while Serb leaders would agree only to limited autonomy.

After negotiations in February and March 1999 went nowhere, on March 24, 1999, NATO began launching airstrikes. Weeks of daily bombings destroyed significant Serbian military targets, yet Milosevic showed no signs of relenting. In fact, Serbian militia stepped up civilian massacres and deportations in Kosovo—by the end of the conflict, the U.N. high commissioner for refugees estimated that at least 850,000 people had fled Kosovo. The refugee crisis put a heavy burden on neighboring countries such as Albania and Macedonia. Many wondered whether the NATO strikes had actually exacerbated the violence. As effective as NATO airpower might be against Serbian targets, it was utterly helpless in preventing Serb soldiers and paramilitaries from wreaking havoc on Kosovo's civilians.

World opinion was divided over the effectiveness of conducting airstrikes without the support of ground troops, but NATO countries remained reluctant to do so, fearing that the inevitable casualties would dampen the public's resolve for troops on foreign soil. The initial reason NATO gave for involvement in Kosovo was to avoid a wider Balkan war, but once Serbia began accelerating their campaign of ethnic cleansing in Kosovo, NATO's reason for fighting changed to preventing a human rights calamity. Yet without a concomitant change in military strategy—sending in ground troops—many wondered whether there would be any Kosovars left to save. NATO's hesitation in committing to a land battle—and therefore putting its troops at greater risk—ultimately paid off. Serbia finally agreed to sign a U.N.-approved peace agreement with NATO on June 3, ending the 11-week war. As Serbian forces withdrew, a five-nation NATO peacekeeping force entered Kosovo and began monitoring the return of refugees. Russia complicated NATO's efforts by demanding a role as a peacekeeper yet refusing to answer to NATO. A new group of refugees, Kosovar's Serbs, began fleeing the province, fearing vengeance from ethnic Albanians. Milosevic, who was indicted as a war criminal by the U.N. tribunal for the deportation of ethnic Albanians from Kosovo, held fast to the presidency as opposition groups and some Serbian Orthodox leaders began calling for his ouster.

Seychelles

REPUBLIC OF SEYCHELLES

President: France-Albert René (1977)
Area: 175 sq. mi. (455 sq. km)
Population (1999 est.): 79,164 (average annual rate of natural increase: 1.28%); birth rate: 19.4/1000; infant mortality rate: 16.7/1000; density per sq. mi.: 452
Capital and largest city (1993 est.): Victoria, 25,000.
Monetary unit: Seychelles rupee. **Languages:** English, French, and Seselwa (a creole). **Ethnicity/race:** Seychellois (mixture of Asians, Africans, Europeans). **Religions:** Roman Catholic, 90%; Anglican, 8%. **Literacy rate:** 58%
Economic summary: GDP/PPP (1997 est.): $550 million; $7,000 per capita. **Real growth rate:** n.a. **Inflation:** –0.3%. **Unemployment:** n.a. **Arable land:**

2%. **Agriculture:** sweet potatoes, cassava (tapioca), bananas, broiler chickens, tuna fishing, vanilla, coconuts, cinnamon. **Labor force:** 26,600 (1996); industry, 19%; services, 57%; government, 14%; agriculture, forestry, and fishing, 10% (1989). **Industry:** fishing, tourism, processing of coconuts and vanilla, coir rope, boat building, printing, furniture, beverages. **Exports:** $56.1 million (f.o.b., 1995): fish, petroleum, copra, cinnamon bark. **Imports:** $238 million (c.i.f., 1995): food, beverages, tobacco, manufactured goods, machinery, petroleum products, transport equipment. **Major trading partners:** EU, Japan, China, Singapore, South Africa. **Member of Commonwealth of Nations**

Geography Seychelles consists of an archipelago of about 100 islands in the Indian Ocean northeast of Madagascar. The principal islands are Mahé (55 sq. mi.; 142 sq. km), Praslin (15 sq. mi.; 38 sq. km), and La Digue (4 sq. mi.; 10 sq. km). The Aldabra, Farquhar, and Desroches groups are included in the territory of the republic.

Government Socialist multiparty state.

History The Seychelles were uninhabited when the British East India Company became the first visitors to the archipelago in 1609. Thereafter, it became a favorite pirate haven. The French claimed the islands in 1756 and administered them as part of the colony of Mauritius. The British gained control of the islands through the Treaty of Paris (1814) and changed the islands' name from the French Séchelles to the Anglicized Seychelles.

The islands became self-governing in 1975 and independent on June 29, 1976. It has remained a member of the Commonwealth of Nations. Its first president, James Mancham, was overthrown in 1977 by the prime minister, France-Albert René. At first René created a socialist state with a one-party system, but later reintroduced a multiparty system as well as various reforms.

To increase revenue the government in 1996 quietly initiated an Economic Citizenship Program that provides foreigners with the opportunity to obtain a Seychelles passport upon payment of $25,000. A new law in late 1995 granted immunity from criminal prosecution to anyone investing $10 million in the country.

In elections held in March 1998, President France-Albert René was reelected with 66.6% of the vote.

Sierra Leone

REPUBLIC OF SIERRA LEONE

President: Ahmad Tejan Kabbah (1998)
Area: 27,925 sq. mi (71,740 sq. km)
Population (1999 est.): 5,296,651 (average annual rate of natural increase: 2.89%); birth rate: 45.6/1000; infant mortality rate: 126.2/1000; density per sq. mi.: 190
Capital and largest city (1994 est.): Freetown, 1,300,000. **Monetary unit:** Leone. **Languages:** English (official), Mende, Temne, Krio. **Ethnicity/race:** 18 native African tribes 99% (Temne 30%, Mende 30%, other 39%), Creole, European, Lebanese, and Asian 1%. **Religions:** Islam, 40%, Christian, 35%; Indigenous, 20%. **Literacy rate:** 21%
Economic summary: GDP/PPP (1997 est.): $2.65

billion; $540 per capita. **Real growth rate:** –27%. **Inflation:** 40% (1997). **Unemployment:** n.a. **Arable land:** 7%. **Agriculture:** coffee, cocoa, palm kernels, rice, palm oil, peanuts, poultry, cattle, sheep, pigs, fish. **Labor force:** 1.369 million (1981 est.); agriculture, 49%; industry, 21%; services, 30% (1995). **Industry:** diamonds, petroleum refining, beverages, cigarettes, textiles, footwear. **Natural resources:** diamonds, bauxite, iron ore. **Exports:** $47 million (f.o.b., 1996): diamonds, rutile, cocoa, coffee, fish. **Imports:** $211 million (c.i.f., 1996): food, machinery and equipment, fuels and lubricants. **Major trading partners:** U.K., U.S., western European countries, Japan, China, Nigeria, India, Côte d'Ivoire. **Member of Commonwealth of Nations**

Geography Sierra Leone, on the Atlantic Ocean in West Africa, is half the size of Illinois. Guinea, in the north and east, and Liberia, in the south, are its neighbors. Mangrove swamps lie along the coast, with wooded hills and a plateau in the interior. The eastern region is mountainous.

Government Constitutional democracy.

History The Bulom people were thought to have been the earliest inhabitants of Sierra Leone, followed by the Mende and Temne peoples in the 15th century, and thereafter the Fulani. The Portuguese were the first Europeans to explore the land, and gave Sierra Leone its name, which means "lion mountains." Freetown, on the coast, was ceded to English settlers in 1787 as a home for blacks discharged from the British armed forces and also for runaway slaves who had found asylum in London. In 1808 the coastal area became a British colony, and in 1896 a British protectorate was proclaimed over the hinterland.

Sierra Leone became an independent nation on April 27, 1961. A military coup overthrew the civilian government in 1967, which was in turn replaced by civilian rule a year later. The country declared itself a republic on April 19, 1971.

A coup attempt early in 1971 led to then prime minister Stevens calling in troops from neighboring Guinea's army who remained for two years. Stevens turned the government into a one-party state under the aegis of the All People's Congress Party in April 1978. In 1992 rebel soldiers overthrew Stevens's successor, Joseph Momoh, calling for a return to a multi-party system. In 1996, another military coup ousted the country's military leader and president. Nevertheless, a multiparty presidential election proceeded in 1996, and People's Party candidate Ahmed Tejan Kabbah won with 59.4% of the vote, becoming Sierra Leone's first democratically elected president.

But a violent military coup ousted President Kabbah's civilian government in May 1997, and in June the leader of the coup, Lieut. Col. Johnny Paul Koroma, assumed the title, "Head of the Armed Forces Revolutionary Council." Koroma began a reign of terror, destroying the economy and murdering enemies. The Commonwealth of Nations demanded the reinstatement of Kabbah and Nigerian troops intervened to this end.

After ten months in exile, Kabbah resumed his rule over Sierra Leone on March 10, 1998, although the ousted junta and other rebel forces continued to wage attacks, many of which include brutal maimings of civilians. In Jan. 1999, rebels and Liberian mercenaries stormed the capital in spite of the Nigerian-led coalition of troops, known as ECOMOG, who are protecting the government. The rebels called for the ouster of Kabbah and the release of imprisoned rebel leader Foday Sankoh. ECOMOG regained control of Freetown but President Kabbah later released Sankoh so he could participate in peace negotiations.

In July 1999, an fragile peace treaty was signed requiring that the ruling government share power with the rebel Revolutionary United Front, the same rebels who had maimed thousands of civilians and had been determined to oust Kabbah. Two previous peace treaties with the rebels had failed.

Singapore

REPUBLIC OF SINGAPORE

President: S. R. Nathan (1999)
Prime Minister: Goh Chok Tong (1990)
Area: 252.9 sq. mi. (647.5 sq. km)
Population (1999 est.): 3,531,600 (average annual rate of natural increase: 0.87%); birth rate: 13.4/1000; infant mortality rate: 3.8/1000; density per sq. mi.: 14,315
Capital (1996 est.): Singapore, 3,044,000. **Monetary unit:** Singapore dollar. **Languages:** Malay, Chinese (Mandarin), Tamil, English. **Ethnicity/race:** Chinese 76.4%, Malay 14.9%, Indian 6.4%, other 2.3%. **Religions:** Islam, Christian, Buddhist, Hindu, Taoist. **Literacy rate:** 90%
Economic summary: GDP/PPP (1997 est.): $84.6 billion; $24,600 per capita. **Real growth rate:** 6.5% (1996). **Inflation:** 1.8% (1997). **Unemployment:** 3%. **Arable land:** 2%. **Agriculture:** poultry, rubber, copra, vegetables, fruits. **Labor force:** (1997 est.), 1.856 million; manufacturing, 25.6%; commerce, 22.9%; financial and business services, 33.5%; construction, 6.6% (1994). **Industry:** petroleum refining, ship repair, electronics, financial and business services, biotechnology, oil drilling equipment, rubber processing and products, processed food and beverages. **Exports:** $125.6 billion (1997 est.): computer equipment, rubber and rubber products, petroleum products, telecommunications equipment. **Imports:** $133.9 billion (1997 est.): aircraft, petroleum, chemicals, foodstuffs. **Major trading partners:** U.S., EU, Hong Kong, Japan, Malaysia. **Member of Commonwealth of Nations**

Geography The Republic of Singapore consists of the main island of Singapore, off the southern tip of the Malay Peninsula between the South China Sea and the Indian Ocean, and 58 nearby islands.

Government Republic.

History Inhabitants of the Malaysian peninsula and the island of Singapore first migrated to the area between 2500 and 1500 B.C.E. (*see* Malaysia). British and Dutch interest in the region grew with the spice trade, and the trading post of Singapore was founded in 1819 by Sir Stamford Raffles. It was made a separate crown colony of Britain in 1946, when the former colony of the Straits Settlements was dissolved. The other two settlements on the peninsula—Penang and Malacca—became part of the Union of Malaya, and the small island of Labuan was transferred to North Borneo. The Cocos (or Keeling) Islands and Christmas Island were transferred to Australia in 1955 and in 1958, respectively.

Singapore attained full internal self-government in 1959, and Lee Kwan Yew, an economic visionary with an authoritarian streak, took the helm as prime minister. On Sept. 16, 1963, Singapore joined Malaya, Sabah (North Borneo), and Sarawak in the

Federation of Malaysia. It withdrew from the Federation on Aug. 9, 1965, and a month later proclaimed itself a republic.

Under Lee, Singapore developed into one of the cleanest, safest, and most economically prosperous cities in Asia. However, Singapore's strict rules of civil obedience also drew criticism from those who said the nation's prosperity was achieved at the expense of individual freedoms. In 1990, Lee stepped down as prime minister but remained "senior minister" with considerable influence over his successor, Goh Chok Tong, who continued to preside over Singapore through difficult economic times in 1998.

The first direct presidential election took place in Aug. 1993. Ong Teng Cheong faced what initially appeared to be only token opposition but which ultimately took 40% of the vote.

In 1998, Singapore and Malaysia's often-strained relations soured again against the backdrop of the Asian financial crisis, which was taking a heavy toll on both economies. Singaporean leaders accused Malaysia of using a newly built $2.3 billion international airport at Kuala Lumpur to supplant the island nation as a regional air hub.

S. R. Nathan was declared president without an election when he was certified as the only candidate eligible to run in the elections originally scheduled for Aug. 28, 1999.

Slovakia

REPUBLIC OF SLOVAKIA

President: Rudolf Schuster (1999)
Prime Minister: Mikulás Dzurinda (1998)
Area: 18,917 sq. mi. (48,845 sq. km)
Population (1999 est.): 5,396,193 (Average annual rate of natural increase: 0.01%); birth rate: 9.5/1000; infant mortality rate: 9.5/1000; density per sq. mi.: 285
Capital and largest city (1993 est.): Bratislava, 446,600. **Other large city (1993 est.):** Kosice, 237,300. **Monetary unit:** Koruna (SKK). **Languages:** Slovak (official), Hungarian. **Ethnicity/race:** Slovak 85.7%, Hungarian 10.7%, Gypsy 1.5%, Czech 1%, Ruthenian 0.3%, Ukrainian 0.3%, German 0.1%, Polish 0.1%. **Religions:** Roman Catholic 60.3%, atheist 9.7%, Protestant 8.4%, Orthodox 4.1%, other 17.5%. **Literacy rate:** 99%
Economic summary: GDP/PPP (1997 est.): $46.3 billion; $8,600 per capita. **Real growth rate:** 5.9%. **Inflation:** 6%. **Unemployment:** 12.8%. **Arable land:** 31%. **Industry:** metal and metal products, food and beverages, electricity, gas, coke, oil, nuclear fuel, chemicals, man-made fibers, machinery, paper, printing, earthenware and ceramics, transport vehicles, textiles, electrical and optical apparatus, rubber products. **Labor force:** 2.352 million; industry, 29.3%; agriculture, 8.9%; services, 45.6%; construction, 8.0%; transport and communication, 8.2% (1994). **Agriculture:** grains, potatoes, sugar beets, fruit, forestry, hops, cattle, poultry, sheep. **Exports:** $8.8 billion (f.o.b., 1996): machinery and transport equipment, chemicals, manufactured goods, raw materials. **Imports:** $11.1 billion (f.o.b., 1996): machinery, transport equipment, fuels, manufactured goods, chemicals, agricultural products. **Major trading partners:** Czech Republic, EU, former Soviet republics, U.S., central and eastern European countries.

Geography Slovakia is located in central Europe. The land has rugged mountains, rich in mineral resources, with vast forests and pastures. The Carpathian Mountains dominate the topography of Slovakia, with lowland areas in the southern region. Slovakia is about twice the size of the state of Maryland.

Government Parliamentary democracy.

History Present-day Slovakia was settled by Slavic Slovaks about the 6th century C.E. They were politically united in the Moravian empire in the 9th century. In 907, the Germans and the Magyars conquered the Moravian state and the Slovaks fell under Hungarian control from the 10th century up until 1918. When the Hapsburg-ruled empire collapsed in 1918 following World War I, the Slovaks joined the Czech lands of Bohemia, Moravia, and part of Silesia to form the new joint state of Czechoslovakia. In March 1939, Germany occupied Czechoslovakia, established a German "protectorate," and created a puppet state out of Slovakia with Monsignor Josef Tiso as premier. The country was liberated from the Germans by the Soviet army in the spring of 1945, and Slovakia was restored to its prewar status and rejoined to a new Czechoslovakian state.

After the Communist Party took power in Feb. 1948, Slovakia was again subjected to a centralized Czech-dominated government and antagonism between the two republics developed. On Jan. 1, 1969, the nation became the Slovak Socialist Republic of Czechoslovakia.

Nearly 42 years of Communist rule for Slovakia ended when Vaclav Havel became president of Czechoslovakia in 1989 and democratic political reform began. However, with the demise of Communist power, a strong Slovak nationalist movement resurfaced and the rival relationship between the two states increased. By the end of 1991, discussions between Slovak and Czech political leaders turned to whether the Czech and Slovak republics should continue to coexist within the federal structure or be divided into two independent states.

After the general election in June 1992, it was decided that two fully independent republics would be created. The Republic of Slovakia came into existence on Jan. 1, 1993. The Parliament in Feb. elected Michal Kovac as president.

Vladimir Meciar, who served three times as Slovakia's prime minister, exhibited increasingly authoritarian behavior, and was cited as the reason Slovakia was eliminated from consideration for both the EU and NATO. A referendum in May 1997 on whether the country should join NATO was boycotted by 90% of the electorate after it turned into a showdown between the prime minister and the president, who wanted a question about direct election of the president placed on the ballot. For more than a year, Slovakia was without a president after Michael Kovac finished his term. Finally, the constitution was changed to allow for direct vote, and Rudolf Schuster was elected in May 1999. Prime Minister Meciar, in the meantime, was defeated as prime minister.

Slovenia

REPUBLIC OF SLOVENIA
President: Milan Kucan (1990)
Prime Minister: Janez Drnovsek (1992)
Area: 7,819 sq. mi. (20,256 sq. km)
Population (1999 est.): 1,970,570 (average annual rate of natural increase: –0.07%); birth rate: 9.0/1000; infant mortality rate: 5.3/1000; density per sq. mi.: 252
Capital and largest city (1996 est.): Ljubljana, 330,000. **Other large city:** Maribor, 103,512. **Monetary unit:** Slovenian tolar. **Languages:** Slovenian; most can also speak Serbo-Croatian. **Ethnicity/race:** Slovene 91%, Serbo-Croation, 6%; other, 3%. **Religions:** Roman Catholic 70.8% (including 2% Uniate), Lutheran 1%, Muslim 1%, other 27.2%. **Literacy rate:** 99%
Economic summary: GDP/PPP (1997 est.): $19.5 billion; $10,000 per capita. **Real growth rate:** 3.25%. **Inflation:** 9.7% (1996). **Unemployment:** 7.1%. **Arable land:** 12%. **Industry:** ferrous metallurgy, rolling mill products, aluminum reduction and rolled products, lead and zinc smelting, electronics, trucks, electric power equipment, wood products, textiles, chemicals, machine tools. **Labor force:** 857,400; services, 62%; industry, 36%; agriculture, 2%. **Agriculture:** potatoes, hops, wheat, sugar beets, corn, grapes, cattle, sheep, poultry. **Manufactured products:** automobiles, iron and steel, cement, chemicals, textiles, furniture, shoes, electrical machinery, pharmaceuticals. **Exports:** $8.3 billion (f.o.b., 1996): machinery and transport equipment, other manufactured goods, chemicals, food. **Imports:** $9.5 billion (f.o.b., 1996): machinery and transport equipment, other manufactured goods, chemicals, fuels, lubricants. **Major trading partners:** EU, former Yugoslav republics, U.S.

Geography Slovenia occupies an area about the size of the state of Massachusetts. It is largely a mountainous republic and almost half of the land is forested, with hilly plains spread across the central and eastern regions. Mount Triglav, the highest peak, rises to 9,393 ft. (2,864 m).

Government Parliamentary democracy.

History Slovenia was originally settled by Illyrian and Celtic peoples. It became part of the Roman empire in the first century B.C.E.

The Slovenes were a south Slavic group that settled in the region during the 6th century C.E. During the 7th century, the Slavs established the Slavic state of Samu, which owed its allegiance to the Avars, who dominated the Hungarian plain until Charlemagne defeated them in the late 8th century.

In the 11th century, Slovenia was a separate province of the kingdom of Hungary. When the Hungarians were defeated by the Turks in 1526, Hungary accepted Austrian Hapsburg rule in order to escape Turkish domination. Thus, Slovenia and Croatia became part of the Austro-Hungarian kingdom when the dual-monarchy was established in 1857. Like Croatia and unlike the other Balkan states, it is primarily Roman Catholic.

Following the defeat and collapse of Austria-Hungary in World War I, Slovenia declared its independence. It formally joined with Montenegro, Serbia, and Croatia on Dec. 4, 1918, to form the new nation called the Kingdom of the Serbs, Croats, and Slovenes. The name was later changed to Yugoslavia in 1929.

During World War II, Germany occupied Yugoslavia and Slovenia was divided among Germany, Italy, and Hungary. For the duration of the war many Slovenes fought a guerrilla war against the Nazis under the leadership of the Croatian-born Communist resistance leader, Marshal Tito. After the final defeat of the Axis powers in 1945, Slovenia was again made into a republic of the newly established Communist nation of Yugoslavia.

In the 1980s, Slovenia agitated for greater autonomy and occasionally threatened to secede. It introduced a multiparty system and in 1990 elected a non-communist government. Slovenia declared its independence from Yugoslavia on June 25, 1991. The Serbian-dominated Yugoslavian army tried to keep Slovenia in line and some brief fighting took place, but the army then withdrew its forces. Unlike Croatia and Bosnia, Slovenia was able to sever itself from Yugoslavia with relatively little violence. With recognition of its independence granted by the European Community in 1992, the country began realigning its economy and society toward western Europe.

Solomon Islands

Sovereign: Queen Elizabeth II (1952)
Governor-General: John Lapli (1999)
Prime Minister: Bartholomew Ulufa'alu (1997)
Area: 11,500 sq. mi. (28,450 sq. km)
Population (1999 est.): 455,429 (average annual rate of natural increase: 3.18%); birth rate: 35.9/1000; Infant mortality rate: 23.0/1000; density per sq. mi.: 40
Capital and largest city (1990 est.): Honiara (on Guadalcanal), 35,288. **Monetary unit:** Solomon Islands dollar. **Languages:** English, Solomon Pijin (an English pidgin), over 60 indigenous Melanesian languages. **Ethnicity/race:** Melanesian 93%, Polynesian 4%, Micronesian 1.5%, European 0.8%, Chinese 0.3%, other 0.4%. **Religions:** Anglican; Roman Catholic; South Seas Evangelical; Seventh-Day Adventist, United (Methodist) Church, other Protestant. **Literacy rate:** 30%
Economic summary: GDP/PPP (1997 est.): $1.27 billion; $3,000 per capita. **Real growth rate:** 3.5%. **Inflation:** 11.8% (1996). **Unemployment:** n.a. **Arable land:** 1%. **Agriculture:** coconuts, palm oil, rice, cocoa, yams, pigs, vegetables, cattle, timber, fish, beans, potatoes. **Labor force:** 26,842; agriculture, forestry, fishing, 23.7%; services, 41.5%; commerce, transport and finance, 21.7%; construction, manufacturing and mining, 13.1% (1992 est.). **Industry:** processed fish, copra. **Natural resources:** fish, timber, gold, bauxite. **Exports:** $168 million (f.o.b., 1995): cocoa, fish, timber, copra, palm oil. **Imports:** $152 million (c.i.f., 1995 est.): machinery and transport equipment, foodstuffs, fuel, live animals, manufactured goods. **Major trading partners:** Japan, EU, Australia, Thailand, Singapore, Hong Kong, China. **Member of British Commonwealth**

Geography A scattered archipelago of mountainous islands and low-lying coral atolls, the Solomon Islands lie east of Papua New Guinea and northeast of Australia in the south Pacific. The islands include: Guadalcanal, Malaita, Santa Isabel, San Cristóbal, Choiseul, New Georgia, Santa Cruz group, and numerous smaller islands.

Government Parliamentary monarchy.

History It is thought that people have lived in the Solomon Islands since at least 2000 B.C.E. Explored in 1568 by Alvaro de Mendana of Spain, the Solomons were not visited again for about 200 years. In 1886, Great Britain and Germany divided the islands between them, but later Britain was given control of the entire territory. The Japanese invaded the islands in World War II, and they became the scene of some of the bloodiest battles in the Pacific theater, most famously, the battle of Guadalcanal. The British gained control of the Solomons again in 1945.

In 1976 the islands became self-governing, and in 1978 they gained independence. The border with Papua New Guinea (PNG) remained a source of tension in the 1990s. Incursions into Solomon Islands territory by PNG forces, who were countering secessionist action on neighboring Bougainville Island, gave rise to formal protests in mid-1997.

Somalia

SOMALI DEMOCRATIC REPUBLIC

National name: Al Jumhouriya As-Somalya al-Dimocradia
President: Vacant, no functioning government in place
Prime Minister: Vacant
Area: 246,199 sq. mi. (637,660 sq. km)
Population (1999 est.): 7,140,643 (average annual rate of natural increase: 2.94%); birth rate: 48.0/1000; infant mortality rate: 125.8/1000; density per sq. mi.: 29
Capital and largest city (1990 est.): Mogadishu, 900,000. **Monetary unit:** Somali shilling. **Languages:** Somali (official), Arabic, English, Italian. **Ethnicity/ race:** Somali 85%, Bantu, Arabs. **Religion:** Islam (Sunni). **Literacy rate:** 24%
Economic summary: Political turmoil in 1991–92 resulted in widespread famine and a substantial drop in economic output. Much of the economy has been devastated by the civil war. Agriculture is most important sector with livestock accounting for about 40% of GDP and about 65% of export earnings. **GDP/PPP** (1996 est.): $8 billion; $600 per capita. **Real growth rate:** 4%. **Inflation:** n.a. **Unemployment:** n.a. **Arable land:** 2%. **Agriculture:** livestock, bananas, sorghum, cereals, sugar cane, maize, sesame seeds, beans. **Labor force:** 3.7 million (1993 est.); very few are skilled laborers; agriculture, 71%; industry and services, 29%. **Natural resources:** uranium. **Exports:** $130 million (1994 est.): livestock, skins and hides, bananas. **Imports:** $269 million (1994 est.): textiles, foodstuffs, construction materials and equipment, petroleum products. **Major trading partners:** Saudi Arabia, Italy, U.S., U.K., Germany.

Geography Somalia, situated in the Horn of Africa, lies along the Gulf of Aden and the Indian Ocean. It is bounded by Djibouti in the northwest, Ethiopia in the west, and Kenya in the southwest. In area it is slightly smaller than Texas. Generally arid and barren, Somalia has two chief rivers, the Shebelle and the Juba.

Government None. Last president was overthrown in Jan. 1991; since then Somalia has been plunged into anarchy.

History From the 7th to the 10th century, Arab and Persian trading posts were established along the coast of present-day Somalia. Nomadic tribes occupied the interior, occasionally pushing into Ethiopian territory. In the 16th century, Turkish rule extended to the northern coast and the Sultans of Zanzibar gained control in the south.

After British occupation of Aden in 1839, the Somali coast became its source of food. The French established a coal mining station in 1862 at the site of Djibouti and the Italians planted a settlement in Eritrea. Egypt, which for a time claimed Turkish rights in the area, was succeeded by Britain. By 1920, a British protectorate and an Italian protectorate occupied what is now Somalia. The British ruled the entire area after 1941, with Italy returning in 1950 to serve as United Nations trustee for its former territory.

By 1960, Britain and Italy granted independence to their respective sectors, enabling the two to join as the Republic of Somalia on July 1, 1960. Somalia broke diplomatic relations with Britain in 1963 when the British granted the Somali-populated Northern Frontier District of Kenya to the Republic of Kenya.

On Oct. 15, 1969, President Abdi Rashid Ali Shermarke was assassinated and the army seized power, dissolving the legislature and arresting all government leaders. Maj. Gen. Mohamed Siad Barre, as president of a renamed Somali Democratic Republic, leaned heavily toward the U.S.S.R. In 1977, Somalia openly backed rebels in the easternmost area of Ethiopia, the Ogaden Desert, which had been seized by Ethiopia at the turn of the century. Somalia acknowledged defeat in an eight-month war against the Ethiopians that year, having lost much of its 32,000-man army and most of its tanks and planes. President Siad Barre fled the country in late Jan. 1991. His departure left Somalia in the hands of a number of clan-based guerrilla groups, none of which trusted each other.

Africa's worst drought occurred in 1992, and coupled with the devastation of civil war, Somalia was plunged into a severe famine—an estimated one-third of the population was in danger of dying from starvation. U.S. troops were sent in to protect the delivery of food in Dec. 1992. In May the U.N. took control of the relief efforts from the U.S. The warlord Mohamed Farah Aidid ambushed U.N. troops and dragged American bodies through the streets, causing an about-face in America's willingness to involve itself in the fate of this anarchic country. Peace talks in Kenya appeared to be moving slowly but steadily toward an agreement on an interim government, at least in principle, when on March 23, 1994, they collapsed. The last of the U.S. troops left in late March, leaving 19,000 U.N. troops behind.

Since 1991 Somalia has been engulfed in anarchy. Over the past seven years peace negotiations between the various factions have been fruitless, and no attempt has been made to rebuild the government. In 1991, a breakaway nation, the Somaliland Republic, proclaimed its independence. Since then several warlords have begun to set up their own ministates—Colonel Abdullahi Yussuf Ahmed is president of breakaway Puntland and Mohamed "General Morgan" Said Hersi began setting up Jubaland in the fall of 1998.

In 1999, Somali warlord Hussein Mohamed Aidid allied himself with Eritrea in the war between Ethiopia and Eritrea, which caused the conflict to move onto Somalian territory.

South Africa

REPUBLIC OF SOUTH AFRICA
National name: Republic of South Africa
President: Thabo Mbeki (1999)
Area: 471,440 sq. mi. (1,219,912 sq. km)
Population (1999 est.): 43,426,386 (average annual rate of natural increase: 1.31%); birth rate: 25.9/1000; infant mortality rate: 52.0/1000; density per sq. mi.: 92
Administrative capital: Pretoria
Legislative capital: Cape Town
Judicial capital: Bloemfontein. No decision has been made to relocate the seat of government. South Africa is demarcated into nine provinces, consisting of the Gauteng, Northern Province, Mpumalanga, North West, KwaZulu/Natal, Eastern Cape, Western Cape, Northern Cape, and Free State. Each province has its own capital. **Largest metropolitan areas (1995):** Cape Peninsula, 2,350,157; Johannesburg 1,916,063; East Rand, 1,378,792; Durban/Pinetown, 1,137,378; Pretoria, 1,080,187. **Monetary unit:** Rand.
Languages: English, Afrikaans, Ndebele, Sesotho sa Leboa, Sesotho, Swati, Xitsonga, Setswana, Tshivenda, Xhosa and Zulu are the official languages of the interim period. **Ethnicity/race:** black 75.2%, white 13.6%, Colored 8.6%, Indian 2.6%. **Religions:** Christian; Hindu; Islam. **Literacy rate:** 76%
Economic summary: GDP/PPP (1997 est.): $270 billion; $6,200 per capita. **Real growth rate:** 3%. **Inflation:** 9.7%. **Unemployment:** 30%, plus 11% underemployed. **Arable land:** 10%. **Agriculture:** corn, wool, wheat, sugarcane, fruits, vegetables, beef, poultry, mutton. **Labor force:** 14.2 million economically active (1996); by occupation: services, 35%, agriculture, 30%, industry, 20%, mining, 9%, other, 6%. **Industry:** gold, chromium, diamonds, assembled automobiles, machinery, textiles, iron and steel, chemicals, fertilizer, metalworking, food stuffs. **Natural resources:** gold, diamonds, platinum, uranium, coal, iron ore, phosphates, manganese. **Exports:** $31.3 billion (f.o.b., 1997): gold, diamonds, minerals and metals, food, chemicals. **Imports:** $28 billion (f.o.b., 1997): transport equipment, machinery, metals, chemicals, textiles, scientific instruments. **Major trading partners:** Germany, U.S., other EU, Japan, U.K., Hong Kong, Taiwan.

Geography South Africa, on the continent's southern tip, is washed by the Atlantic Ocean on the west and by the Indian Ocean on the south and east. Its neighbors are Namibia in the northwest, Zimbabwe and Botswana in the north, and Mozambique and Swaziland in the northeast. The kingdom of Lesotho forms an enclave within the southeastern part of South Africa. Bophuthatswana, Transkei, Ciskei, and Venda are independent states within South Africa, which occupies an area nearly three times that of California.

The southernmost point of Africa is Cape Agulhas, located in the Western Cape Province about 100 miles (161 km) southeast of the Cape of Good Hope.

Government Republic.

History The San people were the first settlers. The Dutch East India Company landed the first European settlers on the Cape of Good Hope in 1652, launching a colony that by the end of the 18th century numbered only about 15,000. Known as Boers or Afrikaners, speaking a Dutch dialect known as Afrikaans, the settlers as early as 1795 tried to establish an independent republic.

After occupying the Cape Colony in that year, Britain took permanent possession in 1814 at the end of the Napoleonic Wars, bringing in 5,000 settlers. Anglicization of government and the freeing of slaves in 1833 drove about 12,000 Afrikaners to make the "great trek" north and east into African tribal territory, where they established the republics of the Transvaal and the Orange Free State.

The discovery of diamonds in 1867 and gold nine years later brought an influx of "outlanders" into the republics and spurred Cecil Rhodes to plot annexation. Rhodes's scheme of sparking an "outlander" rebellion to which an armed party under Leander Starr Jameson would ride to the rescue misfired in 1895, forcing Rhodes to resign as prime minister of the Cape colony. What British expansionists called the "inevitable" war with the Boers eventually broke out on Oct. 11, 1899. The defeat of the Boers in 1902 led in 1910 to the Union of South Africa, composed of four provinces, the two former republics, and the old Cape and Natal colonies. Louis Botha, a Boer, became the first prime minister. Organized political activity among Africans started with the establishment of the African National Congress in 1912.

Jan Christiaan Smuts brought the nation into World War II on the Allied side against Nationalist opposition, and South Africa became a charter member of the United Nations in 1945, but refused to sign the Universal Declaration of Human Rights. Apartheid—racial separation—dominated domestic politics as the Nationalists gained power and imposed greater restrictions on Bantus, Asians, and Coloreds (in South Africa the term meant any nonwhite person). African voters were removed from the voter rolls in 1936.

Afrikaner hostility to Britain triumphed in 1961 with the declaration on May 31 of the Republic of South Africa and the severing of ties with the Commonwealth. Nationalist prime minister H. F. Verwoerd's government in 1963 asserted the power to restrict the freedom of those who opposed rigid racial laws. Three years later, amid increasing racial tension and criticism from the outside world, Verwoerd was assassinated. His Nationalist successor, Balthazar J. Vorster, launched a campaign of conciliation toward conservative black African states, offering development loans and trade concessions.

Elections on May 7, 1987, increased the power of President Botha's Nationalist Party while enabling the far-right Conservative Party to replace the liberal Progressives as the official opposition. The results of the whites-only vote indicated a strong conservative reaction against Botha's policy of limited reform.

A stroke led Botha to step down as leader of his party in 1989 in favor of F. W. de Klerk. De Klerk accelerated the pace of reform. He removed the ban from the African National Congress, the principal anti-apartheid organization, and released Nelson Mandela, the ANC deputy president, after 27 years of imprisonment. Negotiations between the government and the ANC commenced.

On June 5, 1991, the Parliament scrapped the country's apartheid laws concerning property ownership. On June 17 the Parliament did the same for the Population Registration Act of 1950, which classified all South Africans at birth by race. In Feb. 1993 the ANC approved a plan that would allow minority parties to participate in the government for five years after the end of white rule. Also in Feb., the first nonwhites entered the cabinet in an apparent bid to broaden the base of the ruling National Party.

The 1994 election, as expected, resulted in a massive victory for Mandela and his ANC. The new government included six ministers from the National Party and three from the Inkatha Freedom Party.

In 1997 the Truth and Reconciliation Commission, chaired by Desmond Tutu, began hearings regarding human rights violations between 1960 and 1993. The commission promised amnesty to those who confessed their crimes under the apartheid system. In 1998 F. W. de Klerk, P. W. Botha, and leaders of the ANC appeared before the commission, and the nation continued to grapple with its enlightened but often painful and divisive process of national recovery.

Nelson Mandela, whose term as president cemented his reputation as one of the world's most enlightened statesmen, retired in 1999. On June 2, 1999, Thabo Mbeki, the pragmatic deputy president of South Africa and leader of the African National Congress, was elected president in a landslide, having already assumed many of Mandela's governing responsibilities.

Spain

KINGDOM OF SPAIN

National name: Reino de España
Ruler: King Juan Carlos I (1975)
Prime Minister: José María Aznar (1996)
Area: 195,364.5 sq. mi. (504,750 sq. km)[1]
Population (1999 est.): 39,167,744 (average annual growth rate: 0.03%); birth rate: 10.0/1000; infant mortality rate: 6.4/1000; density per sq. mi.: 201
Capital and largest city (1995 est.): Madrid, 2,947,228. **Other large cities:** Barcelona, 1,630,867; Valencia, 764,293; Seville, 714,148. **Monetary units:** Peseta and euro. **Languages:** Castilian Spanish 74%, Catalan 17%, Galician 7%, Basque 2%. **Ethnicity/ race:** composite of Mediterranean and Nordic types. **Religion:** Roman Catholic, 99%. **Literacy rate:** 95%
Economic summary: GDP/PPP (1997 est.): $642.4 billion; $16,400 per capita. **Real growth rate:** 3.3%. **Inflation:** 2.1%. **Unemployment:** (1997 est.), 21%. **Arable land:** 30%. **Agriculture:** grain, vegetables, olives, wine grapes, sugar beets, citrus, beef, pork, poultry, dairy products, fish. **Labor force:** 16.2 million; services, 64%; manufacturing, mining, and construction, 28%; agriculture, 8% (1997). **Industry:** processed foods, textiles, footwear, petro-chemicals, steel, automobiles, ships, machine tools, tourism. **Natural resources:** coal, lignite, water power, uranium, mercury, pyrites, fluorospar, gypsum, iron ore, zinc, lead, tungsten, copper. **Exports:** $94.5 billion (f.o.b., 1995): cars and trucks, semifinished manufactured goods, foodstuffs, machinery and electrical equipment. **Imports:** $118.3 billion (c.i.f., 1995): machinery and transportation equipment, chemicals, petroleum, semifinished goods, consumer goods, machines and electrical equipment. **Major trading partners:** EU, U.S.

1. Including the Balearic and Canary Islands.

Geography Spain occupies 85% of the Iberian Peninsula, which it shares with Portugal, in southwestern Europe. Africa is less than 10 miles (16 km) south at the Strait of Gibraltar. A broad central plateau slopes to the south and east, crossed by a series of mountain ranges and river valleys. Principal rivers are the Ebro in the northeast, the Tajo in the central region, and the Guadalquivir in the south. Off Spain's east coast in the Mediterranean are the Balearic Islands (1,936 sq. mi.; 5,014 sq. km), the largest of which is Majorca. Sixty miles (97 km) west of Africa are the Canary Islands (2,808 sq. mi.; 7,273 sq. km).

Government Parliamentary monarchy.

History Spain, originally inhabited by Celts, Iberians, and Basques, became a part of the Roman Empire in 206 B.C.E., when it was conquered by Scipio Africanus. In C.E. 412, the barbarian Visigothic leader Ataulf crossed the Pyrenees and ruled Spain, first in the name of the Roman emperor and then independently. In 711, the Muslims under Tariq entered Spain from Africa and within a few years completed the subjugation of the country. In 732, the Franks, led by Charles Martel, defeated the Muslims near Poitiers, thus preventing the further expansion of Islam in southern Europe. Internal dissension of Spanish Islam invited a steady Christian conquest from the north.

Aragon and Castile were the most important Spanish states from the 12th to the 15th century, consolidated by the marriage of Ferdinand II and Isabella I in 1469. The last Muslim stronghold, Granada, was captured in 1492. Roman Catholicism was established as the official state religion and most Jews (1492) and Muslims (1502) were expelled. In the era of exploration, discovery, and colonization, Spain amassed tremendous wealth and a vast colonial empire through the conquest of Peru by Pizarro (1532–33) and of Mexico by Cortés (1519–21). The Spanish Hapsburg monarchy became for a time the most powerful in the world. In 1588, Philip II sent his invincible Armada to invade England, but its destruction cost Spain its supremacy on the seas and paved the way for England's colonization of America. Spain then sank rapidly to the status of a second-rate power under the rule of weak Hapsburg kings, and never again played a major role in European politics. The War of the Spanish Succession (1701–14) resulted in Spain's loss of Belgium, Luxembourg, Milan, Sardinia, and Naples. Its colonial empire in the Americas and the Philippines vanished in wars and revolutions during the 18th and 19th centuries.

In World War I, Spain maintained a position of neutrality. In 1923, Gen. Miguel Primo de Rivera became dictator. In 1930, King Alfonso XIII revoked the dictatorship, but a strong antimonarchist and republican movement led to his leaving Spain in 1931. The new constitution declared Spain a workers' republic, broke up the large estates, separated church and state, and secularized the schools. The elections held in 1936 returned a strong Popular Front majority, with Manuel Azaña as president.

On July 18, 1936, a conservative army officer in Morocco, Francisco Franco Bahamonde, led a mutiny against the government. The civil war that followed lasted three years and cost the lives of nearly a million people. Franco was aided by Fascist Italy and Nazi Germany, while Soviet Russia helped the Loyalist side. Several hundred leftist Americans served in the Abraham Lincoln Brigade on the side of the republic. The war ended when Franco took

Madrid on March 28, 1939. Franco became head of the state, national chief of the Falange Party (the governing party), and premier and caudillo (leader). In a referendum in 1947, the Spanish people approved a Franco-drafted succession law declaring Spain a monarchy again. Franco, however, continued as chief of state.

In 1969, Franco and the Cortes designated Prince Juan Carlos Alfonso Víctor María de Borbón (who married Princess Sophia of Greece on May 14, 1962) to become king of Spain when the provisional government headed by Franco came to an end. Franco died of a heart attack on Nov. 20, 1975, after more than a year of ill health, and Juan Carlos was proclaimed king seven days later.

Under pressure from Catalonian and Basque nationalists, Premier Adolfo Suárez granted home rule to these regions in 1979. Basque separatists committed hundreds of terrorist bombings and kidnappings that continue to the present. With the overwhelming election of Prime Minister Felipe González Márquez and his Spanish Socialist Workers Party in the Oct. 20, 1982, parliamentary elections, the Franco past was finally buried.

Spain entered NATO in 1982. A treaty admitting Spain, along with Portugal, to the European Economic Community, now the European Union, took effect on Jan. 1, 1986. Later that year, Spain voted to remain in NATO, but outside of its military command. General elections in March 1996 produced a victory for the conservative Popular Party, which, although lacking an absolute majority in the Cortes, received the backing of regional parties for a coalition government with Aznar as prime minister.

On Oct. 16, 1998, Spain issued a warrant for the extradition of former Chilean dictator Augusto Pinochet, charging him with the genocide, torture, and kidnapping of thousands of people, including Spanish nationals, during his 17-year rule. While the extradition was contested, Pinochet remained under house arrest in England, where had been receiving medical treatment at the time of his arrest.

Sri Lanka

DEMOCRATIC SOCIALIST REPUBLIC OF SRI LANKA

President: Chandrika B. Kumaratunga (1994)
Prime Minister: Sirimavo Bandaranaike (1994)
Area: 25,332 sq. mi. (65,610 sq. km)
Population (1999 est.): 19,144,875 (average annual rate of natural increase: 1.21%); birth rate: 18.2/1000; infant mortality rate: 16.1/1000; density per sq. mi.: 756
Capital and largest city (1992 est.): Sri Jayewardenepura Kotte (Colombo), 1,994,000. **Other large cities (1992 est.):** Gampaha, 1,543,000; Kurunegala, 1,445,000; Kandy, 1,257,000. **Monetary unit:** Sri Lanka rupee. **Languages:** Sinhala, Tamil, English. **Ethnicity/race:** Sinhalese 74%, Tamil 18%, Moor 7%, Burgher, Malay, and Vedda 1%. **Religions:** Buddhist, 69%; Hindu, 15%; Islam, 8%; Christian, 8%. **Literacy rate:** 88%
Economic summary: GDP/PPP (1997 est.): $72.1 billion; $3,800 per capita. **Real growth rate:** 6%. **Inflation:** (1997), 9.6%. **Unemployment:** (1997 est.), 11%. **Arable land:** 14%. **Agriculture:** rice, sugarcane, grains, oilseed, roots, spices, tea, rubber, coconuts, milk, eggs, hides, meat. **Labor force:** 6.2 million (1997); agriculture. 37%; services, 46%; industry, 17%

(1994). **Industry:** processed rubber, tea, coconuts, textiles, cement, refined petroleum, tobacco. **Natural resources:** limestone, graphite, gems. **Exports:** $4.1 billion (f.o.b., 1996): textiles, tea, rubber, petroleum products, gems and jewelry. **Imports:** $5.4 billion (c.i.f., 1996): machinery and equipment, textiles, transport equipment, petroleum, building materials, sugar, wheat. **Major trading partners:** U.S., U.K., Germany, Japan, Singapore, India, Iran, Taiwan, Belgium, Hong Kong, China, South Korea. **Member of Commonwealth of Nations**

Geography An island in the Indian Ocean off the southeast tip of India, Sri Lanka is about half the size of Alabama. Most of the land is flat and rolling; mountains in the south-central region rise to over 8,000 feet (2,438 m).

Government Republic.

History Indo-Aryan emigration from India in the 5th century B.C.E. came to form the largest ethnic group on Sri Lanka today, the Sinhalese. Tamils, the second-largest ethnic group on the island, were originally from the Tamil region of India, and emigrated between the 3rd century B.C.E. and C.E. 1200. Until colonial powers controlled Ceylon (the country's name until 1972), Sinhalese and Tamil rulers fought for dominance over the island. The Tamils, primarily Hindus, claimed the northern section of the island and the Sinhalese, who are predominantly Buddhist, controlled the south. In 1505 the Portuguese took possession of Ceylon until the Dutch India Company usurped control (1658–1796). The British took over in 1796, and Ceylon became an English crown colony in 1802. The British developed coffee, tea, and rubber plantations. On Feb. 4, 1948, after pressure from Ceylonese nationalist leaders (which briefly unified the Tamil and Sinhalese), Ceylon became a self-governing dominion of the Commonwealth of Nations.

S. W. R. D. Bandaranaike became prime minister in 1956 and championed Sinhalese nationalism, making Sinhala the country's only official language and including state support of Buddhism, further marginalizing the Tamil minority. He was assassinated in 1959 by a Buddhist monk. His widow, Sirimavo Bandaranaike, became the world's first female prime minister in 1960. The name *Ceylon* was changed to Sri Lanka on May 22, 1972, which was its original name and means "resplendent island."

The Tamil minority's mounting resentment toward the Sinhalese majority's monopoly on political and economic power, exacerbated by cultural and religious differences, erupted in bloody violence in 1983. The civil war continues today. Tamils make up about 18% of the population in Sri Lanka, whereas approximately three-quarters of Sri Lanka's 18 million people are Sinhalese. Tamil rebel groups, the strongest of which are the Liberation Tigers of Tamil Eelam, or Tamil Tigers, are fighting for a separate nation.

India had sent a peacekeeping force in July 1987 to help maintain an accord granting the Tamil minority limited autonomy. The agreement failed, and Indian troops withdrew at the end of 1989.

President Ranasinghe Premadasa was assassinated at a May Day political rally in 1993 when a Tamil rebel detonated explosives strapped to himself.

Tamil extremists have frequently resorted to terrorist attacks against civilians. The civil war continues unabated and the president has extended the state of emergency to the entire country.

Sudan

REPUBLIC OF THE SUDAN

National name: Jamhuryat es-Sudan
President: Lt. Gen. Omar Hassan Ahmad al-Bashir (1993)
Area: 967,491 sq. mi. (2,505,810 sq. km)
Population (1999 est.): 34,475,690 (average annual rate of natural increase: 2.87%); birth rate: 39.3/1000; infant mortality rate: 70.9/1000; density per sq. mi.: 36
Capital (1993 est.): Khartoum, 924,505. **Largest cities:** Omdurman, 1,267,077; Port Sudan, 305,385.
Monetary unit: Sudanese pound. **Languages:** Arabic, English, tribal dialects. **Ethnicity/race:** black 52%, Arab 39%, Beja 6%, foreigners 2%, other 1%.
Religions: Islam, 70% (Sunni); indigenous, 20%; Christian, 5%. **Literacy rate:** 27%
Economic summary: GDP/PPP (1997 est.): $26.6 billion; $875 per capita. **Real growth rate:** 5%. **Inflation:** 27%. **Unemployment:** 30% (FY 92/93 est.). **Arable land:** 5%. **Agriculture:** cotton, oil seeds, gum arabic, sorghum, wheat, millet, sheep. **Labor force:** 11 million; agriculture, 80%; industry and commerce, 10%; government, 6% (note: labor shortages for almost all categories of skilled employment) (1983 est.). **Industry:** cotton ginning, textiles, cement, edible oils, sugar, soap distilling, shoes, petroleum refining. **Natural resources:** crude oil, some iron ore, copper, chrome, industrial metals. **Exports:** $620 million (f.o.b., 1996): cotton, livestock, meat, gum arabic. **Imports:** $1.5 billion (1996): petroleum products, machinery and equipment, medicines, textiles, manufactured goods, chemicals. **Major trading partners:** Western Europe, Saudi Arabia, eastern Europe, Japan.

Geography The Sudan, in northeast Africa, is the largest country on the continent, measuring about one-fourth the size of the United States. Its neighbors are Chad and the Central African Republic on the west, Egypt and Libya on the north, Ethiopia and Eritrea on the east, and Kenya, Uganda, and Congo on the south. The Red Sea washes about 500 miles of the eastern coast. It is traversed from north to south by the Nile, all of whose great tributaries are partly or entirely within its borders.

Government Military government. Headed by President Omar Hassan Ahmad al-Bashir, the de facto ruler of the country is Hassan el-Turabi, a cleric and political leader who is a major figure in the pan-Arabic Islamic fundamental resurgence.

History What is now northern Sudan was in ancient times the kingdom of Nubia, which came under Egyptian rule after 2600 B.C.E. An Egyptian and Nubian civilization called Kush flourished until C.E. 350. Missionaries converted the region to Christianity in the 6th century, but an influx of Muslim Arabs, who had already conquered Egypt, eventually controlled the area and replaced Christianity with Islam. During the 1500s a people called the Funj conquered much of Sudan, and several other black African groups settled in the south, including the Dinka, Shilluk, Nuer, and Azande. Egyptians again conquered the Sudan in 1874, and after Britain occupied Egypt in 1882, it took over Sudan in 1898, ruling the country in conjunction with Egypt. It was known as the Anglo-Egyptian Sudan between 1898 and 1955.

The 20th century saw the growth of Sudanese nationalism, and in 1953 Egypt and Britain granted the Sudan self-government. Independence was proclaimed on Jan. 1, 1956. Since independence, the Sudan has been ruled by a series of unstable parliamentary governments and military regimes. Under Maj. Gen. Gaafar Mohamed Nimeiri, the Sudan instituted fundamentalist Islamic law in 1983. This exacerbated the rift between the Arab North, the seat of the government, and the black African animists and Christians in the South. Differences in language, religion, ethnicity, and political power erupted in an unending civil war between government forces, strongly influenced by the National Islamic Front (NIF), and the southern rebels, whose most influential faction is the Sudanese People's Liberation Army. Neither side has gained the upper hand, and more than an estimated 1 million people have died in battle or from famines and disease resulting from war. Human rights violations, religious persecution, and allegations that the Sudan has been a safe haven for terrorists have isolated the country from most of the international community.

On Aug. 20, 1998, the United States launched cruise missiles that destroyed a pharmaceutical manufacturing facility in Khartoum that allegedly manufactured chemical weapons. Sudan has close ties with Iraq, which has thwarted the U.N. inspections of its weapons stockpiles that are thought to include biological weapons. The U.S. contended that the Sudanese factory was financed by the wealthy Islamic militant, Osama bin Laden.

In 1999 international attention has been focused on evidence that slavery is widespread throughout Sudan. Arab raiders from the north of the country have enslaved thousands of southerners, who are black. The Dinka people have been the hardest hit. Some sources point out that the raids intensified in the 1980s along with the civil war between north and south. Since the early 1990s, several international human rights organizations have engaged in the controversial practice of buying back slaves from the traders. Some contend this may inadvertently encourage slavery since slave redemption has become profitable. The anti-slavery organizations counter that in the absence of a political solution, buying back slaves is the only hope for thousands of Sudanese.

Suriname

REPUBLIC OF SURINAME

President: Jules Wijdenbosch (1996)
Prime Minister: Pretaapnarian Radhakishun (1996)
Area: 63,251 sq. mi. (163,270 sq. km)
Population (1999 est.): 431,156 (average annual rate of natural increase: 1.60%); birth rate: 21.8/1000; infant mortality rate: 26.5/1000; density per sq. mi.: 7
Capital and largest city (1993 est.): Paramaribo, 200,970. **Monetary unit:** Suriname guilder.
Languages: Dutch, Surinamese (lingua franca), English widely spoken. **Ethnicity/race:** Hindustani (also known locally as "East" Indians; their ancestors emigrated from northern India in the latter part of the 19th century) 37%, Creole (mixed European and African ancestry) 31%, Javanese 15.3%, "Bush Black" (also known as "Bush Creole" whose ancestors were

brought to the country in the 17th and 18th centuries as slaves) 10.3%, Amerindian 2.6%, Chinese 1.7%, Europeans 1%, other 1.1%. **Religions:** Protestant, 25.2%; Roman Catholic, 22.8%; Hindu, 27.4%; Islam, 19.6%; indigenous, about 5%. **Literacy rate:** 95% **Economic summary: GDP/PPP** (1997 est.): $1.44 billion; $3,400 per capita. **Real growth rate:** 4%. **Inflation:** 8%. **Unemployment:** 20% **Arable land:** 0%. **Agriculture:** bananas, palm kernels, coconuts, plantains, peanuts, beef, chicken, forest products, shrimp. **Labor force:** n.a. **Industry:** bauxite and gold mining, alumina and aluminum production, lumbering, food processing, fishing. **Natural resources:** bauxite, iron ore, timber, fish, shrimp. **Exports:** $434.3 million (f.o.b, 1996 est.): bauxite, alumina, aluminum, rice, shrimp and fish, bananas. **Imports:** $490 million (f.o.b., 1997 est.): capital equipment, petroleum, cotton, foodstuffs, consumer goods. **Major trading partners:** U.S., Trinidad, Netherlands, Norway, Germany, Brazil, U.K., Japan, Netherlands Antilles.

Geography Suriname lies on the northeast coast of South America, with Guyana to the west, French Guiana to the east, and Brazil to the south. It is about one-tenth larger than Michigan. The principal rivers are the Corantijn on the Guyana border, the Marowijne in the east, and the Suriname, on which the capital city of Paramaribo is situated.

Government Republic.

History Suriname's earliest inhabitants were the Surinen Indians, after whom the country is named. By the 16th century they had been supplanted by other South American Indians. Spain explored Suriname in 1593, but by 1602 the Dutch began to settle the land, followed by the English. The English transferred sovereignty to the Dutch in 1667 (the Treaty of Breda) in exchange for New Amsterdam (New York). Colonization was confined to a narrow coastal strip, and until the abolition of slavery in 1863, African slaves furnished the labor for the coffee and sugarcane plantation economy. Escaped African slaves fled into the interior, reconstituted their western African culture and government, and came to be called "Bush Negroes" by the Dutch. After 1870, laborers were imported from British India and the Dutch East Indies.

Known as Dutch Guiana, the colony was integrated into the kingdom of the Netherlands in 1948. Two years later Dutch Guiana was granted full home rule in matters other than foreign affairs and defense. After race rioting over unemployment and inflation, The Netherlands granted Suriname complete independence on Nov. 25, 1975. A coup d'état in 1980 brought military rule. During much of the 1980s Suriname was under the control of Lieut. Col. Dési Bouterse, who in late Dec. 1990 resigned as commander of the armed forces. A guerrilla insurgency by the Jungle Commando (a Bush Negro guerrilla group) furthered disruption in the country, and the instability in the region caused some foreign governments to withhold economic aid. Free elections were held on May 25, 1991, depriving the military of much of its political power. In 1992 a peace treaty was signed between the government and several guerrilla groups. In March 1997, the president announced new economic measures, including eliminating import tariffs on most basic goods coupled with strict price controls. Later that year, The Netherlands declared that it would prosecute the former military dictator of Suriname, Dési Bouterse, for large-scale cocaine trafficking.

In May 1999, a financial crisis prompted more than 20,000 people to protest Jules Wijdenbosch's regime, calling for him to step down. In June, Wijdenbosch responded by pledging that elections would take place no later than May 25, 2000. The next elections in Suriname had been scheduled for 2001.

Swaziland

KINGDOM OF SWAZILAND

Ruler: King Mswati III (1986)
Prime Minister: Barnabas Sibusiso Dlamini (1996)
Area: 6,704 sq. mi. (17,360 sq. km)
Population (1999 est.): 985,335 (average annual rate of natural increase: 1.91%); birth rate: 40.8/1000; infant mortality rate: 101.9/1000; density per sq. mi.: 147
Capital and largest city (1990 est.): Mbabane 47,020.
Monetary unit: Lilangeni. **Languages:** English and Swazi (official). **Ethnicity/race:** African 97%, European 3%. **Religions:** Christian, 60%; indigenous, 40%. **Literacy rate:** 70%
Economic summary: GDP/PPP (1997 est.): $3.9 billion; $3,800 per capita. **Real growth rate:** 3%. **Inflation:** 9.5% (1997). **Unemployment:** 22% (1995 est.). **Arable land:** 11%. **Agriculture:** sugarcane, cotton, maize, tobacco, rice, citrus, pineapple, corn, sorghum, peanuts, cattle, goats, sheep. **Labor force:** 135,000 (1996); 70% in the private sector; 30% in the public sector. **Industry:** mining (coal and asbestos), wood pulp, cotton yarn. **Natural resources:** asbestos, diamonds. **Exports:** $893 million (f.o.b., 1996): soft drink concentrates, sugar, wood pulp, cotton, yarn. **Imports:** $1.1 billion (f.o.b., 1996): machinery, motor vehicles, transport equipment, petroleum products, foodstuffs, chemicals. **Major trading partners:** South Africa, U.K., U.S., EU, Japan. **Member of Commonwealth of Nations**

Geography Swaziland, which is 85% the size of New Jersey, is surrounded by South Africa and Mozambique. The country consists of a high veld in the west and a series of plateaus descending from 6,000 feet (1,829 m) to a low veld of 1,500 feet (457 m).

Government Monarchy.

History Bantu peoples migrated southwest to the area of Mozambique in the 16th century. A number of clans broke away from the main body in the 18th century and settled in Swaziland. In the 19th century these clans organized as a tribe, partly because they were in constant conflict with the Zulu. Their ruler, Mswazi, applied to the British in the 1840s for help against the Zulu. The British and the Transvaal governments guaranteed the independence of Swaziland in 1881.

South Africa held Swaziland as a protectorate from 1894 to 1899, but after the Boer War, in 1902, Swaziland was transferred to British administration. The paramount chief was recognized as the native authority in 1941. In 1963, the territory was constituted a protectorate, and on Sept. 6, 1968, it became the independent nation of Swaziland.

Since 1986, King Mswati III has ruled as sub-Saharan Africa's last absolute monarch. Political parties are banned and the king appoints 10 of the 65 members of Parliament as well as the prime minister. King Mswati can veto any law passed by the legislature and frequently rules by decree.

Sweden

KINGDOM OF SWEDEN

National name: Konungariket Sverige
Sovereign: King Carl XVI Gustaf (1973)
Prime Minister: Göran Persson (1996)
Area: 173,800 sq. mi. (449,964 sq. km)
Population (1999 est.): 8,911,296 (average annual rate of natural increase 0.12%); birth rate: 12.0/1000; infant mortality rate: 3.9/1000; density per sq. mi.: 51
Capital and largest city (1994): Stockholm, 703,627.
  Largest cities: Göteborg, 444,553; Malmö, 242,706; Uppsala, 181,191. **Monetary unit:** Krona. **Language:** Swedish. **Ethnicity/race:** white, Lapp (Sami), foreign-born or first-generation immigrants 12% (Finns, Yugoslavs, Danes, Norwegians, Greeks, Turks). **Religions:** Evangelical Lutheran 94%, Roman Catholic 1.5%, Pentecostal 1%, other 3.5%. **Literacy rate:** 99%
Economic summary: GDP/PPP (1997 est.): $176.2 billion; $19,700 per capita. **Real growth rate:** 2.1%. **Inflation:** 2% (1997). **Unemployment:** 6.6%, plus 5% in training programs (Sept. 1996). **Arable land:** 7%. **Agriculture:** dairy products, grains, sugar beets, potatoes. **Labor force:** 4.552 million (84% unionized, 1992); community, social, and personal services, 38.3%; mining and manufacturing, 21.2%; commerce, hotels and restaurants, 14.1%; banking and insurance, 9%; communications, 7.2%; construction, 7%; agriculture, fishing, and forestry, 3.2% (1991). **Industry:** processed foods, iron and steel, precision equipment, wood pulp and paper products, automobiles. **Natural resources:** forests, iron ore, hydroelectric power, zinc, uranium. **Exports:** $84.5 billion (f.o.b., 1996): machinery, motor vehicles, wood pulp, paper products, chemicals, petroleum and petroleum products, iron and steel products. **Imports:** $66.6 billion (c.i.f., 1996): machinery, clothing, petroleum and petroleum products, foodstuffs, iron and steel, chemicals. **Major trading partners:** EU, Finland, Norway, U.S.

Geography Sweden, which occupies the eastern part of the Scandinavian peninsula, is the fourth-largest country in Europe, and is one-tenth larger than California. The country slopes eastward and southward from the Kjólen Mountains along the Norwegian border, where the peak elevation is Kebnekaise at 6,965 feet (2,123 m) in Lapland. In the north are mountains and many lakes. To the south and east are central lowlands and south of them are fertile areas of forest, valley, and plain. Along Sweden's rocky coast, chopped up by bays and inlets, are many islands, the largest of which are Gotland and Öland.

Government Constitutional monarchy.

History The earliest historical mention of Sweden is found in Tacitus's *Germania,* where reference is made to the powerful king and strong fleet of the Sviones. In the 11th century, Olaf Sköttkonung became the first Swedish king to be baptized as a Christian. Around 1400, an attempt was made to unite Sweden, Norway, and Denmark into one kingdom, but this led to bitter strife between the Danes and the Swedes. In 1520, the Danish king, Christian II, conquered Sweden and in the "Stockholm Bloodbath" put leading Swedish personages to death. Gustavus Vasa (1523–60) broke away from Denmark and fashioned the modern Swedish state. He also confiscated property from the Roman Catholic Church in Sweden to pay Sweden's war debts. The

king justified his actions on the basis of the doctrines of Martin Luther, which were being accepted nationwide with royal encouragement. The Lutheran Swedish church was eventually adopted as the state church, a position it still holds.

Sweden played a leading role in the second phase (1630–35) of the Thirty Years' War (1618–48). By the Treaty of Westphalia (1648), Sweden obtained western Pomerania and some neighboring territory on the Baltic. In 1700, a coalition of Russia, Poland, and Denmark united against Sweden and by the Peace of Nystad (1721) forced it to relinquish Livonia, Ingria, Estonia, and parts of Finland. Sweden emerged from the Napoleonic Wars with the acquisition of Norway from Denmark and with a new royal dynasty stemming from Marshal Jean Bernadotte of France, who became king Charles XIV (1818–44). The artificial union between Sweden and Norway led to an uneasy relationship, and the union was finally dissolved in 1905. Sweden maintained a position of neutrality in both world wars.

An elaborate structure of welfare legislation, imitated by many larger nations, began with the establishment of old-age pensions in 1911. Economic prosperity based on its neutralist policy enabled Sweden, together with Norway, to pioneer in public health, housing, and job security programs. Forty-four years of Socialist government were ended in 1976 with the election of a conservative coalition headed by Thorbjörn Fälldin. The Socialists were returned to power in the election of 1982, but Prime Minister Olof Palme, a Socialist, was assassinated by a gunman on Feb. 28, 1986, leaving Sweden stunned. Palme's Socialist domestic policies were carried out by his successor, Ingvar Carlsson. Elections in Sept. 1991 ousted the Social Democrats (Socialists) from power. The new coalition of four conservative parties pledged to reduce taxes and cut back on the welfare state but not alter Sweden's traditional neutrality. In Sept. 1994 the Social Democrats emerged again after three years as the opposition party.

In a 1994 referendum voters approved joining the European Union. Although supportive of a European monetary union, Sweden announced in 1997 that it would not adopt the euro when it debuted in 1999.

Switzerland

SWISS CONFEDERATION

National name: Schweiz/Suisse/Svizzera/Svizra
President: Ruth Dreifuss (1999)
Area: 15,941 sq. mi. (41,290 sq. km)
Population (1999 est.): 7,275,467 (average annual rate of natural increase: 0.15%); birth rate: 10.5/1000; infant mortality rate: 4.9/1000; density per sq. mi.: 456
Capital (1994 est.): Bern, 129,423. **Largest cities:** Zurich, 343,045; Basel, 176,220; Geneva, 171,744; Lausanne, 117,153. **Monetary unit:** Swiss franc. **Languages:** German, French, Italian, Romansch. **Ethnicity/race:** German 65%, French 18%, Italian 10%, Romansch 1%, other 6%. **Religions:** Roman Catholic 49%, Protestant 40%, other 5%, no religion 8.3%. **Literacy rate:** 99%
Economic summary: GDP/PPP (1997 est.): $172.4 billion; $23,800 per capita. **Real growth rate:** 0.4%. **Inflation:** –0.1% (1997). **Unemployment:** 5% (1997). **Arable land:** 10%. **Agriculture:** grains, fruits, vegetables, meat, eggs. **Labor force:** 3.8 million (850,000 foreign workers); services, 67%; manufacturing and construction, 29%; agriculture and

forestry, 4% (1995). **Industry:** watches and clocks, precision instruments, machinery, textiles. **Natural resources:** water power, timber, salt. **Exports:** $99.2 billion (f.o.b., 1997): machinery, chemicals, metals, agricultural products. **Imports:** $86.6 billion (c.i.f., 1997): machinery, chemicals, metals, agricultural products. **Major trading partners:** EU, U.S., Japan.

Geography Switzerland, in central Europe, is the land of the Alps. Its tallest peak is the Dufourspitze at 15,203 feet (4,634 m) on the Swiss side of the Italian border, one of 10 summits of the Monte Rose massif. The tallest peak in all of the Alps, Mont Blanc (15,771 ft.; 4,807 m), is actually in France. Most of Switzerland is composed of a mountainous plateau bordered by the great bulk of the Alps on the south and by the Jura Mountains on the northwest. The country's largest lakes—Geneva, Constance (Bodensee), and Maggiore—straddle the French, German-Austrian, and Italian borders, respectively. The Rhine, navigable from Basel to the North Sea, is the principal inland waterway. Switzerland is twice the size of New Jersey.

Government Federal republic.

History Called Helvetia in ancient times, Switzerland in 1291 was a league of cantons in the Holy Roman Empire. Fashioned around the nucleus of three German forest districts of Schwyz, Uri, and Unterwalden, the Swiss Confederation slowly added new cantons. In 1648 the Treaty of Westphalia gave Switzerland its independence from the Holy Roman Empire.

French revolutionary troops occupied the country in 1798 and named it the Helvetic Republic, but Napoléon in 1803 restored its federal government. By 1815, the French- and Italian-speaking peoples of Switzerland had been granted political equality.

In 1815, the Congress of Vienna guaranteed the neutrality and recognized the independence of Switzerland. In the revolutionary period of 1847, the Catholic cantons seceded and organized a separate union called the *Sonderbund*, but were defeated and rejoined the federation.

In 1848, the new Swiss constitution established a union modeled upon that of the U.S. The federal constitution of 1874 established a strong central government while maintaining large powers of control in each canton. National unity and political conservatism grew as the country prospered from its neutrality. Its banking system became the world's leading repository for international accounts. Strict neutrality was its policy in both world wars. Geneva was the seat of the League of Nations (later the European headquarters of the United Nations) and of a number of international organizations.

Allegations in the 1990s that secret assets of Jewish Holocaust victims were deposited in Swiss banks led to international criticism and the establishment of a fund to reimburse victims and their families.

Surprisingly, women were not given the right to vote or to hold office until 1971. Switzerland's first woman president—as well as the first Jew to assume the position—was Ruth Dreifuss in 1999.

Syria

SYRIAN ARAB REPUBLIC

National name: Al-Jamhouriya al Arabiya As-Souriya
President: Hafez al-Assad (1971)
Prime Minister: Mahmoud al-Zubi (1987)
Area: 71,498 sq. mi. (185,180 sq. km)
Population (1999 est.): 17,213,871 (average annual rate of natural increase: 3.16%); birth rate: 37.0/1000; infant mortality rate: 36.4/1000; density per sq. mi.: 241
Capital (1994 est.): Damascus, 1,549,932. **Largest cities:** Aleppo, 1,591,400; Homs, 644,204; Latakia, 306,535; Hama, 229,000. **Monetary unit:** Syrian pound. **Languages:** Arabic (official), French and English widely understood. **Ethnicity/race:** Arab 90.3%, Kurds, Armenians, and other 9.7%. **Religions:** Islam, 90%; Christian, 10%. **Literacy rate:** 65%
Economic summary: GDP/PPP (1997 est.): $106.1 billion; $6,600 per capita. **Real growth rate:** 4.6%. **Inflation:** 15%–20% (1997 est.). **Unemployment:** 12% (1997 est.). **Arable land:** 28%. **Agriculture:** cotton, wheat, barley, lentils, chickpeas, beef, lamb, poultry, eggs, milk. **Labor force:** 4.7 million (1995 est.): services, 40%; industry, 20%; agriculture, 40% (1996 est.). **Industry:** textiles, phosphate, petroleum, processed food, beverages, tobacco. **Natural resources:** chrome, manganese, asphalt, iron ore, rock salt, phosphate, oil, gypsum. **Exports:** $4.2 billion (f.o.b., 1997): petroleum, textiles, cotton, fruits and vegetables, phosphates, live animals, foodstuffs, manufacturing. **Imports:** $5.7 billion (c.i.f., 1997): machinery and equipment, foodstuffs, animals, metal and metal products, textiles, chemicals, consumer goods. **Major trading partners:** EU, U.S., Canada, Arab countries, former U.S.S.R. nations.

Geography Slightly larger than North Dakota, Syria lies at the eastern end of the Mediterranean Sea. It is bordered by Lebanon and Israel on the west, Turkey on the north, Iraq on the east, and Jordan on the south. Coastal Syria is a narrow plain, in back of which is a range of coastal mountains, and still farther inland a steppe area. In the east is the Syrian Desert, and in the south is the Jebel Druze Range. The highest point in Syria is Mount Hermon (9,232 ft.; 2,814 m) on the Lebanese border.

Government Republic under a military regime since March 1963.

History Ancient Syria was conquered by Egypt about 1500 B.C.E., and after that by Hebrews, Assyrians, Chaldeans, Persians, and Alexander the Great of Macedonia. From 64 B.C.E. until the Arab conquest in C.E. 636, it was part of the Roman Empire except during brief periods. The Arabs made it a trade center for their extensive empire, but it suffered severely from the Mongol invasion in 1260 and fell to the Ottoman Turks in 1516. Syria remained a Turkish province until World War I.

A secret Anglo-French pact of 1916 put Syria in the French zone of influence. The League of Nations gave France a mandate over Syria after World War I, but the French were forced to put down several nationalist uprisings. In 1930, France recognized Syria as an independent republic, but still subject to the mandate. After nationalist demonstrations in 1939, the French high commissioner suspended the Syrian constitution. In 1941, British and Free French forces invaded Syria to eliminate Vichy control. During the rest of World War II, Syria was an Allied base. Again in 1945, nationalist demonstrations broke into actual fighting, and British troops had to restore order. Syrian forces met a series of reverses while participating in the Arab invasion of Palestine in 1948. In 1958, Egypt and Syria formed the United Arab Republic, with Gamal Abdel Nasser of Egypt as president. However, Syria became independent again on Sept. 29, 1961, following a revolution.

In the Arab-Israeli War of 1967, Israel quickly vanquished the Syrian army. Before acceding to the U.N. cease-fire, the Israeli forces took control of the fortified Golan Heights. Syria joined Egypt in attacking Israel in Oct. 1973 in the fourth Arab-Israeli war, but was pushed back from initial successes on the Golan Heights and ended up losing more land. However, in the settlement worked out by U.S. Secretary of State Henry A. Kissinger in 1974, the Syrians recovered all the territory lost in 1973 and a token amount of territory, including the deserted town of Quneitra, lost in 1967.

In the mid-1970s Syria sent some 20,000 troops to support Muslim Lebanese in their armed conflict with Christian militants supported by Israel during the civil war in Lebanon. Syrian troops frequently clashed with Israeli troops during Israel's 1982 invasion of Lebanon and remained thereafter as occupiers of large portions of Lebanon.

The first Arab country to condemn Iraq's invasion of Kuwait, Syria sent troops to help defend Saudi Arabia from possible Iraqi attack. After the Gulf War, hope for peace negotiations between Israel and Arab states, particularly Syria, rose but then foundered. In 1990, President Assad ruled out any possibility of legalizing opposition political parties. In Dec. 1991 voters approved a fourth term for Assad, giving him 99.98% of the vote.

In the 1990s, the slowdown in the Israeli-Palestinian peace process was echoed in the lack of progress in Israeli-Syrian relations. Confronted with a steadily strengthening strategic partnership between Israel and Turkey, Syria took steps to construct a countervailing alliance by improving relations with Iraq, strengthening ties with Iran, and collaborating more closely with Saudi Arabia. The defeat of conservative Israeli prime minister Netanyahu and the election of the Labor Party's Ehud Barak marked a shift in Syrian-Israeli relations. The new Israeli prime minister announced that one of his major goals was to broker peace with Syria and end the low-grade war in Southern Lebanon with the Syrian-backed Hezbollah guerrillas.

Taiwan

REPUBLIC OF CHINA

President: Lee Teng-hui (1988)
Premier: Vincent Siew (1997)
Area: 13,895 sq. mi. (35,980 sq. km)
Population (1999 est.): 22,113,250 (average annual rate of natural increase: 0.93%); birth rate: 14.6/1000; infant mortality rate: 6.0/1000; density per sq. mi.: 1,591
Capital and largest city (1995): Taipei, 2,643,439.
   Largest cities: Kaohsiung, 1,423,163; Tai Chung, 848,320; Tainan, 705,565; Keelung, 367,668.
   Monetary unit: New Taiwan dollar. **Language:** Chinese (Mandarin). **Ethnicity/race:** Taiwanese 84%, mainland Chinese 14%, aborigine 2%. **Religions:** Buddhist, 4.86 million; Taoist, 3.3 million; Protestant, 422,000; Catholic, 304,000. **Literacy rate:** 92%
Economic summary: GNP/PPP (1997 est.): $308 billion; $14,200 per capita income. **Real growth rate:** 6.8% (1997). **Inflation:** 0.9%. **Unemployment:** 2.7%

(1997). **Arable land:** 24%. **Agriculture:** rice, wheat, corn, soybeans, vegetables, fruit, tea, pigs, poultry, beef, milk, fish. **Labor force:** 9.31 million: industry, 38%; agriculture, 10%; services, 52%. **Industry:** electronics, textiles, chemicals, clothing, food processing, plywood, sugar milling, cement, ship building, petroleum refining. **Natural resources:** coal, natural gas, limestone, marble. **Exports:** $122.1 billion (f.o.b., 1997): machinery and electrical equipment, electronic products, information/communications, textile products. **Imports:** $114.4 billion (c.i.f., 1997): machinery and electrical equipment, electronic products, chemicals, precision instruments. **Major trading partners:** U.S., Hong Kong, Japan, Germany.

Geography The Republic of China today consists of the island of Taiwan, an island 100 miles (161 km) off the Asian mainland in the Pacific; two offshore islands, Kinmen (Quemoy) and Matsu; and the nearby islets of the Pescadores chain. It is slightly larger than the combined areas of Massachusetts and Connecticut. Taiwan is divided by a central mountain range that runs from north to south, rising sharply on the east coast and descending gradually to a broad western plain, where cultivation is concentrated.

Government Multiparty democracy.

History Taiwan was inhabited by aborigines of Malayan descent when Chinese from the areas now designated as Fukien and Kwangtung began settling it in the 7th century, becoming the majority. The Portuguese explored the area in 1590, naming it "the Beautiful" (Formosa). In 1624 the Dutch set up forts in the south, the Spanish in the north. The Dutch forced out the Spanish in 1641 and controlled the island until 1661, when Chinese General Koxinga took it over and established an independent kingdom. The Manchus seized the island in 1683 and held it until 1895, when it passed to Japan after the first Sino-Japanese War. Japan developed and exploited Formosa. It was the target of heavy American bombing during World War II, and at the close of the war the island was restored to China.

After the defeat of its armies on the mainland, the Nationalist government of Generalissimo Chiang Kai-shek retreated to Taiwan in Dec. 1949. Chiang dominated the island, even though only 15% of the population consisted of the 1949 immigrants, the Kuomintang. He maintained a 600,000-man army in the hope of eventually recovering the mainland. Beijing viewed the Taiwanese government with suspicion and anger, referring to Taiwan as a breakaway province of China.

The U.N. seat representing all of China was held by the Nationalists for over two decades before being lost in Oct. 1971, when the People's Republic of China was admitted and Taiwan was forced to abdicate its seat to Beijing.

Chiang died at 87 of a heart attack on April 5, 1975. His son, Chiang Ching-kuo, continued as premier and was a dominant figure in the Taipei regime. In April 1991, President Lee Teng-hui formally declared an end to emergency rule, which had existed since Chiang's forces originally occupied the island. In the first full election in many decades, the governing Kuomintang in Dec. 1991 won 71% of the vote, affirming the island's opposition to reunification with China. In Feb. 1993 the president, himself a native Taiwanese, nominated Lien Chan, another native, to be prime minister, marking a further generational shift away from the mainland exiles.

In the island's first free presidential election voters defied mainland intimidation and gave 54% of the vote to incumbent President Lee Teng-hui. The second-place finisher, with 21%, advocated complete independence from China. The ruling Nationalists successfully defeated numerous no-confidence motions raised in response to a crime wave in May 1997. The president made a public apology and promised a new cabinet would be formed. In 1998, Taiwan renewed its push for a separate U.N. seat—its sixth attempt in recent years. The move has been blocked each time by the Beijing government.

President Lee Teng-hui sorely rankled mainland China by announcing in July 1999 that he was abandoning the longstanding "One China" policy that has kept the peace between the small island and its powerful neighbor, and would from now on deal with China on a "state-to-state basis." China, which has vowed to someday unite Taiwan with the mainland, has threatened to use force against Taiwan, and in late Aug. conducted submarine warfare exercises and missile tests near the island in an effort to intimidate its tiny brazen neighbor, as it had once before in 1996.

Tajikistan

REPUBLIC OF TAJIKISTAN

President: Imomali Rakhmonov (1992)
Prime Minister: Yakhyo Azimov (1996)
Area: 55,300 sq. mi. (143,100 sq. km)
Population (1999 est.): 6,102,854 (average annual rate of natural increase: 1.96%); birth rate, 27.5/1000; infant mortality rate: 114.8/1000; density per sq. mi.: 110
Capital and largest city (1994 est.): Dushanbe, 524,000;. **Other large city:** Khodzhent (Leninabad), 164,500.
Monetary unit: Tajik ruble. **Religion:** Sunni Muslim, 80%. **Ethnicity/race:** Tajik 64.9%, Uzbek 25%, Russian 3.5% (declining because of emigration), other 6.6%.
Language: Tajik. **Literacy rate:** 98% (1989)
Economic summary: GNP/PPP (1997 est.): $4.1 billion; $700 per capita. **Real growth rate:** –10%. **Inflation:** 40% (1996). **Unemployment:** 2.4%, also includes large numbers of underemployed, and unregistered unemployed (Dec. 1996). **Arable land:** 6%. **Labor force:** 1.9 million (1996); agriculture and forestry, 52%, services, 31%, manufacturing, mining, and construction, 17% (1995). **Industry:** aluminum, zinc, lead, cement, chemicals and fertilizers, vegetable oil, metal-cutting machine tools, refrigerators and freezers. **Agriculture:** cotton, grain, fruits, and grapes. **Exports:** $768 million (1996 est.): aluminum, cotton, fruits, vegetable oil, textiles. **Imports:** $657 million (1996 est.): fuel, chemicals, machinery and transport equipment, textiles, foodstuffs. **Major trading partners:** Russia, Kazakhstan, Ukraine, Uzbekistan, Turkmenistan.

Geography Ninety-three percent of Tajikistan's territory is mountainous and the mountain glaciers are the source of its rivers. Tajikistan is an earthquake-prone area. The republic is bounded by China in the east, Afghanistan to the south, Uzbekistan and Kirghizia to the west and north. The central Asian republic also includes the Gorno-Badakh Shan Autonomous region. Tajikistan is slightly larger than the state of Illinois.

Government Republic.

History The Tajiks, whose language is nearly identical with Persian, were part of the ancient Persian empire that was ruled by Darius I and later conquered by Alexander the Great (333 B.C.E.). In the 7th and 8th centuries, Arabs conquered the region and brought Islam. The Tajiks were successively ruled by Uzbeks and then Afghans until claimed by Russia in the 1860s. In 1924, Tajikistan was consolidated into a newly formed Tajik Autonomous Soviet Socialist Republic, which was administratively part of the Uzbek S.S.R. until the Tajik A.S.S.R. gained full-fledged republic status in 1929.

Tajikistan declared its sovereignty in Aug. 1990. In 1991, the republic's Communist leadership supported the attempted coup against Soviet president Mikhail Gorbachev. Tajikistan joined with ten other former Soviet republics in the Commonwealth of Independent States on Dec. 21, 1991. A parliamentary republic was proclaimed and presidential rule abolished on Nov. 1992. After independence, Tajikistan experienced sporadic conflict as the Communist-dominated government struggled to combat an insurgency by Islamic and democratic opposition forces. Despite continued international efforts to end the civil war, periodic fighting continued. Tajikistan's civil war ended officially on June 27, 1997, with the signing in Moscow of peace accords between the government of President Imomali Rakhmonov and the United Tajik Opposition (UTO), a coalition of largely Islamic groups. Since then, however, peace has been tenuous, marred regularly by killing sprees by various opposition groups.

Tanzania

UNITED REPUBLIC OF TANZANIA

President: Benjamin William Mkapa (1995)
Prime Minister: Frederick Tluway Sumaye (1995)
Area: 364,879 sq. mi. (945,090 sq. km)[1]
Population (1999 est.): 31,270,820 (average annual rate of natural increase: 2.36%); birth rate: 40.4/1000; infant mortality rate: 95.3/1000; density per sq. mi.: 86
Capital and largest city (1988): Dar es Salaam, 1,360,850[2]. **Monetary unit:** Tanzanian shilling.
Languages: Swahili, English, local languages.
Ethnicity/race: mainland: native African (95% Bantu, consisting of well over 100 tribes) 99%, Asian, European, and Arab 1%. Zanzibar: Arab, mixed Arab and native African, native African. **Religions:** Christian, 40%; Muslim, 33%. **Literacy rate:** 52%
Economic summary: GDP/PPP (1997 est.): $21.1 billion; $700 per capita. **Real growth rate:** 4.3%. **Inflation:** 15%. **Unemployment:** n.a. **Arable land:** 3%. **Agriculture:** tobacco, corn, cassava, wheat, cotton, coffee, sisal, cashew nuts, pyrethrum, cloves, bananas, fruits, vegetables, cattle, sheep, goats. **Labor force:** 13.495 million; agriculture, 90%; industry and commerce, 10% (1995 est.). **Industry:** agricultural processing, diamond and gold mining, oil refining, shoes, cement, textiles, wood products, fertilizer, salt. **Natural resources:** hydroelectric potential, phosphates, iron, and coal. **Exports:** $760 million (f.o.b., 1996): coffee, cotton, sisal, manufactured goods, minerals, cashew nuts, tobacco, tea. **Imports:** $1.4 billion (c.i.f., 1996): machinery and transport equipment, crude oil, consumer goods. **Major trading partners:** Germany, U.K., U.S., Japan, Italy, Denmark, Kenya, Netherlands, Hong Kong, EU, China, India.
Member of Commonwealth of Nations

1. Including Zanzibar. 2. Some government offices have been transferred to Dodoma, which is planned as the new national capital by the end of the 1990s.

Geography Tanzania is in East Africa on the Indian Ocean. To the north are Uganda and Kenya; to the west, Burundi, Rwanda, and Congo; and to the south, Mozambique, Zambia, and Malawi. Its area is three times that of New Mexico. Tanzania contains three of Africa's best-known lakes—Victoria in the north, Tanganyika in the west, and Nyasa in the south. Mount Kilimanjaro in the north, 19,340 feet (5,895 m), is the highest point on the continent. The island of Zanzibar is separated from the mainland by a 22–mile channel.

Government Republic.

History Arab traders first began to colonize the area in C.E. 700. Portuguese explorers reached the coastal regions in 1500 and held some control until the 17th century, when the sultan of Oman took power. With what are now Burundi and Rwanda, Tanganyika became the colony of German East Africa in 1885. After World War I, it was administered by Britain under a League of Nations mandate and later as a U.N. trust territory.

Although not mentioned in old histories until the 12th century, Zanzibar was always believed to have had connections with southern Arabia. The Portuguese made it one of their tributaries in 1503 and later established a trading post, but they were driven from Oman by Arabs in 1698. Zanzibar was declared independent of Oman in 1861 and, in 1890, it became a British protectorate.

Tanganyika became independent on Dec. 9, 1961; Zanzibar on Dec. 10, 1963. On April 26, 1964, the two nations merged into the United Republic of Tanganyika and Zanzibar. The name was changed to Tanzania six months later.

An invasion by Ugandan troops in Nov. 1978 was followed by a counterattack in Jan. 1979, in which 5,000 Tanzanian troops were joined by 3,000 Ugandan exiles opposed to President Idi Amin. Within a month, full-scale war developed. Tanzanian president Julius Nyerere kept troops in Uganda in open support of former Ugandan president Milton Obote, despite protests from opposition groups, until the national elections in Dec. 1980.

In Nov. 1985, Nyerere stepped down as president. Ali Hassan Mwinyi, his vice president, succeeded him. Running unopposed, Mwinyi was elected president in Oct. Shortly thereafter plans were announced to study the benefits of instituting a multiparty democracy.

The crisis in Rwanda in 1994 sent hundreds of thousands of refugees fleeing into Tanzania, taxing the already-meager resources of the country. The government immediately appealed for international aid. In Oct. 1995 the country's first multiparty elections since independence took place.

On Aug. 7, 1998, the U.S. embassy in Dar es Salaam was bombed by terrorists, killing 10. The same day an even more devastating explosion destroyed the U.S. embassy in neighboring Kenya.

Thailand

KINGDOM OF THAILAND

Ruler: King Bhumibol Adulyadej (1946)
Prime Minister: Chuan Leekpai (1997)
Area: 198,455 sq. mi. (514,000 sq. km)
Population (1999 est.): 60,609,046 (average annual rate of natural increase 0.93%); birth rate: 16.5/1000; infant

mortality rate: 29.5/1000; density per sq. mi.: 305
Capital and largest city (1990): Bangkok, 5,882,000.
Other large cities: Nonthanburi, 261,335; Chiang Mai, 170,397. **Monetary unit:** baht. **Languages:** Thai (Siamese), Chinese, English. **Ethnicity/race:** Thai 75%, Chinese 14%, other 11%. **Religions:** Buddhist, 94.4%; Islam, 4%; Hinduism, 1.1%; Christian, 0.5%. **Literacy rate:** 93%
Economic summary: GDP/PPP (1997 est.): $525 billion; $8,800 per capita. **Real growth rate:** –0.4%. **Inflation:** 5.6%. **Unemployment:** 3.5%. **Arable land:** 34%. **Agriculture:** rice, rubber, corn, tapioca, sugarcane, soybeans, coconuts. **Labor force:** (1997) 33.6 million; agriculture, 54%; industry, 15%; services, including government, 31% (1996 est.). **Industry:** tourism (largest source of foreign exchange), textiles and garments, agricultural processing, beverages, tobacco, cement, light manufacturing, electric appliances and components, integrated circuits, furniture, plastics, tungsten, and tin. **Natural resources:** fish, natural gas, forests, fluorite, tin, tungsten. **Exports:** $51.6 billion (f.o.b., 1997): manufactures, agricultural products, and fisheries. **Imports:** $73.5 billion (c.i.f., 1996): capital goods, consumer goods, fuels. **Major trading partners:** Japan, U.S., Singapore, Germany, Taiwan, Malaysia, Hong Kong, South Korea, U.K., France.

Geography Thailand occupies the western half of the Indochinese peninsula and the northern two-thirds of the Malay Peninsula in southeast Asia. Its neighbors are Burma (Myanmar) on the north and west, Laos on the north and northeast, Cambodia on the east, and Malaysia on the south. Thailand is about the size of France.

Government Constitutional monarchy.

History The Thais first began settling their present homeland from the Asian continent in the 6th century C.E., and by the end of the 13th century ruled most of the western portion. During the next 400 years, they fought sporadically with the Cambodians to the east and Burmese to the west. Formerly called Siam, Thailand has never experienced foreign rule. The British gained a colonial foothold in the region in 1824, but by 1896 an Anglo-French accord guaranteed the independence of Thailand. A coup in 1932 demoted the monarchy to titular status and established representative government with universal suffrage.

At the outbreak of World War II, Japanese forces attacked Thailand. After five hours of token resistance Thailand yielded to Japan on Dec. 8, 1941, subsequently becoming a staging area for the Japanese campaign against Malaya. Following the demise of a pro-Japanese puppet government in July 1944, Thailand repudiated the declaration of war it had been forced to make in 1942 against Britain and the U.S.

By the late 1960s the nation's problems largely stemmed from conflicts brewing in neighboring Cambodia and Vietnam. Although Thailand had received $2 billion in U.S. economic and military aid since 1950, and had sent troops (paid by the U.S.) to Vietnam while permitting U.S. bomber bases on its territory, the collapse of South Vietnam and Cambodia in spring 1975 brought rapid changes in the country's diplomatic posture. At the Thai government's insistence, the U.S. agreed to withdraw all 23,000 U.S. military personnel remaining in Thailand by March 1976.

Three years of civilian government ended with a military coup on Oct. 6, 1976. Political parties, banned after the coup, gained limited freedom in 1980. The same year, the National Assembly elected Gen. Prem Tinsulanonda as prime minister. General elections held on April 18, 1983, and July 27, 1986, resulted in Prem continuing as prime minister over a coalition government.

Fleeing from Laos, Vietnam, and the genocidal regime of Cambodia's Pol Pot, refugees flooded into Thailand in 1978 and 1979. Despite efforts by the United States and other Western countries to resettle them, a total of 130,000 Laotians and Vietnamese were living in camps along the Cambodian border in mid-1980.

On April 3, 1981, a military coup against the Prem government failed. Another coup attempt on Sept. 9, 1985, was crushed by loyal troops after 10 hours of fighting in Bangkok. In Feb. 1991 a bloodless putsch led by Gen. Suchinda Kraprayoon overthrew the democratic government on charges of corruption. The new junta declared a state of emergency; under martial law, the houses of Parliament were dismissed and the constitution abolished. Parliamentary elections in March 1992 gave more than half the seats at stake to pro-military parties. In April, the top military commander was appointed prime minister. A scandal over a land-reform program caused the fall of the government in May 1995. The prime minister dissolved Parliament and set a date for new elections. Voters in early July gave the largest number of seats in Parliament to the Thai Nation Party, whose leader moved quickly to form a coalition government. A new draft constitution, calling for cabinet ministers to relinquish their parliamentary seats, came under fire in the early months of 1997 from a number of politicians.

Following several years of unprecedented economic growth, Thailand's economy, once one of the strongest in the region, collapsed under the weight of foreign debt in 1997. The Thai economy's downfall set off a chain reaction in the region, sparking the Asian currency crisis. Although one of the first Asian economies to be ravaged by the currency crisis, the Thai government quickly accepted restructuring guidelines as a condition of the International Monetary Fund's $17 billion bailout. By 1998, Thailand's economy, while far from completely recovered, appeared to be in better condition than that of many of its Asian neighbors, and continued to improve in 1999.

Togo

REPUBLIC OF TOGO

National name: République Togolaise
President: Gen. Gnassingbe Eyadema (1967)
Prime Minister: Koffi Eugene Adoboli (1999)
Area: 21,925 sq. mi. (56,790 sq. km)
Population (1999 est.): 5,081,413 (average annual rate of natural increase: 3.51%); birth rate: 44.8/1000; infant mortality rate: 77.6/1000; density per sq. mi.: 232
Capital and largest city (1983): Lomé, 366,476.
Monetary unit: Franc CFA. **Languages:** Ewé, Mina (south), Kabyé, Cotocoli (north), French (official), and many dialects. **Ethnicity/race:** native African (37 tribes; largest and most important are Ewe, Mina, and Kabre) 99%, European and Syrian-Lebanese less than 1%. **Religions:** Indigenous beliefs, 70%; Christian, 20%; Islam, 10%. **Literacy rate:** 43%

Economic summary: GDP/PPP (1997 est.): $6.2 billion; $1,300 per capita. **Real growth rate:** 4.8%. **Inflation:** 15.7% (1995 est.). **Unemployment:** n.a. **Arable land:** 38%. **Agriculture:** coffee, cocoa, cotton, yams, cassava, corn, beans, rice, millet, sorghum, meat, fish. **Labor force:** (1993 est.), 1.538 million; agriculture, 65%; industry, 5%; services, 30% (1997 est.). **Industry:** phosphate mining, agricultural processing, cement, handicrafts, textiles, beverages. **Natural resources:** marble, phosphate, limestone. **Exports:** $196 million (f.o.b., 1996): phosphate, cocoa, coffee, cotton. **Imports:** $404 million (c.i.f., 1996): consumer goods, petroleum products, machinery and equipment. **Major trading partners:** EU, Japan, U.S., Africa, China, Canada, Taiwan.

Geography Togo, twice the size of Maryland, is on the south coast of West Africa bordering on Ghana to the west, Burkina Faso to the north and Benin to the east. The Gulf of Guinea coastline, only 32 miles long (51 km), is low and sandy. The only port is at Lomé. The Togo hills traverse the central section.

Government Republic.

History The Voltaic peoples and the Kwa were the earliest known inhabitants. The Ewe followed in the 14th century, and the Ane in the 18th century. The Danish claimed the land in the 18th century, but by 1884 it was established as a German colony (Togoland). The area was split between the British and the French as League of Nations mandates after World War I and subsequently administered as U.N. trusteeships. The British portion voted for incorporation with Ghana. The French portion became Togo, which declared its independence on April 27, 1960.

The government of Nicolas Grunitzky was overthrown in a bloodless coup on Jan. 13, 1967, led by Lt. Col. Etienne Eyadema (now Gen. Gnassingbé Eyadema). A National Reconciliation Committee was set up to rule the country. In April, however, Eyadema dissolved the committee and took over as president. The presidential election held in Aug. 1993 gave Eyadema more than 96% of the vote, but only 36% of the electorate went to the polls. Many of the major opposition candidates withdrew prior to the election. In Aug. 1996 Prime Minister Edem Kodjo resigned. The planning minister, Kwassi Klutse, was then appointed prime minister.

Tonga

KINGDOM OF TONGA

Sovereign: King Taufa'ahau Tupou IV (1965)
Prime Minister: Baron Vaea (1991)
Area: 290 sq. mi. (748 sq. km)
Population (1999 est.): 109,082 (average annual rate of natural increase: 1.99%); birth rate: 25.9/1000; infant mortality rate: 37.9/1000; density per sq. mi.: 376
Capital and largest city (1990 est.): Nuku'alofa, 34,000. **Monetary unit:** Pa'anga. **Languages:** Tongan (an Austronesian language), English. **Ethnicity/race:** Polynesian, European (about 300). **Religions:** Christian; Free Wesleyan Church claims over 30,000 adherents. **Literacy rate:** 47%
Economic summary: GDP/PPP (1996 est.): $239 million; $2,250 per capita. **Real growth rate:** 1%. **Inflation:** 2% (1997 est.) **Arable land:** 24%. **Agriculture:** vanilla, coffee, ginger, black pepper, coconuts, bananas, corn. **Labor force:** (1994) 36,665; agriculture, 65% (1997 est.). **Natural resources:** fish, copra. **Exports:** $15.3 million (f.o.b.,

1996): squash, fish, vanilla, root crops, coconut oil.
Imports: $82.9 million (f.o.b., 1996): food products, live animals, machinery and transport equipment, manufactures, fuels, chemicals. **Major trading partners:** New Zealand, Canada, Australia, Fiji, U.S., Japan, EU. **Member of Commonwealth of Nations**

Geography Situated east of the Fiji Islands in the South Pacific, Tonga (also called the Friendly Islands) consists of some 150 islands, of which 36 are inhabited. Most of the islands contain active volcanic craters; others are coral atolls.

Government Constitutional monarchy.

History Polynesians have lived on Tonga for at least 3,000 years. The Dutch were the first to explore the islands, landing on Tafahi in 1616. The current royal dynasty of Tonga was founded in 1831 by Taufa'ahau Tupou, who took the name George I. He consolidated the kingdom by conquest and in 1875 granted a constitution. In 1900, his great-grandson, George II, signed a treaty of friendship with Britain, and the country became a British protected state. The treaty was revised in 1959. Tonga became independent on June 4, 1970.

The continuing challenge to the government—largely controlled by the king, his nominees, and a small group of hereditary nobles—posed by the prodemocracy movement was institutionalized in Sept. 1994 with the formation of the Tonga Democratic Party. In March 1997, Cyclone Hina caused damage to crops and buildings, mostly on Tongatapu; one person was reported killed. In 1999, Tonga was accepted for membership in the U.N.

Trinidad and Tobago

REPUBLIC OF TRINIDAD AND TOBAGO
President: A. N. R. Robinson (1997)
Prime Minister: Basdeo Panday (1995)
Area: 1,980 sq. mi. (5,130 sq. km)
Population (1999 est.): 1,102 096 (average annual rate of natural increase: 0.63%); birth rate: 14.5/1000; infant mortality rate: 18.6/1000; density per sq. mi.: 557
Capital and largest city (1995): Port-of-Spain, 52,451.
Monetary unit: Trinidad and Tobago dollar.
Languages: English (official), Hindi, French, Spanish.
Ethnicity/race: black 43%, East Indian (a local term–primarily immigrants from northern India) 40%, mixed 14%, white 1%, Chinese 1%, other 1%.
Religions: Roman Catholic, 33%; Hindu, 25%; Anglican, 15%; other Christian, 14%; Muslim, 6%.
Literacy rate: 95%
Economic summary: GDP/PPP (1996 est.): $13.2 billion; $10,400 per capita. **Real growth rate:** 3.1%. **Inflation:** 3.4% (1996). **Unemployment:** 16.1% (Dec. 1996). **Arable land:** 15%. **Agriculture:** sugar cane, cocoa, coffee, citrus. **Labor force:** 404,500; manufacturing, mining, and quarrying, 14%; construction and utilities, 13%; agriculture, 11%; services, 62% (1993 est.). **Industry:** petroleum, processed food, cement, tourism. **Natural resources:** petroleum, natural gas, asphalt. **Exports:** $2.5 billion (f.o.b., 1996): including reexports—petroleum and petroleum products, steel products, fertilizer, sugar, cocoa, coffee, citrus fruits, flowers. **Imports:** $2.1 billion (c.i.f., 1996): machinery, transportation equipment, manufactured goods, food, live animals. **Major trading partners:** U.S., Caribbean, Latin America, wstern Europe, U.K., Canada. **Member of Commonwealth of Nations**

Geography Trinidad and Tobago lie in the Caribbean Sea off the northeast coast of Venezuela. Trinidad, the larger at 1,864 sq. mi. (4,828 sq. km), is mainly flat and rolling, with mountains in the north that reach a height of 3,085 feet (940 m) at Mount Aripo. Tobago, at just 116 sq. mi. (300 sq. km), is heavily forested with hardwood trees.

Government Parliamentary democracy.

History When Trinidad was explored by Columbus in 1498, it was inhabited by the Arawaks; the Carib Indians inhabited Tobago. Trinidad remained in Spanish possession, despite raids by other European nations, until it capitulated to the British in 1797 during a war between Britain and Spain. Trinidad was officially ceded to Britain in 1802. Tobago passed between Britain and France several times before it was ultimately ceded to Britain in 1814. In 1845, the immigration of indentured workers from India for the sugarcane plantations began; it continued until 1917. In 1889 Tobago was administratively combined with Trinidad.

Partial self-government was instituted in 1925 and from 1958 to 1962, the nation was part of the West Indies Federation. On Aug, 31, 1962, it became independent and on Aug. 1, 1976, Trinidad and Tobago became a republic, remaining within the Commonwealth. The People's National Movement (PNM) won six consecutive elections and held power from 1956 to 1986. In Dec. 1986 the National Alliance for Reconstruction (NAR), a coalition party, won the majority of parliamentary seats, promising divestment of most state-owned companies, reorganization of the civil service, and structural readjustment of the economy in the light of shrinking oil revenues.

In July 1990 a small, radical Muslim group attempted a coup in which several ministers, including the prime minister, were held hostage for six days.

The NAR was defeated in elections in Dec. 1991, and the PNM returned to power. In the 1995 elections, the United National Congress (UNC), led by Basdeo Panday, teamed up with the NAR and formed a coalition government.

Trinidad hanged several members of a gang of murderers in June 1999, its first executions in five years. There has been growing support for capital punishment among Caribbean Commonwealth members, and anger against Britain, their former colonizer, for urging them to outlaw the death penalty.

Tunisia

REPUBLIC OF TUNISIA
National name: Al-Joumhouria Attunisia
President: Zine El Abidine Ben Ali (1987)
Prime Minister: Hamed Karoui (1989)
Area: 63,170 sq. mi. (163,610 sq. km)
Population (1999 est.): 9,513,603 (average annual rate of natural increase: 1.47%); birth rate: 19.7/1000; infant mortality rate: 31.4/1000; density per sq. mi.: 151
Capital and largest city (1994): Tunis, 887,800.
Monetary unit: Tunisian dinar. **Languages:** Arabic, French. **Ethnicity/race:** Arab-Berber 98%, European

1%, Jewish less than 1%. **Religions:** Islam (Sunni), 98%; Christian, 1%; Jewish, less than 1%. **Literacy rate:** 65%

Economic summary: GDP/PPP (1997 est.): $56.5 billion; $6,100 per capita. **Real growth rate:** 5.6%. **Inflation:** 4.6%. **Unemployment:** 15% (1997 est.). **Arable land:** 19%. **Agriculture:** olives, dates, oranges, almonds, grain, sugar beets, grapes, poultry, beef, dairy products. **Labor force:** 2.917 million (1993 est.); services, 55%; industry, 23%; agriculture, 22% (1995 est.). **Industry:** tourism, textiles, footwear, food, beverages, petroleum mining. **Natural resources:** oil, phosphates, iron ore, lead, zinc. **Exports:** $5.6 billion (f.o.b., 1997 est.): hydrocarbons, textiles, agricultural products, phosphates and chemicals. **Imports:** $7.4 billion (c.i.f., 1997 est.): industrial goods and equipment, hydrocarbons, food, consumer goods. **Major trading partners:** France, Italy, Germany, U.S., Belgium and Luxembourg, Spain, The Netherlands.

Geography Tunisia, at the northernmost bulge of Africa, thrusts out toward Sicily to mark the division between the eastern and western Mediterranean Sea. Twice the size of South Carolina, it is bordered on the west by Algeria and by Libya on the south. Coastal plains on the east rise to a north-south escarpment that slopes gently to the west. The Sahara Desert lies in the most southern part. Tunisia is more mountainous in the north, where the Atlas range continues from Algeria.

Government Republic.

History Tunisia was settled by the Phoenicians in the twelfth century B.C.E. By the sixth and fifth centuries B.C.E., the great city-state of Carthage (derived from the Phoenician name for "new city") dominated much of the western Mediterranean. The three Punic Wars between Rome and Carthage (the second was the most famous, pitting the Roman general Scipio Africanus against Carthage's Hannibal), led to the complete destruction of Carthage by 146 B.C.E.

Except for an interval of Vandal conquest in C.E. 439–533, Carthage was part of the Roman Empire until the Arab conquest of 648–69. It was then ruled by various Arab and Berber dynasties until the Turks took it in 1570–74 and made it part of the Ottoman Empire until the nineteenth century. In the late 16th century, it was a stronghold for the Barbary pirates. French troops occupied the country in 1881, and the bey, the local Tunisian ruler, signed a treaty acknowledging a French protectorate.

Nationalist agitation forced France to recognize Tunisian independence and sovereignty in 1956. The Constituent Assembly deposed the bey on July 25, 1957, declared Tunisia a republic, and elected Habib Bourguiba as president. Bourguiba maintained a pro-Western foreign policy that earned him enemies. Tunisia refused to break relations with the U.S. during the Arab-Israeli war in June 1967. Concerned with Islamic fundamentalist plots against the state, the government stepped up efforts to eradicate the movement, including censorship and frequent detention of suspects.

In 1987, the aged Bourguiba was declared mentally unfit to continue as president and was removed from office. He was succeeded as president by General Zine al-Abidine Ben Ali, whose tenure was marked by a rise in Islamic fundamentalism and growing anti-Western sentiments among the populace.

Turkey

REPUBLIC OF TURKEY

National name: Türkiye Cumhuriyeti
President: Süleyman Demirel (1993)
Prime Minister: Bülent Ecevit (1999)
Area: 300,947 sq. mi. (incl. 9,121 in Europe) (780,580 sq. km)
Population (1999 est.): 65,599,206; average annual rate of natural increase 1.57%; birth rate: 20.9/1000; infant mortality rate: 35.8/1000; density per sq. mi.: 218
Capital (1996 est.): Ankara, 2,890,025. **Largest cities:** Istanbul: city proper (1996 est.) 8,203,329; metro. area (1995 est.) 7,817,000; Izmir, 1,920,807; Adana, 1,010,363; Bursa, 949,810; Gaziantep, 683,557.
Monetary unit: Turkish lira. **Language:** Turkish. **Ethnicity/race:** Turkish 80%, Kurdish 20%. **Religion:** Islam (mostly Sunni), 98%. **Literacy rate:** 81%
Economic summary: GDP/PPP (1997 est.): $388.3 billion; $6,100 per capita. **Real growth rate:** 7.2%. **Inflation:** 99% (1997). **Unemployment:** 5.9%, plus another 5.1% underemployed. **Arable land:** 32%. **Agriculture:** cotton, tobacco, cereals, sugar beets, fruits, olives, pulses, citrus, livestock. **Labor force:** 21.6 million; agriculture, 43.1%; services, 30%; industry, 14.4%; construction, 6% (1995) (note: in 1994 about 1.5 million Turks worked abroad). **Industry:** textiles, food processing, mining, steel, petroleum, construction, lumber, paper. **Natural resources:** coal, chromite, copper, borate, sulfur, petroleum. **Exports:** $26 billion (f.o.b., 1997): agricultural products, textiles, leather, glass, iron, steel, foodstuffs. **Imports:** $46.7 billion (f.o.b., 1997): machinery, raw materials, fuels, foodstuffs, fertilizer, chemicals. **Major trading partners:** EU, U.S., Russia.

Geography Turkey is at the northeastern end of the Mediterranean Sea in southeast Europe and southwest Asia. To the north is the Black Sea and to the west is the Aegean Sea. Its neighbors are Greece and Bulgaria to the west, Russia and Ukraine to the north (through the Black Sea), Georgia, Armenia, Azerbaijain, and Iran to the east, and Syria and Iraq to the south. The Dardanelles, the Sea of Marmara, and the Bosporus divide the country. Turkey in Europe comprises an area about equal to the state of Massachusetts. It is hilly country drained by the Maritsa River and its tributaries. Turkey in Asia, or Anatolia, is about the size of Texas. Its center is a treeless plateau rimmed by mountains.

Government Parliamentary democracy.

History Anatolia (Turkey in Asia) was occupied in about 1900 B.C.E. by the Indo-European Hittites and after the Hittite empire's collapse in 1200 B.C.E., by Phrygians and Lydians. The Persian empire occupied the area in the 6th century B.C.E., giving way to the Roman Empire, then later the Byzantine Empire. The Ottoman Turks first appeared in the early 13th century, subjugating Turkish and Mongol bands pressing against the eastern borders of Byzantium and making the Christian Balkan states their vassals. They gradually spread through the Near East and Balkans, capturing Constantinople in 1453 and storming the gates of Vienna two centuries later. At its height, the Ottoman Empire stretched from the Persian Gulf to western Algeria. Lasting for 600 years, the Ottoman Empire was not only one of the most powerful empires in the history of the Mediterranean region, but generated a great cultural outpouring of Islamic art, architecture, and literature.

After the reign of Sultan Süleyman I the Magnificent (1494–1566), the Ottoman Empire began to decline politically, administratively, and economically. By the 18th century, Russia was seeking to establish itself as the protector of Christians in Turkey's Balkan territories. Russian ambitions were checked by Britain and France in the Crimean War (1854–56), but the Russo-Turkish War (1877–78) gave Bulgaria virtual independence and Romania and Serbia liberation from their nominal allegiance to the sultan. Turkish weakness stimulated a revolt of young liberals known as the Young Turks in 1909. They forced Sultan Abdul Hamid to grant a constitution and install a liberal government. However, reforms were no barrier to further defeats in a war with Italy (1911–12) and the Balkan Wars (1912–13). Under the influence of German military advisers, Turkey signed a secret alliance with Germany on Aug. 2, 1914, that led to a declaration of war by the Allied powers and the ultimate humiliation of the occupation of Turkish territory by Greek and other Allied troops.

Turkey's present boundaries were drawn in 1923 at the Conference of Lausanne, and Turkey became a republic with Kemal Atatürk as the first president. The Ottoman sultanate and caliphate were abolished, and modernization, reform, and industrialization began under Atatürk's direction. He secularized Turkish society, reducing Islam's dominant role and replacing Arabic with the Latin alphabet for writing the Turkish language. After Atatürk's death in 1938, parliamentary government and a multiparty system gradually took root in Turkey, despite periods of instability and brief intervals of military rule. Neutral during most of World War II, Turkey, on Feb. 23, 1945, declared war on Germany and Japan, but took no active part in the conflict. Turkey became a full member of NATO in 1952, was a signatory in the Balkan Entente (1953), joined the Baghdad Pact (1955; later CENTO), joined the Organization for European Economic Co-operation (OEEC) and the Council of Europe, and became an associate member of the European Common Market in 1963.

Turkey invaded Cyprus by sea and air on July 20, 1974, following the failure of diplomatic efforts to resolve conflicts between Turkish and Greek Cypriots. Turkey unilaterally announced a cease-fire on August 16, after having gained control of 40% of the island. Turkish Cypriots established their own state in the north on Feb. 13, 1975. In July 1975, after a 30-day warning, Turkey took control of all the U.S. installations except the big joint defense base at Incirlik, which it reserved for "NATO tasks alone."

The establishment of military government in Sept. 1980 stopped the slide toward anarchy and brought some improvement in the economy. A Constituent Assembly, consisting of the six-member National Security Council and members appointed by them, drafted a new constitution that was approved by an overwhelming (91.5%) majority of the voters in a Nov. 6, 1982, referendum. Martial law was gradually lifted.

About 12 million Kurds live in the southeast region of Turkey, roughly 20% of Turkey's population. Turkey, however, does not officially recognize Kurds as a minority group and is therefore exempted from protecting their rights. Oppression of Kurds and Kurdish culture led to the emergence in 1984 of the Kurdistan Workers' Party (PKK), a militant Kurdish terrorist campaign under the leadership of Abdullah Ocalan. Although the guerrilla movement sought independence at first, by the late 1980s the rebel Kurds were willing to accept an autonomous state or a federation with Turkey. In March 1995, Turkish troops moved into northern Iraq seeking to root out Kurdish rebels, who had used Iraq as a base. About 35,000 have died in clashes between the military and the PKK during the 1980s and '90s. On Feb. 16, 1999, Kurd leader and terrorist Abdullah Ocalan was captured, tried, and convicted of treason and separatism on June 2, 1999, and sentenced to death. On August 17, 1999, western Turkey was devastated by an earthquake that left more than 15,000 dead and 200,000 homeless. The government was decried for lax control of builders whose faulty construction increased the destruction and added to the death toll.

Turkmenistan

TURKMENISTAN

President: Saparmurad A. Niyazov (1990)
Area: 188,500 sq. mi. (488,100 sq. km)
Population (1999 est.): 4,366,383 (average annual rate of natural increase: 1.71%); birth rate: 25.9/1000; infant mortality rate: 73.1/1000; density per sq. mi.: 23
Capital and largest city (1994 est.): Ashgabat, 518,000. **Other large cities:** Chardzhou, 166,400; Tashauz, 117,000. **Monetary unit:** Manat.
Languages: Turkmen, 72%; Russian, 12%; Uzbek, 9%. **Ethnicity/race (1995):** Turkmen 77%, Uzbek 9.2%, Russian 6.7%, Kazak 2%, other 5.1%.
Religions: Muslim 89%, Eastern Orthodox 9%, unknown 2%. **Literacy rate:** 98%
Economic summary: GDP/PPP (1996 est.): $12.5 billion; $3,000 per capita. **Real growth rate:** –0.3%. **Inflation:** 992%. **Unemployment:** n.a. **Arable land:** 3%. **Labor force:** 2.34 million (1996); agriculture and forestry, 44%; industry and construction, 19%; other, 37% (1996). **Industry:** natural gas, oil, petroleum products, textiles, food processing. **Agriculture:** cotton, grain, livestock. **Exports:** $1.7 billion to outside former U.S.S.R. countries (1996): natural gas, petroleum products, electricity, chemicals, cotton, textiles, carpets. **Imports:** $1.5 billion from outside the former U.S.S.R. countries (1996): machinery and parts, plastics and rubber, consumer durables, textiles, grain, foodstuffs. **Major trading partners:** C.I.S. countries, Russia, eastern European countries, Turkey, Argentina.

Geography Turkmenistan (formerly Turkmenia) is bounded by the Caspian Sea in the west, Kazakhstan in the north, Uzbekistan in the east, and Iran and Afghanistan in the south. About nine-tenths of Turkmenistan is desert, chiefly the Kara-Kum; this is one of the world's largest sand deserts at approximately 138,966 sq. mi. (360,000 sq. km) in area. Many irrigation canals and reservoirs have been built, including the Kara-Kum Canal, which runs from the Amu Darya River westward to the Caspian Sea for a distance of 870 miles (1,400 km).

Government Republic.

History Turkmenistan was once part of the ancient Persian empire. The Turkmen people were originally pastoral nomads and some of them continued this way of life up into the 20th century, living in transportable dome-shaped felt tents. The territory was ruled by the Seljuk Turks in the 11th century. The Mongols of Ghenghis Khan conquered the land in the 13th century and dominated the area for the next two centuries until they were deposed in the late 15th century by invading Uzbeks. Prior to the 19th century, Turkmenia was divided into two lands, one belonging to the khanate of Khiva and the other belonging to the khanate of Bukhara. In 1868, the khanate of Khiva was made part of the Russian empire and Turkmenia became known as the Transcaspia Region of Russian Turkistan. Turkmenistan was later formed out of the Turkistan Autonomous Soviet Socialist Republic, founded in 1922, and was made an independent Soviet Socialist Republic on May 13, 1925.

Turkmenistan declared its sovereignty in Aug. 1990 and became a member of the Commonwealth of Independent States on Dec. 21, 1991, together with ten other former Soviet republics. It established a government more authoritarian than those functioning in the other newly independent central Asian republics. President Saparmurad A. Niyazov, also called the Turkmenbashy (Leader of All Turkmens), has attempted to create a cult of personality through heavy-handed self-promotion. Protests against his authoritarian rule and practices notwithstanding, the president extended his term into the next century.

Along with Azerbaijan and Kazakhstan, Turkmenistan is one of the fortunate countries bordering the Caspian Sea, which is estimated to hold 10% of the world's potential oil reserves. In the 1990s, Turkmenistan exported gas through a Russian pipeline, bringing in about $1 billion per year. But in 1993, Russia closed down Turkmenistan's only pipeline because it competed with Russia's own gas exportation. Turkmenistan was limited to exporting gas to its impoverished central Asian neighbors, who were unable to pay their bills. Turkmenistan then opened a pipeline route to Iran, generally agreed to be the most economical route for exporting Caspian oil, which ruffled the feathers of Iran's enemy, the U.S. Thus far, the new plan has not brought in money, and the country is living off loans from Western countries such as Germany, who hope to partner up with the oil-rich, money-poor country.

Tuvalu

Sovereign: Queen Elizabeth II (1952)
Governor-General: Tomasi Puapua (1998)
Prime Minister: Ionatana Ionatana (1999)
Area: 10 sq. mi. (26 sq. km)
Population (1999 est.): 10,588; growth rate: 1.34%; birth rate: 21.9/1000; infant mortality rate: 25.5/1000; density per sq. mi.: 1,059
Capital and largest city (1991): Funafuti, 3,839.
Monetary unit: Tuvaluan dollar, Australian dollar.
Languages: Tuvaluan, English. **Ethnicity/race:** Polynesian 96%. **Religion:** Church of Tuvalu (Congregationalist), 97%. **Literacy rate:** less than 50%
Economic summary: GDP/PPP (1995 est.): $7.8 million; per capita income: $800; **Real growth rate:** 8.7% (1995). **Inflation:** 3.9% (average 1985–93). **Unemployment:** n.a. **Arable land:** 0%. **Agriculture:** fish, coconuts. **Exports:** $165,000 (f.o.b., 1989): copra. **Imports:** $4.4 million (c.i.f., 1989) food, fuels, machinery, animals, manufactured goods. **Major trading partners:** Australia, Fiji, New Zealand.
Member of Commonwealth of Nations

Geography Tuvalu consists of nine small islands scattered over 500,000 square miles of the western Pacific, just south of the equator. The islands include Niulakita, Nukulaelae, Funafuti, Nukufetau, Vaitupu, Nui, Niutao, Nanumaga (Nanumanga), and Nanumea.

Government Constitutional democracy.

History Formerly the Ellice Islands, Tuvalu's first Polynesian settlers were probably Samoans or Tongans. The Ellice Islands became a British protectorate in 1892 and were annexed by Britain in 1915–16 as part of the Gilbert and Ellice Islands Colony. The Ellice Islands were separated from the Gilberts in 1975, given home rule, and renamed Tuvalu. Full independence was granted on Sept. 30, 1978, but it remained part of the Commonwealth.

In 1979, the U.S. gave Tuvalu four islands that had been U.S. territory.

In 1997, the government adopted a strong stance on the need to control emissions of greenhouse gases in order to ensure the survival of low-lying island nations.

Uganda

REPUBLIC OF UGANDA

President: Yoweri Museveni (1986)
Prime Minister: Apolo Nsibambi (1999)
Area: 91,459 sq. mi. (236,040 sq. km)
Population (1999 est.): 22,804,973 (average annual rate of natural increase: 3.01%); birth rate: 48.5/1000; infant mortality rate: 90.7/1000; density per sq. mi.: 249
Capital and largest city (1991 est.): Kampala, 773,463.
Monetary unit: Ugandan shilling. **Languages:** English (official), Swahili, Luganda, Ateso, Luo. **Ethnicity/race:** Baganda 17%, Karamojong 12%, Basogo 8%, Iteso 8%, Langi 6%, Rwanda 6%, Bagisu 5%, Acholi 4%, Lugbara 4%, Bunyoro 3%, Batobo 3%, European, Asian, Arab 1%, other 23%. **Religions:** Christian, 66%; Islam, 16%. **Literacy rate:** 54%
Economic summary: GDP/PPP (1997 est.): $34.6 billion; $1,700 per capita. **Real growth rate:** 5%. **Inflation:** 6% (1997 est.). **Arable land:** 25%. **Agriculture:** tobacco, cassava, potatoes, corn, millet, pulses, beef, goat meat, milk, poultry. **Labor force:** 8.361 million (1993 est.): agriculture, 86%; industry, 4%; services, 10% (1980 est.). **Industry:** refined sugar, brewing, tobacco, textiles. **Natural resources:** copper, cobalt, limestone, salt. **Exports:** $604 million (f.o.b., 1996): gold, coffee, cotton, tea, corn, fish. **Imports:** $1.2 billion (c.i.f., 1996): machinery, transport equipment, chemicals, fuel, cotton, piece goods, food. **Major trading partners:** U.S., U.K., Kenya, Italy, France, Spain, South Africa, India, Japan. **Member of the Commonwealth of Nations**

Geography Uganda, twice the size of Pennsylvania, is in East Africa. It is bordered on the west by Congo, on the north by the Sudan, on the east by Kenya, and on the south by Tanzania and Rwanda. The country, which lies across the equator, is divided into three main areas—swampy lowlands, a fertile plateau with wooded hills, and a desert region. Lake Victoria forms part of the southern border.

Government Multiparty democracy.

History About 500 B.C.E. Bantu-speaking peoples migrated to the area now called Uganda. By the 14th century, three kingdoms dominated, Buganda (meaning "state of the Gandas"), Bunyoro, and Ankole. Uganda was first explored by Europeans as well as Arab traders in 1844. An Anglo-German agreement of 1890 declared it to be in the British sphere of influence in Africa, and the Imperial British East Africa Company was chartered to develop the area. The company did not prosper financially, and in 1894 a British protectorate was proclaimed. Few Europeans permanently settled in Uganda, but it attracted Indians, Pakistanis, and Goans, who became important players in Ugandan commerce.

Uganda became independent on Oct. 9, 1962, and Sir Edward Mutesa, the king of Buganda (Mutesa II), was elected the first president and Milton Obote the first prime minister of the newly independent country. With the help of a young army officer, Col. Idi Amin, Prime Minister Obote seized control of the government from President Mutesa four years later.

On Jan. 25, 1971, Col. Amin deposed president Obote. Obote went into exile in Tanzania. Amin expelled Asian residents and launched a reign of terror against Ugandan opponents, torturing and killing tens of thousands. In 1976, he had himself proclaimed "President for Life." In 1977, Amnesty International estimated that 300,000 may have died under his rule, including church leaders and recalcitrant cabinet ministers.

After Amin held military exercises on the Tanzanian border, angering Tanzania's president Julius Nyerere, a combined force of Tanzanian troops and Ugandan exiles loyal to former president Obote invaded Uganda and chased Amin into exile in Saudi Arabia. After a series of interim administrations, President Obote led his People's Congress Party to victory in 1980 elections that opponents charged were rigged. On July 27, 1985, army troops staged a coup and took over the government. Obote fled into exile. The military regime installed Gen. Tito Okello as chief of state.

The National Resistance Army (NRA), an anti-Obote group led by Yoweri Museveni, kept fighting after it had been excluded from the new regime. They seized Kampala on Jan. 29, 1986, and Museveni was declared president. Museveni has transformed the ruins of Idi Amin and Milton Obote's Uganda into an economic miracle, preaching a philosophy of self-sufficiency and anticorruption. Western countries have flocked to assist him in the country's transformation. Nevertheless, it remains one of Africa's poorest countries. A ban on political parties was lifted in 1996, and the incumbent Museveni won 72% of the vote, reflecting his popularity due to the country's economic recovery.

Uganda continues to battle the extremist Lord's Resistance Army based in Sudan. Close ties with Rwanda (many Rwandan Tutsi exiles helped Museveni come to power) led to the assistance of Uganda and Rwanda in the ousting of Zaire's Mobutu Sese Seko in 1997, and a year later, in efforts to unseat his successor, Laurent Kabila, whom both countries originally supported but from whom they grew estranged. In Aug. 1999, both Uganda and Rwanda signed the Congo peace agreement, along with Kabila, his foreign allies, and the rebel groups who fought against him.

Ukraine

UKRAINE

President: Leonid D. Kuchma (1994)
Prime Minister: Valery Pustovoitenko (1997)
Area: 233,000 sq. mi. (603,700 sq. km)
Population (1999 est.): 49,811,174 (average annual rate of natural increase: –0.68%): birth rate: 9.5/1000; infant mortality rate: 21.7/1000; density per sq. mi.: 214
Capital: Kyiv (Kiev), 2,637,000. **Other large cities:** Kharkiv, 1,622,000; Donetske, 1,121,000; Odessa, 1,104,000; Lviv, 803,000. **Monetary unit:** Hryvnia (since Sept. 2, 1996). **Language:** Ukrainian.
Ethnicity/race: Ukrainian 73%, Russian 22%, Jewish 1%, other 4%. **Religions:** Orthodox, 76%; Ukrainian Catholic (Uniate), 13.5%; Jewish, 2.3%; Baptist, Mennonite, Protestant, and Muslim, 8.2%. **Literacy rate:** 100%
Economic summary: GDP/PPP (1997 est.): $124.9 billion; $2,500 per capita. **Real growth rate:** –3.2% (1997 est.). **Inflation:** 10% (est. 1997). **Unemployment:** 2.6%, plus large numbers of underemployed (Dec. 1997). **Arable land:** 58%. **Labor force:** (est. 1997) 22.8 million; industry and construction, 32%; agriculture and forestry, 24%; health, education and culture, 17%, trade and distribution, 8%; transport and communication, 7%; other, 12% (1996). **Natural resources:** iron ore, coal, manganese, natural gas, oil, salt, sulfur, graphite, titanium, magnesium, kaolin, nickel, mercury, and timber. **Agriculture:** grain, sugar beets, sunflower seeds, vegetables, meat, milk. **Exports:** $15.2 billion (1997 est.): ferrous and nonferrous metals, chemicals, machinery and transportation equipment, food products. **Imports:** $20.2 billion (1997 est.): machinery and parts, transportation equipment, chemicals, energy, plastics, rubber. **Major trading partners:** C.I.S. countries, EU, Poland, Czech Republic, China, Switzerland.

Geography Located in southeastern Europe, the country consists largely of fertile black soil steppes. Mountainous areas include the Carpathians in the southwest and the Crimean chain in the south. There are forest lakes in the north. Ukraine is bordered by Belarus on the north, by Russia on the north, northeast, and east, by the Sea of Azov and the Black Sea on the south, by Moldova and Romania on the southwest, and by Hungary, Slovakia, and Poland on the west.

Government Constitutional republic.

History Ukraine was known as "Kievan Rus" (from which Russia is a derivative) up until the 16th century. In the 9th century, Kiev was the major political and cultural center in eastern Europe. Kievan Rus reached the height of its power in the 10th century and adopted Byzantine Christianity, the Church Slavonic written language, and the Cyrillic alphabet during that period. The Mongol conquest in 1240 ended Kievan power. From the 13th to the 16th century, Kiev was under the influence of Poland and western Europe. The negotiation of the Union of Brest-Litovsk in 1596 divided the Ukrainians into Orthodox and Ukrainian Catholic faithful. In 1654, Ukraine asked the czar of Moscow for protection against Poland and the Treaty of Pereyasav signed that year recognized the suzerainty of Moscow. The agreement was interpreted by Moscow as an invitation to take over Kiev and the Ukrainian state was eventually absorbed into the Russian empire.

After the Russian Revolution, Ukraine declared its independence from Russia on Jan. 28, 1918, and several years of warfare ensued with several groups. The Red Army finally was victorious over Kiev and in 1920, Ukraine became a Soviet republic. In 1922, Ukraine became one of the founders of the United Soviet Socialist Republics. In the 1930s, the Soviet government's enforcement of collectivization met with peasant resistance, which in turn prompted the confiscation of grain from Ukrainian farmers by Soviet authorities; the resulting famine took an estimated 5 million lives. Ukraine was one of the most devastated Soviet republics during World War II. (For details on World War II, see Headline History, World War II.) On April 26, 1986, the nation's nuclear power plant at Chernobyl was the site of the world's worst nuclear accident. On Oct. 29, 1991, the Ukrainian Parliament voted to shut down the reactor within two years' time and asked for international assistance in dismantling it.

When President Leonid Kravchuk was elected by the Ukrainian Parliament in 1990, he vowed to seek Ukrainian sovereignty. Ukraine declared its independence on Aug. 24, 1991. In Dec. 1991, Ukrainian, Russian, and Belarus leaders cofounded a new Commonwealth of Independent States with the new capital to be situated in Minsk, Belarus. The new country's government was slow to reform the Soviet-era state-run economy, which was plagued by declining production, rising inflation, and widespread unemployment in the years following independence. The U.S. announced in Jan. 1994 that an agreement had been reached with Russia and Ukraine for the destruction of Ukraine's entire nuclear arsenal. In Oct. 1994, Ukraine began a program of economic liberalization and moved to reestablish central authority over Crimea. In 1995, Crimea's separatist leader was removed and the Crimean constitution revoked.

In June 1996, the last strategic nuclear warhead was removed to Russia. Also that month Parliament approved a new constitution that allows for private ownership of land. An agreement was signed in May 1997 on the future of the Black Sea fleet, by which Ukrainian and Russian ships will share the port of Sevastopol for 20 years. Ukraine and Russia also signed a 10-year political treaty three days later, by which, among other provisions, Russia recognized the political and territorial integrity of Ukraine, including the Crimean Peninsula.

The Russian financial crisis in fall 1998 led to severe problems for the Ukrainian economy, which is dependent on Russia for 40% of its foreign trade. Ukraine remains saddled with its Soviet-era economy, and all of its major industries are still under state control. Western investors have shown only minimal interest.

United Arab Emirates

President: Sheikh Zayed Bin Sultan Al-Nahyan (1971)
Prime Minister: Sheikh Maktoum Bin Rashid Al-Maktoum (1990)
Area: 32,375 sq. mi. (82,880 sq. km)
Population (1999 est.): 2,344,402 (average annual rate of natural increase: 1.57%); birth rate: 18.9/1000; infant mortality rate: 14.1/1000; density per sq. mi.: 73
Capital and largest city (1989 est.): Abu Dhabi, 363,432. **Monetary unit:** U.A.E. dirham. **Languages:** Arabic, English as a second language. **Ethnicity/race:**

Emiri 19%, other Arab and Iranian 23%, South Asian 50%, other expatriates (includes Westerners and East Asians) 8% (1982). **Religions:** Islam (Sunni 80%, Shi'ite 16%), others 4%. **Literacy rate:** 68%
Economic summary: GDP/PPP (1997 est.): $54.2 billion; $24,000 per capita. **Real growth rate:** 5%. **Inflation:** 3.6%. **Arable land:** 0%. **Agriculture:** vegetables, dates, watermelon, eggs, dairy products, poultry, fish. **Labor force:** 1.05 million (1996 est.); industry and commerce, 30%; services, 65%; agriculture, 5% (note: 75% of the labor force is foreign, July 1997 est.). **Industry:** petroleum, fishing, petrochemicals, construction materials, boat building, handicrafts, pearling. **Natural resource:** oil. **Exports:** $33.2 billion (f.o.b., 1996 est.): oil and gas exports, re-exports, dried fish, dates. **Imports:** $23.5 billion (f.o.b., 1996 est.): manufactured goods, machinery and transport equipment, chemicals, food. **Major trading partners:** Japan, western Europe, U.S., Singapore, Korea, India, Iran, China, Taiwan.

Geography The United Arab Emirates, in the eastern part of the Arabian Peninsula, extends along part of the Gulf of Oman and the southern coast of the Persian Gulf. The nation is the size of Maine. Its neighbors are Saudi Arabia to the west and south, Qatar to the north, and Oman to the east. Most of the land is barren and sandy.

Government Federation formed in 1971 by seven emirates known as the Trucial States—Abu Dhabi (the largest), Dubai, Sharjah, Ajman, Fujairah, Ras al Khaimah, and Umm al-Qaiwain.

History Originally the area was inhabited by a seafaring people who were converted to Islam in the 7th century. Later, a dissident sect, the Carmathians, established a powerful sheikdom and its army conquered Mecca. After the sheikdom disintegrated, its people became pirates. Threatening the Sultanate of Muscat and Oman early in the 19th century, the pirates provoked the intervention of the British, who in 1820 enforced a partial truce and in 1853 a permanent truce. Thus what had been called the Pirate Coast was renamed the Trucial Coast. The British provided the nine Trucial states with protection but did not formally administer them as a colony.

The British withdrew from the Persian Gulf in 1971, and the Trucial states became a federation called the United Arab Emirates (U.A.E.). Two of the Trucial states, Bahrain and Oman, chose not to join the federation, reducing the number of states to seven.

The country signed a military defense agreement with the U.S. in 1994 and one with France in 1995. In 1997, U.A.E. officials protested Iranian military activities in the Persian Gulf, especially in regard to the ownership of three Gulf islands, which had been the subjects of disputes for many years.

United Kingdom

UNITED KINGDOM OF GREAT BRITAIN AND NORTHERN IRELAND
Sovereign: Queen Elizabeth II (1952)
Prime Minister: Tony Blair (1997)
Area: 94,247 sq. mi. (244,820 sq. km)
Population (1999 est.): 59,113,439 (average annual rate of natural increase: 0.13%); birth rate: 11.9/1000; infant mortality rate: 5.8/1000; density per sq. mi.: 627
Capital and largest city (1995 est.): London, 7,007,091. **Other large cities:** Birmingham,

1,009,100; Leeds, 721,800; Glasgow, 681,470; Liverpool, 479,000; Bradford, 477,500; Edinburgh, 441,620; Manchester, 434,600; Bristol, 396,600. **Monetary unit:** Pound sterling (£). **Languages:** English, Welsh, Scots Gaelic. **Ethnicity/race:** English 81.5%; Scottish 9.6%; Irish 2.4%; Welsh 1.9%; Ulster 1.8%; West Indian, Indian, Pakistani, and other 2.8%. **Religions:** Church of England (established church); Church of Wales (disestablished); Church of Scotland (established church—Presbyterian); Church of Ireland (disestablished); Roman Catholic; Methodist; Congregational; Baptist; Jewish. **Literacy rate:** 99% **Economic summary: GDP/PPP** (1997 est.): $1.242 trillion; $21,200 per capita. **Real growth rate:** 3.5%. **Inflation:** 3.1%. **Unemployment:** 5.5% (1997 est.). **Arable land:** 25%. **Agriculture:** cereals, oilseed, potatoes, vegetables, cattle, sheep, poultry, fish. **Labor force:** 28.2 million (1997); services, 68.9%; manufacturing and construction, 17.5%; government, 11.3%; energy, 1.2%; agriculture, 1.1% (1996). **Industry:** production machinery, electric power equipment, automation equipment, railroad equipment, shipbuilding, aircraft, motor vehicles and parts, electronics and communication equipment, metals, chemicals, coal, petroleum, paper and paper products, food processing, textiles, clothing, other consumer goods. **Natural resources:** coal, oil, gas. **Exports:** $268 billion (f.o.b., 1997): machinery, transport equipment, chemicals, petroleum, manufactured goods, semifinished goods. **Imports:** $283.5 billion (f.o.b., 1997): foodstuffs, machinery, manufactured goods, semifinished goods, consumer goods. **Major trading partners:** EU, U.S.

Geography The United Kingdom, consisting of England, Wales, Scotland, and Northern Ireland, is twice the size of New York State. England, in the southeast part of the British Isles, is separated from Scotland on the north by the granite Cheviot Hills; from them the Pennine chain of uplands extends south through the center of England, reaching its highest point in the Lake District in the northwest. To the west along the border of Wales—a land of steep hills and valleys—are the Cambrian Mountains, while the Cotswolds, a range of hills in Gloucestershire, extend into the surrounding shires.

Important rivers flowing into the North Sea are the Thames, Humber, Tees, and Tyne. In the west are the Severn and Wye, which empty into the Bristol Channel and are navigable, as are the Mersey and Ribble.

Government The United Kingdom is a constitutional monarchy and parliamentary democracy, with a queen and a Parliament that has two houses: the House of Lords with about 830 hereditary peers, 26 spiritual peers, about 270 life peers and peeresses, and 9 law lords, also life peers, and the House of Commons, which has 651 popularly elected members. Supreme legislative power is vested in Parliament, which sits for five years unless sooner dissolved. The House of Lords was stripped of most of its power in 1911, and now its main function is to revise legislation. The executive power of the Crown is exercised by the cabinet, headed by the prime minister.

Ruler Queen Elizabeth II, born April 21, 1926, elder daughter of King George VI and Queen Elizabeth, succeeded to the throne on the death of her father on Feb. 6, 1952. On Nov. 20, 1947, she married Prince Philip, duke of Edinburgh, born June 10,

1921. Their children are Prince Charles[1] (heir presumptive), born Nov. 14, 1948; Princess Anne, born Aug. 15, 1950; Prince Andrew, born Feb. 19, 1960; and Prince Edward, born March 10, 1964. Prince William Arthur Philip Louis, son of Prince Charles and the late princess of Wales and second in line to the throne, was born June 21, 1982. A second son, Prince Henry Charles Albert David, was born Sept. 15, 1984, and is third in line.

History Stonehenge and other examples of prehistoric culture are what remains of the earliest inhabitants of Britain. Celtic peoples followed. Roman invasions of the 1st century B.C.E. brought Britain into contact with continental Europe. When the Roman legions withdrew in the 5th century C.E., Britain fell easy prey to the invading hordes of Angles, Saxons, and Jutes from Scandinavia and the Low Countries. The invasions had little effect on the Celtic peoples of Wales and Scotland. Seven large Anglo-Saxon kingdoms were established, and the original Britons were forced into Wales and Scotland. It was not until the 10th century that the country finally became united under the kings of Wessex. Following the death of Edward the Confessor (1066), a dispute about the succession arose, and William, duke of Normandy, invaded England, defeating the Saxon king, Harold II, at the Battle of Hastings (1066). The Norman conquest introduced Norman French law and feudalism.

The reign of Henry II (1154–89), first of the Plantagenets, saw an increasing centralization of royal power at the expense of the nobles, but in 1215 John (1199–1216) was forced to sign the Magna Carta, which awarded the people, especially the nobles, certain basic rights. Edward I (1272–1307) continued the conquest of Ireland, reduced Wales to subjection, and made some gains in Scotland. In 1314, however, English forces led by Edward II were ousted from Scotland after the Battle of Bannockburn. The late 13th and early 14th centuries saw the development of a separate House of Commons with tax-raising powers. Edward III's claim to the throne of France led to the Hundred Years' War (1338–1453) and the loss of almost all the large English territory in France. In England, the great poverty and discontent caused by the war were intensified by the Black Death, a plague that reduced the population by about one-third. The Wars of the Roses (1455–85), a struggle for the throne between the House of York and the House of Lancaster, ended in the victory of Henry Tudor (Henry VII) at Bosworth Field (1485).

During the reign of Henry VIII (1509–47), the church in England asserted its independence from the Roman Catholic Church. Under Edward VI and Mary, the two extremes of religious fanaticism were reached, and it remained for Henry's daughter, Elizabeth I (1558–1603), to set up the Church of England on a moderate basis. In 1588, the Spanish Armada, a fleet sent out by Catholic King Philip II of Spain, was defeated by the English and destroyed during a storm. During Elizabeth's reign, England

---

1. The title Prince of Wales, which is not inherited, was conferred on Prince Charles by his mother on July 26, 1958. The investiture ceremony took place on July 1, 1969. The previous Prince of Wales was Prince Edward Albert, who held the title from 1911 to 1936 before he became Edward VIII.

Rulers of England and Great Britain

Name	Born	Ruled[1]	Name	Born	Ruled[1]
SAXONS[2]			Henry VI	1421	1422–1461[5]
Egbert[3]	c. 775	802–839	**HOUSE OF YORK**		
Ethelwulf	?	839–858	Edward IV	1442	1461–1483[5]
Ethelbald	?	858–860	Edward V	1470	1483–1483
Ethelbert	?	860–865	Richard III	1452	1483–1485
Ethelred I	?	865–871	**HOUSE OF TUDOR**		
Alfred the Great	849	871–899	Henry VII	1457	1485–1509
Edward the Elder	c. 870	899–924	Henry VIII	1491	1509–1547
Athelstan	895	924–939	Edward VI	1537	1547–1553
Edmund I the Deed-doer	921	939–946	Jane (Lady Jane Grey)[6]	1537	1553–1553
Edred	c. 925	946–955	Mary I ("Bloody Mary")	1516	1553–1558
Edwy the Fair	c. 943	955–959	Elizabeth I	1533	1558–1603
Edgar the Peaceful	943	959–975	**HOUSE OF STUART**		
Edward the Martyr	c. 962	975–978	James I[7]	1566	1603–1625
Ethelred II the Unready	968	978–1016	Charles I	1600	1625–1649
Edmund II Ironside	c. 993	1016	**COMMONWEALTH**		
DANES			Council of State	—	1649–1653
Canute	995	1016–1035	Oliver Cromwell[8]	1599	1653–1658
Harold I Harefoot	c.1016	1035–1040	Richard Cromwell[8]	1626	1658–1659[9]
Hardecanute	c.1018	1040–1042	**RESTORATION OF HOUSE OF STUART**		
SAXONS			Charles II	1630	1660–1685
Edward the Confessor	c.1004	1042–1066	James II	1633	1685–
Harold II	c.1020	1066			1688[10]
HOUSE OF NORMANDY			William III[11]	1650	1689–1702
William I the Conqueror	1027	1066–1087	Mary II[11]	1662	1689–1694
William II Rufus	c.1056	1087–1100	Anne	1665	1702–1714
Henry I Beauclerc	1068	1100–1135	**HOUSE OF HANOVER**		
Stephen of Boulogne	c.1100	1135–1154	George I	1660	1714–1727
HOUSE OF PLANTAGENET			George II	1683	1727–1760
Henry II	1133	1154–1189	George III	1738	1760–1820
Richard I Coeur de Lion	1157	1189–1199	George IV	1762	1820–1830
John Lackland	1167	1199–1216	William IV	1765	1830–1837
Henry III	1207	1216–1272	Victoria	1819	1837–1901
Edward I Longshanks	1239	1272–1307	**HOUSE OF SAXE-COBURG[12]**		
Edward II	1284	1307–1327	Edward VII	1841	1901–1910
Edward III	1312	1327–1377	**HOUSE OF WINDSOR[12]**		
Richard II	1367	1377–1399[4]	George V	1865	1910–1936
HOUSE OF LANCASTER			Edward VIII	1894	1936[13]
Henry IV Bolingbroke	1367	1399–1413	George VI	1895	1936–1952
Henry V	1387	1413–1422	Elizabeth II	1926	1952–

1. Year of end of rule is also that of death, unless otherwise indicated. 2. Dates for Saxon kings are still subject of controversy. 3. Became king of West Saxons in 802; considered (from 828) first king of all England. 4. Died 1400. 5. Henry VI reigned again briefly 1470–71. 6. Nominal queen for 9 days; not counted as queen by some authorities. She was beheaded in 1554. 7. Ruled in Scotland as James VI (1567–1625). 8. Lord Protector. 9. Died 1712. 10. Died 1701. 11. Joint rulers (1689–1694). 12. Name changed from Saxe-Coburg to Windsor in 1917. 13. Was known after his abdication as the duke of Windsor, died 1972.

became a world power. Elizabeth's heir was a Stuart—James VI of Scotland—who joined the two crowns as James I (1603–25). The Stuart kings incurred large debts and were forced either to depend on Parliament for taxes or to raise money by illegal means. In 1642, war broke out between Charles I and a large segment of the Parliament; Charles was defeated and executed in 1649, and the monarchy was then abolished. After the death in 1658 of Oliver Cromwell, the lord protector, the Puritan Commonwealth fell to pieces and Charles II was placed on the throne in 1660. The struggle between the king and Parliament continued, but Charles II knew when to compromise. His brother, James II (1685–88), possessed none of his ability and was ousted by the Revolution of 1688, which confirmed the primacy of Parliament. James's daughter, Mary, and her husband, William of Orange, then became the rulers.

Queen Anne's reign (1702–14) was marked by the duke of Marlborough's victories over France at Blenheim, Oudenarde, and Malplaquet in the War of the Spanish Succession. England and Scotland meanwhile were joined by the Act of Union (1707). Upon the death of Anne, the distant claims of the elector of Hanover were recognized, and he became king of Great Britain and Ireland as George I. The unwillingness of the Hanoverian kings to rule resulted in the formation by the royal ministers of a cabinet, headed by a prime minister, which directed all public business. Abroad, the constant wars with France expanded the British Empire all over the globe, particularly in North America and India. This imperial growth was checked by the revolt of the American colonies (1775–81). Struggles with France broke out again in 1793 and during the Napoleonic Wars, which ended at Waterloo in 1815.

The Victorian era, named after Queen Victoria (1837–1901), saw the growth of a democratic system of government that had begun with the Reform Bill of 1832. The two important wars in Victoria's reign were the Crimean War against Russia (1853–56) and

British Prime Ministers since 1770

Name	Term	Name	Term
Lord North (Tory)	1770–1782	William E. Gladstone (Liberal)	1886–1886
Marquis of Rockingham (Whig)	1782–1782	Marquis of Salisbury (Conservative)	1886–1892
Earl of Shelburne (Whig)	1782–1783	William E. Gladstone (Liberal)	1892–1894
Duke of Portland (Coalition)	1783–1783	Earl of Rosebery (Liberal)	1894–1895
William Pitt, the Younger (Tory)	1783–1801	Marquis of Salisbury (Conservative)	1895–1902
Henry Addington (Tory)	1801–1804	Arthur James Balfour (Conservative)	1902–1905
William Pitt, the Younger (Tory)	1804–1806	Sir H. Campbell-Bannerman (Liberal)	1905–1908
Baron Grenville (Whig)	1806–1807	Herbert H. Asquith (Liberal)	1908–1915
Duke of Portland (Tory)	1807–1809	Herbert H. Asquith (Coalition)	1915–1916
Spencer Perceval (Tory)	1809–1812	David Lloyd George (Coalition)	1916–1922
Earl of Liverpool (Tory)	1812–1827	Andrew Bonar Law (Conservative)	1922–1923
George Canning (Tory)	1827–1827	Stanley Baldwin (Conservative)	1923–1924
Viscount Goderich (Tory)	1827–1828	James Ramsay MacDonald (Labor)	1924–1924
Duke of Wellington (Tory)	1828–1830	Stanley Baldwin (Conservative)	1924–1929
Earl Grey (Whig)	1830–1834	James Ramsay MacDonald (Labor)	1929–1931
Viscount Melbourne (Whig)	1834–1834	James Ramsay MacDonald (Coalition)	1931–1935
Sir Robert Peel (Tory)	1834–1835	Stanley Baldwin (Coalition)	1935–1937
Viscount Melbourne (Whig)	1835–1841	Neville Chamberlain (Coalition)	1937–1940
Sir Robert Peel (Tory)	1841–1846	Winston Churchill (Coalition)	1940–1945
Earl Russell (Whig)	1846–1852	Clement R. Attlee (Labor)	1945–1951
Earl of Derby (Tory)	1852–1852	Sir Winston Churchill (Conservative)	1951–1955
Earl of Aberdeen (Coalition)	1852–1855	Sir Anthony Eden (Conservative)	1955–1957
Viscount Palmerston (Liberal)	1855–1858	Harold Macmillan (Conservative)	1957–1963
Earl of Derby (Conservative)	1858–1859	Sir Alec Frederick Douglas-Home (Conservative)	1963–1964
Viscount Palmerston (Liberal)	1859–1865		
Earl Russell (Liberal)	1865–1866	Harold Wilson (Labor)	1964–1970
Earl of Derby (Conservative)	1866–1868	Edward Heath (Conservative)	1970–1974
Benjamin Disraeli (Conservative)	1868–1868	Harold Wilson (Labor)	1974–1976
William E. Gladstone (Liberal)	1868–1874	James Callaghan (Labor)	1976–1979
Benjamin Disraeli (Conservative)	1874–1880	Margaret Thatcher (Conservative)	1979–1990
William E. Gladstone (Liberal)	1880–1885	John Major (Conservative)	1990–1997
Marquis of Salisbury (Conservative)	1885–1886	Tony Blair (Labor)	1997–

the Boer War (1899–1902), the latter enormously extending Britain's influence in Africa. Increasing uneasiness at home and abroad marked the reign of Edward VII (1901–10). Within four years after the accession of George V in 1910, Britain entered World War I when Germany invaded Belgium. The nation was led by coalition cabinets, headed first by Herbert Asquith and then, starting in 1916, by the Welsh statesman David Lloyd George. Postwar labor unrest culminated in the general strike of 1926.

King Edward VIII succeeded to the throne on Jan. 20, 1936, at his father's death, but abdicated on Dec. 11, 1936 (in order to marry an American divorcée, Wallis Warfield Simpson) in favor of his brother, who became George VI.

The efforts of Prime Minister Neville Chamberlain to stem the rising threat of Nazism in Germany failed with the German invasion of Poland on Sept. 1, 1939, which was followed by Britain's entry into World War II on Sept. 3. Allied reverses in the spring of 1940 led to Chamberlain's resignation and the formation of another coalition war cabinet by the Conservative leader, Winston Churchill, who led Britain through most of World War II. Churchill resigned shortly after V-E Day, May 7, 1945, but then formed a "caretaker" government that remained in office until after the parliamentary elections in July, which the Labor Party won overwhelmingly. The new government, formed by Clement R. Attlee, began a moderate socialist program.

(For details of World War II [1939–45], *see* Headline History, World War II.)

In 1951, Churchill again became prime minister at the head of a Conservative government. George VI died on Feb. 6, 1952, and was succeeded by his daughter Elizabeth II. Churchill stepped down in 1955 in favor of Sir Anthony Eden, who resigned on grounds of ill health in 1957, and was succeeded by Harold Macmillan and Sir Alec Douglas-Home. In 1964, Harold Wilson led the Labor Party to victory. A lagging economy brought the Conservatives back to power in 1970. Prime Minister Edward Heath won Britain's admission to the European Community. Margaret Thatcher became Britain's first woman prime minister as the Conservatives won 339 seats on May 3, 1979.

An Argentine invasion of the Falkland Islands on April 2, 1982, involved Britain in a war 8,000 miles from the home islands. Although Argentina had long claimed the Falklands, known as the *Malvinas* in Spanish, negotiations were in progress until a month before the invasion. When more than 11,000 Argentine troops on the Falklands surrendered on June 14, 1982, Thatcher declared her intention to garrison the islands indefinitely, together with a naval presence. Although there were continuing economic problems and foreign policy disputes, an upswing in the economy in 1986–87 led Thatcher to call elections for June 11 in which she won a near-unprecedented third consecutive term. Through much, if not all, of 1990 the Conservatives were losing the confidence of the electorate. The unpopularity of her poll tax together with an uncompromising position toward further European integration eroded support within her own party. When John Major won the Conservative Party leadership in November, Mrs. Thatcher resigned, paving the way for the queen to ask Mr. Major to form a government.

In the middle of a long recession John Major called a national election for April 1992. Confounding many political observers, the Conservatives won but by a far narrower margin than previously. After months of political maneuvering the U.K. ratified the Maastrict Treaty in Aug. 1993.

Eighteen years of Conservative rule ended in May 1997 when Tony Blair and the Labour Party triumphed in the British elections. Blair has been compared to U.S. president Bill Clinton for his youthful, telegenic personality and centrist views. He produced constitutional reform that partially decentralized the U.K., leading to the formation of separate Parliaments in Wales and Scotland by 1999. Britain turned over its colony Hong Kong to China in July 1997.

Blair's controversial meeting in October 1997 with Sinn Fein's political leader, Gerry Adams, was the first meeting in 76 years between a British prime minister and a Sinn Fein leader. It infuriated numerous factions but was a symbolic gesture in support of the nascent peace talks in Northern Ireland. In 1998 the Good Friday Agreement, strongly supported by Tony Blair, held out the promise of peace between Catholics and Protestants, but talks ran aground in 1999.

Along with the U.S., Britain launched airstrikes against Iraq in Dec. 1998 after Saddam Hussein expelled U.N. arms inspectors. Low-grade bombings of Iraq continued throughout 1999. In the spring of 1999, Britain spearheaded the NATO operation in Kosovo, which resulted in Yugoslavian president Slobodan Milosevic's withdrawal from the territory. British peacekeeping forces remain in Kosovo.

Northern Ireland

Status: Part of United Kingdom
Area: 5,452 sq. mi. (14,121 sq. km)
Population (1998 est.): 1,688,600
Capital and largest city (1992): Belfast, 287,500.
Monetary unit: British pound sterling (£). **Language:** English. **Religions:** Presbyterian, Church of Ireland, Roman Catholic, Methodist.

Geography Northern Ireland is composed of 26 districts, derived from the boroughs of Belfast and Londonderry and the counties of Antrim, Armagh, Down, Fermanagh, Londonderry, and Tyrone. Together they are commonly called Ulster, though the territory does not include the entire ancient province of Ulster. Predominantly Protestant, it forms the northern part of the island of Ireland, westernmost of the British Isles. It is slightly larger than Connecticut.

Government Northern Ireland is an integral part of the United Kingdom (it has 12 representatives in the British House of Commons), but under the terms of the Government of Ireland Act in 1920, it had a semi-autonomous government. In 1972, however, after three years of sectarian violence between Protestants and Catholics that resulted in more than 400 dead and thousands injured, Britain suspended the Ulster Parliament. The Ulster counties became governed directly from London after an attempt to return certain powers to an elected assembly in Belfast.

As a result of the Good Friday Agreement of 1998, a coalition government was to be formed by July 16, 1999, after which the transfer of legislative powers from the British Parliament to the assembly was to take place on the 17th, thereby ending three decades of direct rule from London. Peace talks broke down once again just before the government was to be formed. David Trimble, Protestant leader of the Ulster Unionist Party (UUP) and winner of the 1998 Nobel Peace Prize, was to have been first minister.

History Ulster was part of Catholic Ireland until the reign of Elizabeth I (1558–1603) when, after suppressing three Irish rebellions, the Crown confiscated lands in Ireland and settled the Scots Presbyterians in Ulster. Another rebellion in 1641–51, brutally crushed by Oliver Cromwell, resulted in the settlement of Anglican Englishmen in Ulster. Subsequent political policy favoring Protestants and disadvantaging Catholics encouraged further Protestant settlement in Northern Ireland.

Northern Ireland did not separate from the South until William Gladstone presented, in 1886, his proposal for home rule in Ireland. The Protestants in the North feared domination by the Catholic majority. Industry, moreover, was concentrated in the North and dependent on the British market. When World War I began, civil war threatened between the regions. Northern Ireland, however, did not become a political entity until the six counties accepted the Home Rule Bill of 1920. This set up a semiautonomous Parliament in Belfast and a Crown-appointed governor advised by a cabinet of the prime minister and eight ministers, as well as a 12-member representation in the House of Commons in London.

When the Republic of Ireland gained sovereignty in 1922, relations improved between North and South, although the Irish Republican Army (I.R.A.), outlawed in recent years, continued the struggle to end the partition of Ireland. In 1966–69, rioting and street fighting between Protestants and Catholics occurred in Londonderry, fomented by extremist nationalist Protestants, who feared the Catholics might attain a local majority, and by Catholics demonstrating for civil rights. These confrontations became known as "the Troubles."

The religious communities, Catholic and Protestant, became hostile armed camps. British troops were brought in to separate them, but themselves became a target of Catholics, particularly by the I.R.A., which by this time had turned into a full-fledged terrorist movement. The goal of the I.R.A. was to eject the British and unify Northern Ireland with the Irish Republic to the south. The Protestants remained tenaciously loyal to the United Kingdom, and various Protestant terrorist organizations pursued the Unionist cause through violence. Various attempts at representational government and power-sharing foundered during the 1970s, and both sides were further polarized. Direct rule from London and the presence of British troops failed to stop the violence.

In Oct. 1977, the 1976 Nobel Peace Prize was awarded to Mairead Corrigan and Betty Williams, founders of the Community of Peace People, a nonsectarian organization dedicated to creating peace in Northern Ireland. Intermittent violence continued, however, and on Aug. 27, 1979, an I.R.A. bomb killed Lord Mountbatten as he was sailing off southern Ireland, heightening tensions. Catholic protests over the death of I.R.A. hunger striker Bobby Sands in 1981 fueled more violence. Riots, sniper fire, and terrorist attacks killed more than 3,200 people between 1969 and 1998. Among the attempts at reconciliation undertaken during the 1980s was the Anglo-Irish Agreement (1985), which, to the dismay of Unionists, marked the first time the Republic of Ireland had been given an official consultative role in the affairs of the province.

In 1997, Northern Ireland made a significant step in the direction of stemming sectarian strife. The first formal peace talks began on Oct. 6 with representatives of eight major Northern Irish political parties participating, a feat that in itself required three years of negotiations. Two smaller Protestant parties, including hard-liner Ian Paisley's Democratic Unionists, boycotted the talks. For the first time, Sinn Fein, the political wing of the I.R.A., won two seats in the British Parliament, which went to Sinn Fein president Gerry Adams and second-in-command Martin McGuinness. Although the election strengthened the I.R.A.'s political legitimacy, it was the I.R.A.'s resumption of the 17-month cease-fire, which had collapsed in Feb. 1996, that gained them a place at the negotiating table.

A landmark settlement, the Good Friday Agreement of April 10, 1998, came after 19 months of intensive negotiations that involved eight of the ten Northern Irish political parties. Chaired by former U.S. senator George Mitchell, the talks were advanced by a high-profile set of mediators, including British prime minister Tony Blair, Irish prime minister Bertie Ahern, and President Bill Clinton. Two participating groups, the Protestant Ulster Democratic Party and Sinn Fein, were temporarily suspended from the talks because of continued paramilitary activities. The accord called for Protestants to share political power with the minority Catholics, and gave the Republic of Ireland a voice in Northern Irish affairs. In turn, Catholics were to suspend the goal of a united Ireland—a territorial claim that was the raison d'être of the I.R.A. and was written into the Irish Republic's constitution—unless the largely Protestant North voted in favor of such an arrangement, an unlikely occurrence.

The resounding commitment to the settlement was demonstrated in a dual referendum on May 22, 1998: the North approved the accord by a vote of 71% to 29%, and in the Irish Republic 94% favored it. But the deaths of three Catholic boys in July 1998 during the traditional Protestant marches through Catholic neighborhoods was an appalling reminder of the fragility of peace. In October, the Nobel Peace Prize was awarded to John Hume and David Trimble, leaders of the largest Catholic and Protestant political parties, an incentive for all sides to ensure that this time the peace would last.

In Dec. 1998 the rival Northern Ireland politicians agreed on the organization and contents of the new coalition government, but in June 1999 the peace process again hit an impasse when the I.R.A. refused to disarm prior to the assembly of Northern Ireland's new provincial cabinet. Sinn Fein insisted the I.R.A. would only begin giving up its illegal weapons after the formation of the new government; Unionists demanded disarmament first. As a result, the Ulster Unionists boycotted the assembly session that would have nominated the cabinet to run the new coalition government. The embryonic Northern Irish government was stillborn in July 1999, and subsequent talks have not produced results.

Scotland

Status: Part of United Kingdom
First Minister: Donald Dewar (1999)
Area: 30,414 sq. mi. (78,772 sq. km)
Population (1996 est.): 5,128,000; density per sq. mi.: 168.6
Capital (1995 est.): Edinburgh, 441,620. **Largest City:** Glasgow, 681,470. **Monetary unit:** British pound sterling (£). **Languages:** English, Scots Gaelic.
Religions: Church of Scotland (established church—Presbyterian), Roman Catholic, Scottish Episcopal Church, Baptist, Methodist

Geography   Scotland occupies the northern third of the island of Great Britain. It is bounded by England in the south and on the other three sides by water: by the Atlantic Ocean on the west and north and by the North Sea on the east. Scotland is divided into three physical regions—the Highlands; the Central Lowlands, containing two-thirds of the population; and the Southern Uplands. The western Highland coast is intersected throughout by long, narrow sea lochs, or fjords. Scotland also includes the Outer and Inner Hebrides and other islands off the west coast and the Orkney and Shetland Islands off the north coast. The famous Scottish Highlands include a series of lochs (or lakes), the largest of which is Loch Ness, famous for its mythical monster.

Government   England and Scotland have shared a monarch since 1603 and a Parliament since 1707, but in May 1999, Scotland elected its own Parliament for the first time in three centuries. The new Scottish legislature was in part the result of British Prime Minister Tony Blair's campaign promise to permit devolution, the transfer of local powers from London to Edinburgh. In a Sept. 1997 referendum, 74% of Scotland voted in favor of their own Parliament, which will control most domestic affairs, including health, education, and transportation, and will have powers to legislate and raise taxes. Queen Elizabeth opened the new Parliament on July 2, 1999.

History   The first inhabitants of Scotland were the Picts, a Celtic tribe. Between 82 c.e. and 208 c.e., the Romans invaded Scotland, naming it Caledonia. Roman influence over the land, however, was minimal.

The Scots, a Celtic tribe from Ireland, migrated to the west coast of Scotland in about 500. Kenneth McAlpin, King of the Scots, ascended the throne of the Pictish kingdom in about 843, thereby uniting the various Scots and Pictish tribes under one kingdom called Alba. By the 11th century, the monarchy had extended its borders to include much of what is Scotland today.

English influence on the region expanded when Malcolm III, king of Scotland from 1057–93, married an English princess. England's appetite for Scottish land began to grow over 12th and 13th centuries, and in 1296 King Edward I of England successfully invaded Scotland in 1296. The following year Robert the Bruce led a revolt for independence, was crowned king of Scotland (Robert I) in 1306, and after years of battle, defeated the English in 1314 at the Battle of Bannockburn. In 1328 the English finally recognized Scottish independence.

In the 16th century John Knox introduced the Scottish reformation, and the Presbyterian church replaced Catholicism as the official religion. In 1567, Mary, Queen of Scots, a Catholic, was forced to abdicate the Scottish throne, and was later executed by Elizabeth I of England. Mary's son, James VI, was raised as a Protestant, and in 1603 he succeeded Elizabeth on the English throne as King James I of England. James thus became ruler of both Scotland and England, though the countries remained separate. In 1707, after a century of turmoil, Scotland and England passed the Act of Union, which united Scotland, England, and Wales under one rule as the Kingdom of Great Britain. The House of Hanover replaced the Stuart lineage on the throne in 1714, which caused a rebellion among Scots who still supported the Stuarts. The Jacobites, as the rebels were called, led two uprisings, in 1715 and again in 1745.

With the advent of the Industrial Revolution, Scotland, whose chief product had been textiles, began developing in the industries of shipbuilding, coal mining, iron, and steel. In the late 20th century Scotland has concentrated on electronics and high tech industries. The North Sea has also become an important source of oil and gas.

In May 1999, Scotland elected their first separate parliament in three centuries. Labour won the largest number of seats in Parliament, defeating the Scottish National Party (SNP), which supports Scotland's independence from Britain.

Wales

Status: Part of United Kingdom
Secretary of State: Alun Michael (1998)
Area: 8,019 sq. mi. (20,768 sq. km)
Population (1993 est.): 2,906,500
Capital and largest city (1996 est.): Cardiff, 306,600.
  Monetary unit: British pound sterling (£). **Languages:** English, Welsh. **Religions:** Calvinistic Methodist, Church of Wales (disestablished—Anglican), Roman Catholic

Geography Wales lies west of England and is separated from England by the Cambrian Mountains. It is bordered on the northwest, west, and south by the Irish Sea and on the northeast and east by England. Wales is generally hilly; the Snowdon range in the northern part culminates in Mount Snowdon (3,560 ft., 1,085 m), Wales's highest peak.

Government Until 1999, Wales was ruled solely by the U.K. government and a secretary of state. In the referendum of Sept. 18, 1997, Welsh citizens voted to establish a National Assembly. Wales will remain part of the U.K. and the secretary of state for Wales and members of Parliament from Welsh constituencies will continue to have seats in Parliament. Although Wales will control most of its local affairs, unlike Scotland, which voted to have its own Parliament in 1999, the National Assembly will not be able to legislate and raise taxes. The Welsh assembly officially opened on July 1, 1999.

History The prehistoric peoples of Wales left behind megaliths and other impressive monuments. They were followed by settlements of Celts in the region. The Romans occupied the region from the 1st to the 5th century c.e. Thereafter Angles, Saxons, and Jutes invaded the British island, but left Wales virtually untouched. Beginning in the 8th century, the various Welsh tribes fought with their Anglo-Saxon neighbors to the east, but the Welsh were able to thwart attempted invasions. After William the Conqueror subdued England in 1066, however, his Norman armies marched into Wales in 1093 and occupied portions of it. By 1282, the English conquest of Wales was complete, and in 1284, the Statute of Rhuddlan formalized England's sovereignty over Wales. In 1301, King Edward I gave his son, who later became Edward II, the title Prince of Wales, a gesture meant to indicate the unity and relationship between the two lands. With the exception of Edward II, all subsequent British monarchs have given this title to their eldest son.

In 1400, the Welsh prince Owen Glendower led a revolt against the English, expelling them from much of Wales in just four years. By 1410, however, his rebellion was crushed. In 1485, Henry VII became king of England. A Welshman and the first in the Tudor line, Henry's reign made English rule more palatable to the Welsh. His son, King Henry VIII, joined England and Wales under the Act of Union in 1536.

The Industrial Revolution of the 19th century transformed Wales and threatened the traditional livelihood of farmers and shepards. In the 20th century, the economy of Wales was based primarily on coal production. After World War I, coal prices dropped; this, coupled with the Great Depression, fueled high unemployment rates and economic uncertainty.

In recent years, a resurgence of the Welsh language and culture has demonstrated a stronger national identity among the Welsh, and politically the country has moved toward greater self-government (devolution). In 1999, with the strong support of Britain's prime minister Tony Blair, Wales opened the Welsh National Assembly, the first real self-government Wales has had in more than six hundred years.

Dependencies of the United Kingdom

Anguilla

Status: Dependency
Governor: Robert Harris (1997)
Chief Minister: Hubert Hughes (1994)
Area: 35 sq. mi. (91 sq. km)
Population (1999 est.): 11,510; average annual rate of natural increase: 1.14%; birth rate: 16.7/1000; infant mortality rate: 18.7/1000; density per sq. mi.: 329
Capital (1992): The Valley, 1,400. **Monetary unit:** East Caribbean dollar. **Ethnicity/race:** black African.
  Literacy: 95%
Economic summary: GDP/PPP (1996 est.): $75 million; $7,200 per capita. **Real growth rate:** 3.4%. **Inflation:** 3.6%. **Unemployment:** 7% (1992). **Industry:** tourism, boat building, offshore financial services. **Labor force:** (1992): 4,400; commerce, 36%; services, 29%; construction, 18%; transportation and utilities, 10%; manufacturing, 3%; agriculture/forestry/fishing/mining, 4%. **Exports:** $1.3 million (f.o.b., 1995). **Imports:** $39.8 million (f.o.b., 1995).

Anguilla was first colonized in 1650 by English settlers from St. Christopher (St. Kitts) and has since remained a British territory. It was originally part of the West Indies Associated States as a component of the St. Kitts-Nevis-Anguilla Federation. In 1967, Anguilla declared its independence from the Federation but Britain did not recognize this action. In Feb. 1969, Anguilla voted to cut all ties with Britain and become an independent republic. In March, Britain landed troops on the island and, on March 30, a truce was signed. In July 1971,

Anguilla became a dependency of Britain and two months later Britain ordered the withdrawal of all its troops. A new constitution for Anguilla, effective in Feb. 1976, provides for separate administration and a government of elected representatives. The Associated State of St. Kitts-Nevis-Anguilla ended in 1980 and in 1982 a new Anguillan constitution took effect. In 1997, Anguilla announced that it would build a new airport, with almost double the present runway length, in an effort to increase tourism.

Bermuda

Status: Self-governing dependency
Governor: Thorold Masefield (1997)
Premier: Jennifer Smith (1998)
Area: 20 sq. mi. (52 sq. km)
Population (1999 est.): 62,472; average annual rate of natural increase: 0.46%; birth rate: 11.8/1000; infant mortality rate: 9.3/1000; density per sq. mi.: 3,124
Capital (1994 est.): Hamilton, 1,100. **Monetary unit:** Bermuda dollar. **Ethnicity/race:** black African 61%, white and other 39%. **Literacy rate:** 98%
Economic summary: GDP/PPP (1996 est.): $1.8 billion; $29,000 per capita. **Real growth rate:** 2.4%. **Unemployment:** negl. (1995). **Arable land:** n.a. **Agriculture:** bananas, vegetables, citrus fruits, dairy products. **Labor force:** 34,133; clerical, 23%; services, 23%; laborers, 17%; technical and professional, 16%; administrative and managerial, 12%. **Industry:** tourism, finance, insurance, structural concrete products, paints, perfumes, pharmaceuticals, ship repairing. **Natural resources:** limestone, sandy beaches, and clear water. **Exports:** $67.7 million (f.o.b., 1996): reexports of pharmaceuticals. **Imports:** $569 million (f.o.b., 1996): miscellaneous manufactures, machinery and transport equipment, food, live animals, chemicals. **Major trading partners:** U.S., U.K., Canada, Venezuela, Japan.

Bermuda is an archipelago of about 360 small islands, 580 miles (934 km) east of North Carolina. The largest is (Great) Bermuda, or Main Island. Explored by Juan de Bermúdez, a Spaniard, early in the 16th century, the islands were settled in 1612 by an offshoot of the Virginia Company. Bermuda became a crown colony in 1684.

In 1968, Bermuda was granted a new constitution, its first prime minister, and autonomy, except for foreign relations, defense, and internal security. The predominantly white United Bermuda Party has retained power in four elections against the opposition—the black-led Progressive Labor Party—although Bermuda's population is 61% black. U.S. air and navy bases, which had been leased in 1941 for 99-year terms, closed in 1995, along with Canadian, British army, and Royal Navy. In a referendum held in Aug. 1995, nearly three-fourths of those voting opposed independence. The prime minister's unexpected resignation in March 1997 led the ruling United Bermuda Party to name Pamela Gordon the country's first female and youngest premier. She was succeeded in 1998 by Jennifer Smith.

British Antarctic Territory

Status: Dependency
Commissioner: Peter M. Newton (1992)
Area: 500,000 sq. mi. (1,395,000 sq. km)
Population: no permanent residents

The British Antarctic Territory consists of the South Shetland Islands, South Orkney Islands, and nearby Graham Land on the Antarctic continent, largely uninhabited. They are dependencies of the British Crown colony of the Falkland Islands but received a separate administration in 1962, being governed by a British-appointed high commissioner who is governor of the Falklands.

British Indian Ocean Territory

Status: Dependency
Commissioner: David Ross MacLennan (1994)
Administrative headquarters: Victoria, Seychelles
Area: 85 sq. mi. (220 sq. km)

This dependency, consisting of the Chagos Archipelago and other small island groups, was formed in 1965 by agreement with Mauritius and the Seychelles. There is no permanent civilian population in the territory. One of its islands, Diego Garcia (17 sq. mi.), is a joint U.S.-U.K. refueling and support station that was used during the Persian Gulf War (1991).

British Virgin Islands

VIRGIN ISLANDS
Status: Dependency
Governor: Frank Savage (1998)
Chief Minister: Ralph O'Neal (1995)
Area: 59 sq. mi. (153 sq. km)
Population (1999 est.): 19,156; average annual rate of natural increase: 1.13%; birth rate: 15.9/1000; infant mortality rate: 22.2/1000; density per sq. mi.: 325
Capital (1991 census): Road Town (on Tortola): 3,983. **Monetary unit:** U.S. dollar. **Literacy rate:** 98%
Economic summary: GDP/PPP (1995 est.): $135 million; $10,200 per capita. **Real growth rate:** 4%. **Inflation:** 2.5% (1990 est.). **Unemployment:** 3% (1995). **Labor force:** 4,911 (1980). **Exports:** (f.o.b., 1990): $3.4 million: rum, fresh fish, gravel, sand, fruits, animals. **Imports:** (c.i.f., 1988): $11.5 million: building materials, automobiles, foodstuffs, machinery.

Some 36 islands (more than 20 are uninhabited) in the Caribbean Sea northeast of Puerto Rico and west of the Leeward Islands, the British Virgin Islands are economically interdependent with the U.S. Virgin Islands to the south. The principal islands are Tortola, Virgin Gorda, Anegada, and Jost Van Dyke. When Christopher Columbus explored the islands in 1493, he found the Carib people living there. By 1596 most of the Caribs had fled or been killed.

The British Virgin Islands were annexed in 1672. The English planters' slave-based sugar plantations declined after slavery was abolished in the first half of the 19th century. The islands received a separate administration in 1956 as a crown colony. In 1997, the British Virgin Islands' government decided to spend $25 million on a three-year development plan to increase tourist facilities. Tourism are the islands' mainstay.

Cayman Islands

Status: Dependency
Governor: John Wynne Owen (1995)
Area: 100 sq. mi. (259 sq. km)
Population (1999 est.): 39,335; average annual rate of natural increase: 0.87%; birth rate: 13.7/1000; infant mortality rate: 8.4/1000; density per sq. mi.: 393
Capital (1992 est.): George Town (on Grand Cayman), 15,000. **Monetary unit:** Cayman Islands dollar. **Literacy rate:** 98%
Economic Summary: GDP: (1996 est.): $860 million; $23,800 per capita. **Inflation:** 4.5%. **Unemployment:** 7% (1992). **Exports:** $3.4 million (f.o.b., 1995 est.):

turtle products, manufactured goods. **Imports:** $333 million (c.i.f., 1995 est.): foodstuffs, manufactured goods. **Major trading partners:** U.S., Trinidad and Tobago, U.K., Netherland Antilles, Japan.

The Caymans consist of three islands—Grand Cayman (76 sq. mi.; 197 sq. km), Cayman Brac (22 sq. mi.; 57 sq. km), and Little Cayman (20 sq. mi.; 52 sq. km)—situated about 180 miles (290 km) northwest of Jamaica. They were dependencies of Jamaica until 1959, when they became a unit territory within the Federation of the West Indies. In 1962, upon the dissolution of the federation, the Cayman Islands became a British dependency, and a new constitution approved in 1972 provided for a greater degree of autonomy. Tourism and finance are the Cayman Islands' major industries; tourism increased eightfold between the mid-1970s and the early 1990s and there are more than 500 licensed banks and trust companies on the islands.

Channel Islands

Status: Crown dependencies
Lieutenant Governor of Jersey: Sir Michael Wilkes (1995)
Lieutenant Governor of Guernsey: Vice Adm. Sir John Coward (1994)
Area: 120 sq. mi. (311 sq. km)
Populations (1999 est.): Jersey, 89,721; Guernsey, 65,386
Capital of Jersey (1991): St. Helier, 28,123
Capital of Guernsey (1991): St. Peter Port, 16,648.
Monetary units: Guernsey pound; Jersey pound

This group of islands, lying in the English Channel off the northwest coast of France, belonged to the Duchy of Normandy until it passed to the English Crown with the Norman conquest of 1066. It was the only British possession occupied by Germany during World War II. English and French are commonly spoken (though use of the latter is declining), and a Norman-French patois survives.

For administrative purposes, the islands are divided into the Bailiwick of Jersey (45 sq. mi.; 117 sq. km), including the Ecrehous rocks and Les Minquiers, and the Bailiwick of Guernsey (30 sq. mi.; 78 sq. km), including Alderney (3 sq. mi.; 7.8 sq. km); Sark (2 sq. mi.; 5.2 sq. km), Herm, Jethou, Brechou, and other smaller islands. The Channel Islands enjoy tax sovereignty, and their exports are protected by British tariff barriers. Financial services, tourism, market gardening, and dairy farming are important industries.

Falkland Islands and Dependencies

Status: Dependency
Governor: Richard Ralph (1996)
Chief Executive: R. Sampson
Area: 4,700 sq. mi. (12,173 sq. km)
Population (1998 est.): 2,805
Capital (1991): Stanley (on East Falkland), 1,643.
Monetary unit: Falkland Island pound
Exports: $7.6 million (f.o.b., 1995): wool, hides, meat.
Imports: $24.7 million (1995): food, clothing, fuel, building material, and machinery. **Major trading partners:** U.K., The Netherlands, Netherland Antilles, Japan.

This sparsely inhabited dependency consists of a group of islands in the South Atlantic, about 250 miles (402 km) east of the South American mainland. The largest islands are East Falkland and West Falkland. The English captain John Strong made the first recorded landing in the Falklands in 1690. The islands passed between the French, Spanish, and British until 1820, when the Argentine government proclaimed its sovereignty. In 1833 a British force expelled the few remaining Argentine officials from the island without firing a shot, and in 1841 a British civilian lieutenant-governor was appointed for the Falklands. Colonial status was granted to the Falklands in 1892. Argentina, calling the islands *Las Islas Malvinas*, regularly protested Britain's occupation of the islands. On April 2, 1982, Argentina's military government invaded the Falklands. The Falkland Islands war ended 10 weeks later with the surrender of the Argentine forces at Stanley to British troops, who had forcibly reoccupied the islands. Argentina still claims the islands. But an agreement between Argentina and the United Kingdom in 1995 sought to defuse licensing and sovereignty conflicts that would dampen foreign interest in exploiting the Falkland Islands' potential oil reserves.

The Falkland Islands' dependencies are South Georgia Island (1,450 sq. mi.; 3,756 sq. km), the South Sandwich Islands, and other islets. Three former dependencies—Graham Land, the South Shetland Islands, and the South Orkney Islands— were established as a new British dependency, the British Antarctic Territory, in 1962.

Gibraltar

Status: Self-governing dependency
Governor: Sir Richard Luce (1997)
Chief Minister: Peter Caruana (1996)
Area: 2.25 sq. mi. (5.8 sq. km)
Population (1999 est.): 29,165; average annual rate of natural increase: 0.38%; birth rate: 12.7/1000; infant mortality rate: 6.5/1000; density per sq. mi.: 12,962.
Monetary unit: Gibraltar pound. **Literacy rate:** 99% (est.)
Economic summary: GNP/PPP: (1997 est.): $500 million; $17,500 per capita. **Exports:** $83.7 million (f.o.b., 1995): re-exports of tobacco, petroleum, wine. **Imports:** $778 million (c.i.f., 1995): manufactured goods, fuels, foodstuffs. **Major trading partners:** U.K, Morocco, Portugal, The Netherlands, Spain, U.S.

Gibraltar, at the south end of the Iberian Peninsula, is a rocky promontory commanding the western entrance to the Mediterranean. Aside from its strategic importance, it is also a free port, naval base, and coaling station. It was captured by the Moorish leader Tarik, crossing from Africa into Spain in c.e. 711, and its name is derived from the Arabic, *Jabal-al-Tarik* (Mount of Tarik). In the 15th century, it passed to the Moorish ruler of Granada and later became Spanish. It was captured by an Anglo-Dutch force in 1704 during the War of the Spanish Succession and passed to Great Britain by the Treaty of Utrecht in 1713. Since then Spain has continually laid claims to it. Most of the inhabitants of Gibraltar are of Spanish, Italian, and Maltese descent, and in 1981 Gibraltarians were granted full British citizenship.

Spanish efforts to recover Gibraltar culminated in a referendum in 1967 in which the residents voted overwhelmingly to retain their link with Britain. In response, Spain sealed Gibraltar's land border between 1969 and 1985. The last British military battalion on the "Rock" was withdrawn in March 1991.

Isle of Man

Status: Self-governing crown dependency
Lieutenant Governor: Sir Timothy Daunt (1995)
Chief Minister: Donald James Gelling (1996)
Area: 221 sq. mi. (572 sq. km)
Population (1999 est.): 75,686; average annual rate of
natural increase: 0.09%; birth rate: 12.4/1000; infant
mortality rate: 2.5/1000; density per sq. mi.: 342
Capital (1991): Douglas, 22,214. **Monetary unit:** Isle of
Man pound

The Isle of Man is situated in the Irish Sea, equidistant from Scotland, Ireland, and England. Among its earliest inhabitants were Celts, and their language, Manx, which is closely related to Irish and Scottish Gaelic, remained the everyday speech of the people until the first half of the 19th century. Manx now has no native speakers. Norse (Viking) invasions began about C.E. 800, and the island was a dependency of Norway until 1266. During this period the Isle of Man came under a Scandinavian system of government that has remained practically unchanged ever since. The island came under the control of England in 1341. After allowing a succession of feudal lords rule the island, the British Parliament purchased sovereignty over the island in 1765. The Isle of Man continues to be administered according to its own laws by a government composed of the lieutenant-governor, a legislative council, and a House of Keys, one of the most ancient legislative assemblies in the world.

Leeward Islands

SEE BRITISH VIRGIN ISLANDS; MONTSERRAT.

Montserrat

Status: Dependency
Governor: Tony Abbot (1997)
Chief Minister: David Brandt (1997)
Area: 38 sq. mi. (98 sq. km)
Population (1999 est.): 12,853; average annual rate of
natural increase: 0.40%; birth rate: 13.9/1000; infant
mortality rate: 12.0/1000; density per sq. mi.: 338
Capital (1991 est.): Plymouth, 2,500. **Monetary unit:**
East Caribbean dollar
Economic summary: GDP/PPP (1996 est.): $43 million;
$5,000 per capita. **Real growth rate:** −20.2%.
Inflation: 6.2%. **Labor force:** 4,521 (1992). **Exports:**
$12.1 million (f.o.b., 1995 est.): electric parts, plastic
bags, apparel, hot peppers, live plants, cattle.
Imports: $29.9 million (f.o.b., 1994 est.): machinery
and transportation equipment, foodstuffs,
manufactured goods, fuels, lubricants and related
materials.

The island of Montserrat is in the Lesser Antilles of the West Indies. Until 1956, it was a division of the Leeward Islands. In 1958 Montserrat joined the Federation of the West Indies, remaining a member until that organization's dissolution in 1962. Unlike most other British West Indies possessions, Montserrat, with its weak economy, has not vigorously sought independence. The Soufrière Hills volcano began erupting in 1995 and the situation continued to worsen through 1998, with the capital, Plymouth, destroyed and the southern and central parts of the British colony having been evacuated. Only about 4,000 people were left in the northern "safe zone" in 1998 after thousands had moved to nearby Antigua, Britain, or other parts of the Caribbean.

Pitcairn Island

Status: Dependency
Governor: Martin Williams (nonresident) (1998)
Island Magistrate: Jay Warren (1993)
Area: 1.75 sq. mi. (4.5 sq. km)
Population (July 1998 est.): 50; density per sq. mi.: 30
Capital: Adamstown

Pitcairn Island, in the South Pacific about midway between Australia and South America, consists of the island of Pitcairn and the three uninhabited islands of Henderson, Duicie, and Oeno. Pitcairn was settled in 1790 by British mutineers from the ship *Bounty,* commanded by Capt. William Bligh. One of the most remote islands in the world, it was annexed as a British colony in 1838. Overpopulation forced removal of the settlement to Norfolk Island in 1856, but about 40 persons soon returned.

The descendants of First Mate Fletcher Christian, the 8 other mutineers, and the dozen or so Tahitians who accompanied them still inhabit the island. In addition to English, the residents of Pitcairn speak a dialect that is a mixture of Tahitian and 18th-century English.

St. Helena

Status: Dependency
Governor: David Hollamby (1999)
Area: 158 sq. mi. (410 sq. km)
Population (1999 est.): 7,145; average annual rate of
natural increase: 0.74%; birth rate: 13.9/1000; infant
mortality rate: 28.0/1000; density per sq. mi.: 45
Capital (1987): Jamestown, 1,332. **Monetary unit:**
Pound sterling. **Literacy rate:** 97%

St. Helena is a remote volcanic island in the South Atlantic about 1,100 miles (1,770 km) from the west coast of Africa. It is famous as Napoleon's place of exile (1815–21). The island was discovered in 1502 by João da Nova, a Spanish navigator in the service of Portugal. It was taken for England in 1659 by the East India Company and was brought under the direct government of the Crown in 1834. After the opening of the Suez Canal, in 1870, St. Helena's importance as a port of call diminished. About two-thirds of the colony's budget is provided by the United Kingdom in the form of a subsidy.

St. Helena has two dependencies: Ascension (34 sq. mi.; 88 sq. km), an island about 700 miles (1,127 km) northwest of St. Helena; and Tristan da Cunha (40 sq. mi.; 104 sq. km), a group of six islands about 1,500 miles (2,414 km) south-southwest of St. Helena.

Turks and Caicos Islands

Status: Dependency
Governor: John Kelly (1996)
Chief Minister: Derek H. Taylor (1995)
Area: 193 sq. mi. (500 sq. km)
Population (1999 est.): 16,863; average annual rate of
natural increase: 2.15%; birth rate: 26.4/1000; infant
mortality rate: 21.1/1000; density per sq. mi.: 87
Capital (1990): Cockburn Town, 3,720. **Monetary unit:**
U.S. dollar. **Literacy rate:** 98%
Economic summary: GDP/PPP (1996 est.): $110 million;
$7,700 per capita. **Real growth rate:** 3.5%. **Labor
force:** 4,848 (1990 est.); majority engaged in fishing and
tourist industries. **Exports:** $6.8 million (f.o.b., 1993):
lobster, dried and fresh conch, conch shells. **Imports:**
$42.8 million (1993): food and beverages, tobacco,
clothing, manufactures, construction materials. **Major
trading partners:** U.S., U.K.

These two groups of islands are near the Bahamas in the Caribbean. The principal islands in the Turks group are Grand Turk and Salt Cay; the principal islands in the Caicos group are South Caicos, East Caicos, Middle (or Grand) Caicos, North Caicos, Providenciales, and West Caicos. The islands were not settled by Europeans until 1678, when British colonists from Bermuda established a salt-panning industry. The islands were at first placed under the Bahamas government, but in 1874 they became dependencies of the colony of Jamaica. Following Jamaica's independence, they became a British crown colony. The salt production industry, the islands' economic mainstay, ceased in 1964 and gave way to tourism, offshore financial services, and fishing.

United States

THE UNITED STATES OF AMERICA

President: William J. Clinton (1993)
Vice President: Albert A. Gore, Jr. (1993)
Land area: 3,761,363 sq. mi. (9,629,091 sq. km)
Resident population (July 1999 est.): 272,878,000;
(1990 census): 248,709,873 (change 1980–1990: 9.8%).
White: 199,686,070 (80.3%); Black: 29,986,060 (12.1%); American Indian, Eskimo, or Aleut: 1,959,234 (0.8%); Asian or Pacific Islander: 7,273,662 (2.9%); Other Race: 9,804,847 (3.9%); Hispanic origin[1]: 22,354,059 (9.0%); (average annual rate of natural increase: 0.55%); birth rate: 14.3/1000; infant mortality rate: 6.3/1000; density per sq. mi.: 77
Capital (1990 census.): Washington, D.C., 606,900.
Largest cities (1998 est.): New York: city proper, 7,420,166; metro. area (1996 est.), 19,938,492; Los Angeles: city proper, 3,597,556; metro. area (1996 est.), 15,495,155; Chicago, 2,802,079; Houston, 1,786,691; Philadelphia, 1,436,287; San Diego, 1,220,666; Phoenix, 1,198,064; San Antonio, 1,114,130; Dallas, 1,075,894; Detroit, 970,196.
Monetary unit: dollar. **Languages:** predominantly English, sizable Spanish-speaking minority. **Ethnicity/race:** white 83.4%, black 12.4%, Asian 3.3%, Native American 0.8% (1992). **Religions:** Protestant, 61%; Roman Catholic, 25%; Jewish, 2%; other, 5%; none, 7%. **Literacy rate:** 97%
Economic summary: GDP/PPP (1997 est.): $8.083 trillion; $30,200 per capita. **Real growth rate:** 3.8%. **Inflation:** 2%. **Unemployment:** 4.9% (1997). **Arable land:** 19%. **Agriculture:** corn, wheat, barley, oats, sugar, potatoes, soybeans, fruits, beef, veal, pork. **Labor force:** 136.3 million (includes unemployed, 1997); managerial and professional, 29.1%; technical, sales and administrative support, 29.6%; services; 13.5%; manufacturing, mining, transportation and crafts, 25.1%; farming, fishing and forestry, 2.7%. **Industry:** petroleum, steel, motor vehicles, aerospace, telecommunications, chemicals, electronics, food processing, consumer goods, lumber mining. **Natural resources:** coal, oil, copper, gold, silver, minerals, timber. **Exports:** $625.1 billion (f.o.b., 1996): capital goods, automobiles, industrial supplies, raw materials, consumer goods, agricultural products. **Imports:** $822 billion (c.i.f., 1996): crude oil, refined petroleum products, machinery, automobiles, consumer goods, industrial and raw materials, food, beverages. **Major trading partners:** Canada, Japan, western Europe.

1. Persons of Hispanic origin can be of any race.

Government Federal republic.

The president is elected for a four-year term and may be reelected only once. The bicameral Congress consists of the 100-member Senate, elected to a six-year term with one-third of the seats becoming vacant every two years, and the 435-member House of Representatives, elected every two years. The minimum voting age is 18. (*See also* Profile of the United States, U.S. States, U.S. Cities, U.S. Statistics, and U.S. Government and History.)

U.S. Territories and Outlying Areas

Puerto Rico
COMMONWEALTH OF PUERTO RICO

Governor: Pedro Rosselló, New Progressive Party (1993; reelected 1997)
Capital and largest city (1990 pop.): San Juan, 437,745. **Other large cities (1990 pop.):** Bayamón, 220,262; Ponce, 190,900; Carolina, 177,806
Land area: 3,459 sq. mi. (8,959 sq. km)
1999 est. population: 3,887,652; average annual rate of natural increase: 0.80%; birth rate: 15.9/1,000; infant mortality rate: 10.8/1,000; density per sq. mi.: 1,124
Currency: U.S. dollars. **Languages:** Spanish and English (both official). **Ethnicity/race:** Almost entirely Hispanic. **Religions:** Roman Catholic 85%, Protestant denominations and other 15%. **Literacy rate:** 90%
Economic Summary: GDP/PPP (1997): $32.9 billion; per capita: $8,600; **Real growth rate:** 3%. **Inflation:** 5.5% (1997 est.). **Unemployment:** 13% (FY 96/97 est.) **Agriculture:** livestock products, chickens, sugarcane, coffee, pineapples, plantains, bananas. **Labor force:** (1996): 1.3 million; government, 19%; manufacturing, 13%; trade, 17%; construction, 5%; other, 32%. **Industries:** pharmaceuticals, electronics, apparel, food products, tourism. **Natural resources:** some copper and nickel, potential for onshore and offshore oil. **Exports:** $22.9 billion (f.o.b. 1996): pharmaceuticals, electronics, apparel, canned tuna, rum, beverage concentrates, medical equipment. **Imports:** $19.1 billion (c.i.f. 1996): chemicals, clothing, food, fish, petroleum products. **Major trading partner:** U.S.

The Commonwealth of Puerto Rico is located in the Caribbean Sea, about 1,000 miles east southeast of Miami, Fla. A possession of the United States, it consists of the island of Puerto Rico plus the adjacent islets of Vieques, Culebra, and Mona. Puerto Rico has a mountainous tropical ecosystem with very little flat land and few mineral resources.

Puerto Rico's executive power resides in the governor, who is elected directly for a term of four years. A bicameral legislature consists of a 27-member Senate and a 51-member House of Representatives, all elected for four-year terms. From 1940 to 1968, Puerto Rican politics was dominated by a party advocating voluntary association with the U.S. Since then, the New Progressive Party, a party favoring U.S. statehood, has won five of the last eight gubernatorial elections. Puerto Ricans have twice voted to determine their political status. In 1967, the outcome was Commonwealth 60%; statehood 39%; independence 1%. In 1993, Commonwealth dropped to 48.6%; statehood rose to 46.3%; independence polled 4.4%; and 0.6% of the ballots were blank or spoiled.

Under the Commonwealth formula, residents of Puerto Rico lack voting representation in Congress and the right to participate in presidential elections. Also, funding caps limit their access to several key federal programs. As U.S. citizens, Puerto Ricans are subject to military service and most federal laws. Residents of the Commonwealth pay no federal income tax on locally generated earnings, but Puerto

Rico government income tax rates are set at a level that closely parallels federal-plus-state levies on the mainland.

When Christopher Columbus arrived there in 1493, the island was inhabited by the peaceful Arawak Indians, who were being challenged by the warlike Carib Indians. Puerto Rico remained economically undeveloped until 1830, when the island gradually developed a plantation economy founded on three export crops: sugarcane, coffee, and tobacco. After Puerto Ricans began to press for political independence, the island was granted broad powers of self-government by Spain in 1897. But during the Spanish-American War of 1898 American troops invaded the island and Spain ceded it to the U.S. Since then, Puerto Rico has remained an unincorporated U.S. territory. Its people were granted American citizenship under the Jones Act in 1917; were permitted to elect their own governor, beginning in 1948; and now fully administer their internal affairs under a constitution approved by the U.S. Congress in 1952. In spite of broad popular support for the autonomy of the Commonwealth government and a rapidly modernizing industrial society, there were expressions of dissatisfaction. Puerto Rican extremists dramatized their desire for independence with an attempt to assassinate President Truman on Nov. 1, 1950, and on March 1, 1954, they wounded five congressmen in an attack in the U.S. Capitol.

A self-help program of economic development and social welfare (called "Operation Bootstrap") was forged in the 1940s by Puerto Rican leader and subsequent four-time Governor Luis Muñoz Marín. In a little more than four decades, much of the island's crushing poverty was eliminated. This was done partly through emphasis on the development of manufacturing and service industries, the latter related to an enormous growth in tourism. Also during this period, many Puerto Ricans migrated to large cities on the mainland U.S.

Puerto Rico is a major hub of Caribbean commerce, finance, tourism, and communications. San Juan is one of the world's busiest cruise ship ports, and Puerto Rico's standard of living continues to be among the highest in the hemisphere. Its future political status, however, remains unclear. On March 4, 1998, the U.S. House of Representatives passed a bill that called for binding elections in Puerto Rico to decide the island's permanent political status.

Guam

TERRITORY OF GUAM

Governor: Carl T. C. Gutierrez (1995)
Capital: Agaña; population (1990) 1,139
Land area: 212 sq. mi. (549 sq. km)
1999 est. population: 151,716; average annual rate of natural increase: 2.22%; birth rate: 26.5/1,000; infant mortality rate: 7.8/1,000; density per sq. mi.: 716 **1996 est. net migration:** 3 migrants per 1,000 population.
Languages: English and Chamorro, most residents are bilingual; Japanese also widely spoken.. **Ethnicity/race:** Chamorro, 47%; Filipino, 25%; Caucasian, 10%; Chinese, Japanese, Korean, and other, 18%.
Religions: Roman Catholic 98% and other 2%.
Literacy rate: 99%. **Currency:** U.S. dollars
Economic summary: GNP/PPP (1996 est.): $3 billion; **per capita:** $19,000. **Real growth rate:** n.a. **Inflation:** 11% (1995). **Unemployment:** 7.3% (Dec. 1994).
Labor force: (1994): 65,660: government, 31%;

private, 69%; construction, 12%; other, 3%.
Industries: U.S. military, tourism, transshipment services, concrete products, printing and publishing, food processing, textiles. **Exports:** $34 million (f.o.b., 1984); **Imports:** $493 million (c.i.f., 1984).

Guam is the largest and southernmost island in the Marianas Archipelago. The island is sharply divided into a northern coralline limestone plateau and a southern chain of volcanic hills. Today Guam is an unincorporated, organized territory of the United States. The people of Guam have been U.S. citizens since 1950. They have been represented in the U.S. Congress since 1973 by a nonvoting delegate, but do not participate in presidential elections. The executive branch includes a popularly elected governor, who serves a four-year term. The legislative branch is a 21-member unicameral legislature whose members are elected every two years.

Guam was probably visited by the Portuguese navigator Ferdinand Magellan (sailing for Spain) in 1521. The island was formally claimed by Spain in 1565, and its people were forced into submission and conversion to Roman Catholicism, beginning in 1668. After the Spanish-American War of 1898, Spain ceded Guam to the United States. From 1899 to 1949, the U.S. Navy administered Guam, except during 1941–44, when Japanese forces seized and occupied the island. Guam was liberated by American military forces in the summer of 1944. Guam's economy is based on two main sources of revenue: tourism and U.S. military spending (U.S. naval and air force bases occupy one-third of the land on Guam).

U.S. Virgin Islands

VIRGIN ISLANDS OF THE UNITED STATES

Governor: Charles Turnbull (1998)
Capital: Charlotte Amalie (on St. Thomas), population (1990): 12,331
Land area: 140 sq. mi (363 sq. km): St. Croix, 84 sq.. mi. (218 sq. km), St. Thomas, 32 sq. mi (83 sq. km), St. John, 20 sq. mi. (52 sq. km)
Population (est. 1999): 119,827; average annual rate of natural increase: 1.17%; birth rate: 17.1/1,000; infant mortality rate: 10.1/1,000; density per sq. mi.: 856.
Languages: English (official), but Spanish and French are also spoken. . **Ethnicity/race:** West Indian, 74% (45% born in the Virgin Islands and 29% born elsewhere in the West Indies), U.S. mainland, 13%; Puerto Rican, 5%; other, 8%; black, 80%, white, 15%, other, 5%; 14% of Hispanic origin. **Religions:** Baptist 42%, Roman Catholic 34%, Episcopalian 17%, other 7%. **Literacy rate:** 90%. **Currency:** U.S. dollars
Economic summary: GDP/PPP(1989): $1.34 billion.
Per capita: $11,052. **Real growth rate:** n.a. **Inflation:** n.a. **Unemployment:** 6.2% (March 1994). **Labor force:** (1992): 48,620. **Industries:** tourism, petroleum refining, watch assembly, rum distilling, construction, pharmaceuticals, textiles, electronics. **Exports:** $1.8 billion (f.o.b., 1992). **Imports:** $2.2 billion (c.i.f., 1992). **Aid:** Western (non-U.S.) countries, official development assistance and other official flows, and bilateral commitments (1970–89): $42 million.

The Virgin Islands, consisting of nine main islands and some 75 islets, were explored by Columbus in 1493. They were originally inhabited by the Carib Indians. Since 1666, England has held six of the main islands; the remaining three (St. Croix, St. Thomas, and St. John), as well as about

50 of the islets, were eventually acquired by Denmark, which named them the Danish West Indies. In 1917, these islands were purchased by the U.S. from Denmark for $25 million.

Congress granted U.S. citizenship to Virgin Islanders in 1927. Universal suffrage was given in 1936 to all persons who could read and write the English language. The governor was elected by popular vote for the first time in 1970; previously he had been appointed by the president of the U.S. A unicameral 15-person legislature serves the Virgin Islands, and congressional legislation gave the islands a nonvoting representative in Congress. Residents of the islands substantially enjoy the same rights as those enjoyed by mainlanders with one important exception: citizens of the U.S. Virgin Islands who are residents may not vote in presidential elections. Independence appears not to be the goal for the islands, and statehood continues to be only a remote possibility.

Tourism is the primary economic activity, accounting for most of the GDP and 70% of employment. All goods made in the Virgin Islands qualify for duty-free entry into the United States.

American Samoa
TERRITORY OF AMERICAN SAMOA

Governor: Tauese Pita Sunia (1997)
Capital: Pago Pago, population 1990: 3,519
Land area: 77 sq. mi (199 sq. km)
Population (1999 est.): 63,786; average rate of natural increase: 2.25%; birth rate 26.5/1,000; infant mortality rate: 10.2/1,000; density per sq. mi.: 828. **Languages:** Samoan (closely related to Hawaiian and other Polynesian languages) and English; most people are bilingual. **Ethnicity/race:** Samoan (Polynesian), 89%; Tongan, 4%; Caucasian, 2%; other, 6%. **Religions:** Christian Congregationalist 50%, Roman Catholic 20%, Protestant denominations and other 30%. **Literacy rate:** 99%. **Currency:** U.S. dollars
Economic summary: GDP/PPP (1995): $150 million. **Per capita:** $2,600. **Real growth rate:** n.a. **Inflation:** n.a. **Unemployment:** 12% (1991). **Labor force:** 14,400 (1990). **Exports:** $318 million (f.o.b., 1992). **Imports:** $418 million (c.i.f., 1992). **Aid (1991):** $21 million in operational funds and $1,227,000 in construction for capital-improvement projects from the U.S. Department of Interior.

American Samoa, a group of five volcanic islands and two coral atolls located some 2,600 miles south of Hawaii in the South Pacific, is an unincorporated, unorganized territory of the U.S. It includes the eastern Samoan islands of Tutuila, Aunu'u, and Rose; three islands (Ta'u, Olosega, and Ofu) of the Manu'a group; and Swains Island. Around 1000 B.C.E. Proto-polynesians established themselves in the islands, and their descendants are one of the few remaining societies of Polynesians. The Dutch navigator Jacob Roggeveen sighted the Manu'a Islands in 1722. American Samoa has been a territory of the United States since April 17, 1900, when the High Chiefs of Tutuila signed the first of two Deeds of Cession for the islands to the U.S. (Congress ratified the Deeds in 1929). Swains Island, which is privately owned, came under U.S. administration in 1925.

Until World War II the United States operated a coaling station and naval base in Pago Pago. During the war, the islands were an important U.S. Marines staging area. In 1960 American Samoa ratified its territorial constitution and has since developed a modern, self-governing political system. American Samoans elect a governor, lieutenant governor, and legislature. The legislature (Fono) consists of two houses: the Senate, selected by village chiefs (matai) for four-year terms, and the House of Representatives, elected by the general population for two-year terms. The people of American Samoa are U.S. nationals, not U.S. citizens, but many have become naturalized American citizens. Economic activity is strongly linked to the U.S., with which American Samoa does 80%–90% of its foreign trade. Tuna fishing and tuna processing plants are the backbone of the private sector, with canned tuna the primary export ($300 million annually). Transfers from the U.S. government add substantially to American Samoa's economic well-being.

Northern Mariana Islands
THE COMMONWEALTH OF THE NORTHERN MARIANA ISLANDS, OR CNMI

Governor: Pedro P. Tenorio (1998)
Capital: Chalan Kanoa (on Saipan)
Total area: 184.17 sq. mi. (477 sq. km)
Population (1999 est.): 69,398; average annual rate of natural increase: 1.98%; birth rate: 22.2/1,000; infant mortality: 6.8/1,000; density per sq. mi.: 377. Most reside on Saipan, which is also the seat of government; Rota, Agrihan, and Tinian are also inhabited. About half the population are U.S. citizens; the remainder are temporary alien workers. **Languages:** English (official), Chamorro, Carolinian. **Ethnicity/race:** Chamorro, Carolinians, other Micronesians, Caucasian, Japanese, Chinese, Korean. **Religion:** Primarily Roman Catholic. **Literacy rate:** 97%. **Currency:** U.S. dollars
Economic summary: The government of the CNMI benefits substantially from U.S. financial assistance. Gross national product (1994 est.): $524 million. Labor force: 7,476 indigenous; 22,560 foreign workers (1995). Exports (mostly garments to the U.S.): $514 million; Imports: $587 million. The U.S. and Japan are the major trade partners.

The Northern Mariana Islands, east of the Philippines and south of Japan, include the islands of Rota, Saipan, Tinian, Pagan, Guguan, Agrihan, and Aguijan. Although sighted by Ferdinand Magellan in 1521 as he sailed for Spain, the islands were not settled by Europeans until 1668, when missionaries converted the indigenous Chamorro people to Catholicism. They were ruled successively by Spain, Germany, and Japan before they became a U.N. Trusteeship (administered by the U.S.) after World War II. The Commonwealth of the Northern Mariana Islands (CNMI) became part of the United States on November 3, 1986. Spanish cultural traditions are still strong.

In recent years, Saipan's garment industry has been accused of luring thousands of Asians to the island with promises of good pay. Once there, the workers find themselves virtual prisoners forced to work in squalid sweat shops. Because of Saipan's territorial status, it is able to pay low wages and at the same time claim its clothing is "Made in the USA," sidestepping import duties and tariffs.

Midway Islands
Total area: 2 sq. mi. (5 sq. km)
Population (1995 est.): no indigenous inhabitants; 453 U.S. military personnel.

The Midway Islands consist of a circular atoll, 6 miles in diameter, that encloses two islands. Lying about 1,150 miles west-northwest of Hawaii, the islands were first explored by Captain N. C. Brooks on July 5, 1859, in the name of the United States. The atoll was formally declared a U.S. possession in 1867, and in 1903 Theodore Roosevelt made it a naval reservation. The island was renamed "Midway" by the U.S. Navy in recognition of its geographic location on the route between California and Japan. Air traffic across the Pacific increased the island's importance in the mid-1930s; the San Francisco–Manila mail route included a regular stop on Midway. Its military importance was soon recognized, and the navy began building an air and submarine base there in 1940. The Battle of Midway, which took place from June 3–6, 1942, was considered a turning point in World War II. After the war, the strategic importance of the island declined; the Midway stop for commercial air traffic was eliminated in 1950, and the air base closed in 1992.

Wake Island

Total area: 2.5 sq. mi. (6.5 sq. km)
Comparative size: about 11 times the size of the Mall in Washington, D.C.
Population (1995 est.): no indigenous inhabitants; 302 U.S. military personnel and civilian contractors.
Economy: The economic activity is limited to providing services to U.S. military personnel and contractors on the island. All food and manufactured goods must be imported.

Wake Island, about halfway between Midway and Guam, is an atoll consisting of the three islets of Wilkes, Peale, and Wake. They were discovered by the British in 1796 and annexed by the U.S. in 1899. In 1938, Pan American Airways established a seaplane base, and Wake Island was used as a commercial base for several years. On Dec. 8, 1941, it was attacked by the Japanese, who finally took possession on Dec. 23. It was surrendered by the Japanese on Sept. 4, 1945.

Johnston Atoll

Land area: 1.08 sq. mi. (2.8 sq. km); density per sq. mi.: 1,111
Population (July 1997 est.): no indigenous inhabitants; 1,200 U.S. military and civilian personnel

Johnston is a coral atoll about 700 miles southwest of Hawaii. It consists of four small islands—Johnston Island, Sand Island, Hikina Island, and Akau Island—which lie on a 9-mile-long reef. The atoll was discovered by Capt. Charles James Johnston of HMS *Cornwallis* in 1807. In 1858 it was claimed by Hawaii, and later became a U.S. possession. Johnston Atoll is a Naval Defensive Sea Area and Airspace Reservation and is closed to the public. In the early 1990s, the U.S. government opened a facility for destroying chemical weapons on Johnston Atoll.

Baker, Howland, and Jarvis Islands

These Pacific islands were claimed by the United States under the Guano Act of 1856 on May 13, 1936. Guano, composed of phosphates, was used as fertilizer in the 19th century, and its collection was a highly lucrative business. Through the Guano Act the U.S. gained a total of 79 tiny territories around the world; it still controls eight of them. Baker Island is a saucer-shaped atoll with an area of approximately one square mile about 1,650 miles from Hawaii. Howland Island, 36 miles to the northwest, is 1 mile long and half a mile wide. Howland Island is related to the disappearance of Amelia Earhart and Fred J. Noonan during their round-the-world flight in 1937—Howland Island was the destination they were headed for when they disappeared. Jarvis Island is several hundred miles to the east.

Kingman Reef

Kingman Reef, located about 1,000 miles south of Hawaii, was discovered by Capt. E. Fanning in 1798, but named for Capt. W. E. Kingman, who rediscovered it in 1853. Triangular in shape, it is about 9.5 miles long. A United States possession since 1922, Kingman Reef is a Naval Defensive Sea Area and Airspace Reservation, and is closed to the public.

Navassa Island

Navassa Island is located in the Caribbean Sea, 99.4 miles (160 km) south of the U.S. naval base at Guantanamo, Cuba, between Cuba, Haiti, and Jamaica. The island has a total area of 2 sq. mi. (5.2 sq. km). It was claimed for the U.S. under the Guano Act in 1857. The Navassa Phosphate Company mined the island until 1900, enlisting hundreds of freed American slaves to dig out several tons of guano. Working conditions were so brutal that the laborers finally revolted in 1889, killing their supervisors. The island is also claimed by Haiti.

Palmyra Atoll

Palmyra Atoll is an incorporated territory of the U.S. and privately owned. The atoll has a total area of 4.6 sq. mi. (11.9 sq. km) and is located in the North Pacific Ocean, 994 miles (1,600 km) southwest of Honolulu. It was used as a military base by the U.S. during World War II, but was not attacked.

Uruguay

ORIENTAL REPUBLIC OF URUGUAY

National name: República Oriental del Uruguay
President: Julio María Sanguinetti Coirolo (1995)
Area: 68,040 sq. mi. (176,220 sq. km)
Population (1999 est.): 3,308,523 (average annual rate of natural increase: 0.80%); birth rate: 16.8/1000; infant mortality rate: 13.5/1000; density per sq. mi.: 49
Capital and largest city (1998): Montevideo, 1,330,440.
Monetary unit: Peso. **Language:** Spanish. **Ethnicity/race:** white 88%, mestizo 8%, black 4%. **Religions:** Roman Catholic, 66%; Protestant, 2%; Jewish, 2%.
Literacy rate: 96%
Economic summary: GDP/PPP (1997 est.): $29.1 billion; $8,900 per capita. **Real growth rate:** 5.1% (1997). **Inflation:** 15.2% (1997). **Unemployment:** 10.3%. **Arable land:** 7%. **Agriculture:** wheat, rice, corn, sorghum, livestock, fishing. **Labor force:** 1.38 million; government, 25%; manufacturing, 19%; commerce, 12%; utilities, construction, transport and communications, 12%; agriculture, 11%; other services, 21% (1988 est.). **Industry:** processed meats, wool and hides, textiles, shoes, handbags and leather wearing apparel, cement, refined petroleum. **Natural resources:** hydroelectric power potential. **Exports:** $2.7 billion (f.o.b., 1997): wool and textile manufactures, beef and other animal products, rice,

fish, shellfish. **Imports:** $3.7 billion (c.i.f., 1997): machinery and equipment, vehicles, chemicals, minerals, plastics, oil. **Major trading partners:** U.S., Brazil, Argentina, Germany, China, Italy, Nigeria.

Geography Uruguay, on the east coast of South America south of Brazil and east of Argentina, is comparable in size to Oklahoma. The country consists of a low, rolling plain in the south and a low plateau in the north. It has a 120-mile (193 km) Atlantic shoreline, a 235-mile (378 km) frontage on the Rio de la Plata, and 270 miles (435 km) on the Uruguay River, its western boundary.

Government Republic.

History Prior to European settlement, Uruguay was inhabited by groups of indigenous peoples collectively known as the Charrúas. Juan Díaz de Solis, a Spaniard, visited Uruguay in 1516, but the Portuguese were first to settle it when they founded the town of Colonia del Sacramento in 1680. After a long struggle, Spain wrested the country from Portugal in 1778, by which time almost all of the indigenous people had been exterminated. Uruguay revolted against Spain in 1811, only to be conquered in 1817 by the Portuguese from Brazil. Independence was reasserted with Argentine help in 1825, and the republic was set up in 1828.

Independence, however, did not restore order, and a revolt in 1836 touched off nearly 50 years of factional strife, including an inconclusive civil war (1839–51) and a war with Paraguay (1865–70), accompanied by occasional armed intervention by Argentina and Brazil. Uruguay, made prosperous by meat and wool exports, founded a welfare state early in the 20th century under President José Batlle y Ordóñez, who ruled from 1903 to 1929. A decline began in the 1950s as successive governments struggled to maintain a large bureaucracy and costly social benefits. Economic stagnation and left-wing terrorist activity followed.

A military coup ousted the civilian government in 1973. The military dictatorship that followed used fear and terror to demoralize the population, taking thousands of political prisoners. After ruling for 12 years, the brutal military regime permitted election of a civilian government in Nov. 1984 and relinquished rule in March 1985; full political and civil rights were then restored.

Subsequent leaders contended with high inflation and a mammoth national debt. Presidential and legislative elections in Nov. 1994 resulted in a narrow victory for the center-right Colorado Party and its presidential candidate Julio Sanguinetti Cairolo, who had been president in 1985–90. The new president pushed for constitutional and economic reforms aimed at reducing inflation and the size of the public sector, partially through tax increases and privatization. The next national election is scheduled for Nov. 1999.

Uzbekistan

REPUBLIC OF UZBEKISTAN

National name: Uzbekiston Respublikasi
President: Islam A. Karimov (1990)
Prime Minister: Otkir Sultonov (1995)
Area: 172,700 sq. mi. (447,400 sq. km)
Population (1999 est.): 24,102,473; (average annual rate of natural increase: 1.57%); birth rate: 23.4/1000; infant mortality rate: 71.6/1000; density per sq. mi.: 140
Capital and largest city (1992 est.): Tashkent, 2,106,000. **Other large cities:** Samarkand, 372,000; Andijon, 302,000. **Languages:** Uzbek 74.3%, Russian 14.2%, Tajik 4.4%, other 7.1%. **Ethnicity/race (1996 est.):** Uzbek 80%, Russian 5.5%, Tajik 5%, Kazak 3%, Karakalpak 2.5%, Tatar 1.5%, other 2.5%. **Religions:** Muslim (mostly Sunnis), 88%; Eastern Orthodox, 9%; other, 3%. **Literacy rate:** 97%
Economic summary: GDP/PPP (1997 est.): $60.7 billion; $2,500 per capita. **Real growth rate:** 2.4% (1997 est.). **Inflation:** 55%.(1996 est.). **Unemployment:** 5% officially, plus large numbers of underemployed (Dec. 1996 est.). **Arable land:** 9%. **Labor force:** 8.6 million; agriculture and forestry, 44%; industry and construction, 20% (1995). **Natural resources:** natural gas, petroleum, coal, gold, uranium, silver, copper, lead and zinc, tungsten, molybdenum. **Agriculture:** cotton, vegetables, fruits, grain, livestock. **Exports:** $3.8 billion (1996): cotton, gold, textiles, chemicals, mineral fertilizers, vegetable oil, autos. **Imports:** $4.7 billion (1996): machinery and parts, consumer durables, grain, and other food. **Major trading partners:** Russia, Ukraine, eastern Europe, U.S., Czech Republic.

Geography Uzbekistan is situated in central Asia between the Amu Darya and Syr Darya Rivers, the Aral Sea, and the slopes of the Tien Shan Mountains. It is bounded by Kazakhstan in the north and northwest, Kyrgyzstan and Tajikistan in the east and southeast, and Turkmenistan in the southwest. The republic also includes the Karakalpakstan Autonomous Republic with its capital, Nukus (1992 est. pop., 182,000). The country is about one-tenth larger in area than the state of California.

Government Republic; authoritarian presidential rule.

History The Uzbekistan land was once part of the ancient Persian empire and was later conquered by Alexander the Great in the 4th century B.C.E. During the 8th century, the nomadic Turkic tribes living there were converted to Islam by invading Arab forces who dominated the area. The Mongols under Ghengis Khan took over the region from the Seljuk Turks in the 13th century. In the 14th century the region became part of Tamerlane's empire; the city of Samarkand became its capital, reaping the wealth of Tamerlane's many conquests. The Uzbeks invaded the territory in the early 16th century and merged with the other inhabitants in the area. Their empire broke up into separate Uzbek principalities, the khanates of Khiva, Bukhara, and Kokand. These city-states resisted Russian expansion into the area, but were conquered by the Russian forces in the mid-19th century.

The territory was made into the Uzbek Republic in 1924 and became the independent Uzbekistan Soviet Socialist Republic in 1925.

In June 1990, Uzbekistan declared its independence from the Soviet Union, the first of the central Asian republics to do so. Uzbekistan became fully independent and joined with ten other former Soviet republics on Dec. 21, 1991, in the Commonwealth of Independent States.

Vozrozhdeniye, an island in the Aral Sea, was a secret test site for biological weapons during the Soviet era. In 1988, the Soviets attempted to bury the evidence on the island, a frightening legacy that

Uzbekistan inherited upon independence. U.S. scientists have confirmed that the island contains live anthrax and other deadly poisons.

In Feb. 1992, President Karimov, a former Communist Party boss, affirmed his commitment to democracy and human rights, but effectively suppressed opposition parties in mid-1993. The criminal code was amended to impose stricter penalties for antigovernment activity. Opposition groups were largely excluded in future elections while the ruling party continued to post decisive victories.

In 1999, the country battled against militant Islamic groups bent on the overthrow of the secular government. In Feb. 1999, a series of bomb blasts killed 16 and injured hundreds in the capital, Tashkent. Militant Islamic gunmen remain stationed across the border in southern Kyrgyzstan, and Uzbek fighter planes have been unable to rout them.

Vanuatu

REPUBLIC OF VANUATU
President: John Bani (1999)
Prime Minister: Donald Kalpokas (1998)
Area: 5,700 sq. mi. (14,760 sq. km)
Population (1999 est.): 173,000 (average annual rate of natural increase: 2.02%); birth rate: 28.5/1000; infant mortality rate: 59.6/1000; density per sq. mi.: 33
Capital and largest city (1993 est.): Port Vila, 26,100.
Monetary unit: Vatu. **Languages:** Bislama (a Melanesian pidgin English), English, French (all 3 official). **Ethnicity/race:** indigenous Melanesian 94%, French 4%, Vietnamese, Chinese, other Pacific Islanders. **Religions:** Presbyterian, 36.7%; Roman Catholic, 15%; Anglican, 15%; other Christian, 10%; indigenous beliefs, 7.6%; other, 15.7%. **Literacy rate:** 55%
Economic summary: GDP/PPP (1996 est.): $231 million, $1,300 per capita. **Real growth rate:** 3% (1996). **Inflation:** 2.2% (1996). **Labor force:** 66,597 (1989 est.); by occupation: agriculture, 65%; services, 32%; industry, 5%. **Arable land:** 2%. **Agriculture:** copra, cocoa, coffee, coconut, taro, yams, fruits, vegetables, fish, beef. **Exports:** $30 million (f.o.b., 1996): copra, cocoa, coffee, frozen fish, timber, beef. **Imports:** $97 million (f.o.b., 1996): machines and vehicles, food, raw materials, fuel, chemicals. **Major trading partners:** EU, New Zealand, Japan, Australia.

Geography Vanuatu is an archipelago of 83 islands lying between New Caledonia and Fiji in the South Pacific. Largest of the islands is Espiritu Santo (875 sq. mi.; 2,266 sq. km); others are Efate, Malekula, Malo, Pentecost, and Tanna.

Government Republic.

History The first settlers were believed to have arrived approximately 3,500 years ago from New Guinea and the Solomon Islands by canoe. The islands were sighted by Pedro Fernandes de Queiros of Portugal in 1606 and were charted by the British navigator James Cook in 1774, who named the archipelago New Hebrides, after the northern Scottish islands. Competing British and French claims to the islands led to the formation of a condominium government, allowing for joint British-French rule in 1906. The islands' plantation economy, based on imported Vietnamese labor, was prosperous until the 1920s, when markets for its products declined. Diseases brought by missionaries, sandalwood traders, and others helped reduce the population from approximately 1 million in 1800 to

45,000 in 1935. The islands served as a major Allied base in World War II. After World War II, the indigenous Melanesians' began lobbying for independence. In 1980 the country achieved independence and was renamed Vanuatu.

A brief rebellion by French settlers and plantation workers on Espiritu Santo took place in May 1980. Britain sent a company of Royal Marines and France a contingent of 50 policemen to quell the revolt, which the new government said was financed by the Phoenix Foundation, a right-wing U.S. group.

Papua New Guinea also sent aid, and in Aug. the secessionist movement was subdued.

When French nuclear testing resumed in 1995, Vanuatu refused to join the other members of the South Pacific Forum in their condemnation, on the grounds that it was France's domestic matter.

Vatican City (Holy See)

National name: Stato della Città del Vaticano
Ruler: Pope John Paul II (1978)
Area: 0.17 sq. mi. (0.44 sq. km)
Population (July 1998 est.): 860; population growth rate: 1.15%; density per sq. mi.: 5,059. **Monetary unit:** Lira.
Languages: Latin, Italian, and various other languages.
Ethnicity/race: Italians, Swiss. **Religion:** Roman Catholic.
Labor force: High dignitaries, priests, nuns, guards, and 3,000 lay workers who live outside the Vatican.
Budget (1994): Revenues: $175.5 million; Expenditures: $175.5 million, including capital expenditures.

Geography The Vatican City State is situated on the Vatican hill, on the right bank of the Tiber River, within the city of Rome.

Government The pope has full legal, executive, and judicial powers. Executive power over the area is in the hands of a commission of cardinals appointed by the pope. The college of Cardinals is the pope's chief advisory body, and upon his death the cardinals elect his successor for life.

History The Vatican City State, sovereign and independent, is the survivor of the papal states that in 1859 comprised an area of some 17,000 square miles (44,030 sq. km). During the struggle for Italian unification, from 1860 to 1870, most of this area became part of Italy. By an Italian law of May 13, 1871, the temporal power of the pope was abrogated, and the territory of the papacy was confined to the Vatican and Lateran palaces and the villa of Castel Gandolfo. The popes consistently refused to recognize this arrangement and, by the Lateran Treaty of Feb. 11, 1929, between the Vatican and the kingdom of Italy, the exclusive dominion and sovereign jurisdiction of the Holy See over the city of the Vatican was again recognized, thus restoring the pope's temporal authority over the area.

The first session of Ecumenical Council Vatican II was opened by John XXIII on Oct. 11, 1962, to plan and set policies for the modernization of the Roman Catholic Church. Pope Paul VI continued the council, opening the second session on Sept. 29, 1963.

On Aug. 26, 1978, Cardinal Albino Luciani was chosen by the college of cardinals to succeed Paul VI, who had died of a heart attack on Aug. 6. The new pope took the name John Paul I. (For a listing of all the popes, *see* the table in Religion.) Only 34 days after his election, John Paul I died of a heart attack, ending the shortest reign in 373 years. On Oct. 16, Cardinal Karol Wojtyla, 58, was chosen pope and took the name John Paul II.

On May 13, 1981, a Turkish terrorist shot the pope in St. Peter's Square, the first assassination attempt against the pontiff in modern times. On June 3, 1985, the Vatican and Italy ratified a new church-state treaty, known as a concordat, replacing the Lateran Pact of 1929. The new accord affirmed the independence of Vatican City but ended a number of privileges the Catholic Church had in Italy, including its status as the state religion. The treaty ended Rome's status as a "sacred city." Relations, diplomatic and ecclesiastical, with eastern Europe have improved dramatically with the fall of communism. Relations with Russia, while improving, have not yet reached the ambassadorial level. Diplomatic ties were established in March 1994 with Jordan and full relations established with Israel in June. Six months earlier the two nations had accorded each other mutual recognition. The Holy See, calling for closer relations with Orthodoxy, was scheduled to meet with Russian Patriarch Alexy II in June 1997, but differences prevented the encounter from taking place. In Jan. 1998, Pope John Paul II made a historic visit to Cuba, hoping to promote religious freedom in that communist nation. Iranian president Mohammad Khatami met with the pope in 1999, the first state visit by an Iranian leader to a western nation since Iran's 1979 Islamic revolution.

Venezuela

REPUBLIC OF VENEZUELA

National name: Republica de Venezuela
President: Hugo Chavez (1999)
Area: 352,143 sq. mi. (912,050 sq. km)
Population (1999 est.): 23,203,466 (average annual rate of natural increase: 1.73%); birth rate: 22.3/1000; infant mortality rate: 26.5/1000; density per sq. mile: 66
Capital: Caracas. **Largest cities (1990 est.):** Caracas, city, 1,824,892, metro area, 2,784,042; Maracaibo, 1,206,726; Valencia, 616,000; Barquisimento, 723,587.
Monetary unit: bolivar. **Languages:** Spanish, various indigenous languages in the remote interior. **Ethnicity/race:** mestizo 67%, white 21%, black 10%, Amerindian 2%. **Religions:** Roman Catholic, 96%; Protestant, 2%. **Literacy rate:** 91.1%
Economic summary: GDP: (1997 est.): $185 billion, $8,300 per capita. **Real growth rate:** 5% (1997). **Inflation:** 38% (1997). **Unemployment:** 11.5%. **Arable land:** 4%. **Agriculture:** rice, coffee, corn, cacao, sugar, bananas, dairy and meat products. **Labor force:** 9.2 million; services, 64%; industry, 23%; agriculture, 13%. **Industry:** petroleum, iron ore mining, construction materials, food processing, textiles, steel, aluminum, motor vehicle assembly. **Natural resources:** petroleum, natural gas, iron ore, hydroelectric power. **Exports:** $20.8 billion (f.o.b., 1996): petroleum, iron ore, bauxite. **Imports:** $10.5 billion (f.o.b., 1996): raw materials, machinery and equipment, transport equipment, construction materials. **Major trading partners:** U.S., Japan, Germany, Italy, The Netherlands, Canada.

Geography Venezuela, a third larger than Texas, occupies most of the northern coast of South America on the Caribbean Sea. It is bordered by Colombia to the west, Guyana to the east, and Brazil to the south. Mountain systems break Venezuela into four distinct areas: (1) the Maracaibo lowlands; (2) the mountainous region in the north and northwest; (3) the Orinoco basin, with the llanos (vast grass-covered plains) on its northern border and great forest areas in the south and southeast; (4) the Guiana Highlands, south of the Orinoco, accounting for nearly half the national territory.

Government Federal republic.

History The Arawak and Carib Indians were the first inhabitants of Venezuela. Columbus explored Venezuela on his third voyage in 1498. A subsequent Spanish explorer gave the country its name, meaning "Little Venice." There were no important settlements until Caracas was founded in 1567. Simón Bolívar, who led the liberation of much of the continent from Spain, was born in Caracas in 1783. With Bolívar taking part, Venezuela was one of the first South American colonies to revolt against Spain, in 1810, but it was not until 1821 that independence was won. Federated at first with Colombia and Ecuador as the Republic of Greater Colombia, the country set up a republic in 1830 and then sank for many decades into a condition of revolt, dictatorship, and corruption.

From 1908 to 1935, Gen. Juan Vicente Gómez was an absolute dictator. A military junta ruled after his death in 1935. Dr. Rómulo Betancourt and the liberal Acción Democrática Party won a majority of seats in a constituent assembly to draft a new constitution in 1946. A well-known writer, Rómulo Gallegos, candidate of Betancourt's party, easily won the presidential election of 1947. But the army ousted Gallegos the following year and instituted a military junta.

The country overthrew the dictatorship of Marcos Peréz Jiménez in 1958 and thereafter enjoyed a series of stable, democratically elected governments, beginning with that of Rómulo Betancourt, who served from 1959–64. Rafael Caldera Rodríguez, president from 1969 to 1974, legalized the Communist Party and established diplomatic relations with Moscow.

In 1974, President Carlos Andrés Pérez took office and, in 1976, Venezuela nationalized 21 oil companies, mostly subsidiaries of U.S. firms, offering compensation of $1.28 billion. Venezuela's developing market economy (Venezuela has the highest GNP per capita of any country in South America) continues to be supported mainly by the exploitation of petroleum, natural gas, and mineral reserves. President Pérez was reelected to a non-consecutive term in 1988. Venezuela experienced political turbulence in response to a 1989 economic austerity program launched by President Pérez. Disgruntled military officers unsuccessfully mounted two coup attempts in 1992 and, in 1993, Congress impeached Pérez on corruption charges. President Rafael Caldera was elected in December 1993. His administration's primary concerns were economic problems. In June 1994, approximately half of the country's banking sector collapsed and the government dealt with falling oil prices, foreign debt repayment, and high inflation in the mid-1990s. In 1997, the government announced that it planned to permit large-scale gold and diamond mining in the Imataca reserve in order to reap large tax revenues and create new, badly needed jobs. The creation of jobs was still an issue during the first quarter of 1999, when Venezuela's economy shrunk by nearly 10%, mostly due to falling oil prices. President Chavez, who took office on Feb. 2, 1999, made the idea of a new constitution the centerpiece of his governing agenda. Members of a constituent assembly formed to rewrite the Magna Carta on July 25, 1999. In Aug. a constitutional assembly made up of Chavez allies replaced the existing democratically elected congress. Popular with voters, who have been clamoring for the reform of their ailing economy and a stop to the growing chasm between rich and poor, Chavez has gradually garnered more and more power. His critics predict the emergence of a left-wing dictatorship.

Vietnam

SOCIALIST REPUBLIC OF VIETNAM

National name: Công Hòa Xa Hôi Chú Nghia Viêt Nam
President: Tran Duc Luong (1997)
Prime Minister: Phan Van Khai (1997)
Area: 127,246 sq. mi. (329,560 sq. km)
Population (1999 est.): 77,311,210 (average annual rate of natural increase: 1.42%); birth rate: 20.8/1000; infant mortality rate: 34.8/1000; density per sq. mi.: 608
Capital: Hanoi. **Largest cities (1992 est.):** Ho Chi Minh City (Saigon), 3,015,743; Hanoi, 1,073,760. Other large cities (1989): Haiphong, 456,049; Da Nang, 370,670; Nha Trang, 213,687; Qui Nho'n, 160,091; Hué 211,085. **Monetary unit:** Dong. **Languages:** Vietnamese (official), French, English, Khmer, Chinese. **Ethnicity/race:** Vietnamese 85%–90%, Chinese 3%, Muong, Thai, Meo, Khmer, Man, Cham. **Religions:** Buddhist, Roman Catholic, Islam, Taoist, Confucian, Animist. **Literacy rate:** 94%
Economic summary: GDP/PPP (1997 est.): $128 billion; $1,700 per capita. **Real growth rate:** 8.5%. **Inflation:** 5% (1997). **Unemployment:** 25% (1995 est.). **Arable land:** 17%. **Agriculture:** rice, corn, potatoes, rubber, soybeans, coffee, tea, bananas, poultry, pigs, fish. **Labor force:** 32.7 million; agriculture, 65%, industry and services, 35%. **Industry:** food processing, garments, shoes, machine building, mining, cement, chemical fertilizer, glass, tires, oil. **Natural resources:** phosphates, forests, coal. **Exports:** $7.1 billion (f.o.b., 1996 est.): crude oil, machine products, rice, coffee, rubber, tea, garments, shoes. **Imports:** $11.1 billion (f.o.b., 1996 est.): machinery and equipment, petroleum products, fertilizer, steel products, raw cotton, grain, cement, motorcycles. **Major trading partners:** Singapore, Japan, Hong Kong, Thailand, Germany, Indonesia, South Korea, Taiwan.

Geography Vietnam occupies the eastern and southern part of the Indochinese peninsula in Southeast Asia, with the South China Sea along its entire coast. China is to the north and Laos and Cambodia to the west. Long and narrow on a north-south axis, Vietnam is about twice the size of Arizona. The Mekong River delta lies in the south..

Government Communist state.

History The Vietnamese are descendants of nomadic Mongols from China and migrants from Indonesia. According to mythology, the first ruler of Vietnam was Hung Vuong, who founded the nation in 2879 B.C.E. From 111 B.C.E. China ruled the nation then known as Nam Viet as a vassal state until the 15th century, an era of nationalistic expansion, when Cambodians were pushed out of the southern area of what is now Vietnam.

A century later, the Portuguese were the first Europeans to enter the area. France established its influence early in the 19th century, and within 80 years conquered the three regions into which the country was then divided—Cochin-China in the south, Annam in the central region, and Tonkin in the north.

France first unified Vietnam in 1887, when a single governor-generalship was created, followed by the first physical links between north and south—a rail and road system. Even at the beginning of World War II, however, there were internal differences among the three regions. Japan took over military bases in Vietnam in 1940 and a pro-Vichy French administration remained until 1945. Veteran Communist leader Ho Chi Minh organized an independence movement known as the Vietminh to exploit the confusion surrounding France's weakened influence in the region. At the end of the war, Ho's followers seized Hanoi and declared a short-lived republic, which ended with the arrival of French forces in 1946.

Paris proposed a unified government within the French Union under the former Annamite emperor, Bao Dai. Cochin-China and Annam accepted the proposal, and Bao Dai was proclaimed emperor of all Vietnam in 1949. Ho and the Vietminh withheld support, and the revolution in China gave them the outside help needed for a war of resistance against French and Vietnamese troops armed largely by a United States worried about cold war Communist expansion.

A bitter defeat at Dien Bien Phu in northwest Vietnam on May 5, 1954, broke the French military campaign and resulted in the division of Vietnam. In the new South, Ngo Dinh Diem, premier under Bao Dai, deposed the monarch in 1955 and made himself president. Diem used strong U.S. backing to create an authoritarian regime that suppressed all opposition but could not eradicate the Northern-supplied Communist Viet Cong.

Skirmishing grew into a full-scale war, with escalating U.S. involvement. A military coup, U.S.-inspired in the view of many, ousted Diem on Nov. 1, 1963, and a kaleidoscope of military governments followed. The most savage fighting of the war occurred in early 1968 during the Vietnamese New Year, known as Tet. Although the so-called Tet Offensive ended in a military defeat for the North, its psychological impact changed the course of the war.

U.S. bombing and an invasion of Cambodia in the summer of 1970—an effort to destroy Viet Cong bases in the neighboring state—marked the end of major U.S. participation in the fighting. Most American ground troops were withdrawn from combat by mid-1971 when the U.S. conducted heavy bombing raids on the Ho Chi Minh Trail—a crucial North Vietnamese supply line. In 1972, secret peace negotiations led by Secretary of State Henry A. Kissinger took place and peace settlement was signed in Paris on Jan. 27, 1973.

By April 9, 1975, Hanoi's troops marched within 40 miles of Saigon, the South's capital. South Vietnam's president Thieu resigned on April 21 and fled. Gen. Duong Van Minh, the new president, surrendered Saigon on April 30, ending a war that claimed the lives of 1.3 million Vietnamese and 58,000 Americans.

In 1977, border clashes between Vietnam and Cambodia intensified, as well as accusations by its former ally Beijing that Chinese residents of Vietnam were being subjected to persecution. Beijing cut off all aid and withdrew 800 technicians.

Hanoi was also preoccupied with a continuing war in Cambodia, where 60,000 Vietnamese troops had invaded and overthrown the country's Communist leader Pol Pot and his pro-Chinese regime. In early 1979, Vietnam was conducting a two-front war: defending its northern border against a Chinese invasion, and supporting its army in Cambodia, which was still fighting Pol Pot's Khmer Rouge guerrillas. Hanoi's Marxist policies combined with the destruction of the country's infrastructure during the decades of fighting devastated Vietnam's economy. However, it started to pick up in 1986 under *do Maui* (economic renovation), an effort at limited privatization. Vietnamese troops began limited withdrawals from Laos and Cambodia in 1988, and Vietnam supported the Cambodian peace agreement signed in Oct. 1991.

The U.S. lifted a Vietnamese trade embargo in Feb. 1994 that had been in place since its involvement in the war. Full diplomatic relations were announced between the two countries in July 1995. In April 1997, a pact was signed with the U.S. concerning repayment of the $146 million wartime debt incurred by the South Vietnamese government, and the following year the nation began a drive to eliminate inefficient bureaucrats and streamline the approval process for direct foreign investment. Although reform-minded officials have in recent years won key roles in government, Vietnam's ruling Communist Party has adamantly resisted political changes, even as major economic restructuring has been set in motion

(For a Vietnam War chronology, *see* Headline History.)

Western Sahara

WESTERN SAHARA

Head of State: none
Area: 165,185 sq. mi. (266,000 sq. km)
Population (1999): 239,333; growth rate: 2.88%; birth rate: 45.4/1000; infant mortality rate: 136.7/1000; density per sq. mi.: 1.5
Largest cities (1991): El Aaiun (20,010). **Monetary unit:** Moroccan dirham (DH). **Languages:** Hassaniya Arabic, Moroccan Arabic. **Ethnicity/race:** Saharawi, Arab, Berber. **Religion:** Muslim. **Literacy rate:** n.a.
Economic summary: GDP: n.a.; **Labor force:** 12,000; pastoral nomadism, fishing, and phosphate mining are the principal sources of income. **Agriculture:** fruits, vegetables, camels, sheep, goats. **Industry:** phosphates, handicrafts. **Major trading partners:** Morocco claims and administers Western Sahara, so trade partners are included in overall Moroccan accounts.

Geography Located in northern Africa on the Atlantic Ocean, Western Sahara is surrounded by Algeria to the east, Morocco to the north, and Mauritania to the south. About the size of Colorado, it is mostly low, flat desert with some small mountains in the south and northeast.

Government Legal status of the territory is disputed and sovereignty unresolved; a U.N. referendum on the issue is planned. The territory is contested by Morocco and the Polisario Front, which in Feb. 1976 formerly proclaimed a government-in-exile of the Saharawi Arab Democratic Republic, now officially recognized by about 70 countries.

History Little is known about Western Sahara until the 4th century B.C.E. when trade with Europe began. During the Middle Ages it was occupied first by Berbers, and then by the Arabic-speaking Muslim Bedouins. In the 19th century the Spanish lay claim to the southern coastal region, called Rio de Oro, and later occupied the northern interior region, Saguia el Hamra, in 1934. The Spanish formally united the two regions, and it became known as Spanish Sahara in 1958. Both Morocco and Mauritania sought to control the territory, and when the Spanish departed in 1976 they divided the territory between them. In the meantime, the indigenous Saharawis began fighting for independence. In 1976, the insurgents, called the Polisario Front, declared a government-in-exile (the Saharawi Arab Democratic Republic) from their base in Algeria. Mauritania reached a peace agreement with the Polisario in 1979, but Morocco then seized the land given up by Mauritania, and now exerts administrative control over the entire region. The U.N. is attempting to hold a referendum on the issue, and a U.N.-administered cease-fire has been in effect since Sept. 1991, but the issue remains unresolved.

Republic of Yemen

National name: Al Jumhuriyahal Yamaniyah
President: Ali Abdullah Saleh
Prime Minister: Abdul Karim al-Iryani (1998)
Area: 203,850 sq. mi. (527,970 sq. km)
Population (1999 est.): 16,942,230 (average annual rate of natural increase: 3.34%); birth rate: 43.3/1000; infant mortality rate: 69.8/1000; density per sq. mi.: 83
Capital (1995): Sanaá 972,011. **Largest cities (1995):** Tiaz, 2,205,947; Hodiedah, 1,749,944; Aden, 562,162.
Monetary unit: Rial. **Language:** Arabic. **Ethnicity/race:** predominantly Arab; Afro-Arab concentrations in western coastal locations; South Asians in southern regions; small European communities in major metropolitan areas. **Religion:** Islam (Sunni and Shi'ite). **Literacy rate:** 39%
Economic summary: GDP: (1997 est.): $31.8 billion; $2,300 per capita. **Real growth rate:** 5%. **Inflation:** 5%. **Unemployment:** 30% (1995 est.). **Arable land:** 3%. **Agriculture:** grains, fruits, vegetables, coffee, cotton, dairy products, poultry, meat, fish. **Industry:** crude and refined oil, textiles, leather goods, handicrafts, fish, aluminum products. **Exports:** $2.3 billion (f.o.b., 1997 est.): cotton, coffee, hides, vegetables, dried fish. **Imports:** $2.3 billion (f.o.b., 1997 est.): textiles, manufactured consumer goods, foodstuffs, sugar, grain, flour. **Major trading partners:** U.K., Japan, Saudi Arabia, Australia, U.S.

Geography Formerly known as the states of People's Democratic Republic of Yemen and the Yemen Arab Republic, the Republic of Yemen occupies the southwestern tip of the Arabian Peninsula on the Red Sea opposite Ethiopia, and extends along the southern part of the Arabian Peninsula on the Gulf of Aden and the Indian Ocean. Saudi Arabia is to the north and Oman is to the east. The country is about the size of France. A 700-mile (1,130-km) narrow coastal plain in the south gives way to a mountainous region and then a plateau area. Some of the interior highlands in the west attain a height of 12,000 feet (3,660 m).

Government Parliamentary.

History The history of Yemen dates back to the Minaean (1200–650 B.C.E.) and Sabaean (750–115 B.C.E.) kingdoms. Ancient Yemen (centered around the port of Aden) engaged in the lucrative myrrh and frankincense trade. It was invaded by the Romans (1st century C.E.) as well as the Ethiopians and Persians (6th century C.E.). In C.E. 628 it converted to Islam and in the 10th century came under the control of the Rassite dynasty of the Zaidi sect, which remained involved in North Yemeni politics until 1962. The Ottoman Turks nominally occupied the area from 1538 to the decline of their empire in 1918.

The northern portion of Yemen was ruled by imams until a pro-Egyptian military coup took place in 1962. The junta proclaimed the Yemen Arab Republic, and after a civil war in which Egypt's Nasser and the U.S.S.R. supported the revolutionaries, and King Saud of Saudi Arabia and King Hussein of Jordan supported the royalists, the war finally ended with the defeat of the royalists in mid-1969.

The southern port of Aden, strategically located at the opening of the Red Sea, was colonized by Britain in 1839, and by 1937, with an expansion of its territory, was known as the Aden Protectorate. In the 1960s the Nationalist Liberation Front (NLF) fought against British rule, which led to the establishment of the People's Republic of Southern Yemen on Nov. 30, 1967. In 1979, under strong Soviet influence, the People's Democratic Republic of Yemen, the country became the only Marxist state in the Arab world.

The Republic of Yemen was established on May 22, 1990, when pro-Western Yemen and Marxist Yemen Arab Republic merged after 300 years of separation to form the new nation. The poverty and decline in Soviet economic support in the South was an important incentive for the merger. The new president, Ali Abdullah Saleh, was elected by the parliaments of both countries.

Differences over power sharing and the pace of integration between the north and the south came to a head in 1994, resulting in a civil war. The north's superior forces quickly overwhelmed the south in May and early June despite the south's brief declaration of succession. The victorious north presented a reconciliation plan providing for a general amnesty and pledges to protect political democracy.

The president's party, the General People's Congress, won an enormous victory in the April 1997 parliamentary elections, the first since the civil war. In 1998–99, a militant Islamic group, the Aden-Abyan Islamic Army, kidnapped several groups of Western tourists, which led to the deaths of four during a poorly orchestrated rescue attempt. The group's leader, Zein Al-Abidine al-Mihdar, threatened to continue attacks on tourists and government officials. The goal of the militants is to overthrow the government and turn Yemen into an Islamic state.

Yugoslavia

SEE SERBIA AND MONTENEGRO.

Zaire

SEE CONGO, DEMOCRATIC REBUBLIC OF.

Zambia
REPUBLIC OF ZAMBIA

President: Frederick T. J. Chiluba (1991)
Area: 290,586 sq. mi. (752,610 sq. km)
Population (1999 est.): 9,663,535 (average annual rate of natural increase: 2.20%); birth rate: 44.5/1000; infant mortality rate: 91.9/1000; density per sq. mi.: 33
Capital: Lusaka. **Largest cities (1997):** Lusaka, 1.6 million; (1990 est.) Kitwe, 338,207; Ndola, 376,311; Chingola, 167,954. **Monetary unit:** Kwacha.
Languages: English and local dialects. **Ethnicity/race:** African 98.7%, European 1.1%, other 0.2%.
Religions: Christian, 50–75%; Islam and Hindu, 24–49%; remainder indigenous beliefs. **Literacy rate:** 73%
Economic summary: GDP/PPP (1997 est.): $8.8 billion; $950 per capita. **Real growth rate:** 3.5%. **Inflation:** 43.9% (1997 est.). **Unemployment:** 22% (1991). **Arable land:** 7%. **Agriculture:** corn, sorghum, rice, peanuts, sunflower seed, tobacco, cotton, sugarcane, cassava, cattle, goats, pigs, poultry, beef, pork, milk, eggs, hides. **Labor force:** 3.4 million; agriculture 85%. **Industry:** machinery, transportation equipment, foodstuffs, fuels, petroleum products, electricity, miscellaneous manufactured goods. **Natural resources:** copper, zinc, lead, cobalt, coal. **Exports:** $975 million (f.o.b., 1996 est.): copper, zinc, lead, cobalt, tobacco. **Imports:** $990 million (f.o.b., 1996 est.): manufactured goods, machinery and transport equipment, foodstuffs, fuels. **Major trading partners:** Western Europe, Japan, South Africa, U.S., Saudi Arabia, India. **Member of Commonwealth of Nations.**

Geography Zambia, a landlocked country in south-central Africa, is about one-tenth larger than Texas. It is surrounded by Angola, Zaire, Tanzania, Malawi, Mozambique, Zimbabwe, Botswana, and Namibia. The country is mostly a plateau that rises to 8,000 feet (2,434 m) in the east.

Government Republic.

History Early humans inhabited present-day Zambia between one and two million years ago. Today the country is made up almost entirely of Bantu-speaking peoples.

Empire builder Cecil Rhodes obtained mining concessions in 1889 from King Lewanika of the Barotse and sent settlers to the area soon thereafter. The region was ruled by the British South Africa Company, which he established, until 1924, when the British government took over the administration.

From 1953 to 1964, Northern Rhodesia was federated with Southern Rhodesia and Nyasaland (now Malawi) in the Federation of Rhodesia and Nyasaland. On Oct. 24, 1964, Northern Rhodesia became the independent nation of Zambia.

Kenneth Kaunda, the first president, kept Zambia within the Commonwealth of Nations. The country's economy, dependent on copper exports, was threatened when Rhodesia declared its independence from British rule in 1965 and defied U.N. sanctions, which Zambia supported, an action that deprived Zambia of its trade route through Rhodesia. The U.S., Britain, and Canada organized an airlift in 1966 to ship gasoline into Zambia. In 1967, Britain agreed to finance new trade routes for Zambia.

Kaunda visited China in 1967, and China later agreed to finance a 1,000-mile railroad from the copper fields to Dar es Salaam in Tanzania. A pipeline was opened in 1968 from Ndola in Zambia's copper belt to the Indian Ocean at Dar es Salaam, ending the three-year oil drought. In 1969, Kaunda announced the nationalization of the foreign copper-mining industry, with Zambia to take 51% (over $1 billion, estimated). He then announced a similar takeover of foreign oil producers.

With a soaring debt and inflation rate in 1991, riots took place in Lusaka, resulting in a number of killings. Mounting domestic pressure forced Kaunda to move Zambia toward multiparty democracy.

National elections on Oct. 31, 1991, brought a stunning defeat to long-serving President Kaunda and a repudiation of his persistent belief in a one-party state. The newly elected chief executive, Frederick Chiluba, called for sweeping economic reforms, including privatization and the establishment of a stock market. Parliament passed a bill in May 1996 that stated a president may serve only two terms, thus preventing any possible political return of Kenneth Kaunda, a measure criticized by opposition parties. General elections in Nov. 1996 saw the reelection of President Chiluba with 70% of the vote.

In 1999 Angola accused Zambia of supporting the UNITA rebels, who are in the midst of a civil war with the Angolan government. Zambia refuted the charges, claiming that Angola's anger stemmed from Zambia's refusal to allow it to fight against the rebels within Zambian borders.

Zimbabwe

REPUBLIC OF ZIMBABWE

Executive President: Robert Mugabe (1987)
Area: 150,698 sq. mi. (390,580 sq. km)
Population (1999 est.): 11,163,160 (average annual rate of natural increase: 1.02%); birth rate: 30.6/1000; infant mortality rate: 61.2/1000; density per sq. mi.: 74
Capital and largest city (1992): Harare, 1,184,169. **Other large cities:** Bulawayo, 621,000; Chitungwiza, 274,035. **Monetary unit:** Zimbabwean dollar.
Languages: English (official), Ndebele, Shona (85%).
Ethnicity/race: African 98% (Shona 71%, Ndebele 16%, other 11%), white 1%, mixed and Asian 1%.
Religions: Christian, 25%; Animist, 24%; Syncretic, 50%. **Literacy rate:** 85%
Economic summary: GDP/PPP (1996 est.): $24.9 billion; $2,200 per capita. **Real growth rate:** 8.1%. **Inflation:** 21.4%. **Unemployment:** at least 45% (1994 est.). **Arable land:** 7%. **Agriculture:** corn, cotton, tobacco, wheat, coffee, sugarcane, peanuts, cattle, sheep, goats, pigs. **Labor force:** 4.228 million (1993 est.); agriculture, 27%; transport and services, 46%; industry, 27%. **Industry:** mining, copper, steel, nickel, tin, wood products, cement, chemicals, fertilizer, footwear, foodstuffs, beverages, clothes. **Natural resources:** gold, copper, chrome, nickel, tin, asbestos. **Exports:** $2.5 billion (f.o.b., 1996 est.): gold, tobacco, asbestos, copper, meat, chrome, nickel, corn, sugar. **Imports:** $2.2 billion (f.o.b., 1996 est.): machinery, petroleum products, transport equipment. **Major trading partners:** U.K., South Africa, Germany, Japan, U.S.

Geography Zimbabwe, a landlocked country in south-central Africa, is slightly smaller than California. It is bordered by Botswana on the west, Zambia on the north, Mozambique on the east, and South Africa on the south.

Government Parliamentary democracy.

History The remains of early humans, dating back 500,000 years, have been discovered in present-day Zimbabwe. The land's earliest settlers, the Khoisan, date back to 200 B.C.E. After a period of Bantu domination, the Shona people ruled, followed by the Nguni and Zulu peoples. By the mid-19th century the descendents of the Nguni and Zulu, the Ndebele, had established a powerful warrior kingdom.

The first British explorers, colonists, and missionaries arrived in the 1850s, and the massive influx of foreigners led to the establishment of the territory Rhodesia, named after Cecil Rhodes of the British South Africa Company. In 1923, European settlers voted to become the self-governing British colony of Southern Rhodesia. After a brief federation with Northern Rhodesia and Nyasaland (now Malawi) in the post–World War II period, Southern Rhodesia (also known as Rhodesia) chose to remain a colony when its two partners voted for independence in 1963.

On Nov. 11, 1965, the conservative white-minority government of Rhodesia declared its independence from Britain. The country resisted the demands of black Africans, and Prime Minister Ian Smith withstood British pressure, economic sanctions, and guerrilla attacks to uphold white supremacy. On March 1, 1970, Rhodesia formally proclaimed itself a republic. Heightened guerrilla war and a withdrawal of South African military aid in 1976 marked the beginning of the collapse of Smith's 11 years of resistance.

Black nationalist movements were led by Bishop Abel Muzorewa of the African National Congress and Ndabaningi Sithole, who were moderates, and guerrilla leaders Robert Mugabe of the Zimbabwe African National Union (ZANU) and Joshua Nkomo of the Zimbabwe African People's Union (ZAPU), who advocated revolution.

On March 3, 1978, Smith, Muzorewa, Sithole, and Chief Jeremiah Chirau signed an agreement to transfer power to the black majority by Dec. 31, 1978. They constituted themselves an Executive Council, with chairmanship rotating but with Smith retaining the title of prime minister. Blacks were named to each cabinet ministry, serving as co-ministers with the whites already holding these posts. African nations and rebel leaders immediately denounced the action, but Western governments were more reserved, although none granted recognition to the new regime.

The white minority finally consented to hold multiracial elections in 1980, and Robert Mugabe won a landslide victory. The country achieved independence on April 17, 1980, under the name Zimbabwe. Mugabe eventually established a one-party socialist state, but by 1990 he instituted multiparty elections and in 1991 deleted all references to Marxism-Leninism and scientific socialism from the constitution. Parliamentary elections in April 1995 gave Mugabe's party a stunning victory with 63 of the 65 contested seats, and in 1996 Mugabe won another six-year term as president.

Zimbabwe has been hit especially hard by AIDS, reducing the average life expectancy in Zimbabwe to 39 years, down from 65 years prior to the AIDS epidemic.

Zimbabwe has sent troops to assist Laurent Kabila in Congo's civil war and has indicated that it will also support the Angola government in its war against the UNITA rebels.

Preamble of the United Nations Charter

The Charter of the United Nations was adopted at the San Francisco Conference of 1945. The complete text may be obtained by writing to the United Nations Sales Section, United Nations, New York, N.Y. 10017, and enclosing $1.

We the peoples of the United Nations determined to save succeeding generations from the scourge of war, which twice in our lifetime has brought untold sorrow to mankind, and

To reaffirm faith in fundamental human rights, in the dignity and worth of the human person, in the equal rights of men and women and of nations large and small, and

To establish conditions under which justice and respect for the obligations arising from treaties and other sources of international law can be maintained, and

To promote social progress and better standards of life in larger freedom, and for these ends

To practice tolerance and live together in peace with one another as good neighbors, and

To unite our strength to maintain international peace and security, and

To insure, by the acceptance of principles and the institution of methods, that armed force shall not be used, save in the common interest, and

To employ international machinery for the promotion of the economic and social advancement of all peoples, have resolved to combine our efforts to accomplish these aims.

Accordingly, our respective Governments, through representatives assembled in the city of San Francisco, who have exhibited their full powers found to be in good and due form, have agreed to the present Charter of the United Nations and do hereby establish an international organization to be known as the United Nations.

Principal Organs of the United Nations

Secretariat

This is the directorate on UN operations, apart from political decisions. All members contribute to its upkeep. Its headquarters staff of about 4,730 specialists is recruited from member nations on the basis of as wide a geographical distribution as possible. The staff works under the Secretary-General, whom it assists and advises.

Secretaries-General

Kofi Annan, Ghana, Jan. 1, 1997.

Boutros Boutros-Ghali, Egypt, Jan. 1, 1992–Dec. 31, 1996.

Javier Pérez de Cuéllar, Peru, Jan. 1, 1982–Dec. 31, 1991.

Kurt Waldheim, Austria, Jan. 1, 1972–Dec. 31, 1981.

U Thant, Burma (Myanmar), Nov. 3, 1961–Dec. 31, 1971.

Dag Hammarskjöld, Sweden, April 11, 1953–Sept. 17, 1961.

Trygve Lie, Norway, Feb. 1, 1946–April 10, 1953.

General Assembly

The General Assembly is the world's forum for discussing matters affecting world peace and security, and for making recommendations concerning them. It has no power of its own to enforce decisions. It is composed of the 51 original member nations and those admitted since, a total of 185. Each nation has one vote. On important questions including international peace and security, a two-thirds majority of those present and voting is required. Decisions on other questions are made by a simple majority. The assembly's agenda can be as broad as the charter. It can make recommendations to member nations, the Security Council, or both. Emphasis is given on questions relating to international peace and security brought before it by any member, the Security Council, or nonmembers. It also maintains a broad program of international cooperation in economic, social, cultural, educational, and health fields, and for assisting in human rights and freedoms. Among other duties, the assembly has functions relating to the trusteeship system, and considers and approves the UN budget. Every member contributes to operating expenses according to its means.

Security Council

The Security Council is the primary instrument for establishing and maintaining international peace. Its main purpose is to prevent war by settling disputes between nations. Under the charter, the council is permitted to dispatch a UN force to stop aggression. All member nations undertake to make available armed forces, assistance, and facilities to maintain international peace and security. Any member may bring a dispute before the Security Council or the General Assembly. Any nonmember may do so if it accepts the charter obligations of pacific settlement. The Security Council has 15 members. There are five permanent members: the United States, the Russian Federation, Britain, France, and China; and 10 temporary members elected by the General Assembly for two-year terms, from five different regions of the world. Voting on procedural matters requires a nine-vote majority to carry. However, on questions of substance, the vote of each of the five permanent members is required. The ten non-permanent members of the council in 1999 are Brazil (1999), Canada (2000), Gabon (1999), Gambia (1999), Malaysia (2000), Namibia (2000), Netherlands (2000), Slovenia (1999), Argentina (2000), and Bahrain (1999).

Economic and Social Council

This council is composed of 54 members elected by the General Assembly to 3-year terms. It works closely with the General Assembly as a link with groups formed within the UN to help peoples in such fields as education, health, and human rights.

It insures that there is no overlapping and sets up commissions to deal with economic conditions and collect facts and figures on conditions over the world. It issues studies and reports and may make recommendations to the assembly and specialized agencies.

Agencies of the United Nations

Linked to the United Nations through special agreements, the separate, autonomous specialized agencies of the UN family set standards and guidelines, help formulate policies, provide technical assistance, and other forms of practical help in virtually all areas of economic and social endeavor.

The International Labor Organization (ILO) formulates policies and programs to improve working conditions and employment opportunities, and defines international labor standards as guidelines for governments.

The Food and Agriculture Organization of the UN (FAO) works to raise levels of nutrition and standards of living, to improve agricultural productivity and food security, and to better the conditions of rural populations.

The UN Educational, Scientific and Cultural Organization (UNESCO) promotes education for all, cultural development, protection of the world's natural and cultural heritage, press freedom, and communication.

The World Health Organization (WHO) coordinates programs aimed at solving health problems and the attainment by all people of the highest possible level of health; it works in areas such as immunization, health education, and the provision of essential drugs.

The World Bank group provides loans and technical assistance to developing countries to reduce poverty and advance sustainable economic growth.

The International Monetary Fund (IMF) facilitates international monetary cooperation and financial stability, and provides a permanent forum for consultation, advice, and assistance on financial issues.

The International Civil Aviation Organization (ICAO) sets international standards necessary for the safety, security, efficiency, and regularity of air transport, and serves as the medium for cooperation in all areas of civil aviation.

The Universal Postal Union (UPU) establishes international regulations for the organization and improvement of postal services, provides technical assistance, and promotes cooperation in postal matters.

The International Telecommunication Union (ITU) fosters international cooperation for the improvement and use of telecommunications of all kinds, coordinates usage of radio and TV frequencies, promotes safety measures, and conducts research.

The World Meteorological Organization (WMO) promotes scientific research on the atmosphere and on climate change, and facilitates the global exchange of meteorological data and information.

The International Maritime Organization (IMO) works to improve international shipping procedures, encourages the highest standards in marine safety, and seeks to prevent marine pollution from ships.

The World Intellectual Property Organization (WIPO) promotes international protection of intellectual property and fosters cooperation on copyrights, trademarks, industrial designs, and patents.

The International Fund for Agricultural Development (IFAD) mobilizes financial resources for better food production and nutrition among the poor in developing countries.

The UN Industrial Development Organization (UNIDO) promotes the industrial advancement of developing countries through technical assistance, advisory services, and training.

The International Atomic Energy Agency (IAEA), an autonomous intergovernmental organization under the aegis of the UN, works for the safe and peaceful uses of atomic energy.

The UN and the World Trade Organization (WTO), the major entity overseeing international trade, cooperate in assisting developing countries' exports through the Geneva-based International Trade Center.

U.S. Representatives to the United Nations

Year	Ambassador	Year	Ambassador
1946	Edward R. Stettinius, Jr.	1975–76	Daniel P. Moynihan
1946–47	Herschel V. Johnson (acting)	1976–77	William W. Scranton
1947–53	Warren R. Austin	1977–79	Andrew Young
1953–60	Henry Cabot Lodge, Jr.	1979–81	Donald McHenry
1960–61	James J. Wadsworth	1981–85	Jeane J. Kirkpatrick
1961–65	Adlai E. Stevenson	1985–89	Vernon A. Walters
1965–68	Arthur J. Goldberg	1989–92	Thomas J. Pickering
1968	George W. Ball	1992–93	Edward J. Perkins
1968–69	James Russell Wiggins	1993–96	Madeleine K. Albright
1969–71	Charles W. Yost	1997–98	Bill Richardson
1971–73	George Bush	1999–	Richard Holbrooke
1973–75	John A. Scali		

Members of the United Nations

Country	Joined UN[1]	Country	Joined UN[1]	Country	Joined UN[1]
Afghanistan	1946	Georgia	1992	Nigeria	1960
Albania	1955	Germany	1973	Norway	1945
Algeria	1962	Ghana	1957	Oman	1971
Andorra	1993	Greece	1945	Pakistan	1947
Angola	1976	Grenada	1974	Palau	1994
Antigua and Barbuda	1981	Guatemala	1945	Panama	1945
Argentina	1945	Guinea	1958	Papua New Guinea	1975
Armenia	1992	Guinea-Bissau	1974	Paraguay	1945
Australia	1945	Guyana	1966	Peru	1945
Austria	1955	Haiti	1945	Philippines	1945
Azerbaijan	1992	Honduras	1945	Poland	1945
Bahamas	1973	Hungary	1955	Portugal	1955
Bahrain	1971	Iceland	1946	Qatar	1971
Bangladesh	1974	India	1945	Romania	1955
Barbados	1966	Indonesia	1950	Russian Federation	1945
Belarus	1945	Iran	1945	Rwanda	1962
Belgium	1945	Iraq	1945	St. Kitts and Nevis	1983
Belize	1981	Ireland	1955	St. Lucia	1979
Benin	1960	Israel	1949	St. Vincent and the	
Bhutan	1971	Italy	1955	Grenadines	1980
Bolivia	1945	Jamaica	1962	Samoa, Western	1976
Bosnia and Herzegovina	1992	Japan	1956	San Marino	1992
Botswana	1966	Jordan	1955	São Tomé and Príncipe	1975
Brazil	1945	Kazakhstan	1992	Saudi Arabia	1945
Brunei Darussalam	1984	Kenya	1963	Senegal	1960
Bulgaria	1955	Kiribati*	1999	Seychelles	1976
Burkina Faso	1960	North Korea	1991	Sierra Leone	1961
Burma (Myanmar)	1948	South Korea	1991	Singapore	1965
Burundi	1962	Kuwait	1963	Slovakia[4]	1993
Cambodia	1955	Kyrgyzstan	1992	Slovenia	1992
Cameroon	1960	Laos	1955	Solomon Islands	1978
Canada	1945	Latvia	1991	Somalia	1960
Cape Verde	1975	Lebanon	1945	South Africa	1945
Central African Republic	1960	Lesotho	1966	Spain	1955
Chad	1960	Liberia	1945	Sri Lanka	1955
Chile	1945	Libya	1955	Sudan	1956
China[2]	1945	Liechtenstein	1990	Suriname	1975
Colombia	1945	Lithuania	1991	Swaziland	1968
Comoros	1975	Luxembourg	1945	Sweden	1946
Congo	1960	Macedonia[3]	1993	Syria	1945
Congo, Dem. Rep.	1960	Madagascar	1960	Tajikistan	1992
Costa Rica	1945	Malawi	1964	Tanzania	1961
Côte d'Ivoire	1960	Malaysia	1957	Thailand	1946
Croatia	1992	Maldives	1965	Togo	1960
Cuba	1945	Mali	1960	Tonga*	1999
Cyprus	1960	Malta	1964	Trinidad and Tobago	1962
Czech Republic[3]	1993	Marshall Islands	1991	Tunisia	1956
Denmark	1945	Mauritania	1961	Turkey	1945
Djibouti	1977	Mauritius	1968	Turkmenistan	1992
Dominica	1978	Mexico	1945	Uganda	1962
Dominican Republic	1945	Micronesia	1991	Ukraine	1945
Ecuador	1945	Moldova	1992	United Arab Emirates	1971
Egypt	1945	Monaco	1993	United Kingdom	1945
El Salvador	1945	Mongolia	1961	United States	1945
Equatorial Guinea	1968	Morocco	1956	Uruguay	1945
Eritrea	1993	Mozambique	1975	Uzbekistan	1992
Estonia	1991	Namibia	1990	Vanuatu	1981
Ethiopia	1945	Nauru*	1999	Venezuela	1945
Fiji	1970	Nepal	1955	Viet Nam	1977
Finland	1955	Netherlands	1945	Yemen, Republic of	1947
France	1945	New Zealand	1945	Yugoslavia	1945
Gabon	1960	Nicaragua	1945	Zambia	1964
Gambia	1965	Niger	1960	Zimbabwe	1980

*In 1999, the Security Council approved membership for Kiribati, Nauru, and Tonga, but none has yet formally joined the U.N. 1. The UN officially came into existence on Oct. 24, 1945. 2. On Oct. 25, 1971, the UN voted membership to the People's Republic of China, which replaced the Republic of China (Taiwan) in the world body. 3. The General Assembly on April 8, 1993, decided to admit the state provisionally being referred to as "The Former Yugoslav Republic of Macedonia" pending settlement of the difference that has arisen over its name. 4. Czechoslovakia was an original member of the United Nations from Oct. 24, 1945. As of December 31, 1992, it ceased to exist and the Czech Republic and Slovakia as successor states were admitted January 19, 1993.

Selected International Organizations

Arab League (AL)
Members: (21 plus the Palestine Liberation Organization) Algeria, Bahrain, Comoros, Djibouti, Egypt, Iraq, Jordan, Kuwait, Lebanon, Libya, Mauritania, Morocco, Oman, Qatar, Saudi Arabia, Somalia, Sudan, Syria, Tunisia, UAE, Yemen, Palestine Liberation Organization

Association of Southeast Asian Nations (ASEAN)
Members: (9) Brunei, Burma, Indonesia, Laos, Malaysia, Philippines, Singapore, Thailand, Vietnam
Observers: (2) Cambodia, Papua New Guinea.
Consultative partners: (2) China, Russia

Big Seven and Group of 7 (G-7)
Members: (7) Big Six (Canada, France, Germany, Italy, Japan, UK) plus the US

Commonwealth of Nations
Members: (52) Antigua and Barbuda, Australia, The Bahamas, Bangladesh, Barbados, Belize, Botswana, Brunei, Cameroon, Canada, Cyprus, Dominica, Fiji, The Gambia, Ghana, Grenada, Guyana, India, Jamaica, Kenya, Kiribati, Lesotho, Malawi, Malaysia, Maldives, Malta, Mauritius, Mozambique, Namibia, N.Z., Nigeria (suspended), Pakistan, Papua New Guinea, Saint Kitts and Nevis, Saint Lucia, Saint Vincent and the Grenadines, Samoa, Seychelles, Sierra Leone, Singapore, Solomon Islands, South Africa, Sri Lanka, Swaziland, Tanzania, Tonga, Trinidad and Tobago, Uganda, UK, Vanuatu, Zambia, Zimbabwe
Special members: (2) Nauru (soon to become full member), Tuvalu

Commonwealth of Independent States (CIS)
Members: (12) Armenia, Azerbaijan, Belarus, Georgia, Kazakhstan, Kyrgyzstan, Moldova, Russia, Tajikistan, Turkmenistan, Ukraine, Uzbekistan

European Union (EU)
Members: (18) Austria, Belgium, Czech Republic, Denmark, Finland, France, Germany, Greece, Hungary, Ireland, Italy, Luxembourg, Netherlands, Poland, Portugal, Spain, Sweden, UK
Membership applicants: (12) Albania, Bulgaria, Cyprus, Czech Republic, Estonia, Hungary, Latvia, Lithuania, Malta, Poland, Romania, Slovakia

North Atlantic Treaty Organization (NATO)
Members: (16) Belgium, Canada, Denmark, France, Germany, Greece, Iceland, Italy, Luxembourg, Netherlands, Norway, Portugal, Spain, Turkey, UK, US

Organization of Petroleum Exporting Countries (OPEC)
Members: (11) Algeria, Indonesia, Iran, Iraq, Kuwait, Libya, Nigeria, Qatar, Saudi Arabia, UAE, Venezuela

Foreign Embassies in the United States

Source: U.S. Department of State.

Embassy of the Republic of Albania, 2100 S. St., N.W., Washington, D.C. 20008. Phone: 202-223-4942. Fax: 202-628-7342.

Embassy of the Democratic & Popular Republic of Algeria, 2118 Kalorama Rd., N.W., Washington, D.C. 20008. Phone: 202-265-2800. Fax: 202-667-2174.

Embassy of Andorra, 2 United Nations Plaza, 25th flr. New York, N.Y. 10017. Phone: 212-750-8064. Fax: 212-750-6630.

Embassy of the Republic of Angola, 1615 M. St., N.W., Suite 900, Washington D.C. 20036. Phone: 202-785-1156. Fax: 202-785-1258.

Embassy of Antigua & Barbuda, 3216 New Mexico Ave., N.W., Washington, D.C. 20016. Phone: 202-362-5211, 5166, 5122. Fax: 202-362-5225.

Embassy of the Argentine Republic, 1600 New Hampshire Ave., N.W., Washington, D.C. 20009. Phone: 202-238-6400. Fax: 202-238-6471.

Embassy of the Republic of Armenia, 2225 R Street, N.W., Washington, D.C. 20008. Phone: 202-319-1976. Fax: 202-319-2982.

Embassy of Australia, 1601 Massachusetts Ave., N.W., Washington, D.C. 20036. Phone: 202-797-3000. Fax: 202-797-3168.

Embassy of Austria, 3524 International Court, N.W., Washington, D.C. 20008. Phone: 202-895-6700. Fax: 202-895-6750.

Embassy of the Republic of Azerbaijan, 927-15th St., N.W., Suite 700, P.O. Box 28790, Washington, D.C. 20038. Phone: 202-842-0001. Fax: 202-842-0004.

Embassy of The Commonwealth of The Bahamas, 2220 Massachusetts Ave., N.W., Washington, D.C. 20008. Phone: 202-319-2660. Fax: 202-319-2668.

Embassy of the State of Bahrain, 3502 International Dr., N.W., Washington, D.C. 20008. Phone: 202-342-0741, 0742. Fax: 202-362-2192.

Embassy of the People's Republic of Bangladesh, 2201 Wisconsin Ave., N.W., Washington, D.C. 20007. Phone: 202-342-8372 to 8376.

Embassy of Barbados, 2144 Wyoming Ave., N.W., Washington, D.C. 20008. Phone: 202-939-9200 to 9202.

Embassy of the Republic of Belarus, 1619 New Hampshire Ave., N.W., Washington, D.C. 20009. Phone: 202-986-1640. Fax: 202-986-1805.

Embassy of Belgium, 3330 Garfield St., N.W., Washington, D.C. 20008. Phone: 202-333-6900. Fax: 202-333-3079.

Embassy of Belize, 2535 Massachusetts Ave., N.W., Washington, D.C. 20008. Phone: 202-332-9636. Fax: 202-332-6888.

Embassy of the Republic of Benin, 2737 Cathedral Ave., N.W., Washington, D.C. 20008. Phone: 202-232-6656 to 6658. Fax: 202-265-1996.

Embassy of the Republic of Bolivia, 3014 Massachusetts Ave., N.W., Washington, D.C. 20008. Phone: 202-483-4410 to 4412. Fax: 202-328-3712.

Embassy of the Republic of Bosnia and Herzegovina, 2109 E St. N.W., Washington, D.C. 20037. Phone: 202-337-1500. Fax: 202-337-1502.

Embassy of the Republic of Botswana, 1531–1533 New Hampshire Ave., N.W., Washington, D.C. 20036. Phone: 202-244-4990, 4991. Fax: 202-244-4164.

Brazilian Embassy, 3006 Massachusetts Ave., N.W., Washington, D.C. 20008. Phone: 202-238-2700. Fax: 202-238-2827.

Embassy of the State of Brunei Darussalam, 2600 Virginia Ave., N.W., Suite 300, 3rd floor, Washington, D.C. 20037. Phone: 202-342-0159. Fax: 202-342-0158.

Embassy of the Republic of Bulgaria, 1621-22nd St., N.W., Washington, D.C. 20008. Phone: 202-387-7969. Fax: 202-234-7973.

Embassy of Burkina Faso, 2340 Massachusetts Ave., N.W., Washington, D.C. 20008. Phone: 202-332-5577. Fax: 202-667-1882.

Embassy of the Union of Burma, 2300 S. St., N.W., Washington, D.C. 20008. Phone: 202-332-9044, 9045. Fax: 202-332-9046.

Embassy of the Republic of Burundi, 2233 Wisconsin Ave., N.W., Suite 212, Washington, D.C. 20007. Phone: 202-342-2574.

Embassy of the Republic of Cambodia, 4500 16th St., N.W., Washington, D.C. 20011. Phone: 202-726-7742. Fax: 202-726-8381.

Embassy of the Republic of Cameroon, 2349 Massachusetts Ave., N.W., Washington, D.C. 20008. Phone: 202-265-8790. Fax: 202-387-3826.

Embassy of Canada, 501 Pennsylvania Ave., N.W., Washington, D.C. 20001. Phone: 202-682-1740. Fax: 202-682-7726.

Embassy of the Republic of Cape Verde, 3415 Massachusetts Ave., N.W., Washington, D.C. 20007. Phone: 202-965-6820. Fax: 202-965-1207.

Embassy of Central African Republic, 1618-22nd St. N.W., Washington, D.C. 20008. Phone: 202-483-7800, 7801. Fax: 202-332-9893.

Embassy of the Republic of Chad, 2002 R St., N.W., Washington, D.C. 20009. Phone: 202-462-4009. Fax: 202-265-1937.

Embassy of Chile, 1732 Massachusetts Ave., N.W., Washington, D.C. 20036. Phone: 202-785-1746. Fax: 202-887-5579.

Embassy of the People's Republic of China, 2300 Connecticut Ave., N.W., Washington, D.C. 20008. Phone: 202-328-2500 to 2502.

Embassy of Colombia, 2118 Leroy Pl., N.W., Washington, D.C. 20008. Phone: 202-387-8338. Fax: 202-232-8643.

Embassy of the Federal and Islamic Republic of Comoros, c/o Permanent Mission of the Federal and Islamic Republic of Comoros to the United Nations, 420 E. 50th St., New York, N.Y. 10022. Phone: 212-972-8010. Fax: 212-983-4712.

Embassy of the Democratic Republic of Congo, 1800 New Hampshire Ave., N.W., Washington, D.C. 20009. Phone: 202-234-7690, 7691. Fax: 202-237-0748.

Embassy of the Republic of Congo, 4891 Colorado Ave., N.W., Washington, D.C. 20011. Phone: 202-726-5500. Fax: 202-726-1860.

Embassy of Costa Rica, 2114 S St., N.W., Washington, D.C. 20008. Phone: 202-234-2945. Fax: 202-265-4795.

Embassy of the Republic of Côte d'Ivoire, 3421 Massachusetts Ave., N.W., Washington, D.C. 20007. Phone: 202-797-0300.

Embassy of the Republic of Croatia, 2343 Massachusetts Ave., N.W., Washington, D.C. 20008. Phone: 202-588-5899. Fax: 202-588-8936.

Cuban Interests Section, 2630 16th St., N.W., Washington, D.C. 20009. Phone: 202-797-8518 to 8520.

Embassy of the Republic of Cyprus, 2211 R St. N.W., Washington, D.C. 20008. Phone: 202-462-5772. Fax: 202-483-6710.

Embassy of the Czech Republic, 3900 Spring of Freedom St., N.W., Washington, D.C. 20008. Phone: 202-363-6315. Fax: 202-966-8540.

Royal Danish Embassy, 3200 Whitehaven St., N.W., Washington, D.C. 20008. Phone: 202-234-4300. Fax: 202-328-1470.

Embassy of the Republic of Djibouti, 1156-15th St., N.W., Suite 515, Washington, D.C. 20005. Phone: 202-331-0270. Fax: 202-331-0302.

Embassy of the Commonwealth of Dominica, 3216 New Mexico Ave., N.W., Washington, D.C. 20016. Phone: 202-364-6781. Fax: 202-364-6791.

Embassy of the Dominican Republic, 1715-22nd St., N.W., Washington, D.C. 20008. Phone: 202-332-6280, 6281. Fax: 202-265-8057.

Embassy of Ecuador, 2535-15th St., N.W., Washington, D.C. 20009. Phone: 202-234-7200. Fax: 202-667-3482.

Embassy of the Arab Republic of Egypt, 3521 International Court, N.W., Washington, D.C. 20008. Phone: 202-895-5400. Fax: 202-244-4319/5131.

Embassy of El Salvador, 2308 California St., N.W., Washington, D.C. 20008. Phone: 202-265-9671, 9672.

Embassy of Equatorial Guinea, 1712 I St., N.W., Suite 410, Washington, D.C. 20006. Phone: 202-296-4174. Fax: 202-296-4195.

Embassy of the State of Eritrea, 1708 New Hampshire Ave., N.W., Washington, D.C., 20009. Phone: 202-319-1991. Fax: 202-319-1304.

Embassy of Estonia, 2131 Massachusetts Ave., Washington, D.C. 20008. Phone: 202-588-0101. Fax: 202-588-0108.

Embassy of Ethiopia, 2134 Kalorama Rd., N.W., Washington, D.C. 20008. Phone: 202-234-2281, 2282. Fax: 202-328-7950.

Embassy of The Republic of Fiji, 2233 Wisconsin Ave., N.W., Suite 240, Washington, D.C. 20007. Phone: 202-337-8320. Fax: 202-337-1996.

Embassy of Finland, 3301 Massachusetts Ave., N.W., Washington, D.C. 20008. Phone: 202-298-5800. Fax: 202-298-6030.

Embassy of France, 4101 Reservoir Rd., N.W., Washington, D.C. 20007. Phone: 202-944-6000. Fax: 202-944-6166.

Embassy of the Gabonese Republic, 2034-20th St., N.W., Suite 200, Washington, D.C. 20009. Phone: 202-797-1000. Fax: 202-332-0668.

Embassy of The Gambia, 1155-15th St., N.W., Suite 1000, Washington, D.C. 20005. Phone: 202-785-1399, 1379, 1425. Fax: 202-785-1430.

Embassy of the Republic of Georgia, 1615 New Hampshire Ave., N.W., Suite 300, Washington, D.C. 20009. Phone: 202-387-2390. Fax: 202-393-4537.

Embassy of the Federal Republic of Germany, 4645 Reservoir Rd., N.W., Washington, D.C. 20007. Phone: 202-298-8141. Fax: 202-298-4249.

Embassy of Ghana, 3512 International Dr., N.W., Washington, D.C. 20008. Phone: 202-686-4520. Fax: 202-686-4527.

Embassy of Greece, 2221 Massachusetts Ave., N.W., Washington, D.C. 20008. Phone: 202-939-5800. Fax: 202-939-5824.

Embassy of Grenada, 1701 New Hampshire Ave., N.W., Washington, D.C. 20009. Phone: 202-265-2561.

Embassy of Guatemala, 2220 R St., N.W., Washington, D.C. 20008. Phone: 202-745-4952 to 4954. Fax: 202-745-1908.

Embassy of the Republic of Guinea, 2112 Leroy Pl., N.W., Washington, D.C. 20008. Phone: 202-483-9420. Fax: 202-483-8688.

Embassy of the Republic of Guinea-Bissau, 1511 K. St., N.W., Suite 519, Washington, D.C. 20005. Phone: 202-347-3950. Fax: 202-347-3954.

Embassy of Guyana, 2490 Tracy Pl., N.W., Washington, D.C. 20008. Phone: 202-265-6900, 6901.

Embassy of the Republic of Haiti, 2311 Massachusetts Ave., N.W., Washington, D.C. 20008. Phone: 202-332-4090 to 4092. Fax: 202-745-7215.

Apostolic Nunciature of the Holy See, 3339 Massachusetts Ave., N.W., Washington, D.C. 20008. Phone: 202-333-7121.

Embassy of Honduras, 3007 Tilden St., N.W., Suite 4-M, Washington, D.C. 20008. Phone: 202-966-7702, 2604, 5008, 4596. Fax: 202-966-9751.

Embassy of the Republic of Hungary, 3910 Shoemaker St., N.W., Washington, D.C. 20008. Phone: 202-362-6730. Fax: 202-966-8135.

Embassy of Iceland, 1156-15th St., N.W., Suite 1200, Washington, D.C. 20005. Phone: 202-265-6653 to 6655. Fax: 202-265-6656.

Embassy of India, 2107 Massachusetts Ave., N.W., Washington, D.C. 20008. Phone: 202-939-7000. Fax: 202-483-3972.

Embassy of the Republic of Indonesia, 2020 Massachusetts Ave., N.W., Washington, D.C. 20036. Phone: 202-775-5200. Fax: 202-775-5365.

Iranian Interests Section, 2209 Wisconsin Ave., N.W., Washington, D.C. 20007. Phone: 202-965-4990.

Iraqi Interests Section, 1801 P St., N.W., Washington, D.C. 20036. Phone: 202-483-7500.

Embassy of Ireland, 2234 Massachusetts Ave., N.W., Washington, D.C. 20008. Phone: 202-462-3939. Fax: 202-232-5993.

Embassy of Israel, 3514 International Dr., N.W., Washington, D.C. 20008. Phone: 202-364-5500. Fax: 202-364-5610.

Embassy of Italy, 1601 Fuller St., N.W., Washington, D.C. 20009. Phone: 202-328-5500. Fax: 202-483-2187.

Embassy of Jamaica, 1520 New Hampshire Ave., N.W., Washington, D.C. 20036. Phone: 202-452-0660. Fax: 202-452-0081.

Embassy of Japan, 2520 Massachusetts Ave., N.W., Washington, D.C. 20008. Phone: 202-238-6700. Fax: 202-328-2187.

Embassy of the Hashemite Kingdom of Jordan, 3504 International Dr., N.W., Washington, D.C. 20008. Phone: 202-966-2664. Fax: 202-966-3110.

Embassy of the Republic of Kazakhstan, (temporary) 1401 16th St., N.W., Washington, D.C. 20036. Phone: 202-232-5488. Fax: 202-232-5845.

Embassy of the Republic of Kenya, 2249 R St., N.W., Washington, D.C. 20008. Phone: 202-387-6101. Fax: 202-462-3829.

Embassy of the Republic of Korea, 2450 Massachusetts Ave., N.W., Washington, D.C. 20008. Phone: 202-939-5600. Fax: 202-387-0205.

Embassy of the State of Kuwait, 2940 Tilden St., N.W., Washington, D.C. 20008. Phone: 202-966-0702. Fax: 202-966-0517.

Embassy of the Kyrgyz Republic, 1732 Wisconsin Ave., Washington, D.C. 20007. Phone: 202-338-5141. Fax: 202-338-5139.

Embassy of the Lao People's Democratic Republic, 2222 S St., N.W., Washington, D.C. 20008. Phone: 202-332-6416. Fax: 202-332-4923.

Embassy of Latvia, 4325-17th St., N.W., Washington, D.C. 20011. Phone: 202-726-8213, 8214. Fax: 202-726-6785.

Embassy of Lebanon, 2560-28th St., N.W., Washington, D.C. 20008. Phone: 202-939-6300. Fax: 202-939-6324.

Embassy of the Kingdom of Lesotho, 2511 Massachusetts Ave., N.W., Washington, D.C. 20008. Phone: 202-797-5533 to 5536. Fax: 202-234-6815.

Embassy of the Republic of Liberia, 5303 Colorado Ave., N.W., Washington, D.C. 20011. Phone: 202-723-0437. Fax: 202-723-0436.

Embassy of the Republic of Lithuania, 2622 16th St., N.W., Washington, D.C. 20009. Phone: 202-234-5860. Fax: 202-328-0466.

Embassy of the Grand Duchy of Luxembourg, 2200 Massachusetts Ave., N.W., Washington, D.C. 20008. Phone: 202-265-4171. Fax: 202-328-8270.

Embassy of the Former Yugoslav Republic of Macedonia, 3050 K St., N.W., Suite 210, Washington, D.C. 20007. Phone: 202-337-3063. Fax: 202-337-3093.

Embassy of the Republic of Madagascar, 2374 Massachusetts Ave., N.W., Washington, D.C. 20008. Phone: 202-265-5525, 5526.

Embassy of Malawi , 2408 Massachusetts Ave., N.W., Washington, D.C. 20008. Phone: 202-797-1007.

Embassy of Malaysia, 2401 Massachusetts Ave., N.W., Washington, D.C. 20008. Phone: 202-328-2700. Fax: 202-483-7661.

Embassy of the Republic of Mali, 2130 R St., N.W., Washington, D.C. 20008. Phone: 202-332-2249; 202-939-8950. Fax: 202-332-6603.

Embassy of Malta, 2017 Connecticut Ave., N.W., Washington, D.C. 20008. Phone: 202-462-3611, 3612. Fax: 202-387-5470.

Embassy of the Republic of the Marshall Islands, 2433 Massachusetts Ave., N.W., Washington, D.C. 20008. Phone: 202-234-5414. Fax: 202-232-3236.

Embassy of the Islamic Republic of Mauritania, 2129 Leroy Pl., N.W., Washington, D.C. 20008. Phone: 202-232-5700. (202) 319-2623.

Embassy of the Republic of Mauritius, 4301 Connecticut Ave., N.W., Suite 441, Washington, D.C. 20008. Phone: 202-244-1491, 1492. Fax: 202-966-0983.

Embassy of Mexico, 1911 Pennsylvania Ave., N.W., Washington, D.C. 20006. Phone: 202-728-1600. 202-728-1698.

Embassy of the Federated States of Micronesia, 1725 N St., N.W., Washington, D.C. 20036. Phone: 202-223-4383. Fax: 202-223-4391.

Embassy of the Republic of Moldova, 2101 S St., N.W., Washington, D.C. 20008. Phone: 202-667-1130. Fax: 202-667-1204.

Embassy of Mongolia, 2833 M St., N.W., Washington, D.C. 20007. Phone: 202-333-7117. Fax: 202-298-9227.

Embassy of the Kingdom of Morocco, 1601 21st St., N.W., Washington, D.C. 20009. Phone: 202-462-7979 to 7982, inclusive. Fax: 202-265-0161.

Embassy of the Republic of Mozambique, 1990 M St., N.W., Suite 570, Washington, D.C. 20036. Phone: 202-293-7146. Fax: 202-835-0245.

Embassy of the Union of Myanmar, 2300 S St., N.W., Washington, D.C. 20008. Phone: 202-332-9044, 9045.

Embassy of the Republic of Namibia, 1605 New Hampshire Ave., N.W., Washington, D.C. 20009. Phone: 202-986-0540. Fax: 202-986-0443.

Royal Nepalese Embassy, 2131 Leroy Pl., N.W., Washington, D.C. 20008. Phone: 202-667-4550. Fax: 202-667-5534.

Royal Netherlands Embassy, 4200 Linnean Ave., N.W., Washington, D.C. 20008. Phone: 202-244-5300; after 6 p.m. 202-494-8594. Fax: 202-362-3430.

Embassy of New Zealand, 37 Observatory Circle, N.W., Washington, D.C. 20008. Phone: 202-328-4800. Fax: 202-667-5227.

Embassy of Nicaragua, 1627 New Hampshire Ave., N.W., Washington, D.C. 20009. Phone: 202-939-6570. Fax: 939-6542.

Embassy of the Republic of Niger, 2204 R St., N.W., Washington, D.C. 20008. Phone: 202-483-4224 to 4227, inclusive.

Embassy of the Federal Republic of Nigeria, 1333 16th St., N.W., Washington, D.C. 20036. Phone: 202-986-8400. Fax: (202) 775-1385.

Royal Norwegian Embassy, 2720 34th St., N.W., Washington, D.C. 20008. Phone: 202-333-6000. Fax: 202-337-0870.

Embassy of the Sultanate of Oman, 2535 Belmont Rd., N.W., Washington, D.C. 20008. Phone: 202-387-1980 to 1982. Fax: 202-745-4933.

Embassy of Pakistan, 2315 Massachusetts Ave., N.W., Washington, D.C. 20008. Phone: 202-939-6200. Fax: 202-387-0484.

Embassy of the Republic of Palau, 1150 18th St., N.W., Suite 750, Washington, D.C. 20036. Phone: 202-452-6814. Fax: 202-452-6281.

Embassy of the Republic of Panama, 2862 McGill Terrace, N.W., Washington, D.C. 20008. Phone: 202-483-1407.

Embassy of Papua New Guinea, 1779 Massachusetts Ave., N.W., Suite 805, Washington, D.C. 20036. Phone: 202-745-3680. Fax: 202-745-3679.

Embassy of Paraguay, 2400 Massachusetts Ave., N.W., Washington, D.C. 20008. Phone: 202-483-6960 to 6962. Fax: 202-234-4508.

Embassy of Peru, 1700 Massachusetts Ave., N.W., Washington, D.C. 20036. Phone: 202-833-9860 to 9869. Fax: 202-659-8124.

Embassy of the Philippines, 1600 Massachusetts Ave., N.W., Washington, D.C. 20036. Phone: 202-467-9300. Fax: 202-328-7614.

Embassy of the Republic of Poland, 2640 16th St., N.W., Washington, D.C. 20009. Phone: 202-234-3800 to 3802. Fax: 202-328-6271.

Embassy of Portugal, 2125 Kalorama Rd., N.W., Washington, D.C. 20008. Phone: 202-328-8610. Fax: 202-462-3726.

Embassy of the State of Qatar, 4200 Wisconsin Ave., N.W., Washington, D.C. 20016. Phone: 202-274-1600.

Embassy of Romania, 1607 23rd St., N.W., Washington, D.C. 20008. Phone: 202-332-4846, 4848, 4851; after hours 332-4846. Fax: 202-232-4748.

Embassy of the Russian Federation, 2650 Wisconsin Ave., N.W., Washington, D.C. 20007. Phone: 202-298-5700 to 5704 inclusive. Fax: 202-298-5735.

Embassy of the Republic of Rwanda, 1714 New Hampshire Ave., N.W., Washington, D.C. 20009. Phone: 202-232-2882. Fax: 202-232-4544.

Embassy of Saint Kitts and Nevis, 3216 New Mexico Ave., N.W., Washington, D.C. 20016. Phone: 202-686-2636. Fax: 202-686-5740.

Embassy of Saint Lucia, 3216 New Mexico Ave., N.W., Washington, D.C. 20016. Phone: 202-364-6792 to 6795. Fax: 202-364-6728.

Embassy of Saint Vincent and the Grenadines, 3216 New Mexico Ave., N.W., Washington, D.C. 20016. Phone: 202-364-6730. Fax: 202-364-6736.

Embassy of the Independent State of Samoa, 800 Second Ave., Suite 400D, New York, N.Y. 10017. Phone: 212-599-6196, 6197. Fax: 212-599-0797.

Embassy of Saudi Arabia, 601 New Hampshire Ave., N.W., Washington, D.C. 20037. Phone: 202-342-3800.

Embassy of the Republic of Senegal, 2112 Wyoming Ave., N.W., Washington, D.C. 20008. Phone: 202-234-0540, 0541.

Embassy of the Republic of Seychelles, 800 Second Ave., Suite 400C, New York, N.Y. 10017. Phone: 212-972-1785. Fax: 212-972-1786.

Embassy of Sierra Leone, 1701 19th St., N.W., Washington, D.C. 20009. Phone: 202-939-9261/63. Fax: 202-483-1793.

Embassy of the Republic of Singapore, 3501 International Pl., N.W., Washington, D.C. 20008. Phone: 202-537-3100. Fax: 202-537-0876.

Embassy of the Slovak Republic, 2201 Wisconsin Ave., N.W., Suite 250, Washington, D.C. 20007. Phone: 202-965-5161. Fax: 202-965-5166.

Embassy of the Republic of Slovenia, 1525 New Hampshire Ave., N.W., Washington, D.C. 20036. Phone: 202-667-5363. Fax: 202-667-4563.

Embassy of the Solomon Islands, 800 Second Ave., Suite 400L, New York, N.Y. 10017. Phone: 212-599-6192, 6193. Fax: 212-661-8925.

Embassy of the Republic of South Africa, 3051 Massachusetts Ave., N.W., Washington, D.C. 20008. Phone: 202-232-4400. Fax: 202-265-1607.

Embassy of Spain, 2375 Pennsylvania Ave., N.W., Washington, D.C. 20037. Phone: 202-452-0100 and 728-2340. Fax: 202-833-5670.

Embassy of the Democratic Socialist Republic of Sri Lanka, 2148 Wyoming Ave., N.W., Washington, D.C. 20008. Phone: 202-483-4025 to 4028. Fax: 202-232-7181.

Embassy of the Republic of the Sudan, 2210 Massachusetts Ave., N.W., Washington, D.C. 20008. Phone: 202-338-8565 to 8570. Fax: 202-667-2406.

Embassy of the Republic of Suriname, 4301 Connecticut Ave., N.W., Suite 460, Washington, D.C. 20008. Phone: 202-244-7488, 7590 to 7592. Fax: 202-244-5878.

Embassy of the Kingdom of Swaziland, 3400 International Drive, N.W., Washington, D.C. 20008. Phone: 202-362-6683, 6685. Fax: 202-244-8059.

Embassy of Sweden, 1501 M St., N.W., Washington, D.C. 20005. Phone: 202-467-2600. Fax: 202-467-2699.

Embassy of Switzerland, 2900 Cathedral Ave., N.W., Washington, D.C. 20008. Phone: 202-745-7900. Fax: 202-387-2564.

Embassy of the Syrian Arab Republic, 2215 Wyoming Ave., N.W., Washington, D.C. 20008. Phone: 202-232-6313. Fax: 202-234-9548.

Embassy of the United Republic of Tanzania, 2139 R St., N.W., Washington, D.C. 20008. Phone: 202-939-6125. Fax: 202-797-7408.

Royal Thai Embassy, 1024 Wisconsin Ave., N.W., Washington, D.C. 20007. Phone: 202-944-3600. Fax: 202-944-3611.

Embassy of the Republic of Togo, 2208 Massachusetts Ave., N.W., Washington, D.C. 20008. Phone: 202-234-4212, 4213. Fax: 202-232-3190.

Embassy of Trinidad and Tobago, 1708 Massachusetts Ave., N.W., Washington, D.C. 20036. Phone: 202-467-6490. Fax: 202-785-3130.

Embassy of Tunisia, 1515 Massachusetts Ave., N.W., Washington, D.C. 20005. Phone: 202-862-1850.

Embassy of the Republic of Turkey, 1714 Massachusetts Ave., N.W., Washington, D.C. 20036. Phone: 202-659-8200. Fax: 202-659-0744.

Embassy of Turkmenistan, 2207 Massachusetts Ave., N.W., Washington, D.C. 20008. Phone: 202-588-1500. Fax: 202-588-0697.

Embassy of the Republic of Uganda, 5911-16th St., N.W., Washington, D.C. 20011. Phone: 202-726-7100 to 7102, 0416. Fax: 202-726-1727.

Embassy of Ukraine, 3350 M St., N.W., Washington, D.C. 20007. Phone: 202-333-0606. Fax: 202-333-0817.

Embassy of the United Arab Emirates, 1255, 22nd St., N.W., Suite 700, Washington, D.C. 20007. Phone: 202-955-7999.

United Kingdom of Great Britain & Northern Ireland—British Embassy, 3100 Massachusetts Ave., N.W., Washington, D.C. 20008. Phone: 202-588-6500. Fax: 202-588-7870.

Embassy of Uruguay, 2715 M St., N.W., Washington, D.C. 20007. Phone: 202-331-1313 to 1316. Fax: 202-331-8142.

Embassy of the Republic of Uzbekistan, 1746 Massachusetts Ave., N.W., Washington, D.C. 20036. Phone: 202-887-5300. Fax: 202-293-6804.

Embassy of the Republic of Venezuela, 1099 30th St., N.W., Washington D.C. 20007. Phone: 202-342-2214. Fax: 202-342-6820.

Embassy of Vietnam, 1233 20th St., N.W., Washington, D.C. 20036. Phone: 202-861-0737. Fax: 202-861-0917.

Embassy of the Republic of Yemen, 2600 Virginia Ave., N.W., Suite 705, Washington, D.C. 20037. Phone: 202-965-4760, 4761. Fax: 202 337–2017.

Embassy of the Republic of Zambia, 2419 Massachusetts Ave., N.W., Washington, D.C. 20008. Phone: 202-265-9717 to 9719. Fax: 202-332-0826.

Embassy of the Republic of Zimbabwe, 1608 New Hampshire Ave., N.W., Washington, D.C. 20009. Phone: 202-332-7100. Fax: 202-483-9326.

Diplomatic Personnel To and From the U.S.

Country	U.S. Representative to[1]	Rank	Representative from[2]	Rank
Albania	Marisa R. Lino	Amb.	Petnt Bushat I	Amb.
Algeria	Cameron R. Hume	Amb.	Ramtane Lamamra	Amb.
Andorra	Edward L. Romero	Amb.	Juli Minoves Triquell	Amb.
Angola	Joseph Gerard Sullivan	Amb.	Antonio dos Santos Franca	Amb.
Antigua and Barbuda[3]	E. William Crotty	Amb.	Lionel A. Hurst	Amb.
Argentina	—		Diego Ramiro Guelar	Amb.
Armenia	Michael Craig Lemmon	Amb.	Rouben Robert Shugarian	Amb.
Australia	Genta Hawkins Holmes	Amb.	Andrew Sharp Peacock	Amb.
Austria	Kathryn Walt Hall	Amb.	Peter Moser	Amb.
Azerbaijan	Stanley T. Escudero	Amb.	Hafiz Mir Jalal Pashayev	Amb.
Bahamas	Arthur Schechter	Amb.	Sir Arlington Griffith Butler	Amb.
Bahrain	Johnny Young	Amb.	Muhammad Abdul Ghaffar	Amb.
Bangladesh	John C. Holzman	Amb.	K. M. Shehabuddin	Amb.
Barbados[3]	E. William Crotty	Amb.	Sir Courtney N. Blackman	Amb.
Belarus	Daniel V. Speckhard	Amb.	Valery V. Tsepkalo	Amb.
Belgium	Paul L. Cejas	Amb.	Alex Reyn	Amb.
Belize	Carolyn Curiel	Amb.	James S. Murphy	Amb.
Berin	Robert C. Felder	Amb.	Lucien Edgar Tonoukouin	Amb.
Bolivia	Donna Hrinak	Amb.	Maroelo Perez Monasterios	Amb.
Bosnia-Herzegovina	Richard Kauzlarich	Amb.	Sven Alkalaj	Amb.
Botswana	Robert Krueger	Amb.	Archibald Mooketsa Mogwe	Amb.
Brazil	—		Paulo-Tarso Flecha de Lima	Amb.
Brunei	Glen R. Rase	Amb.	Pengiran Anak Dato Puteh	Amb.
Bulgaria	Avis T. Bohlen	Amb.	Philip Dimitrov	Amb.
Burkina Faso	Sharon P. Wilkinson	Amb.	Bruno Zidouemba	Amb.
Burma (Myanmar)	Kent M. Wiedemann	Ch'd	Tin Winn	Amb.
Burundi	Morris N. Hughes, Jr.	Amb.	Thomas Ndikumana	Amb.
Cambodia	Kenneth M. Quinn	Amb.	Vun Yaung Tan	Cd'A
Cameroon	John Melvin Yates	Amb.	Jerome Mendouga	Amb.
Canada	Gordon D. Giffin	Amb.	Raymond A. J. Chretien	Amb.
Cape Verde	Lawrence N. Benedict	Amb.	Amilcar Spencer Lopes	Amb.
Central African Republic	Robert Cephas Perry	Amb.	Henry Koba	Amb.
Chad	David C. Halsted	Amb.	Hassaballah Ahmat Soubiane	Amb.
Chile	John O'Leary	Amb.	Genaro Arriagada	Amb.
China	James R. Sasser	Amb.	Li Zhao Xing	Amb.
Colombia	Curtis W. Kamman	Amb.	Luis Alberto Moreno	Amb.
Comoros	Harold Walter Geisel	Amb.	Ahmed Djabir	Amb.
Congo, Democratic Republic of	William Lacy Swing	Amb.	Faida Mitifu	Cd'A
Congo, Rep. of	—		Serge Mombouli	Min.-Consl.
Costa Rica	Thomas Dodd	Amb.	Jaime Daremblum	Amb.
Côte d'Ivoire	George Mu	Amb.	Koffi Moise Koumoue	Amb.
Croatia	William Montgomery	Amb.	Miomir Zuzul	Amb.
Cuba	Michael Kozak	P.O.	—	—
Cyprus	Kenneth C. Brill	Amb.	Dr, Erato Kozakou Marcoullis	Amb.
Czech Republic	John Shattuck	Amb.	Alexandr Vondra	Amb.
Denmark	Richard N. Swett	Amb.	K. Erik Tygesen	Amb.
Djibouti	Lange Schermerhorn	Amb.	Roble Olhaye	Amb.
Dominica[3]	—		Dr. Nicholas J.O. Liverpool	Amb.
Dominican Republic	—		Bernardo Vega	Amb.
Ecuador	Leslie Alexander	Amb.	Ivonne A-baki	Amb.
Egypt	Daniel Kurtzer	Amb.	Ahmed Maher El Sayed	Amb.
El Salvador	Anne W. Patterson	Amb.	Rene A. Leon	Amb.
Equatorial Guinea	John Melvin Yates	Amb.	Pastor Micha Ondo Bile	Amb.
Eritrea	William David Clarke	Amb.	Semere Russom	Amb.
Estonia	Melissa F. Wells	Amb.	Grigore Kalev Stoicescu	Amb.
Ethiopia	David H. Shinn	Amb.	Berhane Gebre-Christos	Amb.
Fiji [4]	—		Napolioni Masirewa	Amb.
Finland	Eric S. Edelman	Amb.	Jaakko Tapani Laajava	Amb.
France	Felix Rohatyn	Amb.	François V. Bujon	Amb.
Gabon	James Vela Ledesma	Amb.	Paul Bunduku-Latha	Amb.

Country	U.S. Representative to[1]	Rank	Representative from[2]	Rank
Gambia, The	George Williford Boyce Haley	Amb.	Crispin Grey Johnson	Amb.
Georgia	Kenneth Spencer Yalowitz	Amb.	Tedo Japaridze	Amb.
Germany	John Christian Kornblum	Amb.	Juergen Chrobog	Amb.
Ghana	Kathryn Dee Robinson	Amb.	Kobina Arthur Koomson	Amb.
Greece	R. Nicholas Burns	Amb.	Alexandre Phllon	Amb.
Grenada[3]	E. William Crotty	Amb.	Denis G. Antoine	Amb.
Guatemala	Donald Planty	Amb.	William Howard Stixrud	Amb.
Guinea	Tibor P. Nagy, Jr.	Amb.	Mohamed Aly Thiam	Amb.
Guinea-Bissau	—	—	Mario Lopes da Rosa	Amb.
Guyana	James F. Mack	Amb.	Mohammed Ali Odeen Ish-mael	Amb.
Haiti	Timothy Carney	Amb.	Louis Harold Joseph	Amb.
Holy See	Corinne Claiborne Boggs	Amb.	Most Rev. Gabriele Montalvo	Apostolic-Nuncio
Honduras	James F. Creagan	Amb.	Jose Benjamin Zapata	C'd A.
Hong Kong	Richard A. Boucher	Cons. Gen.	—	—
Hungary	Peter Tufo	Amb.	Dr. Geza Jeszenszky	Amb.
Iceland	Day O. Mount	Amb.	John Baldvin Hannibalsson	Amb.
India	Richard F. Celeste	Amb.	Naresh Chandra	Amb.
Indonesia	J. Stapleton Roy	Amb.	Dorodjatun Kuntjoro Jakti	Amb.
Ireland	Michael J. Sullivan	Amb.	Sean O'Huiginn	Amb.
Israel	Edward S. Walker, Jr.	Amb.	Zalman Shoval	Amb.
Italy	Thomas M. Foglietta	Amb.	Ferdinando Salleo	Amb.
Jamaica	Stanley L. McLelland	Amb.	Richard Leighton Bernal	Amb.
Japan	Thomas S. Foley	Amb.	Kunihiko Saito	Amb.
Jerusalem	John E. Herbst	Cons. Gen.	—	—
Jordan	William Joseph Burns	Amb.	Marwan Jamil Muasher	Amb.
Kazakhstan	Richard Henry Jones	Amb.	Bolat K. Nurgaliyev	Amb.
Kenya	Prudence Bushnell	Amb.	Samson Kipkoech Chemai	Amb.
Kiribati, Republic of	Joan Plaisted	Amb.	—	—
South Korea	Stephen W. Bosworth	Amb.	Hong Koo Lee	Amb.
Kuwait	James A. Larocco	Amb.	Mohammed Sabah Al-Salim Al-Sabah	Amb.
Kyrgyzstan	Anne Marie Sigmund	Amb.	Baktybek Abdrissaev	Amb.
Laos	Wendy J. Chamberlin	Amb.	Vang Rattanavong	Amb.
Latvia	James Howard Holmes	Amb.	Ojars Eriks Kalnins	Amb.
Lebanon	David Satterfield	Amb.	Dr. Farid Abboud	Amb.
Lesotho	Katherine Hubay Peterson	Amb.	Ben T. Nteso	C'd A
Liberia	Donald Petterson	C'd A	Rachel Diggs	Amb.
Liechenstein	Madeline May Kunin	Amb.	—	—
Lithuania	Keith Smith	Amb.	Stasys Sakalauskas	Amb.
Luxembourg	James Hormel	Amb.	Arlette Conzemius	Amb.
Macedonia	Christopher R. Hill	Amb.	Lubica Z. Acevska	Amb.
Madagascar	Shirley Elizabeth Barnes	Amb.	Zina Andrianarivelo Razafy	Amb.
Malawi	Amelia Ellen Shippy	Amb.	Willie Chokani	Amb.
Malaysia	B. Lynn Pascoe	Amb.	Dato Sheikh Abdul Khaled Ghazzaii	Amb.
Maldives, Republic of	Shaun Edward Donnelly	Amb.	—	—
Mali	David P. Rawson	Amb.	Cheick Oumar Diarrah	C'dA
Malta	Kathryn Proffitt	Amb.	Anthony Darmanin	Amb.
Marshall Islands	Joan M. Plaisted	Amb.	Banny De Brum	Amb.
Mauritania	Timberlake Foster	Amb.	Abdellahi Ould Kebd	C'dA
Mauritius	Harold W. Geisel	Amb.	Chitmansing Jesseramsing	Amb.
Mexico	Jeffrey Davidow	Amb.	Jesus F. Reyes Heroles G.G.	Amb.
Micronesia	—	—	Jesse B. Marehalau	Amb.
Moldova	Rudolf Vilemk Perina	Amb.	Ceslav Ciobanu	Amb.
Mongolia	Alphonso F. La Porta	Amb.	Jalbuu Choinhor	Amb.
Morocco	Edward M. Gabriel	Amb.	Mohamed Benaissa	Amb.
Mozambique	B. Dean Curran	Amb.	Marcos Geraldo Namashulua	Amb.
Namibia	Peter Graham Kaestner	C'dA	Leonard Nangolo Iipumbu	Amb.
Nepal	Ralph Frank	Amb.	Damodar Prasad Gautam	Amb.
Netherlands	Cynthia Perrin Schneider	Amb.	Joris M. Vos	Amb.
New Zealand	Josiah Horton Beeman	Amb.	James B. Bolger	Amb.
Nicaragua	Lino Gutierrez	Amb.	Francisco Javier Aguirre Sacasa	Amb.
Niger	Charles O. Cecil	Amb.	Joseph Diatta	Amb.
Nigeria	William H. Twaddell	Amb.	Walkili Hassan Adamu	Amb.
Norway	David B. Hermelin	Amb.	Tom Eric Vraalsen	Amb.

Country	U.S. Representative to[1]	Rank	Representative from[2]	Rank
Oman	John G. Craig	Amb.	Abdulla Moh'd Aqueel Al-Dhahab	Amb.
Pakistan	William B. Milam	Amb.	Riaz Khokhar	Amb.
Palau	Thomas C. Hubbard	Amb.	Hersey Kyota	Amb.
Panama	Simon Ferro	Amb.	Dr. Eloy Alfaro	Amb.
Papua New Guinea	Arma Jane Karaer	Amb.	Nagora Y. Bogan	Amb.
Paraguay	Maura Harty	Amb.	Elianne Cibils	C'dA
Peru	Dennis C. Jett	Amb.	Ricardo V. Luna	Amb.
Philippines	Thomas C. Hubbard	Amb.	Raul Chaves Rabe	Amb.
Poland	Daniel Fried	Amb.	Jerzy Kozminski	Amb.
Portugal	Gerald S. McGowan	Amb.	Fernando Andresen Guimaraes	Amb.
Qatar	Elizabeth Davenport McKune	Amb.	Saad Mohamed Al Kobaishe	Amb.
Romania	Jim Rosapepe	Amb.	Mircea Dan Geoana	Amb.
Russia	James Collins	Amb.	Yury Ushakov	Amb.
Rwanda	George McDade Staples	Amb.	Theogene N. Rudasingwa	Amb.
Saint Kitts and Nevis[3]	E. William Crotty	Amb.	Dr. Osbert W. Liburd	Amb.
Saint Lucia[3]	E. William Crotty	Amb.	Sonia Merlyn Johnny	Amb.
Saint Vincent and the Grenadines[3]	E. William Crotty	Amb.	Kingsley C.A. Layne	Amb.
Samoa, Western	Josiah Horton Beeman	Amb.	Tuiloma Neroni Slade	Amb.
Sao Tome and Principe, Democtaric Republic of	James Vela Ledesma	Amb.	—	—
Saudi Arabia	Wyche Fowler, Jr.	Amb.	Prince Bandar Bin Sultan	Amb.
Senegal	Dane F. Smith, Jr.	Amb.	Mamadou Mansour Seck	Amb.
Serbia Montenegro	Richard Miles	C'dA	—	—
Seychelles	Harold Geisel	Amb.	Claude Morel	Cd'A
Sierra Leone	Joseph Melrose. Jr.	Amb.	John Ernest Leigh	Amb.
Singapore	Steven J. Green	Amb.	Heng-Chee Chan	Amb.
Slovakia	Ralph Johnson	Amb.	Martin Butora	Amb.
Slovenia	Nancy Halliday Ely-Raphel	Amb.	Dr. Dimitrij Rupel	Amb.
Solomon Islands	Arma Jane Karser	Amb.	Rex Stephen Horoi	Amb.
Somalia	—	—	—	—
South Africa	James A. Joseph	Amb.	Makate Sheila Sisulu	Amb.
Spain	Edward L. Romero	Amb.	Antonio Oyarzabal	Amb.
Sri Lanka	Shaun E. Donnelly	Amb.	Dr. Warnasena Rasaputram	Amb.
Sudan	—	—	Mahdi Ibrahim Mohamed	Amb.
Suriname	Dennis Hays	Amb.	Arnold T. Halfhide	Amb.
Swaziland	Alan R. McKee	Amb.	Mary M. Kanya	Amb.
Sweden	Lyndon L. Olson, Jr.	Amb.	Rulf Ekeus	Amb.
Switzerland	Madeleine May Kunin	Amb.	Alfred Defago	Amb.
Syria	Ryan Clark Crocker	Amb.	Walid Al-Moualem	Amb.
Tajikistan	Robert P. J. Finn	Amb.	—	—
Tanzania	Charles Richard Stith	Amb.	Mustafa Salim Nyang'anyi	Amb.
Thailand	Richard E. Hecklinger	Amb.	Nitya Pibulsonggram	Amb.
Togo	Brenda Schoonover	Amb.	Akoussoulelou Bodjona	Amb.
Trinidad and Tobago	Edward Shumaker III	Amb.	Michael Arneaud	Amb.
Tunisia	Robin Raphel	Amb.	Noureddine Mejdoub	Amb.
Turkey	Mark R. Parris	Amb.	Baki Ilkin	Amb.
Turkmenistan	Steven R. Mann	Amb.	Halil Ugur	Amb.
Uganda	Nancy Jo Powell	Amb.	Edith Ssempala	Amb.
Ukraine	Steven Karl Pifer	Amb.	Anton Buteiko	Amb.
United Arab Emirates	Theodore H. Kattouf	Amb.	Mohammad bin Hussein Al-Shaali	Amb.
United Kingdom	Philip Lader	Amb.	Sir Christopher Meyer	Amb.
Uruguay	Christopher Ashby	Amb.	Alvaro Diez de Medina	Amb.
Uzbekistan	Joe Presel	Amb.	Sodiq Safaev	Amb.
Venezuela	John F. Maisto	Amb.	Alfredo Toro Hardy	Amb.
Vietnam	Pete Peterson	Amb.	Bang Le	Amb.
Yemen	Barbara K. Bodine	Amb.	Abdulwahab A. Al Hajjri	Amb.
Yugoslavia (former)	—	—	—	—
Zambia	Arlene Render	Amb.	Dunstan Weston Kamana	Amb.
Zimbabwe	Tom McDonald	Amb.	Elita Tinoenda Tundi Sakupwanya	Amb.

1. As of Spring 1999. 2. As of Spring 1999. 3. The U.S. Embassy in Barbados currently serves seven independent nations of the Eastern Caribbean (Barbados, Antigua and Barbuda, Dominica; Grenada, St. Kitts and Nevis, St. Lucia, and St. Vincent and the Grenadines) and provides consular services to American citizens in the nearby European dependent territories. 4. Ambassador to Fiji, Nauru, Tonga, and Tuvalu. NOTE: Amb.=Ambassador; Cd'A=Charge d'Affaires; Secy.=Secretary; Cons. Gen.=Consul General; Consl.=Counselor; Min.=Minister; P.O.=Principal Officer; Dir.=Director; USLO=U.S. Liaison Office. *Source:* U.S. Department of State.

Cruise Lines Go Overboard

A fleet of monster ships is steaming into a high-seas showdown. They're loaded for fun. But can they all make money?

By JOHN GREENWALD TIME

Not since the *Titanic* set sail has the sea seemed so alluring or the cruise industry looked so unsinkable as it does today. With 5 million customers booking passage in 1997—a 10-fold increase from two decades earlier—major carriers such as Carnival and Royal Caribbean have steamed to record sales and profits. They have turned a once snooty form of travel into mass-market vacations for people like Ken and Sherry Nunn and daughter Ashley, an Indiana family that recently spent three nights aboard Royal Caribbean's cozy 2,250-passenger *Sovereign of the Seas.* "Everything's right there, and you don't have to run yourself crazy looking for something to do," says Sherry, who sampled the lavish feedings and reveled in the duty-free shopping. "If I could afford to take a cruise every year, I would gladly do it."

Crowded Waters

Even that film about a seagoing catastrophe has piqued consumer interest. But the danger in the future may not be icebergs on the high seas as much as traffic. Flush with cash, cruise lines have ordered an astonishing $10 billion worth of floating pleasure palaces, some of which will be the largest passenger ships ever built. The new vessels, to be delivered through 2002, will increase the number of berths a whopping 50%. Among them: the $450 million, 2,600-passenger *Grand Princess,* flagship of the Princess line. At a record-breaking 109,353 tons (the *Titanic* displaced, temporarily, 46,328 tons), *Grand Princess* has 15 decks, three show lounges, and the world's largest floating casino.

The Walt Disney Co. is also taking to sea, a move that both scares and encourages this $7.5 billion industry. In 1998, Disney launched a pair of $370 million ships that each carry 1,760 passengers. Backed by a $130 million marketing budget, these floating Mouse traps offer three- and four-day excursions as part of Disney World vacations. The good news is that Disney's money will sell the industry to a new generation of travelers. The bad news is that Disney (sales: $22.5 billion) dwarfs the other companies, it hangs on to customers the way pirates do treasure, and its kid-friendly packages will be tough to match.

Growing Market

For public consumption, the cruise captains have been shouting, "Welcome aboard!" They contend, as they always have, that the seafaring market is still largely untapped, with just 8% of North Americans having taken a cruise. That leaves plenty of room for bookings to continue to grow a robust 9% to 10% a year. "Our philosophy is, 'If you build the ship, they will come,'" says Rich Steck, a spokesman for Royal Caribbean, which is spending more than $2.8 billion to add seven new liners to its 16-ship fleet by 2002. "We're banking on that heavily."

Escaping Reality

The superliners offer everything from towering atriums to nightclubs to conference centers, gymnasiums, and rock-climbing walls designed to keep passengers from ever having to contemplate the ocean. "It's such a fantasy world," gushes Patty Cromie, a New Jersey mother of three who recently cruised on Carnival's new, $330 million *Elation.* "The spa, the shows, the lounges and boutiques, not to mention being waited on hand and foot. I hardly dared go to sleep."

In their quest for synthetic perfection, the cruise lines have created their own ports of call. Disney's Castaway Cay in the Bahamas features three beaches and a 12-acre snorkeling lagoon. At Coco Cay, Royal Caribbean's 140-acre island, aquamarine waters lap at the white sand beach, while snorkelers explore a 16th century sailing ship and a small plane that the company submerged to give divers a sense of adventure.

The new features are designed to lure middle-class travelers who are younger and more active but have less time to spend at sea than the retired blue bloods who once dominated the passenger lists. The big lines offer services including playrooms, golf courses, and virtual-reality games. Such touches have lowered the average age of Royal Caribbean customers to the low 40s from the 60s and 70s not long ago.

The Price of Luxury

Although the accoutrements are new, the economics of cruising aren't changing much. The idea is to attract customers with low daily rates and give them every opportunity to spend freely in the bars, shops, and casino while onboard. According to the Cruise Lines International Association, the average daily rate for the industry is about $200 a day, which includes food and entertainment. Canny passengers can swing discounts by booking at the last minute, when some companies may be desperate to fill empty berths.

Of course, some passengers prefer pure luxury. Retired California businessman Roy Black and his wife have spent $30,000 for the penthouse of Crystal Cruises' 940-passenger ship *Harmony* during a 30-day world tour. The Blacks are so fond of Crystal, a privately owned company, that they've taken 18 *Harmony* cruises. "It's the ultimate in comfort, spaciousness, and décor" Black says of the 950-sq.-ft. penthouse, which comes with a Jacuzzi and private butler service, among other creature comforts. "It's always been our home away from home."

Knut Kloster Jr., the former chairman of the Norwegian Cruise and Royal Viking lines, plans to top even that by launching a ship that will be a permanent home for its passengers. The globe-trotting vessel, called *World of ResidenSea*, will have 286 condominiums when completed in early 2001. Kloster has so far sold 65 units, which go for as much as $6.6 million. And for those who can't get enough *Titanic*, a U.S.-Swiss partnership plans to build a

$500 million replica that will take its maiden voyage on the 90th anniversary of the *Titanic*'s, in 2002. Two thousand passengers may enjoy the same kind of Gilded Age service as the original, and with enough lifeboats for everyone.

But even a new *Titanic* may not be much of a match for the fleets of gigantic new ships. Then again, the sheer number of ships may be no match for the next economic downturn. Right now, that doesn't worry the industry. It's confident it can continue to increase the number of people willing to pay for their sea legs. And if worse ever comes to worst, sailing to the poorhouse will never be so luxe. □

Current Travel Warnings

(for U.S. citizens; as of 9/10/99)

Country	Most recent warning issued	Country	Most recent warning issued
Afghanistan	7/8/99	Iraq	12/17/98
Albania	4/14/99	Lebanon	7/9/99
Algeria	6/8/99	Liberia	3/24/99
Angola	7/27/99	Libya	8/4/99
Bosnia and Herzegovina	7/30/99	Nigeria	4/29/99
Burundi	7/15/99	Pakistan	8/10/99
Central African Republic	6/7/99	Rwanda	3/19/99
Colombia	6/10/99	Serbia and Montenegro	8/6/99
Republic of Congo (Brazzaville)	12/3/98	Sierra Leone	12/24/98
Dem. Rep. of the Congo (formerly Zaire)	4/23/99	Somalia	7/14/98
Eritrea	6/15/99	Sudan	7/28/99
Ethiopia	4/21/99	Tajikistan	9/25/98
Guinea-Bissau	6/14/98	Yemen	1/28/99
Iran	4/2/98		

Source: U.S. Department of State. Web: http://travel.state.gov.

The World's Top 40 Tourism Destinations, 1998

International tourist arrivals (excluding same-day visitors)

Rank 1990	1998	Country	Arrivals 1998	Rank 1990	1998	Country	Arrivals 1998
1	1	France	70,000,000	20	22	Netherlands	6,170,000
3	2	Spain	47,743,000	22	23	Belgium	6,152,000
2	3	United States	47,127,000	26	24	Ireland	6,073,000
4	4	Italy	34,829,000	55	25	South Africa	5,981,000
7	5	United Kingdom	25,475,000	23	26	Singapore	5,600,000
12	6	China	24,000,000	38	27	Indonesia	4,900,000
8	7	Mexico	19,300,000	32	28	Argentina	4,859,000
27	8	Poland	18,820,000	29	29	Tunisia	4,700,000
10	9	Canada	18,659,000	31	30	Korea Republic	4,250,000
6	10	Austria	17,282,000	18	31	Croatia	4,200,000
9	11	Germany	16,504,000	28	32	Japan	4,100,000
16	12	Czech Republic	16,325,000	36	33	Australia	4,012,000
17[1]	13	Russian Federation	15,810,000	35	34	Egypt	3,766,000
5	14	Hungary	14,660,000	37	35	Saudi Arabia	3,700,000
14	15	Portugal	11,800,000	34	36	Macau	3,590,000
13	16	Greece	11,077,000	33	37	Puerto Rico	3,255,000
11	17	Switzerland	11,025,000	25	38	Morocco	3,241,000
19	18	China, Hong Kong SAR	9,600,000	53	39	Brazil	3,135,000
24	19	Turkey	9,200,000	30	40	Romania	3,075,000
21	20	Thailand	7,720,000			Total 1–40	538,571,000
15	21	Malaysia	6,856,000			World Total	625,236,000

1. Former USSR. *Source:* World Tourism Organization (WTO). Web: www.world-tourism.org.

U.S. Passport Information

Source: Department of State. Bureau of Consular Affairs. Web: http://travel.state.gov.

With a few exceptions, a passport is required for all U.S. citizens to depart and enter the United States and to enter most foreign countries. Persons who travel to a country where a U.S. passport is not required should be in possession of documentary evidence of their U.S. citizenship and identity to facilitate reentry into the United States. Travelers should check passport and visa requirements with consular officials of the countries to be visited well in advance of their departure date.

Application for a passport may be made at a passport agency, many Federal and state courts, probate courts, some county and municipal offices, and some post offices. The thirteen major cities with U.S. passport agencies are Boston, Chicago, Honolulu, Houston, Los Angeles, Miami, New Orleans, New York, Philadelphia, San Francisco, Seattle, Stamford, Conn., and Washington, D.C.

All persons are required to obtain individual passports in their own names. Neither spouses nor children may be included in each other's passports. Applicants age 13 years and older must appear in person before the clerk or agent executing the application if it is their first time applying, their passport was lost or stolen, or their passport was issued more than 12 years ago. For children under the age of 13, a parent or legal guardian may execute an application for them.

First-time passport applicants must apply in person. Applicants must present the following items at a passport facility:

• Completed Form DSP-11, Application for Passport (available at facility, many travel agencies, or on the web). This form may be completed in advance; however, it must be signed by you in person before a passport agent.

• Proof of U.S. citizenship. You may use one of the following: previous U.S. passport; certified birth certificate issued by the city, county, or state; Consular Report of Birth Abroad; Naturalization Certificate; or Certificate of Citizenship.

• Proof of identity. Acceptable proof includes: previous U.S. passport; Naturalization Certificate; Certificate of Citizenship; current, valid driver's license; government ID (city, state, or federal); military ID (military and dependents); work ID (must be

currently employed by the company); student ID (must be currently enrolled); Merchant Marines card (also known as a "Seamen's" or "Z" card); pilot or flight attendant ID. *Note:* Social Security cards are NOT acceptable as identification.

• Two passport photographs. Photographs must be 2×2 inches in size. The image size from the bottom of the chin to the top of the head should be between 1 inch and 1⅜ inches. They may be in color or black and white. They must be full face, front view with a plain white or off-white background. Photographs should be taken in normal street attire, without a hat or headgear that obscures the hair or hairline.

• The applicable fee. A fee of $45 plus a $15 execution fee is charged for adults 16 years and older for a passport valid for ten years from the date of issue. The fee for children under 16 years of age is $25 for a five-year passport plus $15 for the execution of the application. Persons of all ages born outside the U.S. are required to pay an additional $100 complex case fee. The fee for passport renewals by mail is $40 (there is no execution fee added).

• DSP-64 Lost or Stolen Passport Form (if necessary). In addition to the items listed above, if your passport was lost or stolen, you will need to complete and submit this form (available at passport facilities and on the web).

Passport renewals can be handled through the mail in some instances. You may apply by mail if: (1) you can submit your most recent passport and it is not mutilated, altered, or damaged; (2) you were at least 16 years old when your most recent passport was issued; (3) you were issued your most recent passport less than 12 years ago; and (4) you use the same name as on your most recent passport, OR, you have had your name changed by marriage or court order and can submit proper documentation to reflect your name changes.

In order to apply for a renewal by mail, you must fill out and submit Form DSP-82, which can be obtained at a passport facility or downloaded from the web site. Attach to it the following: (1) your most recent passport; (2) two identical passport photographs; and (3) the $40 fee. Make your check or money order payable to Passport Services. If your name changed, enclose a certified copy of the Court Order, Adoption Decree, Marriage Certificate, or Divorce Decree specifying another name for you to use. Mail the above items (if possible, in a padded envelope) to: National Passport Center; P.O. Box 371971, Pittsburgh, PA 15250-7971.

Normal processing time for a passport application is 25 working days. However, it is recommended that you apply for your passport several months in advance of your planned departure. If you will need visas from foreign embassies, allow more time. If you need to leave in a hurry, you may expedite the process for an additional fee of $35 per passport. When requesting expedite service, two-way overnight mail for each application is strongly suggested. If you are applying by mail and wish to have your processing expedited, clearly mark the envelope EXPEDITED. You should receive your passport in 7-10 business days if using expedited service

Travel Web Sites

American Automobile Association: www.aaa.com
Amtrak: www.amtrak.com
Bureau of Consular Affairs: travel.state.gov
CIA World Factbook:
  www.odci.gov/cia/publications/factbook
Exchange Rates: www.x-rates.com
Expedia Travel (Microsoft): www.expedia.com
Fodor's Travel Online: www.fodors.com
Frommer's Budget Travel Online:
  www.frommers.com
Greyhound: www.greyhound.com
Hostelling International: www.iyhf.org
Lonely Planet: www.lonelyplanet.com
National Park Service ParkNet: www.nps.gov
Preview Travel: www.previewtravel.com
Rail Connection (Europe): www.railconnection.com
Travelocity: www.travelocity.com
Zagat (restaurants): www.zagat.com

and two-way overnight delivery, depending upon the reliability of your overnight service.

If your passport is lost or stolen report the loss on Form DSP-64 when you apply, in person, for your new passport. If you are abroad, report the loss immediately to local police authorities and the nearest U.S. embassy or consulate. Remember to write your current address in the space provided in your passport, so that, if it is found, it can be returned to you.

Your passport is a valuable citizenship and identity document. It should be carefully safeguarded. Its loss could cause you unnecessary travel complications as well as significant expense. The State Dept. suggests you make two copies of the identification page—one to leave with a friend or relative at home in case of

an emergency, and one to keep with you in the event that your passport is lost or stolen while abroad. This will make it easier to get a new passport, should it be necessary. It is also a good idea to carry two extra passport-size photos with you.

If you have questions or would like more information about obtaining or renewing a passport, visit the State Dept. web site (http://travel.state.gov) or call the National Passport Information Center. Note that the Information Center charges 35 cents per minute for automated information and $1.05 per minute for operator assistance at 1-900-225-5674. (You must speak with an operator to check the status of a pending passport application.) Alternatively, you may call 1-888-362-8668 and pay a flat rate of $4.95 per call.

Consumer Complaints Against U.S. Airlines

Complaint category	1990	1991	1992	1993	1994	1995	1996	1997	1998
TOTAL	**7,703**	**6,106**	**5,639**	**4,438**	**5,179**	**4,629**	**5,782**	**6,394**	**7,994**
Flight problems[1]	3,034	1,877	1,624	1,211	1,586	1,133	1,628	1,699	2,277
Customer service[2]	758	714	695	599	805	667	999	1,418	1,715
Baggage	1,329	883	752	627	761	628	882	826	1,108
Ticketing/boarding[3]	624	659	680	577	598	666	857	904	1,137
Refunds	701	783	721	482	393	576	521	531	602
Oversales[4]	399	301	265	257	301	263	353	414	388
Fares[5]	312	388	573	398	267	185	180	195	277
Advertising	96	96	54	51	94	66	61	57	40
Tours	29	23	12	16	127	18	16	13	23
Smoking	74	30	25	30	20	15	13	5	4
Credit	5	10	10	4	2	4	3	1	1
Other	342	342	228	186	225	408	269	331	422

NOTE: Calendar year data. 1. Cancellations, delays, etc. from schedule. 2. Unhelpful employees, inadequate meals or cabin service, treatment of delayed passengers. 3. Errors in reservations and ticketing; problems in making reservations and obtaining tickets. 4. All bumping problems, whether or not airline complied with DOT regulations. 5. Incorrect or incomplete information about fares, discount fare conditions, and availability, etc. *Source:* U.S. Dept. of Transportation, Office of Consumer Affairs, *Air Travel Consumer Report.*

Passengers Denied Boarding by U.S. Airlines,[1] 1998

		Denied boardings (DB's)		Enplaned passengers	Involuntary DB's per 10,000 passengers
Rank	Airline	Voluntary	Involuntary		
1.	Continental	76,167	574	42,352,892	0.14
2.	U.S. Airways	81,830	1,267	56,564,712	0.22
3.	Northwest	120,045	1,394	46,025,183	0.30
4.	American	221,826	3,387	73,618,441	0.46
5.	United	142,057	4,561	79,813,016	0.57
6.	America West	49,811	2,074	18,174,910	1.14
7.	Delta	233,732	13,449	102,405,802	1.31
8.	Alaska	24,530	1,822	13,028,998	1.40
9.	Southwest	81,201	10,230	59,053,217	1.73
10.	TWA	50,005	6,039	23,132,879	2.61
	Total	**1,081,204**	**44,797**	**514,170,050**	**0.87**

1. Includes U.S. airlines with at least one percent of total domestic scheduled-service passenger revenues. *Source:* Office of Aviation Enforcement and Proceedings, U.S. Dept. of Transportation.

Top 20 U.S. States & Territories Visited by Overseas Travelers[1], 1998

State/Territory	% of total overseas visitors	Overseas visitors (thousands)	State/Territory	% of total overseas visitors	Overseas visitors (thousands)
Florida	25.6%	6,067	Georgia	2.8%	664
California	25.2	5,972	Pennsylvania	2.5	592
New York	22.3	5,285	Washington	2.2	521
Hawaiian Islands	11.8	2,796	Colorado	1.9	450
Nevada	8.1	1,920	Louisiana	1.7	403
Illinois	5.3	1,256	Virginia	1.7	403
Massachusetts	4.9	1,161	Michigan	1.6	379
Texas	4.7	1,114	Ohio	1.6	379
Guam	4.4	1,043	North Carolina	1.5	355
Arizona	3.6	853	Utah	1.5	355
New Jersey	3.6	853			

1. Excludes visitors from Canada and Mexico. *Source:* U.S. Dept. of Commerce, International Trade Administration.

Top 20 U.S. Cities/Hawaiian Islands Visited by Overseas Travelers[1], 1998

City	% of total overseas visitors	Overseas visitors (thousands)	City	% of total overseas visitors	Overseas visitors (thousands)
New York City	21.1%	5,000	Tampa/St. Petersburg	3.1%	735
Los Angeles	15.0	3,555	Atlanta	2.4	569
Miami	13.8	3,270	Anaheim	2.2	521
Orlando	12.1	2,867	Ft. Lauderdale	2.2	521
San Francisco	10.9	2,583	Houston	2.1	498
Oahu/Honolulu	9.4	2,228	San Jose	2.0	474
Las Vegas	7.6	1,801	Seattle	2.0	474
Metro D.C. area	5.9	1,398	Phoenix	1.8	427
Chicago	5.1	1,209	Dallas/Ft. Worth	1.7	403
Boston	4.4	1,043	Maui	1.7	403
San Diego	3.3	782			

1. Excludes visitors from Canada and Mexico. *Source:* U.S. Dept. of Commerce, International Trade Administration.

Top 20 International Destinations of American Tourists

Rank	Country	1996 travelers (000)	1997 travelers (000)	Percent change 1996/1997	Rank	Country	1996 travelers (000)	1997 travelers (000)	Percent change 1996/1997
1.	Mexico	19,616	17,700	-10%	12.	Hong Kong	752	671	-11%
2.	Canada	12,909	13,401	4	12.	Switzerland	693	671	-3
3.	United Kingdom	2,869	3,570	24	14.	South Korea	554	649	17
4.	France	1,860	2,098	13	15.	Republic of China	495	562	14
5.	Germany	1,642	1,796	9		(Taiwan)			
6.	Italy	1,385	1,471	6	16.	Turkey	475	519	9
7.	Jamaica	1,029	1,341	30	17.	Brazil	376	498	32
8.	Japan	871	1,082	24	18.	People's Republic	396	476	20
9.	Bahamas	1,504	1,017	-32		of China			
10.	Netherlands	772	822	7	18.	Philippines	475	476	0
11.	Spain	613	714	16	20.	Australia	534	454	-15

Source: U.S. Dept. of Commerce, International Trade Administration; Statistics Canada; Mexican Ministry of Tourism.

Top 20 Nationalities of Overseas Travelers to the U.S.

Rank	Country of residence	1997 total	1998 total	1997/1998 % change	Rank	Country of residence	1997 total	1998 total	1997/1998 % change
1.	Japan	5,367,578	4,885,369	-9.0%	11.	Switzerland	410,209	410,900	0.2%
2.	United Kingdom	3,720,979	3,974,976	6.8	12.	Taiwan	442,780	386,413	-12.7
3.	Germany	1,994,296	1,901,938	-4.6	13.	Colombia	317,736	367,968	15.8
4.	France	978,327	1,013,222	3.5	14.	South Korea	746,550	364,061	-51.2
5.	Brazil	940,698	909,477	-3.3	15.	Spain	328,024	326,339	-0.5
6.	Italy	580,261	610,796	5.3	16.	Sweden	292,424	300,925	2.9
7.	Venezuela	487,981	540,685	10.8	17.	Israel	260,052	269,752	3.7
8.	Argentina	503,393	523,909	4.1	18.	Bahamas	319,240	251,929	-21.1
9.	Netherlands	473,420	490,198	3.5	19.	Ireland	217,278	232,391	7.0
10.	Australia	500,615	460,705	-8.0	20.	Belgium	241,366	230,190	-4.6

NOTE: Excludes arrivals from Mexico and Canada. *Source:* U.S. Dept. of Commerce, International Trade Administration.

State Tourism Offices

The following is a selected list of state tourism office Web addresses and phone numbers. Where a toll-free 800 or 888 number is available, it is given. However, the numbers are subject to change.

Alabama
334-242-4169 or
1-800-ALABAMA
www.touralabama.org

Alaska
907-465-2010
www.travelalaska.com

Arizona
602-230-7733 or
1-800-842-8257
www.arizona.com

Arkansas
501-682-7777 or
1-800-NATURAL
www.arkansas.com

California
1-800-862-2543
www.gocalif.ca.gov

Colorado
1-800-COLORADO
www.colorado.com

Connecticut
860-270-8081 or
1-800-CT-BOUND
www.ctbound.org

Delaware
302-739-4271 or
1-800-441-8846
www.state.de.us/tourism

**District of Columbia
(Washington, D.C.)**
202-789-7000
www.washington.org

Florida
850-488-5607 or
888-7FLA-USA
www.flausa.com

Georgia
404-656-3590 or
1-800-VISIT-GA
www.georgia.com

Hawaii
808-923-1811 or
1-800-GO-HAWAII
www.gohawaii.com

Idaho
208-334-2470 or
1-800-635-7820
www.visitid.org

Illinois
1-800-2-CONNECT
www.enjoyillinois.com

Indiana
1-800-291-8844
www.indiana.com

Iowa
515-242-4705 or
1-800-345-IOWA
www.state.ia.us/tourism

Kansas
785-296-2009 or
1-800-2-KANSAS
www.kansascommerce.com/
0400travel.html

Kentucky
1-800-225-TRIP Ext. 67
www.kentuckytourism.com

Louisiana
225-342-8100 or
1-800-33-GUMBO
www.louisianatravel.com

Maine
207-623-0363 or
1-888-MAINE-45
www.visitmaine.com

Maryland
410-767-3400 or
1-800-543-1036
www.mdisfun.org

Massachusetts
617-727-3201 or
1-800-227-MASS
www.massvacation.com

Michigan
1-888-78-GREAT
www.michigan.org

Minnesota
651-296-5029 or
1-800-657-3700
www.exploreminnesota.com

Mississippi
228-875-0079 or
1-800-927-6378
www.mississippi.org

Missouri
573-751-4133 or
1-800-MISSOURI
www.missouritourism.org

Montana
406-444-2654 or
1-800-VISIT-MT
www.visitmt.com

Nebraska
402-471-3796 or
1-800-228-4307
www.visitnebraska.org

Nevada
1-800-NEVADA-8
www.travelnevada.com

New Hampshire
603-271-2343 or
1-800-FUN-IN-NH or
1-800-258-3608 (for recorded
weekly events, ski conditions,
foliage reports)
www.visitnh.gov

New Jersey
1-800-JERSEY-7
www.visitnj.org

New Mexico
505-827-7400 or
1-800-SEE-NEWMEX
www.newmexico.org

New York
1-800-225-5697 or
518-474-4116
www.iloveny.state.ny.us

North Carolina
919-733-4171 or
1-800-VISIT-NC
www.visitnc.com

North Dakota
701-328-2525 or
1-800-HELLO-ND
www.ndtourism.com

Ohio
614-466-8844 or
1-800-BUCKEYE
www.ohiotourism.com

Oklahoma
405-521-2409 or
1-800-652-6552
www.touroklahoma.com

Oregon
503-986-0000 or
1-800-547-7842
www.traveloregon.com

Pennsylvania
717-787-5453 or
1-800-VISIT-PA Ext. 257
www.visit.state.pa.us

Puerto Rico
1-800-223-6530
www.travelandsports.com

Rhode Island
401-222-2601 or
1-800-556-2484
www.visitrhodeisland.com

South Carolina
803-734-0122
www.travelsc.com

South Dakota
605-773-3301 or
1-800-S-DAKOTA
www.travelsd.com

Tennessee
1-800-461-TENN
www.state.tn.us/tourdev

Texas
1-800-452-9292
www.traveltex.com

Utah
801-538-1030 or
1-800-200-1160
www.utah.com

Average Daily Temperatures (°F) in Tourist Cities

(For U.S. cities, *see* Climate of Selected U.S. Cities)

Location	January		April		July		October	
	High	Low	High	Low	High	Low	High	Low
Acapulco (Mexico)	87	72	87	73	89	77	89	77
Amsterdam (Netherlands)	41	34	53	40	69	55	57	46
Athens (Greece)	54	42	67	52	90	72	74	60
Auckland (New Zealand)	73	60	67	56	56	46	63	52
Bangkok (Thailand)	89	69	94	78	91	77	89	76
Beijing (China)	35	15	68	44	87	71	67	44
Belgrade (Yugoslavia)	38	28	62	43	81	60	64	46
Berlin (Germany)	35	26	55	38	74	55	55	41
Bombay (India)	83	67	89	76	85	77	89	76
Cairo (Egypt)	65	47	83	57	96	70	86	65
Calcutta (India)	80	55	97	75	89	79	89	74
Cape Town (South Africa)	69	56	66	54	60	50	65	53
Caracas (Venezuela)	75	56	81	60	78	61	79	61
Copenhagen (Denmark)	36	29	50	37	72	55	53	42
Dublin (Ireland)	47	35	54	38	67	51	57	43
Glasgow (Scotland)	43	34	53	38	66	52	54	43
Hamilton (Bermuda)	68	58	71	59	85	73	79	69
Helsinki (Finland)	27	17	43	31	71	57	45	37
Hong Kong (China)	67	51	79	67	90	78	84	70
Istanbul (Turkey)	48	36	59	45	78	64	66	53
Jerusalem (Israel)	55	41	73	50	87	63	81	59
Kingston (Jamaica)	86	67	87	70	90	73	88	73
Lagos (Nigeria)	88	74	89	77	82	74	85	74
Lisbon (Portugal)	56	46	64	52	79	63	69	57
London (United Kingdom)	44	35	56	40	73	55	58	44
Madrid (Spain)	50	34	63	43	89	61	67	48
Mexico City (Mexico)	66	42	77	51	73	53	70	50
Montreal (Canada)	22	6	51	33	79	60	56	39
Moscow (Russia)	21	9	47	31	76	55	46	34
Nairobi (Kenya)	77	53	75	57	69	51	77	54
Nassau (Bahamas)	77	65	81	69	88	75	85	73
Oslo (Norway)	30	20	50	34	73	56	49	37
Paris (France)	42	32	60	41	76	55	59	44
Prague (Czech Republic)	34	25	55	40	74	58	54	44
Quebec (Canada)	19	3	45	30	77	58	51	37
Rio de Janeiro (Brazil)	84	73	80	69	75	63	77	66
Rome (Italy)	54	39	68	46	88	64	73	53
San José (Costa Rica)	75	58	79	62	77	62	77	60
San Juan (Puerto Rico)	81	70	83	72	86	76	86	75
Seoul (Korea)	33	17	62	42	84	70	67	47
Singapore	86	73	89	75	87	75	88	74
Stockholm (Sweden)	31	23	45	32	70	55	48	39
Sydney (Australia)	79	65	73	57	62	44	72	55
Taipei (Taiwan)	66	54	77	63	92	76	81	67
Tokyo (Japan)	48	31	64	48	84	71	70	56
Toronto (Canada)	30	17	51	35	79	60	57	42
Vancouver (Canada)	42	32	55	41	71	55	57	44
Vienna (Austria)	34	26	57	41	75	59	55	44
Zurich (Switzerland)	36	26	60	41	77	56	57	43

Vermont
1-800-VERMONT
www.travel-vermont.com

Virginia
804-786-4484 or
1-800-932-5827
www.virginia.org

Washington
360-753-7426
www.tourism.wa.gov

Washington, D.C.
See District of Columbia

West Virginia
304-558-2200 or
1-800-CALL-WVA
www.state.wv.us/tourism

Wisconsin
608-266-2161 or
1-800-372-2737 or
1-800-432-TRIP
www.travelwisconsin.com

Wyoming
307-777-7777 or
1-800-225-5996
www.wyomingtourism.org

Take Their Word for It: The Kids Are Alright

While parents worry, a new TIME/Nickelodeon poll shows that youngsters find the world a less scary place—and are in no rush to grow up

By CLAUDIA WALLIS TIME

Let's face it, as grownups, it's our job to worry. And for those of us attempting to raise children in the 21st century, there's no shortage of anxieties to gnaw at the nerves. How, we wonder, can our children flourish and stay on course with only a few hours a day of parental devotion? How can kids focus on schoolwork when tempted by a luscious smorgasbord of multimedia junk? Looming larger is a more ominous concern: Will my child's life end in a burst of gunfire and a pool of blood on the cafeteria's cold linoleum floor?

Surely American kids have never faced a more corrupting, corrosive, and threatening environment. Or have they? Given the recent headlines and hand wringing, it is something of a shock to discover that according to a major new kids' survey, children don't see the world that way at all.

From mid-May through June 1, 1999, just a few weeks after the Littleton, Colo., shootings at Columbine High, New York-based pollsters Penn, Schoen & Berland Assoc. sat down with 1,172 kids, ages 6 to 14, in 25 U.S. cities. The poll was conducted for Nickelodeon, the children's TV channel, and TIME. Kids from a sample weighted to match U.S. demographics were interviewed one-on-one and without their parents in a venue where most feel at ease: a shopping mall. Pollsters also interviewed 397 parents.

What emerges loud and clear from the study is that kids are very happy to be kids, and they don't view the world as the nasty place their parents perceive it to be. Nine out of 10 say they feel safe in their schools and neighborhoods. While parents list crime, violence, and guns as the worst aspects of being a child today, such concerns are way down the list for kids.

Modern Times, Traditional Values

As for the much lamented decline of family values—well, has anyone mentioned this to kids? Asked whom they admire most, 79% say it's good old Mom and Dad; an additional 19% name their grandparents. Athletes, musicians, and movie stars don't even come close.

Childhood in the '90s: A TIME/Nickelodeon Poll

How safe do you feel in your school?

Very safe	49%
Pretty safe	44%
Not safe	5%

What are the most important things that kids at your school use to decide who fits in?

AGES 9 - 11	
Being a good friend	45%
Being good at sports	35%
Popularity	31%
Being funny	31%
AGES 12 - 14	
Clothes	44%
Popularity	37%
Being good-looking	34%
Being a good friend	33%

How much respect do you think adults have for kids?

	Kids	Parents
A lot	31%	52%
Some	48%	42%
A little	16%	6%
None	5%	0%

Do you spend more time with your mom, your dad, or both about the same?

Mom	47%
Dad	11%
The same	41%

What is bad about being a kid?

KIDS SAY:	
Getting bossed around	17%
School, homework	15%
Can't do everything I want	11%
Chores	9%
Being grounded	9%
PARENTS SAY:	
Crime	26%
Youth violence, guns	13%
Peer pressure	13%
Drugs	5%
Homework, chores	4%

OLD-FASHIONED VALUES

Of all the people you know or know about, who are the top three you look up to most?

My parents	79%
My grandparents	19%
Athletes	13%

Do you believe in God?

Yes	95%

Percent who pray

Ages 6-8	73%
Ages 9-11	81%
Ages 12-14	84%

How important is it to wait until you are married to have sex?

Very	53%
Somewhat	23%
Not important	22%

At what age do you think pre-marital sex is appropriate?

Kids	23 years old
Parents	18 years old

FUTURE LEADERS?

Would you rather be Bill Gates or Bill Clinton?

Bill Gates	67%
Bill Clinton	21%

Would you like to be President of the U.S.?

KIDS SAY:	
Yes	36%
No	62%

Would you like your child to be President?

PARENTS SAY:	
Yes	31%
No	58%

Methodology: Penn, Schoen & Berland conducted 1,172 interviews with children ages 6 to 14 and 397 interviews with parents at 27 shopping malls in 25 cities throughout the U.S. from May 14 to June 1,1999. Margin of error: all kids +/- 2.9%; age categories and parents +/- 5%.

But God looms large for the younger generation: 95% of the kids surveyed said they were believers. Nearly half claimed to attend religious services every week, and 8 out of 10 say they pray. Sure, they may enjoy dipping into the sultry waters of *Dawson's Creek* on Wednesday nights, but their ideas about sex would cheer William Bennett: 76% of those ages 12 to 14 say it's "somewhat or very important" to wait until marriage before having sex. When the other 24% were asked to name an appropriate age for pre-marital sex, these pubescent puritans settled on 23. The average age mentioned by parents: 18.

So are adults cultivating gray hairs and worry lines for nothing? Could it be that the kids are alright? For the most part, yes, and don't be so sur-prised, say several child psychologists consulted by TIME on the poll results.

"Parents remain the most significant people in children's lives, until age 14 or 15, when they have more fully embraced peer culture," says Jean Bailey, coordinator of child and adolescent mental-health services at Lutheran Medical Center in Brooklyn, N.Y. Personal values about religion, sex, and obey-ing authority are shaped primarily by parents right up until the teenage years, when things suddenly shift. While kids may be exposed to sex in the media, "there's a lot of anxiety about what the whole deal of sexual behavior is," says child psy-chologist Anthony Wolf, author of *Get Out of My Life, but First Could You Drive Me and Cheryl to the Mall?* (1991). Wolf is not surprised that kids are in no rush to become teens: "Teenagers are out there doing all these fast and wild things. Kids see that world as a little scary."

Understanding Our Children

If Americans have the wrong idea about their kids, it may be because of the very disturbed kids who make headlines. "We should be very concerned about those kids, but they are a small minority," notes Johns Hopkins sociologist Andrew Cherlin. Adults also tend to read too much into children's superficial gestures. A five-year-old who wants to dress like Posh Spice still wants to be a kid; after all, only kids get to play dress-up! And if kids seem to be growing up faster than they used to, the fault may lie partly with adults, especially some of those in the entertainment business. Says Nickelodeon president Herb Scannell, who commissioned the poll: "One of the problems we have in this industry is we make assumptions: kids don't want to see movies with kids; they want to see movies with teens, movies with aliens. We're not listening to kids."

The kids have taken note of this disregard, and if there's a lesson for parents in the Nickelodeon/ TIME poll, it's tune in to your kids and show them some respect. While the majority of parents in the study claim to have great respect for kids, only 31% of kids feel that adults actually do respect them "a lot." This "respect gap" is even more glaring among kids in the 12 to 14 age group: 27% said they get little respect from adults or none at all.

"It's true that most adults think they don't have much to learn from children and don't really value their opinions, except on topics like, say, ice cream," says David Elkind, professor of child development at Tufts University and author of *The Hurried Child* (1981). "Kids do have interesting ideas, if you're willing to listen. And I think sometimes adults are not civil enough with kids, saying please, thank you, apologizing for breaking promises."

Sensitive young teens emerge as a particularly interesting group in the poll. The middle school years are perilous. While only 14% of the 9- to 11-year-olds said they had ever tried alcohol, the fig-ure rose to 42% among 12- to 14-year-olds. Drug use rose from zero to 11%; smoking from 11% to 44%.

Peer pressure rears its head in other ways as well. What does it take to "fit in" at school? Kids ages 9 to 11 say it's being a good friend, being good at sports, and being funny or popular. But kids in the 12 to 14 group have different criteria: clothes come first, then "being popular," and third, good looks. "This is a little bit sad," observes Wolf, "but it also shows parents what they're up against if they're try-ing to draw the line on certain clothes."

Signs of the Times

Despite all this, 60% of kids ages 12 to 14 say, as most younger kids do, that they would like to spend more time with their parents. The problem, of course, is finding that time, which is at a premium in the increasing number of two-earner households and those headed by single parents. A clear reflec-tion of how families have changed: 41% of the kids sampled said they spend an equal amount of time with both parents. "This is one of our most signifi-cant cultural changes," says Dr. Leon Hoffman, who co-directs the Parent Child Center at the New York Psychoanalytic Society. In practice for 30 years, Hoffman has found a "very dramatic difference in the involvement of the father—in everything from caretaking to general decision making around kids' lives." Alas, this change has been slower to reach black children: 76% of black kids surveyed said they spend more time with their mom than their dad.

There are other signs of change. The most worri-some: 1 in 6 kids ages 12 to 14 claims to have seen a gun at school. Other studies have also shown that American kids have easy access to guns. That kids in the survey feel safe at school may be because school shootings remain rare. The study did find, however, that black and Hispanic children are a lot more wor-ried than whites about being crime victims.

On the upside, tolerance for diversity seems to be gathering strength. Most kids support the notion that girls and boys can play on the same sports teams. Nine out of 10 say they have friends of a different race. Four out of 10 say that it's not very important, or not important at all, that a future spouse should be someone of the same race. Most expect to see a black President and a woman President in their lifetime.

As an institution, however, the presidency appears to have suffered: 62% of kids ages 9 to 14 say they do not want to grow up to be President. "It's too much pressure, and everyone is watching you," explained a seventh-grade girl. "I don't want to turn out like Bill and Monica," said an 11-year-old. In fact, 67% of 9- to 14-year-olds said they'd rather be Bill Gates than Bill Clinton.

But mostly, and most reassuringly, kids just want to be kids. What's so great about it? Parents in the poll said the boon for kids today is technology and com-puters. They just don't get it. The best things about being a kid, say those who really know, are playing, hanging with friends, and having fun. Well, duh! □

Families by Type and Selected Characteristics, 1998

Characteristics	All families	Married-couple families	Other families	
			Female householder	Male householder
All families	70,880	54,317	12,652	3,911
Size of family[1]				
2 people	30,282	22,042	6,016	2,225
3 people	16,231	11,639	3,628	964
4 people	14,633	12,402	1,777	454
5 people	6,555	5,633	756	167
6 people	2,047	1,746	239	63
7 people or more	1,130	855	237	39
Average size	3.18	3.24	3.04	2.86
Own children under 18				
Without own children under 18	36,120	29,048	4,960	2,113
With own children under 18	34,760	25,269	7,693	1,798
Total own children under 18	64,323	47,931	13,656	2,736
Average per family with own children under 18	1.85	1.90	1.78	1.52
Householder's age				
Under 25 years	3,019	1,373	1,095	551
25 to 34 years	13,639	9,886	2,887	866
35 to 44 years	18,872	14,180	3,637	1,055
45 to 54 years	14,694	11,734	2,260	701
55 to 64 years	9,387	7,936	1,099	352
65 to 74 years	6,989	5,841	938	210
75 years or more	4,282	3,368	738	176
Median age	45.0	46.4	41.4	40.4
Householder's marital status				
Married, spouse present	54,317	54,317		
Married, spouse absent (incl. separated couples)	2,506	—	1,977	529
Widowed	2,698	—	2,325	373
Divorced	5,910	—	4,518	1,391
Never married	5,449	—	3,831	1,618

NOTE: Numbers are in thousands, except averages and medians. 1. Note that "size of family" and "size of household" are different. Household members include all people living in the household, whereas family members include only the householder and his/her relatives. Data applies to U.S. families only. *Source:* U.S. Bureau of the Census, *Current Population Survey.*

Families by Type, 1970–1998

(with children under age 18, for selected years 1970–1998)

Family type	1970	1980	1990	1991	1992	1993	1994	1995	1996	1997	1998
Total											
Two parents[1]	85%	77%	73%	72%	71%	71%	69%	69%	68%	68%	68%
Mother only[1]	11	18	22	22	23	23	23	23	24	24	23
Father only[2]	1	2	3	3	3	3	3	4	4	4	4
No parent	3	4	3	3	3	3	4	4	4	4	4
White											
Two parents[1]	90	83	79	78	77	77	76	76	75	75	74
Mother only[1]	8	14	16	17	18	17	18	18	18	18	18
Father only[2]	1	2	3	3	3	3	3	3	4	4	5
No parent	2	2	2	2	2	2	3	3	3	3	3
Black											
Two parents[1]	58	42	38	36	36	36	33	33	33	35	36
Mother only[1]	30	44	51	54	54	54	53	52	53	52	51
Father only[2]	2	2	4	4	3	3	4	4	4	5	4
No parent	10	12	8	7	7	7	10	11	9	8	9
Hispanic[3]											
Two parents[1]	78	75	67	66	65	65	63	63	62	64	64
Mother only[1]	—	20	27	27	28	28	28	28	29	27	27
Father only[2]	—	2	3	3	4	4	4	4	4	4	4
No parent	—	3	3	4	3	4	5	4	5	5	5

1. Excludes families where parents are not living as a married couple. 2. Includes some families where both parents are present in the household, but living as unmarried partners. 3. Persons of Hispanic origin may be of any race. NOTE: Data applies to U.S. families. *Source:* U.S. Bureau of the Census, *Current Population Reports.*

Young Adults Living at Home, 1960–1998

	Male			Female		
	Total population, 18–24 years old	Number living at home	Percent	Total population, 18–24 years old	Number living at home	Percent
1960	6,842,000	3,583,000	52%	7,876,000	2,750,000	35%
1970	10,398,000	5,641,000	54	11,959,000	4,941,000	41
1980	14,278,000	7,755,000	54	14,844,000	6,336,000	43
1985	13,695,000	8,172,000	60	14,149,000	6,758,000	48
1990	12,450,000	7,232,000	58	12,860,000	6,135,000	48
1995	12,545,000	7,328,000	58	12,613,000	5,896,000	47
1998	12,633,000	7,399,000	59	12,568,000	5,974,000	48

	Male			Female		
	Total population, 25–34 years old	Number living at home	Percent	Total population, 25–34 years old	Number living at home	Percent
1960	10,896,000	1,185,000	11%	11,587,000	853,000	7%
1970	11,929,000	1,129,000	9	12,637,000	829,000	7
1980	18,107,000	1,894,000	10	18,689,000	1,300,000	7
1985	20,184,000	2,685,000	13	20,673,000	1,661,000	8
1990	21,462,000	3,213,000	15	21,779,000	1,774,000	8
1995	20,589,000	3,166,000	15	20,800,000	1,759,000	8
1998	19,526,000	2,845,000	15	19,828,000	1,680,000	8

NOTE: Unmarried college students living in dorms are counted as living at home. *Source:* U.S. Bureau of the Census, *Current Population Reports,* March 1998.

Child Support Payments Due and Actually Received, 1995

Characteristics	Custodial parents	Custodial mothers	Custodial fathers
Custodial parents due child support payments	6,966,000	6,233,000	733,000
Mean payments (dollars)			
Due	$4,057	$4,126	$3,468
Received	2,555	2,631	1,910
Deficit	1,502	1,495	1,558
Aggregate payments (billions of dollars)			
Child support due	$28.3	$25.7	$2.5
Child support received	17.8	16.4	1.4
Aggregate child support deficit	10.5	9.3	1.1
Percent of aggregate due actually received	63.0%	63.8%	55.1%

NOTE: Applies to people 15 years and older with own children under 21 years of age present from an absent parent as of spring 1996. *Source:* U.S. Bureau of the Census, *Current Population Survey,* April 1996.

Teen Birth Rates Decline

Source: Centers for Disease Control and Prevention, National Center for Health Statistics.

An April 1999 report released by the Centers for Disease Control and Prevention (CDC) reveals that a declining trend in teen birth rates since 1991 continued through 1997. The overall birth rate for teens aged 15–19 declined 16% from 1991 to 1997, with drops in all racial categories and in all states.

Also of note in the 1999 report are statistics showing declines in second births to teens and births to unmarried teens. From 1991 to 1996, the rate of teens giving birth for the second time dropped by a solid 21%. Births to unmarried teens ages 15–17 dropped by 12% from 1994 to 1997. For teens ages 18–19, the decline in that time period was 7%.

A number of factors likely contributed to the change. Relevant data from a 1995 study by the Department of Health and Human Services showed a decline in the percentage of females and males aged 15–19 who had ever had intercourse. For females, the percentage dropped from 55% in 1990 to 50% in 1995; for never-married males, from 60% in 1988 to 55% in 1995.

In addition to waiting longer before experiencing intercourse for the first time, people are practicing safer sex. The '90s have seen a heightened awareness among teens of the risks involved with sex, including pregnancy and HIV infection. In 1997, 91.5% of students said they had been taught about HIV and AIDS in school (up from 83.3% in 1991). Perhaps by no coincidence, today's teenagers are more likely than ever to use contraceptives during their first intercourse.

The trends are a positive answer to the call in President Clinton's 1995 State of the Union address for a national initiative to fight teen pregnancy. □

Teen Birth Rates in the U.S., Selected Years
(rates per 1,000 females in specified group)

Age	1980	1985	1990	1991	1993	1995	1997[1]
All races							
10–14 years	1.1	1.2	1.4	1.4	1.4	1.3	1.2
15–19 years	53.0	51.0	59.9	62.1	59.6	56.8	52.9
White, total							
10–14 years	—	—	0.7	0.8	0.8	0.8	0.7
15–19 years	—	—	50.8	52.8	51.1	50.1	46.8
White, non-Hispanic							
10–14 years	0.4	—	0.5	0.5	0.5	0.4	0.4
15–19 years	41.2	—	42.5	43.4	40.7	39.3	36.4
Black							
10–14 years	4.3	4.5	4.9	4.8	4.6	4.2	3.5
15–19 years	97.8	95.4	112.8	115.5	108.6	96.1	89.5
American Indian[2]							
10–14 years	1.9	1.7	1.6	1.6	1.4	1.8	1.7
15–19 years	82.2	79.2	81.9	85.0	83.1	78.0	71.8
Asian/Pacific Islander							
10–14 years	0.3	0.4	0.7	0.8	0.6	0.7	0.5
15–19 years	26.2	23.8	26.4	27.4	27.0	26.1	24.8
Hispanic[3]							
10–14 years	1.7	—	2.4	2.4	2.7	2.7	2.6
15–19 years	82.2	—	100.3	106.7	106.8	106.7	99.1

1. Data for 1997 are preliminary. 2. Includes births to Aleuts and Eskimos. 3. Persons of Hispanic origin may be of any race.
NOTE: Data applies to the U.S. *Source:* Centers for Disease Control and Prevention, National Center for Health Statistics. *National Vital Statistics Report,* Vol. 47, No. 12. Dec. 17, 1998.

Adoption in the U.S., 1973–1995

(Number of ever-married women 18–44 years of age and percent who have ever adopted a child)

Characteristic	1973	1982	1988	1995
All women (thousands)	30,701	34,632	36,689	37,448
Percent who ever adopted[1]	2.1%	2.2%	1.6%	1.3%
Age at interview				
18-24 years	0.4	0.6	—	0.2
25-34 years	1.8	2.0	0.5	0.4
35-39 years	3.1	2.1	2.2	1.9
40-44 years	4.0	4.3	4.3	2.5
Marital status at interview				
Currently married	2.2	2.1	1.8	1.3
Formerly married	1.5	2.4	0.9	1.2
Fecundity status at interview[2]				
Surgically sterile	3.3	2.1	2.1	1.3
Impaired fecundity	5.7	9.2	6.1	4.1
Fecund	0.8	0.8	0.2	0.5
Ever used infertility services				
Yes	—	7.5	6.6	3.7
No	—	1.0	0.6	0.6
Education at interview[3]				
No high school diploma or GED[4]	1.8	1.7	1.8	0.8
High school diploma or GED	2.4	2.4	1.5	1.2
Some college, no bachelor's degree	1.6	2.2	1.2	1.4
Bachelor's degree or higher	4.6	3.1	2.4	1.7
Race and Hispanic origin				
Hispanic	1.2	0.7	0.8	0.6
Non-Hispanic white	2.3	2.4	1.8	1.4
Non-Hispanic black	1.6	1.5	1.6	1.9

1. Total includes women with missing or inapplicable data on some variables. Also includes women of other race and ethnic origins, not shown separately. 2. Fecundity status in 1973 was measured only as surgically sterile, subfecund, and fecund. In 1982, 1988, and 1995, fecundity status differentiated surgically sterile women based on contraceptive versus noncontraceptive reasons. Fecundity status also included three subcategories of impaired fecundity—nonsurgically sterile, subfecund, and long interval. 3. Limited to women 22–44 years at interview. 4. GED is general equivalency diploma. GED was explicitly asked about in only the 1988 and 1995 surveys. *Source:* Centers for Disease Control and Prevention, National Center for Health Statistics. *Advance Data* no. 306, May 11, 1999.

Child Abuse and Neglect

Based on reports alleging child abuse and neglect that were referred for investigation by the respective child-protective services agency in each state. The reporting period may be either calendar year or fiscal year. The majority of states provided duplicated counts. Also, varying number of states reported the various characteristics presented below. A substantiated case represents a type of investigation disposition that determines that there is sufficient evidence under state law to conclude that maltreatment occurred or that the child is at risk of maltreatment. An indicated case represents a type of disposition that concludes that there was a reason to suspect maltreatment had occurred.

	1990		1994		1995		1996	
Item	Number	Percent	Number	Percent	Number	Percent	Number	Percent
Types of substantiated maltreatment								
Victims, total[1, 2]	690,658	—	1,011,595	—	970,285	100.0%	969,018	100.0%
Neglect	338,770	49.1%	520,550	51.5%	507,015	52.3	500,032	51.6
Physical abuse	186,801	27.0	241,338	23.9	237,840	24.5	229,332	23.7
Sexual abuse	119,506	17.3	136,362	13.5	122,964	12.7	119,397	12.3
Emotional maltreatment	45,621	6.6	47,337	4.7	42,051	4.3	55,473	5.7
Medical neglect	n.a.	n.a.	24,593	2.4	28,541	2.9	25,758	2.7
Sex of victim								
Victims, total[2]	794,101	100.0	903,195	100.0	809,634	100.0	808,370	100.0
Male	357,367	45.0	420,817	46.6	381,075	47.1	384,280	47.5
Female	405,409	51.1	472,535	52.3	425,193	52.5	419,656	51.9
Age of victim								
Victims, total[2]	807,965	100.0	901,573	100.0	808,575	100.0	807,854	100.0
1 year and younger	106,507	13.2	119,203	13.2	103,335	12.8	101,055	12.5
2 to 5 years old	192,018	23.8	240,925	26.7	215,303	26.6	208,754	25.8
6 to 9 years old	175,609	21.7	210,334	23.3	195,400	24.2	200,888	24.9
10 to 13 years old	150,507	18.6	172,800	19.2	154,682	19.1	158,247	19.6
14 to 17 years old	116,015	14.4	132,566	14.7	121,548	15.0	123,872	15.3
18 years and over	5,464	0.7	6,821	0.8	7,506	0.9	6,466	0.8

NOTE: n.a. = not available. 1. More than one type of maltreatment may be substantiated per child. Therefore, totals for this category will add up to be more than 100%. Victim totals and maltreatment types are based on subset of states that reported both the number of child victims and maltreatment incidences by type for that year. 2. Includes other and unknown not shown separately. Source: Statistical Abstract of the United States 1998.

Breast-Feeding by Selected Characteristics of Mother, 1972–1994

Breast-feeding, which has gone in and out of fashion over the decades, nearly doubled between 1972 and 1994 and continues to be on the rise. Breast milk contains antibodies that help protect babies against illnesses and allergies, and is considered by doctors to be more beneficial than formula.

Selected characteristics of mother	Percent of babies breast-fed							
	1972–74	1975–77	1978–80	1981–83	1984–86	1987–89	1990–92	1993–94
Total	30.1%	36.7%	47.5%	58.1%	54.5%	52.3%	54.2%	58.1%
Race								
White, non-Hispanic	32.5	38.9	53.2	64.3	59.7	58.3	59.1	61.2
Black, non-Hispanic	12.5	16.8	19.6	26.0	22.9	21.0	22.9	27.5
Hispanic[1]	33.1	42.9	46.3	52.8	58.9	51.3	58.8	67.4
Education[2]								
No high school diploma or GED[3]	14.0	19.4	27.6	31.4	36.8	30.0	38.6	43.0
High school diploma or GED[3]	25.0	33.6	40.2	54.3	46.7	46.6	46.0	51.2
Some college, no bachelor's degree	35.2	43.5	63.2	66.7	66.1	57.8	60.7	65.9
Bachelor's degree or higher	65.5	66.9	71.3	83.2	75.3	79.2	80.8	80.6
Geographic region								
Northeast	29.9	34.7	49.3	68.2	55.3	49.9	54.0	56.7
Midwest	22.3	30.9	34.4	46.0	50.9	50.4	51.6	49.7
South	30.6	33.1	49.5	57.9	45.3	42.5	43.6	49.7
West	47.1	54.5	66.6	69.9	70.9	69.1	70.5	79.3
Age at baby's birth								
Under 20 years	17.0	22.1	31.4	31.0	30.6	26.2	35.2	45.3
20–24 years	28.7	33.5	44.7	50.8	50.2	46.7	44.7	50.9
25–29 years	38.7	45.9	53.6	62.2	59.8	57.1	56.5	55.9
30–44 years	43.1	47.5	55.2	73.1	65.9	65.3	67.5	71.1

NOTE: Years indicate babies' birth years. Based on household interviews of samples of women ages 15–44. 1. Hispanic may be of any race. 2. For women 22–44 years of age. Education is as of year of interview. 3. General equivalency diploma. Source: National Center for Health Statistics.

Gays Enter the Mainstream

What closet? Gay life—and gay politics—comes of age

By **RICHARD LACAYO** TIME

There may well be more openly gay men and women in America now than in any other country at any other time in history. The sexual revolution, gay visibility in the media, the reckonings forced by AIDS—there are any number of reasons for this emergence. It has changed straight America, of course. Just go rent *My Best Friend's Wedding,* or watch *Will & Grace* on NBC. What's less noticed is that it has also changed gay America. The existence of a greater number of visible and comfortable gays has paved the way for more of the same—more visible and comfortable gays.

Gays in the Heartland

"I think we've done a great deal of persuading people that we are not a countercultural force," says Andrew Sullivan, author *(Love Undetectable)* and former *New Republic* editor, who epitomizes the argument that homosexuals should embrace the existing institutions of heterosexual society. "We are a mainstream force." Sullivan likes to point out that the richest gay group in the nation isn't a political group but a religious denomination, the Metropolitan Community Church, whose offerings totaled $17 million in 1997 and whose membership across the nation has grown to 40,000.

The mainstreaming of gays isn't confined to New York City and Los Angeles: 21-year-olds are coming out everywhere, so that, for instance, a gay freshman landing this fall at Western Michigan University in Kalamazoo or at the University of Idaho in Moscow could find a group to join. In little Agency, Mo. (pop. 300), a woman named Liz Jalbert is president of Midland Empire Task Force, a gay group that doubled in size to nearly 100 paid members from 1996 to 1998.

As a consequence, even the anti-gay right has had to shift the tone of its message as more straight Americans become acquainted with their own gay friends and family. Anita Bryant, the singer turned anti-gay campaigner of the 1970s, said that what homosexuals really want is "the right to propose to our children." It says something about the difficulties of demonizing homosexuals these days when Senate majority leader Trent Lott merely compares them to kleptomaniacs, as he did in 1998, or when Christian groups run ad campaigns insisting gays can be cured. While that language may try to throw the debate back more than 20 years, before psychologists concluded that homosexuality is not a mental illness, it represents a recognition that pure contempt is tricky when you are talking about people's children or friends.

America's Attitudes toward Gays: A TIME/CNN Poll

How do you feel about homosexual relationships?

	1998	1978
Acceptable for others, but not self	52%	35%
Acceptable for others and self	12%	6%
Not acceptable at all	33%	59%

Are homosexual relationships between consenting adults morally wrong or not a moral issue?

	1998	1978
Yes, morally wrong	48%	53%
Not a moral issue	45%	38%

Do you have a family member or close friend who is gay or lesbian?

	1998	1994
Yes	41%	32%
No	57%	66%

Is homosexuality something that some people are born with, or is it due to factors such as how they were raised or their environment?

Born with	33%
How raised or environment	40%
Both	11%

Can people who are homosexual change their sexual orientation if they choose to do so?

Yes 51%   No 36%

Do you favor or oppose permitting people who are openly gay or lesbian to serve in the military?

Favor 52%   Oppose 39%

Do you favor or oppose permitting people who are openly gay or lesbian to teach in schools in your community?

Favor 51%   Oppose 42%

From a telephone poll of 1,036 adult Americans taken for TIME/CNN on Oct. 14-15, 1998, by Yankelovich Partners Inc. Margin of error is ± 3%. "Not sures" omitted.

At the same time, lesbian and gay organizations have gone from being outcasts of the left to being an expected presence in politics, or at least in Democratic coalitions, and a presence knocking at the door of the Republican Party. "The whole public attitude on gay issues has become much more mainstream," notes Al From, who runs the Democratic Leadership Council, which breeds centrist New Democrats like Clinton. "A lot of gay businessmen are New Democrats. A lot more people are dealing with gays in their families."

No Longer Fringe Radicals

It has been a long road from there to here. Largely because of opposition from unions, blacks, and church groups, it was not until 1983 that a gay organization, the National Gay and Lesbian Task Force, was admitted to the Leadership Conference on Civil Rights, one of Washington's most liberal legislative coalitions. It was 11 years more before the group took a consensus position on anything involving gay rights. In 1994 it backed a modest change in the Employment Non-Discrimination Act, or ENDA, that would prohibit discrimination on the basis of sexual orientation while permitting an exemption for churches. Two years later that amendment was defeated in the Senate by just a single vote.

For a long time, the most prominent nationwide gay-rights organization was the 35,000-member National Gay and Lesbian Task Force, which grew out of the scruffy radicalism of the old gay-liberation movement. But after 25 years, it still has virtually no lobbying presence on Capitol Hill. In the later 1980s the AIDS epidemic brought forth the street-theater militancy of ACT UP and in 1990 the in-your-face tribalism of Queer Nation. "We're here, we're queer, get used to it" was an interesting statement of the facts. But the cutting edge of gay politics threatened to cut gays off altogether from the give and take of lawmaking.

The election of Bill Clinton was a psychological turning point, even though his support on gay-rights issues has been unsteady. His "Don't ask, don't tell" compromise on gays in the military satisfied no one. He signed the "Defense of Marriage" Act, which denies federal recognition to same-sex unions, then advertised the fact in '96 campaign spots on Christian radio stations. But he was canny about the symbolic gestures. He ended the federal policy of treating gays as security risks and invited gay activists to the White House for the first time. The message he sent was that gays were part of the American family and also part of the political game.

From Street Rallies to D.C. Lobbies

"The Clinton election took the wind out of the sails of street activists," says John Gallagher, national correspondent of the *Advocate*, the gay news monthly. "They used to be outside shouting. Now people have to be inside talking, which is a new experience." And during those years, a new kind of gay lobbying group has emerged. The Human Rights Campaign, founded in 1980, is the group that corresponds to mainstreaming impulses within the gay community. It's also the largest—

membership 250,000 in 1998, up from 85,000 just five years earlier. Sedate and pragmatic, with a name so innocuous it could be transferred intact to a group devoted to fair labor practices, the Human Rights Campaign was established to speak to the middle class in middle-class terms.

There has also been a small, careful movement within the G.O.P. to support some gay initiatives. In 1998, 30 Republicans joined Democrats to defeat a move to ban adoption by gays in the District of Columbia. Earlier, when Republican Joel Hefley of Colorado tried to revoke a Clinton Executive Order banning discrimination against gay federal employees, his measure was defeated, with the astonishing help of 63 Republican votes.

As the G.O.P.'s 2000 presidential campaign began gearing up, prominent Republican presidential hopefuls, including George W. Bush, John McCain, and Elizabeth Dole, have demonstrated a new solicitousness toward gay voters. According to Rich Tafel, executive director of the Log Cabin Republicans, a gay Republican organization, "It looks like Republicans for the first time are saying, 'This is a community I'm not going to alienate and maybe I want to reach out to it.' That's kind of a shocking revelation." And an about-face from the 1996 campaign, when Republican nominee Bob Dole returned a $1,000 donation from the same gay organization. Yet none of these presidential contenders support a broad gay agenda; all oppose gay marriage, adoptions by gays and a change in policy concerning homosexuals in the military.

But at the same time that gay activists have become more sophisticated and accommodating, their opponents on the Christian right have become more militant and more powerful within the Republican Party. Gary Bauer, head of the Family Research Council, and his mentor James Dobson, the Christian broadcaster who heads Focus on the Family, with its 2.3 million-name mailing list, have made opposition to gay rights a defining issue. Republicans trying to bridge the gap complain that while the rhetoric of the Christian right makes compromise difficult, so does some of the language of gay activism. "They've got to get off the stuff about Christians having this conspiracy to incite hate crimes," insists a Republican lawmaker. "When you have people so far apart, it makes it more difficult."

Politics Is Local

In the end and in the beginning, the struggle over gay rights is only partly political in the legislative sense. Much of the real action is in everyday life—from household arrangements to mass media to the simple yet crucial changes wrought by acquaintance and friendship. This debate has been carried on in the culture at large for years, around the ears of gays who, because they lived within it, came out and came out earlier, in a process that may not have been easy but that eventually seemed to them right and essential. If Washington reacts slowly and crudely, turning family dramas and internal dialogues into attack ads and legislative-floor fights, it only proves what conservatism has always argued—that government, even representative government, is a crude representative of ordinary lives. □

Gender of Sexual Partners in the United States
(sexually active only)

| | Same gender | | Both genders | | Opposite genders | |
	Men	Women	Men	Women	Men	Women
1988	2.3%	0.2%	0.3%	0.0%	97.4%	99.8%
1989	1.4	1.2	0.3	0.4	98.3	98.4
1990	1.1	0.5	0.9	0.0	98.0	99.5
1991	2.0	0.3	0.7	0.1	97.3	99.6
1993	1.8	1.8	0.3	0.4	97.9	97.8
1994	2.1	2.1	0.5	0.4	97.5	97.5
1996	3.5	2.1	0.6	0.9	96.0	97.0

Source: General Social Survey (GSS), National Opinion Research Center, University of Chicago, 1996.

Sexual Intercourse[1] by Age of Women[2] and Marital Status, 1995

| | All women | | Never-married women | |
Age	Number in thousands	Percent	Number in thousands	Percent
Women (15–44)[2]	60,201	89.3%	22,679	71.5%
15 years	1,690	22.1	1,674	21.4
16 years	1,874	38.0	1,874	38.0
17 years	1,889	51.1	1,831	49.6
18 years	1,771	65.4	1,641	62.7
19 years	1,737	75.5	1,542	72.4
20–24 years	9,041	88.6	5,939	82.6
25–29 years	9,693	95.9	3,456	88.6
30–44 years	32,506	98.2	4,722	87.4

1. Women who have ever had intercourse. 2. For its "National Survey of Family Growth," the CDC only collects data on women, and only those of childbearing years, roughly considered to be ages 15–44. Comparable statistics on men, older and younger women, not available. Source: Center for Disease Control, National Survey of Family Growth, 1995.

The Equal Pay Act 36 Years Later
Narrowing the wage gap half a penny per year

Rosie the Riveter

Because of the large number of American women taking jobs in the war industries during World War II, the National War Labor Board urged employers in 1942 to voluntarily make "adjustments which equalize wage or salary rates paid to females with the rates paid to males for comparable quality and quantity of work on the same or similar operations."

Not only did employers fail to heed this "voluntary" request, but at the war's end most women lost their new jobs to make room for returning veterans.

Separate and Unequal

Until the early 1960s, newspapers published separate job listings for men and women. Jobs were categorized according to sex, with the higher level jobs listed almost exclusively under "Help Wanted—Male." In some cases the ads ran identical jobs under male and female listings—but with separate pay scales. Separate, of course, meant unequal: between 1950 and 1960, women with full-time jobs earned on average between 59–64 cents for every dollar their male counterparts earned in the same job.

It wasn't until the passage of the Equal Pay Act on June 10, 1963 (effective June 11, 1964) that it became illegal to pay women lower rates for the same job strictly on the basis of their sex. Demonstrable differences in seniority, merit, the quality or quantity of work, or other considerations might merit different pay, but gender could no longer be viewed as a drawback on one's résumé.

The "Going Market Rate" for Women

The act was gradually expanded over the next decade to include a larger segment of the workforce, and between June 1964 and Jan. 1971 back wages totaling more than $26 million were paid to 71,000 women. Two landmark court cases served to strengthen and further define the Equal Pay Act:

- *Schultz v. Wheaton Glass Co.* (1970), U.S. Court of Appeals for the Third Circuit: Ruled that jobs need to be "substantially equal" but not "identical" to fall under the protection of the Equal Pay Act. An employer cannot, for example, change the job titles of women workers in order to pay them less than men.
- *Corning Glass Works v. Brennan* (1974), U.S. Supreme Court: Ruled that employers cannot justify paying women lower wages because that is what they traditionally received under the "going market rate." A wage differential occurring "simply because men would not work at the low rates paid women" was unacceptable.

The blatant discrimination apparent in these court cases seems archaic today, as does the practice of sex-segregated job listings. The workplace has changed radically in the three-and-a-half decades since the passage of the Equal Pay Act.

But what has not changed substantially, however, is women's pay. The wage gap has narrowed, but it is still significant. Women earned 59% of the wages men earned in 1963; in 1997 they earned 74% of men's wages—an improvement of less than half a penny a year. Why is there still such a disparity?

Why Still Such a Wide Gap?

A variety of explanations for the persistent wage gap have been offered. One is that older women are factored into the wage gap equation, and many of these women from an older generation work in jobs still subject to the attitudes and conditions of the past. In contrast, the rates for young women coming of age in the 1990s reflect women's social and legal advances. In 1997, for example, women under 25 working full-time earned 92.1% of men's salaries compared to older women (25–54), who earned 74.4% of what men made.

Equal Pay in the Millennium?

Does this imply that once the oldest generation of women has retired the wage gap will shrink considerably? Perhaps. But even the narrow wage gap of 92.1% that applies to women under 25 looks less rosy when you consider economist Katha Pollitt's take on it:

> Young men and women have always had earnings more compatible than those of their elders: starting salaries are generally low, and do not accurately reflect the advantages that accrue, or fail to accrue, over time as men advance and women stay in place, or as women in mostly female kinds of jobs reach the end of characteristically short career paths. (*The Nation,* April 14, 1997)

Women have made enormous progress in the workforce since the Equal Pay Act, but the stubborn fact remains that 36 years later the basic goal of the act has not been realized.

The Wage Gap

The wage gap is a statistical indicator often used as an index of the status of women's earnings relative to men's. It is also used to compare the earnings of other races and ethnicities to those of white males, a group generally not subject to race- or sex-based discrimination. The wage gap is expressed as a percentage (e.g., in 1996, women earned 74% as much as men) and is calculated by dividing the median annual earnings for women by median annual earnings for men. Since 1963, when the Equal Pay Act was signed, the closing of the wage gap between men and women has been at a rate of less than half a penny a year.

1996 Median Annual Earnings by Race and Sex

Race/gender	Earnings	Wage ratio	Race/gender	Earnings	Wage ratio
White Men	$32,966	100.0%	All Men	$32,144	
White Women	$24,160	73.3	All Women	$23,710	
Black Men	$26,404	80.0	Wage gap		73.8%
Black Women	$21,473	65.1			
Hispanic Men	$21,056	63.9			
Hispanic Women	$18,655	56.6			

Women's Earnings as a Percentage of Men's, 1951–1997
(for year-round full-time work)

Year	Percent	Year	Percent	Year	Percent	Year	Percent	Year	Percent
1951	63.9%	1961	59.2	1971	59.5	1981	59.2	1991	69.9
1952	63.9	1962	59.3	1972	57.9	1982	61.7	1992	70.8
1953	63.9	1963	58.9	1973	56.6	1983	63.6	1993	71.5
1954	63.9	1964	59.1	1974	58.8	1984	63.7	1994	72.0
1955	63.9	1965	59.9	1975	58.8	1985	64.6	1995	71.4
1956	63.3	1966	57.6	1976	60.2	1986	64.3	1996	73.8
1957	63.8	1967	57.8	1977	58.9	1987	65.2	1997	74.2
1958	63.0	1968	58.2	1978	59.4	1988	66.0		
1959	61.3	1969	58.9	1979	59.7	1989	68.7		
1960	60.7	1970	59.4	1980	60.2	1990	71.6		

Source: U.S. Women's Bureau.

Gender Issues Web Sites

Abortion and Reproductive Rights:
  www.caral.org/abortion.html
American Coalition for Fathers and Children:
  www.acfc.org/
The Fatherhood Coalition: fatherhoodcoalition.org/
Gender and Sexuality: eserver.org/gender
Institute for Women's Policy Research:
  www.iwpr.org/index.html
The Men's Center.com: www.themenscenter.com
Men's Health Center: www.drkoop.com/resource/mens
The Men's Issues Page: www.vix.com/men

Men's Rights, Inc.: www.mens-rights.org/index.htm
The National Gay and Lesbian Task Force:
  www.ngltf.org
National Organization for Women: www.now.org
The National Organization on Male Sexual Victimization: www.malesurvivor.org
Violence against Women: www.usdoj.gov/vawo
Women's Bureau: www.dol/dol/wb/
Women's International Center: www.wic.org/
WWWomen: www.wwwomen.com

The Prevalence of Profiling

Guilty of "Driving While Black?" The A.C.L.U. charges that cops across the U.S. often search people just because of their race

By **TAMMERLIN DRUMMOND** TIME

When blacks and Hispanics across the U.S. read headlines about the practice of "racial profiling" by state troopers in New Jersey, it didn't strike them as an obscure practice in a far-off state. It sounded like their own experience. They have long believed it's no coincidence that so many of them have been stopped and frisked by police for no apparent reason. African Americans even coined a term for their supposed offense: DWB, for Driving While Black.

It's Not Just in New Jersey

In June 1999 their suspicions gained supporting evidence. A 43-page report released by the American Civil Liberties Union showed the problem to be of national scope. Citing police statistics, case studies from 23 states, and media reports, the organization asserts that law-enforcement agencies have systematically targeted minority travelers for search—pedestrians, motorists, and airline passengers—based on the belief that they are more likely than whites to commit crimes. Says David Harris, the University of Toledo law professor who wrote the A.C.L.U. study: "It affects blacks and Hispanics from every station in life and every geographic location."

The practice is often a contributing factor in tensions between minorities and police. In 1999 the Justice Department released a 12-city survey in which 24% of the blacks who were polled said they were unhappy with their local police. It was a smaller number than might be expected at a time of prominent police-brutality cases, including the trial of three New York City officers accused of assaulting Haitian immigrant Abner Louima. But it was a far higher number than the 10% of whites unhappy with police.

Most law-enforcement officials have steadfastly denied that their officers engage in racial profiling. And the practice has been difficult to prove because few police agencies record the race of the drivers they pull over. An important exception came in a study in May 1999 by the attorney general of New Jersey, who found that police brass unofficially encouraged state troopers to stop blacks and Hispanics in disproportionate numbers as part of a campaign to increase drug arrests. Two troopers were later suspended and indicted on charges of falsifying records to conceal racial profiling. (They pleaded not guilty.) A judge dismissed charges against 21 people whom the troopers had arrested.

Hispanics Also Targeted

Across the U.S. nonwhite travelers tell similar tales of police harassment. According to the A.C.L.U. report, the stretch of Interstate 95 from Florida to New York is especially notorious. On I-95 in Maryland, blacks made up 17% of motorists but 73% of those stopped and searched. In 1998 a class-action suit accused Maryland state troopers of targeting black drivers. In Illinois, where Hispanics are just 8% of the population, they represented 30% of the drivers stopped by police. "It's really deeply ingrained behavior that is going to be hard to change," says Reggie Shuford, an A.C.L.U. staff attorney.

The civil-liberties group wants federal legislation requiring all law-enforcement agencies to track racial data from traffic stops. Only a few police departments, including those in San Jose, Calif., and San Diego, now do so. The organization is also pushing for an end to so-called pretext stops as a crime-fighting tool and a ban on racial profiling in all federally funded drug-interdiction programs.

Ronald Neubauer, president of the International Association of Chiefs of Police, blasted the A.C.L.U. report for "using an extremely broad brush to portray all of law enforcement as individuals who practice racial profiling." He added that "we recognize a problem exists, but it is an extremely small number of officers conducting themselves illegally."

Flying While Black

Still, when the A.C.L.U. placed ads in the black media asking victims of racial profiling to share their stories, the organization was flooded with thousands of complaints—and not just about traffic stops. The next battleground may be airports. Several recent lawsuits allege that U.S. Customs Service inspectors regularly strip-search minorities solely because of their race. Customs officials deny that they countenance racial profiling, but they have formed a commission to investigate the allegations.

The Supreme Court has upheld the right of law-enforcement officers to stop and search people whom they suspect of even minor infractions. But the courts do not consider race alone to be grounds for suspicion. "You don't have to resort to these techniques to reduce crime," says Hugh Price, president of the National Urban League. "Public safety and civil liberties are not either-or propositions." □

Half the Public Views Police as Unfair to Minorities

Fifty percent of the public believes that law-enforcement officials and the police do not treat whites and minorities alike, according to a poll commissioned by the American Bar Association (2/24/99). Only 39% are confident that the police are impartial when it comes to race.

Population of the United States by Race and Hispanic Origin

(as of July 1999)

	Total population	% of population		Total population	% of population
All races	272,330,000	100.0%	Asian and Pacific Islander	10,861,000	4.0%
White	224,103,000	82.3	Hispanic origin (of any race)	30,461,000	11.2
Black	34,997,000	12.9			
American Indian, Eskimo, and Aleut	2,369,000	0.9			

NOTE: Percentages add up to more than 100% because Hispanics may be of any race and are therefore counted under more than one category. *Source:* U.S. Census Bureau; Web: www.census.gov.

U.S. Asian Population

(Percent distribution)
Total Asians counted in the 1990 Census: 6,908,638

National origin	Percent	National origin	Percent	National origin	Percent
Chinese	23.8%	Laotian	2.2%	Bangladeshi	0.2%
Filipino	20.4	Cambodian	2.1	Malayan	0.2
Japanese	12.3	Thai	1.3	Indonesian	0.4
Asian Indian	11.8	Hmong	1.3	Pakistani	1.2
Korean	11.6	Burmese	0.1	Other Asian	2.1
Vietnamese	8.9	Sri Lankan	0.2		

Source: U.S. Census Bureau, 1990 figures.

U.S. Pacific Islander Population

(Percent distribution)
Total Pacific Islanders counted in the 1990 Census: 365,024

National origin or ancestry	Percent	National origin or ancestry	Percent	National origin or ancestry	Percent
Hawaiian	57.8%	Fijian	1.9%	Tahitian	0.3%
Samoan	17.2	Palauan	0.4	Other Pacific Islander	3.8
Guamanian	13.5	Northern Mariana	0.3		
Tongan	4.8	Islander			

Source: U.S. Census Bureau, 1990 figures.

U.S. Hispanic/Latino Population

(Percent distribution)
Total Hispanics counted in the 1990 Census: 22.3 million

National origin	Percent	National origin	Percent	National origin	Percent
Mexican	61.2%	Central American	6.0%	South American	4.7%
Puerto Rican	12.1	Salvadoran	42.7	Colombian	36.6
Cuban	4.8	Guatemalan	20.3	Ecuadorian	18.5
Dominican	2.4	Nicaraguan	15.3	Peruvian	16.9
Other Hispanic	3.9	Honduran	9.9	Argentinean	9.7
Spaniard[1]	4.4	Panamanian	7.0	Chilean	6.6
		Costa Rican	4.3	Other South American	11.7
		Other Central American	2.1		

NOTE: Hispanics may be of any race. 1. Includes those who reported "Spanish." *Source:* U.S. Census Bureau, 1990 figures.

U.S. States with an African American Population of 1 Million or More, 1997

State	Number (in millions)	State	Number (in millions)	State	Number (in millions)
New York	3.2	North Carolina	1.6	Pennsylvania	1.2
California	2.4	Maryland	1.4	New Jersey	1.2
Texas	2.4	Louisiana	1.4	South Carolina	1.1
Florida	2.3	Michigan	1.4	Alabama	1.1
Georgia	2.1	Virginia	1.3		
Illinois	1.8	Ohio	1.3		

Source: U.S. Census Bureau.

Race of U.S. Couples, 1990

	Total	White	Black	American Indian	Asian	Other race
Same-race couples	97.1%	97.0%	92.8%	26.4%	70.0%	74.7%
Interracial couples:						
Specified group and white race group	2.7	NA	5.8	70.6	28.7	23.2
Specified race group and other race groups [1]	0.2	3.0	1.5	3.1	1.3	2.1

1. Includes all other race groups except whites and the specified group, classified by the race of the male partner. *Source: 1990 Census of Population and Housing,* Public Use Microdata Samples.

Preference for Racial or Ethnic Terminology

Preferred term[1]	Percent	Preferred term[1]	Percent
Hispanic		**Black**	
Hispanic	57.88%	Black	44.15%
Of Spanish origin	12.34	African American	28.07
Latino	11.74	Afro-American	12.12
Some other term	7.85	Negro	3.28
No preference	10.18	Some other term	2.19
White		Colored	1.09
White	61.66%	No preference	9.11
Caucasian	16.53	**American Indian**	
European American	2.35	American Indian	49.76%
Some other term	1.97	Native American	37.35
Anglo	.96	Some other term	3.66
No preference	16.53	Alaska Native	3.51
		No preference	5.72

1. Preferred term by group of people the term is meant to represent. *Source:* U.S. Census Bureau Survey, May 1995.

American Indian Tribes with Populations Greater than 10,000

(1990 U.S. Census figures)

American Indian tribe	Number	Percent distribution	American Indian tribe	Number	Percent distribution
American Indian population, total[1]	**1,878,285**	**100.0%**	Canadian and Latin American tribes	22,379	1.2%
Cherokee	308,132	16.4	Chickasaw	20,631	1.1
Navajo	219,198	11.7	Potawatomi	16,763	0.9
Chippewa	103,826	5.5	Tohono O'Odham	16,041	0.9
Sioux	103,255	5.5	Pima	14,431	0.8
Choctaw	82,299	4.4	Tlingit	13,925	0.7
Pueblo	52,939	2.8	Seminole	13,797	0.7
Apache	50,051	2.7	Alaskan Athabaskans	13,738	0.7
Iroquois	49,038	2.6	Cheyenne	11,456	0.6
Lumbee	48,444	2.6	Comanche	11,322	0.6
Creek	43,550	2.3	Paiute	11,142	0.6
Blackfoot	32,234	1.7	Puget Sound Salish	10,246	0.5

1. Includes other American Indian tribes not shown separately. *Source:* U.S. Census Bureau, *1990 Census of Population, General Population Characteristics, American Indian and Alaska Native Areas* (CP-1-1A); and press releases CB91-232 and CB92-244.

Alaska Native Population

The Alaska Native population, the indigenous peoples of Alaska, include Eskimos, Indians, and Aleuts. Their total population was 85,698 in 1990. More than half of all Alaska Natives are Eskimos. (The term *Eskimo* is used for Alaska Natives; the term *Inuit* is generally used for Eskimos living in Canada.) The two main Eskimo groups, Inupiat and Yupik, are distinguished by their language and geography. The former live in the north and northwest parts of Alaska and speak Inupiaq, while the latter live in the south and southwest and speak Yupik.

About 36% of Alaska Natives are American Indians. The major tribes are the Alaskan Athabaskan (11,696) in the central part of the state, and the Tlingit (9,448), Tsimshian (1,653), and Haida (1,083) in the southeast.

The Aleuts, native to the Aleutian Islands, Kodiak Island, the lower Alaska and Kenai Peninsulas, and Prince William Sound, are physically and culturally related to the Eskimos. About 12% of Alaska Natives are Aleuts, and in 1990, they made up 10,052 of the indigenous population.

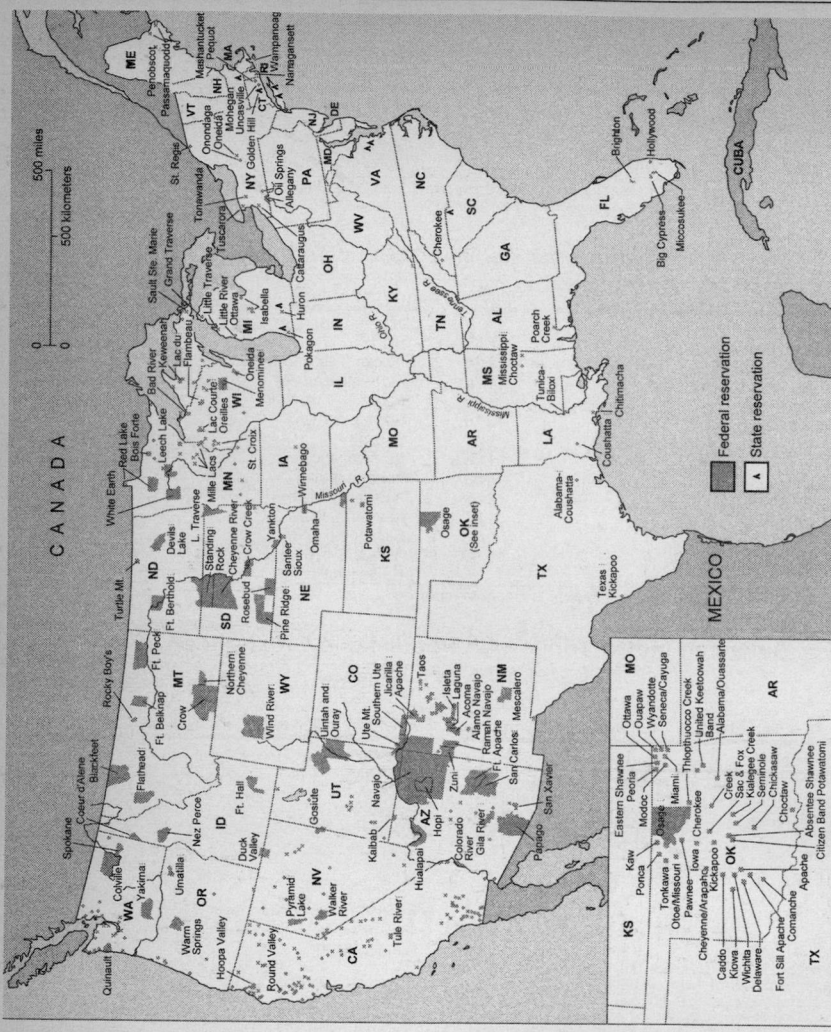

U.S. Federal and State Reservations

Federal reservation

▲ State reservation

Populations of the Ten Largest Reservations
(1990 Census figures)

Name	Population
Navajo (Ariz., N.M., Utah)	143,405
Pine Ridge (Neb., S.D.)	11,182
Fort Apache (Ariz.)	9,825
Gila River (Ariz.)	9,116
Papago (Ariz.)	8,480
Rosebud (S.D.)	8,043
San Carlos (Ariz.)	7,110
Zuni Pueblo (Ariz., N.M.)	7,073
Hopi (Ariz.)	7,061
Blackfeet (Mont.)	7,025

The 218,320 American Indians living on these 10 reservations account for about half of all American Indians living on reservations and trust lands. *Source:* 1990 Census Bureau. *Map source:* Frederick E. Hoxie, ed., *Encyclopedia of North American Indians* (Boston: Houghton Mifflin, 1996). Reprinted with permission.

Ancestry of U.S. Population by Rank, 1990 Census
(Groups with populations exceeding one million)

1990 Rank	Ancestry group	Number	Percent	1990 Rank	Ancestry group	Number	Percent
1	German	57,947,873	23.2%	18	Welsh	2,033,893	0.8%
2	Irish	38,735,539	15.6	19	Spanish	2,024,004	0.8
3	English	32,651,788	13.1	20	Puerto Rican	1,955,323	0.8
4	African	23,777,098	9.6	21	Slovak	1,882,897	0.8
5	Italian	14,664,550	5.9	22	White	1,799,711	0.7
6	American	12,395,999	5.0	23	Danish	1,634,669	0.7
7	Mexican	11,586,983	4.7	24	Hungarian	1,582,302	0.6
8	French	10,320,935	4.1	25	Chinese	1,505,245	0.6
9	Polish	9,366,106	3.8	26	Filipino	1,450,512	0.6
10	American Indian	8,708,220	3.5	27	Czech	1,296,411	0.5
11	Dutch	6,227,089	2.5	28	Portuguese	1,153,351	0.5
12	Scotch-Irish	5,617,773	2.3	29	British	1,119,154	0.4
13	Scottish	5,393,581	2.2	30	Hispanic	1,113,259	0.4
14	Swedish	4,680,863	1.9	31	Greek	1,110,373	0.4
15	Norwegian	3,869,395	1.6	32	Swiss	1,045,495	0.4
16	Russian	2,952,987	1.2	33	Japanese	1,004,645	0.4
17	French Canadian	2,167,127	0.9				

Note: Data are based on a sample and subject to sampling variability. Since persons who reported multiple ancestries were included in more than one group, the sum of the persons reporting the ancestry is greater than the total; for example, a person reporting "English-French" was tabulated in both the "English" and "French" categories. *Source:* U.S. Census Bureau.

Persons Speaking a Language Other than English at Home

Language	Persons five years old and over who speak language	Language	Persons five years old and over who speak language	Language	Persons five years old and over who speak language
Speak only English	198,601,000	Portuguese	430,000	Armenian	150,000
Spanish	17,339,000	Japanese	428,000	Navajo	149,000
French	1,702,000	Greek	388,000	Hungarian	148,000
German	1,547,000	Arabic	355,000	Hebrew	144,000
Italian	1,309,000	Hindi (Urdu)	331,000	Dutch	143,000
Chinese	1,249,000	Russian	242,000	Mon-Khmer (Cambodian)	127,000
Tagalog	843,000	Yiddish	213,000	Gujarathi	102,000
Polish	723,000	Thai (Laotian)	206,000		
Korean	626,000	Persian	202,000		
Vietnamese	507,000	French Creole	188,000		

Source: U.S. Census Bureau, 1990 Census of Population and Housing Data Paper Listing (CPH-L-133).

The Foreign-Born Population in the United States, 1990
25 most common places of birth

1990 rank	Place of birth	Number	Percent	1990 rank	Place of birth	Number	Percent
1	Mexico	4,298,014	21.7%	14	Dominican Republic	347,858	1.8%
2	Philippines	912,674	4.6	15	Jamaica	334,140	1.7
3	Canada	744,830	3.8	16	Soviet Union	333,725	1.7
4	Cuba	736,971	3.7	17	Japan	290,128	1.5
5	Germany	711,929	3.6	18	Colombia	286,124	1.4
6	United Kingdom	640,145	3.2	19	Taiwan	244,102	1.2
7	Italy	580,592	2.9	20	Guatemala	225,739	1.1
8	Korea	568,397	2.9	21	Haiti	225,393	1.1
9	Vietnam	543,262	2.7	22	Iran	210,941	1.1
10	China	529,837	2.7	23	Portugal	210,122	1.1
11	El Salvador	465,433	2.4	24	Greece	177,398	0.9
12	India	450,406	2.3	25	Laos	171,577	0.9
13	Poland	388,328	2.0				

Source: U.S. Census Bureau.

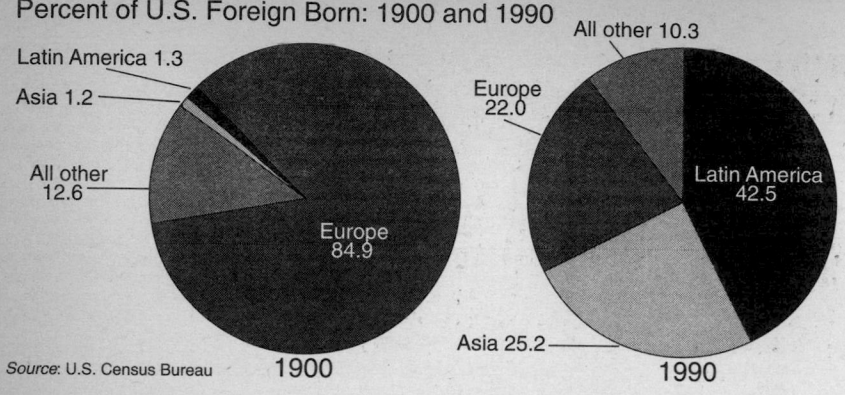

Percent of U.S. Foreign Born: 1900 and 1990

1900
- Latin America 1.3
- Asia 1.2
- All other 12.6
- Europe 84.9

1990
- All other 10.3
- Europe 22.0
- Latin America 42.5
- Asia 25.2

Source: U.S. Census Bureau

Immigration to U.S.: 1850–1930, 1960–1990

| Year | Total[1] | Region of birth reported | | | | | |
		Europe	Asia	Africa	Oceania	Latin America	North America
1990	19,767,316	4,350,403	4,979,037	363,819	104,145	8,407,837	753,917
1980	14,079,906	5,149,572	2,539,777	199,723	77,577	4,372,487	853,427
1970	9,619,302	5,740,891	824,887	80,143	41,258	1,803,970	812,421
1960	9,738,091	7,256,311	490,996	35,355	34,730	908,309	952,500
1930	14,204,149	11,784,010	275,665	18,326	17,343	791,840	1,310,369
1920	13,920,692	11,916,048	237,950	16,126	14,626	588,843	1,138,174
1910	13,515,886	11,810,115	191,484	3,992	11,450	279,514	1,209,717
1900	10,341,276	8,881,548	120,248	2,538	8,820	137,458	1,179,922
1890	9,249,547	8,030,347	113,383	2,207	9,353	107,307	980,938
1880	6,679,943	5,751,823	107,630	2,204	6,859	90,073	717,286
1870	5,567,229	4,941,049	64,565	2,657	4,028	57,871	493,467
1860	4,138,697	3,807,062	36,796	526	2,140	38,315	249,970
1850	2,244,602	2,031,867	1,135	551	588	20,773	147,711

1. The sum of the regions for a particular year will not equal the total. Totals include significant numbers of immigrants for whom no region of birth was reported. *Source*: U.S. Census Bureau, March 9, 1999.

Ethnic Concentrations in the United States

According to the 1990 U.S. Census, ancestry groups show striking differences in where they choose to settle in the United States. These differences often reflect initial settlement patterns, especially for the newer immigrant groups. Of the largest European ancestries, French, Scottish, and Welsh are distributed fairly evenly throughout the country. Other large European groups are more concentrated. For example, more than half of the nation's Italians live in the Northeast, and over half of the Norwegians and Czechs are clustered in the Midwest. About 47% of the Scotch-Irish are concentrated in the South, while 45% of the Danish live in the West.

The regional concentration of persons of Hispanic ancestry depended on their specific country of origin. For instance, the Northeast contained 86% of the country's Dominicans, 66% of Puerto Ricans, and 63% of Ecuadorians. The South was home to 69% of Cubans and 51% of Nicaraguans. About 62% of Salvadorans and Guatemalans and 57% of Mexicans lived in the West.

Persons of West Indian ancestry are concentrated in the Northeast: 59% of the nation's Jamaicans and 55% of Haitians live there.

Among the larger Southwest Asian ancestry groups, over half of the Armenians and Iranians reside in the West, and 43% of the Syrians live in the Northeast.

People of Asian and Pacific Islander ancestry are found largely in the West. The West is home to 87% of the country's Hawaiians, 72% of Japanese, 59% of Cambodians, and 54% of Chinese and Vietnamese.

California—the perennial destination of many migrants—has the largest number of persons of German, Irish, English, African American, Mexican, French, American Indian, Dutch, Scotch-Irish, Scottish, and Swedish ancestry of any state, according to the 1990 Census. New York—the traditional port of entry for large numbers of immigrants—has more Italians and Polish than any other state, and Minnesota ranks first for Norwegians.

About 5% of respondents to the 1990 Census reported their ancestry as "American." Texas has the largest number of persons who considered this to be their ethnic identity.

Life-Saving Skills Summary

Skill	Adult (9 years and older)	Child (1 to 8 years)	Infant (birth to 1 year)
Rescue breathing (used when victim is not breathing)	Give 1 slow breath about every 5 seconds; about 1½ seconds per breath; 1 minute = about 10 to 12 breaths	Give 1 slow breath about every 3 seconds; about 1½ seconds per breath; 1 minute = about 20 breaths	Give 1 slow breath about every 3 seconds; about 1½ seconds per breath; 1 minute = about 20 breaths
CPR (used if victim is not breathing and does not have a heart-beat)	Depth of compression is about 2 inches; compressions are performed with both hands; complete 15 compressions in about 10 seconds; do cycles of 15 compressions and 2 breaths	Depth of compression is about 1½ inches; compressions are performed with 1 hand; complete 5 compressions in about 3 seconds; do cycles of 5 compressions and 1 breath	Depth of compression is about 1 inch; compressions are performed with 2 fingers; complete 5 compressions in about 3 seconds; do cycles of 5 compressions and 1 breath
Choking (conscious)	Determine if person is choking; stand behind person and deliver abdominal thrusts; repeat until object is expelled or victim loses consciousness	Determine if child is choking; stand or kneel behind child and deliver abdominal thrusts; repeat until object is expelled or child loses consciousness	Determine if infant is choking; give 5 back blows; give 5 chest thrusts; repeat until object is expelled or infant loses consciousness
Choking (unconscious)	Give 2 slow breaths; retilt head and give 2 slow breaths; give up to 5 abdominal thrusts; do finger sweep; give 2 slow breaths; repeat abdominal thrusts, finger sweep, and 2 slow breaths	Give 2 slow breaths; retilt head and give 2 slow breaths; give up to 5 abdominal thrusts; check for object in throat; do finger sweep if object is visible; give 2 slow breaths; repeat abdominal thrusts, foreign-body check/finger sweep, and 2 slow breaths	Give 2 slow breaths; retilt head and give 2 slow breaths; give 5 back blows; give 5 chest thrusts; check for object in throat; do finger sweep if object is visible; repeat back blows, chest thrusts, foreign-body check/finger sweep, and 2 slow breaths

Rescue Breathing

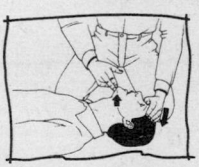

1. With head tilted back, pinch nose shut.

2. ADULT: Give 1 slow breath about every 5 seconds.

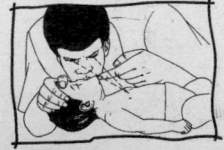

CHILD/INFANT: Give 1 slow breath about every 3 seconds.

CPR (Adult)

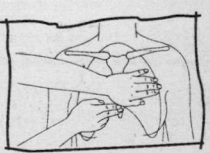

1. Find hand position.

2. Position shoulders over hands. Compress chest 15 times.

3. Give 2 slow breaths. Recheck pulse and breathing. If no pulse, continue sets of 15 compressions and 2 breaths.

Choking

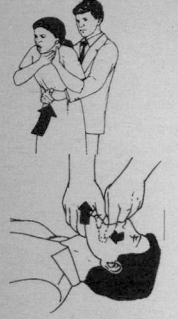

If conscious but choking, give abdominal thrusts until object comes out.

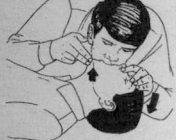

If a person becomes unconscious:

Step 1. Clear any object from mouth.

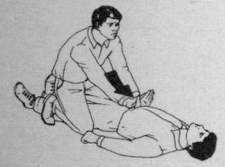

Step 2. Give 2 slow breaths.

If air won't go in, give up to 5 abdominal thrusts.

Other Emergencies

Burns

First Degree: Signs/Symptoms—reddened skin. **Treatment**—Immerse quickly in cold water or apply ice until pain stops.

Second Degree: Signs/Symptoms—reddened skin, blisters. **Treatment**—(1) Cut away loose clothing. (2) Cover with several layers of cold moist dressings or, if limb is involved, immerse in cold water for relief of pain. (3) Treat for shock.

Third Degree: Signs/Symptoms—skin destroyed, tissues damaged, charring. **Treatment**—(1) Cut away loose clothing (do not remove clothing adhered to skin). (2) Cover with several layers of sterile, cold, moist dressings for relief of pain and to stop burning action. (3) Treat for shock.

Poisons

Treatment—(1) Dilute by drinking large quantities of water. (2) Induce vomiting except when poison is corrosive or a petroleum product. (3) Call the poison-control center or a doctor.

Shock

Shock may accompany any serious injury: blood loss, breathing impairment, heart failure, burns. Shock can kill—treat as soon as possible and continue until medical aid is available.

Signs/Symptoms—(1) Shallow breathing. (2) Rapid and weak pulse. (3) Nausea, collapse, vomiting. (4) Shivering. (5) Pale, moist skin. (6) Mental confusion. (7) Drooping eyelids, dilated pupils.

Treatment—(1) Establish and maintain an open airway. (2) Control bleeding. (3) Keep victim lying down. Exception: Head and chest injuries, heart attack, stroke, sun stroke. If no spine injury, victim may be more comfortable and breathe better in a semi-reclining position. If in doubt, keep the victim flat. Elevate the feet unless injury would be aggravated. Maintain normal body temperature. Place blankets under and over victim.

Frostbite

Most frequently frostbitten: toes, fingers, nose, and ears. It is caused by exposure to cold.

Signs/Symptoms—(1) Skin becomes pale or a grayish-yellow color. (2) Parts feel cold and numb. (3) Frozen parts feel doughy.

Treatment—(1) Victim should be wrapped in woolen cloth and kept dry. (2) Do not rub, chafe, or manipulate frostbitten parts. (3) Bring victim indoors. (4) Place affected parts in warm water (102° to 105°) and make sure water remains warm. Never thaw if the victim has to go back out into the cold, which may cause the affected area to be refrozen. (5) Do not use hot water bottles or a heat lamp, and do not place victim near a hot stove. (6) For serious frostbite, seek medical aid for thawing because pain will be intense and tissue damage extensive.

Heat Cramps

Affects people who work or do strenuous exercises in a hot environment. To prevent it, such people should drink large amounts of cool water and add a pinch of salt to each glass of water.

Signs/Symptoms—(1) Painful muscle cramps in legs and abdomen. (2) Faintness. (3) Profuse perspiration.

Treatment—(1) Move victim to a cool place. (2) Give victim sips of salted drinking water (one teaspoon of salt to one quart of water). (3) Apply manual pressure to the cramped muscle.

Heat Exhaustion

Signs/Symptoms—(1) Pale and clammy skin. (2) Profuse perspiration. (3) Rapid and shallow breathing. (4) Weakness, dizziness, and headache.

Treatment—(1) Care for victim as if he or she were in shock. (2) Remove victim to a cool area, do not allow chilling. (3) If body gets too cold, cover victim.

Heat Stroke

Signs/Symptoms—(1) Face is red and flushed. (2) Victim becomes rapidly unconscious. (3) Skin is hot and dry with no perspiration.

Treatment—(1) Lay victim down with head and shoulders raised. (2) Reduce the high body temperature as quickly as possible. (3) Apply cold applications to the body and head. (4) Use ice and fan if available. (5) Watch for signs of shock and treat accordingly. (6) Get medical aid as soon as possible.

NOTE: The almanac is not responsible for actions undertaken by anyone using these first-aid procedures. This information cannot substitute for a CPR or first-aid course. Contact your local Red Cross to find out about a variety of community programs that teach life-saving skills and safety information. *Sources:* "Life-saving Skills Summary" table and graphics from First Aid First © 1995 by the American Red Cross. "Other Emergencies" courtesy of First Aid, Mining Enforcement and Safety Administration, U.S. Dept. of the Interior.

Herbal Healing: The Folklore and the Facts

Herbs have been used for centuries. But they can both heal and harm

By CHRISTINE GORMAN TIME

Perhaps you've nursed a cold with hot tea and honey, jump-started the day with a cappuccino, or soothed a sore throat with a mentholated cough drop. If so, you've practiced herbal medicine. These remedies are so much a part of our daily routine that no one thinks them flaky. Nor do most doctors mind that you use them—as long as you don't overdo it. So why are so many U.S. physicians reluctant to recommend herbal supplements? Is it just a matter of ignorance and provincialism?

No. Physicians have legitimate concerns about the safety, efficacy, and potential misuse of the herbal products that their patients used—to the tune of $13 billion in 1998. More and more M.D.s, like their patients, accept that some herbal products may help when conventional treatments fail. The difference is that doctors are more demanding of proof. As Dr. Yank Coble of the American Medical Association puts it, "In God we trust. All others must have data."

Medical Establishment Takes Note

Fortunately, those data are starting to trickle in. At the urging of its members, in one November week in 1998, the A.M.A. for the first time devoted all its research publications, including the flagship *Journal of the A.M.A.*, to scientific studies on alternative, or complementary, medicine. As with conventional medicine, the results showed that some treatments work, whereas others don't.

One of the more intriguing studies, conducted in Australia, found merit in Chinese herbal treatments for irritable-bowel syndrome, a gastrointestinal disorder that strikes 10% to 20% of the population in many industrialized countries and for which conventional medicine often offers only symptomatic relief. Most of the other studies the A.M.A. reported on yielded mixed results. Researchers at St. Luke's–Roosevelt in New York City determined that *Gar-cinia cambogia* does not, by itself, help patients lose weight. A review of all the studies conducted on saw palmetto found significant improvement in urine flow in men with enlarged prostates. But the reviewers cautioned that the saw-palmetto studies were too hastily conducted to determine long-term results.

Because herbal remedies are not regulated in the U.S., consumers should read the best available studies before trying these medications. With a few notable exceptions, much of the information about herbs on the Internet is unreliable. But authoritative books are available from the American Botanical Council and the Medical Economics Co. Here are a few other tips:

- **Don't assume that "natural" means safe.** Folks have suffered liver damage from sipping teas brewed from comfrey, an herb that is used in poultices and ointments to treat sprains and bruises but should never be taken internally. Special note to pregnant women and nursing mothers: avoid echinacea, senna, comfrey, and licorice.

- **Make sure what you're taking is pure.** In May 1998 the FDA verified industry reports that certain shipments of ginseng were contaminated with high levels of a fungicide. Some imported Chinese remedies have allegedly been doped with Valium or other prescription drugs.

- **Look for standardized preparations to get the same product with each new bottle you buy.** In November 1998 the U.S. Pharmacopeia, a nonprofit organization, published the first American standards for the potency of nine herbs. Manufacturers that adhere to those standards can add the letters NF, for national formulary, to their labels.

- **Buy from companies that research their products.** For example, most studies of ginkgo biloba, which appears to delay the progression of early Alzheimer's disease in some patients, have been conducted on an extract produced by Schwabe of Germany and distributed in the U.S. by Nature's

Some Common Medicinal Herbs

Scientific name	Hypericum perforatum	Panax ginseng	Ginkgo biloba	Echinacea purpurea
Common name:	St. John's wort	Asian ginseng	Ginkgo biloba	Echinacea
Brands:	Sundown, Spring Valley, Your Life	Ginsana, Sundown	Sundown, Ginkoba, Spring Valley	Sundown, Nature's Resource, Your Life
What it does:	Supports a healthy mood; helps relieve mild to moderate depression	Increases stamina	An antioxidant; increases blood circulation and oxygenation; improves memory	Stimulates the immune system; helps fight colds and flus
Precautions:	In high dosages may cause users to be extremely sensitive to sunlight	Avoid if you have hypertension	Do not use with blood thinners	May interfere with immunosuppressive therapy; rare cases of allergic reaction
Where it grows:	Chile, Argentina	Wisconsin	South Carolina	Washington, Oregon

Way (Ginkgold) and Warner-Lambert (the Quanterra line). The best-studied version of St. John's wort, which appears to work for mild to moderate depression, is Kira, produced by Lichtwer.

• **Be sure to tell your doctor what you're taking.** According to the *Journal of the American Medical Association,* 15 million Americans take herbs at the same time as prescription medications. Yet 60% of them don't inform their doctors, which would at least allow the physicians to watch for problematic drug-herb interactions.

• **Don't let herbal preparations lull you into ignoring serious problems.** "A lot of my patients with hepatitis C take milk thistle," says Dr. Melissa Palmer, a liver specialist in Plainview, N.Y. "It seems to normalize their liver-function tests, but it doesn't affect the underlying disease." Finally, don't expect a pill to make up for an unhealthy life-style. No herb can take the place of exercise and good nutrition. Among the most healthful plants you can consume are leafy green vegetables like broccoli and spinach.   □

Use of Alternative Therapies for Common Medical Conditions, 1997

Condition	Percentage reporting condition	Used alternative therapy for condition in past 12 mos.	Saw alternative practitioner for condition in past 12 mos.	Saw M.D. and used alternative therapy in past 12 mos.	Saw M.D. and alternative practitioner in past 12 mos.	Therapies most commonly used
Back problems	24.0%	47.6%	30.1%	58.8%	39.1%	Chiropractic, massage
Allergies	20.7	16.6	4.2	28.0	6.4	Herbal, relaxation
Fatigue	16.7	27.0	6.3	51.6	13.1	Relaxation, massage
Arthritis	16.6	26.7	10.0	38.5	15.9	Relaxation, chiropractic
Headaches	12.9	32.2	13.3	42.0	20.0	Relaxation, chiropractic
Neck problems	12.1	57.0	37.5	66.6	47.5	Chiropractic, massage
High blood pressure	10.9	11.7	0.9	11.9	1.1	Megavitamins, relaxation
Sprains or strains	10.8	23.6	10.3	29.4	15.9	Chiropractic, relaxation
Insomnia	9.3	26.4	7.6	48.4	13.3	Relaxation, herbal
Lung Problems	8.7	13.2	2.5	17.9	3.4	Relaxation, spiritual healing, herbal
Skin problems	8.6	6.7	2.2	6.8	0.0	Imagery, energy healing
Digestive problems	8.2	27.3	9.7	34.1	10.7	Relaxation, herbal
Depression	5.6	40.9	15.6	40.9	26.9	Relaxation, spiritual healing
Anxiety	5.5	42.7	11.6	42.7	21.0	Relaxation, spiritual healing

Source: © copyright 1998. *The Journal of the American Medical Association,* "Alternative Medicine in US, 1990–1997," Table 3, Nov. 11, 1998.

Sugar Consumption Skyrockets

"Sugar consumption is off the charts," reports Michael F. Jacobson, executive director of the Center for Science in the Public Interest. "Added sugars—found largely in junk foods such as soft drinks, cakes, and cookies—squeeze healthier foods out of the diet. Sugar now accounts for 16 percent of the calories consumed by the average American and 20 percent of teenagers' calories." A government study found that back in 1977–78, added sugars provided only 11 percent of the average person's calories.

According to the USDA, people consuming 2,000 calories a day should eat no more than about 10 teaspoons of added sugar. But USDA surveys show that the average American is consuming about 20 teaspoons of sugar per day.

Soft drinks, which contain about nine teaspoons of sugar per 12-ounce can, are a leading contributor to increased sugar consumption.

Since 1942, when the American Medical Association (AMA) expressed concern about sweetened carbonated beverages, candy, and other foods rich in sugar but poor in nutrients, soft-drink consumption has increased about seven-fold (excluding diet soda), and overall sugar consumption has increased by one-third. "With all the focus on fat, we've forgotten about sugar. It's time to rethink our national infatuation with sweets," concludes Jacobson.

Got Milk Substitutes?

Federal Dietary Guidelines recommend two to three servings of milk, yogurt, or cheese daily in order to ingest the necessary amount of calcium. Yet the majority of non-white American adults are lactose intolerant:[1]

• Asian Americans   95%
• African Americans   65%
• American Indians   65%
• Hispanic Americans   50%

• Caucasians   15%
• Entire American pop. 25%
• World population   75%

All children are born with the enzyme lactase, which allows them to digest milk, but by the age of ten many children of non-European descent no longer produce the enzyme. Health and civil rights groups, spearheaded by the Congressional Black Caucus's Health Brain Trust, have urged that the lactose intolerance of non-white Americans be taken into account when preparing the new dietary guidelines that will be issued in 2000. Donna M. Christian-Christensen, head of the Black Caucus's committee, remarked to the *New York Times,* "These are called 'Guidelines for Americans,' so they should reflect all Americans."

1. *Source of statistics:* Richard Grand, M.D., Tufts University Medical School.

Caffeine Content of Selected Foods and Drugs

Product	Serving size[1]	Caffeine (mg)	Product	Serving size[1]	Caffeine (mg)
Over-the-counter			Coca-Cola	12 ounces	45
NoDoz, maximum			Dr. Pepper, regular or		
strength; Vivarin	1 tablet	200	diet	12 ounces	41
Excedrin	2 tablets	130	Sunkist Orange Soda	12 ounces	40
NoDoz, regular strength	1 tablet	100	Pepsi-Cola	12 ounces	37
Anacin	2 tablets	64	7-UP or Diet 7-UP	12 ounces	0
Coffees			Minute Maid Orange		
Coffee, brewed	8 ounces	135	Soda	12 ounces	0
Coffee, instant	8 ounces	95	Sprite or Diet Sprite	12 ounces	0
Coffee, decaffeinated	8 ounces	5	7-Eleven Big Gulp cola	64 ounces	190
Starbucks coffee grande	16 ounces	550	**Frozen desserts and yogurt**		
Teas			Ben & Jerry's No Fat		
Tea, leaf or bag	8 ounces	50	Coffee Fudge Frozen		
Snapple Iced Tea,			Yogurt	1 cup	85
all varieties	16-ounce bottle	48	Häagen-Dazs Coffee Ice		
Lipton Iced Tea,			Cream	1 cup	58
assorted varieties	16-ounce bottle	18–40	Dannon Coffee Yogurt	8 ounces	45
Tea, green	8 ounces	30	Stonyfield Farm		
Tea, instant	8 ounces	15	Cappuccino Yogurt	8 ounces	0
Celestial Seasonings			**Chocolates or candies**		
Herbal Tea, all varieties	8 ounces	0	Hershey Bar, 1 bar	1.5 ounces	10
Soft drinks			Coffee or hot chocolate	8 ounces	5
Mountain Dew	12 ounces	55			
Diet Coke	12 ounces	47			

1. Serving sizes are based on commonly eaten portions, pharmaceutical instructions, or the amount of the leading-selling container size. *Source:* Center for Science in the Public Interest. Reprinted/Adapted from *Nutrition Action Healthletter* (1875 Connecticut Ave., NW., Suite 300, Washington, DC 20009–5728. $24.00 for 10 issues.)

First Federal Obesity Guidelines: More Than Half of All Americans Are Too Fat

Source: National Heart, Lung, and Blood Institute

Overweight and obesity continue to be an alarming public-health problem in the United States, affecting 97 million American adults—an astonishing 55% of the population. Between 1960 and 1994, the prevalence of obesity in adults increased from nearly 13% to 22.5% of the U.S. population, with most of the increase occurring in the 1990s. These findings are recorded in the first federal guidelines on the identification, evaluation, and treatment of overweight and obesity in adults, which was released by the National Heart, Lung, and Blood Institute (NHLBI) in June 1998.

"There are several possible reasons for the increase," asserted Karen Donato, coordinator of the Obesity Education Initiative. "When people read labels, they're more likely to notice what's 'low fat and healthy' but may not be looking at calories. Also, more people are eating out and portion sizes have increased. Another issue is decreased physical activity. So people are consuming more calories and are less active. It doesn't take much to tip the energy balance," she said.

According to the guidelines, assessment of overweight involves evaluation of three key measures—body mass index (BMI), waist circumference, and a patient's risk factors for diseases and conditions associated with obesity. Overweight is defined as having a BMI of 25 to 29.9 and obesity as a BMI of 30 and above, which is consistent with the definitions used in many other countries. BMI describes body weight relative to height and is strongly correlated with total body-fat content in adults. According to the guidelines, a BMI of 30 is about 30 pounds overweight and is equivalent to 221 pounds in a 6' person and to 186 pounds in someone who is 5'6". The BMI numbers apply to both men and women. Some very muscular people may have a high BMI without health risks.

Waist circumference, which is strongly associated with abdominal fat, is another measure of overweight—excess abdominal fat is an independent predictor of disease risk. A waist circumference of over 40 inches in men and over 35 inches in women signifies increased risk in those who have a BMI of 25 to 34.9.

According to the guidelines, the most successful strategies for weight loss include calorie reduction, increased physical activity, and behavior therapy designed to improve eating and physical activity habits.

The guidelines have been reviewed by 115 health experts at major medical and professional societies, and have been endorsed by 54 professional societies, government agencies, and consumer organizations. The published report is available on the NHLBI Web site: http://www.nhlbi.nih.gov/nhlbi/cardio/obes/prof/guidelns/ob_home.htm. Single free copies of the consumer tips referred to above are available by writing to the NHLBI Information Center, P.O. Box 30105, Bethesda, MD 20824–0105.

Measuring Body Mass

The new body mass index (BMI) applies to both men and women. To determine BMI, weight in kilograms is divided by height in meters, squared. To calculate your body mass index from the table below, locate your height in inches in the left-hand column, then follow it across until you locate your weight; the number at the very top is your body mass index. A BMI of 25 to 29.9 is considered overweight and one of 30 or above is considered obese.

Body Mass Index Chart

Height (inches)	19	20	21	22	23	24	25	26	27	28	29	30	31	32	33	34	35
									Body Weight (pounds)								
58	91	96	100	105	110	115	119	124	129	134	138	143	148	153	158	162	167
59	94	99	104	109	114	119	124	128	133	138	143	148	153	158	163	168	173
60	97	102	107	112	118	123	128	133	138	143	148	153	158	163	168	174	179
61	100	106	111	116	122	127	132	137	143	148	153	158	164	169	174	180	185
62	104	109	115	120	126	131	136	142	147	153	158	164	169	175	180	186	191
63	107	113	118	124	130	135	141	146	152	158	163	169	175	180	186	191	197
64	110	116	122	128	134	140	145	151	157	163	169	174	180	186	192	197	204
65	114	120	126	132	138	144	150	156	162	168	174	180	186	192	198	204	210
66	118	124	130	136	142	148	155	161	167	173	179	186	192	198	204	210	216
67	121	127	134	140	146	153	159	166	172	178	185	191	198	204	211	217	223
68	125	131	138	144	151	158	164	171	177	184	190	197	203	210	216	223	230
69	128	135	142	149	155	162	169	176	182	189	196	203	209	216	223	230	236
70	132	139	146	153	160	167	174	181	188	195	202	209	216	222	229	236	243
71	136	143	150	157	165	172	179	186	193	200	208	215	222	229	236	243	250
72	140	147	154	162	169	177	184	191	199	206	213	221	228	235	242	250	258
73	144	151	159	166	174	182	189	197	204	212	219	227	235	242	250	257	265
74	148	155	163	171	179	186	194	202	210	218	225	233	241	249	256	264	272
75	152	160	168	176	184	192	200	208	216	224	232	240	248	256	264	272	279
76	156	164	172	180	189	197	205	213	221	230	238	246	254	263	271	279	287

Source: National Heart, Lung, and Blood Institute.

Self-Perception of Being Overweight

Not only do many Americans struggle with weight problems, but they often harbor misperceptions about their weight—considering themselves in the correct weight range when they are actually unhealthily overweight, or worse still, considering themselves overweight when in fact they are not.

- Almost twice as many women as men who are not overweight think that they are. 25.3% of men and 47.9% of women defined as within their normal weight range think they weigh too much.
- Overweight women are more realistic than overweight men in recognizing themselves as over-

weight. 91.8% of women defined as overweight perceive themselves as such, whereas only 83.4% of overweight men consider themselves to be so.
- The group least forgiving of itself consists of white women between 40 and 59 years who are within their target weight range—a full 59.6% of these women are convinced that they are overweight when they actually aren't.
- Least concerned about their weight are overweight black men 60 years and older—36.3% of these overweight men don't accept being labeled overweight.

Percent of overweight people who think they are overweight

Age	Total[1]		Non-Hispanic white		Non-Hispanic black	
	Male	Female	Male	Female	Male	Female
Total	83.4%	91.8%	86.2%	94.2%	71.9%	87.4%
20 to 39 years old	84.5	94.5	88.8	97.4	73.4	90.9
40 to 59 years old	89.0	95.4	92.1	98.0	74.0	93.4
60 years old and over	73.0	83.6	74.6	86.5	63.7	71.7

Percent of population not overweight who think they are overweight

Age	Total[1]		Non-Hispanic white		Non-Hispanic black	
	Male	Female	Male	Female	Male	Female
Total	25.3%	47.9%	28.1%	50.2%	13.1%	37.5%
20 to 39 years old	24.8	49.5	28.1	51.4	10.1	41.1
40 to 59 years old	27.6	56.5	30.7	59.6	19.6	46.5
60 years old and over	23.2	35.3	24.7	38.6	12.6	13.5

1. Includes other races and persons of Hispanic origin not shown separately. *Source:* U.S. National Center for Health Statistics, unpublished data covering 1988–1994.

Ten Tips for Staying Lean

1. Curb calorie density

Does fat make you fat? For years, popular diet books assured the chubby masses that a low-fat diet was the key to weight loss. They were right . . . and wrong. "Our research shows that it's calorie density—not fat—that determines how many calories people eat," says Susan Roberts of the Jean Mayer U.S. Department of Agriculture Human Nutrition Research Center on Aging at Tufts University in Boston. For 18 days, Roberts offered 14 people meals that were either low-fat (20 percent of calories from fat) or high-fat (40 percent fat). But, unlike other studies comparing high-fat and low-fat diets, these two regimens had the same amount of fiber, palatability, and calorie density (that's a food's calories divided by its weight). "When we kept calorie density constant, people on the high-fat diet ate no more calories than people on the low-fat diet," says Roberts. But her research doesn't let fat off the hook, because it's so calorie-dense. "Fat is important to watch out for, but low-fat foods that are high in sugar like SnackWell's cookies and Entenmann's cakes are also high in calorie density," says Roberts's colleague Megan McCrory. The bottom line is that low-fat diets that are loaded with vegetables and fruits and other high-fiber, low-calorie foods may indeed help keep the pounds off. Diets filled with calorie-dense low-fat cakes, cookies, ice cream—and even bread, pasta, and crackers—may not.

2. Shrink your servings

"When people were served larger portions of lasagna, they ate more than when they were given smaller portions and allowed to get up for more," says Tufts's McCrory. That's what happened in single-meal studies done decades ago. More recent studies show that when people are given larger amounts of "hedonistic" foods like M&Ms, they eat more than people who are given smaller amounts. "When we gave people big buckets of popcorn—the ones you have to hold with two hands—at a movie theater, they ate 40 to 50 percent more popcorn than people who got smaller buckets," says Brian Wansink, director of the Food and Brand Research Lab at the University of Illinois at Urbana-Champaign. The only exception: Women on a date ate the same amount of popcorn, regardless of bucket size, he notes. When they were on their own or with friends, though, watch out. The nation is proving those studies right. "Serving sizes in restaurants have gotten bigger," says Marion Nestle of New York University. "Food is low in cost relative to rent and labor," she explains. "So it's just as easy to throw in more food." And it's tough to change. "People become accustomed to large amounts, so if they're served a normal portion they feel cheated," says Nestle. That could explain why people who frequent restaurants are more likely to be overweight. "We asked people how many times they ate at different restaurants, like Chinese, Mexican, or places that serve pizza, hamburgers, fried chicken, or fried fish," says McCrory. "The more often they ate out, the fatter they were." It may be more than huge portions that make restaurant-goers heavier. "Restaurants serve foods that are calorie-dense, palatable, varied, and in large portions," says McCrory. And that's a recipe for flab. The answer, says Nestle, is simple: Eat less. "Before you put the first fork in, think about how much you're going to eat and have them wrap up the rest for the next day," says Nestle, who recently dropped ten pounds to lower her blood cholesterol. (It fell 60 points.) "It really works."

3. Limit (some) choices

"Eat a variety of foods," says the government's *Dietary Guidelines for Americans,* the American Dietetic Association, and others. "But variety may be the dieter's enemy," says McCrory. "People eat more pasta if they have three shapes to choose from, even if all three are the same color and they're served with plain spaghetti sauce," she says. Lack of variety may help some people lose weight on the Atkins diet or other regimens that limit bread, pasta, rice, potatoes, and other carbohydrates. Suddenly, variety plummets to a much narrower—and more manageable—range. "The instinct to eat a variety of foods is incredibly powerful," says Tufts's Susan Roberts. "We probably wouldn't have survived in Paleolithic times if we weren't programmed to eat meat, fruit, and vegetables instead of just one food." McCrory and Roberts found that people who eat the widest variety of almost any food—including sweets, pizza, sandwiches, salad dressings, pasta, and potatoes—have more body fat. (More variety means typically eating eight rather than three kinds of sandwiches, six rather than two kinds of cookies, etc.) Exceptions: people who eat a variety of fruits and dairy products have no more (or less) body fat. And people who eat the widest variety of vegetables have *less* body fat than others. "Vegetables are good news for people who are trying to reduce their weight," says Roberts. "They're low in calorie density, so they may displace calorie-dense foods, and their bulk may reduce overeating." Yet just five vegetables—fresh potatoes, frozen potatoes, onions, iceberg lettuce, and processed tomatoes—make up half of all the vegetables we eat, says McCrory. Instead of a variety of vegetables, many of us eat a variety of junk. "If you want cookies, you're better off buying three boxes of one kind than one box each of three different kinds," says McCrory. "With just one kind of cookie in the house, you get sick of it after a while."

4. Curb liquid calories

Ate more than you should have? No problem. You'll just eat less later. That's more likely to happen if the extra calories you ate came from solid rather than from liquid foods, says Richard Mattes of Purdue University. He gave 15 normal-weight men and women an extra 450 calories a day as either a liquid (three 12-ounce cans of soda) or solid (45 large jelly beans) for four weeks each. "When they got the solid food, they ate less at other times, so they adjusted for all of the calories," he explains. In contrast, "when they got the liquid food, they just added those calories to their customary diet. They didn't compensate at all." Other studies also suggest that people compensate best for solid foods, less well for semi-solid foods like (non-clear) soup or milkshakes, and worst for liquids, he adds. "Liquid calories don't trip our satiety mechanisms," says Mattes. A recent analysis of a national survey jibes with his findings. "The more (non-diet) sodas children drink, the more calories they consume," he notes. The solution: "Use beverages that have no calories," Mattes suggests.

5. Make movement part of your life

This doesn't necessarily mean tennis or bicycling. Gardening, raking leaves, mowing the lawn, and washing windows also count. "Overweight people are more amenable to increasing lifestyle activities—like using the stairs or parking farther away from the mall—than going to the gym," says Thomas Wadden, an obesity expert at the University of Pennsylvania. And people who boost their lifestyle activity are just as successful at keeping the weight off as people who participate in formal exercise programs. In fact, overweight children lose more weight when told to limit sedentary activities than when told to exercise (or to do both). "Getting kids to turn off the TV or spend less time at the computer works better than urging them to increase their aerobic activity," says Wadden.

6. Exercise for weight *maintenance*

Exercise doesn't make much difference when you're trying to lose weight. "Fairly strenuous exercise—30 to 40 minutes three or four times a week—produces only a two to six pound weight loss over six months," says Wadden. That's because exercise just doesn't burn that many calories and because some people may compensate by eating more. "Most people who participate in an exercise program think, 'I should look like Cindy Crawford by now,'" he says. But that's unrealistic. It's not weight *loss*, but weight *maintenance*, that gets easier when people exercise. "If you find 100 people who have kept the weight off, 90 of them are likely to be exercising enough to burn more than 1,500 calories a week," says Wadden. Rena Wing of the University of Pittsburgh has enrolled 2,000 people in her National Weight Control Registry. These weight-loss champs—who report having lost an average of 66 pounds—expend an average of 2,800 calories a week. That's the equivalent of walking three or four miles a day. Who has the time? "Most of the people in our registry don't do only one thing," says Wing. On average, they spend about 1,000 calories a week walking. That's ten miles. But most combine that with other activities."That's the flip-side of limiting your variety of high-calorie foods," she adds. "For physical activity, we encourage variety" so people don't get bored.

7. Break it up

Note to busy folks: People who exercise in shorter bouts may be more likely to stick with the program. "If you tell people they have to exercise for 40 minutes a day and warm up and cool down, some say they don't have 40 minutes and that's the end of it," says Wing. "But if you say, 'try to find ten minutes four times a day,' they say, 'OK, maybe I can do ten minutes after my lunch break or while I'm waiting for the pasta to cook'." And even if they don't squeeze in all four bouts, they may get in two or three.

8. Find a friend

For many people, eating less and exercising more is easier if they don't go it alone. "It's an old strategy," says Rena Wing. "In some early weight-loss studies, they put people at a worksite on different teams to compete against one another. It works because the people on the team support each other and the competition is fun." Wing does caution, however, that "groups don't always work. When we treated husbands and wives together, we weren't very successful. It seemed to help the wife, but the husband did less well." One can only speculate as to why. But in general, it makes sense that healthy living loves company. Would you rather be watching your weight in a crowd that's munching on baby carrots or pigging out on pizza? And even the most airtight excuse for avoiding exercise can evaporate when someone asks you to go for a walk or run.

9. Set realistic goals

How much weight can you expect to lose? A few years ago, Tom Wadden and colleagues asked 60 obese women—they averaged 218 pounds—their "goal weight," "dream weight," "happy weight," "acceptable weight," and "disappointed weight." After 48 weeks of treatment, the women lost an average of 35 pounds . . . slightly less than their "disappointed" weight loss (37 pounds). Half never even lost that much. Almost all fell far short of their "acceptable" weight loss (55 pounds). "Most people have unrealistic expectations," says Wadden. "People can typically reduce their weight by 10 to 15 percent with the best behavior-modification programs. If you try to lose 20 or 30 percent, you're likely to regain the weight." The body seems to defend its weight, he adds. "But there's a certain amount of wiggle room." Go beyond it and you set yourself up to fail. "Satisfaction is comparing what you expect and what you get," says Wadden. "If you keep ratcheting up your expectations, you'll get dissatisfied and quit."

10. Think healthy, not just skinny

Diet sodas, Wow chips, and artificially sweetened candy bars may help you cut calories, but healthy they're not. Each time you chew on a high- or low-calorie candy bar you miss a chance to swallow some phytochemicals neatly packaged in a wedge of watermelon or a handful of berries. Luckily, the same foods that cut your risk of cancer, heart disease, diabetes, and stroke should help you trim extra padding between your shoulders and knees. Don't think of them as punishment. Dishes like roasted asparagus, stir-fried broccoli, sautéed mushrooms, or broiled pineapple or bananas can be delicacies. Skinny isn't the only point of exercise, either. You can be fit *and* fat . . . if you move enough. "When we looked at overweight men as a group, they were less physically fit and had the highest death rate," says Steven Blair of the Cooper Institute of Aerobics Research in Dallas. "But when we looked separately at the overweight men who were fit, we didn't see much increase in dying." The same probably holds for women. To be fit, you have to accumulate at least 30 minutes of moderate-intensity activity most days.

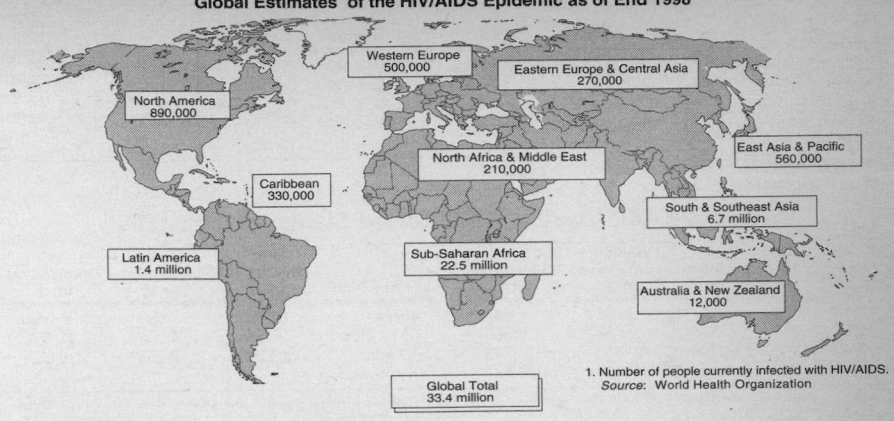

Global Estimates¹ of the HIV/AIDS Epidemic as of End 1998

Western Europe
500,000

Eastern Europe & Central Asia
270,000

North America
890,000

North Africa & Middle East
210,000

East Asia & Pacific
560,000

Caribbean
330,000

South & Southeast Asia
6.7 million

Latin America
1.4 million

Sub-Saharan Africa
22.5 million

Australia & New Zealand
12,000

Global Total
33.4 million

1. Number of people currently infected with HIV/AIDS.
Source: World Health Organization

Understanding AIDS

Acquired Immune Deficiency Syndrome, or AIDS, was first reported in mid-1981 in the United States; it is believed to have originated in Sub-Saharan Africa. The human immunodeficiency virus (HIV) that causes AIDS was identified in 1983, and by 1985 tests to detect the virus were available. The credit for discovering the AIDS virus is jointly shared by Dr. Robert Gallo, a researcher at the National Cancer Institute, and Luc Montagnier of the Pasteur Institute, France.

Although the first reported cases involved homosexual men in Los Angeles who were infected through sexual contact, the principal mode of transmission throughout the world is through the exchange of bodily fluids during heterosexual intercourse. According to the World Health Organization, extensive spread of HIV appears to have begun in the late 1970s and early 1980s among men and women with multiple sexual partners in East and Central Africa and among homosexual and bisexual men in certain urban areas of the Americas, Australasia, and Western Europe.

In addition to sexual contact, AIDS has been spread by intravenous drug users sharing infected hypodermic needles. The virus can also be passed on through transfused blood or its components. It may also be transmitted from infected mother to infant before, during, or shortly after birth.

Two major types of HIV have been recognized, HIV-1 and HIV-2. HIV-1 is the dominant type worldwide. HIV-2 is found principally in West Africa but cases have been reported from East Africa, Europe, Asia, and Latin America. There are at least ten different genetic subtypes of HIV-1, but their biological and epidemiological significance is unclear at present. Both HIV-1 and HIV-2 are transmitted in the same ways.

A fatal and incurable disease caused by the human immunodeficiency virus (HIV), AIDS attacks and destroys the immune system, gradually leaving the individual defenseless against illnesses that lead to death. These illnesses are referred to as "opportunistic" infections or diseases: in AIDS patients the most common are *Pneumocystis carinii* pneumonia (PCP), a parasitic infection of the lungs; and a type of cancer known as Kaposi's sarcoma (KS). Other opportunistic infections include unusually severe infections with yeast, cytomegalovirus, herpes virus, and parasites such as Toxoplasma or Cryptosporidia. Milder infections with these organisms do not suggest immune deficiencies. Symptoms of full-blown AIDS include a persistent cough, fever, and difficulty in breathing. Multiple purplish blotches and bumps on the skin may indicate Kaposi's sarcoma. The virus can also cause brain damage.

People infected with the virus can have a wide range of symptoms—from none to mild to severe. At least a fourth to a half of those infected will develop AIDS within four to ten years. Many experts think the percentage will be much higher.

With no cure at present, prudence could save thousands of people who have yet to be exposed to the virus. Use of condoms lessens the possibility of transmission as does the elimination of sharing hypodermic needles. The fate of many will depend less on science than on the ability of large numbers of human beings to change their behavior in the face of growing danger.

New drugs and tests have given researchers renewed optimism in treating AIDS. As of July 1996, three dozen preventive HIV vaccines were being tested in small-scale clinical trials around the world. In the summer of 1998, the first AIDS vaccine trials began in the United States. Five thousand volunteers are involved in this trial, and the study will last three years. For those already infected, powerful drug combinations are able to decrease the amount of HIV virus in the blood to undetectable levels.

Status of the World AIDS Epidemic, End of 1998

	Total	Adults	Women	Children under 15 years
People newly infected with HIV in 1998	5.8 million	5.2 million	2.1 million	590,000
Number of people living with HIV/AIDS	33.4 million	32.2 million	13.8 million	1.2 million
AIDS deaths in 1998	2.5 million	2.0 million	900,000	510,000
Total number of AIDS deaths since beginning of epidemic	13.9 million	10.7 million	4.7 million	3.2 million

Source: World Health Organization.

Cumulative AIDS Deaths in the United States through 1998[1]

Age at death[2]	Men, cumulative total	Women, cumulative total	Cumulative total	Age at death[2]	Men, cumulative total	Women, cumulative total	Cumulative total
Under 15	2,632	2,352	4,984	45–54	63,966	7,693	71,659
15–24	6,162	2,228	8,390	55 or older	26,855	4,334	31,189
25–34	104,832	19,416	124,248	All ages	352,545	58,255	410,800
35–44	147,815	22,166	169,981				

1. Data for deaths occurring in 1998 are incomplete and not tabulated separately, but are included in the cumulative totals.
2. Data tabulated under "all ages" include 349 persons whose age at death is unknown. Source: Centers for Disease Control, HIV/AIDS Surveillance Report, vol. 10, no. 2.

AIDS Cases Reported in the U.S., by Patient Characteristics

Characteristics	1981–1997 total	1990	1994	1996	1997
Total	620,077	41,549	77,170	66,545	58,493
Age:					
Under 5 years old	6,041	583	751	483	306
5 to 12 years old	1,661	139	221	170	145
13 to 19 years old	992	173	401	378	363
20 to 29 years old	107,302	8,061	12,636	9,770	8,234
30 to 39 years old	280,672	18,801	34,980	29,834	25,795
40 to 49 years old	157,328	9,640	20,309	18,774	16,954
50 to 59 years old	46,602	2,921	5,834	5,278	4,957
Over 60 years old	17,479	1,231	2,038	1,858	1,739
Sex:					
Male	522,430	36,684	63,357	53,009	45,738
Female	97,647	4,865	13,813	13,536	12,755
Race/Ethnic Group:					
Non-Hispanic White	288,422	22,267	32,750	26,189	20,188
Non-Hispanic Black	229,804	13,206	30,954	28,661	27,018
Hispanic	94,719	5,661	12,568	10,804	10,394
Other/unknown	7,132	415	898	891	893
Transmission category:					
Males, 13 years and over	518,443	36,294	62,882	52,677	45,495
Men who have sex with men	305,750	23,809	35,278	27,475	20,912
Injecting drug use	109,858	6,960	15,141	11,806	9,744
Men who have sex with men and injecting drug use	38,993	2,809	4,533	3,154	2,265
Hemophilia/coagulation disorder	4,427	333	482	304	180
Heterosexual contact[1]	11,729	260	1,891	2,349	2,090
Heterosexual contact with injecting drug user	6,847	457	933	827	703
Transfusion[2]	4,604	449	369	272	217
Undetermined[3]	36,235	1,217	4,255	6,490	9,384
Females, 13 years and over	93,932	4,533	13,316	13,215	12,547
Injecting drug use	41,483	2,327	5,911	4,730	4,046
Hemophilia/coagulation disorder	198	16	28	22	16
Heterosexual contact[1]	20,374	506	3,433	3,783	3,295
Heterosexual contact with injecting drug user	15,405	1,036	2,031	1,871	1,349
Transfusion[2]	3,391	335	310	267	182
Undetermined[3]	13,081	313	1,603	2,542	3,659

1. Includes persons who have had heterosexual contact with a person with human immunodeficiency virus (HIV) infection or at risk of HIV infection. 2. Receipt of blood transfusion, blood components, or tissue. 3. Includes persons for whom risk information is incomplete (because of death, refusal to be interviewed, or loss to follow-up), persons still under investigation, men reported only to have had heterosexual contact with prostitutes, and interviewed persons for whom no specific risk is identified. Source: U.S. Centers for Disease Control and Prevention, HIV/AIDS Surveillance Reports. From Statistical Abstract of the United States, 1998.

New Cases of Cancer and Survival Rates in the U.S.

| | Estimated new cases,[1] 1997 (thousands) | | | Five-year relative survival rate (percent) | | | | | | | |
| | | | | White | | | | Black | | | |
Site	Total	Male	Female	1974–78	1979–83	1984–88	1989–92	1974–78	1979–83	1984–88	1989–92
All Sites[2]	1,382	786	597	52.6%	53.8%	57.9%	62.7%	40.4%	40.6%	42.5%	46.7%
Lung	178	98	80	13.7	14.4	14.3	15.1	11.2	12.5	11.6	10.7
Breast[3]	182	1	180	76.1	77.7	83.5	86.9	63.6	65.1	67.9	71.2
Colon and rectum	131	66	65	52.5	56.3	62.0	63.8	45.7	48.7	51.5	53.2
Prostate	335	335	n.a.	71.0	76.2	83.6	94.6	62.8	63.4	68.7	79.6
Bladder	55	40	15	74.8	78.6	81.5	83.0	50.5	58.7	60.1	63.5
Corpus uteri	35	n.a.	35	88.7	84.3	85.9	87.6	60.8	54.3	57.7	56.2
Non-Hodgkin's lymphoma[4]	54	30	23	47.8	52.0	54.1	52.3	48.2	51.1	47.1	42.0
Oral cavity and pharynx	31	21	10	55.2	55.4	56.4	55.5	36.6	32.9	35.0	32.9
Leukemia[4]	28	16	12	36.3	38.5	42.5	43.1	31.6	31.5	34.5	29.1
Melanoma of skin	40	23	17	81.0	83.1	87.1	87.6	57.9	64.2	66.0	69.5
Pancreas	28	13	14	1.9	2.7	2.7	4.1	1.8	4.3	4.8	3.5
Kidney	29	17	12	54.9	56.1	61.6	64.3	53.4	58.4	57.4	59.3
Stomach	22	14	8	15.6	16.8	18.6	19.3	16.3	17.5	19.7	21.6
Ovary	27	n.a.	27	37.6	39.8	41.7	51.0	41.6	39.2	40.8	45.0
Cervix uteri[5]	15	n.a.	15	69.9	68.8	71.5	71.2	63.6	61.4	56.5	60.6

n.a. = not applicable 1. Estimates provided by American Cancer Society are based on rates from the National Cancer Institute's SEER program. 2. Includes other sites not shown separately. 3. Survival rates for women only. 4. All types combined. 5. Invasive cancer only. NOTE: The five-year relative survival rate, which is derived by adjusting the observed survival rate for expected mortality, represents the likelihood that a person will not die from causes directly related to their cancer within five years. *Source:* U.S. National Institutes of Health, National Cancer Institute, *Cancer Statistics Review,* annual.

Leading Causes of Mortality throughout the World

| | All countries | | Africa | | The Americas | | Eastern Mediter- ranean | | Europe | | Southeast Asia | | Western Pacific | |
Deaths	rank	% of total	rank	% of total	rank	% of total	rank	% of total	rank	% of total	rank	% of total	rank	% of total
Ischematic heart disease	1	13.7%	9	2.9%	1	17.9%	1	13.6%	1	25.5%	1	13.8%	3	11.1%
Cerebrovascular disease	2	9.5	7	4.7	2	10.3	5	5.3	2	13.7	4	6.5	1	14.3
Acute lower respiratory infections	3	6.4	3	8.2	3	4.2	2	9.1	4	3.6	2	9.3	4	4.0
HIV/AIDS	4	4.2	1	19.0	13	1.8	27	0.4	42	0.2	8	2.2	42	0.2
Chronic obstructive pulmonary disease	5	4.2	14	1.1	6	2.8	10	1.7	5	2.7	11	1.6	2	12.0
Diarrheal diseases	6	4.1	4	7.6	10	2.0	3	7.4	22	0.7	3	6.6	17	1.2
Perinatal conditions	7	4.0	5	5.5	7	2.6	4	7.3	13	1.2	5	6.0	10	2.2
Tuberculosis	8	2.8	11	2.2	19	1.0	7	3.7	23	0.6	6	5.1	9	2.9
Cancer of trachea/ bronchus/lung	9	2.3	38	0.3	4	3.2	20	1.0	3	4.2	15	1.2	6	3.6
Road traffic accidents	10	2.2	12	1.8	5	3.1	9	1.9	8	1.9	7	2.5	12	2.0

Source: The World Health Report, 1999.

Global Health Trends from The World Health Report, 1999

- **In developed countries, noncommunicable diseases are the leading causes of death.** Heart disease and stroke have declined as causes of death in recent decades, while death rates from some cancers have risen. Leading causes of death from cancers were those of the lung, stomach, colon and rectum, liver, and breast.
- **In developing countries, the five main causes of death are infectious diseases:** acute lower respiratory infections, tuberculosis, diarrhea, HIV/AIDS, and malaria.
- **Almost 300 million cases of malaria occur worldwide annually,** and there are more than 1 million deaths per year from the disease. Almost 90% of these deaths occur in sub-Saharan Africa, where young children are the most affected. Chlo-

roquine was the main drug used to treat malaria for decades, but the disease's increasing resistance to the drug has forced its replacement in parts of the world. Safe, effective, and affordable options are quickly running out.
- **With current smoking patterns, about 500 million people alive today will eventually be killed by tobacco.** While studies in the 1960s suggested that one in four long-term smokers died from their habit, studies in the 1990s suggest that the real ratio is now about one in two.
- **Immunization is the greatest public health success story in history.** Vaccines are available to combat the six major diseases in children: measles, tetanus, pertussis, tuberculosis, poliomyelitis, and diphtheria.

National Transplant Data

Registered Patients Waiting for Transplants
(as of Sept. 1997)

Kidney	37,336	Liver	9,021	Heart-Lung	226
Kidney-Pancreas	1,577	Lung	2,571	Pancreas Islet Cell	78
Heart	3,813	Pancreas	363	Intestine	84
				Total	**55,069**

NOTE: The number of registrants may be greater than the actual number of patients, since some patients are listed with more than one transplant center. Source: National Organ Procurement & Transplantation Network.

Transplants Completed Annually
(as of Sept. 20, 1997)

	1992	1993	1994	1995	1996		1992	1993	1994	1995	1996
Kidney[1]	10,231	11,020	11,390	11,885	12,045	Liver	3,064	3,440	3,653	3,922	4,062
Intestine	22	34	23	45	45	Lung	535	667	723	871	805
Heart	2,171	2,297	2,341	2,360	2,343	Pancreas	557	774	842	1,027	1,021
Heart-Lung	48	60	70	70	39	**Total**	**16,628**	**18,292**	**19,042**	**20,180**	**20,360**

NOTE: Some patients receive simultaneous transplants of more than one organ type (e.g., kidney-pancreas). These cases are included in both organ counts. Double kidney and double lung transplants are only counted once. 1. Includes both cadaveric and living-related transplants. Source: National Organ Procurement & Transplantation Network.

Organ Transplant Reform

Source: Department of Health and Human Services

As of Oct. 1, 1999, the nation's organ transplantation system was reformed, ensuring that allocation of scarce organs will be based on common medical criteria, not accidents of geography.

Under the former system, organs had been first offered to the region in which they become available. If no match is found there, the organ is offered nationwide. But the emphasis on treating local transplant patients means that less ill patients may receive a transplant while patients with more urgent medical need in other locations continue to wait. Today there is a wide variation in waiting times, with patients in some areas waiting five times longer or more for an organ than in other areas. The new criteria would provide for wider sharing to ensure organs are made available to patients with greatest medical need.

The scarcity of transplant organs has remained a chronic problem in the United States. In 1996, some 20,000 Americans—about 55 each day—were able to live healthier lives through transplantation. However, more than 55,000 people are on the transplant waiting list nationwide, and some 4,000 people—10 every day—die in the U.S. while awaiting a donated organ.

For further information on organ donation, contact the U.S. Department of Health and Human Services' organ donation site: www.organdonor.gov.

Percent of Persons Not Covered by Health Insurance, by State, 1997

State	Percent	State	Percent	State	Percent
Alabama	15.5%	Louisiana	14.9%	Oklahoma	17.8%
Alaska	18.1	Maine	14.9	Oregon	13.3
Arizona	24.5	Maryland	13.4	Pennsylvania	10.1
Arkansas	24.4	Massachusetts	12.6	Rhode Island	10.2
California	21.5	Michigan	11.6	South Carolina	16.8
Colorado	15.1	Minnesota	9.2	South Dakota	11.8
Connecticut	12.0	Mississippi	20.1	Tennessee	13.6
Delaware	13.1	Missouri	12.6	Texas	24.5
D.C.	16.2	Montana	19.5	Utah	13.4
Florida	19.6	Nebraska	10.8	Vermont	9.5
Georgia	17.6	Nevada	17.5	Virginia	12.6
Hawaii	7.5	New Hampshire	11.8	Washington	11.4
Idaho	17.7	New Jersey	16.5	West Virginia	17.2
Illinois	12.4	New Mexico	22.6	Wisconsin	8.0
Indiana	11.4	New York	17.5	Wyoming	15.5
Iowa	12.0	North Carolina	15.5	**Total U.S.**	**16.1**
Kansas	11.7	North Dakota	15.2		
Kentucky	15.0	Ohio	11.5		

NOTE: These estimates should not be used to rank the states. Results from different samplings could easily show different estimates and rankings because of small sampling sizes. For example, the high noncoverage for Texas is not statistically different from that of New Mexico. Source: U.S. Census Bureau, March 1997 Current Population Survey.

Mental Illness in America

Source: National Institute of Mental Health

According to a recent study by the World Health Organization, the World Bank, and Harvard University, mental disorders account for 4 of the 10 leading causes of disability in established market economies worldwide. These disorders are: major depression, bipolar (commonly called *manic-depressive*) illness, schizophrenia, and obsessive-compulsive disorder. Other research has estimated that the cost of mental illnesses in the United States, including indirect costs such as days lost from work, was $148 billion in 1990, the last time the total bill was measured.

Depression

More than 19 million adult Americans age 18 and over will suffer from a depressive illness—major depression, bipolar disorder, or dysthymia—each year. Many of them will be unnecessarily incapacitated for weeks or months because their illness is untreated.

- The onset of depression may be occurring earlier in life in people born in recent decades compared to the past.
- Nearly twice as many women (12%) as men (7%) are affected by a depressive illness each year.
- Depression is a frequent and serious complication of heart attack, stroke, diabetes, and cancer, but is very treatable.
- Depression increases the risk of having a heart attack. According to one recent study that covered a 13-year period, individuals with a history of major depression were four times as likely to suffer a heart attack compared to people without such a history.
- Depression costs the nation more than $30 billion per year in direct and indirect costs, according to the most recent data available.
- Major depression is the leading cause of disability in the United States and worldwide, according to a recent study by the World Health Organization, the World Bank, and Harvard University.

Bipolar (Manic-Depressive) Illness

More than 2.3 million Americans ages 18 and over—about 1% of the population—suffer from bipolar illness.

- As many as 20% of people with bipolar illness die by suicide.
- Men and women are equally likely to develop bipolar illness

Suicide

In 1996, approximately 31,000 people died from suicide in the United States. Almost all people who kill themselves have a diagnosable mental disorder, most commonly depression, or a substance abuse problem.

- The highest suicide rates in the United States are found in white men over age 85.
- The suicide rate in young people has increased dramatically in recent years. In 1996, the most recent year for which statistics are available, suicide was the 3rd leading cause of death among 15- to 24-year-olds.
- Men are more than four times as likely as women to commit suicide.

Schizophrenia

More than 2 million adult Americans are affected by schizophrenia.

- In men, schizophrenia usually appears in the late teens or early twenties. The disorder usually shows up when women are in their twenties to early thirties.
- Schizophrenia affects men and women with equal frequency.
- Most people with schizophrenia suffer chronically throughout their lives.
- One of every 10 people with schizophrenia eventually commits suicide.
- Schizophrenia costs the nation $32.5 billion annually according to the most recently available data.

Anxiety Disorders

More than 16 million adults ages 18 to 54 in the United States suffer from anxiety disorders, which include panic disorder, obsessive-compulsive disorder, post-traumatic stress disorder, social phobia, and generalized anxiety disorder.

- Anxiety disorders cost $46.6 billion in 1990.
- Anxiety disorders are frequently complicated by depression, eating disorders, or substance abuse.
- Many people have more than one anxiety disorder.

Panic Disorder

Panic disorder affects about 1.7% of the U.S. adult population ages 18 to 54, or 2.4 million people, in a given year.

- Panic disorder typically strikes in young adulthood. Roughly half of all people who have panic disorder develop the condition before age 24.
- Women are twice as likely as men to develop panic disorder.
- People with panic disorder may also suffer from depression and substance abuse.
- About one-third of all people with panic disorder develop agoraphobia, an illness in which they become afraid of being in any place or situation where escape might be difficult or help unavailable in the event of a panic attack.

Obsessive-Compulsive Disorder (OCD)

About 2.3% of the U.S. adult population ages 18 to 54, approximately 3.3 million Americans, has OCD in a given year.

- OCD affects men and women with equal frequency.
- The nation's social and economic losses due to OCD totaled $8.4 billion in 1990.

Post-Traumatic Stress Disorder (PTSD)

- In the United States, about 3.6% of adults ages 18 to 54, or 5.2 million people, have PTSD during the course of a given year.

- PTSD can develop at any age, including childhood.
- PTSD is more likely to occur in women than in men.
- About 30% of men and women who have spent time in war zones experience PTSD. The disorder also frequently occurs after violent personal assaults, such as rape, mugging, or domestic violence; terrorism; natural or human-caused disasters; and accidents.
- Depression, alcohol, or other substance abuse, or another anxiety disorder often accompany PTSD.

Social Phobia

About 3.7% of American adults ages 18 to 54, or 5.3 million people, have social phobia in a given year.
- Social phobia occurs in women twice as often as men, although a higher proportion of men seek help for this disorder.
- The disorder typically begins in childhood or early adolescence and rarely develops after age 25.

- Social phobia is often accompanied by depression and may lead to alcohol or other drug abuse.

Attention Deficit Hyperactivity Disorder (ADHD)

ADHD is one of the most common mental disorders in children, affecting 3% to 5% of school-age children.
- Two to three times more boys than girls are affected.
- ADHD has long-term adverse affects on success at school, work, and in social relationships.
- National public school expenditures on behalf of students with ADHD exceeded $3 billion in 1995.
- As they grow older, children with untreated ADHD who have a coexisting conduct disorder often experience drug abuse, antisocial behavior, teenage pregnancy, and injuries of all sorts.

Drug Use by Americans, 12 Years and Older

Type of drug	Ever used			Current user		
	1979	1990	1996	1979	1990	1996
Marijuana and hashish	27.9%	30.5%	32.0%	13.2%	5.4%	4.7%
Cocaine	8.6	11.2	10.3	2.6	0.9	0.8
Inhalants	n.a.	5.7	5.6	n.a.	0.4	0.4
Hallucinogens	8.9	7.9	9.7	1.9	0.4	0.6
Heroin	1.3	0.8	1.1	0.1	—	0.1
Stimulants	n.a.	5.5	4.7	n.a.	0.6	0.4
Sedatives	n.a.	2.8	2.3	n.a.	0.2	0.1
Tranquilizers	n.a.	4.0	3.6	n.a.	0.6	0.4
Analgesics	n.a.	6.3	5.5	n.a.	0.9	0.9
Alcohol	88.5	82.2	82.6	63.2	52.6	51.0
Cigarettes	n.a.	75.4	71.6	n.a.	32.6	28.9

Current users are those who used drugs at least once within month prior to this study. *Source:* U.S. Substance Abuse and Mental Health Services Administration, *National Household Survey on Drug Abuse.*

Age of First Marijuana Use, 1965–1996

Year	Number of 1st time users (in 1000s)	Mean age	First time use (per 1,000) by age			Year	Number of 1st time users (in 1000s)	Mean age	First time use (per 1,000) by age		
			12-17	18-25	26-34				12-17	18-25	26-34
1965	617	18.8	9.2	13.4	4.9	1981	2218	17.8	57.0	46.2	4.8
1966	900	20.3	11.2	23.4	2.7	1982	2080	18.2	50.5	45.8	9.1
1967	1467	19.9	15.2	40.9	6.9	1983	2044	17.8	54.9	42.4	3.5
1968	1590	19.1	18.5	44.8	3.7	1984	1994	19.6	51.2	38.8	3.9
1969	2218	19.2	32.2	52.3	5.4	1985	1767	17.8	48.7	39.1	1.5
1970	2668	19.3	35.8	64.8	10.7	1986	1871	19.4	50.4	41.9	3.0
1971	2799	18.8	42.5	66.7	12.5	1987	1817	17.9	49.2	43.2	2.3
1972	2897	18.4	52.0	63.5	9.5	1988	1526	17.3	43.0	37.7	1.7
1973	2782	18.2	55.5	58.4	8.0	1989	1413	17.8	37.6	34.2	2.4
1974	3008	18.2	57.2	62.0	9.9	1990	1401	17.3	37.0	37.0	1.4
1975	3185	18.8	69.4	55.1	12.8	1991	1376	17.5	36.6	33.9	1.7
1976	2824	18.5	61.3	53.4	10.4	1992	1701	17.7	45.5	39.3	2.8
1977	2884	19.3	66.5	48.6	10.1	1993	1949	17.0	53.9	46.3	2.2
1978	2879	17.8	76.9	50.7	7.1	1994	2393	16.7	73.3	47.9	2.7
1979	2585	18.0	61.4	55.4	4.1	1995	2406	16.6	74.6	50.7	2.4
1980	2492	18.6	58.2	57.1	5.3	1996	2540	16.4	83.2	53.6	1.3

Source: SAMHSA, Office of Applied Studies, National Household Survey on Drug Abuse, 1994–1997.

Nationwide Trends in Drug Abuse

Source: National Institute on Drug Abuse

According to the results of the 1996 National Household Survey on Drug Abuse, the number of current illicit-drug users did not change significantly from 1995 (12.8 million) to 1996 (13 million). Below are the report's findings on the extent of drug abuse for 1996, the most recent year for which figures are available.

Cocaine

Cocaine use has stabilized, with the overall number of current cocaine users 1.75 million in 1996. This is down from a peak of 5.7 million in 1985. Nevertheless, there were still an estimated 652,000 Americans who used cocaine for the first time in 1995. Supplies remain abundant in nearly every city. Data indicate a leveling-off in many urban areas: cocaine-related deaths were stable or up slightly in nine of the ten areas where such information was reported; the percentage of treatment admissions for primary cocaine problems declined slightly or remained stable in 12 of the 14 areas where data were available; and prices of cocaine remained stable in most areas. Demographic data continue to show most cocaine users as older, inner-city crack addicts.

Heroin

There has been an increasing trend in new heroin use since 1992, with an estimated 141,000 new heroin users in 1995. The estimated number of heroin users increased from 68,000 in 1993 to 216,000 in 1996. A large portion of these recent new users were smoking, snorting, or sniffing heroin, and most were under age 26. There is increasing incidence of new users (snorters) in the younger age groups, often among women. In some areas, such as San Francisco, the recent initiates increasingly include members of the middle class. In Boston and Newark, heroin users are also found in suburban populations. Purity remains high, as does intranasal use, in the East and in some midwestern cities, notably Chicago and Detroit. Supplies remain abundant. Aggressive marketing and price cutting has intensified in some cities, such as Boston, Detroit, and New York.

Marijuana

There were an estimated 2.4 million people who started using marijuana in 1995. The resurgence in marijuana use continues, especially among adolescents. Two factors may be contributing to a dramatic leap in adverse consequences resulting from marijuana use: higher potency and the use of marijuana mixed with or in combination with other dangerous drugs.

Methamphetamine

In several western and midwestern cities, methamphetamine indicators, which had been steadily increasing for several years, appear mixed. On the West Coast, the area where methamphetamine use is endemic, increased use is evident in San Francisco and Seattle, while in San Diego and Los Angeles indicators show stable or slightly declining trends. However, it is too soon to predict that the indicators in those areas have peaked. All four routes of administration—injecting, snorting, smoking (including "chasing the dragon" in San Francisco), and oral ingestion—are used but vary from city to city. Reports of violence related to methamphetamine persist in Honolulu and are now also occurring in Seattle.

Stimulants

Methcathinone ("cat" or "goobs") use has been reported in Detroit and Michigan's Upper Peninsula. Ephedrine-based products sold at convenience stores, truck stops, and health-food stores are common among adolescents in Atlanta, Detroit, Minneapolis/St. Paul, and Texas. New York State recently banned the sale of such products in an attempt to curb escalating abuse among adolescents. Methylenedioxymethamphetamine (MDMA or "Ecstasy") use was reported most often among young adults and adolescents at clubs, raves, and rock concerts in Atlanta, Miami, St. Louis, Seattle, and areas of Texas.

Depressants

Use of gamma hydroxybutrate (GHB) in the club scene is becoming more widespread throughout the country, notably in Atlanta, Detroit, Honolulu, Miami, New York City (where it is also reportedly used by fashion models), Phoenix, and Texas. Ketamine ("Special K") use in nightclubs has also been reported in several cities. A mixture of GHB, ketamine, and alcohol, called "Special K-lude" because of the similar effects produced by methaqualone (Quaalude), is reported in New York City. Flunitrazepam (Rohypnol) use continues in many areas of the country (with the exception of the Northeast), most notably in Texas and Florida. Its widespread availability has declined, however, since the federal ban on its importation.

Hallucinogens

According to field reports in numerous areas, such as Texas, Boston, Chicago, New York, Philadelphia, St. Louis, and Washington, D.C., phencyclidine (PCP) is often used in combination with other drugs. A frequently reported combination is joints or blunts containing marijuana mixed with or dipped into PCP. In other cities, such as Los Angeles and New Orleans, PCP is commonly purchased as a pre-dipped cigarette. In New York City, PCP is combined with crack in "spaceballs." Lysergic acid diethylamide (LSD) remains widely available, especially in suburban and rural areas.

Heavy Alcohol Use, by Age Group, Race/Ethnicity, and Sex: 1985–1997

Demographic characteristics	1985	1990	1991	1992	1993	1994	1995	1996	1997
Total	8.3%	6.3%	6.8%	6.2%	6.7%	6.2%	5.5%	5.4%	5.4%
Age group									
12–17	9.5	4.4	6.0	3.4	3.4	2.5	2.8	2.9	3.1
18–25	13.8	14.9	15.2	15.1	14.0	13.2	12.0	12.9	11.1
26–34	11.5	8.2	7.9	8.5	8.5	8.0	7.9	7.1	7.5
≥35	5.2	3.7	4.4	3.9	5.0	4.8	3.9	3.8	4.0
Race/Ethnicity									
White	9.1	6.7	7.2	6.8	7.5	6.4	5.7	5.5	5.7
Black	3.5	4.1	4.3	3.5	3.3	4.8	4.6	5.3	3.8
Hispanic	7.1	5.9	6.8	6.3	6.0	7.3	6.3	7.2	6.3
Other	—	—	3.3	2.2	1.9	4.7	2.4	2.1	2.3
Sex									
Male	13.8	10.8	10.8	10.1	11.9	10.3	9.4	13.8	8.9
Female	3.2	2.1	3.1	2.7	1.9	2.5	2.0	1.9	2.1

NOTE: Heavy alcohol use is defined as drinking five or more drinks on the same occasion on each of five or more days in the past 30 days. *Source:* U.S. Substance Abuse and Mental Health Services Administration, Office of Applied Studies, *National Household Survey on Drug Abuse.*

Smoking-Related Mortality

An estimated 47 million adults in the United States smoke cigarettes, even though this behavior will result in death or disability for half of all regular users. Cigarette smoking is the single most preventable cause of premature death in the United States. Each year, more than 430,000 Americans die from cigarette smoking. In fact, one in every five deaths in the United States is smoking related.

• About 10 million people in the United States have died from causes attributed to smoking (including heart disease, emphysema, and other respiratory diseases) since the first Surgeon General's report on smoking and health in 1964—2 million of these deaths were the result of lung cancer alone.

• Between 1960 and 1990, deaths from lung cancer among women have increased by more than 400%—exceeding breast cancer deaths in the mid-1980s. Smoking triples the risk of dying from heart disease among middle-aged men and women.

• On average, smokers die nearly seven years earlier than nonsmokers.

• Annually, exposure to secondhand smoke causes an estimated 3,000 deaths from lung cancer among American adults. Scientific studies also link secondhand smoke with heart disease.

• Approximately 80% of adult smokers started smoking before the age of 18. Every day, nearly 3,000 young people under the age of 18 become regular smokers.

Smoking Prevalence among U.S. Adults, 1955–1994
(as a percent of population, 18 years of age and older)

In 1994, 48 million adults 18 years of age and older (25.3 million men, 22.7 million women) were current smokers in the U.S. Smoking among adults decreased dramatically from 42% in 1965 to 26% in 1994. During this period, smoking among the adult male population declined from 52% to 28%; adult female smoking declined from 34% to 23%.

Year	Overall population	Males	Females	Whites	Blacks
1955	—	56.9%	28.4%	—	—
1965	42.4%	51.9	33.9	42.1%	45.8%
1970	37.4	44.1	31.5	37.0	41.4
1974	37.1	43.1	32.1	36.4	44.0
1978	34.1	38.1	30.7	33.9	37.7
1980	33.2	37.6	29.3	32.9	36.9
1983	32.1	35.1	29.5	31.8	35.9
1985	30.1	32.6	27.9	29.6	34.9
1987	28.8	31.2	26.5	28.5	32.9
1988	28.1	30.8	25.7	27.8	31.7
1990	25.5	28.4	22.8	25.6	26.2
1991	25.7	28.1	23.5	25.5	29.1
1992	26.5	28.6	24.6	26.6	27.8
1993	25.0	27.7	22.5	24.9	26.1
1994	25.5	28.2	23.1	26.3	27.2

Source: Office on Smoking and Health, Centers for Disease Control and Prevention.

Respiratory Conditions in the U.S., 1995
(in thousands)

Type of acute condition	All ages	Under 5 years	5–17 years	18–24 years	25–44 years	45–64 years	65 years and older
Common cold	60,564	10,895	16,633	5,423	15,434	8,349	3,832
Other acute upper respiratory infections	31,687	5,981	10,380	2,251	8,021	3,762	1,290
Influenza	108,009	10,862	29,958	10,742	37,570	14,477	4,401
Acute bronchitis	13,250	2,571	2,570	1,102	3,689	1,651	1,667
Pneumonia	5,113	898	1,071	83	1,171	1,207	684
Other respiratory conditions	4,413	1,125	1,264	279	1,016	340	389
Total	223,037	32,333	61,875	19,880	66,901	29,785	12,262

Source: Centers for Disease Control and Prevention.

The Common Cold

Source: National Institute of Allergy and Infectious Diseases, National Institutes of Health.

The problem. Adults average about two to four colds a year, although the range varies widely. Women, especially those aged 20–30 years, have more colds than men, possibly because of their closer contact with children. On average, individuals older than 60 have fewer than one cold a year. Colds are most prevalent among children, and seem to be related to youngsters' relative lack of resistance to infection and to contacts with other children in day-care centers and schools. Children have about 6–10 colds a year.

The causes: viruses. More than 200 different viruses are known to cause the symptoms of the common cold. **Rhinoviruses** (from the Greek *rhin,* meaning nose) cause an estimated 30 to 35 percent of all adult colds, and are most active in early fall, spring, and summer. **Coronaviruses** are believed to cause a large percentage of all adult colds. They induce colds primarily in the winter and early spring. Of the more than 30 isolated strains, three or four infect humans.

Does cold weather cause a cold? Although many people are convinced that a cold results from exposure to cold weather, or from getting chilled or overheated, these conditions in fact have little or no effect on the development or severity of a cold. Nor is susceptibility apparently related to factors such as exercise, diet, or enlarged tonsils or adenoids.

How cold viruses cause disease. Viruses cause infection by overcoming the body's complex defense system. The body's first line of defense is mucus, produced by the membranes in the nose and throat. Mucus traps the material we inhale: pollen, dust, bacteria, and viruses. When a virus penetrates the mucus and enters a cell, it commandeers the protein-making machinery to manufacture new viruses which, in turn, attack surrounding cells.

Cold symptoms: the body fights back. Cold symptoms are probably the result of the body's immune response to the viral invasion. Virus-infected cells in the nose send out signals that recruit specialized white blood cells to the site of the infection. In turn, these cells emit a range of immune system chemicals such as kinins. These chemicals probably lead to the symptoms of the common cold by causing swelling and inflammation of the nasal membranes, leakage of proteins and fluid from capillaries and lymph vessels, and the increased production of mucus.

How colds are spread. Depending on the virus type, any or all of the following routes of transmission may be common:

• Touching infectious respiratory secretions on skin and on environmental surfaces and then touching the eyes or nose.

• Inhaling relatively large particles of respiratory secretions transported briefly in the air.

• Inhaling droplet nuclei, smaller infectious particles suspended in the air for long periods of time.

Prevention. Handwashing is the simplest and most effective way to keep from getting rhinovirus colds. Not touching the nose or eyes is another. Individuals with colds should always sneeze or cough into a facial tissue, and promptly throw it away. If possible, one should avoid close, prolonged exposure to persons who have colds.

Because rhinoviruses can survive up to three hours outside the nasal passages on inanimate objects and skin, cleaning environmental surfaces with a virus-killing disinfectant might help prevent spread of infection.

Treatment. Only symptomatic treatment is available for uncomplicated cases of the common cold: bed rest, plenty of fluids, gargling with warm salt water, petroleum jelly for a raw nose, and aspirin or acetaminophen to relieve headache or fever.

Nonprescription cold remedies, including decongestants and cough suppressants, may relieve some cold symptoms but will not prevent, cure, or even shorten the duration of illness. Nonprescription antihistamines may have some effect in relieving inflammatory responses such as runny nose and watery eyes.

Antibiotics do not kill viruses. These prescription drugs should be used only for rare bacterial complications, such as sinusitis or ear infections, that can develop as secondary infections. The use of antibiotic "just in case" will not prevent secondary bacterial infections.

Does vitamin C have a role? Many people are convinced that taking large quantities of vitamin C will prevent colds or relieve symptoms. To test this theory, several large-scale, controlled studies involving children and adults have been conducted. To date, no conclusive data has shown that large doses of vitamin C prevent colds. The vitamin may reduce the severity or duration of symptoms, but there is no definitive evidence.

Warfighting 101: The Lessons of Victory

Triumphant in Kosovo, the Pentagon eyes the future—and puts pressure on the army to speed up deployment

By MARK THOMPSON TIME

On paper, Operation Allied Force may be the sharpest-looking war in American history. The numbers are remarkable: 99.6% of allied bombs—NATO dropped 20,000 of them—found their targets. NATO pilots flew some 35,000 sorties, and though two U.S. planes were shot down, it was the kind of war in which a fighter jock could be hit on an overnight raid and by sunrise be sipping coffee in Italy—and praising the Lord for helping him find the ejection handle. Stunningly, in a war that NATO believes killed some 5,000 Yugoslavs, not a single allied pilot died. Western military technology finally seemed to have transformed war into a push-button exercise. And it is on exactly this point that debate is beginning.

An Unprecedented Air War

While Air Force officers were bragging that air power by itself had triumphed for the first time in history, Army officers were quick to note that air power had failed abjectly in attaining the war's key goal—protecting ethnic Albanians from Serbian violence. Says William Odom, a retired Army three-star: "This war didn't do anything to vindicate air power. It didn't stop the ethnic cleansing, and it didn't remove Milosevic." In fact, a ground movement—an offensive by the resurgent Kosovo Liberation Army—played a key role in upping the pressure on Milosevic's army by forcing Serbian

armor out into the open where it was vulnerable to allied attack. Says Army General Henry Shelton, Chairman of the Joint Chiefs of Staff: "As [Milosevic] massed his forces to fight back, he set himself up for B-52 and B-1 bombing."

B-52? B-1? What about the sleek B-2? Not since World War II has the U.S. military hurled three types of heavy bombers—B-1s, B-2s, and B-52s—at an enemy. Ironically, while the B-2 performed well, the success of older aircraft may make it harder for the services to bring costly new planes on line. In the coming decades, the Pentagon planned to spend $300 billion on three new classes of warplanes, including $70 billion for a fleet of 339 F-22 fighters. This fall, however, Congress slashed the defense budget for the first F-22s, which one Congressman called "a billion-dollar cancer eating a hole in the Air Force." If U.S. air forces are so good, the thinking goes, why upgrade?

Smart Bombs—And Cheap, Too

It wasn't just older, cheaper planes that won over Kosovo. The real star of the show was a new but very cheap bomb that allowed U.S. warplanes to drop bombs regardless of the weather, guided to their targets by a constellation of Global Positioning Satellites rather than pilot eyeballs. While the Joint Direct Attack Munition (JDAM) is a pretty low-tech weapon, its satellite-guided tail fins let a plane at any altitude drop it right on target through clouds, smoke, or darkness.

Lessons of Operation Allied Force

Kosovo showed U.S. battle gear at its best and worst. A rundown:

WINNER: AIR POWER

B-2
Believe the hype (and the cost). The $2.2 billion bomber was accurate and reliable.

JDAM
At $20,000 each (cruise missiles average $1 million each) these accurate satellite-guided bombs were a bargain.

DRONES
Unmanned spy planes reduced pilot risk and helped target Serb troops on the move.

LOSER: THE ARMY

APACHES
A molasses-slow deployment and fear of missiles benched the warbirds.

ARMY DIVISIONS
Their inability to move fast into hot spots will raise questions on the Hill.

F-22s
The ease with which today's fighters cleared the skies helped dampen Congress's enthusiasm for this overbudget under-achiever.

At about $20,000 a pop, the JDAM is far cheaper than the $1 million cruise missile that has been the precision-guided weapon of choice for the past decade. "Once you get the air defenses suppressed, you can just fly over and puke out JDAMs," says Merrill McPeak, the retired general who ran the Air Force during the Gulf War. "You can't beat the economics."

This war marks the first time that 90% of all weapons dropped have been so-called smart bombs, guided to their targets either by pilots or satellites. During the Gulf War, only 8% of the bombs dropped were precision-guided. Such weapons had really triumphed in September 1995 during the Bosnian conflict. In a two-week campaign that was 70% smart bombs, the U.S. military helped drive the Bosnian Serbs to the negotiating table.

The air war, though, quickly drained U.S. precision-guided munitions. The B-2 force had less than 1,000 JDAMs before the war began, forcing the Air Force to order up more a week into the conflict. The war highlighted the Pentagon's peculiar priorities: it has budgeted some $350 billion for three new high-tech warplane programs but doesn't have the ammo it needs for its current crop of bombers.

Apaches Grounded

The strength of the allied air performance will also reignite debate over the heft and utility of U.S. Army forces. The lame deployment of the Army's 24 Apache helicopters—slowed by the need to ship humanitarian supplies into the region—created a perception that the Army couldn't get those choppers to war promptly and that the Pentagon was chicken to use them once they got there. Moreover, despite decades of chatter about fast, light forces, the U.S. Army still can't move a major fighting force quickly into place. That's a problem that Shelton, among others, wants fixed quickly.

A small, powerful force that can be quickly moved anywhere around the globe would be a perfect match for problem spots like Kosovo. The Army has been trying to pull this off for two decades, reaching back to the Soviet invasion of Afghanistan, which made Washington planners nervous about conflicts in that part of the world. But the idea died amid Army politics and lean budgets.

Some in the Army argue that building a smaller armored force is foolish until key advances have been made, especially in the areas of fuel and ammo, which armored forces devour. Electromagnetic guns, lasers, and new fuel types could allow the Army to achieve its goal of fielding such a force that could fight for two weeks without resupply. But until then, the speed of deployment is mostly dependent on how quickly the Army can set up logistics links. Napoleon's old dictum that an army travels on its stomach remains true today.

Molasses-Slow Deployment

The Army's current fast-deploying force is the 82nd Airborne's ready brigade, which is set to move within 37 hours. But the Army couldn't deploy such a unit to Kosovo for action. In recent years, the Army scrapped the aging but light Sheridan tank it once used, and canceled the air-droppable Advanced Gun System that was to have replaced it. That means the 82nd has to seize and hold a major airfield within four hours of parachuting in, to allow C-17s carrying M-1 tanks to land. The Army's latest study on the subject isn't much use either. It's titled, "Enabling Rapid and Decisive Strategic Maneuver for the Army After 2010."

But even if the Army is never fast and light, the U.S. military will still possess an unmatchable tactical dominance over its opponents. That worries some Pentagon thinkers. In the next conflict, they fret, a really smart foe won't fight the U.S. in the skies or on the ground—places where victory is unlikely. Instead, it will be smart and strike far away from the war zone—in the heart of a major U.S. city, perhaps—with chemical or biological weapons. Even the slickest Stealth bomber couldn't stop that. □

Post-Vietnam Combat Casualties*

Place	Dates	Casualties	Place	Dates	Casualties
Lebanon	Aug. 1982–Feb. 1984	254	Persian Gulf	Aug. 1990–March 1998, Dec. 1998–present	148
Grenada	Oct.–Nov. 1983	18			
Libya	April 10–16, 1986	2	Somalia	Dec. 1992–May 1993	29
Panama	Dec. 1989–Jan. 1990	23	Haiti	Sept. 1994–April 1996	0
			Yugoslavia	March–June 1999	0

*Does not include deaths from accidents. *Source:* Defense Dept.

Highest Ranking Officers in U.S. History

General and Commander-in-Chief[1]

George Washington (1732–1799), b. Westmoreland County, Va., unanimously voted by Congress on June 15, 1775, to the rank of general and commander-in-chief (of the Continental Army).

General of the Armies[2]

John Joseph Pershing (1860–1948), b. Linn County, Mo., made permanent general of the armies 1919.

General of the Army, General of the Air Force (Five-Stars)

George Catlett Marshall (1880–1959), b. Uniontown, Pa., promoted December 1944.

Douglas MacArthur (1880–1964), b. Little Rock, Ark., promoted December 1944.

Dwight David Eisenhower (1890–1969), b. Denison, Texas, promoted December 1944.

Henry Harley Arnold (1866–1950), b. Gladwyne, Pa. Arnold had the unique distinction of being a five-star general twice—in 1944 as general of the army, and in June 1949 as general of the air force. He is the only air force general to have held the five-star rank.

Omar Nelson Bradley (1893–1981), b. Clark, Mo., promoted September 1950.

Fleet Admiral (Five-Star)

William Daniel Leahy (1875–1959), b. Hampton, Iowa, promoted December 1944.

Ernest Joseph King (1878–1956), b. Lorain, Ohio, promoted December 1944.

Chester William Nimitz (1885–1966), b. Fredericksburg, Texas, promoted December 1944.

William Frederick Halsey (1882–1959), b. Elizabeth, N.J., promoted December 1945.

1. On March 15, 1978, George Washington was promoted posthumously to the newly created rank of General of the Armies of the United States. Congress authorized this title to make it clear that Washington was the army's senior general. 2. General Pershing was given the option of five stars but he declined. *Source:* Department of Defense and U.S. Army Historian, Research and Analysis Center.

The Joint Chiefs of Staff (JCS)

The Joint Chiefs of Staff consist of the chairman, the vice chairman, the chief of staff of the army, the chief of naval operations, the chief of staff of the air force, and the commandant of the Marine Corps.

The collective body of the JCS is headed by the chairman (or vice chairman in the chairman's absence), who sets the agenda and presides over JCS meetings. Their responsibilities take precedence over their duties as the Chiefs of Military Services. The chairman is the principal military adviser to the president, the secretary of defense, and the National Security Council (NSC); however, all JCS members are by law military advisers, and they may respond to a request or voluntarily submit, through the chairman, advice or opinions to the president, the secretary of state, or the NSC. The Joint Chiefs of Staff have no executive authority to commit combatant forces.

In addition to their responsibilities on the JCS, the military service chiefs are responsible to the secretaries of their military departments for management of the services. The service chiefs serve for four years. By custom the vice chiefs of the services act for their chiefs in most matters having to do with day-to-day operation of the services.

Joint Chiefs of Staff, Mid-1999

Chairman of the Joint Chiefs of Staff, General Henry H. Shelton, U.S. Army; vice chairman of the Joint Chiefs of Staff, General Joseph W. Ralston,[1] U.S. Air Force; General Eric K. Shinseki, chief of staff of the army; Admiral Jay L. Johnson, chief of naval operations; General Michael E. Ryan, chief of staff of the U.S. Air Force; and General James L. Jones, commandant of the Marine Corps.

Past Chairmen of the JCS

General of the Army, Omar N. Bradley, 1949–1953
Adm. Arthur W. Radford, U.S. Navy, 1953–1957
Gen. Nathan F. Twining, U.S. Air Force, 1957–1960
Gen. Lyman L. Lemnitzer, U.S. Army, 1960–1962
Gen. Maxwell D. Taylor, U.S. Army, 1962–1964
Gen. Earle G. Wheeler, U.S. Air Force, 1964–1970
Adm. Thomas H. Moorer, U.S. Navy, 1970–1974
Gen. George S. Brown, U.S. Air Force, 1974–1978
Gen. David C. Jones, U.S. Air Force, 1978–1982
Gen. John W. Vessey, Jr., U.S. Army, 1982–1985
Adm. William J. Crowe, U.S. Navy, 1985–1989
Gen. Colin L. Powell, U.S. Army, 1989–1993
Gen. John M. Shalikashvili, U.S. Army, 1993–1997

1. In August 1999, Gen. Ralston was named as the Pentagon's choice to replace Gen. Wesley Clark as supreme commander of NATO forces in Europe. His confirmation is pending.

U.S. Military Pay Grades

Source: U.S. Department of Defense.

Pay Grade	Army	Navy	Marines	Air Force
Commissioned Officers				
O-1	Second Lieutenant	Ensign	Second Lieutenant	Second Lieutenant
O-2	First Lieutenant	Lieutenant Junior Grade	First Lieutenant	First Lieutenant
O-3	Captain	Lieutenant	Captain	Captain
O-4	Major	Lieutenant Commander	Major	Major
O-5	Lieutenant Colonel	Commander	Lieutenant Colonel	Lieutenant Colonel
O-6	Colonel	Captain	Colonel	Colonel
O-7	Brigadier General	Rear Admiral (L)	Brigadier General	Brigadier General
O-8	Major General	Rear Admiral	Major General	Major General
O-9	Lieutenant General	Vice Admiral	Lieutenant General	Lieutenant General
O-10	General	Admiral	General	General

Pay Grade	Army	Navy	Marines	Air Force
Special Grades[1]				
(5 stars)	General of the Army	Fleet Admiral	(none)	General of the Air Force
Warrant Officers				
W-1	Warrant Officer. Grades W-2 to W-5 Chief Warrant Officer			
Enlisted Personnel				
E-1	Private	Seaman Recruit	Private	Airman Basic
E-2	Private	Seaman Apprentice	Private First Class	Airman
E-3	Private First Class	Seaman	Lance Corporal	Airman First Class
E-4	Corporal Specialist 4	Petty Officer, Third Class	Corporal	Sergeant Senior Airman
E-5	Sergeant Specialist 5	Petty Officer, Second Class	Sergeant	Staff Sergeant
E-6	Staff Sergeant Specialist 6	Petty Officer, First Class	Staff Sergeant	Technical Sergeant
E-7	Sergeant First Class Specialist 7	Chief Petty Officer	Gunnery Sergeant	Master Sergeant
E-8	First Sergeant Master Sergeant	Senior Chief Petty Officer	First Sergeant Master Sergeant	Senior Master Sergeant
E-9	Command Sergeant Major Sergeant Major	Master Chief Petty Officer	Sergeant Major Master Gunnery Sergeant	Chief Master Sergeant
Special Grades[2]				
	Sergeant Major of the Army	Master Chief Petty Officer of the Navy	Sergeant Major of the Marine Corps	Chief Master Sergeant of the Air Force

1. There are no living five-star commissioned officers. 2. Senior enlisted advisers. There is only one for each branch of service.

Monthly Basic Pay Rates by Grade, Effective 1999

Grade	<2	>2	>4	>6	>10	>14	>16	>18	>20	>26
Commissioned Officers										
0-10[1]	$7,838.70	$8,114.40	$8,114.40	$8,114.40	$8,425.80	$8,892.60	$9,528.90	$9,528.90	$10,167.00	$10,800.00
0-9	6,947.10	7,129.20	7,129.20	7,129.20	7,466.10	7,776.90	8,425.80	8,425.80	8,892.60	9,528.90
0-8	6,292.20	6,481.20	6,481.20	6,481.20	7,129.20	7,466.10	7,776.90	8,114.40	8,425.80	8,633.70
0-7	5,228.40	5,583.90	5,583.90	5,834.40	6,172.50	6,481.20	7,129.20	7,619.70	7,619.70	7,619.70
0-6	3,875.10	4,257.30	4,536.60	4,536.60	4,536.60	4,690.80	5,432.40	5,709.60	5,834.40	6,694.20
0-5	3,099.60	3,639.30	3,891.00	3,891.00	4,008.00	4,507.50	4,845.00	5,122.20	5,277.90	5,277.90
0-4	2,612.40	3,181.20	3,393.30	3,456.30	3,855.30	4,257.30	4,444.80	4,566.60	4,566.60	4,566.60
0-3	2,427.60	2,714.10	3,210.60	3,364.50	3,673.80	3,949.50	3,949.50	3,949.50	3,949.50	3,949.50
0-2	2,117.10	2,312.10	2,871.30	2,930.40	2,930.40	2,930.40	2,930.40	2,930.40	2,930.40	2,930.40
0-1	1,838.10	1,913.10	2,312.10	2,312.10	2,312.10	2,312.10	2,312.10	2,312.10	2,312.10	2,312.10
Warrant Officers										
W-5	0.00	0.00	0.00	0.00	0.00	0.00	0.00	0.00	$ 4,221.30	$ 4,697.70
W-4	$2,473.20	$2,653.80	$2,714.10	$2,838.00	$3,087.30	$3,456.30	$3,577.80	$3,673.80	3,792.00	4,224.30
W-3	2,247.90	2,438.40	2,469.90	2,498.70	2,838.00	3,023.40	3,114.00	3,210.60	3,335.70	3,577.80
W-2	1,968.90	2,130.30	2,192.10	2,312.10	2,531.10	2,714.10	2,809.90	2,901.90	2,993.10	3,114.00
W-1	1,640.40	1,880.70	2,037.90	2,130.30	2,312.10	2,498.70	2,591.70	2,681.70	2,777.70	2,777.70
Enlisted Members										
E-9	0.00	0.00	0.00	0.00	$2,877.30	$3,008.40	$3,078.00	$3,147.00	$ 3,207.60	$ 3,704.70
E-8	0.00	0.00	0.00	0.00	2,482.50	2,613.60	2,682.90	2,743.80	2,811.30	3,308.40
E-7	$1,684.80	$1,818.90	$1,952.10	$2,018.70	2,149.50	2,316.60	2,382.60	2,448.60	2,480.40	2,976.60
E-6	1,449.30	1,579.80	1,715.40	1,779.90	1,911.60	2,073.30	2,140.20	2,172.60	2,172.60	2,172.60
E-5	1,271.70	1,384.20	1,514.40	1,614.30	1,746.30	1,844.10	1,844.10	1,844.10	1,844.10	1,844.10
E-4	1,185.90	1,252.80	1,428.60	1,485.30	1,485.30	1,485.30	1,485.30	1,485.30	1,485.30	1,485.30
E-3	1,117.80	1,179.00	1,274.70	1,274.70	1,274.70	1,274.70	1,274.70	1,274.70	1,274.70	1,274.70
E-2	1,075.80	1,075.80	1,075.80	1,075.80	1,075.80	1,075.80	1,075.80	1,075.80	1,075.80	1,075.80
E-1>4	959.40	959.40	959.40	959.40	959.40	959.40	959.40	959.40	959.40	959.40

NOTE: E-1 with less than 4 months: $887.70. 1. Basic pay without cap. Actual amount of basic pay received is $9,225.00 per month.

Service Academies

U.S. Military Academy

Established in 1802 by an act of Congress, the U.S. Military Academy is located on the west bank of the Hudson River some 50 miles north of New York City. To gain admission a candidate must first secure a nomination from an authorized source.

Any number of applicants can meet the requirements for a *nomination* in these categories. *Appointments* (offers of admission), however, can only be made to a much smaller number, about 1,150 to 1,200 each year.

Candidates may be nominated for vacancies during the year preceding the day of admission, which occurs in late June or early July. The best time to apply is during the spring of the junior year in high school.

Candidates must be citizens of the U.S. at time of enrollment (except foreign students admitted by agreement between the U.S. and another country), not married, pregnant, nor have a legal obligation to support a child or children, be at least 17 but not yet 23 years old on July 1 of the year admitted. Entrance requirements and procedures for appointment are described in the Admissions Bulletin and the Admissions Prospectus, available without charge from Admissions, U.S. Military Academy, West Point, NY 10996-1797. Phone: 914-938-4041.

Cadets are members of the U.S. Army. As such they receive annual salaries of more than $6,500. This pay covers the cost of their uniforms, textbooks, a personal computer, and living incidentals. There is no tuition and room and board are provided. Upon successful completion of the four-year course, the graduate receives the degree of bachelor of science and is commissioned a second lieutenant in the U.S. Army with a requirement to serve as an officer on active duty for a minimum of five years.

U.S. Naval Academy

The Naval School, established in 1845 at Fort Severn, Annapolis, Md., was renamed the U.S. Naval Academy in 1850. A four-year course was adopted a year later. The "Yard," as the campus is referred to, blends French Renaissance and modern architecture with many new academic, athletic, and laboratory facilities.

Eighteen majors are offered in engineering, science, mathematics, social sciences, and the humanities. Graduates are awarded the bachelor of science or bachelor of science in engineering and are commissioned as officers in the U.S. Navy or Marine Corps.

A nomination is required in order to receive an appointment. You can apply to Congressmen, Senators, and the Vice President for a nomination.

To have basic eligibility for admission, candidates must be citizens of the U.S., of good moral charac-

ter, at least 17 and not more than 23 years of age on July 1 of their entering year, unmarried, not pregnant, and without legal obligation to dependents.

Tuition, board, lodging, and medical and dental care are provided. Midshipmen receive $558.04 a month for books, uniforms, and personal needs. Upon being commissioned as an Ensign in the Navy or a Second Lieutenant in the Marine Corps, the commitment is at least 5 years' active duty. Officers pursuing aviation typically are required to serve 8–9 years depending on the length of aviation training and aircraft type.

For general information or answers to specific questions, write: Director of Candidate Guidance, U.S. Naval Academy, Annapolis, MD 21402-5018, or call 1-800-638-9156.

U.S. Air Force Academy

The bill establishing the U.S. Air Force Academy was signed by President Eisenhower on April 1, 1954. The first class of 306 cadets was sworn in on July 11, 1955, at Lowry Air Force Base, Denver, Colo., the academy's temporary location. The Cadet Wing moved into the academy's permanent home north of Colorado Springs, Colo., in 1958.

Cadets receive four years of academic, military, and physical education to prepare them for leadership as officers in the air force. The academy is authorized a total of 4,000 cadets. Each new class averages 1,200. The candidates for the academy must be at least 17 and not have passed their 23rd birthday on July 1 of the year for which they enter the academy, must be a U.S. citizen, unmarried, have no dependents, be of good moral character, and be able to meet the mental and physical requirements. International students authorized admission are exempt from the U.S. citizenship requirement.

Cadets receive their entire education at government expense and, in addition, receive a monthly salary of $558.00 to pay for supplies, clothing, and personal expenses. Prior to admission, appointees deposit $2,500 to help defray the initial cost of uniforms, a personal computer, and supplies. Upon completion of the four-year program, leading to a bachelor of science degree, a cadet who meets the qualifications is commissioned a second lieutenant in the U.S. Air Force. For details on admissions, call 1-800-443-9266, or write: HQ USAFA/RRS, 2304 Cadet Drive, Suite 200, USAF Academy, Colorado Springs, CO 80840-5025.

U.S. Coast Guard Academy

The U.S. Coast Guard Academy is the only one of the four armed forces service academies that offers appointments based solely on the basis of an annual nationwide competition, with no congressional appointments or geographical quotas. Competition is open to all U.S. citizens who have reached their 17th but not their 22nd birthday by July 1 of the entering year. There is no fee to apply, but candidates who are offered and accept an appointment to the Academy must pay an entrance fee of $3,000. Cadets receive a full scholarship including room and

---

Service Academy Web Sites

U.S. Military Academy: www.usma.edu
U.S. Air Force Academy: www.usafa.af.mil
U.S. Naval Academy: www.nadn.navy.mil
U.S. Coast Guard Academy:
  www.cga.edu
U.S. Merchant Marine Academy: www.usmma.edu

Military & Veterans Web Sites

U.S. Air Force: www.af.mil
U.S. Army: www.army.mil
U.S. Navy: www.navy.mil
MarineLINK: www.usmc.mil
U.S. Coast Guard: www.uscg.mil
DefenseLink (DOD): www.defenselink.mil
Military Woman:
    www.wimsa.org (not a DOD or armed forces site)
Selective Service System: www.sss.gov
Department of Veterans Affairs (VA):
    www.va.gov
BosniaLINK: www.dtic.mil/bosnia/index.html
Gulf War Veterans: www.gulfweb.org
Vietnam Veterans: www.vva.org
WWII U.S. Veterans: ww2.vet.org
Korea War Veterans Memorial:
    www.nps.gov/kwvm/index2.htm
Medal of Honor Museum:
    www.ngeorgia.com/history/sites/mohm.htm
American Legion: www.legion.org
Air America: www.air-america.org
North Atlantic Treaty Organization (NATO):
    www.nato.int

board. In addition, they receive a monthly allowance of approximately $600 to cover the costs of uniforms, textbooks, a new laptop, and other expenses.

Upon graduation, there is a 5-year commitment to serve as a commissioned Coast Guard officer, the first two years of which are on a Coast Guard cutter.

A viewbook or video can be obtained by writing to Director of Admission, U.S. Coast Guard Academy, 15 Mohegan Avenue, New London, CT 06320, or by calling 1-800-883-8724 or 860-444-8500.

U.S. Merchant Marine Academy

The U.S. Merchant Marine Academy, situated at Kings Point, N.Y., on the north shore of Long Island, was dedicated September 30, 1943. It is maintained by the Department of Transportation under direction of the Maritime Administration.

The academy has a complement of approximately 950 men and women representing every state, D.C., the Canal Zone, Puerto Rico, Guam, American Samoa, and the Virgin Islands. It is also authorized to admit up to 12 candidates from the Western Hemisphere and 30 other foreign students at any one time.

Candidates are nominated by senators and members of the House of Representatives. Nominations to the academy are governed by a state and territory quota system based on population and the results of the College Entrance Examination Board tests.

A candidate must be a citizen not less than 17 and not yet 25 years of age by July 1 of the year in which admission is sought.

The course is four years and includes one year of practical training aboard a merchant ship. Study includes marine engineering, navigation, satellite navigation and communications, electricity, ship construction, naval science and tactics, economics, business, languages, history, etc.

Upon completion of the course of study, a graduate receives a bachelor of science degree, a license as a merchant marine officer (issued by the U.S. Coast Guard), and a commission as an ensign in the Naval Reserve.

For additional information, write to Admissions Office, U.S. Merchant Marine Academy, 300 Steamboat Rd., Kings Point, NY, 11024, or call 516-773-5000.

The National Guard

The National Guard consists of citizen-soldiers and airmen who serve on both a federal and a state level. The Army National Guard has units in 2,700 communities in all 50 states, the District of Columbia, Guam, Puerto Rico, and the Virgin Islands. The Air National Guard has 88 flying units at more than 170 installations nationwide. National Guard units are organized, trained, and equipped to the same standards as the U.S. Army and the U.S. Air Force.

The National Guard has two roles—one as part of the nation's military force and the other for state emergencies and community support missions. This dual state/federal role for the National Guard is based on a Constitutional mandate. The relationship is unique and sets the National Guard apart from other military reserve forces.

Currently, the Army National Guard, 367,000 strong, makes up more than one-half of the total army's ground combat forces and one-third of its support forces. Air National Guard units, with a total strength of 109,000, are closely integrated with the U.S. Air Force and perform worldwide operations on a daily basis. ◻

Female Military Personnel on Active Duty by Grade, September 1998

Rank/Grade	Army	Air Force	Navy	Marine Corps	Total
Total officers	10,367	11,971	7,777	854	30,969
Total enlisted	60,787	53,542	42,261	8,928	165,518
Cadets & midshipmen	624	653	656	—	1,933
Grand total	71,778	66,166	50,694	9,782	198,420

Source: Department of Defense.

Female Military Personnel on Active Duty, 1970–1995

Year	Army	% of all personnel	Air Force	% of all personnel	Navy	% of all personnel	Marine Corps	% of all personnel	Total	% of all personnel
1970	16,724	1.3%	13,654	1.7%	8,683	1.3%	2,418	0.9%	41,479	1.4%
1980	69,338	8.9	60,394	10.8	34,980	6.6	6,706	3.6	171,418	8.4
1985	79,247	3.7	70,061	11.6	52,603	9.2	9,695	4.9	211,606	9.8
1989	86,494	n/a	77,103	n/a	59,518	n/a	9,708	n/a	232,823	n/a
1990	83,621	11.4	74,134	13.9	59,907	10.3	9,356	4.8	227,018	11.1
1991	80,306	11.3	72,436	14.2	59,391	10.4	9,005	4.6	221,138	11.1
1992	73,430	12.0	68,789	14.6	59,305	10.9	8,524	4.6	210,048	11.6
1993	71,328	12.5	66,732	15.0	57,601	11.3	7,845	4.4	203,506	11.9
1994	69,878	12.9	66,314	15.6	55,825	11.9	7,671	4.4	199,688	12.4
1995	68,046	13.4	64,147	16.0	55,830	12.8	8,093	4.6	196,116	12.9

Source: Department of Defense.

Veterans of U.S. Wars and Their Dependents
(on the VA Compensation and Pension Rolls as of July 1, 1998)

As of July 1, 1997, there were approximately 25.6 million veterans living in the United States. Nearly 80 of every 100 living veterans served during a period when the U.S. was involved in an armed conflict. Almost one-third of the nation's population—approximately 70 million veterans, their dependents, and survivors of deceased veterans—are potentially eligible for VA benefits and services.

Veterans' benefits have existed since the origins of the nation. The last dependent of a Revolutionary War veteran died in 1911; the War of 1812's last dependent died in 1946; the Mexican War's in 1962. Some 1,131 children and widows of Spanish-American War veterans are receiving VA benefits. There are in fact still a few surviving widows and children of Civil War and Indian War veterans who draw VA benefits.

	Veterans	Children	Parents	Surviving spouses
Civil War	—	15	—	2
Indian Wars	—	1	—	2
Spanish-American War	—	334	—	694
Mexican Border	13	26	—	301
World War I	779	7,021	2	46,311
World War II	797,996	20,236	3,022	298,688
Korean Conflict	272,979	4,592	2,446	67,128
Vietnam Era	815,380	16,787	7,692	102,752
Persian Gulf War	231,271	6,601	345	4,368
Total	2,666,029[1]	65,047[2]	16,562[3]	557,653[4]

1. Includes 547,608 peacetime veterans with service between January 31, 1955, and August 5, 1964; peacetime veterans with service beginning after May 7, 1975, and all other peacetime periods; and 3 World War I Retired Emergency Officers. 2. Includes 9,434 children of deceased peacetime veterans. 3. Includes 3,055 parents of deceased peacetime veterans. 4. Includes 37,407 surviving spouses of deceased peacetime veterans. *Source:* Department of Veterans Affairs.

Last Living Veterans of America's Wars

American Revolution (1775–1784)
- Last veteran, Daniel F. Bakeman, died 4/5/1869, age 109
- Last widow, Catherine S. Damon, died 11/11/06, age 92
- Last dependent, Phoebe M. Palmeter, died 4/25/11, age 90

War of 1812 (1812–1815)
- Last veteran, Hiram Cronk, died 5/13/05, age 105
- Last widow, Carolina King, died 6/28/36, age unknown
- Last dependent, Esther A. H. Morgan, died 3/12/46, age 89

Indian Wars (c. 1817–1898)
- Last veteran, Fredrak Fraske, died 6/18/73, age 101

Mexican War (1846–1848)
- Last veteran, Owen Thomas Edgar, died 9/3/29, age 98
- Last widow, Lena James Theobald, died 6/20/63, age 89
- Last dependent, Jesse G. Bivens, died 11/1/62, age 94

Civil War (1861–1865)
- Last Union veteran, Albert Woolson, died 8/2/56, age 109
- Last Confederate veteran, John Salling, died 3/16/58, age 112

Spanish-American War (1898–1902)
- Last veteran, Nathan E. Cook, died 9/10/92, age 106

Active Military Duty Personnel, 1940–1999[1]

Year	Army[2]	Air Force[2, 3]	Navy	Marine Corps	Total
1940	269,023		160,997	28,345	458,365
1945	8,266,373		3,319,586	469,925	12,055,884
1950	593,167	411,277	380,739	74,279	1,459,462
1955	1,109,296	959,946	660,695	205,170	2,935,107
1960	873,078	814,752	616,987	170,621	2,475,438
1965	969,066	824,662	669,985	190,213	2,653,926
1970	1,322,548	791,349	691,126	259,737	3,064,760
1975	784,333	612,751	535,085	195,951	2,128,120
1980	777,036	557,969	527,153	188,469	2,050,627
1985	780,787	601,515	570,705	198,025	2,151,032
1990	732,403	535,233	579,417	196,652	2,043,705
1991	710,821	510,432	570,262	194,040	1,985,555
1992	610,450	470,315	541,883	184,529	1,807,177
1993	572,423	444,351	509,950	178,379	1,705,103
1994	541,343	426,327	468,662	174,158	1,610,490
1995	508,559	400,409	434,617	174,639	1,518,224
1996	491,103	389,001	416,735	174,883	1,471,722
1997	491,707	377,385	395,564	173,906	1,438,562
1998	483,880	367,470	382,338	173,142	1,406,830
1999[4]	473,595	363,449	370,343	172,369	1,379,756

1. Military personnel on extended or continuous active duty. Excludes reserves on active duty for training. Prior year totals have been corrected. 2. Represents "Command Strength" prior to June 30, 1956. 3. Army Air Forces and its predecessors for period prior to September 18, 1947. 4. Totals as of September 30, except 1999 totals, are for January 31. Figures for 1998 and 1999 include cadets-midshipmen. *Source:* Department of Defense.

The Medal of Honor

Often called the Congressional Medal of Honor, it is the nation's highest military award for "uncommon valor" by men and women in the armed forces. It is given for actions that are above and beyond the call of duty in combat against an armed enemy. The medal was first awarded by the army on March 25, 1863. More than 3,400 men and one woman have been awarded the medal.

Recipients of the medal are awarded $400 per month for life, a right to burial at Arlington National Cemetery, admission for them or their children to a service academy (if they qualify and quotas permit), and free travel on government aircraft to almost anywhere in the world, on a space-available basis.

Medal of Honor Recipients

	Total[1]	Army	Navy	Marines	Air Force	Coast Guard
Civil War	1,520	1,195	308	17	—	—
Indian Wars (1861–1898)	428	428	—	—	—	—
Korea (1871)	15	—	9	6	—	—
Spanish-American War	109	30	64	15	—	—
Philippines/Samoa	91	70	12	9	—	—
Boxer Rebellion	59	4	22	33	—	—
Veracruz (1914)	55	—	46	9	—	—
Haiti (1915)	6	—	—	6	—	—
Dominican Republic	3	—	—	3	—	—
Haiti (1919–1920)	2	—	—	2	—	—
Nicaragua (1927–1933)	2	—	—	2	—	—
Peacetime (1865–1870)	12	—	12	—	—	—
Peacetime (1871–1898)	103	—	101	2	—	—
Peacetime (1899–1911)	51	1	48	2	—	—
Peacetime (1915–1916)	8	—	8	—	—	—
Peacetime (1920–1940)	18	2	15	1	—	—
World War I	124	96	21	7	—	—
World War II	440	301	57	81	—	1
Korean War	131	78	7	42	4	—
Vietnam War	239	155	15	57	12	—
Somalia (1993)	2	2	—	—	—	—
Unknown Soldiers	9					
Total	3,427	2,362	745	294	16	1

1. These totals reflect the total number of Medals of Honor awarded. Nineteen (19) men received a second award. The total number of Medal of Honor recipients is 3,408. As of May 13, 1997, there are 169 living Medal of Honor recipients. *Source:* The Congressional Medal of Honor Society, Mt. Pleasant, S.C.

American Prisoners of War

Congress defines a former prisoner of war as a person who, while serving on active military, naval, or air service, was forcibly detained or interned in the line of duty by an enemy government or a hos- tile force, during a period of war or in situations comparable to war. Less than half (40%) of the Americans held prisoner in the last six conflicts are now living.

	Total	WWI	WWII	Korea	Vietnam	Persian Gulf	Somalia
Captured and interned	142,257	4,120	130,201	7,140	772	23	1
Returned to U.S. military control	125,202	3,973	116,129	4,418	658	23	1
Refused repatriation	21	0	0	21	0	0	0
Died while POW	17,034	147	14,072	2,701	144	0	0
Alive, Jan. 1998	55,999	5	52,531	2,814	625	23	1

Source: U.S. Department of Veterans Affairs

U.S. Casualties in the Major Wars

War	Branch of service	Numbers engaged	Battle deaths	Other deaths	Total deaths	Wounds not mortal	Total casualties[1]
Revolutionary War	Army	n.a.	4,044	n.a.	n.a.	6,004	n.a.
(1775 to 1783)	Navy	n.a.	342	n.a.	n.a.	114	n.a.
	Marines	n.a.	49	n.a.	n.a.	70	n.a.
	Total	**n.a.**	**4,435**	**n.a.**	**n.a.**	**6,188**	**n.a.**
War of 1812	Army	n.a.	1,950	n.a.	n.a.	4,000	n.a.
(1812 to 1815)	Navy	n.a.	265	n.a.	n.a.	439	n.a.
	Marines	n.a.	45	n.a.	n.a.	66	n.a.
	Total	**286,730**	**2,260**	**n.a.**	**n.a.**	**4,505**	**n.a.**
Mexican War	Army	n.a.	1,721	11,550	13,271	4,102	17,373
(1846 to 1848)	Navy	n.a.	1	n.a.	n.a.	3	n.a.
	Marines	n.a.	11	n.a.	n.a.	47	n.a.
	Total	**78,718**	**1,733**	**n.a.**	**n.a.**	**4,152**	**n.a.**
Civil War	Army	2,128,948	138,154	221,374	359,528	280,040	639,568
(1861 to 1865)[2]	Navy	84,415	2,112	2,411	4,523	1,710	6,233
	Marines	148	148	312	460	131	591
	Total	**2,213,363**	**140,414**	**224,097**	**364,511**	**281,881**	**646,392**
Spanish-American War	Army	280,564	369	2,061	2,430	1,594	4,024
(1898)	Navy	22,875	10	0	10	47	57
	Marines	3,321	6	0	6	21	27
	Total	**306,760**	**385**	**2,061**	**2,446**	**1,662**	**4,108**
World War I	Army	4,057,101	50,510	55,868	106,378	193,663	300,041
(1917 to 1918)	Navy	599,051	431	6,856	7,287	819	8,106
	Marines	78,839	2,461	390	2,851	9,520	12,371
	Total	**4,734,991**	**53,402**	**63,114**	**116,516**	**204,002**	**320,518**
World War II	Army[3]	11,260,000	234,874	83,400	318,274	565,861	884,135
(1941 to 1946)	Navy	4,183,466	36,950	25,664	62,614	37,778	100,392
	Marines	669,100	19,733	4,778	24,511	67,207	91,718
	Total	**16,112,566**	**291,557**	**113,842**	**405,399**	**670,846**	**1,076,245**
Korean War	Army	2,834,000	27,709	2,452	30,161	77,596	107,757
(1950 to 1953)	Navy	1,177,000	475	173	648	1,576	2,224
	Marines	424,000	4,270	339	4,609	23,744	28,353
	Air Force	1,285,000	1,198	298	1,496	368	1,864
	Total	**5,720,000**	**33,652**	**3,262**	**36,914**	**103,284**	**140,198**
War in Southeast Asia[4]	Army	4,368,000	30,914	7,275	38,189	96,802	134,991
	Navy	1,842,000	1,631	928	2,559	4,178	6,737
	Marines	794,000	13,082	1,754	14,836	51,392	66,228
	Air Force	1,740,000	1,739	844	2,583	931	3,514
	Total	**8,744,000**	**47,366**	**10,801**	**58,167**	**153,303**	**211,470**

See p. 391 for post-Vietnam casualties. NOTES: All data are subject to revision. For wars before World War I, information represents best data from available records. However, due to incomplete records and possible difference in usage of terminology, reporting systems, etc., figures should be considered estimates. n.a. = not available. 1. Excludes captured or interned and missing in action who were subsequently returned to military control. 2. Union forces only. Totals should probably be somewhat larger as data or disposition of prisoners are far from complete. Final Confederate deaths, based on incomplete returns, were 133,821, to which should be added 26,000–31,000 personnel who died in Union prisons. 178,975 blacks served in the Union Army. 2,894 were killed in battle or mortally wounded, 33,953 died from other causes including 29,658 deaths from disease. 3. Army data include air force. 4. Vietnam figures provided by the U.S. Center of Military History, Reference Division, Washington, D.C., February 1994. Navy figures exclude coast guard, in which there were 5 battle deaths. *Source:* Department of Defense.

Casualties in World War I

Country	Total mobilized forces	Killed or died[1]	Wounded	Prisoners or missing	Total casualties
Austria-Hungary	7,800,000	1,200,000	3,620,000	2,200,000	7,020,000
Belgium	267,000	13,716	44,686	34,659	93,061
British Empire[2]	8,904,467	908,371	2,090,212	191,652	3,190,235
Bulgaria	1,200,000	87,500	152,390	27,029	266,919
France[2]	8,410,000	1,357,800	4,266,000	537,000	6,160,800
Germany	11,000,000	1,773,700	4,216,058	1,152,800	7,142,558
Greece	230,000	5,000	21,000	1,000	27,000
Italy	5,615,000	650,000	947,000	600,000	2,197,000
Japan	800,000	300	907	3	1,210
Montenegro	50,000	3,000	10,000	7,000	20,000
Portugal	100,000	7,222	13,751	12,318	33,291
Romania	750,000	335,706	120,000	80,000	535,706
Russia	12,000,000	1,700,000	4,950,000	2,500,000	9,150,000
Serbia	707,343	45,000	133,148	152,958	331,106
Turkey	2,850,000	325,000	400,000	250,000	975,000
United States	4,734,991	116,516	204,002	—	320,518

1. Includes deaths from all causes. 2. Official figures. NOTE: For additional U.S. figures, *see* the table U.S. Casualties in the Major Wars. *Source:* Department of Defense.

Casualties in World War II

Country	Men in war	Battle deaths	Wounded
Australia	1,000,000	26,976	180,864
Austria	800,000	280,000	350,117
Belgium	625,000	8,460	55,513[1]
Brazil[2]	40,334	943	4,222
Bulgaria	339,760	6,671	21,878
Canada	1,086,343[7]	42,042[7]	53,145
China[3]	17,250,521	1,324,516	1,762,006
Czechoslovakia	—	6,683[4]	8,017
Denmark	—	4,339	—
Finland	500,000	79,047	50,000
France	—	201,568	400,000
Germany	20,000,000	3,250,000[4]	7,250,000
Greece	—	17,024	47,290
Hungary	—	147,435	89,313
India	2,393,891	32,121	64,354
Italy	3,100,000	149,496[4]	66,716
Japan	9,700,000	1,270,000	140,000
Netherlands	280,000	6,500	2,860
New Zealand	194,000	11,625[4]	17,000
Norway	75,000	2,000	—
Poland	—	664,000	530,000
Romania	650,000[5]	350,000[6]	—
South Africa	410,056	2,473	—
U.S.S.R.	—	6,115,000[4]	14,012,000
United Kingdom	5,896,000	357,116[4]	369,267
United States	16,112,566	291,557	670,846
Yugoslavia	3,741,000	305,000	425,000

1. Civilians only. 2. Army and navy figures. 3. Figures cover period July 7, 1937–Sept. 2, 1945, and concern only Chinese regular troops. They do not include casualties suffered by guerrillas and local military corps. 4. Deaths from all causes. 5. Against Soviet Russia; 385,847 against Nazi Germany. 6. Against Soviet Russia; 169,822 against Nazi Germany. 7. National Defense Ctr., Canadian Forces Hq., Director of History. NOTE: The figures in this table are unofficial estimates obtained from various sources.

Merchant Marine Casualties in World War II

In 1988, the U.S. government conferred official veteran status on those who served aboard oceangoing merchant ships in World War II. The officers and crews played a key role in transporting the troops and war matériel that enabled the United States and its allies to defeat the Axis powers.

During the war, merchant seamen died as a result of enemy attacks at a rate that proportionately exceeded all branches of the armed services, with the exception of the U.S. Marine Corps.

Enemy action sank more than 700 U.S.-flag merchant ships and claimed the lives of over 6,000 civilian seafarers. Untold thousands of additional seamen were wounded or injured during these attacks, and nearly 600 were made prisoners of war.

For international military affairs, *see* pp. 164–165.

U.S. Postal Rates and Fees

Domestic Rates as of Jan. 10, 1999

Postal Information Web Sites

United States Postal Service:
http://www.usps.gov/postofc/welcome.htm
ZIP Code Look Up: http://www.usps.gov/ncsc/
U.S. Postal Service Rate Calculators:
http://www.usps.gov/business/calcs.htm

First-Class Mail

Single-Piece Letter/Flat Rates

1st ounce	$0.33
Each additional ounce	0.22

Weight not over (oz.)	Rate	Weight not over (oz.)	Rate
1*	$0.33	9	$2.09
2	0.55	10	2.31
3	0.77	11	2.53
4	0.99	12	2.75
5	1.21	13	2.97
6	1.43	Over 13 ounces, see	
7	1.65	Priority Mail.	
8	1.87		

*Nonstandard surcharge may apply to pieces weighing 1 ounce or less based on size.

Card Rates

Single postal card sold by United States Postal Service	$0.20
Double postal card sold by USPS	0.40
Single postcard (commercial)	0.20

Postcard Dimensions: Not larger than 4¼ by 6 inches by 0.016 inch thick. Not smaller than 3½ by 5 inches by 0.007 inch thick.

Periodicals

Only publishers and registered news agents approved for periodicals mailing privileges may mail at periodicals rates. Publications mailed by the public are charged at the applicable Express Mail, Priority Mail, single-piece First-Class, standard "A," or standard "B" rates.

Standard "A"

Used primarily by retailers, catalogers, and other advertisers to promote products and services. See postmaster for details. **Use**—For mailing certain items—circulars, books, catalogs, other printed matter, merchandise, seeds, cuttings, bulbs, and plants—weighing less than 16 ounces.

Express Mail

Express Mail is the postal service's fastest service. Next-day delivery by 12 noon to most destinations. Delivered 365 days a year with no extra charge for Saturday, Sunday, or holiday delivery. All packages must use an Express Mail label. Items may weigh up to 70 pounds and measure up to 108 inches in combined length and girth. Call 1-800-222-1811 for delivery information between ZIP codes.

Features—Express Mail envelopes, labels, and boxes are available, at no additional charge, at post offices or by calling 1-800-222-1811.

Post Office to Addressee Service

Up to 8 ounces	$11.75
Over 8 ounces, up to 2 pounds	15.75
Up to 3 pounds	17.25
Up to 4 pounds	19.40
Up to 5 pounds	21.55
Up to 6 pounds	25.40
Up to 7 pounds	26.45
Over 7 pounds, see postmaster.	

Flat-Rate Envelope—Post Office to Addressee Service

$15.00, regardless of weight or destination for matter sent in a flat-rate envelope provided by the Postal Service.

Priority Mail

Priority Mail offers two-day service to most domestic destinations. Items may weigh up to 70 pounds and measure up to 108 inches in combined length and girth.

Delivery confirmation for Priority Mail has been introduced. For mailers who apply their own barcodes and access postal information systems for electronic confirmation, the service is free. Manual service is $0.35.

Features—Priority Mail envelopes, labels, and boxes are available, at no additional charge, at post offices or by calling 1-800-222-1811.

Single-Piece Rates[1]

Up to 2 pounds	$3.20
Up to 3 pounds	4.30
Up to 4 pounds	5.40
Up to 5 pounds	6.50
Over 5 pounds, see postmaster.	

1. A parcel weighing less than 15 pounds but measuring more than 84 inches in length and girth combined is chargeable with a minimum rate equal to that for a 15-pound parcel for the zone to which it is addressed.

Flat-Rate Envelope

$3.00, regardless of weight or destination, for matter sent in a flat-rate envelope provided by the Postal Service.

Standard "B"

For mailing circulars, books, catalogs, other printed matter, and packages weighing 16 ounces or more. Enclosed or attached First-Class Mail is charged at First-Class rates. Packages may weigh up to 70 pounds and measure up to 108 inches in combined length and girth.

Parcel Post Zone Rates

For rates priced by distance and weight, see postmaster.

Special Services (Domestic Mail)

Certificate of Mailing

Proves that an item was mailed. Must be purchased at time of mailing. No record kept at the post office.

Fee, in addition to postage—$0.60

Certified Mail

Provides a mailing receipt, and a record is kept at the recipient's post office. A return receipt can also be purchased for an additional fee. Available only with First-Class and Priority Mail.

Fee, in addition to postage—$1.40

Insurance

Provides coverage against loss or damage. Coverage up to $600.00 for standard "A" and standard "B" mail as well as standard "A" and standard "B" matter mailed at Priority Mail or First-Class Mail rate. Insurance up to $25,000 can be purchased by using Registered Mail. Do not insure a package for more than its value.

Liability	Fee, in addition to postage
$.01 to $50.00	$0.75
$50.01 to $100.00	1.60
$100.01 to $200.00	2.50
$200.01 to $300.00	3.40
$300.01 to $400.00	4.30
$400.01 to $500.00	5.20
$500.01 to $600.00	6.10

Money Orders

Provides safe transmission of money. Available in amounts up to $700.00.

Fee, in addition to postage—$0.80

Registered Mail

Provides maximum protection and security for valuables. Available only for Priority Mail and First-Class Mail. May be combined with COD, Restricted Delivery, or Return Receipt. Additional postal insurance available.

	Declared Value	Fee, in addition to postage
Without Insurance	$0.00	$6.00
With Insurance	$0.01 to $100	6.20
	$100.01 to $500.00	6.75
	$500.01 to $1,000.00	7.30
	$1,000.01 to $2,000.00	7.85

For higher values, consult your postmaster.

Restricted Delivery

Available only for Certified Mail, COD, Insured Mail for more than $50.00, or Registered Mail.

Fee, in addition to postage—$2.75

Return Receipt

Available only for Express Mail, Certified Mail, COD, Insured Mail for more than $50.00, or Registered Mail.

Requested at time of mailing:

Showing to whom (signature) and date delivered	$1.25
Showing to whom (signature), date, and addressee's address	1.50

Requested after mailing:

Showing to whom (signature) and date delivered	7.00

Special Delivery

Available for all classes except Express Mail. Provides preferential handling to the extent practicable in dispatch, transportation, and expedited delivery at the destination.

	Fee, in addition to postage		
Class of mail	2 lb. or less	Over 2 lb., but not over 10 lb.	Over 10 lb.
First-Class & Priority Mail	$ 9.95	$10.35	$11.15
Other classes	10.45	11.25	12.10

Collect on Delivery (COD)

Allows mailers to collect the price of goods and/or postage on merchandise ordered by addressee when it is delivered. Fees include insurance. Maximum amount $600.00; see postmaster for details.

Sizes for Domestic Mail

Mail must meet these standards:
- Thickness—No less than 0.007 inch thick. Pieces that are ¼ inch thick or less must be at least 3½ inches high, 5 inches long, and rectangular in shape.
- Combined length and girth—No more than 108 inches.
- Weight—No more than 70 pounds.

Keys and identification devices are exempted from these requirements.

Additional standards apply to bulk mail and mail addressed to APOs and FPOs.

The Mail-Order Merchandise Rule

The mail-order rule adopted by the Federal Trade Commission in October 1975 provides that when you order by mail:
- You must receive the merchandise when the seller says you will.
- If you are not promised delivery within a certain time period, the seller must ship the merchandise to you no later than 30 days after your order comes in.
- If you don't receive it shortly after that 30-day period, you can cancel your order and get your money back.

ZIP Codes

The ZIP code was instituted in 1963 and allows for electronic processing and delivery of mail. An envelope that does not include a ZIP Code in the delivery address must be manually sorted, which increases the cost of sorting the mail and causes mail to be delayed en route to the delivery address. ZIP Code directories are available for use or sale at your local post office, or you can look up ZIP codes on-line: www.usps.gov/ncsc/.

In 1983, the Postal Service began to use an expanded ZIP Code called ZIP+4. It is composed of the original five-digit code plus a four-digit add-on. The four-digit add-on number identifies a geographic segment within the five-digit delivery area such as a city block, an office building, an individual high-volume receiver of mail, or any other unit that would aid efficient mail sorting and delivery.

International Postal Rates
As of August 1999

Letters and Letter Packages— Airmail Rates
All countries except Canada and Mexico

Weight not over (oz.)		Weight not over (oz.)	
0.5	$0.60	9.0	$ 7.40
1.0	1.00	9.5	7.80
1.5	1.40	10.0	8.20
2.0	1.80	10.5	8.60
2.5	2.20	11.0	9.00
3.0	2.60	11.5	9.40
3.5	3.00	12.0	9.80
4.0	3.40	12.5	10.20
4.5	3.80	13.0	10.60
5.0	4.20	13.5	11.00
5.5	4.60	14.0	11.40
6.0	5.00	14.5	11.80
6.5	5.40	15.0	12.20
7.0	5.80	15.5	12.60
7.5	6.20	16.0	13.00
8.0	6.60	16.5	13.40
8.5	7.00		

See postmaster for weights up to 4 lb. Maximum weight: 64 ounces.

Letters and Letter Packages— Canada and Mexico

Weight not over		Can-ada[1]	Mex-ico	Weight not over		Can-ada[1]	Mex-ico
(lb.)	(oz.)			(lb.)	(oz.)		
0	0.5	$0.48	$0.40	0	10	$2.39	$ 4.06
0	1	0.55	0.46	0	11	2.59	4.46
0	1.5	0.67	0.66	0	12	2.79	4.86
0	2	0.76	0.86	1	0	3.59	6.46
0	3	1.00	1.26	1	8	4.52	9.66
0	4	1.20	1.66	2	0	5.44	12.86
0	5	1.40	2.06	2	8	6.36	16.06
0	6	1.60	2.46	3	0	7.29	19.26
0	7	1.80	2.86	3	8	8.21	22.46
0	8	2.00	3.26	4	0	9.14	25.66
0	9	2.19	3.66				

1. A 4-pound maximum applies except for registered items sent to Canada. Canada-bound registered items may weigh up to 66 pounds. For registered items weighing over 4 pounds, the rate is $1.85 for each additional pound up to the 66-pound limit.

Postcards and Postal Rates: Canada—$0.45; Mexico— $0.40; all others—$0.55

All-Time Top 10 Most Popular Commemorative Stamps

Issue	No. saved (millions)
Elvis '93	124.0
Wildflowers '92	76.2
Rock and Roll '93	75.8
Civil War '95	46.6
Legends of the West '94	46.5
Marilyn Monroe '95	46.3
Bugs Bunny '97	45.3
Summer Olympics '92	39.6
The World of Dinosaurs	38.5
Centennial Olympic Games '96	38.1

Source: U.S.P.S., 1998. Popularity of stamps is measured by number saved, not used.

Top 10 Dog Bite Cities for Postal Workers, FY 1998

City	Dog bites
1. Houston	49
2. Chicago	37
3. Miami	35
4. Los Angeles	32
5. Brooklyn	22
6. Cleveland	20
7. Buffalo, Jamaica, New York[1]	17
8. Dallas, Detroit[1]	16
9. Richmond, San Antonio, San Francisco[1]	15
10. Baltimore, Boston, Phoenix[1]	14

1. ties. *Source:* U.S.P.S., 1999. A total of 2,541 postal workers were bitten by dogs in FY1998.

State Abbreviations and State Postal Codes

State	Abbreviation	Postal code	State	Abbreviation	Postal code	State	Abbreviation	Postal code
Alabama	Ala.	AL	Kentucky	Ky.	KY	Ohio	Ohio	OH
Alaska	Alaska	AK	Louisiana	La.	LA	Oklahoma	Okla.	OK
Arizona	Ariz.	AZ	Maine	Maine	ME	Oregon	Ore.	OR
Arkansas	Ark.	AR	Maryland	Md.	MD	Pennsylvania	Pa.	PA
California	Calif.	CA	Massachusetts	Mass.	MA	Puerto Rico	P.R.	PR
Colorado	Colo.	CO	Michigan	Mich.	MI	Rhode Island	R.I.	RI
Connecticut	Conn.	CT	Minnesota	Minn.	MN	South Carolina	S.C.	SC
Delaware	Del.	DE	Mississippi	Miss.	MS	South Dakota	S.D.	SD
Dist. of Columbia	D.C.	DC	Missouri	Mo.	MO	Tennessee	Tenn.	TN
Florida	Fla.	FL	Montana	Mont.	MT	Texas	Tex.	TX
Georgia	Ga.	GA	Nebraska	Nebr.	NE	Utah	Utah	UT
Guam	Guam	GU	Nevada	Nev.	NV	Vermont	Vt.	VT
Hawaii	Hawaii	HI	New Hampshire	N.H.	NH	Virginia	Va.	VA
Idaho	Idaho	ID	New Jersey	N.J.	NJ	Virgin Islands	V.I.	VI
Illinois	Ill.	IL	New Mexico	N.M.	NM	Washington	Wash.	WA
Indiana	Ind.	IN	New York	N.Y.	NY	West Virginia	W.Va.	WV
Iowa	Iowa	IA	North Carolina	N.C.	NC	Wisconsin	Wis.	WI
Kansas	Kans.	KS	North Dakota	N.D.	ND	Wyoming	Wyo.	WY

Should All Be Forgiven?

Giving up that grudge could be good for your health. Researchers are pioneering a science of redemption based on an old form of grace

By DAVID VAN BIEMA TIME

Ask the prodigal son's brother: sometimes the quality of mercy is strained. Of all acknowledged good acts, forgiveness is the one we are most suspicious of. "To err is human, to forgive, supine," punned S. J. Perelman. In a country where the death penalty has been a proven vote getter in recent years, forgiveness is often seen as effete and irresponsible. Sometimes it even seems to condone the offense, as noted centuries ago by Jewish sages:, "He that is merciful to the cruel will eventually be cruel to the innocent."

Out of the Confessional . . .

And yet despite every indignity and scoff, forgiveness does not just endure but thrives. There is not only a religious impetus to forgive but also therapeutic, social, and practical reasons to do so. This applies to victims of crimes as well as to those who must deal with the slings and arrows of more common misfortunes—unfaithfulness, betrayal, ungratefulness, and mere insult. In the past two years, scientists and sociologists have begun to extract forgiveness and the act of forgiving from the confines of the confessional, transforming it into the subject of quantifiable research. In one case, they have even systemized it as a 20-part "intervention" that they claim can be used to treat a number of anger-related ills in a totally secular context. In short, to forgive is no longer just divine.

"The field is just exploding" says Virginia psychologist Everett Worthington, director of the Templeton Foundation Campaign for Forgiveness Research. He should know. His organization, set up by mutual-fund magus Sir John Templeton, has distributed $5 million to scientists studying, among other things, forgiveness among chimpanzees and its physiological effects on the pulse and the sweat glands of humans. A number of psychotherapists are testifying that there is nothing like it for dissipating anger, mending marriages, and banishing depression. Just a few years ago, says Robert Enright, a psychology professor at the University of Wisconsin and a pioneer in the scientific study of forgiveness, most secularly inclined intellectuals "trashed it; they said, 'Only wimps forgive.'" But now, Enright says, "psychiatrists, M.D.s, scientists, lawyers, ministers, and social workers can all be on the same page. We are really on a roll."

. . . Into the Laboratory

Step into a forgiveness laboratory partly funded by a $75,000 Templeton grant. At Hope College in Holland, Mich., Charlotte van Oyen Witvliet puts electrodes on a young volunteer. In a moment he will think about a hurt that has been done him and then "actively rehearse" it for 16 seconds. At the sound of a tone, he will escalate his thoughts to "nursing a grudge" and making the offender feel horrible. Another beep will cue him to shift gears and "empathize with the offender." Finally, he will imagine ways to "wish that person well." Throughout the two-hour session, the four responses occur in different sequences, and Witvliet, a professor of psychology, will measure his heart rate, blood pressure, sweat, and muscle tension.

So far, she has studied 70 subjects, half of them men, half women. Witvliet finds "robust" physiological differences between nonforgiving and forgiving states. Subjects' cardiovascular systems inevitably labor when they remember the person who hurt them. But stress is "significantly greater" when they consider revenge rather than forgiveness. Witvliet suggests that we may be drawn to hold grudges "because that makes us feel like we are more in control and we are less sad." But interviews with her subjects indicate that they felt in even greater control when they tried to empathize with their offenders and enjoyed the greatest sense of power, well-being, and resolution when they managed to grant forgiveness. "If you are willing to exert the effort it takes to be forgiving, there are benefits both emotionally and physically," she concludes.

Evolutionary psychologist David Buss, a professor at the University of Texas in Austin, has pondered the sociobiological logic of forgiveness and concluded that at least in the realm of mating, men and women may be programmed to employ it differently. Males, he suggests, are less likely to forgive a fling because if the woman becomes pregnant, "a man doesn't want to be investing resources in other men's children." In contrast, a woman may be more forgiving of a man's one-time infidelity (assuming

The Unforgiven: A Time/CNN Poll

Would you forgive someone who:

	% FORGIVE	% NOT FORGIVE
Told lies about you?	73	24
Stole money from you?	67	31
Slapped or punched you in the face?	64	32
Held you up with a gun?	42	54
Murdered someone in your community?	33	59
Raped you?*	22	73
Raped a member of your family?	19	77
Murdered your child?	15	81

*asked of women only

From a telephone poll of 1,049 adult Americans taken on March 25, 1999 for TIME/CNN by Yankelovich Partners, Inc. Margin of error is ± 3%. "Not sures" omitted.

that he has already given her a child) but less forgiving of a long-term diversion of material or emotional resources to another woman or a second family. "From an evolutionary perspective," says Buss, "part of the reason a woman marries is to secure all the resources of a man for herself and her children."

A Spineless Nostrum?

For all its feel-good potential, however, forgiveness has more problematic reverberations than, say, Prozac. Can a woman's healing be helped by forgiving a physically abusive ex-husband who continues to savage her verbally among friends? What if they are still married and he is still beating her? Should the unrepentant be forgiven at all? Bruce Kittle, a Wisconsin pastor, warns of misuse: "In religious traditions, there can be a sense of revictimization. They say to themselves, Here I am, and my child has been killed, and my pastor during my grieving period says, Jesus says you need to forgive, and if you don't, you are a sinner."

The definitions of forgiveness are many, but most acknowledge that forgiveness involves a "giving up"

of something, whether it be anger, the right to vengeance or, say some skeptics, the memory of an event the way it really was. In *The Sunflower*, Nazi hunter Simon Wiesenthal asked whether it would be proper for a Jew in a slave-labor camp to grant forgiveness to a dying SS man begging absolution for earlier murders. As part of a symposium that is incorporated into the book, the writer Cynthia Ozick said absolutely not: "Forgiveness is pitiless. It forgets the victim. It blurs over suffering and death. It drowns the past. The face of forgiveness is mild, but how stony to the slaughtered . . . Let the SS man : . . go to hell." How-to books, therapy, and interventions may be useful in dealing with an unfaithful spouse, gossiping colleague, or even some cases of violence. But there are other practices—serial killing, torture, genocide—often regarded as unforgivable.

There are no easy answers to such objections. But for most of us, they will remain in the background so long as—during its journey from sacrament to science experiment to possible nostrum—forgiveness becomes neither a foregone conclusion nor an obligation, but remains a mystery within the heart of the forgiver.   □

Religious Population of the World, 1996
(in thousands)

Statistics of the world's religions are only very rough approximations. Aside from Christianity, few religions, if any, attempt to keep statistical records; and even Protestants and Catholics employ different methods of counting members.

Religion	Total	Percent distri-bution	Africa	Asia[1]	Latin America	North America	Europe[2]	Oceania
Total Religious Population[3]	**5,804,120**	**100.0%**	**748,130**	**3,513,218**	**490,444**	**295,677**	**727,678**	**28,973**
Christians (total)	1,955,229	33.7%	360,874	303,127	455,819	255,542	555,614	24,253
Roman Catholics	981,465	16.9%	125,376	94,250	408,968	75,398	269,021	8,452
Protestants	404,020	7.0%	114,726	45,326	34,816	121,361	79,534	8,257
Orthodox	218,350	3.8%	25,215	13,970	460	6,390	171,665	650
Anglicans	69,136	1.2%	27,200	650	1,089	6,300	28,357	5,540
Other Christians	282,258	4.9%	68,357	148,931	10,486	46,093	7,037	1,354
Muslims[4]	1,126,325	19.4%	308,660	778,362	1,356	5,530	32,032	385
Nonreligious[5]	886,929	15.3%	3,567	752,759	16,053	21,315	90,390	2,845
Hindus[6]	793,076	13.7%	1,986	786,991	760	1,365	1,650	323
Buddhists[7]	325,275	5.6%	38	321,985	569	920	1,563	200
Atheists[8]	222,195	3.8%	440	175,450	3,010	1,850	40,845	600
Chinese folk religionists[9]	220,971	3.8%	13	220,653	68	100	120	17
New Religionists[10]	106,016	1.8%	21	103,361	919	900	803	11
Ethnic Religionists	102,945	1.8%	70,250	30,350	1,042	45	1,150	108
Sikhs	19,508	0.3%	37	18,465	9	496	494	7
Jews	13,866	0.2%	165	4,257	1,084	5,836	2,432	92
Spiritists	10,293	0.2%	5	1,120	8,834	315	18	1
Baha'is	6,404	0.1%	1,923	3,230	722	357	95	77
Confucians	5,086	0.1%	1	5,050	3	27	5	1
Jains	4,920	0.1%	59	4,835	5	5	16	1
Shintoists	2,898	—	—	2,893	1	2	1	1
Other Religionists[11]	1,952	—	90	100	190	1,072	450	50
Parsees	191	—	2	185	1	1	1	1
Mandeans	45	—	—	45	—	—	—	—

1. Asia includes the former U.S.S.R. Central Asian republics. 2. Europe includes the Russian Federation, extending to its easternmost boundaries. 3. Total population figures are the U.N. medium variant figures for mid-1996. 4. Muslims: 83% Sunnis, 16% Shi'ites, 1% other. 5. Persons professing no religion, nonbelievers, agnostics, freethinkers, and formerly religious secularists. 6. Hindus: including 70% Vaishnavites, 25% Shaivites, 2% neo-Hindus and reform Hindus. 7. Buddhists: 56% Mahayana, 38% Theravada (Hinayana), and 6% Tantrayana (Lamaism). 8. Persons professing atheism, skepticism, disbelief, or antireligion (opposed to all religion). 9. Followers of the traditional Chinese religion (local deities, ancestor veneration, Confucian ethics, Taoism, universism, divination, some Buddhist elements). 10. Followers of Asian 20th-century New Religions, New Religious movements, radical new crisis religions, and non-Christian syncretistic mass religions, all founded since 1800 and most since 1945. 11. Including 70 minor world religions and a large number of spiritist religions, New Age religions, quasi-religions, and religious or mystic belief systems. Reprinted with permission from *1997 Britannica Book of the Year.* © 1997 Encyclopædia Britannica, Inc.

Major Religions of the World

Judaism

Judaism is the oldest of the monotheistic faiths. It affirms the existence of one God, Yahweh, who entered into covenant with the descendants of Abraham, God's chosen people. Judaism's holy writings reveal how God has been present with them throughout their history. These writings are known as the Torah, specifically the five books of Moses, but most broadly conceived as the Hebrew Scriptures (traditionally called the Old Testament by Christians) and the compilation of oral tradition known as the Talmud (which includes the Mishnah, the oral law).

According to Scripture, the Hebrew patriarch Abraham (20th century? B.C.E.) founded Judaism. He obeyed the call of God to depart northern Mesopotamia and travel to Canaan. God promised to bless his descendants if they remained faithful in worship. Abraham's line descended through Isaac, then Jacob (also called Israel; his descendants came to be called Israelites). According to Scripture, 12 families that descended from Jacob migrated to Egypt, where they were enslaved. They were led out of bondage (13th century? B.C.E.) by Moses, who united them in the worship of Yahweh. The Hebrews returned to Canaan after a 40-year sojourn in the desert, conquering from the local peoples the "promised land" that God had provided for them.

The 12 tribes of Israel lived in a covenant association during the period of the judges (1200?–1000? B.C.E.), leaders known for wisdom and heroism. Saul first established a monarchy (r. 1025?–1005? B.C.E.); his successor, David (r. 1005?–965? B.C.E.), unified the land of Israel and made Jerusalem its religious and political center. Under his son, Solomon (r. 968?–928? B.C.E.), a golden era culminated in the building of a temple, replacing the portable sanctuary in use until that time. Following Solomon's death, the kingdom was split into Israel in the north and Judah in the south. Political conflicts resulted in the conquest of Israel by Assyria (721 B.C.E.) and the defeat of Judah by Babylon (586 B.C.E.). Jerusalem and its temple were destroyed, and many Judeans were exiled to Babylon.

During the era of the kings, the prophets were active in Israel and Judah. Their writings emphasize faith in Yahweh as God of Israel and of the entire universe, and they warn of the dangers of worshiping other gods. They also cry out for social justice.

The Judeans were permitted to return in 539 B.C.E. to Judea, where they were ruled as a Persian province. Though temple and cult were restored in Jerusalem, during the exile a new class of religious leaders had emerged—the scribes. They became rivals to the temple hierarchy and would eventually evolve into the party known as the Pharisees.

Persian rule ended when Alexander the Great conquered Palestine in 332 B.C.E. After his death, rule of Judea alternated between Egypt and Syria. When the Syrian ruler Antiochus IV Epiphanes tried to prevent the practice of Judaism, a revolt was led by the Maccabees (a Jewish family), winning Jewish independence in 128 B.C.E. The Romans conquered Jerusalem in 63 B.C.E.

During this period the Sadducees (temple priests) and the Pharisees (teachers of the law in the synagogues) offered different interpretations of Judaism. Smaller groups that emerged were the Essenes, a religious order; the Apocalyptists, who expected divine deliverance led by the Messiah; and the Zealots, who were prepared to fight for national independence. Hellenism also influenced Judaism at this time.

When the Zealots revolted, the Roman armies destroyed Jerusalem and its temple (C.E. 70). The Jews were scattered in the Diaspora (dispersion) and experienced much persecution. Rabbinic Judaism, developed according to Pharisaic practice and centered on Torah and synagogue, became the primary expression of faith. The Scriptures became codified, and the Talmud took shape. In the 12th century Maimonides formulated the influential 13 Articles of Faith, including belief in God, God's oneness and lack of physical or other form, the changelessness of Torah, restoration of the monarchy under the Messiah, and resurrection of the dead.

Two branches of European Judaism developed during the Middle Ages: the Sephardic, based in Spain and with an affinity to Babylonian Jews; and the Ashkenazic, based in Franco-German lands and affiliated with Rome and Palestine. Two forms of Jewish mysticism also arose at this time: medieval Hasidism and attention to the Kabbalah (a mystical interpretation of Scripture).

After a respite during the 18th-century Enlightenment, anti-Semitism again plagued European Jews in the 19th century, sparking the Zionist movement that culminated in the founding of the state of Israel in 1948. The Holocaust of World War II took the lives of more than 6 million Jews.

Jews today continue synagogue worship, which includes readings from the Law and the Prophets and prayers, such as the Shema (Hear, O Israel) and the Amidah (the 18 Benedictions). Religious life is guided by the commandments of the Torah, such as circumcision and Sabbath observance.

Present-day Judaism has three main expressions: Orthodox, Conservative, and Reform. Reform movements, resulting from the Haskala (Jewish Enlightenment) of the 18th century, began in western Europe but took root in North America. Reform Jews do not hold the oral law (Talmud) to be a divine revelation, and they emphasize ethical and moral teachings. Orthodox Jews follow the traditional faith and practice with great seriousness. They follow a strict kosher diet and keep the Sabbath with care. Conservative Judaism, which developed in the mid-18th century, holds the Talmud to be authoritative and follows most traditional practices, yet tries to make Judaism relevant for each generation, believing that change and tradition can complement each other. Because the Torah assumes belief in God but does not require it, a strong secular movement also exists within Judaism, including atheist and agnostic elements.

In general, Jews do not proselytize, but they do welcome newcomers to their faith.

Christianity

Christianity is a monotheistic religion founded by the followers of Jesus of Nazareth. Jesus, a Jew, was born in about 7 B.C.E. and assumed his public life, probably after his 30th year, in Galilee. The New Testament Gospels describe Jesus as a teacher and miracle worker. He proclaimed the kingdom of God, a future reality that is at the same time already present. Jesus set the requirements for participation in the kingdom of God as a change of heart and repentance for sins, love of God and neighbor, and concern for justice. Circa C.E. 30 he was executed on a cross in Jerusalem, a brutal form of punishment for those considered a political threat to the Roman Empire.

After his death his followers came to believe in him as the Christ, the Messiah. The Gospels report his resurrection and how the risen Jesus was witnessed by many of his followers. The apostle Paul helped spread the new faith in his missionary travels. Historically, Christianity arose out of Judaism and claims that Jesus fulfilled many of the promises of the Hebrew Scripture (often referred to as the Old Testament).

The new religion spread rapidly throughout the Roman Empire. In its first two centuries, Christianity began to take shape as an organization, developing distinctive doctrine, liturgy, and ministry. By the fourth century the Christian church had taken root in countries stretching from Spain in the West to Persia and India in the East. Christians had been subject to persecution by the Roman state, but gained tolerance under Constantine the Great (C.E. 313). The church became favored under his successors, and in 380 the emperor Theodosius proclaimed Christianity the state religion. Other religions were suppressed.

Because differences in doctrine threatened to divide the church, a standard Christian creed was formulated by bishops at successive ecumenical councils, the first of which was held in C.E. 325 (Nicaea). Important doctrines were defined concerning the Trinity—in other words, that there is one God in three persons: Father, Son, and Holy Spirit (Constantinople, C.E. 381), and the nature of Christ as both divine and human (Chalcedon, C.E. 541). Christians came to accept both Hebrew Scripture and the New Testament as authoritative. The New Testament comprises four Gospels (narratives of Jesus' life), 21 Epistles, The Acts of the Apostles, and Revelation.

Because of differences between Christians of the East and West, the unity of the church was broken in 1054. The religious center for the Eastern Orthodox Church was Constantinople, and the Roman Catholic Church defined doctrine and practice for Christians in the West. In 1517 began the Reformation, which ultimately caused a schism in the Western church. Reformers wished to correct certain practices within the Roman church, but also came to view the Christian faith in a distinctly new way. The major Protestant denominations (Lutheran, Presbyterian, Reformed, and Anglican [Episcopalian]) thus came into being. Over the centuries, numerous denominations have broken with these major traditions, resulting in a spectrum of Christian expression.

In the 20th century, many Christians hope to regain a sense of unity through dialogue and cooperation among different traditions. The ecumenical movement led to the formation of the World Council of Churches in 1948 (Amsterdam), which has since been joined by many denominations.

Through its missionary activity Christianity has spread to most parts of the globe.

Eastern Orthodoxy

Eastern Orthodoxy comprises the faith and practices stemming from ancient churches in the eastern part of the Roman Empire. It encompasses Orthodox churches in communion with the see of Constantinople.

The Orthodox, Catholic, Apostolic Church is the direct descendant of the Byzantine state church and consists of independent national churches that are united by doctrine, liturgy, and hierarchical organization (church leaders include deacons and priests, who may either be married or be monks before ordination, and bishops, who must be celibates). The heads of these churches are called patriarchs or metropolitans. Rivalry between the pope of Rome and the patriarch of Constantinople, as well as differences that existed for centuries between the eastern and western parts of the empire, led to a schism in 1054. The mutual excommunication pronounced in that year was lifted in 1965, however, and a climate of better understanding has been created in the 20th century. Orthodox churches belong to the World Council of Churches.

The Eastern Orthodox churches recognize only the canons of the seven ecumenical councils (325–

U.S. Religious Bodies with More Than 500,000 Members

Religious body	Members
Roman Catholic Church	61,207,914
Southern Baptist Convention	15,891,514
United Methodist Church	8,496,047
National Baptist Convention, U.S.A., Inc.	8,200,000
Church of God in Christ	5,499,875
Evangelical Lutheran Church in America	5,185,055
Church of Jesus Christ of Latter-day Saints	4,923,100
Presbyterian Church (U.S.A.)	3,610,753
African Methodist Episcopal Church	3,500,000
National Baptist Convention of America, Inc.	3,500,000
Lutheran Church—Missouri Synod	2,603,036
Episcopal Church	2,536,550
National Missionary Baptist Convention of America	2,500,000
Progressive National Baptist Convention, Inc.	2,500,000
Assemblies of God	2,494,574
Orthodox Church in America	2,000,000
Greek Orthodox Archdiocese of North and South America	1,954,500
Churches of Christ	1,800,000
United Church of Christ	1,438,181
African Methodist Episcopal Zion Church	1,252,369
Baptist Bible Fellowship International	1,200,000
Christian Churches and Churches of Christ	1,071,616
Pentecostal Assemblies of the World	1,000,000
Jehovah's Witnesses	974,719
Christian Church (Disciples of Christ)	879,436
Seventh-Day Adventist Church	825,654
Church of God (Cleveland, Tenn.)	753,230
Christian Methodist Episcopal Church	718,922
Church of Nazarene	619,576

Source: Yearbook of American & Canadian Churches, 1999.

787) as binding for faith, and they reject doctrines that have been added in the West.

The central worship service is called the Liturgy, which is understood as representing God's acts of salvation. Its center is the celebration of the Eucharist, or Lord's Supper. Icons (sacred pictures) have a special place in Orthodox worship. The Mother of Christ, angels, and saints are venerated. The Orthodox Church and the Western Catholic Church recognize the same number of sacraments.

Orthodox Churches are found in Greece, Turkey, Russia, the Balkans, and other parts of the former Soviet Union. In this century Orthodox faith has spread to western Europe and other parts of the world, particularly America.

Eastern Rite Churches

These include the Uniate Churches that recognize the authority of the pope but keep their own traditional liturgies and those churches dating back to the fifth century that emancipated themselves from the Byzantine state church. They include the Melchites, Syrian Catholics, Maronites (Arab Christians in Lebanon), Catholic Copts and Ethiopians, the autonomous Nestorian Church, and others.

Roman Catholicism

Roman Catholicism comprises the belief and practice of the Roman Catholic Church. It stands under the authority of the bishop of Rome, the pope, and is led by him and bishops who are held to be, through ordination, successors of Peter and the apostles. Doctrine and sacraments are administered by the hierarchy of archbishops, bishops, priests, and deacons. As successor to Peter, the pope is considered the Vicar of Christ. Roman Catholics believe their church to be the one, holy, catholic, and apostolic church, possessing all the properties of the one, true church of Christ.

The faith of the church is understood to be identical with that taught by Christ and his apostles and contained in the Bible and tradition. New definitions of doctrines, such as the Immaculate Conception of Mary (1854) and the bodily Assumption of Mary (1950), have been declared by popes, however. At Vatican Council I (1870) the pope was proclaimed "endowed with infallibility, *ex cathedra,* in other words, when exercising the office of pastor and teacher of all Christians."

The center of Roman Catholic worship is the celebration of the Mass, the Eucharist, which is the commemoration of Christ's sacrificial death and resurrection. Other sacraments are baptism, confirmation, penance, matrimony, anointing of the sick (formerly known as extreme unction), and holy orders. The Virgin Mary and the other saints, and their relics, are venerated, and prayers are made to them to intercede with God, in whose presence they are believed to dwell.

The Roman Catholic Church is the largest Christian organization in the world, found in most countries.

Vatican Council II (1962–1965) sought to "update" the church, bringing about changes in practice and more deeply involving the laity. The immensely popular Pope John Paul II (1978–) has taken a more conservative course and has reached out to Catholics worldwide through his extensive travels.

Protestantism

Protestantism encompasses the Christian churches that separated from Rome during the Reformation in the 16th century. This movement was initiated by an Augustinian monk, Martin Luther. The term "Protestant" was originally applied to followers of Luther, who protested at the Diet of Spires (1529) against the decree that prohibited all further ecclesiastical reforms. Other influential reformers included John Calvin, Ulrich Zwingli, and John Knox. Protestantism rejected attempts to tie God's revelation to earthly institutions and strictly adhered to the Word of God as sole authority in matters of faith and practice *(sola scriptura).* Central in the reformers' understanding of the biblical message is the justification of the sinner by faith alone. The church is understood as a fellowship, and the priesthood of all believers is stressed.

The Augsburg Confession (1530) was the principal statement of Lutheran faith and practice. It became a model for other Protestant confessions of faith. Major Protestant denominations include the Lutheran, Reformed (Calvinist), Presbyterian, and Anglican (Episcopalian). Innumerable sects and denominations sprung from these roots, including Quakers, Baptists, Pentecostals, Congregationalists, Methodists, and nondenominational assemblies. Sects that base their faith on additional revelations or insights gained in the modern period include Mormons, Christian Scientists, and Jehovah's Witnesses.

Since the latter part of the 19th century, national councils of churches have been established in many countries, for example, the Federal Council of Churches of Christ in America in 1908. Churches of a particular denomination have joined in federations and world alliances, beginning with the Anglican Lambeth Conference in 1867.

Protestant missionary activity, particularly strong in the last century, resulted in the founding of many churches in Asia and Africa. The ecumenical movement, which originated with Protestant missions, aims at unity among Christians and churches.

Islam

Islam, one of the three major monotheistic faiths, was founded in Arabia by Muhammad between 610 and 632. There are an estimated 5.5 million Muslims in North America and 1 billion Muslims worldwide.

Muhammad was born in 570 C.E. at Mecca and belonged to the Quraysh tribe, which was active in caravan trade. At the age of 25 he joined the trade from Mecca to Syria in the employment of a rich widow, Khadiji, whom he later married. Critical of the lax moral standards and polytheistic practices of the inhabitants of Mecca, he began to lead a contemplative life in the desert. In a dramatic religious vision, the angel Gabriel announced to Muhammad that he was to be a prophet. Encouraged by Khadiji, he devoted himself to the reform of religion and society. Polytheism was to be abandoned. But leaders of the Quraysh generally rejected his teaching, and Muhammad gained only a small following and suffered persecution. He eventually fled Mecca.

The Hegira *(Hijra,* meaning "emigration") of Muhammad from Mecca, where he was not honored, to Medina, where he was well received, occurred in 622 and marks the beginning of the

Muslim era. After a number of military conflicts with Mecca, in 630 he marched on Mecca and conquered it. Muhammad died at Medina in 632. His grave there has since been a place of pilgrimage.

Muhammad's followers, called Muslims, revered him as the prophet of Allah (God), the only God. Muslims consider Muhammad to be the last in the line of prophets that included Abraham and Jesus. Islam spread quickly, stretching from Spain in the west to India in the east within a century after the prophet's death. Sources of the Islamic faith are the Qur'an (Koran), regarded as the uncreated, eternal Word of God, and tradition (hadith) regarding sayings and deeds of the prophet.

Islam means "surrender to the will of Allah," the all-powerful, who determines humanity's fate. Good deeds will be rewarded at the Last Judgment in paradise, and evil deeds will be punished in hell.

The Five Pillars, or primary duties, of Islam are profession of faith; prayer, to be performed five times a day; almsgiving to the poor and the mosque (house of worship); fasting during daylight hours in the month of Ramadan; and pilgrimage to Mecca at least once in a Muslim's lifetime, if it is physically and financially possible. The pilgrimage includes homage to the ancient shrine of the Ka'aba, the most sacred site in Islam.

Muslims gather for corporate worship on Fridays. Prayers and a sermon take place at the mosque, which is also a center for teaching of the Qur'an. The community leader, the imam, is considered a teacher and prayer leader.

Islam succeeded in uniting an Arab world of separate tribes and castes, but disagreements concerning the succession of the prophet caused a division in Islam between two groups, Sunnis and Shi'ites. The Shi'ites rejected the first three successors to Muhammad as usurpers, claiming the fourth, Muhammad's son-in-law Ali, as the rightful leader. The Sunnis (from the word tradition), the largest division of Islam (today more than 80%), believe in the legitimacy of the first three successors. Among these, other sects arose (such as the conservative Wahhabi of Saudi Arabia), as well as different schools of theology. Another development within Islam, beginning in the eighth and ninth centuries, was Sufism, a form of mysticism. This movement was influential for many centuries and was instrumental in the spread of Islam in Asia and Africa.

Islam has expanded greatly under Muhammad's successors. It is the principal religion of the Middle East, Asia, and the northern half of Africa.

Hinduism

Hinduism is the major religion of India, practiced by more than 80% of the population. In contrast to other religions, it has no founder. Considered the oldest religion in the world, it dates back, perhaps, to prehistoric times.

No single creed or doctrine binds Hindus together. Intellectually there is complete freedom of belief, and one can be monotheist, polytheist, or atheist. Hinduism is a syncretic religion, welcoming and incorporating a variety of outside influences.

The most ancient sacred texts of the Hindu religion are written in Sanskrit and called the Vedas (vedah means "knowledge"). There are four Vedic books, of which the Rig-Veda is the oldest. It discusses multiple gods, the universe, and creation. The dates of these works are unknown (1000 B.C.E.?). Present-day Hindus rarely refer to these texts but do venerate them.

The Upanishads (dated 1000–300 B.C.E.), commentaries on the Vedic texts, speculate on the origin of the universe and the nature of deity, and atman (the individual soul) and its relationship to Brahman (the universal soul). They introduce the doctrine of karma and recommend meditation and the practice of yoga.

Further important sacred writings include the Epics, which contain legendary stories about gods and humans. They are the Mahabharata (composed between 200 B.C.E. and C.E. 200) and the Ramayana. The former includes the Bhagavad-Gita (Song of the Lord), an influential text that describes the three paths to salvation. The Puranas (stories in verse, probably written between the 6th and 13th centuries) detail myths of Hindu gods and heroes and also comment on religious practice and cosmology.

According to Hindu beliefs, Brahman is the principle and source of the universe. This divine intelligence pervades all beings, including the individual soul. Thus the many Hindu deities are manifestations of the one Brahman. Hinduism is based on the concept of reincarnation, in which all living beings, from plants on earth to gods above, are caught in a cosmic cycle of becoming and perishing.

Life is determined by the law of karma—one is reborn to a higher level of existence based on moral behavior in a previous phase of existence. Life on earth is regarded as transient and a burden. The goal of existence is liberation from the cycle of rebirth and death and entrance into the indescribable state of moksha (liberation).

The practice of Hinduism consists of rites and ceremonies centering on birth, marriage, and death. There are many Hindu temples, which are considered to be dwelling places of the deities and to which people bring offerings. Places of pilgrimage include Benares on the Ganges, the most sacred river in India. Of the many Hindu deities, the most popular are the cults of Vishnu, Shiva, and Shakti, and their various incarnations. Also important is Brahma, the creator god. Hindus also venerate human saints.

Orthodox Hindu society in India was divided into four major hereditary classes: (1) the Brahmin (priestly and learned class); (2) the Kshatriya (military, professional, ruling, and governing occupations); (3) the Vaishya (landowners, merchants, and business occupations); and (4) the Sudra (artisans, laborers, and peasants). Below the Sudra was a fifth group, the Untouchables (lowest menial occupations and no social standing). The Indian government banned discrimination against the Untouchables in the constitution of India in 1950. Observance of class and caste distinctions varies throughout India.

In modern times work has been done to reform and revive Hinduism. One of the outstanding reformers was Ramakrishna (1836–1886), who inspired many followers, one of whom founded the Ramakrishna mission. The mission is active both in India and in other countries and is known for its scholarly and humanitarian works.

Buddhism

Buddhism was founded in the fourth or fifth century B.C.E. in northern India by a man known traditionally as Siddhartha (meaning "he who has reached the goal") Gautama, the son of a warrior prince. Some scholars believe that he lived from 563 to 483 B.C.E., though his exact life span is uncertain. Troubled by the inevitability of suffering in human life, he left home and a pampered life at the age of 29 to wander as an ascetic, seeking religious insight and a solution to the struggles of human existence. He passed through many trials and practiced extreme self-denial. Finally, while meditating under the bodhi tree ("tree of perfect knowledge") he reached enlightenment and taught his followers about his new spiritual understanding.

Gautama's teachings differed from the Hindu faith prevalent in India at the time. Whereas in Hinduism the Brahmin caste alone performed religious functions and attained the highest spiritual understanding, Gautama's beliefs were more egalitarian, accessible to all who wished to be enlightened. At the core of his understanding were the Four Noble Truths: (1) all living beings suffer; (2) the origin of this suffering is desire—for material possessions, power, and so on; (3) desire can be overcome; and (4) there is a path that leads to release from desire. This way is called the Noble Eightfold Path: right views, right intention, right speech, right action, right livelihood, right effort, right concentration, and right ecstasy.

Gautama promoted the concept of *anatman* (that a person has no actual self) and the idea that existence is characterized by impermanence. This realization helps one let go of desire for transient things. Still, Gautama did not recommend extreme self-denial, but rather a disciplined life called the Middle Way. Like the Hindus, he believed that existence consisted of reincarnation, a cycle of birth and death. He held that it could be broken only by reaching complete detachment from worldly cares. Then the soul could be released into *nirvana* (literally "blowing out")—an indescribable state of total transcendence. Gautama traveled to preach the *dharma* (sacred truth) and was recognized as the Buddha (enlightened one). After his death his followers continued to develop doctrine and practice, which came to center on the Three Jewels: the *dharma* (the sacred teachings of Buddhism), the *sangha* (the community of followers, which now includes nuns, monks, and laity), and the Buddha. Under the patronage of the Mauryan emperor Ashoka (third century B.C.E.), Buddhism spread throughout India and to other parts of Asia. Monasteries were established, as well as temples dedicated to Buddha; at shrines his relics were venerated. Though by the fourth century C.E. Buddhist presence in India had dwindled, it flourished in other parts of Asia.

Numerous Buddhist sects have emerged. The oldest, called the Theravada (Way of the Elders) tradition, interprets Buddha as a great sage but not a deity. It emphasizes meditation and ritual practices that help the individual become an *arhat*, an enlightened being. Its followers emphasize the authority of the earliest Buddhist scriptures, the Tripitaka (Three Baskets), a compilation of sermons, rules for celibates, and doctrine. This sect is prevalent in Southeast Asia and Sri Lanka. It is sometimes called the Hinayana (Lesser Vehicle) tradition (once considered a pejorative term).

Between the second century B.C.E. and the second century C.E., the Mahayana (Greater Vehicle) tradition refocused Buddhism to concentrate less on individual attainment of enlightenment and more on concern for humanity. It promotes the ideal of the *bodhisattva* (enlightened being), who shuns entering nirvana until all sentient beings can do so as well, willingly remaining in the painful cycle of birth and death to perform works of compassion. Members of this tradition conceive of Buddha as an eternal being to whom prayers can be made; other Buddhas are revered as well, adding a polytheistic dimension to the religion. Numerous sects have developed from the Mahayana tradition, which has been influential in China, Korea, and Japan.

A third broad tradition, variously called Vajrayana (Diamond Vehicle), Mantrayana (Vehicle of the Mantra), or Tantric Buddhism, offers a quicker, more demanding way to achieve nirvana. Because of its level of challenge—enabling one to reach enlightenment in one lifetime—it requires the guidance of a spiritual leader. It is most prominent in Tibet and Mongolia. Zen Buddhism encourages individuals to seek the Buddha nature within themselves and to practice a disciplined form of sitting meditation in order to reach *satori*—spiritual enlightenment.

Confucianism

Confucius (K'ung Fu-tzu), born in the state of Lu (northern China), lived from 551 to 479 B.C.E. He was a brilliant teacher, viewing education not merely as the accumulation of knowledge but as a means of self-transformation. His legacy was a system of thought emphasizing education, proper behavior, and loyalty. His effect on Chinese culture was immense.

The teachings of Confucius are contained in the *Analects*, a collection of his sayings as remembered by his students. They were further developed by philosophers such as Mencius (Meng Tse, fl. 400 B.C.E.). Confucianism is little concerned with metaphysical discussion of religion or with spiritual attainments. It instead emphasizes moral conduct and right relationships in the human sphere.

Cultivation of virtue is a central tenet of Confucianism. Two important virtues are *jen*, a benevolent and humanitarian attitude, and *li*, maintaining proper relationships and rituals that enhance the life of the individual, the family, and the state. The "five relations," between king and subject, father and son, man and wife, older and younger brother, and friend and friend, are of utmost importance. These relationships are reinforced by participation in rituals, including the formal procedures of court life and religious rituals such as ancestor worship.

Confucius revolutionized educational thought in China. He believed that learning was not to be focused only on attaining the skills for a particular profession, but for growth in moral judgment and self-realization. Confucius's standards for the proper conduct of government shaped the statecraft of China for centuries. Hundreds of temples in honor of Confucius testify to his stature as sage and teacher.

Confucianism is far less dominant in 20th-century China, at least on an official level. The state cult of

Confucius was ended in 1911. Still, Confucian traditions and moral standards are part of the cultural essence of China and other East Asian countries.

Shinto

Shinto comprises the religious ideas and practices indigenous to Japan. Ancient Shinto focused on the worship of the *kami*, a host of supernatural beings that could be known through forms (objects of nature, remarkable people, abstract concepts such as justice) but were ultimately mysterious. Shinto has no formal dogma and no holy writ, though early collections of Japanese religious thought and practice (*Kojiki*, "Records of Ancient Matters," C.E. 712, and *Nihon shoki*, "Chronicles of Japan," C.E. 720) are highly regarded.

Shinto has been influenced by Confucianism and by Buddhism, which was introduced in Japan in the 6th century. Syncretic schools (such as Ryobu Shinto) emerged, as did other sects that decried Buddhism (such as Ise Shinto).

Under the reign of the emperor Meiji (1868–1912), Shinto became the official state religion. State Shinto, the national cult, emphasized the divinity of the emperor, whose succession was traced back to the first emperor, Jimmu (660 B.C.E.), and beyond him to the sun goddess Amaterasu-o-mi-kami. State Shinto was disestablished after World War II.

Sect Shinto, deriving from sects that developed during the 19th and 20th centuries, continues to thrive in Japan. Shrines dedicated to particular *kami* are visited by parishioners for prayer and traditional ceremonies, such as presenting a newborn child to the *kami*. Traditional festivals celebrated at the shrines include purification rites, presentation of food offerings, prayer, sacred music and dance, and a feast.

No particular day of the week is set aside for prayer. A person may visit a shrine at will, entering through the *torii* (gateway). It is believed that the *kami* can respond to prayer and can offer protection and guidance.

A variety of Shinto sects and practices exist today. Ten-rikyo emphasizes faith healing. Folk Shinto is characterized by veneration of roadside shrines and rites related to agriculture. Buddhist priests serve at many Shinto shrines, and many families keep a small shrine, or god-shelf, at home. Veneration of ancestors and pilgrimage are also common practices.

Taoism

Taoism, one of the major religions of China, is based on ancient philosophical works, primarily the Tao Te Ching, "Classic of Tao and Its Virtue." Traditionally, this book was thought to be the work of Lao-tzu, a quasi-historical philosopher of the 6th century B.C.E.; scholars now believe that the book dates from about the 3rd century B.C.E.. The philosopher Chuang Tzu (4th–3rd centuries B.C.E.) also contributed to the seminal ideas of Taoism.

Tao, "the Way," is the ultimate reality of the universe, according to Taoism. It is a creative process, and humans can live in harmony with it by clearing the self of obstacles. By cultivating *wu-wei*, a type of inaction characterized by humility and prudence, a person can participate in the simplicity and spontaneity of Tao. Striving to attain virtue or achievement is counterproductive and unnecessary. Taoism values mystical contemplation and balance. The human being is viewed as a microcosm of the universe, and the Chinese principle of *yin-yang*, complementary duality, is a model of harmony.

The religious practices of Taoism emerged from these ancient philosophies and from Chinese shamanistic tradition; by the 2nd century C.E., it constituted an organized religion. Longevity and immortality were sought through regulating the energies of the body through breathing exercises, meditation, use of medicinal plants, talismans, and magical formulas. A cult of immortals, including the divinized Lao Tzu, also developed. Influenced by Buddhism, Taoists organized monastic orders. Temple worship and forms of divination, including the *I ching*, were practiced.

Since its beginnings, many sects have arisen within Taoism. All subscribe to the philosophical origins of the religion; some have emphasized faith healing, exorcism, the worship of the immortals, meditation, or alchemy. Buddhism and Confucianism influenced some sects; some operated as secret societies.

Though the present government has tried to suppress it, Taoism is still practiced in mainland China, Taiwan, and Hong Kong. It profoundly influenced Chinese art and literature, and Taoist ideas have become popular in the West during the twentieth century.

Roman Catholic Pontiffs

St. Peter, of Bethsaida in Galilee, Prince of the Apostles, was the first pope. He lived first in Antioch and then in Rome for 25 years. In C.E. 64 or 67, he was martyred. St. Linus became the second pope.

Name	Birthplace	Reigned		Name	Birthplace	Reigned	
		From	To			From	To
St. Linus	Tuscia	67	76	St. Anicetus	Syria	155	166
St. Anacletus (Cletus)	Rome	76	88	St. Soter	Campania	166	175
				St. Eleutherius	Epirus	175	189
St. Clement	Rome	88	97	St. Victor I	Africa	189	199
St. Evaristus	Greece	97	105	St. Zephyrinus	Rome	199	217
St. Alexander I	Rome	105	115	St. Callistus I	Rome	217	222
St. Sixtus I	Rome	115	125	St. Urban I	Rome	222	230
St. Telesphorus	Greece	125	136	St. Pontian	Rome	230	235
St. Hyginus	Greece	136	140	St. Anterus	Greece	235	236
St. Pius I	Aquileia	140	155	St. Fabian	Rome	236	250

Name	Birthplace	Reigned From	Reigned To	Name	Birthplace	Reigned From	Reigned To
St. Cornelius	Rome	251	253	John VII	Greece	705	707
St. Lucius I	Rome	253	254	Sisinnius	Syria	708	708
St. Stephen I	Rome	254	257	Constantine	Syria	708	715
St. Sixtus II	Greece	257	258	St. Gregory II	Rome	715	731
St. Dionysius	Unknown	259	268	St. Gregory III	Syria	731	741
St. Felix I	Rome	269	274	St. Zachary	Greece	741	752
St. Eutychian	Luni	275	283	Stephen II (III)[4]	Rome	752	757
St. Caius	Dalmatia	283	296	St. Paul I	Rome	757	767
St. Marcellinus	Rome	296	304	Stephen III (IV)	Sicily	768	772
St. Marcellus I	Rome	308	309	Adrian I	Rome	772	795
St. Eusebius	Greece	309[1]	309[1]	St. Leo III	Rome	795	816
St. Meltiades	Africa	311	314	Stephen IV (V)	Rome	816	817
St. Sylvester I	Rome	314	335	St. Paschal I	Rome	817	824
St. Marcus	Rome	336	336	Eugene II	Rome	824	827
St. Julius I	Rome	337	352	Valentine	Rome	827	827
Liberius	Rome	352	366	Gregory IV	Rome	827	844
St. Damasus I	Spain	366	384	Sergius II	Rome	844	847
St. Siricius	Rome	384	399	St. Leo IV	Rome	847	855
St. Anastasius I	Rome	399	401	Benedict III	Rome	855	858
St. Innocent I	Albano	401	417	St. Nicholas I	Rome	858	867
St. Zozimus	Greece	417	418	(the Great)			
St. Boniface I	Rome	418	422	Adrian II	Rome	867	872
St. Celestine I	Campania	422	432	John VIII	Rome	872	882
St. Sixtus III	Rome	432	440	Marinus I	Gallese	882	884
St. Leo I	Tuscany	440	461	St. Adrian III	Rome	884	885
(the Great)				Stephen V (VI)	Rome	885	891
St. Hilary	Sardinia	461	468	Formosus	Portus	891	896
St. Simplicius	Tivoli	468	483	Boniface VI	Rome	896	896
St. Felix III (II)[2]	Rome	483	492	Stephen VI (VII)	Rome	896	897
St. Gelasius I	Africa	492	496	Romanus	Gallese	897	897
Anastasius II	Rome	496	498	Theodore II	Rome	897	897
St. Symmachus	Sardinia	498	514	John IX	Tivoli	898	900
St. Hormisdas	Frosinone	514	523	Benedict IV	Rome	900	903
St. John I	Tuscany	523	526	Leo V	Ardea	903	903
St. Felix IV (III)	Samnium	526	530	Sergius III	Rome	904	911
Boniface II	Rome	530	532	Anastasius III	Rome	911	913
John II	Rome	533	535	Landus	Sabina	913	914
St. Agapitus I	Rome	535	536	John X	Tossignano	914	928
St. Silverius	Campania	536	537	Leo VI	Rome	928	928
Vigilius	Rome	537	555	Stephen VII (VIII)	Rome	928	931
Pelagius I	Rome	556	561	John XI	Rome	931	935
John III	Rome	561	574	Leo VII	Rome	936	939
Benedict I	Rome	575	579	Stephen VIII (IX)	Rome	939	942
Pelagius II	Rome	579	590	Marinus II	Rome	942	946
St. Gregory I	Rome	590	604	Agapitus II	Rome	946	955
(the Great)				John XII[5]	Tusculum	955	964
Sabinianus	Tuscany	604	606	Leo VIII[5]	Rome	963	965
Boniface III	Rome	607	607	Benedict V[5]	Rome	964	966
St. Boniface IV	Marsi	608	615	John XIII	Rome	965	972
St. Deusdedit	Rome	615	618	Benedict VI	Rome	973	974
(Adeodatus I)				Benedict VII	Rome	974	983
Boniface V	Naples	619	625	John XIV	Pavia	983	984
Honorius I	Campania	625	638	John XV	Rome	985	996
Severinus	Rome	640	640	Gregory V	Saxony	996	999
John IV	Dalmatia	640	642	Sylvester II	Auvergne	999	1003
Theodore I	Greece	642	649	John XVII	Rome	1003	1003
St. Martin I	Todi	649	655	John XVIII	Rome	1004	1009
St. Eugene I[3]	Rome	654	657	Sergius IV	Rome	1009	1012
St. Vitalian	Segni	657	672	Benedict VIII	Tusculum	1012	1024
Adeodatus II	Rome	672	676	John XIX	Tusculum	1024	1032
Donus	Rome	676	678	Benedict IX[6]	Tusculum	1032	1044
St. Agatho	Sicily	678	681	Sylvester III	Rome	1045	1045
St. Leo II	Sicily	682	683	Benedict IX	Tusculum	1045	1045
St. Benedict II	Rome	684	685	(2nd time)			
John V	Syria	685	686	Gregory VI	Rome	1045	1046
Conon	Unknown	686	687	Clement II	Saxony	1046	1047
St. Sergius I	Syria	687	701	Benedict IX	Tusculum	1047	1048
John VI	Greece	701	705	(3rd time)			

Name	Birthplace	Reigned From	To	Name	Birthplace	Reigned From	To
Damasus II	Bavaria	1048	1048	Nicholas V	Sarzana	1447	1455
St. Leo IX	Alsace	1049	1054	Callistus III	Jativa	1455	1458
Victor II	Germany	1055	1057	Pius II	Siena	1458	1464
Stephen IX (X)	Lorraine	1057	1058	Paul II	Venice	1464	1471
Nicholas II	Burgundy	1059	1061	Sixtus IV	Savona	1471	1484
Alexander II	Milan	1061	1073	Innocent VIII	Genoa	1484	1492
St. Gregory VII	Tuscany	1073	1085	Alexander VI	Jativa	1492	1503
Bl. Victor III	Benevento	1086	1087	Pius III	Siena	1503	1503
Bl. Urban II	France	1088	1099	Julius II	Savona	1503	1513
Paschal II	Ravenna	1099	1118	Leo X	Florence	1513	1521
Gelasius II	Gaeta	1118	1119	Adrian VI	Utrecht	1522	1523
Callistus II	Burgundy	1119	1124	Clement VII	Florence	1523	1534
Honorius II	Flagnano	1124	1130	Paul III	Rome	1534	1549
Innocent II	Rome	1130	1143	Julius III	Rome	1550	1555
Celestine II	Città di Castello	1143	1144	Marcellus II	Montepulciano	1555	1555
Lucius II	Bologna	1144	1145	Paul IV	Naples	1555	1559
Bl. Eugene III	Pisa	1145	1153	Pius IV	Milan	1559	1565
Anastasius IV	Rome	1153	1154	St. Pius V	Bosco	1566	1572
Adrian IV	England	1154	1159	Gregory XIII	Bologna	1572	1585
Alexander III	Siena	1159	1181	Sixtus V	Grottammare	1585	1590
Lucius III	Lucca	1181	1185	Urban VII	Rome	1590	1590
Urban III	Milan	1185	1187	Gregory XIV	Cremona	1590	1591
Gregory VIII	Benevento	1187	1187	Innocent IX	Bologna	1591	1591
Clement III	Rome	1187	1191	Clement VIII	Florence	1592	1605
Celestine III	Rome	1191	1198	Leo XI	Florence	1605	1605
Innocent III	Anagni	1198	1216	Paul V	Rome	1605	1621
Honorius III	Rome	1216	1227	Gregory XV	Bologna	1621	1623
Gregory IX	Anagni	1227	1241	Urban VIII	Florence	1623	1644
Celestine IV	Milan	1241	1241	Innocent X	Rome	1644	1655
Innocent IV	Genoa	1243	1254	Alexander VII	Siena	1655	1667
Alexander IV	Anagni	1254	1261	Clement IX	Pistoia	1667	1669
Urban IV	Troyes	1261	1264	Clement X	Rome	1670	1676
Clement IV	France	1265	1268	Bl. Innocent XI	Como	1676	1689
Bl. Gregory X	Piacenza	1271	1276	Alexander VIII	Venice	1689	1691
Bl. Innocent V	Savoy	1276	1276	Innocent XII	Spinazzola	1691	1700
Adrian V	Genoa	1276	1276	Clement XI	Urbino	1700	1721
John XXI[7]	Portugal	1276	1277	Innocent XIII	Rome	1721	1724
Nicholas III	Rome	1277	1280	Benedict XIII	Gravina	1724	1730
Martin IV[8]	France	1281	1285	Clement XII	Florence	1730	1740
Honorius IV	Rome	1285	1287	Benedict XIV	Bologna	1740	1758
Nicholas IV	Ascoli	1288	1292	Clement XIII	Venice	1758	1769
St. Celestine V	Isernia	1294	1294	Clement XIV	Rimini	1769	1774
Boniface VIII	Anagni	1294	1303	Pius VI	Cesena	1775	1799
Bl. Benedict XI	Treviso	1303	1304	Pius VII	Cesena	1800	1823
Clement V	France	1305	1314	Leo XII	Genga	1823	1829
John XXII	Cahors	1316	1334	Pius VIII	Cingoli	1829	1830
Benedict XII	France	1334	1342	Gregory XVI	Belluno	1831	1846
Clement VI	France	1342	1352	Pius IX	Senegallia	1846	1878
Innocent VI	France	1352	1362	Leo XIII	Carpineto	1878	1903
Bl. Urban V	France	1362	1370	St. Pius X	Riese	1903	1914
Gregory XI	France	1370	1378	Benedict XV	Genoa	1914	1922
Urban VI	Naples	1378	1389	Pius XI	Desio	1922	1939
Boniface IX	Naples	1389	1404	Pius XII	Rome	1939	1958
Innocent VII	Sul mona	1404	1406	John XXIII	Sotto il Monte	1958	1963
Gregory XII	Venice	1406	1415	Paul VI	Concesio	1963	1978
Martin V	Rome	1417	1431	John Paul I	Forno di Canale	1978	1978
Eugene IV	Venice	1431	1447	John Paul II	Wadowice, Poland	1978	

1. Or 310. 2. He should be called Felix II, and his successors of the same name should be numbered accordingly. The discrepancy was caused by the erroneous insertion in some lists of the name of St. Felix of Rome, Martyr. 3. He was elected during the exile of St. Martin I, who endorsed him as pope. 4. After St. Zachary died, a Roman priest named Stephen was elected but died before his consecration as bishop of Rome. His name is not included in all lists for this reason. In view of this historical confusion, the *National Catholic Almanac* lists the true Stephen II as Stephen II (III), the true Stephen III as Stephen III (IV), etc. 5. Confusion exists concerning the legitimacy of claims. If the deposition of John was invalid, Leo was an antipope until after the end of Benedict's reign. If the deposition of John was valid, Leo was the legitimate pope and Benedict an antipope. 6. If the triple removal of Benedict IX was not valid, Sylvester III, Gregory VI, and Clement II were antipopes. 7. Elimination was made of the name of John XX in an effort to rectify the numerical designation of popes named John. The error dates back to the time of John XV. 8. The names of Marinus I and Marinus II were construed as Martin. In view of these two pontificates and the earlier reign of St. Martin I, this pontiff was called Martin IV. *Source: National Catholic Almanac,* from *Annuarrio Pontificio.*

The Books of the Bible

Below is the Protestant canon of the Bible (New Revised Standard Version). The Roman Catholic canon also includes the Deuterocanonical books as part of the Old Testament (these are considered apocryphal by most Protestants). The Hebrew Bible recognizes the books referred to as the Old Testament in the Protestant Bible, but not the Apocryphal/Deuterocanonical books or the New Testament.

The Old Testament
with the Apocryphal/
Deuterocanonical
Books
The Hebrew
Scriptures
  Genesis
  Exodus
  Leviticus
  Numbers
  Deuteronomy
  Joshua
  Judges
  Ruth
  1 Samuel
  2 Samuel
  1 Kings
  2 Kings
  1 Chronicles
  2 Chronicles
  Ezra
  Nehemiah
  Esther
  Job
  Psalms

  Proverbs
  Ecclesiastes
  Song of Solomon
  Isaiah
  Jeremiah
  Lamentations
  Ezekiel
  Daniel
  Hosea
  Joel
  Amos
  Obadiah
  Jonah
  Micah
  Nahum
  Habakkuk
  Zephaniah
  Haggai
  Zechariah
  Malachi
The Apocryphal/
Deuterocanonical
Books
  Tobit
  Judith

  Additions to the Book
    of Esther
  Wisdom of Solomon
  Ecclesiasticus, or the
    Wisdom of Jesus
    Son of Sirach
  Baruch
  The Letter of Jeremiah
  The Prayer of Azariah
    and the Song of the
    Three Jews
  Susanna
  Bel and the Dragon
  1 Maccabees
  2 Maccabees
  1 Esdras
  Prayer of Manasseh
  Psalm 151
  3 Maccabees
  2 Esdras
  4 Maccabees
The New Testament
  Matthew
  Mark
  Luke

  John
  Acts of the Apostles
  Romans
  1 Corinthians
  2 Corinthians
  Galatians
  Ephesians
  Philippians
  Colossians
  1 Thessalonians
  2 Thessalonians
  1 Timothy
  2 Timothy
  Titus
  Philemon
  Hebrews
  James
  1 Peter
  2 Peter
  1 John
  2 John
  3 John
  Jude
  Revelation

The Ten Commandments

The Ten Commandments, also called the Decalogue (Greek, "ten words"), were divine laws revealed to Moses by God on Mt. Sinai. Appearing in both Exodus (Ex. 20: 2–17) and Deuteronomy (Deut. 5:6–21), the commandments are numbered differently depending on whether they appear in a Catholic, Protestant, or Hebrew Bible. The following is the version given in the Revised Standard Version of the Bible.

You shall have no other gods before me.

You shall not make for yourself a graven image, or any likeness of anything that is in heaven above, or that is in the earth beneath, or that is in the water under the earth; you shall not bow down to them or serve them; for I the Lord your God am a jealous God, visiting the iniquity of the fathers upon the children to the third and the fourth generation of those who hate me, but showing steadfast love to thousands of those who love me and keep my commandments.

You shall not take the name of the Lord your God in vain; for the Lord will not hold him guiltless who takes his name in vain.

Remember the Sabbath day, to keep it holy. Six days you shall labor, and do all your work; but the seventh day is a Sabbath to the Lord your God; in it you shall not do any work, you, or your son, or your daughter, your manservant, or your maidservant, or

your cattle, or the sojourner who is within your gates; for in six days the Lord made heaven and earth, the sea, and all that is in them, and rested the seventh day; therefore the Lord blessed the Sabbath day and hallowed it.

Honor your father and your mother, that your days may be long in the land which the Lord your God gives you.

You shall not kill.

You shall not commit adultery.

You shall not steal.

You shall not bear false witness against your neighbor.

You shall not covet your neighbor's wife, or his manservant, or his maidservant, or his ox, or his ass, or anything that is your neighbor's.

Source: Revised Standard Version of the Bible
(Ex.20: 2–17)

Religion Web Sites

About Islam and Muslims:
    http://www.ummah.org.uk/what-is-islam/index.html
Academic Info: Religion:
    http://www.academicinfo.net/religindex.html
Buddha Net: http://www.buddhanet.net/
Christianity Online: http://www.christianity.net/

Hartford Seminary's Internet Links:
    http://www.hartsem.edu/internet.htm
Hinduism Online: http://www.hinduismtoday.kauai.hi.us/
Judaism and Jewish Resources:
    http://shamash.org/trb/judaism.html
World Council of Churches:
    http://www.wcc-coe.org/wcc/map/index-e.html

See Calendar and Holidays for listings of religious holidays.

2000

January
S	M	T	W	T	F	S
						1
2	3	4	5	6	7	8
9	10	11	12	13	14	15
16	17	18	19	20	21	22
23	24	25	26	27	28	29
30	31					

February
S	M	T	W	T	F	S
		1	2	3	4	5
6	7	8	9	10	11	12
13	14	15	16	17	18	19
20	21	22	23	24	25	26
27	28	29				

March
S	M	T	W	T	F	S
			1	2	3	4
5	6	7	8	9	10	11
12	13	14	15	16	17	18
19	20	21	22	23	24	25
26	27	28	29	30	31	

April
S	M	T	W	T	F	S
						1
2	3	4	5	6	7	8
9	10	11	12	13	14	15
16	17	18	19	20	21	22
23	24	25	26	27	28	29
30						

1—New Year's Day
6—Epiphany
8—Ramadan ends
(Eid al-Fitr)
15—Martin Luther King, Jr.'s
Birthday
17—Martin Luther King, Jr.'s
Birthday observed

2—Groundhog Day
12—Lincoln's Birthday
14—Valentine's Day
21—Washington's Birthday
observed
22—Washington's Birthday

8—Ash Wednesday
17—St. Patrick's Day
21—Purim

2—Daylight Saving Time
begins
16—Palm Sunday
20—1st Day of Passover
21—Good Friday
23—Easter Sunday
30—Orthodox Easter

May
S	M	T	W	T	F	S
	1	2	3	4	5	6
7	8	9	10	11	12	13
14	15	16	17	18	19	20
21	22	23	24	25	26	27
28	29	30	31			

June
S	M	T	W	T	F	S
				1	2	3
4	5	6	7	8	9	10
11	12	13	14	15	16	17
18	19	20	21	22	23	24
25	26	27	28	29	30	

July
S	M	T	W	T	F	S
						1
2	3	4	5	6	7	8
9	10	11	12	13	14	15
16	17	18	19	20	21	22
23	24	25	26	27	28	29
30	31					

August
S	M	T	W	T	F	S
		1	2	3	4	5
6	7	8	9	10	11	12
13	14	15	16	17	18	19
20	21	22	23	24	25	26
27	28	29	30	31		

14—Mother's Day
29—Memorial Day observed

1—Ascension Day
9—1st Day of Shavuot
11—Pentecost
14—Flag Day
18—Father's Day

1—Canada Day
4—Independence Day

September
S	M	T	W	T	F	S
					1	2
3	4	5	6	7	8	9
10	11	12	13	14	15	16
17	18	19	20	21	22	23
24	25	26	27	28	29	30

October
S	M	T	W	T	F	S
1	2	3	4	5	6	7
8	9	10	11	12	13	14
15	16	17	18	19	20	21
22	23	24	25	26	27	28
29	30	31				

November
S	M	T	W	T	F	S
			1	2	3	4
5	6	7	8	9	10	11
12	13	14	15	16	17	18
19	20	21	22	23	24	25
26	27	28	29	30		

December
S	M	T	W	T	F	S
					1	2
3	4	5	6	7	8	9
10	11	12	13	14	15	16
17	18	19	20	21	22	23
24	25	26	27	28	29	30
31						

4—Labor Day
30—Rosh Hashanah

9—Yom Kippur
9—Columbus Day
observed
9—Thanksgiving Day
(Canada)
29—Daylight Saving Time
ends
31—Halloween

1—All Saints' Day
7—Election Day
11—Veterans Day
23—Thanksgiving Day
28—Ramadan begins

3—1st Sunday of Advent
22—1st Day of Hanukkah
25—Christmas Day
27—Ramadan ends
(Eid al-Fitr)

Seasons for the Northern Hemisphere, 2000

Mar. 20, 2:35 A.M. EST (07:35 UT*), sun enters
sign of Aries; spring begins

June 20, 9:48 P.M. EDT (June 21, 01:48 UT*), sun
enters sign of Cancer; summer begins

Sept. 22, 1:27 P.M. EDT (17:27 UT*), sun enters
sign of Libra; fall begins

Dec. 21, 8:37 A.M. EST (13:37 UT*), sun enters
sign of Capricorn; winter begins

*Universal Time (UT), also known as Greenwich Mean Time (GMT). *See* p. 451 for a conversion table of Universal Time.

1999

January						
S	M	T	W	T	F	S
					1	2
3	4	5	6	7	8	9
10	11	12	13	14	15	16
17	18	19	20	21	22	23
24	25	26	27	28	29	30
31						

February						
S	M	T	W	T	F	S
	1	2	3	4	5	6
7	8	9	10	11	12	13
14	15	16	17	18	19	20
21	22	23	24	25	26	27
28						

March						
S	M	T	W	T	F	S
	1	2	3	4	5	6
7	8	9	10	11	12	13
14	15	16	17	18	19	20
21	22	23	24	25	26	27
28	29	30	31			

April						
S	M	T	W	T	F	S
				1	2	3
4	5	6	7	8	9	10
11	12	13	14	15	16	17
18	19	20	21	22	23	24
25	26	27	28	29	30	

May						
S	M	T	W	T	F	S
						1
2	3	4	5	6	7	8
9	10	11	12	13	14	15
16	17	18	19	20	21	22
23	24	25	26	27	28	29
30	31					

June						
S	M	T	W	T	F	S
		1	2	3	4	5
6	7	8	9	10	11	12
13	14	15	16	17	18	19
20	21	22	23	24	25	26
27	28	29	30			

July						
S	M	T	W	T	F	S
				1	2	3
4	5	6	7	8	9	10
11	12	13	14	15	16	17
18	19	20	21	22	23	24
25	26	27	28	29	30	31

August						
S	M	T	W	T	F	S
1	2	3	4	5	6	7
8	9	10	11	12	13	14
15	16	17	18	19	20	21
22	23	24	25	26	27	28
29	30	31				

September						
S	M	T	W	T	F	S
			1	2	3	4
5	6	7	8	9	10	11
12	13	14	15	16	17	18
19	20	21	22	23	24	25
26	27	28	29	30		

October						
S	M	T	W	T	F	S
					1	2
3	4	5	6	7	8	9
10	11	12	13	14	15	16
17	18	19	20	21	22	23
24	25	26	27	28	29	30
31						

November						
S	M	T	W	T	F	S
	1	2	3	4	5	6
7	8	9	10	11	12	13
14	15	16	17	18	19	20
21	22	23	24	25	26	27
28	29	30				

December						
S	M	T	W	T	F	S
			1	2	3	4
5	6	7	8	9	10	11
12	13	14	15	16	17	18
19	20	21	22	23	24	25
26	27	28	29	30	31	

2001

January						
S	M	T	W	T	F	S
	1	2	3	4	5	6
7	8	9	10	11	12	13
14	15	16	17	18	19	20
21	22	23	24	25	26	27
28	29	30	31			

February						
S	M	T	W	T	F	S
				1	2	3
4	5	6	7	8	9	10
11	12	13	14	15	16	17
18	19	20	21	22	23	24
25	26	27	28			

March						
S	M	T	W	T	F	S
				1	2	3
4	5	6	7	8	9	10
11	12	13	14	15	16	17
18	19	20	21	22	23	24
25	26	27	28	29	30	31

April						
S	M	T	W	T	F	S
1	2	3	4	5	6	7
8	9	10	11	12	13	14
15	16	17	18	19	20	21
22	23	24	25	26	27	28
29	30					

May						
S	M	T	W	T	F	S
		1	2	3	4	5
6	7	8	9	10	11	12
13	14	15	16	17	18	19
20	21	22	23	24	25	26
27	28	29	30	31		

June						
S	M	T	W	T	F	S
					1	2
3	4	5	6	7	8	9
10	11	12	13	14	15	16
17	18	19	20	21	22	23
24	25	26	27	28	29	30

July						
S	M	T	W	T	F	S
1	2	3	4	5	6	7
8	9	10	11	12	13	14
15	16	17	18	19	20	21
22	23	24	25	26	27	28
29	30	31				

August						
S	M	T	W	T	F	S
			1	2	3	4
5	6	7	8	9	10	11
12	13	14	15	16	17	18
19	20	21	22	23	24	25
26	27	28	29	30	31	

September						
S	M	T	W	T	F	S
						1
2	3	4	5	6	7	8
9	10	11	12	13	14	15
16	17	18	19	20	21	22
23	24	25	26	27	28	29
30						

October						
S	M	T	W	T	F	S
	1	2	3	4	5	6
7	8	9	10	11	12	13
14	15	16	17	18	19	20
21	22	23	24	25	26	27
28	29	30	31			

November						
S	M	T	W	T	F	S
				1	2	3
4	5	6	7	8	9	10
11	12	13	14	15	16	17
18	19	20	21	22	23	24
25	26	27	28	29	30	

December						
S	M	T	W	T	F	S
						1
2	3	4	5	6	7	8
9	10	11	12	13	14	15
16	17	18	19	20	21	22
23	24	25	26	27	28	29
30	31					

Astrological Signs

♈ **Aries (Ram):** March 21–April 19

♉ **Taurus (Bull):** April 20–May 20

♊ **Gemini (Twins):** May 21–June 20

♋ **Cancer (Crab):** June 21–July 22

♌ **Leo (Lion):** July 23–Aug. 22

♍ **Virgo (Virgin):** Aug. 23–Sept. 22

♎ **Libra (Scales):** Sept. 23–Oct. 22

♏ **Scorpio (Scorpion):** Oct. 23–Nov. 21

♐ **Sagittarius (Archer):** Nov. 22–Dec. 21

♑ **Capricorn (Goat):** Dec. 22–Jan. 19

♒ **Aquarius (Water Bearer):** Jan. 20–Feb. 18

♓ **Pisces (Fish):** Feb. 19–March 20

PERPETUAL CALENDAR

1800...4	1844...9	1888...8	1932.13	1976.12	2020.11
1801...5	1845...4	1889...3	1933...1	1977...7	2021...6
1802...6	1846...5	1890...4	1934...2	1978...1	2022...7
1803...7	1847...6	1891...5	1935...3	1979...2	2023...1
1804...8	1848.14	1892.13	1936.11	1980.10	2024...9
1805...3	1849...2	1893...1	1937...6	1981...5	2025...4
1806...4	1850...3	1894...2	1938...7	1982...6	2026...5
1807...5	1851...4	1895...3	1939...1	1983...7	2027...6
1808.13	1852.12	1896.11	1940...9	1984...8	2028.14
1809...1	1853...7	1897...6	1941...4	1985...3	2029...2
1810...2	1854...1	1898...7	1942...5	1986...4	2030...3
1811...3	1855...2	1899...1	1943...6	1987...5	2031...4
1812.11	1856.10	1900...2	1944.14	1988.13	2032.12
1813...6	1857...5	1901...3	1945...2	1989...1	2033...7
1814...7	1858...6	1902...4	1946...3	1990...2	2034...1
1815...1	1859...7	1903...5	1947...4	1991...3	2035...2
1816...9	1860...8	1904.13	1948.12	1992.11	2036.10
1817...4	1861...3	1905...1	1949...7	1993...6	2037...5
1818...5	1862...4	1906...2	1950...1	1994...7	2038...6
1819...6	1863...5	1907...3	1951...2	1995...1	2039...7
1820.14	1864.13	1908.11	1952.10	1996...9	2040...8
1821...2	1865...1	1909...6	1953...5	1997...4	2041...3
1822...3	1866...2	1910...7	1954...6	1998...5	2042...4
1823...4	1867...3	1911...1	1955...7	1999...6	2043...5
1824.12	1868.11	1912...9	1956...8	2000.14	2044.13
1825...7	1869...6	1913...4	1957...3	2001...2	2045...1
1826...1	1870...7	1914...5	1958...4	2002...3	2046...2
1827...2	1871...1	1915...6	1959...5	2003...4	2047...3
1828.10	1872...9	1916.14	1960.13	2004.12	2048.11
1829...5	1873...4	1917...2	1961...1	2005...7	2049...6
1830...6	1874...5	1918...3	1962...2	2006...1	2050...7
1831...7	1875...6	1919...4	1963...3	2007...2	2051...1
1832...8	1876.14	1920.12	1964.11	2008.10	2052...9
1833...3	1877...2	1921...7	1965...6	2009...5	2053...4
1834...4	1878...3	1922...1	1966...7	2010...6	2054...5
1835...5	1879...4	1923...2	1967...1	2011...7	2055...6
1836.13	1880.12	1924.10	1968...9	2012...8	2056.14
1837...1	1881...7	1925...5	1969...4	2013...3	2057...2
1838...2	1882...1	1926...6	1970...5	2014...4	2058...3
1839...3	1883...2	1927...7	1971...6	2015...5	2059...4
1840.11	1884.10	1928...8	1972.14	2016.13	2060.12
1841...6	1885...5	1929...3	1973...2	2017...1	2061...7
1842...7	1886...6	1930...4	1974...3	2018...2	2062...1
1843...1	1887...7	1931...5	1975...4	2019...3	2063...2

DIRECTIONS: The number given with each year in the key above is the number of the calendar to use for that year.

1

```
      JANUARY                FEBRUARY                 MARCH                  APRIL
S  M  T  W  T  F  S     S  M  T  W  T  F  S     S  M  T  W  T  F  S     S  M  T  W  T  F  S
1  2  3  4  5  6  7              1  2  3  4              1  2  3  4                          1
8  9 10 11 12 13 14     5  6  7  8  9 10 11     5  6  7  8  9 10 11     2  3  4  5  6  7  8
15 16 17 18 19 20 21    12 13 14 15 16 17 18    12 13 14 15 16 17 18    9 10 11 12 13 14 15
22 23 24 25 26 27 28    19 20 21 22 23 24 25    19 20 21 22 23 24 25    16 17 18 19 20 21 22
29 30 31                26 27 28                26 27 28 29 30 31       23 24 25 26 27 28 29
                                                                        30

        MAY                     JUNE                    JULY                  AUGUST
S  M  T  W  T  F  S     S  M  T  W  T  F  S     S  M  T  W  T  F  S     S  M  T  W  T  F  S
   1  2  3  4  5  6              1  2  3                       1                   1  2  3  4  5
7  8  9 10 11 12 13     4  5  6  7  8  9 10     2  3  4  5  6  7  8     6  7  8  9 10 11 12
14 15 16 17 18 19 20    11 12 13 14 15 16 17    9 10 11 12 13 14 15    13 14 15 16 17 18 19
21 22 23 24 25 26 27    18 19 20 21 22 23 24    16 17 18 19 20 21 22   20 21 22 23 24 25 26
28 29 30 31             25 26 27 28 29 30       23 24 25 26 27 28 29   27 28 29 30 31
                                                30 31

      SEPTEMBER                OCTOBER                NOVEMBER               DECEMBER
S  M  T  W  T  F  S     S  M  T  W  T  F  S     S  M  T  W  T  F  S     S  M  T  W  T  F  S
                1  2    1  2  3  4  5  6  7              1  2  3  4                   1  2
3  4  5  6  7  8  9     8  9 10 11 12 13 14     5  6  7  8  9 10 11     3  4  5  6  7  8  9
10 11 12 13 14 15 16   15 16 17 18 19 20 21    12 13 14 15 16 17 18    10 11 12 13 14 15 16
17 18 19 20 21 22 23   22 23 24 25 26 27 28    19 20 21 22 23 24 25    17 18 19 20 21 22 23
24 25 26 27 28 29 30   29 30 31                26 27 28 29 30          24 25 26 27 28 29 30
                                                                        31
```

2

```
      JANUARY                FEBRUARY                 MARCH                  APRIL
S  M  T  W  T  F  S     S  M  T  W  T  F  S     S  M  T  W  T  F  S     S  M  T  W  T  F  S
   1  2  3  4  5  6                 1  2  3                 1  2  3     1  2  3  4  5  6  7
7  8  9 10 11 12 13     4  5  6  7  8  9 10     4  5  6  7  8  9 10     8  9 10 11 12 13 14
14 15 16 17 18 19 20    11 12 13 14 15 16 17    11 12 13 14 15 16 17    15 16 17 18 19 20 21
21 22 23 24 25 26 27    18 19 20 21 22 23 24    18 19 20 21 22 23 24    22 23 24 25 26 27 28
28 29 30 31             25 26 27 28             25 26 27 28 29 30 31    29 30

        MAY                     JUNE                    JULY                  AUGUST
S  M  T  W  T  F  S     S  M  T  W  T  F  S     S  M  T  W  T  F  S     S  M  T  W  T  F  S
      1  2  3  4  5                    1  2    1  2  3  4  5  6  7              1  2  3  4
6  7  8  9 10 11 12     3  4  5  6  7  8  9     8  9 10 11 12 13 14     5  6  7  8  9 10 11
13 14 15 16 17 18 19    10 11 12 13 14 15 16    15 16 17 18 19 20 21    12 13 14 15 16 17 18
20 21 22 23 24 25 26    17 18 19 20 21 22 23    22 23 24 25 26 27 28    19 20 21 22 23 24 25
27 28 29 30 31          24 25 26 27 28 29 30    29 30 31                26 27 28 29 30 31

      SEPTEMBER                OCTOBER                NOVEMBER               DECEMBER
S  M  T  W  T  F  S     S  M  T  W  T  F  S     S  M  T  W  T  F  S     S  M  T  W  T  F  S
                   1       1  2  3  4  5  6                 1  2  3                       1
2  3  4  5  6  7  8     7  8  9 10 11 12 13     4  5  6  7  8  9 10     2  3  4  5  6  7  8
9 10 11 12 13 14 15    14 15 16 17 18 19 20    11 12 13 14 15 16 17     9 10 11 12 13 14 15
16 17 18 19 20 21 22   21 22 23 24 25 26 27    18 19 20 21 22 23 24    16 17 18 19 20 21 22
23 24 25 26 27 28 29   28 29 30 31             25 26 27 28 29 30       23 24 25 26 27 28 29
30                                                                     30 31
```

3

```
      JANUARY                FEBRUARY                 MARCH                  APRIL
S  M  T  W  T  F  S     S  M  T  W  T  F  S     S  M  T  W  T  F  S     S  M  T  W  T  F  S
      1  2  3  4  5                    1  2                    1  2        1  2  3  4  5  6
6  7  8  9 10 11 12     3  4  5  6  7  8  9     3  4  5  6  7  8  9     7  8  9 10 11 12 13
13 14 15 16 17 18 19    10 11 12 13 14 15 16    10 11 12 13 14 15 16    14 15 16 17 18 19 20
20 21 22 23 24 25 26    17 18 19 20 21 22 23    17 18 19 20 21 22 23    21 22 23 24 25 26 27
27 28 29 30 31          24 25 26 27 28          24 25 26 27 28 29 30    28 29 30
                                                31

        MAY                     JUNE                    JULY                  AUGUST
S  M  T  W  T  F  S     S  M  T  W  T  F  S     S  M  T  W  T  F  S     S  M  T  W  T  F  S
            1  2  3  4                       1     1  2  3  4  5  6                 1  2  3
5  6  7  8  9 10 11     2  3  4  5  6  7  8     7  8  9 10 11 12 13     4  5  6  7  8  9 10
12 13 14 15 16 17 18    9 10 11 12 13 14 15    14 15 16 17 18 19 20    11 12 13 14 15 16 17
19 20 21 22 23 24 25    16 17 18 19 20 21 22    21 22 23 24 25 26 27    18 19 20 21 22 23 24
26 27 28 29 30 31       23 24 25 26 27 28 29    28 29 30 31             25 26 27 28 29 30 31
                        30

      SEPTEMBER                OCTOBER                NOVEMBER               DECEMBER
S  M  T  W  T  F  S     S  M  T  W  T  F  S     S  M  T  W  T  F  S     S  M  T  W  T  F  S
1  2  3  4  5  6  7           1  2  3  4  5                    1  2     1  2  3  4  5  6  7
8  9 10 11 12 13 14     6  7  8  9 10 11 12     3  4  5  6  7  8  9     8  9 10 11 12 13 14
15 16 17 18 19 20 21    13 14 15 16 17 18 19    10 11 12 13 14 15 16    15 16 17 18 19 20 21
22 23 24 25 26 27 28    20 21 22 23 24 25 26    17 18 19 20 21 22 23    22 23 24 25 26 27 28
29 30                   27 28 29 30 31          24 25 26 27 28 29 30    29 30 31
```

4

```
      JANUARY                FEBRUARY                 MARCH                  APRIL
S  M  T  W  T  F  S     S  M  T  W  T  F  S     S  M  T  W  T  F  S     S  M  T  W  T  F  S
         1  2  3  4                          1                       1       1  2  3  4  5
5  6  7  8  9 10 11     2  3  4  5  6  7  8     2  3  4  5  6  7  8     6  7  8  9 10 11 12
12 13 14 15 16 17 18    9 10 11 12 13 14 15    9 10 11 12 13 14 15    13 14 15 16 17 18 19
19 20 21 22 23 24 25   16 17 18 19 20 21 22    16 17 18 19 20 21 22   20 21 22 23 24 25 26
26 27 28 29 30 31      23 24 25 26 27 28       23 24 25 26 27 28 29   27 28 29 30
                                                30 31

        MAY                     JUNE                    JULY                  AUGUST
S  M  T  W  T  F  S     S  M  T  W  T  F  S     S  M  T  W  T  F  S     S  M  T  W  T  F  S
            1  2  3    1  2  3  4  5  6  7           1  2  3  4  5                    1  2
4  5  6  7  8  9 10     8  9 10 11 12 13 14     6  7  8  9 10 11 12     3  4  5  6  7  8  9
11 12 13 14 15 16 17   15 16 17 18 19 20 21    13 14 15 16 17 18 19    10 11 12 13 14 15 16
18 19 20 21 22 23 24   22 23 24 25 26 27 28    20 21 22 23 24 25 26    17 18 19 20 21 22 23
25 26 27 28 29 30 31   29 30                   27 28 29 30 31          24 25 26 27 28 29 30
                                                                        31

      SEPTEMBER                OCTOBER                NOVEMBER               DECEMBER
S  M  T  W  T  F  S     S  M  T  W  T  F  S     S  M  T  W  T  F  S     S  M  T  W  T  F  S
   1  2  3  4  5  6              1  2  3  4                          1       1  2  3  4  5  6
7  8  9 10 11 12 13     5  6  7  8  9 10 11     2  3  4  5  6  7  8     7  8  9 10 11 12 13
14 15 16 17 18 19 20    12 13 14 15 16 17 18    9 10 11 12 13 14 15    14 15 16 17 18 19 20
21 22 23 24 25 26 27    19 20 21 22 23 24 25   16 17 18 19 20 21 22    21 22 23 24 25 26 27
28 29 30                26 27 28 29 30 31       23 24 25 26 27 28 29   28 29 30 31
                                                30
```

5

```
      JANUARY                FEBRUARY                 MARCH                  APRIL
S  M  T  W  T  F  S     S  M  T  W  T  F  S     S  M  T  W  T  F  S     S  M  T  W  T  F  S
            1  2  3    1  2  3  4  5  6  7     1  2  3  4  5  6  7              1  2  3  4
4  5  6  7  8  9 10     8  9 10 11 12 13 14     8  9 10 11 12 13 14     5  6  7  8  9 10 11
11 12 13 14 15 16 17   15 16 17 18 19 20 21    15 16 17 18 19 20 21    12 13 14 15 16 17 18
18 19 20 21 22 23 24   22 23 24 25 26 27 28    22 23 24 25 26 27 28    19 20 21 22 23 24 25
25 26 27 28 29 30 31                           29 30 31                26 27 28 29 30

        MAY                     JUNE                    JULY                  AUGUST
S  M  T  W  T  F  S     S  M  T  W  T  F  S     S  M  T  W  T  F  S     S  M  T  W  T  F  S
                1  2       1  2  3  4  5  6              1  2  3  4                       1
3  4  5  6  7  8  9     7  8  9 10 11 12 13     5  6  7  8  9 10 11     2  3  4  5  6  7  8
10 11 12 13 14 15 16   14 15 16 17 18 19 20    12 13 14 15 16 17 18    9 10 11 12 13 14 15
17 18 19 20 21 22 23   21 22 23 24 25 26 27    19 20 21 22 23 24 25   16 17 18 19 20 21 22
24 25 26 27 28 29 30   28 29 30                26 27 28 29 30 31      23 24 25 26 27 28 29
31                                                                     30 31

      SEPTEMBER                OCTOBER                NOVEMBER               DECEMBER
S  M  T  W  T  F  S     S  M  T  W  T  F  S     S  M  T  W  T  F  S     S  M  T  W  T  F  S
      1  2  3  4  5                 1  2  3    1  2  3  4  5  6  7           1  2  3  4  5
6  7  8  9 10 11 12     4  5  6  7  8  9 10     8  9 10 11 12 13 14     6  7  8  9 10 11 12
13 14 15 16 17 18 19   11 12 13 14 15 16 17    15 16 17 18 19 20 21    13 14 15 16 17 18 19
20 21 22 23 24 25 26   18 19 20 21 22 23 24    22 23 24 25 26 27 28    20 21 22 23 24 25 26
27 28 29 30            25 26 27 28 29 30 31    29 30                   27 28 29 30 31
```

6

```
      JANUARY                FEBRUARY                 MARCH                  APRIL
S  M  T  W  T  F  S     S  M  T  W  T  F  S     S  M  T  W  T  F  S     S  M  T  W  T  F  S
                1  2       1  2  3  4  5  6              1  2  3  4                 1  2  3
3  4  5  6  7  8  9     7  8  9 10 11 12 13     5  6  7  8  9 10 11     4  5  6  7  8  9 10
10 11 12 13 14 15 16   14 15 16 17 18 19 20    12 13 14 15 16 17 18    11 12 13 14 15 16 17
17 18 19 20 21 22 23   21 22 23 24 25 26 27    19 20 21 22 23 24 25    18 19 20 21 22 23 24
24 25 26 27 28 29 30   28                      26 27 28 29 30 31       25 26 27 28 29 30
31

        MAY                     JUNE                    JULY                  AUGUST
S  M  T  W  T  F  S     S  M  T  W  T  F  S     S  M  T  W  T  F  S     S  M  T  W  T  F  S
                   1          1  2  3  4  5                 1  2  3    1  2  3  4  5  6  7
2  3  4  5  6  7  8     6  7  8  9 10 11 12     4  5  6  7  8  9 10     8  9 10 11 12 13 14
9 10 11 12 13 14 15    13 14 15 16 17 18 19    11 12 13 14 15 16 17    15 16 17 18 19 20 21
16 17 18 19 20 21 22   20 21 22 23 24 25 26    18 19 20 21 22 23 24    22 23 24 25 26 27 28
23 24 25 26 27 28 29   27 28 29 30             25 26 27 28 29 30 31    29 30 31
30 31

      SEPTEMBER                OCTOBER                NOVEMBER               DECEMBER
S  M  T  W  T  F  S     S  M  T  W  T  F  S     S  M  T  W  T  F  S     S  M  T  W  T  F  S
         1  2  3  4                 1  2    1  2  3  4  5  6              1  2  3  4
5  6  7  8  9 10 11     3  4  5  6  7  8  9     7  8  9 10 11 12 13     5  6  7  8  9 10 11
12 13 14 15 16 17 18   10 11 12 13 14 15 16    14 15 16 17 18 19 20    12 13 14 15 16 17 18
19 20 21 22 23 24 25   17 18 19 20 21 22 23    21 22 23 24 25 26 27    19 20 21 22 23 24 25
26 27 28 29 30         24 25 26 27 28 29 30    28 29 30                26 27 28 29 30 31
                        31
```

7

```
JANUARY               FEBRUARY              MARCH                 APRIL
S  M  T  W  T  F  S    S  M  T  W  T  F  S    S  M  T  W  T  F  S    S  M  T  W  T  F  S
                  1           1  2  3  4  5           1  2  3  4  5                 1  2
 2  3  4  5  6  7  8    6  7  8  9 10 11 12    6  7  8  9 10 11 12    3  4  5  6  7  8  9
 9 10 11 12 13 14 15   13 14 15 16 17 18 19   13 14 15 16 17 18 19   10 11 12 13 14 15 16
16 17 18 19 20 21 22   20 21 22 23 24 25 26   20 21 22 23 24 25 26   17 18 19 20 21 22 23
23 24 25 26 27 28 29   27 28                  27 28 29 30 31         24 25 26 27 28 29 30
30 31

MAY                   JUNE                  JULY                  AUGUST
S  M  T  W  T  F  S    S  M  T  W  T  F  S    S  M  T  W  T  F  S    S  M  T  W  T  F  S
 1  2  3  4  5  6  7           1  2  3  4                    1  2        1  2  3  4  5  6
 8  9 10 11 12 13 14    5  6  7  8  9 10 11    3  4  5  6  7  8  9    7  8  9 10 11 12 13
15 16 17 18 19 20 21   12 13 14 15 16 17 18   10 11 12 13 14 15 16   14 15 16 17 18 19 20
22 23 24 25 26 27 28   19 20 21 22 23 24 25   17 18 19 20 21 22 23   21 22 23 24 25 26 27
29 30 31               26 27 28 29 30         24 25 26 27 28 29 30   28 29 30 31
                                              31

SEPTEMBER             OCTOBER               NOVEMBER              DECEMBER
S  M  T  W  T  F  S    S  M  T  W  T  F  S    S  M  T  W  T  F  S    S  M  T  W  T  F  S
             1  2  3                     1           1  2  3  4  5                 1  2  3
 4  5  6  7  8  9 10    2  3  4  5  6  7  8    6  7  8  9 10 11 12    4  5  6  7  8  9 10
11 12 13 14 15 16 17    9 10 11 12 13 14 15   13 14 15 16 17 18 19   11 12 13 14 15 16 17
18 19 20 21 22 23 24   16 17 18 19 20 21 22   20 21 22 23 24 25 26   18 19 20 21 22 23 24
25 26 27 28 29 30      23 24 25 26 27 28 29   27 28 29 30            25 26 27 28 29 30 31
                       30 31
```

8

```
JANUARY               FEBRUARY              MARCH                 APRIL
S  M  T  W  T  F  S    S  M  T  W  T  F  S    S  M  T  W  T  F  S    S  M  T  W  T  F  S
 1  2  3  4  5  6  7           1  2  3  4                 1  2  3     1  2  3  4  5  6  7
 8  9 10 11 12 13 14    5  6  7  8  9 10 11    4  5  6  7  8  9 10    8  9 10 11 12 13 14
15 16 17 18 19 20 21   12 13 14 15 16 17 18   11 12 13 14 15 16 17   15 16 17 18 19 20 21
22 23 24 25 26 27 28   19 20 21 22 23 24 25   18 19 20 21 22 23 24   22 23 24 25 26 27 28
29 30 31               26 27 28 29            25 26 27 28 29 30 31   29 30

MAY                   JUNE                  JULY                  AUGUST
S  M  T  W  T  F  S    S  M  T  W  T  F  S    S  M  T  W  T  F  S    S  M  T  W  T  F  S
       1  2  3  4  5                 1  2     1  2  3  4  5  6  7           1  2  3  4
 6  7  8  9 10 11 12    3  4  5  6  7  8  9    8  9 10 11 12 13 14    5  6  7  8  9 10 11
13 14 15 16 17 18 19   10 11 12 13 14 15 16   15 16 17 18 19 20 21   12 13 14 15 16 17 18
20 21 22 23 24 25 26   17 18 19 20 21 22 23   22 23 24 25 26 27 28   19 20 21 22 23 24 25
27 28 29 30 31         24 25 26 27 28 29 30   29 30 31               26 27 28 29 30 31

SEPTEMBER             OCTOBER               NOVEMBER              DECEMBER
S  M  T  W  T  F  S    S  M  T  W  T  F  S    S  M  T  W  T  F  S    S  M  T  W  T  F  S
                  1        1  2  3  4  5  6              1  2  3                     1
 2  3  4  5  6  7  8    7  8  9 10 11 12 13    4  5  6  7  8  9 10    2  3  4  5  6  7  8
 9 10 11 12 13 14 15   14 15 16 17 18 19 20   11 12 13 14 15 16 17    9 10 11 12 13 14 15
16 17 18 19 20 21 22   21 22 23 24 25 26 27   18 19 20 21 22 23 24   16 17 18 19 20 21 22
23 24 25 26 27 28 29   28 29 30 31            25 26 27 28 29 30      23 24 25 26 27 28 29
30                                                                   30 31
```

9

```
JANUARY               FEBRUARY              MARCH                 APRIL
S  M  T  W  T  F  S    S  M  T  W  T  F  S    S  M  T  W  T  F  S    S  M  T  W  T  F  S
    1  2  3  4  5  6              1  2  3                    1  2        1  2  3  4  5  6
 7  8  9 10 11 12 13    4  5  6  7  8  9 10    3  4  5  6  7  8  9    7  8  9 10 11 12 13
14 15 16 17 18 19 20   11 12 13 14 15 16 17   10 11 12 13 14 15 16   14 15 16 17 18 19 20
21 22 23 24 25 26 27   18 19 20 21 22 23 24   17 18 19 20 21 22 23   21 22 23 24 25 26 27
28 29 30 31            25 26 27 28 29         24 25 26 27 28 29 30   28 29 30
                                              31

MAY                   JUNE                  JULY                  AUGUST
S  M  T  W  T  F  S    S  M  T  W  T  F  S    S  M  T  W  T  F  S    S  M  T  W  T  F  S
          1  2  3  4                     1        1  2  3  4  5  6              1  2  3
 5  6  7  8  9 10 11    2  3  4  5  6  7  8    7  8  9 10 11 12 13    4  5  6  7  8  9 10
12 13 14 15 16 17 18    9 10 11 12 13 14 15   14 15 16 17 18 19 20   11 12 13 14 15 16 17
19 20 21 22 23 24 25   16 17 18 19 20 21 22   21 22 23 24 25 26 27   18 19 20 21 22 23 24
26 27 28 29 30 31      23 24 25 26 27 28 29   28 29 30 31            25 26 27 28 29 30 31
                       30

SEPTEMBER             OCTOBER               NOVEMBER              DECEMBER
S  M  T  W  T  F  S    S  M  T  W  T  F  S    S  M  T  W  T  F  S    S  M  T  W  T  F  S
 1  2  3  4  5  6  7        1  2  3  4  5                 1  2     1  2  3  4  5  6  7
 8  9 10 11 12 13 14    6  7  8  9 10 11 12    3  4  5  6  7  8  9    8  9 10 11 12 13 14
15 16 17 18 19 20 21   13 14 15 16 17 18 19   10 11 12 13 14 15 16   15 16 17 18 19 20 21
22 23 24 25 26 27 28   20 21 22 23 24 25 26   17 18 19 20 21 22 23   22 23 24 25 26 27 28
29 30                  27 28 29 30 31         24 25 26 27 28 29 30   29 30 31
```

10

```
JANUARY               FEBRUARY              MARCH                 APRIL
S  M  T  W  T  F  S    S  M  T  W  T  F  S    S  M  T  W  T  F  S    S  M  T  W  T  F  S
       1  2  3  4  5                 1  2                     1           1  2  3  4  5
 6  7  8  9 10 11 12    3  4  5  6  7  8  9    2  3  4  5  6  7  8    6  7  8  9 10 11 12
13 14 15 16 17 18 19   10 11 12 13 14 15 16    9 10 11 12 13 14 15   13 14 15 16 17 18 19
20 21 22 23 24 25 26   17 18 19 20 21 22 23   16 17 18 19 20 21 22   20 21 22 23 24 25 26
27 28 29 30 31         24 25 26 27 28 29      23 24 25 26 27 28 29   27 28 29 30
                                              30 31

MAY                   JUNE                  JULY                  AUGUST
S  M  T  W  T  F  S    S  M  T  W  T  F  S    S  M  T  W  T  F  S    S  M  T  W  T  F  S
             1  2  3     1  2  3  4  5  6  7           1  2  3  4  5                 1  2
 4  5  6  7  8  9 10     8  9 10 11 12 13 14    6  7  8  9 10 11 12    3  4  5  6  7  8  9
11 12 13 14 15 16 17   15 16 17 18 19 20 21   13 14 15 16 17 18 19   10 11 12 13 14 15 16
18 19 20 21 22 23 24   22 23 24 25 26 27 28   20 21 22 23 24 25 26   17 18 19 20 21 22 23
25 26 27 28 29 30 31   29 30                  27 28 29 30 31         24 25 26 27 28 29 30
                                                                     31

SEPTEMBER             OCTOBER               NOVEMBER              DECEMBER
S  M  T  W  T  F  S    S  M  T  W  T  F  S    S  M  T  W  T  F  S    S  M  T  W  T  F  S
    1  2  3  4  5  6              1  2  3  4                     1        1  2  3  4  5  6
 7  8  9 10 11 12 13    5  6  7  8  9 10 11    2  3  4  5  6  7  8    7  8  9 10 11 12 13
14 15 16 17 18 19 20   12 13 14 15 16 17 18    9 10 11 12 13 14 15   14 15 16 17 18 19 20
21 22 23 24 25 26 27   19 20 21 22 23 24 25   16 17 18 19 20 21 22   21 22 23 24 25 26 27
28 29 30               26 27 28 29 30 31      23 24 25 26 27 28 29   28 29 30 31
                                              30
```

11

```
JANUARY               FEBRUARY              MARCH                 APRIL
S  M  T  W  T  F  S    S  M  T  W  T  F  S    S  M  T  W  T  F  S    S  M  T  W  T  F  S
          1  2  3  4                     1     1  2  3  4  5  6  7              1  2  3  4
 5  6  7  8  9 10 11    2  3  4  5  6  7  8    8  9 10 11 12 13 14    5  6  7  8  9 10 11
12 13 14 15 16 17 18    9 10 11 12 13 14 15   15 16 17 18 19 20 21   12 13 14 15 16 17 18
19 20 21 22 23 24 25   16 17 18 19 20 21 22   22 23 24 25 26 27 28   19 20 21 22 23 24 25
26 27 28 29 30 31      23 24 25 26 27 28 29   29 30 31               26 27 28 29 30

MAY                   JUNE                  JULY                  AUGUST
S  M  T  W  T  F  S    S  M  T  W  T  F  S    S  M  T  W  T  F  S    S  M  T  W  T  F  S
                1  2        1  2  3  4  5  6              1  2  3  4                     1
 3  4  5  6  7  8  9    7  8  9 10 11 12 13    5  6  7  8  9 10 11    2  3  4  5  6  7  8
10 11 12 13 14 15 16   14 15 16 17 18 19 20   12 13 14 15 16 17 18    9 10 11 12 13 14 15
17 18 19 20 21 22 23   21 22 23 24 25 26 27   19 20 21 22 23 24 25   16 17 18 19 20 21 22
24 25 26 27 28 29 30   28 29 30               26 27 28 29 30 31      23 24 25 26 27 28 29
31                                                                   30 31

SEPTEMBER             OCTOBER               NOVEMBER              DECEMBER
S  M  T  W  T  F  S    S  M  T  W  T  F  S    S  M  T  W  T  F  S    S  M  T  W  T  F  S
       1  2  3  4  5              1  2  3     1  2  3  4  5  6  7           1  2  3  4  5
 6  7  8  9 10 11 12    4  5  6  7  8  9 10    8  9 10 11 12 13 14    6  7  8  9 10 11 12
13 14 15 16 17 18 19   11 12 13 14 15 16 17   15 16 17 18 19 20 21   13 14 15 16 17 18 19
20 21 22 23 24 25 26   18 19 20 21 22 23 24   22 23 24 25 26 27 28   20 21 22 23 24 25 26
27 28 29 30            25 26 27 28 29 30 31   29 30                  27 28 29 30 31
```

12

```
JANUARY               FEBRUARY              MARCH                 APRIL
S  M  T  W  T  F  S    S  M  T  W  T  F  S    S  M  T  W  T  F  S    S  M  T  W  T  F  S
             1  2  3     1  2  3  4  5  6  7        1  2  3  4  5  6              1  2  3
 4  5  6  7  8  9 10     8  9 10 11 12 13 14    7  8  9 10 11 12 13    4  5  6  7  8  9 10
11 12 13 14 15 16 17   15 16 17 18 19 20 21   14 15 16 17 18 19 20   11 12 13 14 15 16 17
18 19 20 21 22 23 24   22 23 24 25 26 27 28   21 22 23 24 25 26 27   18 19 20 21 22 23 24
25 26 27 28 29 30 31   29                     28 29 30 31            25 26 27 28 29 30

MAY                   JUNE                  JULY                  AUGUST
S  M  T  W  T  F  S    S  M  T  W  T  F  S    S  M  T  W  T  F  S    S  M  T  W  T  F  S
                  1        1  2  3  4  5                 1  2  3     1  2  3  4  5  6  7
 2  3  4  5  6  7  8    6  7  8  9 10 11 12    4  5  6  7  8  9 10    8  9 10 11 12 13 14
 9 10 11 12 13 14 15   13 14 15 16 17 18 19   11 12 13 14 15 16 17   15 16 17 18 19 20 21
16 17 18 19 20 21 22   20 21 22 23 24 25 26   18 19 20 21 22 23 24   22 23 24 25 26 27 28
23 24 25 26 27 28 29   27 28 29 30            25 26 27 28 29 30 31   29 30 31
30 31

SEPTEMBER             OCTOBER               NOVEMBER              DECEMBER
S  M  T  W  T  F  S    S  M  T  W  T  F  S    S  M  T  W  T  F  S    S  M  T  W  T  F  S
          1  2  3  4                 1  2        1  2  3  4  5  6           1  2  3  4
 5  6  7  8  9 10 11    3  4  5  6  7  8  9    7  8  9 10 11 12 13    5  6  7  8  9 10 11
12 13 14 15 16 17 18   10 11 12 13 14 15 16   14 15 16 17 18 19 20   12 13 14 15 16 17 18
19 20 21 22 23 24 25   17 18 19 20 21 22 23   21 22 23 24 25 26 27   19 20 21 22 23 24 25
26 27 28 29 30         24 25 26 27 28 29 30   28 29 30               26 27 28 29 30 31
                       31
```

13

```
JANUARY               FEBRUARY              MARCH                 APRIL
S  M  T  W  T  F  S    S  M  T  W  T  F  S    S  M  T  W  T  F  S    S  M  T  W  T  F  S
                1  2        1  2  3  4  5  6        1  2  3  4  5                 1  2
 3  4  5  6  7  8  9    7  8  9 10 11 12 13    6  7  8  9 10 11 12    3  4  5  6  7  8  9
10 11 12 13 14 15 16   14 15 16 17 18 19 20   13 14 15 16 17 18 19   10 11 12 13 14 15 16
17 18 19 20 21 22 23   21 22 23 24 25 26 27   20 21 22 23 24 25 26   17 18 19 20 21 22 23
24 25 26 27 28 29 30   28 29                  27 28 29 30 31         24 25 26 27 28 29 30
31

MAY                   JUNE                  JULY                  AUGUST
S  M  T  W  T  F  S    S  M  T  W  T  F  S    S  M  T  W  T  F  S    S  M  T  W  T  F  S
 1  2  3  4  5  6  7           1  2  3  4                    1  2        1  2  3  4  5  6
 8  9 10 11 12 13 14    5  6  7  8  9 10 11    3  4  5  6  7  8  9    7  8  9 10 11 12 13
15 16 17 18 19 20 21   12 13 14 15 16 17 18   10 11 12 13 14 15 16   14 15 16 17 18 19 20
22 23 24 25 26 27 28   19 20 21 22 23 24 25   17 18 19 20 21 22 23   21 22 23 24 25 26 27
29 30 31               26 27 28 29 30         24 25 26 27 28 29 30   28 29 30 31
                                              31

SEPTEMBER             OCTOBER               NOVEMBER              DECEMBER
S  M  T  W  T  F  S    S  M  T  W  T  F  S    S  M  T  W  T  F  S    S  M  T  W  T  F  S
             1  2  3                     1           1  2  3  4  5              1  2  3
 4  5  6  7  8  9 10    2  3  4  5  6  7  8    6  7  8  9 10 11 12    4  5  6  7  8  9 10
11 12 13 14 15 16 17    9 10 11 12 13 14 15   13 14 15 16 17 18 19   11 12 13 14 15 16 17
18 19 20 21 22 23 24   16 17 18 19 20 21 22   20 21 22 23 24 25 26   18 19 20 21 22 23 24
25 26 27 28 29 30      23 24 25 26 27 28 29   27 28 29 30            25 26 27 28 29 30 31
                       30 31
```

14

```
JANUARY               FEBRUARY              MARCH                 APRIL
S  M  T  W  T  F  S    S  M  T  W  T  F  S    S  M  T  W  T  F  S    S  M  T  W  T  F  S
                  1           1  2  3  4  5           1  2  3  4                     1
 2  3  4  5  6  7  8    6  7  8  9 10 11 12    5  6  7  8  9 10 11    2  3  4  5  6  7  8
 9 10 11 12 13 14 15   13 14 15 16 17 18 19   12 13 14 15 16 17 18    9 10 11 12 13 14 15
16 17 18 19 20 21 22   20 21 22 23 24 25 26   19 20 21 22 23 24 25   16 17 18 19 20 21 22
23 24 25 26 27 28 29   27 28 29              26 27 28 29 30 31       23 24 25 26 27 28 29
30 31                                                                30

MAY                   JUNE                  JULY                  AUGUST
S  M  T  W  T  F  S    S  M  T  W  T  F  S    S  M  T  W  T  F  S    S  M  T  W  T  F  S
    1  2  3  4  5  6              1  2  3                     1           1  2  3  4  5
 7  8  9 10 11 12 13    4  5  6  7  8  9 10    2  3  4  5  6  7  8    6  7  8  9 10 11 12
14 15 16 17 18 19 20   11 12 13 14 15 16 17    9 10 11 12 13 14 15   13 14 15 16 17 18 19
21 22 23 24 25 26 27   18 19 20 21 22 23 24   16 17 18 19 20 21 22   20 21 22 23 24 25 26
28 29 30 31            25 26 27 28 29 30      23 24 25 26 27 28 29   27 28 29 30 31
                                              30 31

SEPTEMBER             OCTOBER               NOVEMBER              DECEMBER
S  M  T  W  T  F  S    S  M  T  W  T  F  S    S  M  T  W  T  F  S    S  M  T  W  T  F  S
                1  2     1  2  3  4  5  6  7           1  2  3  4                 1  2
 3  4  5  6  7  8  9     8  9 10 11 12 13 14    5  6  7  8  9 10 11    3  4  5  6  7  8  9
10 11 12 13 14 15 16   15 16 17 18 19 20 21   12 13 14 15 16 17 18   10 11 12 13 14 15 16
17 18 19 20 21 22 23   22 23 24 25 26 27 28   19 20 21 22 23 24 25   17 18 19 20 21 22 23
24 25 26 27 28 29 30   29 30 31              26 27 28 29 30          24 25 26 27 28 29 30
                                                                     31
```

History of the Calendar

The purpose of a calendar is to reckon time in advance, to show how many days have to elapse until a certain event takes place—the harvest, a religious festival, or whatever. The earliest calendars, naturally, were crude, and they must have been strongly influenced by the geographical location of the people who made them. In the Scandinavian countries, for example, where the seasons are pronounced, the concept of the year was determined by the seasons, specifically by the end of winter. The Norsemen, before becoming Christians, are said to have had a calendar consisting of 10 months of 30 days each.

But in warmer countries, where the seasons are less pronounced, the Moon became the basic unit for time reckoning; an old Jewish book actually makes the statement that "the Moon was created for the counting of the days." All the oldest calendars for which we have reliable information were lunar calendars, based on the time interval from one new moon to the next—a so-called lunation. But even in a warm climate there are annual events that pay no attention to the phases of the Moon. In some areas it was a rainy season; in Egypt it was the annual flooding of the Nile. It was, therefore, necessary to regulate daily life and religious festivals by lunations, but to take care of the annual event in some other manner.

The calendar of the Assyrians was based on the phases of the Moon. The month began with the first appearance of the lunar crescent, and since this can best be observed in the evening, the day began with sunset. They knew that a lunation was 29½ days long, so their lunar year had a duration of 354 days, falling 11 days short of the solar year.[1] After three years such a lunar calendar would be off by 33 days, or more than one lunation. We know that the Assyrians added an extra month from time to time, but we do not know whether they had developed a special rule for doing so or whether the priests proclaimed the necessity for an extra month from observation. If they made every third year a year of 13 lunations, their three-year period would cover 1,091½ days (using their value of 29½ days for one lunation), or just about 4 days too short. In one century this mistake would add up to 133 days by their reckoning (in reality closer to 134 days), requiring four extra lunations per century.

We now know that an eight-year period, consisting of five years with 12 months and three years with 13 months, would lead to a difference of only 20 days per century, but we do not know whether such a calendar was actually used.

The best approximation that was possible in antiquity was a 19-year period, with 7 of these 19 years having 13 months. This means that the period contained 235 months. This, still using the old value for a lunation, made a total of 6,932½ days, while 19 solar years added up to 6,939.7 days, a difference of just one week per period and about five weeks per century. Even the 19-year period required constant adjustment, but it was the period that became the basis of the religious calendar of the Jews. The Arabs used the same calendar at first, but

Muhammed forbade shifting from 12 months to 13 months, so that the Islamic religious calendar, even today, has a lunar year of 354 days. As a result the Islamic religious festivals run through all the seasons of the year three times per century.

The Egyptians had a traditional calendar with 12 months of 30 days each. At one time they added 5 extra days at the end of every year. These turned into a 5-day festival because it was thought to be unlucky to work during that time.

When Rome emerged as a world power, the difficulties of making a calendar were well known, but the Romans complicated their lives because of their superstition that even numbers were unlucky. Hence their months were 29 or 31 days long, with the exception of February, which had 28 days. However, 4 months of 31 days, 7 months of 29 days, and 1 month of 28 days added up to only 355 days. Therefore, the Romans invented an extra month called Mercedonius of 22 or 23 days. It was added every second year.

Even with Mercedonius, the Roman calendar was so far off that Caesar, advised by the astronomer Sosigenes, ordered a sweeping reform in 45 B.C.E. One year, made 445 days long by imperial decree, brought the calendar back in step with the seasons. Then the solar year (with the value of 365 days and 6 hours) was made the basis of the calendar. The months were 30 or 31 days in length, and to take care of the 6 hours, every fourth year was made a 366-day year. Moreover, Caesar decreed the year began with the first of January, not with the vernal equinox in late March.

This was the Julian calendar, named after Julius Caesar. It is still the calendar of the Eastern Orthodox churches. However, the year is 11½ minutes shorter than the figure written into Caesar's calendar by Sosigenes, and after a number of centuries, even 11½ minutes add up.

While Caesar could decree that the vernal equinox should not be used as the first day of the new year, the vernal equinox is still a fact of nature that could not be disregarded. One of the first (as far as we know) to become alarmed about this was Roger Bacon. He sent a memorandum to Pope Clement IV, who apparently was not impressed. But Pope Sixtus IV (who reigned from 1471 to 1484) decided that another reform was needed and called the German astronomer Regiomontanus to Rome to advise him. Regiomontanus arrived in 1475, but one year later he died in an epidemic, one of the recurrent outbreaks of the plague. The pope himself survived, but his reform plans died with Regiomontanus.

Less than a hundred years later, in 1545, the Council of Trent authorized the then pope, Paul III, to reform the calendar once more. Most of the mathematical and astronomical work was done by Father Christopher Clavius, S.J. The immediate correction, advised by Father Clavius and ordered by Pope Gregory XIII, was that Thursday, Oct. 4, 1582, was to be the last day of the Julian calendar. The next day was Friday, with the date of October 15. For long-range accuracy, a formula suggested by the

1. The correct figures are lunation: 29 d, 12 h, 44 min, 2.8 sec (29.530585 d); solar year: 365 d, 5 h, 48 min, 46 sec (365.242216 d); 12 lunations: 354 d, 8 h, 48 min, 34 sec (354.3671 d).

Drift of the Vernal Equinox in the Julian Calendar

Date	Julian year	Date	Julian year	Date	Julian year
March 21	C.E. 325	March 17	C.E. 837	March 13	C.E. 1349
March 20	C.E. 453	March 16	C.E. 965	March 12	C.E. 1477
March 19	C.E. 581	March 15	C.E. 1093	March 11	C.E. 1605
March 18	C.E. 709	March 14	C.E. 1221		

Vatican librarian Aloysius Giglio (latinized into Lilius) was adopted: every fourth year is a leap year *unless* it is a century year like 1700 or 1800. Century years can be leap years *only* when they are divisible by 400 (e.g., 1600). This rule eliminates three leap years in four centuries, making the calendar sufficiently correct for all ordinary purposes.

Unfortunately, all the Protestant princes in 1582 chose to ignore the papal bull; they continued with the Julian calendar. It was not until 1698 that the German professor Erhard Weigel persuaded the Protestant rulers of Germany and of the Netherlands to change to the new calendar. In England the shift took place in 1752, and in Russia it needed the revolution to introduce the Gregorian calendar in 1918.

The average year of the Gregorian calendar, in spite of the leap year rule, is about 26 seconds longer than the earth's orbital period. But this discrepancy will need 3,323 years to build up to a single day.

Modern proposals for calendar reform do not aim at a "better" calendar, but at one that is more convenient to use, especially for commercial purposes. A 365-day year cannot be divided into equal halves or quarters; the number of days per month is haphazard; the months begin or end in the middle of a week; a holiday fixed by date (e.g., the Fourth of July) will wander through a week; a holiday fixed in another manner (e.g., Easter) can fall on 35 possible dates. The Gregorian calendar, admittedly, keeps the calendar dates in reasonable unison with astronomical events, but it still is full of minor annoyances. Moreover, you need a calendar every year to look up dates; an ideal calendar should be one that you can memorize for one year and that is valid for all other years, too.

Time and Calendar

The two natural cycles on which time measurements are based are the year and the day. The year is defined as the time required for Earth to complete one revolution around the Sun, while the day is the time required for Earth to complete one turn upon its axis. Unfortunately Earth needs 365 days plus about six hours to go around the Sun once, so that the year does not consist of so and so many days; the fractional day has to be taken care of by an extra day every fourth year.

But because Earth, while turning upon its axis, also moves around the Sun, there are two kinds of days. A day may be defined as the interval between the highest point of the Sun in the sky on two successive days. This, averaged out over the year, produces the customary 24-hour day. But one might also define a day as the time interval between the moments when a certain point in the sky, say a conveniently located star, is directly overhead. This is called:

Sidereal time. Astronomers use a point which they call the "vernal equinox" for the actual determination. Such a sidereal day is somewhat shorter than the "solar day," namely by about three minutes and 56 seconds of so-called mean solar time.

Apparent solar time is the time based directly on the Sun's position in the sky. In ordinary life the day runs from midnight to midnight. It begins when the Sun is invisible by being 12 hours from its zenith. Astronomers use the so-called Julian day, which runs from noon to noon; the concept was invented by the astronomer Joseph Scaliger, who named it after his father, Julius. To avoid the problems caused by leap-year days and so forth, Scaliger picked a conveniently remote date in the past (4713 B.C.E.) and suggested just counting days without regard to weeks, months, and years. The reason for having the Julian Day run from noon to noon is the practical one that astronomical observations usually extend across the midnight hour, which would require a change in date (or in the Julian Day number) if the astronomical day, like the civil day, ran from midnight to midnight.

Mean solar time, rather than apparent solar time, is what is actually used most of the time. The mean solar time is based on the position of a fictitious "mean sun." The reason why this fictitious sun has to be introduced is the following: Earth turns on its axis regularly; it needs the same number of seconds regardless of the season. But the movement of Earth around the Sun is not regular because Earth's orbit is an ellipse. This has the result (as explained in the section The Seasons) that Earth moves faster in January and slower in July. Though it is Earth that changes velocity, it looks to us as if the Sun does. In January, when Earth moves faster, the *apparent* movement of the Sun looks faster. The mean sun of time measurements, then, is a sun that moves regularly all year round; the real Sun will be either ahead of or behind the mean sun. The difference between the real Sun and the fictitious mean sun is called the *equation of time.*

When the real Sun is west of the mean sun we have the "sun fast" condition, with the real Sun crossing the meridian ahead of the mean sun. The opposite is the "sun slow" situation, when the real Sun crosses the meridian after the mean sun. Of course, what is observed is the real Sun. The equation of time is needed to establish mean solar time, kept by the reference clocks.

But if all clocks were actually set by mean solar time we would be plagued by a welter of time differences that would be "correct" but a major nuisance. A clock on Long Island, correctly showing mean solar time for its location (this would be *local civil time*), would be slightly ahead of a clock in Newark, N.J. The Newark clock would be slightly ahead of a clock in Trenton, N.J., which, in turn, would be ahead of a clock in Philadelphia. This condition prevailed until 1884, when a system of standard time was adopted by the International Meridian Conference. Earth's surface was divided

The Names of the Days of the Week

Latin	Old English	English	German	French	Italian	Spanish
Dies Solis	Sun's Day	Sunday	Sonntag	dimanche	domenica	domingo
Dies Lunae	Moon's Day	Monday	Montag	lundi	lunedì	lunes
Dies Martis	Tiw's Day	Tuesday	Dienstag	mardi	martedì	martes
Dies Mercurii	Woden's Day	Wednesday	Mittwoch	mercredi	mercoledì	miércoles
Dies Jovis	Thor's Day	Thursday	Donnerstag	jeudi	giovedì	jueves
Dies Veneris	Frigg's Day	Friday	Freitag	vendredi	venerdì	viernes
Dies Saturni	Seterne's Day	Saturday	Samstag	samedi	sabato	sábado

NOTE: The seven-day week originated in ancient Mesopotamia and became part of the Roman calendar in C.E. 321. The names of the days are based on the seven celestial bodies (the Sun, the Moon, Mars, Mercury, Jupiter, Venus, and Saturn), believed at that time to revolve around Earth and influence its events. Most of Western Europe adopted the Roman nomenclature. The Germanic languages substituted Germanic equivalents for the names of four of the Roman gods: Tiw, the god of war, replaced Mars; Woden, the god of wisdom, replaced Mercury; Thor, the god of thunder, replaced Jupiter; and Frigg, the goddess of love, replaced Venus.

into 24 zones. The standard time of each zone is the mean astronomical time of one of 24 meridians, 15 degrees apart, beginning at the Greenwich, England, meridian and extending east and west around the globe to the International Date Line. (This system was actually put into use a year earlier by the railroad companies of the U.S. and Canada who, until then, had to contend with some 100 conflicting local sun times observed in terminals across the land.)

For practical purposes, this convention is sometimes altered. For example, Alaska, for a time, consisted of four of the eight U.S. time zones: the Pacific standard time zone (east of Juneau) and the 6th (Juneau), 7th (Anchorage), and 8th (Nome) zones, encompassing the 135°, 150°, and 165° meridians, respectively. In 1983, by act of Congress, the entire state (except the westernmost Aleutians) was united into the 6th zone, Alaska standard time.

The eight U.S. standard time zones are: Atlantic (includes Puerto Rico and the Virgin Islands), eastern, central, mountain, Pacific, Alaska, Hawaii-Aleutian (includes all of Hawaii and those Aleutians west of the Fox Islands), and Samoa standard time.

The Date Line. While the time zones are based on the natural event of the Sun crossing a meridian, the date must be an arbitrary decision. The meridians are traditionally counted from the meridian of the observatory of Greenwich, in England, which is called the zero meridian. The logical place for changing the date is 12 hours, or 180°, from Greenwich. Fortunately, the 180th meridian runs mostly through the open Pacific. The Date Line makes a zigzag in the north to incorporate the eastern tip of Siberia into the Siberian time system and then another one to incorporate a number of islands into the Hawaii-Aleutian time zone. In the south there is a similar zigzag for the purpose of tying a number of British-owned islands to the New Zealand time system. Otherwise, the Date Line is the same as 180° from Greenwich. At points to the east of the Date Line the calendar is one day earlier than at points to the west of it. A traveler going eastward across the Date Line from one island to another would not have to reset his watch because he would stay inside the time zone (provided he does so where the Date Line does *not* coincide with the 180° meridian), but it would be the same time of the *previous* day.

The Seasons

The seasons are caused by the tilt of Earth's axis (23.4°) and not by the fact that Earth's orbit around the Sun is an ellipse. The average distance of Earth from the Sun is 93 million miles; the difference between aphelion (farthest away from the Sun) and perihelion (closest to the Sun) is 3 million miles, so that perihelion is about 91.4 million miles from the Sun. Earth goes through the perihelion point a few days after New Year's Day, just when the Northern Hemisphere has winter. Aphelion is passed during the first days of July. This by itself shows that the distance from the Sun is not important within these limits. What is important is that when Earth passes through perihelion, the northern end of Earth's axis happens to tilt away from the Sun, so that the areas beyond the Tropic of Cancer receive only slanting rays from a Sun low in the sky.

The tilt of Earth's axis is responsible for four lines you find on every globe. When, say, the North Pole is tilted away from the Sun as much as possible, the farthest points in the North which can still be reached by the Sun's rays are 23.5° from the pole. This is the Arctic Circle. The Antarctic Circle is the corresponding limit 23.4° from the South Pole; the Sun's rays cannot reach beyond this point when we have midsummer in the North.

When the Sun is vertically above the equator, the day is of equal length all over Earth. This happens twice a year, and these are the "equinoxes" in March and in September. After having been over the equator in March, the Sun will seem to move northward. The northernmost point where the Sun can be straight overhead is 23.4° north of the equator. This is the Tropic of Cancer; the Sun can never be vertically overhead to the north of this line. Similarly the Sun cannot be vertically overhead to the south of a line 23.4° south of the equator—the Tropic of Capricorn.

This explains the climatic zones. In the belt (the Greek word *zone* means "belt") between the Tropic of Cancer and the Tropic of Capricorn, the Sun can be straight overhead; this is the tropical zone. The two zones where the Sun cannot be overhead but will be above the horizon every day of the year are the two temperate zones; the two areas where the Sun will not rise at all for varying lengths of time are the two polar areas, Arctic and Antarctic. □

The Names of the Months

January: named after Janus, protector of the gateway to heaven

February: named after Februalia, a time period when sacrifices were made to atone for sins

March: named after Mars, the god of war, presumably signifying that the campaigns interrupted by the winter could be resumed

April: from *aperire*, Latin for "to open" (buds)

May: named after Maia, the goddess of growth of plants

June: from *junius*, Latin for the goddess Juno

July: named after Julius Caesar in 44 B.C.E.

August: named after Augustus, the first Roman Emperor, in 8 B.C.E.

September: from *septem*, Latin for "seven"

October: from *octo*, Latin for "eight"

November: from *novem*, Latin for "nine"

December: from *decem*, Latin for "ten"

NOTE: The earliest Latin calendar was a 10-month one, beginning with March; thus, September was the seventh month, October, the eighth, etc. July was originally called Quintilis, meaning fifth; August was originally called Sextilis, meaning sixth.

The Islamic (Hijri) Calendar

The Islamic calendar is based on the lunar year of 354 days. The number of days each month is adjusted according to the lunar cycle, beginning about two days after the new moon. The months drift backwards over the seasons, beginning again on the same day every 32½ years. The Islamic year begins on the first day of Muharram, and is counted from the year of the Hegira *(anno Hegirae)*—the year in which Muhammad emigrated from Mecca to Medina (C.E. 622). The year 2000 translates to A.H. 1420.

Months	Number of days	Months	Number of days	Months	Number of days	Months	Number of days
Muharram	29 or 30	Rabi II	29 or 30	Rajab	29 or 30	Shawwal	29 or 30
Safar	29 or 30	Jumada I	29 or 30	Sha'ban	29 or 30	Dhu'l-Qa'dah	29 or 30
Rabi I	29 or 30	Jumada II	29 or 30	Ramadan	29 or 30	Dhu'l-Hijjah	29 or 30

The Jewish Calendar

The Jewish calendar is based on both solar and lunar years. The average lunar year of 354 days is adjusted to the solar year by the addition of a leap year and an intercalary month. Nisan is considered the first month, although the new year begins with Rosh Hashanah, on the first of Tishri, which is in fact the seventh month—the calendar has different starting points for different purposes. The year 2000 translates to 5760.

Months	Number of days	Months	Number of days	Months	Number of days
Nisan (March-April)*	30	Tishri (Sept.-Oct.)	30	Shevat (Jan.-Feb.)	30
Iyar (April-May)	29	Heshvan (Oct.-Nov.)	29	Adar (Feb.-March)	29
Sivan (May-June)	30	in some years	30	in some years	30
Tammuz (June-July)	29	Kislev (Nov.-Dec.)	29	Adar Sheni	29
Av (July-Aug.)	30	in some years	30	(intercalary month	
Elul (Aug.-Sept.)	29	Tevet (Dec.-Jan.)	29	in leap year only)	

*The months correspond approximately to those of the Gregorian calendar.

The Chinese Calendar

The Chinese lunar year is divided into 12 months of 29 or 30 days. The calendar is adjusted to the length of the solar year by the addition of extra months at regular intervals. The years are arranged in major cycles of 60 years. Each successive year is named after one of 12 animals. These 12-year cycles are continuously repeated. The Chinese New Year is celebrated at the second new moon after the winter solstice and falls between January 21 and February 19 on the Gregorian calendar.

Rat	Ox	Tiger	Cat (Rabbit)	Dragon	Snake	Horse	Sheep (Goat)	Monkey	Rooster	Dog	Pig
1900	1901	1902	1903	1904	1905	1906	1907	1908	1909	1910	1911
1912	1913	1914	1915	1916	1917	1918	1919	1920	1921	1922	1923
1924	1925	1926	1927	1928	1929	1930	1931	1932	1933	1934	1935
1936	1937	1938	1939	1940	1941	1942	1943	1944	1945	1946	1947
1948	1949	1950	1951	1952	1953	1954	1955	1956	1957	1958	1959
1960	1961	1962	1963	1964	1965	1966	1967	1968	1969	1970	1971
1972	1973	1974	1975	1976	1977	1978	1979	1980	1981	1982	1983
1984	1985	1986	1987	1988	1989	1990	1991	1992	1993	1994	1995
1996	1997	1998	1999	2000	2001	2002	2003	2004	2005	2006	2007

Holidays

Religious and Secular, 2000

In the United States, there are 10 federal holidays set by law. Four are set by date (New Year's Day, Independence Day, Veterans Day, and Christmas Day). The other six are set by a day of the week and month: Martin Luther King, Jr.'s Birthday, Washington's Birthday, Memorial Day, Labor Day, Columbus Day, and Thanksgiving. All but the last are celebrated on Mondays to create three-day weekends for federal employees. All Jewish and Islamic holidays begin at sundown the day before they are listed here.

First Day of Ramadan, Fri., Dec. 10, 1999. This day marks the beginning of a month-long fast that all Muslims must keep during the daylight hours. It commemorates the first revelation of the Qur'an. **The last day of Ramadan, Eid al-Fitr,** is celebrated on Sat., Jan. 8, 2000. The next Ramadan (for the year A.H. 1421) will begin on Tues., Nov. 28, 2000.

New Year's Day, Sat., Jan. 1. A federal holiday in the United States, New Year's Day has its origin in Roman times, when sacrifices were offered to Janus, the two-faced Roman deity who looked back on the past and forward to the future.

Epiphany (from Greek *epiphaneia,* "manifestation"), Thurs., Jan. 6. Falls on the 12th day after Christmas and commemorates the manifestation of Jesus Christ to the Gentiles, as represented by the Magi, the baptism of Jesus, and the miracle of the wine at the marriage feast at Cana. One of the 3 major Christian festivals, along with Christmas and Easter. Epiphany originally marked the beginning of the carnival season preceding Lent, and the evening preceding it is known as Twelfth Night.

Martin Luther King, Jr.'s Birthday, Mon., Jan. 17. (The actual date of his birthday is Jan. 15.) A federal holiday observed on the third Monday in January that honors the late civil rights leader. It became a federal holiday in 1986. In 1999, New Hampshire, the last holdout, became the fiftieth state to officially honor the holiday.

Groundhog Day, Wed., Feb. 2. Legend has it that if the groundhog sees his shadow, he'll return to his hole, and winter will last another six weeks.

Lincoln's Birthday, Sat., Feb. 12. A holiday in many states, this day was first formally observed in Washington, D.C., in 1866, when both houses of Congress gathered for a memorial address in tribute to the assassinated president.

St. Valentine's Day, Mon., Feb. 14. This day is the festival of two third-century martyrs, both named St. Valentine. It is not known why this day is associated with lovers. It may derive from an old pagan festival about this time of year, or it may have been inspired by the belief that birds mate on this day.

Washington's Birthday, Mon., Feb. 21. (The actual date of his birthday is Feb. 22.) A federal holiday observed the third Monday in February. It is a common misperception that the federal holiday was changed to "Presidents' Day" and now celebrates both Washington and Lincoln. Only Washington is commemorated by the federal holiday; 12 states, however, officially celebrate "Presidents' Day."

Shrove Tuesday, March 7. Falls the day before Ash Wednesday and marks the end of the carnival season, which once began on Epiphany but is now usually celebrated the last three days before Lent. In France, the day is known as Mardi Gras (Fat Tuesday), and Mardi Gras celebrations are also held in several American cities, particularly in New Orleans. The day is sometimes called Pancake Tuesday by the English because fats, which were prohibited during Lent, had to be used up.

Ash Wednesday, March 8. The seventh Wednesday before Easter and the first day of Lent, which lasts 40 days. Having its origin sometime before C.E. 1000, it is a day of public penance and is marked in the Roman Catholic Church by the burning of the palms blessed on the previous year's Palm Sunday. With the ashes from the palms the priest then marks a cross with his thumb upon the forehead of each worshipper. The Anglican Church and a few Protestant groups in the United States also observe the day, but generally without the use of ashes.

St. Patrick's Day, Fri., March 17. St. Patrick, patron saint of Ireland, has been honored in America since the first days of the nation. Perhaps the most notable part of the observance is the annual St. Patrick's Day parade on Fifth Avenue in New York City.

Purim (Feast of Lots), Tues., March 21. A day of joy and feasting celebrating the deliverance of the Jews from a massacre planned by the Persian minister Haman. According to the Book of Esther, the Jewish queen Esther interceded with her husband, King Ahasuerus, to spare the life of her uncle, Mordecai, and Haman was hanged on the same gallows he had built for Mordecai. The holiday is marked by the reading of the Book of Esther (The Megillah), and by the exchange of gifts, donations to the poor, and the presentation of Purim plays.

Palm Sunday, April 16. Observed the Sunday before Easter to commemorate the entry of Jesus into Jerusalem. The procession and the ceremonies introducing the benediction of palms probably had their origins in Jerusalem.

First Day of Passover (Pesach), Thurs., April 20. The Feast of the Passover, also called the Feast of Unleavened Bread, commemorates the escape of the Jews from Egypt. As the Jews fled, they ate unleavened bread, and from that time the Jews have allowed no leavening in their houses during Passover, bread being replaced by matzoh.

Good Friday, April 21. The Fri. before Easter, it commemorates the Crucifixion, which is retold during services from the Gospel according to St. John. A feature in Roman Catholic churches is the Liturgy of the Passion; there is no Consecration, the Host having been consecrated the previous day. The eating of hot-cross buns on this day is said to have started in England.

Easter Sunday, April 23. Observed in all Western Christian churches, Easter commemorates the Resurrection of Jesus. It is celebrated on the first Sunday after the full moon that occurs on or next after the vernal equinox (fixed at March 21) and is therefore celebrated between March 22 and April 25 inclusive. This date was fixed by the Council of Nicaea in C.E. 325.

Orthodox Easter (Paschal), Sun., April 30. The Orthodox church uses the same formula to calculate Easter as the Western church, but bases it on the traditional Julian calendar instead of the more contemporary Gregorian calendar.

Mother's Day, Sun., May 14. Observed the second Sunday in May, as proposed by Anna Jarvis of Philadelphia in 1907.

Memorial Day, Mon., May 29. Memorial Day became a federal holiday in 1971 that is observed on the last Monday in May. It originated in 1868, when Union General John A. Logan designated a day in which the graves of Civil War soldiers would be decorated. Originally known as Decoration Day, the holiday was changed to Memorial Day within twenty years, becoming a holiday dedicated to the memory of all war dead.

Ascension Day, Thurs., June 1. The Ascension of Jesus took place in the presence of His apostles 40 days after the Resurrection. It is traditionally thought to have occurred on Mount Olivet in Bethany.

First Day of Shavuot (Hebrew Pentecost), Fri., June 9. This festival, sometimes called the Feast of Weeks, or of Harvest, or of the First Fruits, falls 50 days after Passover and originally celebrated the end of the seven-week grain-harvesting season. In later tradition, it also celebrated the giving of the Law to Moses on Mount Sinai.

Pentecost (Whitsunday), June 11. This day commemorates the descent of the Holy Ghost upon the apostles 50 days after the Resurrection. The sermon by the Apostle Peter, which led to the baptism of 3,000 who professed belief, originated the ceremonies that have since been followed. "Whitsunday" is believed to have come from "white Sunday" when, among the English, white robes were worn by those baptized on the day.

Flag Day, Wed., June 14. This day commemorates the adoption by the Continental Congress on June 14, 1777, of the Stars and Stripes as the U.S. flag. Although it is a legal holiday only in Pennsylvania, President Truman, on Aug. 3, 1949, signed a bill requesting the president to call for its observance each year by proclamation.

Father's Day, Sun., June 18. Observed the third Sunday in June, it was first celebrated June 19, 1910.

Independence Day, Tues., July 4. The day of the adoption of the Declaration of Independence in 1776, celebrated in all states and territories. The observance began the next year in Philadelphia.

Labor Day, Mon., Sept. 4. A federal holiday observed the first Monday in September. Labor Day was first celebrated in New York in 1882 under the sponsorship of the Central Labor Union, following

the suggestion of Peter J. McGuire, of the Knights of Labor, that the day be set aside in honor of labor.

First Day of Rosh Hashanah (Jewish New Year), Sat., Sept. 30. This day marks the beginning of the Jewish year 5760 and opens the Ten Days of Penitence, which close with Yom Kippur.

Columbus Day, Mon., Oct. 9. A federal holiday, observed the second Monday in October, it commemorates Christopher Columbus's landing in the New World in 1492. Quite likely the first celebration of Columbus Day was that organized in 1792 by the Society of St. Tammany, or the Columbian Order, widely known as Tammany Hall.

Yom Kippur (Day of Atonement), Mon., Oct. 9. This day marks the end of the Ten Days of Penitence that began with Rosh Hashanah. It is described in Leviticus as a "Sabbath of rest," and synagogue services begin the preceding sundown, resume the following morning, and continue to sundown.

First Day of Sukkot (Feast of Tabernacles), Sat., Oct. 14. This festival, also known as the Feast of the Ingathering, originally celebrated the fruit harvest, and the name comes from the booths or tabernacles in which the Jews lived during the harvest, although one tradition traces it to the shelters used by the Jews in their wandering through the wilderness. During the festival many Jews build small huts in their backyards or on the roofs of their houses.

Simchat Torah (Rejoicing of the Law), Sun., Oct. 22. This joyous holiday falls on the eighth day of Sukkot. It marks the end of the year's reading of the Torah (Five Books of Moses) in the synagogue every Saturday and the beginning of the new cycle of reading.

Halloween, Tues., Oct. 31. Eve of All Saints' Day, formerly called All Hallows and Hallowmass. Halloween is traditionally associated in some countries with customs such as bonfires, masquerading, and the telling of ghost stories. These are old Celtic practices marking the beginning of winter.

All Saints' Day, Wed., Nov. 1. A Roman Catholic and Anglican holiday celebrating all saints, known and unknown.

Election Day (legal holiday in certain states), Tues., Nov. 7. Since 1845, by act of Congress, the first Tuesday after the first Monday in November is the date for choosing presidential electors. State elections are also generally held on this day.

Veterans Day, Sat., Nov. 11. Armistice Day, a federal holiday, was established in 1926 to commemorate the signing on 1918 of the armistice ending World War I. On June 1, 1954, the name was changed to Veterans Day to honor all men and women who have served America in its armed forces.

Thanksgiving, Thurs., Nov. 23. A federal holiday observed the fourth Thursday in November by act of Congress (1941), it was the first such national proclamation issued by President Lincoln in 1863, on the urging of Mrs. Sarah J. Hale, editor of *Godey's*

Lady's Book. Most Americans believe that the holiday dates back to the day of thanks ordered by Governor Bradford of Plymouth Colony in New England in 1621, but scholars point out that days of thanks stem from ancient times.

First Sunday of Advent, Dec. 3. Advent is the season in which the faithful must prepare themselves for the advent of the Savior on Christmas. The four Sundays before Christmas are marked by special church services.

First Day of Hanukkah (Festival of Lights), Fri., Dec. 22. This festival was instituted by Judas Maccabaeus in 165 B.C.E. to celebrate the purification of the Temple of Jerusalem, which had been desecrated three years earlier by Antiochus Epiphanes, who set up a pagan altar and offered sacrifices to Zeus Olympius. In Jewish homes, a light is lighted on each night of the eight-day festival.

Christmas (Feast of the Nativity), Mon., Dec. 25. The most widely celebrated holiday of the Christian year, Christmas is observed as the anniversary of the birth of Jesus. Christmas customs are centuries old. The mistletoe, for example, comes from the Druids, who, in hanging the mistletoe, hoped for peace and good fortune. Use of such plants as holly comes from the ancient belief that such plants blossomed at Christmas.

Comparatively recent is the Christmas tree, first set up in Germany in the 17th century. The use of candles on trees developed from the belief that candles appeared by miracle on the trees at Christmas. Colonial Manhattan Islanders introduced the name Santa Claus, a corruption of the Dutch name St. Nicholas, who lived in fourth-century Asia Minor.

Christian and Secular Holidays, 2000–2002

Year	Ash Wednesday	Easter	Pentecost	Labor Day	Election Day	Thanksgiving	1st Sun. Advent
2000	March 8	April 23	June 11	Sept. 4	Nov. 7	Nov. 23	Dec. 3
2001	Feb. 28	April 15	June 3	Sept. 3	Nov. 6	Nov. 22	Dec. 2
2002	Feb. 13	March 31	May 19	Sept. 2	Nov. 5	Nov. 28	Dec. 1

Shrove Tuesday: 1 day before Ash Wednesday. Palm Sunday: 7 days before Easter. Maundy Thursday: 3 days before Easter. Good Friday: 2 days before Easter. Holy Saturday: 1 day before Easter. Ascension Day: 10 days before Pentecost. Trinity Sunday: 7 days after Pentecost. Corpus Christi: 11 days after Pentecost.

Orthodox Holidays, 1999–2002

Year	Great Lent Begins	Paschal (Easter)	Ascension	Pentecost	Year	Great Lent Begins	Paschal (Easter)	Ascension	Pentecost
1999	Feb. 22	April 11	May 20	May 30	2001	Feb. 26	April 15	May 24	June 3
2000	March 13	April 30	June 8	June 18	2002	March 18	May 5	June 13	June 23

Jewish Holidays, 2000–2002

Year	Purim[1]	1st day Passover[2]	1st day Shavuot[3]	1st day Rosh Hashanah[4]	Yom Kippur[5]	1st day Sukkot[6]	Simchat Torah[7]	1st day Hanukkah[8]
2000	March 21	April 20	June 9	Sept. 30	Oct. 9	Oct. 14	Oct. 22	Dec. 22
2001	March 9	April 8	May 28	Sept. 18	Sept. 27	Oct. 2	Oct. 10	Dec. 10
2002	Feb. 26	April 3	May 17	Sept. 7	Sept. 16	Sept. 21	Sept. 29	Nov. 30

1. Feast of Lots. 2. Feast of Unleavened Bread. 3. Hebrew Pentecost; or Feast of Weeks, or of Harvest, or of First Fruits. 4. Jewish New Year. 5. Day of Atonement. 6. Feast of Tabernacles, or of the Ingathering. 7. Rejoicing of the Law. In Israel, Simchat Torah is celebrated on the day before the date given. 8. Festival of Lights.

Length of Jewish holidays (O=Orthodox, C=Conservative, R=Reform): Passover: O & C, 8 days (holy days: first 2 and last 2); R, 7 days (holy days: first and last). Shavuot: O & C, 2 days; R, 1 day. Rosh Hashanah: O & C, 2 days; R, 1 day. Yom Kippur: All groups, 1 day. Sukkot: All groups, 7 days (holy days: O & C, first 2; R, first only); O & C observe two additional days: Shemini Atseret (Eighth Day of the Feast) and Simchat Torah; R observes Shemini Atseret but not Simchat Torah. Hanukkah: All groups, 8 days. NOTE: All holidays begin at sundown on the evening before the date given.

Islamic Holidays, 1999–2002 (A.H. 1420–1422)

In the Year of the Hegira	Muharram (Islamic New Year)	Mawlid al-Nabi (Muhammed's Birthday)	Ramadan begins	Eid al-Fitr (Ramadan ends)	Eid al-Adha (Festival of Sacrifice)
A.H. 1420	April 17, 1999	June 26, 1999	Dec. 10, 1999	Jan. 8, 2000	March 17, 2000
A.H. 1421	April 6, 2000	June 15, 2000	Nov. 28, 2000	Dec. 27, 2000	March 6, 2001
A.H. 1422	March 26, 2001	June 4, 2001	Nov. 17, 2001	Dec. 17, 2001	Feb. 23, 2002

NOTE: All holidays begin at sundown on the evening before the date given. Islamic holidays are based on the lunar calendar and thus may vary by one or two days. Dates apply to North America.

Hindu Festival Dates, 2000
Source: Jantri 500, by Pal Singh Purewal.

Jan. 14	Makar Sankranti	Aug. 15	Raksha Bandhan
Feb. 10	Vasant Panchami	Aug. 22	Sri Krishna Jayanti
March 4	Maha Shivaratri Vrat (fast)	Sept.1	Ganesh Chaturathi
March 20	Holi (last day)	Sept. 13	Saradhas begin
April 5	Chetra Navratras begin	Sept. 28	Asuj Navratras begin
April 5	Bikarami Samvat 2057 begins	Oct. 7	Dassehra
April 12	Rama Navmi	Oct. 16	Karva Chauth Vrat (fast)
April 13	Vaisakhi (solar new year)	Oct. 26	Diwali (Festival of Lights)

Sikh Festival Dates, 2000
Source: Jantri 500, by Pal Singh Purewal.

Jan. 5	Birthday of Guru Gobind Singh Ji	Sept. 1	First Parkash Granth Sahib Ji
Jan. 13	Maghi	Oct. 20	Installation of Holy Scriptures
March 14	Nanakshahi Samvat 532 begins		as Guru Granth Sahib Ji
	(New Year's Day)	Oct. 26*	Bandichhor Day
March 14	Hola Muhalla	Nov. 11*	Birthday of Guru Nanak Dev Ji
April 14	Vaisakhi	Nov. 24	Martyrdom of Guru Tegh Bahadur Ji
June 16	Martyrdom of Guru Arjan Dev Ji		

*These festivals will continue to be observed according to the lunar calendar. NOTE: Dates for Sikh and Hindu holidays are determined according to the date of their observance in India. The festivals of Maghi and Vaisakhi may differ by one day in the reformed Nanakshahi calendar (followed by Sikhs since 1999) and the Bikarami calendar (followed by Hindus). The Nanakshahi calendar is now a reformed calendar based on the length of the tropical year, while the Bikarami calendar is based on the sidereal year.

Chinese New Year

1999	Feb. 16	**2002**	Feb. 12	**2005**	Feb. 9	**2008**	Feb. 7
2000	Feb. 5	**2003**	Feb. 1	**2006**	Jan. 29	**2009**	Jan. 26
2001	Jan. 24	**2004**	Jan. 22	**2007**	Feb. 18	**2010**	Feb. 14

State Holidays

Jan. 6, Three Kings' Day: P.R.
Jan. 8, Battle of New Orleans Day: La.
Jan. 11, De Hostos's Birthday: P.R.
Jan. 19, Robert E. Lee's Birthday: Ark., Fla., Ky., La., S.C.; (third Mon.): Ala., Miss.
Jan. 19, Confederate Heroes Day: Tex.
Jan. (third Mon.), Lee-Jackson-King Day: Va.
Jan. 30, F. D. Roosevelt's Birthday: Ky.
Feb. 15, Susan B. Anthony's Birthday: Fla., Minn.
March (first Tues.), Town Meeting Day: Vt.
March 2, Texas Independence Day: Tex.
March (first Mon.), Casimir Pulaski's Birthday: Ill.
March 17, Evacuation Day: Mass. (in Suffolk County)
March 20 (first day of spring), Youth Day: Okla.
March 22, Abolition Day: P.R.
March 25, Maryland Day: Md.
March 26, Prince Jonah Kuhio Kalanianaole Day: Hawaii
March (last Mon.), Seward's Day: Alaska
April 2, Pascua Florida Day: Fla.
April 13, Thomas Jefferson's Birthday: Ala., Okla.
April 16, De Diego's Birthday: P.R.
April (third Mon.), Patriots' Day: Maine, Mass.
April 21, San Jacinto Day: Tex.
April 22, Arbor Day: Nebr.
April 22, Oklahoma Day: Okla.
April 26, Confederate Memorial Day: Fla., Ga.
April (fourth Mon.), Fast Day: N.H.
April (last Mon.), Confederate Memorial Day: Ala., Miss.
May 1, Bird Day: Okla.
May 8, Truman Day: Mo.
May 11, Minnesota Day: Minn.
May 20, Mecklenburg Independence Day: N.C.

June (first Mon.), Jefferson Davis's Birthday: Ala., Miss.
June 3, Jefferson Davis's Birthday: Fla., S.C.
June 3, Confederate Memorial Day: Ky., La.
June 9, Senior Citizens Day: Okla.
June 11, King Kamehameha I Day: Hawaii
June 15, Separation Day: Del.
June 17, Bunker Hill Day: Mass. (in Suffolk County)
June 19, Emancipation Day: Tex.
June 20, West Virginia Day: W.Va.
July 17, Muñoz Rivera's Birthday: P.R.
July 24, Pioneer Day: Utah
July 25, Constitution Day: P.R.
July 27, Barbosa's Birthday: P.R.
Aug. (first Sun.), American Family Day: Ariz.
Aug. (first Mon.), Colorado Day: Colo.
Aug. (second Mon.), Victory Day: R.I.
Aug. 16, Bennington Battle Day: Vt.
Aug. (third Friday), Admission Day: Hawaii
Aug. 27, Lyndon B. Johnson's Birthday: Tex.
Aug. 30, Huey P. Long Day: La.
Sept. 9, Admission Day: Calif.
Sept. 12, Defenders' Day: Md.
Sept. 16, Cherokee Strip Day: Okla.
Sept. (first Sat. after full moon), Indian Day: Okla.
Oct. 10, Leif Eriksson Day: Minn.
Oct. 10, Oklahoma Historical Day: Okla.
Oct. 18, Alaska Day: Ala.
Oct. 31, Nevada Day: Nev.
Nov. 4, Will Rogers Day: Okla.
Nov. (week of the 16th), Oklahoma Heritage Week: Okla.
Nov. 19, Discovery Day: P.R.
Dec. 7, Delaware Day: Del.

Birthstones

Month	Stone	Month	Stone	Month	Stone
January	Garnet	June	Pearl, Alexandrite, or Moonstone	October	Opal or Tourmaline
February	Amethyst			November	Topaz or Citrine
March	Aquamarine or Bloodstone	July	Ruby or Star Ruby	December	Turquoise, Lapis Lazuli, Blue Zircon, or Blue Topaz
April	Diamond	August	Peridot or Sardonyx		
May	Emerald	September	Sapphire or Star Sapphire		

Source: Jewelry Industry Council.

Traditional Wedding Anniversary Gift List

Anniv.	Gift	Anniv.	Gift	Anniv.	Gift	Anniv.	Gift
1st	Paper	7th	Copper, wool	13th	Lace	35th	Coral
2nd	Cotton	8th	Bronze, pottery	14th	Ivory	40th	Ruby
3rd	Leather	9th	Pottery, willow	15th	Crystal	45th	Sapphire
4th	Fruit, flowers	10th	Tin	20th	China	50th	Gold
5th	Wood	11th	Steel	25th	Silver	55th	Emerald
6th	Sugar	12th	Silk, linen	30th	Pearl	60th	Diamond

Modern Wedding Anniversary Gift List

Anniv.	Gift	Anniv.	Gift	Anniv.	Gift	Anniv.	Gift
1st	Gold jewelry	8th	Tourmaline	15th	Ruby	30th	Pearl jubilee
2nd	Garnet	9th	Lapis	16th	Peridot	35th	Emerald
3rd	Pearls	10th	Diamond jewelry	17th	Watch	40th	Ruby
4th	Blue topaz	11th	Turquoise	18th	Cat's-eye	45th	Sapphire
5th	Sapphire	12th	Jade	19th	Aquamarine	50th	Golden jubilee
6th	Amethyst	13th	Citrine	20th	Emerald	60th	Diamond jubilee
7th	Onyx	14th	Opal	25th	Silver jubilee		

Source: Jewelry Industry Council.

Selected National Holidays Around the World, 2000

Country	Date	Country	Date	Country	Date	Country	Date
Afghanistan	Aug. 19	Guatemala	Sept. 15	Pakistan	March 23
Albania	Nov. 28	Haiti	Jan. 1	Panama	Nov. 3
Argentina	May 25	Hungary	Aug. 20	Paraguay	May 15
Armenia	Sept. 21	India	Jan. 26	Peru	July 28
Australia	Jan. 26	Indonesia	Aug. 17	Philippines	June 12
Austria	Oct. 26	Iran	Feb. 11	Poland	May 3
Bahamas	July 10	Iraq	July 17	Portugal	June 10
Bangladesh	March 26	Ireland	March 17	Romania	Dec. 1
Barbados	Nov. 30	Israel	May 12[1]	Samoa	June 1
Belarus	July 27	Italy	June 2	Saudi Arabia	Sept. 23
Belgium	July 21	Jamaica	Aug. 7[2]	Senegal	April 4
Belize	Sept. 21	Japan	Dec. 23	Singapore	Aug. 9
Bolivia	Aug. 6	Jordan	May 25	Slovakia	Sept. 1
Brazil	Sept. 7	Kenya	Dec. 12	Slovenia	June 25
Bulgaria	March 3	North Korea	Sept. 9	Somalia	Oct. 21
Canada	July 1	South Korea	Aug. 15	South Africa	May 31
Chile	Sept. 18	Kuwait	Feb. 25	Spain	Oct. 12
China	Oct. 1	Lebanon	Nov. 22	Sri Lanka	Feb. 4
Colombia	July 20	Liberia	July 26	Swaziland	Sept. 6
Congo	Aug. 15	Lithuania	Feb. 16	Sweden	June 6
Croatia	May 30	Luxembourg	June 23	Switzerland	Aug. 1
Cuba	Jan. 1	Macedonia	Aug. 2	Tanzania	April 26
Czech Republic	Oct. 28	Malaysia	Aug. 31	Thailand	Dec. 5
Denmark	April 16	Malta	Sept. 21	Tunisia	March 20
Dominican Republic	Feb. 27	Mexico	Sept. 16	Turkey	Oct. 29
Ecuador	Aug. 10	Monaco	Nov. 19	Uganda	Oct. 9
Egypt	July 23	Mongolia	July 11	United Arab Emirates	Dec. 2
El Salvador	Sept. 15	Morocco	March 3	United Kingdom	June 10[3]
Ethiopia	May 28	Mozambique	June 25	United States	July 4
Finland	Dec. 6	Nepal	Dec. 28	Uruguay	Aug. 25
France	July 14	Netherlands	April 30	Venezuela	July 5
Gabon	Aug. 17	New Zealand	Feb. 6	Vietnam	Sept. 2
Georgia	May 26	Nicaragua	Sept. 15	Yemen, Republic of	May 22
Germany	Oct. 3	Nigeria	Oct. 1	Zambia	Oct. 24
Greece	March 25	Norway	May 17	Zimbabwe	April 18

1. Changes yearly according to Hebrew calendar. 2. Celebrated on first Monday in August. 3. Celebrated the second Saturday in June.

The Expanding Universe Is Accurately Dated

Sources: NASA and Space Science Telescope Institute.

Before the advent of the Hubble Space Telescope, astronomers couldn't decide if the universe was 10 billion or 20 billion years old. The scale size of the universe had a range so vast that it didn't allow astronomers to confront with any certainty many of the most basic questions about the origin and the eventual fate of the universe. The answer to this cosmic puzzle was finally solved in 1999 by NASA's Hubble Space Telescope Key Project team, led by Wendy Freedman of Carnegie Observatories. The team, a group of 27 astronomers from 13 different U.S. and international institutions, announced in May that it had determined the age of the universe with precise accuracy. After an eight-year effort to measure the far-flung galaxies of the expanding universe, the Key Project astronomers confidently concluded that the universe is approximately 12 billion years old.

The team's precise measurements are the key to learning about the universe's rate of expansion, named the Hubble constant (H_0), after the American astronomer Edwin P. Hubble. He was the first to realize that the galaxies were running away from each other at a proportional distance, i.e., the farther away, the faster the recession. It was in 1929 that Hubble discovered this important linear relationship.

Finding the definitive value of Hubble's constant was one of the major goals for the Space Telescope when it was launched in 1990. The constant is one of the most important numbers in cosmology because it is needed to estimate the size and age of the universe. This long-sought number indicates the rate at which the universe has been expanding since the primordial "Big Bang."

The units of the Hubble constant are "kilometers per second, per Megaparsec." A Megaparsec (Mpc) is 3.26 million light-years. For each Megaparsec of distance, the velocity of a distant object appears to increase by some value. The constant can be stated as a simple mathematical expression: $H_0 = v/d$, where H_0 is the current value of the Hubble constant, v is the galaxy's radial outward velocity (in other words, motion along our line-of-sight), and d is the galaxy's distance from Earth. The constant

initially calculated by Hubble was around 500 km/s/Mpc, but this figure has been radically revised during past decades.

For the past 70 years, right up to the launch of the Hubble Telescope, the range of measured values for the expansion of the universe was from 50 to 100 km/s/Mpc. The Key Project team's measurement now gives the precise value of Hubble's constant at 70 km/s/Mpc, with an uncertainty of ten percent. This means that a given galaxy appears to be moving 160,000 miles per hour faster for every 3.3 million light-years away from Earth.

The team used the Hubble Telescope to observe 18 galaxies out to 65 million light-years. They discovered almost 800 Cepheid variable stars, a special class of pulsating stars used for accurate distant measurement. Although Cepheids are rare, they provide a very reliable "standard candle" for estimating intergalactic distances. The team used the stars to calibrate many different methods for measuring distance. Combining Hubble's constant measurement with estimates for the density of the universe, the team determined that the universe is approximately 12 billion years old—similar to the oldest stars. This discovery also cleared up a nagging paradox that arose from previous estimates that the universe appeared to be younger than its oldest stars.

The universe's age is calculated using the expansion rate from precise distance measurements, and the calculated age is refined based on whether the universe appears to be accelerating or decelerating, given the amount of matter observed in space. A rapid expansion rate indicates that the universe did not require as much time to reach its present size, and so it is younger than if it were expanding more slowly.

The researchers emphasize that the age estimate holds true if the universe is below the so-called "critical density," where it is delicately balanced between expanding forever or collapsing. Or, the universe is pervaded by a mysterious force pushing the galaxies farther apart, in which case the Hubble measurements point to an even older universe. □

The Flap Over Pluto

Sources: NASA and the International Astronomical Union.

Misleading reports that Pluto was about to lose its status as a planet in January 1999 caused an unexpected public uproar and a subsequent stir over the planet's standing in the astronomical community. The flap began when some of the national media announced that Pluto was going to be reclassified as a minor planet or, even worse, a lowly asteroid. Although the proposal turned out to be false, the publicity generated by the media hype left many people confused about Pluto's official classification.

Since 1992, a substantial number of smaller objects have been discovered in the outer solar sys-

tem, beyond the orbit of Neptune, with orbits and possibly other properties similar to those of Pluto. These characteristics "Pluto-like" bodies are known as Trans-Neptunian Objects (or TNOs).

The controversy over Pluto's designation began when an astronomer suggested that Pluto be assigned a number in a technical catalog or list of such TNOs so that observations and computations concerning these objects could be conveniently collated. Astronomers know that Pluto does not fit in perfectly as a TNO because it is far larger than any of the other objects discovered in these orbits and it is the only one known to have a moon. This proposal was not in any way intended to change Pluto's standing as a planet. Unfortunately, the purpose of including it in a specialized listing became misinterpreted and was erroneously reported.

The hullabaloo that followed over Pluto's supposed demotion was soon denounced by the Paris-based International Astronomical Union (IAU), the organization that decides the classification of objects in the solar system, which promptly issued a statement confirming that Pluto will remain our ninth planet and that there was no such initiative to reclassify it as some lesser type of heavenly body.

Surprisingly, there is no set scientific law as to what constitutes a planet, but as a rule of thumb, a planet: 1) must directly orbit a star; 2) must be small enough that it has not undergone internal nuclear fusion (i.e., it is not a star or starlike object); and 3) must be large enough that its self-gravity gives it the general shape of a sphere.

Pluto, the smallest planet in the solar system (it's smaller than Earth's moon), has remained enigmatic since its discovery by astronomer Clyde Tombaugh in 1931. It is so unique in comparison to its eight siblings that it almost defies classification. Though it orbits the Sun, Pluto neither qualifies as a terrestrial nor as a gas giant planet. All the other planets in the outer solar system are gaseous giants, whereas Pluto is a small, solid object. Although it behaves like a comet by periodically warming and losing its atmosphere into space, Pluto is far too large for that category. Astronomers speculate that Pluto may be the last survivor of a lost population of objects called "ice dwarfs" that inhabited the primeval solar system.

Pluto's satellite, Charon, discovered in 1978, is larger in proportion to its planet than any other satellite in the solar system. Pluto and its moon are also considered a "double planet system," which occurs when two bodies are reasonably close in mass and so orbit around a common center of gravity (or barycenter), analogous to two children balancing on a teeter-totter. It is thought that Charon may have been born through a head-on collision between Pluto and another large ice body, in much the same way as the Earth–Moon system is believed to have formed.

Pluto is the only planet whose orbit crosses that of another planet (Neptune, normally the eighth planet). Pint-sized Pluto's elliptical orbit takes 248 years, and carries it as close as 2.8 billion miles from the Sun and as far as 4.6 billion miles from the Sun. In September 1979, Pluto crossed within Neptune's orbit again, making Neptune the farthest planet. Pluto remained closer to the Sun than Neptune for most of the 1980s, reaching its closest point (perihelion) to the Sun by late 1989. According to NASA, the last time Pluto was this close to the Sun, George Washington was a boy! In February 1999, Pluto crossed Neptune's orbit again as it headed away from the Sun and regained its status as the most distant planet.   □

Astronomical Terms

Planet is the term used for a body in orbit around a star. Its origin is Greek; even in antiquity it was known that a number of "stars" did not stay in the same relative positions to the others. There were five such restless "stars" known—Mercury, Venus, Mars, Jupiter, and Saturn—and the Greeks referred to them as *planetes,* a word which means "wanderers." That Earth is one of the planets was realized later. The additional planets were discovered after the invention of the telescope.

In 1994, Dr. Alexander Wolszcan, an astronomer at Pennsylvania State University, presented convincing evidence of the first known planets to exist outside our solar system. They circle a pulsar or exploded star in the constellation *Virgo.*

In 1995, several of these *extrasolar planets* were discovered orbiting ordinary stars similar to our Sun as a result of observing gravitational variations of the stars. Swiss astronomers found a planet orbiting star 51 in the constellation *Pegasus,* about 40 light-years away. It is the first planet ever discovered to circle a normal sunlike star. Over the last several years, a total of 21 planets have been discovered (*see* page 450).

Satellite (or *moon*) is the term for a body in orbit around a planet. As long as our own Moon was the only moon known, there was no need for a general term for the moons of planets. But when Galileo Galilei discovered the four main moons of the planet Jupiter, Johannes Kepler (in a letter to Galileo) suggested "satellite" (from the Latin *satelles,* which means attendant) as a general term for such bodies. The word is used interchangeably with "moons:" astronomers speak and write about the moons of Neptune, Saturn, etc. It is also used to describe man-made devices that are launched into orbit. A satellite may be any size.

Orbit is the term for the path traveled by a body in space. It comes from the Latin *orbis,* which means circle or circuit, and *orbita,* which means a rut or a wheel track. Theoretically, there are four mathematical figures that are possible orbits: two are open (hyperbola and parabola) and two are closed (ellipse and circle), but in reality all closed orbits are ellipses. These ellipses can be nearly circular, as are the orbits of most planets, or very elongated, as are the orbits of most comets. In these orbits, the Sun is in one focal point of the ellipse, and the other focal point is empty. In the orbits of satellites, the planet stands in one focal point of the orbit. The *primary* of an orbit is the body in the focal point. For planets, the point of the orbit closest to the Sun is the *perihelion,* and the point farthest from the Sun is the *aphelion.* For orbits around Earth, the corresponding terms are *perigee* and *apogee;* for orbits around other planets, corresponding terms are coined when necessary.

Two heavenly bodies are in *inferior* or *superior conjunction* when they have the same *right ascension,* or are in the same meridian; that is, when one is due north or south of the other. If the bodies appear near each other as seen from Earth, they will rise and set at the same time. They are in *opposition* when they are opposite each other in the heavens: when one rises as the other is setting. *Greatest elongation* is the greatest apparent angular distance from the Sun, when a planet is most favorably suited for observation. Mercury can be seen with the naked eye only at about this time. An *occultation* of a

The Milky Way, the galaxy containing our solar system, is about 100,000 light-years in diameter and about 10,000 light-years thick.

planet or star is an eclipse of it by some other body, usually the Moon.

Stars are the basic units of population in the universe. Our Sun is the nearest star. Stars are very large (our Sun has a diameter of 865,400 miles—a comparatively small star). Stars are composed of intensely hot gasses, deriving their energy from nuclear reactions going on in their interiors.

Galaxies are immense systems containing billions of stars. All that you can see in the sky (with a very few exceptions) belongs to our galaxy—a system of roughly 200 billion stars. The few exceptions are other galaxies. Our own galaxy, the rim of which we see as the "Milky Way," is about 100,000 light-years in diameter and about 10,000 light-years in thickness. Its shape is roughly that of a thick lens; more precisely it is a "spiral nebula," a term first used for other galaxies when they were discovered and before it was realized that these were separate and distinct galaxies. The spiral galaxy nearest to ours is in the constellation *Andromeda*. It is somewhat larger than our own galaxy and is visible to the naked eye. Astronomers have estimated that the universe could contain 40 to 50 billion galaxies.

A *black hole* is the theoretical end-product of the total gravitational collapse of a massive star or group of stars. Crushed even smaller than an incredibly dense neutron star, such a body may become so dense that not even light can escape its gravitational field. It has been suggested that black holes may be detectable in proximity to normal stars when they draw matter away from their visible neighbors. Strong sources of X-rays in our galaxy and beyond may also indicate the presence of black holes.

Quasars ("quasi-stellar" objects), originally thought to be peculiar stars in our own galaxy, are now believed to be the most remote objects in the universe. Quasars emit tremendous amounts of light and microwave radiation. Recent Hubble Space Telescope images suggest that there may be a variety of mechanisms for "turning on" quasars. Although a number of images show collisions between pairs of galaxies, which could trigger the birth of quasars, some pictures reveal apparently normal, undisturbed galaxies possessing quasars.

Quasars are among the most baffling objects in the universe because of their small size and prodigious energy output. Quasars are not much bigger than Earth's solar system but pour out 100 to 1,000 times as much light as an entire galaxy containing a hundred billion stars.

A super massive black hole, gobbling up stars, gas, and dust, is theorized to be the "engine" powering a quasar. Most astronomers agree that an active black hole is the only credible possibility that explains how quasars can be so compact, variable, and powerful. However, no conclusive evidence supports this assumption.

Pulsars are believed to be rapidly spinning neutron stars, so crushed by their own gravity that a million tons of their matter would hardly fill a thimble. Pulsars are so named because they emit bursts of radio waves at regular intervals.

In 1996, astronomers found strong evidence for a massive black hole at the center of the Milky Way. Recent evidence suggests that black holes are so common that they probably exist at the core of nearly all galaxies.

The existence of brown dwarfs, also called failed stars, was confirmed in November 1995 when astronomers at Palomar Observatory in California took the first photograph of this mysterious object. Brown dwarfs lack the mass to generate nuclear fission like true stars but are also too massive and hot to be a planet.

Origin of the Universe

In 1999, a new age for the cosmos was determined by NASA's Hubble Space Telescope Project team to be 12 billion years old. The universe began its existence as a dense, hot globule of gas expanding rapidly outward. At that time, the universe contained nothing but hydrogen and a small amount of helium. There were no stars and no planets. The first stars probably began to condense out of the primordial hydrogen when the universe was about 100 million years old and continued to form as the universe aged. The Sun arose in this way 4.6 billion years ago. Many stars came into being before the Sun was formed; many others formed after the Sun appeared. This process continues, and through telescopes we can now see stars forming out of compressed pockets of hydrogen in outer space.

In 1992, instruments aboard the Cosmic Background Explorer (COBE) satellite, launched in 1989, showed that 99.97% of the radiant energy of the universe was released within the first year of the primeval explosion. This evidence seems to confirm the Big Bang theory, which holds that the universe originated from a single violent explosion (a *big bang*) of a very small agglomeration of matter of extremely high density and temperatures. Astronomers also theorize that 99% of the matter in the universe is invisible or *dark matter* composed of some kind of matter that they cannot yet detect.

In March 1995, astronomers found supporting evidence for the Big Bang when they concluded that data obtained from the space shuttle's *Astro 2* observatory showed that helium was widespread in the early universe. The theory holds that hydrogen and helium were the first elements created when the universe was formed.

Birth and Death of a Star

When a star begins to form as a dense cloud of gas, the individual hydrogen atoms fall toward the center of the cloud under the force of the star's

Astronomical Constants

Light-year (distance traveled by light in one year)	5,880,000,000,000 mi.
Parsec (parallax of one second, or stellar distances)	3.259 light-yrs.
Velocity of light	186,281.7 mi./sec.
Astronomical unit (A.U.), or mean distance Earth to Sun	ca. 93,000,000 mi.[1]
Mean distance, Earth to Moon	238,860 mi.
General precession	50′,.26
Obliquity of the ecliptic	$23° \ 27′8′.26{-}0′.4684(t{-}1900)$[2]
Equatorial radius of Earth	3963.34 statute mi.
Polar radius of Earth	3949.99 statute mi.
Earth's mean radius	3958.89 statute mi.
Oblateness of Earth	1/297
Equatorial horizontal parallax of the moon	57′2′.70
Earth's mean velocity in orbit	18.5 mi./sec.
Sidereal year	365d.2564
Tropical year	365d.2422
Sidereal month	27d.3217
Synodic month	29d.5306
Mean sidereal day	23h56m4s.091 of mean solar time
Mean solar day	24h3m56s.555 of sidereal time

1. Actual mean distance derived from radar bounces: 92,935,700 mi. The value of 92,897,400 mi. (based on parallax of 8″.80) is used in calculations. 2. *t* refers to the year in question, for example, 2000.

gravity. As it falls, it picks up speed, and its energy increases. The increase in energy heats the gas. When this process has continued for some millions of years, the temperature reaches about 20 million degrees Fahrenheit. At this temperature, the hydrogen within the star ignites and burns in a continuing series of nuclear reactions in which all the elements in the universe are manufactured from hydrogen and helium. The onset of these reactions marks the birth of a star. When a star begins to exhaust its hydrogen supply, its life nears an end. The first sign of old age is a swelling and reddening of its outer regions. Such a aging, swollen star is called a red giant. The Sun, a middle-aged star, will probably swell to a red giant in 5 billion years, vaporizing Earth and any creatures that may be left on its surface. When all its fuel has been exhausted, a star cannot generate sufficient pressure at its center to balance the crushing force of gravity. The star collapses under the force of its own weight; if it is a small star, it collapses gently and remains collapsed. Such a collapsed star, at its life's end, is called a white dwarf. The Sun will probably end its life in this way. A different fate awaits a large star. Its final collapse generates a violent explosion, blowing the innards of the star out into space. There, the materials of the exploded star mix with the primeval hydrogen of the universe. Later in the history of the galaxy, other stars are formed out of this mixture. The Sun is one of these stars. It contains the debris of countless other stars that exploded before the Sun was born.

Supernovas

On Feb. 24, 1987, Canadian astronomer Ian Shelter at the Las Campanas Observatory in Chile discovered a supernova—an exploding star—from a photograph taken on Feb. 23 of the Large Magellanic Cloud, a galaxy some 160,000 light-years away from Earth. Astronomers believe that the dying star was Sanduleak −69°202, a 10-million-year-old blue supergiant.

Supernova 1987A was the closest and best-studied supernova in almost 400 years. One was previously observed by Johannes Kepler in 1604, four years before the telescope was invented.

Formation of the Solar System

The Sun's age was calculated in 1989 to be 4.49 billion years old, less than the 4.7 billion years previously believed. It was formed from a cloud of hydrogen mixed with small amounts of other substances that had been manufactured in the bodies of other stars before the Sun was born. This was the parent cloud of the solar system. The dense hot gas at the center of the cloud gave rise to the Sun; the outer regions of the cloud—cooler and less dense—gave birth to the planets.

Our solar system consists of one star (the Sun), nine planets and all their moons, several thousand minor planets called asteroids or planetoids, and an equally large number of comets.

The Sun

All the stars, including our Sun, are gigantic balls of superheated gas, kept hot by atomic reactions in their centers. In our Sun, this atomic reaction is hydrogen fusion: four hydrogen atoms are combined to form one helium atom. The temperature at the core of our Sun must be 20 million degrees centigrade, and the surface temperature averages 6,000° C, or about 11,000° F. The diameter of the Sun is 865,400 miles, and its surface area is approximately 12,000 times that of Earth. Compared with other stars, our Sun is just a bit below average in size and temperature, and is a yellow dwarf star. Its fuel supply (hydrogen) is estimated to be sufficient for another 5 billion years.

Our Sun is not motionless in space; in fact it has two proper motions. One is a seemingly straight-line motion in the direction of the constellation Hercules at the rate of about 12 miles per second. But since the Sun is a part of the Milky Way system and since the whole system rotates slowly around its own center, the Sun also moves at the rate of 175 miles per second as part of the rotating Milky Way system.

A Star's Magnitude

Magnitude is the degree of brightness of a star. In 1856, British astronomer Norman Pogson proposed a quantitative scale of stellar magnitudes, which was adopted by the astronomical community. He noted that we receive 100 times more light from a first magnitude star as from a sixth; thus with a difference of five magnitudes, there is a 100:1 ratio of incoming light energy, which is called *luminous flux*.

Because of the nature of human perception, equal intervals of brightness are actually equal ratios of luminous flux. Pogson's proposal was that one increment in magnitude be the fifth root of 100. This means that each increment in magnitude corresponds to an increase in the amount of energy by 2.512, approximately. A fifth magnitude star is 2.512 times as bright as a sixth, and a fourth magnitude star is 6.310 times as bright as a sixth, and so on. The naked eye, upon optimum conditions, can see down to around the sixth magnitude, that is +6. Under Pogson's system, a few of the brighter stars now have negative magnitudes. For example, Sirius is −1.5. The lower the magnitude number, the brighter the object. The full moon has a magnitude of about −12.5, and the sun is a bright −26.51!

The Brightest Stars

Star	Constellation	Mag.	Dist (l.-y.)	Star	Constellation	Mag.	Dist (l.-y.)
Sirius	Canis Major	-1.6	8	Antares	Scorpius	1.2	170
Canopus	Carina	-0.9	650	Fomalhaut	Piscis Austrinus	1.3	27
Alpha Centauri	Centaurus	+0.1	4	Deneb	Cygnus	1.3	465
Vega	Lyra	0.1	23	Regulus	Leo	1.3	70
Capella	Auriga	0.2	42	Beta Crucis	Crux	1.5	465
Arcturus	Boötes	0.2	32	Eta Carinae	Carina	1-7	—
Rigel	Orion	0.3	545	Alpha-one Crucis	Crux	1.6	150
Procyon	Canis Minor	0.5	10	Castor	Gemini	1.6	44
Achernar	Eridanus	0.6	70	Gamma Crucis	Crux	1.6	—
Beta Centauri	Centaurus	0.9	130	Epsilon Canis Majoris	Canis Major	1.6	325
Altair	Aquila	0.9	18	Epsilon Ursae Majoris	Ursa Major	1.7	50
Betelgeuse	Orion	0.9	600	Bellatrix	Orion	1.7	215
Aldebaran	Taurus	1.1	54	Lambda Scorpii	Scorpius	1.7	205
Spica	Virgo	1.2	190	Epsilon Carinae	Carina	1.7	325
Pollux	Gemini	1.2	31	Mira	Cetus	2-10	250

In addition to this motion, the Sun rotates on its axis. Observing the motion of sunspots (darkish areas that look like enormous whirling storms) and solar flares, which are usually associated with sunspots, has shown that the rotational period of the Sun is just short of 25 days. But this figure is valid for the Sun's equator only; the sections near the Sun's poles seem to have a rotational period of 34 days. Naturally, since the Sun generates its own heat and light, there is no temperature difference between poles and equator.

In 1998, scientists saw for the first time that solar flares produce seismic waves in the Sun's interior that resemble those created by earthquakes. They observed a flare-generated solar quake equivalent to a 11.3 magnitude earthquake. It contained about 40,000 times the energy released in the great 1906 San Francisco earthquake.

What we call the Sun's "surface" is technically known as the photosphere. Since the whole Sun is a ball of very hot gas, there is really no such thing as a surface; it is a question of visual impression. The next layer outside the photosphere is known as the chromosphere, which extends several thousand miles beyond the photosphere. It is in steady motion, and often enormous prominences can be seen to burst from it, extending as much as 100,000 miles into space. Outside the chromosphere is the corona. The corona consists of very tenuous gases (essentially hydrogen) and makes a magnificent sight when the Sun is eclipsed.

As the Sun ages, it gradually expands and heats. In 1994, American astrophysicists studying the eventual fate of the Sun estimated that its brilliancy will increase by 10% over the next 1.1 billion years or more and, in about 6.5 billion years hence, our aging star will have doubled its present luminosity. The extreme heat generated will cause a catastrophic greenhouse effect on Earth and our oceans will boil away, and life on Earth as we know it will end.

The Sun will eventually expand enormously to 166 times its present size and become over 2,000 times as bright. Eight billion years from now, the Sun's radius will engulf the planet Mercury and extend beyond the present orbit of Venus.

However, as the Sun expands, it will also lose considerable mass (as much as one-half) and weaken its gravitational pull on Venus and the other lifeless planets, causing them to orbit further away from the Sun and escape total destruction.

The Moon

Mercury and Venus do not have any moons. Therefore, Earth is closer to the Sun than any other planet orbited by a moon.

The next planet farther out, Mars, has two very small moons. Jupiter has four major moons and twelve minor ones. Saturn, the ringed planet, has 18 known moons (and possibly more), of which one (Titan) is larger than the planet Mercury. Uranus has 18 or possibly 20 moons (four of them large) as well as rings, while Neptune has one large and seven small moons. Pluto has one moon, discovered in 1978. Some astronomers still consider Pluto to be a "runaway moon" of Neptune.

Our Moon, with a diameter of 2,160 miles, is one of the larger moons in our solar system and is especially large when compared with the planet that it orbits. In fact, the common center of gravity of the Earth–Moon system is only about 1,000 miles below Earth's surface. The closest the Moon can come to us (its perigee) is 221,463 miles; the farthest it can go away (its apogee) is 252,710 miles. The period of rotation of the Moon is equal to its period of revolution around Earth. Hence from Earth we can see only one hemisphere of the Moon. Both periods are 27 days, 7 hours, 43 minutes and 11.47 seconds. But while the rotation of the Moon is constant, its velocity in its orbit is not, since it moves more slowly in apogee than in perigee. Consequently, some portions near the rim that are not normally visible will appear briefly. This phenomenon is called "libration," and by taking advantage of the librations, astronomers have succeeded in mapping approximately 59% of the lunar surface. The other 41% can never be seen from Earth but has been mapped by American and Russian Moon-orbiting spacecraft.

Though the Moon goes around Earth in the time mentioned, the interval from new moon to new moon is 29 days, 12 hours, 44 minutes, and 2.78 seconds. This delay of nearly two days is due to the fact that Earth is moving around the Sun, so that the Moon needs two extra days to reach a spot in its orbit where no part is illuminated by the Sun, as seen from Earth.

If the plane of Earth's orbit around the Sun (the ecliptic) and the plane of the Moon's orbit around Earth were the same, the Moon would be eclipsed by Earth every time it is full, and the Sun would be eclipsed by the Moon every time the Moon is "new" (it would be better to call it the "black moon" when it is in this position). But because the two orbits do not coincide, the Moon's shadow normally misses Earth and Earth's shadow misses the Moon. The inclination of the two orbital planes to each other is 5°.

The tides are, of course, caused by the Moon with the help of the Sun, but in the open ocean they are surprisingly low, amounting to about one yard. The very high tides that can be observed near the shore in some places are due to funnelling effects of the shorelines. At new moon and at full moon the tides raised by the Moon are reinforced by the Sun; these are the "spring tides." If the Sun's tidal power acts at right angles to that of the Moon (quarter moons) we get the low "neap tides."

The *Lunar Prospector* spacecraft, launched in January 1998, found that as much as three billion metric tons of water ice is hidden in the permanently shaded craters at the poles. The water probably came from interstellar comets that crashed into the Moon. *Lunar Prospector* also confirmed that the Moon has a small core, supporting the theory that the Moon was ripped away from the early Earth when an object the size of Mars collided with the Earth.

At the end of its mission, on July 31, 1999, the spacecraft was intentionally crashed into a permanently shadowed crater at the Moon's south pole in the hope of detecting a rising plume of water ice, but no cloud of water vapor molecules was observed by powerful Earth telescopes.

Earth

Earth, circling the Sun at an average distance of 93 million miles, is the fifth-largest planet and the third from the Sun. It orbits the Sun at a speed of 67,000 miles per hour, making one revolution in 365 days, 5 hours, 48 minutes, and 45.51 seconds. Earth completes one rotation on its axis every 23 hours, 56 minutes, and 4.09 seconds. Actually a bit pear-shaped rather than a true sphere, Earth has a diameter of 7,927 miles at the equator and a few miles less at the poles. It has an estimated mass of about 6.6 sextillion tons, with an average density of 5.52 grams per cubic centimeter. Earth's surface area encompasses 196,949,970 square miles of which about three-fourths is water.

Origin of Earth

Earth, along with the other planets, is believed to have been born 4.5 billion years ago as a solidified cloud of dust and gases left over from the creation of the Sun. For perhaps 500 million years, the interior of Earth stayed solid and relatively cool, perhaps 2000° F. The main ingredients, according to the best available evidence, were iron and silicates, with small amounts of other elements, some of them radioactive. As millions of years passed, energy released by radioactive decay—mostly of uranium, thorium, and potassium—gradually heated Earth, melting some of its constituents. The iron melted before the silicates, and, being heavier, sank toward the center. This forced up the silicates that it found there. After many years, the iron reached the center, almost 4,000 miles deep, and began to accumulate. No eyes were around at that time to view the turmoil that must have taken place on the face of Earth—gigantic heaves and bubblings on the surface, exploding volcanoes, and flowing lava covering everything in sight. Finally, the iron in the center accumulated as the core. Around it, a thin but fairly stable crust of solid rock formed as Earth cooled. Depressions in the crust were natural basins in which water, rising from the interior of the planet through volcanoes and fissures, collected to form the oceans. Slowly, Earth acquired its present appearance.

Earth Today

As a result of radioactive heating over millions of years, Earth's molten *core* is probably fairly hot today, around 11,000° F. By comparison, lead melts at around 800° F. Most of Earth's 2,100-mile-thick core is liquid, but there is evidence that the center of the core is solid. The liquid outer portion, about 95% of the core, is constantly in motion, causing Earth to have a magnetic field that makes compass needles point north and south. The details are not known, but the latest evidence suggests that planets that have a magnetic field probably have a solid core or a partially liquid one.

Outside the core is Earth's *mantle*, 1,800 miles thick and extending nearly to the surface. The mantle is composed of heavy silicate rock, similar to that brought up by volcanic eruptions. It is somewhere between liquid and solid, slightly yielding, and therefore contributing to an active, moving Earth. Most of Earth's radioactive material is in the thin *crust* that covers the mantle, but some is in the mantle and continues to give off heat. The crust's thickness ranges from 5 to 25 miles.

Scientists recently discovered that Earth's core is not a perfect sphere. X-ray-like images of inside Earth show that there are vast mountains six to seven miles high and deep valleys on the core. These features are in an upside-down relationship to Earth's surface.

In 1996, geophysicists discovered that Earth's solid-iron inner core rotates slightly faster than the rest of the planet and gains a quarter-turn every century. The finding may help explain how Earth's magnetic field periodically reverses its polarity.

Continental Drift

A great deal of recent evidence confirms the theory that the continents of Earth, made mostly of relatively light granite, float in the slightly yielding mantle, like logs in a pond. For many years it had been noticed that if North and South America could be pushed toward western and southern Europe and western Africa, they would fit like pieces in a jigsaw puzzle. Today, there is little question—the continents have drifted widely and continue to do so.

In 10 million years, the world as we know it may be unrecognizable, with California drifting out to sea, Florida joining South America, and Africa moving farther away from Europe and Asia.

Earth's Atmosphere

The thin blanket of atmosphere that envelops Earth extends several hundred miles into space. From sea level—the very bottom of the ocean of air—to a height of about 60 miles, the air in the atmosphere is made up of the same gases in the same ratio: about 78% nitrogen, 21% oxygen, and the remaining 1% being a mixture of argon, carbon dioxide, and tiny amounts of neon, helium, krypton, xenon, and other gases. The atmosphere becomes less dense with increasing altitude: more than three-fourths of Earth's huge envelope is concentrated in the first 5 to 10 miles above the surface. At sea level, a cubic foot of atmosphere weighs about an ounce and a quarter. The entire atmosphere weighs 5,700 trillion tons, and the force with which gravity holds it in place causes it to exert a pressure of nearly 15 pounds per square inch. Going out from Earth's surface, the atmosphere is divided into five regions. The regions, and the heights to which they extend, are: *troposphere,* 0 to 7 miles (at middle latitudes); *stratosphere,* 7 to 30 miles; *mesosphere,* 30 to 50 miles; *thermosphere,* 50 to 400 miles; and *exosphere,* above 400 miles. The boundaries between each of the regions are known respectively as the *tropopause, stratopause, mesopause,* and *thermopause.* Alternative terms often used for the layers above the troposphere are *ozonosphere* (for stratosphere) and *ionosphere* for the remaining upper layers.

The Seasons

Seasons are caused by the 23.4-degree tilt of Earth's axis, which alternately turns the North and South Poles toward the Sun. Times when the Sun's apparent path crosses the equator are known as *equinoxes.* Times when the Sun's apparent path is at the greatest distance from the equator are known as *solstices.* The lengths of the days are most extreme at each solstice. If Earth's axis were perpendicular to the plane of Earth's orbit around the Sun, there would be no seasons, and the days always would be equal in length. Since Earth's axis is at an angle, the Sun strikes Earth directly at the equator only twice a year: in March (vernal equinox) and September (autumnal equinox). In the Northern Hemisphere, spring begins at the vernal equinox, summer at the summer solstice, fall at the autumnal equinox, and winter at the winter solstice. The situation is reversed in the Southern Hemisphere.

Mercury

Mercury is the planet nearest the Sun. Appropriately named for the wing-footed Roman messenger of the gods, Mercury whizzes around the Sun at a speed of 30 miles per second, completing one circuit in 88 days. The days and nights are long on Mercury. It takes 59 Earth days for Mercury to make a single rotation. It spins at a rate of about 6 miles (about 10 kilometers) per hour, measured at the equator, as compared to Earth's spin of about 1,000 miles (about 1,600 kilometers) per hour at the equator.

The photographs *Mariner 10* (1974–1975) radioed back to Earth revealed an ancient, heavily cratered surface on Mercury, closely resembling our own Moon. The pictures showed huge cliffs, or scarps, crisscrossing the planet. These apparently were created when Mercury's interior cooled and shrank, compressing the planet's crust. The cliffs are as high as 1.2 miles (two kilometers) and as long as 932 miles (1,500 kilometers). Another unique feature is the Caloris Basin, a large impact crater about 808 miles (1,300 kilometers) in diameter.

Mercury, like Earth, appears to have a crust of light silicate rock. Scientists believe it has a heavy iron-rich core that makes up about half of its volume.

Instruments onboard *Mariner 10* discovered that the planet has a weak magnetic field and a trace of atmosphere—a trillionth the density of Earth's and composed chiefly of argon, neon, and helium. The spacecraft reported temperatures ranging from 950° F (510° C) on Mercury's sunlit side to –346° F (–210° C) on the dark side. Mercury literally bakes in daylight and freezes at night.

Until the *Mariner 10* probe, little was known about the planet. Even the best telescopic views from Earth showed Mercury as an indistinct object lacking any surface detail. The planet is so close to the Sun that it is usually lost in the Sun's glare.

Radar images taken by astronomers at Jet Propulsion Laboratories and California Institute of Technology during the summer of 1991 suggest that the polar regions of Mercury may be covered with patches of water ice. Although this seems impossible due to the planet's sizzling heat, the polar regions receive very little sunlight and may get as cold as –235° F (–148° C). The radar images showed bright patterns at the poles that are characteristic of ice reflecting radar signals. Other explanations may be offered for this unexpected discovery.

NASA plans to launch a spacecraft to orbit Mercury in 2004. It will map the planet and search for water, a magnetic field, and other phenomena.

Mercury is a naked-eye object at morning or evening twilight when it is at greatest elongation.

Venus

Although Venus is Earth's closest neighbor, very little is known about the planet because it is permanently covered by thick clouds. In 1962, Soviet and

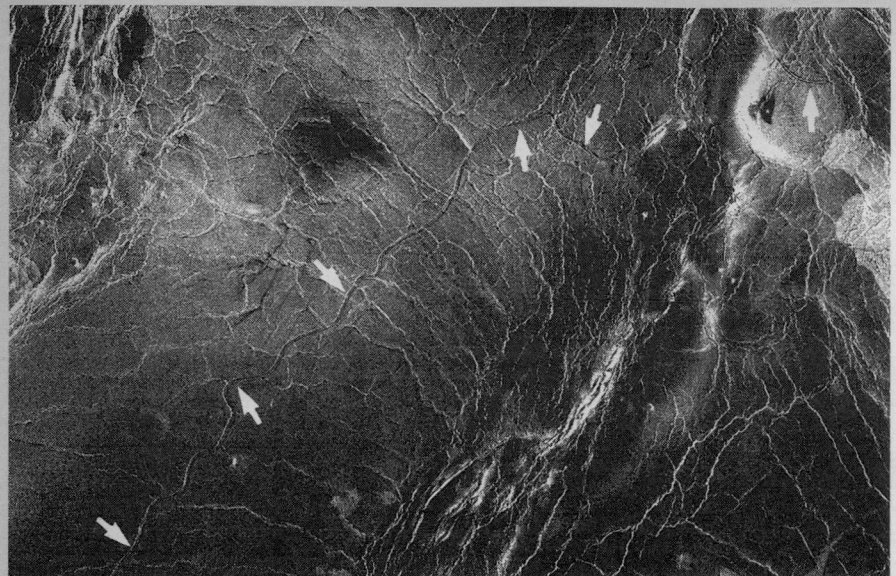

Largest Channel in Solar System. *Magellan* took the above image of the largest known channel on Venus. At 4,200 miles (6,800 kilometers) long and an average of 1.1 miles (1.8 kilometers) wide, it is longer than the Nile River, Earth's longest river, making it the longest known channel in the solar system. The channel was originally discovered by the Soviet *Venery 15* and *16* spacecraft orbiters. *Source:* NASA.

American space probes, coupled with Earth-based radar and infrared spectroscopy, began slowly unraveling some of the mystery surrounding Venus. Twenty-eight years later, the *Magellan* spacecraft, sent by the United States, arrived at Venus in August 1990 and began radar-mapping the planet's surface in greater detail.

According to the latest results, Venus's atmosphere exerts a pressure at the surface 94.5 times greater than Earth's. Walking on Venus would be as difficult as walking a half-mile beneath the ocean. Because of a thick blanket of carbon dioxide, a "greenhouse effect" exists on Venus. Venus intercepts twice as much of the Sun's light as does Earth. The light enters freely through the carbon dioxide gas and is changed to heat radiation in molecular collisions. But carbon dioxide prevents the heat from escaping. Consequently, the temperature of the surface of Venus is over 800° F (427° C), hot enough to melt lead.

The atmospheric composition of Venus is about 96% carbon dioxide, 4% nitrogen, and minor amounts of water, oxygen, and sulfur compounds. There are at least four distinct cloud and haze layers that exist at different altitudes above the planet's surface. The haze layers contain small aerosol particles, possibly droplets of sulfuric acid. A concentration of sulfur dioxide above the cloud tops has been observed to be decreasing since 1978. The source of sulfur dioxide at this altitude is unknown; it may be injected by volcanic explosions or atmospheric overturning.

Measurements of the Venusian atmosphere and its cloud patterns reveal nearly constant high-speed zonal winds, about 220 miles per hour (100 meters per second) at the equator. The winds decrease toward the poles so that the atmosphere at cloud-top

level rotates almost like a solid body. The wind speeds at the equator correspond to Venus's rotation period of four to five days at most latitudes. The circulation is always in the same direction—east to west—as Venus's slow retrograde motion. Earth's winds blow from west to east, the same direction as its rotation.

Venus is quite round, very different from the other planets and from the Moon. Venus has neither polar flattening nor an equatorial bulge. The diameter of Venus is 7,519 miles (12,100 kilometers). Venus has a retrograde axial rotation period of 243.1 Earth days. The surface atmospheric pressure is 1,396 pounds per square inch (95 Earth atmospheres). The planet's mean distance from the Sun is 67.2 million miles (108.2 million kilometers). The period of its revolution around the Sun is 224.7 days.

The highest point on Venus is the summit of Maxwell Montes, 6.71 miles (10.8 kilometers) above the mean level, more than a mile higher than Mount Everest. There is some evidence that this huge mountain is an active volcano. The lowest point is in the rift valley, Diana Chasma, 1.8 miles (2.9 kilometers) below the mean level. This point is about one-fifth the greatest depth on Earth in the Marianas Trench.

Venus has an extreme lowland basin, Atalanta Planitia, which is about the size of Earth's North Atlantic Ocean basin. The smooth surface of the Atalanta Planitia resembles the mare basins of the Moon.

There are only two highland or continental masses on Venus: Ishtar Terra and Aphrodite Terra. Ishtar Terra is 6.8 miles (11 kilometers) at its highest points (the highest peaks on Venus) and those of Aphrodite Terra rise to about 3.10 miles (5 kilometers) above the planet. Ishtar Terra is about the size of the continental United States and Aphrodite Terra is about the size of Africa.

The unmanned NASA spacecraft *Magellan* was launched on May 4, 1989, from the shuttle *Atlantis* and arrived at Venus August 10, 1990, to map most of the planet. Despite some problems with its radio transmissions, the results of the radar mapping delighted scientists and provided them with the sharpest images ever taken of the planet's surface. Images taken from *Magellan* show ten times more detail than ever seen before.

The radar images provided scientists with compelling evidence that the planet has been dominated by volcanism on a global scale. The photos also showed that the planet's second-highest mountain, Maat Mons, rising five miles (eight kilometers) above the Venusian plains, appears to be covered with fresh lava and is possibly an active volcano.

Magellan discovered the longest known channel in the solar system on Venus. It is 4,200 miles (6,800 kilometers) long and averages slightly over a mile (1.8 kilometers) wide. Its origin is puzzling to scientists because high-temperature lava is unlikely to have caused such a long-distance flow on the surface and there are no known substances that could remain liquid long enough under the planet's atmospheric pressure and temperature to have carved out this snakelike feature. The channel is slightly longer than the Nile River, the longest river on Earth. *Magellan* ended its radar and emissions mapping in September 1992 after covering 98% of the planet's surface.

Venus is the brightest of all the planets and is often visible in the morning or evening, when it is frequently referred to as the Morning Star or Evening Star. At its brightest, it can sometimes be seen in full daylight with the naked eye, if one knows where to look.

Mars

Mars, on the other side of Earth from Venus, is Venus's direct opposite in terms of physical properties. Its atmosphere is cold, thin, and transparent, and readily permits observation of the planet's features. We know more about Mars than any other planet except Earth. Mars is a forbidding, rugged planet with huge volcanoes and deep chasms. The largest volcano, Olympus Mons (Olympic Mountain) rises 78,000 feet above the surface, higher than Mount Everest. The plains of Mars are pockmarked by the hits of thousands of meteors over the years.

Until the arrival of *Mars Pathfinder* and *Mars Global Surveyor* in 1997, most of our information about Mars came from the *Mariner* and *Viking* spacecrafts. *Mariner 9* orbited the planet in 1971 and photographed 100% of the planet, uncovering spectacular geological formations, including a Martian "Grand Canyon" that dwarfs the one on Earth. Called Valles Marineris (Mariner Valley), it stretches more than 3,000 miles along the equatorial region of Mars and is over 2.5 miles (4 kilometers) deep in places and 50–62 miles (80 to 100 kilometers) wide. The spacecraft's cameras also recorded what appeared to be dried riverbeds, suggesting the one-time presence of water on the planet. The latter idea gave encouragement to scientists looking for life on Mars, for where there is water, there may be life. However, to date, no evidence of life has been found. Temperatures near the equator range from –17° F in the daytime to –130° F at night.

Mars rotates upon its axis in nearly the same period as Earth—24 hours, 37 minutes—so that a Mars day is almost identical to an Earth day. Mars takes 687 days to make one trip around the Sun. Because of its eccentric orbit, Mars's distance from the Sun can vary by about 36 million miles. Its distance from Earth can vary by as much as 200 million miles. The atmosphere of Mars is much thinner than Earth's; atmospheric pressure is about 1% that of our planet. Its gravity is one-third of Earth's. Major constituents are carbon dioxide and nitrogen. Water vapor and oxygen are minor constituents. Mars's polar caps, composed mostly of frozen carbon dioxide (dry ice), recede and advance according to the Martian seasons.

Mars has four seasons like Earth, but they are much longer. For example, in the northern hemisphere, the Martian spring is 198 days, and the winter season lasts 158 days.

The *Mars Pathfinder* lander and its rover, *Sojourner*, set down on the edge of a boulder-strewn outflow channel known as *Ares Vallis* on July 4, 1997, and provided scientists with a wealth of information on the rocks, soils, and atmosphere of Mars. The lander sent back the first live pictures of the planet's topography and its tiny rover explored a variety of rocks and analyzed their mineral composition with its cameras and on-board X-ray spectrometer.

Analysis of the reddish surface soil pointed to the presence of oxidized iron, indicating that the planet's surface is rusting. *Sojourner* samples of soil taken from several sites found their composition similar to those analyzed by the two *Viking* landers in 1976, indicating that the Martian winds have distributed the soil evenly over the planet.

Scientists were surprised to learn how rapidly the Martian temperature fluctuates due to atmospheric turbulence. It can change by as much as 30°–40° F (17°–22° C) in a matter of minutes, possibly due to strong, gusty winds bringing warm air from one region or cold air from another.

Pictures and subsequent data from *Pathfinder* give the strongest evidence that Mars had an abundance of water millions of years ago. Scientists have inferred from the variety of rocks and sediments found in the *Ares* basin that the spacecraft landed in a channel that was once awash with torrential floods greater than any known on Earth. The diversity of rocks deposited there suggest their different origins, and it appears that they were washed down from the highlands at a time when great floods moved over the surface of Mars.

Before *Pathfinder*, knowledge of the kinds of rocks present on Mars was based mostly on the Martian meteorites found on Earth. Chemical analysis of the Martian rocks and studies of different regions of soil found at *Ares Vallis* confirmed that these rocks have compositions distinct from those of the Martian meteorites found on Earth.

In its three months of operation, the mission returned more than 16,000 images of the Martian landscape from the lander's camera and 550 images from the rover.

The *Sojourner* rover traveled a total of about 328 feet (100 meters) and performed more than 16 chemical analyses of rocks and soil, and explored

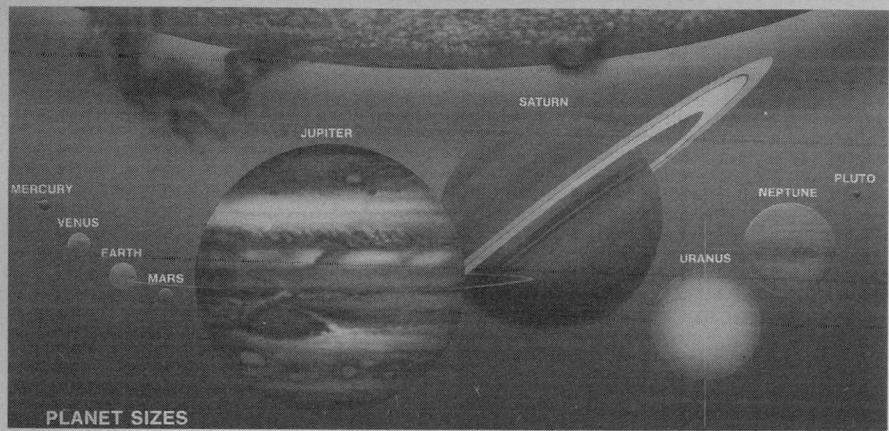

PLANET SIZES. Shown from left to right: Mercury, Venus, Earth, Mars, Jupiter, Saturn, Uranus, Neptune, and Pluto. *Copyright 1990 Hansen Planetarium, Salt Lake City, Utah. Reproduced with permission.*

Basic Planetary Data

	Mercury	Venus	Earth	Mars	Jupiter
Mean distance from sun (millions of kilometers)	57.9	108.2	149.6	227.9	778.3
Mean distance from sun (millions of miles)	36.0	67.24	92.9	141.71	483.88
Period of revolution	88 days	224.7 days	365.2 days	687 days	11.86 yrs
Rotation period	59 days	243 days retrograde	23 hr 56 min 4 sec	24 hr 37 min	9 hr 55 min 30 sec
Inclination of axis	Near 0°	3°	23°27′	25° 12′	3° 5′
Inclination of orbit to ecliptic	7°	3.4°	0°	1.9°	1.3°
Eccentricity of orbit	.206	.007	.017	.093	.048
Equatorial diameter (kilometers)	4,880	12,100	12,756	6,794	142,800
(miles)	3,032.4	7,519	7,926.2	4,194	88,736
Atmosphere (main components)	Virtually none	Carbon dioxide	Nitrogen oxygen	Carbon dioxide	Hydrogen helium
Satellites	0	0	1	2	16
Rings	0	0	0	0	1

	Saturn	Uranus	Neptune	Pluto
Mean distance from sun (millions of kilometers)	1,427	2,870	4,497	5,900
Mean distance from sun (millions of miles)	887.14	1,783.98	2,796.46	3,666
Period of revolution	29.46 yrs	84 yrs	165 yrs	248 yrs
Rotation period	10 hr 40 min 24 sec	16.8 hr(?) retrograde	16 hr 11 min(?)	6 days 9 hr 18 mins retrograde
Inclination of axis	26°44′	97°55′	28°48′	60° (?)
Inclination of orbit to ecliptic	2.5°	0.8°	1.8°	17.2°
Eccentricity of orbit	.056	.047	.009	.254
Equatorial diameter (kilometers)	120,660	51,810	49,528	2,290 (?)
(miles)	74,978	32,193	30,775	1,423 (?)
Atmosphere (main components)	Hydrogen helium	Helium hydrogen methane	Hydrogen helium methane	None detected
Satellites	18[1]	18[2]	8	1
Rings	1,000 (?)	11	4	?

1. Possible additional small moons may orbit Saturn but they have not been confirmed yet. 2. Two additional possible new moons were announced in July 1999. *Source:* Basic NASA data and other sources.

820 square feet (250 square meters) of the planet's surface. Communications were lost with the lander on Sept. 27, 1997, after 83 days of commanding and data return.

NASA launched the *Mars Global Surveyor* spacecraft on Nov. 7, 1996, to provide detailed maps of the planet's surface, its distribution of minerals, and to monitor its weather. The spacecraft entered Mars's orbit on Sept. 11, 1997, and began mapping operations on March 27, 1998. The spacecraft will orbit Mars for 687 days, the length of one Martian year.

Surveyor discovered the first clear evidence of an ancient hydrothermal system near the equator. This implies that water was stable at or near the surface and that a thicker atmosphere existed in Mars's early history.

Most surprising to mission scientists was finding that the planet's northern hemisphere was exceptionally flat—like the Bonneville salt flats in Utah—with slopes and surface roughness increasing towards the equator.

Surveyor's three-dimensional views of the planet's northern polar ice cap showed often striking canyons and spiral troughs in the water and carbon dioxide ice that can reach depths as great as 3,600 feet below the surface. Its data also showed that large areas of the ice cap were extremely smooth, with elevations varying only a few feet over many miles.

In 1999, the *Mars Global Surveyor* discovered magnetic stripes about 100 miles (160 kilometers) wide, the remnants of the planet's ancient magnetism, running east and west on the surface of Mars. At their longest, the band-patterns of magnetic fields extend as far as 1,240 miles (1,996 kilometers) along the surface.

Mars was named for the Roman god of war, because when seen from Earth its distinct red color reminded the ancient people of blood. We know now that the reddish hue reflects the oxidized (rusted) iron in the surface material.

The Martian Moons

Mars has two very small elliptical-shaped moons, Deimos and Phobos—the Greek names for the companions of the God Mars: Deimos (Terror) and Phobos (Fear). They were discovered in August 1877 by the American astronomer Asaph Hall (1829–1907) of the U.S. Naval Observatory in Washington, D.C.

The inner satellite, Phobos, is 16.78 miles (27 kilometers) long and it revolves around the planet in 7.6 hours. The outer moon, Deimos, is 9.32 miles (15 kilometers) long and it circles the planet in 30.35 hours. The short orbital period of Phobos means that the satellite travels around Mars three times in a Martian day.

Recent studies of Phobos indicate that its orbit is slowly decreasing downward and that in approximately 40 million years, it will crash into the planet's surface.

Meteorites from Mars

Thirteen meteorites, almost certainly from Mars, have been discovered. They are known as SNCs[1] (named for the towns where they were found: Shergotty, India, in 1865; Nakhla, Egypt, in 1911; and Chassigny, France, in 1815). This hypothesis was based largely on the composition of noble gases (particularly argon and xenon) trapped in the mete-

1. Pronounced "snick."

orites, and the shergottites in particular, which resemble measurements of the Martian atmosphere made by the *Viking* spacecraft. Major element compositions of the SNCs are also similar to Martian soil analyses made by *Viking*.

The relatively young isotopic ages of the SNC meteorites (1.3 billion years or less) suggest that Mars has been volcanically active during its recent past.

In 1991, a ninth meteorite, LEW 88516, was identified as having reached Earth from Mars some 180 million years ago. It was discovered in December 1988 near Lewis Cliff in Antarctica. The meteorite is very small with a dark pitted surface and weighs less than half an ounce (13.2 grams).

A 4-pound, 7-ounce (1.9 kilograms) meteorite, ALH 84001, found in the Allen Hills of Antarctica in 1984 was reclassified in 1993 as coming from the Red Planet, making it the tenth meteorite known to have originated from Mars. In 1996, NASA announced that meteorite ALH 84001 contained fossils of ancient Martian life forms.

A 40-pound meteorite that crashed to Earth in Nigeria in 1962 has been classified as coming from Mars. It was named Zagami for the region in which it was found.

A 0.38-ounce (12-gram) meteorite (QUE 94201) found in Antarctica in 1995 became the 12th meteorite identified as having a Martian origin.

In 1997, the thirteenth known Martian meteorite, Dar al Gani 476, a 4.8 pound (2.2 kilogram) meteorite, was found in the Sahara Desert.

Jupiter

Jupiter is the largest planet in the solar system—a gaseous world as large as 1,300 Earths. Its equatorial diameter is 88,736 miles (142,800 kilometers), while from pole to pole, Jupiter measures only 84,201 miles (133,500 kilometers). For comparison, the diameter of Earth is 7,926.2 miles (12,756 kilometers). The massive planet rotates at a dizzying speed—once every 9 hours and 55 minutes. It takes Jupiter almost 12 Earth years to complete a journey around the Sun.

The giant planet appears as a banded disk of turbulent clouds with all of its stripes running parallel to its bulging equator. Large dusky gray regions surround each pole. Darker gray or brown stripes called belts intermingle with lighter, yellow-white stripes called zones. The belts are regions of descending air masses and the zones are rising cloudy air masses. The strongest winds—up to 250 miles (400 kilometers) per hour—are found at boundaries between the belts and zones.

This uniquely colorful atmosphere is mainly 89% molecular hydrogen and 11% helium. It contains small amounts of methane, ammonia, ethane, and water.

Cloud-type lightning bolts similar to those on Earth have been found in the Jovian atmosphere. At the polar regions, auroras have been observed. A very thin ring of material less than 0.6 mile (one kilometer) in thickness and about 4,000 miles (6,000 kilometers) in radial extent has been observed circling the planet about 35,000 miles (55,000 kilometers) above the cloud tops.

The most prominent feature on Jupiter is its "Great Red Spot," an oval larger than the planet Earth. It is a tremendous atmospheric storm that rotates counterclockwise with one revolution every six days at the outer edge, while at the center almost no motion can be seen. The spot is about 16,000 miles (25,000 kilometers) on its long axis, and would cover three Earths. The outer rim shows streamline shapes of 225-mile (360-kilometer) winds.

Jupiter is circled by faint rings. They are very tenuous and contain many microscopic-sized particles. The rings are formed by dust kicked up as interplanetary meteoroids smash into the planet's four small inner moons.

Jupiter emits 67% more heat than it absorbs from the Sun. This heat is thought to have been accumulated during the planet's formation several billion years ago.

Twenty-one fragments of comet Shoemaker-Levy 9 bombarded the cloud-covered surface of Jupiter, July 16–22, 1994. It was the most violent event in the recorded history of our solar system. The cometary explosions caused towering plumes of debris and hot gas to rise from the darkened impact sites.

On Dec. 7, 1995, the *Galileo* spacecraft released a probe into Jupiter's atmosphere to study the planet's physical and chemical properties. The probe lasted 57 minutes and early results indicated a lower abundance of water than was expected.

Galileo data has shown that Jupiter has both wet and dry regions, just as Earth has tropics and deserts. This could explain why the probe found less water than anticipated. These dry spots cover less than 1% of the Jovian atmosphere.

Jovian Moons

The four great moons of Jupiter were discovered by Galileo Galilei (1564–1642) in January 1610, and are called the Galilean satellites after their discoverer. Their names are Io, Europa, Ganymede, and Callisto. Like our Moon, the satellites always keep the same face turned toward Earth. Jupiter has 16 known satellites.

Jupiter's four largest moons all have thin atmospheres. A carbon dioxide atmosphere envelopes Callisto; Europa and Ganymede each have thin oxygen atmospheres; and Io's contains sulfur dioxide.

Ganymede

Ganymede, 3,275 miles (5,270 kilometers) in diameter, is Jupiter's largest moon, and it is also the largest satellite in the solar system. Ganymede is about one and one-half times the size of our Moon. It is heavily cratered and probably has the greatest variety of geologic process recorded on its surface. Ganymede is half water and half rock, resulting in a density about two-thirds that of Europa, an ice-coated satellite. No atmosphere has been detected on it.

The first close-up photos of Ganymede taken by the *Galileo* spacecraft, during its June 1996 fly-by, revealed a surface pockmarked with ancient craters and a landscape wrinkled and torn by the same forces that make mountains and move continents on Earth. *Galileo*'s findings also indicated that Ganymede is enveloped in its own magnetic field, possibly created by a molten iron core or even a thin layer of conducting salty water underneath its icy crust.

Ganymede is the first known moon with its own magnetosphere.

Europa

Europa, the brightest of Jupiter's satellites, is about 1,950 miles (3,160 kilometers) in diameter or about the size of Earth's Moon. Its density is about

three times that of water. The moon is covered with a thin ice crust and is crisscrossed with an amazingly complex network of ridges. Some of the fractures on its crust are more than 1,850 miles (3,000 kilometers) long. Very few impact craters are visible on the surface.

Europea is the smoothest object in the solar system. Its mostly flat surface doesn't exceed 0.62 miles (1 kilometer) in height.

Galileo spacecraft photos taken at its closest fly-by on Feb. 20, 1997, at a distance of 363 miles (586 kilometers), showed the existence of ice flows on the surface that strongly suggest that the moon has a hidden subsurface ocean of water or ice-slush. The photos revealed chunky ice rafts that appear to be floating, comparable to icebergs on Earth. The presence of water and enough heat to keep water in a liquid state on Europa enhances the possibility that it could provide an environment for some form of extraterrestrial ocean life. Some researchers think that Europa may have active subsurface volcanoes. Oceanographers have found life near volcanic vents on Earth's sea floors.

NASA scientists have proposed to send a spacecraft called the *Europa Ice Clipper* to the moon in 2001 to determine if it has a global ocean and active volcanoes below its frozen crust. The spacecraft could send an impactor into Europa's surface with such a force that fragments of the moon would be injected into space, to be collected by the *Clipper* and returned to Earth for study.

Callisto

Callisto, 2,400 miles (4,800 kilometers) in diameter, is the outermost and, apparently, the least geologically active of Jupiter's four major satellites. Its density is less than twice that of water. Callisto has the oldest body and most cratered face of any body yet observed in the solar system. Like Ganymede, it seems to have a rocky core surrounded by ice. Unlike Ganymede, the surface of Callisto is completely covered with scars left by tens of thousands of meteoric impacts. Scientist estimate that it would take several billion years to accumulate the number of craters found there. So Callisto is believed to be inactive for at least that long. Although it is the darkest of the Galilean satellites, it is twice as bright as Earth's Moon.

Data from the *Galileo* spacecraft in 1998 suggests that Callisto has a salty ocean beneath its crust, similar to Europa's.

Io

Io, 2,262 miles (3,640 kilometers) in diameter, is the most spectacular of the Galilean moons. Its brilliant colors of red, orange, and yellow set it apart from any other moon or planet. Active volcanoes have been detected on Io, with some plumes extending up to 200 miles (320 kilometers) above the surface. The relative smoothness of Io's surface and its volcanic activity suggest that it has the youngest surface of Jupiter's moons. Its surface is composed of large amounts of sulfur and sulfur-dioxide frost, which account for the primarily yellow-orange surface color.

The volcanoes seem to eject a sufficient amount of sulfur dioxide to form a doughnut-shaped ring (torus) of ionized sulfur and oxygen atoms around Jupiter near Io's orbit. *Galileo* images taken in June

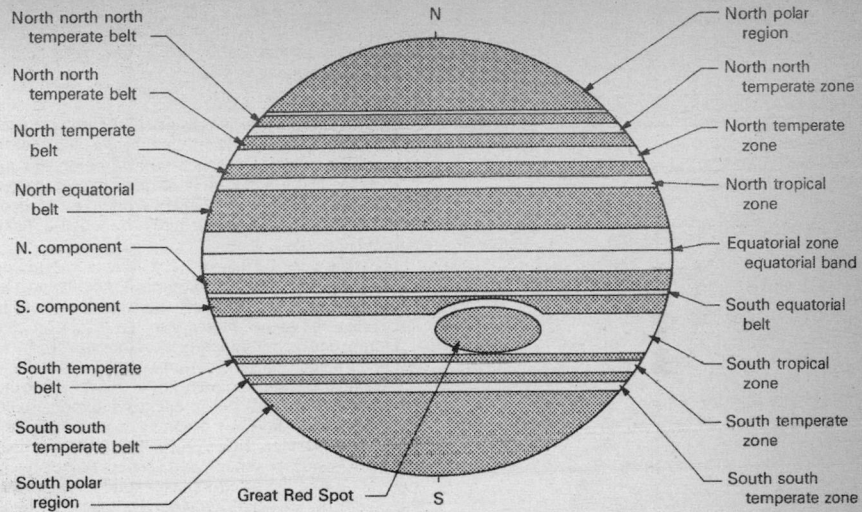

North north north temperate belt

North north temperate belt

North temperate belt

North equatorial belt

N. component

S. component

South temperate belt

South south temperate belt

South polar region

N

North polar region

North north temperate zone

North temperate zone

North tropical zone

Equatorial zone equatorial band

South equatorial belt

South tropical zone

South temperate zone

South south temperate zone

Great Red Spot

S

Schematic diagram of Jupiter's major features. *Source:* NASA.

1996 revealed that Io's landscape undergoes constant change due to the numerous sulfur volcanoes that continuously erupt on its surface.

Observations by *Galileo* during 1998 revealed dozens of volcanic vents on Io where lava is hotter than any surface temperatures recorded on any planetary body in our solar system. At one such volcanic vent, known as Pillan Patera, two of the spacecraft's instruments indicated that the lava temperature may have been 3,140° F.

In 1996, the *Galileo* spacecraft detected a huge iron core within Io that occupies half the moon's diameter. *Galileo* also discovered evidence that Io has its own magnetic field.

Amalthea

Amalthea, Jupiter's innermost satellite, was discovered in 1892. It is so small—165 miles (265 kilometers) long and 90 miles (150 kilometers) wide—that it is extremely difficult to observe from Earth. Amalthea is an elongated, irregularly shaped satellite of reddish color. It orbits the planet every 12 hours and is in synchronous rotation, with its long axis always oriented toward Jupiter.

Amalthea is heavily cratered, with two that are especially large. The largest crater, Pan, is 56 miles (90 kilometers) long and the other large crater, Gaea, is 47 miles (75 kilometers) in length.

Jupiter's other moons are named Adrasta, Metis, Thebe, Leda, Himalia, Lysithea, Elara, Ananke, Carne, Pasiphae, and Sinope.

The Magnetosphere

Perhaps the largest structure in the solar system is the magnetosphere of Jupiter. This is the region of space that is filled with Jupiter's magnetic field and is bounded by the interaction of that magnetic field with the solar wind, which is the Sun's outward flow of charged particles. The plasma of electrically charged particles that exists in the magnetosphere is flattened into a large disk more than 3 million miles

(4.8 million kilometers) in diameter, is coupled to the magnetic field, and rotates around Jupiter. The Galilean satellites are located in the inner regions of the magnetosphere and are subjected to intense radiation bombardment.

The intense radiation field that surrounds Jupiter is fatal to humans. If astronauts were one day able to approach the planet as close as the *Voyager 1* spacecraft did, they would receive a dose of 400,000 rads or roughly 1,000 times the lethal dose for humans.

Even when nearest Earth, Jupiter is still almost 400 million miles away. However, because of its size, it may rival Venus in brilliance when near. Jupiter's four large moons may be seen through field glasses, moving rapidly around Jupiter and changing their positions from night to night.

Saturn

Saturn, the second-largest planet in the solar system, is the least dense. Its mass is 95 times the mass of Earth and its density is 0.70 gram per cubic centimeter, so that it would float in an ocean if there were one big enough to hold it.

Saturn radiates about 80% more energy than it receives from the Sun. However, the excess thermal energy cannot be primarily attributed to Saturn's primordial heat loss, as is speculated for Jupiter.

Saturn's diameter is 74,978 miles (120,660 kilometers) but 10% less at the poles, a consequence of its rapid rotation. Its axis of rotation is tilted by 27 degrees and the length of its day is 10 hours, 39 minutes, and 24 seconds.

Saturn is composed primarily of liquid metallic hydrogen (about 80%) and the second most common element is believed to be helium.

Saturn's atmospheric appearance is very similar to Jupiter's with dark and light cloud markings and swirls, eddies, and curling ribbons; the belts and zones are more numerous and a thick haze mutes the

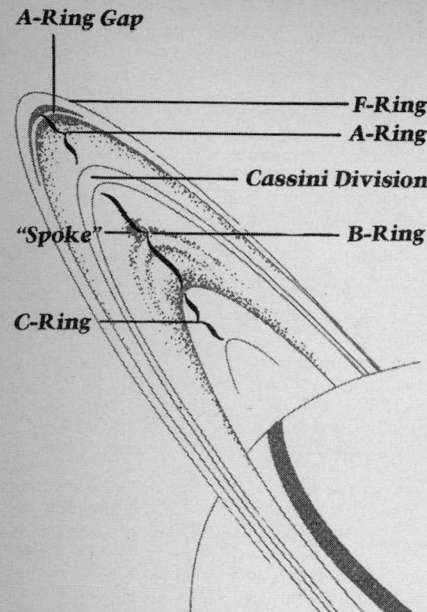

A-Ring Gap

F-Ring

A-Ring

Cassini Division

"Spoke"

B-Ring

C-Ring

NASA illustration of the divisions in Saturn's ring system.

markings. The temperature ranges from 80° K to 90° K (176° F to –203° F).

Winds blow at extremely high speeds on Saturn. Near the equator, the *Voyagers* measured winds of about 1,100 miles per hour (500 meters per second). The winds blow primarily in an eastward direction.

Saturn's Rings

Saturn's spectacular ring system is unique in the solar system, with uncountable billions of tiny particles of water ice (with traces of other material) in orbit around the planet. The ring particles range in size from smaller than grains of sugar to as large as a house. The main rings stretch out from about 4,350 miles (7,000 kilometers) to above the atmosphere of the planet out to the F ring, a total span of 45,984 miles (74,000 kilometers). Saturn's rings can be likened to a phonograph, rings within rings numbering in the hundreds, and spokes in the B rings, and shepherding satellites controlling the F ring.

The main rings are called the A, B, and C rings moving from outside to inside. The gap between the A and B rings is called Cassini's Division and is named for the Italian-French astronomer, Gian Domenico Cassini, who discovered four of Saturn's major moons and the dark, narrow gap, Cassini's Division, splitting the planet's rings.

Saturn's magnetic field has well-defined north and south magnetic poles, and is aligned with Saturn's axis of rotation to within one degree.

Saturn's Moons

Saturn has 18 known moons. There are several possible smaller moons around Saturn but they haven't been confirmed. The five largest moons—

Tethys, Dione, Rhea, Titan, and Iapetus—range from 650 to 3,200 miles (1,060 to 5,150 kilometers) in diameter. The planet's outstanding satellite is Titan, first discovered by the Dutch astronomer Christiaan Huygens in 1656.

Titan

Titan is remarkable because it is the only known moon in the solar system that has a substantial atmosphere—largely nitrogen with a minor amount of methane and a rich variety of other hydrocarbons. Its surface is completely hidden from view (except at infrared and radio wavelengths) by a dense, hazy atmosphere.

The diameter of Titan is 3,200 miles (5,150 kilometers) and it is the second-largest satellite in the solar system after Jupiter's Ganymede. Titan is larger than the planet Mercury.

Titan's surface temperature is about –175° C (–280° F) and its surface pressure is about 50% greater than the surface pressure of Earth. After the *Voyager I* fly-by in 1980, scientists hypothesized that Titan may have an ocean of liquid hydrogen covering its surface. However, in 1990 it was shown that Titan's surface reflects and scatters radio waves, suggesting that the satellite has a solid surface with the possibility of small hydrocarbon lakes or ponds on the surface.

The data were obtained by using NASA's 70-meter antenna in California to transmit powerful radio waves to Titan, and the Very Large Array in New Mexico as the receiver of the reflected waves.

NASA plans to send a scientific probe to the surface of Titan in the summer of 2004 as part of its Cassini Mission. The probe will be provided by the European Space Agency (ESA).

Other Notable Saturnian Moons

The other four largest moons of Saturn are: Tethys, Dione, Rhea, and Iapetus.

Tethys is 650 miles (1,060 kilometers) in diameter. Its surface is heavily cratered and it has a huge, globe-girdling canyon, Ithaca Chasma. Part of the canyon stretches over three-quarters of the satellite's surface. Ithaca Chasma is about 1,550 miles (2,500 kilometers) long. It has an average width of about 62 miles (100 kilometers) and a depth of 1.8 to 3.1 miles (3 to 5 kilometers).

Tethys also has a huge impact crater named Odysseus 244 miles, (4,400 kilometers) in diameter, or more than one-third of the moon's diameter.

Dione is slightly larger than Tethys, 696 miles (1,120 kilometers) in diameter, and is more than half composed of water ice. It has bright, wispy markings resembling thin veils covering its features.

Rhea, the largest of the inner satellites, is 951 miles (1,530 kilometers) in diameter. It is composed mainly of water ice, causing its reflective surface to present an almost uniform white appearance.

Iapetus is the outermost of Saturn's icy satellites. Its appearance is unique because it has one dark and one bright hemisphere. The origin of the black coating of its dark face is unknown. Iapetus has a diameter of 907 miles (1,460 kilometers).

Other notable moons of Saturn are Mimas, Enceladus, Hyperion, Phoebe, and Pan.

Mimas is small, only 244 miles (329 kilometers) in diameter. It has a huge impact crater, Herschel, nearly one-third of its diameter. The crater is about 81 miles (130 kilometers) wide and its icy peak rises almost 6.2 miles (10 kilometers) above the floor.

Mimas is believed to be composed mainly of water and ice and to contain between 20% and 50% rock.

Enceladus is remarkable in that its surface shows signs of extensive and recent geological activity. There may be active water volcanism. The surface is extremely bright, reflecting more than 90% of incident sunlight. This suggests that its surface is composed of extremely pure ice without dust or rocks to contaminate it. Enceladus has a diameter of 310 miles (500 kilometers).

Hyperion orbits between Iapetus and Titan. It is irregular in shape, measuring about 248 by 155 by 124 miles (400 by 250 by 200 kilometers). It may be a remnant of a much larger object that was shattered by impact with another space body. It appears that Hyperion is composed primarily of water ice. Hyperion orbits Saturn in a randomlike motion ("chaotic tumbling").

Phoebe is Saturn's outermost satellite. It travels in a retrograde orbit at a distance of over 6.2 million miles (10 million kilometers) away from the planet. It is the darkest moon of Saturn and is the planet's only known satellite that does not keep the same face always turned to Saturn. It has been speculated that it is an asteroid that was captured by the planet. Phoebe rotates in about nine hours and orbits Saturn in 406 days. It has a diameter of 124 miles (200 kilometers).

Pan was discovered in 1990 from *Voyager 2* photos taken in 1981. The satellite is estimated to be about 12.43 miles (20 kilometers) in diameter, which makes it the planet's smallest known moon. It orbits within the Encke Gap, a 202-mile (325-kilometer) division in Saturn's A ring. It was identified by Johann Franz Encke (1791–1865) in 1837.

The remaining eight moons range from 15 to 120 miles (25 to 190 kilometers) in diameter. They are all non-spherical in shape. Their names are Atlas, Prometheus, Pandora, Epimetheus, Janus, Telesto, Calypso, and Helene.

NASA's Cassini Mission to Saturn, launched in October 1997, will shed more light on the planet's mysteries when it arrives there in June 2004.

Saturn is the last of the planets visible to the naked eye. Saturn is never an object of overwhelming brilliance, but it looks like a bright star. The rings can be seen with a small telescope.

Uranus

Uranus, the first planet discovered in modern times by Sir William Herschel in 1781, is the seventh planet from the Sun, twice as far out as Saturn. Its mean distance from the Sun is 1,783 million miles (2,869 million kilometers). Uranus's equatorial diameter is 32,200 miles (51,810 kilometers). The axis of Uranus is tilted at 97 degrees, so it goes around the Sun nearly lying on its side.

Due to Uranus's unusual inclination, the polar regions receive more sunlight during a Uranus year of 84 Earth years. Scientists had thought that the temperature of its poles would be warmer than that at its equator, but *Voyager 2* discovered that the equatorial temperatures were similar to the temperatures at the poles, –209° C (–344° F), implying that some redistribution of heat toward the equatorial

region must occur within the atmosphere. The wind patterns are much like Saturn's, flowing parallel to the equator in the direction of the planet's rotation.

Ninety-eight percent of the upper atmosphere is composed of hydrogen and helium; the remaining two percent is methane. Scientists speculate that the bulk of the lower atmosphere is composed of water (perhaps as much as 50%), methane, and ammonia. Methane is responsible for Uranus's blue-green color because it selectively absorbs red sunlight and condenses to form clouds of ice crystals in the cooler, higher regions of Uranus's atmosphere.

It was also discovered that the planet's magnetic field was 60 degrees tilted from the planet's axis of rotation and offset from the planet's center by one-third of Uranus's radius. It may be generated at a depth where water is under sufficient pressure to be electrically conductive.

The Uranian Rings

Voyager 2 also expanded the body of information pertaining to the rings and moons of Uranus. *Voyager*'s cameras obtained the first images of 9 previously known narrow rings and discovered at least 2 new rings, one narrow and one broadly diffused, bringing the total known rings to 11. It was found that a highly structured distribution of fine dust exists throughout the ring system.

The outermost (epsilon) ring contains nothing smaller than fist-sized particles. It is flanked by two small moons discovered interior to the orbit of the Uranian moon Miranda. The moons exert a shepherding influence on the epsilon ring and on the outer edges of the gamma and delta rings.

All of the rings lie within one planetary radius[1] of Uranus's cloud tops. Most of Uranus's rings are narrow, ranging in width from 0.6 to 58 miles (1 to 93 kilometers), and are only a few kilometers thick. The Uranian rings are colorless and extremely dark. The dark material may be either irradiated methane ice or organic-rich minerals mixed with water-impregnated, silicon-based compounds. There is evidence that incomplete rings, or "ring arcs," exist at Uranus.

The Uranian Moons

There are 18 known (and possibly two more) moons of Uranus. In order of decreasing distance from the planet, the moons are U16 and U17 (unnamed), Oberon, Titania, Umbriel, Ariel, Miranda, Puck, 1986 U10 (unnamed), Belinda, Cressida, Portia, Rosalind, Desdemona, Juliet, Bianca, Ophelia, and Cordelia. Ten of the moons range in size from 16 to 67 miles (26 to 108 kilometers) in diameter and, being closer to the planet, have faster periods of revolution (8–15 hours) than their more distant relatives.

Oberon and Titania

The two largest moons, Oberon, 942 miles (1,516 kilometers) in diameter, and Titania, 982 miles (1,580 kilometers) in diameter, are less than half the diameter of Earth's moon. Titania, the reddest of Uranus's moons, may have endured global tectonics as evidenced by complex valleys and fault lines etched into its surface. Smooth sections indicate that volcanic resurfacing has taken place.

1. The equatorial radius of Uranus is 15,880 miles (25,560 kilometers) at a pressure of 1 bar.

Umbriel and Ariel

Umbriel and Ariel are roughly three-fourths the size of Oberon and Titania. Umbriel is the darkest of the large moons, with huge craters peppering its surface. Umbriel has a paucity of what are known as bright ray craters, which are formed on an older darker surface when bright submerged ice is excavated and sprayed by meteoroid impacts.

In contrast, the surface of Ariel, the brightest of the Uranian moons, is relatively free of pockmarks due to volcanism that periodically erases the damage done by foreign projectiles. However, there are several extremely deep cuts on Ariel's surface.

Miranda

The smallest of Uranus's large moons, Miranda, 293 miles (472 kilometers) in diameter, has been described as "the most bizarre body in the solar system," with the most geologically complex surface. Miranda's remarkable terrain consists of rolling, heavily cratered plains (the oldest known in the Uranian system) adjoined by three huge, 120- to 180-mile (200- to 300-kilometer) oval-to-trapezoidal regions known as coronae, which are characterized by networks of concentric canyons.

Puck

Puck was the first new moon discovered by *Voyager*, and is 96 miles (154 kilometers) in diameter and makes a trip around Uranus every 18 hours. Puck is shaped somewhat like a potato with a huge impact crater marring roughly one-fourth of its surface.

U16 and U17 (Caliban and Sycorax)

In 1997, two new moons, the first with irregular, non-circular orbits, were discovered around Uranus. These far distant satellites were temporarily designated U16 and U17, and are tentatively named Caliban and Sycorax, respectively. Caliban has a diameter of 37 miles (60 kilometers) and orbits Uranus at an average distance of 4.5 million miles (7.2 million kilometers). Sycorax has a diameter of 74.5 miles (120 kilometers) and a much more elliptical orbit than Caliban, bringing it as close as 3.7 million miles (6 million kilometers) to the planet.

A New Uranian Moon Discovered

On May 18, 1999, the International Astronomical Union announced that Erich Karkoschka, a researcher at the Lunar and Planetary Lab of the University of Arizona in Tucson, had discovered the 18th moon orbiting Uranus. This discovery makes Uranus, along with Saturn, one of only two planets known to have 18 satellites.

It took over 13 years for the new moon to be discovered. The object first appeared as a tiny speck of light on seven images taken by *Voyager 2* when it flew by Uranus in late January 1986, but it went unnoticed. The satellite wasn't recognized until recently, when Karkoschka investigated the old *Voyager* images and compared them with those taken by the Hubble Space Telescope.

Although the moon was found in 1999, it is designated as Satellite 1986 U10 (S/1986 U10). According to its discoverer, the satellite is approximately 25 miles (40 kilometers) in diameter, about the size of Comet Hale-Bopp, and it may have a similar composition to the comet. It orbits 35,000 miles (51,000 kilometers) from Uranus, circling the planet every 15 hours and 18 minutes, similar to the planet's rotational period of about 16.8 hours.

The discovery of two additional probable satellites was announced in July 1999. The candidate moons are about 12 miles (20 kilometers) in diameter and orbit some 6.2 million miles (10 million kilometers) to 15.5 million miles (25 million kilometers) from the planet. If confirmed, the discovery will bring the total up to 20.

Uranus can—on rare occasions—become bright enough to be seen with the naked eye, if one knows exactly where to look; normally, a good set of field glasses or a small portable telescope is required.

Neptune

Little was known about Neptune until August 1989, when NASA's *Voyager 2* became the first spacecraft to observe the planet. Passing about 3,000 miles (4,950 kilometers) above Neptune's north pole, *Voyager 2* made its closest approach to any planet since leaving Earth 12 years prior. The spacecraft passed about 25,000 miles (40,000 kilometers) from Neptune's largest moon, Triton, the last solid body that *Voyager 2* will have studied.

Nearly 3 billion miles (4.5 billion kilometers) from the Sun, Neptune orbits the Sun once in 165 years, and therefore has made not quite a full circle around the Sun since it was discovered.[1]

With an equatorial diameter of 30,775 miles (49,528 kilometers), Neptune is the smallest of our solar system's four gas giants, Jupiter, Saturn, and Uranus.[2] Even so, its volume could hold nearly 60 Earths. Neptune is also denser than the other gas giants, and about 64% heavier than if it were composed entirely of water.

Neptune has a blue color as a result of methane in its atmosphere. Methane preferentially absorbs the longer wavelengths of sunlight (those near the red end of the spectrum). What are left to be reflected are colors at the blue end of the spectrum. The atmosphere of Neptune is mainly composed of hydrogen, with helium and traces of methane and ammonia.

Neptune is a dynamic planet even though it receives only 3% as much sunlight as Jupiter does. *Voyager 2* discovered several large, dark spots that were prominent features on the planet. The largest spot was about the size of Earth and was designated the "Great Dark Spot" by its discoverers. It appeared to be an anticyclone similar to Jupiter's Great Red Spot. While Neptune's Great Dark Spot is comparable in size, relative to the planet, and at the same latitude (22°S latitude) as Jupiter's Great Red Spot, it was far more variable in size and shape than its Jovian counterpart. Bright, wispy "cirrus-type" clouds overlaid the Great Dark Spot at its southern and northeastern boundaries.

At about 42°S latitude, a bright, irregularly shaped, eastward-moving cloud circles much faster

---

1. Astronomers have studied Neptune since Sept. 23, 1846, when Johann Gottfried Galle, of the Berlin Observatory, and Louis d'Arrest, an astronomy student, discovered the eighth planet on the basis of mathematical predictions by Urbain Jean Joseph Le Verrier. Similar predictions were made independently by John Couch Adams. Galileo Galilei had seen Neptune during several nights of observing Jupiter, in January 1613, but didn't realize he was seeing a new planet.
2. These four planets are about 4 to 12 times greater in diameter than Earth. They have no solid surfaces, but possess massive atmospheres that contain substantial amounts of hydrogen and helium with traces of other gases.

than did the Great Dark Spot, "scooting" around Neptune in about 16 hours. This "scooter" may have been a cloud plume rising between cloud decks.

Another spot, designated "D2," was located far to the south of the Great Dark Spot, at 55°S latitude. It is almond-shaped, with a bright central core, and moves eastward around the planet in about 16 hours.

In 1995, images taken by the Hubble Space Telescope showed that the Great Dark Spot has vanished. The great storm center has either dissipated or is obscured by other atmospheric conditions.

The atmosphere above Neptune's clouds is hotter near the equator, cooler in the mid-latitudes, and warm again at the south pole. Temperatures in the stratosphere were measured to be 750° K (900° F), while at the 100 millibar pressure level they were measured to be 55° K (−360° F).

Long, bright clouds, reminiscent of cirrus clouds on Earth, were seen high in Neptune's atmosphere. They appear to form above most of the methane, and consequently are not blue.

At northern low latitudes (27°N), *Voyager* captured images of cloud streaks casting their shadows on cloud decks estimated to be about 30 to 60 miles (50 to 100 kilometers) below. The widths of these cloud streaks range from 30 to 125 miles (50 to 200 kilometers). Cloud streaks were also seen in the southern polar regions (71°S) where the cloud heights were about 30 miles (50 kilometers).

Most of the winds on Neptune blow in a westward direction, which is retrograde, or opposite to the rotation of the planet. Near the Great Dark Spot, there are retrograde winds blowing up to 1,500 miles an hour—the strongest winds measured on any planet.

The Magnetic Field

Neptune's magnetic field is tilted 47 degrees from the planet's rotation axis, and is offset at least 0.55 radii, about 8,500 miles (13,500 kilometers) from the physical center. The dynamo electric currents produced within the planet, therefore, must be relatively closer to the surface than for Earth, Jupiter, or Saturn. Because of its unusual orientation, and the tilt of the planet's rotation axis, Neptune's magnetic field goes through dramatic changes as the planet rotates in the solar wind.

Voyager's planetary radio astronomy instrument measured the periodic radio waves generated by the magnetic field and determined that the rotation rate of the interior of Neptune is 16 hours 7 minutes.

Voyager also detected auroras, similar to the northern and southern lights on Earth, in Neptune's atmosphere. Unlike those on Earth, due to Neptune's complex magnetic field, the auroras are extremely complicated processes that occur over wide regions of the planet, not just near the planet's magnetic poles.

Neptune's Moons

Triton

The largest of Neptune's eight known satellites, Triton is different from all other icy moons that *Voyager* has studied. Triton circles Neptune in a tilted, circular, retrograde orbit, completing an orbit in 5.875 days at an average distance of 205,000 miles (330,000 kilometers) above the planet's cloud tops.

Triton shows evidence of a remarkable geologic history, and *Voyager 2* images show active geyser-like eruptions spewing invisible nitrogen gas and dark dust particles 1 to 5 miles (2 to 8 kilometers) into space.

Triton is about three-quarters the size of Earth's Moon and has a diameter of about 1,680 miles (2,705 kilometers), and a mean density of about 2.066 grams per cubic centimeter. (The density of water is 1.0 grams per cubic centimeter.) This means that Triton contains more rock in its interior than the icy satellites of Saturn and Uranus.

The relatively high density and the retrograde orbit offer strong evidence that Triton did not originate near Neptune, but is a captured object.

An extremely thin atmosphere extends as much as 500 miles (800 kilometers) above the satellite's surface. Tiny nitrogen ice particles may form thin clouds a few kilometers above the surface. Triton is very bright, reflecting 60% to 95% of the sunlight that strikes it. (By comparison, Earth's Moon reflects only 11%.)

The atmospheric pressure at Triton's surface is about 14 microbars, a mere 1/70,000th the surface pressure on Earth. Temperature at the surface is about 38° K (−391° F), making it the coldest surface of any body yet visited in the solar system.

Nereid

Nereid was discovered in 1948 through Earth-based telescopes. Little is known about Nereid, which is slightly smaller than Proteus, having a diameter of 211 miles (340 kilometers). The satellite's surface reflects about 14% of the sunlight that strikes it. Nereid's orbit is the most eccentric in the solar system, ranging from about 841,100 miles (1,353,600 kilometers) to 5,980,200 miles (9,623,700 kilometers).

The Smaller Satellites

In addition to the previously known moons, Triton and Nereid, *Voyager 2* found six more satellites, making the total eight.

Proteus

Like all six of Neptune's recently discovered small satellites, it is one of the darkest objects in the solar system—"as dark as soot" is a good description. It reflects only 6% of the sunlight that strikes it. Proteus is an ellipsoid about 258 miles (416 kilometers) in diameter, larger than Nereid. It circles Neptune at a distance of about 57,700 miles (92,800 kilometers) above the cloud tops, and completes one orbit in 26 hours 54 minutes. Scientists say that it is about as large as a satellite can be without being pulled into a spherical shape by its own gravity.

Proteus and its tiny companions are cratered and irregularly shaped—they are not round—and show no signs of any geologic modifications. All circle the planet in the same direction as Neptune rotates, and remain close to Neptune's equatorial plane.

Larissa

This object is only about 30,300 miles (48,800 kilometers) from Neptune and circles the planet in 13 hours 18 minutes. Its diameter is 120 miles (190 kilometers).

Despina

The satellite is 17,200 miles (27,700 kilometers) from Neptune's clouds and makes one orbit every 8 hours. Its diameter is about 90 miles (150 kilometers).

The First Ten Minor Planets (Asteroids)

Name	Year of discovery	Mean distance from sun (millions of miles)	Orbital period (years)	Diameter (miles)	Magnitude
1. Ceres	1801	257.0	4.60	485	7.4
2. Pallas	1802	257.4	4.61	304	8.0
3. Juno	1804	247.8	4.36	118	8.7
4. Vesta	1807	219.3	3.63	243	6.5
5. Astraea	1845	239.3	4.14	50	9.9
6. Hebe	1847	225.2	3.78	121	8.5
7. Iris	1847	221.4	3.68	121	8.4
8. Flora	1847	204.4	3.27	56	8.9
9. Metis	1848	221.7	3.69	78	8.9
10. Hygeia	1849	222.6	5.59	40(?)	9.5

Galatea

It lies 23,100 miles (37,200 kilometers) from Neptune. Its diameter is 110 miles (180 kilometers) and it completes an orbit in 10 hours 18 minutes.

Thalassa

The satellite appears to be about 50 miles (80 kilometers) in diameter. It orbits Neptune in 7 hours 30 minutes some 15,700 miles (25,200 kilometers) above the cloud tops.

Naiad

The last satellite discovered, it is about 37 miles (60 kilometers) in diameter and orbits Neptune about 14,400 miles (23,200 kilometers) above the clouds in 7 hours 6 minutes.

Neptune's Rings

Voyager found four rings and evidence of ring *arcs* or incomplete rings. The "Main Ring" orbits Neptune at about 23,812.5 miles (38,100 kilometers) above the cloud tops. The "Inner Ring" is about 17,750 miles (28,400 kilometers) from Neptune's cloud tops. An "Inside Diffuse Ring"—a complete ring—is located about 10,687.5 miles (17,100 kilometers) from the planet's cloud tops. Some scientists suspect that this ring may extend all the way down to Neptune's cloud tops. An area called "the Plateau" is a broad, diffuse sheet of fine material just outside the so-called "Inner Ring." The fine material is approximately the size of smoke particles. All other rings contain a greater proportion of larger material.

Pluto

Pluto, the outermost and smallest planet in the solar system, is the only planet not visited by an exploring spacecraft. So little is known about it, that it is difficult to classify. Its distance is so great that the Hubble Space Telescope cannot reveal its surface features. Appropriately named for the Roman god of the underworld, it must be frozen, dark, and dead. Pluto's mean distance from the Sun is 3,687.5 million miles (5,900 million kilometers).

In 1978, light-curve studies gave evidence of a moon revolving around Pluto within the same period as Pluto's rotation. Therefore, it stays over the same point on Pluto's surface. In addition, it keeps the same face toward the planet. The satellite was later named Charon and is estimated to be about 789 miles (1,262.4 kilometers) in diameter. Recent estimates indicate Pluto's diameter is about 1,441.6 miles (2,306.56 kilometers), making the pair more like a double planet than any other in the solar system. Previously, the Earth–Moon system held this distinction. The density of Pluto is slightly greater than that of water.

There is evidence that Pluto has an atmosphere containing methane and polar ice caps that increase and decrease in size with the planet's seasons. It is not known to have water. The Hubble Space Telescope's faint-object camera revealed light and dark regions on Pluto indicating an ice cap at the planet's north pole. It is not known if there is an ice cap at Pluto's south pole.

Pluto was predicted by calculation when Percival Lowell (1855–1916) noticed irregularities in the orbits of Uranus and Neptune. Clyde Tombaugh (1906–1997) discovered the planet in 1930, precisely where Lowell predicted it would be. The name Pluto was chosen because the first two letters represent the initials of Percival Lowell.

Pluto has the most eccentric orbit in the solar system, bringing it at times closer to the Sun than Neptune. Pluto approached the perihelion of its orbit on Sept. 5, 1989, and until February 1999 was closer to the Sun than Neptune. Even then, it could be seen only with a large telescope.

The Asteroids

Between the orbits of Mars and Jupiter are an estimated 30,000 pieces of rocky debris, known collectively as the asteroids, or planetoids. The first and, incidentally, the largest (Ceres), was discovered during the New Year's night of 1801 by the Italian astronomer Father Piazzi (1746–1826), and its orbit was calculated by the German mathematician Karl Friedrich Gauss (1777–1855). Gauss invented a new method of calculating orbits on that occasion. A German amateur astronomer, the physician Olbers (1748–1840), discovered the second asteroid, Pallas. The number now known, catalogued, and named is over 6,000 and could reach 10,000 by the end of the 20th century. A few asteroids do not move in orbits beyond the orbit of Mars, but in orbits that cross the orbit of Mars. The first of them was named Eros because of this peculiar orbit. It had become the rule to bestow female names on the asteroids, but when it was found that Eros crossed the orbit of a major planet, it received a male name. Since then around two dozen orbit-crossers have been discovered, and they are often referred to as the "male asteroids." A few of them—Albert, Adonis, Apollo, Amor, and Icarus—cross the orbit of Earth, and two of them may come closer than our Moon; but the crossing is

A Richter Scale for Close Encounter Asteroids

Sources: NASA and Massachusetts Institute of Technology.

A new tool to help scientists, the media, and the public assess the potential danger of asteroids and comets, collectively called *near-Earth objects (NEOs)*, was created by Dr. Richard P. Binzel, professor of Earth, Atmospheric and Planetary Sciences at the Massachusetts Institute of Technology. His risk-assessment system is similar to the Richter scale used for earthquakes. It is named the Torino Impact Hazard Scale, after the Italian city (Turin), in which the scale was initially adopted by the International Astronomical Union (IAU) in June 1999 and officially endorsed by the IAU on July 22, 1999. Based on the orbit trajectory for a given NEO, the scale takes into account the object's size, speed, and the probability of it striking the Earth.

The Torino Scale uses numbers and color zones that range from 0 to 10, where 0 on the white zone indicates an object has virtually no chance of impact with the Earth. (Zero is also used to categorize any object that is too small to penetrate the Earth's atmosphere, in the event that a collision does occur.) A red 10 indicates that a collision is certain, and the impacting object is so large that it is capable of precipitating a global climatic disaster.

The Torino Scale is color coded as follows:

• White (corresponds to category 0). "Events having no practical consequences," meaning that they are virtually certain to pass the Earth or are so small that any impact would almost certainly dissipate in the atmosphere.

• Green (corresponds to category 1). "Events meriting careful monitoring," refers to objects that have predictable close approaches with some very small, but not seriously concerning, chance of a collision. Nonetheless, prudence dictates their orbits should be tracked closely so that the collision chance will become refined. These objects will almost certainly be reclassified within Torino Scale category zero.

• Yellow (corresponds to categories 2, 3, 4). "Events meriting concern" or close approaches by objects that have higher chances of collision than the Earth typically experiences over a few decades. These are objects for which refinement of the orbits is of high priority.

• Orange (corresponds to categories 5, 6, 7). "Threatening events," refers to close encounters with objects that are large enough to cause regional or global devastation, where the chance of collision greatly exceeds the level that typically occurs within a given century. These are objects for which refinement of the orbits is an extreme priority.

• Red (corresponds to categories 8, 9, 10). "Certain collisions," refers to objects that will definitely hit the Earth. The values of 8, 9, and 10 depend on whether the impact energy is large enough to cause either local damage, regional devastation, or a global climatic catastrophe.

Once an asteroid is detected, scientists use tracking data from a tiny section of its orbit to calculate where it will be in 10, 15, or 100 years. There is some uncertainty in this prediction because the orbit measurements are not perfect and the NEO may be altered by gravity if it passes close to Earth or another planet, but "orbits generally behave like clockwork," Binzel said. As more information is gathered about a particular asteroid, its placement on the scale can be adjusted accordingly.

He pointed out that no asteroid to date has ever had a value greater than one. Large asteroids are rarely a threat to the Earth. An asteroid bigger than a mile across might hit once every 100,000 to one million years on average.

The risk from NEO impacts increases with the size of the projectile. The greatest risk is associated with objects larger than a half-mile to a mile (1 to 2 kilometers), which are large enough to perturb Earth's climate on a global scale by injecting large quantities of dust into the stratosphere. An ocean impact could trigger large ocean waves or tsunamis.

As of July 19, 1999, 304 of the 803 known near-Earth asteroids have a diameter of about 0.6 mile (1 kilometer) or larger. Of these NEOs, 183 have been classified as Potentially-Hazardous Asteroids (PHAs). The potential to make close approaches to Earth does not mean that the PHA will crash into the Earth. It only means that there is a possibility for such a threat. □

---

like a bridge crossing a highway, not like two highways intersecting. Hence there is very little danger of collision from these bodies. They are all small, 3 to 5 miles (4.8 to 8.0 kilometers) in diameter, and therefore very difficult objects to identify, even when quite close. Some scientists believe the asteroids represent the remains of an exploded planet.

On Oct. 29, 1991, the *Galileo* spacecraft took a historic photograph of asteroid 951 Gaspra from a distance of 10,000 miles (16,000 kilometers) away. It was the first close-up photo ever taken of an asteroid in space.

Gaspra is an irregular, potato-shaped object about 12.5 miles (20 kilometers) by 7.5 miles (12 kilometers) by 7 miles (11.2 kilometers) in size. Its surface is covered with a layer of loose rubble and its terrain is covered with several dozen small craters.

Close-up photos of Asteroid 243 Ida taken by the *Galileo* spacecraft on Aug. 28, 1993, revealed that Ida had a tiny egg-shaped moon measuring 0.9 miles by 0.7 miles (1.44 by 1.12 kilometers). The moon has been named Dactyl.

NASA's *Near-Earth Asteroid Rendezvous* spacecraft was launched on Feb. 17, 1996. It flew within 750 miles (1,200 kilometers) of minor planet 253 Mathilde on June 27, 1997, and took spectacular images of the dark, crater-battered world. The asteroid's mean diameter was found to be 33 miles (52.8 kilometers). The *NEAR* spacecraft discovered that the carbon-rich Mathilde is one of the darkest objects in the solar system, only reflecting about 3% of the Sun's light, making it twice as dark as a chunk of charcoal. The asteroid is almost completely cratered, and at least five of its craters just on the lighted side are larger than 12 miles (19.2 kilometers).

The spacecraft reached asteroid 433 Eros in December 1998, but aborted its mission due to engine problems. *NEAR* measured Eros to be 21 miles (33.6 kilometers) long by 8 miles (12.8 kilometers) wide and 8 miles (12.8 kilometers) deep. It rotates once every 5.27 hours and has no visible moons. The spacecraft is scheduled to return to Eros in February 2000 and orbit it for almost one year.

Comets

Comets, according to the noted astronomer Fred L. Whipple (1906–) are enormous "snowballs" of frozen gases (mostly carbon dioxide, methane, and water vapor) and contain very little solid material. The whole behavior of comets can then be explained as the behavior of frozen gas being heated by the Sun. When the comet Kohoutek made its first appearance to man in 1973, its behavior seemed to confirm this theory and later, the international study by five spacecraft that encountered Halley's comet in March 1986 confirmed Whipple's idea of the make-up of comets.

Since comets appear in the sky without any warning, people in classical times and especially during the Middle Ages believed that they had a special meaning, which, of course, was bad. Since a natural catastrophe of some sort of a military conflict occurs every year, it was quite simple to blame the comet that happened to be visible. But even in the past, there were some people who used logical reasoning. When, in Roman times, a comet was blamed for the loss of a battle and hence was called a "bad omen," a Roman writer observed that the victors in the battle probably did not think so.

Up until the middle of the 16th century, comets were believed to be phenomena of the upper atmosphere; they were usually "explained" as "burning vapors" which had risen from "distant swamps." That nobody had ever actually seen burning vapors rise from a swamp did not matter.

But a large comet which appeared in 1577 was carefully observed by Tycho Brahe (1546–1601), a Danish astronomer who is often, and with the best of reasons, called "eccentric," but who insisted on precise measurements for everything. It was Tycho Brahe's accumulation of literally thousands of precise measurements that later enabled his younger collaborator, Johannes Kepler (1571–1630), to discover the laws of planetary motion. Measuring the motion of the comet of 1577, Tycho Brahe could show that it had been far beyond the atmosphere, even though he could not give figures for the distance. Tycho Brahe's work proved that comets were astronomical and not meteorological phenomena.

In 1682, the second Astronomer Royal of Great Britain, Dr. Edmond Halley (1656–1742), checked the orbit of a bright comet that was in the sky then and compared it with earlier comet orbits that were known in part. Halley found that the comet of 1682 was the third to move through what appeared to be the same orbit, and that the three appearances were roughly 76 years apart. Halley concluded that this was the same comet, moving around the Sun in a closed orbit, like the planets. He predicted that it would reappear in 1758 or 1759. Halley himself died in 1742, but a large comet appeared 16 years after his death as predicted and was immediately referred to as "Halley's comet."

Halley's comet appeared again in 1986, sparking a worldwide effort to study it up close. Five satellites in all took readings from the comet at various distances. Two Soviet craft, *Vega 1* and *Vega 2*, went in close to provide detailed pictures of the comet, including the first of the comet's core. The European Space Agency's craft, *Giotto*, entered the comet itself, coming to within 450 miles of the comet's center and successfully passing through its tail. In addition, two Japanese craft, the *Suisei* and the *Sakigake*, passed at a longer distance and analyzed the cloud and tail of the comet and the effect of solar radiation upon it.

Astronomers refer to comets as "periodic" or as "non-periodic" comets, but the latter term does not mean that these comets have no period; it merely means that their period is not known. The actual periods of comets run from 3.3 years (the shortest known) to many thousands of years. Their orbits are elliptical, like those of the planets, but they are very eccentric, long, and narrow ellipses. Only comet Schwassmann-Wachmann has an orbit that has such a low eccentricity (for a cometary orbit) that it could be the orbit of a minor planet.

When a comet, coming from deep space, approaches the Sun, it is at first indistinguishable from a minor planet. Somewhere between the orbits of Mars and Jupiter, its outline becomes fuzzy; it is said to develop a "coma" (the word used here is the Latin word *coma*, which means "hair," not the phonetically identical Greek word that means "deep sleep"). Then, near the orbit of Mars, the comet develops its tail, which at first trails behind. This grows steadily as the comet comes closer and closer to the Sun. As it rounds the Sun (as first noticed by Girolamo Fracastoro, 1483–1553) the tail always points away from the Sun so that the comet, when moving away from the Sun, points its tail ahead like the landing lights of an airplane.

The reason for this behavior is that the tail is pushed in these directions by the radiation pressure of the Sun. It sometimes happens that a comet loses its tail at perihelion; it then grows another one. Although the tail is clearly visible against the black of the sky, it is very tenuous. It has been said that if the tail of Halley's comet could be compressed to the density of iron, it would fit into a small suitcase.

Although very low in mass, comets are among the largest members of the solar system. The nucleus of a comet may be up to 10,000 miles in diameter; its coma between 10,000 and 50,000 miles in diameter; and its tail as long as 28 million miles.

Comet Shoemaker-Levy 9 broke up into 21 fragments in July 1992 and crashed into the surface of Jupiter, July 16–22, 1994, in the most violent event in the recorded history of the solar system.

In 1951, Dutch astronomer Gerard Kuiper first suggested the existence of a disk-shaped swarm of short-period comets that begin beyond the orbit of Neptune and extend past Pluto. In 1995, the Hubble Space Telescope detected the long-sought Kuiper Belt and an estimated 200 million comets were discovered orbiting it.

Meteors and Meteorites

The term *meteor* for what is usually called a *shooting star* bears an unfortunate resemblance to the term *meteorology,* the science of weather and weather forecasting. This resemblance is due to an ancient misunderstanding that wrongly considered meteors an atmospheric phenomenon. Actually, the streak of light in the sky that scientists call a meteor

The 88 Recognized Constellations

In astronomical works, the Latin names of the constellations are used. The letter N or S following the Latin name indicates whether the constellation is located to the north or south of the Zodiac. The letter Z indicates that the constellation is within the Zodiac.

Latin name	Letter	English version	Latin name	Letter	English version	Latin name	Letter	English version
Andromeda	N	Andromeda	Delphinus	N	Dolphin	Pegasus	N	Pegasus
Antlia	S	Airpump	Dorado	S	Swordfish (Gold-fish)	Perseus	N	Perseus
Apus	S	Bird of Paradise				Phoenix	S	Phoenix
Aquarius	Z	Water Bearer	Draco	N	Dragon	Pictor	S	Painter (or his Easel)
Aquila	N	Eagle	Equuleus	N	Filly			
Ara	S	Altar	Eridanus	S	Eridanus (river)	Pisces	Z	Fishes
Aries	Z	Ram	Fornax	S	Furnace	Piscis Austrinus	S	Southern Fish
Auriga	N	Charioteer	Gemini	Z	Twins	Puppis	S	Poop (of Argo)[1]
Boötes	N	Herdsmen	Grus	S	Crane	Pyxis	S	Mariner's Compass
Caelum	S	Sculptor's Tool	Hercules	N	Hercules			
Camelopardalis	N	Giraffe	Horologium	S	Clock	Reticulum	S	Net
Cancer	Z	Crab	Hydra	N	Sea Serpent	Sagitta	N	Arrow
Canes Venatici	N	Hunting Dogs	Hydrus	S	Water Snake	Sagittarius	Z	Archer
Canis Major	S	Great Dog	Indus	S	Indian	Scorpius	Z	Scorpion
Canis Minor	S	Little Dog	Lacerta	N	Lizard	Sculptor	S	Sculptor
Capricornus	Z	Goat (or Sea-Goat)	Leo	Z	Lion	Scutum	N	Shield
			Leo Minor	N	Little Lion	Serpens	N	Serpent
Carina	S	Keel (of Argo)[1]	Lepus	S	Hare	Sextans	S	Sextant
Cassiopeia	N	Cassiopeia	Libra	Z	Scales	Taurus	Z	Bull
Centaurus	S	Centaur	Lupus	S	Wolf	Telescopium	S	Telescope
Cepheus	N	Cepheus	Lynx	N	Lynx	Triangulum	N	Triangle
Cetus	S	Whale	Lyra	N	Lyre (Harp)	Triangulum Australe	S	Southern Triangle
Chameleon	S	Chameleon	Mensa	S	Table (mountain)			
Circinus	S	Compasses	Microscopium	S	Microscope	Tucana	S	Toucan
Columba	S	Dove	Monoceros	S	Unicorn	Ursa Major	N	Big Dipper[2]
Coma Berenices	N	Berenice's Hair	Musca	S	Southern Fly	Ursa Minor	N	Little Dipper[3]
Corona Australis	S	Southern Crown	Norma	S	Rule (straight-edge)	Vela	S	Sail (of Argo)[1]
Corona Borealis	N	Northern Crown				Virgo	Z	Virgin
Corvus	S	Crow (Raven)	Octans	S	Octant	Volans	S	Flying Fish
Crater	S	Cup	Ophiuchus	N	Serpent-Bearer	Vulpecula	N	Fox
Crux	S	Southern Cross	Orion	S	Orion			
Cygnus	N	Swan	Pavo	S	Peacock			

1. The original constellation Argo Navis (the Ship Argo) has been divided into Carina, Puppis, and Vela. Normally the brightest star in each constellation is designated by alpha, the first letter of the Greek alphabet, the second brightest by beta, the second letter of the Greek alphabet, and so forth. But the Greek letters run through Carina, Puppis, and Vela as if it were still one constellation. 2. The Big Dipper is only a part of the constellation Ursa Major (Great Bear) and is not a constellation by itself. 3. The Little Dipper is called Ursa Minor (Little Bear).

is essentially an astronomical phenomenon: the entry of a small piece of cosmic matter into our atmosphere.

The distinction between *meteors* and *fireballs* (formerly also called *bolides*) is merely one of convenience; a fireball is an unusually bright meteor. Incidentally, it also means that a fireball is larger than a faint meteor.

Bodies that enter our atmosphere become visible when they are about 60 miles above the ground. The fact that they grow hot enough to emit light is not due to the "friction" of the atmosphere, as one can often read. The phenomenon responsible for the heating is one of compression. Unconfined air cannot move faster than the speed of sound. Since the entering meteorite moves with 30 to 60 times the speed of sound, the air simply cannot get out of the way. Therefore, it is compressed like the air in the cylinder of a diesel engine and is heated by compression. This heat—or part of it—is transferred to the moving body. The details of this process are now fairly well understood as a result of re-entry tests with ballistic-missile nose cones.

The average weight of a body producing a faint *shooting star* is only a small fraction of an ounce. Even a bright fireball may not weigh more than 2 or 3 pounds. Naturally, the smaller bodies are worn to dust by the passage through the atmosphere; only rather large ones reach the ground. Those that are found are called meteorites. (The *meteor,* to repeat, is the term for the light streak in the sky.) About 1,000 meteorites fall to the Earth each year.

The largest meteorite known is still imbedded in the ground near Grootfontein in southwest Africa and is estimated to weigh 70 tons. The second-largest known is the 34-ton Anighito (on exhibit in the Hayden Planetarium, New York), which was found by Admiral Peary in 1892 at Cape York in Greenland. The largest meteorite found in the United States is the Willamette meteorite (found in Oregon, weight ca. 15 tons), but large portions of this meteorite weathered away before it was found. Its weight as it struck the ground may have been 20 tons.

All these are iron meteorites (an iron meteorite normally contains about 7% nickel), which form one class of meteorites. The other class consists of the stony meteorites, and between them there are the so-called "stony irons." The so-called "tektites" consist of glass similar to our volcanic glass obsidian, and because of the similarity, there is doubt in a number of cases whether the glass is of terrestrial or of extraterrestrial origin.

Though no meteorite larger than the Grootfontein is actually known, we do know that Earth has, on occasion, been struck by much larger bodies. Evidence for such hits are the meteorite craters, of which an especially good example is located near the Cañon Diablo in Arizona. Another meteor crater in the United States is a rather old crater near Odessa, Texas. A large number of others are known, especially in eastern Canada; and for many "probables," meteoric origin has now been proved.

The 13th known lunar meteorite was found in December 1993 by a team from the Antarctic Search for Meteorites project. It is approximately 2 inches long and weighs 0.75 of an ounce.

Some scientists theorize that the mass extermination of dinosaurs from the face of Earth 65 million years ago was due to a large meteor that struck our planet at that time.

Meteor showers are caused by multitudes of very small bodies travelling in swarms. Earth travels in its orbit through these swarms like a car driving through falling snow. The point from which the meteors seem to emanate is called the *radiant* and is named for the constellation in that area. The Perseid meteor shower in August is the most spectacular of the year, boasting, at peak, roughly 60 meteors per hour under good atmospheric conditions. The presence of a bright moon diminishes the number of visible meteors.

The Constellations

Constellations are groupings of stars that form easily recognized and remembered patterns, such as Orion and the Big Dipper. The Big Dipper is actually an asterism, not a constellation, because it is only part of the constellation Ursa Major (the Big Bear). Actually, the stars in the majority of all constellations do not "belong together." Usually they are at greatly varying distances from Earth and just happen to lie more or less in the same line of sight as seen from our solar system. But in a few cases, the stars of a constellation are actually associated; most of the bright stars of the Big Dipper travel together and form what astronomers call an *open cluster.*

If you observe a planet, say Mars, for one complete revolution, you will see that it passes successively through 12 constellations. All planets (except Pluto at certain times) can be observed only in these 12 constellations, which form the so-called zodiac, and the Sun also moves through the zodiacal signs, though the Sun's apparent movement is actually caused by the movement of Earth.

Although the constellations are due mainly to the optical accident of line of sight and have no real significance, astronomers have retained them as reference areas. It is much easier to speak of a star in Orion than to give its geometrical position in the sky. During the Astronomical Congress of 1928, it was decided to recognize 88 constellations. A description of their agreed-upon boundaries was published at Cambridge, England, in 1930, under the title *Atlas Céleste.*

The Auroras

The "northern lights" *(Aurora borealis)* as well as the "southern lights" *(Aurora australis)* are upper-atmosphere phenomena of astronomical origin. The auroras center around the magnetic (not the geographical) poles of Earth, which explains why, in the Western Hemisphere, they have been seen as far to the south as New Orleans and Florida, while the equivalent latitude in the Eastern Hemisphere never

sees an aurora. The northern magnetic pole happens to be in the Western Hemisphere.

The lower limit of an aurora is at about 50 miles (80 kilometers). Upper limits have been estimated to be as high as 400 miles (640 kilometers). Since about 1880, a connection between the auroras on Earth and sunspots has been suspected and has gradually come to be accepted. It was said that the sunspots probably eject "particles" (later the word *electrons* was substituted), which on striking Earth's atmosphere cause the auroras. But this explanation suffered from certain difficulties. Sometimes a very large sunspot group on the Sun, with individual spots bigger than Earth itself, would not cause an aurora. Moreover, even if a sunspot caused an aurora, the time that passed between the appearance of the one and the occurrence of the other was highly unpredictable.

This problem of the time lag is, in all probability, solved by the discovery of the Van Allen layer by artificial satellite *Explorer I.* The Van Allen layer[1] is a double layer of charged subatomic particles around Earth. The inner layer, with its center some 1,500 miles (2,400 kilometers) from the ground, reaches from about 40°N to about 40°S and does not touch the atmosphere. The outer layer, much larger and with its center several thousand miles from the ground, does touch the atmosphere in the vicinity of the magnetic poles.

It seems probable that the "leakage" of electrons from the outer Van Allen layer causes the auroras. A new burst of electrons from the Sun seems to be caught in the outer layer first. Under the assumption that all electrons are first caught in the outer layer, the time lag can be understood. There has to be an "overflow" from the outer layer to produce an aurora.

The Atmosphere

Though reasonably transparent to visible light, the atmosphere may absorb as much as 60% of the visible and near-visible light. It is opaque to most other wavelengths, except certain fairly short radio waves. In addition to absorbing much light, our atmosphere bends light rays entering at a slant (for a given observer) so that the true position of a star close to the horizon is not what it seems to be. One effect is that we see the Sun above the horizon before it actually is. And the unsteady movement of the atmosphere causes the "twinkling" of the stars, which may be romantic, but is a nuisance when it comes to observing.

The composition of our atmosphere near the ground is 78% nitrogen and 21% oxygen, the remaining 1% consisting of other gases, most of it argon. The composition stays the same to an altitude of at least 70 miles (112 kilometers) (except that higher up two impurities, carbon dioxide and water vapor, are missing), but the pressure drops very fast. At 18,000 feet, half of the total mass of the atmosphere is below, and at 100,000 feet, 99% of the mass of the atmosphere is below. The upper limit of the atmosphere is usually given as 120 miles (192 kilometers); no definitive figure is possible, since there is no boundary line between the incredibly attenuated gases 120 miles (192 kilometers) up and space.

1. Named after the American physicist, James Alfred Van Allen (1914–) who discovered the broad bands of intense radiation surrounding Earth in 1958.

Astronomy Web Sites

American Astronomical Society:
www.aas.org/AAS-homepage.html
Asteroid and Comet Impact Hazards:
impact.arc.nasa.gov/index.html
Astronomical Society of the Pacific:
www.aspsky.org
AstroWeb (internet resources):
www.stsci.edu/science/net-resources.html
Center for Earth and Planetary Studies:
www.nasm.edu/ceps
The International Astronomical Union: www.iau.org
NASA Home Page: www.nasa.gov
Space Telescope Science Institute (home of Hubble): www.stsci.edu
U.S. Naval Observatory: www.usno.navy.mil

Some Giant Telescopes

• The world's largest fixed-dish radio telescope (1963) is located near Arecibo, Puerto Rico. It is 1,000 feet (35 meters) in diameter and spans some 25 acres.
• The Very Large Array (VLA) telescope (1980) near Socorro, N.M., is the world's most powerful radio telescope. It is Y-shaped and has 27 separate mobile antennas (each 82 feet in diameter) and is spread out over about a 25-mile (40-kilometer) area.
• The world's largest fully steerable radio telescope (1972), located at Effelsberg, Germany, has a 328-feet (100-meter) antenna.
• The 200-inch (5-meter) Hale telescope at Mount Palomar, Calif. (1948), is the second largest reflector in use.
• The 236-inch (6-meter) Special Astrophysical Observatory (1976) at Zelenchukskaya, on the northern slopes of the Caucasus Mountains in the Russian Federation, is the world's largest reflector telescope in use. However, problems with it make it less useful than the 200-inch Hale.
• The Green Bank Telescope (scheduled for operation in late 1999) at the National Radio Astronomy Observatories site at Green Bank, W.Va., will be the world's largest fully-steerable radio telescope when completed. Described as a 328 feet (100-meter) telescope, its actual surface dimensions are 328 by 360.89 feet (100 by 110 meters).
• The W. M. Keck Telescope (1991) at Mauna Kea, Hawaii, is the world's most powerful reflector telescope. It has a primary mirror composed of 36 hexagonal segments, each 5.9 feet (1.8 meters) in size. The Keck Telescope has a light gathering power four times greater than the 200-inch Hale.
• The Very Large European Space Observatory (ESO) Telescope (VLT) (under construction), located at Cerro Paranal, Chile, will consist of four telescopes that can work independently or in a combined mode. In the combined mode, the VLT provides the total light-collecting power of a 52.5-feet (16-meter) single telescope, making it the largest optical telescope in the world.

• The 40-inch (1.01 meter) telescope at Yerkes Observatory (1897) at Williams Bay, Wis., is the world's largest refracting telescope.
• The Sabaru 27.23-feet (8.3-meter) optical-infrared monolithic-mirror telescope (scheduled for operation in 2000) of the National Observatory of Japan (NADJ), located at Mauna Kea, Hawaii, will be the world's largest single mirror telescope.

Hubble Space Telescope

The $2 billion Edwin P. Hubble Space Telescope (HST) is the most complex and sensitive space observatory ever constructed. It was placed into orbit by the space shuttle *Discovery* on April 25, 1990. HST is 43.3 feet (13 meters) long and 14 feet (4 meters) wide, about the size of a bus or truck. Hubble weighs 25,500 pounds (11,000 kg) and orbits 335 nautical miles (536 kilometers) above Earth.

Since being lifted into orbit, HST has become the principal tool for exploring the universe through this decade and the next.

Astronomers discovered in June 1990 that there was a spherical aberration in one of the telescope's mirrors. In 1991, two of the craft's six gyroscopes failed, and a third failed on Nov. 18, 1993, causing additional problems. NASA successfully repaired the space telescope during the Dec. 2–13, 1993, mission of the *Endeavour*.

Crew members of the space shuttle *Discovery* made fresh repairs to the telescope during an upgrade mission in February 1997, and installed two powerful new scientific instruments—the Near Infrared Camera and Multi-Object Spectrometer (NICMOS)—giving HST still sharper and more distant views of the universe.

The Near Infrared Camera can see the universe at near infrared wavelengths more sensitively that any other existing or planned telescope.

Hubble's Space Telescope Imagery Spectrograph (STIS) is sensitive to light in ultraviolet wavelengths and employs two-dimensional detectors that allow the instrument to gather 30 times more spectral data than the first-generation Hubble spectrographs. STIS is considered to be the most complex scientific instrument built for space science.

A third Space Telescope servicing mission by the crew of *Discovery* is scheduled for October 1999. Although Hubble is operating normally, only three of the spacecraft's six gyroscopes, which allow the telescope to point at the stars and other celestial objects, are working properly. Two have failed and another is acting abnormally. If fewer than three gyroscopes are operating, Hubble cannot control its science mission and automatically places itself in a protective "safe mode." In addition to replacing all six gyroscopes, the crew will replace a guidance sensor and the spacecraft's computer.

The Next Generation Space Telescope (NGST), now in the design stage, will be the successor to the Hubble Space Telescope. It is scheduled for launch in 2007. □

Chandra: Exploring the Invisible Universe

Sources: NASA and Harvard-Smithsonian Center for Astrophysics.

NASA's newest and most powerful X-ray telescope, called the Chandra X-ray Observatory (CXO), was launched on a five-year mission from the space shuttle *Columbia* on July 23, 1999.

Named in honor of the late Indian-American Nobel laureate Subrahmanyan Chandrasekhar, it was formerly known as the Advance X-ray Astrophysics Facility (AXAF).

X-rays are a high energy, invisible form of light. They are produced in the cosmos when gas is heated to millions of degrees by violent and extreme conditions. Much of the matter in the universe is so hot that it can be observed only with X-ray telescopes. The CXO is designed to study some of the great mysteries of the universe such as flaring stars, exploding stars, black holes, and vast clouds of hot gas in galaxy clusters. The telescope has eight times greater resolution and is 20 to 50 times more sensitive than any previous X-ray telescope.

Unlike the Hubble Space Telescope's circular orbit that is relatively close to the Earth, the Chandra X-ray Observatory has been placed in a highly ellip-

tical (oval-shaped) orbit. At its closest approach to Earth, the observatory travels at an altitude of about 6,200 miles (9,978 kilometers). At its farthest, 87,000 miles (140,013 kilometers), it travels almost one-third of the way to the Moon. Due to this elliptical orbit, the telescope circles the Earth every 64 hours, carrying it far outside the belts of radiation that surround our planet. This radiation, while harmless to life on Earth, can overwhelm the observatory's sensitive instruments. The X-ray observatory is outside this radiation long enough to take 55 hours of uninterrupted observations during each orbit. During periods of interference from Earth's radiation belts, scientific observations are not taken. □

A Plethora of Extrasolar Planets

Since Swiss astronomers discovered the first extrasolar planet around a star similar to our Sun—51 Pegasi in the constellation Pegasus—at least 20 others have been identified outside our solar system. Most of these planetary companions are huge gas giants like Jupiter, the largest planet in our solar system. The smallest (lightest) extrasolar planet discovered to date was found in 1999. It circles the star HD 75289 in the southern sky located in the constellation Vela (the Sails) and has a mass less than half (0.42) the mass of Jupiter. By comparison, our Earth has a Jupiter mass of only 0.003.

Many extrasolar planets have masses far greater than Jupiter. For example, the planet around the star 70 Virginis in the constellation Virgo, some 60 light-years from Earth, has a mass almost seven times as great as Jupiter.

In April 1999, astronomers announced having discovered the first multiple-planet solar system that mimics our own. They disclosed that three Jupiter-sized planets orbit the star Upsilon Andromedae, 44 light years from Earth. Upsilon Andromedae is a bright star in the constellation Andromeda visible to the naked eye from the Northern Hemisphere, starting roughly in June.

The innermost, planet "B" (there is no "A"), was discovered in 1996 by astronomers at San Francisco State University. It traverses a circular orbit every 4.6 days and is at least three-quarters of Jupiter's

mass. The other two of the trio were independently found by astronomers from the Harvard-Smithsonian Center for Astrophysics in Cambridge, Mass., and the High Altitude Observatory in Boulder, Colo. The middle planet, "C," is at least twice the mass of Jupiter and takes 242 days to orbit the star. The outermost planet, "D," has a mass of at least four Jupiters and completes one orbit every 3.5 to 4 years. The two latter planets orbit the star in elliptical (oval) patterns, as in previously discovered extrasolar planets.

In July 1999, astronomers at the European Southern Observatory in La Silla, Chile, announced finding a planet circling the star iota Horologii (iota Hor) in the southern constellation Horologium, some 56 light-years away. The planet, designated iota Hor b, has an orbital period of 320 days and a mass of at least 2.26 times that of Jupiter.

Extrasolar planets can't be seen even with the most sophisticated telescopes, and are detected by indirect means. Astronomers use a technique that tracks the wobble in the motion of the stars caused by the gravitational pull of the planets orbiting them. This enables them to infer its mass and orbit, but not the size of the planet being observed.

This first planetary system was found during a survey of 107 stars and suggests that planetary systems like our own are abundant in our Milky Way Galaxy, which contains approximately 200 billion stars. □

The Unusual Planetary Alignment of May 2000

On May 5, 2000, the planets Mercury, Venus, Earth, Mars, Jupiter, and Saturn will be more or less positioned in a line with the Sun. Additionally, the Moon will be almost lined up between the Earth and Sun. Although this has led to many dire predictions of global catastrophes such as melting ice caps, floods, hurricanes, and earthquakes, there is absolutely no scientific basis for these claims. In fact, we won't be able to see this alignment because all the planets will be on the opposite side of the Sun from Earth.

According to NASA, while each planet has a minute and virtually undetectable gravitational pull

on the Earth, and with the planets on the opposite side of the Sun, the force from each body will actually be at its absolute minimum during the alignment. Also, gravitational effects do not somehow multiply simply due to a geometric arrangement. For example, the combined gravitational effect of all the planets together is much less than the effect of the Sun or Moon on the Earth.

Depending on how strictly you define "alignment," the inner six planets are aligned every few hundred years. While unusual, such alignments have happened in the past without any consequences. □

When Is a Blue Moon?

Source: NASA and Sky & Telescope, May 1999.

According to research by folklorist Philip Hiscock, the term "blue moon" is at least 400 years old, but its popular meaning has shifted many times. The earliest known references to a blue moon were intended as examples of obvious

absurdities. As time passed the expression evolved to mean something that rarely or never happens. Hence, the expression "once in a blue moon," which is still popular today.

Another definition of a blue moon that is in common use today—the second full moon in a calendar month—was introduced into popular culture by a mistake in a 1946 *Sky & Telescope* article. The author of the article misinterpreted some information he had read in a 1943 *Sky & Telescope* article that was based on the 1937 *Maine Farmers' Almanac*. It wasn't realized until recently that the editors of the almanac understood a blue moon to be the third full moon when there are four full moons in a season (calculated by a formula related to the solstices and equinoxes) and not the current twice-in-one-month definition.

The 53-year-old error was discovered by astronomers Donald W. Olson and Roger Sinnott, who questioned the modern interpretation of the 1937 almanac's calendar data. Olson deduced the original formula and revealed the mistake in a 1999 article he wrote for *Sky & Telescope* magazine.

Both of the calendar definitions are events that occur approximately every two to three years. The next time we will see two full moons within one month is November 2001, while the next "real" blue moon (in the *Maine Farmers' Almanac* sense) will happen in February 2000.   □

Phenomena, 2000

Configurations of Sun, Moon, and Planets

NOTE: The hour listings are in Universal Time. For conversion to United States time zones, *see* Conversion of Universal Time to Civil Time, p. 453.

JANUARY

d	hr.	
3	04	Venus 3° S of Moon
3	05	Earth at perihelion
3	12	Vesta 0°2 S of Moon (Occn.)
4	12	Moon at apogee
6	18	NEW MOON
7	10	Venus 7° N of Antares
8	06	Neptune 0°2 N of Moon (Occn.)
9	05	Uranus 0°4 N of Moon (Occn.)
10	19	Mars 1°9 N of Moon (Occn.)
13	02	Saturn stationary
14	14	FIRST QUARTER
14	15	Jupiter 4° N of Moon
15	17	Saturn 3° N of Moon
16	01	Mercury in superior conjunction
17	20	Aldebaran 1°2 S of Moon (Occn.)
19	23	Moon at perigee
21	05	FULL MOON (Eclipse)
24	18	Neptune in conjunction with Sun
27	03	Pallas at opposition
28	08	LAST QUARTER

FEBRUARY

d	hr.	
1	00	Vesta 0°4 N of Moon (Occn.)
1	01	Moon at apogee
2	15	Venus 1°4 S of Moon
5	13	NEW MOON (Eclipse)
6	07	Uranus in conjunction with Sun
6	19	Mercury 1°8 N of Moon
8	17	Mars 4° N of Moon
10	15	Ceres stationary
11	02	Jupiter 4° N of Moon
12	00	Saturn 3° N of Moon
12	23	FIRST QUARTER
14	03	Aldebaran 1°2 S of Moon (Occn.)

d	hr.	
15	01	Mercury greatest elong. E (18°)
17	03	Moon at perigee
19	16	FULL MOON
20	22	Mercury stationary
22	06	Venus 0°5 S of Neptune
26	09	Pallas stationary
27	04	LAST QUARTER
28	21	Moon at apogee

MARCH

d	hr.	
1	15	Mercury in inferior conjunction
3	00	Neptune 0°4 N of Moon (Occn.)
4	00	Venus 0°07 S of Uranus
4	01	Uranus 0°7 N of Moon (Occn.)
4	01	Venus 0°6 N of Moon (Occn.)
6	05	NEW MOON
8	14	Mars 5° N of Moon
9	17	Jupiter 4° N of Moon
10	09	Saturn 3° N of Moon
13	07	FIRST QUARTER
13	23	Mercury stationary
15	00	Mercury 2° N of Venus
15	00	Moon at perigee
16	12	Pluto stationary
20	05	FULL MOON
20	08	Equinox
22	09	Ceres at opposition
27	17	Moon at apogee
28	00	LAST QUARTER
28	21	Mercury greatest elong. W (28°)
30	10	Neptune 0°7 N of Moon (Occn.)
31	12	Uranus 1°0 N of Moon (Occn.)

APRIL

d	hr.	
2	12	Mercury 1°6 N of Moon
3	06	Venus 3° N of Moon
4	18	NEW MOON
6	10	Mars 5° N of Moon
6	11	Jupiter 4° N of Moon
6	21	Saturn 3° N of Moon
6	23	Mars 1°1 N of Jupiter
8	22	Moon at perigee
11	14	FIRST QUARTER
16	23	Mars 2° N of Saturn
18	18	FULL MOON
24	12	Moon at apogee
26	18	Neptune 1°0 N of Moon (Occn.)
26	19	LAST QUARTER
27	22	Uranus 1°3 N of Moon
28	09	Mercury 0°3 S of Venus

MAY

d	hr.	
4	04	NEW MOON
5	06	Mars 5° N of Moon
6	09	Moon at perigee
8	04	Jupiter in conjunction with Sun
8	13	Neptune stationary
9	04	Mercury in superior conjunction
10	20	FIRST QUARTER
10	20	Saturn in conjunction with Sun
14	13	Ceres stationary
18	08	FULL MOON
19	03	Mars 6° N of Aldebaran
19	11	Mercury 7° N of Aldebaran
19	15	Mercury 1°1 N of Mars
22	04	Moon at apogee
24	02	Neptune 1°2 N of Moon
25	06	Uranus 1°5 N of Moon
25	15	Uranus stationary
26	12	LAST QUARTER
31	10	Jupiter 1°2 N of Saturn

JUNE

d	hr.	
1	04	Saturn 3° N of Moon
1	05	Jupiter 4° N of Moon
1	18	Pluto at opposition
2	12	NEW MOON
3	13	Moon at perigee
4	04	Mercury 4° N of Moon
4	14	Vesta stationary
9	03	FIRST QUARTER
9	13	Mercury greatest elong. E (24°)
11	11	Venus in superior conjunction
16	22	FULL MOON
18	13	Moon at apogee
19	20	Vesta 0°04 N of Moon (Occn.)
20	07	Neptune 1°3 N of Moon
21	02	Solstice
21	12	Uranus 1°6 N of Moon
22	20	Mercury stationary
23	22	Juno stationary
25	01	LAST QUARTER
28	20	Saturn 3° N of Moon
29	01	Jupiter 4° N of Moon

JULY

d	hr.	
1	16	Mars in conjunction with Sun
1	19	NEW MOON (Eclipse)
1	22	Moon at perigee
4	00	Earth at aphelion
6	12	Mercury in inferior conjunction
8	13	FIRST QUARTER
15	16	Moon at apogee
16	14	FULL MOON (Eclipse)
16	18	Vesta at opposition
17	10	Mercury stationary
17	12	Neptune 1°2 N of Moon
18	16	Uranus 1°6 N of Moon
24	11	LAST QUARTER
26	09	Saturn 2° N of Moon
26	20	Jupiter 3° N of Moon
27	09	Mercury greatest elong. W (20°)
27	23	Neptune at opposition
29	17	Mercury 0°8 S of Moon (Occn.)
30	08	Moon at perigee
31	02	NEW MOON (Eclipse)

AUGUST

d	hr.	
2	17	Pallas 0°008 N of Moon (Occn.)
3	22	Mercury 7° S of Pollux
6	07	Venus 1°1 N of Regulus
7	01	FIRST QUARTER
10	13	Mercury 0°09 S of Mars
11	05	Uranus at opposition

d	hr.	
11	22	Moon at apogee
12	08	Juno at opposition
13	17	Neptune 1°1 N of Moon (Occn.)
14	20	Uranus 1°4 N of Moon
15	05	FULL MOON
22	01	Mercury in superior conjunction
22	19	LAST QUARTER
22	19	Saturn 2° N of Moon
22	20	Pluto stationary
23	10	Jupiter 3° N of Moon
27	14	Moon at perigee
28	03	Mars 0°9 S of Moon (Occn.)
28	06	Vesta stationary
29	10	NEW MOON
30	23	Venus 4° S of Moon

SEPTEMBER

d	hr.	
1	22	Ceres 0°4 N of Moon (Occn.)
5	16	FIRST QUARTER
7	18	Jupiter 5° N of Aldebaran
8	13	Moon at apogee
9	23	Neptune 1°2 N of Moon
11	01	Uranus 1°4 N of Moon
12	20	Saturn stationary
13	20	FULL MOON
16	07	Mars 0°8 N of Regulus
18	19	Venus 3° N of Spica
19	01	Saturn 1°8 N of Moon
19	19	Jupiter 2° N of Moon
21	01	LAST QUARTER
22	17	Equinox
23	15	Mercury 0°7 N of Spica
24	08	Moon at perigee
25	17	Mars 2° S of Moon
27	03	Juno stationary
27	20	NEW MOON
29	13	Mercury 8° S of Moon
29	14	Jupiter stationary
30	00	Venus 5° S of Moon
30	04	Ceres 0°5 S of Moon (Occn.)

OCTOBER

d	hr.	
5	11	FIRST QUARTER
6	07	Moon at apogee
6	10	Mercury greatest elong. E (26°)
7	06	Neptune 1°3 N of Moon
8	08	Uranus 1°5 N of Moon
9	22	Pallas in conjunction with Sun
13	09	FULL MOON
15	11	Neptune stationary
16	06	Saturn 1°6 N of Moon
17	00	Jupiter 2° N of Moon
18	18	Mercury stationary

d	hr.	
19	22	Moon at perigee
20	08	LAST QUARTER
21	05	Jupiter 5° N of Aldebaran
24	05	Mars 3° S of Moon
26	20	Uranus stationary
26	22	Venus 3° N of Antares
27	08	NEW MOON
30	02	Mercury in inferior conjunction
30	08	Venus 4° S of Moon

NOVEMBER

d	hr.	
3	03	Moon at apogee
3	14	Neptune 1°6 N of Moon
4	07	FIRST QUARTER
4	16	Uranus 1°8 N of Moon
7	18	Mercury stationary
11	21	FULL MOON
12	11	Saturn 1°6 N of Moon
13	03	Jupiter 2° N of Moon
14	23	Moon at perigee
15	06	Mercury greatest elong. W (19°)
18	15	LAST QUARTER
19	13	Saturn at opposition
21	10	Ceres in conjunction with Sun
21	18	Mars 4° S of Moon
24	11	Mercury 3° S of Moon
25	23	NEW MOON
28	02	Jupiter at opposition
29	18	Venus 2° S of Moon
30	22	Neptune 1°8 N of Moon

DECEMBER

d	hr.	
1	00	Moon at apogee
2	01	Uranus 2° N of Moon
4	04	FIRST QUARTER
4	14	Pluto in conjunction with Sun
9	17	Saturn 1°8 N of Moon
10	08	Jupiter 3° N of Moon
11	01	Mars 4° N of Spica
11	09	FULL MOON
11	21	Venus 3° S of Neptune
12	22	Moon at perigee
18	01	LAST QUARTER
20	07	Mars 4° S of Moon
21	14	Solstice
23	21	Venus 1°3 S of Uranus
23	23	Ceres 0°9 S of Moon (Occn.)
25	17	NEW MOON (Eclipse)
25	19	Mercury in superior conjunction
28	07	Neptune 2° N of Moon
28	15	Moon at apogee
29	10	Uranus 2° N of Moon
29	22	Venus 1°8 N of Moon

Conversion of Universal Time (U.T.) to Civil Time

U.T.	E.D.T.[1]	E.S.T.[2]	C.S.T.[3]	M.S.T.[4]	P.S.T.[5]
00	*8P	*7P	*6P	*5P	*4P
01	*9P	*8P	*7P	*6P	*5P
02	*10P	*9P	*8P	*7P	*6P
03	*11P	*10P	*9P	*8P	*7P
04	M	*11P	*10P	*9P	*8P
05	1A	M	*11P	*10P	*9P
06	2A	1A	M	*11P	*10P
07	3A	2A	1A	M	*11P
08	4A	3A	2A	1A	M
09	5A	4A	3A	2A	1A
10	6A	5A	4A	3A	2A
11	7A	6A	5A	4A	3A
12	8A	7A	6A	5A	4A
13	9A	8A	7A	6A	5A
14	10A	9A	8A	7A	6A
15	11A	10A	9A	8A	7A
16	N	11A	10A	9A	8A
17	1P	N	11A	10A	9A
18	2P	1P	N	11A	10A
19	3P	2P	1P	N	11A
20	4P	3P	2P	1P	N
21	5P	4P	3P	2P	1P
22	6P	5P	4P	3P	2P
23	7P	6P	5P	4P	3P

NOTES: * denotes previous day. N = noon. M = midnight. 1. Eastern Daylight Time. 2. Eastern Standard Time, same as Central Daylight Time. 3. Central Standard Time, same as Mountain Daylight Time. 4. Mountain Standard Time, same as Pacific Daylight Time. 5. Pacific Standard Time.

Eclipses of the Sun and Moon, 2000

Note: The day of an eclipse is given in Universal Time (U.T.) and may start a day earlier or later depending on your time zone. (*See* Phenomena, 2000 table, pp. 451–452, to find time of eclipse in your area.)

January 31. Total eclipse of the Moon. The beginning of the umbral phase visible in North America except the Aleutian Islands, Central America, South America, most of Africa, Europe, western Asia, Greenland, the arctic region, the Palmer Peninsula of Antarctica, the Atlantic Ocean, and the eastern Pacific Ocean; the end visible in North America, Hawaii, Central America, South America, extreme western Africa, Europe except the southeastern portion, Greenland, the Arctic region, the Palmer Peninsula of Antarctica, the North Pacific Ocean except the southwestern portion, the eastern South Pacific Ocean, the North Atlantic Ocean, and the South Atlantic Ocean except the southeastern portion.

February 5. Partial eclipse of the Sun. Visible in Antarctica and central southern Indian Ocean.

July 1. Partial eclipse of the Sun. Visible in the central southern Pacific Ocean and the southern part of Chile and Argentina.

July 16. Total eclipse of the Moon. The beginning of the umbral phase visible in the western United States, Hawaii, the southern half of Alaska, the west coast of Canada, most of Mexico, extreme southern South America, Australia, New Zealand, the east coast of Asia, Antarctica, the Pacific Ocean, and the southeastern Indian Ocean; the end visible in Asia except the extreme western portion and the north coast, Australia, New Zealand, Hawaii, the extreme western Aleutian Islands, the east coast of Africa, Antarctica, the Indian Ocean, and the western Pacific Ocean.

July 31. Partial eclipse of the Sun. Visible in northern and western Russia, the northern parts of Scandinavia and Greenland, Arctic Ocean, and northwest North America.

December 25. Partial eclipse of the Sun. Visible in Mexico, West Indies, North America except the North West, west Atlantic Ocean, and South Greenland.

Visibility of Planets in Morning and Evening Twilight, 2000

	Morning		Evening
Venus	January 1–May 5	Venus	July 18–December 31
Mars	August 20–December 31	Mars	January 1–May 8
Jupiter	May 22–November 28	Jupiter	January 1–April 24
Saturn	May 29–November 19		November 28–December 31
		Saturn	January 1–April 23
			November 19–December 31

Who Needs the International Space Station?

Critics say the new outpost in space is overdue, overhyped, and overbudget. NASA and ISS fans say: "Get over it!"

By JEFFREY KLUGER TIME

If Russian cosmonauts aboard the International Space Station find themselves running short of borscht, there is a very good reason: the technicians on the ground ate it all. The Russian space agency has been running on fumes since the end of the cold war, but never more so than in the past few years. Employees at the Baikonur space center in Kazakhstan often go unpaid and sometimes slip away at the end of their shifts taking pilfered electrical components with them. Some of those employees, less interested in fencing stolen goods than simply eating a decent meal, have even broken into provisions intended for cosmonauts and made off with as many cans of borscht—and as many rations of vodka—as they could carry.

There's something darkly comical in watching the once feared Russian space agency reduced to such pratfalls, and there was a time when U.S. officials might have enjoyed the show. But Washington is not laughing, and with good reason. On Nov. 20, 1998, the first piece of the 16-nation, NASA-led International Space Station was launched from Baikonur—marking the start of an eight-year construction project that ranks as the greatest peacetime engineering job in history—and a bankrupt Russia is only one of the problems it faces.

Fourteen Years Behind Schedule

The station is three or five or 12 times over budget, depending on who's counting the fiscal beans, and while everything from rubles to yen to pounds is supposedly bankrolling the work, it's American dollars that are really keeping it going. The project is also 14 years behind schedule and will probably slip further before construction on the 360-ft.-long, 460-ton skyliner is done. Worst of all, once the ISS gets into orbit, there are very real concerns about whether it will have anything truly useful to do.

Barring a catastrophe, there is little likelihood that the space station won't fly. Too much money has been spent and too much metal has been cut for it to be scrapped now. But however much work the ISS eventually does, the lessons it yields will probably be less scientific than bureaucratic—lessons about how, and how not, to get a project like this done. "Most of the functions of the space station have disappeared," says Alex Roland, chairman of the department of history at Duke University and a former NASA historian. "NASA is mortgaging its future for the next 20 years."

The International Space Station wasn't always so complex a beast. The idea of a permanent U.S. orbital platform was first proposed by Ronald Reagan in his State of the Union address in January 1984. For all the station's great size, Reagan envisioned it as a fairly fat-free piece of engineering: a lean, $8 billion cluster of modules that could be manufactured on the ground, be assembled in space, and go into service by 1992. Orbiting Earth 200 miles up, it would serve as a flying laboratory for inventing new materials and conducting pharmaceutical work. More important, it would help scientists study the physical effects of extended periods of weightlessness, a necessary prelude to interplanetary missions. "Our principal goal," says Daniel Goldin, NASA's current administrator, "is getting to Mars."

Enter the Russians

What Ronald Reagan could envision and what engineers could build were two different things, however, and when 1992 arrived, NASA had spent $10 billion basically drawing up—and tearing up—space-station blueprints. It fell to the Clinton Administration, which came to town the next year, to set things right. The new White House team decided that while the space station had always been a global enterprise—with Japan, Europe and Canada all contributing parts—NASA would fling the doors open even wider, inviting the Russians, with their wobbly new democracy, to join. With Russia sharing the work, the Administration figured, the overall costs would plummet, holding the U.S. contribution to no more than an additional $17.4 billion.

The Administration figured wrong. Russia agreed to construct two principal components of the ISS: the Zarya, a 40-ft. power-and-propulsion pod that was launched in Dec. 1998 after a year's delay; and the Service Module, a school bus-size assembly that will serve as living quarters for at least part of the six-person multinational crew. Although Russia has the know-how to get both jobs done, it has not had the cash. To jump-start things, the U.S. agreed to pitch in, sending Moscow financial aid that was little more than a handout intended to be used for space-station construction. "Russia's participation was supposed to save us $2 billion," complains Democratic Congressman Timothy Roemer of Indiana. "We've sent $2 billion to Russia."

Especially worrisome has been the Service Module. The Russians pledged to have that station component ready for launch by April 1998. But April came and went, and no Service Module appeared. Moscow missed its second target date, in July 1999, as well, and the launch was again rescheduled—this time for mid-November.

What makes things especially dicey is that if the Service Module doesn't go aloft, nothing else can stay aloft. On Dec. 4, 1998, NASA sent up a shuttle to deploy the Unity node—a 22-ft.-long pod with six portholes that connects to Zarya and will serve as the station's central docking hub. Neither Unity nor Zarya is equipped with adequate propulsion systems, though, and without the Service Module, their orbits will decay. To prevent this, NASA wants to send an additional $660 million Russia's way. In the event that even this isn't enough to get the Service Module built, NASA is looking into modifying the shuttle so it can nudge Zarya and Unity into a more stable orbit. The space agency is also considering other contingency plans, such as building its own emergency-return vehicle for the ISS, replacing an off-the-shelf piece of hardware that Russia had originally agreed to provide. "It's not as though we're ignoring the situation," Goldin says.

Out-of-Orbit Expenses

But all those plans take money—American money—and NASA is being hit from all sides. Prime contractor Boeing admits that it erred in its estimates by as much as $800 million. This, along with other overruns, pushes the ISS cost to $21 billion—and that's on top of the $10 billion spent on research and development before 1992. Moreover, none of this includes the 28 to 38 shuttle launches it will take to truck the station into orbit between now and 2006—launches that will start at a cool $400 million each. When the annual expense of maintaining the ISS during its 10-to-20-year life is included, the Government Accounting Office frets that the project's total price tag could reach $96 billion. Goldin disputes that, stressing that the space agency is spending only one-seventh of its total budget on the ISS.

Money isn't all that's giving station critics night sweats. Years ago, NASA estimated that building a ship this big would require astronauts to make some 80 space walks—a proposition so dangerous it was one of the reasons Congress almost killed the project. NASA pledged to change that figure, and it did—in the wrong direction. Last week the agency admitted that astronaut construction crews may have to venture outside a hair-raising 162 times.

No matter what the numbers are, a simple, low-cost project the space station isn't, and calls have gone up to cancel it altogether—or at the very least show the Russians the door. That, however, is unlikely. Having climbed up into the ISS treehouse, Washington officials seem to have kicked over the ladder that would have let them climb back down. Moscow's promised modules, after all, are vital ones, and if the Russians go, so would their hardware. Political considerations play a role too. A

project this big inevitably turns into budgetary pork, and the ISS has been nothing short of a flying ham. In July 1998, the Senate overwhelmingly killed a proposal to scrap the station, in part because that would mean canceling contracts in vote-rich California, Texas, Florida, and Virginia. "Machiavelli could not have designed it better," says Indiana's Roemer. "The bread crumbs have been spread out in the congressional districts."

Questionable Scientific Merit

If the country is stuck with the ISS, will the new outpost at least return enough science to justify all the trouble? It's debatable. Pressed to explain just what astronauts will be doing up there for the next two decades, NASA points again and again to the same few areas of research, particularly protein-crystal growth and materials manufacturing. But the value of this is disputed. Protein crystals, which grow more uniformly in zero-G and can help scientists develop drugs, are fragile, and can be deformed by a mere bump—something that can happen a lot when astronauts are onboard. Materials manufacturing is similarly subject to human error. A cheaper solution would be to conduct those studies aboard unstaffed spacecraft.

Weightlessness research is a far better argument for the ISS. Even a few days in zero-G can be hard on the body; a three-year Mars mission would be murder. But with reams of data in hand from Russian and American stays aboard the Mir space station, is more zero-G research the best way to spend $96 billion?

None of this has moved Washington, and since the first ISS piece was launched in November 1998, it has become harder still to pull the plug on the project. No one doubts that NASA could finance plenty of other missions—both staffed and unstaffed—if the station were canceled. Just $1 billion of ISS funding, after all, could pay for four missions of a robot spacecraft like the Mars Pathfinder—the little rover that so electrified the country in 1997. The ISS, however, appears to be here to stay, and could dominate NASA's exploratory agenda for a generation. Over the past 40 years, the space agency has shown itself capable of flying brilliant, even transcendent, missions. The space station, sad to say, is not likely to be one of them. □

Earth Microbes on the Moon

Did you know that one inadvertent stowaway from Earth, the common bacteria *Streptococcus mitis*, is the only known survivor of unprotected space travel? In 1991, as *Apollo 12* Commander Pete Conrad reviewed the transcripts of his conversations relayed from the Moon back to Earth, he said, "I always thought the most significant thing that we ever found on the whole . . . Moon was that little bacteria who came back and lived, and nobody ever said [anything] about it."

In November 1969, microorganisms were recovered from inside the camera of the *Surveyor 3*

spacecraft that had been brought back to Earth under sterile conditions by the *Apollo 12* crew. Amazed scientists discovered that 50 to 100 of the organisms survived the launch, space vacuum, three years of radiation exposure, deep-freeze at an average temperature of only 20 degrees above absolute zero, and no nutrients, water, or energy source. *Streptococcus mitis* is a harmless bacterium from the nose, mouth, and throat in humans. How this remarkable feat was accomplished by a colony of space-faring *Strep* bacteria remains speculative.

Major Space Explorations

Ongoing Missions

Galileo (U.S.)

Destination: Jupiter. **Launched:** Oct. 18, 1989. **Achieved Orbit:** Dec. 7, 1995. **Mission:** To study the chemical composition and physical state of the largest planet in the solar system, its atmosphere, and four of its moons, for almost two years. The spacecraft encountered the asteroid 951 Gaspera on Oct. 29, 1991, and took the first close-up photographs ever of an asteroid in space. On Aug. 28, 1993, it passed by asteroid 243 Ida and took close-up photographs, which revealed that Ida has a tiny moon. Upon arrival at Jupiter, *Galileo* released a probe into the planet's atmosphere that descended for 57 minutes before it was destroyed by the planet's extreme temperature and pressure. In 1996, *Galileo* visited and photographed Jupiter's large moons Io, Callisto, and Europa and made fly-bys of Io, Ganymede, Europa, and Callisto in 1997. *Galileo* was named for the Italian astronomer Galileo Galilei, who discovered the four great moons of Jupiter that were the major targets of this mission.

Galileo Europa Mission (GEM):

A two-year continuation of the original Galileo Mission, which was completed in December 1997. GEM will include eight fly-bys of Europa, four fly-bys of Callisto, and two fly-bys of Io by late 1999, as long as the spacecraft remains healthy.

Ulysses (U.S. and European Space Agency)

Destination: The Sun. **Launched:** Oct. 6, 1990. **Flew by Jupiter:** Feb. 8, 1992. **Achieved Highest Southern Latitude:** Sept. 13, 1994 (−80.2 degrees). **Achieved Highest Northern Latitude:** July 31, 1995 (+80.2 degrees). **Mission:** An international project to study the Sun and interstellar space above and below its poles. The spacecraft was put into orbit at right angles to the solar system's ecliptic plane. This special orbit enabled *Ulysses* to examine for the first time the Sun's north and south polar regions. Besides investigating the Sun, the spacecraft is also studying phenomena from the Milky Way and beyond. The spacecraft completed its first full orbit around the Sun on April 17, 1998. *Ulysses* will continue to orbit the Sun and will pass over the north and south poles again in 2000 and 2001.

Near-Earth Asteroid Rendezvous (NEAR) (U.S.)

Destination: Asteroid 433 Eros. **Launched:** Feb. 17, 1996. **Arrival:** Feb. 14, 2000. **Mission:** To rendezvous with Eros and orbit the asteroid for almost one year. It will take comprehensive measurements of its surface, size, volume, mass, spin, and magnetic field. *NEAR* passed by and photographed minor planet 253 Mathilde on June 27, 1997. A planned 1999 rendezvous with the asteroid was aborted due to engine problems and was rescheduled for 2000.

Mars Global Surveyor (U.S.)

Destination: Mars. **Launched:** Nov. 7, 1996. **Arrival:** Sept. 11, 1997. **Mission:** An orbiting spacecraft designed to provide detailed maps of the planet's surface and distribution of minerals, and to monitor the Martian weather. Six instruments are studying Martian surface, atmosphere, and gravitational and magnetic fields. *Surveyor*'s cameras are able to distinguish features as small as 10 feet across.

The primary mapping mission was delayed until March 1999, due to problems with the craft's solar panels. Mapping operations will continue until January 2000. The spacecraft will orbit Mars for 687 days, the length of one Martian year.

Cassini (U.S., the European Space Agency, and the Italian Space Agency)

Destination: Saturn. **Launched:** Oct. 15, 1997. **Arrival:** July 1, 2004. **Mission:** Will orbit Saturn for four years. Before reaching Saturn, *Cassini* will encounter Jupiter and fly down the giant planet's magnetotail, performing studies complementing the Galileo Mission. While orbiting Saturn, *Cassini* will send a small probe named *Huygens* (after the Dutch astronomer Christiaan Huygens, who discovered Titan) to the surface of Saturn's largest moon, Titan, to learn more about its dense atmosphere and its surface state and composition. After relaying data to Earth from Titan, *Cassini* will continue with orbits of Saturn and fly-bys of the planet's 16 or more moons. The spacecraft will also examine Saturn's equatorial zone and study the planet's polar regions. The Cassini mission is named for the Italian-French astronomer Gian Domenico Cassini, who discovered four of Saturn's major moons.

Nozomi ("Hope") (Japan)

Destination: Mars. **Launched:** July 4, 1998, from Kagoshima Space Center. **Arrival:** Dec. 2003. Engine problems delayed its arrival at Mars in 1999. **Mission:** To send an orbiter around Mars to study the effect of the solar wind on the planet's atmosphere for one Martian year (687 days). Its cameras will provide photographic data on cloud distribution, polar haze, dust storms, polar ice, and the planet's surface. After its successful launch, the Planet-B spacecraft was renamed *Nozomi* (hope). Japan's new effort made it the third nation after the United States and Russia to conduct a mission to another planet.

Mars Surveyor '98 (U.S.)

Destination: Mars. **Launched:** *Orbiter*—Dec. 11, 1998; *Lander*—Jan. 3, 1999. Two spacecraft were launched separately but will compose a single mission. **Arrival:** *(Mars Climate Orbiter)*—Sept. 23, 1999; *(Mars Polar Lander)*—Dec. 3, 1999. **Mission:** Dual spacecraft will study the planet's weather-related changes in the atmosphere and on the surface. The *Mars Surveyor Lander* will be the first probe to land in the polar region of Mars. It will photograph the surface of the south polar region as it descends. After landing, it will deploy a package of stereo cameras, and analyze soil samples with a robotic arm. The lander will carry a microphone, funded by the Planetary Society, to detect sounds on Mars. The lander will also carry two microprobes (a.k.a. *Deep Space 2*) that will plunge into the Martian surface prior to the spacecraft's entry into the planet's atmosphere. The probes will test for subsurface water ice and conduct soil experiments.

Stardust (U.S.)

Destination: Comet Wild 2. **Launched:** Feb. 7, 1999. **Mission:** To fly through coma of Comet Wild 2 in 2004, capture particles spewing out of comet, and return comet dust samples to Earth in 2006. *Stardust* will be the first mission to return with comet samples. Enroute to Wild 2, the spacecraft will also collect particles from the interstellar dust stream.

Deep Space 1 (U.S.)

Launched: Oct. 24, 1998. **Mission:** First launch of NASA's New Millennium program, a series of missions to test new technologies. *Deep Space 1* is the first craft to employ an ion-propulsion system. It flew past near-Earth asteroid Braille on July 28, 1999, took photos, and collected scientific data. The primary mission ends Sept. 18, 1999, and if an extended mission is funded, *Deep Space 1* could fly past two comets in 2001.

Future Missions
(Note: Dates are tentative.)

Genesis (U.S.)

Destination: The Sun. **Launch:** Jan. 2001. **Mission:** Gather and return samples of charged particles of the solar wind and return them to Earth in August 2003 for detailed analysis. The reentry vehicle will separate from the spacecraft and parachute its sample return capsule to a location in the Utah desert, The data to be obtained are crucial for improving theories about the origin of the Sun and planets that formed from the same primordial dust cloud.

Mars Surveyor 2001 (U.S.)

Destination: Mars. **Launch:** *Orbiter*—March 2001; *Lander*—April 2001. **Arrival:** *(Mars Surveyor Orbiter)*—Dec. 2001; *(Mars Lander)*—Jan. 2002. **Mission:** The *Mars Surveyor 2001 Orbiter* will conduct a mineralogical mapping of the entire planet and characterize its orbital radiation environment. The lander will conduct scientific experiments and will include a microrover, named *Marie Curie*, similar to the *Pathfinder Sojourner* rover. The rover will be designed to travel 62 miles (100 kilometers) and operate for one year. It will analyze the surface materials and collect samples for return to Earth by a future robotic mission.

Future Mars Surveyors

Destination: Mars. **Launch:** 2003, 2005. **Missions:** Small orbiters will capitalize on the experience of the *Mars Pathfinder* lander mission and will serve as relay stations for international missions of the future. A high-tech rover that will be capable of traveling long distances is under construction for use in the 2003 mission.

A search for water is being considered in 2001, and another planned mission will have a rover investigate an ancient highland bed to study the climate history of the planet. The *Mars Surveyor 2005* mission will be an attempt to bring back a sample of Martian rocks and soil.

Contour (U.S.)

Destination: Comet Nucleus Tour. **Launch:** July 2002. **Mission:** To fly by Comet Encke at 60 miles (100 kilometers), followed by encounters with Comet Schwassmann-Wachmann-3 in June 2006, and Comet d'Arrest in August 2008. The spacecraft will take images and spectral maps of nuclei and analyze dust flowing from them. The mission will help scientists to learn more about the composition and structure of comets, which are believed to be quite individual in their properties.

Selene SELenological and Engineering Explorer (Japan)

Destination: The Moon. **Launch:** 2003. **Mission:** An orbiting spacecraft to study the origin and evolution of the Moon for one year. It will map the entire surface and gather data on chemical and mineralogical composition, magnetic fields, and interior structure. After a year, the propulsion module of the orbiter will separate from the spacecraft and soft-land on the lunar surface to continue the mission for two more months.

U.S. Unstaffed Planetary and Lunar Programs

Lunar Orbiter. Series of spacecraft designed to orbit the Moon, taking pictures and obtaining data in support of the subsequent staffed *Apollo* landings. The U.S. launched five *Lunar Orbiters* between Aug. 10, 1966 and Aug. 2, 1967.

Mariner. Designation for a series of spacecraft designed to fly past or orbit the planets, particularly Mercury, Venus, and Mars. *Mariners* provided the early information on Venus and Mars. *Mariner 9,* orbiting Mars in 1971, returned the most revealing photographs of that planet and helped pave the way for a *Viking* landing in 1976. *Mariner 10* explored Venus and Mercury in 1973 and was the first probe to use a planet's gravity to propel it toward another.

Pioneer. Designation for the United States' first series of sophisticated interplanetary spacecraft. *Pioneers 10* and *11* reached Jupiter in 1973 and 1974 and continued on to explore Saturn and the other outer planets. *Pioneer 11,* renamed *Pioneer Saturn,* examined the Saturn system in September 1979. Significant discoveries were the finding of a small new moon and a narrow new ring. In 1986, *Pioneer 10* was the first man-made object to escape the solar system. *Pioneer Venus 1* and *2* reached Venus in 1978 and provided detailed information about that planet's surface and atmosphere.

Ranger. NASA's earliest Moon-exploration program. Spacecraft were designed for a crash landing on the Moon, taking pictures and returning scientific data up to the moment of impact. Provided the first close-up views of the lunar surface. The *Rangers* provided more than 17,000 close-up pictures, giving us more information about the Moon in a few years than in all the time that had gone before.

Surveyor. Series of unstaffed spacecraft designed to land gently on the Moon and provide information on the surface in preparation for the staffed lunar landings. Their legs were instrumented to return data on the surface hardness of the Moon. *Surveyor* dispelled the fear that *Apollo* spacecraft might sink several feet or more into the lunar dust.

Viking. Designation for two spacecraft designed to conduct detailed scientific examination of the planet Mars, including a search for life. *Viking 1* landed on July 20, 1976; *Viking 2*, Sept. 3, 1976. More was learned about the red planet in a few short months than in all previous missions, but the question of whether there is life on Mars remains unresolved.

Voyager. Designation for two spacecraft designed to explore Jupiter and the other outer planets. *Voyager 1* and *Voyager 2* passed Jupiter in 1979 and sent back surprising color TV images of that planet and its moons. They took a total of about 33,000 pictures. *Voyager 1* passed Saturn in November 1980. *Voyager 2* passed Saturn in August 1981 and Uranus in January 1986.

It encountered Neptune on Aug. 29, 1989, and made many discoveries. It found four rings around the planet, six new moons, a giant spot, and evidence of volcanic-like activity on its largest moon, Triton. The spacecraft sent back over 9,000 pictures of the planet and its system.

On Feb. 13, 1990, at a distance of 3.7 billion miles, *Voyager 1* took its final pictures—the Sun and six of its planets as seen from deep space. NASA released the extraordinary images to the public on June 6, 1990. Only Mercury, Mars, and Pluto were not seen.

Notable Unstaffed Lunar and Interplanetary Probes

Spacecraft	Launch date	Destination	Remarks
Pioneer 3 (U.S.)	Dec. 6, 1958	Moon	Max. alt.: 66,654 mi. Discovered outer Van Allen layer.
Luna 2 (U.S.S.R.)	Sept. 12, 1959	Moon	Impacted on Sept. 14. First space vehicle to reach Moon.
Luna 3 (U.S.S.R.)	Oct. 4, 1959	Moon	Flew around Moon and transmitted first pictures of lunar far side, Oct. 7.
Mariner 2 (U.S.)	Aug. 27, 1962	Venus	Venus probe. Successful mid-course correction. Passed 21,648 mi. from Venus Dec. 14, 1962. Reported 800°F. surface temp. Contact lost Jan. 3, 1963, at 54 million mi.
Ranger 7 (U.S.)	July 28, 1964	Moon	Impacted near Crater Guericke 68.5 hr. after launch. Sent 4,316 pictures during last 15 min. of flight as close as 1,000 ft. above lunar surface.
Mariner 4 (U.S.)	Nov. 28, 1964	Mars	Transmitted first close-up pictures on June 14, 1965, from altitude of 6,000 mi.
Luna 9 (U.S.S.R.)	Jan. 31, 1966	Moon	3,428 lb. Instrument capsule of 220 lb. soft-landed Feb. 3, 1966. Sent back about 30 pictures.
Surveyor 1 (U.S.)	May 30, 1966	Moon	Landed June 2, 1966. Sent almost 10,400 pictures, a number after surviving the 14-day lunar night.
Lunar Orbiter 1 (U.S.)	Aug. 10, 1966	Moon	Orbited Moon Aug. 14. 21 pictures sent.
Surveyor 3 (U.S.)	April 17, 1967	Moon	Soft-landed 65 hr. after launch on Oceanus Procellarum. Scooped and tested lunar soil.
Venera 4 (U.S.S.R.)	June 12, 1967	Venus	Arrived Oct. 17. Instrument capsule sent temperature and chemical data.
Surveyor 5 (U.S.)	Sept. 8, 1967	Moon	Landed near lunar equator Sept. 10. Radiological analysis of lunar soil. Mechanical claw for digging soil.
Surveyor 7 (U.S.)	Jan. 6, 1968	Moon	Landed near Crater Tycho Jan. 10. Soil analysis. Sent 3,343 pictures.
Pioneer 9 (U.S.)	Nov. 8, 1968	Sun	Achieved orbit. Six experiments returned solar radiation data.
Venera 5 (U.S.S.R.)	Jan. 5, 1969	Venus	Landed May 16, 1969. Returned atmospheric data.
Mariner 6 (U.S.)	Feb. 24, 1969	Mars	Came within 2000 mi. of Mars July 31, 1969. Sent back data and TV pictures.
Luna 16 (U.S.S.R.)	Sept. 12, 1970	Moon	Soft-landed Sept. 20, scooped up rock, returned to Earth Sept. 24.
Luna 17 (U.S.S.R.)	Nov. 10, 1970	Moon	Soft-landed on Sea of Rains Nov. 17. *Lunokhod 1*, self-propelled vehicle, used for first time. Sent TV photos, made soil analysis, etc.
Mariner 9 (U.S.)	May 30, 1971	Mars	First craft to orbit Mars, Nov. 13. 7,300 pictures, 1st close-ups of one of Mars' moons. Transmission ended Oct. 27, 1972.
Luna 20 (U.S.S.R.)	Feb. 14, 1972	Moon	Soft-landed Feb. 21 in Sea of Fertility. Returned Feb. 25 with rock samples.

Spacecraft	Launch date	Destination	Remarks
Pioneer 10 (U.S.)	March 3, 1972	Jupiter	620-million-mile flight path through asteroid belt passed Jupiter Dec. 3, 1973, to give man first close-up of planet. In 1986, it became first man-made object to escape solar system.
Luna 21 (U.S.S.R.)	Jan. 8, 1973	Moon	Soft-landed Jan. 16. Lunokhod 2 (moon-car) scooped up soil samples, returned them to Earth Jan. 27.
Mariner 10 (U.S.)	Nov. 3, 1973	Venus, Mercury	Passed Venus Feb. 5, 1974. Arrived Mercury March 29, 1974, for man's first close-up look at planet. First time gravity of one planet (Venus) used to propel spacecraft toward another (Mercury).
Viking 1 (U.S.)	Aug. 20, 1975	Mars	Carrying life-detection labs. Landed July 20, 1976, for detailed scientific research, including pictures. Designed to work for only 90 days, it operated for almost 6½ years before it went silent in November 1982.
Viking 2 (U.S.)	Sept. 9, 1975	Mars	Like Viking 1. Landed Sept. 3, 1976. Functioned 3½ years.
Luna 24 (U.S.S.R.)	Aug. 9, 1976	Moon	Soft-landed Aug. 18, 1976. Returned soil samples Aug. 22, 1976.
Voyager 2 (U.S.)	Aug. 20, 1977	Jupiter, Saturn, Uranus	Launched before Voyager 1. Encountered Jupiter in July 1979; flew by Saturn August 1981; passed Uranus January 1986; and passed Neptune in August 1989.
Voyager 1 (U.S.)	Sept. 5, 1977	Jupiter, Saturn	Fly-by mission. Reached Jupiter in March 1979; passed Saturn November 1980; passed Uranus 1986.
Pioneer Venus 1 (U.S.)	May 20, 1978	Venus	Arrived Dec. 4 and orbited Venus, photographing surface and atmosphere. Crashed into planet's surface mid-October 1992 after circling Venus for 14 years.
Pioneer Venus 2 (U.S.)	Aug. 8, 1978	Venus	Four-part multiprobe, landed Dec. 9.
Venera 13 (U.S.S.R.)	Oct. 30, 1981	Venus	Landed March 1, 1982. Took first X-ray fluorescence analysis of the planet's surface. Transmitted data 2 hours, 7 minutes.
VEGA 1 (U.S.S.R.)	Deployed on Venus, June 10, 1985	Halley's Comet	In fly-by over Venus while en route to encounter Halley's Comet, VEGA 1 and 2 dropped scientific capsules onto Venus to study atmosphere and surface material. Encountered Halley's Comet on March 6 and March 9, 1986. Took TV pictures and studied comet's dust particles.
VEGA 2 (U.S.S.R.)	Deployed on Venus, June 14, 1985	Halley's Comet	See VEGA 1 above.
Suisei (Japan)	Encountered Halley's Comet March 8, 1986	Halley's Comet	Spacecraft made fly-by of comet and studied atmosphere with ultraviolet camera. Observed rotation nucleus.
Sakigake (Japan)	Encountered Halley's Comet March 10, 1986	Halley's Comet	Spacecraft made fly-by to study solar wind and magnetic fields. Detected plasma waves.
Giotto (E.S.A.)	Encountered Halley's Comet March 13, 1986	Halley's Comet	European Space Agency spacecraft made closest approach to comet. Studied atmosphere and magnetic fields. Sent back best pictures of nucleus. Flew by comet Grigg-Skjellerup July 10, 1992. Unable to send pictures.
Phobos Mission (U.S.S.R.)	July 7 and July 12, 1988	Mars and Phobos	Two spacecraft to probe Martian moon Phobos starting April 1989. Were to study orbit and soil chemistry, and send TV pictures and data of planet. Contact was lost with Phobos 1 in August 1988 and later with Phobos 2 in March 1989 after it reached the Martian moon.
Magellan (U.S.)	May 4, 1989	Venus	Arrived at Venus on Aug. 10, 1990, and made a geologic map of planet with a powerful radar. Crashed into Venus Oct. 12, 1994.
Galileo (U.S.)	Oct. 18, 1989	Jupiter	To study Jupiter's atmosphere and its moons during 22-month mission.
Hubble Space Telescope (U.S., E.S.A.)	April 25, 1990	Earth orbit	Studies distant stars and galaxies and searches for evidence of planets in other solar systems. The telescope was repaired by space-shuttle crews in December 1993 and February 1997.
Ulysses (U.S., E.S.A.)	Oct. 6, 1990	Sun	To study the poles of the Sun and interstellar space above and below the poles. First solar encounter was in 1994, second encounter in 1995.

Spacecraft	Launch date	Destination	Remarks
Gamma-Ray Observatory (U.S.)	April 7, 1991	Earth orbit	To make first survey of gamma-ray sources across the whole sky, studying explosive energic sources such as supernovae, quasars, neutron stars, pulsars, and black holes.
Clementine (U.S.)	Jan. 25, 1994	Moon and asteroid Geographos 1620	Entered lunar orbit Feb. 21 and took close-up photos of lunar surface for two months. Computer malfunction prevented planned rendezvous with Geographos.
Mars Pathfinder (U.S.)	Dec. 5, 1996	Ares Vallis, Mars	Landed July 4, 1997. The spacecraft lander and its rover, Sojourner, provided a wealth of information on the Martian rocks, soil, and atmosphere. Sent back the first live pictures. All Pathfinder's objectives were fulfilled and communications failed on Sept. 27, 1997.
Lunar Prospector (U.S.)	Jan. 6, 1998	Moon	Orbited Moon for one year, mapped chemical composition of lunar surface. Found frozen water at north and south poles. At end of its mission on July 31, 1999, it was intentionally crashed into south polar crater in hope of detecting plume of water ice, but no cloud of molecular water vapor was observed by powerful Earth telescopes.

U.S. Staffed Space Flights

Mercury. *Project Mercury,* initiated in 1958 and completed in 1963, was the United States' first human-in-space program. It was designed to further knowledge about humanity's capabilities in space.

In April 1959, seven military-jet test pilots were introduced to the public as America's first astronauts. They were: Lt. M. Scott Carpenter, USN; Capt. L. Gordon Cooper, Jr., USAF; Lt. Col. John H. Glenn, Jr., USMC; Cap. Virgil I. Grissom, USAF; Lt. Cdr. Walter M. Schirra, Jr., USN; Lt. Cdr. Alan B. Shepard, Jr., USN; and Capt. Donald K. Slayton, USAF. Six of the original seven would make a Mercury flight. Slayton was grounded for medical reasons, but remained a director of the astronaut office. He returned to flight status in 1975 as Docking Module Pilot on the *Apollo-Soyuz* flight.

Flight Summary

Each astronaut named his capsule and added the numeral 7 to denote the teamwork of the original astronauts.

May 5, 1961. Alan B. Shepard, Jr., made a suborbital flight in *Freedom 7* and became the first American in space. Time: 15 minutes, 22 seconds.

July 21, 1961. Virgil I. Grissom made the second successful suborbital flight in *Liberty Bell 7,* but spacecraft sank shortly after splashdown. Time: 15 minutes, 37 seconds. Grissom was later killed in *Apollo 1* fire, Jan. 27, 1967.

February 20, 1962. John H. Glenn, Jr., made a three-orbit flight and became the first American in orbit. Time: 4 hours, 55 minutes.

May 24, 1962. M. Scott Carpenter duplicated Glenn's flight in *Aurora 7.* Time: 4 hours, 56 minutes.

October 3, 1962. Walter M. Schirra, Jr., made a six-orbit engineering test flight in *Sigma 7.* Time: 9 hours, 13 minutes.

May 15–16, 1963. L. Gordon Cooper, Jr., performed the last *Mercury* mission and completed 22 orbits in *Faith 7* to evaluate effects of one day in space. Time: 34 hours, 19 minutes.

The Women in Space Program

In 1960, NASA also tested the first female trainees for astronaut duty in the *Mercury* program.

Thirteen out of America's twenty-five top female civilian pilots (women weren't allowed to be military pilots then) passed the same rigorous testing that male candidates underwent in the *Mercury 7* space program. Although they all proved fit to become *Mercury* astronauts, NASA suddenly canceled its testing of qualified women in July 1961, claiming that they required jet test pilot training at Edwards Air Force Base. Unfortunately, instruction at Edwards was closed to women. This new requirement ended America's chance to put the first women in space.

It is ironic that unlike her skilled American counterparts, Valentina Tereshkova, the first woman to fly in space, was a textile factory worker when she entered the Soviet space program. She had no experience as a pilot and her only qualification was that of an amateur parachute jumper before being trained as a cosmonaut in 1962.

These outstanding "Mercury 13" candidates deserve much credit for preparing the way for American women in space. They were: Jerrie Cobb, Rhea Allison, Jane Hart, Mary Wallace Funk, Jean Hixson, Myrtle Cagle, Irene Leverton, Sarah Gorelick, twins Jan and Marion Dietrich, Gene Stumbough, Bernice Steadman, and Gerry Sloan Truhill.

Gemini. *Gemini* was an extension of *Project Mercury,* to determine the effects of prolonged space flight on humans for two weeks or longer—the time it would take to reach the Moon and return. "Walks in space" provided invaluable information for astronauts' later walks on the Moon. The *Gemini* spacecraft, twice as large as the *Mercury* capsule, accommodated two astronauts. Its crew named the project *Gemini* for the third constellation of the Zodiac and its twin stars, Castor and Pollux. The capsule differed from the *Mercury* spacecrafts in that it had hatches above the capsules so that the astronauts could leave the spacecraft and perform spacewalks or extra-vehicular activities (EVAs).

There were 10 staffed flights in the *Gemini* program, starting with *Gemini 3* on March 23, 1965, and ending with the *Gemini 12* mission on Nov. 15, 1966. *Gemini 1* and *2* were unstaffed test flights of the equipment.

Apollo. *Apollo* was the designation for the United States' effort to land a person on the Moon and return him safely to Earth. The goal was successfully accomplished with *Apollo 11* on July 20, 1969, culminating eight years of rehearsal and centuries of dreaming. Astronauts Neil A. Armstrong and Col. Edwin E. Aldrin, Jr., scooped up and brought back the first lunar rocks ever seen on Earth—about 47 pounds.

Tragedy struck Jan. 27, 1967, on the launch pad during a preflight test of what would have become *Apollo 1*, the first staffed mission. Astronauts Lt. Col. Virgil "Gus" Grissom, Lt. Col. Edward H. White, and Lt. Cdr. Roger Chafee lost their lives when a fire swept through the command module.

Six *Apollo* flights followed, ending with *Apollo 17* in December 1972. The last three *Apollos* carried mechanized vehicles called lunar rovers for wideranging surface exploration of the Moon by astronauts. The rendezvous and docking of an *Apollo* spacecraft with a Russian *Soyuz* craft in Earth orbit on July 18, 1975, closed out the *Apollo* program.

During the Apollo project, the following 12 astronauts explored the lunar terrain: Col. Edwin E. "Buzz" Aldrin, Jr., and Neil A. Armstrong, *Apollo 11;* Cdr. Alan L. Bean and Cdr. Charles "Pete" Conrad, Jr., *Apollo 12;* Edgar D. Mitchell and Alan B. Shepard, *Apollo 14;* Lt. Col. James B. Irwin and Col. David R. Scott, *Apollo 15;* Col. Charles M. Duke, Jr., and Capt. John W. Young, *Apollo 16;* and Capt. Eugene A. Cernan and Dr. Harrison H. Schmitt, *Apollo 17*.

Apollo was a three-part spacecraft: the command module (CM), the crew's quarters and flight control section; the service modules (SM) for the propulsion and spacecraft support systems (when together, the two modules were called CSM); and the lunar module (LM) that took two of the crew to the lunar surface, supported them on the Moon, and returned them to the CSM in orbit.

The third lunar attempt, *Apollo 13,* April 11–17, 1970, 5 days, 22.9 hours, was aborted after the service module oxygen tank ruptured. The *Apollo 13* crew members were James A. Lovell, Jr., John L. Swigert, Jr., and Fred W. Haise, Jr. The mission was classified as a "successful failure," because the crew was rescued.

Skylab. America's first Earth-orbiting space station. *Project Skylab* was designed to demonstrate that men can work and live in space for prolonged periods without ill effects. Originally the spent third stage of a *Saturn 5* Moon rocket, *Skylab* measured 118 feet from stem to stern, and carried the most varied assortment of experimental equipment ever assembled in a single spacecraft. Three three-man crews visited the space stations, spending more than 740 hours observing the Sun and bringing home more than 175,000 solar pictures. These were the first recordings of solar activity above Earth's obscuring atmosphere. *Skylab* also evaluated systems designed to gather information on Earth's resources and environmental conditions. *Skylab*'s biomedical findings indicated that humans adapt well to space for at least a period of three months, provided they have a proper diet and adequately

programmed exercise, sleep, work, and recreation periods. *Skylab* orbited Earth at a distance of about 300 miles. Five years after the last *Skylab* mission, the 77-ton space station's orbit began to deteriorate faster than expected, owing to unexpectedly high sunspot activity. On July 11, 1979, the parts of *Skylab* that did not burn up in the atmosphere came crashing down on parts of Australia and the Indian Ocean. No one was hurt.

Space Shuttle. The space shuttle *Columbia* was successfully launched on April 12, 1981. It made five flights (the first four were test runs), the last completed on Nov. 16, 1982. The second shuttle, *Challenger,* made its maiden flight on April 4, 1983. The third shuttle, *Discovery,* made its first flight on Aug. 30, 1984. The fourth space shuttle, *Atlantis,* made its maiden flight on Oct. 3, 1985.

A tragedy occurred on Jan. 28, 1986, when the shuttle *Challenger* exploded, killing the crew of seven 73 seconds after takeoff. It was the world's worst space flight disaster.

The crew members who were killed were: Francis R. Scobee, shuttle commander; Cdr. Michael J. Smith, pilot; mission specialists Judith A. Resnik, Lt. Col. Ellison S. Onizuka, and Ronald E. McNair; and payload specialists Gregory B. Jarvis and Christa McAuliffe (who was to be the first civilian schoolteacher in space).

The cause of the explosion was a rupture in a seal on one of the booster rockets that let a jet of flame escape, igniting the fuel. The weakness in the seal was caused by the cold air temperature when the shuttle was launched.

The first U.S. space mission since the *Challenger* disaster was launched 32 months later, on Sept. 29, 1988, with the flight of *Discovery*. It had a crew of five and deployed a communications satellite.

The fifth and last orbiter, *Endeavour,* was built as a replacement for *Challenger*. It was named after the 16th-century British explorer James Cook's first ship. *Endeavour* was launched on its maiden voyage on May 7, 1992, with a crew of seven astronauts. They made four spacewalks and retrieved a disabled *Intelsat-6* communications satellite. During the mission, Dr. Kathryn Thornton became the second American woman to walk in space.

The shuttle *Columbia* spent a record 17 days, 15 hours in space, Nov. 19–Dec. 7, 1996.

The crew of the 50th mission aboard the *Endeavour,* launched Sept. 12, 1992, included the first black woman astronaut, Dr. Mae C. Jemison, and the first married couple to fly together in space, Air Force Lt. Col. Mark C. Lee and Dr. N. Jan Davis.

Lt. Col. Eileen M. Collins became the first woman to pilot a shuttle, *Discovery,* during the spacecraft's historic rendezvous with the Russian space station *Mir* on Feb. 6, 1995. The shuttle *Atlantis* made the first link-up with the *Mir* on June 29, 1995.

Lt. Col. Collins became the first woman to command a space shuttle when *Columbia* was launched in July 1999 on a mission to deploy the Chandra X-ray Observatory (formerly called AXAF).

Senator John Glenn, 76, the first American to orbit the Earth, flew as a payload specialist on the October 1998 *Discovery* mission. He studied the effects of aging and microgravity on the human body.

Soviet Staffed Space Flight Programs

Vostok. The Soviets' first staffed capsule, roughly spherical, used to place the first six cosmonauts in Earth orbit (1961–1965).

Voskhod. Adaptation of the *Vostok* capsule to accommodate two and three cosmonauts. *Voskhod 1* orbited three persons, and *Voskhod 2* orbited two persons, performing the world's first staffed extra-vehicular activity.

Soyuz. Late-model staffed spacecraft with provisions for three cosmonauts and a "working compartment" accessible through a hatch. Soyuz is the Russian word for "union." The *Soyuz* spacecraft can carry three cosmonauts, and routinely brings cosmonauts and their foreign "guests" to the *Mir* space station. *Soyuz 19,* launched July 15, 1975, docked with the American *Apollo* spacecraft.

Salyut. Earth-orbiting space station intended for prolonged occupancy and re-visitation by cosmonauts. They are usually launched by Soviet Proton rockets. *Salyut 1* was launched April 19, 1971. *Salyut 2,* launched April 3, 1973, malfunctioned in orbit and was never occupied. *Salyut 3* was launched June 25, 1974. *Salyut 4* was launched Dec. 26, 1974. *Salyut 5* was launched June 22, 1976. *Salyut 6* was launched on Sept. 29, 1977. *Salyut 7* was launched on April 19, 1982. A record breaking Russian endurance flight

was set (Feb. 8, 1984–Oct. 2, 1985) when Soviet astronauts spent 237 days in orbit aboard *Salyut 7*. *Salyut 7* re-entered the atmosphere and crashed into the Atlantic Ocean on Feb. 6, 1991.

Mir. The former Soviet Union's space station was launched into orbit on Feb. 20, 1986. Since that time, several space endurance records have been set in *Mir*. On Dec. 29, 1987, Col. Yuri Romanenko set a single-mission record of 326.5 days in space. On Dec. 21, 1989, Col. Vladimir Titov and Musa Manarov returned to Earth after spending 366 days aboard the orbiting space station. On March 22, 1995, Russian cosmonaut Valeriy Polyakov set a new record for the longest human flight in space— 439 days. U.S. astronaut Dr. Shannon W. Lucid set the American and women's space endurance records of 188 days and five hours aboard *Mir* before returning to Earth on Sept. 26, 1996.

Russian hopes to keep *Mir* staffed until 2002 died in 1999, because the Russian government could no longer afford the $250 million annual funding needed to keep the 13-year old space station operating. Attempts to get financing from private investors were unsuccessful. Russian space agency officials reluctantly announced that they would gradually deorbit the unstaffed *Mir* after the last crew left in August 1999. Ground controllers will try to guide the space station's fiery descent through the atmosphere so that it will crash into a desolate area of the Pacific Ocean sometime in early 2000.   □

Notable Staffed Space Flights

Designation and country	Date	Astronauts	Flight time (hr./min)	Remarks
Vostok 1 (U.S.S.R.)	April 12, 1961	Yuri A. Gagarin	1/48	First person in space.
MR III (U.S.)	May 5, 1961	Alan B. Shepard, Jr.	0/15	Range 486 km (302 mi.), peak 187 km (116.5 mi); capsule recovered. First American in space.
Vostok 2 (U.S.S.R.)	Aug. 6–7, 1961	Gherman S. Titov	25/18	First long-duration flight.
MA VI (U.S.)	Feb. 20, 1962	John H. Glenn, Jr.	4/55	First American in orbit.
MA IX (U.S.)	May 15–16, 1963	L. Gordon Cooper, Jr.	34/20	Longest *Mercury* flight.
Vostok 6 (U.S.S.R.)	June 16–19, 1963	Valentina V. Tereshkova	70/50	First woman in space.
Voskhod 1 (U.S.S.R.)	Oct. 12, 1964	Vladimir M. Komarov, Konstantin P. Feoktistov, Boris G. Yegorov	24/17	First 3-person orbital flight; also first flight without space suits.
Voskhod 2 (U.S.S.R.)	March 18, 1965	Alexei A. Leonov, Pavel I. Belyayev	26/2	First "space walk" (by Leonov), 10 min.
GT III (U.S.)	March 23, 1965	Virgil I. Grissom, John W. Young	4/53	First American 2-person crew.
GT IV (U.S.)	June 3–7, 1965	James A. McDivitt, Edward H. White, II	97/48	First American "space walk" (by White), lasting slightly over 20 min.
GT VIII (U.S.)	March 16–17, 1966	Neil A. Armstrong, David R. Scott	10/42	First docking between staffed spacecraft and an unstaffed space vehicle (an orbiting *Agena* rocket).
Apollo 7 (U.S.)	Oct. 11–22, 1968	Walter M. Schirra, Jr., Donn F. Eisele, R. Walter Cunningham	260/9	First staffed test of *Apollo* command module; first live TV transmissions from orbit.
Soyuz 3 (U.S.S.R.)	Oct. 26–30, 1968	Georgi T. Bergeovoi	94/51	First staffed rendezvous and possible docking by Soviet cosmonaut.
Apollo 8 (U.S.)	Dec. 21–27, 1968	Frank Borman, James A. Lovell, Jr., William A. Anders	147/00	First spacecraft in circumlunar orbit; TV transmissions from this orbit. The three astronauts were also the first astronauts to view the whole Earth.
Apollo 9 (U.S.)	Mar. 3–13, 1969	James A. McDivitt, David R. Scott, Russell L. Schweikart	241/1	First staffed flight of Lunar Module.

Designation and country	Date	Astronauts	Flight time (hr./min)	Remarks
Apollo 10 (U.S.)	May 18–26, 1969	Thomas P. Stafford, Eugene A. Cernan, John W. Young	192/3	First descent to within nine miles of Moon's surface by staffed craft.
Apollo 11 (U.S.)	July 16–24, 1969	Neil A. Armstrong, Edwin E. Aldrin, Jr., Michael Collins	195/18	First staffed landing and EVA on Moon; soil and rock samples collected; experiments left on lunar surface.
Soyuz 6 (U.S.S.R.)	Oct. 11–16, 1969	Gorgiy Shonin, Valriy Kabasov	118/42	Three spacecraft and seven men put into Earth orbit simultaneously for first time.
Apollo 12 (U.S.)	Nov. 14–24, 1969	Charles Conrad, Jr., Richard F. Gordon, Jr., Alan Bean	244/36	Staffed lunar landing mission; investigated *Surveyor 3* spacecraft; collected lunar samples. EVA time: 15 hr. 30 min.
Apollo 13 (U.S.)	April 11–17, 1970	James A. Lovell, Jr., Fred W. Haise, Jr., John L. Swigert, Jr.	142/54	Third staffed lunar landing attempt; aborted due to pressure loss in liquid oxygen in service module and failure of fuel cells.
Apollo 14 (U.S.)	Jan. 31–Feb. 9, 1971	Alan B. Shepard, Stuart A. Roosa, Edgar D. Mitchell	216/42	Third staffed lunar landing: returned largest amount of lunar material.
Soyuz 11 (U.S.S.R.)	June 6–30, 1971	Georgiy Tomofeyevich Dobrovolskiy, Vladislav Nikolayevich Volkov, Viktor Ivanovich Patsyev	569/40	Longest stay in space. Linked up with first space station, *Salyut 1*. Astronauts died just before reentry due to loss of pressurization in spacecraft.
Apollo 15 (U.S.)	July 26–Aug. 7, 1971	David R. Scott, James B. Irwin, Alfred M. Worden	295/12	Fourth staffed lunar landing; first use of lunar rover propelled by Scott and Irwin; first live pictures of LM lift-off from Moon; exploration time: 18 hours.
Apollo 16 (U.S.)	April 16–27, 1972	John W. Young, Thomas K. Mattingly, Charles M. Duke, Jr.	265/51	Fifth staffed lunar landing; second use of lunar rover vehicle, propelled by Young and Duke. Total exploration time on the Moon was 20 hr. 14 min, setting new record. Mattingly's in-flight "walk in space" was 1 hr. 23 min. Approximately 213 lb of lunar rock returned.
Apollo 17 (U.S.)	Dec. 7–19, 1972	Eugene A. Cernan, Ronald E. Evans, Harrison H. Schmitt	301/51	Sixth and last staffed lunar landing; third to carry lunar rover. Cernan and Schmitt, during three EVA's, completed total of 22 hr. 05 min 3 sec. USS *Ticonderoga* recovered crew and about 250 lbs of lunar samples.
Skylab SL-2 (U.S.)	May 25–June 22, 1973	Charles Conrad, Jr., Joseph P. Kerwin, Paul J. Weitz	672/50	First staffed *Skylab* launch. Established Skylab Orbital Assembly and conducted scientific and medical experiments.
Skylab SL-3 (U.S.)	July 28–Sept. 25, 1973	Alan L. Bean, Jr., Jack R. Lousma, Owen K. Garriott	1427/9	Second staffed *Skylab* launch. New crew remained in space for 59 days, continuing scientific and medical experiments and Earth observations from orbit.
Skylab SL-4 (U.S.)	Nov. 16, 1973– Feb. 8, 1974	Gerald Carr, Edward Gibson, William Pogue	2017/16	Third staffed *Skylab* launch; obtained medical data on crew for use in extending the duration of staffed space flight; crews "walked in space" 4 times, totaling 44 hr., 40 min. Longest space mission yet: 84 d 1 hr. 16 min. Splashdown in Pacific, Feb. 9, 1974.
Apollo/Soyuz Test Project (U.S. and U.S.S.R.)	July 15–24, 1975 (U.S.)	U.S.: Brig. Gen. Thomas P. Stafford, Vance D. Brand, Donald K. Slayton	216/05	World's first international staffed rendezvous and docking in space; aimed at developing a space rescue capability.
Apollo/Soyuz Test Project (U.S. and U.S.S.R.)	July 15–21, 1975 (U.S.S.R.)	U.S.S.R.: Col. A. A. Leonov, V. N. Kubasov	223/35	*Apollo* and *Soyuz* docked and crewmen exchanged visits on July 17, 1975. Mission duration for *Soyuz:* 142 hr. 31 min. For *Apollo:* 217 hr., 28 min.
Columbia (U.S.)	April 12–14, 1981	Capt. Robert L. Crippen, John W. Young	54/20	Maiden voyage of Space Shuttle.
Mir (U.S.S.R.)	Dec. 21, 1987– Dec. 21, 1988	Col. Vladimir Titov, Musa Manarov	366 days	Set current record for Soviet team endurance flight in orbiting space station.
Endeavour (U.S.)	May 7–16, 1992	Richard J. Hieb, Maj. Thomas D. Akers, Cdr. Pierre J. Thugt	8 days, 23 hr., 17 min.	The three mission specialists remained free of the *Endeavour* for 8 hours and 20 minutes on May 13 during the repair of communications satellite, setting an absolute record for extravehicular duration in space. First capture of a satellite using hands only.

Designation and country	Date	Astronauts	Flight time (hr./min)	Remarks
Endeavour (U.S.)	Dec. 2–13, 1993	Col. Richard O. Covey, Cdr. Kenneth D. Bowersox, Lt. Col. Tom Akers,* Dr. Jeffrey A. Hoffman,** Dr. Story Musgrave,** Claude Nicollier, Dr. Kathryn C. Thornton* (*two space walks; **three space walks)	10 days, 19 hr., 59 min.	Repaired Hubble Space Telescope. Replaced gyroscopes, solar arrays, camera, electronics, and hardware. Installed COSTAR corrective optics to compensate for flaw in Hubble's primary mirror. Record five space walks in a single mission.
Mir-17 (Russia)	Jan. 8, 1994– Mar. 22, 1995	Dr. Valery Polyakov	439[1] days	Record single endurance flight in orbiting space station. Returned to earth with crewmates cosmonaut Helena Kondakova and commander Alexander Viktorenko, who spent 169 days each in *Mir*.
Discovery (U.S.)	Feb. 3–11, 1995	Cdr. James D. Wetherbee, Lt. Col. Eileen M. Collins, Dr. Janice Voss, Dr. Bernard A. Harris, Jr.,* Dr. C. Michael Foale,* Russian cosmonaut Co. Vladimir G. Titov *performed spacewalks.	8 days 6 hr., 29 min.	First rendezvous of U.S. spacecraft with a Russian space station *(Mir)*, Feb. 6. Lt. Col. Collins was first female shuttle pilot. Deployed and retrieved solar observatory satellite. Extra-vehicular activity to test new space suit modifications and practice space station assembly techniques. EVA time: 4 hr., 35 min.
Soyuz TM-21 (Russia)	March 14–22, 1995	Russian cosmonauts Lieut. Col. Vladimir N. Dezhurov and Gennady M. Strekalov, and U.S. astronaut Dr. Norman E. Thagard		Dr. Thagard became the first American astronaut to fly aboard a *Soyuz* spacecraft with a Russian crew launched from Baikonur Space Center in Kazakhstan. He also became the first American to enter the *Mir* space station on March 16.
Atlantis (U.S.)	June 27–July 7, 1995	Lt. Col. Charles J. Prescourt, Capt. Robert L. (Hoot) Gibson, Dr. Eileen S. Baker, Gregory J. Harbaugh, Dr. Bonnie Dunbar, Russian cosmonauts: *Mir-19* commander Anatoly Y. Solovyev, Nikolai M. Budarin	10 days	Marked 100th human mission in U.S. space program and first shuttle link-up with *Mir:* docked June 29, undocked July 4. Joined spacecraft held a record 10 people: 6 Americans and 4 Russians. Three *Mir* crew (*Mir-18* commander Lieut. Col. Vladimir N. Dezhurov, cosmonaut Grennady M. Strekalov, and U.S. astronaut Dr. Norman E. Thagard) returned to Earth aboard the *Atlantis.* Dr. Thagard set a U.S. space record of 112 days in space aboard *Mir.* Cosmonauts Solovyev and Budarin remained aboard *Mir.*
Atlantis (U.S.)	Nov. 12–20, 1995	Col. Kenneth D. Cameron, Lieut. Col. James D. Halsell, Jr., Col. Jerry L. Ross, Lieut. Col. William S. McArthur, Jr., Canadian Major Chris A. Hadfield, who operated the robot arm	8 days, 4 hr., 31 min.	Second docking with *Mir.* Carried 15-foot-long Russian-made docking module and attached it to *Mir.* Brought 2 new solar-powered panels for *Mir* and also supplies and scientific equipment. U.S. and Russian astronauts spent 3 days together on *Mir* conducting experiments.
Endeavour (U.S.)	Jan. 11–20, 1996	Col. Brian Duffy, Brent Jett, Dr. Leroy Chiao,** Capt. Winston E. Scott,* Dr. Daniel T. Berry,* and Japanese astronaut Koichi Wakata, who operated robot arm (*one spacewalk; **two spacewalks)	8 days, 22 hr., 01 min.	Deployed and retrieved NASA satellite, retrieved Japanese satellite. Two spacewalks performed to test spacesuit components and practice space station construction, tools, and techniques. Total EVA time: 13 hours.
Atlantis (U.S.)	March 22–31, 1996	Col. Kevin P. Chilton, Lieut. Col. Richard A. Searfoss, Dr. Ronald M. Sega, Dr. Linda M. Goodwin, Lieut. Col. Michael R. Clifford, Shannon W. Lucid	9 days, 5 hr., 15 min.	Third linkup with *Mir.* (March 22–27). Clifford and Goodwin conducted 6-hour spacewalk in shuttle cargo bay while docked with *Mir.* Lucid remained on board *Mir* for scheduled 140-day tour to conduct biomedical and material science experiments. Booster problems delayed her return until mid-September. Lucid is first American woman to live on *Mir.* On July 15, 1996, she broke the previous record for the longest U.S. manned space flight.
Endeavour (U.S.)	May 19–29, 1996	Col. John H. Casper, Lieut. Col. Curtis L. Brown, Jr., Cdr. Daniel W. Bursch, Mario Runco, Jr., Dr. Andrew S.W. Thomas, Canadian astronaut Dr. Marc Garneau	10 days, 0 hr., 40 min.	Made record of four satellite rendezvous, including three with small PAMS satellite to test the concept of a self-stabilizing satellite in orbit. Deployed and retrieved a Spartan satellite that carried an experimental inflatable antenna.

Designation and country	Date	Astronauts	Flight time (hr./min)	Remarks
Columbia (U.S.)	June 20–July 7, 1996	Col. Terence T. Henricks, Kevin R. Kregel, Lieut. Col. Susan J. Helms, Richard M. Linnehan, Cdr. Charles E. Brady, Jr., Dr. Jean-Jacques Favier (France), Dr. Robert Brent Thirsk (Canada)	16 days, 21 hr., 48 min.	Second-longest mission to date. Studied the effects of weightlessness on people, plants, and animals, and material manufacturing in near-zero gravity.
Atlantis (U.S.)	Sept. 16–26, 1996	William F. Readdy, Terrence W. Wilcutt, Thomas D. Akers, John E. Blaha, Jerome Apt, Carl E. Waltz. Download: Shannon W. Lucid	10 days, 3hr., 19 min.	Fourth *Mir* docking. Carried a Spacelab module. Transferred supplies and equipment to *Mir*. After breaking all American and women's space endurance records (188 days, 5 hr., 0 min), Lucid returned with *Atlantis* crew. John E. Blaha remained on *Mir* for a four-month stay.
Columbia (U.S.)	Nov. 19–Dec. 7, 1996	Kenneth D. Cockrell, Cdr. Kent V. Romingel, Tamara E. Jernigan, Thomas D. Jones, Dr. F. Story Musgrave	17 days, 15 hr., 53 min.	Deployed and recovered two free-flying satellites during mission: an ultraviolet telescope and Wake Shield (semiconductor processing) Facility. A jammed airlock hatch canceled two scheduled spacewalks. Is longest mission to date. Dr. Musgrave, 61, became first person to fly on all five space shuttles.
Atlantis (U.S.)	Jan. 12–22, 1997	Capt. Michael A. Baker, Cdr. Brent W. Jett, Jr., John M. Grunsfeld, Marsha S. Ivins, Peter J.K. Wiscoff, Dr. Jerry L. Linenger. Download: John E. Blaha	10 days, 04 hr., 6 min.	Fifth *Mir* docking (Jan.14–19). Carried Spacehab double module. Transferred supplies to *Mir*. Conducted experiments in Spacehab and *Mir*. John E. Blaha returned with *Atlantis* crew after 128 days in space, 118 aboard *Mir*. Jerry Linenger remained aboard *Mir* for 4.5-month stay.
Discovery (U.S.)	Feb. 11–21, 1997	Cdr. Kenneth Bowersox, Lt. Col. Scott J. Harowitz, Col. Mark C. Lee,* Steven A. Hawley, Gregory J. Harbaugh,* Steven L. Smith,* Joseph R. Tanner* (*spacewalks)	9 days, 2 3 hr., 38 min.	Second space telescope servicing mission. Installed new imaging spectrograph and infrared camera. Also patched torn telescope insulating cover. Deployed telescope at higher altitude: 335 x 321 nautical mile orbit. Mission required five spacewalks totaling 33 hr., 11 min.
Columbia (U.S.)	April 4–8, 1997	Lt. Col. James D. Halsell, Jr., Lt. Cdr. Susan L. Still, Janice E.Voss, Michael L. Gernhardt, Donald A. Thomas, Roger K. Crouch, Gregory T. Linteris	3 days, 23 hr., 13 min.	Planned 12-day mission to study behavior of metals, materials, and fluids in the absence of gravity and microgravity effects on fires. Was cut short due to a fuel-cell generator problem. Susan Still became second female shuttle pilot.
Atlantis (U.S.)	May 15–24,1997	Col. Charles J. Precourt, Lt. Col. Eileen M. Collins, Edward T. Lu, Maj. Carlos I. Noriega, Jean-Francois Clervoy (France), Elena V. Kondakova (Russia), C. Michael Foale. Download: Dr. Jerry M. Linenger	9 days, 5 hr., 20 min.	Sixth *Mir* docking (May 16–21). Carried a Spacehab double module. Transferred supplies and equipment. Jerry M. Linenger returned with *Atlantis* after 132 days in space. Michael Foale remained on *Mir* for a 4.5-month stay.
Columbia (U.S.)	July 1–17, 1997	Lt. Col. James D. Halsell, Jr., Lt. Cdr. Susan L. Still, Janice E.Voss, Donald A. Thomas, Michael L. Gernhard, Roger K. Crouch, Gregory T. Linteris	15 days, 16 hr., 45 min.	Successful reflight of the uncompleted Microgravity Science Mission (*Columbia*, April 4–8, 1997). Is first time the same crew flies together again to complete a previous mission.
Atlantis (U.S.)	Sept. 25–Oct. 6, 1997	James T. Wetherbee, Michael J. Boomfield, Col. Vladimir G Titov,* Scott E. Parazynski,* Jean-Loup J.M. Chretien (France), Wendy B. Lawrence. Up: Dr. David Wolf. Down: C. Michael Foale after 145 days in space, 134 days on *Mir* (*spacewalks)	10 days, 19 hr., 22 min.	7th Mir docking (Sept. 27–Oct. 3). 5 hr. spacewalks (Oct.1) retrieved U.S. experimental packages from *Mir* for return to Earth. Transferred supplies. Tested emergency jet packs for space station workers. Dr. David Wolf replaced Michael Foale on *Mir* for 4-month stay.
Columbia (U.S.)	Nov. 19–Dec. 5, 1997	Kevin R. Kregel, Maj. Steven W. Lindsey, Takao Doi* (Japan), Winston E. Scott,* Kalpana Chawla, Col. Leonid K. Kadenyuk* (Ukraine) (*spacewalks)	15 days, 6 hr., 35 min.	Deployed (Nov. 21) and retrieved (Nov. 24 spacewalk) malfunctioning Spartan solar-observation satellite. A second spacewalk (Dec. 3) tested space station assembly tools and techniques. Total EVA by Doi and Scott: 12 hr., 44 min.

Designation and country	Date	Astronauts	Flight time (hr./min)	Remarks
Endeavour (U.S.)	Jan. 22–31, 1998	Lt. Col. Terrence W. Wilcutt, Joe F. Edwards, Bonnie J. Dunbar, Maj. Michael P. Anderson, James F. Reilly, II, Salizhan S. Sharipov (Kirghizia), Andrew S.W. Thomas. Down: Dr. David Wolf	8 days, 19 hr., 48 min.	8th Mir docking (Jan. 24–29). Thomas replaced David Wolf after 128 days in orbit. Thomas is the seventh and last American to live aboard Mir.
Discovery (U.S.)	June 2–12, 1998	Col. Charles J. Precourt, Cmdr. Dominic L. Gorie, Cmdr. Wendy B. Lawrence, Franklin R. Chang-Diaz, Janet Kavandi, Valeriy Ruymin (Russia) Down: Andrew S.W. Thomas	9 days, 19 hr., 54 min.	Ninth and final Mir docking mission concluded the joint U.S.–Russian program as a precursor to the International Space Station partnership. Thomas returned to Earth after a 4.5-month stay.
Discovery (U.S.)	Oct. 29–Nov.7, 1998	Lt. Col. Curtis L. Brown, Maj. Steven W. Lindsey, Stephen K. Robinson, Dr. Scott E. Parazynski, Pedro Duque (Spain), Dr. Chiaki Mukai (Japan), Senator John H. Glenn, Jr	8 days, 21 hr., 56 min.	Deployed and retrieved Spartan solar observing satellite. Did research with Hubble Telescope Optical Systems Test Platform (HOST). Studied the effects of aging and microgravity in space.
Endeavour (U.S.)	Dec. 4–15, 1998	Capt. Robert D. Cabana, Capt. Frederick W. Sturckow, Lt. Col. Nancy Currie, Col. Jerry L. Ross, Jim H. Newman, Sergei K. Krikalev (Russia)	11 days, 19 hr., 18 min.	International Space Station assembly mission. Connected Node 1, "Unity," to Functional Cargo Block, "Zarya." Ross and Newman made three spacewalks, total EVA: 21 hr., 22 min.
Discovery (U.S.)	May 27–June 6, 1999	Cmdr. Ken V. Rominger, Rick D. Husband, Ellen Ochoa, Tamara E. Jernigan, Daniel T. Barry, Julie Payette (Canada), Valery Tokarev (Russia)	9 days, 19 hr., 13 min.	Docked 5 days, 18 hr. with uninhabited International Space Station. Readied it for arrival of first resident crew. Jernigan and Barry conducted space walks (7 hr., 55 min.) for assembly work.
Columbia (U.S.)	July 23–27, 1999	Lt. Col. Eileen M. Collins, Capt. Jeffrey S. Ashby, Steven A. Hawley, Lt. Col. Catherine G. Coleman, Col. Michel Tognini (France)	4 days, 22 hr., 50 min.	Deployed Chandra X-ray Observatory (formerly AXAF). Eileen Collins became the first female shuttle commander.
Endeavour (U.S.)	Tentatively no later than Oct. 7, 1999[2]	Kevin R. Kregel, Cmdr. Dominic L. Pudwill Gorie, Janet L. Kavandi, Janice Voss, Momoru Mohri (Japan), Gerhard P. J. Thiele (Germany)	Est. 11 days, 4 hr., 5 min.	Shuttle radar topography mission (SRTM). Will map Earth's surface with three-dimensional imaging radar.
Discovery (U.S.)	Tentatively late Oct. or Nov. 1999.[2]	Lt. Col. Curtis L. Brown, Jr., Lt. Cmdr. Scott J. Kelly, Steven L. Smith, C. Michael Foale, John M. Grunsfeld, Claude Nicollier (Switzerland), Jean-Francois Clervoy (France)	Est. 10 days, 21 hr., 38 min.	Third Hubble Space Telescope servicing mission.
Atlantis (U.S.)	Tentatively Dec. 2–13, 1999[2]	Col. James D. Halsell, Jr., Lt. Col. Scott J. Horowitz, Mary E. Webber, Edward Tsang Lu, Lt. Col Jeffrey N. Williams, Lt. Col. Yuri I. Malenchenko (Russia), Boris W. Morukov (Russia).	Est. 11 days	Third International Space Station flight. Spacehab double module.

1. From launch to landing. 2. Official dates are set approximately two weeks prior to the targeted liftoff date. For recorded launch information, call 407-867-4636. NOTES: EVA = Extravehicular Activity. The letters MR stand for Mercury (capsule) and Redstone (rocket); MA, for Mercury and Atlas (rocket); GT, for Gemini (capsule) and Titan-II (rocket). The first astronaut listed in the Gemini and Apollo flights is the command pilot. The Mercury capsules had names: MR-III was Freedom 7, MR-IV was Liberty Bell 7, MA-VI was Friendship 7, MA-VII was Aurora 7, MA-VIII was Sigma 7, and MA-IX was Faith 7. The figure 7 referred to the fact that the first group of U.S. astronauts numbered seven men. Only one Gemini capsule had a name: GT-III was called Molly Brown (after the Broadway musical The Unsinkable Molly Brown); thereafter the practice of naming the capsules was discontinued.

Around the World in Twenty Days

After two decades of failed attempts, a balloon sails into history with the help of technology and the weather

By NADYA LABI TIME

In the novel *Around the World in Eighty Days*, Phileas Fogg employed all manner of transport—steamers, railways, yachts, carriages, trading vessels, sledges, and even elephants. But no balloon. It was Hollywood, not Jules Verne, that sent the intrepid Brit off in that lighter-than-air craft. Fantasy piled upon fantasy, you say? Well, quixotic dreams became triumphant reality in March 1999. In a 180-ft.-high balloon, a silvery dare in the air, two adventurers—Swiss psychiatrist Bertrand Piccard, 41, and British balloon instructor Brian Jones, 51—completed their tour of the world in 20 days. The stakes were different (a purse of $1 million, courtesy of Anheuser-Busch, as opposed to £20,000 in Verne), but their intent was the same. They sought to prove a point—to themselves and the world.

Twenty Failures Since 1981

The *Breitling Orbiter 3* crossed the finish line (9.27° west longitude) over Mauritania on March 20, 1999. Piccard was ecstatic: "I am with the angels and just completely happy," he said over satellite relay. Jones, for his part, said calmly, "I am going to have a cup of tea, like any good Englishman." They had sailed into history. And they decided to sail on a little more. "We do not land. We go to Egypt," Piccard radioed air-traffic control in Senegal. "We are a balloon flying around the world." "I will be tearing their eyes out when I see them," their erstwhile rival Richard Branson, founder of Virgin Atlantic, told TIME. "But apart from that, I think a hug and a bottle of champagne will be appropriate."

Since 1981 there have been nearly 20 attempts to circumnavigate the globe in a balloon. Steve Fossett, a Chicago millionaire who attempted the feat five times, plunged into the Coral Sea after traveling 14,236 mi. in August 1998. And on Christmas Day he went down again near the coast of Hawaii, taking along his partners, Per Lindstrand of Sweden and Branson. The U.S. Coast Guard fished them out at a cost—to taxpayers—of about $130,000. Setting the elusive record was worth the trouble to Fossett. "I can't tell you how it ranks with the others, like climbing Mount Everest or making the first transatlantic airplane flight," said Fossett. "But it's one of the great explorations."

The Last Frontier

It's tough for pioneers to make a name for themselves these days. Both poles have been reached, the Atlantic has been crossed and recrossed, and the eagle has landed. So why not do it in a balloon? Well, what can you say about a pastime whose first

passengers were, in an experiment by the French Montgolfier brothers in 1783, a duck, a rooster, and a sheep? No wonder Piccard has a complex. "The way the public sees it is this," he explained before lift-off. "If we don't leave, we are idiots. If we do leave but don't succeed in our mission, we are incompetent. But if we do succeed, it's because it was easy and anyone could have done it."

But you see, the psychiatrist has a legacy to uphold: his grandfather Auguste was the first to reach the stratosphere in a balloon, and his father, Jacques, dove to the deepest point of the ocean in a bathyscaphe. "Bertrand believes it is his destiny to fly a balloon around the world," said his rival Andy Elson, as the *Orbiter 3* pushed the world record further and further.

Brian Jones was the Mr. Fix-It of the expedition. He was quietly overseeing the construction of the gondola for Cameron Balloons when he was nominated to be a reserve pilot in the *Breitling* attempt. "Of course, reserves in any activity assume they will always remain reserves," he says. But he found himself, as he puts it, "in the hot seat" when Piccard had a falling out with his first copilot, Tony Brown. "He's not an adventurer," says Joanna Jones of her husband. "He's a professional pilot who approaches things in a judged manner." Jones quickly fell into a comfortable rhythm with his copilot. Brian "made me a cup of tea while I was preparing his bed," said Piccard.

High-Tech Circumnavigation

As pioneering craft go, the *Breitling Orbiter 3* outclasses the *Niña,* the *Pinta,* and the *Santa Maria*—and the *Spirit of St. Louis,* for that matter. It is a high-tech combination of hot air and gas, equipped not only with simple necessities like a bunk, toilet, and desks but also with a fax machine and satellite telephones. The journey began on March 1, Piccard's birthday, in the snowcapped mountains of Château-d'Oex, Switzerland. Piccard and Jones cruised toward Italy at an altitude of 21,000 ft., crossed over the Mediterranean at night, and enjoyed a meal of emu. On a satellite phone, Jones chatted with his wife, who spent most of her time at mission control at Geneva's Cointrin Airport, which was manned around the clock by a meteorologist and an air-traffic controller. Piccard's wife, Michele, preferred to stay at home with their three daughters.

Propelled by Hot Air and Gas

The pilots headed toward Morocco, over Mauritania, and then turned northeast to catch a jet stream blowing toward India. In theory, balloons can't be steered, but pilots improvise by dropping up and down between different altitudes in search of the right wind pattern. Like surfers trying to catch a wave, balloonists try to ride jet streams, high-altitude currents that usually move from west to east. "It's magical what pilots can achieve," says balloonmaker Don Cameron. "In competitions with hot-air balloons, they'll set a target 10 mi. away and ask pilots to drop a marker on it, and the pilots will get within a meter of it." The *Orbiter 3* crew hit its target on the fourth day of the journey and sped along in a jet stream at 60 mph They ventured outside the cabin once, when the balloon descended to 10,000 ft., so that Piccard could chip away at ice that had formed on the cables and the capsule. There were few surprises, and the only irritant was a mysterious buzzing in the cabin. On Day 5, Piccard located—and dispatched—its source: a stowaway mosquito.

On March 7 Piccard and Jones heard of a misfortune—and it was good news for their quest. On that day their competitors, the British team of Andy Elson and Colin Prescot, ditched over the Pacific Ocean. After setting an endurance record of 17 days, 18 hrs., 25 min. aloft, the duo, in the *Cable & Wireless* balloon, was knocked out by what amounted to a one-two punch. First, peeved that Branson's December flight had infringed upon its airspace, China denied entry to his countrymen, forcing them to follow a more convoluted route. And then, while traveling over Thailand, Elson and Prescot were hit by a thunderstorm that shredded their balloon's envelope. They survived, after a harrowing dunking in the Pacific.

Riding the Jet Stream to Glory

Piccard and Jones had better luck with China. On March 10 the Beijing government allowed the Swiss-licensed *Breitling* access to its skies, so long as the craft stayed south of the 26th parallel. Nevertheless, morale on the *Orbiter 3* started to flag soon after, as Piccard and Jones flew over the endless expanse of the Pacific Ocean. Progress toward Hawaii was slow, and they lost contact with mission control for four days. "I realized that the worst desert wasn't made of sand but of water," Piccard said when communications were re-established. Then the balloon popped out of its jet stream over Mexico and drifted in the wrong direction. They were using up precious fuel without making much headway. Even worse, a heater faltered, and temperatures on board plummeted to 46°F. Both pilots were exhausted, and Piccard had to resort to self-hypnosis to calm himself. But the duo pulled it together in the homestretch. Catching a 100-mph jet stream over the Atlantic all but assured victory.

At its end, Verne's novel asks of Fogg: "What had he brought back from this long and weary journey? Nothing, say you?" The names Piccard and Jones may not strike the same chords as Columbus or Magellan or Lindbergh or Armstrong. Indeed, their achievement is literally lighter than air. But Piccard and Jones have won the last world-spanning contest of our era. And now they are history.   □

Famous Firsts in Aviation

1783 **First balloon flight.** Jacques and Joseph Montgolfier of Annonay, France, sent up a small smoke-filled balloon about mid-November.

First hydrogen-filled balloon flight. Jacques A. C. Charles, Paris physicist, supervised construction by A. J. and M. N. Robert of a 13-ft.-in-diameter balloon that was filled with hydrogen. It got up to about 3,000 ft. and traveled about 16 mi. in a 45-min. flight (Aug. 27).

First human balloon flights. A Frenchman, Jean Pilâtre de Rozier, made the first captive-balloon ascension (Oct. 15). With the Marquis d'Arlandes, Pilâtre de Rozier, made the first free flight, reaching a peak altitude of about 500 ft., and traveling about 5½ mi. in 20 min. (Nov. 21).

1784 **First powered balloon.** Gen. Jean Baptiste Marie Meusnier developed the first propeller-driven and elliptically shaped balloon—the crew cranking three propellers on a common shaft to give the craft a speed of about 3 mph.

First balloon flight by a woman. Mme. Thible, a French opera singer (June 4).

1793 **First balloon flight in America.** Jean Pierre Blanchard, a French pilot, made it from Philadelphia to near Woodbury, N.J., in just over 45 min. (Jan. 9).

1794 **First military use of the balloon.** Jean Marie Coutelle, using a balloon built for the French Army, made two 4-hr. observation ascents. The military purpose of the ascents seems to have been to damage the enemy's morale.

1797 **First parachute jump.** André-Jacques Garnerin dropped from about 6,500 ft. over Monceau Park in Paris in a 23-ft.-diameter parachute made of white canvas with a basket attached (Oct. 22).

1843 **First air transport company.** In London, William S. Henson and John Stringfellow filed articles of incorporation for the Aerial Transit Company (March 24). It failed.

1852 **First dirigible.** Henri Giffard, a French engineer, flew in a controllable (more or less) steam-engine powered balloon, 144 ft. long and 39 ft. in diameter, inflated with 88,000 cu. ft. of coal gas. It reached 6.7 mph on a flight from Paris to Trappe (Sept. 24).

1860 **First aerial photographers.** Samuel Archer King and William Black made two photos of Boston, which are still in existence.

1872 **First gas-engine-powered dirigible.** Paul Haenlein, a German engineer, flew in a semi-rigid-frame dirigible, powered by a 4-cylinder internal-combustion engine running on coal gas drawn from the supporting bag.

1873 **First transatlantic attempt.** *The New York Daily Graphic* sponsored the attempt with a 400,000 cu. ft. balloon carrying a lifeboat. A rip in the bag during inflation brought collapse of the balloon and the project.

1897 **First successful metal dirigible.** An all-metal dirigible, designed by David Schwarz, a Hungarian, took off from Berlin's Tempelhof Field and, powered by a 16-hp Daimler engine, got several miles before leaking gas caused it to crash (Nov. 13).

1900 **First Zeppelin flight.** Germany's Count Ferdinand von Zeppelin flew the first of his long series of rigid-frame airships. It attained a speed of 18 mph and got 3½ mi. before its steering gear failed (July 2).

1903 **First successful heavier-than-air machine flight.** Aviation was really born on the sand dunes at

Kitty Hawk, N.C., when Orville Wright crawled to his prone position between the wings of the biplane he and his brother Wilbur had built, opened the throttle of their home-made 12-hp engine, and took to the air. He covered 120 ft. in 12 sec. Later that day, in one of four flights, Wilbur stayed up 59 sec. and covered 852 ft. (Dec. 17).

1904 First airplane maneuvers. Orville Wright made the first turn with an airplane (Sept. 15); five days later his brother Wilbur made the first complete circle.

1905 First airplane flight over half an hour. Orville Wright kept his craft up 33 min., 17 sec. (Oct. 4).

1906 First European airplane flight. Alberto Santos-Dumont, a Brazilian, flew a heavier-than-air machine at Bagatelle Field, Paris (Sept. 13).

1908 First airplane fatality. Lt. Thomas E. Selfridge, U.S. Army Signal Corps, was in a group evaluating the Wright plane at Fort Myer, Va. He was up 75 ft. with Orville Wright when the propeller hit a bracing wire and was broken, throwing the plane out of control, killing Selfridge and seriously injuring Wright (Sept. 17).

1909 First cross-Channel flight. Louis Blériot flew in a 25-hp Blériot VI monoplane from Les Baraques near Calais, France, and landed near Dover Castle, England, in a 26.61-mi. (38-km) 37-min. flight across the English Channel (July 25).
First International Aviation Competition Meeting. American Glenn Curtis narrowly beat France's Louis Blériot in the main event and won the Gordon Bennett Cup. Meet held at Rheims, France (Aug. 22–28).

1910 First licensed woman pilot. Baroness Raymonde de la Roche of France, who learned to fly in 1909, received ticket No. 36 on March 8.
First flight from shipboard. Lt. Eugene Ely, USN, took a Curtiss plane off from the deck of the cruiser *Birmingham* at Hampton Roads, Va., and flew to Norfolk (Nov. 14). The following January he reversed the process, flying from Camp Selfridge to the deck of the armored cruiser *Pennsylvania* in San Francisco Bay (Jan. 18).
First aircraft to take off from water. Henri Fabrer in a Gnome-powered floatplane, at Martigues, France (March 28).

1911 First U.S. woman pilot. Harriet Quimby, a magazine writer, got ticket No. 37, making her her second licensed female pilot in the world.

1912 First woman's cross-Channel flight. Harriet Quimby flew from Dover, England, across the English Channel and landed at Hardelot, France, in a Blériot monoplane loaned to her by Louis Blériot (April 16). She was later killed in a flying accident over Dorchester Bay during a Harvard-Boston aviation meet on July 1, 1912.
First parachute jump from a powered airplane. Albert Berry jumped in a test over Jefferson Barracks military post, St. Louis (March 1). Some sources credit Grant Morton as making first jump in 1911.

1913 First multi-engined aircraft. Built and flown by Igor Ivan Sikorsky while still in his native Russia.

1914 First aerial combat. In Aug., Allied and German pilots and observers started shooting at each other with pistols and rifles—with negligible results.

1915 First air raids on England. German Zeppelins started dropping bombs on four English communities (Jan. 19).

1918 First U.S. air squadron. The U.S. Army Air Corps made its first independent raids over enemy lines, in DH-4 planes (British-designed) powered with 400-hp American-designed Liberty engines (April 8).

First regular airmail service. Operated for the Post Office Department by the Army, the first regular service was inaugurated with one roundtrip a day (except Sunday) between Washington, D.C., and New York City (May 15).

1919 First transatlantic flight. The NC-4, one of four Curtiss flying boats commanded by Lt. Comdr. Albert C. Read, reached Lisbon, Portugal (May 27), after hops from Trepassy Bay, Newfoundland, to Horta, Azores (May 16–17), to Ponta Delgada (May 20). The Liberty-powered craft was piloted by Walter Hinton.

First nonstop transatlantic flight. Capt. John Alcock and Lt. Arthur Whitten Brown, British World War I flyers, made the 1,900 mi. trip from St. John's, Newfoundland, to Clifden, Ireland, in 16 hr., 12 min. in a Vickers-Vimy bomber with two 350-hp Rolls-Royce engines (June 15–16).

First lighter-than-air transatlantic flight. The British dirigible R-34, commanded by Maj. George H. Scott, left Firth of Forth, Scotland (July 2), and touched down at Mineola, L.I., 108 hr. later. The eastbound trip was made in 75 hr. (completed July 13).

First scheduled London-Paris passenger service (using airplanes). Aircraft Travel and Transport inaugurated London-Paris service (Aug. 25). Later the company started the first trans-Channel mail service on the same route (Nov. 10).

First free-fall parachute jump. Leslie Irvin jumped over McCook Field, Dayton, Ohio, to prove that one won't lose consciousness during a delayed free-fall using a manually operated parachute (April 28).

1921 First U.S. black female pilot. Bessie Coleman received license June 15. Was killed April 30, 1926, in flying accident.

First naval vessel sunk by aircraft. Two battleships being scrapped by treaty were sunk by bombs dropped from Army planes in demonstration put on by Brig. Gen. William S. Mitchell (July 21).

First helium balloon. The C-7, non-rigid Navy dirigible was first to use non-inflammable helium as lifting gas, making a flight from Hampton Roads, Va., to Washington, D.C. (Dec. 1).

1922 First member of Caterpillar Club. Lt. (later Maj. Gen.) Harold Harris bailed out of a crippled plane he was testing at McCook Field, Dayton, Ohio (Oct. 20), and became the first man to join the Caterpillar Club—those whose lives have been saved by parachutes.

1923 First nonstop transcontinental flight. Lts. John A. Macready and Oakley Kelly flew a single-engine Fokker T-2 nonstop from New York to San Diego, a distance of just over 2,500 mi. in 26 hr., 50 min. (May 2–3).

First autogyro flight. Juan de la Cierva, a brilliant Spanish mathematician, made the first successful flight in a rotary wing aircraft in Madrid (June 9).

1924 First round-the-world flight. Four Douglas Cruiser biplanes of the U.S. Army Air Corps took off from Seattle under command of Maj. Frederick Martin (April 6). 175 days later, two of the planes (Lt. Lowell Smith's and Lt. Erik Nelson's) landed in Seattle after a circuitous route—one source saying 26,345 mi., another saying 27,553 mi.

1926 First polar flight. Then–Lt. Cmdr. Richard E. Byrd, acting as navigator, and Floyd Bennett as pilot, flew a trimotor Fokker from Kings Bay, Spitsbergen, over the North Pole and back in 15½ hr. (May 8–9).

1927 First solo nonstop transatlantic flight. Charles Augustus Lindbergh lifted his Wright-powered Ryan monoplane, *Spirit of St. Louis*, from Roosevelt Field, N.Y., to stay aloft 33 hr. 39 min and travel 3,600 mi. to Le Bourget Field outside Paris (May 20–21). Although 91 persons in 13 separate flights crossed the Atlantic before him, he flew directly between two great world cities and did it alone.

First transatlantic passenger. Charles A. Levine was piloted by Clarence D. Chamberlin from Roosevelt Field, N.Y., to Eisleben, Germany, in a Wright-powered Bellanca (June 4–5).

1928 First east-west transatlantic crossing. Baron Guenther von Huenefeld, piloted by German Capt. Hermann Koehl and Irish Capt. James Fitzmaurice, left Dublin for New York City (April 12) in a single-engine all-metal Junkers-monoplane. Some 37 hr. later, they crashed on Greely Island, Labrador. Rescued.

First U.S.–Australia flight. Sir Charles Kingsford-Smith and Capt. Charles T. P. Ulm, Australians, and two American navigators, Harry W. Lyon and James Warner, crossed the Pacific from Oakland to Brisbane. They went via Hawaii and the Fiji Islands in a trimotor Fokker (May 31–June 8).

First transarctic flight. Sir Hubert Wilkins, an Australian explorer, and Carl Ben Eielson, who served as pilot, flew from Point Barrow, Alaska, to Spitsbergen (mid-April).

1929 First of the endurance records. With Air Corps Maj. Carl Spaatz in command and Capt. Ira Eaker as chief pilot, an Army Fokker, aided by refueling in the air, remained aloft 150 hr. 40 min. at Los Angeles (Jan. 1–7).

First round-the-world airship flight. The LZ-127, known as the *Graf Zeppelin*, flew 21,300 mi. in 20 days and 4 hr. Also set distance record (Aug.).

First blind flight. James H. Doolittle proved the feasibility of instrument-guided flying when he took off and landed entirely on instruments (Sept. 24).

First rocket-engine flight. Fritz von Opel, a German auto maker, stayed aloft in his small rocket-powered craft for 75 sec., covering nearly 2 mi. (Sept. 30).

First South Pole flight. Comdr. Richard E. Byrd, with Bernt Balchen as pilot, Harold I. June, radio operator, and Capt. A. C. McKinley, photographer, flew a trimotor Fokker from the Bay of Whales, Little America, over the South Pole and back (Nov. 28–29).

1930 First Paris–New York nonstop flight. Dieudonné Coste and Maurice Bellonte, French pilots, flew a Hispano-powered Breguet biplane from Le Bourget Field to Valley Stream, L.I., in 37 hr., 18 min. (Sept. 2–3).

1931 First flight into the stratosphere. Auguste Piccard, a Swiss physicist, and Charles Knipfer ascended in a balloon from Augsburg, Germany, and reached a height of 51,793 ft. in a 17-hr. flight that terminated on a glacier near Innsbruck, Austria (May 27).

First nonstop transpacific flight. Hugh Herndon and Clyde Pangborn took off from Sabishiro Beach, Japan, dropped their landing gear, and flew 4,860 mi. to near Wenatchee, Wash., in 41 hr. 13 min. (Oct. 4–5).

1932 First woman's transatlantic solo. Amelia Earhart, flying a Pratt & Whitney Wasp-powered Lockheed Vega, flew alone from Harbor Grace, Newfoundland, to Ireland in approximately 15 hr. (May 20–21).

First westbound transatlantic solo. James A. Mollison, a British pilot, took a de Havilland Puss Moth from Portmarnock, Ireland, to Pennfield, New Brunswick (Aug. 18).

First woman airline pilot. Ruth Rowland Nichols, first woman to hold three international records at the same time—speed, distance, and altitude—was employed by N.Y.–New England Airways.

1933 First round-the-world solo. Wiley Post took a Lockheed Vega, *Winnie Mae*, 15,596 mi. around the world in 7 days, 18 hr., 49½ min. (July 15–22).

1937 First successful helicopter flight. Hanna Reitsch, a German pilot, flew Dr. Heinrich Focke's FW-61 in free, fully controlled flight at Bremen (July 4). Ms. Reitsch was also the first woman civil and military aviation test pilot.

1939 First turbojet flight. Just before their invasion of Poland, the Germans flew a Heinkel He-178 plane powered by a Heinkel S3B turbojet (Aug. 27).

1940 First wartime use of military gliders. German commandos made a successful glider assault on Belgium's Fort Eben-Emael during WWII (May 10).

1941–1945 Most combat missions flown by a pilot in any war. Captain Hans-Ulrich Rudel of Germany flew 2,530 combat missions during WWII while flying a JU-87 Stuka dive bomber. He survived the war.

1942–1945 Top-scoring fighter pilot of any war. German Luftwaffe ace Maj. Erich Hartmann scored 352 victories all while flying a Messerschmitt BF 109 during WWII. He was involved in 800 dogfights, and flew 1,425 missions. Maj. Hartmann survived the war.

World's 25 Busiest Airports by Passengers and Cargo, 1998

ACI 1998 Worldwide Airport Traffic Statistics

Airport	Total passengers	1997–1998 % change	Airport	Total cargo	1997–1998 % change
1. Atlanta, Hartsfield (ATL)	73,474,298	7.7 %	Memphis (MEM)	2,368,975	6.1%
2. Chicago, O'Hare (ORD)	72,485,228	3.0	Los Angeles (LAX)	1,861,050	–0.7
3. Los Angeles (LAX)	61,215,712	1.8	Miami (MIA)	1,793,009	1.5
4. London, Heathrow (LHR)	60,659,593	4.3	Hong Kong (HKG)	1,654,356	–8.8
5. Dallas/Ft. Worth (DFW)	60,482,700	n.a.	Tokyo, Narita (NRT)	1,637,521	–5.8
6. Tokyo, Haneda (HND)	51,240,704	3.9	New York (JFK)	1,604,422	–3.7
7. Frankfurt-Main (FRA)	42,716,270	6.1	Frankfurt-Main (FRA)	1,464,955	–3.3
8. San Francisco (SFO)	40,060,326	–1.1	Chicago, O'Hare (ORD)	1,441,829	2.5
9. Paris, Charles de Gaulle (CDG)	38,628,926	9.5	Seoul (SEL)	1,425,009	–9.1
10. Denver (DEN)	36,831,400	5.3	Louisville (SDF)	1,394,999	3.7
11. Amsterdam, Schiphol (AMS)	34,420,143	9.0	Singapore (SIN)	1,305,592	–3.9
12. Miami (MIA)	33,935,491	–1.7	London, Heathrow (LHR)	1,301,251	3.3
13. Newark (EWR)	32,512,106	5.2	Anchorage (ANC)	1,289,266	2.3
14. Phoenix, Sky Harbor (PHX)	31,769,113	3.6	Amsterdam, Schiphol (AMS)	1,218,746	0.9
15. Detroit (DTW)	31,544,426	n.a.	Newark (EWR)	1,094,383	4.5
16. New York (JFK)	31,436,478	–2.8	Paris, Charles de Gaulle (CDG)	1,067,255	–0.5
17. Houston (IAH)	31,026,369	8.1	Taipei (TPE)	916,881	0.4
18. Minneapolis/St. Paul (MSP)	30,347,920	0.5	Atlanta, Hartsfield (ATL)	907,208	4.9
19. Las Vegas (LAS)	30,227,287	–0.3	Datyon (DAY)	893,239	9.8
20. Seoul (SEL)	29,429,044	–19.9	Indianapolis (IND)	812,664	22.6
21. London, Gatwick (LGW)	29,173,196	8.2	Dallas/Ft. Worth (DFW)	801,968	–1.1
22. St. Louis (STL)	28,700,622	3.7	San Francisco (SFO)	771,931	–1.0
23. Hong Kong (HKG)	27,919,935	–3.7	Osaka (KIX)	766,607	2.9
24. Orlando (MCO)	27,748,571	1.6	Bangkok (BKK)	719,255	–6.7
25. Toronto (YYZ)	26,744,530	2.5	Oakland (OAK)	698,771	3.1

NOTE: Total passengers enplaned and deplaned, passengers in transit counted once. Cargo loaded and unloaded freight and mail (in metric tons). *Source:* Airport Council International, Geneva, Switzerland.

1942 First and only enemy bombing of U.S. mainland. During WWII, a floatplane launched from a Japanese submarine off Cape Blanco, Oregon, dropped incendiary bombs on the Oregon forest in two attempts to start forest fires and terrorize American civilians, but the bombs did little damage (Sept. 9 and 29).

First American jet plane flight. Robert Stanley, chief pilot for Bell Aircraft Corp., flew the Bell XP-59 *Airacomet* at Muroc Army Base, Calif. (Oct. 1).

First woman fighter pilot to shoot down an enemy aircraft. Soviet Lieutenant Lilya Litvyak, flying a Yak-1 fighter of the women's 586th Fighter Aviation Regiment, shot down two German planes over Stalingrad on Sept. 13, 1942.

1944 First production stage rocket-engine fighter plane. The German Messerschmitt Me 163B *Komet* (test flown 1941) became operational in June 1944. Some 350 of these delta-wing fighters were built before WWII in Europe ended.

1947 First piloted supersonic flight in an airplane. Capt. Charles E. Yeager, U.S. Air Force, flew the X-1 rocket-powered research plane built by Bell Aircraft Corp., faster than the speed of sound at Muroc Air Force Base, California (Oct. 14).

1949 First round-the-world nonstop flight. Capt. James Gallagher and USAF crew of 13 flew a Boeing B-50A Superfortress around the world nonstop from Ft. Worth, returning to same point: 23,452 mi. in 94 hr., 1 min., with four aerial refuelings enroute (Feb. 27–March 2).

1950 First nonstop transatlantic jet flight. Col. David C. Schilling (USAF) flew 3,300 mi. from England to Limestone, Maine, in 10 hr., 1 min. (Sept. 22).

1951 First solo across North Pole. Charles F. Blair, Jr., flew a converted P-51 (May 29).

1952 First jetliner service. The De Havilland Comet flight was inaugurated by BOAC between London and Johannesburg, South Africa (May 2). Flight, including stops, took 23 hr., 38 min.

First transatlantic helicopter flight. Capt. Vincent H. McGovern and 1st Lt. Harold W. Moore piloted two Sikorsky H-19s from Westover, Mass., to Prestwick, Scotland (3,410 mi.). Trip was made in five steps, with a flying time of 42 hr., 25 min. (July 15–31).

First transatlantic roundtrip in same day. A British Canberra twin-jet bomber flew from Aldergrove, Northern Ireland, to Gander, Newfoundland, and back in 7 hr., 59 min. flying time (Aug. 26).

1955 First transcontinental roundtrip in same day. Lt. John M. Conroy piloted an F-86 Sabrejet across U.S. (Los Angeles–New York) and back—5,085 mi.—in 11 hr., 33 min., 27 sec. (May 21).

1957 First round-the-world nonstop jet plane flight. Maj. Gen. Archie J. Old, Jr., USAF, led a flight of three Boeing B-52 bombers, powered with eight 10,000-lb.-thrust Pratt & Whitney Aircraft J57 engines around the world in 45 hr., 19 min; distance 24,325 mi.; average speed 525 mph (completed Jan. 18).

1958 First transatlantic jet passenger service. BOAC, New York to London (Oct. 4). Pan American started daily service, New York to Paris (Oct. 26).

First domestic jet passenger service. National Airlines inaugurated service between New York and Miami (Dec. 10).

1968 Prototype of world's first supersonic airliner. The Soviet-designed Tupolev Tu-144 made its first flight, Dec. 31. It first achieved supersonic speed on June 5, 1969.

Active Pilot Certificates Held

Year	Total	Airline transport	Commercial	Private
1970	720,028	31,442	176,585	299,491
1980	814,667	63,652	182,097	343,276
1985	722,376	79,192	155,929	320,086
1990	702,659	107,732	149,666	299,111
1995	639,184	123,877	133,980	261,399
1996	622,261	127,486	129,187	254,002
1997	616,342	130,858	125,300	247,604
1998	618,298	134,612	122,053	247,226

NOTE: Includes other pilot categories—student, 97,738; helicopter, 6,964; glider, 9,402; and recreational, 305. Also nonpilot, i.e., mechanic, parachute rigger, etc. (nonpilot total, 618,298). Data as of Dec. 31, 1998. *Source:* Department of Transportation, Federal Aviation Administration.

1973 First female pilot of a major U.S. scheduled airline. Emily H. Warner became employed by Frontier Airlines on Jan. 29 as second officer on a Boeing 737.

1976 First regularly scheduled commercial supersonic transport (SST) flights begin. Air France and British Airways inaugurated service (Jan. 21). Air France flew the Paris–Rio de Janeiro route; B.A., the London–Bahrain. Both airlines began SST service to Washington, D.C. (May 24).

1977 First successful human-powered aircraft. Paul MacCready, an aeronautical engineer from Pasadena, Calif., was awarded the Kremer Prize for creating the world's first successful human-powered aircraft. The *Gossamer Condor* was flown by Bryan Allen over the required 3-mi. course on Aug. 23.

1978 First successful transatlantic balloon flight. Three Albuquerque, N.M., men, Ben Abruzzo, Larry Newman, and Maxie Anderson, completed the crossing (Aug. 16.; landed, Aug. 17) in their helium-filled balloon, *Double Eagle II.*

1979 First man-powered aircraft to fly across the English Channel. The Kremer Prize for the Channel crossing was won by Bryan Allen who flew the *Gossamer Albatross* from Folkestone, England, to Cap Gris-Nez, France, in 2 hr., 55 min. (June 12).

1980 First successful balloon flight over the North Pole. Sidney Conn and his wife, Eleanor, in hot-air balloon *Joy of Sound* (April 11).

First nonstop transcontinental balloon flight, and also record for longest overland voyage in a balloon. Maxie Anderson and his son, Kris, completed four-day flight from Fort Baker, Calif., to successful landing outside Matane, Quebec, on May 12 in their helium-filled balloon, *Kitty Hawk.*

First long-distance solar-powered flight. Janice Brown, a 98-lb. former teacher, flew a tiny experimental solar-powered aircraft, *Solar Challenger*, six mi. in 22 min. near Marana, Ariz. (Dec. 3). The craft was powered by a 2.75-hp engine.

First solar-powered aircraft to fly across the English Channel. Stephen R. Ptacek flew the 210-lb. *Solar Challenger* at an average speed of 30 mph from Cormeilles-en-Vexin near Paris to the Royal Manston Air Force Base on England's southeastern coast in 5 hr., 30 min. (July 7).

1984 First solo transatlantic balloon flight. Joe W. Kittinger landed Sept. 18 near Savona, Italy, in his helium-filled balloon *Rosie O'Grady's Balloon of Peace* after a flight of 3,535 mi. from Caribou, Me.

1986 First nonstop flight around the world without refueling. From Edwards AFB, Calif., Dick Rutan and Jeana Yeager flew in *Voyager* around the world (24,986.727 mi.), returning to Edwards in 216 hr., 3 min., 44 sec. (Dec. 14–23).

1987 First transatlantic hot-air balloon flight. Richard Branson and Per Lindstrand flew 2,789.6 mi. from Sugarloaf Mt., Maine, to Ireland in the hot-air balloon *Virgin Atlantic Flyer* (July 2–4).

1991 First transpacific hot-air balloon flight. Richard Branson and Per Lindstrand flew about 6,700 mi. from Miyakonyo, Japan, to 150 mi. west of Yellowknife, Northwest Territories, Canada (Jan. 15–17).

1993 First woman to co-pilot a commercial supersonic plane. Barbara Harmer, British Airways, flew as first officer on the Concorde from London to New York City (March 25).

1995 First solo transpacific balloon flight. Steve Fossett made a flight of more than 5,430 mi. from Seoul, South Korea, to Leader, Saskatchewan, Canada, in a helium-filled balloon. Also set record for distance (Feb. 18–21, 1995).

1999 First nonstop, non-refueled around-the-world balloon flight. Brian Jones (UK) and Bertrand Piccard (Switzerland), *Breitling Orbiter 3*, Château d'Oex, Switzerland, to 9.27° west longitude over Mauritania, North Africa, March 1–20, 1999 (19 days 21 hr., 49 min.).

World-Class Helicopter Records

Selected records. *Source:* National Aeronautic Association.

Great Circle Distance without Landing
International: 2,213.04 mi.; 3,561.55 km.
Robert G. Ferry (U.S.) in Hughes YOH-6A helicopter powered by Allison T-63-A-5 engine; from Culver City, Calif., to Ormond Beach, Fla., April 6–7, 1966.

Distance, Closed Circuit
International: 1,739.96 mi.; 2,800.20 km.
Jack Schweibold (U.S.) in Hughes YOH-6A helicopter powered by Allison T-62-A-5 engine; Edwards Air Force Base, Calif., March 26, 1966.

Altitude without Payload
International: 40,820 ft.; 12,442 m.
Jean Boulet (France) in Alouette SA 315-001 *Lama* powered by Artouste IIIB 735 KW engine; Istres, France, June 21, 1972.

Speed around the World, Eastbound
40.99 mph; 65.97 kph.
Joe Ronald Bower (U.S.) pilot, in Bell JetRanger III, powered by one Allison 250-C20J (317 shp), covered 23,800 mi. in 24 days, 4 hr., 36 min. June 28–July 22, 1994.

Speed around the World, Westbound
57.01 mph; 91.75 kph.
Joe Ronald Bower (U.S.) pilot, John W. Williams (U.S.), co-pilot in Bell 430 powered by 2 Allison 250–C40, (811 shp), Aug. 17–Sept. 3, 1996.

Absolute World Records, Balloons

Selected records. *Source:* National Aeronautic Association.

Altitude
113,739.9 ft.; 34,668 m.
Cmdr. M.D. Ross (U.S.) and Lt. Cmdr. V.A. Prather, *Lee Lewis Memorial*, Gulf of Mexico, May 4, 1961.

Distance
29,056 mi.; 46,759 km.
Bertrand Piccard (Switzerland) and Brian Jones (UK), *Breitling Orbiter 3*, Château d'Oex, Switzerland, to near town of Mut, southern Egypt, March 1–21, 1999.

Duration
19 days, 21 hr., 55 min.
Bertrand Piccard (Switzerland) and Brian Jones (UK), *Breitling Orbiter 3*, Château d'Oex, Switzerland, to near town of Mut, southern Egypt, March 1–21, 1999.

First nonstop non-refueled around-the-world flight
19 days, 1 hr., 49 min.
Bertrand Piccard (Switzerland) and Brian Jones (UK), *Breitling Orbiter 3*, Château d'Oex, Switzerland, to long. 9.27° west over Maurtania, North Africa, March 1–20, 1999.

Absolute World Records

(maximum performance in any class)

Source: National Aeronautic Association

Speed around the World, Nonstop, Nonrefueled

Speed (mph)	Date	Plane	Pilots	Place
115.65	Dec. 14–23, 1986	*Voyager*	Dick Rutan & Jeana Yeager (U.S.)	Edwards AFB, Calif.—Edwards AFB, Calif.

Distance, Great Circle without Landing, also Distance, Closed Circuit without Landing

Distance (mi.)	Date	Plane	Pilots	Place
24,986.727	Dec. 14–23, 1986	*Voyager*	Dick Rutan & Jeana Yeager (U.S.)	Edwards AFB, Calif.—Edwards AFB, Calif.

Speed over a Straight Course

Speed (mph)	Date	Plane type	Pilot	Place
2,193.16	July 28, 1976	Lockheed SR-71A	Capt. Eldon W. Joersz (USAF)	Beale AFB, Calif.

Speed over a Closed Circuit

Speed (mph)	Date	Plane type	Pilot	Place
2,092.294	July 27, 1976	Lockheed SR-71A	Maj. Adolphus H. Bledsoe, Jr. (USAF)	Beale AFB, Calif.

Altitude

Height (ft.)	Date	Plane type	Pilot	Place
123,523.58	Aug. 31, 1977	MIG-25, E-266M	Alexander Fedotov (U.S.S.R.)	U.S.S.R.

Altitude in Horizontal Flight

Height (ft.)	Date	Pilot	Place
85,068.997	July 28, 1976	Capt. Robert C. Helt (USAF)	Beale AFB, Calif.

Altitude, Aircraft Launched from a Carrier Airplane

Height (ft.)	Date	Plane type	Pilot	Place
314,750.00	July 17, 1962	N. American X-15-1	Maj. Robert White (USAF)	Edwards AFB, Calif.

Recreating the Wright Stuff

A full-scale replica of the historic 1903 Wright Flyer was constructed and delivered to NASA's Ames Research Center at Moffett Field, Calif., for wind-tunnel testing during the spring of 1999. During the tests, engineers studied the biplane's stability, control, and handling at speeds up to 27 knots (30 mph) in the wind tunnel. The data obtained will be used to build a second Wright Flyer, yet to be constructed, which will be flown at Kitty Hawk, N.C., on Dec. 17, 2003, on the 100th anniversary of the first flight. During the recreation of the world's first powered flight, the pilot will fly the replica low and travel at only 30 mph, the same speed flown by the Wright brothers, and control it while lying on his stomach just as Orville did a century before.

Constructed by a team of volunteers from the Los Angeles section of the American Institute of Aeronautics and Astronautics (AIAA), using plans provided by the Smithsonian, the replica features a 40-foot, 4-inch wingspan reinforced with piano wire, cotton wing coverings, spruce propellers, and a double rudder. The second Flyer, with some modi-

fications for safety, will also be built by the team of volunteers from the AIAA.

Although others had created "flying machines" before them that could barely lift off the ground and were incapable of true flight, the Wright brothers painstakingly worked four years to construct the first power-driven, human-carrying craft that was heavier than air and capable of controlled, sustained flight. After many trials and setbacks, the former bicycle mechanics from Dayton, Ohio, flew into history in their double-winged craft on Dec. 17, 1903, with Orville at the controls and Wilbur running alongside him. The era of the air age began, and the world was never the same. Their invention would create a new industry and revolutionize transportation, commerce, and communication throughout the globe.

In December 1998, President Clinton signed into law the Centennial of Flight Commemoration Act, which established a commission to coordinate the celebration in 2003 of the 100th anniversary of the Wright Brothers' first flight.

The Seven Wonders of the World

Since ancient times, people have put together many "seven wonders" lists; examples include the Seven Wonders of the Natural World, the Seven Wonders of the Modern World, and the Seven Natural Wonders of the U.S. The content of these lists tends to vary, and none is definitive. The original list of seven wonders is the Seven Wonders of the Ancient World, which is made up of a selection of ancient architectural and sculptural accomplishments. The seven wonders that are most widely agreed upon as being in the original list are outlined below. (* indicates photo can be found in the Headline History section.)

The Pyramids of Egypt. * A group of three pyramids, *Khufu, Khafra,* and *Menkaura* at Giza, outside modern Cairo, is often called the first wonder of the world. The largest pyramid, built by Khufu (Cheops), a king of the fourth dynasty, had an original estimated height of 482 ft. (now approximately 450 ft.). The base has sides 755 ft. long. It contains 2,300,000 blocks; the average weight of each is 2.5 tons. Estimated date of completion is 2680 B.C.E. Of all the Ancient Wonders, the pyramids alone survive.

Hanging Gardens of Babylon. Often listed as the second wonder, these gardens were supposedly built by Nebuchadnezzar around 600 B.C.E. to please his queen, Amuhia. They are also associated with the mythical Assyrian queen, Semiramis. Archeologists surmise that the gardens were laid out atop a vaulted building, with provisions for raising water. The terraces were said to rise from 75 to 300 ft.

The Walls of Babylon, also built by Nebuchadnezzar, are sometimes referred to as the second (or the seventh) wonder instead of the Hanging Gardens.

Statue of Zeus (Jupiter) at Olympia. The work of Phidias (5th century B.C.E.), this colossal figure in gold and ivory was reputedly 40 ft. high. All trace of it is lost, except for reproductions on coins.

Temple of Artemis (Diana) at Ephesus. A beautiful structure, begun about 350 B.C.E., in honor of a non-Hellenic goddess who later became identified with the Greek goddess of the same name. The temple, with Ionic columns 60 ft. high, was destroyed by invading Goths in C.E. 262.

Mausoleum at Halicarnassus. This famous monument was erected by Queen Artemisia in memory of her husband, King Mausolus of Caria in Asia Minor, who died in 353 B.C.E. Some remains of the structure are in the British Museum. This shrine is the source of the modern word "mausoleum."

Colossus at Rhodes. This bronze statue of Helios (Apollo), about 105 ft. high, was the work of the sculptor Chares, who reputedly labored for 12 years before completing it in 280 B.C.E. It was destroyed during an earthquake in 224 B.C.E.

Pharos of Alexandria. The seventh wonder was the Pharos (lighthouse) of Alexandria, built by Sostratus of Cnidus during the 3rd century B.C.E. on the island of Pharos off the coast of Egypt. It was destroyed by an earthquake in the 13th century.

Famous Structures

Ancient

The *Great Sphinx of Egypt,* one of the wonders of ancient Egyptian architecture, adjoins the pyramids of Giza and has a length of 240 ft. Built in the 4th dynasty, it is approximately 4,500 years old. A 10-year, $2.5 million restoration project was completed in 1998. Other Egyptian buildings of note include the *Temples of Karnak, Edfu,* and the *Tombs at Beni Hassan.*

The *Parthenon of Greece,** built on the Acropolis in Athens, was the chief temple to the goddess Athena. It was believed to have been completed by 438 B.C.E. The present temple remained intact until the 5th century C.E. Today, though the Parthenon is in ruins, its majestic proportions are still discernible.

Other great structures of ancient Greece were the *Temples at Paestum* (about 540 and 420 B.C.E.); the *Temple of Poseidon* (about 460 B.C.E.); the *Temple of Apollo* at Corinth (about 540 B.C.E.); the *Temple of Apollo* at Bassae (about 450–420 B.C.E.); the famous *Erechtheum* atop the Acropolis (about 421–405 B.C.E.); the *Temple of Athena Niké* at Athens (about 426 B.C.E.); the *Olympieum* at Athens (174 B.C.E.–C.E. 131); the *Athenian Treasury* at Delphi (about 515 B.C.E.); the *Propylaea* of the Acropolis at Athens (437–432 B.C.E.); the *Theater of Dionysus* at Athens (about 350–325 B.C.E.); the *House of Cleopatra* at Delos (138 B.C.E.); and the *Theater* at Epidaurus (about 325 B.C.E.).

The *Colosseum (Flavian Amphitheater) of Rome,* the largest and most famous of the Roman amphitheaters, was opened for use C.E. 80. Elliptical in shape, it consisted of three stories and an upper gallery, rebuilt in stone in its present form in the third century C.E. Its seats rise in tiers, which in turn are buttressed by concrete vaults and stone piers. It could seat between 40,000 and 50,000 spectators. It was principally used for gladiatorial combat.

The *Pantheon* at Rome, begun by Agrippa in 27 B.C.E. as a temple, was rebuilt in its present circular form by Hadrian (C.E. 118–128). Literally the Pantheon was intended as a temple of "all the gods." It is remarkable for its perfect preservation today, and it has served continuously for 20 centuries as a place of worship.

Famous Roman arches include the *Arch of Constantine* (about C.E. 315) and the *Arch of Titus* (about C.E. 80).

Later European

St. Mark's Cathedral in Venice (1063–1071), one of the great examples of Byzantine architecture, was begun in the 9th century. Partly destroyed by fire in 976, it was later rebuilt as a Byzantine edifice.

Other famous examples of Byzantine architecture are St. Sophia in Istanbul (532–537); San Vitale in Ravenna (542); St. Paul's Outside the Walls, Rome (5th century); Assumption Cathedral in the Kremlin, Moscow (begun in 1475); and St. Lorenzo Outside the Walls, Rome, begun in 588.

The Cathedral Group at Pisa (1067–1173), one of the most celebrated groups of structures built in Romanesque-style, consists of the cathedral, the cathedral's baptistery, and the Leaning Tower.* This trio forms a group by itself in the northwest corner of the city. The cathedral and baptistery are built in varicolored marble. The campanile (Leaning Tower) is 179 ft. high and leans more than 16 ft. out of the perpendicular. There is little reason to believe that the architects intended to have the tower lean.

Other examples of Romanesque architecture include the Vézelay Abbey in France (1130); the Church of Notre-Dame-du-Port at Clermont-Ferrand in France (1100); the Church of San Zeno (begun in 1138) at Verona; and Durham Cathedral in England.

The Alhambra (1248–1354), located in Granada, Spain, is universally esteemed as one of the greatest masterpieces of Muslim architecture. Designed as a palace and fortress for the Moorish monarchs of Granada, it is surrounded by a heavily fortified wall more than a mile in perimeter. The location of the Alhambra in the Sierra Nevada provides a magnificent setting for this jewel of Moorish Spain.

The Tower of London is a group of buildings and towers covering 13 acres along the north bank of the Thames. The central White Tower, begun in 1078 during the reign of William the Conqueror, was originally a fortress and royal residence, but was later used as a prison. The Bloody Tower is associated with Anne Boleyn and other notables.

Westminster Abbey, in London, was begun in 1050 and completed in 1065. It was rebuilt and enlarged in several phases, beginning in 1245.

Notre-Dame de Paris (begun in 1163), one of the great examples of Gothic architecture, is a twin-towered church with a steeple over the crossing and immense flying buttresses supporting the masonry at the rear of the church.

Other famous Gothic structures are Chartres Cathedral* (France; 12th century); Sainte Chapelle (Paris, France; 1246–1248); Laon Cathedral (France; 1160–1205); Reims Cathedral (France; 13th–14th centuries; rebuilt after its almost complete destruction in World War I); Rouen Cathedral (France; 13th–16th centuries); Amiens Cathedral (France; 1218–1269); Beauvais Cathedral (France; begun 1247); Salisbury Cathedral (England; 1220–1260); York Minster or the Cathedral of St. Peter (England; begun in the 7th century); Milan Cathedral (Italy; begun 1386); and Cologne Cathedral (Germany; 13th–19th centuries; badly damaged in World War II).

The Duomo* (cathedral) in Florence was founded in 1296, completed by Brunelleschi, and consecrated in 1436. The oval-shaped dome dominates the entire structure.

The Vatican is a group of buildings in Rome comprising the official residence of the pope. The Basilica of St. Peter, the largest church in the Christian world, was begun in 1452. However, it was rebuilt between 1506 and 1626. The Sistine Chapel, begun in 1473, is noted for the art masterpieces of Michelangelo, Botticelli, and others. The Basilica of the Savior (known as St. John Lateran) is the first-ranking Catholic Church in the world, for it is the cathedral of the pope.

Other examples of Renaissance architecture are the Palazzo Riccardi, the Palazzo Pitti, and the Palazzo Strozzi in Florence; the Farnese Palace in Rome; Palazzo Grimani (completed about 1550) in Venice; the Escorial (1563–93) near Madrid; the Town Hall of Seville (1527–32); the Louvre, Paris; the Château at Blois, France; St. Paul's Cathedral, London (1675–1710; badly damaged in World War II); the École Militaire, Paris (1752); the Pazzi Chapel, Florence, designed by Brunelleschi (1429); and the Palace of Fontainebleau and the Château de Chambord in France.

The Palace of Versailles in France, containing the famous Hall of Mirrors, was built during the reign of Louis XIV in the 17th century and served as the royal palace until 1793.

Outstanding European buildings of the 18th and 19th centuries are the Superga at Turin (Italy); the Hôtel-Dieu in Lyons; the Belvedere Palace at Vienna; the Royal Palace of Stockholm; the Bank of England, the British Museum, the University of London, and the Houses of Parliament, all in London; and the Panthéon, the Church of the Madeleine, the Bourse, the Palais de Justice, and the Opera House, all in Paris.

The Eiffel Tower, in Paris, was built for the Exposition of 1889 by Alexandre Eiffel. It is 984-ft. high (1,056 ft., including the television tower).

Asian and African

The Taj Mahal* (1632–1650), at Agra, India, built by Shah Jahan as a tomb for his wife, is considered by some as the most perfect example of the Mogul style and by others as the most beautiful building in the world. Four slim white minarets flank the building, which is topped by a white dome; the entire structure is made of marble. Other examples of Indian architecture are the temples at Benares and Tanjore.

Among famed Muslim edifices are the Dome of the Rock or Mosque of Omar, Jerusalem (C.E. 691); the Citadel (1166) and the Tombs of the Mamelukes (15th century), in Cairo; the Tomb of Humayun in Delhi; the Blue Mosque (1468) at Tabriz; and the Tamerlane Mausoleum at Samarkand.

Angkor Wat, outside the city of Angkor Thom, Cambodia, is one of the most beautiful examples of Cambodian or Khmer architecture. The sanctuary was built during the 12th century.

The Great Wall of China (begun c. 214 B.C.E.), designed specifically as a defense against nomadic tribes, has large watch towers that could be called buildings. It was erected by Emperor Ch'in Shih Huang Ti and is 1,400 miles long. Built mainly of earth and stone, it varies in height between 18 and 30 ft.

Typical of Chinese architecture are the pagodas or temple towers. Among some of the better-known pagodas are the *Great Pagoda of the Wild Geese* at Sian (founded in 652) and *Nan t'a* (11th century) at Fang Shan.

Other well-known Chinese buildings are the *Drum Tower* (1273), the *Three Great Halls* in the Purple Forbidden City (1627), *Buddha's Perfume Tower* (19th century), the *Porcelain Pagoda,* and the *Summer Palace,* all at Beijing.

United States

Rockefeller Center, in New York City, extends from 5th Ave. to the Avenue of the Americas between 48th and 52nd Sts. (and halfway to 7th Ave. between 47th and 51st Sts.). It occupies more than 22 acres and has 19 buildings.

The Cathedral of St. John the Divine, at 112th St. and Amsterdam Ave. in New York City, was begun in 1892 and is now in the final stages of completion. When completed, it will be the largest cathedral in the world: 601-ft. long, 146-ft. wide at the nave, 320-ft. wide at the transept. The east end is designed in Romanesque-Byzantine style, and the nave and west end are Gothic.

The World Trade Center, in New York City, was dedicated in 1973. Its twin towers are 110 stories high (about 1,365 ft.), and the complex contains over 9-million sq.-ft. of office space. A restaurant is on the 107th floor of the North Tower.

San Francisco's *Golden Gate Bridge,* completed in 1937, is one of the most recognizable structures in the U.S. Designed by Joseph B. Strauss, this elegant suspension bridge has a main span of 4,200 ft.

The Statue of Liberty* was designed by Frédéric Auguste Bartholdi of Alsace as a gift to Americans from the people of France. The statue of a female figure holding a torch in her raised hand was accepted on Oct. 28, 1886, by President Grover Cleveland. The 225-ton, steel-reinforced copper structure stands on Liberty Island in New York Harbor. It is 152 feet tall and stands on a 150-foot pedestal.

Mount Rushmore (6,000 ft.), in South Dakota, became a celebrated American landmark after sculptor Gutzon Borglum took on the project of carving into the side of it the heads of four great presidents. From 1927 until his death in 1941, Borglum worked on chiseling the 60-ft. likenesses of Washington, Jefferson, Lincoln, and Theodore Roosevelt. His son, Lincoln, finished the sculpture later that year.

* Photos of these structures can be found in the Headline History section.

Famous Ship Canals

Name	Location	Length (miles)[1]	Width (feet)	Depth (feet)	Locks	Year opened
Albert	Belgium	80.0	53.0	16.5	6	1939
Amsterdam-Rhine	Netherlands	45.0	164.0	41.0	3	1952
Beaumont-Port Arthur	United States	40.0	200.0	34.0	—	1916
Canal du Midi	France	149.0	n.a.	n.a.	100	1692
Chesapeake and Delaware	United States	19.0	250.0	27.0	—	1927
Erie Canal	United States	363.0	70	7	82	1825
Grand Canal	China	1,085.0	n.a.	n.a.	n.a.	7th cent.
Göta Canal	Sweden	240.0	n.a.	n.a.	58	1832
Houston	United States	50.0	([2])	40.0	—	1914
Kiel (Nord-Ostsee Kanal)	Germany	61.3	144.0	36.0	4	1895
Panama	Panama	50.7	110.0	41.0	12	1914
St. Lawrence Seaway	U.S. and Canada	2,400.0[3]	([4])	—	—	1959
Montreal to Prescott	U.S. and Canada	11.5	80.0	30.0	7	1959
Welland	Canada	27.5	80.0	27.0	8	1931
Sault Ste. Marie	Canada	1.2	60.0	16.8	1	1895
Sault Ste. Marie	United States	1.6	80.0	25.0	4	1915
Suez	Egypt	100.6[5]	197.0	36.0	—	1869

1. Statute miles. 2. 300–400 feet. 3. From Montreal to Duluth. 4. 442–550 feet; there are 11.5 miles of locks, 80-feet wide and 30-feet deep. 5. From Port Said lighthouse to entrance channel in Suez roads. *Source:* American Society of Civil Engineers.

World's Largest Subway Systems
(by 1997 usage)

City	Date system completed	Number of riders in 1997 (in millions)	Length (km)
Moscow	1935	3,160	200+
Tokyo	1927	2,740	169.3
Mexico City	n.a.	1,420	n.a.
Seoul	n.a.	1,390	n.a.
New York City	1904	1,130	320.0
Paris	1900	1,120	200.9
Osaka	1933	1,000	99.1
Hong Kong	n.a.	779	28.2
London	1863	770	391.0
São Paulo	n.a.	701	n.a.

NOTE: n.a. = not available.

Notable Modern Bridges

Name	Location	Length of main span feet	meters	Year completed
Suspension	**United States**			
Verrazano-Narrows	Lower New York Bay	4,260	1,298	1964
Golden Gate	San Francisco Bay	4,200	1,280	1937
Mackinac Straits	Michigan	3,800	1,158	1957
George Washington	Hudson River at New York City	3,500	1,067	1931
Tacoma Narrows II	Puget Sound at Tacoma, Wash.	2,800	853	1950
San Francisco–Oakland Bay[1]	San Francisco Bay	2,310	704	1936
Bronx-Whitestone	East River, New York City	2,300	701	1939
Delaware Memorial[1]	Delaware River near Wilmington, Del.	2,150	655	1951, 1968
Seaway Skyway	St. Lawrence River at Ogdensburg, N.Y.	2,150	655	1960
Walt Whitman	Delaware River at Philadelphia	2,000	610	1957
Ambassador International	Detroit River at Detroit	1,850	564	1929
Throgs Neck	East River, New York City	1,800	549	1961
Benjamin Franklin	Delaware River at Philadelphia	1,750	533	1926
Brooklyn Bridge	East River, New York City	1,596	486	1883
Royal Gorge	Arkansas River, Colo.	1,053	321	1929
Wheeling Bridge	Ohio River, Wheeling, W.Va.	1,010	308	1847
	International			
Akashi Kaikyo	Hyogo, Japan	6,529	1,990	1998
Izmit Bay	Marmara Sea, Turkey	5,472	1,668	UC
Storebælt	Denmark	5,328	1,624	1998
Humber	Hull, England	4,626	1,410	1981
Jiangyin Yangtze	China	4,543	1,385	UC
Tsing Ma Bridge	Hong Kong	4,518	1,377	1997
Hardanger Fjord	Norway	4,347	1,324	n.a.
Hoga Kusten	400 km N. Stockholm, Sweden	3,970	1,210	1997
High Coast Bridge	Västernorrland, Sweden	3,969	1,210	1997
Minami Bisan-Seto	Japan	3,668	1,118	1988
Second Bosporus	Istanbul, Turkey	3,576	1,090	1988
First Bosporus	Istanbul, Turkey	3,524	1,074	1973
Third Kurushima	Japan	3,379	1,030	UC
Second Kurushima	Japan	3,346	1,020	UC
Ponte 25 de Abril	Tagus River at Lisbon, Portugal	3,323	1,013	1966
Forth Road	Queensferry, Scotland	3,300	1,006	1964
Kita Bisan-Seto	Japan	3,248	990	1988
Severn	Severn River at Beachley, England	3,240	988	1966
Yicang Bridge	Yangtze River, Hubei Province, China	3,150	960	UC
Shimotsui Straits	Japan	3,084	940	1988
Xiling Yangtze	Three Gorges Dam, China	2,952	900	1996
Tigergate (Humen)	Pearl River, Guangdon Province, China	2,913	888	1997
Ohnaruto	Japan	2,874	876	1988
Pierre Laporte	Quebec, Canada	2,190	668	1970
Cantilever	**United States**			
Commodore John Barry	Chester, Pa.	1,644	501	1974
Greater New Orleans[1]	Mississippi River, La.	1,576	480	1958
Transbay Bridge	San Francisco Bay	1,400	427	1936
	International			
Quebec Railway	St. Lawrence River at Quebec, Canada	1,800	549	1917
Forth Railway[1]	Queensferry, Scotland	1,710	521	1890
Minato Ohashi	Osaka, Japan	1,673	510	1974
Howrah	Hooghly River at Calcutta, India	1,500	457	1943
Steel Arch	**United States**			
New River Gorge	Fayetteville, W. Va.	1,700	518	1977
Bayonne	Kill Van Kull at Bayonne, N.J.	1,675	510	1931
Hell Gate Bridge	East River (Hell Gate), New York City	978	298	1916
	International			
Sydney Harbor	Sydney, Australia	1,670	509	1932
Zdákov	Vltava River, Czech Republic	1,244	380	1967
Port Mann	Fraser River at Vancouver, British Columbia	1,200	366	1964
Cable-Stayed	**United States**			
Dame Point	Jacksonville, Fla.	1,300	396	1988
Houston Ship Channel	Baytown, Tex.	1,250	381	1995

| Name | Location | Length of main span | | Year completed |
		feet	meters	
Sidney Lanier Bridge	Brunswick River, Ga.	1,250	381	UC
Hale Boggs Memorial	Luling, La.	1,222	373	1983
Sunshine Skyway	Tampa, Fla.	1,200	366	1987
	International			
Tatara	Ehime, Japan	2,920	890	UC
Ponte de Normandie	Le Havre, France	2,808	856	1995
Second Nanjing	Yangtze River, Nanjing, China	2,060	628	UC
Wuhan Third Yangtze	Wuhan, Hubei Province, China	2,028	618	UC
Qingzhou Minjiang	Fuzhou, China	1,985	605	1996
Yang Pu	Shanghai, China	1,975	602	1993
Xupu	Shanghai, China	1,936	590	1997
Meiko Chuo	Aichi, Japan	1,936	590	1997
Patras Bridge	Greece	1,837	560	UC
Skarnsundet Bridge	near Trondheim, Norway	1,739	530	1991
Quishi Bridge	Guangdong Province, China	1,700	518	UC
Tsurumi Tsubasa	Kanagawa, Japan	1,673	510	1995
Jingsha Bridge	Yangtze River, Hubei Province, China	1,640	500	UC
Oresund	Denmark/Sweden	1,614	492	UC
Ikuchi	Honshu-Shikoku, Japan	1,608	490	1991
Higashi Kobe	Hyogo, Japan	1,591	485	1994
Zhanjiang Bay Bridge	Guangdong Province, China	1,575	480	1998
Ting Kau	Hong Kong	1,558	475	1997
Seohae	Korea	1,542	470	UC
Alex Fraser	Vancouver, B.C., Canada	1,525	465	1986
Yokohama-ko-odan	Kanagawa, Japan	1,509	460	1989
Second Hooghly	Calcutta, India	1,500	457	1992
Second Severn Crossing	Severn River, England	1,496	456	1996
Dartford	Thames River, Dartford, England	1,476	450	1992
Dao Kanong	Chao Phraya River, Bangkok, Thailand	1,476	450	1987
Queen Elizabeth II	Thames River, Dartford, England	1,476	450	1991
Chongqing 2nd Bridge	Sichuan Province, China	1,457	444	1996
Continuous Truss	**United States**			
Astoria	Columbia River at Astoria, Oregon	1,232	376	1966
Croton Reservoir	Croton, N.Y.	1,052	321	1970
Ravenswood	Ohio River, Ravenswood, W. Va.	902	275	1981
	International			
Oshima	Oshima Island, Japan	1,066	325	1976
Tenmon	Kumamoto, Japan	984	300	1966
Kuronoseto	Nagashima-Kyushu, Japan	984	300	1974
Graf Spee	Germany	839	256	1936
Concrete Arch	**United States**			
Natchez Trace Pkwy.	Franklin, Tenn.	582	177	1994
Westinghouse	Pittsburgh, Pa.	460	140	1931
Jack's Run	Pittsburgh, Pa.	400	120	1930
Cappelen	Minneapolis, Minn.	400	120	1923
	International			
Krk (I)	Krk, Croatia	1,280	390	1979
Gladesville	Parramatta River at Sydney, Australia	1,000	305	1964
Amizade	Paraná River at Foz do Iguassu, Brazil	951	290	1964
Arrábida	Porto, Portugal	886	270	1963
Sandö	Angerman River at Kramfors, Sweden	866	264	1943
Confederation Bridge	Northumberland Strait, Canada	820	250	1997
Sibenik	Sibenik, Yugoslavia	808	246	1966
Krk (II)	Krk, Croatia	800	244	1979
Fiumarella	Catanzaro, Italy	758	231	1961
Zaporozhe	Old Dnepr River, Ukraine	748	228	1952
Esla Bridge	Esla River at Zamora, Spain	645	197	1940
Segmental Construction	**United States**			
Jesse H. Jones Memorial	Houston Ship Channel, Texas	750	228	1982

NOTES: UC = under construction in 1999. n.a. = not available. 1. Twin span. *Source:* Federal Highway Administration.

World's Tallest Buildings

Building, city	Year	Stories	Height m	Height ft.
Petronas Tower 1, Kuala Lumpur, Malaysia	1998	88	452	1,483
Petronas Tower 2, Kuala Lumpur, Malaysia	1998	88	452	1,483
Sears Tower, Chicago	1974	110	442	1,450
Jin Mao Building, Shanghai	1999	88	421	1,381
World Trade Center One, New York	1972	110	417	1,368
World Trade Center Two, New York	1973	110	415	1,362
Empire State Building, New York	1931	102	381	1,250
Central Plaza, Hong Kong	1992	78	374	1,227
Bank of China Tower, Hong Kong	1989	70	369	1,209
T & C Tower, Kaoshiung, Taiwan	1997	85	348	1,140
Amoco Building, Chicago	1973	80	346	1,136
The Center, Hong Kong	1998	79	346	1,135
John Hancock Center, Chicago	1969	100	344	1,127
Shun Hing Square, Shenzhen, China	1996	69	325	1,066
Citic Plaza, Guangzhou, China	1997	80	322	1,056
Chicago Beach Tower Hotel, Dubai	1998	60	321	1,053
Baiyoke Tower II, Bangkok	1997	90	320	1,050
Chrysler Building, New York	1930	77	319	1,046
NationsBank Plaza, Atlanta	1993	55	312	1,023
Library Tower, Los Angeles	1990	75	310	1,018
AT&T Corporate Center, Chicago	1989	60	307	1,007
Texas Commerce Tower, Houston	1982	75	305	1,000
Two Prudential Plaza, Chicago	1990	64	303	995
Ryugyong Hotel, Pyongyang, N. Korea	1995	105	300	984
Commerzbank Tower, Frankfurt	1997	56	299	981
First Interstate Bank Plaza, Houston	1983	71	296	972
Landmark Tower, Yokohama, Japan	1993	70	296	971
311 South Wacker Drive, Chicago	1990	65	293	961
American International Building, New York	1932	67	290	952
First Canadian Place, Toronto	1975	72	290	951
Society Tower, Cleveland	1991	57	290	950
One Liberty Place, Philadelphia	1987	61	287	945
Columbia Seafirst Center, Seattle	1984	76	287	943
40 Wall Street, New York	1930	72	283	927
NationsBank Plaza, Dallas	1985	72	281	921
Overseas Union Bank Centre, Singapore	1986	66	280	919
United Overseas Bank Plaza, Singapore	1992	66	280	919
Republic Plaza, Singapore	1995	66	280	919
Citicorp Center, New York	1977	59	279	915
Scotia Plaza, Toronto	1989	68	275	902
Transco Tower, Houston	1983	64	275	901
Renaissance Tower, Dallas	1975	56	270	886
900 North Michigan Ave., Chicago	1989	66	265	871
NationsBank Corporate Center, Charlotte	1992	60	265	871
SunTrust Plaza, Atlanta	1992	60	265	871
Water Tower Place, Chicago	1976	74	262	859
First Interstate Tower, Los Angeles	1974	62	262	858
Canada Trust Tower, Toronto	1990	51	261	856
Transamerica Corporate Headquarters, San Francisco	1972	48	260	853
G.E. Building, New York	1933	70	259	850
One First National Plaza, Chicago	1969	60	259	850
Two Liberty Place, Philadelphia	1990	58	258	848
Messeturm, Frankfurt	1990	63	257	843
USX Tower, Pittsburgh	1970	64	256	841
Rinku Gate Tower, Osaka	1996	56	256	840
World Trade Center, Osaka	1995	55	252	827
IBM Tower, Atlanta	1988	50	250	820
BNI City Tower, Jakarta	1995	46	250	820
Korea Life Insurance Company, Seoul	1985	60	249	817
CitySpire, New York	1989	75	248	814
Rialto Tower, Melbourne	1985	63	248	814
One Chase Manhattan Plaza, New York	1961	60	248	813
MetLife, New York	1963	59	246	808
Shin Kong Life Tower, Taipei, Taiwan	1993	51	244	801
Malayan Bank, Kuala Lumpur, Malaysia	1988	50	244	799
Tokyo City Hall, Tokyo	1991	48	243	797
Woolworth Building, New York	1913	57	241	792
Mellon Bank Center, Philadelphia	1991	54	241	792
John Hancock Tower, Boston	1976	60	240	788
Bank One Center, Dallas	1987	60	240	787
Commerce Court West, Toronto	1973	57	239	784
Moscow State University, Moscow	1953	26	239	784
Empire Tower, Kuala Lumpur, Malaysia	1994	62	238	781
NationsBank Center, Houston	1984	56	238	780
Bank of America Center, San Francisco	1969	52	237	779
Worldwide Plaza, New York	1989	47	237	778
One Canada Square, London	1991	50	237	777
IDS Center, Minneapolis	1973	52	236	775
U.S. Bank Place, Minneapolis	1992	58	236	774
Norwest Center, Minneapolis	1988	57	235	773
Treasury Building, Singapore	1986	52	235	770
One Ninety One Peachtree Tower, Atlanta	1991	50	235	770
Opera City Tower, Tokyo	1997	54	234	768
Shinjuku Park Tower, Tokyo	1994	52	233	764
Heritage Plaza, Houston	1987	52	232	762
Kompleks Tun Abdul Razak Building, Penang, Malaysia	1985	65	232	760
Palace of Culture and Science, Warsaw	1955	42	231	758
Carnegie Hall Tower, New York	1991	60	231	757
Three First National Plaza, Chicago	1981	57	230	753
Equitable Tower, New York	1986	51	229	752
MLC Centre, Sydney	1978	65	229	751
One Penn Plaza, New York	1972	57	229	750
1251 Avenue of the Americas, New York	1972	54	229	750

NOTE: Height is measured from sidewalk level of main entrance to structural top of building. Antennas and flag poles are not included. *Source:* Council on Tall Buildings and Urban Habitat, Lehigh University.

World's Highest Dams

| Name | River, state, and country | Structural height | | Gross reservoir capacity | | Year completed |
		feet	meters	thousands of acre feet	millions of cubic meters	
Rogun	Vakhsh, Tajikistan	1099	335	9,404	11,600	1985
Nurek	Vakhsh, Tajikistan	984	300	8,512	10,500	1980
Grande Dixence	Dixence, Switzerland	935	285	324	400	1962
Inguri	Inguri, Georgia	892	272	801	1,100	1984
Vaiont	Vaiont, Italy	859	262	137	169	1961
Manuel M. Torres	Grijalva, Mexico	856	261	1,346	1,660	1981
Tehri	Bhagirathi, India	856	261	2,869	3,540	UC
Alvaro Obregon	Mextiquic, Mexico	853	260	n.a.	n.a.	1926
Mauvoisin	Drance de Bagnes, Switzerland	820	250	146	180	1957
Alberto Lleras	Orinoco, Colombia	797	243	811	1,000	1989
Mica	Columbia, Canada	797	243	20,000	24,670	1972
Sayano-Shushensk	Yenisei, Russia	794	242	25,353	31,300	1980
Ertan	Yangtze/Yalong, China	787	240	4,702	5,800	1999
La Esmeralda	Batá, Colombia	778	237	661	815	1975
Kishau	Tons, India	774	236	1,946	2,400	1985
Oroville	Feather, Calif., U.S.	770	235	3,538	4,299	1968
El Cajón	Humuya, Honduras	768	234	4,580	5,650	1984
Chirkey	Sulak, Russia	764	233	2,252	2,780	1977
Bhakra	Sutlej, India	741	226	8,002	9,870	1963
Luzzone	Brenno di Luzzone, Switzerland	738	225	71	87	1963
Hoover	Colorado, Ariz./Nev., U.S.	732	223	28,500	35,154	1936
Contra	Verzasca, Switzerland	722	220	70	86	1965
Mratinje	Piva, Herzegovina	722	220	713	880	1973
Dworshak	N. Fk. Clearwater, Idaho, U.S.	717	219	3,453	4,259	1974
Glen Canyon	Colorado, Ariz., U.S.	710	216	27,000	33,304	1964

NOTES: UC = under construction in 1999. n.a. = not available. *Source: World Register of Dams 1998,* International Commission on Large Dams.

World's Largest Dams

| Dam | Location | Volume (thousands) | | Year completed |
		Cubic meters	Cubic yards	
Syncrude Tailings	Canada	540,000	706,320	UC
Chapetón	Argentina	296,200	311,539	UC
Pati	Argentina	238,180	274,026	UC
New Cornelia Tailings	United States	209,500	274,026	1973
Tarbela	Pakistan	121,720	159,210	1976
Kambaratinsk	Kyrgyzstan	112,200	146,758	UC
Fort Peck	Montana	96,049	125,628	1940
Lower Usuma	Nigeria	93,000	121,644	1990
Cipasang	Indonesia	90,000	117,720	UC
Atatürk	Turkey	84,500	110,522	1990
Yacyretá-Apipe	Paraguay/Argentina	81,000	105,944	UC
Guri (Raul Leoni)	Venezuela	78,000	102,014	1986
Rogun	Tajikistan	75,500	98,750	1985
Oahe	South Dakota	70,339	92,000	1963
Mangla	Pakistan	65,651	85,872	1967
Gardiner	Canada	65,440	85,592	1968
Afsluitdijk	Netherlands	63,400	82,927	1932
Oroville	California	59,639	78,008	1968
San Luis	California	59,405	77,700	1967
Nurek	Tajikistan	58,000	75,861	1980
Garrison	North Dakota	50,843	66,500	1956
Cochiti	New Mexico	48,052	62,850	1975
Tabka (Thawra)	Syria	46,000	60,168	1976
Bennett W.A.C.	Canada	43,733	57,201	1967
Tucuruí	Brazil	43,000	56,242	1984

NOTE: UC = under construction in 1999. *Source:* Department of the Interior, Bureau of Reclamation and *International Water Power and Dam Construction.*

World's Largest Hydroelectric Plants
(over 4,000 MW capacity)

Name of dam	Location	Rated capacity (MW)		Year of initial operation
		Present	Ultimate	
Itaipu	Brazil/Paraguay	12,600	14,000	1983
Guri	Venezuela	10,000	10,000	1986
Grand Coulee	Washington	6,494	6,494	1942
Sayano-Shushensk	Russia	6,400	6,400	1989
Krasnoyarsk	Russia	6,000	6,000	1968
Churchill Falls	Canada	5,428	6,528	1971
La Grande 2	Canada	5,328	5,328	1979
Bratsk	Russia	4,500	4,500	1961
Moxoto	Brazil	4,328	4,328	n.a.
Ust-Ilim	Russia	4,320	4,320	1977
Tucurui	Brazil	4,245	8,370	1984

NOTES: MW = megawatts. n.a. = not available. *Source: International Journal on Hydropower and Dams,* official journal of the International Hydropower Association, Sutton, England.

Notable Tunnels

Name	Location	Length		Year completed
		mi.	km	
Railroad, excluding subways				
Seikan	Tsugaru Strait, Japan	33.5	53.9	1988
Channel Tunnel[1]	English Channel, England–France	31.1	50.0	1994
Simplon (I and II)	Alps, Switzerland–Italy	12.3	19.8	1906 & 1922
Apennine	Bologna–Florence, Italy	11.5	18.5	1934
St. Gotthard	Swiss Alps	9.3	15.0	1880
Lötschberg	Swiss Alps	9.1	14.6	1911
Mont Cénis	French Alps	8.5[2]	13.7	1871
New Cascade	Cascade Mountains, Washington	7.8	12.6	1929
Vosges	Vosges, France	7.0	11.3	1940
Flathead	Rocky Mountains, Montana	7.0	11.3	1970
Arlberg	Austrian Alps	6.3	10.1	1884
Moffat	Rocky Mountains, Colorado	6.2	9.9	1928
Shimizu	Shimizu, Japan	6.1	9.8	1931
Rimutaka	Wairarapa, New Zealand	5.5	8.9	1955
Vehicular				
St. Gotthard	Alps, Switzerland	10.2	16.4	1980
Pinglin Highway	near Taipei, Taiwan	8.0	12.9	UC
Mt. Blanc	Alps, France–Italy	7.0	11.3	1965
Aqualine Expressway	Tokyo Bay, Japan	5.9	9.5	1997
Mt. Ena	Japan Alps, Japan	5.3	8.5	1976[3]
Store Baelt	Great Belt, Denmark	5.0	8.0	1995
Great St. Bernard	Alps, Switzerland–Italy	3.4	5.5	1964
Mount Royal	Montreal, Canada	3.2	5.1	1918
Queensway Road	Mersey River, Liverpool, England	2.2	3.5	1934
Brooklyn-Battery	East River, New York City	1.7	2.7	1950
Fort McHenry	Baltimore, Maryland	1.7	2.7	1985
Holland	Hudson River, New York–New Jersey	1.6	2.6	1927
Lincoln	Hudson River, New York–New Jersey	1.6	2.6	1937
Hampton Roads	Norfolk, Virginia	1.4	2.3	1957
Queens-Midtown	East River, New York City	1.3	2.1	1940
Liberty Tubes	Pittsburgh, Pennsylvania	1.2	1.9	1923
Baltimore Harbor	Baltimore, Maryland	1.2	1.9	1957
Allegheny Tunnels	Pennsylvania Turnpike	1.2	1.9	1940[4]
Yerba	Yerba Buena Island, Calif.	0.5	0.8	1936

NOTE: UC = Under construction in 1999. 1. Three-tunnel system including two rail tunnels (one carries passengers from England to France, the other from France to England) and a central service tunnel. 2. Lengthened to its present 8.5 miles in 1881. 3. Parallel tunnel begun in 1976. 4. Parallel tunnel built in 1965, twin tunnel in 1966. *Source:* American Society of Civil Engineers and International Bridge, Tunnel & Turnpike Association, Wittiker's.

Some World-Famous Cathedrals

Cathedral	Location	Style	Date built	Height ft	Height m
Canterbury	Canterbury, England	various	1070–1089, 1175–1184, 1379–1503	235.0	72.0
Chartres (Notre Dame)	Chartres, France	Gothic	12th–13th centuries	375.0 350.0	114.0 107.0
Church of Christ and Blessed Mary the Virgin	Durham, England	Norman	1093–1133	n.a.	n.a.
Cologne	Cologne, Germany	Gothic	1248–1560, 1842–1880	515.0	157.0
Hagia Sophia	Istanbul, Turkey	Byzantine	532–537	184.0	56.0
Imperial	Speyer, Germany	Romanesque	c. 1030–1061	n.a.	n.a.
Lincoln	Lincoln, England	originally Norman	1075–1501	271.0	83.0
Liverpool	Liverpool, England	n.a.	1904–1978	n.a.	n.a.
Lund	Lund, Sweden	Romanesque	11th century	n.a.	n.a.
Milan	Milan, Italy	various (esp. Gothic)	1386–1813	354.0	108.0
Mosque/Cathedral of Córdoba	Cordoba, Spain	Islamic	784–786, 9th–10th centuries	300.0	90.0
Notre Dame	Amiens, France	Gothic	1220–c. 1270, 14th century, 16th century	370.0	113.0
Notre Dame	Antwerp, Belgium	Gothic	14th–16th centuries	400.0	122.0
Notre Dame	Rouen, France	Gothic	12th–15th centuries	495.0	151.0
Notre-Dame de Paris	Paris, France	Gothic	1163–14th century, 1845–	223.0	68.0
Orvieto	Orvieto, Italy	Gothic	1290–1580	n.a.	n.a.
Our Lady of Peace of Yamoussoukro Basilica	Yamoussoukro, Côte d'Ivoire	n.a.	1986–1989	489.0	149.0
Palatine Chapel of Charlemagne	Aachen, Germany	Carolingian	790–805	101.5	30.9
Reims	Reims, France	French Gothic	13th–14th centuries	n.a.	n.a.
Rochester	Rochester, England	Norman, Gothic	1125–1130	n.a.	n.a.
St. Basil the Blessed (Church of the Intercession)	Moscow, Russia	n.a.	1554–1560	n.a.	n.a.
St. David's	Saint David's, Wales	Norman	12th century	n.a.	n.a.
St.-Étienne	Caen, France	Norman Romanesque	1060s	295.0	90.0
St. Isaac's	St. Petersburg, Russia	Russian Empire	1818–1858	n.a.	n.a.
St. John the Divine	New York, N.Y.	Byzantine-Romanesque, French-Gothic	1892–	n.a.	n.a.
St. Julien du Mans	Le Mans, France	Gothic, Romanesque	11th–15th centuries	210.0	64.0
St. Patrick's	New York, N.Y.	Gothic	1858–1879	n.a.	n.a.
St. Paul's	London, England	Classical English Baroque	1675–1710	365.0	111.3
St. Peter (York Minster)	York, England	Norman, Gothic	13th–15th centuries	n.a.	n.a.
St. Peter's Basilica	Rome, Italy	n.a.	1506–1626	404.0	123.0
St. Pierre	Beauvais, France	Gothic	1227 (never completed)	157.0	48.0
St. Stephen's	Vienna, Austria	Romanesque, Gothic	1147, 1304–1450, 1952	n.a.	n.a.
Salisbury	Salisbury, England	Early English	1220–1260	404.0	123.0
San Marco Basilica	Venice, Italy	Byzantine	completed 1071	324.0	99.0
Santa Maria	Seville, Spain	Gothic, Moorish, Plateresque, Baroque	1402–1506	n.a.	n.a.
Santa Maria del Fiore	Florence, Italy	Gothic	1296–1436	138.0	42.0
Santiago	Santiago, Spain	Romanesque, Plateresque, Baroque	1078–1211	n.a.	n.a.
Siena	Siena, Italy	Italian Gothic	12th–14th centuries	n.a.	n.a.
Strasbourg	Strasbourg, France	Rhenish	1015–1439	475.0	144.0
Toledo	Toledo, Spain	Gothic	13th century	n.a.	n.a.
Ulm	Ulm, Germany	Gothic	14th century	528.0	161.0
Washington National	Washington, D.C.	English Gothic	1907–1990	n.a.	n.a.
Westminster Abbey	Westminster, England	Gothic, Perpendicular	1050–1065, 1245–16th century	n.a.	n.a.
Winchester	Winchester, England	Norman, Gothic	1093, 14th century	n.a.	n.a.
Worms	Worms, Germany	Romanesque	1018–12th century, 13th–14th centuries	n.a.	n.a.

NOTES: n.a. = not available. For more cathedrals, *see* Famous Structures on pp. 474–476.

Explorations

Country or place	Event	Explorer	Date
AFRICA			
Sierra Leone	Explored	Hanno, Carthaginian seaman	c. 520 B.C.E.
Zaire River (Congo)	Mouth visited[1]	Diogo Cão, Portuguese explorer	c. 1484
Cape of Good Hope	Rounded	Bartolomeu Diaz, Portuguese explorer	1488
Gambia River	Explored	Mungo Park, Scottish explorer	1795
Sahara	Crossed	Dixon Denham and Hugh Clapperton, English explorers	1822–1823
Zambezi River	Explored[1]	David Livingstone, Scottish explorer	1851
Sudan	Explored	Heinrich Barth, German explorer	1852–1855
Victoria Falls	Explored[1]	David Livingstone, Scottish explorer	1855
Lake Tanganyika	Explored[1]	Richard Burton and John Speke, British explorers	1858
Lake Victoria, identified as the source of the Nile	Explored	John Speke, British explorer	1858
Zaire River (Congo)	Traced	Sir Henry M. Stanley, British explorer	1877
ASIA			
Punjab (India)	Invaded	Alexander the Great, King of Macedonia	327 B.C.E.
China	Explored	Marco Polo, Italian traveler	c. 1272
Tibet	Visited	Odoric of Pordenone, Italian monk	c. 1325
Southern China	Explored	Niccolò dei Conti, Venetian traveler	c. 1440
India	Explored (Cape route)	Vasco da Gama, Portuguese navigator	1498
Japan	Visited	St. Francis Xavier of Spain, missionary	1549
Arabia	Explored	Carsten Niebuhr, German explorer	1762
China	Explored	Ferdinand Richthofen, German scientist	1868
Mongolia	Explored	Nikolai M. Przhevalsky, Russian explorer	1870–1873
Central Asia	Explored	Sven Hedin, Swedish scientist	1890–1908
EUROPE			
Shetland Islands	Visited	Pytheas of Massilia (Marseille), Greek navigator and geographer	c. 325 B.C.E.
North Cape	Rounded	Ottar, Norwegian explorer	c. 870
Iceland	Colonized	Norwegian noblemen	c. 890–900
NORTH AMERICA			
Greenland	Colonized	Eric the Red, Norwegian	c. 985
Labrador; Nova Scotia (?)	Explored[1]	Leif Ericson, Norse explorer	1000
West Indies	Explored[1]	Christopher Columbus, Italian	1492
North America	Coast explored[1]	Giovanni Caboto (John Cabot), for British	1497
Pacific Ocean	Sighted[1]	Vasco Núñez de Balboa, Spanish explorer	1513
Florida	Explored	Ponce de León, Spanish explorer	1513
Mexico	Conquered	Hernando Cortés, Spanish adventurer	1519–1521
St. Lawrence River	Explored[1]	Jacques Cartier, French navigator	1534
Southwest United States	Explored	Francisco Coronado, Spanish explorer	1540–1542
Colorado River	Explored[1]	Hernando de Alarcón, Spanish explorer	1540
Mississippi River	Explored[1]	Hernando de Soto, Spanish explorer	1541
Frobisher Bay	Explored[1]	Martin Frobisher, English seaman	1576
Maine Coast	Explored	Samuel de Champlain, French explorer	1604
Jamestown, Va.	Settled	John Smith, English colonist	1607
Hudson River	Explored	Henry Hudson, English navigator	1609
Hudson Bay (Canada)	Explored[1]	Henry Hudson	1610
Baffin Bay	Explored[1]	William Baffin, English navigator	1616
Lake Michigan	Navigated	Jean Nicolet, French explorer	1634
Arkansas River	Explored[1]	Jacques Marquette and Louis Jolliet, French explorers	1673
Mississippi River	Explored	Sieur de La Salle, French explorer	1682
Bering Strait	Explored[1]	Vitus Bering, Danish explorer	1728
Alaska	Explored[1]	Vitus Bering	1741
Mackenzie River (Canada)	Explored[1]	Sir Alexander Mackenzie, Scottish-Canadian explorer	1789
Northwest United States	Explored	Meriwether Lewis and William Clark, American explorers	1804–1806
Northeast Passage (Arctic Ocean)	Navigated	Nils Nordenskjöld, Swedish explorer	1879
Greenland	Explored	Robert Peary, American explorer	1892
Northwest Passage	Navigated	Roald Amundsen, Norwegian explorer	1906

Country or place	Event	Explorer	Date
SOUTH AMERICA			
Continent	Explored	Christopher Columbus, Italian	1498
Brazil	Explored[1]	Pedro Alvarez Cabral, Portuguese	1500
Peru	Conquered	Francisco Pizarro, Spanish explorer	1532–1533
Amazon River	Explored	Francisco Orellana, Spanish explorer	1541
Cape Horn	Explored[1]	Willem C. Schouten, Dutch navigator	1615
OCEANIA			
Papua New Guinea	Explored	Jorge de Menezes, Portuguese explorer	1526
Australia	Explored	Abel Janszoon Tasman, Dutch navigator	1642
Tasmania	Explored[1]	Abel Janszoon Tasman	1642
Australia	Explored	John McDouall Stuart, English explorer	1828
Australia	Explored	Robert Burke and William Willis, Australian explorers	1861
New Zealand	Sighted (and named)	Abel Janszoon Tasman, Dutch navigator	1642
New Zealand	Explored	James Cook, English navigator	1769
ARCTIC, ANTARCTIC, AND MISCELLANEOUS			
Africa, Middle East, South and Southeast Asia, and Europe	Explored	Ibn Batuta, greatest Arab traveler	1325–1349
Ocean exploration	Expedition	Ferdinand Magellan's ships circled globe for Spain	1519–1522
Galápagos Islands	Explored	Diego de Rivadeneira, Spanish captain	1535
Spitsbergen	Explored	Willem Barents, Dutch navigator	1596
Antarctic Circle	Crossed	James Cook, English navigator	1773
Antarctica	Explored[1]	Nathaniel Palmer, American whaler (archipelago) and Fabian Gottlieb von Bellingshausen, Russian admiral (mainland)	1820–1821
Antarctica	Explored	Charles Wilkes, American explorer	1840
North Pole	Reached[2]	Robert E. Peary, American explorer	1909
South Pole	Reached	Roald Amundsen, Norwegian explorer	1911

1. First European to reach the area. 2. Admiral Peary's claim to have reached the pole has been disputed from the beginning—as was the claim made by his former colleague, Dr. Frederick Cook, who has been generally dismissed as a charlatan. The credit ultimately went to Peary, a claim officially backed by the U.S. Congress. But recent scholarship, including evidence culled from the journals and diaries of both Cook and Peary, has cast doubt on both explorers' veracity. If it is the case that neither reached the pole, then the credit goes to Joseph Fletcher, who landed a U.S. Air Force C-47 plane there in 1952.

The Continents

A continent is defined as a large unbroken land mass completely surrounded by water, although in some cases continents are (or were in part) connected by land bridges. The seven continents are North America, South America, Europe, Asia, Africa, Australia, and Antarctica. The island groups in the Pacific are often called "Oceania," but this name does *not* imply that scientists consider them the remains of a continent.

Political considerations have often overridden geographical facts when it came to naming continents. Geographically, Europe, including the British Isles, is a large western peninsula of the continent of Asia; and many geographers, when referring to Europe and Asia, speak of the Eurasian continent. But traditionally, Europe is counted as a separate continent, with the Ural and the Caucasus mountains forming the line of demarcation between Europe and Asia. To the south of Europe, Asia has an odd-shaped peninsula jutting westward, which has a large number of political subdivisions. The northern section is taken up by Turkey; to the south of Turkey there are Syria, Iraq, Israel, Jordan, Saudi Arabia, and a number of smaller Arab countries. All these are part of Asia. Traditionally, the island of Cyprus in the Mediterranean is also considered to be part of Asia.

Continental Drift and Plate-Tectonics Theory

Source: U.S. Dept. of the Interior, Geological Survey

According to the theory of continental drift, the world was made up of a single continent through most of geologic time. That continent eventually separated and drifted apart, forming into the seven continents we have today. The first comprehensive theory of continental drift was suggested by the German meteorologist Alfred Wegener in 1912. The hypothesis asserts that the continents consist of lighter rocks that rest on heavier crustal material—similar to the manner in which icebergs float on water. Wegener contended that the relative positions of the continents are not rigidly fixed but are slowly moving—at a rate of about one yard per century.

According to the generally accepted plate-tectonics theory, scientists believe that Earth's surface is broken into a number of shifting slabs or plates, which average about 50 miles in thickness. These plates move relative to one another above a hotter, deeper, more mobile zone at average rates as great as a few inches per year. Most of the world's active volcanoes are located along or near the boundaries between shifting plates and are called plate-boundary volcanoes. However, some active volcanoes are not associated with plate boundaries, and many of these so-called intra-plate volcanoes form roughly linear chains in the interior of some oceanic plates. The Hawaiian Islands provide perhaps the best example of an intra-plate volcanic chain, developed by the northwest-moving Pacific plate passing over an inferred "hot spot" that ini-

tiates the magma-generation and volcano-formation process. The peripheral areas of the Pacific Ocean Basin, containing the boundaries of several plates, are dotted by many active volcanoes that form the so-called Ring of Fire. The Ring provides excellent examples of plate-boundary volcanoes, including Mt. St. Helens.

World Land Areas and Elevations

Area	Approximate land area sq km	Approximate land area sq mi.	Percent of total land area	Elevation, feet and meters Highest	Lowest
WORLD	148,429,000	57,308,738	100.0%	Mt. Everest, Asia, 29,028 ft. (8,848 m)	Dead Sea, Israel-Jordan, 1,312 ft. below sea level (−400 m)
ASIA (includes the Middle East)	44,579,000	17,212,041	30.0	Mt. Everest, Tibet-Nepal, 29,028 ft. (8,848 m)	Dead Sea, Israel-Jordan, 1,312 ft. below sea level (−400 m)
AFRICA	30,065,000	11,608,156	20.3	Mt. Kilimanjaro, Tanzania, 19,340 ft. (5,895 m)	Lake Assal, Djibouti, 512 ft. below sea level (−156 m)
NORTH AMERICA	24,256,000	9,365,290	16.3	Mt. McKinley, Alaska, 20,320 ft. (6,194 m)	Death Valley, Calif., 282 ft. below sea level (−86 m)
SOUTH AMERICA (includes Central America and the Caribbean)	17,819,000	6,879,952	8.9	Mt. Aconcagua, Argentina, 22,834 ft. (6,960 m)	Valdes Peninsula, Argentina 131 ft. below sea level (−40 m)
ANTARCTICA	13,209,000	5,100,021	8.9	Vinson Massif, Ellsworth Mts., 16,066 ft. (4,897 m)	Ice covered 8,327 ft. below sea level (−2,538 m)
EUROPE (includes the recently independent states of the former Soviet Union)	9,938,000	3,837,082	6.7	Elbrus, Russia/Georgia, 18,510 ft. (5,642 m)	Caspian Sea, Russia/Kazakhstan 92 ft. below sea level (−28 m)
AUSTRALIA (includes Oceania)	7,687,000	2,967,966	5.2	Kosciusko, Australia 7,316 ft. (2,228 m)	Lake Eyre, Australia, 52 ft. below sea level (−16 m)

Source: National Geographic Society.

Volcanoes of the World

Source: United States Geological Survey

About 550 volcanoes have erupted on Earth's surface since recorded history; far more have erupted unobserved on the ocean floor. Almost two-thirds of volcanoes are located in the Northern Hemisphere. About 60 volcanoes are active each year. Most volcanoes exist at the boundaries of Earth's crustal plates, such as the famous Ring of Fire that surrounds the Pacific Ocean plate. Of the world's active volcanoes, about 60% are along the perimeter of the Pacific, about 17% on mid-oceanic islands, about 14% in an arc along the south of the Indonesian islands, and about 9% in the Mediterranean area, Africa, and Asia Minor. Fifty volcanoes have erupted in the United States since recorded history, and the United States ranks third, behind Indonesia and Japan, in the number of historically active volcanoes.

The Nature of Volcanoes

Volcanoes are built by the accumulation of their own eruptive products—lava, bombs (crusted over ash flows), and tephra (airborne ash and dust). A volcano is most commonly a conical hill or mountain built around a vent that connects with reservoirs of molten rock below the surface of Earth. The term volcano also refers to the opening or vent through which the molten rock and associated gases are expelled.

Driven by buoyancy and gas pressure, the molten rock, which is lighter than the surrounding solid rock, forces its way upward and may ultimately break though zones of weaknesses in Earth's crust. If so, an eruption begins, and the molten rock may pour from the vent as nonexplosive lava flows, or it may shoot violently into the air as dense clouds of lava fragments. Larger fragments fall back around the vent, and accumulations of fall-back fragments may move downslope as ash flows under the force of gravity. Some of the finer ejected materials may be carried by the wind and fall to the ground many miles away. The finest ash particles may be injected miles into the atmosphere and carried many times around the world by stratospheric winds before settling out.

Magma, Lava, and Pumice

Molten rock below the surface of Earth that rises in volcanic vents is known as magma, but after it erupts from a volcano it is called lava. Originating many tens of miles beneath the ground, the ascending magma commonly contains some crystals, fragments of surrounding (unmelted) rocks, and dissolved gases, but it is primarily a liquid composed of oxygen, silicon, aluminum, iron, magnesium, calcium, sodium, potassium, titanium, and manganese. Magmas also contain many other chemical elements in trace quantities. Upon cooling, the liquid magma may precipitate crystals of various minerals until solidification is complete to form an igneous or magmatic rock.

Lava is red-hot when it pours or blasts out of a vent but soon changes to dark red, gray, black, or some other color as it cools and solidifies. Very hot, gas-rich lava containing abundant iron and magnesium is fluid and flows like hot tar, whereas cooler, gas-poor lava high in silicon, sodium, and potassium

flows sluggishly, like thick honey, or in other cases, like pasty, blocky masses.

All magmas contain dissolved gases, and as they rise to the surface to erupt, the confining pressures are reduced and the dissolved gases are liberated either quietly or explosively. If the lava is a thin fluid (not viscous), the gases may escape easily. But if the lava is thick and pasty (highly viscous), the gases will not move freely but will build up tremendous pressure, and ultimately escape with explosive violence. Gases in lava may be compared with the gas in a bottle of a carbonated soft drink. If you put your thumb over the top of the bottle and shake it vigorously, the gas separates from the drink and forms bubbles. When you remove your thumb abruptly, there is a miniature explosion of gas and liquid. The gases in lava behave in somewhat the same way. Their sudden expansion causes the terrible explosions that throw out great masses of solid rock as well as lava, dust, and ashes.

The violent separation of gas from lava may produce rock froth called pumice. Some of this froth is so light—because of the many gas bubbles—that it floats on water. In many eruptions, the froth is shattered explosively into small fragments that are hurled high into the air in the form of volcanic cinders (red or black), volcanic ash (commonly tan or gray), and volcanic dust.   □

Recent Volcanic Activity
(**Bold** indicates activity in 1999)

Volcano	Date of last eruption or activity	Volcano	Date of last eruption or activity
Adatara, Honshu, Japan	Sept. 7, 1997	Merapi, Indonesia	July 20, 1998
Akutan, Alaska	March 10, 1996	Metis Shoal, Tonga	June 6, 1995
Amukta, Alaska	Sept. 17, 1996	Momotombo, Nicaragua	April 4, 1996
Arenal, Costa Rica	May 5, 1998	Monowai Seamount,	Dec. 5, 1997
Axial Seamount	Jan. 25–28, 1998	Kermadec Islands	
Barren Island, Indian Ocean	Dec. 20, 1994	**Montserrat, West Indies**	**Aug. 13–20, 1999**
Bezymianny, Kamchatka, Russia	**Feb. 24, 1999**	Northern Gorda Ridge	Feb. 28, 1996
Mount Cameroon, Cameroon	**June 8, 1999**	Okmok, Alaska	May. 2, 1997
Cerro Negro, Nicaragua	**Aug. 6, 1999**	Pacaya, Guatemala	May 21, 1998
Chiginagak, Alaska	Nov. 7, 1997	Papandayan, Java, Indonesia	July 1, 1998
Colima, Mexico	**July 29, 1999**	Pavlof, Alaska	June 3, 1997
Eastern Gemini Seamount, Vanuatu	Feb. 23, 1996	Peuet Sague, Indonesia	April 27, 1998
Etna, Sicily, Italy	**Sept. 7, 1999**	Piparo, Trinidad	Feb. 22, 1997
Fernandina, Galápagos	Jan. 25, 1995	**Piton de la Fournaise, Réunion,**	**July 19, 1999**
Fogo, Cape Verde	April 2, 1995	Indian Ocean	
Fuego, Guatemala	**July 29, 1999**	**Popocatepetl, Mexico**	**Aug. 19, 1999**
Grimsvotn Volcano, Iceland	Dec. 18–28, 1998	Rabaul, Papua New Guinea	May 28, 1997
Guagua Pichincha, Ecuador	**Sept. 3–4, 1999**	Rincon de la Vieja, Costa Rica	Feb. 16, 1998
Hakkoda, Japan	July 12, 1997	Ruapehu, New Zealand	Oct. 1997
Mount Hili Aludo, Indonesia	May 13, 1997	Ruby Seamount, Mariana Islands	Oct. 25, 1995
Hosho, Kyushu, Japan	Oct. 12, 1995	Sakura-Jima, Japan	Jan. 24, 1998
Iwate-san, Honshu, Japan	July 10, 1998	San Cristobal, Nicaragua	May 20, 1997
Mount Karangetang, Indonesia	April 19, 1997	Semeru, Java, Indonesia	1967–continuing
Karymsky, Kamchatka, Russia	**Aug. 5, 1999**	Sheveluch, Kamchatka, Russia	July 31, 1997
Kilauea, Hawaii	1983–continuing	**Shin-dake, Kuchinoerabujima**	**Aug. 26, 1999**
Kliuchevskoi, Russia	**June 26, 1999**	Island, Japan	
Komaga-take, Hokkaido, Japan	March 5, 1996	**Shishaldin, Alaska**	**April 19, 1999**
Korovin, Alaska	June 30, 1998	Mount St. Helens, Washington	July 1, 1998
Krakatau, Indonesia	**Feb. 5–7, 1999**	Stromboli, Italy	Aug. 23, 1998
Mount Lewotobi, Indonesia	**July 1, 1999**	**Taal, Philippines**	**July 29, 1999**
Loihi Seamount, Hawaii	July 26, 1996	**Telica, Nicaragua**	**Aug. 11, 1999**
Long Valley caldera, California	April 2, 1996	**Terceira, Azores**	**Jan. 8, 1999**
Maderas, Nicaragua	Sept. 27, 1996	**Tonga (unnamed volcano)**	**Jan. 18, 1999**
Manam, Papua New Guinea	May 28, 1997	**White Island, New Zealand**	**July 23, 1999**
Mayon, Philippines	**July 6, 1999**	Yellowstone, Wyoming	Jan. 9, 1998
McDonald Island, Australia	Dec. 1996	Zacatecas, Mexico	June 1997

Source: Volcano World, University of North Dakota (http://volcano.und.nodak.edu).

The Deadliest Volcanic Eruptions

Deaths	Volcano	Year	Major cause of deaths
92,000	Tambora, Indonesia	1815	Starvation
36,417	Krakatau, Indonesia	1883	Tsunami
29,025	Mt. Pelee, Martinique	1902	Ash flows
25,000	Ruiz, Colombia	1985	Mudflows
14,300	Unzen, Japan	1792	Volcano collapse, tsunami
9,350	Laki, Iceland	1783	Starvation
5,110	Kelut, Indonesia	1919	Mudflows
4,011	Galunggung, Indonesia	1882	Mudflows
3,500	Vesuvius, Italy	1631	Mudflows, lava flows
3,360	Vesuvius, Italy	79	Ash flows and falls
2,957	Papandayan, Indonesia	1772	Ash flows
2,942	Lamington, Papua New Guinea	1951	Ash flows
2,000	El Chichon, Mexico	1982	Ash flows
1,680	Soufriere, St. Vincent	1902	Ash flows
1,475	Oshima, Japan	1741	Tsunami
1,377	Asama, Japan	1783	Ash flows, mudflows
1,335	Taal, Philippines	1911	Ash flows
1,200	Mayon, Philippines	1814	Mudflows
1,184	Agung, Indonesia	1963	Ash flows
1,000	Cotopaxi, Ecuador	1877	Mudflows
800	Pinatubo, Philippines	1991	Roof collapses and disease
700	Komagatake, Japan	1640	Tsunami
700	Ruiz, Colombia	1845	Mudflows
500	Hibok-Hibok, Philippines	1951	Ash flows

Source: Volcano World, University of North Dakota (http://volcano.und.nodak.edu).

Principal Types of Volcanoes

Source: U.S. Dept. of Interior, Geological Survey

Geologists generally group volcanoes into four main kinds—cinder cones, composite volcanoes, shield volcanoes, and lava domes.

Cinder Cones

Cinder cones are the simplest type of volcano. They are built from particles and blobs of congealed lava ejected from a single vent. As the gas-charged lava is blown violently into the air, it breaks into small fragments that solidify and fall as cinders around the vent to form a circular or oval cone. Most cinder cones have a bowl-shaped crater at the summit and rarely rise more than a thousand feet or so above their surroundings. Cinder cones are numerous in western North America as well as throughout other volcanic terrains of the world.

Composite Volcanoes

Composite volcanoes, sometimes called *stratovolcanoes,* are typically deep-sided, symmetrical cones of large dimension built of alternating layers of lava flows, volcanic ash, cinders, blocks, and bombs and may rise as much as 8,000 feet above their bases. Some of the most beautiful mountains in the world are composite volcanoes, including Mt. Fuji in Japan, Mt. Cotopaxi in Ecuador, Mt. Shasta in California, Mt. Hood in Oregon, and Mt. St. Helens and Mt. Rainier in Washington.

Most composite volcanoes have a crater at the summit that contains a central vent or a clustered group of vents. Lavas either flow through breaks in the crater wall or issue from fissures on the flanks of the cone. Lava, solidified within the fissures, forms *dikes* that act as ribs which greatly strengthen the cone.

The essential feature of a composite volcano is a conduit system through which magma from a reservoir deep in Earth's crust rises to the surface. The volcano is built up by the accumulation of material erupted through the conduit and increases in size as lava, cinders, and ash are added to its slopes.

Shield Volcanoes

Shield volcanoes are built almost entirely of fluid lava flows. Flow after flow pours out in all directions from a central summit vent, or group of vents, building a broad, gently sloping cone of flat, domical shape, with a profile much like that of a warrior's shield. They are built up slowly by the accretion of thousands of flows of highly fluid basaltic (from *basalt,* a hard, dense dark volcanic rock) lava that spread widely over great distances, and then cool as thin, gently dipping sheets. Lavas also commonly erupt from vents along fractures (rift zones) that develop on the flanks of the cone. Some of the largest volcanoes in the world are shield volcanoes. In northern California and Oregon, many shield volcanoes have diameters of 3 or 4 miles and heights of 1,500 to 2,000 feet. The Hawaiian Islands are composed of linear chains of these volcanoes, including Kilauea and Mauna Loa on the island of Hawaii.

In some shield volcano eruptions, basaltic lava pours out quietly from long fissures instead of central vents and floods the surrounding countryside with lava flow upon lava flow, forming broad plateaus. Lava plateaus of this type can be seen in Iceland, southeastern Washington, eastern Oregon, and southern Idaho.

Lava Domes

Volcanic or lava domes are formed by relatively small, bulbous masses of lava too viscous to flow any great distance; consequently, on extrusion, the lava piles over and around its vent. A dome grows largely by expansion from within. As it grows its outer surface cools and hardens, then shatters, spilling loose fragments down its sides. Some domes form craggy knobs or spines over the volcanic vent, whereas others form short, steep-sided lava flows known as *coulees*. Volcanic domes commonly occur within the craters or on the flanks of large composite volcanoes. The nearly circular Novarupta Dome that formed during the 1912 eruption of Katmai Volcano, Alaska, measures 800 feet across and 200 feet high. The internal structure of this dome—defined by layering of lava fanning upward and outward from the center—indicates that it grew largely by expansion from within. Mt. Pelée in Martinique, West Indies, and Lassen Peak and Mono domes in California, are examples of lava domes.

Submarine Volcanoes

Submarine volcanoes and volcanic vents are common features on certain zones of the ocean floor. Some are active at the present time and, in shallow water, disclose their presence by blasting steam and rock-debris high above the surface of the sea. Many others lie at such great depths that the tremendous weight of the water above them results in high, confining pressure and prevents the formation and release of steam and gases. Even very large, deepwater eruptions may not disturb the ocean floor.

The famous black sand beaches of Hawaii were created virtually instantaneously by the violent interaction between hot lava and seawater.

Earthquakes

The Severity of an Earthquake

Source: National Earthquake Information Center, U.S. Geological Survey

The severity of an earthquake can be expressed in terms of both intensity and magnitude. The two terms are quite different, however, and they are often confused. Intensity is based on the observed effects of ground shaking on people, buildings, and natural features. It varies from place to place within the disturbed region depending on the location of the observer with respect to the earthquake epicenter. Magnitude is related to the amount of seismic energy released at the hypocenter of the earthquake. It is based on the amplitude of the earthquake waves recorded on instruments, which have a common calibration. The magnitude of an earthquake is thus represented by a single, instrumentally determined value.

Earthquakes are the result of forces deep within Earth's interior that continuously affect its surface. The energy from these forces is stored in a variety of ways within the rocks. When this energy is released suddenly—by shearing movements along faults in the crust of Earth, for example—an earthquake results. The area of the fault where the sudden rupture takes place is called the focus or hypocenter of the earthquake. The point on Earth's surface directly above the focus is called the epicenter of the earthquake.

The Richter Magnitude Scale

Seismic waves are the vibrations from earthquakes that travel through Earth; they are recorded on instruments called seismographs. Seismographs record a zigzag trace that shows the varying amplitude of ground oscillations beneath the instrument. Sensitive seismographs, which greatly magnify these ground motions, can detect strong earthquakes from sources anywhere in the world. The time, location, and magnitude of an earthquake can be determined from the data recorded by seismograph stations.

The Richter magnitude scale was developed in 1935 by Charles F. Richter of the California Institute of Technology as a mathematical device to compare the size of earthquakes. The magnitude of an earthquake is determined from the logarithm of the amplitude of waves recorded by seismographs. Adjustments are included in the magnitude formula to compensate for the variation in the distance between the various seismographs and the epicenter of the earthquakes. On the Richter Scale, magnitude is expressed in whole numbers and decimal fractions. For example, a magnitude of 5.3 might be computed for a moderate earthquake, and a strong earthquake might be rated as magnitude 6.3. Because of the logarithmic basis of the scale, each whole number increase in magnitude represents a tenfold increase in measured amplitude; as an estimate of energy, each whole number step in the magnitude scale corresponds to the release of about 31 times more energy than the amount associated with the preceding whole number value. Great earthquakes, such as the 1964 Good Friday earthquake in Alaska, have magnitudes of 8.0 or higher. On the average, one earthquake of such size occurs somewhere in the world each year. Although the Richter Scale has no upper limit, the largest known shocks have had magnitudes in the 8.8 to 8.9 range.

Why Are There So Many Earthquake Magnitude Scales?

Earthquake size, as measured by the Richter Scale, is a well known, but not well understood, concept. What is even less well understood is the proliferation of magnitude scales and their relation to Richter's original magnitude scale. Richter's magnitude scale was first created for measuring the size of earthquakes occurring in southern California, using relatively high-frequency data from nearby seismograph stations. This magnitude scale was referred to as ML, with the L standing for local. This is what was to eventually become known as the Richter magnitude.

As more seismograph stations were installed around the world, it became apparent that the method developed by Richter was strictly valid only for certain frequency and distance ranges. In order to take advantage of the growing number of globally distributed seismograph stations, new magnitude scales that are an extension of Richter's original idea were developed. These include body-wave magnitude, "mb," and surface-wave magnitude, "MS." Each is valid for a particular frequency range and type of seismic signal. In its range of validity each is equivalent to the Richter magnitude.

Because of the limitations of all three magnitude scales, ML, mb, and MS, a new, more uniformly applicable extension of the magnitude scale, known as moment magnitude, or "MW," was developed. In particular, for very large earthquakes moment magnitude gives the most reliable estimate of earthquake size. New techniques that take advantage of modern telecommunications have recently been implemented, allowing reporting agencies to obtain rapid estimates of moment magnitude for significant earthquakes. So nowadays, when most seismologists announce a magnitude number, they are rarely referring to the Richter Scale.

The Modified Mercalli Intensity Scale

The effect of an earthquake on Earth's surface is called the intensity. The intensity scale consists of a series of certain key responses such as people awakening, movement of furniture, damage to chimneys, and finally—total destruction. Although numerous intensity scales have been developed over the last several hundred years to evaluate the effects of

earthquakes, the one currently used in the United States is the Modified Mercalli (MM) Intensity Scale. It was developed in 1931 by the American seismologists Harry Wood and Frank Neumann. This scale, composed of 12 increasing levels of intensity that range from imperceptible shaking to catastrophic destruction, is designated by Roman numerals. It does not have a mathematical basis; instead it is an arbitrary ranking based on observed effects. The Modified Mercalli Intensity value assigned to a specific site after an earthquake has a more meaningful measure of severity to the nonscientist than the magnitude because intensity refers to the effects actually experienced at that place. □

Frequency of Earthquakes Worldwide[1]

Descriptor	Magnitude	Annual Average	Descriptor	Magnitude	Annual Average
Great	8 or higher	1	Light	4–4.9	c.6,200
Major	7–7.9	18	Minor	3–3.9	c.49,000
Strong	6–6.9	120	Very minor	2–3	c.1,000[2]
Moderate	5–5.9	800	Very minor	1–2	c.8,000[2]

1. Since 1900. 2. Per day. *Source:* National Earthquake Information Center, U.S. Geological Survey.

Number of Earthquakes Worldwide, 1987–1998, and Mortality Figures

Magnitude	1987	1990	1991	1992	1993	1994	1995	1996	1997	1998
8.0–9.9	0	0	0	0	1	2	3	1	0	2
7.0–7.9	11	12	11	23	15	13	22	21	20	10
6.0–6.9	112	115	105	104	141	161	185	160	125	113
5.0–5.9	1,437	1,635	1,469	1,541	1,449	1,542	1,327	1,223	1,118	832
4.0–4.9	4,146	4,493	4,372	5,196	5,034	4,544	8,140	8,794	7,938	6,943
3.0–3.9	1,806	2,457	2,952	4,643	4,263	5,000	5,002	4,869	4,467	5,639
2.0–2.9	1,037	2,364	2,927	3,068	5,390	5,369	3,838	2,388	2,397	3,851
1.0–1.9	102	474	801	887	1,177	779	645	295	388	752
0.1–0.9	0	0	1	2	9	17	19	1	4	9
No magnitude	2,639	5,062	3,878	4,084	3,997	1,944	1,826	2,186	3,415	2,380
Total	11,290	16,612	16,516	19,548	21,476	19,371	21,007	19,938	19,872	20,531
Estimated deaths	**1,080**	**51,916**	**2,326**	**3,814**	**10,036**	**1,038**	**7,949**	**419**	**2,907**	**8,928**

Source: National Earthquake Information Center, U.S. Geological Survey.

Major Earthquakes around the World, 1999

Date	Location	Magnitude[1]	Date	Location	Magnitude[1]
Jan. 19	New Ireland, Papua New Guinea	7.0	May 10	New Britain, Papua New Guinea	7.1
Feb. 6	Santa Cruz Islands	7.3	May 16	New Britain, Papua New Guinea	7.1
	(S. Pacific Sea)		Aug. 17	Izmit region, western Turkey	7.4
March 4	Celebes Sea, Indonesia	7.1	Sept. 21	Taiwan	7.6
April 5	New Britain, Papua New Guinea	7.4	Sept. 30	Oaxaca, Mexico	7.4
April 8	E. Russia/N.E. China border	7.1			

NOTE: A major earthquake is defined here as having a magnitude of 7.0 or more. 1. Unless otherwise indicated, magnitudes listed are moment magnitudes, the newest, more uniformly applicable magnitude scale. *Source:* National Earthquake Information Center, U.S. Geological Survey.

The Ten Largest Earthquakes of the Century

Country or place	Date	Magnitude[1]	Country or place	Date	Magnitude[1]
Chile	May 22, 1960	9.5	Kuril Islands	Nov. 6, 1958	8.7
Alaska	March 27, 1964	9.2	Alaska	Feb. 4, 1965	8.7
Russia	Nov. 4, 1952	9.0	India	Aug. 15, 1950	8.6
Ecuador	Jan. 31, 1906	8.8	Argentina	Nov. 11, 1922	8.5
Alaska	March 9, 1957	8.8	Indonesia	Feb. 1, 1938	8.5

1. Moment magnitude. *Source:* National Earthquake Information Center, U.S. Geological Survey.

The Fifteen Largest Earthquakes in the United States

Rank	Magnitude	Date	Location
1.	9.2	March 27, 1964	Prince William Sound, Alaska
2.	8.8	March 9, 1957	Andreanof Islands, Alaska
3.	8.7	Feb. 4, 1965	Rat Islands, Alaska
4.	8.3	Nov. 10, 1938	East of Shumagin Islands, Alaska
5.	8.3	July 10, 1958	Lituya Bay, Alaska
6.	8.2	Sept. 10, 1899	Yakutat Bay, Alaska
7.	8.2	Sept. 4, 1899	Near Cape Yakataga, Alaska
8.	8.0	May 7, 1986	Andreanof Islands, Alaska
9.	7.9	Feb. 7, 1812	New Madrid, Missouri
10.	7.9	Jan. 9, 1857	Fort Tejon, California
11.	7.9	April 3, 1868	Ka'u District, Island of Hawaii
12.	7.9	Oct. 9, 1900	Kodiak Island, Alaska
13.	7.9	Nov. 30, 1987	Gulf of Alaska
14.	7.8	March 26, 1872	Owens Valley, California
15.	7.8	Feb. 24, 1892	Imperial Valley, California

Source: National Earthquake Information Center, U.S. Geological Survey.

The Fifteen Largest Earthquakes in the Contiguous United States

Rank	Magnitude	Date	Location
1.	7.9	Feb. 7, 1812	New Madrid, Missouri
2.	7.9	Jan. 9, 1857	Fort Tejon, California
3.	7.8	March 26, 1872	Owens Valley, California
4.	7.8	Feb. 24, 1892	Imperial Valley, California
5.	7.7	Dec. 16, 1811	New Madrid, Missouri area
6.	7.7	April 18, 1906	San Francisco, California
7.	7.7	Oct. 3, 1915	Pleasant Valley, Nevada
8.	7.6	Jan. 23, 1812	New Madrid, Missouri
9.	7.6	June 28, 1992	Landers, California
10.	7.5	July 21, 1952	Kern County, California
11.	7.3	Nov. 4, 1927	West of Lompoc, California
12.	7.3	Dec. 16, 1954	Dixie Valley, Nevada
13.	7.3	Aug. 18, 1959	Hebgen Lake, Montana
14.	7.3	Oct. 28, 1983	Borah Peak, Idaho
15.	7.3	Jan. 31, 1922	West of Eureka, California

Source: National Earthquake Information Center, U.S. Geological Survey. NOTE: Widely differing magnitudes have been computed for some of these earthquakes; the values differ according to the methods and data used.

The World's 14 Highest Mountain Peaks (above 8,000 meters)

All 14 of the world's 8,000-meter peaks are located in the Himalaya or the Karakoram ranges in Asia. Thus far, only six climbers have reached the summits of all 14: Reinhold Messner (Italian) was first, followed by Jerzy Kukuczka (Poland), Ehardt Loretan (Switzerland), Carlos Carsolio (Mexico), Krzysztof Wielicki (Poland), and Juan Oiarzabal (Spain).

Mountain	Height Meters	Height Feet	First to summit	Date	Nationality
1. Everest	8,848	29,028	Edmund Hillary, Tenzing Norgay	May 29, 1953	New Zealand (Great Britain)
2. K2 (Mt. Godwin Austen)	8,611	28,250	A. Compagnoni, L. Lacedelli	July 31, 1954	Italy
3. Kangchenjunga	8,586	28,169	G. Band, J. Brown, N. Hardie, S. Streather	May 25, 1955	Great Britain
4. Lhotse	8,516	27,940	F. Luchsinger, E. Reiss	May 18, 1956	Switzerland
5. Makalu	8,463	27,766	J. Couzy, L. Terray, J. Franco, G. Magnone-Gialtsen, J. Bouier, S. Coupé, P. Leroux, A. Vialatte	May 15, 1955	France
6. Cho Oyu	8,201	26,906	H. Tichy, S. Jöchler, Pasang Dawa Lama	Oct. 19, 1954	Germany
7. Dhaulagiri	8,167	26,795	A. Schelbert, E. Forrer, K. Diemberger, P. Diener, Nyima Dorji, Nawang Dorji	May 13, 1960	Switzerland
8. Manaslu	8,163	26,781	T. Iminaschi Gialtsen, K. Kato, M. Higeta	May 9, 1956	Japan
9. Nanga Parbat	8,125	26,660	Hermann Buhl	July 3, 1953	Germany
10. Annapurna	8,091	26,545	M. Herzog, L. Lachenal	June 3, 1950	France
11. Gasherbrum I	8,068	26,470	P. K. Schoeing, A. J. Kauffman	July 4, 1958	United States
12. Broad Peak	8,047	26,400	M. Schmuck, F. Wintersteller, K. Diemberger, H. Buhl	June 9, 1957	Germany
13. Shisha Pangma	8,046	26,397	Hsu Chin and team of 9	May 2, 1964	China
14. Gasherbrum II	8,035	26,360	F. Moravec, S. Larch, H. Willenpart	July 7, 1956	Austria

Highest Mountain Peaks of the World (continued from p. 490)

(*See* p. 500 for U.S. peaks.)

Mountain peak	Range	Location	Height ft.	Height m
Annapurna II	Himalayas	Nepal	26,041	7,937
Gyachung Kang	Himalayas	Nepal	25,910	7,897
Disteghil Sar	Karakoram	Pakistan	25,858	7,882
Himalchuli	Himalayas	Nepal	25,801	7,864
Nuptse	Himalayas	Nepal	25,726	7,841
Nanda Devi	Himalayas	India	25,663	7,824
Masherbrum	Karakoram	Kashmir[1]	25,660	7,821
Rakaposhi	Karakoram	Pakistan	25,551	7,788
Kanjut Sar	Karakoram	Pakistan	25,461	7,761
Kamet	Himalayas	India/Tibet	25,446	7,756
Namcha Barwa	Himalayas	Tibet	25,445	7,756
Gurla Mandhata	Himalayas	Tibet	25,355	7,728
Ulugh Muztagh	Kunlun	Tibet	25,340	7,723
Kungur	Muztagh Ata	China	25,325	7,719
Tirich Mir	Hindu Kush	Pakistan	25,230	7,690
Saser Kangri	Karakoram	India	25,172	7,672
Makalu II	Himalayas	Nepal	25,120	7,657
Minya Konka (Gongga Shan)	Daxue Shan	China	24,900	7,590
Kula Kangri	Himalayas	Bhutan	24,783	7,554
Chang-tzu	Himalayas	Tibet	24,780	7,553
Muztagh Ata	Muztagh Ata	China	24,757	7,546
Skyang Kangri	Himalayas	Kashmir	24,750	7,544
Ismail Samani Peak (formerly Communism Peak)	Pamirs	Tajikistan	24,590	7,495
Jongsong Peak	Himalayas	Nepal	24,472	7,459
Pobeda Peak	Tien Shan	Kyrgyzstan	24,406	7,439
Sia Kangri	Himalayas	Kashmir	24,350	7,422
Haramosh Peak	Karakoram	Pakistan	24,270	7,397
Istoro Nal	Hindu Kush	Pakistan	24,240	7,388
Tent Peak	Himalayas	Nepal	24,165	7,365
Chomo Lhari	Himalayas	Tibet/Bhutan	24,040	7,327
Chamlang	Himalayas	Nepal	24,012	7,319
Kabru	Himalayas	Nepal	24,002	7,316
Alung Gangri	Himalayas	Tibet	24,000	7,315
Baltoro Kangri	Himalayas	Kashmir	23,990	7,312
Muztagh Ata (K-5)	Kunlun	China	23,890	7,282
Mana	Himalayas	India	23,860	7,273
Baruntse	Himalayas	Nepal	23,688	7,220
Nepal Peak	Himalayas	Nepal	23,500	7,163
Amne Machin	Kunlun	China	23,490	7,160
Gauri Sankar	Himalayas	Nepal/Tibet	23,440	7,145
Badrinath	Himalayas	India	23,420	7,138
Nunkun	Himalayas	Kashmir	23,410	7,135
Lenin Peak	Pamirs	Tajikistan/Kyrgyzstan	23,405	7,134
Pyramid	Himalayas	Nepal	23,400	7,132
Api	Himalayas	Nepal	23,399	7,132
Pauhunri	Himalayas	India/China	23,385	7,128
Trisul	Himalayas	India	23,360	7,120
Korzhenevski Peak	Pamirs	Tajikistan	23,310	7,105
Kangto	Himalayas	Tibet	23,260	7,090
Nyainqentanglha	Nyainqentanglha Shan	China	23,255	7,088
Trisuli	Himalayas	India	23,210	7,074
Dunagiri	Himalayas	India	23,184	7,066
Revolution Peak	Pamirs	Tajikistan	22,880	6,974
Aconcagua	Andes	Argentina	22,834	6,960
Ojos del Salado	Andes	Argentina/Chile	22,664	6,908
Bonete	Andes	Argentina/Chile	22,546	6,872
Ama Dablam	Himalayas	Nepal	22,494	6,856
Tupungato	Andes	Argentina/Chile	22,310	6,800
Moscow Peak	Pamirs	Tajikistan	22,260	6,785
Pissis	Andes	Argentina	22,241	6,779
Mercedario	Andes	Argentina/Chile	22,211	6,770
Huascarán	Andes	Peru	22,205	6,768
Llullaillaco	Andes	Argentina/Chile	22,057	6,723
El Libertador	Andes	Argentina	22,047	6,720
Cachi	Andes	Argentina	22,047	6,720
Kailas	Himalayas	Tibet	22,027	6,714
Incahuasi	Andes	Argentina/Chile	21,720	6,620
Yerupaja	Andes	Peru	21,709	6,617
Kurumda	Pamirs	Tajikistan	21,686	6,610
Galan	Andes	Argentina	21,654	6,600
El Muerto	Andes	Argentina/Chile	21,463	6,542
Sajama	Andes	Bolivia	21,391	6,520
Nacimiento	Andes	Argentina	21,302	6,493
Illampu	Andes	Bolivia	21,276	6,485
Illimani	Andes	Bolivia	21,201	6,462
Coropuna	Andes	Peru	21,083	6,426
Laudo	Andes	Argentina	20,997	6,400
Ancohuma	Andes	Bolivia	20,958	6,388
Cuzco (Ausangate)	Andes	Peru	20,945	6,384

1. Kashmir is divided between India and Pakistan, with both countries disputing the boundaries. *Source:* National Geographic Society.

Climbing the Seven Summits

Less than fifty mountaineers have climbed all "Seven Summits"—the highest peak on each of the seven continents. The first was Dick Bass, an American businessman, on April 30, 1985. The seven summits are Mt. Everest (Asia) 29,028 ft., Mt. Aconcagua (South America) 22,834 ft., Mt. McKinley (North America) 20,320 ft., Mt. Kilimanjaro (Africa) 19,340 ft., Mt. Elbrus (Europe) 18,510 ft., Vinson Massif (Antarctica) 16,066 ft., and Kosciusko (Australia) 7,316 ft.

World's Greatest Man-Made Lakes[1]

Name of dam	Location	Millions of cu. m	Thousands of acre-feet	Year completed	Name of dam	Location	Millions of cu. m	Thousands of acre-feet	Year completed
Owen Falls	Uganda	204,800	166,000	1954	Pati (Chapetón)	Argentina	53,700	43,535	UC
Kariba	Zimbabwe	181,592	147,218	1959	Upper Wainganga	India	50,700	41,103	1987
Bratsk	Siberia	169,270	137,220	1964	Sáo Felix	Brazil	50,600	41,022	1986
High Aswan (Sadd-el-Aali)	Egypt	168,000	136,200	1970	Bukhtarma	Former U.S.S.R.	49,740	40,325	1960
Akosombo	Ghana	148,000	120,000	1965	Atatürk (Karababa)	Turkey	48,700	39,482	1990
Daniel Johnson	Canada	141,852	115,000	1968	Cerros Colorados	Argentina	48,000	38,914	1973
Guri (Raul Leoni)	Venezuela	136,000	110,256	1986	Irkutsk	Russia	46,000	37,290	1956
Krasnoyarsk	Siberia	73,300	59,425	1967	Tucuruí	Brazil	36,375	29,489	1984
Bennett W.A.C.	Canada	70,309	57,006	1967	Vilyuy	Russia	35,900	29,104	1967
Zeya	Russia	68,400	55,452	1978	Sanmenxia	China	35,400	28,700	1960
Cabora Bassa	Mozambique	63,000	51,075	1974	Hoover	Nevada/Arizona	35,154	28,500	1936
LaGrande 2	Canada	61,720	50,037	1982	Sobridinho	Brazil	34,200	27,726	1981
LaGrande 3	Canada	60,020	48,659	1982	Glen Canyon	Arizona	33,304	27,000	1964
Ust'-Ilimsk	Russia	59,300	48,075	1980	Jenpeg	Canada	31,790	25,772	1975
Volga-V.I. Lenin	Russia	58,000	47,020	1955					
Caniapiscau	Canada	53,790	43,608	1981					

1. Formed by construction of dams. NOTE: UC = under construction. *Source:* Department of the Interior, Bureau of Reclamation and *International Water Power and Dam Construction.*

Oceans and Seas

Name	Area sq. mi.	Area sq. km	Average depth ft.	Average depth m	Greatest known depth ft.	Greatest known depth m	Place of greatest known depth
Pacific Ocean	64,000,000	165,760,000	13,215	4,028	36,198	11,033	Mariana Trench
Atlantic Ocean	31,815,000	82,400,000	12,880	3,926	30,246	9,219	Puerto Rico Trench
Indian Ocean	25,300,000	65,526,700	13,002	3,963	24,460	7,455	Sunda Trench
Arctic Ocean	5,440,200	14,090,000	3,953	1,205	18,456	5,625	77°45′N; 175°W
Mediterranean Sea[1]	1,145,100	2,965,800	4,688	1,429	15,197	4,632	Off Cape Matapan, Greece
Caribbean Sea	1,049,500	2,718,200	8,685	2,647	22,788	6,946	Off Cayman Islands
South China Sea	895,400	2,319,000	5,419	1,652	16,456	5,016	West of Luzon
Bering Sea	884,900	2,291,900	5,075	1,547	15,659	4,773	Off Buldir Island
Gulf of Mexico	615,000	1,592,800	4,874	1,486	12,425	3,787	Sigsbee Deep
Okhotsk Sea	613,800	1,589,700	2,749	838	12,001	3,658	146°10′E; 46°50′N
East China Sea	482,300	1,249,200	617	188	9,126	2,782	25°16′N; 125°E
Hudson Bay	475,800	1,232,300	420	128	600	183	Near entrance
Japan Sea	389,100	1,007,800	4,429	1,350	12,276	3,742	Central Basin
Andaman Sea	308,100	797,700	2,854	870	12,392	3,777	Off Car Nicobar Island
North Sea	222,100	575,200	308	94	2,165	660	Skagerrak
Red Sea	169,100	438,000	1,611	491	7,254	2,211	Off Port Sudan
Baltic Sea	163,000	422,200	180	55	1,380	421	Off Gotland

1. Includes Black Sea and Sea of Azov. NOTE: For Caspian Sea, *see* Large Lakes of the World.

Large Lakes of the World

(area more than 1,600 sq miles)

Name and location	Area sq. mi.	Area km	Length mi.	Length km	Maximum depth ft.	Maximum depth m
Caspian Sea, Azerbaijan-Russia-Kazakhstan-Turkmenistan-Iran[1]	152,239	394,299	745	1,199	3,104	946
Superior, U.S.-Canada	31,820	82,414	383	616	1,333	406
Victoria, Tanzania-Uganda	26,828	69,485	200	322	270	82
Aral, Kazakhstan-Uzbekistan	25,659	66,457	266	428	223	68
Huron, U.S.-Canada	23,010	59,596	247	397	750	229
Michigan, U.S.	22,400	58,016	321	517	923	281
Tanganyika, Tanzania-Congo	12,700	32,893	420	676	4,708	1,435
Baikal, Russia	12,162	31,500	395	636	5,712	1,741
Great Bear, Canada	12,000	31,080	232	373	270	82
Nyasa, Malawi-Mozambique-Tanzania	11,600	30,044	360	579	2,316	706

Name and location	Area		Length		Maximum depth	
	sq. mi.	km	mi.	km	ft.	m
Great Slave, Canada	11,170	28,930	298	480	2,015	614
Chad,[2] Chad-Niger-Nigeria	9,946	25,760	—	—	23	7
Erie, U.S.-Canada	9,930	25,719	241	388	210	64
Winnipeg, Canada	9,094	23,553	264	425	204	62
Ontario, U.S.-Canada	7,520	19,477	193	311	778	237
Balkhash, Kazakhstan	7,115	18,428	376	605	87	27
Ladoga, Russia	7,000	18,130	124	200	738	225
Onega, Russia	3,819	9,891	154	248	361	110
Titicaca, Bolivia-Peru	3,141	8,135	110	177	1,214	370
Nicaragua, Nicaragua	3,089	8,001	110	177	230	70
Athabaska, Canada	3,058	7,920	208	335	407	124
Rudolf, Kenya	2,473	6,405	154	248	—	—
Reindeer, Canada	2,444	6,330	152	245	—	—
Eyre, South Australia	2,400[3]	6,216	130	209	varies	varies
Issyk-Kul, Kyrgyzstan	2,394	6,200	113	182	2,297	700
Urmia,[2] Iran	2,317	6,001	81	130	49	15
Torrens, South Australia	2,200	5,698	130	209	—	—
Vänern, Sweden	2,141	5,545	87	140	322	98
Winnipegosis, Canada	2,086	5,403	152	245	59	18
Mobutu Sese Seko, Uganda	2,046	5,299	100	161	180	55
Nettilling, Baffin Island, Canada	1,950	5,051	70	113	—	—
Nipigon, Canada	1,870	4,843	72	116	—	—
Manitoba, Canada	1,817	4,706	140	225	22	7
Great Salt, U.S.	1,800	4,662	75	121	15–25	5–8
Kioga, Uganda	1,700	4,403	50	80	about 30	9
Koko-Nor, China	1,630	4,222	66	106		

1. The Caspian Sea is called "sea" because the Romans, finding it salty, named it *Mare Caspium*. Many geographers, however, consider it a lake because it is land-locked. 2. Figures represent high-water data. 3. Varies with the rainfall of the wet season. It has been reported to dry up almost completely on occasion.

Principal Rivers of the World

(*See* pp. 498–499 for other U.S. rivers.)

River	Source	Outflow	Approx. length	
			mi.	km
Nile	Tributaries of Lake Victoria, Africa	Mediterranean Sea	4,180	6,690
Amazon	Glacier-fed lakes, Peru	Atlantic Ocean	3,912	6,296
Mississippi-Missouri-Red Rock	Source of Red Rock, Montana	Gulf of Mexico	3,710	5,970
Yangtze Kiang	Tibetan plateau, China	China Sea	3,602	5,797
Ob	Altai Mts., Russia	Gulf of Ob	3,459	5,567
Huang Ho (Yellow)	Eastern part of Kunlan Mts., west China	Gulf of Chihli	2,900	4,667
Yenisei	Tannu-Ola Mts., western Tuva, Russia	Arctic Ocean	2,800	4,506
Paraná	Confluence of Paranaiba and Grande rivers	Río de la Plata	2,795	4,498
Irtish	Altai Mts., Russia	Ob River	2,758	4,438
Zaire (Congo)	Confluence of Lualab and Luapula rivers, Congo	Atlantic Ocean	2,716	4,371
Heilong (Amur)	Confluence of Shilka (Russia) and Argun (Manchuria) rivers	Tatar Strait	2,704	4,352
Lena	Baikal Mts., Russia	Arctic Ocean	2,652	4,268
Mackenzie	Head of Finlay River, British Columbia, Canada	Beaufort Sea (Arctic Ocean)	2,635	4,241
Niger	Guinea	Gulf of Guinea	2,600	4,184
Mekong	Tibetan highlands	South China Sea	2,500	4,023
Mississippi	Lake Itasca, Minnesota	Gulf of Mexico	2,348	3,779
Missouri	Confluence of Jefferson, Gallatin, and Madison rivers, Montana	Mississippi River	2,315	3,726
Volga	Valdai plateau, Russia	Caspian Sea	2,291	3,687
Madeira	Confluence of Beni and Maumoré rivers, Bolivia-Brazil boundary	Amazon River	2,012	3,238
Purus	Peruvian Andes	Amazon River	1,993	3,207
São Francisco	Southwest Minas Gerais, Brazil	Atlantic Ocean	1,987	3,198
Yukon	Junction of Lewes and Pelly rivers, Yukon Territory, Canada	Bering Sea	1,979	3,185
St. Lawrence	Lake Ontario	Gulf of St. Lawrence	1,900	3,058
Rio Grande	San Juan Mts., Colorado	Gulf of Mexico	1,885	3,034
Brahmaputra	Himalayas	Ganges River	1,800	2,897

River	Source	Outflow	Approx. length mi.	km
Indus	Himalayas	Arabian Sea	1,800	2,897
Danube	Black Forest, Germany	Black Sea	1,766	2,842
Euphrates	Confluence of Murat Nehri and Kara Su rivers, Turkey	Shatt-al-Arab	1,739	2,799
Darling	Central part of Eastern Highlands, Australia	Murray River	1,702	2,739
Zambezi	11°21′S, 24°22′E, Zambia	Mozambique Channel	1,700	2,736
Tocantins	Goiás, Brazil	Pará River	1,677	2,699
Murray	Australian Alps, New South Wales	Indian Ocean	1,609	2,589
Nelson	Head of Bow River, western Alberta, Canada	Hudson Bay	1,600	2,575
Paraguay	Mato Grosso, Brazil	Paraná River	1,584	2,549
Ural	Southern Ural Mts., Russia	Caspian Sea	1,574	2,533
Ganges	Himalayas	Bay of Bengal	1,557	2,506
Amu Darya (Oxus)	Nicholas Range, Pamir Mts., Turkmenistan	Aral Sea	1,500	2,414
Japurá	Andes, Colombia	Amazon River	1,500	2,414
Salween	Tibet, south of Kunlun Mts.	Gulf of Martaban	1,500	2,414
Arkansas	Central Colorado	Mississippi River	1,459	2,348
Colorado	Grand County, Colorado	Gulf of California	1,450	2,333
Dnieper	Valdai Hills, Russia	Black Sea	1,419	2,284
Ohio-Allegheny	Potter County, Pennsylvania	Mississippi River	1,306	2,102
Irrawaddy	Confluence of Nmai and Mali rivers, northeast Burma	Bay of Bengal	1,300	2,092
Orange	Lesotho	Atlantic Ocean	1,300	2,092
Orinoco	Serra Parima Mts., Venezuela	Atlantic Ocean	1,281	2,062
Pilcomayo	Andes Mts., Bolivia	Paraguay River	1,242	1,999
Xi Jiang (Si Kiang)	Eastern Yunnan Province, China	China Sea	1,236	1,989
Columbia	Columbia Lake, British Columbia, Canada	Pacific Ocean	1,232	1,983
Don	Tula, Russia	Sea of Azov	1,223	1,968
Sungari	China-North Korea boundary	Amur River	1,215	1,955
Saskatchewan	Canadian Rocky Mts.	Lake Winnipeg	1,205	1,939
Peace	Stikine Mts., British Columbia, Canada	Great Slave River	1,195	1,923
Tigris	Taurus Mts., Turkey	Shatt-al-Arab	1,180	1,899

Large Islands of the World

Island	Location and political affiliation	Area sq. mi.	sq. km
Greenland	North Atlantic (Danish)	839,999	2,175,597
New Guinea	Southwest Pacific (Irian Jaya, Indonesia, western part; Papua New Guinea, eastern part)	316,615	820,033
Borneo	West mid-Pacific (Indonesian, south part, Brunei and Malaysian, north part)	286,914	743,107
Madagascar	Indian Ocean (Malagasy Republic)	226,657	587,042
Baffin	North Atlantic (Canadian)	183,810	476,068
Sumatra	Northeast Indian Ocean (Indonesian)	182,859	473,605
Honshu	Sea of Japan-Pacific (Japanese)	88,925	230,316
Great Britain	Off coast of NW Europe (England, Scotland, and Wales)	88,758	229,883
Ellesmere	Arctic Ocean (Canadian)	82,119	212,688
Victoria	Arctic Ocean (Canadian)	81,930	212,199
Sulawesi (Celebes)	West mid-Pacific (Indonesian)	72,986	189,034
South Island	South Pacific (New Zealand)	58,093	150,461
Java	Indian Ocean (Indonesian)	48,990	126,884
North Island	South Pacific (New Zealand)	44,281	114,688
Cuba	Caribbean Sea (republic)	44,218	114,525
Newfoundland	North Atlantic (Canadian)	42,734	110,681
Luzon	West mid-Pacific (Philippines)	40,420	104,688
Iceland	North Atlantic (republic)	39,768	102,999
Mindanao	West mid-Pacific (Philippines)	36,537	94,631
Ireland	West of Great Britain (republic, south part; United Kingdom, north part)	32,597	84,426
Hokkaido	Sea of Japan—Pacific (Japanese)	30,372	78,663
Hispaniola	Caribbean Sea (Dominican Republic, east part; Haiti, west part)	29,355	76,029
Tasmania	South of Australia (Australian)	26,215	67,897
Sri Lanka (Ceylon)	Indian Ocean (republic)	25,332	65,610
Sakhalin (Karafuto)	North of Japan (Russian)	24,560	63,610
Banks	Arctic Ocean (Canadian)	23,230	60,166
Devon	Arctic Ocean (Canadian)	20,861	54,030
Tierra del Fuego	Southern tip of South America (Argentinian, east part; Chilean, west part)	18,605	48,187
Kyushu	Sea of Japan—Pacific (Japanese)	16,223	42,018

Highest Waterfalls of the World

Waterfall	Location	Height ft.	Height m	Waterfall	Location	Height ft.	Height m
Angel	Venezuela	3,281	1,000	Cascata delle	Italy	650	198
Tugela	Natal, South Africa	3,000	914	Marmore			
Cuquenán	Venezuela	2,000	610	Maradalsfos	Norway	643	196
Sutherland	South Island, New	1,904	580	Feather	California	640	195
	Zealand			Maletsunyane	Lesotho	630	192
Takkakaw	British Columbia	1,650	503	Bridalveil (Yosemite)	California	620	189
Ribbon (Yosemite)	California	1,612	491	Multnomah	Oregon	620	189
Upper Yosemite	California	1,430	436	Vøringsfos	Norway	597	182
Gavarnie	Southwest France	1,384	422	Nevada (Yosemite)	California	594	181
Vettisfoss	Norway	1,200	366	Skjeggedal	Norway	525	160
Widows' Tears	California	1,170	357	Marina	Guyana	500	152
(Yosemite)				Tequendama	Colombia	425	130
Basaseachic	Mexico	1,020	311	King George's	Cape of Good Hope,	400	122
Staubbach	Switzerland	984	300		South Africa		
Middle Cascade	California	909	277	Illilouette (Yosemite)	California	370	113
(Yosemite)				Victoria	Zimbabwe-Zambia	355	108
King Edward VIII	Guyana	850	259		boundary		
Gersoppa	India	829	253	Handöl	Sweden	345	105
Kaieteur	Guyana	822	251	Lower Yosemite	California	320	98
Skykje	Norway	820	250	Comet (Mt. Rainier	Washington	320	98
Kalambo	Tanzania-Zambia	720	219	Park)			
Fairy (Mt. Rainier	Washington	700	213	Vernal (Yosemite)	California	317	97
Park)				Virginia	Northwest Territories,	315	96
Trummelbach	Switzerland	700	213		Canada		
Aniene (Teverone)	Italy	680	207	Lower Yellowstone	Wyoming	310	94

NOTE: Niagara Falls (New York-Ontario), though of great volume, has parallel drops of only 158 and 167 feet.

Interesting Caves and Caverns of the World

Aggtelek. In village of same name, northern Hungary. Large stalactitic cavern about five miles long.

Altamira Cave. Near Santander, Spain. Contains Stone Age animal paintings on roof and walls.

Antiparos. On island of same name in the Grecian Archipelago. Some stalactites are 20 ft. long. Brilliant colors and fantastic shapes.

Blue Grotto. On island of Capri, Italy. Sea cavern hollowed out in limestone by constant wave action. Now half filled with water because of sinking coast. Name derived from unusual blue light permeating the cave. Source of light is a submerged opening allowing light to pass through the water.

Carlsbad Caverns. Southeast New Mexico. Contains some of the largest and most impressive stalactities and stalagmites, particularly in the Lechuguilla Cave.

Fingal's Cave. On island of Staffa off coast of western Scotland. Penetrates about 200 ft. inland. Contains basaltic columns almost 40 ft. high.

Jenolan Caves. In Blue Mountain plateau, New South Wales, Australia. Beautiful stalactitic formations.

Kent's Cavern. Near Torquay, England. Source of much information on Paleolithic humans.

Lascaux Cave. Southwestern France. Features prehistoric cave paintings estimated to be tens of thousands of years old. Closed to the public.

Lubang Nasib Bagus. Sarawak, Malaysia. World's largest cave chamber: 2,300 ft. long, 1,480 ft. wide, and everywhere at least 230 ft. high.

Luray Caverns. Near Luray, Va. Has large stalactitic and stalagmitic columns of many colors.

Mogao Caves. Located along the old Silk Route in China, Mogao is composed of 492 cells and cave sanctuaries that are famous for their statues and wall paintings, spanning a thousand years of Buddhist art.

Mammoth Cave. This limestone cavern in central Kentucky is the longest cave system in the world. Cave area is about 10 mi. in diameter but has 345 mi. of irregular subterranean passageways at various levels, plus underground lakes and rivers.

Peak Cavern or Devil's Hole. Derbyshire, England. About 2,250 ft. into a mountain. Lowest part is about 600 ft. below the surface.

Postojna Grotto. Postojna, Slovenia. Largest tavern in Europe; numerous beautiful stalactites. Famous example of a karst cave—grooved and irregularly eroded limestone formations carved out by underground streams. Pivka River flows through part of it.

Singing Cave. Iceland. A lava cave; name derived from echoes of people singing in it.

Waitomo Cave. North Island, New Zealand. Glowworms on cave ceiling look like thousands of stars in the night sky.

Wind Cave. In Black Hills of South Dakota. Limestone caverns with stalactites and stalagmites almost entirely missing. Variety of crystal formations called "boxwork."

Wyandotte Cave. In Crawford County, southern Indiana. A limestone cavern with five levels of passages; one of the largest in North America. "Monumental Mountain," approximately 135 ft. high, is believed to be one of the world's largest underground "mountains."

Principal Deserts of the World

Deserts are arid regions, generally receiving less than 10 inches of precipitation a year, or regions where the potential evaporation rate is twice as great as the precipitation.

The world's deserts are divided into four categories. **Subtropical deserts** are the hottest, with parched terrain and rapid evaporation. Although **cool coastal deserts** are located within the same latitudes as subtropical deserts, the average temperature is much cooler because of frigid offshore ocean currents. **Cold winter deserts** are marked by stark temperature differences from season to season, ranging from 100° F (38° C) in the summer to 10° F (−12° C) in the winter. **Polar regions** are also considered to be deserts because nearly all moisture in these areas is locked up in the form of ice.

Desert	Location	Size	Topography
SUBTROPICAL DESERTS			
Sahara	Morocco, Western Sahara, Algeria, Tunisia, Libya, Egypt, Mauritania, Mali, Niger, Chad, Ethiopia, Eritrea, Somalia	3.5 million sq. mi.,	70% gravel plains, sand, and dunes. Contrary to popular belief, the desert is only 30% sand. The world's largest desert gets its name from the Arabic word *Sahra'*, meaning desert
Arabian	Saudi Arabia, Kuwait, Qatar, United Arab Emirates, Oman, Yemen	1 million sq. mi.	Gravel plains, rocky highlands; one-fourth is the Rub al-Khali ("Empty Quarter"), the world's largest expanse of unbroken sand
Kalahari	Botswana, South Africa, Namibia	220,000 sq. mi.	Sand sheets, longitudinal dunes
Gibson	Australia (southern portion of the Western Desert)	120,000 sq. mi.	Sandhills, gravel, grass. These three regions of desert are collectively referred to as the Great Western Desert— otherwise known as "the Outback." Contains Ayers Rock, or Uluru, one of the world's largest monoliths
Great Sandy	Australia (northern portion of the Western Desert)	150,000 sq. mi.	
Great Victoria	Australia (southernmost portion of the Western Desert)	250,000 sq. mi.	
Simpson and Sturt Stony	Australia (eastern half of the continent)	56,000 sq. mi.	Simpson's straight, parallel sand dunes are the longest in the world—up to 125 mi. Encompasses the Stewart Stony Desert, named for the Australian explorer
Mojave	U.S.: Arizona, Colorado, Nevada, Utah	54,000 sq. mi.	Mountain chains, dry alkaline lake beds, calcium carbonate dunes
Sonoran	U.S.: Arizona, California; Mexico	120,000 sq. mi.	Basins and plains bordered by mountain ridges; home to the Saguaro cactus
Chihuahuan	Mexico	175,000 sq. mi.	Shrub desert
Thar	India, Pakistan	175,000 sq. mi.	Rocky sand and sand dunes
COOL COASTAL DESERTS			
Namib	Angola, Namibia, South Africa	13,000 sq. mi.	Gravel plains
Atacama	Chile	54,000 sq. mi.	Salt basins, sand, lava; world's driest desert
COLD WINTER DESERTS			
Great Basin	U.S.: Nevada, Oregon, Utah	190,000 sq. mi.	Mountain ridges, valleys, 1% sand dunes
Colorado Plateau	U.S.: Arizona, Colorado, New Mexico, Utah, Wyoming	130,000 sq. mi.	Sedimentary rock, mesas, and plateaus— includes the Grand Canyon and is also called the "Painted Desert" because of the spectacular colors in its rocks and canyons
Patagonian	Argentina	260,000 sq. mi.	Gravel plains, plateaus, basalt sheets
Kara-Kum	Uzbekistan, Turkmenistan	135,000 sq. mi.	90% gray layered sand—name means "black sand"
Kyzyl-Kum	Uzbekistan, Turkmenistan, Kazakhstan	115,000 sq. mi.	Sands, rock —name means "red sand"
Iranian	Iran	100,000 sq. mi.	Salt, gravel, rock
Taklamakan	China	105,000 sq. mi.	Sand, dunes, gravel
Gobi	China, Mongolia	500,000 sq. mi.	Stony, sandy soil, steppes (dry grasslands)
POLAR			
Arctic	U.S., Canada, Greenland, Iceland, Norway, Sweden, Finland, Russia		Snow, glaciers, tundra
Antarctic	Antarctica	5.4 million sq. mi.	Ice, snow, bedrock

Latitude and Longitude of World Cities
(and time corresponding to 12:00 noon, Eastern Standard Time)

City	Latitude ° ′	Longitude ° ′	Time
Aberdeen, Scotland	57 9 N	2 9 W	5:00 p.m.
Adelaide, Australia	34 55 S	138 36 E	2:30 a.m.[1]
Algiers, Algeria	36 50 N	3 0 E	6:00 p.m.
Amsterdam, Netherlands	52 22 N	4 53 E	6:00 p.m.
Ankara, Turkey	39 55 N	32 55 E	7:00 p.m.
Asunción, Paraguay	25 15 S	57 40 W	1:00 p.m.
Athens, Greece	37 58 N	23 43 E	7:00 p.m.
Auckland, New Zealand	36 52 S	174 45 E	5:00 a.m.[1]
Bangkok, Thailand	13 45 N	100 30 E	midnight
Barcelona, Spain	41 23 N	2 9 E	6:00 p.m.
Beijing, China	39 55 N	116 25 E	1:00 a.m.[1]
Belém, Brazil	1 28 S	48 29 W	2:00 p.m.
Belfast, Northern Ireland	54 37 N	5 56 W	5:00 p.m.
Belgrade, Yugoslavia	44 52 N	20 32 E	6:00 p.m.
Berlin, Germany	52 30 N	13 25 E	6:00 p.m.
Birmingham, England	52 25 N	1 55 W	5:00 p.m.
Bogotá, Colombia	4 32 N	74 15 W	12:00 noon
Bombay, India	19 0 N	72 48 E	10:30 p.m.
Bordeaux, France	44 50 N	0 31 W	6:00 p.m.
Bremen, Germany	53 5 N	8 49 E	6:00 p.m.
Brisbane, Australia	27 29 S	153 8 E	3:00 a.m.[1]
Bristol, England	51 28 N	2 35 W	5:00 p.m.
Brussels, Belgium	50 52 N	4 22 E	6:00 p.m.
Bucharest, Romania	44 25 N	26 7 E	7:00 p.m.
Budapest, Hungary	47 30 N	19 5 E	6:00 p.m.
Buenos Aires, Argentina	34 35 S	58 22 W	2:00 p.m.
Cairo, Egypt	30 2 N	31 21 E	7:00 p.m.
Calcutta, India	22 34 N	88 24 E	10:30 p.m.
Canton, China	23 7 N	113 15 E	1:00 a.m.[1]
Cape Town, South Africa	33 55 S	18 22 E	7:00 p.m.
Caracas, Venezuela	10 28 N	67 2 W	1:00 p.m.
Cayenne, French Guiana	4 49 N	52 18 W	1:00 p.m.
Chihuahua, Mexico	28 37 N	106 5 W	11:00 a.m.
Chongqing, China	29 46 N	106 34 E	1:00 a.m.[1]
Copenhagen, Denmark	55 40 N	12 34 E	6:00 p.m.
Córdoba, Argentina	31 28 S	64 10 W	2:00 p.m.
Dakar, Senegal	14 40 N	17 28 W	5:00 p.m.
Darwin, Australia	12 28 S	130 51 E	2:30 a.m.[1]
Djibouti, Djibouti	11 30 N	43 3 E	8:00 p.m.
Dublin, Ireland	53 20 N	6 15 W	5:00 p.m.
Durban, South Africa	29 53 S	30 53 E	7:00 p.m.
Edinburgh, Scotland	55 55 N	3 10 W	5:00 p.m.
Frankfurt, Germany	50 7 N	8 41 E	6:00 p.m.
Georgetown, Guyana	6 45 N	58 15 W	1:15 p.m.
Glasgow, Scotland	55 50 N	4 15 W	5:00 p.m.
Guatemala City, Guatemala	14 37 N	90 31 W	11:00 a.m.
Guayaquil, Ecuador	2 10 S	79 56 W	12:00 noon
Hamburg, Germany	53 33 N	10 2 E	6:00 p.m.
Hammerfest, Norway	70 38 N	23 38 E	6:00 p.m.
Havana, Cuba	23 8 N	82 23 W	12:00 noon
Helsinki, Finland	60 10 N	25 0 E	7:00 p.m.
Hobart, Tasmania	42 52 S	147 19 E	3:00 a.m.[1]
Iquique, Chile	20 10 S	70 7 W	1:00 p.m.
Irkutsk, Russia	52 30 N	104 20 E	1:00 a.m.
Jakarta, Indonesia	6 16 S	106 48 E	0:30 a.m.[1]
Johannesburg, South Africa	26 12 S	28 4 E	7:00 p.m.
Kingston, Jamaica	17 59 N	76 49 W	12:00 noon
Kinshasa, Congo	4 18 S	15 17 E	6:00 p.m.
La Paz, Bolivia	16 27 S	68 22 W	1:00 p.m.
Leeds, England	53 45 N	1 30 W	5:00 p.m.
Lima, Peru	12 0 S	77 2 W	12:00 noon
Lisbon, Portugal	38 44 N	9 9 W	5:00 p.m.
Liverpool, England	53 25 N	3 0 W	5:00 p.m.
London, England	51 32 N	0 5 W	5:00 p.m.
Lyons, France	45 45 N	4 50 E	6:00 p.m.
Madrid, Spain	40 26 N	3 42 W	6:00 p.m.
Manchester, England	53 30 N	2 15 W	5:00 p.m.
Manila, Philippines	14 35 N	120 57 E	1:00 a.m.[1]
Marseilles, France	43 20 N	5 20 E	6:00 p.m.
Mazatlán, Mexico	23 12 N	106 25 W	10:00 a.m.
Mecca, Saudi Arabia	21 29 N	39 45 E	8:00 p.m.
Melbourne, Australia	37 47 S	144 58 E	3:00 a.m.[1]
Mexico City, Mexico	19 26 N	99 7 W	11:00 a.m.
Milan, Italy	45 27 N	9 10 E	6:00 p.m.
Montevideo, Uruguay	34 53 S	56 10 W	2:00 p.m.
Moscow, Russia	55 45 N	37 36 E	8:00 p.m.
Munich, Germany	48 8 N	11 35 E	6:00 p.m.
Nagasaki, Japan	32 48 N	129 57 E	2:00 a.m.[1]
Nagoya, Japan	35 7 N	136 56 E	2:00 a.m.[1]
Nairobi, Kenya	1 25 S	36 55 E	8:00 p.m.
Nanjing (Nanking), China	32 3 N	118 53 E	1:00 a.m.[1]
Naples, Italy	40 50 N	14 15 E	6:00 p.m.
Newcastle-on-Tyne, England	54 58 N	1 37 W	5:00 p.m.
Odessa, Ukraine	46 27 N	30 48 E	8:00 p.m.
Osaka, Japan	34 32 N	135 30 E	2:00 a.m.[1]
Oslo, Norway	59 57 N	10 42 E	6:00 p.m.
Panama City, Panama	8 58 N	79 32 W	12:00 noon
Paramaribo, Suriname	5 45 N	55 15 W	1:30 p.m.
Paris, France	48 48 N	2 20 E	6:00 p.m.
Perth, Australia	31 57 S	115 52 E	1:00 a.m.[1]
Plymouth, England	50 25 N	4 5 W	5:00 p.m.
Port Moresby, Papua New Guinea	9 25 S	147 8 E	3:00 a.m.[1]
Prague, Czech Republic	50 5 N	14 26 E	6:00 p.m.
Rangoon, Burma	16 50 N	96 0 E	11:30 p.m.
Reykjavik, Iceland	64 4 N	21 58 W	4:00 p.m.
Rio de Janeiro, Brazil	22 57 S	43 12 W	2:00 p.m.
Rome, Italy	41 54 N	12 27 E	6:00 p.m.
Salvador, Brazil	12 56 S	38 27 W	2:00 p.m.
Santiago, Chile	33 28 S	70 45 W	1:00 p.m.
St. Petersburg, Russia	59 56 N	30 18 E	8:00 p.m.
São Paulo, Brazil	23 31 S	46 31 W	2:00 p.m.
Shanghai, China	31 10 N	121 28 E	1:00 a.m.[1]
Singapore, Singapore	1 14 N	103 55 E	0:30 a.m.[1]
Sofia, Bulgaria	42 40 N	23 20 E	7:00 p.m.
Stockholm, Sweden	59 17 N	18 3 E	6:00 p.m.
Sydney, Australia	34 0 S	151 0 E	3:00 a.m.[1]
Tananarive, Madagascar	18 50 S	47 33 E	8:00 p.m.
Teheran, Iran	35 45 N	51 45 E	8:30 p.m.
Tokyo, Japan	35 40 N	139 45 E	2:00 a.m.[1]
Tripoli, Libya	32 57 N	13 12 E	7:00 p.m.
Venice, Italy	45 26 N	12 20 E	6:00 p.m.
Veracruz, Mexico	19 10 N	96 10 W	11:00 a.m.
Vienna, Austria	48 14 N	16 20 E	6:00 p.m.
Vladivostok, Russia	43 10 N	132 0 E	3:00 a.m.[1]
Warsaw, Poland	52 14 N	21 0 E	6:00 p.m.
Wellington, New Zealand	41 17 S	174 47 E	5:00 a.m.[1]
Zürich, Switzerland	47 21 N	8 31 E	6:00 p.m.

1. On the following day.

Miscellaneous Data for the United States

Highest point: Mt. McKinley, Alaska	20,320 ft. (6,198 m)
Lowest point: Death Valley, Calif.	282 ft. (86 m) below sea level
Approximate mean elevation	2,500 ft. (763 m)
Points farthest apart (50 states): Log Point, Elliot Key, Fla., and Kure Island, Hawaii	5,859 mi. (9,429 km)
Geographic center (50 states): in Butte County, S.D. (west of Castle Rock)	44°58′N lat.103°46′W long.
Geographic center (48 conterminous states): In Smith County, Kan. (near Lebanon)	39°50′N lat. 98°35′W long.
Boundaries:	
Between Alaska and Canada	1,538 mi. (2,475 km)
Between the 48 conterminous states and Canada (incl. Great Lakes)	3,987 mi. (6,416 km)
Between the United States and Mexico	1,933 mi. (3,111 km)

Source: U.S. Geological Survey.

Extreme Points of the United States (50 States)

Extreme point	Latitude	Longitude	Distance[1] mi.	Distance[1] km
Northernmost point: Point Barrow, Alaska	71°23′ N	156°29′ W	2,507	4,034
Easternmost point: West Quoddy Head, Me.	44°49′ N	66°57′ W	1,788	2,997
Southernmost point: Ka Lae (South Cape), Hawaii	18°55′ N	155°41′ W	3,463	5,573
Westernmost point: Cape Wrangell, Alaska (Attu Island)	52°55′ N	172°27′ E	3,625	5,833

1. From geographic center of United States (incl. Alaska and Hawaii), west of Castle Rock, S.D., 44°58′ lat., 103°46′ W long. If measured from the prime meridian in Greenwich, England, Cape Wrangell, Attu Island, Alaska, would be the easternmost point.

The Continental Divide

The Continental Divide is a ridge of high ground that runs irregularly north and south through the Rocky Mountains and separates eastward-flowing from westward-flowing streams. The waters that flow eastward empty into the Atlantic Ocean, chiefly by way of the Gulf of Mexico; those that flow westward empty into the Pacific.

Rivers of the United States
(350 or more miles long)

Alabama-Coosa (600 mi.; 966 km): From junction of Oostanula and Etowah R. in Georgia to Mobile R.

Altamaha-Ocmulgee (392 mi.; 631 km): From junction of Yellow R. and South R., Newton Co. in Georgia to Atlantic Ocean.

Apalachicola-Chattahoochee (524 mi.; 843 km): From Towns Co. in Georgia to Gulf of Mexico in Florida.

Arkansas (1,459 mi.; 2,348 km): From Lake Co. in Colorado to Mississippi R. in Arkansas.

Brazos (923 mi.; 1,490 km): From junction of Salt Fork and Double Mountain Fork in Texas to Gulf of Mexico.

Canadian (906 mi.; 1,458 km): From Las Animas Co. in Colorado to Arkansas R. in Oklahoma.

Cimarron (600 mi.; 966 km): From Colfax Co. in New Mexico to Arkansas R. in Oklahoma.

Colorado (1,450 mi.; 2,333 km): From Rocky Mountain National Park in Colorado to Gulf of California in Mexico.

Colorado (862 mi.; 1,387 km): From Dawson Co. in Texas to Matagorda Bay.

Columbia (1,243 mi.; 2,000 km): From Columbia Lake in British Columbia to Pacific Ocean (entering between Oregon and Washington).

Colville (350 mi.; 563 km): From Brooks Range in Alaska to Beaufort Sea.

Connecticut (407 mi.; 655 km): From Third Connecticut Lake in New Hampshire to Long Island Sound in Connecticut.

Cumberland (720 mi.; 1,159 km): From junction of Poor and Clover Forks in Harlan Co. in Kentucky to Ohio R.

Delaware (390 mi.; 628 km): From Schoharie Co. in New York to Liston Point, Delaware Bay.

Gila (649 mi.; 1,044 km): From Catron Co. in New Mexico to Colorado R. in Arizona.

Green (360 mi.; 579 km): From Lincoln Co. in Kentucky to Ohio R. in Kentucky.

Green (730 mi.; 1,175 km): From Sublette Co. in Wyoming to Colorado R. in Utah.

Illinois (420 mi.; 676 km): From St. Joseph Co. in Indiana to Mississippi R. at Grafton in Illinois.

James (sometimes called *Dakota*) (710 mi.; 1,143 km): From Wells Co. in North Dakota to Missouri R. in South Dakota.

Kanawha-New (352 mi.; 566 km): From junction of North and South Forks of New R. in North Carolina, through Virginia and West Virginia (New River becoming Kanawha River), to Ohio River.

Kansas (743 mi.; 1,196 km): From source of Arikaree R. in Elbert Co., Colorado, to Missouri R. at Kansas City, Kansas.

Koyukuk (470 mi.; 756 km): From Brooks Range in Alaska to Yukon R.

Kuskokwim (724 mi.; 1,165 km): From Alaska Range in Alaska to Kuskokwim Bay.

Coastline of the United States

State	Lengths, statute miles		State	Lengths, statute miles	
	General coastline[1]	Tidal shoreline[2]		General coastline[1]	Tidal shoreline[2]
Atlantic Coast:			**Gulf Coast:**		
Maine	228	3,478	Florida (Gulf)	770	5,095
New Hampshire	13	131	Alabama	53	607
Massachusetts	192	1,519	Mississippi	44	359
Rhode Island	40	384	Louisiana	397	7,721
Connecticut	—	618	Texas	367	3,359
New York	127	1,850	Total Gulf coast	1,631	17,141
New Jersey	130	1,792	**Pacific Coast:**		
Pennsylvania	—	89	California	840	3,427
Delaware	28	381	Oregon	296	1,410
Maryland	31	3,190	Washington	157	3,026
Virginia	112	3,315	Hawaii	750	1,052
North Carolina	301	3,375	Alaska (Pacific)	5,580	31,383
South Carolina	187	2,876	Total Pacific coast	7,623	40,298
Georgia	100	2,344	**Arctic Coast:**		
Florida (Atlantic)	580	3,331	Alaska (Arctic)	1,060	2,521
Total Atlantic coast	2,069	28,673	Total Arctic coast	1,060	2,521
			States Total	**12,383**	**88,633**

1. Figures are lengths of general outline of seacoast. Measurements made with unit measure of 30 minutes of latitude on charts as near scale of 1:1,200,000 as possible. Coastline of bays and sounds is included to point where they narrow to width of unit measure, and distance across at such point is included. 2. Figures obtained in 1939-1940 with recording instrument on largest-scale maps and charts then available. Shoreline of outer coast, offshore islands, sounds, bays, rivers, and creeks is included to head of tidewater, or to point where tidal waters narrow to width of 100 feet. *Source:* Department of Commerce, National Oceanic and Atmospheric Administration, National Ocean Service.

Licking (350 mi.; 563 km): From Magoffin Co. in Kentucky to Ohio R. at Cincinnati in Ohio.

Little Missouri (560 mi.; 901 km): From Crook Co. in Wyoming to Missouri R. in North Dakota.

Milk (625 mi.; 1,006 km): From junction of forks in Alberta Province to Missouri R.

Mississippi (2,348 mi.; 3,779 km): From Lake Itasca in Minnesota to mouth of Southwest Pass in Louisiana.

Mississippi-Missouri-Red Rock (3,710 mi.; 5,970 km): From source of Red Rock R. in Montana to mouth of Southwest Pass in Louisiana.

Missouri (2,315 mi.; 3,726 km): From junction of Jefferson R., Gallatin R., and Madison R. in Montana to Mississippi R. near St. Louis.

Missouri-Red Rock (2,540 mi.; 4,090 km): From source of Red Rock R. in Montana to Mississippi R. near St. Louis.

Mobile-Alabama-Coosa (645 mi.; 1,040 km): From junction of Etowah R. and Oostanula R. in Georgia to Mobile Bay.

Neosho (460 mi.; 740 km): From Morris Co. in Kansas to Arkansas R. in Oklahoma.

Niobrara (431 mi.; 694 km): From Niobrara Co. in Wyoming to Missouri R. in Nebraska.

Noatak (350 mi.; 563 km): From Brooks Range in Alaska to Kotzebue Sound.

North Canadian (800 mi.; 1,290 km): From Union Co. in New Mexico to Canadian R. in Oklahoma.

North Platte (618 mi.; 995 km): From Jackson Co. in Colorado to junction with So. Platte R. in Nebraska to form Platte R.

Ohio (981 mi.; 1,579 km): From junction of Allegheny R. and Monongahela R. at Pittsburgh to Mississippi R. between Illinois and Kentucky.

Ohio-Allegheny (1,306 mi.; 2,102 km): From Potter Co. in Pennsylvania to Mississippi R. at Cairo in Illinois.

Osage (500 mi.; 805 km): From east-central Kansas to Missouri R. near Jefferson City in Missouri.

Ouachita (605 mi.; 974 km): From Polk Co. in Arkansas to Red R. in Louisiana.

Pearl (411 mi.; 661 km): From Neshoba County in Mississippi to Gulf of Mexico (Mississippi-Louisiana).

Pecos (926 mi.; 1,490 km): From Mora Co. in New Mexico to Rio Grande in Texas.

Pee Dee-Yadkin (435 mi.; 700 km): From Watauga Co. in North Carolina to Winyah Bay in South Carolina.

Pend Oreille-Clark Fork (531 mi.; 855 km): Near Butte in Montana to Columbia R. on Washington-Canada border.

Platte (990 mi.; 1593 km): From source of Grizzly Creek in Jackson Co., Colorado, to Missouri R. south of Omaha, Nebraska.

Porcupine (569 mi.; 916 km): From Yukon Territory, Canada, to Yukon R. in Alaska.

Potomac (383 mi.; 616 km): From Garrett Co. in Maryland to Chesapeake Bay at Point Lookout in Maryland.

Powder (375 mi.; 603 km): From junction of forks in Johnson Co. in Wyoming to Yellowstone R. in Montana.

Red (1,290 mi.; 2,080 km): From source of Tierra Blanca Creek in Curry County, New Mexico to Mississippi R. in Louisiana.

Red (also called *Red River of the North*) (545 mi.; 877 km): From junction of Otter Tail R. and Bois de Sioux R. in Minnesota to Lake Winnipeg in Manitoba, Canada.

Republican (445 mi.; 716 km): From junction of North Fork and Arikaree R. in Nebraska to junction with Smoky Hill R. in Kansas to form the Kansas R.

Rio Grande (1,900 mi.; 3,060 km): From San Juan Co. in Colorado to Gulf of Mexico.

Roanoke (380 mi.; 612 km): From junction of forks in Montgomery Co. in Virginia to Albemarle Sound in North Carolina.

Sabine (380 mi.; 612 km): From junction of forks in Hunt Co. in Texas to Sabine Lake between Texas and Louisiana.

Sacramento (377 mi.; 607 km): From Siskiyou Co. in California to Suisun Bay.

Saint Francis (425 mi.; 684 km): From Iron Co. in Missouri to Mississippi R. in Arkansas.

Salmon (420 mi.; 676 km): From Custer Co. in Idaho to Snake R.

San Joaquin (350 mi.; 563 km): From junction of forks in Madera Co. in California to Suisun Bay.

San Juan (360 mi.; 579 km): From Archuleta Co. in Colorado to Colorado R. in Utah.

Santee-Wateree-Catawba (538 mi.; 866 km): From McDowell Co. in North Carolina to Atlantic Ocean in South Carolina.

Smoky Hill (540 mi.; 869 km): From Cheyenne Co. in Colorado to junction with Republican R. in Kansas to form Kansas R.

Snake (1,038 mi.; 1,670 km): From Ocean Plateau in Wyoming to Columbia R. in Washington.

South Platte (424 mi.; 682 km): From Park Co. in Colorado to junction with North Platte R. in Nebraska to form Platte R.

Stikine (379 mi.; 610 km): From British Columbia in Canada to Stikine Strait near Wrangell, Alaska.

Susquehanna (444 mi.; 715 km): From Otsego Lake in New York to Chesapeake Bay in Maryland.

Tanana (659 mi.; 1,060 km): From Wrangell Mts. in Yukon Territory, Canada, to Yukon R. in Alaska.

Tennessee (652 mi.; 1,049 km): From junction of Holston R. and French Broad R. in Tennessee to Ohio R. in Kentucky.

Tennessee-French Broad (886 mi.; 1,417 km): From Transylvania Co. in North Carolina to Ohio R. at Paducah in Kentucky.

Tombigbee (525 mi.; 845 km): From junction of forks in Itawamba Co. in Mississippi to Mobile R. in Alabama.

Trinity (360 mi.; 579 km): From junction of forks in Dallas Co. in Texas to Galveston Bay.

Wabash (512 mi.; 824 km): From Darke Co. in Ohio to Ohio R. between Illinois and Indiana.

Washita (500 mi.; 805 km): From Hemphill Co. in Texas to Red R. in Oklahoma.

White (722 mi.; 1,160 km): From Madison Co. in Arkansas to Mississippi R.

Wisconsin (430 mi.; 692 km): From Vilas Co. in Wisconsin to Mississippi R.

Yellowstone (692 mi.; 1,110 km): From Park Co. in Wyoming to Missouri R. in North Dakota.

Yukon (1,979 mi.; 3,185 km): From source of McNeil R. in Yukon Territory, Canada, to Bering Sea in Alaska.

Mountain Peaks in the United States Higher Than 14,000 Feet

Name	State	Height (ft.)	Name	State	Height (ft.)	Name	State	Height (ft.)
Mt. McKinley	Alaska	20,320	Castle Peak	Colo.	14,265	Mt. Eolus	Colo.	14,083
Mt. St. Elias	Alaska	18,008	Quandary Peak	Colo.	14,265	Windom Peak	Colo.	14,082
Mt. Foraker	Alaska	17,400	Mt. Evans	Colo.	14,264	Mt. Columbia	Colo.	14,073
Mt. Bona	Alaska	16,500	Longs Peak	Colo.	14,255	Mt. Augusta	Alaska	14,070
Mt. Blackburn	Alaska	16,390	Mt. Wilson	Colo.	14,246	Missouri Mtn.	Colo.	14,067
Mt. Sanford	Alaska	16,237	White Mtn.	Calif.	14,246	Humboldt Peak	Colo.	14,064
Mt. Vancouver	Alaska	15,979	North Palisade	Calif.	14,242	Mt. Bierstadt	Colo.	14,060
South Buttress	Alaska	15,885	Mt. Cameron	Colo.	14,238	Sunlight Peak	Colo.	14,059
Mt. Churchill	Alaska	15,638	Mt. Shavano	Colo.	14,229	Split Mtn.	Calif.	14,058
Mt. Fairweather	Alaska	15,300	Crestone Needle	Colo.	14,197	Handies Peak	Colo.	14,048
Mt. Hubbard	Alaska	14,950	Mt. Belford	Colo.	14,197	Culebra Peak	Colo.	14,047
Mt. Bear	Alaska	14,831	Mt. Princeton	Colo.	14,197	Mt. Lindsey	Colo.	14,042
East Buttress	Alaska	14,730	Mt. Yale	Colo.	14,196	Ellingwood Point	Colo.	14,042
Mt. Hunter	Alaska	14,573	Mt. Bross	Colo.	14,172	Middle Palisade	Calif.	14,040
Browne Tower	Alaska	14,530	Kit Carson Mtn.	Colo.	14,165	Little Bear Peak	Colo.	14,037
Mt. Alverstone	Alaska	14,500	Mt. Wrangell	Alaska	14,163	Mt. Sherman	Colo.	14,036
Mt. Whitney	Calif.	14,494[1]	Mt. Sill	Calif.	14,163	Redcloud Peak	Colo.	14,034
University Peak	Alaska	14,470	Mt. Shasta	Calif.	14,162	Mt. Langley	Calif.	14,027
Mt. Elbert	Colo.	14,433	El Diente Peak	Colo.	14,159	Conundrum Peak	Colo.	14,022
Mt. Massive	Colo.	14,421	Point Success	Wash.	14,158	Mt. Tyndall	Calif.	14,019
Mt. Harvard	Colo.	14,420	Maroon Peak	Colo.	14,156	Pyramid Peak	Colo.	14,018
Mt. Rainier	Wash.	14,410	Tabeguache Mtn.	Colo.	14,155	Wilson Peak	Colo.	14,017
Mt. Williamson	Calif.	14,370	Mt. Oxford	Colo.	14,153	Wetterhorn Peak	Colo.	14,015
La Plata Peak	Colo.	14,361	Mt. Sill	Calif.	14,153	North Maroon Peak	Colo.	14,014
Blanca Peak	Colo.	14,345	Mt. Sneffels	Colo.	14,150	San Luis Peak	Colo.	14,014
Uncompahgre Peak	Colo.	14,309	Mt. Democrat	Colo.	14,148	Middle Palisade	Calif.	14,012
Crestone Peak	Colo.	14,294	Capitol Peak	Colo.	14,130	Mt. Muir	Calif.	14,012
Mt. Lincoln	Colo.	14,286	Liberty Cap	Wash.	14,112	Mt. of the Holy Cross	Colo.	14,005
Grays Peak	Colo.	14,270	Pikes Peak	Colo.	14,110	Huron Peak	Colo.	14,003
Mt. Antero	Colo.	14,269	Snowmass Mtn.	Colo.	14,092	Thunderbolt Peak	Calif.	14,003
Torreys Peak	Colo.	14,267	Mt. Russell	Calif.	14,088	Sunshine Peak	Colo.	14,001

1. National Geodetic Survey. *Source:* Department of the Interior, U.S. Geological Survey.

Highest, Lowest, and Mean Elevations in the United States

State	Elevation (ft.)[1]	Highest point	Elevation (ft.)	Lowest point	Elevation (ft.)
Alabama	500	Cheaha Mountain	2,405	Gulf of Mexico	Sea level
Alaska	1,900	Mt. McKinley	20,320	Pacific Ocean	Sea level
Arizona	4,100	Humphreys Peak	12,633	Colorado River	70
Arkansas	650	Magazine Mountain	2,753	Ouachita River	55
California	2,900	Mt. Whitney	14,494	Death Valley	−282[2]
Colorado	6,800	Mt. Elbert	14,433	Arkansas River	3,350
Connecticut	500	Mt. Frissell, on south slope	2,380	Long Island Sound	Sea level
Delaware	60	Ebright Road, Del.–Pa. state line	448	Atlantic Ocean	Sea level
D.C.	150	Tenleytown, at Reno Reservoir	410	Potomac River	1
Florida	100	Sec. 30, T6N, R20W, Walton County	345	Atlantic Ocean	Sea level
Georgia	600	Brasstown Bald	4,784	Atlantic Ocean	Sea level
Hawaii	3,030	Puu Wekiu, Mauna Kea	13,796	Pacific Ocean	Sea level
Idaho	5,000	Borah Peak	12,662	Snake River	710
Illinois	600	Charles Mound	1,235	Mississippi River	279
Indiana	700	Franklin Township, Wayne County	1,257	Ohio River	320
Iowa	1,100	Sec. 29, T100N, R41W, Osceola County	1,670	Mississippi River	480
Kansas	2,000	Mt. Sunflower	4,039	Verdigris River	679
Kentucky	750	Black Mountain	4,139	Mississippi River	257
Louisiana	100	Driskill Mountain	535	New Orleans	−8[2]
Maine	600	Mt. Katahdin	5,267	Atlantic Ocean	Sea level
Maryland	350	Backbone Mountain	3,360	Atlantic Ocean	Sea level
Massachusetts	500	Mt. Greylock	3,487	Atlantic Ocean	Sea level
Michigan	900	Mt. Arvon	1,979	Lake Erie	572
Minnesota	1,200	Eagle Mountain	2,301	Lake Superior	600
Mississippi	300	Woodall Mountain	806	Gulf of Mexico	Sea level
Missouri	800	Taum Sauk Mountain	1,772	St. Francis River	230
Montana	3,400	Granite Peak	12,799	Kootenai River	1,800
Nebraska	2,600	Johnson Township, Kimball County	5,424	Missouri River	840
Nevada	5,500	Boundary Peak	13,140	Colorado River	479
New Hampshire	1,000	Mt. Washington	6,288	Atlantic Ocean	Sea level
New Jersey	250	High Point	1,803	Atlantic Ocean	Sea level
New Mexico	5,700	Wheeler Peak	13,161	Red Bluff Reservoir	2,842
New York	1,000	Mt. Marcy	5,344	Atlantic Ocean	Sea level
North Carolina	700	Mt. Mitchell	6,684	Atlantic Ocean	Sea level
North Dakota	1,900	White Butte	3,506	Red River	750
Ohio	850	Campbell Hill	1,549	Ohio River	455
Oklahoma	1,300	Black Mesa	4,973	Little River	289
Oregon	3,300	Mt. Hood	11,239	Pacific Ocean	Sea level
Pennsylvania	1,100	Mt. Davis	3,213	Delaware River	Sea level
Rhode Island	200	Jerimoth Hill	812	Atlantic Ocean	Sea level
South Carolina	350	Sassafras Mountain	3,560	Atlantic Ocean	Sea level
South Dakota	2,200	Harney Peak	7,242	Big Stone Lake	966
Tennessee	900	Clingmans Dome	6,643	Mississippi River	178
Texas	1,700	Guadalupe Peak	8,749	Gulf of Mexico	Sea level
Utah	6,100	Kings Peak	13,528	Beaverdam Wash	2,000
Vermont	1,000	Mt. Mansfield	4,393	Lake Champlain	95
Virginia	950	Mt. Rogers	5,729	Atlantic Ocean	Sea level
Washington	1,700	Mt. Rainier	14,410	Pacific Ocean	Sea level
West Virginia	1,500	Spruce Knob	4,861	Potomac River	240
Wisconsin	1,050	Timms Hill	1,951	Lake Michigan	579
Wyoming	6,700	Gannett Peak	13,804	Belle Fourche River	3,099
United States	**2,500**	**Mt. McKinley (Alaska)**	**20,320**	**Death Valley (California)**	**−282**[2]

1. Approximate mean elevation. 2. Below sea level. *Source:* U.S. Geological Survey.

Latitude and Longitude of U.S. and Canadian Cities
(and time corresponding to 12:00 noon, Eastern Standard Time)

City	Lat. °	Lat. ′	Long. °	Long. ′	Time
Albany, N.Y.	42	40	73	45	12:00 noon
Albuquerque, N.M.	35	05	106	39	10:00 a.m.
Amarillo, Tex.	35	11	101	50	11:00 a.m.
Anchorage, Alaska	61	13	149	54	8:00 a.m.
Atlanta, Ga.	33	45	84	23	12:00 noon
Austin, Tex.	30	16	97	44	11:00 a.m.
Baker, Ore.	44	47	117	50	9:00 a.m.
Baltimore, Md.	39	18	76	38	12:00 noon
Bangor, Maine	44	48	68	47	12:00 noon
Birmingham, Ala.	33	30	86	50	11:00 a.m.
Bismarck, N.D.	46	48	100	47	11:00 a.m.
Boise, Idaho	43	36	116	13	10:00 a.m.
Boston, Mass.	42	21	71	5	12:00 noon
Buffalo, N.Y.	42	55	78	50	12:00 noon
Calgary, Alberta	51	1	114	1	10:00 a.m.
Carlsbad, N.M.	32	26	104	15	10:00 a.m.
Charleston, S.C.	32	47	79	56	12:00 noon
Charleston, W. Va.	38	21	81	38	12:00 noon
Charlotte, N.C.	35	14	80	50	12:00 noon
Cheyenne, Wyo.	41	9	104	52	10:00 a.m.
Chicago, Ill.	41	50	87	37	11:00 a.m.
Cincinnati, Ohio	39	8	84	30	12:00 noon
Cleveland, Ohio	41	28	81	37	12:00 noon
Columbia, S.C.	34	0	81	2	12:00 noon
Columbus, Ohio	40	0	83	1	12:00 noon
Dallas, Tex.	32	46	96	46	11:00 a.m.
Denver, Colo.	39	45	105	0	10:00 a.m.
Des Moines, Iowa	41	35	93	37	11:00 a.m.
Detroit, Mich.	42	20	83	3	12:00 noon
Dubuque, Iowa	42	31	90	40	11:00 a.m.
Duluth, Minn.	46	49	92	5	11:00 a.m.
Eastport, Maine	44	54	67	0	12:00 noon
El Centro, Calif.	32	38	115	33	9:00 a.m.
El Paso, Tex.	31	46	106	29	10:00 a.m.
Eugene, Ore.	44	3	123	5	9:00 a.m.
Fargo, N.D.	46	52	96	48	11:00 a.m.
Flagstaff, Ariz.	35	13	111	41	10:00 a.m.
Fort Worth, Tex.	32	43	97	19	11:00 a.m.
Fresno, Calif.	36	44	119	48	9:00 a.m.
Grand Junction, Colo.	39	5	108	33	10:00 a.m.
Grand Rapids, Mich.	42	58	85	40	12:00 noon
Havre, Mont.	48	33	109	43	10:00 a.m.
Helena, Mont.	46	35	112	2	10:00 a.m.
Honolulu, Hawaii	21	18	157	50	7:00 a.m.
Hot Springs, Ark.	34	31	93	3	11:00 a.m.
Houston, Tex.	29	45	95	21	11:00 a.m.
Idaho Falls, Idaho	43	30	112	1	10:00 a.m.
Indianapolis, Ind.	39	46	86	10	12:00 noon
Jackson, Miss.	32	20	90	12	11:00 a.m.
Jacksonville, Fla.	30	22	81	40	12:00 noon
Juneau, Alaska	58	18	134	24	8:00 a.m.
Kansas City, Mo.	39	6	94	35	11:00 a.m.
Key West, Fla.	24	33	81	48	12:00 noon
Kingston, Ont., Can.	44	15	76	30	12:00 noon
Klamath Falls, Ore.	42	10	121	44	9:00 a.m.
Knoxville, Tenn.	35	57	83	56	12:00 noon
Las Vegas, Nev.	36	10	115	12	9:00 a.m.
Lewiston, Idaho	46	24	117	2	10:00 a.m.
Lincoln, Neb.	40	50	96	40	11:00 a.m.
London, Ont.	43	2	81	34	12:00 noon
Long Beach, Calif.	33	46	118	11	9:00 a.m.
Los Angeles, Calif.	34	3	118	15	9:00 a.m.
Louisville, Ky.	38	15	85	46	12:00 noon
Manchester, N.H.	43	0	71	30	12:00 noon
Memphis, Tenn.	35	9	90	3	11:00 a.m.
Miami, Fla.	25	46	80	12	12:00 noon
Milwaukee, Wis.	43	2	87	55	11:00 a.m.
Minneapolis, Minn.	44	59	93	14	11:00 a.m.
Mobile, Ala.	30	42	88	3	11:00 a.m.
Montgomery, Ala.	32	21	86	18	11:00 a.m.
Montpelier, Vt.	44	15	72	32	12:00 noon
Montreal, Que., Can.	45	30	73	35	12:00 noon
Moose Jaw, Sask., Can.	50	37	105	31	10:00 a.m.
Nashville, Tenn.	36	10	86	47	11:00 a.m.
Nelson, B.C., Can.	49	30	117	17	9:00 a.m.
Newark, N.J.	40	44	74	10	12:00 noon
New Haven, Conn.	41	19	72	55	12:00 noon
New Orleans, La.	29	57	90	4	11:00 a.m.
New York, N.Y.	40	47	73	58	12:00 noon
Nome, Alaska	64	25	165	30	8:00 a.m.
Oakland, Calif.	37	48	122	16	9:00 a.m.
Oklahoma City, Okla.	35	26	97	28	11:00 a.m.
Omaha, Neb.	41	15	95	56	11:00 a.m.
Ottawa, Ont., Can.	45	24	75	43	12:00 noon
Philadelphia, Pa.	39	57	75	10	12:00 noon
Phoenix, Ariz.	33	29	112	4	10:00 a.m.
Pierre, S.D.	44	22	100	21	11:00 a.m.
Pittsburgh, Pa.	40	27	79	57	12:00 noon
Port Arthur, Ont., Can.	48	30	89	17	12:00 noon
Portland, Maine	43	40	70	15	12:00 noon
Portland, Ore.	45	31	122	41	9:00 a.m.
Providence, R.I.	41	50	71	24	12:00 noon
Quebec, Que., Can.	46	49	71	11	12:00 noon
Raleigh, N.C.	35	46	78	39	12:00 noon
Reno, Nev.	39	30	119	49	9:00 a.m.
Richfield, Utah	38	46	112	5	10:00 a.m.
Richmond, Va.	37	33	77	29	12:00 noon
Roanoke, Va.	37	17	79	57	12:00 noon
Sacramento, Calif.	38	35	121	30	9:00 a.m.
St. John, N.B., Can.	45	18	66	10	1:00 p.m.
St. Louis, Mo.	38	35	90	12	11:00 a.m.
Salt Lake City, Utah	40	46	111	54	10:00 a.m.
San Antonio, Tex.	29	23	98	33	11:00 a.m.
San Diego, Calif.	32	42	117	10	9:00 a.m.
San Francisco, Calif.	37	47	122	26	9:00 a.m.
San Jose, Calif.	37	20	121	53	9:00 a.m.
San Juan, P.R.	18	30	66	10	1:00 p.m.
Santa Fe, N.M.	35	41	105	57	10:00 a.m.
Savannah, Ga.	32	5	81	5	12:00 noon
Seattle, Wash.	47	37	122	20	9:00 a.m.
Shreveport, La.	32	28	93	42	11:00 a.m.
Sioux Falls, S.D.	43	33	96	44	11:00 a.m.
Sitka, Alaska	57	10	135	15	8:00 a.m.
Spokane, Wash.	47	40	117	26	9:00 a.m.
Springfield, Ill.	39	48	89	38	11:00 a.m.
Springfield, Mass.	42	6	72	34	12:00 noon
Springfield, Mo.	37	13	93	17	11:00 a.m.
Syracuse, N.Y.	43	2	76	8	12:00 noon
Tampa, Fla.	27	57	82	27	12:00 noon
Toledo, Ohio	41	39	83	33	12:00 noon
Toronto, Ont., Can.	43	40	79	24	12:00 noon
Tulsa, Okla.	36	09	95	59	11:00 a.m.
Victoria, B.C., Can.	48	25	123	21	9:00 a.m.
Virginia Beach, Va.	36	51	75	58	12:00 noon
Washington, D.C.	38	53	77	02	12:00 noon
Wichita, Kan.	37	43	97	17	11:00 a.m.
Wilmington, N.C.	34	14	77	57	12:00 noon
Winnipeg, Man., Can.	49	54	97	7	11:00 a.m.

Mason and Dixon's Line

Mason and Dixon's Line (often called the Mason-Dixon Line) is the boundary between Pennsylvania and Maryland, running at a north latitude of 39°43′19.11″. The greater part of it was surveyed from 1763–1767 by Charles Mason and Jeremiah Dixon, English astronomers who had been appointed to settle a dispute between the colonies. As the line was partly the boundary between the free and the slave states, it has come to signify the division between the North and the South.

Geysers in the United States

Geysers are natural hot springs that intermittently eject a column of water and steam into the air. They exist in many parts of the volcanic regions of the world such as Japan and South America but their greatest development is in Iceland, New Zealand, and Yellowstone National Park.

There are 120 named geysers in Yellowstone National Park, Wyoming, and perhaps half that number unnamed. Most of the geysers and the 4,000 or more hot springs are located in the western portion of the park. The most important are the following:

Norris Geyser Basin has 24 or more active geysers; the number varies. There are scores of steam vents and hot springs. *Steamboat* is the largest active geyser in the world, sending water more than 300 ft. into the air for 3 to 20 minutes. It emits water every few minutes, but its major eruptions are infrequent and erratic. *Valentine* erupts 50–75 ft. at intervals varying from 18 hr. to 3 days or more. *Minuté* erupts 15–20 ft. high, several hours apart. Others include: *Fearless, Veteran, Vixen, Corporal, Whirligig, Little Whirligig,* and *Pinwheel.*

Lower Geyser Basin has at least 18 active geysers. *Fountain* throws water 50–75 ft. in all directions at unpredictable intervals. *Clepsydra* erupts violently from 4 vents up to 30 ft. *Great Fountain* plays every 8 to 15 hr. in spurts from 30 to 90 ft. high.

Midway Geyser Basin has vast steaming terraces of red, orange, pink and other colors; there are pools and springs, including the beautiful *Grand Prismatic Spring. Excelsior* crater discharges boiling water into Firehole River at the rate of 6 cu. ft. per second.

Giant erupts up to 200 ft. at intervals of 2½ days to 3 mo; eruptions last about 1½ hr. *Daisy* sends water up to 75 ft. but is irregular and frequently inactive.

Old Faithful, the most famous geyser in the park, sends up a column varying from 116 to 175 ft. at intervals of about 65 min, varying from 33 to 90 min. Eruptions last about 4 min, during which time about 12,000 gal. are discharged.

Giantess seldom erupts, but during its active period sends up streams 150–200 ft.

Lion plays up to 60 ft. every 2–4 days when active; *Little Cub* up to 10 ft. every 1–2 hr. *Big Cub* and *Lioness* seldom erupt.

There are no geysers in the Mammoth Hot Springs area. The formation is travertine. Sides of a hill are steps and terraces over which flow the steaming waters of hot springs laden with minerals. Each step is tinted by algae to many shades of orange, pink, yellow, brown, green, and blue. Terraces are white where no water flows.

Michigan and Huron: One Lake or Two?

It is a widely accepted fact that Lake Superior, with an area of 31,820 square miles, is the world's largest freshwater lake. However, this fact is based on a historical inaccuracy in the naming of Lake Huron and Lake Michigan. What should have been considered one body of water, Lake Michigan-Huron with an area of 45,410 square miles, was mistakenly given two names, one for each lobe. The explorers in colonial times incorrectly believed each lobe to be a separate lake because of their great size.

Why should the two lakes be considered one? The Huron Lobe and the Michigan Lobe are at the same elevation and are connected by the 120-foot-deep Mackinac Strait, also at the same elevation. Lakes are separated from each other by streams and rivers. The Strait of Mackinac is not a river. It is 3.6 to 5 miles wide, wider than most lakes are long. In essence, it is just a narrowing, not a separation of the two lobes of Lake Michigan-Huron.

The flow between the two lakes can reverse. Because of the large connecting channel, the two can equalize rapidly whenever a water level imbalance occurs. Gauge records for the lakes clearly show them to have identical water level regimes and mean long-term behavior; that is, they are hydrologically considered to be one lake.

Historical names are not easily changed. The separate names for the lake are a part of history and are also legally institutionalized since Lake Michigan is treated as American and Lake Huron is bisected by the international boundary between the United States and Canada.

Of all the world's freshwater lakes, North America's Great Lakes are unique. Their five basins combine to form a single watershed with one common outlet to the ocean. The total volume of the lakes is about 5,475 cubic miles, more than 6,000 trillion gallons.

The Great Lakes are Superior, with an area of 31,820 square miles (82,414 km) shared by the United States and Canada; Huron, with an area of 23,010 square miles (59,596 sq. km) shared by the United States and Canada; Michigan, with an area of 22,400 square miles (58,016 sq. km) entirely in the United States; Erie, with an area of 9,930 square miles (25,719 km) shared by the United States and Canada; and Ontario, with an area of 7,520 square miles (19,477 km) shared by the United States and Canada.

World Heritage Sites in the United States

The United Nations Educational, Scientific, and Cultural Organization (UNESCO) has identified 582 World Heritage sites that it considers of "outstanding universal value." In the United States, there are 22 of these sites; the 17 that are natural sites are listed below. The World Heritage Web site is as follows: http://www.unesco.org/whc/nwhc/pages/home/pages/homepage.htm.

Cahokia Mounds State Historic Site, Illinois: Between C.E. 900 and C.E. 1500 the Cahokia site was the regional center for the Mississippian Indian culture. Named for the Cahokia Indians who came after them, Cahokia features the largest prehistoric earthen constructions in the Americas, a testament to the sophisticated engineering skills of Mississippian culture.

Carlsbad Caverns National Park, New Mexico: Carlsbad Caverns National Park is a network of more than 80 limestone caves, including the nation's deepest—1,597 feet—and third longest. The Lechuguilla Cave is particularly noteworthy for its beautiful stalagtites and stalagmites.

Chaco Culture National Historical Park, New Mexico: Between C.E. 900 and C.E. 1100, the Anasazi built large multistory stone villages and an impressive 400-mile road system in Chaco canyon exemplifying their engineering and construction talents.

Everglades National Park, Florida: The Everglades, or "River of Grass" as the Seminoles called it, is formed by a river of fresh water 6 inches deep and 50 miles wide that flows slowly across the expanse of land of sawgrass marshes, pine forests, and mangrove islands. More than 300 species of birds live in the park as well as alligators, manatees, and Florida panthers.

Glacier Bay National Park and Preserve, Alaska: The park is made up of a huge chain of great tidewater glaciers and a dramatic range of landscapes, from rocky terrain recently covered by ice to lush temperate rain forest. Brown and black bears, mountain goats, whales (including humpbacks), seals, and eagles can be found within the park.

Grand Canyon National Park, Arizona: The Grand Canyon is among Earth's greatest ongoing geological spectacles. About 65 million years ago in Earth's shifting, a huge area of land was lifted a mile and a half above sea level, forming what is now the Colorado Plateau. For the last 6 to 10 million years, the Colorado River has been slowly carving its way down through the center, exposing the many colorful strata of rock.

Great Smoky Mountains National Park, North Carolina/Tennessee: "Place of Blue Smoke" was the name given by the Cherokee Indians to these Appalachian Highlands. The forest here exudes water vapor and oily residues which create a smoke-like haze that surrounds the peaks and fills the valleys. The park is one of the world's finest temperate deciduous forests.

Hawaii Volcanoes National Park, Hawaii: It is thought that the Hawaiian islands were created when molten rock pushed through Earth's crust, forming volcanoes. The two most spectacular live volcanoes are Kilauea and Mauna Loa.

Mammoth Cave National Park, Kentucky: Mammoth Cave, as its name suggests, is the world's most extensive cave system, with 345 miles of passages. Water seeping into the cave creates stalactites, stalagmites, and white gypsum crystal formations. Rare and unusual animals, such as blind fish and colorless spiders, demonstrate adaptation to the absolute blackness and isolation.

Mesa Verde National Park, Colorado: In the sixth century, the Anasazi, or "Ancient Ones," established villages on the high, flat land in southwestern Colorado. In the late 1100s they began constructing multistory stone apartment houses, or pueblos, tucked on ledges and under rock overhangs.

Olympic National Park, Washington: The park encompasses not only snow-capped Mount Olympus, glaciers, alpine meadows, and rocky Pacific Mountain coastline, but also one of the few temperate rain forests in the world. The luxuriant forest is created by the warm, moisture-laden air from the Pacific meeting the mountains, resulting in a dense, green, jungle-like world.

Redwood National Park, California: Redwood National Park contains the tallest living things on Earth, evergreen trees that grow to 350 feet. Descendants of the giant evergreens that grew during the age of the dinosaurs, redwoods take 400 years to mature. Some of the survivors are more than 2,000 years old.

Taos Pueblo, New Mexico: Pueblo de Taos is thought to have appeared before C.E. 1400 and is the best preserved of the pueblos (communal housing) north of the border. Taos is a remarkable example of a traditional type of architectural ensemble from the pre-Hispanic period of the Americas and is unique to this region. Today Taos is inhabited by the Taos Pueblo Indians, and it is still an active community.

Waterton-Glacier International Peace Park, Montana: The two parks sustain an exceptionally diverse habitat, including wolves, bears, and mountain lions. It also features a wide variety of wild flowers and wildlife, including bighorn sheep and bald eagles.

Wrangell–St. Elias National Park and Preserve, Alaska: The park is made up of gargantuan icefields and about 2,000 glaciers that have created a sculpted landscape of valleys, peaks, and lakes. This premier wilderness contains extensive bird, animal, and marine mammal habitats where trumpeter swans, Daal sheep, bisons, and sea lions dwell.

Yosemite National Park, California: Yosemite, located in California's Sierra Nevada Mountains, contains breathtaking panoramas of rugged scenery and a huge variety of plant and animal life. During the last Ice Age the granite bedrock was gouged and shaped into bare peaks, sheer cliffs, rounded domes, and huge monoliths.

HISTORIC FLIGHT: As the century drew to a close, one of the final barriers in aviation was broken, as balloonists Bertrand Piccard of Switzerland and Brian Jones of Britain successfully circumnavigated the earth in their *Breitling Orbiter 3* craft. The 180-ft.-high balloon launched from the Swiss Alps on March 1 and landed 20 days later in Egypt.

AMERICA UNDER THE GUN: A deadly trio of rampages by heavily armed gunmen in Colorado, Georgia and California left Americans shaken, and intensified the nation's ongoing debate over the need for gun control.

The first—and deadliest—incident occurred on April 20 at Columbine High School in Littleton, Colorado, a well-to-do suburb southwest of Denver. Students Dylan Klebold, below left, and Eric Harris, below right, who considered themselves outcasts from the school community, entered the building carrying a small arsenal of guns and bombs and opened fire on their fellow students, concentrating on minorities and athletes.

After a three-hour siege, 13 people lay dead and 25 were injured. At right, young women flee the school during the rampage. Klebold and Harris killed themselves as police entered the building.

ATLANTA: Workers flee an office building on July 29, after Mark Barton opened fire in two buildings, killing nine people and wounding 12 others. Barton, a frustrated day-trading stock investor, killed his wife and children at home, then continued his rampage.

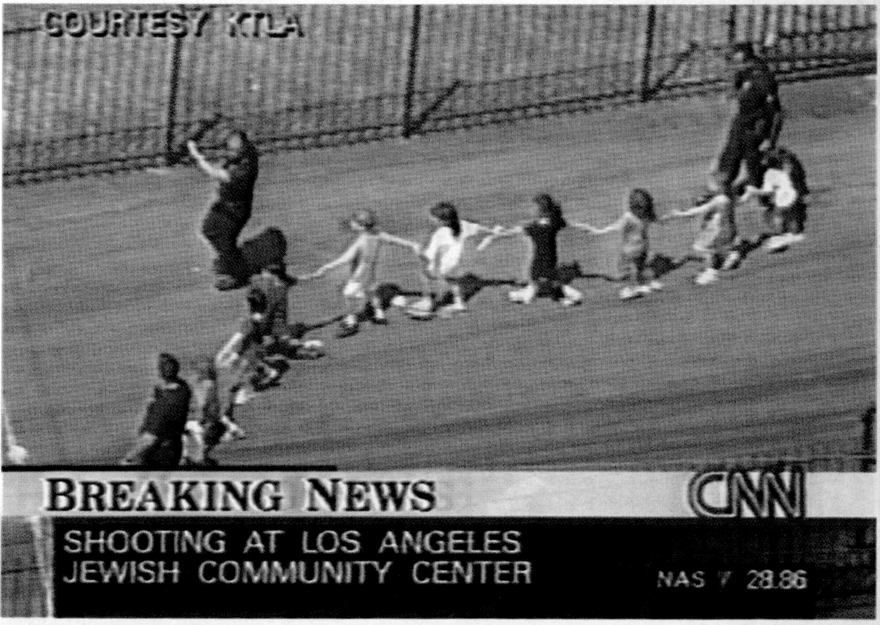

LOS ANGELES: Police lead children from a Jewish day-care center, where Buford Furrow opened fire on Aug. 10, wounding three people. Furrow, an avowed white supremacist, later killed a Filipino-American mail carrier before quietly surrendering to the FBI in Nevada.

CLINTON ACQUITTED: Chief Justice William Rehnquist presides over the impeachment trial of President Clinton, only the second such trial in U.S. history. On Feb. 12 the Senate voted for acquittal on two articles of impeachment, ending the long sex scandal.

ON THE STUMP: Candidates geared up for the November 2000 elections. Vice President Al Gore, left, long expected to be the Democratic nominee, faced a challenge from former Senator Bill Bradley. Meanwhile First Lady Hillary Rodham Clinton held a "listening tour" as she pondered a Senate race in New York.

ON THE RUN: Democratic candidate and onetime hoop star Bill Bradley autographs a ball, top left. Meanwhile, a number of candidates vied for the G.O.P. nomination. The front runner was Texas Governor George W. Bush, top right, son of the ex-President, who said in June he had raised more than $36 million in campaign funds, and who handily won the Iowa straw poll in August. Fighting Bush were millionaire publisher Steve Forbes, above left, and Elizabeth Dole, wife of 1996 G.O.P. nominee Bob Dole, above right.

CRISIS IN KOSOVO: A group of ethnic Albanians cross the border from the Yugoslav province of Kosovo into Macedonia. When Yugoslav President Slobodan Milosevic defied a NATO demand to stop persecuting Kosovo's Albanian majority, NATO planes began to bomb Yugoslavia on March 24. In response, Yugoslav troops drove more than 850,000 Kosovars into exile. After 78 days of NATO bombing, Milosevic signed a peace deal.

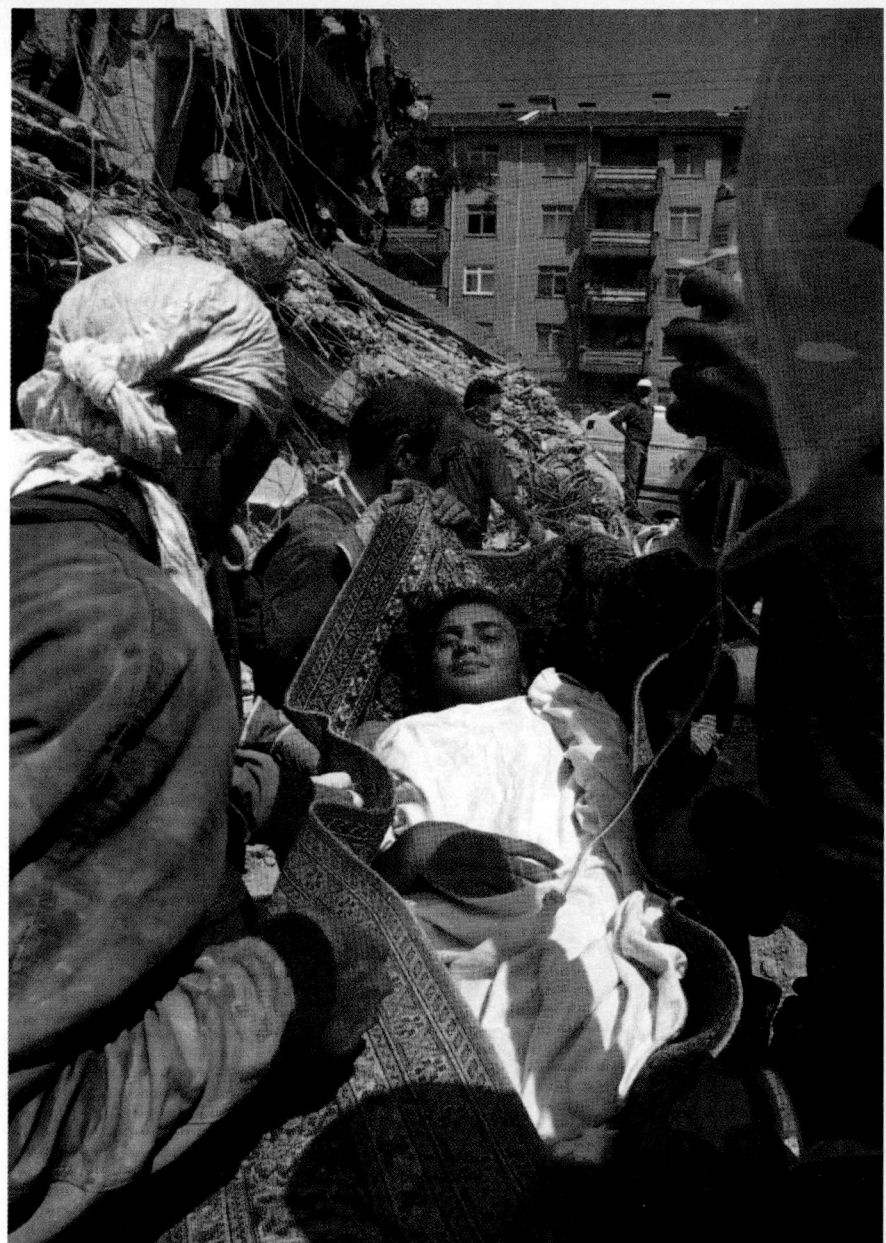

DISASTER IN TURKEY: A team of Russian rescue workers uses a rug as a makeshift stretcher as they carry teenager Ayfer Sirin out of an apartment building in the Turkish town of Golcuk. After an earthquake with a magnitude measuring 7.4 struck northwest Turkey at 3:02 a.m. on Aug. 17, aid teams from around the globe raced to Turkey to assist overwhelmed local authorities. The final toll: more than 15,000 dead.

CLASH IN INDONESIA: After voters in the province of East Timor endorsed independence from Jakarta in August, local militias terrorized the public as government troops
stood by. In September, President B.J. Habibie agreed to let the U.N. police the region.

PROTEST IN CHINA: In a surprising show of dissent against Beijing's iron-fisted rulers,
some 10,000 followers of a meditation cult known as Falun Gong gathered by the
government compound on April 25. The regime quickly cracked down on the movement.

TRANSITION IN SOUTH AFRICA: Former President Nelson Mandela, left, celebrates with his hand-picked successor, Thabo Mbeki, at Mbeki's inauguration ceremony in Pretoria on June 16. Mbeki, former Deputy President, cruised to victory at the polls on June 2.

CHAOS IN THE KREMLIN: President Boris Yeltsin, right, meets with his suitably wary new Prime Minister, Vladimir Putin, on Aug. 10. Putin, a little-known former KGB agent, replaced Sergei Stepashin—and became Yeltsin's fourth Prime Minister in 17 months.

TWISTER! A mother shelters her children under a highway overpass in Oklahoma as a huge funnel cloud moves toward them. A series of tornadoes roared through the state May 3, leaving four dead. The mother and children escaped unharmed.

SHUTTLE FIRST: Eileen Collins, right, the first woman to command a shuttle mission, leads her crew aboard the *Columbia* in June. Weathering a fuel leak at lift-off, the crew successfully put the X-ray telescope Chandra into orbit.

CRESCENT SUN: The century's last full solar eclipse cast an eerie shadow over a swath of the earth's surface from northern Europe, across central Asia and into India on Aug. 17. Here the moon's transit creates a crescent sun, seen between the minarets of the historic Blue Mosque in Istanbul. Though some eclipse watchers in northern Europe were frustrated by clouds, other viewers, including the Pope, enjoyed a clear view of the event.

WHEELING TO GLORY: In a heroic comeback from cancer, American Lance Armstrong pumps past the Arc de Triomphe in Paris on his way to victory in the Tour de France.

HOMER DERBY, PART II: For the second year in a row, sluggers Mark McGwire, left, and Sammy Sosa assaulted Roger Maris' record of 61 home runs in a season. The St. Louis Cardinals' McGwire hit 70 home runs in 1998; Sosa of the Chicago Cubs slammed 66.

LACY ATKINS/THE SAN FRANCISCO EXAMINER

VICTORY! Americans succumbed to soccer fever as the country played host to the Women's World Cup. Fans packed giant stadiums coast to coast as the U.S. team, led by veterans Mia Hamm, Michelle Akers and Julie Foudy, marched to victory. In the final, held in Pasadena's Rose Bowl, the U.S. team beat China 5-4 in overtime. When Brandi Chastain scored the winning goal on a penalty kick, she celebrated by doffing her jersey.

KING HUSSEIN: After a long reign of 47 years, Jordan's King succumbed to cancer in February, shortly after naming his little-known son Abdullah to succeed him.

JOHN KENNEDY, CAROLYN BESSETTE: The President's son, his wife and her sister died at sea when their plane crashed on July 16 with Kennedy at the controls.

JOE DIMAGGIO: The great "Yankee Clipper" died of cancer on March 8 at 84. In the picture above, DiMaggio lines a single on June 29, 1941, to set a new record of hitting safely in 42 consecutive games; his streak was finally stopped at 56 games.

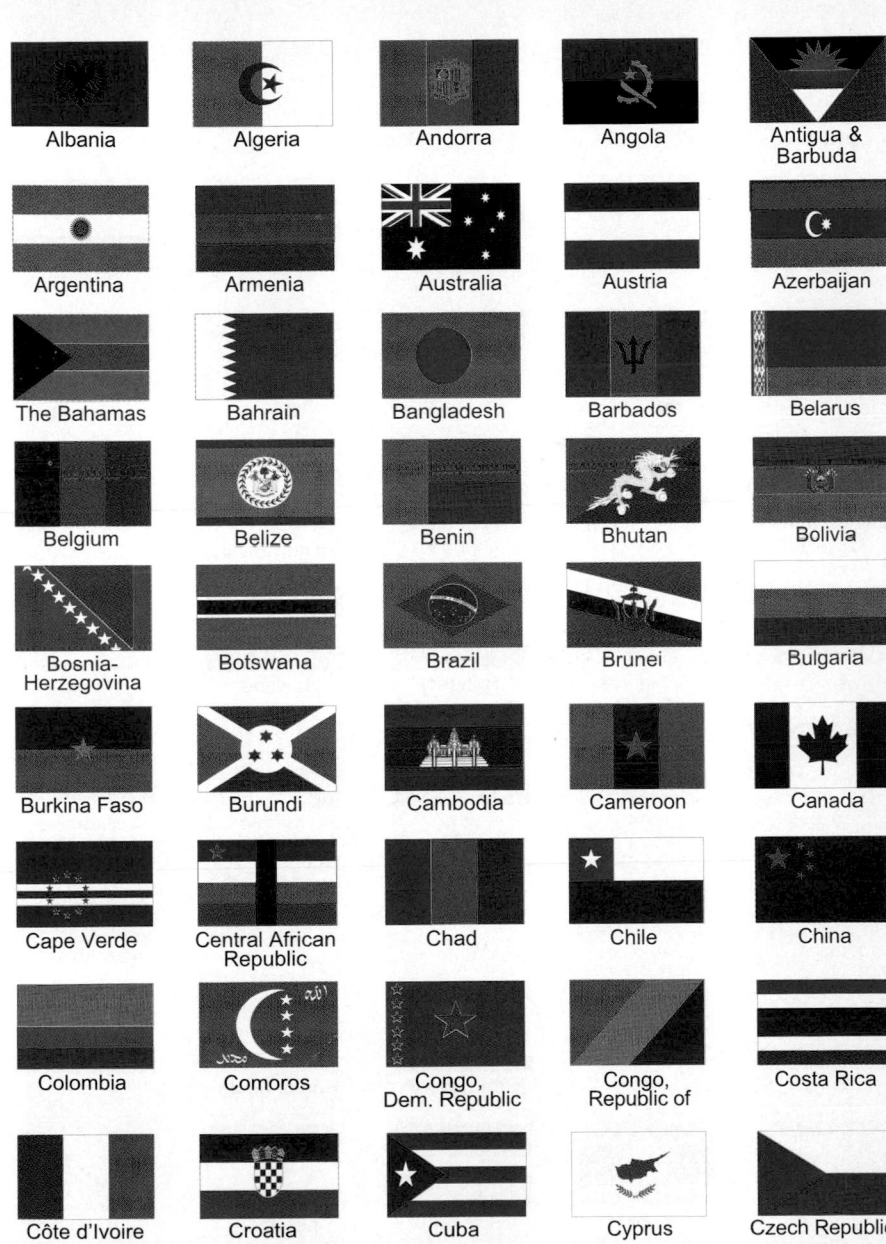

Albania

Algeria

Andorra

Angola

Antigua & Barbuda

Argentina

Armenia

Australia

Austria

Azerbaijan

The Bahamas

Bahrain

Bangladesh

Barbados

Belarus

Belgium

Belize

Benin

Bhutan

Bolivia

Bosnia-Herzegovina

Botswana

Brazil

Brunei

Bulgaria

Burkina Faso

Burundi

Cambodia

Cameroon

Canada

Cape Verde

Central African Republic

Chad

Chile

China

Colombia

Comoros

Congo, Dem. Republic

Congo, Republic of

Costa Rica

Côte d'Ivoire

Croatia

Cuba

Cyprus

Czech Republic

Denmark

Djibouti

Dominica

Dominican Rep.

Ecuador

Egypt	El Salvador	Equitorial Guinea	Eritrea	Estonia
Ethiopia	Fiji	Finland	France	Gabon
The Gambia	Georgia	Germany	Ghana	Greece
Grenada	Guatemala	Guinea	Guinea-Bissau	Guyana
Haiti	Honduras	Hungary	Iceland	India
Indonesia	Iran	Iraq	Ireland	Israel
Italy	Jamaica	Japan	Jordan	Kazakhstan
Kenya	Kiribati	Korea, North	Korea, South	Kuwait
Kyrgyzstan	Laos	Latvia	Lebanon	Lesotho
Liberia	Libya	Liechtenstein	Lithuania	Luxembourg

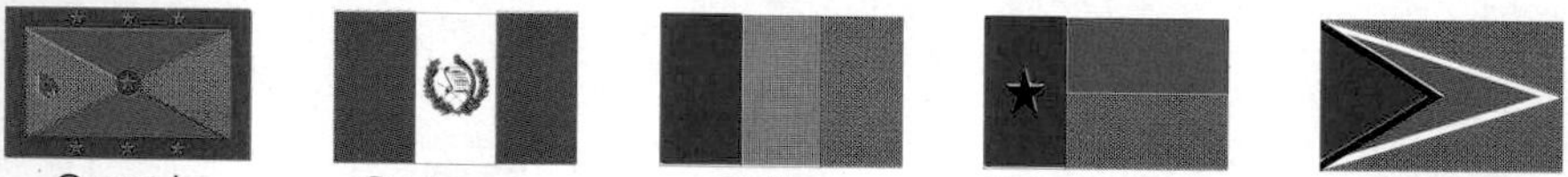

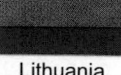

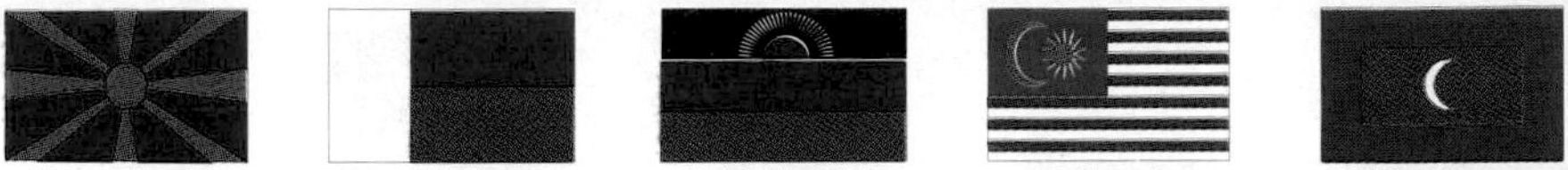

Macedonia	Madagascar	Malawi	Malaysia	Maldives
Mali	Malta	Marshall Is.	Mauritania	Mauritius
Mexico	Micronesia	Moldova	Monaco	Mongolia
Morocco	Mozambique	Myanmar	Namibia	Nauru
Nepal	The Netherlands	New Zealand	Nicaragua	Niger
Nigeria	Norway	Oman	Pakistan	Palau
Panama	Papua New Guinea	Paraguay	Peru	The Philippines
Poland	Portugal	Qatar	Romania	Russia
Rwanda	St. Kitts & Nevis	St. Lucia	St. Vincent & The Grenadines	Samoa
San Marino	São Tomé & Príncipe	Saudi Arabia	Senegal	Seychelles

Sierra Leone	Singapore	Slovakia	Slovenia	Solomon Is.
Somalia	South Africa	Spain	Sri Lanka	The Sudan
Suriname	Swaziland	Sweden	Switzerland	Syria
Taiwan	Tajikistan	Tanzania	Thailand	Togo
Tonga	Trinidad & Tobago	Tunisia	Turkey	Turkmenistan
Tuvalu	Uganda	Ukraine	United Arab Emirates	United Kingdom
United States	Uruguay	Uzbekistan	Vanuatu	Vatican City
Venezuela	Vietnam	Yemen	Yugoslavia	Zambia
Zimbabwe				

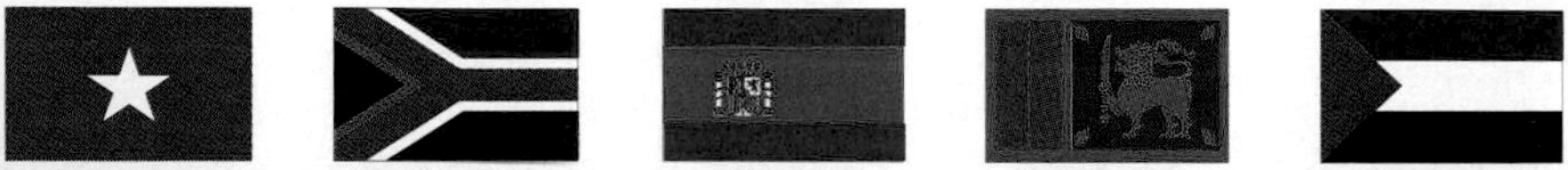

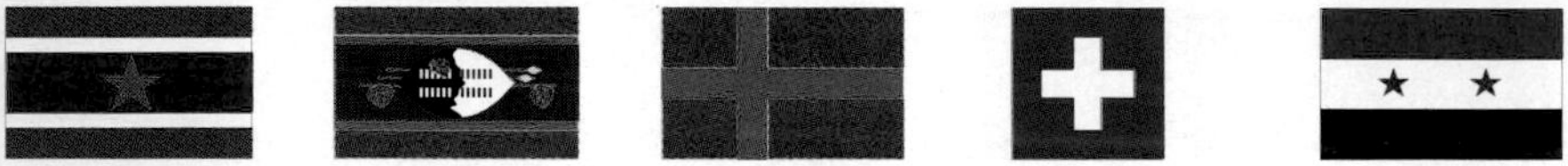

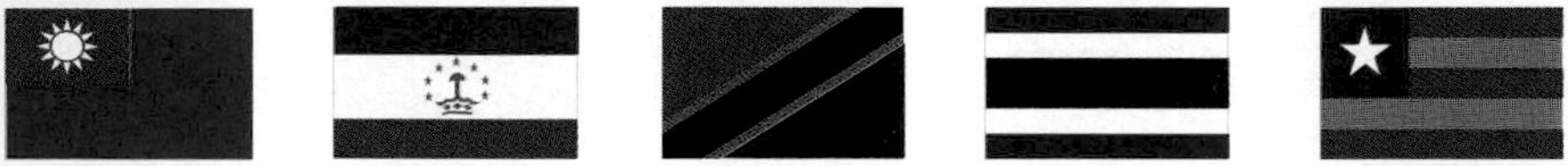

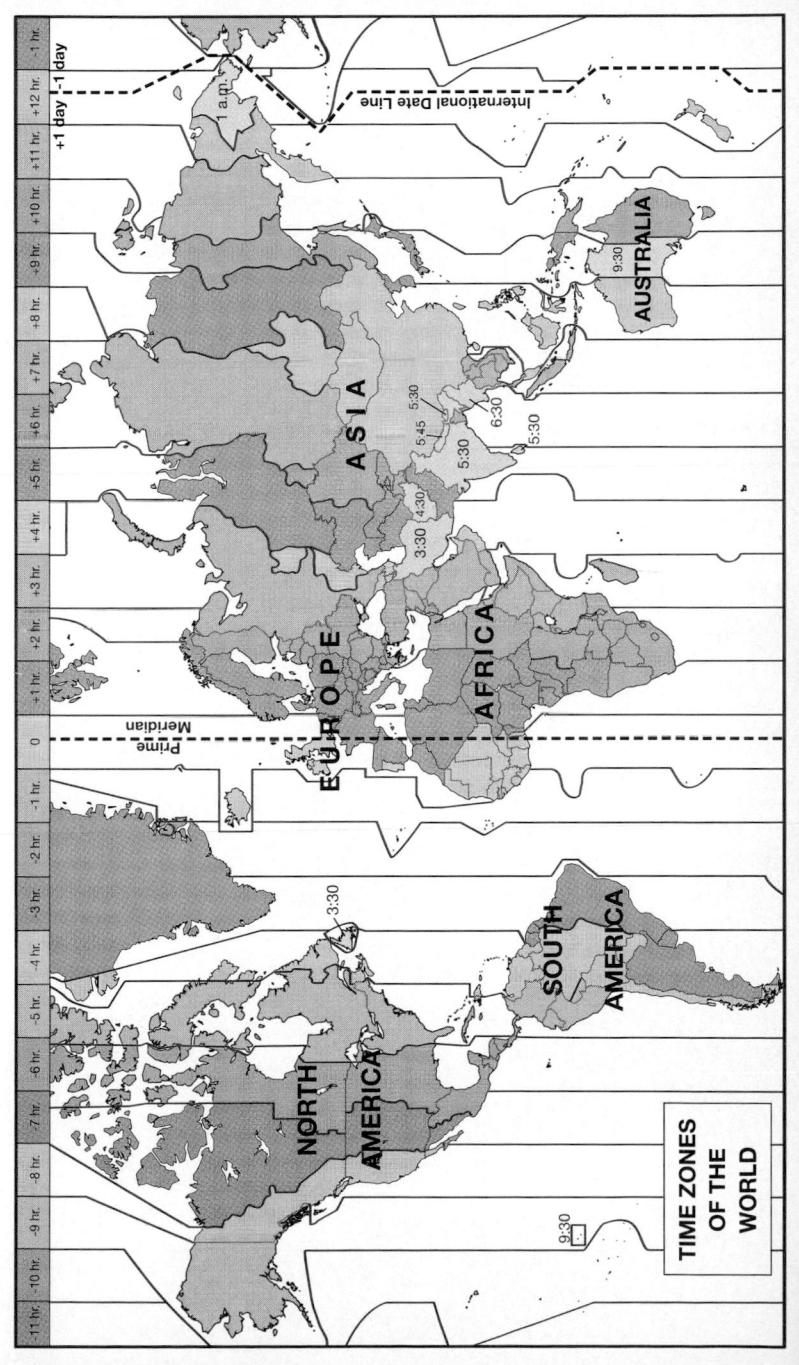

TIME ZONES
OF THE
WORLD

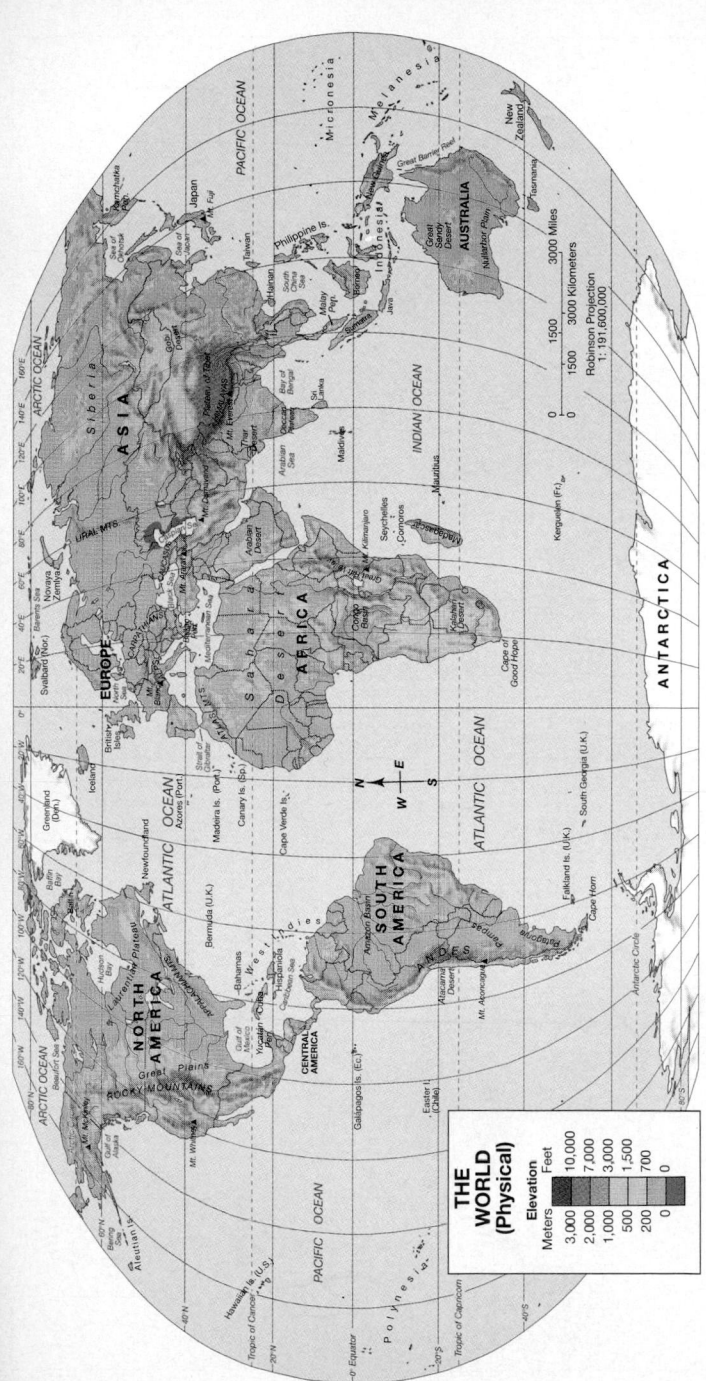

THE
WORLD
(Physical)

Elevation

Meters	Feet
3,000	10,000
2,000	7,000
1,000	3,000
500	1,500
200	700
0	0

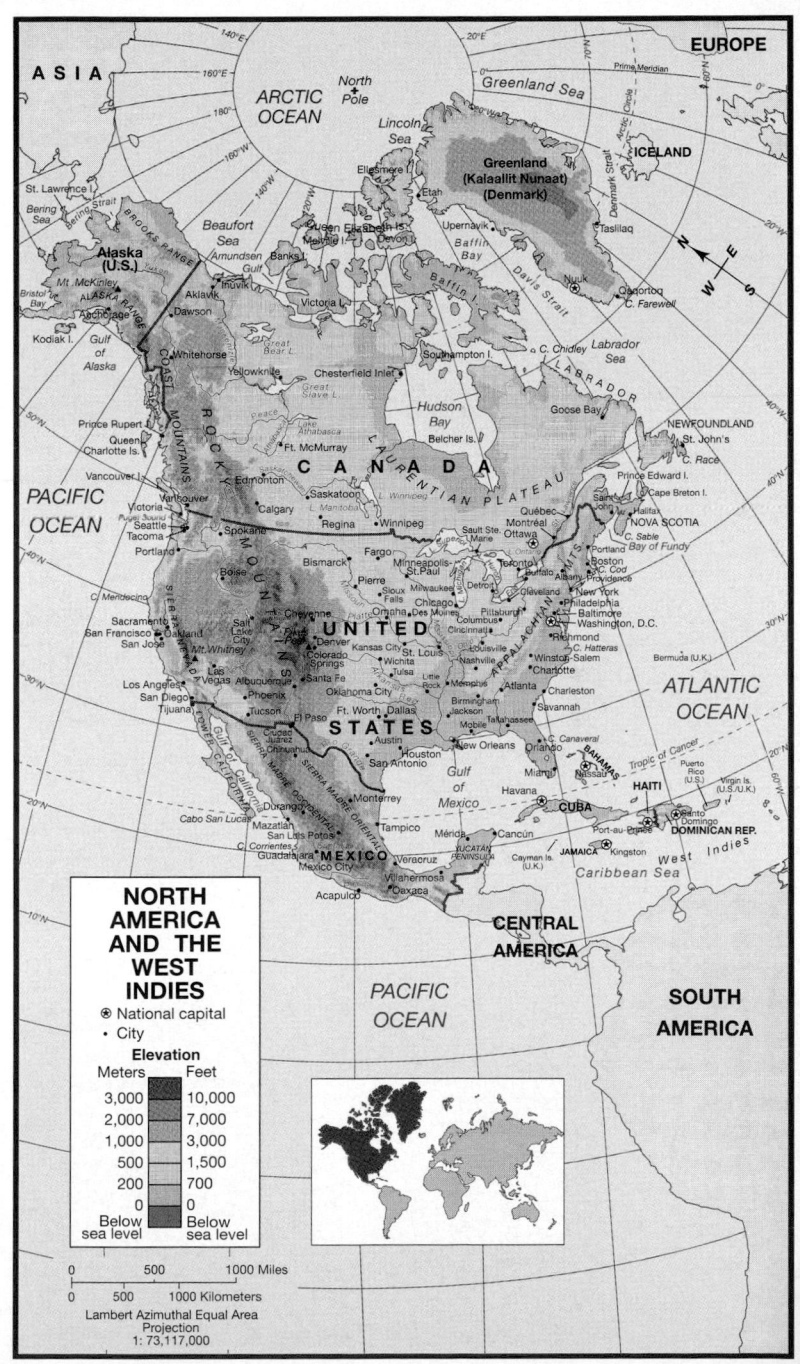

NORTH AMERICA AND THE WEST INDIES

⊛ National capital
• City

Elevation

Meters		Feet
3,000		10,000
2,000		7,000
1,000		3,000
500		1,500
200		700
0		0
Below sea level		Below sea level

| 0 | 500 | 1000 Miles |
| 0 | 500 | 1000 Kilometers |

Lambert Azimuthal Equal Area Projection
1: 73,117,000

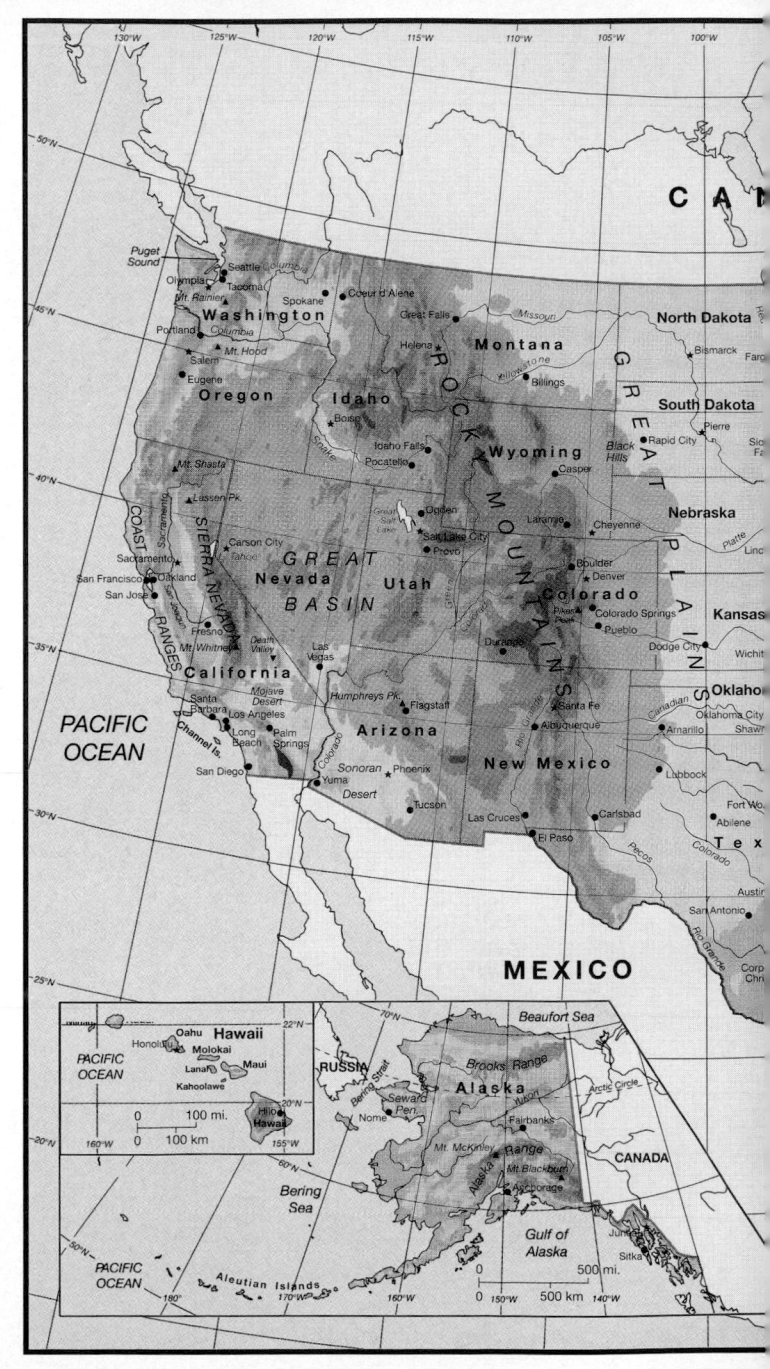

UNITED
STATES
⊗ National capital
★ State capital
● City

Elevation
Meters   Feet
3,000   10,000
2,000   7,000
1,000   3,000
500   1,500
200   700
0   0

0   200   400 Miles
0   200   400 Kilometers
Albers Equal-Area Projection
1: 26,044,000

CANADA

Lake Superior
Minnesota
Duluth
Superior
St. Paul
Minneapolis
Eau Claire
Rochester
Wisconsin
Madison
Green Bay
Milwaukee
Kenosha
Iowa
Cedar Rapids
Rockford
Sioux City
Omaha
Des Moines
Illinois
Champaign
Springfield
Missouri
Springfield
Kansas City
Jefferson City
St. Louis
Topeka

Michigan
Lake Huron
Sault Ste. Marie
Grand Rapids
Flint
Lansing
Ann Arbor
Detroit
Chicago
Gary
Fort Wayne
Muncie
Indianapolis
Indiana
Dayton
Cincinnati
Louisville
Frankfort
Lexington
Kentucky
Bowling Green
Nashville
Tennessee
Chattanooga
Knoxville

L. Ontario
L. Erie
Toledo
Ohio
Cleveland
Akron
Columbus
Springfield
Wheeling
Clarksburg
Charleston
W. Va.
Pittsburgh
Harrisburg

L. Champlain
Maine
Augusta
Montpelier
Mt. Washington
Vt.
N.H.
Concord
Portland
Portsmouth
Manchester
New York
Albany
Boston
Mass.
Worcester
Cape Cod
Rochester
Syracuse
Buffalo
Hartford
Conn.
R.I.
Providence
New Haven
Newark
Long Island
New York
New Jersey
Trenton
Reading
Pennsylvania
Philadelphia
Atlantic City
Baltimore
Md.
Delaware
Dover
Annapolis
Washington, D.C.
Chesapeake Bay
Virginia
Richmond
Williamsburg
Norfolk
Virginia Beach
Lynchburg
Winston-Salem
Durham
Raleigh
Cape Hatteras

Gulf of Maine

Rock Island

Iowa
Missouri

Arkansas
Fort Smith
Little Rock
Memphis
Tulsa

Mississippi
Birmingham
Alabama
Montgomery
Jackson
Mississippi
Louisiana
Shreveport
Baton Rouge
Mobile
Pensacola
New Orleans
Port Arthur
Houston
Galveston

North Carolina
Charlotte
Wilmington
South Carolina
Columbia
Charleston
Athens
Atlanta
Augusta
Georgia
Macon
Savannah
Albany
Tallahassee
Jacksonville
St. Augustine
Daytona Beach
Florida
Orlando
Cape Canaveral
Tampa
St. Petersburg
L. Okeechobee
Fort Lauderdale
Miami

APPALACHIAN MTS.

ATLANTIC
OCEAN

N
W   E
S

Gulf of Mexico

Straits of Florida
Florida Keys
BAHAMAS
CUBA

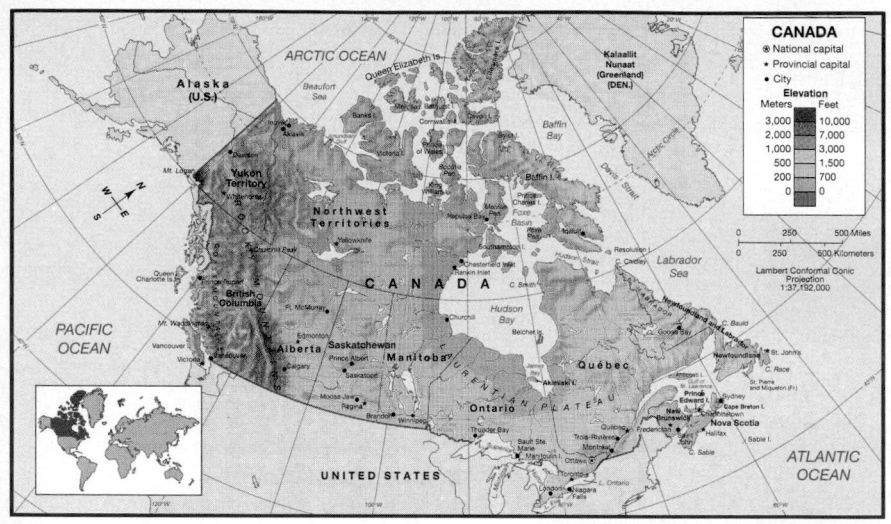

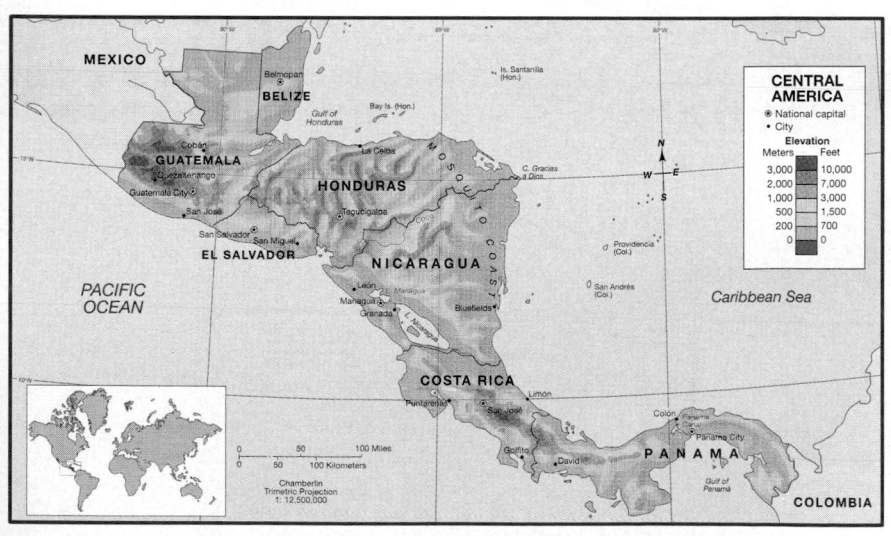

SOUTH AMERICA

⊛ National capital
• City

Elevation

Meters	Feet
3,000	10,000
2,000	7,000
1,000	3,000
500	1,500
200	700
0	0

Galápagos Is. (Ecuador)

I. Marchena
I. San Salvador
I. Isabela
I. Santa Cruz
I. Fernandina
I. San Cristóbal
I. Sta.María
I. Española

WEST INDIES

Caribbean Sea

CENTRAL AMERICA

Neth. Antilles (Neth.)
I. de Margarita
Gulf of Venezuela
Curaçao
Gulf of Paria

Barranquilla
Cartagena
Gulf of Urabá
Maracaibo
Caracas

VENEZUELA

Montería
Cúcuta
San Cristóbal
Ciudad Bolívar
Medellín
Bucaramanga
Manizales
Alto Pilcomayo
Bogotá

Morawhanna
Georgetown
New Amsterdam
Paramaribo

GUYANA
SURINAME

Devil's I.
Cayenne
French Guiana (Fr.)

ATLANTIC OCEAN

Gulf of Panamá
I. Malpelo (Colombia)

C. Corrientes
Buenaventura
Cali
Mt. Huila

COLOMBIA

Guayaquil
Cuenca
Iquitos
Piura

ECUADOR

Mt. Cotopaxi
Quito
Ambato
Mt. Chimborazo
Gulf of Guayaquil

PERU

Trujillo
Mt. Huascarán

Callao
Lima

Cuzco

La Paz
Trinidad

BOLIVIA

El Misti
Arequipa
Cochabamba
Santa Cruz

Iquique

PARAGUAY

Antofagasta

San Félix (Chile)
San Ambrosio (Chile)

Potosí
Sucre

Asunción

Brasília

Belo Horizonte

São Tomé
Rio de Janeiro

São Paulo
Santos
Tropic of Capricorn

Curitiba
I. de Santa Catarina
Pôrto Alegre

CHILE

San Miguel de Tucumán
Mt. Ojos del Salado

Córdoba

Rivera
Salto
Paysandú
L. dos Patos

Viña del Mar
Mt. Aconcagua
Valparaíso
Santiago
Mendoza
Rosario
Buenos Aires
Juan Fernández Is. (Chile)
I. Robinson Crusoe
Vol. Maipo
La Plata
Río de la Plata

URUGUAY
Montevideo
L. Mirí

I. Alejandro Selkirk

ARGENTINA

Concepción

C. San Antonio
Mar del Plata

Bahía Blanca

Negro

Gulf of San Matías
Pen. Valdés

ATLANTIC OCEAN

I. de Chiloé
Gulf of Corcovado
Archipiélago de los Chonos
Pen. Taitao
C. Tres Montes
Gulf of Penas

Gulf of San Jorge

ANDES

Falkland Islands
(U.K.; claimed by Arg.)

Strait of Magellan
Stanley

Tierra del Fuego
I. de los Estados

I. Sta. Inés
Cape Horn

South Georgia (U.K.)

PACIFIC OCEAN

Tropic of Cancer

Gulf of Mexico

Manaus
Amazon

BRAZIL

Belém
I. São Luís
Fortaleza
C. São Roque
Recife

Equator

Salvador

I. de Maracá
I. Caviana

ATLANTIC OCEAN

Antarctic Circle

| 0 | 300 | 600 Miles |
| 0 | 300 | 600 Kilometers |

Lambert Azimuthal Equal-Area Projection
1: 43,697,000

WESTERN EUROPE

⊛ National capital
• City

Elevation

Meters		Feet
3,000		10,000
2,000		7,000
1,000		3,000
500		1,500
200		700
0		0

0   200   400 Miles

0   200   400 Kilometers

Azimuthal Equal-Area Projection
1: 31,019,000

EASTERN EUROPE

⊛ National capital
· City

Elevation

Meters	Feet
3,000	10,000
2,000	7,000
1,000	3,000
500	1,500
200	700
0	0

0   200   400 Miles

0   200   400 Kilometers

Azimuthal Equal-Area Projection
1: 31,019,000

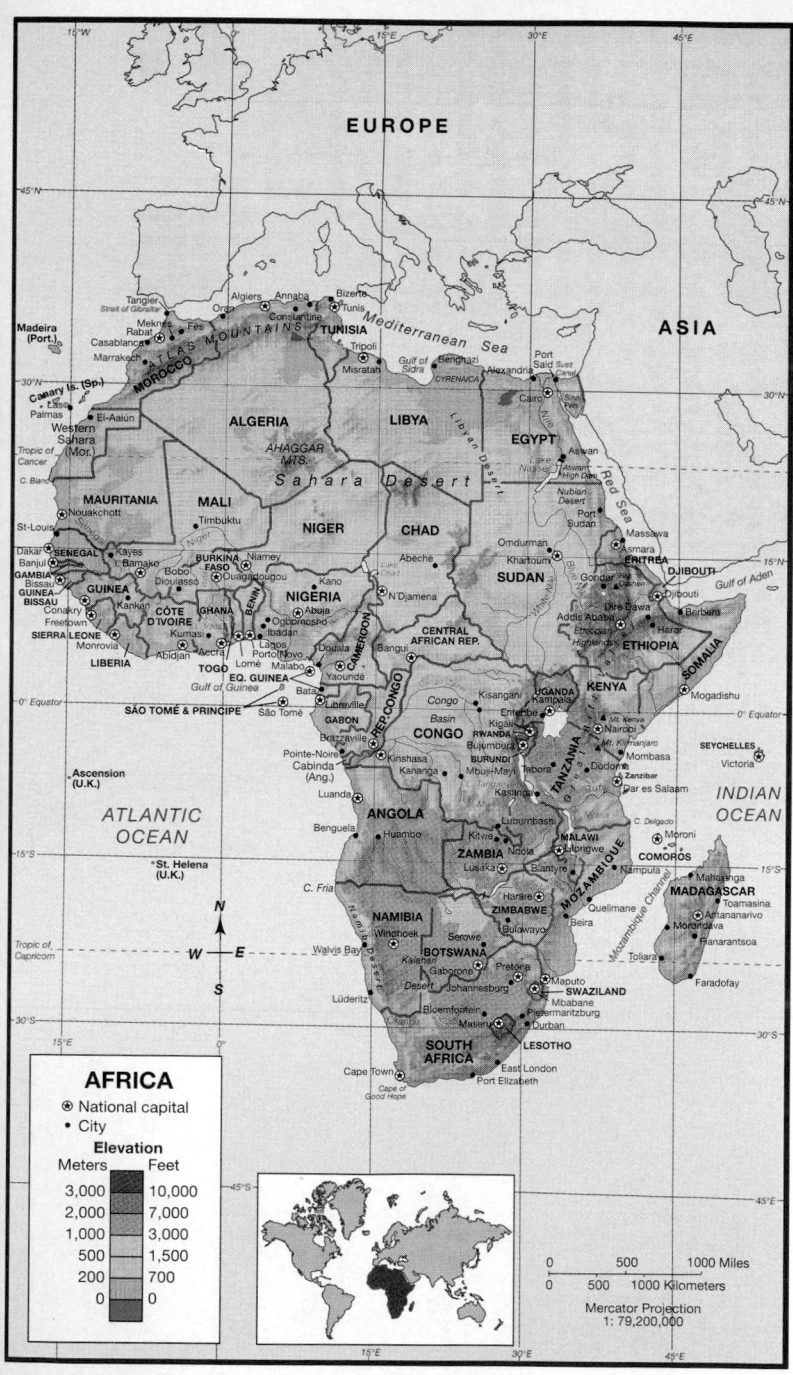

AFRICA

⊛ National capital
• City

Elevation

Meters	Feet
3,000	10,000
2,000	7,000
1,000	3,000
500	1,500
200	700
0	0

0   500   1000 Miles
0   500   1000 Kilometers

Mercator Projection
1: 79,200,000

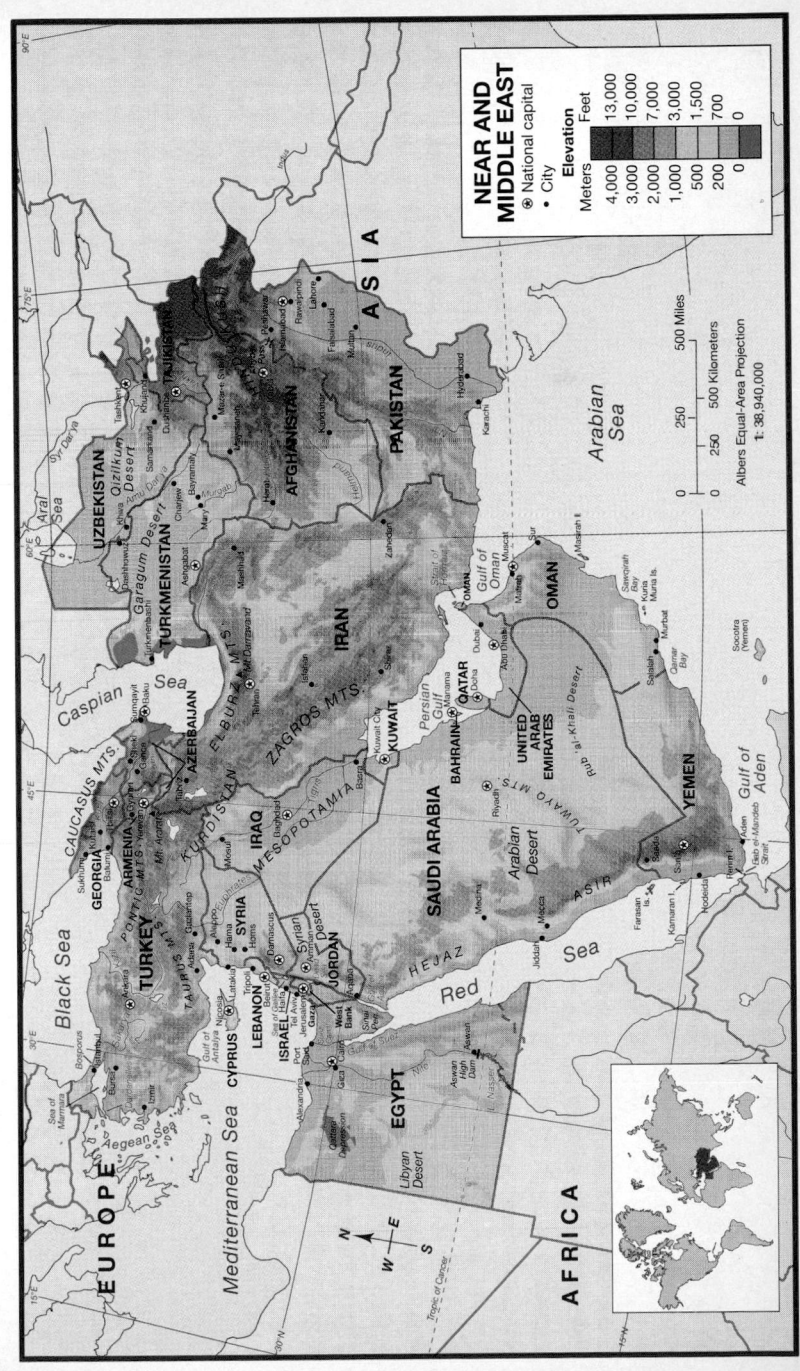

NEAR AND
MIDDLE EAST

⊛ National capital
• City

Elevation
Meters   Feet
          13,000
4,000   10,000
3,000   7,000
2,000   3,000
1,000   1,500
500   700
200
0   0

500 Miles
0   250   500 Kilometers
0   250

Albers Equal-Area Projection
⚹: 38,940,000

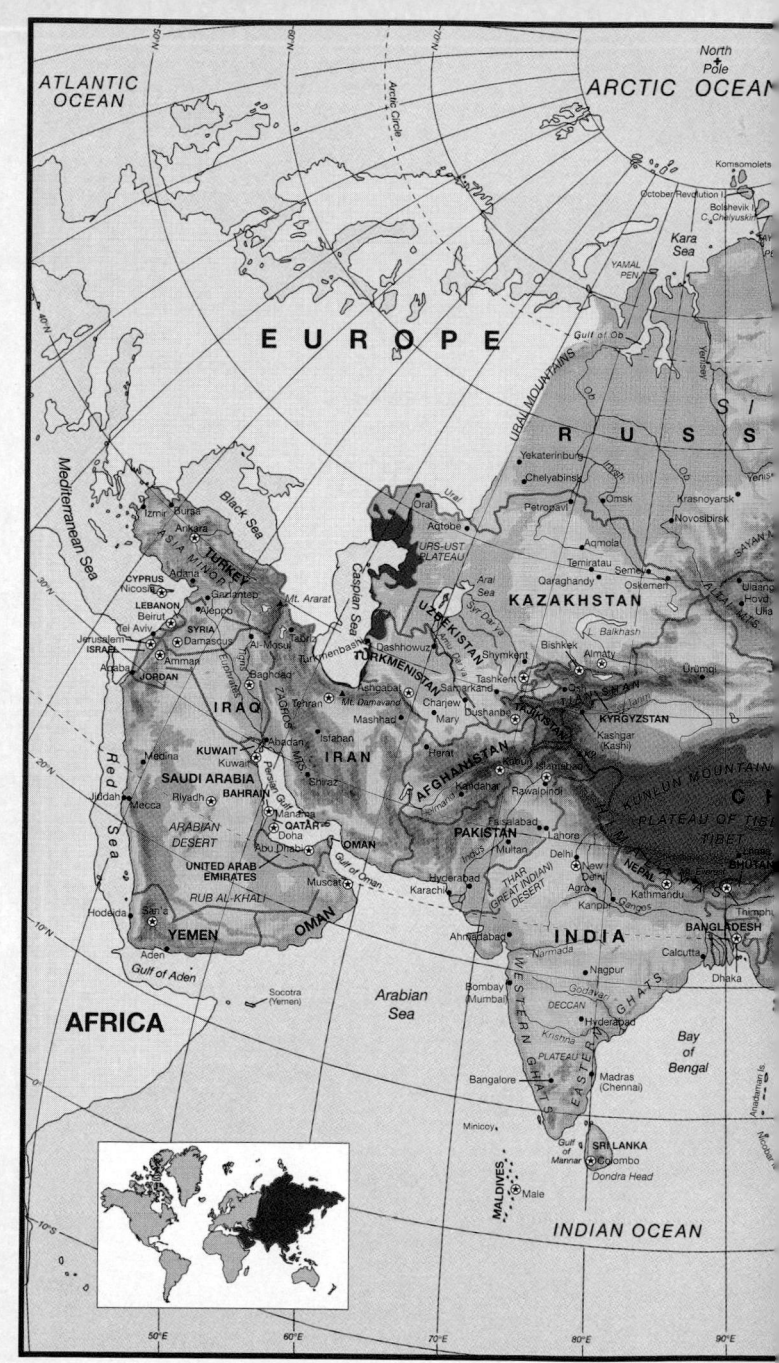

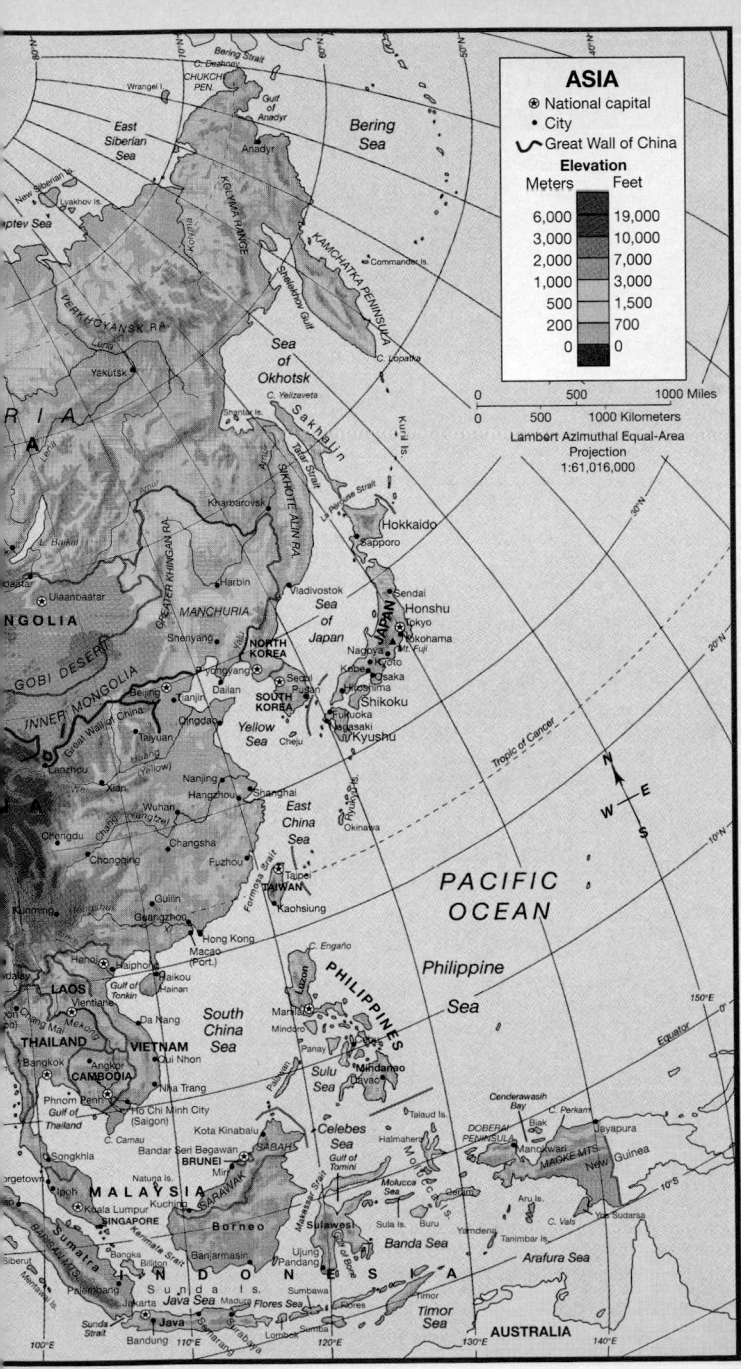

ASIA

⊗ National capital
• City
〰 Great Wall of China

Elevation

Meters	Feet
6,000	19,000
3,000	10,000
2,000	7,000
1,000	3,000
500	1,500
200	700
0	0

0   500   1000 Miles
0   500   1000 Kilometers

Lambert Azimuthal Equal-Area
Projection
1:61,016,000

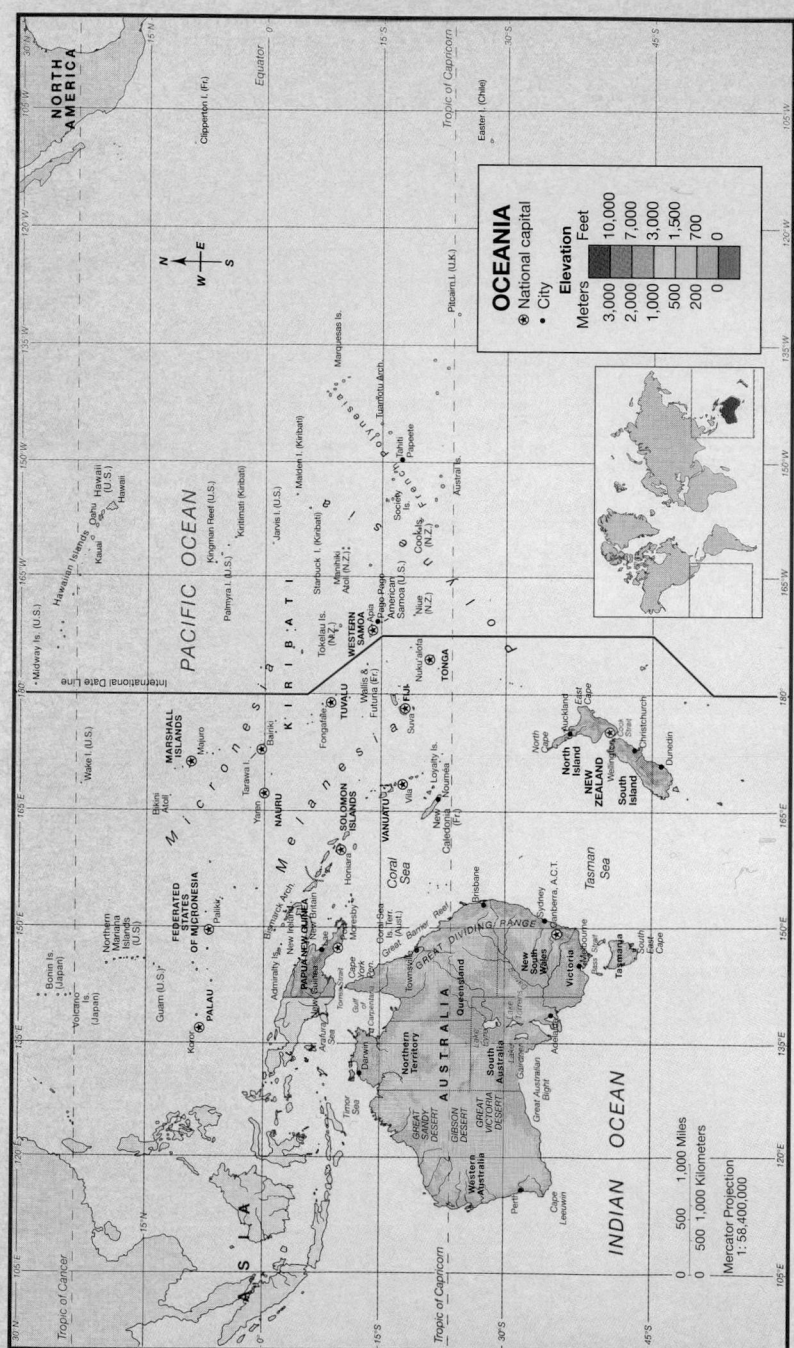

The Elements

Elements are the building blocks of nature. Water, for example, is a compound consisting of the elements hydrogen and oxygen. Each element is a pure substance that cannot be split up into any simpler pure substance.

The smallest particle of an element that can exist is an atom. An atom consists of subatomic particles. The most important of these are protons, which have positive electrical charges; electrons, which have negative electrical charges; and neutrons, which are electrically neutral.

The atomic number of an element is the number of protons in one atom of the element. Each element has a different atomic number. For example, the atomic numbers of hydrogen and oxygen are 1 and 8, respectively.

Elements with atomic numbers 1 (hydrogen) to 94 (plutonium) occur naturally on Earth. The remaining artificial elements have been created since 1940 by using nuclear reactors and particle accelerators. Element 100 is named fermium. Elements with atomic numbers 101 onward are known as the transfermium elements. They are also known as heavy elements because their atoms have very large masses compared with atoms of hydrogen, the lightest of all elements.

Chemical Elements

Element	Symbol	Atomic no.	Atomic wt.	Specific gravity	Melting point °C	Boiling point °C	No. of isotopes[1]	Discoverer	Year
Actinium	Ac	89	227^2	10.07^2	1050	3200±300	11	Debierne	1899
Aluminum	Al	13	26.9815	2.6989	660.37	2467	8	Wöhler	1827
Americium	Am	95	243^6	13.67	994±4	2607	13^3	Seaborg et al.	1944
Antimony	Sb	51	121.75	6.61	630.74	1750	29	Early historic times	—
Argon	Ar	18	39.948	1.7837^4	−189.2	−185.7	8	Rayleigh and Ramsay	1894
Arsenic (gray)	As	33	74.9216	5.73	817	613^5	14	Albertus Magnus	1250?
Astatine	At	85	210	—	302	337	21	Corson et al.	1940
Barium	Ba	56	137.34	3.5	725	1640	25	Davy	1808
Berkelium	Bk	97	247^6	14.00^7	—	—	8^3	Seaborg et al.	1949
Beryllium	Be	4	9.01218	1.848	1278±5	2970	6	Vauquelin	1798
Bismuth	Bi	83	208.9806	9.747	271.3	1560±5	19	Geoffroy	1753
Bohrium	Bh	107	262	—	—	—	—	Armbruster and Münzenberg	1981
Boron	B	5	10.81	2.37^8	2300	2550^5	6	Gay-Lussac and Thénard; Davy	1808
Bromine	Br	35	79.904	3.12^4	−7.2	58.78	19	Balard	1826
Cadmium	Cd	48	112.40	8.65	320.9	765	22	Stromeyer	1817
Calcium	Ca	20	40.08	1.55	839±2	1484	14	Davy	1808
Californium	Cf	98	251^6	—	—	—	12^3	Seaborg et al.	1950
Carbon	C	6	12.011	$1.8-3.5^9$	−3550	4827	7	Prehistoric	—
Cerium	Ce	58	140.12	6.771	798±3	3257	19	Berzelius and Hisinger; Klaproth	1803
Cesium	Cs	55	132.9055	1.873	28.40	678.4	22	Bunsen and Kirchoff	1860
Chlorine	Cl	17	35.453	1.56^4	−100.98	−34.6	11	Scheele	1774
Chromium	Cr	24	51.996	7.18-7.20	1857±20	2672	9	Vauquelin	1797
Cobalt	Co	27	58.9332	8.9	1495	2870	14	Brandt	c.1735
Copper	Cu	29	63.546	8.96	1083.4±0.2	2567	11	Prehistoric	—
Curium	Cm	96	247^6	13.51^2	1340±40	—	13^3	Seaborg et al.	1944
Dubnium	Db	105	262	—	—	—	—	Ghiorso et al.	1970
Dysprosium	Dy	66	162.50	8.540	1409	2335	21	Boisbaudran	1886
Einsteinium	Es	99	254^6	—	—	—	12^3	Ghiorso et al.	1952
Erbium	Er	68	167.26	9.045	1522	2510	16	Mosander	1843
Europium	Eu	63	151.96	5.283	822±5	1597	21	Demarcay	1896
Fermium	Fm	100	257^6	—	—	—	10^3	Ghiorso et al.	1953
Fluorine	F	9	18.9984	1.108^4	−219.62	−188.14	6	Moissan	1886
Francium	Fr	87	223^6	—	27^2	677^2	21	Perey	1938
Gadolinium	Gd	64	157.25	7.898	1311±1	3233	17	Marignac	1880
Gallium	Ga	31	69.72	5.904	29.78	2403	14	Boisbaudran	1875
Germanium	Ge	32	72.59	5.323	937.4	2830	17	Winkler	1886
Gold	Au	79	196.9665	19.32	1064.43	2807	21	Prehistoric	—
Hafnium	Hf	72	178.49	13.31	2227±20	4602	17	Coster and von Hevesy	1923
Hassium	Hs	108	265	—	—	—	—	Armbruster and Münzenberg	1983
Helium	He	2	4.00260	0.1785^4	−272.2	−268.934	5	Janssen	1868
Holmium	Ho	67	164.9303	8.781	1470	2720	29	Delafontaine and Soret	1878
Hydrogen	H	1	1.0080	0.070^4	−259.14	−252.87	3	Cavendish	1766
Indium	In	49	114.82	7.31	156.61	2080	34	Reich and Richter	1863
Iodine	I	53	126.9045	4.93	113.5	184.35	24	Cortois	1811
Iridium	Ir	77	192.22	22.42	2410	4130	25	Tennant	1803
Iron	Fe	26	55.847	7.894	1535	2750	10	Prehistoric	—
Krypton	Kr	36	83.80	3.733^4	−156.6	−152.30±0.10	23	Ramsay and Travers	1898
Lanthanum	La	57	138.9055	6.166	920±5	3454	19	Mosander	1839

Element	Symbol	Atomic no.	Atomic wt.	Specific gravity	Melting point °C	Boiling point °C	No. of isotopes[1]	Discoverer	Year
Lawrencium	Lr	103	257[6]	—	—	—	20[3]	Ghiorso et al.	1961
Lead	Pb	82	207.2	11.35	327.502	1740	29	Prehistoric	—
Lithium	Li	3	6.941	0.534	180.54	1347	5	Arfvedson	1817
Lutetium	Lu	71	174.97	9.835	1656±5	3315	22	Urbain	1907
Magnesium	Mg	12	24.305	1.738	648.8±0.5	1090	8	Black	1755
Manganese	Mn	25	54.9380	7.21-7.44[10]	1244±3	1962	11	Gahn, Scheele, and Bergman	1774
Meitnerium	Mt	109	266	—	—	—	—	GSI, Darmstadt, West Germany	1982
Mendelevium	Md	101	256[6]	—	—	—	3[3]	Ghiorso et al.	1955
Mercury	Hg	80	200.59	13.546	−38.87	356.58	26	Prehistoric	—
Molybdenum	Mo	42	95.94	10.22	2617	4612	20	Scheele	1778
Neodymium	Nd	60	144.24	6.80 & 7.004[10]	1010	3127	16	von Welsbach	1885
Neon	Ne	10	20.179	0.89990 (g/10°C/1 atm)	−248.67	−246.048	8	Ramsay and Travers	1898
Neptunium	Np	93	237.0482	20.25	6400±1	3902	15[3]	McMillan and Abelson	1940
Nickel	Ni	28	58.71	8.902	1453	2732	11	Cronstedt	1751
Niobium (Columbium)	Nb	41	92.9064	8.57	2468±10	4742	24	Hatchett	1801
Nitrogen	N	7	14.0067	0.808[4]	−209.86	−195.8	8	Rutherford	1772
Nobelium	No	102	254[6]	—	—	—	7[3]	Ghiorso et al.	1957
Osmium	Os	76	190.2	22.57	3045±30	5027±100	19	Tennant	1803
Oxygen	O	8	15.9994	1.14[4]	−218.4	−182.962	8	Priestley	1774
Palladium	Pd	46	106.4	12.02	1552	3140	21	Wollaston	1803
Phosphorous (white)	P	15	30.9738	1.82	44.1	280	7	Brand	1669
Platinum	Pt	78	195.09	21.45	1772	3827±100	32	Ulloa	1735
Plutonium	Pu	94	244[6]	19.84	641	3232	16[3]	Seaborg et al.	1940
Polonium	Po	84	210[6]	9.32	254	962	34	Curie	1898
Potassium	K	19	39.102	0.862	63.65	774	10	Davy	1807
Praseodymium	Pr	59	140.9077	6.772	931±4	3212	15	von Weisbach	1885
Promethium	Pm	61	145[6]	—	≈1080	2460	14	Marinsky et al.	1945
Protactinium	Pa	91	231.0359	15.37[2]	<1600	—	14	Hahn and Meitner	1917
Radium	Ra	88	226.0254	5.0?	700	1140	15	Pierre and Marie Curie	1898
Radon	Rn	86	222[6]	4.4[4]	−71	−61.8	20	Dorn	1900
Rhenium	Re	75	186.2	21.02	3180	5627[7]	21	Noddack, Berg, and Tacke	1925
Rhodium	Rh	45	102.9055	12.41	1966±3	3727±100	20	Wollaston	1803
Rubidium	Rb	37	85.4678	1.532	38.89	688	20	Bunsen and Kirchoff	1861
Rutherfordium	Rf	104	261	—	—	—	—	Ghiorso et al.	1969
Ruthenium	Ru	44	101.07	12.44	2310	3900	16	Klaus	1844
Samarium	Sm	62	150.4	7.536	1072±5	1778	17	Boisbaudran	1879
Scandium	Sc	21	44.9559	2.989	1539	2832	15	Nilson	1879
Seaborgium	Sg	106	263	—	—	—	—	Ghiorso et al.	1974
Selenium (gray)	Se	34	78.96	4.79	217	684.9±1	20	Berzelius	1817
Silicon	Si	14	28.086	2.33	1410	2355	8	Berzelius	1824
Silver	Ag	47	107.868	10.5	961.93	2212	27	Prehistoric	—
Sodium	Na	11	22.9898	0.971	97.81±0.03	882.9	7	Davy	1807
Strontium	Sr	38	87.62	2.54	769	1384	18	Davy	1808
Sulfur	S	16	32.06	2.07[11]	112.8	444.674	10	Prehistoric	—
Tantalum	Ta	73	180.9479	16.654	2996	5425±100	19	Ekeberg	1801
Technetium	Tc	43	98.062	11.50[2]	2172	4877	23	Perrier and Segré	1937
Tellurium	Te	52	127.60	6.24	449.5±0.3	989.8±3.8	29	von Reichenstein	1782
Terbium	Tb	65	158.9254	8.234	1360±4	3041	24	Mosander	1843
Thallium	Tl	81	204.37	11.85	303.5	1457±10	28	Crookes	1861
Thorium	Th	90	232.0381	11.72	1750	4790	12	Berzelius	1828
Thulium	Tm	69	168.9342	9.314	1545±15	1727	18	Cleve	1879
Tin (white)	Sn	50	118.69	7.31	231.9681	2270	28	Prehistoric	—
Titanium	Ti	22	47.90	4.55	1660±10	3287	9	Gregor	1791
Tungsten	W	74	183.85	19.3	3410±20	5660	22	J. and F. d'Elhuyar	1783
Uranium	U	92	238.029	19.05	1132.3±0.8	3818	15	Peligot	1841
Vanadium	V	23	50.9414	6.11	1890±10	3380	9	del Rio	1801
Xenon	Xe	54	131.30	3.52[4]	−111.9	−107.1±3	31	Ramsay and Travers	1898
Ytterbium	Yb	70	173.04	6.972	824±5	1193	16	Marignac	1878
Yttrium	Y	39	88.9059	4.457	1523±8	3337	21	Gadolin	1794
Zinc	Zn	30	65.38	7.133	419.58	907	15	Prehistoric	—
Zirconium	Zr	40	91.22	6.506[2]	1852±2	4377	20	Klaproth	1789

NOTES: Elements 110, 111, 112, 114, 116, and 118 have not yet been named and are thus not included. ≈ means "approximately." < means "less than." 1. Isotopes are different forms of the same element having the same atomic number but different atomic weights. 2. Calculated figure. 3. Artificially produced. 4. Liquid. 5. Sublimation point. 6. Mass number of the isotope of longest known life. 7. Estimated. 8. Amorphous. 9. Depending on whether amorphous, graphite, or diamond. 10. Depending on allotropic form.

Three New Elements Discovered in 1999

In 1999 physicists discovered three new "superheavy" elements, one of which has confirmed a theory they had speculated about for the past thirty years.

In January a team of Russian and American physicists at the Joint Institute for Nuclear Research at Dubna, Russia, announced the creation of element 114. The physicists were able to produce just a single atom of the new element, an isotope containing 114 protons and 184 neutrons in its nucleus. Element 114 lasted an unprecedented "stable" 30 seconds, long enough to enable its detection, before breaking down (decaying) into lighter elements. Until this discovery, "superheavy" elements found had been unstable, with lifetimes measured in fractions of a second. For example, element 112, the last element discovered, has a life of just 280 milliseconds. The heavier the element, it seemed, the shorter its life.

But for the last 30 years, theorists had predicted the existence of "an island of stability" occurring among the heavier elements—a group of stable elements living long enough to allow for studies of their nuclear behavior and chemistry. The significance of element 114 is its confirmation that scientists have finally landed upon the shores of the "island of stability" they had only hypothesized about.

In April and June of 1999, another two elements were discovered, this time by scientists at the U.S. Department of Energy's Lawrence Berkeley National Laboratory in California: element 118 and its immediate decay product, element 116. The short-lived isotope of element 118 has a mass number of 293, which contains 118 protons and 175 neutrons in its nucleus. By comparison, the heaviest element found in nature in sizable quantities is uranium which in its common form contains 92 protons and 146 neutrons.

Within less than a millisecond after its creation, the nucleus of element 118 radioactively decays by emitting an alpha particle (a positive charged particle with two protons and two neutrons), leaving behind an isotope of element 116. The second element, 116, has a mass number of 289, which contains 116 protons and 173 neutrons. This "daughter" element is also radioactive and alpha-decays into an isotope of element 114. The chain of successive alpha decays continues until at least element 106, Seaborgium.

Table of Geological Periods

It is now generally assumed that planets are formed by the accretion of gas and dust in a cosmic cloud, but there is no way of estimating the length of this process. Our Earth acquired its present size, more or less, between 4 billion and 5 billion years ago. Life on Earth originated about 2 billion years ago, but there are no good fossil remains from periods earlier than the Cambrian, which began about 550 million years ago. The largely unknown past before the Cambrian Period is referred to as the Pre-Cambrian and is subdivided into the Lower (or older) and Upper (or younger) Pre-Cambrian—also called the Archaeozoic and Proterozoic Eras.

The known geological history of Earth since the beginning of the Cambrian Period is subdivided into three eras, each of which includes a number of periods. They, in turn, are subdivided into subperiods. In a subperiod, a certain section may be especially well known because of rich fossil finds. Such a section is called a formation, and it is usually identified by a place name.

Paleozoic Era

This era began 570 million years ago and lasted for 325 million years. The name was compounded from Greek *palaios* (old) and *zoön* (animal).

Period	Duration[1]	Subperiods	Events
Cambrian (from *Cambria*, Latin name for Wales)	60	Lower Cambrian Middle Cambrian Upper Cambrian	Invertebrate sea life of many types, proliferating during this and the following period
Ordovician (from Latin *Ordovices*, people of early Britain)	70	Lower Ordovician Upper Ordovician	First known fishes
Silurian (from Latin *Silures*, people of early Wales)	30	Lower Silurian Upper Silurian	Gigantic sea scorpions
Devonian (from Devonshire in England)	50	Lower Devonian Upper Devonian	Proliferation of fishes and other forms of sea life; land still largely lifeless
Carboniferous (from Latin *carbo* = coal + *fero* = to bear)	70	Lower or Mississippian Upper or Pennsylvanian	Period of maximum coal formation in swampy forests; early insects and first known amphibians
Permian (from district of Perm in Russia)	45	Lower Permian Upper Permian	Early reptiles and mammals; earliest form of turtles

1. In millions of years.

Mesozoic Era

This era began 245 million years ago and lasted for 180 million years. The name was compounded from Greek *mesos* (middle) and *zoön* (animal). Popular name: Age of Reptiles.

Period	Duration[1]	Subperiods	Events
Triassic (from *trias* = triad)	37	Lower or Buntsandstein (from German *bunt* = colorful + *sandstein* = sandstone). Middle or Muschelkalk (from German *muschel* = shell + *kalk* = limestone). Upper or Keuper (old miner's term)	Early saurians
Jurassic (from Jura Mountains)	62	Lower or Black Jurassic, or Lias (from French *liais* = hard stone) Middle or Brown Jurassic, or Dogger (old provincial English for ironstone) Upper or White Jurassic, or Malm (Middle English for sand)	Many seagoing reptiles; early large dinosaurs; somewhat later, flying reptiles (pterosaurs), earliest known birds
Cretaceous (from Latin *creta* = chalk)	81	Lower Cretaceous Upper Cretaceous	Maximum development of dinosaurs; birds proliferating; opossumlike mammals

1. In millions of years.

Cenozoic Era

This era began 65 million years ago and includes the geological present. The name was compounded from Greek *kainos* (new) and *zoön* (animal). Popular name: Age of Mammals.

Period	Duration[1]	Subperiods	Events
Tertiary (originally thought to be the third of only three periods)	c. 65	Paleocene (from Greek *palaios* = old + *kainos* = new). Eocene (from Greek *eos* = dawn + *kainos* = new). Oligocene (from Greek *oligos* = few + *kainos* = new). Miocene (from Greek *meios* = less + *kainos* = new). Pliocene (from Greek *pleios* = more + *kainos* = new)	First mammals other than marsupials. Formation of amber, rich insect fauna, early bats, steady increase of large mammals. Mammals closely resembling present types; protohumans
Pleistocene (from Greek *pleistos* = most + *kainos* = new) (popular name: Ice Age)	2.0	Four major glaciations, named Günz, Mindel, Riss, and Würm, originally the names of rivers. Last glaciation ended 10,000 to 15,000 years ago	Various forms of early humans
Holocene (from Greek *holos* = entire + *kainos* = new)	0.01	The last 10,000 years to the present	Earliest written documents c. 3200 B.C.E., Sumer

1. In millions of years.

Classification of the Dinosaurs

Dinosaurs ("terrible lizards") belong to a large group of reptiles called Archosauria ("ruling reptiles"). They are classified into two distinct orders, which are distinguished by their pelvic differences.

Saurischia ("lizard hipped"). All members of this order had modern lizardlike pelvises and clawed feet. Saurischians roamed Earth from the Middle Triassic to the end of the Cretaceous period. They included carnivores and plant eaters. Members of the order included Allosaurus ("different lizard"), Apatosaurus ("deceptive lizard"), which was formerly called Brontosaurus, and Tyrannosaurus ("tyrant lizard"). The group is divided into two suborders: **Theropoda** ("beast footed") and **Sauropodomorpha** ("lizard-footed forms"). The Velociraptor ("swift robber") was a theropod.

Ornithiscia ("bird hipped"). All Ornithischian dinosaurs had pelvises similar to those of modern birds, and hoofed toes. All were herbivores. These dinosaurs lived throughout the world from the Middle Triassic to the end of the Cretaceous period. Members of the order included Iguanodon ("iguana tooth"), Stegosaurus ("plated lizard"), and Triceratops ("three-horned face"). The order is divided into four suborders: **Ornithopoda** ("bird footed"), **Stegosauria** ("plated lizards"), **Ankylosauria** ("armored lizards"), and **Certopsia** ("horned faces").

Scientific Classification

Classification, or taxonomy, is a system of categorizing living things. There are seven divisions in the system: (1) Kingdom; (2) Phylum or Division; (3) Class; (4) Order; (5) Family; (6) Genus; (7) Species.

Kingdom is the broadest division. There is no consensus about the number of kingdoms, though most scientists support a four-kingdom (Animalia, Plantae, Protista, and Monera) or five-kingdom (Animalia, Plantae, Protista, Monera, and Fungi) system. The lowest, most basic division is species, which consists of organisms that resemble each other and are capable of interbreeding to produce fertile offspring. Species are identified by two names (binomial nomenclature). The first is the genus, the second is the species.   □

New Human Ancestor Found in Ethiopia

In April 1999, a team of Ethiopian, American, and Japanese researchers announced their discovery of the cranial and tooth remains of a previously unknown hominid that may be a direct human ancestor and an evolutionary link between the ape-man of Africa, *Australopithecus* ("southern ape"), and the genus *Homo* ("man"). The 2.5-million-year-old fossils were unearthed between 1996 and December 1998 outside the Afar village of Bouri, in the desert region of Ethiopia called the Middle Awash. The new species was named *Australopithecus garhi*. The word "garhi" means "surprise" in the Afar language.

In addition to the *garhi* fossils, the team also found the arm and leg bones of several other hominid individuals in the same geological layer. Although they cannot be reliably assigned to *A. gahri* or another species, their relative limb proportions are between those of apes and humans. While the famous "Lucy" fossil (3.2 million years ago) had upper arms that were long relative to her legs, and *Homo erectus*, "upright man" (1.7 million years ago) had the shortened forearms and the longer femurs of modern humans, these new unidentified primates had an intermediary set of limbs: long forearms and human-like legs. This indicates that the thighbone (femur) lengthened at least one million years before the forearm shortened. These bipedal creatures used stone tools to fillet meat and scrape marrow from large animals, the earliest known evidence of animal butchering with stone tools, which marks the transition from a heretofore strict vegetarian diet to a carnivorous one. This "dietary revolution" opened up a whole new world of food and may have paved the way for emigration out of Africa to new habitats and continents.

Analyses of the *A. garhi* fossils show mixed traits that sharply distinguish them from the "Lucy" species *Australopithecus afarensis* (southern ape of Afar) and the other hominid species known to be alive around the same time. The new species' braincase, face, and palate are more primitive than *Homo* and lack the specialized cranial characters of the robust ape-men of eastern and southern Africa. Its features are most like its ancestor *A. afarensis*. The face projects forward, the braincase is crested and small, but the premolars and molars are enormous. This combination of features has never been seen before and scientists say that it is very possible that *A. garhi* was the direct ancestor of *Homo*, which includes modern humans. □

Major Discoveries about Human Ancestors

Living and extinct human beings and their near human ancestors are called "hominids" and belong to the *Hominidae* family of primates. They are not to be confused with "hominoids," which belong to the *Hominoidea* family of primates and include apes and humans. Scientists theorize that the human and ape lines branched off from a common ancestor 8 million to 6 million years ago.

Years ago	Species	Discovered	Remarks
c. 4.4 million	*Ardipithecus ramidus*	1994 in Aramis, Ethiopia	Oldest known human ancestor. Had chimpanzee-like skull
c. 4.2 million	*Australopithecus anamensis*	1995, two sites at Lake Turkana in Kenya: Kanapoi and Allia Bay	Possible ancestor of *A. afarensis* (Lucy). Walked upright
c. 3.2 million	*Australopithecus afarensis*	1974 at Hadar in the Afar triangle of eastern Ethiopia; Laetoli, Tanzania	Nicknamed "Lucy." Her skeleton was 3.5 feet (100 cm.) tall. Had apelike skull. Walked fully upright. Lived in family groups throughout eastern Africa
c. 2.5 million	*Australopithecus africanus*	1924 at Taung, northern Cape Province, South Africa	Descendant of "Lucy." Lived in social groups
c. 2 million	*Australopithecus robustus*	1938 in Kromdraai, South Africa	Was related to *A. africanus*
c. 2 million	*Homo habilis* ("skillful man")	1960 in Olduvai Gorge, Tanzania	First brain expansion; is believed to have used stone tools
c. 1.8 million	*Homo erectus* ("upright man")	1891 at Trinil, Java, Indonesia	Brain size twice that of *australopithecine* species. Controversy exists whether "Java Man," as he was called, is a direct ancestor of *Homo sapiens* or instead developed on a separate evolutionary tract. He is, however, the first hominid to use fire and the hand axe, and to live in caves
c. 100,000(?)	*Homo sapiens* ("knowing or wise man")	1868, Cro-Magnon, France	Anatomically modern humans

The Nation's Highest Science and Technology Honors

The National Medal of Science

The National Medal of Science, established by Congress in 1959, is administered by the National Science Foundation. The medal honors the contributions made by outstanding individuals who have significantly advanced knowledge in the following fields: physics, biology, chemistry, mathematics, engineering, and sociology and other behavioral sciences.

The 1998 National Medal of Science and Medal of Technology recipients were announced by President Clinton on December 8, 1998. The 1999 Science and Technology Medal recipients will be announced in late 1999.

1998 National Medal of Science Recipients

Bruce N. Ames, Professor of Biochemistry and Molecular Biology and Director of the National Institute of Environmental Health Sciences at the University of California, Berkeley, for changing the direction of basic and applied research on mutation, cancer, and aging. His simple, inexpensive test for environmental and natural mutagens identified causes and effects of oxidative DNA damage, and he translated these findings into intelligible public policy recommendations on diet and cancer risk for the American people.

Don L. Anderson, Professor of Geophysics at the California Institute of Technology Seismological Laboratory, Pasadena, Calif., for advancing the understanding of the composition, structure, and dynamics of Earth and Earth-like planets, and for his national and international influence on the advancement of earth sciences over the past three decades.

John N. Bahcall, Professor of Natural Sciences, Institute for Advanced Study, Princeton, N.J., for his pioneering efforts in neutrino astrophysics and his contributions to the development and planning of the Hubble Space Telescope.

John W. Cahn, Fellow at the National Institute of Standards and Technology, Gaithersburg, Md., for his profound influence on the course of materials and mathematics research, and for his enormous contributions to three generations of materials scientists, solid-state physicists, and mathematicians.

Cathleen S. Morawetz, Professor Emerita at the Courant Institute of Mathematical Sciences, New York University, New York, N.Y., for pioneering advances in partial differential equations and wave propagation resulting in application to aerodynamics, acoustics, and optics.

Janet D. Rowley, Professor at the University of Chicago, Chicago, Ill., for revolutionizing cancer research, diagnosis, and treatment through her discovery of chromosomal translocations in cancer, and for her pioneering work on the relationship of prior treatment to recurring chromosome abnormalities.

Eli Ruckenstein, Professor of Chemical Engineering, State University of New York, Buffalo, N.Y., for his world-class pioneering theories and experimental achievements in colloidal and surface phenomena, catalysts, and advanced materials.

George M. Whitesides, Professor of Chemistry at Harvard University, Cambridge, Mass., for his innovative and far-ranging research in chemistry, biology, biochemistry, and material science that has brought breakthroughs to transition metal chemistry, heterogeneous reactions, organic surface chemistry, and enzyme-mediated synthesis.

William Julius Wilson, Professor at the John F. Kennedy School of Government, Harvard University, Cambridge, Mass., for his pioneering methods of interdisciplinary social science research that have advanced understanding of the interaction between the macroeconomic, social structural, cultural, and behavioral forces that cause and reproduce inner-city poverty.

The National Medal of Technology

The National Medal of Technology, established by Congress in 1980, is administered by the U.S. Department of Commerce. The medal is awarded for technological innovation and the advancement of U.S. global competitiveness. The medal also recognizes groundbreaking contributions that commercialize a technology, create jobs, improve productivity, or stimulate the nation's growth and development in other ways. President Clinton announced the 1998 recipients of the Medal of Technology on December 8, 1998.

1998 National Medal of Technology Recipients

Denton A. Cooley, M.D., Founder, President, and Surgeon-in-Chief, Texas Heart Institute, Houston, Tex., for his inspirational skill, leadership, and technical accomplishments during six decades of practicing cardiovascular surgery, including having performed the first successful human heart transplant in the United States, and the world's first implantation of an artificial heart in a man as a bridge to heart transplantation, and for founding the Texas Heart Institute, which has served more heart patients than any other institution in the world.

Team Award (Jointly): Robert T. Fraley, Robert B. Horsch, Ernest G. Jaworski, and Stephen G. Rogers (Monsanto) in St. Louis, Mo., for their pioneering achievements in plant biology and agricultural biotechnology, and for global leadership in the development and commercialization of genetically modified crops to enhance agricultural productivity and sustainability. Robert Fraley is Co-President of the Agricultural Sector; Robert Horsch is Co-President of the Sustainable Development Sector and General Manager of the Agracetus Research Campus; Ernest Jaworski is the retired Director of the Biological Sciences Program; and Stephen Rogers is Director of Biotechnology Projects at Monsanto's European Center for Crop Research, Brussels, Belgium.

Biogen, Inc., Cambridge, Mass., for its leadership in applying breakthroughs in biology to the development of life-saving and life-enhancing pharmaceutical products designed to treat large, previously underserved patient populations throughout the world; and for the development of hepatitis B vaccines, the first vaccines using recombinant DNA technology.

Bristol-Myers Squibb Company, New York, N.Y., for extending and enhancing human life through innovative pharmaceutical research and development, and for redefining the science of clinical study through groundbreaking and extremely complex clinical trials that are now recognized as industry models.

1999 Intel Science Talent Search Winners

The Intel Science Talent Search (Intel STS), now in its 58th year, is America's oldest and most prestigious pre-college science scholarship competition. Intel Corporation assumed sponsorship of the contest, formerly known as the "Westinghouse Science Talent Search," from Westinghouse Electric Corporation in 1998. Intel and Science News Service announced the top ten winners at the National Academy of Sciences, March 8, 1999, in Washington D.C. Science News Service, a nonprofit organization, has administered the competition since its inception. Awards are given to 40 finalists. The remaining 30 finalists receive awards of $3,000 each.

Top Ten Winners

First Place: $50,000 scholarship, Natalia Toro, 14, Fairview High School, Boulder, Colo., for her physics project "Independent Analysis of Evidence for nu_mu < - - > nu_tau Oscillations in the Super-Kamiokande Atmospheric Neutrino Data." Ms. Toro is the youngest student ever to win the top prize. Her project studied oscillations of neutrinos, the most elusive of subatomic particles.

Second Place: $40,000 scholarship, David Moore, 18, Montgomery Blair High School, Silver Springs, Md., for his physics project "Quantum Calculations to Determine Electrical Properties for Molecular Electronic Rectifying Diodes." He used detailed quantum modeling techniques to determine the electrical properties of a newly proposed design for molecular electronic switches.

Third Place: $30,000 scholarship, Keith Winstein, 17, Illinois Mathematics and Science Academy (IMSA), Aurora, Ill., for his computer science project "Lexical Steganography through Adaptive Modulation of the Word Choice Hash." His research focused on steganography, techniques for embedding information in computerized data without making any perceptible change to the original material.

Fourth Place: $20,000 scholarship, Carol Anne Fassbinder, 18, Valley Community High School, Elgin, Iowa, for her biology project "Analysis of Monoterpenoids for Control of the *Varroa jacobsoni*." Her work uncovered a new control for *Varroa jacobsoni*, a parasitic mite that is crippling beekeeping in the state of Iowa.

Fifth Place: $20,000 scholarship, Rio Gabriel Bennin, 17, a home-schooled senior from Berkeley, Calif., who presented a mathematics project, "N-Dimensional Equalizers and Pythagorean Quadrilaterals," which obtained a method for dividing a geometric figure, such as a triangle, into two equal parts.

Sixth Place: $20,000 scholarship, Lisa Beth Schwartz, 17, Roslyn High School, Roslyn Heights, N.Y., whose mathematics project explored patterns in two-way sequences of positive integers.

Seventh Place: $15,000 scholarship, Scott Alexander Fruhan, 17, Roxbury Latin School, West Roxbury, Mass., who presented a biology study on T cells in multiple sclerosis patients. Mononuclear T cells control the body's immune response.

Eighth Place: $15,000 scholarship, Kurt Elliott Mitman, 16, Thomas Jefferson High School for Science and Technology, Alexandria, Va. He presented an astrophysics study on the highly energetic astronomical phenomena known as gamma ray bursts (GRBs) at the Naval Research Laboratory.

Ninth Place: $15,000 scholarship, Diana Barnard Townsend-Butterworth, 17, Chapin School, New York, N.Y., for her biology project that investigated Alzheimer's disease. She focused on the effects on the human brain cells of cadmium, a potentially lethal heavy metal found in cigarettes and many household items.

Tenth Place: $15,000 scholarship, Alexander David Wissner-Gross, 17, Great Neck High School, Great Neck, N.Y. He combined physics, chemistry, computers, and engineering for his study of ionized C60 molecules, called fullerenes or "buckyballs," as a nanoscopic, granular medium.

Oldest Human Remains in North America Found

In 1959, the partial skeletal remains of an ancient woman estimated to be 10,000 years old were unearthed in Arlington Springs on Santa Rosa Island, one of the eight Channel Islands off the southern California coast. They were discovered by Phil C. Orr, curator of anthropology and natural history at the Santa Barbara Museum of Natural History. The remains of the so-called Arlington Springs woman were recently reanalyzed by the latest radiocarbon dating techniques and were found to be approximately 13,000 years old. The new date makes her remains older than any other known human skeleton found so far in North America.

The discovery challenges the popular belief that the first colonists to North America arrived at the end of the last ice age about 11,500 years ago by crossing a Bering land bridge that connected Siberia to Alaska and northwestern Canada. The earlier date and the location of the woman's remains on the island adds weight to an alternative theory that some early settlers may have constructed boats and migrated from Asia by sailing down the Pacific coast.

The Arlington Springs woman lived during the end of the Pleistocene era when large herds of bison and woolly mammoths roamed the grassy plains and other extinct native American animals such as camels, horses, and saber-toothed cats were still around.

The remains of Pleistocene-era animals have been discovered on Santa Rosa Island where the Arlington Springs woman was found. In 1994, the world's most complete skeleton of a pygmy mammoth, a dwarf species, was also excavated here. ☐

Roundup of Recent Discoveries

Ancestor of Mammals Discovered

The fossil skull of a 260-million-year-old sheep-sized animal was found near Williston on the Northern Cape, South Africa. It is the most primitive member yet discovered of a group of plant-eaters on the evolutionary line to mammals. Called *Anomodonts*, they were the dominant land creatures during the Permian period, long before the dinosaurs appeared on Earth.

The new species was named *Anomocephalus africanus*, which means "Lawless-headed one of Africa." The name makes reference to the fact that characteristics common to the *Anomodont* group were not uniform throughout all its members. Before this discovery, it was thought that *Anomodonts* and other creatures associated with the group known as *therapsids*, or mammal-like reptiles, originated in Russia. The new find has reinforced the idea that the distant ancestors of mammals might actually have come from South Africa.

An Antigravity Contraption?

NASA researchers are attempting to validate a controversial gravity modification experiment that Russian scientist Eugene Podklentov conducted several years ago. Podklentov claimed to have shielded objects from Earth's gravitational pull by the use of a ceramic superconductor disc spinning in a magnetic field. He reported that samples of nonconducting and nonmagnetic objects suspended over the rotating disc lost up to 2% of their gravitational pull. Although the gravitational shielding effect of Podklentov's achievement was weak, it is still significant, and its effect may prove to be cumulative for a stack of superconductive discs. If researchers could develop a device that would manipulate gravity waves, it would have a tremendous economic impact on space launches and other forms of transportation.

Fish-Eating Dinosaur Found

A new species of a predatory dinosaur was discovered in the Sahara by an international team led by Paul Sereno of the University of Chicago. The new species, *tenerensis*, was excavated in the Tenere desert of Niger and named *Suchomimus tenerensis* ("crocodile mimic from Tenere"). *Souchos* is Greek for crocodile.

The 100-million-year-old skeleton measures 36 feet in length and is 12 feet at the hip. Its skull has an extremely long and narrow snout with large teeth near its end, similar to that of specialized fish-eating crocodiles. The jaws are studded with over 100 conical teeth that functioned like hooks rather than sliding blades. The huge two-legged creature's powerful forearms were used to snare fish and other prey as it waded in rivers.

Suchomimus belongs to a peculiar group of fish-eating predators called *Spinosaurids* (Spiny Lizards) that grew to the size of *Tyrannosaurus*.

A Collision Split Earth and Moon

Analysis of data from the Lunar Prospector spacecraft supports the theory, first proposed in the Apollo era, that the bulk of the Moon was ripped away from early Earth when an object the size of Mars collided with it. Similarities in the mineral composition of Earth and the Moon indicate that they share a common origin. In the past, some had interpreted this finding to indicate that Earth and the Moon had formed separately from the same cloud of rocks and dust. But new data shows that the Moon has a small core that contains less than 4% of the Moon's total mass, whereas Earth's iron core contains approximately 30% of the planet's mass. If Earth and the Moon had simply formed from the same cloud of rocks and dust, the Moon would have a core similar in proportion to Earth's. A more likely synopsis is that a large body struck Earth, forcing an ejection of rocky, iron-poor material from the outer shell into orbit, which collected to form the Moon.

Medical Maggots

According to researchers at Princess of Wales Hospital, Bridgend, Wales, *Lucilia sericata*, the larvae of the common greenbottle fly, could help to address the problem of antibiotic resistance. Over the past three years, the clinical use of such maggots has been reintroduced into the UK and elsewhere (to well over 400 centers) with considerable success.

Maggots clean wounds by eating only the dead or dying tissue, thus promoting nature's healing process. (Some other fly species do eat healthy flesh.) The mechanism by which the larvae kill bacteria in wounds are not fully understood, but among the explanations offered are the production of natural antibiotic-like agents, the modification of the pH of the wound, or the ingestion and destruction of bacteria as part of the normal feeding process.

Many patients receive this anachronistic larval treatment as a last resort when conventional treatments, including antibiotics, have failed. The research did conclude, however, that using maggots earlier in combating infection may often avert the need for antibiotics.

"S" Marks the Solar Storm

After analyzing daily images taken by the Japanese Yohkoh ("sunbeam") spacecraft over a two-year period, NASA-sponsored scientists have discovered that an S-shaped structure called a sigmoid often appears on the Sun in advance of a coronal mass ejection. Coronal mass ejections (CMEs) are violent discharges of electrically charged gas from the Sun's corona, or outer atmosphere, that are as powerful as billions of nuclear explosions.

The largest explosions in the solar system, CMEs hurl up to 10 billion tons of gas into space at speeds of one to two million miles an hour. The outbursts occur several times in a day, but only those shot toward Earth are dangerous. The solar blasts travel the 93 million miles between the Sun and Earth in about four days and can damage satellites, disrupt communications networks, and cause power outages. The new findings may give space weather forecasters a reliable tool to predict approaching solar storms before they erupt.

It's All in Your Head

A University of Iowa study found new evidence that people may be shy or outgoing because of the way their brains are structured. Researchers at IU used PET scans to study the brain activity of their subjects. The PET scans revealed that introverts have more activity in the frontal lobes of the brain and anterior, or front, thalamus. These areas are activated when a person's brain takes on internal processing such as remembering, problem solving, and planning. Extroverts exhibit more activity in the anterior cingulate gyrus, temporal lobes, and posterior thalamus. These areas are typically thought to be more involved in sensory processing such as listening, watching, or driving.

Differences in cognitive style and sensory-processing relate to characteristics associated with introversion and extroversion. True introverts are quiet, inwardly focused, and reclusive. Extroverts are gregarious, socially active, and sensation seeking. Introverts get more of their stimulation internally, whereas extroverts seek outside sources. These variations in brain activity suggest that a lot of our individual differences have an underlying biological cause.

Brightest Gamma Burst Ever Seen

On Jan. 23, 1999, astronomers saw visible light emitted from a gamma-ray burst. Previously, only the faint, fading afterglow of the event had been detected. Although the catastrophic explosion (called GRB 990123 for the day it occurred) was 9 billion light-years away, the light from it was so bright that observers on Earth could have seen it in the night sky with a pair of binoculars. It was the brightest burst seen so far.

Gamma-ray bursts are brief emissions of high-energy photons traveling to Earth from violent explosions in the deepest reaches of space and typically last a few seconds. The amount of energy released from a gamma-ray burst boggles the mind. Exploding with the power of ten million billion suns, only collisions between objects like super-dense neutron stars and black holes have enough energy potential to create such a cataclysmic event. No one is sure what causes a gamma-ray burst.

Fantastic Inca Mummy Find

In March 1999, an international archeological team found the frozen mummies of two girls and a boy, who had been killed in an Inca sacrificial ritual. Buried about 500 years ago under 5 feet of rock and earth, their remains are in an unprecedented state of preservation and appear as if they just died. CT scans made a few days after the discovery revealed two "perfect mummies" with all their internal organs intact. No cause of death was evident. The American-Peruvian-Argentine-team that made the remarkable find was funded by the National Geographic Society.

The burial platform also contained an elaborate offering to the Inca gods, including some 35 gold, silver, and spondulus shell statues, half of them clothed; moccasins; and exquisite Inca pottery, some of it still containing food. Most of the artifacts are in pristine condition.

The Inca empire once extended 2,500 miles (4,023 kilometers) from Colombia to central Chile, but ended after only nine decades with the Spanish conquest in 1532.

Behemoth Bacterium

A team of German, Spanish, and American marine scientists studying samples of sediment dredged up off the coast of Walvis Bay, Namibia, discovered the largest bacterium ever seen. Some of the record-size organisms were as large as the period at the end of this sentence (up to ¾ of a millimeter wide). They feed on sulfide produced in the sea floor and store nitrate from the seawater in a central sac or "anaerobic lung" which they oxidize for energy.

The new bacteria strain shines white because the microscopic sulfur granules stored within them reflect light. Held in strands by a common mucus sheath, they look like a thin string of pearls, which inspired researchers at the Max Planck Institute for Marine Microbiology to name them *Thiomargarita namibiensis* (Sulfur Pearl of Namibia).

Not-So-Strange Bedfellows

A Washington University anthropologist claims that the characteristics of a 24,500-year-old Neanderthal skeleton of a four-year-old boy show that Neanderthals and early humans cohabited and produced children. If the skeleton is indeed evidence of interbreeding, it contradicts the dominant hypothesis among scientists that Neanderthals were a separate branch of the evolutionary line from early modern humans (Cro-Magnons). According to this theory, early humans were believed to have migrated from Africa and wiped out the Neanderthal population in Europe, either through warfare or because the supposedly more intelligent Cro-Magnons adapted more successfully to their environment.

The child's skeleton was found on a hillside in the Lapedo Valley north of Lisbon, Portugal, in December 1998. It possesses characteristics of both species, such as the stocky trunk and sturdy leg bones of Neanderthals and the prominent jaw and small teeth of modern humans. Radiocarbon dating of the skeleton in 1999 confirmed that the child lived 4,000 years after the arrival of early modern humans (Cro-Magnons) on the Iberian Peninsula where Neanderthals already resided—offering possible evidence that the two groups intermixed, interbred, and produced offspring over several millennia. If this extensive interbreeding did occur, then Neanderthals may not have been a separate species after all. Neanderthals may have disappeared not because they were wiped out from war, but because their traits may have eventually been "bred out." This would also mean that their human descendants—us—carry a little bit of Neanderthal in our gene pool.

A Freakish Frog Mystery

Since 1995, alarming sightings of large numbers of frogs born with extra limbs, missing eyes, and other bizarre abnormalities have been reported more and more often, raising public fears that these ecologically sensitive amphibians are bellwethers of some larger environmental catastrophe. Speculation about the causes of the frog abnormalities included pesticides, chemical pollution, or DNA damage to frog embryos as a result of too much ultraviolet radiation passing through the thinning ozone layer.

Now researchers have partially answered this puzzle. In April 1999, two studies released by scientists from Hartwick College and the Stanford Center for Conservation Biology provided strong evidence that some of the weird disfigurements are caused by small parasitic flatworms called *Riberoria trematodes*. These creatures burrow into the hindquarters of tadpoles where they physically rearrange the limb bud cells and thereby interfere with limb development. Although parasite infections appear to be the direct cause of multiple limb deformities, other kinds of abnormalities, including missing or malformed limbs and eyes, may be caused by something other than parasites, and more research is needed before scientists can draw any conclusions.

Rethinking Long-Necked Dinosaurs

The popular conception of giant long-necked dinosaurs eating leaves from treetops like giraffes is probably more fiction than fact according to the latest research. Scientists at Northern Illinois University and the University of Oregon used specially developed computer software to study the bone structure and simulate the neck mobility of *Diplodocus* and *Apatosaurus* (formerly known as *Brontosaurus*). These two long-necked, long-tailed, plant-eating *sauropods* lived about 120 million years ago during the Jurassic period. *Sauropods* grew over 130 feet (40 m) long and weighed up to 100 tons. They were the largest animals ever to live on land.

The researchers determined that the necks of both creatures were significantly less limber than traditionally assumed. *Diplodocus* could barely lift its head higher than its back and *Apatosaurs* had only a little more flexibility. The study infers that the dinosaurs held their necks horizontally or even curved downward a lot of the time while feeding on water plants, ferns, or low shrubs, and couldn't lift their heads to the vertical position.

Another Menacing Asteroid

Remember the short-lived doomsday asteroid scare of 1997 that turned out to be false? Now there's another one heading our way. Astronomers are cautiously observing the orbits of a potentially hazardous asteroid discovered in January 1999. Researchers at the Minor Planet Center (MPC) have calculated that near-Earth asteroid 1999 AN 10 will pass within 24,000 miles (39,000 kilometers) of Earth in 2027, with the potential for even closer approaches in 2044 and 2048. Six more close flybys of the kilometer-wide rock have been identified, and while astronomers cannot predict all future approaches for more than a few decades after any close encounter, they say that AN 10's orbit will remain dangerously close to the orbit of Earth for the next 600 years. But there's no need to panic. Astronomers advise that its chances of colliding with Earth are very small.

The Mother Lobe of Genius

When Albert Einstein died in 1955 at the age of 76, his brain was removed and preserved for scientific study. Recently, Prof. Sandra F. Witelson and her colleagues at McMaster University, Canada, compared anatomical measurements of Einstein's brain with a control group of men and women whose brains were of normal intelligence, and reported their findings in June 1999.

In general, Einstein's brain was similar to other brains except for one area called the inferior parietal region, which was 15% wider than those of the other brains studied. The inferior parietal lobe is important for processing visual and spatial cognition, mathematical thought, and imagery of movement. The unusual development of this lobe may have been a contributing factor to his genius.

In addition, Einstein's brain was unique in that it did not have a groove, called a sulcus, that normally runs through part of this area. The absence of the groove may have increased his mental power by allowing more neurons in this area to establish connections between each other and work together more easily.   □

Inventions & Discoveries

See also Famous Firsts in Aviation, Nobel Prizes.

Adrenaline: (isolation of) John Jacob Abel, U.S., 1897.

Aerosol can: Erik Rotheim, Norway, 1926.

Air brake: George Westinghouse, U.S., 1868.

Air conditioning: Willis Carrier, U.S., 1911.

Airship: (non-rigid) Henri Giffard, France, 1852; (rigid) Ferdinand von Zeppelin, Germany, 1900.

Aluminum manufacture: (by electrolytic action) Charles M. Hall, U.S., 1866.

Anatomy, human: (*De fabrica corporis humani*, an illustrated systematic study of the human body) Andreas Vesalius, Belgium, 1543; (comparative: parts of an organism are correlated to the functioning whole) Georges Cuvier, France, 1799–1805.

Anesthetic: (first use of anesthetic—ether—on humans) Crawford W. Long, U.S., 1842.

Antibiotics: (first demonstration of antibiotic effect) Louis Pasteur, Jules-François Joubert, France, 1887; (discovery of penicillin, first modern antibiotic) Alexander Fleming, England, 1928; (penicillin's infection-fighting properties) Howard Florey, Ernst Chain, England, 1940.

Antiseptic: (surgery) Joseph Lister, England, 1867.

Antitoxin, diphtheria: Emil von Behring, Germany, 1890.

Appliances, electric: (fan) Schuyler Wheeler, U.S., 1882; (flatiron) Henry W. Seely, U.S., 1882; (stove) Hadaway, U.S., 1896; (washing machine) Alva Fisher, U.S., 1906.

Aqualung: Jacques-Yves Cousteau, Emile Gagnan, France, 1943.

Aspirin: Dr. Felix Hoffman, Germany, 1899.

Astronomical calculator: The Antikythera device, first century B.C.E., Greece. Found off island of Antikythera in 1900.

Atom: (nuclear model of) Ernest Rutherford, England, 1911.

Atomic theory: (ancient) Leucippus, Democritus, Greece, c. 500 B.C.E.; Lucretius, Rome c.100 B.C.E.; (modern) John Dalton, England, 1808.

Atomic structure: (formulated nuclear model of atom, Rutherford model) Ernest Rutherford, England, 1911; (proposed current concept of atomic structure, the Bohr model) Niels Bohr, Denmark, 1913.

Automobile: (first with internal combustion engine, 250 rpm) Karl Benz, Germany, 1885; (first with practical high-speed internal combustion engine, 900 rpm) Gottlieb Daimler, Germany, 1885; (first true automobile, not carriage with motor) René Panhard, Emile Lavassor, France, 1891; (carburetor, spray) Charles E. Duryea, U.S., 1892.

Autopilot: (for aircraft) Elmer A. Sperry, U.S., c.1910, first successful test, 1912, in a Curtiss flying boat.

Avogadro's law: (equal volumes of all gases at the same temperature and pressure contain equal number of molecules) Amedeo Avogadro, Italy, 1811.

Bacteria: Anton van Leeuwenhoek, The Netherlands, 1683.

Balloon, hot-air: Joseph and Jacques Montgolfier, France, 1783.

Barbed wire: (most popular) Joseph E. Glidden, U.S., 1873.

Bar codes: (computer-scanned binary signal code): (retail trade use) Monarch Marking, U.S. 1970; (industrial use) Plessey Telecommunications, England, 1970.

Barometer: Evangelista Torricelli, Italy, 1643.

Bicycle: Karl D. von Sauerbronn, Germany, 1816; (first modern model) James Starley, England, 1884.

Big Bang theory: (the universe originated with a huge explosion) George LeMaitre, Belgium, 1927; (modified LeMaitre theory labeled "Big Bang") George A. Gamow, U.S., 1948; (cosmic microwave background radiation discovered, confirms theory) Arno A. Penzias and Robert W. Wilson, U.S., 1965.

Blood, circulation of: William Harvey, England, 1628.

Boyle's law: (relation between pressure and volume in gases) Robert Boyle, Ireland, 1662.

Braille: Louis Braille, France, 1829.

Bridges: (suspension, iron chains) James Finley, Pa., 1800; (wire suspension) Marc Seguin, Lyons, 1825; (truss) Ithiel Town, U.S., 1820.

Bullet: (conical) Claude Minié, France, 1849.

Calculating machine: (logarithms: made multiplying easier and thus calculators practical) John Napier, Scotland, 1614; (slide rule) William Oughtred, England, 1632; (digital calculator) Blaise Pascal, 1642; (multiplication machine) Gottfried Leibniz, Germany, 1671; (important 19th-century contributors to modern machine) Frank S. Baldwin, Jay R. Monroe, Dorr E. Felt, W. T. Ohdner, William Burroughs, all U.S.; ("analytical engine" design, included concepts of programming, taping) Charles Babbage, England, 1835.

Calculus: Isaac Newton, England, 1669; (differential calculus) Gottfried Leibniz, Germany, 1684.

Camera: (hand-held) George Eastman, U.S., 1888; (Polaroid Land) Edwin Land, U.S., 1948.

"Canals" of Mars: Giovanni Schiaparelli, Italy, 1877.

Carpet sweeper: Melville R. Bissell, U.S., 1876.

Car radio: William Lear, Elmer Wavering, U.S., 1929, manufactured by Galvin Manufacturing Co., "Motorola."

Cells: (word used to describe microscopic examination of cork) Robert Hooke, England, 1665; (theory: cells are common structural and functional unit of all living organisms) Theodor Schwann, Matthias Schleiden, 1838–1839.

Cement, Portland: Joseph Aspdin, England, 1824.

Chewing gum: (spruce-based) John Curtis, U.S., 1848; (chicle-based) Thomas Adams, U.S., 1870.

Cholera bacterium: Robert Koch, Germany, 1883.

Circuit, integrated: (theoretical) G.W.A. Dummer, England, 1952; (phase-shift oscillator) Jack S. Kilby, Texas Instruments, U.S., 1959.

Classification of plants: (first modern, based on comparative study of forms) Andrea Cesalpino, Italy, 1583; (classification of plants and animals by genera and species) Carolus Linnaeus, Sweden, 1737–1753.

Clock, pendulum: Christian Huygens, The Netherlands, 1656.

Coca-Cola: John Pemberton, U.S., 1886.

Combustion: (nature of) Antoine Lavoisier, France, 1777.

Compact disk: RCA, U.S., 1972.

Computers: (first design of analytical engine) Charles Babbage, England, 1830s; (ENIAC, Electronic Numerical Integrator and Calculator, first all-electronic, completed) 1945; (dedicated at University of Pennsylvania) 1946; (UNIVAC, Universal Automatic Computer, handled both numeric and alphabetic data) 1951.

Concrete: (reinforced) Joseph Monier, France, 1877.

Condensed milk: Gail Borden, U.S., 1853.

Conditioned reflex: Ivan Pavlov, Russia, c.1910.

Conservation of electric charge: (the total electric charge of the universe or any closed system is constant) Benjamin Franklin, U.S., 1751–1754.

Contagion theory: (infectious diseases caused by living agent transmitted from person to person) Girolamo Fracastoro, Italy, 1546.

Continental drift theory: (geographer who pieced together continents into a single land mass on maps) Antonio Snider-Pellegrini, France, 1858; (first proposed in lecture) Frank Taylor, U.S.; (first comprehensive detailed theory) Alfred Wegener, Germany, 1912.

Contraceptive, oral: Gregory Pincus, Min Chuch Chang, John Rock, Carl Djerassi, U.S., 1951.

Converter, Bessemer: William Kelly, U.S., 1851.

Cosmetics: Egypt, c. 4000 B.C.E.

Cosamic string theory: (first postulated) Thomas Kibble, 1976.

Cotton gin: Eli Whitney, U.S., 1793.

Crossbow: China, c. 300 B.C.E.

Cyclotron: Ernest O. Lawrence, U.S., 1931.

Deuterium: (heavy hydrogen) Harold Urey, U.S., 1931.

Disease: (chemicals in treatment of) crusaded by Philippus Paracelsus, 1527–1541; (germ theory) Louis Pasteur, France, 1862–1877.

DNA: (deoxyribonucleic acid) Friedrich Meischer, Germany, 1869; (determination of double-helical structure) Rosalind Elsie Franklin, F. H. Crick, England, James D. Watson, U.S., 1953.

Dye: (aniline, start of synthetic dye industry) William H. Perkin, England, 1856.

Science Web Sites

National Science Foundation: www.nsf.gov
National Academy of Sciences: www.nas.edu
American Association for the Advancement of Science: www.aaas.org/
Federation of American Scientists: www.fas.org
The Franklin Institute Science Museum: http://sln.fi.edu
Science News Online: www.sciencenews.org
Popular Science: www.popsci.com
Periodic Table of Elements: WebElements Periodic Table: www.webelements.com
Dinosauria Online: www.dinosauria.com/
Discovery Channel Online: www.discovery.com
Fermilab: www.fnal.gov/
Argonne National Laboratory: www.anl.gov/
American Geophysical Union: www.agu.org
Artificial Life Online: http://alife.santafe.edu/
Newton (for K–12 teachers and students): www.newton.dep.anl.gov
Field Museum (Chicago): www.fmnh.org
Santa Barbara Museum of Natural History: www.sbnature.org
Inventors Hall of Fame: www.invent.org/
The Smithsonian Web: www.si.edu

Dynamite: Alfred Nobel, Sweden, 1867.

Electric cooking utensil: (first) patented by St. George Lane-Fox, England, 1874.

Electric generator (dynamo): (laboratory model) Michael Faraday, England, 1832; Joseph Henry, U.S., c.1832; (hand-driven model) Hippolyte Pixii, France, 1833; (alternating-current generator) Nikola Tesla, U.S., 1892.

Thomas Alva Edison
(1847–1931) *Library of Congress*

Electric lamp: (arc lamp) Sir Humphrey Davy, England, 1801; (fluorescent lamp) A.E. Becquerel, France, 1867; (incandescent lamp) Sir Joseph Swann, England, Thomas A. Edison, U.S., contemporaneously, 1870s; (carbon arc street lamp) Charles F. Brush, U.S., 1879; (first widely marketed incandescent lamp) Thomas A. Edison, U.S., 1879; (mercury vapor lamp) Peter Cooper Hewitt, U.S., 1903; (neon lamp) Georges Claude, France, 1911; (tungsten filament) Irving Langmuir, U.S., 1915.

Electrocardiography: Demonstrated by Augustus Waller, 1887; (first practical device for recording activity of heart) Willem Einthoven, 1903, Dutch physiologist.

Electromagnet: William Sturgeon, England, 1823.

Electron: Sir Joseph J. Thompson, England, 1897.

Elevator, passenger: (safety device permitting use by passengers) Elisha G. Otis, U.S., 1852; (elevator utilizing safety device) 1857.

E = mc²: (equivalence of mass and energy) Albert Einstein, Switzerland, 1907.

Engine, internal combustion: No single inventor. Fundamental theory established by Sadi Carnot, France, 1824; (two-stroke) Etienne Lenoir, France, 1860; (ideal operating cycle for four-stroke) Alphonse Beau de Roche, France, 1862; (operating four-stroke) Nikolaus Otto, Germany, 1876; (diesel) Rudolf Diesel, Germany, 1892; (rotary) Felix Wankel, Germany, 1956.

Evolution: (organic) Jean-Baptiste Lamarck, France, 1809; (by natural selection) Charles Darwin, England, 1859.

Exclusion principle: (no two electrons in an atom can occupy the same energy level) Wolfgang Pauli, Germany, 1925.

Expanding universe theory: (first proposed) George LeMaitre, Belgium, 1927; (discovered first direct evidence that the universe is expanding) Edwin P. Hubble, U.S., 1929; (Hubble constant: a measure of the rate at which the universe is expanding) Edwin P. Hubble, U.S., 1929.

Falling bodies, law of: Galileo Galilei, Italy, 1590.

Fermentation: (microorganisms as cause of) Louis Pasteur, France, c.1860.

Fiber optics: Narinder Kapany, England, 1955.

Fibers, man-made: (nitrocellulose fibers treated to change flammable nitrocellulose to harmless cellulose, precursor of rayon) Sir Joseph Swann, England, 1883; (rayon) Count Hilaire de Chardonnet, France, 1889; (Celanese) Henry and Camille Dreyfuss, U.S., England, 1921; (research on polyesters and polyamides, basis for modern man-made fibers) U.S., England, Germany, 1930s; (nylon) Wallace H. Carothers, U.S., 1935.

Frozen food: Clarence Birdseye, U.S., 1924.

Gene transfer: (human) Steven Rosenberg, R. Michael Blaese, W. French Anderson, U.S., 1989.

Geometry, elements of: Euclid, Alexandria, Egypt, c. 300 B.C.E.; (analytic) René Descartes, France; and Pierre de Fermat, Switzerland, 1637.

Gravitation, law of: Sir Isaac Newton, England, c.1665 (published 1687).

Gunpowder: China, c.700.

Gyrocompass: Elmer A. Sperry, U.S., 1905.

Gyroscope: Léon Foucault, France, 1852.

Halley's Comet: Edmund Halley, England, 1705.

Heart implanted in human, permanent artificial: Dr. Robert Jarvik, U.S., 1982.

Heart, temporary artificial: Willem Kolff, 1957.

Helicopter: (double rotor) Heinrich Focke, Germany, 1936; (single rotor) Igor Sikorsky, U.S., 1939.

Helium first observed on sun: Sir Joseph Lockyer, England, 1868.

Heredity, laws of: Gregor Mendel, Austria, 1865.

Holograph: Dennis Gabor, England, 1947.

Home videotape systems (VCR): (Betamax) Sony, Japan, 1975; (VHS) Matsushita, Japan, 1975.

Ice age theory: Louis Agassiz, Swiss-American, 1840.

Induction, electric: Joseph Henry, U.S., 1828.

Insulin: (first isolated) Sir Frederick G. Banting and Charles H. Best, Canada, 1921; (discovery first published) Banting and Best, 1922; (Nobel Prize awarded for purification for use in humans) John Macleod and Banting, 1923; (first synthesized), China, 1966.

Intelligence testing: Alfred Binet, Theodore Simon, France, 1905.

Interferon: Alick Isaacs, Jean Lindemann, England, Switzerland, 1957.

Isotopes: (concept of) Frederick Soddy, England, 1912; (stable isotopes) J. J. Thompson, England, 1913; (existence demonstrated by mass spectrography) Francis W. Ashton, 1919.

Jet propulsion: (engine) Sir Frank Whittle, England, Hans von Ohain, Germany, 1936; (aircraft) *Heinkel He 178,* 1939.

Kinetic theory of gases: (molecules of a gas are in a state of rapid motion) Daniel Bernoulli, Switzerland, 1738.

Laser: (theoretical work on) Charles H. Townes, Arthur L. Schawlow, U.S., N. Basov, A. Prokhorov, U.S.S.R., 1958; (first working model) T. H. Maiman, U.S., 1960.

Lawn mower: Edwin Budding, John Ferrabee, England, 1830–1831.

LCD (liquid crystal display): Hoffmann-La Roche, Switzerland, 1970.

Lens, bifocal: Benjamin Franklin, U.S., c.1760.

Leyden jar: (prototype electrical condenser) Canon E. G. von Kleist of Kamin, Pomerania, 1745; independently evolved by Cunaeus and P. van Musschenbroek, University of Leyden, Holland, 1746, from where name originated.

Light, nature of: (wave theory) Christian Huygens, The Netherlands, 1678; (electromagnetic theory) James Clerk Maxwell, England, 1873.

Light, speed of: (theory that light has finite velocity) Olaus Roemer, Denmark, 1675.

Lightning rod: Benjamin Franklin, U.S., 1752.

Locomotive: (steam powered) Richard Trevithick, England, 1804; (first practical, due to multiple-fire-tube boiler) George Stephenson, England, 1829; (largest steam-powered) Union Pacific's "Big Boy," U.S., 1941.

Lock, cylinder: Linus Yale, U.S., 1851.

Loom: (horizontal, two-beamed) Egypt, c. 4400 B.C.E.; (Jacquard drawloom, pattern controlled by punch cards) Jacques de Vaucanson, France, 1745, Joseph-Marie Jacquard, 1801; (flying shuttle) John Kay, England, 1733; (power-driven loom) Edmund Cartwright, England, 1785.

Machine gun: James Puckle, England, 1718; Richard J. Gatling, U.S., 1861.

Magnet, Earth is: William Gilbert, England, 1600.

Match: (phosphorus) François Derosne, France, 1816; (friction) Charles Sauria, France, 1831; (safety) J. E. Lundstrom, Sweden, 1855.

Measles vaccine: John F. Enders, Thomas Peebles, U.S., 1953.

Metric system: revolutionary government of France, 1790–1801.

Microphone: Charles Wheatstone, England, 1827.

Microscope: (compound) Zacharias Janssen, The Netherlands, 1590; (electron) Vladimir Zworykin et al., U.S., Canada, Germany, 1932–1939.

Microwave oven: Percy Spencer, U.S., 1947.

Motion, laws of: Isaac Newton, England, 1687.

Motion pictures: Thomas A. Edison, U.S., 1893.

Motion pictures, sound: Product of various inventions. First picture with synchronized musical score: *Don Juan,* 1926; with spoken dialogue: *The Jazz Singer,* 1927; both Warner Bros.

Motor, electric: Michael Faraday, England, 1822; (alternating-current) Nikola Tesla, U.S., 1892.

Motorcycle: (motor tricycle) Edward Butler, England, 1884; (gasoline-engine motorcycle) Gottlieb Daimler, Germany, 1885.

Moving assembly line: Henry Ford, U.S., 1913.

Neptune: (discovery of) Johann Galle, Germany, 1846.

Neptunium: (first transuranic element, synthesis of) Edward M. McMillan, Philip H. Abelson, U.S., 1940.

Neutron: James Chadwick, England, 1932.

Neutron-induced radiation: Enrico Fermi et al., Italy, 1934.

Nitroglycerin: Ascanio Sobrero, Italy, 1846.

Nuclear fission: Otto Hahn, Fritz Strassmann, Germany, 1938.

Nuclear reactor: Enrico Fermi, Italy, et al., 1942.

Ohm's law: (relationship between strength of electric current, electromotive force, and circuit resistance) Georg S. Ohm, Germany, 1827.

Oil well: Edwin L. Drake, U.S., 1859.

Oxygen: (isolation of) Joseph Priestley, 1774; Carl Scheele, 1773.

Ozone: Christian Schönbein, Germany, 1839.

Pacemaker: (internal) Clarence W. Lillehie, Earl Bakk, U.S., 1957.

Paper China, c.100 C.E.

Parachute: Louis S. Lenormand, France, 1783.

Pen: (fountain) Lewis E. Waterman, U.S., 1884; (ball-point, for marking on rough surfaces) John H. Loud, U.S., 1888; (ball-point, for handwriting) Lazlo Biro, Argentina, 1944.

Periodic law: (that properties of elements are functions of their atomic weights) Dmitri Mendeleev, Russia, 1869.

Periodic table: (arrangement of chemical elements based on periodic law) Dmitri Mendeleev, Russia, 1869.

Phonograph: Thomas A. Edison, U.S., 1877.

Photography: (first paper negative, first photograph, on metal) Joseph Nicéphore Niepce, France, 1816–1827; (discovery of fixative powers of hyposulfite of soda) Sir John Herschel, England, 1819; (first direct positive image on silver plate, the daguerreotype) Louis Daguerre, based on work with Niepce, France, 1839; (first paper negative from which a number of positive prints could be made) William Talbot, England, 1841. Work of these four men, taken together, forms basis for all modern photography. (First color images) Alexandre Becquerel, Claude Niepce de Saint-Victor, France, 1848–1860; (commercial color film with three emulsion layers, Kodachrome) U.S., 1935.

Photovoltaic effect: (light falling on certain materials can produce electricity) Edmund Becquerel, France, 1839.

Piano: (Hammerklavier) Bartolommeo Cristofori, Italy, 1709; (pianoforte with sustaining and damper pedals) John Broadwood, England, 1873.

Planetary motion, laws of: Johannes Kepler, Germany, 1609, 1619.

Plant respiration and photosynthesis: Jan Ingenhousz, Holland, 1779.

Plastics: (first material, nitrocellulose softened by vegetable oil, camphor, precursor to Celluloid) Alexander Parkes, England, 1855; (Celluloid, involving recognition of vital effect of camphor) John W. Hyatt, U.S., 1869; (Bakelite, first completely synthetic plastic) Leo H. Baekeland, U.S., 1910; (theoretical background of macromolecules and process of polymerization on which modern plastics industry rests) Hermann Staudinger, Germany, 1922.

Plate tectonics: Alfred Wegener, Germany, 1912–1915.

Plow, forked: Mesopotamia, before 3000 B.C.E.

Plutonium, synthesis of: Glenn T. Seaborg, Edwin M. McMillan, Arthur C. Wahl, Joseph W. Kennedy, U.S., 1941.

Polio, vaccine: (experimentally safe dead-virus vaccine) Jonas E. Salk, U.S., 1952; (effective large-scale field trials) 1954; (officially approved) 1955; (safe oral live-virus vaccine developed) Albert B. Sabin, U.S., 1954; (available in the U.S.) 1960.

Positron: Carl D. Anderson, U.S., 1932.

Pressure cooker: (early version) Denis Papin, France, 1679.

Printing: (block) Japan, c.700; (movable type) Korea, c.1400; Johann Gutenberg, Germany, c.1450 (lithography, offset) Aloys Senefelder, Germany, 1796; (rotary press) Richard Hoe, U.S., 1844; (linotype) Ottmar Mergenthaler, U.S., 1884.

Probability theory: René Descartes, France; and Pierre de Fermat, Switzerland, 1654.

Johann Gutenberg (c. 1400–1468)

Proton: Ernest Rutherford, England, 1919.

Prozac: (antidepressant fluoxetine) Bryan B. Malloy, Scotland, and Klaus K. Schmiegel, U.S., 1972; (released for use in U.S.) Eli Lilly & Company, 1987.

Psychoanalysis: Sigmund Freud, Austria, c.1904.

Pulsars: Antony Hewish and Jocelyn Bell Burnel, England, 1967.

Quantum theory: (general) Max Planck, Germany, 1900; (sub-atomic) Niels Bohr, Denmark, 1913; (quantum mechanics) Werner Heisenberg, Erwin Schrödinger, Germany, 1925.

Quarks: Jerome Friedman, Henry Kendall, Richard Taylor, U.S., 1967.

Quasars: Marten Schmidt, U.S., 1963.

Rabies immunization: Louis Pasteur, France, 1885.

Radar: (limited to one-mile range) Christian Hulsmeyer, Germany, 1904; (pulse modulation, used for measuring height of ionosphere) Gregory Breit, Merle Tuve, U.S., 1925; (first practical radar—radio detection and ranging) Sir Robert Watson-Watt, England, 1934–1935.

Radio: (electromagnetism, theory of) James Clerk Maxwell, England, 1873; (spark coil, generator of electromagnetic waves) Heinrich Hertz, Germany, 1886; (first practical system of wireless telegraphy) Gugliemo Marconi, Italy, 1895; (first long-distance telegraphic radio signal sent across the Atlantic) Marconi, 1901; (vacuum electron tube, basis for radio telephony) Sir John Fleming, England, 1904; (triode amplifying tube) Lee de Forest, U.S., 1906; (regenerative circuit, allowing long-distance sound reception) Edwin H. Armstrong, U.S., 1912; (frequency modulation—FM) Edwin H. Armstrong, U.S., 1933.

Radioactivity: (X-rays) Wilhelm K. Roentgen, Germany, 1895; (radioactivity of uranium) Henri Becquerel, France, 1896; (radioactive elements, radium and polonium in uranium ore) Marie Sklodowska-Curie, Pierre Curie, France, 1898; (classification of alpha and beta particle radiation) Pierre Curie, France, 1900; (gamma radiation) Paul-Ulrich Villard, France, 1900.

Radiocarbon dating, carbon-14 method: (discovered) 1947, Willard F. Libby, U.S.; (first demonstrated) U.S., 1950.

Radio signals, extraterrestrial: first known radio noise signals were received by U.S. engineer, Karl Jansky, originating from the Galactic Center, 1931.

Radio waves: (cosmic sources, led to radio astronomy) Karl Jansky, U.S., 1932.

Razor: (safety, successfully marketed) King Gillette, U.S., 1901; (electric) Jacob Schick, U.S., 1928, 1931.

Reaper: Cyrus McCormick, U.S., 1834.

Refrigerator: Alexander Twining, U.S., James Harrison, Australia, 1850; (first with a compressor device) the Domelse, Chicago, U.S., 1913.

Refrigerator ship: (first) the *Frigorifique*, cooling unit designed by Charles Teller, France, 1877.

Relativity: (special and general theories of) Albert Einstein, Switzerland, Germany, U.S., 1905–1953.

Revolver: Samuel Colt, U.S., 1835.

Richter scale: Charles F. Richter, U.S., 1935.

Rifle: (muzzle-loaded) Italy, Germany, c.1475; (breech-loaded) England, France, Germany, U.S., c.1866; (bolt-action) Paul von Mauser, Germany, 1889; (automatic) John Browning, U.S., 1918.

Rocket: (liquid-fueled) Robert Goddard, U.S., 1926.

Roller bearing: (wooden for cartwheel) Germany or France, c.100 B.C.E.

Rotation of earth: Jean Bernard Foucault, France, 1851.

Royal Observatory, Greenwich: established in 1675 by Charles II of England; John Flamsteed first Astronomer Royal.

Rubber: (vulcanization process) Charles Goodyear, U.S., 1839.

Saccharin: Constantine Fuhlberg, Ira Remsen, U.S., 1879.

Safety pin: Walter Hunt, U.S., 1849.

Saturn, ring around: Christian Huygens, The Netherlands, 1659.

"Scotch" tape: Richard Drew, U.S., 1929.

Screw propeller: Sir Francis P. Smith, England, 1836; John Ericsson, England, worked independently of and simultaneously with Smith, 1837.

Seismograph: (first accurate) John Milne, England, 1880.

Sewing machine: Elias Howe, U.S., 1846; (continuous stitch) Isaac Singer, U.S., 1851.

Solar energy: First realistic application of solar energy using parabolic solar reflector to drive caloric engine on steam boiler, John Ericsson, U.S., 1860s.

Solar system, universe: (sun-centered universe) Nicolaus Copernicus, Warsaw, 1543; (establishment of planetary orbits as elliptical) Johannes Kepler, Germany, 1609; (infinity of universe) Giordano Bruno, Italian monk, 1584.

Spectrum: (heterogeneity of light) Sir Isaac Newton, England, 1665–1666.

Spectrum analysis: Gustav Kirchhoff, Robert Bunsen, Germany, 1859.

Spermatozoa: Anton van Leeuwenhoek, The Netherlands, 1683.

Spinning: (spinning wheel) India, introduced to Europe in Middle Ages; (Saxony wheel, continuous spinning of wool or cotton yarn) England, c.1500–1600; (spinning jenny) James Hargreaves, England, 1764; (spinning frame) Sir Richard Arkwright, England, 1769; (spinning mule, completed mechanization of spinning, permitting production of yarn to keep up with demands of modern looms) Samuel Crompton, England, 1779.

Star catalog: (first modern) Tycho Brahe, Denmark, 1572.

Steam engine: (first commercial version based on principles of French physicist Denis Papin) Thomas Savery, England, 1639; (atmospheric steam engine) Thomas Newcomen, England, 1705; (steam engine for pumping water from collieries) Savery, Newcomen, 1725; (modern condensing, double acting) James Watt, England, 1782.

Steamship: Claude de Jouffroy d'Abbans, France, 1783; James Rumsey, U.S., 1787; John Fitch, U.S., 1790. All preceded Robert Fulton, U.S., 1807, credited with launching first commercially successful steamship.

Stethoscope: René Laënnec, France, 1819.

Sulfa drugs: (parent compound, para-aminobenzenesulfanomide) Paul Gelmo, Austria, 1908; (antibacterial activity) Gerhard Domagk, Germany, 1935.

Superconductivity: (theory) Bardeen, Cooper, Scheiffer, U.S., 1957.

Symbolic logic: George Boule, 1854; (modern) Bertrand Russell, Alfred North Whitehead, England, 1910–1913.

Tank, military: Sir Ernest Swinton, England, 1914.

Tape recorder: (magnetic steel tape) Valdemar Poulsen, Denmark, 1899.

Teflon: DuPont, U.S., 1943.

Samuel F. B. Morse (1791–1872)
Library of Congress

Telegraph: Samuel F. B. Morse, U.S., 1837.

Telephone: Alexander Graham Bell, U.S., 1876.

Telescope: Hans Lippershey, The Netherlands, 1608; (astronomical) Galileo Galilei, Italy, 1609; (reflecting) Isaac Newton, England, 1668.

Television: (Iconoscope–T.V. camera table), Vladimir Zworkin, U.S., 1923, and also kinescope (cathode ray tube), 1928; (mechanical disk-scanning method) successfully demonstrated by J.K. Baird, England, C.F. Jenkins, U.S., 1926; (first all-electric television image), 1927, Philo T. Farnsworth, U.S; (color, mechanical disk) Baird, 1928; (color, compatible with black and white) George Valensi, France, 1938; (color, sequential rotating filter) Peter Goldmark, U.S., first introduced, 1951; (color, compatible with black and white) commercially introduced in U.S., National Television Systems Committee, 1953.

Thermodynamics: (first law: energy cannot be created or destroyed, only converted from one form to another) Julius von Mayer, Germany, 1842; James Joule, England, 1843; (second law: heat cannot of itself pass from a colder to a warmer body) Rudolph Clausius, Germany, 1850; (third law: the entropy of ordered solids reaches zero at the absolute zero of temperature) Walter Nernst, Germany, 1918.

Thermometer: (open-column) Galileo Galilei, c.1593; (clinical) Santorio Santorio, Padua, c.1615; (mercury, also Fahrenheit scale) Gabriel D. Fahrenheit, Germany, 1714; (centigrade scale) Anders Celsius, Sweden, 1742; (absolute-temperature, or Kelvin, scale) William Thompson, Lord Kelvin, England, 1848.

Tire, pneumatic: Robert W. Thompson, England, 1845; (bicycle tire) John B. Dunlop, Northern Ireland, 1888.

Toilet, flush: Product of Minoan civilization, Crete, c. 2000 B.C.E. Alleged invention by "Thomas Crapper" is untrue.

Tractor: Benjamin Holt, U.S., 1900.

Transformer, electric: William Stanley, U.S., 1885.

Transistor: John Bardeen, Walter H. Brattain, William B. Shockley, U.S., 1947.
Tuberculosis bacterium: Robert Koch, Germany, 1882.
Typewriter: Christopher Sholes, Carlos Glidden, U.S., 1867.
Uncertainty principle: (that position and velocity of an object cannot both be measured exactly, at the same time) Werner Heisenberg, Germany, 1927.
Uranus: (first planet discovered in recorded history) William Herschel, England, 1781.
Vaccination: Edward Jenner, England, 1796.
Vacuum cleaner: (manually operated) Ives W. McGaffey, 1869; (electric) Hubert C. Booth, England, 1901; (upright) J. Murray Spangler, U.S., 1907.
Van Allen (radiation) Belt: (around Earth) James Van Allen, U.S., 1958.
Video disk: Philips Co., The Netherlands, 1972.
Vitamins: (hypothesis of disease deficiency) Sir F. G. Hopkins, Casimir Funk, England, 1912; (vitamin A) Elmer V. McCollum, M. Davis, U.S., 1912–1914; (vitamin B) McCollum, U.S., 1915–1916; (thiamin, B_1) Casimir Funk,

England, 1912; (riboflavin, B_2) D. T. Smith, E. G. Hendrick, U.S., 1926; (niacin) Conrad Elvehjem, U.S., 1937; (B_6) Paul Gyorgy, U.S., 1934; (vitamin C) C. A. Hoist, T. Froelich, Norway, 1912; (vitamin D) McCollum, U.S., 1922; (folic acid) Lucy Wills, England, 1933.
Voltaic pile: (forerunner of modern battery, first source of continuous electric current) Alessandro Volta, Italy, 1800.
Wallpaper: Europe, 16th and 17th century.
Wassermann test: (for syphilis) August von Wassermann, Germany, 1906.
Wheel: (cart, solid wood) Mesopotamia, c.3800–3600 B.C.E.
Windmill: Persia, c.600.
World Wide Web: (developed while working at CERN) Tim Berners-Lee, England, 1989; (development of Mosaic browser makes WWW available for general use) Marc Andreeson, U.S., 1993.
Xerography: Chester Carlson, U.S., 1938.
Zero: India, c.600; (absolute zero temperature, cessation of all molecular energy) William Thompson, Lord Kelvin, England, 1848.
Zipper: W. L. Judson, U.S., 1891.

The National Inventors Hall of Fame

The Inventors Hall of Fame, located in Akron, Ohio, was established in 1973 by the National Council of Patent Law Associations, now the National Council of Intellectual Property Law Associations, and the Patent and Trademark Office of the U.S. Department of Commerce.

The 1999 Class of Inductees

Campbell, Donald L., 1904– (Clinton, Iowa); **Martin, Homer Z.,** 1910–1993 (Chicago, Ill.); **Tyson, Charles W.,** 1900–1977; and **Murphree, Eger V.,** 1898–1962 (Bayonne, N.J.), FLUID CATALYTIC CRACKING. Over half the world's gasoline is currently produced by a process developed in 1942 by a group called the "Four Horsemen" of Exxon Research and Engineering Company. The world's first commercial Fluid Catalytic Cracking facility began production for Exxon on May 25, 1942. The process revolutionized the petroleum industry by more efficiently transforming higher boiling oils into lighter, usable products.

Mestral, George de, 1907–1990 (Lake Leman, Switzerland), VELCRO. He got the idea for Velcro while on a walk in the woods. Observing that his wool socks and jacket were covered with burrs, he returned home and, in examining the burrs under a microscope, saw that their barbed, hook-like seed pods meshed with the lopped fibers in his clothes. He realized that this gripping adherence of the burrs worked better than zippers and attempted to simulate the manner with which the burrs clung to his fabric with a synthetic material. By trial and error, de Mestral realized that nylon, when sewn under infrared light, formed tough hooks for the burr side of the fastener. Once he succeeded in mechanizing the production process of weaving 300 hooks and loops per square inch, he patented his "hook and loop fastener" in 1955 under the name Velcro, which was derived from the two French words *velour* and *crochet*.

Molloy, Bryan B., 1939– (Broughty Ferry, Scotland) and **Schmiegel, Klaus K.,** 1939– (Chemnitz, Germany), PROZAC. Molloy and Schmiegel headed the chemistry team at Eli Lilly & Co. that searched for an effective antidepressant that was safer than past medications. They started by examining a group of compounds call "aryloxphenylpropyl-

amines." In 1972, one of the compounds, *Fluoxetine hydrochloride,* was found to be highly selective, targeting only the neurotransmitter serotonin. The compound works by increasing brain levels of serotonin, a neurotransmitter and one of several substances that the brain uses to regulate a person's mood. Years of development and testing finally led to the approval of the drug and in 1988, Eli Lilly introduced it under the brand name Prozac.

Spencer, Percy L., 1894–1970 (Howland, Maine), RADAR and MICROWAVE OVEN. During World War II, Spencer produced working models of improved combat radar equipment at MIT for the Raytheon Corporation. Next to the Manhattan Project, his work on radar sets had the highest priority in World War II.
In 1945, Spencer made his best-known discovery. Waves from a magnetron he was testing melted a candy bar in his pocket. Intrigued, he placed a bag of uncooked popcorn in front of the waves emanating from the magnetron, and the popcorn began to pop. He successfully experimented with other foods, and was prompted to create a device that cooked food through microwave radiation. His first microwave ovens, which he called Radarange, were used mostly by restaurants.

Sessler, Gerhard, 1931– (Rosenfield, Germany) and **West, James E.,** 1931– (Prince Edward County, Virginia) FOIL ELECTRET MICROPHONE. Nearly 90% of all microphones used today are based on the Foil Electret principle. The microphone is based on the understanding of the properties of charge storage in polymers (electrets), an electrical analog of the more familiar magnet. Thin sheets of certain polymer films can be made into electrets by charging them permanently. They are metal coated on one side and placed on a back plate leaving a thin air gap. The sound waves deflect the electret film, which in turn generates an output voltage of the microphone. Thus, sound is converted into electrical signals with high fidelity.

Roots Mania: Genealogy on the Internet

Spurred by new resources on the Internet, the ranks of amateur genealogists are growing, and millions of family trees are flourishing

By MARGOT HORNBLOWER TIME

Once the hobby of self-satisfied blue bloods tracing their families back to the *Mayflower*, genealogy is fast becoming a national obsession—for new parents basking in the glow of family life, baby boomers wrestling with their first intimations of mortality, and various ethnic groups exploring their pride and place in a multicultural society. Powering the phenomenon are the new tools of the digital age: computer programs that turn the search for family trees into an addiction; Web sites that make it easy to find and share information; and chat rooms filled with folks seeking advice and swapping leads. "The Internet has helped democratize genealogy," says Stephen Kyner, editor of *The Computer Genealogist* magazine.

Root-seeking ranks with sex, finance, and sports as a leading subject on the Internet. In March 1999, more than 160 million messages flowed through RootsWeb (http://www.rootsweb.com), a vast electronic trading post for genealogical information. There are at least seven treemaking computer programs currently selling well, and according to Nielsen/NetRatings, the three top genealogy Web sites in March had an audience of 1.3 million devotees.

A Wealth of Data

In April 1999, the Mormon Church, officially known as the Church of Jesus Christ of Latter-day Saints, began testing a new Web site, http://www.familysearch.org. A major contribution to the field, it eventually will be a repository of 600 million names, extracted from vital records worldwide. The Mormons consider genealogy part of their mission and have the world's most extensive records. With the promise that the church's vast trove of well-checked data will eventually be available online comes the potential for another burst in genealogical activity.

The Internet has already made the task easier. Cyndi Howells, 35, a Puyallup, Wash., housewife, got interested as a teenager when she read some old family letters and records for a high school genealogy project. "It was fascinating to see all these names and places and think this was all connected to me," she said. In 1992 she quit her job at a bank, bought a computer and began collecting Web site addresses. In 1996 she posted her list on the Internet. Today http://www.cyndislist.com has grown to 300 pages with links to 41,700 genealogical sites worldwide—from ships' passenger lists to prison rolls.

Be forewarned: much of what is on the Web now is akin to signposts—lists of documents but rarely the documents themselves. The National Archives provides a description of its material online—but only 120,000 of its 4 billion records have been digitized. Much of the Net's information is posted by volunteers who transcribe cemetery headstones or newspaper obituaries—with predictable human error. "People think because it's on the computer, it's the gospel truth. But it's only as good as the person doing it," says Cliff Collier of the Ontario Genealogical Society.

Starting to get interested? If you are willing to forgo leisurely weekends for a search that is bound to be alternately tedious and exhilarating, here's how.

Starting Up

Whether you read a how-to book, click on a Web site with beginner's tips, take a course on family-history research, or join a genealogical club, you must first decide on a collection system. You can use notecards, three-ring binders, or software, but each new twig on the family tree must be documented, with notes on its source. That's why computers, which can organize massive amounts of data, are ideal. Remember that for each generation back, the number of parents doubles; by the time you hit 20 generations, it's up to more than a million.

The first step is to write down everything you know about your family. Then interview relatives, oldest ones first. Videotape or tape-record them if possible. Ask for exact names, dates, and places, and as many details of your ancestors' lives as they can remember. Copy all documents: birth, christening, marriage, and death certificates, school and medical records, family-Bible inscriptions, military papers, old letters. "Everyone has a little piece of the puzzle," says Estelle Guzik, director of the New York Jewish Genealogical Society, who set out to trace relatives killed in the Holocaust. In one family a cousin had saved a 20-year-old invitation list to a son's bar mitzvah. An elderly invitee from Israel still lived at the same address and referred Guzik to her son, a rabbi, who provided a family tree stretching from Australia to France.

One happy by-product of your search is that it's likely to open new avenues of communication. Says Carl Davidson, a Chicago computer consultant: "You didn't used to talk much with older folks at family reunions, except maybe 'Pass the potato salad.' Now they take you home, get out these old Bibles, and dig out ancient maps, and you get to know them in a whole new way."

Roots Surfing

Genealogists disagree on whether to begin by searching the many rich Web sites devoted to genealogy or by traveling directly to a source for documents, whether it's the local branch of the National Archives, a well-stocked genealogical library such as the Newberry in Chicago or the Clayton in Houston, or the closest Mormon Family History Center. In some cases, the Web is a clear time saver. George Warholic, a Rockville, Md., economic consultant, set out in 1983 to trace his Ukrainian relatives. "It was a chore," he remembers. "I spent weeks at the Library of Congress, searching hundreds of telephone books for people with the same name. Now this information can be gotten in a few hours on the Internet."

Like the Internet as a whole, online genealogy information is a chaotic hodgepodge. The scope can be as broad as the U.S. Social Security Death Index, which draws on some 60 million records of those for whom a lump-sum death benefit was paid, mostly between 1963 and 1997; and as specific as the street maps of Eastern Europe on the Shtetl-seeker page of the JewishGen Web site. Click onto Historical Records of Dukes County, Mass., to see who lived on Martha's Vineyard in 1790. Survey the resources of the Trinidad and Tobago National Library on its Web site. Contact the Newfoundland and Labrador Genealogical Society, which has a database of more than 500,000 names, including headstone inscriptions from 300 cemeteries in the Canadian province, and for a small fee the group will do a search and mail back the results. A Salt Lake City entrepreneur offers wills from nine states for $7 each.

Beyond research, the Web is a genealogist's agora, invaluable for trading information and connecting with living relatives. Dave Distler, who works at an electronics firm in Greenwood, Ind., lost track of a great-great-great-grandfather, Friedrich Jakob Distler, who was born in 1814 in Germany, Prussia, Rhineland, or Northern Bavaria, according to vague records. Surfing the Net, he found an organization, Palatines to America, which referred him to a German genealogist who found his grandfather's hometown, Hinterweidenthal. When he entered the village name in a search engine, he found a private email address. Three weeks after emailing, he got a response from a local resident with the phone numbers of two Distler families in the town. In May 1996, three New World and 14 Old World Distlers met at a cozy German inn to celebrate. "Old Uncle Fritz had told me about the mysterious Distlers who journeyed to the other side of the Atlantic," says Brigitte Schubert, a newfound German cousin. "I was so glad to sit beside Dave, I didn't want to let go of his hand."

In the days when your relatives mostly stayed put, they knew more about one another's lives and deaths. But in today's mobile society, as nuclear families splinter, loneliness and alienation are the order of the day. "We are witnessing the atomization of the family," says David Altshuler, director of Manhattan's Museum of Jewish Heritage. "The coming of the millennium focuses people's attention on the disappearance of an era." That nostalgia, the sense of lost roots, has fired a thirst for connection that genealogy seems to satisfy. Middle-aged and older people, who form the majority of root-seekers, talk about leaving a legacy for their children—a guide to their children's identity, a family deeper and broader than ever imagined. With genealogy, says Hank Jones, a San Diego character actor who writes and lectures on the subject, "you have a feeling of belonging again when, in daily life, sometimes you don't." □

Web Sites

($ indicates a fee for access or membership)

General:
National Archives and Records Administration:
www.nara.gov
National Genealogical Society:
www.ngsgenealogy.org $
Federation of Genealogical Societies:
www.fgs.org $
Cyndi's List: www.cyndislist.com
Ancestry.Com: www.ancestry.com $
U.S. GenWeb Project: www.usgenweb.org
Switchboard: www.switchboard.com
Rootsweb: www.rootsweb.com
Brøderbund: www.genealogy.com

Sites for Specific Heritage:
African: www.nypl.org/research/sc/sc.html
www.afrigeneas.com
www.ccharity.com
Australian: www.slnsw.gov.au
www.naa.gov.au
www.alphalink.com.au/~aigs $
British: www.visitbritain.com/activities/wtd%2D9.htm
Canadian: www.archives.ca
Chinese: www.nara.gov/regional/findaids/chirip.html
www.columbia.edu/cu/libraries/indiv/eastasia
Dutch: www.cbg.nl
Jewish: www.jewishgen.org
www.yadvashem.org
Scottish: www.origins.net/GRO
www.open.gov.uk/gros/groshome.htm
Ukrainian: www.carpatho-rusyn.org

U.S. Computer Ownership Up Sharply in the 1990s

Source: U.S. Dept. of Labor, Bureau of Labor Statistics.

Between 1990 and 1997, the percentage of households owning computers increased from 15 to 35 percent, and the amount spent by the average household on computers and associated hardware more than tripled. The ownership rate and change over the period varied by education and demographic group.

Households with the highest levels of education had the highest levels of computer ownership. In 1997, 66 percent of households whose reference person had attended graduate school owned a computer, compared with less than 12 percent of those headed by a person who did not graduate from high school. From 1990 to 1997, college graduates had the largest increase in ownership (from 24 to 56 percent); high school graduates also reported a significant ownership increase (from 9 to 23 percent).

Among racial groups, Asians had the highest computer ownership share (49 percent), followed by whites (36 percent) and blacks (18 percent). Between 1990 and 1997, Asians also showed the largest percentage point change in ownership, growing from 25 to 49 percent. Computer ownership among whites grew from 16 to 36 percent and the ownership rate among blacks rose from 7 to 18 percent.

Computers in Use, 1985–2000

(in millions)

Country[1]	1985	1988	1989	1991	1992	1993	1994	1995	2000[2]
United States	21.50	40.80	47.60	62.00	68.20	76.50	85.80	96.20	160.50
Japan	2.10	5.10	6.40	9.20	10.80	12.60	14.90	18.30	46.80
Germany	1.90	4.20	5.20	7.30	8.70	10.40	12.30	14.20	29.80
United Kingdom	2.10	4.30	5.20	7.20	8.40	9.60	10.90	12.60	26.00
France	1.30	3.10	4.00	5.70	6.50	7.50	8.60	10.00	21.80
Canada	0.90	2.00	2.50	3.70	4.30	5.20	6.20	7.20	15.30
Italy	0.90	2.10	2.60	3.70	4.30	5.00	5.90	6.70	17.50
Australia	0.34	0.95	1.24	2.10	2.70	3.40	4.00	4.80	10.20
South Korea	0.13	0.28	0.43	1.00	1.40	1.90	2.60	3.50	10.60
Spain	0.20	0.50	0.79	1.44	1.80	2.30	2.90	3.50	8.10
Netherlands	0.32	0.76	1.02	1.65	2.00	2.40	2.80	3.30	7.10
China	0.12	0.28	0.40	0.67	0.92	1.34	2.00	2.90	13.30
Russia	0.10	0.23	0.34	0.65	0.93	1.37	1.90	2.70	9.20
Mexico	0.15	0.37	0.49	0.87	1.21	1.61	2.05	2.60	6.30
Brazil	0.10	0.24	0.31	0.62	0.91	1.27	1.76	2.40	7.80
Worldwide Total	**38.10**	**79.40**	**97.00**	**136.90**	**159.20**	**186.90**	**218.80**	**257.20**	**556.90**

1. List represents the fifteen countries with the most computers. 2. Projected. *Source:* Computer Industry Almanac Inc., Arlington Heights, Ill., 847-718-0423; Web: www.c-i-a.com.

Computers Per Capita, 1985–2000

Computers/1000 People	1985	1988	1989	1991	1992	1993	1994	1995	2000[1]
United States	90.1	166.0	191.7	245.4	266.9	296.6	329.2	364.7	580.0
Australia	21.5	58.4	75.3	120.5	155.0	191.9	222.7	264.3	525.7
Norway	28.4	61.2	77.7	120.7	148.2	180.5	218.5	259.5	515.4
Canada	36.4	77.4	96.2	136.6	157.5	189.0	219.2	254.8	511.9
Denmark	25.9	58.6	76.7	127.3	153.8	184.6	217.2	252.5	510.2
Finland	25.4	56.2	76.0	119.3	146.2	178.8	211.0	245.5	505.0
Sweden	24.5	58.5	77.0	114.2	139.6	169.9	204.0	241.1	508.9
New Zealand	25.7	57.2	73.5	115.6	136.4	159.8	191.2	224.8	499.2
United Kingdom	36.4	74.8	90.7	125.7	144.8	164.8	187.4	216.5	441.1
Netherlands	22.4	51.9	69.2	109.7	131.1	156.9	184.3	214.8	450.3
Switzerland	24.2	53.0	70.2	109.0	126.6	149.5	174.3	201.6	443.7
Singapore	17.8	46.5	59.7	84.7	104.8	126.9	153.8	188.8	412.0
Belgium	20.1	47.0	63.2	100.2	117.3	138.3	161.2	188.6	405.2
Ireland	23.8	54.1	68.3	102.0	117.4	136.1	159.1	186.4	404.1
Germany	24.0	54.2	67.6	91.5	108.6	129.2	151.3	174.6	361.8
Europe	**14.3**	**31.7**	**40.8**	**60.2**	**71.0**	**83.5**	**97.3**	**113.4**	**248.9**
Worldwide	**7.8**	**15.4**	**18.5**	**25.2**	**29.1**	**33.6**	**38.8**	**44.9**	**90.3**

1. Projected. *Source:* Computer Industry Almanac Inc., Arlington Heights, Ill., 847-718-0423; Web: www.c-i-a.com.

Internet Resource Guide

The Internet has become a convenient tool for finding information on just about anything. These days it's hard to find a company or organization that doesn't have its own home page. Because sifting through search engine returns can be more time-consuming than a trek to the library, we've compiled a list of Web sites that we've found to be especially useful and informative.

Arts and Literature

Library of Congress: *www.loc.gov*
The Louvre: *mistral.culture.fr/louvre/louvrea.htm*
National Endowment for the Arts: *www.arts.endow.gov*
National Humanities Institute: *www.nhumanities.org*
National Museum of American Art: *www.nmaa.si.edu:80*
New York Times Books: *www.nytimes.com/books*
World Wide Arts Resources: *www.wwar.com*

Business and Investing

Better Business Bureau: *www.bbb.org*
Commodity Futures Trading Commission: *www.cftc.gov*
E*TRADE: *www.etrade.com*

New York Stock Exchange: *www.nyse.com*
Securities and Exchange Commission (SEC): *www.sec.gov*
Small Business Administration (SBA): *www.sba.gov*
Standard & Poor's: *www.standardpoor.com*

Computers and the Internet

Shareware.com: *www.shareware.com*
TechWeb: *www.techweb.com*
World Wide Web Consortium: *www.w3.org*
ZDNet: *www.zdnet.com*

Education

College Board Online: *www.collegeboard.org*
College Edge: *www.collegeedge.com/Default.asp*
FamilyEducation.com: *www.familyeducation.com*
FinAid: *www.finaid.org*
National Center for Education Statistics: *www.nces.ed.gov*
Peterson's: *www.petersons.com*
U.S. News Online Education Page: *www.usnews.com/usnews/edu*

Entertainment

All-Media Guide: *www.allmusic.com*
Entertainment Drive: *www.edrive.com*
Internet Movie Database: *www.imdb.com*
Movielink: *www.movielink.com*
SonicNet: *www.sonicnet.com*
Ultimate Band List: *www.ubl.com*

Government

White House: *www.whitehouse.gov*
Senate: *www.senate.gov*
House of Representatives: *www.house.gov*
Supreme Court Collection: *supct.law.cornell.edu/supct*
Department of Agriculture: *www.usda.gov*
Department of Commerce: *www.doc.gov*
Department of Defense: *www.defenselink.mil*
Department of Education: *www.ed.gov*
Department of Energy: *home.doe.gov*
Department of Health and Human Services: *www.dhhs.gov*
Department of Housing and Urban Development:
www.hud.gov
Department of the Interior: *www.doi.gov*
Department of Justice: *www.usdoj.gov*
Department of Labor: *www.dol.gov*
Department of State: *www.state.gov*
Department of Transportation: *www.dot.gov*
Department of the Treasury: *www.ustreas.gov*
Department of Veterans' Affairs: *www.va.gov*

Other Government Resources

Census Bureau: *www.census.gov*
Central Intelligence Agency (CIA): *www.odci.gov/cia*
Consumer Product Safety Commission: *www.cpsc.gov*
Environmental Protection Agency (EPA): *www.epa.gov*
Equal Employment Opportunity Commission (EEOC):
www.eeoc.gov
Federal Bureau of Investigation: *www.fbi.gov*
Federal Communications Commission: *www.fcc.gov*
Federal Deposit Insurance Corporation (FDIC):
www.fdic.gov
Federal Election Commission (FEC): *www.fec.gov*
Federal Emergency Management Agency: *www.fema.gov*
Federal Housing Finance Board: *www.fhfb.gov*
Federal Reserve System (FRS), Board of Governors of
(the Federal Reserve Board): *www.federalreserve.gov*
Federal Trade Commission (FTC): *www.ftc.gov*
National Transportation Safety Board: *www.ntsb.gov*
Postal Rate Commission: *www.prc.gov*
Social Security Administration: *www.ssa.gov*
U.S. Arms Control and Disarmament Agency:
www.acda.gov
U.S. Commission on Civil Rights: *www.usccr.gov*
U.S. Information Agency: *www.usia.gov*
U.S. International Trade Commission: *www.usitc.gov*
U.S. Postal Service: *www.usps.gov*

Health and Fitness

Centers for Disease Control and Prevention: *www.cdc.gov*
MedExplorer: *www.medexplorer.com*
National Institutes of Health: *www.nih.gov*
New England Journal of Medicine: *www.nejm.org*
President's Council on Physical Fitness and Sports:
www.indiana.edu/~preschal/council.html
ReutersHealth: *www.reutershealth.com*
World Health Organization: *www.who.ch*

Jobs

CareerMosaic: *www.careermosaic.com*
CareerPath.com: *new.careerpath.com*
Monster Board: *www.monster.com*

Kids

Information Please Kids' Almanac:
www.kids.infoplease.com

Interesting Places for Kids:
www.starport.com/places/forKids
Sports Illustrated Kids: *www.sikids.com*
TIME for Kids: *pathfinder.com/TFK/index.html*
Yahooligans!: *www.yahooligans.com*

Labor

Federal Labor Relations Authority: *www.flra.gov*
National Labor Relations Board (NLRB): *www.nlrb.gov*
Occupational Safety and Health Review Commission:
www.oshrc.gov
President's Committee on Employment of People with Disabilities: *www50.pcepd.gov/pcepd*

Magazines

Fortune: *www.pathfinder.com/fortune*
People: *www.pathfinder.com/people/web/index.html*
TIME: *cgi.pathfinder.com/time*
U.S. News & World Report:
www.usnews.com/usnews/home.htm
Wired: *www.wired.com/news*

Military

MarineLINK: *www.usmc.mil*
Selective Service System: *www.sss.gov*
U.S. Air Force: *www.af.mil*
U.S. Army: *www.army.mil*
U.S. Coast Guard: *www.uscg.mil*
U.S. Navy: *www.navy.mil*

News/Media

Associated Press: *wire.ap.org*
BBC TV & Radio: *www.bbc.co.uk*
CNN Interactive: *www.cnn.com*
National Public Radio Online: *www.npr.org*
Newspapers Online: *www.newspapers.com*
New York Times: *www.nytimes.com*
PointCast: *www.pointcast.com*
Reuters: *www.reuters.com/news*
USA Today: *www.usatoday.com*
Wall Street Journal: *www.wsj.com*
The Washington Post: *www.washingtonpost.com*

Public Service

Corporation for National Service: *www.cns.gov*
Peace Corps: *www.peacecorps.gov*

Reference

Ask Jeeves: *www.askjeeves.com*
CIA World Factbook:
www.odci.gov/cia/publications/factbook
FedStats (gov't. statistics): *www.fedstats.gov*
Information Please: *www.infoplease.com*
Internet Public Library: *www.ipl.org*
Learn2: *www.learn2.com*
MapQuest: *www.mapquest.com*

Science

National Aeronautics and Space Administration (NASA):
www.nasa.gov
National Science Foundation (NSF): *www.nsf.gov*
Science Magazine: *www.sciencemag.org*

Search Engines

Excite: *www.excite.com*
HotBot: *www.hotbot.com*
Lycos: *www.lycos.com*
Yahoo!: *www.yahoo.com*

Shopping

Amazon.com: *www.amazon.com*
Barnes and Noble: *www.barnesandnoble.com*
CDNow: *www.cdnow.com*
Florists' Transworld Delivery, Inc.: *www.ftd.com*
iMALL: *www.imall.com*
Powell's Books: *www.powells.com*
Shopping.com: *www.shopping.com*

Sports

CNN Sports Illustrated: *www.CNNSI.com*
ESPN: *espn.go.com*
Major League Baseball: *www.majorleaguebaseball.com*
Major League Soccer: *www.majorleaguesoccer.com*
National Basketball Association: *www.nba.com*
National Football League: *www.nfl.com*
National Hockey League: *www.nhl.com*

Travel

Centers for Disease Control Home Travel Information
Page: *www.cdc.gov/travel/travel.html*
Europe Through the Back Door: *www.ricksteves.com*
Expedia.com: *www.expedia.com*

Flight Tracker:
 www.thetrip.com/usertools/flighttracking/0,1325,1-1,00.html
Fodor's: *www.fodors.com*
Frommer's BudgetTravel Online: *www.frommers.com*
Hostelling International: *www.iyhf.org/index.html*
Lonely Planet Online: *www.lonelyplanet.com*
Preview Travel: *www.previewtravel.com*
Priceline.com: *www.priceline.com*
Travelocity.com: *www.travelocity.com*

Weather

IntelliCast: *www.intellicast.com*
National Weather Service: *www.nws.noaa.gov*
The Weather Channel: *www.weather.com*

Top 15 Countries in Internet Usage Per Capita, 1998

1998 rank	Country	Internet users (per 1,000 people)	1998 rank	Country	Internet users (per 1,000 people)
1.	Iceland	320.3	9.	Denmark	178.6
2.	Finland	305.4	10.	Singapore	140.0
3.	Norway	304.1	11.	Switzerland	138.2
4.	Sweden	289.8	12.	United Kingdom	137.3
5.	United States	283.0	13.	Netherlands	124.8
6.	Australia	234.1	14.	Hong Kong	98.7
7.	Canada	211.5	15.	Israel	95.7
8.	New Zealand	190.1			

NOTE: Includes adult Internet users with weekly usage in businesses and homes. Note that these numbers are 15% to 30% higher when occasional Internet users are included. *Source:* Computer Industry Almanac Inc., Arlington Heights, Ill., 847-718-0423, Web: www.c-i-a.com.

Internet Timeline

1969 ARPA (Advanced Research Projects Agency) goes online in December, connecting four major U.S. universities. Designed for research, education, and government organizations, it provides a communications network linking the country in the event that a military attack destroys conventional communications systems.

1972 Electronic mail is introduced. Queen Elizabeth sends her first email in 1976.

1973 Transmission Control Protocol/Internet Protocol (TCP/IP) is designed and in 1983 it becomes the standard for communicating between computers over the Internet. One of these protocols, FTP (file transfer protocol), allows users to log onto a remote computer, list the files on that computer, and download files from that computer.

1989 The first effort to index the Internet is created by Peter Deutsch at McGill University in Montreal, who devises Archie, an archive of FTP sites. Another indexing system, WAIS (Wide Area Information Server), is developed by Brewster Kahle of Thinking Machines Corp. Tim Berners-Lee of CERN (European Laboratory for Particle Physics) develops a new technique for distributing information on the Internet, which eventually is called the World Wide Web. The Web is based on hypertext, which permits the user to connect from one document to another at different sites on the Internet via hyperlinks (specially programmed words, phrases, buttons, or graphics). Unlike other Internet protocols, such as FTP and email, the Web is accessible through a graphical user interface.

1991 Gopher, the first user-friendly interface, is created at the University of Minnesota and named after the school mascot. Gopher becomes the most popular interface for several years.

1993 Mosaic is developed by Marc Andreeson at the National Center for Supercomputing Applications (NCSA). It becomes the dominant navigating system for the World Wide Web, which at this time accounts for merely 1% of all Internet traffic.

1994 White House launches Web page. Initial commerce sites are established and mass marketing campaigns are launched via email, introducing the term "spamming" to the Internet vocabulary.

1996 Approximately 45 million people are using the Internet, with roughly 30 million of those in North America (United States and Canada), 9 million in Europe, and 6 million in Asia/Pacific (Australia, Japan, etc.). 43.2 million (44%) of U.S. households own a personal computer, and 14 million of them are online.

1997 On July 8, 1997, Internet traffic records are broken as the NASA Web site broadcasts images taken by *Pathfinder* on Mars. The broadcast generates 46 million hits in one day.

1999 The number of Internet users worldwide reaches 150 million by the beginning of 1999. Over 50% are from the United States.

Sources for this timeline include International Data Corporation, the W3C Consortium, and the Internet Society.

Top Retail Software Titles Overall by Units, 1994–1998

Rank	Title	Publisher	Total units	Total dollars
1.	MS Windows 95 Upgrade	Microsoft	5,036,795	$443,568,599
2.	Quicken	Intuit	4,231,565	141,913,851
3.	TurboTax Final	Intuit	4,054,918	126,927,290
4.	Myst	Learning Company	4,031,807	143,180,064
5.	Quicken Deluxe	Intuit	2,967,471	172,332,648
6.	MS Flight Simulator	Microsoft	2,158,685	97,308,253
7.	MS Windows 98 Upgrade	Microsoft	1,896,858	167,291,928
8.	TurboTax Deluxe Final	Intuit	1,816,551	81,249,140
9.	Taxcut—Final	Block Financial	1,561,891	33,127,889
10.	Doom II	GT Interactive	1,554,390	62,704,365
11.	MS Encarta Encyclopedia	Microsoft	1,530,825	82,012,870
12.	QuickBooks	Intuit	1,511,452	151,098,860
13.	MS Plus	Microsoft	1,456,779	64,009,519
14.	Norton Utilities	Symantec	1,339,516	128,723,580
15.	Norton Antivirus	Symantec	1,296,664	87,101,236
16.	UnInstaller	Network Associates	1,257,759	46,231,004
17.	Riven: The Sequel to Myst	Learning Company	1,199,613	50,854,986
18.	MS Publisher	Microsoft	1,198,090	93,922,998
19.	Doom Shareware	Id Software	1,154,522	7,284,897
20.	Warcraft II	Havas Interactive	1,142,001	41,641,690
21.	Monopoly Game	Hasbro Interactive	1,069,212	34,506,547
22.	MS DOS 6.x Step Up Upgrade	Microsoft	1,054,946	9,925,120
23.	MS Works	Microsoft	1,039,340	61,382,846
24.	Sim City 2000	Electronic Arts	1,032,984	41,846,059
25.	Diablo	Havas Interactive	1,022,527	39,549,905

Source: PC Data, Reston, Va. Web: www.pcdata.com.

Top Selling Software, 1998

Rank	Title	Publisher	Average price	Rank	Title	Publisher	Average price
1.	Microsoft Windows 98 Upgrade	Microsoft	$88	12.	Microsoft Plus 98	Microsoft	$35
2.	TurboTax	Intuit	30	13.	Microsoft Flight Simulator	Microsoft	44
3.	TurboTax Deluxe	Intuit	44	14.	Quicken	Intuit	28
4.	Starcraft	Havas Interactive	42	15.	Deer Hunter II 3-D	GT Interactive	18
5.	Quicken Deluxe	Intuit	58	16.	Norton Antivirus 4	Symantec	40
6.	Deer Hunter	GT Interactive	18	17.	Titanic: Adventure Out of Time	Havas Interactive	24
7.	VirusScan 3	Network Associates	30	18.	Lego Island	Learning Company	25
8.	TaxCut	Block Financial	18	19.	Frogger	Hasbro Interactive	31
9.	TurboTax Multi State	Intuit	29	20.	Microsoft Encarta Encyclopedia	Microsoft	29
10.	Myst	Learning Company	18				
11.	Microsoft Windows 95 Upgrade	Microsoft	92				

Source: PC Data, Reston, Va. Web: www.pcdata.com.

Top Selling Home Education Software, 1998

Rank	Title	Publisher	Average price	Rank	Title	Publisher	Average price
1.	Blue's ABC Time Activities	Humongous (GT Interactive)	$18	6.	Jumpstart Second Grade	Havas Interactive	$23
2.	Jumpstart First Grade	Havas Interactive	23	7.	Rugrats Movie Activity Challenge	Learning Company	24
3.	Jumpstart Kindergarten II	Havas Interactive	23	8.	Jumpstart Third Grade	Havas Interactive	23
4.	Blue's Birthday Adventure	Humongous (GT Interactive)	23	9.	I Spy	Scholastic	23
5.	Sesame Street Elmo's Preschool	Learning Company	16	10.	Clue Finders 3rd Grade Adventures Ages 7–9	Learning Company	24

Source: PC Data, Reston, Va. Web: www.pcdata.com.

Top Selling Business Software, 1998

Rank	Title	Publisher	Average price		Rank	Title	Publisher	Average price
1.	Microsoft Windows 98 Upgrade	Microsoft	$ 88		12.	Mac OS 8	Apple Computer	$ 92
2.	VirusScan 3	Network Associates	30		13.	Microsoft FrontPage 98	Microsoft	133
3.	Microsoft Windows 95 Upgrade	Microsoft	92		14.	First Aid 98	Network Associates	35
4.	Microsoft Plus 98	Microsoft	35		15.	Norton Uninstaller Deluxe	Symantec	36
5.	Norton Antivirus 4	Symantec	40		16.	Norton Antivirus 4 Deluxe	Symantec	69
6.	Norton Utilities 3.0	Symantec	65					
7.	Norton Antivirus 5.0	Symantec	40		17.	Dr. Solomon's Anti-Virus	Network Associates	40
8.	pcAnywhere 32 Host/Remote	Symantec	127		18.	VirusScan 3 Deluxe	Network Associates	51
9.	UnInstaller	Network Associates	28		19.	Norton Utilities	Symantec	93
10.	Microsoft Office 97 Upgrade	Microsoft	213		20.	Winfax Pro	Symantec	90
11.	Microsoft Office Pro 97 Upgrade	Microsoft	303					

Source: PC Data, Reston, Va. Web: www.pcdata.com.

Electronic Commerce Users in North America, 1999

Shopping categories	Shoppers (millions)		Purchasing categories	Purchasers (millions)
Total online shoppers	**55.0**		**Total online purchasers**	**28.0**
Gender composition			**Gender composition**	
Female	41%		Female	38%
Male	59%		Male	62%
Overall top shopping categories			**Overall top purchasing categories**	
Cars/car parts	18.2		Books	9.2
Books	12.6		CDs & videos	7.2
Computers	12.4		Computers	5.4
Clothing	11.6		Clothing	4.5
CDs & videos	11.4		Software	4.0
Top shopping categories for male users			**Top purchasing categories for male users**	
Cars/car parts	12.6		Books	5.1
Computers	9.4		CDs & videos	4.5
CDs & videos	7.0		Computers	4.1
Books	6.4		Software	3.1
Home electronics	6.3		Clothing	2.1
Top shopping categories for female users			Travel	2.1
Clothing	6.9		**Top purchasing categories for female users**	
Books	6.2		Books	4.1
Cars/car parts	5.6		CDs & videos	2.7
CDs & videos	4.4		Clothing	2.4
	4.0		Travel	1.3
Travel			Computers	1.3

NOTES: "Shoppers" is defined as people researching and comparing the price and features of products and services online, regardless of whether or not an actual online purchase was made. "Purchasers" is defined as people who actually purchase items online. Based on spring 1999 survey. *Source:* CommerceNet/Nielsen Media Research Demographics of the Internet Survey.

Top Shopping Web Sites, May 1999

Rank	Web site	Unique visitors (thousands)		Rank	Web site	Unique visitors (thousands)
1	AOL Shopping	10,297		6	Barnesandnoble.com	4,330
2	Bluemountainarts.com	10,089		7	Mypoints.com	3,491
3	Amazon.com	9,933		8	Cdnow.com	3,345
4	Ebay.com	8,227		9	Valupage.com	3,244
5	Cnet software download svcs	4,709		10	Freeshop.com	2,719

NOTE: "Unique visitors" refers to the actual number of total users who visited the Web site once in the given month. All unique visitors are unduplicated (counted only once). *Source:* Media Metrix.

Top Web Sites, May 1999

Rank	Web site	Unique visitors (thousands)	Rank	Web site	Unique visitors (thousands)
1	Yahoo.com	31,118	26	Pathfinder.com	5,463
2	AOL.com	28,947	27	About.com	5,337
3	Msn.com	22,209	28	Weather.com	5,153
4	Geocities.com	19,514	29	Simplenet.com	5,127
5	Go.com	18,935	30	Goto.com	4,945
6	Netscape.com	18,537	31	CNN.com	4,771
7	Microsoft.com	16,031	32	CNET software download svcs	4,709
8	Excite.com	15,167	33	Fortunecity.com	4,575
9	Lycos.com	14,891	34	Sidewalk.com	4,496
10	Angelfire.com	12,601	35	Sony Online	4,411
11	Hotmail.com	12,377	36	Barnesandnoble.com	4,330
12	Tripod.com	11,526	37	Earthlink.net	4,299
13	Bluemountainarts.com	10,089	38	Expedia	3,933
14	Amazon.com	9,933	39	Warner Bros. Online	3,911
15	Altavista search services	9,491	40	Digitalcity.com	3,896
16	Snap.com search and services	8,872	41	Hypermart.net	3,847
17	Xoom.com	8,548	42	Ivillage: The Women's Network	3,822
18	Real.com	8,519	43	Travelocity.com	3,813
19	Ebay.com	8,227	44	Preview Travel	3,729
20	Hotbot.com	7,100	45	Att.net	3,671
21	Infospace.com	6,775	46	Porncity.net	3,600
22	Zdnet	6,630	47	Mypoints.com	3,491
23	Icq.com	5,852	48	Go2net.com	3,424
24	Looksmart.com	5,582	49	Broadcast.com Inc.	3,414
25	Msnbc.com	5,531	50	Cnet.com	3,386

NOTE: "Unique visitors" refers to the actual number of total users who visited the Web site once in the given month. All unique visitors are unduplicated (counted only once). *Source:* Media Metrix.

Top News/Information/Entertainment Web Sites, May 1999

Rank	Web site	Unique visitors (thousands)	Rank	Web site	Unique visitors (thousands)
1	AOL News Channel	14,611	6	Msnbc.com	5,531
2	AOL Entertainment Channel	12,049	7	Pathfinder.com	5,463
3	AOL Sports Channel	8,506	8	About.com	5,337
4	AOL Computing Channel	8,005	9	Weather.com	5,153
5	Zdnet	6,630	10	CNN.com	4,771

NOTE: "Unique visitors" refers to the actual number of total users who visited the Web site once in the given month. All unique visitors are unduplicated (counted only once). *Source:* Media Metrix.

Top Education Web Sites, May 1999

Rank	Web site	Unique visitors (thousands)	Rank	Web site	Unique visitors (thousands)
1	Berkeley.edu (U. of Calif. at Berkeley)	1,971	6	Uiuc.edu (U. of Ill. at Urbana-Champaign)	1,411
2	Umich.edu (U. of Mich.)	1,552	7	Unc.edu (U. of N.C. at Chapel Hill)	1,163
3	Msu.edu (Mich. State U.)	1,465	8	Ohio-state.edu (Ohio State U.)	1,127
4	Utexas.edu (U. of Texas at Austin)	1,456	9	Wisc.edu (U. of Wisc.)	1,082
5	Mit.edu (Mass. Inst. of Tech.)	1,428	10	Cmu.edu (Carnegie Mellon U.)	1,055

NOTE: "Unique visitors" refers to the actual number of total users who visited the Web site once in the given month. All unique visitors are unduplicated (counted only once). *Source:* Media Metrix.

Top Travel Web Sites, May 1999

Rank	Web site	Unique visitors (thousands)	Rank	Web site	Unique visitors (thousands)
1	AOL Travel	6,913	6	Mapquest.com	3,268
2	Sidewalk.com	4,496	7	City.net	1,838
3	Expedia	3,933	8	AA.com	1,441
4	Travelocity.com	3,813	9	Delta-Air.com	1,232
5	Preview Travel	3,729	10	SouthWest.com	1,161

NOTE: "Unique visitors" refers to the actual number of total users who visited the Web site once in the given month. All unique visitors are unduplicated (counted only once). *Source:* Media Metrix.

Internet Users in North America, 1995–1999
(in millions)

	Aug. 1995	Apr. 1996	Jan. 1997	Sept. 1997	June 1998	Apr. 1999
Total online	18.0	34.0	51.0	58.0	79.0	92.0
Gender composition						
Female	33%	34%	42%	43%	43%	46%
Male	67%	66%	58%	57%	57%	54%
Shoppers	8.0	19.0	30.0	35.0	48.0	55.0
Purchasers	2.0	4.0	6.0	10.0	20.0	28.0

NOTES: "Shoppers" is defined as people researching and comparing the price and features of products and services online, regardless of whether or not an actual online purchase was made. "Purchasers" is defined as people who actually purchase items online. Based on spring 1999 survey. *Source:* CommerceNet/Nielsen Media Research Demographics of the Internet Survey.

Internet Scams: Don't Believe Everything You Read

When you receive an alarmist chain letter in the mail or see an outrageous article on the cover of a supermarket tabloid, you may easily recognize these as false. Some readers do not automatically question similar information on the Web or in an email forwarded by a friend. The Internet is still relatively new as a widespread method of communication, and many people are not yet savvy about identifying electronic hoaxes.

The Internet contains a wealth of valuable information, but it is often difficult to tell the good from the bad. With easy accessibility, low cost, and wide distribution, the Internet is a great medium for disseminating falsehoods and inaccuracies. Keep in mind that your 13-year-old neighbor can publish on the Web as easily as the *New York Times* can!

While most false information is not malicious, beware of scams intended to frighten or cheat you. Some common email scams are familiar from other media: get rich quick schemes; fad diets; and threatening email chain letters. But new technology begets new scams, from the scare over the nonexistent "Good Times" virus to an email circulated in 1998 that supposedly generated contributions for the American Cancer Society each time it was forwarded—in fact, it collected senders' email addresses so they could be sold for mailing lists.

What can you do to protect yourself from these types of scams? Here are a few simple tips:
- Be a critical reader. Question what you see, and remember that Internet information is no more likely to be true than what you read in print media.
- Check the source. Try to determine the origin of any information you read, and make sure the source is reliable. Email without an author or a source is probably worthless.
- Don't download any software or .exe files from web sites or email unless you are sure of the source. You could be inviting a virus onto your computer.
- Beware of supposedly true stories that happened to "a friend of a friend." This is a common technique in urban myths to add credibility to a story. Similarly, don't assume that references legitimize a mailing—they may be part of the scam.
- Don't reply to emails that contain a link to an unfamiliar email address or URL. There may be a hidden fee.
- Don't perpetuate scams or contribute to Internet traffic congestion by forwarding email of dubious origin.
- If it seems too good to be true, it probably is. Using your common sense is the best protection against scams.

How to Spot A Virus Hoax

Along with rampant warnings about the devastating effects of viruses, frequent email chain letters circulate on the Internet warning readers that certain email messages are dangerous. This is not true. Email virus warnings are just scare tactics. Although it's possible to catch a virus by opening attachments within email messages, you will not catch one in opening the message itself. Fortunately, the hoaxes share many similarities and are easy to recognize. Common traits of virus hoax emails are:

- Overstating the destructive potential of viruses. Real viruses are generally more annoying than harmful. Virus hoaxes usually claim that the virus will destroy computers or hard drives.

- Invoking a respected authority. The claim that a reputable corporation or government agency has issued a warning about the virus gives the hoax credibility. Don't believe it. If in doubt, contact the cited organization.

- Encouraging the reader to send the warning to as many people as possible. This propagates the myth, thus increasing the hysteria.

So what should you do?
- If you get an email virus warning, **do not** pass it on! This behavior only serves to spread unnecessary panic.
- **Do not** be afraid to open an email message. No virus can infect your computer just from opening an email.
- **Do** be wary of attachments. Running or launching an .EXE or .COM file in an attachment could legitimately infect your computer with a virus. Word documents can also be infected with macro viruses, so beware of downloading and especially opening an attached Word document from an unknown source without scanning it first.

If you follow these guidelines, you should be safe from the genuine threats—and you'll save others from the imaginary ones.

Conversion Factors

To change	To	Multiply by	To change	To	Multiply by
acres	square feet	43,560	liters	quarts (liquid)	1.0567
acres	square miles	.001562	meters	feet	3.2808
atmospheres	cms. of mercury	76	meters	miles	.0006214
Btu	kilowatt-hour	.0002928	meters	yards	1.0936
Btu/hour	watts	.2931	metric tons	tons (long)	.9842
bushels	cubic inches	2150.4	metric tons	tons (short)	1.1023
centimeters	inches	.3937	miles	kilometers	1.6093
centimeters	feet	.03281	miles	feet	5280
cubic feet	cubic meters	.0283	miles (nautical)	miles (statute)	1.1516
cubic meters	cubic feet	35.3145	miles (statute)	miles (nautical)	.8684
cubic meters	cubic yards	1.3079	miles/hour	feet/minute	88
cubic yards	cubic meters	.7646	millimeters	inches	.0394
fathoms	feet	6.0	ounces avdp.	grams	28.3495
feet	meters	.3048	ounces	pounds	.0625
feet	miles (nautical)	.0001645	ounces (troy)	ounces (avdp)	1.09714
feet	miles (statute)	.0001894	pecks	liters	8.8096
feet/second	miles/hour	.6818	pints (dry)	liters	.5506
furlongs	feet	660.0	pints (liquid)	liters	.4732
furlongs	miles	.125	pounds ap or t	kilograms	.3782
gallons (U.S.)	liters	3.7853	pounds avdp	kilograms	.4536
grains	grams	.0648	pounds	ounces	16
grams	ounces avdp	.0353	quarts (dry)	liters	1.1012
grams	pounds	.002205	quarts (liquid)	liters	.9463
hectares	acres	2.4710	radians	degrees	57.30
hectoliters	bushels (U.S.)	2.8378	rods	meters	5.029
horsepower	watts	745.7	rods	feet	16.5
hours	days	.04167	square feet	square meters	.0929
inches	millimeters	25.4000	square kilometers	square miles	.3861
inches	centimeters	2.5400	square meters	square feet	10.7639
kilograms	pounds avdp or t	2.2046	square miles	square kilometers	2.5900
kilometers	miles	.6214	square yards	square meters	.8361
kilowatts	horsepower	1.341	tons (long)	metric tons	1.016
knots	nautical miles/hour	1.0	tons (short)	metric tons	.9072
knots	statute miles/hour	1.151	tons (long)	pounds	2240
liters	gallons (U.S.)	.2642	tons (short)	pounds	2000
liters	pints (dry)	1.8162	watts	Btu/hour	3.4129
liters	pints (liquid)	2.1134	watts	horsepower	.001341
liters	quarts (dry)	.9081	yards	meters	.9144
			yards	miles	.0005682

Fahrenheit and Celsius (Centigrade) Scales

°Celsius	°Fahrenheit	°Celsius	°Fahrenheit
−273.15	−459.67	30	86
−250	−418	35	95
−200	−328	40	104
−150	−238	45	113
−100	−148	50	122
−50	−58	55	131
−40	−40	60	140
−30	−22	65	149
−20	−4	70	158
−10	14	75	167
0	32	80	176
5	41	85	185
10	50	90	194
15	59	95	203
20	68	100	212
25	77		

Zero on the Fahrenheit scale represents the temperature produced by the mixing of equal weights of snow and common salt.

	°Fahrenheit	°Celsius
Boiling point of water	212°	100°
Freezing point of water	32°	0°
Absolute zero	−459.6°	−273.1°

Absolute zero is theoretically the lowest possible temperature, the point at which all molecular motion would cease.

To convert Fahrenheit to Celsius (Centigrade), subtract 32 and multiply by ⁵⁄₉.

To convert Celsius (Centigrade) to Fahrenheit, multiply by ⁹⁄₅ and add 32.

Kelvin Scale

Absolute zero, −273.15° on the Celsius (Centigrade) scale, is 0° Kelvin. Thus, Kelvin is equivalent to Celsius plus 273.15. The freezing point of water, 0°C and 32°F, is 273.15°K. The conversion formula is K° = C° + 273.15.

Roman Numerals

Roman numerals are expressed by letters of the alphabet and are rarely used today except for formality or variety.

There are four basic principles for reading Roman numerals:

1. A letter repeated once or twice repeats its value that many times (XXX = 30, CC = 200, etc.).
2. One or more letters placed after another letter of greater value increases the greater value by the amount of the smaller (VI = 6, LXX = 70, MCC = 1200, etc.).
3. A letter placed before another letter of greater value decreases the greater value by the amount of the smaller (IV = 4, XC = 90, CM = 900, etc.).
4. A bar placed on top of a letter or string of letters increases the numeral's value by 1,000 times (XV = 15, $\overline{\text{XV}}$ = 15,000).

Letter	Value	Letter	Value	Letter	Value	Letter	Value	Letter	Value
I	1	VII	7	XL	40	C	100	$\overline{\text{C}}$	100,000
II	2	VIII	8	L	50	D	500	$\overline{\text{D}}$	500,000
III	3	IX	9	LX	60	$\overline{\text{M}}$	1,000	$\overline{\text{M}}$	1,000,000
IV	4	X	10	LXX	70	$\overline{\text{V}}$	5,000		
V	5	XX	20	LXXX	80	$\overline{\text{X}}$	10,000		
VI	6	XXX	30	XC	90	$\overline{\text{L}}$	50,000		

Mean and Median

The arithmetic mean, also called the average, of a series of quantities is obtained by finding the sum of the quantities and dividing it by the number of quantities. In the series 1, 3, 5, 18, 19, 20, 25, the mean or average is 13—in other words, 91 divided by 7.

The median of a series is that point which so divides it that half the quantities are on one side, half on the other. In the above series, the median is 18.

The median often better expresses the common-run, since it is not, as is the mean, affected by an excessively high or low figure. In the series 1, 3, 4, 7, 55, the median of 4 is a truer expression of the common-run than is the mean of 14.

Prime Numbers between 1 and 1,000

	2	3	5	7	11	13	17	19	23
29	31	37	41	43	47	53	59	61	67
71	73	79	83	89	97	101	103	107	109
113	127	131	137	139	149	151	157	163	167
173	179	181	191	193	197	199	211	223	227
229	233	239	241	251	257	263	269	271	277
281	283	293	307	311	313	317	331	337	347
349	353	359	367	373	379	383	389	397	401
409	419	421	431	433	439	443	449	457	461
463	467	479	487	491	499	503	509	521	523
541	547	557	563	569	571	577	587	593	599
601	607	613	617	619	631	641	643	647	653
659	661	673	677	683	691	701	709	719	727
733	739	743	751	757	761	769	773	787	797
809	811	821	823	827	829	839	853	857	859
863	877	881	883	887	907	911	919	929	937
941	947	953	967	971	977	983	991	997	(1009)

New Quarters and Dollar Coin

In December 1998 President Clinton approved the 50 State Quarters Program Act. The program is scheduled to run from 1999 until 2008, with five new quarters released every year over ten years. The quarters are being released in the order that the states joined the union. In 1999, the Delaware, Pennsylvania, New Jersey, Georgia, and Connecticut quarters were released; in 2000, the Massachusetts, Maryland, South Carolina, New Hampshire, and Virginia will be released. 700 million copies of each quarter will be produced.

In 2000, a new dollar coin, featuring the Shoshone guide Sacagawea, will replace the Susan B. Anthony coin, whose reserves are running low.

Portraits and Designs of U.S. Paper Currency

Currency[1]	Portrait	Design on back	Currency[1]	Portrait	Design on back
$1	Washington	ONE between obverse and reverse of Great Seal of U.S.	$50[5]	Grant	U.S. Capitol
			$100[6]	Franklin	Independence Hall
$2[2]	Jefferson	Monticello	$500	McKinley	Ornate FIVE HUNDRED
$2[3]	Jefferson	"The Signing of the Declaration of Independence"	$1,000	Cleveland	Ornate ONE THOUSAND
			$5,000	Madison	Ornate FIVE THOUSAND
$5	Lincoln	Lincoln Memorial	$10,000	Chase	Ornate TEN THOUSAND
$10	Hamilton	U.S. Treasury Building	$100,000[7]	Wilson	Ornate ONE HUNDRED THOUSAND
$20[4]	Jackson	White House			

1. Denominations of $500 and higher were discontinued in 1969. 2. Discontinued in 1966. 3. New issue, April 1976. 4. New issue, September 1998. 5. New issue, Fall 1997. 6. New issue, March 1996. 7. For use only in transactions between Federal Reserve System and Treasury Department.

Customary U.S. Weights and Measures

Linear Measure

12 inches (in.) = 1 foot (ft.)
3 feet = 1 yard (yd)
5½ yards = 1 rod (rd), pole, or perch (16½ ft.)
40 rods = 1 furlong (fur) = 220 yds = 660 ft.
8 furlongs = 1 statute mile (mi.) = 1,760 yds
= 5,280 ft.
3 land miles = 1 league
5,280 feet = 1 statute or land mile
6,076.11549 feet = 1 international nautical mile

Area Measure

144 square inches = 1 sq ft.
9 square feet = 1 sq yd = 1,296 sq in.
30¼ square yards = 1 sq rd = 272¼ sq ft.
160 square rods = 1 acre = 4,840 sq yds
= 43,560 sq ft.
640 acres = 1 sq mi.
1 mile square = 1 section (of land)
6 miles square = 1 township = 36 sections
= 36 sq mi.

Cubic Measure

1,728 cubic inches = 1 cu ft.
27 cubic feet = 1 cu yd

Liquid Measure

When necessary to distinguish the liquid pint or quart from the dry pint or quart, the word "liquid" or the abbreviation "liq" should be used in combination with the name or abbreviation of the liquid unit.

4 gills (gi) = 1 pint (pt) (= 28.875 cu in.)
2 pints = 1 quart (qt) (= 57.75 cu in.)
4 quarts = 1 gallon (gal) (= 231 cu in.)
= 8 pts = 32 gills

Apothecaries' Fluid Measure

60 minims (min.) = 1 fluid dram (fl dr) (= 0.2256 cu in.)
8 fluid drams = 1 fluid ounce (fl oz) (= 1.8047 cu in.)
16 fluid ounces = 1 pt (= 28.875 cu in.) = 128 fl drs
2 pints = 1 qt (= 57.75 cu in.) = 32 fl oz
= 256 fl drs
4 quarts = 1 gal (= 231 cu in.) = 128 fl oz
= 1,024 fl drs

Dry Measure

When necessary to distinguish the dry pint or quart from the liquid pint or quart, the word "dry" should be used in combination with the name or abbreviation of the dry unit.

2 pints = 1 qt (= 67.2006 cu in.)
8 quarts = 1 peck (pk) (= 537.605 cu in.) = 16 pts
4 pecks = 1 bushel (bu) (= 2,150.42 cu in.) = 32 qts

Avoirdupois Weight

When necessary to distinguish the avoirdupois dram from the apothecaries' dram, or to distinguish the avoirdupois dram or ounce from the fluid dram or ounce, or to distinguish the avoirdupois ounce or pound from the troy or apothecaries' ounce or pound, the word "avoirdupois" or the abbreviation "avdp" should be used in combination with the name or abbreviation of the avoirdupois unit. (The "grain" is the same in avoirdupois, troy, and apothecaries' weights.)

27 11/32 grains = 1 dram (dr)
16 drams = 1 oz = 437½ grains
16 ounces = 1 lb = 256 drams = 7,000 grains
100 pounds = 1 hundredweight (cwt)[1]
20 hundredweights = 1 ton (tn) = 2,000 lbs[1]

In "gross" or "long" measure, the following values are recognized:

112 pounds = 1 gross or long cwt[1]
20 gross or long hundredweights = 1 gross or long ton
= 2,240 lbs[1]

1. When the terms "hundredweight" and "ton" are used unmodified, they are commonly understood to mean the 100-pound hundredweight and the 2,000-pound ton, respectively; these units may be designated "net" or "short" when necessary to distinguish them from the corresponding units in gross or long measure.

Units of Circular Measure

Second (″) = —
Minute (′) = 60 seconds
Degree (°) = 60 minutes
Right angle = 90 degrees
Straight angle = 180 degrees
Circle = 360 degrees

Troy Weight

24 grains = 1 pennyweight (dwt)
20 pennyweights = 1 ounce troy (oz t) = 480 grains
12 ounces troy = 1 pound troy (lb t)
= 240 pennyweights
= 5,760 grains

Apothecaries' Weight

20 grains = 1 scruple (s ap)
3 scruples = 1 dram apothecaries' (dr ap)
= 60 grains
8 drams apothecaries' = 1 ounce apothecaries' (oz ap)
= 24 scruples = 480 grains
12 ounces apothecaries' = 1 pound apothecaries' (lb ap)
= 96 drams apothecaries'
= 288 scruples
= 5,760 grains

Gunter's or Surveyor's Chain Measure

7.92 inches = 1 link (li)
100 links = 1 chain (ch) = 4 rods = 66 ft.
80 chains = 1 statute mile = 320 rods = 5,280 ft.

The International System (Metric)

Source: Department of Commerce, National Bureau of Standards.

The International System of Units is a modernized version of the metric system, established by international agreement, that provides a logical and interconnected framework for all measurements in science, industry, and commerce. The system is built on a foundation of seven basic units, and all other units are derived from them. (Use of metric weights and measures was legalized in the United States in 1866, and our customary units of weights and measures are defined in terms of the meter and kilogram.)

Length. Meter. Up until 1983, the meter was defined as 1,650,763.73 wavelengths in a vacuum of the orange-red line of the spectrum of krypton-86. Since then, it is equal to the distance traveled by light in a vacuum in 1/299,792,45 of a second.

Time. Second. The second is defined as the duration of 9,192,631,770 cycles of the radiation associated with a specified transition of the cesium-133 atom.

Mass. Kilogram. The standard for the kilogram is a cylinder of platinum-iridium alloy kept by the International Bureau of Weights and Measures at Paris. A duplicate at the National Bureau of Standards serves as the mass standard for the United States. The kilogram is the only base unit still defined by a physical object.

Temperature. Kelvin. The Kelvin is defined as the fraction 1/273.16 of the thermodynamic temperature of the triple point of water; that is, the point at which water forms an interface of solid, liquid, and vapor. This is defined as 0.01°C on the Centigrade or Celsius scale and 32.02°F on the Fahrenheit scale. The temperature 0°K is called "absolute zero."

Electric Current. Ampere. The ampere is defined as that current that, if maintained in each of two long parallel wires separated by one meter in free space, would produce a force between the two wires (due to their magnetic fields) of 2×10^{-7} newton for each meter of length. (A newton is the unit of force that when applied to one kilogram mass would experience an acceleration of one meter per second per second.)

Luminous Intensity. Candela. The candela is defined as the luminous intensity of 1/600,000 of a square meter of a cavity at the temperature of freezing platinum (2,042°K).

Amount of Substance. Mole. The mole is the amount of substance of a system that contains as many elementary entities as there are atoms in 0.012 kilogram of carbon-12.

Tables of Metric Weights and Measures

Linear Measure

10 millimeters (mm) = 1 centimeter (cm)
  10 centimeters = 1 decimeter (dm) = 100 millimeters
  10 decimeters = 1 meter (m) = 1,000 millimeters
  10 meters = 1 dekameter (dam)
  10 dekameters = 1 hectometer (hm) = 100 meters
  10 hectometers = 1 kilometer (km) = 1,000 meters

Area Measure

100 square millimeters (mm²) = 1 sq centimeter (cm²)
  10,000 square centimeters = 1 sq meter (m²) =
    1,000,000 sq millimeters
  100 square meters = 1 are (a)
  100 ares = 1 hectare (ha) =
    10,000 sq meters
  100 hectares = 1 sq kilometer (km²) =
    1,000,000 sq meters

Volume Measure

10 milliliters (ml) = 1 centiliter (cl)
  10 centiliters = 1 deciliter (dl) = 100 milliliters
  10 deciliters = 1 liter (l) = 1,000 milliliters

10 liters = 1 dekaliter (dal)
  10 dekaliters = 1 hectoliter (hl) = 100 liters
  10 hectoliters = 1 kiloliter (kl) = 1,000 liters

Cubic Measure

1,000 cubic millimeters (mm³) = 1 cu centimeter (cm³)
  1,000 cubic centimeters = 1 cu decimeter (dm³) =
    1,000,000 cu millimeters
  1,000 cubic decimeters = 1 cu meter (m³) =
    1 stere = 1,000,000 cu
    centimeters =
    1,000,000,000 cu
    millimeters

Weight

10 milligrams (mg) = 1 centigram (cg)
  10 centigrams = 1 decigram (dg) = 100 milligrams
  10 decigrams = 1 gram (g) = 1,000 milligrams
  10 grams = 1 dekagram (dag)
  10 dekagrams = 1 hectogram (hg) = 100 grams
  10 hectograms = 1 kilogram (kg) = 1,000 grams
  1,000 kilograms = 1 metric ton (t)

Metric and U.S. Equivalents

1 angstrom[1](light wave measurement)	0.1 millimicron 0.000 1 micron 0.000 000 1 millimeter 0.000 000 004 inch
1 cable's length	120 fathoms 720 feet 219.456 meters
1 centimeter	0.3937 inch
1 decimeter	3.937 inches
1 dekameter	32.808 feet
1 fathom	6 feet 1.8288 meters
1 foot	0.3048 meter
1 furlong	10 chains (surveyor's) 660 feet 220 yards ⅛ statute mile 201.168 meters
1 inch	2.54 centimeters
1 kilometer	0.621 mile
1 league (land)	3 statute miles 4.828 kilometers
1 meter	39.37 inches 1.094 yards
1 micron	0.001 millimeter 0.000 039 37 inch
1 mil	0.001 inch 0.025 4 millimeter
1 mile (statute or land)	5,280 feet 1.609 kilometers
1 mile (nautical international)	1.852 kilometers 1.151 statute miles 0.999 U.S. nautical miles
1 millimeter	0.03937 inch
1 millimicron (m+GRKm)	0.001 micron 0.000 000 039 37 inch
1 nanometer	0.001 micrometer or 0.000 000 039 37 inch
1 point (typography)	0.013 837 inch 1/72 inch (approximately) 0.351 millimeter
1 rod, pole, or perch	16½ feet 5.0292 meters
1 yard	0.9144 meter

Areas or Surfaces

1 acre	43,560 square feet 4,840 square yards 0.405 hectare
1 are	119.599 square yards 0.025 acre
1 hectare	2.471 acres
1 square centimeter	0.155 square inch
1 square decimeter	15.5 square inches
1 square foot	929.030 square centimeters
1 square inch	6.4516 square centimeters
1 square kilometer	0.386 square mile 247.105 acres
1 square meter	1.196 square yards 10.764 square feet
1 square mile	258.999 hectares
1 square millimeter	0.002 square inch
1 square rod, square pole or square perch	25.293 square meters
1 square yard	0.836 square meters

Capacities or Volumes

1 barrel, liquid	31 to 42 gallons[2]
1 bushel (U.S.) struck measure[3]	2,150.42 cubic inches 35.238 liters
1 bushel, heaped (U.S.)	2,747.715 cubic inches 1.278 bushels, struck measure[4]
1 cord (firewood)	128 cubic feet
1 cubic centimeter	0.061 cubic inch
1 cubic decimeter	61.024 cubic inches
1 cubic foot	7.481 gallons 28.316 cubic decimeters
1 cubic inch	0.554 fluid ounce 4.433 fluid drams 16.387 cubic centimeters
1 cubic meter	1.308 cubic yards
1 cubic yard	0.765 cubic meter

1 cup, measuring	8 fluid ounces ½ liquid pint	1 teaspoon, measuring	⅓ tablespoon 1⅓ fluid drams
1 dram, fluid or liquid (U.S.)	⅛ fluid ounces 0.226 cubic inch 3.697 milliliters 1.041 British fluid drachms	1 carat	200 milligrams 3.086 grains
1 dekaliter	2.642 gallons 1.135 pecks	1 dram, apothecaries'	60 grains 3.888 grams
1 gallon (U.S.)	231 cubic inches 3.785 liters 0.833 British gallon 128 U.S. fluid ounces	1 dram, avoirdupois	27 1½₂ (=27.344) grains 1.772 grams
1 gallon (British Imperial)	277.42 cubic inches 1.201 U.S. gallons 4.546 liters 160 British fluid ounces	1 grain	64.798 91 milligrams
		1 gram	15.432 grains 0.035 ounce, avoirdupois
1 hectoliter	26.418 gallons 2.838 bushels	1 kilogram	2.205 pounds
1 liter	1.057 liquid quarts 0.908 dry quart 61.024 cubic inches	1 microgram (µg— the Greek letter mu in combination with the letter g)	0.000 001 gram
1 milliliter	0.271 fluid dram 16.231 minims 0.061 cubic inch	1 milligram	0.015 grain
1 ounce, fluid or liquid (U.S.)	1.805 cubic inch 29.574 milliliters 1.041 British fluid ounces	1 ounce, avoirdupois	437.5 grains 0.911 troy or apothecaries', ounce 28.350 grams
1 peck	8.810 liters	1 ounce, troy or apothecaries'	480 grains 1.097 avoirdupois ounces 31.103 grams
1 pint, dry	33.600 cubic inches 0.551 liter	1 pennyweight	1.555 grams
1 pint, liquid	28.875 cubic inches 0.473 liter	1 point	0.01 carat 2 milligrams
1 quart, dry (U.S.)	67.201 cubic inches 1.101 liters 0.969 British quart	1 pound, avoirdupois	7,000 grains 1.215 troy or apothecaries' pounds 453.592 37 grams
1 quart, liquid (U.S.)	57.75 cubic inches 0.946 liter 0.833 British quart	1 pound, troy or apothecaries'	5,760 grains 0.823 avoirdupois pound 373.242 grams
1 quart (British)	69.354 cubic inches 1.032 U.S. dry quarts 1.201 U.S. liquid quarts	1 ton, gross or long[5]	2,240 pounds 1.12 net tons 1.016 metric tons
1 tablespoon, measuring	3 teaspoons 4 fluid drams ½ fluid ounce	1 ton, metric	2,204.623 pounds 0.984 gross ton 1.102 net tons
		1 ton, net or short	2,000 pounds 0.893 gross ton 0.907 metric ton

1. The angstrom is basically defined as 10^{-10} meter. 2. There is a variety of "barrels" established by law or usage. For example, federal taxes on fermented liquors are based on a barrel of 31 gallons; many state laws fix the "barrel for liquids" at 31½ gallons; one state fixes a 36-gallon barrel for cistern measurement; federal law recognizes a 40-gallon barrel for "proof spirits"; by custom, 42 gallons compose a barrel of crude oil or petroleum products for statistical purposes, and this equivalent is recognized "for liquids" by four states. 3. "Struck measure" refers to a struck, or level, bushel. It is the only official bushel measure in the U.K. 4. Frequently recognized as 1¼ bushels, struck measure. 5. The gross or long ton is used commercially in the United States to only a limited extent, usually in restricted industrial fields. These units are the same as the British "ton."

Definitions of Gold Terminology

The term "fineness" defines a gold content in parts per thousand. For example, a gold nugget containing 885 parts of pure gold, 100 parts of silver, and 15 parts of copper would be considered 885-fine.

The word "karat" indicates the proportion of solid gold in an alloy based on a total of 24 parts. Thus, 14-karat (14K) gold indicates a composition of 14 parts of gold and 10 parts of other metals.

The term "gold-filled" is used to describe articles of jewelry made of base metal that are covered on one or more surfaces with a layer of gold alloy. No article having a gold alloy portion of less than one twentieth by weight may be marked "gold-filled." Articles may be marked "rolled gold plate" provided the proportional fraction and fineness designations are also shown.

Electroplated jewelry items carrying at least 7 millionths of an inch of gold on significant surfaces may be labeled "electroplate." Plate thicknesses less than this may be marked "gold-flashed" or "gold-washed."

Bolts and Screws: Conversion from Fractions of an Inch to Millimeters

Inch	mm	Inch	mm	Inch	mm	Inch	mm
1/64	0.40	17/64	6.75	33/64	13.10	49/64	19.45
1/32	0.79	9/32	7.14	17/32	13.50	25/32	19.84
3/64	1.19	19/64	7.54	35/64	13.90	51/64	20.24
1/16	1.59	5/16	7.94	9/16	14.29	13/16	20.64
5/64	1.98	21/64	8.33	37/64	14.69	53/64	21.03
3/32	2.38	11/32	8.73	19/32	15.08	27/32	21.43
7/64	2.78	23/64	9.13	39/64	15.48	55/64	21.83
1/8	3.18	3/8	9.53	5/8	15.88	7/8	22.23
9/64	3.57	25/64	9.92	41/64	16.27	57/64	22.62
5/32	3.97	13/32	10.32	21/32	16.67	29/32	23.02
11/64	4.37	27/64	10.72	43/64	17.06	59/64	23.42
3/16	4.76	7/16	11.11	11/16	17.46	15/16	23.81
13/64	5.16	29/64	11.51	45/64	17.86	61/64	24.21
7/32	5.56	15/32	11.91	23/32	18.26	31/32	24.61
15/64	5.95	31/64	12.30	47/64	18.65	63/64	25.00
1/4	6.35	1/2	12.70	3/4	19.05	1	25.40

Cooking Measurement Equivalents

16 tablespoons = 1 cup
12 tablespoons = 3/4 cup
10 tablespoons + 2 teaspoons = 2/3 cup
8 tablespoons = 1/2 cup
6 tablespoons = 3/8 cup
5 tablespoons + 1 teaspoon = 1/3 cup
4 tablespoons = 1/4 cup

2 tablespoons = 1/8 cup
2 tablespoons + 2 teaspoons = 1/6 cup
1 tablespoon = 1/16 cup
2 cups = 1 pint
2 pints = 1 quart
3 teaspoons = 1 tablespoon
48 teaspoons = 1 cup

U.S.–Metric Cooking Conversions

U.S. to Metric

Capacity		Weight	
1/5 teaspoon	1 milliliter	1 oz	28 grams
1 teaspoon	5 ml	1 pound	454 grams
1 tablespoon	15 ml		
1 fluid oz	30 ml		
1/5 cup	50 ml		
1 cup	240 ml		
2 cups (1 pint)	470 ml		
4 cups (1 quart)	.95 liter		
4 quarts (1 gal.)	3.8 liters		

Metric to U.S.

Capacity		Weight	
1 milliliter	1/5 teaspoon	1 gram	.035 ounce
5 ml	1 teaspoon	100 grams	3.5 ounces
15 ml	1 tablespoon	500 grams	1.10 pounds
100 ml	3.4 fluid oz	1 kilogram	2.205 pounds
240 ml	1 cup		35 oz
1 liter	34 fluid oz		
	4.2 cups		
	2.1 pints		
	1.06 quarts		
	0.26 gallon		

Prefixes and Multiples

Prefix	Suffix	Equivalent	Multiple/submultiple	Prefix	Suffix	Equivalent	Multiple/submultiple
atto	a	quintillionth part	10^{-18}	deci	d	tenth part	10^{-1}
femto	f	quadrillionth part	10^{-15}	deka	da	tenfold	10
pico	p	trillionth part	10^{-12}	hecto	h	hundredfold	10^2
nano	n	billionth part	10^{-9}	kilo	k	thousandfold	10^3
micro	μ	millionth part	10^{-6}	mega	M	millionfold	10^6
milli	m	thousandth part	10^{-3}	giga	G	billionfold	10^9
centi	c	hundredth part	10^{-2}	tera	T	trillionfold	10^{12}

Common Formulas

Circumference
Circle: $C = \pi d$, in which π is 3.1416 and d the diameter.

Area
Triangle: $A = \dfrac{ab}{2}$, in which a is the base and b the height.

Square: $A = a^2$, in which a is one of the sides.

Rectangle: $A = ab$, in which a is the base and b the height.

Trapezoid: $A = \dfrac{h(a+b)}{2}$, in which h is the height, a the longer parallel side, and b the shorter.

Regular pentagon: $A = 1.720a^2$, in which a is one of the sides.

Regular hexagon: $A = 2.598a^2$, in which a is one of the sides.

Regular octagon: $A = 4.828a^2$, in which a is one of the sides.

Circle: $A = \pi r^2$, in which π is 3.1416 and r the radius.

Volume
Cube: $V = a^3$, in which a is one of the edges.

Rectangular prism: $V = abc$, in which a is the length, b is the width, and c the depth.

Pyramid: $V = \dfrac{Ah}{3}$, in which A is the area of the base and h the height.

Cylinder: $V = \pi r^2 h$, in which π is 3.1416, r the radius of the base, and h the height.

Cone: $V = \dfrac{\pi r^2 h}{3}$, in which π is 3.1416, r the radius of the base, and h the height.

Sphere: $V = \dfrac{4 \pi r^3}{3}$, in which π is 3.1416 and r the radius.

Temperature Scales
Degrees Fahrenheit to Degrees Celsius:
$$T_C = \frac{5}{9}(T_F - 32)$$

Degrees Celsius to Degrees Fahrenheit:
$$T_F = \frac{9}{5} T_C + 32$$

Degrees Celsius to Kelvin:
$$T_K = T_C + 273.15$$

Miscellaneous
Distance in feet traveled by falling body:
$d = 16t^2$, in which t is the time in seconds.

Speed of sound in feet per second through any given temperature of air:
$$V = \frac{1087 \sqrt{273 + t}}{16.52}$$, in which t is the temperature Celsius.

Cost in cents of operation of electrical device:
$C = \dfrac{Wtc}{1000}$, in which W is the number of watts, t the time in hours, and c the cost in cents per kilowatt-hour.

Conversion of matter into energy (Einstein's Theorem): $E = mc^2$, in which E is the energy in ergs, m the mass of the matter in grams, and c the speed of light in centimeters per second:
$$(c^2 = 9 \times 10^{20})$$

Decimal Equivalents of Common Fractions

½	.5000	1/10	.1000	2/7	.2857	3/11	.2727	5/9	.5556	7/11	.6364
⅓	.3333	1/11	.0909	2/9	.2222	4/5	.8000	5/11	.4545	7/12	.5833
¼	.2500	1/12	.0833	2/11	.1818	4/7	.5714	5/12	.4167	8/9	.8889
⅕	.2000	1/16	.0625	¾	.7500	4/9	.4444	6/7	.8571	8/11	.7273
⅙	.1667	1/32	.0313	⅗	.6000	4/11	.3636	6/11	.5455	9/10	.9000
1/7	.1429	1/64	.0156	3/7	.4286	⅚	.8333	⅞	.8750	9/11	.8182
⅛	.1250	⅔	.6667	⅜	.3750	5/7	.7143	7/9	.7778	10/11	.9091
1/9	.1111	2/5	.4000	3/10	.3000	⅝	.6250	7/10	.7000	11/12	.9167

What Global Warming?

As the world heats up, the public simply goes cold

By DICK THOMPSON TIME

If you wanted to question whether global warming is indeed upon us, the spring of 1999 was not the time to do it. Two weeks before the official beginning of summer, a heat wave baked the eastern third of the U.S. and Canada, driving temperatures high into the 90s and even 100s. At the same time, a flurry of scientific papers was released that seemed to explain all the late-spring suffering. In one study, French researchers reported that heat-trapping greenhouse gases are at their highest levels in 420,000 years. In another, U.S. scientists found that 57 species of butterfly may be altering their migratory patterns in response to changing heat patterns.

In light of all this, a sweltering public must have been convinced at last that it's time to do something to cool off the overheated planet, right? Wrong. Even as the temperature was climbing, a new survey by the American Geophysical Union found that Americans are less concerned than ever about combatting global warming. "The more we talk about warming," says the study's director, John Immerwahr, "the [more the] public's concern goes down."

Corporate Culprits?

Such an environmental disconnect may not be much of a mystery. Environmentalists complain that over the past two years industry groups have launched a coordinated advertising campaign to torpedo the 1997 Kyoto treaty, which requires industrial nations to reduce greenhouse emissions. More than $13 million has been spent on ads to block ratification of the treaty by the U.S. Senate. "The purpose of the ads was to convince most Americans that there isn't a problem or that it's too expensive to fix," says National Environmental Trust spokesman Peter Kelly.

Environmentalists also criticize President Clinton for what they believe is his failure to press the issue. In June, Clinton moved for Kyoto treaty changes that environmental groups see as industry-pleasing loopholes. Says Daniel Weiss, the Sierra Club's political director: "Timid leaders communicate hopelessness." And hopelessness breeds indifference.

False Comfort

If such popular so-whating persists, Immerwahr warns, the public may begin grasping at phony solutions to global warming. In June, some people took comfort from the report of a vast haze of pollutants that collects over the Indian Ocean in the winter, but that researchers only recently studied. Filthy as the cloud is, it does deflect solar radiation, and that could lead to cooling. But scientists warn that we cannot simply pollute our way out of global warming. The soot drops from the hazy atmosphere in weeks, whereas greenhouse gases remain for centuries.

The way out of this gridlock, environmentalists say, is to show it's possible to reduce greenhouse gases without sinking the economy. Solutions include cleaner cars and better wind- and solar-power technologies. Says Greg Wetstone, program director for the Natural Resources Defense Council: "When these kinds of options become available, people will feel less hopeless." Of course, it's also possible that only when people feel less hopeless will they press their leaders to make the solutions available. □

Estimated U.S. Emissions of Greenhouse Gases, 1990–1997
(million metric tons of gas)

Gas	1990	1991	1992	1993	1994	1995	1996	P1997
Carbon dioxide	4,971.7	4,916.3	4,988.8	5,109.8	5,183.9	5,236.4	5,422.3	5,503.0
Methane	30.2	30.4	30.4	29.7	29.9	30.0	29.1	29.1
Nitrous oxide	1.0	1.0	1.0	1.0	1.1	1.0	1.0	1.0
Halocarbons and other gases								
CFC-11, CFC-12, CFC-113	0.2	0.2	0.1	0.1	0.1	0.1	0.1	*
HCFC-22	0.1	0.1	0.1	0.1	0.1	0.1	0.1	0.1
HFCs, PFCs, and SF_6	*	*	*	*	*	*	*	*
Methyl chloroform	0.2	0.2	0.1	0.1	0.1	*	*	*
Carbon monoxide	87.4	89.2	86.2	86.3	90.3	81.3	80.4	n.a.
Nitrogen oxides	21.6	21.5	21.9	22.2	22.5	21.7	21.3	n.a.
Nonmethane VOCs	18.9	19.1	18.7	18.9	19.5	18.6	17.2	n.a.

NOTES: * Less than 50,000 metric tons of gas. P = preliminary data. n.a. = not available. *Sources:* Carbon dioxide, methane, nitrous oxide emissions: EIA estimates. Halocarbons and other gases: U.S. Environmental Protection Agency, *Inventory of U.S. Greenhouse Gas Emissions and Sinks 1990–1996,* (March 1998). Criteria pollutants: U.S. Environmental Protection Agency, Office of Air Quality Planning and Standards, *National Air Pollutant Emission Trends, 1900–1996,* EPA-454-R-97-011 (Dec. 1997).

Energy

World Energy Consumption and Carbon Emissions, 1990–2020

Region	Energy consumption (quadrillion btu)				Carbon emissions (million metric tons)			
	1990	1996	2010	2020	1990	1996	2010	2020
Industrialized nations[1]	182.7	202.5	240.4	262.8	2,850	2,980	3,535	3,907
Eastern Europe/Former Soviet Union	73.6	52.4	61.0	69.8	1,290	842	935	1,024
Developing nations								
Asia[2]	51.4	74.5	127.6	177.9	1,065	1,474	2,426	3,377
Middle East[3]	13.1	17.3	27.0	34.7	229	283	434	555
Africa	9.2	11.1	15.5	18.9	178	198	270	325
Central and South America[4]	13.7	17.7	32.6	47.7	174	206	418	629
Total developing	87.4	120.6	202.8	279.2	1,646	2,161	3,547	4,886
Total world	343.8	375.5	504.2	611.8	5,786	5,983	8,018	9,817

1. Includes the U.S., Canada, Mexico, Japan, France, Germany, Italy, the Netherlands, and the United Kingdom. 2. China, India, and South Korea are represented in developing Asia. 3. Turkey is represented in the Middle East. 4. Brazil is represented in Central and South America. *Source:* Energy Information Administration (EIA), *International Energy Annual 1996,* DOE/EIA-0219(96), and EIA, World Energy Projection System (1999).

World Energy Overview

Source: Energy Information Administration, Dept. of Energy. Web: www.eia.doe.gov/emeu/iea/overview.html.

World Primary Energy Production Trends

Between 1988 and 1997, the world's total output of primary energy—petroleum, natural gas, coal, and electric power (hydro, nuclear, geothermal, solar, and wind)—increased at an average annual rate of 1.4%. World production increased from 336 quadrillion Btu in 1988 to 381 quadrillion Btu in 1997.

In 1997, petroleum (crude oil and natural gas plant liquids) continued to be the world's most important primary energy source, accounting for 39.5%, or 151 quadrillion Btu, of world primary energy production. Between 1988 and 1997, petroleum production increased by 9.0 million barrels per day, or 14.2%, rising from 63.2 to 72.2 million barrels per day. The Middle East had the largest production gain, followed by Central and South America, and Western Europe. Their combined gains over the period from 1988 to 1997 were 11.1 million barrels per day. In North America, and in the Eastern Europe and Former U.S.S.R. region, average daily production fell by 0.4 and 5.4 million barrels per day, respectively.

Coal ranked second as a primary energy source in 1997, accounting for 24.2% of world primary energy production. World coal production totaled 5.22 billion short tons—92 quadrillion Btu—in 1997, but it was down by 0.3% from the 1988 level of 5.23 billion short tons.

Dry natural gas ranked third as a primary energy source, accounting for 22.1% of world primary energy production in 1997. Production of dry natural gas was 82 trillion cubic feet, or 84 quadrillion Btu, in 1997. Production increased by 11.9 trillion cubic feet from 69.8 trillion cubic feet in 1988, a gain of 17%.

Hydro, nuclear, and other (geothermal, solar, and wind) electric power generation ranked fourth, fifth, and sixth, respectively, as primary energy sources in 1997, accounting for 6.9, 6.3, and 0.5%, respectively, of world primary energy production. Together they accounted for a combined total of 4.9 trillion kilowatthours—52 quadrillion Btu—in 1997. Nuclear

electric power generation increased significantly between 1988 and 1997, rising from 1.8 trillion kilowatthours to 2.3 trillion kilowatthours, a 26.4% increase. Geothermal, solar, and wind electric power generation also increased significantly over the same period, rising from 35 billion kilowatthours to 131 billion kilowatthours, a 276% increase. (Note: Part of this increase is a result of a discontinuity in the geothermal, solar, and wind electric power time series for the U.S. between 1989 and 1990. Beginning in 1990, the generation of biomass, geothermal, solar, and wind electric power by nonutility power producers is included.) Hydroelectric power continued to represent the largest share of primary electric power generation, contributing 2.5 trillion kilowatthours in 1997, up 20.4% from 2.1 trillion kilowatthours in 1988.

In 1997, the 2.1 quadrillion Btu of biomass, geothermal energy, and solar energy produced in the U.S. and not used for generating electricity accounted for about 0.6% of world's primary energy production.

Major Energy Producers and Consumers

In 1997, three countries—the U.S., Russia, and China—were the leading producers and consumers of world energy. These three countries produced 39% and consumed 41% of the world's total energy.

The U.S., Russia, China, Saudi Arabia, and Canada were the world's five largest producers of energy in 1997, supplying 49.3% of the world's total energy. The next five leading producers of primary energy were the United Kingdom, Iran, Venezuela, Norway, and India, and together they supplied an additional 13% of the world's total energy. The U.S. supplied 72.3 quadrillion Btu of primary energy, significantly more than the 40.9 quadrillion Btu produced by Russia or the 36.2 quadrillion Btu produced by China.

The U.S., China, Russia, Japan, and Germany were the world's five largest consumers of primary energy in 1997, accounting for 50.8% of world energy consumption. They were followed by Canada, India, the United Kingdom, France, and

Italy, which together accounted for an additional 13.6% of world energy consumption. The U.S. consumed 94.2 quadrillion Btu, more than two and one-half times the 36.6 quadrillion Btu consumed by China, while Russia consumed 26.6 quadrillion Btu.

Regional Energy Production and Consumption

Comparisons of energy production and consumption by region help to highlight key energy trends since 1988. In North America, the overall production of energy rose by 11.9 quadrillion Btu between 1988 and 1997. The supply of natural gas and coal increased significantly, by 4.4 quadrillion Btu and 2.7 quadrillion Btu, respectively, more than offsetting a 1.9-quadrillion-Btu decrease in crude oil production. Energy consumption in North America increased by 16.3 quadrillion Btu between 1988 and 1997, the second largest increase for any region. The largest North American increases occurred in the consumption of natural gas, 4.9 quadrillion Btu, petroleum, 2.9 quadrillion Btu, and coal, 2.6 quadrillion Btu.

Overall production of energy in the Central and South America region increased by 8.9 quadrillion Btu between 1988 and 1997, led by increases in crude oil production, 5.3 quadrillion Btu, hydroelectric power generation, 1.7 quadrillion Btu, and natural gas production, 1.2 quadrillion Btu. Energy consumption in the Central and South America region increased by 5.1 quadrillion Btu over the same period. The largest increases occurred in the consumption of petroleum, 2.1 quadrillion Btu, hydroelectric power, 1.7 quadrillion Btu, and natural gas, 1.2 quadrillion Btu.

Energy production in Western Europe, which had fluctuated in a narrow range between 1988 and 1992, finally began to grow in 1993. In 1997, the level was 4.8 quadrillion Btu higher than in 1988. Gains between 1988 and 1997 were greatest for crude oil, 4.7 quadrillion Btu, natural gas, 3.1 quadrillion Btu, and nuclear electric power generation, 1.8 quadrillion Btu. These increases more than offset a decrease of 5.0 quadrillion Btu in coal production. Western European energy consumption increased by 5.5 quadrillion Btu between 1988 and 1997. The increase was led by natural gas, 4.6 quadrillion Btu, petroleum, 3.2 quadrillion Btu, and nuclear electric power, 1.8 quadrillion Btu, which

together more than offset a sharp, 4.1-quadrillion-Btu drop in coal consumption.

Between 1988 and 1997, both energy production and energy consumption in the Eastern Europe and Former U.S.S.R. region declined by more than 24 quadrillion Btu. As a result, this was the only region to experience declines in either total energy production or consumption over the period. The 25.2-quadrillion-Btu decline in energy production was concentrated in crude oil, 11.4 quadrillion Btu, coal, 8.7 quadrillion Btu, and natural gas, 4.7 quadrillion Btu. The 24.2-quadrillion-Btu decline in energy consumption included declines in petroleum, 10.3 quadrillion Btu, coal, 8.2 quadrillion Btu, and natural gas, 5.4 quadrillion Btu.

Since 1988, energy production in the Middle East increased by 15.9 quadrillion Btu, the second largest increase for any region. The increase was concentrated in crude oil. 12.4 quadrillion Btu, and natural gas, 2.9 quadrillion Btu. The increase in energy consumption in the Middle East between 1988 and 1997 was much smaller, only 4.8 quadrillion Btu. The largest consumption increases were in natural gas, 2.5 quadrillion Btu, and petroleum, 2.2 quadrillion Btu.

Energy production in Africa increased by 6.8 quadrillion Btu between 1988 and 1997, led by increases in the production of crude oil, 4.2 quadrillion Btu, and natural gas, 1.4 quadrillion Btu. Energy consumption in Africa grew more slowly over the same period, rising by only 2.2 quadrillion Btu, with petroleum consumption accounting for 1.3 quadrillion Btu of the increase and natural gas for 0.6 quadrillion Btu.

The largest regional increase in primary energy production between 1988 and 1997 occurred in the Far East and Oceania region, where production increased by 22.5 quadrillion Btu. 55% of this increase, 12.4 quadrillion Btu, was accounted for by coal production, with smaller contributions from natural gas, 4.1 quadrillion Btu, and crude oil, 2.7 quadrillion Btu. Consumption in this region increased by 33 quadrillion Btu over the same period, also the largest increase for any region. 78% of this increase occurred in the combined consumption of petroleum, 14.5 quadrillion Btu, and coal, 11.4 quadrillion Btu. At the same time, natural gas consumption increased by 4.2 quadrillion Btu.

Petroleum

Global production of petroleum (crude oil and natural gas plant liquids) increased by 9.0 million barrels per day between 1988 and 1997, an average annual rate of growth of 1.5%. Saudi Arabia, the U.S., and Russia were the three largest producers of petroleum in 1997. Together, they produced 32.8% of the world's petroleum. Production from Iran and Venezuela accounted for an additional 10.0%.

In 1997, the U.S. consumed 18.6 million barrels per day of petroleum—almost 26% of world consumption. Japan ranked a distant second in consumption, with 5.7 million barrels per day, followed by China, Germany, and Russia.

Natural Gas

World production of dry natural gas increased by 11.9 trillion cubic feet, or at an average annual rate of 1.8%, over the period from 1988 to 1997. Russia was the leading producer in 1997 at 20.2 trillion cubic feet, followed by the U.S. at 18.9 trillion cubic

---

Energy Web Sites

U.S. Department of Energy: www.doe.gov
Energy Efficiency and Renewable Energy Network (EREN): www.eren.doe.gov
Federal Energy Regulatory Commission: www.ferc.fed.us
Energy Information Administration (EIA): www.eia.doe.gov
Nuclear Regulatory Commission (NRC): www.nrc.gov
National Renewable Energy Laboratory (NREL): www.nrel.gov
Alliance to Save Energy: www.ase.org
Natural Resources Defense Council: www.nrdc.org
American Council for an Energy-Efficient Economy: www.aceee.org
Center for Renewable Energy and Sustainable Technology (CREST)–Solstice: www.solstice.crest.org

feet. Together these two countries produced 48% of the world total. Canada ranked a distant third in production at 5.9 trillion cubic feet, followed by the United Kingdom and the Netherlands, with 3.2 and 3.0 trillion cubic feet, respectively. These three countries accounted for 15% of the world total.

In 1997, the U.S., which was the leading consumer of dry natural gas at 22.0 trillion cubic feet, and Russia, which ranked second at 13.4 trillion cubic feet, together accounted for 43% of world consumption. Germany ranked a distant third in consumption, with 3.4 trillion cubic feet, followed by the United Kingdom and Canada, at 3.2 and 3.0 trillion cubic feet, respectively.

Coal

Coal was the only primary energy source to experience a production decline between 1988 and 1997. Production decreased by 16 million short tons over the period. China was the leading producer in 1997 at 1.55 billion short tons—equivalent to 26.6 quadrillion Btu. The U.S. was the second leading producer in 1997 with 1.09 billion short tons—equivalent to 23.2 quadrillion Btu. India ranked a distant third at 329 million short tons—equivalent to 6.0 quadrillion Btu, followed by Australia, at 293 million short tons—equivalent to 5.4 quadrillion Btu, and Russia at 288 million short tons—equivalent to 4.7 quadrillion Btu. Together, these five countries accounted for 68% of world coal production in 1997.

China was also the largest consumer of coal in 1997, using 1.53 billion short tons, followed by the U.S., which consumed 1.03 billion short tons, India, Russia, and Germany. These five countries together accounted for 66% of world coal consumption.

Hydroelectric Power

The generation of hydroelectric power increased by 430 billion kilowatthours between 1988 and 1997, or at an average annual rate of 2.1%. The U.S., Canada, Brazil, China, and Russia, were the five largest producers of hydroelectric power in

1997. Their combined hydroelectric power generation accounted for 51% of the world total. The U.S. led the world with 356 billion kilowatthours or 3.7 quadrillion Btu. Canada was a close second with 348 billion kilowatthours or 3.6 quadrillion Btu. Brazil ranked third with 276 billion kilowatthours or 2.9 quadrillion Btu. China was fourth with 175 billion kilowatthours or 1.8 quadrillion Btu, followed by Russia with 151 billion kilowatthours or 1.6 quadrillion Btu.

Nuclear Electric Power

The generation of nuclear electric power increased by 473 billion kilowatthours between 1988 and 1997, or at an average annual rate of 2.6%. The U.S. led the world in nuclear electric power generation in 1997 with 629 billion kilowatthours or 6.7 quadrillion Btu. France was second with 374 billion kilowatthours or 3.9 quadrillion Btu and Japan ranked third with 306 billion kilowatthours or 3.1 quadrillion Btu. In 1997, these three countries generated 58% of the world's nuclear electric power.

Geothermal, Solar, and Wind Electric Power

The generation of geothermal, solar, and wind electric power increased by 96 billion kilowatthours between 1988 and 1997, or at an average annual rate of 16%. (Note: Part of this increase is a result of a discontinuity in the geothermal, solar, and wind electric power time series for the U.S. between 1989 and 1990. Beginning in 1990, the generation of biomass, geothermal, solar,and wind electric power by nonutility power producers is included.) The U.S. led the world in geothermal, solar, and wind electric power generation in 1997 with 86.8 billion kilowatthours. Brazil was second with 9.4 billion kilowatthours, followed by the Philippines with 5.9 billion kilowatthours, Mexico with 5.2 billion kilowatthours, and Italy with 4.5 billion kilowatthours. These five countries accounted for 85% of the world's geothermal, solar, and wind electric power generation in 1997.

Renewable Energy Consumption in the U.S. by Source, 1990–1997
(quadrillion Btu)

Year	Biofuels[1]	Geothermal energy[2]	Conventional hydroelectric power[3, 4]	Solar energy[5]	Wind energy[6]	Total
1990	2.632	r0.355	r3.123	r0.063	0.023	r6.197
1991	2.642	r0.365	r3.205	r0.066	0.027	r6.304
1992	2.788	r0.379	r2.863	0.068	0.030	r6.128
1993	2.784	r0.393	r3.147	r0.071	0.031	r6.426
1994	2.838	r0.395	r2.969	r0.072	0.036	r6.309
1995	r2.846	r0.339	r3.472	r0.073	0.033	r6.763
1996	r2.938	r0.352	r3.914	0.075	r0.035	r7.315
1997e	2.723	0.366	3.942	0.075	0.039	7.145

1. Wood, wood waste, wood liquors, peat, railroad ties, wood sludge, spent sulfite liquors, agricultural waste, straw, tires, fish oils, tall oil, sludge waste, waste alcohol, municipal solid waste, landfill gases, other waste, and ethanol blended into motor gasoline. 2. Includes electricity imports from Mexico that are derived from geothermal energy. Includes grid-connected electricity, and geothermal heat pump and direct use energy. Excludes shaft power and remote electrical power. 3. Hydroelectricity generated by pumped storage is not included in renewable energy. 4. Includes electricity net imports from Canada that are derived from hydroelectric power. 5. Includes solar thermal and photovoltaic energy. 6. Includes only grid-connected electricity. Excludes direct heat applications. r = revised. e = estimated. Source: Energy Information Administration (EIA), Office of Coal, Nuclear, Electric and Alternative Fuels estimates, and Oregon Institute of Technology.

World Net Electricity Consumption by Region, 1990–2020
(billion kilowatthours)

Region	History		Projections					Average annual percent change, 1996–2020
	1990	1996	2000	2005	2010	2015	2020	
Industrialized countries	**6,248**	**7,194**	**7,529**	**8,298**	**9,001**	**9,749**	**10,485**	**1.6%**
United States	2,713	3,243	3,333	3,585	3,843	4,113	4,345	1.2
Eastern Europe/	1,908	1,535	1,396	1,536	1,673	1,813	1,965	1.0
Former Soviet Union								
Developing countries	**2,274**	**3,324**	**3,895**	**5,033**	**6,282**	**7,695**	**9,422**	**4.4**
Developing Asia	1,268	2,002	2,350	3,105	3,937	4,918	6,122	4.8
China	551	925	1,107	1,520	2,030	2,672	3,486	5.7
India	257	378	493	644	802	981	1,192	4.9
South Korea	95	181	190	237	285	335	387	3.2
Other developing Asia	365	519	560	704	819	930	1,056	3.0
Central and South America	449	604	735	950	1,182	1,421	1,728	4.5
Total world	**10,431**	**12,053**	**12,821**	**14,868**	**16,956**	**19,257**	**21,872**	**2.5**

Sources: Energy Information Administration (EIA): *International Energy Annual 1996,* DOE/EIA-0219(96), and World Energy Projection System (1999).

World Natural Gas Reserves by Country as of Jan. 1, 1999

Country	Reserves (trillion cubic feet)	Percent of world total	Country	Reserves (trillion cubic feet)	Percent of world total
World	**5,145**	**100.0%**	Turkmenistan	101	2.0%
Top 20 countries	**4,579**	**89.0**	Malaysia	82	1.6
Russian Federation	1,700	33.0	Indonesia	72	1.4
Iran	812	15.8	Uzbekistan	66	1.3
Qatar	300	5.8	Kazakhstan	65	1.3
United Arab Emirates	212	4.1	Canada	64	1.2
Saudi Arabia	204	4.0	Mexico	63	1.2
United States	167	3.3	Netherlands	63	1.2
Venezuela	143	2.8	Kuwait	52	1.0
Algeria	130	2.5	China	48	0.9
Nigeria	124	2.4	**Rest of world**	**566**	**11.0**
Iraq	110	2.1			

Source: "Worldwide Look at Reserves and Production," *Oil & Gas Journal,* Vol. 96, No. 52 (Dec. 28, 1998), pp. 38–39.

Motor Vehicle Fuel Consumption and Travel in the U.S.

	1960	1965	1970	1975	1980	1985	1990	1995	1996
Number registered (thousands)[1]									
Passenger car	61,671	75,258	89,244	106,706	121,601	127,885	133,700	128,387	129,728
Total	73,858	90,358	111,242	137,913	161,490	177,133	193,057	205,427	210,236
Vehicle-miles traveled (millions)									
Passenger car	587,000	723,000	917,000	1,034,000	1,112,000	1,247,000	1,408,000	1,438,000	1,468,000
Total	719,000	888,000	1,110,000	1,328,000	1,527,000	1,775,000	2,144,000	2,423,000	2,482,000
Fuel consumed (million gallons)									
Passenger car	41,171	49,723	67,819	74,140	69,982	71,518	69,568	68,072	68,897
Total	57,880	71,104	92,329	108,984	114,960	121,301	130,755	143,834	146,676
Average miles traveled per vehicle (thousands)									
Passenger car	9.5	9.6	10.3	9.7	9.1	9.7	10.5	11.2	11.3
Total	9.7	9.8	10.0	9.6	9.5	10.0	11.1	11.8	11.8
Average miles traveled per gallon									
Passenger car	14.3	14.5	13.5	13.9	15.9	17.4	20.2	21.1	21.3
Total	12.4	12.5	12.0	12.2	13.3	14.6	16.4	16.8	16.9
Average fuel consumed per vehicle (gallons)									
Passenger car	668	661	760	695	576	559	520	530	531
Total	784	787	830	790	712	685	677	700	698

1. Includes personal passenger vehicles, buses, and motor trucks. *Source:* U.S. Department of Transportation.

Major Air Pollutants

Pollutant	Sources	Effects
Ozone. A gas that can be found in two places. Near the ground (the troposphere), it is a major part of smog. Higher in the air (the stratosphere), it helps block radiation from the sun.	Ozone is not created directly, but is formed when nitrogen oxides and volatile organic compounds mix in sunlight. That is why ozone is mostly found in the summer. Nitrogen oxides come from burning gasoline, coal, or other fossil fuels. There are many types of volatile organic compounds, and they come from sources ranging from factories to trees.	Ozone near the ground can cause a number of health problems. Ozone can lead to more frequent asthma attacks in people who have asthma and can cause sore throats, coughs, and breathing difficulty. It may even lead to premature death. Ozone can also hurt plants and crops.
Carbon monoxide. A gas that comes from the burning of fossil fuels, mostly in cars. It cannot be seen or smelled.	Carbon monoxide is released when engines burn fossil fuels. Emissions are higher when engines are not tuned properly, and when fuel is not completely burned. Cars emit a lot of the carbon monoxide found outdoors. Furnaces and heaters in the home can emit high concentrations of carbon monoxide, too, if they are not properly maintained.	Carbon monoxide makes it hard for body parts to get the oxygen they need to run correctly. Exposure to carbon monoxide makes people feel dizzy and tired, and gives them headaches. Elderly people with heart disease are hospitalized more often when they are exposed to higher amounts of carbon monoxide.
Nitrogen dioxide. A reddish-brown gas that comes from the burning of fossil fuels. It has a strong smell at high levels.	Nitrogen dioxide mostly comes from power plants and cars. Nitrogen dioxide is formed in two ways—when nitrogen in the fuel is burned, or when nitrogen in the air reacts with oxygen at very high temperatures. Nitrogen dioxide can also react in the atmosphere to form ozone, acid rain, and particles.	High levels of nitrogen dioxide exposure can give people coughs and can make them feel short of breath. People who are exposed to nitrogen dioxide for a long time have a higher chance of getting respiratory infections. Acid rain can hurt plants and animals, and can make lakes dangerous to swim in or fish in.
Particulate matter. Solid or liquid matter that is suspended in the air. To remain in the air, particles are usually less than 0.1 mm wide, and can be as small as 0.00005 mm.	Particulate matter can be divided into two types—coarse particles and fine particles. Coarse particles are bigger than 0.002 mm, and are formed from sources like road dust, sea spray, and construction. Fine particles are smaller than 0.002 mm, and are formed when fuel is burned in automobiles and power plants.	Particulate matter that is small enough can enter the lungs and cause health problems. Some of these problems include: more frequent asthma attacks, more trips to the hospital for respiratory problems, and premature death. Particulate matter can also make clothes and other materials dirty.
Sulfur dioxide. A corrosive gas that cannot be seen or smelled at low levels but can have a "rotten egg" smell at high levels.	Sulfur dioxide mostly comes from the burning of coal or oil in power plants. It also comes from plants that make chemicals, paper, or fuel. Like nitrogen dioxide, sulfur dioxide also reacts in the atmosphere to form acid rain and particles.	Sulfur dioxide exposure can affect people who have asthma or emphysema by making it more difficult for them to breathe. It can also irritate people's eyes, noses, and throats. Sulfur dioxide can harm trees and crops, damage buildings, and make it harder for people to see long distances.
Lead. A blue-gray metal that is very toxic and is found in a number of forms and locations.	Outside, lead comes from cars in areas where unleaded gasoline is not used. Lead can also come from power plants and other industrial sources. Inside, lead paint is an important source of lead, especially in houses where paint is peeling. Lead in old pipes can also be a source of lead in drinking water.	High amounts of lead can be dangerous for small children, and can lead to lower IQs and kidney problems. For adults, exposure to lead can increase the chance of having heart attacks or strokes.
Toxic air pollutants. A large number of chemicals that are known or suspected to cause cancer. Some important pollutants in this category include arsenic, asbestos, benzene, and dioxin.	Each toxic air pollutant comes from a slightly different source, but many are created in chemical plants or are emitted when fossil fuels are burned. Some toxic air pollutants, like asbestos and formaldehyde, can be found in building materials and can lead to indoor air problems. Many toxic air pollutants can also enter the food and water supply, and people can be exposed when they eat or drink.	Toxic air pollutants can cause cancer. Some toxic air pollutants can also cause birth defects. Other effects depend on the pollutant, but can include skin and eye irritation and breathing problems.

Pollutant	Sources	Effects
Stratospheric ozone depleters. Chemicals that can destroy the ozone in the stratosphere. These chemicals include chlorofluorocarbons (CFCs), halons, and other compounds that include chlorine or bromine.	CFCs are used in air conditioners and refrigerators, since they work well as coolants. They can also be found in aerosol cans and fire extinguishers. Other stratospheric ozone depleters are used as solvents in industry.	If the ozone in the stratosphere is destroyed, people are exposed to more radiation from the sun (ultraviolet radiation). This can lead to skin cancer and eye problems. Higher ultraviolet radiation can also harm plants and animals.
Greenhouse gases. Gases that stay in the air for a long time, and warm up the planet by trapping sunlight. This is called the "greenhouse effect" because the gases act like the glass in a greenhouse. Some of the important greenhouse gases are carbon dioxide, methane, and nitrous oxide.	Carbon dioxide is the most important greenhouse gas, and it comes from the burning of fossil fuels in cars, power plants, houses, and industry. Methane is released during the processing of fossil fuels, and also comes from natural sources like cows and rice paddies. Nitrous oxide comes from industrial sources and decaying plants.	The greenhouse effect can lead to changes in the climate of the planet. Some of these changes might include more temperature extremes, higher sea levels, changes in forest composition, and damage to land near the coast. Human health might be affected by diseases that are related to temperature, or by damage to land and water.

Source: Jonathan Levy, Harvard School of Public Health. Based on information provided by the Environmental Protection Agency.

Largest Nuclear Power Plants in the U.S.

Plant	Operating utility	Capacity (net MWe)	Year operative
Palo Verde 3, Ariz.	Arizona Public Service	1262	1987
Palo Verde 1, Ariz.	Arizona Public Service	1258	1985
Palo Verde 2, Ariz.	Arizona Public Service	1258	1986
South Texas 1, Tex.	Houston Lighting & Power	1250	1988
South Texas 2, Tex.	Houston Lighting & Power	1250	1989
Grand Gulf 1, Miss.	System Energy Resources	1200	1984
Washington 2, Wash.	General Electric Company	1170	1984
Perry 1, Ohio	Cleveland Electric Illuminating	1169	1986
Vogtle 2, Ga.	Georgia Power	1169	1989
Vogtle 1, Ga.	Georgia Power	1164	1987
Wolf Creek, Kans.	Wolf Creek Nuclear Operating	1163	1985
Seabrook 1, N.H.	Public Service of N.H.	1162	1990
Comanche Peak 1, Tex.	Texas Utilities	1150	1990
Comanche Peak 2, Tex.	Texas Utilities	1150	1993
Callaway, Mo.	Union Electric	1143	1984
Nine Mile Point 2, N.Y.	Niagara Mohawk	1136	1987
Catawba 1, S.C.	Duke Power Co.	1129	1985
Catawba 2, S.C.	Duke Power Co.	1129	1986
McGuire 1, N.C.	Duke Power Co.	1129	1981
McGuire 2, N.C.	Duke Power Co.	1129	1983
Byron 1, Ill.	Commonwealth Edison	1120	1985
Byron 2, Ill.	Commonwealth Edison	1120	1987
Millstone 3, Conn.	Northeast Nuclear Energy	1120	1986
Sequoyah 1, Tenn.	Tennessee Valley Authority	1119	1980
Sequoyah 2, Tenn.	Tennessee Valley Authority	1119	1981

Source: Department of Energy, Energy Information Administration.

Oil in the Caspian Region

Source: Based on data from the Dept. of Energy, Energy Information Administration.

To members of the energy industry, the breakup of the Soviet Union in 1991 had implications that extended far beyond politics. Lying under and around the Caspian Sea is an expanse of oil reserves that will bring big profits to those who are crafty enough to position themselves in the region. High-ranking political figures and oil executives alike are jumping into the game as the nations comprising this new frontier explore their many lucrative options.

The nations in the Caspian region—notably Azerbaijan, Kazakhstan, and Turkmenistan, and to a lesser degree Russia, Iran, and Uzbekistan—are believed to be sitting on what amounts to 10% of the earth's potential oil reserves. Proven reserves total approximately 16–32 billion barrels of oil, with a possible additional 100–300 billion barrels not yet proven. Thanks to the Soviet Union's collapse, the world has gained the opportunity to share in one of the planet's greatest supplies of natural resources.

Major operations cannot get under way in Azerbaijan, Kazakhstan, and Turkmenistan without expensive improvements in the infrastructure and equipment. To help defray costs, the countries are busy scouting out international partners for development of the reserves and for construction of much-needed new pipelines.

Turkmenistan, in desperate need of money and at odds with Russia, has begun negotiations for the construction of an oil pipeline to Turkey. Iranian, British, and Chinese companies have begun developing some oil reserves, and American companies are working on development plans. Turkmenistan has also been granted loans by foreign banks to modernize the country's domestic natural gas pipeline network.

Economic woes have plagued Kazakhstan in the late 1990s as well, forcing the country to relinquish a great deal of control over its oil development to foreign companies. A consortium of American and Russian oil companies is currently producing about one third of Kazakhstan's oil.

While the construction of a pipeline to Russia is expected to be completed in 2001, Kazakhstan hopes to be able to extend its interests beyond the Russian influence by building a second new pipeline to another nearby country. The U.S. and its Western friends have that same hope, which may yet be realized.

Azerbaijan has attracted the most attention from foreign investors, largely due to the efforts of shrewd, pro-Western President Haydar Aliyev to fortify his nation's role on the world stage. In September 1994, the Azerbaijan International Oil Consortium signed an $8 billion, 30-year contract that some labeled "the deal of the century." Under the contract, three Caspian Sea oil fields with reserves of about 3–5 billion barrels are being developed.

Where this Azeri oil will end up is perhaps the hottest question being thrown around in the Caspian region and on the world stage.

One faction in the oil debate argues that a line to Iran is the most economical solution, given the short distance and the nation's well developed oil production and exporting capabilities. The U.S. has adamantly opposed this option, though, due to existing American sanctions that would make it difficult for the Western giant to claim a stake in Caspian oil. Politically speaking, many world leaders would also like to see the oil distributed away from the volatile Middle East, which already controls the bulk of the world's supply.

The alternatives, however, are not much more attractive. The plan for Azerbaijan that has been heavily pushed by the Clinton administration involves building a pipeline through Georgia and NATO ally Turkey to the Mediterranean. Such a long pipeline would be very costly and less efficient than constructing one through a country closer to Azerbaijan. The option of building a new line to Russia has also received resistance from the U.S., which would like to keep Russian dominance over the region to a minimum. Another plan on the drawing board involves building a long pipeline east to China.

As world leaders squabble and oil companies compete for development rights, three young nations enjoy their good fortune and a newfound influence brought on by their Caspian treasure.

Animals and Nature

Gestation, Incubation, and Longevity of Certain Animals

Animal	Gestation or incubation, in days & (average)	Longevity, in years & (record exceptions)	Animal	Gestation or incubation, in days & (average)	Longevity, in years & (record exceptions)
Ass	365	18-20 (63)	Horse	329-345 (336)	20-25 (50+)
Bear	180-240[1]	15-30 (47)	Human	253-303	([2])
Cat	52-69 (63)	10-12 (26+)	Kangaroo	32-39[1]	4-6 (23)
Chicken	22	7-8 (14)	Lion	105-113 (108)	10 (29)
Cow	280	9-12 (39)	Monkey	139-270[1]	12-15[1] (29)
Deer	197-300[1]	10-15 (26)	Mouse	19-31[1]	1-3 (4)
Dog	53-71 (63)	10-12 (24)	Parakeet (Budgerigar)	17-20 (18)	8 (12+)
Duck	21-35[1] (28)	10 (15)	Pig	101-130 (115)	10 (22)
Elephant	510-730[1] (624)	30-40 (71)	Pigeon	11-19	10-12 (39)
Fox	51-63[1]	8-10 (14)	Rabbit	30-35 (31)	6-8 (15)
Goat	136-160 (151)	12 (17)	Rat	21	3 (5)
Groundhog	31-32	4-9	Sheep	144-152[1]	12 (16)
Guinea pig	58-75 (68)	3 (6)	Squirrel	44	8-9 (15)
Hamster, golden	15-17	2 (8)	Whale	365-547[1]	—
Hippopotamus	220-255 (240)	30 (49+)	Wolf	60-63	10-12 (16)

1. Depending on kind. 2. For life expectancy charts, *see* Expectation of Life by Sex. *Source:* James G. Doherty, General Curator, The Wildlife Conservation Society.

Animal Names: Male, Female, and Young

Animal	Male	Female	Young	Animal	Male	Female	Young	Animal	Male	Female	Young
Ass	Jack	Jenny	Foal	Duck	Drake	Duck	Duckling	Sheep	Ram	Ewe	Lamb
Bear	Boar	Sow	Cub	Elephant	Bull	Cow	Calf	Swan	Cob	Pen	Cygnet
Cat	Tom	Queen	Kitten	Fox	Dog	Vixen	Cub	Swine	Boar	Sow	Piglet
Cattle	Bull	Cow	Calf	Goose	Gander	Goose	Gosling	Tiger	Tiger	Tigress	Cub
Chicken	Rooster	Hen	Chick	Horse	Stallion	Mare	Foal	Whale	Bull	Cow	Calf
Deer	Buck	Doe	Fawn	Lion	Lion	Lioness	Cub	Wolf	Dog	Bitch	Pup
Dog	Dog	Bitch	Pup	Rabbit	Buck	Doe	Bunny				

Source: James G. Doherty, General Curator, The Wildlife Conservation Society.

Animal Group Terminology

Source: James G. Doherty, General Curator, The Wildlife Conservation Society.

ants: colony
bears: sleuth, sloth
bees: grist, hive, swarm
birds: flight, volery
cattle: drove
cats: clutter, clowder
chicks: brood, clutch
clams: bed
cranes: sedge, seige
crows: murder
doves: dule
ducks: brace, team
elephants: herd
elks: gang
finches: charm
fish: school, shoal, draught
foxes: leash, skulk
geese: flock, gaggle, skein
gnats: cloud, horde
goats: trip

gorillas: band
hares: down, husk
hawks: cast
hens: brood
hogs: drift
horses: pair, team
hounds: cry, mute, pack
kangaroos: troop
kittens: kindle, litter
larks: exaltation
lions: pride
locusts: plague
magpies: tidings
mules: span
nightingales: watch
oxen: yoke
oysters: bed
parrots: company
partridges: covey

peacocks: muster, ostentation
pheasants: nest, bouquet
pigs: litter
ponies: string
quail: bevy, covey
rabbits: nest
seals: pod
sheep: drove, flock
sparrows: host
storks: mustering
swans: bevy, wedge
swine: sounder
toads: knot
turkeys: rafter
turtles: bale
vipers: nest
whales: gam, pod
wolves: pack, route
woodcocks: fall

Speed of Animals

Most of the following measurements are for maximum speeds over approximate quarter-mile distances. Exceptions—which are included to give a wide range of animals—are the lion and elephant, whose speeds were clocked in the act of charging; the whippet, which was timed over a 200-yard course; the cheetah over a 100-yard distance; humans for a 15-yard segment of a 100-yard run; and the black mamba, six-lined race runner, spider, giant tortoise, three-toed sloth, and garden snail, which were measured over various small distances.

Animal	Speed (mph)	Animal	Speed (mph)	Animal	Speed (mph)
Cheetah	70.00	Mongolian wild ass	40.00	Human	27.89
Pronghorn antelope	61.00	Greyhound	39.35	Elephant	25.00
Wildebeest	50.00	Whippet	35.50	Black mamba snake	20.00
Lion	50.00	Rabbit (domestic)	35.00	Six-lined race runner	18.00
Thomson's gazelle	50.00	Mule deer	35.00	Squirrel	12.00
Quarter horse	47.50	Jackal	35.00	Pig (domestic)	11.00
Elk	45.00	Reindeer	32.00	Chicken	9.00
Cape hunting dog	45.00	Giraffe	32.00	Spider (Tegenearia atrica)	1.17
Coyote	43.00	White-tailed deer	30.00	Giant Tortoise	0.17
Gray fox	42.00	Wart hog	30.00	Three-toed sloth	0.15
Hyena	40.00	Grizzly bear	30.00	Garden snail	0.03
Zebra	40.00	Cat (domestic)	30.00		

Source: Natural History Magazine, March 1974, copyright 1974. The American Museum of Natural History; and James G. Doherty, General Curator, The Wildlife Conservation Society.

America's 10 Most Endangered Rivers of 1999

Rank	River	State(s)	Threat(s)
1.	Lower Snake River	Wash.	Federal dams
2.	Missouri River	Mont., N.D., S.D., Neb., Iowa, Kans., Mo.	Channelization, dams, bank stabilization, poor grazing practices
3.	Alabama-Coosa-Tallapoosa River Basin	Ga., Ala.	Sprawl, water withdrawals, pollution, dams
4.	Upper San Pedro River	Ariz. and Sonora, Mex.	Sprawl, groundwater pumping
5.	Yellowstone River	Mont., N.D.	Bank stabilization, flood control
6.	Cedar River	Wash.	Sprawl, water withdrawals
7.	Fox River	Ill., Wis.	Sprawl, pollution, state agency inaction
8.	Carmel River	Calif.	Sprawl, water withdrawals, dams
9.	Coal River	W.Va.	Mountaintop removal coal mining
10.	Bear River	Utah	Sprawl, water withdrawals, proposed dam

Source: American Rivers, *America's Most Endangered Rivers of 1999* (annual report).

Threatened and Endangered Species

Source: U.S. Fish and Wildlife Service, Dept. of the Interior.

Group	Endangered[1] U.S.	Endangered[1] Foreign	Threatened[2] U.S.	Threatened[2] Foreign	Total listings[3]	Species with recovery plans[4]
Mammals	61	251	8	16	336	49
Birds	75	178	15	6	274	77
Reptiles	14	65	21	14	114	30
Amphibians	9	8	8	1	26	11
Fishes	69	11	41	0	121	88
Snails	18	1	10	0	29	20
Clams	61	2	8	0	71	45
Crustaceans	17	0	3	0	20	12
Insects	28	4	9	0	41	27
Arachnids	5	0	0	0	5	5
Flowering plants	540	1	132	0	673	494
Conifers	2	0	1	2	5	2
Ferns & others	26	0	2	0	28	26
Total	**925**	**521**	**258[5]**	**39**	**1,743**	**886**

NOTE: As of June 30, 1999. 1. *Endangered species* are those in danger of extinction. 2. *Threatened species* are those likely to become an endangered species within the foreseeable future. 3. Separate populations of a species listed both as endangered and threatened are tallied only once, for the endangered population (except the olive ridley sea turtle, for which only the threatened U.S. population is tallied). Those species are the argali, leopard, gray wolf, piping plover, roseate tern, chimpanzee, green sea turtle, Stellar sea lion, saltwater crocodile, bull trout, chinook salmon, and steelhead. 4. There are 519 approved recovery plans sponsored by the endangered species program of the U.S. Fish and Wildlife Service. They are dedicated to restoring species to a secure status in the wild. Some recovery plans cover more than one species, and a few species have separate plans covering different parts of their ranges. Recovery plans are drawn up only for species in the United States. 5. Nine U.S. animal species have dual status (eight within the U.S.).

Water Supply of the World

The Antarctic Icecap is the largest supply of fresh water, nearly 2% of the world's total of fresh and salt water. As can be seen from the table below, the amount of water in our atmosphere is over ten times as large as the water in all the rivers taken together.

The fresh water actually available for human use in lakes and rivers and the accessible ground water amounts to only about one third of one percent of the world's total water supply.

	Surface area (square miles)	Volume (cubic miles)	Percentage of total[1]
Salt Water			
The oceans	139,500,000	317,000,000	97.2
Inland seas and saline lakes	270,000	25,000	0.008
Fresh Water			
Freshwater lakes	330,000	30,000	0.009
All rivers (average level)	—	300	0.0001
Antarctic Icecap	6,000,000	6,300,000	1.9
Arctic Icecap and glaciers	900,000	680,000	0.21
Water in the atmosphere	197,000,000	3,100	0.001
Ground water within half a mile from surface	—	1,000,000	0.31
Deep-lying ground water	—	1,000,000	0.31
Total (rounded)	—	**326,000,000**	**100.00**

1. All figures are estimated. *Source:* Department of the Interior, Geological Survey.

National Forest System, 1900–1997

Year	Number of forests	Area (million acres)	Year	Number of forests	Area (million acres)
1900	38	46.52	1960	151	180.84
1905	83	75.35	1965	154	182.14
1910	149	168.03	1970	154	182.57
1915	162	162.77	1975	155	183.28
1920	152	156.03	1980	155	183.06
1925	159	158.40	1985	156	186.32
1930	149	160.09	1992	156	187.11
1935	142	163.31	1993	155	187.23
1940	160	174.77	1994	155	187.27
1945	155	177.64	1995	155	187.24
1950	151	179.69	1996	155	187.28
1955	149	180.30	1997	155	187.42

Source: U.S. Dept. of Agriculture, Forest Service. *Land Areas of the National Forest System.*

Top Twenty Most Visited National Park Sites, 1998

Rank	Name and location	Number of visitors	Rank	Name and location	Number of visitors
1.	Blue Ridge Parkway, Va.-N.C.	19,026,498	10.	Cape Cod National Seashore, Mass.	4,804,185
2.	Golden Gate National Recreation Area, Calif.	14,046,590	11.	Vietnam Veterans Memorial, D.C.	4,687,299
3.	Great Smoky Mountains National Park, Tenn.	9,989,395	12.	Castle Clinton National Monument, N.Y.	4,390,268
4.	Lake Mead National Recreation Area, Nev.-Az.	8,788,055	13.	Lincoln Memorial, D.C.	4,368,912
5.	Gateway National Recreation Area, N.Y.-N.J.	7,124,022	14.	Gulf Islands National Seashore, Fla.-Miss.	4,293,301
6.	George Washington Memorial Parkway, Va.-M.D.-D.C.	6,584,802	15.	Franklin Delano Roosevelt Memorial, D.C.	4,258,807
7.	Natchez Trace Parkway, Miss.-Ala.-Tenn.	5,810,094	16.	Grand Canyon National Park, Ariz.	4,239,682
8.	Statue of Liberty National Monument, N.Y.-N.J.	5,200,633	17.	Yosemite National Park, Calif.	3,657,132
			18.	Olympic National Park, Wash.	3,577,007
9.	Delaware Water Gap National Recreation Area, Pa.-N.J.	5,019,175	19.	San Francisco Maritime National Historical Park, Calif.	3,535,081
			20.	Cuyahoga Valley National Recreation Area, Ohio	3,467,107

Source: Department of the Interior, National Park Service. www.nps.gov

The National Park System

Source: Department of the Interior, National Park Service.

The National Park System of the United States is administered by the National Park Service, a bureau of the Department of the Interior. Started with the establishment of Yellowstone National Park on March 1, 1872, the system includes not only the most extraordinary and spectacular scenic exhibits in the United States, but also a large number of sites distinguished either for their historic or prehistoric importance or scientific interest, or for their superior recreational assets. The National Park System is made up of 375 areas covering more than 83 million acres in every state except Delaware. It also includes areas in the District of Columbia, American Samoa, Guam, Puerto Rico, and the Virgin Islands. A list of the areas follows. Note that the National Park System does not include the Affiliated Areas, National Heritage Areas, Wild and Scenic Rivers System, and the National Trails System. See also the excellent Web site of the Park Service: www.nps.gov.

NOTE: n.a. means "not available."

NATIONAL PARKS

Name, location, and year authorized	Acreage	Outstanding characteristics
Acadia (Maine), 1919	46,998.43	Rugged seashore on Mt. Desert Island and adjacent mainland
Arches (Utah), 1971	73,378.98	Unusual stone arches, windows, pedestals caused by erosion (Park was a National Monument 1929–1971)
Badlands (S.D.), 1978	242,755.94	Arid land of fossils, prairie, bison, deer, bighorn sheep, antelope (Park was a National Monument 1929–1978)
Big Bend (Tex.), 1935	801,163.21	Mountains and desert bordering the Rio Grande
Biscayne (Fla.), 1980	172,924.07	Aquatic, coral reef park south of Miami (Park was a National Monument, 1968–1980)
Bryce Canyon (Utah), 1924	35,835.08	Area of grotesque eroded rocks brilliantly colored
Canyonlands (Utah), 1964	337,570.43	Colorful wilderness with impressive red-rock canyons, spires, arches
Capitol Reef (Utah), 1971	241,904.26	Highly colored sedimentary rock formations in high, narrow gorges (Park was a National Monument 1937–1971)
Carlsbad Caverns (N.M.), 1930	46,766.45	One of the world's largest known caves
Channel Islands (Calif.), 1980	249,353.77	Area is rich in marine mammals, sea birds, endangered species, and archeology (Park was a National Monument 1938–1980)
Crater Lake (Ore.), 1902	183,224.05	Deep blue lake in heart of inactive volcano
Death Valley (Calif.-Nev.), 1994	3,367,627.68	Largest desert, surrounded by high mountains, containing the lowest point in the Western hemisphere (Park was a National Monument 1933–1994)
Denali (Alaska), 1917	4,741,800.00	Contains Mt. McKinley, N. America's highest mountain (20,320 ft.) (Formerly Mt. McKinley National Park, 1917–1980)
Dry Tortugas (Fla.), 1992	64,700.00	Located 70 miles off Key West. Features an underwater nature trail (Formerly Ft. Jefferson National Monument 1935–1992)
Everglades (Fla.), 1934	1,507,850.00	Subtropical area with abundant bird and animal life
Gates of the Arctic (Alaska), 1980	7,523,898.00	Diverse north central wilderness contains part of Brooks Range
Glacier (Mont.), 1910	1,013,572.42	Rocky Mountain scenery with many glaciers and lakes

Name, location, and year authorized	Acreage	Outstanding characteristics
Glacier Bay (Alaska), 1980	3,224,794.00	Popular for wildlife, whale-watching, glacier-calving, and scenery (Park was a National Monument 1925–1980)
Grand Canyon (Ariz.), 1919	1,217,158.32	Mile-deep gorge, 4 to 18 miles wide, 217 miles long
Grand Teton (Wyo.), 1929	309,994.72	Picturesque range of high mountain peaks
Great Basin (Nev.), 1986	77,180.00	Exceptional scenic, biologic, and geologic attractions (Formerly Lehman Caves National Monument 1922–1986)
Great Smoky Mts. (N.C.-Tenn), 1926	521,621.00	Highest mountain range east of Black Hills; luxuriant plant life
Guadalupe Mountains (Tex.), 1966	86,415.97	Contains highest point in Texas: Guadalupe Peak (8,751 ft.)
Haleakala (Hawaii), 1960	28,091.14	World-famous 10,023-ft. Haleakala volcano (dormant) (Formerly Hawaii National Park 1916–1960)
Hawaii Volcanoes (Hawaii), 1961	209,695.38	Spectacular volcanic area; luxuriant vegetation at lower levels (Formerly Hawaii National Park 1916–1961)
Hot Springs (Ark.), 1921	5,549.46	47 mineral hot springs said to have therapeutic value
Isle Royale (Mich.), 1931	571,790.11	Largest wilderness island in Lake Superior; moose, wolves, lakes
Joshua Tree (Calif.), 1994	792,749.87	Desert region featuring Joshua trees and a great variety of plants and animals. (Park was a National Monument 1936–1994)
Katmai (Alaska), 1980	3,674,540.87	Expansion may assure brown bear's preservation,. Park is known for fishing, 1912 eruption, bears (Park was a National Monument 1918–1980)
Kenai Fjords (Alaska), 1980	670,642.79	Mountain goats, marine mammals, birdlife are features at this seacoast park near Seward (Park was a National Monument 1978–1980)
Kings Canyon (Calif.), 1890	461,901.20	Huge canyons; high mountains; giant sequoias (Formerl;y General Grant National Park 1890–1940)
Kobuk Valley (Alaska), 1980	1,750,736.86	Native culture and anthropology center around the broad Kobuk River in northwest Alaska (Park was a National Monument 1978–1980)
Lake Clark (Alaska), 1980	2,619,858.50	Park provides scenic and wilderness recreation across Cook Inlet from Anchorage. (Park was a National Monument 1978–1980)
Lassen Volcanic (Calif.), 1916	106,372.36	Exhibits of impressive volcanic phenomena
Mammoth Cave (Ky.), 1926	52,830.19	Vast limestone labyrinth with underground river
Mesa Verde (Colo.), 1906	52,121.93	Best-preserved prehistoric cliff dwellings in United States
Mount Rainier (Wash.), 1899	235,612.50	Single-peak glacial system; dense forests, flowered meadows
National Park of American Samoa, 1988	9,000.00	Samoa National Park, American Samoa: two rain forest preserves and a coral reef on the island of Ofu are home to unique tropical animals. The park also includes several thousand acres on the islands of Tutuila and Ta'u
North Cascades (Wash.), 1968	504,780.94	Roadless Alpine landscape; jagged peaks; mountain lakes; glaciers
Olympic (Wash.), 1938	922,651.01	Finest Pacific Northwest rain forest; scenic mountain park
Petrified Forest (Ariz.), 1962	93,532.57	Extensive natural exhibit of petrified wood (Park was a National Monument 1906–1962)
Redwood (Calif.), 1968	110,232.40	Coastal redwood forests; contains world's tallest known tree (369.2 ft.)
Rocky Mountain (Colo.), 1915	265,727.15	Section of the Rocky Mountains; 107 named peaks over 10,000 ft.
Saguaro (Ariz.), 1994	91,452.95	Giant saguaro cacti, unique to the Sonoran Desert, sometimes reach a height of 50 ft. in this cactus forest. (Park was a National Monument 1933–1994)
Sequoia (Calif.), 1890	402,482.38	Giant sequoias; magnificent High Sierra scenery, including Mt. Whitney
Shenandoah (Va.), 1926	197,388.98	Tree-covered mountains; scenic Skyline Drive
Theodore Roosevelt (N.D.), 1978	70,446.89	Scenic valley of Little Missouri River; T.R. Ranch; wildlife (Theodore Roosevelt National Memorial Park 1947–1978)
Virgin Islands (U.S. V.I.), 1956	14,688.87	Beaches; lush hills; prehistoric Carib Indian relics
Voyageurs (Minn.), 1971	218,035.33	Wildlife, canoeing, fishing, and hiking
Wind Cave (S.D.), 1903	28,295.03	Limestone caverns in Black Hills; buffalo herd
Wrangell-St. Elias (Alaska), 1980	8,323,617.68	Largest Park System area has abundant wildlife, second highest peak in U.S. (Mt. St. Elias); adjoins Canadian park. (Park was a National Monument 1978–1980)
Yellowstone (Wyo.-Mont.-Idaho), 1872	2,219,790.71	World's greatest geyser area; abundant falls, wildlife, and canyons
Yosemite (Calif.), 1890	761,236.20	Mountains; inspiring gorges and waterfalls; giant sequoias
Zion (Utah), 1919	146,597.61	Multicolored gorge in heart of southern Utah desert

Name and location	Total acreage
National Historical Parks	
Appomattox Court House (Va.)	1,774.81
Boston (Mass.)	41.03
Cane River Creole (La.)	206.86
Chaco Culture (N.M.)	33,974.29
Chesapeake and Ohio Canal (Md.-W.Va.-D.C.)	19,236.60
Colonial (Va.)	9,352.60
Cumberland Gap (Ky.-Tenn.-Va.)	20,454.02
Dayton Aviation Heritage (Ohio)	85.65
George Rogers Clark (Ind.)	26.17
Harpers Ferry (W.Va.-Md.)	2,287.48
Hopewell Culture (Ohio)	1,134.44
Independence (Pa.)	44.88
Jean Lafitte (La.)	20,020.00
Kalaupapa (Hawaii)	10,778.88
Kaloko-Honokohau (Hawaii)	1,160.91
Keewenaw (Mich.)	1,870.00
Klondike Goldrush (Alaska-Wash.)	13,191.35
Lowell (Mass.)	136.86
Lyndon B. Johnson (Tex.)	1,570.15
Marsh-Billings (Vt.)	643.07
Minuteman (Mass.)	935.55
Morristown (N.J.)	1,683.61
Natchez (Miss.)	108.26
New Bedford Whaling (Mass.)	20.00
New Orleans Jazz (La.)	n.a.
Nez Perce (Idaho)	2,122.75
Pecos (N.M.)	6,670.65
Pu'uhonua a Honaunau (Hawaii)	181.80
Salt River Bay and Ecological Preserve (U.S. V.I.)	945.00
San Antonio Missions (Tex.)	819.19
San Francisco Maritime (Calif.)	31.18
San Juan Island (Wash.)	1,751.99
Saratoga (N.Y.)	3,392.42
Sitka (Alaska)	106.83
Tumacacori (Ariz.)	46.52
Valley Forge (Pa.)	3,466.47
War in the Pacific (Guam)	1,960.07
Women's Rights (N.Y.)	6.80
National Monuments	
Agate Fossil Beds (Neb.)	3,055.22
Alibates Flint Quarries (Tex.)	1,370.97
Aniakchak (Alaska)	137,176.00
Aztec Ruins (N.M.)	319.73
Bandelier (N.M.)	32,737.20
Black Canyon of the Gunnison (Colo.)	20,766.14
Booker T. Washington (Va.)	223.92
Buck Island Reef (U.S. V.I.)	880.00
Cabrillo (Calif.)	137.06
Canyon de Chelly (Ariz.)	83,840.00
Cape Krusenstern (Alaska)	650,000.00
Capulin Volcano (N.M.)	792.84
Casa Grande (Ariz.)	472.50
Castillo de San Marcos (Fla.)	20.51
Castle Clinton (N.Y.)	1.00
Cedar Breaks (Utah)	6,154.60
Chiricahua (Ariz.)	11,984.73
Colorado (Colo.)	20,453.93
Congaree Swamp (S.C.)	22,200.00
Craters of the Moon (Idaho)	53,440.05
Devils Postpile (Calif.)	798.46
Devils Tower (Wyo.)	1,346.91
Dinosaur (Utah-Colo.)	210,844.02

Name and location	Total acreage
Effigy Mounds (Iowa)	1,481.39
El Malpais (N.M.)	114,276.95
El Morro (N.M.)	1,278.72
Florissant Fossil Beds (Colo.)	5,998.09
Fort Frederica (Ga.)	241.42
Fort Matanzas (Fla.)	227.76
Fort McHenry (Md.)	43.26
Fort Pulaski (Ga.)	5,623.10
Fort Stanwix (N.Y.)	15.52
Fort Sumter (S.C.)	194.60
Fort Union (N.M.)	720.60
Fossil Butte (Wyo.)	8,198.00
George Washington Birthplace (Va.)	550.23
George Washington Carver (Mo.)	210.00
Gila Cliff Dwellings (N.M.)	533.13
Grand Portage (Minn.)	709.97
Great Sand Dunes (Colo.)	38,662.18
Hagerman Fossil Beds (Idaho)	4,345.59
Hohokam Pima (Ariz.)	1,690.00
Homestead (Neb.)	195.11
Hovenweep (Utah-Colo.)	784.93
Jewel Cave (S.D.)	1,273.51
John Day Fossil Beds (Ore.)	14,014.10
Lava Beds (Calif.)	46,559.87
Little Big Horn Battlefield (Mont.)	765.34
Montezuma Castle (Ariz.)	857.69
Muir Woods (Calif.)	553.55
Natural Bridges (Utah)	7,636.49
Navajo (Ariz.)	360.00
Ocmulgee (Ga.)	701.54
Oregon Caves (Ore.)	487.98
Organ Pipe Cactus (Ariz.)	330,688.86
Petroglyph (N.M.)	7,240.33
Pinnacles (Calif.)	16,265.44
Pipe Spring (Ariz.)	40.00
Pipestone (Minn.)	281.78
Poverty Point (La.)	910.85
Rainbow Bridge (Utah)	160.00
Russell Cave (Ala.)	310.45
Salinas Pueblo Missions (N.M.)	1,071.42
Scotts Bluff (Neb.)	3,003.03
Statue of Liberty (N.Y.-N.J.)	58.38
Sunset Crater Volcano (Ariz.)	3,040.00
Timpanogos Cave (Utah)	250.00
Tonto (Ariz.)	1,120.00
Tuzigoot (Ariz.)	800.62
Walnut Canyon (Ariz.)	3,541.46
White Sands (N.M.)	143,732.92
Wupatki (Ariz.)	35,442.13
Yucca House (Colo.)	33.87
National Preserves	
Aniakchak (Alaska)	465,603.00
Bering Land Bridge (Alaska)	2,698,000.00
Big Cypress (Fla.)	716,000.00
Big Thicket (Tex.)	96,679.68
Denali (Alaska)	1,334,200.00
Gates of the Arctic (Alaska)	948,629.00
Glacier Bay (Alaska)	58,406.00
Katmai (Alaska)	418,699.30
Lake Clark (Alaska)	1,410,641.50
Little River Canyon (Ala.)	13,669.00
Mojave (Calif.)	1,450,000.00
Noatak (Alaska)	6,570,000.00
Tallgrass Prairie (Kans.)	10,894.00

Name and location	Total acreage
Timucuan Ecological and Historic Preserve (Fla.)	46,000.00
Wrangell-St. Elias (Alaska)	4,852,773.31
Yukon-Charley (Alaska)	2,526,509.46

National Reserves

Name and location	Total acreage
City of Rocks (Idaho)	14,407.19
Ebey's Landing (Wash.)	19,000.00

National Military Parks

Name and location	Total acreage
Chickamauga and Chattanooga (Ga.-Tenn.)	8,119.11
Fredericksburg and Spotsylvania (Va.)	7,787.26
Gettysburg Nat. Mil. Park (Pa.)	5,906.30
Guilford Courthouse (N.C.)	220.25
Horseshoe Bend (Ala.)	2,040.00
Kings Mountain (S.C.)	3,945.29
Pea Ridge (Ark.)	4,300.35
Shiloh Nat. Park (Tenn.)	3,972.87
Vicksburg Nat. Mil. Park (Miss.)	1,736.47

National Battlefields

Name and location	Total acreage
Antietam (Md.)	3,255.89
Big Hole (Mont.)	655.61
Cowpens (S.C.)	841.56
Fort Donelson (Tenn.)	551.69
Fort Necessity (Pa.)	902.80
Monocacy (Md.)	1,647.01
Moores Creek (N.C.)	86.52
Petersburg (Va.)	2,744.10
Stones River (Tenn.)	708.32
Tupelo (Miss.)	1.00
Wilson's Creek (Mo.)	1,749.91

National Battlefield Parks

Name and location	Total acreage
Kennesaw Mountain (Ga.)	2,884.14
Manassas (Va.)	5,071.62
Richmond (Va.)	820.59

National Battlefield Site

Name and location	Total acreage
Brices Cross Roads (Miss.)	1.00

National Historic Sites

Name and location	Total acreage
Abraham Lincoln Birthplace (Ky.)	116.50
Adams (Mass.)	13.74
Allegheny Portage Railroad (Pa.)	1,249.20
Andersonville (Ga.)	494.61
Andrew Johnson (Tenn.)	16.68
Bent's Old Fort (Colo.)	799.80
Boston African-American (Mass.)	n.a.
Brown v. Board of Education (Kans.)	1.85
Carl Sandburg Home (N.C.)	263.65
Charles Pinckney (S.C.)	28.45
Christiansted (U.S. V.I.)	27.15
Clara Barton (Md.)	8.59
Edgar Allan Poe (Pa.)	0.52
Edison (N.J.)	21.25
Eisenhower (Pa.)	690.46
Eleanor Roosevelt (N.Y.)	180.50
Eugene O'Neill (Calif.)	13.19
Ford's Theatre (Lincoln Museum) (D.C.)	0.29
Fort Bowie (Ariz.)	1,000.00
Fort Davis (Tex.)	460.00
Fort Laramie (Wyo.)	832.85

Name and location	Total acreage
Fort Larned (Kan.)	718.39
Fort Point (Calif.)	29.00
Fort Raleigh (N.C.)	512.93
Fort Scott (Kan.)	16.69
Fort Smith (Ark.-Okla.)	75.00
Fort Union Trading Post (N.D.-Mont.)	443.80
Fort Vancouver (Wash.)	208.89
Frederick Douglass Home (D.C.)	8.53
Frederick Law Olmsted (Mass.)	1.75
Friendship Hill (Pa.)	674.56
Golden Spike (Utah)	2,735.28
Grant-Kohrs Ranch (Mont.)	1,498.38
Hampton (Md.)	62.04
Harry S. Truman (Mo.)	6.67
Herbert Hoover (Iowa)	186.80
Home of F. D. Roosevelt (N.Y.)	290.34
Hopewell Furnace (Pa.)	848.06
Hubbell Trading Post (Ariz.)	160.09
James A. Garfield (Ohio)	7.82
Jimmy Carter (Ga.)	70.54
John F. Kennedy (Mass.)	0.09
John Muir (Calif.)	344.73
Knife River Indian Villages (N.D.)	1,758.35
Lincoln Home (Ill.)	12.24
Longfellow (Mass.)	1.98
Maggie L. Walker (Va.)	1.29
Manzanar National Historic Site (Calif.)	800.00
Martin Luther King, Jr. (Ga.)	36.95
Martin Van Buren (N.Y.)	39.58
Mary McLeod Bethune Council House (D.C.)	0.07
Nicodemus (Kans.)	161.35
Ninety Six (S.C.)	989.14
Palo Alto Battlefield (Tex.)	3,357.42
Pennsylvania Avenue (D.C.)	20.6
Puukohola Heiau (Hawaii)	86.24
Sagamore Hill (N.Y.)	83.02
Saint-Gaudens (N.H.)	148.23
Saint Paul's Church (N.Y.)	6.13
Salem Maritime (Mass.)	9.02
San Juan (P.R.)	75.13
Saugus Iron Works (Mass.)	8.51
Springfield Armory (Mass.)	54.93
Steamtown (Pa.)	62.48
Theodore Roosevelt Birthplace (N.Y.)	0.11
Theodore Roosevelt Inaugural (N.Y.)	1.03
Thomas Stone (Md.)	328.25
Tuskegee Institute (Ala.)	57.92
Ulysses S. Grant (Mo.)	9.60
Vanderbilt Mansion (N.Y.)	211.65
Washita Battlefield (Okla.)	330.28
Weir Farm (Conn.)	60.76
Whitman Mission (Wash.)	98.15
William Howard Taft (Ohio)	3.07

National Memorials

Name and location	Total acreage
Arkansas Post (Ark.)	389.18
Arlington House, the Robert E. Lee Memorial (Va.)	27.91
Chamizal (Tex.)	54.90
Coronado (Ariz.)	4,750.22
De Soto (Fla.)	26.84
Federal Hall (N.Y.)	0.45

Name and location	Total acreage
Fort Caroline (Fla.)	138.39
Fort Clatsop (Ore.)	125.20
Franklin Delano Roosevelt Memorial (D.C.)	7.50
General Grant (N.Y.)	0.76
Hamilton Grange (N.Y.)	0.11
Jefferson National Expansion Memorial (Mo.)	90.96
Johnstown Flood (Pa.)	164.12
Korean War Veterans (D.C.)	2.20
Lincoln Boyhood (Ind.)	199.65
Lincoln Memorial (D.C.)	107.43
Lyndon Baines Johnson Memorial Grove on the Potomac (D.C.)	17.00
Mount Rushmore (S.D.)	1,278.45
Perry's Victory and International Peace Memorial (Ohio)	25.38
Roger Williams (R.I.)	4.56
Thaddeus Kosciuszko (Pa.)	0.02
Theodore Roosevelt Island (D.C.)	88.50
Thomas Jefferson Memorial (D.C.)	18.36
USS *Arizona* Memorial (Hawaii)	10.50
Vietnam Veterans Memorial (D.C.)	2.00
Washington Monument (D.C.)	106.01
Wright Brothers (N.C.)	428.44

National Seashores

Assateague Island (Md.-Va.)	39,721.85
Canaveral (Fla.)	57,661.69
Cape Cod (Mass.)	43,569.09
Cape Hatteras (N.C.)	30,319.43
Cape Lookout (N.C.)	28,243.36
Cumberland Island (Ga.)	36,415.39
Fire Island (N.Y.)	19,578.55
Gulf Islands (Fla.-Miss.)	135,607.15
Padre Island (Tex.)	130,434.27
Point Reyes (Calif.)	71,057.03

National Parkways

Blue Ridge (Va.-N.C.)	87,992.21
George Washington Memorial (Va.-Md.)	7,247.63
John D. Rockefeller, Jr., Memorial (Wyo.)	23,777.22
Natchez Trace (Miss.-Tenn.-Ala.)	51,747.59

National Lakeshores

Apostle Islands (Wis.)	69,371.89
Indiana Dunes (Ind.)	15,139.02
Pictured Rocks (Mich.)	73,235.53
Sleeping Bear Dunes (Mich.)	71,189.40

National Rivers

Big South Fork National River & Recreation Area (Ky.-Tenn.)	125,000.00
Buffalo (Ark.)	94,309.49
Mississippi National River & Recreation Area (Minn.)	53,775.00
New River Gorge (W.Va.)	70,911.69
Niobrara National Scenic Riverways (Neb.)	21,074.00
Ozark National Scenic Riverways (Mo.)	80,790.04

Name and location	Total acreage
National Recreation Areas	
Amistad (Tex.)	58,500.00
Bighorn Canyon (Wyo.-Mont.)	120,296.22
Boston Harbor Islands (Mass.)	1,482.25
Chattahoochee River (Ga.)	9,238.81
Chickasaw (Okla.)	9,888.83
Curecanti (Colo.)	41,972.42
Cuyahoga Valley (Ohio)	32,524.76
Delaware Water Gap (Pa.-N.J.)	67,191.66
Gateway (N.Y.-N.J.)	26,601.27
Gauley River (W. Va.)	11,145.07
Glen Canyon (Ariz.-Utah)	1,236,880.00
Golden Gate (Calif.)	74,441.36
Lake Chelan (Wash.)	61,886.98
Lake Mead (Ariz.-Nev.)	1,495,665.52
Lake Meredith (Tex.)	44,977.63
Lake Roosevelt (Wash.)	100,390.31
Ross Lake (Wash.)	117,574.59
Santa Monica Mountains (Calif.)	150,050.00
Whiskeytown-Shasta-Trinity (Calif.)	42,503.46

National Scenic Trails

Appalachian (Maine-N.H.-Vt.-Mass.-Conn.-N.Y.-N.J.- Pa.-Md.-W.Va.-Va.-N.C.-Tenn., Ga.)	172,109.93
Natchez Trace (Ala.-Miss.-Tenn.)	11,995.00
Potomac Heritage (D.C.-Md.-Va.-Pa.)	n.a.

International Historic Site

Saint Croix Island (Maine)	35.39

National Cemeteries[1]

Andersonville (Ga.)	494.61
Andrew Johnson (Tenn.)	16.68
Antietam (Md.)	11.36
Battleground (D.C.)	1.03
Fort Donelson (Tenn.)	15.30
Fredericksburg (Va.)	12.00
Gettysburg (Pa.)	20.58
Little Big Horn (Mont.)	765.34
Poplar Grove (Va.)	8.72
Shiloh (Tenn.)	10.05
Stones River (Tenn.)	719.81
Vicksburg (Miss.)	116.28
Yorktown (Va.)	2.91

1. The National Cemeteries are not independent areas of the National Park System; each is part of a military park, battlefield, etc., except Battleground. Their acreage is kept separately. Arlington National Cemetery is under the Department of the Army.

Other Parks

Catoctin Mountain (Md.)	5,770.22
Constitution Gardens (D.C.)	52.00
Fort Washington Park (Md.)	341.00
Greenbelt (Md.)	1,175.99
National Capital Parks (D.C.)	6,546.92
National Mall (D.C.)	146.35
Piscataway (Md.)	4,440.52
Prince William Forest (Va.)	18,571.55
Rock Creek Park (D.C.)	1,754.37
White House (D.C.)	18.07
Wolf Trap Farm Park for the Performing Arts (Va.)	130.28

A Mean Season for Hurricanes

And researchers predict that more monster storms are on the way

By ERIC LARSON TIME

The 1998 Atlantic hurricane season was the deadliest in more than 200 years. Not since the "Great Hurricane" of 1780 that struck Martinique, St. Eustatius, and Barbados (Oct. 10–16, 1780), killing an estimated 22,000 people, has the Atlantic hurricane basin seen storm-related fatalities like those of Hurricane Mitch (Oct. 21–Nov. 5, 1998). More than 11,000 people were estimated dead in the battered countries of Nicaragua and Honduras, while some 2 million were left homeless. In all, the storm caused a staggering $3 billion in damage—more than half the combined Nicaraguan and Honduran gross domestic products. As the gravity of the disaster reached around the world, millions of dollars in aid poured in. But Central America's development, which lagged far behind the rest of the world before Hurricane Mitch struck, has been set back decades.

In 1998's mean season, Mitch, a Category 5 monster (the Saffir/Simpson Hurricane Scale rates hurricanes from 1–5 according to intensity), registered average sustained winds near 180 mph (Oct. 25) with gusts well over 200 mph. Based on barometric pressure, Mitch was the fourth most intense hurricane observed in the Atlantic basin this century.

Ten Storms in One Month

"The season started a little late with Tropical Storm Alex on July 27, but made up for lost time," said Jerry Jarrell, director of the National Weather Service's National Hurricane Center. "In a remarkable span of 35 days between Aug. 19 and Sept. 22, ten named tropical storms formed. That's nearly a whole year's worth of activity crammed into little more than a month."

The year tallied seven landfalling storms in the continental United States, including Hurricanes Bonnie, Earl, Georges, Frances, and Mitch (the last two were downgraded to a tropical storm on landfall) and tropical storms Charley and Hermine.

With 50% more hurricanes and 30% more tropical storms than normal in 1998, many researchers believe we have entered a period of increased hurricane intensity, more like the period from 1940 through 1969 when monster storms swept ashore with greater frequency.

Cycles of activity and relative quiet occur every several decades and no one really knows why. According to Bill Gray, a hurricane expert from Colorado State University, one reason may be a phenomenon known as the "Atlantic conveyor." The subject of much recent research, the conveyor is a gigantic oceanic flywheel that transports cold water from the seas off Iceland and Greenland in a majestic, slow current along the bottom of the ocean to Antarctica, where it surfaces several decades later and flows back north, absorbing heat as it passes the equator. The conveyor seems to have kicked into a faster gear lately, bringing warm equatorial water north before it can cool. Hurricanes draw their energy from warm water.

Researchers emphasize that both phases, active and quiet, are normal, but that's not very reassuring. Even if the next high-intensity phase of hurricane activity is simply a replay of the last such period, it will wreak far more destruction on the mainland U.S. than ever before. Reason: a frenzy of coastal construction has brought huge populations to live at America's beaches and barrier islands—people with no conception of what it's like to sustain a direct hit from a truly powerful hurricane.

Hurricane Fodder

The trend toward more damaging hurricanes was made explicit in a study done by Christopher Landsea, a research meteorologist with the National Oceanic and Atmospheric Administration's Hurricane Research Division in Miami, and Roger A. Pielke, Jr., a social scientist with the National Center for Atmospheric Research in Boulder, Colo. They looked at the most destructive hurricanes in U.S. history and then, says Pielke, posed the question: "If

Costliest Hurricanes of the Century

(U.S. Mainland)

Rank	Year	Name	Damage then (in millions)	Damage now (in millions)	Dead	Rank	Year	Name	Damage then (in millions)	Damage now (in millions)	Dead
1.	1926	Unnamed	$ 105	$77,490	243	6.	1938	Unnamed	$ 306	$17,821	600
2.	1992	Andrew	$26,500	$35,468	15	7.	1928	Unnamed	$ 25	$14,785	1,836
3.	1900	Unnamed (Galveston)	$ 30	$28,528	8,000	8.	1965	Betsy	$1,420	$13,326	75
4.	1915	Unnamed	$ 50	$24,171	275	9.	1960	Donna	$ 387	$12,913	50
5.	1944	Unnamed	$ 63	$18,074	18	10.	1969	Camille	$1,421	$11,752	256

Sources: Normalized Hurricane Damages in the United States by Roger Pielke, Jr., and Christopher Landsea; National Oceanic and Atmospheric Administration.

history repeats itself, and it certainly will, what might we expect?" To answer it, the researchers did not simply adjust the original damage totals for inflation. They also included data on the great increase in population, wealth, and development that had occurred over the decades in the places where the storms struck.

Looked at in this light, 1992's Hurricane Andrew, officially the costliest hurricane on record with damage, in today's dollars, of $35.5 billion, dropped to second place. The first was a Category 4 hurricane (wind speeds above 130 m.p.h.) that struck southeast Florida in 1926 and skipped into Alabama. (It has no name because the custom of naming storms began only in the early '50s.) If that storm took the same path today, it would cause damage totaling $77.5 billion. Of the ten costliest hurricanes of the century, 9 occurred before 1970. The only recent hurricane to make Pielke's and Landsea's Top-10 list was Andrew.

Mean and Unpredictable

Another reason that future hurricane seasons may be more damaging than ever before: hurricanes have the capacity for sudden changes in intensity. For Jerry Jarrell, who is director of the federal Tropical Prediction Center as well as the National Hurricane Center, the most frightening near miss was not Andrew but Hurricane Opal, which hit the Gulf Coast in October 1995. Opal had been a weak storm, but just before it struck, it underwent what forecasters call "rapid deepening," leaping from Category 2 to nearly Category 5, with winds at 150 m.p.h. It also started moving faster. Such rapid change is the thing emergency managers most fear. Says Tom Millwee, coordinator of the Texas Division of Emergency Management: "You go to bed thinking you've got a Cat 1 moving at 10 m.p.h. You wake up, it's a Cat 5 moving at 20 m.p.h."

The sudden change threw evacuation plans into chaos. Most people waited until morning to evacuate, and did so in a vast crush of cars. Road construction further slowed progress. By morning the scene along Interstate 10 outside Pensacola was like something from a grade-B disaster film. Jarrell estimates 10,000 people were stranded on the highways, listening to ever more urgent broadcasts on their radios. Some drivers abandoned their cars and fled for high ground. Then, just before landfall, Opal had another change of heart. She fizzled. By the time the storm crossed the coast, its winds diminished by at least a third. With more and more people moving to coastal areas, their sheer number makes the unpredictability and ever changing strength of hurricanes that much more difficult to cope with.

Calm before the Storm

Despite Mitch's ferociousness and the army of lesser demons that plagued the 1998 Atlantic hurricane season, those inhabiting America's coastal regions seem impervious to the possibility of future disaster. Homes still rise on the barrier islands off North Carolina. On Galveston's westernmost beaches, where the land is barely above sea level, luxurious new mansions stand atop stilts so tall the scene is almost comical.

Just a few minutes up the road, however, there's a poignant monument to this sort of denial. Near bright blue signs marking Galveston's primary evacuation route, a small plaque commemorates the site where the hurricane of 1900 destroyed an orphanage and took the lives of 87 children. Just across the street stands a brand new Wal-Mart. ☐

Most Deadly Western Hemisphere Hurricanes on Record

Hurricane	Date	Areas struck	Deaths
1. "The Great Hurricane"	Oct. 10–16, 1780	Martinique, St. Eustatius, Barbados, ships	22,000
2. Hurricane Mitch	Oct. 26–Nov. 4, 1998	Central America: Honduras, Nicaragua	11,000+
3. Galveston, Texas	Sept. 8, 1900	Galveston Island	8,000
4. Hurricane Fifi	Sept. 14–19, 1974	Honduras	8,000
5. Dominican Republic	Sept. 1–6, 1930	Dominican Republic	8,000
6. Hurricane Flora	Sept. 30, 1963–Oct. 8, 1963	Haiti, Cuba	7,200
7. Martinique	Sept. 6, 1776	Point Petre Bay	>6,000

Source: National Oceanic and Atmospheric Administration.

Strongest Atlantic Hurricanes on Record

Hurricane	Date	Pressure	Peak winds	Total no. of hours at Cat 5	Total no. of hours winds 155+ knots
1. Gilbert	Sept. 13, 1988	888 mb (26.22 in.)	160 knots	18 hours	6 hours
2. Florida Keys	Sept. 3, 1935	892 mb (26.34 in.)	140 knots	3 hours	0 hours
3. Allen	Aug. 7, 1980	899 mb (26.55 in.)	165 knots	24/24/12 hours[1]	3/12/3 hours[1]
4. Mitch	Oct. 26, 1998	905 mb (26.73 in.)	155 knots	33 hours	15 hours
5. Camille	Aug. 17, 1969	905 mb (26.73 in.)	165 knots	24 hours	18 hours

1. Hurricane Allen attained Category 5 status three times during its life history: first on Aug. 5, second on Aug. 7, and third on Aug. 9. Source: National Oceanic and Atmospheric Administration.

Climate of 100 Selected U.S. Cities

| City | Average monthly temperature (°F)[1] | | | | Precipitation | | Snowfall | |
	Jan.	April	July	Oct.	Average annual (in.)[1]	Average annual (days)[2]	Average annual (in.)[2]	Years[2]
Albany, N.Y.	21.1	46.6	71.4	50.5	35.74	134	65.5	38
Albuquerque, N.M.	34.8	55.1	78.8	57.4	8.12	59	10.6	45
Anchorage, Alaska	13.0	35.4	58.1	34.6	15.20	115	69.2	41[3]
Asheville, N.C.	36.8	55.7	73.2	56.0	47.71	124	17.5	20
Atlanta, Ga.	41.9	61.8	78.6	62.2	48.61	115	1.9	50
Atlantic City, N.J.	31.8	51.0	74.4	55.5	41.93	112	16.4	40[3]
Austin, Texas	49.1	68.7	84.7	69.8	31.50	83	0.9	43
Baltimore, Md.	32.7	54.0	76.8	56.9	41.84	113	21.8	34
Baton Rouge, La.	50.8	68.4	82.1	68.2	55.77	108	0.1	34[3]
Billings, Mont.	20.9	44.6	72.3	49.3	15.09	96	57.2	50
Birmingham, Ala.	42.9	62.8	80.1	62.6	54.52	117	1.3	41
Bismark, N.D.	6.7	42.5	70.4	46.1	15.36	96	40.3	45
Boise, Idaho	29.9	48.6	74.6	51.9	11.71	92	21.4	45
Boston, Mass.	29.6	48.7	73.5	54.8	43.81	127	41.8	49[3]
Bridgeport, Conn.	29.5	48.6	74.0	56.0	41.56	117	26.0	36
Buffalo, N.Y.	23.5	45.4	70.7	51.5	37.52	169	92.2	41
Burlington, Vt.	16.6	42.7	69.6	47.9	33.69	153	78.2	41
Caribou, Maine	10.7	37.3	65.1	43.1	36.59	160	113.3	45
Casper, Wyo.	22.2	42.1	70.9	47.1	11.43	95	80.5	34
Charleston, S.C.	47.9	64.3	80.5	65.8	51.59	113	0.6	42
Charleston, W.Va.	32.9	55.3	74.5	55.9	42.43	151	31.5	37
Charlotte, N.C.	40.5	60.3	78.5	60.7	43.16	111	6.1	45
Cheyenne, Wyo.	26.1	41.8	68.9	47.5	13.31	98	54.1	49
Chicago, Ill.	21.4	48.8	73.0	53.5	33.34	127	40.3	26
Cleveland, Ohio	25.5	48.1	71.6	53.2	35.40	156	53.6	43
Columbia, S.C.	44.7	63.8	81.0	63.4	49.12	109	1.9	37
Columbus, Ohio	27.1	51.4	73.8	53.9	36.97	137	28.3	37[3]
Concord, N.H.	19.9	44.1	69.5	48.3	36.53	125	64.5	43
Dallas-Ft. Worth, Texas	44.0	65.9	86.3	67.9	29.46	78	3.1	31
Denver, Colo.	29.5	47.4	73.4	51.9	15.31	88	59.8	50
Des Moines, Iowa	18.6	50.5	76.3	54.2	30.83	107	34.7	45
Detroit, Mich.	23.4	47.3	71.9	51.9	30.97	133	40.4	26
Dodge City, Kan.	29.5	54.3	80.0	57.7	20.66	78	19.5	42
Duluth, Minn.	6.3	38.3	65.4	44.2	29.68	135	77.4	41[3]
El Paso, Texas	44.2	63.6	82.5	63.6	7.82	47	5.2	45
Fairbanks, Alaska	-12.7	30.2	61.5	25.1	10.37	106	67.5	33
Fargo, N.D.	4.3	42.1	70.6	46.3	19.59	100	35.9	42
Grand Junction, Colo.	25.5	51.7	78.9	54.9	8.00	72	26.1	38
Grand Rapids, Mich.	22.0	46.3	71.4	50.9	34.35	143	72.4	21
Hartford, Conn.	25.2	48.8	73.4	52.4	44.39	127	50.0	30
Helena, Mont.	18.1	42.3	67.9	45.1	11.37	96	47.9	44
Honolulu, Hawaii	72.6	75.7	80.1	79.5	23.47	100	0.0	38[3]
Houston, Texas	51.4	68.7	83.1	69.7	44.76	105	0.4	50
Indianapolis, Ind.	26.0	52.4	75.1	54.8	39.12	125	23.1	53[3]
Jackson, Miss.	45.7	65.1	81.9	65.0	52.82	109	1.2	21
Jacksonville, Fla.	53.2	67.7	81.3	69.5	52.76	116	T	43
Juneau, Alaska	21.8	39.1	55.7	41.8	53.15	220	102.8	41
Kansas City, Mo.	28.4	56.9	80.9	59.6	29.27	98	20.0	43
Knoxville, Tenn.	38.2	59.6	77.6	59.5	47.29	127	12.3	42
Las Vegas, Nev.	44.5	63.5	90.2	67.5	4.19	26	1.4	36
Lexington, Ky.	31.5	55.1	75.9	56.8	45.68	131	16.3	40
Little Rock, Ark.	39.9	62.4	82.1	63.1	49.20	104	5.4	42
Long Beach, Calif.	55.2	60.9	72.8	67.5	11.54	32	T	41[3]
Los Angeles, Calif.	56.0	59.5	69.0	66.3	12.08	36	T	49
Louisville, Ky.	32.5	56.6	77.6	57.7	43.56	125	17.5	37
Madison, Wisc.	15.6	45.8	70.6	49.5	30.84	118	40.8	36
Memphis, Tenn.	39.6	62.6	82.1	62.9	51.57	107	5.5	34
Miami, Fla.	67.1	75.3	82.5	77.9	57.55	129	0.0	42
Milwaukee, Wisc.	18.7	44.6	70.5	50.9	30.94	125	47.0	44
Minneapolis-St. Paul, Minn.	11.2	46.0	73.1	49.6	26.36	115	48.9	46
Mobile, Ala.	50.8	68.0	82.2	68.5	64.64	123	0.3	43
Montgomery, Ala.	46.7	65.2	81.7	65.3	49.16	108	0.3	40
Mt. Washington, N.H.	5.1	22.4	48.7	30.5	89.92	209	246.8	52
Nashville, Tenn.	37.1	59.7	79.4	60.2	48.49	119	11.1	43
Newark, N.J.	31.2	52.1	76.8	57.2	42.34	122	28.2	43
New Orleans, La.	52.4	68.7	82.1	69.2	59.74	114	0.2	38[3]
New York, N.Y.	31.8	51.9	76.4	57.5	42.82	119	26.1	40[3]

| City | Average monthly temperature (°F)[1] | | | | Precipitation | | Snowfall | |
	Jan.	April	July	Oct.	Average annual (in.)[1]	(days)[2]	Average annual (in.)[2]	Years[2]
Norfolk, Va.	39.9	58.2	78.4	61.3	45.22	115	7.9	36
Oklahoma City, Okla.	35.9	60.2	82.1	62.3	30.89	82	9.0	45
Olympia, Wash.	37.2	47.3	63.0	50.1	50.96	164	18.0	43
Omaha, Neb.	20.2	52.2	77.7	54.5	30.34	98	31.1	49[3]
Philadelphia, Pa.	31.2	52.9	76.5	56.5	41.42	117	21.9	42[3]
Phoenix, Ariz.	52.3	68.1	92.3	73.4	7.11	36	T	47[3]
Pittsburgh, Pa.	26.7	50.1	72.0	52.5	36.30	154	44.6	32
Portland, Maine	21.5	42.8	68.1	48.5	43.52	128	72.4	44
Portland, Ore.	38.9	50.4	67.7	54.3	37.39	154	6.8	44
Providence, R.I.	28.2	47.9	72.5	53.2	45.32	124	37.1	31
Raleigh, N.C.	39.6	59.4	77.7	59.7	41.76	112	7.7	40
Reno, Nev.	32.2	46.4	69.5	50.3	7.49	51	25.3	42
Richmond, Va.	36.6	57.9	77.8	58.6	44.07	113	14.6	47
Roswell, N.M.	41.4	61.9	81.4	61.7	9.70	52	11.4	37[3]
Sacramento, Calif.	45.3	58.2	75.6	63.9	17.10	58	0.1	36[3]
Salt Lake City, Utah	28.6	49.2	77.5	53.0	15.31	90	59.1	56
San Antonio, Texas	50.4	69.6	84.6	70.2	29.13	81	0.4	42
San Diego, Calif.	56.8	61.2	70.3	67.5	9.32	43	T	44
San Francisco, Calif.	48.5	54.8	62.2	60.6	19.71	63	T	57
Savannah, Ga.	49.1	66.0	81.2	66.9	49.70	111	0.3	34
Seattle-Tacoma, Wash.	39.1	48.7	64.8	52.4	38.60	158	12.8	40
Sioux Falls, S.D.	12.4	46.4	74.0	49.4	24.12	96	39.9	39
Spokane, Wash.	25.7	45.8	69.7	47.5	16.71	114	51.5	37
Springfield, Ill.	24.6	53.3	76.5	56.0	33.78	114	24.5	37
St. Louis, Mo.	28.8	56.1	78.9	57.9	33.91	111	19.8	48[3]
Tampa, Fla.	59.8	71.5	82.1	74.4	46.73	107	T	38
Toledo, Ohio	23.1	47.8	71.8	51.7	31.78	137	38.3	29
Tucson, Ariz.	51.1	64.9	86.2	70.4	11.14	52	1.2	44
Tulsa, Okla.	35.2	61.0	83.2	62.6	38.77	89	9.0	46
Vero Beach, Fla.	61.9	71.7	81.1	75.2	51.41	n.a.	n.a.	0
Washington, D.C.	35.2	56.7	78.9	59.3	39.00	112	17.0	41[3]
Wichita, Kan.	29.6	56.3	81.4	59.1	28.61	85	16.4	31
Wilmington, Del.	31.2	52.4	76.0	56.3	41.38	117	20.9	37

1. Based on 30-year period 1951–80. Data latest available. 2. Data through 1984 based on number of years as indicated in Years column. 3. For snowfall data where number of years differs from that for precipitation data. T = trace. n.a. = not available. *Source:* National Oceanic and Atmospheric Administration.

Wind Chill Factors

| Wind speed (mph) | Thermometer reading (°F) | | | | | | | | | | | | | | | | |
	35	30	25	20	15	10	5	0	−5	−10	−15	−20	−25	−30	−35	−40	−45
5	33	27	21	19	12	7	0	−5	−10	−15	−21	−26	−31	−36	−42	−47	−52
10	22	16	10	3	−3	−9	−15	−22	−27	−34	−40	−46	−52	−58	−64	−71	−77
15	16	9	2	−5	−11	−18	−25	−31	−38	−45	−51	−58	−65	−72	−78	−85	−92
20	12	4	−3	−10	−17	−24	−31	−39	−46	−53	−60	−67	−74	−81	−88	−95	−103
25	8	1	−7	−15	−22	−29	−36	−44	−51	−59	−66	−74	−81	−88	−96	−103	−110
30	6	−2	−10	−18	−25	−33	−41	−49	−56	−64	−71	−79	−86	−93	−101	−109	−116
35	4	−4	−12	−20	−27	−35	−43	−52	−58	−67	−74	−82	−89	−97	−105	−113	−120
40	3	−5	−13	−21	−29	−37	−45	−53	−60	−69	−76	−84	−92	−100	−107	−115	−123
45	2	−6	−14	−22	−30	−38	−46	−54	−62	−70	−78	−85	−93	−102	−109	−117	−125

NOTE: This chart gives equivalent temperatures for combinations of wind speed and temperature. For example, the combination of a temperature of 10° Fahrenheit and a wind blowing at 10 mph has a cooling power equal to −9° F. Wind speeds of higher than 45 mph have little additional cooling effect.

Recorded Weather Extremes

Highest average annual mean temperature (world): Dallol, Ethiopia (Oct. 1960–Dec. 1966), 94° F (35° C). **(U.S.):** Key West, Fla. (30-year normal), 78.2° F (25.7° C).

Lowest average annual mean temperature (world): Plateau Station, Antarctica, −70° F (−7° C). **(U.S.):** Barrow, Alaska (30-year normal), 9.3° F (−13° C).

Greatest average yearly rainfall (world): Cherrapunji, India (74-year avg), 450 in. (1,143 cm). **(U.S.):** Mt. Waialeale, Kauai, Hawaii (32-year avg), 460 in. (1,168 cm).

Minimum average yearly rainfall (world): Arica, Chile (59-year avg), 0.03 in. (0.08 cm) (no rainfall for 14 consecutive

years). **(U.S.):** Death Valley, Calif. (42-year avg), 1.63 in. (4.14 cm). Bagdad, Calif., holds the U.S. record for the longest period with no measurable rain, 767 days, from Oct. 3, 1912 to Nov. 8, 1914.

Hottest summer average in Western Hemisphere (U.S.): Death Valley, Calif., 98° F (36.7° C).

Longest hot spell (world): Marble Bar, W. Australia, 100° F (38° C) (or above) for 162 consecutive days, Oct. 30, 1923 to Apr. 7, 1924.

Largest hailstone (U.S.): Coffeyville, Kans., 17.5 in. (44.5 cm), Sept. 3, 1979.

World and U.S. Extremes of Climate

Highest Recorded Temperatures

	Place	Date	Degrees Fahrenheit	Degrees Centigrade
World (Africa)	El Azizia, Libya	Sept. 13, 1922	136	58
North America (U.S.)	Death Valley, Calif.	July 10, 1913	134	57
Asia	Tirat Tsvi, Israel	June 21, 1942	129	54
Australia	Cloncurry, Queensland	Jan. 16, 1889	128	53
Europe	Seville, Spain	Aug. 4, 1881	122	50
South America	Rivadavia, Argentina	Dec. 11, 1905	120	49
Canada	Midale and Yellow Grass, Saskatchewan, Canada	July 5, 1937	113	45
Persian Gulf (sea-surface)		Aug. 5, 1924	96	36
Antarctica	Vanda Station	Jan. 5, 1974	59	15
South Pole		Dec. 27, 1978	7.5	−14

Lowest Recorded Temperatures

	Place	Date	Degrees Fahrenheit	Degrees Centigrade
World (Antarctica)	Vostok	July 21, 1983	−129	−89
Asia	Verkhoyansk/Oimekon	Feb. 6, 1933	−90	−68
Greenland	Northice	Jan. 9, 1954	−87	−66
North America (excl. Greenland)	Snag, Yukon, Canada	Feb. 3, 1947	−81	−63
United States	Prospect Creek, Alaska	Jan. 23, 1971	−80	−62
U.S. (excl. Alaska)	Rogers Pass, Mont.	Jan. 20, 1954	−70	−56.5
Europe	Ust 'Shchugor, Russia	n.a.	−67	−55
South America	Sarmiento, Argentina	June 1, 1907	−27	−33
Africa	Ifrane, Morocco	Feb. 11, 1935	−11	−24
Australia	Charlotte Pass, N.S.W.	June 29, 1994	−9	−22

Greatest Rainfalls

	Place	Date	Inches	Centimeters
1 minute (World)	Unionville, Md.	July 4, 1956	1.23	3.1
20 minutes (World)	Curtea-de-Arges, Romania	July 7, 1889	8.1	20.5
42 minutes (World)	Holt, Mo.	June 22, 1947	12	30.5
12 hours (World)	Grand Ilet, La Réunion	Jan. 26, 1980	46	114
24 hours (World)	Foc-Foc, La Réunion	Jan. 7–8, 1966	72	182.5
24 hours (N. Hemisphere)	Paishih, Taiwan	Sept. 10–11, 1963	49	125
24 hours (Australia)	Bellenden Ker, Queensland	Jan. 4, 1979	44	114
24 hours (U.S.)	Alvin, Tex.	July 25–26, 1979	43	109
24 hours (Canada)	Ucluelet Brynnor Mines, British Columbia	Oct. 6, 1967	19	49
5 days (World)	Commerson, La Réunion	Jan. 23–28, 1980	156	395
1 month (World)	Cherrapunji, India	July 1861	366	930
12 months (World)	Cherrapunji, India	Aug. 1860–Aug. 1861	1,042	2,647
12 months (U.S.)	Kukui, Maui, Hawaii	Dec. 1981–Dec. 1982	739	1878

Greatest Snowfalls

	Place	Date	Inches	Centimeters
1 month (U.S.)	Tamarack, Calif.	Jan. 1911	390	991
24 hours (N. America)	Silver Lake, Colo.	April 14–15, 1921	76	195.6
24 hours (Alaska)	Thompson Pass	Dec. 29, 1955	62	157.5
19 hours (France)	Bessans	April 5–6, 1969	68	173
1 storm (N. America)	Mt. Shasta Ski Bowl, Calif.	Feb. 13–19, 1959	189	480
1 storm (Alaska)	Thompson Pass	Dec. 26–31, 1955	175	445.5
1 season (N. America)	Mount Baker, Wash.	1998–1999	1,140	2,895.6
1 season (Alaska)	Thompson Pass	1952–1953	974.5	2,475
1 season (Canada)	Revelstoke Mt. Copeland, British Columbia	1971–1972	964	2,446.5

Source: U.S. Army Corps of Engineers, Engineer Topographic Laboratories.

Apparent Temperature for Values of Room Temperature and Relative Humidity

Relative Humidity (%)

Room temperature (°F)	0	10	20	30	40	50	60	70	80	90	100
75	68	69	71	72	74	75	76	76	77	78	79
74	66	68	69	71	72	73	74	75	76	77	78
73	65	67	68	70	71	72	73	74	75	76	77
72	64	65	67	68	70	71	72	73	74	75	76
71	63	64	66	67	68	70	71	72	73	74	75
70	63	64	65	66	67	68	69	70	71	72	73
69	62	63	64	65	66	67	68	69	70	71	72
68	61	62	63	64	65	66	67	68	69	70	71
67	60	61	62	63	64	65	66	67	68	68	69
66	59	60	61	62	63	64	65	66	67	67	68
65	59	60	61	61	62	63	64	65	65	66	67
64	58	59	60	60	61	62	63	64	64	65	66
63	57	58	59	59	60	61	62	62	63	64	64
62	56	57	58	58	59	60	61	61	62	63	63
61	56	57	57	58	59	59	60	60	61	61	62
60	55	56	56	57	58	58	59	59	60	60	61

Source: National Oceanic and Atmospheric Administration, Environmental Data and Information Service and National Climatic Center.

Yes, It's Sure Getting Warmer

In May 1999, British and American scientists published information based on extensive research that confirms a commonly held conception—it is getting warmer. According to these experts, annual global surface temperatures have risen 1.03°F (0.57°C) over the past 136 years (1861–1997), establishing the 20th century as the warmest era of the millennium.

In fact, researchers at the Universities of Massachusetts and Arizona, as well as scientists at both NASA and the National Oceanic and Atmospheric Administration, have concluded that the 1990s has been the warmest decade of the millennium, with 1998 the warmest year so far. The years 1997, 1995, and 1990 fall into close 2nd, 3rd, and 4th places behind sizzling 1998.

Yet despite the fact that in 1998 the *average* temperature for the 48 contiguous states was the highest since 1896, ironically, no all-time-high individual state temperature records were broken in that same year.

Record Highest Temperatures by State

State	Temp. °F	Temp. °C	Date	Station	Elevation in feet
Alabama	112	44	Sept. 5, 1925	Centerville	345
Alaska	100	38	June 27, 1915	Fort Yukon	est. 420
Arizona	128	53	June 29, 1994	Lake Havasu	785
Arkansas	120	49	Aug. 10, 1936	Ozark	396
California	134	57	July 10, 1913	Greenland Ranch	-178
Colorado	118	48	July 11, 1888	Bennett	5,484
Connecticut	106	41	July 15, 1995	Danbury	457
Delaware	110	43	July 21, 1930	Millsboro	20
D.C.	106	41	July 20, 1930	Washington	410
Florida	109	43	June 29, 1931	Monticello	207
Georgia	113	45	May 27, 1978	Greenville	860
Hawaii	100	38	Apr. 27, 1931	Pahala	850
Idaho	118	48	July 28, 1934	Orofino	1,027
Illinois	117	47	July 14, 1954	E. St. Louis	410
Indiana	116	47	July 14, 1936	Collegeville	672
Iowa	118	48	July 20, 1934	Keokuk	614
Kansas	121	49	July 24, 1936*	Alton (near)	1,651
Kentucky	114	46	July 28, 1930	Greensburg	581
Louisiana	114	46	Aug. 10, 1936	Plain Dealing	268
Maine	105	41	July 10, 1911*	North Bridgton	450
Maryland	109	43	July 10, 1936*	Cumberland & Frederick	623; 325
Massachusetts	107	42	Aug. 2, 1975	New Bedford & Chester	120; 640
Michigan	112	44	July 13, 1936	Mio	963
Minnesota	114	46	July 6, 1936*	Moorhead	904
Mississippi	115	46	July 29, 1930	Holly Springs	600
Missouri	118	48	July 14, 1954*	Warsaw & Union	687; 560
Montana	117	47	July 5, 1937	Medicine Lake	1,950
Nebraska	118	48	July 24, 1936*	Minden	2,169
Nevada	125	52	June 29, 1994	Laughlin	680
New Hampshire	106	41	July 4, 1911	Nashua	125
New Jersey	110	43	July 10, 1936	Runyon	18
New Mexico	122	50	June 27, 1994	Lakewood	3,418
New York	108	42	July 22, 1926	Troy	35
North Carolina	110	43	Aug. 21, 1983	Fayetteville	81
North Dakota	121	49	July 6, 1936	Steele	1,857
Ohio	113	45	July 21, 1934*	Gallipolis (near)	673
Oklahoma	120	49	June 29, 1994*	Tipton	1,251
Oregon	119	48	Aug. 10, 1898	Pendleton	1,074
Pennsylvania	111	44	July 10, 1936*	Phoenixville	100
Rhode Island	104	40	Aug. 2, 1975	Providence	51
South Carolina	111	44	June 28, 1954*	Camden	170
South Dakota	120	49	July 5, 1936	Gannvalley	1,750
Tennessee	113	45	Aug. 9, 1930*	Perryville	377
Texas	120	49	Aug. 12, 1936	Seymour	1,291
Utah	117	47	July 5, 1895	Saint George	2,880
Vermont	105	41	July 4, 1911	Vernon	310
Virginia	110	43	July 15, 1954	Balcony Falls	725
Washington	118	48	Aug. 5, 1961*	Ice Harbor Dam	475
West Virginia	112	44	July 10, 1936*	Martinsburg	435
Wisconsin	114	46	July 13, 1936	Wisconsin Dells	900
Wyoming	114	46	July 12, 1900	Basin	3,500

* Also on earlier dates at the same or other places. *Source:* National Climatic Data Center, Asheville, N.C., and Storm Phillips, STORMFAX, INC.

Record Lowest Temperatures by State

State	Temp. °F	Temp. °C	Date	Station	Elevation in feet
Alabama	−27	−33	Jan. 30, 1966	New Market	760
Alaska	−80	−62	Jan. 23, 1971	Prospect Creek	1,100
Arizona	−40	−40	Jan. 7, 1971	Hawley Lake	8,180
Arkansas	−29	−34	Feb. 13, 1905	Pond	1,250
California	−45	−43	Jan. 20, 1937	Boca	5,532
Colorado	−61	−52	Feb. 1, 1985	Maybell	5,920
Connecticut	−32	−36	Feb. 16, 1943	Falls Village	585
Delaware	−17	−27	Jan. 17, 1893	Millsboro	20
D.C.	−15	−26	Feb. 11, 1899	Washington	410
Florida	−2	−19	Feb. 13, 1899	Tallahassee	193
Georgia	−17	−27	Jan. 27, 1940	CCC Camp F-16	est. 1,000
Hawaii	7	−14	Jan. 23, 1997	Mauna Kea	13,770
Idaho	−60	−51	Jan. 18, 1943	Island Park Dam	6,285
Illinois	−36	−38	Jan. 5, 1999	Elizabeth	880
Indiana	−36	−38	Jan. 19, 1994	New Whiteland	785
Iowa	−47	−44	Feb. 3, 1996	Elkader	745
Kansas	−40	−40	Feb. 13, 1905	Lebanon	1,812
Kentucky	−37	−38	Jan. 19, 1994	Shelbyville	730
Louisiana	−16	−27	Feb. 13, 1899	Minden	194
Maine	−48	−44	Jan. 19, 1925	Van Buren	510
Maryland	−40	−40	Jan. 13, 1912	Oakland	2,461
Massachusetts	−35	−37	Jan. 12, 1981	Chester	640
Michigan	−51	−46	Feb. 9, 1934	Vanderbilt	785
Minnesota	−60	−51	Feb. 2, 1996	Tower	1,400
Mississippi	−19	−28	Jan. 30, 1966	Corinth	420
Missouri	−40	−40	Feb. 13, 1905	Warsaw	700
Montana	−70	−57	Jan. 20, 1954	Rogers Pass	5,470
Nebraska	−47	−44	Feb. 12, 1899	Camp Clarke	3,700
Nevada	−50	−46	Jan. 8, 1937	San Jacinto	5,200
New Hampshire	−46	−43	Jan. 28, 1925	Pittsburg	1,575
New Jersey	−34	−37	Jan. 5, 1904	River Vale	70
New Mexico	−50	−46	Feb. 1, 1951	Gavilan	7,350
New York	−52	−47	Feb. 18, 1979*	Old Forge	1,720
North Carolina	−34	−37	Jan. 21, 1985	Mt. Mitchell	6,525
North Dakota	−60	−51	Feb. 15, 1936	Parshall	1,929
Ohio	−39	−39	Feb. 10, 1899	Milligan	800
Oklahoma	−27	−33	Jan. 18, 1930	Watts	958
Oregon	−54	−48	Feb. 10, 1933*	Seneca	4,700
Pennsylvania	−42	−41	Jan. 5, 1904	Smethport	est. 1,500
Rhode Island	−25	−32	Feb. 5, 1996	Greene	425
South Carolina	−20	−28	Jan. 18, 1977	Caesars Head	3,100
South Dakota	−58	−50	Feb. 17, 1936	McIntosh	2,277
Tennessee	−32	−36	Dec. 30, 1917	Mountain City	2,471
Texas	−23	−31	Feb. 8, 1933*	Seminole	3,275
Utah	−69	−56	Feb. 1, 1985	Peters Sink	8,095
Vermont	−50	−46	Dec. 30, 1933	Bloomfield	915
Virginia	−30	−34	Jan. 22, 1985	Mountain Lake	3,870
Washington	−48	−44	Dec. 30, 1968	Mazama & Winthrop	2,120; 1,765
West Virginia	−37	−38	Dec. 30, 1917	Lewisburg	2,200
Wisconsin	−54	−48	Jan. 24, 1922	Danbury	908
Wyoming	−63	−53	Feb. 9, 1933	Moran	6,770

* Also on earlier dates at the same or other places. *Source:* National Climatic Data Center, Asheville, N.C., and Storm Phillips, STORMFAX, INC.

Record Monthly High and Low Temperatures in the United States

Source: National Climatic Data Center, Asheville, N.C., and Storm Phillips, STORMFAX, Inc.

January

The highest temperature ever recorded for the month of January occurred on January 17, 1936, and again in 1954, in Laredo, Tex. (elevation 421 ft.), where the temperature reached 98° F.

The lowest temperature ever recorded for the month of January occurred on January 20, 1954, in Rogers Pass, Mont. (elevation 5,470 ft.), where the temperature fell to –70° F.

February

The highest temperature ever recorded for the month of February occurred on February 3, 1963, in Montezuma, Ariz. (elevation 735 ft.), where the temperature reached 105° F.

The lowest temperature ever recorded for the month of February occurred on February 1, 1985, at the Peters Sink station in Utah (elevation 8,095 ft.), where the temperature fell to –69° F.

March

The highest temperature ever recorded for the month of March occurred on March 31, 1954, in Rio Grande City, Tex. (elevation 168 ft.), where the temperature reached 108° F.

The lowest temperature ever recorded for the month of March occurred on March 17, 1906, in Snake River, Wyo. (elevation 6,862 ft.), where the temperature dropped to –50° F.

April

The highest temperature ever recorded for the month of April occurred on April 25, 1898, at Volcano Springs, Calif. (elevation –220 ft.), where the temperature reached 118° F.

The lowest temperature ever recorded for the month of April occurred on April 5, 1945, in Eagle Nest, N.M. (elevation 8,250 ft.), where the temperature dropped to –36° F.

May

The highest temperature ever recorded for the month of May occurred on May 27, 1896, in Salton, Calif. (elevation –263 ft.), where the temperature reached 124° F.

The lowest temperature ever recorded for the month of May occurred on May 7, 1964, in White Mountain 2, Calif. (elevation 12,470 ft.), where the temperature dropped to –15° F.

June

The highest temperature ever recorded for the month of June occurred on June 23, 1902, at Volcano Springs, Calif. (elevation –220 ft.), where the temperature reached 129° F.

The lowest temperature ever recorded for the month of June occurred on June 13, 1907, in Tamarack, Calif. (elevation 8,000 ft.), where the temperature dropped to 2° F.

July

The highest temperature ever recorded for the month of July occurred on July 10, 1913, at Greenland Ranch, Calif. (elevation –178 ft.), where temperature reached 134° F.

The lowest temperature ever recorded for the month of July occurred on July 21, 1911, at Painter, Wyo. (elevation 6,800 ft.), where the temperature fell to 10° F.

August

The highest temperature ever recorded for the month of August occurred on August 12, 1933, at Greenland Ranch, Calif. (elevation –178 ft.), where the temperature reached 127° F.

The lowest temperature ever recorded for the month of August occurred on August 25, 1910, in Bowen, Mont. (elevation 6,080 ft.), where the temperature fell to 5° F.

September

The highest temperature ever recorded for the month of September occurred on September 2, 1950, in Mecca, Calif. (elevation –175 ft.), where the temperature reached 126° F.

The lowest temperature ever recorded for the month of September occurred on September 24, 1926, at Riverside Ranger Station, Mont. (elevation 6,700 ft.), where the temperature fell to –9° F.

October

The highest temperature ever recorded for the month of October occurred on October 5, 1917, in Sentinel, Ariz. (elevation 685 ft.), where the temperature reached 116° F.

The lowest temperature ever recorded for the month of October occurred on October 29, 1917, in Soda Butte, Wyo. (elevation 6,600 ft.), where the temperature fell to –33° F.

November

The highest temperature ever recorded for the month of November occurred on November 12, 1906, in Craftonville, Calif. (elevation 1,759 ft.), where the temperature reached 105° F.

The lowest temperature ever recorded for the month of November occurred on November 16, 1959, at Lincoln, Mont. (elevation 5,130 ft.), where the temperature fell to –53° F.

December

The highest temperature ever recorded for the month of December occurred on December 8, 1938, in La Mesa, Calif. (elevation 539 ft.), where the temperature reached 100° F.

The lowest temperature ever recorded for the month of December occurred on December 19, 1924, at Riverside Ranger Station, Mont. (elevation 6,700 ft.), where the temperature fell to –59° F.

Temperature Extremes in the United States

Source: National Oceanic and Atmospheric Administration, Environmental Data and Information Service, and National Climatic Center

The Highest Temperature Extremes

Greenland Ranch, California, with 134° F on July 10, 1913, holds the record for the highest temperature ever officially observed in the United States. This station was located in barren Death Valley, 178 feet below sea level. Death Valley is about 140 miles long, four to six miles wide, and oriented north to south in southwestern California. Much of the valley is below sea level and is flanked by towering mountain ranges with Mt. Whitney, the highest landmark in the 48 conterminous states, rising to 14,495 feet above sea level, less than 100 miles to the west. Death Valley has the hottest summers in the Western Hemisphere, and is the only known place in the United States where nighttime temperatures sometimes remain above 100° F.

The highest annual normal (1941–1970 mean) temperature in the United States, 78.2° F, and the highest summer (June–August) normal temperature, 92.8° F, are for Death Valley, California. The highest winter (December–February) normal temperature is 72.8° F for Honolulu, Hawaii.

Amazing temperature rises of 40° to 50° F in a few minutes occasionally may be brought about by chinook winds.[1]

---

1. A warm, dry wind that descends from the eastern slopes of the Rocky Mountains, causing a rapid rise in temperature.

The Lowest Temperature Extremes

The lowest temperature on record in the United States, –79.8° F, was observed at Prospect Creek Camp in the Endicott Mountains of northern Alaska (latitude 66°48′N, longitude 150°40′W) on Jan. 23, 1971. The lowest ever recorded in the conterminous 48 states, –69.7° F, occurred at Rogers Pass, in Lewis and Clark County, Mont., on Jan. 20, 1954. Rogers Pass is in mountainous and heavily forested terrain about one half of a mile east of and 140 feet below the summit of the Continental Divide.

The lowest annual normal (1941–1970 mean) temperature in the United States is 9.3° F for Barrow, Alaska, which lies on the Arctic coast. Barrow also has the coolest summers (June–August) with a normal temperature of 36.4° F. The lowest winter (December–February) normal temperature, is –15.7° F for Barter Island on the Arctic coast of northeast Alaska.

In the 48 conterminous states, Mt. Washington, N.H. (elevation 6,262 feet), has the lowest annual normal temperature, 26.9° F, and the lowest normal summer temperature, 46.8° F. A few stations in the northeastern United States and in the upper Rocky Mountains have normal annual temperatures in the 30s; summer normal temperatures at these stations are in the low 50s. Winter normal temperatures are lowest in northeastern North Dakota, 5.6° F for Langdon Experiment Farm, and in northwestern Minnesota, 5.3° F for Hallock.

Some Outstanding Temperature Rises

In 12 hours: 83° F, Granville, N.D., Feb. 21, 1918, from –33° F to 50° F from early morning to late afternoon.

In 15 minutes: 42° F, Fort Assiniboine, Mont., Jan. 19, 1892, from –5° F to 37° F.

In seven minutes: 34° F, Kipp, Mont., Dec. 1, 1896. The observer also reported that a total rise of 80° F occurred in a few hours and that 30 inches of snow disappeared in half a day.

In two minutes: 49° F, Spearfish, S.D., Jan. 22, 1943, from –4° F at 7:30 A.M. to 45° F at 7:32 A.M.

Some Outstanding Temperature Falls

In 24 hours: 100° F, Browing, Mont., Jan. 23–24, 1916, from 44° F to –56° F.

In 12 hours: 84° F, Fairfield, Mont., Dec. 24, 1924, from 63° F at noon to –21° F at midnight.

In 2 hours: 62° F, Rapid City, S.D., Jan. 12, 1911, from 49° F at 6:00 A.M. to –13° F at 8:00 A.M.

In 27 minutes: 58° F, Spearfish, S.D., Jan. 22, 1943, from 54° F at 9:00 A.M. to –4° F at 9:27 A.M.

In 15 minutes: 47° F, Rapid City, S.D., Jan. 10, 1911, from 55° F at 7:00 A.M. to 8° F. at 7:15 A.M.

Tornado Facts and Myths

Tornadoes, violently rotating columns of air extending from a thunderstorm to the ground, are among nature's most virulent storms. In an average year, 800 tornadoes are reported across the United States, resulting in 80 deaths and more than 1,500 injuries. The worst tornadoes are capable of tremendous destruction with wind speeds of 250 miles per hour or more.

Tornadoes can occur anywhere in the U.S. at any time of the year. In the southern states, the peak tornado season is March through May, while peak months in the northern states are during the summer.

Myth: Areas near rivers, lakes, and mountains are safe from tornadoes.

Fact: No place is safe. In the late 1980s, a tornado swept through Yellowstone National Park leaving a path of destruction up and down a 10,000-foot mountain.

Myth: The low pressure in a tornado causes buildings to "explode" as the tornado passes overhead.

Fact: Violent winds exceeding 200 miles per hour and debris slamming into buildings cause most structural damage.

Myth: Windows should be opened before a tornado approaches to equalize pressure and minimize damage.

Fact: Opening windows allows damaging winds to enter the structure and wastes precious time. Leave the windows alone; instead, immediately go to a safe place.

GREAT DISASTERS

The following lists are not all-inclusive due to space limitations. Only disasters involving great loss of life and/or property, historical interest, or unusual circumstances are listed. Data as of late August 1999. For other disasters *see* Current Events: What Happened in 1999.

WORST UNITED STATES DISASTERS

AIRCRAFT

1979 **May 25, Chicago:** American Airlines DC-10 lost left engine upon take-off and crashed seconds later, killing all 272 persons aboard and three on the ground in worst U.S. air disaster.

DAM

1928 **March 12, Santa Paula, Calif.:** collapse of St. Francis Dam left 450 dead.

DROUGHT

1930s **Many states:** longest drought of 20th century. Peak periods were 1930, 1934, 1936, 1939, and 1940. During 1934, dry regions stretched solidly from N.Y. and Pa. across the Great Plains to the Calif. coast. A great "dust bowl" covered 50 million acres in south central plains during winter of 1935-1936.

EARTHQUAKE

1906 **April 18, San Francisco:** earthquake accompanied by fire razed more than 4 sq mi.; more than 500 dead or missing.

EPIDEMIC

1918 **Nationwide:** Spanish influenza killed over 500,000 Americans.

EXPLOSION

1947 **April 16–18, Texas City, Tex.** most of the city destroyed by a fire and subsequent explosion on the French freighter *Grandcamp* carrying a cargo of ammonium nitrate. At least 516 were killed and over 3,000 injured.

FIRE

1871 **Oct. 8, Peshtigo, Wis.:** over 1,200 lives lost and 2 billion trees burned in forest fire.

FLOOD

1889 **May 31, Johnstown, Pa.:** more than 2,200 died in flood.

HURRICANE

1900 **Aug. 27–Sept. 15, Galveston, Tex.:** the "Galveston Hurricane" killed over 6,000 from devastation due to both winds and tidal wave.

MARINE

1865 **April 27, Mississippi River, Tenn.:** boiler explosion on Mississippi River steamboat *Sultana,* near Memphis; 1,547 killed.

MINE

1907 **Dec. 6, Monongha, W. Va.:** coal mine explosion killed 361.

OIL SPILL

1989 **Mar. 24, Prince William Sound, Alaska:** tanker *Exxon Valdez* hit an undersea reef and released 10 million plus gallons of oil into the waters.

RAILROAD

1918 **July 9, Nashville, Tenn.:** 101 killed in a two-train collision near Nashville.

SUBMARINE

1963 **April 10, North Atlantic:** atomic-powered submarine *Thresher* sank; 129 dead.

TERRORIST ATTACK

1995 **April 19, Oklahoma City:** car bomb exploded outside Federal office building, collapsing wall and floors. 168 persons were killed, including 19 children and one person who died in rescue effort. Over 220 buildings sustained damage. Timothy McVeigh and Terry Nichols later convicted in the antigovernment plot to avenge the Branch Davidian standoff in Waco, Tex. exactly two years earlier. (*See* Miscellaneous Disasters.)

TORNADO

1925 **March 18, Mo., Ill., and Ind.:** great "Tri-State Tornado;" 689 deaths. Over 2,000 injured. Property damage estimated at $16.5 million.

WINTER STORM

1888 **March 11–14, East Coast:** the "Blizzard of 1888." 400 people died; as much as five feet of snow. Damage was estimated at $20 million.

EARTHQUAKES AND VOLCANIC ERUPTIONS

C.E. 79 **Aug. 24, Italy:** eruption of Mt. Vesuvius buried cities of Pompeii and Herculaneum, killing thousands.

856 **Dec. 22, Damghan, Iran:** 200,000 were killed in one of the deadliest earthquakes on record.

893 **March 23, Ardabil, Iran:** earthquake killed about 150,000 people.

1138 **Aug. 9, Aleppo, Syria:** deadly earthquake claimed lives of 230,000 people.

1290 **Sept., Chihli, China:** earthquake killed about 100,000 people.

1556 **Jan. 23, Shaanxi (Shensi) Province, China:** most deadly earthquake in history; 830,000 killed.

1667 **Nov., Shemakha, Caucasia:** earthquake killed about 80,000 people.

1727 **Nov. 18, Tabriz, Iran:** about 77,000 victims killed in deadly earthquake.

1755 **Nov. 1, Portugal:** one of the most severe of recorded earthquakes leveled Lisbon and was felt as far away as southern France and North Africa; 70,000 killed.

1811 **Dec. 16, Mississippi Valley nr. New Madrid, Mo.:** earthquake reversed the course of the Mississippi River. Fatalities unknown due to sparse population in area. Aftershocks and tremors continued into 1812. It has been estimated that three of the series of earthquakes had surface-wave magnitudes of 8.6, 8.4, and 8.8 on the Richter scale. It is the largest series of earthquakes known to have occurred in North America.

1883 Aug. 26–28, Netherlands Indies: eruption of Krakatau; violent explosions destroyed two-thirds of island. Sea waves occurred as far away as Cape Horn, and possibly England. Estimated 36,000 dead.

1886 Aug. 31, Charleston, S.C.: 60 persons killed and damage to city extensive. Earthquake's magnitude was 7.7 on the Richter scale.

1902 May 8, Martinique, West Indies: Mt. Pelée erupted and wiped out city of St. Pierre; 40,000 dead.

1906 April 18, San Francisco: earthquake accompanied by fire razed more than 4 sq mi.; more than 500 dead or missing.

1908 Dec. 28, Messina, Sicily: about 85,000 killed and city totally destroyed by earthquake.

1915 Jan. 13, Avezzano, Italy: earthquake left 29,980 dead.

1920 Dec. 16, Gansu (Kansu) Province, China: earthquake killed 200,000.

1923 Sept. 1, Japan: earthquake destroyed third of Tokyo and most of Yokohama. More than 140,000 killed in magnitude 8.3 quake.

1927 May 22, nr. Xining, China: magnitude 8.3 earthquake claimed approximately 200,000 victims.

1932 Dec. 25, Gansu, China: magnitude 7.6 earthquake rattled China, killing approximately 70,000.

1933 March 10, Long Beach, Calif.: 117 left dead by earthquake.

1935 May 30, Pakistan: earthquake at Quetta killed 30,000–60,000.

1939 Jan. 24, Chile: earthquake razed 50,000 sq mi.; about 30,000 killed.
Dec. 27, Northern Turkey: severe quakes destroyed city of Erzingan; about 100,000 casualties.

1950 Aug. 15, India: earthquake affected 30,000 sq mi. in Assam; 20,000–30,000 believed killed.

1964 March 28, Alaska: strongest earthquake ever to strike North America hit 80 miles east of Anchorage; followed by seismic wave 50 feet high that traveled 8,445 miles at 450 miles per hour; 117 killed.

1970 May 31, Peru: earthquake left more than 50,000 dead, 17,000 missing.

1972 Dec. 22, Managua, Nicaragua: earthquake devastated city, leaving up to 6,000 dead.

1976 Feb. 4, Guatemala: quake left over 23,000 dead.
July 28, Tangshan, China: earthquake devastated 20-sq-mi. area of city, leaving 242,000 confirmed dead, with estimates placing toll as high as 655,000.
Aug. 17, Mindanao, Philippines: earthquake and tidal wave left up to 8,000 dead or missing.

1978 Sept. 16, Tabas, Iran: earthquake destroyed city in eastern Iran, leaving 25,000 dead.

1985 Sept. 19–20, Mexico: earthquake registering 8.1 on Richter scale struck central and southwestern regions, devastating part of Mexico City and three coastal states. An estimated 25,000 killed.
Nov. 14–16, Colombia: eruption of Nevada del Ruiz, 85 miles northwest of Bogotá. Mud slides buried most of the town of Armero and devastated Chinchiná. About 25,000 killed.

1988 Dec. 7, Armenia: earthquake measuring 6.9 on the Richter scale killed nearly 25,000, injured 15,000, and left at least 400,000 homeless.

1989 Oct. 17, San Francisco Bay Area: earthquake measuring 7.1 on Richter scale killed 67 and injured over 3,000. Over 100,000 buildings damaged or destroyed; damage cost city billions of dollars.

1990 June 21, Northwestern Iran: earthquake measuring 7.7 on Richter scale destroyed cities and villages in Caspian Sea area. At least 50,000 dead, over 60,000 injured, and 400,000 homeless.

1994 Jan. 17, San Fernando Valley, Calif.: earthquake measuring 6.6 on Richter scale killed 61 and injured over 8,000. Damage estimated at $13–20 billion.

1995 Jan.17, Osaka, Kyoto, and Kobe, Japan: 5,100 killed and 26,800 injured, estimated damage $100 billion. Epicenter 12 miles under Awaji Island in the Inland Sea. Magnitude: 7.2.

1997 May 12, Northeastern Iran: severe earthquake measuring 7.1 on Richter scale left more than 1,500 people dead and at least 4,460 injured.
June–Sept., Southern Montserrat: ongoing eruption of Soufriere Hills volcano since July 1995; killed 20 persons in major eruption on June 25, 1997, rendered southern two-thirds of Montserrat uninhabitable, and forced some 8,000 of the island's 12,000 residents to abandon the island.

1998 May 30, Northern Afghanistan: magnitude 7.1 earthquake and aftershocks killed an estimated 5,000 and injured at least 1,500. A Feb. 4th quake in same area killed about 2,300.

1999 Jan. 25, Western Colombia: 1,124 dead and 4,000 injured in magnitude 6 earthquake in and around the city of Armenia. More than 200,000 left homeless; city plagued by looting and violence among desperate survivors.
Aug. 17, Turkey: magnitude 7.4 earthquake devastated the northwest portion of the country. Nearly 14,000 confirmed dead, with thousands more missing. Additional 43,000 were injured.

MAJOR U.S. EPIDEMICS

1793 Philadelphia: more than 4,000 residents died from yellow fever.

1832 July–Aug., New York City: over 3,000 people killed in a cholera epidemic.
Oct., New Orleans: cholera took the lives of 4,340 people.

1848 New York City: more than 5,000 deaths caused by cholera.

1853 New Orleans: yellow fever killed 7,790.

1867 New Orleans: 3,093 perished from yellow fever.

1878 Southern States: over 13,000 people died from yellow fever in lower Mississippi Valley.

1916 Nationwide: over 7,000 deaths occurred and 27,363 cases were reported of polio (infantile paralysis) in America's worst polio epidemic.

1918 March–Nov., Nationwide: outbreak of Spanish influenza killed over 500,000 people in the worst single U.S. epidemic.

1949 Nationwide: 2,720 deaths occurred from polio, and 42,173 cases were reported.

1952 Nationwide: polio killed 3,300; 57,628 cases reported; worst epidemic since 1916.

1981 1981 to Dec. 1998: total U.S. AIDS cases reported to Centers for Disease Control: 688,200; total AIDS deaths reported: 405,816.

FLOODS, AVALANCHES, AND TIDAL WAVES

1228 Holland: 100,000 people reputedly drowned by sea flood in Friesland.

1642 China: rebels destroyed Kaifeng seawall; 300,000 drowned.

1896 June 15, Sanriku, Japan: earthquake and tidal wave killed 27,000.

1889 May 31, Johnstown, Pa.: more than 2,200 died in flood.

1953 Northwest Europe: storm followed by floods devastated North Sea coastal areas. Netherlands was hardest hit with 1,794 dead.

1959 Dec. 2, Frejus, France: flood caused by collapse of Malpasset Dam left 412 dead.

1960 Agadir, Morocco: 10,000–12,000 dead as earthquake set off tidal wave and fire, destroying most of city.

1962 Jan. 10, Peru: avalanche down Huascaran, extinct Andean volcano, killed more than 3,000.

1963 Oct. 9, Italy: landslide into the Vaiont Dam; flood killed about 2,000.

1966 Oct. 21, Aberfan, Wales: avalanche of coal, waste, mud, and rocks killed 144 people, including 116 children in school.

1969 Jan. 18–26, Southern Calif.: floods and mudslides from heavy rains caused widespread property damage; at least 100 dead. Another downpour (Feb. 23–26) caused further floods and mudslides; at least 18 dead.

1970 Nov. 13, East Pakistan: 200,000 killed by cyclone-driven tidal wave from Bay of Bengal. Over 100,000 missing.

1972 Feb. 26, Man, W. Va.: more than 118 died when slag-pile dam collapsed under pressure of torrential rains and flooded 17-mile valley.

    June 9–10, Rapid City, S.D.: flash flood caused 237 deaths and $160 million in damage.

    June 20, Eastern Seaboard: tropical storm Agnes, in ten-day rampage, caused widespread flash floods. Death toll 129; 115,000 left homeless; damage estimated at $3.5 billion.

1976 Aug. 1, Loveland, Colo.: flash flood along Route 34 in Big Thompson Canyon left 139 dead.

1988 Aug.–Sept., Bangladesh: heaviest monsoon in 70 years inundated three-fourths of country, killing more than 1,300 and leaving 30 million homeless. Damage estimated at over $1 billion.

1993 June–Aug., Ill., Iowa, Kan., Ky., Minn., Mo., Neb., N.D., S.D., Wis.: two months of heavy rain caused Mississippi River and tributaries to flood in ten states, causing almost 50 deaths and about $12 billion in damage to property and agriculture in Midwest. Almost 70,000 left homeless.

1997 Dec. 1996–Jan. 1997, U.S. West Coast: torrential rains and snowmelt produced severe floods in parts of Calif., Ore., Wash., Idaho, Nev., and Mont., causing 36 deaths and about $2–3 billion in damage.

    March, Ohio and Mississippi Valleys: flooding and tornadoes plagued Ark., Mo., Miss., Tenn., Ill., Ind., Ky., Ohio, and W.Va. 67 were killed and damage totaled approximately $1 billion.

1998 July 17, Papua New Guinea: spurred by undersea earthquake, three tsunamis wiped out entire villages in the northwestern province of Sepik. One tidal wave reported by survivor to be 30 ft. high. At least 2,000 found or presumed dead. Many who were injured by the tsunamis were later killed by deadly gangrene infections.

    Summer, Central and Northeast China: heaviest flooding of Yangtze and other rivers since 1954. More than 3,000 killed and 14 million left homeless. Estimated damages exceed $20 billion.

1999 Summer, Asia: flooding plagued Asia again after weeks of torrential downpours. More than 950 killed and millions left homeless in S. Korea, China, Japan, the Philippines, and Thailand.

TROPICAL STORMS

Cyclones, hurricanes, and typhoons are the same kind of tropical storm but are called by different names in different areas of the world.

CYCLONES

1864 Oct. 5, India: most of Calcutta denuded by cyclone; 70,000 killed.

1942 Oct. 16, India: cyclone devastated Bengal; about 40,000 lives lost.

1960 Oct. 10, East Pakistan: cyclone and tidal wave killed about 6,000.

1963 May 28–29, East Pakistan: cyclone killed about 22,000 along coast.

1965 May 11–12 and June 1–2, East Pakistan: cyclones killed about 47,000.

    Dec. 15, Karachi, Pakistan: cyclone killed about 10,000.

1970 Nov. 12–13, East Pakistan: cyclone and tidal waves killed 200,000 and another 100,000 were reported missing.

1971 Sept. 29, Orissa state, India: cyclone and tidal wave off the Bay of Bengal killed as many as 10,000.

1974 Dec. 25, Darwin, Australia: cyclone destroyed nearly the entire city, causing mass evacuation; 50 reported dead.

1977 Nov. 19, Andhra Pradesh, India: cyclone and tidal wave claimed lives of 20,000.

1991 April 30, southeastern Bangladesh: cyclone killed over 131,000 and left as many as 9 million homeless. Thousands of survivors died from hunger and water-borne disease.

U.S. HURRICANES

(U.S. deaths only, except where noted)

1776 Sept. 2–Sept. 9, N.C. to Nova Scotia: called the "Hurricane of Independence", it is believed that 4,170 in the U.S. and Canada died in the storm.

1856 Aug. 11, Last Island, La.: 400 died.

1893 Aug. 28, Savannah, Ga., Charleston, S.C., Sea Islands, S.C.: at least 1,000 died.

1900 Aug. 27–Sept. 15, Galveston, Tex. and Texas Gulf Coast: more than 8,000 died in hurricane and tidal wave. The "Galveston Hurricane" is considered the deadliest in U.S. history.

1909 Sept. 10–21, La. and Miss.: 350 deaths.

1915 Aug. 5–23, East Tex. and La.: 275 killed.

1919 Sept. 2–15, Fla., La., and Tex.: 287 deaths, and 488 deaths at sea.

1926 Sept. 11–22, Fla. and Ala.: 243 deaths.

1928 Sept. 6–20, Southern Fla.: 1,836 died and 1,870 injured.

1935 **Aug. 29–Sept. 10, Southern Fla.:** 408 killed.

1938 **Sept. 10–22, Long Island and southern New England:** 600 deaths; 1,764 injured.

1944 **Sept. 9–16, N.C. to New England:** 46 deaths, and 344 deaths at sea.

1947 **Sept. 4–21, Fla. and mid-Gulf Coast:** 51 killed.

1954 **Aug. 25–31, N.C. to New England:** "Carol" killed 60 and injured 1,000 in Long Island–New England area.

Oct. 5–18, S.C. to N.Y.: "Hazel" killed 95 in U.S.; about 400–1,000 in Haiti; 78 in Canada.

1955 **Aug. 7–21, N.C. to New England:** "Diane" took 184 lives.

1957 **June 25–28. Tex. to Ala.:** "Audrey" wiped out Cameron, La., causing 390 deaths.

1960 **Aug. 29–Sept. 13, Fla. to New England:** "Donna" killed 50 in the U.S. 115 deaths in Antilles— mostly from flash floods in Puerto Rico.

1961 **Sept. 3–15, Tex. coast:** "Carla" devastated Texas gulf cities, taking 46 lives.

1965 **Aug. 27–Sept. 12, southern Fla. and La.:** "Betsy" killed 75 people.

1969 **Aug. 14–22, Miss., La., Ala., Va., and W. Va.:** 256 killed and 68 persons missing as a result of "Camille."

1972 **June 14–23, Fla. to N.Y.:** "Agnes" caused 117 deaths (50 in Pa.).

1979 **Aug. 25–Sept. 7, Caribbean Islands to New England:** "David" caused five U.S. deaths; 1,200 in the Dominican Republic.

1980 **Aug. 3–10, Caribbean Islands to Tex. Gulf:** "Allen" killed 28 in U.S.; over 200 in Caribbean.

1985 **Oct.–Nov.:** "Juan" struck La. and the Southeast. Though only a category 1 hurricane, it caused severe flooding and $1.5 billion in damages. 63 lives were lost.

1989 **Sept. 10–22, Caribbean Sea, S.C., and N.C.:** "Hugo" claimed 49 U.S. lives (71 killed overall); $4.2 billion paid in insurance claims.

1992 **Aug. 22–26, South Fla., La., and Bahamas:** Gulf Coast hurricane "Andrew," with damage estimated at $15–$20 billion, is most costly hurricane in U.S. history.

1996 **Sept. 5, N.C. and Va.:** "Fran," a category 3 hurricane, took 37 lives and caused $5.0 billion in damage.

OTHER HURRICANES

1780 **Oct. 10–16, Barbados, West Indies:** "The Great Hurricane of 1780" killed 20–22,000 persons and completely flattened the islands of Barbados, Martinique, and St. Eustatius; is the deadliest western hemisphere hurricane on record.

1926 **Oct. 20, Cuba:** powerful hurricane killed 650.

1930 **Sept. 3, Santo Domingo:** hurricane killed about 8,000 people.

1934 **Sept. 21, Japan:** hurricane killed more than 4,000 on Honshu.

1955 **Sept. 19, Mexico:** "Hilda" took 200 lives.

Sept. 22–28, Caribbean: "Janet" killed 200 in Honduras and 300 in Mexico.

1961 **Oct. 31, British Honduras:** "Hattie" devastated capital Belize, killed at least 400.

1963 **Oct. 2–7, Caribbean:** "Flora" killed about 7,200 in Haiti and Cuba.

1966 **Sept. 24–30, Caribbean area:** "Inez" killed 293.

1974 **Sept. 14–19, Honduras:** "Fifi" struck northern section of country, leaving 8,000 dead, 100,000 homeless.

1988 **Sept. 12–17, Caribbean Sea and Gulf of Mexico:** "Gilbert" took at least 260 lives and caused some 39 tornadoes in Tex.

1997 **Oct. 8–10, southern Mexico:** "Pauline" devastated resort city of Acapulco and villages along the coast in states of Oaxaca and Guerrero, leaving 217 dead and 20,000 homeless.

1998 **Sept. 20–29, Caribbean, Fla. Keys, and Gulf Coast:** "Georges" killed about 600 people, mostly in Dominican Republic. Damage estimated to be $5 billion, including $2 billion in Puerto Rico.

Oct. 26–Nov. 4, Central America (notably, Honduras and Nicaragua): "Mitch" killed more than 11,000 people in Central America, becoming the deadliest Atlantic storm in 200 years. Winds reached as high as 180 m.p.h. Two to three million people were left homeless and more than $5 billion in damage was done to crops and infrastructure in Honduras, Nicaragua, and Guatemala.

TYPHOONS

1906 **Sept. 18, Hong Kong:** typhoon with tsunami killed an estimated 10,000 persons.

1949 **Dec. 5, off Korea:** typhoon struck fishing fleet; several thousand men reported dead.

1959 **Aug. 20, Fukien province, China:** "Iris" killed 2,334.

Sept. 27, Honshu, Japan: "Vera" killed an estimated 4,464.

1960 **June 9, Fukien province, China:** "Mary" caused at least 1,600 deaths.

1984 **Sept. 2–3, Philippines:** "Ike" hit seven major islands, leaving 1,300 dead.

1991 **Nov. 5, Central Philippines:** flash floods triggered by tropical storm "Thelma" killed about 3,000 people. Leyte city of Ormoc was worst hit.

U. S. TORNADOES

1840 **May 6, Natchez, Miss.:** tornado struck heart of the city, killing 317 and injuring over 1,000.

1880 **April 18, Marshfield, Mo.:** series of 24 tornadoes demolished city, killing 99 people.

1884 **Feb. 19, Miss., Ala., N.C., S.C., Tenn., Ky., Ind.:** tornadoes caused estimated 800 deaths.

1890 **March 27, Louisville, Ky.:** twister hit community and caused 76 deaths.

1896 **May 27, St. Louis, Mo.:** tornado destroyed large section of the city, killing 255.

1899 **June 12, New Richmond, Wis.:** tornado struck while circus was in town, causing 117 deaths.

1902 **May 18, Goliad, Tex.:** tornado killed 114.

1903 **June 1, Gainesville, Holland, Ga.:** twister caused 98 deaths.

1905 **May 10, Snyder, Okla.:** tornado killed 97.

1908 **April 24, Amite, La.; Purvis, Miss.:** tornado killed 143.

April 24, Natchez, Miss.: twister struck, causing 91 deaths.

1913 **March 23, Omaha, Neb.:** tornado devastated city Easter Sunday evening, killing 103.

1917 **May 26, Mattoon, Ill.:** tornado smashed area, causing 101 deaths.

1920 **April 20, Starkville, Miss.; Waco, Ala.:** tornado killed 88.

1924 **June 28, Lorain, Sandusky, Ohio:** tornado swept through cities, causing 85 deaths.

1925 **March 18, Mo., Ill., Ind.:** the "Tri-State Tornado" was the most violent single twister in U.S. history. It caused the deaths of 689 people and injured over 2,000. Property damage was estimated at $16.5 million.

1927 **May 9, Poplar Bluff, Mo.:** twister killed 98.
Sept. 29, St. Louis, Mo.: a five-minute tornado ripped through the city and caused 79 deaths.

1932 **March 21, Ala., Miss., Ga., Tenn.:** outbreak of tornadoes killed 268.

1936 **April 5, Tupelo, Miss.:** tornado ripped through the town, killing 216.
April 6, Gainesville, Ga.: twister obliterated the small mill town, causing 203 deaths.

1944 **June 23, Shinnston, W.Va.:** tornadoes caused 100 deaths.

1947 **April 9, Woodward, Okla.:** tornado demolished town, killing 181.

1952 **March 21–22, Ark., Tenn., Mo., Miss., Ala., Ky.:** tornadoes caused 343 deaths.

1953 **May 11, Waco, Tex.:** a single tornado struck, killing 114.
June 8, Flint, Mich.: tornado killed 116.
June 9, Worcester, Mass.: tornado hit town, causing 90 deaths.

1955 **May 25, Udall, Kans.:** tornado killed 80.

1965 **April 11, Iowa, Ind., Ohio, Mich:** tornadoes in Iowa, Ill., Ind., Ohio, Mich., and Wis. caused 256 deaths.

1974 **April 3–4:** a series of 148 twisters comprised the deadly 1974 "Super Tornado Outbreak" that struck 13 states in the East, South, and Midwest. Before it was over, 330 died and 5,484 were injured in a damage path covering more than 2,500 miles. It was the worst tornado outbreak in U.S. history.

1999 **Jan. 17–22:** a series of tornadoes swept through Tenn. and Ark., leaving 17 dead. Damages were estimated at $1.3 billion.

May 3: unusually large twister, thought to have been a mile wide at times, killed 41 people and injured at least 748 others in Okla. A separate tornado killed another 5 and injured about 150 in Kans. Damages totaled at least $1 billion.

NUCLEAR POWER PLANT ACCIDENTS

1952 **Dec. 12, Chalk River, nr. Ottawa, Canada:** a partial meltdown of the reactor's uranium fuel core resulted after the accidental removal of four control rods. Although millions of gallons of radioactive water accumulated inside the reactor, there were no injuries.

1957 **Oct. 7, Windscale Pile No. 1, north of Liverpool, England:** fire in a graphite-cooled reactor spewed radiation over the countryside, contaminating a 200-sq-mi area.

South Ural Mountains: explosion of radioactive wastes at Soviet nuclear weapons factory 12 miles from city of Kyshtym forced the evacuation of over 10,000 people from a contaminated area. No casualties were reported by Soviet officials.

1976 **nr. Greifswald, East Germany:** radioactive core of reactor in the Lubmin nuclear power plant nearly melted down due to the failure of safety systems during a fire.

1979 **March 28, Three Mile Island, nr. Harrisburg, Pa.:** one of two reactors lost its coolant, which caused the radioactive fuel to overheat and caused a partial meltdown. Some radioactive material was released.

1986 **April 26, Chernobyl, nr. Kiev, former U.S.S.R.:** explosion and fire in the graphite core of one of four reactors released radioactive material that spread over part of the Soviet Union, Eastern Europe, Scandinavia, and later Western Europe. 31 claimed dead. Total casualties are unknown and estimates run into the thousands. Worst such accident to date.

FIRES AND EXPLOSIONS

1666 **Sept. 2, England:** "Great Fire of London" destroyed St. Paul's Church, etc. Damage £10 million.

1835 **Dec. 16, New York City:** 530 buildings destroyed by fire.

1871 **Oct. 8, Chicago:** the "Chicago Fire" burned 17,450 buildings, killed 250 persons; $196 million damage.

1872 **Nov. 9, Boston:** fire destroyed 800 buildings; $75 million damage.

1876 **Dec. 5, New York City:** fire in Brooklyn Theater killed more than 300.

1881 **Dec. 8, Vienna:** at least 620 died in fire at Ring Theatre.

1900 **May 1, Scofield, Utah:** explosion of blasting powder in coal mine killed 200.
June 30, Hoboken, N.J.: piers of North German Lloyd Steamship line burned; 326 dead.

1903 **Dec. 30, Chicago:** Iroquois Theatre fire killed 602.

1906 **March 10, France:** explosion in coal mine in Courrières killed 1,060.

1907 **Dec. 6, Monongha, W. Va.:** coal mine explosion killed 361.
Dec. 19, Jacobs Creek, Pa.: explosion in coal mine left 239 dead.

1909 **Nov. 13, Cherry, Ill.:** explosion in coal mine killed 259.

1911 **March 25, New York City:** fire in Triangle Shirtwaist Factory fatal to 145.

1913 **Oct. 22, Dawson, N.M.:** coal mine explosion left 263 dead.

1917 **April 10, Eddystone, Pa.:** explosion in munitions plant killed 133.

1930 **April 21, Columbus, Ohio:** fire in Ohio State Penitentiary killed 320 convicts.

1937 **March 18, New London, Tex.:** explosion destroyed schoolhouse; 294 killed.

1942 **April 26, Manchuria:** explosion in Honkeiko Colliery killed 1,549.
Nov. 28, Boston: Coconut Grove nightclub fire killed 491.

1944 **July 6, Hartford, Conn.:** fire and ensuing stampede in main tent of Ringling Brothers Circus killed 168, injured 487.
July 17, Port Chicago, Calif.: 322 killed when ammunition ships exploded.
Oct. 20, Cleveland: liquid-gas tanks exploded, killing 130.

1946 **Dec. 7, Atlanta:** fire in Winecoff Hotel killed 119.

1947 **April 16–18, Texas City, Tex.:** most of the city destroyed by a fire and subsequent explosion on the French freighter *Grandcamp* carrying a cargo of ammonium nitrate. At least 516 were killed and over 3,000 injured.

1949 **Sept. 2, China:** fire on Chongqing (Chungking) waterfront killed 1,700.

1954 **May 26, off Quonset Point, R.I.:** explosion and fire aboard aircraft carrier *Bennington* killed 103 crewmen.

1956 **Aug. 7, Colombia:** about 1,100 reported killed when seven army ammunition trucks exploded at Cali.

Aug. 8, Belgium: 262 died in coal mine fire at Marcinelle.

1960 **Jan. 21, Coalbrook, South Africa:** coal mine explosion killed 437.

Nov. 13, Syria: 152 children killed in moviehouse fire.

1961 **Dec. 17, Niteroi, Brazil:** circus fire fatal to 323.

1962 **Feb. 7, Saarland, West Germany:** coal mine gas explosion killed 298.

1963 **Nov. 9, Japan:** explosion in coal mine at Omuta killed 447.

1965 **May 28, India:** coal mine fire in state of Bihar killed 375.

June 1, near Fukuoka, Japan: coal mine explosion killed 236.

1967 **May 22, Brussels:** fire in L'Innovation, major department store, left 322 dead.

July 29, off North Vietnam: fire on U.S. carrier *Forrestal* killed 134.

1969 **Jan. 14, Pearl Harbor, Hawaii:** nuclear aircraft carrier *Enterprise* ripped by explosions; 27 dead, 82 injured.

1970 **Nov. 1, Saint-Laurent-du-Pont, France:** fire in dance hall killed 146 young people.

1972 **May 13, Osaka, Japan:** 118 people died in fire in nightclub on top floor of Sennichi department store.

June 6, Wankie, Rhodesia: explosion in coal mine killed 427.

1973 **Nov. 29, Kumamoto, Japan:** fire in Taiyo department store killed 101.

1974 **Feb. 1, Sao Paulo, Brazil:** fire in upper stories of bank building killed 189 persons, many of whom leaped to their deaths.

1975 **Dec. 27, Dhanbad, India:** explosion in coal mine followed by flooding from nearby reservoir left 372 dead.

1977 **May 28, Southgate, Ky.:** fire in Beverly Hills Supper Club; 167 dead.

1978 **July 11, Tarragona, Spain:** 140 killed at coastal campsite when tank truck carrying liquid gas overturned and exploded.

Aug. 20, Abadan, Iran: nearly 400 killed when arsonists set fire to crowded theater.

1982 **Dec. 18–21, Caracas, Venezuela:** power-plant fire left 128 dead.

1986 **Dec. 31, San Juan, P.R.:** arson fire in Dupont Plaza Hotel was set by three employees, killing 96 people.

1989 **June 3, Ural Mountains:** liquefied petroleum gas leaking from a pipeline running alongside the Trans-Siberian railway near Uta, 72 miles east of Moscow, exploded and destroyed two passing passenger trains. About 500 travelers were killed and 723 injured of an estimated 1,200 passengers on both trains.

Oct. 23, Pasadena, Tex.: a huge explosion followed by a series of others and a raging fire at a plastics manufacturing plant owned by Phillips Petroleum Co. killed 22 and injured more than 80 persons. A large leak of ethylene was presumed to be the cause.

1990 **March 25, New York City:** arson fire in the illegal Happy Land Social Club, in the Bronx, killed 87 people.

1993 **May 10, near Bangkok, Thailand:** fire in doll factory killed at least 187 persons and injured 500 others. World's deadliest factory fire.

1999 **March 24, Chamonix, France:** Belgian truck carrying margarine and flour broke out into flames in the Mont Blanc tunnel, trapping dozens of cars. Death toll was at least 42.

WORST U.S. FOREST FIRES

1871 **Oct. 8–14, Peshtigo, Wis:** over 1,200 lives lost and 4 million acres burned in nation's worst forest fire.

1894 **Sept. 1, Minn.:** forest fires ravaged over 160,000 acres and destroyed six towns, killing 600, including 413 in town of Hinckley.

1889 **June 6, Seattle, Wash.:** fire destroyed 64 acres of the city and killed 2 persons. Damage was estimated at $15 million.

1910 **Aug. 10, Idaho:** fires burned 2 million acres of woods and killed over 70 people.

1918 **Oct. 13–15, Minn. and Wis.:** forest fire struck towns in both states; 1,000 died, including 400 in town of Cloquet, Minn. About $1 million in losses.

1947 **Oct. 25–27, Maine:** forest fire destroyed part of Bar Harbor and damaged Acadia National Park.

1956 **Nov. 25, Calif.:** raging fire destroyed 40,000 acres in Cleveland National Forest and caused 11 deaths.

1988 **Aug.–Sept., Western U.S.:** fires destroyed over 1.2 million acres in Yellowstone National Park and damaged Alaska woodlands.

1991 **Oct. 20–23, Oakland–Berkeley, Calif.:** brush fire in drought-stricken area destroyed over 3,000 homes and apartments. At least 24 persons died; damage estimated at $1.5 billion.

SHIPWRECKS

1833 **May 11, *Lady of the Lake:*** bound from England to Quebec, struck iceberg; 215 perished.

1853 **Sept. 29, *Annie Jane:*** emigrant vessel off coast of Scotland; 348 died.

1865 **April 27, *Sultana:*** boiler explosion on Mississippi River steamboat, near Memphis, 1,547 killed.

1898 **Nov. 26, *City of Portland:*** 157 died nr. Cape Cod.

1904 **June 15, *General Slocum:*** excursion steamer burned in East River, N.Y.; 1,021 perished.

1912 **March 5, *Principe de Asturias:*** Spanish steamer struck rock off Sebastien Point; 500 drowned.

April 15, *Titanic:* sank after colliding with iceberg; 1,513 died.

1914 **May 29, *Empress of Ireland:*** sank after collision in St. Lawrence River; 1,024 perished.

1915 **July 24, *Eastland:*** Great Lakes excursion steamer overturned in Chicago River; 812 died.

1917 **Dec. 6, *Mont Blanc:*** French ammunition ship collided with Belgian steamer in Halifax Harbor, Canada; 1,600 people died.

1928 **Nov. 12, *Vestris:*** British steamer sank in gale off Va.; 110 died.

1934 **Sept. 8, *Morro Castle:*** 134 killed in fire off Asbury Park, N.J.

1939 **May 23, *Squalus:*** submarine with 59 men sank off Hampton Beach, N.H.; 33 saved.

June 1, Submarine *Thetis:* sank in Liverpool Bay, England; 99 perished.

1942 **Oct. 2, *Queen Mary:*** rammed and sank a British cruiser; 338 aboard the cruiser died.

1945 **April 9:** U.S. ship, loaded with aerial bombs, exploded at Bari, Italy; at least 360 killed.

1948 **Nov.:** unidentified Chinese troopship evacuating Nationalist troops from Manchuria sank nr. Yingkow, killing an estimated 6,000 persons.

Dec. 3, *Kiangya:* Chinese passenger ship carrying refugees fleeing Communist troops during civil war, struck an old mine, exploded, and sank off Shanghai; over 3,000 believed to have been killed.

1949 **Sept. 17, *Noronic:*** Canadian Great Lakes cruise ship burned at Toronto dock; about 130 died.

1952 **April 26, *Hobson:*** minesweeper collided with aircraft carrier *Wasp* and sank during night maneuvers in mid-Atlantic; 176 persons lost.

1953 **Jan. 9, *Chang Tyong-Ho:*** South Korean ferry foundered off Pusan; 249 reported dead.

Jan. 31, *Princess Victoria:* British ferry sank in Irish Sea; 133 lost.

1954 **Sept. 26, *Toya Maru:*** more than 1,000 killed when commercial ferry sank in Tsugaru Strait, Japan.

1956 **July 25, *Andrea Doria:*** Italian liner collided with Swedish liner *Stockholm* off Nantucket Island, Mass., sank next day. At least 52 died or were unaccounted for.

1962 **April 8, *Dara:*** British liner exploded and sank in Persian Gulf; 236 dead. Caused by time bomb.

1963 **April 10, *Thresher:*** atomic-powered submarine sank in North Atlantic; 129 dead.

May 4: United Arab Republic ferry capsized and sank in upper Nile; over 200 died.

1968 **Late May, *Scorpion:*** nuclear submarine sank in Atlantic 400 miles S.W. of Azores; 99 dead.

1970 **Dec. 15:** ferry in Korean Strait capsized; 261 lost.

1976 **Oct. 20, *George Prince:*** Mississippi River ferry rammed by Norwegian tanker *Frosta* nr. Luling, La.; 77 dead.

1983 **May 25, *10th of Ramadan:*** Nile steamer caught fire and sank in Lake Nasser, near Aswan, Egypt; 272 dead and 75 missing.

1987 **March 9:** British ferry capsized after leaving Belgian port of Zeebrugge with 500 aboard; 134 drowned. Water rushing through open bow is believed to be probable cause.

Dec. 20.: over 4,000 killed when passenger ferry *Dona Paz* collided with oil tanker *Victor* off Mindoro Is., 110 miles south of Manila.

1990 **April 7, *Scandinavian Star:*** suspected arson fire aboard Danish-owned North Sea ferry killed at least 110 passengers in Skagerrak Strait off Norway.

April 7: double-decker ferry sank in Gyaing River in Myanmar (Burma) during a storm and 215 persons were believed drowned.

1991 **Dec. 14:** ferry carrying 569 passengers sank in Red Sea off coast of Safaga, Egypt, after hitting a coral reef. Over 460 people believed drowned.

1993 **Feb. 17, *Neptune:*** triple-deck ferry capsized off southern peninsula of Haiti during a squall. Over 1,000 passengers believed drowned. About 300 survived the sinking.

1994 **Sept. 28, *Estonia:*** passenger ferry capsized off coast of Southwest Finland and sank in a stormy Baltic Sea. Only about 140 of the estimated 1,040 passengers aboard survived.

1996 **Jan. 21, *Gurita:*** overloaded ferry sank off the coast of northern Sumatra, killing 340.

1999 **Feb., *Harta Rimba:*** ship sank in the South China Sea, killing about 325 people. The ship had not been licensed for passenger use.

MYSTERIOUS DISAPPEARANCES

1872 ***Mary Celeste:*** the brigantine set sail from New York harbor for Genoa, Italy, on Nov. 5. A British brigantine, the *DeGratia,* discovered the ship derelict on Dec. 5 and boarded her. Everyone aboard the *Mary Celeste* had vanished—her captain, his family, and its 14-man crew. The ship was in perfect order with ample supplies and there was no sign of violence or trouble. The fate of the crew remains unknown.

1928 **Dec. 22, *Köbenhavn:*** the five-masted Danish steel barque, a sail-training ship with a crew of 75 including 45 boy cadets, sailed from the River Plate for Melbourne, Australia, on Dec. 14. The last radio contact with the ship was made on Dec. 22 and all was well. The *Köbenhavn* and its crew disappeared without a trace and no one knows what happened to it.

AIRCRAFT CRASHES

(150 deaths or more, with exceptions)

1921 **Aug. 24, England:** British dirigible *AR-2* broke in two on trial trip near Hull; 62 died.

1925 **Sept. 3, Caldwell, Ohio:** U.S. dirigible *Shenandoah* broke apart; 14 dead.

1930 **Oct. 5, Beauvais, France:** British dirigible *R 101* crashed, killing 47.

1933 **April 4, N.J.:** U.S. dirigible *Akron* crashed; 73 died.

1937 **May 6, Lakehurst, N.J.:** German zeppelin *Hindenburg* destroyed by fire at tower mooring; 36 killed.

1945 **July 28, New York City:** U.S. Army bomber B-25 crashed into Empire State Building; 13 dead.

1960 **Dec. 16, New York City:** United DC-8 and Trans World Super Constellation collided then crashed in two boroughs, killing 134 in air and on ground.

1961 **Feb. 15, nr. Brussels:** 72 on board and farmer on ground killed in crash of Sabena plane; U.S. figure skating team wiped out.

1966 **Dec. 24, Binh Thai, South Vietnam:** crash of military-chartered plane into village killed 129.

1971 **July 30, Morioka, Japan:** Japanese Boeing 727 and F-86 fighter collided in mid-air; 162 died.

1972 **Aug. 14, East Berlin, East Germany:** Soviet-built East German Ilyushin plane crashed, killing 156.

Dec. 3, Santa Cruz de Tenerife, Canary Islands: Spanish charter jet carrying West German tourists crashed on take-off; all 155 aboard killed.

1973 **Jan. 22, Kano, Nigeria:** 171 Nigerian Muslims returning from Mecca and five crewmen died in crash.

Feb. 21, Sinai: civilian Libyan Arab Airlines Boeing 727 shot down by Israeli fighters after it had strayed off course; 108 died, five survived.

Officials claimed that the pilot had ignored fighters' warnings to land.

1974 March 3, Paris: Turkish DC-10 jumbo jet crashed in forest shortly after take-off; all 346 passengers and crew killed.

Dec. 4, Colombo, Sri Lanka: Dutch DC-8 carrying Muslims to Mecca crashed on landing approach, killing all 191 persons aboard.

1975 April 4, near Saigon, Vietnam: Air Force Galaxy C-5A crashed after take-off, killing 172, mostly Vietnamese children.

Aug. 3, Agadir, Morocco: Chartered Boeing 707, returning Moroccan workers home after vacation in France, plunged into mountainside; all 188 aboard killed.

1976 Sept. 10, Zagreb, Yugoslavia: midair collision between British Airways Trident and Yugoslav charter DC-9 fatal to all 176 persons aboard.

1977 March 27, Santa Cruz de Tenerife, Canary Islands: Pan American and KLM Boeing 747s collided on runway. All 249 on KLM plane and 333 of 394 aboard Pan Am jet killed. Total of 582 is highest for any type of aviation disaster.

1978 Jan. 1, Bombay: Air India 747 with 213 aboard exploded and plunged into sea minutes after takeoff.

Sept. 25, San Diego, Calif.: Pacific Southwest plane collided in midair with Cessna. All 135 on airliner, 2 in Cessna, and 7 on ground killed for total of 144.

Nov. 15, Colombo, Sri Lanka: chartered Icelandic Airlines DC-8, carrying 249 Muslim pilgrims from Mecca, crashed in thunderstorm during landing approach; 183 killed.

1979 May 25, Chicago: American Airlines DC-10 lost left engine upon take-off and crashed seconds later, killing all 272 persons aboard and three on the ground in worst U.S. air disaster.

Nov. 26, Jidda, Saudi Arabia: Pakistan International Airlines 707 carrying pilgrims returning from Mecca crashed on takeoff; all 156 aboard killed.

Nov. 28, Mt. Erebus, Antarctica: Air New Zealand DC-10 crashed on sightseeing flight; 257 killed.

1980 Aug. 19, Riyadh, Saudi Arabia: all 301 aboard Saudi Arabian jet killed when burning plane made safe landing but passengers were unable to escape.

1981 Dec. 1, Ajaccio, Corsica: Yugoslav DC-9 Super 80 carrying tourists crashed into mountain on landing approach, killing all 178 aboard.

1983 Aug. 30, nr. island of Sakhalin off Siberia: South Korean civilian jetliner Boeing 747, flight KAL-007, shot down by Soviet fighter after it strayed off course into Soviet airspace. All 269 aboard killed. Secret Soviet documents released in Oct. 1992 reveal that the plane was flying a straight course for two hours with its navigational lights on and did not take evasive action. Crew was unaware of its location and never saw the Soviet fighter that downed them. The Soviet fighter did not give a warning by firing tracer bullets as originally claimed. Recorded conversations indicated that the crew members did not know what hit them.

Nov. 26, Madrid: a Colombian Avianca Boeing 747 crashed near Mejorada del Campó Airport killing 183 persons aboard. Eleven people survived the accident.

1985 June 23, off coast of Ireland: Air-India Boeing 747 exploded over Atlantic; all 329 aboard were killed.

Aug. 12, Japan: Japan Air Lines Boeing 747 crashed into a mountain, killing 520 of the 524 aboard.

Dec. 12, Gander, Newfoundland: a chartered Arrow Air DC-8, bringing American soldiers home for Christmas, crashed on takeoff. All 256 aboard died.

1987 May 9, Poland: Polish airliner Ilyushin 62M, on charter flight to N.Y., crashed after takeoff from Warsaw, killing 183.

Aug. 16, Detroit: Northwest Airlines McDonnell Douglas MD-30 plunged to heavily traveled boulevard, killing 156. Girl, 4, only survivor.

Nov. 26, south of Mauritius: South African Airways Boeing 747 went down in rough seas; 160 died.

Nov. 29, Burma: Korean Air Boeing 747 jetliner exploded from bomb planted by North Korean agents and crashed into sea, killing all 115 aboard.

1988 July 3, Persian Gulf: U.S. Navy cruiser *Vincennes* shot down Iran Air A300 Airbus, killing 290 persons, after mistaking it for an attacking jet fighter.

Aug. 28, Ramstein Air Force Base, West Germany: three jets from Italian Air Force acrobatic team collided in mid-air during air show and crashed, killing 70 persons, including the pilots and spectators on the ground. It is worst air-show disaster in history.

Dec. 21, Lockerbie, Scotland: a N.Y.-bound Pan-Am Boeing 747 exploded in flight from a terrorist bomb and crashed into Scottish village, killing all 259 aboard and 11 on the ground. Passengers included 35 Syracuse University students and many U.S. military personnel.

1989 June 7, Paramaribo, Suriname: a Surinam Airways DC-8 carrying 174 passengers and nine crew members crashed into the jungle while making a third attempt to land in a thick fog, killing 168 aboard.

1991 July 11, Jedda, Saudi Arabia: Canadian-chartered DC-8 carrying pilgrims returning to Nigeria crashed after takeoff, killing 261 persons.

1994 April 14, Northern Iraq: two American F-15C fighter aircraft mistook two U.S. Army blackhawk helicopters for Russian-made Iraqi MI-24 helicopters and shot them down over no-fly zone, killing all 26 on board.

April 26, Nagoya, Japan: a China Airlines A-300 Airbus from Taiwan crash-landed and exploded on the tarmac. Only seven of the 271 passengers aboard survived.

June 6, Xian, China: a Russian-built Tupolev-154 airliner of China Northwest Airlines crashed 10 minutes after takeoff, killing all 160 aboard.

1995 Dec. 20, near Cali, Colombia: 160 people killed when American Airlines Boeing 757 crashed in Andean Mountains.

1996 Jan. 8, Kinshasa, Zaire: a Russian-built Antonov-32 cargo plane crashed after takeoff from Kinshasa into the center of the city, killing over 350 people and injuring at least 470.

Feb. 5, off coast of Puerto Plata, Dominican Republic: a Boeing 737 crashed into Atlantic Ocean after takeoff, killing 189.

July 17, off coast of Long Island, N.Y.: a TWA Boeing 747-100 bound for Paris from New York exploded over waters of eastern L.I. and crashed into Atlantic Ocean, killing all 230 aboard.

Nov. 12, near New Delhi, India: shortly after takeoff, Saudi Arabian Airlines Boeing 747 collided in midair with Kazak Airlines Ilyushin 76 plane approaching the New Delhi airport. All 349 passengers and crew were killed; the world's worst midair collision.

1997 **Aug. 6, Guam:** South Korean Air Boeing 747-300 from Seoul crashed into jungle near Agana International Airport killing 227 persons; 27 survived.
Sept. 26, nr. northern Indonesia: Indonesian Garuda Airlines A-300 Airbus jetliner crashed while approaching Medan Airport, Sumatra, killing all 234 persons aboard.

1998 **Feb. 3, Mt. Cermis, Italy:** low-flying U.S. Marine surveillance jet on training flight accidentally cut

ski-lift cable-car line, causing all 20 people aboard to fall some 260 feet to their deaths.
Feb. 16, Taipei, Taiwan: China Airlines Airbus 300 jumbo jet crashed while trying to land in fog at Chiang Ki-Shek International Airport, killing all 196 passengers and crew and at least six persons on the ground.
Sept. 2, Nova Scotia, Canada: Swissair flight from New York to Geneva crashed off Canadian coast, killing all 229 aboard. 136 Americans were on the McDonnell Douglas MD-11.

SPACE ACCIDENTS

1967 **Jan. 27, *Apollo 1*:** a fire aboard the space capsule on the ground at Cape Kennedy, Fla. killed astronauts Virgil I. Grissom, Edward H. White, and Roger Chaffee.
April 23–24, *Soyuz 1*: Vladimir M. Komarov was killed when his craft crashed after its parachute lines, released at 23,000 feet for reentry, became snarled.

1971 **June 6–30, *Soyuz 11*:** three cosmonauts, Georgi T. Dolrovolsky, Vladislav N. Volkov, and Viktor I. Patsayev, found dead in the craft after its automatic landing. Apparent cause of death was loss

of pressurization in the space craft during reentry into the earth's atmosphere.

1980 **March 18, U.S.S.R.** a Vostok rocket exploded on its launch pad while being refueled, killing 50 at the Plesetsk Space Center.

1986 **Jan 28, *Challenger* Space Shuttle:** exploded 73 seconds after lift off, killing all seven crew members. They were: Francis R. Scobee, Michael J. Smith, Judith A. Resnick, Ronald E. McNair, Ellison S. Onizuka, Gregory B. Jarvis, and schoolteacher Christa McAuliffe. A booster leak ignited the fuel, causing the explosion.

RAILROAD ACCIDENTS

NOTE: Very few passengers were killed in a single U.S. train wreck up until 1853. These early trains ran slowly and made short trips, night travel was rare, and there were not many of them in operation.

1831 **June 17:** the boiler exploded on America's first passenger locomotive, *The Best Friend of Charleston*, killing the fireman. He was the first person in America to be killed in a railroad accident.

1833 **Nov. 8, nr. Heightstown, N.J.:** world's first train wreck and first passenger fatalities recorded. A 24-passenger Camden & Amboy train derailed due to a broken axle, killing two passengers and injuring all others. Former President John Quincy Adams and Cornelius Vanderbilt, who later made a fortune in railroads, were aboard the train.

1853 **May 6, Norwalk, Conn:** a New Haven Railroad train ran through an open drawbridge and plunged into the Norwalk River. Forty-six passengers were crushed to death or drowned. This was the first major drawbridge accident.

1856 **July 17, Camp Hill, Pa.:** two Northern Penn trains crashed head-on. Sixty-six church school children bound for a picnic died in the flaming wreckage.

1876 **Dec. 29, Ashtabula, Ohio:** a Lake Shore train fell into the Ashtabula River when the bridge it was crossing collapsed during a snowstorm. Ninety-two were killed.

1887 **Aug. 10, nr. Chatsworth, Ill.:** a burning railroad trestle collapsed while a Toledo, Peoria & Western train was crossing, killing 81 and injuring 372.

1904 **Aug. 7, Eden, Colo.:** train derailed on bridge during flash flood; 96 killed.

1910 **March 1, Wellington, Wash.:** two trains swept into canyon by avalanche; 96 dead.

1915 **May 22, Gretna, Scotland:** two passenger trains and troop train collided; 227 killed.

1917 **Dec. 12, Modane, France:** nearly 550 killed in derailment of troop train near mouth of Mt. Cenis tunnel.

1918 **July 9, Nashville, Tenn.:** 101 killed in a two-train collision near Nashville.

Nov. 1, New York City: derailment of subway train in Malbone St. tunnel in Brooklyn left 92 dead.

1926 **March 14, Virilla River Canyon, Costa Rica:** an over-crowded train carrying pilgrims derailed while crossing the Colima Bridge, killing over 300 people and injuring hundreds more.

1939 **Dec. 22, nr. Magdeburg, Germany:** more than 125 killed in collision; 99 killed in another wreck near Friedrichshafen.

1943 **Dec. 16, nr. Rennert, N.C.:** 72 killed in derailment and collision of two Atlantic Coast Line trains.

1944 **March 2, nr. Salerno, Italy:** 521 suffocated when Italian train stalled in tunnel.

1949 **Oct. 22, nr. Nowy Dwor, Poland:** more than 200 reported killed in derailment of Danzig-Warsaw express.

1950 **Nov. 22, Richmond Hill, N.Y.:** 79 died when one Long Island Rail Road commuter train crashed into rear of another.

1951 **Feb. 6, Woodbridge, N.J.:** 85 died when Pennsylvania Railroad commuter train plunged through temporary overpass.

1952 **Oct. 8, Harrow-Wealdstone, England:** two express trains crashed into commuter train; 112 dead.

1957 **Sept. 1, nr. Kendal, Jamaica:** about 175 killed when train plunged into ravine.
Sept. 29, nr. Montgomery, West Pakistan: express train crashed into standing oil train; nearly 300 killed.
Dec. 4, St. John's, England: 92 killed, 187 injured as one commuter train crashed into another in fog.

1960 **Nov. 14, Pardubice, Czechoslovakia:** two trains collided; 110 dead, 106 injured.

1962 May 3, nr. Tokyo: 163 killed and 400 injured when train crashed into wreckage of collision between inbound freight train and outbound commuter train.

1963 Nov. 9, nr. Yokohama, Japan: two passenger trains crashed into derailed freight train, killing 162.

1964 July 26, Custoias, Portugal: passenger train derailed; 94 dead.

1970 Feb. 4, nr. Buenos Aires: 236 killed when express train crashed into standing commuter train.

1972 July 21, Seville, Spain: head-on crash of two passenger trains killed 76.

Oct. 6, nr. Saltillo, Mexico: train carrying religious pilgrims derailed and caught fire, killing 204 and injuring over 1,000.

Oct. 30, Chicago: two Illinois Central commuter trains collided during morning rush hour; 45 dead and over 200 injured.

1974 Aug. 30, Zagreb, former Yugoslavia: train entering station derailed, killing 153 and injuring over 60.

1981 June 6, nr. Mansi, India: driver of train carrying over 500 passengers braked to avoid hitting a cow, causing train to plunge off a bridge into the Baghmati River; 268 passengers were reported killed, but at least 300 more were missing.

1982 July 11, Tepic, Mexico: Nogales-Guadalajara train plunged down mountain gorge, killing 120.

1989 Jan. 15, Maizdi Khan, Bangladesh: a train carrying Muslim pilgrims crashed head-on with a mail train, killing at least 110 persons and injuring as many as 1,000. Many people were riding on the roof of the trains and between the cars.

Aug. 10, nr. Los Mochis, Mexico: a second-class passenger train traveling from Mazatlán to Mexicali, plunged off a bridge at Puente del Rio Bamoa into the river and killed an estimated 85 people and injured 107.

1990 Jan. 4, Sangi village, Sindh province, Pakistan: an overcrowded sixteen-car passenger train was switched to the wrong track and rammed into a standing freight train. At least 210 persons were killed and 700 were believed injured in what is said to be Pakistan's worst train disaster.

1993 Sept. 22, nr. Mobile, Ala.: Amtrak's *Sunset Limited,* en route to Miami, jumped rails on weakened bridge that had been damaged by a barge, and plunged in Big Bayou Canot, killing 47 persons.

1995 Aug. 20, Firozabad, Northern India: a speeding passenger train rammed another train that was stalled after hitting a cow. About 300 persons were killed and over 400 injured.

1997 March 3, Punjab province, Pakistan: passenger train crashed due to failed brakes, killing 119 and injuring at least 80 persons.

1998 June 3, nr. Eschede, Germany: Inter City Express passenger train traveling at 125 m.p.h. crashed into support pier of an overpass, killing 98. Is nation's worst postwar train accident. Crash may have been caused by a defective wheel.

OIL SPILLS

1978 March 16, off Portsall, France: wrecked supertanker *Amoco Cadiz* spilled 68 million gallons, causing widespread environmental damage over 100 miles of Brittany coast—world's largest tanker disaster.

1979 June 3, Gulf of Mexico: exploratory oil well Ixtoc 1 blew out, spilling an estimated 140 million gallons of crude oil into the open sea. Although it is the largest known oil spill, it had a low environmental impact.

1989 Mar. 24, Prince William Sound, Alaska: tanker *Exxon Valdez* hit an undersea reef and spilled 10 million plus gallons of oil into the waters, causing the worst oil spill in U.S. history.

Dec. 19, off Las Palmas, the Canary Islands: explosion in Iranian supertanker, the *Kharg-5,* tore through its hull and caused 19 million gallons of crude oil to spill out into the Atlantic Ocean about 400 miles north of Las Palmas, forming a 100-square-mile oil slick.

1991 Jan. 25, Southern Kuwait: during the Persian Gulf War, Iraq deliberately released an estimated 460 million gallons of crude oil into the Persian Gulf from tankers at Mina al-Ahmadi and Sea Island Terminal 10 miles off Kuwait. Spill had little military significance. On Jan. 27, U.S. warplanes bombed pipe systems to stop the flow of oil.

1994 Aug. 12, nr. Ursinsk, Russia: huge oil spill from ruptured pipeline.

Sept. 8, Russia: a dam built to contain oil burst and spilled oil into Kolva River tributary. U.S. Energy Department estimated spill at 2 million barrels. Russian state-owned oil company claimed spill was only 102,000 barrels.

1996 Feb. 15, off Welsh coast: supertanker *Sea Empress* ran aground at port of Milford Haven, Wales, spewed out 70,000 tons of crude oil, and created a 25-mile slick.

SPORTS DISASTERS

1955 June 11, Le Mans, France: racing car in Grand Prix hurtled into grandstand, killing 82 spectators.

1964 May 24, Lima, Peru: more than 300 soccer fans killed and over 500 injured during riot and panic following unpopular ruling by referee in Peru vs. Argentina soccer game. It is worst soccer disaster on record.

1971 Jan. 2, Glasgow, Scotland: 66 killed in crush at Glasgow Rangers home stadium when soccer fans trying to leave encountered fans trying to return to stadium after hearing that a late goal had been scored.

1982 Oct. 20, Moscow: according to *Sovietsky Sport,* as many as 340 died at Lenin Stadium when exiting soccer fans collided with returning fans after final goal was scored. All the fans had been crowded into one section of stadium by police.

1985 May 11, Bradford, England: 56 burned to death and over 200 injured when fire engulfed main grandstand at Bradford's soccer stadium.

May 29, Brussels, Belgium: drunken group of British soccer fans supporting Liverpool club stormed stand filled with Italian supporters of Juventus team before European Champion's Cup final. While British fans attacked rival spectators at the Heysel Stadium, concrete retaining wall collapsed and 39 persons were crushed or trampled to death, 32 of them Italians. More than 400 persons were injured.

1988 March 12, Katmandu, Nepal: some 80 soccer fans seeking cover during a violent hail storm at the national stadium were trampled to death in a stampede because the stadium doors were locked.

1989 April 15, Sheffield, England: 94 killed and 170 injured at Hillsborough stadium when throngs of Liverpool soccer fans, many without tickets, col-

lapsed a stadium barrier in a mad rush to see the game between Liverpool and Nottingham Forest. It is Britain's worst soccer disaster.

1996 Oct. 16, Guatemala City: at least 84 killed and 147 injured by stampeding soccer fans before a 1998 World Cup qualifying match between Guatemala and Peru held at Mateo Flores National Stadium.

TERRORIST ATTACKS IN U.S.

1920 Sept. 16, New York City: TNT bomb planted in unattended horse-drawn wagon exploded on Wall Street opposite House of Morgan, killing 35 persons and injuring hundreds more. Bolshevist or anarchist terrorists believed responsible but crime never solved.

1975 Jan. 24, New York City: bomb set off in historical Fraunces Tavern killed four and injured more than 50 persons. Puerto Rican nationalist group (FALN) claimed responsibility and police tied 13 other bombings to it.

1993 Feb. 26, New York City: bomb exploded in basement garage of World Trade Center; killed six and injured at least 1,040 others. Six Middle

Eastern men were later convicted in this act of vengeance for the Palestinian people. They claimed to be retaliating against U.S. support for the Israeli government.

1995 April 19, Oklahoma City: car bomb exploded outside Federal office building, collapsing wall and floors. 168 persons were killed, including 19 children and one person who died in rescue effort. Over 220 buildings sustained damage. Timothy McVeigh and Terry Nichols later convicted in the antigovernment plot to avenge the Branch Davidian standoff in Waco, Tex. exactly two years earlier. (*See* Miscellaneous Disasters.)

WARTIME DISASTERS

1915 May 6, off the coast of Ireland: despite German warnings in newspapers, the Cunard Liner *Lusitania* sailed from N.Y. for Liverpool, England, on May 1st and was sunk by a German submarine. 1,198 passengers and crew, 128 of them Americans, died. Unknown to the passengers, the ship was carrying a cargo of small arms. Disaster contributed to entry of the U.S. into World War I.

1916 Feb. 26, Mediterranean: 3,100 people died when the French cruiser *Provence* was sunk by a German submarine.

1940 Sept. 13, Atlantic Ocean: luxury liner S.S. *City of Benares* sailed from Liverpool with over 90 British children who were being evacuated to Canada to escape harm during World War II. About 600 miles out to sea, the ship was torpedoed by a German submarine during the night and only 13 of the children survived the disaster.[1]

1941 Dec. 7, Pearl Harbor, Hawaii: 1,177 crewmen killed when U.S. Battleship *Arizona* was sunk during a surprise attack on the American naval base by Japanese warplanes. The devastating air strike, which damaged or destroyed every battleship in the U.S. Pacific fleet, is the worst naval catastrophe in U.S. history.

1943 Nov. 26, Mediterranean Sea: 1,105 U.S. soldiers died when the British troopship HMT *Rohna* was sunk by a German air-to-surface guided missile. It is the worst U.S. troopship disaster.

Dec., Bari Harbor, Italy: U.S. ship, damaged during German bombing attack, leaked mustard gas into harbor, killing 83 U.S. servicemen and nearly 1,000 civilians.

1944 Sept. 12, South China Sea: U.S. submarines torpedoed and sank two Japanese troop ships, the *Kachidoki Maru* and the *Rakuyo Maru.* Unknown to the submarines, the Japanese, in

disregard for the rules of treatment of prisoners of war, had forced 2,000 British, Australian, and American POWs into the holds of the ships, which were designed to hold only 300 troops. Later, when the subs discovered the tragedy, they sought to rescue as many survivors as possible. Japanese vessels picked up most of *Kachidoki Maru*'s prisoners but abandoned those from the *Rakuyo Maru,* taking only the Japanese survivors. Of the 1,300 POWs aboard the *Rakuyo Maru,* 159 were rescued, but only seven lived.

Oct. 24, South China Sea: the *Arisan Maru* carrying 1,800 American prisoners was torpedoed by a U.S. submarine and sunk. The Japanese destroyer escort rescued Japanese military and civilian personnel and left the POWs to their fate. It is estimated that only ten prisoners survived the disaster.

Dec. 17–18, Philippine Sea: a typhoon struck U.S. Third Fleet's Task Force 38, sank three destroyers, damaged seven other ships, destroyed 186 aircraft, and killed 800 officers and men.

1945 Jan. 30, Baltic Sea: 7,700 persons died in world's largest marine disaster when the Nazi passenger ship *Wilhelm Gustoff* carrying Germans fleeing Poland was torpedoed by a Soviet submarine.

May 3: several days before World War II ended in Europe, the German passenger ship, *Cap Arcona,* carrying about 6,000, of which an estimated 5,000 were concentration camp prisoners, was sunk by British aircraft. An estimated 5,000 persons were killed.

May 4, Gearhart Mountain, south-central Ore.: six people on a picnic, including a mother and her unborn child, were the only persons ever killed by a balloon-carried bomb launched from Japan. During the war, Japan launched some 6,000 FUGO ("windship weapon") balloons to drift across the Pacific to the U.S. and Canada, each carrying bombs and incendiaries for starting forest fires and creating death and havoc among the American people. Although over 200

---

1. During the war (1939–1945), some 10,000 children were evacuated to stay with foster parents in the United States and Canada. The sinking of the *City of Benares* ended the British government's evacuation program.

of the deadly balloons floated to the U.S. before the war ended, the government kept it a secret from the American people.

July 29, nr. Leyte Gulf, Philippines: heavy cruiser *Indianapolis* torpedoed and sunk by a Japanese submarine. Of the crew of 1,199 men, only 316 survived. Due to Navy blundering, the warship was not reported missing when it did not arrive at Leyte on July 31 as scheduled and therefore no search was ever made for crew. The survivors were discovered by a Navy patrol plane 82 hours after the ship had gone down.

1991 Feb., Kuwait: during Persian Gulf War, Iraqi troops systematically dynamited and set fire to 650 of Kuwait's 950 oil wells, causing world's worst man-made environmental disaster. Total of 749 wells damaged. Last of oil fires extinguished on Nov. 6, 1991.

MISCELLANEOUS DISASTERS

1888 March 11–14, East Coast: the "Blizzard of 1888." 400 people died; as much as five feet of snow. Damage was estimated at $20 million.

1928 March 12, Santa Paula, Calif.: collapse of St. Francis Dam left 450 dead.

1930s Many states: longest drought of the 20th century. Peak periods were 1930, 1934, 1936, 1939, and 1940. During 1934, dry regions stretched solidly from N.Y. and Pa. across the Great Plains to the Calif. coast. A great "dust bowl" covered some 50 million acres in the south central plains during the winter of 1935–1936.

1958 Jan.–Oct., Austria, France, Germany, Italy, and Switzerland: 283 people were killed in mountain climbing accidents in Alps Mountains.

1980 Jan. 20, Sincelejo, Colombia: bleachers at a bull-ring collapsed, leaving 222 dead.

March 30, Stavanger, Norway: floating hotel in North Sea collapsed, killing 123 oil workers.

June–Sept., Central and Eastern U.S.: an estimated 10,000 people were killed during the summer in a long heat wave and drought. Damages totaled about $20 billion.

1981 July 18, Kansas City, Mo.: suspended walkway in Hyatt Regency Hotel collapsed; 113 dead, 186 injured.

1982 Sept. 29–Oct. 1: seven people in the Chicago area were killed after taking Extra-Strength Tylenol capsules laced with cyanide. 31 million bottles of Tylenol were eventually taken off the market. The murderer was never caught.

1984 Dec. 3, Bhopal, India: toxic gas, methyl isocyanate, seeped from Union Carbide insecticide plant, killed more than 2,000, injured about 150,000.

1987 Sept. 18. Goiânia, Brazil: 244 people contaminated with cesium-137 that was removed from a steel cylinder taken from a cancer-therapy machine in an abandoned clinic and sold as scrap. Four people died in worst radiation disaster in Western Hemisphere.

1988 Summer, Central and Eastern U.S.: a severe drought and heat wave killed an estimated 5,000–10,000 people, including heat stress-related deaths. Damages reached $40 billion.

July 6, North Sea off Scotland: 166 workers killed in explosion and fire on Occidental Petroleum's *Piper Alpha* rig in North Sea; 64 survivors. It is the world's worst offshore oil disaster.

1990 July 2, Mecca, Saudi Arabia: a stampede in a 1,800 foot-long pedestrian tunnel leading from Mecca to a tent city for pilgrims killed 1,426 pilgrims who were trampled to death.

1991 Nov. 29, near Coalinga, Calif.: a massive traffic accident occurred during a severe dust storm involving 104 vehicles in a pileup on Interstate 5; 17 persons killed.

1993 April 19, Waco, Tex.: 51-day stalemate between federal agents and members of Christian Branch Davidian cult ended in a fiery tragedy after federal agents botched their assault on the sect's compound. About 80 Branch Davidians, including at least 17 children, died when the compound burned to the ground in a suspicious blaze. Earlier, on Feb. 28, four agents were shot to death in failed attack on heavily armed compound. Jurors in the criminal trial of surviving cult members were unable to determine who fired the first shot. The incident was reopened for investigation in Aug. 1999.

March 12–14, Eastern U.S.: "storm of the century" struck the eastern seaboard, killing approximately 270. Record snowfalls (with rates of 2-3 inches per hour) and high winds caused $3–6 billion in damage.

1995 June 29, Seoul, Korea: five-story wing of Sampoong Department Store collapsed, killing at least 206 people, injuring 910 others.

July 12–17, U.S. Midwest and Northeast: over 800 persons, including 560 in Chicago, died in record heat wave.

1996 Jan. 6–8, Eastern U.S.: heavy snow paralyzed the Appalachians, the mid-Atlantic, and the Northeast. 187 were killed in the blizzard and in the floods that resulted after a sudden warm-up. Damages reached $3 billion.

May 10–11, Mt. Everest, Nepal: eight climbers died near summit during storm on mountain. Is worst single loss of lives to occur in a season on Mt. Everest. Another four died over the remaining course of the month.

1997 April 15, Mecca, Saudia Arabia: fire and stampede in pilgrim's encampment killed 217 and injured at least 1,300.

1998 Summer, Southern U.S.: severe heat and drought spread across Tex. and Okla., all the way to North and South Carolina. At least 200 were left dead and $6–9 billion of damage was estimated.

Aug. 7, Nairobi, Kenya, and Dar es Salaam, Tanzania: U.S. embassies bombed by terrorists, killing 243 in Kenya and 10 in Tanzania; more than 1,000 injured.

1999 Summer, Eastern U.S.: rainfall shortages resulted in what was the worst drought on record for Md., Del., N.J., and R.I. The state of W.Va. was declared a Disaster Area. 3.81 million acres were consumed by fire as of mid-Aug. Crops were severely damaged in many states, putting losses in the mid-Atlantic region at at least $800 million.

Summer, Continental U.S.: record heat continued throughout the country, resulting in drought, crop damage, and 282 deaths nationwide.

U.S. Societies and Associations

Source: Questionnaires to organizations. Names are listed alphabetically according to key word in title; figure in parentheses is year of founding; other figure is membership.

The following is a partial list selected for general readership interest. A comprehensive listing of approximately 23,000 national and international organizations can be found in the *Encyclopedia of Associations*, 31st ed., 1996, published by Gale Research Company, 835 Penobscot Building, 645 Griswold St., Detroit, Mich. 48226-4049, available in most public libraries.

AARP (American Association of Retired Persons) (1958): 601 E. St. N.W., Washington, D.C. 20049. 33,000,000. Phone: (202) 434-2277. www.aarp.org.

Abortion Federation, National (1977): 1755 Mass. Ave., Ste. 600, Washington, D.C. 20036. Phone: (202) 667-5881 (Communications Director) or (800) 772-9100. www.prochoice.org.

Accountants, American Institute of Certified Public (1887): 1211 Avenue of the Americas, New York, N.Y. 10036-8775. 330,000. Phone: (212) 596-6200. www.aicpa.org.

ACSM: American Congress on Surveying and Mapping (1941): 5410 Grosvenor Lane, Ste. 100, Bethesda, Md. 20814-2144. 8,000. Phone: (301) 493-0200. www.survmap.org.

Actors' Equity Association (1913): 165 W. 46th St., New York, N.Y. 10036. Phone: (212) 869-8530. www.actorsequity.org.

Actuaries, Society of (1949): 475 N. Martingale Rd., Ste. 800, Schaumburg, Ill. 60173-2226. 16,900. Phone: (847) 706-3557. www.soa.org.

Aeronautic Association, National (1905): 1815 N. Fort Myer Dr., Ste. 700, Arlington, Va. 22209. 300,000. Phone: (703) 527-0226. www.naa.ycg.org.

African-American Institute, The (1953): 380 Lexington Ave., New York, N.Y. 10168-4298. Phone: (212) 949-5666. www.aaionline.org.

AFS Intercultural Programs—USA (American Field Service) (1947): 198 Madison Avenue, 8th Flr., New York, N.Y. 10016. 100,000. Phone: (212) 299-9000 (or (800) AFS-INFO). www.afs.org.

Agricultural History Society (1919): 1301 New York Ave. N.W., Washington, D.C. 20005-4788. 1,400. Phone: (202) 219-0786. www.iastate.edu/~history_info/aghissoc.htm.

Agronomy, American Society of (1907): 677 S. Segoe Rd., Madison, Wis. 53711-1086. 11,400. Phone: (608) 273-8080; fax: (608) 273-2021. www.agronomy.org.

Aircraft Association, Experimental (1953): P.O. Box 3086, Oshkosh, Wis. 54903-3086. 170,000. Phone: (920) 426-4800. www.eaa.org.

Aircraft Owners and Pilots Association (1939): 421 Aviation Way, Frederick, Md. 21701-4798. 340,000. Phone: (301) 695-2000; fax: (301) 695-2375. www.aopa.org.

Air Force Association (1946): 1501 Lee Highway, Arlington, Va. 22209-1198. 170,000. Phone: (703) 247-5800. www.afa.org.

Air Line Pilots Association (1931): 1625 Massachusetts Ave. N.W., Washington, D.C. 20036 and 535 Herndon Pkwy., Herndon, Va. 20170. 49,000. Phone: (703) 689-2270. www.alpa.org.

Al-Anon Family Group Headquarters, Inc. For families and friends of alcoholics. (1951): 1600 Corporate Landing Pkwy., Virginia Beach, Va. 23454-5617. 33,000 groups worldwide. Phone: (757) 563-1600. www.al-anon.org.

Alcoholics Anonymous (1935): A.A. World Services, Inc., P.O. Box 459, New York, N.Y. 10163. 2,000,000. Phone: (212) 870-3400. www.aa.org.

Alexander Graham Bell Association for the Deaf (1890): 3417 Volta Place N.W., Washington, D.C. 20007-2778. 6,200. Phone: (202) 337-5220 V, TTY. www.agbell.org.

Alzheimer's Association (1980): 919 N. Michigan Ave., Ste. 1000, Chicago, Ill. 60611-1676. Phone: (312) 335-8700; (800) 272-3900. www.alz.org.

American Academy of Allergy, Asthma and Immunology (1943): 611 E. Wells St., Milwaukee, Wis. 53202. 5,000. Phone: (414) 272-6071. www.aaaai.org.

American Alliance for Health, Physical Education, Recreation and Dance (1885): 1900 Association Dr., Reston, Va. 20191. 25,000. Phone: (703) 476-3400. www.aahperd.org.

American Automobile Association (1902): 1000 AAA Dr., Heathrow, Fla. 32746-5063. Phone: (407) 444-7000. www.aaa.com.

American Civil Liberties Union (1920): 125 Broad St., 18th Flr., New York, N.Y. 10004-2400. 275,000. www.aclu.org.

American Contract Bridge League (1927): 2990 Airways Blvd., Memphis, Tenn. 38116-3847. Phone: (901) 332-5586; fax: (901) 398-7754. www.acbl.org.

American Federation of Labor and Congress of Industrial Organizations (AFL-CIO) (1955): 815 16th St. N.W., Washington, D.C. 20006. 14,500,000. Phone: (202) 637-5000. www.aflcio.org.

American Federation of Musicians of the United States and Canada (1896): 1501 Broadway, Ste. 600, Paramount Bldg., New York, N.Y. 10036. Phone: (212) 869-1330. www.afm.org.

American Forests (1875): P.O. Box 2000, Washington, D.C. 20013. 115,000. Phone: (202) 955-4500. www.amfor.org.

American Foundrymen's Society, Inc. (1896): 505 State St., Des Plaines, Ill. 60016-8399. 13,000. Phone: (847) 824-0181; (800) 537-4237. www.afsinc.org.

American Friends Service Committee (1917): 1501 Cherry St., Philadelphia, Pa. 19102-1479. Phone: (215) 241-7000. www.afsc.org.

American Geographical Society, The (1851): 120 Wall St., Ste. 100, New York, N.Y. 10005-3904. 1,500. Phone: (212) 422-5456; fax: (212) 422-5480. email: amgeosoc@earthlink.net. www.personal.umich.edu/~sarhaus/isss/ags.html.

American Geriatrics Society (1942): 770 Lexington Ave., Ste. 300, New York, N.Y. 10021. 6,000. Phone: (212) 308-1414; fax: (212) 832-8646. www.americangeriatrics.org.

American Heart Association (1924): 7272 Greenville Ave., Dallas, Tex. 75231-4596. 4,200,000 volunteers. Phone: (800) AHA-USA1. www.amhrt.org.

American Historical Association (1884): 400 A St. S.E., Washington, D.C. 20003-3889. 15,000. Phone: (202) 544-2422. email: aha@theaha.org. www.theaha.org.

American Indian Affairs, Association on (1923): Tekakwitha Complex, Agency Road #7, Box 268, Sisseton, S.D. 57262. 40,000. Phone: (605) 698-3998 or 3787. www.indian-affairs.org.

American Institute of Planners (1917) and American Society of Planning Officials (1934): Administrative

Offices: 122 S. Michigan Ave., Chicago, Ill. 60603. 30,000. Phone: (312) 431-9100. Headquarters: 1776 Massachusetts Ave. N.W., Washington, D.C. 20036. Phone: (202) 872-0611. www.planning.org.

American Jewish Committee (1906): Jacob Blaustein Building, 165 East 56th Street, New York, N.Y. 10022. 70,000. Phone: (212) 751-4000; fax: (212) 838-2120. www.ajc.org.

American Kennel Club (1884): 260 Madison Ave., New York, N.Y. 10016. 505 member clubs. Phone: (212) 696-8200; (919) 233-9767 (customer service). www.akc.org.

American Legion, The (1919): 700 N. Pennsylvania St., Indianapolis, Ind. 46206. 2,900,000. Phone: (317) 630-1200. www.legion.org.

American Legion Auxiliary (1919): 777 N. Meridian St., 3rd Flr., Indianapolis, Ind. 46204. 1,000,000. Phone: (317) 635-6291. www.legion-aux.org.

American Mensa, Ltd. (1960): 1229 Corporate Drive West, Arlington, Texas 76006–6103. 50,000. Phone: (817) 607-0060. www.us.mensa.org.

American Montessori Society (1960): 281 Park Avenue South, 6th Flr., New York, N.Y. 10010-6102. Phone: (212) 358-1250; fax: (212) 358-1256. www.amshq.org.

American Museum of Natural History (1869): Central Park West at 79th St., New York, N.Y. 10024-5192. 500,000. Phone: (212) 769-5606. www.amnh.org.

Americans for Democratic Action, Inc. (1947): 1625 K St. N.W., Ste. 210, Washington, D.C. 20006. 70,000. Phone: (202) 785-5980. www.adaction.org.

American Society for Nutritional Sciences (1928): 9650 Rockville Pike, Bethesda, Md. 20814-3990. 3,600. Phone: (301) 530-7050. www.faseb.org/asns.

American Society for Public Administration (ASPA) (1939): 1120 G St. N.W., Ste. 700, Washington, D.C. 20005. 12,000. Phone: (202) 393-7878. www.aspanet.org.

American Universities, Association of (1900): 1200 New York Avenue NW, Ste. 550, Washington, D.C. 20005. Phone: (202) 408-7500. www.tulane.edu/~aau.

American Water Resources Association (1964): 950 Herndon Parkway, Ste. 300, Herndon, Va. 20170– 5531. 4,000. Phone: (703) 904-1225. fax: (703) 904-1228. email: awrahq@aol.com. www.awra.org.

Amnesty International USA (1961): 322 Eighth Ave., New York, N.Y. 10001. 300,000. Phone: (212) 807-8400. www.amnesty-usa.org.

AMVETS (American Veterans of World War II, Korea, and Vietnam) (1943): 4647 Forbes Blvd., Lanham, Md. 20706-4380. 250,000. Phone: (301) 459-9600. www.amvets.org.

Animals, The American Society for the Prevention of Cruelty to (ASPCA) (1866): 424 E. 92nd St., New York, N.Y. 10128-6804. 400,000+. Phone: (212) 876-7700. www.aspca.org.

Animals, The Fund For, Inc. (1967): 200 W. 57th St., New York, N.Y. 10019. 175,000. Phone: (212) 246-2096. www.arrs.envirolink.org/fund.

Anthropological Association, American (1902): 4350 N. Fairfax Dr., Ste. 640, Arlington, Va. 22203-1620. 11,500. Phone: (703) 528-1902. www.aaanet.org.

Anti-Defamation League (1913): 823 United Nations Plaza, New York, N.Y. 10017-3560. Phone: (212) 885-7700. www.adl.org.

Anti-Vivisection Society, The American (1883): 801 Old York Rd., #204, Jenkintown, Pa. 19046-1685. 15,000. Phone: (215) 887-0816; fax: (215) 887-2088. www.aavs.org.

Appraisers, American Society of (1936): 555 Herndon Parkway, Ste. 125, Herndon, VA 20170. 6,500. Phone: (800) ASA-VALU or (703) 478-2228. www.appraisers.org.

Arboriculture, International Society of (1924): P.O. Box 3129, Champaign, Ill. 61826-3129. 8,000.

Archaeological Institute of America (1879): 656 Beacon St., Boston, Mass. 02215-2006. 11,000. Phone: (617) 353-9361. email: aia@bu.edu. www.archaeological.org.

Architects, The American Institute of (1857): 1735 New York Ave. N.W., Washington, D.C. 20006-5292. 59,000. Phone: (202) 626-7300. www.aiaonline.com.

Architectural Historians, Society of (1940): 1365 N. Astor St., Chicago, Ill. 60610-2144. 4,000. Phone: (312) 573-1365; fax: (312) 573-1141. www.upenn.edu/sah.

Army, Association of the United States (1950): 2425 Wilson Blvd., Arlington, Va. 22201-3385. 100,000+. Phone: (703) 841-4300. www.ausa.org.

Arthritis Foundation (1948): 1330 West Peachtree St., Atlanta, Ga. 30309. Over 150 local offices. Phone: (404) 872-7100; (800) 283-7800. www.arthritis.org.

Arts, National Endowment for the (1965): 1100 Pennsylvania Ave. N.W., Washington, D.C. 20506. Phone: (202) 682-5400. arts.endow.gov.

ASM International ® (1913): 9639 Kinsman Rd., Materials Park, Ohio 44073-0002. 44,000. Phone: (440) 338-5151; fax: (440) 338-4634. www.asm-intl.org.

Association for Investment Management and Research (1990): 5 Boar's Head Lane, P.O. Box 3668, Charlottesville, Va. 22903-0668. 36,000. Phone: (804) 980-3668. www.aimr.com.

Astronomical Society, American (1899): 2000 Florida Ave. ,Ste. 400, Washington, D.C. 20009. 6,300. Phone: (202) 328-2010. www.aas.org.

Atheists, American (1963): P.O. Box 5733, Parsippany, N.J. 07054-6733. 40,000 families. Phone: (908) 276-7300. www.atheists.org.

Audubon Society, National (1905): 700 Broadway, New York, N.Y. 10003-9562. 550,000. Phone: (212) 979-3000. www.audubon.org.

Authors League of America (1912): 330 W. 42nd St., 29th Flr., New York, N.Y. 10036-6902. 14,000. Phone: (212) 564-8350.

Autism Society of America (1965): 7910 Woodmont Ave., Ste. 300, Bethesda, Md. 20814-3015. 18,000+. Phone: (301) 657-0881; (800) 3AUTISM. www.autism-society.org.

Automobile Club, National (1924): 1151 East Hillsdale Blvd., Foster City, Calif. 94404. 200,000. Phone: (650) 294-7000. www.nationalautoclub.com.

Bar Association, American (1878): 750 N. Lake Shore Dr., Chicago, Ill. 60611-4497. 371,000. Phone: (312) 988-5000. www.abanet.org.

Barber Shop Quartet Singing in America, Society for the Preservation and Encouragement of (SPEBSQSA, Inc.) (1938): 6315 Third Ave., Kenosha, Wis. 53143. 34,000. Phone: (800) 876-SING. www.spebsqsa.org.

Better Business Bureaus, Council of (1912): 4200 Wilson Blvd., Ste. 800, Arlington, Va. 22203-1804. Phone: (703) 276-0100; fax: (703) 525-8277. www.bbb.org.

Bible Society, American (1816): 1865 Broadway, New York, N.Y. 10023-7505. Phone: (800) 32-BIBLE; (212) 408-1200. www.americanbible.org.

Biblical Literature, Society of (1880): 825 Houston Mill Road, Ste. 350, Atlanta, Ga. 30329. 7,000 members, 1,200 subscribers. Phone: (404) 727-3100; fax: (404) 727-3101. www.sbl-site.org.

Big Brothers Big Sisters of America (1977): 230 N. 13th St., Philadelphia, Pa. 19107. Phone: (215) 567-7000. www.bbbsa.org.

Biochemistry and Molecular Biology, American Society for (1906): 9650 Rockville Pike, Bethesda, Md. 20814. 10,000. Phone: (301) 530-7145. www.faseb.org/asbmb.

Biological Sciences, American Institute of (1947): 1444 I St. N.W., Ste. 200, Washington, D.C. 20005. 6,000. Phone: (202) 628-1500, (800) 424-8666. www.aibs.org.

Blind, American Council of the (1961): 1155 15th St. N.W., Ste. 720, Washington, D.C. 20005. 40,000. Phone: (202) 467-5081. www.acb.org.

Blind, National Federation of the (1940): 1800 Johnson St., Baltimore, Md. 21230. 50,000. Phone: (410) 659-9314. www.nfb.org.

B'nai B'rith International (1843): 1640 Rhode Island Ave. N.W., Washington, D.C. 20036-3278. 500,000. Phone: (202) 857-6600. www.bnaibrith.org.

Booksellers Association, American (1900): 828 So. Broadway, Tarrytown, N.Y. 10591. 4,500. Phone: (914) 591-2665, (800) 637-0037. www.bookweb.org.

Boys & Girls Clubs of America (1906): 1230 West Peachtree St. N.W., Atlanta, Ga., 30309. 2,800,000 youth served. Phone: (404) 815-5700; fax: (404) 815-5757. www.bgca.org.

Boy Scouts of America (1910): 1325 W. Walnut Hill Lane, P.O. Box 152079, Irving, Tex. 75015-2079. 4.8 mil. Phone: (972) 580-2000. www.bsa.scouting.org.

Broadcasters, National Association of (1922): 1771 N St. N.W., Washington, D.C. 20036-2891. Phone: (202) 429-5490. www.nab.org.

Brookings Institution, The (1916): 1775 Massachusetts Ave. N.W., Washington, D.C. 20036-2188. Phone: (202) 797-6000. www.brookings.org.

Business Education Association, National (1946): 1914 Association Dr., Reston, Va. 20191-1596. 16,000. Phone: (703) 860-8300; fax: (703) 620-4483. email: nbea@nbea.org; www.nbea.org.

Business Women's Association, American (1949): 9100 Ward Parkway, P.O. Box 8728, Kansas City, Mo. 64114-0728. 80,000. Phone: (816) 361-6621; (800) 228-0007. fax: (816) 361-4991. email: abwa@abwahq.org. www.abwahq.org.

Camp Fire Boys and Girls (1910): 4601 Madison Ave., Kansas City, Mo. 64112-1278. 667,000. Phone: (816) 756-1950. www.campfire.org.

Camping Association, The American (1910): 5000 State Rd. 67 N., Martinsville, Ind. 46151-7902. 5,500, 2,000+ camps. Phone: (765) 342-8456. www.aca-camps.org.

Cancer Society, American (1913): 1599 Clifton Rd. N.E., Atlanta, Ga. 30329. Over 2 million volunteers. Phone: (800) ACS-2345 or check local listings. www.cancer.org.

CARE, Inc. (1945): 151 Ellis St. NE, Atlanta, Ga. 30303-2439. Programs in 62 developing countries. Phone: (800) 521-CARE. www.care.org.

Carnegie Endowment for International Peace (1910): 1779 Massachusetts Ave., N.W., Washington, D.C. 20036–2103. Phone: (202) 483-7600; fax: (202) 483-1840. www.ceip.org.

Catholic Charities USA (1910): 1731 King St., Ste. 200, Alexandria, Va. 22314. 1,400 agencies and institutions. Phone: (703) 549-1390. www.catholiccharitiesusa.org.

Catholic Daughters of the Americas (1903): 10 W. 71st St., New York, N.Y. 10023. 115,000. Phone: (212) 877-3041. www.catholicdaughters.org.

Catholic War Veterans of the U.S.A. Inc. (1935): 441 N. Lee St., Alexandria, Va. 22314. 35,000. Phone: (703) 549-3622. www.va.gov/vso/cwv.htm.

Cerebral Palsy Associations, Inc., United (1949): 1660 L St. N.W., Ste. 700, Washington, D.C. 20036. 153 affiliates. Phone: (202) 973-7197/TT, (800) 872-5827. www.ucpa.org.

Chamber of Commerce of the U.S. (1912): 1615 H St. N.W., Washington, D.C. 20062. 220,000. Phone: (202) 659-6000. www.uschamber.org.

Chemical Engineers, American Institute of (1908): 3 Park Ave., New York, N.Y. 10016-5991. 52,000. Phone: (212) 591-7338; (800) 242-4363. www.aiche.org.

Chemical Society, American (1876): 1155 16th St. N.W., Washington, D.C. 20036. 151,024. Phone: (202) 872-4600. www.acs.org.

Chess Federation, United States (1939): 3054 NYS Rte. 9W, New Windsor, N.Y. 12553. 50,000+. Phone: (914) 562-8350; (800) 388-KING. www.uschess.org.

Child Labor Committee, National (1904): 1501 Broadway, Rm. 1111, New York, N.Y. 10036. Phone: (212) 840-1801.

Children's Book Council (1945): 568 Broadway, Ste. 404, New York, N.Y. 10012. 80. Phone: (212) 966-1990; fax: (212) 966-2073. email: staff@cbcbooks.org. www.cbcbooks.org.

Child Welfare League of America (1920): 440 First St. N.W., Ste. 310, Washington, D.C. 20001-2085. 1,000 agencies. Phone: (202) 638-2952. www.cwla.org.

Chiropractic Association, American (1963): 1701 Clarendon Blvd., Arlington, Va. 22209. 22,000. Phone: (703) 276-8800, (800) 986-4636; fax: (703) 243-2593. www.amerchiro.org.

Cities, National League of (1924): 1301 Pennsylvania Ave. N.W., Washington, D.C. 20004-1763. 18,000 cities and towns. Phone: (202) 626-3000. www.nlc.org.

Civil Air Patrol, National Headquarters (1941): 105 S. Hansell St., Bldg. 714, Maxwell AFB, Ala. 36112-6332. 53,000. Phone: (334) 953-4287. www.cap.af.mil.

Civil Engineers, American Society of (1852): 1801 Alexander Bell Dr., Reston, Va. 20191-4400. 120,000. Phone: (800) 548–ASCE (2723); (703) 295-6300. www.asce.org.

Clinical Pathologists, American Society of (1922): 2100 W. Harrison St., Chicago, Ill. 60612. 77,200. Phone: (312) 738-1336; fax: (312) 738-9798. www.ascp.org.

The College Fund/UNCF (1944): 8260 Willow Oaks Corporate Dr., P.O. Box 10444, Fairfax, Va. 22031. 39 member institutions. Phone: (703) 205-3400, (800) 331-2244; fax: (703) 205-3576. www.uncf.org.

Colleges and Employers, National Association of (formerly College Placement Council) (1956): 62 E. Highland Ave., Bethlehem, Pa. 18017. 3,200. Phone: (800) 544-5272. www.jobweb.org.

Common Cause (1970): 1250 Connecticut Ave. N.W., Washington, D.C. 20036. 250,000. Phone: (202) 833-1200; fax: (202) 659-3716. www.commoncause.org.

Community Cultural Center Association, American (1978): 149 Cannongate 3, Nashua, N.H. 03063. Phone: (603) 886-2748.

Composer/USA, National Association of (1933): P.O. Box 49256, Barrington Station, Los Angeles, Calif. 90049. 600. Phone: (310) 541-8213. www.thebook.com/nacusa.

Congress of Racial Equality (CORE) (1942): 817 Broadway, 3rd Flr., New York, N.Y. 10003. Nationwide network of chapters. Phone: (212) 598-4000; fax: (212) 598-4000. www.core-online.org.

Conscientious Objectors, Central Committee for (1948): 1515 Cherry St., Philadelphia, Pa. 19102. Phone: (215) 563-8787. 655 Sutter St., Ste. 514, San Francisco, Calif. 94102. Phone: (415) 474-3002. www.libertynet.org/ccco.

Conservation Engineers, Association of (1961): Attn: Jim Price, Secretary, c/o Arkansas Game & Fish Commission, #2 Natural Resources Drive, Little Rock, Ark. 72205. Phone: (501) 219-4300.

Consumer Federation of America (1968): 1424 16th St. N.W., Ste. 604, Washington, D.C. 20036. 260 member organizations. Phone: (202) 387-6121. www.consumerfed.org.

Consumers League, National (1899): 1701 K St. N.W., Ste. 1200, Washington, D.C. 20006. Phone: (202) 835-3323. www.natlconsumersleague.org.

Consumers Union (1936): 101 Truman Ave., Yonkers, N.Y. 10703-1057. 4.6 million subscribers to *Consumer Reports Magazine*. Phone: (914) 378-2000. www.consumersunion.org.

Country Music Association (1958): One Music Circle South, Nashville, Tenn. 37203. 7,000+. Phone: (615) 244-2840. www.cmaworld.org.

Credit Management, National Association of (1896): 8815 Centre Park Dr., Ste. 200, Columbia, Md. 21045-2158. 30,000+ members. Phone: (410) 740-5560. www.nacm.org.

Credit Union National Association (1934): P.O. Box 431, Madison, Wis. 53701-0431. 51 state leagues representing 12,400 credit unions. Phone: (800) 356-9655. www.cuna.org.

Crime and Delinquency, National Council on (1907): 685 Market St., #620, San Francisco, Calif. 94105. Criminal justice research, nationwide membership. Phone: (415) 896-6223. http://solar.rtd.utk.edu/ccsi/csusa/cnme/crimedel.html.

CSA/USA, Celiac Sprue Association/United States of America, Inc., (1978): P.O. Box 31700, Omaha, Neb. 68131-0700. 6 regions in U.S., 74 chapters, 36 active resource units. Phone: (402) 558-0600; fax: (402) 558-1347. www.csaceliac.org.

Dairy Council, National (1915): 10255 W. Higgins Rd., Ste. 900 Rosemont, Ill. 60018-5616. Phone: (847) 803-2000; fax: (847) 803-2077. www.ndc.org.

Daughters of the American Revolution, National Society (1896): 1776 D St. N.W., Washington, D.C. 20006-5392. 180,000. Phone: (202) 628-1776. www.dar.org.

Deaf, National Association of the (1880): 814 Thayer Ave., Silver Spring, Md. 20910-4500. 51 state association affiliates. Phone: (301) 587-1788 V; (301) 587-1789 TTY. www.nad.org.

Defenders of Wildlife (1947): 1101 14th St. N.W., #1400, Washington, D.C. 20005. 200,000 members and supporters. Phone: (202) 682-9400. www.defenders.org.

Dental Association, American (1859): 211 E. Chicago Ave., Chicago, Ill. 60611. 141,000. Phone: (312) 440-2500. www.ada.org.

Diabetes Association, American (1940): 1660 Duke St., Alexandria, Va. 22314. Phone: (703) 549-1500; (800) 342-2383. www.diabetes.org/default.asp.

Dignity (1969): 1500 Massachusetts Ave. N.W., Ste. 11, Washington, D.C. 20005. 5,000. Phone: (202) 861-0017 and (800) 877-8797. www.dignityusa.org.

Disabled American Veterans (1920): 807 Maine Ave. S.W., Washington, D.C. 20024. 1,400,000. Phone: (202) 554-3501. www.dav.org.

Dowsers, Inc., The American Society of (1961): P.O. Box 24, Danville, Vt. 05828. 5,000. Phone: (800) 711-9530; fax: (802) 748-8565. email: ASD@dowsers.org. www.newhampshire.com/dowsers.org.

Ducks Unlimited, Inc. (1937): One Waterfowl Way, Memphis, Tenn. 38120. 600,000. Phone: (901) 758-3825. www.ducks.org.

Earthwatch (1971): 680 Mt. Auburn St., Box 9104, Watertown, Mass. 02471. 75,000. Phone: (800) 776-0188; fax: (617) 926-8532. www.earthwatch.org.

Eastern Star, Order of, General Grand Chapter (1876): 1618 New Hampshire Ave. N.W., Washington, D.C. 20009-2549. 1,207,301. Phone: (202) 667-4737. www.easternstar.org.

Easter Seal Society, The National (1919): 230 W. Monroe, Ste. 1800, Chicago, Ill. 60606. 109 state and local affiliate societies operating 500 service sites. Phone: (312) 726-6200; (312) 726-4258 TDD. www.seals.com.

Economic Association, American (1885): 2014 Broadway, Ste. 305, Nashville, Tenn. 37203. 22,000. 5,500 inst. subscribers. Phone: (615) 322-2595. www.vanderbilt.edu/AEA.

Edison Electric Institute (1933): 701 Pennsylvania Ave. N.W., Washington, D.C. 20004-2696. www.eei.org.

Education, American Council on (ACE), (1918): One Dupont Circle N.W., Washington, D.C. 20036-1193. 1,600+ colleges and universities and 200+ higher education associations. Phone: (202) 939-9300. www.acenet.edu.

Educational Exchange, Council on International (1947): 205 E. 42nd St., New York, N.Y. 10017-5706. Phone: (212) 822-2600. www.ciee.org.

Educational Research Association, American (1916): 1230 17th St. N.W., Washington, D.C. 20036-3078. 22,000. Phone: (202) 223-9485. www.aera.net.

Education Association, National (1857): 1201 16th St. N.W., Washington, D.C. 20036-3290. 2.3 million. Phone: (202) 833-4000. www.nea.org.

Electrochemical Society, The (1902): 10 S. Main St., Pennington, N.J. 08534-2896. 7,000. Phone: (609) 737-1902; fax: (609) 737-2743. email: ecs@electrochem.org. www.electrochem.org.

Elks of the U.S.A., Benevolent and Protective Order of the (1868): 2750 N. Lakeview Ave., Chicago, Ill. 60614-1889. 1,300,000. Phone: (773) 755-4700. www.elks.org/default.cfm.

Energy Engineers, Association of (1977): 4025 Pleasantdale Rd., Ste. 420, Atlanta, Ga. 30340. 8,500. Phone: (770) 447-5083; fax: (770) 446-3969. email: info@aeecenter.org. www.aeecenter.org.

English-Speaking Union of the United States (1920): 16 E. 69th St., New York, N.Y. 10021. 18,000. Phone: (212) 879-6800. www.english-speakingunion.org.

Entomological Society of America (1889): 9301 Annapolis Rd., Lanham, Md. 20706-3115. 7,400+. Phone: (301) 731-4535; fax: (301) 731-4538. email: esa@entsoc.org. www.entsoc.org.

Esperanto League for North America, The (1952): P.O. Box 1129, El Cerrito, Calif. 94530. Over 1,000. Phone: (800) 377-3726. www.esperanto-usa.org.

Exceptional Children, The Council for (1922): 1920 Association Dr., Reston, Va. 20191-1589. 54,000. Voice phone: (800) CEC-SPED; TTY: (703) 264-9446; fax: (703) 264-9494. email: cec@cec.sped.org. www.cec.sped.org.

Exploration Geophysicists, Society of (1930): P.O. Box 702740, Tulsa, Okla. 74170-2740. 16,536. Phone: (918) 497-5500. www.seg.org.

Family and Consumer Sciences, American Association of (1909): 1555 King St., Alexandria, Va. 22314. 14,500. Phone: (703) 706-4600. www.aafcs.org.

Family Campers & RVers (1949): 4804 Transit Rd., Bldg. 2, Depew, N.Y. 14043. 42,000 families. Phone: (800) 245-9755; fax: (716) 668-6242. www.fcrv.org.

Family, Career, and Community Leaders of America [evolved from Future Homemakers of America, Inc. (1945)]: 1910 Association Dr., Reston, Va. 20191-1584. 230,000. Phone: (703) 476-4900. www.fhahero.org.

Family Physicians, American Academy of (1947): 8880 Ward Pkwy., Kansas City, Mo. 64114. 88,000. Phone: (816) 333-9700. www.aafp.org.

Family Relations, National Council on (1938): 3989 Central Ave. N.E., #550, Minneapolis, Minn. 55421. 42,000 families. Phone: (612) 781-9331. www.ncfr.com.

Farm Bureau Federation, American (1919): 225 Touhy Ave., Park Ridge, Ill. 60068. 4.7 million member families. Phone: (847) 685-8600. www.fb.com.

Federal Bar Association (1920): 2215 M St. N.W., Washington, D.C. 20037. 15,000. Phone: (202) 785-1614; fax: (202) 785-1568. www.fedbar.org.

Federal Employees, National Federation of (1917): 1016 16th St. N.W., Washington, D.C. 20036. Rep. 150,000. Phone: (202) 862-4400.

Fellowship of Reconciliation (1915): Box 271, Nyack, N.Y. 10960. 20,000. Phone: (914) 358-4601. www.nonviolence.org/for.

Female Executives, National Association for (1972): 30 Irving Place, New York, N.Y. 10003. 150,000+. Phone: (800) 634-6233. www.nafe.com.

FFA Organization, National (1928): 6060 FFA Drive, P.O. Box 68960, Indianapolis, Ind., 46268-0960. Phone: (317) 802-6060. www.ffa.agriculture.com.

Fire Protection Association, National (1896): One Batterymarch Park, P.O. Box 9101, Quincy, Mass. 02269-9101. 65,000+. Phone: (617) 770-3000. www.nfpa.org.

Flag Foundation, National (1968): Flag Plaza, Pittsburgh, Pa. 15219-3630. 3,000+. Phone: (412) 261-1776. www.icss.com/usflag/nff.html.

Fleet Reserve Association (1924): 125 N. West St., Alexandria, Va. 22314-2754. 162,000. Phone: (703) 683-1400; (800) 372-1924. email: news-fra@fra.org. www.fra.org.

Foreign Policy Association (1918): 470 Park Ave. So., New York, N.Y. 10016-6819. Phone: (212) 481-8100. www.fpa.org.

Foreign Relations, Council on (1921): 58 E. 68th St., New York, N.Y. 10021. 3,400. Phone: (212) 734-0400. www.foreignrelations.org.

Foreign Study, American Institute for (1964): 102 Greenwich Ave., Greenwich, Conn. 06830. Phone: (203) 869-9090; (800) 727-AIFS. www.aifs.org.

Forensic Sciences, American Academy of (1948): 410 N. 21st St., Ste. 203/80904, P.O. Box 669, Colorado Springs, Colo. 80901-0669. 4,315. Phone: (719) 636-1100; fax: (719) 636-1993. www.aafs.org.

Foresters, Society of American (1900): 5400 Grosvenor Lane, Bethesda, Md. 20814. 18,000. Phone: (301) 897-8720. www.safnet.org.

4-H Program (early 1900s): Room 3441-S, U.S. Department of Agriculture, Washington, D.C. 20250. 5.6 million. Phone: (202) 720-2908. www.4h-usa.org.

Freedom of Information Center (1958): 127 Neff Annex, Univ. of Missouri, Columbia, Mo. 65211. Phone: (573) 882-4856. www.missouri.edu/~foiwww/

French Institute/Alliance Française (1898): 22 E. 60th St., New York, N.Y. 10022. 9,000. Phone: (212) 355-6100. www.fiaf.org.

Friends of Animals Inc. (1957): 777 Post Rd., Ste. 205, Darien, Conn. 06820. 120,000. Phone: (203) 656-1522. www.envirolink.org/orgs/foa.

Friends of the Earth (1969): 1025 Vermont Ave. N.W., 3rd Flr., Washington, D.C. 20005. 35,000. Phone: (202) 783-7400. www.foe.org.

Gamblers Anonymous: Box 17173, Los Angeles, Calif. 90017. Phone: (213) 386-8789. www.gamblersanonymous.org.

Gay and Lesbian Task Force, National (1973): 1700 Kalorama Rd. N.W., Washington, D.C. 20009-2624. 35,000 members. Phone: (202) 332-6483. www.ngltf.org.

Genealogical Society, National (1903): 4527 17th St. N., Arlington, Va. 22207-2399. 17,000+. Phone: (703) 525-0050; fax: (703) 525-0052. www.ngsgenealogy.org.

Geographers, Association of American (1904): 1710 16th St. N.W., Washington, D.C. 20009-3198. 7,000. Phone: (202) 234-1450; fax: (202) 234-2744. email: gaia@aag.org. www.aag.org.

Geographic Education, National Council for (1915): 16A Leonard Hall, Indiana University of Pennsylvania, Indiana, Pa. 15705. 3,700. Phone: (724) 357-6290.

Geographic Society, National (1888): 1145 17th St. N.W., Washington, D.C. 20036-4688. 9,200,000. Phone: (800) 647-5463. www.nationalgeographic.com.

Geological Institute, American (1948): 4220 King St., Alexandria, Va. 22302-1502. 34 geoscience societies representing 100,000 geoscientists. Phone: (703) 379-2480. www.agiweb.org/.

Geological Society of America, Inc. (1888): 3300 Penrose Pl., P.O. Box 9140, Boulder, Colo. 80301-9140. 15,000. Phone: (303) 447-2020. www.geosociety.org.

German American National Congress, The (Deutsch-Amerikanischer National Kongress— D.A.N.K.) (1958): 4740 N. Western Ave., Executive Office, Chicago, Ill. 60625-2097. Phone: (773) 275-1100. www.dank.org.

Gideons International, The (1889): 2900 Lebanon Rd., Nashville, Tenn. 37214-2540. 130,000. Phone: (615) 883-8533. www.gideons.org.

Gifted, The Association for the (1958): The Council for Exceptional Children, 1920 Association Dr., Reston, Va. 20191-1589. 2,200. Phone: (703) 620-3660.

Girl Scouts of the U.S.A. (1912): 420 Fifth Ave., New York, N.Y. 10018-2798. 2,500,000. Phone: (212) 852-6559. www.gsusa.org.

Girls Incorporated (1945): 120 Wall St., 3rd. Flr., New York, N.Y. 10005. 350,000. Phone: (212) 509-2000. www.girlsinc.org.

Graphoanalysis Society, International (1929): 111 N. Canal St., Chicago, Ill. 60606. 10,000. Phone: (312) 930-9446; www.igas.com.

Gray Panthers (1970): 733 15th St. N.W., Ste. 437, Washington, D.C. 20005. Over 50 chapters (networks). Phone: (202) 737-1160. www.graypanthers.org.

Greenpeace (1971): 1436 U St. N.W., Washington, D.C. 20009. 600,000. Phone: (800) 326-0959. www.greenpeaceusa.org.

Guide Dog Foundation for the Blind, Inc.® (1946): 371 E. Jericho Turnpike, Smithtown, N.Y. 11787-2976. 100,000. Phone: (516) 265-2121; (800) 548-4337; fax: (516) 361-5192. www.guidedog.org.

Hadassah, The Women's Zionist Organization of America (1912): 50 W. 58th St., New York, N.Y. 10019. 385,000. Phone: (212) 355-7900. www.hadassah.org.

Handgun Control, Inc. (1974): 1225 Eye St. N.W., Ste. 100, Washington, D.C. 20005. 380,000. Phone: (202) 898-0792. www.handguncontrol.org.

Heating, Refrigerating and Air-Conditioning Engineers, Inc., American Society of (1959): 1791 Tullie Circle N.E., Atlanta, Ga. 30329. 50,000. Phone: (404) 636-8400. www.ashrae.org.

Helicopter Association International (1948): 1635 Prince St., Alexandria, Va. 22314. Phone: (703) 683-4646; fax: (703) 683-4745. www.rotor.com.

Historians, The Organization of American (1907): Indiana Univ., 112 N. Bryan St., Bloomington, Ind. 47408-4199. 12,000. Phone: (812) 855-7311. www.indiana.edu/~oah.

Historic Preservation, National Trust for (1949): 1785 Massachusetts Ave. N.W., Washington, D.C. 20036. 275,000. Phone: (202) 588-6000. www.nationaltrust.org.

Horse Council, Inc., American (1969): 1700 K St. N.W., #300, Washington, D.C. 20006. More than 190 organizations and 2,400 individuals. Phone: (202) 296-4031. www.horsecouncil.org/ahc.html.

Horse Shows Association, Inc., American (1917): 4047 Iron Works Parkway, Lexington, Ky. 40511. 70,000+. Phone: (212) 972-2473. www.ahsa.org.

Horticultural Association, National Junior (1935): c/o Bill Fountain, 318 Ag Science North, University of Kentucky, Lexington, Ky. 40546. 12,500. Phone: (606) 257-3320.

Horticultural Society, American (1922): 7931 East Boulevard Dr., Alexandria, Va. 22308. 22,000. Phone: (703) 768-5700 or (800) 777-7931; fax: (703) 768-8700. www.ahs.org.

Hostelling International—American Youth Hostels (1934): 733 15th St. N.W., Ste. 840, Washington, D.C. 20005. 124,000. Phone: (202) 783-6161 for membership and reservations. www.hiayh.org.

Humane Association, American (1877): 63 Inverness Drive East, Englewood, Colo. 80112-5117. Phone: (303) 792-9900. www.americanhumane.org.

Humane Society of the United States (1954): 2100 L St. N.W., Washington, D.C. 20037. 5,000,000. Phone: (202) 452-1100. www.hsus.org.

Humanities, National Endowment for the (1965): 1100 Pennsylvania Ave. N.W., Washington, D.C. 20506. Phone: (202) 606-8400. www.neh.fed.us.

Hydrogen Energy, International Association for (1975): P.O. Box 248266, Coral Gables, Fla. 33124. 2,500. Phone: (305) 284-4666. www.iahe.org.

Industrial Engineers, Institute of (1948): 25 Technology Park/Atlanta, Norcross, Ga. 30092. 24,000. Phone: (770) 449-0461.

International Credit Association (ICA) (1912): P.O. Box 15945-314, Lenexa, Kans. 66285-5945. 7,500 members, 100 local associations. Phone: (913) 307-9432; fax: (314) 991-3029. email: icahdqtrs@stlnet.com. www.ica-credit.org.

Izaak Walton League of America (1922): 707 Conservation Lane, Gaithersburg, Md. 20878-2983. 50,000+. Phone: (800) 453-5403. www.iwla.org.

Jewish Community Centers Association (JCC) of North America (1917): 15 E. 26th St., New York, N.Y. 10010-1579. 275+ affiliated Jewish Community Centers, YM-YWHAs, and camps serving 1 million+ members. Phone: (212) 532-4958; fax: (212) 481-4158. email: info@jcca.org. www.jcca.org.

Jewish Congress, American (1918): 15 E. 84th St., New York, N.Y. 10028. 50,000. Phone: (212) 879-4500. www.ajcongress.org.

Jewish Historical Society, American (1892): 2 Thornton Rd., Waltham, Mass. 02154. 3,500. Phone: (781) 891-8110; fax: (617) 899-9208. email: ajhs@ajhs.org. www.ajhs.org.

Jewish War Veterans of the U.S.A. (1896): 1811 R St. N.W., Washington, D.C. 20009-1659. Phone: (202) 265-6280. www.penfed.org/jwv/home.htm.

Jewish Women, National Council of (1893): 53 W. 23rd St., 6th Flr., New York, N.Y. 10010. 90,000. Phone: (212) 645-4048; fax: (212) 645-7466. www.ncjw.org.

John Birch Society (1958): P.O. Box 8040, Appleton, Wis. 54912. Under 100,000. Phone: (920) 749-3780; fax: (920) 749-5062. www.jbs.org.

Journalists, Society of Professional, (1909): 16 S. Jackson, Greencastle, Ind. 46135-1514. 13,500. Phone: (765) 653-3333. www.spj.org.

Judaism, American Council for (1943): P.O. Box 9009, Alexandria, Va. 22304. Phone: (703) 836-2546. www.acjna.org.

Junior Achievement Inc. (1919): One Education Way, Colorado Springs, Colo. 80906. 3 million+. Phone: (719) 540-8000. www.ja.org.

Junior Chamber of Commerce, The United States, Jaycees (1920): 4 West 21 Street, Tulsa, Okla. 74114-1116. 113,000. Phone: (918) 584-2481; fax: (918) 584-4422. www.ajli.org.

Junior Leagues International, Inc., Association of (1921): 660 First Ave., New York, N.Y. 10016-3241. 295 Leagues, 193,000+ members. Phone: (212) 683-1515. www.ajli.org.

Junior State of America (1934): 60 E. Third Ave., Ste. 320, San Mateo, Calif. 94401-4302. 15,000. Phone: (650) 347-1600 or (800) 334-5353. www.jsa.org.

Kiwanis International (1915): 3636 Woodview Trace, Indianapolis, Ind. 46268. 316,000. Phone: (317) 875-8755. email: kiwanismail@kiwanis.org. www.kiwanis.org.

Knights of Columbus (1852): One Columbus Plaza, New Haven, Conn. 06510. 1,600,000. Phone: (203) 772-2130. www.kofc.org.

Knights Templar, Grand Encampment of (1816): 5097 N. Elston Ave., Ste. 101, Chicago, Ill. 60630-2460. 220,000. Phone: (773) 777-3300.

La Leche League International (1956): 1400 N. Meacham Rd., Schaumburg, Ill. 60168-4079. 50,000. Phone: (847) 519-7730. www.lalecheleague.org.

Law, American Society of International (1906): 2223 Massachusetts Ave. N.W., Washington, D.C. 20008. 4,300. Phone: (202) 939-6000. www.asil.org.

League of Women Voters of the U.S. (1920): 1730 M St. N.W., Washington, D.C. 20036-4508. Phone: (202) 429-1965; fax: (202) 429-0854. www.lwv.org.

Legal Aid and Defender Association, National (1911): 1625 K St. N.W., Ste. 800, Washington, D.C. 20006-1604. 2,400. Phone: (202) 452-0620. www.nlada.org.

Legal Secretaries, National Association of (1949): 314 East 3rd St., Ste. 210, Tulsa, Okla. 74120-2409. 6,000. Phone: (918) 582-5188. www.nals.org.

Leukemia Society of America (1949): 600 Third Ave., New York, N.Y. 10016. Phone: (212) 573-8484. www.leukemia.org.

Library Association, American (1876): 50 E. Huron St., Chicago, Il. 60611. 57,000. Phone: (800) 545-2433. www.ala.org.

Lions Clubs International (1917): 300 22nd St., Oak Brook, Ill. 60521-8842. 1,419,408. Phone: (708) 571-5466. www.lr.net/lions/lci.html.

Lung Association, American (1904): 1740 Broadway, New York, N.Y. 10019-4374. 99 constituent and affiliate associations. Phone: (800) LUNG-USA; (800) 586-4872. www.lungusa.org.

Magazine Editors, American Society of (1963): 919 Third Ave., 22nd Flr., New York, N.Y. 10022. 900. Phone: (212) 872-3700. www.asme.magazine.org

Management Accountants, Institute of (1919): 10 Paragon Dr., Montvale, N.J. 07645-1759. 80,000. Phone: (201) 573-9000. www.rutgers.edu/accounting/raw/ima.

Management Association, American (1923): 1601 Broadway, New York, N.Y. 10019-7420. 70,000. Phone: (212) 586-8100. www.tregistry.com/ama.htm.

Management Consultants, Institute of (1968): 1200 19th St. N.W., Ste. 300, Washington, D.C. 20036–2422. 25 chapters. Phone: (202) 857-5334; (800) 221-2557. www.imcusa.org/imc.html.

Manufacturers, National Association of (1895): 1331 Pennsylvania Ave. N.W., Washington, D.C. 20004-1790. Approx. 14,000. Phone: (202) 637-3000. www.nam.org.

March of Dimes Birth Defects Foundation (1938): 1275 Mamaroneck Ave., White Plains, N.Y. 10605. 104 chapters. Phone: (914) 428-7100, (888) 663-4637; tty: (914) 997-4764; fax: (914) 997-4763. email: resourcecenter@modimes.org. www.modimes.org.

Marine Conservation, Center for (1972): 1725 De Sales St. N.W., Ste. 600, Washington, D.C. 20036. 120,000. Phone: (202) 429-5609. www.cmc-ocean.org.

Marine Corps Association (1913): P.O. Box 1775, 715 Broadway, Quantico, Va. 22134. 100,723. Phone: (703) 640-6161; (800) 336-0291. www.mca-marines.org.

Marine Technology Society (1963): 1828 L St. N.W., Ste. 906, Washington, D.C. 20036. 2,000+. Phone: (202) 775-5966; fax: (202) 429-9417. www.cms.udel.edu/mts.

Masons, Royal Arch, General Grand Chapter International (1797): P.O. Box 489, Danville, Ky. 40423-0489. 230,000. Phone: (606) 236-0757.

Mathematical Association of America (1915): 1529 18th St. N.W., Washington, D.C. 20036-1368. 30,000. Phone: (202) 387-5200. www.maa.org.

Mathematical Society, American (1888): P.O. Box 6248, Providence, R.I. 02940-6248. 30,000. Phone: (401) 455-4000. email: ams@ams.org. www.ams.org.

Mayflower Descendants, General Society of (1897): 4 Winslow St., P.O. Box 3297, Plymouth, Mass.

02361. 24,500+. Phone: (508) 746-3188. www.mayflower.org.

Mechanical Engineers, American Society of (1880): 3 Park Ave., New York, N.Y. 10016-5990. 125,000. Phone: (800) THE-ASME. www.asme.org.

Medical Association, American (1847): 515 N. State St., Chicago, Ill. 60610. 300,000 physicians. Phone: (312) 464-5000. www.ama-assn.org.

Mental Health Association, National (1909): 1021 Prince St., Alexandria, Va., 22314-2971. 340 affiliates. Phone: (703) 684-7722; (800) 969-NMHA; TDD (800) 433-5959; fax: (703) 684-5968. email: nmhainfo@aol.com. www.nmha.org

Meteorological Society, American (1919): 45 Beacon St., Boston, Mass. 02108-3693. 10,000+. Phone: (617) 227-2425. www.ametsoc.org/ams.

Military Chaplains Association of the U.S.A. (1925): P.O. Box 42660, Washington, D.C. 20015-0660. 1,500. Phone: (202) 574-2423. www.wrldnet.net/~cma.

Mining, Metallurgical, and Petroleum Engineers, The American Institute of (1871): 3 Park Ave., New York, N.Y. 10016-5998. 4 Member Societies: Society for Mining, Metallurgy and Exploration, The Minerals, Metals & Materials Society, Iron & Steel Society, Society of Petroleum Engineers. Phone: (212) 419-7679; fax: (212) 419-7671. email: AIMENY@aol.com. www.idis.com/aime.

Model Aeronautics, Academy of (1936): 5151 East Memorial Dr., Muncie, Ind. 47302. 150,000. Phone: (765) 287-1256. www.modelaircraft.org.

Modern Language Association of America (1883): 10 Astor Place, New York, N.Y. 10003-6981. 30,000+. Phone: (212) 475-9500. www.mla.org.

Moose International, Inc. (1888): Mooseheart, Ill. 60539. 1,600,000+. Phone: (630) 859-2000. www.mooseintl.org.

Mothers Against Drunk Driving (MADD) (1980): P.O. Box 541688, Dallas, Tex. 75354-1688. 3 million members and supporters. Victim hotline: (800) GET-MADD. www.madd.org.

Motion Picture Arts & Sciences, Academy of (1927): 8949 Wilshire Blvd., Beverly Hills, Calif. 90211-1972. Phone: (310) 247-3000. www.ampas.org.

Multiple Sclerosis Society, National (1946): 733 Third Ave., New York, N.Y. 10017. 350,000. Phone: (800) FIGHT-MS (344-4867). www.nmss.org.

Muscular Dystrophy Association (1950): 3300 East Sunrise Dr., Tucson, Ariz. 85718. 2,300,000 volunteers. Phone: (800) 572-1717. www.mdausa.org.

Museums, American Association of (1906): 1575 Eye St., NW, Ste. 400, Washington, D.C. 20005. 16,000+. Phone: (202) 289-1818; fax: (202) 289-6578, tty: (202) 289-8439. www.aam-us.org.

Muzzle Loading Rifle Association, National (1933): P.O. Box 67, Friendship, Ind. 47021-0067. 25,000. Phone: (812) 667-5131. www.ool.com/nmlra/.

NAFSA: Association of International Educators (1948): 1307 New York Ave. N.W., 8th Flr., Washington, D.C. 20005-4701. 7,500. Phone: (202) 737-3699. www.nafsa.org.

National Abortion and Reproductive Rights Action League (NARAL) (1969): 1156 15th St. N.W., Washington, D.C. 20005. 500,000. Phone: (202) 973-3000. www.naral.org.

National Association for the Advancement of Colored People (1909): 4805 Mt. Hope Dr., Baltimore, Md. 21215. 500,000+. Phone: (410) 358-8900. www.naacp.org.

National Conference for Community and Justice, The (founded as The Natl. Conf. of Christians & Jews) (1927): 475 Park Avenue South, 19th Flr., New York, N.Y. 10016-6901. Phone: (212) 545-1300. www.nccj.org.

National Cooperative Business Association (formerly Cooperative League of the U.S.A.)

(1916): 1401 New York Ave. N.W., Ste. 1100, Washington, D.C. 20005. Phone: (202) 638-6222. www.cooperative.org.

National Council of the Churches of Christ in the USA (1950): 475 Riverside Drive, Rm. 850, New York, N.Y. 10115. 35 Protestant and Orthodox communions. Phone: (212) 870-2227. www.ncccusa.org.

National Grange of the Order of Patrons of Husbandry, (1867): 1616 H St. N.W., Washington, D.C. 20006-4999. 300,000. Phone: (202) 628-3507; fax: (202) 347-1091. www.grange.org.

National Press Club (1908): National Press Bldg., 529 14th St. N.W., 13th Flr., Washington, D.C. 20045. 4,200+. Phone: (202) 662-7500. npc.press.org.

National PTA (National Congress of Parents and Teachers) (1897): 330 N. Wabash Ave., Ste. 2100, Chicago, Ill. 60611. 6.5 million. Phone: (800) 307-4782. email: info@pta.org. www.pta.org.

National Rifle Association of America (1871): 11250 Waples Mill Rd., Fairfax, Va. 22030. 3,300,000. Phone: (703) 267-1000. www.nra.org.

National Urban League, Inc. (1910): 120 Wall St., New York, N.Y. 10005. 115 affiliates in 34 states and D.C. Phone: (212) 558-5300. www.nul.org.

National Wildlife Federation (1936): 8925 Leesburg Pike, Vienna, VA 22184. 4,000,000+. Phone: (703) 790-4000. www.nwf.org.

Nature Conservancy, The (1951): 4245 N. Fairfax Dr., Ste. 100, Arlington, Va. 22203-1606. 900,000. Phone: (703) 841-5300. www.tnc.org.

Naval Architects and Marine Engineers, The Society of (1893): 601 Pavonia Ave., Jersey City, N.J. 07306. 10,000+. Phone: (201) 798-4800; fax: (201) 798-4975. www.sname.org.

Naval Engineers, American Society of (1888): 1452 Duke St., Alexandria, Va. 22314. 6,800. Phone: (703) 836-6727; fax: (703) 836-7491. www.navalengineers.org.

Naval Institute, United States (1873): 291 Wood Rd., Annapolis, Md. 21402. 80,000+. Phone: (410) 268-6110. www.usni.org.

Navigation, The Institute of (1945): 1800 Diagonal Rd., Ste. 480, Alexandria, Va. 22314. 3,800. Phone: (703) 683-7101; fax: (703) 683-7105. email: membership@ion.org. www.ion.org.

Navy League of the United States (1902): 2300 Wilson Blvd., Arlington, Va. 22201-3308. 71,500. Phone: (703) 528-1775. www.navyleague.org.

NDIA (National Defense Industrial Association) (1997): 2111 Wilson Blvd., Ste. 400, Arlington, Va. 22201. 28,000 individual, 900 companies. Phone: (703) 522-1820. www.ndia.org.

Neurofibromatosis Foundation, Inc., The National (1978): 95 Pine St., 16th Flr., New York, NY 10005. 38,000. Phone: (800) 323-7938; in NY State (212) 344-NNFF; fax: (212) 747-0004. email: nnff@aol.com. www.nf.org.

Newspaper Association of America (1992): 1921 Gallows Rd., Ste. 600, Vienna, Va. 22182. Phone (703) 902-1600. www.naa.org.

Nondestructive Testing, Inc., The American Society for (1941): 1711 Arlingate Lane, P.O. Box 28518, Columbus, Ohio 43228-0518. 10,240. Phone: (800) 222-ASNT. www.asnt.org.

NOT SAFE (National Organization Taunting Safety and Fairness Everywhere) (1980) (Humor Group): P.O. Box 5743, Montecito, Calif. 93150. 975. Phone: (805) 969-6217.

Nuclear Society, American (1954): 555 N. Kensington Ave., La Grange Park, Ill. 60526. 13,000. Phone: (708) 352-6611. www.ans.org.

Numismatic Association, American (1891): 818 N. Cascade Ave., Colorado Springs, Colo. 80903-3279. 28,000. Phone: (719) 632-2646. email: ana@money.org. www.money.org.

Nurses Association, American (1897): 600 Maryland Ave. S.W., Ste. 100, Washington, D.C. 20024.

180,000. Phone: (800) 274-4ANA.
www.nursingworld.org.

Odd Fellows, Sovereign Grand Lodge, Independent Order of (1819): 422 North Trade St., Winston-Salem, N.C. 27101. 460,000. Phone: (336) 725-5955. 128.125.109.137/IOOF.shtml

Olympic Committee, United States (1921): One Olympic Plaza, Colorado Springs, Colo. 80909-5760. Phone: (719) 632-5551. www.olympic-usa.org.

Optimist International (1919): 4494 Lindell Blvd., St. Louis, Mo. 63108. 130,000+. Phone: (314) 371-6000. www.optimist.org.

Optometric Association, American (1898): 243 N. Lindbergh Blvd., St. Louis, Mo. 63141. 32,000. Phone: (314) 991-4100. www.aoanet.org.

Ornithologists' Union, American (1883): c/o Division of Birds, National Museum of Natural History, MRC-116, Washington, D.C. 20560. 4,000. Phone: (202) 357-2051. pica.wru.umt.edu/aou/aou.html.

Overeaters Anonymous, Inc. (1960): P.O. Box 44020, Rio Rancho, N. Mex. 87124-4020. 150,000. Phone: (505) 891-2664. www.overeatersanonymous.org.

Parents, Families and Friends of Lesbians and Gays (1981): 1101 14th St. N.W., Ste. 1030, Washington, D.C. 20005. 77,000 households. Phone: (202) 638-4200. www.pflag.org.

Parents Without Partners (1957): 401 N. Michigan Ave., Chigaco, Ill. 60611-4267. 50,000. Phone: (312) 644-6610. www.parentswithoutpartners.org.

Peace Action (a merger of SANE and the Nuclear Weapons Freeze Campaign) (1957): 1819 H St. N.W., Ste. 420, Washington D.C. 20006. 55,000. Phone: (202) 862-9740. www.webcom.com/peaceact.

People For the American Way (1980): 2000 M St. N.W., Ste. 400, Washington, D.C. 20036. 300,000. Phone: (202) 467-4999. www.pfaw.org.

Petroleum Geologists, American Association of (1917): P.O. Box 979, Tulsa, Okla. 74101-0979. 31,500. Phone: (918) 584-2555. www.geobyte.com.

Pharmaceutical Association, American (1852): 2215 Constitution Ave. N.W., Washington, D.C. 20037-2985. 50,000+. Phone: (202) 628-4410. www.aphanet.org.

Philatelic Society, American (1886): P.O. Box 8000, State College, Pa. 16803. 55,000+. Phone: (814) 237-3803. www.west.net/~stamps1/aps.html.

Photogrammetry and Remote Sensing, American Society for (1934): 5410 Grosvenor Lane, Ste. 210, Bethesda, Md. 20814-2160. 7,000+. Phone: (301) 493-0290; fax: (301) 493-0208. email: asprs@asprs.org. www.asprs.org.

Photographic Society of America (1934): 3000 United Founders Blvd., Ste. 103, Oklahoma City, Okla. 73112-3940. Phone: (405) 843-1437. www.psa-photo.org.

Physical Society, The American (1899): One Physics Ellipse, College Park, Md. 20740-3200. 41,000. Phone: (301) 209-3200. www.aps.org.

Physical Therapy Association, American (APTA) (1921): 1111 N. Fairfax St., Alexandria, Va. 22314-1488. 75,000. Phone: (703) 684-2782. www.apta.org.

Physics, American Institute of (1931): One Physics Ellipse, College Park, Md. 20740-3843. 125,000. Phone: (301) 209-3100. www.aip.org.

Pilot International (1921): Pilot International Headquarters, 244 College St., P.O. Box 4844, Macon, Ga. 31208-4844. 25,000. Phone: (912) 743-7403. www.pilotinternational.org.

Planetary Society, The (1980): 65 N. Catalina Ave., Pasadena, Calif. 91106-2301. 100,000. Phone: (626) 793-5100. www.planetary.org.

Planned Parenthood® Federation of America, Inc., (1916): 810 Seventh Ave., New York, N.Y. 10019. 150 affiliates. Phone: (212) 541-7800; fax: (212) 261-4560. www.plannedparenthood.org.

Plastics Engineers, Society of (1942): P.O. Box 403, 14 Fairfield Dr., Brookfield, Conn. 06804-0403. 32,000+. Phone: (203) 775-0471. www.4spe.org.

Police, American Federation of (1966): Records Center, 3801 Biscayne Blvd., Miami, Fla. 33137. 100,000. Phone: (305) 573-0070. www.aphf.org.

Police, International Association of Chiefs of (1893): 515 N. Washington St., Alexandria Va. 22314-2357. 14,000. Phone: (703) 836-6767. www.theiacp.org.

Political and Social Science, American Academy of (1889): 3937 Chestnut St., Philadelphia, Pa. 19104. Phone: (215) 386-4594.

Political Science, Academy of (1880): 475 Riverside Dr., Ste. 1274, New York, N.Y. 10115-1274. 8,500. Phone: (212) 870-2500.

Prevent Blindness America (1908): 500 E. Remington Rd., Schaumburg, Ill. 60173. 21 affiliates and divisions. Phone: (847) 843-2020; (800) 331-2020. www.preventblindness.org.

Professional Engineers, National Society of (1934): 1420 King St., Alexandria, Va. 22314-2794. 60,000. Phone: (703) 684-2800; fax: (703) 836-4875. www.nspe.org.

Professional Photographers of America, Inc. (1880): 299 Peachtree St. N.W., #2200, Atlanta, Ga. 30303-2206. 14,000. Phone: (404) 522-8600. www.ppa-world.org.

Psychiatric Association, American (1844): 1400 K St. N.W., Washington, D.C. 20005. 40,537. Phone: (202) 682-6000. www.psych.org.

Psychoanalytic Association, The American (1911): 309 E. 49th St., New York, N.Y. 10017. 3,116 psychoanalysts. Phone: (212) 752-0450; fax: (212) 593-0571. email: apsaorg@compuserve.com. www.apsa.org.

Psychological Association, American (1892): 750 First St. N.E., Washington, D.C. 20002. 159,000. Phone: (202) 336-5500; TDD: (202) 336-5662. www.apa.org.

Public Health Association, American (1872): 800 I St. N.W., Washington, D.C. 20001-3710. 50,000+. Phone: (202) 777-2742. www.apha.org.

Puppeteers of America (1937): 5 Cricklewood Path, Pasadena, Calif. 91107-1002. Phone: (626) 797-5748. www.puppeteers.org

Quality, The American Society for (1946): 611 E. Wisconsin Ave., P.O. Box 3005, Milwaukee, Wis. 53201-3005. 135,000+. Phone: (414) 272-8575. www.asq.org.

Railroads, Association of American (1934): 50 F St. N.W., Washington, D.C. 20001-1564. Phone: (202) 639-2100. www.aar.org.

Recording Arts & Sciences, Inc., National Academy of (1957): 3402 Pico Blvd., Santa Monica, Calif. 90405. 13,000. Phone: (310) 392-3777. www.grammy.com.

Red Cross, American (1881): 1621 N. Kent St., Arlington Va. 22209. Approx. 1,650 chapters. Phone: (703) 248-4222. www.redcross.org.

Rehabilitation Association, National (1925): 633 S. Washington St., Alexandria, Va. 22314. 12,000. Phone: (703) 836-0850. www.nationalrehab.org.

Reserve Officers Association of the United States (1922): 1 Constitution Ave. N.E., Washington, D.C. 20002-5655. 93,000. Phone: (202) 479-2200. www.roa.org.

Retired Federal Employees, National Association (1921): 606 N. Washington St., Alexandria, Va. 22314. 400,000+. Phone: (703) 838-7760. www.narfe.org.

Reye's Syndrome Foundation, National (1974): P.O. Box 829, Bryan, Ohio 43506-0829. Phone: (800) 233-7393; fax: (419) 636-3366. email: reyessyn@mail.bright.net. www.bright.net/~reyessyn.

RID-USA (Remove Intoxicated Drivers) (1978): Box 520, Schenectady, N.Y. 12301. Over 150/41 state chapters. Phone: (518) 372-0034/(518) 393-HELP;

fax: (518) 370-4917.
www.crisny.org/not–for–profit/ridusa/.

Right to Life, Committee, Inc., National (1973): 419
7th St. N.W., Ste. 500, Washington, D.C. 20004.
Phone: (202) 626-8800. www.nrlc.org

Rotary International (1905): One Rotary Center, 1560
Sherman Ave., Evanston, Ill. 60201. 1.2 million in
161 countries and 35 geographical regions. Phone:
(847) 866-3000. www.rotary.org.

SAE (Society of Automotive Engineers) (1905): 400
Commonweatlh Dr., Warrendale, Pa. 15096-0001.
75,000+. Phone: (724) 776-4841. www.sae.org.

Safety Council, National (1913): 1121 Spring Lake
Dr., Itasca, Ill. 60143-3201. Phone: (630) 285-1121.
www.nsc.org.

Salvation Army, The (1865): National Headquarters,
615 Slaters Lane, P.O. Box 269, Alexandria, Va.
22313. 453,150. Phone: (703) 684-5500.
www.salvationarmy.org.

Save-the-Redwoods League (1918): 114 Sansome
St., Ste. 605, San Francisco, Calif. 94104-3814.
45,000. Phone: (415) 362-2352.
www.savetheredwoods.org.

**Science, American Association for the
Advancement of (1848):** 1200 New York Ave. N.W.,
Washington, D.C. 20005. 143,000. Phone: (202)
326-6400. www.aaas.org.

Science and Health, American Council on (1978):
1995 Broadway, 2nd Flr., New York, N.Y.
10023-5860. Phone: (212) 362-7044; fax: (212)
362-4919. email: acsh@acsh.org. www.acsh.org.

Science Fiction Society, World (1939): P.O. Box
426159, Kendall Square Station, Cambridge, Mass.
02142. email: mpc@wsfs.org www.wsfs.org.

Scientists, Federation of American (FAS) (1945):
307 Massachusetts Ave. N.E., Washington, D.C.
20002. 4,000. Phone: (202) 546-3300. www.fas.org.

SCRABBLE® Association, National (1978): P.O. Box
700, 120 Front Street Garden, Greenport, N.Y.
11944. 10,000. Phone: (516) 477-0033.
www.scrabble-assoc.com

Screen Actors Guild (1933): 5757 Wilshire Blvd., Los
Angeles, Calif. 90036-3600. 96,000. Phone: (323)
954-1600. www.sag.com.

Sculpture Society, National (1893): 1177 Ave. of the
Americas, New York, N.Y. 10036. 3,000. Phone:
(212) 764-5645. www.sculptor.org/NSS

Seeing Eye Inc., The (1929): P.O. Box 375,
Morristown, N.J. 07963-0375. Phone: (973)
539-4425. www.seeingeye.org.

Senior Citizens, National Alliance of (1974): 1744
Riggs Place, N.W., 3rd Flr., Washington, D.C. 20006.
117,000. Phone: (202) 986-0117.

**Shriners of North America and Shriners Hospitals
for Children, The (1872 and 1922):** 2900 Rocky
Point Drive, Tampa, Fla. 33607-1400. 550,000.
Phone: (813) 281-0300. www.shrinershq.org.

Sierra Club (1892): 85 2nd Street, San Francisco,
Calif. 94105-3441. 550,000. Phone: (415) 977-5500.
www.sierraclub.org.

**SIETAR INTERNATIONAL (The International Society
for Intercultural Education, Training and
Research) (1974):** P.O. Box 467, Putney, Vt. 05345.
2,000+. Phone: (802) 387-4785.
www.sietarinternationl.org.

Simon Wiesenthal Center (1977): 9786 W. Pico
Blvd., Los Angeles, Calif. 90035. 400,000 member
families. Phone: (310) 553-9036.
www.wiesenthal.com.

Small Business United, National (1937): 1156 15th
St. N.W., Washington, D.C. 20005. 65,000+. Phone:
(202) 293-8830; fax: (202) 872-8543. email:
nsbu@nsbu.org. www.nsbu.org.

Social Work Education, Council on (1952): 1600
Duke St., Alexandria, Va. 22314. Phone: (703)
683-8080; fax: (703) 683-8099. www.cswe.org.

Social Workers, National Association of (1955): 750
First St. N.E., Ste. 700, Washington, D.C. 20002-4241.
Phone: (202) 408-8600. www.naswdc.org.

**Society for Integrative and Comparitive Biology
(formerly the American Society of Zoologists)
(1890):** 401 N. Michigan Ave., Chicago, Ill. 60611.
2,200. Phone: (312) 527-6697; (800) 955-1236; fax:
(312) 245-1085. email: sicb@sba.com www.sicb.org.

Soil and Water Conservation Society (1945): 7515
N.E. Ankeny Rd., Ankeny, Iowa 50021. 10,000.
Phone: (515) 289-2331; fax: (515) 289-1227. email:
swcs@swcs.org. www.swcs.org.

Songwriters Guild of America, The (1931): 1500
Harbor Blvd., Weehawken, N.J. 07087-6732. Phone:
(201) 867-7603. www.songwriters.org.

Sons of Italy in America, Order (1905): 219 E St.
N.E., Washington, D.C. 20002. 500,000. Phone:
(202) 547-2900. www.osia.org.

**Sons of the American Revolution, National Society
of the (1889):** 1000 S. 4th St., Louisville, Ky. 40203.
26,000. Phone: (502) 589-1776. www.sar.org.

Soroptimist International of the Americas (1921):
Two Penn Center Plaza, Ste. 1000, Philadelphia, Pa.
19102-1883. 50,000. Phone: (215) 557-9300.
www.siahq.com.

**Southern Early Childhood Association (formerly
SACUS) (1948):** P.O. Box 55930, Little Rock, Ark.
72215-5930. 19,300. Phone: (501) 663-0353; fax:
(501) 663-2114. email: seca@aristotle.net.
www.seca50.org.

Space Education Association, U.S. (1973): Global
Operations Center, 231 School Lane, P.O. Box 249,
Rheems, Pa. 17570-0249. Voice/Fax: (717)
367-5196.

Space Society, National (1974): 600 Pennsylvania
Ave., S.E., Ste. 201, Washington, D.C. 20003.
Phone: (202) 543-1900; fax: (202) 546-4189.
www.nss.org/.

Special Olympics International, Inc. (1968): 1325 G
St. N.W., Ste. 500, Washington, D.C., 20005.
1,000,000. Phone: (202) 628-3630.
www.specialolympics.org.

**Speech-Language-Hearing Association, American
(1925):** 10801 Rockville Pike, Rockville, Md. 20852.
96,000. Phone: (301) 897-5700. www.asha.org.

Sports Car Club of America Inc. (1944): 9033 E.
Easter Place, P.O. Box 3278, Englewood, Colo.
80112. 55,000. Phone: (303) 694-7222.
www.scca.org/index.html.

Statistical Association, American (1839): 1429 Duke
St., Alexandria, Va. 22314-3402. 19,000.

Student Association, United States (1947): 1413 K
Street, NW, 9th Flr., Washington, D.C. 20005. 350
schools (3.5 million students). Phone: (202)
347-8772. www.essential.org/ussa.

Surgeons, American College of (1913): 633 North
Saint Clair, Chicago, Ill. 60611-3211. 56,000+.
Phone: (312) 202-5000. www.facs.org.

Symphony Orchestra League, American (1942):
1156 15th St. N.W., Ste. 800, Washington, D.C.
20005. 5,500. Phone: (202) 776-0212.
www.symphony.org.

**TASH: The Association for Persons with Severe
Handicaps (1974):** 29 W. Susquehanna Ave., Ste.
210, Baltimore, Md. 21204. 8,500. Phone: (410)
828-TASH. www.tash.org.

Teachers, American Federation of (1916): 555 New
Jersey Ave. N.W., Washington, D.C., 20001.
900,000+. Phone: (202) 879-4400. www.aft.org.

Testing & Materials, American Society for (1898):
100 Barr Harbor Dr., W. Conshohocken, Pa.
19428-2959. 35,000. Phone: (610) 832-9585.
www.astm.org.

The Arc (1950): 500 E. Border St., Ste. 300, Arlington,
Texas 76010. A national organization on mental
retardation. 140,000 members, 1,200 state and local
chapters. Phone: (817) 261-6003. www.thearc.org.

Theatre Guild, Inc. (1919): 226 W. 47th St., New York, N.Y. 10036. 72,000. Phone: (212) 873-0676.

Theosophical Society in America, The (1875): P.O. Box 270, Wheaton, Ill. 60189-0270. 4,400. Phone: (630) 668-1571. www.theosophical.org.

Tin Can Sailors, Inc. (1976): P.O. Box 100, Somerset, Mass. 02726. 19,300. Phone: (800) 223-5535. www.destroyers.org.

Toastmasters International (1924): P.O. Box 9052, Mission Viejo, Calif. 92690-7052, and 23182 Arroyo Vista, Rancho Santa Margarita, Calif. 92688. 170,000. Phone: (949) 858-8255; fax: (949) 858-1207. email: tminfo@toastmasters.org. www.toastmasters.org.

TOUGHLOVE International (1977): P.O. Box 1069, Doylestown, Pa. 18901. 500 registered groups. Phone: (215) 348-7090; (800) 333-1069. www.toughlove.org.

TransAfrica Forum (1981): 1744 R. St. N.W., Washington, D.C. 20009. Phone: (202) 797-2301; fax: (202) 797-2382. email: transforum@igc.org. www.igc.apc.org/transafrica.

Travel Agents, American Society of (ASTA) (1931): 1101 King St., Alexandria, Va. 22314. 26,500. Phone: (703) 739-2782. www.astanet.com.

Travelers Aid International (1851): 1612 K St. N.W., Ste. 506, Washington, D.C. 20006. Phone: (202) 546-1127; fax: (202) 546-1127. www.travelersaid.org.

Tuberous Sclerosis Association, Inc., National (1974): 8181 Professional Place, Ste. 110, Landover, Md. 20785-2226. 5,000. Phone: (301) 459-9888; (800) 225-6872; fax: (301) 459-0394. email: ntsa@aol.com. www.ntsa.org.

UFOs, National Investigations Committee on (1967): 14617 Victory Blvd., Ste. 4, Van Nuys, Calif. 91411. Phone: (818) 989-5942; fax: (818) 989-2165. www.nicufo.com.

UNICEF, U.S. Committee for (1947): 333 E. 38th St., New York, N.Y. 10016. 20,000 volunteers. Phone: (212) 686-5522. www.unicefusa.org.

Union of Concerned Scientists (1969): 2 Brattle Square, Cambridge, Mass. 02238. 70,000. Phone: (617) 547-5552. www.ucsusa.org.

United Daughters of the Confederacy® (1894): 328 N. Boulevard, Richmond, Va. 23220-4057. 24,000. Phone: (804) 355-1636. www.hqudc.org.

United Jewish Communities (formerly United Jewish Appeal) (1939): Ste. 11E, 111 Eighth Ave., New York, N.Y. 10011. Phone: (212) 284-6500. www.uja.org.

United Way of America (1918): 701 N. Fairfax St., Alexandria, Va. 22314-2045. 1,400 local United Ways. Phone: (703) 836-7100; fax: (703) 683-7840. www.unitedway.org.

University Foundation, International (1973): 1301 S. Noland Rd., Independence, Mo. 64055. 67,000. Phone: (816) 461-3633.

University Women, American Association of (1881): 1111 16th St. N.W., Washington, D.C. 20036. 150,000. Phone: (800) 326-AAUW (2289). www.aauw.org.

USO (United Service Organizations) (1941): World Headquarters, Washington Navy Yard, 1008 Eberle Place SE, Ste. 301, Washington, D.C. 20374-5096. Phone: (800) 876-7469. www.uso.org.

Veterans Committee, American (AVC) (1944): Bethesda, Md. 20817. 15,000. Phone & fax: (301) 320-6490. www.va.gov/vso/avc.htm.

Veterans of Foreign Wars of the U.S. (1899): 406 W. 34th St., Kansas City, Mo. 64111. VFW and Auxiliary, 2.1 million. Phone: (816) 756-3390. www.vfw.org.

Veterinary Medical Association, American (1863): 1931 N. Meacham Rd., Ste. 100, Schaumburg, Ill. 60173. 57,700. Phone: (847) 925-8070. www.avma.org.

Volunteers of America (1896): 110 South Union Street, 2nd Flr., Alexandria, Va. 22314-3324. Provides human services in more than 400 communities. Phone: (703) 548-2288; 1-800-899-0089. www.voa.org.

War Resisters League (1923): 339 Lafayette St., New York, N.Y. 10012. 12,000. Phone: (212) 228-0450; fax: (212) 228-6193. email: wrl@igc.apc.org. www.nonviolence.org/wrl.

Washington Legal Foundation (1977): 2009 Massachusetts Ave., N.W., Washington, D.C. 20036. 100,000. Phone: (202) 588-0302. www.wlf.org.

Water Quality Association (1974): 4151 Naperville Rd., Lisle, Ill. 60532. 2,200. Phone: (630) 505-0160; fax: (630) 505-9637. www.wqa.org.

Welding Society, American (1919): 550 N.W. LeJeune Rd., Miami, Fla. 33126. 50,000. Phone: (305) 443-9353; (800) 443-9353. www.aws.org.

Wildlife Fund, World (1961): 1250 24th St. N.W., Washington, D.C. 20037. 1.2 million. Phone: (800) 225-5993. www.wwf.org.

Woman's Christian Temperance Union, National (1874): 1730 Chicago Ave., Evanston, Ill. 60201-4585. Under 20,000. Phone: (847) 864-1396, (800) 755-1321. www.wctu.org.

Women, National Organization for (NOW) (1966): 1000 16th St. N.W., Ste. 700, Washington, D.C. 20036. 500,000. Phone: (202) 331-0066. www.now.org.

Women Police, The International Association of (1915): Box 149, Deer Isle, Me. 04627-9700. 3,000. Phone: (207) 348-6976; fax: (207) 348-6171. www.iawp.org.

Women's American ORT (1927): 315 Park Ave. South, New York, N.Y. 10010. Chapters throughout the U.S. Phone: (212) 505-7700. www.waort.org.

Women's Educational and Industrial Union (1877): 356 Boylston St., Boston, Mass. 02116. 1,500. Phone: (617) 536-5651; fax: (617) 247-8826.

Women's International League for Peace and Freedom (1915): 1213 Race St., Philadelphia, Pa. 19107. 10,000. Phone: (215) 563-7110. www.wilpf.org.

World Future Society (1966): 7910 Woodmont Ave., Ste. 450, Bethesda, Md. 20814. 30,000. Phone: (301) 656-8274; fax: (301) 951-0394. www.wfs.org.

World Health, American Association for (1953): 1825 K St. N.W., Washington, D.C. 20006. Phone: (202) 466-5883, fax: (202) 466-5896. email: AAWHstaff@aol.com. www.aawhworldhealth.org.

World Peace, International Association of Educators for (1967): P.O. Box 3282, Mastin Lake Station, Huntsville, Ala. 35810-0282. 25,000. Phone: (256) 534-5501. www.homeplanet.org/iaewp.

World Peace Foundation (1910): 104 Mt. Auburn St., Cambridge, Mass. 02138. Phone: (617) 491-5085; fax: (617) 491-8588. www.hiid.harvard.edu/programs/wpeace/index.html.

Worldwatch Institute (1974): 1776 Massachusetts Ave. N.W., Washington, D.C. 20036-1904. Global environmental research organization. Phone: (202) 452-1999; fax: (202) 296-296-7365. email: worldwatch@worldwatch.org. www.worldwatch.org.

Writers Union, National (1981): 113 University Place, 6th Flr., New York, N.Y. 10003. 5,000. Phone: (212) 254-0279. www.nwu.org.

YMCA of the USA (1844): 101 N. Wacker Dr., Chicago, Ill. 60606. 16.9 million. Phone: (312) 977-0031. www.ymca.net.

Young Women's Christian Association of the U.S.A. (1858 in U.S.A., 1855 in England): Empire State Building, 350 Fifth Ave., 3rd Flr., New York, N.Y. 10118. 2,000,000. Phone: (212) 273-7800. www.ywca.org.

Zionist Organization of America (1897): 4 E. 34th St., New York, N.Y. 10016. 50,000. Phone: (212) 481-1500; fax: (212) 481-1515. www.zoa.org.

First Aid for Crossword Puzzlers

We cannot begin to list all the odd words you might encounter in your daily and Sunday crossword puzzles, for such words run into the many thousands. But we have tried to include those that turn up most frequently, as well as many others that should be of help to you when you are unable to go any further.

We do not guarantee that the definitions in your puzzle will be exactly the same as ours, although we have checked every word with a standard dictionary and have followed its definition.

In nearly every case, we have used as the key word the principal noun of the definition, rather than any adjective, adjective phrase, or noun used as an adjective. And, to simplify your searching, we have grouped the words according to the number of spaces you have to fill.

Words of Two Letters

Ambary, DA
And (French, Latin), ET
Article (Arabic), AL
  (French), LA, LE, UN
  (Spanish), EL, LA, UN
At the (French), AU
  (Spanish), AL
Behold, LO
Bird: Hawaiian, OO
Birthplace: Abraham's, UR
Bone, OS
Buddha, FO
Butterfly: Peacock, IO
Champagne, AY
Chaos, NU
Chief: Burmese, BO
Coin: Roman, AS
  Siamese, AT
Concerning, RE
Dialect: Chinese, WU
Double (Egy. relig.), KA
Drama: Japanese, NO
Egg (comb. form), OO
Esker, OS

Eye (Scotch), EE
Factor: Amplification, MU
Fifty (Greek), NU
Fish: Carplike, ID
Force, OD
Forty (Greek), MU
From (French, Latin, Spanish), DE
  (Latin prefix), AB
From the (French), DU
God: Babylonian, EA, ZU
  Egyptian sun, RA
  Hindu unknown, KA
  Semitic, EL
Goddess: Babylonian, AI
  Greek earth, GE
Gold (heraldry), OR
Gulf: Arctic, OB
Heart (Egy. relig.), AB
Indian: South American, GE
King: Of Bashan, OG
Language: Artificial, RO
  Assamese, AO
Lava: Hawaiian, AA

Letter: Greek, MU, NU, PI, XI
  Hebrew, HE, PE
Lily: Palm, TI
Measure: Vietnamese, LY
  Chinese, HO, HU, KO, LI,
  MU, PU, TO, TU
  Japanese, GO, JO, MO, RI,
  SE, TO
  Metric land, AR
  Netherlands, EL
  Portuguese, PE
  Siamese, WA
  Swedish, AM
  Type, EM, EN
Monk: Buddhist, BO
Month: Jewish, AB
Mouth, OS
Mulberry: Indian, AL
Native: Burmese, WA
Note: Of Scale, DO, FA, MI,
  LA, RE, TI
Of (French, Latin, Spanish), DE
Of the (French), DU

One (Scotch), AE
Pagoda: Chinese, TA
Plant: East Indian fiber, DA
Ridge: Sandy, AS, OS
River: Russian, OB
Sloth: Three-toed, AI
Soul (Egy. relig.), BA
Sound: Hindu mystic, OM
Suffix: Comparative, ER
To the: French, AU
  Spanish, AL
Tree: Buddhist sacred, BO
Tribe: Assamese, AO
Type: Jumbled, PI
Weight: Vietnamese, TA
  Chinese, LI
  Danish, ES
  Japanese, MO
  Roman, AS
Whirlwind: Faeroe Is., OE
Yes (German), JA
  (Italian, Spanish), SI
  (Russian), DA

Words of Three Letters

Adherent, IST
Again, BIS
Age, ERA
Antelope: African, GNU, KOB
Apricot: Japanese, UME
Article (German), DAS, DEM,
  DEN, DER, DES, DIE, EIN
  (French), LES, UNE
  (Spanish), LAS, LOS, UNA
Banana: Polynesian, FEI
Barge, HOY
Bass: African, IYO
Beak, NEB, NIB
Beard: Grain, AWN
Beetle: June, DOR
Being, ENS
Berry: Hawthorn, HAW
Beverage: Hawaiian, AVA
Bird: Australian, EMU
  Crowlike, JAY
  Extinct, MOA
  Fabulous, ROC
  Frigate, IWA
  Parson, POE, TUE, TUI
  Sea, AUK
Blackbird, ANI, ANO
Born, NEE
Bronze: Roman, AES
Bugle: Yellow, IVA
By way of, VIA
Canton: Swiss, URI
Cap: Turkish, FEZ
Catnip, NEP
Character: In "Faerie Queene,"
  UNA
Coin (Money of account):
  Afghan, PUL
  Albanian, LEK
  Guyanese, BIT

Bulgarian, LEV, LEW
French, ECU, SOU
Indian, PIE
Japanese, SEN, YEN
Korean, WON
Lithuanian, LIT
Macao, Timor, AVO
Palestinian, MIL
Persian, PUL
Peruvian, SOL
Rumanian, BAN, LEU, LEY
Scandinavian, ORE
Siamese, ATT
Collection: Facts, ANA
Commune: Belgian, ANS, ATH
  Netherlands, EDE, EPE
Community: Russian, MIR
Constellation: Southern, ARA
Contraction: Poetic, EEN, EER,
  OER
Covering: Apex of roof, EPI
Crab: Fiddler, UCA
Crag: Rocky, TOR
Cry: Crow, rook, raven, CAW
Cup: Wine, AMA
Cymbal, Oriental, TAL, ZEL
Disease: Silkworm, UJI
Division: Danish territorial, AMT
  Geologic, EON
Doctrine, ISM
Dowry, DOT
Dry (French), SEC
Dynasty: Chinese, CHI, HAN,
  SUI, WEI, YIN
Eagle: Sea, ERN
Earth (comb. form), GEO
Egg: Louse, NIT
Eggs: Fish, ROE
Emmet, ANT

Enzyme, ASE
Equal (comb. form), ISO
Extension: building, ELL
Far (comb. form), TEL
Farewell, AVE
Fiber: Palm, TAL
Finial, EPI
Fish: Carplike, IDE
  Pikelike, GAR
Flatfish, DAB
Fleur-de-lis, LIS, LYS
Food: Hawaiian, POI
Formerly, NEE
Friend (French), AMI
Game: Card, LOO
Garment: Camel-hair, ABA
Gateway, DAR
Gazelle: Tibetan, GOA
Genus: Ducks, AIX
  Grasses, POA
  Grasses (maize), ZEA
  Herbs or shrubs, IVA
  Lizards, UTA
  Rodents (incl. house mice),
  MUS
  Ruminants (incl. cattle), BOS
  Swine, SUS
Gibbon: Malay, LAR
God: Assyrian, SIN
  Babylonian, ABU, ANU, BEL,
  HEA, SIN, UTU
  Irish sea, LER
  Phrygian, MEN
  Polynesian, ORO
Goddess: Babylonian, AYA
  Etruscan, UNI
  Hindu, SRI, UMA, VAC
  Teutonic, RAN

Governor: Algerian, DEY
  Turkish, BEY
Grampus, ORC
Grape, UVA
Grass: Meadow, POA
Gypsy, ROM
Hail, AVE
Hare: Female, DOE
Hawthorn, HAW
Hay: Spread for drying, TED
Herb: Japanese, UDO
  Perennial, PIA
  Used for blue dye, WAD
Herd: Whales, GAM, POD
Hero: Spanish, CID
High (music), ALT
Honey (pharm.), MEL
Humorist: American, ADE
I (Latin), EGO
I love (Latin), AMO
Indian: Algonquin, FOX, SAC,
  WEA
  Chimakuan, HOH
  Keresan, SIA
  Mayan, MAM
  Shoshonean, UTE
  Siouan, KAW, OTO
  South American, ITE, ONA,
  URO, URU, YAO
  Tierra del Fuego, ONA
  Wakashan, AHT
Ingot, PIG
Inlet: Narrow, RIA
Island: Cyclades, IOS
  Dodecanese, COS, KOS
  (French), ILE
  River, AIT
Jackdaw, DAW

John (Gaelic), IAN
Keelbill: ANI, ANO
Kiln, OST
King: British legendary LUD
Kobold, NIS
Lace: To make, TAT
Lamprey, EEL
Language: Artificial, IDO
 Bantu, ILA
 Siamese, LAO, TAI
Leaf: Palm, OLA, OLE
Leaving, ORT
Left: Cause to turn, HAW
Letter: Greek, CHI, ETA, PHI,
 PSI, RHO, TAU
 Hebrew, MEM, NUN, SIN,
 TAV, VAU
Lettuce, COS
Life (comb. form), BIO
Lily: Palm, TOI
Lizard, EFT
Louse: Young, NIT
Love (Anglo-Irish), GRA
Lute: Oriental, TAR
Macaw: Brazilian, ARA
Marble, TAW
Match: Shooting (French), TIR
Meadow, LEA
Measure: Abyssinian, TAT
 Algerian, PIK
 Vietnamese, GON, MAU,
 NGU, VUO, SAO, TAO, TAT
 Arabian, DEN, SAA
 Belgian, VAT
 Bulgarian, OKA, OKE
 Chinese, FEN, TOU, YIN
 Cloth, ELL
 Cyprus, OKA, OKE, PIK
 Czech, LAN, SAH
 Danish, FOD, MIL, POT
 Dominican Republic, ONA
 Dutch, old, AAM
 East Indian, KIT
 Egyptian, APT, HEN, PIK,
 ROB
 Electric, MHO, OHM
 Energy, ERG
 English, PIN
 Estonian, TUN
 French, POT
 German, AAM
 Greek, PIK
 Hebrew, CAB, HIN, KOR,
 LOG
 Hungarian, AKO
 Icelandic, FET
 Indian, GAZ, GUZ, JOW,
 KOS
 Japanese, BOO, CHO, KEN,
 RIN, SHO, SUN, TAN
 Malabar, ADY
 Metric land, ARE
 Netherlands, KAN, KOP,
 MUD, VAT, ZAK
 Norwegian, FOT, POT
 Persian, GAZ, GUZ, MOU,
 ZAR, ZER
 Polish, CAL
 Rangoon, DHA, LAN
 Roman, PES, URN

Russian, FUT, LOF
Scotch, COP
Siamese, KEN, NIU, RAI,
 SAT, SEN, SOK, WAH, YOT
Somaliland, TOP
Spanish, PIE
Straits Settlements, PAU,
 TUN
Swedish, ALN, FOT, MIL,
 REF, TUM
Swiss, POT
Tunisian, SAA
Turkish, OKA, OKE, PIK
Wire, MIL
Württemberg, IMI
Yarn, LEA
Yugoslav, OKA, RIF
Milk, LAC
Milkfish, AWA
Moccasin, PAC
Money: Yap stone, FEI
Money of Account (also Coin):
 Anglo-Saxon, ORA, ORE
 French, SOU
 Indian, LAC
 Japanese, RIN
 Oman, GAJ
 Virgin Islands, BIT
Monkey: Capuchin, SAI
Morsel, ORT
Mother: Peer Gynt's, ASE
Mountain: Asia Minor, IDA
Mulberry: Indian, AAL, ACH,
 AWL
Muttonbird: New Zealand, OII
Nahoor, SNA
Native: Mindanao, ATA
Neckpiece, BOA
Newt, EFT
No (Scotch), NAE
Note: Guido's highest, ELA
 Of scale, SOL
Nursemaid: Oriental, AMA, IYA
Ocher: Yellow, SIL
One (Scotch), YIN
Ornament: Pagoda, TEE
Oven: Polynesian, UMU
Ox: Tibetan, YAK
Pagoda: Chinese, TAA
Parrot: Hawk, HIA
 New Zealand, KEA
Part: Footlike, PES
Particle: Electrified, ION
Pasha, DEY
Pass: Mountain, COL
Paste: Rice, AME
Pea: Indian split, DAL
Peasant: Philippine, TAO
Penpoint, NEB, NIB
Piece out, EKE
Pigeon, NUN
Pine: Textile screw, ARA
Pistol (slang), GAT
Pit: Baking, IMU
Plant: Pepper, AVA
Play: By Capek, RUR
Poem: Old French, DIT
Porgy: Japanese, TAI
Priest: Biblical high, ELI
Prince: Ethiopian, RAS

Pseudonym: Dickens', BOZ
Queen: Fairy, MAB
Quince: Bengal, BEL
Record: Ship's, LOG
Refuse: Flax (Scotch), PAB,
 POB
Resin, LAC
Resort, SPA
Revolver (slang), GAT
Right: Cause to turn, GEE
River: Scotch or English, DEE
 (Spanish), RIO
 Swiss, AAR
Room: Harem, ODA
Rootstock: Fern, ROI
Rose (Persian), GUL
Ruff: Female, REE
Rule: Indian, RAJ
Sailor, GOB, TAR
Saint: Female (abbr.), STE
 Islamic, PIR
Salt, SAL
Sash: Japanese, OBI
Scrap, ORT
Seed: Poppy, MAW
 Small, PIP
Self, EGO
Serpent: Vedic sky, AHI
Sesame, TIL
Sheep: Female, EWE
 Indian, SHA
 Male, RAM
Sheepfold (Scotch), REE
Shelter, LEE
Shield, ECU
Shooting match (French), TIR
Shrew: European, ERD
Shrub: Evergreen, YEW
Silkworm, ERI
Snake, ASP, BOA
Soak, RET
Son-in-law: Mohammed's, ALI
Sorrel: Wood, OCA
Spade: Long, narrow, LOY
Spirit: Malignant, KER
Spot: Playing-card, PIP
Spread for drying, TED
Spring: Mineral, SPA
Sprite: Water, NIX
Statesman: Japanese, ITO
Stern: Toward, AFT
Stomach: Bird's, MAW
Street (French), RUE
Summer (French), ETE
Sun, SOL
Swamp, BOG, FEN
Swan: Male, COB
Tea: Chinese, CHA
Temple: Shinto, SHA
Thing (law), RES
Title: Etruscan, LAR
 Monk's, FRA
 Portuguese, DOM
 Spanish, DON
 Turkish, AGA, BEY
Tool: Cutting, ADZ, AXE
 Mining, GAD
 Piercing, AWL
Tree: Candlenut, AMA
 Central American, EBO

East Indian, SAJ, SAL
Evergreen, YEW
Hawaiian, KOA, KOU
Indian, BEL, DAR
Linden, LIN
New Zealand, AKE
Philippine, DAO, TUA, TUI
Rubber, ULE
South American, APA
Tribe: New Zealand, ATI
Turmeric, REA
Twice, BIS
Twin: Siamese, ENG
Uncle (dialect), EAM, EME
Veil: Chalice, AER, AIR
Vessel: Wine, AMA
Vestment: Ecclesiastical, ALB
Vetch: Bitter, ERS
Victorfish, AKU
Vine: New Zealand, AKA
 Philippine, IYO
Wallaba, APA
Wapiti, ELK
Water (French), EAU
Waterfall, LIN
Watering place: Prussian, EMS
Weave: Designating plain,
 UNI
Weight: Vietnamese, CAN
 Bulgarian, OKA, OKE
 Burmese, MOO, VIS
 Chinese, FEN, HAO, KIN,
 SSU, TAN, YIN
 Cyprus, OKA, OKE
 Danish, LOD, ORT, VOG
 East Indian, TJI
 Egyptian, KAT, OKA, OKE
 English, for wool, TOD
 German, LOT
 Greek, MNA, OKA, OKE
 Indian, SER
 Japanese, FUN, KIN, RIN,
 SHI
 Korean, KON
 Malacca, KIP
 Mongolian, LAN
 Netherlands, ONS
 Norwegian, LOD
 Polish, LUT
 Rangoon, PAI
 Roman, BES
 Russian, LOT
 Siamese, BAT, HAP, PAI
 Swedish, ASS, ORT
 Turkish, OKA, OKE
 Yugoslav, OKA, OKE
Whales: Herd, GAM, POD
Wildebeest, GNU
Wing, ALA
Witticism, MOT
Wolframite, CAL
Worm: African, LOA
Wreath: Hawaiian, LEI
Yale, ELI
Yam: Hawaiian, HOI
Yes (French), OUI
Young: Bring forth, EAN
Z (letter), ZED

Words of Four Letters

Aborigine: Borneo, DYAK
Agave, ALOE
Animal: Footless, APOD
Ant: White, ANAI, ANAY
Antelope: African, ASSE, BISA, GUIB,
 KOBA, KUDU, ORYX, POKU, PUKU,
 TOPI, TORA
Apoplexy: Plant, ESCA
Apple, POME
Apricot, ANSU
Ardor, ELAN
Armadillo, APAR, PEBA, PEVA, TATU
Ascetic: Islamic, SUFI
Association: Chinese, TONG

Astronomer: Persian, OMAR
Avatar: Of Vishnu, RAMA
Axillary, ALAR
Band: Horizontal (heraldry), FESS
Barracuda, SPET
Bark: Mulberry, TAPA
Base: Column, DADO
Bearing (heraldry), ORLE
Beer: Russian, KVAS
Beige, ECRU
Being, ESSE
Beverage: Japanese rice, SAKE
Bird: Asian, MINA, MYNA
 Egyptian sacred, IBIS

Extinct, DODO, MAMO
Flightless, KIWI
Gull-like, TERN
Hawaiian, IIWI, MAMO
Parson, KOKO
Unfledged, EYAS
Birds: As class, AVES
Black, EBON
 (French), NOIR
Blackbird: European, MERL
Boat: Flat-bottomed, DORY
Bone: Forearm, ULNA
Bones, OSSA
Box, Japanese, INRO

Bravo (rare), EUGE
Buffalo: Indian wild, ARNA
Bull (Spanish), TORO
Burden, ONUS
Cabbage: Sliced, SLAW
Caliph: Islamic, OMAR
Canoe: Malay, PRAU, PROA
Cap: Military, KEPI
Cape, NESS
Capital: Ancient Irish, TARA
Case: Article, ETUI
Cat: Wild, BALU, EYRA
Chalcedony, SARD
Chamber: Indian ceremonial, KIVA
Channel: Brain, ITER
Cheese: Dutch, EDAM
Chest: Sepulchral stone, CIST
Chieftain: Arab, EMIR
Church: Part of, APSE, NAVE
  (Scotch), KIRK
Claim (law), LIEN
Cluster: Flower, CYME
Coin: Chinese, TAEL, YUAN
  German, MARK
  Indian, ANNA
  Iranian, RIAL
  Italian, LIRA
  Moroccan, OKIA
  Siamese, BAHT
  South American, PESO
  Spanish, DURO, PESO
  Turkish, PARA
Commune: Belgian, AATH
Composition: Musical, OPUS
Compound: Chemical, DIOL
Constellation: Southern, PAVO
Council: Russian, DUMA
Counsel, REDE
Covering: Seed, ARIL
Cross: Egyptian, ANKH
Cry: Bacchanalian, EVOE
Cup (Scotch), TASS
Cupbearer, SAKI
Dagger: DIRK
  Malay, KRIS
Dam: River, WEIR
Dash, ELAN
Date: Roman, IDES
Dawn: Pertaining to, EOAN
Dean: English, INGE
Decay: In fruit, BLET
Deer: Sambar, MAHA
Disease: Skin, ACNE
Disk: Solar, ATEN
Dog: Hunting, ALAN
Drink: Hindu intoxicating, SOMA
Duck, SMEE, SMEW, TEAL
Dynasty: Chinese, CHEN, CHIN, CHOU,
  CHOW, HSIA, MING, SUNG, TANG,
  TSIN
  Mongol, YUAN
Eagle: Biblical, GIER
  Sea, ERNE
Egyptian: Christian, COPT
Ear: Pertaining to, OTIC
Entrance: Mine, ADIT
Esau, EDOM
Escutcheon: Voided, ORLE
Eskers, OSAR
Evergreen: New Zealand, TAWA
Fairy: Persian, PERI
Family: Italian, ESTE
Far (comb. form), TELE
Farewell, VALE
Father (French), PERE
Fennel: Philippine, ANIS
Fever: Malarial, AGUE
Fiber: East Indian, JUTE
Firn, NEVE
Fish: Carplike, DACE
  Hawaiian, ULUA
  Herringlike, SHAD
  Mackerellike, CERO
  Marine, HAKE
  Sea, LING, MERO, OPAH
  Spiny-finned, GOBY

Food: Tropical, TARO
Foot: Metric, IAMB
Formerly, ERST
Founder: Of Carthage, DIDO
France: Southern, MIDI
Furze, ULEX
Gaelic, ERSE
Gaiter, SPAT
Game: Card, FARO, SKAT
Garlic: European wild, MOLY
Garment: Hindu, SARI
  Roman, TOGA
Gazelle, CORA
Gem, JADE, ONYX, OPAL, RUBY
Genus: Amphibians (incl. frogs), RANA
  Amphibians (incl. tree toads), HYLA
  Antelopes, ORYX
  Auks, ALCA, URIA
  Bees, APIS
  Birds (American ostriches), RHEA
  Birds (cranes), CRUS
  Birds (magpies), PICA
  Birds (peacocks), PAVO
  Cetaceans, INIA
  Ducks (incl. mallards), ANAS
  Fishes (burbots), LOTA
  Fishes (incl. bowfins), AMIA
  Geese (snow geese), CHEN
  Gulls, XEMA
  Herbs, ARUM, GEUM
  Insects (water scorpions), NEPA
  Lilies, ALOE
  Mammals (mankind), HOMO
  Orchids, DISA
  Owls, ASIO, BUBO, OTUS
  Palms, NIPA
  Sea birds, SULA
  Sheep, OVIS
  Shrubs, Eurasian, ULEX
  Shrubs (hollies), ILEX
  Shrubs (incl. Virginia Willow), ITEA
  Shrubs, tropical, EVEA
  Snakes (sand snakes), ERYX
  Swans, OLOR
  Trees, chocolate, COLA
  Trees (ebony family), MABA
  Trees (incl. maples), ACER
  Trees (olives), OLEA
  Trees, tropical, EVEA
  Turtles, EMYS
Goat: Wild, IBEX, KRAS, TAHR, TAIR,
  THAR
God: Assyrian, ASUR
  Babylonian, ADAD, ADDU, ENKI,
  ENZU, IRRA, NABU, NEBO, UTUG
  Celtic, LLEU, LLEW
  Hindu, AGNI, CIVA, DEVA, DEWA,
  KAMA, RAMA, SIVA, VAYU
  Phrygian, ATYS
  Semitic, BAAL
  Teutonic, HLER
Goddess: Babylonian, ERUA, GULA
  Hawaiian, PELE
  Hindu, DEVI, KALI, SHRI, VACH
Gooseberry: Hawaiian, POHA
Gourd, PEPO
Grafted (heraldry), ENTE
Grandfather (obsolete), AIEL
Grandparents: Pertaining to, AVAL
Grass: Hawaiian, HILO
Gray (French), GRIS
Green (heraldry), VERT
Groom: Indian, SYCE
Half (prefix), DEMI, HEMI, SEMI
Hamlet, DORP
Hammerhead: Part of, PEEN
Handle, ANSA
Harp: Japanese, KOTO
Hartebeest, ASSE, TORA
Hautboy, OBOE
Hawk: Taken from nest (falconry), EYAS
Hearing (law), OYER
Heater: For liquids, ETNA
Herb: Aromatic, ANET, DILL
  Fabulous, MOLY
  Perennial, GEUM, SEGO

Pot, WORT
  Used for blue dye, WADE, WOAD
Hill: Flat-topped, MESA
  Sand, DENE, DUNE
Hoarfrost, RIME
Hog: Immature female, GILT
Holly, ILEX
House: Cow, BYRE
  (Spanish), CASA
Ice: Floating, FLOE
Image, ICON, IKON
Incarnation: Of Vishnu, RAMA
Indian: Algonquin, CREE, SAUK
  Central American, MAYA
  Iroquoian, ERIE
  Mexican, CORA
  Peruvian, CANA, INCA, MORO
  Shoshonean, HOPI
  Siouan, OTOE
  Southwestern, HOPI, PIMA, YUMA,
  ZUNI
Insect: Immature, PUPA
Instrument: Stringed, LUTE, LYRE
Ireland, EIRE, ERIN
Jacket: English, ETON
Jail (British), GAOL
Jar, OLLA
Judge: Islamic, CADI
Juniper: European, CADE
Kiln, OAST, OVEN
King: British legendary, LUDD, NUDD
Kiss, BUSS
Knife: Philippine, BOLO
Koran: Section of, SURA
Laborer: Spanish American, PEON
Lake: Mountain, TARN
  (Scotch), LOCH
Lamp: Miner's, DAVY
Landing place: Indian, GHAT
Language: Buddhist, PALI
  Japanese, AINU
Latvian, LETT
Layer: Of iris, UVEA
Leaf: Palm, OLAY, OLLA
Legislature: Ukrainian, RADA
Lemur, LORI
Leopard, PARD
Let it stand, STET
Letter: Greek, BETA, IOTA, ZETA
  Hebrew, AYIN, BETH, CAPH, KOPH,
  RESH, SHIN, TETH, YODH
  Papal, BULL
Lily, ALOE
Literature: Hindu sacred, VEDA
Lizard, GILA
  Monitor, URAN
Loquat, BIWA
Magistrate: Genoese or Venetian, DOGE
Man (Latin), HOMO
Mark: Omission, DELE
Marmoset: South American, MICO
Meadow: Fertile, VEGA
Measure: Electric, VOLT, WATT
  Force, DYNE
  Hebrew, OMER
  Printing, PICA
  Spanish or Portuguese, VARA
  Swiss land, IMMI
Medley, OLIO
Merganser, SMEW
Milk (French), LAIT
Molding, GULA
  Curved, OGEE
Mongoose: Crab-eating, URVA
Monk: Tibetan, LAMA
Monkey: African, MONA, WAAG
  Ceylonese, MAHA
  Cochin-China, DOUC
  South American, SAKI, TITI
Monkshood, ATIS
Month: Jewish, ADAR, ELUL, IYAR
Mother (French), MERE
Mountain: Thessaly, OSSA
Mouse: Meadow, VOLE
Mythology: Norse, EDDA
Nail (French), CLOU

Native: Philippine, MORO
Nest: Of pheasants, NIDE
Network, RETE
No (German), NEIN
Noble: Islamic, AMIR
Notice: Death, OBIT
Novel: By Zola, NANA
Nursemaid: Oriental AMAH, AYAH, EYAH
Nut: Philippine, PILI
Oak: Holm, ILEX
Oil (comb. form), OLEO
Ostrich: American, RHEA
Oven, KILN, OAST
Owl: Barn, LULU
Ox: Celebes wild, ANOE
   Extinct wild, URUS
Palm, ATAP, NIPA, SAGO
Parliament, DIET
Parrot: New Zealand, KAKA
Pass: Indian mountain, GHAT
Passage: Closing (music), CODA
Peach: Clingstone, PAVY
Peasant: Indian, RYOT
   Old English, CARL
Pepper: Australasian, KAVA
Perfume, ATAR
Persia, IRAN
Person: Extraordinary, ONER
Pickerel or pike, ESOX
Pitcher, EWER
Plant: Aromatic, NARD
   Century, ALOE
   Indigo, ANIL
   Pepper, KAVA
Platform: Raised, DAIS
Plum: Wild, SLOE
Pods: Vegetable, OKRA, OKRO
Poem: Epic, EPOS
Poet: Persian, OMAR
   Roman, OVID
Poison, BANE
   Arrow, INEE
Porkfish, SISI
Portico: Greek, STOA
Premium, AGIO
Priest: Islamic, IMAM
Prima donna, DIVA
Prong: Fork, TINE
Pseudonym: Lamb's, ELIA
Queen: Carthaginian, DIDO
   Hindu, RANI
Rabbit, CONY
Race: Of Japan, AINU
Rail: Ducklike, COOT
   North American, SORA
Redshank, CLEE
Refuse: After pressing, MARC
Regiment: Turkish, ALAI
Reliquary, ARCA
Resort: Italian, LIDO
Ridges: Sandy, ASAR, OSAR
River: German, ELBE, ODER
   Italian, ADDA
   Siberian, LENA
Road: Roman, ITER

Abode of dead: Babylonian, ARALU
Aborigine: Borneo DAYAK
Aftersong, EPODE
Aloe, AGAVE
Animal: Footless, APODE
Ant, EMMET
Antelope: African, ADDAX, BEISA,
   CAAMA, ELAND, GUIBA, ORIBI,
   TIANG
   Goat, GORAL, SEROW
   Indian, SASIN
   Siberian, SAIGA
Arch: Pointed, OGIVE
Armadillo, APARA, POYOU, TATOU
Arrowroot, ARARU
Artery: Trunk, AORTA
Association: Russian, ARTEL
   Secret, CABAL
Author: English, READE

Rockfish: California, RENA
Rodent: Mouselike, VOLE
   South American, PACA
Rootstock, TARO
Salamander, NEWT
Salmon: Silver, COHO
   Young, PARR
Same (Greek), HOMO
   (Latin), IDEM
Sauce: Fish, ALEC
School: English, ETON
Seaweed, AGAR, ALGA, KELP
Secular, LAIC
Sediment, SILT
Seed: Dill, ANET
   Of vetch, TARE
Serf, ILOT
Sesame, TEEL
Settlement: Eskimo, ETAH
Shark: Atlantic, GATA
   European, TOPE
Sheep: Wild, UDAD
Sheltered, ALEE
Shield, EGIS
Ship: Jason's, ARGO
   Left side of, PORT
   Two-masted, BRIG
Shrine: Buddhist, TOPE
Shrub: New Zealand, TUTU
Sign: Magic, RUNE
Silkworm, ERIA
Skin: Beaver, PLEW
Skink: Egyptian, ADDA
Slave, ESNE
Sloth: Two-toed, UNAU
Smooth, LENE
Snow: Glacial, NEVE
Soapstone, TALC
Society: African secret, EGBO, PORO
Son: Of Seth, ENOS
Song (German), LIED
   Unaccompanied, GLEE
Sound: Lung, RALE
Sour, ACID
Sow: Young, GILT
Spike: Brad-shaped, BROB
Spirit: Buddhist evil, MARA
Stake: Poker, ANTE
Star: Temporary, NOVA
Starch: East Indian, SAGO
Stone: Precious, OPAL
Strap: Bridle, REIN
Strewn (heraldry), SEME
Sweetsop, ATES, ATTA
Sword: Fencing, EPEE, FOIL
Tambourine: African, TAAR
Tapir: Brazilian, ANTA
Tax, CESS
Tea: South American, MATE
Therefore (Latin), ERGO
Thing: Extraordinary, ONER
Three (dice, cards, etc.), TREY
Thrush: Hawaiian, OMAO
Tide, NEAP

Words of Five Letters

Automaton, GOLEM, ROBOT
Award: Motion-picture, OSCAR
Basket: Fishing, CREEL
Beer: Russian, KVASS
Bible: Islamic, KORAN, QUR'AN
Bird: Asian, MINAH, MYNAH
   Indian, SHAMA
   Larklike, PIPIT
   Loonlike, GREBE
   Oscine, VIREO
   South American, AGAMI
   Swimming, GREBE
Black: (French), NOIRE
   (Heraldry), SABLE
Blackbird: European, MERLE, OUSEL,
   OUZEL
Block: Glacial, SERAC
Blue (heraldry), AZURE
Boat: Eskimo, BIDAR, UMIAK

Tipster: Racing, TOUT
Tissue, TELA
Title: Etruscan, LARS
   Hindu, BABU
   Indian, RAJA
   Islamic, EMIR, IMAM
   Persian, BABA
   Spanish, DONA
   Turkish, AGHA, BABA
Toad: Largest-known, AGUA
   Tree, HYLA
Tool: Cutting, ADZE
Track: Deer, SLOT
Tract: Sandy, DENE
Tree: Apple, SORB
   Central American, EBOE
   East Indian, TEAK
   Eucalyptus, YATE
   Guyanese and Trinidadian, MORA
   Javanese, UPAS
   Linden, LIME, LINN, TEIL, TILL
   Sandarac, ARAR
   Sassafras, AGUE
   Tamarisk salt, ATLE
Tribe: Moro, SULU
Trout, CHAR
Vessel: Arab, DHOW
Vestment: Ecclesiastical, COPE
Vetch, TARE
Vine: East Indian, SOMA
Violinist: Famous, AUER
Vortex, EDDY
Wampum, PEAG
Wapiti, STAG
Waste: Allowance for, TRET
Watchman: Indian, MINA
Water (Spanish), AGUA
Waterfall, LINN
Wavy (heraldry), ONDE, UNDE
Wax, CERE
   Chinese, PELA
Weed: Biblical, TARE
Weight: Ancient, MINA
   Danish (pl.), ESER
   East Asian, TAEL
   Greek, MINA
   Siamese, BAHT
Well done (rare), EUGE
Whale, CETE
   Killer, ORCA
   White, HUSE, HUSO
Whirlpool, EDDY
Wife: Of Geraint, ENID
Willow: Virginia, ITEA
Wine, PORT
Winged, ALAR
   (Heraldry), AILE
Wings, ALAE
Withered, SERE
Without (French), SANS
Wool: To comb, CARD
Work, OPUS
Wrong: Civil, TORT
Young: Bring forth, YEAN

Bobwhite, COLIN, QUAIL
Bone (comb. form), OSTEO
   Leg, TIBIA
   Thigh, FEMUR
Broom: Twig, BESOM
Brother (French), FRERE
   Moses, AARON
Canoe: Eskimo, BIDAR, KAYAK
Cape: Papal, FANON, ORALE
Caravansary, SERAI
Card: Old playing, TAROT
Caterpillar: New Zealand, AWETO
Catkin, AMENT
Cavity: Stone, GEODE
Cephalopod, SQUID
Cetacean, WHALE
Chariot, ESSED
Cheek: Pertaining to, MALAR
Chieftain: Arab, EMEER

Child (Scotch), BAIRN
Cigar, CLARO
Coating: Seed. TESTA
Cockatoo: Palm, ARARA
Coin: Costa Rican, COLON
 Danish, KRONE
 Ecuadorian, SUCRE
 English, GROAT, PENCE
 French, FRANC
 German, KRONE, TALER
 Hungarian, PENGO
 Icelandic, KRONA
 Indian, RUPEE
 Iraqi, DINAR
 Norwegian, KRONE
 Polish, ZLOTY
 Russian, COPEC, KOPEK, RUBLE
 Swedish, KRONA
 Turkish, ASPER
 Yugoslav, DINAR
Collar: Papal, FANON, ORALE
 Roman, RABAT
Commune: Italian, TREIA
Composition: Choral, MOTET
Compound: Chemical, ESTER
Conceal (law), ELOIN
Council: Ecclesiastical, SYNOD
Court: Anglo-Saxon, GEMOT
 Inner, PATIO
Crest: Mountain, ARETE
Crown: Papal, TIARA
Cuttlefish, SEPIA
Date: Roman, NONES
Decree: Islamic, IRADE
 Russian, UKASE
Deposit: Loam, LOESS
Desert: Gobi, SHAMO
Devilfish, MANTA
Disease: Cereals, ERGOT
Disk, PATEN
Dog: Wild, DHOLE, DINGO
Dormouse, LEROT
Drum, TABOR
Duck: Sea, EIDER
Dynasty: Chinese, CHING, LIANG,
 SHANG
Earthquake, SEISM
Eel, ELVER, MORAY
Ermine: European, STOAT
Ether: Crystalline, APIOL
Fabric: Velvetlike, PANNE
Fabulist, AESOP
Family: Italian, CENCI
Fiber: West Indian, SISAL
Fig: Smyrna, ELEME, ELEMI
Figure: Of speech, TROPE
Finch: European, SERIN
Fish: American small, KILLY
Flower: Garden, ASTER
Friend (Spanish), AMIGO
Fruit: Tropical, MANGO
Fungus: Rye, ERGOT
Furze, GORSE
Gateway, TORAN, TORII
Gem, AGATE, BERYL, PEARL, TOPAZ
Genus: Barnacles, LEPAS
 Bears, URSUS
 Birds (loons), GAVIA
 Birds (nuthatches), SITTA
 Cats, FELIS
 Dogs, CANIS
 Fishes (chiros), ELOPS
 Fishes (perch), PERCA
 Geese, ANSER
 Grasses, STIPA
 Grasses (incl. oats), AVENA
 Gulls, LARUS
 Hares, rabbits, LEPUS
 Hawks, BUTEO
 Herbs, old world, INULA
 Herbs, trailing or climbing, APIOS
 Herbs, tropical, TACCA, URENA
 Horses, EQUUS
 Insects (olive flies), DACUS
 Lice, plant, APHIS
 Lichens, USNEA

Lizards, AGAMA
Moles, TALPA
Mollusks, OLIVA
Monkeys, CEBUS
Palms, ARECA
Pigeons, GOURA
Plants (amaryllis family), AGAVE
Ruminants (goats), CAPRA
Shrubs, Asiatic, SABIA
Shrubs (heath), ERICA
Shrubs (incl. raspberry), RUBUS
Shrubs, tropical, IXORA, TREMA,
 URENA
Ticks, ARGAS
Trees (of elm family), TREMA, ULMUS
Trees, tropical, IXORA, TREMA
Goat: Bezoar, PASAN
God: Assyrian, ASHIR, ASHUR, ASSUR
 Babylonian, DAGAN, SIRIS
 Gaelic, DAGDA
 Hindu, BHAGA, INDRA, SHIVA
 Japanese, EBISU
 Philistine, DAGON
 Phrygian, ATTIS
 Teutonic, AEGIR, GYMIR
 Welsh, DYLAN
Goddess: Babylonian, ISTAR, NANAI
 Hindu, DURGA, GAURI, SHREE
Group: Of six, HEXAD
Grove: Sacred to Diana, NEMUS
Growing out, ENATE
Guitar: Hindu, SITAR
Gull: PEWEE, PEWIT
Hartebeest, CAAMA
Headdress: Jewish or Persian, TIARA
 Liturgical, MITER, MITRE
Heath, ERICA
Herb: Grasslike marsh, SEDGE
Heron, EGRET
Hog: Young, SHOAT, SHOTE
Image, EIKON
Indian: Cariban, ARARA
 Iroquoian, HURON
 Mexican, AZTEC, OPATA, OTOMI
 Muskhogean, CREEK
 Siouan, OSAGE, TETON
 Spanish American, ARARA, CARIB
Inflorescence: Racemose, AMENT
Insect: Immature, LARVA
Intrigue, CABAL
Iris: Yellow, SEDGE
Juniper, GORSE, RETEM
Kidneys: Pertaining to, RENAL
King: British legendary, LLUDD
Kite: European, GLEDE
Kobold, NISSE
Land: Cultivated, ARADA, ARADO
Landholder (Scotch), LAIRD, THANE
Language: Dravidian, TAMIL
Lariat, LASSO, REATA
Laughing, RIANT
Lawgiver: Athenian, DRACO, SOLON
Leaf: Calyx, SEPAL
 Fern, FROND
Lemur, LORIS
Letter: English, AITCH
 Greek, ALPHA, DELTA, GAMMA,
 KAPPA, OMEGA, SIGMA, THETA
 Hebrew, ALEPH, CHETH, GIMEL,
 SADHE, ZAYIN
Lichen, USNEA
Lighthouse, PHARE
Lizard: Old World, AGAMA
Loincloth, DHOTI
Louse: Plant, APHID
Macaw: Brazilian, ARARA
Mahogany: Philippine, ALMON
Mammal: Badgerlike, RATEL
 Civetlike, GENET
 Giraffelike, OKAPI
 Raccoonlike, COATI
Man (French), HOMME
Marble, AGATE
Mark: Insertion, CARET
Market place: Greek, AGORA
Marsupial: Australian, KOALA

Measure: Electric, FARAD, HENRY
 Energy, JOULE
 Metric, LITER, STERE
 Printing, AGATE
 Russian, VERST
Mixture: Smelting, MATTE
Mohicans: Last of, UNCAS
Molding: Convex, OVOLO, TORUS
Mole, TALPA
Monkey: African, PATAS
 Capuchin, SAJOU
 Howling, ARABA
Monkshood, ATEES
Month: Jewish, NISAN, SIVAN, TEBET
Museum (French), MUSEE
Musketeer, ATHOS
Native: Aleutian, ALEUT
 New Zealand, MAORI
Neckpiece: Ecclesiastical, AMICE
Nerve (comb. form), NEURO
Nest: Eagle's or hawk's, AERIE
 Insect's, NIDUS
Net: Fishing, SEINE
Newsstand, KIOSK
Nitrogen, AZOTE
Noble: Islamic, AMEER
Nodule: Stone, GEODE
Nostrils, NARES
Notched irregularly, EROSE
Nymph: Islamic, HOURI
Official: Roman, EDILE
Oleoresin, ELEMI
Opening: Mouthlike, STOMA
Oration: Funeral, ELOGE
Ostiole, STOMA
Page: Left-hand, VERSO
 Right-hand, RECTO
Palm, ARECA, BETEL
Park: Colorado, ESTES
Perfume, ATTAR
Philosopher: Greek, PLATO
Pillar: Stone, STELA, STELE
Pinnacle: Glacial, SERAC
Plain, LLANO
Plant: Century, AGAVE
 Climbing, LIANA
 Dwarf, CUMIN
 East Asian perennial, RAMIE
 Medicinal, SENNA
 Mustard family, CRESS
Plate: Communion, PATEN
Poem: Lyric, EPODE
Point: Lowest, NADIR
Poplar, ABELE, ALAMO, ASPEN
Porridge: Spanish American, ATOLE
Post: Stair, NEWEL
Priest: Islamic, IMAUM
Protozoan, AMEBA
Queen: (French), REINE
 Hindu, RANEE
Rabbit, CONEY
Rail, CRAKE
Red (heraldry), GULES
Religion: Moslem, Muslim, ISLAM
Resin, ELEMI
Revoke (law), ADEEM
Rich man, MIDAS, NABOB
Ridge: Sandy, ESKAR, ESKER
River: French, LOIRE, SEINE
Rockfish: California, REINA
Rootstock: Fragrant, ORRIS
Ruff: Female, REEVE
Sack: Pack, KYACK
Salt: Ethereal, ESTER
Saltpeter, NITER, NITRE
Salutation: Eastern, SALAM
Sandpiper: Old World, TEREK
Scented, OLENT
School: Fish, SHOAL
 French public, LYCEE
Scriptures: Islamic, KORAN
Seaweeds, ALGAE
Seed: Aromatic, ANISE
Seraglio, HAREM, SERAI
Serf, HELOT
Sheep: Wild, AUDAD

Sheeplike, OVINE
Shield, AEGIS
Shoe: Wooden, SABOT
Shoots: Pickled bamboo, ACHAR
Shot: Billiard, CAROM, MASSE
Shrine: Buddhist, STUPA
Shrub: Burning bush, WAHOO
  Ornamental evergreen, TOYON
  Used in tanning, SUMAC
Silk: Watered, MOIRE
Sister (French), SOEUR
  (Latin), SOROR
Six: Group of, HEXAD
Skeleton: Marine, CORAL
Slave, HELOT
Snake, ABOMA, ADDER, COBRA,
  RACER
Soldier: French, POILU
  Indian, SEPOY
Sour, ACERB
Spirit: Air, ARIEL
Staff: Shepherd's, CROOK
Starwort, ASTER
Steel (German), STAHL
Stockade: Russian, ETAPE

Stop (nautical), AVAST
Storehouse, ETAPE
Subway: Parisian, METRO
Tapestry, ARRAS
Tea: Paraguayan, YERBA
Temple: Hawaiian, HEIAU
Terminal: Positive, ANODE
Theater: Greek, ODEON, ODEUM
Then (French), ALORS
Thread: Surgical, SETON
Thrush: Wilson's, VEERY
Title: Hindu, BABOO
  Indian, RAJAH, SAHEB, SAHIB
  Islamic, EMEER, IMAUM
Tree: Buddhist sacred, PIPAL
  East Indian cotton, SIMAL
  Hickory, PECAN
  Light-wooded, BALSA
  Malayan, TERAP
  Mediterranean, CAROB
  Mexican, ABETO
  Mexican pine, OCOTE
  New Zealand, MAIRE
  Philippine, ALMON
  Rain, SAMAN

South American, UMBRA
Tamarack, LARCH
Tamarisk salt, ATLEE
West Indian, ACANA
Trout, CHARR
Troy, ILION, ILIUM
Twin: Siamese, CHANG
Vestment: Ecclesiastical, STOLE
Violin: Famous, AMATI, STRAD
Volcano: Mud, SALSE
Wampum, PEAGE
War cry: Greek, ALALA
Wavy (heraldry), UNDEE
Weight: Jewish, GERAH
Wen, TALPA
Wheat, SPELT
Wheel: Persian water, NORIA
Whitefish, CISCO
Willow, OSIER
Window: Bay, ORIEL
Wine, MEDOC, RHINE, TINTA, TOKAY
Winged, ALATE
Woman (French), FEMME
Year: Excess of solar over lunar, EPACT
Zoroastrian, PARSI

Words of Six or More Letters

Agave, MAGUEY
Alkaloid: Crystalline, ESERIN, ESERINE
Alligator, CAYMAN
Amphibole, EDENITE, URALITE
Ant: White, TERMITE
Antelope: African, DIKDIK, DUIKER,
  GEMSBOK, IMPALA, KOODOO
  European, CHAMOIS
  Indian, NILGAI, NILGAU, NILGHAI,
  NILGHAU
Ape: Asian or East Indian, GIBBON
Appendage: Leaf, STIPEL, STIPULE
Armadillo, PELUDO, TATOUAY
Arrowroot, ARARAO
Ascetic: Jewish, ESSENE
Ass: Asian wild, ONAGER
Avatar: Of Vishnu, KRISHNA
Babylonian, ELAMITE
Badge: Shoulder, EPAULET
Baldness, ALOPECIA
Barracuda, SENNET
Bark: Aromatic, SINTOC
Bearlike, URSINE
Beetle, ELATER
Bible: Zoroastrian, AVESTA
Bird: Sea, PETREL
  South American, SERIEMA
  Wading, AVOCET, AVOSET
Bone: Leg, FIBULA
Branched, RAMATE
Brother (Latin), FRATER
Bunting: European, ORTOLAN
Call: Trumpet, SENNET
Canoe: Eskimo, BAIDAR, OOMIAK
Caravansary, IMARET
Cat: Asian or African, CHEETAH
  Leopardlike, OCELOT
Cenobite: Jewish, ESSENE
Centerpiece: Table, EPERGNE
Cetacean, DOLPHIN, PORPOISE
Chariot, ESSEDA, ESSEDE
Chief: Seminole, OSCEOLA
Claim: Release as (law), REMISE
Clock: Water, CLEPSYDRA
Cloud, CUMULUS, NIMBUS
Coach: French hackney, FIACRE
Coin: Czech, KORUNA
  Ethiopian, TALARI
  Finnish, MARKKA
  German, THALER
  Greek, DRACHMA
  Haitian, GOURDE
  Honduran, LEMPIRA
  Hungarian, FORINT
  Indo-Chinese, PIASTER
  Netherlands, GUILDER
  Panamanian, BALBOA
  Paraguayan, GUARANI
  Portuguese, ESCUDO

Russian, COPECK, KOPECK,
  ROUBLE
  Spanish, PESETA
  Venezuelan, BOLIVAR
Communion: Last holy, VIATICUM
Conceal (law), ELOIGN
Confection, PRALINE
Construction: Sentence, SYNTAX
Convexity: Shaft of column, ENTASIS
Court: Anglo-Saxon, GEMOTE
Cow: Sea, DUGONG, MANATEE
Cylindrical, TERETE
Dagger, STILETTO
  Malay, CREESE, KREESE
Date: Roman, CALENDS, KALENDS
Deer, CARIBOU, WAPITI
Disease: Plant, ERINOSE
Doorkeeper, OSTIARY
Dragonflies: Order of, ODANATA
Drink: Of gods, NECTAR
Drum: TABOUR
  Moorish, ATABAL, ATTABAL
Duck: Fish-eating, MERGANSER
  Sea, SCOTER
Dynasty: Chinese, MANCHU
Eel, CONGER
Edit, REDACT
Envelope: Flower, PERIANTH
Eskimo, AMERIND
Ether: Crystalline, APIOLE
Excuse (law), ESSOIN
Eyespots, OCELLI
Fabric, ESTAMENE, ESTAMIN,
  ETAMINE
Falcon: European, KESTREL
Figure: Used as column, CARYATID,
  TELAMON
Fine: For punishment, AMERCE
Fish: Asian fresh-water, GOURAMI
  Pikelike, BARRACUDA
Five: Group of, PENTAD
Fly: African, TSETSE
Foot: Metric, ANAPEST, IAMBUS
Foxlike, VULPINE
Frying pan, SPIDER
Fur, KARAKUL
Galley: Greek or Roman, BIREME,
  TRIREME
Game: Card, ECARTE
Garment: Greek, CHLAMYS
Gateway, GOPURA, TORANA
Genus: Birds (ravens, crows), CORVUS
  Eels, CONGER
  Fishes, ANABAS
  Foxes, VULPES
  Herbs, ANEMONE
  Insects, CICADA
  Lemurs, GALAGO
  Mints (incl. catnip), NEPETA

Mollusks, ANOMIA, ASTARTE,
  TEREDO
  Mollusks (incl. oysters), OSTREA
  Monkeys (spider monkeys), ATELES
  Thrushes (incl. robins), TURDUS
  Trees (of elm family), CELTIS
  Trees (inc. dogwood), CORNUS
  Trees, tropical American, SAPOTA
  Wrens, NANNUS
Gibbon, SIAMANG, WOUWOU
Gland: Salivary, RACEMOSE
Goat: Bezoar, PASANG
Goatlike, CAPRINE
God: Assyrian, ASHSHUR, ASSHUR
  Babylonian, BABBAR, MARDUK,
  MERODACH, NANNAR, NERGAL,
  SHAMASH
  Hindu, BRAHMA, KRISHNA, VISHNU
  Tahitian, TAAROA
Goddess: Babylonian, ISHTAR
  Hindu, CHANDI, HAIMAVATI, LAK-
  SHMI, PARVATI, SARASVATI, SARAS-
  WATI
Government, POLITY
Governor: Persian, SATRAP
Grandson (Scotch), NEPOTE
Group: Of five, PENTAD
  Of nine, ENNEAD
  Of seven, HEPTAD
Hare: in first year, LEVERET
Harpsichord, SPINET
Herb: Alpine, EDELWEISS
  Chinese, GINSENG
  South African, FREESIA
Hermit, EREMITE
Hero: Legendary, PALADIN
Heron, BITTERN
Horselike, EQUINE
Hound: Short-legged, BEAGLE
House (French), MAISON
Idiot, CRETIN
Implement: Stone, NEOLITH
Incarnation: Hindu, AVATAR
Indian, APACHE, COMANCHE, PAIUTE,
  SENECA
Inn: Turkish, IMARET
Insects: Order of, DIPTERA
Instrument: Japanese banjolike,
  SAMISEN
  Musical, CLAVIER, SPINET
Interstice, AREOLA
Ironwood, COLIMA
Juniper: Old Testament, RAETAM
Kettledrum, ATABAL
King: Fairy, OBERON
Kneecap, PATELLA
Knife, MACHETE
Langur: Sumatran, SIMPAI
Legislature: Spanish, CORTES

Lemur: African, GALAGO
   Madagascar, AYEAYE
Letter: Greek, EPSILON, LAMBDA, OMI-
   CRON, UPSILON
   Hebrew, DALETH, LAMEDH, SAMEKH
Lighthouse, PHAROS
Lizard, IGUANA
Llama, ALPACA
Lockjaw, TETANUS
Locust, CICADA, CICALA
Macaw: Brazilian, MARACAN
Maid: Of Astolat, ELAINE
Mammal: Madagascar, TENDRAC, TEN-
   REC
Man (Spanish), HOMBRE
Marmoset: South American, TAMARIN
Marsupial, BANDICOOT, WOMBAT
Massacre, POGROM
Mayor: Spanish, ALCALDE
Measure: Electric, AMPERE, COULOMB,
   KILOWATT
Medicine: Quack, NOSTRUM
Member: Religious order, CENOBITE
Molasses, TREACLE
Monkey: African, GRIVET, NISNAS
   Asian, LANGUR
   Philippine, MACHIN
   South American, PINCHE, SAIMIRI,
   SAMIRI, SAPAJOU
Monster, CHIMERA, GORGON
   (Comb. form), TERATO
   Cretan, MINOTAUR
Month: Jewish, HESHVAN, KISLEV, SHE-
   BAT, TAMMUZ, TISHRI, VEADAR
Mountain: Asia Minor, ARARAT
Mulct, AMERCE
Musketeer, ARAMIS, PORTHOS
Nearsighted, MYOPIC
Net, TRAMMEL
New York City, GOTHAM
Nine: Group of, ENNEAD
Nobleman: Spanish, GRANDEE
Official: Roman, AEDILE
Onyx: Mexican, TECALI
Order: Dragonflies, ODANATA
   Insects, DIPTERA
Organ: Plant, PISTIL

Ornament: Shoulder, EPAULET
Overcoat: Military, CAPOTE
Ox: Wild, BANTENG
Oxidation: Bronze or copper, PATINA
Paralysis: Incomplete, PARESIS
Pear: Alligator, AVOCADO
Persimmon: Mexican, CHAPOTE
Pipe: Peace, CALUMET
Plaid (Scotch), TARTAN
Plain, PAMPAS, STEPPE, TUNDRA
Plant: Buttercup family, ANEMONE
   Century, MAGUEY
   On rocks, LICHEN
Plowing: Fit for, ARABLE
Poem: Heroic, EPOPEE
   Six-lined, SESTET
Point: Highest, ZENITH
Potion: Love, PHILTER, PHILTRE
Protozoan, AMOEBA
Punish, AMERCE
Purple (heraldry), PURPURE
Queen: Fairy, TITANIA
Race: Skiing, SLALOM
Rat, BANDICOOT, LEMMING
Retort, RIPOST, RIPOSTE
Ring: Harness, TERRET
   Little, ANNULET
Rodent: Jumping, JERBOA
   Spanish American, AGOUTI, AGOUTY
Sailor: East Indian, LASCAR
Salmon: Young, GRILSE
Salutation: Eastern, SALAAM
Sandpiper, PLOVER
Sandy, ARENOSE
Sapodilla, SAPOTA, SAPOTE
Saw: Surgical, TREPAN
Seven: Group of, HEPTAD
Sexes: Common to both, EPICENE
Shawl: Mexican, SERAPE
Sheathing: Flower, SPATHE
Sheep: Wild, AOUDAD, ARGALI
Shipworm, TEREDO
Shoes: Mercury's winged, TALARIA
Shortening: Syllable, SYSTOLE
Shrub, SPIRAEA
Sickle-shaped, FALCATE

Silver (heraldry), ARGENT
Snake, ANACONDA
Speech: Loss of, APHASIA
Spiral, HELICAL
Staff: Bishop's, CROSIER, CROZIER
Stalk: Plant, PETIOLE
State: Swiss, CANTON
Studio, ATELIER
Swan: Young, CYGNET
Swimming, NATANT
Sword-shaped, ENSATE
Terminal: Negative, CATHODE
Third (music), TIERCE
Thrust: Fencing, RIPOST, RIPOSTE
Tile: Pertaining to, TEGULAR
Tomb: Empty, CENOTAPH
Tooth (comb. form), ODONTO
Tower: Islamic, MINARET
Tree: African timber, BAOBAB
   Black gum, TUPELO
   East Indian, MARGOSA
   Locust, ACACIA
   Malayan, SINTOC
   Marmalade, SAPOTE
Urn: Tea, SAMOVAR
Vehicle, LANDAU, TROIKA
Verbose, PROLIX
Viceroy: Egyptian, KHEDIVE
Vulture: American, CONDOR
Warehouse (French), ENTREPOT
Whale: White, BELUGA
Whirlpool, VORTEX
Will: Addition to, CODICIL
   Having left, TESTATE
Wind, CHINOOK, MONSOON, SIMOOM,
   SIMOON, SIROCCO
Window: In roof, DORMER
Wine, BARBERA, BURGUNDY, CABER-
   NET, CHABLIS, CHIANTI, CLARET,
   MUSCATEL, RIESLING, SAUTERNE,
   SHERRY, ZINFANDEL
Wolfish, LUPINE
Woman: Boisterous, TERMAGANT
Woolly, LANATE
Workshop, ATELIER
Zoroastrian, PARSEE

Old Testament Names

We do not pretend that this list is all-inclusive. We list only those names that occur most often in crossword puzzles.

Aaron: First high priest of Jews; son of Amram; brother of Miriam and Moses; father of Abihu, Eleazer, Ithamar, and Nadab.
Abel: Son of Adam; slain by Cain.
Abigail: Wife of Nabal; later, wife of David.
Abihu: Son of Aaron.
Abimelech: King of Gerar.
Abner: Commander of army of Saul and Ishbosheth; slain by Joab.
Abraham (or Abram): Patriarch; forefather of the Jews; son of Terah; husband of Sarah; father of Isaac and Ishmael.
Absalom: Son of David and Maacah; revolted against David; slain by Joab.
Achish: King of Gath; gave refuge to David.
Achsa (or Achsah): Daughter of Caleb; wife of Othniel.
Adah: Wife of Lamech.
Adam: First man; husband of Eve; father of Cain, Abel, and Seth.
Adonijah: Son of David and Haggith.
Agag: King of Amalek; spared by Saul; slain by Samuel.
Ahasuerus: King of Persia; husband of Vashti and, later, Esther; sometimes identified with Xerxes the Great.
Ahijah: Prophet; foretold accession of Jeroboam.
Ahinoam: Wife of David.
Amasa: Commander of army of David; slain by Joab.
Amnon: Son of David and Ahinoam; ravished Tamar; slain by Absalom.
Amram: Husband of Jochebed; father of Aaron, Miriam and Moses.
Asenath: Wife of Joseph.
Asher: Son of Jacob and Zilpah.
Balaam: Prophet; rebuked by his donkey for cursing God.

Barak: Jewish captain; associated with Deborah.
Baruch: Secretary to Jeremiah.
Bathsheba: Wife of Uriah; later, wife of David.
Belshazzar: Crown prince of Babylon.
Benaiah: Warrior of David; proclaimed Solomon King.
Ben-Hadad: Name of several kings of Damascus.
Benjamin: Son of Jacob and Rachel.
Bezaleel: Chief architect of Tabernacle.
Bilhah: Servant of Rachel; mistress of Jacob.
Bildad: Comforter of Job.
Boaz: Husband of Ruth; father of Obed.
Cain: Son of Adam and Eve; slayer of Abel; father of Enoch.
Cainan: Son of Enos.
Caleb: Spy sent out by Moses to visit Canaan; father of Achsa.
Canaan: Son of Ham.
Chilion: Son of Elimelech; husband of Orpah.
Cush: Son of Ham; father of Nimrod.
Dan: Son of Jacob and Bilhah.
Daniel: Prophet; saved from lions by God.
Deborah: Hebrew prophetess; helped Israelites conquer Canaanites.
Delilah: Mistress and betrayer of Samson.
Elam: Son of Shem.
Eleazar: Son of Aaron; succeeded him as high priest.
Eli: High priest and judge; teacher of Samuel; father of Hophni and Phinehas.
Eliakim: Chief minister of Hezekiah.
Eliezer: Servant of Abraham.
Elihu: Comforter of Job.
Elijah (or Elias): Prophet; went to heaven in chariot of fire.
Elimelech: Husband of Naomi; father of Chilion and Mahlon.
Eliphaz: Comforter of Job.

Elisha (or Eliseus): Prophet; successor of Elijah.
Elkanah: Husband of Hannah; father of Samuel.
Enoch: Son of Cain.
Enoch: Father of Methuselah.
Enos: Son of Seth; father of Cainan.
Ephraim: Son of Joseph.
Esau: Son of Isaac and Rebecca; sold his birthright to his brother Jacob.
Esther: Jewish wife of Ahasuerus; saved Jews from Haman's plotting.
Eve: First woman; created from rib of Adam.
Ezra (or Esdras): Hebrew scribe and priest.
Gad: Son of Jacob and Zilpah.
Gehazi: Servant of Elisha.
Gideon: Israelite hero; defeated Midianites.
Goliath: Philistine giant; slain by David.
Hagar: Handmaid of Sarah; concubine of Abraham; mother of Ishmael.
Haggith: Mother of Adonijah.
Ham: Son of Noah; father of Cush, Mizraim, Phut, and Canaan.
Haman: Chief minister of Ahasuerus; hanged on gallows prepared for Mordecai.
Hannah: Wife of Elkanah; mother of Samuel.
Hanun: King of Ammonites.
Haran: Brother of Abraham; father of Lot.
Hazael: King of Damascus.
Hephzi-Bah: Wife of Hezekiah; mother of Mannaseh.
Hiram: King of Tyre.
Holofernes: General of Nebuchadnezzar; slain by Judith.
Hophni: Son of Eli.
Isaac: Hebrew patriarch; son of Abraham and Sarah; half brother of Ishmael; husband of Rebecca; father of Esau and Jacob.
Ishmael: Son of Abraham and Hagar; half brother of Isaac.
Issachar: Son of Jacob and Leah.
Ithamar: Son of Aaron.
Jabal: Son of Lamech and Adah.
Jabin: King of Hazor.
Jacob: Hebrew patriarch; founder of Israel; son of Isaac and Rebecca; husband of Leah and Rachel; father of Asher, Benjamin, Dan, Gad, Issachar, Joseph, Judah, Levi, Naphtali, Reuben, Simeon, and Zebulun.
Jael: Slayer of Sisera.
Japheth: Son of Noah.
Jehoiada: High priest; husband of Jehoshabeath; revolted against Athaliah and made Joash King of Judah.
Jehoshabeath (or Jehosheba): Daughter of Jehoram of Judah; wife of Jehoiada.
Jephthah: Judge in Israel; sacrificed his only daughter because of vow.
Jesse: Son of Obed; father of David.
Jethro: Midianite priest; father of Zipporah.
Jezebel: Phoenician princess; wife of Ahab; mother of Ahaziah, Athaliah, and Jehoram.
Joab: Commander in chief under David; slayer of Abner, Absalom, and Amasa.
Job: Patriarch; underwent many afflictions; comforted by Bildad, Elihu, Eliphaz and Zophar.
Jochebed: Wife of Amram.
Jonah: Prophet; cast into sea and swallowed by great fish.
Jonathan: Son of Saul; friend of David.
Joseph: Son of Jacob and Rachel; sold into slavery by his brothers; husband of Asenath; father of Ephraim and Manasseh.
Joshua: Successor of Moses; son of Nun.
Jubal: Son of Lamech and Adah.
Judah: Son of Jacob and Leah.
Judith: Slayer of Holofernes.
Kish: Father of Saul.

Laban: Father of Leah and Rachel.
Lamech: Son of Methuselah; father of Noah.
Lamech: Husband of Adah and Zillah; father of Jabal, Jubal, and Tubal-Cain.
Leah: Daughter of Laban; wife of Jacob.
Levi: Son of Jacob and Leah.
Lot: Son of Haran; escaped destruction of Sodom.
Maacah: Mother of Absalom and Tamar.
Mahlon: Son of Elimelech; first husband of Ruth.
Manasseh: Son of Joseph.
Melchizedek: King of Salem.
Methuselah: Patriarch; son of Enoch; father of Lamech.
Michal: Daughter of Saul; wife of David.
Miriam: Prophetess; daughter of Amram; sister of Aaron and Moses.
Mizraim: Son of Ham.
Mordecai: Uncle of Esther; with her aid, saved Jews from Haman's plotting.
Moses: Prophet and lawgiver; son of Amram; brother of Aaron and Miriam; husband of Zipporah.
Naaman: Syrian captain; cured of leprosy by Elisha.
Nabal: Husband of Abigail.
Naboth: Owner of vineyard; stoned to death because he would not sell it to Ahab.
Nadab: Son of Aaron.
Nahor: Father of Terah.
Naomi: Wife of Elimelech; mother-in-law of Ruth.
Naphtali: Son of Jacob and Bilhah.
Nathan: Prophet; reproved David for causing Uriah's death.
Nebuchadnezzar (or Nebuchadrezzar): King of Babylon; destroyer of Jerusalem.
Nehemiah: Jewish leader; empowered by Artaxerxes to rebuild Jerusalem.
Nimrod: Mighty hunter; son of Cush.
Noah: Patriarch; son of Lamech; escaped Deluge by building Ark; father of Ham, Japheth and Shem.
Nun (or Non): Father of Joshua.
Obed: Son of Boaz; father of Jesse.
Og: King of Bashan.
Orpah: Wife of Chilion.
Othniel: Kenezite; judge of Israel; husband of Achsa.
Phinehas: Son of Eleazer.
Phinehas: Son of Eli.
Phut (or Put): Son of Ham.
Potiphar: Egyptian official; bought Joseph.
Rachel: Wife of Jacob.
Rebecca (or Rebekah): Wife of Isaac.
Reuben: Son of Jacob and Leah.
Ruth: Wife of Mahlon, later of Boaz; daughter-in-law of Naomi.
Samson: Judge of Israel; famed for strength; betrayed by Delilah.
Samuel: Hebrew judge and prophet; son of Elkanah.
Sarah (or Sara, Sarai): Wife of Abraham.
Sennacherib: King of Assyria.
Seth: Son of Adam; father of Enos.
Shem: Son of Noah; father of Elam.
Simeon: Son of Jacob and Leah.
Sisera: Canaanite captain; slain by Jael.
Tamar: Daughter of David and Maachah; ravished by Amnon.
Terah: Son of Nahor; father of Abraham.
Tubal-Cain: Son of Lamech and Zillah.
Uriah: Husband of Bathsheba; sent to death in battle by David.
Vashti: Wife of Ahasuerus; set aside by him.
Zadok: High priest during David's reign.
Zebulun (or Zabulon): Son of Jacob and Leah.
Zillah: Wife of Lamech.
Zilpah: Servant of Leah; mistress of Jacob.
Zipporah: Daughter of Jethro; wife of Moses.
Zophar: Comforter of Job.

Kings of Judah and Israel

Kings Before Division of Kingdom

Saul: First King of Israel; son of Kish; father of Ish-Bosheth, Jonathan and Michal.
Ish-Bosheth (or Eshbaal): King of Israel; son of Saul.
David: King of Judah; later of Israel; son of Jesse; husband of Abigail, Ahinoam, Bathsheba, Michal, etc.; father of Absalom, Adonijah, Amnon, Solomon, Tamar, etc.
Solomon: King of Israel and Judah; son of David; father of Rehoboam.
Rehoboam: Son of Solomon; during his reign the kingdom was divided into Judah and Israel.

Kings of Judah (Southern Kingdom)

Rehoboam: First King.
Abijah (or Abijam or Abia): Son of Rehoboam.
Asa: Probably son of Abijah.
Jehoshaphat: Son of Asa.
Jehoram (or Joram): Son of Jehoshaphat; husband of Athaliah.
Ahaziah: Son of Jehoram and Athaliah.
Athaliah: Daughter of King Ahab of Israel and Jezebel; wife of Jehoram.
Joash (or Jehoash): Son of Ahaziah.

Amaziah: Son of Joash.
Uzziah (or Azariah): Son of Amaziah.
Jotham: Regent, later King; son of Uzziah.
Ahaz: Son of Jotham.
Hezekiah: Son of Ahaz; husband of Hephzi-Bah.
Manasseh: Son of Hezekiah and Hephzi-Bah.
Amon: Son of Manasseh.
Josiah (or Josias): Son of Amon.
Jehoahaz (or Joahaz): Son of Josiah.
Jehoiakim: Son of Josiah.
Jehoiachin: Son of Jehoiakim.
Zedekiah: Son of Josiah; kingdom overthrown by Babylonians under Nebuchadnezzar.

Kings of Israel (Northern Kingdom)

Jeroboam I: Led secession of Israel.
Nadab: Son of Jeroboam I.
Baasha: Overthrew Nadab.
Elah: Son of Baasha.
Zimri: Overthrew Elah.
Omri: Overthrew Zimri.

Ahab: Son of Omri; husband of Jezebel.
Ahaziah: Son of Ahab.
Jehoram (or Joram): Son of Ahab.
Jehu: Overthrew Jehoram.
Jehoahaz (or Joahaz): Son of Jehu.
Jehoash (or Joash): Son of Jehoahaz.
Jeroboam II: Son of Jehoash.
Zechariah: Son of Jeroboam II.
Shallum: Overthrew Zechariah.
Menahem: Overthrew Shallum.
Pekahiah: Son of Menahem.
Pekah: Overthrew Pekahiah.
Hoshea: Overthrew Pekah; kingdom overthrown by Assyrians under Sargon II.

Prophets

Major. Isaiah, Jeremiah, Ezekiel, Daniel.
Minor. Hosea, Obadiah, Nahum, Haggai, Joel, Jonah, Habakkuk, Zechariah, Amos, Micah, Zephaniah, Malachi.

Greek and Roman Mythology

Most of the Greek deities were adopted by the Romans, although in many cases there was a change of name. In the list below, information is given under the Greek name; the name in parentheses is the Roman equivalent. In addition, there are several deities that are exclusively Roman.

Acheron: One of several **Rivers of Underworld:** Acheron (woe), Cocytus (wailing), Lethe (forgetfulness), Phlegethon (fire), Styx (across which souls of dead were ferried by Charon).
Achilles: Greek warrior; slew Hector at Troy; slain by Paris, who wounded him in his vulnerable heel.
Actaeon: Hunter; surprised Artemis bathing; changed by her to stag; and killed by his dogs.
Admetus: King of Thessaly; his wife, Alcestis, offered to die in his place.
Adonis: Beautiful youth loved by Aphrodite.
Aeacus: One of three judges of dead in Hades; son of Zeus.
Aeëtes: King of Colchis; father of Medea; keeper of Golden Fleece.
Aegeus: Father of Theseus; believing Theseus killed in Crete, he drowned himself; Aegean Sea named for him.
Aegisthus: Son of Thyestes; slew Atreus; with Clytemnestra, his paramour, slew Agamemnon; slain by Orestes.
Aegyptus: Brother of Danaus; his sons, except Lynceus, slain by Danaides.
Aeneas: Trojan; son of Anchises and Aphrodite; after fall of Troy, led his followers eventually to Italy; loved and deserted Dido.
Aeolus: One of several **Winds:** Aeolus (keeper of winds), Boreas (Aquilo) (north wind), Eurus (east wind), Notus (Auster) (south wind), Zephyrus (Favonius) (west wind).
Aeson: King of Ioclus; father of Jason; overthrown by his brother Pelias; restored to youth by Medea.
Aether: Personification of sky.
Aethra: Mother of Theseus.
Agamemnon: King of Mycenae; son of Atreus; brother of Menelaus; leader of Greeks against Troy; slain on his return home by Clytemnestra and Aegisthus.
Aglaia: One of several **Graces:** Beautiful goddesses: Aglaia (Brilliance), Euphrosyne (Joy), and Thalia (Bloom); daughters of Zeus.
Ajax: Greek warrior; killed himself at Troy because Achilles's armor was awarded to Odysseus.
Alcestis: Wife of Admetus; offered to die in his place but saved from death by Hercules.
Alcmene: Wife of Amphitryon; mother by Zeus of Hercules.
Alcyone: One of several **Pleiades:** Alcyone, Celaeno, Electra, Maia, Merope, Sterope or Asterope, Taygeta; seven daughters of Atlas; transformed into heavenly constellation, of which six stars are visible (Merope is said to have hidden in shame for loving a mortal).
Alecto: One of several **Furies:** Avenging spirits; Alecto, Megaera, and Tisiphone; known also as Erinyes or Eumenides.
Alectryon: Youth changed by Ares into cock.
Althaea: Wife of Oeneus; mother of Meleager.
Amazons: Female warriors in Asia Minor; supported Troy against Greeks.
Amphion: Musician; husband of Niobe; charmed stones to build fortifications for Thebes.
Amphitrite: Sea goddess; wife of Poseidon.
Amphitryon: Husband of Alcmene.
Anchises: Father of Aeneas.

Ancile: Sacred shield that fell from heavens; palladium of Rome.
Andraemon: Husband of Dryope.
Andromache: Wife of Hector.
Andromeda: Daughter of Cepheus; chained to cliff for monster to devour; rescued by Perseus.
Anteia: Wife of Proetus; tried to induce Bellerophon to elope with her.
Anteros: God who avenged unrequited love.
Antigone: Daughter of Oedipus; accompanied him to Colonus; performed burial rite for Polynices and hanged herself.
Antinoüs: Leader of suitors of Penelope; slain by Odysseus.
Aphrodite (Venus): Goddess of love and beauty; daughter of Zeus; mother of Eros.
Apollo: God of beauty, poetry, music; later identified with Helios as Phoebus Apollo; son of Zeus and Leto.
Aquilo: One of several **Winds:** Aeolus (keeper of winds), Boreas (Aquilo) (north wind), Eurus (east wind), Notus (Auster) (south wind), Zephyrus (Favonius) (west wind).
Arachne: Maiden who challenged Athena to weaving contest; changed to spider.
Ares (Mars): God of war; son of Zeus and Hera.
Argo: Ship in which Jason and followers sailed to Colchis for Golden Fleece.
Argus: Monster with hundred eyes; slain by Hermes; his eyes placed by Hera into peacock's tail.
Ariadne: Daughter of Minos; aided Theseus in slaying Minotaur; deserted by him on island of Naxos and married to Dionysus.
Arion: Musician; thrown overboard by pirates but saved by dolphin.
Artemis (Diana): Goddess of moon; huntress; twin sister of Apollo.
Asclepius (Aesculapius): Mortal son of Apollo; slain by Zeus for raising dead; later deified as god of medicine. Also known as Asklepios.
Astarte: Phoenician goddess of love; variously identified with Aphrodite, Selene, and Artemis.
Astraea: Goddess of Justice; daughter of Zeus and Themis.
Atalanta: Princess who challenged her suitors to a foot race; Hippomenes won race and married her.
Athena (Minerva): Goddess of wisdom; known poetically as Pallas Athene; sprang fully armed from head of Zeus.
Atlas: Titan; held world on his shoulders as punishment for warring against Zeus; son of Iapetus.
Atreus: King of Mycenae; father of Menelaus and Agamemnon; brother of Thyestes, three of whose sons he slew and served to him at banquet; slain by Aegisthus.
Atropos: One of several **Fates:** Goddesses of destiny; Clotho (Spinner of thread of life), Lachesis (Determiner of length), and Atropos (Cutter of thread); also called Moirae. Identified by Romans with their goddesses of fate, Nona, Decuma, and Morta; called Parcae.
Auster: One of several **Winds:** Aeolus (keeper of winds), Boreas (Aquilo) (north wind), Eurus (east wind), Notus (Auster) (south wind), Zephyrus (Favonius) (west wind).

Avernus: Infernal regions; name derived from small vaporous lake near Vesuvius which was fabled to kill birds and vegetation.

Bellerophon: Corinthian hero; killed Chimera with aid of Pegasus; tried to reach Olympus on Pegasus and was thrown to his death.

Bellona: Roman goddess of war.

Boreas: One of several **Winds:** Aeolus (keeper of winds), Boreas (Aquilo) (north wind), Eurus (east wind), Notus (Auster) (south wind), Zephyrus (Favonius) (west wind).

Briareus: Monster of hundred hands; son of Uranus and Gaea.

Briseis: Captive maiden given to Achilles; taken by Agamemnon in exchange for loss of Chryseis, which caused Achilles to cease fighting, until death of Patroclus.

Cadmus: Brother of Europa; planter of dragon seeds from which first Thebans sprang.

Calliope: One of several **Muses,** Goddesses presiding over arts and sciences: Calliope (epic poetry), Clio (history), Erato (lyric and love poetry), Euterpe (music), Melpomene (tragedy), Polymnia or Polyhymnia (sacred poetry), Terpsichore (choral dance and song), Thalia (comedy and bucolic poetry), Urania (astronomy); daughters of Zeus and Mnemosyne.

Calypso: Sea nymph; kept Odysseus on her island Ogygia for seven years.

Cassandra: Daughter of Priam; prophetess who was never believed; slain with Agamemnon.

Castor: One of **Dioscuri,** Twins Castor and Pollux; sons of Leda by Zeus.

Celaeno: One of several **Pleiades:** Alcyone, Celaeno, Electra, Maia, Merope, Sterope or Asterope, Taygeta; seven daughters of Atlas; transformed into heavenly constellation, of which six stars are visible (Merope is said to have hidden in shame for loving a mortal).

Centaurs: Beings half man and half horse; lived in mountains of Thessaly.

Cephalus: Hunter; accidentally killed his wife Procris with his spear.

Cepheus: King of Ethiopia; father of Andromeda.

Cerberus: Three-headed dog guarding entrance to Hades.

Chaos: Formless void; personified as first of gods.

Charon: Boatman on Styx who carried souls of dead to Hades; son of Erebus.

Charybdis: Female monster; personification of whirlpool.

Chimera: Female monster with head of lion, body of goat, tail of serpent; killed by Bellerophon.

Chiron: Most famous of centaurs.

Chronos: Personification of time.

Chryseis: Captive maiden given to Agamemnon; his refusal to accept ransom from her father Chryses caused Apollo to send plague on Greeks besieging Troy.

Circe: Sorceress; daughter of Helios; changed Odysseus's men into swine.

Clio: One of several **Muses:** Goddesses presiding over arts and sciences: Calliope (epic poetry), Clio (history), Erato (lyric and love poetry), Euterpe (music), Melpomene (tragedy), Polymnia or Polyhymnia (sacred poetry), Terpsichore (choral dance and song), Thalia (comedy and bucolic poetry), Urania (astronomy); daughters of Zeus and Mnemosyne.

Clotho: One of several **Fates:** Goddesses of destiny; Clotho (Spinner of thread of life), Lachesis (Determiner of length), and Atropos (Cutter of thread); also called Moirae. Identified by Romans with their goddesses of fate; Nona, Decuma, and Morta; called Parcae.

Clytemnestra: Wife of Agamemnon, whom she slew with aid of her paramour, Aegisthus; slain by her son Orestes.

Cocytus: One of several **Rivers of Underworld:** Acheron (woe), Cocytus (wailing), Lethe (forgetfulness), Phlegethon (fire), Styx (across which souls of dead were ferried by Charon).

Creon: Father of Jocasta; forbade burial of Polynices; ordered burial alive of Antigone.

Creüsa: Princess of Corinth, for whom Jason deserted Medea; slain by Medea, who sent her poisoned robe; also known as Glaüke.

Creusa: Wife of Aeneas; died fleeing Troy.

Cronus (Saturn): Titan; god of harvests; son of Uranus and Gaea; dethroned by his son Zeus.

Cybele: Anatolian nature goddess; adopted by Greeks and identified with Rhea.

Cyclopes: Race of one-eyed giants (singular: Cyclops).

Daedalus: Athenian artificer; father of Icarus; builder of Labyrinth in Crete; devised wings attached with wax for him and Icarus to escape Crete.

Danae: Princess of Argos; mother of Perseus by Zeus, who appeared to her in form of golden shower.

Danaïdes: Daughters of Danaüs; at his command, all except Hypermnestra slew their husbands, the sons of Aegyptus.

Danaüs: Brother of Aegyptus; father of Danaïdes; slain by Lynceus.

Daphne: Nymph; pursued by Apollo; changed to laurel tree.

Decuma: One of several **Fates:** Goddesses of destiny; Clotho (Spinner of thread of life), Lachesis (Determiner of length), and Atropos (Cutter of thread); also called Moirae. Identified by Romans with their goddesses of fate; Nona, Decuma, and Morta; called Parcae.

Deino: One of several **Graeae:** Sentinels for Gorgons; Deino, Enyo, and Pephredo; had one eye among them, which passed from one to another.

Demeter (Ceres): Goddess of agriculture; mother of Persephone.

Dido: Founder and queen of Carthage; stabbed herself when deserted by Aeneas.

Diomedes: Greek hero; with Odysseus, entered Troy and carried off Palladium, sacred statue of Athena.

Diomedes: Owner of man-eating horses, which Hercules, as ninth labor, carried off.

Dione: Titan goddess; mother by Zeus of Aphrodite.

Dionysus (Bacchus): God of wine; son of Zeus and Semele.

Dioscuri: Twins Castor and Pollux; sons of Leda by Zeus.

Dryads: Wood nymphs.

Dryope: Maiden changed to Hamadryad.

Echo: Nymph who fell hopelessly in love with Narcissus; faded away except for her voice.

Electra: Daughter of Agamemnon and Clytemnestra; sister of Orestes; urged Orestes to slay Clytemnestra and Aegisthus.

Electra: One of several **Pleiades:** Alcyone, Celaeno, Electra, Maia, Merope, Sterope or Asterope, Taygeta; seven daughters of Atlas; transformed into heavenly constellation, of which six stars are visible (Merope is said to have hidden in shame for loving a mortal).

Elysium: Abode of blessed dead.

Endymion: Mortal loved by Selene.

Enyo: One of several **Graeae:** Sentinels for Gorgons; Deino, Enyo, and Pephredo; had one eye among them, which passed from one to another.

Eos (Aurora): Goddess of dawn.

Epimetheus: Brother of Prometheus; husband of Pandora.

Erato: One of several **Muses:** Goddesses presiding over arts and sciences: Calliope (epic poetry), Clio (history), Erato (lyric and love poetry), Euterpe (music), Melpomene (tragedy), Polymnia or Polyhymnia (sacred poetry), Terpsichore (choral dance and song), Thalia (comedy and bucolic poetry), Urania (astronomy); daughters of Zeus and Mnemosyne.

Erebus: Spirit of darkness; son of Chaos.

Erinyes: One of several **Furies:** Avenging spirits; Alecto, Megaera, and Tisiphone; known also as Erinyes or Eumenides.

Eris: Goddess of discord.

Eros (Amor or Cupid): God of love; son of Aphrodite.

Eteocles: Son of Oedipus, whom he succeeded to rule alternately with Polynices; refused to give up throne at end of year; he and Polynices slew each other.

Eumenides: One of several **Furies:** Avenging spirits; Alecto, Megaera, and Tisiphone; known also as Erinyes or Eumenides.

Euphrosyne: One of several **Graces:** Beautiful goddesses: Aglaia (Brilliance), Euphrosyne (Joy), and Thalia (Bloom); daughters of Zeus.

Europa: Mortal loved by Zeus, who, in form of white bull, carried her off to Crete.

Eurus: One of several **Winds:** Aeolus (keeper of winds), Boreas (Aquilo) (north wind), Eurus (east wind), Notus (Auster) (south wind), Zephyrus (Favonius) (west wind).

Euryale: One of several **Gorgons:** Female monsters; Euryale, Medusa, and Stheno; had snakes for hair; their glances turned mortals to stone.

Eurydice: Nymph; wife of Orpheus.

Eurystheus: King of Argos; imposed twelve labors on Hercules.

Euterpe: One of several **Muses:** Goddesses presiding over arts and sciences: Calliope (epic poetry), Clio (history), Erato (lyric and love poetry), Euterpe (music), Melpomene (tragedy), Polymnia or Polyhymnia (sacred poetry), Terpsichore (choral dance and song), Thalia (comedy and bucolic poetry), Urania (astronomy); daughters of Zeus and Mnemosyne.

Fates: Goddesses of destiny; Clotho (Spinner of thread of life), Lachesis (Determiner of length), and Atropos (Cutter of thread); also called Moirae. Identified by Romans with their goddesses of fate; Nona, Decuma, and Morta; called Parcae.

Fauns: Roman deities of woods and groves.

Favonius: One of several **Winds:** Aeolus (keeper of winds), Boreas (Aquilo) (north wind), Eurus (east wind), Notus (Auster) (south wind), Zephyrus (Favonius) (west wind).

Flora: Roman goddess of flowers.

Fortuna: Roman goddess of fortune.

Furies: Avenging spirits; Alecto, Megaera, and Tisiphone; known also as Erinyes or Eumenides.

Gaea: Goddess of earth; daughter of Chaos; mother of Titans; known also as Ge, Gea, Gaia, etc.

Galatea: Statue of maiden carved from ivory by Pygmalion; given life by Aphrodite.

Galatea: Sea nymph; loved by Polyphemus.

Ganymede: Beautiful boy; successor to Hebe as cupbearer of gods.

Glaucus: Mortal who became sea divinity by eating magic grass.

Golden Fleece: Fleece from ram that flew Phrixos to Colchis; Aeëtes placed it under guard of dragon; carried off by Jason.

Gorgons: Female monsters; Euryale, Medusa, and Stheno; had snakes for hair; their glances turned mortals to stone.

Graces: Beautiful goddesses: Aglaia (Brilliance), Euphrosyne (Joy), and Thalia (Bloom); daughters of Zeus.

Graeae: Sentinels for Gorgons; Deino, Enyo, and Pephredo; had one eye among them, which passed from one to another.

Hades (Dis): Name sometimes given Pluto; also, abode of dead, ruled by Pluto.

Haemon: Son of Creon; promised husband of Antigone; killed himself in her tomb.

Hamadryads: Tree nymphs.

Harpies: Monsters with heads of women and bodies of birds.

Hebe (Juventas): Goddess of youth; cupbearer of gods before Ganymede; daughter of Zeus and Hera.

Hecate: Goddess of sorcery and witchcraft.

Hector: Son of Priam; slayer of Patroclus; slain by Achilles.

Hecuba: Wife of Priam.

Helen: Fairest woman in world; daughter of Zeus and Leda; wife of Menelaus; carried to Troy by Paris, causing Trojan War.

Heliades: Daughters of Helios; mourned for Phaëthon and were changed to poplar trees.

Helios (Sol): God of sun; later identified with Apollo.

Helle: Sister of Phrixos; fell from ram of Golden Fleece; water where she fell named Hellespont.

Hephaestus (Vulcan): God of fire; celestial blacksmith; son of Zeus and Hera; husband of Aphrodite.

Hera (Juno): Queen of heaven; wife of Zeus.

Hercules: Hero and strong man; son of Zeus and Alcmene; performed twelve labors or deeds to be free from bondage under Eurystheus; after death, his mortal share was destroyed, and he became immortal. Also known as Herakles or Heracles. Labors: (1) killing Nemean lion; (2) killing Lernaean Hydra; (3) capturing Erymanthian boar; (4) capturing Cerynean hind; (5) killing man-eating Stymphalian birds; (6) procuring girdle of Hippolyte; (7) cleaning Augean stables; (8) capturing Cretan bull; (9) capturing man-eating horses of Diomedes; (10) capturing cattle of Geryon; (11) procuring golden apples of Hesperides; (12) bringing Cerberus up from Hades.

Hermes (Mercury): God of physicians and thieves; messenger of gods; son of Zeus and Maia.

Hero: Priestess of Aphrodite; Leander swam Hellespont nightly to see her; drowned herself at his death.

Hesperus: Evening star.

Hestia (Vesta): Goddess of hearth; sister of Zeus.

Hippolyte: Queen of Amazons; wife of Theseus.

Hippolytus: Son of Theseus and Hippolyte; falsely accused by Phaedra of trying to kidnap her; slain by Poseidon at request of Theseus.

Hippomenes: Husband of Atalanta, whom he beat in race by dropping golden apples, which she stopped to pick up.

Hyacinthus: Beautiful youth accidentally killed by Apollo, who caused flower to spring up from his blood.

Hydra: Nine-headed monster in marsh of Lerna; slain by Hercules.

Hygeia: Personification of health.

Hyman: God of marriage.

Hyperion: Titan; early sun god; father of Helios.

Hypermnestra: Daughter of Danaüs; refused to kill her husband Lynceus.

Hypnos (Somnus): God of sleep.

Iapetus: Titan; father of Atlas, Epimetheus, and Prometheus.

Icarus: Son of Daedalus; flew too near sun with wax-attached wings and fell into sea and was drowned.

Io: Mortal maiden loved by Zeus; changed by Hera into heifer.

Iobates: King of Lycia; sent Bellerophon to slay Chimera.

Iphigenia: Daughter of Agamemnon; offered as sacrifice to Artemis at Aulis; carried by Artemis to Tauris where she became priestess; escaped from there with Orestes.

Iris: Goddess of rainbow; messenger of Zeus and Hera.

Ismene: Daughter of Oedipus; sister of Antigone.

Iulus: Son of Aeneas.

Ixion: King of Lapithae; for making love to Hera he was bound to endlessly revolving wheel in Tartarus.

Janus: Roman god of gates and doors; represented with two opposite faces.

Jason: Son of Aeson; to gain throne of Ioclus from Pelias, went to Colchis and brought back Golden Fleece; married Medea; deserted her for Creüsa.

Jocasta: Wife of Laius; mother of Oedipus; unwittingly became wife of Oedipus; hanged herself when relationship was discovered.

Lachesis: One of several **Fates:** Goddesses of destiny; Clotho (Spinner of thread of life), Lachesis (Determiner of length), and Atropos (Cutter of thread); also called Moirae. Identified by Romans with their goddesses of fate; Nona, Decuma, and Morta; called Parcae.

Laius: Father of Oedipus, by whom he was slain.

Laocoön: Priest of Apollo at Troy; warned against bringing wooden horse into Troy; destroyed with his two sons by serpents sent by Athena.

Lares: Roman ancestral spirits protecting descendants and homes.

Lavinia: Wife of Aeneas after defeat of Turnus.

Leander: Swam Hellespont nightly to see Hero; drowned in storm.

Leda: Mortal loved by Zeus in form of swan; mother of Helen, Clytemnestra, Dioscuri.

Lethe: One of several **Rivers of Underworld:** Acheron (woe), Cocytus (wailing), Lethe (forgetfulness), Phlegethon (fire), Styx (across which souls of dead were ferried by Charon).

Leto (Latona): Mother by Zeus of Artemis and Apollo.

Lucina: Roman goddess of childbirth; identified with Juno.

Lynceus: Son of Aegyptus; husband of Hypermnestra; slew Danaüs.

Maia: Daughter of Atlas; mother of Hermes.

Maia: One of several **Pleiades:** Alcyone, Celaeno, Electra, Maia, Merope, Sterope or Asterope, Taygeta; seven daughters of Atlas; transformed into heavenly constellation, of which six stars are visible (Merope is said to have hidden in shame for loving a mortal).

Manes: Souls of dead Romans, particularly of ancestors.

Marsyas: Shepherd; challenged Apollo to music contest and lost; flayed alive by Apollo.

Medea: Sorceress; daughter of Aeëtes; helped Jason obtain Golden Fleece; when deserted by him for Creüsa, killed her children and Creüsa.

Medusa: Gorgon; slain by Perseus, who cut off her head.

Megaera: One of several **Furies:** Avenging spirits; Alecto, Megaera, and Tisiphone; known also as Erinyes or Eumenides.

Meleager: Son of Althaea; his life would last as long as brand burning at his birth; Althaea quenched and saved it but destroyed it when Meleager slew his uncles.

Melpomene: One of several **Muses:** Goddesses presiding over arts and sciences: Calliope (epic poetry), Clio (history), Erato (lyric and love poetry), Euterpe (music), Melpomene (tragedy), Polymnia or Polyhymnia (sacred poetry), Terpsichore (choral dance and song), Thalia (comedy and bucolic poetry), Urania (astronomy); daughters of Zeus and Mnemosyne.

Memnon: Ethiopian king; made immortal by Zeus; son of Tithonus and Eos.

Menelaus: King of Sparta; son of Atreus; brother of Agamemnon; husband of Helen.

Merope: One of several **Pleiades:** Alcyone, Celaeno, Electra, Maia, Merope, Sterope or Asterope, Taygeta; seven daughters of Atlas; transformed into heavenly constellation, of which six stars are visible; said to have hidden in shame for loving a mortal.

Mezentius: Cruel Etruscan king; ally of Turnus against Aeneas; slain by Aeneas.

Midas: King of Phrygia; given gift of turning to gold all he touched.

Minos: King of Crete; after death, one of three judges of dead in Hades; son of Zeus and Europa.

Minotaur: Monster, half man and half beast, kept in Labyrinth in Crete; slain by Theseus.

Mnemosyne: Goddess of memory; mother by Zeus of Muses.

Moirae: One of several **Fates:** Goddesses of destiny; Clotho (Spinner of thread of life), Lachesis (Determiner of length), and Atropos (Cutter of thread); also called Moirae. Identified by Romans with their goddesses of fate; Nona, Decuma, and Morta; called Parcae.

Momus: God of ridicule.

Morpheus: God of dreams.

Morta: One of several **Fates:** Goddesses of destiny; Clotho (Spinner of thread of life), Lachesis (Determiner of length), and Atropos (Cutter of thread); also called Moirae. Identified by Romans with their goddesses of fate; Nona, Decuma, and Morta; called Parcae.

Muses: Goddesses presiding over arts and sciences: Calliope (epic poetry), Clio (history), Erato (lyric and love poetry), Euterpe (music), Melpomene (tragedy), Polymnia or Polyhymnia (sacred poetry), Terpsichore (choral dance and song), Thalia (comedy and bucolic poetry), Urania (astronomy); daughters of Zeus and Mnemosyne.

Naiads: Nymphs of waters, streams, and fountains.

Napaeae: Wood nymphs.

Narcissus: Beautiful youth loved by Echo; in punishment for not returning her love, he was made to fall in love with his image reflected in pool; pined away and became flower.

Nemesis: Goddess of retribution.

Neoptolemus: Son of Achilles; slew Priam; also known as Pyrrhus.

Nereids: Sea nymphs; attendants on Poseidon.

Nestor: King of Pylos; noted for wise counsel in expedition against Troy.

Nike: Goddess of victory.

Niobe: Daughter of Tantalus; wife of Amphion; her children slain by Apollo and Artemis; changed to stone but continued to weep her loss.

Nona: One of several **Fates:** Goddesses of destiny; Clotho (Spinner of thread of life), Lachesis (Determiner of length), and Atropos (Cutter of thread); also called Moirae. Identified by Romans with their goddesses of fate; Nona, Decuma, and Morta; called Parcae.

Notus: One of several **Winds:** Aeolus (keeper of winds), Boreas (Aquilo) (north wind), Eurus (east wind), Notus (Auster) (south wind), Zephyrus (Favonius) (west wind).

Nymphs: Beautiful maidens; inferior deities of nature.

Nyx (Nox): Goddess of night.

Oceanids: Ocean nymphs; daughters of Oceanus.

Oceanus: Eldest of Titans; god of waters.

Odysseus (Ulysses): King of Ithaca; husband of Penelope; wandered ten years after fall of Troy before arriving home.

Oedipus: King of Thebes; son of Laius and Jocasta; unwittingly murdered Laius and married Jocasta; tore his eyes out when relationship was discovered.

Oenone: Nymph of Mount Ida; wife of Paris, who abandoned her; refused to cure him when he was poisoned by arrow of Philoctetes at Troy.

Oreads: Mountain nymphs.

Orestes: Son of Agamemnon and Clytemnestra; brother of Electra; slew Clytemnestra and Aegisthus; pursued by Furies until his purification by Apollo.

Orion: Hunter; slain by Artemis and made heavenly constellation.

Orpheus: Famed musician; son of Apollo and Muse Calliope; husband of Eurydice.

Pales: Roman goddess of shepherds and herdsmen.

Palinurus: Aeneas' pilot; fell overboard in his sleep and was drowned.

Pan (Faunus): God of woods and fields; part goat; son of Hermes.

Pandora: Opener of box containing human ills; mortal wife of Epimetheus.

Parcae: One of several **Fates:** Goddesses of destiny; Clotho (Spinner of thread of life), Lachesis (Determiner of length), and Atropos (Cutter of thread); also called Moirae. Identified by Romans with their goddesses of fate; Nona, Decuma, and Morta; called Parcae.

Paris: Son of Priam; gave apple of discord to Aphrodite, for which she enabled him to carry off Helen; slew Achilles at Troy; slain by Philoctetes.

Patroclus: Great friend of Achilles; wore Achilles' armor and was slain by Hector.

Pegasus: Winged horse that sprang from Medusa's body at her death; ridden by Bellerophon when he slew Chimera.

Pelias: King of Ioclus; seized throne from his brother Aeson; sent Jason for Golden Fleece; slain unwittingly by his daughters at instigation of Medea.

Pelops: Son of Tantalus; his father cooked and served him to gods; restored to life; Peloponnesus named for him.

Penates: Roman household gods.

Penelope: Wife of Odysseus; waited faithfully for him for ten years while putting off numerous suitors.

Pephredo: One of several **Graeae:** Sentinels for Gorgons; Deino, Enyo, and Pephredo; had one eye among them, which passed from one to another.

Periphetes: Giant; son of Hephaestus; slain by Theseus.

Persephone (Proserpine): Queen of infernal regions; daughter of Zeus and Demeter; wife of Pluto.

Perseus: Son of Zeus and Danaë; slew Medusa; rescued Andromeda from monster and married her.

Phaedra: Daughter of Minos; wife of Theseus; caused the death of her stepson, Hippolytus.

Phaethon: Son of Helios; drove his father's sun chariot and was struck down by Zeus before he set world on fire.

Philoctetes: Greek warrior who possessed Hercules' bow and arrows; slew Paris at Troy with poisoned arrow.

Phineus: Betrothed of Andromeda; tried to slay Perseus but turned to stone by Medusa's head.

Phlegethon: One of several **Rivers of Underworld:** Acheron (woe), Cocytus (wailing), Lethe (forgetfulness), Phlegethon (fire), Styx (across which souls of dead were ferried by Charon).

Phosphor: Morning star.

Phrixos: Brother of Helle; carried by ram of Golden Fleece to Colchis.

Pirithous: Son of Ixion; friend of Theseus; tried to carry off Persephone from Hades; bound to enchanted rock by Pluto.

Pleiades: Alcyone, Celaeno, Electra, Maia, Merope, Sterope or Asterope, Taygeta; seven daughters of Atlas; transformed into heavenly constellation, of which six stars are visible (Merope is said to have hidden in shame for loving a mortal).

Pluto (Dis): God of Hades; brother of Zeus.

Plutus: God of wealth.

Pollux: One of **Dioscuri:** Twins Castor and Pollux; sons of Leda by Zeus.

Polymnia: One of several **Muses:** Goddesses presiding over arts and sciences: Calliope (epic poetry), Clio (history), Erato (lyric and love poetry), Euterpe (music), Melpomene (tragedy), Polymnia or Polyhymnia (sacred poetry), Terpsichore (choral dance and song), Thalia (comedy and bucolic poetry), Urania (astronomy); daughters of Zeus and Mnemosyne.

Polynices: Son of Oedipus; he and his brother Eteocles killed each other; burial rite, forbidden by Creon, performed by his sister Antigone.

Polyphemus: Cyclops; devoured six of Odysseus's men; blinded by Odysseus.

Polyxena: Daughter of Priam; betrothed to Achilles, whom Paris slew at their betrothal; sacrificed to shade of Achilles.

Pomona: Roman goddess of fruits.

Pontus: Sea god; son of Gaea.

Poseidon (Neptune): God of sea; brother of Zeus.

Priam: King of Troy; husband of Hecuba; ransomed Hector's body from Achilles; slain by Neoptolemus.

Priapus: God of regeneration.

Procris: Wife of Cephalus, who accidentally slew her.

Procrustes: Giant; stretched or cut off legs of victims to make them fit iron bed; slain by Theseus.

Proetus: Husband of Anteia; sent Bellerophon to Iobates to be put to death.

Prometheus: Titan; stole fire from heaven for man. Zeus punished him by chaining him to rock in Caucasus where vultures devoured his liver daily.

Proteus: Sea god; assumed various shapes when called on to prophesy.

Psyche: Beloved of Eros; punished by jealous Aphrodite; made immortal and united with Eros.

Pygmalion: King of Cyprus; carved ivory statue of maiden which Aphrodite gave life as Galatea.

Pyramus: Babylonian youth; made love to Thisbe through hole in wall; thinking Thisbe slain by lion, killed himself.

Python: Serpent born from slime left by Deluge; slain by Apollo.

Quirinus: Roman war god.

Remus: Brother of Romulus; slain by him.

Rhadamanthus: One of three judges of dead in Hades; son of Zeus and Europa.

Rhea (Ops): Daughter of Uranus and Gaea; wife of Cronus; mother of Zeus; identified with Cybele.

Rivers of Underworld: Acheron (woe), Cocytus (wailing), Lethe (forgetfulness), Phlegethon (fire), Styx (across which souls of dead were ferried by Charon).

Romulus: Founder of Rome; he and Remus suckled in infancy by she-wolf; slew Remus; deified by Romans.

Sarpedon: King of Lycia; son of Zeus and Europa; slain by Patroclus at Troy.

Satyrs: Hoofed demigods of woods and fields; companions of Dionysus.

Sciron: Robber; forced strangers to wash his feet, then hurled them into sea where tortoise devoured them; slain by Theseus.

Scylla: Female monster inhabiting rock opposite Charybdis; menaced passing sailors.

Selene: Goddess of moon.

Semele: Daughter of Cadmus; mother by Zeus of Dionysus; demanded Zeus appear before her in all his splendor and was destroyed by his lightning bolts.

Sibyis: Various prophetesses; most famous, Cumaean sibyl, accompanied Aeneas into Hades.

Sileni: Minor woodland deities similar to satyrs (singular: silenus). Sometimes Silenus refers to eldest of satyrs, son of Hermes or of Pan.

Silvanus: Roman god of woods and fields.

Sinis: Giant; bent pines, with which he hurled victims against side of mountain; slain by Theseus.

Sirens: Minor deities who lured sailors to destruction with their singing.

Sisyphus: King of Corinth; condemned in Tartarus to roll huge stone to top of hill; it always rolled back down again.

Sphinx: Monster of Thebes; killed those who could not answer her riddle; slain by Oedipus. Name also refers to other monsters having body of lion, wings, and head and bust of woman.

Sterope: One of several **Pleiades:** Alcyone, Celaeno, Electra, Maia, Merope, Sterope or Asterope, Taygeta; seven daughters of Atlas; transformed into heavenly constellation, of which six stars are visible (Merope is said to have hidden in shame for loving a mortal).

Stheno: One of several **Gorgons:** Female monsters; Euryale, Medusa, and Stheno; had snakes for hair; their glances turned mortals to stone.

Styx: One of several **Rivers of Underworld:** Acheron (woe), Cocytus (wailing), Lethe (forgetfulness), Phlegethon (fire), Styx (across which souls of dead were ferried by Charon).

Symplegades: Clashing rocks at entrance to Black Sea; Argo passed through, causing them to become forever fixed.

Syrinx: Nymph pursued by Pan; changed to reeds, from which he made his pipes.

Tantalus: Cruel king; father of Pelops and Niobe; condemned in Tartarus to stand chin-deep in lake surrounded by fruit branches; as he tried to eat or drink, water or fruit always receded.

Tartarus: Underworld below Hades; often refers to Hades.

Taygeta: One of several **Pleiades:** Alcyone, Celaeno, Electra, Maia, Merope, Sterope or Asterope, Taygeta; seven daughters of Atlas; transformed into heavenly constellation, of which six stars are visible (Merope is said to have hidden in shame for loving a mortal).

Telemachus: Son of Odysseus; made unsuccessful journey to find his father.

Tellus: Roman goddess of earth.

Terminus: Roman god of boundaries and landmarks.

Terpsichore: One of several **Muses:** Goddesses presiding over arts and sciences: Calliope (epic poetry), Clio (history), Erato (lyric and love poetry), Euterpe (music), Melpomene (tragedy),

Polymnia or Polyhymnia (sacred poetry), Terpsichore (choral dance and song), Thalia (comedy and bucolic poetry), Urania (astronomy); daughters of Zeus and Mnemosyne.

Terra: Roman earth goddess.

Thalia: One of several **Graces:** Beautiful goddesses: Aglaia (Brilliance), Euphrosyne (Joy), and Thalia (Bloom); daughters of Zeus. Also one of several **Muses:** Goddesses presiding over arts and sciences: Calliope (epic poetry), Clio (history), Erato (lyric and love poetry), Euterpe (music), Melpomene (tragedy), Polymnia or Polyhymnia (sacred poetry), Terpsichore (choral dance and song), Thalia (comedy and bucolic poetry), Urania (astronomy); daughters of Zeus and Mnemosyne.

Thanatos (Mors): God of death.

Themis: Titan goddess of laws of physical phenomena; daughter of Uranus; mother of Prometheus.

Theseus: Son of Aegeus; slew Minotaur; married and deserted Ariadne; later married Phaedra.

Thisbe: Beloved of Pyramus; killed herself at his death.

Thyestes: Brother of Atreus; Atreus killed three of his sons and served them to him at banquet.

Tiresias: Blind soothsayer of Thebes.

Tisiphone: One of several **Furies:** Avenging spirits; Alecto, Megaera, and Tisiphone; known also as Erinyes or Eumenides.

Titans: Early gods from which Olympian gods were derived; children of Uranus and Gaea.

Tithonus: Mortal loved by Eos; changed into grasshopper.

Triton: Demigod of sea; son of Poseidon.

Turnus: King of Rutuli in Italy; betrothed to Lavinia; slain by Aeneas.

Urania: One of several **Muses:** Goddesses presiding over arts and sciences: Calliope (epic poetry), Clio (history), Erato (lyric and love poetry), Euterpe (music), Melpomene (tragedy), Polymnia or Polyhymnia (sacred poetry), Terpsichore (choral dance and song), Thalia (comedy and bucolic poetry), Urania (astronomy); daughters of Zeus and Mnemosyne.

Uranus: Personification of Heaven; husband of Gaea; father of Titans; dethroned by his son Cronus.

Vertumnus: Roman god of fruits and vegetables; husband of Pomona.

Winds: Aeolus (keeper of winds), Boreas (Aquilo) (north wind), Eurus (east wind), Notus (Auster) (south wind), Zephyrus (Favonius) (west wind).

Zephyrus: One of several **Winds:** Aeolus (keeper of winds), Boreas (Aquilo) (north wind), Eurus (east wind), Notus (Auster) (south wind), Zephyrus (Favonius) (west wind).

Zeus (Jupiter): Chief of Olympian gods; son of Cronus and Rhea; husband of Hera.

Norse Mythology

Aesir: Chief gods of Asgard.

Andvari: Dwarf; robbed of gold and magic ring by Loki.

Angerbotha (Angrbotha): Giantess; mother by Loki of Fenrir, Hel, and Midgard serpent.

Asgard (Asgarth): Abode of gods.

Ask (Aske, Askr): First man; created by Odin, Hoenir, and Lothur.

Asynjur: Goddesses of Asgard.

Atli: Second husband of Gudrun; invited Gunnar and Hogni to his court, where they were slain; slain by Gudrun.

Audhumla (Audhumbla): Cow that nourished Ymir; created Buri by licking ice cliff.

Balder (Baldr, Baldur): God of light, spring, peace, joy; son of Odin; slain by Hoth at instigation of Loki.

Bifrost: Rainbow bridge connecting Midgard and Asgard.

Bragi (Brage): God of poetry; husband of Ithunn.

Branstock: Great oak in hall of Volsungs; into it, Odin thrust Gram, which only Sigmund could draw forth.

Brynhild: Valkyrie; wakened from magic sleep by Sigurd; married Gunnar; instigated death of Sigurd; killed herself and was burned on pyre beside Sigurd.

Bur (Bor): Son of Buri; father of Odin, Hoenir, and Lothur.

Buri (Bori): Progenitor of gods; father of Bur; created by Audhumla.

Embla: First woman; created by Odin, Hoenir, and Lothur.

Fafnir: Son of Rodmar, whom he slew for gold in Otter's skin; in form of dragon, guarded gold; slain by Sigurd.

Fenrir: Wolf; offspring of Loki; swallows Odin at Ragnarok and is slain by Vitharr.

Forseti: Son of Balder.

Frey (Freyr): God of fertility and crops; son of Njorth; originally one of Vanir.

Freya (Freyja): Goddess of love and beauty; sister of Frey; originally one of Vanir.

Frigg (Frigga): Goddess of sky; wife of Odin.

Garm: Watchdog of Hel; slays, and is slain by, Tyr at Ragnarok.

Gimle: Home of blessed after Ragnarok.

Giuki: King of Nibelungs; father of Gunnar, Hogni, Guttorm, and Gudrun.

Glathsheim (Gladsheim): Hall of gods in Asgard.

Gram (meaning "Angry"): Sigmund's sword; rewelded by Regin; used by Sigurd to slay Fafnir.

Greyfell: Sigmund's horse; descended from Sleipnir.

Grimhild: Mother of Gudrun; administered magic potion to Sigurd which made him forget Brynhild.

Gudrun: Daughter of Giuki; wife of Sigurd; later wife of Atli and Jonakr.

Gunnar: Son of Giuki; in his semblance Sigurd won Brynhild for him; slain at hall of Atli.

Guttorm: Son of Giuki; slew Sigurd at Brynhild's request.

Heimdall (Heimdallr): Guardian of Asgard.

Hel: Goddess of dead and queen of underworld; daughter of Loki.

Hiordis: Wife of Sigmund; mother of Sigurd.

Hoenir: One of creators of Ask and Embla; son of Bur.

Hogni: Son of Giuki; slain at hall of Atli.

Hoth (Hoder, Hodur): Blind god of night and darkness; slayer of Balder at instigation of Loki.

Ithunn (Ithun, Iduna): Keeper of golden apples of youth; wife of Bragi.

Jonakr: Third husband of Gudrun.

Jormunrek: Slayer of Swanhild; slain by sons of Gudrun.
Jotunnheim (Jotunheim): Abode of giants.
Lif and Lifthrasir: First man and woman after Ragnarok.
Loki: God of evil and mischief; instigator of Balder's death.
Lothur (Lodur): One of creators of Ask and Embla.
Midgard (Midgarth): Abode of mankind; the earth.
Midgard Serpent: Sea monster; offspring of Loki; slays, and is slain by, Thor at Ragnarok.
Mimir: Giant; guardian of well in Jotunnheim at root of Yggdrasill; knower of past and future.
Mjollnir: Magic hammer of Thor.
Nagifar: Ship to be used by giants in attacking Asgard at Ragnarok; built from nails of dead men.
Nanna: Wife of Balder.
Nibelungs: Dwellers in northern kingdom ruled by Giuki.
Niflheim (Nifelheim): Outer region of cold and darkness; abode of Hel.
Njorth: Father of Frey and Freya; originally one of Vanir.
Norns: Demigoddesses of fate: Urth (Urdur) (past), Verthandi (Verdandi) (present), Skuld (future).
Odin (Othin): Head of Aesir; creator of world with Vili and Ve; equivalent to Woden (Wodan, Wotan) in Teutonic mythology.
Otter: Son of Rodmar; slain by Loki; his skin filled with gold hoard of Andvari to appease Rodmar.
Ragnarok: Final destruction of present world in battle between gods and giants; some minor gods will survive, and Lif and Lifthrasir will repeople world.
Regin: Blacksmith; son of Rodmar; foster-father of Sigurd.
Rerir: King of Huns; son of Sigi.
Rodmar: Father of Regin, Otter, and Fafnir; demanded Otter's skin be filled with gold; slain by Fafnir, who stole gold.
Sif: Wife of Thor.
Siggeir: King of Goths; husband of Signy; he and his sons slew Volsung and his sons, except Sigmund; slain by Sigmund and Sinflotli.
Sigi: King of Huns; son of Odin.
Sigmund: Son of Volsung; brother of Signy, who bore him Sinflotli; husband of Hiordis, who bore him Sigurd.
Signy: Daughter of Volsung; sister of Sigmund; wife of Siggeir; mother by Sigmund of Sinflotli.

Sigurd: Son of Sigmund and Hiordis; wakened Brynhild from magic sleep; married Gudrun; slain by Guttorm at instigation of Brynhild.
Sigyn: Wife of Loki.
Sinflotli: Son of Sigmund and Signy.
Skuld: One of several **Norns:** Demigoddesses of fate: Urth (Urdur) (Past), Verthandi (Verdandi) (Present), Skuld (Future).
Sleipnir (Sleipner): Eight-legged horse of Odin.
Surt (Surtr): Fire demon; slays Frey at Ragnarok.
Svartalfaheim: Abode of dwarfs.
Swanhild: Daughter of Sigurd and Gudrun; slain by Jormunrek.
Thor: God of thunder; oldest son of Odin; equivalent to Germanic deity Donar.
Tyr: God of war; son of Odin; equivalent to Tiu in Teutonic mythology.
Ull (Ullr): Son of Sif; stepson of Thor.
Urth: One of several **Norns:** Demigoddesses of fate: Urth (Urdur) (past), Verthandi (Verdandi) (present), Skuld (future).
Valhalla (Valhall): Great hall in Asgard where Odin received souls of heroes killed in battle.
Vali: Odin's son: Ragnarok survivor.
Valkyries: Virgins, messengers of Odin, who selected heroes to die in battle and took them to Valhalla; generally considered as nine in number.
Vanir: Early race of gods; three survivors, Njorth, Frey, and Freya, are associated with Aesir.
Ve: Brother of Odin; one of creators of world.
Verthandi: One of several **Norns:** Demigoddesses of fate: Urth (Urdur) (past), Verthandi (Verdandi) (present), Skuld (future).
Vili: Brother of Odin; one of creators of world.
Vingolf: Abode of goddesses in Asgard.
Vitharr (Vithar): Son of Odin; survivor of Ragnarok.
Volsung: Descendant of Odin, and father of Signy, Sigmund; his descendants were called Volsungs.
Yggdrasill: Giant ash tree springing from body of Ymir and supporting universe; its roots extended to Asgard, Jotunnheim, and Niffheim.
Ymir (Ymer): Primeval frost giant killed by Odin, Vili, and Ve; world created from his body; also, from his body sprang Yggdrasill.

Egyptian Mythology

Aaru: Abode of the blessed dead.
Amen (Amon, Ammdn): One of chief Theban deities; united with sun god under form of Amen-Ra.
Amenti: Region of dead where souls were judged by Osiris.
Anubis: Guide of souls to Amenti; son of Osiris; jackal-headed.
Apis: Sacred bull, an embodiment of Ptah; identified with Osiris as Osiris-Apis or Serapis.
Geb (Keb, Seb): Earth god; father of Osiris; represented with goose on head.
Hathor (Athor): Goddess of love and mirth; cow-headed.
Horus: God of day; son of Osiris and Isis; hawk-headed.
Isis: Goddess of motherhood and fertility; sister and wife of Osiris.
Khepera: God of morning sun.
Khnemu (Khnum, Chnuphis, Chnemu, Chnum): Ram-headed god.
Khonsu (Khensu, Khuns): Son of Amen and Mut.
Mentu (Ment): Solar deity, sometimes considered god of war; falcon-headed.

Min (Khem, Chem): Principle of physical life.
Mut (Maut): Wife of Amen.
Nephthys: Goddess of the dead; sister and wife of Set.
Nu: Chaos from which world was created, personified as a god.
Nut: Goddess of heavens; consort of Geb.
Osiris: God of underworld and judge of dead; son of Geb and Nut.
Ptah (Phtha): Chief deity of Memphis.
Ra: God of the Sun, the supreme god; son of Nut; Pharaohs claimed descent from him; represented as lion, cat, or falcon.
Serapis: God uniting attributes of Osiris and Apis.
Set (Seth): God of darkness or evil; brother and enemy of Osiris.
Shu: Solar deity; son of Ra and Hathor.
Tem (Atmu, Atum, Tum): Solar deity.
Thoth (Dhouti): God of wisdom and magic; scribe of gods; ibis-headed

American Crossword Puzzle Tournament
March 12–14, 1999, Stamford, Connecticut

The oldest and largest crossword puzzle tournament in the United States is directed by Will Shortz, the crossword puzzle editor of *The New York Times.* Competitors face eight puzzles and are scored on accuracy and speed.

1978	Nancy Schuster, Rego Park, N.Y.		1989	Jon Delfin, New York, N.Y.
1979	Miriam Raphael, Port Chester, N.Y.		1990	Jon Delfin, New York, N.Y.
1980	Daniel Pratt, Fort Meade, Md.		1991	Jon Delfin, New York, N.Y.
1981	Philip Cohen, Aliquippa, Pa.		1992	Douglas Hoylman, Chevy Chase, Md.
1982	Stanley Newman, Brooklyn, N.Y.		1993	Trip Payne, Atlanta, Ga.
1983	David Rosen, Buffalo, N.Y.		1994	Douglas Hoylman, Chevy Chase, Md.
1984	John McNeill, Austin, Tex.		1995	Jon Delfin, New York, N.Y.
1985	David Rosen, Buffalo, N.Y.		1996	Douglas Hoylman, Chevy Chase, Md.
1986	David Rosen, Buffalo, N.Y.		1997	Douglas Hoylman, Chevy Chase, Md.
1987	David Rosen, New York, N.Y.		1998	Trip Payne, Atlanta, Ga.
1988	Douglas Hoylman, Chevy Chase, Md.		1999	Jon Delfin, New York, N.Y.

A Concise Guide to Style

From *Webster's II New Riverside University Dictionary.* © 1984 by Houghton Mifflin Company.

This section discusses and illustrates the basic conventions of American capitalization, punctuation, and italicization.

Capitalization

Capitalize the following:

1. The first word of a sentence: Some spiders are poisonous; others are not. Are you my new neighbor?

2. The first word of a direct quotation, except when the quotation is split: Joyce asked, "Do you think that the lecture was interesting?" "No," I responded, "it was very boring." Tom Paine said, "The sublime and the ridiculous are often so nearly related that it is difficult to class them separately."

3. The first word of each line in a poem in traditional verse: Half a league, half a league,/Half a league onward,/All in the valley of Death/Rode the six hundred.—Alfred, Lord Tennyson

4. The names of people, of organizations and their members, of councils and congresses, and of historical periods and events: Marie Curie, Benevolent and Protective Order of Elks, an Elk, Protestant Episcopal Church, an Episcopalian, the Democratic Party, a Democrat, the Nuclear Regulatory Commission, the U.S. Senate, the Middle Ages, World War I, the Battle of Britain.

5. The names of places and geographic divisions, districts, regions, and locales: Richmond, Vermont, Argentina, Seventh Avenue, London Bridge, Arctic Circle, Eastern Hemisphere, Continental Divide, Middle East, Far North, Gulf States, East Coast, the North, the South Shore.

   Do not capitalize words indicating compass points unless a specific region is referred to: Turn north onto Interstate 91.

6. The names of rivers, lakes, mountains, and oceans: Ohio River, Lake Como, Rocky Mountains, Atlantic Ocean.

7. The names of ships, aircraft, satellites, and space vehicles: U.S.S. *Arizona*, *Spirit of St. Louis*, the spy satellite *Ferret-D*, *Voyager II*, the space shuttle *Challenger*.

8. The names of nationalities, races, tribes, and languages: Spanish, Maori, Bantu, Russian.

9. Words derived from proper names, except in their extended senses: the Byzantine Empire. *But:* byzantine office politics.

10. Words indicating family relationships when used with a person's name as a title: Aunt Toni and Uncle Jack. *But:* my aunt and uncle, Toni and Jack Walker.

11. A title (i.e., civil, judicial, military, royal and noble, religious, and honorary) when preceding a name: Justice Marshall, General Jackson, Mayor Daley, Queen Victoria, Lord Mountbatten, Pope John Paul II, Professor Jacobson, Senator Byrd.

12. References to specific presidents and vice presidents of the United States, *but* lower case references that are general: Vice President John Adams went on to become our second president.

13. All key words in titles of literary, dramatic, artistic, and musical works: the novel *The Old Man and the Sea,* the short story "Notes from Underground," an article entitled "On Passive Verbs," James Dickey's poem "In the Tree House at Night," the play *Cat on a Hot Tin Roof,* Van Gogh's *Wheat Field and Cypress Trees,* Beethoven's *Emperor Concerto.*

14. *The* in the title of a newspaper if it is a part of the title: *The Wall Street Journal. But:* the New York *Daily News.*

15. The first word in the salutation and in the complimentary close of a letter: My dear Carol, Yours sincerely.

16. Epithets and substitutes for the names of people and places: Old Hickory, Old Blood and Guts, The Oval Office, the Windy City.

17. Words used in personifications: When is not Death at watch/Within those secret waters?/What wants he but to catch/Earth's heedless sons and daughters?—Edmund Blunden

18. The pronoun *I:* I told them that I had heard the news.

19. Names for the Deity and sacred works: God, the Almighty, Jesus, Allah, the Supreme Being, the Bible, the Qu'ran, the Talmud.

20. Days of the week, months of the year, holidays, and holy days: Tuesday, May, Independence Day, Passover, Ramadan, Christmas.

21. The names of specific courts: the Supreme Court of the United States, the Massachusetts Appeals Court, the United States Court of Appeals for the First Circuit.

22. The names of treaties, accords, pacts, laws, and specific amendments: Panama Canal Treaty, Treaty of Paris, Geneva Accords, Warsaw Pact countries, Sherman Antitrust Law, Labor Management Relations Act, took the Fifth Amendment.

23. Registered trademarks and service marks: Day-Glo®, Comsat®.

24. The names of geologic eras, periods, epochs, and strata and the names of prehistoric divisions: Paleozoic Era, Precambrian, Pleistocene, Age of Reptiles, Bronze Age, Stone Age.

25. The names of constellations, planets, and stars: Milky Way, Southern Crown, Saturn, Jupiter, Uranus, Polaris.

26. Genus but not species names in binomial nomenclature: *Rana pipiens.*

27. New Latin names of classes, families, and all groups higher than genera in botanical and zoological nomenclature: Nematoda.
    Do not capitalize derivatives from such names: nematodes.

28. Many abbreviations and acronyms: Dec., Tues., Lt. Gen., M.F.A., UNESCO, MIRV.

Italicization

Use italics to:

1. Indicate titles of books, plays, and epic poems: *War and Peace, The Importance of Being Earnest, Paradise Lost.*

2. Indicate titles of magazines and newspapers: *New York* magazine, *The Wall Street Journal,* the New York *Daily News.*

3. Set off the titles of motion pictures and radio and television programs: *Star Wars, All Things Considered, Masterpiece Theater.*

4. Indicate titles of major musical compositions: Handel's *Messiah,* Adam's *Giselle.*

5. Set off the names of paintings and sculpture: *Mona Lisa, Pietà.*

6. Indicate words, letters, or numbers that are referred to: The word *hiss* is onomatopoeic. *Can't* means *won't* in your lexicon. You form your *n*'s like *u*'s. A *6* looks like an inverted *9.*

7. Indicate foreign words and phrases not yet assimilated into English: *C'est la vie* was the response to my complaint.

8. Indicate the names of plaintiff and defendant in legal citations: *Roe* v. *Doe.*

9. Emphasize a word or phrase: When you appear on the national news, you are *somebody.*
    Use this device sparingly.

10. Distinguish New Latin names of genera, species, subspecies, and varieties in botanical and zoological nomenclature: *Homo sapiens.*

11. Set off the names of ships and aircraft: U.S.S. *Arizona, Spirit of St. Louis.*

Punctuation

Apostrophe

1. Indicates the possessive case of singular and plural nouns, indefinite pronouns, and surnames combined with designations such as *Jr., Sr.,* and *II:* my sister's husband, my three sisters' husbands, anyone's guess, They answer each other's phones, John Smith, Jr.'s car.

2. Indicates joint possession when used with the last of two or more nouns in a series: Doe and Roe's report.

3. Indicates individual possession or authorship when used with each of two or more nouns in a series: Smith's, Roe's, and Doe's reports.

4. Indicates the plurals of words, letters, and figures used as such: *x*'s, *y*'s, and *z*'s.

5. Indicates omission of letters in contractions: aren't, that's, o'clock.

6. Indicates omission of figures in dates: the class of '63.

Brackets

1. Enclose words or passages in quoted matter to indicate insertion of material written by someone other than the author: A tough but nervous, tenacious but restless race [the Yankees]; materially ambitious, yet prone to introspection. ... —Samuel Eliot Morison

2. Enclose material inserted within matter already in parentheses: (Vancouver [B.C.] January 1, 19—).

Colon

1. Introduces words, phrases, or clauses that explain, amplify, or summarize what has gone before: Suddenly I realized where we were: Rome.
    "There are two cardinal sins from which all the others spring: impatience and laziness." —Franz Kafka

2. Introduces a long quotation: In his original draft of the *Declaration of Independence,* Jefferson wrote: "We hold these truths to be sacred and undeniable; that all men are created equal and independent, that from that equal creation they derive rights inherent and inalienable. ..."

3. Introduces a list: We need the following items: pens, paper, pencils, blotters, and erasers.

4. Separates chapter and verse numbers in Biblical references: James 1:4.

5. Separates city from publisher in footnotes and bibliographies: Chicago: Riverside Press, 1983.

6. Separates hour and minute(s) in time designations: 9:30 a.m., a 9:30 meeting.

7. Follows the salutation in a business letter: Sir or Madam:

Comma

1. Separates the clauses of a compound sentence connected by a coordinating conjunction: A difference exists between the musical works of Handel and Haydn, and it is a difference worth noting.
    The comma may be omitted in short compound sentences: I heard what you said and I am furious. I got out of the car and I walked and walked.

2. (optional) Separates *and* or *or* from the final item in a series of three or more: Red, yellow, and blue may be mixed to produce all colors.

3. Separates two or more adjectives modifying the same noun if *and* could be used between them without altering the meaning: a solid, heavy gait. *But:* a polished mahogany dresser.

4. Sets off nonrestrictive clauses or phrases (i.e., those that if eliminated would not affect the meaning of the sentences): The burglar, who had entered through the patio, went straight to the silver chest.
    The comma should not be used when a clause is restrictive (i.e., essential to the meaning of the sentence): The burglar who had entered through the patio went straight to the silver chest; the other burglar searched for the wall safe.

5. Sets off words or phrases in apposition to a noun or noun phrase: Plato, the famous Greek philosopher, was a student of Socrates.
    The comma should not be used if such words or phrases precede the noun: The Greek philosopher Plato was a student of Socrates.

6. Sets off transitional words and short expressions that require a pause in reading or speaking: Unfortunately, my friend was not well traveled. Did you, after all, find what you were looking for? I live with my family, of course.

7. Sets off words used to introduce a sentence: No, I haven't been to Paris. Well, what do you think we should do now?

8. Sets off a subordinate clause or a long phrase that precedes a principal clause: By the time we found the restaurant, we were starved. Of all the illustrations in the book, the most striking are those of the tapestries.

9. Sets off short quotations and sayings: The candidate said, "Actions speak louder than words." "Talking of axes," said the Duchess, "chop off her head."—Lewis Carroll

10. Indicates omission of a word or words: To err is human; to forgive, divine.

11. Sets off the year from the month in full dates: Nicholas II of Russia was shot on July 16, 1918.
    Note that when only the month and the year are used, no comma appears: Nicholas II of Russia was shot in July 1918.

12. Sets off city and state in geographic names: Atlanta, Georgia, is the transportation center of the South. 34 Beach Drive, Bedford, VA 24523.

13. Separates series of four or more figures into thousands, millions, etc.: 67,000; 200,000.

14. Sets off words used in direct address: "I tell you, folks, all politics is applesauce."—Will Rogers. Thank you for your expert assistance, Dolores.

15. Separates a tag question from the rest of a sentence: You forgot your keys again, didn't you?

16. Sets off sentence elements that could be misunderstood if the comma were not used: Some time after, the actual date for the project was set.

17. Follows the salutation in a personal letter and the complimentary close in a business or personal letter: Dear Jessica, Sincerely yours, Fred.

18. Sets off titles and degrees from surnames and from the rest of a sentence: Walter T. Prescott, Jr.; Gregory A. Rossi, S.J.; Susan P. Green, M.D., presented the case.

Dash

1. Indicates a sudden break or abrupt change in continuity: "If—if you'll just let me explain—" the student stammered. And the problem—if there really is one—can then be solved.

2. Sets apart an explanatory, a defining, or an emphatic phrase: Foods rich in protein—meat, fish, and eggs—should be eaten on a daily basis.
    More important than winning the election, is governing the nation. That is the test of a political party—the acid, final test.—Adlai E. Stevenson

3. Sets apart parenthetical matter: Wolsey, for all his faults—and he had many—was a great statesman, a man of natural dignity with a generous temperament. . . .—Jasper Ridley

4. Marks an unfinished sentence: "But if my bus is late—" he began.

5. Sets off a summarizing phrase or clause: The vital measure of a newspaper is not its size but its spirit—that is its responsibility to report the news fully, accurately, and fairly.—Arthur H. Sulzberger

6. Sets off the name of an author or source, as at the end of a quotation: A poet can survive everything but a misprint.—Oscar Wilde

Ellipses

1. Indicate, by three spaced points, omission of words or sentences within quoted matter: Equipped by education to rule in the nineteenth century, . . . he lived and reigned in Russia in the twentieth century.—Robert K. Massie

2. Indicate, by four spaced points, omission of words at the end of a sentence: The timidity of bureaucrats when it comes to dealing with . . . abuses is easy to explain. . . . —*New York*

3. Indicate, when extended the length of a line, omission of one or more lines of poetry:
    Roll on, thou deep and dark blue ocean—roll!
    . . . .
    Man marks the earth with ruin—his control
    Stops with the shore.—Lord Byron

4. Are sometimes used as a device, as for example, in advertising copy:
    To help you Move and Grow
        with the Rigors of
    Business in the 1980s . . .
        and Beyond.—*Journal of Business Strategy*

Exclamation Point

1. Terminates an emphatic or exclamatory sentence: Go home at once! You've got to be kidding!

2. Terminates an emphatic interjection: Encore!

Hyphen

1. Indicates that part of a word of more than one syllable has been carried over from one line to the next:
    During the revolution, the nation was beset with problems—looting, fighting, and famine.

2. Joins the elements of some compounds: greatgrandparent, attorney-at-law, ne'er-do-well.

3. Joins the elements of compound modifiers preceding nouns: high-school students, a fire-and-brimstone lecture, a two-hour meeting.

4. Indicates that two or more compounds share a single base: four- and six-volume sets, eight-and nine-year olds.

5. Separates the prefix and root in some combinations; check a dictionary when in doubt about the spelling: anti-Nazi, re-elect, co-author, re-form/reform, re-cover/recover, re-creation/recreation.

6. Punctuates written-out compound numbers from 21 through 99: forty-six years of age, a person who is forty-six, two hundred fifty-nine dollars.

Parentheses

1. Enclose material that is not essential to a sentence and that if not included would not alter its meaning: After a few minutes (some say less) the blaze was extinguished.

2. Often enclose letters or figures to indicate subdivisions of a series: A movement in sonata form consists of the following elements: (1) the exposition, (2) the development, and (3) the recapitulation.

3. Enclose figures following and confirming written-out numbers, especially in legal and business documents: The fee for my services will be two thousand dollars ($2,000.00).

4. Enclose an abbreviation for a term following the written-out term, when used for the first time in a text: The patient is suffering from acquired immune deficiency syndrome (AIDS).

Period

1. Terminates a complete declarative or mild imperative sentence: There could be no turning back as war's dark shadow settled irrevocably across the continent of Europe.—W. Bruce Lincoln. Return all the books when you can. Would you kindly affix your signature here.

2. Terminates sentence fragments: Gray clouds— and what looks like a veil of rain falling behind the East German headland. A pair of ducks. A tired or dying swan, head buried in its back feathers, sits on the sand a few feet from the water's edge.—Anthony Bailey

3. Follows some abbreviations: Dec., Rev., St., Blvd., pp., Co.

Question Mark

1. Punctuates a direct question: Have you seen the new play yet? Who goes there? *But:* I wonder who said "Nothing is easy in war." I asked if they planned to leave.

2. Indicates uncertainty: Ferdinand Magellan (1480?–1521), Plato (427?–347 B.C.E.).

Quotation Marks

1. Double quotation marks enclose direct quotations: "What was Paris like in the Twenties?" our daughter asked. "Ladies and Gentlemen," the Chief Usher said, "the President of the United States." Robert Louis Stevenson said that "it is better to be a fool than to be dead." When advised not to become a lawyer because the profession was already overcrowded, Daniel Webster replied, "There is always room at the top."

2. Double quotation marks enclose words or phrases to clarify their meaning or use or to indicate that they are being used in a special way: This was the border of what we often call "the West" or "the Free World." "The Windy City" is a name for Chicago.

3. Double quotation marks set off the translation of a foreign word or phrase: *die Grenze,* "the border."

4. Double quotation marks set off the titles of series of books, of articles or chapters in publications, of essays, of short stories and poems, of individual radio and television programs, and of songs and short musical pieces: "The Horizon Concise History" series; an article entitled "On Reflexive Verbs in English"; Chapter Nine, "The Prince and the Peasant"; Pushkin's "The Queen of Spades"; Tennyson's "Ode on the Death of the Duke of Wellington"; "The Bob Hope Special"; Schubert's "Death and the Maiden."

5. Single quotation marks enclose quotations within quotations: The blurb for the piece proclaimed, "Two years ago at Geneva, South Vietnam was virtually sold down the river to the Communists. Today the spunky little . . . country is back on its own feet, thanks to 'a mandarin in a sharkskin suit who's upsetting the Red timetable'."—Frances FitzGerald

Put commas and periods inside quotation marks; put semicolons and colons outside. Other punctuation, such as exclamation points and question marks, should be put inside the closing quotation marks only if part of the matter quoted.

Semicolon

1. Separates the clauses of a compound sentence having no coordinating conjunction: Do not let us speak of darker days; let us rather speak of sterner days.—Winston Churchill

2. Separates the clauses of a compound sentence in which the clauses contain internal punctuation, even when the clauses are joined by conjunctions: Skis in hand, we trudged to the lodge, stowed our lunches, and donned our boots; and the rest of our party waited for us at the lifts.

3. Separates elements of a series in which items already contain commas: Among those at the diplomatic reception were the Secretary of State; the daughter of the Ambassador to the Court of St. James's, formerly of London; and two United Nations delegates.

4. Separates clauses of a compound sentence joined by a conjunctive adverb, such as *however, nonetheless,* or *hence:* We insisted upon a hearing; however, the Grievance Committee refused.

5. May be used instead of a comma to signal longer pauses for dramatic effect: But I want you to know that when I cross the river my last conscious thought will be of the Corps; and the Corps; and the Corps.—General Douglas MacArthur

Virgule

1. Separates successive divisions in an extended date: fiscal year 1998/99.

2. Represents *per:* 35 km/hr, 1,800 ft./sec.

3. Means *or* between the words *and* and *or:* Take water skis and/or fishing equipment when you visit the beach this summer.

4. Separates two or more lines of poetry that are quoted and run in on successive lines of a text: The student actress had a memory lapse when she came to the lines "Double, double, toil and trouble/Fire burn and cauldron bubble/Eye of newt and toe of frog/Wool of bat and tongue of dog" and had to leave the stage in embarrassment.

Forms of Address

Source: Webster's II New Riverside University Dictionary. © 1984 by Houghton Mifflin Company.

Academics

Dean, college or university. *Address:* Dean _____.
Salutation: Dear Dean_____
President. *Address:* President _____ _____.
Salutation: Dear President _____.
Professor, college or university. *Address:* Professor
_____ _____. *Salutation:* Dear Professor
_____.

Clerical and Religious Orders

Abbot. *Address:* The Right Reverend _____
_____, O.S.B. Abbot of _____.
Salutation: Right Reverend Abbot or Dear Father Abbot.
Archbishop, Eastern Orthodox. *Address:* The Most Reverend [Joseph], Archbishop of _____. *Salutation:*
Your Eminence.
Archbishop, Roman Catholic. *Address:* The Most Reverend _____ _____, Archbishop of _____.
Salutation: Your Excellency.
Archdeacon, Episcopal. *Address:* The Venerable
_____ _____, Archdeacon of _____.
Salutation: Venerable Sir or Dear Archdeacon
_____.
Bishop, Episcopal. *Address:* The Right Reverend
_____ _____, Bishop of _____.
Salutation: Right Reverend Sir or Dear Bishop
_____.
Bishop, other Protestant. *Address:* The Reverend
_____ _____. *Salutation:* Dear Bishop
_____.
Bishop, Roman Catholic. *Address:* The Most Reverend
_____ _____, Bishop of _____.
Salutation: Your Excellency or Dear Bishop _____.
Brotherhood, Roman Catholic. *Address:* Brother
_____ _____, C.F.C. *Salutation:* Dear Brother
or Dear Brother [Joseph].
Brotherhood, superior of. *Address:* Brother [Joseph]
C.F.C. Superior. *Salutation:* Dear Brother [Joseph].
Cardinal. *Address:* His Eminence [Joseph] Cardinal
[Stone]. *Salutation:* Your Eminence.
Clergyman/woman, Protestant. *Address:* The Reverend
_____ _____ or The Reverend _____
_____, D.D. *Salutation:* Dear Mr./Ms. _____ or
Dear Dr. _____.
Dean of a cathedral, Episcopal. *Address:* The Very Reverend _____ _____, Dean of _____.
Salutation: Dear Dean _____.
Monsignor. *Address:* The Right Reverend Monsignor
_____ _____. *Salutation:* Dear Monsignor.
Patriarch, Greek Orthodox. *Address:* His All Holiness
Patriarch [Joseph]. *Salutation:* Your All Holiness.
Patriarch, Russian Orthodox. *Address:* His Holiness the
Patriarch of _____. *Salutation:* Your Holiness.
Pope. *Address:* His Holiness The Pope. *Salutation:* Your
Holiness or Most Holy Father.
Priest, Roman Catholic. *Address:* The Reverend
_____ _____, S.J. *Salutation:* Dear Reverend
Father or Dear Father.
Rabbi, man or woman. *Address:* Rabbi _____
_____ or _____ _____, D.D. *Salutation:*
Dear Rabbi _____ or Dear Dr. _____.
Sisterhood, Roman Catholic. *Address:* Sister _____
_____, C.S.J. *Salutation:* Dear Sister or Dear Sister
_____.
Sisterhood, superior of. *Address:* The Reverend Mother
Superior, S.C. *Salutation:* Reverend Mother.

Diplomats

Ambassador, U.S. *Address:* The Honorable _____
_____ The Ambassador of the United States.
Salutation: Sir/Madam or Dear Mr./Madam Ambassador.

Ambassador to the U.S. *Address:* His/Her Excellency
_____ _____, The Ambassador of _____.
Salutation: Excellency or Dear Mr./Madam Ambassador.
Chargé d'Affaires, U.S. *Address:* The Honorable
_____ _____, United States Chargé d'Affaires.
Salutation: Dear Mr./Ms. _____.
Consul, U.S. *Address:* _____ _____, Esq.,
United States Consul. *Salutation:* Dear Mr./Ms.
_____.
Minister, U.S. or to U.S. *Address:* The Honorable
_____ _____, The Minister of _____.
Salutation: Sir/Madam or Dear Mr./Madame Minister.
Secretary General, United Nations. *Address:* His/Her
Excellency _____ _____, Secretary General of
the United Nations. *Salutation:* Dear Mr./Madam/
Madame Secretary General.
United Nations Representative (Foreign). *Address:* His/
Her Excellency _____ _____, Representative
of _____ to the United Nations. *Salutation:* Excellency or My dear Mr./Madame _____.
United Nations Representative (U.S.) *Address:* The Honorable _____ _____, United States Representative to the United Nations. *Salutation:* Sir/Madam or
Dear Mr./Ms. _____.

Government Officials

Assemblyman. *Address:* The Honorable _____
_____. *Salutation:* Dear Mr./Ms. _____.
Associate Justice, U.S. Supreme Court. *Address:* Mr./
Madam Justice _____ _____. *Salutation:* Dear
Mr./Madam Justice or Sir/Madam.
Attorney General, U.S. *Address:* The Honorable
_____ _____, Attorney General of the United
States. *Salutation:* Dear Mr./Madam or Attorney General.
Cabinet member. *Address:* The Honorable _____
_____, Secretary of _____. *Salutation:* Sir/
Madam or Dear Mr./Madam Secretary.
Chief Justice, U.S. Supreme Court. *Address:* The Chief
Justice of the United States. *Salutation:* Dear Mr./
Madame Chief Justice.
Commissioner (federal, state, local). *Address:* The Honorable _____ _____. *Salutation:* Dear Mr./Ms.
_____.
Governor. *Address:* The Honorable _____
_____, Governor of _____. *Salutation:* Dear
Governor _____.
Judge, federal. *Address:* The Honorable _____
_____, Judge of the United States District Court for
the _____, District of _____. *Salutation:* Sir/
Madam or Dear Judge _____.
Judge, state or local. *Address:* The Honorable _____
_____ _____, Judge of the Court of
_____. *Salutation:* Dear Judge _____.
Lieutenant Governor. *Address:* The Honorable _____
_____ _____, Lieutenant Governor of
_____. *Salutation:* Dear Mr./Ms. _____.
Mayor. *Address:* The Honorable _____ _____,
Mayor of _____. *Salutation:* Dear Mayor _____.
President, U.S. *Address:* The President. *Salutation:* Dear
Mr./Madam President.
President, U.S., former. *Address:* The Honorable
_____ _____. *Salutation:* Dear Mr./Madam
_____.
Representative, state. *Address:* The Honorable
_____ _____. *Salutation:* Dear Mr./Ms.
_____.
Representative, U.S. *Address:* The Honorable _____
_____, United States House of Representatives.
Salutation: Dear Mr./Ms. _____.

Senator, state. *Address:* The Honorable _____
_____. The State Senate, State Capitol. *Salutation:* Dear Senator _____.

Senator, U.S. *Address:* The Honorable _____
_____, United States Senate. *Salutation:* Dear Senator _____.

Speaker, U.S. House of Representatives. *Address:* The Honorable _____ _____, Speaker of the House of Representatives. *Salutation:* Dear Mr./Madam Speaker.

Vice President, U.S. *Address:* The Vice President of the United States. *Salutation:* Sir/Madam or Dear Mr./Madam Vice President.

Military and Naval Officers

Rank. *Address:* Full rank, USN (or USCG, USAF, USA, USMC). *Salutation:* Dear (full rank) _____.

Professions

Attorney. *Address:* Mr./Ms. _____ _____, Attorney at law or _____ _____, Esq. *Salutation:* Dear Mr./Ms. _____.

Dentist. *Address:* _____ _____, D.D.S. *Salutation:* Dear Dr. _____.

Physician. *Address:* _____ _____, M.D. *Salutation:* Dear Dr. _____.

Veterinarian. *Address:* _____ _____, D.V.M. *Salutation:* Dear Dr. _____.

Foreign Words and Phrases

The English meanings given below are not necessarily literal translations. Foreign words and phrases should be set in italics (or underlined if written in long-hand) if their meanings are likely to be unknown to the reader. Whether the expression is familiar or unfamiliar, however, is a matter of judgment. Below, all foreign words have been italicized for the sake of emphasis.

ad absurdum (ad ab-sir'dum) [Lat.]: to the point of absurdity. "He tediously repeated his argument *ad absurdum.*"

ad infinitum (ad in-fun-eye'tum) [Lat.]: to infinity. "The lecture seemed to drone on *ad infinitum.*"

ad nauseam (ad noz'ee-um) [Lat.]: to a sickening degree. "The politician uttered one platitude after another *ad nauseam.*"

aficionado (uh-fish'ya-nah'doh) [Span.]: an ardent devotee. "I was surprised at what a baseball *aficionado* she had become."

annus mirabilis (an'us muh-ra'buh-lis) [Lat.]: wonderful year. "Last year was the *annus mirabilis* for my company."

au courant (oh' koo-rahn') [Fr.]: up-to-date. "The shoes, the hair, the clothes—every last detail of her dress, in fact—was utterly *au courant.*"

beau geste (boh zhest') [Fr.]: a fine or noble gesture, often futile. "My fellow writers supported me by writing letters of protest to the publisher, but their *beau geste* could not prevent the inevitable."

beau monde (boh' mond') [Fr.]: high society. "Such elegant decor would impress even the *beau monde.*"

bête noire (bet nwahr') [Fr.]: something or someone particularly disliked. "Talk of the good old college days way back when had become his *bête noire,* and he began to avoid his school friends."

bona fide (boh'na fide) [Lat.]: in good faith; genuine. "For all her reticence and modesty, it was clear that she was a *bona fide* expert in her field."

bon mot (bon moe') [Fr.]: a witty remark or comment. "One *bon mot* after another flew out of his mouth, charming the audience."

bon vivant (bon vee-vahnt') [Fr.]: a person who lives luxuriously and enjoys good food and drink. "It's true he's quite the *bon vivant,* but when he gets down to business he conducts himself like a Spartan."

carpe diem (kar'pay dee'um) [Lat.]: seize the day. "So what if you have an 8:00 a.m. meeting tomorrow and a full day of appointments? *Carpe diem!*"

carte blanche (kart blonsh') [Fr.]: unrestricted power to act on one's own. "I may have *carte blanche* around the office, but at home I'm a slave to my family's demands."

caveat emptor (kav'ee-ot emp'tor) [Lat.]: let the buyer beware. "Before you leap at that real estate deal, *caveat emptor!*"

comme ci comme ça (kom see' kom sah') [Fr.]: so-so. "The plans for the party strike me as *comme ci comme ça.*"

comme il faut (kom eel foe') [Fr.]: as it should be; fitting. "His end was truly *comme il faut.*"

coup de grâce (koo de grahss') [Fr.]: finishing blow. "After an already wildly successful day, the *coup de grâce* came when she won best all-around athlete."

cri de coeur (kree' de kur') [Fr.]: heartfelt appeal. "About to leave the podium, he made a final *cri de coeur* to his people to end the bloodshed."

de rigueur (duh ree-gur') [Fr.]: strictly required, as by etiquette, usage, or fashion. "Loudly proclaiming one's support for radical causes had become *de rigueur* among her crowd."

deus ex machina (day'us ex mahk'uh-nuh) [Lat.]: a contrived device to resolve a situation. "Stretching plausibility, the movie concluded with a *deus ex machina* ending in which everyone was rescued at the last minute."

dolce vita (dole'chay vee'tuh) [Ital.]: sweet life; the good life perceived as one of physical pleasure and self-indulgence. "My vacation this year is going to be two uninterrupted weeks of *dolce vita.*"

Doppelgänger* (dop'pul-gang-ur) [Ger.]: a ghostly double or counterpart of a living person. "I could not shake the sense that some shadowy *Doppelgänger* echoed my every move."

ecce homo (ek'ay ho'mo) [Lat.]: behold the man. "The painting depicted the common Renaissance theme, *ecce homo*—Christ wearing the crown of thorns."

enfant terrible (ahn-fahn' tay-reeb'luh) [Fr.]: an incorrigible child; an outrageously outspoken or bold person. "Again he played the role of *enfant terrible,* jolting us with his blunt assessment; yet I was secretly thrilled that the truth had come out in such a flagrant manner."

entre nous (ahn'truh noo') [Fr.]: between ourselves; confidentially. "*Entre nous,* their marriage is on the rocks."

ex cathedra (ex kuh-thee′druh) [Lat.]: with authority; used especially of those pronouncements of the pope that are considered infallible. "I resigned myself to obeying; my father's opinions were *ex cathedra* in our household."

ex post facto (ex′ post fak′toh) [Lat.]: retroactively. "I certainly hope that the change in policy will be honored *ex post facto.*"

fait accompli (fate ah-kom-plee′) [Fr.]: an accomplished fact, presumably irreversible. "There's no use protesting—it's a *fait accompli.*"

faux pas (foh pah′) [Fr.]: a social blunder. "Suddenly, she realized she had unwittingly committed yet another *faux pas.*"

Feinschmecker* (fine′shmek-er) [Ger.]: gourmet. "No, I don't think McDonald's will do; he's much too much of a *Feinschmecker.*"

flagrante delicto (fla-grahn′tee di-lik′toh) [Lat.]: in the act. "The detective realized that without hard evidence he had no case; he would have to catch the culprit *flagrante delicto.*"

glasnost (glaz′nohst) [Rus.]: open and frank discussion: initiated by Mikhail Gorbachev in 1985 in the Soviet Union. "Once the old chairman retired, the spirit of *glasnost* pervaded the department."

hoi polloi (hoy′ puh-loy′) [Gk.]: the common people. "Marie Antoinette recommended cake to the *hoi polloi.*"

in loco parentis (in loh′koh pa-ren′tiss) [Lat.]: in the place of a parent. "Put those cigarettes away young man; while you're with me consider my word *in loco parentis.*"

in situ (in sit′too) [Lat.]: situated in the original or natural position. "I prefer seeing statues *in situ* rather than in the confines of a museum."

in vino veritas (in vee′no vare′i-toss) [Lat.]: in wine there is truth. "By the end of the drunken banquet, several of the guests had made a good deal of their private lives public, prompting the host to murmur to his wife, '*in vino veritas.*'"

ipso facto (ip′soh fak′toh) [Lat.]: by the fact itself. "An extremist, *ipso facto,* cannot become part of a coalition."

je ne sais quoi (zhun say kwah′) [Fr.]: I know not what; an elusive quality. "She couldn't explain it, but there was something *je ne sais quoi* about him that she found devastatingly attractive."

mano a mano (mah′no ah mah′no) [Span.]: a direct confrontation or conflict. "'Stay out of it,' he admonished his friends, 'I want to handle this guy *mano a mano.*'"

mea culpa (may′uh kul′puh) [Lat.]: I am to blame. "His *mea culpa* was so offhand that I hardly think he meant it."

memento mori (muh-men′toh more′ee) [Lat.]: a reminder that you must die. "The skull rested on the mantlepiece as a *memento mori.*"

modus operandi (moh′dus op-er-an′dee) [Lat.]: a method of operating. "Her *modus operandi* is to sugar-coat the truth so thoroughly that the news almost seems welcome."

mot juste (moh zhoost′) [Fr.]: the exact, appropriate word. "'Rats!' screamed the defiant three-year-old, immensely proud of his *mot juste.*"

ne plus ultra (nee′ plus ul′truh) [Lat.]: the most intense degree of a quality or state. "Pulling it from the box, he realized he was face to face with the *ne plus ultra* of computers."

nom de guerre (nom duh gair′) [Fr.]: pseudonym. "He went by his *nom de guerre* when frequenting trendy nightclubs."

nom de plume (nom duh ploom′) [Fr.]: pen name. "Deciding it was time to sit down and begin a novel, the would-be writer spent the first several hours deciding upon a suitably dashing *nom de plume.*"

nota bene (noh′tuh ben′nee) [Ital.]: note well; take notice. "She appended her suggestions to the manuscript, underlining the words *nota bene* for added emphasis."

persona non grata (per-soh′nuh non grah′tuh) [Lat.]: unacceptable or unwelcome person. "Once I was cut out of the will, I became *persona non grata* among my relatives."

pro bono (pro boh′noh) [Lat.]: done or donated without charge; free. "The lawyer's *pro bono* work gave him a sense of value that his work on behalf of the corporation could not."

quid pro quo (kwid′ pro kwoh′) [Lat.]: something for something; an equal exchange. "She vowed that when she had the means, she would return his favors *quid pro quo.*"

sans souci (sahn soo-see′) [Fr.]: carefree. "Their mood was definitely *sans souci.*"

savoir-faire (sav′wahr fair′) [Fr.]: the ability to say and do the correct thing. "She presided over the gathering with impressive *savoir faire.*"

sic transit gloria mundi (sick tran′sit glor′ee-uh mun′dee) [Lat.]: thus passes away the glory of the world. "Watching the aging former football quarterback lumber down the street, potbellied and dissipated, his friend shook his head in disbelief and muttered, '*sic transit gloria mundi.*'"

sine qua non (sin′ay kwah nohn′) [Lat.]: indispensable. "Lemon is the *sine qua non* of this recipe."

terra incognita (tare′uh in-kog-nee′tuh) [Lat.]: unknown territory. "When the conversation suddenly switched from contemporary fiction to medieval Albanian playwrights, he felt himself entering *terra incognita.*"

tout le monde (too luh mond′) [Fr.]: everybody; everyone of importance. "Don't miss the event; it's bound to be attended by *tout le monde.*"

veni, vidi, vici (ven′ee vee′dee vee′chee) [Lat.]: I came, I saw, I conquered. "After the takeover the business mogul gloated, '*veni, vidi, vici.*'"

verboten (fer-boh′ten) [Ger.]: forbidden, as by law; prohibited. "That topic, I am afraid, is *verboten* in this household."

vox populi (voks pop′yoo-lie) [Lat.]: the voice of the people. "My sentiments echo those of the *vox populi.*"

Wanderjahr* (vahn′der-yahr) [Ger.]: a year or period of travel, especially following one's schooling. "The trio took off on their *Wanderjahr* soon after they graduated, planning to circle the globe by bicycle."

Weltanschauung* (velt´an-shou´ung) [Ger.]: a comprehensive conception or image of the universe and of humanity's relation to it. "His *Weltanschauung* gradually metamorphized from a grim and pessimistic one to a sunny, but no less complex, view."

Zeitgeist* (zite´guyst) [Ger.]: the spirit of the time; general trend of thought or feeling characteristic of a particular period of time. "She blamed it on the *Zeitgeist,* which encouraged hedonistic excess."

---

*German nouns are capitalized. A familiar German expression that is not italicized, however, should be lowercased, following the English conventions of not capitalizing common nouns. "His proclivities leaned more to the occult than to the philosophical: a poltergeist he could understand; the *Zeitgeist* he could not."

Easily Confused Words

allusion / illusion *Allusion* is a noun that means an indirect reference: "The speech made allusions to the final report." *Illusion* is a noun that means a misconception: "The policy is designed to give an illusion of reform."

alternately / alternatively *Alternately* is an adverb that means in turn; one after the other: "We alternately spun the wheel in the game." *Alternatively* is an adverb that means on the other hand; one or the other: "You can choose a large bookcase or, alternatively, you can buy two small ones."

beside / besides *Beside* is a preposition that means next to: "Stand here beside me." *Besides* is an adverb that means also: "Besides, I need to tell you about the new products my company offers."

bimonthly / semimonthly *Bimonthly* is an adjective that means every two months: "I brought the cake for the bimonthly office party." *Bimonthly* is also a noun that means a publication issued every two months: "The bimonthly magazine will soon become a monthly publication." *Semimonthly* is an adjective that means happening twice a month: "We have semimonthly meetings on the 1st and the 15th."

cite / site *Cite* is a verb that means to quote as an authority or example: "I cited several eminent scholars in my study of water resources." It also means to recognize formally: "The public official was cited for service to the city." It can also mean to summon before a court of law: "Last year the company was cited for pollution violations." *Site* is a noun meaning location: "They chose a new site for the factory just outside town."

complement / compliment *Complement* is a noun or verb that means something that completes or makes up a whole: "The red sweater is a perfect complement to the outfit." *Compliment* is a noun or verb that means an expression of praise or admiration: "I received many compliments about my new outfit."

concurrent / consecutive *Concurrent* is an adjective that means simultaneous or happening at the same time as something else: "The concurrent strikes of several unions crippled the economy." *Consecutive* means successive or following one after the other: "The union called three consecutive strikes in one year."

connote / denote *Connote* is a verb that means to imply or suggest: "The word 'espionage' connotes mystery and intrigue." *Denote* is a verb that means to indicate or refer to specifically: "The symbol for 'pi' denotes the number 3.14159."

discreet / discrete *Discreet* is an adjective that means prudent, circumspect, or modest: "Their discreet comments about the negotiations led the reporters to expect an early settlement." *Discrete* is an adjective that means separate or individually distinct: "Each company in the conglomerate operates as a discrete entity."

disinterested / uninterested *Disinterested* is an adjective that means unbiased or impartial: "We appealed to the disinterested mediator to facilitate the negotiations." *Uninterested* is an adjective that means not interested or indifferent: "They seemed uninterested in our offer."

effect / affect *Effect* is usually a noun that means a result or the power to produce a result: "The sound of the falling rain had a calming effect, nearly putting me to sleep." *Affect* is usually a verb that means to have an influence on: "His loud humming was affecting my ability to concentrate." Note that *effect* can also be a verb meaning to bring about or execute: "The speaker's somber tone effected a dampening in the general mood of the audience."

emigrant / immigrant / migrant *Emigrant* is a noun that means one who leaves one's native country to settle in another: "The emigrants spent four weeks aboard ship before landing in Los Angeles." *Immigrant* is a noun that means one who enters and settles in a new country: "Most of the immigrants easily found jobs." *Migrant* is a noun that means one who travels from one region to another, especially in search of work: "The migrants worked in the strawberry fields on the west coast, then traveled east to harvest wheat."

foreword / forward *Foreword* is a noun that means an introductory note or preface: "In my foreword I explained my reasons for writing the book." *Forward* is an adjective or adverb that means toward the front: "I sat in the forward section of the bus. Please step forward when your name is called." *Forward* is also a verb that means to send on: "Forward the letter to the customer's new address."

farther / further *Farther* is an adjective and adverb that means to or at a more distant point: "We drove 50 miles today; tomorrow, we will travel 100 miles farther." *Further* is an adjective and adverb that means to or at a greater extent or degree: "We won't be able to suggest a solution until we are further along in our evaluation of the problem." It can also mean in addition or moreover: "They stated further that they would not change the policy."

few / less *Few* is an adjective that means small in number. It is used with countable objects: "This department has few employees." *Less* is an adjective that means small in amount or degree. It is used with objects of indivisible mass: "Which jar holds less water?"

figuratively / literally *Figuratively* is an adverb that means metaphorically or symbolically: "Happening upon the shadowy figure, they figuratively jumped out of their shoes." *Literally* is an adverb that means word for word or according to the exact meaning of the words: "I translated the Latin passage literally."

hanged / hung *Hanged* is the past tense and past participle of hang when the meaning is to execute by suspending by the neck: "They hanged the prisoner for treason." "The convicted killer was hanged at dawn." *Hung* is the past tense and participle of hang when the meaning is to suspend from above with no support from below: "I hung the painting on the wall." "The painting was hung at a crooked angle."

it's / its *It's* is a contraction for it is, whereas *its* is the possessive form of it: "It's a shame that we cannot talk about its size."

laid / lain / lay *Laid* is the past tense and the past participle of the verb lay and not the past tense of lie. *Lay* is the past tense of the verb lie and *lain* is the past participle: "He laid his books down and lay down on the couch, where he has lain for an hour."

principal / principle *Principal* is a noun that means a person who holds a high position or plays an important role: "The school principal has 20 years of teaching experience. The principals in the negotiations will meet tomorrow at 10 o'clock." It also means a sum of money on which interest accrues: "The depositors were guaranteed they would not lose their principal." *Principal* is also an adjective that means chief or leading: "The necessity of moving to another city was the principal reason I turned down the job offer." *Principle* is a noun that means a rule or standard: "They refused to compromise their principles."

stationary / stationery *Stationary* is an adjective that means fixed or unmoving: "They maneuvered around the stationary barrier in the road." *Stationery* is a noun that means writing materials: "We printed the letters on company stationery."

American Sign Language and the Manual Alphabet

Sign language for the deaf was first systematized in France during the eighteenth century by Abbot Charles-Michel l'Epée. French Sign Language (FSL) was brought to the United States in 1816 by Thomas Gallaudet, founder of the American School for the Deaf in Hartford, Connecticut. He developed American Sign Language (ASL), a language of gestures and hand symbols that express words and concepts. It is the fourth most used language in the United States today.

Along with sign language and lip reading, many deaf people communicate with the manual alphabet, which uses finger positions that correspond to the letters of the alphabet to spell out words.

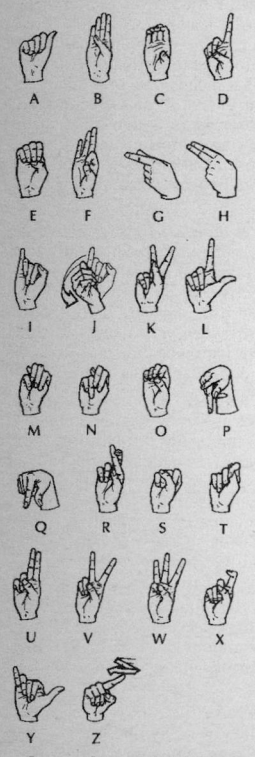

American Manual Alphabet

"You give it to me." or "Give it to me."

"How many?" or "How many do you want?"

"What's up?"

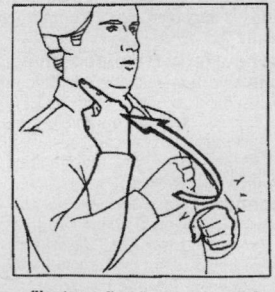

"last year" or "one year ago"

Baker-Shenk, C., and Cokely, D., *American Sign Language: A Teacher's Resource Text on Grammar and Culture* (1980). Washington, D.C.: Gallaudet University Press. Copyright © 1980 Charlotte Baker and Dennis Cokely. Reprinted with permission of the publisher.

The 50 Most Widely Spoken Languages[1] in the World

Rank, language	Countries[2]	Population[3] (in millions)
1. Chinese, Mandarin	Brunei, Cambodia, China, Indonesia, Malaysia, Mongolia, Philippines, Singapore, S. Africa, Taiwan, Thailand	885.0
2. Spanish	Andorra, Argentina, Belize, Bolivia, Chile, Colombia, Costa Rica, Cuba, Dominican Rep., Ecuador, El Salvador, Eq. Guinea, Guatemala, Honduras, Mexico, Nicaragua, Panama, Paraguay, Peru, Spain, Uruguay, U.S., Venezuela	332.0
3. English	Australia, Botswana, Brunei, Cameroon, Canada, Eritrea, Ethiopia, Fiji, The Gambia, Guyana, Ireland, Israel, Lesotho, Liberia, Malaysia, Micronesia, Namibia, Nauru, New Zealand, Palau, Papua New Guinea, Samoa, Seychelles, Sierra Leone, Singapore, Solomon Islands, Somalia, S. Africa, Suriname, Swaziland, Tonga, U.K., U.S., Vanuatu, Zimbabwe, many Caribbean states	322.0
4. Bengali	Bangladesh, India, Singapore	189.0
5. Hindi	India, Nepal, Singapore, S. Africa, Uganda	182.0
6. Portuguese	Brazil, Cape Verde, France, Guinea-Bissau, Portugal, São Tomé and Príncipe	170.0
7. Russian	China, Israel, Mongolia, Russia, U.S.	170.0
8. Japanese	Japan, Singapore, Taiwan	125.0
9. German, Standard	Austria, Belgium, Bolivia, Czech Rep., Denmark, Germany, Hungary, Italy, Kazakhstan, Liechtenstein, Luxembourg, Paraguay, Poland, Romania, Slovenia, Switzerland	98.0
10. Chinese, Wu	China	77.2
11. Javanese	Indonesia, Malaysia, Singapore	75.5
12. Korean	China, Japan, N. Korea, S. Korea, Singapore, Thailand	75.0
13. French	Andorra, Belgium, Burkina Faso, Burundi, Cameroon, Canada, Comoros, Congo, Congo (Dem. Rep. of), Djibouti, France, Gabon, Guinea, Haiti, Luxembourg, Mauritania, Monaco, Rwanda, Senegal, Seychelles, Switzerland, Vanuatu	72.0
14. Vietnamese	China, Vietnam	67.7
15. Telugu	India, Singapore	66.4
16. Chinese, Yue (Cantonese)	Brunei, China, Costa Rica, Indonesia, Malaysia, Panama, Philippines, Singapore, Thailand, Vietnam	66.0
17. Marathi	India	64.8
18. Tamil	India, Malaysia, Mauritius, Singapore, S. Africa, Sri Lanka	63.1
19. Turkish	Bulgaria, Cyprus, Greece, Macedonia, Romania, Turkey, Uzbekistan	59.0
20. Urdu	Afghanistan, India, Mauritius, Pakistan, S. Africa, Thailand	58.0
21. Chinese, Min Nan	Brunei, China, Indonesia, Malaysia, Philippines, Singapore, Taiwan, Thailand	49.0
22. Chinese, Jinyu	China	45.0
23. Gujarati	India, Kenya, Pakistan, Singapore, S. Africa, Tanzania, Uganda, Zambia, Zimbabwe	44.0
24. Polish	Czech Rep., Germany, Israel, Poland, Romania, Slovakia	44.0
25. Arabic, Egyptian	Egypt	42.5
26. Ukrainian	Poland, Slovakia, Ukraine	41.0
27. Italian	Croatia, Eritrea, France, Italy, San Marino, Slovenia, Switzerland	37.0
28. Chinese, Xiang	China	36.0
29. Malayalam	India, Singapore	34.0
30. Chinese, Hakka	Brunei, China, Indonesia, Malaysia, Panama, Singapore, Suriname, Taiwan, Thailand	34.0
31. Kannada	India	33.7
32. Oriya	India	31.0
33. Panjabi, Western	India, Pakistan	30.0
34. Sunda	Indonesia	27.0
35. Panjabi, Eastern	India, Kenya, Singapore	26.0
36. Romanian	Hungary, Israel, Moldova, Romania, Serbia and Montenegro, Ukraine	26.0
37. Bhojpuri	India, Mauritius, Nepal	25.0
38. Azerbaijani, South	Afghanistan, Iran, Iraq, Syria, Turkey	24.4
39. Farsi, Western	Iran, Iraq, Oman, Qatar, Tajikistan, United Arab Emirates	24.3
40. Maithili	India, Nepal	24.3
41. Hausa	Benin, Burkina Faso, Cameroon, Ghana, Niger, Nigeria, Sudan, Togo	24.2
42. Arabic, Algerian	Algeria	22.4
43. Burmese	Bangladesh, Myanmar	22.0
44. Serbo-Croatian[4]	Bosnia and Herzegovina, Croatia, Macedonia, Serbia and Montenegro, Slovakia	21.0
45. Chinese, Gan	China	20.6
46. Awadhi	India, Nepal	20.5
47. Thai	Singapore, Thailand	20.0
48. Dutch	Belgium, France, Netherlands, Suriname	20.0
49. Yoruba	Benin, Nigeria	20.0
50. Sindhi	Afghanistan, India, Pakistan, Singapore	19.7

1. Many of the languages listed are technically dialects, not separate languages. They are listed separately because they differ from each other enough to be mutually unintelligible. 2. The countries listed under Spanish, English, Portuguese, French, and Serbo-Croatian do not include those in which less than 1% of the population speaks the language as a first language. 3. The population figures refer to first language speakers in all countries and are general estimates. 4. Serbo-Croatian is now known variously as Serbian, Croatian, or Bosnian, depending on the speaker's ethnic or political affiliation. *Source: Ethnologue,* 13th Edition, Barbara F. Grimes, Editor. © 1996, Summer Institute of Linguistics, Inc.

PEOPLE

Many public figures not listed here may be found elsewhere in the almanac.

U.S. Presidents
U.S. Vice Presidents
Families of U.S. Presidents
U.S. Governors
U.S. Congress
U.S. Supreme Court Justices
U.S. Government Officials

British Prime Ministers
Rulers of England
Rulers of France
Rulers of Judah and Israel
Rulers of Prussia
Rulers of Russia
Sports Personalities

Names in parentheses indicate a person's original name or nickname. Locations in parentheses are the present-day name of the birthplace. Dates of birth appear as month/day/year. **Boldface** years in parentheses are dates of **(birth–death)**.

Information has been gathered from many sources, including the individuals themselves. However, the almanac cannot guarantee the accuracy of every item.

A

Aalto, Alvar (architect); Kuortane, Finland **(1898–1976)**
Abbado, Claudio (orchestra conductor); Milan, Italy, 1933
Abbott, Bud (William Abbott) (comedian); Asbury Park, N.J. **(1898–1974)**
Abbott, George (stage producer); Forestville, N.Y. **(1887–1995)**
Abelard, Peter (theologian); nr. Nantes, France **(1079–1142)**
Abernathy, Ralph (civil rights leader); Linden, Ala. **(1926–1990)**
Abraham, F(ahrid) Murray (actor); Pittsburgh, 10/24/39
Achebe, Chinua (writer); Ogidi, Nigeria, 11/16/30
Acheson, Dean (statesman); Middletown, Conn. **(1893–1971)**
Acuff, Roy Claxton (musician); nr. Maynardsville, Tenn. **(1903–1992)**
Adams, Abigail (First Lady, writer); Weymouth, Mass. **(1744–1818)**
Adams, Bryan (singer, songwriter); Kingston, Ontario, Canada, 11/5/59
Adams, Charles Francis (diplomat); Boston **(1807–1886)**
Adams, Don (actor); New York City, 4/19/26
Adams, Edie (Edie Enke) (actress); Kingston, Pa., 4/16/29
Adams, Franklin Pierce (columnist, author); Chicago **(1881–1960)**
Adams, Gerry (political leader); West Belfast, Northern Ireland, 10/6/48
Adams, Henry Brooks (historian); Boston **(1838–1918)**
Adams, Joey (comedian); New York City, 1/6/11
Adams, John (2nd U.S. president); Braintree (Quincy), Mass. **(1735–1826)**
Adams, John Quincy (6th U.S. president); Braintree (Quincy), Mass. **(1767–1848)**
Adams, Maude (Maude Kiskadden) (actress); Salt Lake City **(1872–1953)**
Adams, Samuel (American Revolutionary patriot); Boston **(1722–1803)**
Adams, Scott (cartoonist); Catskill, N.Y., 6/8/57
Adamson, Joy (naturalist, writer); Troppau, Silesia **(1910–1980)**
Addams, Charles (cartoonist); Westfield, N.J. **(1912–1988)**
Addams, Jane (social worker, Nobel laureate); Cedarville, Ill. **(1860–1935)**
Adderley, Julian "Cannonball" (jazz saxophonist); Tampa, Fla. **(1928–1975)**
Ade, George (humorist); Kentland, Ind. **(1866–1944)**
Adenauer, Konrad (statesman); Cologne, Germany **(1876–1967)**
Adler, Alfred (psychoanalyst); Vienna **(1870–1937)**
Adler, Larry (musician); Baltimore, 2/10/14
Adler, Richard (songwriter); New York City, 8/3/21
Aeschylus (dramatist); Eleusis, Greece **(525–456 B.C.E.)**
Aesop (fabulist); Samos?, Greece, fl. c. 500 B.C.E.
Agnew, Spiro (political figure); Baltimore **(1905–1996)**
Aiello, Danny (actor); New York City, 6/20/33
Aiken, Conrad (poet); Savannah, Ga. **(1889–1973)**
Ailey, Alvin (choreographer); Rogers, Tex. **(1931–1989)**
Akhmatova, Anna (poet); Odessa, Ukraine **(1889–1966)**
Akihito, Tsugunomiya (Emperor of Japan); Tokyo, 12/23/33
Albanese, Licia (operatic soprano); Bari, Italy, 7/22/13
Albee, Edward (playwright); Washington, D.C., 3/12/28
Albers, Josef (painter); Bottrop, Germany **(1888–1976)**
Albert, Eddie (Edward Albert Heimberger) (actor); Rock Island, Ill., 4/22/08
Albert, Edward (actor); Los Angeles, 2/20/51
Albertson, Jack (actor); Malden, Mass. **(1907–1981)**

Albright, Madeleine (diplomat, U.S. Secretary of State); Prague, Czechoslovakia, 5/15/37
Alcott, Louisa May (novelist); Germantown, Pa. **(1832–1888)**
Alda, Alan (actor); New York City, 1/28/36
Alden, John (American Pilgrim); England **(c. 1599–1687)**
Alexander, Jane (Quigley) (actress); Boston, 10/28/39
Alexander, Jason (Jay Scott Greenspan) (actor); Newark, N.J., 9/23/59
Alexander the Great (monarch, conqueror); Pella, Macedonia, Greece **(356–323 B.C.E.)**
Alger, Horatio (author); Revere, Mass. **(1834–1899)**
Algren, Nelson (novelist); Detroit **(1909–1981)**
Allen, Debbie (dancer-choreographer, actress); Houston, 1/16/50
Allen, Ethan (American Revolutionary soldier); Litchfield, Conn. **(1738–1789)**
Allen, Fred (John Florence Sullivan) (comedian); Cambridge, Mass. **(1894–1956)**
Allen, Gracie (Grace Ethel Cecile Rosalie Allen) (comedienne); San Francisco **(1906–1964)**
Allen, Joan (actress); Rochelle, Ill., 8/20/56
Allen, Mel (Melvin Israel) (sportscaster); Birmingham, Ala. **(1913–1996)**
Allen, Peter (actor, songwriter); Tenterfield, Australia **(1944–1992)**
Allen, Steve (TV entertainer); New York City, 12/26/21
Allen, Woody (Allen Stewart Konigsberg) (actor, writer, director); Brooklyn, N.Y., 12/1/35
Allende, Isabel (novelist); Lima, Peru, 8/2/42
Alley, Kirstie (actress); Wichita, Kans., 1/12/55
Allison, Fran (actress); LaPorte City, Iowa **(1908?–1989)**
Allman, Gregg (singer); Nashville, Tenn., 12/8/47
Allyson, June (Ella Geisman) (actress); New York City, 10/7/17
Alonso, Alicia (ballet dancer); Havana, 12/21/21?
Alpert, Herb (band leader); Los Angeles, 3/31/35?
Alsop, Joseph W., Jr. (journalist); Avon, Conn. **(1910–1989)**
Alsop, Stewart (journalist); Avon, Conn. **(1914–1974)**
Alt, Carol (model); Flushing, New York, 12/1/60
Altman, Robert (director); Kansas City, Mo., 2/20/25
Amanpour, Christiane (broadcast journalist); London, 1958
Amati, Nicola (violin maker); Cremona, Italy **(1596–1684)**
Ambler, Eric (suspense writer); London **(1909–1998)**
Ameche, Don (Dominic Amici) (actor); Kenosha, Wis. **(1908–1993)**
Amis, Kingsley (novelist); London **(1922–1995)**
Amory, Cleveland (writer, conservationist); Nahant, Mass. **(1917–1998)**
Amos (Freeman F. Gosden) (radio comedian); Richmond, Va. **(1899–1982)**
Amos, John (actor); Newark, N.J., 12/27/41
Amos, Tori (singer); Newton, N.C., 8/22/63
Amsterdam, Morey (actor); Chicago **(1914–1996)**
Andersen, Hans Christian (author of fairy tales); Odense, Denmark **(1805–1875)**
Anderson, Eddie (Rochester) (actor); Oakland, Calif. **(1905–1977)**
Anderson, Gillian (actress); Chicago, 8/9/68
Anderson, Harry (actor); Newport, R.I., 10/14/52
Anderson, Ib (ballet dancer); Copenhagen, 12/14/54
Anderson, Jack (journalist); Long Beach, Calif., 10/19/22
Anderson, Dame Judith (actress); Adelaide, Australia **(1898–1992)**
Anderson, Lindsay (Gordon) (director); Bangalore, India **(1923–1994)**
Anderson, Loni (actress); St. Paul, Minn., 8/5/45
Anderson, Lynn (singer); Grand Forks, N.D., 9/26/47

Anderson, Marian (contralto); Philadelphia **(1897–1993)**
Anderson, Maxwell (dramatist); Atlantic, Pa. **(1888–1959)**
Anderson Lee, Pamela (Pamela Anderson) (model, actress); Ladysmith, British Columbia, Canada, 7/1/67
Anderson, Richard Dean (actor); Minneapolis, Minn., 1/23/50
Anderson, Robert (playwright); New York City, 4/28/17
Anderson, Sherwood (novelist); Camden, Ohio **(1876–1941)**
Andress, Ursula (actress); Bern, Switzerland, 3/19/38
Andrews, Julie (Julia Wells) (actress, singer); Walton-on-Thames, England, 10/1/35
Andrews, La Verne (singer); Minneapolis **(1916–1967)**
Andrews, Maxene (singer); Minneapolis **(1918–1995)**
Andrews, Patti (singer); Minneapolis, 2/16/20
Andy (Charles J. Correll) (radio comedian); Peoria, Ill. **(1890–1972)**
Angeles, Victoria de los (Victoria Gamez Cima) (operatic soprano); Barcelona, 11/1/24
Angelico, Fra (Guido di Pietro; Giovanni de Fiesole) (painter); nr. Florence **(c. 1400–1455)**
Angelou, Maya (Marguerite Johnson) (poet, novelist); St. Louis, 4/4/28
Aniston, Jennifer (Jennifer Anistonapoulos) (actress); Sherman Oaks, Calif., 2/11/69
Anka, Paul (singer, composer); Ottawa, Ont., Canada, 7/30/41
Annan, Kofi (diplomat, U.N. Secretary General); Kumasi, Ghana, 4/8/38
Ann-Margret (Ann-Margaret Olsson) (actress); Valsjobyn, Sweden, 4/28/41
Anouilh, Jean (playwright); Bordeaux, France **(1910–1987)**
Anthony, Susan Brownell (woman suffragist); Adams, Mass. **(1820–1906)**
Antonioni, Michelangelo (director); Ferrara, Italy, 9/29/12
Antony, Mark (Marcus Antonius) (statesman); Rome **(c. 83–30 B.C.E.)**
Anuszkiewicz, Richard (painter); Erie, Pa., 5/23/30
Apple, Fiona (singer); New York City, 4/8/68
Applegate, Christina (actress); Los Angeles, Calif., 11/25/71
Aquinas, St. Thomas (philosopher); nr. Aquino, Italy **(1225–1274)**
Arafat, Yasir (Mohammed Abdel-Raouf Arafat al Qudwa al Husseini) (Chairman of the Palestine Liberation Organization); Cairo, Egypt, 8/24/29
Arbuckle, Roscoe "Fatty" (actor, director); Smith Center, Kans. **(1887–1933)**
Archimedes (physicist, mathematician); Syracuse, Sicily **(287–212 B.C.E.)**
Archipenko, Alexandre (sculptor); Kiev, Ukraine **(1887–1964)**
Arden, Elizabeth (Florence Nightingale Graham) (cosmetics executive); Woodbridge, Canada **(1891–1966)**
Arden, Eve (Eunice Quedens) (actress); Mill Valley, Calif. **(1912–1990)**
Arendt, Hannah (historian); Hanover, Germany **(1906–1975)**
Aristophanes (dramatist); Athens **(c. 448–c. 385 B.C.E.)**
Aristotle (philosopher); Stagirus, Macedonia **(384–322 B.C.E.)**
Arkin, Adam (actor); New York City, 8/19/57
Arkin, Alan (actor, director); New York City, 3/26/34
Arledge, Roone (TV executive); Forest Hills, N.Y., 7/8/31
Arlen, Harold (Hyman Arluck) (composer); Buffalo, N.Y. **(1905–1986)**
Armani, Georgio (fashion designer); Piacenza, Italy, 7/11/34
Armstrong, Louis ("Satchmo") (musician); New Orleans **(1900–1971)**
Arnaz, Desi (Desiderio Arnaz) (actor, producer); Santiago, Cuba **(1917–1986)**
Arness, James (James Aurness) (actor); Minneapolis, 5/26/23
Arno, Peter (cartoonist); New York City **(1904–1968)**
Arnold, Benedict (American Revolutionary War general, charged with treason); Norwich, Conn. **(1741–1801)**
Arnold, Eddy (singer); Henderson, Tenn., 5/15/18
Arnold, Matthew (poet, critic); Laleham, England **(1822–1888)**
Arp, Jean (sculptor, painter); Strasbourg, France **(1887–1966)**
Arpino, Gerald (choreographer); Staten Island, N.Y., 1/14/28
Arquette, Cliff (actor); Toledo, Ohio **(1905–1974)**
Arquette, Patricia (actress); Chicago, 4/8/68
Arquette, Rosanna (actress); New York City, 8/10/59
Arrau, Claudio (pianist); Chillán, Chile **(1903–1991)**
Arroyo, Martina (soprano); New York City, 2/2/40
Arthur, Bea (Bernice Frankel) (actress); New York City, 5/13/23
Arthur, Chester Alan (21st U.S. president); Fairfield, Vt. **(1830–1886)**
Ashcroft, Dame Peggy (actress); Croydon, England **(1907–1991)**
Ashkenazy, Vladimir (concert pianist); Gorki, U.S.S.R., 7/6/37
Ashley, Elizabeth (actress); Ocala, Fla., 8/30/39
Ashton, Sir Frederick William Mallandaine (choreographer); Guayaquil, Ecuador **(1904–1988)**

Asimov, Isaac (author); Petrovichi, Russia **(1920–1992)**
Asner, Edward (actor); Kansas City, Mo., 11/15/29
Assante, Armand (actor); New York City, 10/4/49
Astaire, Fred (Frederick Austerlitz) (dancer, actor); Omaha, Neb. **(1899–1987)**
Astin, John (actor, director); Baltimore, 3/30/30
Astor, Brooke (socialite, philanthropist); Portsmouth, N.H., 3/16/05
Astor, John Jacob (financier); Waldorf, Germany **(1763–1848)**
Astor, Mary (Lucile Langhanke) (actress); Quincy, Ill. **(1906–1987)**
Atatürk, Kemal (Mustafa Kemal) (Turkish soldier, statesman); Salonika, Greece **(1881–1938)**
Atkins, Chet (guitarist); nr. Luttrell, Tenn., 6/20/24
Atkinson, Rowan (actor); Newcastle-Upon-Tyne, England, 1/6/55
Attenborough, Richard (actor, director); Cambridge, England, 8/29/23
Attila (King of Huns); **(406?–453)**
Attucks, Crispus (American Revolutionary Patriot); Boston **(c. 1723–1770)**
Auberjonois, Rene (actor); New York City, 6/1/40
Auchincloss, Louis (author); Lawrence, N.Y., 9/27/17
Auden, W(ystan) H(ugh) (poet); York, England **(1907–1973)**
Audubon, John James (naturalist, painter); Haiti **(1785–1851)**
Auer, Leopold (violinist, teacher); Veszprém, Hungary **(1845–1930)**
Augustine, Saint (Aurelius Augustinus) (theologian); Tagaste, Numidia, Algeria **(354–430)**
Augustus (Gaius Octavius) (Roman emperor); Rome **(63 B.C.E.–c.E. 14)**
Aung, San Suu Kyi (human rights activist); Rangoon, Burma, 6/19/45
Austen, Jane (novelist); Steventon, England **(1775–1817)**
Autry, Gene (singer, actor); Tioga, Tex. **(1907–1998)**
Avalon, Frankie (singer); Philadelphia, 9/18/39
Avedon, Richard (photographer); New York City, 5/15/23
Avery, Milton (painter); Altmar, N.Y. **(1893–1965)**
Ax, Emanuel (pianist); Lvov, Ukraine, 6/8/49
Axelrod, George (playwright); New York City, 6/9/22
Ayckbourn, Alan (playwright); London, 4/12/39
Aykroyd, Dan (actor); Ottawa, Ont., Canada, 7/1/52
Ayres, Lew (actor); Minneapolis **(1908–1996)**
Aznavour, Charles (singer, composer); Paris, 5/22/24

B

Bacall, Lauren (Betty Joan Perske) (actress); New York City, 9/16/24
Bach, Carl Phillipp Emanuel (composer); Weimar, Germany **(1714–1788)**
Bach, Johann Sebastian (composer); Eisenach, Germany **(1685–1750)**
Bacharach, Burt (songwriter); Kansas City, Mo., 5/12/29
Backus, Jim (actor); Cleveland **(1913–1989)**
Bacon, Francis (philosopher, essayist); London **(1561–1626)**
Bacon, Francis (painter); Dublin **(1910–1992)**
Bacon, Kevin (actor); Philadelphia, 7/8/58
Bacon, Roger (philosopher, scientist); Ilchester, England **(c. 1214–1294?)**
Badu, Erykah (Erykah Wright) (singer); Dallas, 1971
Baez, Joan (folk singer); Staten Island, N.Y., 1/9/41
Bailey, F. Lee (lawyer); Waltham, Mass., 6/10/33
Bailey, Pearl (singer); Newport News, Va. **(1918–1990)**
Bain, Conrad (actor); Lethbridge, Alberta, Canada, 2/4/23
Baio, Scott (actor); Brooklyn, N.Y., 9/22/61
Baird, Bil (William B. Baird) (puppeteer); Grand Island, Neb. **(1904–1987)**
Baker, Anita (singer); Toledo, Ohio, 1958
Baker, Carroll (actress); Johnstown, Pa., 5/28/31
Baker, Josephine (singer, dancer); St. Louis **(1906–1975)**
Baker, Russell (columnist); Loudoun County, Va., 8/14/25
Balanchine, George (choreographer); St. Petersburg, Russia **(1904–1983)**
Balboa, Vasco Nuñez de (explorer); Jerez de los Caballeros, Spain **(1475–1517)**
Baldwin, Alec (actor); Massapequa, N.Y., 4/3/58
Baldwin, James (novelist); New York City **(1924–1987)**
Bale, Christian (actor); Pembrokeshire, Wales, 1/30/74
Balenciaga, Cristóbal (fashion designer); Guetaria, Spain **(1895–1972)**
Ball, Lucille (Lucille Désirée Ball) (actress, producer); Celoron (nr. Jamestown), N.Y. **(1911–1989)**
Balmain, Pierre (fashion designer); St.-Jean-de-Maurienne, France **(1914–1982)**
Balsam, Martin (actor); Bronx, New York **(1919–1996)**
Balzac, Honoré de (novelist); Tours, France **(1799–1850)**

Bancroft, Anne (Annemarie Italiano) (actress); New York City, 9/17/31

Banderas, Antonio (José Antonio Dominguez Banderas) (actor, model); Málaga, Spain, 8/10/60

Bankhead, Tallulah (actress); Huntsville, Ala. **(1903–1968)**

Banks, Tyra (model); Los Angeles, 12/4/73

Banting, Fredrick Grant (physiologist); Alliston, Ont., Canada **(1891–1941)**

Bara, Theda (Theodosia Goodman) (actress); Cincinnati **(1890–1955)**

Barak, Ehud (Israeli Prime Minister); Kibbutz Mishmar Hasharon, Israel, 2/12/42

Barbera, Joseph (animator, producer); New York City, 1911

Baraka, Imamu Amiri (LeRoi Jones) (playwright); Newark, N.J., 10/7/34

Baranski, Christine (actress); Buffalo, N.Y., 5/2/52

Barber, Red (Walter Lanier) (sportscaster); Columbus, Miss. **(1908–1992)**

Barber, Samuel (composer); West Chester, Pa. **(1910–1981)**

Barbie, Klaus (Nazi, "The Butcher of Lyon"); Bad Godesberg, Germany **(1913–1991)**

Bardot, Brigitte (Camille Javal) (actress); Paris, 9/28/34

Barenboim, Daniel (concert pianist, conductor); Buenos Aires, 11/15/42

Barker, Bob (game-show host); Darrington, Wash., 12/12/23

Barkin, Ellen (actress); Bronx, N.Y., 4/16/54

Barnard, Christiaan N. (heart surgeon); Beauford West, South Africa, 10/8/22

Barnum, Phineas Taylor (showman); Bethel, Conn. **(1810–1891)**

Barrie, Sir James Matthew (author); Kirriemuir, Scotland **(1860–1937)**

Barry, John (naval officer); County Wexford, Ireland **(1745–1803)**

Barrymore, Diana (actress); New York City **(1921–1960)**

Barrymore, Drew (actress); Los Angeles, 2/22/75

Barrymore, Ethel (Ethel Blythe) (actress); Philadelphia **(1879–1959)**

Barrymore, Georgiana Drew (actress); Philadelphia **(1856–1893)**

Barrymore, John (John Blythe) (actor); Philadelphia **(1882–1942)**

Barrymore, Lionel (Lionel Blythe) (actor); Philadelphia **(1878–1954)**

Barrymore, Maurice (Herbert Blythe) (actor, playwright); Agra, India **(1847–1905)**

Barth, John (novelist); Cambridge, Md., 5/27/30

Barthelme, Donald (novelist); Philadelphia **(1931 –1989)**

Bartók, Béla (composer); Nagyszentmiklo, Hungary **(1881–1945)**

Barton, Clara (founder of American Red Cross); Oxford, Mass. **(1821–1912)**

Baruch, Bernard Mannes (statesman); Camden, S.C. **(1870–1965)**

Baryshnikov, Mikhail Nikolayevich (ballet dancer, artistic director); Riga, Latvia, 1/27/48

Basie, Count (William Basie) (band leader); Red Bank, N.J. **(1904–1984)**

Basinger, Kim (actress); Athens, Ga., 12/8/53

Bassett, Angela (actress); New York City, 8/16/58

Bassey, Shirley (singer); Cardiff, Wales, 1/8/37

Batchelor, Clarence Daniel (political cartoonist); Osage City, Kans. **(1888–1977)**

Bateman, Jason (actor); Rye, N.Y., 1/14/69

Bateman, Justine (actress); Rye, N.Y., 2/19/66

Bates, Alan (actor); Allestree, England, 2/17/34

Bates, Kathy (Kathleen Doyle Bates) (actress); Memphis, Tenn., 6/28/48

Battle, Kathleen (soprano); Portsmouth, Ohio, 8/13/48

Baudelaire, Charles Pierre (poet); Paris **(1821–1867)**

Baxter, Anne (actress); Michigan City, Ind. **(1923–1985)**

Baxter, Meredith (actress); Los Angeles, 6/21/47

Beardsley, Aubrey Vincent (illustrator); Brighton, England **(1872–1898)**

Beaton, Cecil (photographer, designer); London **(1904–1980)**

Beatty, Clyde (animal trainer); Chillicothe, Ohio **(1903–1965)**

Beatty, Warren (Henry Warren Beaty) (actor, producer); Richmond, Va., 3/30/37

Beaumont, Francis (dramatist); Grace-Dieu, England **(1584–1616)**

Becket, Thomas à (Archbishop of Canterbury); London **(1118?–1170)**

Beckett, Samuel (playwright); Dublin **(1906–1989)**

Beckmann, Max (painter); Leipzig, Germany **(1884–1950)**

Bede, Saint ("The Venerable Bede") (scholar); Monkwearmouth, England **(673–735)**

Beecham, Sir Thomas (conductor); St. Helens, England **(1879–1961)**

Beecher, Henry Ward (clergyman); Litchfield, Conn. **(1813–1887)**

Beerbohm, Sir Max (author); London **(1872–1956)**

Beery, Noah (actor); Kansas City, Mo. **(1884–1946)**

Beery, Noah, Jr. (actor); New York City **(1913–1994)**

Beery, Wallace (actor); Kansas City, Mo. **(1886–1949)**

Beethoven, Ludwig van (composer); Bonn, Germany **(1770–1827)**

Begin, Menachem (Israeli Prime Minister); Brest-Litovsk, Belarus **(1913–1992)**

Begley, Ed (actor); Hartford, Conn. **(1901–1970)**

Beiderbecke, Bix (jazz musician); Davenport, Iowa **(1903–1931)**

Beineix, Jean-Jacques (director, producer, screenwriter) 1946

Belafonte, Harry (singer, actor); New York City, 3/1/27

Belafonte-Harper, Shari (actress); New York City, 9/22/54

Belasco, David (dramatist, producer); San Francisco **(1854–1931)**

Bel Geddes, Barbara (actress); New York City, 10/31/22

Bell, Alexander Graham (inventor); Edinburgh, Scotland **(1847–1922)**

Bell, Quentin (author, artist); England **(1910–1996)**

Bellamy, Edward (author); Chicopee Falls, Mass. **(1850–1898)**

Bellamy, Ralph (actor); Chicago **(1904–1991)**

Bellini, Giovanni (painter); Venice **(c. 1430–1516)**

Bellow, Saul (novelist); Lachine, Que., Canada, 6/10/15

Bellows, George Wesley (painter, lithographer); Columbus, Ohio **(1882–1925)**

Belmondo, Jean-Paul (actor); Neuilly-sur-Seine, France, 4/9/33

Belushi, Jim (actor); Chicago, 6/15/54

Belushi, John (comedian, actor); Chicago **(1949–1982)**

Benchley, Peter Bradford (novelist); New York City, 5/8/40

Benchley, Robert Charles (humorist); Worcester, Mass. **(1889–1945)**

Bendix, William (actor); New York City **(1906–1964)**

Benedict, Ruth Fulton (anthropologist); New York City **(1887–1948)**

Benes, Eduard (statesman); Kozlany, former Czechoslovakia **(1884–1948)**

Benét, Stephen Vincent (poet, story writer); Bethlehem, Pa. **(1898–1943)**

Benét, William Rose (poet, novelist); Ft. Hamilton, Brooklyn, N.Y. **(1886–1950)**

Ben-Gurion, David (David Green) (statesman); Plónsk, Poland **(1886–1973)**

Benigni, Roberto (actor, director, screenwriter); Misericordia, Arezzo, Italy, 10/27/52

Bening, Annette (actress); Topeka, Kans., 5/29/58

Bennett, Enoch Arnold (novelist, dramatist); Hanley, England **(1867–1931)**

Bennett, James Gordon (editor); Keith, Scotland **(1795–1872)**

Bennett, Joan (actress); Palisades, N.J. **(1910–1990)**

Bennett, Robert Russell (composer); Kansas City, Mo. **(1894–1981)**

Bennett, Tony (Anthony Benedetto) (singer); Astoria, Queens, N.Y., 8/3/26

Benny, Jack (Benjamin Kubelsky) (comedian); Chicago **(1894–1974)**

Benson, Robby (actor); Dallas, 1/21/56

Bentham, Jeremy Heinrich (economist); London **(1748–1832)**

Benton, Thomas Hart (painter); Neosho, Mo. **(1889–1975)**

Berendt, John (writer); Syracuse, N.Y., 12/5/39

Berenger, Tom (actor); Chicago, 5/31/50

Berg, Alban (composer); Vienna **(1885–1935)**

Berg, Gertrude (writer, actress); New York City **(1899–1966)**

Bergen, Candice (actress); Beverly Hills, Calif., 5/9/46

Bergen, Edgar (ventriloquist); Chicago **(1903–1978)**

Bergen, Polly (Nellie Paulina Burgin) (actress, singer); Knoxville, Tenn., 7/14/30

Bergerac, Cyrano de (poet); Paris **(1619–1655)**

Bergman, Ingmar (film director); Uppsala, Sweden, 7/14/18

Bergman, Ingrid (actress); Stockholm **(1918–1982)**

Bergson, Henri (philosopher); Paris **(1859–1941)**

Berkeley, Busby (William Berkeley Enos) (choreographer, director); Los Angeles **(1895–1976)**

Berle, Milton (Milton Berlinger) (comedian); New York City, 7/12/08

Berlin, Irving (Israel Baline) (songwriter); Temum, Russia **(1888–1989)**

Berlioz, Louis Hector (composer); La Côte-Saint-André, France **(1803–1869)**

Berman, Lazar (concert pianist); Leningrad (St. Petersburg), Russia, 2/26/30

Bernardin, Joseph Cardinal (prelate); Columbia, S.C. **(1928–1996)**

Bernhard, Sandra (actress, comedian); Flint, Mich., 6/6/55

Bernhardt, Sarah (Rosine Bernard) (actress); Paris **(1844–1923)**

Bernini, Gian Lorenzo (sculptor, painter); Naples, Italy **(1598–1680)**

Bernoulli, Jacques (scientist); Basel, Switzerland **(1654–1705)**

Bernsen, Corbin (actor); North Hollywood, Calif., 7/7/54

Bernstein, Leonard (conductor); Lawrence, Mass. **(1918–1990)**

Berry, Chuck (Charles Edward Berry) (singer, guitarist); San Jose, Calif., 1/15/26

Berry, Halle (actress, model); Cleveland, Ohio, 8/14/68
Berry, Ken (actor); Moline, Ill., 11/3/30
Berry, Richard (songwriter); Extension, S.C. (1935–1997)
Berryman, John (poet); McAlester, Okla. (1914–1972)
Bertinelli, Valerie (actress); Wilmington, Del., 4/23/60
Bertolucci, Bernardo (actor); Parma, Italy, 3/16/40
Bethune, Mary McLeod (educator); Mayesville, S.C. (1875–1955)
Betjeman, Sir John (Poet Laureate); London (1906–1984)
Bettelheim, Bruno (psychoanalyst); Vienna (1903–1990)
Bierce, Ambrose Gwinnett (journalist); Meigs County, Ohio (1842–1914?)
Bikel, Theodore (actor, folk singer); Vienna, 5/2/24
Bing, Sir Rudolf (opera manager); Vienna (1902–1997)
Bingham, George Caleb (painter); Augusta Co., Va. (1811–1879)
Binoche, Juliette (actress); Paris, 3/9/64
Bishop, Joey (Joseph Gottlieb) (comedian); New York City, 2/3/19
Bismarck-Schönhausen, Prince Otto Eduard Leopold von (statesman); Schönhausen, Germany (1815–1898)
Bisset, Jacqueline (actress); Weybridge, England, 9/13/44
Bixby, Bill (actor); San Francisco (1934–1993)
Bizet, Georges (Alexandre César Léopold Bizet) (composer); Paris (1838–1875)
Bjoerling, Jussi (tenor); Stora Tuna, Sweden (1911–1960)
Björk (Björk Gudmundsdottir) (pop musician, singer); Reykjavik, Iceland, 11/21/65
Black, Clint (singer, songwriter); Long Branch, N.J., 2/4/62
Black, Karen (actress); Park Ridge, Ill., 7/1/42
Black, Shirley Temple (child actress, former ambassador); Santa Monica, Calif., 4/23/28
Blackstone, Sir William (jurist); London (1723–1780)
Blackwell, Elizabeth (physician, educator); England (1821–1910)
Blades, Ruben (actor, musician, composer); Panama City, Panama, 7/16/48
Blair, Tony (British prime minister); Edinburgh, Scotland, 3/6/53
Blake, Amanda (Beverly Louise Neill) (actress); Buffalo, N.Y. (1929–1989)
Blake, Eubie (James Hubert) (pianist); Baltimore (1883–1983)
Blake, Robert (Michael Gubitosi) (actor); Nutley, N.J., 9/18/33
Blake, William (poet, artist); London (1757–1827)
Blanc, Mel (Melvin Jerome) (actor, voice specialist); San Francisco (1908–1989)
Blass, Bill (fashion designer); Fort Wayne, Ind., 6/22/22
Bleeth, Yasmine (model, actress); New York City, 6/14/68
Blige, Mary J. (hip-hop singer); Bronx, N.Y. , 1/11/71
Bloch, Ernest (composer); Geneva (1880–1959)
Bloom, Claire (actress); London, 2/15/31
Bloomgarden, Kermit (producer); Brooklyn, N.Y. (1904–1976)
Blume, Judy (Judy Sussman) (young adult novelist); Elizabeth, N.J., 2/12/38
Bly, Nellie (pseud. for Elizabeth Seaman) (journalist); Cochrane Mills, Pa. (1867–1922)
Bly, Robert (poet, critic); Madison, Minn., 12/23/26
Boccaccio, Giovanni (author); Paris (1313–1375)
Boccherini, Luigi (Rodolfo) (composer); Lucca, Italy (1743–1805)
Boccioni, Umberto (painter, sculptor); Reggio di Calabria, Italy (1882–1916)
Bochco, Steven (TV producer, writer); New York City, 12/16/43
Bock, Jerry (composer); New Haven, Conn., 11/23/28
Bogarde, Dirk (Derek Van den Bogaerde) (film actor, director); London (1921–1999)
Bogart, Humphrey DeForest (actor); New York City (1899–1957)
Bogdanovich, Peter (producer, director); Kingston, N.Y., 7/30/39
Bogosian, Eric (playwright, screenwriter, actor, monologuist); Woburn, Mass., 4/24/53
Bohlen, Charles E. (diplomat); Clayton, N.Y. (1904–1974)
Bohr, Niels (atomic physicist); Copenhagen (1885–1962)
Bok, Sissela (Sissela Ann Myrdal) (scholar); Stockholm, 12/2/34
Bolger, Ray (dancer, actor); Dorchester, Mass (1904–1987)
Bolívar, Simón (South American liberator); Caracas, Venezuela (1783–1830)
Bologna, Giovanni da (sculptor); Douai, France (1529–1608)
Bombeck, Erma (author, columnist); Dayton, Ohio (1927–1996)
Bonaparte, Napoleon (Emperor of the French); Ajaccio, Corsica, France (1769–1821)
Bond, Julian (Georgia legislator); Nashville, Tenn., 1/14/40
Bonet, Lisa (actress); San Francisco, 11/16/67
Bonham Carter, Helena (actress); London, 5/23/66
Bon Jovi, Jon (musician, songwriter); Sayreville, N.J., 3/2/62
Bonnard, Pierre (painter); Fontenayaux-Roses, France (1867–1947?)
Bono (Paul Hewson) (singer, songwriter); Dublin, Ireland, 5/10/60
Bono, Sonny (Salvatore Bono) (singer, politician); Detroit (1935–1998)

Boone, Daniel (frontiersman); nr. Reading, Pa. (1734–1820)
Boone, Pat (Charles Boone) (singer); Jacksonville, Fla., 6/1/34
Boone, Richard (actor); Los Angeles (1917–1981)
Boorstin, Daniel (historian); Atlanta, 10/1/14
Booth, Edwin Thomas (actor); Bel Air, Md. (1833–1893)
Booth, Evangeline Cory (religious leader); London (1865–1950)
Booth, John Wilkes (actor; assassin of Lincoln); Harford County, Md. (1838–1865)
Booth, Shirley (Thelma Booth Ford) (actress); New York City (1907–1992)
Borden, Lizzie (Elizabeth Andrew Borden) (accused murderer); Fall River, Mass. (1860–1927)
Borge, Victor (pianist, comedian); Copenhagen, 1/3/09
Borgia, Cesare (nobleman, soldier); Rome (1476–1507)
Borgia, Lucrezia (Duchess of Ferrara); Rome (1480–1519)
Borgnine, Ernest (actor); Hamden, Conn., 1/24/17
Borromini, Francesco (architect); Bissone, Italy (1599–1667)
Bosch, Hieronymus (Hieronymus van Aeken) (painter); Hertogenbosch, Netherlands (c. 1450–1516)
Bosley, Tom (actor); Chicago, 10/1/27
Bostwick, Barry (actor); San Mateo, Calif., 2/24/45
Boswell, James (diarist, biographer); Edinburgh, Scotland (1740–1795)
Botticelli, Sandro (Alessandro di Mariano dei Filipepi) (painter); Florence, Italy (1444–1510)
Bottoms, Timothy (actor); Santa Barbara, Calif., 8/30/50
Boulez, Pierre (conductor); Montbrison, France, 3/26/25
Bourke-White, Margaret (photographer); New York City (1906–1971)
Boutros-Ghali, Boutros (ex-Secretary General of the U.N.); Cairo, Egypt, 11/14/22
Bow, Clara (actress); Brooklyn, N.Y. (1905–1965)
Bowen, Catherine Drinker (biographer); Haverford, Pa. (1897–1973)
Bowie, David (David Robert Jones) (actor, musician); London, 1/8/47
Bowie, James (soldier); Burke County, Ga. (1799–1836)
Bowles, Chester (diplomat); Springfield, Mass. (1901–1986)
Boxleitner, Bruce (actor); Elgin, Ill., 5/12/50
Boyce, William (composer); London? (1710–1779)
Boyd, Bill ("Hopalong Cassidy") (actor); Cambridge, Ohio (1895–1972)
Boyd, Stephen (Stephen Millar) (actor); Belfast, Northern Ireland (1928–1977)
Boyer, Charles (actor); Figeac, France (1897–1978)
Boy George (George Alan O'Dowd) (singer); London, 6/14/61
Boyle, Peter (actor); Philadelphia, 10/18/33
Boyle, Robert (scientist); Lismore Castle, Munster, Ireland (1627–1691)
Bradbury, Ray Douglas (science-fiction writer); Waukegan, Ill., 8/22/20
Bradlee, Benjamin C. (editor); Boston, 8/26/21
Bradley, Ed (broadcast journalist); Philadelphia, 6/22/41
Bradley, Omar N. (5-star general); Clark, Mo. (1893–1981)
Bradley, Thomas (mayor of Los Angeles); Calvert, Tex. (1917–1998)
Brady, Mathew (early photographer); Warren Co., N.Y. (c. 1823–1896)
Brahe, Tycho (astronomer); Knudstrup, Denmark (1546–1601)
Bragg, Billy (singer, songwriter); Barking, England, 12/20/57
Brahms, Johannes (composer); Hamburg (1833–1897)
Braille, Louis (teacher of blind); Coupvray, France (1809–1862)
Brailowsky, Alexander (pianist); Kiev, Ukraine (1896–1976)
Bramante, Donato D'Agnolo (architect); Monte Asdrualdo (now Fermignano, Italy) (1444–1514)
Branagh, Kenneth (actor, director, writer, producer); Belfast, Northern Ireland, 12/10/60
Brancusi, Constantin (sculptor); Pestisansi, Romania (1876–1957)
Brandauer, Klaus Maria (Klaus Maria Steng) (actor); Bad Aussee, Steiermark, Austria , 6/22/44
Brando, Marlon (actor); Omaha, Neb., 4/3/24
Brandt, Willy (Herbert Frahm) (ex-Chancellor); Lübeck, Germany (1913– 1992)
Brandy (Brandy Norwood) (actress, singer); McComb, Miss., 2/11/79
Braque, Georges (painter); Argenteuil, France (1882–1963)
Bratt, Benjamin (actor); San Francisco, 12/16/63
Braugher, André (actor); Chicago, 7/1/62
Braxton, Toni (R&B singer); Severn, Maryland, 10/7/67
Brazelton, T(homas) Berry II (pediatrician, writer); Waco, Tex., 5/10/18
Brecht, Bertolt (dramatist, poet); Augsburg, Bavaria (1898–1956)
Brel, Jacques (singer, composer); Brussels (1929–1978)

Brennan, Walter (actor); Lynn, Mass. **(1894–1974)**
Brennan, William J., Jr. (Supreme Court Justice); Newark, N.J. **(1906–1997)**
Breslin, Jimmy (journalist); Jamaica, Queens, N.Y., 10/17/30
Breton, André (writer); Tinchebray, France **(1896–1966)**
Breuer, Marcel (architect, designer); Pécs, Hungary **(1902–1981)**
Brewster, Kingman, Jr. (ex-president of Yale); Longmeadow, Mass. **(1919–1988)**
Brezhnev, Leonid I. (Communist Party Secretary); Dneprodzerzhinsk, Ukraine **(1906–1982)**
Brice, Fanny (Fannie Borach) (comedienne); New York City **(1892–1951)**
Bridges, Beau (actor); Los Angeles, 12/9/41
Bridges, Jeff (actor); Los Angeles, 12/4/49
Bridges, Lloyd (actor); San Leandro, Calif. **(1913–1998)**
Brinkley, Christie (model, actress); Malibu, California, 2/2/54
Brinkley, David (TV newscaster); Wilmington, N.C., 7/10/20
Britten, Benjamin (composer); Lowestoft, England **(1913–1976)**
Broderick, Matthew (actor); New York City, 3/21/62
Brodsky, Joseph Alexandrovitch (poet); St. Petersburg, Russia **(1940–1996)**
Brody, Jane (journalist); Brooklyn, N.Y., 5/19/41
Brokaw, Tom (TV newscaster); Webster, S.D., 2/6/40
Brolin, James (actor); Los Angeles, 7/18/40
Bromfield, Louis (novelist); Mansfield, Ohio **(1896–1956)**
Bronson, Charles (Charles Buchinsky) (actor); Ehrenfield, Pa., 11/3/21
Brontë, Charlotte (novelist); Thornton, England **(1816–1855)**
Brontë, Emily Jane (novelist); Thornton, England **(1818–1848)**
Bronzino, Agnolo (painter); Monticelli, Italy **(1503–1572)**
Brook, Peter (director); London, 3/21/25
Brooke, Rupert (poet); Rugby, England **(1887–1915)**
Brooks, Albert (Albert Einstein) (actor, writer, director); Beverly Hills, Calif., 7/22/47
Brooks, Avery (actor) 4/18/49
Brooks, Gwendolyn (poet); Topeka, Kans., 6/7/17
Brooks, James L. (film and television producer); New York City, 5/9/40
Brooks, Mel (Melvin Kaminsky) (writer, film director); Brooklyn, N.Y., 6/28/26
Brosnan, Pierce (actor); County Meath, Ireland, 5/16/52
Brothers, Joyce (Bauer) (psychologist, author, radio-TV personality); New York City, 9/20/28
Broun, Matthew Heywood Campbell (journalist); Brooklyn, N.Y. **(1888–1939)**
Brown, Charles Brockden (novelist); Philadelphia **(1771–1810)**
Brown, Helen Gurley (editor, author); Green Forest, Ark., 2/18/22
Brown, James (singer); Augusta, Ga., 5/3/34
Brown, Joe E. (comedian); Holgate, Ohio **(1892–1973)**
Brown, John (abolitionist); Torrington, Conn. **(1800–1859)**
Brown, Les (band leader); Reinerton, Pa., 3/14/12
Brown, Margaret Wise (children's author); Brooklyn, N.Y. **(1910–1962)**
Brown, Trisha (choreographer); Aberdeen, Wash., 11/25/36
Browne, Jackson (singer, guitarist); Heidelberg, Germany, 10/9/48
Browning, Elizabeth Barrett (poet); Durham, England **(1806–1861)**
Browning, Robert (poet); London **(1812–1889)**
Brubeck, Dave (musician); Concord, Calif., 12/6/20
Bruce, Lenny (comedian); Long Island, N.Y. **(1926–1966)**
Bruce, Nigel (actor); Ensenada, Mexico **(1895–1953)**
Brueghel, Pieter (painter); nr. Breda, Flanders, Netherlands **(c. 1520–1569)**
Bruhn, Erik (Belton Evers) (ballet dancer); Copenhagen **(1928–1986)**
Brunelleschi, Filippo (architect); Florence, Italy **(1377–1446)**
Bruno, Giordano (philosopher); Nola, Italy **(1548–1600)**
Brutus, Marcus Junius (Roman politician) **(85–42 B.C.E.)**
Bryan, William Jennings (orator, politician); Salem, Ill. **(1860–1925)**
Bryant, Anita (singer); Barnsdall, Okla., 3/25/40
Bryant, William Cullen (poet, editor); Cummington, Mass. **(1794–1878)**
Brynner, Yul (Taidje Khan) (actor); Sakhalin Island, Russia **(1920–1985)**
Brzezinski, Zbigniew (ex-presidential adviser); Warsaw, 3/28/28
Buber, Martin (philosopher, theologian); Vienna **(1878–1965)**
Buchanan, Pat (politician); Washington, D.C., 11/2/38
Buchholz, Horst (actor); Berlin, 12/4/33
Büchner, Georg (dramatist); Goddelau, Germany **(1813–1837)**
Buchwald, Art (Arthur Buchwald) (columnist); Mount Vernon, N.Y., 10/20/25
Buck, Pearl S(ydenstricker) (author); Hillsboro, W. Va. **(1892–1973)**
Buckley, Christopher (writer); New York City, 1952

Buckley, Jeff (singer, songwriter); Orange County, Calif. **(1966–1997)**
Buckley, William F., Jr. (journalist); New York City, 11/24/25
Buffalo Bill (William Frederick Cody) (scout); Scott County, Iowa **(1846–1917)**
Buffett, Jimmy (singer, writer); Mobile, Ala., 12/25/46
Buffett, Warren (investment expert); Omaha, Neb., 8/30/30
Bujold, Genevieve (actress); Montreal, 7/1/42
Bujones, Fernando (ballet dancer); Miami, Fla., 3/9/55
Bulgakov, Mikhail (novelist); Kiev, Ukraine **(1891–1940)**
Bullins, Ed (playwright); Philadelphia, 7/2/35
Bullock, Sandra (actress); Washington D.C., 7/26/65
Bumbry, Grace (mezzo-soprano); St. Louis, 1/4/37
Bunche, Ralph J. (statesman); Detroit **(1904–1971)**
Bundy, McGeorge (educator); Boston **(1919–1996)**
Bundy, William Putnam (editor); Washington, D.C., 9/24/17
Buñuel, Luis (film director); Calanda, Spain **(1900–1983)**
Bunyan, John (preacher, author); Elstow, England **(1628–1688)**
Burbank, Luther (horticulturist); Lancaster, Mass. **(1849–1926)**
Burke, Adm. Arleigh A. (ex-Chief of Naval Operations); Boulder, Colo. **(1901–1996)**
Burke, Billie (comedienne); Washington, D.C. **(1885–1970)**
Burke, Delta (actress); Orlando, Fla., 7/30/56
Burke, Edmund (statesman); Dublin **(1729–1797)**
Burne-Jones, Edward Coley (painter); Birmingham, England **(1833–1898)**
Burnett, Carol (comedienne); San Antonio, 4/26/33
Burney, Fanny (Frances) (writer); King's Lynn, England **(1752–1840)**
Burns, Edward (actor, film director, screenwriter, producer); Long Island, N.Y., 1/29/68
Burns, George (Nathan Birnbaum) (comedian); New York City **(1896–1996)**
Burns, Ken (documentary filmmaker); Brooklyn, N.Y., 7/29/53
Burns, Robert (poet); Alloway, Scotland **(1759–1796)**
Burr, Aaron (political leader); Newark, N.J. **(1756–1836)**
Burr, Raymond (William Stacey Burr) (actor); New Westminster, British Columbia, Canada **(1917–1993)**
Burroughs, Edgar Rice (novelist); Chicago **(1875–1950)**
Burroughs, William S. (writer); St. Louis **(1914–1997)**
Burrows, Abe (playwright, director); New York City **(1910–1985)**
Burstyn, Ellen (Edna Rae Gillooly) (actress); Detroit, 12/7/32
Burton, LeVar (actor, director); Landsthul, Germany, 2/16/57
Burton, Richard (Richard Jenkins) (actor); Pontrhydfen, Wales **(1925–1984)**
Burton, Tim (filmmaker); Burbank, Calif., 8/25/58
Buscemi, Steve (actor); Brooklyn, New York, 12/13/57
Bush, George Herbert Walker (41st U.S. president); Milton, Mass., 6/12/24
Butkus, Dick (NFL linebacker, actor); Chicago, 12/9/42
Butler, Samuel (author); Langar, England **(1835–1902)**
Butterworth, Charles (actor); South Bend, Ind. **(1896–1946)**
Buttons, Red (Aaron Chwatt) (actor); New York City, 2/5/19
Buzzi, Ruth (comedienne); Westerly, R.I., 7/24/36
Byrd, Richard Evelyn (polar explorer); Winchester, Va. **(1888–1957)**
Byrne, David (composer, musician, director, actor); Dumbarton, Scotland, 5/14/52
Byrne, Gabriel (actor); Dublin, 5/12/50
Byron, George Gordon (6th Baron Byron) (poet); London **(1788–1824)**

C

Caan, James (actor); Queens, New York, 3/26/39
Caballé, Montserrat (soprano); Barcelona, Spain, 4/12/33
Cabot, John (Giovanni Caboto) (navigator); Genoa **(1450–1498)**
Cabot, Sebastian (navigator); Venice **(c. 1476–1557)**
Cadmus, Paul (painter, etcher); New York City, 12/17/04
Caesar, Irving (lyricist); New York City **(1895–1996)**
Caesar, Gaius Julius (statesman); Rome **(100–44 B.C.E.)**
Caesar, Sid (comedian); Yonkers, N.Y., 9/8/22
Cage, Nicolas (Nicolas Coppola) (actor); Long Beach, Calif., 1/7/64
Cagney, James (actor); New York City **(1899–1986)**
Cahn, Sammy (songwriter); New York City **(1913–1993)**
Caine, Michael (Maurice J. Micklewhite) (actor); London, 3/14/33
Calder, Alexander (sculptor); Lawnton, Pa. **(1898–1976)**
Calderón del al Barca, Pedro (dramatist); Madrid **(1600–1681)**
Caldwell, Erskine (novelist); White Oak, Ga. **(1903–1987)**
Caldwell, Sarah (opera director, conductor); Maryville, Mo., 3/6/24
Caldwell, Taylor (novelist); Manchester, England **(1900–1985)**
Caldwell, Zoe (actress); Hawthorn, Australia, 9/14/33
Calhoun, John Caldwell (statesman); nr. Calhoun Mills, S.C. **(1782–1850)**

Caligula Gaius Caesar (Roman emperor); Antium, Latium (12–41)

Calisher, Hortense (novelist); New York City, 12/20/11

Callas, Maria (Maria Calogeropoulos) (dramatic soprano); New York City (1923–1977)

Calloway, Cab (Cabell Calloway) (band leader); Rochester, N.Y. (1907–1994)

Calvin, John (Jean Chauvin) (religious reformer); Noyon, Picardy (1509–1564)

Calvin, Melvin (chemist, Nobel laureate); St. Paul, Minn. (1911–1997)

Cambridge, Godfrey (comedian); New York City (1933–1976)

Cameron, James (director); Kapuskasing, Ont., Canada, 8/16/54

Cameron, Rod (Rod Cox) (actor); Calgary, Alberta, Canada (1912–1983)

Campbell, Glen (singer); nr. Delight, Ark., 4/22/38

Campbell, Naomi (model); London, England, 5/22/70

Campbell, Neve (actress); Guelph, Ont., Canada, 10/3/73

Campion, Jane (director, screenwriter); Waikanae, New Zealand, 1954

Camus, Albert (author); Mondovi, Algeria (1913–1960)

Canaletto (Giovanni Antonio Canale) (painter); Venice (1697–1768)

Candy, John (actor, comedian); Toronto (1950–1994)

Caniff, Milton (cartoonist); Hillsboro, Ohio (1907–1988)

Cannon, Dyan (Samille Diane Friesen) (actress); Tacoma, Wash., 1/4/37

Cantinflas (Mario Moreno-Reyes) (comedian); Mexico City (1911–1993)

Cantor, Eddie (Edward Iskowitz) (actor); New York City (1892–1964)

Capone, Al(fonse) (gangster); Brooklyn, N.Y. (1899–1947)

Capote, Truman (novelist); New Orleans (1924–1984)

Capp, Al (Alfred Gerald Caplin) (cartoonist); New Haven, Conn. (1909–1979)

Capra, Frank (film producer, director); Palermo, Italy (1897–1991)

Caputo, Phil (Philip Joseph Caputo) (author, journalist); Chicago, 6/10/41

Caravaggio, Michelangelo Merisi da (painter); Caravaggio, Italy (1573–1610)

Cardin, Pierre (fashion designer); nr. Venice, 7/7/22

Cardinale, Claudia (actress); Tunis, Tunisia, 4/15/39

Carey, Drew (actor, producer); Cleveland, 5/23/58

Carey, Harry (actor); New York City (1878–1947)

Carey, Macdonald (actor); Sioux City, Iowa (1913–1994)

Carlin, George (comedian); Bronx, N.Y., 5/12/37

Carlisle, Kitty (singer, actress); New Orleans, 9/3/15

Carlyle, Thomas (essayist, historian); Ecclefechan, Scotland (1795–1881)

Carmichael, Hoagy (Hoagland Howard) (songwriter); Bloomington, Ind. (1899–1981)

Carne, Judy (Joyce Botterill) (singer, actress); Northampton, England, 4/27/39

Carnegie, Andrew (industrialist); Dunfermline, Scotland (1835–1919)

Carney, Art (actor); Mt. Vernon, N.Y., 11/4/18

Caron, Leslie (actress); Paris, 7/1/31

Carpenter, Mary Chapin (singer, songwriter); Princeton, New Jersey, 2/21/58

Carr, Vikki (Florencia Bisenta de Casillas Martinez Cardona) (singer); El Paso, Tex., 7/19/42

Carracci, Annibale (painter); Bologna, Italy (1560–1609)

Carracci, Lodovico (painter); Bologna, Italy (1555–1619)

Carradine, David (actor); Hollywood, Calif., 12/8/36

Carradine, John (actor); New York City (1906–1988)

Carradine, Keith (actor); San Mateo, Calif., 8/8/49

Carreras, José (tenor); Barcelona, Spain, 12/5/46

Carroll, Diahann (Carol Diahann Johnson) (singer, actress); Bronx, N.Y., 7/17/35

Carroll, Leo G. (actor); Weedon, England (1892–1972)

Carroll, Lewis (Charles Lutwidge Dodgson) (author, mathematician); Daresbury, England (1832–1898)

Carson, Jack (actor); Carmen, Man., Canada (1910–1963)

Carson, Johnny (TV entertainer); Corning, Iowa, 10/23/25

Carson, Kit (Christopher Carson) (scout); Madison County, Ky. (1809–1868)

Carson, Rachel (biologist, author); Springdale, Pa. (1907–1964)

Carter, Betty (jazz singer, composer); Flint, Mich. (1930–1998)

Carter, Chris (television and film writer, director, producer); Bellflower, Calif., 10/13/57

Carter, Dixie (actress); McLemoresville, Tenn., 5/25/39

Carter, Jack (comedian); New York City, 6/24/23

Carter, James Earl, Jr. (39th U.S. president); Plains, Ga., 10/1/24

Carter, Lynda (actress); Phoenix, Ariz., 7/24/51

Cartier, Jacques (explorer); Saint-Malo, Brittany, France (1491–1557)

Cartier-Bresson, Henri (photographer); Chanteloup, France, 8/22/08

Cartland, Barbara (author); England, 7/9/01

Caruso, Enrico (Errico Caruso) (tenor); Naples, Italy (1873–1921)

Carver, George Washington (botanist); Diamond Grove, Mo. (1864–1943)

Cary, Arthur Joyce Lunel (novelist); Londonderry, Ireland (1888–1957)

Casals, Pablo (cellist); Vendrell, Spain (1876–1973)

Casanova de Seingalt, Giovanni Jacopo (adventurer); Venice (1725–1798)

Case, Steve (business executive); Honolulu, 8/21/58

Cash, Johnny (singer); nr. Kingsland, Ark., 2/26/32

Cass, Peggy (comedienne); Boston (1924–1999)

Cassatt, Mary (painter); Allegheny, Pa. (1844–1926)

Cassavetes, John (director); New York City (1929–1989)

Cassidy, David (singer); New York City, 4/12/50

Cassidy, Jack (actor); Richmond Hill, Queens, N.Y. (1927–1976)

Cassidy, Shaun (actor, television producer, singer); Los Angeles, 9/27/58

Cassini, Oleg (Oleg Lolewski-Cassini) (fashion designer); Paris, 4/11/13

Castagno, Andrea del (painter); San Martino a Corella, Italy (c. 1421–1457)

Castaneda, Carlos (cultural anthropologist, author); Sao Paulo, Brazil (1931–1998)

Castle, Irene (Irene Foote) (actress, dancer); New Rochelle, N.Y. (1893–1969)

Castle, Vernon Blythe (dancer, aviator); Norwich, England (1887–1918)

Castro Ruz, Fidel (Premier); Mayari, Oriente, Cuba, 8/13/26

Cather, Willa Sibert (novelist); Winchester, Va. (1876–1947)

Cato, Marcus Porcius (called Cato the Elder) (statesman); Tusculum, Italy (234–149 B.C.E.)

Catt, Carrie Lane Chapman (woman suffragist); Ripon, Wis. (1859–1947)

Catton, Bruce (historian); Petoskey, Mich. (1899–1978)

Catullus, Gaius Valerius (poet); Verona (c. 84–c. 54 B.C.E.)

Cavallaro, Carmen (band leader); New York City (1913–1989)

Cavett, Dick (Richard Cavett) (TV entertainer); Gibbon, Neb., 11/19/36

Ceausescu, Nicolae (head of state); Scorniscesti, Romania (1918–1989)

Céline, Louis Ferdinand (pseud. of Louis Fuch Destouches) (novelist); Paris (1894–1961)

Cellini, Benvenuto (goldsmith, sculptor); Florence, Italy (1500–1571)

Cervantes Saavedra, Miguel de (novelist); Alcalá de Henares, Spain (1547–1616)

Cézanne, Paul (painter); Aix-en-Provence, France (1839–1906)

Chagall, Marc (painter); Vitebsk, Russia (1887–1985)

Chaliapin, Feodor Ivanovitch (operatic basso); Kazan, Russia (1873–1938)

Chamberlain, Arthur Neville (statesman); Edgbaston, England (1869–1940)

Chamberlain, Richard (actor, producer); Los Angeles, 3/31/35

Champion, Gower (choreographer); Geneva, Ill. (1921–1980)

Champion, Marge (actress, dancer); Los Angeles, 9/2/23

Champlain, Samuel de (explorer); nr. Rochefort, France (1567–1635)

Chan, Jackie (Chan Kwong Sang) (actor); Hong Kong, 4/7/54

Chancellor, John (TV commentator); Chicago (1927–1996)

Chandler, Jeff (actor); Brooklyn, N.Y. (1918–1961)

Chandler, Raymond (writer); Chicago (1883–1959)

Chanel, "Coco" (Gabriel Bonheur) (fashion designer); Issoire, France (1883–1971)

Chaney, Lon (actor); Colorado Springs, Colo. (1883–1930)

Channing, Carol (actress); Seattle, 1/31/23

Channing, Stockard (Susan Stockard) (actress); New York City, 2/13/44

Chaplin, Geraldine (actress); Santa Monica, Calif., 7/31/44

Chaplin, Sir Charles (actor); London (1889–1977)

Charisse, Cyd (Tula Finklea) (dancer, actress); Amarillo, Tex., 3/8/21

Charlemagne (Holy Roman Emperor); birthplace unknown (742–814)

Charles, Ray (Ray Charles Robinson) (pianist, singer, songwriter); Albany, Ga., 9/23/30

Charo (Maria Rosario Pilar Martinez) (actress); Murcia, Spain, 1/15/51

Chase, Chevy (Cornelius Crane Chase) (comedian); New York City, 10/8/43

Chase, Lucia (founder Ballet Theatre [now American Ballet Theatre]); Waterbury, Conn. **(1907–1986)**

Chateaubriand, François René de (writer, statesman); St. Malo, France **(1768–1848)**

Chaucer, Geoffrey (poet); London **(c. 1340–1400)**

Chuan, Leekpai (Prime Minister of Thailand); Muang District, Thailand, 7/28/38

Chávez, Carlos (composer); nr. Mexico City **(1899–1978)**

Chavez, Cesar (labor leader); nr. Yuma, Ariz. **(1927–1993)**

Chayefsky, Paddy (Sidney Chayefsky) (playwright); New York City **(1923–1981)**

Checker, Chubby (Ernest Evans) (performer); Philadelphia, 10/3/41

Cheever, John (novelist); Quincy, Mass. **(1912–1982)**

Chekhov, Anton Pavlovich (dramatist, short-story writer); Taganrog, Russia **(1860–1904)**

Cher (Cherilyn Sarkisian La Piere) (actress, singer); El Centro, Calif., 5/20/46

Cherubini, Luigi (composer); Florence **(1760–1842)**

Chesterton, Gilbert Keith (author); Kensington, England **(1874–1936)**

Chesnutt, Charles Waddell (author); Cleveland **(1858–1932)**

Chevalier, Maurice (entertainer); Paris **(1888–1972)**

Chiang Kai-shek (Chief of State); Feng-hwa, China **(1887–1975)**

Child, Julia (food expert); Pasadena, Calif., 8/15/12

Chippendale, Thomas (cabinet-maker); Otley, England **(1718–1779)**

Chirac, Jacques (President of France); Paris, 11/29/32

Chirico, Giorgio de (painter); Vólos, Greece **(1888–1978)**

Chisholm, Shirley Anita St. Hill (U.S. Representative); Brooklyn, N.Y., 11/30/24

Chlumsky, Anna (actress); Chicago, 12/3/80

Chomsky, (Avram) Noam (linguist, educator, activist); Philadelphia, 12/7/28

Chopin, Frédéric François (composer); nr. Warsaw **(1810–1849)**

Chopin, Kate O'Flaherty (author); St. Louis **(1851–1904)**

Chow, Yun-Fat (actor); Hong Kong, 5/18/55

Chrétien, Jean Joseph-Jacques (Prime Minister of Canada); Shawinigan, Quebec, 1/11/34

Christie, Agatha (mystery writer); Torquay, England **(1890–1976)**

Christie, Julie (actress); Chukua, India, 4/14/41

Chung, Connie (broadcast journalist); Washington, D.C., 8/20/46

Churchill, Sir Winston Leonard Spencer (statesman); Blenheim Palace, Oxfordshire, England **(1874–1965)**

Cicero, Marcus Tullius (orator, statesman); Arpinum, Italy **(106–43 B.C.E.)**

Cid, El (Rodrigo [or Ruy] Diez de Bivar) (Spanish national hero); nr. Burgos, Spain **(c. 1043–1099)**

Cilento, Diane (actress); Queensland, Australia, 10/5/33

Cimabue, Giovanni (painter); Florence, Italy **(c. 1240–c. 1302)**

Cimino, Michael (director, writer, producer); New York City, 11/16/43

Claire, Ina (Ina Fagan) (actress); Washington, D.C. **(1895–1985)**

Clancy, Tom (novelist); Baltimore, 4/12/47

Clapton, Eric (singer, guitarist); Ripley, England, 3/30/45

Clark, Dick (TV personality); Mt. Vernon, N.Y., 11/30/29

Clark, Mary Higgins (writer); New York City, 12/24/31

Clark, Petula (singer); Epsom, England, 11/15/34

Clark, Roy (country music artist); Meherrin, Va., 4/15/33

Clark, William (explorer); Caroline County, Va. **(1770–1838)**

Clarke, Arthur C. (science fiction writer); Minehead, England, 12/16/17

Claude Lorrain (Claude Gellée) (painter); Champagne, France **(1600–1682)**

Clausewitz, Karl von (military strategist); Burg, Germany **(1780–1831)**

Clay, Henry (statesman); Hanover County, Va. **(1777–1852)**

Clay, Lucius D. (banker, ex-general); Marietta, Ga. **(1897–1978)**

Clayburgh, Jill (actress); New York City, 4/30/44

Cleary, Beverly (Beverly Atlee Bunn) (children's author); McMinnville, Ore., 1916

Cleaver, Eldridge (Leroy) (author, activist); Wabbaseka, Ark. **(1935–1998)**

Cleese, John (writer, actor); Weston-super-Mare, England, 10/27/39

Clemenceau, Georges (statesman); Mouilleron-en-Pareds, Vondée, France **(1841–1929)**

Cleopatra (Queen of Egypt); Alexandria, Egypt **(69–30 B.C.E.)**

Cleveland, Stephen Grover (22nd & 24th U.S. president); Caldwell, N.J. **(1837–1908)**

Cliburn, Van (Harvey Lavan Cliburn, Jr.) (concert pianist); Shreveport, La., 7/12/34

Clift, Montgomery (actor); Omaha, Neb. **(1920–1966)**

Cline, Patsy (singer); Winchester, Va. **(1933–1963)**

Clinton, Hillary Rodham (First Lady); Park Ridge, Ill., 10/26/47

Clinton, William Jefferson (42nd U.S. president); Hope, Ark., 8/19/46

Clooney, George (actor); Lexington, Ky., 5/6/61

Clooney, Rosemary (singer); Maysville, Ky., 5/23/28

Close, Glenn (actress); Greenwich, Conn., 3/19/47

Clurman, Harold (stage producer); New York City **(1901–1980)**

Cobain, Kurt (musician); Hoquiam, Washington **(1967–1994)**

Cobb, Irvin Shrewsbury (humorist); Paducah, Ky. **(1876–1944)**

Cobb, Lee J. (Leo Jacob Cobb) (actor); New York City **(1911–1976)**

Coburn, Charles Douville (actor); Savannah, Ga. **(1877–1961)**

Coburn, James (actor); Laurel, Neb., 8/31/28

Coca, Imogene (comedienne); Philadelphia, 11/18/08

Cocker, Jarvis (singer, songwriter); Sheffield, England, 9/19/63

Cocker, Joe (John Robert Cocker) (singer); Sheffield, England, 5/20/44

Coco, James (actor); New York City **(1929–1987)**

Cocteau, Jean (author); Maison-Lafitte, France **(1891–1963)**

Cohan, George Michael (actor, dramatist); Providence, R.I. **(1878–1942)**

Cohen, Leonard (composer); Montreal, Quebec, Canada, 9/21/34

Colbert, Claudette (Lily Chauchoin) (actress); Paris **(1903–1996)**

Cole, Nat "King" (singer); Montgomery, Ala. **(1919–1965)**

Cole, Natalie (singer); Los Angeles, 2/6/50

Cole, Paula (singer, songwriter); Rockport, Mass., 4/15/68

Cole, Thomas (painter); Lancashire, England **(1801–1848)**

Coleman, Dabney (actor); Austin, Tex., 1/3/32

Coleridge, Samuel Taylor (poet); Ottery St. Mary, England **(1772–1834)**

Colette (Sidonie-Gabrielle Colette) (novelist); St.-Sauveur, France **(1873–1954)**

Collingwood, Charles (TV commentator); Three Rivers, Mich. **(1917–1985)**

Collins, Joan (actress); London, 5/23/33

Collins, Judy (singer); Seattle, 5/1/39

Colman, Ronald (actor); Richmond, England **(1891–1958)**

Colonna, Jerry (comedian); Boston **(1905–1986)**

Coltrane, John (jazz musician); Hamlet, N.C. **(1926–1967)**

Columbo, Russ (singer, bandleader); San Francisco **(1908–1934)**

Columbus, Chris (director, screenwriter); Spangler, Pa., 9/10/58

Columbus, Christopher (Cristoforo Colombo) (explorer); Genoa, Italy **(1451–1506)**

Colvin, Shawn (folk singer); Vermillion, S.D., 1/10/58

Combs, Sean "Puffy" (singer, record producer); New York City, 11/9/69

Comden, Betty (writer); New York City, 5/3/19

Comenius, Johann Amos (educational reformer); Nivnice, Moravia, Czech Republic **(1592–1670)**

Commager, Henry Steele (historian); Pittsburgh **(1902–1998)**

Como, Perry (Pierino Como) (singer); Canonsburg, Pa., 5/18/12

Compton, Karl Taylor (physicist); Wooster, Ohio **(1887–1954)**

Comte, Auguste (philosopher); Montpellier, France **(1798–1857)**

Conant, James B. (educator, statesman); Dorchester, Mass. **(1893–1978)**

Condon, Eddie (jazz musician); Goodland, Ind. **(1905–1973)**

Confucius (K'ung Fu-tzu) (philosopher); Shantung province, China **(c. 551– 479 B.C.E.)**

Congreve, William (dramatist); nr. Leeds, England **(1670–1729)**

Connelly, Marc (playwright); McKeesport, Pa. **(1890–1980)**

Connery, Sean (actor); Edinburgh, Scotland, 8/25/30

Connick, Jr., Harry (musician, actor); New Orleans, La., 9/11/67

Conniff, Ray (band leader); Attleboro, Mass., 11/6/16

Connors, Chuck (actor); Brooklyn, N.Y. **(1921–1992)**

Connors, Mike (Krekor Ohanian) (actor); Fresno, Calif., 8/15/25

Conrad, Joseph (Teodor Jozef Konrad Korzeniowski) (novelist); Berdichev, Ukraine **(1857–1924)**

Conrad, Robert (Conrad Robert Falk) (actor); Chicago, 3/1/35

Conrad, William (actor); Louisville, Ky. **(1920–1994)**

Conried, Hans (Frank Foster) (actor); Baltimore **(1915–1982)**

Conroy, Pat (author); Atlanta, 10/26/45

Constable, John (painter); East Bergholt, Suffolk, England **(1776–1837)**

Constantine II (ex-king of Greece); Athens, 6/2/40

Constantine, Michael (actor); Reading, Pa., 5/22/27

Conte, Richard (actor); New York City **(1916–1975)**

Conti, Tom (actor); Paisley, Scotland, 11/22/41

Convy, Bert (actor, host); St. Louis **(1933–1991)**

Conway, Tim (comedian); Chagrin Falls, Ohio, 12/15/33

Coogan, Jackie (actor); Los Angeles **(1914–1984)**

Cook, Peter (actor, writer); Torquay, England **(1937–1995)**

Cooke, Alistair (Alfred Alistair) (TV narrator, journalist); Manchester, England, 11/20/08

Cooke, Jack Kent (business executive); Hamilton, Ont., Canada **(1912–1997)**

Cooley, Denton A(rthur) (heart surgeon); Houston, 8/22/20

Coolidge, (John) Calvin (30th U.S. president); Plymouth, Vt. **(1872–1933)**

Coolidge, Rita (singer); Nashville, Tenn., 5/1/45

Coolio (Artis Ivey, Jr.) (rap artist); Los Angeles, California, 8/1/63

Cooper, Alice (Vincent Furnier) (rock musician); Detroit, 2/4/48

Cooper, Gary (Frank James Cooper) (actor); Helena, Mont. **(1901–1961)**

Cooper, Dame Gladys (actress); Lewisham, England **(1898–1971)**

Cooper, Jackie (actor, director); Los Angeles, 9/15/22

Cooper, James Fenimore (novelist); Burlington, N.J. **(1789–1851)**

Cooper, Peter (industrialist, philanthropist); New York City **(1791–1883)**

Copernicus, Nicolaus (Mikolaj Kopernik) (astronomer); Thorn, Poland **(1473–1543)**

Copland, Aaron (composer); Brooklyn, N.Y. **(1900–1990)**

Copley, John Singleton (painter); Boston **(1738–1815)**

Copperfield, David (David Kotkin) (illusionist); Metuchen, N.J., 9/16/56

Coppola, Francis Ford (film director); Detroit, 4/7/39

Corelli, Arcangelo (composer); Fusignano, Italy **(1653–1713)**

Corelli, Franco (operatic tenor); Ancona, Italy, 4/8/23

Corgan, Billy (musician); Elk Grove, Ill., 3/17/67

Corneille, Pierre (dramatist); Rouen, France **(1606–1684)**

Cornell, Katharine (actress); Berlin **(1893–1974)**

Corot, Jean Baptiste Camille (painter); Paris **(1796–1875)**

Corella, Angel (ballet dancer); Madrid, Spain, 11/8/75

Correggio, Antonio Allegri da (painter); Correggio, Italy **(1494–1534)**

Corsaro, Frank (opera director); New York harbor, 12/22/24

Cortés (or Cortez), Hernando (explorer); Medellin, Spain **(1485–1547)**

Cosby, Bill (actor); Philadelphia, 7/12/37

Cosell, Howard (Howard Cohen) (sportscaster); Winston-Salem, N.C. **(1918–1995)**

Costello, Elvis (Declan Patrick McManus) (singer, musician, songwriter); London, 1954

Costello, Lou (comedian); Paterson, N.J. **(1908–1959)**

Costner, Kevin (actor); Los Angeles, 1/18/55

Cotten, Joseph (actor); Petersburg, Va. **(1905–1994)**

Couperin, François (composer); Paris **(1668–1733)**

Courbet, Gustave (painter); Ornans, France **(1819–1877)**

Couric, Katie (TV host); Arlington, Va., 1/7/57

Courtenay, Tom (actor); Hull, England, 2/25/37

Cousins, Norman (publisher); Union Hill, N.J. **(1915–1990)**

Cousteau, Jacques-Yves (marine explorer); St. André-de-Cubzac, France **(1910–1997)**

Covey, Stephen R. (author); Salt Lake City, 10/24/32

Coward, Sir Noel (playwright, actor); Teddington, England **(1899–1973)**

Cowles, Gardner, Jr. (newspaper publisher); Algona, Iowa **(1903–1985)**

Cowper, William (poet); Great Berkhamstead, England **(1731–1800)**

Cox, Archibald (Watergate prosecutor); Plainfield, N.J., 5/17/12

Cox, Courteney (actress); Birmingham, Ala., 6/15/64

Coyote, Peter (actor); New York City, 10/10/41

Cozzens, James Gould (novelist); Chicago **(1903–1978)**

Crabbe, Buster (Clarence Crabbe) (actor); Oakland, Calif. **(1908–1983)**

Cranach, Lucas, the elder (painter); Kronach, Germany **(1472–1553)**

Crane, Hart (poet); Garrettsville, Ohio **(1899–1932)**

Crane, Stephen (novelist, poet); Newark, N.J. **(1871–1900)**

Cranmer, Thomas (churchman); Aslacton, England **(1489–1556)**

Craven, Wes (director, producer, screenwriter); Cleveland, 8/2/39

Crawford, Broderick (actor); Philadelphia **(1911–1986)**

Crawford, Cheryl (stage producer); Akron, Ohio **(1902–1986)**

Crawford, Cindy (model, actress); De Kalb, Illinois, 2/20/66

Crawford, Joan (Lucille LeSueur) (actress, business executive); San Antonio **(1908–1977)**

Crazy Horse (Lakota Indian leader); nr. Bear Butte, S.D. **(1840?–1877)**

Crenna, Richard (actor); Los Angeles, 11/30/27

Crespin, Régine (operatic soprano); Marseilles, France, 2/23/29

Crichton, (John) Michael (novelist, film producer); Chicago, 10/23/42

Crick, Francis Harry Compton (scientist, Nobel laureate); Northampton, England, 6/8/16

Crisp, Donald (actor); London **(1880–1974)**

Croce, Benedetto (philosopher); Peseasseroli, Aquila, Italy **(1866–1952)**

Croce, Jim (singer); Philadelphia **(1942–1973)**

Crockett, Davy (David) (frontiersman); Greene County, Tenn. **(1786–1836)**

Cromwell, Oliver (statesman); Huntingdon, England **(1599–1658)**

Cronenberg, David (film director); Toronto, Canada, 3/15/43

Cronin, A. J. (Archibald J. Cronin) (novelist); Cardross, Scotland **(1896–1981)**

Cronkite, Walter (TV newscaster); St. Joseph, Mo., 11/4/16

Cronyn, Hume (actor); London, Ont., Canada, 7/18/11

Crosby, Bing (Harry Lillis) (singer, actor); Tacoma, Wash. **(1904–1977)**

Crosby, Bob (musician); Spokane, Wash. **(1913–1993)**

Crosby, Cathy Lee (actress); Los Angeles, 12/2/48

Crosby, Norm (comedian); Boston, 9/15/27

Cross, Ben (Bernard) (actor); Paddington, England, 12/16/47

Cross, Milton (opera commentator); New York City **(1897–1975)**

Crouse, Russel (playwright); Findlay, Ohio **(1893–1966)**

Crow, Sheryl (musician, record producer); Kennett, Mo., 2/11/62

Crowe, Russell (actor, musician); Auckland, New Zealand , 4/7/64

Crudup, Billy (actor); Manhasset, N.Y., 7/8/68

Cruise, Tom (Thomas Mapother IV) (actor, producer); Syracuse, N.Y., 7/3/62

Crystal, Billy (comedian, actor); Long Beach, N.Y., 3/14/47

Cugat, Xavier (band leader); Barcelona, Spain **(1900–1990)**

Cukor, George (film director); New York City **(1899–1983)**

Culkin, Macaulay (actor); New York City, 8/26/80

Cullen, Bill (William Lawrence Cullen) (radio and TV entertainer); Pittsburgh **(1920–1990)**

Cullen, Countee (poet); New York City **(1903–1946)**

Culp, Robert (actor); Berkeley, Calif., 8/16/30

cummings, e. e. (Edward Estlin Cummings) (poet); Cambridge, Mass. **(1894–1962)**

Cummings, Robert (actor); Joplin, Mo. **(1908–1990)**

Cunningham, Merce (choreographer); Centralia, Wash., 4/16/19

Curie, Marie (Marja Sklodowska) (physical chemist, Nobel laureate); Warsaw **(1867–1934)**

Curie, Pierre (physicist); Paris **(1859–1906)**

Curtin, Jane (actress); Cambridge, Mass., 9/6/47

Curtin, Phyllis (soprano); Clarksburg, W. Va., 12/3/27

Curtis, Jamie Lee (actress); Los Angeles, 11/22/58

Curtis, Tony (Bernard Schwartz) (actor); Bronx, N.Y., 6/3/25

Curzon, Clifford (concert pianist); London **(1907–1982)**

Cusaok, Joan (actress); New York City, 10/11/62

Cusack, John (actor); Chicago, 6/28/66

Custer, George Armstrong (army officer); New Rumley, Ohio **(1839–1876)**

D

Dafoe, Willem (William Dafoe, Jr.) (actor); Appleton, Wis., 7/22/55

da Gama, Vasco (explorer); Sines, Portugal **(1460–1524)**

Daguerre, Louis (photographic pioneer); nr. Paris **(1787–1851)**

Dahl, Arlene (actress); Minneapolis, 8/11/28

Dalai Lama (Tenzin Gyatso) (spiritual and temporal head of Tibet); Taktser, China, 1935

Daley, Richard J. (Mayor of Chicago); Chicago **(1902–1976)**

Dali, Salvador (painter); Figueras, Spain **(1904–1989)**

Dalton, John (chemist); nr. Cockermouth, England **(1766–1844)**

Dalton, Timothy (actor); Colwyn Bay, Wales, U.K., 3/21/46

Daly, Tyne (actress); Madison, Wis., 2/21/46

d'Amboise, Jacques (ballet dancer); Dedham, Mass., 7/28/34

Damone, Vic (Vito Farinola) (singer); Brooklyn, N.Y., 6/12/28

Damrosch, Walter Johannes (orchestra conductor); Breslau, Poland **(1862–1950)**

Dana, Charles Anderson (editor); Hinsdale, N.H. **(1819–1897)**

Dandridge, Dorothy (actress); Cleveland **(1923–1965)**

Danes, Claire (actress); New York City, 4/12/79

Dangerfield, Rodney (Jacob Cohen) (actor, comedian); Babylon, N.Y., 11/22/22

Daniels, Jeff (actor); Chelsea, Mich., 2/19/55

Daniels, William (actor); Brooklyn, N.Y., 3/31/27

Danilova, Alexandra (ballet dancer); Peterhof, Russia **(1904–1997)**

Dannay, Frederic (novelist, pseudonym Ellery Queen); Brooklyn, N.Y. **(1905–1982)**

Danner, Blythe (actress); Philadelphia, 2/3/43

D'Annunzio, Gabriele (soldier, author); Francaville at Mare, Pescara, Italy **(1863–1938)**

Danson, Ted (actor); San Diego, Calif., 12/29/47

Dante (or Durante) Alighieri (poet); Florence, Italy **(1265–1321)**

Danton, Georges Jacques (French Revolutionary leader); Arcis-sur-Aube, France **(1759–1794)**

Danza, Tony (actor); Brooklyn, N.Y., 4/21/51
Darren, James (actor); Philadelphia, 6/8/36
Darrow, Clarence Seward (lawyer); Kinsman, Ohio **(1857–1938)**
Darwin, Charles Robert (naturalist); Shrewsbury, England **(1809–1882)**
Dassin, Jules (film director); Middletown, Conn., 12/18/11
Daumier, Honoré (caricaturist); Marseilles, France **(1808–1879)**
David, Jacques-Louis (painter); Paris **(1748–1825)**
David (King of Israel and Judah;) died c. 973 B.C.E.
Davidson, John (singer, actor); Pittsburgh, 12/13/41
Davies, Marion (Marion Douras) (actress); New York City **(1897–1961)**
Davies, (William) Robertson (writer); Thamesville, Ont., Canada **(1913–1996)**
Davis, Angela (social activist); Birmingham, Ala., 1/26/44
Davis, Ann B. (actress); Schenectady, N.Y., 5/5/26
Davis, Lt. Gen. Benjamin O., Jr. (Air Force general); Washington, D.C., 12/18/12
Davis, Brig. Gen. Benjamin O., Sr. (U.S. Army general); Washington, D.C. **(1877–1970)**
Davis, Bette (actress); Lowell, Mass. **(1908–1989)**
Davis, Geena (Virginia Davis) (actress); Wareham, Mass., 1/21/57
Davis, Jefferson (President of the Confederacy); Christian (now Todd) County, Ky. **(1808–1889)**
Davis, Judy (actress); Perth, Australia, 1955
Davis, Mac (singer); Lubbock, Tex., 1/21/42
Davis, Miles (jazz trumpeter); Alton, Ill. **(1926–1991)**
Davis, Ossie (actor, writer); Cogdell, Ga., 12/18/17
Davis, Sammy, Jr. (actor, singer); New York City **(1925–1990)**
Davis, Stuart (painter); Philadelphia **(1894–1964)**
Dawson, Richard (actor, host); Gosport, Hampshire, England, 11/20/32
Day, Doris (Doris von Kappelhoff) (singer, actress); Cincinnati, 4/3/24
Dayan, Moshe (ex-Defense Minister of Israel); Dagania, Palestine **(1915–1981)**
Day-Lewis, Daniel (actor); London, 4/29/58
Dean, James (actor); Marion, Ind. **(1931–1955)**
Dean, Jimmy (singer); Seth Ward, nr. Plainview, Tex., 8/10/28
De Bakey, Michael E. (heart surgeon); Lake Charles, La., 9/7/08
de Beauvoir, Simone (novelist, philosopher); Paris **(1908–1986)**
Debs, Eugene Victor (Socialist leader); Terre Haute, Ind. **(1855–1926)**
Debussy, Claude Achille (composer); St. Germain-en-Laye, France **(1862–1918)**
De Carlo, Yvonne (Peggy Yvonne Middleton) (actress); Vancouver, B.C., Canada, 9/1/24
de Chirico, Giorgio (painter); Volos, Greece **(1888–1978)**
Dee, Ruby (Ruby Ann Wallace) (actress); Cleveland, 10/27/24
Dee, Sandra (Alexandra Zuck) (actress); Bayonne, N.J., 4/23/42
Degas, Hilaire Germain Edgar (painter); Paris **(1834–1917)**
de Gaulle, Charles André Joseph Marie (soldier, statesman); Lille, France **(1890–1970)**
de Havilland, Olivia (actress); Tokyo, 7/1/16
de Kooning, Willem (artist); Rotterdam **(1904–1997)**
Delacroix, Eugène (painter); Charenton-St. Maurice, France **(1798–1863)**
Delany, Dana (actress); New York City, 3/15/56
de la Renta, Oscar (fashion designer); Santo Domingo, Dominican Republic, 7/22/32
Delaunay, Robert (painter); Paris **(1885–1941)**
De Laurentiis, Dino (film producer); Torre Annunziata, Bay of Naples, Italy, 8/8/18
della Robbia, Andrea (sculptor); Florence **(1435–1525)**
della Robbia, Luca (sculptor); Florence **(1400–1482)**
Delon, Alain (actor); Sceaux, France, 11/8/35
Del Toro, Benicio (actor); Santurce, Puerto Rico, 2/19/67
DeLuise, Dom (actor, comedian); Brooklyn, N.Y., 8/1/33
Demarest, William (actor); St. Paul, Minn. **(1892–1983)**
de Mille, Agnes (choreographer); New York City **(1905–1993)**
De Mille, Cecil Blount (film director); Ashfield, Mass. **(1881–1959)**
Demme, Jonathan (director, producer, screenwriter); Baldwin, New York, 2/22/44
Demosthenes (orator); Athens **(384?–322 B.C.E.)**
Dench, Dame Judi (film and stage actress); York, England, 12/9/34
Deneuve, Catherine (actress); Paris, 10/22/43
Deng Xiaoping (Chinese leader); Sichuan province, China **(1904–1997)**
De Niro, Robert (actor, director); New York City, 8/17/43
Dennehy, Brian (actor); Bridgeport, Conn., 7/9/39
Denning, Richard (actor); Poughkeepsie, N.Y. **(1914–1998)**
Dennis, Sandy (actress); Hastings, Neb. **(1937–1992)**
Denny, Reginald (actor); Richmond, England **(1891–1967)**

Denver, John (Henry John Deutschendorf, Jr.) (singer, actor); Roswell, N.M. **(1943–1997)**
De Palma, Brian (film director); Newark, N.J., 9/11/40
Depp, Johnny (actor); Owensboro, Ky., 6/9/63
Derain, André (painter); Chatou, Seine-et-Oise, France **(1880–1954)**
Derek, John (actor, director); Los Angeles **(1926–1998)**
Dern, Bruce (actor); Winnetka, Ill., 6/4/36
Dern, Laura (actress); Los Angeles, 2/10/67
Dershowitz, Alan (lawyer); Brooklyn, N.Y., 9/1/38
Derrida, Jacques (philosopher); El-Biar, Algeria, 7/15/30
Descartes, René (philosopher, mathematician); La Haye, France **(1596–1650)**
De Seversky, Alexander P. (aviator); Tiflis (Tilisi), Georgia **(1894–1974)**
De Sica, Vittorio (film director); Sora, Italy **(1901–1974)**
Desmond, Johnny (composer); Detroit **(1921–1985)**
De Soto, Hernando (explorer); Barcarrota, Spain **(c. 1500–1542)**
De Valera, Eamon (ex-President of Ireland); New York City **(1882–1975)**
Devane, William (actor); Albany, N.Y., 9/5/39
Devine, Andy (actor); Flagstaff, Ariz. **(1905–1977)**
DeVito, Danny (Daniel Michael DeVito) (actor, director, producer); Neptune, N.J., 11/17/44
De Vries, Peter (novelist); Chicago **(1910–1993)**
de Waart, Edo (conductor); Amsterdam, the Netherlands, 6/1/41
Dewey, George (admiral); Montpelier, Vt. **(1837–1917)**
Dewey, John (philosopher, educator); Burlington, Vt. **(1859–1952)**
Dewey, Thomas E. (political figure); Owosso, Mich. **(1902–1971)**
Dewhurst, Colleen (actress); Montreal **(1926–1991)**
Dey, Susan (actress); Pekin, Ill., 12/10/52
Diaghilev, Sergei (ballet impressario); Novgorod, Russia **(1872–1929)**
Diamond, Neil (singer); Brooklyn, N.Y., 1/24/41
Diana (Diana Frances Spencer) (Princess of Wales); Sandringham, England **(1961–1997)**
Diaz, Cameron (actress, model); San Diego, Calif., 8/30/72
DiCaprio, Leonardo (actor); Los Angeles, 11/11/74
Dichter, Misha (pianist); Shanghai, 9/27/45
Dickens, Charles John Huffam (novelist); Portsea, England **(1812–1870)**
Dickey, James (writer); Atlanta **(1923–1997)**
Dickinson, Angie (Angeline Brown) (actress); Kulm, N.D., 9/30/31
Dickinson, Emily Elizabeth (poet); Amherst, Mass. **(1830–1886)**
Diddley, Bo (Elias McDaniel) (guitarist); McComb, Miss., 12/30/28
Diderot, Denis (encyclopedist); Langres, France **(1713–1784)**
Dietrich, Marlene (Maria Magdalena von Losch) (actress); Berlin **(1901–1992)**
DiFranco, Ani (singer, songwriter); Buffalo, New York, 9/23/70
Diller, Phyllis (Phyllis Driver) (comedienne); Lima, Ohio, 7/17/17
Dillon, Matt (actor); New Rochelle, N.Y., 2/18/64
Dine, Jim (painter); Cincinnati, 6/16/35
Dinesen, Isak (Karen Blixen) (author); Rungsted, Denmark **(1885–1962)**
Dinkins, David (ex-Mayor of New York City); Trenton, N.J., 7/10/27
Diogenes (philosopher); Sinope, Turkey **(c. 412–323 B.C.E.)**
Dion (Dion DiMucci) (singer); Bronx, N.Y., 7/18/39
Dion, Celine (musician); Charlemagne, Que., Canada, 3/30/68
Dior, Christian (fashion designer); Granville, France **(1905–1957)**
Disney, Walt(er) Elias (film animator, producer); Chicago **(1901–1966)**
Disraeli, Benjamin (Earl of Beaconsfield) (statesman); London **(1804–1881)**
Dix, Dorothea (civil rights reformer); Hampden, Maine **(1802–1887)**
Dixon, Jeane (Jeane Pinckert) (seer); Medford, Wis. **(1918–1997)**
Dobbs, Mattiwilda (soprano); Atlanta, 7/11/25
Doctorow, E(dgar) L(aurence) (novelist); New York City, 1/6/31
Dogg, Snoop Doggy (Calvin Broadus) (musician); Long Beach, California , 10/20/72
Doherty, Shannen (actress); Memphis, Tenn., 4/21/71
Dole, Elizabeth Hanford (public official); Salisbury, N.C., 7/29/36
Dole, Robert (political figure); Russell, Kans., 7/22/23
Dolin, Anton (dancer); Slinfold, England **(1904–1983)**
Domingo, Placido (tenor); Madrid, 1/21/41
Domino, Fats (Antoine) (musician); New Orleans, 2/26/28
Donahue, Phil (TV host); Cleveland, 12/21/35
Donahue, Troy (Merle Johnson) (actor); New York City, 1/27/36
Donaldson, Sam (broadcast journalist); El Paso, Tex., 3/11/34
Donat, Robert (actor); Withington, England **(1905–1958)**
Donatello (Donato Niccolò di Betto Bardi) (sculptor); Florence **(c. 1386–1466)**
Donlevy, Brian (actor); Portadown, Ireland **(1899–1972)**
Donne, John (poet); London **(1573–1631)**

Donner, Richard (director, producer); New York City, 1939
D'Onofrio, Vincent (actor); Brooklyn, N.Y., 6/30/59
Donovan (Donovan Leitch) (singer, songwriter); Glasgow, Scotland, 2/10/46
Doolittle, James H. (ex-Air Force general); Alameda, Calif. **(1896–1993)**
Doohan, James (actor); Vancouver, B.C., 3/20/20
Dorati, Antal (orchestra conductor); Budapest **(1906–1988)**
Dorn, Michael (actor); Luling, Tex., 12/9/52
Dorris, Michael (anthropologist, writer); Louisville, Ky. **(1945–1997)**
Dorsey, Jimmy (band leader); Shenandoah, Pa. **(1904–1957)**
Dorsey, Thomas Andrew (father of gospel music); Villa Rice, Ga. **(1899–1993)**
Dorsey, Tommy (band leader); Mahanoy Plane, Pa. **(1905–1956)**
Dos Passos, John (author); Chicago **(1896–1970)**
Dostoevski, Fyodor Mikhailovich (novelist); Moscow **(1821–1881)**
Dotrice, Roy (actor); Guernsey, Channel Islands, England, 5/26/23
Douglas, Aaron (painter); Topeka, Kans. **(1900–1979)**
Douglas, Helen Gahagan (ex-Representative); Boonton, N.J. **(1900–1980)**
Douglas, Kirk (Issur Danielovitch) (actor); Amsterdam, N.Y., 12/9/16
Douglas, Melvyn (Melvyn Hesselberg) (actor); Macon, Ga. **(1901–1981)**
Douglas, Michael (actor, producer); New Brunswick, N.J., 9/25/44
Douglas, Mike (Michael D. Dowd, Jr.) (TV host); Chicago, 8/11/25
Douglas, Stephen Arnold (politician); Brandon, Vt. **(1813–1861)**
Douglass, Frederick (abolitionist, author, orator); Tuckahoe, Md. **(1817–1895)**
Dow, Charles (financier); Sterling, Conn. **(1851–1902)**
Down, Lesley-Ann (actress); London, 3/17/54
Downey, Robert, Jr. (actor, director); New York City, 4/4/65
Downs, Hugh (broadcast journalist); Akron, Ohio, 2/14/21
Doyle, Sir Arthur Conan (novelist, spiritualist); Edinburgh, Scotland **(1859–1930)**
Doyle, David (actor); Lincoln, Neb. **(1929–1997)**
Drake, Sir Francis (navigator); Tavistock, England **(1545–1596)**
Dr. Dre (Andre Young) (rap singer); Los Angeles, 2/18/66
Dreiser, Theodore (writer); Terre Haute, Ind. **(1871–1945)**
Drescher, Fran (television and film actress); New York City, 9/30/57
Dreyfus, Alfred (French army officer); Mulhouse, France **(1859–1935)**
Dreyfuss, Richard (actor); Brooklyn, N.Y., 10/29/47
Drury, Allen (novelist); Houston **(1918–1998)**
Dryden, John (poet); Northamptonshire, England **(1631–1700)**
Dryer, Fred (ex-NFL player, actor); Hawthorne, Calif., 7/6/46
Dubček, Alexander (ex-President of Czechoslovakia); Uhroved, former Czechoslovakia **(1921–1992)**
Dubinsky, David (David Dobnievski) (labor leader); Brest-Litovsk, Belarus **(1892–1982)**
Du Bois, W(illiam) E(dward) B(urghardt) (scholar, civil rights activist); Great Barrington, Mass. **(1868–1963)**
Duchamp, Marcel (painter); Blainville, France **(1887–1968)**
Duchin, Eddy (pianist, bandleader); Cambridge, Mass. **(1909–1951)**
Duchin, Peter (pianist, band leader); New York City, 7/28/37
Duchovny, David (actor); New York City, 8/7/60
Dufay, Guillaume (composer); Cambrai, France **(c. 1400–1474)**
Duffy, Julia (actress); Minneapolis, Minn., 6/27/50
Dufy, Raoul (painter); Le Havre, France **(1877–1953)**
Dukakis, Olympia (actress); Lowell, Mass., 6/20/31
Duke, James B. (industrialist); nr. Durham, N.C. **(1856–1925)**
Duke, Patty (Anna Marie Duke) (actress); New York City, 12/14/46
Dulles, Allen Welsh (ex-Director of CIA); Watertown, N.Y. **(1893–1969)**
Dulles, John Foster (political figure); Washington, D.C. **(1888–1959)**
Dumas, Alexandre (called Dumas fils) (novelist); Paris **(1824–1895)**
Dumas, Alexandre (called Dumas père) (novelist); Villers-Cotterets, France **(1802–1870)**
du Maurier, Daphne (novelist); London **(1907–1989)**
du Maurier, George Louis Palmella Busson (novelist); Paris **(1834–1896)**
Dumont, Margaret (actress); Brooklyn, N.Y. **(1889–1965)**
Dunaway, Faye (actress); Bascom, Fla., 1/14/41
Dunbar, Paul Laurence (poet); Dayton, Ohio **(1872–1906)**
Duncan, Isadora (dancer); San Francisco **(1878–1927)**
Duncan, Sandy (actress); Henderson, Tex., 2/20/46
Dunham, Katherine (dancer, choreographer); Chicago, 6/22/09
Dunne, Irene (actress); Louisville, Ky. **(1898–1990)**
Duns Scotus, John (theologian); Duns, Scotland **(1265–1303)**
Du Pont, Pierre S. (economist); Paris **(1739–1817)**
Durante, Jimmy (comedian); New York City **(1893–1980)**

Duras, Marguerite (Donnadieu) (novelist, dramatist); Gia Dinh, Vietnam **(1914–1996)**
Durbin, Deanna (Edna Mae) (actress); Winnipeg, Canada, 12/4/22
Dürer, Albrecht (painter, engraver); Nürnberg, Germany **(1471–1528)**
Durning, Charles (actor); Highland Falls, N.Y., 2/28/23
Durrell, Lawrence George (novelist); Julundur, India **(1912–1990)**
Duse, Eleonora (actress); Chioggia, Italy **(1859–1924)**
Dussault, Nancy (actress); Pensacola, Fla., 6/30/36
Duvall, Robert (actor, director, producer); San Diego, Calif., 1/5/31
Duvall, Shelley (actress); Houston, 7/7/49
Dvořák, Antonin (composer); Nelahozeves, Czechoslovakia **(1841–1904)**
Dylan, Bob (Robert Zimmerman) (singer, songwriter, guitarist); Duluth, Minn., 5/24/41
Dysart, Richard (actor); Brighton, Mass., 3/30/29

E

Eakins, Thomas (painter, sculptor); Philadelphia **(1844–1916)**
Earhart, Amelia (aviator); Atchison, Kans. **(1898–1937)**
Earp, Wyatt (Berry Stapp) (sheriff, gunfighter); Monmouth, Ill. **(1848–1929)**
Eastman, George (camera inventor); Waterville, N.Y. **(1854–1932)**
Eastwood, Clint (actor, director, producer); San Francisco, 5/31/30
Ebert, Roger (film critic); Urbana, Ill., 6/18/42
Ebsen, Buddy (Christian Ebsen, Jr.) (actor); Belleville, Ill., 4/2/08
Eckstine, Billy (singer); Pittsburgh **(1914–1993)**
Eddy, Mary Baker (founder of Christian Science Church); Bow, N.H. **(1821–1910)**
Eddy, Nelson (baritone, actor); Providence, R.I. **(1901–1967)**
Edel, Leon (author); Pittsburgh **(1907–1997)**
Edelman, Marian Wright (social activist); Bennettsville, S.C., 6/6/39
Eden, Sir Anthony (Earl of Avon) (ex-Prime Minister); Durham, England **(1897–1977)**
Eden, Barbara (actress); Tucson, Ariz., 8/23/34
Edison, Thomas Alva (inventor); Milan, Ohio **(1847–1931)**
Edwards, Anthony (actor); Santa Barbara, Calif., 7/19/62
Edwards, Blake (film writer, producer); Tulsa, Okla., 7/26/22
Edwards, Jonathan (theologian); East Windsor, Conn. **(1703–1758)**
Edwards, Ralph (TV and radio producer); Merino, Colo., 6/13/13
Edwards, Vincent (Vincent Edward Zoino) (actor); Brooklyn, N.Y. **(1928–1996)**
Eglevsky, André (ballet dancer); Moscow **(1917–1977)**
Egoyan, Atom (film director, writer, editor); Cairo, 7/19/60
Ehrlich, Paul (bacteriologist); Strzelin, Poland **(1854–1915)**
Eichmann, (Karl) Adolf (Nazi, mass murderer); Solingen, Germany **(1906–1962)**
Eikenberry, Jill (actress); New Haven, Conn., 1/21/47
Einstein, Albert (physicist); Ulm, Germany **(1879–1955)**
Eisner, Michael (entertainment executive); Mt. Kisco, N.Y., 3/7/42
Eisenhower, Dwight David (34th U.S. president); Denison, Tex. **(1890–1969)**
Eisenhower, Milton S. (educator); Abilene, Kans. **(1899–1985)**
Eisenstaedt, Alfred (photographer, photojournalist); Dirschau (Prussia, now Tczew), Poland **(1898–1995)**
Ekland, Britt (Britt-Marie) (actress); Stockholm, 10/6/42
Electra, Carmen (Tara Patrick) (model, actress); Cincinnati, Ohio, 4/20/73
Elfman, Jenna (Jennifer Mary Butala) (actress); Los Angeles, 9/30/71
Elgar, Sir Edward (composer); Worcester, England **(1857–1934)**
Elgart, Larry (band leader); New London, Conn., 3/20/22
El Greco (Domenicos Theotocopoulos) (painter); Candia, Crete, Greece **(c. 1541–1614)**
Elion, Gertrude B. (chemist, Nobel laureate); New York City **(1918–1999)**
Eliot, George (Mary Ann Evans) (novelist); Chilvers Coton, England **(1819–1880)**
Eliot, Thomas Stearns (poet); St. Louis **(1888–1965)**
Elizabeth I (Queen of England); Greenwich, England **(1533–1603)**
Elizabeth II (Queen of England); London, 4/21/26
Elizondo, Hector (actor); New York City, 12/22/36
Ellington, Duke (Edward Kennedy) (jazz musician); Washington, D.C. **(1899–1974)**
Elliot, "Mama" Cass (Ellen Naomi Cohen) (singer); Baltimore **(1941–1974)**
Elliott, Sam (actor); Sacramento, Calif., 8/9/44
Ellison, Lawrence J. (computer industry executive); New York City, 1944
Ellison, Ralph (novelist); Oklahoma City, Okla. **(1914–1994)**
Ellsberg, Daniel (activist); Chicago, 4/7/31
Elman, Mischa (violinist); Stalnoye, Ukraine **(1891–1967)**

Emerson, Ralph Waldo (philosopher, poet); Boston **(1803–1882)**

Enesco, Georges (composer); Dorohoi, Romania **(1881–1955)**

Engels, Friedrich (Socialist writer); Barmen, Germany **(1820–1895)**

Englund, Robert (actor); Glendale, Calif., 6/6/49

Entremont, Philippe (concert pianist); Rheims, France, 6/7/34

Ephron, Nora (writer, director); New York City, 5/19/41

Epicurus (philosopher); Samos, Greece **(341–270 B.C.E.)**

Epstein, Sir Jacob (sculptor); New York City **(1880–1959)**

Erasmus, Desiderius (Gerhard Gerhards) (scholar); Rotterdam **(1469–1536)**

Erdrich, (Karen) Louise (writer); Little Falls, Minn., 7/6/54

Erickson, Leif (actor); Alameda, Calif. **(1911–1986)**

Ericson, Leif (navigator) c. 10th century C.E.

Erikson, Erik H. (psychoanalyst); Frankfurt, Germany **(1902–1994)**

Ernst, Max (painter); Bruhl, Germany **(1891–1976)**

Erté (Romain de Tirtoff) (artist, designer); St. Petersburg, Russia **(1892–1990)**

Estevez, Emilio (actor, director, screenwriter); New York City, 5/12/62

Eszterhas, Joe (screenwriter); Csakanydorosло, Hungary, 11/23/44

Euclid (mathematician); Megara, Greece, fl. 300 B.C.E.

Euler, Leonhard (mathematician); Basel, Switzerland **(1707–1783)**

Euripides (dramatist); Salamis, Greece **(c. 484–407 B.C.E.)**

Evangelista, Linda (model); St. Catharines, Ont., Canada, 5/10/65

Evans, Dale (born Lucille Wood Smith but raised as Frances Octavia Smith) (actress, singer); Uvalde, Tex., 10/30/12

Evans, Dame Edith (actress); London **(1888–1976)**

Evans, Linda (actress); Hartford, Conn., 11/18/42

Evans, Maurice (actor); Dorchester, England **(1901–1989)**

Everett, Chad (Raymond Lee Cramton) (actor); South Bend, Ind., 6/11/36

Everett, Rupert (actor, model, musician); Norfolk, England, 5/29/59

Everhart, Angie (model, actress); Akron, Ohio, 9/6/69

Evers, Charles (civil rights leader); Decatur, Miss., 9/14/22

Evers, Medgar (civil rights leader); Decatur, Miss. **(1925–1963)**

Evers-Williams, Myrlie (civil rights leader); Vicksburg, Miss., 3/17/33

F

Fabares, Shelley (actress); Santa Monica, Calif., 1/19/44

Fabian (Fabian Anthony Forte) (singer); Philadelphia, 2/6/43

Fabray, Nanette (Nanette Fabarés) (actress); San Diego, Calif., 10/27/22

Fahrenheit, Gabriel (German physicist); Danzig, Poland **(1686–1736)**

Fairbanks, Douglas (Douglas Ulman) (actor); Denver **(1883–1939)**

Fairbanks, Douglas, Jr. (actor); New York City, 12/9/09

Fairchild, Morgan (Patsy Ann McClenny) (actress); Dallas, 2/3/50

Faith, Percy (conductor); Toronto **(1908–1976)**

Falk, Peter (actor); New York City, 9/16/27

Falla, Manuel de (composer); Cadiz, Spain **(1876–1946)**

Faludi, Susan (journalist, writer); New York City, 4/18/59

Falwell, Jerry (fundamentalist preacher); Lynchburg, Va., 8/11/33

Faraday, Michael (physicist); Newington, England **(1791–1867)**

Farentino, James (actor); Brooklyn, N.Y., 2/24/38

Farley, Chris (actor, comedian); Madison, Wis. **(1964–1997)**

Farmer, James (civil rights leader); Marshall, Tex. **(1920–1999)**

Farr, Jamie (actor); Toledo, Ohio, 7/1/34

Farrar, Geraldine (soprano, actress); Melrose, Mass. **(1882–1967)**

Farrell, Eileen (operatic soprano); Willimantic, Conn., 2/13/20

Farrell, James T. (novelist); Chicago **(1904–1979)**

Farrell, Mike (actor); St. Paul, Minn., 2/6/39

Farrell, Perry (Perry Bernstein) (lead singer); Queens, New York, 3/29/59

Farrell, Suzanne (Roberta Sue Ficker) (ballet dancer); Cincinnati, 8/16/45

Farrow, Mia (actress); Los Angeles, 2/9/46

Fasanella, Ralph (painter); New York City **(1914–1997)**

Fassbinder, Rainer Werner (film, stage director); Bad Wörishofen, Germany **(1946–1982)**

Fast, Howard (novelist); New York City, 11/11/14

Faubus, Orval E(ugene) (governor of Arkansas); Combs, Ark. **(1910–1994)**

Faulkner, William (novelist); New Albany, Miss. **(1897–1962)**

Fauré, Gabriel Urbain (composer); Pamiers, France **(1845–1924)**

Fawcett, Farrah (Mary Farrah Leni Fawcett) (actress); Corpus Christi, Tex., 2/2/47

Faye, Alice (Ann Leppert) (actress); New York City **(1912–1998)**

Feiffer, Jules (cartoonist); New York City, 1/26/29

Feininger, Lyonel (painter); New York City **(1871–1956)**

Feldman, Marty (actor, screenwriter, director); London **(1938–1982)**

Feldon, Barbara (actress); Pittsburgh, 3/12/41

Feliciano, José (singer); Larez, Puerto Rico, 9/10/45

Felker, Clay S. (editor, publisher); St. Louis, 10/2/25

Fell, Norman (actor); Philadelphia **(1923–1998)**

Fellini, Federico (film director); Rimini, Italy **(1920–1993)**

Fender, Freddie (Baldemar Huerta) (singer); San Benito, Tex., 6/4/37

Ferber, Edna (novelist); Kalamazoo, Mich. **(1885–1968)**

Ferguson, Maynard (jazz trumpeter); Verdun, Que., Canada, 5/4/28

Ferlinghetti, Lawrence (poet, writer, translator); Yonkers, N.Y., 3/24/19

Fermi, Enrico (atomic physicist); Rome **(1901–1954)**

Fernandel (Fernand Joseph Desire Contandin) (actor); Marseilles, France **(1903–1971)**

Ferraro, Geraldine Anne (political figure); New York City, 8/26/35

Ferrer, José (actor, director); Santurce, Puerto Rico **(1912–1992)**

Ferrer, Mel (actor); Elberon, N.J., 8/25/17

Fetchit, Stepin (Lincoln Theodore Perry) (comedian); Key West, Fla. **(1902–1985)**

Fiedler, Arthur (conductor); Boston **(1894–1979)**

Field, Eugene (poet); St. Louis **(1850–1895)**

Field, Marshall (merchant); nr. Conway, Mass. **(1834–1906)**

Field, Sally (actress); Pasadena, Calif., 11/6/46

Fielding, Henry (novelist); nr. Glastonbury, England **(1707–1754)**

Fields, W. C. (William Claude Dukenfield) (comedian); Philadelphia **(1880–1946)**

Fiennes, Joseph (actor); Salisbury, England, 5/27/70

Fiennes, Ralph (actor); Suffolk, England, 12/22/62

Fierstein, Harvey (Forbes) (playwright, actor); Brooklyn, 6/6/54

Figgis, Mike (director, screenwriter, composer, actor); Carlisle, England, 2/28/48

Filene, Edward A. (merchant) **(1860–1937)**

Fillmore, Millard (13th U.S. president); Locke, Cayuga County, N.Y. **(1800–1874)**

Finch, Peter (actor); Kensington, England **(1916–1977)**

Finney, Albert (actor); Salford, England, 5/9/36

Fiorentino, Linda (Clorinda Fiorentino) (actress); Philadelphia, 3/9/60

Firkusny, Rudolf (pianist); Napajedia, former Czechoslovakia **(1912–1994)**

Firth, Colin (actor); Grayshot, England, 9/10/60

Fischer-Dieskau, Dietrich (baritone); Berlin, 5/28/25

Fishburne, Laurence (actor); Augusta, Ga., 7/30/61

Fisher, Carrie (actress); Los Angeles, 10/21/56

Fisher, Eddie (Edwin) (singer); Philadelphia, 8/10/28

Fitzgerald, Barry (William Joseph Shields) (actor); Dublin **(1888–1961)**

Fitzgerald, Ella (singer); Newport News, Va. **(1918–1996)**

Fitzgerald, F. Scott (Francis Scott Key Fitzgerald) (novelist); St. Paul, Minn. **(1896–1940)**

Fitzgerald, Geraldine (actress); Dublin, 11/24/14

Fitzgerald, Pegeen (radio broadcaster); Norcatur, Kans. **(1910–1989)**

Flack, Roberta (singer); Black Mountain, N.C., 2/10/40

Flagstad, Kirsten (Wagnerian soprano); Hamar, Norway **(1895–1962)**

Flatt, Lester Raymond (bluegrass musician); Overton County, Tenn. **(1914–1979)**

Flaubert, Gustave (novelist); Rouen, France **(1821–1880)**

Fleming, Sir Alexander (bacteriologist); Lochfield, Scotland **(1881–1955)**

Fletcher, John (dramatist); Rye, Sussex, England **(1579–1625)**

Flockhart, Calista (actress); Freeport, Illinois, 11/11/64

Flynn, Errol (actor); Hobart, Tasmania **(1909–1959)**

Fodor, Eugene (violinist); Turkey Creek, Colo., 3/5/50

Fokine, Michel (dancer, choreographer); St. Petersburg, Russia **(1880–1942)**

Fonda, Bridget (actress); Los Angeles, 1/27/64

Fonda, Henry (actor); Grand Island, Neb. **(1905–1982)**

Fonda, Jane (actress); New York City, 12/21/37

Fonda, Peter (actor); New York City, 2/23/39

Fontaine, Frank (singer, comedian); Cambridge, Mass. **(1920–1979)**

Fontaine, Joan (Joan de Havilland) (actress); Tokyo, 10/22/17

Fontanne, Lynn (actress); London **(1887–1983)**

Fonteyn, Dame Margot (Margaret Hookham) (ballet dancer); Reigate, England **(1919–1991)**

Foote, Shelby (historian); Greenville, Miss., 11/17/16

Forbes, Malcolm S(tevenson) (publisher, sportsman); Brooklyn, N.Y. **(1919–1990)**

Ford, Gerald Rudolph (38th U.S. president); Omaha, Neb., 7/14/13

Ford, Glenn (Gwyllyn Ford) (actor); Ste.-Christine, Que., Canada, 5/1/16

Ford, Harrison (actor); Chicago, 7/13/42

Ford, Henry (industrialist); Greenfield, Mich. **(1863–1947)**
Ford, John (film director); Cape Elizabeth, Maine **(1895–1973)**
Ford, Tennessee Ernie (Ernie Jennings Ford) (singer); Bristol, Tenn. **(1919–1991)**
Foreman, George (boxer, actor); Marshall, Texas, 1/10/49
Forrester, Maureen (contralto); Montreal, 7/25/30
Forsythe, John (actor); Penn's Grove, N.J., 1/29/18
Fosdick, Harry Emerson (clergyman); Buffalo, N.Y. **(1878–1968)**
Fosse, Bob (Robert Louis Fosse) (choreographer, director); Chicago **(1927–1987)**
Foster, Jodie (Alicia Christian Foster) (actress, director, producer); Los Angeles, 11/19/62
Foster, Stephen Collins (composer); nr. Pittsburgh **(1826–1864)**
Fountain, Pete (jazz musician); New Orleans, 7/3/30
Fox, Matthew (actor); Crowheart, Wy., 7/14/66
Fox, Michael J. (actor, producer); Edmonton, Alta., Canada, 6/9/61
Foxx, Redd (John Elroy Sanford) (actor, comedian); St. Louis **(1922–1991)**
Foy, Eddie, Jr. (dancer, actor); New Rochelle, N.Y. **(1905–1983)**
Fra Angelico (Giovanni da Fiesole) (painter); Vicchio in the Mugello, Tuscany, Italy **(c. 1387–1455)**
Fracci, Carla (ballet dancer); Milan, Italy, 8/20/36
Fragonard, Jean Honoré (painter); Grasse, France **(1732–1806)**
Frakes, Jonathan (actor); Bethlehem, Pa., 8/19/52
Frampton, Peter (rock musician); Beckenham, England, 4/20/50
France, Anatole (Jacques Anatole François Thibault) (author); Paris **(1844–1924)**
Francescatti, Zino (violinist); Marseilles, France **(1902–1991)**
Franciosa, Anthony (Anthony Papaleo) (actor); New York City, 10/25/28
Francis, Anne (actress); Ossining, N.Y., 7/16/30
Francis, Connie (Concetta Franconero) (singer); Newark, N.J., 12/12/38
Francis, Genie (actress); Englewood, N.J., 5/26/62
Francis of Assisi, Saint (Giovanni Francesco Barnardone) (founder of Franciscans); Assisi, Italy **(1182–1226)**
Franck, César Auguste (composer); Liège, Belgium **(1822–1890)**
Franco Bahamonde, Francisco (Chief of State); El Ferrol, Spain **(1892–1975)**
Frankenheimer, John (movie director, producer); New York City, 2/19/30
Frankenthaler, Helen (artist); New York City, 12/12/28
Frankl, Victor E. (psychiatrist); Vienna **(1905–1997)**
Franklin, Aretha (singer); Memphis, Tenn., 3/25/42
Franklin, Benjamin (statesman, scientist); Boston **(1706–1790)**
Franklin, Bonnie (actress); Santa Monica, Calif., 1/6/44
Franklin, John Hope (historian); Rentiesville, Okla., 1/2/15
Frann, Mary (actress); St. Louis **(1943–1998)**
Franz, Dennis (Dennis Schlachta) (actor); Chicago, 10/28/44
Fraser, Brendan (actor); Indianapolis, Indiana, 12/3/67
Frazer, Sir James George (anthropologist); Glasgow, Scotland **(1854–1941)**
Freeman, Morgan (actor); Memphis, Tenn., 6/1/37
Freud, Sigmund (psychoanalyst); Moravia, Czech Repubic **(1856–1939)**
Frey, Glenn (musician); Detroit, 11/6/48
Frick, Henry Clay (industrialist); Westmoreland Co., Pa. **(1849–1919)**
Friedan, Betty (Betty Naomi Goldstein) (feminist, writer); Peoria, Ill., 2/4/21
Fromm, Erich (psychoanalyst); Frankfurt-am-Main, Germany **(1900–1980)**
Frost, David (TV entertainer); Tenterden, England, 4/7/39
Frost, Robert Lee (poet); San Francisco **(1874–1963)**
Fry, Christopher (playwright); Bristol, England, 12/18/07
Fugard, Athol (playwright); Middleburg, South Africa, 6/11/32
Fulbright, J. William (politician); Sumner, Mo. **(1905–1995)**
Fuller, Charles (playwright); Philadelphia, 3/5/39
Fuller, R(ichard) Buckminster (Jr.) (architect, educator); Milton, Mass. **(1895–1983)**
Fulton, Robert (inventor); Lancaster County, Pa. **(1765–1815)**
Funicello, Annette (actress); Utica, N.Y., 10/22/42
Funt, Allen (TV producer); Brooklyn, N.Y., 9/16/14

G

Gabin, Jean (actor); Paris **(1904–1976)**
Gable, (William) Clark (actor); Cadiz, Ohio **(1901–1960)**
Gabo, Naum (sculptor); Briansk, Russia **(1890–1977)**
Gabor, Eva (actress); Budapest **(1920–1995)**
Gabor, Zsa Zsa (Sari) (actress); Budapest, 2/6/17
Gabriel, Peter (musician); Cobham, England, 2/13/50
Gabrieli, Giovanni (composer); Venice **(c. 1557–1612)**

Gaddis, William (novelist); New York City, 12/29/22
Gainsborough, Thomas (painter); Sudbury, Suffolk, England **(1727–1788)**
Galbraith, John Kenneth (economist); Iona Station, Ont., Canada, 10/15/08
Galilei, Galileo (astronomer, physicist); Pisa, Italy **(1564–1642)**
Gallico, Paul (novelist); New York City **(1897–1976)**
Gallup, George H. (poll taker); Jefferson, Iowa **(1901–1984)**
Galsworthy, John (novelist, dramatist); Coombe, England **(1867–1933)**
Galway, James (flutist); Belfast, Northern Ireland, 12/8/39
Gambling, John A. (radio broadcaster); New York City, 1930
Gandhi, Indira (Indira Nehru) (former prime minister); Allahabad, India **(1917– 1984)**
Gandhi, Mohandas Karamchand (called Mahatma Gandhi) (Hindu leader); Porbandar, India **(1869–1948)**
Gannett, Frank E. (editor, publisher) **(1876–1957)**
Garagiola, Joe (Joseph Henry Garagiola) (sportscaster); St. Louis, 2/12/26
Garbo, Greta (Greta Gustafsson) (actress); Stockholm **(1905–1990)**
Garcia, Andy (Andres Arturo Garcia-Menendez) (actor); Havana, Cuba, 4/12/56
Garcia, Jerry (rock musician); San Francisco **(1942–1995)**
Garcia Lorca, Frederico (poet, dramatist); Fuente Vaqueros, Spain **(1898–1936)**
Garden, Mary (soprano); Aberdeen, Scotland **(1874–1967)**
Gardenia, Vincent (actor); Naples, Italy **(1922–1992)**
Gardner, Ava (actress); Smithfield, N.C. **(1922–1990)**
Gardner, Erle Stanley (novelist); Malden, Mass. **(1889–1970)**
Garfield, James Abram (20th U.S. president); Cuyahoga County, Ohio **(1831–1881)**
Garfunkel, Art (Arthur) (singer); Newark, N.J., 11/5/41
Garibaldi, Giuseppe (Italian nationalist leader); Nice, France **(1807–1882)**
Garland, Judy (Frances Gumm) (actress, singer); Grand Rapids, Minn. **(1922–1969)**
Garner, Erroll (jazz pianist); Pittsburgh **(1921–1977)**
Garner, James (James Bumgarner) (actor); Norman, Okla., 4/7/28
Garofalo, Janeane (actress, comedienne); Newton, New Jersey, 9/28/64
Garr, Teri (actress); Lakewood, Ohio, 12/11/49
Garrison, William Lloyd (abolitionist); Newburyport, Mass. **(1805–1879)**
Garroway, Dave (TV host); Schenectady, N.Y. **(1913–1982)**
Garson, Greer (actress); County Down, Northern Ireland **(1903–1996)**
Garth, Jennie (actress); Urbana, Ill., 4/3/72
Garvey, Marcus Moziah (black nationalist leader); Jamaica **(1887–1940)**
Gassman, Vittorio (film actor, director); Genoa, Italy, 9/1/22
Gates, Bill (William Henry Gates III) (software pioneer); Seattle, 10/28/55
Gates, Henry Louis, Jr. (scholar); Keyser, W. Va., 9/16/50
Gaudí, Antonio (architect); Reus, Spain **(1852–1926)**
Gauguin, (Eugène Henri) Paul (painter); Paris **(1848–1903)**
Gautama Buddha (Prince Siddhartha) (philosopher); Kapilavastu, India **(c. 563–c. 483 B.C.E.)**
Gavin, John (actor, diplomat); Los Angeles, 4/8/35
Gavras, Konstantinos (Costa-Gavras) (film director); Loutra-Iraias, Greece, 2/13/33
Gaye, Marvin (singer); Washington, D.C. **(1939–1984)**
Gayle, Crystal (Brenda Gayle Webb) (singer); Paintsville, Ky., 1/9/51
Gaynor, Janet (actress); Philadelphia **(1906–1984)**
Gaynor, Mitzi (Francesca Mitzi Marlene de Czanyi von Gerber) (actress); Chicago, 9/4/31
Gazzara, Ben (Biagio Anthony Gazzara) (actor); New York City, 8/28/30
Gedda, Nicolai (tenor); Stockholm, 7/11/25
Gellar, Sarah Michelle (actress); New York City, 4/14/77
Genet, Jean (playwright); Paris **(1910–1986)**
Genghis Khan (Temujin) (conqueror); nr. Lake Baikal, Russia **(1162–1227)**
Gentry, Bobbie (Roberta Streeter) (singer); Chickasaw Co., Miss., 7/27/44
George, David Lloyd (statesman); Manchester, England **(1863–1945)**
George, Henry (economist, reformer); Philadelphia **(1839–1897)**
Gere, Richard (actor); Philadelphia, 8/29/49
Gericault, Jean Louis (painter); Rouen, France **(1791–1824)**
Geronimo (Goyathlay) (Apache chieftain); Arizona **(1829–1909)**
Gershwin, George (composer); Brooklyn, N.Y. **(1898–1937)**

Gershwin, Ira (lyricist); New York City (1896–1983)

Getty, J. Paul (oil executive); Minneapolis (1892–1976)

Getz, Stan (saxophonist); Philadelphia (1927–1991)

Ghiberti, Lorenzo (goldsmith, sculptor); Florence (1378–1455)

Ghostley, Alice (actress); Eve, Mo., 8/14/26

Giacometti, Alberto (sculptor); Switzerland (1901–1966)

Giannini, Giancarlo (actor); La Spezia, Italy, 8/1/42

Gibbon, Edward (historian); Putney, England (1737–1794)

Gibson, Charles Dana (illustrator); Roxbury, Mass. (1867–1944)

Gibson, Henry (actor, comedian); Germantown, Pa., 9/21/35

Gibson, Mel (actor, director, producer); Peekskill, N.Y., 1/3/56

Gide, André (author); Paris (1869–1951)

Gielgud, Sir John (actor); London, 4/14/04

Gifford, Kathie Lee (Kathie Lee Epstein) (talk show host); Paris, 8/16/53

Gilbert, Melissa (actress); Los Angeles, 5/8/64

Gilbert, Walter (chemist, Nobel laureate); Boston, 3/21/32

Gilbert, Sir William Schwenck (librettist); London (1836–1911)

Gilels, Emil (concert pianist); Odessa, Ukraine (1916–1985)

Gillespie, Dizzy (John Birks Gillespie) (jazz trumpeter); Cheraw, S.C. (1917–1993)

Gilligan, Carol (Friedman) (psychologist); New York City, 11/28/36

Gilpin, Peri (actress); Waco, Tex., 5/27/61

Gimbel, Bernard F. (merchant); Vincennes, Ind. (1885–1966)

Gingrich, Newt (politician); Harrisburg, Pa., 6/17/43

Ginsberg, Allen (poet); Newark, N.J. (1926–1997)

Giordano, Luca (painter); Naples, Italy (1632–1705)

Giorgione (painter); Castelfranco, Italy (c. 1477–1510)

Giotto di Bondone (painter); Vespignamo, Italy (c. 1266–1337)

Giovanni, Nikki (poet); Knoxville, Tenn., 6/7/43

Giroud, Françoise (French government official); Geneva, 9/21/16

Gish, Dorothy (actress); Massillon, Ohio (1898–1968)

Gish, Lillian (Lillian de Guiche) (actress); Springfield, Ohio (1893–1993)

Givenchy, Hubert (fashion designer); Beauvais, France, 2/21/27

Gladstone, William Ewart (statesman); Liverpool, England (1809–1898)

Glaser, Paul Michael (actor, director); Cambridge, Mass., 3/25/43

Glass, Philip (composer); Baltimore, 1/31/37

Gleason, Jackie (comedian); Brooklyn, N.Y. (1916–1987)

Glenn, John (legislator, astronaut); Cambridge, Ohio, 7/18/21

Gless, Sharon (actress); Los Angeles, 5/31/43

Glover, Danny (actor); San Francisco, 7/22/47

Gluck, Christoph Willibald (composer); Erasbach, Germany (1714–1787)

Gobel, George (comedian); Chicago (1920–1991)

Godard, Jean Luc (film director); Paris, 12/3/30

Goddard, Paulette (Marion Levy) (actress); Great Neck, N.Y. (1911–1990)

Goddard, Robert Hutchings (father of modern rocketry); Worcester, Mass. (1882–1945)

Godfrey, Arthur (entertainer); New York City (1903–1983)

Goebbels, Joseph Paul (Nazi leader); Rheydt, Germany (1897–1945)

Goering, Hermann (Nazi leader); Rosenheim, Germany (1893–1946)

Goethals, George Washington (engineer); Brooklyn, N.Y. (1858–1928)

Goethe, Johann Wolfgang von (poet, playwright, novelist); Frankfurt-am-Main, Germany (1749–1832)

Gogol, Nikolai Vasilievich (novelist); nr. Mirgorod, Ukraine (1809–1852)

Goldberg, Rube (cartoonist); San Francisco (1883–1970)

Goldberg, Whoopi (Caryn Johnson) (actress); New York City, 11/13/49

Goldblum, Jeff (actor); Pittsburgh, 10/22/52

Golden, Harry (Harry Goldhurst) (author); New York City (1902–1981)

Goldman, Emma (anarchist); Kovno, Lithuania (1869–1940)

Goldsmith, Oliver (dramatist, poet); County Longford, Ireland (1728–1774)

Goldwyn, Samuel (Schmuel Gelbfisz) (film producer); Warsaw (1879–1974)

Gompers, Samuel (labor leader); London (1850–1924)

Goodall, Jane (Baroness van Lawick-Goodall) (ethologist); London, 4/3/34

Gooding, Jr., Cuba (actor); Bronx, New York, 1/2/68

Goodman, Benny (clarinetist); Chicago (1909–1986)

Goodman, John (actor); St. Louis, 6/20/52

Goodwin, Doris (Helen) Kearns (historian); Rockville Center, N.Y., 1/4/43

Goodyear, Charles (inventor); New Haven, Conn. (1800–1860)

Gorbachev, Mikhail Sergeyevich (Soviet leader); Privolnoye, Russia, 3/2/31

Gordimer, Nadine (novelist, short-story writer); Springs, South Africa, 12/20/23

Gordon, Dexter (jazz musician); Los Angeles (1923–1990)

Gordon, Ruth (actress); Wollaston, Mass. (1896–1985)

Gore, Albert, Jr. (Vice President of the U.S.); Washington, D.C., 3/31/48

Gordy, Berry, Jr. (record company executive); Detroit, 11/28/29

Gorey, Edward (St. John) (illustrator, author); Chicago, 2/22/25

Gorki, Maxim (Alexei Maximovich Peshkov) (author); Nizhni Novgorod, Russia (1868–1936)

Gorky, Arshile (painter); Armenia (1904–1948)

Gormé, Eydie (singer); Bronx, N.Y., 8/16/32

Gorshin, Frank (actor); Pittsburgh, 4/5/34

Gossett, Louis, Jr. (actor); Brooklyn, N.Y., 5/27/36

Gottschalk, Louis Moreau (pianist, composer); New Orleans (1829–1869)

Gould, Chester (cartoonist); Pawnee, Okla. (1900–1985)

Gould, Elliott (Elliott Goldstein) (actor); Brooklyn, N.Y., 8/29/38

Gould, Glenn (concert pianist); Toronto (1932–1982)

Gould, Morton (composer); Richmond Hill, Queens, N.Y. (1913–1996)

Gould, Stephen Jay (paleontologist, science writer); New York City, 9/10/41

Goulet, Robert (singer); Lawrence, Mass., 11/26/33

Gounod, Charles François (composer); Paris (1818–1893)

Goya y Lucientes, Francisco José de (painter); Fuendetodos, Spain (1746–1828)

Grable, Betty (actress); St. Louis (1916–1973)

Grace, Princess of Monaco (Grace Kelly) (ex-actress); Philadelphia (1929–1982)

Graham, Bill (Wolfgang Grajonca) (rock impresario); Berlin (1930–1991)

Graham, Billy (William F. Graham) (evangelist); Charlotte, N.C., 11/7/18

Graham, Katharine Meyer (newspaper publisher); New York City, 6/16/17

Graham, Martha (choreographer); Pittsburgh (1894–1991)

Grainger, Percy Aldridge (pianist, composer); Melbourne, Australia (1882–1961)

Gramm, Donald (Grambach) (bass-baritone); Milwaukee (1927–1983)

Grammer, Kelsey (actor); St. Thomas, V.I., 2/21/55

Granger, Stewart (James Stewart) (actor); London (1913–1993)

Grant, Cary (Alexander Archibald Leach) (actor); Bristol, England (1904–1986)

Grant, Hugh (actor); London, England, 9/9/60

Grant, Lee (Lyova Haskell Rosenthal) (actress); New York City, 10/31/30

Grant, Ulysses Simpson (18th U.S. president); Point Pleasant, Ohio (1822–1885)

Grass, Günter (novelist); Danzig, Poland, 10/16/27

Graves, Nancy (Stevenson) (artist); Pittsfield, Mass. (1940–1996)

Graves, Peter (Peter Aurness) (actor); Minneapolis, 3/18/26

Graves, Robert (writer); London (1895–1985)

Gray, Linda (actress); Santa Monica, Calif., 9/12/40

Gray, Thomas (poet); London (1716–1771)

Greco, José (dancer); Montorio nei Frentani, Italy, 12/23/18

Greeley, Horace (journalist, politician); Amherst, N.H. (1811–1872)

Green, Adolph (actor, lyricist); New York City, 12/2/15

Green, Al (singer); Forrest City, Ark., 4/13/46

Greene, Graham (novelist); Berkhamsted, England (1904–1991)

Greene, Lorne (actor); Ottawa, Ont., Canada (1915–1987)

Greene, Shecky (comedian, actor); Chicago, 4/8/25

Greenstreet, Sydney (actor); Sandwich, England (1879–1954)

Greenspan, Alan (chairman of the Federal Reserve); New York City, 3/6/26

Greer, Germaine (feminist, writer); Melbourne, Australia, 1/29/39

Gregory, Cynthia (ballet dancer); Los Angeles, 7/8/46

Gregory, Dick (comedian); St. Louis, 10/12/32

Gregory, Lady (Isabella) Augusta (playwright); Roxborough, Ireland (1852–1932)

Greuze, Jean-Baptiste (painter); Tournus, France (1725–1805)

Grey, Joel (Joel Katz) (actor, dancer); Cleveland, 4/11/32

Grey, Zane (author); Zanesville, Ohio (1875–1939)

Grieg, Edvard Hagerup (composer); Bergen, Norway (1843–1907)

Grier, Pam (actress); Winston-Salem, N.C., 5/26/49

Griffin, Merv (TV host, producer); San Mateo, Calif., 7/6/25

Griffith, Andy (actor); Mount Airy, N.C., 6/1/26

Griffith, David Lewelyn Wark (film producer); La Grange, Ky. (1875–1948)

Griffith, Melanie (actress); New York City, 8/9/57

Grigorovich, Yuri (choreographer); Leningrad (St. Petersburg), Russia, 1/1/27

Grimes, Tammy (actress); Lynn, Mass., 1/30/34

Grimm, Jacob (author of fairy tales); Hanau, Germany **(1785–1863)**

Grimm, Wilhelm (author of fairy tales); Hanau, Germany **(1786–1859)**

Gris, Juan (José Victoriano González) (painter); Madrid **(1887–1927)**

Grisham, John (attorney, author); Jonesboro, Ark., 2/8/55

Grodin, Charles (actor); Pittsburgh, 4/21/35

Groening, Matt (animator, producer); Portland, Ore., 2/14/54

Gromyko, Andrei A. (diplomat); Starye Gromyki, Russia **(1909–1989)**

Gropius, Walter (architect); Berlin **(1883–1969)**

Gropper, William (painter, illustrator); New York City **(1897–1977)**

Gross, Michael (actor); Chicago, 6/21/47

Grosz, George (painter); Germany **(1893–1959)**

Grove, Andrew (Andras Grof) (computer industry executive); Budapest, Hungary, 9/2/36

Grünewald, Matthias (Mathis Gothart Neithart) (painter); Würzburg, Germany **(c. 1470–1528)**

Guest, Christopher (Christopher Haden-Guest) (actor, writer, director); New York City, 2/5/48

Guggenheim, Meyer (capitalist); Langnau, Switzerland **(1828–1905)**

Guillaume, Robert (actor); St. Louis, 11/30/27

Guinness, Sir Alec (actor); London, 4/2/14

Guitry, Sacha (Alexandre Guitry) (actor, film director); St. Petersburg, Russia **(1885–1957)**

Gumbel, Bryant Charles (TV newscaster); New Orleans, 9/29/48

Gunther, John (author); Chicago **(1901–1970)**

Gutenberg, Johann (printer); Mainz, Germany **(c. 1397–1468)**

Guthrie, Arlo (singer); New York City, 7/10/47

Guthrie, Woody (folk singer, composer); Okemah, Okla. **(1912–1967)**

Gwenn, Edmund (actor); London **(1875–1959)**

Gwynne, Fred (actor); New York City **(1926–1993)**

H

Habibie, Bacharuddin, Jusuf (President of Indonesia); Pare-Pare, Indonesia, 6/25/36

Hackett, Bobby (trumpeter); Providence, R.I. **(1915–1976)**

Hackett, Buddy (Leonard Hacker) (comedian, actor); Brooklyn, N.Y., 8/31/24

Hackman, Gene (actor); San Bernardino, Calif., 1/30/31

Hagen, Uta (actress); Göttingen, Germany, 6/12/19

Haggard, Merle (songwriter, singer); Bakersfield, Calif., 4/6/37

Hagman, Larry (Larry Hageman) (actor); Weatherford, Tex., 9/21/31

Haig, Alexander Meigs, Jr. (ex-Secretary of State, ex-general); Bala-Cynwyd, Pa., 12/2/24

Haile Selassie (Ras Tafari Makonnen) (ex-Emperor); Ethiopia **(1892–1975)**

Hailey, Arthur (novelist); Luton, England, 4/5/20

Halberstam, David (journalist); New York City, 4/10/34

Hale, Alan (actor, director); Washington, D.C. **(1892–1950)**

Hale, Barbara (actress); DeKalb, Ill., 4/18/21

Hale, Edward Everett (clergyman, author); Boston **(1822–1909)**

Hale, Nathan (American Revolutionary officer); Coventry, Conn. **(1755–1776)**

Halevi, Judah (Jewish poet); Toledo, Spain **(1085–1140)**

Haley, Alex (writer); Ithaca, N.Y. **(1921–1992)**

Haley, Jack (actor); Boston **(1899–1979)**

Hall, Anthony Michael (Michael Anthony Thomas Charles Hall) (actor, singer); Boston, 4/14/68

Hall, Arsenio (comedian, talk-show host); Cleveland, 2/12/58

Hall, Donald (Andrew, Jr.) (poet); New Haven, Conn., 9/20/28

Hall, Huntz (actor); New York City **(1919–1999)**

Hall, Monty (TV personality); Winnipeg, Canada, 8/25/23

Halley, Edmund (astronomer); London **(1656–1742)**

Hals, Frans (painter); Antwerp, Netherlands (c. 1580–1666)

Halsey, William Frederick, Jr. (naval officer); Elizabeth, N.J. **(1882–1959)**

Hamel, Veronica (actress); Philadelphia, 11/20/43

Hamill, Mark (actor); Oakland, 9/25/52

Hamilton, Alexander (statesman); Nevis, British West Indies **(1755–1804)**

Hamilton, Alice (physician, reformer); New York City **(1869–1970)**

Hamilton, Edith (scholar); Dresden, Germany **(1867–1963)**

Hamilton, George (actor); Memphis, Tenn., 8/12/39

Hamlin, Harry (actor); Pasadena, Calif., 10/30/51

Hamlisch, Marvin (composer, pianist); New York City, 6/2/44

Hammarskjöld, Dag (U.N. Secretary-General); Jönköping, Sweden **(1905–1961)**

Hammerstein, Oscar, II (librettist, stage producer); New York City **(1895–1960)**

Hampton, Lionel (vibraharpist, band leader); Birmingham, Ala., 4/12/13

Hamsun, Knut (Knut Pedersen) (novelist); Lom, Norway **(1859–1952)**

Hancock, Herbie (jazz musician); Chicago, 4/12/40

Hancock, John (statesman); Braintree, Mass. **(1737–1793)**

Hand, Learned (jurist); Albany, N.Y. **(1872–1961)**

Handel, George Frederick (Georg Friedrich Händel) (composer); Halle, Germany **(1685–1759)**

Handy, William Christopher (blues composer); Florence, Ala. **(1873–1958)**

Hanks, Tom (actor, director, writer); Concord, Calif., 7/9/56

Hannah, Daryl (actress); Chicago, 12/19/60

Hannibal (Carthaginian general); North Africa **(247–182 B.C.E.)**

Hansberry, Lorraine (playwright); Chicago **(1930–1965)**

Hanson, Howard (conductor); Wahoo, Neb. **(1896–1981)**

Harburg, E. Y. "Yip" (songwriter); New York City **(1896–1981)**

Harding, Warren Gamaliel (29th U.S. president); Morrow County, Ohio **(1865–1923)**

Hardwicke, Sir Cedric (actor); Stourbridge, England **(1893–1964)**

Hardy, Oliver (comedian); Atlanta **(1892–1957)**

Hardy, Thomas (novelist); Dorsetshire, England **(1840–1928)**

Harkness, Edward S. (business executive); Cleveland **(1874–1940)**

Harlow, Jean (Harlean Carpentier) (actress); Kansas City, Mo. **(1911–1937)**

Harlow, Shalom (model, TV personality); Oshawa, Ontario, Canada, 12/5/73

Harmon, Mark (actor); Burbank, Calif., 9/2/51

Harnick, Sheldon (lyricist); Chicago, 4/30/24

Harper, Valerie (actress); Suffern, N.Y., 8/22/40

Harrell, Lynn (cellist); New York City, 1/30/44

Harrelson, Woody (actor); Midland, Tex., 7/23/61

Harriman, Pamela (ambassador); Farnborough, England **(1920–1997)**

Harriman, W. (William) Averell (ex-Governor of New York); New York City **(1891–1986)**

Harrington, Pat, Jr. (actor, comedian); New York City, 8/13/29

Harris, Barbara (Sandra Markowitz) (actress); Evanston, Ill., 7/25/35

Harris, Ed (actor); Englewood, N.J., 11/28/50

Harris, Emmylou (singer); Birmingham, Ala., 4/2/47

Harris, Julie (actress); Grosse Pointe Park, Mich., 12/2/25

Harris, Phil (actor, band leader); Linton, Ind. **(1906–1995)**

Harris, Richard (actor); Limerick, Ireland, 10/1/33

Harris, Rosemary (actress); Ashby, England, 9/19/30

Harris, Roy (composer); Lincoln County, Okla. **(1898–1979)**

Harrison, Benjamin (23rd U.S. president); North Bend, Ohio **(1833–1901)**

Harrison, George (singer, songwriter); Liverpool, England, 2/25/43

Harrison, Gregory (actor); Avalon, Catalina Island, Calif., 5/31/50

Harrison, Sir Rex (Reginald Carey) (actor); Huyton, England **(1908–1990)**

Harrison, William Henry (9th U.S. president); Charles City County, Va. **(1773–1841)**

Harry, Deborah (Blondie) (musician); Miami, Fla., 7/1/45

Hart, Lorenz (lyricist); New York City **(1895–1943)**

Hart, Mary (Mary Johanna Harum) (host); Sioux Falls, S.D., 11/8/50

Hart, Melissa Joan (actress); Sayville, N.Y., 4/18/76

Hart, Moss (playwright); New York City **(1904–1961)**

Harte, Bret (Francis Brett Harte) (author); Albany, N.Y. **(1836–1902)**

Hartford, Huntington (George Huntington Hartford II) (A.&P. heir); New York City, 4/18/11

Hartford, John (singer, banjoist); New York City, 12/30/37

Hartley, Mariette (actress); New York City, 6/21/40

Hartman, David Downs (TV newscaster); Pawtucket, R.I., 5/19/35

Hartman, Phil (actor, comedian); Brantford, Ont., Canada **(1948–1998)**

Hartman Black, Lisa (actress); Houston, 6/1/56

Harvey, Laurence (Larushka Skikne) (actor); Joniskis, Lithuania **(1928–1973)**

Harvey, Polly Jean (PJ Harvey) (singer, songwriter); Yeovil, England, 10/9/69

Harvey, William (physician); Folkestone, England **(1578–1657)**

Hasselhoff, David (actor, producer); Baltimore, 7/17/52

Hatcher, Teri (actress); Sunnyvale, Calif., 12/8/64

Havel, Vaclav (political leader, dramatist, poet); Prague, 10/5/36

Havens, Richie (musician); Brooklyn, N.Y., 1/21/41

Hawke, Ethan (actor); Austin, Tex., 11/6/70

Hawking, Stephen (physicist, astronomer); Oxford, England, 1/8/42

Hoover, Herbert Clark (31st U.S. president); West Branch, Iowa **(1874–1964)**
Hoover, J. Edgar (FBI director); Washington, D.C. **(1895–1972)**
Hope, Bob (Leslie Townes Hope) (comedian); London, 5/29/03
Hopkins, Sir Anthony (actor); Port Talbot, Wales, 12/31/37
Hopkins, Gerald Manley (poet); Stratford, England **(1844–1899)**
Hopkins, Johns (financier); Anne Arundel County, Md. **(1795–1873)**
Hopper, Dennis (actor); Dodge City, Kans., 5/17/36
Hopper, Edward (painter); Nyack, N.Y. **(1882–1967)**
Horace (Quintus Horatius Flaccus) (poet); Venosa, Italy **(65–8 B.C.E.)**
Horne, Lena (singer); Brooklyn, N.Y., 6/30/17
Horne, Marilyn (mezzo-soprano); Bradford, Pa., 1/16/34
Horowitz, Vladimir (pianist); Kiev, Ukraine **(1903–1989)**
Horsley, Lee (actor); Muleshoe, Tex., 5/15/55
Horton, Edward Everett (comedian); Brooklyn, N.Y. **(1887–1970)**
Hoskins, Bob (actor); Bury St. Edmunds, England, 10/26/42
Houdini, Harry (Ehrich Weiss) (magician); Appleton, Wis. **(1874–1926)**
Houseman, John (Jacques Haussmann) (producer, director, actor); Bucharest **(1902–1988)**
Housman, A(lfred) E(dward) (poet); Fockburg, England **(1859–1936)**
Houston, Charles Hamilton (civil rights lawyer); Washington, D.C. **(1895–1950)**
Houston, Samuel (political leader); Rockbridge County, Va. **(1793–1863)**
Houston, Whitney (singer); Newark, N.J., 8/9/63
Howard, Ken (actor); El Centro, Calif., 3/28/44
Howard, Leslie (Leslie Stainer) (actor); London **(1893–1943)**
Howard, Ron (actor, producer, director); Duncan, Okla., 3/1/54
Howard, Trevor (actor); Kent, England **(1916–1988)**
Howe, Elias (inventor); Spencer, Mass. **(1819–1867)**
Howe, Irving (literary critic); New York City **(1920–1993)**
Howe, Julia Ward (poet, reformer); New York City **(1819–1910)**
Hudson, Henry (English navigator) **(fl. 1607–1611)**
Hudson, Rock (born Roy Scherer, Jr.; took Roy Fitzgerald as legal name) (actor); Winnetka, Ill. **(1925–1985)**
Huggins, Nathan Irvin (historian); Chicago **(1927–1989)**
Hughes, Charles Evans (jurist); Glens Falls, N.Y. **(1862–1948)**
Hughes, Howard (industrialist, film producer); Houston **(1905–1976)**
Hughes, Langston (poet); Joplin, Mo. **(1902–1967)**
Hughes, Ted (poet); Mytholmroyd, England **(1930–1998)**
Hugo, Victor Marie (author); Besançon, France **(1802–1885)**
Hulce, Tom (actor); Detroit, 12/6/53
Hume, David (philosopher); Edinburgh, Scotland **(1711–1776)**
Hume, Kirsty (model); Glasgow, Scotland, 9/4/76
Humperdinck, Engelbert (composer); Siegburg, Germany **(1854–1921)**
Humperdinck, Engelbert (Arnold Dorsey) (singer); Madras, India, 5/2/36
Hunt, Helen (actress); Los Angeles, 6/15/63
Hunt, Linda (actress); Morristown, New Jersey, 4/2/45
Hunter, Holly (actress); Atlanta, 3/20/58
Hunter, Kim (Janet Cole) (actress); Detroit, 11/12/22
Hunter, Tab (Arthur Andrew Gelien) (actor); New York City, 7/11/31
Hunter-Gault, Charlayne (activist, broadcast journalist); Due West, S.C., 2/27/42
Huntley, Chet (TV newscaster); Cardwell, Mont. **(1911–1974)**
Hurley, Elizabeth (actress, model); Backingstoke, England, 6/10/65
Hurok, Sol (Solomon Hurok) (impresario); Pogar, Russia **(1884–1974)**
Hurst, Fannie (novelist); Hamilton, Ohio **(1889–1968)**
Hurston, Zora Neale (author); Eatonville, Fla. **(1901–1960)**
Hurt, John (actor); Shirebrook, England, 1/22/40
Hurt, William (actor); Washington, D.C., 3/20/50
Hus, Jan (Bohemian religious reformer); Husinetz, nr. Budweis, Czech Republic **(c. 1369–1415)**
Husing, Ted (sportscaster); New York City **(1901–1962)**
Hussein I (King); Jordan **(1935–1999)**
Hussein, Saddam (al-Tikriti) (Iraqi President); Tikrit, Iraq, 4/28/37
Huston, Anjelica (actress); Los Angeles, 7/8/51
Huston, John (actor, director, writer); Nevada, Mo. **(1906–1987)**
Huston, Walter (Walter Houghston) (actor); Toronto **(1884–1950)**
Hutchins, Robert M. (educator); Brooklyn, N.Y. **(1899–1977)**
Hutton, Betty (Betty Thornburg) (actress); Battle Creek, Mich., 2/26/21
Hutton, Lauren (actress, model); Charleston, S.C., 11/17/43
Hutton, Timothy (actor); Los Angeles, 8/16/60
Huxley, Aldous (author); Godalming, England **(1894–1963)**
Huxley, Sir Julian S. (biologist, author); London **(1887–1975)**
Huxley, Thomas Henry (biologist); Ealing, England **(1825–1895)**
Hynde, Chrissie (singer); Akron, Ohio, 9/7/51

I

Iacocca, Lee (Lido Anthony) (business executive); Allentown, Pa., 10/15/24
Ian, Janis (singer); New York City, 5/7/51
Ibsen, Henrik (dramatist); Skien, Norway **(1828–1906)**
Ice Cube (O'Shea Jackson) (musician, actor); Los Angeles, 6/15/69
Ice-T (Tracy Morrow) (rap musician, actor); Newark, N.J., 2/16/68
Inge, William (playwright); Independence, Kans. **(1913–1973)**
Ingres, Jean Auguste Dominique (painter); Montauban, France **(1780–1867)**
Inness, George (painter); nr. Newburgh, N.Y. **(1825–1894)**
Ionesco, Eugene (playwright); Slatina, Romania **(1912–1994)**
Ireland, Jill (actress); London **(1936–1990)**
Ireland, Kathy (model, actress); Glendale, California, 3/8/63
Ireland, Patricia (feminist, social activist); Oak Park, Ill., 10/19/45
Irons, Jeremy (actor); Cowes, Isle of Wight, England, 9/19/48
Irving, Amy (actress); Palo Alto, Calif., 9/10/53
Irving, John (Winslow) (writer); Exeter, N.H., 3/2/42
Irving, Washington (author); New York City **(1783–1859)**
Isaak, Chris (musician, actor); Stockton, California, 6/26/56
Isherwood, Christopher (novelist, playwright); nr. Dilsey and High Lane, England **(1904–1986)**
Iturbi, José (concert pianist); Valencia, Spain **(1895–1980)**
Ives, Burl (Icle Ivanhoe) (singer); Hunt, Ill. **(1909–1995)**
Ives, Charles E(dward) (composer); Danbury, Conn. **(1874–1954)**
Ivins, Molly (journalist); Monterey, Calif., 8/30/44
Ivory, James (director, producer); Berkeley, Calif., 6/7/28

J

Jackson, Andrew (7th U.S. president); Waxhaw, S.C. **(1767–1845)**
Jackson, Anne (actress); Millvale, Pa., 9/3/26
Jackson, Glenda (actress); Cheshire, England, 5/9/36
Jackson, Janet (singer); Gary, Ind., 5/16/66
Jackson, Rev. Jesse (civil rights leader); Greenville, S.C., 10/8/41
Jackson, Kate (actress); Birmingham, Ala., 10/29/49
Jackson, Mahalia (gospel singer); New Orleans **(1911–1972)**
Jackson, Maynard (mayor of Atlanta); Dallas, 3/23/38
Jackson, Michael (singer); Gary, Ind., 8/29/58
Jackson, Samuel L. (actor); Washington, D.C., 12/21/48
Jackson, Thomas Jonathan ("Stonewall") (general); Clarksburg, Va. (now W. Va.) **(1824–1863)**
Jacobi, Derek (actor); Leytonstone, England, 10/22/38
Jacobs, Jane (urbanologist); Scranton, Pa., 5/1/16
Jagger, Mick (Michael Phillip Jagger) (singer); Dartford, England, 7/26/43
James, Harry (trumpeter); Albany, Ga. **(1916–1983)**
James, Henry (novelist); New York City **(1843–1916)**
James, Jesse Woodson (outlaw); Clay County, Mo. **(1847–1882)**
James, William (psychologist); New York City **(1842–1910)**
Jameson, (Margaret) Storm (novelist); Whitby, England **(1897–1986)**
Janis, Byron (pianist); McKeesport, Pa., 3/24/28
Janis, Conrad (actor, musician); New York City, 2/11/28
Janssen, David (David Meyer) (actor); Naponee, Neb. **(1930–1980)**
Jaworkski, Leon (Watergate special prosecutor); Waco, Tex. **(1905–1982)**
Jay, John (statesman, jurist); New York City **(1745–1829)**
Jeanmaire, Renée (dancer); Paris, 4/29/24
Jefferson, Thomas (3rd U.S. president); Shadwell, Va. **(1743–1826)**
Jemison, Mae C. (astronaut, physician); Decatur, Ala., 10/17/56
Jenner, Edward (physician); Berkeley, England **(1749–1823)**
Jennings, Peter (news anchor); Toronto, 7/29/38
Jennings, Waylon (singer); Littlefield, Tex., 6/15/37
Jessel, George (entertainer); New York City **(1898–1981)**
Jessup, Philip C. (diplomat); New York City **(1897–1986)**
Jillian, Ann (actress); Cambridge, Mass., 1/29/51
Joan of Arc (Jeanne d'Arc) (saint, patriot); Domremy-la-Pucelle, France **(1412–1431)**
Jobs, Steven Paul (computer industry pioneer); San Francisco, 1955
Joel, Billy (singer); New York City, 5/9/49
Joffrey, Robert (Abdullah Jaffa Bey Khan) (choreographer); Seattle **(1930–1988)**
John, Elton (Reginald Kenneth Dwight) (singer, pianist); Pinner, England, 3/25/47
Johns, Jasper (painter, sculptor); Augusta, Ga., 5/15/30
Johnson, Andrew (17th U.S. president); Raleigh, N.C. **(1808–1875)**
Johnson, Don (actor); Flatt Creek, Mo., 12/15/49
Johnson, James Weldon (author, educator); Jacksonville, Fla. **(1871–1938)**

Johnson, Lyndon Baines (36th U.S. president); Stonewall, Tex. **(1908–1973)**
Johnson, Philip Cortelyou (architect); Cleveland, 7/8/06
Johnson, Samuel (lexicographer, author); Lichfield, England **(1709–1784)**
Johnson, Van (actor); Newport, R.I., 8/20/16
Johnson, Virginia (human sexuality expert); Springfield, Mo., 2/11/25
Joliot-Curie, Frédéric (chemist, Nobel laureate); Paris **(1900–1958)**
Joliot-Curie, Irène (Irène Curie) (chemist, Nobel laureate); France **(1897–1956)**
Jolliet, Louis (Louis Joliet) (explorer); Beaupré, Canada **(1645–1700)**
Jolson, Al (Asa Yoelson) (actor, singer); St. Petersburg, Russia **(1886–1950)**
Jones, Dean (actor); Morgan County, Ala., 1/25/35
Jones, George (singer); Saratoga, Tex., 9/12/31
Jones, Inigo (architect); London **(1573–1652)**
Jones, James (novelist); Robinson, Ill. **(1921–1977)**
Jones, James Earl (actor); Arkabutla, Miss., 1/17/31
Jones, Jennifer (Phylis Isley) (actress); Tulsa, Okla., 3/2/19
Jones, John Paul (John Paul) (naval officer); Scotland **(1747–1792)**
Jones, Quincy (composer); Chicago, 3/14/33
Jones, Shirley (singer, actress); Smithtown, Pa., 3/31/34
Jones, Spike (host, orchestra leader); Long Beach, Calif. **(1911–1965)**
Jones, Tom (Thomas Jones Woodward) (singer); Pontypridd, Wales, 6/7/40
Jones, Tommy Lee (actor); San Saba, Tex., 9/15/46
Jong, Erica (writer); New York City, 3/26/42
Jonson, Ben (Benjamin Jonson) (poet, dramatist); Westminster, England **(1572–1637)**
Joplin, Janis (singer); Port Arthur, Tex. **(1943–1970)**
Joplin, Scott (ragtime pianist, composer); Texarkansas, Tex. **(1868–1917)**
Jordan, Barbara (U.S. Representative); Houston **(1936–1996)**
Jordan, Neil (film director, screenwriter); Sligo, Ireland, 2/25/50
Joseph (Chief Joseph) (Nez Perce Indian leader); eastern Ore. **(1841–1904)**
Josquin des Prés (usually known as Josquin) (composer); Conde-sur-L'Escaut?, Hainaut, Belgium **(c. 1445–1521)**
Jourdan, Louis (Louis Gendre) (actor); Marseilles, France, 6/19/19
Jovovich, Milla (actress, model, singer); Kiev, Ukraine, 12/19/75
Joyce, James (novelist); Dublin **(1882–1941)**
Juárez, Benito Pablo (statesman); Guelatao, Mexico **(1806–1872)**
Judd, Ashley (actress); Los Angeles, 4/19/68
Julia, Raul (Raúl Rafael Carlos Julia y Arcelay) (actor); San Juan, P.R. **(1940–1994)**
Jung, Carl Gustav (psychoanalyst); Basel, Switzerland **(1875–1961)**

K

Kabalevsky, Dmitri (composer); St. Petersburg, Russia **(1904–1987)**
Kafka, Franz (author); Prague **(1883–1924)**
Kádár, János (Communist Party leader); Hungary **(1912–1989)**
Kahn, Gus (songwriter); Coblenz, Germany **(1886–1941)**
Kahn, Louis I. (architect); Oesel Island, Estonia **(1901–1974)**
Kahn, Madeline (actress); Boston, 9/29/42
Kandinsky, Wassily (painter); Moscow **(1866–1944)**
Kanin, Garson (playwright); Rochester, N.Y. **(1912–1999)**
Kant, Immanuel (philosopher); Königsberg (Kaliningrad), Russia **(1724–1804)**
Kantor, MacKinlay (novelist); Webster City, Iowa **(1904–1977)**
Kaplan, Justin (writer, editor); New York City, 9/5/25
Karan, Donna (fashion designer); Forest Hills, N.Y., 10/2/48
Karloff, Boris (William Henry Pratt) (actor); London **(1887–1969)**
Kasdan, Lawrence (film director, writer, actor, producer); Miami, 1/14/49
Kasem, Casey (disc jockey); Detroit, 4/27/32
Kaufman, Andy (actor, comedian); New York City **(1949–1984)**
Kaufman, George S. (playwright); Pittsburgh **(1889–1961)**
Kavner, Julie (actress); Los Angeles, 9/7/51
Kaye, Danny (David Daniel Kominski) (comedian); Brooklyn, N.Y. **(1913–1987)**
Kaye, Sammy (band leader); Cleveland **(1910–1987)**
Kazan, Elia (director); Constantinople, Turkey, 9/7/09
Kazan, Lainie (Levine) (singer); New York City, 5/15/40
Kazantzakis, Nikos (writer); Herakleion, Crete **(1883–1957)**
Keach, Stacy (actor); Savannah, Ga., 6/2/41
Keaton, Buster (Joseph Frank Keaton) (comedian); Piqua, Kans. **(1896–1966)**
Keaton, Diane (actress); Los Angeles, 1/5/46

Keaton, Michael (Michael Douglas) (actor); Robinson Township, Pa., 9/9/51
Keats, John (poet); London **(1795–1821)**
Keel, Howard (Harold Clifford Leek) (singer, actor); Gillespie, Ill., 4/13/19
Keeler, Ruby (Ethel Hilde Keeler) (actress, dancer); Halifax, Nova Scotia, Canada **(1910–1993)**
Kefauver, Estes (legislator); Madisonville, Tenn **(1903–1963)**
Keitel, Harvey (actor); Brooklyn, N.Y., 5/13/39
Keith, Brian (Robert Brian Keith, Jr.) (actor); Bayonne, N.J. **(1921–1997)**
Keller, Helen Adams (author, educator); Tuscumbia, Ala. **(1880–1968)**
Kelley, DeForest (actor); Atlanta **(1920–1999)**
Kelly, Emmett (clown); Sedan, Kans. **(1898–1979)**
Kelly, Gene (dancer, actor); Pittsburgh **(1912–1996)**
Kelly, R. (Robert Kelly) (singer, record producer, actor); Chicago, 1969
Kempis, Thomas à (mystic); Kempis, Prussia (Germany) **(1380–1471)**
Kendall, Henry W. (physicist, Nobel laureate); Boston **(1926–1999)**
Kennan, George F. (diplomat); Milwaukee, 2/16/04
Kennedy, Arthur (actor); Worcester, Mass. **(1914–1990)**
Kennedy, Caroline Bessette (socialite); White Plains, N.Y. **(1966–1999)**
Kennedy, George (actor); New York City, 2/18/25
Kennedy, John Fitzgerald (35th U.S. president); Brookline, Mass. **(1917–1963)**
Kennedy, John F., Jr. (publisher); Washington, D.C. **(1960–1999)**
Kennedy, Joseph P. (financier); Boston **(1888–1969)**
Kennedy, Robert Francis (legislator); Brookline, Mass. **(1925–1968)**
Kennedy, Rose Fitzgerald (President's mother); Boston **(1890–1995)**
Kent, Allegra (ballet dancer); Santa Monica, Calif., 8/11/38
Kent, Rockwell (painter); Tarrytown Heights, N.Y. **(1882–1971)**
Kenton, Stan (Stanley Newcomb) (jazz musician); Wichita, Kans. **(1912–1979)**
Kepler, Johannes (astronomer); Weil, Germany **(1571–1630)**
Kercheval, Ken (actor); Wolcottville, Ind., 7/15/35
Kerensky, Alexander Fedorovich (statesman); Simbirsk, Russia **(1881–1970)**
Kern, Jerome David (composer); New York City **(1885–1945)**
Kerns, Joanna (actress); San Francisco, 2/12/53
Kerouac, Jack (Jean-Louis Kerouac) (writer); Lowell, Mass. **(1922–1969)**
Kerr, Deborah (actress); Helensburgh, Scotland, 9/30/21
Kettering, Charles F. (engineer, inventor); nr. Loudonville, Ohio **(1876–1958)**
Kevorkian, Jack (medical pathologist); Pontiac, Mich., 3/26/28
Key, Francis Scott (lawyer, author of national anthem); Frederick (Carroll) County, Md. **(1779– 1843)**
Keyes, Frances Parkinson (novelist); Charlottesville, Va. **(1885–1970)**
Keynes, John Maynard (1st Baron of Tilton) (economist); Cambridge, England **(1883–1946)**
Khachaturian, Aram (composer); Tiflis, Russia **(1903–1978)**
Khomeini, Ayatollah Ruhollah (Islamic religious leader); Iran **(1900–1989)**
Khrushchev, Nikita S. (Soviet leader); Kalinovka, nr. Kursk, Ukraine **(1894–1971)**
Kidd, Michael (choreographer); Brooklyn, N.Y., 8/12/19
Kidd, William (called Captain Kidd) (pirate); Greenock, Scotland **(c. 1645–1701)**
Kidder, Margot (actress); Yellowknife, N.W.T., Canada, 10/17/48
Kidman, Nicole (actress); Honolulu, 6/20/67
Kiepura, Jan (tenor); Sosnowiec, Poland **(1902–1966)**
Kieran, John (writer); New York City **(1892–1981)**
Kierkegaard, Sören Aalys (philosopher); Copenhagen **(1813–1855)**
Kiesinger, Kurt Georg (diplomat); Ebingen, Germany **(1904–1988)**
Kiley, Richard (actor, singer); Chicago **(1922–1999)**
Kilmer, Alfred Joyce (poet); New Brunswick, N.J. **(1886–1918)**
Kilmer, Val (actor); Los Angeles,, 12/31/59
King, Alan (Irwin Alan Kniberg) (entertainer); Brooklyn, N.Y., 12/26/27
King, B.B. (Riley King) (guitarist); Itta Bena, Miss., 9/16/25
King, Carole (singer, songwriter); Brooklyn, N.Y., 2/9/41
King, Coretta Scott (civil rights leader); Marion, Ala., 4/27/27
King, Larry (TV host); New York City, 11/19/33
King, Martin Luther, Jr. (civil rights leader); Atlanta **(1929–1968)**
King, Stephen (writer); Portland, Maine, 9/21/47
Kingsley, Ben (Krishna Bhanji) (actor); Snainton, England, 12/31/43
Kingsley, Sidney (Sidney Kirschner) (playwright); New York City **(1906–1995)**

Kingsolver, Barbara (writer); Annapolis, Md., 4/8/55
Kingston, Maxine Hong (novelist); Stockton, Calif., 10/27/40
Kinsey, Alfred Charles (human sexuality expert); Hoboken, N.J. (1894–1956)
Kinski, Nastassja (Nastassja Nakszynski) (actress); West Berlin, 1/24/61
Kipling, Rudyard (author); Bombay (Mumbai) (1865–1936)
Kipnis, Alexander (basso); Ukraine (1891–1978)
Kirby, George (comedian); Chicago (1923–1995)
Kirchner, Ernst Ludwig (painter); Aschaffenburg, Germany (1880–1938)
Kirk, Grayson (educator); Jeffersonville, Ohio (1903–1997)
Kirkland, Gelsey (ballet dancer); Bethlehem, Pa., 12/29/52
Kirkpatrick, Jeane Jordan (educator-public affairs); Duncan, Okla., 11/19/26
Kirkpatrick, Ralph (harpsichordist); Leominster, Mass. (1911–1984)
Kirstein, Lincoln (dance, theater executive); Rochester, N.Y. (1907–1996)
Kirsten, Dorothy (soprano); Montclair, N.J. (1910–1992)
Kissinger, Henry (Heinz Alfred Kissinger) (ex-U.S. Secretary of State); Furth, Germany, 5/27/23
Kitt, Eartha (singer); North, S.C., 1/26/28
Klee, Paul (painter); Münchenbuchsee, nr. Bern, Switzerland (1879–1940)
Klein, Calvin (fashion designer); Bronx, N.Y., 11/19/42
Klein, Robert (comedian); New York City, 2/8/42
Kleist, Henrich von (poet); Frankfurt an der Oder, Germany (1777–1811)
Klemperer, Otto (conductor); Breslau, Poland (1885–1973)
Klemperer, Werner (actor); Cologne, Germany, 3/22/20
Klimt, Gustav (painter); Vienna (1862–1918)
Kline, Kevin (actor); St. Louis, 10/24/47
Klugman, Jack (actor); Philadelphia, 4/27/22
Knight, Gladys (singer); Atlanta, 5/28/44
Knight, John S. (publisher); Bluefield, W. Va. (1894–1981)
Knight, Ted (Tadeus Wladyslaw Konopka) (actor); Terryville, Conn. (1923–1986)
Knight, Wayne (actor); Cartersville, Ga., 8/7/55
Knopf, Alfred A. (publisher); New York City (1892–1984)
Knopfler, Mark (musician); Glasgow, Scotland, 8/12/49
Knotts, Don (actor); Morgantown, W. Va., 7/21/24
Knox, John (religious reformer); Haddington, East Lothian, Scotland (1505–1572)
Koch, Robert (physician); Klausthal, Germany (1843–1910)
Koenig, Walter (actor); Chicago, 9/14/36
Koestler, Arthur (novelist); Budapest (1905–1983)
Kokoschka, Oskar (painter); Póchlarn Austria (1886–1980)
Kollwitz, Käthe (graphic artist, sculptor); Königsberg, Russia (1867–1945)
Koop, C. Everett (ex-Surgeon General); Brooklyn, N.Y., 10/14/16
Kooper, Al (singer, pianist); Brooklyn, N.Y., 2/5/44
Kopell, Bernie (actor); New York City, 6/21/33
Koppel, Ted (broadcast journalist); Lancashire, England, 2/8/40
Korman, Harvey (actor); Chicago, 2/15/27
Kosciusko, Thaddeus (Tadeusz Andrzej Bonawentura Kosciuszko) (military officer; Grand Duchy of Lithuania) (1746–1817)
Kossuth, Lajos (patriot); Monok, Hungary (1802–1894)
Kostelanetz, André (orchestra conductor); St. Petersburg, Russia (1901–1980)
Kosygin, Aleksei N. (Premier); St. Petersburg, Russia (1904–1980)
Kotto, Yaphet (actor); New York City, 11/15/37
Koussevitzky, Serge (Sergei) Alexandrovitch (orchestra conductor); Vishni Volochek, Tver, Russia (1874–1951)
Kramer, Stanley E. (film producer, director); New York City, 9/29/13
Kràus, Lili (pianist); Budapest (1905–1986)
Kravitz, Lenny (musician); New York City, 5/26/64
Kreisler, Fritz (violinist, composer); Vienna (1875–1962)
Kresge, S. S. (merchant); Bald Mount, Pa. (1867–1966)
Krips, Josef (orchestra conductor); Vienna (1902–1974)
Kristofferson, Kris (singer); Brownsville, Tex., 6/22/36
Krupa, Gene (drummer); Chicago (1909–1973)
Krupp, Alfred (munitions magnate); Essen, Germany (1812–1887)
Kubelik, Rafael (conductor); Bychory, former Czechoslovakia (1914–1996)
Kublai Khan (Mongol conqueror) (1216–1294)
Kubrick, Stanley (film director, producer); New York City (1928–1999)
Kudrow, Lisa (actress); Encino, Calif., 7/30/63
Kuralt, Charles (TV journalist); Wilmington, N.C. (1934–1997)
Kurosawa, Akira (film director); Tokyo (1910–1998)
Kurtz, Efrem (conductor); St. Petersburg, Russia (1900–1995)
Kurtz, Swoosie (actress); Omaha, Neb. 9/6/44

L

LaBelle, Patti (singer, actress); Philadelphia, 5/24/44
Ladd, Cheryl (Cheryl Stoppelmoor) (actress); Huron, S.D., 7/12/51
Ladd, Diane (actress); Meridian, Miss., 11/29/32
Lafayette, Marquis de (Marie Joseph Paul Yves Roch Gilbert du Motier) (military officer); Auvergne, France (1757–1834)
Lafitte, Jean (pirate); Bayonne?, France (1780–1826)
La Follette, Robert Marin (politician); Primrose, Wis. (1855–1925)
La Fontaine, Jean de (poet); Château-Thierry, France (1621–1695)
La Guardia, Fiorello Henry (Mayor of New York); New York City (1882–1947)
Lahti, Christine (actress, director); Birmingham, Mich., 4/4/50
Laine, Frankie (Frank Paul LoVecchio) (singer); Chicago, 3/30/13
Laird, Melvin (ex-Secretary of Defense); Omaha, Neb., 9/1/22
Lamarck, Chevalier de (Jean Baptiste Pierre Antoine de Monet) (naturalist); Bazantin, France (1744–1829)
Lamas, Lorenzo (actor); Los Angeles, 1/20/58
Lamb, Charles (Elia) (essayist); London (1775–1834)
L'Amour, Louis (author); Jamestown, N.D. (1908–1988)
Lancaster, Burt (actor); New York City (1913–1994)
Landau, Martin (actor); Brooklyn, N.Y., 6/20/31
Landers, Ann (Esther Pauline Friedman) (columnist); Sioux City, Iowa, 7/4/18
Landon, Michael (Eugene Maurice Orowitz) (actor, director, producer); Forest Hills, Queens, N.Y. (1936–1991)
Lane, Abbe (Abigail Francine Lassman) (singer); New York City, 1933
Lane, Burton (songwriter); New York City (1912–1997)
Lane, Nathan (Joseph Lane) (actor, singer); Jersey City, New Jersey, 2/3/56
Lang, Fritz (film director); Vienna (1890–1976)
Lang, Paul Henry (music critic); Budapest (1901–1991)
Lange, Hope (actress); Redding Ridge, Conn., 11/28/33
Lange, Jessica (actress); Cloquet, Minn., 4/20/49
Langella, Frank (actor); Bayonne, N.J., 1/1/40
Langmuir, Irving (chemist); Brooklyn, N.Y. (1881–1957)
Langtry, Lillie (Emily Le Breton) (actress); Island of Jersey (1852–1929)
Lansbury, Angela (actress, producer); London, 10/16/25
Lansing, Robert (Robert Howell Brown) (actor); San Diego, Calif. (1928–1994)
Lanza, Mario (Alfred Arnold Cocozza) (singer, actor); Philadelphia (1921–1959)
Lao-tse (Li Erh) (philosopher); Honan Province, China (c. 604–531 b.c.e.)
Lardner, Ring (Ringgold Wilmar Lardner) (story writer); Niles, Mich. (1885–1933)
La Rouchefoucauld, Francois duc de (author); Paris (1613–1680)
Larroquette, John (actor); New Orleans, 11/25/47
Larson, Gary (cartoonist); Tacoma, Wash., 8/14/50
La Salle, Eriq (actor); Hartford, Conn., 7/23/62
La Salle, Sieur de (Robert Cavelier) (explorer); Rouen, France (1643–1687)
Lasch, Christopher (historian, social critic); Omaha, Neb. (1932–1994)
La Tour, Georges de (painter); Vic-sur-Seille, France (1593–1652)
Lauder, Sir Harry (Harry MacLennan) (singer); Portobello, Scotland (1870–1950)
Lauer, Matt (TV host); New York City, 12/20/57
Laughton, Charles (actor); Scarborough, England (1899–1962)
Lauper, Cyndi (singer); New York City, 6/20/53
Laurel, Stan (Arthur Jefferson) (comedian); Ulverston, England (1890–1965)
Laurents, Arthur (playwright); New York City, 7/14/18
Laurie, Piper (Rosetta Jacobs) (actress); Detroit, 1/22/32
Lavin, Linda (actress); Portland, Maine, 10/15/37
Lavoisier, Antoine-Laurent (chemist); Paris (1743–1794)
Lawford, Peter (actor); London (1923–1984)
Lawless, Lucy (Lucy Ryan) (actress); Auckland, New Zealand, 3/29/68
Lawrence, David Herbert (novelist); Nottingham, England (1885–1930)
Lawrence, Jacob (painter); Atantic City, N.J., 9/7/17
Lawrence, Martin (actor); Frankfurt, Germany, 4/16/65
Lawrence, Sharon (actress); Charlotte, N.C., 6/29/62
Lawrence, Steve (Sidney Leibowitz) (singer); Brooklyn, N.Y., 7/8/35
Lawrence of Arabia (Thomas Edward Lawrence, later changed to Shaw) (author, soldier); Tremadoc, Wales (1888–1935)
Lawrence, Vicki (actress); Inglewood, Calif., 3/26/49
Leach, Penelope (Balchin) (child psychologist, writer); London, 11/19/37

Leach, Robin (host, producer); London, 8/29/41

Leachman, Cloris (actress); Des Moines, Iowa, 4/30/26

Leadbelly, (Huddie Ledbetter) (blues singer, guitarist); Mooringsport, La. **(1885–1949)**

Leakey, Louis Seymour Bazett (anthropologist); Kabete, Kenya **(1903–1972)**

Leakey, Mary (anthropologist); London **(1913–1996)**

Leakey, Richard (paleoanthropologist, wildlife conservationist); Kenya, 12/19/44

Lean, David (film director); Croydon, England **(1908–1991)**

Lear, Edward (nonsense poet); London **(1812–1888)**

Lear, Evelyn (Shulman) (soprano); Brooklyn, N.Y., 1/8/26

Lear, Norman (TV producer); New Haven, Conn., 7/27/22

Learned, Michael (actress); Washington, D.C., 4/9/39

Leary, Denis (actor, screenwriter, film director); Worcester, Mass., 8/18/57

Leary, Timothy (psychologist, LSD advocate); Springfield, Mass. **(1920–1996)**

Le Blanc, Matt (actor); Newton, Mass., 7/25/67

le Carré, John (David John Moore Cornwell) (novelist); Poole, England, 10/19/31

Le Corbusier (Charles Edouard Jeanneret) (architect); La Chauxde-Fonds, Switzerland **(1887–1965)**

Lee, Ang (film director); Pingtung, Taiwan, 10/23/54

Lee, Christopher (actor); London, 5/27/22

Lee, Manfred B. (pseudonym Ellery Queen) (novelist); Brooklyn, N.Y. **(1905–1971)**

Lee, Michele (actress, singer); Los Angeles, 6/24/42

Lee, Peggy (Norma Engstrom) (singer); Jamestown, N.D., 5/26/20

Lee, Robert E(dward) (Confederate general); Stratford Estate, Va. **(1807–1870)**

Lee, Spike (Shelton Jackson Lee) (actor, director, writer, producer); Atlanta, 3/20/57

Leeuwenhoek, Anton van (zoologist); Delft, Netherlands **(1632–1723)**

Lehár, Franz (composer); Komárom, Hungary **(1870–1948)**

Lehman, Herbert H. (Governor, Senator); New York City **(1878–1963)**

Lehmann, Lotte (soprano); Perleberg, Germany **(1888–1976)**

Lehrer, Jim (TV newscaster); Wichita, Kans., 5/19/34

Leibniz, Gottfried W. von (scientist); Leipzig, Germany **(1646–1716)**

Leibovitz, Annie (photographer); Westbury, Conn., 10/2/49

Leigh, Janet (Jeanette Helen Morrison) (actress); Merced, Calif., ,7/6/27

Leigh, Jennifer Jason (Jennifer Morrow) (actress); Los Angeles, 2/5/62

Leigh, Mike (film director, screenwriter); Manchester, England, 2/20/43

Leigh, Vivien (Vivian Mary Hartley) (actress); Darjeeling, India **(1913–1967)**

Leinsdorf, Erich (conductor); Vienna **(1912–1993)**

Lemmon, Jack (actor); Boston, 2/8/25

Lenin, Vladimir (Vladimir Ilich Ulyanov) (Soviet leader); Simbirsk, Russia **(1870–1924)**

Lennon, John (singer, songwriter); Liverpool, England **(1940–1980)**

Leno, Jay (comedian, TV host); New Rochelle, N.Y., 4/28/50

Leonard, Sheldon (Sheldon Leonard Bershad) (actor, producer); New York City **(1907–1997)**

Leonardo da Vinci, (painter, scientist); Vinci, Tuscany, Italy **(1452–1519)**

Leoni, Téa (actress); New York City, 2/25/66

Lerner, Alan Jay (lyricist); New York City **(1918–1986)**

Lerner, Max (columnist); Minsk, Russia **(1902–1992)**

Lessing, Doris (novelist); Kermanshah, Iran, 10/22/19

Leto, Jared (actor); Bossier City, La., 12/26/71

Letterman, David (TV host, producer); Indianapolis, 4/12/47

Levant, Oscar (pianist); Pittsburgh **(1906–1972)**

Levenson, Sam (humorist); New York City **(1911–1980)**

Levi, Carlo (novelist); Turin, Italy **(1902–1975)**

Levine, James (music director, Metropolitan Opera); Cincinnati, 6/23/43

Levine, Joseph E. (film producer); Boston **(1905–1987)**

Levinson, Barry (screenwriter, director, producer, actor); Baltimore, 4/6/42

Lewis, C(live) S(taples) (author); Belfast, Northern Ireland **(1898–1963)**

Lewis, Gilbert Newton (chemist, Nobel laureate); Weymouth, Mass. **(1875–1946)**

Lewis, Jerry (Joseph Levitch) (comedian, film director); Newark, N.J., 3/16/26

Lewis, Jerry Lee (singer); Ferriday, La., 9/29/35

Lewis, John Llewellyn (labor leader); Lucas, Iowa **(1880–1969)**

Lewis, Juliette (actress); Los Angeles, 12/21/73

Lewis, Meriwether (explorer); Albemarle Co., Va. **(1774–1809)**

Lewis, (Percy) Wyndham (artist, writer); Bay of Fundy, Maine (at sea) **(1884–1957)**

Lewis, Shari (Shari Hurwitz) (puppeteer); New York City **(1934–1998)**

Lewis, Sinclair (novelist); Sauk Centre, Minn. **(1885–1951)**

Ley, Willy (science writer); Berlin **(1906–1969)**

Liberace (Wladziu Liberace) (pianist); West Allis, Wis. **(1919–1987)**

Lichtenstein, Roy (painter); New York City **(1923–1997)**

Lie, Trygve Halvdan (first U.N. Secretary-General); Oslo **(1896–1968)**

Light, Judith (actress); Trenton, N.J., 2/9/49

Lightfoot, Gordon (singer, songwriter); Orillia, Ont., Canada, 11/17/38

Limbaugh, Rush (political commentator); Cape Girardeau, Mo., 1/12/51

Lin, Maya (architect, sculptor); Athens, Ohio, 10/5/59

Lin Yutang (author); Changchow, China **(1895–1976)**

Lincoln, Abraham (16th U.S. president); Hardin (Larue) County, Ky. **(1809–1865)**

Lind, Jenny (Johanna Maria Lind) (soprano); Stockholm **(1820–1887)**

Lindbergh, Anne Morrow (author); Englewood, N.J., 6/22/06

Lindbergh, Charles A. (aviator); Detroit **(1902–1974)**

Linden, Hal (Harold Lipshitz) (actor); New York City, 3/20/31

Lindsay, Howard (playwright); Waterford, N.Y. **(1889–1968)**

Linkletter, Art (radio-TV personality); Moose Jaw, Sask., Canada, 7/17/12

Linnaeus, Carolus (Carl von Linné) (botanist); Råshult, Sweden **(1707–1778)**

Liotta, Ray (actor); Union, N.J., 12/18/55

Lipchitz, Jacques (sculptor); Druskieniki, Latvia **(1891–1973)**

Lippi, Fra Filippo (painter); Florence **(1406–1469)**

Lippmann, Walter (columnist, author, political analyst); New York City **(1889–1974)**

Lister, Joseph (1st Baron of Lyme Regis) (surgeon); Upton, England **(1827–1912)**

Liszt, Franz (composer, pianist); Raiding, Hungary **(1811–1886)**

Lithgow, John (actor); Rochester, N.Y., 6/6/45

Little, Rich (impressionist); Ottawa, Ont., Canada, 11/26/38

Livingstone, David (missionary, explorer); Lanarkshire, Scotland **(1813–1873)**

L. L. Cool J (James Todd Smith) (rap artist); New York City, 1/14/68

Llewellyn, Richard (novelist); St. David's, Wales **(1906–1983)**

Lloyd Webber, Andrew (composer); London, 3/22/48

Lloyd George, David (Earl of Dwyfor) (statesman); Manchester, England **(1863–1945)**

Lloyd, Jake (actor); Fort Collins, Colo., 3/5/89

Locke, Alain L. (philosopher); Philadelphia **(1886–1954)**

Locke, John (philosopher); Somersetshire, England **(1632–1704)**

Lockhart, June (actress); New York City, 6/25/25

Locklear, Heather (actress); Los Angeles, 9/25/61

Lodge, Henry Cabot (legislator); Boston **(1850–1924)**

Lodge, Henry Cabot, Jr. (diplomat); Nahant, Mass. **(1902–1985)**

Loesser, Frank (composer); New York City **(1910–1969)**

Loewe, Frederick (composer); Vienna **(1901–1988)**

Logan, Joshua (director, producer); Texarkana, Tex. **(1908–1988)**

Lollobrigida, Gina (Luigina Lollobrigida) (actress); Subiaco, Italy, 7/4/27

Lombard, Carole (Jane Alice Peters) (actress); Ft. Wayne, Ind. **(1908–1942)**

Lombardo, Guy (band leader); London, Ont., Canada **(1902–1977)**

London, George (baritone); Montreal **(1920–1985)**

London, Jack (John Griffith London) (novelist); San Francisco **(1876–1916)**

Long, Huey Pierce (politician); Winnfield, La. **(1893–1935)**

Long, Shelley (actress); Fort Wayne, Ind., 8/23/49

Longfellow, Henry Wadsworth (poet); Portland, Maine **(1807–1882)**

Longworth, Alice Roosevelt (social figure); New York City **(1884–1980)**

Loos, Anita (novelist); Sissons, Calif. **(1888–1981)**

Lopez, Jennifer (actress, singer); Bronx, N.Y., 12/24/70

Lopez, Trini (singer); Dallas, 5/15/37

Lopez, Vincent (band leader); Brooklyn, N.Y. **(1895–1975)**

Lord, Jack (John Joseph Ryan) (actor); New York City **(1920–1998)**

Loren, Sophia (Sofia Scicolone) (actress); Rome, 9/20/34

Lorenz, Konrad (ethologist); Vienna **(1903–1989)**

Lorre, Peter (Laszlo Löewenstein) (actor); Rosenberg, former Czechoslovakia **(1904–1964)**

Loudon, Dorothy (actress, singer); Boston, 9/17/33

Louis-Dreyfus, Julia (actress); New York City, 1/13/61

Louis XIV (King of France); St.-Germain-en-Laye, France **(1638–1715)**

Louise, Tina (actress); New York City, 2/11/37
Love, Susan (surgeon, oncologist, activist); Long Branch, N.J., 2/9/48
Lovecraft, Howard Phillips (author); Providence, R.I. **(1890–1937)**
Lovett, Lyle (country singer, songwriter); Klein, Tex., 11/1/56
Lowe, Rob (actor); Charlottesville, Va., 3/17/64
Lowell, Amy (poet); Brookline, Mass. **(1874–1925)**
Lowell, James Russell (poet); Cambridge, Mass. **(1819–1891)**
Lowell, Robert (poet); Boston **(1917–1977)**
Loy, Myrna (Myrna Williams) (actress); nr. Helena, Mont. **(1905– 1993)**
Loyola, St. Ignatius of (Iñigo de Oñez y Loyola) (founder of Jesuits); Gúipuzcoa Province, Spain **(1491– 1556)**
Lubitsch, Ernst (film director); Berlin **(1892–1947)**
Lucas, George (film director); Modesto, Calif., 5/14/44
Lucci, Susan (actress); Scarsdale, N.Y., 12/23/46
Luce, Clare Boothe (playwright, former Ambassador); New York City **(1903–1987)**
Luce, Henry Robinson (editor, publisher); Tengchow, China **(1898– 1967)**
Ludlum, Robert (author); New York City, 5/25/27
Lugosi, Béla (Béla Blasko) (actor); Lugos, Hungary **(1888–1956)**
Lukas, J. Anthony (author); New York City **(1933–1997)**
Lukas, Paul (actor); Budapest **(1895–1971)**
Lully, Jean Baptiste (French composer); Florence **(1639–1687)**
Lumet, Sidney (director); Philadelphia, 6/25/24
Lunden, Joan (TV host); Fair Oaks, Calif., 9/19/50
Lunt, Alfred (actor); Milwaukee **(1892–1977)**
Lupino, Ida (actress, director); London **(1918–1995)**
LuPone, Patti (actress, singer); Northport, N.Y., 4/21/49
Luther, Martin (religious reformer); Eisleben, East Germany **(1483– 1546)**
Lynch, David (film director); Missoula, Mont., 1/20/46
Lynn, Loretta (singer); Butcher's Hollow, Ky., 4/14/35

M

Ma, Yo-Yo (cellist); Paris, 10/7/55
Maazel, Lorin (conductor); Neuilly, France, 3/5/30
MacArthur, Charles (playwright); Scranton, Pa. **(1895–1956)**
MacArthur, Douglas (five-star general); Little Rock Barracks, Ark. **(1880–1964)**
MacArthur, James (actor); Los Angeles, 12/8/37
Macaulay, Thomas Babington (author); Rothley Temple, England **(1800–1859)**
MacDermot, Galt (composer); Montreal, 12/19/28
MacDonald, James Ramsay (statesman); Lossiemouth, Scotland **(1866–1937)**
MacDonald, Jeanette (actress, soprano); Philadelphia **(1907–1965)**
Macdonald, Ross (Kenneth Millar) (mystery writer); Los Gatos, Calif. **(1915–1983)**
MacDowell, Edward Alexander (composer); New York City **(1861– 1908)**
MacDowell, Andie (Rosalie Anderson MacDowell) (actress); Gaffney, S.C., 4/21/58
MacFadden, Bernarr (physical culturist); nr. Mill Spring, Mo. **(1868– 1955)**
Machaut, Guillaume de (composer); Marchault, France **(1300– 1377)**
Machiavelli, Niccolò (political philosopher); Florence, Italy **(1469– 1527)**
Mackie, Bob (designer); Monterey Park, Calif., 3/24/40
MacLaine, Shirley (Shirley MacLean Beaty) (actress); Richmond, Va., 4/24/34
MacLeish, Archibald (poet); Glencoe, Ill. **(1892–1982)**
Macmillan, Harold (ex-Prime Minister); London **(1894–1986)**
MacMurray, Fred (actor); Kankakee, Ill. **(1908–1991)**
MacNeil, Cornell (baritone); Minneapolis, 9/24/22
MacNeil, Robert (TV newscaster); Montreal, 1/19/31
MacNicol, Peter (actor); Dallas, 4/10/54
Macpherson, Elle (Eleanor Gow) (model, actress); Sydney, Australia, 3/29/64
MacRae, Gordon (singer, actor); East Orange, N.J. **(1921–1986)**
MacRae, Sheila (comedienne); London, 9/24/24
Madison, James (4th U.S. president); Port Conway, Va. **(1751– 1836)**
Madonna (Madonna Louise Ciccone) (singer, actress); Bay City, Mich., 8/16/58
Maeterlinck, Count Maurice (author); Ghent, Belgium **(1862–1949)**
Magellan, Ferdinand (Fernando de Magalhaes) (navigator); Sabrosa, Portugal (**c. 1480–1521)**
Magliozzi, Ray ("Car Talk" host); Cambridge, Mass., 3/30/49
Magliozzi, Tom ("Car Talk" host); Cambridge, Mass., 6/28/37

Magritte, René (painter); Belgium **(1898–1967)**
Magsaysay, Ramón (statesman); Iba, Luzon, Philippines **(1907– 1957)**
Mahan, Alfred Thayer (naval historian); West Point, N.Y. **(1840– 1914)**
Mahler, Gustav (composer, conductor); Kalischt, Czechoslovakia **(1860–1911)**
Mahoney, John (actor); Manchester, England, 6/20/40
Mailer, Norman (novelist); Long Branch, N.J., 1/31/23
Maillol, Aristide (sculptor); Banyuls-sur-Mer, Rousillion, France **(1861–1944)**
Maimonides, Moses (Jewish philosopher); Cordoba, Spain **(1135– 1204)**
Mainbocher (Main Rousseau Bocher) (fashion designer); Chicago **(1891–1976)**
Majors, Lee (Harvey Lee Yeary) (actor); Wyandotte, Mich., 4/23/40
Makarova, Natalia (ballet dancer); Leningrad (St. Petersburg), Russia, 11/21/40
Makeba, Miriam (singer); Johannesburg, South Africa, 3/4/32
Malamud, Bernard (novelist); Brooklyn, N.Y. **(1914–1986)**
Malcolm X (Malcolm Little; el Hajj Ma lik el-Shabazz) (Black nationalist, religious leader); Omaha, Neb. **(1925–1965)**
Malden, Karl (Karl Mladen Sekulovich) (actor); Chicago, 3/22/13
Malkovich, John (actor); Christopher, Ill., 12/9/53
Mallarmé, Stephane (poet, essayist); Paris **(1842–1898)**
Malle, Louis (director); Thumeries, France **(1932–1995)**
Malraux, André (author); Paris **(1901–1976)**
Malthus, Thomas Robert (economist); nr. Dorking, England **(1766– 1834)**
Maltin, Leonard (film critic and historian); New York City, 12/18/50
Mamet, David (playwright); Chicago, 11/30/47
Manchester, Melissa (singer); Bronx, N.Y., 2/15/51
Manchester, William (writer); Attleboro, Mass., 4/1/22
Mancini, Henry (composer, conductor); Cleveland **(1924–1994)**
Mandela, Nelson (Rolihlahla) (former president of South Africa); Umtata, Transkei, 7/18/18
Mandela, Winnie (Nomzamo) (South African political activist); Pondoland district of the Transkei, 1936?
Mandrell, Barbara (singer); Houston, 12/25/48
Manet, Edouard (painter); Paris **(1832–1883)**
Mangione, Chuck (hornist, pianist, composer); Rochester, N.Y., 11/29/40
Manheim, Camryn (actress); New York City, 3/8/61
Manilow, Barry (singer); Brooklyn, N.Y., 6/17/46
Mankiewicz, Frank F. (columnist); New York City, 5/16/24
Mankiewicz, Joseph L. (film writer, director); Wilkes-Barre, Pa. **(1909–1993)**
Mann, Horace (educator); Franklin, Mass. **(1796–1859)**
Mann, Thomas (novelist); Lübeck, Germany **(1875–1955)**
Mannes, Marya (writer); New York City **(1904–1990)**
Mansfield, Jayne (Jayne Palmer) (actress); Bryn Mawr, Pa. **(1932– 1967)**
Mansfield, Katherine (story writer); Wellington, New Zealand **(1888–1923)**
Manson, Marilyn (Brian Warner) (rock musician); Canton, Ohio, 1/5/69
Mantegna, Andrea (painter); Isola di Carturo, Italy **(1431–1506)**
Mantegna, Joe (actor); Chicago, 11/13/47
Mantovani, Annunzio (conductor); Venice **(1905–1980)**
Mao Zedong (Tse-tung) (Chinese leader); Shao Shan, China **(1893– 1976)**
Mapplethorpe, Robert (photographer); Floral Park, Queens, N.Y. **(1946–1989)**
Marat, Jean Paul (French revolutionist); Boudry, Neuchâtel, Switzerland **(1743–1793)**
Marceau, Marcel (mime); Strasbourg, France, 3/22/23
Marceau, Sophie (actress); Paris, 11/17/66
March, Fredric (Frederick Bickel) (actor); Racine, Wis. **(1897–1975)**
Marchand, Nancy (actress); Buffalo, N.Y., 6/19/28
Marconi, Guglielmo (inventor); Bologna, Italy **(1874–1937)**
Marcus Aurelius (Marcus Annius Verus) (Roman emperor); Rome **(121–180)**
Marcus, Rudolph Arthur (chemist, Nobel laureate); Montreal, 7/21/23
Marcuse, Herbert (philosopher); Berlin **(1898–1979)**
Margaret Rose (Princess of England); Glamis Castle, Angus, Scotland, 8/21/30
Margrethe II (Queen of Denmark); Copenhagen, 4/16/40
Margulies, Julianna (actress); Spring Valley, N.Y., 6/8/65
Marie Antoinette (Josephe Jeanne Marie Antoinette) (Queen of France); Vienna **(1755 –1793)**
Marisol (Escobar) (Venezuelan-American sculptor); Paris, 1930
Markham, Edwin (poet); Oregon City, Ore. **(1852–1940)**

Markova, Dame Alicia (Lilian Alice Marks) (ballet dancer); London, 12/1/10

Marley, Bob (singer, songwriter); Kingston, Jamaica **(1945–1981)**

Marlowe, Christopher (dramatist); Canterbury, England **(1664–1593)**

Marquand, J(ohn) P(hillips) (novelist); Wilmington, Del. **(1893–1960)**

Marquette, Jacques (missionary, explorer); Laon, France **(1637–1675)**

Marriner, Neville (conductor); Lincoln, England, 4/15/24

Marsalis, Wynton (musician); New Orleans, 10/18/61

Marshall, E.G. (actor); Owatonna, Minn. **(1910–1998)**

Marshall, Garry (director, producer, screenwriter, actor); New York City, 11/13/34

Marshall, George Catlett (general); Uniontown, Pa. **(1880–1959)**

Marshall, Herbert (actor); London **(1890–1968)**

Marshall, John (jurist); nr. Germantown, Va. **(1755–1835)**

Marshall, Penny (Penny Marscharelli) (actress, director, producer); Bronx, N.Y., 10/15/42

Marshall, Thurgood (U.S. Supreme Court justice); Baltimore **(1908–1993)**

Martin, Dean (Dino Crocetti) (singer, actor); Steubenville, Ohio **(1917–1995)**

Martin, Mary (singer, actress); Weatherford, Tex. **(1913–1990)**

Martin, Steve (actor, writer, producer); Waco, Tex., 8/14/45

Martin, Tony (Alvin Morris) (singer); San Francisco, 12/25/13

Martinelli, Giovanni (tenor); Montagnana, Italy **(1885–1969)**

Martins, Peter (dancer, choreographer); Copenhagen, 10/27/45

Marvell, Andrew (poet); Winestead, England **(1621–1678)**

Marvin, Lee (actor); New York City **(1924–1987)**

Marx, Chico (Leonard) (comedian); New York City **(1891–1961)**

Marx, Groucho (Julius) (comedian); New York City **(1890–1977)**

Marx, Harpo (Arthur) (comedian); New York City **(1893–1964)**

Marx, Karl (Socialist writer); Treves, Germany **(1818–1883)**

Marx, Zeppo (Herbert) (comedian); New York City **(1901–1979)**

Mary Stuart (Mary, Queen of Scots) (Queen of Scotland); Linlithgow, Scotland **(1542–1587)**

Masaccio, (Tommaso di Giovanni di Simone Cassai) (painter); San Giovanni Valdarno, Tuscany **(1401–c. 1428)**

Masaryk, Jan Garrigue (statesman); Prague **(1886–1948)**

Masaryk, Thomas Garrigue (statesman); Hodonin, Czech Republic **(1850–1937)**

Masefield, John (poet); Ledbury, England **(1878–1967)**

Masekela, Hugh (trumpeter); Wilbank, South Africa, 4/4/39

Mason, Jackie (Jacob Moshe Maza) (comedian); Sheboygan, Wis., 6/9/31

Mason, James (actor); Huddersfield, England **(1909–1984)**

Mason, Marsha (actress); St. Louis, 4/3/42

Massenet, Jules Emile Frédéric (composer); Montaud, France **(1842–1912)**

Massine, Léonide (choreographer); Moscow **(1895–1979)**

Masters, Edgar Lee (poet); Garnett, Kans. **(1869–1950)**

Masters, William (human sexuality expert); Cleveland, 12/27/15

Masterson, Mary Stuart (actress, writer, director); New York City, 6/28/66

Mastroianni, Marcello (actor); Fontana Liri, Italy **(1924–1996)**

Mather, Cotton (clergyman); Boston **(1663–1728)**

Mathis, Johnny (singer); San Francisco, 9/30/35

Matisse, Henri (painter); Le Cateau, France **(1869–1954)**

Matthau, Walter (Walter Matuschanskayasky) (actor); New York City, 10/1/20

Mature, Victor (actor); Louisville, Ky., 1/29/15

Maugham, W(illiam) Somerset (author); Paris **(1874–1965)**

Mauldin, Bill (political cartoonist); Mountain Park, N.M., 10/29/21

Maupassant, Henri René Albert Guy de (story writer); Normandy, France **(1850–1893)**

Maurois, André (Emile Herzog) (author); Elbauf, France **(1885–1967)**

Maximilian (Ferdinand Maximilian Joseph) (Emperor of Mexico); Vienna (**1832–1867)**

Maxwell, James Clerk (physicist); Edinburgh, Scotland **(1831–1879)**

Maxwell, (Ian) Robert (publisher); Selo Slatina, Czechoslavakia **(1923–1991)**

May, Elaine (Elaine Berlin) (entertainer, writer); Philadelphia, 4/21/32

May, Rollo (psychologist); Ada, Ohio **(1909–1994)**

Mayer, Louis B. (movie executive); Minsk, Russia **(1885–1957)**

Mayo, Charles H. (surgeon); Rochester, Minn. **(1865–1939)**

Mayo, Charles W. (surgeon); Rochester, Minn. **(1898–1968)**

Mayo, Virginia (Jones) (actress); St. Louis, 11/30/20

Mayo, William J. (surgeon); Le Sueur, Minn. **(1861–1939)**

Mayron, Melanie (actress); Philadelphia, 10/20/52

Mazzini, Giuseppe (patriot); Genoa **(1805–1872)**

McBride, Patricia (ballet dancer); Teaneck, N.J., 8/23/42

McCallum, David (actor); Glasgow, Scotland, 9/19/33

McCambridge, Mercedes (actress); Joliet, Ill., 3/17/18

McCarthy, Eugene J. (ex-Senator); Watkins, Minn., 3/29/16

McCarthy, Joseph Raymond (Senator); Grand Chute, Wis. **(1908–1957)**

McCarthy, Mary (novelist); Seattle **(1912–1989)**

McCartney, Linda (photographer, singer); New York City **(1941–1998)**

McCartney, Paul (singer, songwriter); Liverpool, England, 6/18/42

McClanahan, Rue (actress); Healdton, Okla., 2/21/35

McClellan, George Brinton (general); Philadelphia **(1826–1885)**

McClintock, Barbara (geneticist, Nobel laureate)

McCloy, John J. (lawyer, banker); Philadelphia **(1895–1989)**

McCormack, John (tenor); Athlone, Ireland **(1884–1945)**

McCormack, John W. (ex-Speaker of House); Boston **(1891–1980)**

McCormick, Cyrus Hall (inventor); Rockbridge County, Va. **(1809–1884)**

McCracken, James (dramatic tenor); Gary, Ind. **(1926–1988)**

McCrea, Joel (actor); Los Angeles **(1905–1990)**

McCullers, Carson (novelist); Columbus, Ga. **(1917–1967)**

McDermott, Dylan (actor); Waterbury, Conn., 10/26/62

McDormand, Frances (actress); Illinois, 6/23/57

McDowall, Roddy (actor); London **(1928–1998)**

McDowell, Malcolm (actor); Leeds, England, 6/15/43

McFadden, Gates (actress); Cuyahoga Falls, Ohio, 3/2/49

McGavin, Darren (actor); San Joaquin, Calif., 5/7/22

McGillis, Kelly (actress); Newport Beach, Calif., 7/9/57

McGinley, Phyllis (poet, writer); Ontario, Ore. **(1905–1978)**

McGoohan, Patrick (actor); Astoria, Queens, N.Y., 3/19/28

McGovern, Elizabeth (actress); Evanston, Ill., 7/18/61

McGovern, Maureen (singer); Youngstown, Ohio, 7/27/49

McGregor, Ewan (actor); Crieff, Scotland, 3/31/71

McKellen, Ian (actor); Burnley, England, 5/25/39

McKinley, William (25th U.S. president); Niles, Ohio **(1843–1901)**

McKuen, Rod (singer, composer); Oakland, Calif., 4/29/33

McLachlan, Sarah (singer, songwriter); Halifax, Nova Scotia, 1/28/68

McLaughlin, John (guitarist); Yorkshire, England, 1/4/42

McLean, Don (singer, songwriter); New Rochelle, N.Y., 10/2/45

McLuhan, Marshall (Herbert Marshall) (communications writer); Edmonton, Alta., Canada **(1911–1980)**

McMahon, Ed (TV personality); Detroit, 3/6/23

McMurtry, Larry (novelist); Wichita Falls, Tex., 6/3/36

McQueen, Butterfly (Thelma) (actress); Tampa, Fla. **(1911–1995)**

McQueen, Steve (Terence Stephen McQueen) (actor); Beech Grove, Indiana **(1930–1980)**

McRaney, Gerald (actor); Collins, Miss., 8/19/47

Mead, Margaret (anthropologist); Philadelphia **(1901–1978)**

Meadows, Audrey (actress); Wu Chang, China **(1924–1996)**

Meadows, Jayne (actress); Wu Chang, China, 9/27/26

Meaney, Colm (actor); Dublin, 5/30/53

Meany, George (labor leader); New York City **(1894–1980)**

Meara, Anne (actress); New York City, 9/20/29

Medici, Lorenzo de' (called Lorenzo the Magnificent) (Florentine ruler); Florence, Italy **(1449–1492)**

Mehta, Zubin (conductor); Bombay (Mumbai), 4/29/36

Meir, Golda (Golda Myerson, nee Mabovitz) (ex-Premier of Israel); Kiev, Ukraine **(1898–1978)**

Melba, Dame Nellie (Helen Porter Mitchell) (soprano); nr. Melbourne, Australia **(1861–1931)**

Melchior, Lauritz (Lebrecht Hommel) (heroic tenor); Copenhagen **(1890–1973)**

Mellon, Andrew William (financier); Pittsburgh **(1855–1937)**

Melville, Herman (novelist); New York City **(1819–1891)**

Mencken, Henry Louis (writer); Baltimore **(1880–1956)**

Mendel, Gregor Johann (geneticist); Heinzendorf, Austrian Silesia **(1822–1884)**

Mendeleyev, Dmitri Ivanovich (chemist); Tobolsk, Russia **(1834–1907)**

Mendelssohn-Bartholdy, Jakob Ludwig Felix (composer); Hamburg **(1809–1847)**

Mendès-France, Pierre (ex-Premier); Paris **(1905–1982)**

Mengele, Josef (Nazi, "Angel of Death"); Günzberg, Germany **(1911–1979)**

Mennin, Peter (Peter Mennini) (composer); Erie, Pa. **(1923–1983)**

Menninger, Karl A. (psychiatrist); Topeka, Kans. **(1899–1966)**

Menotti, Gian Carlo (composer); Cadegliano, Italy, 7/7/11

Menuhin, Yehudi (violinist, conductor); New York City **(1916–1999)**

Menzies, Robert Gordon (ex-Prime Minister); Jeparit, Australia **(1894–1978)**

Mercer, Johnny (songwriter); Savannah, Ga. **(1909–1976)**

Mercer, Mabel (singer); Burton-on-Trent, England **(1900–1984)**
Merchant, Ismail (Ismail Noormohamed Abdul Rehman) (film producer); Bombay (Mumbai), 12/25/36
Merchant, Natalie (singer, songwriter); Jamestown, N.Y., 10/26/63
Mercury, Freddie (Farookh Bulsara) (musician, singer); Zanzibar **(1946–1991)**
Meredith, Burgess (actor); Cleveland **(1908–1997)**
Merman, Ethel (Ethel Zimmerman) (singer, actress); Astoria, Queens, N.Y. **(1909–1984)**
Merrick, David (David Margulois) (stage producer); St. Louis, 11/27/12
Merrill, Robert (baritone); Brooklyn, N.Y., 6/4/19
Merton, Thomas (clergyman, writer); France **(1915–1968)**
Mesmer, Franz Anton (physician); Itzmang, nr. Constance, Germany **(1733–1815)**
Mesta, Perle (social figure); Sturgis, Mich. **(1889–1975)**
Metacom, (King Philip) (Wampanoag Indian sachem); southeastern Mass. **(1640–1676)**
Metternich, Prince Klemens Wenzel Nepomuk Lothar von (statesman); Coblenz, Germany **(1773–1859)**
Mfume, Kweisi (Frizzell Gray) (politician, NAACP leader); Baltimore, 10/24/48
Michaels, Lorne (producer); Toronto, 11/17/44
Michelangelo Buonarroti (painter, sculptor, architect); Caprese, Italy **(1475–1564)**
Michener, James A. (novelist); New York City **(1907–1997)**
Mickiewicz, Adam (Polish poet); Zozie, Belorussia (Belarus) **(1798–1855)**
Midler, Bette (singer, actress, producer); Honolulu, 12/1/45
Mielziner, Jo (stage designer); Paris **(1901–1976)**
Mifune, Toshiro (actor, film producer); Tsingtao, China **(1920–1997)**
Mies van der Rohe, Ludwig (architect, designer); Aachen, Germany **(1886–1969)**
Mikoyan, Anastas I. (diplomat); Sanain, Armenia **(1895–1978)**
Milano, Alyssa (actress); Brooklyn, New York, 12/19/72
Milhaud, Darius (composer); Aix-en-Provence, France **(1892–1974)**
Mill, John Stuart (philosopher); London **(1806–1873)**
Milland, Ray (Reginald Truscott-Jones) (actor); Neath, Wales **(1907–1986)**
Millay, Edna St. Vincent (poet); Rockland, Maine **(1892–1950)**
Miller, Ann (Lucille Ann Collier) (dancer, actress); Cherino, Tex., 4/12/23
Miller, Arthur (playwright); New York City, 10/17/15
Miller, Glenn (band leader); Clarinda, Iowa **(1904–1944)**
Miller, Henry (novelist); New York City **(1891–1980)**
Miller, Jason (John Miller) (playwright, actor); New York City, 4/22/39
Miller, Mitch (Mitchell) (musician); Rochester, N.Y., 7/4/11
Miller, Roger (singer); Fort Worth **(1936–1992)**
Millet, Jean François (painter); Gruchy, France **(1814–1875)**
Millett, Kate (feminist, writer); St. Paul, Minn., 9/14/34
Millikan, Robert A. (physicist); Morrison, Ill. **(1869–1953)**
Mills, Donna (actress); Chicago, 12/11/41
Mills, Hayley (actress); London, 4/18/46
Mills, Juliet (actress); London, 11/21/41
Milne, A(lan) A(lexander) (author); London **(1882–1956)**
Milner, Martin (actor); Detroit, 12/28/31
Milnes, Sherrill (baritone); Downers Grove, Ill., 1/10/35
Milosevic, Slobodan (Yugoslav President); Pozarevac, Serbia, 8/29/41
Milstein, Nathan (concert violinist); Odessa, Ukraine **(1904–1992)**
Milton, John (poet); London **(1608–1674)**
Mingus, Charles (jazz composer); Nogales, Ariz. **(1922–1979)**
Minnelli, Liza (singer, actress); Hollywood, Calif., 3/12/46
Minnelli, Vincente (film director); Chicago **(1913–1986)**
Minuit, Peter (Governor of New Amsterdam); Wesel, Germany **(1580–1638)**
Miranda, Carmen (Maria do Carmo da Cunha) (singer, dancer); Lisbon **(1909–1955)**
Miró, Joan (painter); Barcelona **(1893–1983)**
Mirren, Helen (Ilynea Lydia Mironoff) (actress); London, 7/26/45
Mitchell, John N. (former Attorney General); Detroit **(1913–1988)**
Mitchell, Joni (Roberta Joan Anderson) (singer, songwriter); Ft. Macleod, Alb., Canada, 11/7/43
Mitchell, Margaret (novelist); Atlanta **(1900–1949)**
Mitchell, Maria (astronomer); Nantucket, Mass. **(1818–1889)**
Mitchum, Robert (actor); Bridgeport, Conn. **(1917–1997)**
Mitropoulos, Dimitri (orchestra conductor); Athens **(1896–1960)**
Mitterand, François (Maurice) (ex-prime minister of France); Jarnac, France **(1916–1996)**
Mix, Tom (actor); Mix Run, Pa. **(1880–1940)**
Mobutu Sese Seko (Zairean dictator); Lisala, Congo **(1930–1997)**
Modigliani, Amedeo (painter); Leghorn, Italy **(1884–1920)**

Moffo, Anna (soprano); Wayne, Pa., 6/27/34
Mohammed (prophet); Mecca, Saudi Arabia **(570–632)**
Molière (Jean Baptiste Poquelin) (dramatist); Paris **(1622–1673)**
Molina, Mario (chemist, Nobel laureate); Mexico City, 3/19/43
Moll, Richard (actor); Pasadena, Calif., 1/13/43?
Molnar, Ferenc (dramatist); Budapest **(1878–1952)**
Molotov, Vyacheslav M. (V. M. Skryabin) (diplomat); Kukarka, Russia **(1890–1986)**
Mondrian, Piet (painter); Amersfoort, Netherlands **(1872–1944)**
Monet, Claude (painter); Paris **(1840–1926)**
Monica Monica Arnold (singer); Atlanta, Ga., 10/24/80
Monk, Meredith (choreographer, composer, performing artist); Lima, Peru, 11/20/42
Monk, Thelonious (pianist); Rocky Mount, N.C. **(1918–1982)**
Monroe, James (5th U.S. president); Westmoreland County, Va. **(1758–1831)**
Monroe, Marilyn (Norma Jean Mortenson or Baker) (actress); Los Angeles **(1926–1962)**
Monsarrat, Nicholas (novelist); Liverpool, England **(1910–1979)**
Montaigne, Michel Eyquem de (essayist); nr. Bordeaux, France **(1533–1592)**
Montalban, Ricardo (actor); Mexico City, 11/25/20
Montand, Yves (Ivo Livi) (actor, singer); Florence, Italy **(1921–1991)**
Montesquieu, Charles-Louis de Secondat, baron de La Brède and de, (philosopher); nr. Bordeaux, France **(1689–1755)**
Montessori, Maria (physician, educator); Chiaravalle, Italy **(1870–1952)**
Monteux, Pierre (conductor); Paris **(1875–1964)**
Monteverdi, Claudio (composer); Cremona Italy **(1567–1643)**
Montezuma II (Aztec emperor); Mexico **(1466–1520)**
Montgomery, Elizabeth (actress); Hollywood, Calif. **(1933–1995)**
Montgomery, Robert (Henry, Jr.) (actor); Beacon, N.Y. **(1904–1981)**
Montgomery of Alamein, 1st Viscount of Hindhead (Sir Bernard Law Montgomery) (military leader); London **(1887–1976)**
Montoya, Carlos (guitarist); Madrid **(1903–1993)**
Moore, Clayton (Jack Moore) (actor); Chicago, 9/14/14
Moore, Clement Clarke (author); New York City **(1779–1863)**
Moore, Demi (actress); Roswell, N.M., 11/11/62
Moore, Dudley (actor, writer, musician); Dagenham, England, 4/19/35
Moore, Grace (soprano); Jellico, Tenn. **(1901–1947)**
Moore, Henry (sculptor); Castleford, England **(1898–1986)**
Moore, Julianne (actress); Boston, 12/3/60
Moore, Marianne (poet); Kirkwood, Mo. **(1887–1972)**
Moore, Mary Tyler (actress); Brooklyn, N.Y., 12/29/36
Moore, Melba (Beatrice) (singer, actress); New York City, 10/27/45
Moore, Roger (actor); London, 10/14/27
Moore, Thomas (poet); Dublin **(1779–1852)**
Moorehead, Agnes (actress); Clinton, Mass. **(1906–1974)**
Moranis, Rick (actor); Toronto, 4/18/53
More, Henry (philosopher); Grantham, England **(1614–1687)**
More, Sir Thomas (statesman, author); London **(1478–1535)**
Moreno, Rita (Rosita Dolores Alverio) (actress); Humacao, P.R., 12/11/31
Morgan, Harry (Harry Bratsburg) (actor); Detroit, 4/10/15
Morgan, John Pierpont (financier); Hartford, Conn. **(1837–1913)**
Moriarty, Michael (actor); Detroit, 4/5/41
Morini, Erica (concert violinist); Vienna **(1904–1995)**
Morison, Samuel Eliot (historian); Boston **(1887–1976)**
Morita, Pat (Noriyuki Morita) (actor); Berkeley, California, 8/28/32
Morley, Christopher Darlington (novelist); Haverford, Pa. **(1890–1957)**
Morris, Mark (choreographer); Seattle, 8/29/56
Morris, William (poet, craftsman); Walthamstow, England **(1834–1896)**
Morrison, Jim (James Douglas Morrison) (singer, songwriter); Melbourne, Fla. **(1943–1971)**
Morrison, Toni (Chloe Anthony Wofford) (novelist); Lorain, Ohio, 2/18/31
Morrison, Van (singer); Belfast, Northern Ireland, 8/31/45
Morse, Marston (mathematician); Waterville, Maine **(1892–1977)**
Morse, Samuel Finley Breese (painter, inventor); Charlestown, Mass. **(1791–1872)**
Morton, Jelly Roll (Ferdinand Joseph La Menthe) (jazz composer); New Orleans **(1890–1941)**
Moseley-Braun, Carol (U.S. Senator); Chicago, 8/16/47
Moses, Grandma (Mrs. Anna Mary Robertson Moses) (painter); Greenwich, N.Y. **(1860–1961)**
Moses, Robert (urban planner); New Haven, Conn. **(1888–1981)**
Moss, Kate (model); London, England, 1/16/74
Mostel, Zero (Samuel Joel Mostel) (actor); Brooklyn, N.Y. **(1915–1977)**

Mother Teresa (Agnes Gonxha Bojaxhíu) (nun); Skopje, Macedonia **(1910–1997)**

Motherwell, Robert (artist, "action" painter); Aberdeen, Wash. **(1915–1991)**

Mott, Lucretia (Coffin) (feminist, reformer, abolitionist); Nantucket, Mass. **(1793–1880)**

Moussorgsky, Modest Petrovich (composer); Karev, Russia **(1839–1881)**

Moyers, Bill D. (Billy Don) (journalist); Hugo, Okla., 6/5/34

Moynihan, Daniel Patrick (New York Senator); Tulsa, Okla., 3/16/27

Mozart, Wolfgang Amadeus (Johannes Chrysostomus Wolfgangus Theophilus Mozart) (composer); Salzburg, Austria **(1756–1791)**

Mudd, Roger (TV newscaster); Washington, D.C., 2/9/28

Muggeridge, Malcolm (Thomas) (writer); Croydon, England **(1903–1990)**

Muhammad (founder of Islam); Mecca, Saudi Arabia **(c. 570–632)**

Muhammad, Elijah (Elijah Poole) (religious leader); Sandersville, Ga. **(1897–1975)**

Mulgrew, Kate (actress); Dubuque, Iowa, 4/29/55

Mulhare, Edward (actor); Ireland **(1923–1997)**

Mulliken, Robert Sanderson (chemist, Nobel laureate); Newburyport, Mass. **(1896–1986)**

Mulroney, Dermot (actor, musician, producer); Alexandria, Va., 10/31/63

Mumford, Lewis (cultural historian, city planner); Flushing, Queens, N.Y. **(1895–1990)**

Munch, Edvard (painter); Löten, Norway **(1863–1944)**

Munchhausen, Karl Friedrich Hieronymus, baron von (anecdotist); Hannover, Germany **(1720–1797)**

Muni, Paul (Muni Weisenfreund) (actor); Lemburg, Ukraine **(1895–1967)**

Muñoz Marin, Luis (ex-governor of Puerto Rico); San Juan, P.R. **(1898–1980)**

Munsel, Patrice (soprano); Spokane, Wash., 5/14/25

Murdoch, Iris (novelist); Dublin **(1919–1999)**

Murdoch, Rupert (publisher); Melbourne, Australia, 3/11/31

Murillo, Bartolomé Esteban (painter); Seville, Spain **(1617–1682)**

Murphy, Audie (actor, war hero); Kingston, Tex. **(1924–1971)**

Murphy, Eddie (actor, comedian); Brooklyn, N.Y., 4/3/61

Murphy, George (actor, dancer, ex-Senator); New Haven, Conn. **(1902–1992)**

Murray, Arthur (dance teacher); New York City **(1895–1991)**

Murray, Bill (actor, comedian); Wilmette, Ill., 9/21/50

Murray, Kathryn (dance teacher); Jersey City, N.J., 1906

Murrow, Edward R. (commentator, government official); Greensboro, N.C. **(1908–1965)**

Musil, Robert (novelist); Klagenfurt, Austria **(1880–1942)**

Muskie, Edmund (political figure); Rumford, Maine **(1914–1996)**

Mussolini, Benito (Italian dictator); Dovia, Forli, Italy **(1883–1945)**

Muti, Riccardo (orchestra conductor); Naples, Italy, 7/28/41

Mutter, Anne-Sophie (violinist); Rheinfelden, Germany, 6/29/63

Myers, Mike (actor, writer, comedian); Scarborough, Ont., Canada, 5/25/63

Myerson, Bess (consumer advocate); Bronx, N.Y., 7/16/24

Myrdal, Gunnar (sociologist, economist); Gustaf Parish, Sweden **(1898–1987)**

N

Nabokov, Vladimir (novelist); St. Petersburg, Russia **(1899–1977)**

Nabors, Jim (actor, singer); Sylacauga, Ala., 6/12/32

Nader, Ralph (consumer advocate); Winsted, Conn., 2/27/34

Nair, Mira (director, screenwriter); Bhubaneswar, India, 10/15/57

Nash, Graham (singer); Blackpool, England, 1942

Nash, Ogden (poet); Rye, N.Y. **(1902–1971)**

Nasser, Gamal Abdel (statesman); Beni Mor, Egypt **(1918–1970)**

Nast, Thomas (cartoonist); Landau, Germany **(1840–1902)**

Nation, Carry Amelia (temperance leader); Garrard County, Ky. **(1846–1911)**

Natta, Giulio (chemist, Nobel laureate); Imperia, Italy **(1903–1979)**

Natwick, Mildred (actress); Baltimore **(1905–1994)**

Neagle, Anna (Marjorie Robertson) (actress); London **(1908–1986)**

Neal, Patricia (actress); Packard, Ky., 1/20/26

Neeson, Liam (William John) (actor); Ballymena, Northern Ireland, 6/7/52

Negri, Pola (Apolina Mathias-Chalupec) (actress); Bromberg, Poland **(1899–1987)**

Nehru, Jawaharlal (first Prime Minister of India); Allahabad, India **(1889–1964)**

Neill, Sam (Nigel Neill) (actor); Omagh, Northern Ireland, 9/14/47

Nelligan, Kate (actress); London, Ont., Canada, 3/16/51

Nelson, Barry (Robert Haakon Nielsen) (actor); San Francisco, 4/16/20

Nelson, David (actor); New York City, 10/24/36

Nelson, Harriet Hilliard (Peggy Lou Snyder) (actress); Des Moines, Iowa **(1909–1994)**

Nelson, Ozzie (Oswald) (actor); Jersey City, N.J. **(1907–1975)**

Nelson, Ricky (Eric) (singer, actor); Teaneck, N.J. **(1940–1985)**

Nelson, Viscount Horatio (naval officer); Burnham Thorpe, England **(1758–1805)**

Nelson, Willie (singer); Waco, Tex., 4/30/33

Nenni, Pietro (Socialist leader); Faenza, Italy **(1891–1980)**

Nero (Nero Claudius Caesar Drusus Germanicus) (Roman emperor); Antium, Italy **(37–68)**

Nero, Peter (pianist); New York City, 5/22/34

Netanyahu, Benjamin (Binyamin) (former Israeli Prime Minister); Tel Aviv, Israel, 10/21/49

Neuwirth, Bebe (Beatrice Neuwirth) (actress); Newark, N.J., 12/31/58

Nevelson, Louise (sculptor); Kiev, Russia **(1899–1988)**

Neville, Aaron (singer); New Orleans, 1/24/41

Newhart, Bob (actor); Chicago, 9/5/29

Newhouse, Samuel I. (publisher); New York City **(1895–1979)**

Newley, Anthony (actor, songwriter); London **(1931–1999)**

Newman, Edwin (news commentator); New York City, 1/25/19

Newman, John Henry (prelate); London **(1801–1890)**

Newman, Paul (actor, director); Cleveland, 1/26/25

Newman, Randy (singer); Los Angeles, 11/28/43

Newton, Huey (black activist); New Orleans **(1942–1989)**

Newton, Sir Isaac (mathematician, scientist); nr. Grantham, England **(1642–1727)**

Newton, Wayne (singer); Norfolk, Va., 4/3/42

Newton-John, Olivia (singer); Cambridge, England, 9/26/48

Nichols, Nichelle (actress); Robbins, Ill., 12/28/33

Nichols, Mike (Michael Peschkowsky) (stage and film director); Berlin, 11/6/31

Nicholson, Jack (actor, director, writer); Neptune, N.J., 4/22/37

Nicks, Stevie (Stephanie Lynn Nicks) (singer, songwriter); Phoenix, Arizona, 5/26/48

Nielsen, Leslie (actor); Regina, Sask., Canada, 2/11/26

Nietzsche, Friedrich Wilhelm (philosopher); nr. Lützen, Saxony, Germany **(1844–1900)**

Nightingale, Florence (nurse); Florence, Italy **(1820–1910)**

Nijinsky, Vaslav (ballet dancer); Warsaw **(1890–1950)**

Nilsson, Birgit (soprano); West Karup, Sweden, 5/17/23

Nilsson, Harry (singer, songwriter); Brooklyn, N.Y. **(1941–1994)**

Nimitz, Chester W. (naval officer); Fredericksburg, Tex. **(1885–1966)**

Nimoy, Leonard (actor, director, writer, producer); Boston, 3/26/31

Nin, Anais (author, diarist); Neuilly, France **(1903–1977)**

Niven, David (actor); Kirriemuir, Scotland **(1910–1983)**

Nixon, Richard Milhous (37th U.S. president); Yorba Linda, Calif. **(1913–1994)**

Nizer, Louis (lawyer, author); London **(1902–1994)**

Nobel, Alfred Bernhard (industrialist); Stockholm **(1833–1896)**

Noguchi, Isamu (sculptor); Los Angeles **(1904–1988)**

Nolan, Lloyd (actor); San Francisco **(1902–1985)**

Nolte, Nick (actor); Omaha, Neb., 2/8/40

Norell, Norman (Norman Levinson) (fashion designer); Noblesville, Ind. **(1900–1972)**

Norman, Jessye (soprano); Augusta, Ga., 9/15/45

Norman, Marsha (Marsha Williams) (playwright); Louisville, Ky., 9/21/47

Normand, Mabel (actress); Boston **(1894–1930)**

Norris, Chuck (Carlos Ray Norris) (actor, athlete); Ryan, Oklahoma, 3/10/40

Norstad, Gen. Lauris (ex-commander of NATO forces); Minneapolis **(1907–1988)**

Norton, Edward (actor); Columbia, Md., 8/18/69

North, John Ringling (circus director); Baraboo, Wis. **(1903–1985)**

North, Oliver (ex-military officer); San Antonio, 10/7/43

North, Sheree (actress); Los Angeles, 1/17/33

Norton, Eleanor Holmes (New York City government official, lawyer); Washington, D.C., 6/13/37

Nostradamus (Michel de Notredame) (astrologer); St. Rémy, France **(1503–1566)**

Novaes, Guiomar (pianist); São João de Boa Vista, Brazil **(1895–1979)**

Novak, Kim (Marilyn Novak) (actress); Chicago, 2/13/33

Novarro, Ramon (Ramon Samaniegoes) (actor); Durango, Mexico **(1899–1968)**

Novello, Ivor (actor, playwright, composer); Cardiff, Wales **(1893–1951)**

Nugent, Elliott (actor, director); Dover, Ohio **(1899–1980)**

Nureyev, Rudolf (ballet dancer); Siberia **(1938–1993)**

Nyro, Laura (singer, songwriter); Bronx, N.Y. **(1947–1997)**

O

Oakie, Jack (actor); Sedalia, Mo. **(1903–1978)**

Oakley, Annie (Phoebe Anne Oakley Mozee) (markswoman); Darke County, Ohio **(1860–1926)**

Oates, Joyce Carol (novelist); Lockport, N.Y., 6/16/38

Oberon, Merle (Estelle Merle O'Brien Thompson) (actress); Calcutta, India **(1911–1979)**

Oberth, Hermann (rocketry and space flight pioneer); Nagyszeben, Austria-Hungary (Sibiu, Romania) **(1894–1989)**

O'Brian, Hugh (Hugh J. Krampe) (actor); Rochester, N.Y., 4/19/25

O'Brien, Conan (TV personality); Brookline, Mass., 4/18/63

O'Brien, Edmond (actor); New York City **(1915–1985)**

O'Brien, Margaret (Angela Maxine O'Brien) (actress); San Diego, Calif., 1/15/37

O'Brien, Pat (William Joseph O'Brien, Jr.) (actor); Milwaukee **(1899–1983)**

O'Brien, Tim (novelist); Austin, Minn., 10/1/46

Obuchi, Keizo (Prime Minister of Japan); Nakanojo, Japan, 6/25/37

O'Casey, Sean (playwright); Dublin **(1881–1964)**

Ochs, Adolph Simon (publisher); Cincinnati **(1858–1935)**

O'Connor, Carroll (actor); New York City, 8/2/24

Odets, Clifford (playwright); Philadelphia **(1906–1963)**

Odetta (Odetta Holmes) (folk singer, actress); Birmingham, Ala., 12/31/30

O'Donnell, Chris (actor); Winnetka, Ill., 6/26/70

O'Donnell, Rosie (actress, talk show host); Commack, N.Y., 3/21/62

Offenbach, Jacques (composer); Cologne, Germany **(1819–1880)**

O'Hara, John (novelist); Pottsville, Pa. **(1905–1970)**

O'Hara, Maureen (Maureen FitzSimons) (actress); Dublin, 8/17/20

Ohlsson, Garrick (pianist); Bronxville, N.Y., 4/3/48

Ohrbach, Jerry (actor, singer); Bronx, N.Y., 10/20/35

Oistrakh, David (concert violinist); Odessa, Russia **(1908–1974)**

O'Keeffe, Georgia (painter); Sun Prairie, Wis. **(1887–1986)**

Oland, Warner (actor); Umea, Sweden **(1880–1938)**

Oldenburg, Claes (painter); Stockholm, 1/28/29

Oldman, Gary (actor, director); London, 3/21/58

Olin, Lena (actress); Stockholm, 3/22/55

Oliphant, Patrick B. (editorial cartoonist); Adelaide, Australia, 7/24/35

Oliver, Edna May (actress); Malden, Mass. **(1883–1942)**

Olivier, Sir Laurence (actor); Dorking, England **(1907–1989)**

Olmos, Edward James (actor); East Los Angeles, 2/24/47

Olmsted, Frederick Law (landscape architect); Hartford, Conn. **(1822–1903)**

Olsen, Ole (John Sigvard Olsen) (comedian); Peru, Ind. **(1892–1963)**

Omar Khayyam (poet, astronomer); Nishapur, Iran (died c. 1123)

Onassis, Aristotle (shipping executive); Smyrna, Turkey **(1906–1975)**

Onassis, Christina (shipping executive); New York City **(1950–1988)**

Onassis, Jacqueline Kennedy (Jacqueline Bouvier) (First Lady); Southampton, N.Y. **(1929–1994)**

O'Neal, Ryan (Patrick) (actor); Los Angeles, 4/20/41

O'Neal, Tatum (actress); Los Angeles, 11/5/63

O'Neill, Eugene Gladstone (playwright); New York City **(1888–1953)**

O'Neill, Jennifer (actress); Rio de Janeiro, 2/20/49

Oppenheimer, J. Robert (nuclear physicist); New York City **(1904–1967)**

Orbach, Jerry (actor); New York City, 10/20/35

Orff, Carl (composer); Munich, Germany **(1895–1982)**

Orlando, Tony (Michael Anthony Orlando Cassavitis) (singer); New York City, 4/3/44

Ormandy, Eugene (conductor); Budapest **(1899–1985)**

Ormond, Julia (actress); Epsom, Surrey, England, 1/4/65

Orozco, José Clemente (painter); Zapotlán, Jalisco, Mexico **(1883–1949)**

Orwell, George (Eric Arthur Blair) (British author); Motihari, India **(1903–1950)**

Osborn, Paul (playwright); Evansville, Ind. **(1901–1988)**

Osborne, John (playwright); London **(1929–1994)**

Osbourne, Ozzy (John Osbourne) (singer); Birmingham, England, 12/3/48

Osler, Sir William (physician); Bondhead, Ont., Canada **(1849–1919)**

Osmond, Donny (singer, actor); Ogden, Utah, 12/9/57

Osmond, Marie (Olive Marie) (singer, actress); Ogden, Utah, 10/13/59

O'Sullivan, Maureen (actress); County Roscommon, Ireland **(1911–1998)**

Oswald, Lee Harvey (presumed assassin); New Orleans **(1939–1963)**

Otis, Elisha (inventor); Halifax, Vt. **(1811–1861)**

O'Toole, Peter (actor); Connemara, Ireland, 8/2/32

Ovid (Publius Ovidius Naso) (poet); Sulmona, Italy **(43 b.c.e.–c.e. 17)**

Ovitz, Michael (entertainment executive); Chicago, 12/14/46

Owens, Buck (Alvis Edgar Owens) (singer); Sherman, Tex., 8/12/29

Ozawa, Seiji (orchestra conductor); Fentian (Shenyan), Manchuria, 7/1/35

P

Paar, Jack (TV personality); Canton, Ohio, 5/1/18

Pacino, Al (Alfred) (actor); New York City, 4/25/40

Packard, Vance (author); Granville Summit, Pa. **(1914–1996)**

Paderewski, Ignace Jan (pianist, statesman); Kurylowka, Russian Podolia **(1860–1941)**

Paganini, Nicolò (violinist); Genoa, Italy **(1782–1840)**

Page, Geraldine (actress); Kirksville, Mo. **(1924–1987)**

Page, Jimmy (musician); Heston, Ireland, 1/9/44

Page, Patti (Clara Ann Fowler) (singer, entertainer); Claremore, Okla., 11/8/27

Pagels, Elaine Hiesey (religious scholar); Palo Alto, Calif., 2/13/43

Paglia, Camille (writer, social critic); Endicott, N.Y., 4/2/47

Paine, Thomas (political philosopher); Thetford, England **(1737–1809)**

Pakula, Alan J. (film director); New York City **(1928–1998)**

Palance, Jack (Walter Palanuik) (actor); Lattimer, Pa., 2/18/19

Palestrina, Giovanni Pierluigi da (composer); Palestrina, Italy **(1526–1594)**

Paley, William S. (broadcasting executive); Chicago **(1901–1990)**

Palladio, Andrea (architect); Padua or Vicenza, Italy **(1508–1580)**

Palmer, Robert (rock musician); Batley, England, 1/19/49

Palmerston, Henry John Templeton (3rd Viscount) (statesman); Broadlands, England **(1784–1865)**

Palminteri, Chazz (Calogero Lorenzo Palminteri) (actor, writer); Bronx, New York, 5/15/51

Paltrow, Gwyneth (actress); Los Angeles, 9/28/73

Papanicolaou, George N. (physician); Coumi, Greece **(1883–1962)**

Papas, Irene (Lelekou) (actress); Chiliomodian, Greece, 3/9/26

Papp, Joseph (Joseph Papirofsky) (stage producer, director); Brooklyn, N.Y. **(1921–1991)**

Paracelsus, Philippus (Aureolus Theophrastus Bombastus von Hohenheim) (physican); Einsiedeln, Switzerland **(1493–1541)**

Park, Chung Hee (President of South Korea); Sangmo-ri, Korea **(1917–1979)**

Parker, Charlie "Bird" (jazz musician); Kansas City, Kans. **(1920–1955)**

Parker, Dorothy (Dorothy Rothschild) (author); West End, N.J. **(1893–1967)**

Parker, Fess (actor); Fort Worth, Tex., 8/16/25

Parker, Sarah Jessica (actress); Nelsonville, Ohio, 3/25/65

Parker, Suzy (model, actress); San Antonio, 10/28/33

Parkinson, C(yril) Northcote (historian); Durham, England **(1909–1993)**

Parkman, Francis (historian); Boston **(1823–1893)**

Parks, Bert (Bert Jacobson) (entertainer); Atlanta **(1914–1992)**

Parks, Gordon (film director); Ft. Scott, Kans., 11/30/12

Parks, Rosa (civil rights activist); Tuskegee, Ala., 2/4/13

Parnell, Charles Stewart (statesman); Avondale, Ireland **(1846–1891)**

Parnis, Mollie (Mollie Parnis Livingston) (fashion designer); New York City **(1905?–1992)**

Parsons, Estelle (actress); Marblehead, Mass., 11/20/27

Parton, Dolly (singer); Locust Ridge, Tenn., 1/19/46

Pascal, Blaise (philosopher); Clermont, France **(1623–1662)**

Pasternak, Boris Leonidovich (author); Moscow **(1890–1960)**

Pasternak, Joseph (film producer); Silagy-Somlyo, Romania **(1901–1991)**

Pasteur, Louis (chemist); Dôle, France **(1822–1895)**

Pastor, Tony (Antonio) (actor, theater manager); New York City **(1837–1908)**

Pater, Walter (Horatio) (writer); London **(1839–1894)**

Patinkin, Mandy (Mandel) (actor, singer); Chicago, 11/30/52

Paton, Alan (author); Pietermaritzburg, South Africa **(1903–1988)**

Patric, Jason (actor); Queens, N.Y., 6/17/66

Patti, Adelina (soprano); Madrid **(1843–1919)**

Patton, George Smith, Jr. (general); San Gabriel, Calif. **(1885–1945)**

Paul, Alice (feminist, woman suffragist); Moorestown, N.J. **(1885–1977)**

Paul, Les (Lester William Polfus) (guitarist); Waukesha, Wis., 6/9/15

Paul VI (Giovanni Battista Montini) (Pope); Concesio, nr. Brescia, Italy **(1897–1978)**

Pauley, Jane (Margaret Jane Pauley) (TV newscaster); Indianapolis, 10/31/50

Pauling, Linus Carl (chemist, Nobel laureate); Portland, Ore. **(1901–1994)**

Pavarotti, Luciano (tenor); Modena, Italy, 10/12/35

Pavlov, Ivan Petrovich (physiologist); Ryazan district, Russia **(1849–1936)**

Pavlova, Anna (ballet dancer); St. Petersburg, Russia **(1885–1931)**

Paxton, Bill (actor); Fort Worth, Texas, 5/17/55

Peale, Norman Vincent (clergyman); Bowersville, Ohio **(1898–1993)**

Pearl, Minnie (Sarah Ophelia Colley Cannon) (comedienne, singer); Centerville, Tenn. **(1912–1996)**

Pears, Peter (tenor); Farnham, England **(1910–1986)**

Pearson, Drew (Andrew Russel Pearson) (columnist); Evanston, Ill. **(1897–1969)**

Pearson, Lester B. (statesman); Toronto **(1897–1972)**

Peary, Robert Edwin (explorer); Cresson, Pa. **(1856–1920)**

Peck, Gregory (Eldred Gregory Peck) (actor); La Jolla, Calif., 4/5/16

Peckinpah, Sam (film director); Fresno, Calif. **(1925–1984)**

Peerce, Jan (tenor); New York City **(1904–1984)**

Pegler, (James) Westbrook (columnist); Minneapolis **(1894–1969)**

Pei, I(eoh) M(ing) (architect); Canton, China, 4/26/17

Penn, Arthur (director); Philadelphia, 9/27/22

Penn, Sean (actor, filmmaker); Los Angeles, 8/17/60

Penn, William (American colonist); London **(1644–1718)**

Penney, James C. (merchant); Hamilton, Mo. **(1875–1971)**

Peppard, George (actor); Detroit **(1928–1994)**

Pepys, Samuel (diarist); Bampton, England **(1633–1703)**

Perelman, S(idney) J(oseph) (writer); Brooklyn, N.Y. **(1904–1979)**

Perez, Rosie (actress, dancer, choreographer); Brooklyn, New York, 5/16/63

Pergolesi, Giovanni Battista (composer); Jesi, Italy **(1710–1736)**

Pericles (statesman); Athens died 429 B.C.E.

Perkins, Anthony (actor); New York City **(1932–1992)**

Perkins, Frances (social reformer); Boston **(1882–1965)**

Perlman, Itzhak (violinist); Tel Aviv, Israel, 8/31/45

Perlman, Rhea (actress); Brooklyn, N.Y., 3/31/48

Perón, Isabel (María Estela Martínez Cartas) (former chief of state); La Rioja, Argentina, 2/4/31

Perón, Juan D. (statesman); nr. Lobos, Argentina **(1895–1974)**

Perón, Maria Eva Duarte de (political leader); Los Toldos, Argentina **(1919–1952)**

Perot, H. Ross (business executive); Texarkana, Tex., 6/27/30

Perrine, Valerie (actress, dancer); Galveston, Tex., 9/3/43

Perry, Luke (Coy Luther Perry III) (actor); Fredericktown, Ohio, 10/11/66

Perry, Matthew (actor); Williamstown, Mass., 8/19/69

Pershing, John Joseph (general); Linn County, Mo. **(1860–1948)**

Pestalozzi, Johann (educator); Zurich, Switzerland **(1746–1827)**

Peters, Bernadette (Bernadette Lazzara) (actress); New York City, 2/28/48

Peters, Brock (actor, singer); New York City, 7/2/27

Peters, Jean (actress); Canton, Ohio, 10/15/26

Peters, Roberta (Roberta Peterman) (soprano); New York City, 5/4/30

Petit, Roland (choreographer, dancer); Villemombe, France, 1924

Petrarch (Francesco Petrarca) (poet); Arezzo, Italy **(1304–1374)**

Petty, Tom (folk/rock musician); Gainesville, Florida, 10/20/50

Pfeiffer, Michelle (actress); Santa Ana, Calif., 4/29/58

Philbin, Regis (talk show host); New York City, 8/25/33

Philip (Philip Mountbatten) (Duke of Edinburgh); Corfu, Greece, 6/10/21

Phillippe, Ryan (actor); New Castle, Del., 9/10/75

Phoenix, Joaquin (actor); Puerto Rico, 10/28/74

Phoenix, River (actor); Madras, Ore. **(1970–1993)**

Piaf, Edith (Edith Gassion) (singer); Paris **(1916–1963)**

Piatigorsky, Gregor (cellist); Ekaterinoslav, Russia **(1903–1976)**

Piazza, Marguerite (soprano); New Orleans, 5/6/26

Picasso, Pablo (painter, sculptor); Málaga, Spain **(1881–1973)**

Pickett, Wilson (singer); Prattville, Ala., 3/18/41

Pickford, Mary (Gladys Mary Smith) (actress); Toronto **(1893–1979)**

Picon, Molly (actress); New York City **(1898–1992)**

Pidgeon, Walter (actor); East St. John, N.B., Canada **(1898–1984)**

Hyde Pierce, David (actor); Saratoga Springs, N.Y., 4/3/59

Pierce, Franklin (14th U.S. president); Hillsboro, N.H. **(1804–1869)**

Pilegg, Mitch (actor); Portland, Ore., 4/5/52

Pinkett-Smith, Jada (actress); Baltimore, 9/18/71

Pinsky, Robert (Poet Laureate of the U.S.); Long Branch, N.J., 10/20/40

Pinochet (Ugarte), Augusto (former leader of Chile's military government); Valparaíso, Chile, 11/25/15

Pinter, Harold (playwright); London, 10/10/30

Pinza, Ezio (basso); Rome **(1892–1957)**

Pirandello, Luigi (dramatist, novelist); nr. Girgenti, Italy **(1867–1936)**

Piranesi, Giambattista (artist); Mestre, Italy **(1720–1778)**

Pissaro, Camille Jacob (painter); St. Thomas, U.S. Virgin Islands **(1830–1903)**

Piston, Walter (composer); Rockland, Maine **(1894–1976)**

Pitman, Sir [Isaac] James (educator, publisher); Bath, England **(1901–1985)**

Pitt, Brad (actor); Shawnee, Okla., 12/18/63

Pitt, William ("Younger Pitt") (statesman); nr. Bromley, England **(1759–1806)**

Pitts, ZaSu (actress); Parsons, Kans. **(1898–1963)**

Pius XII (Eugenio Pacelli) (Pope); Rome **(1876–1958)**

Pizarro, Francisco (explorer); Trujillo, Spain **(c. 1476–1541)**

Planck, Max (physicist); Kiel, Germany **(1858–1947)**

Plant, Robert (musician, singer, song writer); West Bromwich, Staffordshire, England , 8/20/48

Plath, Sylvia (poet); Boston **(1932–1963)**

Plato (Aristocles) (philosopher); Athens **(c. 427–347 B.C.E.)**

Pleasence, Donald (actor); Worksop, England **(1919–1995)**

Pleshette, Suzanne (actress); New York City, 1/31/37

Plimpton, George (author); New York City, 3/18/27

Plimpton, Martha (actress); New York City, 11/16/70

Plisetskaya, Maya (ballet dancer); Moscow, 11/20/25

Plowright, Joan (actress); Brigg, England, 10/28/29

Plummer, Christopher (actor); Toronto, 12/13/29

Plutarch (biographer); Chaeronea, Greece **(c. 46–c. 120)**

Pocahontas (Matoaka) (American Indian princess); (Virginia) **(c. 1595–1617)**

Podhoretz, Norman (author); Brooklyn, N.Y., 1/16/30

Poe, Edgar Allan (poet, story writer); Boston **(1809–1849)**

Poitier, Sidney (actor, director); Miami, Fla., 2/20/24

Polanski, Roman (director); Paris, 8/18/33

Polk, James Knox (11th U.S. president); Mecklenburg County, N.C. **(1795–1849)**

Pollack, Sydney (film director, producer, actor); Lafayette, Ind., 7/1/34

Pollard, Michael J. (actor); Passaic, N.J., 5/30/39

Pollock, Jackson (painter); Cody, Wyo. **(1912–1956)**

Polo, Marco (traveler); Venice **(c. 1254–1324)**

Pol Pot (Cambodian dictator); Kompong Thom, Cambodia **(1925–1998)**

Pompadour, Mme. de (Jeanne Antoinette Poisson) (courtesan); Versailles **(1721–1764)**

Pompey (Gnaeus Pompeius Magnus) (general); Rome **(106–48 B.C.E.)**

Ponce de León, Juan (explorer); Servas, Spain **(c. 1460–1521)**

Pons, Lily (coloratura soprano); Cannes, France **(1904–1976)**

Ponselle, Rosa (soprano); Meriden, Conn. **(1897–1981)**

Ponti, Carlo (director); Milan, Italy, 12/11/13

Pontormo, Jacopo da (painter); Pontormo, Italy **(1492–1557)**

Pope, Alexander (poet); London **(1688–1744)**

Porter, Cole (songwriter); Peru, Ind. **(1891–1964)**

Porter, Katherine Anne (novelist); Indian Creek, Tex. **(1891–1980)**

Portman, Natalie (actress); Jerusalem, 6/9/81

Posey, Parker (actress); Baltimore, 11/8/68

Post, Wiley (aviator); Grand Plain, Tex. **(1900–1935)**

Poston, Tom (actor); Columbus, Ohio, 10/17/27

Potëmkin, Grigori Aleksandrovich, Prince (statesman); Khizovo (Khizov), Belarus **(1739–1791)**

Potok, Chaim (author); New York City, 2/17/29

Potter, (Helen) Beatrix (author, illustrator); South Kensington, Middlesex, England **(1866–1943)**

Potts, Annie (actress); Nashville, Tenn., 10/28/52

Poulenc, Francis (composer); Paris **(1899–1963)**

Pound, Ezra (poet); Hailey, Idaho **(1885–1972)**

Poussin, Nicolas (painter); Villers, France **(1594–1665)**

Powell, Adam Clayton, Jr. (Congressman); New Haven, Conn. **(1908–1972)**

Powell, Colin L. (retired general); New York City, 4/5/37

Powell, Dick (actor); Mt. View, Ark. **(1904–1963)**

Powell, Eleanor (actress, tap dancer); Springfield, Mass. **(1912–1982)**

Powell, Jane (Suzanne Burce) (actress, singer); Portland, Ore., 4/1/29

Powell, William (actor); Pittsburgh **(1892–1984)**

Power, Tyrone (actor); Cincinnati, Ohio **(1914–1958)**

Powers, Stefanie (Stefania Zofia Federkiewcz) (actress); Hollywood, Calif., 11/12/42

Praxiteles (sculptor); Athens **(c. 370–c. 330 B.C.E.)**

Preminger, Otto (director, producer); Vienna **(1906–1986)**

Prentiss, Paula (Paula Ragusa) (actress); San Antonio, 3/4/39

Presley, Elvis (singer, actor); Tupelo, Miss. **(1935–1977)**

Presley, Priscilla (actress); Brooklyn, N.Y., 5/24/45

Preston, Robert (Robert Preston Meservey) (actor); Newton Highlands, Mass. **(1918–1987)**

Previn, André (conductor); Berlin, 4/6/29

Previn, Dory (singer); Rahway, N.J., 10/22/29?

Price, Leontyne (Mary) (soprano); Laurel, Miss., 2/10/27

Price, Ray (country music artist); Perryville, Tex., 1/12/26

Price, Vincent (actor); St. Louis **(1911–1993)**

Pride, Charley (singer); Sledge, Miss., 3/18/38?

Priestley, Jason (actor, producer); Vancouver, B.C., Canada, 8/28/69

Priestley, J. B. (John B.) (author); Bradford, England **(1894–1984)**

Priestley, Joseph (chemist); nr. Leeds, England **(1733–1804)**

Primakov, Yevgeny (Russian political leader); Kiev, Ukraine, 10/29/29

Primrose, William (violist); Glasgow, Scotland **(1904–1982)**

Prince (Prince Roger Nelson) (singer); Minneapolis, 6/7/58

Prince, Harold (stage producer); New York City, 1/30/28

Principal, Victoria (actress); Fukuoka, Japan, 1/3/45

Prinze, Freddie (actor); New York City **(1954–1977)**

Pritchett, V(ictor) S(awdon) (literary critic); Ipswich, England **(1900–1997)**

Procter, William (scientist); Cincinnati **(1872–1951)**

Prokofiev, Sergei Sergeevich (composer); St. Petersburg, Russia **(1891–1953)**

Proulx, E. Annie (novelist); Norwich, Conn., 8/22/35

Proust, Marcel (novelist); Paris **(1871–1922)**

Provine, Dorothy (actress); Deadwood, S. Dak., 1/20/37

Prowse, Juliet (actress, dancer); Bombay (Mumbai) **(1936–1996)**

Pryce, Jonathan (actor); Holywell, Wales, 6/1/47

Pryor, Richard (comedian); Peoria, Ill., 12/1/40

Ptolemy (Claudius Ptolemaeus) (astronomer, geographer); Ptolemais Hermii, Egypt, fl. 2nd cent.

Pucci, Emilio (Marchese di Barsento) (fashion designer); Naples, Italy **(1914–1992)**

Puccini, Giacomo (composer); Lucca, Italy **(1858–1924)**

Puente, Tito (band leader); New York City, 4/20/23

Pulaski, Casimir (military officer); Podolia, Poland **(1748–1779)**

Pulitzer, Joseph (publisher); Makó, Hungary **(1847–1911)**

Pullman, Bill (actor); Delphi, N.Y., 12/17/53

Pullman, George (inventor); Brockton, N.Y. **(1831–1897)**

Purcell, Henry (composer); London **(1658–1695)**

Pusey, Nathan M. (educator); Council Bluffs, Iowa, 4/4/07

Pushkin, Alexander Sergeevich (poet, dramatist); Moscow **(1799–1837)**

Puzo, Mario (novelist); New York City **(1921–1999)**

Pyle, Ernest Taylor (journalist); Dana, Ind. **(1900–1945)**

Pythagoras (mathematician, philosopher); Samos, Greece **(c. 582–c. 507C.E.)**

Q

Qaddafi, Muammar al- (Libyan leader); Libya, 1942

Quaid, Dennis (actor); Houston, 4/9/54

Quaid, Randy, (actor); Houston, 10/1/50

Quayle, Anthony (actor); Ainsdale, England **(1913–1989)**

Queen, Ellery: pen name of Frederic Dannay and Manfred B. Lee

Queen Latifah (Dana Owens) (rap musician, actress); Newark, New Jersey, 3/18/70

Queler, Eve (conductor); New York City, 1/1/36

Quennell, Sir Peter Courtney (biographer); Bromley, England **(1905–1993)**

Quindlen, Anna (writer); Philadelphia, 7/8/53

Quinn, Aidan (actor); Chicago, 3/8/59

Quinn, Anthony (Antonio Quiñones) (actor); Chihuahua, Mexico, 4/21/16

R

Rabe, David (playwright); Dubuque, Iowa, 3/10/40

Rabelais, François (satirist); nr. Chinon, France **(c. 1490–1553)**

Rabi, I(sidor) I(saac) (physicist); Rymanow, Poland **(1898–1988)**

Rabin, Yitzhak (former Israeli Prime Minister); Jerusalem **(1922–1995)**

Rachmaninoff, Sergei Wassilievitch (pianist, composer); Oneg Estate, Novgorod, Russia **(1873–1943)**

Racine, Jean Baptiste (dramatist); La Ferté-Milon, France **(1639–1699)**

Radner, Gilda (comedienne); Detroit **(1946–1989)**

Raft, George (actor); New York City **(1895–1980)**

Rainier III (Prince); Monaco, 5/31/23

Rains, Claude (actor); London **(1889–1967)**

Raitt, Bonnie (singer); Burbank, Calif., 11/8/49

Raitt, John (actor, singer); Santa Ana, Calif., 1/19/17

Raleigh, Sir Walter (courtier, navigator); London **(1552?–1618)**

Rambeau, Marjorie (actress); San Francisco **(1889–1970)**

Rameau, Jean-Philippe (composer); Dijon, France **(1683–1764)**

Rampal, Jean-Pierre (Louis) (flutist); Marseilles, France, 7/1/22

Rand, Ayn (novelist, philosopher); St. Petersburg, Russia **(1905–1982)**

Randall, Tony (Leonard Rosenberg) (actor); Tulsa, Okla., 2/26/20

Randolph, A(sa) Philip (labor leader); Crescent City, Fla. **(1889–1979)**

Rankin, Jeannette (politician, pacifist); Missoula, Mont. **(1880–1973)**

Raphael (Raffaello Santi) (painter, architect); Urbino, Italy **(1483–1520)**

Rasputin, Grigori Efimovich (monk); Tobolsk Province, Russia **(1872–1916)**

Rathbone, Basil (Philip St. John Basil Rathbone) (actor); Johannesburg, South Africa **(1892–1967)**

Rather, Dan (TV newscaster); Wharton, Tex., 10/31/31

Rattigan, Terence (playwright); London **(1911–1977)**

Rauschenberg, Robert (painter); Port Arthur, Tex., 10/22/25

Ravel, Maurice Joseph (composer); Ciboure, France **(1875–1937)**

Ray, Aldo (DaRe) (actor); Pen Argyl, Pa. **(1926–1991)**

Ray, Gene Anthony (actor, dancer); Harlem, N.Y., 5/24/63

Ray, Man (painter); Philadelphia **(1890–1976)**

Ray, Satyajat (film director); Calcutta **(1921–1992)**

Raye, Martha (Margie Yvonne Reed) (comedienne, actress); Butte, Mont. **(1916–1994)**

Reagan, Ronald Wilson (40th U.S. president, actor); Tampico, Ill., 2/6/11

Reasoner, Harry (TV commentator); Dakota City, Iowa **(1923–1991)**

Redding, Otis (singer); Dawson, Ga. **(1941–1967)**

Reddy, Helen (singer); Melbourne, Australia, 10/25/41

Redford, Robert (Charles Robert Redford, Jr.) (actor); Santa Monica, Calif., 8/18/37

Redgrave, Lynn (actress); London, 3/8/43

Redgrave, Sir Michael (actor); Bristol, England **(1908–1985)**

Redgrave, Vanessa (actress); London, 1/30/37

Redon, Odilon (artist); Bordeaux, France **(1840–1916)**

Reed, Donna (Donna Belle Mullenger) (actress); Denison, Iowa **(1921–1986)**

Reed, Lou (Lewis Allen Reed) (musician, guitarist, singer, song writer); Freeport, New York, 3/ 2/42

Reed, Rex (critic); Ft. Worth, 10/2/40

Reed, Walter (army surgeon); Belroi, Va. **(1851–1902)**

Reese, Della (Deloreese Patricia Early) (singer, actress); Detroit, 7/6/32

Reeve, Christopher (actor, activist); New York City, 9/25/52

Reeves, Jim (singer); Panola County, Tex. **(1923–1964)**

Reeves, Keanu (actor, musician); Beirut, Lebanon, 9/2/64

Reich, Robert (Clinton Cabinet Member); Scranton, Pa., 6/24/46

Reich, Steve (composer); New York City, 10/3/36

Reid, Wallace (actor); St. Louis **(1891–1923)**

Reiner, Carl (actor); New York City, 3/20/22

Reiner, Fritz (conductor); Budapest **(1888–1963)**

Reiner, Robert (actor, director, writer, producer); Bronx, N.Y., 3/6/45

Reinhardt, Max (Max Goldmann) (theater producer); nr. Vienna **(1873–1943)**

Reiser, Paul (actor, producer); New York City, 3/30/57

Remarque, Erich Maria (novelist); Osnabrük, Germany **(1898–1970)**

Rembrandt (Rembrandt Harmensz van Rijn) (painter); Leyden, Netherlands **(1605–1669)**

Remick, Lee (Ann) (actress); Boston **(1935–1991)**

Remnick, David (writer, editor); Hackensack, N.J., 10/29/58

Renfro, Brad (actor); Knoxville, Tenn., 7/25/82

Rennert, Günther (opera director, producer); Essen, Germany, 4/1/11

Rennie, Michael (actor); Bradford, England **(1909–1971)**

Reno, Janet (U.S. Attorney General); Miami, Fla., 7/21/38

Renoir, Jean (film director, writer); Paris **(1894–1979)**

Renoir, Pierre Auguste (painter); Limoges, France **(1841–1919)**

Resnais, Alain (film director); Vannes, France, 6/3/22

Resnik, Regina (mezzo-soprano); New York City, 8/30/22

Respighi, Ottorino (composer); Bologna, Italy **(1879–1936)**

Reston, James (journalist); Clydebank, Scotland **(1909–1995)**

Reuther, Walter (labor leader); Wheeling, W. Va. **(1907–1970)**
Revere, Paul (silversmith, hero of famous ride); Boston **(1735–1818)**
Revson, Charles (business executive); Boston **(1906–1975)**
Reynolds, Burt (actor, director, producer); Lansing, Mich., 2/11/36
Reynolds, Debbie (Marie Frances Reynolds) (actress); El Paso, Tex., 4/1/32
Reynolds, Sir Joshua (painter); nr. Plymouth, England **(1723–1792)**
Reynolds, Marjorie (Marjorie Goodspeed) (actress); Buhl, Idaho **(1921–1997)**
Reznor, Trent (musician); Mercer, Pa., 5/17/65
Rhodes, Cecil John (South African statesman); Bishop Stortford, England **(1853–1902)**
Ricci, Christina (actress); Santa Monica, Calif., 2/12/80
Rice, Anne (novelist); New Orleans, 10/14/41
Rice, Elmer (Elmer Leopold Reizenstein) (playwright); New York City **(1892–1967)**
Rice, Grantland (sports writer); Murfreesboro, Tenn. **(1880–1954)**
Rich, Buddy (Bernard) (drummer); Brooklyn, N.Y. **(1917–1987)**
Rich, Charlie (singer); Colt, Ark. **(1932–1995)**
Richard I the Lion-hearted (King of England); Oxford, England **(1157–1199)**
Richards, Ann (Dorothy Ann Willis) (ex-governor of Texas); Lakeview, Tex., 9/1/33
Richards, Keith (rock singer); Dartford, England, 12/18/43
Richards, Michael (actor); California, 7/21/48
Richardson, Elliot L. (ex-Cabinet member); Boston, 7/20/20
Richardson, Sir Ralph (actor); Cheltenham, England **(1902–1983)**
Richardson, Tony (director); Shipley, England **(1928–1991)**
Richelieu, Duc de (Armand Jean du Plessis) (cardinal); Paris **(1585–1642)**
Richie, Lionel (singer, songwriter); Tuskegee, Ala., 6/20/49
Richter, Charles Francis (seismologist); Hamilton, Ohio **(1900–1985)**
Richter, Sviatoslav (pianist); Zhitomir, Ukraine, 3/20/14
Rickenbacker, Eddie (Edward V.) (aviator); Columbus, Ohio **(1890–1973)**
Rickles, Don (comedian); New York City, 5/8/26
Rickover, Vice Admiral Hyman G. (atomic energy expert); Russia **(1900–1986)**
Riddle, Nelson (composer); Hackensack, N.J. **(1921–1985)**
Ride, Sally K(risten) (astronaut, astrophysicist); Encino, Calif., 5/26/51
Ridgway, General Matthew B. (ex-Army Chief of Staff); Ft. Monroe, Va. **(1895–1993)**
Riemenschneider, Tilman (sculptor); Osterode, Germany **(c. 1460–1531)**
Rigg, Diana (actress); Doncaster, England, 7/20/38
Riley, James Whitcomb (poet); Greenfield, Ind. **(1849–1916)**
Rilke, Rainer Maria (poet); Prague **(1875–1926)**
Rimbaud, (Jean Nicolas) Arthur (poet); Charleville, France **(1854–1891)**
Rimes, LeAnn (singer); Jackson, Miss., 8/28/82
Rimsky-Korsakov, Nikolai Andreevich (composer); Tikhvin, Russia **(1844–1908)**
Rinehart, Mary (née Roberts) (novelist); Pittsburgh **(1876–1958)**
Ringwald, Molly (actress); Sacramento, California, 2/18/68
Ritchard, Cyril (actor, director); Sydney, Australia **(1898–1977)**
Ritter, John (Jonathan) (actor); Burbank, Calif., 9/17/48
Ritter, Tex (Woodward Maurice Ritter) (singer); Panola County, Tex. **(1905–1973)**
Ritter, Thelma (actress); Brooklyn, N.Y. **(1905–1969)**
Rivera, Chita (Dolores Conchita Figuero del Rivero) (dancer, actress, singer); Washington, D.C., 1/23/33
Rivera, Diego (painter); Guanajuato, Mexico **(1886–1957)**
Rivera, Geraldo (Miguel Rivera) (TV host); New York City, 7/4/43
Rivers, Joan (comedienne); Brooklyn, N.Y., 6/8/33
Rivers, Larry (Yitzroch Loiza Grossberg) (painter); New York City, 8/17/23
Roach, Hal (film producer); Elmira, N.Y. **(1892–1992)**
Robards, Jason, Jr. (actor); Chicago, 7/22/22
Robards, Jason, Sr. (actor); Hillsdale, Mich. **(1892–1963)**
Robbins, Harold (Harold Rubin) (novelist); New York City **(1916–1997)**
Robbins, Jerome (Jerome Rabinowitz) (choreographer); New York City **(1918–1998)**
Robbins, Marty (singer); Glendale, Ariz. **(1925–1982)**
Robbins, Tim (Timothy Francis) (actor, director); West Covina, Calif., 10/16/58
Roberts, Cokie (Mary Martha Corinne Morrison Claiborne Boggs) (broadcast journalist); New Orleans, 12/27/43
Roberts, Eric (actor); Biloxi, Miss., 4/18/56
Roberts, Julia (actress); Smyrna, Ga., 10/28/67

Roberts, Oral (Granville) (evangelist, publisher); nr. Ada, Okla., 1/24/18
Robertson, Cliff (Clifford Parker Robertson III) (actor); La Jolla, Calif., 9/9/25
Robertson, Dale (Dayle) (actor); Oklahoma City, 7/14/23
Robeson, Paul (singer, actor); Princeton, N.J. **(1898–1976)**
Robespierre, Maximilien François Marie Isidore de (French Revolutionist); Arras, France **(1758–1794)**
Robinson, Bill "Bojangles" (Luther) (dancer); Richmond, Va. **(1878–1949)**
Robinson, Edward G. (Emanuel Goldenberg) (actor); Bucharest **(1893–1973)**
Robinson, Edwin Arlington (poet); Head Tide, Maine **(1869–1935)**
Robinson Peete, Holly (Holly Robinson) (actress); Philadelphia, Pennsylvania, 9/18/64
Robinson, Robert (chemist, Nobel laureate); Chesterfield, Derbyshire, England **(1885–1975)**
Robinson, Smokey (singer, songwriter); Detroit, 2/19/40
Rock, Chris (comedian, actor); Brooklyn, New York, 2/7/66
Rockefeller, David (banker); New York City, 6/12/15
Rockefeller, John Davison (business executive); Richford, N.Y. **(1839–1937)**
Rockefeller, John Davison, Jr. (industrialist); Cleveland **(1874–1960)**
Rockefeller, John D., 3rd (philanthropist); New York City **(1906–1978)**
Rockefeller, Laurance S. (conservationist); New York City, 5/26/10
Rockwell, Norman (painter, illustrator); New York City **(1894–1978)**
Roddenberry, Gene (creator of *Star Trek*); El Paso, Tex. **(1921–1991)**
Rodgers, Jimmie (singer); Meridian, Miss. **(1897–1933)**
Rodgers, Richard (composer); New York City **(1902–1979)**
Rodin, François Auguste René (sculptor); Paris **(1840–1917)**
Rodzinski, Artur (conductor); Spalato, Dalmatia **(1894–1958)**
Roeg, Nicolas (film director); London, 8/15/28
Roentgen, Wilhelm Konrad (physicist); Lennep, Prussia **(1845–1923)**
Roethke, Theodore (poet); Saginaw, Mich. **(1908–1963)**
Rogers, Buddy (Charles Rogers) (actor); Olathe, Kans. **(1904–1999)**
Rogers, Carl (psychologist); Oak Park, Ill. **(1902–1987)**
Rogers, Fred (TV producer, host); Latrobe, Pa., 3/20/28
Rogers, Ginger (Virginia McMath) (dancer, actress); Independence, Mo. **(1911–1995)**
Rogers, Kenny (singer); Houston, 8/21/38
Rogers, Mimi (actress); Coral Gables, Florida, 1/27/56
Rogers, Roy (Leonard Frank Sly) (actor, singer); Cincinnati **(1911–1998)**
Rogers, Wayne (actor); Birmingham, Ala., 4/7/33
Rogers, Will (William Penn Adair Rogers) (humorist); Oologah, Okla. **(1879–1935)**
Rogers, William P. (ex-Secretary of State); Norfolk, N.Y., 6/23/13
Roland, Gilbert (actor); Juarez, Mexico **(1905–1994)**
Rolland, Romain (author); Clamecy, France **(1866–1944)**
Rollins, Sonny (saxophonist); New York City, 9/7/30
Romberg, Sigmund (composer); Szeged, Hungary **(1887–1951)**
Rome, Harold (composer); Hartford, Conn. **(1908–1993)**
Romero, Cesar (actor); New York City **(1907–1994)**
Romney, George W. (automobile executive, governor); Chihuahua, Mexico **(1907–1995)**
Romulo, Carlos P. (diplomat, educator); Manila **(1899–1985)**
Ronsard, Pierre de (poet); La Possonnière nr. Couture, France **(1524–1585)**
Ronstadt, Linda (singer); Tucson, Ariz., 7/30/46
Rooney, Andy (TV personality); Albany, N.Y., 1/14/19
Rooney, Mickey (Joe Yule, Jr.) (actor); Brooklyn, N.Y., 9/23/20
Roosevelt, (Anna) Eleanor (reformer, humanitarian); New York City **(1884–1962)**
Roosevelt, Franklin Delano (32nd U.S. president); Hyde Park, N.Y. **(1882–1945)**
Roosevelt, Theodore (26th U.S. president); New York City **(1858–1919)**
Rorem, Ned (composer); Richmond, Ind., 10/23/23
Rose, Billy (showman); New York City **(1899–1966)**
Rose, Leonard (concert cellist); Washington, D.C. **(1918–1984)**
Roseanne (Roseanne Barr) (actress); Salt Lake City, 11/3/52
Rosenberg, Ethel (spy); New York City **(1915–1953)**
Rosenberg, Julius (spy); New York City **(1918–1953)**
Ross, Betsy (Betsey Griscom) (flagmaker); Philadelphia **(1752–1836)**
Ross, Diana (singer); Detroit, 3/26/44
Ross, Katharine (actress); Hollywood, Calif., 1/29/42
Rossellini, Isabella (model, actress); Rome, Italy, 6/18/52

Rossellini, Roberto (film director); Rome (1906–1977)

Rossetti, Christina Georgina (poet); London (1830–1894)

Rossetti, Dante Gabriel (painter, poet); London (1828–1882)

Rossini, Gioacchino Antonio (composer); Pesaro, Italy (1792–1868)

Rosten, Leo (writer); Lodz, Poland (1908–1997)

Rostand, Edmond (dramatist); Marseilles, France (1868–1918)

Rostow, Walt Whitman (economist); New York City, 10/7/16

Rostropovich, Mstislav (cellist, conductor); Baku, Azerbaijan, 3/27/27

Roth, Henry (writer); Tysmenica, Ukraine (1906–1995)

Roth, Philip (novelist); Newark, N.J., 3/19/33

Roth, Tim (actor); London, 5/14/64

Rothko, Mark (Marcus Rothkovich) (painter); Russia (1903–1970)

Rouault, Georges (painter); Paris (1871–1958)

Roundtree, Richard (actor); New Rochelle, N.Y., 9/7/42

Rousseau, Henri (painter); Laval, France (1844–1910)

Rousseau, Jean Jacques (philosopher); Geneva (1712–1778)

Rovere, Richard H. (journalist); Jersey City, N.J., 5/5/15

Rowan, Carl Thomas (journalist); Ravenscroft, Tenn., 8/11/25

Rowan, Dan (comedian); Beggs, Okla. (1922–1987)

Rowlands, Gena (actress); Cambria, Wis., 6/19/30

Royko, Mike (columnist); Chicago (1932–1997)

Rubens, Sir Peter Paul (painter); Siegen, Germany (1577–1640)

Rubinstein, Arthur (concert pianist); Lódz, Poland (1887–1982)

Rubinstein, Helena (cosmetics executive); Krakow, Poland (1882?–1965)

Rubinstein, John (actor, composer); Los Angeles, 12/8/46

Rucker, Darius (musician, singer, songwriter); Charleston, S.C., 5/13/66

Rudel, Julius (conductor); Vienna, 3/6/21

Ruffo, Titta (baritone); Italy (1878–1953)

Runyon, (Alfred) Damon (journalist); Manhattan, Kans. (1884–1945)

Rushdie, (Ahmed) Salman (novelist); Bombay (Mumbai), 6/19/47

Rusk, Dean (ex-Sec. of State); Cherokee County, Ga. (1909–1994)

Ruskin, John (art critic); London (1819–1900)

Russell, Keri (actress); Fountain Valley, Calif., 3/23/76

Russell, Lord Bertrand (Arthur William) (mathematician, philosopher); Trelleck, Wales (1872–1970)

Russell, Jane (actress); Bemidji, Minn., 6/21/21

Russell, Ken (film director); Southhampton, England, 4/3/27

Russell, Kurt (actor); Springfield, Mass., 3/17/51

Russell, Leon (pianist, singer); Lawton, Okla., 4/2/41

Russell, Lillian (Helen Louise Leonard) (soprano); Clinton, Iowa (1861–1922)

Russell, Mark (satirist); Buffalo, N.Y., 8/23/32

Russell, Nipsy (comedian); Atlanta, 10/13/24

Russell, Rosalind (actress); Waterbury, Conn. (1912–1976)

Russell, Theresa (Theresa Paup) (actress); San Diego, Calif., 3/20/57

Russo, Rene (actress); Burbank, California, 2/17/54

Rustin, Bayard (civil rights leader); West Chester, Pa. (1910–1987)

Rutherford, Dame Margaret (actress); London (1892–1972)

Ryan, Jeri (actress); Munich, Germany, 2/22/68

Ryan, Meg (Margaret Mary Emily Anne Hyra) (actress); Fairfield, Conn., 11/19/61

Ryan, Robert (actor); Chicago (1909–1973)

Rydell, Bobby (Robert Ridarelli) (singer); Philadelphia, 4/26/42

Ryder, Winona (Winona Horowitz) (actress); Winona, Minn., 10/29/71

Rysanek, Leonie (dramatic soprano); Vienna (1928–1998)

S

Saarinen, Eero (architect); Finland (1910–1961)

Sabin, Albert B. (polio researcher); Bialystok, Poland (1906–1993)

Sabu (Dastagir) (actor); Karapur, India (1924–1963)

Sacagawea (Shoshone Indian guide); Lemhi River valley (Idaho) (c. 1786–1812)

Sachs, Jeffrey D. (economist, educator); Michigan, 1954

Sadat, Anwar el- (former president); Egypt (1918–1981)

Sade, Marquis de (Donatien Alphonse François, Comte de Sade) (libertine, writer); Paris (1740–1814)

Safer, Morley (TV newscaster); Toronto, 11/8/31

Sagan, Carl (Edward) (astronomer, science writer); New York City (1934–1996)

Sagan, Françoise (novelist); Cajarc, France, 6/21/35

Sahl, Mort (Morton Lyon Sahl) (comedian); Montreal, 5/11/27

Saint, Eva Marie (actress); Newark, N.J., 7/4/24

St. Denis, Ruth (dancer, choreographer); Newark, N.J. (1878–1968)

St. James, Susan (Susan Miller) (actress); Los Angeles, 8/14/46

St. John, Jill (actress); Los Angeles, 8/19/40

St. Johns, Adela Rogers (journalist, author); Los Angeles (1894–1988)

Sainte-Marie, Buffy (Beverly) (folk singer); Craven, Sask., Canada, 2/20/41

Saint-Gaudens, Augustus (sculptor); Dublin (1848–1907)

Saint-Laurent, Yves (Henri Donat Mathieu) (fashion designer); Oran, Algeria, 8/1/36

Saint-Saens, Charles Camille (composer); Paris (1835–1921)

Sakharov, Andrei Dmitriyevich (nuclear physicist, peace activist); Russia (1921–1989)

Sales, Soupy (Milton Hines) (television entertainer); Franklinton, N.C., 1/6/26

Salinger, J(erome) D(avid) (novelist); New York City, 1/1/19

Salisbury, Harrison E. (journalist); Minneapolis (1908–1993)

Salk, Jonas (polio researcher); New York City (1914–1995)

Salk, Lee (psychologist); New York City (1926–1992)

Salomon, Haym (American Revolution financier); Leszno, Poland (1740–1785)

Sand, George (Amandine Lucille Aurore Dudevant, née Dupin) (novelist); Paris (1804–1876)

Sandburg, Carl (poet, biographer); Galesburg, Ill. (1878–1967)

Sanders, George (actor); St. Petersburg, Russia (1906–1972)

Sandler, Adam (comedian, musician, actor, screenwriter, singer); Brooklyn, New York, 9/9/66

Sands, Tommy (singer); Chicago, 8/27/37

Sanger, Margaret (birth-control advocate); Corning, N.Y. (1879–1966)

San Giacomo, Laura (actress); Hoboken, N.J., 11/14/62

Santayana, George (philosopher); Madrid (1863–1952)

Sappho (poet); Lesbos, Greece (610 B.C.E.–580 B.C.E.)

Sarandon, Susan (Susan Tomalin) (actress); New York City, 10/4/46

Sargent, John Singer (painter); Florence, Italy (1856–1925)

Sarnoff, David (radio executive); Minsk, Belarus (1891–1971)

Saroyan, William (novelist); Fresno, Calif. (1908–1981)

Sarrazin, Michael (actor); Que., Canada, 5/22/40

Sarto, Andrea del (Andrea Domenico d'Agnolo di Francesco) (painter); Florence, Italy (1486–1531)

Sartre, Jean-Paul (existentialist writer); Paris (1905–1980)

Sassoon, Vidal (hair stylist); London, 1/17/28

Satie, Erik (Alfred Leslie) (composer); Paris (1866–1925)

Saul (King of Israel) fl. 11th cent. B.C.E.

Savage, Fred (actor); Highland Park, Illinois, 7/9/76

Savalas, Telly (Aristoteles) (actor); Garden City, N.Y. (1924–1994)

Savonarola, Girolamo (religious reformer); Ferrara, Italy (1452–1498)

Sawyer, Diane (broadcast journalist); Glasgow, Ky., 12/22/45

Sayão, Bidú (soprano); Rio de Janeiro (1904–1999)

Sayles, John (director, screenwriter, actor); Schenectady, N.Y., 9/28/50

Scarlatti, Alessandro (composer); Palermo, Italy (1659–1725)

Scarlatti, Domenico (composer); Naples, Italy (1685–1757)

Scavullo, Francesco (photographer); Staten Island, N.Y., 1/16/29

Schama, Simon (historian); London, 2/13/45

Schapiro, Meyer (Meir) (art historian); Siauliai, Lithuania (1904–1906)

Schary, Dore (producer, writer); Newark, N.J. (1905–1980)

Schell, Maximilian (actor); Vienna, 12/8/30

Schiaparelli, Elsa (fashion designer); Rome (1890–1973)

Schiff, Dorothy (newspaper publisher); New York City (1903–1989)

Schiffer, Claudia (model, actress); Rheinberg/Dusseldorf, Germany, 8/25/70

Schiller, Johann Christoph Friedrich von (dramatist, poet); Marbach, Germany (1759–1805)

Schipa, Tito (tenor); Lecce, Italy (1890–1965)

Schippers, Thomas (conductor); Kalamazoo, Mich. (1930–1977)

Schlegel, Friedrich von (philosopher); Hanover, Germany (1772–1829)

Schlesinger, Arthur M., Jr. (historian); Columbus, Ohio, 10/15/17

Schnabel, Artur (pianist, composer); Lipnik, Austria (1882–1951)

Schneider, Romy (Rose-Marie Albach-Retty) (actress); Vienna (1938–1982)

Schoenberg, Arnold (composer); Vienna (1874–1951)

Schomberg, Arthur (bibliophile, antiquarian); San Juan, P.R. (1874–1938)

Schopenhauer, Arthur (philosopher); Danzig, Poland (1788–1860)

Schröder, Gerhard (Chancellor of Germany); Mossenberg, Germany, 4/7/44

Schubert, Franz Peter (composer); Vienna (1797–1828)

Schulberg, Budd (novelist); New York City, 3/27/14

Schulz, Charles M. (cartoonist); Minneapolis, 11/26/22

Schumacher, Joel (film director, producer, screenwriter); New York City, 8/29/39
Schuman, Robert (statesman); Luxembourg **(1886–1963)**
Schuman, William (composer); New York City **(1910–1992)**
Schumann, Robert Alexander (composer); Zwickau, Germany **(1810–1856)**
Schumann-Heink, Ernestine (contralto); nr. Prague **(1861–1936)**
Schwartz, Arthur (songwriter); Brooklyn, N.Y. **(1900–1984)**
Schwarzenegger, Arnold (bodybuilder, actor); Graz, Austria, 7/30/47
Schwarzkopf, Elisabeth (soprano); Poznán, Poland, 12/9/15
Schwarzkopf, H. Norman (retired general); Trenton, N.J., 8/22/34
Schweitzer, Albert (humanitarian, Nobel laureate); Kaysersburg, Upper Alsace **(1875–1965)**
Schwimmer, David (actor); New York City, 11/12/66
Scofield, Paul (actor); Hurstpierpoint, England, 1/21/22
Scorsese, Martin (actor, writer, director, producer); Flushing, N.Y., 11/17/42
Scott, George C. (actor); Wise, Va. **(1927–1999)**
Scott, Hazel (singer, pianist); Port of Spain, Trinidad **(1920–1981)**
Scott, Lizabeth (Emma Matzo) (actress); Scranton, Pa., 9/29/23
Scott, Randolph (Randolph Crane) (actor); Orange County, Va. **(1898–1987)**
Scott, Robert Falcon (explorer); Devonport, England **(1868–1912)**
Scott, Sir Walter (novelist); Edinburgh, Scotland **(1771–1832)**
Scott, Zachary (actor); Austin, Tex. **(1914–1965)**
Scotto, Renata (operatic soprano); Savona, Italy, 2/24/36
Scruggs, Earl Eugene (bluegrass musician); Cleveland County, N.C., 1/6/24
Seaborg, Glenn Theodore (chemist, Nobel laureate); Ishpeming, Mich. **(1912–1999)**
Seagal, Steven (actor); Lansing, Mich., 4/10/52
Seal (Sealhenry Olumide Samuel) (singer, songwriter); London, England, 2/19/63
Seattle (Chief Seattle) (Suquamish Indian leader); Blake Island (Wash.) **(c. 1786–1866)**
Sebastian, John (composer, singer); New York City, 3/17/44
Seberg, Jean (actress); Marshalltown, Iowa **(1938–1979)**
Sedaka, Neil (singer); Brooklyn, N.Y., 3/13/39
Sedgwick, Kyra (actress); New York City, 8/19/65
Seeger, Pete (folk singer); New York City, 5/3/19
Segal, Erich (novelist); Brooklyn, N.Y., 6/16/37
Segal, George (actor); New York City, 2/13/36
Segovia, Andrés (guitarist); Linares, Spain **(1893–1987)**
Seinfeld, Jerry (comedian); Brooklyn, N.Y., 4/29/54
Selena (Selena Quintanilla Perez) (singer); Lake Jackson, Tex. **(1971–1995)**
Selleck, Tom (actor); Detroit, 1/29/45
Sellars, Peter (theater director); Pittsburgh, 1958?
Sellers, Peter (actor); Southsea, England **(1925–1980)**
Selznick, David O. (producer); Pittsburgh **(1902–1965)**
Sendak, Maurice (Bernard) (children's book author, illustrator); Brooklyn, N.Y., 6/10/28
Sennett, Mack (Michael Sinnott) (film producer); Richmond, Que., Canada **(1880–1960)**
Sequoyah (Cherokee linguist); Taskigi, Tenn. **(c. 1770–1843)**
Serkin, Peter (pianist); New York City, 7/24/47
Serkin, Rudolf (pianist); Eger, Czech Republic **(1903–1991)**
Serling, Rod (writer, TV host); Syracuse, N.Y. **(1924–1975)**
Sessions, Roger (composer); Brooklyn, N.Y. **(1896–1985)**
Seurat, Georges (painter); Paris **(1859–1891)**
Seuss, Dr. (Theodor Seuss Geisel) (author, illustrator); Springfield, Mass. **(1904–1991)**
Sevareid, Eric (TV commentator); Velva, N.D. **(1912–1991)**
Severinsen, Doc (Carl) (band leader); Arlington, Ore., 7/7/27
Sewell, Rufus (actor, musician); London, 10/29/67
Sexton, Anne (poet); Newton, Mass. **(1928–1974)**
Seymour, Jane (Joyce Penelope Wilhelmina Frankenburg) (actress); Wimbledon, England, 2/15/51
Shabazz, Betty (Betty Sanders) (civil rights activist); Detroit **(1936–1997)**
Shaffer, Peter (playwright); Liverpool, England, 5/15/26
Shaham, Gil (violinist); Urbana, Ill., 1971
Shahn, Ben(jamin) (painter); Kaunas, Lithuania **(1898–1969)**
Shakespeare, William (dramatist); Stratford on Avon, England **(1564–1616)**
Shakur, Tupac (Amaru Shakur) (singer, actor); Brooklyn, N.Y. **(1971–1996)**
Shandling, Garry (comedian, actor, producer); Chicago, 11/29/49
Shange, Ntozake (Paulette Williams) (poet, playwright); Trenton, N.J., 10/18/48
Shankar, Ravi (sitar player); Benares, India, 4/7/20

Sharif, Omar (Michael Shalhoub) (actor); Alexandria, Egypt, 4/10/32
Shatner, William (actor); Montreal, 3/22/31
Shaw, Artie (Arthur Arshawsky) (band leader); New York City, 5/23/10
Shaw, George Bernard (dramatist); Dublin **(1856–1950)**
Shaw, Irwin (novelist); Brooklyn, N.Y. **(1913–1984)**
Shaw, Robert (actor); Lancashire, England **(1927–1978)**
Shaw, Robert (chorale conductor); Red Bluff, Calif. **(1916–1999)**
Shawn, Ted (Edwin Myers Shawn) (dancer, choreographer); Kansas City, Mo. **(1891–1972)**
Shearer, Moira (ballet dancer); Dunfermline, Scotland, 1/17/26
Shearer, Norma (actress); Montreal **(1900–1983)**
Shearing, George (pianist); London, 8/13/20
Sheedy, Ally (Alexandra Sheedy) (actress, writer); New York City, 6/12/62
Sheen, Charlie (actor); Los Angeles, 9/3/65
Sheen, Fulton J. (Peter Sheen) (Roman Catholic bishop); El Paso, Ill. **(1895–1979)**
Sheen, Martin (Ramon Estevez) (actor); Dayton, Ohio, 8/3/40
Shelley, Mary Wollstonecraft Godwin (writer); London **(1797–1851)**
Shelley, Percy Bysshe (poet); nr. Horsham, England **(1792–1822)**
Shelton, Henry (Chairman of the Joint Chiefs of Staff); Tarboro, N.C., 1/2/42
Shepard, Sam (Samuel Shepard Rogers) (playwright); Ft. Sheridan, Ill., 11/5/43
Shepherd, Cybill (actress); Memphis, Tenn., 2/18/50
Sheraton, Thomas (furniture designer); Stockton-on-Tees, England **(1751–1806)**
Sheridan, Ann (Clara Lou Sheridan) (actress); Denton, Tex. **(1915–1967)**
Sheridan, Philip (army officer); Albany, N.Y. **(1831–1888)**
Sheridan, Richard Brinsley (dramatist); Dublin **(1751–1816)**
Sherman, William Tecumseh (army officer); Lancaster, Ohio **(1820–1891)**
Sherwood, Robert Emmet (playwright); New Rochelle, N.Y. **(1896–1955)**
Shevardnadze, Eduard Amvrosiyevich (State Council Chairman, Georgia); Mamati, Georgia, 1/25/28
Shields, Brooke (actress); New York City, 5/31/65
Shire, Talia (Coppola) (actress); Lake Success, N.Y., 4/25/46
Shirer, William L. (journalist, historian); Chicago **(1904–1993)**
Sholokhov, Mikhail (novelist); Veshenskaya, Russia **(1905–1984)**
Shore, Dinah (Frances Rose Shore) (singer); Winchester,Tenn. **(1917–1994)**
Short, Bobby (Robert Waltrip Short) (singer, pianist); Danville, Ill., 9/15/24
Short, Martin (actor); Hamilton, Ont., Canada, 3/26/50
Shostakovich, Dmitri (composer); St. Petersburg, Russia **(1906–1975)**
Shriner, Herb (humorist, host); Toledo, Ohio **(1918–1970)**
Shriver, Maria (TV co-host); Chicago, 11/6/55
Shriver, Sargent (Robert Sargent Shriver, Jr.) (business executive); Westminster, Md., 11/9/15
Shue, Andrew (actor, soccer player); South Orange, N.J., 2/20/67
Shue, Elisabeth (actress); Wilmington, Del., 6/10/63
Shulman, Max (novelist); St. Paul, Minn. **(1919–1988)**
Sibelius, Jean (Johann Julius Christian Sibelius) (composer); Tavastehus, Finland **(1865–1957)**
Sidney, Sir Philip (poet); Penshurst, England **(1554–1586)**
Sidney, Sylvia (Sophia Kosow) (actress); New York City **(1910–1999)**
Siegfried and Roy (illusionists) **Siegfried Fischbacher;** Rosenheim, Bavaria, Germany, 1939 **Roy Uwe Ludwig Horn;** Nordenham, nr. Bremen, Germany, 1944
Siepi, Cesare (basso); Milan, Italy, 2/10/23
Signoret, Simone (Simone Kaminker) (actress); Wiesbaden, Germany **(1921–1985)**
Sihanouk, Norodom (King of Cambodia); Cambodia, 10/31/22
Sikorsky, Igor I. (inventor); Kiev, Ukraine **(1889–1972)**
Sills, Beverly (Belle Silverman) (soprano, opera director); Brooklyn, N.Y., 5/25/29
Sills, Milton (actor); Chicago **(1882–1930)**
Silone, Ignazio (Secondo Tranquilli) (novelist); Pescina del Marsi, Italy **(1900–1978)**
Silver, Ron (Ron Zimelman) (actor); New York City, 7/2/46
Silverheels, Jay (Harold J. Smith) (actor); Brantford, Ont., Canada **(1919–1980)**
Silverman, Fred (broadcasting executive); New York City, 9/13/37
Silvers, Phil (Philip Silversmith) (comedian); Brooklyn, N.Y. **(1912–1985)**
Silverstein, Shel (writer, poet); Chicago **(1932–1999)**
Silverstone, Alicia (actress); San Francisco, 10/4/76

Sim, Alastair (actor); Edinburgh, Scotland (1900–1976)

Simenon, Georges (Georges Sim) (mystery writer); Liège, Belgium (1903–1989)

Simmons, Jean (actress); Crouch Hill, London, 1/31/29

Simon, Carly (singer, songwriter); New York City, 6/25/45

Simon, Neil (playwright); Bronx, N.Y., 7/4/27

Simon, Norton (business executive); Portland, Ore. (1907–1993)

Simon, Paul (singer, songwriter); Newark, N.J., 11/5/42

Simon, Simone (actress); Marseilles, France, 4/23/14

Simone, Nina (Eunice Kathleen Waymoa) (singer, pianist); Tryon, N.C., 2/21/33

Sinatra, Frank (Francis Albert Sinatra) (singer, actor); Hoboken, N.J. (1915–1998)

Sinbad (David Adkins) (actor, comedian); Benton Harbor, Michigan, 11/10/56

Sinclair, Upton Beall (novelist); Baltimore (1878–1968)

Singer, Isaac Bashevis (novelist); Radzymin, Poland (1904–1991)

Singleton, John (writer, director); Los Angeles, 1/6/68

Sinise, Gary (actor, director); Chicago, 3/17/55

Siqueiros, David (painter); Chihuahua, Mexico (1896–1974)

Sirtis, Marina (actress); London, 3/29/59

Siskel, Gene (film critic); Chicago (1946–1999)

Sisley, Alfred (painter); Paris (1839–1899)

Sitting Bull (Prairie Sioux Indian Chief); on Grand River, S.D. (c. 1835–1890)

Skelton, Red (Richard) (comedian); Vincennes, Ind. (1913–1997)

Skerritt, Tom (actor); Detroit, 8/25/43

Skinner, B(urrhus) F(rederic) (psychologist); Susquehanna, Pa. (1904–1990)

Skinner, Otis (actor); Cambridge, Mass. (1858–1942)

Slater, Christian (Christopher Hawkins) (actor); New York City, 8/18/69

Slatkin, Leonard (conductor); Los Angeles, 9/1/44

Sloan, Alfred P., Jr. (industrialist); New Haven, Conn. (1875–1965)

Sloan, John (painter); Lock Haven, Pa. (1871–1951)

Smalley, Richard E. (chemist, Nobel laureate); Akron, Ohio, 6/6/43

Smetana, Bedrich (composer); Litomysl, Czech Republic (1824–1884)

Smith, Adam (economist); Kirkaldy, Scotland (1723–1790)

Smith, Alexis (actress); Penticon, Canada (1921–1993)

Smith, Alfred Emanuel (politician); New York City (1873–1944)

Smith, Bessie (blues singer); Chattanooga, Tenn. (1894–1937)

Smith, Sir C. Aubrey (actor); London (1863–1948)

Smith, David (sculptor); Decatur, Ind. (1906–1965)

Smith, Harry (TV co-anchor); Hammond, Ind., 8/21/51

Smith, Howard K. (TV commentator); Ferriday, La., 5/12/14

Smith, Jaclyn (actress); Houston, 10/26/47

Smith, John (American colonist); Willoughby, Lincolnshire, England (1580–1631)

Smith, Joseph (religious leader); Sharon, Vt. (1805–1844)

Smith, Kate (Kathryn) (singer); Greenville, Va. (1909–1986)

Smith, Kevin (director, screenwriter); Red Bank, N.J., 8/2/70

Smith, Dame Maggie (actress); Ilford, England, 12/28/34

Smith, Patti Lee (singer, songwriter); Chicago, 12/30/46

Smith, Red (Walter) (sports columnist); Green Bay, Wis. (1905–1982)

Smith, Will (actor, rap singer); Philadelphia, 9/25/68

Smits, Jimmy (actor); New York City, 7/9/55

Smollet, Tobias (novelist); Dalquhurn, Scotland (1721–1771)

Smothers, Dick (Richard) (comedian); New York City, 11/20/39

Smothers, Tom (Thomas) (comedian); New York City, 2/2/37

Snipes, Wesley (actor); Orlando, Fla., 7/31/62

Snow, Lord (Charles Percy) (author); Leicester, England (1905–1980)

Snowdon, Earl of (Anthony Armstrong-Jones) (photographer); London, 3/7/30

Snyder, Tom (TV personality); Milwaukee, 5/12/36

Socrates (philosopher); Athens (469–399 B.C.E.)

Soderbergh, Steven (film director, screenwriter); Baton Rouge, La., 1/14/63

Solomon (King of Israel); Jerusalem, fl. 950 B.C.E.

Solon (lawgiver); Salamis, Greece (c. 630–559 B.C.E.)

Solti, Sir Georg (conductor); Budapest (1912–1997)

Solzhenitsyn, Aleksandr (novelist); Kislovodsk, Russia, 12/11/18

Somers, Suzanne (Suzanne Mahoney) (actress); San Bruno, Calif., 10/16/46

Somes, Michael (ballet dancer); Horsley, England (1917–1994)

Sommer, Elke (Elke Schletz) (actress); Berlin, 11/5/42

Sondheim, Stephen (composer); New York City, 3/22/30

Sonnenfeld, Barry (cinematographer, film director); New York City, 4/1/53

Sontag, Susan (author, film director); New York City, 1/28/33

Sophocles (dramatist); nr. Athens (c. 496–406 B.C.E.)

Sorbo, Kevin (actor); Mound, Minn., 9/24/58

Sorvino, Mira (actress); Tenafly, N.J., 9/28/67

Sorvino, Paul (actor); Brooklyn, N.Y., 4/13/39

Sothern, Ann (Harriette Lake) (actress); Valley City, N.D., 1/22/09

Soul, David (David Solberg) (actor); Chicago, 8/28/43

Sousa, John Philip (composer); Washington, D.C. (1854–1932)

Soyer, Raphael (painter); Borisoglebsk, Russia (1899–1987)

Spaak, Paul-Henri (statesman); Brussels (1899–1972)

Spacek, Sissy (Mary Elizabeth Spacek) (actress); Quitman, Tex., 12/25/49

Spacey, Kevin (actor); South Orange, N.J., 7/28/59

Spade, David (actor; comedian); Birmingham, Mich., 7/22/65

Spader, James (actor); Boston, 2/7/60

Spark, Muriel (novelist); Edinburgh, Scotland, 2/1/18

Spector, Phil (rock producer); Bronx, N.Y., 12/25/40

Spelling, Aaron (producer); Dallas, 4/22/28

Spelling, Tori (Victoria) (actress); Los Angeles, 5/16/73

Spencer, Herbert (philosopher); Derby, England (1820–1903)

Spender, Stephen (poet); nr. London (1909–1995)

Spengler, Oswald (philosopher); Blankenburg, Germany (1880–1936)

Spenser, Edmund (poet); London (1552?–1599)

Spewack, Bella (playwright); Hungary (1899–1990)

Spiegel, Sam (producer); Jaroslaw, Poland (1901–1985)

Spielberg, Steven (director, producer, writer, actor); Cincinnati, 12/18/47

Spillane, Mickey (Frank Spillane) (mystery writer); Brooklyn, N.Y., 3/9/18

Spiner, Brent (actor); Houston, 2/2/49

Spinoza, Baruch (philosopher); Amsterdam, Netherlands (1632–1677)

Spitalny, Phil (orchestra leader) (1890–1970)

Spivak, Lawrence (TV producer); Brooklyn, N.Y. (1900–1994)

Spock, Benjamin (pediatrician, writer); New Haven, Conn. (1903–1998)

Springsteen, Bruce (singer, songwriter); Freehold, N.J., 9/23/49

Sproul, Robert G. (educator); San Francisco (1891–1975)

Squanto (Wampanoag Indian emissary); Patuxet (Plymouth Bay, Mass.) (c. 1590–1622)

Stack, Robert (Robert Modini) (actor); Los Angeles, 1/13/19

Stafford, Jo (singer); Coalinga, Calif., 11/12/18

Stahl, Lesley (broadcast journalist); Lynn, Mass., 12/16/41

Stalin, Joseph Vissarionovich (Iosif V. Dzhugashvili) (Soviet leader); nr. Tbilisi, Tbilisi, Georgia (1879–1953)

Stallone, Sylvester (actor, writer, director); New York City, 7/6/46

Stamp, Terence (actor); London, 1938

Stander, Lionel (actor); New York City (1908–1994)

Stanislavski (Konstantin Sergeevich Alekseev) (stage producer); Moscow (1863–1938)

Stanley, Sir Henry Morton (John Rowlands) (explorer); Denbigh, Wales (1841–1904)

Stanley, Kim (Patricia Reid) (actress); Tularosa, N.M., 2/11/25

Stans, Maurice H. (ex-Secretary of Commerce); Shakope, Minn. (1908–1998)

Stanton, Elizabeth Cady (woman suffragist); Johnstown, N.Y. (1815–1902)

Stanton, Frank (broadcasting executive); Muskegon, Mich., 3/20/08

Stanwyck, Barbara (Ruby Stevens) (actress); Brooklyn, N.Y. (1907–1990)

Stapleton, Jean (Jeanne Murray) (actress); New York City, 1/19/23

Stapleton, Maureen (actress); Troy, N.Y., 6/21/25

Starker, János (cellist); Budapest, 7/5/26

Starr, Kay (Starks) (singer); Dougherty, Okla., 7/21/22

Starr, Kenneth (independent counsel for Whitewater investigation); Vernon, Tex., 7/21/46

Starr, Ringo (Richard Starkey) (singer, songwriter); Liverpool, England, 7/7/40

Stassen, Harold E. (ex-government official); West St. Paul, Minn., 4/13/07

Staudinger, Hermann (chemist, Nobel laureate); Worms, Germany (1881–1965)

Steber, Eleanor (soprano); Wheeling, W. Va. (1916–1990)

Steegmuller, Francis (biographer); New Haven, Conn. (1906–1994)

Steel, Danielle (Danielle Fernande Schuelein-Steel) (novelist); New York City, 8/14/47

Steele, Tommy (singer); London, 12/17/36

Stefani, Gwen (singer); Orange County, Calif., 10/3/69

Stegner, Wallace (Earle) (novelist, critic); Lake Mills, Iowa (1909–1993)

Steichen, Edward Jean (photographer, artist); Luxembourg (1879–1973)

Steiger, Rod (Rodney) (actor); Westhampton, N.Y., 4/14/25

Stein, Gertrude (author); Allegheny, Pa. (1874–1946)

Steinbeck, John Ernst (novelist); Salinas, Calif. **(1902–1968)**
Steinberg, David (comedian); Winnipeg, Man., Canada, 8/19/42
Steinberg, William (conductor); Cologne, Germany **(1899–1978)**
Steinem, Gloria (feminist, publisher); Toledo, Ohio, 3/25/34
Steinmetz, Charles (electrical engineer); Breslau, Poland **(1865– 1923)**
Steenburgen, Mary (actress); Newport, Ark., 2/8/53
Stendhal (Marie Henri Beyle) (novelist); Grenoble, France **(1783– 1842)**
Stern, Howard (radio personality); New York City, 1/2/54
Stern, Isaac (concert violinist); Kreminlecz, Russia, 7/21/20
Sterne, Laurence (novelist); Clonmel, Ireland **(1713–1768)**
Stevens, Cat (Steven Georgiou) (singer, songwriter); London, 7/21/47
Stevens, Connie (Concetta Ingolia) (singer); Brooklyn, N.Y., 8/8/38
Stevens, George (film director); Oakland, Calif. **(1905–1975)**
Stevens, Risë (mezzo-soprano); New York City, 6/11/13
Stevens, Wallace (poet); Reading, Pa. **(1879–1955)**
Stevenson, Adlai Ewing (statesman); Los Angeles **(1900–1965)**
Stevenson, McLean (actor); Bloomington, Ill. **(1929–1996)**
Stevenson, Parker (actor); Philadelphia, 6/4/52
Stevenson, Robert Louis Balfour (novelist, poet); Edinburgh, Scotland **(1850–1894)**
Stewart, James (actor); Indiana, Pa. **(1908–1997)**
Stewart, Jon (Jonathan Stewart Leibowitz) (comedian, actor); Trenton, New Jersey, 11/28/62
Stewart, Martha (entrepreneurial home stylist); Nutley, N.J., 8/3/41
Stewart, Patrick (actor); Mirfield, England, 7/13/40
Stewart, Rod (Roderick David) (singer); London, 1/10/45
Stieglitz, Alfred (photographer); Hoboken, N.J. **(1864–1946)**
Stiers, David Ogden (actor); Peoria, Ill., 10/31/42
Stiller, Ben (actor, director, comic); New York City, 11/30/65
Stiller, Jerry (actor); Brooklyn, N.Y., 6/8/29
Stills, Stephen (singer, songwriter); Dallas, 1/3/45
Stine, R.L. (Robert Lawrence Stine) (writer); Columbus, Ohio, 10/8/43
Sting (Gordon Matthew Sumner) (singer, composer); Wallsend, England, 10/2/51
Stipe, Michael (singer); Decatur, Ga., 1/4/60
Stockwell, Dean (actor); North Hollywood, Calif., 3/5/36
Stoker, Bram (novelist); Dublin **(1847–1912)**
Stokes, Carl (TV newscaster); Cleveland, 6/21/27
Stokowski, Leopold (conductor); London **(1882–1977)**
Stoltz, Eric (actor); Whittier, California, 9/30/61
Stone, Edward Durell (architect); Fayetteville, Ark. **(1902–1978)**
Stone, I(sidor) F(einstein) (journalist); Philadelphia **(1907–1989)**
Stone, Irving (Irving Tennenbaum) (novelist); San Francisco **(1903– 1989)**
Stone, Lucy (woman suffragist); nr. West Brookfield, Mass. **(1818– 1893)**
Stone, Oliver (director, writer, producer); New York City, 9/15/46
Stone, Robert (novelist); Brooklyn, N.Y., 8/21/37
Stone, Sharon (actress); Meadville, Pa., 3/10/58
Stone, Sly (Sylvester Stone) (rock musician) 1944
Stooges, The Three (comedy team) **Moe Howard** (Moses Horwitz); Brooklyn, N.Y. **(1897–1975;) Shemp Howard** (Samuel Horwitz); Brooklyn, N.Y. **(1900–1955;) Larry Fine** (Laurence Feinburg); Philadelphia **(1911–1974;) Curly Howard** (Jerome Horwitz); Brooklyn, N.Y. **(1906 –1952)**
Stoppard, Tom (Thomas Straussler) (playwright); Zlin, Slovakia, 7/3/37
Stout, Rex (mystery writer); Noblesville, Ind. **(1886–1975)**
Stowe, Harriet Elizabeth Beecher (novelist); Litchfield, Conn. **(1811–1896)**
Stowe, Madeleine (actress); Eagle Rock, Calif., 8/18/58
Strachey, (Giles) Lytton (biographer); London **(1880–1932)**
Stradivari, Antonio (violinmaker); Cremona, Italy **(1644–1737)**
Straight, Beatrice (actress); Old Westbury, N.Y., 8/2/18
Strasberg, Lee (stage director); Budanov, Austria **(1901–1982)**
Strasberg, Susan (actress); New York City, 5/22/38
Stratas, Teresa (soprano); Toronto, 5/26/38
Straus, Oskar (composer); Vienna **(1870–1954)**
Strauss, Johann (composer); Vienna **(1825–1899)**
Strauss, Lewis L. (naval officer, scientist); Charleston, W. Va. **(1896–1974)**
Strauss, Peter (actor); New York City, 2/20/47
Strauss, Richard (composer); Munich, Germany **(1864–1949)**
Stravinsky, Igor (composer); Orlenbaum, Russia **(1882–1971)**
Streep, Meryl (Mary Louise) (actress); Summit, N.J., 6/22/49
Streisand, Barbra (singer, actress, director, producer, writer); Brooklyn, N.Y., 4/24/42
Strindberg, (Johan) August (dramatist); Stockholm **(1849–1912)**
Stritch, Elaine (actress); Detroit, 2/2/25

Struthers, Sally Ann (actress); Portland, Ore., 7/28/48
Stuart, Gilbert Charles (painter); Rhode Island **(1755–1828)**
Stuart, Gloria (film actress); Santa Monica, Calif., 7/4/10
Stuart, James Ewell Brown (known as Jeb) (Confederate army officer); Patrick County, Va. **(1833–1864)**
Sturges, Preston (Edmond P. Biden) (director, screenwriter, playwright); Chicago **(1898–1959)**
Stuyvesant, Peter (Governor of New Amsterdam); West Friesland, Netherlands **(1592–1672)**
Styne, Jule (Julius Kerwin Stein) (songwriter); London **(1905–1994)**
Styron, William (William Clark Styron, Jr.) (novelist); Newport News, Va., 6/11/25
Suharto (President of Indonesia); Sedaju-Godean, Java, 2/20/21
Sukarno (Indonesian leader); Surabaja, Java **(1901–1970)**
Sullavan, Margaret Brooke (actress); Norfolk, Va. **(1911–1960)**
Sullivan, Sir Arthur Seymour (composer); London **(1842–1900)**
Sullivan, Barry (Patrick Barry) (actor); New York City **(1912–1994)**
Sullivan, Ed (columnist, TV personality); New York City **(1901– 1974)**
Sullivan, Frank (Francis John) (humorist); Saratoga Springs, N.Y. **(1892–1976)**
Sullivan, Louis Henry (architect); Boston **(1856–1924)**
Sulzberger, Arthur Ochs (newspaper publisher); New York City, 2/5/26
Sumac, Yma (singer); Ichocan, Peru, 9/10/27
Summer, Donna (La Donna Andrea Gaines) (singer); Boston, 12/31/48
Sun Ra (Herman "Sunny" Blount) (jazz composer); Birmingham, Ala. **(1914?–1993)**
Sun Tzu (writer, military strategist); China **(fl. c. 500–320 B.C.E.)**
Sun Yat-sen (statesman); nr. Macao **(1866–1925)**
Susann, Jacqueline (novelist); Philadelphia **(1918–1974)**
Susskind, David (TV producer); New York City **(1920–1987)**
Sutherland, Donald (actor); St. John, N.B., Canada, 7/17/34
Sutherland, Joan (soprano); Sydney, Australia, 11/7/26
Sutherland, Kiefer (actor); London, 12/18/66
Suzuki, Pat (actress); Cressey, Calif., 1931
Swados, Elizabeth (composer, playwright); Buffalo, N.Y., 2/5/51
Swanson, Gloria (Gloria May Josephine Svensson) (actress); Chicago **(1899–1983)**
Swarthout, Gladys (soprano); Deepwater, Mo. **(1904–1969)**
Swayze, John Cameron (news commentator); Wichita, Kans. **(1906–1995)**
Swayze, Patrick (actor, dancer); Houston, 8/18/54
Swenenborg, Emanuel (scientist, philosopher, mystic); Stockholm **(1688–1772)**
Swift, Jonathan (satirist); Dublin **(1667–1745)**
Swinburne, Algernon Charles (poet); London **(1837–1909)**
Swit, Loretta (actress); Passaic, N.J., 11/4/37
Swope, Herbert Bayard (journalist); St. Louis **(1882–1958)**
Sydow, Max von (Carl Adolf von Sydow) (actor); Lund, Sweden, 4/10/29
Symons, Arthur (poet, critic); Milford Haven, Wales **(1865–1945)**
Synge, John Millington (dramatist); nr. Dublin **(1871–1909)**
Szilard, Leo (physicist); Budapest **(1898–1964)**

T

Taft, Robert Alphonso (legislator); Cincinnati **(1889–1953)**
Taft, William Howard (27th U.S. president); Cincinnati **(1857–1930)**
Tagore, Sir Rabindranath (poet); Calcutta **(1861–1941)**
Tallchief, Maria (ballet dancer); Fairfax, Okla., 1/24/25
Talleyrand-Pèrigord, Charles Maurice de (statesman); Paris **(1754–1838)**
Talmadge, Norma (actress); Niagara Falls, N.Y. **(1897–1957)**
Talvela, Martti (basso); Hiitola, Finalnd **(1935–1989)**
Tamerlane (Timur) (Mongol conqueror); nr. Samarkand, Turkestan **(c. 1336–1405)**
Tamiroff, Akim (actor); Baku, Azerbaijan **(1899–1972)**
Tan, Amy (novelist); Oakland, Calif., 2/19/52
Tanaka, Tomoyuki (film producer); Osaka, Japan **(1910–1997)**
Tandy, Jessica (actress); London **(1909–1994)**
Tarbell, Ida Minerva (author, muckraker); Erie Co., Pa. **(1857–1944)**
Tarkington, (Newton) Booth (novelist); Indianapolis **(1869–1946)**
Tartikoff, Brandon (television executive); Freeport, N.Y. **(1949– 1997)**
Tate, Allen (John Orley) (poet, critic); Winchester, Ky. **(1899–1979)**
Tate, Sharon (actress); Dallas **(1943–1969)**
Tati, Jacques (Jacques Tatischeff) (actor); Pecq, France **(1908– 1982)**
Taylor, Deems (composer); New York City **(1885–1966)**
Taylor, Elizabeth (actress); London, 2/27/32
Taylor, Harold (educator); Toronto, 9/28/14

Taylor, James (singer, songwriter); Boston, 3/12/48
Taylor, Laurette (Laurette Cooney) (actress); New York City (1884–1946)
Taylor, Lili (actress); Glenco, Ill., 2/20/67
Taylor, Gen. Maxwell D. (former Army Chief of Staff); Keytesville, Mo. (1901–1987)
Taylor, Niki (model); Pembroke Pines, Florida, 3/5/75
Taylor, Paul (choreographer); Wilkinsburg, Pa., 7/29/30
Taylor, Rod (actor); Sydney, Australia, 1/11/30
Taylor, Zachary (12th U.S. president); Montebello, Orange County, Va. (1784–1850)
Tchaikovsky, Peter (Pëtr) Ilich (composer); Votkinsk, Russia (1840–1893)
Teasdale, Sara (poet); St. Louis (1884–1933)
Tebaldi, Renata (lyric soprano); Pesaro, Italy, 1/2/22
Tecumseh (Shawnee Indian chief); nr. Springfield, Ohio (1768–1813)
Te Kanawa, Kiri (soprano); Gisborne, New Zealand, 3/6/44
Telemann, Georg Philipp (composer); Magdeburg, Germany (1681–1767)
Teller, Edward (atomic physicist); Budapest, 1/15/08
Templeton, Alec Andrew (pianist, composer); Cardiff, Wales (1910–1963)
Tennille, Toni (singer); Montgomery, Ala., 5/8/43
Tennyson, Alfred (1st Baron Tennyson) (poet); Somersby, England (1809–1892)
Tenskwatawa (Shawnee prophet); Old Piqua, Ohio (c. 1770–c. 1835)
Terhune, Albert Payson (novelist, journalist); Newark, N.J. (1872–1942)
Terkel, Studs (writer, interviewer); New York City, 5/16/12
Terry, Ellen Alicia (actress); Coventry, England (1848–1928)
Terry-Thomas (Thomas Terry Hoar Stevens) (actor); London (1911–1990)
Tesla, Nikola (electrical engineer, inventor); Smiljan, Croatia (1856–1943)
Thackeray, William Makepeace (novelist); Calcutta (1811–1863)
Thalberg, Irving G. (producer); Brooklyn, N.Y. (1899–1936)
Thant, U (U.N. statesman); Pantanaw, Burma (1909–1974)
Tharp, Twyla (dancer, choreographer); Portland, Ind., 7/1/42
Thatcher, Margaret (former Prime Minister); Grantham, England, 10/13/25
Thebom, Blanche (mezzo-soprano); Monessen, Pa., 9/19/19
Theodorakis, Mikis (composer); Chios, Greece, 7/29/25
Thicke, Alan (actor, composer); Kirland Lake, Ont., Canada, 3/1/47
Thieu, Nguyen Van (ex-President of South Vietnam); Trithuy, Vietnam, 4/5/23
Thomas, Danny (Amos Jacobs) (entertainer, TV producer); Deerfield, Mich. (1912–1991)
Thomas, Dylan Marlais (poet); Carmarthenshire, Wales (1914–1953)
Thomas, JonathanTaylor (actor); Bethlehem, Pa., 9/8/81
Thomas, Kristen Scott (actress); Redruth, Cornwall, England, 1960
Thomas, Lowell (explorer, commentator); Woodington, Ohio (1892–1981)
Thomas, Marlo (actress); Detroit, 11/21/43
Thomas, Michael Tilson (conductor); Hollywood, Calif., 12/21/44
Thomas, Norman Mattoon (Socialist leader); Marion, Ohio (1884–1968)
Thomas, Philip Michael (actor); Columbus, Ohio, 5/26/49
Thomas, Richard (actor); New York City, 6/13/51
Thompson, Dorothy (writer); Lancaster, N.Y. (1894–1961)
Thompson, Emma (actress); London, 4/15/59
Thompson, Hunter (Stockton) (writer); Louisville, Ky., 7/18/39
Thompson, Lea (actress); Rochester, Minn., 5/31/61
Thompson, Sada (actress); Des Moines, Iowa, 9/27/29
Thomson, Virgil (Garnett) (composer); Kansas City, Mo. (1896–1989)
Thoreau, Henry David (naturalist, author); Concord, Mass. (1817–1862)
Thorndike, Dame Sybil (actress); Gainsborough, England (1882–1976)
Thorne-Smith, Courtney (actress); San Francisco, 11/8/67
Thornton, Billy Bob (actor, screenwriter); Hot Springs, Arkansas, 8/4/55
Thurber, James Grover (author, cartoonist); Columbus, Ohio (1894–1961)
Thurman, Robert A. F. (scholar, Indo-Tibetan Buddhist studies); New York City, 8/6/40
Thurman, Uma (actress); Boston, 4/29/70
Thurmond, (James) Strom (U.S. Senator); Edgefield, S.C., 12/5/02
Tibbett, Lawrence (baritone); Bakersfield, Calif. (1896–1960)

Tiberius Caesar Augustus (Roman emperor); Capri (42 B.C.E.–C.E. 37)
Tiegs, Cheryl (model, actress); Minnesota, 9/25/47
Tierney, Gene (actress); Brooklyn, N.Y. (1920–1991)
Tillich, Paul (philosopher, theologian); Starzeddel, Germany (1886–1965)
Tillstrom, Burr (puppeteer); Chicago (1917–1985)
Tilly, Meg (Margaret Tilly) (actress); Texada Island, B.C., Canada, 2/14/60
Tintoretto, Il (Jacopo Robusti) (painter); Venice (1518–1594)
Tiny Tim (Herbert Khaury) (entertainer); New York City (1932–1996)
Tiomkin, Dmitri (composer); St. Petersburg, Russia (1894–1979)
Titian (Tiziano Vecelli) (painter); Pieve di Cadore, Italy (1477–1576)
Tito (Josip Broz or Brozovich) (President of Yugoslavia); Croatia (former Yugoslavia) (1892–1980)
Tocqueville, Alexis de (writer); Verneuil, France (1805–1859)
Todd, Michael (producer); Minneapolis (1907–1958)
Todd, Richard (actor); Dublin, 6/11/19
Todd, Thelma (actress); Lawrence, Mass. (1905–1935)
Tolkien, J(ohn) R(onald) R(euel) (fantasy writer); Bloemfontein, South Africa (1892–1973)
Tolstoy, Count Leo (Lev) Nikolaevich (novelist); Tula Province, Russia (1828–1910)
Tomei, Marisa (actress); Brooklyn, N.Y., 12/4/64
Tomlin, Lily (actress, comedienne); Detroit, 9/1/36
Tone, Franchot (actor); Niagara Falls, N.Y. (1905–1968)
Tormé, Mel (Melvin) (singer); Chicago (1925–1999)
Torn, Rip (Elmore Torn, Jr.) (actor, director); Temple, Tex., 2/6/31
Torquamada, Tomásde (Spanish Inquisitor); Valladolid, Spain (1420–1498)
Toscanini, Arturo (orchestra conductor); Parma, Italy (1867–1957)
Totenberg, Nina (broadcast journalist); New York City, 1/14/44
Toulouse-Lautrec (Henri Marie Raymond de Toulouse-Lautrec Monfa) (painter); Albi, France (1864–1901)
Toynbee, Arnold J. (historian); London (1889–1975)
Tracy, Spencer (actor); Milwaukee (1900–1967)
Traubel, Helen (Wagnerian soprano); St. Louis (1903–1972)
Travanti, Daniel J. (actor); Kenosha, Wis., 3/7/40
Travolta, John (actor); Englewood, N.J., 2/18/54
Treacher, Arthur (actor); Brighton, England (1894–1975)
Tree, Sir Herbert Beerbohm (actor, manager); London (1853–1917)
Trevor, Claire (Wemlinger) (actress); New York City, 3/9/09
Trigère, Pauline (fashion designer); Paris, 11/4/12
Trilling, Diana (writer); New York City (1905–1996)
Trilling, Lionel (author, educator); New York City (1905–1975)
Trollope, Anthony (novelist); London (1815–1882)
Trotsky, Leon (Lev Davidovich Bronstein) (statesman); Elisavetgrad, Russia (1879–1940)
Troyanos, Tatiana (mezzo-soprano); New York City (1938–1993)
Trudeau, Garry (cartoonist); New York City, 1948
Trudeau, Pierre Elliott (former Prime Minister); Montreal, 10/18/19
Truffaut, François (film director); Paris (1932–1984)
Trujillo y Molina, Rafael Leonidas (dictator); San Cristóbal, Dominican Republic (1891–1961)
Truman, Harry S. (33rd U.S. president); near Lamar, Mo. (1884–1972)
Truman, Margaret (author); Independence, Mo., 2/17/24
Trump, Donald (business executive); New York City, 6/14/46
Truth, Sojourner (Isabella) (preacher, abolitionist); Ulster Co., N.Y. (c. 1797–1883)
Tryon, Thomas (actor, novelist); Hartford, Conn. (1926–1991)
Tsiolkovsky, Konstantin E. (father of cosmonautics); Izhevskoye, Russia (1857–1935)
Tsongas, Paul E. (politician); Lowell, Mass. (1941–1997)
Tubman, Harriet (Araminta) (abolitionist); Dorchester Co., Md. (c. 1820–1913)
Tuchman, Barbara (Wertheim) (historian, author); New York City (1912–1989)
Tucker, Forrest (actor); Plainfield, Ind. (1919–1986)
Tucker, Richard (tenor); New York City (1914–1975)
Tucker, Sophie (Sophia Kalish) (singer); Russia (1884–1966)
Tudor, Antony (choreographer); London (1909–1987)
Tune, Tommy (dancer, choreographer); Wichita Falls, Tex., 2/28/39
Turgenev, Ivan Sergeevich (novelist); Orel, Russia (1818–1883)
Turlington, Christy (model); San Francisco, 1/2/69
Turner, Frederick J. (historian); Portage, Wis. (1861–1932)
Turner, Ike (singer); Clarksdale, Miss., 11/5/31
Turner, Janine (actress); Lincoln, Neb., 12/6/62
Turner, Joseph M.W. (painter); London (1775–1851)
Turner, Kathleen (actress); Springfield, Mo., 6/19/54
Turner, Lana (Julia Jean Mildred Frances Turner) (actress); Wallace, Idaho (1920–1995)

Turner, Nat (civil rights leader); Southampton County, Va. (1800–1831)
Turner, Ted (business executive); Cincinnati, 11/19/38
Turner, Tina (Annie Mae Bullock) (singer); Nut Bush, Tenn., 11/26/39
Turpin, Ben (comedian); New Orleans (1874–1940)
Turturro, John (actor); Brooklyn, N.Y., 2/28/57
Twain, Mark (Samuel Langhorne Clemens) (author); Florida, Mo. (1835–1910)
Twain, Shania (Eileen Regina Twain) (country singer); Windsor, Ontario, Canada, 8/28/65
Tweed, William Marcy (politician); New York City (1823–1878)
Twiggy (Leslie Hornby) (model); London, 9/19/49
Twining, Gen. Nathan F. (former Air Force Chief of Staff); Monroe, Wis. (1897–1982)
Twitty, Conway (Harold Lloyd Jenkins) (singer, guitarist); Friars Point, Miss. (1933–1993)
Tyler, John (10th U.S. president); Charles City County, Va. (1790–1862)
Tyler, Liv (actress, model); Portland, Maine, 7/1/77
Tyler, Steven (singer); New York City, 3/26/48
Tyson, Cicely (actress); New York City, 12/19/33

U

Uccello, Paolo (painter); Florence (1397–1475)
Udall, Stewart L. (ex-Secretary of the Interior); St. Johns, Ariz., 1/31/20
Uggams, Leslie (singer, actress); New York City, 5/25/43
Ulanova, Galina (ballet dancer); St. Petersburg, Russia (1910–1998)
Ullman, Tracey (actress, singer); Slough, England, 12/30/59
Ullmann, Liv (actress); Tokyo, 12/16/39
Ulrich, Skeet (actor, model); North Carolina, 1/20/70
Untermeyer, Louis (anthologist, poet); New York City (1885–1977)
Updike, John (novelist); Shillington, Pa., 3/18/32
Urey, Harold C. (chemist, Nobel laureate); Walkerton, Ind. (1893–1981)
Uris, Leon (novelist); Baltimore, 8/3/24
Ustinov, Peter (actor, producer); London, 4/16/21
Utrillo, Maurice (painter); Paris (1883–1955)

V

Vaccaro, Brenda (actress); Brooklyn, N.Y., 11/18/39
Vadim, Roger (Roger Vadim Plemiannikov) (film director); Paris, 1/26/28
Valentine, Karen (actress); Santa Rosa, Calif., 5/25/47
Valentino, Rudolph (Rodolpho d'Antonguolla) (actor); Castellaneta, Italy (1895–1926)
Valentino (Valentino Garavani) (fashion designer); nr. Milan, Italy, 5/11/32
Valéry, Paul (Ambroise Toussaint Jules) (poet, critic); Sète, France (1871–1945)
Vallee, Rudy (Hubert Prior Rudy Vallée) (band leader, singer); Island Pond, Vt. (1901–1986)
Valli, Frankie (Frank Castellaccio) (singer); Newark, N.J., 5/3/37
Van Allen, James Alfred (space physicist); Mt. Pleasant, Iowa, 9/7/14
Van Buren, Abigail (Pauline Esther Friedman) (columnist); Sioux City, Iowa, 7/4/18
Van Buren, Martin (8th U.S. president); Kinderhook, N.Y. (1782–1862)
Vance, Vivian (Vivian Jones) (actress); Cherryvale, Kans. (1912–1979)
Van Der Beek, James (actor); Cheshire, Conn., 3/8/77
Vanderbilt, Alfred G. (sportsman); London, 9/22/12
Vanderbilt, Cornelius (financier); Port Richmond, N.Y. (1794–1877)
Vanderbilt, Gloria (fashion designer); New York City, 2/20/24
Van Doren, Carl (writer, educator); Hope, Ill. (1885–1950)
Van Doren, Mamie (actress); Rowena, S.D., 2/6/33
Vandross, Luther (R&B singer); New York City, 4/20/51
Van Dyke, Dick (actor); West Plains, Mo., 12/13/25
Vandyke (or Van Dyck), Sir Anthony (painter); Antwerp, Belgium (1599–1641)
Van Eyck, Jan (painter); Maeseyck, Belgium (c. 1390–1441)
Van Fleet, Jo (actress); Oakland, Calif. (1915–1996)
van Gogh, Vincent (painter); Groot Zundert, Brabant, Belgium (1853–1890)
van Hamel, Martine (ballet dancer); Brussels, 11/16/45
Van Heusen, Jimmy (Edward Chester Babcock) (songwriter); Syracuse, N.Y. (1913–1990)
Van Patten, Dick (actor); Richmond Hill, N.Y., 12/9/28

Van Peebles, Melvin (playwright); Chicago, 9/21/32
Vasari, Giorgio (art historian); Arezzo, Italy (1511–1574)
Vaughan, Sarah (singer); Newark, N.J. (1924–1990)
Vaughan Williams, Ralph (composer); Down Ampney, England (1872–1958)
Vaughn, Robert (actor); New York City, 11/22/32
Vaughn, Vince (actor); Minneapolis, 3/28/70
Veblen, Thorstein (economist, social critic); Cato Township, Wis. (1857–1929)
Veidt, Conrad (actor); Potsdam, Germany (1893–1943)
Velázquez, Diego Rodriguez de Silva y (painter); Seville, Spain (1599–1660)
Venturi, Robert (Charles) (architect); Philadelphia, 6/25/25
Verdi, Giuseppe (composer); Roncole, Italy (1813–1901)
Verdon, Gwen (actress); Culver City, Calif., 1/13/25
Vereen, Ben (actor, singer); Miami, Fla., 10/10/46
Verlaine, Paul (poet); Metz, France (1844–1896)
Vermeer, Jan (or Jan van der Meer van Delft) (painter); Delft, Netherlands (1632–1675)
Verne, Jules (author); Nantes, France (1828–1905)
Veronese, Paolo (Paolo Cagliari) (painter); Verona (1528–1588)
Verrazano, Giovanni da (navigator); Florence, Italy (c. 1485–1528)
Verrett, Shirley (mezzo-soprano); New Orleans, 5/31/33
Versace, Gianni (fashion designer); Reggio, Italy (1946–1997)
Vesalius, Andreas (anatomist); Brussels (1515–1564)
Vespucci, Amerigo (navigator); Florence, Italy (1454–1512)
Vickers, Jon (tenor); Prince Albert, Sask., Canada, 10/29/26
Vico, Giovanni Battista (philosopher); Naples, Italy (1668–1744)
Victoria (Queen of England); London (1819–1901)
Vidal, Gore (novelist); West Point, N.Y., 10/3/25
Vidor, King (film director, producer); Galveston, Tex. (1895–1982)
Vigoda, Abe (actor); New York City, 2/24/21
Villa, Pancho (Doroteo Arango) (revolutionary); Hacienda de Rio Grande, San Juan del Rio, Mexico (1877–1923)
Villella, Edward (ballet dancer); Bayside, Queens, N.Y., 10/1/36
Villon, François (François de Montcorbier) (poet); Paris (1431–1463)
Vinton, Bobby (singer); Canonsburg, Pa., 4/16/35
Virgil (or Vergil) (Publius Vergilius Maro) (poet); nr. Mantua, Italy (70–19 B.C.E.)
Vishnevskaya, Galina (soprano); St. Petersburg, Russia, 10/25/26
Vivaldi, Antonio (composer); Venice (1678–1741)
Vlaminck, Maurice de (painter); Paris (1876–1958)
Voight, Jon (actor); Yonkers, N.Y., 12/29/38
Volta, Alessandro (scientist); Como, Italy (1745–1827)
Voltaire (François Marie Arouet) (author); Paris (1694–1778)
von Aroldingen, Karin (Karin Awny Hannelore Reinbold von Aroedingen and Eltzinger) (ballet dancer); Greiz, Germany, 7/9/41
von Braun, Wernher (rocket scientist); Wirsitz, Germany (1912–1977)
von Furstenberg, Betsy (Elizabeth Caroline Maria Agatha Felicitas Therese von Furstenberg-Hedringen) (actress); Nelheim-Hagen, Germany, 8/16/35
von Fürstenberg, Diane (Diane Simone Michelle Halfin) (fashion designer); Brussels, 12/31/46
von Hindenburg, Paul (statesman); Posen, Poland (1847–1934)
von Karajan, Herbert (conductor); Salzburg, Austria (1908–1989)
Vonnegut, Kurt, Jr. (novelist); Indianapolis, 11/11/22
Von Stade, Frederica (mezzo-soprano); Somerville, N.J., 6/1/45
Von Stroheim, Erich Oswald Hans Carl Maria von Nordenwall (actor, director); Vienna (1885–1957)
Von Zell, Harry (announcer); Indianapolis (1906–1981)
Vreeland, Diana (Diana Da Iziel) (fashion journalist, museum consultant); Paris (1903?–1989)

W

Wagner, Lindsay (actress); Los Angeles, 6/22/49
Wagner, Robert (actor); Detroit, 2/10/30
Wagner, Robert F. (ex-Mayor of New York City); New York City (1910–1991)
Wagner, Wilhelm Richard (composer); Leipzig, Germany (1813–1883)
Wahlberg, Mark (actor, model, musician); Dorchester, Mass., 6/5/71
Waits, Tom (blues singer); Pomona, Calif., 12/7/49
Waldheim, Kurt (ex-U.N. Secretary-General); St. Andrae-Wörden, Austria, 12/21/18
Walesa, Lech (Polish labor leader and ex-president); Popowo, Poland, 9/29/43
Walken, Christopher (actor); Queens, N.Y., 3/31/43
Walker, Alice (novelist, poet); Eatonon, Ga., 2/9/44
Walker, Nancy (Ann Myrtle Swoyer) (actress, comedienne); Philadelphia (1922–1992)

Walker, Robert (actor); Salt Lake City (1918–1951)
Walker, T-Bone (blues singer); Linden, Tex. (1910–1975)
Wallace, DeWitt (publisher); St. Paul, Minn. (1889–1981)
Wallace, George C. (ex-governor); Clio, Ala. (1919–1998)
Wallace, Irving (novelist); Chicago (1916–1990)
Wallace, Mike (Myron Wallace) (TV interviewer, commentator); Brookline, Mass., 5/9/18
Wallach, Eli (actor); Brooklyn, N.Y., 12/7/15
Wallenberg, Raoul (diplomat, humanitarian); Stockholm (1912–1947)
Wallenstein, Alfred (conductor); Chicago (1898–1983)
Waller, Thomas "Fats" (pianist); New York City (1904–1943)
Wallis, Hal (film producer); Chicago (1899–1986)
Walpole, Horace (statesman, novelist); London (1717–1797)
Walsh, J. T. (actor); San Francisco, Calif. (1944–1998)
Waltari, Mika (novelist); Helsinki (1903–1979)
Walter, Bruno (Bruno Walter Schlesinger) (orchestra conductor); Berlin (1876–1962)
Walters, Barbara (TV commentator); Boston, 9/25/31
Walton, Izaak (author); Stafford, England (1593–1683)
Wambaugh, Joseph (author, screenwriter); East Pittsburgh, 1/22/37
Wanamaker, John (merchant); Philadelphia (1838–1922)
Wanamaker, Sam (actor, director); Chicago (1919–1993)
Ward, Barbara (economist); York, England (1914–1981)
Ward, Rachel (actress); Cornwall Manor, England, 9/12/57
Warhol, Andy (Warhola) (artist); McKeesport, Pa. (1928–1987)
Waring, Fred (band leader); Tyrone, Pa. (1900–1984)
Warner, H. B. (Henry Bryan Warner Lickford) (actor); London (1876–1958)
Warren, Lesley Ann (actress); New York City, 8/16/46
Warren, Robert Penn (novelist); Guthrie, Ky. (1905–1989)
Warrick, Ruth (actress); St. Joseph, Mo., 6/29/15
Warwick, Dionne (singer); East Orange, N.J., 12/12/41
Washington, Booker T(aliaferro) (educator); Franklin County, Va. (1856–1915)
Washington, Denzel (actor); Mt. Vernon, N.Y., 12/28/54
Washington, George (1st U.S. president); Westmoreland County, Va. (1732–1799)
Washington, Harold (ex-mayor of Chicago); Chicago (1922–1987)
Waters, Ethel (actress, singer); Chester, Pa. (1896–1977)
Waters, Muddy (McKinley Morganfield) (singer, guitarist); Rolling Fork, Miss. (1915–1983)
Waterston, Sam (actor); Cambridge, Mass., 11/15/40
Watson, James Dewey (scientist, Nobel laureate); Chicago, 4/6/28
Watson, Thomas John (industrialist); Campbell, N.Y. (1874–1956)
Watt, James (inventor); Greenock, Scotland (1736–1819)
Watteau, Jean-Antoine (painter); Valanciennes, France (1684–1721)
Wattleton, Faye (family planning advocate); St. Louis, 7/8/43
Watts, André (concert pianist); Nuremberg, Germany, 6/20/46
Waugh, Alec (Alexander Raban Waugh) (novelist); London (1898–1981)
Waugh, Evelyn (novelist); London (1903–1966)
Wayans, Damon (actor, comedian, writer, producer); New York City, 9/4/60
Wayans, Keenan Ivory (actor, comedian, writer, director); New York City, 6/8/58
Wayne, Anthony (military officer); Waynesboro (family farm), nr. Paoli, Pa. (1745–1796)
Wayne, David (David McMeekan) (actor); Traverse City, Mich. (1914–1995)
Wayne, John (Marion Michael Morrison) (actor); Winterset, Iowa (1907–1979)
Weaver, Dennis (actor); Joplin, Mo., 6/4/25
Weaver, Fritz (actor); Pittsburgh, 1/19/26
Weaver, Sigourney (actress); New York City, 10/8/49
Webb, Clifton (Webb Parmelee Hollenbeck) (actor); Indianapolis (1893–1966)
Webb, Jack (actor, producer); Santa Monica, Calif. (1920–1982)
Weber, Karl Maria Friedrich Ernst von (composer); nr. Lübeck, Germany (1786–1826)
Webster, Daniel (statesman); Salisbury, N.H. (1782–1852)
Webster, Margaret (producer, director, actress); New York City (1905–1973)
Webster, Noah (lexicographer); West Hartford, Conn. (1758–1843)
Weill, Kurt (composer); Dessau, Germany (1900–1950)
Weir, Peter (director); Sydney, Australia, 8/21/44
Weissmuller, Johnny (Peter John Weissmuller) (actor, swimmer); Freidorf, Romania (1904–1984)
Weizmann, Chaim (statesman); Grodno Province, Russia (1874–1952)
Welch, Raquel (Raquel Tejada) (actress); Chicago, 9/5/40
Weld, Tuesday (Susan Ker Weld) (actress); New York City, 8/27/43
Welk, Lawrence (band leader); Strasburg, N.D. (1903–1992)

Welles, Orson (actor, director, producer); Kenosha, Wis. (1915–1985)
Wellington, Duke of (Arthur Wellesley) (statesman); Ireland (1769–1852)
Wells, H(erbert) G(eorge) (author); Bromley, England (1866–1946)
Wells, Ida Bell (Barnett) (journalist); Holly Springs, Miss. (1862–1931)
Welty, Eudora (novelist); Jackson, Miss., 4/13/09
Wenner, Jann (publisher); New York City, 1/7/46
Werfel, Franz (novelist); Prague (1890–1945)
Werner, Oskar (Josef Schliessmayer) (actor, director); Vienna (1922–1984)
Wertheimer, Linda (radio journalist); Carlsbad, N.M., 3/19/43
Wertmueller, Lina (Arcanguela Felice Assunta W. von Elgg) (director); Rome, 8/14/28
Wesley, John (religious leader); Epworth Rectory, Lincolnshire, England (1703–1791)
West, Benjamin (painter); Springfield, Pa. (1738–1820)
West, Dame Rebecca (Cicily Fairfield) (novelist); County Kerry, Ireland (1892–1983)
West, Jessamyn (novelist); nr. North Vernon, Ind. (1902–1984)
West, Mae (actress); Brooklyn, N.Y. (1893–1980)
West, Nathanael (Nathan Weinstein) (novelist); New York City (1902–1940)
Westheimer, Dr. Ruth (Karola Ruth Siegel) (human sexuality expert); Frankfurt, Germany, 1928
Westinghouse, George (inventor); Central Bridge, N.Y. (1846–1914)
Westmoreland, William Childs (ex-Army Chief of Staff); Saxon, S.C., 3/26/14
Weyden, Roger van der (painter); Tournai, Belgium (c. 1400–1464)
Wharton, Edith Newbold (née Jones) (novelist); New York City (1862–1937)
Wheatley, Phillis (poet); Senegal (c. 1753–1784)
Wheeler, Bert (Albert Jerome Wheeler) (comedian); Paterson, N.J. (1895–1968)
Whistler, James Abbott McNeill (painter, etcher); Lowell, Mass. (1834–1903)
Whitaker, Forest (actor); Longview, Tex., 7/15/61
White, Betty (actress); Oak Park, Ill., 1/17/22
White, Edmund (writer); Cincinnati, Ohio, 1/13/40
White, E(lwyn) B(rooks) (author); Mt. Vernon, N.Y. (1899–1985)
White, Pearl (actress); Green Ridge, Mo. (1889–1938)
White, Stanford (architect); New York City (1853–1906)
White, Theodore H. (historian); Boston (1915–1986)
White, Vanna (TV personality); Conway, S.C., 2/18/57
White, William Allen (journalist); Emporia, Kans. (1868–1944)
Whitehead, Alfred North (mathematician, philosopher); Isle of Thanet, England (1861–1947)
Whiteman, Paul (band leader); Denver (1891–1967)
Whiting, Margaret (singer, actress); Detroit, 7/22/24
Whitman, Walt (Walter) (poet); West Hills, N.Y. (1819–1892)
Whitmore, James (actor); White Plains, N.Y., 10/1/21
Whitney, Cornelius Vanderbilt (sportsman); New York City (1899–1992)
Whitney, Eli (inventor); Westboro, Mass. (1765–1825)
Whitney, John Hay (publisher); Ellsworth, Maine (1904–1982)
Whittier, John Greenleaf (poet); Haverhill, Mass. (1807–1892)
Wideman, John Edgar (writer); Washington, D.C., 6/14/41
Widmark, Richard (actor); Sunrise, Minn., 12/26/14
Wiesel, Elie (Eliezer) (author); Signet, Romania, 9/30/28
Wiesenthal, Simon (Nazi hunter); Buchach, Ukraine, 12/31/08
Wilde, Cornel (film actor, producer); New York City (1915–1989)
Wilde, Oscar Fingal O'Flahertie Wills (author); Dublin (1854–1900)
Wilder, Billy (Samuel Wilder) (film producer, director); Vienna, 6/22/06
Wilder, Gene (Jerome Silberman) (actor, writer, director, producer); Milwaukee, 6/11/35
Wilder, Thornton (author); Madison, Wis. (1897–1975)
Wilding, Michael (actor); Westcliff, England (1912–1979)
Wilkins, Roy (civil rights leader); St. Louis (1901–1981)
William, Prince (heir to British throne); London, 6/21/82
Williams, Andy (singer); Wall Lake, Iowa, 12/3/30
Williams, Anson (actor, director); Los Angeles, 9/25/49
Williams, Billy Dee (actor); New York City, 4/6/37
Williams, Cindy (actress); Van Nuys, Calif., 8/22/47
Williams, Edward Bennett (lawyer); Hartford, Conn. (1920–1988)
Williams, Emlyn (actor, playwright); Mostyn, Wales (1905–1987)
Williams, Esther (actress, swimmer); Los Angeles, 8/8/23
Williams, Gluyas (cartoonist); San Francisco (1888–1982)
Williams, Hank, Sr. (Hiram King Williams) (singer); Georgiana, Ala. (1923–1953)
Williams, Joe (singer); Cordele, Ga. (1918–1999)
Williams, John T. (composer, conductor); Queens, N.Y., 2/8/32

Nobel Prizes

(For years not listed, no award was made. *See* p. 48 for 1999 winners.)

PEACE

1901	Henri Dunant (Switzerland); Frederick Passy (France)
1902	Elie Ducommun and Albert Gobat (Switzerland)
1903	Sir William R. Cremer (U.K.)
1904	Institut de Droit International (Belgium)
1905	Bertha von Suttner (Austria)
1906	Theodore Roosevelt (U.S.)
1907	Ernesto T. Moneta (Italy) and Louis Renault (France)
1908	Klas P. Arnoldson (Sweden) and Frederik Bajer (Denmark)
1909	Auguste M. F. Beernaert (Belgium) and Baron Paul H. B. B. d'Estournelles de Constant de Rebecque (France)
1910	Bureau International Permanent de la Paix (Switzerland)
1911	Tobias M. C. Asser (Holland) and Alfred H. Fried (Austria)
1912	Elihu Root (U.S.)
1913	Henri La Fontaine (Belgium)
1917	International Red Cross
1919	Woodrow Wilson (U.S.)
1920	Léon Bourgeois (France)
1921	Karl H. Branting (Sweden) and Christian L. Lange (Norway)
1922	Fridtjof Nansen (Norway)
1925	Sir Austen Chamberlain (U.K.) and Charles G. Dawes (U.S.)
1926	Aristide Briand (France) and Gustav Stresemann (Germany)
1927	Ferdinand Buisson (France) and Ludwig Quidde (Germany)
1929	Frank B. Kellogg (U.S.)
1930	Lars O. J. Söderblom (Sweden)
1931	Jane Addams and Nicholas M. Butler (U.S.)
1933	Sir Norman Angell (U.K.)
1934	Arthur Henderson (U.K.)
1935	Karl von Ossietzky (Germany)
1936	Carlos de S. Lamas (Argentina)
1937	Lord Cecil of Chelwood (U.K.)
1938	Office International Nansen pour les Réfugiés (Switzerland)
1944	International Red Cross
1945	Cordell Hull (U.S.)
1946	Emily G. Balch and John R. Mott (U.S.)
1947	American Friends Service Committee (U.S.) and British Society of Friends' Service Council (U.K.)
1949	Lord John Boyd Orr (Scotland)
1950	Ralph J. Bunche (U.S.)
1951	Léon Jouhaux (France)
1952	Albert Schweitzer (French Equatorial Africa)
1953	George C. Marshall (U.S.)
1954	Office of U.N. High Commissioner for Refugees
1957	Lester B. Pearson (Canada)
1958	Rev. Dominique Georges Henri Pire (Belgium)
1959	Philip John Noel-Baker (U.K.)

1960	Albert John Luthuli (South Africa)
1961	Dag Hammarskjöld (Sweden)
1962	Linus Pauling (U.S.)
1963	Intl. Comm. of Red Cross; League of Red Cross Societies (both Geneva)
1964	Rev. Dr. Martin Luther King, Jr. (U.S.)
1965	UNICEF (United Nations Children's Fund)
1968	René Cassin (France)
1969	International Labour Organization
1970	Norman E. Borlaug (U.S.)
1971	Willy Brandt (West Germany)
1973	Henry A. Kissinger (U.S.); Le Duc Tho (North Vietnam)[1]
1974	Eisaku Sato (Japan); Sean MacBride (Ireland)
1975	Andrei D. Sakharov (U.S.S.R.)
1976	Mairead Corrigan and Betty Williams (both Northern Ireland)
1977	Amnesty International
1978	Menachem Begin (Israel) and Anwar el-Sadat (Egypt)
1979	Mother Teresa of Calcutta (India)
1980	Adolfo Pérez Esquivel (Argentina)
1981	Office of the United Nations High Commissioner for Refugees
1982	Alva Myrdal (Sweden) and Alfonso García Robles (Mexico)
1983	Lech Walesa (Poland)
1984	Bishop Desmond Tutu (South Africa)
1985	International Physicians for the Prevention of Nuclear War
1986	Elie Wiesel (U.S.)
1987	Oscar Arias Sánchez (Costa Rica)
1988	U.N. Peacekeeping Forces
1989	Dalai Lama (Tibet)
1990	Mikhail S. Gorbachev (U.S.S.R.)
1991	Daw Aung San Suu Kyi (Burma)
1992	Rigoberta Menchú (Guatemala)
1993	F. W. de Klerk and Nelson Mandela (both South Africa)
1994	Yasir Arafat (Palestine), Shimon Peres, and Yitzhak Rabin (both Israel)
1995	Joseph Rotblat and Pugwash Conference on Science and World Affairs (U.K.)
1996	Carlos Filipe Ximenes Belo and José Ramos-Horta (East Timor)
1997	International Campaign to Ban Landmines and Jody Williams (U.S.)
1998	John Hume and David Trimble (Northern Ireland)

1. Le Duc Tho refused prize, charging that peace had not yet really been established in South Vietnam.

LITERATURE

1901	René F. A. Sully Prudhomme (France)
1902	Theodor Mommsen (Germany)
1903	Björnstjerne Björnson (Norway)
1904	Frédéric Mistral (France) and José Echegaray (Spain)
1905	Henryk Sienkiewicz (Poland)
1906	Giosuè Carducci (Italy)

1907 Rudyard Kipling (U.K.)
1908 Rudolf Eucken (Germany)
1909 Selma Lagerlöf (Sweden)
1910 Paul von Heyse (Germany)
1911 Maurice Maeterlinck (Belgium)
1912 Gerhart Hauptmann (Germany)
1913 Rabindranath Tagore (India)
1915 Romain Rolland (France)
1916 Verner von Heidenstam (Sweden)
1917 Karl Gjellerup (Denmark) and Henrik
     Pontoppidan (Denmark)
1919 Carl Spitteler (Switzerland)
1920 Knut Hamsun (Norway)
1921 Anatole France (France)
1922 Jacinto Benavente (Spain)
1923 William B. Yeats (Ireland)
1924 Wladyslaw Reymont (Poland)
1925 George Bernard Shaw (Ireland)
1926 Grazia Deledda (Italy)
1927 Henri Bergson (France)
1928 Sigrid Undset (Norway)
1929 Thomas Mann (Germany)
1930 Sinclair Lewis (U.S.)
1931 Erik A. Karlfeldt (Sweden)
1932 John Galsworthy (U.K.)
1933 Ivan G. Bunin (Russia)
1934 Luigi Pirandello (Italy)
1936 Eugene O'Neill (U.S.)
1937 Roger Martin du Gard (France)
1938 Pearl S. Buck (U.S.)
1939 Frans Eemil Sillanpää (Finland)
1944 Johannes V. Jensen (Denmark)
1945 Gabriela Mistral (Chile)
1946 Hermann Hesse (Switzerland)
1947 André Gide (France)
1948 Thomas Stearns Eliot (U.K.)
1949 William Faulkner (U.S.)
1950 Bertrand Russell (U.K.)
1951 Pär Lagerkvist (Sweden)
1952 François Mauriac (France)
1953 Sir Winston Churchill (U.K.)
1954 Ernest Hemingway (U.S.)
1955 Halldór Kiljan Laxness (Iceland)
1956 Juan Ramón Jiménez (Spain)
1957 Albert Camus (France)
1958 Boris Pasternak (U.S.S.R.) (declined)
1959 Salvatore Quasimodo (Italy)
1960 St. John Perse (Alexis St.-Léger Léger)
     (France)
1961 Ivo Andric (Yugoslavia)
1962 John Steinbeck (U.S.)
1963 Giorgios Seferis (Seferiades) (Greece)
1964 Jean-Paul Sartre (France) (declined)
1965 Mikhail Sholokhov (U.S.S.R.)
1966 Shmuel Yosef Agnon (Israel) and Nelly Sachs
     (Sweden)
1967 Miguel Angel Asturias (Guatemala)
1968 Yasunari Kawabata (Japan)
1969 Samuel Beckett (Ireland)
1970 Aleksandr Solzhenitsyn (U.S.S.R.)
1971 Pablo Neruda (Chile)
1972 Heinrich Böll (Germany)
1973 Patrick White (Australia)
1974 Eyvind Johnson and Harry Martinson (both
     Sweden)
1975 Eugenio Montale (Italy)
1976 Saul Bellow (U.S.)
1977 Vicente Aleixandre (Spain)
1978 Isaac Bashevis Singer (U.S.)
1979 Odysseus Elytis (Greece)

1980 Czeslaw Milosz (U.S.)
1981 Elias Canetti (Bulgaria)
1982 Gabriel García Márquez (Colombia)
1983 William Golding (U.K.)
1984 Jaroslav Seifert (Czechoslovakia)
1985 Claude Simon (France)
1986 Wole Soyinka (Nigeria)
1987 Joseph Brodsky (U.S.)
1988 Naguib Mahfouz (Egypt)
1989 Camilo José Cela (Spain)
1990 Octavio Paz (Mexico)
1991 Nadine Gordimer (South Africa)
1992 Derek Walcott (Trinidad)
1993 Toni Morrison (U.S.)
1994 Kenzaburo Oe (Japan)
1995 Seamus Heaney (Ireland)
1996 Wislawa Szymborska (Poland)
1997 Dario Fo (Italy)
1998 José Saramago (Portugal)

PHYSICS

1901 Wilhelm K. Roentgen (Germany), for
     discovery of Roentgen rays
1902 Hendrik A. Lorentz and Pieter Zeeman
     (Netherlands), for work on influence of
     magnetism upon radiation
1903 A. Henri Becquerel (France), for work on
     spontaneous radioactivity; and Pierre and
     Marie Curie (France), for study of radiation
1904 John Strutt (Lord Rayleigh) (U.K.), for
     discovery of argon in investigating gas
     density
1905 Philipp Lenard (Germany), for work with
     cathode rays
1906 Sir Joseph Thomson (U.K.), for investigations
     on passage of electricity through gases
1907 Albert A. Michelson (U.S.), for spectroscopic
     and metrologic investigations
1908 Gabriel Lippmann (France), for method of
     reproducing colors by photography
1909 Guglielmo Marconi (Italy) and Ferdinand
     Braun (Germany), for development of
     wireless
1910 Johannes D. van der Waals (Netherlands),
     for work with the equation of state for gases
     and liquids
1911 Wilhelm Wien (Germany), for his laws
     governing the radiation of heat
1912 Gustaf Dalén (Sweden), for discovery of
     automatic regulators used in lighting
     lighthouses and light buoys
1913 Heike Kamerlingh-Onnes (Netherlands), for
     work leading to production of liquid helium
1914 Max von Laue (Germany), for discovery of
     diffraction of Roentgen rays passing through
     crystals
1915 Sir William Bragg and William L. Bragg
     (U.K.), for analysis of crystal structure by
     X-rays
1917 Charles G. Barkla (U.K.), for discovery of
     Roentgen radiation of the elements
1918 Max Planck (Germany), discoveries in
     connection with quantum theory
1919 Johannes Stark (Germany), discovery of
     Doppler effect in Canal rays and
     decomposition of spectrum lines by electric
     fields
1920 Charles E. Guillaume (Switzerland), for
     discoveries of anomalies in nickel-steel alloys

1921 Albert Einstein (Germany), for discovery of the law of the photoelectric effect

1922 Niels Bohr (Denmark), for investigation of structure of atoms and radiations emanating from them

1923 Robert A. Millikan (U.S.), for work on elementary charge of electricity and photoelectric phenomena

1924 Karl M. G. Siegbahn (Sweden), for investigations in X-ray spectroscopy

1925 James Franck and Gustav Hertz (Germany), for discovery of laws governing impact of electrons upon atoms

1926 Jean B. Perrin (France), for work on discontinuous structure of matter and discovery of the equilibrium of sedimentation

1927 Arthur H. Compton (U.S.), for discovery of Compton phenomenon; and Charles T. R. Wilson (U.K.), for method of perceiving paths taken by electrically charged particles

1928 In 1929, the 1928 prize was awarded to Sir Owen Richardson (U.K.), for work on the phenomenon of thermionics and discovery of the Richardson Law

1929 Prince Louis Victor de Broglie (France), for discovery of the wave character of electrons

1930 Sir Chandrasekhara Raman (India), for work on diffusion of light and discovery of the Raman effect

1932 In 1933, the prize for 1932 was awarded to Werner Heisenberg (Germany), for creation of the quantum mechanics

1933 Erwin Schrödinger (Austria) and Paul A. M. Dirac (U.K.), for discovery of new fertile forms of the atomic theory

1935 James Chadwick (U.K.), for discovery of the neutron

1936 Victor F. Hess (Austria), for discovery of cosmic radiation; and Carl D. Anderson (U.S.), for discovery of the positron

1937 Clinton J. Davisson (U.S.) and George P. Thomson (U.K.), for discovery of diffraction of electrons by crystals

1938 Enrico Fermi (Italy), for identification of new radioactivity elements and discovery of nuclear reactions effected by slow neutrons

1939 Ernest Orlando Lawrence (U.S.), for development of the cyclotron

1943 Otto Stern (U.S.), for detection of magnetic momentum of protons

1944 Isidor Isaac Rabi (U.S.), for work on magnetic movements of atomic particles

1945 Wolfgang Pauli (Austria), for work on atomic fissions

1946 Percy Williams Bridgman (U.S.), for studies and inventions in high-pressure physics

1947 Sir Edward Appleton (U.K.), for discovery of layer that reflects radio short waves in the ionosphere

1948 Patrick M. S. Blackett (U.K.), for improvement on Wilson chamber and discoveries in cosmic radiation

1949 Hideki Yukawa (Japan), for mathematical prediction, in 1935, of the meson

1950 Cecil Frank Powell (U.K.), for method of photographic study of atom nucleus, and for discoveries about mesons

1951 Sir John Douglas Cockcroft (U.K.) and Ernest T. S. Walton (Ireland), for work in 1932 on transmutation of atomic nuclei

1952 Edward Mills Purcell and Felix Bloch (U.S.), for work in measurement of magnetic fields in atomic nuclei

1953 Fritz Zernike (Netherlands), for development of "phase contrast" microscope

1954 Max Born (U.K.), for work in quantum mechanics; and Walther Bothe (Germany), for work in cosmic radiation

1955 Polykarp Kusch and Willis E. Lamb, Jr. (U.S.), for atomic measurements

1956 William Shockley, Walter H. Brattain, and John Bardeen (all U.S.), for developing electronic transistor

1957 Tsung Dao Lee and Chen Ning Yang (China), for disproving principle of conservation of parity

1958 Pavel A. Cherenkov, Ilya M. Frank, and Igor E. Tamm (all U.S.S.R.), for work resulting in development of cosmic-ray counter

1959 Emilio Segre and Owen Chamberlain (both U.S.), for demonstrating the existence of the anti-proton

1960 Donald A. Glaser (U.S.), for invention of "bubble chamber" to study subatomic particles

1961 Robert Hofstadter (U.S.), for determination of shape and size of atomic nucleus; Rudolf Mössbauer (Germany), for method of producing and measuring recoil-free gamma rays

1962 Lev D. Landau (U.S.S.R.), for his theories about condensed matter

1963 Eugene Paul Wigner, Maria Goeppert Mayer (both U.S.), and J. Hans D. Jensen (Germany), for research on structure of atom and its nucleus

1964 Charles Hard Townes (U.S.), Nikolai G. Basov, and Aleksandr M. Prochorov (both U.S.S.R.), for developing maser and laser principle of producing high-intensity radiation

1965 Richard P. Feynman, Julian S. Schwinger (both U.S.), and Shinichiro Tomonaga (Japan), for research in quantum electrodynamics

1966 Alfred Kastler (France), for work on energy levels inside atom

1967 Hans A. Bethe (U.S.), for work on energy production of stars

1968 Luis Walter Alvarez (U.S.), for study of subatomic particles

1969 Murray Gell-Mann (U.S.), for study of subatomic particles

1970 Hannes Alfvén (Sweden), for theories in plasma physics; and Louis Néel (France), for discoveries in antiferromagnetism and ferromagnetism

1971 Dennis Gabor (U.K.), for invention of holographic method of three-dimensional imagery

1972 John Bardeen, Leon N. Cooper, and John Robert Schrieffer (all U.S.), for theory of superconductivity, where electrical resistance in certain metals vanishes above absolute zero temperature

1973 Ivar Giaever (U.S.), Leo Esaki (Japan), and Brian D. Josephson (U.K.), for theories that have advanced and expanded the field of miniature electronics

1974 Antony Hewish (U.K.), for discovery of pulsars; Martin Ryle (U.K.), for using radiotelescopes to probe outer space with high degree of precision

1975 James Rainwater (U.S.), Ben Mottelson, and Aage N. Bohr (both Denmark), for showing that the atomic nucleus is asymmetrical

1976 Burton Richter and Samuel C. C. Ting (both U.S.), for discovery of subatomic particles known as J and psi

1977 Philip W. Anderson, John H. Van Vleck (both U.S.), and Nevill F. Mott (U.K.), for work underlying computer memories and electronic devices

1978 Arno A. Penzias and Robert W. Wilson (both U.S.), for work in cosmic microwave radiation; Piotr L. Kapitsa (U.S.S.R.), for basic inventions and discoveries in low-temperature physics

1979 Steven Weinberg, Sheldon L. Glashow (both U.S.), and Abdus Salam (Pakistan), for developing theory that electromagnetism and the "weak" force, which causes radioactive decay in some atomic nuclei, are facets of the same phenomenon

1980 James W. Cronin and Val L. Fitch (both U.S.), for work concerning the asymmetry of subatomic particles

1981 Nicolaas Bloembergen, Arthur L. Schawlow (both U.S.), and Kai M. Siegbahn (Sweden), for developing technologies with lasers and other devices to probe the secrets of complex forms of matter

1982 Kenneth G. Wilson (U.S.), for analysis of changes in matter under pressure and temperature

1983 Subrahmanyam Chandrasekhar and William A. Fowler (both U.S.), for complementary research on processes involved in the evolution of stars

1984 Carlo Rubbia (Italy) and Simon van der Meer (Netherlands), for their role in discovering three subatomic particles, a step toward developing a single theory to account for all natural forces

1985 Klaus von Klitzing (Germany), for developing an exact way of measuring electrical conductivity

1986 Ernst Ruska, Gerd Binnig (both Germany), and Heinrich Rohrer (Switzerland), for work on microscopes

1987 K. Alex Müller (Switzerland) and J. Georg Bednorz (Germany), for their discovery of high-temperature superconductors

1988 Leon M. Lederman, Melvin Schwartz, and Jack Steinberger (all U.S.), for research that improved the understanding of elementary particles and forces

1989 Norman F. Ramsey (U.S.), for work leading to development of the atomic clock, and Hans G. Dehmelt (U.S.) and Wolfgang Paul (Germany), for developing methods to isolate atoms and subatomic particles

1990 Richard E. Taylor (Canada), Jerome I. Friedman, and Dr. Henry W. Kendall (both U.S.), for their "breakthrough in our understanding of matter" that confirmed the reality of quarks

1991 Pierre-Gilles de Gennes (France), for his discoveries about the ordering of molecules in substances ranging from "super" glue to an exotic form of liquid helium

1992 George Charpak (France), for his inventions of particle detectors

1993 Joseph H. Taylor and Russell A. Hulse (both U.S.), for their discovery of a binary pulsar

1994 Clifford G. Shull (U.S.) and Bertram N. Brockhouse (Canada), for adapting beams of neutrons as probes to explore the atomic structure of matter

1995 Martin L. Perl and Frederick Reines (both U.S.), for their discoveries of "two of nature's most remarkable subatomic particles"—the tau and the neutrino

1996 David M. Lee, Robert C. Richardson, and Douglas D. Osheroff (all U.S.), for their discovery of superfluity in helium-3

1997 Steven Chu, William D. Phillips (both U.S.), and Claude Cohen-Tannoudji (France), for developing a method to cool and trap atoms using light from lasers

1998 Robert B. Laughlin (U.S.), Horst L. Störmer (Germany), and Daniel C. Tsui (U.S.), for their discovery of a new form of quantum fluid with fractionally charged excitations

CHEMISTRY

1901 Jacobus H. van't Hoff (Netherlands), for laws of chemical dynamics and osmotic pressure in solutions

1902 Emil Fischer (Germany), for experiments in sugar and purin groups of substances

1903 Svante A. Arrhenius (Sweden), for his electrolytic theory of dissociation

1904 Sir William Ramsay (U.K.), for discovery and determination of place of inert gaseous elements in air

1905 Adolf von Baeyer (Germany), for work on organic dyes and hydroaromatic combinations

1906 Henri Moissan (France), for isolation of fluorine, and introduction of electric furnace

1907 Eduard Buchner (Germany), discovery of cell-less fermentation and investigations in biological chemistry

1908 Sir Ernest Rutherford (U.K.), for investigations into disintegration of elements

1909 Wilhelm Ostwald (Germany), for work on catalysis and investigations into chemical equilibrium and reaction rates

1910 Otto Wallach (Germany), for work in the field of alicyclic compounds

1911 Marie Curie (France), for discovery of elements radium and polonium

1912 Victor Grignard (France), for reagent discovered by him; and Paul Sabatier (France), for methods of hydrogenating organic compounds

1913 Alfred Werner (Switzerland), for linking up atoms within the molecule

1914 Theodore W. Richards (U.S.), for determining atomic weight of many chemical elements

1915 Richard Willstätter (Germany), for research into coloring matter of plants, especially chlorophyll

1918 Fritz Haber (Germany), for synthetic production of ammonia

1920 Walther Nernst (Germany), for work in thermochemistry

1921 Frederick Soddy (U.K.), for investigations into origin and nature of isotopes

1922 Francis W. Aston (U.K.), for discovery of isotopes in nonradioactive elements and for discovery of the whole number rule

1923 Fritz Pregl (Austria), for method of microanalysis of organic substances discovered by him

1925 In 1926, the 1925 prize was awarded to Richard Zsigmondy (Germany), for work on the heterogeneous nature of colloid solutions

1926 Theodor Svedberg (Sweden), for work on disperse systems

1927 In 1928, the 1927 prize was awarded to Heinrich Wieland (Germany), for investigations of bile acids and kindred substances

1928 Adolf Windaus (Germany), for investigations on constitution of the sterols and their connection with vitamins

1929 Sir Arthur Harden (U.K.) and Hans K. A. S. von Euler-Chelpin (Sweden), for research of fermentation of sugars

1930 Hans Fischer (Germany), for work on coloring matter of blood and leaves and for his synthesis of hemin

1931 Karl Bosch and Friedrich Bergius (both Germany), for invention and development of chemical high-pressure methods

1932 Irving Langmuir (U.S.), for work in realm of surface chemistry

1934 Harold C. Urey (U.S.), for discovery of heavy hydrogen

1935 Frédéric and Irène Joliot-Curie (both France), for synthesis of new radioactive elements

1936 Peter J. W. Debye (Netherlands), for investigations on dipole moments and diffraction of X-rays and electrons in gases

1937 Walter N. Haworth (U.K.), for research on carbohydrates and vitamin C; and Paul Karrer (Switzerland), for work on carotenoids, flavins, and vitamins A and B

1938 Richard Kuhn (Germany), for carotenoid study and vitamin research (declined)

1939 Adolf Butenandt (Germany), for work on sexual hormones (declined the prize); and Leopold Ruzicka (Switzerland), for work with polymethylenes

1943 Georg Hevesy De Heves (Hungary), for work on use of isotopes as indicators

1944 Otto Hahn (Germany), for work on atomic fission

1945 Artturi Illmari Virtanen (Finland), for research in the field of conservation of fodder

1946 James B. Sumner (U.S.), for crystallizing enzymes; John H. Northrop and Wendell M. Stanley (both U.S.), for preparing enzymes and virus proteins in pure form

1947 Sir Robert Robinson (U.K.), for research in plant substances

1948 Arne Tiselius (Sweden), for biochemical discoveries and isolation of mouse paralysis virus

1949 William Francis Giauque (U.S.), for research in thermodynamics, especially effects of low temperature

1950 Otto Diels and Kurt Alder (both Germany), for discovery of diene synthesis enabling scientists to study structure of organic matter

1951 Glenn T. Seaborg and Edwin H. McMillan (both U.S.), for discovery of plutonium

1952 Archer John Porter Martin and Richard Laurence Millington Synge (both U.K.), for development of partition chromatography

1953 Hermann Staudinger (Germany), for research in giant molecules

1954 Linus C. Pauling (U.S.), for study of forces holding together protein and other molecules

1955 Vincent du Vigneaud (U.S.), for work on pituitary hormones

1956 Sir Cyril Hinshelwood (U.K.) and Nikolai N. Semenov (U.S.S.R.), for parallel research on chemical reaction kinetics

1957 Sir Alexander Todd (U.K.), for research with chemical compounds that are factors in heredity

1958 Frederick Sanger (U.K.), for determining molecular structure of insulin

1959 Jaroslav Heyrovsky (Czechoslovakia), for development of polarography, an electrochemical method of analysis

1960 Willard F. Libby (U.S.), for "atomic time clock" to measure age of objects by measuring their radioactivity

1961 Melvin Calvin (U.S.), for establishing chemical steps during photosynthesis

1962 Max F. Perutz and John C. Kendrew (U.K.), for mapping protein molecules with X-rays

1963 Carl Ziegler (Germany) and Giulio Natta (Italy), for work in uniting simple hydrocarbons into large molecule substances

1964 Dorothy Mary Crowfoot Hodgkin (U.K.), for determining structure of compounds needed in combatting pernicious anemia

1965 Robert B. Woodward (U.S.), for work in synthesizing complicated organic compounds

1966 Robert Sanderson Mulliken (U.S.), for research on bond holding atoms together in molecule

1967 Manfred Eigen (Germany), Ronald G. W. Norrish, and George Porter (both U.K.), for work in high-speed chemical reactions

1968 Lars Onsager (U.S.), for development of system of equations in thermodynamics

1969 Derek H. R. Barton (U.K.) and Odd Hassel (Norway), for study of organic molecules

1970 Luis F. Leloir (Argentina), for discovery of sugar nucleotides and their role in biosynthesis of carbohydrates

1971 Gerhard Herzberg (Canada), for contributions to knowledge of electronic structure and geometry of molecules, particularly free radicals

1972 Christian Boehmer Anfinsen, Stanford Moore, and William Howard Stein (all U.S.), for pioneering studies in enzymes

1973 Ernst Otto Fischer (W. Germany) and Geoffrey Wilkinson (U.K.), for work that could solve problem of automobile exhaust pollution

1974 Paul J. Flory (U.S.), for developing analytic methods to study properties and molecular structure of long-chain molecules

1975 John W. Cornforth (Australia) and Vladimir Prelog (Switzerland), for research on structure of biological molecules such as antibiotics and cholesterol

1976 William N. Lipscomb, Jr. (U.S.), for work on the structure and bonding mechanisms of boranes

1977 Ilya Prigogine (Belgium), for contributions to nonequilibrium thermodynamics, particularly the theory of dissipative structures

1978 Peter Mitchell (U.K.), for contributions to the understanding of biological energy transfer

1979 Herbert C. Brown (U.S.) and Georg Wittig (West Germany), for developing a group of substances that facilitate very difficult chemical reactions

1980 Paul Berg, Walter Gilbert (both U.S.), and Frederick Sanger (U.K.), for developing methods to map the structure and function of DNA, the substance that controls the activity of the cell

1981 Roald Hoffmann (U.S.) and Kenichi Fukui (Japan), for applying quantum-mechanics theories to predict the course of chemical reactions

1982 Aaron Klug (U.K.), for research in the detailed structures of viruses and components of life

1983 Henry Taube (U.S.), for research on how electrons transfer between molecules in chemical reactions

1984 R. Bruce Merrifield (U.S.), for research that revolutionized the study of proteins

1985 Herbert A. Hauptman and Jerome Karle (both U.S.), for their outstanding achievements in the development of direct methods for the determination of crystal structures

1986 Dudley R. Herschback, Yuan T. Lee (both U.S.), and John C. Polanyi (Canada), for their work on "reaction dynamics"

1987 Donald J. Cram, Charles J. Pedersen (both U.S.), and Jean-Marie Lehn (France), for wide-ranging research that has included the creation of artificial molecules that can mimic vital chemical reactions of the processes of life

1988 Johann Deisenhofer, Robert Huber, and Hartmut Michel (all West Germany), for unraveling the structure of proteins that play a crucial role in photosynthesis

1989 Thomas R. Cech and Sidney Altman (both U.S.), for their discovery, independently, that RNA could actively aid chemical reactions in the cells

1990 Elias James Corey (U.S.), for developing new ways to synthesize complex molecules ordinarily found in nature

1991 Richard R. Ernst (Switzerland), for refinements he developed in nuclear magnetic-resonance spectroscopy

1992 Rudolph A. Marcus (U.S.), for his mathematical analysis of how the overall energy in a system of interacting molecules changes and induces an electron to jump from one molecule to another

1993 Kary B. Mullis (U.S.) and Michael Smith (Canada), for their contributions to the science of genetics

1994 George A. Olah (U.S.), University of Southern California in Los Angeles, for research that opened new ways to break apart and rebuild compounds of carbon and hydrogen

1995 F. Sherwood Rowland, Mario Molina (both U.S.), and Paul Crutzen (Netherlands), for their pioneering work in explaining the chemical processes that deplete the earth's ozone shield

1996 Richard E. Smalley, Robert F. Curl, Jr. (both U.S.), and Harold W. Kroto (U.K.), for discovery of a new class of carbon molecule

1997 Paul D. Boyer (U.S.), Jens C. Skou (Denmark), and John E. Walker (U.K.), for discoveries about a molecule that allows the human body to store and transfer energy between cells

1998 Walter Kohn (U.S.) and John A. Pople (U.K.), for their developments in the study of the properties of molecules and the chemical processes in which they are involved

PHYSIOLOGY OR MEDICINE

1901 Emil A. von Behring (Germany), for work on serum therapy against diphtheria

1902 Sir Ronald Ross (U.K.), for work on malaria

1903 Niels R. Finsen (Denmark), for his treatment of lupus vulgaris with concentrated light rays

1904 Ivan P. Pavlov (U.S.S.R.), for work on the physiology of digestion

1905 Robert Koch (Germany), for work on tuberculosis

1906 Camillo Golgi (Italy) and Santiago Ramón y Cajal (Spain), for work on structure of the nervous system

1907 Charles L. A. Laveran (France), for work with protozoa in the generation of disease

1908 Paul Ehrlich (Germany) and Elie Metchnikoff (U.S.S.R.), for work on immunity

1909 Theodor Kocher (Switzerland), for work on the thyroid gland

1910 Albrecht Kossel (Germany), for achievements in the chemistry of the cell

1911 Allvar Gullstrand (Sweden), for work on the dioptrics of the eye

1912 Alexis Carrel (France), for work on vascular ligature and grafting of blood vessels and organs

1913 Charles Richet (France), for work on anaphylaxy

1914 Robert Bárány (Austria), for work on physiology and pathology of the vestibular system

1919 Jules Bordet (Belgium), for discoveries in connection with immunity

1920 August Krogh (Denmark), for discovery of regulation of capillaries' motor mechanism

1922 In 1923, the 1922 prize was shared by Archibald V. Hill (U.K.), for discovery relating to heat-production in muscles; and Otto Meyerhof (Germany), for correlation between consumption of oxygen and production of lactic acid in muscles

1923 Sir Frederick Banting (Canada) and John J. R. Macleod (Scotland), for discovery of insulin

1924 Willem Einthoven (Netherlands), for discovery of the mechanism of the electrocardiogram

1926 Johannes Fibiger (Denmark), for discovery of the Spiroptera carcinoma

1927 Julius Wagner-Jauregg (Austria), for use of malaria inoculation in treatment of dementia paralytica

1928 Charles Nicolle (France), for work on typhus exanthematicus

1929 Christiaan Eijkman (Netherlands), for discovery of the antineuritic vitamins; and Sir Frederick Hopkins (U.K.), for discovery of growth-promoting vitamins

1930 Karl Landsteiner (U.S.), for discovery of human blood groups

1931 Otto H. Warburg (Germany), for discovery of the character and mode of action of the respiratory ferment

1932 Sir Charles Sherrington (U.K.) and Edgar D. Adrian (U.S.), for discoveries of the function of the neuron

1933 Thomas H. Morgan (U.S.), for discoveries on hereditary function of the chromosomes

1934 George H. Whipple, George R. Minot, and William P. Murphy (U.S.), for discovery of liver therapy against anemias

1935 Hans Spemann (Germany), for discovery of the organizer effect in embryonic development

1936 Sir Henry Dale (U.K.) and Otto Loewi (Germany), for discoveries on chemical transmission of nerve impulses

1937 Albert Szent-Györgyi von Nagyrapolt (Hungary), for discoveries on biological combustion

1938 Corneille Heymans (Belgium), for determining importance of sinus and aorta mechanisms in the regulation of respiration

1939 Gerhard Domagk (Germany), for antibacterial effect of prontocilate

1943 Henrik Dam (Denmark) and Edward A. Doisy (U.S.), for analysis of vitamin K

1944 Joseph Erlanger and Herbert Spencer Gasser (both U.S.), for work on functions of the nerve threads

1945 Sir Alexander Fleming, Ernst Boris Chain, and Sir Howard Florey (all U.K.), for discovery of penicillin

1946 Herman J. Muller (U.S.), for hereditary effects of X-rays on genes

1947 Carl F. and Gerty T. Cori (U.S.), for work on animal starch metabolism; Bernardo A. Houssay (Argentina), for study of pituitary

1948 Paul Mueller (Switzerland), for discovery of insect-killing properties of DDT

1949 Walter Rudolf Hess (Switzerland), for research on brain control of body; and Antonio Caetano de Abreu Freire Egas Moniz (Portugal), for development of brain operation

1950 Philip S. Hench, Edward C. Kendall (both U.S.), and Tadeus Reichstein (Switzerland), for discoveries about hormones of adrenal cortex

1951 Max Theiler (South Africa), for development of anti-yellow-fever vaccine

1952 Selman A. Waksman (U.S.), for co-discovery of streptomycin

1953 Fritz A. Lipmann (Germany-U.S.) and Hans Adolph Krebs (Germany-U.K.), for studies of living cells

1954 John F. Enders, Thomas H. Weller, and Frederick C. Robbins (all U.S.), for work with cultivation of polio virus

1955 Hugo Theorell (Sweden), for work on oxidation enzymes

1956 Dickinson W. Richards, Jr., André F. Cournand (both U.S.), and Werner Forssmann (Germany), for new techniques in treating heart disease

1957 Daniel Bovet (Italy), for development of drugs to relieve allergies and relax muscles during surgery

1958 Joshua Lederberg (U.S.), for work with genetic mechanisms; George W. Beadle and Edward L. Tatum (both U.S.), for discovering how genes transmit hereditary characteristics

1959 Severo Ochoa and Arthur Kornberg (both U.S.), for discoveries related to compounds within chromosomes that play a vital role in heredity

1960 Sir Macfarlane Burnet (Australia) and Peter Brian Medawar (U.K.), for discovery of acquired immunological tolerance

1961 Georg von Bekesy (U.S.), for discoveries about physical mechanisms of stimulation within cochlea

1962 James D. Watson (U.S.), Maurice H. F. Wilkins, and Francis H. C. Crick (both U.K.), for determining structure of deoxyribonucleic acid (DNA)

1963 Alan Lloyd Hodgkin, Andrew Fielding Huxley (both U.K.), and Sir John Carew Eccles (Australia), for research on nerve cells

1964 Konrad E. Bloch (U.S.) and Feodor Lynen (Germany), for research on mechanism and regulation of cholesterol and fatty-acid metabolism

1965 François Jacob, André Lwolff, and Jacques Monod (all France), for study of regulatory activities in body cells

1966 Charles Brenton Huggins (U.S.), for studies in hormone treatment of cancer of prostate; Francis Peyton Rous (U.S.), for discovery of tumor-producing viruses

1967 Haldan K. Hartline, George Wald, and Ragnar Granit (all U.S.), for work on human eye

1968 Robert W. Holley, Har Gobind Khorana, and Marshall W. Nirenberg (all U.S.), for studies of genetic code

1969 Max Delbruck, Alfred D. Hershey, and Salvador E. Luria (all U.S.), for study of mechanism of virus infection in living cells

1970 Julius Axelrod (U.S.), Ulf S. von Euler (Sweden), and Sir Bernard Katz (U.K.), for studies of how nerve impulses are transmitted within the body

1971 Earl W. Sutherland, Jr. (U.S.), for research on how hormones work

1972 Gerald M. Edelman (U.S.), and Rodney R. Porter (U.K.), for research on the chemical structure and nature of antibodies

1973 Karl von Frisch, Konrad Lorenz (both Austria), and Nikolaas Tinbergen (Netherlands), for their studies of individual and social behavior patterns

1974 George E. Palade, Christian de Duve (both U.S.), and Albert Claude (Belgium), for contributions to understanding inner workings of living cells

1975 David Baltimore, Howard M. Temin, and Renato Dulbecco (all U.S.), for work in interaction between tumor viruses and genetic material of the cell

1976 Baruch S. Blumberg and D. Carleton Gajdusek (both U.S.), for discoveries concerning new mechanisms for the origin and dissemination of infectious diseases

1977 Rosalyn S. Yalow, Roger C. L. Guillemin, and Andrew V. Schally (all U.S.), for research in role of hormones in chemistry of the body

1978 Daniel Nathans, Hamilton Smith (both U.S.), and Werner Arber (Switzerland), for discovery of restriction enzymes and their application to problems of molecular genetics

1979 Allan McLeod Cormack (U.S.) and Godfrey Newbold Hounsfield (U.K.), for developing computed axial tomography (CAT scan) X-ray technique

1980 Baruj Benacerraf, George D. Snell (both U.S.), and Jean Dausset (France), for discoveries that explain how the structure of cells relates to organ transplants and diseases

1981 Roger W. Sperry, David H. Hubel (both U.S.), and Torsten N. Wiesel (Sweden), for studies vital to understanding the organization and functioning of the brain

1982 Sune Bergstrom, Bengt Samuelsson (both Sweden), and John R. Vane (U.K.), for research in prostaglandins, hormonelike substances involved in a wide range of illnesses

1983 Barbara McClintock (U.S.), for her discovery of mobile genes in the chromosomes of a plant that change the future generations of plants they produce

1984 Cesar Milstein (U.K./Argentina), Georges J. F. Kohler (West Germany), and Niels K. Jerne (U.K./Denmark), for their work in immunology

1985 Michael S. Brown and Joseph L. Goldstein (both U.S.), for their work, which has drastically widened our understanding of the cholesterol metabolism and increased our possibilities to prevent and treat atherosclerosis and heart attacks

1986 Rita Levi-Montalcini (dual U.S./Italy) and Stanley Cohen (U.S.), for their contributions to the understanding of substances that influence cell growth

1987 Susumu Tonegawa (Japan), for his discoveries of how the body can suddenly marshal its immunological defenses against millions of different disease agents that it has never encountered before

1988 Gertrude B. Elion, George H. Hitchings (both U.S.), and Sir James Black (U.K.), for their discoveries of important principles for drug treatment

1989 J. Michael Bishop and Harold E. Varmus (both U.S.), for their unifying theory of cancer development

1990 Joseph E. Murray and E. Donnall Thomas (both U.S.), for their pioneering work in transplants

1991 Erwin Neher and Bert Sakmann (both Germany), for their research, particularly for the development of a technique called patch clamp

1992 Edmond H. Fischer and Edwin G. Krebs (both U.S.), for their discovery of a regulatory mechanism affecting almost all cells

1993 Phillip A. Sharp (U.S.) and Richard J. Roberts (U.K.), for their independent discovery in 1977 of "split genes"

1994 Alfred G. Gilman and Martin Rodbell (both U.S.), for discovery of G-proteins that help cells respond to outside signals

1995 Edward B. Lewis, Eric F. Wieschaus (both U.S.), and Christiane Nüsslein-Volhard (Germany), for studies of the fruit fly that will help explain congenital malformations in humans

1996 Peter C. Doherty (Australia) and Rolf M. Zinkernagel (Switzerland), for discoveries about how the immune system recognizes virus-infected cells

1997 Stanley B. Prusiner (U.S.), for discovery of a new type of germ, called prions, that causes degenerative brain disorders

1998 Robert F. Furchgott, Louis J. Ignarro, and Ferid Murad (all U.S.), for discovering that nitric oxide acts as a signal in the cardiovascular system

ECONOMIC SCIENCE

1969 Ragnar Frisch (Norway) and Jan Tinbergen (Netherlands), for work in econometrics (application of mathematics and statistical methods to economic theories and problems)

1970 Paul A. Samuelson (U.S.), for efforts to raise the level of scientific analysis in economic theory

1971 Simon Kuznets (U.S.), for developing concept of using a country's gross national product to determine its economic growth

1972 Kenneth J. Arrow (U.S.) and Sir John R. Hicks (U.K.), for theories that help to assess business risk and government economic and welfare policies

1973 Wassily Leontief (U.S.), for devising the input-output technique to determine how different sectors of an economy interact

1974 Gunnar Myrdal (Sweden) and Friedrich A. von Hayek (U.K.), for pioneering analysis of the interdependence of economic, social, and institutional phenomena

1975 Leonid V. Kantorovich (U.S.S.R.) and Tjalling C. Koopmans (U.S.), for work on the theory of optimum allocation of resources

1976 Milton Friedman (U.S.), for work in consumption analysis and monetary history and theory, and for demonstration of complexity of stabilization policy

1977 Bertil Ohlin (Sweden) and James E. Meade (U.K.), for contributions to theory of international trade and international capital movements

1978 Herbert A. Simon (U.S.), for research into the decision-making process within economic organizations

1979 Sir Arthur Lewis (U.K.) and Theodore Schultz (U.S.), for work on economic problems of developing nations

1980 Lawrence R. Klein (U.S.), for developing models for forecasting economic trends and shaping policies to deal with them

1981 James Tobin (U.S.), for analyses of financial markets and their influence on spending and saving by families and businesses

1982 George J. Stigler (U.S.), for work on government regulation in the economy and the functioning of industry

1983 Gerard Debreu (U.S.), in recognition of his work on the basic economic problem of how prices operate to balance what producers supply with what buyers want

1984 Sir Richard Stone (U.K.), for his work to develop the systems widely used to measure the performance of national economics

1985 Franco Modigliani (U.S.), for his pioneering work in analyzing the behavior of household savers and the functioning of financial markets

1986 James M. Buchanan (U.S.), for his development of new methods for analyzing economic and political decision-making

1987 Robert M. Solow (U.S.), for seminal contributions to the theory of economic growth

1988 Maurice Allais (France), for his pioneering development of theories to better understand market behavior and the efficient use of resources

1989 Trygve Haavelmo (Norway), for his pioneering work in methods for testing economic theories

1990 Harry M. Markowitz, William F. Sharpe, and Merton H. Miller (all U.S.), whose work provided new tools for weighing the risks and rewards of different investments and for valuing corporate stocks and bonds

1991 Ronald Coase (U.S.), for his pioneering work in how property rights and the cost of doing business affect the economy

1992 Gary S. Becker (U.S.), for "having extended the domain of economic theory to aspects of human behavior which had previously been dealt with—if at all—by other social science disciplines"

1993 Robert W. Fogel and Douglass C. North (both U.S.), for their work in economic history

1994 John F. Nash, John C. Harsanyi (both U.S.), and Reinhard Selten (Germany), for their pioneering work in game theory

1995 Robert E. Lucas, Jr. (U.S.), for having had the greatest influence on macroeconomic research since 1970

1996 James A. Mirrlees (U.K.) and William Vickrey (U.S.), for "their fundamental contributions to the economic theory of incentives"

1997 Robert C. Merton and Myron S. Scholes (both U.S.), for developing a formula that determines the value of stock options and other derivatives

1998 Amartya Sen (India), for his contributions to welfare economics

Pulitzer Prizes

(For years not listed, no award was made.)

PULITZER PRIZES IN JOURNALISM

Meritorious Public Service

1918 *New York Times;* also special award to Minna Lewinson and Henry Beetle Hough
1919 *Milwaukee Journal*
1921 *Boston Post*
1922 *New York World*
1923 *Memphis Commercial Appeal*
1924 *New York World*
1926 *Columbus* (Ga.) *Enquirer Sun*
1927 *Canton* (Ohio) *Daily News*
1928 *Indianapolis Times*
1929 *New York Evening World*
1931 *Atlanta Constitution*
1932 *Indianapolis News*
1933 *New York World-Telegram*
1934 *Medford* (Ore.) *Mail Tribune*
1935 *Sacramento Bee*
1936 *Cedar Rapids* (Iowa) *Gazette*
1937 *St. Louis Post-Dispatch*
1938 *Bismarck* (N.D.) *Tribune*
1939 *Miami Daily News*
1940 *Waterbury* (Conn.) *Republican* and *American*
1941 *St. Louis Post-Dispatch*
1942 *Los Angeles Times*
1943 *Omaha World-Herald*
1944 *New York Times*
1945 *Detroit Free Press*
1946 *Scranton* (Pa.) *Times*
1947 *Baltimore Sun*
1948 *St. Louis Post-Dispatch*
1949 (Lincoln) *Nebraska State Journal*
1950 *Chicago Daily News;* and *St. Louis Post-Dispatch*
1951 *Miami Herald;* and *Brooklyn Eagle*
1952 *St. Louis Post-Dispatch*
1953 *Whiteville* (N.C.) *News Reporter;* and *Tabor City* (N.C.) *Tribune*
1954 *Newsday* (Garden City, N.Y.)

1955 *Columbus* (Ga.) *Ledger* and *Sunday Ledger-Enquirer*
1956 *Watsonville* (Calif.) *Register-Pajaronian*
1957 *Chicago Daily News*
1958 (Little Rock) *Arkansas Gazette*
1959 *Utica* (N.Y.) *Observer Dispatch* and *Utica Daily Press*
1960 *Los Angeles Times*
1961 *Amarillo* (Tex.) *Globe-Times*
1962 *Panama City* (Fla.) *News-Herald*
1963 *Chicago Daily News*
1964 *St. Petersburg* (Fla.) *Times*
1965 *Hutchinson* (Kan.) *News*
1966 *Boston Globe*
1967 *Louisville Courier-Journal* and *Milwaukee Journal*
1968 *Riverside* (Calif.) *Press-Enterprise*
1969 *Los Angeles Times*
1970 *Newsday* (Garden City, N.Y.)
1971 *Winston–Salem* (N.C.) *Journal and Sentinel*
1972 *New York Times*
1973 *Washington Post*
1974 *Newsday* (Garden City, N.Y.)
1975 *Boston Globe*
1976 *Anchorage* (Alaska) *Daily News*
1977 *Lufkin* (Tex.) *News*
1978 *Philadelphia Inquirer*
1979 *Point Reyes* (Calif.) *Light*
1980 *Gannett News Service*
1981 *Charlotte* (N.C.) *Observer*
1982 *Detroit News*
1983 *Jackson* (Miss.) *Clarion-Ledger*
1984 *Los Angeles Times*
1985 *The Fort Worth Star-Telegram*
1986 *Denver Post*
1987 *Pittsburgh Press,* reporting by Andrew Schneider and Matthew Brelis
1988 *Charlotte* (N.C.) *Observer*
1989 *Anchorage Daily News*

1990 *Philadelphia Inquirer* and *Washington* (N.C.) *Daily News*
1991 *Des Moines Register,* reporting by Jane Schorer
1992 *Sacramento Bee* for "The Sierra in Peril" series by Tom Knudson
1993 *Miami Herald*
1994 *The Akron* (Ohio) *Beacon Journal*
1995 *The Virgin Islands Daily News*
1996 *The News and Observer* (Raleigh, N.C.)
1997 *The Times-Picayune* (New Orleans, La.)
1998 *Grand Forks* (N.D.) *Herald*
1999 *Washington Post*

Editorial

1917 *New York Tribune*
1918 *Louisville Courier-Journal*
1920 Harvey E. Newbranch *(Omaha Evening World-Herald)*
1922 Frank M. O'Brien *(New York Herald)*
1923 William Allen White *(Emporia* [Kan.] *Gazette)*
1924 *Boston Herald*; special prize: Frank I. Cobb *(New York World)*
1925 *Charleston* (S.C.) *News and Courier*
1926 Edward M. Kingsbury *(New York Times)*
1927 F. Lauriston Bullard *(Boston Herald)*
1928 Grover Cleveland Hall *(Montgomery* [Ala.] *Advertiser)*
1929 Louis Isaac Jaffe *(Norfolk Virginian-Pilot)*
1931 Charles S. Ryckman *(Fremont* [Neb.] *Tribune)*
1933 *Kansas City* (Mo.) *Star*
1934 E. P. Chase *(Atlantic* [Iowa] *News Telegraph)*
1936 Felix Morley *(Washington Post);* George B. Parker (Scripps–Howard Newspapers)
1937 John W. Owens *(Baltimore Sun)*
1938 W. W. Waymack *(Des Moines Register and Tribune)*
1939 Ronald G. Callvert *(Portland Oregonian)*
1940 Bart Howard *(St. Louis Post-Dispatch)*
1941 Reuben Maury *(New York Daily News)*
1942 Geoffrey Parsons *(New York Herald Tribune)*
1943 Forrest W. Seymour *(Des Moines Register and Tribune)*
1944 Henry J. Haskell *(Kansas City* [Mo.] *Star)*
1945 George W. Potter *(Providence* [R.I.] *Journal-Bulletin)*
1946 Hodding Carter ([Greenville, Miss.] *Delta Democrat-Times)*
1947 William H. Grimes *(Wall Street Journal)*
1948 Virginius Dabney *(Richmond Times-Dispatch)*
1949 John H. Crider *(Boston Herald);* Herbert Elliston *(Washington Post)*
1950 Carl M. Saunders *(Jackson* [Mich.] *Citizen Patriot)*
1951 William H. Fitzpatrick *(New Orleans States)*
1952 Louis LaCoss *(St. Louis Globe-Democrat)*
1953 Vermont C. Royster *(Wall Street Journal)*
1954 Don Murray *(Boston Herald)*
1955 Royce Howes *(Detroit Free Press)*
1956 Lauren K. Soth *(Des Moines Register and Tribune)*
1957 Buford Boone *(Tuscaloosa* [Ala.] *News)*
1958 Harry S. Ashmore *(Arkansas Gazette)*
1959 Ralph McGill *(Atlanta Constitution)*
1960 Lenoir Chambers *(Virginian-Pilot)*
1961 William J. Dorvillier *(San Juan* [P.R.] *Star)*
1962 Thomas M. Storke *(Santa Barbara* [Calif.] *News-Press)*
1963 Ira B. Harkey, Jr. *(Pascagoula* [Miss.] *Chronicle)*

1964 Hazel Brannon Smith *(Lexington* [Miss.] *Advertiser)*
1965 John R. Harrison *(Gainesville* [Fla.] *Daily Sun)*
1966 Robert Lasch *(St. Louis Post-Dispatch)*
1967 Eugene Patterson *(Atlanta Constitution)*
1968 John S. Knight (Knight Newspapers)
1969 Paul Greenberg *(Pine Bluff* [Ark.] *Commercial)*
1970 Phillip L. Geyelin *(Washington Post)*
1971 Horance G. Davis, Jr. *(Gainesville* [Fla.] *Sun)*
1972 John Strohmeyer *(Bethlehem* [Pa.] *Globe Times)*
1973 Roger Bourne Linscott *(Berkshire Eagle* [Pittsfield, Mass.])
1974 F. Gilman Spencer *(Trenton* [N.J.] *Trentonian)*
1975 John Daniell Maurice *(Charleston* [W. Va.] *Daily Mail)*
1976 Philip P. Kerby *(Los Angeles Times)*
1977 Warren L. Lerude, Foster Church, and Norman F. Cardoza *(Reno* [Nev.] *Gazette* and *Nevada State Journal)*
1978 Meg Greenfield *(Washington Post)*
1979 Edwin M. Yoder, Jr. *(Washington Star)*
1980 Robert L. Bartley *(Wall Street Journal)*
1982 Jack Rosenthal *(New York Times)*
1983 *Miami Herald*
1984 Albert Scardino *(Georgia Gazette)*
1985 Richard Aregood *(Philadelphia Daily News)*
1986 Jack Fuller *(Chicago Tribune)*
1987 Jonathan Freedman *(San Diego Tribune)*
1988 Jane E. Healy *(Orlando Sentinel)*
1989 Lois Wille *(Chicago Tribune)*
1990 Thomas J. Hylton *(Pottstown* [Pa.] *Mercury)*
1991 Ron Casey, Harold Jackson, and Joey Kennedy *(Birmingham* [Ala.] *News)*
1992 Maria Henson *(Lexington* [Ky.] *Herald-Leader)*
1994 R. Bruce Dold *(Chicago Tribune)*
1995 Jeffrey Good *(St. Petersburg* [Fla.] *Times)*
1996 Robert B. Semple, Jr. *(New York Times)*
1997 Michael Gartner *(Daily Tribune* [Ames, Iowa])
1998 Bernard L. Stein *(The Riverdale Press* [Bronx, N.Y.])
1999 Editorial Board *(Daily News* [New York, N.Y.])

Correspondence

1929 Paul Scott Mowrer *(Chicago Daily News)*
1930 Leland Stowe *(New York Herald Tribune)*
1931 H. R. Knickerbocker *(Philadelphia Public Ledger* and *New York Evening Post)*
1932 Walter Duranty *(New York Times);* Charles G. Ross *(St. Louis Post-Dispatch)*
1933 Edgar Ansel Mowrer *(Chicago Daily News)*
1934 Frederick T. Birchall *(New York Times)*
1935 Arthur Krock *(New York Times)*
1936 Wilfred C. Barber *(Chicago Tribune)*
1937 Anne O'Hare McCormick *(New York Times)*
1938 Arthur Krock *(New York Times)*
1939 Louis P. Lochner (Associated Press)
1940 Otto D. Tolischus *(New York Times)*
1941 Group award[1]
1942 Carlos P. Romulo *(Philippines Herald)*
1943 Hanson W. Baldwin *(New York Times)*
1944 Ernie Pyle (Scripps–Howard Newspaper Alliance)
1945 Harold V. (Hal) Boyle (Associated Press)
1946 Arnaldo Cortesi *(New York Times)*
1947 Brooks Atkinson *(New York Times)*

1. For the public services and the individual achievements of American news reporters in the war zones.

Editorial Cartooning

1922 Rollin Kirby (New York World)
1924 Jay Norwood Darling (New York Tribune)
1925 Rollin Kirby (New York World)
1926 D. R. Fitzpatrick (St. Louis Post-Dispatch)
1927 Nelson Harding (Brooklyn Eagle)
1928 Nelson Harding (Brooklyn Eagle)
1929 Rollin Kirby (New York World)
1930 Charles R. Macauley (Brooklyn Eagle)
1931 Edmund Duffy (Baltimore Sun)
1932 John T. McCutcheon (Chicago Tribune)
1933 H. M. Talburt (Washington Daily News)
1934 Edmund Duffy (Baltimore Sun)
1935 Ross A. Lewis (Milwaukee Journal)
1937 C. D. Batchelor (New York Daily News)
1938 Vaughn Shoemaker (Chicago Daily News)
1939 Charles G. Werner (Daily Oklahoman [Oklahoma City])
1940 Edmund Duffy (Baltimore Sun)
1941 Jacob Burck (Chicago Times)
1942 Herbert L. Block (NEA Service)
1943 Jay Norwood Darling (New York Herald Tribune)
1944 Clifford K. Berryman (Washington Evening Star)
1945 Bill Mauldin (United Features Syndicate)
1946 Bruce Alexander Russell (Los Angeles Times)
1947 Vaughn Shoemaker (Chicago Daily News)
1948 Reuben L. Goldberg (New York Sun)
1949 Lute Pease (Newark Evening News)
1950 James T. Berryman (Washington Evening Star)
1951 Reg (Reginald W.) Manning (Arizona Republic [Phoenix])
1952 Fred L. Packer (New York Mirror)
1953 Edward D. Kuekes (Cleveland Plain Dealer)
1954 Herbert L. Block (Washington Post and Times-Herald)
1955 Daniel R. Fitzpatrick (St. Louis Post-Dispatch)
1956 Robert York (Louisville Times)
1957 Tom Little (Nashville Tennessean)
1958 Bruce M. Shanks (Buffalo Evening News)
1959 Bill Mauldin (St. Louis Post-Dispatch)
1961 Carey Orr (Chicago Tribune)
1962 Edmund S. Valtman (Hartford Times)
1963 Frank Miller (Des Moines Register)
1964 Paul Conrad (formerly of Denver Post, later on Los Angeles Times)
1966 Don Wright (Miami News)
1967 Patrick B. Oliphant (Denver Post)
1968 Eugene Gray Payne (Charlotte [N.C.] Observer)
1969 John Fischetti (Chicago Daily News)
1970 Thomas F. Darcy (Newsday [Garden City, N.Y.])
1971 Paul Conrad (Los Angeles Times)
1972 Jeffrey K. MacNelly (Richmond [Va.] News Leader)
1974 Paul Szep (Boston Globe)
1975 Garry Trudeau (Universal Press Syndicate)
1976 Tony Auth (Philadelphia Inquirer)
1977 Paul Szep (Boston Globe)
1978 Jeffrey K. MacNelly (Richmond [Va.] News Leader)
1979 Herbert L. Block (Washington Post)
1980 Don Wright (Miami News)
1981 Mike Peters (Dayton [Ohio] Daily News)
1982 Ben Sargent (Austin [Tex.] American-Statesman)
1983 Richard Locher (Chicago Tribune)

1984 Paul Conrad (Los Angeles Times)
1985 Jeff MacNelly (Chicago Tribune)
1986 Jules Feiffer (Village Voice)
1987 Berke Breathed (Washington Post Writers Group)
1988 Doug Marlette (Atlanta Constitution and Charlotte [N.C.] Observer)
1989 Jack Higgins (Chicago Sun-Times)
1990 Tom Toles (Buffalo News)
1991 Jim Borgman (Cincinnati Inquirer)
1992 Signe Wilkinson (Philadelphia Daily News)
1993 Stephen R. Benson (Arizona Republic)
1994 Michael P. Ramirez (The Commercial Appeal, Memphis)
1995 Mike Luckovich (The Atlanta Constitution)
1996 Jim Morin (The Miami Herald)
1997 Walt Handelsman (The Times-Picayune)
1998 Stephen P. Breen (The Asbury Park [N.J.] Press)
1999 David Horsey (Seattle Post-Intelligencer)

News Photography

1942 Milton Brooks (Detroit News)
1943 Frank Noel (Associated Press)
1944 Frank Filan (Associated Press); Earle L. Bunker (Omaha World-Herald)
1945 Joe Rosenthal (Associated Press)
1947 Arnold Hardy
1948 Frank Cushing (Boston Traveler)
1949 Nat Fein (New York Herald Tribune)
1950 Bill Crouch (Oakland Tribune)
1951 Max Desfor (Associated Press)
1952 John Robinson and Don Ultang (Des Moines Register & Tribune)
1953 William M. Gallagher (Flint [Mich.] Journal)
1954 Mrs. Walter M. Schau
1955 John L. Gaunt, Jr. (Los Angeles Times)
1956 New York Daily News
1957 Harry A. Trask (Boston Traveler)
1958 William C. Beall (Washington Daily News)
1959 William Seaman (Minneapolis Star)
1960 Andrew Lopez (United Press International)
1961 Yasushi Nagao (Mainichi Newspapers, Tokyo)
1962 Paul Vathis (Harrisburg [Pa.] bureau of Associated Press)
1963 Hector Rondon (La Republica, Caracas, Venezuela)
1964 Robert H. Jackson (Dallas Times Herald)
1965 Horst Faas (Associated Press)
1966 Kyoichi Sawada (United Press International)
1967 Jack R. Thornell (Associated Press)
1968 News: Rocco Morabito (Jacksonville [Fla.] Journal); features: Toshio Sakai (United Press International)
1969 Spot news: Edward T. Adams (Associated Press); features: Moneta Sleet, Jr.
1970 Spot news: Steve Starr (Associated Press); features: Dallas Kinney (Palm Beach Post)
1971 Spot news: John Paul Filo (Valley Daily News and Daily Dispatch [Tarentum and New Kensington, Pa.]); features: Jack Dykinga (Chicago Sun-Times)
1972 Spot news: Horst Faas and Michel Laurent (Associated Press); features: Dave Kennerly (United Press International)
1973 Spot news: Huynh Cong Ut (Associated Press); features: Brian Lanker (Topeka Capital-Journal)
1974 Spot news: Anthony K. Roberts (Associated Press); features: Slava Veder (Associated Press)

1975 Spot news: Gerald H. Gay *(Seattle Times);* features: Matthew Lewis *(Washington Post)*

1976 Spot news: Stanley J. Forman *(Boston Herald-American);* features: photographic staff of *Louisville Courier-Journal* and *Times*

1977 Spot news: Neal Ulevich (Associated Press) and Stanley J. Forman *(Boston Herald-American);* features: Robin Hood *(Chattanooga News-Free Press)*

1978 Spot news: John Blair, freelance, Evansville, Ind.; features: J. Ross Baughman (Associated Press)

1979 Spot news: Thomas J. Kelly, 3rd *(Pottstown* [Pa.] *Mercury);* features: photographic staff of *Boston Herald-American*

1980 Features: Erwin H. Hagler *(Dallas Times Herald)*

1981 Spot news: Larry C. Price *(Fort Worth Star-Telegram);* features: Taro M. Yamasaki *(Detroit Free Press)*

1982 Spot news: Ron Edmonds (Associated Press); features: John H. White *(Chicago Sun-Times)*

1983 Spot news: Bill Foley (Associated Press); features: James B. Dickman *(Dallas Times Herald)*

1984 Spot news: Stan Grossfeld *(Boston Globe);* features: Anthony Suau *(Denver Post)*

1985 Spot news: photographic staff of *Register,* Santa Ana, Calif.; features: Stan Grossfeld *(Boston Globe)*

1986 Spot news: Michel duCille and Carol Guzy *(Miami Herald);* features: Tom Gralish *(Philadelphia Inquirer)*

1987 Spot news: Kim Komenich *(San Francisco Examiner);* features: David Peterson *(Des Moines Register)*

1988 Spot news: Scott Shaw *(Odessa* [Texas] *American);* features: Michel duCille *(Miami Herald)*

1989 Spot news: Ron Olshwanger *(St. Louis Post-Dispatch);* features: Manny Crisostomo *(Detroit Free Press)*

1990 Spot news: *Oakland Tribune;* features: David C. Turnley *(Detroit Free Press)*

1991 Spot news: Greg Marinovich (Associated Press); features: William Snyder *(Dallas Morning News)*

1992 Spot news: Associated Press staff; features: John Kaplan *(Herald* [Monterey, Calif.] and *Pittsburgh Post–Gazette)*

1993 Spot news: William Snyder and Ken Geiger *(Dallas Morning News);* features: Associated Press

1994 Spot news: Paul Watson *(Toronto Star);* features: Kevin Carter, freelancer for *New York Times*

1995 Spot news: Carol Guzy *(Washington Post);* features: Associated Press Staff

1996 Spot news: Charles Porter IV, freelance photographer for Associated Press; features: Stephanie Walsh, freelance photographer for Newhouse News Service

1997 Spot news: Annie Wells *(The Press Democrat* [Santa Rosa, Calif.]); features: Alexander Zemlianichenko (Associated Press)

1998 Spot news: Martha Rial *(The Pittsburgh Post–Gazette);* features: Clarence Williams *(The Los Angeles Times)*

1999 Spot news: Associated Press photo staff; features: Associated Press photo staff

National Telegraphic Reporting
1942 Louis Stark *(New York Times)*
1944 Dewey L. Fleming *(Baltimore Sun)*
1945 James Reston *(New York Times)*
1946 Edward A. Harris *(St. Louis Post-Dispatch)*
1947 Edward T. Folliard *(Washington Post)*

National Reporting
1948 Bert Andrews *(New York Herald Tribune);* Nat S. Finney *(Minneapolis Tribune)*
1949 C. P. Trussell *(New York Times)*
1950 Edwin O. Guthman *(Seattle Times)*
1952 Anthony Leviero *(New York Times)*
1953 Don Whitehead (Associated Press)
1954 Richard Wilson (Cowles Newspapers)
1955 Anthony Lewis *(Washington Daily News)*
1956 Charles L. Bartlett *(Chattanooga Times)*
1957 James Reston *(New York Times)*
1958 Relman Morin (Associated Press) and Clark Mollenhoff *(Des Moines Register & Tribune)*
1959 Howard Van Smith *(Miami News)*
1960 Vance Trimble (Scripps-Howard Newspaper Alliance)
1961 Edward R. Cony *(Wall Street Journal)*
1962 Nathan G. Caldwell and Gene S. Graham *(Nashville Tennessean)*
1963 Anthony Lewis *(New York Times)*
1964 Merriman Smith (United Press International)
1965 Louis M. Kohlmeier *(Wall Street Journal)*
1966 Haynes Johnson *(Washington Evening Star)*
1967 Stanley Penn and Monroe Karmin *(Wall Street Journal)*
1968 Howard James *(Christian Science Monitor);* Nathan K. (Nick) Kotz *(Des Moines Register* and *Minneapolis Tribune)*
1969 Robert Cahn *(Christian Science Monitor)*
1970 William J. Eaton *(Chicago Daily News)*
1971 Lucinda Franks and Thomas Powers (United Press International)
1972 Jack Anderson *(United Feature Syndicate)*
1973 Robert Boyd and Clark Hoyt *(Knight Newspapers)*
1974 Jack White *(Providence* [R.I.] *Journal-Bulletin);* James R. Polk *(Washington Star-News)*
1975 Donald L. Barlett and James B. Steele *(Philadelphia Inquirer)*
1976 James Risser *(Des Moines Register)*
1977 Walter Mears (Associated Press)
1978 Gaylord D. Shaw *(Los Angeles Times)*
1979 James Risser *(Des Moines Register)*
1980 Bette Swenson Orsini and Charles Stafford *(St. Petersburg Times)*
1981 John M. Crewdson *(New York Times)*
1982 Rick Atkinson *(Kansas City* [Mo.] *Times)*
1983 *Boston Globe*
1984 John N. Wilford *(New York Times)*
1985 Thomas J. Knudson *(Des Moines Register)*
1986 Craig Flournoy and George Rodrigue *(Dallas Morning News)* and Arthur Howe *(Philadelphia Inquirer)*
1987 *Miami Herald,* staff; *New York Times,* staff
1988 Tim Weiner *(Philadelphia Inquirer)*
1989 Donald L. Barlett and James B. Steele *(Philadelphia Inquirer)*
1990 Ross Anderson, Bill Dietrich, Mary Ann Gwinn, and Eric Nalder *(Seattle Times)*

1991 Marjie Lundstrom and Rochelle Sharpe (Gannett News Service)
1992 Jeff Taylor and Mike McGraw *(Kansas City Star)*
1993 David Maranniss *(Washington Post)*
1994 Eileen Welsome *(Albuquerque* [N.M.] *Tribune)*
1995 Tony Horwitz *(Wall Street Journal)*
1996 Alix M. Freedman *(Wall Street Journal)*
1997 *Wall Street Journal* staff
1998 Russell Carollo and Jeff Nesmith *(Dayton* [Ohio] *Daily News)*
1999 *The New York Times* staff

International Telegraphic Reporting

1942 Laurence Edmund Allen (Associated Press)
1943 Ira Wolfert (North American Newspaper Alliance, Inc.)
1944 Daniel De Luce (Associated Press)
1945 Mark S. Watson *(Baltimore Sun)*
1946 Homer W. Bigart *(New York Herald Tribune)*
1947 Eddy Gilmore (Associated Press)

International Reporting

1948 Paul W. Ward *(Baltimore Sun)*
1949 Price Day *(Baltimore Sun)*
1950 Edmund Stevens *(Christian Science Monitor)*
1951 Keyes Beech and Fred Sparks *(Chicago Daily News)*; Homer Bigart and Marguerite Higgins *(New York Herald Tribune)*; Relman Morin and Don Whitehead (Associated Press)
1952 John M. Hightower (Associated Press)
1953 Austin C. Wehrwein *(Milwaukee Journal)*
1954 Jim G. Lucas (Scripps-Howard Newspapers)
1955 Harrison E. Salisbury *(New York Times)*
1956 William Randolph Hearst, Jr., and Frank Conniff (Hearst Newspapers); Kingsbury Smith (INS)
1957 Russell Jones (United Press)
1958 *New York Times*
1959 Joseph Martin and Philip Santora *(New York Daily News)*
1960 A. M. Rosenthal *(New York Times)*
1961 Lynn Heinzerling (Associated Press)
1962 Walter Lippmann (New York Herald Tribune Syndicate)
1963 Hal Hendrix *(Miami News)*
1964 Malcolm W. Browne (Associated Press); David Halberstam *(New York Times)*
1965 J. A. Livingston *(Philadelphia Bulletin)*
1966 Peter Arnett (Associated Press)
1967 R. John Hughes *(Christian Science Monitor)*
1968 Alfred Friendly *(Washington Post)*
1969 William Tuohy *(Los Angeles Times)*
1970 Seymour M. Hersh (Dispatch News Service)
1971 Jimmie Lee Hoagland *(Washington Post)*
1972 Peter R. Kann *(Wall Street Journal)*
1973 Max Frankel *(New York Times)*
1974 Hedrick Smith *(New York Times)*
1975 William Mullen and Ovie Carter *(Chicago Tribune)*
1976 Sydney H. Schanberg *(New York Times)*
1978 Henry Kamm *(New York Times)*
1979 Richard Ben Cramer *(Philadelphia Inquirer)*
1980 Joel Brinkley and Jay Mather *(Louisville Courier-Journal)*
1981 Shirley Christian *(Miami Herald)*
1982 John Darnton *(New York Times)*
1983 Thomas L. Friedman *(New York Times)*
1984 Karen E. House *(Wall Street Journal)*
1985 Josh Friedman, Dennis Bell, and Ozier Muhammad *(Newsday)*

1986 Lewis M. Simons, Pete Carey, and Katherine Ellison *(San Jose Mercury News)*
1987 Michael Parks *(Los Angeles Times)*
1988 Thomas L. Friedman *(New York Times)*
1989 Bill Keller *(New York Times)*; Glenn Frankel *(Washington Post)*
1990 Nicholas D. Kristof and Sheryl WuDunn *(New York Times)*
1991 Caryle Murphy *(Washington Post)*; Serge Schmemann *(New York Times)*
1992 Patrick J. Sloyan *(Newsday)*
1993 John F. Burns *(New York Times)*; Roy Gutman *(Newsday)*
1994 *Dallas Morning News* team
1995 Mark Fritz (Associated Press)
1996 David Rohde *(Christian Science Monitor)*
1997 John F. Burns *(New York Times)*
1998 *New York Times* staff
1999 *Wall Street Journal* staff

Reporting

1917 Herbert B. Swope *(New York World)*
1918 Harold A. Littledale *(New York Evening Post)*
1920 John J. Leary, Jr. *(New York World)*
1921 Louis Seibold *(New York World)*
1922 Kirke L. Simpson (Associated Press)
1923 Alva Johnston *(New York Times)*
1924 Magner White *(San Diego Sun)*
1925 James W. Mulroy and Alvin H. Goldstein *(Chicago Daily News)*
1926 William Burke Miller *(Louisville Courier-Journal)*
1927 John T. Rogers *(St. Louis Post-Dispatch)*
1929 Paul Y. Anderson *(St. Louis Post-Dispatch)*
1930 Russell D. Owen *(New York Times)*; special award: W. O. Dapping *(Auburn* [N.Y.] *Citizen)*
1931 A. B. MacDonald *(Kansas City* [Mo.] *Star)*
1932 W. C. Richards, D. D. Martin, J. S. Pooler, F. D. Webb, and J. N. W. Sloan *(Detroit Free Press)*
1933 Francis A. Jamieson (Associated Press)
1934 Royce Brier *(San Francisco Chronicle)*
1935 William H. Taylor *(New York Herald Tribune)*
1936 Lauren D. Lyman *(New York Times)*
1937 John J. O'Neill *(New York Herald Tribune)*; William Leonard Laurence *(New York Times)*; Howard W. Blakeslee (Associated Press); Gobind Behari Lal (Universal Service); David Dietz (Scripps–Howard Newspapers)
1938 Raymond Sprigle *(Pittsburg Post-Gazette)*
1939 Thomas L. Stokes *(New York World-Telegram)*
1940 S. Burton Heath *(New York World-Telegram)*
1941 Westbrook Pegler *(New York World-Telegram)*
1942 Stanton Delaplane *(San Francisco Chronicle)*
1943 George Weller *(Chicago Daily News)*
1944 Paul Schoenstein and associates *(New York Journal-American)*
1945 Jack S. McDowell *(San Francisco Call-Bulletin)*
1946 William Leonard Laurence *(New York Times)*
1947 Frederick Woltman *(New York World-Telegram)*
1948 George E. Goodwin *(Atlanta Journal)*
1949 Malcolm Johnson *(New York Sun)*
1950 Meyer Berger *(New York Times)*
1951 Edward S. Montgomery *(San Francisco Examiner)*
1952 George de Carvalho *(San Francisco Chronicle)*

1953 Editorial staff *(Providence Journal and Evening Bulletin);*[1] Edward J. Mowery *(New York World-Telegram and Sun)*[2]

1954 *Vicksburg* (Miss.) *Sunday Post-Herald;*[1] Alvin Scott McCoy *(Kansas City* [Mo.] *Star)*[2]

1955 Mrs. Caro Brown *(Alice* [Tex.] *Daily Echo);*[1] Roland Kenneth Towery *(Cuero* [Tex.] *Record)*[2]

1956 Lee Hills *(Detroit Free Press);*[1] Arthur Daley *(New York Times)*[2]

1957 *Salt Lake Tribune;*[1] Wallace Turner and William Lambert *(Portland Oregonian)*[2]

1958 *Fargo* [N.D.] *Forum;*[1] George Beveridge *(Washington* [D.C.] *Evening Star)*[2]

1959 Mary Lou Werner *(Washington* [D.C.] *Evening Star);*[1] John Harold Brislin *(Scranton* [Pa.] *Tribune & Scrantonian)*[2]

1960 Jack Nelson *(Atlanta Constitution);*[1] Miriam Ottenberg *(Washington Evening Star)*[2]

1961 Sanche de Gramont *(New York Herald Tribune);*[1] Edgar May *(Buffalo Evening News)*[2]

1962 Robert D. Mullins *(Deseret News,* Salt Lake City);[1] George Bliss *(Chicago Tribune)*[2]

1963 Sylvan Fox, Anthony Shannon, and William Longgood *(New York World-Telegram and Sun);*[1] Oscar Griffin, Jr. (former editor of *Pecos* [Tex.] *Independent and Enterprise,* now on staff of *Houston Chronicle)*[2]

1. Reporting under pressure of edition deadlines.
2. Reporting not under pressure of edition deadlines.

General Local Reporting

1964 Norman C. Miller *(Wall Street Journal)*

1965 Melvin H. Ruder (*Hungry Horse News,* Columbia Falls, Mont.)

1966 *Los Angeles Times* staff

1967 Robert V. Cox *(Chambersburg* [Pa.] *Public Opinion)*

1968 *Detroit Free Press* staff

1969 John Fetterman *(Louisville Times and Courier-Journal)*

1970 Thomas Fitzpatrick *(Chicago Sun-Times)*

1971 Akron (Ohio) *Beacon* staff

1972 Richard Cooper and John Machacek *(Rochester* [N.Y.] *Times-Union)*

1973 *Chicago Tribune*

1974 Arthur M. Petacque and Hugh F. Hough *(Chicago Sun-Times)*

1975 *Xenia* (Ohio) *Daily Gazette*

1976 Gene Miller *(Miami Herald)*

1977 Margo Huston *(Milwaukee Journal)*

1978 Richard Whitt *(Louisville Courier-Journal)*

1979 Staff of *San Diego* (Calif.) *Evening Tribune*

1980 Staff of *Philadelphia Inquirer*

1981 *Longview* (Wash.) *Daily News*

1982 *Kansas City* (Mo.) *Star* and *Kansas City* (Mo.) *Times*

1983 *Fort Wayne* (Ind.) *News-Sentinel*

1984 *Newsday*

General News Reporting

1985 Thomas Turcol *(Virginian-Pilot and Ledger-Star)*

1986 Edna Buchanan *(Miami Herald)*

1987 *Akron Beacon Journal* staff

1988 *Alabama Journal* (Montgomery) staff; *Lawrence* (Mass.) *Eagle-Tribune* staff

1989 *Louisville Courier-Journal* staff

1990 *San Jose* (Calif.) *Mercury News*

Spot News Reporting

1991 *Miami Herald* staff

1992 *New York Newsday* staff

1993 *Los Angeles Times* staff

1994 *New York Times* staff

1995 *Los Angeles Times* staff

1996 Robert D. McFadden *(New York Times)*

1997 *Newsday* staff (Long Island, N.Y.)

1998 Discontinued

Breaking News Reporting

1998 *Los Angeles Times* staff

1999 *The Hartford Courant* staff

Special Local Reporting

1964 James V. Magee, Albert V. Gaudiosi, and Frederick A. Meyer *(Philadelphia Bulletin)*

1965 Gene Goltz *(Houston Post)*

1966 John A. Frasca *(Tampa Tribune)*

1967 Gene Miller *(Miami Herald)*

1968 J. Anthony Lukas *(New York Times)*

1969 Albert L. Delugach and Denny Walsh *(St. Louis Globe-Democrat)*

1970 Harold Eugene Martin *(Montgomery Advertiser)*

1971 William Hugh Jones *(Chicago Tribune)*

1972 Timothy Leland, Gerard N. O'Neill, Stephen A. Kurkjian, and Ann DeSantis *(Boston Globe)*

1973 Sun Newspapers of Omaha, Neb.

1974 William Sherman *(New York Daily News)*

1975 *Indianapolis Star*

1976 *Chicago Tribune*

1977 Acel Moore and Wendell Rawls, Jr. *(Philadelphia Inquirer)*

1978 Anthony R. Dolan *(Stamford* [Conn.] *Advocate)*

1979 Gilbert M. Gaul and Elliot G. Jaspin *(Pottsville* [Pa.] *Republican)*

1980 Nils J. Bruzelius, Alexander B. Hawes, Jr., Stephen A. Kurkjian, Robert M. Porterfield, and Joan Vennochi *(Boston Globe)*

1981 Clark Hallas and Robert B. Lowe (*Arizona Daily Star,* Tucson)

1982 Paul Henderson *(Seattle Times)*

1983 Loretta Tofani *(Washington Post)*

1984 Kenneth Cooper, Joan FitzGerald, Jonathan Kaufman, Norman Lockman, Gary McMillan, Kirk Scharfenberg, and David Wessel *(Boston Globe)*

Investigative Reporting

1985 Lucy Morgan, Jack Reed *(St. Petersburg* [Fla.] *Times),* and William K. Marimow *(Philadelphia Inquirer)*

1986 Jeffrey A. Marx and Michael M. York *(Lexington* [Ky.] *Herald Leader)*

1987 Daniel R. Biddle, H. G. Bissinger, and Fredric N. Tulsky *(Philadelphia Inquirer)*

1988 Dean Baquet, William C. Gaines, and Ann Marie Lipinski *(Chicago Tribune)*

1989 Bill Dedman *(Atlanta Journal and Constitution)*

1990 Lou Kilzer and Chris Ison *(Minneapolis-St. Paul Star Tribune)*

1991 Joseph T. Hallinan and Susan M. Headden *(Indianapolis Star)*

1992 Lorraine Adams and Dan Malone *(Dallas Morning News)*

1993 Jeff Brazil and Steve Berry *(Orlando* [Fla.] *Sentinel)*

1994 *Providence* (R.I.) *Journal-Bulletin* staff
1995 Stephanie Saul and Brian Donovan
     (Newsday)
1996 *Orange County Register* staff (Santa Ana, Calif.)
1997 Eric Nalder, Deborah Nelson, and Alex Tizon *(Seattle Times)*
1998 Gary Cohn and Will Englund (*The Sun* [Baltimore, Md.])
1999 *The Miami Herald* staff

Feature Writing
1979 Jon D. Franklin *(Baltimore Evening Sun)*
1980 Madeleine Blais *(Miami Herald)*
1981 Teresa Carpenter (*Village Voice,* New York)
1982 Saul Pett (Associated Press)
1983 Nan Robertson *(New York Times)*
1984 Peter M. Rinearson *(Seattle Times)*
1985 Alice Steinbach *(Baltimore Sun)*
1986 John Camp *(St. Paul Pioneer Press and Dispatch)*
1987 Steve Twomey *(Philadelphia Inquirer)*
1988 Jacqui Banaszynski *(St. Paul Pioneer Press Dispatch)*
1989 David Zucchino *(Philadelphia Inquirer)*
1990 Dave Curtin *(Colorado Springs Gazette Telegraph)*
1991 Sheryl James *(St. Petersburg* [Fla.] *Times)*
1992 Howell Raines *(New York Times)*
1993 George Lardner, Jr. *(Washington Post)*
1994 Isabel Wilkerson *(New York Times)*
1995 Ron Suskind *(Wall Street Journal)*
1996 Rick Bragg *(New York Times)*
1997 Lisa Pollak *(Baltimore Sun)*
1998 Thomas French *(St. Petersburg* [Fla.] *Times)*
1999 Angelo B. Henderson *(Wall Street Journal)*

Commentary
1970 Marquis W. Childs *(St. Louis Post-Dispatch)*
1971 William A. Caldwell (*Record* [Hackensack, N.J.])
1972 Mike Royko *(Chicago Daily News)*
1973 David S. Broder *(Washington Post)*
1974 Edwin A. Roberts, Jr. *(National Observer)*
1975 Mary McGrory *(Washington Star)*
1976 Walter W. (Red) Smith *(New York Times)*
1977 George F. Will (*Washington Post* Writers Group)
1978 William Safire *(New York Times)*
1979 Russell Baker *(New York Times)*
1980 Ellen H. Goodman *(Boston Globe)*
1981 Dave Anderson *(New York Times)*
1982 Art Buchwald (*Los Angeles Times* Syndicate)
1983 Claude Sitton (*Raleigh* [N.C.] *News & Observer)*
1984 Vermont Royster *(Wall Street Journal)*
1985 Murray Kempton *(Newsday)*
1986 Jimmy Breslin *(New York Daily News)*
1987 Charles Krauthammer (*Washington Post* Writers Group)
1988 Dave Barry *(Miami Herald)*
1989 Clarence Page *(Chicago Tribune)*
1990 Jim Murray *(Los Angeles Times)*
1991 Jim Hoagland *(Washington Post)*
1992 Anna Quindlen *(New York Times)*
1993 Liz Balmaseda *(Miami Herald)*
1994 William Raspberry *(Washington Post)*
1995 Jim Dwyer *(New York Newsday)*
1996 E. R. Shipp *(New York Daily News)*
1997 Eileen McNamara *(Boston Globe)*
1998 Mike McAlary *(New York Daily News)*
1999 Maureen Dowd *(New York Times)*

Criticism
1970 Ada Louise Huxtable *(New York Times)*
1971 Harold C. Schonberg *(New York Times)*
1972 Frank Peters, Jr. *(St. Louis Post-Dispatch)*
1973 Ronald Powers *(Chicago Sun-Times)*
1974 Emily Genauer (Newsday Syndicate)
1975 Roger Ebert *(Chicago Sun-Times)*
1976 Alan M. Kriegsman *(Washington Post)*
1977 William McPherson *(Washington Post)*
1978 Walter Kerr *(New York Times)*
1979 Paul Gapp *(Chicago Tribune)*
1980 William A. Henry, 3rd *(Boston Globe)*
1981 Jonathan Yardley *(Washington Star)*
1982 Martin Bernheimer *(Los Angeles Times)*
1983 Manuela Hoelterhoff *(Wall Street Journal)*
1984 Paul Goldberger *(New York Times)*
1985 Howard Rosenberg *(Los Angeles Times)*
1986 Donal Henahan *(New York Times)*
1987 Richard Eder *(Los Angeles Times)*
1988 Tom Shales *(Washington Post)*
1989 Michael Skube *(News and Observer* [Raleigh, N.C.])
1990 Allan Temko *(San Francisco Chronicle)*
1991 David Shaw *(Los Angeles Times)*
1993 Michael Dirda *(Washington Post)*
1994 Lloyd Schwartz *(Boston Phoenix)*
1995 Margo Jefferson *(New York Times)*
1996 Robert Campbell *(Boston Globe)*
1997 Tim Page *(Washington Post)*
1998 Michiko Kakutani *(New York Times)*
1999 Blair Kamin *(Chicago Tribune)*

Explanatory Journalism
1985 Jon Franklin *(Baltimore Evening Sun)*
1986 *New York Times*
1987 Jeff Lyon and Peter Gorner *(Chicago Tribune)*
1988 Daniel Hertzberg and James B. Stewart *(Wall Street Journal)*
1989 David Hanners, William Snyder, and Karen Blessen *(Dallas Morning News)*
1990 David A. Vise and Coll *(Washington Post)*
1991 Susan C. Faludi *(Wall Street Journal)*
1992 Robert S. Capers and Eric Lipton *(Hartford Courant)*
1993 Mike Toner *(Atlanta Journal–Constitution)*
1994 Ronald Kotulak *(Chicago Tribune)*
1995 Leon Dash and Lucian Perkins *(Washington Post)*
1996 Laurie Garrett *(Newsday* [Long Island, N.Y.])
1997 Michael Vitez, Ron Cortes, and April Saul *(Philadelphia Inquirer)*
1998 Paul Salopek *(Chicago Tribune)*
1999 Richard Read *(Oregonian* [Portland, Ore.])

Specialized Reporting
1985 Randall Savage and Jackie Crosby *(Macon* [Ga.] *Telegraph and News)*
1986 Andrew Schneider and Mary Pat Flaherty *(Pittsburgh Press)*
1987 Alex S. Jones *(New York Times)*
1988 Walt Bogdanich *(Wall Street Journal)*
1989 Edward Humes *(Orange County Register)*
1990 Tamar Stieber *(Albuquerque* (N.M.) *Journal)*

Beat Reporting
1991 Natalie Angier *(New York Times)*
1992 Deborah Blum *(Sacramento Bee)*
1993 Paul Ingrassia and Joseph B. White *(Wall Street Journal)*

1994   Eric Freedman and Jim Mitzelfeld *(Detroit News)*
1995   David M. Shribman *(Boston Globe)*
1996   Bob Keeler *(Newsday* [Long Island, N.Y.])
1997   Byron Acohido *(Seattle Times)*
1998   Linda Greenhouse *(New York Times)*
1999   Chuck Philips and Michael A. Hiltzik *(Los Angeles Times)*

PULITZER PRIZES IN LETTERS

Fiction[1]

1918   *His Family,* Ernest Poole
1919   *The Magnificent Ambersons,* Booth Tarkington
1921   *The Age of Innocence,* Edith Wharton
1922   *Alice Adams,* Booth Tarkington
1923   *One of Ours,* Willa Cather
1924   *The Able McLaughlins,* Margaret Wilson
1925   *So Big,* Edna Ferber
1926   *Arrowsmith,* Sinclair Lewis
1927   *Early Autumn,* Louis Bromfield
1928   *The Bridge of San Luis Rey,* Thornton Wilder
1929   *Scarlet Sister Mary,* Julia Peterkin
1930   *Laughing Boy,* Oliver La Farge
1931   *Years of Grace,* Margaret Ayer Barnes
1932   *The Good Earth,* Pearl S. Buck
1933   *The Store,* T. S. Stribling
1934   *Lamb in His Bosom,* Caroline Miller
1935   *Now in November,* Josephine Winslow Johnson
1936   *Honey in the Horn,* Harold L. Davis
1937   *Gone With the Wind,* Margaret Mitchell
1938   *The Late George Apley,* John Phillips Marquand
1939   *The Yearling,* Marjorie Kinnan Rawlings
1940   *The Grapes of Wrath,* John Steinbeck
1942   *In This Our Life,* Ellen Glasgow
1943   *Dragon's Teeth,* Upton Sinclair
1944   *Journey in the Dark,* Martin Flavin
1945   *A Bell for Adano,* John Hersey
1947   *All the King's Men,* Robert Penn Warren
1948   *Tales of the South Pacific,* James A. Michener
1949   *Guard of Honor,* James Gould Cozzens
1950   *The Way West,* A. B. Guthrie, Jr.
1951   *The Town,* Conrad Richter
1952   *The Caine Mutiny,* Herman Wouk
1953   *The Old Man and the Sea,* Ernest Hemingway
1955   *A Fable,* William Faulkner
1956   *Andersonville,* MacKinlay Kantor
1958   *A Death in the Family,* James Agee
1959   *The Travels of Jaimie McPheeters,* Robert Lewis Taylor
1960   *Advise and Consent,* Allen Drury
1961   *To Kill a Mockingbird,* Harper Lee
1962   *The Edge of Sadness,* Edwin O'Connor
1963   *The Reivers,* William Faulkner
1965   *The Keepers of the House,* Shirley Ann Grau
1966   *Collected Stories of Katherine Anne Porter,* Katherine Anne Porter
1967   *The Fixer,* Bernard Malamud
1968   *The Confessions of Nat Turner,* William Styron
1969   *House Made of Dawn,* N. Scott Momaday
1970   *Collected Stories,* Jean Stafford
1972   *Angle of Repose,* Wallace Stegner
1973   *The Optimist's Daughter,* Eudora Welty
1975   *The Killer Angels,* Michael Shaara
1976   *Humboldt's Gift,* Saul Bellow
1978   *Elbow Room,* James Alan McPherson
1979   *The Stories of John Cheever,* John Cheever
1980   *The Executioner's Song,* Norman Mailer

1981   *A Confederacy of Dunces,* John Kennedy Toole
1982   *Rabbit Is Rich,* John Updike
1983   *The Color Purple,* Alice Walker
1984   *Ironweed,* William Kennedy
1985   *Foreign Affairs,* Alison Lurie
1986   *Lonesome Dove,* Larry McMurtry
1987   *A Summons to Memphis,* Peter Taylor
1988   *Beloved,* Toni Morrison
1989   *Breathing Lessons,* Anne Tyler
1990   *The Mambo Kings Play Songs of Love,* Oscar Hijeulos
1991   *Rabbit at Rest,* John Updike
1992   *A Thousand Acres,* Jane Smiley
1993   *A Good Scent From a Strange Mountain,* Robert Olen Butler
1994   *The Shipping News,* E. Annie Proulx
1995   *The Stone Diaries,* Carol Shields
1996   *Independence Day,* Richard Ford
1997   *Martin Dressler: The Tale of an American Dreamer,* Steven Millhauser
1998   *American Pastoral,* Philip Roth
1999   *The Hours,* Michael Cunningham

1. Before 1948, award was for novels only.

History of United States

1917   *With Americans of Past and Present Days,* J. J. Jusserand, Ambassador of France to United States
1918   *A History of the Civil War, 1861–1865,* James Ford Rhodes
1920   *The War With Mexico,* Justin H. Smith
1921   *The Victory at Sea,* William Sowden Sims, in collaboration with Burton J. Hendrick
1922   *The Founding of New England,* James Truslow Adams
1923   *The Supreme Court in United States History,* Charles Warren
1924   *The American Revolution—A Constitutional Interpretation,* Charles Howard McIlwain
1925   *A History of the American Frontier,* Frederic L. Paxson
1926   *The History of the United States,* Edward Channing
1927   *Pinckney's Treaty,* Samuel Flagg Bemis
1928   *Main Currents in American Thought,* Vernon Louis Parrington
1929   *The Organization and Administration of the Union Army, 1861–1865,* Fred Albert Shannon
1930   *The War of Independence,* Claude H. Van Tyne
1931   *The Coming of the War: 1914,* Bernadotte E. Schmitt
1932   *My Experiences in the World War,* John J. Pershing
1933   *The Significance of Sections in American History,* Frederick J. Turner
1934   *The People's Choice,* Herbert Agar
1935   *The Colonial Period of American History,* Charles McLean Andrews
1936   *The Constitutional History of the United States,* Andrew C. McLaughlin
1937   *The Flowering of New England,* Van Wyck Brooks
1938   *The Road to Reunion, 1865–1900,* Paul Herman Buck
1939   *A History of American Magazines,* Frank Luther Mott
1940   *Abraham Lincoln: The War Years,* Carl Sandburg

1941 *The Atlantic Migration, 1607–1860,* Marcus Lee Hansen
1942 *Reveille in Washington,* Margaret Leech
1943 *Paul Revere and the World He Lived In,* Esther Forbes
1944 *The Growth of American Thought,* Merle Curti
1945 *Unfinished Business,* Stephen Bonsal
1946 *The Age of Jackson,* Arthur M. Schlesinger, Jr.
1947 *Scientists Against Time,* James Phinney Baxter, 3rd
1948 *Across the Wide Missouri,* Bernard DeVoto
1949 *The Disruption of American Democracy,* Roy Franklin Nichols
1950 *Art and Life in America,* Oliver W. Larkin
1951 *The Old Northwest, Pioneer Period 1815–1840,* R. Carlyle Buley
1952 *The Uprooted,* Oscar Handlin
1953 *The Era of Good Feelings,* George Dangerfield
1954 *A Stillness at Appomattox,* Bruce Catton
1955 *Great River: The Rio Grande in North American History,* Paul Horgan
1956 *The Age of Reform,* Richard Hofstadter
1957 *Russia Leaves the War: Soviet–American Relations, 1917–1920,* George F. Kennan
1958 *Banks and Politics in America: From the Revolution to the Civil War,* Bray Hammond
1959 *The Republican Era: 1869–1901,* Leonard D. White, assisted by Jean Schneider
1960 *In the Days of McKinley,* Margaret Leech
1961 *Between War and Peace: The Potsdam Conference,* Herbert Feis
1962 *The Triumphant Empire: Thunder-Clouds Gather in the West,* Lawrence H. Gipson
1963 *Washington, Village and Capital, 1800–1878,* Constance McLaughlin Green
1964 *Puritan Village: The Formation of a New England Town,* Sumner Chilton Powell
1965 *The Greenback Era,* Irwin Unger
1966 *Life of the Mind in America,* Perry Miller
1967 *Exploration and Empire: The Explorer and Scientist in the Winning of the American West,* William H. Goetzmann
1968 *The Ideological Origins of the American Revolution,* Bernard Bailyn
1969 *Origins of the Fifth Amendment,* Leonard W. Levy
1970 *Present at the Creation: My Years in the State Department,* Dean Acheson
1971 *Roosevelt: The Soldier of Freedom,* James McGregor Burns
1972 *Neither Black Nor White: Slavery and Race Relations in Brazil and the United States,* Carl N. Degler
1973 *People of Paradox: An Inquiry Concerning the Origin of American Civilization,* Michael Kammen
1974 *The Americans: The Democratic Experience, Vol. 3,* Daniel J. Boorstin
1975 *Jefferson and His Time,* Dumas Malone
1976 *Lamy of Santa Fe,* Paul Horgan
1977 *The Impending Crisis: 1841–1861,* David M. Potter
1978 *The Invisible Hand: The Managerial Revolution in American Business,* Alfred D. Chandler, Jr.
1979 *The Dred Scott Case: Its Significance in Law and Politics,* Don E. Fehrenbacher
1980 *Been in the Storm So Long,* Leon F. Litwack

1981 *American Education: The National Experience; 1783–1876,* Lawrence A. Cremin
1982 *Mary Chesnut's Civil War,* C. Vann Woodward, editor
1983 *The Transformation of Virginia, 1740–1790,* Rhys L. Isaac
1985 *The Prophets of Regulation,* Thomas K. McCraw
1986 *The Heavens and the Earth: A Political History of the Space Age,* Walter A. McDougall
1987 *Voyagers to the West: A Passage in the Peopling of America on the Eve of the Revolution,* Bernard Bailyn
1988 *The Launching of Modern American Science 1846–1876,* Robert V. Bruce
1989 *Parting the Waters,* Taylor Branch; *Battle Cry of Freedom,* James M. McPherson
1990 *In Our Image: America's Empire in the Philippines,* Stanley Karnow
1991 *A Midwife's Tale: The Life of Martha Ballard, Based on Her Diary 1785–1812,* Laurel Thatcher Ulrich
1992 *The Fate of Liberty: Abraham Lincoln and Civil Liberties,* Mark E. Neely, Jr.
1993 *The Radicalism of the American Revolution,* Gordon S. Wood
1995 *No Ordinary Time: Franklin and Eleanor Roosevelt: The Home Front in World War II,* Doris Kearns Goodwin
1996 *William Cooper's Town: Power and Persuasion on the Frontier of the Early American Republic,* Alan Taylor
1997 *Original Meanings: Politics and Ideas in the Making of the Constitution,* Jack N. Rakove
1998 *Summer for the Gods: The Scopes Trial and America's Continuing Debate Over Science and Religion,* Edward J. Larson
1999 *Gotham: A History of New York City to 1898,* Edwin G. Burrows and Mike Wallace

Biography or Autobiography

1917 *Julia Ward Howe,* Laura E. Richards and Maude Howe Elliott, assisted by Florence Howe Hall
1918 *Benjamin Franklin, Self-Revealed,* William Cabell Bruce
1919 *The Education of Henry Adams,* Henry Adams
1920 *The Life of John Marshall,* Albert J. Beveridge
1921 *The Americanization of Edward Bok,* Edward Bok
1922 *A Daughter of the Middle Border,* Hamlin Garland
1923 *The Life and Letters of Walter H. Page,* Burton J. Hendrick
1924 *From Immigrant to Inventor,* Michael Idvorsky Pupin
1925 *Barrett Wendell and His Letters,* M. A. DeWolfe Howe
1926 *The Life of Sir William Osler,* Harvey Cushing
1927 *Whitman,* Emory Holloway
1928 *The American Orchestra and Theodore Thomas,* Charles Edward Russell
1929 *The Training of an American: The Earlier Life and Letters of Walter H. Page,* Burton J. Hendrick
1930 *The Raven,* Marquis James
1931 *Charles W. Eliot,* Henry James
1932 *Theodore Roosevelt,* Henry F. Pringle
1933 *Grover Cleveland,* Allan Nevins

1934	John Hay, Tyler Dennett
1935	R. E. Lee, Douglas S. Freeman
1936	The Thought and Character of William James, Ralph Barton Perry
1937	Hamilton Fish, Allan Nevins
1938	Pedlar's Progress, Odell Shepard; Andrew Jackson, Marquis James
1939	Benjamin Franklin, Carl Van Doren
1940	Woodrow Wilson: Life and Letters, Vols. VII and VIII, Ray Stannard Baker
1941	Jonathan Edwards, Ola E. Winslow
1942	Crusader in Crinoline, Forrest Wilson
1943	Admiral of the Ocean Sea, Samuel Eliot Morison
1944	The American Leonardo: The Life of Samuel F. B. Morse, Carleton Mabee
1945	George Bancroft: Brahmin Rebel, Russel Blaine Nye
1946	Son of the Wilderness, Linnie Marsh Wolfe
1947	The Autobiography of William Allen White
1948	Forgotten First Citizen: John Bigelow, Margaret Clapp
1949	Roosevelt and Hopkins, Robert E. Sherwood
1950	John Quincy Adams and the Foundations of American Foreign Policy, Samuel Flagg Bemis
1951	John C. Calhoun: American Portrait, Margaret Louise Coit
1952	Charles Evans Hughes, Merlo J. Pusey
1953	Edmund Pendleton, 1721–1803, David J. Mays
1954	The Spirit of St. Louis, Charles A. Lindbergh
1955	The Taft Story, William S. White
1956	Benjamin Henry Latrobe, Talbot F. Hamlin
1957	Profiles in Courage, John F. Kennedy
1958	George Washington, Douglas Southall Freeman (Vols. 1–6) and John Alexander Carroll and Mary Wells Ashworth (Vol. 7)
1959	Woodrow Wilson, American Prophet, Arthur Walworth
1960	John Paul Jones, Samuel Eliot Morison
1961	Charles Sumner and the Coming of the Civil War, David Donald
1963	Henry James: Vol. II, The Conquest of London, 1870–1881; Vol. III, The Middle Years, 1881–1895, Leon Edel
1964	John Keats, Walter Jackson Bate
1965	Henry Adams (3 Vols.), Ernest Samuels
1966	A Thousand Days, Arthur M. Schlesinger, Jr.
1967	Mr. Clemens and Mark Twain, Justin Kaplan
1968	Memoirs, 1925–1950, George F. Kennan
1969	The Man From New York, B. L. Reid
1970	Huey Long, T. Harry Williams
1971	Robert Frost: The Years of Triumph, 1915–1938, Lawrence Thompson
1972	Eleanor and Franklin: The Story of Their Relationship Based on Eleanor Roosevelt's Private Papers, Joseph P. Lash
1973	Luce and His Empire, W. A. Swanberg
1974	O'Neill, Son and Artist, Louis Sheaffer
1975	The Power Broker: Robert Moses and the Fall of New York, Robert A. Caro
1976	Edith Wharton: A Biography, Richard W. B. Lewis
1977	A Prince of Our Disorder, John E. Mack
1978	Samuel Johnson, Walter Jackson Bate
1979	Days of Sorrow and Pain: Leo Baeck and the Berlin Jews, Leonard Baker
1980	The Rise of Theodore Roosevelt, Edmund Morris

1981	Peter the Great, Robert K. Massie
1982	Grant: A Biography, William S. McFeely
1983	Growing Up, Russell Baker
1984	Booker T. Washington, Louis R. Harlan
1985	The Life and Times of Cotton Mather, Kenneth Silverman
1986	Louise Bogan: A Portrait, Elizabeth Frank
1987	Bearing the Cross: Martin Luther King, Jr., and the Southern Christian Leadership Conference, David J. Garrow
1988	Look Homeward: A Life of Thomas Wolfe, David Herbert Donald
1989	Oscar Wilde, Richard Ellmann
1990	Machiavelli in Hell, Sebastian de Grazia
1991	Jackson Pollock: An American Saga, Steven Naifeh and Gregory White Smith
1992	Fortunate Son: The Healing of a Vietnam Vet, Lewis B. Puller, Jr.
1993	Truman, David McCullough
1994	W. E. B. DuBois: Biography of a Race, 1868–1919, David Levering Lewis
1995	Harriet Beecher Stowe: A Life, Joan D. Hedrick
1996	God: A Biography, Jack Miles
1997	Angela's Ashes: A Memoir, Frank McCourt
1998	Personal History, Katharine Graham
1999	Lindbergh, A. Scott Berg

Poetry[1]

1918	Love Songs, Sara Teasdale
1919	Old Road to Paradise, Margaret Widdemer; Corn Huskers, Carl Sandburg
1922	Collected Poems, Edwin Arlington Robinson
1923	The Ballad of the Harp-Weaver; A Few Figs from Thistles; eight sonnets in American Poetry, 1922, A Miscellany, Edna St. Vincent Millay
1924	New Hampshire: A Poem With Notes and Grace Notes, Robert Frost
1925	The Man Who Died Twice, Edwin Arlington Robinson
1926	What's O'Clock, Amy Lowell
1927	Fiddler's Farewell, Leonora Speyer
1928	Tristram, Edwin Arlington Robinson
1929	John Brown's Body, Stephen Vincent Benét
1930	Selected Poems, Conrad Aiken
1931	Collected Poems, Robert Frost
1932	The Flowering Stone, George Dillon
1933	Conquistador, Archibald MacLeish
1934	Collected Verse, Robert Hillyer
1935	Bright Ambush, Audrey Wurdemann
1936	Strange Holiness, Robert P. T. Coffin
1937	A Further Range, Robert Frost
1938	Cold Morning Sky, Marya Zaturenska
1939	Selected Poems, John Gould Fletcher
1940	Collected Poems, Mark Van Doren
1941	Sunderland Capture, Leonard Bacon
1942	The Dust Which Is God, William Rose Benét
1943	A Witness Tree, Robert Frost
1944	Western Star, Stephen Vincent Benét
1945	V-Letter and Other Poems, Karl Shapiro
1947	Lord Weary's Castle, Robert Lowell
1948	The Age of Anxiety, W. H. Auden
1949	Terror and Decorum, Peter Viereck
1950	Annie Allen, Gwendolyn Brooks
1951	Complete Poems, Carl Sandburg
1952	Collected Poems, Marianne Moore
1953	Collected Poems, 1917–1952, Archibald MacLeish
1954	The Waking, Theodore Roethke
1955	Collected Poems, Wallace Stevens

1956 *Poems—North & South*, Elizabeth Bishop
1957 *Things of This World*, Richard Wilbur
1958 *Promises: Poems, 1954–1956*, Robert Penn Warren
1959 *Selected Poems, 1928–1958*, Stanley Kunitz
1960 *Heart's Needle*, William Snodgrass
1961 *Times Three: Selected Verse From Three Decades*, Phyllis McGinley
1962 *Poems*, Alan Dugan
1963 *Pictures From Breughel*, William Carlos Williams
1964 *At the End of the Open Road*, Louis Simpson
1965 *77 Dream Songs*, John Berryman
1966 *Selected Poems*, Richard Eberhart
1967 *Live or Die*, Anne Sexton
1968 *The Hard Hours*, Anthony Hecht
1969 *Of Being Numerous*, George Oppen
1970 *Untitled Subjects*, Richard Howard
1971 *The Carrier of Ladders*, William S. Merwin
1972 *Collected Poems*, James Wright
1973 *Up Country*, Maxine Winokur Kumin
1974 *The Dolphin*, Robert Lowell
1975 *Turtle Island*, Gary Snyder
1976 *Self-Portrait in a Convex Mirror*, John Ashbery
1977 *Divine Comedies*, James Merrill
1978 *Collected Poems*, Howard Nemerov
1979 *Now and Then: Poems, 1976–1978*, Robert Penn Warren
1980 *Selected Poems*, Donald Rodney Justice
1981 *The Morning of the Poem*, James Schuyler
1982 *The Collected Poems*, Sylvia Plath
1983 *Selected Poems*, Galway Kinnell
1984 *American Primitive*, Mary Oliver
1985 *Yin*, Carolyn Kizer
1986 *The Flying Change*, Henry Taylor
1987 *Thomas and Beulah*, Rita Dove
1988 *Partial Accounts: New and Selected Poems*, William Meredith
1989 *New and Collected Poems*, Richard Wilbur
1990 *The World Doesn't End*, Charles Simic
1991 *Near Changes*, Mona Van Duyn
1992 *Selected Poems*, James Tate
1993 *The Wild Iris*, Louise Gluck
1994 *Neon Vernacular*, Yusef Komunyakaa
1995 *Simple Truth*, Philip Levine
1996 *The Dream of the Unified Field*, Jorie Graham
1997 *Alive Together: New and Selected Poems*, Lisel Mueller
1998 *Black Zodiac*, Charles Wright
1999 *Blizzard of One*, Mark Strand

1. The poetry prize was established in 1922. The 1918 and 1919 awards were made from gifts provided by the Poetry Society.

General Nonfiction

1962 *The Making of the President, 1960*, Theodore H. White
1963 *The Guns of August*, Barbara W. Tuchman
1964 *Anti-Intellectualism in American Life*, Richard Hofstadter
1965 *O Strange New World*, Howard Mumford Jones
1966 *Wandering Through Winter*, Edwin Way Teale
1967 *The Problem of Slavery in Western Culture*, David Brion Davis
1968 *Rousseau and Revolution*, Will and Ariel Durant
1969 *So Human an Animal*, Rene Jules Dubos; *The Armies of the Night*, Norman Mailer
1970 *Gandhi's Truth*, Erik H. Erikson

1971 *The Rising Sun*, John Toland
1972 *Stilwell and the American Experience in China, 1911–1945*, Barbara W. Tuchman
1973 *Fire in the Lake: The Vietnamese and the Americans in Vietnam*, Frances FitzGerald; *Children of Crisis* (Vols. 1 and 2), Robert M. Coles
1974 *The Denial of Death*, Ernest Becker
1975 *Pilgrim at Tinker Creek*, Annie Dillard
1976 *Why Survive? Being Old in America*, Robert N. Butler
1977 *Beautiful Swimmers: Watermen, Crabs and the Chesapeake Bay*, William W. Warner
1978 *The Dragons of Eden*, Carl Sagan
1979 *On Human Nature*, Edward O. Wilson
1980 *Gödel, Escher, Bach: An Eternal Golden Braid*, Douglas R. Hofstadter
1981 *Fin-de-Siecle Vienna: Politics and Culture*, Carl E. Schorske
1982 *The Soul of a New Machine*, Tracy Kidder
1983 *Is There No Place on Earth for Me?*, Susan Sheehan
1984 *Social Transformation of American Medicine*, Paul Starr
1985 *The Good War: An Oral History of World War II*, Studs Terkel
1986 *Move Your Shadow: South Africa, Black and White*, Joseph Lelyveld; *Common Ground: A Turbulent Decade in the Lives of Three American Families*, J. Anthony Lukas
1987 *Arab and Jew: Wounded Spirits in a Promised Land*, David K. Shipler
1988 *The Making of the Atomic Bomb*, Richard Rhodes
1989 *A Bright Shining Lie*, Neil Sheehan
1990 *And Their Children After Them*, Dale Maharidge and Michael Williamson
1991 *The Ants*, Bert Holldobler and Edward O. Wilson
1992 *The Prize: The Epic Quest for Oil, Money and Power*, Daniel Yergin
1993 *Lincoln at Gettysburg: The Words That Remade America*, Garry Wills
1994 *Lenin's Tomb: The Last Days of the Soviet Empire*, David Remick
1995 *The Beak of the Finch: A Story of Evolution in Our Time*, Jonathan Weiner
1996 *The Haunted Land: Facing Europe's Ghosts After Communism*, Tina Rosenberg
1997 *Ashes to Ashes: America's Hundred-Year Cigarette War, the Public Health, and the Unabashed Triumph of Philip Morris*, Richard Kluger
1998 *Guns, Germs, and Steel: The Fates of Human Societies*, Jared Diamond
1999 *Annals of the Former World*, John McPhee

PULITZER PRIZES IN MUSIC

1943 *Secular Cantata No. 2, A Free Song*, William Schuman
1944 *Symphony No. 4 (Op. 34)*, Howard Hanson
1945 *Appalachian Spring*, Aaron Copland
1946 *The Canticle of the Sun*, Leo Sowerby
1947 *Symphony No. 3*, Charles Ives
1948 *Symphony No. 3*, Walter Piston
1949 *Louisiana Story* music, Virgil Thomson
1950 *The Consul*, Gian Carlo Menotti
1951 Music for opera *Giants in the Earth*, Douglas Stuart Moore
1952 *Symphony Concertante*, Gail Kubik

1954	*Concerto for Two Pianos and Orchestra,* Quincy Porter
1955	*The Saint of Bleecker Street,* Gian Carlo Menotti
1956	*Symphony No. 3,* Ernst Toch
1957	*Meditations on Ecclesiastes,* Norman Dello Joio
1958	*Vanessa,* Samuel Barber
1959	*Concerto for Piano and Orchestra,* John La Montaine
1960	*Second String Quartet,* Elliott Carter
1961	*Symphony No. 7,* Walter Piston
1962	*The Crucible,* Robert Ward
1963	*Piano Concerto No. 1,* Samuel Barber
1966	*Variations for Orchestra,* Leslie Bassett
1967	*Quartet No. 3,* Leon Kirchner
1968	*Echoes of Time and the River,* George Crumb
1969	*String Quartet No. 3,* Karel Husa
1970	*Time's Encomium,* Charles Wuorinen
1971	*Synchronisms No. 6 for Piano and Electronic Sound,* Mario Davidowsky
1972	*Windows,* Jacob Druckman
1973	*String Quartet No. 3,* Elliott Carter
1974	*Notturno,* Donald Martino
1975	*From the Diary of Virginia Woolf,* Dominick Argento
1976	*Air Music,* Ned Rorem
1977	*Visions of Terror and Wonder,* Richard Wernick
1978	*Déjà Vu for Percussion Quartet and Orchestra,* Michael Colgrass
1979	*Aftertones of Infinity,* Joseph Schwantner
1980	*In Memory of a Summer Day,* David Del Tredici
1982	*Concerto for Orchestra,* Roger Sessions
1983	*Three Movements for Orchestra,* Ellen T. Zwilich
1984	*Canti del Sole,* Bernard Rands
1985	*Symphony RiverRun,* Stephen Albert
1986	*Wind Quintet IV,* George Perle
1987	*The Flight Into Egypt,* John Harbison
1988	*12 New Etudes for Piano,* William Bolcom
1989	*Whispers Out of Time,* Roger Reynolds
1990	*Duplicates: A Concerto for Two Pianos and Orchestra,* Mel Powell
1991	*Symphony,* Shulamit Ran
1992	*The Face of the Night, The Heart of the Dark,* Wayne Peterson
1993	*Trombone Concerto,* Christopher Rouse
1994	*Of Reminiscences and Reflections,* Gunther Schuller
1995	*Stringmusic,* Morton Gould
1996	*Lilacs,* George Walker
1997	*Blood on the Field,* Wynton Marsalis
1998	*String Quartet No. 2, Musica Instrumentalis,* Aaron Jay Kernis
1999	*Concerto for Flute, Strings and Percussion,* Melinda Wagner

PULITZER PRIZES IN DRAMA

1918	*Why Marry?,* Jesse Lynch Williams
1920	*Beyond the Horizon,* Eugene O'Neill
1921	*Miss Lulu Bett,* Zona Gale
1922	*Anna Christie,* Eugene O'Neill
1923	*Icebound,* Owen Davis
1924	*Hell-Bent Fer Heaven,* Hatcher Hughes
1925	*They Knew What They Wanted,* Sidney Howard
1926	*Craig's Wife,* George Kelly
1927	*In Abraham's Bosom,* Paul Green

1928	*Strange Interlude,* Eugene O'Neill
1929	*Street Scene,* Elmer L. Rice
1930	*The Green Pastures,* Marc Connelly
1931	*Alison's House,* Susan Glaspell
1932	*Of Thee I Sing,* George S. Kaufman, Morrie Ryskind, and Ira Gershwin
1933	*Both Your Houses,* Maxwell Anderson
1934	*Men in White,* Sidney Kingsley
1935	*The Old Maid,* Zöe Akins
1936	*Idiot's Delight,* Robert E. Sherwood
1937	*You Can't Take It With You,* Moss Hart and George S. Kaufman
1938	*Our Town,* Thornton Wilder
1939	*Abe Lincoln in Illinois,* Robert E. Sherwood
1940	*The Time of Your Life,* William Saroyan
1941	*There Shall Be No Night,* Robert E. Sherwood
1943	*The Skin of Our Teeth,* Thornton Wilder
1945	*Harvey,* Mary Chase
1946	*State of the Union,* Russel Crouse and Howard Lindsay
1948	*A Streetcar Named Desire,* Tennessee Williams
1949	*Death of a Salesman,* Arthur Miller
1950	*South Pacific,* Richard Rodgers, Oscar Hammerstein II, and Joshua Logan
1952	*The Shrike,* Joseph Kramm
1953	*Picnic,* William Inge
1954	*The Teahouse of the August Moon,* John Patrick
1955	*Cat on a Hot Tin Roof,* Tennessee Williams
1956	*The Diary of Anne Frank,* Frances Goodrich and Albert Hackett
1957	*Long Day's Journey Into Night,* Eugene O'Neill
1958	*Look Homeward, Angel,* Ketti Frings
1959	*J. B.* Archibald MacLeish
1960	*Fiorello!* George Abbott, Jerome Weidman, Jerry Bock, and Sheldon Harnick
1961	*All the Way Home,* Tad Mosel
1962	*How to Succeed in Business Without Really Trying,* Frank Loesser and Abe Burrows
1965	*The Subject Was Roses,* Frank D. Gilroy
1967	*A Delicate Balance,* Edward Albee
1969	*The Great White Hope,* Howard Sackler
1970	*No Place to Be Somebody,* Charles Gordone
1971	*The Effect of Gamma Rays on Man-in-the-Moon Marigolds,* Paul Zindel
1973	*That Championship Season,* Jason Miller
1975	*Seascape,* Edward Albee
1976	*A Chorus Line,* Conceived by Michael Bennett
1977	*The Shadow Box,* Michael Cristofer
1978	*The Gin Game,* Donald L. Coburn
1979	*Buried Child,* Sam Shepard
1980	*Talley's Folly,* Lanford Wilson
1981	*Crimes of the Heart,* Beth Henley
1982	*A Soldier's Play,* Charles Fuller
1983	*'Night, Mother,* Marsha Norman
1984	*Glengarry Glen Ross,* David Mamet
1985	*Sunday in the Park with George,* Stephen Sondheim and James Lapine
1987	*Fences,* August Wilson
1988	*Driving Miss Daisy,* Alfred Uhry
1989	*The Heidi Chronicles,* Wendy Wasserstein
1990	*The Piano Lesson,* August Wilson
1991	*Lost in Yonkers,* Neil Simon
1992	*The Kentucky Cycle,* Robert Schenkkan
1993	*Angels in America: Millennium Approaches,* Tony Kushner
1994	*Three Tall Women,* Edward Albee
1995	*The Young Man from Atlanta,* Horton Foote
1996	*Rent,* Jonathan Larson

1998 *How I Learned to Drive,* Paula Vogel
1999 *Wit,* Margaret Edson

SPECIAL CITATIONS

1938 *Edmonton* [Alberta] *Journal,* special bronze plaque for editorial leadership in defense of freedom of the press in province of Alberta
1941 *New York Times,* for the public educational value of its foreign news report
1944 Byron Price, director of the Office of Censorship, for the creation and administration of the newspaper and radio codes; Mrs. William Allen White, for her husband's interest and services during the past seven years as a member of the Advisory Board of the Graduate School of Journalism, Columbia University; Richard Rodgers and Oscar Hammerstein II, for their musical *Oklahoma!*
1945 The cartographers of the American press, for their war maps
1947 (Pulitzer centennial year.) Columbia University and the Graduate School of Journalism, for their efforts to maintain and advance the high standards governing the Pulitzer Prize awards; the *St. Louis Post-Dispatch,* for its unswerving adherence to the public and professional ideals of its founder and its leadership in American journalism
1948 Dr. Frank D. Fackenthal, for his interest and service
1951 Cyrus L. Sulzberger *(New York Times),* for his exclusive interview with Archbishop Stepinac in a Yugoslav prison
1952 *Kansas City Star,* for coverage of 1951 floods; Max Kase *(New York Journal–American),* for exposures of bribery in basketball
1953 *New York Times,* for its 17-year publication of "Review of the Week," and Lester Markel, its founder

1957 Kenneth Roberts, for his historical novels
1958 Walter Lippmann *(New York Herald Tribune),* for his "wisdom, perception and high sense of responsibility" in his commentary on national and international affairs
1960 Garrett Mattingly, for *The Armada*
1961 *American Heritage Picture History of the Civil War,* as a distinguished example of American book publishing
1964 Gannett Newspapers, Rochester, N.Y.
1973 James Thomas Flexner, for his biography *George Washington*
1974 Roger Sessions, for his "life's work in music"
1976 John Hohenberg, for "services for 22 years as Administrator of the Pulitzer Prizes"; Scott Joplin, for his contributions to American music
1977 Alex Haley, for his novel, *Roots*
1978 E. B. White of *New Yorker* magazine and Richard L. Strout of *The Christian Science Monitor*
1982 Milton Babbitt, "for his life's work as a distinguished and seminal American composer"
1984 Theodor Seuss Geisel (Dr. Seuss), for "books full of playful rhymes, nonsense words and strange illustrations"
1985 William Schuman, for "more than half a century of contribution to American music as a composer and educational leader"
1987 Joseph Pulitzer Jr., "for extraordinary services to American journalism and letters during his 31 years as chairman of the Pulitzer Prize Board and for his accomplishments as an editor and publisher"
1992 *Maus,* Art Spiegelman
1996 Herb Caen *(San Francisco Chronicle),* "for his extraordinary and continuing contribution as a voice and conscience of his city"
1998 George Gershwin
1999 Edward Kennedy "Duke" Ellington, who "made an indelible contribution to art and culture"

Academy Awards (Oscars)

1928

Picture: *Wings,* Paramount
Director: Frank Borzage, *Seventh Heaven;* Lewis Milestone, *Two Arabian Nights*
Actress: Janet Gaynor, *Seventh Heaven, Street Angel, Sunrise*
Actor: Emil Jannings, *The Way of All Flesh, The Last Command*

1929

Picture: *The Broadway Melody,* MGM
Director: Frank Lloyd, *The Divine Lady*
Actress: Mary Pickford, *Coquette*
Actor: Warner Baxter, *In Old Arizona*

1930

Picture: *All Quiet on the Western Front,* Universal
Director: Lewis Milestone, *All Quiet on the Western Front*
Actress: Norma Shearer, *The Divorcee*
Actor: George Arliss, *Disraeli*

1931

Picture: *Cimarron,* RKO Radio
Director: Norman Taurog, *Skippy*
Actress: Marie Dressler, *Min and Bill*
Actor: Lionel Barrymore, *A Free Soul*

1932

Picture: *Grand Hotel,* MGM
Director: Frank Borzage, *Bad Girl*
Actress: Helen Hayes, *The Sin of Madelon Claudet*
Actor: Fredric March, *Dr. Jekyll and Mr, Hyde,* and Wallace Beery, *The Champ*

1933

Picture: *Cavalcade,* Fox
Director: Frank Lloyd, *Cavalcade*
Actress: Katharine Hepburn, *Morning Glory*
Actor: Charles Laughton, *The Private Life of Henry VIII*

1934

Picture: *It Happened One Night,* Columbia
Director: Frank Capra, *It Happened One Night*
Actress: Claudette Colbert, *It Happened One Night*
Actor: Clark Gable, *It Happened One Night*

1935

Picture: *Mutiny on the Bounty,* MGM
Director: John Ford, *The Informer*
Actress: Bette Davis, *Dangerous*
Actor: Victor McLaglen, *The Informer*

1936

Picture: *The Great Ziegfeld,* MGM
Director: Frank Capra, *Mr. Deeds Goes to Town*
Actress: Luise Rainer, *The Great Ziegfeld*
Actor: Paul Muni, *The Story of Louis Pasteur*
Supporting Actress: Gale Sondergaard, *Anthony Adverse*
Supporting Actor: Walter Brennan, *Come and Get It*

1937

Picture: *The Life of Emile Zola,* Warner Bros.
Director: Leo McCarey, *The Awful Truth*
Actress: Luise Rainer, *The Good Earth*
Actor: Spencer Tracy, *Captains Courageous*
Supporting Actress: Alice Brady, *In Old Chicago*
Supporting Actor: Joseph Schildkraut, *The Life of Emile Zola*

1938

Picture: *You Can't Take It with You,* Columbia
Director: Frank Capra, *You Can't Take It with You*
Actress: Bette Davis, *Jezebel*
Actor: Spencer Tracy, *Boys Town*
Supporting Actress: Fay Bainter, *Jezebel*
Supporting Actor: Walter Brennan, *Kentucky*

1939

Picture: *Gone with the Wind,* Selznick MGM
Director: Victor Fleming, *Gone with the Wind*
Actress: Vivien Leigh, *Gone with the Wind*
Actor: Robert Donat, *Goodbye, Mr. Chips*
Supporting Actress: Hattie McDaniel, *Gone with the Wind*
Supporting Actor: Thomas Mitchell, *Stagecoach*

1940

Picture: *Rebecca,* Selznick-United Artists
Director: John Ford, *The Grapes of Wrath*
Actress: Ginger Rogers, *Kitty Foyle*
Actor: James Stewart, *The Philadelphia Story*
Supporting Actress: Jane Darwell, *The Grapes of Wrath*
Supporting Actor: Walter Brennan, *The Westerner*

1941

Picture: *How Green Was My Valley,* 20th Century-Fox
Director: John Ford, *How Green Was My Valley*
Actress: Joan Fontaine, *Suspicion*
Actor: Gary Cooper, *Sergeant York*
Supporting Actress: Mary Astor, *The Great Lie*
Supporting Actor: Donald Crisp, *How Green Was My Valley*

1942

Picture: *Mrs. Miniver,* MGM
Director: William Wyler, *Mrs. Miniver*
Actress: Greer Garson, *Mrs. Miniver*
Actor: James Cagney, *Yankee Doodle Dandy*
Supporting Actress: Teresa Wright, *Mrs. Miniver*
Supporting Actor: Van Heflin, *Johnny Eager*

1943

Picture: *Casablanca,* Warner Bros.
Director: Michael Curtiz, *Casablanca*
Actress: Jennifer Jones, *The Song of Bernadette*
Actor: Paul Lukas, *Watch on the Rhine*
Supporting Actress: Katina Paxinou, *For Whom the Bell Tolls*
Supporting Actor: Charles Coburn, *The More the Merrier*

1944

Picture: *Going My Way,* Paramount
Director: Leo McCarey, *Going My Way*
Actress: Ingrid Bergman, *Gaslight*
Actor: Bing Crosby, *Going My Way*
Supporting Actress: Ethel Barrymore, *None But the Lonely Heart*
Supporting Actor: Barry Fitzgerald, *Going My Way*

1945

Picture: *The Lost Weekend,* Paramount
Director: Billy Wilder, *The Lost Weekend*
Actress: Joan Crawford, *Mildred Pierce*
Actor: Ray Milland, *The Lost Weekend*
Supporting Actress: Anne Revere, *National Velvet*
Supporting Actor: James Dunn, *A Tree Grows in Brooklyn*

1946

Picture: *The Best Years of Our Lives,* Goldwyn-RKO Radio
Director: William Wyler, *The Best Years of Our Lives*
Actress: Olivia de Havilland, *To Each His Own*
Actor: Fredric March, *The Best Years of Our Lives*
Supporting Actress: Anne Baxter, *The Razor's Edge*
Supporting Actor: Harold Russell, *The Best Years of Our Lives*

1947

Picture: *Gentleman's Agreement,* 20th Century-Fox
Director: Elia Kazan, *Gentleman's Agreement*
Actress: Loretta Young, *The Farmer's Daughter*
Actor: Ronald Colman, *A Double Life*
Supporting Actress: Celeste Holm, *Gentleman's Agreement*
Supporting Actor: Edmund Gwenn, *Miracle on 34th Street*

1948

Picture: *Hamlet,* Rank-Two Cities-UI
Director: John Huston, *Treasure of Sierra Madre*
Actress: Jane Wyman, *Johnny Belinda*
Actor: Laurence Olivier, *Hamlet*
Supporting Actress: Claire Trevor, *Key Largo*
Supporting Actor: Walter Huston, *Treasure of Sierra Madre*

1949

Picture: *All the King's Men,* Rossen-Columbia
Director: Joseph L. Mankiewicz, *A Letter to Three Wives*
Actress: Olivia de Havilland, *The Heiress*
Actor: Broderick Crawford, *All the King's Men*
Supporting Actress: Mercedes McCambridge, *All the King's Men*
Supporting Actor: Dean Jagger, *Twelve O'Clock High*

1950

Picture: *All About Eve,* 20th Century-Fox
Director: Joseph L. Mankiewicz, *All About Eve*
Actress: Judy Holliday, *Born Yesterday*
Actor: José Ferrer, *Cyrano de Bergerac*
Supporting Actress: Josephine Hull, *Harvey*
Supporting Actor: George Sanders, *All About Eve*

1951

Picture: *An American in Paris,* MGM
Director: George Stevens, *A Place in the Sun*
Actress: Vivien Leigh, *A Streetcar Named Desire*
Actor: Humphrey Bogart, *The African Queen*
Supporting Actress: Kim Hunter, *A Streetcar Named Desire*
Supporting Actor: Karl Malden, *A Streetcar Named Desire*

1952

Picture: *The Greatest Show on Earth,* DeMille-Paramount
Director: John Ford, *The Quiet Man*
Actress: Shirley Booth, *Come Back, Little Sheba*
Actor: Gary Cooper, *High Noon*
Supporting Actress: Gloria Grahame, *The Bad and the Beautiful*
Supporting Actor: Anthony Quinn, *Viva Zapata!*

1953

Picture: *From Here to Eternity,* Columbia
Director: Fred Zinnemann, *From Here to Eternity*
Actress: Audrey Hepburn, *Roman Holiday*
Actor: William Holden, *Stalag 17*
Supporting Actress: Donna Reed, *From Here to Eternity*
Supporting Actor: Frank Sinatra, *From Here to Eternity*

1954

Picture: *On the Waterfront,* Horizon-American Corp., Columbia
Director: Elia Kazan, *On the Waterfront*
Actress: Grace Kelly, *The Country Girl*
Actor: Marlon Brando, *On the Waterfront*
Supporting Actress: Eva Marie Saint, *On the Waterfront*
Supporting Actor: Edmond O'Brien, *The Barefoot Contessa*

1955

Picture: *Marty,* Hecht and Lancaster, United Artists
Director: Delbert Mann, *Marty*
Actress: Anna Magnani, *The Rose Tattoo*
Actor: Ernest Borgnine, *Marty*
Supporting Actress: Jo Van Fleet, *East of Eden*
Supporting Actor: Jack Lemmon, *Mister Roberts*

1956

Picture: *Around the World in 80 Days,* Michael Todd Co., Inc.-United Artists
Director: George Stevens, *Giant*
Actress: Ingrid Bergman, *Anastasia*
Actor: Yul Brynner, *The King and I*
Supporting Actress: Dorothy Malone, *Written on the Wind*
Supporting Actor: Anthony Quinn, *Lust for Life*

1957

Picture: *The Bridge on the River Kwai,* Horizon Films, Columbia
Director: David Lean, *The Bridge on the River Kwai*
Actress: Joanne Woodward, *The Three Faces of Eve*
Actor: Alec Guinness, *The Bridge on the River Kwai*
Supporting Actress: Miyoshi Umeki, *Sayonara*
Supporting Actor: Red Buttons, *Sayonara*

1958

Picture: *Gigi,* Arthur Freed Productions, Inc., MGM
Director: Vincente Minnelli, *Gigi*
Actress: Susan Hayward, *I Want to Live!*
Actor: David Niven, *Separate Tables*
Supporting Actress: Wendy Hiller, *Separate Tables*
Supporting Actor: Burl Ives, *The Big Country*

1959

Picture: *Ben-Hur,* MGM
Director: William Wyler, *Ben-Hur*
Actress: Simone Signoret, *Room at the Top*
Actor: Charlton Heston, *Ben-Hur*
Supporting Actress: Shelley Winters, *The Diary of Anne Frank*
Supporting Actor: Hugh Griffith, *Ben-Hur*

1960

Picture: *The Apartment,* Mirisch Co., Inc., United Artists
Director: Billy Wilder, *The Apartment*
Actress: Elizabeth Taylor, *Butterfield 8*
Actor: Burt Lancaster, *Elmer Gantry*
Supporting Actress: Shirley Jones, *Elmer Gantry*
Supporting Actor: Peter Ustinov, *Spartacus*

1961

Picture: *West Side Story,* Mirisch Pictures, Inc., and B and P Enterprises, Inc., United Artists
Director: Robert Wise and Jerome Robbins, *West Side Story*
Actress: Sophia Loren, *Two Women*
Actor: Maximillian Schell, *Judgment at Nuremberg*
Supporting Actress: Rita Moreno, *West Side Story*
Supporting Actor: George Chakiris, *West Side Story*

1962

Picture: *Lawrence of Arabia,* Horizon Pictures, Ltd.-Columbia
Director: David Lean, *Lawrence of Arabia*
Actress: Anne Bancroft, *The Miracle Worker*
Actor: Gregory Peck, *To Kill a Mockingbird*
Supporting Actress: Patty Duke, *The Miracle Worker*
Supporting Actor: Ed Begley, *Sweet Bird of Youth*

1963

Picture: *Tom Jones,* A Woodfall Production, United Artists-Lopert Pictures
Director: Tony Richardson, *Tom Jones*
Actress: Patricia Neal, *Hud*
Actor: Sidney Poitier, *Lilies of the Field*
Supporting Actress: Margaret Rutherford, *The V.I.P.s*
Supporting Actor: Melvyn Douglas, *Hud*

1964

Picture: *My Fair Lady,* Warner Bros.
Director: George Cukor, *My Fair Lady*
Actress: Julie Andrews, *Mary Poppins*
Actor: Rex Harrison, *My Fair Lady*
Supporting Actress: Lila Kedrova, *Zorba the Greek*
Supporting Actor: Peter Ustinov, *Topkapi*

1965

Picture: *The Sound of Music,* Argyle Enterprises Production, 20th Century-Fox
Director: Robert Wise, *The Sound of Music*
Actress: Julie Christie, *Darling*
Actor: Lee Marvin, *Cat Ballou*
Supporting Actress: Shelley Winters, *A Patch of Blue*
Supporting Actor: Martin Balsam, *A Thousand Clowns*

1966

Picture: *A Man for All Seasons,* Highland Films, Ltd., Production, Columbia
Director: Fred Zinnemann, *A Man for All Seasons*
Actress: Elizabeth Taylor, *Who's Afraid of Virginia Woolf?*
Actor: Paul Scofield, *A Man for All Seasons*
Supporting Actress: Sandy Dennis, *Who's Afraid of Virginia Woolf?*
Supporting Actor: Walter Matthau, *The Fortune Cookie*

1967

Picture: *In the Heat of the Night,* Mirisch Corp. Productions, United Artists
Director: Mike Nichols, *The Graduate*
Actress: Katharine Hepburn, *Guess Who's Coming to Dinner*
Actor: Rod Steiger, *In the Heat of the Night*
Supporting Actress: Estelle Parsons, *Bonnie and Clyde*
Supporting Actor: George Kennedy, *Cool Hand Luke*

1968

Picture: *Oliver!,* Columbia Pictures
Director: Sir Carol Reed, *Oliver!*
Actress: Katharine Hepburn, *The Lion in Winter* and Barbra Streisand, *Funny Girl*
Actor: Cliff Robertson, *Charly*
Supporting Actress: Ruth Gordon, *Rosemary's Baby*
Supporting Actor: Jack Albertson, *The Subject Was Roses*

1969

Picture: *Midnight Cowboy,* Jerome Hellman-John Schlesinger Production, United Artists
Director: John Schlesinger, *Midnight Cowboy*
Actress: Maggie Smith, *The Prime of Miss Jean Brodie*
Actor: John Wayne, *True Grit*
Supporting Actress: Goldie Hawn, *Cactus Flower*
Supporting Actor: Gig Young, *They Shoot Horses, Don't They?*

1970

Picture: *Patton,* Frank McCarthy-Franklin J. Schaffner Production, 20th Century-Fox
Director: Franklin J. Schaffner, *Patton*
Actress: Glenda Jackson, *Women in Love*
Actor: George C. Scott, *Patton*
Supporting Actress: Helen Hayes, *Airport*
Supporting Actor: John Mills, *Ryan's Daughter*

1971

Picture: *The French Connection,* D'Antoni Productions, 20th Century-Fox
Director: William Friedkin, *The French Connection*
Actress: Jane Fonda, *Klute*
Actor: Gene Hackman, *The French Connection*
Supporting Actress: Cloris Leachman, *The Last Picture Show*
Supporting Actor: Ben Johnson, *The Last Picture Show*

1972

Picture: *The Godfather,* Albert S. Ruddy Production, Paramount
Director: Bob Fosse, *Cabaret*
Actress: Liza Minnelli, *Cabaret*

Actor: Marlon Brando, *The Godfather*
Supporting Actress: Eileen Heckart, *Butterflies Are Free*
Supporting Actor: Joel Gray, *Cabaret*

1973

Picture: *The Sting,* Universal-Bill/Phillips-George Roy Hill Production, Universal
Director: George Roy Hill, *The Sting*
Actress: Glenda Jackson, *A Touch of Class*
Actor: Jack Lemmon, *Save the Tiger*
Supporting Actress: Tatum O'Neal, *Paper Moon*
Supporting Actor: John Houseman, *The Paper Chase*

1974

Picture: *The Godfather, Part II,* Coppola Co. Production, Paramount
Director: Francis Ford Coppola, *The Godfather, Part II*
Actress: Ellen Burstyn, *Alice Doesn't Live Here Anymore*
Actor: Art Carney, *Harry and Tonto*
Supporting Actress: Ingrid Bergman, *Murder on the Orient Express*
Supporting Actor: Robert De Niro, *The Godfather, Part II*

1975

Picture: *One Flew Over the Cuckoo's Nest,* Fantasy Films Production, United Artists
Director: Milos Forman, *One Flew Over the Cuckoo's Nest*
Actress: Louise Fletcher, *One Flew Over the Cuckoo's Nest*
Actor: Jack Nicholson, *One Flew Over the Cuckoo's Nest*
Supporting Actress: Lee Grant, *Shampoo*
Supporting Actor: George Burns, *The Sunshine Boys*

1976

Picture: *Rocky,* Robert Chartoff-Irwin Winkler Production, United Artists
Director: John G. Avildsen, *Rocky*
Actress: Faye Dunaway, *Network*
Actor: Peter Finch, *Network*
Supporting Actress: Beatrice Straight, *Network*
Supporting Actor: Jason Robards, *All the President's Men*

1977

Picture: *Annie Hall,* Jack Rollins-Charles H. Joffe Production, United Artists
Director: Woody Allen, *Annie Hall*
Actress: Diane Keaton, *Annie Hall*
Actor: Richard Dreyfuss, *The Goodbye Girl*
Supporting Actress: Vanessa Redgrave, *Julia*
Supporting Actor: Jason Robards, *Julia*

1978

Picture: *The Deer Hunter,* Michael Cimino Film Production, Universal
Director: Michael Cimino, *The Deer Hunter*
Actress: Jane Fonda, *Coming Home*
Actor: Jon Voight, *Coming Home*
Supporting Actress: Maggie Smith, *California Suite*
Supporting Actor: Christopher Walken, *The Deer Hunter*

1979

Picture: *Kramer vs. Kramer,* Stanley Jaffe Production, Columbia Pictures
Director: Robert Benton, *Kramer vs. Kramer*
Actress: Sally Field, *Norma Rae*
Actor: Dustin Hoffman, *Kramer vs. Kramer*
Supporting Actress: Meryl Streep, *Kramer vs. Kramer*
Supporting Actor: Melvyn Douglas, *Being There*

1980

Picture: *Ordinary People,* Wildwood Enterprises Production, Paramount
Director: Robert Redford, *Ordinary People*
Actress: Sissy Spacek, *Coal Miner's Daughter*
Actor: Robert De Niro, *Raging Bull*
Supporting Actress: Mary Steenburgen, *Melvin and Howard*
Supporting Actor: Timothy Hutton, *Ordinary People*

1981

Picture: *Chariots of Fire,* Enigma Productions, Ladd Company/Warner Bros.
Director: Warren Beatty, *Reds*
Actress: Katharine Hepburn, *On Golden Pond*
Actor: Henry Fonda, *On Golden Pond*
Supporting Actress: Maureen Stapleton, *Reds*
Supporting Actor: John Gielgud, *Arthur*

1982

Picture: *Gandhi,* Indo-British Films Production/Columbia
Director: Richard Attenborough, *Gandhi*
Actress: Meryl Streep, *Sophie's Choice*
Actor: Ben Kingsley, *Gandhi*
Supporting Actress: Jessica Lange, *Tootsie*
Supporting Actor: Louis Gossett, Jr., *An Officer and a Gentleman*

1983

Picture: *Terms of Endearment,* Paramount
Director: James L. Brooks, *Terms of Endearment*
Actress: Shirley MacLaine, *Terms of Endearment*
Actor: Robert Duvall, *Tender Mercies*
Supporting Actress: Linda Hunt, *The Year of Living Dangerously*
Supporting Actor: Jack Nicholson, *Terms of Endearment*

1984

Picture: *Amadeus,* Orion
Director: Milos Forman, *Amadeus*
Actress: Sally Field, *Places in the Heart*
Actor: F. Murray Abraham, *Amadeus*
Supporting Actress: Dame Peggy Ashcroft, *A Passage to India*
Supporting Actor: Haing S. Ngor, *The Killing Fields*

1985

Picture: *Out of Africa,* Universal
Director: Sydney Pollack, *Out of Africa*
Actress: Geraldine Page, *The Trip to Bountiful*
Actor: William Hurt, *Kiss of the Spider Woman*
Supporting Actress: Anjelica Huston, *Prizzi's Honor*
Supporting Actor: Don Ameche, *Cocoon*

1986

Picture: *Platoon,* Orion
Director: Oliver Stone, *Platoon*
Actress: Marlee Matlin, *Children of a Lesser God*
Actor: Paul Newman, *The Color of Money*
Supporting Actress: Dianne Wiest, *Hannah and Her Sisters*
Supporting Actor: Michael Caine, *Hannah and Her Sisters*

1987

Picture: *The Last Emperor,* Columbia Pictures
Director: Bernardo Bertolucci, *The Last Emperor*
Actress: Cher, *Moonstruck*
Actor: Michael Douglas, *Wall Street*
Supporting Actress: Olympia Dukakis, *Moonstruck*
Supporting Actor: Sean Connery, *The Untouchables*

1988

Picture: *Rain Man,* United Artists
Director: Barry Levinson, *Rain Man*
Actress: Jodie Foster, *The Accused*
Actor: Dustin Hoffman, *Rain Man*
Supporting Actress: Geena Davis, *The Accidental Tourist*
Supporting Actor: Kevin Kline, *A Fish Called Wanda*

1989

Picture: *Driving Miss Daisy,* Warner Bros.
Director: Oliver Stone, *Born on the Fourth of July*
Actress: Jessica Tandy, *Driving Miss Daisy*
Actor: Daniel Day-Lewis, *My Left Foot*
Supporting Actress: Brenda Fricker, *My Left Foot*
Supporting Actor: Denzel Washington, *Glory*

1990

Picture: *Dances With Wolves,* Orion
Director: Kevin Costner, *Dances With Wolves*
Actress: Kathy Bates, *Misery*
Actor: Jeremy Irons, *Reversal of Fortune*

Supporting Actress: Whoopi Goldberg, *Ghost*
Supporting Actor: Joe Pesci, *Goodfellas*

1991

Picture: *The Silence of the Lambs*, Orion
Director: Jonathan Demme, *The Silence of the Lambs*
Actress: Jodie Foster, *The Silence of the Lambs*
Actor: Anthony Hopkins, *The Silence of the Lambs*
Supporting Actress: Mercedes Ruehl, *The Fisher King*
Supporting Actor: Jack Palance, *City Slickers*

1992

Picture: *Unforgiven*, Warner Bros.
Director: Clint Eastwood, *Unforgiven*
Actress: Emma Thompson, *Howards End*
Actor: Al Pacino, *Scent of a Woman*
Supporting Actress: Marisa Tomei, *My Cousin Vinny*
Supporting Actor: Gene Hackman, *Unforgiven*

1993

Picture: *Schindler's List*, Universal
Director: Steven Spielberg, *Schindler's List*
Actress: Holly Hunter, *The Piano*
Actor: Tom Hanks, *Philadelphia*
Supporting Actress: Anna Paquin, *The Piano*
Supporting Actor: Tommy Lee Jones, *The Fugitive*

1994

Picture: *Forrest Gump*, Paramount
Director: Robert Zemeckis, *Forrest Gump*
Actress: Jessica Lange, *Blue Sky*
Actor: Tom Hanks, *Forrest Gump*
Supporting Actress: Dianne Wiest, *Bullets Over Broadway*
Supporting Actor: Martin Landau, *Ed Wood*

1995

Picture: *Braveheart*, Paramount
Director: Mel Gibson, *Braveheart*
Actress: Susan Sarandon, *Dead Man Walking*
Actor: Nicolas Cage, *Leaving Las Vegas*
Supporting Actress: Mira Sorvino, *Mighty Aphrodite*
Supporting Actor: Kevin Spacey, *The Usual Suspects*

1996

Picture: *The English Patient*, Miramax
Director: Anthony Minghella, *The English Patient*
Actress: Frances McDormand, *Fargo*
Actor: Geoffrey Rush, *Shine*
Supporting Actress: Juliette Binoche, *The English Patient*
Supporting Actor: Cuba Gooding, Jr., *Jerry Maguire*

1997

Picture: *Titanic*, 20th Century Fox and Paramount
Director: James Cameron, *Titanic*
Actress: Helen Hunt, *As Good As It Gets*
Actor: Jack Nicholson, *As Good As It Gets*
Supporting Actress: Kim Basinger, *L.A. Confidential*
Supporting Actor: Robin Williams, *Good Will Hunting*

1998

Picture: *Shakespeare in Love*, Miramax
Director: Steven Spielberg, *Saving Private Ryan*
Actress: Gwyneth Paltrow, *Shakespeare in Love*
Actor: Roberto Benigni, *Life Is Beautiful*
Supporting Actress: Judi Dench, *Shakespeare in Love*
Supporting Actor: James Coburn, *Affliction*

Other Academy Awards for 1998

Art Direction: Martin Childs and Jill Quertier, *Shakespeare in Love*
Cinematography: Janusz Kaminski, *Saving Private Ryan*
Costume Design: Sandy Powell, *Shakespeare in Love*
Documentary (feature): James Moll and Ken Lipper, *The Last Days;* **(short subject):** Keiko Ibi, *The Personals: Improvisations on Romance in the Golden Years*
Editing: Michael Kahn, *Saving Private Ryan*
Foreign-Language Film: *Life Is Beautiful*, Italy
Makeup: Jenny Shircore, *Elizabeth*
Music (original musical or comedy score): Stephen Warbeck, *Shakespeare in Love;* **(original dramatic score):** Nicola Piovani, *Life Is Beautiful;* **(original song):** "When You Believe," *The Prince of Egypt*, Stephen Schwartz
Adapted Screenplay: Bill Condon, *Gods and Monsters*

Original Screenplay: Marc Norman and Tom Stoppard, *Shakespeare in Love*
Short Subject (live action): Kim Magnusson and Anders Thomas Jensen, *Election Night (Valgaften);* **(animated):** Chris Wedge, *Bunny*
Sound: Gary Rydstrom, Gary Summers, Andy Nelson, and Ronald Judkins, *Saving Private Ryan*
Sound Effects Editing: Gary Rydstrom and Richard Hymns, *Saving Private Ryan*
Visual Effects: Joel Hynek, Nicholas Brooks, Stuart Robertson and Kevin Mack, *What Dreams May Come*
Lifetime Achievement: Director Elia Kazan
Irving G. Thalberg Memorial Award: Producer-director Norman F. Jewison
Scientific and Technical: Avid Technology Inc.

1998 National Society of Film Critics Awards

Best Picture: *Out of Sight*
Best Actor: Nick Nolte, *Affliction*
Best Actress: Ally Sheedy, *High Art*
Best Supporting Actor: Bill Murray, *Rushmore*
Best Supporting Actress: Judi Dench, *Shakespeare in Love*

Best Director: Steven Soderbergh, *Out of Sight*
Best Screenplay: Scott Frank, *Out of Sight*
Best Cinematography: John Toll, *The Thin Red Line*
Best Foreign Film: *Taste of Cherry* (Iran)
Best Documentary: *The Farm*
Special Award: *Mother and Son*, Experimental Film

1998 Broadcast Film Critics Association Awards

Best Picture: *Saving Private Ryan*
Best Actor: Ian McKellen, *Gods and Monsters* and *Apt Pupil*
Best Actress: Cate Blanchett, *Elizabeth*
Best Supporting Actor: Billy Bob Thornton, *A Simple Plan* and *Primary Colors*
Best Supporting Actress (tie): Joan Allen, *Pleasantville* Kathy Bates, *Primary Colors*
Best Director: Steven Spielberg, *Saving Private Ryan*
Best Original Screenplay: Marc Norman and Tom Stoppard, *Shakespeare in Love*
Best Adapted Screenplay: Scott A. Smith, *A Simple Plan*

Best Song: "When You Believe," *The Prince of Egypt*
Best Score: John Williams, *Saving Private Ryan*
Best Foreign-Language Film: *Life Is Beautiful*
Best Documentary: *Wild Man Blues*
Best Animated Feature (tie): *A Bug's Life* and *The Prince of Egypt*
Best Family Film: *A Bug's Life*
Best Made-for-TV Picture: *From the Earth to the Moon* (HBO)
Best Child Performance: Ian Michael Smith, *Simon Birch*
Breakthrough Performer: Joseph Fiennes, *Elizabeth* and *Shakespeare in Love*

1998 National Board of Review Awards

Best Picture: *Gods and Monsters*
Best Actor: Ian McKellen, *Gods and Monsters*
Best Actress: Fernanda Montenegro, *Central Station*
Best Supporting Actor: Ed Harris, *The Truman Show* and *Stepmom*
Best Supporting Actress: Christina Ricci, *The Opposite of Sex, Buffalo 66,* and *Pecker*
Best Director: Shekhar Kapur, *Elizabeth*

Best Foreign Film: *Central Station*
Best Documentary: *Wild Man Blues*
Career Achievement Award: Michael Caine
Special Achievement in Filmmaking: Roberto Benigni
Freedom of Expression Award: Bernardo Bertolucci
Director's Debut Award: Kasi Lemmons, *Eve's Bayou*
Best Breakthrough Performer: Bai Ling, *Red Corner*

1998 Golden Globe Awards

Film Awards

Best Motion Picture—Drama: *Saving Private Ryan*
Best Actor in a Drama: Jim Carrey, *The Truman Show*
Best Actress in a Drama: Cate Blanchett, *Elizabeth*
Best Motion Picture—Musical or Comedy: *Shakespeare in Love*
Best Actor in a Musical or Comedy: Michael Caine, *Little Voice*
Best Actress in a Musical or Comedy: Gwyneth Paltrow, *Shakespeare in Love*
Best Supporting Actor: Ed Harris, *The Truman Show*
Best Supporting Actress: Lynn Redgrave, *Gods and Monsters*
Best Director: Steven Spielberg, *Saving Private Ryan*
Best Screenplay: Marc Norman and Tom Stoppard, *Shakespeare in Love*
Best Original Score: Burkhard Dallwitz; additional music by Philip Glass, *The Truman Show*
Best Original Song: "The Prayer," *Quest for Camelot*
Best Foreign Film: *Central Station* (Brazil)

Television Awards

Best Series—Drama: *The Practice* (ABC)
Best Actor in a Drama: Dylan McDermott, *The Practice*
Best Actress in a Drama: Keri Russell, *Felicity*
Best Series—Musical or Comedy: *Ally McBeal* (Fox)
Best Actor in a Musical or Comedy Series: Michael J. Fox, *Spin City*
Best Actress in a Musical or Comedy Series: Jenna Elfman, *Dharma and Greg*
Best Miniseries or Movie Made for Television: *From the Earth to the Moon* (HBO)
Best Actor in a Miniseries or Movie Made for Television: Stanley Tucci, *Winchell*
Best Actress in a Miniseries or Movie Made for Television: Angelina Jolie, *Gia*
Best Supporting Actor in a Series, Miniseries, or Movie Made for Television (tie): Don Cheadle, *The Rat Pack,* and Gregory Peck, *Moby Dick*
Best Supporting Actress in a Series, Miniseries, or Movie Made for Television (tie): Faye Dunaway, *Gia,* and Camryn Manheim, *The Practice*

1999 Tony (Antoinette Perry) Awards

Play: *Side Man*
Musical: *Fosse*
Revival—Play: *Death of a Salesman*
Revival—Musical: *Annie Get Your Gun*
Actor—Play: Brian Dennehy, *Death of a Salesman*
Actress—Play: Judi Dench, *Amy's View*
Actor—Musical: Martin Short, *Little Me*
Actress—Musical: Bernadette Peters, *Annie Get Your Gun*
Featured Actor—Play: Frank Wood, *Side Man*
Featured Actress—Play: Elizabeth Franz, *Death of a Salesman*
Featured Actor—Musical: Roger Bart, *You're a Good Man Charlie Brown*
Featured Actress—Musical: Kristin Chenoweth, *You're a Good Man Charlie Brown*

Director—Play: Robert Falls, *Death of a Salesman*
Director—Musical: Matthew Bourne, *Swan Lake*
Book—Musical: *Parade*
Score—Musical: *Parade*
Orchestration: Ralph Burns and Douglas Besterman, *Fosse*
Scenic Designer: Richard Hoover, *Not About Nightingales*
Costume Designer: Lez Brotherston, *Swan Lake*
Choreographer: Matthew Bourne, *Swan Lake*
Lighting Designer: Andrew Bridge, *Fosse*
Regional Theater: Crossroads Theater Company, New Brunswick, N.J.
Special Awards: Uta Hagen, Arthur Miller, Isabelle Stevenson, and the production of *Fool Moon*

1999 New York Drama Critics Circle Awards

Best New Play: *Wit*
Best Musical: *Parade*

Best Foreign Play: *Closer*
Special Citation: David Hare

1999 Obie Awards

The Obie Awards, presented by *The Village Voice,* honor superior off-Broadway theater.

Best Production: The Wooster Group, *House/Lights*
Playwriting: W. David Hancock, *The Race of the Ark Tattoo;* Dare Clubb; *Oedipus;* Christopher Durang, *Betty's Summer Vacation*
Direction: Jim Simpson, *Benten Kozo;* Melia Bensussen, *The Turn of the Screw;* Nicholas Martin, *Betty's Summer Vacation;* Declan Donnellan, *Le Cid*
Performance: Liev Schreiber, *Cymbeline;* Kathleen Chalfant, *Wit;* Daniel Gerroll, sustained excellence of performance; Matthew Maher, *The Race of the Ark Tattoo;* Randall Duk Kim, sustained excellence of performance; Mina Bern, sustained excellence of performance; Darius de Haas, *Running Man;* Viola

Davis, *Everybody's Ruby;* Kristine Nielson, *Betty's Summer Vacation;* Swoosie Kurtz, *The Mineola Twins*
Design: Thomas Lynch, for sustained excellence of set design; Michael Chybowski, for sustained excellence of lighting design; Martin Pakledinaz, costume design for *The Misanthrope;* Diedre Murray, score for *Running Man*
Special Citations: Peggy Shaw, *Menopausal Gentleman;* Richard Maxwell, *House;* Carmelita Tropicana; David Cale, *Lillian;* Kim Hughes, *Sakina's Restaurant;* Aasif Mandvi, *Sakina's Restaurant;* Ronnie Burkett; *Tinka's New Dress;* Lisa Kron; *2.5 Minute Ride;* Basil Twist; *Symphonie Fantastique*
Sustained Achievement: Wynn Handman
Ross Wetzsteon Award: Ellie Covan-Dixon Place

Major Grammy Awards for Recording in 1998

Record: "My Heart Will Go On," Celine Dion
Album: *The Miseducation of Lauryn Hill*, Lauryn Hill
Song: "My Heart Will Go On," James Horner and Will Jennings, songwriters
New Artist: Lauryn Hill
Female Pop Vocal: "My Heart Will Go On," Celine Dion
Male Pop Vocal: "My Father's Eyes," Eric Clapton
Pop Duo or Group with Vocals: "Jump Jive An' Wail," The Brian Setzer Orchestra
Pop Collaboration with Vocals: "I Still Have That Other Girl,"Elvis Costello and Burt Bacharach
Pop Instrumental: "Sleepwalk," The Brian Setzer Orchestra
Dance Recording: "Ray of Light," Madonna
Pop Album: *Ray of Light,* Madonna
Traditional Pop Album: *Live at Carnegie Hall—The 50th Anniversary Concert,* Patti Page
Female Rock Vocal: "Uninvited," Alanis Morissette
Male Rock Vocal: "Fly Away," Lenny Kravitz
Rock Duo or Group with Vocals: "Pink,"Aerosmith
Hard Rock: "Most High," Jimmy Page and Robert Plant
Metal: "Better Than You," Metallica
Rock Instrumental: "The Roots of Coincidence," Pat Metheny Group
Rock Song: "Uninvited," Alanis Morissette, songwriter
Rock Album: *The Globe Sessions*, Sheryl Crow
Alternative Album: *Hello Nasty,* Beastie Boys
Female R&B Vocal: "Doo Wop (That Thing)," Lauryn Hill
Male R&B Vocal: "St. Louis Blues," Stevie Wonder
R&B Duo or Group with Vocals: "The Boy Is Mine," Brandy & Monica
R&B Song: "Doo Wop (That Thing)," Lauryn Hill, songwriter
R&B Album: *The Miseducation of Lauryn Hill,* Lauryn Hill
Traditional R&B Vocal Performance: *Live! One Night Only,* Patti LaBelle
Rap Solo: "Gettin' Jiggy Wit It," Will Smith
Rap Duo or Group: "Intergalactic," Beastie Boys
Rap Album: *Vol. 2 . . . Hard Knock Life,* Jay-Z
Female Country Vocal: "You're Still the One," Shania Twain
Male Country Vocal: "If You Ever Have Forever in Mind," Vince Gill
Country Duo or Group with Vocals: "There's Your Trouble," Dixie Chicks
Country Collaboration with Vocals: "Same Old Train,"Clint Black, Joe Diffie, Merle Haggard, Emmylou Harris, Alison Krauss, Patty Loveless, Earl Scruggs, Ricky Skaggs, Marty Stuart, Pam Tillis, Randy Travis, Travis Tritt, and Dwight Yoakam
Country Instrumental: "A Soldier's Joy," Randy Scruggs and Vince Gill
Country Song: "You're Still the One," Robert John "Mutt" Lange and Shania Twain, songwriters
Country Album: *Wide Open Spaces,* Dixie Chicks
Bluegrass Album: *Bluegrass Rules!,* Ricky Skaggs and Kentucky Thunder
New Age Album: *Landmarks,* Clannad
Contemporary Jazz: *Imaginary Day,* Pat Metheny Group
Jazz Vocal: *I Remember Miles,* Shirley Horn
Jazz Instrumental, Solo: "Rhumbata," Chick Corea and Gary Burton
Jazz Instrumental, Individual or Group: *Gershwin's World,* Herbie Hancock
Large Jazz Ensemble: *Count Plays Duke,* Count Basie Orchestra
Latin Jazz: *Hot House,* Arturo Sandoval
Rock Gospel Album: *You Are There,* Ashley Cleveland
Pop/Contemporary Gospel Album: *This Is My Song,* Deniece Williams
Southern Gospel, Country Gospel, or Bluegrass Gospel Album: *The Apostle—Music From and Inspired by the Motion Picture,* various artists
Traditional Soul Gospel Album: *He Leadeth Me,* Cissy Houston
Contemporary Soul Gospel Album: *The Nu Nation Project,* Kirk Franklin
Gospel Album by a Choir or Chorus: *Reflections,* The Associates; O'Landa Draper, Choir Director

Latin Pop: *Vuelve,* Ricky Martin
Latin Rock/Alternative: *Sueños Liquidos,* Mana
Tropical Latin: *Contra la Corriente,* Marc Anthony
Mexican-American: *Los Super Seven,* Los Super Seven
Tejano: *Said and Done,* Flaco Jimenez
Traditional Blues: *Any Place I'm Going,* Otis Rush
Contemporary Blues: *Slow Down,* Keb' Mo'
Traditional Folk: *Long Journey Home,* The Chieftains with various artists
Contemporary Folk: *Car Wheels on a Gravel Road,* Lucinda Williams
Reggae Album: *Friends,* Sly and Robbie
World Music Album: *Quanta Live,* Gilberto Gil
Polka Album: *Dance with Me,* Jimmy Sturr and His Orchestra
Musical Album for Children: *Elmopalooza!,* The Sesame Street Muppets with various artists
Spoken Word Album for Children: *The Children's Shakespeare,* various artists
Spoken Word or Non-Musical Album: *Still Me (Christopher Reeve),* Christopher Reeve
Spoken Comedy Album: *The 2000 Year Old Man in the Year 2000,* Mel Brooks and Carl Reiner
Musical Show Album: *The Lion King*
Instrumental Composition: "Almost 12," Bela Fleck, Future Man, and Victor Lemonte Wooten, composers
Instrumental Composition for a Motion Picture or for Television: *Saving Private Ryan,* John Williams, composer
Song Written Specifically for a Motion Picture or for Television: "My Heart Will Go On" (from *Titanic*), James Horner and Will Jennings, songwriters
Instrumental Arrangement: "Waltz for Debby," Don Sebesky, arranger
Instrumental Arrangement with Accompanying Vocals: "St. Louis Blues," Herbie Hancock, Robert Sadin, and Stevie Wonder, arrangers
Historical Album: *The Complete Hank Williams*
Producer, Non-Classical: Rob Cavallo
Classical Producer: Steven Epstein
Classical Album: *Barber: Prayers of Kierkegaard/ Vaughan Williams: Dona Nobis Pacem/Bartok: Cantata Profana,* Atlanta Symphony Orchestra and Chorus, Robert Shaw, conductor
Orchestral: *Mahler: Sym. No. 9,* Pierre Boulez conducting the Chicago Symphony Orchestra
Opera: *Bartok: Bluebeard's Castle,* Pierre Boulez, conducting the Chicago Symphony Orchestra
Choral: *Barber: Prayers of Kierkegaard/Vaughan Williams: Dona Nobis Pacem/Bartok: Cantata Profana,* Robert Shaw, conductor
Instrumental Soloist with Orchestra: *Penderecki: Violin Con. No. 2 "Metamorphosen",* Anne-Sophie Mutter, violin; Krzysztof Penderecki, conductor
Instrumental Soloist without Orchestra: *Bach: English Suites Nos. 1, 3 & 6,* Murray Perahia, piano
Chamber Music: *American Scenes (Works of Copland, Previn, Barber, Gershwin),* Andre Previn, piano; Gil Shaham, violin
Small Ensemble Performance (with or without Conductor): "Reich: Music for 18 Musicians," Steve Reich and Musicians
Classical Vocal: *The Beautiful Voice (Works of Charpentier, Gounod, Massenet, Flotow, Etc.),* Renee Fleming, soprano
Classical Contemporary Composition: *Penderecki: Violin Con. No. 2 "Metamorphosen,"* Krzysztof Penderecki, composer
Classical Crossover Album: "Soul of the Tango—The Music of Astor Piazzolla," Yo-Yo Ma, cello; Jorge Calandrelli, conductor
Music Video, Short Form: "Ray of Light," Jonas Akerlund, video director
Music Video, Long Form: *American Masters: Lou Reed: Rock & Roll Heart,* Timothy Greenfield-Sanders, video director

1998 Country Music Association Awards

Entertainer of the Year: Garth Brooks
Single of the Year: "Holes in the Floor of Heaven," Steve Wariner
Album of the Year: *Everywhere,* Tim McGraw
Song of the Year: "Holes in the Floor of Heaven," Steve Wariner
Male Vocalist of the Year: George Strait
Female Vocalist of the Year: Trisha Yearwood

Vocal Group of the Year: Dixie Chicks
Vocal Duo of the Year: Brooks & Dunn
Vocal Event of the Year: "You Don't Seem to Miss Me," Patty Loveless
Horizon Award: Dixie Chicks
Musician of the Year: Brett Mason
Music Video of the Year: "This Kiss," Faith Hill

1999 Jazz Awards

Musician of the Year: Dave Douglas
Composer of the Year: Dave Douglas
Innovator/Explorer: Dave Douglas
Trumpeter: Dave Douglas
Big Band: The Mingus Big Band
Band on Tour: The Mingus Big Band

Album: *Gershwin's World,* Herbie Hancock
Recording Debut: *A Cloud of Red Dust,* Stefon Harris
Male Singer: Andy Bey
Female Singer: Cassandra Wilson
Combo: Dave Holland Quintet
Lifetime Achievement: Sonny Rollins

1998 National Book Awards

The National Book Awards are presented by the Association of American Publishers. (Called the American Book Awards 1980–1986; reverted to original name in 1987.)

Fiction: *Charming Billy,* Alice McDermott (Farrar, Straus & Giroux)
Nonfiction: *Slaves in the Family,* Edward Ball (Farrar, Straus & Giroux)

Poetry: *This Time: New and Selected Poems,* Gerald Stern (W.W. Norton)
Young People's Literature: *Holes,* Louis Sachar (Frances Foster Books/Farrar, Straus & Giroux)

Booker Prize

Officially the "Booker McConnell Prize," this is Britain's most prestigious literary award. The $34,000 prize is presented each Oct. or Nov. by the National Book League in the United Kingdom, for the best full-length novel written in English by a citizen of a current or former British Commonwealth country. (Book's current publisher is listed in parentheses.)

1969 *Something to Answer For,* P. H. Newby (out of print)
1970 *The Elected Member,* Bernice Rubens (Abacus [Little Brown U.K.])
1971 *In a Free State,* V. S. Naipaul (Random House) paper
1972 *G.: A Novel,* John Berger (Vintage) paper
1973 *The Siege of Krishnapur,* J. G. Farrell (Carroll & Graf) paper
1974 (tie) *The Conservationist,* Nadine Gordimer (Viking) paper
Holiday, Stanley Middleton (out of print)
1975 *Heat and Dust,* Ruth Prawer Jhabvala (Peter Smith)
1976 *Saville,* David Storey (Vintage) U.K.
1977 *Staying On,* Paul Scott (Univ. of Chicago Press) paper
1978 *The Sea, The Sea,* Iris Murdoch (Viking) paper
1979 *Offshore,* Penelope Fitzgerald (Mariner) paper
1980 *Rites of Passage,* William Golding (Farrar, Straus & Giroux)
1981 *Midnight's Children,* Salman Rushdie (Knopf)
1982 *Schindler's List,* Thomas Keneally (Simon & Schuster)
1983 *Life & Times of Michael K,* J. M. Coetzee (Viking) paper

1984 *Hotel du Lac,* Anita Brookner (Vintage) paper
1985 *The Bone People,* Keri Hulme (Viking) paper
1986 *The Old Devils,* Kingsley Amis (Penguin) U.K.
1987 *Moon Tiger,* Penelope Lively (Grove/Atlantic) paper
1988 *Oscar and Lucinda,* Peter Carey (Vintage) paper
1989 *The Remains of the Day,* Kazuo Ishiguro (Vintage) paper
1990 *Possession: A Romance,* A. S. Byatt (Vintage) paper
1991 *The Famished Road,* Ben Okri (Anchor) paper
1992 *The English Patient,* Michael Ondaatje (Knopf)
Sacred Hunger, Barry Unsworth (W. W. Norton & Company) paper
1993 *Paddy Clarke, Ha Ha Ha,* Roddy Doyle (Penguin USA) paper
1994 *How Late It Was, How Late,* James Kelman (Delta) paper
1995 *The Ghost Road,* Pat Barker (Dutton)
1996 *Last Orders,* Graham Swift (Knopf)
1997 *The God of Small Things,* Arundhati Roy (Random House)
1998 *Amsterdam,* Ian McEwan (Doubleday)

1998 National Book Critics Circle Awards

Fiction: *The Love of a Good Woman,* Alice Munro (Knopf)
General Nonfiction: *We Wish to Inform You That Tomorrow We Will Be Killed with Our Families: Stories from Rwanda,* Philip Gourevitch (Farrar, Straus & Giroux)
Biography or Autobiography: *A Beautiful Mind,* Sylvia Nasar (Simon & Schuster)

Poetry: *The Bird Catcher,* Marie Ponsot (Knopf)
Criticism: *Visions of Jazz: The First Century,* Gary Giddins (Oxford University Press)
Nona Balakian Citation for Excellence in Reviewing: Albert Mobilio, a New York-based critic and poet

Newbery Medal

The Newbery Medal is awarded annually by the American Library Association for the most distinguished contribution to American literature for children.

1999 Newbery Medal and Honor Books

Newbery Medal for Best Book: *Holes*, Louis Sachar (Frances Foster Books/Farrar Straus & Giroux)
Newbery Honor Book: *A Long Way from Chicago*, Richard Peck (Dial Books for Young Readers)

1922–1998

1922   *The Story of Mankind*, Hendrick Willem Van Loon
1923   *The Voyages of Dr. Doolittle*, Hugh A. Lofting
1924   *The Dark Frigate*, Charles Boardman Hawes
1925   *Tales from Silver Lands*, Charles Joseph Finger
1926   *Shen of the Sea*, Arthur Bowie Chrisman
1927   *Smoky, the Cow Horse*, Will James
1928   *Gay-Neck, the Story of a Pigeon*, Dhan Gopal Mukerji
1929   *The Trumpeter of Krakow*, Eric P. Kelly
1930   *Hitty, Her First Hundred Years*, Rachel Field
1931   *The Cat Who Went to Heaven*, Elizabeth Jane Coatsworth
1932   *Waterless Mountain*, Laura Adams Armer
1933   *Young Fu of the Upper Yangtze*, Elizabeth Foreman Lewis
1934   *Invincible Louisa*, Cornelia Meigs
1935   *Dobry*, Monica Shannon
1936   *Caddie Woodlawn*, Carol Ryrie Brink
1937   *Roller Skates*, Ruth Sawyer
1938   *The White Stag*, Kate Seredy
1939   *Thimble Summer*, Elizabeth Enright
1940   *Daniel Boone*, James Henry Daugherty
1941   *Call it Courage*, Armstrong Sperry
1942   *The Matchlock Gun*, Walter Dumax Edmonds
1943   *Adam of the Road*, Elizabeth Janet Gray
1944   *Johnny Tremain*, Esther Forbes
1945   *Rabbit Hill*, Robert Lawson
1946   *Strawberry Girl*, Lois Lenski
1947   *Miss Hickory*, Carolyn Sherwin Bailey
1948   *The Twenty-One Balloons*, William Pène du Bois
1949   *King of the Wind*, Marguerite Henry
1950   *The Door in the Wall*, Marguerite de Angeli
1951   *Amos Fortune, Free Man*, Elizabeth Yates
1952   *Ginger Pye*, Eleanor Estes
1953   *Secret of the Andes*, Ann Nolan Clark
1954   *. . . And Now Miguel*, Joseph Krumgold
1955   *The Wheel on the School*, Meindert DeJong
1956   *Carry On, Mr. Bowditch*, Jean Lee Latham
1957   *Miracles on Maple Hill*, Virginia Eggertsen Sorensen
1958   *Rifles for Watie*, Harold Keith

1959   *The Witch of Blackbird Pond*, Elizabeth George Speare
1960   *Onion John*, Joseph Krumgold
1961   *Island of the Blue Dolphins*, Scott O'Dell
1962   *The Bronze Bow*, Elizabeth George Speare
1963   *A Wrinkle in Time*, Madeleine L'Engle
1964   *It's Like This, Cat*, Emily Cheney Neville
1965   *Shadow of a Bull*, Maia Wojciechowska
1966   *I, Juan de Pareja*, Elizabeth Borton de Treviño
1967   *Up a Road Slowly*, Irene Hunt
1968   *From the Mixed-Up Files of Mrs. Basil E. Frankweiler*, E. L. Konigsburg
1969   *The High King*, Lloyd Alexander
1970   *Sounder*, William H. Armstrong
1971   *Summer of the Swans*, Betsy Cromer Byars
1972   *Mrs. Frisby and the Rats of NIMH*, Robert C. O'Brien
1973   *Julie of the Wolves*, Jean Craighead George
1974   *The Slave Dancer*, Paula Fox
1975   *M. C. Higgins, the Great*, Virginia Hamilton
1976   *The Grey King*, Susan Cooper
1977   *Roll of Thunder, Hear My Cry*, Mildred D. Taylor
1978   *Bridge to Terabithia*, Katherine Paterson
1979   *The Westing Game*, Ellen Raskin
1980   *A Gathering of Days: A New England Girl's Journal, 1830–32*, Joan W. Blos
1981   *Jacob Have I Loved*, Katherine Paterson
1982   *A Visit to William Blake's Inn: Poems for Innocent and Experienced Travelers*, Nancy Willard
1983   *Dicey's Song*, Cynthia Voigt
1984   *Dear Mr. Henshaw*, Beverly Cleary
1985   *The Hero and the Crown*, Robin McKinley
1986   *Sarah, Plain and Tall*, Patricia MacLachlan
1987   *The Whipping Boy*, Sid Fleischman
1988   *Lincoln: A Photobiography*, Russell Freedman
1989   *Joyful Noise: Poems for Two Voices*, Paul Fleischman
1990   *Number the Stars*, Lois Lowry
1991   *Maniac Magee: a Novel*, Jerry Spinelli
1992   *Shiloh*, Phyllis Reynolds Naylor
1993   *Missing May*, Cynthia Rylant
1994   *The Giver*, Lois Lowry
1995   *Walk Two Moons*, Sharon Creech
1996   *The Midwife's Apprentice*, Karen Cushman
1997   *The View from Saturday*, E. L. Konigsburg
1998   *Out of the Dust*, Karen Hesse

Caldecott Medal

The Caldecott Medal is awarded annually by the American Library Association for the most distinguished American picture book for children.

1999 Caldecott Medal and Honor Books

Caldecott Medal for Best Picture Book: *Snowflake Bentley*, illustrated by Mary Azarian, written by Jacqueline Briggs Martin (Houghton Mifflin)
Caldecott Honor Books: *Duke Ellington: The Piano Prince and His Orchestra*, illustrated by Brian Pinkney, written by Andrea Davis Pinkney (Hyperion Books for Children); *No, David!*, illustrated and written by David Shannon (Blue Sky Press/Scholastic); *Snow*, illustrated and written by Uri Shulevitz (Farrar Straus & Giroux); *Tibet through the Red Box*, illustrated and written by Peter Sís (Frances Foster Books/Farrar Straus & Giroux)

1938–1998

1938   *Animals of the Bible, a Picture Book*, text selected by Helen Dean Fish, illustrated by Dorothy P. Lathrop
1939   *Mei Li*, written and illustrated by Thomas Handforth

1940 *Abraham Lincoln*, written and illustrated by Ingrid and Edgar Parin D'Aulaire

1941 *They Were Strong and Good*, written and illustrated by Robert Larson

1942 *Make Way for Ducklings*, written and illustrated by Robert McCloskey

1943 *The Little House*, written and illustrated by Virginia Lee Burton

1944 *Many Moons*, written by James Thurber, illustrated by Louis Slobodkin

1945 *Prayer for a Child*, written by Elizabeth Orton Jones

1946 *The Rooster Crows*, written and illustrated by Maud and Miska Petersham

1947 *The Little Island*, written by Golden MacDonald, illustrated by Leonard Weisgard

1948 *White Snow, Bright Snow*, written by Alvin Tresselt, illustrated by Roger Duvoisin

1949 *The Big Snow*, written and illustrated by Berta and Elmer Hader

1950 *Song of the Swallows*, written and illustrated by Leo Politi

1951 *The Egg Tree*, written and illustrated by Katherine Milhous

1952 *Finders Keepers*, written by William Lipkind, illustrated by Nicolas Mordivinoff

1953 *The Biggest Bear*, written and illustrated by Lynd Ward

1954 *Madeline's Rescue*, written and illustrated by Ludwig Bemelmans

1955 *Cinderella, or, The Little Glass Slipper*, translated and illustrated by Marcia Brown

1956 *Frog Went A-Courtin'*, retold by John Langstaff, illustrated by Feodor Rojankovsky

1957 *A Tree is Nice*, written by Janice May Udry, Illustrated by Marc Simont

1958 *Time of Wonder*, written and illustrated by Robert McCloskey

1959 *Chanticleer and the Fox*, adapted and illustrated by Barbara Cooney

1960 *Nine Days to Christmas*, written by Marie Hall Ets and Aurora Labastida, illustrated by Marie Hall Ets

1961 *Baboushka and the Three Kings*, written by Ruth Robbins, illustrated by Nicolas Sidjakov

1962 *Once a Mouse*, retold and illustrated by Marcia Brown

1963 *The Snowy Day*, written and illustrated by Ezra Jack Keats

1964 *Where the Wild Things Are*, written and illustrated by Maurice Sendak

1965 *May I Bring a Friend?*, written by Beatrice Schenk de Regniers, illustrated by Beni Montresor

1966 *Always Room for One More*, written by Sorche Nic Leodhas, illustrated by Nonny Hogrogian

1967 *Sam, Bangs and Moonshine*, written and illustrated by Evaline Ness

1968 *Drummer Hoff*, written by Barbara Emberley, illustrated by Ed Emberley

1969 *The Fool of the World and the Flying Ship*, retold by Arthur Ransome, illustrated by Uri Shulevitz

1970 *Sylvester and the Magic Pebble*, written and illustrated by William Steig

1971 *A Story, A Story: An African Tale*, retold and illustrated by Gail E. Haley

1972 *One Fine Day*, written and illustrated by Nonny Hogrogian

1973 *The Funny Little Woman*, retold by Arlene Mosel, illustrated by Blair Lent

1974 *Duffy and the Devil*, retold by Harve Zemach, illustrated by Margot Zemach

1975 *Arrow to the Sun: A Pueblo Indian Tale*, adapted and illustrated by Gerald H. McDermott

1976 *Why Mosquitos Buzz in People's Ears (An African Tale)*, retold by Verna Aardema, illustrated by Leo and Diane Dillon

1977 *Ashanti to Zulu: African Traditions*, written by Margaret Musgrove, illustrated by Leo and Diane Dillon

1978 *Noah's Ark*, written by Jacob Revius, illustrated by Peter Spier

1979 *The Girl Who Loved Wild Horses*, written and illustrated by Paul Goble

1980 *Ox-Cart Man*, written by Donald Hall, illustrated by Barbara Cooney

1981 *Fables*, written and illustrated by Arnold Lobel

1982 *Jumanji*, written and illustrated by Chris Van Allsburg

1983 *Shadow*, translated and illustrated by Marcia Brown

1984 *The Glorious Flight: Across the Channel with Louise Blériot*, written and illustrated by Alice and Martin Provensen

1985 *St. George and the Dragon*, retold by Margaret Hodges, illustrated by Trina Schart Hyman

1986 *The Polar Express*, written and illustrated by Chris Van Allsburg

1987 *Hey, Al*, written by Arthur Yorinks, illustrated by Richard Egielski

1988 *Owl Moon*, written by Jane Yolen, illustrated by John Schoenherr

1989 *Song and Dance Man*, written by Karen Ackerman, illustrated by Stephen Gammell

1990 *Lon Po Po: A Red-Riding Hood Story from China*, translated and illustrated by Ed Young

1991 *Black & White*, written and illustrated by David Macaulay

1992 *Tuesday*, written and illustrated by David Wiesner

1993 *Mirette on the High Wire*, written and illustrated by Emily Arnold McCully

1994 *Grandfather's Journey*, written and illustrated by Allen Say

1995 *Smoky Night*, written by Eve Bunting, illustrated by David Diaz

1996 *Officer Buckle and Gloria*, written and illustrated by Peggy Rathmann

1997 *Golem*, written and illustrated by David Wisniewski

1998 *Rapunzel*, illustrated and retold by Paul O. Zelinsky

Other American Library Association Awards for Children's Books, 1999

1998 Coretta Scott King Awards, honoring black authors and illustrators: (author): *Heaven,* Angela Johnson (Simon & Schuster); **(illustrator):** *i see the rhythm,* Michele Wood (Children's Book Press)

1998 Coretta Scott King Honor Books: (author): *Jazmin's Notebook,* Nikki Grimes (Dial Books for Young Readers); *Breaking Ground, Breaking Silence: The Story of New York's African Burial Ground,* Joyce Hansen and Gary McGowan (Henry Holt); *The Other Side: Shorter Poems,* Angela Johnson (Orchard Books); **(illustrator):** *I Have Heard of a Land,* Floyd Cooper (Joanna Cotler Books/HarperCollins); *The Bat Boy & His Violin,* E. B. Lewis (Simon & Schuster); *Duke Ellington: The Piano Prince and His Orchestra,* illustrated by Brian Pinkney, written by Andrea Davis Pinkney (Hyperion Books for Children)

1998 Pura Belpre Awards, honoring Latino writers and illustrators (awarded biennially): (author): *Parrot in the Oven,* Victor Martinez (Joanna Cotler Books); **(illustrator):** *Snapshots from the Wedding,* illustrated by Stephanie Garcia, written by Gary Soto (Putnam)

1998 Pura Belpre Honor Awards, honoring Latino writers and illustrators (awarded biennially): (author): *Spirits of the High Mesa,* Floyd Martinez (Arte Publico); *Laughing Tomatoes and Other Spring Poems* (Children's Book Press); **(illustrator):** *The Golden Flower,* Enrique Sanchez (Simon & Schuster); *My Family,* Carmen Lomas Garza (Children's Book Press); *Gathering the Sun,* Simon Silva (Lee & Shepard)

1999 Mildred L. Batchelder Award, for best book originally published in a foreign language in a foreign country: *Thanks to My Mother,* by Schoschana Rabinovici, originally published in Hebrew (Dial Books for Young Readers)

1999 Margaret A. Edwards Award, lifetime achievement award for outstanding literature for young adults: Anne McCaffrey

1999 National Magazine Awards

General Excellence:
I.D. Magazine (circulation less than 100,000)
Fast Company (circulation 100,000 to 400,000)
Condé Nast Traveler (circulation 400,000 to 1,000,000)
Vanity Fair (circulation more than 1,000,000)
Personal Service: *Good Housekeeping*
Special Interests: *PC Computing*
Reporting: *Newsweek*

Essays and Criticism: *The Atlantic Monthly*
Feature Writing: *The American Scholar*
Public Interest: *TIME*
Design: *ESPN The Magazine*
Fiction: *Harper's Magazine*
Single-Topic Issue: *The Oxford American*
Photography: *Martha Stewart Living*
General Excellence in New Media: *Cigar Aficionado*

Bollingen Prize in Poetry

This $50,000 award is given biennially. It is administered by Yale University and the Bollingen Foundation.

1949	Ezra Pound	1967	Robert Penn Warren
1950	Wallace Stevens	1969	John Berryman and Karl Shapiro
1951	John Crowe Ransom	1971	Richard Wilbur and Mona Van Duyn
1952	Marianne Moore	1973	James Merrill
1953	Archibald MacLeish and William Carlos Williams	1975	Archie Randolph Ammons
1954	W. H. Auden	1977	David Ignatow
1955	Léonie Adams and Louise Bogan	1979	W. S. Merwin
1956	Conrad Aiken	1981	Howard Nemerov and May Swenson
1957	Allen Tate	1983	Anthony Hecht and John Hollander
1958	e. e. cummings	1985	John Ashbery and Fred Chappell
1959	Theodore Roethke	1987	Stanley Kunitz
1960	Delmore Schwartz	1989	Edgar Bowers
1961	Yvor Winters	1991	Laura Riding Jackson and Donald Justice
1962	John Hall Wheelock and Richard Eberhart	1993	Mark Strand
1963	Robert Frost	1995	Kenneth Koch
1965	Horace Gregory	1997	Gary Snyder
		1999	Robert White Creeley

Kingsley Tufts Poetry Prize

This $50,000 award is given to a poet for a book published in the previous year. Established in 1992, it is administered by the Claremont (California) Graduate School.

1993	Susan Mitchell, *Rapture*	1997	Campbell McGrath, *Spring Comes to Chicago*
1994	Yusef Komunyakaa, *Neon Vernacular*	1998	John Koethe, *Falling Water*
1995	Thomas Lux, *Split Horizon*	1999	B. H. Fairchild, *The Art of the Lathe*
1996	Deborah Digges, *Rough Music*		

1998 George Foster Peabody Awards for Broadcasting

Coverage of Africa: National Public Radio
Sisterhood of Hope: WHAS Radio, Louisville, Ky.
I Must Keep Fightin': The Art of Paul Robeson: National Public Radio
Performance Today: National Public Radio

The Reckoning: CBS News/Public Eye with Bryant Gumbel
Christiane Amanpour: International Reporting on Cable News Network and CBS News: *60 Minutes*

The Olympic Bribery Scandal: KTVX-TV, Salt Lake City, Utah

Frontline: Washington's Other Scandal: WGBH/Frontline, Washington Media Associates and Public Affairs Television

About Race: KRON-TV, San Francisco

The Human Body: BBC and The Learning Channel

Africans in America: America's Journey Through Slavery: WGBH-TV, Boston

Travis: ITVS and City People Productions

Frank Lloyd Wright: Florentine Films and WETA-TV, Washington, D.C.

When Good Men Do Nothing: BBC, London, and WGBH-TV, Boston

American Masters: Alexander Calder: Thirteen/WNET, New York and Florentine Films/Sherman Pictures

Cold War: Jeremy Isaacs Productions and CNN Productions, Atlanta

The American Experience: Riding the Rails: The American Experience and The American History Project/Out of the Blue Productions Inc. and WGBH Educational Foundation

Dateline NBC: Checks and Balances: NBC News, New York

The American Experience: America 1900: The American Experience, David Grubin Productions Inc., and WGBH Educational Foundation

Christopher: WANE-TV, Fort Wayne, Ind.

The Bear: TVC and Channel 4, London

HBO Sports Documentaries: Home Box Office, New York

Dr. Katz: Professional Therapist: Comedy Central, Tom Snyder Productions Inc. and Popular Arts Entertainment, in association with HBO Downtown Productions

Mobil Masterpiece Theatre: King Lear: A Chestermead Production for the BBC, London and WGBH-TV, Boston

Shot through the Heart: Home Box Office, New York

The Baby Dance: Showtime Networks Inc, Egg Pictures and Pacific Motion Pictures

The Practice: ABC, David E. Kelley Productions

NYPD Blue: "Raging Bulls," ABC, Steven Bochco Productions

Ally McBeal: Fox, David E. Kelley Productions

The Larry Sanders Show: "Flip," Home Box Office and Brillstein-Grey Entertainment

Linda Ellerbee, Host of *Nick News*: As host of *Nick News*, Linda Ellerbee provides important explanations and interpretations of news events for children that are instructive for adults as well, and reflect only the most recent examples of the consistent excellence achieved by this leading broadcast journalist.

Jac Venza: For more than four decades, Jac Venza has been a driving force in the presentation of cultural and arts programming on television. His growing list of accomplishments includes *Dance in America, Theater in America, Great Performances,* and *American Masters,* of which he is one.

Robert Halmi, Sr.: Perhaps the last of the great network television impresarios, Robert Halmi, Sr. is recognized for his uncompromising vision and for his commitment to excellence in the presentation of classic and contemporary drama on commercial television.

1998 Alfred I. du Pont–Columbia University Broadcast News Awards

GOLD BATON
Nova, for five programs and consistently outstanding science reporting, as exemplified by: "Everest: The Death Zone," "The Brain Eater," "Supersonic Spies," "China's Mysterious Mummies," and "Coma" (WGBH-TV, Boston)

SILVER BATONS
Television Awards:
ABC News *Nightline* and Ted Koppel for "Crime & Punishment," a four-part series on how prisoners live in maximum-security prisons

WEWS-TV, Cleveland, and Bill Sheil for "Final Mission"

Mike Wallace and CBS News *60 Minutes,* for an investigation of the international pharmaceutical industry

Eric Engberg, Vince Gonzales, and *CBS Evening News:* "Tomb of the Unknowns," a seven-part series that helped identify the remains of a Vietnam War serviceman buried at Arlington National Cemetery

Raymond Henderson, Tony Buba, and Independent Television Service for *Struggles in Steel: A Story of African-American Steelworkers* (PBS)

Laura Angelica Simón, Tracey Trench, and *P.O.V.:* "Fear and Learning at Hoover Elementary," about the impact of California's immigration policy on a school

WRAL-TV, Raleigh, and Stuart Wilson for a series of investigative reports on military medicine

WBBM-TV, Chicago, and Carol Marin for coverage of Congressman William Lipinski's primary campaign

WMAQ-TV, Chicago, and Renee Ferguson for *Strip-Searched* at O'Hare

Vanessa Roth and Thirteen/WNET, New York, for *Taken In: The Lives of America's Foster Children* (PBS)

Radio Awards:
Dan Collison, Rebecca Perl, Tom Jennings, and *This American Life* for "Scenes from a Transplant," a radio documentary tracing the treatment of a cancer patient (Public Radio International)

1999 Major Emmy Awards

Drama Series: *The Practice* (ABC)
　Actress: Edie Falco, *The Sopranos*
　Actor: Dennis Franz, *N.Y.P.D. Blue*
　Supporting Actress: Holland Taylor, *The Practice*
　Supporting Actor: Michael Badalucco, *The Practice*
　Guest Actor: Edward Herrmann, *The Practice*
　Guest Actress: Debra Monk, *N.Y.P.D. Blue*
Comedy Series: *Ally McBeal* (Fox)
　Actress: Helen Hunt, *Mad About You*
　Actor: John Lithgow, *3rd Rock from the Sun*
　Supporting Actress: Kristen Johnston, *3rd Rock from the Sun*
　Supporting Actor: David Hyde Pierce, *Frasier*
　Guest Actress: Tracey Ullman, *Ally McBeal*
　Guest Actor: Mel Brooks, *Mad About You*
Variety, Music, or Comedy Series: *Late Show with David Letterman* (CBS)
Variety, Music, or Comedy Special: *The 1998 Tony Awards* (CBS)

Miniseries or Special: *Horatio Hornblower* (A&E)
　Actress: Helen Mirren, *The Passion of Ayn Rand*
　Actor: Stanley Tucci, *Winchell*
　Supporting Actress: Anne Bancroft, *Deep in My Heart*
　Supporting Actor: Peter O'Toole, *Joan of Arc*
Made-for-TV Movie: *A Lesson Before Dying* (HBO)
Individual Performance, Variety or Music Program: John Leguizamo, *John Leguizamo's Freak*
Outstanding Nonfiction Series (possibility of one or more than one award): *The American Experience* (PBS) and *American Masters* (PBS)
Outstanding Nonfiction Special: *Thug Life in D.C.* (HBO)
Outstanding Children's Program: *The Truth about Drinking: The Teen Files* (syndicated)
Outstanding Animated Program (one hour or less): *King of the Hill:* "And They Call It Bobby Love" (Fox)

1999 Daytime Emmy Awards

Outstanding Drama Series: *General Hospital* (ABC)
Lead Actress in a Drama Series: Susan Lucci, *All My Children*
Lead Actor in a Drama Series: Anthony Geary, *General Hospital*
Supporting Actress in a Drama Series: Sharon Case, *The Young and the Restless*
Supporting Actor in a Drama Series: Stuart Damon, *General Hospital*
Younger Actress in a Drama Series: Heather Tom, *The Young and the Restless*
Younger Actor in a Drama Series: Jonathan Jackson, *General Hospital*
Drama Series Writing Team: *The Young and the Restless*
Outstanding Children's Series: *Disney Presents: Bill Nye the Science Guy* (syndicated)
Outstanding Children's Special: *The Island on Bird Street* (SHO)
Outstanding Children's Animated Program: *Arthur* (PBS)
Outstanding Children's Animated Program (special class): *Steven Spielberg Presents: Pinky and the Brain* (WB)

Performer in a Children's Series: Fred Rogers, *Mister Rogers' Neighborhood*
Performer in a Children's Special: Jordan Kiziuk, *The Island on Bird Street*
Performer in an Animated Program: Rob Paulsen, *Steven Spielberg Presents: Pinky and the Brain*
Outstanding Preschool Children's Series: *Sesame Street* (PBS)
Special Class Program: *1998 Macy's Thanksgiving Day Parade* (NBC)
Outstanding Game Show: *Win Ben Stein's Money* (COM)
Outstanding Game-Show Host: Ben Stein and Jimmy Kimmel, co-hosts, *Win Ben Stein's Money*
Outstanding Talk Show: *The Rosie O'Donnell Show* (syndicated)
Outstanding Talk-Show Host: Rosie O'Donnell, *The Rosie O'Donnell Show*
Outstanding Service Show (tie): *Better Homes and Gardens Television* (syndicated) and *Martha Stewart Living* (syndicated)
Outstanding Service-Show Host: Ming Tsai, *East Meets West with Ming Tsai*

1999 NAACP Image Awards

MOTION PICTURE

Outstanding Motion Picture: *How Stella Got Her Groove Back*
Outstanding Actress in a Motion Picture: Angela Bassett, *How Stella Got Her Groove Back*
Outstanding Actor in a Motion Picture: Danny Glover, *Beloved*

TELEVISION

Outstanding Comedy Series: *Cosby*
Outstanding Actress in a Comedy Series: Tia and Tamera Mowry, *Sister, Sister*
Outstanding Actor in a Comedy Series: Steve Harvey, *The Steve Harvey Show*
Outstanding Drama Series: *Touched by an Angel*
Outstanding Actress in a Drama Series: Della Reese, *Touched by an Angel*
Outstanding Actor in a Drama Series: Eriq La Salle, *ER*

LITERARY WORK

Outstanding Literary Work, Fiction: *Mama Flora's Family: A Novel*, Alex Haley and David Stevens

Outstanding Literary Work, Nonfiction: *With Ossie & Ruby: In This Life Together*, Ossie Davis and Ruby Dee
Outstanding Literary Work, Children's: *Let My People Go: Bible Stories Told by a Freeman of Color*, written by Patricia and Frederick McKissack, illustrated by E. Ransome

RECORDING

Outstanding New Artist: Lauryn Hill, *The Miseducation of Lauryn Hill*
Outstanding Female Artist: Lauryn Hill, *The Miseducation of Lauryn Hill*
Outstanding Male Artist: Luther Vandross, *I Know*
Outstanding Duo or Group: Whitney Houston and Mariah Carey, *When You Believe*
Outstanding Rap Artist: Will Smith, *Just the Two of Us*
Outstanding Jazz Artist: Lena Horne, *Being Myself*
Outstanding Gospel Artist: Kirk Franklin, *The Nu Nation Project*
Outstanding Song: Kirk Franklin, "Lean on Me"
Outstanding Album: Lauryn Hill, *The Miseducation of Lauryn Hill*

1999 MacArthur Foundation Awards

The MacArthur Foundation awards monetary prizes each year in order to provide financial assistance for selected innovators.

Jillian Banfield, 39, mineralogist; Madison, Wisc.
Carolyn Bertozzi, 32, chemist; Albany, Calif.
Bruce Blair, 51, foreign policy analyst; Washington
John Bonifaz, 33, public interest lawyer; Boston
Shawn Carlson, 39, physicist and educator; San Diego
Mark Danner, 40, journalist; Berkeley, Calif. and New York
Alison Des Forges, 56, writer, researcher, and human rights advocate; Buffalo, N.Y.
Elizabeth Diller, 45, architect; New York and **Ricardo Scofidio,** 64, architect; New York
Saul Friedlander, 66, historian; Los Angeles
Jennifer Gordon, 33, lawyer and community organizer; Brooklyn, N.Y.
David Hillis, 40, molecular biologist; Austin, Tex.
Sara Horowitz, 36, executive director, Working Today; New York
Jacqueline Jones, 51, social historian; Wellesley, Mass.
Laura Kiessling, 38, chemist and biochemist; Madison, Wisc.
Leslie Kurke, 39, literature professor; Berkeley, Calif.

David Levering Lewis, 63, historian; New York
Juan Martin Maldacena, physicist; Cambridge, Mass.
Gay McDougall, 51, attorney; Washington
Campbell McGrath, 37, poet; Miami Beach, Fla.
Dennis Moore, 54, anthropological linguist; Belem-Para, Brazil
Elizabeth Murray, 58, painter; New York
Pepón Osorio, 44, installation artist; New York
Peter Shor, 39, computer scientist; Florham Park, N.J.
Eva Silverstein, 28, theoretical physicist; Stanford, Calif.
Wilma Subra, 55, chemist and environmentalist; New Iberia, La.
Ken Vandermark, 34, musician; Chicago
Naomi Wallace, 38, playwright; Otterburn, England
Jeffrey Weeks, 42, mathematician; Canton, N.Y.
Fred Wilson, 44, installation artist; New York
Xu Bing, 44, artist; New York
Ofelia Zepeda, linguist, poet, editor, and community leader; Tucson

Presidential Medal of Freedom

The nation's highest civilian award, the Presidential Medal of Freedom recognizes exceptional meritorious service. The medal was established by President Truman in 1945 to recognize notable service in the war. In 1963, President Kennedy reintroduced it as an honor for distinguished civilian service in peace time. Shown below are only those medals awarded during President Clinton's administration.

1993*	Arthur Ashe, Jr. (athlete, tennis)
1993	William J. Brennan, Jr. (jurist)
1993	Marjory Stoneman Douglas (conservationist)
1993	J. William Fulbright (public servant)
1993*	Thurgood Marshall (jurist)
1993	General Colin L. Powell [1](soldier)
1993*	Joseph L. Raugh, Jr. (civil-rights and labor activist)
1993	Martha Raye (entertainer)
1993	John Minor Wisdom (public servant)
1994	Herbert Block (cartoonist)
1994*	Cesar Chavez (labor leader)
1994	Arthur Flemming (government servant)
1994	James Grant (executive director, UNICEF)
1994	Dorothy Height (civil-rights leader)
1994	Barbara Jordan (public servant)
1994	Lane Kirkland (labor leader)
1994	Robert H. Michel (public servant)
1994	R. Sargent Shriver (government servant)
1995	Peggy Charren (children's television advocate)
1995	William Thaddeus Coleman, Jr. (public servant and civil-rights advocate)
1995	Joan Ganz Cooney (children's television advocate)
1995	John Hope Franklin (historian)
1995	A. Leon Higginbotham, Jr. (jurist and civil-rights advocate)
1995	Frank M. Johnson, Jr. (jurist)
1995	C. Everett Koop (public health worker)
1995	Gaylord A. Nelson (public servant and conservationist)
1995	Walter P. Reuther (labor leader)
1995	James W. Rouse (urban planner)
1995*	William C. Velasquez (voting rights advocate)
1995	Lew R. Wasserman (media executive)
1996	James Scott Brady (gun control advocate)
1996	Cardinal Joseph Bernadin (Catholic leader)
1996	Millard D. Fuller (founder, Habitat for Humanity)
1996	David Alan Hamburg (physician and children's advocate)
1996	John H. Johnson (founder, *Ebony* and *Jet*)
1996	Eugene M. Lang (founder, "I Have a Dream" Foundation)
1996	Jan Nowak-Jezioranski (WWII Polish resistence fighter)

1996	Antonia Pantoja (Puerto Rican educational and economic advocate)
1996	Rosa Parks (civil-rights leader)
1996	Ginetta Sagan (advocate for political prisoners)
1996	Morris Udall (public servant)
1997	Robert Dole (public servant)
1997	William J. Perry (soldier)
1998	Arnold Aronson (civil-rights advocate)
1998	Brooke Astor (philanthropist)
1998	Robert Coles (psychiatrist and author)
1998	Justin Dart, Jr. (founder of Americans with Disabilities Act)
1998	James Farmer (civil-rights leader)
1998	Dante B. Fascell (public servant)
1998	Zachary Fisher (philanthropist)
1998	Frances Hesselbein (former leader of the Girl Scouts of America)
1998	Fred Korematsu (activist redressing Japanese-American internment in WWII)
1998	Sol M. Linowitz (jurist)
1998	Wilma Mankiller (former Cherokee Nation leader)
1998	Margaret Murie (environmentalist)
1998	Mario G. Obledo (activist for Mexican-American civil rights)
1998	Elliot L. Richardson (public servant)
1998	David Rockefeller (philanthropist)
1998*	Albert Shanker (educator)
1998	Adm. Elmo R. Zumwalt, Jr. (soldier)
1999	Lloyd M. Bentsen (public servant)
1999	Edgar M. Bronfman, Sr. (president of World Jewish Congress)
1999	President Jimmy Carter (public servant, activist)
1999	Rosalynn Carter (human-rights activist)
1999	Evelyn Dubrow (lobbyist)
1999	Sister Isolina Ferre (advocate for the poor)
1999	President Gerald Ford (public servant)
1999	Oliver White Hill (civil-rights lawyer)
1999	Max Kampelman (arms-control expert)
1999	Helmut Kohl (former German chancellor)
1999	Edgar Wayburn (Sierra Club leader)

1. With Distinction. NOTE: An asterisk following a year denotes a posthumous award.

Enrico Fermi Award

The $100,000 award is given in recognition of scientific and technical achievement in atomic energy. Awarded by the president, it is the U.S. government's oldest science and technology award.

1954	Enrico Fermi
1956	John von Neumann
1957	Ernest O. Lawrence
1958	Eugene P. Wigner
1959	Glenn T. Seaborg
1961	Hans A. Bethe
1962	Edward Teller
1963	J. Robert Oppenheimer
1964	Hyman G. Rickover
1966	Otto Hahn, Lise Meitner, and Fritz Strassman
1968	John A. Wheeler
1969	Walter H. Zinn
1970	Norris E. Bradbury
1971	Shields Warren and Stafford L. Warren

1972	Manson Benedict
1976	William L. Russell
1978	Harold M. Agnew and Wolfgang K. H. Panofsky
1980	Alvin M. Weinberg and Rudolf E. Peirls
1981	W. Bennett Lewis
1982	Herbert Anderson and Seth Neddermeyer
1983	Alexander Hollaender and John Lawrence
1984	Robert R. Wilson and Georges Vendryès
1985	Norman C. Rasmussen and Marshall N. Rosenblath
1986	Ernest D. Courant and M. Stanley Livingston
1987	Luis W. Alvarez and Gerald F. Tape
1988	Richard B. Setlow and Victor F. Weisskopf

1989 Award not given
1990 George A. Cowan and Robley D. Evans
1991 Award not given
1992 Leon M. Lederman, Harold Brown, and John S. Foster, Jr.
1993 Freeman J. Dyson and Liane B. Russell

1994 Award not given
1995 Ugo Fano and Martin Kamen
1996 Richard Garwin, Mortimer Elkind, and H. Rodney Withers
1997 Award not given
1998 Maurice Goldhaber and Michael E. Phelps

Fields Medal Winners

The Fields Medal has been awarded since 1936 by the International Congress of Mathematicians in Toronto to recognize outstanding mathematics achievement.

1936 Lars Valerian Ahlfors (Harvard University) and Jesse Douglas (Massachusetts Institute of Technology)

(Fields Medals were not awarded during World War II)

1950 Laurent Schwarts (University of Nancy) and Alte Selberg (Institute for Advanced Study, Princeton)

1954 Kunihiko Kodaira (Princeton University) and Jean-Pierre Serre (University of Paris)

1958 Klaus Friedrich Roth (University of London) and René Thom (University of Strasbourgh)

1962 Lars V. Hörmander (University of Stockholm) and John Willard Milnor (Princeton University)

1966 Michael Francis Atiyah (Oxford University), Paul Joseph Cohen (Stanford University), Alexander Grothendieck (University of Paris), and Stephen Smale (University of California, Berkeley)

1970 Alan Baker (Cambridge University), Heisuke Hironaka (Harvard University), Serge P. Novikov (Moscow University), and John Griggs Thompson (Cambridge University)

1974 Enrico Bombieri (University of Pisa) and David Bryant Mumford (Harvard University)

1978 Pierre René Deligne (Institut des Hautes Études Scientifiques), Charles Louis Fefferman (Princeton University), Gregori

Alexandrovitch Margulis (Moscow University), and Daniel G. Quillen (Massachusetts Institute of Technology)

1982 Alain Connes (Institut des Hautes Études Scientifiques), William P. Thurston (Princeton University), and Shing-Tung Yau (Institute for Advanced Study, Princeton)

1986 Simon Donaldson (Oxford University), Gerd Faltings (Princeton University), and Michael Freedman (University of California, San Diego)

1990 Vladimir Drinfeld (Phys. Inst. Kharkov), Vaughan Jones (University of California, Berkeley), Shigefumi Mori (University of Kyoto), and Edward Witten (Institute for Advanced Study, Princeton)

1994 Pierre-Louis Lions (Université de Paris–Dauphine), Jean-Christophe Yoccoz (Université de Paris–Sud), Jean Bourgain (Institute for Advanced Study, Princeton), and Efim Zelmanov (University of Wisconsin)

1998 Richard E. Borcherds (Cambridge University), William T. Gowers (Cambridge University), Maxim Kontsevich (Institut des Hautes Études Scientifiques and Rutgers University), and Curtis T. McMullen (Harvard University)

Recipients of Kennedy Center Honors

The Kennedy Center Honors recognize the lifetime achievements of selected American performing artists.

1978 Marian Anderson (contralto), Fred Astaire (dancer-actor), Richard Rodgers (Broadway composer), Arthur Rubinstein (pianist), George Balanchine (choreographer)

1979 Ella Fitzgerald (jazz singer), Henry Fonda (actor), Martha Graham (choreographer), Tennessee Williams (playwright), Aaron Copland (composer)

1980 James Cagney (actor), Leonard Bernstein (composer-conductor), Agnes de Mille (choreographer), Lynn Fontanne (actress), Leontyne Price (soprano)

1981 Count Basie (jazz composer-pianist), Cary Grant (actor), Helen Hayes (actress), Jerome Robbins (choreographer), Rudolf Serkin (pianist)

1982 George Abbott (Broadway producer), Lillian Gish (actress), Benny Goodman (jazz clarinetist), Gene Kelly (dancer-actor), Eugene Ormandy (conductor)

1983 Katherine Dunham (dancer-choreographer), Elia Kazan (director-author), James Stewart (actor), Virgil Thomson (music critic-composer), Frank Sinatra (singer)

1984 Lena Horne (singer), Danny Kaye (comedian-actor), Gian Carlo Menotti (composer), Arthur Miller (playwright), Isaac Stern (violinist)

1985 Merce Cunningham (dancer-choreographer), Irene Dunne (actress), Bob Hope (comedian), Alan Jay Lerner (lyricist-playwright), Frederick Loewe (composer), Beverly Sills (soprano)

1986 Lucille Ball (comedienne), Ray Charles (musician), Yehudi Menuhin (violinist), Antony Tudor (choreographer), Hume Cronyn and Jessica Tandy (husband-and-wife acting team)

1987 Perry Como (singer), Bette Davis (actress), Sammy Davis, Jr., (entertainer), Nathan Milstein (violinist), Alwin Nikolais (choreographer)

1988 Alvin Ailey (choreographer), George Burns (comedian-actor), Myrna Loy (actress), Alexander Schneider (violinist), Roger L. Stevens (theatrical producer and the Kennedy Center's founding chairman)

1989 Harry Belafonte (singer-actor), Claudette Colbert (actress), Alexandra Danilova (ballerina), Mary Martin (actress), William Schuman (composer)

1990 Dizzy Gillespie (jazz trumpeter), Katharine Hepburn (actress), Risë Stevens (mezzo-soprano), Jule Styne (composer), Billy Wilder (director)

1991 Roy Acuff (country songwriter and singer), Betty Comden and Adolph Green (co-authors of books and lyrics of musicals), the brothers Fayard and Harold Nicholas (dancers), Gregory Peck (actor), Robert Shaw (choral director)

1992 Lionel Hampton (jazz musician), Paul Newman (actor), Joanne Woodward (actress), Ginger Rogers (dancer-actress), Mstislav Rostropovich (cellist-conductor), Paul Taylor (choreographer)

1993 Johnny Carson (talk-show host), Arthur Mitchell (dancer and choreographer), Georg Solti (conductor), Stephen Sondheim (composer and lyricist), Marion Williams (gospel singer)

1994 Kirk Douglas (actor), Aretha Franklin (singer), Morton Gould (composer), Harold Prince (producer and director), Pete Seeger (folk singer)

1995 Jacques D'Ambroise (choreographer), Marilyn Horne (mezzo soprano), B. B. King (blues singer), Sidney Poitier (actor), Neil Simon (playwright)

1996 Edward Albee (playwright), Benny Carter (jazz musician), Johnny Cash (musician), Jack Lemmon (actor), Maria Tallchief (ballerina)

1997 Lauren Bacall (actress), Bob Dylan (songwriter and singer), Charlton Heston (actor), Jessye Norman (soprano), Edward Villella (ballet dancer and director)

1998 Bill Cosby (actor and comedian), John Kander and Fred Ebb (Broadway composer and lyricist team), Willie Nelson (singer and songwriter), André Previn (composer and conductor), Shirley Temple Black (actress)

The Spingarn Medal

The Spingarn Medal is awarded annually by the National Association for the Advancement of Colored People for outstanding achievement by a black American.

1915 Ernest E. Judd	**1944** Charles Drew	**1972** Gordon Parks
1916 Charles Young	**1945** Paul Robeson	**1973** Wilson C. Riles
1917 Harry T. Burleigh	**1946** Thurgood Marshall	**1974** Damon Keith
1918 William Stanley Braithwaite	**1947** Percy Julian	**1975** Hank Aaron
1919 Archibald H. Grimke	**1948** Channing H. Tobias	**1976** Alvin Ailey
1920 W. E. B. Du Bois	**1949** Ralph J. Bunche	**1977** Alex Haley
1921 Charles S. Gilpin	**1950** Charles Hamilton Houston	**1978** Andrew Young
1922 Mary B. Talbert	**1951** Mabel Keaton Staupers	**1979** Rosa L. Parks
1923 George Washington Carver	**1952** Harry T. Moore	**1980** Rayford W. Logan
1924 Roland Hayes	**1953** Paul R. Williams	**1981** Coleman Young
1925 James Weldon Johnson	**1954** Theodore K. Lawless	**1982** Benjamin E. Mays
1926 Carter G. Woodson	**1955** Carl Murphy	**1983** Lena Horne
1927 Anthony Overton	**1956** Jackie Robinson	**1984** Tom Bradley
1928 Charles W. Chesnutt	**1957** Martin Luther King. Jr.	**1985** Bill Cosby
1929 Mordecai Wyatt Johnson	**1958** Daisy Bates and the Little Rock Nine	**1986** Benjamin L. Hooks
1930 Henry A. Hunt	**1959** Edward Kennedy (Duke) Ellington	**1987** Percy Ellis Sutton
1931 Richard Berry Harrison	**1960** Langston Hughes	**1988** Frederick Douglass Patterson
1932 Robert Russa Moton	**1961** Kenneth B. Clark	**1989** Jesse Jackson
1933 Max Yergan	**1962** Robert C. Weaver	**1990** L. Douglas Wilder
1934 William T. B. Williams	**1963** Medgar Evers	**1991** Colin T. Powell
1935 Mary McLeod Bethune	**1964** Roy Wilkins	**1992** Barbara Jordan
1936 John Hope	**1965** Leontyne Price	**1993** Dorothy Irene Height
1937 Walter White	**1966** John H. Johnson	**1994** Maya Angelou
1938 No award	**1967** Edward W. Brooke III	**1995** John Hope Franklin
1939 Marian Anderson	**1968** Sammy Davis, Jr.	**1996** A. Leon Higginbotham, Jr.
1940 Louis T. Wright	**1969** Clarence M. Mitchell, Jr.	**1997** Carl Rowan
1941 Richard Wright	**1970** Jacob Lawrence	**1998** Myrlie Evers-Williams
1942 A. Philip Randolph	**1971** Leon Howard Sullivan	**1999** Earl G. Graves, Sr.
1943 William H. Hastie		

1998 Cool Site of the Year Awards

Cool Site: *How Stuff Works*, www.howstuffworks.com
Cool Book Site: *Best Book Buys*, www.bestbookbuys.com
Cool Community on the Web: *Talk City*, www.talkcity.com
Cool Design: *The Fray*, www.fray.com
Cool Game Site: *Uproar*, www.uproar.com
Cool Humor Site: *Brunching Shuttlecocks*, www.brunching.com
Cool Innovation: *Thing World*, www.thingworld.com
Cool Money Site: *Motley Fool*, www.fool.com
Cool Music Site: *Spinner*, www.spinner.com

Cool Movie Site: *Countdown*, www.countingdown.com
Cool Personal Site: *Chunk*, www.chunk.com
Cool Reference Site: *How Stuff Works*, www.howstuffworks.com
Cool Science Site: *The True Witness*, library.advanced.org/17049
Cool Shopping Site: *eBay*, www.ebay.com
Cool Sports Site: *Formula 1*, www.formula1.com
Cool Zine Site: *Slashdot.Org*, www.slashdot.org

U.S. Symphony Orchestras and Their Music Directors

(with expenses over $1,050,000)

Akron Symphony Orchestra: Jeffrey K. Sperry[1]
Alabama Symphony Ochestra: Richard Westerfield
American Composers Orchestra: Dennis Russell Davies
American Symphony Orchestra: Leon Botstein
Arkansas Symphony Orchestra: David Itkin
Aspen Chamber Symphony: David Zinman
Atlanta Symphony: Yoel Levi
Austin Symphony: Peter Bay
Baltimore Symphony: Yuri Temirkanov
Baton Rouge Symphony: James Paul
Boca Pops (Florida Symphonic Pops): Crafton Beck[2, 3]
Boston Symphony: Seiji Ozawa
Boston Symphony Chamber Players: Malcolm Lowe
Boulder Philharmonic Orchestra: Theodor Kuchar
Brooklyn Philharmonic: Robert Spano
Buffalo Philharmonic Orchestra: JoAnn Falletta
Cedar Rapids Symphony: Christian Tiemeyer[2]
Charleston Symphony: David Stahl
Charlotte Symphony: Peter McCoppin
Chattanooga Symphony & Opera Association: Robert Bernhardt
Chicago Sinfonietta: Paul Freeman
Chicago Symphony: Daniel Barenboim
Cincinnati Symphony: Jesus Lopez-Cobos
Cleveland Orchestra: Christoph von Dohnanyi
Colorado Springs Symphony: Yaacov Bergman
Colorado Symphony (Denver): Marin Alsop
Columbus Symphony: Alessandro Siciliani
Dallas Symphony: Andrew Litton
Dayton Philharmonic: Neal Gittleman
Delaware Symphony: Stephen Gunzenhauser
Des Moines Symphony: Joseph Giunta
Detroit Symphony: Neeme Jarvi
Elgin Symphony Orchestra: Robert L. Hanson[2]
El Paso Symphony Orchestra: Gurer Aykal
Erie Philharmonic: Peter Bay
Evansville Philharmonic Orchestra: Alfred Savia
Florida Orchestra: Jahja Ling
Florida Philharmonic Orchestra: James Judd
Florida West Coast Symphony Orchestra: Leif Bjaland[2, 3]
Fort Wayne Philharmonic: Edvard Tchivzhel
Fort Worth Symphony: John Giordano
Fresno Philharmonic Orchestra: Raymond Harvey
Grand Rapids Symphony: Catherine Comet
Grant Park Symphony (Chicago): Hugh Wolff[4]
Greensboro Symphony Orchestra: Stuart Malina
Greenville Symphony Orchestra: Edvard Tchivzhel
Handel & Haydn Society: Christopher Hogwood[3]
Harrisburg Symphony Orchestra: Richard Westerfield
Hartford Symphony: Michael Lankester
Honolulu Symphony Society: Samuel Wong
Houston Symphony: Christopher Eschenbach
Hudson Valley Philharmonic (Poughkeepsie): Randall Craig Fleischer
Indianapolis Symphony: Raymond Leppard
Jacksonville Symphony: Roger Nierenberg
Kalamazoo Symphony Orchestra: Yoshimi Takeda
Kansas City Symphony: Anne Manson
Kennedy Center Opera House Orchestra: Heinze Frickle
Knoxville Symphony: Kirk Trevor
Little Orchestra Society of New York: Dino Anagnost
Long Beach Symphony: JoAnn Falletta

Long Island Philharmonic: David Lockington
Los Angeles Chamber Orchestra: Jeffrey Kahane
Los Angeles Philharmonic: Esa-Pekka Salonen
Louisiana Philharmonic Orchestra: Klauspeter Seibel
Louisville Orchestra: Max Bragado-Darman
Madison Symphony Orchestra: John De Main
Memphis Symphony: Alan Balter
Milwaukee Symphony Orchestra: Andreas Delfs
Minnesota Orchestra: Eiji Oue
Mississippi Symphony: Colman Pearce
Monterey County Symphony: Joan Devisser[1]
Music Academy of the West Summer Festival Orchestra: Carleen Landes[3]
Music of the Baroque: Thomas S. Wikman
Naples Philharmonic: Christopher Seaman
Nashville Symphony: Kenneth D. Schermerhorn
National Sininietta: Burton A. Zipser[3]
National Symphony (D.C.): Leonard Slatkin
New Haven Symphony: Michael Palmer
New Jersey Symphony: Zdenek Macal[2, 3]
New Mexico Symphony: David Lockington
New West Symphony: Boris Brott[2]
New World Symphony (Fla.): Michael Tilson Thomas[3]
New York Chamber Symphony of the 92nd St. Y: Gerard Schwarz
New York Philharmonic: Kurt Masur
New York Pops: Skitch Henderson
North Carolina Symphony: Gerhardt Zimmermann
Northeastern Pennsylvania Philharmonic: Hugh Keelan
Ohio Chamber Orchestra: David Lockington[1]
Oklahoma City Philharmonic: Joel A. Levine
Omaha Symphony: Victor Yampolsky
Omaha Symphony Chamber Orchestra: Victor Yampolsky
Oregon Symphony: James DePreist
Pacific Symphony (Calif.): Carl St. Clair
Palm Beach Pops: Bob Lappin
Philadelphia Orchestra: Wolfgang Sawallisch
Philharmonia Baroque Orchestra: Nicholas McGegan
Phoenix Symphony: Hermann Michael
Pittsburgh Symphony Orchestra: Mariss Jansons
Portland Symphony: Toshiyuki Shimada
Quad City Symphony Orchestra Association: Kim Allen Kluge
Rhode Island Philharmonic: Larry Rachleff
Richmond Symphony: George Manahan
River City Brass Band: Denis Colwell
Rochester Philharmonic: Christopher Seaman
Sacramento Symphony Orchestra: Geoffrey Simon
St. Louis Symphony: Hans Vonk
St. Paul Chamber Orchestra: Hugh Wolff
San Antonio Symphony: Christopher Wilkins
San Francisco Symphony: Michael Tilson Thomas
San Jose Symphony: Leonid Grin[2]
Santa Barbara Symphony Orchestra: Gisele Ben-Dor
Santa Rosa Symphony: Jeffrey Kahane
Savannah Symphony: Philip Greenberg
Seattle Symphony: Gerard Schwarz
Shreveport Symphony: Dennis Simons
Spokane Symphony: Fabio Mechetti
Springfield Symphony (Mass.): Mark Russell Smith
Stamford Symphony Orchestra: Roger Nierenberg[2]
Symphony of United Nations: Joseph Eger

Syracuse Symphony: Fabio Mechetti
Toledo Symphony: Andrew Massey
Tucson Symphony: George Hanson
Tulsa Philharmonic: Bernard Rubenstein
Utah Symphony: Keith Lockhart
Virginia Symphony: JoAnn Falletta

Westchester Philharmonic: Paul Lustig Dunkel[2]
West Virginia Symphony: Thomas B. Conlin[3]
Wichita Symphony: Zuohuang Chen
Winston-Salem Piedmont Triad Symphony:
Peter J. Perret
Youngstown Symphony Orchestra: Isaiah Jackson

1. Executive Director. 2. Conductor. 3. Artistic Director. 4. Principal Conductor. 5. Music Conductor.

U.S. Opera Companies
(budgets $2,000,000 and over)

American Musical Theatre of San Jose (Calif.), Dianna Shuster, Art. Dir.
Arizona Opera Company (Tucson, Phoenix), Glynn Ross, Gen. Dir.
Aspen Opera Theater Center (Colo.), Robert Harth, Pres. and CEO
Atlanta Opera, The (Ga.), William Fred Scott, Art. Dir.
Austin Lyric Opera (Tex.), Joseph McClain, Gen. Dir.
Baltimore Opera Company (Md.), Michael Harrison, Gen. Dir.
Boston Lyric Opera Company (Mass.), Janice Mancini Del Sesto, Gen. Dir.
Central City Opera House Association (Colo.), Daniel R. Rule, Gen. Mgr.
Cincinnati Opera Association (Ohio), James de Blasis, Art. Dir.
Civic Light Opera (Pittsburgh), Charles Gray, Exec. Dir.
Cleveland Opera (Ohio), David Bamberger, Gen. Dir.
Dallas Opera, The (Tex.), Plato S. Karayanis, Gen. Dir.
Florentine Opera Company (Milwaukee), Dennis W. Hanthorn, Gen. Dir.
Florida Grand Opera (Miami), Robert M. Heuer, Gen. Mgr. and CEO
Glimmerglass Opera (Cooperstown, N.Y.), Paul Kellogg, Art. Dir.
Goodspeed Opera House (East Haddam, Conn.), Michael Price, Exec. Dir.
Hawaii Opera Theatre (Honolulu), J. Mario Ramos, Gen. Dir. and Art. Dir.
Houston Grand Opera Association (Tex.), R. David Gockley, Gen. Dir.
Kentucky Opera (Louisville), Thomson Smillie, Gen. Dir.
Long Beach Civic Light Opera (Calif.), J. Phillip Keene III, Exec. Dir.
Los Angeles Music Center Opera (Calif.), Peter Hemmings, Gen. Dir.
Lyric Opera of Chicago (Ill.), Ardis Krainik, Gen. Dir.
Lyric Opera of Kansas City (Mo.), Evan R. Luskin, Gen. Dir.
Metro Lyric Opera (Allenhurst, N.J.), Era M. Tognoli, Gen. Dir. and Art. Dir.

Metropolitan Opera Association, (N.Y.), James Levine, Art. Dir.
Michigan Opera Theatre (Detroit), David DiChiera, Gen. Dir.
Minnesota Opera, The (Minneapolis), Kevin Smith, Pres. and Gen. Dir.
New York City Opera (N.Y.), Paul Kellogg, Gen. Dir.
New York City Opera National Company (N.Y.), Clifford Kellas, Tour Coord.
Ohio Light Opera (Wooster), James Stuart, Art. Dir.
Opera Colorado (Denver), Nathaniel Merrill, Pres. and Gen. Dir.
Opera Company of Philadelphia (Pa.), Robert B. Driver, Gen. Dir.
Opera Pacific (Irvine, Calif.), David DiChiera, Art. Dir.
Opera Theatre of St. Louis (Mo.), Charles MacKay, Gen. Dir.
Orlando Opera Company Inc. (Fla.), Robert Swedberg, Gen. Dir.
Palm Beach Opera Inc. (Fla.), Herbert P. Benn, Gen. Dir.
Pittsburgh Opera, Inc. (Pa.), Tito Capobianco, Art. Dir.
Portland Opera Association (Ore.), Robert Bailey, Gen. Dir.
San Diego Civic Light Opera Association (Calif.), Leon Drew, Gen. Mgr.
San Diego Opera (Calif.), Ian D. Campbell, Gen. Dir.
San Francisco Opera (Calif.), Lotfi Mansouri, Gen. Dir.
San Francisco Opera Center (Calif.), Richard Harrell, Gen. Dir.
Santa Barbara Civic Light Opera (Calif.), Paul Iannacone, Exec. Prod.
Santa Fe Opera (N.M.), John Crosby, Gen. Dir.
Sarasota Opera Association (Fla.), Deane Carroll Allyn, Exec. Dir.
Seattle Opera Association (Wash.), Speight Jenkins, Gen. Dir.
Virginia Opera (Norfolk), Peter Mark, Gen. Dir.
Utah Opera Company (Salt Lake City), Anne Ewers, Gen. Dir.
Washington Opera, The (D.C.), Placido Domingo, Art. Dir. Designate

U.S. Dance Companies
(budgets $2,500,000 and over)

Alvin Ailey American Dance Theatre (1958): Judith Jamison, Art. Dir.
American Ballet Theatre (1940): Kevin McKenzie, Art. Dir.
Atlanta Ballet Company (1929): John McFall, Art. Dir. and CEO
Ballet Florida (1986): Marie Hale, Art. Dir.
BalletMet Columbus (1978): David Nixon, Art. Dir.
Ballet West (1968[1]): Jonas Kåge, Art. Dir.
Boston Ballet (1964): Anna-Marie Holmes, Art. Dir.
Cincinnati Ballet (1955): Victoria Morgan, Art. Dir.
Cleveland San Jose Ballet (1976): Dennis Nahat, Art. Dir.
Colorado Ballet (1961): Martin Fredmann, Art. Dir.
Merce Cunningham Dance Company (1952): Merce Cunningham, Art. Dir.

Dance Theater of Harlem (1968): Arthur Mitchell, Art. Dir.
Feld Ballet New York (1974): Eliot Feld, Dir.
Martha Graham Dance Company (1927): Ron Protas, Art. Dir.
Houston Ballet (1968): Ben Stevenson, Art. Dir.
Joffrey Ballet of Chicago (1954): Gerald Arpino, Art. Dir.
Los Angeles Ballet (1995[2]): Andrew Deneau, Gen. Dir.
Miami City Ballet (1986): Edward Villella, Art. Dir.
Milwaukee Ballet (1970): Basil Thompson, Art. Dir.
New York City Ballet (1948): Peter Martins, Ballet-Master-in-Chief
Ocheami-Afrikan Dance Company (1978): Kofe Anang, Art. Dir.
Pacific Northwest Ballet (1972): Kent Stowell and Francia Russell, Art. Dirs.

Pittsburgh Ballet Theater (1970): Terrence S. Orr, Art. Dir.
San Francisco Ballet (1933): Helgi Tomasson, Art. Dir.

Paul Taylor Dance Company (1954): Paul Taylor, Dir.
Streb/Ringside (1985): Elizabeth Streb, Art. Dir.

NOTE: Year founded appears in parentheses after name. 1. Prior company founded 1963, name changed to Ballet West in 1968. 2. Originally founded 1954, survived several reincarnations, the most recent of which was begun in 1995.

Best-Selling Books, 1998

Source: Publishers Weekly

Hardcover Fiction

1. *The Street Lawyer,* John Grisham
2. *Rainbow Six,* Tom Clancy
3. *Bag of Bones,* Stephen King
4. *A Man in Full,* Tom Wolfe
5. *Mirror Image,* Danielle Steel
6. *The Long Road Home,* Danielle Steel
7. *The Klone and I,* Danielle Steel
8. *Point of Origin,* Patricia Cornwell
9. *Paradise,* Toni Morrison
10. *All Through the Night,* Mary Higgins Clark

Hardcover Nonfiction

1. *The 9 Steps to Financial Freedom,* Suze Orman
2. *The Greatest Generation,* Tom Brokaw
3. *Sugar Busters!,* H. Leighton Steward, Morrison C. Bethea, Sam S. Andrews, and Luis A. Balart
4. *Tuesdays with Morrie,* Mitch Albom
5. *The Guinness Book of Records 1999,* Guinness Media
6. *Talking to Heaven,* James Van Praagh
7. *Something More: Excavating Your Authentic Self,* Sarah Ban Breathnach
8. *In the Meantime,* Iyanla Vanzant
9. *A Pirate Looks at Fifty,* Jimmy Buffett
10. *If Life Is a Game These Are the Rules,* Cherie Carter-Scott, Ph.D.

Trade Paperbacks

1. *Don't Sweat the Small Stuff . . . and it's all small stuff,* Richard Carlson, Ph.D.
2. *Divine Secrets of the Ya-Ya Sisterhood,* Rebecca Wells
3. *Chicken Soup for the Teenage Soul,* Jack Canfield, Mark Victor Hansen, et al.
4. *Don't Sweat the Small Stuff with Your Family,* Richard Carlson, Ph.D.
5. *Chicken Soup for the Kid's Soul,* Jack Canfield, Mark Victor Hansen, et al.
6. *Chicken Soup for the Pet Lover's Soul,* Jack Canfield, Mark Victor Hansen, et al.
7. *Chicken Soup for the Mother's Soul,* Jack Canfield, Mark Victor Hansen, et al.
8. *A Second Chicken Soup for the Woman's Soul,* Jack Canfield, Mark Victor Hansen, et al.
9. *Here on Earth,* Alice Hoffman
10. *Prescription for Nutritional Healing: A Practical A-Z Reference to Drug-Free Remedies Using Vitamins, Minerals, Herbs & Food Supplements,* James F. Balch, M.D., and Phyllis A. Balch, C.N.C.

Mass Market Paperbacks

1. *The Partner,* John Grisham
2. *The Ghost,* Danielle Steel
3. *The Ranch,* Danielle Steel
4. *Special Delivery,* Danielle Steel
5. *Unnatural Exposure,* Patricia Cornwell
6. *Pretend You Don't See Her,* Mary Higgins Clark
7. *Power Plays: ruthless.com,* Tom Clancy
8. *Rising Tides,* Nora Roberts
9. *Wizard and Glass,* Stephen King
10. *Dr. Atkins' New Diet Revolution,* Robert C. Atkins, M.D.

All-Time Children's Best-Selling Books

From the date of publication (in parentheses) through the end of 1995.

Source: Publishers Weekly

Hardcovers

1. *The Poky Little Puppy,* Janette Sebring Lowrey (1942)
2. *The Tale of Peter Rabbit,* Beatrix Potter (1902)
3. *Tootle,* Gertrude Crampton (1945)
4. *Saggy Baggy Elephant,* Kathryn and Byron Jackson (1955)
5. *Scuffy the Tugboat,* Gertrude Crampton (1955)
6. *Pat the Bunny,* Dorothy Kunhardt (1940)
7. *Green Eggs and Ham,* Dr. Seuss (1960)
8. *The Cat in the Hat,* Dr. Seuss (1957)
9. *The Littlest Angel,* Charles Tazewell (1946)
10. *One Fish, Two Fish, Red Fish, Blue Fish,* Dr. Seuss (1960)

Paperbacks

1. *Charlotte's Web,* E. B. White, illus. by Garth Williams (1974)
2. *The Outsiders,* S. E. Hinton (1968)
3. *Tales of a Fourth Grade Nothing,* Judy Blume (1976)
4. *Shane,* Jack Schaeffer (1983)
5. *Are You There, God? It's Me, Margaret,* Judy Blume (1972)
6. *Where the Red Fern Grows,* Wilson Rawls (1974)
7. *A Wrinkle in Time,* Madeleine L'Engle (1973)
8. *Island of the Blue Dolphins,* Scott O'Dell (1971)
9. *Little House on the Prairie,* Laura Ingalls Wilder, illus. by Garth Williams (1971)
10. *Little House in the Big Woods,* Laura Ingalls Wilder, illus. by Garth Williams (1971)

The 100 Best Novels of the 20th Century

The Board of the Modern Library, a division of Random House, published its selections in July 1998. The list was criticized for not including enough women and minorities, and several alternative lists quickly followed.

1. *Ulysses*, James Joyce
2. *The Great Gatsby*, F. Scott Fitzgerald
3. *A Portrait of the Artist as a Young Man*, James Joyce
4. *Lolita*, Vladimir Nabokov
5. *Brave New World*, Aldous Huxley
6. *The Sound and the Fury*, William Faulkner
7. *Catch-22*, Joseph Heller
8. *Darkness at Noon*, Arthur Koestler
9. *Sons and Lovers*, D. H. Lawrence
10. *The Grapes of Wrath*, John Steinbeck
11. *Under the Volcano*, Malcolm Lowry
12. *The Way of All Flesh*, Samuel Butler
13. *1984*, George Orwell
14. *I, Claudius*, Robert Graves
15. *To the Lighthouse*, Virginia Woolf
16. *An American Tragedy*, Theodore Dreiser
17. *The Heart Is a Lonely Hunter*, Carson McCullers
18. *Slaughterhouse-Five*, Kurt Vonnegut
19. *Invisible Man*, Ralph Ellison
20. *Native Son*, Richard Wright
21. *Henderson the Rain King*, Saul Bellow
22. *Appointment in Samarra*, John O'Hara
23. *U.S.A. (trilogy)*, John Dos Passos
24. *Winesburg, Ohio*, Sherwood Anderson
25. *A Passage to India*, E. M. Forster
26. *The Wings of the Dove*, Henry James
27. *The Ambassadors*, Henry James
28. *Tender Is the Night*, F. Scott Fitzgerald
29. *The Studs Lonigan Trilogy*, James T. Farrell
30. *The Good Soldier*, Ford Madox Ford
31. *Animal Farm*, George Orwell
32. *The Golden Bowl*, Henry James
33. *Sister Carrie*, Theodore Dreiser
34. *A Handful of Dust*, Evelyn Waugh
35. *As I Lay Dying*, William Faulkner
36. *All the King's Men*, Robert Penn Warren
37. *The Bridge of San Luis Rey*, Thornton Wilder
38. *Howards End*, E. M. Forster
39. *Go Tell It on the Mountain*, James Baldwin
40. *The Heart of the Matter*, Graham Greene
41. *Lord of the Flies*, William Golding
42. *Deliverance*, James Dickey
43. *A Dance to the Music of Time (series)*, Anthony Powell
44. *Point Counter Point*, Aldous Huxley
45. *The Sun Also Rises*, Ernest Hemingway
46. *The Secret Agent*, Joseph Conrad
47. *Nostromo*, Joseph Conrad
48. *The Rainbow*, D. H. Lawrence
49. *Women in Love*, D. H. Lawrence
50. *Tropic of Cancer*, Henry Miller
51. *The Naked and the Dead*, Norman Mailer
52. *Portnoy's Complaint*, Philip Roth
53. *Pale Fire*, Vladimir Nabokov
54. *Light in August*, William Faulkner
55. *On the Road*, Jack Kerouac
56. *The Maltese Falcon*, Dashiell Hammett
57. *Parade's End*, Ford Madox Ford
58. *The Age of Innocence*, Edith Wharton
59. *Zuleika Dobson*, Max Beerbohm
60. *The Moviegoer*, Walker Percy
61. *Death Comes for the Archbishop*, Willa Cather
62. *From Here to Eternity*, James Jones
63. *The Wapshot Chronicles*, John Cheever
64. *The Catcher in the Rye*, J. D. Salinger
65. *A Clockwork Orange*, Anthony Burgess
66. *Of Human Bondage*, W. Somerset Maugham
67. *Heart of Darkness*, Joseph Conrad
68. *Main Street*, Sinclair Lewis
69. *The House of Mirth*, Edith Wharton
70. *The Alexandria Quartet*, Lawrence Durell
71. *A High Wind in Jamaica*, Richard Hughes
72. *A House for Mr. Biswas*, V. S. Naipaul
73. *The Day of the Locust*, Nathanael West
74. *A Farewell to Arms*, Ernest Hemingway
75. *Scoop*, Evelyn Waugh
76. *The Prime of Miss Jean Brodie*, Muriel Spark
77. *Finnegans Wake*, James Joyce
78. *Kim*, Rudyard Kipling
79. *A Room with a View*, E. M. Forster
80. *Brideshead Revisited*, Evelyn Waugh
81. *The Adventures of Augie March*, Saul Bellow
82. *Angle of Repose*, Wallace Stegner
83. *A Bend in the River*, V. S. Naipaul
84. *The Death of the Heart*, Elizabeth Bowen
85. *Lord Jim*, Joseph Conrad
86. *Ragtime*, E. L. Doctorow
87. *The Old Wives' Tale*, Arnold Bennett
88. *The Call of the Wild*, Jack London
89. *Loving*, Henry Green
90. *Midnight's Children*, Salman Rushdie
91. *Tobacco Road*, Erskine Caldwell
92. *Ironweed*, William Kennedy
93. *The Magus*, John Fowles
94. *Wide Sargasso Sea*, Jean Rhys
95. *Under the Net*, Iris Murdoch
96. *Sophie's Choice*, William Styron
97. *The Sheltering Sky*, Paul Bowles
98. *The Postman Always Rings Twice*, James M. Cain
99. *The Ginger Man*, J. P. Donleavy
100. *The Magnificent Ambersons*, Booth Tarkington

The 100 Best Nonfiction Books of the 20th Century

The Board of the Modern Library, a division of Random House, published its selections in April 1999.

1. *The Education of Henry Adams*, Henry Adams
2. *The Varieties of Religious Experience*, William James
3. *Up from Slavery*, Booker T. Washington
4. *A Room of One's Own*, Virginia Woolf
5. *Silent Spring*, Rachel Carson
6. *Selected Essays, 1917–1932*, T. S. Eliot
7. *The Double Helix*, James D. Watson
8. *Speak, Memory*, Vladimir Nabokov
9. *The American Language*, H. L. Mencken
10. *The General Theory of Employment, Interest, and Money*, John Maynard Keynes
11. *The Lives of a Cell*, Lewis Thomas
12. *The Frontier in American History*, Frederick Jackson Turner
13. *Black Boy*, Richard Wright
14. *Aspects of the Novel*, E. M. Forster
15. *The Civil War*, Shelby Foote

16. *The Guns of August*, Barbara Tuchman
17. *The Proper Study of Mankind*, Isaiah Berlin
18. *The Nature and Destiny of Man*, Reinhold Niebuhr
19. *Notes of a Native Son*, James Baldwin
20. *The Autobiography of Alice B. Toklas*, Gertrude Stein
21. *The Elements of Style*, William Strunk and E. B. White
22. *An American Dilemma*, Gunnar Myrdal
23. *Principia Mathematica*, Alfred North Whitehead and Bertrand Russell
24. *The Mismeasure of Man*, Stephen Jay Gould
25. *The Mirror and the Lamp*, Meyer Howard Abrams
26. *The Art of the Soluble*, Peter B. Medawar
27. *The Ants*, Bert Hoelldobler and Edward O. Wilson
28. *A Theory of Justice*, John Rawls
29. *Art and Illusion*, Ernest H. Gombrich
30. *The Making of the English Working Class*, E. P. Thompson
31. *The Souls of Black Folk*, W. E. B. DuBois
32. *Principia Ethica*, G. E. Moore
33. *Philosophy and Civilization*, John Dewey
34. *On Growth and Form*, D'Arcy Thompson
35. *Ideas and Opinions*, Albert Einstein
36. *The Age of Jackson*, Arthur Schlesinger, Jr.
37. *The Making of the Atomic Bomb*, Richard Rhodes
38. *Black Lamb and Grey Falcon*, Rebecca West
39. *Autobiographies*, W. B. Yeats
40. *Science and Civilization in China*, Joseph Needham
41. *Goodbye to All That*, Robert Graves
42. *Homage to Catalonia*, George Orwell
43. *The Autobiography of Mark Twain*, Mark Twain
44. *Children of Crisis*, Robert Coles
45. *A Study of History*, Arnold J. Toynbee
46. *The Affluent Society*, John Kenneth Galbraith
47. *Present at the Creation*, Dean Acheson
48. *The Great Bridge*, David McCullough
49. *Patriotic Gore*, Edmund Wilson
50. *Samuel Johnson*, Walter Jackson Bate
51. *The Autobiography of Malcolm X*, Alex Haley and Malcolm X
52. *The Right Stuff*, Tom Wolfe
53. *Eminent Victorians*, Lytton Strachey
54. *Working*, Studs Terkel
55. *Darkness Visible*, William Styron
56. *The Liberal Imagination*, Lionel Trilling
57. *The Second World War*, Winston Churchill

58. *Out of Africa*, Isak Dinesen
59. *Jefferson and His Time*, Dumas Malone
60. *In the American Grain*, William Carlos Williams
61. *Cadillac Desert*, Marc Reisner
62. *The House of Morgan*, Ron Chernow
63. *The Sweet Science*, A. J. Liebling
64. *The Open Society and Its Enemies*, Karl Popper
65. *The Art of Memory*, Frances A. Yates
66. *Religion and the Rise of Capitalism*, R. H. Tawney
67. *A Preface to Morals*, Walter Lippmann
68. *The Gate of Heavenly Peace*, Jonathan D. Spence
69. *The Structure of Scientific Revolutions*, Thomas S. Kuhn
70. *The Strange Career of Jim Crow*, C. Vann Woodward
71. *The Rise of the West*, William H. McNeill
72. *The Gnostic Gospels*, Elaine Pagels
73. *James Joyce*, Richard Ellmann
74. *Florence Nightingale*, Cecil Woodham-Smith
75. *The Great War and Modern Memory*, Paul Fussell
76. *The City in History*, Lewis Mumford
77. *Battle Cry of Freedom*, James M. McPherson
78. *Why We Can't Wait*, Martin Luther King, Jr.
79. *The Rise of Theodore Roosevelt*, Edmund Morris
80. *Studies in Iconology*, Erwin Panofsky
81. *The Face of Battle*, John Keegan
82. *The Strange Death of Liberal England*, George Dangerfield
83. *Vermeer*, Lawrence Gowing
84. *A Bright Shining Lie*, Neil Sheehan
85. *West with the Night*, Beryl Markham
86. *This Boy's Life*, Tobias Wolff
87. *A Mathematician's Apology*, G. H. Hardy
88. *Six Easy Pieces*, Richard P. Feynman
89. *Pilgrim at Tinker Creek*, Annie Dillard
90. *The Golden Bough*, James George Frazer
91. *Shadow and Act*, Ralph Ellison
92. *The Power Broker*, Robert A. Caro
93. *The American Political Tradition*, Richard Hofstadter
94. *The Contours of American History*, William Appleman Williams
95. *The Promise of American Life*, Herbert Croly
96. *In Cold Blood*, Truman Capote
97. *The Journalist and the Murderer*, Janet Malcolm
98. *The Taming of Chance*, Ian Hacking
99. *Operating Instructions*, Anne Lamott
100. *Melbourne*, Lord David Cecil

Best American Journalism of the 20th Century

The following works were chosen as the 20th century's best American journalism by a panel of experts assembled by the New York University school of journalism:

1. **John Hersey:** "Hiroshima," *The New Yorker,* 1946
2. **Rachel Carson:** *Silent Spring,* book, 1962
3. **Bob Woodward and Carl Bernstein:** Investigation of the Watergate break-in, *The Washington Post,* 1972
4. **Edward R. Murrow:** *Battle of Britain,* CBS radio, 1940
5. **Ida Tarbell:** "The History of the Standard Oil Company," *McClure's,* 1902–1904
6. **Lincoln Steffens:** "The Shame of the Cities," *McClure's,* 1902–1904

7. **John Reed:** *Ten Days That Shook the World,* book, 1919
8. **H. L. Mencken:** Scopes "Monkey" trial, *The Sun* of Baltimore, 1925
9. **Ernie Pyle:** Reports from Europe and the Pacific during World War II, Scripps-Howard newspapers, 1940-45
10. **Edward R. Murrow and Fred Friendly:** Investigation of Sen. Joseph McCarthy, CBS, 1954
11. **Edward R. Murrow, David Lowe, and Fred Friendly:** documentary "Harvest of Shame,"

CBS television, 1960

12. **Seymour Hersh:** Investigation of massacre by American soldiers at My Lai in Vietnam, Dispatch News Service, 1969

13. **The New York Times:** Publication of the Pentagon Papers, 1971

14. **James Agee and Walker Evans:** *Let Us Now Praise Famous Men,* book, 1941

15. **W. E. B. DuBois:** *The Souls of Black Folk,* collected articles, 1903

16. **I. F. Stone:** *I. F. Stone's Weekly,* 1953-67

17. **Henry Hampton:** "Eyes on the Prize," documentary, 1987

18. **Tom Wolfe:** *The Electric Kool-Aid Acid Test* book, 1968

19. **Norman Mailer:** *The Armies of the Night,* book, 1968

20. **Hannah Arendt:** *Eichmann in Jerusalem: A Report on the Banality of Evil,* collected articles, 1963

21. **William Shirer:** *Berlin Diary: The Journal of a Foreign Correspondent, 1939–1941,* collected articles, 1941

22. **Truman Capote:** *In Cold Blood: A True Account of a Multiple Murder and Its Consequences,* book, 1965

23. **Joan Didion:** *Slouching Towards Bethlehem,* collected articles, 1968

24. **Tom Wolfe:** *The Kandy-Kolored Tangerine-Flake Streamline Baby,* collected articles, 1965

25. **Michael Herr:** *Dispatches,* book, 1977

26. **Theodore White:** *The Making of the President: 1960,* book, 1961

27. **Robert Capa:** Ten photographs from D-Day, 1944

28. **J. Anthony Lukas:** *Common Ground: A Turbulent Decade in the Lives of Three American Families,* book, 1985

29. **Richard Harding Davis:** Coverage of German march into Belgium, Wheeler Syndicate and magazines, 1914

30. **Dorothy Thompson:** Reports on the rise of Hitler, *Cosmopolitan* and *Saturday Evening Post,* 1931–1934

31. **John Steinbeck:** Reports on Okie migrant camp life, *The San Francisco News,* 1936

32. **A. J. Liebling:** *The Road Back to Paris,* collected articles, 1944

33. **Ernest Hemingway:** Reports on the Spanish Civil War, *The New Republic,* 1937–1938

34. **Martha Gellhorn:** *The Face of War,* collected articles, 1959

35. **James Baldwin:** *The Fire Next Time,* book, 1963

36. **Joseph Mitchell:** *Up in the Old Hotel and Other Stories,* Collection of much older articles, 1992

37. **Betty Friedan:** *The Feminine Mystique,* book, 1963

38. **Ralph Nader:** *Unsafe at Any Speed: The Designed-In Dangers of the American Automobile,* book, 1965

39. **Herblock (Herbert Block):** Cartoons on McCarthyism, *The Washington Post,* 1950

40. **James Baldwin:** "Letter from the South: Nobody Knows My Name," *The Partisan Review,* 1959

41. **Nick Ut:** Photograph of a burning girl running from a napalm attack, The Associated Press, 1972

42. **Pauline Kael:** "Trash, Art, and the Movies," *Harper's,* 1969

43. **Gay Talese:** *Fame and Obscurity: Portraits by Gay Talese,* collected articles, 1970

44. **Randy Shilts:** Reports on AIDS, *The San Francisco Chronicle,* 1981–1985

45. **Janet Flanner (Genet):** *Paris Journals* chronicling Paris' emergence from the Occupation, *The New Yorker,* 1944–1945

46. **Neil Sheehan:** *A Bright Shining Lie: John Paul Vann and America in Vietnam,* book, 1988

47. **A. J. Liebling:** *The Wayward Pressman,* collected articles, 1947

48. **Tom Wolfe:** *The Right Stuff,* book, 1979

49. **Murray Kempton:** *America Comes of Middle Age: Columns 1950–1962,* collected articles, 1963

50. **Murray Kempton:** *Part of Our Time: Some Ruins and Monuments of the Thirties,* book, 1955

51. **Donald L. Barlett and James B. Steele:** "America: What Went Wrong?" *The Philadelphia Inquirer,* 1991

52. **Taylor Branch:** *Parting the Waters: America in the King Years, 1954–63,* book, 1988

53. **Harrison Salisbury:** Reporting from the Soviet Union, *The New York Times,* 1949–1954

54. **John McPhee:** *The John McPhee Reader,* collected articles, 1976

55. **ABC:** Live television broadcast of Army-McCarthy hearings, 1954

56. **Frederick Wiseman:** *Titicut Follies,* documentary, 1967

57. **David Remnick:** *Lenin's Tomb: The Last Days of the Soviet Empire,* book, 1993

58. **Richard Ben Cramer:** *What It Takes: The Way to the White House,* book, 1992

59. **Jonathan Schell:** *The Fate of the Earth,* book, 1982

60. **Russell Baker:** "Francs and Beans," *The New York Times,* 1975

61. **Homer Bigart:** Account of being over Japan in a bomber when World War II came to an end, The New York *Herald-Tribune,* 1945

62. **Ben Hecht:** *1,001 Afternoons in Chicago,* collected articles, 1922

63. **Walter Cronkite:** documentary on Vietnam, CBS television, 1968

64. **Walter Lippmann:** Early essays, *The New Republic.* 1914

65. **Margaret Bourke-White:** Photographs following the defeat of Germany, *Life* magazine, 1945

66. **Lillian Ross:** *Reporting,* collected articles, 1964

67. **Nicholas Lemann:** *The Promised Land: The Great Black Migration and How It Changed America,* book, 1991

68. **Joe Rosenthal:** Photograph of Marines raising an American flag on Mount Suribachi on the island of Iwo Jima, The Associated Press, 1945

69. **Hodding Carter Jr.:** "Go for Broke," editorial, Carter's *Delta Democrat-Times* (Greenville, Miss.), 1945

70. **The New Yorker:** *The New Yorker Book of War Pieces,* collected articles, 1947

71. **Meyer Berger:** Report on the murderer Howard Unruh, *The New York Times,* 1949

72. **Norman Mailer:** *The Executioner's Song,* book, 1979

73. **Robert Capa:** Spanish Civil War photos, *Life* magazine, 1936
74. **Susan Sontag:** "Notes on 'Camp'," *The Partisan Review,* 1964
75. **Bob Woodward and Carl Bernstein:** *All the President's Men,* book, 1974
76. **John Hersey:** *Here to Stay,* collected articles, 1963
77. **A. J. Liebling:** *The Earl of Louisiana,* book, 1961
78. **Mike Davis:** *City of Quartz: Excavating the Future in Los Angeles,* book, 1990
79. **Melissa Fay Greene:** *Praying for Sheetrock,* book, 1991
80. **J. Anthony Lukas:** "The Two Worlds of Linda Fitzpatrick," *The New York Times,* 1967
81. **Herbert Bayard Swope:** "Klan Exposed," *The New York World,* 1921
82. **William Allen White:** "To an Anxious Friend," *The Emporia* (Kan.) *Gazette,* 1922
83. **Edward R. Murrow:** Report of the liberation of Buchenwald, CBS radio, 1945
84. **Joseph Mitchell:** *McSorley's Wonderful Saloon,* collected articles, 1943
85. **Lillian Ross:** *Picture,* book, 1952
86. **Earl Brown:** Series of articles on race, *Harper's* and *Life* magazines, 1942–1944
87. **Greil Marcus:** *Mystery Train: Images of America in Rock 'n' Roll Music,* book, 1975

88. **Morley Safer:** Atrocities committed by American soldiers on the hamlet of Cam Ne in Vietnam, CBS television, 1965
89. **Ted Poston:** Coverage of the "Little Scottsboro" trial, *The New York Post,* 1949
90. **Leon Dash:** "Rosa Lee's Story," *The Washington Post,* 1994
91. **Jane Kramer:** *Europeans,* collected articles, 1988
92. **Eddie Adams and Vo Suu:** Associated Press photograph and NBC television footage of a Saigon execution, 1968
93. **Grantland Rice:** "Notre Dame's 'Four Horsemen'," The New York *Herald-Tribune,* 1924
94. **Jane Kramer:** *The Politics of Memory: Looking for Germany in the New Germany,* collected articles, 1996
95. **Frank McCourt:** *Angela's Ashes,* book, 1996
96. **Vincent Sheean:** *Personal History,* book, 1935
97. **W. E. B. DuBois:** Columns on race during his tenure as editor of *The Crisis,* 1910–1934
98. **Damon Runyon:** Crime reporting, *The New York American,* 1926
99. **Joe McGinniss:** *The Selling of the President 1968,* book, 1969
100. **Hunter S. Thompson:** *Fear and Loathing on the Campaign Trail,* book, 1973

Poets Laureate of the United States

Robert Penn Warren	1986–1987	Mona Van Duyn	1992–1993
Richard Wilbur	1987–1988	Rita Dove	1993–1995
Howard Nemerov	1988–1990	Robert Hass	1995–1997
Mark Strand	1990–1991	Robert Pinsky	1997–
Joseph Brodsky	1991–1992		

NOTE: The post was established in 1985. Appointment is for a one-year term, but is renewable.

Poets Laureate of England

Edmund Spenser	1591–1599	Laurence Eusden	1718–1730	Alfred Austin	1896–1913
Samuel Daniel	1599–1619	Colley Cibber	1730–1757	Robert Bridges	1913–1930
Ben Jonson	1619–1637	William Whitehead	1757–1785	John Masefield	1930–1967
William Davenant	1638–1668	Thomas Warton	1785–1790	Cecil Day-Lewis	1967–1972
John Dryden[1]	1670–1689	Henry James Pye	1790–1813	Sir John Betjeman	1972–1984
Thomas Shadwell	1689–1692	Robert Southey	1813–1843	Ted Hughes	1984–1998
Nahum Tate	1692–1715	William Wordsworth	1843–1850	Andrew Motion	1999–
Nicholas Rowe	1715–1718	Alfred Lord Tennyson	1850–1892		

1. First to bear the title officially.

Longest Broadway Runs

Show	Dates	Performances[1]	Show	Dates	Performances[1]
1. *Cats*	10/82–present	6,949	14. *Annie*	4/77–1/83	2,377
2. *A Chorus Line*	10/75–4/90	6,137	15. *Man of La Mancha*	11/65–6/71	2,329
3. *Oh! Calcutta*	9/76–8/89	5,962	16. *Abie's Irish Rose*	5/22–10/27	2,327
4. *Les Misérables*	3/87–present	5,031	17. *Oklahoma!*	3/43–5/48	2,212
5. *The Phantom of the Opera*	1/88–present	4,734	18. *Beauty and the Beast*	4/94–present	2,136
6. *42nd Street*	8/80–1/89	3,485	19. *Pippin*	10/72–6/77	1,944
7. *Miss Saigon*	4/91–present	3,396	20. *South Pacific*	4/49–1/54	1,925
8. *Grease*	2/72–4/80	3,388	21. *The Magic Show*	5/74–12/78	1,920
9. *Fiddler on the Roof*	9/64–7/72	3,242	22. *Gemini*	6/77–9/81	1,819
10. *Life with Father*	11/39–7/47	3,224	23. *Deathtrap*	2/78–6/82	1,793
11. *Tobacco Road*	12/33–5/41	3,182	24. *Harvey*	11/44–1/49	1,775
12. *Hello Dolly*	1/64–12/70	2,844	25. *Dancin'*	3/78–6/82	1,774
13. *My Fair Lady*	3/56–9/62	2,717	26. *Smokey Joe's Cafe*	3/95–present	1,773
			27. *La Cage Aux Folles*	6/83–11/87	1,761

1. As of 5/30/99. *Source:* League of American Theatres and Producers, Inc.

Top 10 Classical Albums, 1998

1. *Aria—The Opera Album,* Andrea Bocelli (Philips/PolyGram Classics)
2. *Viaggio Italiano,* Andrea Bocelli (Philips/PolyGram Classics)
3. *The 3 Tenors: Paris 1998,* Carreras, Domingo, Pavarotti (Levine) (Atlantic/AG)
4. *My Secret Passion—The Arias,* Michael Bolton (Sony Classical)
5. *Piazzolla: The Soul of the Tango,* Yo-Yo Ma (Sony Classical)
6. *Paul McCartney's Standing Stone,* London Symphony Orchestra (Foster) (MPL/EMI Classics/Angel Records)
7. *Bach: The Cello Suites,* Yo-Yo Ma (Sony Classical)
8. *The Vienna I Love,* Andre Rieu (Philips/PolyGram Classics)
9. *Pavarotti's Greatest Hits—The Ultimate Collection,* Luciano Pavarotti (London/PolyGram Classics)
10. *In Concert,* Andre Rieu (Philips/PolyGram Classics)

Source: © 1999 BPI Communications Inc. Used with permission from *Billboard*/SoundScan/BDS.

Top 10 Country Singles, 1998

1. "Just to See You Smile," Tim McGraw (Curb)
2. "Bye Bye," Jo Dee Messina (Curb)
3. "This Kiss," Faith Hill (Warner Bros.)
4. "I'm Alright," Joe Dee Messina (Curb)
5. "There's Your Trouble," Dixie Chicks (Monument)
6. "I'm from the Country," Tracy Byrd (MCA Nashville)
7. "I Just Want to Dance with You," George Strait (MCA Nashville)
8. "I Can Still Feel You," Collin Raye (Epic)
9. "There Goes My Baby," Trisha Yearwood (MCA Nashville)
10. "Love of My Life," Sammy Kershaw (Mercury)

Source: © 1999 BPI Communications Inc. Used with permission from *Billboard*/SoundScan/BDS.

Top 10 Country Albums, 1998

1. *Sevens,* Garth Brooks (Capitol)
2. *Come on Over,* Shania Twain (Mercury)
3. *You Light Up My Life—Inspirational Songs,* LeAnn Rimes (Curb)
4. *Hope Floats,* Soundtrack (Capitol)
5. *The Limited Series,* Garth Brooks (Capitol)
6. *Everywhere,* Tim McGraw (Curb)
7. *The Greatest Hits Collection,* Brooks & Dunn (Arista Nashville)
8. *Wide Open Spaces,* Dixie Chicks (Monument/Sony)
9. *Faith,* Faith Hill (Warner Bros.)
10. *Sittin' on Top of the World,* LeAnn Rimes (Curb)

Source: © 1999 BPI Communications Inc. Used with permission from *Billboard*/SoundScan/BDS.

Top 10 Pop Singles, 1998

1. "Too Close," Next (Arista)
2. "The Boy Is Mine, " Brandy & Monica (Atlantic)
3. "You're Still the One," Shania Twain (Mercury Nashville)
4. "Truly Madly Deeply," Savage Garden (Columbia)
5. "How Do I Live," LeAnn Rimes (Curb)
6. "Together Again," Janet Jackson (Virgin)
7. "All My Life/Don't Rush (Take Love Slowly)," K-Ci & JoJo (MCA)
8. "Candle in the Wind 1997/Something About the Way You Look Tonight," Elton John (Rocket/A&M)
9. "Nice & Slow," Usher (LaFace/Arista)
10. "I Don't Want to Wait," Paula Cole (Imago/Warner Bros.)

Source: © 1999 BPI Communications Inc. Used with permission from *Billboard*/SoundScan/BDS.

Top 10 Pop Albums, 1998

1. *Titanic,* Soundtrack (Sony Classical)
2. *Let's Talk About Love,* Celine Dion (550 Music/Epic)
3. *Sevens,* Garth Brooks (Capitol Nashville)
4. *Backstreet Boys,* Backstreet Boys (Jive)
5. *Come on Over,* Shania Twain (Mercury Nashville)
6. *Yourself or Someone Like You,* matchbox 20 (Lava/Atlantic/Warner Bros.)
7. *City of Angels,* Soundtrack (Warner Sunset/Reprise/Warner Bros.)
8. *Big Willie Style,* Will Smith (Columbia)
9. *Savage Garden,* Savage Garden (Columbia)
10. *Spiceworld,* Spice Girls (Virgin)

Source: © 1999 BPI Communications Inc. Used with permission from *Billboard*/SoundScan/BDS.

Top 10 R&B Singles, 1998

1. "Too Close," Next (Arista)
2. "They Don't Know/Are U Still Down," Jan B. (Yab Yum/550 Music/Epic)
3. "The Boy Is Mine," Brandy & Monica (Atlantic)
4. "No, No, No," Destiny's Child (Columbia)
5. "Nice & Slow," Usher (LaFace/Arista)
6. "Let's Ride," Montell Jordan featuring Master P & Silkk the Shocker (Def Jam)
7. "My Body," LSG (EastWest/EEG)
8. "All My Life/Don't Rush (Take Love Slowly)," K-Ci & JoJo (MCA)
9. "I Don't Ever Want to See You Again," Uncle Sam (Stonecreek/Epic)
10. "Friend of Mine," Kelly Price (T-Neck/Island)

Source: © 1999 BPI Communications Inc. Used with permission from *Billboard*/SoundScan/BDS.

Top R&B Albums, 1998

1. *The Miseducation of Lauryn Hill,* Lauryn Hill (Ruffhouse/Columbia)
2. *It's Dark and Hell Is Hot,* DMX (Ruff Ryders/Def Jam/Mercury)
3. *Vol. 2 . . . Hard Knock Life,* Jay Z (Roc-A-Fella/Def Jam/Mercury)
4. *Anytime,* Brian McKnight (Motown)
5. *Levert.Sweat.Gill,* LSG (EastWest/EEG)
6. *My Way,* Usher (LaFace/Arista)
7. *MP Da Last Don,* Master P (No Limit/Priority)
8. *Charge It 2 Da Game,* Silkk the Shocker (No Limit/Priority)
9. *Live,* Erykah Badu (Kedar/Universal)
10. *R U Still Down? (Remember Me),* 2Pac (Amaru/Jive)

Source: © 1999 BPI Communications Inc. Used with permission from *Billboard*/SoundScan/BDS.

Top 15 Concert Grosses of 1998

Amusement Business annually ranks domestic and international concert grosses and touring acts.

(Headliner, supporting act, dates; gross ticket sales in U.S. dollars; total attendance; venue)

1. **The Rolling Stones (3/29–4/5)**, $14,819,850; 271,766; River Plate Stadium, Buenos Aires, Argentina
2. **The Rolling Stones, Dave Matthews Band (6/29, 7/1–7/2, 7/5–7/6)**, $11,094,308; 261,277; Amsterdam (The Netherlands) Arena
3. **The Rolling Stones, Pearl Jam (11/14–11/15, 11/18–11/19)**, $10,955,527; 186,220; Network Associates Stadium, Oakland, Calif.
4. **The Rolling Stones (3/12–3/17)**, $10,025,470; 130,020; Tokyo (Japan) Dome
5. **U2 (2/5–2/7)**, $8,668,840; 160,478; River Plate Stadium, Buenos Aires, Argentina
6. **Luis Miguel (10/9–10/30, 11/1–11/2)**, $6,766,336; 159,878; National Auditorium, Mexico City, Mexico
7. **The Rolling Stones, Fiona Apple (1/14, 1/16–1/17)**, $6,395,815; 53,626; Madison Square Garden, New York, N.Y.
8. **U2 (1/30–1/31)**, $6,103,065; 154,056; Morumbi Stadium, Sao Paulo, Brazil
9. **The Rolling Stones (3/20–3/21)**, $5,317,800; 69,427; Osaka (Japan) Dome
10. **U2 (12/2–12/3)**, $4,595,225; 106,966; Foro Sol, Mexico City, Mexico
11. **The Rolling Stones, The Corrs (9/12)**, $4,448,942; 85,913; Maimankt, Mannheim, Germany
12. **The Rolling Stones, Jean Louis Aubert (7/25)**, $4,406,313; 76,716; Stade De France, Paris, France
13. **The Rolling Stones, Jonny Lang (6/13)**, $4,366,698; 91,590; Zeppelinfeld, Nuremberg, Germany
14. **Billy Joel (2/5–2/6, 2/18–2/19, 11/6–11/8)**, $4,312,294; 116,837; First Union Center, Philadelphia, Pa.
15. **The Rolling Stones, Hothouse Flowers (7/13)**, $4,303,476; 74,588; Olympia Stadium, Munich, Germany

Source: © 1998 BPI Communications Inc. Used with permission from *Amusement Business*.

The Recording Industry Association of America's Diamond Awards
Top-Selling Certified Albums of All Time

The RIAA certifies recordings that sell 10,000,000 or more copies as diamond. The Diamond Awards were established in March 1999.

25 Million
Their Greatest Hits 1971–1975, Eagles (Elektra)
Thriller, Michael Jackson (Epic)

23 Million
The Wall, Pink Floyd (Columbia)

18 Million
Rumours, Fleetwood Mac (Warner Bros.)
Greatest Hits Volumes I & II, Billy Joel (Columbia)

17 Million
The Beatles, The Beatles (Capitol)
Led Zeppelin IV, Led Zeppelin (Atlantic)

16 Million
Back in Black, AC/DC (Atlantic)
Boston, Boston (Epic)
No Fences, Garth Brooks (Capitol)
The Bodyguard (Soundtrack), Whitney Houston and Various Artists (Arista)
Jagged Little Pill, Alanis Morissette (Warner)

15 Million
Saturday Night Fever (Soundtrack), Bee Gees and Various Artists (RSO)
Hotel California, Eagles (Elektra)
Appetite for Destruction, Guns N' Roses (Geffen)
Cracked Rear View, Hootie & the Blowfish (Atlantic)
Elton John—Greatest Hits, Elton John (Polygram)
The Dark Side of the Moon, Pink Floyd (Capitol)
Born in the U.S.A., Bruce Springsteen (Columbia)

14 Million
The Beatles/1967–1970, The Beatles (Capitol)
Ropin' the Wind, Garth Brooks (Capitol)

13 Million
The Beatles/1962–1966, The Beatles (Capitol)
Bat Out of Hell, Meat Loaf (Epic)
Purple Rain (Soundtrack), Prince and the Revolution (Warner Bros.)

12 Million
II, Boyz II Men (Motown)

Slippery When Wet, Bon Jovi (Mercury)
Double Live, Garth Brooks (Capitol Nashville)
Hysteria, Def Leppard (Mercury)
Breathless, Kenny G (Arista)
Whitney Houston, Whitney Houston (Arista)
Kenny Rogers' Greatest Hits, Kenny Rogers (Capitol)
Bruce Springsteen & the E Street Band Live 1975–85, (Box set), Bruce Springsteen & the E Street Band (Columbia)

11 Million
Abbey Road, The Beatles (Capitol)
Sgt. Pepper's Lonely Hearts Club Band, The Beatles (Capitol)
Metallica, Metallica (Elektra)
Greatest Hits, James Taylor (Warner Bros.)
The Woman in Me, Shania Twain (Polygram)
Dirty Dancing (Soundtrack) (RCA)
Candle in the Wind 1997/Something About the Way You Look Tonight (Single), Elton John (Rocket)

10 Million
Backstreet Boys, Backstreet Boys (Jive)
The Hits, Garth Brooks (Capitol)
Music Box, Mariah Carey (Columbia)
Daydream, Mariah Carey (Columbia)
Unplugged, Eric Clapton (Warner)
Falling into You, Celine Dion (Sony)
Best of the Doobies, Doobie Brothers (Warner Bros.)
Dookie, Green Day (Reprise)
Please Hammer Don't Hurt 'Em, M. C. Hammer (Capitol)
Greatest Hits, Journey (Columbia)
Tapestry, Carole King (Ode)
Like a Virgin, Madonna (Sire)
Faith, George Michael (Columbia)
Tragic Kingdom, No Doubt (Trauma)
Ten, Pearl Jam (Sony)
Can't Slow Down, Lionel Richie (Motown)
CrazySexyCool, TLC (LaFace)
The Joshua Tree, U2 (Island)
Van Halen, Van Halen (Warner Bros.)
1984 (MCMLXXXIV), Van Halen (Warner Bros.)
Eliminator, ZZ Top (Warner Bros.)
The Lion King (Soundtrack) (Walt Disney)
Titanic (Soundtrack) (Sony Classical)

The Country Music Hall of Fame

1961
Jimmie Rodgers
Fred Rose
Hank Williams

1962
Roy Acuff

1963
No candidate received enough votes to qualify for induction.

1964
Tex Ritter

1965
Ernest Tubb

1966
Eddy Arnold
James R. Denny
George D. Hay
Uncle Dave Macon

1967
Red Foley
J. L. Frank
Jim Reeves
Stephen H. Sholes

1968
Bob Wills

1969
Gene Autry
Bill Monroe

1970
Original Carter Family

1971
Arthur Edward Satherley

1972
Jimmie H. Davis

1973
Chet Atkins
Patsy Cline

1974
Owen Bradley
Frank "Pee Wee" King

1975
Minnie Pearl

1976
Paul Cohen
Kitty Wells

1977
Merle Travis

1978
Grandpa Jones

1979
Hubert Long
Hank Snow

1980
Johnny Cash
Connie B. Gay
Original Sons of the Pioneers

1981
Vernon Dalhart
Grant Turner

1982
Lefty Frizzell
Ray Horton
Marty Robbins

1983
Little Jimmy Dickens

1984
Ralph Sylvester Peer
Floyd Tillman

1985
Lester Flatt and Earl Scruggs

1986
Whitey Ford
Wesley H. Rose

1987
Rod Brasfield

1988
Loretta Lynn
Roy Rogers

1989
Jack Stapp
Cliffie Stone
Hank Thompson

1990
Tennessee Ernie Ford

1991
Boudleaux and Felice Bryant

1992
George Jones
Frances Williams Preston

1993
Willie Nelson

1994
Merle Haggard

1995
Roger Miller
Jo Walker-Meador

1996
Patsy Montana
Buck Owens
Ray Price

1997
Cindy Walker
Harlan Howard
Brenda Lee

1998
Tammy Wynette
Elvis Presley
George Morgan

Top 10 Video Sales, 1998

1. *Austin Powers,* (New Line Home Video/Warner Home Video)
2. *Hercules,* (Walt Disney Home Video/Buena Vista Home Entertainment)
3. *As Good As It Gets,* (Columbia TriStar Home Video)
4. *Men in Black,* (Columbia TriStar Home Video)
5. *Spice World,* (Columbia TriStar Home Video)
6. *The Little Mermaid: The Special Edition,* (Walt Disney Home Video/Buena Vista Home Entertainment)
7. *My Best Friend's Wedding,* (Columbia TriStar Home Video)
8. *Grease 20th Anniversary Edition,* (Paramount Home Video)
9. *Air Force One,* (Columbia TriStar Home Video)
10. *Titanic,* (Paramount Home Video)

Source: © 1999 BPI Communications Inc. Used with permission from *Billboard*/SoundScan/BDS.

Top 10 Video Rentals, 1998

1. *L.A. Confidential,* (Warner Home Video)
2. *Face/Off,* (Paramount Home Video)
3. *As Good As It Gets,* (Columbia TriStar Home Video)
4. *Good Will Hunting,* (Miramax Home Entertainment/Buena Vista Home Entertainment)
5. *The Devil's Advocate,* (Warner Home Video)
6. *Boogie Nights,* (New Line Home Video/Warner Home Video)
7. *The Full Monty,* (FoxVideo)
8. *The Game,* (PolyGram Video)
9. *Wag the Dog,* (New Line Home Video/Warner Home Video)
10. *Austin Powers,* (New Line Home Video/Warner Home Video)

Source: © 1999 BPI Communications Inc. Used with permission from *Billboard*/SoundScan/BDS.

Consumer Spending on Entertainment in 1998

Film	$6.68 billion[1]	Books	1.04 billion books sold[3]
Music	$13.7 billion[2]	Video games	$6.3 billion[4]

Sources: 1. Variety 2. RIAA 3. Book Industry Study Group 4. NPD Group

The Rock and Roll Hall of Fame

1986
Chuck Berry
James Brown
Ray Charles
Sam Cooke
Fats Domino
The Everly Brothers
Buddy Holly
Jerry Lee Lewis
Elvis Presley
Little Richard
Nonperformers
Alan Freed
Sam Phillips
Early Influences
Robert Johnson
Jimmie Rodgers
Jimmy Yancey
Lifetime Achievement
John Hammond

1987
The Coasters
Eddie Cochran
Bo Diddley
Aretha Franklin
Marvin Gaye
Bill Haley
B.B. King
Clyde McPhatter
Ricky Nelson
Roy Orbison
Carl Perkins
Smokey Robinson
Joe Turner
Muddy Waters
Jackie Wilson
Nonperformers
Leonard Chess
Ahmet Ertegun
Jerry Leiber and Mike Stoller
Jerry Wexler
Early Influences
Louis Jordan
T-Bone Walker
Hank Williams

1988
The Beach Boys
The Beatles
The Drifters
Bob Dylan
The Supremes
Nonperformer
Berry Gordy, Jr.

Early Influences
Woody Guthrie
Leadbelly
Les Paul

1989
Dion
Otis Redding
The Rolling Stones
The Temptations
Stevie Wonder
Nonperformer
Phil Spector
Early Influences
The Ink Spots
Bessie Smith
The Soul Stirrers

1990
Hank Ballard
Bobby Darin
The Four Seasons
The Four Tops
The Kinks
The Platters
Simon and Garfunkel
The Who
Nonperformers
Gerry Goffin and Carole King
Brian Holland, Eddie Holland,
 and Lamont Dozier
Early Influences
Louis Armstrong
Charlie Christian
Ma Rainey

1991
LaVern Baker
The Byrds
John Lee Hooker
The Impressions
Wilson Pickett
Jimmy Reed
Ike and Tina Turner
Nonperformers
Dave Bartholomew
Ralph Bass
Early Influence
Howlin' Wolf
Lifetime Achievement
Nesuhi Ertegun

1992
Bobby "Blue" Bland
Booker T. and the MG's
Johnny Cash

Jimi Hendrix Experience
Isley Brothers
Sam and Dave
The Yardbirds
Nonperformers
Leo Fender
Bill Graham
Doc Pomus
Early Influences
Elmore James
Professor Longhair

1993
Ruth Brown
Cream
Creedence Clearwater
 Revival
The Doors
Etta James
Frankie Lymon and
 the Teenagers
Van Morrison
Sly and the Family Stone
Nonperformers
Dick Clark
Milt Gabler
Early Influence
Dinah Washington

1994
The Animals
The Band
Duane Eddy
The Grateful Dead
Elton John
John Lennon
Bob Marley
Rod Stewart
Nonperformer
Johnny Otis
Early Influence
Willie Dixon

1995
The Allman Brothers Band
Al Green
Janis Joplin
Led Zeppelin
Martha and the Vandellas
Neil Young
Frank Zappa
Nonperformer
Paul Ackerman
Early Influence
The Orioles

1996
David Bowie
Jefferson Airplane
Little Willie John
Gladys Knight and the Pips
Pink Floyd
The Shirelles
The Velvet Underground
Nonperformer
Tom Donahue
Early Influence
Pete Seeger

1997
The Bee Gees
Buffalo Springfield
Crosby, Stills and Nash
The Jackson Five
Joni Mitchell
Parliament-Funkadelic
The (Young) Rascals
Nonperformer
Syd Nathan
Early Influences
Mahalia Jackson
Bill Monroe

1998
The Eagles
Fleetwood Mac
Mamas and Papas
Lloyd Price
Santana
Gene Vincent
Nonperformer
Allen Toussaint
Early Influence
"Jelly Roll" Morton

1999
Billy Joel
Curtis Mayfield
Paul McCartney
Del Shannon
Dusty Springfield
Bruce Springsteen
The Staple Singers
Nonperformer
George Martin
Early Influences
Charles Brown
Bob Wills and His Texas
 Playboys

Top Television Specials 1998–1999[1]

Rank	Program name (network) [first telecast]	Rating (% of TV households)	Rank	Program name (network) [first telecast]	Rating (% of TV households)
1.	Academy Awards (ABC) [3/21/99]	28.6%	4.	Golden Globe Awards (NBC) [1/24/99]	16.1%
2.	Oscar Preview Show (ABC) [3/21/99]	18.1	5.	Mad About You Special (NBC) [5/13/99]	13.8
3.	Grammy Awards (CBS) [2/24/99]	16.6			

NOTES: Each rating point represents 994,000 households using television. Does not include sports telecasts. 1. Sept. 21, 1998–May 26, 1999. *Source:* Nielsen Media Research. © 1999, Nielsen Media Research.

Top 25 Regularly Scheduled Network Programs, 1998–1999[1]

Rank	Program name (network)	Rating (% of TV households)	Rank	Program name (network)	Rating (% of TV households)
1.	ER (NBC)	17.8%	14.	Law & Order (NBC)	10.1%
2.	Friends (NBC)	15.7	15.	Drew Carey Show (ABC)	9.9
3.	Frasier (NBC)	15.6	15.	20/20 (Fri.) (ABC)	9.9
4.	NFL Monday Night Football (ABC)	13.9	17.	JAG (CBS)	9.8
5.	Jesse (NBC)	13.7	17.	NFL Monday Showcase (ABC)	9.8
5.	Veronica's Closet (NBC)	13.7	17.	Providence (NBC)	9.8
7.	60 Minutes (CBS)	13.2	17.	Dateline (Fri.) (NBC)	9.8
8.	Touched by an Angel (CBS)	13.1	21.	Ally McBeal (Fox)	9.7
9.	CBS Sunday Movie (CBS)	12.1	21.	Becker (CBS)	9.7
10.	20/20 (Wed.) (ABC)	11.2	21.	CBS Tuesday Movie (CBS)	9.7
11.	Home Improvement (ABC)	11.0	21.	Dateline NBC (Mon.) (NBC)	9.7
12.	Everybody Loves Raymond (CBS)	10.6	21.	Dateline NBC (Tues.) (NBC)	9.7
13.	NYPD Blue (ABC)	10.5			

NOTE: Each rating point represents 994,000 households using television. 1. 1998–1999 season through May 26, 1999. *Source:* Nielsen Media Research. © 1999, Nielsen Media Research.

Top 15 Syndicated TV Programs 1998–1999 Season[1]

Rank	Program name[2]	Rating (% of TV households)	Rank	Program name[2]	Rating (% of TV households)
1.	Wheel of Fortune	11.4%	9.	Entertainment Tonight	5.9%
2.	Jeopardy	9.5	10.	Buena Vista I	5.8
3.	ESPN NFL Regular Season	6.9	11.	Frasier	5.5
4.	Judge Judy (AT)	6.8	12.	Home Improvement (AT)	5.3
5.	Jerry Springer (AT)	6.7	12.	The X-Files (AT)	5.3
6.	Friends (AT)	6.6	14.	Wheel of Fortune (Weekend)	5.1
7.	Oprah Winfrey Show (AT)	6.4	15.	National Geographic on Assignment	4.4
7.	Seinfeld	6.4			

NOTES: Each rating point represents 994,000 households using television. (AT) = Additional Telecasts. 1. Aug. 31, 1998–May 30, 1999. 2. Programs airing three or less weeks have been excluded from this ranking. *Source:* Nielsen Media Research. © 1999, Nielsen Media Research.

Top 10 Sports Telecasts 1998–1999[1]

Rank	Program name (network)	Description	Rating (% of TV households)
1.	Super Bowl XXXIII (Fox)	Denver vs. Atlanta	40.2%
2.	AFC Championship on CBS (CBS)	N.Y. Jets at Denver	26.6
3.	Fox NFC Championship (Fox)	Atlanta at Minnesota	25.7
4.	Fox NFC Wildcard Game (Fox)	Green Bay at San Francisco	23.6
5.	Fox NFC Playoff–Sun. (Fox)	Arizona at Minnesota	21.4
6.	AFC/NFC Playoff Game 2 (ABC)	Arizona at Dallas	21.2
7.	AFC Divisional Playoff (CBS)	Jacksonville at N.Y. Jets	20.1
8.	AFC Divisional Playoff (CBS)	Miami at Denver	18.4
9.	AFC Wildcard Playoff (CBS)	New England at Jacksonville	18.3
10.	Fox NFC Playoff–Sat. (Fox)	San Francisco at Atlanta	18.2

NOTE: Each rating point represents 994,000 households using television. 1. Sept. 21, 1998–May 26, 1999. *Source:* Nielsen Media Research. © 1999, Nielsen Media Research.

Top-Rated TV Movies 1998–1999[1]

Rank	Episode title (network)	Rating (% of TV households)	Rank	Episode title (network)	Rating (% of TV households)
1.	Noah's Ark, Part 1 (NBC)	20.9%	10.	Marriage of Convenience (CBS)	14.6%
2.	Noah's Ark, Part 2 (NBC)	17.0	11.	Saint Maybe (CBS)	14.4
3.	The Christmas Wish (CBS)	16.3	12.	Mama Flora's Family, Part 1 (CBS)	14.3
4.	Joan of Arc, Part 1 (CBS)	15.2			
5.	Forever Love (CBS)	15.1	12.	Cab to Canada (CBS)	14.3
5.	The '60s, Part 1 (NBC)	15.1	12.	Too Rich: Secret Life of Doris Duke, Part 1 (CBS)	14.3
7.	The Temptations, Part 1 (NBC)	15.0			
8.	Alice in Wonderland (NBC)	14.8	15.	Sabrina (CBS)	14.0
9.	The Secret Path (CBS)	14.7	15.	The Temptations, Part 2 (NBC)	14.0

NOTE: Each rating point represents 994,000 households using television. 1. Sept. 21, 1998–May 23, 1999. *Source:* Nielsen Media Research. © 1999, Nielsen Media Research.

Television Set Ownership

(January 1999)
Total number of U.S. households: 101,240,000 (100.0%)
Total number of TV households: 99,400,000 (98.2%)

Households with	Number	Percent[1]	Households with	Number	Percent[1]
Color TV sets	98,406,000	99%	One set	25,844,000	26%
Black and white only	994,000	1	Cable	74,550,000	75
Two or more sets	73,556,000	74			

1. Number reflects percent of total number of TV households. *Source:* Nielsen Media Research. © 1999, Nielsen Media Research.

Weekly TV Viewing by Age

(in hours and minutes)

	Time per week				Time per week		
	Nov. 1998	Nov. 1997	Nov. 1996		Nov. 1998	Nov. 1997	Nov. 1996
Women 18–24 years old	22 hr. 11 min.	25 hr. 22 min.	24 hr. 32 min.	**Female teens 12–17**	19 hr. 40 min.	19 hr. 60 min.	18 hr. 19 min.
Women 25–54	30 hr. 35 min.	31 hr. 45 min.	30 hr. 44 min.	**Male teens 12–17**	20 hr. 16 min.	19 hr. 60 min.	19 hr. 59 min.
Women 55 and over	42 hr 00 min.	41 hr. 50 min.	41 hr. 50 min.	**Children 2–5**	23 hr. 01 min.	26 hr. 02 min.	23 hr. 21 min.
Men 18–24	19 hr. 29 min.	20 hr. 30 min.	20 hr. 20 min.	**Children 6–11**	18 hr. 59 min.	19 hr. 49 min.	19 hr. 59 min.
Men 25–54	27 hr. 53 min.	28 hr. 44 min.	28 hr. 04 min.				
Men 55 and over	36 hr. 47 min.	36 hr. 17 min.	37 hr. 08 min.				

Source: Nielsen Media Research. © 1999, Nielsen Media Research.

Top 100 Daily Newspapers in the United States

By circulation, as of September 30, 1998

Rank	Newspaper	Circulation	Rank	Newspaper	Circulation
1.	*Wall Street Journal* (New York, N.Y.)	1,740,450	34.	*Star* (Kansas City, Mo.)	281,596
2.	*USA Today* (Arlington, Va.)	1,653,428	35.	*Herald* (Boston)	271,425
3.	*Times* (Los Angeles)	1,067,540	36.	*Times-Picayune* (New Orleans)	259,317
4.	*Times* (New York, N.Y.)	1,066,658	37.	*Sun-Sentinel* (Fort Lauderdale, Fla.)	258,726
5.	*Post* (Washington, D.C.)	759,122	38.	*Sentinel* (Orlando, Fla.)	258,726
6.	*Daily News* (New York, N.Y.)	723,143	39.	*Investor's Business Daily* (Los Angeles)	251,172
7.	*Tribune* (Chicago)	673,508	40.	*Dispatch* (Columbus, Ohio)	246,528
8.	*Newsday* (Long Island, N.Y.)	572,444	41.	*News* (Detroit)	245,351
9.	*Chronicle* (Houston)	550,763	42.	*Observer* (Charlotte, N.C.)	243,818
10.	*Sun-Times* (Chicago)	485,666	43.	*Post-Gazette* (Pittsburgh, Pa.)	243,453
11.	*Morning News* (Dallas)	479,863	44.	*News* (Buffalo, N.Y.)	237,229
12.	*Chronicle* (San Francisco)	475,324	45.	*Tribune* (Tampa, Fla.)	235,786
13.	*Globe* (Boston)	470,825	46.	*Star-Telegram* (Fort Worth, Tex.)	232,112
14.	*Post* (New York, N.Y.)	437,467	47.	*Star* (Indianapolis)	230,223
15.	*Arizona Republic* (Phoenix)	435,330	48.	*Courier-Journal* (Louisville, Ky.)	228,144
16.	*Inquirer* (Philadelphia)	428,895	49.	*Times* (Seattle)	227,715
17.	*Star-Ledger* (Newark, N.J.)	407,026	50.	*World-Herald* (Omaha, Neb.)	219,891
18.	*Plain Dealer* (Cleveland)	382,933	51.	*Express-News* (San Antonio, Tex.)	218,661
19.	*Free Press* (Detroit)	378,256	52.	*Courant* (Hartford, Conn.)	211,041
20.	*Union-Tribune* (San Diego)	378,112	53.	*Times-Dispatch* (Richmond, Va.)	207,175
21.	*Register* (Orange County, Calif.)	356,953	54.	*Daily Oklahoman* (Oklahoma City)	204,963
22.	*Herald* (Miami)	349,114	55.	*Daily News* (Los Angeles)	201,107
23.	*Oregonian* (Portland)	346,593	56.	*Pioneer Press* (St. Paul, Minn.)	199,119
24.	*Times* (St. Petersburg, Fla.)	344,784	57.	*Virginian-Pilot* (Norfolk, Va.)	197,773
25.	*Post* (Denver)	341,554	58.	*Post-Intelligencer* (Seattle)	196,271
26.	*Star Tribune* (Minneapolis)	334,751	59.	*Enquirer* (Cincinnati)	196,181
27.	*Rocky Mountain News* (Denver)	331,978	60.	*Tennessean* (Nashville)	184,979
28.	*Post-Dispatch* (St. Louis)	329,582	61.	*American-Statesman* (Austin, Tex.)	183,319
29.	*Sun* (Baltimore)	314,033	62.	*Daily News* (Philadelphia)	175,448
30.	*Constitution* (Atlanta)	303,698	63.	*Democrat and Chronicle* (Rochester, N.Y.)	174,579
31.	*Mercury News* (San Jose, Calif.)	290,885			
32.	*Journal Sentinel* (Milwaukee)	285,776	64.	*Democrat-Gazette* (Little Rock, Ark.)	173,316
33.	*Bee* (Sacramento, Calif.)	283,589			

Rank	Newspaper	Circulation
65.	*Palm Beach Post* (West Palm Beach, Fla.)	173,074
66.	*Times-Union* (Jacksonville, Fla.)	172,511
67.	*Journal* (Providence, R.I.)	167,381
68.	*Commercial Appeal* (Memphis)	163,603
69.	*Register* (Des Moines, Iowa)	163,292
70.	*World* (Tulsa, Okla.)	162,186
71.	*Press-Enterprise* (Riverside, Calif.)	161,612
72.	*Asbury Park Press* (Neptune, N.J.)	159,472
73.	*News & Observer* (Raleigh, N.C.)	157,634
74.	*Bee* (Fresno, Calif.)	155,931
75.	*Daily News* (Dayton, Ohio)	152,308
76.	*Journal News* (White Plains, N.Y.)	151,695
77.	*Review-Journal* (Las Vegas)	151,162
78.	*News* (Birmingham, Ala.)	148,835
79.	*Blade* (Toledo, Ohio)	146,138
80.	*Beacon Journal* (Akron, Ohio)	143,199
81.	*Daily Herald* (Arlington Heights, Ill.)	141,703
82.	*Record* (Bergen County, N.J.)	141,368

Rank	Newspaper	Circulation
83.	*Press* (Grand Rapids, Mich.)	139,703
84.	*Tribune* (Salt Lake City)	129,612
85.	*Morning Call* (Allentown, Pa.)	129,522
86.	*News Tribune* (Tacoma, Wash.)	129,247
87.	*News Journal* (Wilmington, Del.)	125,401
88.	*State* (Columbia, S.C.)	120,433
89.	*News-Sentinel* (Knoxville, Tenn.)	115,248
90.	*Spokesman-Review* (Spokane, Wash.)	114,475
91.	*Examiner* (San Francisco)	113,198
92.	*Herald-Leader* (Lexington, Ky.)	113,036
93.	*Journal* (Albuquerque)	112,751
94.	*Herald-Tribune* (Sarasota, Fla.)	109,438
95.	*Post & Courier* (Charleston, S.C.)	109,272
96.	*Journal* (Atlanta)	106,896
97.	*Telegram & Gazette* (Worcester, Mass.)	105,896
98.	*Clarion-Ledger* (Jackson, Miss.)	105,382
99.	*Press-Telegram* (Long Beach, Calif.)	105,167
100.	*Advertiser* (Honolulu)	102,358

Source: *Editor & Publisher's* International Yearbook.

Top 100 Daily Newspapers in the World According to 1998 Circulation

Rank	Newspaper	Circulation
1.	*Yomiuri Shimbun* (Japan)	14,532,694
2.	*Asahi Shimbun* (Japan)	12,601,375
3.	*Sichuan Ribao* (China)	8,000,000
4.	*Mainichi Shimbun* (Japan)	5,845,857
5.	*Bild* (Germany)	5,674,400
6.	*Chunichi Shimbun* (Japan)	4,323,144
7.	*Sun* (England)	3,718,354
8.	*Renmin Ribao* (China)	3,000,000
9.	*Sankei Shimbun* (Japan)	2,890,835
10.	*Nihon Keizai Shimbun* (Japan)	2,705,877
11.	*Gongren Ribao* (China)	2,500,000
12.	*Daily Mail* (England)	2,387,867
13.	*Daily Mirror* (England)	2,339,001
14.	*Chosun Ilbo* (South Korea)	2,225,000
15.	*Dong-A Ilbo* (South Korea)	2,150,000
16.	*Hokkaido Shimbun* (Japan)	1,962,666
17.	*Eleftherotypia* (Greece)	1,858,316
18.	*Xin Min Wan Bao* (China)	1,750,000
19.	*Wall Street Journal* (United States)	1,740,450
20.	*Yangcheng Wanbao* (China)	1,730,000
21.	*Kerala Kaumudi* (India)	1,720,000
22.	*Wen Hui Bao Daily* (China)	1,700,000
23.	*USA Today* (United States)	1,653,428
24.	*Joong-Ang Daily News* (South Korea)	1,550,000
25.	*Economic Daily* (China)	1,500,000
26.	*Rodong Sinmun* (North Korea)	1,500,000
27.	*Kyung-Hyang Daily News* (South Korea)	1,478,537
28.	*Sports Nippon* (Japan)	1,452,699
29.	*Shizuoka Shimbun* (Japan)	1,442,310
30.	*Sankei Sports* (Japan)	1,367,734
31.	*West Deutche Allgemeine* (Germany)	1,313,400
32.	*United Daily News* (Taiwan)	1,300,000
33.	*China Times* (Taiwan)	1,270,000
34.	*O Estado de Sao Paulo* (Brazil)	1,230,160
35.	*Jang Daily* (Pakistan)	1,200,000
36.	*Jang Lahore* (Pakistan)	1,200,000
37.	*Akhbar El Yom/Al Akhbar* (Egypt)	1,159,339
38.	*Hankook Ilbo* (South Korea)	1,156,000
39.	*Hochi Shimbun* (Japan)	1,119,031
40.	*Daily Express* (England)	1,118,981
41.	*Los Angeles Times* (United States)	1,067,540
42.	*New York Times* (United States)	1,066,540
43.	*Tokyo Shimbun* (Japan)	1,062,080

Rank	Newspaper	Circulation
44.	*Daily Telegraph* (England)	1,047,861
45.	*Nishinippon Shimbun* (Japan)	1,041,104
46.	*Jiefang Ribao* (China)	1,000,000
47.	*Nanfang Ribao* (China)	1,000,000
48.	*Nongmin Ribao* (China)	1,000,000
49.	*Zhongguo Qingnian Ribao* (China)	1,000,000
50.	*Nikkan Sports* (Japan)	984,058
51.	*Al Akhbar* (Egypt)	980,000
52.	*Guangming Ribao* (China)	950,000
53.	*Al Ahram* (Egypt)	900,000
54.	*Al Goumhouriya* (Egypt)	900,000
55.	*Seoul Shinmun* (South Korea)	900,000
56.	*Xin Hua Ribao* (China)	900,000
57.	*Verdens Gang* (Norway)	870,267
58.	*Corriere della Sera* (Italy)	868,266
59.	*Kyoto Shimbun* (Japan)	839,499
60.	*Chugoku Shimbun* (Japan)	831,165
61.	*Jang* (Pakistan)	820,000
62.	*Times of India* (India)	813,000
63.	*Kobe Shimbun* (Japan)	810,353
64.	*Beijing Wanbao* (China)	800,000
65.	*Hubei Ribao* (China)	800,000
66.	*Jiefangjun Ribao* (China)	800,000
67.	*Trybuna Slaska* (Poland)	800,000
68.	*La Gazzetta dello Sport* (Italy)	798,243
69.	*Ouest-France* (France)	790,133
70.	*Holos Ukrainy* (Ukraine)	768,000
71.	*The Times* (England)	766,999
72.	*ABC* (Spain)	765,668
73.	*Washington Post* (United States)	759,122
74.	*La Repubblica* (Italy)	754,930
75.	*De Telegraf* (Netherlands)	751,400
76.	*Gazeta Wyborcza* (Poland)	750,000
77.	*Zero Hora* (Brazil)	727,188
78.	*Diario dos Campos* (Brazil)	725,000
79.	*New York Daily News* (United States)	723,143
80.	*Sabah* (Turkey)	722,950
81.	*Jornal da Tarde* (Brazil)	709,793
82.	*Beijing Ribao* (China)	700,000
83.	*Chongqing Ribao* (China)	700,000
84.	*Clarin* (Argentina)	700,000
85.	*Thai Rath* (Thailand)	700,000
86.	*Zhejiang Ribao* (China)	700,000
87.	*Diario Insular* (Portugal)	684,143

Rank	Newspaper	Circulation	Rank	Newspaper	Circulation
88.	Granma Internacional (Cuba)	675,000	95.	La Nacion (Argentina)	630,000
89.	Chicago Tribune (United States)	673,508	96.	Hurriyet (Turkey)	615,579
90.	Daily Record (Scotland)	671,267	97.	Herald Sun (Australia)	600,000
91.	China Daily News (Taiwan)	670,000	98.	Hurriyet (Pakistan)	600,000
92.	The Daily Star (England)	650,406	99.	Liaoning Ribao (China)	600,000
93.	Guangxi Ribao (China)	650,000	100.	Oriental Daily News (Hong Kong)	600,000
94.	Malayala Manorama (India)	630,068			

Source: Editor & Publisher's International Yearbook.

Top 100 Consumer Magazines, 1998

Rank	Magazine	Circulation[1]	Rank	Magazine	Circulation[1]
1.	Modern Maturity	20,468,227	51.	Cooking Light	1,424,254
2.	NRTA/AARP Bulletin	20,359,318	52.	Outdoor Life	1,362,418
3.	Reader's Digest	14,221,558	53.	Boys' Life	1,330,814
4.	TV Guide	12,832,942	54.	American Rifleman	1,276,633
5.	National Geographic Magazine	8,697,927	55.	Consumers Digest	1,272,381
6.	Better Homes & Gardens	7,614,682	56.	Rolling Stone	1,251,646
7.	Family Circle	5,004,998	57.	Scholastic Parent & Child	1,246,791
8.	Good Housekeeping	4,551,296	58.	Parenting	1,239,152
9.	Ladies' Home Journal	4,548,983	59.	Car & Driver	1,234,824
10.	McCall's	4,221,216	60.	Discover	1,224,117
11.	Woman's Day	4,156,126	61.	In Style	1,207,777
11.	Time	4,091,631	62.	Motor Trend	1,192,991
13.	People	3,676,704	63.	The Elks Magazine	1,192,468
14.	Sports Illustrated	3,267,131	64.	New Woman	1,180,898
15.	Playboy	3,243,854	65.	PC Magazine	1,179,186
16.	Newsweek	3,189,775	66.	Mademoiselle	1,174,997
17.	Prevention	3,148,299	67.	Vogue	1,168,678
18.	Home & Away	3,038,968	68.	PC World	1,147,925
19.	Redbook	2,861,200	69.	Weight Watchers Magazine	1,146,216
20.	The American Legion Magazine	2,701,377	70.	Self	1,145,326
21.	Cosmopolitan	2,675,123	71.	Endless Vacation	1,136,093
22.	Avenues	2,613,967	72.	Shape	1,125,097
23.	Via Magazine	2,498,973	73.	The Family Handyman	1,117,911
24.	Southern Living	2,494,467	74.	Us	1,103,232
25.	Seventeen	2,426,461	75.	Soap Opera Digest	1,101,146
26.	Martha Stewart Living	2,295,004	76.	Vanity Fair	1,097,523
27.	National Enquirer	2,225,480	77.	Sesame Street Magazine	1,085,703
28.	U.S. News & World Report	2,191,377	78.	Bon Appetit	1,073,013
29.	Glamour	2,186,283	79.	Scouting	1,072,575
30.	YM	2,178,697	80.	Health	1,071,808
31.	Smithsonian	2,064,717	81.	FamilyFun	1,071,248
32.	Teen	1,964,045	82.	Country Home	1,058,145
33.	AAA Going Places	1,961,032	83.	Kiplinger's Personal Finance	1,046,924
34.	Money	1,918,938	84.	PC/Computing	1,026,712
35.	Star	1,860,912	85.	Home	1,018,690
36.	V.F.W. Magazine	1,824,943	86.	Michigan Living	1,013,828
37.	Ebony	1,798,900	87.	American Health—for Women	1,006,139
38.	Field & Stream	1,760,642	88.	American Homestyle & Gardening	1,003,046
39.	Parents	1,742,226	89.	Travel & Leisure	1,001,998
40.	Country Living	1,676,007	90.	Essence	1,000,608
41.	Men's Health	1,605,908	91.	Penthouse	996,323
42.	First for Women	1,591,198	92.	Fitness	980,131
43.	Woman's World	1,572,020	93.	Victoria	967,122
44.	Popular Science	1,563,066	94.	Elle	958,295
45.	Life	1,558,823	95.	Today's Homeowner	954,525
46.	Golf Digest	1,548,161	96.	Jet	934,260
47.	Sunset	1,461,631	97.	The American Hunter	933,323
48.	Entertainment Weekly	1,442,430	98.	Business Week (North America)	911,156
49.	Golf Magazine	1,435,375	99.	Country America	904,675
50.	Popular Mechanics	1,428,849	100.	Gourmet	885,564

NOTE: Average paid circulation for year ending Dec. 31, 1998. 1. Figure includes subscriptions and single-copy sales.
Source: Magazine Audit Bureau of Circulation.

Movie Revenues

All-Time Box Office Grosses[1]	
1. Titanic (1997)	$600,788,188
2. Star Wars (1977)[2]	460,998,007
3. E.T.—the Extra-Terrestrial (1982)[2]	399,804,539
4. Jurassic Park (1993)	357,067,947
5. Forrest Gump (1994)[2]	329,690,974
6. The Lion King (1994)[2]	312,855,561
7. Return of the Jedi (1983)[2]	309,161,884
8. Independence Day (1996)	306,169,255
9. The Empire Strikes Back (1980)[2]	290,268,568
10. Home Alone (1990)	285,016,000
11. Jaws (1975)[2]	260,000,000
12. Star Wars Episode One: The Phantom Menace (1999)	255,758,124[3]
13. Batman (1989)	251,188,924
14. Men in Black (1997)	250,690,539
15. Raiders of the Lost Ark (1981)[2]	245,034,358
16. Twister (1996)	241,708,908
17. Beverly Hills Cop (1984)	234,760,478
18. The Lost World: Jurassic Park (1997)	229,074,524
19. Ghostbusters (1984)	220,858,490
20. Mrs. Doubtfire (1993)	219,194,773
21. Ghost (1990)	217,631,306
22. Aladdin (1992)	217,350,219
23. Saving Private Ryan (1998)	216,119,491
24. Back to the Future (1985)	210,609,762
25. Terminator 2 (1991)	204,466,562

Top 25 Movies of 1998[4]	
1. Armageddon (Buena Vista)	$201,578,182
2. Saving Private Ryan (DreamWorks)	190,805,259
3. There's Something About Mary (Fox)	176,101,937
4. The Waterboy (Buena Vista)	155,523,746
5. A Bug's Life (Buena Vista)	154,152,003
6. Doctor Dolittle (Fox)	144,158,464
7. Rush Hour (New Line)	140,754,711
8. Deep Impact (Paramount)	140,464,664
9. Godzilla (Sony/TriStar)	136,036,753
10. Lethal Weapon 4 (Warner Bros.)	129,734,803
11. The Truman Show (Paramount)	125,619,201
12. Mulan (Buena Vista)	120,620,254
13. Patch Adams (Universal)	116,507,970
14. You've Got Mail (Warner Bros.)	108,174,879
15. Enemy of the State (Buena Vista)	107,221,416
16. The Rugrats Movie (Paramount)	94,269,189
17. The Mask of Zorro (Sony)	93,771,072
18. The Prince of Egypt (DreamWorks)	90,829,789
19. Antz (DreamWorks)	90,484,950
20. The X-Files (Fox)	83,892,374
21. Stepmom (Sony)	83,619,126
22. The Wedding Singer (New Line)	80,224,502
23. City of Angels (Warner Bros.)	78,647,175
24. The Horse Whisperer (Buena Vista)	75,383,563
25. Six Days, Seven Nights (Buena Vista)	74,339,294

1. As of June 6, 1999. 2. Including reissues. 3. Still tracking. 4. As of Jan. 31, 1999. Including reissues. *Source:* Exhibitor Relations Co. Inc.

American Film Institute's Greatest 100 Movies of All Time

1. Citizen Kane (1941)
2. Casablanca (1942)
3. The Godfather (1972)
4. Gone With the Wind (1939)
5. Lawrence of Arabia (1962)
6. The Wizard of Oz (1939)
7. The Graduate (1967)
8. On the Waterfront (1954)
9. Schindler's List (1993)
10. Singin' in the Rain (1952)
11. It's a Wonderful Life (1946)
12. Sunset Boulevard (1950)
13. The Bridge on the River Kwai (1957)
14. Some Like It Hot (1959)
15. Star Wars (1977)
16. All About Eve (1950)
17. The African Queen (1951)
18. Psycho (1960)
19. Chinatown (1974)
20. One Flew Over the Cuckoo's Nest (1975)
21. The Grapes of Wrath (1940)
22. 2001: A Space Odyssey (1968)
23. The Maltese Falcon (1941)
24. Raging Bull (1980)
25. E.T.—the Extra-Terrestrial (1982)
26. Dr. Strangelove (1964)
27. Bonnie and Clyde (1967)
28. Apocalypse Now (1979)
29. Mr. Smith Goes to Washington (1939)
30. The Treasure of the Sierra Madre (1948)
31. Annie Hall (1977)
32. The Godfather Part II (1974)
33. High Noon (1952)
34. To Kill a Mockingbird (1962)
35. It Happened One Night (1934)
36. Midnight Cowboy (1969)
37. The Best Years of Our Lives (1946)
38. Double Indemnity (1944)
39. Doctor Zhivago (1965)
40. North by Northwest (1959)
41. West Side Story (1961)
42. Rear Window (1954)
43. King Kong (1933)
44. The Birth of a Nation (1915)
45. A Streetcar Named Desire (1951)
46. A Clockwork Orange (1971)
47. Taxi Driver (1976)
48. Jaws (1975)
49. Snow White and the Seven Dwarfs (1937)
50. Butch Cassidy and the Sundance Kid (1969)
51. The Philadelphia Story (1940)
52. From Here to Eternity (1953)
53. Amadeus (1984)
54. All Quiet on the Western Front (1930)
55. The Sound of Music (1965)
56. M*A*S*H (1970)
57. The Third Man (1949)
58. Fantasia (1940)
59. Rebel without a Cause (1955)
60. Raiders of the Lost Ark (1981)
61. Vertigo (1958)
62. Tootsie (1982)
63. Stagecoach (1939)
64. Close Encounters of the Third Kind (1977)
65. The Silence of the Lambs (1991)
66. Network (1976)
67. The Manchurian Candidate (1962)
68. An American in Paris (1951)
69. Shane (1953)
70. The French Connection (1971)

71. *Forrest Gump* (1994)
72. *Ben-Hur* (1959)
73. *Wuthering Heights* (1939)
74. *The Gold Rush* (1925)
75. *Dances with Wolves* (1990)
76. *City Lights* (1931)
77. *American Graffiti* (1973)
78. *Rocky* (1976)
79. *The Deer Hunter* (1978)
80. *The Wild Bunch* (1969)
81. *Modern Times* (1936)
82. *Giant* (1956)
83. *Platoon* (1986)
84. *Fargo* (1996)
85. *Duck Soup* (1933)

86. *Mutiny on the Bounty* (1935)
87. *Frankenstein* (1931)
88. *Easy Rider* (1969)
89. *Patton* (1970)
90. *The Jazz Singer* (1927)
91. *My Fair Lady* (1964)
92. *A Place in the Sun* (1951)
93. *The Apartment* (1960)
94. *GoodFellas* (1990)
95. *Pulp Fiction* (1994)
96. *The Searchers* (1956)
97. *Bringing Up Baby* (1938)
98. *Unforgiven* (1992)
99. *Guess Who's Coming to Dinner* (1967)
100. *Yankee Doodle Dandy* (1942)

American Film Institute's 50 Greatest Screen Legends

Men
1. Humphrey Bogart
2. Cary Grant
3. James Stewart
4. Marlon Brando
5. Fred Astaire
6. Henry Fonda
7. Clark Gable
8. James Cagney
9. Spencer Tracy
10. Charlie Chaplin
11. Gary Cooper
12. Gregory Peck
13. John Wayne
14. Laurence Olivier
15. Gene Kelly
16. Orson Welles
17. Kirk Douglas
18. James Dean
19. Burt Lancaster
20. The Marx Brothers
21. Buster Keaton
22. Sidney Poitier
23. Robert Mitchum
24. Edward G. Robinson
25. William Holden

Women
1. Katharine Hepburn
2. Bette Davis
3. Audrey Hepburn
4. Ingrid Bergman
5. Greta Garbo
6. Marilyn Monroe
7. Elizabeth Taylor
8. Judy Garland
9. Marlene Dietrich
10. Joan Crawford
11. Barbara Stanwyck
12. Claudette Colbert
13. Grace Kelly
14. Ginger Rogers
15. Mae West
16. Vivien Leigh
17. Lillian Gish
18. Shirley Temple
19. Rita Hayworth
20. Lauren Bacall
21. Sophia Loren
22. Jean Harlow
23. Carole Lombard
24. Mary Pickford
25. Ava Gardner

Miss America Winners

1921 Margaret Gorman, Washington, D.C.
1922–23 Mary Campbell, Columbus, Ohio
1924 Ruth Malcolmson, Philadelphia, Pa.
1925 Fay Lamphier, Oakland, Calif.
1926 Norma Smallwood, Tulsa, Okla.
1927 Lois Delaner, Joliet, Ill.
1933 Marion Bergeron, West Haven, Conn.
1935 Henrietta Leaver, Pittsburgh, Pa.
1936 Rose Coyle, Philadelphia, Pa.
1937 Bette Cooper, Bertrand Island, N.J.
1938 Marilyn Meseke, Marion, Ohio
1939 Patricia Donnelly, Detroit, Mich.
1940 Frances Marie Burke, Philadelphia, Pa.
1941 Rosemary LaPlanche, Los Angeles, Calif.
1942 JoCaroll Dennison, Tyler, Texas
1943 Jean Bartel, Los Angeles, Calif.
1944 Venus Ramey, Washington, D.C.
1945 Bess Myerson, New York, N.Y.
1946 Marilyn Buferd, Los Angeles, Calif.
1947 Barbara Walker, Memphis, Tenn.
1948 BeBe Shopp, Hopkins, Minn.
1949 Jacque Mercer, Litchfield, Ariz.
1951 Yolande Betbeze, Mobile, Ala.
1952 Coleen Kay Hutchins, Salt Lake City, Utah
1953 Neva Jane Langley, Macon, Ga.
1954 Evelyn Margaret Ay, Ephrata, Pa.
1955 Lee Meriwether, San Francisco, Calif.
1956 Sharon Ritchie, Denver, Colo.
1957 Marian McKnight, Manning, S.C.
1958 Marilyn Van Derbur, Denver, Colo.
1959 Mary Ann Mobley, Brandon, Miss.
1960 Lynda Lee Mead, Natchez, Miss.
1961 Nancy Fleming, Montague, Mich.
1962 Maria Fletcher, Asheville, N.C.
1963 Jacquelyn Mayer, Sandusky, Ohio
1964 Donna Axum, El Dorado, Ark.
1965 Vonda Kay Van Dyke, Phoenix, Ariz.

1966 Deborah Irene Bryant, Overland Park, Kan.
1967 Jane Anne Jayroe, Laverne, Okla.
1968 Debra Dene Barnes, Moran, Kan.
1969 Judith Anne Ford, Belvidere, Ill.
1970 Pamela Anne Eldred, Birmingham, Mich.
1971 Phyllis Ann George, Denton, Texas
1972 Laurie Lea Schaefer, Columbus, Ohio
1973 Terry Anne Meeuwsen, DePere, Wis.
1974 Rebecca Ann King, Denver, Colo.
1975 Shirley Cothran, Fort Worth, Texas
1976 Tawney Elaine Godin, Yonkers, N.Y.
1977 Dorothy Kathleen Benham, Edina, Minn.
1978 Susan Perkins, Columbus, Ohio
1979 Kylene Baker, Galax, Va.
1980 Cheryl Prewitt, Ackerman, Miss.
1981 Susan Powell, Elk City, Okla.
1982 Elizabeth Ward, Russellville, Ark.
1983 Debra Maffett, Anaheim, Calif.
1984 Vanessa Williams, Milwood, N.Y.[1]
1984 Suzette Charles, Mays Landing, N.J.
1985 Sharlene Wells, Salt Lake City, Utah
1986 Susan Akin, Meridian, Miss.
1987 Kellye Cash, Memphis, Tenn.
1988 Kaye Lani Rae Rafko, Monroe, Mich.
1989 Gretchen Elizabeth Carlson, Anoka, Minn.
1990 Debbye Turner, Mexico, Mo.
1991 Marjorie Judith Vincent, Oak Park, Ill.
1992 Carolyn Suzanne Sapp, Honolulu, Hawaii
1993 Leanza Cornett, Jacksonville, Fla.
1994 Kimberly Clarice Aiken, Columbia, S.C.
1995 Heather Whitestone, Birmingham, Ala.
1996 Shawntel Smith, Muldrow, Okla.
1997 Tara Dawn Holland, Overland Park, Kan.
1998 Katherine Shindle, Evanston, Ill.
1999 Nicole Johnson, Roanoke, Va.

1. Resigned July 23, 1984.

States

Data for state populations are the latest available from the U.S. Census Bureau. NOTE: Persons of Hispanic origin can be of any race. "American Indian" includes American Indians, Eskimos, and Aleuts. "Asian" includes Asians and Pacific Islanders. Largest cities include incorporated places only, as defined by the U.S. Census Bureau. They do not include adjacent or suburban areas.

For secession and readmission dates of the former Confederate states, *see* U.S. Government & History: The Confederate States of America. For lists of governors, senators, and representatives, *see* U.S. Government & History: The Governors of the Fifty States, The Senate, and The House of Representatives. For U.S. Territories, *see* Countries of the World: United States.

Alabama

Capital: Montgomery
Governor: Don Siegelman, D (to Jan. 2003)
Lieut. Governor: Steve Windom, R (to Jan. 2003)
Senators: Jeff Sessions, R (to Jan. 2003); Richard C. Shelby, R (to Jan. 2005)
Secy. of State: Jim Bennett, R (to Jan. 2003)
Treasurer: Lucy Baxley, D (to Jan. 2003)
Atty. General: William Pryor, R (to Jan. 2003)
Auditor: Susan D. Parker, D (to Jan. 2003)
Organized as territory: March 3, 1817
Entered Union (rank): Dec. 14, 1819 (22)
Present constitution adopted: 1901
Motto: *Audemus jura nostra defendere* (We dare defend our rights)
State symbols: flower, camellia (1959); **bird,** yellowhammer (1927); **song,** "Alabama" (1931); **tree,** Southern longleaf pine (1949, 1997); **salt water fish,** fighting tarpon (1955); **fresh water fish,** largemouth bass (1975); **horse,** racking horse (1975); **mineral,** hematite (1967); **rock,** marble (1969); **game bird,** wild turkey (1980); **dance,** square dance (1981); **nut,** pecan (1982); **fossil,** species *Basilosaurus Cetoides* (1984); **official mascot and butterfly,** eastern tiger swallowtail (1989); **insect,** monarch butterfly (1989); **reptile,** Alabama red-bellied turtle (1990); **gemstone,** star blue quartz (1990); **shell,** *scaphella junonia johnstoneae* (1990)
Nickname: Yellowhammer State
Origin of name: May come from Choctaw meaning "thicket-clearers" or "vegetation-gatherers"
10 largest cities (1998 est.): Birmingham, 252,997; Mobile, 202,181; Montgomery, 197,014; Huntsville, 175,979; Tuscaloosa, 83,376; Hoover, 59,551; Dothan, 57,069; Decatur, 54,694; Gadsden, 42,158; Auburn, 40,425
Land area: 50,750 sq mi. (131,443 sq km)
Geographic center: In Chilton Co., 12 mi. SW of Clanton
Number of counties: 67
Largest county (area): Jefferson, 659,524 sq. mi
State forests: 21 (48,000 ac.)
State parks: 22 (45,614 ac.)
1998 resident population est.: 4,351,999
1990 resident census population (rank): 4,040,587 (22). **Male:** 1,936,162; **Female:** 2,104,425. **White:** 2,975,797 (73.6%); **Black:** 1,020,705 (25.3%); **American Indian:** 16,506 (0.4%); **Asian:** 21,797 (0.5%); **Other race:** 5,782 (0.1%); **Hispanic:** 24,629 (0.6%). **1990 percent population under 18:** 26.2; **65 and over:** 12.9; **median age:** 32.9.

Spanish explorers are believed to have arrived at Mobile Bay in 1519, and the territory was visited in 1540 by the explorer Hernando de Soto. The first permanent European settlement in Alabama was founded by the French at Fort Louis de la Mobile in 1702. The British gained control of the area in 1763 by the Treaty of Paris, but had to cede almost all the Alabama region to the U.S. and Spain after the American Revolution. The Confederacy was founded at Montgomery in February 1861 and, for a time, the city was the Confederate capital.

During the last part of the 19th century, the economy of the state slowly improved. At Tuskegee Institute, founded in 1881 by Booker T. Washington, Dr. George Washington Carver carried out his famous agricultural research.

In the 1950s and '60s, Alabama was the site of such landmark civil-rights actions as the bus boycott in Montgomery (1955–56) and the "Freedom March" from Selma to Montgomery (1965).

Today paper, chemicals, rubber and plastics, apparel and textiles, primary metals, and automobile manufacturing constitute the leading industries of Alabama. Continuing as a major manufacturer of coal, iron, and steel, Birmingham is also noted for its world-renowned medical center, especially for heart surgery. The state ranks high in the production of poultry, soybeans, milk, vegetables, livestock, wheat, cattle, cotton, peanuts, fruits, hogs, and corn.

Points of interest include the Helen Keller birthplace "Ivy Green" at Tuscumbia, the Space and Rocket Center at Huntsville, the White House of the Confederacy, the restored state Capitol, the Civil Rights Memorial, the Shakespeare Festival Theater Complex in Montgomery, the Civil Rights Institute in Birmingham, the Russell Cave near Bridgeport, the Bellingrath Gardens at Theodore, the USS *Alabama* at Mobile, Mound State Monument near Tuscaloosa, and the Gulf Coast area.

Famous natives and residents: Hank Aaron, baseball player; Ralph Abernathy, civil rights activist; Tallulah Bankhead, actress; Hugo L. Black, jurist; George Washington Carver, educator, agricultural chemist; Nat "King" Cole, entertainer; Marva Collins, educator; Kenneth Gibson, first black mayor of major eastern city (Newark); Lionel Hampton, jazz musician; W. C. Handy, composer; Kate Jackson, actress; Helen Keller, author and educator; Coretta Scott King, civil rights leader; Harper Lee, writer; Joe Louis, boxer; Willie Mays, baseball player; Jim Nabors, actor; Jesse Owens, athlete; Rosa Parks, civil rights activist; Wayne Rogers, actor; Tascaluza, Choctaw chief; George Wallace, former governor; William Weatherford (Red Eagle), Creek leader; Heather Whitestone, Miss America (1995).

Alaska

Capital: Juneau
Governor: Tony Knowles, D (to Dec. 2002)
Lieut. Governor: Fran Ulmer, D (to Dec. 2002)
Senators: Frank H. Murkowski, R (to Jan. 2005); Ted Stevens, R (to Jan. 2003)
Commissioner of Administration: Bob Poe
Atty. General: Bruce M. Bothelho, D
Organized as territory: 1912
Entered Union (rank): Jan. 3, 1959 (49)
Constitution ratified: April 24, 1956
Motto: North to the Future
State symbols: flower, forget-me-not (1949); **tree,** sitka spruce (1962); **bird,** willow ptarmigan (1955); **fish,** king salmon (1962); **song,** "Alaska's Flag" (1955); **gem,** jade (1968); **marine mammal,** bowhead whale (1983); **fossil,** woolly mammoth (1986); **mineral,** gold (1968); **sport,** dog mushing (1972)
Nickname: The state is commonly called "The Last Frontier" or "Land of the Midnight Sun"
Origin of name: Corruption of Aleut word meaning "great land" or "that which the sea breaks against"
10 largest cities (1998 est.): Anchorage, 254,982; Fairbanks, 33,295; Juneau, 30,191; Sitka, 8,338; Kenai, 7,943; Kodiak, 7,720; Ketchikan, 7,543; Bethel, 6,342; Wasilla, 5,791; Homer, 4,794
Land area: 570,374 sq mi. (1,477,267 sq km)
Geographic center: 60 mi. NW of Mt. McKinley
Number of boroughs: 16
Largest borough (1998 pop. est.): Anchorage, 254,982
State parks: more than 100 (3.5 million acres)
1998 resident population: 614,010
1990 resident census population (rank): 550,043 (49). **Male:** 289,867; **Female:** 260,176. **White:** 415,492 (75.5%); **Black:** 22,451 (4.1%); **American Indian:** 85,698 (15.6%); **Asian:** 19,728 (3.6%); **Other race:** 6,675 (1.2%); **Hispanic:** 17,803 (3.2%). **1990 percent population under 18:** 31.3; **65 and over:** 4.1; **median age:** 29.3.

Vitus Bering, a Dane working for the Russians, and Alexei Chirikov discovered the Alaskan mainland and the Aleutian Islands in 1741. The tremendous land mass of Alaska—equal to one-fifth of the continental U.S.—was unexplored in 1867 when Secretary of State William Seward arranged for its purchase from the Russians for $7,200,000. The transfer of the territory took place on Oct. 18, 1867. Despite a price of about two cents an acre, the purchase was widely ridiculed as "Seward's Folly." The first official census (1880) reported a total of 33,426 Alaskans, all but 430 being of aboriginal stock. The Gold Rush of 1898 resulted in a mass influx of more than 30,000 people. Since then, Alaska has contributed billions of dollars' worth of products to the U.S. economy.

In 1968, a large oil and gas reservoir near Prudhoe Bay on the Arctic Coast was found. The Prudhoe Bay reservoir, with an estimated recoverable 10 billion barrels of oil and 27 trillion cubic feet of gas, is twice as large as any other oil field in North America. The Trans-Alaska pipeline was completed in 1977 at a cost of $7.7 billion. On June 20, oil started flowing through the 800-mile-long pipeline from Prudhoe Bay to the port of Valdez.

Other industries important to Alaska's economy are fisheries, wood and wood products, furs, and tourism.

Denali National Park and Mendenhall Glacier in North Tongass National Forest are of interest, as is the large totem pole collection at Sitka National Historical Park. The Katmai National Park includes the "Valley of Ten Thousand Smokes," an area of active volcanoes.

The Alaska Native population, the indigenous peoples of Alaska, include Eskimos, Indians, and Aleuts. More than half of all Alaska Natives are Eskimos. (The term *Eskimo* is used for Alaska Natives; the term *Inuit* is generally used for Eskimos living in Canada.) The two main Eskimo groups, Inupiat and Yupik, are distinguished by their language and geography. The former live in the north and northwest parts of Alaska and speak Inupiaq, while the latter live in the south and southwest and speak Yupik.

About 36% of Alaska Natives are American Indians. The major tribes are the Alaskan Athabaskan (11,696) in the central part of the state, and the Tlingit (9,448), Tsimshian (1,653), and Haida (1,083) in the southeast.

The Aleuts, native to the Aleutian Islands, Kodiak Island, the lower Alaska and Kenai Peninsulas, and Prince William Sound, are physically and culturally related to the Eskimos. About 12% of Alaska Natives are Aleuts, and in 1990, they made up 10,052 of the indigenous population.

Famous natives and residents: Clarence L. Andrews, author; Aleksandr Baranov, first governor of Russian America; Margaret Elizabeth Bell, author; Benny Benson, designed state flag at age 13; Vitus Bering, explorer; Charles E. Bunnell, educator; Susan Butcher, sled-dog racer; William A. Egan, first state governor; Carl Ben Eielson, pioneer pilot; Henry E. Gruennig, political leader; B. Frank Heintzleman, territorial governor; Walter J. Hickel, former governor; Sheldon Jackson, educator and missionary; Joe Juneau, prospector; Austin Lathrop, industrialist; Sydney Lawrence, painter; Ray Mala, actor; Virgil F. Partch, cartoonist; Joe Redington, Sr., sled-dog musher and promoter; Peter Trinble Rowe, first Episcopal bishop; Ivan Popov-Veniaminov (St. Innocent), Russian Orthodox missionary; Ferdinand Wrangel, educator; Samuel Hall Young, founder of first American church.

Arizona

Capital: Phoenix
Governor: Jane Dee Hull, R (to Jan. 2003)
Senators: Jon Kyl, R (to Jan. 2001); John McCain (to Jan. 2005)
Secy. of State: Betsey Bayless, R (to Jan. 2003)
Atty. General: Janet Napolitano, D (to Jan. 2003)
Treasurer: Carol Springer, R (to Jan. 2003))
Organized as territory: Feb. 24, 1863
Entered Union (rank): Feb. 14, 1912 (48)
Present constitution adopted: 1911
Motto: *Ditat Deus* (God enriches)
State symbols: flower: flower of saguaro cactus (1931); **bird:** cactus wren (1931); **colors:** blue and old gold (1915); **song:** "Arizona March Song" (1919); **tree:** palo verde (1954); **neckwear:** bola tie (1971); **fossil:** petrified wood (1988); **gemstone:** turquoise (1974); **animals: mammal,** ringtail (1986); **reptile,** Arizona ridgenose rattlesnake (1986); **fish,** Arizona trout (1986); **amphibian,** Arizona tree frog (1986)
Nickname: Grand Canyon State
Origin of name: From the Indian "Arizonac," meaning "little spring" or "young spring"
10 largest cities (1998 est.): Phoenix, 1,198,064; Tucson, 460,466; Mesa, 360,076; Scottsdale, 195,394; Glendale, 193,482; Tempe, 167,622; Chandler, 160,329; Gilbert, 88,840; Peoria, 87,048; Yuma, 62,433
Land area: 113,642 sq mi. (296,400 sq km)
Geographic center: In Yavapai Co., 55 mi. ESE of Prescott

Number of counties: 15
Largest county (1998 est.): Maricopa, 2,784,075
State parks: 24
1998 resident population est.: 4,668,631
1990 resident census population (rank): 3,665,228 (24). **Male:** 1,810,691; **Female:** 1,854,537. **White:** 2,963,186 (80.8%); **Black:** 110,524 (3.0%); **American Indian:** 203,527 (5.6%); **Asian:** 55,206 (1.5%); **Other race:** 332,785 (9.1%); **Hispanic:** 688,338 (18.8%). **1990 percent population under 18:** 26.8; **65 and over:** 13.1; **median age:** 32.0.

Marcos de Niza, a Spanish Franciscan friar, was the first European to explore Arizona. He entered the area in 1539 in search of the mythical Seven Cities of Gold. Although he was followed a year later by another gold seeker, Francisco Vásquez de Coronado, most of the early settlement was for missionary purposes. In 1775 the Spanish established Fort Tucson. In 1848, after the Mexican War, most of the Arizona territory became part of the U.S., and the southern portion of the territory was added by the Gadsden Purchase in 1853.

In 1973 one of the world's most massive dams, the New Cornelia Tailings, was completed near Ajo.

Arizona history is rich in legends of America's Old West. It was here that the great Indian chiefs Geronimo and Cochise led their people against the frontiersmen. Tombstone, Ariz., was the site of the West's most famous shoot-out—the gunfight at the O.K. Corral. Today, Arizona has one of the largest U.S. Indian populations; more than 14 tribes are represented on 20 reservations.

Manufacturing has become Arizona's most important industry. Principal products include electrical, communications, and aeronautical items. The state produces over half of the country's copper. Agriculture is also important to the state's economy.

State attractions include the Grand Canyon, the Petrified Forest, and the Painted Desert. Hoover Dam, Lake Mead, Fort Apache, and the reconstructed London Bridge at Lake Havasu City are of particular interest.

Famous natives and residents: Apache Kid, Indian outlaw; Erma Bombeck, humorist and writer; Lynda Carter, actress; Cesar Chavez, labor leader; Cochise, Apache chief; Alice Cooper, singer and songwriter; Wyatt Earp, marshall; Max Ernst, painter; Geronimo (Goyathlay), Apache chief; Barry Goldwater, politician; Zane Grey, novelist; Carl Trumbull Hayden, politician; George W. P. Hunt, first state governor; Bill Keane, cartoonist; Eusebio Kino, missionary; Percival Lowell, astronomer; Frank Luke, Jr., WWI fighter ace; Charles Mingus, jazz musician and composer; Carlos Montezuma, doctor and Indian spokesman; Sandra Day O'Connor, jurist; William O'Neill, frontier sheriff; Alexander M. Patch, general; William H. Pickering, astronomer; Linda Ronstadt, singer; Paolo Soleri, architect; Clyde W. Tombaugh, astronomer; Tanya Tucker, singer; Stewart Udall, former Secretary of the Interior; Pauline Weaver, frontier person; Frank Lloyd Wright, architect.

Arkansas

Capital: Little Rock
Governor: Mike Huckabee, R (to Jan. 2003)
Lieut. Governor: Winthrop Rockefeller, R (to 2002)
Senators: Tim Hutchinson, R (to Jan. 2003); Blanche Lambert Lincoln (to Jan. 2005)
Secy. of State: Sharon Priest, D (to Jan. 2003)
Atty. General: Mark Pryor (to Jan. 2003)
Auditor of State: Gus Wingfield, D (to Jan. 2003)
Treasurer of State: Jimmie Lou Fisher, D (to Jan. 2003)

Land Commissioner: Charles Daniels, D (to Jan. 2003)
Organized as territory: March 2, 1819
Entered Union (rank): June 15, 1836 (25)
Present constitution adopted: 1874
Motto: *Regnat populus* (The people rule)
State symbols: flower, apple blossom (1901); **tree,** pine (1939); **bird,** mockingbird (1929); **insect,** honeybee (1973); **song,** "Arkansas" (1963)
Nickname: The Natural State
Origin of name: From the Quapaw Indians
10 largest cities (1998 est.): Little Rock, 175,303; Fort Smith, 75,637; North Little Rock, 59,184; Fayetteville, 53,300; Pine Bluff, 52,968; Jonesboro, 52,250; Springdale, 40,287; Conway, 39,164; Hot Springs, 37,961; Rogers, 37,073
Land area: 52,075 sq mi. (134,874 sq km)
Geographic center: In Pulaski Co., 12 mi. NW of Little Rock
Number of counties: 75
Largest county (1998 pop. est.): Pulaski, 350,345
State parks: 50
1998 resident population est.: 2,538,303
1990 resident census population(rank): 2,350,725 (33). **Male:** 1,133,076; **Female:** 1,217,649. **White:** 1,944,744 (82.7%); **Black:** 373,912 (15.9%); **American Indian:** 12,773 (0.5%); **Asian:** 12,530 (0.5%); **Other race:** 6,766 (0.3%); **Hispanic:** 19,876 (0.8%). **1990 percent population under 18:** 26.4; **65 and over:** 14.9; **median age:** 33.7.

Hernando de Soto, in 1541, was among the early European explorers to visit the territory. It was a Frenchman, Henri de Tonti, who in 1686 founded the first permanent white settlement—the Arkansas Post. In 1803 the area was acquired by the U.S. as part of the Louisiana Purchase.

Food products are the state's largest employing sector, with lumber and wood products a close second. Arkansas is also a leader in the production of cotton, rice, and soybeans. It also has the country's only active diamond mine; located near Murfreesboro, it is operated as a tourist attraction.

Hot Springs National Park, and Buffalo National River in the Ozarks are major state attractions.

Blanchard Springs Caverns, the Arkansas Territorial Restoration at Little Rock, and the Arkansas Folk Center in Mountain View are of interest.

Famous natives and residents: G. M. "Broncho Billy" Anderson, actor; Maya Angelou, author and poet; Katharine Susan Anthony, author; Helen Gurley Brown, editor; Glen Campbell, singer; Hattie Caraway, first elected woman senator; Johnny Cash, singer; Eldridge Cleaver, black activist; William Jefferson Clinton, 42nd President; Dizzy Dean, baseball player; Orval Faubus, former governor; John Gould Fletcher, writer; James W. Fulbright, former senator; John H. Johnson, publisher; Alan Ladd, actor; Douglas MacArthur, 5-star general; John Paul McConnell, U.S. Air Force officer; Ben Murphy, actor; Frank Pace, Jr., public official; Ben Piazza, actor; Albert Pike, pioneer teacher and lawyer; Dick Powell, actor; Opie P. Read, writer; Jenny D. Rice-Meyrowitz, painter; Brehon Burke Somervell, World Wars I and II U.S. Army officer; Mary Steenburgen, actress; Edward Durrell Stone, architect; William C. Warfield, concert singer and actor.

California

Capital: Sacramento
Governor: Gray Davis, D (to Jan. 2003)
Lieut. Governor: Cruz M. Bustamante, D (to Jan. 2003)
Senators: Barbara Boxer, D (to Jan. 2005); Dianne Feinstein, D (to Jan. 2001)
Secy. of State: Bill Jones, R (to Jan. 2003)
Controller: Kathleen Connell, D (to Jan. 2003)

Atty. General: Bill Lockyer, D (to Jan. 2003)
Treasurer: Phil Angelides, D (to Jan. 2003)
Supt. of Public Instruction: Delaine Eastin
Entered Union (rank): Sept. 9, 1850 (31)
Present constitution adopted: 1879
Motto: *Eureka* (I have found it)
State symbols: flower, golden poppy (1903); **tree,** California redwoods (*Sequoia sempervirens & Sequoia gigantea*) (1937 % 1953); **bird,** California valley quail (1931); **animal,** California grizzly bear (1953); **fish,** California golden trout (1947); **colors,** blue and gold (1951); **song,** "I Love You, California" (1951)
Nickname: Golden State
Origin of name: From a book, *Las Sergas de Esplandián,* by Garcia Ordóñez de Montalvo, c. 1500
10 largest cities (1998 est.): Los Angeles, 3,597,556; San Diego, 1,220,666; San Jose, 861,284; San Francisco, 745,774; Long Beach, 430,905; Sacramento, 404,168; Fresno, 398,133; Oakland, 365,874; Santa Ana, 305,955; Anaheim, 295,153
Land area: 155,973 sq mi. (403,970 sq km)
Geographic center: In Madera Co., 35 mi. NE of Madera
Number of counties: 58
Largest county (1998 pop. est.): Los Angeles, 9,213,533
National forests: 18
State parks and beaches: 264
1998 resident population est.: 32,666,550
1990 resident census population(rank): 29,760,021 (1). **Male:** 14,897,627; **Female:** 14,862,394. **White:** 20,524,327 (69.9%); **Black:** 2,208,801 (7.4%); **American Indian:** 242,164 (0.8%); **Asian:** 2,845,659 (9.6%); **Other race:** 3,939,070 (13.2%); **Hispanic:** 7,687,938 (25.8%). **1990 percent population under 18:** 26.0; **65 and over:** 10.5; **median age:** 31.3.

Although California was sighted by Spanish navigator Juan Rodríguez Cabrillo in 1542, its first Spanish mission (at San Diego) was not established until 1769. California became a U.S. territory in 1847 when Mexico surrendered it to John C. Frémont. On Jan. 24, 1848, James W. Marshall discovered gold at Sutter's Mill, starting the California Gold Rush and bringing settlers to the state in large numbers.

In 1964, the U.S. Census Bureau estimated that California had become the most populous state, surpassing New York. California also leads the country in personal income and consumer expenditures.

Leading industries include manufacturing (transportation equipment, machinery, and electronic equipment), agriculture, biotechnology, and tourism. Principal natural resources include timber, petroleum, cement, and natural gas.

More immigrants settle in California than any other state—more than one-third of the nation's total in 1994. Asians and Pacific Islanders led the influx.

Death Valley, in the southeast, is 282 feet below sea level, the lowest point in the nation. Mt. Whitney (14,491 ft.) is the highest point in the contiguous 48 states. Lassen Peak is one of two active U.S. volcanoes outside of Alaska and Hawaii; its last eruptions were recorded in 1917. The General Sherman Tree in Sequoia National Park is estimated to be 3,500 years old and a stand of bristlecone pine trees in the White Mountains may be over 4,000 years old.

Other points of interest include Yosemite National Park, Disneyland, Hollywood, the Golden Gate Bridge, San Simeon State Park, and Point Reyes National Seashore.

Famous natives and residents: Gertrude Atherton, author; David Belasco, playwright and producer; Shirley Temple Black, actress, ambassador; Dave Brubeck, musician; Luther Burbank, horticulturalist; Julia Child, chef; Joe DiMaggio, baseball player; James H. Doolittle, air force general; Isadora Duncan, dancer; John Frémont, explorer; Robert Frost, poet; Henry George, economist; Richard "Pancho" Gonzales, tennis player; George E. Hale, astronomer; Bret Harte, writer; William Randolph Hearst, publisher; Sidney Howard, playwright; Collis Potter Huntington, financier; Helen Hunt Jackson, writer; Robinson Jeffers, poet; Anthony M. Kennedy, jurist; Jack London, author; James W. Marshall, first discoverer gold; Aimee Semple McPherson, evangelist; Marilyn Monroe, actress; John Muir, naturalist; Richard M. Nixon, President; Isamu Noguchi, sculptor; Frank Norris, novelist; Kathleen Norris, novelist; George S. Patton, Jr., general; Robert Redford, actor; Sally K. Ride, astronaut; William Saroyan, author; Junípero Serra, missionary; Upton Sinclair, novelist; Leland Stanford, railroad magnate; Lincoln Steffens, journalist, author; John Steinbeck, author; Adlai Stevenson, statesman; Johann Sutter, pioneer; Michael Tilson Thomas, conductor; Earl Warren, jurist.

Colorado

Capital: Denver
Governor: Bill Owens, R (to Jan. 2003)
Lieut. Governor: Joe Rogers, D (to Jan. 2003)
Senators: Wayne A. Allard (to Jan. 2003); Ben Nighthorse Campbell (to Jan. 2005)
Secy. of State: Vikki Buckley, R (to Jan 2003)
Treasurer: Mike Coffman, R (to Jan. 2003)
Controller: Arthur Barnhart
Atty. General: Ken Salazar, D (to Jan. 2003)
Organized as territory: Feb. 28, 1861
Entered Union (rank): Aug. 1, 1876 (38)
Present constitution adopted: 1876
Motto: *Nil sine Numine* (Nothing without Providence)
State symbols: flower, Rocky Mountain columbine (1899); **tree,** Colorado blue spruce (1939); **bird,** lark bunting (1931); **animal,** Rocky Mountain bighorn sheep (1961); **gemstone,** aquamarine (1971); **colors,** blue and white (1911); **song,** "Where the Columbines Grow" (1915); **fossil,** stegosaurus (1991)
Nickname: Centennial State
Origin of name: From the Spanish, "ruddy" or "red"
10 largest cities (1998 est.): Denver, 499,055; Colorado Springs, 344,987; Aurora, 250,604; Lakewood, 136,883; Fort Collins, 108,905; Pueblo, 107,301; Arvada, 97,610; Westminster, 95,691; Boulder, 90,543; Thornton, 74,139
Land area: 103,730 sq mi. (268,660 sq km)
Geographic center: In Park Co., 30 mi. NW of Pikes Peak
Number of counties: 63
Largest county (1998 pop. est.): Jefferson, 501,591
State forests: 1 (71,000 ac.)
State parks: 44 (160,000 ac.)
1998 resident population est.: 3,970,971
1990 resident census population (rank): 3,294,394 (26). **Male:** 1,631,295; **Female:** 1,663,099. **White:** 2,095,474 (88.2%); **Black:** 133,146 (4.0%); **American Indian:** 27,776 (0.8%); **Asian:** 59,862 (1.8%); **Other race:** 168,136 (5.1%); **Hispanic:** 424,302 (12.9%). **1990 percent population under 18:** 26.1; **65 and over:** 10.0; **median age:** 32.4.

First visited by Spanish explorers in the 1500s, the territory was claimed for Spain by Juan de Ulibarri in 1706. The U.S. obtained eastern Colorado as part of the Louisiana Purchase in 1803, the central portion in 1845 with the admission of Texas as a state, and the western part in 1848 as a result of the Mexican War.

Colorado has the highest mean elevation of any state, with more than 1,000 Rocky Mountain peaks over 10,000 feet high and 54 towering above 14,000 feet. Pikes Peak, the most famous of these mountains, was discovered by U.S. Army Lieut. Zebulon M. Pike in 1806.

Once primarily a mining and agricultural state, Colorado's economy is now driven by the service-producing industries, which provide jobs for approximately 82.4 percent of the state's non-farm work force. Tourism expenditures in the state total approximately 6 billion dollars annually. Tourist expenditures on the ski industry account for 1.8 billion dollars annually, approximately a third of the total tourist expenditures. The main tourist attractions in the state include Rocky Mountain National Park, Curecanti National Recreation Area, Mesa Verde National Park, the Great Sand Dunes and Dinosaur National Monuments, Colorado National Monument, and the Black Canyon of the Gunnison National Monument.

The two primary facets of Colorado's manufacturing industry are food and kindred products, and printing and publishing.

The mining industry, which includes oil and gas, coal, and metal mining, was important to Colorado's economy, but it now employs only 1.2 percent of the state's workforce. Denver is home to companies that control half of the nation's gold production. The farm industry, which is primarily concentrated in livestock, is also an important element of the state's economy. The primary crops in Colorado are corn, hay, and wheat.

Famous natives and residents: William E. Barrett, writer; William Bent, fur trader and pioneer; Charles F. Brannan, lawyer and public official; M. Scott Carpenter, astronaut; Lon Chaney, actor; Mary Coyle Chase, playwright; Jack Dempsey, boxer; Ralph Edwards, entertainer; John Evans, physician, educator; Douglas Fairbanks, actor; John Thomas Fante, writer; Eugene Fodor, violinist; Gene Fowler, writer; Erick Hawkins, choreographer; Homer Lea, soldier, writer; Ted Mack, TV host; Jaye P. Morgan, singer; Peg Murray, actress; Ouray, Ute Indian chief; Anne Parrish, writer; Barbara Rush, actress; Horace A. Tabor, silver king and lieut. governor; Lowell Thomas, commentator and author; Dalton Trumbo, screenwriter, novelist; Byron R. White, jurist; Paul Whiteman, conductor; Don Wilson, announcer.

Connecticut

Capital: Hartford
Governor: John G. Rowland, R (to Jan. 2003)
Lieut. Governor: M. Jodi Rell, R (to Jan. 2003)
Senators: Christopher J. Dodd, D (to Jan. 2005); Joseph I. Lieberman, D (to Jan. 2001)
Secy. of the State: Susan Bysiewicz, D (to Jan. 2003)
Comptroller: Nancy Wyman, D (to Jan. 2003)
Treasurer: Denise Nappier, D (to Jan. 2003)
Atty. General: Richard Blumenthal, D (to Jan. 2003)
Entered Union (rank): Jan. 9, 1788 (5)
Present constitution adopted: Dec. 30, 1965
Motto: *Qui transtulit sustinet* (He who transplanted still sustains)
State symbols: flower, mountain laurel (1907); **tree,** white oak (1947); **animal,** sperm whale (1975); **bird,** American robin (1943); **hero,** Nathan Hale (1985); **heroine,** Prudence Crandall (1995); **insect,** praying mantis (1977); **mineral,** garnet (1977); **song,** "Yankee Doodle" (1978); **ship,** USS *Nautilus* (SSN571) (1983); **shellfish,** eastern oyster (1989); **fossil,** *Eubrontes Giganteus* (1991); **composer,** Charles Edward Ives (1991)

Official designation: *Constitution State* (1959)
Nickname: Nutmeg State
Origin of name: From an Indian word (Quinnehtukqut) meaning "beside the long tidal river"
10 largest cities (1998 est.): Bridgeport, 137,425; Hartford, 131,523; New Haven, 123,189; Stamford, 110,689; Waterbury, 105,346; Norwalk, 78,064; New Britain, 70,492; Danbury, 65,829; Bristol, 59,158; Meriden, 56,667
Land area: 4,845 sq mi. (12,550 sq km)
Geographic center: In Hartford Co., at East Berlin
Number of counties: 8
Largest county (1998 pop. est.): Fairfield, 838,362
State forests: 30 (145,529 ac.)
State parks: 91 (31,884 ac.)
1998 resident population est.: 3,274,069
1990 resident census population(rank): 3,287,116 (27). **Male:** 1,592,873; **Female:** 1,694,243. **White:** 2,859,353 (87.0%); **Black:** 274,269 (8.3%); **American Indian:** 6,654 (0.2%); **Asian:** 50,698 (1.5%); **Other race:** 96,142 (2.9%); **Hispanic:** 213,116 (6.5%). **1990 percent population under 18:** 22.8; **65 and over:** 13.6; **median age:** 34.3.

The Dutch navigator, Adriaen Block, was the first European of record to explore the area, sailing up the Connecticut River in 1614. In 1633, Dutch colonists built a fort and trading post near present-day Hartford, but soon lost control to English Puritans migrating south from the Massachusetts Bay Colony.

English settlements, established in the 1630s at Windsor, Wethersfield, and Hartford, united in 1639 to form the Connecticut Colony and adopted the *Fundamental Orders.*

The colony's royal charter of 1662 was exceptionally liberal. When Gov. Edmund Andros tried to seize it in 1687, it was hidden in the Hartford Oak, commemorated in Charter Oak Place.

Connecticut played a prominent role in the Revolutionary War, serving as the Continental Army's major supplier. Sometimes called the "Arsenal of the Nation," the state became one of the most industrialized in the nation.

Today, Connecticut factories produce weapons, sewing machines, jet engines, helicopters, motors, hardware and tools, cutlery, clocks, locks, silverware, and submarines. Hartford has the oldest U.S. newspaper still being published—the *Hartford Courant,* established 1764—and is the insurance capital of the nation.

Poultry, fruit, and dairy products account for the largest portion of farm income, and Connecticut's shade-grown tobacco is acknowledged to be the state's most valuable crop per acre.

Connecticut is a popular resort area with its 250-mile Long Island Sound shoreline and many inland lakes. Among the major points of interest are Yale University's Gallery of Fine Arts and Peabody Museum. Other famous museums include the P. T. Barnum, Winchester Gun, and American Clock and Watch. The town of Mystic features a recreated 19th-century New England seaport and the Mystic Marinelife Aquarium.

Famous natives and residents: Dean Acheson, statesman; Ethan Allan, American Revolutionary soldier; Benedict Arnold, American Revolutionary general; P. T. Barnum, showman; Henry Ward Beecher, clergyman; John Brown, abolitionist; Oliver Ellsworth, jurist; Eileen Farrell, soprano; Charles Goodyear, inventor; Nathan Hale, American Revolutionary officer; Dorothy Hamill, ice skater; Katharine Hepburn, actress; Charles Ives, composer; Edwin H. Land, inventor; John Pierpont Morgan, financier; Frederick Law Olmsted, landscape designer; Rosa Ponselle, soprano; Adam Clayton Powell, Jr., congressman; Benjamin Spock, pediatrician; Harriet Beecher Stowe, author; Mark Twain, author; Morris R. Waite, jurist; Noah Webster, lexicographer.

Delaware

Capital: Dover
Governor: Thomas R. Carper, D (to Jan. 2001)
Lieut. Governor: Ruth Ann Minner, D (to Jan. 2001)
Senators: Joseph R. Biden, Jr., D (to Jan. 2003); William V. Roth, Jr., R (to Jan. 2001)
Secy. of State: Edward J. Freel, D (Pleasure of Governor)
State Treasurer: Jack Markell, D. (to Jan. 2002)
Atty. General: M. Jane Brady, R (to Jan. 2002)
Entered Union (rank): Dec. 7, 1787 (1)
Present constitution adopted: 1897
Motto: Liberty and independence
State symbols: colors, colonial blue and buff; **flower,** peach blossom (1895); **tree,** American holly (1939); **bird,** blue hen chicken (1939); **insect,** ladybug (1974); **fish,** weakfish, *cynoscion regalis* (1981); **song,** "Our Delaware"
Nicknames: Diamond State; First State; Small Wonder
Origin of name: From Delaware River and Bay; named in turn for Sir Thomas West, Baron De La Warr
10 largest cities (1998 est.): Wilmington, 71,678; Dover, 30,369; Newark, 28,000; Milford, 6,665; Seaford, 6,600; Elsmere, 5,764; Smyrna, 5,652; New Castle 4,888; Middletown, 4,434; Georgetown, 4,185
Land area: 1,955 sq mi. (5,153 sq km)
Geographic center: In Kent Co., 11 mi. S of Dover
Number of counties: 3
Largest county (1998 pop. est.): New Castle, 482,807
State forests: 3 (9,353 ac.)
State parks: 13
1998 resident population est.: 743,603
1990 resident census population (rank): 666,168 (46). **Male:** 322,968; **Female:** 343,200. **White:** 535,094 (80.3%); **Black:** 112,460 (16.9%); **American Indian:** 2,019 (0.3%); **Asian:** 9,057 (1.4%); **Other race:** 7,538 (1.1%); **Hispanic:** 15,820 (2.4%). **1990 percent population under 18:** 24.5; **65 and over:** 12.1; **median age:** 32.7.

Henry Hudson, sailing under the Dutch flag, is credited with Delaware's discovery in 1609. The following year, Capt. Samuel Argall of Virginia named Delaware for his colony's governor, Thomas West, Baron De La Warr. An attempted Dutch settlement failed in 1631. Swedish colonization began at Fort Christina (now Wilmington) in 1638, but New Sweden fell to Dutch forces led by New Netherlands' Gov. Peter Stuyvesant in 1655.

England took over the area in 1664 and it was transferred to William Penn as the southern Three Counties in 1682. Semiautonomous after 1704, Delaware fought as a separate state in the American Revolution and became the first state to ratify the Constitution in 1787.

During the Civil War, although a slave state, Delaware did not secede from the Union.

In 1802, Éleuthère Irénée du Pont established a gunpowder mill near Wilmington that laid the foundation for Delaware's huge chemical industry. Delaware's manufactured products now also include vulcanized fiber, textiles, paper, medical supplies, metal products, machinery, machine tools, and automobiles.

Delaware also grows a great variety of fruits and vegetables and is a U.S. pioneer in the food-canning industry. Corn, soybeans, potatoes, and hay are important crops. Delaware's broiler-chicken farms supply the big Eastern markets, and fishing and dairy products are other important industries.

Points of interest include the Fort Christina Monument, Hagley Museum, Holy Trinity Church (erected in 1698, the oldest Protestant church in the United States still in use) and Winterthur Museum, in and near Wilmington; central New Castle, an almost unchanged late 18th-century capital; and the Delaware Museum of Natural History.

Popular recreation areas include Cape Henlopen, Delaware Seashore, Trapp Pond State Park, and Rehoboth Beach.

Famous natives and residents: Richard Allen, founder of the African Methodist Episcopal Church; Valerie Bertinelli, actress; Robert Montgomery Bird, playwright and novelist; Henry S. Canby, editor and author; Annie Jump Cannon, astronomer; Elizabeth Margaret Chandler, author; Felix Darley, artist; John Dickinson, statesman; E. I. du Pont, industrialist; Oliver Evans, inventor; Thomas Garrett, abolitionist; Henry Heimlich, surgeon, inventor; Wilham Julius "Judy" Johnson, basketball player; J. P. Marquand, novelist; Howard Pyle, artist and author; George Read, jurist, signer of Declaration of Independence; Jay Saunders Redding, educator and author; Caesar Rodney, patriot, signer of Declaration of Independence; Frank Stephens, sculptor; Estelle Taylor, actress; George Alfred Townsend, journalist and author.

District of Columbia

See Washington, D.C., listing in U.S. Cities.

Florida

Capital: Tallahassee
Governor: Jeb Bush, R (to Jan. 2003)
Lieut. Governor: Frank Brogan, R (to Jan. 2003)
Senators: Bob Graham, D (to Jan. 2005); Connie Mack III, R (to Jan. 2001)
Secy. of State: Katherine Harris, R (to Jan. 2003)
Comptroller: Bob Milligan, R (to Jan. 2003)
Commissioner of Agriculture: Bob Crawford, D (to Jan. 2003)
Atty. General: Bob Butterworth, D (to Jan. 2003)
Organized as territory: March 30, 1821
Entered Union (rank): March 3, 1845 (27)
Present constitution adopted: 1969
Motto: In God we trust (1868)
State symbols: flower, orange blossom (1909); **bird,** mockingbird (1927); **song,** "Suwannee River" (1935)
Nickname: Sunshine State (1970)
Origin of name: From the Spanish, meaning "feast of flowers" (Easter)
10 largest cities (1998 est.): Jacksonville (CC[1]), 693,630; Miami, 368,624; Tampa, 289,156; St. Petersburg, 236,029; Hialeah, 211,392; Orlando, 181,175; Fort Lauderdale, 153,728; Tallahassee, 136,628; Hollywood, 130,026; Pembroke Pines, 115,361
Land area: 53,997 sq mi. (139,852 sq km)
Geographic center: In Hernando Co., 12 mi. NNW of Brooksville
Number of counties: 67
Largest county (1998 pop. est.): Dade, 2,152,437
State forests: 35 (550,000 ac.)
State parks: 147 (456,972 ac.)
1998 resident population est.: 14,915,980
1990 resident census population (rank): 12,937,926 (4). **Male:** 6,261,719; **Female:** 6,676,207. **White:** 10,749,285 (83.1%); **Black:** 1,759,534 (13.6%); **American Indian:** 36,335 (0.3%); **Asian:** 154,302 (1.2%); **Other race:** 238,470 (1.8%); **Hispanic:** 1,574,143 (12.2%). **1990 percent population under 18:** 22.2; **65 and over:** 18.3; **median age:** 36.2.

1. Consolidated City (Coextensive with Duval County).

In 1513, Ponce De Leon, seeking the mythical "Fountain of Youth," discovered and named Florida, claiming it for Spain. Later, Florida would be held at different times by Spain and England until Spain finally sold it to the United States in 1819. (Incidentally, France established a colony named Fort Caroline in 1564 in the state that was to become Florida.)

Florida's early-19th-century history as a U.S. territory was marked by wars with the Seminole Indians that did not end until 1842, although a treaty was actually never signed.

Today Florida is one of the nation's fastest-growing states. It's population went from 2.8 million in 1950 to more than 12.9 million in 1990.

Florida's economy rests on a solid base of tourism (in 1992 the state entertained more than 40.5 million visitors from all over the world), manufacturing, agriculture, and international trade.

In recent years, oranges, grapefruit, and tomatoes led Florida's agricultural-product list, followed by vegetables, potatoes, melons, strawberries, sugar cane, dairy products, cattle and calves, and forest products.

Major tourist attractions are Miami Beach, Palm Beach, St. Augustine (founded in 1565, thus the oldest permanent city in the U.S.), Daytona Beach, and Fort Lauderdale on the East Coast. West Coast resorts include Sarasota, Tampa, Key West, and St. Petersburg. The Orlando area, where Disney World is located on a 27,000-acre site, is Florida's most popular tourist destination.

Also drawing many visitors are the NASA Kennedy Space Center's Spaceport USA, located in the town of Kennedy Space Center, Everglades National Park, and the Epcot Center.

Famous natives and residents: Julian "Cannonball" Adderley, jazz saxophonist; Pat Boone, singer; Fernando Bujones, ballet dancer; Steve Carlton, baseball player; Fay Dunaway, actress; Stepin Fetchit (Lincoln Theodore Perry), comedian; Lue Gim Gong, horticulturist; Dwight Gooden, baseball player; Zora Neale Hurston, writer; Daniel James, four-star general; James Weldon Johnson, author and educator; Frances Langford, singer; Little Richard, singer; Butterfly McQueen, actress; Jim Morrison, singer; Osceola, Seminole Indian leader; Sidney Poitier, actor; A. Philip Randolph, labor leader; Marjorie Kinnan Rawlings, author; Burt Reynolds, actor; Charles and John Ringling, circus entrepreneurs; Joseph W. Stilwell, army general; Norman E. Thargard, astronaut; Clarence Thomas, jurist; Ben Vereen, actor.

Georgia

Capital: Atlanta
Governor: Roy E. Barnes, D (to Jan. 2003)
Lieut. Governor: Mark Taylor, D (to Jan. 2003)
Senators: Max Cleland, D (to Jan. 2003);
   Paul Coverdell, R (to Jan. 2005)
Secy. of State: Cathy Cox, D (to Jan. 2003)
Insurance Commissioner: John Oxendine, D
   (to Jan. 2003)
Atty. General: Thurbert Baker, D (to Jan. 2003)
Entered Union (rank): Jan. 2, 1788 (4)
Present constitution adopted: 1977
Motto: Wisdom, justice, and moderation
State symbols: flower, Cherokee rose (1916); **tree,** live oak (1937); **bird,** brown thrasher (1935); **song,** "Georgia on My Mind" (1922)
Nicknames: Peach State, Empire State of the South
Origin of name: In honor of George II of England
10 largest cities (1998 est.): Atlanta, 403,819; Columbus[1], 182,219; Savannah, 131,674; Macon, 114,336; Athens-Clarke County, 89,361; Albany,

77,545; Roswell, 57,102; Marietta, 51,362; Warner Robins, 46,698; Valdosta, 41,390
Land area: 57,919 sq mi. (150,010 sq km)
Geographic center: In Twiggs Co., 18 mi. SE of Macon
Number of counties: 160
Largest county (1998 pop. est.): Fulton, 739,367
State forests: 25,258,000 ac. (67% of total state area)
State parks: 53 (42,600 ac.)
1998 resident population est.: 7,642,207
1990 resident census population (rank): 6,478,216 (11). **Male:** 3,144,503; **Female:** 3,333,713. **White:** 4,600,148 (71.0%); **Black:** 1,746,565 (27.0%); **American Indian:** 13,348 (0.2%); **Asian:** 75,781 (1.2%); **Other race:** 42,374 (0.7%); **Hispanic:** 108,922 (1.7%). **1990 percent population under 18:** 26.7; **65 and over:** 10.1; **median age:** 31.4.

1. Consolidated City (Coextensive with Muscogee County).

Hernando de Soto, the Spanish explorer, first traveled parts of Georgia in 1540. British claims later conflicted with those of Spain. After obtaining a royal charter, Gen. James Oglethorpe established the first permanent settlement in Georgia in 1733 as a refuge for English debtors. In 1742, Oglethorpe defeated Spanish invaders in the Battle of Bloody Marsh.

A Confederate stronghold, Georgia was the scene of extensive military action during the Civil War. Union General William T. Sherman burned Atlanta and destroyed a 60-mile-wide path to the coast, where he captured Savannah in 1864.

The largest state east of the Mississippi, Georgia is typical of the changing South with an ever-increasing industrial development. Atlanta, largest city in the state, is the communications and transportation center for the Southeast and the area's chief distributor of goods.

Georgia leads the nation in the production of paper and board, tufted textile products, and processed chicken. Other major manufactured products are transportation equipment, food products, apparel, and chemicals.

Important agricultural products are corn, cotton, tobacco, soybeans, eggs, and peaches. Georgia produces twice as many peanuts as the next leading state. From its vast stands of pine come more than half of the world's resins and turpentine and 74.4 percent of the U.S. supply. Georgia is also a leader in the production of marble, kaolin, barite, and bauxite.

Principal tourist attractions in Georgia include the Okefenokee National Wildlife Refuge, Andersonville Prison Park and National Cemetery, Chickamauga and Chattanooga National Military Park, the Little White House at Warm Springs where Pres. Franklin D. Roosevelt died in 1945, Sea Island, the enormous Confederate Memorial at Stone Mountain, Kennesaw Mountain National Battlefield Park, and Cumberland Island National Seashore.

Famous natives and residents: Conrad Aiken, poet; James Bowie, soldier; James Brown, singer; Jim Brown, actor and athlete; Erskine Caldwell, writer; James E. Carter, former president; Ray Charles, singer; Lucius D. Clay, banker and former general; Ty Cobb, baseball player; Ossie Davis, actor and writer; James Dickey, poet; Mattiwilda Dobbs, soprano; Melvyn Douglas, actor; Rebecca Latimer Felton, first appointed woman U.S. senator; Roosevelt Grier, entertainer and former athlete; Oliver Hardy, comedian; Joel Chandler Harris, journalist and author; Larry Holmes, boxer; Miriam Hopkins, actress; Harry James, trumpeter; Jasper Johns, painter and sculptor; Bobby Jones, golfer; Stacy Keach, actor; DeForest Kelley, actor; Martin Luther King, Jr., civil rights leader; Gladys Knight, singer; Joseph

R. Lamar, jurist; Juliette Gordon Low, U.S. Girl Scouts founder; Carson McCullers, novelist; Johnny Mercer, songwriter; Margaret Mitchell, novelist; Elijah Muhammad, religious leader; Jessye Norman, soprano; Otis Redding, singer; Burt Reynolds, actor; Jackie Robinson, baseball player; Dean Rusk, former secretary of state; Nipsey Russell, comedian; Alice Walker, author; Joanne Woodward, actress.

Hawaii

Capital: Honolulu (on Oahu)
Governor: Benjamin Cayetano, D (to Dec. 2002)
Lieut. Governor: Mazie Hirono, D
Senators: Daniel K. Akaka, D (to Jan. 2001); Daniel K. Inouye, D (to Jan. 2005)
Comptroller: Raymond Sato
Atty. General: Earl Anzai
Organized as territory: 1900
Entered Union (rank): Aug. 21, 1959 (50)
Motto: Ua Mau Ke Ea O Ka Aina I Ka Pono (The life of the land is perpetuated in righteousness)
State symbols: flower, hibiscus (yellow) (1988); **song,** "Hawaii Ponoi" (1967); **bird,** nene (hawaiian goose) (1957); **tree,** kukui (candlenut) (1959)
Nickname: Aloha State (1959)
Origin of name: Uncertain. The islands may have been named by Hawaii Loa, their traditional discoverer. Or they may have been named after Hawaii or Hawaiki, the traditional home of the Polynesians.
10 largest cities[1] **(1996 est.):** Honolulu, 377,059; Hilo, 37,808; Kailua, 36,818; Kaneohe, 35,448; Waipahu, 31,435; Pearl City, 30,993; Waimalu, 29,967; Mililani Town, 29,359; Schofield Barracks, 19,597; Wahiawa, 17,386
Land area: 6,423 sq mi. (16,637 sq km)
Geographic center: Between islands of Hawaii and Maui
Number of counties: Four plus one non-functioning county (Kalawao)
Largest county (1998 pop. est.): Honolulu, 872,478
State parks and historic sites: 19
1998 resident population est.: 1,193,001
1990 resident census population (rank): 1,108,229 (41). **Male:** 563,891; **Female:** 544,338. **White:** 369,616 (33.4%); **Black:** 27,195 (2.5%); **American Indian:** 5,099 (0.5%); **Asian and Pacific Islander:** 685,236 (61.8%); **Other race:** 21,083 (1.9%); **Hispanic:** 81,390 (7.3%). **1990 percent population under 18:** 25.3; **65 and over:** 11.3; **median age:** 32.5.

1. Census Designated Place. There are no political boundaries to Honolulu or any other place, but statistical boundaries are assigned under state law.

First settled by Polynesians sailing from other Pacific islands between c.e. 300 and 600, Hawaii was visited in 1778 by British Captain James Cook, who called the group the Sandwich Islands.

Hawaii was a native kingdom throughout most of the 19th century, when the expansion of the vital sugar industry (pineapple came after 1898) meant increasing U.S. business and political involvement. In 1893, Queen Liliuokalani was deposed and a year later the Republic of Hawaii was established with Sanford B. Dole as president. Then, following its annexation in 1898, Hawaii became a U.S. territory in 1900.

The Japanese attack on the naval base at Pearl Harbor on Dec. 7, 1941, was directly responsible for U.S. entry into World War II.

Hawaii, 2,397 miles west-southwest of San Francisco, is a 1,523-mile chain of islets and eight main islands—Hawaii, Kahoolawe, Maui, Lanai, Molokai, Oahu, Kauai, and Niihau. The Northwestern Hawaiian Islands, other than Midway, are administratively part of Hawaii.

The temperature is mild and Hawaii's soil is fertile for tropical fruits and vegetables. Cane sugar, pineapple, and flowers and nursery products are the chief products. Hawaii also grows coffee beans, bananas, and macadamia nuts. The tourist business is Hawaii's largest source of outside income.

Hawaii's highest peak is Mauna Kea (13,796 ft.). Mauna Loa (13,679 ft.) is the largest volcanic mountain in the world in cubic content.

Among the major points of interest are Hawaii Volcanoes National Park (Hawaii), Haleakala National Park (Maui), Puuhonua o Honaunau National Historical Park (Hawaii), Polynesian Cultural Center (Oahu), the USS *Arizona* and USS *Missouri* Memorial at Pearl Harbor, The National Memorial Cemetery of the Pacific (Oahu), and Iolani Palace (the only royal palace in the U.S.), Bishop Museum, and Waikiki Beach (all in Honolulu).

Famous natives and residents: Salevaa Atisanoe (Konishiki), sumo wrestler; George Ariyoshi, first Japanese-American elected governor; Hiram Bingham, missionary; Charles R. Bishop, banker and philanthropist; Tia Carrere, singer, actress; Samuel N. Castle, missionary, founder of Castle & Cooke Ltd. with Amos S. Cooke, missionary and educator; Father Damien, priest and philanthropist; Sanford B. Dole, territorial governor; Jean Erdman, dancer, choreographer; Hiram L. Fong, first Chinese-American senator; Don Ho, entertainer; Gerrit P. Judd, advisor to the Hawaiian king; Kaahumanu, Hawaiian queen; Duke Paoa Kahanamoku, Olympic swimming champion; Kamehameha I, first Hawaiian king; Kamehameha V, last of the dynasty; George Parsons Lathrop, journalist and poet; Liliuokalani, queen, last Hawaiian monarch; Bette Midler, singer; Ellison Onizuka, astronaut; Kawaipuna Prejean, Hawaiian activist, proponent of Hawaiian sovereignty; Chad Rowan (Akebono), sumo wrestler; Harold Sakata, actor; Carolyn Suzanne Sapp, Miss America (1991); James Shigeta, actor; Claus Spreckels, developer of Hawaiian sugar industry; Don Stroud, actor; John Waihee, first Hawaiian elected Governor.

Idaho

Capital: Boise
Governor: Dirk Kempthorne, R (to Jan. 2003)
Lieut. Governor: C. L. "Butch" Otter, R (to Jan. 2003)
Senators: Larry E. Craig, R (to Jan. 2003); Mike Crapo, R (to Jan. 2005)
Secy. of State: Pete T. Cenarrusa, R (to Jan. 2003)
State Controller: J. D. Williams, D (to Jan. 2003)
Atty. General: Alan G. Lance, R (to Jan. 2003)
Treasurer: Ron G. Crane, R (to Jan. 2003)
Organized as territory: March 3, 1863
Entered Union (rank): July 3, 1890 (43)
Present constitution adopted: 1890
Motto: Esto perpetua (It is forever)
State symbols: flower, syringa (1931); **tree,** white pine (1935); **bird,** mountain bluebird (1931); **horse,** Appaloosa (1975); **gem,** star garnet (1967); **song,** "Here We Have Idaho"; **folk dance,** square dance; **fish,** cutthroat trout (1990); **fossil,** Hagerman horse fossil (1988)
Nickname: Gem State
Origin of name: Unknown. Though popularly believed to be an Indian word, it is an invented name whose meaning is unknown.
10 largest cities (1998 est.): Boise, 157,452; Pocatello, 53,074; Idaho Falls, 48,122; Nampa, 41,951; Twin Falls, 33,296; Coeur d'Alene, 32,565; Lewiston, 30,363; Meridian, 25,377; Caldwell, 22,340; Moscow, 19,312
Land area: 82,751 sq mi. (214,325 sq km)
Geographic center: In Custer Co., at Custer, SW of Challis

Number of counties: 44, plus small part of Yellowstone National Park
Largest county (1998 pop. est.): Ada, 275,687
State forests: 881,000 ac.
State parks: 21
1998 resident population est.: 1,228,684
1990 resident census population (rank): 1,006,749 (42). **Male:** 500,956; **Female:** 505,793. **White:** 950,451 (94.4%); **Black:** 3,370 (0.3%); **American Indian:** 13,780 (1.4%); **Asian:** 9,365 (0.9%); **Other race:** 29,783 (3.0%); **Hispanic:** 52,927 (5.3%). **1990 percent population under 18:** 30.6; **65 and over:** 12.0; **median age:** 31.5.

After its acquisition by the U.S. as part of the Louisiana Purchase in 1803, the region was explored by Meriwether Lewis and William Clark in 1805–06. Northwest boundary disputes with Great Britain were settled by the Oregon Treaty in 1846 and the first permanent U.S. settlement in Idaho was established by the Mormons at Franklin in 1860.

After gold was discovered on Orofino Creek in 1860, prospectors swarmed into the territory, but left little more than a number of ghost towns.

In the 1870s, growing white occupation of Indian lands led to a series of battles between U.S. forces and the Nez Percé, Bannock, and Sheepeater tribes.

Mining, lumbering, and irrigation farming have been important for years. Idaho produces more than one fifth of all the silver mined in the U.S. It also ranks high among the states in antimony, lead, cobalt, garnet, phosphate rock, vanadium, zinc, mercury, and gold.

Idaho's most impressive growth began when World War II military needs made processing agricultural products a big industry, particularly the dehydrating and freezing of potatoes. The state produces about one fourth of the nation's potato crop, as well as wheat, apples, corn, barley, sugar beets, and hops.

With the growth of winter sports, tourism now outranks mining in dollar revenue. Idaho's many streams and lakes provide fishing, camping, and boating sites. The nation's largest elk herds draw hunters from all over the world and the famed Sun Valley resort attracts thousands of visitors to its swimming and skiing facilities.

Other points of interest are the Craters of the Moon National Monument; Nez Percé National Historic Park, which includes many sites visited by Lewis and Clark; and the State Historical Museum in Boise.

Famous natives and residents: Joe Albertson, grocery chain founder; Cecil Andrus, former governor; T. H. Bell, educator; Ezra Taft Benson, Eisenhower's Secretary of Agriculture, pres. LDS church, marketing specialist; William E. Borah, former senator; Gutzon Borglum, Mt. Rushmore sculptor; Carol R. Brink, author; Frank F. Church, former senator; Fred Dubois, senator; Vardis Fisher, novelist; Lawrence H. Gipson, historian; Ernest Hemingway, author; Mariel Hemingway, actress; Chief Joseph, Nez Percé chief; Harmon Killebrew, baseball player; Jerry Kramer, football player, author; Ezra Pound, poet; Sacagawea, Shoshonean guide; J. R. Simplot, industrialist; Robert E. Smylie, political leader; Henry Spalding, missionary; Frank Steunenberg, former governor; Picabo Street, skier; David Tompson, founded first trading post; Lana Turner, actress.

Illinois

Capital: Springfield
Governor: George H. Ryan, R (to Jan. 2003)
Lieut. Governor: Corinne G. Wood, R (to Jan. 2003)
Senators: Richard J. Durbin, D (to Jan. 2003); Peter G. Fitzgerald, R (to Jan. 2005)

Atty. General: Jim Ryan, R (to Jan. 2003)
Secy. of State: Jesse White, D (to Jan. 2003)
Comptroller: Daniel W. Hynes, D (to Jan. 2003)
Treasurer: Judith Barr Topinka, R (to Jan. 2003)
Organized as territory: Feb. 3, 1809
Entered Union (rank): Dec. 3, 1818 (21)
Present constitution adopted: 1970
Motto: State sovereignty, national union
State symbols: flower, violet (1908); **tree,** white oak (1973); **bird,** cardinal (1929); **animal,** white-tailed deer (1982); **fish,** bluegill (1987); **insect,** monarch butterfly (1975); **song,** "Illinois" (1925); **mineral,** fluorite (1965)
Nickname: Prairie State
Origin of name: Algonquin for "tribe of superior men"
10 largest cities (1998 est.): Chicago, 2,802,079; Rockford, 143,656; Aurora, 124,736; Springfield, 117,098; Naperville, 117,091; Peoria, 111,148; Joliet, 92,285; Elgin, 87,507; Decatur, 79,972; Arlington Heights, 76,522
Land area: 55,593 sq mi. (143,987 sq km)
Geographic center: Chestnut, on Illinois route 54 between Mt. Pulaski and Clinton.
Number of counties: 102
Largest county (1998 pop. est.): Cook, 5,189,689
Public use areas: 187 (275,000 ac.), incl. state parks, memorials, forests and conservation areas
1998 resident population est.: 12,045,326
1990 resident census population (rank): 11,430,602 (6). **Male:** 5,552,233; **Female:** 5,878,369. **White:** 8,952,978 (78.3%); **Black:** 1,694,273 (14.8%); **American Indian:** 21,836 (0.2%); **Asian:** 285,311 (2.5%); **Other race:** 476,204 (4.2%); **Hispanic:** 904,446 (7.9%). **1990 percent population under 18:** 25.8; **65 and over:** 12.6; **median age:** 32.7.

French explorers Jacques Marquette and Louis Joliet, in 1673, were the first Europeans of record to visit the region. In 1699 French settlers established the first permanent settlement at Cahokia, near present-day East St. Louis.

Great Britain obtained the region at the end of the French and Indian Wars in 1763. The area figured prominently in frontier struggles during the Revolutionary War and in Indian wars during the early 19th century.

Significant episodes in the state's early history include the growing migration of Eastern settlers following the opening of the Erie Canal in 1825; the Black Hawk War, which virtually ended the Indian troubles in the area; and the rise of Abraham Lincoln from farm laborer to president.

Today, Illinois stands high in manufacturing, coal mining, agriculture, and oil production. The sprawling Chicago district (including a slice of Indiana) is a great iron and steel producer, meat packer, grain exchange, and railroad center. Chicago is also famous as a Great Lakes port.

Illinois ranks third in the nation in export of agricultural products, first in corn and soybeans, and third in hog production. An important dairy state, Illinois is also a leader in corn, oats, wheat, barley, rye, truck vegetables, and the nursery products.

The state manufactures a great variety of industrial and consumer products: railroad cars, clothing, furniture, tractors, liquor, watches, and farm implements are just some of the items made in its factories and plants.

Central Illinois is noted for shrines and memorials associated with the life of Abraham Lincoln. In Springfield are the Lincoln Home, the Lincoln Tomb, and the restored Old State Capitol. Other points of interest are the home of Mormon leader Joseph Smith in Nauvoo and, in Chicago: the Art Institute, Field Museum, Museum of Science and Industry, Shedd Aquarium, Adler Planetarium, Merchandise Mart, and Chicago Portage National Historic Site.

Famous natives and residents: Franklin Pierce Adams, author; Jane Addams, social worker; Mary Astor, actress; Jack Benny, comedian; Black Hawk, Sauk Indian chief; Harry A. Blackmun, jurist; Ray Bradbury, author; William Jennings Bryan, orator and politician; Edgar Rice Burroughs, novelist; Gower Champion, choreographer; John Chancellor, TV commentator; Raymond Chandler, writer; Jimmy Connors, tennis champion; James Gould Cozzens, novelist; Richard J. Daley, former mayor of Chicago; Miles Davis, musician; Peter DeVries, novelist; Walt Disney, film animator and producer; John Dos Passos, author; James T. Farrell, novelist; Betty Friedan, feminist; Benny Goodman, musician; John Gunther, author; Ernest Hemingway, author; Charlton Heston, actor; Wild Bill Hickok, scout; William Holden, actor; Rock Hudson, actor; Burl Ives, singer; James Jones, novelist; John Jones, civil rights leader; Quincy Jones, composer; Keokuk (Watchful Fox), chief of the Sac and Fox Indians; Walter Kerr, drama critic; Archibald MacLeish, poet; David Mamet, playwright; Robert A. Millikan, physicist; Sherrill Milnes, baritone; Bill Murray, actor; Bob Newhart, actor and comedian; William S. Paley, broadcasting executive; Drew Pearson, columnist; Richard Pryor, comedian and actor; Ronald Reagan, former President and actor; Carl Sandburg, poet; Sam Shepard, playwright; William L. Shirer, author and historian; John Paul Stevens, jurist; McLean Stevenson, actor; Preston Sturges, director; Gloria Swanson, actress; Carl Van Doren, writer and educator; Melvin Van Peebles, playwright; Irving Wallace, novelist; Alfred Wallenstein, conductor; Raquel Welch, actress; Florenz Ziegfield, theatrical producer.

Indiana

Capital: Indianapolis
Governor: Frank O'Bannon, D (to Jan. 2001)
Lieut. Governor: Joseph E. Kernan, D (to Jan. 2001)
Senators: Evan Bayh, D (to Jan. 2005); Richard G. Lugar, R (to Jan. 2001)
Secy. of State: Sue Anne Gilroy, R (to Dec. 2002)
Treasurer: Tim Berry, R (to Feb. 2003)
Atty. General: Jeffrey A. Modisett, D (to Jan. 2001)
Auditor: Connie Kay Nass, R (to Dec. 2002)
Organized as territory: May 7, 1800
Entered Union (rank): Dec. 11, 1816 (19)
Present constitution adopted: 1851
Motto: The Crossroads of America
State symbols: flower, peony (1957); **tree,** tulip tree (1931); **bird,** cardinal (1933); **song,** "On the Banks of the Wabash, Far Away" (1913); **river,** Wabash; **stone,** limestone
Official language: English
Nickname: Hoosier State
Origin of name: Meaning "land of Indians"
10 largest cities (1998 est.): Indianapolis, 741,304; Fort Wayne, 185,716; Evansville, 122,779; Gary, 108,469; South Bend, 99,417; Hammond, 78,212; Muncie, 67,476; Bloomington, 65,065; Anderson, 58,528; Terre Haute, 53,355
Land area: 35,870 sq mi. (92,904 sq km)
Geographic center: In Boone Co., 14 mi. NNW of Indianapolis
Number of Counties: 92
Largest county (1998 pop. est.): Marion, 813,405
State parks: 23 (56,409 ac.)
State historic sites: 17 (2,007 ac.)
1998 resident population est.: 5,899,195
1990 resident census population(rank): 5,544,159 (14). **Male:** 2,688,281; **Female:** 2,855,878. **White:** 5,020,700 (90.6%); **Black:** 432,092 (7.8%); **American Indian:** 12,720 (0.2%); **Asian:** 37,617 (0.7%); **Other race:** 41,030 (0.7%); **Hispanic:** 98,788 (1.8%). **1990 percent population under 18:** 26.3; **65 and over:** 12.6; **median age:** 32.7.

First explored for France by sieur de la Salle in 1679–1680, the region figured importantly in the Franco-British struggle for North America that culminated with British victory in 1763.

George Rogers Clark led American forces against the British in the area during the Revolutionary War and, prior to becoming a state, Indiana was the scene of frequent Indian uprisings until the victory of Gen. William Henry Harrison at Tippecanoe in 1811.

Indiana's 41-mile Lake Michigan waterfront—one of the world's great industrial centers—turns out iron, steel, and oil products. Products include automobile parts and accessories, mobile homes and recreational vehicles, truck and bus bodies, aircraft engines, farm machinery, and fabricated structural steel. Wood office furniture and pharmaceuticals are also manufactured.

The state is a leader in agriculture with corn the principal crop. Hogs, soybeans, wheat, oats, rye, tomatoes, onions, and poultry also contribute heavily to Indiana's agricultural output. Much of the building limestone used in the U.S. is quarried in Indiana, which is also a large producer of coal.

Wyandotte Cave, one of the largest in the U.S., is located in Crawford County in southern Indiana, and West Baden and French Lick are well known for their mineral springs. Other attractions include Indiana Dunes National Lakeshore, Indianapolis Motor Speedway, Lincoln Boyhood National Memorial, and the George Rogers Clark National Historical Park.

Famous natives and residents: George Ade, humorist; Leon Ames, actor; Anne Baxter, actress; Albert J. Beveridge, political leader; Larry Bird, basketball player; Bill Blass, fashion designer; Frank Borman, astronaut; Hoagy Carmichael, songwriter; James Dean, actor; Eugene V. Debs, Socialist leader; Lloyd C. Douglas, author; Theodore Dreiser, writer; Bernard F. Gimbel, merchant; Virgil Grissom, astronaut; Phil Harris, actor and band leader; John Milton Hay, statesman; James R. Hoffa, labor leader; Michael Jackson, singer; Buck Jones, actor; Alfred C. Kinsey, zoologist; David Letterman, TV host and comedian; Eli Lilly, pharmaceuticals manufacturer; Carole Lombard, actress; Shelley Long, actress; Marjorie Main, actress; James McCracken, tenor; Joaquin Miller, poet; Paul Osborn, playwright; Cole Porter, songwriter; Gene Stratton Porter, naturalist and author; Ernest Taylor Pyle, journalist; J. Danforth Quayle, former vice president; James Whitcomb Riley, poet; Knute Rockne, football coach; Ned Rorem, composer; Red Skelton, comedian; Rex Stout, mystery writer; Booth Tarkington, author; Twyla Tharp, dancer and choreographer; Forrest Tucker, actor; Harold C. Urey, physicist; Kurt Vonnegut, Jr., author; Dan Wakefield, author; Robert Wise, director; Jessamyn West, novelist; Wendell Willkie, lawyer; Wilbur Wright, inventor.

Iowa

Capital: Des Moines
Governor: Tom Vilsack, D (to Jan. 2003)
Lieut. Governor: Sally Pederson, D (to Jan. 2003)
Senators: Chuck Grassley, R (to Jan. 2005); Tom Harkin, D (to Jan. 2003)
Secy. of State: Chet Culver, D (to Jan. 2003)
Treasurer: Michael L. Fitzgerald, D (to Jan. 2003)
Atty. General: Tom Miller, D (to Jan. 2003)
Organized as territory: June 12, 1838
Entered Union (rank): Dec. 28, 1846 (29)
Present constitution adopted: 1857
Motto: Our liberties we prize and our rights we will maintain
State symbols: flower, wild rose (1897); **bird,** eastern goldfinch (1933); **colors,** red, white, and blue (in state flag); **song,** "Song of Iowa"
Nickname: Hawkeye State
Origin of name: Probably from an Indian word meaning

"this is the place," or "the Beautiful Land"

10 largest cities (1998 est.): Des Moines, 191,293; Cedar Rapids, 114,563; Davenport, 96,842; Sioux City, 82,697; Waterloo, 63,703; Iowa City, 60,897; Dubuque, 56,467; Council Bluffs, 56,312; Ames, 48,415; West Des Moines, 42,333

Land area: 55,875 sq mi. (144,716 sq km)

Geographic center: In Story Co., 5 mi. NE of Ames

Number of counties: 99

Largest county (1998 pop. est.): Polk, 359,826

State forests: 5 (28,000 ac.)

State parks: 84 (49,237)

1998 resident population est.: 2,862,447

1990 resident census population (rank): 2,776,755 (30). **Male:** 1,344,802; **Female:** 1,431,953. **White:** 2,683,090 (96.6%); **Black:** 48,090 (1.7%); **American Indian:** 7,349 (0.3%); **Asian:** 25,476 (0.9%); **Other race:** 12,750 (0.5%); **Hispanic:** 32,647 (1.2%). **1990 percent population under 18:** 25.9; **65 and over:** 15.3; **median age:** 34.0.

The first Europeans to visit the area were the French explorers Father Jacques Marquette and Louis Joliet in 1673. The U.S. obtained control of the area in 1803 as part of the Louisiana Purchase.

During the first half of the 19th century, there was heavy fighting between white settlers and Indians. Lands were taken from the Indians after the Black Hawk War in 1832 and again in 1836 and 1837.

When Iowa became a state in 1846, its capital was Iowa City; the more centrally located Des Moines became the new capital in 1857. At that time, the state's present boundaries were also drawn.

Although Iowa produces a tenth of the nation's food supply, the value of Iowa's manufactured products is twice that of its agriculture. Major industries are food and associated products, non-electrical machinery, electrical equipment, printing and publishing, and fabricated products.

Iowa stands in a class by itself as an agricultural state. Its farms sell over $10 billion worth of crops and livestock annually. Iowa leads the nation in all corn, soybean, livestock, and hog marketings, with about 25% of the pork supply and 6% of the grain-fed cattle. Iowa's forests produce hardwood lumber, particularly walnut, and its mineral products include cement, limestone, sand, gravel, gypsum, and coal.

Tourist attractions include the Herbert Hoover birthplace and library near West Branch; the Amana Colonies; Fort Dodge Historical Museum, Fort, and Stockade; the Iowa State Fair at Des Moines in August; and the Effigy Mounds National Monument, a prehistoric Indian burial site at Marquette.

Famous natives and residents: Bix Beiderbecke, jazz musician; Norman Borlaug, plant pathologist, geneticist, and Nobel Peace Prize winner; William "Buffalo Bill" F. Cody, scout; Johnny Carson, TV entertainer; Gardner Cowles, Jr., publisher; Simon Estes, bass-baritone; William Frawley, actor; George H. Gallup, poll taker; Susan Glaspell, writer; Herbert Hoover, former president; MacKinlay Kantor, novelist; Charles A. Kettering, inventor; Ann Landers, columnist; Cloris Leachman, actress; John L. Lewis, labor leader; Glenn L. Martin, aviator and manufacturer; Elsa Maxwell, writer; Frederick L. Maytag, inventor and manufacturer; Glenn Miller, bandleader; Kate Mulgrew, actress; Harriet Nelson, actress; Nathan M. Pusey, educator; David Rabe, playwright; Harry Reasoner, TV commentator; Donna Reed, actress; Lillian Russell, soprano; Robert Schiller, evangelist; Wallace Stegner, novelist and critic; Billy Sunday, evangelist; James A. Van Allen, space physicist; Abigail Van Buren, columnist; Henry A. Wallace, statesman and vice president; John Wayne, actor; Andy Williams, singer; Meredith Willson, composer; Grant Wood, painter.

Kansas

Capital: Topeka

Governor: Bill Graves, R (to Jan. 2003)

Lieut. Governor: Gary Sherrer, R (to Jan. 2003)

Senators: Sam Brownback, R (to Jan. 2005); Pat Roberts, R (to Jan. 2003)

Secy. of State: Ron Thornburgh, R (to Jan. 2003)

Treasurer: Tim Shallenburger, R (to Jan. 2003)

Atty. General: Carla Stovall, R (to Jan. 2003)

Commission of Insurance: Kathleen Sebelius, D (to Jan. 2003)

Organized as territory: May 30, 1854

Entered Union (rank): Jan. 29, 1861 (34)

Present constitution adopted: 1859

Motto: *Ad astra per aspera* (To the stars through difficulties)

State symbols: flower, sunflower (1903); **tree,** cottonwood (1937); **bird,** western meadowlark (1937); **animal,** buffalo (1955); **song,** "Home on the Range" (1947)

Nicknames: Sunflower State; Jayhawk State

Origin of name: From a Sioux word meaning "people of the south wind"

10 largest cities (1998 est.): Wichita, 329,211; Kansas City, 141,297; Overland Park, 139,685; Topeka, 118,977; Olathe, 85,035; Lawrence, 74,244; Shawnee, 45,250; Salina, 44,022; Manhattan, 41,318; Leavenworth, 39,227

Land area: 81,823 sq mi. (211,922 sq km)

Geographic center: In Barton Co., 15 mi. NE of Great Bend

Number of counties: 105

Largest county (1998 pop. est.): Sedgwick, 448,050

State parks: 22 (14,394 ac.)

1998 resident population est.: 2,629,067

1990 resident census population (rank): 2,477,574 (32). **Male:** 1,214,645; **Female:** 1,262,929. **White:** 2,231,986 (90.1%); **Black:** 143,076 (5.8%); **American Indian:** 21,965 (0.9%); **Asian:** 31,750 (1.3%); **Other race:** 48,797 (2.0%); **Hispanic:** 93,670 (3.8%). **1990 percent population under 18:** 26.7; **65 and over:** 13.8; **median age:** 32.8.

Spanish explorer Francisco de Coronado, in 1541, is considered the first European to have traveled this region. Sieur de la Salle's extensive land claims for France (1682) included present-day Kansas. Ceded to Spain by France in 1763, the territory reverted to France in 1800 and was sold to the U.S. as part of the Louisiana Purchase in 1803.

Lewis and Clark, Zebulon Pike, and Stephen H. Long explored the region between 1803 and 1819. The first permanent settlements in Kansas were outposts—Fort Leavenworth (1827), Fort Scott (1842), and Fort Riley (1853)—established to protect travelers along the Santa Fe and Oregon Trails.

Just before the Civil War, the conflict between the pro- and anti-slavery forces earned the region the grim title of Bleeding Kansas.

Today, wheat fields, oil-well derricks, herds of cattle, and grain-storage elevators are chief features of the Kansas landscape. A leading wheat-growing state, Kansas also raises corn, sorghum, oats, barley, soybeans, and potatoes. Kansas stands high in petroleum production and mines zinc, coal, salt, and lead. It is also the nation's leading producer of helium.

Wichita is one of the nation's leading aircraft-manufacturing centers, ranking first in production of private aircraft. Kansas City is an important transportation, milling, and meat-packing center.

Points of interest include the Kansas History Center at Topeka, the Eisenhower boyhood home and the new Eisenhower Memorial Museum and Presidential Library at Abilene, John Brown's cabin at Osawatomie, recreated Front Street in Dodge City, Fort Larned (once the most important military post on the Santa Fe Trail), and Fort Leavenworth and Fort Riley.

Famous natives and residents: Roscoe "Fatty" Arbuckle, actor; Clarence D. Batchelor, political cartoonist; Gwendolyn Brooks, poet; Walter P. Chrysler, auto manufacturer; Clark M. Clifford, former secretary of defense; John Steuart Curry, painter; Amelia Earhart, aviator; Milton S. Eisenhower, educator; Gary Hart, politician; William Inge, playwright; Walter Johnson, baseball pitcher; Osa L. Johnson, documentary film producer; Buster Keaton, comedian; Emmett Kelly, clown; Stan Kenton, jazz musician; James Lehrer, broadcast journalist; Edgar Lee Masters, poet; Mary McCarthy, actress; Hattie McDaniel, actress; Karl Menninger, psychiatrist; Gordon Parks, film director; Zasu Pitts, actress; Samuel Ramey, opera singer; Charles Robinson, statesman and first governor; Charles (Buddy) Rogers, actor; Damon Runyon, journalist; Eugene W. Smith, photojournalist; Milburn Stone, actor; John Cameron Swayze, news commentator; William Allen White, journalist; Charles E. Whittaker, jurist; Jess Willard, boxer.

Kentucky

Capital: Frankfort
Governor: Paul E. Patton, D (to Dec. 1999)
Lieut. Governor: Stephen L. Henry, D (to Dec. 1999)
Senators: Jim Bunning, R (to Jan. 2005);
Mitch McConnell, R (to Jan. 2003)
Secy. of State: John Y. Brown III, D (to Dec. 1999)
Treasurer: Ed Hatchett, D (to Dec. 1999)
Auditor: John Kennedy Hamilton, D
(to Dec. 1999)
Atty. General: A.B. Chandler III, D (to Dec. 1999)
Entered Union (rank): June 1, 1792 (15)
Present constitution adopted: 1891
Motto: United we stand, divided we fall
State symbols: tree, tulip poplar (1994); **flower,** goldenrod; **bird,** Kentucky cardinal; **song,** "My Old Kentucky Home"
Nickname: Bluegrass State
Origin of name: From an Iroquoian word "Ken-tah-ten" meaning "land of tomorrow"
10 largest cities (1998 est.): Louisville, 255,045; Lexington-Fayette, 241,749; Owensboro, 54,041; Bowling Green, 44,822; Covington, 40,389; Hopkinsville, 32,045; Richmond, 27,644; Henderson, 26,457; Frankfort, 26,418; Paducah, 25,883
Land area: 39,732 sq mi. (102,907 sq km)
Geographic center: In Marion Co., 3 mi. NNW of Lebanon
Number of counties: 120
Largest county (1998 pop. est.): Jefferson, 672,104
State forests: 9 (44,173 ac.)
State parks: 49
1998 resident population est.: 3,936,499
1990 resident census population (rank): 3,685,296 (23). **Male:** 1,785,235; **Female:** 1,900,061. **White:** 3,391,832 (92.0%); **Black:** 262,907 (7.1%); **American Indian:** 5,769 (0.2%); **Asian:** 17,812 (0.5%); **Other race:** 6,976 (0.2%); **Hispanic:** 21,984 (0.6%). **1990 percent population below age 18:** 25.9; **65 and over:** 12.7; **median age:** 32.9.

Kentucky was the first region west of the Allegheny Mountains to be settled by American pioneers. James Harrod established the first permanent settlement at Harrodsburg in 1774; the following year Daniel Boone, who had explored the area in 1767, blazed the Wilderness Trail and founded Boonesboro.

Politically, the Kentucky region was originally part of Virginia, but early statehood was gained in 1792. During the Civil War, as a slaveholding state with a considerable abolitionist population, Kentucky was caught in the middle of the conflict, supplying both Union and Confederate forces with thousands of troops.

In recent years, manufacturing has shown important gains, particularly in automotive assembly and parts manufacturing. Kentucky also prides itself on producing some of the nation's best tobacco, horses, and whiskey. Corn, soybeans, wheat, fruit, hogs, cattle, and dairy products are among the agricultural items produced.

Among the manufactured items produced in the state are motor vehicles, furniture, aluminum ware, brooms, apparel, lumber products, machinery, textiles, and iron and steel products. Kentucky also produces significant amounts of petroleum, natural gas, fluorspar, clay, and stone. However, coal accounts for 90% of the total mineral income.

Louisville, the largest city, famed for the Kentucky Derby at Churchill Downs, is also the location of a large state university, whiskey distilleries, and cigarette factories. The Bluegrass country around Lexington is the home of some of the world's finest race horses. Other attractions are Mammoth Cave, the George S. Patton, Jr., Military Museum at Fort Knox, and Old Fort Harrod State Park.

Famous natives and residents: John Adair, pioneer and political leader; Muhammad Ali, boxer; Alben W. Barkley, former vice president; Louis D. Brandeis, jurist; John Mason Brown, critic; Kit Carson, scout; Champ Clark, politician; Rosemary Clooney, singer; Irvin S. Cobb, humorist; Jefferson Davis, president of the Confederacy; Irene Dunne, actress; Crystal Gayle, singer; David W. Griffith, film producer; John M. Harlan, jurist; Elizabeth Hardwick, writer; Casey Jones, celebrated locomotive engineer; Abraham Lincoln, former president; Loretta Lynn, singer; Carry Amelia Nation, temperance leader; Patricia Neal, actress; George Reeves, actor; Wiley B. Rutledge, jurist; Diane Sawyer, broadcast journalist; Phil Simms, football player; Adlai Stevenson, former vice president; Allen Tate, poet and critic; Hunter Thompson, writer; Frederick M. Vinson, jurist; Robert Penn Warren, novelist.

Louisiana

Capital: Baton Rouge
Governor: Murphy J. "Mike" Foster, D (to Jan. 2000)
Lieut. Governor: Kathleen Blanco, D (to Jan. 2000)
Senators: John B. Breaux, D (to Jan. 2005);
Mary Landrieu, D (to Jan. 2003)
Secy. of State: W. Fox McKeithen, R (to Jan. 2000)
Treasurer: Ken Duncan, D (to Jan. 2000)
Atty. General: Richard P. Ieyoub, D (to Jan. 2000)
Organized as territory: March 26, 1804
Entered Union (rank): April 30, 1812 (18)
Present constitution adopted: 1974
Motto: Union, justice, and confidence
State symbols: flower, magnolia (1900); **tree,** bald cypress (1963); **bird,** eastern brown pelican (1958); **songs,** "Give Me Louisiana" and "You Are My Sunshine"
Nickname: Pelican State
Origin of name: In honor of Louis XIV of France
10 largest cities (1998 est.): New Orleans, 465,538; Baton Rouge, 211,551; Shreveport, 188,319; Lafayette, 113,615; Kenner, 71,641; Lake Charles, 70,766; Bossier City, 56,637; Monroe, 53,612; Alexandria, 45,800; New Iberia, 32,664
Land area: 43,566 sq mi. (112,836 sq km)
Geographic center: In Avoyelles Parish, 3 mi. SE of Marksville
Number of parishes (counties): 64
Largest parish (1998 pop. est.): Orleans, 465,538

State forests: 1 (8,000 ac.)
State parks: 30 (13,932 ac.)
1998 resident population est.: 4,368,967
1990 resident census population (rank): 4,219,973 (21). **Male:** 2,031,386; **Female:** 2,188,587. **White:** 2,839,138 (67.3%); **Black:** 1,299,281 (30.8%); **American Indian:** 18,541 (0.4%); **Asian:** 41,099 (1.0%); **Other race:** 21,914 (0.5%); **Hispanic:** 93,044 (2.2%). **1990 percent population under 18:** 29.1; **65 and over:** 11.1; **median age:** 30.9.

Louisiana has a rich, colorful historical background. Early Spanish explorers were Alvárez Piñeda, 1519; Álvar Núñez Cabeza de Vaca, 1528; and Hernando De Soto in 1541. Sieur de la Salle reached the mouth of the Mississippi and claimed all the land drained by it and its tributaries for Louis XIV of France in 1682.

Louisiana became a French crown colony in 1731, was ceded to Spain in 1763, returned to France in 1800, and was sold by Napoleon to the U.S. as part of the Louisiana Purchase (with large territories to the north and northwest) in 1803.

In 1815, Gen. Andrew Jackson's troops defeated a larger British army in the Battle of New Orleans, neither side aware that the treaty ending the War of 1812 had been signed.

Louisiana is a leader in natural gas, salt, petroleum, and sulfur production. Much of the oil and sulfur comes from offshore deposits. The state also produces large crops of sweet potatoes, rice, sugar cane, pecans, soybeans, corn, and cotton.

Leading manufactured items include chemicals, processed food, petroleum and coal products, paper, lumber and wood products, transportation equipment, and apparel.

Louisiana marshes supply most of the nation's muskrat fur as well as that of opossum, raccoon, mink, and otter, and large numbers of game birds.

Major points of interest include New Orleans with its French Quarter and Superdome, plantation homes near Natchitoches and New Iberia, Cajun country in the Mississippi Delta region, Chalmette National Historical Park, and the state capital at Baton Rouge.

Famous natives and residents: Louis Armstrong, musician; Geoffrey Beene, fashion designer; Truman Capote, writer; Kitty Carlisle, singer and actress; Van Cliburn, concert pianist; Michael De Bakey, heart surgeon; Fats Domino, musician; Louis Moreau Gottschalk, pianist and composer; Bryant Gumbel, TV newscaster; Lillian Hellman, playwright; Al Hirt, trumpeter; Mahalia Jackson, gospel singer; Jean Laffite, privateer; Dorothy Lamour, actress; John A. Lejeune, Marine Corps general; Elmore Leonard, author; Jerry Lee Lewis, singer; Huey P. Long, politician; Wynton Marsalis, musician; Jelly Roll Morton, jazz musician and composer; Huey Newton, black activist; Marguerite Piazza, soprano; Paul Prudhomme, chef; Howard K. Smith, TV commentator; Ben Turpin, comedian; Ray Walston, actor; Edward Douglas White, jurist.

Maine

Capital: Augusta
Governor: Angus S. King, Jr., I (to Jan. 2003)
Senators: Susan Collins, R (to Jan. 2003); Olympia J. Snowe, R (to Jan. 2001)
Secy. of State: Dan A. Gwadosky, D (to Jan. 1999)
Controller: Carol Whitney, R (to Jan. 1999)
Atty. General: Andrew Ketterer, D (to Jan. 1999)
Entered Union (rank): March 15, 1820 (23)
Present constitution adopted: 1820
Motto: *Dirigo* (I lead)

State symbols: flower, white pine cone and tassel (1895); **tree,** white pine tree (1945); **bird,** chickadee (1927); **fish,** landlocked salmon (1969); **mineral,** tourmaline (1971); **song,** "State of Maine Song" (1937); **animal,** moose (1979); **cat,** Maine coon cat (1985); **fossil,** *pertica quadrifaria* (1985); **insect,** honeybee (1975)
Nickname: Pine Tree State
Origin of name: First used to distinguish the mainland from the offshore islands. It has been considered a compliment to Henrietta Maria, queen of Charles I of England. She was said to have owned the province of Mayne in France.
10 largest cities (1998 est.): Portland, 62,786; Lewiston, 36,186; Bangor, 30,508; South Portland, 22,810; Auburn, 22,617; Biddeford, 20,851; Augusta, 19,978; Westbrook, 16,679; Waterville, 16,263; Saco, 16,068
Largest town (1990 census): Brunswick, 20,906
Land area: 30,865 sq mi. (79,939 sq km)
Geographic center: In Piscataquis Co., 18 mi. N of Dover-Foxcroft
Number of counties: 16
Largest county (1998 pop. est.): Cumberland, 253,582
State forests: 1 (21,000 ac.)
State parks: 26 (247,627 ac.)
State historic sites: 18 (403 ac.)
1998 resident population est.: 1,244,250
1990 resident census population (rank): 1,227,928 (38). **Male:** 597,850; **Female:** 630,078. **White:** 1,208,360 (98.4%); **Black:** 5,138 (0.4%); **American Indian:** 5,998 (0.5%); **Asian:** 6,683 (0.5%); **Other race:** 1,749 (0.1%); **Hispanic:** 6,829 (0.6%).; **median age:** 33.8

John Cabot and his son, Sebastian, are believed to have visited the Maine coast in 1498. However, the first permanent English settlements were not established until more than a century later, in 1623.

The first naval action of the Revolutionary War occurred in 1775 when colonials captured the British sloop *Margaretta* off Machias on the Maine coast. In that same year, the British burned Falmouth (now Portland).

Long governed by Massachusetts, Maine became the 23rd state as part of the Missouri Compromise in 1820.

Maine produces 98% of the nation's low-bush blueberries. Farm income is also derived from apples, potatoes, dairy products, and vegetables, with poultry and eggs the largest selling items.

The state is one of the world's largest pulp-paper producers. It ranks second in boot-and-shoe manufacturing. With almost 89% of its area forested, Maine turns out wood products from boats to toothpicks.

Maine leads the world in the production of the familiar flat tins of sardines, producing more than 75 million of them annually. Lobstermen normally catch 50% of the nation's total of lobsters. The 1996 catch was 16,435 metric tons, the second-largest lobster catch in history.

A scenic seacoast, beaches, lakes, mountains, and resorts make Maine a popular vacationland. There are more than 2,500 lakes and 5,000 streams, plus 26 state parks to attract hunters, fishermen, skiers, and campers.

Major points of interest are Bar Harbor, Acadia National Park, Allagash National Wilderness Waterway, the Wadsworth-Longfellow House in Portland, Roosevelt Campobello International Park, and the St. Croix Island National Monument.

Famous natives and residents: F. Lee Bailey, defense attorney; Charles F. Browne (Artemus Ward), humorist; Cyrus Curtis, publisher; Dorothea Dix, civil rights reformer; John Ford, film director; Melville Fuller, jurist; Marsden Hartley, painter; Henry Wadsworth Longfellow, poet; Sarah Orne Jewett, author; Stephen King, writer; Linda Lavin, actress; Edna St. Vincent Millay, poet; Marston Morse, mathematician; Frank Munsey, publisher; Walter Piston, composer; George Putnam, publisher; Kenneth Roberts, historical novelist; Edwin Arlington Robinson, poet; Margaret Chase Smith, politician; Samantha Smith, peacemaker and actress; John Hay Whitney, publisher.

Maryland

Capital: Annapolis
Governor: Parris N. Glendening, D (to Jan. 2003)
Lieut. Gov.: Kathleen Kennedy Townsend, D (to Jan. 2003)
Senators: Barbara A. Mikulski, D (to Jan. 2005); Paul S. Sarbanes, D (to Jan. 2001)
Secy. of State: John T. Willis, D (to Jan. 1999)
Comptroller of the Treasury: William Donald Schaefer, D (to Jan. 2003)
Treasurer: Richard N. Dixon, D (to Jan. 2003)
Atty. General: J. Joseph Curran, Jr., D (to Jan. 2003)
Entered Union (rank): April 28, 1788 (7)
Present constitution adopted: 1867
Motto: *Fatti maschii, parole femine* (Manly deeds, womanly words)
State symbols: bird, Baltimore oriole (1947); **boat,** skipjack (1985); **crustacean,** Maryland blue crab (1989); **dinosaur,** Astrodon johnstoni (1998); **dog,** Chesapeake Bay retriever (1964); **drink,** milk (1998); **flower,** black-eyed susan (1918); **fish,** rockfish (1965); **folk dance,** square dance (1994); **fossil shell,** ecphora gardnerae gardnerae (Wilson) (1994); **insect,** Baltimore checkerspot butterfly (1973); **reptile,** Diamondback terrapin (1994); **song,** "Maryland! My Maryland!" (1939); **sport,** jousting (1962); **tree,** white oak (1941).
Nicknames: Free State; Old Line State
Origin of name: In honor of Henrietta Maria (queen of Charles I of England)
10 largest cities (1998 est.): Baltimore, 645,593; Frederick, 47,468; Gaithersburg, 46,980; Rockville, 46,788; Bowie, 40,704; Hagerstown, 34,105; Annapolis, 33,585; College Park, 25,855; Greenbelt, 22,076; Cumberland, 21,521
Land area: 9,775 sq mi. (25,316 sq km)
Geographic center: In Prince Georges Co., 4½ mi. NW of Davidsonville
Number of counties: 23, and 1 independent city
Largest county (1998 pop. est.): Montgomery, 840,879
State forests: 13 (132,944 ac.)
State parks: 47 (87,670 ac.)
1998 resident population est.: 5,134,808
1990 resident census population (rank): 4,781,468 (19). **Male:** 2,318,671; **Female:** 2,462,797. **White:** 3,393,964 (71.0%); **Black:** 1,189,899 (24.9%); **American Indian:** 12,972 (0.3%); **Asian:** 139,719 (2.9%); **Other race:** 44,914 (0.9%); **Hispanic:** 125,102 (2.6%). **1990 percent population under 18:** 24.3; **65 and over:** 10.8; **median age:** 32.9.

Maryland was inhabited by Indians as early as circa 10,000 B.C.E. Permanent Indian villages were established by circa C.E. 1000.

In 1608, Capt. John Smith explored Chesapeake Bay. Charles I granted a royal charter for Maryland to Cecil Calvert, Lord Baltimore, in 1632, and English settlers, many of whom were Roman Catholic, landed on St. Clement's (now Blakistone) Island in 1634. Religious freedom, granted all Christians in the Toleration Act passed by the Maryland assembly in 1649, was ended by a Puritan revolt, 1654–58.

From 1763 to 1767, Charles Mason and Jeremiah Dixon surveyed Maryland's northern boundary line with Pennsylvania. In 1791, Maryland ceded land to form the District of Columbia.

In 1814, when the British unsuccessfully tried to capture Baltimore, the bombardment of Fort McHenry inspired Francis Scott Key to write the words to "The Star-Spangled Banner."

The Baltimore clipper-ship trade developed during the 19th century. During the Civil War, Maryland remained a Union state even while the battles of South Mountain (1862), Antietam (1862), and Monocacy (1864) were fought on her soil.

In 1904, the Great Fire of Baltimore occurred. In 1937, the City of Greenbelt, a New Deal model community, was chartered.

Maryland's Eastern Shore and Western Shore embrace the Chesapeake Bay, and the many estuaries and rivers create one of the longest waterfronts of any state. The Bay produces more seafood—oysters, crabs, clams, fin fish—than any comparable body of water. Important agricultural products, in order of cash value, are greenhouse and nursery products, chickens, dairy products, soybeans, corn, eggs, vegetables, melons, and wheat. Maryland is a leader in vegetable canning. Stone, coal, sand, gravel, cement, and clay are the chief mineral products.

Manufacturing industries produce food and kindred products, instruments, chemicals, printing and publishing, transportation equipment, and primary metals. Baltimore, home of the Johns Hopkins University and Hospital, ranks as the nation's second port in foreign tonnage. Annapolis, site of the U.S. Naval Academy, has one of the earliest state houses (1772–79) still in regular use by a state government.

Among the popular attractions in Maryland are the Fort McHenry National Monument; Harpers Ferry and Chesapeake and Ohio Canal National Historic Parks; Antietam National Battlefield; National Aquarium, USS *Constellation,* and Maryland Science Center at Baltimore's Inner Harbor; Historic St. Mary's City; Jefferson Patterson Historical Park and Museum at St. Leonard; U.S. Naval Academy in Annapolis; Goddard Space Flight Center at Greenbelt; Assateague Island National Park Seashore; Ocean City beach resort; and Catoctin Mountain, Fort Frederick, and Piscataway parks.

Famous natives and residents: Benjamin Banneker, almanacker and mathematician-astronomer; John Barth, writer; Eubie Blake, musician; John Wilkes Booth, actor and Lincoln assassin; Francis X. Bushman, actor; James M. Cain, writer; Samuel Chase, jurist; Frederick Douglass, abolitionist; John Hurst Fletcher, Methodist bishop and educator; Christopher Gist, frontiersman; Philip Glass, composer; Matthew Henson, reached North Pole with Peary; Billie Holiday, jazz-blues singer; Johns Hopkins, financier; Reverdy Johnson, lawyer and statesman; Thomas Johnson, political leader; Francis Scott Key, laywer and author of the words to the national anthem; Thurgood Marshall, jurist; H. L. Mencken, writer; Hezekiah Niles, journalist; Charles Wilson Peale, painter; Frank Perdue, farmer, businessman; James R. Randall, journalist and writer of the state song; Babe Ruth, baseball player; Upton Sinclair, novelist; Roger B. Taney, jurist; George Alfred Townsend (Gath), journalist; Harriet Tubman, abolitionist; Leon Uris, novelist; Frank Zappa, singer.

Massachusetts

Capital: Boston
Governor: Argeo Paul Cellucci, R (to Jan. 2003)
Lieut. Governor: Jane Swift, R (to Jan. 2003)
Senators: Edward M. Kennedy, D (to Jan. 2001); John F. Kerry, D (to Jan. 2003)
Secy. of the Commonwealth: William F. Galvin, D (to Jan. 2003)
Treasurer & Receiver-General: Shannon P. O'Brien, D (to Jan. 2003)
Auditor of the Commonwealth: A. Joseph DeNucci, D (to Jan. 2003)
Atty. General: Thomas F. Reilly, D (to Jan. 2003)
Present constitution drafted: 1780 (oldest U.S. state constitution in effect today)
Entered Union (rank): Feb. 6, 1788 (6)
Motto: *Ense petit placidam sub libertate quietem* (By the sword we seek peace, but peace only under liberty)
State symbols: flower, mayflower (1918); **tree,** American elm (1941); **bird,** chickadee (1941); **song,** "All Hail to Massachusetts" (1966); **beverage,** cranberry juice (1970); **insect,** ladybug (1974); **muffin,** corn muffin; **dessert,** Boston cream pie
Nicknames: Bay State; Old Colony State
Origin of name: From Massachusett tribe of Native Americans, meaning "at or about the great hill"
10 largest cities (1998 est.): Boston, 555,447; Worcester, 166,535; Springfield, 148,144; Lowell, 101,075; New Bedford, 96,353; Cambridge, 96,352; Brockton, 93,173; Fall River, 90,654; Quincy, 85,752; Lynn, 81,075
Land area: 7,838 sq mi. (20,300 sq km)
Geographic center: In Worcester Co., in S part of city of Worcester
Number of counties: 14
Largest county (1998 pop. est.): Middlesex, 1,424,116
State forests and parks: 129 (242,000 ac.)[1]
1998 resident population est.: 6,147,132
1990 resident census population (rank): 6,016,425 (13). **Male:** 2,888,745; **Female:** 3,127,680. **White:** 5,405,374 (89.8%); **Black:** 300,130 (5.0%); **American Indian:** 12,241 (0.2%); **Asian:** 143,392 (2.4%); **Other race:** 155,288 (2.6%); **Hispanic:** 287,549 (4.8%). **1990 percent population under 18:** 22.5; **65 and over:** 13.6; **median age:** 33.4.

1. The Metropolitan District Commission, an agency of the Commonwealth serving municipalities in the Boston area, has about 14,000 acres of parkways and reservations under its jurisdiction.

Massachusetts has played a significant role in American history since the Pilgrims, seeking religious freedom, founded Plymouth Colony in 1620. As one of the most important of the 13 colonies, Massachusetts became a leader in resisting British oppression. In 1773, the Boston Tea Party protested unjust taxation. The Minute Men started the American Revolution by battling British troops at Lexington and Concord on April 19, 1775.

During the 19th century, Massachusetts was famous for the vigorous intellectual activity of its renowned writers and educators and for its expanding commercial fishing, shipping, and manufacturing interests.

Massachusetts pioneered the manufacture of textiles and shoes. Today, these industries have been replaced in importance by activity in the electronics and communications equipment fields.

The state's cranberry crop is the nation's largest. Also important are dairy and poultry products, nursery and greenhouse produce, vegetables, and fruit.

Tourism has become an important factor in the economy of the state because of its numerous recreational areas and historical landmarks. Cape Cod has summer theaters, water sports, and an artists' colony at Provincetown. Tanglewood, in the Berkshires, features the summer concerts of the Boston Symphony.

Among the many other points of interest are Old Sturbridge Village in Sturbridge in central Massachusetts, Minute Man National Historical Park between Lexington and Concord, and, in Boston: Old North Church, Old State House, Faneuil Hall, the USS *Constitution,* and the John F. Kennedy Library and Museum.

Famous natives and residents: John Adams, former president; John Quincy Adams, former president; Samuel Adams, patriot; Horatio Alger, novelist; Susan B. Anthony, woman suffragist; Clara Barton, American Red Cross founder; Leonard Bernstein, conductor; George Bush, former president; William Cullen Bryan, poet and editor; Luther Burbank, horticulturalist; John Cheever, novelist; John Singleton Copley, painter; e.e. cummings, poet; Jacques d'Amboise, ballet dancer; Bette Davis, actress; Cecil B. DeMille, film director; Emily Dickinson, poet; Ralph Waldo Emerson, philosopher and poet; Geraldine Farrar, soprano, actress; Benjamin Franklin, statesman and scientist; Buckminster Fuller, architect and educator; Robert Goddard, father of modern rocketry; John Hancock, statesman; Nathaniel Hawthorne, novelist; Oliver Wendell Holmes, jurist; Winslow Homer, painter; Elias Howe, inventor; John F. Kennedy, former president; Amy Lowell, poet; James Russell Lowell, poet; Robert Lowell, poet; Horace Mann, educator; Cotton Mather, clergyman; Samuel F. B. Morse, painter and inventor; Edgar Allan Poe, writer; Paul Revere, silversmith and Revolutionary War figure; Dr. Seuss (Theodore Geisel), author and illustrator; David Souter, jurist; Lucy Stone, woman suffragist; Louis Henry Sullivan, architect; Henry David Thoreau, author; Barbara Walters, TV commentator; James McNeill Whistler, painter; Eli Whitney, inventor; John Greenleaf Whittier, poet.

Michigan

Capital: Lansing
Governor: John Engler, R (to Jan. 2003)
Lieut. Governor: Dick Posthumus, R (to Jan. 2003)
Senators: Spencer Abraham, R (to Jan. 2001); Carl Levin, D (to Jan. 2003)
Secy. of State: Candace S. Miller, R (to Jan. 2003)
Atty. General: Jennifer Granholm, D (to Jan. 2003)
Organized as territory: Jan. 11, 1805
Entered Union (rank): Jan. 26, 1837 (26)
Present constitution adopted: April 1, 1963, (effective Jan. 1, 1964)
Motto: *Si quaeris peninsulam amoenam circumspice* (If you seek a pleasant peninsula, look around you)
State symbols: flower, apple blossom (1897); **bird,** robin (1931); **mammal,** white-tailed deer (1997) **fishes,** trout (1965), brook trout (1988); **gem,** isle royal greenstone (chlorastrolite) (1972); **stone,** petoskey stone (1965); **tree,** white pine (1955); **soil,** kalkaska soil series (1990); **reptile,** painted turtle (1996); **flag,** "Blue charged with the arms of the state" (1911); **wildflower,** Dwarf Lake iris (1998).
Nickname: Wolverine State
Origin of name: From Indian word "Michigana" meaning "great or large lake"
10 largest cities (1998 est.): Detroit, 970,196; Grand Rapids, 185,437; Warren, 142,455; Flint, 131,668; Lansing, 127,825; Sterling Heights, 124,339; Ann Arbor, 109,967; Livonia, 101,358; Dearborn, 91,691; Westland, 86,227
Land area: 56,809 sq mi.
Geographic center: In Wexford Co., 5 mi. NNW of Cadillac

Number of counties: 83
Largest county (1998 pop. est.): Wayne, 2,118,129
State parks and recreation areas: 96 (265,000 ac.)
1998 resident population est.: 9,817,242
1990 resident census population (rank): 9,295,297
(8). **Male:** 4,512,781; **Female:** 4,782,516. **White:**
7,756,086 (83.4%); **Black:** 1,291,706 (13.9%); **American Indian:** 55,638 (0.6%); **Asian:** 104,983 (1.1%);
Other race: 86,884 (0.9%); **Hispanic:** 201,596
(2.2%). **1990 percent population under 18:** 26.5; **65
and over:** 11.9; **median age:** 32.5.

Indian tribes were living in the Michigan region when the first European, Étienne Brulé of France, arrived in 1618. Other French explorers, including Jacques Marquette, Louis Joliet, and sieur de la Salle, followed, and the first permanent settlement was established in 1668 at Sault Ste. Marie. France was ousted from the territory by Great Britain in 1763, following the French and Indian Wars.

After the Revolutionary War, the U.S. acquired most of the region, which remained the scene of constant conflict between the British and U.S. forces and their respective Indian allies through the War of 1812.

Bordering on four of the five Great Lakes, Michigan is divided into Upper and Lower peninsulas by the Straits of Mackinac, which link lakes Michigan and Huron. The two parts of the state are connected by the Mackinac Bridge, one of the world's longest suspension bridges. To the north, connecting lakes Superior and Huron, are the busy Sault Ste. Marie Canals.

While Michigan ranks first among the states in production of motor vehicles and parts, it is also a leader in many other manufacturing and processing lines, including prepared cereals, machine tools, airplane parts, refrigerators, hardware, steel springs, and furniture.

The state produces important amounts of iron, copper, iodine, gypsum, bromine, salt, lime, gravel, and cement. Michigan's farms grow apples, cherries, beans, pears, grapes, potatoes, and sugar beets. Michigan's forests contribute significantly to the state's economy. Forest-based industries (wood product industry, tourism, and recreation) support nearly 200,000 jobs and contribute over $12 billion to the state economy. With 10,083 inland lakes and 3,288 miles of Great Lakes shoreline, Michigan is a prime area for both commercial and sport fishing.

Points of interest are the automobile plants in Dearborn, Detroit, Flint, Lansing, and Pontiac; Mackinac Island; Pictured Rocks and Sleeping Bear Dunes National Lakeshores; Greenfield Village in Dearborn; and the many summer resorts along both the inland lakes and Great Lakes.

Famous natives and residents: Nelson Algren, novelist; Ralph J. Bunche, statesman, Ellen Burstyn, actress; Bruce Catton, historian; Roger Chaffee, astronaut; Francis Ford Coppola, film director; Thomas E. Dewey, politician; Edna Ferber, novelist; Henry Ford, industrialist; Ali Haji-Sheikh, football player; Julie Harris, actress; Earvin "Magic" Johnson, basketball player; Ring Lardner, writer; Charles A. Lindbergh, aviator; Madonna, singer; Dick Martin, comedian; Terry McMillan, author; John N. Mitchell, former attorney general; Ted Nugent, singer; Gilda Radner, comedienne; Della Reese, singer; Jason Robards, Sr., actor; Diana Ross, singer; Steven Seagal, actor; Bob Seger, singer; Tom Selleck, actor; Thomas Schippers, conductor; Potter Stewart, jurist; Lily Tomlin, actress; Danny Thomas, entertainer; Margaret Whiting, singer; Robin Williams, comedian and actor; Stevie Wonder, singer.

Minnesota

Capital: St. Paul
Governor: Jesse Ventura, Reform Party (to Jan. 2003)
Lieut. Governor: Mae Schunk, Reform Party (to Jan. 2003)
Senators: Rod Grams, R (to Jan. 2001);
Paul Wellstone, D (to Jan. 2003)
Secy. of State: Mary Kiffmeyer, R
(to Jan. 2003)
State Auditor: Judi Dutcher, R (to Jan. 2003)
Atty. General: Mike Hatch, D
(to Jan. 2003)
State Treasurer: Carol Johnson, D (to Jan. 2003)
Organized as territory: March 3, 1849
Entered Union (rank): May 11, 1858 (32)
Present constitution adopted: 1858
Motto: L'Étoile du Nord (The North Star)
State symbols: flower, lady slipper (1902); **tree,** red (or Norway) pine (1953); **bird,** common loon (also called great northern diver) (1961); **song,** "Hail Minnesota" (1945); **fish,** walleye (1965); **mushroom,** morel (1984)
Nicknames: North Star State; Gopher State; Land of 10,000 Lakes
Origin of name: From a Dakota Indian word meaning "sky-tinted water"
10 largest cities (1998 est.): Minneapolis, 351,731; St. Paul, 257,284; Bloomington, 86,186; Duluth, 81,228; Rochester, 78,173; Coon Rapids, 63,674; Brooklyn Park, 63,115; Plymouth, 61,509; Eagan, 60,042; Burnsville, 59,334
Land area: 79,617 sq mi. (206,207 sq km)
Geographic center: In Crow Wing Co., 10 mi. SW of Brainerd
Number of counties: 87
Largest county (1998 pop. est.): Hennepin, 1,059,669
State forests: 55
State parks: 66 (226,000 ac.)
1998 resident population est.: 4,725,419
1990 resident census population (rank): 4,375,099 (20). **Male:** 2,145,183; **Female:** 2,229,916. **White:** 4,130,395 (94.4%); **Black:** 94,944 (2.2%); **American Indian:** 49,909 (1.1%); **Asian:** 77,886 (1.8%); **Other race:** 21,965 (0.5%); **Hispanic:** 53,884 (1.2%) **1990 percent population under 18:** 26.7; **65 and over:** 12.5; **median age:** 32.4.

Following the visits of several French explorers, fur traders, and missionaries, including Jacques Marquette, Louis Joliet, and sieur de la Salle, the region was claimed for Louis XIV by Daniel Greysolon, sieur Duluth, in 1679.

The U.S. acquired eastern Minnesota from Great Britain after the Revolutionary War and 20 years later bought the western part from France in the Louisiana Purchase of 1803. Much of the region was explored by U.S. Army Lt. Zebulon M. Pike before the northern strip of Minnesota bordering Canada was ceded by Britain in 1818.

The state is rich in natural resources. A few square miles of land in the north in the Mesabi, Cuyuna, and Vermillion ranges produce more than 75% of the nation's iron ore. The state's farms rank high in yields of corn, wheat, rye, alfalfa, and sugar beets. Other leading farm products include butter, eggs, milk, potatoes, green peas, barley, soybeans, oats, and livestock.

Minnesota's factory production includes nonelectrical machinery, fabricated metals, flour-mill products, plastics, electronic computers, scientific instruments, and processed foods. It is also one of the nation's leaders in the printing and paper-products industries.

Minneapolis is the trade center of the Midwest, and the headquarters of the world's largest super-computer and grain distributor. St. Paul is the nation's biggest publisher of calendars and law books. These "twin cities" are the nation's third-largest trucking center. Duluth has the nation's largest inland harbor and now handles a significant amount of foreign trade. Rochester is the home of the Mayo Clinic, an internationally famous medical center.

Today, tourism is a major revenue producer in Minnesota, with arts, fishing, hunting, water sports, and winter sports bringing in millions of visitors each year.

Among the most popular attractions are the St. Paul Winter Carnival; the Tyrone Guthrie Theatre, the Institute of Arts, Walker Art Center, and Minne-haha Park, in Minneapolis; Boundary Waters Canoe Area; Voyageurs National Park; North Shore Drive; the Minnesota Zoological Gardens; and the state's more than 10,000 lakes.

Famous natives and residents: LaVerne, Maxene, and Patti Andrews, singers; Warren E. Burger, jurist; William E. Colby, former director of the CIA; William Demarest, actor; William O. Douglas, jurist; Bob Dylan, singer and composer; F. Scott Fitzgerald, novelist; Judy Garland, singer and actress; J. Paul Getty, oil executive; Cass Gilbert, architect; Duane Hanson, sculptor; Hubert H. Humphrey, senator and vice president; Jessica Lange, actress; Sinclair Lewis, novelist; Cornell MacNeil, baritone; Roger Maris, baseball player; E. G. Marshall, actor; Charles H. Mayo, surgeon; William J. Mayo, surgeon; Eugene J. McCarthy, former senator; Kate Millett, feminist; Walter F. Mondale, former U.S. vice president; Gen. Lauris Norstad, former commander of NATO forces; Westbrook Pegler, columnist; John Sargent Pillsbury, businessman; Marion Ross, actress; Jane Russell, actress; Harrison E. Salisbury, journalist; Charles M. Schulz, cartoonist; Max Shulman, novelist; Maurice H. Stans, former secretary of commerce; Harold E. Stassen, former government official; Michael Todd, producer; Frederick Weyerhaeuser, businessman; Gig Young, actor.

Mississippi

Capital: Jackson
Governor: Kirk Fordice, R (to Jan. 2000)
Lieut. Governor: Ronnie Musgrove, D (to Jan. 2000)
Senators: Thad Cochran, R (to Jan. 2003);
Trent Lott, R (to Jan. 2001)
Secy. of State: Eric Clark, D (to Jan. 2000)
Treasurer: Marshall Bennett, D (to Jan. 2000)
Auditor: Phil Bryant, R (to Jan. 2000)
Atty. General: Mike Moore, D (to Jan. 2000)
Agriculture and Commerce Commissioner:
Lester Spell, D (to Jan. 2000)
Insurance Commissioner: George Dale, D (to Jan. 2000)
Organized as territory: April 7, 1798
Entered Union (rank): Dec. 10, 1817 (20)
Present constitution adopted: 1890
Motto: *Virtute et armis* (By valor and arms)
State symbols: flower, flower or bloom of the magnolia or evergreen magnolia (1952); **wildflower,** coreopsis (1991); **tree,** magnolia (1938); **bird,** mockingbird (1944); **song,** "Go, Mississippi" (1962); **stone,** petrified wood (1976); **fish,** largemouth or black bass (1974); **insect,** honeybee (1980); **shell,** oyster shell (1974); **water mammal,** bottlenosed dolphin or porpoise (1974); **fossil,** prehistoric whale (1981); **land mammal,** white-tailed deer (1974), red fox (1997); **waterfowl,** wood duck (1974); **beverage,** milk (1984); **butterfly,** spicebush swallowtail (1991); **dance,** square dance (1995)
Nickname: Magnolia State
Origin of name: From an Indian word meaning "Father of Waters"

10 largest cities (1998 est.): Jackson, 188,419; Gulfport, 64,762; Hattiesburg, 48,806; Biloxi, 47,316; Greenville, 42,042; Meridian, 40,255; Tupelo, 35,589; Vicksburg, 27,221; Pascagoula, 27,163; Southaven, 23,434
Land area: 46,914 sq mi. (121,506 sq km)
Geographic center: In Leake Co., 9 mi. WNW of Carthage
Number of counties: 82
Largest county (1998 pop. est.): Hinds, 247,144
State forests: 1 (1,760 ac.)
State parks: 29 (24,521 ac.)
1998 resident population est.: 2,752,092
1990 resident census population (rank): 2,573,216 (31). **Male:** 1,230,617; **Female:** 1,342,599. **White:** 1,633,461 (63.5%); **Black:** 915,057 (35.6%); **American Indian:** 8,525 (0.3%); **Asian:** 13,016 (0.5%); **Other race:** 3,157 (0.1%); **Hispanic:** 15,931 (0.6%). **1990 percent population under 18:** 29.0; **65 and over:** 12.5; **median age:** 31.1.

First explored for Spain by Hernando De Soto, who discovered the Mississippi River in 1540, the region was later claimed by France. In 1699, a French group under Sieur d'Iberville established the first permanent settlement near present-day Ocean Springs.

Great Britain took over the area in 1763 after the French and Indian Wars, ceding it to the U.S. in 1783 after the Revolution. Spain did not relinquish its claims until 1798, and in 1810 the U.S. annexed West Florida from Spain, including what is now southern Mississippi.

For a little more than one hundred years, from shortly after the state's founding through the Great Depression, cotton was the undisputed king of Mississippi's largely agrarian economy. Over the last half-century, however, Mississippi has progressively deepened its commitment to diversification by balancing agricultural output with increased industrial activity.

Today, agriculture continues as a major segment of the state's economy. While the most acreage is devoted to soybeans, cotton is the largest cash crop—Mississippi remains third in the nation in cotton production. The state's farmlands yield important harvests of corn, peanuts, pecans, rice, sugar cane, sweet potatoes, soybeans, and food grains as well as poultry, eggs, meat animals, dairy products, feed crops, and horticultural crops. Mississippi remains the world's leading producer of pond-raised catfish. Mississippi boasts 100,000 of the 140,000 total acres nationwide of catfish ponds.

The state abounds in historical landmarks and is the home of the Vicksburg National Military Park. Other National Park Service areas are Brices Cross Roads National Battlefield Site, Tupelo National Battlefield, and part of Natchez Trace National Parkway. Pre–Civil War mansions are the special pride of Natchez, Oxford, Columbus, Vicksburg, and Jackson.

Famous natives and residents: Red Barber, sportscaster; Jimmy Buffett, singer and songwriter; Craig Claiborne, columnist and restaurant critic; Bo Diddley, guitarist; Charles Evers, civil rights leader; Medgar Evers, civil rights leader; William Faulkner, novelist; Shelby Foote, historian; Richard Ford, novelist; John Grisham, novelist; Barry Hannah, novelist; Beth Henley, playwright and actress; Jim Henson, puppeteer; James Earl Jones, actor; B. B. King, guitarist; Mary Ann Mobley, actress; Willie Morris, writer; Elvis Presley, singer and actor; Leontyne Price, soprano; William Raspberry, columnist; Jerry Rice, football player; Jimmie Rodgers, singer; Sela Ward, actress; Muddy Waters, singer and guitarist; Eudora Welty, novelist; Tennessee Williams, playwright; Oprah Winfrey, talk-show host and actress; Richard Wright, novelist; Tammy Wynette, country music star; Zig Ziglar, speaker and author.

Missouri

Capital: Jefferson City
Governor: Mel Carnahan, D (to Jan. 2001)
Lieut. Governor: Roger Wilson, D (to Jan. 2001)
Senators: John Ashcroft, R (to Jan. 2001); Christopher S. Bond, R (to Jan. 2005)
Secy. of State: Rebecca ("Bekki") McDowell Cook, D (to Jan. 2001)
Auditor: Claire C. McCaskill, D (to Jan. 2003)
Treasurer: Bob Holden, D (to Jan. 2001)
Atty. General: Jeremiah "Jay" W. Nixon, D (to Jan. 2001)
Organized as territory: June 4, 1812
Entered Union (rank): Aug. 10, 1821 (24)
Present constitution adopted: 1945
Motto: *Salus populi suprema lex esto* (The welfare of the people shall be the supreme law)
State symbols: flower, hawthorn (1923); **bird,** bluebird (1927); **fish,** paddlefish (1997), channel catfish (1997); **song,** "Missouri Waltz" (1949); **fossil,** crinoid (1989); **musical instrument,** fiddle (1987); **rock,** mozarkite (1967); **mineral,** galena (1967); **insect,** honeybee (1985); **tree,** flowering dogwood (1955); **tree nut,** eastern black walnut (1990); **animal,** mule (1995); **dance,** square dance (1995); **Missouri Day,** third Wednesday in October (1915)
Nickname: Show-me State
Origin of name: Named after the Missouri Indian tribe. "Missouri" means "town of the large canoes."
10 largest cities (1998 est.): Kansas City, 441,574; St. Louis, 339,316; Springfield, 142,898; Independence, 116,832; Columbia, 78,915; St. Joseph, 69,622; Lee's Summit, 66,623; St. Charles, 58,166; St. Peter's, 50,297; Florissant, 47,069
Land area: 68,898 sq mi. (178,446 sq km)
Geographic center: In Miller Co., 20 mi. SW of Jefferson City
Number of counties: 114, plus 1 independent city
Largest county (1998 pop. est.): St. Louis, 998,696
Conservation areas[1]**:** leased, 287 (194,381 ac.); owned, 785 (761,863 ac.)
Conservation accesses: leased, 72; owned, 251
State parks and historic sites: 80
1998 resident population est.: 5,438,559
1990 resident census population (rank): 5,117,073 (15). **Male:** 2,464,315; **Female:** 2,652,758. **White:** 4,486,228 (87.7%); **Black:** 548,208 (10.7%); **American Indian:** 19,835 (0.4%); **Asian:** 41,277 (0.8%); **Other race:** 21,525 (0.4%); **Hispanic:** 61,702 (1.2%).
1990 percent population under 18: 25.7; **65 and over:** 14.0; **median age:** 33.4.

1. Includes wildlife areas, natural history areas, state forests, and tower sites.

Hernando De Soto visited the Missouri area in 1541. France's claim to the entire region was based on sieur de la Salle's travels in 1682. French fur traders established Ste. Genevieve in 1735 and St. Louis was first settled in 1764.

The U.S. gained Missouri from France as part of the Louisiana Purchase in 1803, and the territory was admitted as a state following the Missouri Compromise of 1820. Throughout the pre–Civil War period and during the war, Missourians were sharply divided in their opinions about slavery and in their allegiances, supplying both Union and Confederate forces with troops. However, the state itself remained in the Union.

Historically, Missouri played a leading role as a gateway to the West, St. Joseph being the eastern starting point of the Pony Express, while the much-traveled Santa Fe and Oregon trails began in Independence. Now a popular vacationland, Missouri has 11 major lakes and numerous fishing streams, springs, and caves. Bagnell Dam, across the Osage River in the Ozarks, completed in 1931, created one of the largest man-made lakes in the world, covering 65,000 acres.

Missouri's economy relies on a diversified industrial base. Service industries provide more income and jobs than any other segment, and include a growing tourism and travel sector. Wholesale and retail trade, manufacturing, and agriculture also play significant roles in the state's economy. Missouri is a leading producer of transportation equipment (including automobile manufacturing and auto parts), beer and beverages, and defense and aerospace technology. Food processing is the state's fastest-growing industry, well suited to the state's blend of agricultural, natural, energy, and transportation resources. Missouri mines produce 90% of the nation's principal (non-recycled) lead supply.

Missouri's largest corporate employers include McDonnell-Douglas/Boeing, Wal-Mart, Washington University, Schnuck Markets, Barnes Hospital, Chrysler Corporation, Ford Motor Company, May Department Stores, Trans World Airlines, and Southwestern Bell. The state's top agricultural products include grain, sorghum, hay, corn, soybeans, wheat, oats, barley, tobacco, and rice. A well-established grape and wine program brings together aspects of agriculture, manufacturing, and tourism to support a vibrant vintner industry.

Tourism draws hundreds of thousands of visitors to a number of Missouri points of interest: the country-music shows of Branson; Bass Pro Shops national headquarters (Springfield); the Gateway Arch at the Jefferson National Expansion (St. Louis); Mark Twain's boyhood home and cave (Hannibal); the Harry S Truman home and library (Independence); the scenic beauty of the Ozark National Scenic Riverways; and the Pony Express and Jesse James museums (St. Joseph). The state's different lake regions also attract fishermen and sun-seekers from throughout the Midwest.

Famous natives and residents: Robert Altman, film director; Burt Bacharach, songwriter; Josephine Baker, singer and dancer; Wallace Beery, actor; Robert Russell Bennett, composer; Yogi Berra, baseball player; Thomas Hart Benton, painter; Bill Bradley, basketball player and former N.J. senator; Omar N. Bradley, five-star general; Grace Bumbry, soprano; William Burroughs, writer; Sarah Caldwell, opera director and conductor; Martha Jane Canary (Calamity Jane), frontierswoman; George Washington Carver, scientist; Walter Cronkite, TV newscaster; Robert Cummings, actor; Jane Darwell, actress; Walt Disney, artist; T. S. Eliot, poet; Redd Foxx, actor and comedian; Betty Grable, actress; Dick Gregory, comic and activist; Jean Harlow, actress; George Hearn, actor; Edwin Hubble, astronomer; Langston Hughes, poet; John Huston, film director; Jesse James, outlaw; Scott Joplin, composer; Marianne Moore, poet; Geraldine Page, actress; James C. Penney, merchant; John Joseph Pershing, general; Vincent Price, actor; Joseph Pulitzer, journalist; Ginger Rogers, dancer and actress; Sacajawea, Indian guide for Lewis and Clark; Casey Stengel, baseball player; Gladys Swarthout, soprano; Sara Teasdale, poet; Virgil Thomson, composer; Harry S Truman, former president; Mark Twain, author; Dick Van Dyke, actor; Ruth Warrick, actress; Dennis Weaver, actor; Mary Wickes, actress; Laura Ingalls Wilder, author; Roy Wilkins, civil rights leader.

Montana

Capital: Helena
Governor: Marc Racicot, R (to Jan. 2001)
Lieut. Governor: Judy Martz, R (to Jan. 2001)
Senators: Max Baucus, D (to Jan. 2003);
Conrad R. Burns, R (to Jan. 2001)
Secy. of State: Mike Cooney, D (to Jan. 2001)
Auditor: Mark O'Keefe, D (to Jan. 2001)
Atty. General: Joe Mazurek, D (to Jan. 2001)
Organized as territory: May 26, 1864
Entered Union (rank): Nov. 8, 1889 (41)
Present constitution adopted: 1972
Motto: *Oro y plata* (Gold and silver)
State symbols: flower, bitterroot (1895); **tree,**
ponderosa pine (1949); **stones,** sapphire and agate
(1969); **bird,** Western meadowlark (1981); **song,**
"Montana" (1945)
Nickname: Treasure State
Origin of name: Chosen from Latin dictionary by J. M.
Ashley. It is a Latinized Spanish word meaning
"mountainous."
10 largest cities (1998 est.): Billings, 91,750; Great
Falls, 56,395; Missoula, 52,239; Butte-Silver Bow[1],
33,994; Bozeman, 29,936; Helena, 28,306; Kalispell,
16,089; Haure, 10,015; Anaconda–Deer Lodge County,
9,999; Miles City, 8,685
Land area: 145,556 sq mi. (376,991 sq km)
Geographic center: In Fergus Co., 12 mi. W
of Lewistown
Number of counties: 56, plus small part of Yellowstone
National Park
Largest county (1998 pop. est.): Yellowstone, 126,158
State forests: 7 (214,000 ac.)
State parks and recreation areas: 110 (18,273 ac.)
1998 resident population est.: 880,453
1990 resident census population (rank): 799,065 (44).
Male: 395,769; **Female:** 403,296. **White:** 741,111
(92.7%); **Black:** 2,381 (0.3%); **American Indian:**
47,679 (6.0%); **Asian:** 4,259 (0.5%); **Other race:**
3,635 (0.5%); **Hispanic:** 12,174 (1.5%). **1990 percent
population under 18:** 27.8; **65 and over:** 13.3;
median age: 33.8.

1. Consolidated City.

First explored for France by François and Louis-
Joseph Verendrye in the early 1740s, much of the
region was acquired by the U.S. from France as part
of the Louisiana Purchase in 1803. Before western
Montana was obtained from Great Britain in the
Oregon Treaty of 1846, American trading posts and
forts had been established in the territory.

The major Indian Wars (1867–1877) included the
famous 1876 Battle of the Little Big Horn, better
known as "Custer's Last Stand," in which Cheyenne
and Sioux defeated George A. Custer and more than
200 of his men in southeastern Montana.

Much of Montana's early history was concerned
with mining, with copper, lead, zinc, silver, coal,
and oil as principal products. Butte is the center of
the area that once supplied half of the U.S. copper.

Fields of grain cover much of Montana's plains. It
ranks high among the states in wheat and barley,
with rye, oats, flaxseed, sugar beets, and potatoes as
other important crops. Sheep and cattle raising make
significant contributions to the economy.

Tourist attractions include hunting, fishing, skiing,
and dude ranching. Glacier National Park, on the
Continental Divide, is a scenic and vacation wonderland with 60 glaciers, 200 lakes, and many
streams with good trout fishing.

Other major points of interest include the Little
Bighorn Battlefield National Monument, Virginia

City, Yellowstone National Park, Museum of the
Plains Indians at Browning, and the Fort Union
Trading Post and Grant-Kohr's Ranch National His-
toric Sites.

Famous natives and residents: Dorothy Baker, author; Dirk
Benedict, actor; W. A. (Tony) Boyle, labor union official;
Gary Cooper, actor; John Cowan, prospector and founder
of Last Chance Gulch (now Helena); Alfred Bertram
Guthrie, Pulitzer Prize–winning author; Chet Huntley, TV
newscaster; Will James, writer and artist; Dorothy
Johnson, author; Evel Knievel, daredevil motorcyclist;
Myrna Loy, actress; David Lynch, filmmaker; Mike
Mansfield, former senator; George Montgomery, actor;
Jeannette Rankin, first woman elected to Congress;
Martha Raye, actress; Charles M. Russell, Old West
painter; Michael Smuin, choreographer; Lester C. Thurow,
economist and educator.

Nebraska

Capital: Lincoln
Governor: Mike Johanns, R (to Jan. 2003)
Lieut. Governor: Dave Maurstad, R (to Jan. 2003)
Senators: Chuck Hagel, R (to Jan. 2003);
J. Robert Kerrey, D (to Jan. 2001)
Secy. of State: Scott Moore, R (to Jan. 2003)
Atty. General: Don Stenberg, R (to Jan. 2003)
Auditor: Kate Witek, R (to Jan. 2003)
Treasurer: David Heineman, R (to Jan. 2003)
Organized as territory: May 30, 1854
Entered Union (rank): March 1, 1867 (37)
Present constitution adopted: Oct. 12, 1875 (exten-
sively amended 1919–20)
Motto: Equality before the law
State symbols: flower, goldenrod (1895); **fish,** channel
catfish (1997); **American folk dance,** square dance
(1997); **ballad,** "A Place Like Nebraska" (1997); **tree,**
cottonwood (1972); **bird,** Western meadowlark (1929);
insect, honeybee (1975); **gemstone,** blue agate
(1967); **rock,** prairie agate (1967); **fossil,** mammoth
(1967); **song,** "Beautiful Nebraska" (1967); **soil,** typic
argiustolls, holdreges series (1979); **mammal,** whitetail
deer (1981); **grass,** little bluestem (1969); **drink,** milk
(1998).
Nicknames: Cornhusker State (1945); Beef State
Origin of name: From an Oto Indian word meaning
"flat water"
10 largest cities (1998 est.): Omaha, 371,291; Lincoln,
213,088; Bellevue, 44,047; Grand Island, 41,392;
Kearney, 27,968; Fremont, 24,429; Norfolk, 23,476;
North Platte, 23,307; Hastings, 21,356; Columbus,
20,898
Land area: 76,878 sq mi. (199,113 sq km)
Geographic center: In Custer Co., 10 mi. NW of
Broken Bow
Number of counties: 93
Largest county (1998 pop. est.): Douglas, 443,794
State parks: 85 areas, historical and recreational;
8 major areas
1998 resident population est.: 1,662,719
1990 resident census population (rank): 1,578,417
(36). **Male:** 769,439; **Female:** 808,946. **White:**
1,480,558 (93.8%); **Black:** 57,404 (3.6%); **American
Indian:** 12,410 (0.8%); **Asian:** 12,422 (0.8%); **Other
race:** 15,591 (1.0%); **Hispanic:** 36,969 (2.3%). **1990
percent population under 18:** 27.2; **65 and over:**
14.1; **median age:** 32.9.

French fur traders first visited Nebraska in the late
1600s. Part of the Louisiana Purchase in 1803, eastern Nebraska was explored by Lewis and Clark in
1804–1806.

Robert Stuart pioneered the Oregon Trail across
Nebraska in 1812–1813 and the first permanent
white settlement was established at Bellevue in 1823.
Western Nebraska was acquired by treaty following

the Mexican War in 1848. The Union Pacific began its transcontinental railroad at Omaha in 1865. In 1937, Nebraska became the only state in the Union to have a unicameral (one-house) legislature. Members are elected to it without party designation.

Nebraska is a leading grain-producer with bumper crops of grain, sorghum, corn, and wheat. More varieties of grass, valuable for forage, grow in this state than in any other in the nation. The state's sizable cattle and hog industries make Dakota City and Lexington among the nation's largest meat-packing centers.

Manufacturing has become diversified in Nebraska, strengthening the state's economic base. Firms making electronic components, auto accessories, pharmaceuticals, and mobile homes have joined such older industries as clothing, farm machinery, chemicals, and transportation equipment. Oil was discovered in 1939 and natural gas in 1949.

Among the principal attractions are Agate Fossil Beds, Homestead, and Scotts Bluff National Monuments; Chimney Rock National Historic Site; a re-created pioneer village at Minden; SAC Museum near Ashland; the Stuhr Museum of the Prairie Pioneer with 57 original 19th-century buildings near Grand Island; Boys Town; the Sheldon Memorial Art Gallery and the Lied Center for the Performing Arts located on the University of Nebraska campus in Lincoln; the State Capitol in Lincoln; the Joslyn Art Museum in Omaha; the Henry Doorly Zoo in Omaha; Museum of Nebraska Art in Kearney; Museum of Nebraska History in Lincoln; and the University of Nebraska State Museum in Lincoln.

Famous natives and residents: Grace Abbott, social worker; Bess Streeter Aldrich, author; Grover Cleveland Alexander, Hall of Fame pitcher; Fred Astaire, dancer and actor; Max Baer, boxer; Bil Baird, puppeteer; George Beadle, geneticist; Marlon Brando, actor; William Jennings Bryan, three-time U.S. presidential candidate; Warren Buffett, investor; Johnny Carson, TV host; Willa Cather, author; Dick Cavett, TV entertainer; Richard B. Cheney, former secretary of Defense; Montgomery Clift, actor; James Coburn, actor; William "Buffalo Bill" Cody, showman of the Old West; Sandy Dennis, actress; Mignon Eberhart, author; Harold "Doc" Edgerton, inventor; Ruth Etting, singer and actress; Fr. Edward J. Flanagan, founder of Boys Town; Henry Fonda, actor; Gerald Ford, former president; Bob Gibson, baseball player; Howard Hanson, conductor; Leland Hayward, producer; Robert Henri, painter; David Janssen, actor; Francis La Flesche, ethnologist; Melvin Laird, politician and former secretary of defense; Frank W. Leahy, football coach; Harold Lloyd, actor; Malcolm X, civil rights advocate; Dorothy McGuire, actress; Julius Sterling Morton, politician and journalist; John G. Neihardt, epic poet; Nick Nolte, actor; George W. Norris, U.S. Senator; John J. Pershing, Army leader and founder of Pershing Rifles; Nathan Roscoe Pound, dean of Harvard Law School and botanist; Red Cloud, Indian rights advocate; Mari Sandoz, author; Standing Bear, Indian rights advocate; Robert Taylor, actor; Susette La Flesche Tibbles, Omaha Indian activist; Paul Williams, singer, composer, and actor; Julie Wilson, singer and actress; Darryl F. Zanuck, film producer.

Nevada

Capital: Carson City
Governor: Kenny Guinn, R (to Jan. 2003)
Lieut. Governor: Lorraine Hunt, R (to Jan. 2003)
Senators: Richard Bryan, D (to Jan. 2001);
   Harry Reid, D (to Jan. 2005)
Secy. of State: Dean Heller, R (to Jan. 2003)
Treasurer: Brian Krolicki, R (to Jan. 2003)
Controller: Kathy Augustine, R (to Jan. 2003)
Atty. General: Frankie Sue Del Papa, D (to Jan. 2003)

Organized as territory: March 2, 1861
Entered Union (rank): Oct. 31, 1864 (36)
Present constitution adopted: 1864
Motto: All for Our Country
State symbols: flower, sagebrush (1959); **trees,** single-leaf pinon (1953) and bristlecone pine (1987); **bird,** mountain bluebird (1967); **animal,** desert bighorn sheep (1973); **colors,** silver and blue (1983); **song,** "Home Means Nevada" (1933); **rock,** sandstone (1987); **precious gemstone,** virgin valley black fire opal (1987); **semiprecious gemstone,** Nevada turquoise (1987); **grass,** Indian ricegrass (1977); **metal,** silver (1977); **fossil,** ichthyosaur (1977); **fish,** lahontan cutthroat trout (1981); **reptile,** desert tortoise (1989); **state artifact,** tule duck decoy (1995)
Nicknames: Sagebrush State; Silver State; Battle Born State
Origin of name: Spanish: "snowcapped"
10 largest cities (1998 est.): Las Vegas, 404,288; Reno, 163,334; Henderson, 152,717; North Las Vegas, 94,218; Sparks, 62,432; Carson, 49,301; Elko, 19,204; Boulder City, 14,166; Mesquite, 10,125; Winnemucca, 9,404
Land area: 109,806 sq mi. (284,397 sq km)
Geographic center: In Lander Co., 26 mi. SE of Austin
Number of counties: 16, plus 1 independent city
Largest county (1998 est.): Clark, 1,162,129
State parks: 20 (150,000 ac., including leased lands)
1998 resident population est.: 1,746,898
1990 resident census population (rank): 1,201,833 (39). **Male:** 611,880; **Female:** 589,953. **White:** 1,012,695 (84.3%); **Black:** 78,771 (6.6%); **American Indian:** 19,637 (1.6%); **Asian:** 38,127 (3.2%); **Other race:** 52,603 (4.4%); **Hispanic:** 124,419 (10.4%). **1990 percent population under 18:** 24.7; **65 and over:** 10.6; **median age:** 33.2.

Trappers and traders, including Jedediah Smith and Peter Skene Ogden, entered the Nevada area in the 1820s. In 1843–1845, John C. Fremont and Kit Carson explored the Great Basin and Sierra Nevada.

In 1848 following the Mexican War, the U.S. obtained the region and the first permanent settlement was a Mormon trading post near present-day Genoa.

The driest state in the nation, with an average annual rainfall of only about 7 inches, much of Nevada is uninhabited, sagebrush-covered desert. The wettest part of the state receives about 40 inches of precipitation per year, while the driest spot has less than four inches per year.

Nevada was made famous by the discovery of the fabulous Comstock Lode in 1859 and its mines have produced large quantities of gold, silver, copper, lead, zinc, mercury, barite, and tungsten. Oil was discovered in 1954. Gold now far exceeds all other minerals in value of production.

In 1931, the state created two industries, divorce and gambling. For many years, Reno and Las Vegas were the "divorce capitals of the nation." More liberal divorce laws in many states have ended this distinction, but Nevada is the gambling and entertainment capital of the U.S. State gambling taxes account for 37.7% of general fund tax revenues. Although Nevada leads the nation in per capita gambling revenue, it ranks only fourth in total gambling revenue.

Near Las Vegas, on the Colorado River, stands Hoover Dam, which impounds the waters of Lake Mead, one of the world's largest artificial lakes.

The state's agricultural crop consists mainly of hay, alfalfa seed, barley, wheat, and potatoes.

Nevada manufactures gaming equipment; lawn and garden irrigation devices; titanium products; seismic and machinery monitoring devices; and specialty printing.

Major resort areas flourish in Lake Tahoe, Reno, and Las Vegas. Recreation areas include those at Pyramid Lake, Lake Tahoe, and Lake Mead and Lake Mohave, both in Lake Mead National Recreation Area. Among the other attractions are Hoover Dam, Virginia City, and Great Basin National Park (includes Lehman Caves).

Famous natives and residents: Eva Adams, former director of U.S. Mint; Andre Agassi, tennis player; Raymond T. Baker, former director of U.S. Mint; Helen Delich Bentley, government official and newspaperwoman; Robert Caples, painter; Walter Van Tilburg Clark, writer; Henry Comstock, prospector of "Comstock Lode" fame; Abby Dalton, actress; Michele Greene, actress; Sarah Winnemucca Hopkins, author and Paiute interpreter and peacemaker; Jack Kramer, tennis player; Paul Laxalt, politician; William Lear, aviation inventor; Robert C. Lynch, surgeon; John W. Mackay, benefactor, one of Big Four of Comstock Lode; Emma Nevada, opera singer; Thelma "Pat" Nixon, former First Lady; James W. Nye, territory governor and former senator; Lute Pease, cartoonist and Pulitzer Prize winner; Edna Purviance, actress; Patty Sheehan, golfer; Jack Wilson, Paiute Indian prophet; George Wingfield, mining millionaire.

New Hampshire

Capital: Concord
Governor: Jeanne Shaheen, D (to Jan. 2001)
Senators: Judd Gregg, R (to Jan. 2005); Bob Smith, R (to Jan. 2003)
Treasurer: Georgie A. Thomas, R (to Dec. 1998)
Secy. of State: William M. Gardner, D (to Dec. 1998)
Atty. General: Philip T. McLaughlin (to March 2001)
Entered Union (rank): June 21, 1788 (9)
Present constitution adopted: 1784
Motto: Live free or die
State symbols: flower, purple lilac (1919); **tree,** white birch (1947); **animal,** white-tailed deer (1983); **insect,** ladybug (1977); **saltwater fish,** striped bass (1994); **freshwater fish,** brook trout (1995); **amphibian,** spotted newt (1985); **butterfly,** karner blue (1992); **bird,** purple finch (1957); **songs,** "Old New Hampshire" (1949) and "New Hampshire, My New Hampshire" (1963)
Nickname: Granite State
Origin of name: From the English county of Hampshire
10 largest cities (1998 est.): Manchester, 102,524; Nashua, 82,169; Concord, 37,444; Rochester, 27,869; Dover, 25,953; Portsmouth, 25,388; Keene, 22,313; Laconia, 16,435; Claremont, 13,868; Lebanon, 12,461
Land area: 8,969 sq mi. (23,231 sq km)
Geographic center: In Belknap Co., 3 mi. E of Ashland
Number of counties: 10
Largest county (1998 pop. est.): Hillsborough, 363,031
State parks: 42 (50,000+ ac.)
1998 resident population est.: 1,185,048
1990 resident census population (rank): 1,109,252 (41). **Male:** 543,544; **Female:** 565,708. **White:** 1,087,433 (98.0%); **Black:** 7,198 (0.6%); **American Indian:** 2,134 (0.2%); **Asian:** 9,343 (0.8%); **Other race:** 3,144 (0.3%); **Hispanic:** 11,333 (1.0%). **1990 percent population under 18:** 25.1; **65 and over:** 11.3; **median age:** 32.7.

Under an English land grant, Capt. John Smith sent settlers to establish a fishing colony at the mouth of the Piscataqua River, near present-day Rye and Dover, in 1623. Capt. John Mason, who partici-

pated in the founding of Portsmouth in 1630, gave New Hampshire its name.

After a 38-year period of union with Massachusetts, New Hampshire was made a separate royal colony in 1679. As leaders in the revolutionary cause, New Hampshire delegates received the honor of being the first to vote for the Declaration of Independence on July 4, 1776. New Hampshire is the only state that ever played host at the formal conclusion of a foreign war when, in 1905, Portsmouth was the scene of the treaty ending the Russo-Japanese War.

Abundant water power early turned New Hampshire into an industrial state, and manufacturing is the principal source of income in the state. The most important industrial products are electrical and other machinery, textiles, pulp and paper products, and stone and clay products.

Dairy and poultry farming and growing fruit, truck vegetables, corn, potatoes, and hay are the major agricultural pursuits.

Tourism, because of New Hampshire's scenic and recreational resources, now brings over $3.5 billion into the state annually.

Vacation attractions include Lake Winnipesaukee, largest of 1,300 lakes and ponds; the 724,000-acre White Mountain National Forest; Daniel Webster's birthplace near Franklin; Strawbery Banke, restored building of the original settlement at Portsmouth; and the famous "Old Man of the Mountain" granite head profile, the state's official emblem, at Franconia.

Famous natives and residents: Sherman Adams, former governor and presidential advisor; Salmon P. Chase, jurist; Charles Anderson Dana, editor; Mary Baker Eddy, founder of the Christian Science Church; Dustin Farnum, actor; Thomas Green Fessenden, journalist and satirical poet; Daniel Chester French, sculptor; Horace Greeley, journalist and politician; Sarah J. Hale, editor; John Irving, writer; Benjamin F. Keith, theater entrepreneur; Jackson Hall Kelly, promoter of Oregon settlement; John Langdon, political leader; Sharon Christa McAuliffe, teacher and astronaut; Franklin Pierce, former president; Augustus Saint-Gaudens, sculptor; Alan Shepard, astronaut; Harlan F. Stone, jurist; Daniel Webster, statesman; Henry Wilson, politician and former vice president; Noah Worcester, clergyman and pacifist.

New Jersey

Capital: Trenton
Governor: Christine Todd Whitman, R (to Jan. 2002)
Senators: Robert Torricelli, D (to Jan. 2003); Frank R. Lautenberg, D (to Jan. 2001)
Secy. of State: DeForest B. Soaries, Jr., R (to Jan. 2002)
Treasurer: James A. DiEleuterio, Jr., R (to Jan. 2002)
Atty. General: John Farmer, Jr., R (to Jan. 2002)
Chief Justice: Deborah T. Poritz, R
Entered Union (rank): Dec. 18, 1787 (3)
Present constitution adopted: 1947
Motto: Liberty and prosperity
State symbols: flower, purple violet (1913); **bird,** eastern goldfinch (1935); **insect,** honeybee (1974); **tree,** red oak (1950); **animal,** horse (1977); **colors,** buff and blue (1965); **folk dance,** square dance; **dinosaur,** hadrosaurus foulkii; **fish,** brook trout; **shell,** knobbed whelk
Nickname: Garden State
Origin of name: From the Channel Isle of Jersey
10 largest cities (1998 est.)[1]: Newark, 267,823; Jersey City, 232,429; Paterson, 148,212; Elizabeth, 110,661; Trenton, 84,494; Camden, 83,546; Clifton, 76,180; East Orange, 69,598; Bayonne, 61,051; Passaic, 60,817

Land area: 7,419 sq mi. (19,215 sq km)
Geographic center: In Mercer Co., 5 mi.
 SE of Trenton
Number of counties: 21
Largest county (1998 pop. est.): Bergen, 858,529
State forests: 11
State parks: 35 (67,111 ac.)
1998 resident population est.: 8,115,011
1990 resident census population (rank): 7,730,188
 (9). **Male:** 3,735,685; **Female:** 3,994,503. **White:**
 6,130,465 (79.3%); **Black:** 1,036,825 (13.4%); **American Indian:** 14,970 (0.2%); **Asian:** 272,521 (3.5%);
 Other race: 275,407 (3.6%); **Hispanic:** 739,861
 (9.6%). **1990 percent population under 18:** 23.3; **65 and over:** 13.4; **median age:** 34.3.

New Jersey's early colonial history was involved with that of New York (New Netherlands), of which it was a part. One year after the Dutch surrender to England in 1664, New Jersey was organized as an English colony under Gov. Philip Carteret.

In 1676 the colony was divided between Carteret and a company of English Quakers who had obtained the rights belonging to John, Lord Berkeley. New Jersey became a united, crown colony in 1702, administered by the royal governor of New York. Finally, in 1738, New Jersey was separated from New York under its own royal governor, Lewis Morris.

Because of its key location between New York City and Philadelphia, New Jersey saw much fighting during the American Revolution.

Today, New Jersey, an area of wide industrial diversification, is known as the Crossroads of the East. Products from over 15,000 factories can be delivered overnight to almost 60 million people, representing 12 states and the District of Columbia. The greatest single industry is chemicals; New Jersey is one of the foremost research centers in the world. Many large oil refineries are located in northern New Jersey. Other important manufactured items are pharmaceuticals, instruments, machinery, electrical goods, and apparel.

Of the total land area, 36% is forested (1992). Farmland is declining. In 1995 there were about 9,000 farms, with over 850,000 acres under harvest. The state ranks high in the production of almost all garden vegetables. Tomatoes, asparagus, corn, and blueberries are important crops, and poultry and dairy farming make significant contributions to the state's economy.

Tourism is the second-largest industry in New Jersey. The state has numerous resort areas on 127 miles of Atlantic coastline. In 1977, New Jersey voters approved legislation allowing legalized casino gambling in Atlantic City. Points of interest include the Delaware Water Gap, the Edison National Historic Site in West Orange, Princeton University, Liberty State Park, Jersey City, and the N.J. State Aquarium in Camden (opened 1992).

Famous natives and residents: Bud Abbott, comedian; Charles Addams, cartoonist; Edwin Aldrin, astronaut; Count Basie, band leader; Joan Bennett, actress; Jon Bon Jovi, musician; William J. Brennan, jurist; Aaron Burr, political leader; James Fenimore Cooper, novelist; Lou Costello, comedian; Stephen Crane, writer; Helen Gahagan Douglas, former representative; Allen Ginsberg, poet; William Frederick Halsey, Jr., admiral; Alfred Joyce Kilmer, poet; Ernie Kovacs, comedian; Jerry Lewis, comedian and film director; Anne Morrow Lindbergh, author; Norman Mailer, novelist; Patricia McBride, ballerina; Richard Nixon, former president; Dorothy Parker, author; Joe Piscopo, comedian and actor; Paul Robeson, singer and actor; Philip Roth,

novelist; Ruth St. Denis, dancer and choreographer; Antonin Scalia, jurist; H. Norman Schwarzkopf, general; Frank Sinatra, singer and actor; Bruce Springsteen, musician; Alfred Stieglitz, photographer; Albert Payson Terhune, journalist and novelist; Sarah Vaughan, singer; William Carlos Williams, physician and poet; Edmund Wilson, literary critic and author.

New Mexico

Capital: Santa Fe
Governor: Gary E. Johnson, R (to Jan. 2003)
Lieut. Governor: Walter Bradley, R (to Jan. 2003)
Senators: Jeff Bingaman, D (to Jan. 2001);
 Pete V. Domenici, R (to Jan. 2003)
Secy. of State: Rebecca Vigil-Giron, D (to Jan. 2003)
Atty. General: Patricia A. Madrid, D (to Jan. 2003)
State Auditor: Domingo P. Martinez, D (to Jan. 2003)
State Treasurer: Michael A. Montoya, D (to Jan. 2003)
Commissioner of Public Lands: Ray Powell, D
 (to Jan. 2003)
Organized as territory: Sept. 9, 1850
Entered Union (rank): Jan. 6, 1912 (47)
Present constitution adopted: 1911
Motto: *Crescit eundo* (It grows as it goes)
State symbols: flower, yucca (1927); **tree,** piñon
 (1949); **animal,** black bear (1963); **bird,** roadrunner
 (1949); **fish,** cutthroat trout (1955); **vegetables,** chili
 and frijol (1965); **gem,** turquoise (1967); **song,** "O Fair
 New Mexico" (1917); **Spanish-language song,** "Asi
 Es Nuevo Méjico" (1971); **poem,** A Nuevo México
 (1991); **grass,** blue gramma (1973); **fossil,**
 coelophysis (1981); **cookie,** bizcochito (1989); **insect,**
 tarantula hawk wasp (1989); **ballad,** "Land of
 Enchantment" (1989); **bilingual song,** "New Mexico—
 Mi Lindo Nuevo Mexico", (1995); **question,** "Red or
 Green?", (1999).
Nickname: Land of Enchantment (1999)
Origin of name: From the country of Mexico
10 largest cities (1998 est.): Albuquerque, 419,311; Las
 Cruces, 76,102; Santa Fe, 67,879; Rio Rancho,
 50,041; Roswell, 47,624; Farmington, 39,028; Clovis,
 32,394; Alamogordo, 28,312; Hobbs, 27,156;
 Carlsbad, 26,315
Land area: 121,365 sq mi. (314,334 sq km)
Geographic center: In Torrance Co., 12 mi. SSW of
 Willard
Number of counties: 33
Largest county (1998 pop. est.): Bernalillo, 525,958
State-owned forested land: 933,000 ac.
State parks: 31 (267,302 ac.)
1998 resident population est.: 1,736,931
1990 resident census population (rank): 1,515,069
 (37). **Male:** 745,253; **Female:** 769,816. **White:**
 1,146,028 (75.6%); **Black:** 30,210 (2.0%); **American Indian:** 134,355 (8.9%); **Asian:** 14,124 (0.9%); **Other race:** 190,352 (12.6%); **Hispanic:** 579,224 (38.2%).
 1990 percent population under 18: 29.5; **65 and over:** 10.8; **median age:** 31.1.

Francisco Vásquez de Coronado, a Spanish explorer searching for gold, traveled the region that became New Mexico in 1540–42. In 1598 the first Spanish settlement was established on the Rio Grande River by Juan de Onate; in 1610 Santa Fe was founded and made the capital of New Mexico.

The U.S. acquired most of New Mexico in 1848, as a result of the Mexican War, and the remainder in the 1853 Gadsden Purchase. Union troops captured the territory from the Confederates during the Civil War. With the surrender of Geronimo in 1886, the Apache Wars and most of the Indian conflicts in the area were ended.

Since 1945, New Mexico has been a leader in energy research and development with extensive experiments conducted at Los Alamos Scientific Laboratory and Sandia Laboratories in the nuclear, solar, and geothermal areas.

Minerals are the state's richest natural resource and New Mexico is one of the U.S. leaders in output of uranium and potassium salts. Petroleum, natural gas, copper, gold, silver, zinc, lead, and molybdenum also contribute heavily to the state's income.

The principal manufacturing industries include food products, chemicals, transportation equipment, lumber, electrical machinery, and stone-clay-glass products. More than two-thirds of New Mexico's farm income comes from livestock products, especially sheep. Cotton, pecans, and sorghum are the most important field crops. Corn, peanuts, beans, onions, chilies, and lettuce are also grown.

Tourist attractions in New Mexico include the Carlsbad Caverns National Park, Inscription Rock at El Morro National Monument, the ruins at Fort Union, Billy the Kid mementos at Lincoln, the White Sands and Gila Cliff Dwellings National Monuments, and the Chaco Culture National Historical Park.

Famous natives and residents: Kathy Baker, actress; Judy Blume, author; Ernest L. Blumenshein, artist; William "Billy the Kid" Bonney, outlaw; Richard Bradford, author; Ralph Bunche, Nobel Peace Prize winner; Bruce Cabot, actor; Glen Campbell, singer; Kit Carson, army scout and trapper; Dennis Chavez, former senator; John Chisum, cattle king; Mangus Coloradas, Apache leader; Edward Condon, physicist; Bill Daily, actor; John Denver, singer; Bo Diddley, blues guitarist; Patrick Garrett, lawman; Greer Garson, actress; Sid Gutierrez, astronaut; William Hanna, animator; Neil Patrick Harris, actor; Carl Hatch, former senator; Tony Hillerman, author; Conrad Hilton, hotel executive; Dennis Hopper, actor; Peter Hurd, artist; Preston Jones, playwright and actor; Ralph Kiner, baseball player and sportscaster; Nancy Lopez, golfer; Maria Martínez, San Ildefonso Pueblo potter; Demi Moore, actress; Jim Morrison, singer and songwriter; Bill Mauldin, political cartoonist; Popé, San Juan Pueblo medicine man and leader; Georgia O'Keeffe, painter; Harrison Schmitt, astronaut and U.S. representative; Kim Stanley, actress; Slim Summerville, actor; Clyde Tombaugh, astronomer; Al Unser, Bobby Unser, auto racers; Victorio, Apache chief; Linda Wertheimer, NPR correspondent; Kathy Whitworth, golfer.

New York

Capital: Albany
Governor: George E. Pataki, R (to Jan. 2003)
Lieut. Governor: May Donohue, R (to Jan. 2003)
Senators: Charles E. Schumer, D (to Jan. 2005); Daniel P. Moynihan, D (to Jan. 2001)
Secy. of State: Alexander Treadwell, R (to Jan. 1999)
Comptroller: Carl McCall, D (to Jan. 2003)
Atty. General: Eliot Spitzer, D (to Jan. 2003)
Entered Union (rank): July 26, 1788 (11)
Present constitution adopted: 1777 (last revised 1938)
Motto: *Excelsior* (Ever upward)
State symbols: animal, beaver (1975); **fish,** brook trout (1975); **gem,** garnet (1969); **flower,** rose (1955); **tree,** sugar maple (1956); **bird,** bluebird (1970); **insect,** ladybug (1989); **song,** "I Love New York" (1980)
Nickname: Empire State
Origin of name: In honor of the Duke of York
10 largest cities (1998 est.): New York, 7,420,166; Buffalo, 300,717; Rochester, 216,887; Yonkers, 190,153; Syracuse, 152,215; Albany, 94,305; New Rochelle, 67,225; Mount Vernon, 66,824; Schenectady, 61,698; Utica, 59,334
Land area: 47,224 sq mi. (122,310 sq km)
Geographic center: In Madison Co., 12 mi. S of Oneida and 26 mi. SW of Utica
Number of counties: 62

Largest county (1998 pop. est.): Kings, 2,267,942
State forest preserves: Adirondacks, 2,500,000 ac.; Catskills, 250,000 ac.
State parks: 152
1998 resident population est.: 18,175,301
1990 resident census population (rank): 17,990,455 (2). **Male:** 8,625,673; **Female:** 9,364,782. **White:** 13,385,255 (74.4%); **Black:** 2,859,055 (15.9%); **American Indian:** 62,651 (0.3%); **Asian:** 693,760 (3.9%); **Other race:** 989,734 (5.5%); **Hispanic:** 2,214,026 (12.3%). **1990 percent population under 18:** 23.7; **65 and over:** 13.1; **median age:** 33.7.

Giovanni da Verrazano, an Italian-born navigator sailing for France, discovered New York Bay in 1524. Henry Hudson, an Englishman employed by the Dutch, reached the bay and sailed up the river now bearing his name in 1609, the same year that northern New York was explored and claimed for France by Samuel de Champlain.

In 1624 the first permanent Dutch settlement was established at Fort Orange (now Albany); one year later Peter Minuit is said to have purchased Manhattan Island from the Indians for trinkets worth about $24 and founded the Dutch colony of New Amsterdam (now New York City), which was surrendered to the English in 1664.

For a short time, New York City was the U.S. capital and George Washington was inaugurated there as the first president on April 30, 1789.

New York's extremely rapid commercial growth may be partly attributed to Governor De Witt Clinton, who pushed through the construction of the Erie Canal (Buffalo to Albany), which was opened in 1825. Today, the 559-mile Governor Thomas E. Dewey Thruway connects New York City with Buffalo and with Connecticut, Massachusetts, and Pennsylvania express highways. Two toll-free superhighways, the Adirondack Northway (linking Albany with the Canadian border) and the North-South Expressway (crossing central New York from the Pennsylvania border to the Thousand Islands), have been opened.

New York, with the great metropolis of New York City, is the spectacular nerve center of the nation. It is a leader in manufacturing, foreign trade, commercial and financial transactions, book and magazine publishing, and theatrical production.

New York City is not only a national but an international leader. A leading seaport, its John F. Kennedy International Airport is one of the busiest airports in the world. New York is the largest manufacturing center in the country. The apparel industry is the city's largest manufacturing employer, with printing and publishing second.

Nearly all the rest of the state's manufacturing is done on Long Island, along the Hudson River north to Albany, and through the Mohawk Valley, Central New York, and Southern Tier regions to Buffalo. The St. Lawrence seaway and power projects have opened the North Country to industrial expansion and have given the state a second seacoast.

The state ranks fourth in the nation in manufacturing, with 982,000 employees in 1995. The principal industries are apparel, printing and publishing, leather products, instruments, and electronic equipment. The convention and tourist business is one of the state's most important sources of income.

New York farms raise cattle and calves, produce corn and poultry, and raise vegetables and fruits. The state is a leading wine producer.

Among the major points of interest are Castle Clinton, Fort Stanwix, and Statue of Liberty National Monuments; Niagara Falls; U.S. Military Academy at West Point; National Historic Sites that include homes of Franklin D. Roosevelt at Hyde Park and Theodore Roosevelt in Oyster Bay and New York City; the Women's Rights National Historic Park in Seneca Falls; National Memorials, including Grant's Tomb and Federal Hall in New York City; Fort Ticonderoga; the Baseball Hall of Fame in Cooperstown; and the United Nations, skyscrapers, museums, theaters, and parks in New York City.

Famous natives and residents: Kareem Abdul-Jabbar, basketball player; Lucille Ball, actress; Humphrey Bogart, actor; James Cagney, actor; Maria Callas, soprano; Benjamin N. Cardozo, jurist; Paddy Chayefsky, playwright; Peter Cooper, industrialist and philanthropist; Aaron Copland, composer; Sammy Davis, Jr., actor and singer; Agnes de Mille, choreographer; Eamon De Valera, former president of Ireland; George Eastman, inventor; Millard Fillmore, former president; Lou Gehrig, baseball player; George Gershwin, composer; Learned Hand, jurist; Edward Hopper, painter; Julia Ward Howe, poet and reformer; Charles Evans Hughes, jurist; Washington Irving, author; Henry James, novelist; John Jay, jurist; Michael Jordan, basketball player; Jerome Kern, composer; Rockwell Kent, painter; Vince Lombardi, football coach; Chico, Groucho, Harpo, and Zeppo Marx, comedians; Herman Melville, author; Ethel Merman, singer and actress; Ogden Nash, poet; Eugene O'Neill, playwright; Red Jacket, Seneca chief; John D. Rockefeller, industrialist; Norman Rockwell, painter and illustrator; Mickey Rooney, actor; Anna Eleanor Roosevelt, reformer and humanitarian; Franklin D. Roosevelt, former president; Theodore Roosevelt, former president; Jonas Salk, polio researcher; Margaret Sanger, birth control leader; Barbara Stanwyck, actress; Risë Stevens, mezzo-soprano; Richard Tucker, tenor; Martin Van Buren, former president; Mae West, actress; Walt Whitman, poet; Edith Wharton, novelist.

North Carolina

Capital: Raleigh
Governor: James B. Hunt, Jr., D (to Jan. 2001)
Lieut. Governor: Dennis A. Wicker, D (to Jan. 2001)
Senators: John Edwards, D (to Jan. 2005); Jesse Helms, R (to Jan. 2003)
Secy. of State: Elaine F. Marshall, D (to Jan. 2001)
Treasurer: Harlan E. Boyles, D (to Jan. 2001)
Auditor: Ralph Campbell, D (to Jan. 2001)
Atty. General: Michael Easley, D (to Jan. 2001)
Entered Union (rank): Nov. 21, 1789 (12)
Present constitution adopted: 1971
Motto: *Esse quam videri* (To be rather than to seem)
State symbols: flower, dogwood (1941); **tree,** pine (1963); **bird,** cardinal (1943); **mammal,** gray squirrel (1969); **insect,** honeybee (1973); **reptile,** eastern box turtle (1979); **gemstone,** emerald (1973); **shell,** scotch bonnet (1965); **historic boat,** shad boat (1987); **beverage,** milk (1987); **rock,** granite (1979); **dog,** plott hound (1989); **song,** "The Old North State" (1927); **colors,** red and blue (1945)
Nickname: Tar Heel State
Origin of name: In honor of Charles I of England
10 largest cities (1998 est.): Charlotte, 504,637; Raleigh, 259,423; Greensboro, 197,910; Winston-Salem, 164,316; Durham, 153,513; Cary, 82,071; Fayetteville, 77,295; High Point, 76,117; Jacksonville, 68,380; Wilmington, 68,062
Land area: 48,718 sq mi. (126,180 sq km)

Geographic center: In Chatham Co., 10 mi. NW of Sanford
Number of counties: 100
Largest county (1998 pop. est.): Mecklenburg, 630,848
State forests: 1
State parks: 30 (125,000 ac.)
1998 resident population est.: 7,546,493
1990 resident census population (rank): 6,628,637 (10). **Male:** 3,214,290; **Female:** 3,414,347. **White:** 5,008,491 (75.6%); **Black:** 1,456,323 (22.0%); **American Indian:** 80,155 (1.2%); **Asian:** 52,166 (0.8%); **Other race:** 31,502 (0.5%); **Hispanic:** 76,726 (1.2%). **1990 percent population under 18:** 24.2; **65 and over:** 12.1; **median age:** 33.0.

English colonists, sent by Sir Walter Raleigh, unsuccessfully attempted to settle Roanoke Island in 1585 and 1587. Virginia Dare, born there in 1587, was the first child of English parentage born in America.

In 1653 the first permanent settlements were established by English colonists from Virginia near the Roanoke and Chowan rivers. The region was established as an English proprietary colony in 1663–65 and its early history was the scene of Culpepper's Rebellion (1677), the Quaker-led Cary Rebellion of 1708, the Tuscarora Indian War of 1711–13, and many pirate raids.

During the American Revolution, there was relatively little fighting within the state, but many North Carolinians saw action elsewhere. Despite considerable pro-Union, anti-slavery sentiment, North Carolina joined the Confederacy during the Civil War.

North Carolina is the nation's largest furniture, tobacco, brick, and textile producer. It holds second place in the Southeast in population and first place in the value of its industrial and agricultural production. This production is highly diversified, with metalworking, chemicals, and paper constituting enormous industries. Tobacco, corn, cotton, hay, peanuts, and vegetable crops are of major importance. It is the country's leading producer of mica and lithium.

Tourism is also important, with travelers and vacationers spending more than $1 billion annually in North Carolina. Sports include year-round golfing, skiing at mountain resorts, both fresh- and salt-water fishing, and hunting.

Among the major attractions are the Great Smoky Mountains, the Blue Ridge National Parkway, the Cape Hatteras and Cape Lookout National Seashores, the Wright Brothers National Memorial at Kitty Hawk, Guilford Courthouse and Moores Creek National Military Parks, Carl Sandburg's home near Hendersonville, and the Old Salem Restoration in Winston-Salem.

Famous natives and residents: David Brinkley, TV newscaster; Howard Cosell, sportscaster; Virginia Dare, first person born in America to English parents; James B. Duke, industrialist; Roberta Flack, singer; Ava Gardner, actress; Richard Gatling, inventor; Billy Graham, evangelist; Kathryn Grayson, singer and actress; Jesse Helms, politician; O. Henry, writer; Barbara Howar, broadcaster and writer; Andrew Johnson, former president; Charles Kuralt, TV journalist; Sugar Ray Leonard, boxer; Dolley Madison, former first lady; Ronni Milsap, country music singer; Thelonious Monk, pianist; Alfred Moore, jurist; Edward R. Murrow, commentator and government official; Walter Hines Page, commentator and ambassador; Floyd Patterson, boxer; Richard Petty, auto racer; James K. Polk, former president; Soupy Sales, comedian; Earl Scruggs, bluegrass musician; Randy Travis, musician; John Scott Trotter, orchestra leader; Thomas Wolfe, novelist.

North Dakota

Capital: Bismarck
Governor: Edward T. Schafer, R (to Dec. 15, 2000)
Lieut. Governor: Rosemarie Myrdal, R (to Dec. 15, 2000)
Senators: Kent Conrad, D (to Jan. 2001);
Byron L. Dorgan, D (to Jan. 2005)
Secy. of State: Alvin A. Jaeger, R (to Dec. 31, 2000)
Auditor: Robert R. Peterson, R (to Dec. 31, 2000)
Treasurer: Kathi Gilmore, D (to Dec. 31, 2000)
Atty. General: Heidi Heitkamp, D (to Dec. 31, 2000)
Organized as territory: March 2, 1861
Entered Union (rank): Nov. 2, 1889 (39)
Present constitution adopted: 1889
Motto: Liberty and union, now and forever: one and inseparable
State symbols: tree, American elm (1947); **bird,** western meadowlark (1947); **song,** "North Dakota Hymn" (1947); **fish,** northern pike (1969); **grass,** western wheatgrass (1977); **fossil,** teredo petrified wood (1967); **beverage,** milk (1983); **state march,** Spirit of the Land (1975); **flower,** wild prairie rose (1907); **equine,** Nokota horse (1993); **dance,** square dance (1995)
Nickname: Sioux State; Flickertail State; Peace Garden State
Origin of name: From the Sioux tribe, meaning "allies"
10 largest cities (1998 est.): Fargo, 86,718; Bismarck, 54,040; Grand Forks, 47,327; Minot, 35,286; Dickinson, 16,221; Mandan, 15,860; Jamestown, 14,713; West Fargo, 14,091; Williston, 12,446; Wahpeton, 9,322
Land area: 68,994 sq mi. (178,695 sq km)
Geographic center: In Sheridan Co., 5 mi. SW of McClusky
Number of counties: 53
Largest county (1998 pop. est.): Cass, 116,832
State parks: 18 (15,773 ac.)
1998 resident population est.: 638,244
1990 resident census population (rank): 638,800 (47). **Male:** 318,201; **Female:** 320,599. **White:** 604,142 (94.6%); **Black:** 3,524 (0.6%); **American Indian:** 25,917 (4.1%); **Asian:** 3,462 (0.5%); **Other race:** 1,755 (0.3%); **Hispanic:** 4,665 (0.7%). **1990 percent population under 18:** 27.5; **65 and over:** 14.3; **median age:** 32.3.

North Dakota was explored in 1738–40 by French Canadians led by sieur de la Verendrye. In 1803, the U.S. acquired most of North Dakota from France in the Louisiana Purchase. Lewis and Clark explored the region in 1804–06 and the first settlements were made at Pembina in 1812 by Scottish and Irish families while this area was still in dispute between the U.S. and Great Britain.

In 1818, the U.S. obtained the northeastern part of North Dakota by treaty with Great Britain and took possession of Pembina in 1823.

North Dakota is the most rural of all the states, with farms covering more than 90% of the land. North Dakota ranks first in the nation's production of spring and durum wheat, and the state's coal and oil reserves are plentiful.

Other agricultural products include barley, rye, sunflowers, dry edible beans, honey, oats, flaxseed, sugar beets, hay, beef cattle, sheep, and hogs.

Recently, manufacturing industries have grown, especially food processing and farm equipment. The state also produces natural gas, lignite, salt, clay, sand, and gravel.

The Garrison Dam on the Missouri River provides extensive irrigation and produces 400,000 kilowatts of electricity for the Missouri Basin areas.

Known for its waterfowl, grouse, and deer hunting and bass, trout, and northern pike fishing, North Dakota has 18 state parks and recreation areas.

Points of interest include the International Peace Garden near Dunseith, Fort Union Trading Post National Historic Site, the State Capitol at Bismarck, the Badlands, Theodore Roosevelt National Park, and Fort Lincoln, now a state park, from which Gen. George Custer set out on his last campaign in 1876.

Famous natives and residents: Lynn Anderson, singer; Maxwell Anderson, playwright; Dr. Robert H. Bahmer, U.S. archivist; Elizabeth Bodine, humanitarian; Dr. Anne Carlsen, educator; Warren Christopher, former U.S. Secretary of State; Ronald N. Davies, jurist; Angie Dickinson, actress; Ivan Dmitre, artist; Carl Ben Eielson, aviator; Phyllis Frelich, actress; Bertin C. Gamble, founder of Gamble-Skogmo; William H. Gass, writer and philosopher; Rev. Richard C. Halverson, U.S. Senate chaplain; Brynhild Haugland, state legislator; Phil D. Jackson, basketball player and coach; Dr. Leon O. Jacobson, researcher and educator; Harold K. Johnson, former army general and U.S. Army Chief of Staff; David C. Jones, former Chairman, Joint Chiefs of Staff; Louis L'Amour, author; Peggy Lee, singer; William Lemke, former representative; Roger Maris, baseball player; Marquis de Mores, cattleman who established Medora; Gerald P. Nye, former senator; Casper Oimoen, skier; William A. Owens, former Vice Chairman, Joint Chiefs of Staff; Arthur Peterson, radio and TV actor; Cliff (Fido) Purpur, hockey player and coach; James Rosenquist, painter; Harold Schafer, founder of Gold Seal Co.; Eric Sevareid, TV commentator; Ann Sothern, actress; Dorothy Stickney, actress; Edward K. Thompson, *Life* magazine editor; Era Bell Thompson, *Ebony* magazine editor; Tommy Tucker, band leader; Bobby Vee, entertainer; Lawrence Welk, band leader; Larry Woiwode, writer.

Ohio

Capital: Columbus
Governor: Bob Taft, R (to Jan. 2003)
Lieut. Governor: Maureen O'Connor, R (to Jan. 2003)
Senators: Mike DeWine, R (to Jan. 2001); George V. Voinovich, R (to Jan. 2005)
Secy. of State: J. Kenneth Blackwell, R (to Jan. 2003)
Auditor: Jim Petro, R (to Jan. 2003)
Treasurer: Joseph P. Deters, R (to Jan. 2003)
Atty. General: Betty D. Montgomery, R (to Jan. 2003)
Entered Union (rank): March 1, 1803 (17)
Present constitution adopted: 1851
Motto: With God, all things are possible
State symbols: flower, scarlet carnation (1904); **tree,** buckeye (1953); **bird,** cardinal (1933); **insect,** ladybug (1975); **gemstone,** flint (1965); **song,** "Beautiful Ohio" (1969); **drink,** tomato juice (1965)
Nickname: Buckeye State
Origin of name: From an Iroquoian word meaning "great river"
10 largest cities (1998 est.): Columbus, 670,234; Cleveland, 495,817; Cincinnati, 336,400; Toledo, 312,174; Akron, 215,712; Dayton, 167,475; Youngstown, 84,650; Parma, 83,347; Canton, 79,259; Lorain, 68,857
Land area: 40,953 sq mi. (106,067 sq km)
Geographic center: In Delaware Co., 25 mi. NNE of Columbus
Number of counties: 88
Largest county (1998 pop. est.): Cuyahoga, 1,380,696
State forests: 19 (172,744 ac.)
State parks: 71 (198,027 ac.)
1998 resident population est.: 11,209,493
1990 resident census population (rank): 10,847,115 (7). **Male:** 5,226,340; **Female:** 5,620,775. **White:** 9,521,756 (87.8%); **Black:** 1,154,826 (10.6%); **American Indian:** 20,358 (0.2%); **Asian:** 91,179 (0.8%); **Other race:** 58,996 (0.5%); **Hispanic:** 139,696 (1.3%). **1990 percent population under 18:** 25.8; **65 and over:** 13.0; **median age:** 33.3.

First explored for France by sieur de la Salle in 1669, the Ohio region became British property after the French and Indian Wars. Ohio was acquired by the U.S. after the Revolutionary War in 1783. In 1788, the first permanent settlement was established at Marietta, capital of the Northwest Territory.

The 1790s saw severe fighting with the Indians in Ohio; a major battle was won by Maj. Gen. Anthony Wayne at Fallen Timbers in 1794. In the War of 1812, Commodore Oliver H. Perry defeated the British in the Battle of Lake Erie on Sept. 10, 1813.

Ohio is one of the nation's industrial leaders, ranking third in the value of manufactured products. Important manufacturing centers are located in or near Ohio's major cities. Akron is known for rubber; Canton for roller bearings; Cincinnati for jet engines and machine tools; Cleveland for auto assembly and parts, refining, and steel; Dayton for office machines, refrigeration, and heating and auto equipment; Youngstown and Steubenville for steel; and Toledo for glass and auto parts.

The state's thousands of factories almost overshadow its importance in agriculture and mining. Its fertile soil produces soybeans, corn, oats, grapes, and clover. More than half of Ohio's farm receipts come from dairy farming and sheep and hog raising. Ohio is the top state in lime production and among the leaders in coal, clay, salt, sand, and gravel. Petroleum, gypsum, cement, and natural gas are also important.

Tourism is a valuable revenue producer, bringing in $9.9 billion in 1996, and ranking 7th among the 50 states. Attractions include the Rock and Roll Hall of Fame, Indian burial grounds at Mound City Group National Monument, Perry's Victory International Peace Memorial, the Pro Football Hall of Fame at Canton, and the homes of presidents Grant, Taft, Hayes, Harding, and Garfield.

Famous natives and residents: Neil Armstrong, astronaut; Kathleen Battle, soprano; George Bellows, painter and lithographer; Ambrose Bierce, journalist; Erma Bombeck, columnist; Bill Boyd (Hopalong Cassidy), actor; Milton Caniff, cartoonist; Hart Crane, poet; George Armstrong Custer, army officer; Dorothy Dandridge, actress; Doris Day, singer and actress; Clarence Darrow, lawyer; Ruby Dee, actress; Rita Dove, former U.S. poet laureate; Hugh Downs, TV broadcaster; Thomas A. Edison, inventor; Clark Gable, actor; James A. Garfield, former president; Lillian Gish, actress; John Glenn, astronaut and senator; Ulysses S. Grant, former president; Warren G. Harding, former president; Rutherford Hayes, former president; Benjamin Harrison, former president; William Dean Howells, novelist and critic; Zane Grey, author; Robert Henri, painter; Kenisaw Mountain Landis, first baseball commissioner; Dean Martin, singer and actor; William McKinley, former president; Paul Newman, actor; Jack Nicklaus, golfer; Annie Oakley, markswoman; Norman Vincent Peale, clergyman; Tyrone Power, actor; Judith Resnik, astronaut; Eddie Rickenbacker, aviator; Arthur M. Schlesinger, Jr., historian; William Tecumseh Sherman, army general; Gloria Steinem, feminist; William H. Taft, former president; Tecumseh, Shawnee Indian chief; Lowell Thomas, explorer and commentator; James Thurber, author and cartoonist; Orville Wright, inventor; Cy Young, baseball player.

Oklahoma

Capital: Oklahoma City
Governor: Frank Keating, R (to Jan. 2003)
Lieut. Governor: Mary Fallin, R (to Jan. 2003)
Senators: James M. Inhofe, R (to Jan. 2003); Don Nickles, R (to Jan. 2005)
Secy. of State: Mike Hunter, R (to Jan. 2003)
Treasurer: Robert Butkin, D (to Jan. 2003)

Atty. General: Drew Edmondson, D (to Jan. 2003)
Organized as territory: May 2, 1890
Entered Union (rank): Nov. 16, 1907 (46)
Present constitution adopted: 1907
Motto: *Labor omnia vincit* (Labor conquers all things)
State symbols: flower, mistletoe (1893); **tree,** redbud (1937); **bird,** scissor-tailed flycatcher (1951); **animal,** bison (1972); **reptile,** mountain boomer lizard (1969); **stone,** rose rock (barite rose) (1968); **colors,** green and white (1915); **song,** "Oklahoma" (1953); **beverage,** milk; **butterfly,** black swallowtail; **fish,** white or sand bass; **folk dance,** square dance; **furbearer,** raccoon; **game animal,** white-tailed deer; **grass,** Indiangrass; **insect,** honeybee; **musical instrument,** fiddle; **poem,** "Howdy Folks," David Randolph Milsten; **waltz,** "Oklahoma Wind"; **wildflower,** Indian blanket
Nickname: Sooner State
Origin of name: From two Choctaw Indian words meaning "red people"
10 largest cities (1998 est.): Oklahoma City, 472,221; Tulsa, 381,393; Norman, 93,019; Lawton, 81,107; Broken Arrow, 72,564; Edmond, 64,962; Midwest City, 54,037; Moore, 45,318; Enid, 45,234; Stillwater, 38,765
Land area: 68,679 sq mi. (177,877 sq km)
Geographic center: In Oklahoma Co., 8 mi. N of Oklahoma City
Number of counties: 77
Largest county (1998 pop. est.): Oklahoma, 632,988
State parks: 51 (72,000 ac.)
1998 resident population est.: 3,346,713
1990 resident census population (rank): 3,145,585 (28). **Male:** 1,530,819; **Female:** 1,614,766. **White:** 2,583,512 (82.1%); **Black:** 233,801 (7.4%); **American Indian:** 252,420 (8.0%); **Asian:** 33,563 (1.1%); **Other race:** 42,289 (1.3%); **Hispanic:** 86,160 (2.7%). **1990 percent population under 18:** 26.6; **65 and over:** 13.5; **median age:** 33.1.

Francisco Vásquez de Coronado first explored the region for Spain in 1541. The U.S. acquired most of Oklahoma in 1803 in the Louisiana Purchase from France; the Western Panhandle region became U.S. territory with the annexation of Texas in 1845.

Set aside as Indian Territory in 1834, the region was divided into Indian Territory and Oklahoma Territory on May 2, 1890. The two were combined to make a new state, Oklahoma, on Nov. 16, 1907.

On April 22, 1889, the first day homesteading was permitted, 50,000 people swarmed into the area. Those who tried to beat the noon starting gun were called "Sooners," hence the state's nickname.

Oil made Oklahoma a rich state, but natural-gas production has now surpassed it. Oil refining, meat packing, food processing, and machinery manufacturing (especially construction and oil equipment) are important industries.

Other minerals produced in Oklahoma include helium, gypsum, zinc, cement, coal, copper, and silver.

Oklahoma's rich plains produce bumper yields of wheat, as well as large crops of sorghum, hay, cotton, and peanuts. More than half of Oklahoma's annual farm receipts are contributed by livestock products, including cattle, dairy products, swine, and broilers.

Tourist attractions include the National Cowboy Hall of Fame in Oklahoma City, the Will Rogers Memorial in Claremore, the Cherokee Cultural Center with a restored Cherokee village, the restored Fort Gibson Stockade near Muskogee, the Lake Texoma recreation area, Pari-Mutuel horse racing at

Remington Park in Oklahoma City, and Blue Ribbon Downs in Sallisaw.

Famous natives and residents: Johnny Bench, baseball player; John Berryman, poet; Garth Brooks, singer; Iron Eyes Cody, Cherokee actor; L. Gordon Cooper, astronaut; Ralph Ellison, writer; James Garner, actor; Owen K. Garriott, astronaut; Vince Gill, singer; Chester Gould, cartoonist; Woody Guthrie, singer and composer; Roy Harris, composer; Paul Harvey, broadcaster; Van Heflin, actor; Ron Howard, actor and director; Ben Johnson, actor; Jennifer Jones, actress; Jeane Kirkpatrick, educator and public-affairs spokesperson; Shannon Lucid, astronaut; Wilma P. Mankiller, principal chief of the Cherokee Nation of Oklahoma; Mickey Mantle, baseball player; Reba McEntire, singer; Shannon Miller, Olympic gymnast; Bill Moyers, journalist; Daniel Patrick Moynihan, N.Y. senator; Patti Page, singer; Mary Kay Place, actress and writer; Tony Randall, actor; Oral Roberts, evangelist; Dale Robertson, actor; Will Rogers, humorist; Dan Rowan, comedian; Thomas P. Stafford, astronaut; Maria Tallchief, ballerina; Jim Thorpe, athlete; Alfre Woodard, actress.

Oregon

Capital: Salem
Governor: John A. Kitzhaber, D (to Jan. 2003)
Senators: Gordon Smith, R (to Jan. 2003);
   Ron Wyden, D (to Jan. 2005)
Secy. of State: Phil Keisling, D (to Jan. 2001)
Treasurer: James A. Hill, D (to Jan. 2001)
Atty. General: Hardy Myers, D (to Jan. 2001)
Organized as territory: Aug. 14, 1848
Entered Union (rank): Feb. 14, 1859 (33)
Present constitution adopted: 1859
Motto: Alis volat Propriis (She flies with her own wings) (1987)
State symbols: flower, Oregon grape (1899); **tree,** douglas fir (1939); **animal,** beaver (1969); **bird,** western meadowlark (1927); **fish,** chinook salmon (1961); **rock,** thunderegg (1965); **colors,** navy blue and gold (1959); **song,** "Oregon, My Oregon" (1927); **insect,** swallowtail butterfly (1979); **dance,** square dance (1997); **nut,** hazelnut (1989); **gemstone,** sunstone (1987)
Nickname: Beaver State
Origin of name: Unknown. However, it is generally accepted that the name, first used by Jonathan Carver in 1778, was taken from the writings of Maj. Robert Rogers, an English army officer.
10 largest cities (1998 est.): Portland, 503,891; Eugene, 128,240; Salem, 126,702; Gresham, 85,021; Beaverton, 62,111; Hillsboro, 61,111; Medford, 57,156; Springfield, 50,682; Corvallis, 50,202; Albany, 38,832
Land area: 96,003 sq mi. (248,647 sq km)
Geographic center: In Crook Co., 25 mi. SSE of Prineville
Number of counties: 36
Largest county (1998 pop. est.): Multnomah, 631,082
State forests: 820,000 ac.
State parks: 240 (93,330 ac.)
1998 resident population est.: 3,281,974
1990 resident census population (rank): 2,842,321 (29). **Male:** 1,397,073; **Female:** 1,445,248. **White:** 2,636,787 (92.8%); **Black:** 46,178 (1.6%); **American Indian:** 38,496 (1.4%); **Asian:** 69,269 (2.4%); **Other race:** 51,591 (1.8%); **Hispanic:** 112,707 (4.0%). **1990 percent population under 18:** 25.5; **65 and over:** 13.8; **median age:** 34.5.

Spanish and English sailors are believed to have sighted the Oregon coast in the 1500s and 1600s. Capt. James Cook, seeking the Northwest Passage, charted some of the coastline in 1778. In 1792, Capt. Robert Gray, in the *Columbia*, discovered the river named after his ship and claimed the area for the U.S.

In 1805 the Lewis and Clark expedition explored the area. John Jacob Astor's fur depot, Astoria, was founded in 1811. Disputes for control of Oregon between American settlers and the Hudson Bay Company were finally resolved in the 1846 Oregon Treaty in which Great Britain gave up claims to the region.

Oregon has a $3.3 billion lumber and wood products industry, and an $859 million paper and allied manufacturing industry. Its salmon-fishing industry is one of the world's largest.

In agriculture, the state leads in growing peppermint, cover seed crops, blackberries, boysenberries, loganberries, black raspberries, and hazelnuts. It is second in raising hops, raspberries, sweet cherries, prunes, snap beans, and onions. Oregon has the only nickel smelter in the United States.

With the low-cost electric power provided by Bonneville Dam, McNary Dam, and other dams in the Pacific Northwest, Oregon has developed steadily as a manufacturing state. Leading manufactured items are lumber and plywood, metalwork, machinery, aluminum, chemicals, paper, food packing, and electronic equipment.

Crater Lake National Park, Mount Hood, and Bonneville Dam on the Columbia are major tourist attractions. Oregon Dunes National Recreation Area has been established near Florence. Other points of interest include the Oregon Caves National Monument, Cape Perpetua in Siuslaw National Forest, Columbia River Gorge between The Dalles and Troutdale, Hells Canyon, Newberry Volcanic National Monument, and John Day Fossil Beds National Monument.

Famous natives and residents: James Beard, food expert; Raymond Carver, writer and poet; Homer C. Davenport, political cartoonist; David Douglas, botanist; Abigail Scott Duniway, women's suffrage advocate; John E. Frohnmeyer, former chairman of the National Endowment for the Arts; Robert Gray, sea captain and discoverer of Columbia River; Matt Groening, cartoonist; Mark Hatfield, senator; Donald P. Hodel, former secretary of the Interior; Chief Joseph, Nez Percé chief; Dave Kingman, baseball player; Ursula LeGuin, writer; Edwin Markham, poet; Phyllis McGinley, author; Linus Pauling, chemist; Jane Powell, actress and singer; John Reed, poet and author; Harvey W. Scott, editor; Doc Severinsen, band leader; Norton Simon, business executive; Paul M. Simon, Illinois senator; William E. Stafford, poet; Sally Struthers, actress.

Pennsylvania

Capital: Harrisburg
Governor: Tom Ridge, R (to Jan. 2003)
Lieut. Governor: Mark Schweiker, R (to Jan. 2003)
Senators: Rick Santorum, R (to Jan. 2001);
   Arlen Specter, R (to Jan. 2005)
Acting Secy. of the Commonwealth: Kim Pizzingrilli, R (at the pleasure of the governor)
Auditor General: Robert P. Casey, Jr., D (to Jan. 2001)
Atty. General: D. Michael Fisher, R (to Jan. 2001)
Entered Union (rank): Dec. 12, 1787 (2)
Present constitution adopted: 1968
Motto: Virtue, liberty, and independence
State symbols: flower, mountain laurel (1933); **tree,** hemlock (1931); **bird,** ruffed grouse (1931); **dog,** Great Dane (1965); **colors,** blue and gold (1907); **song,** "Pennsylvania" (1990)
Nickname: Keystone State
Origin of name: In honor of Adm. Sir William Penn, father of William Penn. It means "Penn's Woodland."
10 largest cities (1998 est.): Philadelphia, 1,436,287; Pittsburgh, 340,520; Erie, 102,640; Allentown,

100,757; Reading, 74,762; Scranton, 74,683;
Bethlehem, 69,383; Lancaster, 52,951; Harrisburg,
49,502; Altoona, 49,226
Land area: 44,820 sq mi. (116,083 sq km)
Geographic center: In Centre Co., 2½ mi. SW
of Bellefonte
Number of counties: 67
Largest county (1998 pop. est.): Philadelphia,
1,436,287
State forests: over 2 mil. ac.
State parks: 116
1998 resident population est.: 12,001,451
1990 resident census population (rank): 11,881,643
(5). **Male:** 5,694,265; **Female:** 6,187,378. **White:**
10,520,201 (88.5%); **Black:** 1,089,795 (9.2%); **American Indian:** 14,733 (0.1%); **Asian:** 137,438 (1.2%);
Other race: 119,476 (1.0%); **Hispanic:** 232,262
(2.0%). **1990 percent population under 18:** 23.5; **65
and over:** 15.4; **median age:** 34.9.

Rich in historic lore, Pennsylvania territory was
disputed in the early 1600s among the Dutch, the
Swedes, and the English. England acquired the
region in 1664 with the capture of New York and in
1681 Pennsylvania was granted to William Penn, a
Quaker, by King Charles II.

Philadelphia was the seat of the federal government almost continuously from 1776 to 1800; there
the Declaration of Independence was signed in 1776
and the U.S. Constitution drawn up in 1787. Valley
Forge, of Revolutionary War fame, and Gettysburg,
site of the pivotal battle of the Civil War, are both
in Pennsylvania. The Liberty Bell is located in a
glass pavilion across from Independence Hall in
Philadelphia.

With the decline of the coal, steel, and railroad
industries, Pennsylvania's industry has diversified,
although the state still leads the country in the production of specialty steel. Pennsylvania is a leader
in the production of chemicals, food, and electrical
machinery and produces 10% of the nation's
cement. Also important are brick and tiles, glass,
limestone, and slate. Data processing is also increasingly important.

Pennsylvania's 9 million agricultural acres (6 million acres for crops and pasture, 3 million acres in
farm woodlands) produce a wide variety of crops,
and its 55,535 farms are the backbone of the state's
economy. Leading products are milk, poultry, eggs,
a variety of fruits, sweet corn, potatoes, mushrooms,
cheese, beans, hay, maple syrup, and even Christmas trees.

Pennsylvania has the largest rural population in
the nation. The state's farmers sell more than $3.3
billion in crops and livestock annually, and agribusiness and food-related industries account for another
$35 billion in economic activity annually.

Tourists now spend approximately $6 billion in
Pennsylvania annually. Among the chief attractions
are the Gettysburg National Military Park, Valley
Forge National Historical Park, Independence
National Historical Park in Philadelphia, the Pennsylvania Dutch region, the Eisenhower farm near Gettysburg, and the Delaware Water Gap National Recreation Area.

Famous natives and residents: Louisa May Alcott, novelist;
Marian Anderson, contralto; Maxwell Anderson, dramatist;
Samuel Barber, composer; John Barrymore, actor; Donald
Barthelme, author; Stephen Vincent Benet, poet and story
writer; Daniel Boone, frontiersman; Ed Bradley, TV
anchorman; James Buchanan, former president; Alexander
Calder, sculptor; Rachel Carson, biologist and author;

Mary Cassatt, painter; Henry Steele Commager, historian;
Bill Cosby, actor; Stuart Davis, painter; Jimmy and Tommy
Dorsey, band leaders; W. C. Fields, comedian; Stephen
Foster, composer; Robert Fulton, inventor; Grace, Princess
of Monaco; Martha Graham, choreographer; Alexander
Haig, former secretary of state; Marilyn Horne,
mezzo-soprano; Lee Iacocca, auto executive; Reggie
Jackson, baseball player; Gene Kelly, dancer and actor;
Gelsey Kirkland, ballerina; S. S. Kresge, merchant; Mario
Lanza, actor and singer; George C. Marshall, five-star
general; George McClellan, former general; Margaret
Mead, anthropologist; Andrew Mellon, financier; Tom Mix,
actor; Arnold Palmer, golfer; Robert E. Peary, explorer;
Man Ray, painter; Mary Roberts Rinehart, novelist; Betsy
Ross, flagmaker; B. F. Skinner, psychologist; John Sloan,
painter; Gertrude Stein, author; James Stewart, actor;
John Updike, novelist; Honus Wagner, baseball player;
Fred Waring, band leader; Ethel Waters, singer and
actress; Anthony Wayne, military officer; August Wilson,
poet, writer, and playwright; Wallis Warfield, Duchess of
Windsor; Andrew Wyeth, painter.

Rhode Island

Capital: Providence
Governor: Lincoln C. Almond, R (to Jan. 2003)
Lieut. Governor: Charles J. Fogarty, D (to Jan. 2003)
Senators: John H. Chafee, R (to Jan. 2001);
Jack Reed, D (to Jan. 2003)
Secy. of State: Jim Langevin, D (to Jan. 2003)
Atty. General: Sheldon Whitehouse, D (to Jan. 2003)
General Treasurer: Paul J. Tavares, D (to Jan. 2003)
Entered Union (rank): May 29, 1790 (13)
Present constitution adopted: 1843
Motto: Hope
State symbols: flower, violet (unofficial) (1968); **tree,**
red maple (official) (1964); **bird,** Rhode Island red hen
(official) (1954); **shell,** quahog (official); **mineral,**
bowenite (1966); **stone,** cumberlandite (1966); **colors,**
blue, white, and gold (in state flag); **song,** "Rhode
Island" (1946)
Nickname: The Ocean State
Origin of name: From the Greek Island of Rhodes
Largest cities (1998 est.): Providence, 150,890;
Warwick, 84,094; Cranston, 74,521; Pawtucket,
68,169; East Providence, 47,882; Woonsocket,
41,034; Newport, 24,279; Central Falls, 16,364
Land area: 1,045 sq mi. (2,706 sq km)
Geographic center: In Kent Co., 1 mi. SSW
of Compton
Number of counties: 5
Largest county (1998 pop. est.): Providence, 574,038
State forests: 11 (20,900 ac.)
State parks: 14
1998 resident population est.: 988,480
1990 resident census population (rank): 1,003,464
(43). **Male:** 481,496; **Female:** 521,968. **White:**
917,375 (91.4%); **Black:** 38,861 (3.9%); **American
Indian:** 4,071 (0.4%); **Asian:** 18,325 (1.8%); **Other
race:** 24,832 (2.5%); **Hispanic:** 45,752 (4.6%). **1990
percent population under 18:** 22.5; **65 and over:**
15.0; **median age:** 33.8.

From its beginnings, Rhode Island has been distinguished by its support for freedom of conscience
and action, started by Roger Williams, who was
exiled by the Massachusetts Bay Colony Puritans in
1636, and was the founder of the present state capital, Providence. Williams was followed by other
religious exiles who founded Pocasset, now Portsmouth, in 1638 and Newport in 1639.

Rhode Island's rebellious, authority-defying
nature was further demonstrated by the burnings of
the British revenue cutters *Liberty* and *Gaspee* prior
to the Revolution, by its early declaration of independence from Great Britain in May 1776, its
refusal to participate actively in the War of 1812,

and by Dorr's Rebellion of 1842, which protested property requirements for voting.

Rhode Island, smallest of the fifty states, is densely populated and highly industrialized. It is a primary center for jewelry manufacturing in the U.S. Electronics, metal, plastic products, and boat and ship construction are other important industries. Non-manufacturing employment includes research in health, medicine, and the ocean environment. Providence is a wholesale distribution center for New England.

Two of New England's fishing ports are at Galilee and Newport. Rural areas of the state support small-scale farming, including grapes for local wineries, turf grass, and nursery stock. Tourism is one of Rhode Island's largest industries, generating over a billion dollars a year in revenue.

Newport became famous as the summer capital of society in the mid–19th century. Touro Synagogue (1763) is the oldest in the U.S. Other points of interest include the Roger Williams National Memorial in Providence, Samuel Slater's Mill in Pawtucket, the General Nathanael Greene Homestead in Coventry, and Block Island.

Famous natives and residents: Harry Anderson, actor; George M. Cohan, actor and dramatist; Eddie Dowling, actor and stage producer; Nelson Eddy, baritone and actor; Ann Smith Franklin, printer and almanac publisher; Charles Gorham, silversmith; Spalding Gray, writer, performance artist; Bobby Hackett, trumpeter; David Hartman, TV newscaster; Ruth Hussey, actress; Anne Hutchinson, religious leader; Thomas H. Ince, film producer; Wilbur John, Quaker leader; Van Johnson, actor; Clarence King, first director of the U.S. Geological Survey; Galway Kinnell, poet; Oliver LaFarge, writer; Irving R. Levine, news correspondent; H. P. Lovecraft, author; Ida Lewis, lighthouse keeper; John McLaughlin, political commentator, broadcaster; Dana C. Munro, educator and historian; Matthew C. Perry, naval officer; Oliver Hazard Perry, naval officer; King Philip (Metacomet), Indian leader; Anthony Quinn, actor; Gilbert Stuart, painter; Sarah Helen (Power) Whitman, poet; Jemima Wilkinson, religious leader; Roger Williams, clergyman and founder of Rhode Island; Leonard Woodcock, labor union official; James Woods, actor.

South Carolina

Capital: Columbia
Governor: Jim Hodges, D (to Jan. 2003)
Lieut. Governor: Robert L. Peeler, R (to Jan. 2003)
Senators: Ernest Hollings, D (to Jan. 2005); Strom Thurmond, R (to Jan. 2003)
Secy. of State: Jim Miles, R (to Jan. 2003)
Comptroller General: Jim Lander, D (to Jan. 2003)
Atty. General: Charles M. Condon, R (to Jan. 2003)
Entered Union (rank): May 23, 1788 (8)
Present constitution adopted: 1895
Mottoes: *Animis opibusque parati* (Prepared in mind and resources) and *Dum spiro spero* (While I breathe, I hope)
State symbols: flower, Carolina yellow jessamine (1924); **tree,** palmetto tree (1939); **bird,** Carolina wren (1948); **song,** "Carolina" (1911)
Nickname: Palmetto State
Origin of name: In honor of Charles I of England
10 largest cities (1998 est.): Columbia, 110,840; Charleston, 87,044; North Charleston, 68,072; Greenville, 56,436; Rock Hill, 46,218; Mount Pleasant, 41,330; Spartanburg, 40,954; Sumter, 40,518; Hilton Head Island, 30,377; Florence, 29,511
Land area: 30,111 sq mi. (77,988 sq km)
Geographic center: In Richland Co., 13 mi. SE of Columbia

Number of counties: 46
Largest county (1998 pop. est.): Greenville, 353,845
State forests: 4 (124,052 ac.)
State parks: 50 (61,726 ac.)
1998 resident population est.: 3,835,962
1990 resident census population (rank): 3,486,703 (25). **Male:** 1,688,510; **Female:** 1,798,193. **White:** 2,406,974 (69.0%); **Black:** 1,039,884 (29.8%); **American Indian:** 8,246 (0.2%); **Asian:** 22,382 (0.6%); **Other race:** 9,217 (0.3%); **Hispanic:** 30,551 (0.9%) **1990 percent population under 18:** 26.4; **65 and over:** 11.4; **median age:** 31.9.

Following exploration of the coast in 1521 by Francisco de Gordillo, the Spanish tried unsuccessfully to establish a colony near present-day Georgetown in 1526 and the French also failed to colonize Parris Island near Fort Royal in 1562.

The first English settlement was made in 1670 at Albemarle Point on the Ashley River, but poor conditions drove the settlers to the site of Charleston (originally called Charles Town). South Carolina, officially separated from North Carolina in 1729, was the scene of extensive military action during the Revolution and again during the Civil War. The Civil War began in 1861 as South Carolina troops fired on federal Fort Sumter in Charleston Harbor and the state was the first to secede from the Union.

Once primarily agricultural, South Carolina has built so many large textile and other mills that today its factories produce eight times the output of its farms in cash value. Charleston makes asbestos, wood, pulp, and steel products; chemicals, machinery, and apparel are also important.

Farms have become fewer but larger in recent years. South Carolina grows more peaches than any other state except California; it ranks fifth in overall tobacco production. Other farm products include cotton, peanuts, sweet potatoes, soybeans, corn, and oats. Poultry and dairy products are also important revenue producers.

Points of interest include Fort Sumter National Monument, Fort Moultrie, Fort Johnson, and aircraft carrier USS *Yorktown* in Charleston Harbor; the Middleton, Magnolia, and Cypress Gardens in Charleston; Cowpens National Battlefield; the Hilton Head resorts; and the Riverbanks 200 and Botanical Garden in Columbia.

Famous natives and residents: Bernard Baruch, statesman; Mary McLeod Bethune, educator; James F. Byrnes, senator, jurist and secretary of state; John C. Calhoun, statesman; Mark Clark, general; Joe Frazier, prize fighter; Althea Gibson, tennis champion; Dizzy Gillespie, jazz trumpeter; DuBose Heyward, poet, playwright, and novelist; Andrew Jackson, former president; Jesse Jackson, civil rights leader; Eartha Kitt, singer; Francis Marion ("Swamp Fox"), Revolutionary general; Ronald McNair, astronaut; John Rutledge, jurist; Strom Thurmond, politician; Charles Townes, physicist; William Westmoreland, former army chief of staff; Vanna White, TV personality.

South Dakota

Capital: Pierre
Governor: William J. Janklow, R (to Jan. 2003)
Lieut. Governor: Carole Hillard, R (to Jan. 3003)
Senators: Thomas A. Daschle, D (to Jan. 2005); Tim Johnson, D (to Jan. 2003)
Atty. General: Mark Barnett, R (to Jan. 2003)
Secy. of State: Joyce Hazeltine, R (to Jan. 2003)
Auditor: Vern Larson, R (to Jan. 2003)
Treasurer: Richard Butler, D (to Jan. 2003)
Organized as territory: March 2, 1861

Entered Union (rank): Nov. 2, 1889 (40)
Present constitution adopted: 1889
Motto: Under God the people rule
State symbols: flower, American pasqueflower (1903);
grass, Western wheat grass (1970); **soil,** houdek
(1990); **tree,** black hills spruce (1947); **bird,**
ring-necked pheasant (1943); **insect,** honeybee
(1978); **animal,** coyote (1949); **mineral stone,** rose
quartz (1966); **gemstone,** fairburn agate (1966);
colors, blue and gold (in state flag); **song,** "Hail!
South Dakota" (1943); **fish,** walleye (1982); **musical
instrument,** fiddle (1989)
Nicknames: Mount Rushmore State; Coyote State
Origin of name: From the Sioux tribe, meaning "allies"
10 largest cities (1998 est.): Sioux Falls, 116,762;
Rapid City, 57,513; Aberdeen, 24,865; Watertown,
19,909; Brookings, 17,138; Mitchell, 14,386;
Yankton, 14,325; Pierre, 13,267; Vermillion, 11,967;
Huron, 11,778
Land area: 75,898 sq mi. (196,575 sq km)
Geographic center: In Hughes Co., 8 mi. NE of Pierre
Number of counties: 67 (64 county governments)
Largest county (1998 pop. est.): Minnehaha, 143,011
State forests: None[1]
State parks: 13 plus 39 recreational areas (87,269 ac.)[2]
1998 resident population est.: 738,171
1990 resident census population (rank): 696,004 (45).
Male: 342,498; **Female:** 353,506. **White:** 637,515
(91.6%); **Black:** 3,258 (0.5%); **American Indian:**
50,575 (7.3%); **Asian:** 3,123 (0.4%); **Other race:**
1,533 (0.2%); **Hispanic:** 5,252 (0.8%). **1990 percent
population under 18:** 28.5; **65 and over:** 14.7;
median age: 32.4.

1. No designated state forests; about 13,000 ac. of
state land is forestland. 2. Acreage includes 39 recreation areas and 80 roadside parks, in addition to 12
state parks.

Exploration of this area began in 1743 when
Louis-Joseph and François Verendrye came from
France in search of a route to the Pacific.

The U.S. acquired the region as part of the Louisiana Purchase in 1803 and it was explored by
Lewis and Clark in 1804–06. Fort Pierre, the first
permanent settlement, was established in 1817. In
1831, the first Missouri River steamboat reached the
fort.

Settlement of South Dakota did not begin in earnest
until the arrival of the railroad in 1873 and the discovery of gold in the Black Hills the following year.

South Dakota's economy in recent years has ben-
efitted from an expanding and diversifying industrial
base. Agriculture is a cultural and economic mainstay, but it no longer leads the state in employment
or share of gross state product. Durable-goods
manufacturing and private services have evolved as
the drivers of the economy. Tourism is also a booming industry in the state, generating approximately
$1.25 billion worth of economic activity each year.

South Dakota is the second largest producer of
flaxseed and sunflower seed in the nation. It is the
third largest producer of hay and rye.

South Dakota is the nation's second leading
producer of gold and the Homestake Mine is the
richest in the U.S. Other minerals produced
include berylium, bentonite, granite, silver, and
uranium.

The Black Hills are the highest mountains east of
the Rockies. Mt. Rushmore, in this group, is famous
for the likenesses of Washington, Jefferson, Lincoln,
and Theodore Roosevelt, which were carved in

granite by Gutzon Borglum. A memorial to Crazy
Horse is also being carved in granite near Custer.

Other tourist attractions include the Badlands; the
World's Only Corn Palace, in Mitchell; and the city
of Deadwood, where Wild Bill Hickok was killed in
1876 and where gambling was recently legalized to
truly recapture the city's Old West flavor.

Famous natives and residents: Sparky Anderson, baseball
manager; Gertrude Bonnin (Zitkala-Sa), Sioux writer and
pan-Indian activist; Tom Brokaw, TV newscaster; Robert
Casey, writer; Myron Floren, accordionist; Joseph J. Foss,
WW II Marine fighter ace; Mary Hart, TV host; Crazy
Horse, Oglala chief; Oscar Howe, Sioux artist; Hubert H.
Humphrey, former vice president; Cheryl Ladd, actress;
Ernest Orlando Lawrence, physicist; Russell Means,
American Indian activist; George McGovern, politician;
Arthur C. Mellette, first governor; Dorothy Provine, actress;
Rain-in-the-Face, Hunkpapa Sioux chief; Red Cloud, chief
of the Oglala Sioux; Ben Reifel, Brulé Sioux congressman;
Ole Edvart Rölvaag, writer; Sitting Bull, chief of
Hunkpappa Sioux; Norm Van Brocklin, football player;
Mamie Van Doren, actress.

Tennessee

Capital: Nashville
Governor: Don Sundquist, R (to Jan. 2003)
Lieut. Governor: John S. Wilder, D (to Jan. 2000)
Senators: William Frist, R (to Jan. 2001);
Fred Thompson, R (to Jan. 2003)
Secy. of State: Riley C. Darnell, D (to Jan. 2001)
Atty. General: Paul G. Summers, D (to Aug. 2005)
Treasurer: Steve Adams, D (to Jan. 2001)
Comptroller: John G. Morgan (to Jan. 2001)
Entered Union (rank): June 1, 1796 (16)
Present constitution adopted: 1870; amended 1953,
1960, 1966, 1972, 1978
Motto: Agriculture and Commerce (1987)
Slogan: Tennessee—America at its best! (1965)
State symbols: flower, iris (1933); **tree,** tulip poplar
(1947); **bird,** mockingbird (1933); **horse,** Tennessee
walking horse; **animal,** raccoon (1971); **wild flower,**
passion flower (1973); **songs,** "Tennessee Waltz"
(1965); "My Homeland, Tennessee" (1925); "When It's
Iris Time in Tennessee" (1935); "My Tennessee"
(1955); "Rocky Top" (1982); "Tennessee" (1992)
Nickname: Volunteer State
Origin of name: Of Cherokee origin; the exact meaning
is unknown
10 largest cities (1998 est.): Memphis, 603,507;
Nashville-Davidson (CC[1]), 510,274; Knoxville,
165,540; Chattanooga, 147,790; Clarksville, 97,978;
Murfreesboro, 58,430; Johnson City, 57,079; Jackson,
51,115; Kingsport, 41,139; Hendersonville, 38,625
Land area: 41,220 sq mi. (106,759 sq km)
Geographic center: In Rutherford Co., 5 mi. NE
of Murfreesboro
Number of counties: 95
Largest county (1998 pop. est.): Shelby, 868,825
State forests: 13 (155,000 ac.)
State parks: 50 (133,000 ac.)
1998 resident population est.: 5,430,621
1990 resident census population (rank): 4,877,185
(17). **Male:** 2,348,928; **Female:** 2,528,257. **White:**
4,048,068 (83.0%); **Black:** 778,035 (16.0%); **American Indian:** 10,039 (0.2%); **Asian:** 31,839 (0.7%);
Other race: 9,204 (0.2%); **Hispanic:** 32,741 (0.7%).
1990 percent population under 18: 24.9; **65 and
over:** 12.7; **median age:** 33.5.

1. Consolidated City.

First visited by the Spanish explorer Hernando de
Soto in 1540, the Tennessee area would later be
claimed by both France and England as a result of

the 1670s and 1680s explorations of Jacques Marquette and Louis Joliet, sieur de la Salle, and the Englishmen James Needham and Gabriel Arthur.

Great Britain obtained the region following the French and Indian Wars in 1763. It was rapidly occupied by settlers moving in from Virginia and the Carolinas.

During 1784–87, the settlers formed the "state" of Franklin, which was disbanded when the region was allowed to send representatives to the North Carolina legislature. In 1790 Congress organized the territory south of the Ohio River, and Tennessee joined the Union in 1796.

Although Tennessee joined the Confederacy during the Civil War, there was much pro-Union sentiment in the state, which was the scene of extensive military action.

The state is now predominantly industrial; the majority of its population lives in urban areas. Among the most important products are chemicals, textiles, apparel, electrical machinery, furniture, and leather goods. Other lines include food processing, lumber, primary metals, and metal products. The state is known as the U.S. hardwood-flooring center and ranks first in the production of marble, zinc, pyrite, and ball clay.

Tennessee is one of the leading tobacco-producing states in the nation. Its farming income is derived from livestock and dairy products, as well as corn, cotton, and soybeans.

With six other states, Tennessee shares the extensive federal reservoir developments on the Tennessee and Cumberland River systems. The Tennessee Valley Authority operates a number of dams and reservoirs in the state.

Among the major points of interest are the Andrew Johnson National Historic Site at Greenville, the American Museum of Atomic Energy at Oak Ridge, Great Smoky Mountains National Park, the Hermitage (home of Andrew Jackson near Nashville), Rock City Gardens near Chattanooga, and three National Military Parks.

Famous natives and residents: James Agee, writer; Eddy Arnold, singer; Chet Atkins, guitarist; Julian Bond, Georgia legislator; Davy Crockett, frontiersman; David G. Farragut, first American admiral; Lester Flatt, bluegrass musician; Tennessee Ernie Ford, singer; Abe Fortas, jurist; Aretha Franklin, singer; Nikki Giovanni, poet; Al Gore, Jr., vice president; Red Grooms, artist; Isaac Hayes, composer; Benjamin L. Hooks, civil rights activist; Cordell Hull, former secretary of state; Andrew Jackson, former president; Andrew Johnson, former president; Estes Kefauver, legislator; Anita Kerr, singer; Grace Moore, soprano; Dolly Parton, singer; Minnie Pearl, singer and comedienne; James K. Polk, president; Grantland Rice, sportswriter; Carl Rowan, journalist; Wilma Rudolph, sprinter; Sequoia, Cherokee scholar and educator; Cybil Shepherd, actress; Dinah Shore, actress and singer; Tina Turner, singer; Alvin York, World War I hero.

Texas

Capital: Austin
Governor: George W. Bush, R (to Jan. 2003)
Lieut. Governor: Rick Perry, R (to Jan. 2003)
Senators: Phil Gramm, R (to Jan. 2003);
  Kay Bailey Hutchison, R (to Jan. 2001)
Secy. of State: Alberto Gonzales (apptd. by gov.)
Comptroller: Carole Keeton Rylander, R (to Jan. 2003)
Atty. General: John Cornyn, R (to Jan. 2003)
Entered Union (rank): Dec. 29, 1845 (28)
Present constitution adopted: 1876
Motto: Friendship

State symbols: flower, bluebonnet (1901); **tree,** pecan (1919); **bird,** mockingbird (1927); **song,** "Texas, Our Texas" (1929); **fish,** guadalupe bass (1989); **seashell,** lightning whelk (1987); **dish,** chili (1977); **folk dance,** square dance (1991); **fruit,** Texas red grapefruit (1993); **gem,** Texas blue topaz (1969); **gemstone cut,** Lone Star cut (1977); **grass,** sideoats grass (1971); **reptile,** horned lizard (1993); **stone,** petrified palmwood (1969); **plant,** prickly pear cactus; **insect,** monarch butterfly; **pepper,** jalapeño pepper; **mammal,** longhorn; **small mammal,** armadillo; **flying mammal,** Mexican free-tailed bat
Nickname: Lone Star State
Origin of name: From an Indian word meaning "friends"
10 largest cities (1998 est.): Houston, 1,786,691; San Antonio, 1,114,130; Dallas, 1,075,894; El Paso, 615,032; Austin, 552,434; Fort Worth, 491,801; Arlington, 306,497; Corpus Christi, 281,453; Plano, 219,486; Garland, 193,408
Land area: 261,914 sq mi. (678,358 sq km)
Geographic center: In McCulloch Co., 15 mi. NE of Brady
Number of counties: 254
Largest county (1998 pop. est.): Harris, 3,206,063
State forests: 5 (7,609 ac.)
State parks: 123
1998 resident population est.: 19,759,614
1990 resident census population (rank): 16,986,510 (3). **Male:** 8,365,963; **Female:** 8,620,547. **White:** 12,774,762 (75.2%); **Black:** 2,021,632 (11.9%); **American Indian:** 65,877 (0.4%); **Asian:** 319,459 (1.9%); **Other race:** 1,804,780 (10.6%); **Hispanic:** 4,339,905 (25.5%). **1990 percent population under 18:** 28.5; **65 and over:** 10.1; **median age:** 30.6.

Spanish explorers, including Álvar Núñez Cabeza de Vaca and Francisco Vásquez de Coronado, were the first to visit the region in the 16th and 17th centuries, settling at Ysleta near El Paso in 1682. In 1685, sieur de la Salle established a short-lived French colony at Matagorda Bay.

Americans, led by Stephen F. Austin, began to settle along the Brazos River in 1821 when Texas was controlled by Mexico, recently independent from Spain. In 1836, following a brief war between the American settlers in Texas and the Mexican government, the Independent Republic of Texas was proclaimed with Sam Houston as president. This war was famous for the battles of the Alamo and San Jacinto. After Texas became the 28th U.S. state in 1845, border disputes led to the Mexican War of 1846–48.

Today, Texas, second only to Alaska in land area, leads all other states in such categories as oil, cattle, sheep, and cotton. Possessing enormous natural resources, Texas is a major agricultural state and an industrial giant.

Sulfur, salt, helium, asphalt, graphite, bromine, natural gas, cement, and clays are among the state's valuable resources. Chemicals, oil refining, food processing, machinery, and transportation equipment are among the major Texas manufacturing industries.

Texas ranches and farms produce beef cattle, poultry, rice, pecans, peanuts, sorghum, and an extensive variety of fruits and vegetables.

Millions of tourists spend well over $20.6 billion annually visiting 123 state parks, recreation areas, and points of interest such as the Gulf Coast resort area, the Lyndon B. Johnson Space Center in Houston, the Alamo in San Antonio, the state capital in Austin, and the Big Bend and Guadalupe Mountains National Park.

Famous natives and residents: Alvin Ailey, choreographer; Mary Kay Ash, cosmetics entrepreneur; Steven Fuller Austin, founding father of Texas; Gene Autry, singer and actor; Carol Burnett, comedienne; Cyd Charisse, actress and dancer; Denton A. Cooley, heart surgeon; Joan Crawford, actress; Dwight David Eisenhower, former president and general; A. J. Foyt, auto racer; Ben Hogan, golfer; Howard Hughes, industrialist and film producer; Jack Johnson, boxer; Lyndon B. Johnson, former president; George Jones, singer; Tommy Lee Jones, actor; Scott Joplin, composer; Trini Lopez, singer; Mary Martin, singer and actress; Spanky McFarland, actor; Audie Murphy, actor and war hero; Chester Nimitz, admiral; Sandra Day O'Connor, jurist; Buck Owens, singer; Selena Pérez, singer; Lou Diamond Phillips, actor; Katherine Anne Porter, novelist; Wiley Post, aviator; Dan Rather, TV newscaster; Robert Rauschenberg, painter; Tex Ritter, singer; Rip Torn, actor and director; Tommy Tune, dancer and choreographer; Lupe Velez, actress; Dooley Wilson, actor and musician; Babe Didrikson Zaharias, athlete and golfer.

Utah

Capital: Salt Lake City
Governor: Michael O. Leavitt, R (to Jan. 2001)
Lieut. Governor: Olene Walker, R (to Jan. 2001)
Senators: Robert F. Bennett, R (to Jan. 2005);
   Orrin G. Hatch, R (to Jan. 2001)
Atty. General: Jan Graham, D (to Jan. 2001)
Organized as territory: Sept. 9, 1850
Entered Union (rank): Jan. 4, 1896 (45)
Present constitution adopted: 1896
Motto: Industry
State symbols: flower, sego lily (1911); **tree,** blue spruce (1933); **bird,** California gull (1955); **emblem,** beehive (1959); **song,** "Utah, We Love Thee" (1953); **gem,** topaz; **animal,** Rocky Mountain elk (1971); **insect,** honeybee (1983); **grass,** Indian rice grass (1990); **fossil,** allosaurus (1988); **cooking pot,** dutch oven (1997); **fish,** Bonneville cutthroat trout (1997); **fruit,** cherry (1997); **mineral,** copper; **rock,** coal (1991)
Nickname: Beehive State
Origin of name: From the Ute tribe, meaning "people of the mountains"
10 largest cities (1998 est.): Salt Lake City, 174,348; Provo, 110,419; West Valley City, 99,372; Sandy, 99,186; Orem, 78,937; Ogden, 66,507; West Jordan, 60,804; Taylorsville, 56,753; Layton, 55,112; St. George, 46,186
Land area: 82,168 sq mi. (212,816 sq km)
Geographic center: In Sanpete Co., 3 mi. N. of Manti
Number of counties: 29
Largest county (1998 pop. est.): Salt Lake, 850,667
National parks: 5
National monuments: 7
State parks/forests: 45 (64,097 ac.)
1998 resident population est.: 2,099,758
1990 resident census population (rank): 1,722,850 (35). **Male:** 855,759; **Female:** 867,091. **White:** 1,615,845 (93.8%); **Black:** 11,576 (0.7%); **American Indian:** 24,283 (1.4%); **Asian:** 33,371 (1.9%); **Other race:** 37,775 (2.2%); **Hispanic:** 84,597 (4.9%). **1990 percent population under 18:** 36.4; **65 and over:** 8.7; **median age:** 26.2.

The region was first explored for Spain by Franciscan friars Escalante and Dominguez in 1776. In 1824 the famous American frontiersman Jim Bridger discovered the Great Salt Lake.

Fleeing the religious persecution encountered in eastern and middle-western states, the Mormons reached the Great Salt Lake in 1847 and began to build Salt Lake City. The U.S. acquired the Utah region in the treaty ending the Mexican War in 1848, and the first transcontinental railroad was completed with the driving of a golden spike at Promontory Summit in 1869.

Mormon difficulties with the federal government about polygamy did not end until the Mormon Church renounced the practice in 1890, six years before Utah became a state.

Rich in natural resources, Utah has long been a leading producer of copper, gold, silver, lead, zinc, and molybdenum. Oil has also become a major product. Utah shares rich oil shale deposits with Colorado and Wyoming. Utah also has large deposits of low sulphur coal.

Ranked eighth among the states in number of sheep in 1989, Utah also produces large crops of alfalfa, winter wheat, and beans.

Utah's traditional industries of agriculture and mining are complemented by increased tourism business and growing aerospace, biomedical, and computer-related businesses. Utah is home to computer software giant Novell.

Utah is a great vacationland with 11,000 miles of fishing streams and 147,000 acres of lakes and reservoirs. Among the many tourist attractions are Arches, Bryce Canyon, Canyonlands, Capitol Reef, and Zion National Parks; Cedar Breaks, Dinosaur, Howenweeg, Natural Bridges, Rainbow Bridge, Timpanogos Cave, and Grand Staircase (Escalante) National Monuments; the Mormon Tabernacle in Salt Lake City; and Monument Valley. Salt Lake City will be the site of the 2002 Winter Olympics.

Famous natives and residents: Maude Adams, actress; Roseanne, actress; Frank Borzage, film director and producer; John M. Browning, inventor; Butch Cassidy, outlaw; Laraine Day, actress; Bernard De Voto, writer; Avard Fairbanks, sculptor; Philo Farnsworth, television pioneer; Jake Garn, senator; John Gilbert, actor; J. Willard Marriott, restaurant and hotel chain founder; Peter Skene Ogden, fur trader and trapper; Merlin Olsen, football player; Donny Osmond, Marie Osmond, singers; Ivy Baker Priest, former U.S. treasurer; Lee Greene Richards, painter; Leroy Robertson, composer; Brent Scowcroft, business executive and consultant; Reed Smoot, first Mormon elected to U.S. Senate; Mack Swain, actor; Everett Thorpe, painter; Robert Walker, actor; James Woods, actor; Brigham Young, territory governor and religious leader; Loretta Young, actress.

Vermont

Capital: Montpelier
Governor: Howard Dean, D (to Jan. 2001)
Lieut. Governor: Douglas A. Racine, D (to Jan. 2001)
Senators: James M. Jeffords, R (to Jan. 2001);
   Patrick Leahy, D (to Jan. 2005)
Secy. of State: Deb Markowitz, D (to Jan. 2001)
Treasurer: James H. Douglas, R (to Jan. 2001)
Auditor of Accounts: Edward S. Flanagan, D (to Jan. 2001)
Atty. General: William Sorrell, D (to Jan. 2001)
Entered Union (rank): March 4, 1791 (14)
Present constitution adopted: 1793
Motto: Vermont, Freedom and Unity
State symbols: flower, red clover (1894); **tree,** sugar maple (1949); **bird,** hermit thrush (1941); **animal,** Morgan horse (1961); **insect,** honeybee (1978); **song,** "Hail, Vermont!" (1938)
Nickname: Green Mountain State
Origin of name: From the French "vert mont," meaning "green mountain"
10 largest cities (1998): Burlington, 38,453; Rutland, 17,348; South Burlington, 14,037; Barre, 9,066; Essex Junction, 8,705; Montpelier, 7,734; St. Albans, 7,308; Winooski, 6,619; Newport, 4,537; Bellows Falls, 3,231

Land area: 9,249 sq mi. (23,956 sq km)
Geographic center: In Washington Co., 3 mi.
E of Roxbury
Number of counties: 14
Largest county (1998 pop. est.): Chittenden, 142,642
State forests: 34 (113,953 ac.)
State parks: 45 (31,325 ac.)
1998 resident population est.: 590,883
1990 resident census population (rank): 562,758 (48).
Male: 275,492; **Female:** 287,266. **White:** 555,088
(98.6%); **Black:** 1,951 (0.3%); **American Indian:**
1,696 (0.3%); **Asian:** 3,215 (0.6%); **Other race:** 808
(0.1%); **Hispanic:** 3,661 (0.7%). **1990 percent population under 18:** 25.4; **65 and over:** 11.8;
median age: 32.9.

The Vermont region was explored and claimed for
France by Samuel de Champlain in 1609 and the first
French settlement was established at Fort Ste. Anne
in 1666. The first English settlers moved into the
area in 1724 and built Fort Dummer on the site of
present-day Brattleboro. England gained control of
the area in 1763 after the French and Indian Wars.

First organized to drive settlers from New York
out of Vermont, the Green Mountain Boys, led by
Ethan Allen, won fame by capturing Fort Ticonderoga from the British on May 10, 1775, in the early
days of the Revolutionary War.

In 1777 Vermont adopted its first constitution abolishing slavery and providing for universal male suffrage without property qualifications. In 1791 Vermont became the fourteenth state to join the Union.

Vermont leads the nation in the production of
monument granite, marble, and maple syrup. It is
also a leader in the production of talc.

Vermont's rugged, rocky terrain discourages
extensive agricultural farming, but is well suited to
raising fruit trees, and to dairy farming. Vermont has
the highest proportion of dairy cows to humans in
the nation.

Principal industrial products include electrical
equipment, fabricated metal products, printing and
publishing, and paper and allied products.

Tourism is a major industry in Vermont. Vermont's
many famous ski areas include Stowe, Killington,
Mt. Snow, Bromley, Jay Peak, and Sugarbush. Hunting and fishing also attract many visitors to Vermont
each year. Among the many points of interest are the
Green Mountain National Forest, Bennington Battle
Monument, the Calvin Coolidge Homestead at Plymouth, and the Marble Exhibit in Proctor.

Famous natives and residents: Chester A. Arthur, former
president; Orson Bean, actor; Calvin Coolidge, former
president; George Dewey, admiral; John Dewey,
philosopher and educator; Stephen A. Douglas, politician;
James Fisk, financial speculator; Wilbur Fisk, clergyman
and educator; Richard Morris Hunt, architect; William
Morris Hunt, painter; Elisha Otis, inventor; Moses
Pendleton, choreographer; Joseph Smith, religious leader;
Ernest Thompson, actor and writer; Rudy Vallee, singer
and band leader; Henry Wells, pioneer entrepreneur (Wells
Fargo & Co.); Brigham Young, religious leader.

Virginia

Capital: Richmond
Governor: James S. Gilmore, R (to Jan. 2002)
Lieut. Governor: John H. Hager, R (to Jan. 2002)
Senators: Charles Robb, D (to Jan. 2001);
John Warner, R (to Jan. 2003)
Secy. of the Commonwealth: Anne P. Petera (apptd. by
governor)
Comptroller: William E. Landsidle (apptd. by governor)

Atty. General: Mark L. Earley
Entered Union (rank): June 25, 1788 (10)
Present constitution adopted: 1970
Motto: *Sic semper tyrannis* (Thus always to tyrants)
State symbols: flower, American dogwood (1918); **bird,**
cardinal (1950); **dog,** American foxhound (1966);
shell, oyster shell (1974); **tree,** dogwood (1956)
Nicknames: The Old Dominion; Mother of Presidents
Origin of name: In honor of Elizabeth "Virgin Queen" of
England
10 largest cities (1998 est.): Virginia Beach, 432,380;
Norfolk, 215,215; Chesapeake, 199,564; Richmond,
194,173; Newport News, 178,615; Arlington CDP,
177,275; Hampton, 136,968; Alexandria, 118,300;
Portsmouth, 98,936; Roanoke, 93,749
Land area: 39,598 sq mi. (102,558 sq km)
Geographic center: In Buckingham Co., 5 mi. SW of
Buckingham
Number of counties: 95, plus 40 independent cities
Largest county (1998 pop. est.): Fairfax, 929,239
State forests: 11 (50,636 ac.)
State parks and recreational parks: 43
1998 resident population est.: 6,791,345
1990 resident census population (rank): 6,187,358
(12). **Male:** 3,033,974; **Female:** 3,153,384. **White:**
4,791,739 (77.4%); **Black:** 1,162,994 (18.8%); **American Indian:** 15,282 (0.2%); **Asian:** 159,053 (2.6%);
Other race: 58,290 (0.9%); **Hispanic:** 160,288 (2.6%).
1990 percent population under 18: 24.3; **65 and
over:** 10.7; **median age:** 32.5.

The history of America is closely tied to that of
Virginia, particularly in the Colonial period.
Jamestown, founded in 1607, was the first permanent English settlement in North America and slavery was introduced there in 1619. The surrenders
ending both the American Revolution (Yorktown)
and the Civil War (Appomattox) occurred in Virginia. The state is called the "Mother of Presidents"
because eight chief executives of the United States
were born there.

Today, Virginia has a large number of diversified
manufacturing industries, including transportation
equipment, textiles, food processing, and printing.
Other important lines are electronic and other electrical equipment, chemicals, apparel, lumber and
wood products, furniture, and industrial machinery
and equipment.

Agriculture remains an important sector in the
Virginia economy and the state ranks among the top
10 in the U.S. in tomatoes, tobacco, peanuts, summer potatoes, turkeys, apples, broilers, and sweet
potatoes. Other crops include corn, vegetables, and
barley. Famous for Smithfield hams, Virginia also
has a large dairy industry.

Coal mining accounts for roughly 75% of Virginia's mineral output, and lime, kyanite, and stone are
also mined.

Points of interest include Mt. Vernon and other
places associated with George Washington; Monticello, home of Thomas Jefferson; Stratford, home
of the Lees; Richmond, capital of the Confederacy
and of Virginia; and Williamsburg, the restored
Colonial capital.

The Chesapeake Bay Bridge-Tunnel spans the
mouth of Chesapeake Bay, connecting Cape Charles
with Norfolk. Consisting of a series of low trestles,
two bridges and two mile-long tunnels, the complex
is 18 miles (29 km) long. It was opened in 1964.

Other attractions are the Shenandoah National
Park, Fredericksburg and Spotsylvania National

Military Park, the Booker T. Washington birthplace near Roanoke, Arlington House (the Robert E. Lee Memorial), the Skyline Drive, and the Blue Ridge National Parkway.

Famous natives and residents: Richard Arlen, actor; Arthur Ashe, tennis player; Pearl Bailey, singer; Russell Baker, columnist; Warren Beatty, actor; George Bingham, painter; Richard E. Byrd, polar explorer; Willa Cather, novelist; Roy Clark, country music artist; William Clark, explorer; Henry Clay, statesman; Joseph Cotten, actor; Ella Fitzgerald, singer; William H. Harrison, former president; Patrick Henry, statesman; Sam Houston, political leader; Thomas Jefferson, former president; Robert E. Lee, Confederate general; Meriwether Lewis, explorer; Shirley MacLaine, actress; James Madison, former president; John Marshall, jurist; Cyrus McCormick, inventor; James Monroe, former president; Opechancanough, Powhatan leader; John Payne, actor; Walter Reed, army surgeon; Matthew Ridgway, former Army Chief of Staff; Bill "Bojangles" Robinson, dancer; George C. Scott, actor; Sam Snead, golfer; James "Jeb" Stuart, Confederate army officer; Zachary Taylor, former president; Nat Turner, leader of slave uprising; John Tyler, former president; Booker T. Washington, educator; George Washington, first president; Woodrow Wilson, former president; Tom Wolfe, journalist.

Washington

Capital: Olympia
Governor: Gary Locke, D (to 2001)
Lieut. Governor: Brad Owen, D (to 2001)
Senators: Slade Gorton, R (to Jan. 2001);
 Patty Murray, D (to Jan. 2005)
Secy. of State: Ralph Munro, R (to 2001)
State Treasurer: Michael J. Murphy (to 2001)
Atty. General: Christine Gregoire, D (to 2001)
Organized as territory: March 2, 1853
Entered Union (rank): Nov. 11, 1889 (42)
Present constitution adopted: 1889
Motto: Al-Ki (Indian word meaning "by and by")
State symbols: flower, coast rhododendron (1949); **tree,** western hemlock (1947); **bird,** willow goldfinch (1951); **fish,** steelhead trout (1969); **gem,** petrified wood (1975); **colors,** green and gold (1925); **song,** "Washington, My Home" (1959); **folk song,** "Roll On Columbia, Roll On" (1987); **dance,** square dance (1979)
Nicknames: Evergreen State; Chinook State
Origin of name: In honor of George Washington
10 largest cities (1998 est.): Seattle, 536,978; Spokane, 184,058; Tacoma, 179,814; Bellevue, 104,052; Everett, 88,625; Federal Way, 74,254; Vancouver, 73,526; Lakewood, 65,933; Yakima, 64,967; Bellingham, 61,894
Land area: 66,582 sq mi. (172,447 sq km)
Geographic center: In Chelan Co., 10 mi. WSW of Wenatchee
Number of counties: 39
Largest county (1998 pop. est.): King, 1,654,876
State forest lands: 1,922,880 ac.
State parks: 215 (231,861 ac.)[1]
1998 resident population est.: 5,689,263
1990 resident census population (rank): 4,866,692 (18). **Male:** 2,413,747; **Female:** 2,452,945. **White:** 4,308,937 (88.5%); **Black:** 149,801 (3.1%); **American Indian:** 81,483 (1.7%); **Other race:** 115,513 (2.4%); **Hispanic:** 214,570 (4.4%). **1990 percent population under 18:** 25.9; **65 and over:** 11.8; **median age:** 33.0.

1. Parks and undeveloped areas administered by State Parks and Recreation Commission. Dept. of Wildlife administers wildlife and recreation areas totaling 428,989.5 acres.

As part of the vast Oregon Country, Washington territory was visited by Spanish, American, and British explorers—Bruno Heceta for Spain in 1775, the American Capt. Robert Gray in 1792, and Capt. George Vancouver for Britain in 1792–1794. Lewis and Clark explored the Columbia River region and coastal areas for the U.S. in 1805–1806.

Rival American and British settlers and conflicting territorial claims threatened war in the early 1840s. However, in 1846 the Oregon Treaty set the boundary at the 49th parallel and war was averted.

Washington is a leading lumber producer. Its rugged surface is rich in stands of Douglas fir, hemlock, ponderosa and white pine, spruce, larch, and cedar. The state holds first place in apples, lentils, dry edible peas, hops, pears, red raspberries, spearmint oil, and sweet cherries, and ranks high in apricots, asparagus, grapes, peppermint oil, and potatoes. Livestock and livestock products make important contributions to total farm revenue and the commercial fishing catch of salmon, halibut, and bottomfish makes a significant contribution to the state's economy.

Manufacturing industries in Washington include aircraft and missiles, shipbuilding and other transportation equipment, lumber, food processing, metals and metal products, chemicals, and machinery.

The Columbia River contains one-third of the potential water power in the U.S., harnessed by such dams as the Grand Coulee, one of the greatest power producers in the world. Washington has over 1,000 dams built for a variety of purposes including irrigation, power, flood control, and water storage. Its abundance of electrical power makes Washington one of the nation's major producers of refined aluminum.

Among the major points of interest: Mt. Rainier, Olympic, and North Cascades National Parks. In 1980, Mount St. Helens, a peak in the Cascade Range in Southwestern Washington, erupted on May 18th. Also of interest are Whitman Mission and Fort Vancouver National Historic Sites; and the Pacific Science Center and the Space Needle, in Seattle.

Famous natives and residents: Bob Barker, TV host; Dyan Cannon, actress; Carol Channing, actress; Judy Collins, singer; Bing Crosby, singer and actor; Bob Crosby, musician; Merce Cunningham, choreographer; Howard Duff, actor; Frances Farmer, actress; Bill Gates, software executive; Jimi Hendrix, guitarist; Frank Herbert, writer; Robert Joffrey, choreographer; Gypsy Rose Lee, entertainer; Hank Ketcham, cartoonist; Mary McCarthy, novelist; Guthrie McClintic, theatrical producer and director; John McIntire, actor; Robert Motherwell, artist; Patrice Munsel, soprano; Ella Raines, actress; Jimmy Rogers, singer; Francis Scobee, astronaut; Seattle, Dwamish, Suquamish chief; Jeff Smith, TV cook; Smohalla, Indian prophet and chief; Adam West, actor; Martha Wright, singer; Audrey Wurdemann, poet.

West Virginia

Capital: Charleston
Governor: Cecil H. Underwood, R (to Jan. 2001)
Senators: Robert C. Byrd, D (to Jan. 2001);
 John D. "Jay" Rockefeller IV, D (to Jan. 2003)
Secy. of State: Ken Heckler, D
State Auditor: Glen Gainer
Atty. General: Darrell McGraw, D
Entered Union (rank): June 20, 1863 (35)
Present constitution adopted: 1872
Motto: Montani semper liberi (Mountaineers are always free)
State symbols: flower, rhododendron (1903); **tree,** sugar maple (1949); **bird,** cardinal (1949); **animal,** black bear (1973); **colors,** blue and gold (official) (1863); **songs,** "West Virginia, My Home Sweet Home," "The West Virginia Hills," and "This Is My West Virginia" (adopted by Legislature in 1947, 1961, and 1963 as official state songs)
Nickname: Mountain State

Origin of name: In honor of Elizabeth, "Virgin Queen" of England
10 largest cities (1998 est.): Charleston, 55,056; Huntington, 52,571; Wheeling, 32,541; Parkersburg, 31,715; Morgantown, 26,751; Weirton, 21,206; Fairmont, 19,088; Beckley, 18,187; Clarksburg, 17,011; Martinsburg, 15,049
Land area: 24,087 sq mi. (62,384 sq km)
Geographic center: In Braxton Co., 4 mi. E of Sutton
Number of counties: 55
Largest county (1998 pop. est.): Kanawha, 202,011
State forests: 9 (79,502 ac.)
State parks: 35 (74,508 ac.)
1998 resident population est.: 1,811,156
1990 resident census population (rank): 1,793,477 (34). **Male:** 861,536; **Female:** 931,941. **White:** 1,725,523 (96.2%); **Black:** 56,295 (3.1%); **American Indian:** 2,458 (0.1%); **Asian:** 7,459 (0.4%); **Other race:** 1,742 (0.1%); **Hispanic:** 8,489 (0.5%). **1990 percent population under 18:** 24.7; **65 and over:** 15.0; **median age:** 35.3.

West Virginia's early history from 1609 until 1863 is largely shared with Virginia, of which it was a part until Virginia seceded from the Union in 1861. Then the delegates of 40 western counties formed their own government, which was granted statehood in 1863.

First permanent settlement dates from 1731 when Morgan Morgan founded Mill Creek. In 1742 coal was discovered on the Coal River, an event that would be of great significance in determining West Virginia's future.

The state usually ranks third in total coal production with about 15% of the U.S. total. It also is a leader in steel, glass, aluminum, and chemical manufactures; natural gas; oil; quarry products; and hardwood lumber.

Major cash farm products are poultry and eggs, dairy products, apples, and feed crops. Nearly 75% of West Virginia is covered with forests.

Tourism is increasingly popular in mountainous West Virginia and visitors spent $2.475 billion in 1990. More than a million acres have been set aside in 35 state parks and recreation areas and in 9 state forests and national forests.

Major points of interest include Harpers Ferry and New River Gorge National River, The Greenbrier and Berkeley Springs resorts, the scenic railroad at Cass, and the historic homes in the Eastern Panhandle.

Famous natives and residents: George Brett, baseball player; Pearl S. Buck, author; Phyllis Curtin, soprano; Martin R. Delany, first Black Army major; Billy Dixon, frontiersman and scout; Joanne Dru, actress; Thomas "Stonewall" Jackson, Confederate general; John S. Knight, publisher; Don Knotts, actor; Peter Marshall, TV host; Kathy Mattea, country music superstar; Whitney D. Morrow, banker and diplomat; Mary Lou Retton, gymnast; Walter Reuther, labor leader; Eleanor Steber, soprano; Lewis L. Strauss, naval officer and scientist; Cyrus Vance, government official; William Lyne Wilson, legislator and university president; Chuck Yeager, test pilot and Air Force general.

Wisconsin

Capital: Madison
Governor: Tommy G. Thompson, R (to Jan. 2003)
Lieut. Governor: Scott McCallum, R (to Jan. 2003)
Senators: Russell D. Feingold, D (to Jan. 2005); Herb Kohl, D (to Jan. 2001)
Secy. of State: Douglas J. La Follette, D (to Jan. 2003)
State Treasurer: Jack C. Voight, R (to Jan. 2003)
Atty. General: James E. Doyle, D (to Jan. 2003)
Superintendent of Public Instruction: John Benson, Nonpartisan (to July 2001)
Organized as territory: July 4, 1836
Entered Union (rank): May 29, 1848 (30)
Present constitution adopted: 1848
Motto: Forward
State symbols: flower, wood violet (1949); **tree,** sugar maple (1949); **grain,** corn (1990); **bird,** robin (1949); **animal,** badger; **wild life animal,** white-tailed deer (1957); **domestic animal,** dairy cow (1971); **insect,** honeybee (1977); **fish,** musky (muskellunge) (1955); **song,** "On Wisconsin"; **mineral,** galena (1971); **rock,** red granite (1971); **symbol of peace:** mourning dove (1971); **soil,** antigo silt loam (1983); **fossil,** trilobite (1985); **dog,** American Water Spaniel (1986); **beverage,** milk (1988); **dance,** polka (1994)
Nickname: Badger State
Origin of name: French corruption of an Indian word whose meaning is disputed
10 largest cities (1998 est.): Milwaukee, 578,364; Madison, 209,306; Green Bay, 97,789; Kenosha, 87,849; Racine, 81,095; Appleton, 65,514; Waukesha, 61,989; West Allis, 59,974; Eau Claire, 59,200; Janesville, 59,149
Land area: 54,314 sq mi. (140,673 sq km)
Geographic center: In Wood Co., 9 mi. SE of Marshfield
Number of counties: 78
Largest county (1998 pop. est.): Milwaukee, 911,713
State forests: 9 (476,004 ac.)
State parks & scenic trails: 45 parks, 14 trails (66,185 ac.)
1998 resident population est.: 5,223,500
1990 resident census population (rank): 4,891,769 (16). **Male:** 2,392,935; **Female:** 2,498,834. **White:** 4,512,523 (92.2%); **Black:** 244,539 (5.0%); **American Indian:** 39,387 (0.8%); **Asian:** 53,583 (1.1%); **Other race:** 41,737 (0.9%); **Hispanic:** 93,194 (1.9%). **1980 percent population under 18:** 26.4; **65 and over:** 13.3; **median age:** 32.8.

The Wisconsin region was first explored for France by Jean Nicolet, who landed at Green Bay in 1634. In 1660 a French trading post and Roman Catholic mission were established near present-day Ashland.

Great Britain obtained the region in settlement of the French and Indian Wars in 1763; the U.S. acquired it in 1783 after the Revolutionary War. However, Great Britain retained actual control until after the War of 1812. The region was successively governed as part of the territories of Indiana, Illinois, and Michigan between 1800 and 1836, when it became a separate territory.

Wisconsin is a leading state in milk and cheese production. In 1996 the state ranked first in the number of milk cows (1,410,000) and produced 29% of the nation's total output of cheese. Other important farm products are peas, beans, beets, corn, potatoes, oats, hay, and cranberries.

The chief industrial products of the state are automobiles, machinery, furniture, paper, beer, and processed foods. Wisconsin ranks second among the 47 paper-producing states.

Wisconsin is a pioneer in social legislation, providing pensions for the blind (1907), aid to dependent children (1913), and old-age assistance (1925). In labor legislation, the state was the first to enact an unemployment compensation law (1932) and the first in which a workman's compensation law actually took effect. Wisconsin had the first state-wide primary-election law and the first successful income-tax law. In April 1984, Wisconsin became the first state to adopt the Uniform Marital Property Act. The act took effect on January 1, 1986.

The state has over 14,000 lakes, of which Winnebago is the largest. Water sports, ice-boating, and fishing are popular, as are skiing and hunting. Public parks and forests take up one-seventh of the land, with 45 state parks, 9 state forests, 14 state trails, 3 recreational areas, and 2 national forests.

Among the many points of interest are the Apostle Islands National Lakeshore; Ice Age National Scientific Reserve; the Circus World Museum at Baraboo; the Wolf, St. Croix, and Lower St. Croix national scenic riverways; and the Wisconsin Dells.

Famous natives and residents: Don Ameche, actor; Ray Chapman Andrews, naturalist and explorer; Walter Annenberg, media tycoon and philanthropist; Carrie Catt, woman suffragist; John R. Commons, economist; Tyne Daly, actress; August Derleth, author; Jeanne Dixon, seer; Zona Gale, novelist; Eric Heiden, skater; Woody Herman, band leader; Hildegarde, singer; Harry Houdini, magician; Hans V. Kaltenborne, journalist; Pee Wee King, singer; George F. Kennan, diplomat; Robert La Follette, politician; William D. Leahy, Fleet Admiral; Liberace, pianist; Charles Litel, actor; Allen Ludden, TV host; Alfred Lunt, actor; Frederic March, actor; Jackie Mason, comedian; John Ringling North, circus director; Pat O'Brien, actor; Georgia O'Keeffe, painter; Charlotte Rae, actress; William H. Rehnquist, jurist; Gena Rowlands, actress; Tom Snyder, newscaster; Spencer Tracy, actor; Thorstein Veblen, economist; Orson Welles, actor and producer; Thornton Wilder, author; Charles Winninger, actor; Frank Lloyd Wright, architect.

Wyoming

Capital: Cheyenne
Governor: Jim Geringer, R (to Jan. 2003)
Senators: Michael B. Enzi, R (to Jan. 2003); Craig Thomas, R (to Jan. 2001)
Secy. of State: Joe Meyer, R (to Jan. 2003)
Auditor: Max Maxfield, R (to Jan. 2003)
Supt. of Public Instruction: Judy Catchpole, R (to Jan. 2003)
Treasurer: Cynthia M. Lummis, R (to Jan. 2003)
Atty. General: Bill Hill, R (apptd. by Governor)
Organized as territory: May 19, 1869
Entered Union (rank): July 10, 1890 (44)
Present constitution adopted: 1890
Motto: Equal rights (1955)
State symbols: flower, Indian paintbrush (1917); **tree,** cottonwood (1947); **bird,** meadowlark (1927); **gemstone,** jade (1967); **insignia,** bucking horse (unofficial); **song,** "Wyoming" (1955)
Nickname: Equality State
Origin of name: From the Delaware Indian word, meaning "mountains and valleys alternating"; the same as the Wyoming Valley in Pennsylvania
10 largest cities (1998 est.): Cheyenne, 53,640; Casper, 48,283; Laramie, 25,035; Gillette, 19,463; Rock Springs, 19,408; Sheridan, 14,591; Green River, 13,059; Evanston, 11,475; Riverton, 10,126; Cody, 8,807
Land area: 97,105 sq mi. (251,501 sq km)
Geographic center: In Fremont Co., 58 mi. ENE of Lander
Number of counties: 23, plus Yellowstone National Park

Largest county (1998 pop. est.): Laramie, 78,872
State parks and historic sites: 23 (58,498 ac.)
1998 resident population est.: 480,907
1990 resident census population (rank): 453,588 (50). **Male:** 227,007; **Female:** 226,581. **White:** 427,061 (94.2%); **Black:** 3,606 (0.8%); **American Indian:** 9,479 (2.1%); **Asian:** 2.806 (0.6%); **Other race:** 10,636 (2.3%); **Hispanic:** 25,751 (5.7%). **1990 percent population under 18:** 29.9; **65 and over:** 10.4; **median age:** 32.0.

The U.S. acquired the land comprising Wyoming from France as part of the Louisiana Purchase in 1803. John Colter, a fur-trapper, is the first white man known to have entered present Wyoming. In 1807 he explored the Yellowstone area and brought back news of its geysers and hot springs.

Robert Stuart pioneered the Oregon Trail across Wyoming in 1812–13 and, in 1834, Fort Laramie, the first permanent trading post in Wyoming, was built. Western Wyoming was obtained by the U.S. in the 1846 Oregon Treaty with Great Britain and as a result of the treaty ending the Mexican War in 1848.

When the Wyoming Territory was organized in 1869 Wyoming women became the first in the nation to obtain the right to vote. In 1925 Mrs. Nellie Tayloe Ross was elected first woman governor in the United States.

Wyoming's towering mountains and vast plains provide spectacular scenery, grazing lands for sheep and cattle, and rich mineral deposits.

Mining, particularly oil and natural gas, is the most important industry. Wyoming has the world's largest sodium carbonate (natrona) deposits and has the nation's second largest uranium deposits.

Wyoming ranks second among the states in wool production. In January 1995, it ranked third in sheep and lambs, exceeded only by Texas and California; it also had 1,410,000 cattle. Principal crops include wheat, oats, sugar beets, corn, potatoes, barley, and alfalfa.

Second in mean elevation to Colorado, Wyoming has many attractions for the tourist trade, notably Yellowstone National Park. Cheyenne is famous for its annual "Frontier Days" celebration. Flaming Gorge, the Fort Laramie National Historic Site, and Devils Tower and Fossil Butte National Monuments are other points of interest.

Famous natives and residents: James Bridger, trapper, guide and storyteller; Dick Cheney, former Secretary of Defense; Buffalo Bill Cody, scout; John Colter, trader and first white man to enter Wyoming; June E. Downey, educator; Thomas Fitzpatrick, mountain man and guide; Curt Gowdy, sportscaster; Tom Horn, detective; Isabel Jewell, actress; Velma Linford, writer; Esther Morris, first woman judge; Ted Olson, writer; John "Portugee" Phillips, frontiersman; Jackson Pollock, painter; Nellie Tayloe Ross, first woman elected governor of a state; Alan K. Simpson, senator; Jedediah S. Smith, mountain man and first American to reach California from the East; Alan Swallow, publisher and author; Willis Van Devanter, Supreme Court justice; Francis E. Warren, first state governor; Chief Washakie, chief of the Shoshone; James G. Watt, former secretary of the Interior.

Tabulated Data on State Governments

State	Governor Term, years	Governor Annual salary	Legislature[1] Membership U[3]	Legislature[1] Membership L[4]	Legislature[1] Term, years U[3]	Legislature[1] Term, years L[4]	Legislature[1] Salaries of members[5]		Highest Court[2] Members	Highest Court[2] Term, years	Highest Court[2] Annual salary
Alabama	4[6]	$ 87,643	35	105	4	4	$ 10	per diem	9	6	$115,695[7]
Alaska	4	81,648	20	40	4	2	24,012[8]	per annum	5	3[9]	99,996[7]
Arizona	4	75,000	30	60	2	2	15,000	per annum	5	6	114,257[7]
Arkansas	4	60,000	35	100	4	2	12,500	per annum	7	8	95,216[7]
California	4	114,000	40	80	4	2	72,500	per annum	7	12	127,276[7]
Colorado	4	70,000	35	65	4	2	17,500	per annum	7	10	91,000[7]
Connecticut	4	78,000	36	151	2	2	16,760	per annum	7	8	113,042[7]
Delaware	4[10]	107,000	21	41	4	2	28,300	per annum	5	12	121,200[7]
Florida	4[6]	110,962	40	120	4[6]	2[11]	26,388	per annum	7	6	137,314
Georgia[6]	4	111,480	56	180	2	2	11,348	per annum	7	6	124,310
Hawaii	4	94,780	25	51	4	2	32,000	per annum	5	10	93,780[7]
Idaho	4	92,500	35	70	2	2	12,360[8]	per annum	5	6	90,791[7]
Illinois	4	114,439	59	118	4-2	2	50,802	per annum	7	10	122,892
Indiana	4[6]	77,200	50	100	4	2	11,600	per annum	5	2[9]	81,000
Iowa	4	98,300	50	100	4	2	20,120	per annum	9	8	106,700[7]
Kansas	4	80,355	40	125	4	2	138	per diem[12]	7	6	82,005[7]
Kentucky	4	95,525	38	100	4	2	151	per diem[13]	7	8	103,741[7]
Louisiana	4	95,000	39	105	4	4	16,800	per annum	7	10	85,000
Maine	4	70,000	35	151	2	2	18,000	per biennium	7	7	80,392
Maryland	4[6]	120,000	47	141	4	4	29,700	per annum	7	10	107,300[7]
Massachusetts	4	100,000	40	160	2	2	46,410	per annum	7	(15)	95,880[7]
Michigan	4	127,300	38	110	4	2	53,192	per annum	7	8	124,770
Minnesota	4	114,000	67	134	4[15]	2	27,979	per annum	7	6	83,494
Mississippi	4	83,160	52	122	4	4	10,000	per session	9	8	90,800[7]
Missouri	4[10]	107,269	34	163	4[16]	2	27,580	per annum	7	12	108,783[7]
Montana	4	59,310	50	100	4	2	55	per diem	7	8	68,874
Nebraska	4[6]	65,000	49[17]	—	4[17]	—	12,000	per annum	7	6	101,649
Nevada	4	90,000	21	42	4	2	7,800	per biennium	5	6	107,600
New Hampshire	2	86,235	24	(18)	2	2	200	per biennium	5	(14)	95,628[7]
New Jersey	4[6]	130,000[19]	40	80	4[16]	2	35,000	per annum	7	7[20]	128,800[7]
New Mexico	4[6]	90,000	42	70	4	2	104	per diem	5	8	79,567[7]
New York	4	130,000	61	150	2	2	57,500	per annum	7	14	125,000[7]
North Carolina	4[6]	91,938	50	120	2	2	13,026	per annum	7	8	89,532[7]
North Dakota	4	75,372	49	98	4	4	111	per diem[21]	5	10	82,164[7]
Ohio	4	115,752	33	99	4	2	42,427	per annum	7	6	101,150[7]
Oklahoma	4	101,140	48	101	4	2	38,400	per annum	(22)	6	97,807[7]
Oregon	4[6]	80,000	30	60	4	2	1,092	per month	7	6	83,700
Pennsylvania	4[6]	125,000	50	203	4	2	47,000	per annum	7	10	119,750[7]
Rhode Island	4	69,900	50	100	2	2	10,000	per annum	5	(23)	104,403
South Carolina	4	106,078	46	124	4	2	10,400	per annum	5	10	106,061[7]
South Dakota	4[6]	84,739	35	70	2	2	6,000	per biennium	5	3[24]	82,701[7]
Tennessee	4	85,000	33	99	4	2	16,500	per annum	5	8	101,820
Texas	4	99,122	31	150	4	2	7,200	per annum	9	6	94,686[7]
Utah	4	90,700	29	75	4	2	100	per diem	5	3[8]	98,500[7]
Vermont	2	96,661	30	150	2	2	510[25]	per week	5	6	83,072[7]
Virginia	4[13]	110,000	40	100	4	2	17,640[26]	per annum	7	12	112,044[7]
Washington	4[27]	121,000	49	98	4[11]	2	28,300	per annum	9	6	112,078
West Virginia	4[6]	72,000	34	100	4	2	15,000	per annum	5	12	72,000
Wisconsin	4	102,882	33	99	4	2	39,211	per annum	7	10	100,690[7]
Wyoming	4	95,000	30	60	4	2	125	per diem	5	8	85,000

NOTE: Salaries are rounded to nearest dollar. 1. Known as *General Assembly* in Ark., Colo., Conn., Del., Ga., Ill., Iowa, Ind., Ky., Md., Mo., N.C., Ohio, Pa., R.I., S.C., Tenn., Vt., Va.; *Legislative Assembly* in N.D., Ore.; *General Court* in Mass., N.H.; *Legislature* in other states. Meets biennially in Calif., Ky., Maine, Mont., Nev., N.J., N.D., Ore., Pa., Texas. Wyoming Legislature has regular general session on odd-numbered years and a budget session on even-numbered years. Arkansas General Assembly meets every other year for 60 days in odd numbered years. Ohio General Assembly meets when deemed necessary. Legislative bodies meet annually in other states. 2. Known as *Court of Appeals* in Md., N.Y.; *Supreme Court of Virginia* in Va.; *Supreme Judicial Court* in Maine, Mass.; *Supreme Court* in other states. 3. Upper house: *Senate* in all states except Neb., which has a single-house legislative body, "the Legislature." 4. Lower house: *Assembly* in Calif., Nev., N.Y., Wis.; *House of Delegates* in Md., Va., W.Va.; *General Assembly* in N.J.; *House of Representatives* in other states. 5. Base salary. Does not include additional payments for expenses, mileage, special sessions, etc., or additional per diem payments. 6. May not serve third consecutive term. 7. Chief justice receives a higher salary. 8. Leaders receive a higher salary. 9. Initial term; thereafter elected popularly for 10-year term. 10. May serve only two terms, consecutive or otherwise. 11. Have term limitations. 12. When in session, plus $600/mo. when not in session. 13. $1,435 per month when not in session. 14. Until 70 years old. 15. Every 10 years after election (census) term is only for 2 years. 16. Legislators may serve only 8 years in each house, 16 combined. 17. Unicameral legislature. 18. Constitutional number: 375-400. 19. Legislated salary; salary received is $85,000. 20. Second term receive tenure, mandatory retirement at 70. 21. When in session, plus $250 per month when not in session. 22. Nine members in Supreme Court, highest in civil cases; five in Court of Criminal Appeals. 23. Term of good behavior. 24. Subsequent terms, eight years. 25. To limit of $13,000 per biennium; $100 per diem for Special Session. 26. Upper house receives higher salary. 27. No person is eligible who would have served during 8 of the previous 14 years. *Source:* questionnaires to the states.

Land and Water Area of States, 1990

(in square miles)

State	Rank (total area)	Land[1] area	Water[2] area	Total area	State	Rank (total area)	Land[1] area	Water[2] area	Total area
Alabama	30	50,750.23	1,672.71	52,422.94	Montana	4	145,556.34	1,489.82	147,046.16
Alaska	1	570,373.55	86,050.59	656,424.14	Nebraska	16	76,877.73	480.67	77,358.40
Arizona	6	113,642.26	364.00	114,006.26	Nevada	7	109,805.89	761.02	110,566.91
Arkansas	29	52,075.29	1,107.07	53,182.36	New Hampshire	46	8,969.36	381.57	9,350.93
California	3	155,973.09	7,734.06	163,707.15	New Jersey	47	7,418.84	1,303.11	8,721.95
Colorado	8	103,729.54	370.78	104,100.32	New Mexico	5	121,364.54	233.69	123,598.23
Connecticut	48	4,845.39	698.26	5,543.65	New York	27	47,223.85	7,250.71	54,474.56
Delaware	49	1,954.62	534.76	2,489.38	North Carolina	28	48,718.08	5,103.27	53,821.35
Dist. of Columbia	—	61.41	6.95	68.36	North Dakota	19	68,994.24	1,709.59	70,703.83
Florida	22	53,997.08	11,761.00	65,758.08	Ohio	34	40,952.59	3,874.94	44,827.53
Georgia	24	57,918.73	1,522.49	59,441.22	Oklahoma	20	68,678.57	1,224.33	69,902.90
Hawaii	43	6,423.34	4,508.24	10,931.58	Oregon	9	96,002.58	2,383.17	98,385.75
Idaho	14	82,750.93	822.84	83,573.77	Pennsylvania	33	44,819.61	1,238.63	46,058.24
Illinois	25	55,593.29	2,324.55	57,917.84	Rhode Island	50	1,044.98	500.12	1,545.10
Indiana	38	35,870.18	549.91	36,420.09	South Carolina	40	30,111.12	1,895.99	32,007.11
Iowa	26	55,874.90	400.64	56,275.54	South Dakota	17	75,897.74	1,223.72	77,121.46
Kansas	15	81,823.02	458.98	82,282.00	Tennessee	36	41,219.52	926.49	42,146.01
Kentucky	37	39,732.31	678.93	40,411.24	Texas	2	261,914.26	6,686.70	268,600.96
Louisiana	31	43,566.03	8,277.44	51,843.47	Utah	13	82,168.15	2,735.97	84,904.12
Maine	39	30,864.55	4,522.78	35,387.33	Vermont	45	9,249.33	365.67	9,615.00
Maryland	42	9,774.65	2,632.80	12,407.45	Virginia	35	39,597.79	3,171.09	42,768.88
Massachusetts	44	7,837.98	2,716.81	10,554.79	Washington	18	66,581.95	4,720.70	71,302.65
Michigan	11	56,809.18	40,001.04	96,810.22	West Virginia	41	24,086.55	144.89	24,231.44
Minnesota	12	79,616.66	7,326.05	86,942.71	Wisconsin	23	54,313.71	11,189.50	65,503.21
Mississippi	32	46,913.64	1,519.95	48,433.59	Wyoming	10	97,104.55	713.56	97,818.11
Missouri	21	68,898.01	810.80	69,708.81	**U.S. Total**		3,536,341.73	251,083.35	3,787,425.08

1. Dry land and land temporarily or partially covered by water, such as marshland, swamps, etc.; streams and canals under one-eighth statute mile wide; and lakes, reservoirs, and ponds under 40 acres. 2. Permanent inland water surface, such as lakes, reservoirs, and ponds having an area of 40 acres or more; streams, sloughs, estuaries, and canals one-eighth statute mile or more in width; deeply indented embayments and sounds, and other coastal waters behind or sheltered by headlands or islands separated by less than 1 nautical mile of water; and islands under 40 acres in area. Excludes areas of oceans, bays, sounds, etc. lying within U.S. jurisdiction but not defined as inland water. *Source:* Department of Commerce, Bureau of the Census.

State Capitals and Largest Cities

State	Capital	Largest city	State	Capital	Largest city
Alabama	Montgomery	Birmingham	Montana	Helena	Billings
Alaska	Juneau	Anchorage	Nebraska	Lincoln	Omaha
Arizona	Phoenix	Phoenix	Nevada	Carson City	Las Vegas
Arkansas	Little Rock	Little Rock	New Hampshire	Concord	Manchester
California	Sacramento	Los Angeles	New Jersey	Trenton	Newark
Colorado	Denver	Denver	New Mexico	Santa Fe	Albuquerque
Connecticut	Hartford	Bridgeport	New York	Albany	New York City
Delaware	Dover	Wilmington	North Carolina	Raleigh	Charlotte
Florida	Tallahassee	Jacksonville	North Dakota	Bismarck	Fargo
Georgia	Atlanta	Atlanta	Ohio	Columbus	Columbus
Hawaii	Honolulu	Honolulu	Oklahoma	Oklahoma City	Oklahoma City
Idaho	Boise	Boise	Oregon	Salem	Portland
Illinois	Springfield	Chicago	Pennsylvania	Harrisburg	Philadelphia
Indiana	Indianapolis	Indianapolis	Rhode Island	Providence	Providence
Iowa	Des Moines	Des Moines	South Carolina	Columbia	Columbia
Kansas	Topeka	Wichita	South Dakota	Pierre	Sioux Falls
Kentucky	Frankfort	Louisville	Tennessee	Nashville	Memphis
Louisiana	Baton Rouge	New Orleans	Texas	Austin	Houston
Maine	Augusta	Portland	Utah	Salt Lake City	Salt Lake City
Maryland	Annapolis	Baltimore	Vermont	Montpelier	Burlington
Massachusetts	Boston	Boston	Virginia	Richmond	Virginia Beach
Michigan	Lansing	Detroit	Washington	Olympia	Seattle
Minnesota	St. Paul	Minneapolis	West Virginia	Charleston	Charleston
Mississippi	Jackson	Jackson	Wisconsin	Madison	Milwaukee
Missouri	Jefferson City	Kansas City	Wyoming	Cheyenne	Cheyenne

Source: U.S. Bureau of the Census, 1990 figures.

50 Largest Cities of the United States

(According to 1998 Census Bureau data)

Data supplied by Bureau of the Census and by the cities in response to questionnaires. Ranking of 50 largest cities based on June 30, 1998, census estimates. Per capita personal income data is given for the Metropolitan Statistical Area (MSA), the Primary Metropolitan Statistical Area (PMSA), the New England County Metropolitan Area (NECMA), or the Consolidated Metropolitan Statistical Area (CMSA), as noted. Average daily temperature data is from *County and City Data Book.* Population breakdown figures available only for original 1990 census data. For the revised 1990 census total population figures, see "Top 50 Cities in the U.S. by Estimated 1998 Population and Rank," p. 789. NOTE: Persons of Hispanic origin may be of any race.

Albuquerque, N.M.

Mayor: Jim Baca (to Dec. 2001)
1998 est. population (rank): 419,311 (36)
1990 census population (rank): 384,736 (38); **% change,** 8.9; **Male,** 186,584; **Female,** 198,152; **White,** 301,010 (78.3%); **Black,** 11,484 (3.0%); **American Indian, Eskimo, or Aleut,** 11,708 (3.0%); **Asian or Pacific Islander,** 6,660 (1.7%); **Other race,** 53,874; **Hispanic origin,** 132,706 (34.5%). **1990 population under 18:** 25.0%; **65 and over:** 11.1%; **median age:** 32.5.
Land area: 163 sq mi. (422 sq km); **Alt.:** 4,958 ft.
Avg. daily temp. (1998): Jan., 34.8° F; July, 78.8° F
Churches: 211; **City-owned parks:** 189; **Radio stations:** 43 (AM, 17; FM, 26); **Television stations:** 11
Civilian Labor Force: 224,003; **Unemployed:** 10,305, **Percent:** 4.6; **Per capita personal income (MSA) 1992:** $17,758
Chamber of Commerce: Greater Albuquerque Chamber of Commerce, 401 2nd St., N.W., Albuquerque, N.M. 87125. Albuquerque Hispanic Chamber of Commerce, 202 Central Ave., S.E., Albuquerque, N.M. 87102

Albuquerque is the largest city in New Mexico and the seat of Bernalillo County. It is situated in west central New Mexico on the upper Rio Grande River. Early Spanish settlers arrived there in the mid-1600s. The old town was founded in 1706 by Don Francisco Cuervo y Valdés, the governor of New Mexico, and named after the Duke of Albuquerque, the viceroy of New Spain. During the Civil War, Confederate forces briefly occupied the city in 1862. The new town section was founded in 1880. In 1883, Albuquerque became the county seat and was incorporated as a city in 1891.

The city is noted as a center for health and medical services in the region, and government agencies, nuclear research, banking, and tourism are important to the economy. There is a growing high-tech center in Albuquerque and Intel Corp.'s largest manufacturing facility is located there.

Famous natives: Erna Fergusson, author; Annabeth Gish, actress; Fred Haney, baseball player, executive; Ernie Pyle, World War II war correspondent; Slim Summerville, actor; Al and Bobby Unser, auto racers.

Atlanta, Ga.[1]

Mayor: Bill Campbell (to Jan. 2002)
1998 est. population (rank): 403,819 (39)[2]
1990 census population (rank): 394,017 (36); **% change,** 2.5; **Male,** 187,877; **Female,** 206,140; **White,** 122,327 (31.1%); **Black,** 264,262 (67.1%); **American Indian, Eskimo, or Aleut,** 563 (0.1%); **Asian or Pacific Islander,** 3,498 (0.9%); **Other race,** 3,367; **Hispanic origin,** 7,525 (1.9%).

1990 population under 18: 24.1%; **65 and over:** 11.3%; **median age:** 31.5.
City land area: 136 sq mi. (352.2 sq km); **Alt.:** Highest, 1,050 ft.; lowest, 940 ft.
Avg. daily temp.: Jan., 41.9° F; July, 78.6° F
Churches: 1,500; **City-owned parks:** 277 (3,178 ac.); **Radio stations:** AM, 7; FM, 20; **Television stations:** 8 commercial; 2 PBS
Civilian Labor Force (1996): 1,976,970; **Unemployed:** 75,260, **Percent:** 3.8; **Per capita personal income (MSA) 1996:** $25,563
Chamber of Commerce: Metro Atlanta Chamber of Commerce, 235 International Blvd., Atlanta, Ga. 30303

1. Information is gathered on the 20-county MSA.
2. 1996 est. population: 3,505,970 (metro area).

Atlanta, the largest city and capital of Georgia, is the seat of Fulton County. It is situated in the northwest part of the state at the base of the Blue Ridge Mountains near the Chattahoochee River. The first European settler was Hardy Ivy, who built a cabin there in 1833.

The town was founded as Terminus in 1837 as the end of the Georgia railroad line (Western and Atlantic Railroad) and became incorporated as Marthasville in 1843 in honor of ex-governor Lumpkin's daughter Martha. It was renamed Atlanta in 1845 and incorporated as a city in 1847. The name was suggested by the railroad's chief engineer, J. Edgar Thomson, and was derived from its location at the end of the Georgia and Atlantic railroad line. The city later became the capital of Georgia in 1868.

During the Civil War, the city was burned and almost completely destroyed while occupied by General W. T. Sherman's troops in November 1864. It was quickly rebuilt after the war and it grew rapidly due to the expansion of the railroads in the southwest. Atlanta's diverse economy is led by the service, communications, retail trade, manufacturing, finance, and insurance industries. The convention business is also important, and the 1996 Summer Olympic Games were held there.

Famous natives: Hank Aaron, baseball player; Arrested Development, recording artists; Jimmy Carter, former president; Ray Charles, singer; James Dickey, poet; Mattivilda Dobbs, soprano; Walt Frazier, basketball player; Oliver Hardy, comedian; Evander Holyfield, boxer; Allan Jackson, singer; Bobby Jones, golfer; DeForest Kelley, actor; Martin Luther King, Jr., civil rights leader and Nobel Peace Prize winner; Gladys Knight, singer; Kriss Kross, recording artists; Margaret Mitchell, novelist; Bert Parks, entertainer; Eric Roberts, actor; Julia Roberts, actress; Doug Stone, singer; Gwen Torrence, Olympic athlete; Lee Tracy, actor; Travis Tritt, singer; Ted Turner, TBS and CNN founder; Jane Withers, actress; Joanne Woodward, actress; Andrew Young, civil rights activist.

Austin, Tex.

Mayor: Kirk Watson (to May 2000)
1998 est. population (rank): 552,434 (21)[1]
1990 census population (rank): 465,622
(27); **% change,** 17.0; **Male,** 232,473; **Female,**
233,149; **White,** 328,542 (70.6%); **Black,** 57,868
(12.4%); **American Indian, Eskimo, or Aleut:,** 1,756
(0.4%); **Asian or Pacific Islander,** 14,141 (3.0%);
Other race, 63,315; **Hispanic origin,** 106,868
(23.0%). **1990 population under 18:** 23.1%; **65 and
over:** 7.4%; **median age:** 28.9
Land area: 252.3 sq mi. (653 sq km); **Alt.:** From 425 ft.
to over 1000 ft.
Avg. daily temp.: Jan., 49.1° F; July, 84.7° F
Churches: 353 churches, representing 45 denominations; **City-owned parks and playgrounds:** 169
(11,800 ac.); **Radio stations:** AM, 12; FM, 27;
Television stations: 7 commercial; 1 PBS;
1 independent
Civilian Labor Force (1998): 681,732; **Unemployed:**
17,899, **Percent:** 2.6; **Per capita personal income
(MSA) 1992:** $26,700, Austin–San Marcos
Chamber of Commerce: Greater Austin Chamber of
Commerce, P.O. Box 1967, Austin, Tex. 78767

1. 1997 est. population 561,045.

Austin, the state capital of Texas and seat of
Travis County, is the fifth-largest city in Texas. It is
situated in the south central part of the state on the
Colorado River. The site was called Waterloo in
1838 and in 1839 was incorporated as a city and
chosen as the capital of the independent Republic of
Texas. Waterloo was renamed Austin in honor of
Stephen F. Austin, the founder of the Texas Repub-
lic. It became the permanent capital of the state of
Texas in 1870.

Austin's growth was spurred by several developments after the Civil War—the railroads reached the
city in the 1870s; it was crossed by the important
Chisholm cattle trail; and it became the seat of the
state university in 1883.

Austin has a growing commercial and diversified
manufacturing sector. Civilian government employment is 20% of the labor force and is important to
the economy. As home to the University of Texas,
Austin is a major center for research and development, and is nationally recognized as a high-
technology center. The city has a new convention
center downtown.

Famous natives: Don Baylor, baseball player and
manager; Earl Campbell, football player; Liz Carpenter,
author; Dabney Coleman, actor; Ben Crenshaw, golfer;
Michael Dell, founder Dell Computer Corp.; Tobe Hooper,
film director; Lady Bird Johnson, former First Lady; Tom
Kite, golfer; James Michener, author; Willie Nelson,
musician; Amado Pena, artist; Darrell Royal, football
coach; Zachary Scott, actor; Jerry Jeff Walker, musician;
Dalhart Windberg, artist.

Baltimore, Md.

Mayor: Kurt L. Schmoke (to Dec. 1999)
1998 est. population (rank): 645,593 (16)
1990 census population (rank): 736,014
(13); **% change,** –12.3; **Male,** 343,513; **Female:**
392,501; **White,** 287,753 (39.1%); **Black,** 435,768
(59.2%); **American Indian, Eskimo, or Aleut:** 2,555
(0.3%); **Asian or Pacific Islander:** 7,942 (1.1%);
Other race: 1,996; **Hispanic origin:** 7,602 (1.0%).
1990 population under 18: 24.4%; **65 and over:**
13.7%; **Median age:** 32.6.
Land area: 80.3 sq mi. (208 sq km); **Alt.:** Highest,
490 ft.; lowest, sea level

Avg. daily temp.: Jan., 35.5° F; July, 79.9° F
Churches: Roman Catholic, 72; Jewish, 50; Protestant
and others, 344; **City-owned parks:** 347 park areas
and tracts (6,314 ac.); **Radio stations:** AM, 10; FM,
11; **Television stations:** 7 (including Home
Shopping Network)
Civilian Labor Force: 333,043; **Unemployed:** 35,531,
Percent: 10.7; **Per capita personal income (PMSA)
1992:** $22,412
Chamber of Commerce: Greater Baltimore Committee,
111 S. Calvert St., Ste. 1500, Baltimore, Md. 21202

Baltimore is the largest city in Maryland and is
situated in the northern part of the state on the
Patapsco River estuary, an arm of Chesapeake Bay.
The city is independent and is in no county.

The site was settled in the early 17th century and
founded as a town in 1729. The town was named
after Lord Baltimore, the founder of Maryland, and
was incorporated as a city in 1797. It has an excellent harbor and has been a principal port since the
18th century. Baltimore was a pioneer ship-building
center and the Baltimore clipper, one of the best
sailing ships of its day, was used extensively in
world trade.

Baltimore's economy is focused on manufacturing, in steel, heavy and light industries; ship construction; and scientific research and development.

Famous natives: Larry Adler, musician; John Astin, actor;
Eubie Blake, pianist; Francis X. Bushman, actor; Charlie
Chase, actor; Hans Conried, actor; Mildred Dunnock,
actress; "Mama" Cass Elliot, singer; Barry Farber,
broadcaster; Paul Ford, actor; Philip Glass, composer;
Billie Holiday, singer; Barry Levinson, director; H. L.
Mencken, writer; Babe Ruth, baseball player; Upton
Sinclair, novelist; Leon Uris, novelist; Frank Zappa,
musician.

Boston, Mass.

Mayor: Thomas Menino (to Dec. 2001)
1998 est. population (rank): 555,447 (20)
1990 census population (rank): 574,283
(20); **% change,** –3.3; **Male,** 275,972; **Female,**
298,311; **White,** 360,875 (62.8%); **Black,** 146,945
(25.6%); **American Indian, Eskimo, or Aleut,** 1,884
(0.3%); **Asian or Pacific Islander,** 30,388 (5.3%);
Other race, 34,191; **Hispanic origin,** 61,955 (10.8%).
1990 population under 18: 19.1%; **65 and over:**
11.5%; **median age:** 30.3.
Land area: 47.2 sq mi. (122 sq km); **Alt.:** Highest, 330
ft.; lowest, sea level
Avg. daily temp.: Jan., 29.6° F; July, 73.5° F
Churches: Protestant, 187; Roman Catholic, 71; Jewish,
13; others, 100; **City-owned parks, playgrounds,
etc.:** 2,276.36 ac.; **Radio stations:** AM, 7; FM, 17;
Television stations: 8
Civilian Labor Force (Jan. 1999): 295,689;
Unemployed: 9,951, **Percent:** 3.4; **Per capita per-
sonal income (1996):** $32,150[1]
Chamber of Commerce: Boston Chamber of Com-
merce, 600 Atlantic Ave., Boston, Mass. 02210

1. Suffolk County.

Boston is the state capital and seat of Suffolk
County, and the largest city in Massachusetts. It is
located in the eastern part of the state at the head of
Boston Bay. It was incorporated as a city in 1822.
No city in the U.S. is richer in historical associations
than Boston, and no city has retained more of its
original buildings as memorials to America's past.

Puritans from England settled at Boston in 1630,
only ten years after the Pilgrims had landed at Plymouth in 1620. They named their new town Boston,
after the former home of many of the Pilgrims in

Lincolnshire, England. Fourteen years later, the pioneer Bostonians set aside the first public park in the U.S.—the Boston Common. The following year, 1635, they opened the first free public school in America. Today, the Boston metropolitan area is home to 68 colleges and universities.

Boston is a major industrial, financial, and educational hub and has one of the finest ports in the world. The port of Boston handled more than 16.8 million tons of cargo in 1999.

The city's banking and financial services, insurance, and real estate sectors continue to drive Boston's economy. Boston is also a leading city in health care, with 25 inpatient hospitals and numerous community health centers. The city's unique cultural and historic heritage makes it a center of tourism and its hotel industry ranks first in the nation in occupancy. Boston's other businesses are in high technology, biotechnology, software, and electronics.

Famous natives: Samuel Adams, patriot; John Singleton Copley, painter; Ralph Waldo Emerson, philosopher and poet; Arthur Fiedler, conductor; Benjamin Franklin, statesman and scientist; Edward Everett Hale, clergyman and author; Oliver Wendell Holmes, Supreme Court justice; Winslow Homer, painter; Joseph P. Kennedy, financier; Jack Lemmon, actor; Robert Lowell, poet; Edgar Allan Poe, writer; Paul Revere, patriot and silversmith; John L. Sullivan, boxer; Barbara Walters, TV journalist.

Charlotte, N.C.

Mayor: Pat McCrory (to Nov. 1999)
1998 est. population: 504,637 (25)[1]
1990 census population (rank): 395,934 (35);
    % change, 20.3; **Male,** 188,088; **Female,** 207,846;
    White, 259,760 (65.6%); **Black,** 125,827 (31.8%);
    American Indian, Eskimo, or Aleut: 1,425 (0.4%);
    Asian or Pacific Islander: 7,211 (1.8%); **Other race,**
    1,711; **Hispanic origin,** 5,571 (1.4%). **1990 population under 18:** 24.2%; **65 and over:** 9.8%;
    median age: 32.1.
Land area: 234 sq mi. (606.2 sq km); **Alt.:** 765 ft.
Avg. daily temp.: Jan., 40.5° F; July, 78.5° F
Churches: Protestant, over 400; Roman Catholic, 8;
    Jewish, 3; Greek Orthodox, 1; **City-owned parks and parkways:** 130; **Radio stations:** AM, 10; FM, 17;
    Television stations: 4 commercial; 2 PBS
Civilian Labor Force (1997): 341,010; **Unemployed:**
    9,200, **Percent:** 3.0; **Per capita personal income (MSA) 1997:** $15,586[2]
Chamber of Commerce: Charlotte Chamber, P.O. Box
    32785, Charlotte, N.C., 28232

1. 1997 est. population: 470,553. 2. Charlotte–Gastonia Rock Hill, N.C.–S.C.

Charlotte, North Carolina's largest city and the seat of Mecklenburg County, is located in the southern part of the state near the South Carolina border. It was named for King George III of England's wife, Charlotte Sophia of Mecklenburg-Strelitz.

Settled about 1750, Charlotte was incorporated as a city in 1768 and made the county seat in 1774. Charlotte was a leading Confederate city during the Civil War and was the last meeting place of the full Confederate cabinet.

From 1800 to 1848, Charlotte was the center of U.S. gold production. A branch of the U.S. mint operated from there from 1837 to 1913.

The city has a highly diversified economy and is a foremost center for distribution, retailing, technology, and manufacturing. It is the second-largest banking center in the U.S. It is the seat of the University of North Carolina at Charlotte.

Famous natives: Romare Bearden, artist; Richard G. Darman, government official; Billy Graham, evangelist; Charles Gwathmey, architect; Hamilton Jordan, government official; Donald Schollander, swimmer; Randolph Scott, actor.

Chicago, Ill.

Mayor: Richard M. Daley (to April 2003)
1998 est. population (rank): 2,802,079 (3)
1990 census population (rank): 2,783,726 (3);
    % change, 0.7; **Male,** 1,334,705; **Female,** 1,449,021;
    White, 1,263,524 (45.4%); **Black,** 1,087,711 (39.1%);
    American Indian, Eskimo, or Aleut, 7,064 (0.3%);
    Asian or Pacific Islander, 104,118 (3.7%); **Other race,** 321,309; **Hispanic origin,** 545,852 (19.6%).
    1990 population under 18: 26.0%; **65 and over:**
    11.9%; **median age:** 31.3.
Land area: 228.469 sq mi. (592 sq km); **Alt.:** Highest,
    672 ft.; lowest, 578.5 ft.
Avg. daily temp. (1998): Jan., 29.6° F; July, 74.5° F
Churches: Protestant, 850; Roman Catholic, 252; Jewish, 51; **City-owned parks:** 551; **Radio stations (1998):** AM, 15; FM, 28; **Television stations:** 14
Civilian Labor Force (PMSA 1996): 4,120,400;
    Unemployed: 194,400, **Percent:** 4.7; **Per capita personal income (PMSA) 1994:** $25,865
Chamber of Commerce: Chicagoland Chamber of
    Commerce, 200 N. LaSalle, Chicago, Ill. 60601

Chicago is the largest city in Illinois and the seat of Cook County. Built directly on the lake front, it stretches for 22 miles along the southwestern shore of Lake Michigan.

The first white men known to have visited Chicago were Louis Joliet and Jacques Marquette in 1673. The first permanent white settler in the area was John Kinzie, who is sometimes called the Father of Chicago. He took over a trading post in 1796 that had been established in 1791 by Jean-Baptiste Point du Sable, a black fur trapper. Fort Dearborn, a blockhouse and stockade, was built in 1804, but was evacuated in 1812, with more than half of its garrison massacred at what is now the foot of 18th Street. Not until 1830 was the town laid out. The name Chicago is thought to come from the Algonquian word "Chicagou" meaning strong or powerful. Some early Frenchmen believed that the name was derived from the Algonquian word for "onion place" because wild onions grew there.

Chicago was incorporated as a village in 1833 and as a city in 1837. Thirty-four years later it was destroyed in the great Chicago fire of 1871.

Chicago is a major Great Lakes port and the commercial, financial, industrial, and cultural center of the Midwest. The manufacturing industries dominate the wholesale and retail trade, and trade in agricultural commodities is important to the economy. The Chicago Board of Trade is the largest agricultural futures market in the world.

Famous natives: Jack Benny, comedian; Edgar Rice Burroughs, author; Raymond Chandler, author; Hillary Rodham Clinton, lawyer and First Lady; Michael Crichton, author; Walt Disney, filmmaker; John Dos Passos, author; Bobby Fischer, chess player; Bob Fosse, choreographer and director; Benny Goodman, clarinetist; Dorothy Hamill, figure skater; Quincy Jones, composer; Gene Krupa, drummer; David Mamet, playwright; Bob Newhart, comedian; Kim Novak, actress; Donald O'Connor, actor; William L. Shirer, journalist and historian; Gloria Swanson, actress; Melvin Van Peebles, playwright; Alfred Wallenstein, conductor; Robin Williams, comedian and actor; Robert Young, actor.

Cleveland, Ohio

Mayor: Michael R. White (to Dec. 2001)
1998 est. population (rank): 495,817 (28)
1990 census population (rank): 505,616 (24);
% change, –1.9; **Male,** 237,211; **Female,** 268,405;
White, 250,234 (49.5%); **Black,** 235,405 (46.6%);
American Indian, Eskimo, or Aleut, 1,562 (0.3%);
Asian or Pacific Islander, 5,115 (1.0%); **Other race,**
13,300; **Hispanic origin,** 23,197 (4.6%). **1990 population under 18:** 26.9%; **65 and over:** 14.0%; **median age:** 31.9.
Land area: 79 sq mi. (205 sq km); **Alt.:** Highest, 1048 ft.; lowest, 573 ft.
Avg. daily temp.: Jan., 25.5° F; July, 71.6° F
Churches [1]**:** Protestant, 980; Roman Catholic, 187; Jewish, 31; Eastern Orthodox, 22; **City-owned parks:** 41 (1,930 ac.); **Radio stations:** AM, 15; FM, 17;
Television stations: 7
Civilian Labor Force: 209,700; **Unemployed:** 19,900, **Percent:** 9.7; **Per capita personal income (PMSA) 1992:** $21,533[1]
Chamber of Commerce: Greater Cleveland Growth Association, 200 Tower City Center, Cleveland, Ohio 44113

1. Cleveland–Lorain–Elyria.

Cleveland is the second-largest city in Ohio and the seat of Cuyahoga County. It is located in the northeastern part of the state on Lake Erie. In the colonial era, the Cleveland area was known as the Connecticut Western Reserve, part of a land grant made to Connecticut by King Charles II in 1662. The city was founded in 1796 by Gen. Moses Cleaveland, who was the head surveyor of the Connecticut Land Company. This company had bought three million acres in what is now northern Ohio. A permanent settlement was founded in 1799, named after the general, and the spelling was shortened to Cleveland. The city was incorporated in 1836.

Cleveland's industrial growth was stimulated by the opening of the Ohio and Erie canals in 1832 and, later, the advent of the Civil War with the corresponding demand for machinery, railroad equipment, ships, and other items.

The port of Cleveland is the largest overseas general cargo port on Lake Erie. Greater Cleveland has long been famous as a diversified durable goods manufacturing area. Following the national trend, Cleveland has been shifting to a more services-based economy. Greater Cleveland is a world corporate center for leading national and multinational companies in industries ranging from transportation, insurance, retailing, and utilities, to commercial banking and finance.

Famous natives: Jim Backus, actor; Drew Carey, actor and comedian; Dorothy Dandridge, actress; Ruby Dee, actress; Phil Donahue, talk-show host; Joel Grey, actor; Arsenio Hall, talk-show host; Margaret Hamilton, actress; Philip Johnson, architect; Henry Mancini, composer; Burgess Meredith, actor; Paul Newman, actor; Carl Stokes, jurist.

Colorado Springs, Colo.

Mayor: Mary Lou Makepeace (to 2001)
1998 est. population (rank): 344,987 (48)
1990 census population (rank): 281,140
(54); **% change,** 23.0; **Male,** 137,611; **Female,**
143,529; **White,** 241,513 (85.9%); **Black,** 19,746
(7.0%); **American Indian, Eskimo, or Aleut,** 2,335
(0.8%); **Asian or Pacific Islander,** 6,845 (2.4%);
Other race, 10,701; **Hispanic origin,** 25,662 (9.1%).
1990 population under 18: 26.7%; **65 and over:**
9.2%; **median age:** 31.1.
Land area: 183.2 sq mi. (474.49 sq km); **Alt.:** 6,035 ft.
Avg. daily temp.: Jan., 28.8° F; July, 71.2° F
Churches: Protestant, 400+; Roman Catholic, 20; Jewish, 3; others, **City parks and playgrounds:** 156 (10,762 ac.); **Radio stations:** AM, 7; FM, 17;
Television stations: 7
Civilian Labor Force: 138,239; **Unemployed:** 10,084, **Percent:** 6.68; **Per capita personal income (1989):** $14,243
Chamber of Commerce: Colorado Springs Chamber of Commerce, 2 N. Cascade Ave., Suite 110, Colorado Springs, Colo. 80903

Colorado Springs is the second-largest city in Colorado, after Denver. It is the seat of El Paso County, making up about three-quarters of the county's population. It is located on the edge of the Rocky Mountains, with Pikes Peak (14,110 feet) towering beside it to the west. To the east begin the Great Plains.

The city was founded in 1871. General William Jackson Palmer, a Pennsylvania-born Civil War veteran, came across the scenic spot in his railroad travels and was inspired to begin a new resort community there. The subsequent development of Colorado Springs was influenced in part by an influx of English tourists later in the 1870s and by the discovery of gold in nearby Cripple Creek in the 1890s. Millionaire businessmen and philanthropists, such as Spencer Penrose, Charles Tutt, and Winfield Scott Stratton, helped to establish the city's infrastructure and shape its popularity as a tourist destination.

During World War II, Colorado Springs sold a large amount of land just south of the city to the military. The U.S. Army established Fort Carson as a training facility. The military presence in Colorado Springs would continue to grow, with the establishment of the United States Air Force Academy there in the 1950s, and later, the construction of Peterson Air Force Base, Falcon Air Force Base, and Cheyenne Mountain Air Force Base. The bases are all home to space command centers (with Cheyenne Mountain housing the headquarters for the North American Aerospace Defense Command [NORAD]) and have collectively earned Colorado Springs its national reputation as the leading center for military space operations.

The city's economy is still based heavily on tourism. In more recent years, Colorado Springs has gained a strong foothold in the electronics, high-technology, and manufacturing industries. The city is also a large center for amateur sports, as it is home to the headquarters of the U.S. Olympic Committee and Olympic Training Center facility.

Famous natives: Bert Andrews, journalist; Kelly Bishop, actress; Spring Byington, actress; Lon Chaney, actor; Marjorie Daw, actress; Marceline Day, actress; Rich "Goose" Gossage, baseball player; Helen Hunt Jackson, writer and poet; Chase Masterson, actress; Sherry Stringfield, actress.

Columbus, Ohio

Mayor: Gregory S. Lashutka (to Nov. 1999)
1998 est. population (rank): 670,234 (15)
1990 census population (rank): 632,910 (16);
% change, 5.9; **Male,** 305,574; **Female,** 327,336;
White, 471,025 (74.4%); **Black,** 142,748 (22.6%);
American Indian, Eskimo, or Aleut, 1,469 (0.2%);
Asian or Pacific Islander, 14,993 (2.4%); **Other race,**
2,675; **Hispanic origin,** 6,741 (1.1%). **1990 population under 18:** 23.7%; **65 and over:** 9.2%; **median age:** 29.4.

Land area: 209 sq mi. (541.5 sq km); **Alt.:** Highest, 902 ft.; lowest, 702 ft.
Avg. daily temp.: Jan., 27.1° F; July, 73.8° F
Churches: Protestant, 436; Roman Catholic, 62; Jewish, 5; Other, 8; **City-owned parks:** 203 (12,891 ac.);
   Radio stations: AM, 10; FM, 16; **Television stations:** 9 commercial, 3 PBS
Civilian Labor Force (1995): 554,733; **Unemployed:** 18,233, **Percent:** 3.3; **Per capita personal income (1992):** $13,151
Chamber of Commerce: Columbus Area Chamber of Commerce, P.O. Box 1527, Columbus, Ohio 43216

Columbus, the largest city in Ohio, is the state capital and the seat of Franklin County. It is located in central Ohio on the Scioto River.

The first structures near downtown Columbus were earthen mounds constructed by Indian tribes known as Mound Builders. The Indians lived alone in Central Ohio until the 1700s, when the first explorers entered the Midwest. The first permanent settlement was founded by a surveyor from Kentucky, Lucas Sullivant, in 1797 and was named Franklinton. The site was laid out as the state capital in 1812 and named to honor Christopher Columbus. It became the capital in 1816. Columbus was chartered as a city in 1834 and annexed Franklinton in 1870. The city's growth was stimulated by the development of transportation facilities—a feeder to the Ohio Canal completed in 1832, the National Road in 1833, and the arrival of the railroad in 1850.

Columbus is a port of entry and a major industrial, commercial, manufacturing, and cultural center. It is the seat of Ohio State University. The city has enjoyed steady growth over the years due to its economic diversity—no single activity dominates the economy.

Famous natives: Warner Baxter, actor; George Bellows, painter; Michael Feinstein, singer and pianist; Eileen Heckart, actress; Jack Nicklaus, golfer; Tom Poston, actor; Eddie Rickenbacker, aviator; Arthur M. Schlesinger, historian; James Thurber, writer; Nancy Wilson, singer.

Dallas, Tex.

Mayor: Ron Kirk (to May 1999)
City Manager: Teodoro J. Benavides
1998 est. population (rank): 1,075,894 (9)
1990 census population (rank): 1,006,877 (8);
   % change, 6.8; **Male,** 495,141; **Female,** 511,736;
   White, 556,760 (55.3%); **Black,** 296,994 (29.5%);
   American Indian, Eskimo, or Aleut, 4,792 (0.5%);
   Asian or Pacific Islander, 21,952 (2.2%); **Other race,** 126,379; **Hispanic origin,** 210,240 (20.9%). **1990 population under 18:** 25.0%; **65 and over:** 9.7%; **median age:** 30.6.
Land area: 378 sq mi. (979 sq km); **Alt.:** Highest, 750 ft.; lowest, 375 ft.
Avg. daily temp.: Jan., 45.0° F; July, 86.3° F
Churches: 1,974 (in Dallas Co.); **City-owned parks:** 296 (47,025 ac.); **Radio stations:** AM, 19; FM, 30; **Television stations:** 10 commercial, 1 PBS
Civilian Labor Force: 570,661; **Unemployed:** 50,526, **Percent:** 8.9; **Per capita personal income (PMSA) 1992:** $22,424
Chamber of Commerce: Dallas Chamber of Commerce, 1201 Elm, Dallas, Tex. 75270

Dallas is the second-largest city in Texas and is the seat of Dallas County. It is situated 185 miles northeast of Austin on the Trinity River near the junction of its three forks. It was first settled by Tennessee lawyer John Neely Bryan as a trading post on the Trinity River in 1841. Many historians believe that Bryan named the city after George Mifflin Dallas, vice president under James K. Polk, but there is no official agreement on this. It was incorporated as a town in 1856 and a city in 1871. The city developed as a cotton market in the 1870s and became the chief cotton-producing region of Texas.

The economy is highly diversified and the city is the leading commercial, marketing, and industrial center of the southwest. The insurance business is important, and the service sector has experienced rapid growth. Dallas is also a popular tourist and convention city.

Famous natives: Tex Avery, animator and director; Robby Benson, actor; Ernie Banks, baseball player; Bebe Daniels, actress; Linda Darnell, actress; Lee Elder, golfer; Morgan Fairchild, actress; Trini Lopez, singer; Aaron Spelling, producer; Stephen Stills, singer; Sharon Tate, actress; Lee Trevino, golfer.

Denver, Colo.

Mayor: Wellington Webb (to June 30, 2003)
1998 est. population (rank): 499,055 (27)
1990 census population (rank): 467,610 (26);
   % change, 6.7; **Male,** 227,517; **Female,** 240,093;
   White, 337,198 (72.1%); **Black,** 60,046 (12.8%);
   American Indian, Eskimo, or Aleut, 5,381 (1.2%);
   Asian or Pacific Islander, 11,005 (2.4%); **Other race,** 53,980; **Hispanic origin,** 107,382 (23.0%); **1990 population under 18:** 22.0%; **65 and over:** 13.9%; **median age:** 33.9.
Land area: 154.63 sq mi. (400.5 sq km); **Alt.:** Highest, 5,494 ft.; lowest, 5,140 ft.
Avg. daily temp.: Jan., 29.5° F; July, 73.3° F
Churches:[1] Protestant, 859; Roman Catholic, 60; Jewish, 13; **City-owned parks:** 205 (4,166 ac.); **City-owned mountain parks:** 40 (13,600 ac.); **Radio stations:** AM, 23; FM, 20[1]; **Television stations:** 17[1]
Civilian Labor Force: 245,495[2], **Unemployed:** 17,527[2]; **Percent:** 7.1[2]; **Per capita personal income (PMSA) 1992:** $22,930
Chamber of Commerce: Greater Denver Chamber of Commerce, 1445 Market Street, Denver, Colo. 80202

1. Metropolitan area. 2. Denver City/County.

Denver is the largest city in Colorado. It is the state capital and the seat of Denver County. It lies at the foot of the Rocky Mountains and is situated at the junction of the South Platte River and Cherry Creek. The city was born in 1858, when gold was discovered in the sands of Cherry Creek, and it began as a tough village of cabins, shacks, and tents. It was incorporated as a city in 1861 and became the territorial capital in 1867. The city is named for James W. Denver, governor of the Kansas Territory, which included part of Colorado. The city prospered from the famous gold and silver mines of the 1870s and the 1880s.

Denver International Airport, the first major new airport constructed in the U.S. in 21 years, opened to passenger traffic on Feb. 28, 1995, at a cost of $4.9 billion. At 53 square miles, it is the largest airport in North America.

Denver is an important cultural, industrial, transportation, tourist, and marketing center. It is also a regional center for many federal government agencies and a leader in the development of western energy resources.

Denver's fastest-growing industries include contract construction, real estate, retail trade, and government.

Famous natives: Tim Allen, comedian and actor; Ward Bond, actor; Douglas Fairbanks, Sr., actor; John Hart, newsman; Pat Hingle, actor; Ted Mack, TV host; Barbara Rush, actress; Alan K. Simpson, senator; Paul Whiteman, bandleader; Don Wilson, announcer.

Detroit, Mich.

Mayor: Dennis W. Archer (to 2002)
1998 est. population (rank): 970,196 (10)
1990 census population (rank): 1,027,974 (7);
 % change, –5.6; **Male,** 476,814; **Female,** 551,160;
 White, 222,316 (21.6%); **Black,** 777,916 (75.7%);
 American Indian, Eskimo, or Aleut, 3,655 (0.4%);
 Asian or Pacific Islander, 8,461 (0.8%); **Other race,**
 15,626; **Hispanic origin,** 28,473 (2.8%). **1990 population under 18:** 29.4%; **65 and over:** 12.2%; **median
 age:** 30.8.
Land area: 143 sq mi. (370 sq km); **Alt.:** Highest, 685
 ft.; lowest, 574 ft.
Avg. daily temp.: Jan., 23.4° F; July, 71.9° F
Churches:[1] Protestant, 1,165; Roman Catholic, 89; Jewish, 2; **City-owned parks:** 56 parks (3,843 ac.); 393
 sites (5,838 ac.); **Radio stations:** AM, 27; FM, 30
 (includes 3 in Windsor, Ont.); **Television stations:** 8[2]
 (includes 1 in Windsor, Ont.)
Civilian Labor Force (1997): 394,050; **Unemployed:**
 31,100; **Percent:** 7.9; **Per capita personal
 income (1992):** $21,000
Chamber of Commerce: Detroit Regional Chamber of
 Commerce, One Woodward Avenue, P.O. Box 33840,
 Detroit MI 48232-0840

1. Six-county metropolitan area. 2. Within four counties of Metro Detroit.

Detroit, the largest city in Michigan, is situated in the southeastern part of the state on the Detroit River. It is the seat of Wayne County. Detroit was incorporated as a city in 1815 and reincorporated in 1824.

Detroit is the oldest city of any size west of the seaboard colonies, having been founded by Antoine de la Mothe Cadillac on July 24, 1701, more than a century before Chicago was founded. The French were the first settlers and they gave the city its name from their word meaning "strait," referring to the 27-mile-long Detroit River, which connects Lake Erie and Lake St. Clair. The river forms part of the international boundary, and marks the only point where Canada lies directly south of U.S. territory.

Because of its strategic location, Detroit was fought over by the French, the British, and the Indians. It was the headquarters for the British forces in the Northwest Territory during the American Revolutionary War.

The first steam vessel, the *Walk-in-the-Water*, made its appearance on the Great Lakes in 1818, and Detroit was the western terminus for most of its voyages from Buffalo. Its link to all the important cities on the Great Lakes made it a major exporting port.

Detroit is one of the largest manufacturing cities in the U.S. and is the center of the automobile manufacturing industry, which has experienced a decline to foreign competition in the past decade. The health and medical care sector is important to the economy, and employment in the finance, insurance, and real-estate industries has inched up in the Detroit metropolitan area since 1991.

Famous natives: Ralph Bunche, statesman; Francis Ford Coppola, director; Charles Lindbergh, aviator; Madonna, singer and actress; John Mitchell, former U.S. Attorney General; George Peppard, actor; Gilda Radner, comedian; Della Reese, singer; Sugar Ray Robinson, boxer; Diana Ross, singer; Tom Selleck, actor; Margaret Whiting, singer.

El Paso, Tex.

Mayor: Carlos Ramirez (to May 2001)
1998 est. population (rank): 615,032 (17)[1]
1990 census population (rank): 515,342 (22);
 % change, 19.3; **Male,** 247,163; **Female,** 268,179;
 White, 396,122 (76.9%); **Black,** 17,708 (3.4%);
 American Indian, Eskimo, or Aleut, 2,239 (0.4%);
 Asian or Pacific Islander, 5,956 (1.2%); **Other race,**
 93,317; **Hispanic origin,** 355,669 (69.0%). **1990
 population under 18:** 31.9%; **65 and over:** 8.7%;
 median age: 28.7
Land area: 247.4 sq mi. (641 sq km); **Alt.:** 4,000 ft.
Avg. daily temp.: Jan., 44.2° F; July, 82.5° F
Churches: Protestant, 320; Roman Catholic, 39; Jewish,
 3; others, 20; **City-owned parks:** 116[2] (1,180 ac.);
 Radio Stations: AM, 18; FM, 17; **Television
 stations:** 6
Civilian Labor Force (1995): 285,100; **Unemployed:**
 31,100, **Percent:** 10.9; **Per capita personal
 income (1992):** $12,790
Chamber of Commerce: El Paso Chamber of Commerce and El Paso Hispanic Chamber of Commerce,
 10 Civic Center Plaza, El Paso, Tex. 79944

1. 1997 est. population: 596,804. 2. Includes 109 developed and 7 undeveloped parks.

El Paso, the fourth-largest city in Texas and the seat of El Paso County, is located in the far western part of the state on the north bank of the Rio Grande River, opposite the Mexican city of Ciudad Juárez on the south bank.

In 1581, Spanish explorers came through the Pass of the North to test the missionary and mining possibilities of New Mexico. The area had been inhabited for centuries by various Indian groups. On April 30, 1598, Juan de Onate took formal possession of the area for King Philip II of Spain and subsequently crossed the Rio Grande River near a site west of the present downtown El Paso that he called "El Paso del Rio del Norte," meaning the crossing of the river—the first use of the name "El Paso." In 1659, the mission of Nuestra Senora de Guadalupe was founded on a site that is present-day downtown Ciudad Juárez; the mission is still in use today. In 1682, Spanish colonists from Mexico founded the settlement of Ysleta on the site of the present-day city. However, it wasn't until 1827 that the first permanent settlement at El Paso was established by Juan María Ponce de León. The city's real growth started with the arrival of the Southern Pacific Railroad in 1881. El Paso was incorporated as a city in 1873.

In 1888, Mexico changed the name of Paso del Norte to Ciudad Juárez in honor of Benito Juárez. Later, in 1967, the U.S. agreed to cede a long-disputed part of El Paso to Mexico due to changes in the course of the Rio Grande, which forms the international boundary between the two countries. El Paso and its sister city of Ciudad Juárez across the U.S./Mexico border are inexorably joined by culture and economy. El Paso and Juárez make up the largest international metroplex in the world.

El Paso is an important port of entry to the U.S. from Mexico. The apparel industry plays a major role in the El Paso area. The high technology, medical device manufacturing, plastics, refining, automotive, food processing, and defense-related industries are important to the economy. El Paso's service sector has experienced the healthiest growth since 1983. El Paso is also a major tourist resort.

Famous natives: Manuel Acosta, artist; Don Bluth, animation director; Vicki Carr, singer; Sam Donaldson, newsman; Judith Ivey, actress; Guy Kibbee, actor; Sandra Day O'Connor, Supreme Court justice; Debbie Reynolds, actress; Irene Ryan, actress.

Fort Worth, Tex.

Mayor: Kenneth Barr (to May 2001)
City Manager: Bob Terrell
1998 est. population (rank): 491,801 (29)[1]
1990 census population (rank): 447,619 (28);
  % change, 9.9; **Male,** 220,268; **Female:** 227,351;
  White, 285,549 (63.8%); **Black,** 98,532 (22.0%);
  American Indian, Eskimo, or Aleut, 1,914 (0.4%);
  Asian or Pacific Islander, 8,910 (2.0%); **Other race,**
  52,714; **Hispanic origin,** 87,345 (19.5%). **1990 popu-
  lation under 18:** 26.6%; **65 and over:** 11.2%; **median
  age:** 30.3.
Land area: 300.6 sq mi. (778.8 sq km); **Alt.:** Highest,
  780 ft.; lowest, 520 ft.
Avg. daily temp.: Jan., 44.2° F; July, 82.5° F
Churches: 941, representing 72 denominations; **City-
  owned parks:** 200 (9,906.7 ac.); **Radio stations:**
  AM, 12; FM, 18; **Television stations:** 13
Civilian Labor Force (1999): 273,484; **Unemployed:**
  11,015, **Percent:** 4; **Per capita personal income
  (MSA) 1997:** $25,818 [2]
Chamber of Commerce: Fort Worth Chamber of Com-
  merce, 777 Taylor Street, Suite 900, Fort Worth,
  Tex. 76102

1. 1997 est. population: 484,500. 2. Tarrant County.

Fort Worth, seat of Tarrant County, is situated in the north central part of Texas on the Trinity River.

The city was founded by Major Ripley Arnold in 1849 as a military outpost on the Trinity River to protect settlers moving westward from frequent Indian attacks. It was named after Gen. William J. Worth, the commander of the Texas army. Fort Worth was incorporated in 1873. Its growth was stimulated in the 1870s by the proximity to the Chisholm cattle trail. It prospered as a meat-packing and shipping center when the Texas and Pacific Railway arrived in 1876, and later experienced a new boom when oil was discovered nearby in 1917. The establishment of military installations in the area during both world wars also spurred the economy.

Fort Worth has traditionally been a diverse center of manufacturing and is not dependent on the oil or financial sectors. The city's industries range from clothing and food products to jet fighters, helicopters, computers, pharmaceuticals, and plastics. Fort Worth is a national leader in aviation products, electronic equipment, and refrigeration equipment. It is home to a multitude of major corporate headquarters, offices, and distribution centers.

Famous natives: Robert Bass, financier; Mark Brooks, golfer; Betty Buckley, singer and actress; Kate Capshaw, actress; Ornette Coleman, composer; Sandra Haynie, golfer; Patricia Highsmith, writer; Spanky McFarland, actor; R. Bruce Merrifield, Nobelist in chemistry; Roger Miller, singer; Fess Parker, actor; Bill Paxton, actor; Rex Reed, critic; Johnny Rutherford, auto racer; Liz Smith, columnist.

Fresno, Calif.

Mayor: Jim Patterson (to Jan. 2001)
City Manager: Jeffrey M. Reid
1998 est. population (rank): 398,133 (40)
1990 census population (rank): 354,202 (47);
  % change, 12.4; **Male,** 172,241; **Female,** 181,961;
  White, 209,604 (59.2%); **Black,** 29,409 (8.3%);
  American Indian, Eskimo, or Aleut, 3,729 (1.1%);
  Asian or Pacific Islander, 44,358 (12.5%); **Other**
race, 67,102; **Hispanic origin,** 105,787 (29.9%). **1990
  population under 18:** 31.7%; **65 and over:** 10.1%;
  median age: 28.4.
Land area: 99.38 sq mi. (257.39 sq km); **Alt.:** 328 ft.
Avg. daily temp.: Jan., 45.5° F; July, 81.0° F
Churches: 450 (approximate); **City-owned parks:** 38
  (690 ac.); **Radio stations:** AM 11[1]; FM 13[1]; Bilin-
  gual 1; **Television stations:** 8[1]
Civilian Labor Force: 174,496; **Unemployed:** 22,708,
  Percent: 13.0; **Per capita personal income (MSA)
  1992:** $16,376
Chamber of Commerce: Fresno County and City
  Chamber of Commerce, P.O. Box 1469, 2331 Fresno
  St., Fresno, Calif. 93716

1. Metropolitan area.

Fresno is located in central California, 184 miles southeast of San Francisco and 222 miles northwest of Los Angeles. It is the seat of Fresno County. Fresno was incorporated as a city in 1885.

Fresno began as a station for the Central Pacific Railroad in 1872 and was made the seat of Fresno County in 1874. The city's name is Spanish for the ash trees that the early explorers found in the area.

Fresno is the world capital of agribusiness, with 250 different crops produced by 7,500 farmers on 1.9 million irrigated acres, worth $3 billion a year. Fresno county's top five agricultural products are grapes, cotton, tomatoes, cattle and calves, and turkeys. The city is also a trade, financial, media, and commercial center. Its diverse industries include agricultural chemicals, farm equipment, canned fruit and vegetables, clothing, computer software, electric wire, pumps, glass, and plastic products.

Famous natives: Mike Connors, actor; Maynard Dixon, painter; Bruce Furniss, swimmer; Jon Hall, actor; Daryle Lamonica, football player; Sam Peckinpah, director; William Saroyan, novelist; Tom Seaver, baseball player.

Honolulu, Hawaii

Mayor: Jeremy Harris (to Jan. 2001)
1998 est. population (rank): 395,789 (41)
1990 census population (rank): 365,272 (44)[1];
  % change, 5.0; **Male,** 186,371; **Female,** 190,688;
  White, 104,038 (27.6%); **Black,** 7,371 (1.95%);
  American Indian, Eskimo, or Aleut, 1,197 (0.3%);
  Asian or Pacific Islander, 259,629 (68.9%); **Other
  race,** 4,824 (1.3%); **Hispanic origin,** 18,017 (4.8%).
  1990 population under 18: 19.8%; **65 and over:**
  15.5%; **median age:** n.a.
Land area: 600 sq mi. (1554 sq km); **Alt.:** Highest,
  4,003 ft.; lowest, sea level
Avg. daily temp.: Jan., 72.6° F; July, 81° F
Churches: Roman Catholic, 39; Buddhist, 51; Jewish, 2;
  Protestant and others, 402; **City-owned parks:** 6,146
  ac.; **Radio stations:** AM, 17; FM, 14; **Television
  stations:** 9
Civilian Labor Force (1998): 429,050[2]; **Unemployed:**
  22,950[2], **Percent:** 5.4[2]; **Per capita personal income
  (1997):** $27,259
Chamber of Commerce: Chamber of Commerce of
  Hawaii, 1132 Bishop St., Suite 200, Honolulu,
  Hawaii 96813

1. Census Designated Place; the census bureau does not include the entire city and county in its census of Honolulu. If it did, the 1990 census and rank would be 836,231 (12). 2. City and county.

Honolulu is the capital (on Oahu) and largest city in Hawaii. It is also the seat of Honolulu County. The City and County of Honolulu is the seat of the state government and includes the entire island of Oahu and most of the Northwestern Hawaiian

Islands, from Nihoa to Kure Atoll, except Midway. The population of Oahu makes up 73% of the state's total population. The City and County of Honolulu is the only metropolitan statistical area in the state of Hawaii. It is situated in the central Pacific Ocean 2,397 miles west-southwest of San Francisco. Honolulu's name means "sheltered harbor" and derives from the native words hono, meaning "a bay," and lulu, meaning "sheltered."

Honolulu's early history was one of turbulence and conflict. One of the last areas on the globe to be explored and exploited by Europeans (it was first visited by British Captain James Cook in 1778), Hawaii was subject to strong pressures from many forces, including American missionaries, who arrived in 1820, and opportunistic whalers. These whalers were among those who built Honolulu originally, bringing trade, commerce, and prosperity that led to expansion into the sugar and pineapple industries.

As early as 1814, Russia tried to move in and Russian soldiers built a bastion at the harbor's edge. The British flag was raised in 1843 and French forces occupied Honolulu in 1849. Each time control was given back to the independent kingdom without bloodshed. In 1898, a group of Americans completed a project attempted at intervals during the previous 65 years—annexation to the United States. Honolulu was incorporated as a city in 1907.

Honolulu was bombed by Japan in a surprise attack on the unprepared U.S. naval base at Pearl Harbor on Dec. 7, 1941. This action forced the United States to enter World War II. "Remember Pearl Harbor" became a famous American wartime slogan.

Hawaiian statehood in 1959 and the viability of commercial air travel to the island brought boom times to Honolulu. Tourism is the city's principal industry, followed by federal defense expenditures and agricultural exports (chiefly pineapples).

Famous natives: Hiram Bingham, explorer; Jean Erdman, dancer and choreographer; Hiram Fong, senator; Daniel Inouye, senator; Duke Kahanamoku, surfer and Olympian swimmer; Bette Midler, actress and singer; Kelly Preston, actress; Louise Morgan Sill, author; Don Stroud, actor; Merlin D. Tuttle, biologist and wildlife photographer.

Houston, Tex.

Mayor: Lee P. Brown (to Dec. 1999)
1998 est. population (rank): 1,786,691 (4)
1990 census population (rank): 1,630,553 (4);
  % change, 8.0; **Male,** 809,048; **Female,** 821,505;
  White, 859,069 (52.7%); **Black,** 457,990 (28.1%);
  American Indian, Eskimo, or Aleut, 4,126 (0.3%);
  Asian or Pacific Islander, 67,113 (4.1%); **Other race,**
  242,255; **Hispanic origin,** 450,483 (27.6%). **1990**
  population under 18: 26.7%; **65 and over:** 8.3%;
  median age: 30.4.
Land area: 617.48 sq mi. (1,521 sq km); **Alt.:** Highest,
  120 ft.; lowest, sea level
Avg. daily temp.: Jan., 50.4° F; July, 82.6° F
Churches: 1,750[1]; **City-owned parks:** 311 (32,655 ac.);
  Radio stations: AM, 22; FM, 32[1]; **Television sta-**
  tions: 14 commercial, 1 PBS
Civilian Labor Force: 2,172,600[2]; **Unemployed:**
  98,300[2], **Percent:** 4.5[2]; **Per capita personal income**
  1997: $28,977[2]
Chamber of Commerce: Greater Houston Partnership,
  1200 Smith, Suite 700, Houston, Tex. 77002

1. Harris County. 2. Primary Metropolitan Statistical Area.

Houston, the largest city in Texas and seat of Harris County, is located in the southeastern part of the state near the Gulf of Mexico.

Sam Houston was the commander-in-chief of the Texas troops who fought a successful war of rebellion against domination by Mexico, which had been in possession of Texas. On April 21, 1836, Houston's men won a decisive victory in which the Mexican dictator, Gen. Santa Anna, was taken prisoner and forced to sign the treaty that launched the Republic of Texas. In September, a constitution was ratified, and Houston was elected president. The Texas Republic was recognized by the U.S. and by the major European powers. The present city of Houston was incorporated in 1837 and named after Sam Houston; it was the Republic's first capital.

The port of Houston ranks first among U.S. ports in foreign tonnage handled. The city is a major business, financial, science, and technology center. Houston is outstanding in oil and natural-gas production and is the energy capital of the world. It is the home of one of the largest medical facilities in the world—the Texas Medical Center—and the focus of the aerospace industry. The Lyndon B. Johnson Space Center is the nation's headquarters for staffed spaceflight.

Famous natives: Debbie Allen, choreographer; Lance Alworth, football player; Denton Cooley, heart surgeon; Jim Demaret, golfer; Allen Drury, novelist; Shelly Duvall, actress; A. J. Foyt, auto racer; Howard Hughes, industrialist; Barbara C. Jordan, educator, lawyer and politician; Barbara Mandrell, singer; Annette O'Toole, actress; Dennis and Randy Quaid, actors; Kenny Rogers, singer; Patrick Swayze, actor and dancer.

Indianapolis, Ind.

Mayor: Stephen Goldsmith (to Dec. 31, 1999)
1998 est. population (rank): 741,304 (13)
1990 census population (rank)[2]: 741,952 (12);
  % change, 1.4; **Male,** 352,309; **Female,** 389,643;
  White, 564,447 (77.2%); **Black,** 166,031 (22.4%);
  American Indian, Eskimo, or Aleut, 1,580 (0.2%);
  Asian or Pacific Islander, 6,943 (0.9%); **Other race,**
  2,951; **Hispanic origin,** 7,790 (1.0%). **1990 popula-**
  tion under 18: 25.6%; **65 and over:** 11.5%; **median**
  age: 31.8.
Land area: 352 sq mi. (912 sq km); **Alt.:** Highest, 840
  ft.; lowest, 700 ft.
Avg. daily temp.: Jan., 25.5 F; July, 75.4° F
Churches: 1,191[1]; **City-owned parks:** 211 (9,866 ac.);
  Radio stations: AM, 8[3]; FM, 17[3]; **Television**
  stations: 7[1]
Civilian Labor Force (1999): 453,890[1] **Unemployed:**
  13,160[1], **Per capita personal income (MSA) 1997:**
  $26,577
Chamber of Commerce: Indianapolis Chamber of Com-
  merce, 320 N. Meridian St., Indianapolis, Ind. 46204

1. Marion County. 2. Consolidated city. 3. Metropolitan area.

Indianapolis, the largest city in Indiana and seat of Marion County, is located in the central part of the state on the West Fork of the White River. Its name derives from combining "Indiana" with "polis," the Greek word for city.

Indianapolis was settled in 1820, and in 1825 its site was chosen as the state capital. It was incorporated as a city in 1832 and reincorporated in 1838. The city's growth began when the railroad reached it in 1847. Toward the end of the 19th century, the discovery of nearby natural gas and the start of the automobile industry hastened its industrial expansion. On Jan. 1, 1970, Indianapolis merged with surrounding Marion County.

Indianapolis is an important center of a rich agricultural region and a major grain and livestock market. It is also a focal point of commerce, transportation, and manufacturing for the region. Some leading industries are electronics, pharmaceuticals, and food processing. The financial sector, and service and insurance industries are growing rapidly.

Indianapolis is the site of the world-famous 500-mile automobile race and the Indiana State Fair.

Famous natives: Monte Blue, actor; David Letterman, TV host; Steve McQueen, actor; Jane Pauley, TV newscaster; Booth Tarkington, author; Kurt Vonnegut, Jr., author; Harry Von Zell, announcer; Clifton Webb, actor.

Jacksonville, Fla.

Mayor: John Delaney (to June 30, 2003)
1998 est. population (rank): 693,630 (14)
1990 census population (rank)[1]: 672,971 (15);
  % change, 9.2; **Male,** 328,737; **Female,** 344,234;
  White, 489,604 (77.1%); **Black,** 163,902 (24.4%);
  American Indian, Eskimo, or Aleut, 1,904 (0.3%);
  Asian or Pacific Islander, 12,940 (1.9%); **Other race,**
  4,621; **Hispanic origin,** 17,333 (2.6%). **1990 population under 18:** 25.9%; **65 and over:** 10.7%; **median age:** 31.5.
Land area: 759.6 sq mi. (1,967 sq km), **Alt.:** Highest, 71 ft.; lowest, sea level
Avg. daily temp.: Jan., 53.2° F; July, 81.3° F
Churches: Protestant, 794; Roman Catholic, 21; Jewish, 5; others, 22; **City-owned parks and playgrounds:** 19 (7,404 ac.); **Radio stations:** AM, 14; FM, 16;
  Television stations: 6 commercial, 1 PBS, 1 religious
Civilian Labor Force: 328,211; **Unemployed:** 24,051, **Percent:** 7.3; **Per capita personal income (MSA) 1992:** $19,146
Chamber of Commerce: Jacksonville Area Chamber of Commerce, Jacksonville, Fla. 32202

1. Consolidated city.

Jacksonville, Florida's largest city, is located in Duval County in the northeast corner of Florida, on the banks of the St. Johns River and adjacent to the Atlantic Ocean. It is the largest metropolitan area in northeast Florida and southeast Georgia.

Starting in the 16th century, French, Spanish, and English explorers and colonists were attracted to the region by the St. Johns River. The site was settled by Lewis Hogans in 1816. Jacksonville was laid out in 1822 and was named after Gen. Andrew Jackson, the first military governor of Florida. It was incorporated as a city in 1832.

During the Civil War, much of the city was destroyed by Union forces who occupied Jacksonville four times. The city was rebuilt and, following the development of its harbor and the railroads, fast became the transportation hub and leading industrial city in Florida by the 1880s. In 1968, the city and county governments consolidated.

Jacksonville is the transportation hub and distribution focal point in the state. The strength of the city's economy lies in its broad diversification. The area's economy is balanced among distribution, financial services, biomedical, consumer goods, information services, manufacturing, and other industries. Jacksonville has the largest deepwater port in the South Atlantic and is the leading port in the U.S. for automobile imports.

Famous natives: Mae Axton, songwriter; Pat Boone, singer; Judy Canova, comedian; Harold Carmichael, football player; Merion C. Cooper, producer and director; Billy Daniels, vocalist; Storm Davis, athlete; Bob Hayes, athlete; Wanda Hendrix, actress; James Weldon Johnson, author and educator; John Rosamond Johnson, musician and composer; Mark McCumber, pro golfer; Ray Mercer, boxer; Charles "Hoss" Singleton, songwriter; Bill Terry, member of Baseball Hall of Fame; Donnie Van Zant, rock musician; Ronnie Van Zant, rock musician; Leeroy Yarbrough, auto racer.

Kansas City, Mo.

Mayor: Kay Barnes (to April 2003)
City Manager: Robert L. Collins (apptd. July 1997)
1998 est. population (rank): 441,574 (33)
1990 census population (rank): 435,146 (31);
  % change: 1.6; **Male,** 206,965; **Female,** 228,181;
  White, 290,572 (66.8%); **Black,** 128,768 (29.6%);
  American Indian, Eskimo, or Aleut, 2,144 (0.5%);
  Asian or Pacific Islander, 5,239 (1.2%); **Other race,**
  8,423; **Hispanic origin,** 17,017 (3.9%). **1990 population under 18:** 24.8%; **65 and over:** 12.9%; **median age:** 32.8.
Land area: 317 sq mi. (821 sq km); **Alt.:** Highest, 1,014 ft.; lowest, 722 ft.
Avg. daily temp.: Jan., 28.4° F; July, 80.9 F
Churches: 1,100 churches of all denominations[1]; **City-owned parks and playgrounds:** 189 (10,647 ac.); **Radio stations:** AM, 14; FM, 19[1]; **Television stations:** 7[1]
Civilian Labor Force: 239,600; **Unemployed:** 15,400, **Percent:** 6.4; **Per capita personal income (MSA) 1992:** $24,576[2]
Chamber of Commerce: Chamber of Commerce of Greater Kansas City, 911 Main St., Kansas City, Mo. 64105

1. Metropolitan area. 2. Kansas City, Mo.–Kan.

Kansas City is the largest city in Missouri. It is located in the western part of the state, at the junction of the Missouri and Kansas rivers. Kansas City is located in Jackson, Clay, Platte, and Cass counties.

In 1821, the year Missouri entered the Union, French trader François Chouteau came from St. Louis to establish a trading post on the site of the present city to take advantage of the growing fur trade with the Kansa, Osage, Wyandotte, and other tribes. In 1833, a settlement was laid out by John Calvin McCoy and developed, called the town of Westport Landing. The community became the Town of Kansas and was incorporated as a city in 1850 and renamed Kansas City in 1889. The city's name reflects its Native American heritage—its site was within the territory of the Kansa or Kaw Indians.

The city grew rapidly in the mid-1880s as the starting point for gold prospectors and settlers heading westward. The coming of the Missouri-Pacific Railroad in 1865 and the spanning of the Missouri River by the Hannibal Bridge in 1869 also contributed to the city's growth, and it prospered as a center for the nation's cattle business.

The Kansas City metropolitan area, once known primarily for agriculture and manufacturing, has expanded its economic base to include strong growth in areas of telecommunications, banking and finance, and the service industry. A transportation hub since the 1800s, the area enjoys a national and regional prominence as a distribution and manufacturing center. Kansas City ranks nationally as first in greeting-card publishing, frozen food storage and distribution, and hard winter-wheat marketing; second in wheat flour production; and third in auto and truck assembly. The area is one of ten federal regional centers and employs over 25,000 in local, state, and federal government. The city is also a regional center for health care, employing over 55,000 in this industry.

Famous natives: Robert Altman, director; Edward Asner, actor; Burt Bacharach, composer; Noah and Wallace Beery, actors; Robert Russell Bennett, composer; Jeanne Eagels, actress; Jean Harlow, actress; Ted Shawn, dancer and choreographer; Casey Stengel, baseball player; Virgil Thompson, composer; Tom Watson, golfer.

Las Vegas, Nev.

Mayor: Oscar Goodman (to May 2003)
1998 est. population (rank): 404,288 (37)
1990 census population (rank): 258,295 (63);
  % change: 56.2; **Male,** 130,981; **Female,** 127,314;
  White, 202,549 (78.4%); **Black,** 29,529 (11.4%);
  American Indian, Eskimo, or Aleut, 2,282 (0.9%);
  Asian or Pacific Islander, 9,325 (3.6%); **Other race,**
  14,610; **Hispanic origin,** 32,369 (12.5%); **1990 population under 18:** 25.0%; **65 and over:** 10.3%; **median age:** 32.5.
Land area: 83.3 sq mi. (1,215.7 sq km); **Alt.:** 2,174 ft.
Avg. daily temp.: Jan., 45.5° F; July, 91° F
Churches: over 500 churches and synagogues; **Radio stations:** AM 8; FM 18; **Television stations:** 7
Civilian Labor Force: (1990 census): 131,001;
  Unemployed: 19,043, **Percent:** 4.9; **Per capita personal income (MSA) 1992:** $19,994
Chamber of Commerce: 3720 Howard Hughes Parkway, Las Vegas, NV 89109

Las Vegas, seat of Clark County in southeastern Nevada, is the largest city in the state and one of the fastest-growing cities in the United States. Between April 1990 and July 1994, the Las Vegas metropolitan area population increased by 26%, growing from 852,646 to 1,076,267.

The area was discovered by Spanish explorers in 1829. The site of Las Vegas ("The Meadows" in Spanish) was originally a watering place for travelers on their way to southern California. It was first settled by Mormons in 1855, who were attracted by its artesian springs. They abandoned their settlement two years later in 1857 and the U.S. Army established Fort Baker there in 1864. In 1867, Las Vegas was detached from the Arizona Territory and joined with Nevada.

The town was established in 1905 and started to grow with the arrival of the San Pedro, Los Angeles, and Salt Lake Railroad in 1905. However, its growth did not really begin until shortly after 1931, when the Nevada legislature legalized gambling in an effort to lift the state from the Great Depression. The construction of nearby Hoover Dam economically aided the area as well.

The Las Vegas that we know today basically began after World War II when the idea of large hotels along the brand new "Strip" was developed. Las Vegas is the Marriage Capital of America. There are 50 wedding chapels in the city. Tourism and the convention industry are the city's major sources of income. In addition, manufacturing, government, warehousing, and trucking are major sources of employment. Many high-technology companies are also located there. Three of the reasons for that are the city's proximity to sophisticated military technology centers like Nellis Air Force Base, the top-secret Nuclear Testing Grounds, and the College of Engineering at the University of Nevada, Las Vegas.

Las Vegas has a favorable business climate: taxes are relatively low, and there are neither city nor state income taxes. This is because gambling and sales taxes, paid by tourists, have allowed the city and state governments to avoid personal and corporate income taxes.

Popular nearby tourist attractions are Hoover Dam and Lake Mead (the largest man-made lake in the U.S.), Lake Mojave, the Mt. Charleston Recreation Area, Red Rock Canyon, and the Death Valley National Monument.

Famous natives: Andre Agassi, tennis player; Clara Bow, actress; Howard Hughes, industrialist and film producer; Jack Kramer, tennis player; Phyllis McGuire, singer; Benjamin Siegel, hotel-casino promoter; Orson Welles, actor and producer; Joe Williams, jazz singer.

Long Beach, Calif.

Mayor: Beverly O'Neill (to April 2002)
City Manager: Henry Taboada
1998 est. population (rank): 430,905 (35)
1990 census population (rank): 429,433 (32);
  % change, 0.4; **Male,** 216,685; **Female,** 212,748;
  1996 est. population breakdown: **White,** 168,074
  (39.1%); **Black,** 63,376 (14.8%); **American Indian,
  Eskimo, or Aleut,** 2,322 (0.5%); **Asian or Pacific
  Islander,** 66,767 (15.6%); **Hispanic origin,** 125,269
  (29.3%). **1990 population under 18:** 25.5%; **65 and
  over:** 10.8%; **median age:** 30.0.
Land area: 49.8 sq mi. (129 sq km); **Alt.:** Highest,
  170 ft.; lowest, sea level
Avg. daily temp.: Jan., 55.2° F; July, 72.8° F
Churches: 236; **City-owned parks:** 58 (plus 5 golf
  courses); **Radio stations:** AM, 2; FM, 2; **Television
  stations:** 8 (metro area)
Civilian Labor Force: 212,700; **Unemployed:** 11,800,
  Percent: 5.6; **Per capita personal income (MSA)
  1992:** $21,434[1]
Chamber of Commerce: Long Beach Area Chamber of
  Commerce, One World Trade Center, Suite 350, Long
  Beach, Calif. 90831-0350

1. Los Angeles–Long Beach MSA.

Long Beach is the fifth-largest city in California and is situated on San Pedro Bay, south of Los Angeles, in Los Angeles County.

The town was laid out and settled in 1881 by developer W. E. Willmore, who sold lots in the site as a seaside resort community called Willmore City. It was renamed Long Beach for its 8½-mi. beach in 1884. The city was incorporated in 1888 and reincorporated in 1897.

Long Beach is a major industrial port. The services and manufacturing industries together account for over 50% of the local economy. Retail trade and government are the next largest sectors, accounting for an additional 30% of employment. Tourism is also important to the economy. The Aquarium of the Pacific opened June 20, 1998. Minor industries include transportation, communication and utilities, wholesale trade, finance, insurance, and real estate. Long Beach's economy has been adversely affected by cutbacks in the defense and aircraft production industries.

Famous natives: Jack Anderson, journalist; Jennifer Bartlett, artist; Barbara Britton, actress; Nicholas Cage, actor; Spike Jones, orchestra leader; Sally Kellerman, actress; Billie Jean King, tennis player; Martha Rae Watson, track star; Heather Watts, dancer.

Los Angeles, Calif.

Mayor: Richard Riordan (to June 2001)
1998 est. population (rank): 3,597,556 (2)
1990 census population (rank): 3,485,398 (2);
   % change, 3.2; **Male,** 1,750,055; **Female,** 1,735,343;
   White, 1,841,182 (52.8%); **Black,** 487,674 (14.0%);
   American Indian, Eskimo, or Aleut, 16,379 (0.5%);
   Asian or Pacific Islander, 341,807 (9.8%); **Other**
   race, 798,356; **Hispanic origin,** 1,391,411 (39.9%).
   1990 population under 18: 24.8%; **65 and over:**
   10.0%; **median age:** 30.7.
Land area: 467.4 sq mi. (1,210.57 sq km); **Alt.:** Highest,
   5,081 ft.; lowest, sea level
Avg. daily temp.: Jan., 57.2° F; July, 74.1° F
Churches: 2,000 of all denominations; **City-owned**
   parks: 355 (15,357 ac.); **Radio stations:** AM, 35; FM,
   53; **Television stations:** 19
Civilian Labor Force: 1,827,505; **Unemployed:**
   198,626, **Percent:** 10.9; **Per capita personal income**
   (PMSA) 1992: $21,434[1]
Chamber of Commerce: Los Angeles Chamber of
   Commerce, 404 S. Bixel St., Los Angeles, Calif. 90017
1. Los Angeles–Long Beach.

Los Angeles is the largest city in California and
the second-largest urban area in the nation. It is
located in the southern part of the state on the
Pacific Ocean. It is the seat of Los Angeles County.
Geographically, it extends more than 40 miles from
the mountains to the sea.

The Spanish explorer Gaspar de Portolá visited
the site in 1769. On Sept. 4, 1781, the Mexican provincial governor, Filipe de Neve, founded "El
Pueblo de Nuestra Señora la Reina de Los Angeles,"
meaning "The Village of Our Lady, the Queen of the
Angels." The pueblo became the capital of the
Mexican province, Alta California, and it was the
last place to surrender to the U.S. at the time of the
American occupation in 1847. By the Treaty of
Guadalupe Hidalgo in 1848, Mexico ceded California to the United States and Los Angeles was incorporated as a city in 1850.

The city's phenomenal growth was brought about
by its equable climate, which attracted people and
industry from all parts of the nation; the development of its citrus-fruit industry; the discovery of oil
in the area during the early 1890s; the development
of its man-made harbor—its port is one of the busiest in the U.S.; and the growth of the motion picture
industry in the early 20th century. Today, Hollywood is a suburb of Los Angeles.

Los Angeles is a major hub of shipping, manufacturing, industry, and finance, and is world-renowned
in the entertainment and communications fields. It is
a favorite vacation destination and attracts millions of
tourists to the area each year from all over the world.

Los Angeles County is the nation's largest manufacturing center, surpassing Chicago, New York, and
Detroit. The ports of Los Angeles and Long Beach
are second only to New York as the largest customs
district in the United States.

Major employers in the Los Angeles Five-County
area are in the business and management sector.
Growth in the key wholesale industries—apparel and
textiles, furniture, jewelry, and toys—and the boom
in industrial trade were the trend for the region in the
1990s. Other important sectors are health services
and international trade and investment. The aerospace and technology industries have declined due to

defense cutbacks but are projected to remain a viable
part of the region's economy.

Famous natives: Busby Berkeley, choreographer and
director; Marge Champion, dancer and choreographer;
Jackie Coogan, actor; Jackie Cooper, actor; Linda
Fratianne, figure skater; Jodie Foster, actress and director;
John Gavin, actor and diplomat; Pancho Gonzalez, tennis
player; Cynthia Gregory, ballerina; Jerome Hines, basso;
Dustin Hoffman, actor; Theodore Harold Maiman, laser
inventor; Marilyn Monroe, actress; Isamu Noguchi,
sculptor; Leonard Slotkin, conductor; Duke Snider,
baseball player; Adlai E. Stevenson, statesman; Madeleine
Stowe, actress; Darryl Strawberry, baseball player.

Memphis, Tenn.

Mayor: W. W. Herenton (to Dec. 1999)
1998 est. population (rank): 603,507 (18)
1990 census population (rank): 610,337 (18);
   % change, −2.4; **Male,** 285,010; **Female,** 325,327;
   White, 268,600 (43.4%); **Black,** 334,737 (54.8%);
   American Indian, Eskimo, or Aleut, 960 (0.2%);
   Asian or Pacific Islander, 4,805 (0.8%); **Other race,**
   1,235; **Hispanic origin,** 4,455 (0.7%). **1990 popula-**
   tion under 18: 26.9%; **65 and over:** 12.2%; **median**
   age: 31.5.
Land area: 277 sq mi. (702 sq km); **Alt.:** Highest, 417 ft.
Avg. daily temp.: Jan., 39.6° F; July, 82.1° F
Churches: 2000+; **Parks and playgrounds:** 230
   (13,291 ac.); **Radio stations:** AM, 14; FM, 15;
   Television stations: 6
Civilian Labor Force: 292,819; **Unemployed:** 25,640,
   Percent: 8.8; **Per capita personal income (MSA)**
   1992: $19,517
Chamber of Commerce: Memphis Area Chamber of
   Commerce, P.O. Box 224, Memphis, Tenn. 38103

Memphis, the largest city in Tennessee and the
seat of Shelby County, is located in the southwestern corner of the state, on the Mississippi River.

The first settlers of Memphis were the Chickasaw
Indians, who had a village named Chisca there on
the bluffs overlooking the Mississippi River. Hernando de Soto, in 1541, is said to have had his first
glimpse of the Mississippi from the site of Memphis; in the next century, Louis Joliet and Jacques
Marquette stopped there to trade with the Indians.
The French explorer Sieur de La Salle tried to claim
the region for France in 1682 and built Fort Prudhomme there. The area was ceded to the United
States by the Chickasaw Indians in 1818. Memphis
was officially established in 1819 by three enterpris-
ing businessmen from Nashville, James Winchester,
John Overton, and future president Andrew Jackson.
Jackson named it after the ancient Egyptian city
because of its Nilelike site on the Mississippi River.
Memphis was incorporated as a city in 1826 and
became an important Mississippi River port.

During the Civil War, Memphis was a Confederate military center. In 1862, Federal forces won a
gunboat battle on the river at Memphis and General
Sherman was enabled to take the city.

Memphis's population was devastated by several
yellow-fever epidemics during the 1870s. The city
did not recover its prosperity until the end of the
19th century.

Memphis is one of the country's largest inland
ports and is known as "America's Distribution Center," serving the northeast, southeast, and southwest
regions of the country. Memphis is a leader in agribusiness, cultivating soybeans, rice, grain sorghum,
winter wheat, and corn, and raising livestock. The
city is the world's largest trading center for spot

cotton, handling over 40% of the nation's crops annually. It is the largest hardwood lumber trading and processing center in the world and is estimated to be the nation's third-largest total food processor.

Health care and related activities such as medical education and biomedical research are Memphis's largest industries, bringing over $2.5 billion a year to the local economy. Also important are high-technology communications.

Famous natives: Kathy Bates, actress; Dixie Carter, actress; Rosalind Cash, singer; Aretha Franklin, singer; Morgan Freeman, actor; Al Green, singer; George Hamilton, actor; Anfernee "Penny" Hardaway, basketball player; Isaac Hayes, singer; Hal Holbrook, actor; Benjamin Hooks, organization official; Hal Needham, director; Charlie Rich, singer; Cybill Shepherd, actress; Robert Siodmak, director; Fred Smith, business executive; Rufus Thomas, singer; Kemmons Wilson, business executive.

Mesa, Arizona

Mayor: Wayne Brown (to June 5, 2000)
City Manager: Charles K. Luster
1998 est. population (rank): 360,076 (46)
1990 census population (rank): 288,091 (53);
  % change, 25; **Male,** 141,470; **Female,** 146,621;
  White, 259,472 (90.1%); **Black,** 5,342 (19.0%);
  American Indian, Eskimo, or Aleut, 3,018 (1.0%);
  Asian or Pacific Islander, 4,355 (1.5%); **Other race,**
  15,904 (5.5%); **Hispanic origin,** 31,357 (10.9%). **1990
  population under 18:** 28.5%; **65 and over:** 12.4%;
  median age: 32.
Land area: over 123 sq mi. (319 sq km); **Alt.:** 1,241 ft.
Avg. daily temp.: Jan., 52.9° F; July, 84.9° F
  City-owned parks: 52; **Radio stations:** AM, 20;
  FM, 17; **Television stations:** 7
Civilian Labor Force: 194,569; **Unemployed:** 4,401,
  Percent: 2.3; **Per capita personal income (1989):**
  $13,506
Chamber of Commerce: 120 N. Center St., P.O. Box
  5820, Mesa, AZ 85211–5820

Mesa is the third-largest city in Arizona and is located in the south central portion of the state in Maricopa County. Sitting atop a plateau overlooking the Valley of the Sun, the city gets its name from Spanish word for "tabletop."

The site was settled in 1878 by Mormons, who utilized existing Hohokum Indian canals for irrigation. The population of the area grew rapidly after World War II as the manufacturing, tourism, and retail trades became increasingly important.

With 313 days of sunshine a year, Mesa was an ideal choice for several major-league baseball spring training camps. It is also the winter home of the Chicago Cubs.

Currently, Mesa is one of the fastest-growing cities in the U.S. due to its excellent climate and strong local economy, which boasts some of the country's top manufacturers. Electronics, automotive testing, propulsion equipment, aerospace, and heavy machinery firms are among the most significant in the region.

Famous natives: Danielle Fishel, actress; Liz Reney, actress

Miami, Fla.

Mayor: Joe Carollo (to Nov. 2001)
City manager: Edward Marquez (apptd. Nov. 1996)
1998 est. population (rank): 368,624 (44)
1990 census population (rank): 358,548 (46);
  % change, 2.8; **Male,** 173,223; **Female,** 185,325;
  White, 235,358 (65.6%); **Black,** 98,207 (27.4%);
  American Indian, Eskimo, or Aleut, 545 (0.2%);
  Asian or Pacific Islander, 2,272 (0.6%); **Other race,**
  22,166; **Hispanic origin,** 223,964 (62.5%). **1990
  population under 18:** 23.0%; **65 and over,** 16.6%;
  median age: 36.0.
Land area: 34.3 sq mi. (89 sq km); **Water area:** 19.5 sq
  mi.; **Alt.:** Average, 12 ft.
Avg. daily temp.: Jan., 67.1° F; July, 82.4° F
Churches (Dade County): Protestant, 850; Roman
  Catholic, 61; Jewish, 64; **City-owned parks (Miami):**
  109; **Radio stations (Dade County):** 29; **Television
  stations (Dade County):** 9 TV, 1 Cable
Civilian Labor Force: 181,684; **Unemployed:** 21,348,
  Percent: 11.8; **Per capita personal income (PMSA)
  1992:** $17,124
Chamber of Commerce: Greater Miami Chamber of
  Commerce, 1601 Biscayne Blvd., Miami, Fla. 33132

Miami, the second-largest city in Florida and seat of Dade County, is located in the southeastern part of the state, on Biscayne Bay.

The area was once the home of the Tequesta Indians until they were nearly wiped out by European diseases and warfare brought on by two centuries of Spanish control of Florida. Miami was founded in 1870 near the site of Ft. Dallas, built in 1835 during the Seminole Indian wars. The city's name is probably derived from "Mayaimi," an Indian word for "big water."

Miami is the only U.S. city to have been conceived by a woman. Julia Tuttle, a Clevelander, arrived there in 1891 and bought several hundred acres on the bank of the Miami River. She convinced New York financier Henry M. Flagler of the area's vast potential and persuaded him to extend his Florida East Coast Railroad to Miami in 1896, the year the city was incorporated. Flagler dredged Miami Harbor, built the renowned Royal Palm Hotel, which opened Jan. 1, 1897, and promoted the area as a winter playground. Tourists flocked there and, by 1910, the city was a thriving recreational area. Miami survived the collapse of a land speculation boom in the 1920s, and severe hurricanes in 1926 and 1935, and continued to grow in the aftermath of these disasters.

Miami experienced one of its most monumental population boosts during the 1960s when about 260,000 Cuban refugees arrived on its shore seeking freedom. They made a great impact on Miami, now a bilingual metropolis, and spurred economic growth.

Miami is an international banking and finance center and the city has the greatest concentration of international and Edge Act banks[1] in North America; these constitute a major employment base. Greater Miami[2] has a highly diversified economy with over 170 multinational Miami-based companies, a bevy of Fortune 500 companies, and a rapidly growing manufacturing and distribution center. Miami ranks number one in Florida for total manufacturing income, employment, and number of manufacturing establishments. Greater Miami is the nation's leader in biomedical technology and the health care sector is a major industry. It is also part of an area known as the Computer Coast of Florida, and its growing technologies include computers, electrical engineering, and plastics manufacturing.

Miami is one of the world's leading year-round resort centers with tourism contributing over 60% of

the area's economy. The city is a major transportation hub and the port of Miami is the world's largest cruise port and a major seaport for cargo. The famous island resort of Miami Beach, incorporated in 1915, is part of Greater Miami and is connected to Miami by four causeways.
1. Edge Act banks may make only foreign loans and accept foreign deposits. 2. Greater Miami is made up of 27 municipalities of which the city of Miami is the largest.

Famous natives: Fernando Bujones, dancer; Steve Carlton, baseball player; Debbie Harry, singer; Dick Howser, baseball player and manager; Sidney Poitier, actor; Janet Reno, attorney general of the U.S.; Ben Vereen, actor; Ellen Zwilich, composer.

Milwaukee, Wis.

Mayor: John O. Norquist (to April 2000)
1998 est. population (rank): 578,364 (19)
1990 census population (rank): 628,088 (17);
 % change, –7.9; **Male,** 296,837; **Female,** 331,251;
 White, 398,033 (63.4%); **Black,** 191,255 (30.5%);
 American Indian, Eskimo, or Aleut, 5,858 (0.9%);
 Asian or Pacific Islander, 11,817 (1.9%); **Other race,** 21,125; **Hispanic origin,** 39,409 (6.3%). **1990 population under 18:** 27.4%; **65 and over:** 12.4%; **median age:** 30.3.
Land area: 95.8 sq mi. (248 sq km); **Alt.:** 580.60 ft.
Avg. daily temp.: Jan., 26.9° F; July, 72.4° F
Churches: 411; **County-owned parks:** 14,785 ac.;
 Radio stations: AM, 6; FM, 12; **Television stations:** 11
Civilian Labor Force (1999): 297,707; **Unemployed:** 15,859; **Percent:** 5.3; **Per capita personal income (PMSA) 1995:** $23,822
Chamber of Commerce: Metropolitan Milwaukee Association of Commerce, 756 N. Milwaukee St., Milwaukee, Wis. 53202; Milwaukee Minority Chamber of Commerce, 509 W. Wisconsin Ave. #606, Milwaukee, Wis. 53203; Hispanic Chamber of Commerce, 816 W. National Ave., Milwaukee, Wis. 53204

Milwaukee, the largest city in Wisconsin and seat of Milwaukee County, is located in the southeastern part of the state on Lake Michigan.

French missionaries visited the site of Milwaukee in the seventeenth century, but it was not until 1795 that Jacques Vieau established a fur-trading post there. The first permanent white settler, Vieau's son-in-law, Solomon Juneau, an agent of the American Fur Company, made his home there in 1818. The settlement merged with several neighboring villages in 1838 to form Milwaukee, and the city was incorporated in 1846. The origins of the word "Milwaukee" are disputed; it may come from the Potawatomi "Mahn-ah-wauk," meaning council grounds of the Patawatomi; "Mah-an-wauk-seepe," meaning gathering place of rivers, or the Algonquian "Miloaki," meaning beautiful land. A large wave of German immigrants arrived after 1848 and contributed greatly to the city's political, economic, and cultural development.

Milwaukee is one of the great industrial centers in the country and one of the largest Great Lakes ports. Currently, port commerce runs almost 3 million tons per year.

Its economy was forged by heavy industries but is now diversified. Manufacturing remains strong and Milwaukee manufacturers are national leaders in lithographic commercial printing and the production of medical diagnostic instruments, small gasoline engines, malt beverages, iron and steel forgings, mining and construction machinery, robotics, speed changers and drives, and electronic controls. Milwaukee's high-tech manufacturing community is the ninth-largest among the nation's 31 major metropolitan areas. Though Milwaukee was once known as a "beer town," less than 1% of its workforce is now involved in beer production. However, beer still plays an important role and almost 11% of the nation's malt beverage is produced there.

Tourism is important to the economy. About 5 million people visit Milwaukee every year.

Famous natives: Donald Gramm, bass-baritone; Woody Herman, band leader; Al Jarreau, singer; Kristen Johnston, actress; George F. Kennan, diplomat; Alfred Lunt, actor; Douglas MacArthur, army general; Pat O'Brien, actor; Tom Snyder, TV personality; Speech, member of the rap group "Arrested Development;" Spencer Tracy, actor; Gene Wilder, actor; Jerry and David Zucker, film producers.

Minneapolis, Minn.

Mayor: Sharon Sayles Belton (to Jan. 2002)
1998 est. population (rank): 351,731 (47)
1990 census population (rank): 368,383 (42);
 % change, –4.5; **Male,** 178,671; **Female,** 189,712;
 White, 288,967 (78.4%); **Black,** 47,948 (13.0%);
 American Indian, Eskimo, or Aleut, 12,335 (3.3%);
 Asian or Pacific Islander, 15,723 (4.3%); **Other race,** 3,410; **Hispanic origin,** 7,900 (2.1%). **1990 population under 18:** 20.6%; **65 and over:** 13.0%; **median age:** 31.7
Land area: 58.7 sq mi. (143 sq km); **Alt.:** Highest, 945 ft.; lowest, 695 ft.
Avg. daily temp.: Jan., 11.2° F; July, 73.1° F
Churches: 419; **City-owned parks:** 153; **Radio stations:** AM, 17; FM, 15 (metro area); **Television stations:** 6 (metro area)
Civilian Labor Force: 204,477; **Unemployed:** 9,905, **Percent:** 4.8; **Per capita personal income (MSA) 1992:** $23,284[1]
Chamber of Commerce: Greater Minneapolis Chamber of Commerce, Young Quinlan Building, 81 S. Ninth Street, Suite 200, Minneapolis, Minn. 55402-3223

1. Minneapolis–St. Paul Minn.–Wis.

Minneapolis, the largest city in Minnesota and the seat of Hennepin County, is located in the southeast central part of the state on the Mississippi River. It is adjacent to its "twin city" of St. Paul. The Minneapolis–St. Paul Standard Metropolitan Statistical Area is the 15th-largest in the United States.

In 1680, Father Louis Hennepin visited the future site of Minneapolis and gave the Falls of St. Anthony their name. Lieutenant Zebulon Pike made a treaty with the Sioux Indians in 1805–1806 by which they ceded to the whites land, including the Falls of St. Anthony and the site of Minneapolis. Fort Snelling was built in 1819–1820 and, in 1823, the government built a lumber and flour mill. Flour milling became the major industry of early Minneapolis and made the city the milling capital of the world. The town of St. Anthony was established on the east bank of the Mississippi in 1848 and the town of Minneapolis grew up on the opposite bank of the river. The name Minneapolis is a combination of the Dakota Sioux word "minna," for water, and the Greek word "polis," for city. Minneapolis was incorporated as a city in 1867, and in 1872 the city of St. Anthony (chartered in 1860) was annexed to it. After the spread of the railroads in the 1870s, Minneapolis became the gateway to the Northern Great Plains.

Minneapolis is a center of industry and commerce serving a large agricultural region. During the 20th century, manufacturing, food processing, milling, computers, health services, and graphic arts developed as Minneapolis's major industries. Sixteen Fortune 500 industrial and 17 Fortune service companies are headquartered there. The city is the home of the world's largest cash grain market and is the headquarters of the Ninth Federal Reserve Bank.

Famous natives: La Verne, Maxene, and Patti Andrews, singers; James Arness, actor; Lew Ayres, actor; Patty Berg, golfer; Virginia Bruce, actress; J. Paul Getty, oil executive; Peter Graves, actor; George Roy Hill, director; Cornell MacNeil, baritone; Ralph Meeker, actor; Westbrook Pegler, columnist; Prince, singer; Harrison Salisbury, journalist; Charles Schulz, cartoonist; Anne Tyler, writer; Bud Wilkinson, football coach; David Winfield, baseball player.

Nashville-Davidson, Tenn.

Mayor: Philip N. Bredesen (to Aug. 1999)
1998 est. population (rank): 510,274 (24)[1]
1990 census population (rank)[2]: 510,784 (23);
  % change, 4.5; **Male,** 242,492; **Female,** 268,292;
  White, 381,740 (78.2%); **Black,** 119,273 (23.4%);
  American Indian, Eskimo, or Aleut, 1,162 (0.2%);
  Asian or Pacific Islander, 7,081 (1.4%); **Other race,**
  1,528; **Hispanic origin,** 4,775 (0.9%). **1990 population under 18:** 22.8%; **65 and over:** 11.6%; **median age:** 32.6.
Land area: 533 sq mi. (1,380 sq km); **Altitude:** Highest, 1,100 ft.; lowest, approx. 400 ft.
Avg. daily temp.: Jan., 36.7° F; July, 76.6° F
Churches: Protestant, 781; Roman Catholic, 18; Jewish, 3; **City-owned parks:** 76 (6,650 ac.); **Radio stations:** AM, 15; FM, 19; **Television stations:** 11
Civilian Labor Force (1997): 313,636; **Unemployed:** 9,225, **Percent:** 2.9; **Per capita personal income (1995):** $23,655
Chamber of Commerce: Nashville Area Chamber of Commerce, 161 Fourth Ave. North, Nashville, Tenn. 37219

1. 1997 est. population: 536,650. 2. Consolidated city.

The consolidated city of Nashville-Davidson is the capital of and second-largest city in Tennessee and is located in the north central part of the state on the Cumberland River. It is the seat of Davidson County.

During the winter of 1779–1780, James Robertson and John Donelson founded a settlement at Big Salt Lick by the Cumberland River at the present site of the city. They built forts on both sides of the river, naming one of them Fort Nashborough in honor of Francis Nash, a Revolutionary War general. In 1784, the town was named Nashville and was incorporated as a city in 1806.

Nashville became the capital of Tennessee in 1843 and was the seat of Davidson County until 1963, when it merged with the county to become Nashville-Davidson.

Nashville's best-known industries are recording, publishing, and the distribution of music, especially country music. The city is a port of entry and an important industrial and commercial center serving the Upper South. Its diverse economy includes automobiles, apparel, publishing, insurance, and banking. Health care services is the largest industry. Nashville is the home of several religious organizations and is a major tourist attraction and convention center.

Famous natives: Roy Acuff, singer; Gregg Allman, singer; Pat Boone, singer; Rita Coolidge, singer; Jeff Gordon, race car driver; Al Gore, vice president; Red Grooms, artist; Alex Haley, author; Barbara Howar, hostess and writer; Brenda Lee, singer; Minnie Pearl, comedienne; Annie Potts, actress; Paula Robeson, flutist; Wilma Rudolph, athlete; Dinah Shore, actress and singer; Tina Turner, singer; Oprah Winfrey, entertainer.

New Orleans, La.

Mayor: Marc H. Morial (to Feb. 2002)
1998 est. population (rank): 465,538 (31)
1990 census population (rank): 496,938 (25);
  % change, –6.3; **Male,** 230,883; **Female,** 266,055;
  White, 173,554 (34.9%); **Black,** 307,728 (61.9%);
  American Indian, Eskimo, or Aleut, 759 (0.2%);
  Asian or Pacific Islander, 9,678 (1.9%); **Other race,**
  5,219; **Hispanic origin,** 17,238 (3.5%). **1990 population under 18:** 27.5%; **65 and over,** 13.0%; **median age:** 31.6.
Land area: 199.4 sq mi. (516 sq km); **Alt.:** Highest, 15 ft.; lowest, –4 ft.
Avg. daily temp.: Jan., 52.4° F; July, 77° F
Churches: 712; **City-owned parks:** 165 (299 ac.); **Radio stations:** AM, 12; FM, 14; **Television stations:** 7
Civilian Labor Force: 205,610[1]; **Unemployed:** 15,055[1], **Percent:** 7.3[1]; **Per capita personal income (MSA) 1992:** $18,087
Chamber of Commerce: The Chamber/New Orleans and the River Region, 301 Camp Street, New Orleans, La. 70130

1. New Orleans City/Orleans Parish.

New Orleans, the largest city in Louisiana and seat of Orleans Parish, is located in the southeastern part of the state, between the Mississippi River and Lake Ponchartrain.

One of the few cities of the nation that has been under three flags, New Orleans has belonged to Spain, France, and the U.S. The French founded it in 1718 and named it in honor of the Duke of Orleans. In 1762, France ceded the city and the territory to Spain. In 1800, the territory was returned to France, but government authorities did not take over until 1803, only 20 days before the region became part of the U.S. in the Louisiana Purchase.

New Orleans is famous for its French Quarter. The Mardi Gras—a week of carnival held in New Orleans before the beginning of Lent—is the most spectacular festival in the U.S., and is a popular tourist attraction. Tourism has grown rapidly in recent years, and New Orleans hosts more than seven million visitors annually.

New Orleans is one of the world's greatest international ports, one of the largest in the nation, and a major focus of the city's economy. New Orleans is home to the corporate offices of oil companies with major offshore operations in the Gulf of Mexico, as well as the distribution and service centers of offshore equipment suppliers and fabricators.

The manufacturing industry is a significant part of the economy, with petroleum, petrochemical, shipbuilding, and aerospace industries all playing a role. The New Orleans region also functions as a mining, processing, and transportation center for other minerals, principally sulfur. Service industries are playing a larger role, with health care and telecommunications leading the way. The information services sector is one of the fastest-growing, and the New Orleans region is widely regarded as a leading center of medicine and health care in the South.

Famous natives: Louis Armstrong, musician; Truman Capote, author; Fats Domino, musician; Louis Gottschalk, pianist and composer; Bryant Gumbel, TV personality; Lillian Hellman, playwright and author; Al Hirt, musician; Mahalia Jackson, singer; Dorothy Lamour, actress; Wynton Marsalis, musician; Huey Newton, activist; Marguerite Piazza, soprano; Rusty Staub, baseball player; Ben Turpin, comedian; Shirley Verrett, mezzo-soprano; Carl Weathers, actor; Del Williams, football player.

New York, N.Y.

Mayor: Rudolph W. Giuliani (to Dec. 2001)
Borough Presidents: Bronx, Fernando Ferrer; Brooklyn, Howard Golden; Manhattan, C. Virginia Fields; Queens, Claire Shulman; Staten Island, Guy V. Molinari
1998 est. population (rank): 7,420,166 (1)
1990 census population (rank): 7,322,564 (1)[1]; **% change,** 1.3; **Male,** 3,437,687; **Female,** 3,884,877; **White,** 3,827,088 (52.2%); **Black,** 2,102,512 (28.7%); **American Indian, Eskimo, or Aleut,** 27,531 (0.4%); **Asian or Pacific Islander,** 512,719 (7.0%); **Other race,** 852,714; **Hispanic origin,** 1,783,511 (24.4%).[1] **1990 population under 18:** 23.0%; **65 and over:** 13.0%; **median age:** 33.7.
Land area: 321.8 sq mi. (826.68 sq km) (Queens, 112.1; Brooklyn, 81.8; Staten Island, 60.2; Bronx, 44.0; Manhattan, 23.7); **Alt.:** Highest, 410 ft.; lowest, sea level
Avg. daily temp.: Jan., 31.8° F; July, 76.7° F
Churches: Protestant, 1,766; Jewish, 1,256; Roman Catholic, 437; Orthodox, 66; **City-owned parks:** 1,701 (27,944.4 ac.); **Radio stations:** AM, 13; FM, 18; **Television stations:** 6 commercial, 1 public
Civilian Labor Force: 3,311,000; **Unemployed:** 359,000, **Percent:** 10.8; **Per capita personal income (PMSA) 1992:** $27,039
Chamber of Commerce: New York Chamber of Commerce and Industry, One Battery Park Plaza, New York, N.Y. 10004

1. Race breakdown figures according to N.Y.C. Dept. of City Planning: White, non-Hispanic, 3,163,125; Black, non-Hispanic, 1,847,049; American Indian, non-Hispanic, 17,871; Asian, non-Hispanic, 489,157; Hispanic, 1,783,511.

New York City is the largest city in the United States. It is located in the southern part of New York State, at the mouth of the Hudson River (also known as North River as it passes Manhattan Island).

In 1609, Henry Hudson, who worked for the Dutch East India Company, sailed up the river that now bears his name and went as far as Albany. Five years later, a permanent settlement was established at what is now New York, but it was originally called New Amsterdam by the Dutch governors. One of them, Peter Minuit, was said to have bought Manhattan Island from the Indians for $24 worth of beads, buttons, and trinkets. In 1664, Great Britain's Duke of York sent a fleet that quietly seized the settlement from the Dutch, without bloodshed, and rechristened the colony in honor of the duke.

Control of New York passed to the young U.S. at the end of the Revolutionary War, and George Washington was inaugurated president in New York's old City Hall. Congress met in New York from 1785 to 1790.

In 1898, when Greater New York was chartered, the city expanded to include the following five boroughs, which are also counties in New York State: Manhattan (New York County); Brooklyn (Kings County); Bronx (Bronx County); Queens (Queens County); and Staten Island (Richmond County). There is a growing effort among Staten Island residents to separate from Greater New York and become an independent city of Staten Island.

"The Big Apple" is the most populous city in the United States, a major world capital, and a world leader in finance, the arts, and communications. The city is also the center of advertising, fashion, publishing, and radio broadcasting in the United States.

New York has many museums, art galleries, and educational institutions. The port of New York is one of the finest in the world. The city is the home of the United Nations and is headquarters for some of the world's largest corporations.

Famous natives: Kareem Abdul-Jabbar, basketball player; Woody Allen, actor and director; Martina Arroyo, soprano; Lauren Bacall, actress; James Baldwin, novelist; Harry Belafonte, singer and actor; Humphrey Bogart, actor; James Cagney, actor; Maria Callas, soprano; Aaron Copland, composer; Sammy Davis, Jr., singer and actor; Agnes de Mille, choreographer; Robert De Niro, actor; Eamon De Valera, former president of Ireland; Gertrude Elion, Nobel Prize winner in medicine; Lou Gehrig, baseball player; George Gershwin, composer; Ira Gershwin, lyricist; Jackie Gleason, actor; Rita Hayworth, actress; Lena Horne, singer; Julia Ward Howe, poet and reformer; Washington Irving, author; Henry James, novelist; Michael Jordan, basketball player; Sandy Koufax, baseball player; Roy Lichtenstein, painter; Vince Lombardi, football player and coach; Chico, Groucho, Harpo, and Zeppo Marx, comedians; Herman Melville, novelist; Yehudi Menuhin, violinist; James Michener, novelist; Arthur Miller, playwright; Eugene O'Neill, playwright; J. Robert Oppenheimer, nuclear physicist; Al Pacino, actor; Jerome Robbins, choreographer; Eleanor Roosevelt, reformer and humanitarian; Theodore Roosevelt, former president; Jonas Salk, polio researcher; Beverly Sills, soprano; Neil Simon, playwright; Barbra Streisand, singer and actress; Ed Sullivan, TV personality; Mae West, actress; Edith Wharton, novelist; Rosalyn Yalow, Nobel Prize winner in medicine.

Oakland, Calif.

Mayor: Jerry Brown
City Manager: Robert C. Bobb
1998 est. population (rank): 365,874 (45)[1]
1990 census popultion (rank): 372,242 (39); **% change,** –1.7; **Male,** 178,824; **Female,** 193,418; **White,** 120,849 (32.5%); **Black,** 163,335 (43.9%); **American Indian, Eskimo, or Aleut,** 2,371 (0.6%); **Asian or Pacific Islander,** 54,931 (14.8%); **Other race,** 30,756; **Hispanic origin,** 51,771 (13.9%). **1990 population under 18,** 24.9%; **65 and over,** 12.0%; **median age:** 32.7.
Land area: 53.9 sq mi. (140 sq km); **Alt.:** Highest, 1,700 ft.; lowest, sea level
Avg. daily temp.: Jan., 49.0° F; July, 63.7° F
Churches: 374, representing over 78 denominations in the City; over 500 churches in Alameda County; **City-owned parks:** 2,196 ac.; **Radio stations:** AM, 1; **Television stations:** 1 commercial
Civilian Labor Force: 180,624; **Unemployed:** 18,148, **Percent:** 10.0; **Per capita personal income (PMSA) 1992:** $24,359
Chamber of Commerce: Oakland Chamber of Commerce, 475 Fourteenth St., Oakland, Calif. 94612-1903

1. 1997 est. population: 386,100

Oakland is located in the west central part of California on the east side of San Francisco Bay. It is the seat of Alameda County.

Don Luis Peralta first settled the site of Oakland in 1820 when he established the Rancho San Antonio. The gold rush of 1849 attracted more people to the area and the city's population continued to grow after a ferry service to San Francisco was started in 1851. Oakland was incorporated as a town in 1852 and as a city in 1854. It was named after the numerous oak trees found in the area. Oakland became the western terminus of the Central Pacific Railroad in 1869 and the seat of Alameda County in 1873.

In the latter part of the 19th century and also in 1910, additional territory was annexed to Oakland

and the city assumed its present size. In 1906, thousands of people fled to Oakland in the aftermath of the San Francisco earthquake and settled there permanently, furthering the city's growth. Oakland's economic development continued to rise with the opening of the San Francisco–Oakland Bay Bridge in 1936.

Oakland is a major center of culture and commerce. It is an important container shipping port and the terminus of three transcontinental railroads. Oakland's industries include shipbuilding, food processing, chemicals, pharmaceuticals, electrical and high technology manufacturing. Oakland is also a leading importer of foreign cars. The city is the headquarters of many national and international corporations.

Famous natives: Buster Crabbe, actor; Frederick Cottrell, inventor; Dennis Eckersley, athlete; Hammer, singer, dancer, and songwriter; Rod McKuen, singer and composer; Russ Meyer, producer and director; Eddie (Anderson) Rochester, actor; George Stevens, director; Amy Tan, writer; Jo Van Fleet, actress.

Oklahoma City, Okla.

Mayor: Kirk Humphreys (to April 2002)
City Manager: Glen E. Deck
1998 est. population (rank): 472,221 (30)
1990 census population (rank): 444,719 (29);
  % change, 6.2; **Male,** 214,466; **Female,** 230,253;
  White, 332,539 (74.8%); **Black,** 71,064 (16.0%);
  American Indian, Eskimo, or Aleut, 14,794 (4.2%);
  Asian or Pacific Islander, 10,491 (2.4%); **Other race,**
  11,831; **Hispanic origin,** 22,033 (5.0%). **1990 population under 18:** 26.0%; **65 and over:** 11.9%; **median age:** 32.4.
Land area: 608.2 sq mi. (1,575 sq km); **Alt.:** Highest, 1,320 ft.; lowest, 1,140 ft.
Avg. daily temp.: Jan., 35.9° F; July, 82.1° F
Churches: Roman Catholic, 25; Jewish, 2; Protestant and others, 741; **City-owned parks:** 138 (3,944 ac.); **Television stations:** 8; **Radio stations:** AM, 10; FM, 14
Civilian Labor Force (1998): 534,110; **Unemployed:** 20,260; **Percent:** 3.8; **Per capita personal income (MSA) 1997:** $21,659
Chamber of Commerce: Greater Oklahoma City Chamber of Commerce, 123 Park Ave., Oklahoma City, Okla. 73102

Oklahoma City, the state capital and seat of Oklahoma County, is the largest city in Oklahoma. It is located in the central part of the state on the North Canadian River.

Oklahoma City sprang into being almost overnight. On April 22, 1889, the government threw open the territory for settlement, and there was a classic rush across the line to stake claims. Within a short time, a sprawling tent city sprang up near the Santa Fe railroad tracks and Oklahoma City was a bustling town of 10,000. The city was incorporated in 1890 and replaced Guthrie as the state capital in 1910. Oil was discovered in the city in 1928 and petroleum production became a mainstay of the city's economy.

Oklahoma City is the wholesale and distributing center for the state, and the city's stockyards are the largest stocker and feeder cattle market in the world. Following the decline of the energy sector, Oklahoma City is fostering a private entrepreneurial environment and a more diversified economy.

Within the service sector, health services are projected to grow, followed by retail trade and business services. Aerospace, distribution, and telecommunications have been targeted for business attraction. Nearby Tinker Air Force Base, one of the world's largest air depots, is a major city employer.

Famous natives: Johnny Bench, baseball; Lon Chaney, Jr., actor; Ralph Ellison, writer; Kay Francis, actress; Dale Robertson, actor; Ted Shackleford, actor; Pamela Tiffin, actress; Vince Gill, country singer.

Omaha, Neb.

Mayor: Hal Daub (to 2001)
1998 est. population (rank): 371,291 (43)
1990 census population (rank): 335,795 (48);
  % change, 7.8; **Male,** 160,392; **Female,** 175,403;
  White, 281,603 (83.9%); **Black,** 43,989 (13.1%);
  American Indian, Eskimo, or Aleut, 2,274 (0.7%);
  Asian or Pacific Islander, 3,412 (1.0%); **Other race,**
  4,517; **Hispanic origin,** 10,288 (3.1%). **1990 population under 18:** 25.4%; **65 and over:** 12.9%; **median age:** 32.2.
Land area: 113 sq mi. (290 sq km); **Alt.:** Highest, 1,270 ft.
Avg. daily temp.: Jan., 20.2° F; July, 77.7° F
Churches: Protestant, 246; Roman Catholic, 44; Jewish, 4; **City-owned parks:** 164 (over 7,400 ac.); **Radio stations:** AM, 7; FM, 13; **Television stations:** 6
Civilian Labor Force: 177,387; **Unemployed:** 8,298, **Percent:** 4.7; **Per capita personal income (MSA) 1992:** $20,242[1]
Chamber of Commerce: Omaha Chamber of Commerce, 1301 Harney St., Omaha, Neb. 68102

1. Omaha, Neb.–Iowa.

Omaha, the largest city in Nebraska and the seat of Douglas County, is located in the eastern part of the state on the west bank of the Missouri River, opposite Council Bluffs, Iowa.

The Lewis and Clark expedition visited the area in 1804, and the U.S. Army built Ft. Atkinson nearby in 1819. Pierre Cabanne established a fur-trading post at the site in 1825. The first Mormon migrants wintered there in 1846–1847 on their way to Utah. The city grew rapidly as the most northerly supply point for overland wagons to the Far West.

The city was officially founded in 1854 after the Nebraska Territory was opened for settlement. It was named for the Omaha Indians living nearby, whose tribal name means "those who go upstream or against the current." Omaha was incorporated as a city in 1857 and was the capital of the Nebraska Territory from 1855 to 1867. The city continued to thrive as a point of entry and a major transportation center when the Union Pacific trans-continental railroad arrived in 1869.

Omaha is a major market for food processing, telecommunications, and insurance. Other important industries include electrical equipment and finance as well as printing and publishing.

Famous natives: Fred Astaire, dancer and actor; Max Baer, boxer; Ronald Boone, former NBA professional; Robert Boozer, former NBA professional; Marlon Brando, actor; Montgomery Clift, actor; Gerald Ford, former president; Bob Gibson, baseball player; Swoosie Kurtz, actress; Melvin Laird, former secretary of defense; Dorothy McGuire, actress; Nick Nolte, actor; Gale Sayers, football player; Malcolm X, political activist; Paul Williams, singer and composer.

Philadelphia, Pa.

Mayor: Edward G. Rendell (to Jan. 2000)
1998 est. population (rank): 1,436,287 (5)
1990 census population (rank): 1,585,577 (5);
  % change, –9.4; **Male,** 737,763; **Female,** 847,814;
  White, 848,586 (53.5%); **Black,** 631,936 (39.9%);
  American Indian, Eskimo, or Aleut, 3,454 (0.2%);
  Asian or Pacific Islander, 43,522 (2.7%); **Other race,**
  58,079; **Hispanic origin,** 89,193 (5.6%). **1990 population under 18:** 23.9%; **65 and over:** 15.2%; **median
  age:** 33.2.
Land area: 136 sq mi. (352 sq km); **Alt.:** Highest, 440
  ft.; lowest, sea level
Avg. daily temp.: Jan., 31.2° F; July, 76.5° F
Churches: Roman Catholic, 133; Jewish, 55; Protestant
  and others, 830; **City-owned parks:** 630 (10,252 ac.);
  Radio stations: AM, 40[1]; FM, 43[1]; **Television
  stations:** 14[1]
Civilian Labor Force (1997 est.): 652,126[1];
  Unemployed: 41,085[1], **Percent:** 8.8[2]; **Per capita per-
  sonal income (PMSA) 1994:** $25,220[1]
Chamber of Commerce: Philadelphia Chamber of Com-
  merce, 1234 Market Street, Suite 1800, Philadelphia,
  Pa. 19107

1. Philadelphia City/County.

Philadelphia, the largest city in Pennsylvania and seat of Philadelphia County (coterminous), is located in the southeastern part of the state at the junction of the Schuylkill and Delaware Rivers.

Philadelphia, the City of Brotherly Love, was settled in 1681 by Capt. William Markham, who, with a small band of colonists, was sent out by his cousin, William Penn. Penn arrived the following year.

In the period before the American Revolution, the city outstripped all others in the colonies in educa-tion, arts, science, industry, and commerce. In 1774–1776, the First and Second Continental Congresses met in Philadelphia; and, from 1781–1783, the city was the capital of the U.S. under the Articles of Confederation. In 1790, it became the nation's capi-tal under the Constitution and remained so until the seat of the federal government moved to Washing-ton in 1800.

Within a half-century of the founding of the nation at Independence Hall, Philadelphia had emerged as the "world's greatest workshop." The steam locomotives and hat factories of the 19th cen-tury have been replaced by diverse manufacturing specialties such as chemicals (including pharmaceu-ticals), medical devices, transportation equipment, and printing and publishing. In the services sector, Philadelphia is a major net "exporter" in subsectors such as health services, insurance carriers, legal ser-vices, and architecture and engineering services.

The city abounds in landmarks of early Ameri-can history, including Independence Hall and the Liberty Bell.

Famous natives: Marian Anderson, contralto; Frankie Avalon, singer and actor; John, Lionel, and Ethel Barrymore, actors; Kevin Bacon, actor; Boyz II Men, R&B group; Mary Cassatt, artist; Wilt Chamberlain, basketball player; Chubby Checker, singer; Bill Cosby, actor; Stuart Davis, painter; Thomas Eakins, painter and sculptor; W. C. Fields, comedian; Benjamin Franklin, inventor and statesman; Grace (Kelly), actress and Princess of Monaco; Walt Kelly, cartoonist; Patti LaBelle, singer; Mario Lanza, singer and actor; George McClellan, general; Margaret Mead, anthropologist; Edgar Allen Poe, author; Anna Quindlen, writer and Pulitzer Prize winner; Man Ray, painter; Betsy Ross, flagmaker; Will Smith, actor; Jacqueline Susann, novelist; Robert Venturi, architect.

Phoenix, Ariz.

Mayor: Skip Rimsza (to Oct. 1999)
City Manager: Frank Fairbanks (apptd. May 1990)
1998 est. population (rank): 1,198,064 (7)[1]
1990 census population (rank): 983,403 (9);
  % change, 21.3; **Male,** 487,589; **Female,** 495,814;
  White, 803,332 (81.6%); **Black,** 51,053 (5.2%);
  American Indian, Eskimo, or Aleut, 18,225 (1.9%);
  Asian or Pacific Islander, 16,303 (1.7%); **Other race,**
  94,490; **Hispanic origin,** 197,103 (20.0%). **1990
  population under 18:** 27.2%; **65 and over,** 9.7%;
  median age: 31.1.
Land area: 476.7 sq mi. (1,216.8 sq km); **Alt.:** Highest,
  2,740 ft..; lowest, 1,017 ft.
Avg. daily temp.: Jan., 53.6° F; July, 93.5° F
City-owned parks: 170 (25,235 ac.); **Radio stations:**
  AM, 20; FM, 20; **Television stations:** 9 commercial;
  1 PBS
Civilian Labor Force: 1,482,000; **Unemployed:** 51,200,
  Percent: 3.3; **Per capita personal income (MSA)
  1992:** $19,018
Chamber of Commerce: Phoenix Chamber of Com-
  merce, 201 N. Central, Phoenix, Ariz. 85073

1. 1997 est. population: 1,187,944.

Phoenix, the capital of Arizona and seat of Mari-copa County, is the largest city in the state. It is located in the center of Arizona, on the Salt River.

The prehistoric Hohokam Indians first settled the area about 300 B.C.E. and dug a system of extensive irrigation canals for farming. The Indian culture mysteriously broke up in the 1400s. The site was permanently resettled again by Jack Swilling and "Lord Darrell" Duppa about 1867. Because the city was founded on the ruins of the ancient civilization, it was named Phoenix after the legendary Phoenix bird that could regenerate itself. The irrigation canals were restored for farming, and ranching and prospecting began in the surrounding area. The city quickly grew as an important trading center.

Phoenix was incorporated as a city in 1881 and was made the territorial capital in 1889. It became the state capital when Arizona was admitted to the Union in 1912.

Phoenix is a center of agriculture and commerce. Major industries include government, agricultural products, aerospace technology, electronics, air-conditioning, leather goods, and Indian arts and crafts. The city of Phoenix is renowned as a leader in local government management and received the 1993 Bertelsmann Foundation award for the best-managed city in the world.

Famous natives: Lynda Carter, actress; Joan Ganz Cooney, TV executive; Alice Cooper, musician; Arthur A. Fletcher, government official; Barry Goldwater, politician; Stevie Nicks, musician; Charles S. Robb, politician; Mare Winningham, actress.

Pittsburgh, Pa.

Mayor: Tom Murphy (to Jan. 2002)
1998 est. population (rank): 340,520 (49)
1990 census population (rank): 369,879 (40);
  % change, –7.9; **Male,** 171,722; **Female,** 198,157;
  White, 266,791 (72.1%); **Black,** 95,362 (25.8%);
  American Indian, Eskimo, or Aleut, 671 (0.2%);
  Asian or Pacific Islander, 5,937 (1.6%); **Other race,**
  1,118; **Hispanic origin,** 3,468 (0.9%). **1990 population under 18:** 19.8%; **65 and over,** 17.9%; **median
  age:** 34.6.
Land area: 55.5 sq mi. (144 sq km); **Alt.:** Highest, 1,240
  ft.; lowest, 715 ft.
Avg. daily temp.: Jan., 26.7° F; July, 72.0° F

Churches: Protestant, 348; Roman Catholic, 86; Jewish, 28; Orthodox, 26; **City-owned parks and playgrounds:** 270 (2,572 ac.); **Radio stations:** AM, 12; FM, 20; **Television stations:** 11
Civilian Labor Force: 164,600; **Unemployed:** 7,400, **Percent:** 4.5; **Per capita personal income (MSA) 1996 :** $24,957
Chamber of Commerce: The Chamber of Commerce of Greater Pittsburgh, 3 Gateway Center, Pittsburgh, Pa. 15222

Pittsburgh, the second-largest city in Pennsylvania and seat of Allegheny County, is located in the southwestern part of the state at the junction where the Allegheny and Monongahela rivers join to form the Ohio River.

Some of the first inhabitants of the area were the Shawnee, Seneca, Delaware, and Iroquois Indians, who had left the area by 1754. That year a detachment of troops from Virginia put a fort on the site of present Pittsburgh (Ft. Prince George), considering it a strategic spot. Following the original Virginia settlers, the French seized the spot and named it Ft. Duquesne; in 1758, the British took it away from the French. The British built a new fort and named it after the British prime minister, William Pitt. A town developed around the fort and was incorporated as the City of Pittsburgh in 1816.

By the late 1800s, Pittsburgh had become a world leader in iron and steelmaking, and it remained so for nearly a century. In the early 1980s, the country's domestic steel industry collapsed, causing major upheavals in Pittsburgh's manufacturing sector.

The Pittsburgh region underwent a successful diversified economic transition, shifting from heavy industries to light manufacturing, advanced technologies such as industrial automation, advanced materials, software engineering, and biomedical technology, medicine, education, finance, and corporate services. Pittsburgh is a national leader in health care services and is the world's leading center for organ transplantation.

Pittsburgh is also a major U.S. transportation center and is one of the nation's largest inland ports in terms of tonnage.

Famous natives: Rachel Carson, ecologist and writer; Henry Steele Commager, historian; Bill Cullen, radio and TV entertainer; John Davidson, singer and actor; Billy Eckstine, singer; Erroll Garner, jazz pianist; Scott Glenn, actor; Martha Graham, dancer and choreographer; George S. Kaufman, playwright; Michael Keaton, actor; Gene Kelly, actor and dancer; Oscar Levant, pianist; Andrew Mellon, financier; Adolphe Menjou, actor; William Powell, actor; Mary Roberts Rinehart, novelist; Peter Sellars, theater director; David O. Selznick, producer; Joseph Wambaugh, novelist; Andy Warhol, artist; August Wilson, playwright.

Portland, Ore.

Mayor: Vera Katz (to Jan. 2001)
1998 est. population (rank).: 503,891 (26)
1990 census population (rank): 437,319 (30); **% change,** 3.7; **Male,** 211,914; **Female,** 225,405; **White,** 370,135 (84.4%); **Black,** 33,530 (7.7%); **American Indian, Eskimo, or Aleut,** 5,399 (1.2%); **Asian or Pacific Islander,** 23,185 (5.3%); **Other race,** 5,070; **Hispanic origin,** 13,874 (3.2%). **1990 population under 18:** 21.9%; **65 and over,** 14.6%; **median age:** 34.5.
Land area: 137.8 sq mi. (357 sq km); **Alt.:** Highest, 1073 ft.; lowest, sea level
Avg. daily temp.: Jan., 38.9° F; July, 67.7° F
Churches: Protestant, 450; Roman Catholic, 48; Jewish, 9; Buddhist, 6; other, 190; **City-owned parks:** 200 (over 9,400 ac.);

Radio stations: AM: 14, FM: 14; **Television stations:** 5 commercial, 1 public
Civilian Labor Force: 248,724; **Unemployed:** 18,372, **Percent:** 7.4; **Per capita personal income (PMSA) 1992:** $20,681
Chamber of Commerce: Portland Chamber of Commerce, 221 NW 2nd Ave., Portland, Ore. 97209

Portland, the largest city in Oregon and seat of Multnomah County, is located in the northwestern part of the state on the Willamette River.

Lewis and Clark camped at the site of Portland in 1805 on their expedition across the continent. Portland was founded in 1845 and was almost called Boston after the city in Massachusetts. Founders Amos Lovejoy from Massachusetts and Francis Pettygrove from Maine flipped a coin to decide the name of the new town. Pettygrove won the toss and named the place Portland after his hometown. Portland was incorporated as a city in 1851.

Portland's growth was stimulated during the 1850s as a supply base for the California gold rush, by the development of its salmon and lumber industries, and by the arrival of the railroad in 1883. The city continued to grow during 1879 to 1900 as a supply point for the Alaska gold rush and as the site of the Lewis and Clark Centennial Exposition in 1905.

The port of Portland leads the west in grain exports and is among the top five auto-import centers in the United States. The port ranks third in overall volume behind Los Angeles and Long Beach.

Portland has a diverse economy with a broad base of manufacturing, distribution, wholesale and retail trade, regional government, and business services. Major manufacturing industries include machinery, electronics, metals, transportation equipment, and lumber and wood products. Technology is a thriving part of Portland's economy, with over 500 high-tech companies located in the metropolitan area. Tourism is also important to Portland's economy.

Famous natives: James Beard, food expert; Pietro Belluschi, architect; Richard Fosbury, high jumper; Matt Groening, cartoonist; Margaux Hemingway, actress; Phil Knight, founder of Nike; Terrance Knox, actor; Jeff Lorber, jazz musician; Linus Pauling, chemist; Jane Powell, singer and actress; Ahmad Rashad, football player and sportscaster; Susan Ruttan, actress; Doc Severinson, band leader; Norton Simon, business executive; Sally Ann Struthers, actress; Gus Van Sant, film director; Lindsay Wagner, actress; Mitch Williams, baseball pitcher.

Sacramento, Calif.

Mayor: Joe Serna, Jr. (to March 2000)
1998 est. population (rank): 404,168 (38)
1990 census population (rank): 369,365 (42); **% change,** 9.4; **Male,** 178,737; **Female,** 190,628; **White,** 221,963 (60.1%); **Black,** 56,521 (15.3%); **American Indian, Eskimo, or Aleut,** 4,561 (1.2%); **Asian or Pacific Islander,** 55,426 (15.0%); **Other race,** 30,894; **Hispanic origin,** 60,007 (16.2%). **1990 population under 18:** 26.2%; **65 and over,** 12.1%; **median age:** 31.8.
Land area: 123 sq mi. (318.7 sq km)
Avg. daily temp.: Jan., 53.5° F; July, 88.4° F
City park & recreational facilities: 134+ (1,427+ ac.); **Television stations:** 7
Civilian Labor Force: 188,670; **Unemployed:** 13,070, **Percent:** 6.9; **Per capita personal income (PMSA) 1992:** $23,038
Chamber of Commerce: Sacramento Chamber of Commerce, 917 7th St., Sacramento, Calif. 95814; West Sacramento Chamber of Commerce, 834-C Jefferson Blvd., Sacramento, Calif. 95691

Sacramento is the capital of and seventh-largest city in Calif. and is the seat of Sacramento County. It is located in the north central part of the state at the confluence of the Sacramento and American rivers.

In 1839, German-born Swiss citizen John Augustus Sutter obtained a grant from the Mexican governor to establish a colony for fellow Swiss emigrants on a large tract of land in the vicinity that he named New Helvetia (New Switzerland), and established Fort Sutter there as a trading post.

After gold was discovered on Sutter's property in 1848, the settlement rapidly expanded as the prominent supply point for gold prospectors coming from the East. Sacramento was laid out in 1848 and named after California's principal river, which ran beside it. The river's name in Spanish honors the Holy Sacrament. It became incorporated as a city in 1849 and was made the state capital in 1854. Sacramento was the terminus of the first railroad in 1856 and the western terminus of the Pony Express in 1860.

The city has always been a hub of river transportation and is a major deep-water port connected to the Pacific Ocean. Sacramento's economy is highly diversified and, along with state government and military installations, its industries include aerospace, high technology, furniture, chemicals, pharmaceuticals, meat packing, and food processing of crops from the Central Valley.

The defense sector of the economy declined and Mather Air Force Base and the Army Depot were closed in 1995.

Famous natives: Joan Didion, author; Mark Goodson, TV producer; Tom Hanks, actor; Henry Hathaway, director; Anthony M. Kennedy, Supreme Court justice; Molly Ringwald, actress.

St. Louis, Mo.

Mayor: Clarence Harmon (to April 2001)
1998 est. population (rank): 339,316 (50)
1990 census population (rank): 396,685 (34);
% change, –14.5; **Male,** 180,680; **Female,** 216,005;
White, 202,085 (50.9%); **Black,** 188,408 (47.5%);
American Indian, Eskimo, or Aleut, 950 (0.2%);
Asian or Pacific Islander, 3,733 (0.9%); **Other race,** 1,509; **Hispanic origin,** 5,124 (1.3%). **1990 population under 18:** 25.2%; **65 and over:** 16.6%; **median age:** 32.8.
Land area: 61.4 sq mi. (159 sq km); **Alt.:** Highest, 616 ft.; lowest, 413 ft.
Avg. daily temp.: Jan., 28.8° F; July, 78.9° F
Churches: 900[1]; **City-owned parks:** 89 (2,639 ac.);
Radio stations: AM, 21; FM 27[1]; **Television stations:** 6 commercial; 1 PBS
Civilian Labor Force: 179,278; **Unemployed:** 14,379, **Percent:** 8.0; **Per capita personal income (MSA)** 1992: $22,700[2]
Chamber of Commerce: St. Louis Regional Commerce and Growth Association, 100 S. Fourth St., Ste. 500, St. Louis, Mo. 63102

1. Metropolitan area. 2. St. Louis, Mo.–Ill.

St. Louis, the second-largest city in Missouri, is located in the east central part of the state on the Mississippi River. The city is independent and is not part of any county.

St. Louis was founded by the French in 1764 when Auguste Chouteau established a fur-trading post and Pierre Laclède Liguest, a New Orleans merchant, founded a town in February 1764 at the present site. They named it after King Louis XV of France and

his patron saint, Louis IX. From 1770 to 1803, St. Louis was a Spanish possession and retroceded to France in 1803 in accordance with the Treaty of San Ildefonso (1800), only to be acquired by the U.S. as part of the Louisiana purchase that year.

The town was incorporated in 1809. From 1812 to 1821, St. Louis was the capital of the Missouri Territory and was incorporated as a city in 1822.

John Jacob Astor opened the Western branch of the American Fur Company in 1819 and the city prospered during the early part of the 19th century as a center for the transportation of the fur trade. St. Louis's commercial growth continued as a major transportation hub with the development of steamboat traffic and the later expansion of the railroads in the 1850s. The world-famous Louisiana Purchase Exposition was held here in 1904.

Manufacturing is important to the city's economy, and its highly developed industries include automobiles, aircraft and space technology, metal fabrication, beer, steelmaking, chemicals, food processing, and storage and distribution.

The giant stainless steel Gateway Arch, 630 feet high, standing on the banks of the Mississippi symbolizes St. Louis as the Gateway to the West.

Famous natives: Josephine Baker, singer; Yogi Berra, baseball player; Grace Bumbry, mezzo-soprano; Morris Carnovsky, actor; T. S. Eliot, poet; Eugene Field, poet; Redd Foxx, comedian; Joe Garagiola, baseball player; John Goodman, actor; Betty Grable, actress; Dick Gregory, comedian; Al Hirschfeld, cartoonist; Kevin Kline, actor; David Merrick, producer; Vincent Price, actor; Judy Rankin, golfer; Leon Spinks, boxer; Herbert Bayard Swope, journalist; Sara Teasdale, poet; Helen Traubel, soprano; Roy Wilkins, civil rights leader.

San Antonio, Tex.

Mayor: Howard Peak (to June 1999)
City Manager: Alexander E. Briseno (apptd. April 27, 1990)
1998 est. population (rank): 1,114,130 (8)[1]
1990 census population (rank): 935,933 (10);
% change, 14.1; **Male,** 450,695; **Female,** 485,238;
White, 676,082 (72.3%); **Black,** 65,884 (7.0%);
American Indian, Eskimo, or Aleut, 3,303 (0.4%);
Asian or Pacific Islander, 10,703 (1.1%); **Other race,** 179,961; **Hispanic origin,** 520,282 (55.6%). **1990 population under 18:** 29.0%; **65 and over:** 10.5%; **median age:** 29.8.
Land area: 399.7 sq mi. (1035.5 sq km); **Alt.:** 700 ft.
Avg. daily temp.: Jan., 51.2° F; July, 86.1° F
City-owned parks: 6,717 ac.; **Radio stations:** AM, 20; FM, 22; **Television stations:** 9
Civilian Labor Force: 695,110; **Unemployed:** 32,177, **Percent:** 4.6; **Per capita personal income (MSA)** 1992: $17,282
Chamber of Commerce: Greater San Antonio Chamber of Commerce, P.O. Box 1628, 602 E. Commerce, San Antonio, Tex. 78296

1. 1997 est. population: 1,115,600.

San Antonio, the third-largest city in Texas and the seat of Bexar County, is located in the south central part of the state, on the San Antonio River.

The site of San Antonio was first visited in 1691 by a Franciscan friar on the feast day of St. Anthony and was named San Antonio de Padua in his honor. San Antonio was permanently settled on May 1, 1718, when the Spanish governor of Coahuila and Texas, Martin de Alarcón, founded the presidio (a fort) of San Antonio de Bejar (Bexar) and the mission of San Antonio de Valero (later called the

Alamo[1]) on the site of a Coahuiltecan Indian village. San Antonio remained almost continuously under Spanish rule until 1812, when Mexico won its independence from Spain.

During the outbreak of the Texas revolution (1835) against the tyranny of Mexican dictator General Santa Anna, San Antonio was captured by a small band of rebels who occupied the fortified mission of the Alamo in December 1835. The historic battle of the Alamo was fought there (Feb. 24 to March 6, 1836) and its 183 besieged defenders were massacred by Santa Anna's troops. Their heroism aroused the anger and fighting spirit of Texans to shout their famous battle cry "Remember the Alamo!" and defeat the Mexicans six weeks later (April 21, 1836) at the battle of San Jacinto. Texas became an independent republic in 1836 and San Antonio was incorporated as a city on Jan. 5, 1837.

After the Civil War, San Antonio prospered as a major shipping point for cattle with the arrival of the railroad in 1877. The city has been an important military center since World War II and is the home to five of the largest military installations in the nation, including Fort Sam Houston, constructed in 1876. San Antonio is a leading livestock center and one of the largest produce exchange markets. The city's industries are highly diversified and tourism is important to the economy.

1. Spanish for the cottonwood tree.

Famous natives: Carol Burnett, comedienne; Cody Carlson, football player; Henry G. Cisneros, secretary of HUD; Joan Crawford, actress; Cito Gaston, baseball manager; Ann Harding, actress; Jesse James Leija, boxer; Emilio Navaira, Tejano music singer; Oliver North, military officer and government official; Suzy Parker, model and actress; Paula Prentiss, actress; Kyle Rote, football player; David R. Scott, astronaut; John Silber, university president; Patsy Torres, Tejano music singer; Edward H. White, astronaut.

San Diego, Calif.

Mayor: Susan Golding (to 2000)
City Manager: Michael Uberuaga (apptd. Nov. 1997)
1998 est. population (rank): 1,220,666 (6)
1990 census population (rank): 1,110,549 (6);
% change, 9.9; **Male,** 566,464; **Female,** 544,085;
White, 745,406 (67.1%); **Black,** 104,261 (9.4%);
American Indian, Eskimo, or Aleut, 6,800 (0.6%);
Asian or Pacific Islander, 130,945 (11.8%); **Other race,** 123,137; **Hispanic origin,** 229,519 (20.7%).
1990 population under 18: 23.1%; **65 and over:** 10.2%; **median age:** 30.5.
Land area: 330.7 sq miles (857 sq km); **Alt.:** Highest, 1,591 ft.; lowest, sea level
Avg. daily temp.: Jan., 56.8° F; July, 70.3° F
Churches: Roman Catholic, 39; Jewish, 9; Protestant, 334; Eastern Orthodox, 8; other, 18; **City park and recreation facilities:** 164 (17,207 ac.); **Radio stations:** AM, 8; FM, 18; **Television stations:** 9
Civilian Labor Force: 548,687; **Unemployed:** 41,301, **Percent:** 7.5; **Per capita personal income (MSA) 1992:** $20,384
Chamber of Commerce: San Diego Chamber of Commerce, 402 West Broadway, Suite 1000, San Diego, Calif. 92101

San Diego is the second-largest city in California. It is located in the southwestern part of the state, on San Diego Bay.

Portuguese navigator Juan Rodríguez Cabrillo claimed the bay in 1542 for Spain. The site was named San Miguel by Cabrillo. On Nov. 12, 1602, Don Sebastian de Viscaíno came ashore with his party on the day of St. Didacus (San Diego in Spanish) and celebrated a mass in the saint's honor. By coincidence, Viscaíno's flagship was named *San Diego*. He renamed the place San Diego after the 15th-century saint.

In 1769, Franciscan Father Junípero Serra established the first California mission there—San Diego del Alcala. In 1822, Mexico won control of the town after it declared its independence from Spain. In 1846, during the Mexican War, San Diego was seized by the United States and incorporated into a city in 1850 after California joined the Union that same year.

Today, San Diego's excellent natural harbor is a busy commercial port and a hub of U.S. naval operations. However, the naval training center at San Diego is slated to be closed due to defense cutbacks. Other leading industries are electronics, aerospace and missiles, medical and scientific research, oceanography, and agriculture. Its magnificent climate and proximity to Mexico have made tourism a significant part of the city's economy.

Famous natives: Billy Casper, golfer; Florence Chadwick, swimmer; Dennis Conner, yacht racer; Ted Danson, actor; Robert Duvall, actor; Nanette Fabray, actress; Robert Lansing, actor; Margaret O'Brien, actress; Carol Vaness, soprano; Ted Williams, baseball player; Mickey Wright, golfer.

San Francisco, Calif.

Mayor: Willie L. Brown, Jr. (to Jan. 2000)
1998 est. population (rank): 745,774 (12)
1990 census population (rank): 723,959 (14);
% change, 3.0; **Male,** 362,497; **Female,** 361,462;
White, 387,783 (53.6%); **Black,** 79,039 (10.9%);
American Indian, Eskimo, or Aleut, 3,456 (0.5%);
Asian or Pacific Islander, 210,876 (29.1%); **Other race,** 42,805; **Hispanic origin,** 100,717 (13.9%). **1990 population under 18:** 16.1%; **65 and over:** 14.6%; **median age:** 35.8.
Land area: 46.1 sq mi. (120 sq km); **Alt.:** Highest, 925 ft.; lowest, sea level
Avg. daily temp.: Jan., 48.5° F; July, 62.2° F
Churches: 540 of all denominations; **City-owned parks and squares:** 225; **Radio stations:** 29; **Television stations:** 10
Civilian Labor Force (1995): 398,000[1]; **Unemployed (S.F. residents):** 26,000[1], **Percent:** 6.4[1]; **Per capita personal income (PMSA) 1992:** $31,262
Chamber of Commerce: Greater San Francisco Chamber of Commerce, 465 California St., San Francisco, Calif. 94104

1. San Francisco City/County.

San Francisco, the fourth-largest city in California, is coextensive with San Francisco County. It is located in the northern part of the state between the Pacific Ocean and San Francisco Bay. A narrow arm of land embraces San Francisco Bay, the largest land-locked harbor in the world, and shelters it from the Pacific Ocean. On this arm of land is San Francisco, a city on hills, almost surrounded by water.

A Franciscan father who was sailing with Sebastián Rodríguez Cermeño named the bay San Francisco on Nov. 7, 1595. In 1776, the Spaniards established a presidio, or military post, and a Franciscan mission on the end of the beautiful peninsula. In the following year, a little town called Yerba Buena, Spanish for "Good Herb," because mint grew in abundance, was founded around the mission.

In 1846, during the Mexican War, Yerba Buena was taken over by the United States. It was renamed San Francisco in 1847 and became incorporated as a city in 1850.

When gold was discovered in California in 1848, the city's population jumped to 10,000, and it experienced turbulent years until order was established by Vigilance Committees, first in 1851, and again in 1856. Then followed a period of more orderly growth and the foundations of the great commerce and industry of today were laid.

In 1906, San Francisco experienced the nation's most destructive earthquake, which, together with the fire that followed, practically destroyed the city. The city was quickly rebuilt and grew rapidly as a leading transportation, industrial, and cultural center. In the 19th century, the American explorer and soldier John C. Frémont, known as The Pathfinder, named the entrance to the bay the Golden Gate, and the famous bright orange Golden Gate Bridge was dedicated in May 1937.

A vital part of the economic and cultural fabric of northern California, the port of San Francisco covers 7½ miles of waterfront. The port is home to a broad range of commercial, maritime, and public activities. Its major shipping terminals serve shipping lines from around the world. Fisherman's Wharf, Alcatraz, Hyde St. Pier, and Pier 39 all make the port of San Francisco one of the world's leading visitor destinations.

Small businesses have a very important place in the economy. More than 80% of the city's 33,800 businesses have fewer than 15 employees. The high-technology industries of electronics and biotechnology are well represented throughout the Bay Area. With nearly 30% of the worldwide biotechnology labor force, and 360 biotech firms, the Bay Area has been appropriately called "Bionic Bay." Tourism is one of San Francisco's largest industries and the largest employer of city residents. Nearly 13.4 million persons visit San Francisco each year and annual visitor spending is $231 million, providing 66,400 jobs.

The military has played an important role in San Francisco and the Bay Area's economies, but its impact will decline due to defense cutbacks. San Francisco is also the banking and financial center of the West and is home to a Federal Reserve Bank and a United States Mint. More than 60 foreign banks maintain offices there.

Famous natives: Gracie Allen, comedienne; Luis Walter Alvarez, Nobel Prize winner in physics; David Belasco, dramatist and producer; Mel Blanc, actor and voice specialist; Rosemary Casals, tennis player; Isadora Duncan, dancer; Clint Eastwood, actor; Robert Frost, poet; Rube Goldberg, cartoonist; William Randolph Hearst, publisher; Bruce Lee, actor; Mervyn LeRoy, director; Jack London, novelist; Johnny Mathis, singer; Lloyd Nolan, actor; O. J. Simpson, football player; Robert G. Sproul, educator; Irving Stone, novelist; Natalie Wood, actress.

San Jose, Calif.

Mayor: Ron Gonzales
Acting City Manager: Debra Figone
1998 population (est): 861,284 (11)[1]
1990 census population (rank): 782,248 (11);
 % change, 10.1; **Male,** 397,709; **Female,** 384,539;
 White, 491,280 (62.8%); **Black,** 36,790 (4.7%);
 American Indian, Eskimo, or Aleut, 5,416 (0.7%);
 Asian or Pacific Islander, 152,815 (19.5%); **Other**

race, 95,947; **Hispanic origin,** 208,388 (26.6%). **1990 population under 18:** 26.7%; **65 and over:** 7.2%; **median age:** 30.4.
Land area: 180.8 sq mi. (468.27 sq km); **Alt.:** Highest, 4,372 ft.; lowest, sea level
Avg. daily temp.: Jan., 49.5° F; July, 68.8° F
Churches: 403; **City-owned parks and playgrounds:** 152 (3,136 ac.); **Radio stations:** 14; **Television stations:** 4
Civilian Labor Force: 420,686; **Unemployed:** 33,484, **Percent:** 8.0; **Per capita personal income (PMSA) 1992:** $25,924[1]
Chamber of Commerce: San Jose Chamber of Commerce, One Paseo de San Antonio, San Jose, Calif. 95113

1. 1999 est. population: 909,100

San Jose, the third-largest city in California and seat of Santa Clara County, is located in the northern part of the state in the Santa Clara Valley near San Francisco Bay, 50 miles south of downtown San Francisco.

San Jose was founded on Nov. 29, 1777, by Spanish colonizers who named the settlement Pueblo de San José de Guadalupe in honor of Saint Joseph and after the Guadalupe River on which the pueblo (town) was situated. San Jose was the first city to be established in California.

After California became a U.S. territory in 1847, San Jose was the state capital from 1849 to 1852 and was incorporated as a city in 1850. It developed commercially as a supply base for gold prospectors and, when the railroad connected it with San Francisco in 1864, became the distribution point for agricultural products from the Santa Clara Valley.

Today, the city continues to be the distribution and food-processing center for the surrounding rich agricultural region, which produces seasonal fruits and grapes. More than 50 wineries grace the valley.

San Jose is the capital of Silicon Valley (Santa Clara), the nation's center of high technology, where more than 3,000 high-tech companies are located. Silicon Valley is also one of the world's leading centers for medical treatment and research. Heart transplants, gene splicing, and transportable baby incubators were developed there.

San Jose has healthy retail, transportation, and tourism industries as well, and is the primary center for real estate and industrial development in the area.

Famous natives: "Fatty" Arbuckle, actor; Chuck Berry, singer and guitarist; Cesar Chavez, labor leader; Peggy Fleming, figure skater; Farley Granger, actor; Edmund Lowe, actor; Jim Plunkett, football player.

Seattle, Wash.

Mayor: Paul Schell (to Dec. 31, 2001)
1998 est. population (rank): 536,978 (22)
1990 census population (rank): 516,259 (21);
 % change, 4.0; **Male,** 252,042; **Female,** 264,217;
 White, 388,858 (75.3%); **Black,** 51,948 (10.1%);
 American Indian, Eskimo, or Aleut, 7,326 (1.4%);
 Asian or Pacific Islander, 60,819 (11.8%); **Other race,** 7,308 (1.4%); **Hispanic origin,** 18,349 (3.6%).
 1990 population under 18: 16.5%; **65 and over:** 15.2%; **median age:** 34.9.
Land area: 144.6 sq mi. (375 sq km); **Alt.:** Highest, 521 ft.; lowest, sea level
Avg. daily temp.: Jan., 42.2° F; July, 67.6° F
Churches: Roman Catholic, 35; Jewish, 12; Protestant, 447; others, 42; **City-owned parks, playgrounds, etc.:** 397 (6,000+ ac.); **Radio stations:** AM, 15; FM, 22; **Television stations:** 6

Civilian Labor Force (1999): (3 counties) 1,206,089;
Unemployed: 37,389, **Percent:** 3.1; **Per capita
personal income:** $35,019
Chamber of Commerce: Greater Seattle Chamber of
Commerce, 1301 5th Ave., Suite 2400, Seattle, Wash.
98101-2603

Seattle is the largest city in Washington and the
seat of King County. A city of steep hills, Seattle
lies in western Washington between two bodies of
water—Puget Sound on the west and Lake Washington on the east. Its fine landlocked harbor has made
Seattle one of the major ports in the United States.

Seattle was first settled by five pioneer families
from Illinois at Alki Point at the south end of Elliott
Bay in 1851. They moved in 1852 to the eastern
shore of the bay and laid out a town in 1853. It was
named Seattle after a friendly Suquamish Indian
Chief (Seattle is only an approximation of his name).

Seattle successfully withstood an Indian attack in
1856 and was incorporated as a city in 1869. A
disastrous fire almost destroyed the entire business
district in 1889. When the Great Northern Railway
arrived in 1893, the city became a major rail terminus and it grew rapidly. It was a boom town during
the Alaska gold rush of 1897 and continued to prosper as a major Pacific port of entry with the opening
of the Panama Canal in 1914.

Seattle is the region's commercial and transportation hub and the center of manufacturing, trade, and
finance. Its important diversified industries include
aircraft, lumber and forest products, fishing, high
technology, food processing, boat building, machinery, fabricated metals, chemicals, pharmaceuticals,
and apparel.

Famous natives: Chester Carlson, Xerox inventor; Carol
Channing, actress; Judy Collins, singer; Fred Couples,
golfer; Gail Devers, athlete; Frances Farmer, actress;
William Gates, Microsoft founder; June Havoc, actress;
Jimi Hendrix, guitarist; Robert Joffrey, choreographer;
Gypsy Rose Lee, entertainer; Mary Livingstone,
comedienne; Kevin McCarthy, actor; Mary McCarthy,
novelist; Jeff Smith, food expert; Martha Wright, singer.

Tucson, Ariz.

Mayor: George Miller (to Dec. 1999)
1998 est. population (rank): 460,466 (32)[1]
1990 census population (rank): 405,390 (33);
% change, 10.8; **Male,** 197,319; **Female,** 208,071;
White, 305,055 (74.6%); **Black,** 17,366 (4.3%);
American Indian, Eskimo, or Aleut, 6,464 (1.6%);
Asian or Pacific Islander, 8,901 (2.2%); **Other race,**
67,604; **Hispanic origin,** 118,595 (29.3%). **1990
population under 18:** 24.5%; **65 and over:** 12.6%;
median age: 30.6.
Land area: 162 sq mi. (419 sq km); **Alt.:** 2,400 ft.
Avg. daily temp.: Jan., 51.1° F; July, 86.2° F
Churches: Protestant, 340; Roman Catholic, 42; other,
150; **City-owned parks and parkways:** (25,349 ac.);
Radio stations: AM, 15; FM, 17; **Television stations:**
3 commercial; 1 educational; 3 other
Civilian Labor Force (1997): 364,700; **Unemployed:**
10,300, **Percent:** 2.8; **Per capita personal income
(1997):** $22,307
Chamber of Commerce: Tucson Metropolitan Chamber
of Commerce, P.O. Box 991, Tucson, Ariz. 85702

1. 1997 est. population: 452,298.

Tucson is the second-largest city in Arizona and
the seat of Pima County. It is located in the southeastern part of the state on the Santa Cruz River.

The site was originally settled by the prehistoric
Hohokam Indians (300 B.C.E.–C.E.1400s). The first

Europeans to visit the area were Spanish missionaries in the 17th century. In 1700, the Jesuit missionary explorer Father Eusebio Fancisco Kino founded
the mission of San Xavier del Bac close by the
Papago Indian village of Stjukshon (later called
Tucson). Stjukshon is an Indian word meaning "village of the dark spring at the foot of the mountain."
The Papago Indians are descendants of the ancient
Hohokam peoples.

In 1776, Spanish colonists from Mexico constructed a presidio (fort) at Tucson as protection
against the hostile Apache Indians and also established the mission of San Jose de Tucson nearby.
Tucson remained a military outpost under Spanish
rule and later Mexican control until the area was sold
to the United States as part of the Gadsden Purchase
in 1853. Tucson was the capital of the Arizona Territory from 1867 to 1877. It was incorporated as a
city in 1877. The town grew rapidly when the Southern Pacific Railroad arrived in 1880 and silver and
copper deposits were discovered nearby.

Tucson is a popular vacation and health resort due
to its sunny, mild, and dry climate and unique desert
location. Tourism is important to the city's economy.
Major industries include aerospace and missile production, high technology, optics, biotechnology,
environmental technology, software, and electronics.
Tucson is also the commercial center for the surrounding area's agriculture and mining industries.
The city is the home of the University of Arizona.

Famous natives: Rose E. Bird, jurist; Dennis De Concini,
senator; Barbara Eden, actress; Linda Ronstadt, singer.

Tulsa, Okla.

Mayor: M. Susan Savage (to May 2002)
1998 est. population (rank): 381,393 (42)
1990 census population (rank): 367,302 (43);
% change, 3.8; **Male,** 175,538; **Female,** 191,764;
White, 291,444 (79.3%); **Black,** 49,825 (13.6%);
American Indian, Eskimo, or Aleut, 17,091 (4.7%);
Asian or Pacific Islander, 5,133 (1.4%); **Other race,**
3,809; **Hispanic origin,** 9,564 (2.6%). **1990 population under 18:** 24.4%; **65 and over:** 12.7%; **median
age:** 33.1.
Land area: 191.5 sq mi. (497.1 sq km); **Alt.:** 674 ft.
Avg. daily temp.: Jan., 35.2° F; July, 83.2° F
Churches: Protestant, 593; Roman Catholic, 32; Jewish,
2; others, 4; **City parks and playgrounds:** 121 (6,050
ac.); **Radio stations:** AM, 9; FM, 21; **Television stations:** 7 commercial; 1 PBS; 1 cable
Civilian Labor Force (1997): 398,700; **Unemployed:**
12,200, **Percent:** 3.1; **Per capita personal income
(1995):** $20,479
Chamber of Commerce: Metropolitan Tulsa Chamber of
Commerce, 616 S. Boston, Tulsa, Okla. 74119

Tulsa, the second-largest city in Oklahoma and
seat of Tulsa County, is located in the northeastern
part of the state on the Arkansas River.

Tulsa was settled in the 1830s by Creek Indians
from Alabama who were forcibly sent to the area
(then part of Indian Territory) under the Indian
Removal Act of 1830. Creek medicine men planted
ashes from their old home at the new site and the
Creeks named their new village "Tulsy," meaning old
town, in memory of their former home in Tallassee,
Ala. In time, the village became the town of Tulsa.

The coming of the first railroad in 1882 attracted
white settlers to Tulsa and the town developed into
a cattle-shipping center. When enormous oil deposits were discovered at nearby Red Fork in 1901 and

at Glenn Pool in 1905, the city experienced rapid growth as a center of a booming petroleum industry. Tulsa was incorporated as a city in 1898 and chartered in 1908.

Tulsa is the center of the state's petroleum industry and has a diversified economy. Important industries include aerospace, chemicals, computer parts, automobile glass, fabricated metals, and industrial machinery. The city became a major inland port when the Tulsa Port of Catoosa opened in 1971.

Famous natives: Garth Brooks, singer; Blake Edwards, director; Paul Harvey, commentator; Jennifer Jones, actress; Henry R. Kravis, investment banker; Daniel Patrick Moynihan, senator; Tony Randall, actor; Alfre Woodard, actress; Judy Woodruff, journalist.

Virginia Beach, Va.

Mayor: Meyera E. Obendorf (to June 2000)
1998 est. population (rank): 432,380 (34)
1990 census population (rank): 393,069 (37);
% change, 10.0; **Male,** 199,571; **Female,** 193,498;
White, 316,408 (80.5%); **Black,** 54,671 (13.9%);
American Indian, Eskimo, or Aleut, 1,384 (0.4%);
Asian or Pacific Islander, 17,025 (4.3%); **Other race,**
3,581; **Hispanic origin,** 12,137 (3.1%); **1990 population under 18:** 28.0%; **65 and over:** 5.9%; **median age:** 28.9.
Land area: 258.7 sq mi. (670 sq km); **Alt.:** 12 ft.
Avg. daily temp.: Jan., 39.9° F; July, 78.4° F
Churches: Protestant, 235; Catholic, 13; Jewish, 5;
City-owned parks: 182 (1,748 ac.); **Radio stations:**
AM 18, FM 26; **Television stations:** 4 commercial, 1 PBS, 1 cable
Civilian Labor Force: 194,579; **Unemployed:** 11,541,
Percent: 5.9; **Per capita personal income (MSA)**
1992: $18,077[1]
Chamber of Commerce: Hampton Roads Chamber of Commerce, 4512 Virginia Beach Blvd., Virginia Beach, Va., 23463

1. Norfolk–Virginia Beach–Newport News.

Virginia Beach, the largest city in Virginia, is located in the southeasternmost portion of the state on the Atlantic coastline. It is independent and is not part of any county.

The first English settlers to set foot in America landed at Cape Henry at the tip of Virginia Beach on April 29, 1607. They were led by John Smith on his way to establishing Jamestown. The first permanent settlement within the city limits was made at Lynnhaven Bay in 1621. Cape Henry became an important port for British merchant ships calling on America, and it was here that the French Fleet led by Admiral Comte de Grasse blockaded the British Fleet during the American Revolution.

Virginia Beach gained its reputation as a famous vacation resort in the 19th century, following the building of a railroad connecting its oceanfront with Norfolk and the construction of its first hotel in 1883. Virginia Beach was incorporated as a town in 1906 and as a city in 1952. In 1963, Princess Anne County and Virginia Beach merged and gave the present city an area of 310 square miles of oceanfront.

Tourism is the mainstay of the economy and 2.5 million people visit Virginia Beach overnight each year. Virginia Beach's economy is supported by four nearby military bases and diverse industries, including agriculture (165 farms), computer software, engineering, and technical services.

Famous natives and residents: V. C. Andrews, novelist; Raymond Brian Buckland, occult writer; Ann Woodruff Compton, news correspondent; D. J. Dozier, football and baseball player; George Eastman, inventor; Juice Newton, singer; Kenneth S. Reightler, Jr., astronaut; Pat Robertson, evangelist; Henry Walke, naval officer in Mexican and Civil wars; Pernell "Sweet Pea" Whitaker, boxer; Skip Wilkins, wheelchair athlete.

Washington, D.C.

Created municipal corporation: Feb. 21, 1871
Mayor: Anthony Williams
Motto: *Justitia omnibus* (Justice to all)
Flower: American beauty rose; **Tree:** Scarlet oak
1998 est. population: 523,124 (23)
1990 census population (rank): 606,900 (19);
% change, –13.8; **Male,** 282,970; **Female,** 323,930;
White, 179,667 (29.6%); **Black,** 399,604 (65.8%);
American Indian, Eskimo, or Aleut, 1,466 (0.2%);
Asian or Pacific Islander, 11,214 (1.8%); **Other race,** 14,949; **Hispanic origin,** 32,710 (5.4%)
Land area: 68.25 sq mi. (177 sq km); **Alt.:** Highest, 420 ft.; lowest, sea level
Avg. daily temp.: Jan., 35.2° F; July, 78.9° F
Churches: Protestant, 610; Roman Catholic, 132; Jewish, 9; **City parks:** 753 (7,725 ac.); **Radio stations:**
AM, 9; FM, 38; **Television stations:** 19
Civilian Labor Force: 276,000; **Unemployed:** 23,000,
Percent: 8.4; **Per capita personal income (PMSA)**
1992: $26,817[1]
Board of Trade: Greater Washington Board of Trade, 1129 20th Street, N.W., Washington, D.C. 20036
Chamber of Commerce: D.C. Chamber of Commerce, 1319 F St., NW, Washington, D.C. 20004

1. Washington, D.C.–Md.–Va.–W.Va.

The District of Columbia—identical with the City of Washington—is the capital of the United States. It is located between Virginia and Maryland on the Potomac River. The district is named after Columbus.

D.C. history began in 1790 when Congress directed selection of a new capital site, 100 square miles, along the Potomac. When the site was determined, it included 30.75 square miles on the Virginia side of the river. In 1846, however, Congress returned that area to Virginia, leaving the 68.25 square miles ceded by Maryland in 1788. The seat of government was transferred from Philadelphia to Washington on Dec. 1, 1800, and President John Adams became the first resident in the White House.

The city was planned and partly laid out by Major Pierre Charles L'Enfant, a French engineer. This work was perfected and completed by Major Andrew Ellicott and Benjamin Banneker, a freeborn black man, who was an astronomer and mathematician. In 1814, during the War of 1812, a British force burned the capital including the White House.

Until Nov. 3, 1967, the District of Columbia was administered by three commissioners appointed by the president. On that day, a government consisting of a mayor-commissioner and a 9-member council, all appointed by the president with the approval of the Senate, took office. On May 7, 1974, the citizens of the District of Columbia approved a Home Rule Charter, giving them an elected mayor and 13-member council—their first elected municipal government in more than a century. The district also has one non-voting member in the House of Representatives and an elected Board of Education.

On Aug. 22, 1978, Congress passed a proposed constitutional amendment to give Washington, D.C., voting representation in the Congress. The amendment had to be ratified by at least 28 state legislatures within seven years to become effective. As of 1985 it died.

A petition asking for the district's admission to the Union as the 51st state was filed in Congress on September 9, 1983. The district is continuing this drive for statehood.

The federal government and tourism are the mainstays of the city's economy, and many unions, business, professional, and nonprofit organizations are headquartered there.

Famous natives: Edward Albee, playwright; Billie Burke, comedienne; Ina Claire, actress; John Foster Dulles, statesman; Duke Ellington, musician; Jane Greer, actress; Goldie Hawn, actress; Helen Hayes, actress; J. Edgar Hoover, former director of the F.B.I.; William Hurt, actor; Noor al-Hussein, queen of Jordan; Michael Learned, actress; Roger Mudd, newscaster; Eleanor Holmes Norton, government official; Chita Rivera, dancer and actress; Leonard Rose, cellist; John Philip Sousa, composer; Frances Sternhagen, actress.

Top 50 Cities in the U.S. by Estimated 1998 Population and Rank

	7/1/98 population estimate	4/1/90 population census	Numeric population change 1990–1998	Percent population change 1990–1998	Size rank 1990	Size rank 1998
New York, N.Y.	7,420,166	7,322,564	97,602	1.3%	1	1
Los Angeles, Calif.	3,597,556	3,485,557	111,999	3.2	2	2
Chicago, Ill.	2,802,079	2,783,726	18,353	0.7	3	3
Houston, Tex.	1,786,691	1,654,348	132,343	8.0	4	4
Philadelphia, Pa.	1,436,287	1,585,577	−149,290	−9.4	5	5
San Diego, Calif.	1,220,666	1,110,623	110,043	9.9	6	6
Phoenix, Ariz.	1,198,064	988,015	210,049	21.3	9	7
San Antonio, Tex.	1,114,130	976,514	137,616	14.1	10	8
Dallas, Tex.	1,075,894	1,007,618	68,276	6.8	8	9
Detroit, Mich.	970,196	1,027,974	−57,778	−5.6	7	10
San Jose, Calif.	861,284	782,224	79,060	10.1	11	11
San Francisco, Calif.	745,774	723,959	21,815	3.0	14	12
Indianapolis (remainder),[1] Ind.	741,304	731,278	10,026	1.4	13	13
Jacksonville (remainder),[1] Fla.	693,630	635,230	58,400	9.2	15	14
Columbus, Ohio	670,234	632,945	37,289	5.9	16	15
Baltimore, Md.	645,593	736,014	−90,421	−12.3	12	16
El Paso, Tex.	615,032	515,342	99,690	19.3	22	17
Memphis, Tenn.	603,507	618,652	−15,145	−2.4	18	18
Milwaukee, Wis.	578,364	628,088	−49,724	−7.9	17	19
Boston, Mass.	555,447	574,283	−18,836	−3.3	20	20
Austin, Tex.	552,434	472,020	80,414	17.0	27	21
Seattle, Wash.	536,978	516,259	20,719	4.0	21	22
Washington, D.C.	523,124	606,900	−83,776	−13.8	19	23
Nashville-Davidson (remainder),[1] Tenn.	510,274	488,366	21,908	4.5	25	24
Charlotte, N.C.	504,637	419,558	85,079	20.3	33	25
Portland, Ore.	503,891	485,975	17,916	3.7	26	26
Denver, Colo.	499,055	467,610	31,445	6.7	28	27
Cleveland, Ohio	495,817	505,616	−9,799	−1.9	23	28
Fort Worth, Tex.	491,801	447,619	44,182	9.9	29	29
Oklahoma City, Okla.	472,221	444,724	27,497	6.2	30	30
New Orleans, La.	465,538	496,938	−31,400	−6.3	24	31
Tucson, Ariz.	460,466	415,444	45,022	10.8	34	32
Kansas City, Mo.	441,574	434,829	6,745	1.6	31	33
Virginia Beach, Va.	432,380	393,089	39,291	10.0	37	34
Long Beach, Calif.	430,905	429,321	1,584	0.4	32	35
Albuquerque, N.M.	419,311	384,915	34,396	8.9	38	36
Las Vegas, Nev.	404,288	258,877	145,411	56.2	63	37
Sacramento, Calif.	404,168	369,365	34,803	9.4	42	38
Atlanta, Ga.	403,819	393,929	9,890	2.5	36	39
Fresno, Calif.	398,133	354,091	44,042	12.4	47	40
Honolulu CDP,[2] Hawaii	395,789	377,059	18,730	5.0	39	41
Tulsa, Okla.	381,393	367,302	14,091	3.8	44	42
Omaha, Neb.	371,291	344,463	26,828	7.8	48	43
Miami, Fla.	368,624	358,648	9,976	2.8	46	44
Oakland, Calif.	365,874	372,242	−6,368	−1.7	40	45
Mesa, Ariz.	360,076	289,199	70,877	24.5	53	46
Minneapolis, Minn.	351,731	368,383	−16,652	−4.5	43	47
Colorado Springs, Colo.	344,987	280,430	64,557	23.0	54	48
Pittsburgh, Pa.	340,520	369,879	−29,359	−7.9	41	49
St. Louis, Mo.	339,316	396,685	−57,369	−14.5	35	50

1. "Remainder" indicates that the city is part of a consolidated city-county government and that the populations of other incorporated places in the county have been excluded from the totals shown here. 2. Honolulu CDP (census designated place) is not incorporated as a city but is recognized for census purposes as a large urban place. Honolulu CDP is coextensive with Honolulu Judicial District within the city and county of Honolulu. NOTE: 1990 population figures in this table reflect most recent revisions by the Census Bureau. They are not the same as those used in the individual city profiles. *Source:* U.S. Census Bureau.

Tabulated Data on City Governments

City	Mayor Term, years	Mayor Salary[1]	City manager's salary[1,2]	Council or Commission Name	Members	Term, years	Salary[1,3]
Albuquerque, N.M.	4	$ 73,500	—	Council	9	4	$ 7,028
Atlanta, Ga.	4	100,000	—	Council	18	4	22,000
Austin, Tex.	3	35,000	$125,000	Council	7	3	30,000
Baltimore, Md.	4	95,000	—	Council	19	4	37,000
Boston, Mass.	4	110,000	—	Council	13	2	54,500
Charlotte, N.C.	2	20,000	129,728	Council	11	2	12,000
Chicago, Ill.	4	192,100	—	Council	50	4	85,000
Cincinnati, Ohio	2	50,121	148,800	Council	9	2	46,621
Cleveland, Ohio	4	101,286	—	Council	21	4	47,751
Colorado Springs, Colo.	4	6,250	137,000	Council	9	4	6,200
Columbus, Ohio	4	98,000	—	Council	7	4	25,000
Dallas, Tex.	2	50[4]	179,001	Council	15	2	50[4]
Denver, Colo.	4	109,992	—	Council	13	4	55,800
Detroit, Mich.	4	143,000	—	Council	9	4	66,000
El Paso, Tex.	2	25,000	—	Council	9[5]	2	15,000
Fort Worth, Tex.	2	75[4]	147,204	Council	9[5]	2	75[4]
Fresno, Calif.	4	99,000	120,000	Council	8[5]	4	28,800
Honolulu, Hawaii	4	100,000	95,000[6]	Council	9	4	38,500
Houston, Tex.	2	160,500	—	Council	14	2	42,800
Indianapolis, Ind.	4	83,211	—	Council	29	4	14,817
Jacksonville, Fla.	2	110,000	105,000[7]	Council	19	4	24,000
Kansas City, Mo.	4	80,000	133,500	Council	13[5]	4	39,996
Las Vegas, Nev.	4	75,800	112,499	Council	4	4	33,480
Long Beach, Calif.	4	88,228	173,500	Council	9	4	22,057
Los Angeles, Calif.	4[8]	139,607	193,224[6]	Council	15	4	107,390
Memphis, Tenn.	4	110,000	98,000[6]	Council	13	4	20,100
Mesa, Ariz.	4	43,200	140,000	Council	6	4	28,800
Miami, Fla.	4	97,000	96,000	Commission	5	4	5,000
Milwaukee, Wis.	4	115,851	—	Council	17	4	54,159
Minneapolis, Minn.	4	73,486	95,888	Council	13	4	54,578
Nashville, Tenn.	4	75,000	8,900[9]	Council	40	4	6,900
New Orleans, La.	4	90,000	57,900	Council	7	4	42,500
New York, N.Y.	4	165,000	142,140[9]	Council	51	4	70,500
Oakland, Calif.	4	97,740	147,090[10]	Council	9[5]	4	47,880[8,11]
Oklahoma City, Okla.	4	2,000	100,000	Council	8	4	20[12]
Omaha, Neb.	4	88,408	—	Council	7	4	25,779
Philadelphia, Pa.	4	110,000	95,000[7]	Council	17	4	65,000
Phoenix, Ariz.	4	37,500	161,372	Council	9[5]	4	35,000
Pittsburgh, Pa.	4	83,253	—	Council	9	4	47,470
Portland, Ore.	4	83,416	—	Council	4	4	70,261
Sacramento, Calif,	4	1,652[13]	124,963	Council	9	4	1,251[13]
St. Louis, Mo.	4	71,266	—	Board of Alderman	29	4	18,500
San Antonio, Tex.	2	3,000[14]	115,000	Council	11[5]	2	20[4]
San Diego, Calif.	4	75,268	166,056	Council	8	4	56,479
San Francisco, Calif.	4	150,414	149,866	Bd. of Supvrs.	11	4	37,584
San Jose, Calif.	4	87,550	158,000	Council	10	4	58,240
Seattle, Wash.	4	122,691	—	Council	9	4	75,505
Tucson, Ariz.	4	36,000	127,000	Council	7[5]	4	18,000
Tulsa, Okla.	4	70,000	—	Council	9	2	12,000
Virginia Beach, Va.	4	20,000	125,000	Council	11	4	18,000
Washington, D.C.	4	90,705	115,700	Council	13	4	71,885

1. Annual salary unless otherwise indicated; does not include additional payments for expenses, special sessions, etc. 2. City manager's term is indefinite and at will of council (or mayor). 3. In some cities, leaders receive a higher salary. 4. Per council meeting, with an annual cap. 5. Including mayor. 6. Appointed by mayor, approved by council. 7. Appointed by mayor; not subject to council confirmation. 8. At mayor's request; limited to 2 terms. 9. No city manager; salary is for deputy or vice mayor. 10. Denotes average based on range. 11. Council also serves as the Redevelopment Agency for which there is additional compensation. 12. Per council meeting; not to exceed 5 meetings a month. 13. Per month. 14. Plus council pay. Source: Questionnaires to the cities.

U.S. Cities with Population Over 50,000

ZIP codes provided below indicate the primary ZIP code for each city; please consult a ZIP code directory to find the appropriate ZIP code for a particular address.

City	ZIP code	1998 pop. est.	1998 rank
Alabama			
Birmingham	35203	252,997	66
Decatur	35601	54,694	508
Dothan	36302	57,069	480
Hoover	35216	59,551	448
Huntsville	35813	175,979	109
Mobile	36601	202,181	82
Montgomery	36119	197,014	85
Tuscaloosa	35401	83,376	286
Alaska			
Anchorage	99501	254,982	65
Arizona			
Chandler	85225	160,329	121
Flagstaff	86004	56,657	489
Gilbert	85234	88,840	261
Glendale	85301	193,482	89
Mesa	85201	360,076	46
Peoria	85345	87,048	268
Phoenix	85026	1,198,064	7
Scottsdale	85251	195,394	86
Tempe	85282	167,622	114
Tucson	85726	460,466	32
Yuma	85364	62,433	419
Arkansas			
Fayetteville	72701	53,300	529
Fort Smith	72917	75,637	329
Jonesboro	72401	52,250	541
Little Rock	72231	175,303	111
North Little Rock	72114	59,184	454
Pine Bluff	71601	52,968	532
California			
Alameda	94501	78,695	311
Alhambra	91715	84,124	280
Anaheim	92803	295,153	57
Antioch	94509	81,428	292
Apple Valley	92307	56,440	492
Arcadia	91006	50,157	570
Bakersfield	93380	210,284	79
Baldwin Park	91706	71,953	353
Bellflower	90706	63,609	410
Berkeley	94704	108,101	204
Buena Park	90622	73,373	346
Burbank	91505	97,430	232
Camarillo	93010	59,348	450
Carlsbad	92008	74,732	333
Carson	90745	87,647	266
Cerritos	90703	53,883	518
Chino	91710	65,766	392
Chula Vista	92010	160,553	120
Clovis	93612	63,962	407
Compton	90221	92,269	249
Concord	94520	117,708	174
Corona	91720	112,815	186
Costa Mesa	92628	102,348	211
Daly City	94015	99,231	224
Davis	95616	54,405	511
Diamond Bar	91765	54,470	510
Downey	90241	93,653	242
El Cajon	92020	94,259	239
El Monte	91731	111,653	188
Encinitas	92024	59,943	444
Escondido	92025	120,578	169
Fairfield	94533	89,854	257
Fontana	92335	109,777	199
Fountain Valley	92708	56,679	487
Fremont	94537	204,298	81
Fresno	93706	398,133	40
Fullerton	92634	121,954	167
Garden Grove	92642	151,264	129
Gardena	90247	53,642	519
Glendale	92109	185,086	100
Hawthorne	90250	73,413	345
Hayward	94544	128,872	155
Hemet	92543	52,781	537
Hesperia	92345	62,309	422
Huntington Beach	92647	195,316	87
Huntington Park	90255	58,209	466
Inglewood	90311	111,618	189
Irvine	92713	136,446	147
Laguna Niguel	92607	53,615	522
La Habra	90631	54,294	512
La Mesa	90241	55,986	498
Lake Forest	92630	79,923	303
Lakewood	90714	76,222	323
Lancaster	93534	118,518	172
Livermore	94550	72,284	351
Lodi	95240	56,173	497
Long Beach	90809	430,905	35
Los Angeles	90052	3,597,556	2
Lynwood	90262	63,360	412
Merced	95340	59,380	449
Milpitas	95035	60,738	437
Mission Viejo	92690	95,440	237
Modesto	95350	182,016	103
Montebello	90640	60,530	440
Monterey Park	91754	62,531	418
Moreno Valley	92388	144,613	135
Mountain View	94041	72,192	352
Napa	94558	66,548	386
National City	92050	54,994	507
Newport Beach	92658	72,416	350
Norwalk	90650	97,518	231
Oakland	94615	365,874	45
Oceanside	92054	152,367	127
Ontario	91761	147,188	134
Orange	92613	123,820	164
Oxnard	93030	154,622	123
Palmdale	93550	100,157	218
Palo Alto	94303	59,098	457
Paramount	90723	51,131	551
Pasadena	91109	134,587	149
Petaluma	94952	50,913	557
Pico Rivera	90660	60,683	439
Pittsburg	94565	52,796	536
Pleasanton	94566	64,039	406
Pomona	91768	135,659	148
Rancho Cucamonga	91739	120,047	170
Redding	96049	77,944	315
Redlands	92373	67,309	382
Redondo Beach	92077	63,075	414
Redwood City	94063	73,438	344
Rialto	92376	83,933	283
Richmond	94802	93,470	243
Riverside	92517	262,140	61
Rosemead	91770	53,186	530
Roseville	95678	71,609	358
Sacramento	95813	404,168	38
Salinas	93907	121,458	168
San Bernardino	92403	186,402	97
San Buenaventura (Ventura)	93001	98,366	227
San Diego	92199	1,220,666	6
San Francisco	94188	745,774	12
San Jose	95101	861,284	11
San Leandro	94577	74,387	337
San Mateo	94402	91,282	253
San Rafael	94901	51,057	553
Santa Ana	92799	305,955	55
Santa Barbara	93102	86,645	271
Santa Clara	95050	100,370	217
Santa Clarita	91380	127,001	159
Santa Cruz	95060	52,853	535
Santa Maria	93454	68,121	375
Santa Monica	90406	89,522	258
Santa Rosa	95402	126,891	160
Santee	92071	57,740	471
Simi Valley	93065	110,463	195
South Gate	90280	88,384	263
South San Francisco	94080	58,829	459
Stockton	95213	240,143	69
Sunnyvale	94086	127,444	158

City	ZIP code	1998 pop. est.	1998 rank
Thousand Oaks	91359	117,199	175
Torrance	90510	137,533	142
Turlock	95380	50,266	568
Tustin	92681	64,370	401
Union City	94587	64,085	405
Upland	91786	67,826	379
Vacaville	95687	83,362	287
Vallejo	94590	111,539	190
Victorville	92392	68,914	369
Visalia	93277	89,308	260
Vista	92083	80,909	298
Walnut Creek	94596	64,306	402
West Covina	91790	99,455	220
Westminster	92684	84,042	282
Whittier	90605	79,135	308
Yorba Linda	92686	60,156	441
Colorado			
Arvada	80001	97,610	230
Aurora	80010	250,604	67
Boulder	80302	90,543	256
Colorado Springs	80910	344,987	48
Denver	80201	499,055	27
Fort Collins	80521	108,905	200
Greeley	80631	70,434	362
Lakewood	80215	136,883	145
Longmont	80501	62,078	424
Pueblo	81003	107,301	205
Thornton	80229	74,139	341
Westminster	80030	95,691	236
Connecticut			
Bridgeport	06602	137,425	143
Bristol	06010	59,158	455
Danbury	06810	65,829	391
Hartford	06101	131,523	153
Meriden	06450	56,667	488
New Britain	06050	70,492	361
New Haven	06511	123,189	165
Norwalk	06856	78,064	314
Stamford	06910	110,689	193
Waterbury	06701	105,346	207
West Haven	06616	51,639	546
Delaware			
Wilmington	19850	71,678	356
District of Columbia			
Washington	20066	523,124	23
Florida			
Boca Raton	33431	71,761	355
Boynton Beach	33436	53,607	524
Cape Coral	33990	91,180	254
Clearwater	34618	101,474	212
Coral Springs	33075	111,744	187
Davie	33329	62,061	425
Daytona Beach	32114	65,136	396
Deerfield Beach	33441	50,921	556
Delray Beach	33444	53,618	521
Deltona	32725	58,168	468
Fort Lauderdale	33310	153,728	124
Gainesville	32602	92,648	247
Hialeah	33010	211,392	78
Hollywood	33022	130,026	154
Jacksonville (remainder)	32203	693,630	14
Lakeland	33805	74,204	340
Largo	34640	66,264	388
Lauderhill	33152	50,814	559
Margate	33063	51,268	550
Melbourne	32901	69,057	367
Miami	33152	368,624	44
Miami Beach	33119	97,053	233
Miramar	33023	57,215	475
North Miami	33261	50,772	560
Orlando	32862	181,175	104
Palm Bay	32901	77,486	317
Pembroke Pines	33084	115,361	180
Pensacola	32501	58,193	467
Plantation	33318	81,424	293
Pompano Beach	33060	75,982	328
Port St. Lucie	34985	79,351	305
Sarasota	34230	51,035	554
St. Petersburg	33730	236,029	70
Sunrise	33322	80,338	301

City	ZIP code	1998 pop. est.	1998 rank
Tallahassee	32301	136,628	146
Tamarac	33309	52,929	534
Tampa	33630	289,156	58
West Palm Beach	33406	76,308	321
Georgia			
Albany	31706	77,545	316
Athens–Clarke County (remainder)	30601	89,361	259
Atlanta	30304	403,819	39
Augusta-Richmond County (remainder)	30901	187,689	96
Columbus (remainder)	31908	182,219	102
Macon	31201	114,336	183
Marietta	30060	51,362	548
Roswell	30075	57,102	478
Savannah	31402	131,674	151
Hawaii			
Honolulu CDP	96820	395,789	41
Idaho			
Boise City	83708	157,452	122
Pocatello	83201	53,074	531
Illinois			
Arlington Heights	60005	76,522	320
Aurora	60505	124,736	162
Bloomington	61701	58,841	458
Bolingbrook	60440	54,288	513
Champaign	61820	64,280	404
Chicago	60607	2,802,079	3
Cicero	60650	71,289	359
Decatur	62523	79,972	302
Des Plaines	60018	55,272	504
Downers Grove	60515	51,716	545
Elgin	60120	87,507	267
Evanston	60201	71,928	354
Joliet	60436	92,285	248
Mount Prospect	60056	53,581	525
Naperville	60540	117,091	177
Oak Lawn	60455	57,730	472
Oak Park	60301	50,646	563
Peoria	61601	111,148	191
Rockford	61125	143,656	136
Schaumburg	60194	74,481	336
Skokie	60077	58,628	461
Springfield	62703	117,098	176
Waukegan	60085	75,999	327
Wheaton	60187	55,308	503
Indiana			
Anderson	46011	58,528	463
Bloomington	47408	65,065	397
Evansville	47708	122,779	166
Fort Wayne	46802	185,716	98
Gary	46401	108,469	201
Hammond	46320	78,212	312
Indianapolis (remainder)	46206	741,304	13
Muncie	47302	67,476	380
South Bend	46624	99,417	221
Terre Haute	47808	53,355	528
Iowa			
Cedar Rapids	52401	114,563	182
Council Bluffs	51501	56,312	495
Davenport	52802	96,842	234
Des Moines	50318	191,293	91
Dubuque	52001	56,467	491
Iowa City	52240	60,897	434
Sioux City	51101	82,697	289
Waterloo	50703	63,703	408
Kansas			
Kansas City	66106	141,297	139
Lawrence	66044	74,244	339
Olathe	66061	85,035	276
Overland Park	66204	139,685	140
Topeka	66603	118,977	171
Wichita	67276	329,211	52
Kentucky			
Lexington-Fayette	40511	241,749	68
Louisville	40231	255,045	64
Owensboro	42301	54,041	515
Louisiana			
Baton Rouge	70821	211,551	77
Bossier City	71111	56,637	490
Kenner	70062	71,641	357

City	ZIP code	1998 pop. est.	1998 rank
Lafayette	70501	113,615	184
Lake Charles	70601	70,766	360
Monroe	71203	53,612	523
New Orleans	70113	465,538	31
Shreveport	71102	188,319	95
Maine			
Portland	04101	62,786	416
Maryland			
Baltimore	21233	645,593	16
Massachusetts			
Boston	02205	555,447	20
Brockton	02402	93,173	245
Cambridge	02139	93,352	244
Chicopee	01020	54,049	514
Fall River	02720	90,654	255
Haverhill	01830	55,321	502
Lawrence	01842	69,420	365
Lowell	01853	101,075	214
Lynn	01901	81,075	297
Malden	02148	52,644	538
Medford	02155	55,981	499
New Bedford	02740	96,353	235
Newton	02164	80,345	300
Quincy	02369	85,752	275
Somerville	02143	74,100	342
Springfield	01101	148,144	132
Taunton	02780	52,553	540
Waltham	02154	58,540	462
Worcester	01613	166,535	116
Michigan			
Ann Arbor	48103	109,967	197
Battle Creek	49016	53,496	527
Dearborn	48120	91,691	251
Dearborn Heights	48127	59,805	445
Detroit	48283	970,196	10
Farmington Hills	48333	79,784	304
Flint	48502	131,668	152
Grand Rapids	49501	185,437	99
Kalamazoo	49001	76,241	322
Lansing	48924	127,825	157
Livonia	48150	101,358	213
Pontiac	48343	68,916	368
Rochester Hills	48309	67,413	381
Roseville	48066	51,390	547
Royal Oak	48068	64,290	403
Saginaw	48605	63,464	411
Southfield	48037	75,104	331
St. Clair Shores	48080	66,056	389
Sterling Heights	48311	124,339	163
Taylor	48180	72,551	348
Troy	48099	79,303	306
Warren	48090	142,455	138
Westland	48185	86,227	272
Wyoming	49509	68,671	371
Minnesota			
Bloomington	55431	86,186	273
Brooklyn Park	55429	63,115	413
Burnsville	55337	59,334	452
Coon Rapids	55433	63,674	409
Duluth	55806	81,228	294
Eagan	55121	60,042	442
Eden Prairie	55343	50,279	567
Minneapolis	55401	351,731	47
Minnetonka	55345	50,952	555
Plymouth	55441	61,509	431
Rochester	55901	78,173	313
St. Cloud	56301	50,745	561
St. Paul	55101	257,284	63
Mississippi			
Gulfport	39500	64,762	400
Jackson	39205	188,419	94
Missouri			
Columbia	65201	78,915	310
Independence	64050	116,832	178
Kansas City	64108	441,574	33
Lee's Summit	64063	66,623	385
Springfield	65801	142,898	137
St. Charles	63301	58,166	469
St. Joseph	64501	69,622	363
St. Louis	63155	339,316	50

City	ZIP code	1998 pop. est.	1998 rank
St. Peters	63303	50,297	566
Montana			
Billings	59101	91,750	250
Great Falls	59401	56,395	494
Missoula	59801	52,239	542
Nebraska			
Lincoln	68501	213,088	76
Omaha	68108	371,291	43
Nevada			
Henderson	89015	152,717	126
Las Vegas	89199	404,288	37
North Las Vegas	89030	94,218	240
Reno	89510	163,334	119
Sparks	89431	62,432	420
New Hampshire			
Manchester	03103	102,524	210
Nashua	03060	82,169	290
New Jersey			
Bayonne	07002	61,051	433
Camden	08101	83,546	285
Clifton	07015	76,180	324
East Orange	07019	69,598	364
Elizabeth	07201	110,661	194
Jersey City	07303	232,429	71
Newark	07101	267,823	60
Passaic	07055	60,817	435
Paterson	07510	148,212	131
Trenton	08650	84,494	279
Union City	07087	57,621	473
Vineland	08360	55,484	501
New Mexico			
Albuquerque	87101	419,311	36
Las Cruces	88001	76,102	326
Rio Rancho	87124	50,041	572
Santa Fe	87501	67,879	378
New York			
Albany	12288	94,305	238
Buffalo	14240	300,717	56
Mount Vernon	10551	66,824	384
New Rochelle	10802	67,225	383
New York	10199	7,420,166	1
Niagara Falls	14302	56,768	485
Rochester	14692	216,887	73
Schenectady	12305	61,698	430
Syracuse	13220	152,215	128
Troy	12180	51,320	549
Utica	13504	59,334	452
Yonkers	10702	190,153	93
North Carolina			
Asheville	28801	63,031	415
Cary	27511	82,071	291
Charlotte	28228	504,637	25
Durham	27701	153,513	125
Fayetteville	28302	77,295	318
Gastonia	28052	56,977	482
Greensboro	27420	197,910	84
Greenville	27833	57,005	481
High Point	27260	76,117	325
Jacksonville	28540	68,380	373
Raleigh	27611	259,423	62
Rocky Mount	27801	56,901	483
Wilmington	28402	68,062	377
Winston-Salem	27102	164,316	118
North Dakota			
Bismarck	58501	54,040	516
Fargo	58102	86,718	270
Ohio			
Akron	44309	215,712	74
Canton	44711	79,259	307
Cincinnati	45234	336,400	51
Cleveland	44101	495,817	28
Cleveland Heights	44118	53,533	526
Columbus	43216	670,234	15
Dayton	45401	167,475	115
Elyria	44035	56,278	496
Euclid	44117	50,644	564
Hamilton	45011	61,808	429
Kettering	45429	57,205	476
Lakewood	44107	55,682	500
Lorain	44052	68,857	370

City	ZIP code	1998 pop. est.	1998 rank
Parma	44129	83,347	288
Springfield	45501	65,568	393
Toledo	43601	312,174	53
Youngstown	44501	84,650	278
Oklahoma			
Broken Arrow	74012	72,564	347
Edmond	73034	64,962	399
Lawton	73501	81,107	295
Midwest City	73125	54,037	517
Norman	73069	93,019	246
Oklahoma City	73125	472,221	30
Tulsa	74103	381,393	42
Oregon			
Beaverton	97005	62,111	423
Corvallis	97330	50,202	569
Eugene	97401	128,240	156
Gresham	97030	85,021	277
Hillsboro	97123	61,111	432
Medford	97501	57,156	477
Portland	97208	503,891	26
Salem	97301	126,702	161
Springfield	97477	50,682	562
Pennsylvania			
Allentown	18101	100,757	215
Bethlehem	18016	69,383	366
Erie	16515	102,640	209
Lancaster	17604	52,951	533
Philadelphia	19104	1,436,287	5
Pittsburgh	15290	340,520	49
Reading	19612	74,762	332
Scranton	18505	74,683	334
Rhode Island			
Cranston	02920	74,521	335
Pawtucket	02860	68,169	374
Providence	02904	150,890	130
Warwick	02886	84,094	281
South Carolina			
Charleston	29423	87,044	269
Columbia	29292	110,840	192
Greenville	29602	56,436	493
North Charleston	29406	68,072	376
South Dakota			
Rapid City	57701	57,513	474
Sioux Falls	57101	116,762	179
Tennessee			
Chattanooga	37421	147,790	133
Clarksville	37040	97,978	228
Jackson	38301	51,115	552
Johnson City	37601	57,079	479
Knoxville	37950	165,540	117
Memphis	38101	603,507	18
Murfreesboro	37130	58,430	464
Nashville-Davidson (remainder)	37229	510,274	24
Texas			
Abilene	79604	108,257	203
Amarillo	79120	171,207	113
Arlington	76010	306,497	54
Austin	78710	552,434	21
Baytown	77520	68,588	372
Bedford	76021	50,148	571
Beaumont	77707	109,841	198
Brownsville	78520	137,883	141
Bryan	77801	58,763	460
Carrollton	75006	100,463	216
College Station	77840	59,742	446
Corpus Christi	78469	281,453	59
Dallas	75260	1,075,894	9
Denton	76201	76,933	319
El Paso	79910	615,032	17
Fort Worth	76161	491,801	29
Galveston	77550	59,567	447
Garland	75040	193,408	90
Grand Prairie	75051	113,329	185
Harlingen	78550	58,210	465
Houston	77201	1,786,691	4
Irving	75015	178,253	107
Killeen	76541	80,720	299

City	ZIP code	1998 pop. est.	1998 rank
Laredo	78041	175,783	110
Lewisville	75067	72,466	349
Longview	75602	75,576	330
Lubbock	79402	190,974	92
McAllen	78501	106,822	206
Mesquite	75149	114,632	181
Midland	79711	99,621	219
Missouri City	77459	62,371	421
North Richland Hills	76182	54,622	509
Odessa	79761	91,572	252
Pasadena	77501	133,964	150
Plano	75075	219,486	72
Port Arthur	77640	56,827	484
Richardson	75080	86,020	274
Round Rock	78664	60,686	438
San Angelo	76902	88,233	264
San Antonio	78284	1,114,130	8
Sugar Land	77478	51,725	544
Tyler	75712	83,908	284
Victoria	77901	61,882	428
Waco	76702	108,272	202
Wichita Falls	76307	99,236	223
Utah			
Layton	84040	55,112	505
Ogden	84401	66,507	387
Orem	84057	78,937	309
Provo	84601	110,419	196
Salt Lake City	84199	174,348	112
Sandy	84070	99,186	225
Taylorsville	84118	56,753	486
West Jordan	84084	60,804	436
West Valley City	84199	99,372	222
Virginia			
Alexandria	22313	118,300	173
Arlington CDP	22210	177,275	108
Chesapeake	23320	199,564	83
Danville	24541	50,868	558
Hampton	23670	136,968	144
Lynchburg	24506	65,473	395
Newport News	23607	178,615	106
Norfolk	23501	215,215	75
Portsmouth	23707	98,936	226
Richmond	23232	194,173	88
Roanoke	24022	93,749	241
Suffolk	23434	62,703	417
Virginia Beach	23450	432,380	34
Washington			
Bellevue	98009	104,052	208
Bellingham	98225	61,894	427
Everett	98201	88,625	262
Federal Way	98063	74,254	338
Kennewick	99336	50,316	565
Lakewood	98439	65,933	390
Seattle	98109	536,978	22
Shoreline	98133	52,116	543
Spokane	99210	184,058	101
Tacoma	98413	179,814	105
Vancouver	98661	73,526	343
Yakima	98903	64,967	398
West Virginia			
Charleston	25301	55,056	506
Huntington	25704	52,571	539
Wisconsin			
Appleton	54911	65,514	394
Eau Claire	54703	59,200	453
Green Bay	54303	97,789	229
Janesville	53545	59,149	456
Kenosha	53140	87,849	265
Madison	53714	209,306	80
Milwaukee	53203	578,364	19
Oshkosh	54901	57,955	470
Racine	53403	81,095	296
Waukesha	53186	61,989	426
West Allis	53214	59,974	443
Wyoming			
Cheyenne	82001	53,640	520

U.S. Telephone Area Codes and Time Zones

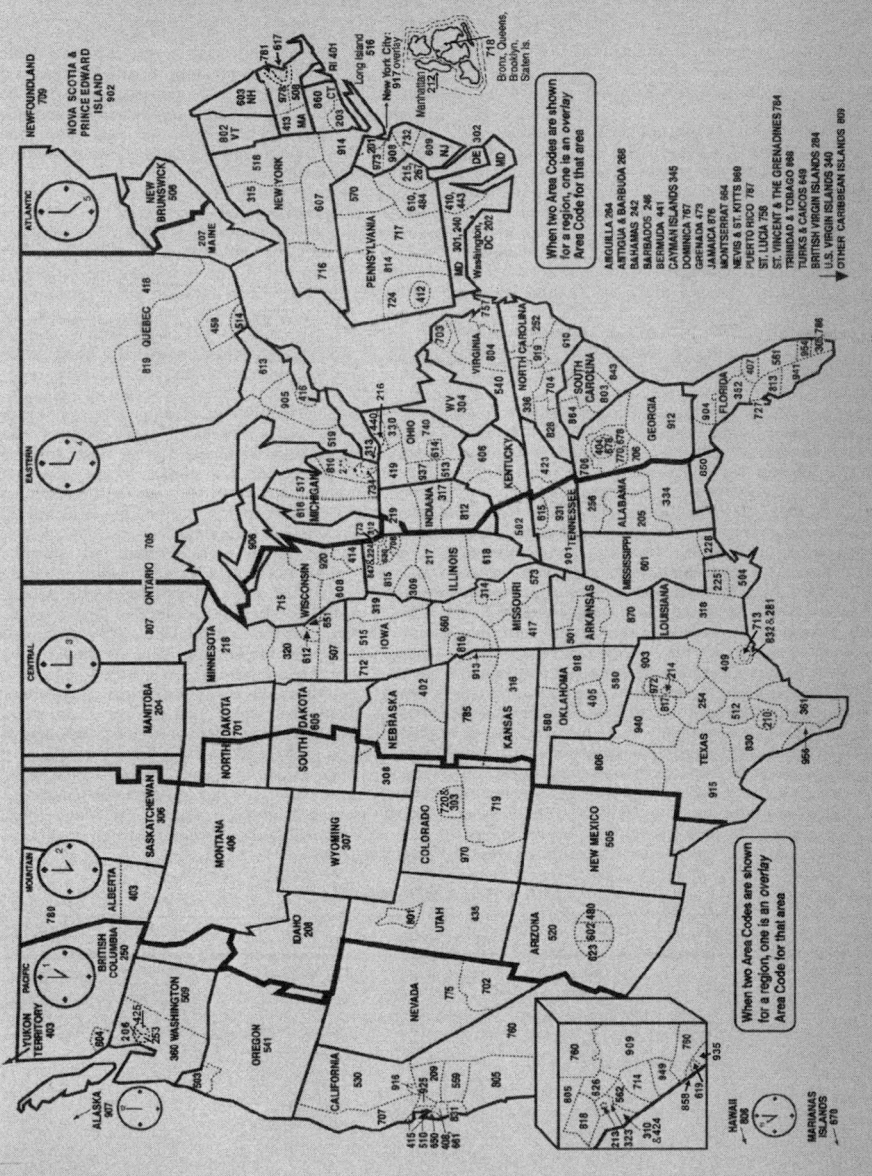

NOTES: Data as of July 29, 1999. "Overlay" area codes span across geographical areas that may already include one or more other area codes. *Source:* Bell Atlantic Yellow Pages Company, with additional information from the North American Numbering Plan Administration.

Census 2000

Can the 2000 census be pulled off smoothly, avoiding the quagmire of criticism that followed the 1990 census? Don't count on it. Tallying up the inhabitants of the third most populous country in the world is no small feat.

The Census Bureau has not been idly standing by since the nation's ill-fated 1990 census, in which more than 8.4 million people were missed and 4.4 million others were counted twice. That operation proved that tracking down every individual in our ever-growing population is perhaps a larger task than our forefathers envisioned when they mandated a decennial headcount in the Constitution. With ten years to tinker, though, surely the Census Bureau has come up with a foolproof plan to achieve more accurate results? According to Census director Kenneth Prewitt, it's not that simple: "All the factors that made it difficult to count Americans in prior censuses are today even more present."

Specifically, there are more people around to disregard the census questionnaire. In 1990, 30 million households did not respond to the Bureau's mailing. Census Bureau employees had to be sent out to America's neighborhoods to ascertain the number of people living in those households. The Bureau explained that many of these census delinquents simply could not read their mailings. The number of Americans who do not speak English has grown significantly over the past two decades. Many other Americans, inundated with junk mail, probably lost their census questionnaires in the shuffle. And then there are the homeless, the illiterate, and the people who just plain refuse to participate for one politically inspired reason or another.

Steps are being taken to curb some of these factors in 2000. Questionnaires will be available in English, Spanish, Korean, Chinese, Vietnamese, and Tagalog (which is spoken in the Philippines) in order to generate a higher response level from the immigrant population. The Census Bureau also plans to tap into the nation's passion for technology. People who receive the standard short form, which consists of just seven questions, will be able to fill it out online rather than having to mail it back. Online filing will be more convenient for many citizens and should help streamline the counting process for the Bureau by reducing the amount of time required for data entry. Those who receive the long form (one out of every six households) will still be required to respond by mail.

In addition to being a massive operation, involving some 860,000 temporary workers, the 2000 census will be an expensive one. Total cost estimates have climbed to a mind-blowing $6 billion. The Census Bureau was forced to request more funding after the Supreme Court ruled in a 5–4 decision in January 1999 that the use of statistical sampling for redistributing Congressional seats among the 50 states is unconstitutional. Census data, however, is also used in distributing funding for education, highways, and other needs, among the nation's communities. Statistical sampling, which is believed to produce data that more accurately reflect the demographic make-up of the nation, tends to be a better way to get financial support to the areas that need it most. The Census Bureau had little choice but to devise a two-fold plan involving both a head count and statistical sampling.

Because the Supreme Court ruling left open the possiblity that statistical sampling results could be used to redraw the district lines within state boundaries, Census 2000 became a source of heated political debate on Capitol Hill in 1999. Statistical sampling attempts to fill in gaps in head-count results with people that are most likely to be missed in the count—including immigrants, minorities, and poor people. Many Democrats favor the use of statistical sampling in redrawing districts because the support they tend to pick up from these groups would give the party a good shot at gaining Congressional seats. Republicans, who have not traditionally received a strong backing from these groups, have fought tooth and nail against redistricting based on statistical sampling data.

National Censuses[1]

Year	Resident population[2]	Land area, sq mi.	Pop. per sq mi.	Year	Resident population[2]	Land area, sq mi.	Pop. per sq mi.
1790	3,929,214	864,746	4.5	1900	75,994,575	2,969,834	25.6
1800	5,308,483	864,746	6.1	1910	91,972,266	2,969,565	31.0
1810	7,239,881	1,681,828	4.3	1920	105,710,620	2,969,451	35.6
1820	9,638,453	1,749,462	5.5	1930	122,775,046	2,977,128	41.2
1830	12,866,020	1,749,462	7.4	1940	131,669,275	2,977,128	44.2
1840	17,069,453	1,749,462	9.8	1950	150,697,361	2,974,726	50.7
1850	23,191,876	2,940,042	7.9	1960	179,323,175	3,540,911	50.6
1860	31,443,321	2,969,640	10.6	1970	203,302,031	3,540,023	57.4
1870	39,818,449	2,969,640	13.4	1980	226,545,805	3,539,289	64.0
1880	50,155,783	2,969,640	16.9	1990	248,709,873	3,536,278	70.3
1890	62,947,714	2,969,640	21.2				

1. Beginning with 1960, figures include Alaska and Hawaii. 2. Excludes armed forces overseas. *Source:* U.S. Bureau of the Census; Web: www.census.gov.

Profile of the United States

This profile was created by the editors of the almanac from many data sources. Most figures are approximate. For additional details about the U.S., please refer to the appropriate sections of the almanac.

Geography

Number of states: 50
Land area (1990): 3,536,338 sq. mi. Share of world land area (1990): 6.2%
Population density (1990): 70.3 people per sq. mi.
Northernmost point: Point Barrow, Alaska
Easternmost point: West Quoddy Head, Maine
Southernmost point: Ka Lae (South Cape), Hawaii
Westernmost point: Cape Wrangell, Alaska[1]
Geographic center (50 states): in Butte County, S.D. (44' 58' N. lat., 103' 46' W. long.)
Highest point: Mt. McKinley, Alaska (20,320 ft.)
Lowest point: Death Valley, Calif. (282 ft. below sea level)
1. The extreme points are measured from the geographic center of the United States (incl. Alaska and Hawaii), west of Castle Rock, S.D., 44° 58' N. lat., 103° 46' W. long. If measured from the prime meridian in Greenwich, England, Cape Wrangell, Alaska, would be the easternmost point.

Population

Total Resident Pop.[1] (July 1999): 272,878,000
Mean center of population (1990): 10 miles southeast of Steelville in Crawford County, Mo.
Males (July 1999): 133,352,000
Females (July 1999): 139,526,000
White (July 1999): 224,692,000 (82.3% of pop.)
Black (July 1999): 34,903,000 (12.8% of pop.)
Asian and Pacific Islander (July 1999): 10,887,000 (4.0% of pop.)
American Indian, Eskimo, and Aleut (July 1999): 2,396,000 (0.9% of pop.)
Hispanic origin (can be of any race) (July 1999): 31,365,000 (11.5% of pop.)
Median age (July 1999): 35.5
Baby boomers (1992): 77,000,000
Rural population (1990): 66,964,000
Metropolitan population (1990): 192,725,741
Families (1998): 70,880,000
Average family size (1998): 3.18
Home ownership (1995): 64.7% of pop.
Married (March 1997): 117,965,000
Never married (March 1997): 58,303,000
Divorced (March 1997) 19,424,000
Unmarried couples (1995): 3,661,000
Single parents (1995): female, 12,514,000; male, 3,513,000
Widowed (March 1998): 13,599,000
1. Excludes the United States Armed Forces overseas.

Vital Statistics

Births (1998): 3,946,000 (14.6 per 1,000)
Deaths (1998): 2,331,000 (8.6 per 1,000)
Marriages (1998): 2,244,000 (8.3 per 1,000)
Divorces (1998): 1,135,000 (4.2 per 1,000)
Infant mortality rate (1998): 7.0 per 1,000
Legal abortions (1995): 1,210,883
Life expectancy (1997): Total U.S., both sexes, 76.5; total men, 73.6; total women, 79.4; white men, 74.3; white women, 79.9; black men, 67.2; black women, 74.7

Civilian Labor Force

All (1998): 137,673 (4.5% are unemployed)
Males (1998): 73,959,000 (4.4% are unemployed)
Females (1998): 63,714,000 (4.6% are unemployed)
Work at home (telecommuters, est. 1997): 21.5 million
Farms (1997): 1,911,859; total acres (1997): 931,795,255
Avg. hourly earnings of workers (1998): $12.78
Avg. weekly hours of workers (1998): 34.6

Income and Credit

Gross Domestic Product (1998): $8,508.9 billion
Federal budget (est. 1999): total receipts, $1,806.3 billion; total outlays, $1,727.1 billion
Personal income per capita (1998): $26,412
Median four-person family income (1997): $53,350
Individual shareholders (1992): 51,300,000
Number below poverty level (1997): total, 35,574,000; white, 24,396,000; black, 9,116,000; Hispanic, 8,308,000

Education

Elementary school pupils, grades K–8 (1999)[1]: 38,789,000
Secondary school pupils, grades 9–12 (1999)[1]: 15,148,000
Dropout rate, grades 10–12 (1997): 4.6%
College enrollment (1996): 15,200,000
Number of college students age 25 and older (1996): 6,200,000 (40.9%)
Money spent on public elementary and secondary education (1994–95): $260,142,000
Public school teachers (1996): 2,611,000; elementary, 1,535,000; secondary, 1,077,000; private elementary and secondary school teachers (1994): 378,000
Average salary for public school teachers (1997): $39,580
1. Projected.

Conveniences

Radio stations (July 1999): AM, 4,782; FM, 5,745
Television stations (July 1999): 1,599
Registered automobiles (1997): 129,749,000
Newspaper circulation (1995): 58,193,391
Cable TV households (1998): 74,550,000
Total TV households (Jan. 1999): 99,400,000
Percent of TV households with two or more sets (Jan. 1999): 74
TV Homes with VCRs (est. 1997): 74%
Internet users per 1,000 people (1998): 283

Crime

Total arrests (est. 1997): 10,544,624; Under 18 years, 1,969,407
Prisoners under sentence of death (1996): 3,219
Law enforcement officers killed (1996): 100
Total murder victims (1997): 18,209
Violent crime (1997): 1,634,773
Property crimes (1997): 11,540,297
Homicides per 100,000 people (1998): 6.2
Persons executed under civil authority (1997): 432
Hate crime victims (1997): 10,255

Population

Colonial Population Estimates

(in round numbers)

Year	Population	Year	Population
1610	350	1700	250,900
1620	2,300	1710	331,700
1630	4,600	1720	466,200
1640	26,600	1730	629,400
1650	50,400	1740	905,600
1660	75,100	1750	1,170,800
1670	111,900	1760	1,593,600
1680	151,500	1770	2,148,100
1690	210,400	1780	2,780,400

Covers years before the establishment of the U.S. Census in 1790. See following page for National Census figures, 1790 to 1990.

Total Population

Area	1990	1980	1970
50 states of U.S.	248,709,873	226,545,805	203,302,031
48 conterminous	247,051,601	225,179,263	202,229,535
Alaska	550,043	401,851	302,583
Hawaii	1,108,229	964,691	769,913
American Samoa	46,773	32,297	27,159
Canal Zone	(1)	(1)	44,198
Corn Islands	—	—	(2)
Guam	133,152	105,979	84,996
Johnston Atoll	n.a.	327	1,007
Midway	(3)	453	2,220
Puerto Rico	3,522,037	3,196,520	2,712,033
Swan Islands	n.a.	n.a.	22
Trust Ter. of Pac. Is.	15,122[5]	132,929[4]	90,940
Virgin Is. of U.S.	101,809	96,569	62,468
Wake Island	(3)	302	1,647
Population abroad	922,819	995,546	1,737,836
Armed forces	910,611	515,408	1,057,776
Total	253,451,585	231,106,727	208,066,557

1. Reverted to Panama. 2. Returned to Nicaragua April 25, 1971. 3. No indigenous population. 4. Includes Northern Mariana Islands. 5. Palau only Trust Territory remaining. NOTE: n.a. = not available. Source: U.S. Bureau of the Census; Web: www.census.gov.

Population Distribution by Age, Race, Nativity, and Sex Ratio

Year	Total	Under 5	5–19	20–44	45–64	65 and over	Total	Native born	Foreign born	Black	Other races[1]
Percent Distribution											
1860[2]	100.0%	15.4%	35.8%	35.7%	10.4%	2.7%	85.6%	72.6 %	13.0 %	14.1%	0.3%
1870[2]	100.0	14.3	35.4	35.4	11.9	3.0	87.1	72.9	14.2	12.7	0.2
1880[2]	100.0	13.8	34.3	35.9	12.6	3.4	86.5	73.4	13.1	13.1	0.3
1890[3]	100.0	12.2	33.9	36.9	13.1	3.9	87.5	73.0	14.5	11.9	0.3
1900	100.0	12.1	32.3	37.7	13.7	4.1	87.9	74.5	13.4	11.6	0.5
1910	100.0	11.6	30.4	39.0	14.6	4.3	88.9	74.4	14.5	10.7	0.4
1920	100.0	10.9	29.8	38.4	16.1	4.7	89.7	76.7	13.0	9.9	0.4
1930	100.0	9.3	29.5	38.3	17.4	5.4	89.8	78.4	11.4	9.7	0.5
1940	100.0	8.0	26.4	38.9	19.8	6.8	89.8	81.1	8.7	9.8	0.4
1950	100.0	10.7	23.2	37.6	20.3	8.1	89.5	82.8	6.7	10.0	0.5
1960	100.0	11.3	27.1	32.2	20.1	9.2	88.6	83.4	5.2	10.5	0.9
1970[2]	100.0	8.4	29.5	31.7	20.6	9.8	87.6	83.4	4.3	11.1	1.4
1980	100.0	7.2	24.8	37.1	19.6	11.3	83.1	n.a.	n.a.	11.7	5.2
1990	100.0	7.6	21.3	40.1	18.6	12.5	83.9	n.a.	n.a.	12.3	3.8
Males per 100 Females											
1860[2]	104.7	102.4	101.2	107.9	111.5	98.3	105.3	103.7	115.1	99.6	260.8
1870[2]	102.2	102.9	101.2	99.2	114.5	100.5	102.8	100.6	115.3	96.2	400.7
1880[2]	103.6	103.0	101.3	104.0	110.2	101.4	104.0	102.1	115.9	97.8	362.2
1890[3]	105.0	103.6	101.4	107.3	108.3	104.2	105.4	102.9	118.7	99.5	165.2
1900	104.4	102.1	100.9	105.8	110.7	102.0	104.9	102.8	117.4	98.6	185.2
1910	106.0	102.5	101.3	108.1	114.4	101.1	106.6	102.7	129.2	98.9	185.6
1920	104.0	102.5	100.8	102.8	115.2	101.3	104.4	101.7	121.7	99.2	156.6
1930	102.5	103.0	101.4	100.5	109.1	100.5	102.9	101.1	115.8	97.0	150.6
1940	100.7	103.2	102.0	98.1	105.2	95.5	101.2	100.1	111.1	95.0	140.5
1950	98.6	103.9	102.5	96.2	100.1	89.6	99.0	98.8	102.0	93.7	129.7
1960	97.1	103.4	102.7	95.6	95.7	82.8	97.4	97.6	94.2	93.3	109.7
1970[2]	94.8	104.0	103.3	95.1	91.6	72.1	95.3	95.9	83.8	90.8	100.2
1980	94.5	104.7	104.0	98.1	90.7	67.6	94.8	n.a.	n.a.	89.6	100.3
1990	95.1	104.8	105.0	99.8	92.5	67.2	95.9	n.a.	n.a.	89.8	96.5

NOTES: Data exclude armed forces overseas. Beginning in 1960, includes Alaska and Hawaii. n.a. = not available. 1. The 1980 and 1990 census data for white and other races categories are not directly comparable to those shown for the preceding years because of changes in the way some persons reported their race, as well as changes in procedures relating to racial classification. 2. Excludes persons for whom age is not available. 3. Excludes persons enumerated in the Indian Territory and on Indian reservations. Source: U.S. Bureau of the Census; Web: www.census.gov.

Resident Population—Selected Characteristics, 1790–1999

(in thousands)

Date	Male	Female	White	Black	Total other	Other — American Indian, Eskimo, Aleut	Other — Asian and Pacific Islanders	Hispanic origin[1]
1790 (Aug. 2)[2]	n.a.	n.a.	3,172	757	n.a.	n.a.	n.a.	n.a.
1800 (Aug. 4)[2]	n.a.	n.a.	4,306	1,002	n.a.	n.a.	n.a.	n.a.
1850 (June 1)[2]	11,838	11,354	19,553	3,639	n.a.	n.a.	n.a.	n.a.
1900 (June 1)[2]	38,816	37,178	66,809	8,834	351	n.a.	n.a.	n.a.
1910 (Apr. 15)[2]	47,332	44,640	81,732	9,828	413	n.a.	n.a.	n.a.
1920 (Jan. 1)[2]	53,900	51,810	94,821	10,463	427	n.a.	n.a.	n.a.
1930 (Apr. 1)[2]	62,137	60,638	110,287	11,891	597	n.a.	n.a.	n.a.
1940 (Apr. 1)[2]	66,062	65,608	118,215	12,866	589	n.a.	n.a.	n.a.
1950 (Apr. 1)[2]	74,833	75,864	134,942	15,042	713	n.a.	n.a.	n.a.
1950 (Apr. 1)	75,187	76,139	135,150	15,045	1,131	n.a.	n.a.	n.a.
1960 (Apr. 1)	88,331	90,992	158,832	18,872	1,620	n.a.	n.a.	n.a.
1970 (Apr. 1)[3]	98,926	104,309	178,098	22,581	2,557	n.a.	n.a.	n.a.
1980 (Apr. 1)[4, 5]	110,053	116,493	194,713	26,683	5,150	1,420	3,729	14,609
1990 (Apr. 1)[4, 6]	121,271	127,494	208,727	30,511	9,527	2,065	7,462	22,372
1991 (July 1)[7]	122,943	129,184	210,961	31,131	10,035	2,110	7,925	23,384
1992 (July 1)[7]	124,404	130,590	212,860	31,667	10,467	2,148	8,319	24,275
1993 (July 1)[7]	125,767	131,979	214,677	32,179	10,890	2,185	8,705	25,214
1994 (July 1)[7]	127,028	133,261	216,365	32,654	11,271	2,221	9,050	26,152
1995 (July 1)[7]	128,272	134,493	218,010	33,098	11,657	2,254	9,403	27,099
1996 (July 1)[7]	129,483	135,707	219,623	33,518	12,050	2,289	9,761	28,092
1997 (July 1)[7]	130,760	136,984	221,317	33,973	12,454	2,324	10,130	29,160
1998 (July 1)[7]	132,046	138,252	223,001	34,431	12,867	2,360	10,507	30,250
1999 (July 1)[7]	133,352	139,526	224,692	34,903	13,283	2,396	10,887	31,365

NOTES: n.a. = not available. 1. Persons of Hispanic origin may be of any race. 2. Excludes Alaska and Hawaii. 3. The revised 1970 resident population count is 203,302,031, which incorporates changes due to errors found after tabulations were completed. The race and sex data shown here reflect the official 1970 census count. 4. The race data shown have been modified to be consistent with the guidelines in Federal Statistical Directive No. 15 issued by the Office of Management and Budget. Figures are not comparable to the 1990 census race categories. 5. Total population count has been revised since the 1980 census publications. Numbers by age, race, Hispanic origin, and sex have not been corrected. 6. The April 1, 1990, census count (248,765,170) includes count resolution corrections processed through Aug. 1997, and does not include adjustments for census coverage errors except for adjustments estimated for the 1995 Census Test in Oakland, Calif.; Paterson, N.J.; and six Louisiana parishes. These adjustments amounted to a total of 55,297 persons. 7. Estimated. *Source: Statistical Abstract of the United States 1998.*

Population Trends by Region

	July 1990	July 1994	July 1995	July 1996	July 1997	July 1998
United States	249,439,545	260,292,437	262,760,639	265,179,411	267,636,061	270,298,524
Northeast[1]	50,873,469	51,349,083	51,428,139	51,502,371	51,588,281	51,721,625
New England	13,219,210	13,241,007	13,280,586	13,326,211	13,378,545	13,429,862
Middle Atlantic	37,654,259	38,108,076	38,147,553	38,176,160	38,209,736	38,291,763
Midwest[2]	59,763,595	61,452,399	61,837,876	62,181,664	62,460,453	62,889,382
East North Central	42,075,499	43,228,928	43,483,513	43,713,327	43,889,857	44,194,756
West North Central	17,688,096	18,223,471	18,354,363	18,468,337	18,570,596	18,694,626
South[3]	85,731,322	90,606,513	91,824,747	93,009,528	94,187,161	95,429,486
South Atlantic	43,756,608	46,337,861	46,962,293	47,588,515	48,230,168	48,944,678
East South Central	15,208,424	15,877,321	16,044,096	16,187,380	16,325,977	16,471,211
West South Central	26,766,290	28,391,331	28,818,358	29,233,633	29,631,016	30,013,597
West[4]	53,071,159	56,884,442	57,669,877	58,485,848	59,400,166	60,258,031
Mountain	13,716,651	15,314,473	15,752,130	16,124,450	16,482,103	16,813,233
Pacific	39,354,508	41,569,969	41,917,747	42,361,398	42,918,063	43,444,798

NOTES: These population estimates incorporate revisions of estimates from previous years and the results of special censuses and test censuses conducted by the Bureau of the Census. Data released to public in Dec. 1998. 1. The Northeast region includes the New England division: Conn., Maine, Mass., N.H., R.I., and Vt.; and the Middle Atlantic division: N.J., N.Y., and Pa. 2. The Midwest region includes the East North Central division: Ill., Ind., Mich., Ohio, and Wis.; and the West North Central division: Iowa, Kans., Minn., Mo., Nebr., N.D., and S.D. 3. The South region includes the South Atlantic division: Del., D.C., Fla., Ga., Md., N.C., S. C., Va., and W.Va.; the East South Central division: Ala., Ky., Miss., Tenn.; and the West South Central division: Ark., La., Okla., and Tex. 4. The West region includes the Mountain division: Ariz., Colo., Idaho, Mont., Nev., N.M., Utah, Wyo.; and the Pacific division: Alaska, Calif., Hawaii, Ore., and Wash. *Source:* Population Estimates Program, Population Division, U.S. Bureau of the Census; Web: www.census.gov/population.

Population by State

State	1990	Percent change, 1980–1990	Pop. per sq mi., 1990	Pop. rank, 1990	1980	1950	1900	1790
Alabama	4,040,587	3.8%	79.6	22	3,893,888	3,061,743	1,828,697	—
Alaska	550,403	36.8	1.0	49	401,851	128,643	63,592	—
Arizona	3,665,228	34.9	32.3	24	2,718,215	749,587	122,931	—
Arkansas	2,350,725	2.8	45.1	33	2,286,435	1,909,511	1,311,564	—
California	29,786,021	25.8	191.4	1	23,667,902	10,586,223	1,485,053	—
Colorado	3,294,394	14.0	31.8	26	2,889,964	1,325,089	539,700	—
Connecticut	3,287,116	5.8	678.5	27	3,107,576	2,007,280	908,420	237,946
Delaware	666,168	12.1	340.8	46	594,338	318,085	184,735	59,096
D.C.	606,900	−4.9	884.4	—	638,333	802,178	278,718	—
Florida	12,937,926	32.8	239.9	4	9,746,324	2,771,305	528,542	—
Georgia	6,478,216	18.6	111.8	11	5,463,105	3,444,578	2,216,331	82,548
Hawaii	1,108,229	14.8	172.5	41	964,691	499,794	154,001	—
Idaho	1,006,749	6.6	12.2	42	943,935	588,637	161,772	—
Illinois	11,430,602	0.0	205.6	6	11,426,518	8,712,176	4,821,550	—
Indiana	5,544,159	1.0	154.6	14	5,490,224	3,934,224	2,516,462	—
Iowa	2,776,755	−4.7	49.7	30	2,913,808	2,621,073	2,231,853	—
Kansas	2,477,574	4.8	30.3	32	2,363,679	1,905,299	1,470,495	—
Kentucky	3,687,000	0.7	92.8	23	3,660,777	2,944,806	2,147,174	73,677
Louisiana	4,222,000	0.4	96.9	21	4,205,900	2,683,516	1,381,625	—
Maine	1,227,928	9.1	39.8	38	1,124,660	913,774	694,466	96,540
Maryland	4,781,468	13.4	489.1	19	4,216,975	2,343,001	1,188,044	319,728
Massachusetts	6,016,425	4.9	767.6	13	5,737,037	4,690,514	2,805,346	378,787
Michigan	9,295,297	0.4	163.6	8	9,262,078	6,371,766	2,420,982	—
Minnesota	4,375,099	7.4	55.0	20	4,075,970	2,982,483	1,751,394	—
Mississippi	2,575,000	2.2	54.9	31	2,520,638	2,178,914	1,551,270	—
Missouri	5,117,073	4.1	74.3	15	4,916,686	3,954,653	3,106,665	—
Montana	799,065	1.5	5.5	44	786,690	591,024	243,329	—
Nebraska	1,578,385	0.5	20.6	36	1,569,825	1,325,510	1,066,300	—
Nevada	1,201,833	50.2	10.9	39	800,493	160,083	42,335	—
New Hampshire	1,109,252	20.4	123.7	40	920,610	533,242	411,588	141,885
New Jersey	7,748,000	5.2	1,044.3	9	7,364,823	4,835,329	1,883,669	184,139
New Mexico	1,515,069	16.3	12.5	37	1,302,894	681,187	195,310	—
New York	17,990,455	2.5	384.1	2	17,558,072	14,830,192	7,268,894	340,120
North Carolina	6,632,000	12.8	136.1	10	5,881,766	4,061,929	1,893,810	393,751
North Dakota	638,800	−2.2	9.3	47	652,717	619,636	319,146	—
Ohio	10,847,115	0.5	264.9	7	10,797,630	7,946,627	4,157,545	—
Oklahoma	3,145,585	4.0	45.8	28	3,025,290	2,233,351	790,391[1]	—
Oregon	2,842,321	8.0	29.6	29	2,633,105	1,521,341	413,536	—
Pennsylvania	11,883,000	0.2	265.1	5	11,863,895	10,498,012	6,302,115	434,373
Rhode Island	1,003,464	6.0	960.3	43	947,154	791,896	428,556	68,825
South Carolina	3,486,703	11.7	115.4	25	3,121,820	2,117,027	1,340,316	249,073
South Dakota	696,004	0.7	9.2	45	690,768	652,740	401,570	—
Tennessee	4,877,185	6.2	118.3	17	4,591,120	3,291,718	2,020,616	35,691
Texas	16,986,510	19.4	64.9	3	14,229,191	7,711,194	3,048,710	—
Utah	1,722,850	17.9	21.0	35	1,461,037	688,862	276,749	—
Vermont	562,758	10.1	60.8	48	511,456	377,747	343,641	85,425
Virginia	6,189,000	15.8	156.3	12	5,346,818	3,318,680	1,854,184	747,610[2]
Washington	4,866,692	17.8	73.1	18	4,132,156	2,378,963	518,103	—
West Virginia	1,793,477	−8.0	74.5	34	1,949,644	2,005,552	958,800	—
Wisconsin	4,891,769	3.9	90.1	16	4,705,767	3,434,575	2,069,042	—
Wyoming	453,588	−3.5	4.7	50	469,557	290,529	92,531	—
Total U.S.	**248,709,873**	**9.8**	**—**	**—**	**226,545,805**	**151,325,798**	**76,212,168**	**3,929,214**

1. Includes population of Indian Territory, 1900: 392,960. 2. Until 1863, Virginia included what is now West Virginia. *Source:* U.S. Bureau of the Census; Web: www.census.gov.

Resident Population of the United States:
Estimates, by Sex, Race, and Hispanic Origin, with Median Age, 1999
(in thousands)

	Total population	% of population	Median age	Male population	Female population
All races	272,878	100.0%	35.5	133,352	139,526
White	224,692	82.3	36.6	110,372	114,320
Black	34,903	12.8	30.1	16,573	18,329
American Indian, Eskimo, and Aleut	2,396	0.9	27.6	1,186	1,211
Asian and Pacific Islander	10,887	4.0	31.7	5,221	5,667
Hispanic origin (of any race)	31,365	11.5	26.5	15,774	15,591

NOTES: As of July 1, 1999. Percentages add up to more than 100% because Hispanics may be of any race and are therefore counted under more than one category. *Source:* U.S. Bureau of the Census; Web: www.census.gov.

Resident Population Estimates by Age and Sex, 1999

	Both sexes	Male	Female
Population, all ages	272,878,000	133,352,000	139,526,000
Median age	35.5	34.3	36.6
Five-year age groups			
Under 5 years	18,918,000	9,668,000	9,250,000
5 to 9 years	19,957,000	10,213,000	9,744,000
10 to 14 years	19,554,000	10,015,000	9,540,000
15 to 19 years	19,762,000	10,159,000	9,603,000
20 to 24 years	18,061,000	9,197,000	8,864,000
25 to 29 years	18,240,000	9,067,000	9,174,000
30 to 34 years	19,750,000	9,780,000	9,970,000
35 to 39 years	22,556,000	11,221,000	11,335,000
40 to 44 years	22,278,000	11,045,000	11,233,000
45 to 49 years	19,363,000	9,505,000	9,858,000
50 to 54 years	16,452,000	8,001,000	8,451,000
55 to 59 years	12,883,000	6,186,000	6,697,000
60 to 64 years	10,526,000	4,973,000	5,553,000
65 to 69 years	9,455,000	4,339,000	5,116,000
70 to 74 years	8,779,000	3,866,000	4,914,000
75 to 79 years	7,337,000	3,060,000	4,277,000
80 to 84 years	4,823,000	1,816,000	3,007,000
85 to 89 years	2,629,000	848,000	1,781,000
90 to 94 years	1,151,000	308,000	843,000
95 to 99 years	344,000	76,000	269,000
100 years and over	60,000	11,000	49,000
Special age categories			
18 years and over	202,682,000	97,395,000	105,287,000
65 years and over	34,578,000	14,323,000	20,255,000

NOTE: As of July 1, 1999. *Source:* U.S. Bureau of the Census. Web: www.census.gov.

Population Explosion among Older Americans

The United States has seen a rapid growth in its elderly population during the 20th century. The number of Americans aged 65 and older climbed above 34.6 million in 1999, compared with 3.1 million in 1900. For the same years, the ratio of elderly Americans to the total population jumped from one in 25 to one in eight. The trend is guaranteed to continue in the coming century as the baby-boom generation grows older. Between 1990 and 2020, the population aged 65 to 74 is projected to grow 74 percent.

The elderly population explosion is a result of impressive increases in life expectancy. When the nation was founded, the average American could expect to live to the age of 35. Life expectancy at birth had increased to 47.3 by 1900 and in 1997 stood at 76.5.

Along with the growth of the general elderly population has come a remarkable increase in the number of Americans reaching age 100. The 1990 census found that there were 37,306 centenarians in the U.S. Current projections estimate that the number will reach 72,000 in the year 2000 and as many 834,000 by 2050.

Source: Based on U.S. Census Bureau data.

Persons 65 Years Old and Over—Characteristics by Sex, 1980–1997

Characteristic	Total			Male			Female		
	1980	1990	1997	1980	1990	1997	1980	1990	1997
Total[1] (million)	**24.2**	**29.6**	**31.9**	**9.9**	**12.3**	**13.4**	**14.2**	**17.2**	**18.5**
White (million)	21.9	26.5	28.5	9.0	11.0	12.0	12.9	15.4	16.4
Black (million)	2.0	2.5	2.6	0.8	1.0	1.0	1.2	1.5	1.6
Percent below poverty level[2]	15.2%	11.4%	10.8%	11.1%	7.8%	6.8%	17.9%	13.9%	13.6%
Percent distribution									
Marital status:									
Single	5.5%	4.6%	4.2%	4.9%	4.2%	4.1%	5.9%	4.9%	4.3%
Married	55.4	56.1	55.6	78.0	76.5	74.2	39.5	41.4	42.1
Spouse present	53.6	54.1	53.3	76.1	74.2	71.8	37.9	39.7	39.9
Spouse absent	1.8	2.0	2.3	1.9	2.3	2.4	1.7	1.7	2.2
Widowed	35.7	34.2	33.4	13.5	14.2	15.7	51.2	48.6	46.3
Divorced	3.5	5.0	6.8	3.6	5.0	6.0	3.4	5.1	7.4
Family status:									
In families[3]	67.6%	66.7%	67.2%	83.0%	81.9%	79.6%	56.8%	55.8%	56.8%
Nonfamily householders	31.2	31.9	32.2	15.7	16.6	18.4	42.0	42.8	42.2
Secondary individuals	1.2	1.4	1.1	1.3	1.5	2.0	1.1	1.4	0.9
Living arrangements:									
Living in household	99.8%	99.7%	100.0%	99.9%	99.9%	100.0%	99.7%	99.5%	100.0%
Living alone	30.3	31.0	31.2	14.9	15.7	17.3	41.0	42.0	41.2
Spouse present	53.6	54.1	53.5	76.1	74.3	71.8	37.9	39.7	39.9
Living with someone else	15.9	14.6	15.3	8.9	9.9	10.9	20.8	17.8	18.9
Not in household[4]	0.2	0.3	—	0.1	0.1	—	0.3	0.5	—
Years of school completed:									
8 years or fewer	43.1%	28.5%	18.8%	45.3%	30.0%	19.5%	41.6%	27.5%	18.3%
1 to 3 years of high school	16.2	16.1	15.7[5]	15.5	15.7	14.6[5]	16.7	16.4	16.4[5]
4 years of high school	24.0	32.9	34.3[6]	21.4	29.0	29.6[6]	25.8	35.6	37.7[6]
1 to 3 years of college	8.2	10.9	16.5[7]	7.5	10.8	16.3[7]	8.6	11.0	16.6[7]
4 years or more of college	8.6	11.6	14.8[8]	10.3	14.5	19.9[8]	7.4	9.5	11.1[8]
Labor force participation:[9]									
Employed	12.2%	11.5%	11.8%	18.4%	15.9%	16.5%	7.8%	8.4%	8.3%
Unemployed	0.4	0.4	0.4	0.6	0.5	0.5	0.3	0.3	0.3
Not in labor force	87.5	88.1	87.8	81.0	83.6	82.9	91.9	91.3	91.4

NOTE: (—) Represents zero. 1. Includes other races, not shown separately. 2. Poverty status based on income in preceding year. 3. Excludes those living in unrelated subfamilies. 4. In group quarters other than institutions. 5. Represents those who completed 9th to 12th grade, but have no high school diploma. 6. High school graduate. 7. Some college or associate degree. 8. Bachelor's or advanced degree. 9. Annual averages of monthly figures (from U.S. Bureau of Labor Statistics, *Employment and Earnings*, January issues. Data beginning 1994 not directly comparable with earlier years). *Source:* Except as noted, U.S. Bureau of the Census, *Current Population Reports.*

Population Aged 100 and Over, 1990

	Total	White	Black	American Indian, Eskimo, and Aleut	Asian and Pacific Islander	Other	Hispanic[1]	Non-Hispanic	
								White	All other races
Both sexes	37,306	30,105	5,874	264	492	571	1,642	29,130	6,534
100 to 104 years	30,947	25,881	4,208	180	357	321	1,051	25,186	4,710
105 years and over	6,359	4,224	1,666	84	135	250	591	3,944	1,824
Males	7,901	5,799	1,587	99	175	241	581	5,490	1,830
100 to 104 years	5,944	4,616	1,025	68	122	113	317	4,421	1,206
105 years and over	1,957	1,183	562	31	53	128	264	1,069	624
Females	29,405	24,306	4,287	165	317	330	1,061	23,640	4,704
100 to 104 years	25,003	21,265	3,183	112	235	208	734	20,765	3,504
105 years and over	4,402	3,041	1,104	53	82	122	327	2,875	1,200

1. Persons of Hispanic origin may be of any race. *Source:* U.S. Bureau of the Census, *1990 Census of Population—General Population Characteristics, United States.*

Estimated 1996 Population of Metro Areas Over One Million

Metropolitan statistical area (MSA) or Consolidated metropolitan statistical area (CMSA)	July 1996
New York City–Northern N.J.–Long Island, N.Y.–Conn.–Pa. (CMSA)	19,938,492
Los Angeles–Riverside–Orange County, Calif. (CMSA)	15,495,155
Chicago–Gary–Kenosha, Ill.–Ind.–Wis. (CMSA)	8,599,774
Washington–Baltimore, D.C.–Md.–Va.–W.Va. (CMSA)	7,164,519
San Francisco–Oakland–San Jose, Calif. (CMSA)	6,605,428
Philadelphia–Wilmington–Atlantic City, Pa.–N.J.–Del.–Md. (CMSA)	5,973,463
Boston–Worcester–Lawrence, Mass.–N.H.–Maine–Conn. (CMSA)	5,563,475
Detroit–Ann Arbor–Flint, Mich. (CMSA)	5,284,171
Dallas–Fort Worth, Tex. (CMSA)	4,574,561
Houston–Galveston–Brazoria, Tex. (CMSA)	4,253,428
Atlanta, Ga. (MSA)	3,541,230
Miami–Fort Lauderdale, Fla. (CMSA)	3,514,403
Seattle–Tacoma–Bremerton, Wash. (CMSA)	3,320,829
Cleveland–Akron, Ohio (CMSA)	2,913,430
Minneapolis–St. Paul, Minn.–Wis. (MSA)	2,765,116
Phoenix–Mesa, Ariz. (MSA)	2,746,703
San Diego, Calif. (MSA)	2,655,463
St. Louis, Mo.–Ill. (MSA)	2,548,238
Pittsburgh, Pa. (MSA)	2,379,411
Denver–Boulder–Greeley, Colo. (CMSA)	2,277,401
Tampa–St. Petersburg–Clearwater, Fla. (MSA)	2,199,231

Metropolitan statistical area (MSA) or Consolidated metropolitan statistical area (CMSA)	July 1996
Portland–Salem, Ore.–Wash. (CMSA)	2,078,357
Cincinnati–Hamilton, Ohio–Ky.–Ind. (CMSA)	1,920,931
Kansas City, Mo.–Kans. (MSA)	1,690,343
Milwaukee–Racine, Wis. (CMSA)	1,642,658
Sacramento–Yolo, Calif. (CMSA)	1,632,133
Norfolk–Virginia Beach–Newport News, Va.–N.C. (MSA)	1,540,252
Indianapolis, Ind. (MSA)	1,492,297
San Antonio, Tex. (MSA)	1,490,111
Columbus, Ohio (MSA)	1,447,646
Orlando, Fla. (MSA)	1,417,291
Charlotte–Gastonia–Rock Hill, N.C.–S.C. (MSA)	1,321,068
New Orleans, La. (MSA)	1,312,890
Salt Lake City–Ogden, Utah (MSA)	1,217,842
Las Vegas, Nev.–Ariz.	1,201,073
Buffalo–Niagara Falls, N.Y. (MSA)	1,175,240
Hartford, Conn. (MSA)	1,144,574
Greensboro–Winston-Salem–High Point, N.C. (MSA)	1,141,238
Providence–Fall River–Warwick, R.I.–Mass. (MSA)	1,124,044
Nashville, Tenn. (MSA)	1,117,178
Rochester, N.Y. (MSA)	1,088,037
Memphis, Tenn.–Ark.–Miss. (MSA)	1,078,151
Oklahoma City, Okla. (MSA)	1,026,657

Source: U.S. Bureau of the Census; Web: www.census.gov.

Marital Status and Household Characteristics

Marriages and Divorces, 1900–1998

Year	Marriage Number	Rate[2]	Divorce[1] Number	Rate[2]	Year	Marriage Number	Rate[2]	Divorce[1] Number	Rate[2]
1900	709,000	9.3	55,751	0.7	1985	2,425,000	10.2	1,187,000	5.0
1910	948,166	10.3	83,045	0.9	1986	2,400,000	10.0	1,159,000	4.8
1920	1,274,476	12.0	170,505	1.6	1987	2,421,000	9.9	1,157,000	4.8
1930	1,126,856	9.2	195,961	1.6	1988	2,389,000	9.7	1,183,000	4.8
1940	1,595,879	12.1	264,000	2.0	1989	2,404,000	9.7	1,163,000	4.7
1950	1,667,231	11.1	385,144	2.6	1990	2,448,000	9.8	1,175,000	4.7
1960	1,523,000	8.5	393,000	2.2	1991	2,371,000	9.4	1,187,000	4.7
1965	1,800,000	9.3	479,000	2.5	1992	2,362,000	9.2	1,215,000	4.8
1970	2,158,802	10.6	708,000	3.5	1993	2,334,000	9.0	1,187,000	4.6
1975	2,152,662	10.1	1,036,000	4.9	1994	2,362,000	9.1	1,191,000	4.6
1980	2,406,708	10.6	1,182,000	5.2	1995	2,336,000	8.9	1,169,000	4.4
1982	2,495,000	10.8	1,180,000	5.1	1996	2,344,000	8.8	1,150,000	4.3
1983	2,444,000	10.5	1,179,000	5.0	1997	2,384,000	8.9	1,163,000	4.3
1984	2,487,000	10.5	1,155,000	4.9	1998	2,256,000	8.4	955,000	3.5

1. Includes annulments. 2. Per 1,000 population. Divorce rates for 1941–1946 are based on population including armed forces overseas. Marriage rates are based on population excluding armed forces overseas. NOTE: Marriage and divorce figures for most years include some estimated data. Alaska is included beginning 1959, Hawaii beginning 1960. *Source:* Department of Health and Human Services, National Center for Health Statistics; Web: www.dhhs.gov.

Households, Families, and Married Couples, 1890–1998

Date	Households Number	Households Average population per household	Families Number	Families Average population per family	Married couples Number
June 1890	12,690,000	4.93	—	—	—
April 1930	29,905,000	4.11	—	—	25,174,000
April 1940	34,949,000	3.67	32,166,000	3.76	26,571,000
March 1950	43,554,000	3.37	39,303,000	3.54	34,075,000
April 1955	47,874,000	3.33	41,951,000	3.59	36,251,000
March 1960[1]	52,799,000	3.35	45,111,000	3.67	39,254,000
March 1965	57,436,000	3.32	47,956,000	3.70	41,689,000
March 1970	63,401,000	3.14	51,586,000	3.58	44,728,000
March 1975	71,120,000	2.94	55,712,000	3.42	46,951,000
March 1980	80,776,000	2.76	59,550,000	3.29	49,112,000
March 1985	86,789,000	2.69	62,706,000	3.23	50,350,000
March 1990	93,347,000	2.63	66,090,000	3.17	52,317,000
March 1995	98,990,000	2.65	69,305,000	3.19	53,858,000
March 1996	99,627,000	2.65	69,594,000	3.20	53,567,000
Dec. 1997	101,018,000	2.64	70,241,000	3.19	53,604,000
Dec. 1998	102,528,000	2.62	70,880,000	3.18	54,317,000

1. First year in which figures for Alaska and Hawaii were included. *Source:* U.S. Bureau of the Census; Web: www.census.gov.

Singles in the United States

The ratio of unmarried men per 100 unmarried women in U.S. Metro Areas, 1990

Highest Ratio Men to Women

Rank	Metro Area	Ratio
1	Jacksonville, N.C. MSA	223.64
2	Killeen–Temple, Tex. MSA	122.75
3	Fayetteville, N.C. MSA	117.66
4	Brazoria, Tex. PMSA	116.71
5	Lawton, Okla. MSA	115.63
6	State College, Pa. MSA	112.98
7	Clarksville–Hopkinsville, Tenn.–Ky. MSA	112.71
8	Anchorage, Alaska MSA	112.45
9	Salinas–Seaside–Monterey, Calif. MSA	112.01
10	Bryan–College Station, Tex. MSA	111.40
11	Bremerton, Wash. MSA	108.30
12	San Diego, Calif. MSA	105.33
13	Honolulu, Hawaii MSA	105.22
14	Las Vegas, Nev. MSA	104.65
15	Yuma, Ariz. MSA	104.64
16	Grand Forks, N.D. MSA	104.19
17	San Jose, Calif. PMSA	103.63
18	Reno, Nev. MSA	103.52
19	Lafayette–West Lafayette, Ind. MSA	102.01
20	Fort Walton Beach, Fla. MSA	101.70
21	Vallejo–Fairfield–Napa, Calif. PMSA	101.68
22	Lake County, Ill. PMSA	101.56
23	Champaign–Urbana–Rantoul, Ill. MSA	101.33
24	Jackson, Miss. MSA	101.24
25	Colorado Springs, Colo. MSA	99.42

Lowest Ratio Men to Women

Rank	Metro Area	Ratio
1	Sarasota, Fla. MSA	65.57
2	Bradenton, Fla. MSA	68.41
3	Altoona, Pa. MSA	69.42
4	Springfield, Ill. MSA	69.63
5	Jacksonville, Tenn. MSA	69.72
6	Gadsden, Ala. MSA	69.86
7	Wheeling, W.Va.–Ohio MSA	70.48
8	Charleston, W.Va. MSA	70.65
9	St. Joseph, Mo. MSA	70.93
10	Lynchburg, Va. MSA	71.04
11	Roanoke, Va. MSA	71.09
12	Asheville, N.C. MSA	71.14
13	Shreveport, La. MSA	71.54
14	Birmingham, Ala. MSA	71.63
15	Danville, Va. MSA	71.72
16	Pittsburgh, Pa. PMSA	72.04
17	Monroe, La. MSA	72.06
18	Owensboro, Ky. MSA	72.14
19	Pittsburgh–Beaver Valley, Pa. (CMSA)	72.16
20	Florence, Ala. MSA	72.20
21	Sherman–Denison, Tex. MSA	72.27
22	Florence, S.C. MSA	72.32
23	Huntington–Ashland, W.Va.–Ky.–Ohio MSA	72.67
24	Cumberland, Md.–W.Va. MSA	72.73
25	Steubenville–Weirton, Ohio–W.Va. MSA	72.87

NOTE: Unmarried includes never-married, widowed, and divorced persons, 15 years or older. Metro Areas as defined June 30, 1990. The presence of a military base, college or university, etc. in a metropolitan area may have a significant impact on the size of the ratio. MSA—Metropolitan Statistical Area. CMSA—Consolidated Metropolitan Statistical Area. PMSA—Primary Metropolitan Statistical Area. *Source:* U.S. Bureau of the Census; Web: www.census.gov.

Percent Never Married, 1970 and 1998

Age	1970	1998	Age	1970	1998
Male:			Female:		
20 to 24 years	35.8%	83.4%	20 to 24 years	54.7%	70.3%
25 to 29 years	10.5	51.0	25 to 29 years	19.1	38.6
30 to 34 years	6.2	29.2	30 to 34 years	9.4	21.6
35 to 39 years	5.4	21.6	35 to 39 years	7.2	14.3
40 to 44 years	4.9	15.6	40 to 44 years	6.3	9.9

NOTE: Data applies to the U.S. *Source:* U.S. Bureau of the Census, *Current Population Reports.*

Median Age at First Marriage

Year	Males	Females	Year	Males	Females	Year	Males	Females
1890	26.1	22.0	1950	22.8	20.3	1994	26.7	24.5
1900	25.9	21.9	1960	22.8	20.3	1995	26.9	24.5
1910	25.1	21.6	1970	23.2	20.8	1996	27.1	24.8
1920	24.6	21.2	1980	24.7	22.0	1997	26.8	25.0
1930	24.3	21.3	1990	26.1	23.9	1998	26.7	25.0
1940	24.3	21.5	1993	26.5	24.5			

Source: U.S. Bureau of the Census; Web: www.census.gov.

Persons Living Alone, by Sex and Age
(in thousands)

Sex and Age[1]	1997 Number	1997 Percent	1994 Number	1994 Percent	1990 Number	1990 Percent	1980 Number	1980 Percent	1970 Number	1970 Percent
Both sexes										
15 to 24 years	1,083	4.0%	1,126	4.8%	1,210	5.3%	1,726	9.4%	556	5.1%
25 to 44 years	7,508	29.0	7,235	30.6	7,110	30.9	4,729	25.8	1,604	14.8
45 to 64 years	6,877	27.0	5,967	25.3	5,502	23.9	4,514	24.7	3,622	33.4
65 years and over	9,934	39.0	9,285	39.3	9,176	39.9	7,328	40.1	5,071	46.7
Total, 15 years and over	**25,402**	**100.0**	**23,613**	**100.0**	**22,999**	**100.0**	**18,296**	**100.0**	**10,851**	**100.0**
Male										
15 to 24 years	566	2.0	570	6.0	674	7.4	947	13.6	274	2.5
25 to 44 years	4,615	18.0	4,359	46.2	4,231	46.8	2,920	41.9	933	8.6
45 to 64 years	2,947	12.0	2,473	26.2	2,203	24.3	1,613	23.2	1,152	10.6
65 years and over	2,314	9.0	2,037	21.6	1,942	21.5	1,486	21.3	1,174	10.8
Total, 15 years and over	**10,442**	**41.0**	**9,439**	**100.0**	**9,049**	**100.0**	**6,966**	**100.0**	**3,532**	**100.0**
Female										
15 to 24 years	519	2.0	557	3.9	536	3.8	779	6.9	282	2.6
25 to 44 years	2,893	11.0	2,872	20.3	2,881	20.7	1,809	16.0	671	6.2
45 to 64 years	3,931	15.0	3,493	24.6	3,300	23.7	2,901	25.6	2,470	22.8
65 years and over	7,619	30.0	7,248	51.1	7,233	51.8	5,842	51.6	3,897	35.9
Total, 15 years and over	**14,961**	**59.0**	**14,171**	**100.0**	**13,950**	**100.0**	**11,330**	**100.0**	**7,319**	**100.0**

1. Prior to 1980, data are for persons 14 years and older. NOTE: Details may not add up to 100% because of rounding. *Source:* U.S. Bureau of the Census; Web: www.census.gov.

Female Family Householders with No Spouse Present, 1980–1997

	White 1980	White 1990	White 1997	Black 1980	Black 1990	Black 1997	Hispanic origin[1] 1980	Hispanic origin[1] 1990	Hispanic origin[1] 1997
Total (in thousands):	6,052	7,306	8,339	2,495	3,275	3,947	610	1,116	1,617
Marital Status:									
Never married (single)	11%	15%	20%	27%	39%	46%	23%	27%	39%
Married, spouse absent	17	16	16	29	21	19	32	29	23
Widowed	33	26	20	22	17	13	15	16	11
Divorced	40	43	44	22	23	22	30	29	27
Presence of children under age 18:									
No children	41	43	40	28	32	34	25	33	30
With own children	59	58	60	72	68	66	75	67	70
One child	28	30	30	26	30	30	28	25	31
Two children	20	19	21	23	22	21	23	22	24
Three children	7	7	7	11	9	10	15	13	10
Four or more children	3	2	2	11	7	6	9	6	5
Children per family	1.03	0.95	1.01	1.51	1.26	1.22	1.56	1.37	1.40

NOTES: As of March. Covers persons 15 years old and over. 1. Persons of Hispanic origin my be of any race. *Source:* U.S. Bureau of the Census, *Current Population Reports,* pp. 20–506, and earlier reports.

Households with Two Unrelated Adults, March 1998

(in thousands)

	Total	Age of Householder				
		Under 25 years	25 to 34 years	35 to 44 years	45 to 64 years	65 years and over
All householders	5,911	1,183	2,190	1,196	1,059	283
Partner of opposite sex	4,236	776	1,618	857	797	188
No children under 15 years in household	2,716	452	883	509	695	177
With children under 15 years in household	1,520	325	735	348	102	11
Partner of same sex	1,674	407	571	339	263	95
No children under 15 years in household	1,508	387	484	301	243	93
With children under 15 years in household	167	20	88	38	19	2
Male householders	3,217	612	1,200	695	580	129
Partner of opposite sex	2,352	408	891	514	441	98
No children under 15 years in household	1,556	237	544	318	366	90
With children under 15 years in household	796	170	347	196	75	8
Partner of same sex	865	204	309	181	140	31
No children under 15 years in household	833	201	292	176	134	29
With children under 15 years in household	32	3	17	4	6	2
Female householders	2,694	571	989	501	479	154
Partner of opposite sex	1,885	369	727	343	356	90
No children under 15 years in household	1,161	215	340	191	329	87
With children under 15 years in household	724	154	387	153	27	3
Partner of same sex	810	203	262	158	123	64
No children under 15 years in household	675	186	192	124	109	64
With children under 15 years in household	135	17	70	34	13	—

Source: U.S. Bureau of the Census. Web: www.census.gov.

Births

Live Births by Age and Race of Mother

Year[1]/race	Total	Age of Mother							
		Under 15	15–19	20–24	25–29	30–34	35–39	40–44	45–49
1940	2,558,647	3,865	332,667	799,537	693,268	431,468	222,015	68,269	7,558
1945	2,858,449	4,028	298,868	832,746	785,299	554,906	296,852	78,853	6,897
1950	3,631,512	5,413	432,911	1,155,167	1,041,360	610,816	302,780	77,743	5,322
1955	4,014,112	6,181	493,770	1,290,939	1,133,155	732,540	352,320	89,777	5,430
1960	4,257,850	6,780	586,966	1,426,912	1,092,816	687,722	359,908	91,564	5,182
1965	3,760,358	7,768	590,894	1,337,350	925,732	529,376	282,908	81,716	4,614
1970	3,731,386	11,752	644,708	1,418,874	994,904	427,806	180,244	49,952	3,146
1975	3,144,198	12,642	582,238	1,093,676	936,786	375,500	115,409	26,319	1,628
1980	3,612,258	10,169	552,161	1,226,200	1,108,291	550,354	140,793	23,090	1,200
1985	3,760,561	10,220	467,485	1,141,320	1,201,350	696,354	214,336	28,334	1,162
1990	4,158,212	11,657	521,826	1,093,730	1,277,108	886,063	317,583	48,607	1,638
1995	3,899,589	12,242	499,873	965,547	1,063,539	904,666	383,745	67,250	2,727
1996	3,914,953	11,242	494,272	951,247	1,078,411	904,329	400,810	71,663	2,980
1997	3,880,894	10,121	483,220	942,048	1,069,436	886,798	409,710	76,084	3,333
White	3,072,640	5,021	338,272	720,546	871,636	735,571	337,423	61,417	2,633
Black	599,913	4,712	128,539	182,600	135,529	94,123	45,069	8,981	357
American Indian[2]	38,572	202	7,810	12,316	9,168	5,812	2,694	542	28
Asian or Pacific Islander	169,769	186	8,599	26,586	53,103	51,292	24,524	5,144	315
Hispanic origin[3]	709,767	2,833	118,122	216,152	188,669	121,539	51,601	10,405	439

NOTE: Data refer only to births occurring within the U.S. 1. Data for 1940–55 are adjusted for under-registration. Beginning 1960, only registered births are shown. Data for 1960–70 based on a 50% sample of births. For 1972–84, based on 100% of births in selected states and on 50% sample in all other states. Beginning 1989, births are tabulated by race of mother; previously based on race of child. 2. Includes births to Aleuts and Eskimos. 3. Persons of Hispanic origin may be any race.
Source: Department of Health and Human Services, National Center for Health Statistics; Web: www.dhhs.gov.

Live Births by Sex and Sex Ratio

Year	Total[1,2] Male	Female	Males per 1,000 females	White Male	Female	Males per 1,000 females	Black Male	Female	Males per 1,000 females
1985	1,927,983	1,832,578	1,052	1,536,646	1,454,727	1,056	308,575	299,618	1,030
1986	1,924,868	1,831,679	1,051	1,523,914	1,446,525	1,053	315,788	305,433	1,034
1987	1,951,153	1,858,241	1,050	1,535,517	1,456,971	1,054	325,259	316,308	1,028
1988	2,002,424	1,907,086	1,050	1,562,675	1,483,487	1,053	341,441	330,535	1,033
1989	2,069,490	1,971,468	1,050	1,606,757	1,525,234	1,053	360,131	349,264	1,031
1990	2,129,495	2,028,717	1,050	1,654,928	1,570,415	1,054	367,455	357,121	1,029
1991	2,101,518	2,009,389	1,046	1,659,077	1,582,196	1,049	346,455	336,147	1,031
1992	2,082,097	1,982,917	1,050	1,641,811	1,559,867	1,053	342,726	330,907	1,036
1993	2,048,861	1,951,379	1,050	1,616,332	1,533,501	1,054	333,984	324,891	1,028
1994	2,022,589	1,930,178	1,048	1,599,803	1,521,401	1,051	322,554	313,837	1,028
1995	1,996,355	1,930,234	1,049	1,588,427	1,510,458	1,052	308,115	297,024	1,031
1996	1,990,480	1,901,014	1,047	—	—	1,050	—	—	1,028
1997	1,985,596	1,895,298	1,048	—	—	1,050	—	—	1,031

NOTE: (—) Data not available. 1. Excludes births to nonresidents of U.S. 2. Includes races other than white and black. *Source:* Department of Health and Human Services, National Center for Health Statistics; Web: www.dhhs.gov.

Selected Characteristics of Births by Race of Mother, 1997

Characteristic	All races	White	Black	American Indian[1]	Asian or Pacific Islander	Hispanic origin[2]
Percentage of mothers who:						
Had prenatal care beginning in the first trimester	82.5%	84.7%	72.3%	68.1%	82.1%	73.7%
Had late or no prenatal care	3.9	3.2	7.3	8.6	3.8	6.2
Were tobacco users[3]	13.2	14.3	9.7	20.8	3.2	4.1
Were alcohol users[4]	1.2	1.1	1.7	3.6	0.4	0.7
Gained less than 16 lbs[5]	11.1	10.0	16.6	15.3	9.9	13.4
Had Caesarean births	20.8	20.7	21.8	18.0	19.0	20.2
Median weight gain[5]	30.5	30.6	29.7	30.2	30.0	29.8
Percentage of infants who:						
Were born prior to 37 full weeks	11.4%	10.2%	17.5%	12.2%	10.2%	11.2%
Weighed less than 1,500 grams (3 lb 4 oz.)	1.4	1.1	3.0	1.2	1.1	1.1
Weighed less than 2,500 grams (5 lb 8 oz.)	7.5	6.5	13.0	6.8	7.2	6.4
Weighed 4,000 grams (8 lb 4 oz.) or more	10.1	11.2	5.3	12.4	5.8	8.9
Had five-minute Apgar scores of less than 7[6]	1.4	1.2	2.4	1.4	1.0	1.2

1. Includes births to Aleuts and Eskimos. 2. Hispanic origin may be of any race. 3. Excludes data for Calif., Ind., N.Y. (but includes N.Y.C.), and S.D., which did not report tobacco use on birth certificate. 4. Excludes data for Calif. and S.D., which did not report alcohol use on birth certificate. 5. Excludes data for Calif., which did not report weight gain on birth certificate. 6. Excludes data for Calif. and Tex., which did not report Apgar scores on birth certificate. Apgar scores are derived from evaluations of five major signs at one minute and five minutes after birth. Each sign is given a score of 0–2 for a total of ten possible points; scores of 7–10 are considered normal, 4–7 may require resuscitative measures, and 0–3 require immediate resuscitation. The signs and scores (0-1-2) are as follows: Activity or muscle tone (absent—arms and legs flexed—active movement); Pulse (absent—below 100 bpm—above 100 bpm); Grimace or reflex irritability (no response—grimace—sneeze, cough, pulls away); Appearance or skin color (blue-gray, pale all over—normal, except for extremities—normal over entire body); Respiration (absent—slow, irregular—good, crying). *Source:* U.S. Department of Health and Human Services; Web: www.dhhs.gov.

Births, Birth Rates, and Fertility Rates by State, 1997

State	Number of births	Birth rate[1]	Fertility rate[2]	State	Number of births	Birth rate[1]	Fertility rate[2]
United States[3]	3,903,260	14.6	65.4	Hawaii	17,793	15.0	70.1
Alabama	60,766	14.2	62.4	Idaho	18,601	15.6	71.2
Alaska	9,993	16.5	71.4	Illinois	183,141	15.5	69.0
Arizona	74,430	16.8	76.2	Indiana	81,010	13.9	60.9
Arkansas	36,573	14.6	67.5	Iowa	37,014	13.0	60.3
California	532,561	16.7	73.8	Kansas	37,000	14.4	65.7
Colorado	56,313	14.7	64.2	Kentucky	53,199	13.7	60.0
Connecticut	45,832	14.0	63.6	Louisiana	65,535	15.1	65.4
Delaware	10,273	14.2	60.5	Maine	13,717	11.0	49.3
D.C.	8,332	15.3	61.9	Maryland	71,061	14.0	59.7
Florida	192,438	13.4	65.6	Massachusetts	82,029	13.5	58.3
Georgia	116,888	15.9	66.1	Michigan	133,366	13.9	61.1

State	Number of births	Birth rate[1]	Fertility rate[2]	State	Number of births	Birth rate[1]	Fertility rate[2]
Minnesota	64,726	13.9	61.5	Rhode Island	12,464	12.6	56.1
Mississippi	41,409	15.2	66.3	South Carolina	51,615	14.0	60.1
Missouri	73,301	13.7	61.7	South Dakota	10,681	14.6	67.9
Montana	10,875	12.4	58.6	Tennessee	74,391	14.0	61.4
Nebraska	23,531	14.2	64.8	Texas	332,874	17.4	75.6
Nevada	24,924	15.5	72.0	Utah	43,893	21.9	92.9
New Hampshire	14,422	12.4	52.9	Vermont	6,708	11.4	49.8
New Jersey	116,214	14.5	65.9	Virginia	92,732	13.9	58.7
New Mexico	27,306	15.9	71.9	Washington	78,585	14.2	62.5
New York	265,382	14.6	65.0	West Virginia	21,252	11.6	53.7
North Carolina	107,763	14.7	64.9	Wisconsin	66,842	13.0	58.0
North Dakota	8,412	13.1	61.0	Wyoming	6,377	13.2	60.6
Ohio	152,519	13.7	60.6	Puerto Rico	64,421	17.0	72.2
Oklahoma	46,865	14.2	65.9	Virgin Islands	2,063	18.2	82.4
Oregon	43,907	13.7	63.1	Guam	4,370	30.2	138.6
Pennsylvania	145,427	12.1	55.9				

NOTE: Data by place of residence. 1. Birth rates per 1,000 total population. 2. Fertility rates per 1,000 women aged 15-44. 3. Excludes data for Puerto Rico, Virgin Islands, and Guam. *Source:* Department of Health and Human Services, National Center for Health Statistics; Web: www.dhhs.gov.

Contraceptive Use by Women, 15 to 44 Years Old, 1995

Contraceptive status and method	All women	Age			Marital status		
		15–24 years	25–34 years	35–44 years	Never married	Currently married	Formerly married
All women (in thousands)	**60,201**	**18,002**	**20,758**	**21,440**	**22,679**	**29,673**	**7,849**
Percent distribution							
Sterile[1]	29.7%	2.6%	25.0%	57.0%	6.9%	43.2%	45.1%
Surgically sterile	27.9	1.8	23.6	54.0	5.7	41.1	42.5
Nonsurgically sterile[2]	1.7	0.7	1.3	2.8	1.1	2.0	2.2
Pill	17.3	23.1	23.7	6.3	20.4	15.6	14.6
IUD	0.5	0.1	0.6	0.8	0.3	0.7	0.4
Diaphragm	1.2	0.2	1.2	2.0	0.5	1.8	0.9
Condom	13.1	13.9	15.0	10.7	13.9	13.3	10.1
Periodic abstinence	1.5	0.5	1.8	2.0	0.6	2.3	0.7
Withdrawal	2.0	1.6	2.3	1.9	1.5	2.3	1.8
Other methods[3]	3.9	5.6	4.2	2.1	4.6	3.3	3.9

1. Total sterile includes male sterile for unknown reasons. 2. Persons sterile from illness, accident, or congenital conditions. 3. Includes implants, injectables, morning-after-pill, suppository, Today(TM) sponge, and less frequently used methods. *Source:* U.S. National Center for Health Statistics. From *Statistical Abstract of the United States 1997.*

Abortion Statistics, 1972–1995

	1972	1980	1985	1990	1995
Reported no. legal abortions	586,760	1,297,606	1,328,570	1,429,577	1,210,883
Abortion ratio[1]	180	359	354	345	311
Abortion rate[2]	13	25	24	24	20
	Percentage distribution				
Age group (yrs)					
≤19	32.6%	29.2%	26.3%	22.4%	20.1%
20–24	32.5	35.5	34.7	33.2	32.5
≥25	34.9	35.3	39.0	44.4	47.4
Marital status					
Married	29.7	23.1	19.3	21.7	20.3
Unmarried	70.3	76.9	80.7	78.3	79.7

1. Number of legal induced abortions per 1,000 live births. 2. Number of legal induced abortions per 1,000 women aged 15–44 years. *Source:* U.S. Department of Health and Human Services, *Morbidity and Mortality Weekly Report,* vol. 46, no. 48.

Mortality

15 Leading Causes of Death in the U.S., 1998

Rank[1]	Causes of death	Number	Deaths per 100,000 pop.	Age-adjusted death rate		
				1998	1997	Percent change
	All causes	2,329,520	865.8	473.8	485.8	−2.5%
1	Diseases of heart	727,624	270.4	128.1	132.6	−3.4
2	Malignant neoplasms, including neoplasms of lymphatic and hematopoietic tissues	540,702	201.0	124.3	126.5	−1.7
3	Cerebrovascular diseases	159,059	59.1	25.4	26.2	−3.0
4	Chronic obstructive pulmonary diseases and allied conditions	111,823	41.6	21.3	21.4	−0.4
5	Accidents and adverse effects	94,266	35.0	29.2	30.1	−3.0
	Motor vehicle accidents	42,693	15.9	15.4	16.1	−4.3
	All other accidents and adverse effects	51,572	19.2	13.7	14.1	−2.8
6	Pneumonia and influenza	92,048	34.2	13.3	13.2	0.8
7	Diabetes mellitus	63,813	23.7	13.5	13.6	−0.7
8	Suicide	29,732	11.1	10.2	10.7	−4.7
9	Nephritis, nephrotic syndrome, and nephrosis	25,755	9.6	4.4	4.4	n.a.
10	Chronic liver disease and cirrhosis	24,981	9.3	7.2	7.4	−2.7
11	Septicemia	22,817	8.5	4.2	4.2	n.a.
12	Alzheimer's disease	22,467	8.3	2.7	2.8	−3.6
13	Homicide and legal intervention	18,890	7.0	7.5	8.2	−8.5
14	Atherosclerosis	15,563	5.8	2.0	2.1	−4.8
15	Human immunodeficiency virus infection	13,930	5.2	4.9	7.8	−37.2
	All other causes	366,050	136.0	n.a.	n.a.	n.a.

NOTES: n.a. = not applicable. Deaths and death rates for 12 months ending June 1998. 1. Rank based on number of deaths. *Source:* U.S. National Center for Health Statistics, *National Vital Statistics Report,* vol. 47, no. 22.

Life Expectancy at Birth by Race and Sex, 1940–1997

	All races			White			Black		
Year	Both sexes	Male	Female	Both sexes	Male	Female	Both sexes	Male	Female
1997	76.5	73.6	79.4	77.1	74.3	79.9	71.1	67.2	74.7
1996	76.1	73.1	79.1	76.8	73.9	79.7	70.2	66.1	74.2
1995	75.8	72.5	78.9	76.5	73.4	79.6	69.6	65.2	73.9
1994	75.7	72.4	79.0	76.5	73.3	79.6	69.5	64.9	73.9
1993	75.5	72.2	78.8	76.3	73.1	79.5	69.2	64.6	73.7
1992	75.8	72.3	79.1	76.5	73.2	79.8	69.6	65.0	73.9
1991	75.5	72.0	78.9	76.3	72.9	79.6	69.3	64.6	73.8
1990	75.4	71.8	78.8	76.1	72.7	79.4	69.1	64.5	73.6
1989	75.1	71.7	78.5	75.9	72.5	79.2	68.8	64.3	73.3
1988	74.9	71.4	78.3	75.6	72.2	78.9	68.9	64.4	73.2
1987	74.9	71.4	78.3	75.6	72.1	78.9	69.1	64.7	73.4
1986	74.7	71.2	78.2	75.4	71.9	78.8	69.1	64.8	73.4
1985	74.7	71.1	78.2	75.3	71.8	78.7	69.3	65.0	73.4
1984	74.7	71.1	78.2	75.3	71.8	78.7	69.5	65.3	73.6
1983	74.6	71.0	78.1	75.2	71.6	78.7	69.4	65.2	73.5
1982	74.5	70.8	78.1	75.1	71.5	78.7	69.4	65.1	73.6
1981	74.1	70.4	77.8	74.8	71.1	78.4	68.9	64.5	73.2
1980	73.7	70.0	77.4	74.4	70.7	78.1	68.1	63.8	72.5
1979	73.9	70.0	77.8	74.6	70.8	78.4	68.5	64.0	72.9
1978	73.5	69.6	77.3	74.1	70.4	78.0	68.1	63.7	72.4
1977	73.3	69.5	77.2	74.0	70.2	77.9	67.7	63.4	72.0
1976	72.9	69.1	76.8	73.6	69.9	77.5	67.2	62.9	71.6
1975	72.6	68.8	76.6	73.4	69.5	77.3	66.8	62.4	71.3
1974	72.0	68.2	75.9	72.8	69.0	76.7	66.0	61.7	70.3
1973	71.4	67.6	75.3	72.2	68.5	76.1	65.0	60.9	69.3
1972[1]	71.2	67.4	75.1	72.0	68.3	75.9	64.7	60.4	69.1
1971	71.1	67.4	75.0	72.0	68.3	75.8	64.6	60.5	68.9
1970	70.8	67.1	74.7	71.7	68.0	75.6	64.1	60.0	68.3
1960	69.7	66.6	73.1	70.6	67.4	74.1	—	—	—
1950	68.2	65.6	71.1	69.1	66.5	72.2	—	—	—
1940	62.9	60.8	65.2	64.2	62.1	66.6	—	—	—

(—) Data not available. 1. Deaths based on a 50-percent sample. *Source:* U.S. National Center for Health Statistics, *Monthly Vital Statistics Report;* Web: www.dhhs.gov.

Life Expectancy by Age, 1850–1997

Calendar period	Age								
	0	10	20	30	40	50	60	70	80
White males									
1850[1]	38.3	48.0	40.1	34.0	27.9	21.6	15.6	10.2	5.9
1890[1]	42.50	48.45	40.66	34.05	27.37	20.72	14.73	9.35	5.40
1900–1902[2]	48.23	50.59	42.19	34.88	27.74	20.76	14.35	9.03	5.10
1909–1911[2]	50.23	51.32	42.71	34.87	27.43	20.39	13.98	8.83	5.09
1919–1921[3]	56.34	54.15	45.60	37.65	29.86	22.22	15.25	9.51	5.47
1929–1931	59.12	54.96	46.02	37.54	29.22	21.51	14.72	9.20	5.26
1939–1941	62.81	57.03	47.76	38.80	30.03	21.96	15.05	9.42	5.38
1949–1951	66.31	58.98	49.52	40.29	31.17	22.83	15.76	10.07	5.88
1959–1961[5]	67.55	59.78	50.25	40.98	31.73	23.22	16.01	10.29	5.89
1969–1971[6]	67.94	59.69	50.22	41.07	31.87	23.34	16.07	10.38	6.18
1979–1981	70.82	61.98	52.45	43.31	34.04	25.26	17.56	11.35	6.76
1990	72.7	63.5	54.0	44.7	35.6	26.7	18.7	12.1	7.1
1995	73.4	64.1	54.5	45.2	36.1	27.3	19.3	12.5	7.2
1997	74.3	65.0	55.3	45.9	36.7	27.7	19.6	12.7	7.4
White females									
1850[1]	40.5	47.2	40.2	35.4	29.8	23.5	17.0	11.3	6.4
1890[1]	44.46	49.62	42.03	35.36	28.76	22.09	15.70	10.15	5.75
1900–1902[2]	51.08	52.15	43.77	36.42	29.17	21.89	15.23	9.59	5.50
1909–1911[2]	53.62	53.57	44.88	36.96	29.26	21.74	14.92	9.38	5.35
1919–1921[3]	58.53	55.17	46.46	38.72	30.94	23.12	15.93	9.94	5.70
1929–1931	62.67	57.65	48.52	39.99	31.52	23.41	16.05	9.98	5.63
1939–1941	67.29	60.85	51.38	42.21	33.25	24.72	17.00	10.50	5.88
1949–1951	72.03	64.26	54.56	45.00	35.64	26.76	18.64	11.68	6.59
1959–1961[5]	74.19	66.05	56.29	46.63	37.13	28.08	19.69	12.38	6.67
1969–1971[6]	75.49	66.97	57.24	47.60	38.12	29.11	20.79	13.37	7.59
1979–1981	78.22	69.21	59.44	49.76	40.16	30.96	22.45	14.89	8.65
1990	79.4	70.1	60.3	50.6	41.0	31.6	23.0	15.4	9.0
1995	79.6	70.2	60.4	50.6	41.0	31.7	23.0	15.4	8.9
1997	79.9	70.5	60.7	50.9	41.3	32.0	23.2	15.5	9.1
All other males[4]									
1900–1902[2]	32.54	41.90	35.11	29.25	23.12	17.34	12.62	8.33	5.12
1909–1911[2]	34.05	40.65	33.46	27.33	21.57	16.21	11.67	8.00	5.53
1919–1921[3]	47.14	45.99	38.36	32.51	26.53	20.47	14.74	9.58	5.83
1929–1931	47.55	44.27	35.95	29.45	23.36	17.92	13.15	8.78	5.42
1939–1941	52.33	48.54	39.74	32.25	25.23	19.18	14.38	10.06	6.46
1949–1951	58.91	52.96	43.73	35.31	27.29	20.25	14.91	10.74	7.07
1959–1961[5]	61.48	55.19	45.78	37.05	28.72	21.28	15.29	10.81	6.87
1969–1971[6]	60.98	53.67	44.37	36.20	28.29	21.24	15.35	10.68	7.57
1979–1981	65.63	57.40	47.87	39.13	30.64	22.92	16.54	11.36	7.22
1990	67.0	58.5	49.0	40.3	31.9	23.9	17.0	11.4	7.0
1995	67.9	59.1	49.6	40.8	32.4	24.6	17.6	11.7	7.0
1997	69.8	60.9	51.4	42.5	33.7	25.5	18.3	12.4	7.9
All other females[4]									
1900–1902[2]	35.04	43.02	36.89	30.70	24.37	18.67	13.60	9.62	6.48
1909–1911[2]	37.67	42.84	36.14	29.61	23.34	17.65	12.78	9.22	6.05
1919–1921[3]	46.92	44.54	37.15	31.48	25.60	19.76	14.69	10.25	6.58
1929–1931	49.51	45.33	37.22	30.67	24.30	18.60	14.22	10.38	6.90
1939–1941	55.51	50.83	42.14	34.52	27.31	21.04	16.14	11.81	8.00
1949–1951	62.70	56.17	46.77	38.02	29.82	22.67	16.95	12.29	8.15
1959–1961[5]	66.47	59.72	50.07	40.83	32.16	24.31	17.83	12.46	7.66
1969–1971[6]	69.05	61.49	51.85	42.61	33.87	25.97	19.02	13.30	9.01
1979–1981	74.00	65.64	55.88	46.39	37.16	28.59	20.49	14.44	9.17
1990	75.2	66.6	56.8	47.3	38.1	29.2	21.3	14.5	8.8
1995	75.7	66.8	57.0	47.5	38.3	29.6	21.5	14.5	8.7
1997	76.7	67.8	58.0	48.4	39.1	30.3	22.1	15.1	9.4

1. Massachusetts only; white and nonwhite combined, the latter being about 1% of the total. 2. Original Death Registration States. 3. Death Registration States of 1920. 4. Data for periods 1900–1902 to 1929–1931 relate to blacks only. 5. Alaska and Hawaii included beginning in 1959. 6. Deaths of nonresidents of the United States excluded starting in 1970. *Sources:* Department of Health and Human Services, National Center for Health Statistics; Web: www.dhhs.gov.

U.S. Annual Death Rates per 1,000 Population

Year	Rate	Year	Rate	Year	Rate	Year	Rate	Year	Rate	Year	Rate
1900	17.2	1937	11.3	1950	9.6	1964	9.4	1977	8.6	1990	8.6
1905	15.9	1938	10.6	1951	9.7	1965	9.4	1978	8.7	1991	8.5
1910	14.7	1939	10.6	1952	9.6	1966	9.5	1979	8.5	1992	8.5
1915	13.2	1940	10.8	1953	9.6	1967	9.4	1980	8.7	1993	8.8
1920	13.0	1941	10.5	1954	9.2	1968	9.7	1981	8.6	1994	8.8
1925	11.7	1942	10.3	1955	9.3	1969	9.5	1982	8.5	1995	8.8
1930	11.3	1943	10.9	1956	9.4	1970[1]	9.5	1983	8.6	1996	8.8
1931	11.1	1944	10.6	1957	9.6	1971	9.3	1984	8.6	1997	8.6
1932	10.9	1945	10.6	1958	9.5	1972	9.4	1985	8.7	1998	8.6
1933	10.7	1946	10.0	1959	9.4	1973	9.3	1986	8.7		
1934	11.1	1947	10.1	1960	9.5	1974	9.1	1987	8.7		
1935	10.9	1948	9.9	1962	9.5	1975	8.8	1988	8.8		
1936	11.6	1949	9.7	1963	9.6	1976	8.8	1989	8.7		

NOTES: Includes only deaths occurring within the registration states. Beginning with 1933, area includes entire U.S.; with 1959 includes Alaska, and with 1960 includes Hawaii. Excludes fetal deaths. Rates as of April 1 for 1940, 1950, 1960, 1970, and 1980, and estimated as of July 1 for all other years. 1. First year for which deaths of nonresidents are excluded. *Sources:* Department of Health and Human Services, National Center for Health Statistics. Web: www.dhhs.gov.

Infant Mortality Rates, 1950–1996

		Deaths per 1,000 live births				
		Neonatal			Fetal mortality rate[1]	Late fetal mortality rate[2]
Year	Infant	Under 28 days	Under 7 days	Postneonatal		
1950[3]	29.2	20.5	17.8	8.7	18.4	14.9
1960[3]	26.0	18.7	16.7	7.3	15.8	12.1
1970	20.0	15.1	13.6	4.9	14.0	9.5
1980	12.6	8.5	7.1	4.1	9.1	6.2
1985	10.6	7.0	5.8	3.7	7.8	4.9
1988	10.0	6.3	5.2	3.6	7.5	4.5
1989	9.8	6.2	5.1	3.6	7.5	4.5
1990	9.2	5.8	4.8	3.4	7.5	4.3
1991	8.9	5.6	4.6	3.4	7.3	4.1
1992	8.5	5.4	4.4	3.1	7.4	4.1
1993	8.4	5.3	4.3	3.1	7.1	3.8
1994	8.0	5.1	4.2	2.9	7.0	3.7
1995	7.6	4.9	4.0	2.7	7.0	3.6
1996	7.3	4.8	3.8	2.6	6.9	3.6

NOTES: "Infant" is defined as under 1 year of age; "neonatal" is under 28 days; "postneonatal" is 28–365 days. 1. Number of fetal deaths of 20 weeks or more gestation per 1,000 live births plus fetal deaths. 2. Number of fetal deaths of 28 weeks or more gestation per 1,000 live births plus late fetal deaths. 3. Includes birth and deaths of persons who were not residents of the 50 states and the District of Columbia. *Sources:* Centers for Disease Control and Prevention, National Center for Health Statistics.

Improper Driving as a Factor in Accidents

	Fatal accidents		Injury accidents		All accidents	
Kind of improper driving	1995	1994	1995	1994	1995	1994
Improper driving	**68.1%**	**63.7%**	**73.5%**	**65.7%**	**75.5%**	**67.2%**
Speed too fast or unsafe	19.8	19.5	13.9	11.2	14.0	11.9
Right of way	15.2	15.1	25.5	24.1	22.9	21.3
Failed to yield	10.2	9.1	18.1	15.0	17.0	14.5
Passed stop sign	2.2	2.6	2.4	3.1	1.9	2.5
Disregarded signal	3.0	3.4	5.0	6.0	4.0	4.3
Drove left of center	9.1	9.4	2.4	2.5	2.2	2.3
Improper overtaking	1.5	1.6	1.3	1.2	1.5	1.4
Made improper turn	2.3	2.6	2.8	2.9	4.2	4.1
Followed too closely	0.5	0.5	7.0	5.9	7.2	5.6
Other improper driving	19.7	15.0	20.7	17.9	23.6	20.6
No improper driving stated	**31.9**	**36.3**	**26.5**	**34.3**	**24.5**	**32.8**
Total	**100.0%**	**100.0%**	**100.0%**	**100.0%**	**100.0%**	**100.0%**

NOTE: Figures are latest available. *Source:* Motor-vehicle reports from 11 (1993) and 17 (1994) state traffic authorities to National Safety Council.

Alcohol-Related Traffic Fatalities (by Holiday), 1997

Holiday 1997	Total traffic fatalities	Total fatalities alcohol-related	Percent fatalities alcohol-related	Time period monitored
New Year's Eve & Day	192	129	67.2%	6 p.m. 12/31/96–5:59 a.m. 1/2/97
St. Patrick's Day	72	21	29.2	6 p.m. 3/17/97–5:59 a.m. 3/18/97
Memorial Day weekend	513	239	46.6	6 p.m. 5/23/97–5:59 a.m. 5/27/97
Fourth of July weekend	508	253	49.8	6 p.m. 7/3/97–5:59 a.m. 7/7/97
Labor Day weekend	507	254	50.1	6 p.m. 8/29/97–5:59 a.m. 9/2/97
Halloween	138	54	39.1	6 p.m. 10/31/97–5:59 a.m. 11/1/97
Thanksgiving weekend	570	231	40.5	6 p.m. 11/26/97–5:59 a.m. 12/2/97
Christmas weekend	478	208	43.5	6 p.m. 12/24/97–5:59 a.m. 12/29/97

Source: Mothers Against Drunk Driving (MADD).

Deaths and Death Rates from Accidents, by Type: 1980–1995

Type of accident	Deaths (number)					Rate per 100,000 population				
	1980	1990	1993	1994	1995	1980	1990	1993	1994	1995
Motor vehicle accidents	53,172	46,814	41,893	42,524	43,363	23.5	18.8	16.3	16.3	16.5
Traffic	51,930	45,827	40,899	41,507	42,331	22.9	18.4	15.9	15.9	16.1
Nontraffic	1,242	987	994	1,017	1,032	0.5	0.4	0.4	0.4	0.4
Water-transport accidents	1,429	923	763	723	762	0.6	0.4	0.3	0.3	0.3
Air and space transport accidents	1,494	941	859	1,075	851	0.7	0.4	0.3	0.4	0.3
Railway accidents	632	663	670	635	569	0.3	0.3	0.3	0.2	0.2
Accidental falls	13,294	12,313	13,141	13,450	13,986	5.9	5.0	5.1	5.2	5.3
Accidental drowning	6,043	3,979	3,807	3,404	3,790	2.7	1.6	1.5.	1.3	1.4
Accidents caused by—										
Fires and flames	5,822	4,175	3,900	3,986	3,761	2.6	1.7	1.5	1.5	1.4
Firearms, unspecified and other	1,667	1,175	1,261	1,123	992	0.7	0.5	0.5	0.4	0.4
Handguns	288	241	260	233	233	0.1	0.1	0.1	0.1	0.1
Electric current	1,095	670	548	561	559	0.5	0.3	0.2	0.2	0.2
Accidental poisoning by—										
Drugs and medicines	2,492	4,506	7,382	7,828	8,000	1.1	1.8	2.9	3.0	3.0
Other solid and liquid substances	597	549	495	481	461	0.3	0.2	0.2	0.2	0.2
Gases and vapors	1,242	748	660	685	611	0.5	0.3	0.3	0.3	0.2
Complications due to medical procedures	2,282	2,669	2,724	2,616	2,712	1.0	1.1	1.1	1.0	1.0
Inhalation and ingestion of objects	3,249	3,303	3,160	3,065	3,185	1.4	1.3	1.2	1.2	1.2

NOTE: Excludes deaths of nonresidents of the United States. *Source: Statistical Abstract of the United States 1998.*

Deaths by Firearms, 1979–1997

(per 100,000 population in specified group)

Year	All races		White		Black	
	Number of deaths	Death rate[1]	Number of deaths	Death rate[1]	Number of deaths	Death rate[1]
1979	33,019	14.7	24,234	12.5	8,304	31.6
1980	33,780	14.9	24,849	12.8	8,505	31.9
1981	34,050	14.8	25,237	12.8	8,324	30.7
1982	32,957	14.2	25,071	12.7	7,415	27.0
1983	31,099	13.3	24,038	12.1	6,589	23.6
1984	31,331	13.3	24,419	12.2	6,449	22.9
1985	31,566	13.3	24,507	12.1	6,565	23.0
1986	33,373	13.9	25,339	12.5	7,494	25.9
1987	32,895	13.6	24,789	12.1	7,586	25.9
1988	33,989	13.9	24,892	12.1	8,475	28.5
1989	34,776	14.1	25,023	12.1	9,077	30.1
1990	37,155	14.9	26,299	12.6	10,175	33.4
1991	38,317	15.2	26,455	12.5	11,025	35.4
1992	37,776	14.8	26,120	12.3	10,906	34.5
1993	39,595	15.4	26,948	12.5	11,763	36.6
1994	38,505	14.8	26,403	12.2	11,223	34.4
1995	35,957	13.7	25,438	11.7	9,643	29.1
1996	34,040	12.8	24,114	11.0	9,175	27.4
1997	32,436	12.1	23,270	10.5	8,389	24.7

1. On an annual basis, per 100,000 population in specified group. *Source:* Centers for Disease Control and Prevention, *Monthly Vital Statistics Report,* vol. 47, no. 19.

Death Rates for Suicide, 1950–1996
(deaths per 100,000 resident population)

Characteristic	1950[1]	1960[1]	1970	1980	1985	1990	1996
All ages[2]	11.0	10.6	11.8	11.4	11.5	11.5	10.8
5 to 14 years	0.2	0.3	0.3	0.4	0.8	0.8	0.8
15 to 24 years	4.5	5.2	8.8	12.3	12.8	13.2	12.0
25 to 34 years	9.1	10.0	14.1	16.0	15.3	15.2	14.5
35 to 44 years	14.3	14.2	16.9	15.4	14.6	15.3	15.5
45 to 54 years	20.9	20.7	20.0	15.9	15.7	14.8	14.9
55 to 64 years	27.0	23.7	21.4	15.9	16.8	16.0	13.7
65 to 74 years	29.3	23.0	20.8	16.9	18.7	17.9	15.0
75 to 84 years	31.1	27.9	21.2	19.1	23.9	24.9	20.0
85 years and over	28.8	26.0	19.0	19.2	19.4	22.2	20.2
Male, all ages[2]	17.3	16.6	17.3	18.0	18.8	19.0	18.0
Female, all ages[2]	4.9	5.0	6.8	5.4	4.9	4.5	4.0

1. Includes deaths of persons who were not residents of the 50 states and the District of Columbia. 2. Data is age-adjusted. *Sources:* Centers for Disease Control and Prevention, National Center for Health Statistics.

Miscellaneous
Top 20 Charities in the U.S., 1998

1998 Rank	Charity	Private support	1997 rank
1.	Salvation Army (Alexandria, Va.)[1, 2]	$1,171,801,000	1
2.	YMCA of the USA (Chicago)[1, 3]	493,874,000	7
3.	American Red Cross (Falls Church, Va.)[1]	490,158,993	2
4.	American Cancer Society (Atlanta)[1]	488,512,000	3
5.	Fidelity Investments Charitable Gift Fund (Boston)	456,176,185	11
6.	Harvard University (Cambridge, Mass.)	427,603,792	10
7.	Catholic Charities USA (Alexandria, Va.)[1]	425,262,180	5
8.	Second Harvest (Chicago)[4]	400,598,748	6
9.	Boys & Girls Clubs of America (Atlanta)[1]	382,767,534	8
10.	Stanford University (Palo Alto, Calif.)	312,284,937	9
11.	American Heart Association (Dallas)[1]	301,514,000	12
12.	YWCA of the USA (New York)[2]	297,664,036	13
13.	Gifts in Kind International (Alexandria, Va.)[4]	289,610,113	16
14.	World Vision (Federal Way, Wash.)[1]	279,577,000	14
15.	Boy Scouts of America (Irving, Tex.)[1]	247,529,000	15
16.	Campus Crusade for Christ International (Orlando, Fla.)	236,153,000	19
17.	Nature Conservancy (Arlington, Va.)	235,107,172	20
18.	Habitat for Humanity International (Americus, Ga.)	233,335,000	21
19.	Shriners Hospitals for Children (Tampa, Fla.)[1]	225,401,000	17
20.	Cornell University (Ithaca, N.Y.)	220,627,995	18

"Top charities" is defined as the charities that raised the most money from Americans. 1. Includes affiliates. 2. Figures are estimates. 3. Affiliates have varying fiscal years. 4. Non-cash-gifts make up 50 percent or more of private support. *Source: The Chronicle of Philanthropy,* Nov. 5, 1998. Reprinted with permission.

Most Common Names in the U.S.

Rank	Name	Frequency[1]	Rank	Name	Frequency[1]	Rank	Name	Frequency[1]
Last names			**Female first names**			**Male first names**		
1.	Smith	1.00%	1.	Mary	2.63%	1.	James	3.32%
2.	Johnson	0.81	2.	Patricia	1.07	2.	John	3.27
3.	Williams	0.70	3.	Linda	1.04	3.	Robert	3.14
4.	Jones	0.62	4.	Barbara	0.98	4.	Michael	2.63
5.	Brown	0.62	5.	Elizabeth	0.94	5.	William	2.45
6.	Davis	0.48	6.	Jennifer	0.93	6.	David	2.36
7.	Miller	0.42	7.	Maria	0.83	7.	Richard	1.70
8.	Wilson	0.34	8.	Susan	0.79	8.	Charles	1.52
9.	Moore	0.31	9.	Margaret	0.77	9.	Joseph	1.40
10.	Taylor	0.31	10.	Dorothy	0.73	10.	Thomas	1.38

NOTE: Based on 1990 Census data. Numbers are rounded. 1. Percent of U.S. population sample. *Source:* U.S. Census Bureau.

Percent of Adult Population Doing Volunteer Work, 1995

Age, sex, race, and Hispanic origin	Percent of population volunteering	Average hours volunteered per week	Educational attainment and household income	Percent of population volunteering	Average hours volunteered per week
Total	48.8%	4.2	Elementary school	18.7%	(B)
			Some high school	26.1	3.3
18–24 years	38.4	2.8	High-school graduate	43.1	4.0
25–34 years	50.8	4.3	Technical, trade, or	51.2	4.4
35–44 years	55.0	4.3	business school		
45–54 years	55.3	4.5	Some college	56.3	3.9
55–64 years	47.9	4.8	College graduate	70.7	4.8
65–74 years	44.7	4.1			
75 years and over	33.7	4.4	Under $10,000	34.7	3.6
			10,000–19,999	34.3	3.2
Male	45.1	4.2	20,000–29,999	45.2	3.7
Female	52.2	4.2	30,000–39,999	46.0	3.7
			40,000–49,999	52.7	5.8
White	51.9	4.2	50,000–59,999	64.1	5.1
Black	35.3	4.5	60,000–74,999	56.4	4.4
Hispanic[1]	40.4	4.3	75,000–99,999	64.8	4.0
			100,000 or more	69.4	4.4

Type of activity	Percent of population involved in activity	Type of activity	Percent of population involved in activity
Arts, culture, humanities	6.2%	Political organizations	3.8%
Education	17.5	Private, community foundations	2.7
Environment	7.1	Public and societal benefit	6.7
Health	13.2	Recreation—adults	7.3
Human services	12.7	Religion	25.8
Informal	20.3	Work-related organizations	7.9
International, foreign	1.6	Youth development	15.4

(B) = Base figure too small to meet statistical standards for reliability. 1. Hispanic persons may be of any race. NOTE: Covers persons 18 years and over. Volunteers are persons who worked in some way to help others for no monetary pay during the previous year. Based on a sample survey conducted during the spring of the following year and subject to sampling variability. Source: *Statistical Abstract of the United States 1998.*

Participation in Various Leisure Activities, 1997

		Attendance at			Participation in				
	Adult population (mil.)	Movies	Sports events	Amuse-ment park	Exercise program	Playing sports	Charity work	Home improvement/ repair	Computer hobbies
Total	195.6	66%	41%	57%	76%	45%	43%	66%	40%
Sex: Male	94.2	66	49	58	75	56	40	71	44
Female	101.4	65	34	57	77	35	46	61	37
Race or ethnicity									
Hispanic[1]	19.1	59	35	66	69	35	31	61	25
White	146.1	68	44	56	78	48	45	70	43
Black	22.1	60	35	55	74	34	44	51	37
American Indian	3.0	65	34	59	83	49	34	58	37
Asian	5.3	76	29	58	70	48	41	58	62
Age: 18 to 24 years	23.7	88	51	76	85	67	35	57	68
25 to 34 years	40.1	79	51	70	82	63	41	63	51
35 to 44 years	45.3	73	46	68	79	52	50	76	47
45 to 54 years	33.7	65	42	53	77	40	46	75	40
55 to 64 years	20.9	46	33	40	69	19	44	71	23
65 to 74 years	19.6	38	21	29	65	23	40	55	11
75 years and over	12.3	28	16	18	56	13	40	44	7
Education: Grade school	13.7	14	13	34	46	13	20	40	1
Some high school	26.9	52	25	54	66	30	31	59	19
High-school graduate	62.0	62	38	58	74	41	36	65	35
Some college	50.3	78	48	64	81	54	50	71	52
College graduate	25.2	82	59	61	87	61	55	76	63
Graduate school	17.4	81	55	53	88	57	67	73	59

NOTE: Covers activities engaged in at least once in the prior 12 months. 1. People of Hispanic origin may be of any race. Source: U.S. National Endowment for the Arts, *1997 Survey of Public Participation in the Arts.*

Household Pet Ownership, 1996

Item	Dog	Cat	Pet bird	Horse
Households owning companion pets[1] (millions)	31.20	27.00	4.60	1.50
Percent of all households	31.60%	27.30%	4.60%	1.50%
Average number owned	1.70	2.20	2.70	2.70
Total companion pet population[1] (millions)	52.90	59.10	12.60	4.00
Households obtaining veterinary care[2]	88.70%	72.90%	15.80%	66.30%
Average visits per household per year	2.60	1.90	0.20	2.30
Average annual costs per household	$ 186.80	$ 112.24	$10.95	$226.26
Total expenditures (millions)	$5,828.00	$3,030.00	$50.00	$339.00
Percent distribution of households owning pets				
Annual household income: Under $12,500	12.70%	13.90%	17.30%	9.50%
$12,500 to $24,999	19.10	19.70	20.90	20.30
$25,000 to $39,999	21.60	21.50	22.00	21.80
$40,000 to $59,999	21.50	21.20	17.50	23.10
$60,000 and over	25.20	23.70	22.30	25.40
Family size:[1] One person	13.20%	16.80%	12.70%	12.10%
Two persons	31.00	32.60	27.90	29.10
Three persons	21.40	20.60	20.40	22.00
Four or more persons	34.50	29.90	38.90	36.70

NOTE: Based on a sample survey of 80,000 households in 1996. 1. As of December. 2. During 1996. *Source:* American Veterinary Medical Association, Schaumburg, Ill., *U.S. Pet Ownership and Demographics Sourcebook, 1997*. Reprinted with permission.

Adult Literacy

In a 1994 assessment of adult literacy skills, 21 percent of the adult population had only basic, or "level one," reading and writing skills. Compared to most of the other countries assessed in 1994, the United States showed a greater concentraion of adults scoring at the lowest literacy level (level one). However, the United States had one of the highest concentrations of adults scoring at or above level four on the reading and writing scale.

Country	Percentage of adults scoring on four levels of the prose literacy scale			
	Level 1	Level 2	Level 3	Level 4/5
Canada	16.6%	25.6%	35.1%	22.7%
Germany	14.4	34.2	38.0	13.4
Netherlands	10.5	30.1	44.1	15.3
Poland	42.6	34.5	19.8	3.1
Sweden	7.5	20.3	39.7	32.4
Switzerland (French)	17.6	33.7	38.6	10.0
Switzerland (German)	19.3	35.7	36.1	8.9
United States	**20.7**	**25.9**	**32.4**	**21.1**

NOTE: Prose literacy relates to the knowledge and skills required to understand and use information from texts, including editorials, news stories, poems, and fiction. Most of the tasks at **Prose Level 1** require the reader to locate and match a single piece of information that is identical to, or nearly identical to, the information given in the text. **Prose Level 2** requires the reader to locate one or more pieces of information from the text and to compare and contrast information. The tasks at **Prose Level 3** require readers to search the text to match information and make low-level inferences. **Prose Level 4/5** measures how well readers perform mulitple-feature matching, use specialized knowledge, and make text-based inferences from more abstract text sources. *Source:* National Center for Education Statistics, U.S. Dept. of Education, *The Condition of Education, 1997*.

Top 15 States for Rearing Children, 1999

Each year the Children's Rights Council, a national child advocacy organization, ranks the states (plus the District of Columbia) based upon conditions for rearing children. Criteria include abuse and neglect rates, immunization, high school dropout rate, poverty level, child death rate, infant mortality rate, prenatal care, juvenile arrests, birth rate, and divorce rate.

Rank 1999	Rank 1998	State	Rank 1999	Rank 1998	State	Rank 1999	Rank 1998	State
1	8	Maine	6	6	North Dakota	11	2	Minnesota
2	5	Massachusetts	7	26	Maryland	12	18	Rhode Island
3	17	Connecticut	8	14	Kansas	13	11	Hawaii
4	10	Vermont	9	13	Wisconsin	14	28	Alaska
5	3	New Hampshire	10	1	Iowa	15	4	Nebraska

Source: Children's Rights Council, Washington, D.C., Web: www.vix.com/crc.

Homeownership by State, 1990

State	Homeownership rate (%)	State	Homeownership rate (%)	State	Homeownership rate (%)
U.S. total	64.2%	Louisiana	65.9%	Oklahoma	68.1%
Alabama	70.5	Maine	70.5	Oregon	63.1
Alaska	56.1	Maryland	65.0	Pennsylvania	70.6
Arizona	64.2	Massachusetts	59.3	Rhode Island	59.5
Arkansas	69.6	Michigan	71.0	South Carolina	69.8
California	55.6	Minnesota	71.8	South Dakota	66.1
Colorado	62.2	Mississippi	71.5	Tennessee	68.0
Connecticut	65.6	Missouri	68.8	Texas	60.9
Delaware	70.2	Montana	67.3	Utah	68.1
Florida	67.2	Nebraska	66.5	Vermont	69.0
Georgia	64.9	Nevada	54.8	Virginia	66.3
Hawaii	53.9	New Hampshire	68.2	Washington	62.6
Idaho	70.1	New Jersey	64.9	Washington, D.C.	38.9
Illinois	64.2	New Mexico	67.4	West Virginia	74.1
Indiana	70.2	New York	52.2	Wisconsin	66.7
Iowa	70.0	North Carolina	68.0	Wyoming	67.8
Kansas	67.9	North Dakota	65.6		
Kentucky	69.6	Ohio	67.5		

Source: U.S. Census Bureau. Web:www.census.gov/hhes/www/housing/census/historic/ownrate.html.

Homeownership Rates by Select Characteristics, 1950–1990

Characteristic	1950	1960	1970	1980	1990
U.S. total	55.0%	61.9%	62.9%	64.4%	64.2%
Mobile home owners	79.4	88.3	84.5	79.8	79.8
One-person households	42.1	40.8	42.4	43.5	48.7
Recent movers	n.a.	34.0	31.4	33.5	28.8
Age of householder					
Under 35	n.a.	n.a.	41.2	43.8	39.6
65 and over	67.9	68.8	67.5	70.1	75.2
Black householder	34.5	n.a.	41.6	44.4	43.4
Hispanic householder[1]	n.a.	n.a.	43.7	43.4	42.4

NOTES: n.a. = not available. 1. Persons of Hispanic origin may be of any race. *Source:* U.S. Census Bureau. Web: www.census.gov/hhes/www/housing/census/historic/ownrate.html.

Employment Status of Persons with Disabilities, 1994–1995

	Total (thousands)	Employed	
		Number (thousands)	Percent
All persons aged 21-64	149,369	113,832	76.2%
With no disability	119,902	98,396	82.1
With any disability	29,467	15,436	52.4
Severe	14,219	3,707	26.1
Not severe	15,248	11,729	76.9
With a mental disability	6,012	2,484	41.3
Uses a wheelchair	685	151	22.0
Does not use a wheelchair, has used a cane, crutches, or a walker for 6 months or more	1,609	442	27.5
Unable to perform one or more functional activities	6,841	2,205	32.2
Unable to see words and letters	568	175	30.8
Unable to hear normal conversation	358	214	59.7
Unable to have speech understood	119	33	(1)
Unable to lift/carry 10 pounds	3,017	813	27.0
Unable to climb stairs without resting	3,736	952	25.5
Unable to walk three city blocks	3,547	798	22.5

1. Base less than 150,000. *Source:* U.S. Census Bureau. Data from the Survey of Income and Program Participation.

Families Living in Cities, March 1998
(in thousands)

Metropolitan-nonmetropolitan residence	All families Total	All families Married-couple families	Owner Total	Owner Married-couple families	Renter Total	Renter Married-couple families
Total	70,880	54,317	52,109	43,964	18,771	10,352
In MSAs	56,346	42,773	40,566	34,100	15,780	8,673
Central cities	19,592	13,099	11,578	9,138	8,014	3,962
Ring	36,754	29,674	28,988	24,962	7,766	4,712
MSAs of 2,500,000 or more	25,051	18,793	17,205	14,403	7,846	4,391
Central cities	8,256	5,220	4,205	3,186	4,051	2,033
Ring	16,795	13,574	13,000	11,216	3,795	2,357
MSAs of 1,000,000 to 2,499,000	12,362	9,385	9,029	7,656	3,332	1,730
Central cities	4,130	2,775	2,599	2,079	1,531	696
Ring	8,232	6,610	6,431	5,576	1,801	1,034
MSAs of 250,000 to 999,999	13,557	10,403	10,243	8,593	3,314	1,810
Central cities	4,950	3,463	3,265	2,631	1,685	832
Ring	8,607	6,940	6,978	5,962	1,629	978
MSAs of 249,999 or fewer	5,377	4,192	4,089	3,449	1,288	743
Central cities	2,256	1,642	1,509	1,241	747	401
Ring	3,121	2,550	2,579	2,208	541	342
Not in MSAs	14,533	11,543	11,543	9,864	2,991	1,679

NOTE: MSA = Metropolitan Statistical Area. *Source:* U.S. Bureau of the Census. Web: www.census.gov.

Median Years of Tenure with Current Employer, 1983–1996

Age and sex	Jan. 1983	Jan. 1987	Jan. 1991	Feb. 1996	Age and sex	Jan. 1983	Jan. 1987	Jan. 1991	Feb. 1996
Both sexes	3.5	3.4	3.6	3.8	35 to 44 years	7.3	7.0	6.5	6.1
16 to 17 years	.7	.6	.7	.7	45 to 54 years	12.8	11.8	11.2	10.1
18 to 19 years	.8	.7	.8	.7	55 to 64 years	15.3	14.5	13.4	10.5
20 to 24 years	1.5	1.3	1.3	1.2	65 years and over	8.3	8.3	7.0	8.3
25 to 34 years	3.0	2.9	2.9	2.8	Women	3.1	3.0	3.2	3.5
35 to 44 years	5.2	5.5	5.4	5.3	16 to 17 years	.7	.6	.7	.7
45 to 54 years	9.5	8.8	8.9	8.3	18 to 19 years	.8	.7	.8	.7
55 to 64 years	12.2	11.6	11.1	10.2	20 to 24 years	1.5	1.3	1.3	1.2
65 years and over	9.6	9.5	8.1	8.4	25 to 34 years	2.8	2.6	2.7	2.7
Men	4.1	4.0	4.1	4.0	35 to 44 years	4.1	4.4	4.5	4.8
16 to 17 years	.7	.6	.7	.6	45 to 54 years	6.3	6.8	6.7	7.0
18 to 19 years	.8	.7	.8	.7	55 to 64 years	9.8	9.7	9.9	10.0
20 to 24 years	1.5	1.3	1.4	1.2	65 years and over	10.1	9.9	9.5	8.4
25 to 34 years	3.2	3.1	3.1	3.0					

NOTES: For workers age 16 and over. Data for 1996 are not strictly comparable with data for 1991 and earlier years because the 1996 data incorporate population controls from the 1990 census, adjusted for the estimated undercount. Figures for the 1983–1991 period are based on population controls from the 1980 census. *Source:* Bureau of Labor Statistics.

Getting to Work in the City
Commuting characteristics for the 15 largest cities by population, 1990

City of residence	Total workers 16 years and over	Means of transportation (%) Drove alone	Means of transportation (%) Carpool	Means of transportation (%) Public transit	Means of transportation (%) Other Means[1]	Average travel time to work (min.)
New York, N.Y.	3,183,088	24.0%	8.5%	53.4%	14.0%	36.5
Los Angeles, Calif.	1,629,096	65.2	15.4	10.5	8.9	26.5
Chicago, Ill.	1,181,677	46.3	14.8	29.7	9.2	31.5
Houston, Tex.	772,957	71.7	15.5	6.5	6.3	24.7
Philadelphia, Pa.	640,577	44.7	13.2	28.7	13.5	27.4
San Diego, Calif.	560,913	70.7	12.8	4.2	12.2	20.4
Dallas, Tex.	500,566	72.5	15.2	6.7	5.7	24.0
Phoenix, Ariz.	473,966	73.7	15.1	3.3	7.9	23.0
San Jose, Calif.	400,932	76.9	14.6	3.5	5.1	25.5
San Antonio, Tex.	395,551	73.4	15.5	4.9	6.2	21.7
San Francisco, Calif.	382,309	38.5	11.5	33.5	16.5	26.9
Indianapolis, Ind.	362,777	78.0	13.4	3.3	5.2	20.8
Detroit, Mich.	325,054	67.8	16.1	10.7	5.3	24.7
Jacksonville, Fla.	312,958	75.5	14.2	2.7	7.6	21.6
Baltimore, Md.	307,679	50.9	16.8	22.0	10.2	26.0
Total for U.S.	115,070,274	73.2	13.4	5.3	0.7	n.a.

NOTES: n.a. = not available. Percentages may not add up to 100%, due to rounding. 1. Includes commuting by motorcycle, bicycle, walking, and all other means. Also includes those who worked at home. *Source:* U.S. Bureau of the Census; Web: www.census.gov.

Has Asia Recovered?

After a devastating slump, the region's economies are on the mend. But a brand-new set of problems may pose more peril ahead

By PAUL KRUGMAN TIME

In 1997, a nasty fiscal flu emerged in Bangkok. It spread rapidly through Asia and beyond, and before hitting bottom in late summer 1998, it had claimed a host of seemingly robust economies as victims. But no new cases had been reported in the few months leading up to July 1999, and most of the original victims seemed to be past the worst. Like anyone who has been very sick and starts to feel better, they felt relieved, even euphoric.

But were they celebrating too soon? Pundits who want to sound judicious are fond of warning against generalizing. Each country is different, they say, and no one story fits all of Asia.

This is, of course, silly. All of these economies imploded within a few months of one another, and the logic of catastrophe—a combined banking and currency crisis, as panicked investors tried both to convert long-term assets into cash and to convert baht or rupiah into dollars—was pretty much the same everywhere.

Governments had no good options. If they let their currencies plunge, inflation would soar, and companies that had borrowed in dollars would go bankrupt. If they tried to support their currencies by pushing up interest rates, the same firms would go bust from the combination of debt burden and recession. In practice, countries split the difference—and still paid a heavy price.

Crony Capitalism

In hindsight it is easy to find reasons why the countries deserved their punishment. Like most clichés, the catchphrase "crony capitalism" has prospered because it gets at something real: excessively cozy relationships between government and business really did lead to a lot of bad investments.

Suppose the U.S., which is pulling in overseas money at the rate of about $300 billion annually, were to see that inflow suddenly become a trillion-dollar outflow—which, on a relative basis, is what happened to Asia's crisis-hit countries. How solid would our financial system look?

Given that there were no good options, was the policy response mainly on the right track? There was frantic blame-shifting when everything in Asia seemed to be going wrong; now there is a race to claim credit when some things have started to go right.

The truth is that an impartial observer would probably conclude that none of the policies adopted either on or in defiance of advice given by the International Monetary Fund—which "suggested" that client countries tighten their belts and raise interest rates—made much of a difference. Whatever countries tried, just about all the capital that could flee, did. And when there was no more money to run, the natural recuperative powers of the economies began to prevail. At best, the money doctors who purported to offer cures provided a helpful bedside manner; at worst, they were like medieval physicians who prescribed bleeding as a remedy for all ills.

Will the patients stage a full recovery? As President Bill Clinton might say, it depends on exactly what you mean by "full." If by recovery you mean not just a return to growth, but a recovery that resembles what people used to regard as the Asian norm, the answer is almost surely no.

For one thing, the region's entrepreneurs are not what they used to be. Asian institutions that looked on paper like modern corporations were really overgrown family firms, whose growth depended on the wealth of their owners and their ability to leverage that wealth through bank loans. Well, it will be a long time before Asian banks are able or willing to provide the funding they used to—and, in any case, the entrepreneurs, their fortunes slashed by the crisis, cannot provide the necessary collateral.

Even before the crisis there were indications that Asia was facing diminishing returns—that rapid growth was being sustained only by ever more massive infusions of foreign capital. Foreign investors may have stopped fleeing, but they are not going to pour in funds the way they did a few years ago.

Could the recovery be aborted, with an actual relapse? Not just yet. It would take several years of irresponsible borrowing to create the conditions for a repeat of 1997. Such things can be arranged, but the prospect does not seem imminent.

The Japan Syndrome

Inevitably, worries about Japan color the prospects of the whole region. And Japan was in trouble long before anyone even imagined that the words Asia and crisis could be used in the same sentence.

If developing Asia suffered from an acute, potentially lethal but short-lived fever, Japan suffers from a slow, wasting disease, the result not of the nation's vices but of its virtues. While there are many things wrong with Japan, the immediate problem is excessive thrift: Japanese households simply save more than the country's businesses can be persuaded to invest, even at a zero interest rate.

The classic response to such a trap is a fiscal jump start: use deficit spending to get the economy moving, and hope that this motivates investors and consumers. But after years of ever widening deficits—Japan will run the largest peacetime budget deficit in history this year—the economic engine still shows no sign of catching. True, official statistics say the economy grew an astonishing 1.9% in the first quarter of 1999, a number that has mystified observers who look at other indicators and see no evidence of a boom. But there is no sign of a genuine, self-sustaining recovery, and it is all too easy to see how things could get considerably worse—indeed, how Japan could plunge into a nasty deflationary spiral if consumers keep their hands in their pockets.

Bizarrely, the Japan syndrome seems to have spread to Asia's other giant. China never caught the Asian flu, because foreign-exchange regulations—though they fostered inefficiency and corruption—prevented hot money from leaving and deterred it from coming in the first place. Instead, the problem is, believe it or not, excessive thrift. Incredibly for a developing country, China is experiencing pronounced deflation. In the end, China, like Japan, may be forced to roll the printing presses—a move that would not be possible without a devaluation of the renminbi, which would make the lives of the country's neighbors considerably more difficult.

Did the Crisis Help?

Adversity is supposed to come with a silver lining. Has Asia's crisis laid the foundation for sounder economic growth in the future? The answer is a definite maybe. The crisis has curbed some of the worst abuses of crony capitalism, and it has tempered the dangerous belief that "Asian values" somehow made the region's economies bulletproof. The crisis has also probably done some good by softening free-market fundamentalism: countries are less likely to be pressured into throwing their capital markets open to the world before their financial markets are ready, and Washington is less likely to view the main purpose of economic diplomacy as making the world safe for hedge funds. Above all, the crisis has reinforced democratic tendencies and made it much harder for paternalistic strongmen to claim they know best.

Still, it is hard to escape the feeling that a dangerous complacency is setting in. When Mexico started to recover from its 1995 "tequila" crisis, policymakers and investors alike acted as if it had been a one-time event, never to be repeated. But it turned out to be a dress rehearsal for the Asian crisis a year later. Because the world didn't end this time around, everyone is starting to believe that the situation is under control—even though proposals for international reform have been watered down to homeopathic levels. Could investors and countries really be foolish enough to make the same mistakes yet again? Of course they could. □

Economic Outlook Through 2006

The Bureau of Labor Statistics (BLS) released its biennial update of the employment outlook for the coming decade in the Nov. 1997 issue of *Monthly Labor Review*. Highlights of the report follow.

Slower Growth in the Labor Force

The gradual slowdown in the rate of labor-force expansion continues to be one of the fundamental forces shaping the employment outlook. The slowdown is itself a reflection of very long-term swings in fertility. At the same time, immigration has become an increasingly important source of population and labor-force growth, moderating to some degree the slowing of population and labor-force growth.

The labor force will increase by about 15 million persons (or 11 percent) over the next 10 years, reaching 149 million by 2006. By comparison, the labor force expanded by some 16 million persons (or 14 percent) over the past 10 years. Significant shifts are expected in its demographic structure. The result will be a continuation of the aging of the labor force seen in the previous decade. By 2006, the median age of the labor force will approach 41 years, a level not seen in the United States since the 1960s.

Changing Complexion of the Labor Force

Women will continue to increase their share of the labor force, although at a slower rate than in the past. Labor force participation for women overall is projected to rise by about 2 percentage points, half the increase of the preceding decade. By 2006, women's share of the labor force will increase by just 1.2 percentage points, to 47.4 percent, compared with increases of 1.7 points between 1986 and 1996, and 4 points between 1976 and 1986.

Significant compositional shifts are also expected along racial/ethnic lines. Although white non-Hispanics are expected to continue to account for by far the largest share of the labor force in 2006 (73 percent, compared with 75 percent in 1996 and 80 percent in 1986), their rate of growth is considerably below that of the black, Asian, and Hispanic groups. Continued rapid growth of the Hispanic population makes it likely that this group will become the second-largest ethnic grouping, replacing blacks, by 2006 or shortly thereafter.

Output

As the natural increase of the population slows, immigration has become a major factor in determining the prospects for labor-force growth. The results are a labor force that is not only larger, but one that is younger and has a different ethnic mix and higher overall participation rate.

The moderating growth in the labor force will also affect potential output and total employment. Overall, real gross domestic product is projected to increase 2.1 percent per year over the projection period, compared with 2.3 percent over the preceding 10-year period. The slowdown reflects lower employment growth, partially offset by a modest improvement in productivity.

One of the most striking features of the macroeconomic outlook is the growing internationalization of the U.S. economy. By 2006, exports and imports are each expected to approach 20 percent of gross domestic product. Investment spending also shows strong growth, nearly 50 percent faster than the overall economy. Both of these trends are fueled in large part by strong demand for computers and a broad array of other high technology products.

Unemployment

The projected growth of gross domestic product, slower labor-force growth, and a favorable inflation outlook combine to allow the unemployment rate to remain at relatively low levels. The trade and federal budget deficits also respond favorably to projected economic conditions, with the trade deficit reduced substantially in real terms and the federal budget deficit virtually eliminated.

Mirroring the slowdown in labor-force growth, total employment is expected to expand more slowly in the 1996–2006 period than it did in the preceding 10 years. The economy is expected to add 18.6 million new jobs by 2006, compared with a gain of 21 million between 1986 and 1996. As was the case in the previous BLS projection, all of this growth occurs in the service-producing sector, including net gains of 3.6 million in business services, 3.2 million in health services, and 2.3 million in retail trade. Although manufacturing shows a slight decline overall, some industries, particularly those benefiting from strong exports and capital spending, show moderation or even reversal of previously projected employment declines.

Industry

While the overall picture of industrial structure has not changed dramatically, a number of sectors do show significant changes from previous projections. The computer and data-processing services sector, for example, is now expected to add 1.3 million jobs, twice the number previously projected.

The growth and shifting industrial structure of the U.S. economy has major implications for the pattern of occupational demand over the next 10 years. At the major group level, professionals; managers; technicians; and service, marketing, and sales workers are all expected to increase their share of total employment. Meanwhile, occupational groups such as administrative support; precision production, craft and repair; and fabricators, laborers and operators will experience a declining share.

The shifting industrial structure has a major impact on the relative growth of occupations. The three fastest growing occupations, for example, are computer specialties, reflecting, in large part, the expected rapid expansion of the computer and data-processing services industry. Similarly, as a result of rapid employment growth in health services, half of the 30 fastest growing occupations are health-care related.

Education and Training

The projections also show that differing growth prospects among occupations have important implications for education. While the economy will continue to generate large numbers of jobs at all educational levels, the results also show that employment in occupations requiring an associate degree or higher will grow considerably faster than those with lesser educational requirements.

The new BLS projections describe an economy that is gradually slowing in response to demographic factors, but is nevertheless expected to produce 18 million new jobs by 2006—as well as a much larger number of job openings to meet replacement needs. The effects of the long-term trend toward sevice-producing activities is evident, as computer and health-related occupations dominate the list of the fastest growing jobs. On the other hand, the decline in manufacturing jobs seems to have come to at least a temporary halt, as the growing internationalization and computerization of the economy provides significant demand for technology-related manufactured products. Finally, while the economy will generate job opportunities at all educational and skill levels, the increasing role of technology means that the fastest-growing jobs are most likely to be those requiring relatively more extensive education and training.   □

Industry Output and Employment Projections to 2006

Over the 1996–2006 period, total employment in the United States is projected to increase by 18.6 million to 151 million. The projected annual average rate of growth is 1.3 percent, slower than the 1.7 percent annual average rate of growth from 1986 to 1996. Most of the increase (95 percent) comes from nonfarm wage and salary jobs, as agricultural employment is expected to decline by 24,000. Private household wage and salary jobs also are projected to decline, by 153,000. The remaining portion of growth in total jobs is accounted for by an increase of 1.2 million in nonagricultural self-employed and unpaid family workers.

The macroeconomic factors whose combined influence most affects the growth of total employment are increases in the labor force, in productivity, and in the nation's gross domestic product, or GDP. In the latest round of Bureau of Labor Statistics (BLS) projections, the labor force grows at an annual average rate of 1.1 percent during the 1996–2006 projection period. This is a slowing in the rate of growth compared to the 1.3-percent annual average rate of increase posted over the 1986–96 period. The growth rate of the nonfarm labor productivity index is projected to average 1.1 percent per year

from 1996 through 2006, an increase from the 0.7 percent rate of change during the previous 10 years. The rate of growth for GDP during the projection period is 2.1 percent, a slight decline from the 2.3 percent average annual increase during the 1986–96 period. The overall picture, then, is one of an economy in which the rate of growth of both the labor force and GDP is slowing, but output, as measured by GDP, continues to outpace labor force growth because of productivity gains.

Services

The service-producing sector, excluding private households, has a projected increase of 17.6 million nonfarm wage and salary jobs, from 94.3 million in 1996 to 111.9 million by 2006. Within the service-producing sector, employment growth is highly concentrated. During the 1986–96 period, 11.2 million, or 56 percent, of the 20.1 million increase in service-producing sector employment was concentrated in the services division. The projected 11.3 million gain in wage and salary jobs in the services division over the 1996–2006 period accounts for almost two thirds of the projected 17.6 million increase in employment in the service-producing sector. The addition of job growth for retail trade (2.3 million) and for state and local government (1.8 million) to that for the services division accounts for 87 percent of the projected job gains in the service-producing sector.

Goods

The goods-producing sector, excluding agricultural products, has a slight projected increase of 20,000 wage and salary jobs, with employment remaining essentially stable at 24.4 million over the 1996–2006 period. However, strong productivity gains allow real gross duplicated output to grow at a projected 2.3 percent annual rate. At the major

industry level on the goods-producing side, only construction is projected to post an employment gain. From the 1996 level of 5.4 million, construction is expected to add 500,000 jobs to reach a projected 2006 jobs level of 5.9 million. Employment in mining is projected to decline by 131,000, from a level of 574,000 in 1996 to 443,000 in 2006. Over the 1986–96 period, mining lost 204,000 jobs. Manufacturing is expected to decline by 350,000 jobs, from 18.5 million in 1996 to 18.2 million in 2006. The decline for manufacturing is about 30 percent less than the reduction of 493,000 jobs recorded over the previous 10-year period, 1986–96.

Fastest Growing Occupations, 1996–2006

(in thousands)

Occupation	Employment		Change	
	1996	2006	Number	Percent
Database administrators, computer support specialists, and all other computer scientists	212	461	249	118%
Computer engineers	216	451	235	109
Systems analysts	506	1,025	520	103
Personal and home care aides	202	374	171	85
Physical and corrective therapy assistants and aides	84	151	66	79
Home health aides	495	873	378	76
Medical assistants	225	391	166	74
Desktop publishing specialists	30	53	22	74
Physical therapists	115	196	81	71
Occupational therapy assistants and aides	16	26	11	69

Source: U.S. Department of Labor, Bureau of Labor Statistics, *Monthly Labor Review*, November 1997.

Projected Rate of Employment Growth or Decline by Industry, 1996–2006

Industry description	Change (in thousands of jobs)	Average annual rate of change	Industry description	Change (in thousands of jobs)	Average annual rate of change
	1996–2006	1996–2006		1996–2006	1996–2006
Fastest growing			**Most rapidly declining**		
Computer and data-processing services	1,301.2	7.6%	Coal mining	−44.4	−6.0%
Health services	796.4	5.3	Watches, clocks, and parts	−2.6	−4.0
Management and public relations	526.8	4.8	Footwear, except rubber and plastic	−15.7	−4.0
Misc. transportation services	123.1	4.8	Search and navigation equipment	−51.2	−3.8
Residential care	397.7	4.8	Crude petroleum, natural gas, and gas liquids	−46.7	−3.7
Personnel supply services	1,393.3	4.3	Luggage, handbags, and leather products	−15.0	−3.6
Water and sanitation	118.2	4.2	Tobacco products	−11.1	−3.1
Individual and misc. social services	419.6	4.1	Metal cans and shipping containers	−10.4	−3.1
Offices of health practitioners	1,294.5	3.9	Apparel	−167.8	−3.0
Amusement and recreation services	456.7	3.5	Tires and inner tubes	−20.2	−2.9
Automobile parking, repair, and services	345.9	3.3	Photographic equipment and supplies	−19.8	−2.6
Nursing and personal care facilities	644.8	3.2	Electrical industrial apparatus	−33.6	−2.4
Producers, orchestras, and entertainers	52.9	3.0	Petroleum refining	−20.7	−2.3
Misc. equipment rental and leasing	82.4	3.0	Household appliances	−24.6	−2.2
Security and commodity brokers	189.0	3.0	Blast furnaces and basic steel products	−43.6	−2.0
Passenger transportation arrangement	64.3	2.7	State and local government enterprises	−108.0	−2.0
Child day-care services	164.2	2.6	Electric distribution equipment	−14.2	−1.9
Misc. business services	576.5	2.5	Private households	−152.8	−1.8

Source: U.S. Department of Labor, Bureau of Labor Statistics, *Monthly Labor Review*. Web: stats.bls.gov.

Employed and Unemployed Workers by Sex and Age

(in thousands)

	1998[1]	1997[1]	1996[1]	1995[1]	1994[1]	1993[2]	1990[2]	1985	1980	1970
Men, 20 yr. and over										
Employed	67,134	66,524	64,897	64,085	63,294	62,335	61,678	56,562	53,101	45,581
Full time	61,837	61,057	59,543	58,707	57,707	57,010	57,055	52,425	49,699	43,138
Part time	5,297	5,467	5,354	5,377	5,587	5,345	4,623	4,137	3,403	2,444
Unemployed	2,580	2,826	3,147	3,239	3,627	4,287	3,239	3,715	3,353	1,638
Full time[3]	2,366	2,623	2,899	2,988	3,359	4,011	3,000	3,479	3,167	1,502
Part time[4]	214	203	248	251	269	276	239	236	186	137
Women, 20 yr. and over										
Employed	57,278	57,647	53,310	54,396	53,606	52,099	50,535	44,154	38,492	26,952
Full time	44,045	43,698	41,953	40,943	40,183	40,209	39,138	33,604	29,391	20,654
Part time	13,233	13,949	13,357	13,453	13,423	11,890	11,397	10,550	9,102	6,297
Unemployed	2,424	2,187	2,783	2,819	3,049	3,288	2,596	3,129	2,615	1,349
Full time[3]	1,966	1,785	2,258	2,265	2,506	2,670	2,079	2,536	2,135	1,077
Part time[4]	458	402	525	554	543	619	517	593	480	271
Total 16 yr. and over										
Employed	131,463	130,785	126,707	124,900	123,060	120,259	118,793	107,150	99,303	78,678
Full time	108,202	106,618	103,537	101,679	99,772	99,114	98,666	88,535	82,564	66,752
Part time	23,261	24,167	23,170	23,220	23,288	21,145	20,128	18,615	16,742	11,924
Unemployed	6,209	5,957	7,236	7,404	7,996	8,940	7,047	8,312	7,637	4,093
Full time[3]	4,916	4,846	5,803	5,909	6,513	7,305	5,677	6,793	6,269	3,206
Part time[4]	1,293	1,111	1,433	1,495	1,483	1,635	1,369	1,519	1,369	889
Total 16–19 yr.										
Employed	7,051	6,614	6,499	6,419	6,161	5,805	6,581	6,434	7,710	6,144
Full time	2,320	1,863	2,041	2,029	1,883	1,895	2,473	2,507	3,474	2,960
Part time	4,731	4,751	4,458	4,390	4,278	3,910	4,107	3,927	4,237	3,183
Unemployed	1,205	944	1,307	1,346	1,320	1,365	1,212	1,468	1,669	1,106
Full time[3]	584	438	646	657	648	625	598	777	966	626
Part time[4]	621	506	661	689	672	740	614	690	701	480

1. Data beginning in 1994 are not directly comparable with earlier years due to the introduction of a major redesign of the Current Population Survey. 2. Revised; data beginning in 1990 are not directly comparable with earlier years due to the introduction of 1990 census-based population controls, adjusted for the estimated under-count. 3. Persons seeking full-time work. 4. Persons seeking part-time work. Source: Current Population Survey. Web: stats.bls.gov/cpsaatab.htm.

Unemployment Rate by Race, Age, and Sex, 1996–1998

Age and race	Men			Women			Age and race	Men			Women		
	1996	1997	1998	1996	1997	1998		1996	1997	1998	1996	1997	1998
Total, 16 and over	5.4%	4.9%	4.4%	5.4%	5.0%	4.6%	Total, 25 and over	4.1%	3.6%	3.2%	4.3%	3.9%	3.6%
White	4.7	4.2	3.9	4.7	4.2	3.9	White	3.6	3.2	2.8	3.8	3.3	3.1
Black	11.1	10.2	8.9	10.0	9.9	9.0	Black	8.0	6.9	6.0	7.4	7.6	6.8

Source: Bureau of Labor Statistics, U.S. Department of Labor. Web: stats.bls.gov.

Unemployment Rate in the Civilian Labor Force

Year	Rate	Year	Rate	Year	Rate	Year	Rate	Year	Rate	Year	Rate
1920	5.2%	1948	3.8%	1970	4.9%	1989	5.3%	Feb.	4.6%	1999	
1928	4.2	1950	5.3	1972	5.6	1990	5.6	March	4.7	Jan.	4.3%
1930	8.7	1952	3.0	1974	5.6	1991	6.8	April	4.3	Feb.	4.4
1932	23.6	1954	5.5	1976	7.7	1992	7.5	May	4.4	March	4.2
1934	21.7	1956	4.1	1978	6.1	1993	6.9	June	4.5	April	4.3
1936	16.9	1958	6.8	1980	7.1	1994	6.1	July	4.5	May	4.2
1938	19.0	1960	5.5	1982	9.7	1995	5.6	Aug.	4.5	June	4.3
1940	14.6	1962	5.5	1984	7.5	1996	5.4	Sept.	4.5	July	4.3
1942	4.7	1964	5.2	1986	7.0	1997	4.9	Oct.	4.5		
1944	1.2	1966	3.8	1987	6.2	1998	4.5	Nov.	4.4		
1946	3.9	1968	3.6	1988	5.5	Jan.	4.6	Dec.	4.3		

NOTES: Estimates prior to 1940 are based on sources other than direct enumeration. Data prior to 1948 is for persons age 14 and over. Data beginning in 1948 is for persons age 16 and over. Source: U.S. Department of Labor, Bureau of Labor Statistics. Web: stats.bls.gov.

Full-Time Workers by Occupation and Sex, 1998

Occupation	Total		Men		Women	
	Number of workers (in thousands)	Median weekly earnings	Number of workers (in thousands)	Median weekly earnings	Number of workers (in thousands)	Women's earnings as a percent of men's
Total, 16 years and over	95,595	$523	54,313	$598	41,282	76.3%
Managerial and professional specialty	29,304	759	14,941	905	14,363	72.4
Executive, administrative, and managerial	14,451	755	7,746	915	6,705	68.4
Professional specialty	14,853	763	7,195	895	7,658	76.2
Mathematical and computer scientists	1,544	938	1,105	986	438	87.1
Health assessment and treating occupations	2,102	738	363	791	1,739	92.3
Teachers, except college and university	3,974	671	1,022	746	2,952	86.3
Technical, sales, and administrative support	27,372	477	10,439	606	16,933	69.1
Technicians and related support	3,507	599	1,773	701	1,734	72.9
Sales occupations	9,636	502	5,299	622	4,338	59.8
Administrative support, including clerical	14,229	438	3,368	518	10,862	80.7
Service occupations	10,592	327	5,291	389	5,301	76.1
Private household	381	223	19	—	362	$220[1]
Protective services	2,140	598	1,817	613	323	78.5
Service occupations, except private household and protective services	8,070	307	3,455	325	4,616	90.8
Food preparation and service occupations	3,032	288	1,581	303	1,451	89.4
Precision production, craft, and repair	11,691	572	10,741	587	949	69.5
Mechanics and repairers	4,081	597	3,926	599	155	86.6
Construction trades	4,054	543	3,989	545	64	74.9
Operators, fabricators, and laborers	15,082	415	11,564	456	3,518	71.7
Machine operators, assemblers, and inspectors	6,987	406	4,482	472	2,505	69.5
Transportation and material-moving occupations	4,322	510	3,977	519	345	71.9
Handlers, equipment cleaners, helpers, and laborers	3,773	351	3,105	362	669	85.9
Farming, forestry, and fishing	1,555	302	1,337	307	218	88.6

Dash indicates base is less than 50,000, so no data are provided. 1. Since the men's earnings are effectively zero, it is not possible to calculate a percentage. The number is the median weekly earnings for women. *Source:* U.S. Department of Labor, Bureau of Labor Statistics, *Employment & Earnings,* January 1999. Web: stats.bls.gov.

Employment Status by Industry

(in millions of persons unless specified)

Category	1998	1997	1996	1995	1990	1985	1980	1970	1950	1945	1932	1929
Employment Status[1]												
Civilian noninstitutional population	205.2	203.1	200.6	198.6	189.2	178.2	167.7	137.1	105.0	94.1	—	—
Civilian labor force	137.7	136.3	133.9	132.3	125.8	115.5	106.9	82.8	62.2	53.9	—	—
Civilian labor force participation rate (percent)	67.1	67.1	66.8	66.6	66.5	64.8	63.8	60.4	59.2	57.2	—	—
Employed	131.5	129.6	126.7	124.9	118.8	107.2	99.3	78.7	58.9	52.8	38.9	47.6
Employment-population ratio	64.1	63.8	63.2	62.9	62.8	60.1	59.2	57.4	56.1	56.1	—	—
Agriculture	3.4	3.4	3.4	3.4	3.2	3.2	3.4	3.5	7.2	8.6	10.2	10.5
Nonagricultural industries	128.1	126.2	123.3	121.5	115.6	104.0	95.9	75.2	51.8	44.2	28.8	37.2
Unemployed	6.2	6.7	7.2	7.4	7.1	8.3	7.6	4.1	3.3	1.0	12.1	1.6
Unemployment rate (percent)	4.5	4.9	5.4	5.6	5.6	7.2	7.1	4.9	5.3	1.9	23.6	3.2
Not in labor force	67.6	66.8	66.7	66.3	63.3	62.7	60.8	54.3	42.8	40.2	—	—
Industry												
Total nonfarm employment	128.0	122.3	119.5	117.2	109.4	97.4	90.4	70.9	45.2	40.4	23.6	31.3
Goods-producing industries	33.2	24.7	24.3	24.2	24.9	24.8	25.7	23.6	18.5	17.5	8.6	13.3
Mining	0.6	0.6	0.6	0.6	0.7	0.9	1.0	0.6	0.9	0.8	0.7	1.1
Construction	8.5	5.6	5.4	5.2	5.1	4.7	4.3	3.6	2.4	1.1	1.0	1.5
Manufacturing: durable goods	12.6	10.9	10.7	10.7	10.7	11.5	12.2	11.2	8.1	9.1	—	—
Nondurable goods	8.2	7.6	7.8	7.8	7.8	7.8	8.1	8.2	7.2	6.4	—	—
Services-producing industries	98.2	97.5	95.3	93.0	84.5	72.5	64.7	47.3	26.7	22.9	15.0	18.0
Transportation and public utilities	7.5	6.4	6.3	6.2	5.8	5.2	5.1	4.5	4.0	3.9	2.8	3.9
Trade, wholesale	5.1	6.7	6.6	6.4	6.2	5.7	5.3	4.0	2.6	2.0	—	—

Category	1998	1997	1996	1995	1990	1986	1980	1970	1950	1945	1932	1929
Retail	22.1	22.1	21.6	21.2	19.6	17.3	15.0	11.0	6.7	5.4	—	—
Finance, insurance, and real estate	8.6	7.1	7.0	6.8	6.7	5.9	5.2	3.6	1.9	1.5	—	—
Services	47.2	35.6	34.4	33.1	27.9	21.9	17.9	11.5	5.4	4.2	—	—
Federal government	—	2.7	2.8	2.8	2.8	2.9	2.9	2.7	1.9	2.8	—	—
State and local government	—	17.0	16.7	16.5	15.2	13.5	13.4	9.8	4.1	3.1	2.7	2.5
Public Administration	5.9	—	—	—	—	—	—	—	—	—	—	—

1. For 1929–45, figures on employment status relate to persons 14 years and over; beginning in 1950, 16 years and over. Data beginning in 1990, 1994, and 1998 are not directly comparable with earlier years due to the introduction of census-based population controls, the introduction of a major redesign of the Current Population Survey, and new composite estimation procedures, respectively. *Source:* U.S. Department of Labor, *Monthly Labor Review.*

Employment Status by Race and Major Occupational Groups

	1998		1997		1996	
Race and occupational group	Number (thousands)	Percent distribution	Number (thousands)	Percent distribution	Number (thousands)	Percent distribution
White						
Managerial and professional specialty	34,063	30.7%	33,089	30.1%	32,127	29.8%
Executive, administrative, and managerial	16,903	15.2	16,420	14.9	15,848	14.7
Professional specialty	17,160	15.5	16,669	15.2	16,279	15.1
Technical, sales, and administrative support	32,490	29.3	32,624	29.7	32,127	29.8
Technicians and related support	3,557	3.2	3,571	3.3	3,342	3.1
Sales occupations	13,704	12.4	13,730	12.5	13,476	12.5
Administrative support, including clerical	15,229	13.7	15,323	13.9	15,309	14.2
Service occupations	13,807	12.4	13,604	12.4	13,476	12.5
Precision production, craft, and repair	12,729	11.5	12,472	11.4	11,967	11.1
Operators, fabricators, and laborers	14,609	13.2	14,813	13.5	14,662	13.6
Farming, forestry, fishing	3,233	2.9	3,254	3.0	3,342	3.1
Total	**110,931**	**100.0**	**109,856**	**100.0**	**107,808**	**100.0**
Black						
Managerial and professional specialty	2,947	20.2%	2,764	19.8%	2,708	20.0%
Executive, administrative, and managerial	1,368	9.4	1,267	9.1	1,219	9.0
Professional specialty	1,579	10.9	1,497	10.7	1,490	11.0
Technical, sales, and administrative support	4,264	29.3	4,032	28.9	3,873	28.6
Technicians and related support	441	3.0	410	2.9	366	2.7
Sales occupations	1,415	9.7	1,271	9.1	1,219	9.0
Administrative support, including clerical	2,408	16.5	2,352	16.8	2,289	16.9
Service occupations	3,148	21.6	3,092	22.1	2,966	21.9
Precision production, craft, and repair	1,158	8.0	1,144	8.2	1,070	7.9
Operators, fabricators, and laborers	2,866	19.7	2,781	19.9	2,790	20.6
Farming, forestry, and fishing	172	1.2	156	1.1	135	1.0
Total	**14,556**	**100.0**	**13,969**	**100.0**	**13,542**	**100.0**

Note: Workers are 16 years or older. *Source:* U.S. Department of Labor, Bureau of Labor Statistics. Web: stats.bls.gov.

Persons in the Labor Force

	Labor force[1]		Percent in labor force in[2]			Labor force[1]		Percent in labor force in[2]	
Year	Number (thousands)	Percent of working-age population	Farm occupation	Nonfarm occupation	Year	Number (thousands)	Percent of working-age population	Farm occupation	Nonfarm occupation
1840	5,420	46.6%	68.6%	31.4%	1920	42,434	51.3%	27.0%	73.0%
1850	7,697	46.8	63.7	36.3	1930	48,830	49.5	21.4	78.6
1860	10,533	47.0	58.9	41.1	1940	52,789	52.2	17.4	82.6
1870	12,925	45.8	53.0	47.0	1950	60,054	53.5	11.6	88.4
1880	17,392	47.3	49.4	50.6	1960	69,877	55.3	6.0	94.0
1890	23,318	49.2	42.6	57.4	1970	82,049	58.2	3.1	96.9
1900	29,073	50.2	37.5	62.5	1980	106,085	62.0	2.2	97.8
1910	37,371	52.2	31.0	69.0	1990	125,182	65.3	1.6	98.4

1. For 1830 to 1930, the data relate to the population and gainful workers at ages 10 and over. For 1940 to 1960, the data relate to the population and labor force at ages 14 and over; for 1970 and 1980, the data relate to the population and labor force at age 16 and over. For 1940 to 1980, the data include the Armed Forces. 2. The farm and nonfarm percentages relate only to the experienced civilian labor force. *Source:* U.S. Bureau of the Census. Web: www.census.gov.

Mothers Participating in Labor Force

	Percentage of mothers with children		
Year	Under 18 years	6 to 17 years	Under 6 years[1]
1955	27.0%	38.4%	18.2%
1965	35.0	45.7	25.3
1975	47.3	54.8	38.8
1980	56.6	64.3	46.8
1985	62.1	69.9	53.5
1986	62.8	70.4	54.4
1987	64.7	72.0	56.7
1988	65.1	73.3	56.1
1989	65.7	74.2	56.7
1990	66.7	74.7	58.2
1991	66.6	74.4	58.4
1992	67.2	75.9	58.0
1993	67.0	75.4	57.9
1994	68.4	76.0	60.3
1995	69.7	76.4	62.3
1996	70.2	77.2	62.3
1997	72.1	78.1	65.0
1998	72.3	78.4	65.2

1. May also have older children. NOTE: 1955 data are for April; 1965 and 1975–94 data are for March. Data for 1994 and subsequent years are not directly comparable to previous years because of major revisions to the survey questionnaire and the data collection methodology, and the introduction of 1990 census-based population controls into the estimation process. *Source:* U.S. Department of Labor, Bureau of Labor Statistics. Web: stats.bls.gov.

Women in the Civilian Labor Force

Year	Number[1] (thousands)	% Female population aged 16 and over[1]	% of Labor force population aged 16 and over[1]
1900	5,319	18.8%	18.3%
1910	7,445	21.5	19.9
1920	8,637	21.4	20.4
1930	10,752	22.0	22.0
1940	12,845	25.4	24.3
1950	18,389	33.9	29.6
1960	23,240	37.7	33.4
1970	31,543	43.3	38.1
1980	45,487	51.5	42.5
1990[2]	56,829	57.5	45.2
1993	58,795	57.9	45.5
1994[3]	60,239	58.8	46.0
1996	61,857	59.3	46.2
1997	63,036	59.8	46.2
1998	63,714	59.8	46.3

1. For 1900–1930, data relate to population and labor force aged 10 and over; for 1940, to population and labor force aged 14 and over; beginning 1950, to civilian population and labor force aged 16 and over. 2. Data beginning in 1990 are not strictly comparable with data for prior years because population controls were adjusted. 3. Data beginning 1994 are not strictly comparable with data for prior years because of a major redesign of the Current Population Survey (household survey) questionnaire and collection methodology. *Source:* U.S. Department of Labor, Women's Bureau.

Percent of Employed Women in Select Occupations

Occupations	1998	1997	1996	1995	1994	1990	1988	1986
Technical, sales, administrative support	40.7%	41.0%	41.4%	41.9%	42.4%	44.4%	44.6%	45.6%
Managerial and professional	31.4	30.8	30.3	29.4	28.7	26.2	25.2	23.7
Service occupations	17.5	17.4	17.5	17.7	17.8	17.7	17.9	18.3
Precision production, craft and repair	2.0	2.1	2.1	2.1	2.2	2.2	2.3	2.4
Operators, fabricators, laborers	7.4	7.6	7.6	7.6	7.7	8.5	8.9	8.9
Farming, forestry, fishing	1.1	1.1	1.2	1.3	1.2	1.0	1.1	1.1

NOTE: Percentage of female labor force (16 years of age and over) employed in each occupation, annual averages. Details may not add up to totals because of rounding. *Source:* U.S. Dept. of Labor, Bureau of Labor Statistics. Web: stats.bls.gov.

Earnings Distribution of Full-Time Workers by Sex, 1996

	Number (in thousands)			Distribution (% of total)			Women as a % of each earnings level
	Total	Men	Women	Total	Men	Women	
$7,499 or less	10,323	4,876	5,447	9.2%	7.5%	11.6%	52.8%
$7,500 to $12,499	10,978	5,168	5,810	9.8	7.9	12.4	52.9
$12,500 to $19,999	17,966	8,424	9,541	16.0	12.9	20.3	53.1
$20,000 to $29,999	24,098	12,735	11,363	21.4	19.5	24.2	47.2
$30,000 to $39,999	17,120	10,545	6,575	15.2	16.1	14.0	38.4
$40,000 to $49,999	10,401	7,068	3,336	9.3	10.8	7.1	32.1
$50,000 to $59,999	6,048	4,454	1,597	5.4	6.8	3.4	26.4
$60,000 to $74,999	4,879	3,835	1,044	4.3	5.9	2.2	21.4
$75,000 to $99,999	2,225	791	203	2.0	1.2	0.4	9.1
$100,000 and Over	2,733	2,338	395	2.4	3.6	0.8	14.5
Total	112,387	65,409	46,978				

Source: U.S. Bureau of the Census. Web: www.census.gov.

Earnings by Sex and Race, 1948–1997

Year	Median earnings (All races)		Earnings as a percentage of men's (all races)							
			All races	White		Black[1]		Hispanic origin[2]	
	Men	Women	Women	Men	Women	Men	Women	Men	Women
1997	$25,212	$13,703	54.4%	103.6%	54.7%	71.8%	51.8%	64.3%	40.7%
1996	24,381	13,109	53.8	104.7	54.4	69.2	49.4	64.8	39.8
1995	23,761	12,775	53.8	105.9	54.6	70.9	48.6	65.8	39.6
1994	23,523	12,418	52.8	104.4	53.5	69.0	48.5	66.8	39.7
1993	23,439	12,269	52.3	104.2	53.4	69.2	45.1	64.9	38.4
1988	25,653	12,053	47.0	105.6	48.1	63.7	38.9	68.9	37.0
1983	23,577	10,183	43.2	105.3	43.9	61.3	37.9	77.1	36.9
1978	26,001	9,673	37.2	104.7	37.6	62.7	33.9	76.6	34.6
1973	27,394	9,508	34.7	104.9	35.0	63.5	31.6	77.0	32.9
1968	25,459	8,595	33.8	104.8	34.8	62.2	27.6	—	—
1963	21,742	6,613	30.4	106.5	31.9	55.4	21.3	—	—
1958	19,132	6,011	31.4	106.2	34.2	52.9	20.0	—	—
1953	17,827	6,453	36.2	105.2	40.1	58.1	23.5	—	—
1948	14,678	6,181	42.1	104.8	47.3	56.9	20.5	—	—

Year-round, full-time workers, aged 15 years and over. Income in 1997 dollars. Dash indicates data are not available. 1. Prior to 1967, data are for black and other races. 2. Persons of Hispanic origin may be of any race. *Source:* Current Population Reports, Series P60, U.S. Bureau of the Census. Web: www.census.gov/hhes/income/histinc/p02.html.

Nonmanufacturing Industries—Weekly Earnings and Hours

Industry	1998		1990		1970	
	Earnings	Hours worked	Earnings	Hours worked	Earnings	Hours worked
General building contracting	$601.47	37.9	$487.08	37.7	$184.40	36.3
Local and transportation	452.79	38.7	376.65	38.2	142.30	42.1
Telephone communications	756.08	42.5	578.74	40.9	131.60	39.4
Radio and TV broadcasting	633.32	35.6	438.61	34.7	147.45	38.2
Electric, gas, and sanitary services	842.73	42.2	636.76	41.7	172.64	41.5
Wholesale trade	537.98	38.4	411.48	38.1	137.60	40.0
Retail trade	254.63	29.1	195.26	28.8	82.47	33.8
Services	419.87	32.7				
Hotels, tourist courts, motels	279.20	31.3	214.68	30.8	68.16	34.6
Laundries and dry cleaning plants	286.44	34.1	232.22	34.0	77.47	35.7
Business services	420.43	33.5	n.a.	n.a.	n.a.	n.a.
Advertising	646.58	36.8	n.a.	n.a.	n.a.	n.a.
Computer and data-processing services	814.66	38.5	n.a.	n.a.	n.a.	n.a.
Auto repair, services, parking	395.95	35.8	n.a.	n.a.	n.a.	n.a.
Health services	454.13	33.1	n.a.	n.a.	n.a.	n.a.
Mining						
Metal mining	812.13	44.5	602.07	42.7	165.68	42.7
Bituminous coal and lignite mining	867.63	44.7	740.52	44.0	186.41	40.8
Nonmetallic minerals	683.01	46.4	524.12	45.3	155.11	44.7

Source: U.S. Department of Labor, Bureau of Labor Statistics, *Employment & Earnings*, March 1999. Web: http://stats.bls.gov/ceshome.htm.

Manufacturing Industries—Weekly Earnings and Hours

Industry	1998		1980		1970	
	Earnings	Hours worked	Earnings	Hours worked	Earnings	Hours worked
All manufacturing	$562.53	41.7	$288.62	39.7	$133.73	39.8
Durable goods	591.78	42.3	310.78	40.1	143.07	40.3
Lumber and wood products	456.62	41.1	252.18	38.5	117.51	39.7
Furniture and fixtures	441.05	40.5	209.17	38.1	108.58	39.2
Primary metal industries	684.22	44.2	391.78	40.1	159.17	40.5
Iron and steel foundries	622.62	44.6	328.00	40.0	151.03	40.6
Nonferrous foundries	529.82	42.9	291.27	39.9	138.16	39.7
Fabricated metal products	552.86	42.3	300.98	40.4	143.67	40.7
Hardware, cutlery, hand tools	518.64	42.2	275.89	39.3	132.33	40.1
Structural metal products	527.50	42.2	291.85	40.2	142.61	40.4

Industry	1998		1980		1970	
	Earnings	Hours worked	Earnings	Hours worked	Earnings	Hours worked
Industrial machinery and equipment	$618.46	42.8	$328.00	41.0	$154.95	41.1
Electric and electronic equipment	542.75	41.4	276.21	39.8	130.54	39.8
Transportation equipment	762.10	43.4	379.61	40.6	163.22	40.3
Motor vehicles and equipment	780.39	43.5	394.00	40.0	170.07	40.3
Nondurable goods	521.48	40.9	255.45	39.0	120.43	39.1
Food and kindred products	492.06	41.7	271.95	39.7	127.98	40.5
Tobacco manufactures	713.19	38.2	294.89	38.1	110.00	37.8
Textile mill products	425.99	41.0	203.31	40.1	97.76	39.9
Apparel and other textile products	317.80	37.3	161.42	35.4	84.37	35.3
Paper and allied products	672.70	43.4	330.85	42.2	144.14	41.9
Printing and publishing	514.75	38.3	279.36	37.1	147.78	37.7
Chemicals and allied products	740.02	43.2	344.45	41.5	153.50	41.6
Petroleum and allied products	911.24	43.6	422.18	41.8	182.76	42.7
Leather and leather products	351.18	37.6	169.09	36.7	92.63	37.2

Source: U.S. Dept. of Labor, Bureau of Labor Statistics, *Employment & Earnings*, January 1999. Web: http://stats.bls.gov/ceshome.htm.

National Labor Organizations with Membership Over 100,000

Members[1]	Union
775,000	United International Union of Automobile, Aerospace, and Agricultural Implement Workers of America[2]
110,000	Bakery, Confectionery, and Tobacco Workers International Union
123,041	International Association of Bridge, Structural, Ornamental, and Reinforcing Iron Workers
510,000	United Brotherhood of Carpenters and Joiners of America
630,000	Communications Workers of America
2,400,000	National Education Association (Ind.)
750,000	International Brotherhood of Electrical Workers
180,000	International Union of Electronic, Electrical, Salaried, Machine, and Furniture Workers
214,000	International Association of Fire Fighters
1,400,000	United Food and Commercial Workers International Union
600,000	American Federation of Government Employees
150,000	Graphic Communications International Union
300,000	Hotel Employees and Restaurant Employees International Union
750,000	Laborers' International Union of North America
315,000	National Association of Letter Carriers
600,000	International Association of Machinists and Aerospace Workers[2]
200,000	United Mine Workers of America
250,000	Union of Needletrades, Industrial, and Textile Employees[3]
182,000	American Nurses Association (Ind.)
130,000	Office and Professional Employees International Union
400,000	International Union of Operating Engineers
130,000	International Brotherhood of Painters and Allied Trades
250,000	United Paperworkers International Union
291,000	United Association of Journeymen and Apprentices of the Plumbing and Pipe Fitting Industry of the United States and Canada
366,000	American Postal Workers Union
100,000	Retail, Wholesale, and Department Store Union
1,300,000	Service Employees International Union
150,000	Sheet Metal Workers' International Association
1,300,000	American Federation of State, County, and Municipal Employees
700,000	United Steelworkers of America[2]
940,000	American Federation of Teachers
1,400,000	International Brotherhood of Teamsters
162,000	Amalgamated Transit Union
100,000	Transportation • Communications International Union
125,000	United Transportation Union

NOTE: List is arranged alphabetically by keyword. 1. Unless otherwise noted, unions are AFL-CIO affiliated. 2. The United Int'l Union of Automobile, Aerospace, and Agricultural Implement Workers of America; the Int'l Assoc. of Machinists and Aerospace Workers; and the United Steelworkers of America announced on July 27, 1995, they will merge over a five-year period. 3. Merger of the International Ladies Garment Workers' Union and the Amalgamated Clothing and Textile Workers Union. Source: mailings to labor organzations.

Work Stoppages Involving 1,000 Workers or More

Year	Work stoppages	Workers involved (thousands)	Days idle (thousands)	Year	Work stoppages	Workers involved (thousands)	Days idle (thousands)
1950	424	1,698	30,390	1989	51	452	16,996
1960	222	896	13,260	1990	44	185	5,926
1970	381	2,468	52,761	1991	40	392	4,584
1975	235	965	17,563	1992	35	364	3,989
1980	187	795	20,844	1993	35	184	3,981
1983	81	909	17,461	1994	45	322	5,020
1984	68	391	8,499	1995	28	176	5,736
1985	61	584	7,079	1996	37	273	4,887
1986	72	900	11,861	1997	29	339	4,497
1987	46	174	4,456	1998	34	387	5,116
1988	40	118	4,381				

NOTE: Refers to stoppages that began in the year. Days idle is total for all stoppages in effect. Workers are counted more than once if they were involved in more than one stoppage during the year. *Source:* U.S. Department of Labor, Bureau of Labor Statistics, *Monthly Labor Review,* March 1999. Web: stats.bls.gov.

Federal Minimum Wage Rates, 1955–1997

	Value of the minimum wage			Value of the minimum wage	
Year	Current dollars	Constant (1996) dollars[1]	Year	Current dollars	Constant (1996) dollars[1]
1955	$0.75	$4.39	1977	$2.30	$5.95
1956	1.00	5.77	1978	2.65	6.38
1957	1.00	5.58	1979	2.90	6.27
1958	1.00	5.43	1980	3.10	5.90
1959	1.00	5.39	1981	3.35	5.78
1960	1.00	5.30	1982	3.35	5.45
1961	1.15	6.03	1983	3.35	5.28
1962	1.15	5.97	1984	3.35	5.06
1963	1.25	6.41	1985	3.35	4.88
1964	1.25	6.33	1986	3.35	4.80
1965	1.25	6.23	1987	3.35	4.63
1966	1.25	6.05	1988	3.35	4.44
1967	1.40	6.58	1989	3.35	4.24
1968	1.60	7.21	1990	3.80	4.56
1969	1.60	6.84	1991	4.25	4.90
1970	1.60	6.47	1992	4.25	4.75
1971	1.60	6.20	1993	4.25	4.61
1972	1.60	6.01	1994	4.25	4.50
1973	1.60	5.65	1995	4.25	4.38
1974	2.00	6.37	1996	4.75	4.75
1975	2.10	6.12	1997	5.15	5.03
1976	2.30	6.34			

1. Adjusted for inflation using the CPI-U. *Source:* U.S. Employment Standards Admin. Web: www.dol.gov/esa/public/minwage.

Median Four-Person Family Income
(in current dollars)

Year	Income	Percent change	Year	Income	Percent change	Year	Income	Percent change
1997	$53,350	3.6%	1989	$40,763	4.4%	1981	$26,274	8.0%
1996	51,518	3.7	1988	39,051	6.1	1980	24,332	8.6
1995	49,687	5.7	1987	36,812	6.0	1979	22,395	9.6
1994	47,012	4.1	1986	34,716	5.9	1978	20,428	9.1
1993	45,161	2.1	1985	32,777	5.4	1977	18,723	8.1
1992	44,251	2.8	1984	31,097	6.6	1976	17,315	9.3
1991	43,056	3.9	1983	29,184	5.7	1975	15,848	7.5
1990	41,151	1.7	1982	27,619	5.1			

Source: Income Statistics Branch/HHES Division, U.S. Bureau of the Census. Web: www.census.gov.

Median Income of Households with Selected Characteristics, 1997

Characteristic	White		Black		Hispanic Origin[1]		All Races	
	As a % of all white households	Median income	As a % of all black households	Median income	As a % of all Hispanic households	Median income	As a % of all households	Median income
Overall		$38,972		$25,050		$26,628		$37,005
Region								
Northeast	20%	41,214	18%	23,312	17%	24,023	19%	38,929
Midwest	25	40,040	18	23,861	7	31,009	24	38,316
South	34	36,681	55	25,074	34	26,207	36	34,345
West	22	39,479	9	29,989	41	27,276	21	39,162
Type of household								
Family households	69	47,454	67	29,915	81	29,253	69	45,347
Married-couple families	56	52,199	31	45,372	56	34,317	53	51,681
Single-father household	4	38,511	5	28,593	6	28,249	4	36,634
Single-mother household	10	25,670	31	17,962	19	16,393	12	23,040
Nonfamily households	31	22,380	33	17,073	19	16,807	31	21,705
Male living alone	10	25,415	13	17,139	7	16,524	11	23,871
Female living alone	15	15,818	16	13,738	7	9,666	15	15,530
Size of household								
One person	26	19,288	29	15,258	14	12,222	26	18,762
Two persons	33	40,954	25	26,870	21	26,390	32	39,343
Three persons	17	50,269	19	28,047	20	26,396	17	47,115
Four persons	15	55,819	15	35,529	21	33,053	15	53,165
Five persons	7	52,493	7	36,525	14	31,586	7	50,407
Six persons	2	48,974	3	32,050	5	30,185	2	46,465
Seven persons or more	1	46,044	2	30,799	4	36,088	1	42,343
Number of earners								
No earners	21	15,324	21	8,172	15	7,842	21	14,142
One	33	31,412	44	21,319	36	20,464	34	29,780
Two	36	55,474	28	44,728	36	37,106	35	54,192
Three	7	68,363	6	57,599	9	47,569	7	67,182
Four or more	2	86,319	1	77,190	4	58,360	2	84,816

1. Persons of Hispanic origin may be of any race. *Source:* U.S. Bureau of the Census, *Money Income in the United States: 1997.* Web: www.census.gov.

Total Household Income by Race

Income range	White			Black			Hispanic[1]		
	1997	1980	1967	1997	1980	1967	1997	1980	1972
Number of households (thousands)	86,106	71,872	54,188	12,474	8,847	5,728	8,590	3,906	2,655
Percent distribution									
Under $5,000	2.8%	2.7%	5.4%	7.4%	7.9%	11.6%	5.5%	5.0%	3.9%
$5,000 to $9,999	6.7	8.6	8.6	14.0	18.0	16.4	11.3	11.7	8.7
$10,000 to $14,999	7.8	7.7	7.2	10.5	12.9	13.6	10.7	10.7	12.4
$15,000 to $24,999	14.6	16.0	15.7	17.9	19.8	22.6	19.7	21.2	21.8
$25,000 to $34,999	13.2	14.5	19.2	14.2	13.2	15.9	15.0	16.2	19.8
$35,000 to $49,999	16.5	19.7	21.6	14.9	14.4	11.7	16.6	16.9	19.0
$50,000 to $74,999	18.8	18.9	15.2	13.1	10.0	5.8	12.2	12.8	10.7
$75,000 to $99,999	9.5	7.3	4.2	4.6	2.8	1.5	5.0	3.6	2.4
$100,000 and over	10.2	4.8	2.8	3.3	1.0	0.9	4.1	1.9	1.5
Median income	$38,972	$35,620	$32,197	$25,050	$20,521	$18,694	$26,628	$26,025	$27,129

NOTE: Households as of March of the following year. 1. Persons of Hispanic origin may be of any race. *Source:* U.S. Bureau of the Census. Web: www.census.gov.

Per Capita Personal Income

Year	Amount	Year	Amount	Year	Amount	Year	Amount	Year	Amount	Year	Amount
1935	$ 474	1965	$2,773	1981	$10,949	1986	$15,122	1991	$19,652	1996[1]	$24,164
1945	1,223	1970	3,893	1982	11,731	1987	15,968	1992	20,576	1997[1]	25,288
1950	1,501	1975	5,851	1983	12,352	1988	17,052	1993	21,231	1998[1]	26,482
1955	1,881	1979	8,638	1984	13,585	1989	18,176	1994	22,086		
1960	2,219	1980	9,910	1985	14,427	1990	19,188	1995	23,059		

1. Revised. *Source:* U.S. Bureau of Economic Analysis, *Survey of Current Business.* Web: www.bea.doc.gov.

Per Capita Personal Income by State

State	1980	1990	1997	1998[1]	State	1980	1990	1997	1998[1]
Alabama	$ 7,465	$14,899	$20,672	$21,500	Montana	$ 8,342	$14,743	$19,660	$20,247
Alaska	13,007	20,887	24,969	25,771	Nebraska	8,895	17,379	23,618	24,786
Arizona	8,854	16,262	21,998	23,152	Nevada	10,848	20,248	26,514	27,360
Arkansas	7,113	13,779	19,595	20,393	New Hampshire	9,150	20,231	27,766	29,219
California	11,021	20,656	26,314	27,579	New Jersey	10,966	24,182	32,356	33,953
Colorado	10,143	18,818	27,015	28,821	New Mexico	7,940	14,213	19,298	20,008
Connecticut	11,532	25,426	35,863	37,700	New York	10,179	22,322	30,250	31,679
Delaware	10,059	19,719	28,493	29,932	North Carolina	7,780	16,284	23,168	24,122
Dist. of Columbia	12,251	24,643	35,704	37,325	North Dakota	8,642	15,320	20,103	21,708
Florida	9,246	18,785	24,799	25,922	Ohio	9,399	17,547	24,163	25,239
Georgia	8,021	17,121	23,822	25,106	Oklahoma	9,018	15,117	20,305	21,056
Hawaii	10,129	20,905	25,598	26,210	Oregon	9,309	17,201	23,920	24,775
Idaho	8,105	15,304	20,392	21,080	Pennsylvania	9,353	18,884	25,670	26,889
Illinois	10,454	20,159	27,688	28,976	Rhode Island	9,227	19,035	25,667	26,924
Indiana	8,914	16,815	23,202	24,302	South Carolina	7,392	15,101	20,508	21,387
Iowa	9,226	16,683	23,120	24,007	South Dakota	7,800	15,628	21,076	22,201
Kansas	9,880	17,639	23,972	25,049	Tennessee	7,711	15,903	22,699	23,615
Kentucky	7,679	14,751	20,570	21,551	Texas	9,439	16,747	23,707	25,028
Louisiana	8,412	14,279	20,458	21,385	Utah	7,671	14,063	20,185	21,096
Maine	7,760	17,041	21,937	23,002	Vermont	7,957	17,444	23,017	24,217
Maryland	10,394	22,088	28,674	30,023	Virginia	9,413	19,543	26,109	27,489
Massachusetts	10,103	22,248	31,239	32,902	Washington	10,256	19,268	26,451	28,066
Michigan	9,801	18,239	24,956	25,979	West Virginia	7,764	13,964	18,724	19,373
Minnesota	9,673	18,784	26,243	27,667	Wisconsin	9,364	17,399	24,048	25,184
Mississippi	6,573	12,578	18,098	18,998	Wyoming	11,018	16,905	22,596	23,225
Missouri	8,812	17,407	23,629	24,447	**United States**	**9,494**	**18,667**	**25,288**	**26,482**

NOTE: Per capita personal income was computed using midyear population estimates of the Bureau of the Census. 1. Revised. *Source:* U.S. Department of Commerce, Bureau of Economic Analysis, *Survey of Current Business.* Web: www.bea.doc.gov.

Per Capita Income and Personal Consumption Expenditures
(in current dollars)

Year	Gross national product	Personal income	Disposable personal income	Personal Consumption Expenditures			
				Durable goods	Nondurable goods	Services	Total
1950	$ 1,900	$ 1,504	$ 1,368	$ 203	$ 648	$ 416	$ 1,267
1955	2,456	1,901	1,687	235	755	570	1,560
1960	2,851	2,265	1,986	240	847	741	1,829
1965	3,268	2,840	2,505	327	987	954	2,268
1970	4,951	4,056	3,489	418	1,318	1,385	3,121
1975	7,401	6,081	5,291	627	1,927	2,135	4,689
1980	11,985	9,916	8,421	963	2,992	3,653	7,607
1985	16,776	13,895	11,861	1,555	3,807	5,622	10,985
1990	21,737	18,477	15,695	1,910	4,748	7,888	14,547
1991	22,500	19,100	16,700	1,800	5,000	8,700	15,400
1992	23,340	19,802	17,346	1,881	5,053	9,101	16,035
1993	24,576	20,810	18,153	2,083	5,185	9,683	16,951
1994	27,119	22,589	19,711	2,290	5,555	10,574	18,419
1995	28,060	23,413	20,316	2,358	5,631	11,072	19,061
1996	29,378	24,578	21,127	2,443	5,885	11,610	19,938
1997	30,634	25,686	21,871	2,538	6,001	12,268	20,807
1998	n.a.	26,240[1]	22,212[2]	2,661[2]	6,143[2]	12,581[2]	21,385[2]

NOTE: n.a. = not available. 1. Revised. 2. Preliminary. *Source:* U.S. Department of Commerce, *Survey of Current Business,* May 1998. Web: www.doc.gov.

Credit Card Use, 1989–1995

General purpose credit cards include Mastercard, Visa, Optima, and Discover cards. All dollar figures are given in constant 1995 dollars based on consumer price index data as published by U.S. Bureau of Labor Statistics.

Age of family head and family income[1]	Percent having a general purpose credit card	Percent having a balance after last month's bills	Median balance[2]	Percent of cardholding families who—		
				Almost always pay off the balance	Sometimes pay off the balance	Hardly ever pay off the balance
1989, total	55.8%	52.0%	$1,200	53.1%	21.5%	25.4%
1992, total	62.2	52.8	1,100	52.8	19.6	27.6
1995, total	**66.4**	**56.3**	**1,500**	**51.9**	**20.4**	**27.7**
Under 35 years old	59.0	69.2	1,500	40.2	23.5	36.3
35 to 44 years old	68.5	68.1	1,900	40.7	26.9	32.4
45 to 54 years old	75.4	64.8	1,800	47.1	22.5	30.4
55 to 64 years old	71.9	48.0	1,800	59.3	18.4	22.3
65 to 74 years old	68.3	30.8	800	72.0	12.9	15.1
75 years old and over	54.6	18.2	700	85.8	2.5	11.7
Less than $10,000	26.3	55.8	1,000	56.4	12.4	31.2
$10,000 to $24,999	53.3	57.0	1,500	50.9	17.2	31.9
$25,000 to $49,999	75.0	59.2	1,500	47.6	20.9	31.5
$50,000 to $99,999	93.1	59.4	2,000	49.7	25.3	25.1
$100,000 and more	97.1	35.4	2,100	73.7	17.2	9.1

1. Families include one-person units. 2. Among families having a balance. *Source:* Board of Governors of the Federal Reserve System, *Statistical Abstract of the U.S., 1997,* www.census.gov/stat_abstract/.

Consumer Credit
(installment credit outstanding; in billions of dollars, not seasonally adjusted)

Holder	1998[4]	1997	1996	1995	1990	1985	1980	1975
Commercial banks	$ 499.5	$ 511.6	$ 529.4	$ 507.8	$ 347.1	$ 245.1	$ 147.0	$ 82.9
Finance companies	153.2	154.9	154.5	152.6	133.3	111.7	62.3	32.7
Credit unions	149.8	146.7	144.1	131.9	93.1	72.7	44.0	25.7
Retailers[1]	65.1	67.7	79.7	85.1	43.5	43.0	28.7	18.2
Other[2]	47.0	46.3	44.7	40.1	57.0	53.8	20.1	9.2
Pools[3]	326.8	272.1	271.9	214.4	77.9	—	—	—
Total	**1,241.4**	**1,199.3**	**1,224.4**	**1,131.9**	**751.9**	**526.3**	**302.1**	**168.7**

1. Starting in 1994, source includes retailers and gasoline companies in nonfinancial business category. 2. Includes mutual savings banks, savings and loan associations, and gasoline companies (until 1994). 3. Beginning 1989, outstanding balances of pools upon which securities have been issued; these balances are no longer on the balance sheets for the loan originators. 4. Preliminary data as of May 1998. *Source:* Federal Reserve Board. Web http://www.bog.frb.fed.us.

Financial Debt Held by Families, 1992 and 1995

Age of family head and family income	Any debt	Mortgage, home equity	Installment	Other lines of credit	Credit card	Investment real estate	Other debt[1]
Percent of families holding debt							
1992 total	73.6%	39.1%	46.2%	2.4%	43.8%	7.8%	8.8%
1995 total	74.9	41.0	46.2	1.9	47.4	6.4	8.5
Under 35 years old	83.7	32.9	62.6	2.7	54.8	2.8	7.6
35 to 44 years old	87.2	54.2	60.2	2.1	56.1	6.8	10.5
45 to 54 years old	86.6	61.9	53.7	2.2	56.6	10.8	12.9
55 to 64 years old	74.1	45.3	34.8	1.6	43.4	11.6	7.7
65 to 74 years old	54.3	25.1	16.7	1.3	30.8	5.3	5.3
75 years old and over	28.7	6.8	9.0	(2)	17.7	1.7	2.9
Less than $10,000	48.1	9.2	25.8	(3)	24.7	2.0	6.1
$10,000 to $24,999	67.7	25.2	40.7	1.3	42.0	2.3	8.5
$25,000 to $49,999	83.6	47.3	54.2	2.0	55.8	5.9	8.3
$50,000 to $99,999	89.2	68.0	60.2	3.2	63.1	10.1	8.9
$100,000 and more	85.8	73.1	38.7	4.3	38.9	25.9	14.1

1. Includes loans on insurance policies, loans against pension accounts, and other unclassified loans. 2. Represents or rounds to zero. 3. Base figure too small. *Source: Statistical Abstract of the United States 1998.*

Poverty and Income in the United States

Source: U.S. Bureau of the Census, *Poverty in the United States: 1997* and *Money Income in the United States: 1997.*

Poverty

In 1997, the poverty rate was 13.3%, significantly lower than the 13.7% reported for 1996. The number of people with family incomes below their official poverty level in 1997 was 35.6 million, not statistically different from the 36.5 million in 1996.

Age

The poverty rate in 1997 for people under 18 years of age was 19.9%, significantly higher than the rate for adults aged 18 to 64 (10.9%) and those aged 65 and over (10.5%). None of the age groups had any significant changes in their poverty rates between 1996 and 1997.

In addition to having the highest poverty rate of all age groups, children continued to represent a large share of the poor population (40%) even though they were only about one-fourth of the total population.

Children under age six were particularly vulnerable. In 1997, the overall poverty rate for related children under six years of age was 21.6%. Related children under age six living in families with single mothers had a poverty rate (59.1%) that was more than five times the rate for their counterparts in married-couple families (10.6%).

Race and Hispanic Origin

Both the number of poor and the poverty rate for blacks and people of Hispanic origin decreased significantly in 1997. The number of poor blacks dropped from 9.7 million in 1996 to 9.1 million in 1997, and their poverty rate dropped from 28.4% in 1996 to 26.5% in 1997. The number of poor and the poverty rate for people of Hispanic origin (who may be of any race) dropped as well: from 29.4% (8.7 million) in 1996 to 27.1% (8.3 million) in 1997. These declines in the poverty rates of blacks and Hispanics accounted for most of the decrease in the overall poverty rate between 1996 and 1997.

Although the poverty rates dropped for blacks and people of Hispanic origin, their rates remained significantly higher than the rates for people in other racial and ethnic groups. In 1997, the poverty rate was 11.0% for whites, and 14.0% for Asians and Pacific Islanders, compared with 26.5% for blacks. The poverty rate was 8.6% for non-Hispanic whites and 27.1% for Hispanics.

Even though the poverty rates for whites (11.0%) and non-Hispanic whites (8.6%) were lower than those for the other racial and ethnic groups, the majority of poor people in 1997 were white. Among the poor, 69% were white and 46% were non-Hispanic white.

Families

Both the number of poor families and the poverty rate for families declined between 1996 and 1997. In 1997, 7.3 million families were in poverty, yielding a family poverty rate of 10.3%. Both figures were significantly lower than the 7.7 million families and 11.0% reported for 1996.

More than half of the decline in the number of poor families occurred among black families. In 1997 the poverty rate of black families dropped to 23.6% (2.0 million), down from 26.1% (2.2 million) in 1996. Black families headed by a single mother experienced a similar drop in the percentage of

families who were poor: 39.8% (1.6 million), down from 43.7% (1.7 million) poor in 1996.

Across all racial and ethnic groups, female householder families contrasted most starkly with married-couple families. Families headed by a single mother had the highest poverty rate (31.6%) and comprised the majority of poor families (55%). Married-couple families, by contrast, had the lowest poverty rate (5.2%), yet still comprised a large share of poor families (39%) since they were the most common type of family.

Income

Between 1996 and 1997, real median household income increased by 1.9%, from $36,306 to $37,005. This is the third consecutive year households in the United States experienced an increase in real annual median income.

Race and Hispanic Origin

Asians and Pacific Islanders continued to have the highest median household income ($45,249) among the race groups in 1997. White households had the second highest ($38,972) followed by black households ($25,050). White, non-Hispanic households had a median income of $40,577 in 1997, and Hispanic-origin households had a median income of $26,628.

Most racial and ethnic groups fared well between 1996 and 1997. Specifically, white households experienced an increase in real median income of 2.5%, and black households experienced a 4.3% increase. Households maintained by a person of Hispanic origin experienced a 4.5% increase in median income between 1996 and 1997; households maintained by a white, non-Hispanic person experienced a 2.3% increase.

Year-Round, Full-Time Workers

The real median earnings of both men and women working full time, year round, increased between 1996 and 1997. The median earnings of men increased by 2.4%, going from $32,882 to $33,674; the median earnings of women increased by 3.0%, going from $24,254 to $24,973. In 1997, as in 1996, women earned about 74 cents for every dollar men earned.

Per Capita Income

Real per capita income increased significantly (by 3.7%) between 1996 and 1997, going from $18,552 to $19,241. The per capita income of the white population increased by 4.1%, going from $19,621 to $20,425. The Hispanic-origin population also experienced an increase in per capita income between 1996 and 1997 of 4.8%, going from $10,279 to $10,773. Per capita income for blacks and Asian and Pacific Islanders was not significantly changed.

Poverty Thresholds

The poverty thresholds in 1997 were as follows: one person under 65: $8,350; age 65 and over, $7,698; two persons: householder under 65, $10,805; householder 65 and over, $9,712; three persons, $12,802; four persons, $16,400; five persons, $19,380 six persons, $21,886; seven persons, $24,802; eight persons, $27,593; nine or more persons, $32,566.

Persons Below the Poverty Level, 1975–1997

(in thousands)

Year	All persons	White	Black	Hispanic origin[1]	Year	All persons	White	Black	Hispanic origin[1]
1975	25,877	17,770	7,545	2,991	1987	32,221	21,195	9,520	5,422
1976	24,975	16,713	7,595	2,783	1988	31,745	20,715	9,356	5,357
1977	24,720	16,416	7,726	2,700	1989	32,415	21,294	9,525	6,086
1978	24,497	16,259	7,625	2,607	1990	33,585	22,326	9,837	6,006
1979	26,072	17,214	8,050	2,921	1991	35,708	23,747	10,242	6,339
1980	29,272	19,699	8,579	3,491	1992	38,014	25,259	10,827	7,592
1981	31,822	21,553	9,173	3,713	1993	39,265	26,226	10,877	8,126
1982	34,398	23,517	9,697	4,301	1994	38,059	25,379	10,196	8,416
1983	35,303	23,984	9,882	4,633	1995	36,425	24,423	9,872	8,574
1984	33,700	22,955	9,490	4,806	1996	36,529	24,650	9,694	8,697
1985	33,064	22,860	8,926	5,236	1997	35,574	24,396	9,116	8,308
1986	32,370	22,183	8,983	5,117					

1. Persons of Hispanic origin may be of any race. *Source:* U.S. Bureau of the Census. Web: www.census.gov.

Percent of Persons in Poverty by State, 1991–1997

State	1997 Percent	1995 Percent	1993 Percent	1991 Percent	State	1997 Percent	1995 Percent	1993 Percent	1991 Percent
Alabama	14.8%	20.1%	17.4%	19.0%	Montana	16.3%	15.3%	14.9%	15.5%
Alaska	8.5	7.1	9.1	12.0	Nebraska	10.0	9.6	10.3	9.8
Arizona	18.8	16.1	15.4	15.5	Nevada	9.6	11.1	9.8	11.6
Arkansas	18.4	14.9	20.0	17.4	New Hampshire	7.7	5.3	9.9	7.4
California	16.8	16.7	18.2	16.3	New Jersey	9.2	7.8	10.9	10.0
Colorado	9.4	8.8	9.9	10.6	New Mexico	23.4	25.3	17.4	23.0
Connecticut	10.1	9.7	8.5	9.0	New York	16.6	16.5	16.4	15.7
Delaware	9.1	10.3	10.2	7.7	North Carolina	11.8	12.6	14.4	14.6
D.C.	23.0	22.2	26.4	18.6	North Dakota	12.3	12.0	11.2	14.7
Florida	14.3	16.2	17.8	15.7	Ohio	11.8	11.5	13.0	13.5
Georgia	14.7	12.1	13.5	17.1	Oklahoma	15.2	17.1	19.9	17.2
Hawaii	13.0	10.3	8.0	7.8	Oregon	11.7	11.2	11.8	13.6
Idaho	13.3	14.5	13.1	14.1	Pennsylvania	11.4	12.2	13.2	11.2
Illinois	11.6	12.4	13.6	13.8	Rhode Island	11.9	10.6	11.2	10.7
Indiana	8.2	9.6	12.2	15.8	South Carolina	13.1	19.9	18.7	16.5
Iowa	9.6	12.2	10.3	9.8	South Dakota	14.1	14.5	14.2	14.3
Kansas	10.4	10.8	13.1	12.4	Tennessee	15.1	15.5	19.6	15.5
Kentucky	16.4	14.7	20.4	18.8	Texas	16.7	17.4	17.4	18.0
Louisiana	18.4	19.7	26.4	19.2	Utah	8.3	8.4	10.7	13.0
Maine	10.7	11.7	15.4	14.2	Vermont	10.9	10.3	10.0	12.7
Maryland	9.3	10.1	9.7	9.3	Virginia	12.5	10.2	9.7	10.0
Massachusetts	11.2	11.0	10.7	11.3	Washington	10.5	12.5	12.1	9.7
Michigan	10.7	12.2	15.4	14.2	West Virginia	17.5	16.7	22.2	17.9
Minnesota	9.7	9.2	11.6	13.1	Wisconsin	8.5	8.5	12.6	10.0
Mississippi	18.6	23.5	24.7	23.8	Wyoming	12.7	12.2	13.3	9.9
Missouri	10.6	9.4	16.1	14.9					

Source: Poverty in the United States, 1997, Current Population Reports, Bureau of the Census. Web: www.census.gov.

Characteristics of Persons Below Poverty Level in 1997

(in thousands)

	Number	Percent		Number	Percent
Total[1]	35,574	13.3%	45 to 54 years	2,439	7.2%
White	24,396	11.0	55 to 59 years	1,092	9.0
Black	9,116	26.5	60 to 64 years	1,127	11.2
Asian and Pacific Islander	1,468	14.0	65 years and over	3,376	10.5
Hispanic origin[2]	8,308	27.1	Northeast	6,474	12.6
Under 18 years	14,113	19.9	Midwest	6,493	10.4
18 to 24 years	4,416	17.5	South	13,748	14.6
25 to 34 years	4,759	12.1	West	8,858	14.6
35 to 44 years	4,251	9.6			

1. Includes races not shown separately. 2. Persons of Hispanic origin may be of any race. *Source:* "Income, Poverty, and Valuation of Noncash Benefits," *Current Population Reports,* U.S. Bureau of the Census. Web: www.census.gov.

Weighted Average Poverty Thresholds for Families of Specified Size, 1960–1998

Calendar year	Individual	2 persons	Families of 3 persons or more					
			3 persons	4 persons	5 persons	6 persons	7 persons
1960	$1,490	$ 1,924	$ 2,359	$ 3,022	$ 3,560	$ 4,002	$ 4,921
1965	1,582	2,048	2,514	3,223	3,797	4,264	5,248
1970	1,954	2,525	3,099	3,968	4,680	5,260	6,468
1975	2,724	3,506	4,293	5,500	6,499	7,316	9,022
1980	4,190	5,363	6,565	8,414	9,966	11,269	12,761
1985	5,469	6,998	8,573	10,989	13,007	14,696	16,656
1990	6,652	8,509	10,419	13,359	15,792	17,839	20,241
1995	7,763	9,933	12,158	15,569	18,408	20,804	23,552
1997	8,183	10,473	12,802	16,400	19,380	21,886	24,802
1998[1]	8,480	10,915	12,750	16,813	20,275	23,320	26,833

1. Householder under 65 years old. *Source:* U.S. Bureau of the Census. Web: www.census.gov.

Social Welfare Expenditures Under Public Programs
(in millions of dollars)

Year and source of funds	Social insurance	Public aid	Health and medical programs[1]	Veterans' programs	Education	Housing	Other social welfare	All health and medical care[2]	Total social welfare	Total social welfare as:	
										% of gross domestic product	% of total govt. outlays
Federal											
1982	$250,551	$52,485	$14,598	$24,463	$11,917	$7,176	$6,500	$90,776	$367,691	11.8%	52.5%
1984	288,743	58,480	16,622	25,970	13,010	10,226	7,349	103,927	420,399	11.4	50.2
1986	326,588	65,615	19,926	27,072	15,022	10,164	7,977	125,730	472,364	11.2	47.6
1988	358,412	74,137	22,681	28,845	16,952	14,006	8,112	149,102	523,144	11.0	49.1
1990	422,257	92,858	27,204	30,428	18,374	16,612	8,905	190,616	616,639	11.2	51.4
1992	495,710	138,704	31,872	34,212	20,188	17,950	10,677	249,528	749,312	12.6	57.1
1994	557,389	162,675	34,770	37,262	24,084	24,724	11,718	n.a.	852,622	12.5	51.4
State and Local											
1982	52,481	28,367	19,195	245	121,957	778	5,154	40,738	228,178	7.4	62.6
1984	52,378	32,206	20,383	301	139,046	1,306	5,946	44,540	251,569	7.0	58.9
1986	63,816	37,464	24,408	373	163,495	1,872	6,728	53,884	298,158	7.3	58.2
1988	73,783	46,237	29,859	409	202,416	2,550	7,368	70,511	362,622	7.5	60.1
1990	91,565	53,953	36,263	488	240,011	2,856	9,012	85,775	434,148	7.9	68.0
1992	121,266	69,241	39,163	555	272,011	2,668	10,855	104,559	515,758	8.7	70.6
1994	126,458	75,351	44,526	633	320,112	2,045	12,899	n.a.	582,023	8.5	74.0
Total											
1982	303,033	80,852	33,793	24,708	133,874	7,954	11,654	131,514	595,869	19.2	55.7
1984	341,120	90,685	37,006	26,275	152,056	11,532	13,295	148,467	671,969	18.3	52.8
1986	390,404	103,079	44,334	27,445	178,518	12,036	14,705	179,614	770,522	18.5	47.9
1988	432,195	120,375	52,540	29,254	219,368	16,556	15,480	219,613	885,766	18.5	52.8
1990	513,823	146,811	63,467	30,916	258,385	19,468	17,918	276,391	1,050,788	19.2	56.7
1992	616,975	207,945	71,035	34,767	292,198	20,617	21,532	354,058	1,265,070	21.3	61.6
1994	683,847	238,025	79,296	37,895	344,196	26,769	24,617	407,910	1,434,645	21.0	58.2
Percent of total, by type											
1986	50.7%	13.4%	5.8%	3.6%	23.2%	1.6%	1.9%	23.3%	100.0%	(3)	(3)
1988	48.8	13.6	5.9	3.3	24.8	1.9	1.7	24.8	100.0	(3)	(3)
1990	49.0	14.0	6.0	3.0	25.0	2.0	1.0	26.0	100.0	(3)	(3)
1992	48.8	16.4	5.6	2.7	23.1	1.6	1.7	28.0	100.0	(3)	(3)
1994	47.7	16.6	5.5	2.6	24.0	1.9	1.7	28.4	100.0	(3)	(3)
Federal spending as a percent of total											
1986	83.6%	63.7%	44.9%	98.6%	8.4%	84.4%	54.2%	70.0%	61.3%	(3)	(3)
1988	82.9	61.6	43.2	98.6	7.7	84.6	52.4	67.9	59.1	(3)	(3)
1990	82.0	63.0	43.0	98.0	7.0	85.0	50.0	69.0	59.0	(3)	(3)
1992	80.3	66.7	44.9	98.4	6.9	87.1	49.6	70.5	59.2	(3)	(3)
1994	81.5	68.3	43.8	98.3	7.0	92.4	47.6	72.0	59.4	(3)	(3)

NOTE: n.a. = not available. 1. Excludes program parts of social insurance, public aid, veterans, and other social welfare. 2. Combines health and medical programs with medical services provided in connection with social insurance, public aid, veterans, and other social welfare programs. 3. Not applicable. *Source:* Social Security Admin. Web: www.ssa.gov.

Drop in Welfare Rolls Since January 1993

	Number of families on welfare March 1999	Percent reduction 1993–1998		Number of families on welfare March 1999	Percent reduction 1993–1998
Alabama	20,009	−61%	Nebraska	11,653	−30
Alaska	9,059	−22	Nevada	8,030	−38
Arizona	34,851	−49	New Hampshire	6,563	−39
Arkansas	12,095	−55	New Jersey	65,341	−48
California	630,301	−25	New Mexico	25,995	−16
Colorado	14,609	−66	New York	297,897	−30
Connecticut	35,823	−37	North Carolina	60,720	−53
Delaware	6,574	−42	North Dakota	3,132	−52
Dist. of Columbia	19,148	−22	Ohio	110,817	−57
Florida	81,957	−68	Oklahoma	20,200	−60
Georgia	55,720	−61	Oregon	17,271	−59
Guam	2,532	80	Pennsylvania	113,193	−45
Hawaii	16,565	−7	Puerto Rico	36,539	−40
Idaho	1,435	−82	Rhode Island	18,918	−14
Illinois	128,700	−44	South Carolina	17,942	−67
Indiana	32,987	−55	South Dakota	3,314	−54
Iowa	22,284	−39	Tennessee	58,690	−48
Kansas	12,932	−57	Texas	115,600	−59
Kentucky	42,682	−49	Utah	9,996	−46
Louisiana	39,868	−56	Vermont	6,656	−34
Maine	12,922	−46	Virgin Islands	932	−13
Maryland	34,901	−57	Virginia	36,713	−50
Massachusetts	54,356	−52	Washington	63,202	−37
Michigan	97,089	−57	West Virginia	9,653	−77
Minnesota	46,798	−27	Wisconsin	8,723	−89
Mississippi	16,478	−73	Wyoming	836	−87
Missouri	51,843	−42	**U.S. total**	**2,668,364**	**−46**
Montana	5,320	−55			

Source: U.S. Dept. of Health and Human Services, Admin. for Children and Families. Web: www.acf.dhhs.gov.

Social Security

The original Social Security Act was passed in 1935 and is administered by the Social Security Administration and other agencies within the Department of Health and Human Services.

What Does Social Security Offer?

The Social Security contribution you pay gives you four different kinds of protection: (1) retirement benefits, (2) survivors' benefits, (3) disability benefits, and (4) Medicare hospital insurance benefits.

Retirement Benefits

Currently, as a worker you become eligible for the full amount of your retirement benefits at age 65. You may retire at age 62 and get 80% of your full benefit. The closer you are to age 65 when you start collecting your benefit, the larger the fraction of your full benefit you will get.

The amount of the retirement benefit you are entitled to at age 65 is the key to all other benefits under the program. The retirement benefit is based on covered earnings, which will be updated (indexed) to reflect the increases in average wages that have occurred since the earnings were paid. Your largest 35 years of adjusted earnings are averaged together and a formula is applied to the adjusted average to figure the benefit rate.

In general, the highest retirement check that can be paid to a worker who retired at 65 in January 1997 is about $1,327.60 a month. Maximum pay-

ment to the family of this retired worker is about $2,324.40 as of January 1997.

Survivor Benefits

This feature of the Social Security program gives your family valuable life-insurance protection. The amount of protection is again geared to what the worker would be entitled to if he had been age 65 when he died. Total family survivor benefits were estimated to be as high as $2,534.00 a month if the worker died in 1995. Your survivors could get:

1. A one-time cash payment of $255 for your spouse or minor children if you have enough work credits.

2. A benefit for each child until he or she reaches 18 (or 19, if the child is in full-time attendance at an elementary or secondary school), or at any age if disabled before 22. "Child" includes biological or legally adopted children, or dependent stepchildren or grandchildren.

3. A benefit for your widow(er), at any age, if she/he has your entitled children under 16 or disabled in care.

4. Your spouse or divorced spouse can get a widow's, widower's, or surviving divorced spouse's benefit starting at age 60. A widow, or widower, who first becomes entitled at 65 or later will get 100% of his or her deceased spouse's basic amount (or the amount of the deceased spouse's reduced benefits).

5. Dependent parents can sometimes collect survivors' benefits. They are usually eligible if: (a) they were getting at least half their support from the deceased worker; (b) they have reached 62; (c) they are not eligible for a greater retirement benefit based on their own earnings; and (d) they have not married since the worker's death.

Disability Benefits

Disability benefits can be paid to several groups of people:

• Disabled workers under age 65 and their families.

• Persons disabled before age 22 who continue to be disabled. These benefits are payable as early as age 18 when a parent (or step-parent or grandparent under certain circumstances) receives Social Security retirement or disability benefits or when an insured parent dies.

• Disabled widows and widowers and (under certain conditions) disabled, surviving, divorced spouses of workers who were insured at death. These benefits are payable as early as 50. Consult your local Social Security office for the latest disability information.

The SSA determines whether or not you qualify for disability benefits based on criteria including the severity of your condition and the earnings you continue to receive after you become disabled. To be considered for disability benefits, you should file a claim with a Social Security office as soon as you become disabled. However, even if you are approved, benefits will not begin until after a waiting period of six months after the beginning of your disability.

Medicare Program

Medicare is the nation's largest health insurance program. Generally, you are eligible for Medicare if you or your spouse worked for at least 10 years in Medicare-covered employment and you are 65 years old and a citizen or permanent resident of the United States. You might also qualify for coverage if you are a younger person with a disability or with chronic kidney disease.

Medicare-covered services include:

• **Hospital insurance.** Financial assistance is available for necessary medical care and services furnished by Medicare-certified hospitals, skilled nursing facilities, home health agencies, and hospices.

• **Inpatient hospital care.** Medicare helps pay for up to 90 days of inpatient hospital care in each benefit period. Covered services include your semi-private room and meals, general nursing services, operating and recovery room costs, intensive care, drugs, laboratory tests, X-rays, and all other necessary medical services and supplies.

• **Skilled nursing facility care.** You may need inpatient skilled nursing or rehabilitation services after a hospital stay. If you meet certain conditions, Medicare will help pay for up to 100 days in a participating skilled nursing facility in each benefit period.

• **Home health care.** If you meet certain conditions, Medicare pays the full approved cost of covered home health care services. This includes part-time or intermittent skilled nursing services prescribed by a physician for treatment or rehabilitation of homebound patients.

• **Hospice care.** Medicare helps pay for hospice care for terminally ill beneficiaries who select the hospice care benefit.

• **Medical insurance (Part B).** Medicare Part B helps pay for doctor's services, outpatient hospital services (including emergency room visits), ambulance transportation, diagnostic tests, laboratory services, some preventive care like mammography and Pap smear screening, outpatient therapy services, durable medical equipment and supplies, and a variety of other health services.

Additional benefits are available through the Medicare program. For further information contact the Social Security Administration at 1-800-772-1213.

Monthly Social Security Benefits and Average Amount

Type of beneficiary	Number of beneficiaries				Average amount, 1996
	1940	1960	1980	1996	
All beneficiaries	222,488	14,844,589	35,618,840	43,736,836	$672.80
Retirement program	148,490	10,599,021	23,243,078	30,310,865	703.58
Retired workers	112,331	8,061,469	19,582,625	26,898,072	744.96
Wives and husbands	29,749	2,269,384	3,018,008	2,970,226	383.50
Children	6,410	268,168	642,445	442,567	337.07
Survivor program	73,998	3,558,117	7,600,836	7,353,284	637.95
Nondisabled widows and widowers	4,437	1,543,843	4,287,930	5,027,901	706.85
Disabled widows and widowers	—	—	126,659	181,911	470.95
Widowed mothers and fathers	20,499	401,358	562,798	242,135	514.91
Children	48,238	1,576,802	2,608,653	1,897,667	487.17
Parents	824	36,114	14,796	3,670	613.54
Disability program	—	687,451	4,682,172	6,072,034	561.36
Disabled workers	—	455,371	2,861,253	4,385,623	703.94
Wives and husbands	—	76,599	462,204	223,854	171.39
Children	—	155,481	1,358,715	1,462,557	193.51
Special age-72 beneficiaries	—	—	92,754	653	197.27

NOTE: Data as of December for each year. *Source:* Social Security Administration.

Distribution of Federal Funds by State and Territory, Fiscal Year 1998

(in millions of dollars)

State and outlying area	Total	Retirement and disability	Other direct payments	Grants	Procurement	Salaries and wages
United States, total	$1,484,177	$507,202	$328,417	$269,128	$209,260	$170,171
Alabama	25,297	9,483	5,606	4,161	3,104	2,944
Alaska	4,767	756	438	1,427	863	1,282
Arizona	24,067	9,086	4,509	4,147	3,793	2,533
Arkansas	13,016	5,607	3,441	2,440	475	1,054
California	161,571	49,217	37,554	32,090	25,365	17,344
Colorado	21,009	6,648	3,516	3,048	4,300	3,496
Connecticut	19,424	6,245	4,355	3,653	3,814	1,357
Delaware	3,553	1,479	814	678	215	367
District of Columbia	24,034	1,683	1,615	4,101	5,200	11,436
Florida	83,558	36,235	22,179	10,320	7,128	7,696
Georgia	37,144	12,764	7,560	6,233	4,603	5,984
Hawaii	8,442	2,348	1,293	1,190	1,053	2,557
Idaho	5,961	2,135	1,100	1,055	1,019	652
Illinois	55,467	20,579	14,667	10,156	4,576	5,490
Indiana	26,098	10,750	7,046	4,152	2,233	1,917
Iowa	14,535	5,571	4,670	2,424	930	941
Kansas	13,426	5,086	3,411	1,934	1,316	1,680
Kentucky	23,161	7,984	4,604	4,236	3,850	2,488
Louisiana	22,900	7,622	6,217	4,708	2,351	2,002
Maine	7,463	2,659	1,429	1,602	1,025	748
Maryland	41,565	10,508	7,575	5,022	10,417	8,042
Massachusetts	37,173	11,484	9,380	8,019	5,451	2,840
Michigan	41,917	17,544	11,069	8,618	1,871	2,814
Minnesota	20,399	7,572	5,129	4,199	1,795	1,704
Mississippi	15,314	5,443	3,733	3,025	1,613	1,500
Missouri	32,682	10,842	7,379	5,065	6,341	3,055
Montana	5,465	1,809	1,528	1,139	376	614
Nebraska	8,253	3,187	2,105	1,511	487	963
Nevada	7,566	3,287	1,559	1,081	805	835
New Hampshire	5,272	2,232	1,026	1,042	524	448
New Jersey	40,373	15,174	10,541	7,108	4,091	3,458
New Mexico	12,933	3,375	1,661	2,547	3,769	1,581
New York	99,766	33,295	25,169	28,066	5,995	7,240
North Carolina	35,677	14,346	7,299	7,133	2,064	4,833
North Dakota	4,131	1,169	1,084	1,067	258	554
Ohio	52,006	21,075	12,588	9,733	4,368	4,242
Oklahoma	18,205	7,038	4,090	3,059	1,381	2,637
Oregon	15,119	6,307	3,339	3,275	728	1,471
Pennsylvania	67,350	26,507	17,994	12,381	5,163	5,306
Rhode Island	6,039	2,129	1,515	1,368	313	715
South Carolina	19,870	7,785	3,826	3,525	2,489	2,246
South Dakota	4,319	1,414	1,073	1,007	317	508
Tennessee	30,497	10,656	6,582	5,510	5,116	2,633
Texas	92,019	30,388	20,764	15,809	13,893	11,164
Utah	8,728	3,069	1,361	1,727	1,180	1,392
Vermont	2,895	1,066	593	803	154	278
Virginia	55,830	14,769	6,756	4,423	18,523	11,360
Washington	31,186	10,716	5,516	5,422	4,920	4,612
West Virginia	10,697	4,498	2,372	2,480	488	859
Wisconsin	21,883	9,330	5,096	4,697	1,295	1,464
Wyoming	2,743	909	434	850	175	376
American Samoa	135	29	6	91	7	3
Guam	998	155	66	266	167	344
Northern Marianas	63	11	8	39	3	2
Puerto Rico	11,119	4,031	2,080	3,895	374	739
Virgin Islands	482	104	71	256	11	40
Undistributed	28,615	11	27	116	25,126	3,336

Source: Consolidated Federal Funds Report, Fiscal Year 1998.

The Rich Get Richer

In September 1999, the Center on Budget and Policy Priorities (CBPP) released a report examining the distribution of after-tax income among Americans in 1977 and 1999. The report, which is based on data from the Congressional Budget Office, shows that despite tax increases on high-income households in 1990 and 1993, this group has received large tax cuts overall since 1977. The result has been a widening of the gap between the rich and the poor.

The CBPP report breaks the U.S. population into fifths based on after-tax household income level. According to the report, the top one percent of Americans made an average gain of 115% in after-tax income between 1977 and 1999. The top one-fifth also fared well, gaining 43%. In contrast, the middle fifth made only 8% more and the bottom fifth in fact saw its average income decline by 9%. The next-to-bottom fifth did not change significantly.

Average After-Tax Income in 1997 and 1999

| | 1999[1] | | 1977 | |
Income group	Average income	Share of all income (percent)	Average income	Share of all income (percent)
Lowest fifth	$ 8,800	4.2%	$ 10,000	5.7%
Second fifth	20,000	9.7	22,100	11.5
Middle fifth	31,400	14.7	32,400	16.4
Fourth fifth	45,100	21.3	42,600	22.8
Highest fifth	102,300	50.4	74,000	44.2
Top one percent	515,600	12.9	234,700	7.3

NOTE: Figures rounded to nearest hundred dollars. 1. Projected. *Source:* Center on Budget and Policy Priorities. Web: www.cbpp.org. (Based on data from the Congressional Budget Office.)

The Public Debt

| | Gross debt | | | Gross debt | |
Year	Amount (in millions)	Per capita	Year	Amount (in millions)	Per capita
1800 (Jan. 1)	$ 83	$ 15.87	1965	$ 313,819[1]	$ 1,612.70
1860 (June 30)	65	2.06	1970	370,094[1]	1,807.09
1865	2,678	75.01	1975	533,189	2,496.90
1900	1,263	16.60	1980	907,701	3,969.55
1920	24,299	228.23	1985	1,823,103	7,598.51
1925	20,516	177.12	1990	3,233,313	12,823.28
1930	16,185	131.51	1994	4,643,711	17,805.64
1935	28,701	225.55	1995	4,973,983	18,928.53
1940	42,968	325.23	1996	5,217,305	19,681.26
1945	258,682	1,848.60	1997	5,355,085	20,006.08
1950	256,087[1]	1,688.30	1998	5,529,921	20,474.79
1955	272,807[1]	1,650.63	1999	5,638,656	20,663.65
1960	284,093[1]	1,572.31			

Note: Figures as of July for each year. 1. Adjusted to exclude issues to the International Monetary Fund and other international lending institutions to conform to the budget presentation. *Source:* U.S. Department of the Treasury, Financial Management Service. Web: www.publicdebt.treas.gov/opd/opdpenny.htm.

National Income by Type
(in billions of dollars)

Type of income	1998	1995	1990	1985	1980	1975	1970	1965	1960
National income	$6,994.7	$5,828.9	$4,611.9	$3,351.5	$2,216.1	$1,295.5	$836.6	$587.8	$426.2
Compensation of employees	4,981.0	4,222.7	3,352.8	2,425.7	1,653.9	951.3	618.1	399.8	296.7
Wages and salaries	4,153.9	3,433.2	2,757.5	1,995.7	1,377.6	814.7	551.5	363.7	272.8
Supplements to wages and salaries	827.1	789.5	595.2	430.0	276.3	136.6	66.6	36.1	23.8
Proprietors' income[1,2]	577.2	486.1	361.0	257.4	167.9	116.5	78.0	63.5	50.5
Farm	28.7	27.9	36.3	24.5	13.8	24.2	14.8	13.0	11.5
Business and professional	548.5	458.2	324.6	232.5	154.1	92.3	63.2	50.4	39.1
Rental income[1]	162.6	111.7	61.4	49.1	35.3	26.6	24.7	22.5	19.1
Corporate profits[1,2]	824.6	604.8	369.5	282.2	167.1	121.1	75.7	80.9	48.8
Net interest	449.3	403.6	467.3	337.2	191.9	80.0	40.0	21.1	11.2

1. Includes capital consumption adjustment. 2. Includes inventory valuation adjustment. *Source:* U.S. Department of Commerce, Bureau of Economic Analysis, *Survey of Current Business*, May 1999. Web: www.bea.doc.gov.

The Federal Budget, 1995–2000
(in billions of dollars)

	Actual			Estimate	
	1995	1997	1998	1999	2000
Receipts by Source					
Individual income taxes	$ 590.2	$ 737.5	$ 828.6	$ 868.9	$ 899.7
Corporation income taxes	157.0	182.3	188.7	182.2	189.4
Social insurance and retirement receipts	484.5	539.4	571.8	608.8	636.5
Excise taxes	57.5	56.9	57.7	68.1	69.9
Estate and gift taxes	15.6	19.8	24.1	25.9	27.0
Customs duties	20.9	17.9	18.4	17.7	18.4
Miscellaneous receipts	28.6	25.5	32.7	34.7	42.1
Total receipts	1,355.2	1,579.3	1,721.8	1,806.3	1,883.0
Outlays by Function					
National defense	272.1	270.5	268.5	276.7	274.1
Human resources	923.8	1,002.3	1,033.4	1,087.4	1,142.8
Education, training, employment, and social services	54.3	53.0	54.9	60.1	63.4
Health	115.4	123.8	131.4	143.1	152.3
Medicare	159.9	190.0	192.8	205.0	216.6
Income security	220.5	230.9	233.2	243.1	258.0
Social security	335.8	365.3	379.2	392.6	408.6
Veterans benefits and services	37.9	39.3	41.8	43.5	44.0
Physical resources	59.2	60.0	74.7	77.8	84.8
Energy	4.9	1.5	1.3	0.05	(2.0)
Natural resources and environment	22.1	21.4	22.4	24.3	23.7
Commerce and housing credit	(17.8)	(14.6)	1.0	0.5	6.4
Transportation	39.4	40.8	40.3	42.6	46.4
Community and regional development	10.6	11.0	9.7	10.4	10.2
Net interest	232.2	244.0	243.4	227.2	215.2
Other functions	73.0	74.4	79.8	97.9	94.5
International affairs	16.4	15.2	13.1	15.5	16.1
General science, space and technology	16.7	17.2	18.2	18.5	18.6
Agriculture	9.8	9.0	12.2	21.4	15.1
Administration of justice	16.2	20.2	22.8	24.5	27.5
General government	13.8	12.8	13.4	14.9	14.5
Allowances	—	—	—	3.1	2.6
Undistributed offsetting receipts	(44.5)	(50.0)	(47.2)	(40.0)	(45.7)
Total Outlays	1,515.7	1,601.2	1,652.6	1,727.1	1,765.7
Reserve Pending Social Security Reform	—	—	69.2	79.3	117.3
Total Deficit or Surplus	−160.5	−21.9	—	—	—

NOTE: The fiscal year is from October 1 to September 30. *Source:* Budget of the United States Government, Fiscal Year 2000. Web: www.access.gpo.gov/usbudget/fy2000/summary.html.

Receipts and Outlays of the Federal Government, 1789–1999
(in millions of dollars)

From 1789 to 1842, the federal fiscal year ended December 31; from 1844 to 1976, on June 30; and beginning 1977, on September 30.

		Receipts				
	Customs (including tonnage tax)[1]	Internal revenue		Miscellaneous taxes and receipts	Total receipts	Net receipts[2]
		Income and profits tax	Other			
1789–1791	$ 4	—	—	—	$ 4	$ 4
1800	9	—	$ −1	$ 1	11	11
1810	9	—	—	1	9	9
1820	15	—	—	3	18	18
1830	22	—	—	3	25	25
1840	14	—	—	6	20	20
1850	40	—	—	4	44	44
1860	53	—	—	3	56	56
1870	195	—	185	32	411	411
1880	187	—	124	23	334	334
1890	230	—	143	31	403	403
1900	233	—	295	39	567	567
1910	334	—	290	52	675	675
1915	210	$ 80	335	72	698	683
1929	602	2,331	607	493	4,033	3,862
1939	319	2,189	2,972	188	5,668	4,979
1944	431	34,655	7,030	3,325	45,441	43,563

Receipts

	Customs (including tonnage tax)[1]	Internal revenue		Miscellaneous taxes and receipts	Total receipts	Net receipts[2]
		Income and profits tax	Other			
1945	$ 355	$ 35,173	$ 8,729	$ 3,494	$ 47,750	$ 44,362
1950	423	28,263	11,186	1,439	41,311	36,422
1956	705	56,639	20,564	389	78,297	74,547
1960	1,123	67,151	28,266	1,190	97,730	92,492
1965	1,478	79,792	39,996	1,598	122,863	116,833
1970	2,494	138,689	65,276	3,424	209,883	193,743
1975	3,782	202,146	108,371	6,711	321,010	280,997
1980	7,482	359,927	192,436	12,797	572,641	520,050
1985	12,079	474,074	311,092	18,576	815,821	733,996
1988	16,198	495,376	377,469	19,909	([4])	908,953
1990	16,707	560,391	426,893	27,470	([4])	1,031,462
1991	15,949	565,913	449,577	22,846	([4])	1,054,265
1992	17,359	576,234	470,401	26,459	([4])	1,090,453
1993	18,802	627,200	488,934	18,290	([4])	1,153,226
1994	20,099	683,123	531,924	22,041	([4])	1,257,187
1995	19,300	747,247	556,721	27,309	([4])	1,350,578
1996	18,670	828,241	534,948	25,534	([4])	1,407,393
1997	17,928	919,759	539,371	25,465	([4])	1,579,292
1998	18,297	1,017,263	653,580	32,658	([4])	1,721,798
1999	17,654	1,051,155	702,831	34,694	([4])	1,806,334

Outlays

Year	Department of Defense (Army, 1789–1950)	Department of the Navy	Interest on public debt	All other	Net outlays[3]	Surplus (+) or deficit (−)
1789–1791	$ 1	—	$ 2	$ 1	$ 4	—
1800	3	$ 3	3	1	11	—
1810	2	2	3	1	8	$ +1
1820	3	4	5	6	18	—
1830	5	3	2	5	15	+10
1840	7	6	—	11	24	−4
1850	9	8	4	18	40	+4
1860	16	12	3	32	63	−7
1870	58	22	129	101	310	+101
1880	38	14	96	120	268	+66
1890	45	22	36	215	318	+85
1900	135	56	40	290	521	+46
1910	190	123	21	359	694	−19
1915	202	142	23	379	746	−63
1929	426	365	678	1,658	3,127	+734
1939	695	673	941	6,533	8,841	−3,862
1944	49,438	26,538	2,609	16,401	94,986	−51,423
1945	50,490	30,047	3,617	14,149	98,303	−53,941
1950	5,789	4,130	5,750	23,875	39,544	−3,122
1956	35,693	—	6,787	27,981	70,460	+4,087
1960	43,969	—	9,180	39,075	92,223	+269
1965	47,179	—	11,346	59,904	118,430	−1,596
1970	78,360	—	19,304	98,924	196,588	−2,845
1975	87,471	—	32,665	205,969	326,105	−45,108
1980	136,138	—	74,860	368,013	579,011	−58,961
1985	244,054	—	178,945	513,810	936,809	−202,813
1988	290,349	—	151,711	621,995	1,064,055	−155,102
1990	299,355	—	183,790	768,725	1,251,850	−220,388
1991	273,292	—	194,541	855,924	1,323,757	−269,492
1992	298,350	—	199,439	883,005	1,380,794	−290,340
1993	291,186	—	198,811	918,635	1,408,632	−255,406
1994	281,451	—	202,957	976,149	1,460,557	−203,370
1995	271,895	—	232,175	1,010,364	1,514,434	−163,856
1996	265,748	—	241,090	1,053,674	1,560,512	−153,119
1997	270,473	—	244,013	1,086,749	1,601,235	−21,943
1998	268,456	—	243,359	1,140,737	1,652,552	+69,246[5]
1999	276,730	—	227,244	1,223,097	1,727,071	+79,263[5]

1. Beginning 1933, tonnage tax is included in "Other receipts." 2. Net receipts equal total receipts less (a) appropriations to federal old-age and survivors' insurance trust fund beginning fiscal year 1939 and (b) refunds of receipts beginning fiscal year 1933. 3. Includes Air Force 1950–65 (in millions): 1950, $3,521; 1956, $16,750; 1960, $19,065; 1965, $18,471. 4. Net receipts are now the total receipts. Public Law 99-177 moved two social security trust funds off-budget. 5. Surplus is actually a reserve pending Social Security Reform. *Source:* Budget of the United States Government, Fiscal Year 2000. Web: www.access.gpo.gov/su_docs/budget/index.html.

U.S. Contributions to International Organizations

Organization	1999 (est.)	1998
United Nations and affiliated agencies:		
Food and Agriculture Org.	$ 81	$ 81
International Atomic Energy Agency	51	56
International Civil Aviation Org.	13	13
International Labor Org.	64	57
International Maritime Org.	1	1
International Telecommunications Union	8	7
United Nations	277	259
U.N. War Crimes Tribunals	25	14
Universal Postal Union	2	1
World Health Org.	108	107
World Intellectual Property Org.	1	1
World Meteorological Org.	12	11
Subtotal	643	607
Inter-American organizations:		
Inter-American Institute for Cooperation on Agriculture	17	17
Org. of American States	55	55
Pan American Health Org.	50	50
Subtotal	122	122
Regional organizations:		
Asia Pacific Economic Cooperation	1	1
North Atlantic Assembly	1	1
North Atlantic Treaty Org.	48	36
Org. for Economic Cooperation and Development	63	55
South Pacific Commission	1	1
Subtotal	114	94
Other international organizations:		
World Trade Org./General Agreement on Tariffs and Trade	14	13
Customs Cooperation Council	4	3
International Agency for Research on Cancer	2	2
International Center for Study of Preservation & Restoration of Cultural Properties	1	1

Organization	1999 (est.)	1998
International Bureau of Weights and Measures	$ 1	$ 1
International Grains Council	1	1
Interparliamentary Union	0	0
Org. for Prohibition of Chemical Weapons	17	24
Other international organizations	2	1
Subtotal	42	46
U.N. Buydown	0	19
Chemical Weapons/Biological Weapons Center	2	n.a.
Total	**$922**	**$889**
International peacekeeping activities:		
U.N. Disengagement Observer Force	8	8
U.N. Interim Force in Lebanon	30	36
U.N. Operations in Angola	14	37
U.N. Iraq–Kuwait Observer Mission	5	4
U.N. Mission for the Referendum in the Western Sahara	24	13
War Crimes Tribunal–Rwanda	12	7
U.N. Operations in the Former Yugoslavia	105	80
War Crimes Tribunal–Yugoslavia	12	7
U.N. Peacekeeping Operation in Guatemala	0	0
U.N. Observer Mission in Georgia	8	5
U.N. Mission in Haiti	0	0
U.N. Observer Mission in Liberia	0	0
U.N. Assistance Mission for Rwanda	0	0
U.N. Force in Cyprus	7	6
U.N. Mission in Tajikistan	3	5
U.N. Observer Mission in Sierra Leone	3	3
Payment of Prior Year Balances	138	78
Total	**$369**	**$289**

NOTE: All years are fiscal years. All amounts in millions. *Source:* Budget of the United States Government Fiscal Year 2000.

U.S. Direct Investment in Other Countries, 1997
(in millions of dollars)

	All industries	Petro-leum	Manu-facturing	Wholesale trade	Banking	Finance, insurance, real estate	Services	Other industries
All countries	$860,723	$85,726	$288,290	$69,080	$34,359	$280,920	$40,874	$61,475
Canada	99,859	12,738	45,892	7,307	1,047	19,050	4,667	9,159
Europe	420,934	29,793	142,528	34,620	17,312	153,625	24,824	18,232
Belgium	17,403	237	8,788	2,102	252	4,066	1,364	594
France	34,615	1,045	15,887	2,857	781	8,996	4,118	930
Germany	43,931	2,648	20,462	2,538	1,065	13,816	1,713	1,689
Ireland	14,476	(*)	8,462	352	(*)	5,113	321	22
Italy	17,749	(*)	12,223	2,122	379	842	1,089	(*)
Netherlands	64,648	2,623	14,682	4,936	(*)	35,732	4,617	(*)
Spain	11,642	194	6,432	1,472	2,031	639	432	442
Switzerland	35,203	1,144	3,723	8,151	3,341	16,786	1,880	177
United Kingdom	138,765	14,228	38,267	7,389	6,886	54,023	7,569	10,402
Latin America and Other Western Hemisphere	172,481	9,462	47,496	8,358	4,939	81,403	5,424	15,399
South America	67,112	6,824	31,005	2,297	3,851	9,395	2,779	10,962
Brazil	35,727	1,769	22,584	656	1,489	4,711	1,602	2,915
Central America	48,881	1,264	15,919	2,475	622	23,758	971	3,873
Mexico	25,395	109	15,119	862	510	4,079	924	3,792
Panama	20,958	724	102	509	89	19,585	33	83
Other Western Hemisphere	56,489	1,374	572	3,587	466	48,250	1,674	565

	All industries	Petroleum	Manufacturing	Wholesale trade	Banking	Finance, insurance, real estate	Services	Other industries
Bermuda	$ 33,092	$ 150	(*)	$ 1,607	$ 0	$29,822	$1,407	(*)
United Kingdom Islands, Caribbean	12,143	236	(*)	102	634	11,040	24	(*)
Africa	10,253	5,872	1,899	198	299	834	115	1,038
Middle East	8,959	3,438	1,744	271	741	1,878	408	479
Asia and Pacific	142,704	20,442	48,731	18,327	10,020	24,131	5,437	15,616
Australia	26,125	1,206	7,506	2,569	2,181	4,779	1,805	6,080
China	5,013	899	2,696	363	107	636	63	250
Hong Kong	19,065	624	2,755	5,237	1,859	3,049	1,155	4,387
Japan	35,569	4,686	14,293	5,628	565	8,839	1,177	380
Singapore	17,514	3,329	7,851	1,874	694	3,154	528	85

* Suppressed to avoid disclosure of data of individual companies. Source: U.S. Department of Commerce, Bureau of Economic Analysis. Web: www.bea.doc.gov.

Balance of International Payments
(in billions of dollars)

Item	1998[1]	1995	1990	1985	1980	1975	1970	1965	1960
Exports of goods, services, and income	$1,192.2	$969.2	$652.9	$366.0	$343.2	$157.9	$68.4	$42.7	$30.5
Goods, adjusted, excluding military	670.2	575.9	389.5	214.4	224.0	107.1	42.5	26.5	19.7
Services	263.7	210.6	133.1	54.0	44.7	23.2	11.4	7.2	4.6
Transfers under U.S. military agency sales contracts	17.2	13.4	9.8	9.0	8.2	3.9	1.5	0.8	0.3
Receipts of income on U.S. assets abroad	256.5	182.7	130.0	90.0	75.9	25.4	11.8	7.4	4.6
Imports of goods and services	−1,098.2	−1,082.3	−722.7	−461.2	−333.9	−132.6	−60.0	−32.8	−23.7
Goods, adjusted, excluding military	−917.2	−749.4	−497.6	−339.0	−249.3	−98.0	−39.9	−21.5	−14.8
Services	−181.0	−142.2	−106.9	−58.0	−41.4	−22.0	−14.7	−9.2	−7.7
Direct defense expenditures	−12.8	−9.8	−17.1	−12.0	−10.7	−4.8	−4.9	−3.0	−3.1
Payments of income on foreign assets in U.S.	−263.4	−190.7	−118.1	−65.0	−43.2	−12.6	−5.5	−2.1	−1.2
Unilateral transfers, excluding military grants, net	−44.1	−35.1	−22.3	−15.0	−7.0	−4.6	−3.3	−2.9	−2.3
U.S. assets abroad, net	−292.8	−307.9	−57.7	−27.7	−86.1	−39.7	−9.3	−5.7	−4.1
U.S. government assets abroad, net	−0.4	−0.3	2.9	−2.8	−5.2	−3.5	−1.6	−1.6	−1.1
U.S. private assets abroad, net	−285.6	−297.8	−58.5	−26.0	−71.5	−35.4	−10.2	−5.3	−5.1
Foreign assets in U.S., net	502.6	424.5	86.3	127.1	50.3	15.6	6.4	0.7	2.3
Statistical discrepancy	10.1	31.5	63.5	23.0	29.6	5.5	−0.2	−0.5	−1.0
Balance on goods, services, and income	−176.5	−113.1	−69.7	−106.8	9.5	25.2	8.5	10.0	6.9
Balance on current account	−220.6	−148.2	−92.1	−118.0	3.7	18.4	2.4	5.4	2.8

NOTE: − denotes debits. Only selected items within each category are shown. 1. Revised. Source: U.S. Department of Commerce, Bureau of Economic Analysis, Survey of Current Business, April 1998. Web: www.bea.doc.gov.

Gross Domestic Product or Expenditure[1]
(in billions of dollars)

Item	1998	1997	1996	1995	1994	1990	1980	1970
Gross domestic product	$8,508.9	$8,110.9	$7,636.0	$7,245.8	$6,931.4	$5,513.8	$2,708.0	$1,010.7
GDP in chained (1992) dollars	7,549.9	7,269.8	6,928.4	6,739.0	6,604.2	6,138.7	4,611.9	3,388.2
Personal consumption expenditures	5,806.0	5,493.7	5,207.6	4,924.3	4,698.7	3,742.6	1,748.1	646.5
Durable goods	723.5	673.0	634.5	606.4	580.9	465.9	212.5	85.3
Nondurable goods	1,662.0	1,600.6	1,534.7	1,486.1	1,429.7	1,217.7	682.9	270.4
Services	3,420.5	3,220.1	3,038.4	2,831.8	2,688.1	2,059.0	852.7	290.8
Gross private domestic investment	1,369.2	1,256.0	1,116.5	1,065.3	1,014.4	802.6	467.6	150.3
Residential	369.4	327.9	309.2	289.8	287.7	215.7	123.3	41.4
Nonresidential	939.4	860.7	781.4	738.5	667.2	587.0	353.8	106.7
Change in business inventories	60.4	67.4	25.9	37.0	59.5	0	−9.5	2.3
Net export of goods and services	−154.1	−93.4	−94.8	−102.3	−96.4	−74.4	−14.7	1.2
Government purchases	1,487.8	1,454.6	1,406.7	1,358.5	1,314.7	1,042.9	507.1	212.7
Federal	520.7	520.2	520.0	516.7	516.3	424.9	209.1	100.1
State and local	967.1	934.4	886.7	841.7	798.4	618.0	298.0	112.6

1. Current dollars except as noted. Source: U.S. Bureau of Economic Analysis, Survey of Current Business, February 1999. Web: www.bea.doc.gov.

Per Capita Consumption of Principal Foods[1]

Food	1996	1994	1992	1990	Food	1996	1994	1992	1990
Red meat[2]	112.8	114.8	114.1	112.3	Fruits[4]	283.2	277.9	261.0	266.8
Poultry[2]	64.4	63.3	60.8	56.3	Peanuts	5.7	5.8	6.2	6.0
Fish and shellfish[2]	14.7	15.1	14.7	15.0	Vegetables	412.5	404.7	394.8	386.4
Eggs	30.5	30.6	30.3	30.2	Sugar	66.2	65.0	64.6	64.4
Fluid milk and cream[3]	223.6	226.3	230.5	233.4	Corn sweeteners[5]	84.5	81.0	76.2	71.1
Ice cream	15.9	16.1	16.3	15.8	Flour and cereal products	198.5	194.1	186.2	182.0
Cheese	27.7	26.8	26.0	24.8	Soft drinks (gal)	52.0	51.3	48.5	46.3
Butter	4.3	4.8	4.4	4.4	Coffee bean equivalent	9.0	8.2	10.0	10.3
Margarine	11.1	11.4	10.6	9.7	Cocoa (chocolate liquor				
Total fats and oils[3]	65.8	68.6	67.4	62.8	equivalent)	n.a.	3.9	4.6	4.3

NOTE: n.a. = not available. 1. Data are on a retail-weight basis unless otherwise indicated. Final consumer products from a combination of primary food groups, such as bakery products, are measured and reported in the form of their primary ingredients, such as flour, shortening, and eggs. 2. Boneless, trimmed equivalent. 3. Fat-content basis. 4. Excludes wine grapes. 5. Dry basis. *Source:* U.S. Department of Agriculture, Economic Research Service. Web: www.usda.gov.

Consumer Price Index for All Urban Consumers
(1982–84 = 100)

Group	July 1999	March 1998	March 1997	March 1996	Group	July 1999	March 1998	March 1997	March 1996
All items	166.7	158.8	160.0	155.7	Housing, total	164.7	155.6	155.9	151.7
Food	163.8	158.9	156.6	151.6	Rent	177.5	169.9	165.1	160.6
Alcoholic beverages	169.9	163.8	162.1	157.4	Gas and electricity	124.0	118.8	123.4	118.2
Men's and boys' apparel	128.3	132.7	129.2	129.1	Fuel oil, coal, bottled gas	87.5	94.5	105.5	99.3
Women's and girls' apparel	116.1	126.0	130.1	129.9	House operation[1]	126.8	124.5	125.4	124.6
					Transportation	144.7	139.9	144.9	141.2
Footwear	125.2	127.7	127.0	128.1	Medical care	251.1	239.3	233.4	226.6
Tobacco products	356.0	254.0	238.2	230.8	Personal care	161.1	155.6	151.8	149.4

1. Combines house furnishings and operation. *Source:* U.S. Department of Labor, Bureau of Labor Statistics, *Monthly Labor Review,* May 1998. Web: stats.bls.gov.

Producer Price Indexes by Major Commodity Groups
(1982 = 100)

Commodity	1998	1997	1995	1990	1985	1980	1975	1970
All commodities	**124.4**	**126.7**	**124.7**	**116.3**	**103.2**	**89.8**	**58.4**	**38.1**
Farm products	104.6	110.1	107.4	112.2	95.1	102.9	77.0	45.8
Processed foods and feeds	131.6	132.9	127.0	121.9	103.5	95.9	72.6	44.6
Textile products and apparel	126.7	122.5	120.8	114.9	102.9	89.7	67.4	52.4
Hides, skins, and leather products	n.a.	153.5	153.7	141.7	108.9	94.7	56.5	42.0
Fuels and related products and power	89.1	82.8	78.0	82.2	91.4	82.8	35.4	15.3
Chemicals and allied products	n.a.	143.5	142.5	123.6	103.7	89.0	62.0	35.0
Rubber and plastic products	n.a.	123.1	124.3	113.6	101.9	90.1	62.2	44.9
Lumber and wood products	179.5	181.9	178.1	129.7	106.6	101.5	62.1	39.9
Pulp, paper, and allied products	171.7	171.2	172.2	141.3	113.3	86.3	59.0	37.5
Metals and metal products	122.5	130.6	134.5	123.0	104.4	95.0	61.5	38.7
Machinery and equipment	147.2	125.4	126.6	120.7	107.2	86.0	57.9	40.0
Furniture and household durables	148.4	130.7	128.2	119.1	107.1	90.7	67.5	51.9
Nonmetallic mineral products	n.a.	133.7	129.0	114.7	108.6	88.4	54.4	35.3
Transportation equipment	141.2	141.5	139.7	121.5	107.9	82.9	56.7	41.9

NOTE: n.a. = not available. *Source:* U.S. Department of Labor, Bureau of Labor Statistics, Division of Industrial Prices and Price Indexes. Web: stats.bls.gov

Imports and Exports of Leading Commodities
by Principal SITC Groupings (in millions of dollars)

Item	Cumulative 1998 Exports	Cumulative 1998 Imports	Cumulative 1997 Exports	Cumulative 1997 Imports
Selected commodities[1]				
ADP equipment; office machines	$40,745	$76,846	$43,698	$74,993
Airplanes and airplane parts	50,284	12,638	38,818	9,474
Alcoholic beverages, distilled	385	2,295	385	2,186
Aluminum	3,599	5,962	3,768	5,558
Animal feeds	4,050	606	4,621	648
Artwork/antiques	1,149	3,977	1,120	3,587
Basketware, etc.	2,583	3,835	2,494	3,364
Cereal flour	1,272	1,460	1,241	1,328

Item	Cumulative 1998		Cumulative 1997	
	Exports	Imports	Exports	Imports
Chemicals	$ 68,040	$ 54,621	$ 69,483	$ 50,348
Cigarettes and tobacco	5,625	883	5,965	1,204
Clothing	8,508	53,743	8,396	48,408
Coal	3,191	726	3,586	655
Coffee	10	3,063	7	3,575
Copper	1,276	3,063	1,441	3,254
Cork, wood, lumber	4,093	7,625	5,146	8,179
Corn	4,617	142	5,426	103
Cotton, raw, and linters	2,563	19	2,716	20
Crude fertilizers	1,599	1,298	1,621	1,334
Crude oil	670	37,534	1,040	54,226
Fish and preparations	2,170	8,105	2,624	7,687
Footwear	720	13,879	800	14,026
Furniture and bedding	4,408	13,338	3,942	11,144
Gem diamonds	124	8,489	108	7,595
Glass	1,998	1,774	2,125	1,750
Glassware	714	1,607	813	1,553
Gold, nonmonetary	5,393	3,571	5,673	3,035
Hides and skins	1,126	110	1,503	130
Iron and steel mill production	5,475	17,161	5,637	14,285
Jewelry	761	5,273	729	4,588
Lighting, plumbing	1,406	3,391	1,535	2,944
Liquefied propane/butane	204	931	298	1,158
Live animals	678	1,718	685	1,655
Machinery	156,611	167,198	158,504	159,799
Meat and preparations	6,411	2,847	6,885	2,656
Metal manufactures, n.e.s.	10,657	13,505	10,309	12,242
Metal ores; scrap	3,592	4,101	4,662	4,156
Mineral fuels, other	2,609	1,132	3,355	1,864
Natural gas	243	5,338	275	5,477
Nickel	365	894	347	1,144
Oils/fats, vegetable	1,825	1,324	1,398	1,381
Optical goods	1,907	2,727	1,697	2,493
Paper and paperboard, printed matter, and pulp	18,016	18,311	18,756	17,207
Petroleum preparations	2,855	10,945	3,899	13,904
Photographic equipment	3,477	5,656	3,865	5,759
Plastic articles, n.e.s.	5,548	6,140	5,092	5,676
Platinum	392	3,057	437	1,973
Pottery	103	1,719	101	1,683
Records/magnetic media	6,053	4,387	6,815	4,137
Rice	1,208	182	933	217
Rubber articles, n.e.s.	1,290	1,645	1,256	1,553
Rubber tires and tubes	2,549	4,095	2,394	3,417
Scientific instruments	24,143	15,505	24,039	13,969
Ships, boats	1,716	1,134	1,366	875
Silver and bullion	624	662	641	472
Soybeans	4,878	54	7,479	86
Spacecraft	1,102	142	994	239
Sugar	3	709	3	956
Televisions, VCRs, etc.	23,401	42,462	24,093	36,771
Textile yarn, fabric	8,973	12,890	8,975	11,951
Toys/games/sporting goods	3,342	18,691	3,827	17,374
Travel goods	304	3,944	330	3,841
Vegetables and fruits	7,321	8,372	7,472	7,752
Vehicles	53,398	121,310	55,669	112,926
Watches/clocks/parts	311	3,207	310	2,838
Wheat	3,712	284	4,196	359
Wood manufactures	1,692	5,634	1,958	4,668
Total, selected categories:				
Manufactured goods[1]	551,368	792,422	550,529	728,928
Agricultural commodities[1]	50,608	35,741	55,639	35,164
Mineral fuels[1]	9,957	57,646	12,682	78,277
Total[2]	682,977	913,828	689,182	870,671

NOTES: SITC = Standard International Trade Classification; n.e.s. = not elsewhere specified. 1. Domestic exports. 2. Total exports (domestic and foreign). Details may not equal totals due to rounding. Data not seasonally adjusted. *Source:* U.S. Bureau of the Census, Foreign Trade Division. Web: http://www.census.gov/foreign-trade/Press-Release/current_press_release/exh15.txt.

Agricultural Output by State, 1998 Crops

State	Corn (1,000 bu)	Wheat (1,000 bu)	Cotton[2] (1,000 ba[3])	Potatoes (1,000 cwt)	Tobacco (1,000 lb)	Cattle (1,000 head)	Swine (1,000 head)
Alabama	12,600	3,570	570	780		229	91
Arizona	5,250	15,840	604	2,284		463	9
Arkansas	21,500	45,900	1,220			21	
California	41,600	38,550	1,495	13,703		1,019	2,212
Colorado	155,150	103,710		28,230		2,417	41
Connecticut					4,573	(1)	(1)
Delaware	15,500	3,723		1,012		36 [4]	279 [4]
Florida	3,410	559	68	8,798	17,102	51	141
Georgia	22,525	10,320	1,550		92,400	359	297
Hawaii						18	37
Idaho	7,800	102,410		139,650		743	
Illinois	1,473,450	57,600		1,421		1,019	9,197
Indiana	760,350	35,750		1,600	17,000	43	6,327
Iowa	1,769,000	1,280		306		932	28,906
Kansas	418,950	494,900	13			7,541	
Kentucky	135,700	24,750			460,910	50	2,530
Louisiana	43,740	3,960	645			26	38
Maine		10,750	1,450	18,060		(1)	(1)
Maryland	43,600			1,081	9,100	(4)	(4)
Massachusetts				660	1,764	(1)	(1)
Michigan	227,550	30,780		14,725		395	
Minnesota	1,032,750	80,444		21,170		685	7,940
Mississippi	43,000	6,750					
Missouri	285,000	57,500	350	1,892	6,300	76	3,927
Montana	2,070	168,790		3,180		22	28
Nebraska	1,239,750	82,800		9,781		7,300	6,286
Nevada				2,726		1	
New Hampshire		1,240				(1)	(1)
New Jersey	9,016	2,288		702		24	96
New Mexico	14,025	7,950	101	3,204		21	3
New York	66,120	7,020	1,005	7,290		87	53
North Carolina	53,900	27,880		3,430	566,890	162	9,786
North Dakota	88,275	310,650		28,670			72
Ohio	470,940	74,240		1,200	17,934	150	1,261
Oklahoma	28,600	198,900	140			35	4,119
Oregon	6,270	57,490		26,229		15	189
Pennsylvania	116,550	9,690		3,360	15,720	959	2,428
Rhode Island				147		(1)	(1)
South Carolina	11,000	7,680	350		96,750		
South Dakota	429,550	120,884		1,248		249	4,452
Tennessee	59,520	15,170	545		117,969		
Texas	185,000	136,500	3,550	4,867		6,767	324
Utah	3,384	8,834		728			27
Vermont						(1)	(1)
Virginia	25,200	11,025	140	1,380	98,625	19	4,173
Washington	19,000	157,425		93,225		925	
West Virginia	2,720	456			2,380	14	11
Wisconsin	404,150	7,635		30,895	4,230	1,650	375
Wyoming	7,620	6,790		120		6	6
Total U.S.	9,761,085	2,550,383	13,796	477,754	1,529,647	35,465	101,029

1. The cattle and pig estimates for New England states have been aggregated. 2. Production ginned and to be ginned. 3. 480-lb net weight bales. 4. The cattle and pig totals for Maryland are included with those for Delaware. *Source:* U.S. Department of Agriculture, National Agricultural Statistics Service. Web: www.usda.gov/nass.

Farm Indexes
(1990–1992 = 100)

Year	Prices paid by farmers[1]	Prices rec'd by farmers[2]	Ratio[3]	Year	Prices paid by farmers[1]	Prices rec'd by farmers[2]	Ratio[3]
1975	47	73	155	1993	104	101	97
1980	75	98	137	1994	106	100	94
1985	86	91	106	1995	109	102	93
1990	99	104	105	1996	115	112	98
1991	100	100	99	1997	118	107	90
1992	101	98	97	1998	117	101	87

1. Commodities and services, interest, taxes, and wage rates. 2. All crops and livestock. 3. Ratio of index of prices received by farmers to index of prices paid by farmers. May not compute directly due to rounding. *Source:* U.S. Department of Agriculture, National Agricultural Statistics Service. Web: www.usda.gov/nass.

Farm Income
(in millions of dollars)

Year	Cash receipts from marketings Crops[1]	Livestock, livestock products	Government payments	Total cash income[2]	Year	Cash receipts from marketings Crops[1]	Livestock, livestock products	Government payments	Total cash income[2]
1930	$ 3,868	$ 5,187	—	$ 9,055	1985	74,293	69,822	$ 7,705	$ 157,854
1935	2,977	4,143	$ 573	7,693	1990	80,131	89,843	9,298	186,824
1940	3,469	4,913	723	9,105	1991	82,060	86,735	8,214	184,858
1945	9,655	12,008	742	22,405	1992	84,853	86,350	9,169	188,160
1950	12,356	16,105	283	28,764	1993	87,500	90,200	13,402	200,100
1955	13,523	15,967	229	29,842	1994	93,100	88,200	7,900	198,300
1960	15,023	18,989	703	34,958	1995	101,000	87,100	7,300	205,900
1965	17,479	21,886	2,463	42,215	1996	106,200	93,000	7,300	217,400
1970	20,977	29,532	3,717	54,768	1997	111,100	96,500	7,500	227,500
1975	45,813	43,089	807	90,707	1998	102,200	94,500	12,200	222,800
1980	71,746	67,991	1,285	143,295	1999[2]	96,900	93,700	16,600	221,200

1. Includes items not listed. 2. Forecast. *Source:* U.S. Department of Agriculture, Economic Research Service. Web: www.usda.gov.

Largest U.S. Businesses

Rank 1996	1997	1998	Company	Revenues ($ millions)	Rank 1996	1997	1998	Company	Revenues ($ millions)
1	1	1	General Motors Corp.	$161,315.0	28	36	36	Kroger	$28,203.3
1	2	2	Ford Motor Co.	144,416.0	48	46	37	Merck & Co. Inc.	26,898.2
4	4	3	Wal-Mart Stores, Inc.	139,208.0	15	19	38	Chevron Corp.	26,801.0
3	3	4	Exxon Corp.	100,697.0	35	43	39	Metropolitan Life Insurance	26,735.0
5	5	5	General Electric Co.	100,469.0					
6	6	6	Intl. Business Machines Corp.	81,667.0	43	38	40	Intel Corp.	26,273.0
					26	32	41	Lockheed Martin	26,266.0
20	21	7	Citigroup	76,431.0	32	39	42	Allstate Corp.	25,879.0
10	9	8	Philip Morris Cos. Inc.	57,813.0	34	41	43	United Technologies	25,715.0
36	11	9	Boeing Co.	56,154.0	—	—	44	Bank One Corp.	25,595.0
7	10	10	AT&T Corp.	53,588.0	41	48	45	GTE Corp.	25,473.0
38	47	11	BankAmerica Corp.	50,777.0	37	52	46	United Parcel Service	24,788.0
12	13	12	State Farm Insurance Cos.	48,113.9	42	55	47	USX	24,754.0
					65	50	48	Safeway	24,484.2
8	8	13	Mobil Corp.	47,678.0	49	53	49	Costco	24,269.9
16	14	14	Hewlett-Packard Co.	47,061.0	31	45	50	ConAgra	23,840.5
17	16	15	Sears Roebuck	41,322.0	39	49	51	Johnson & Johnson	23,657.0
14	15	16	E.I. du Pont de Nemours and Co.	39,130.0	53	56	52	BellSouth Corp.	23,123.0
					55	51	53	Walt Disney Co.	22,976.0
18	20	17	Procter & Gamble Co.	37,154.0	21	31	54	PepsiCo, Inc.	22,348.0
88/86	30	18	TIAA-CREF	35,889.1	—	79	55	Ingram Micro	22,034.0
30	24	19	Merrill Lynch and Co.	35,853.0	—	96	56	First Union Corp.	21,543.0
13	18	20	Prudential Ins. Co. of America	34,427.0	54	59	57	Cigna	21,437.0
					68	66	58	Caterpillar	20,977.0
22	23	21	Kmart Corp.	33,674.0	—	—	59	McKesson HBOC	20,857.3
23	26	22	American International Group	33,296.0	46	63	60	Loews	20,713.0
25	27	23	Chase Manhattan Corp.	32,379.0	67	71	61	Aetna	20,604.1
11	12	24	Texaco	31,707.0	—	—	62	Wells Fargo	20,482.0
99	28	25	Bell Atlantic Corp.	31,565.9	51	72	63	Xerox Corp.	20,019.0
29	33	26	Federal Natl. Mortgage Assoc. (Fannie Mae)	31,498.8	57	61	64	Sara Lee	20,011.0
					—	85	65	PG&E Corp.	19,942.0
94	57	27	Enron	31,260.0	80	77	66	Lehman Brothers Holdings	19,894.0
60	42	28	Compaq Computer Corp.	31,169.0	56	65	67	American Stores	19,866.7
—	35	29	Morgan Stanley Dean Witter Discover	31,131.0	63	67	68	New York Life Insurance	19,848.9
27	34	30	Dayton Hudson	30,951.0	—	100	69	Raytheon	19,530.0
33	25	31	J.C. Penney	30,678.0	44	58	70	International Paper	19,500.0
50	44	32	Home Depot	30,219.0	61	70	71	AMR Corp.	19,205.0
—	37	33	Lucent Technologies Inc.	30,147.0	64	73	72	American Express Co.	19,132.0
					58	68	73	Coca-Cola Co.	18,813.0
24	29	34	Motorola Inc.	29,398.0	47	69	74	Columbia/HCA Healthcare	18,681.0
85	40	35	SBC Communications Inc.	28,777.0	45	60	75	Dow Chemical	18,441.0
					73	74	76	J.P. Morgan & Co.	18,425.0

1996	Rank 1997	1998	Company	Revenues ($ millions)	1996	Rank 1997	1998	Company	Revenues ($ millions)
76	78	77	Bristol-Myers Squibb Co.	$18,283.6	82	90	88	Sprint	$17,134.3
—	—	78	Dell Computer Corp.	18,243.0	66	76	89	RJR Nabisco Holdings	17,037.0
—	95	79	Federal Home Loan Mortgage Corp. (Freddie Mac)	18,048.0	—	—	90	Electronic Data Systems	16,891.0
					93	99	91	Archer Daniels Midland	16,108.6
					89	92	92	Albertson's	16,005.1
59	62	80	MCI WorldCom	17,678.0	—	—	93	Cardinal Health	15,918.1
—	81	81	Duke Energy	17,610.0	—	—	94	FDX	15,872.8
71	75	82	UAL	17,561.0	75	83	95	Federated Department Stores	15,833.0
—	—	83	Republic Industries	17,487.3	—	—	96	Alcoa	15,489.4
—	—	84	United HealthCare	17,355.0	92	94	97	Sysco	15,327.5
—	—	85	Halliburton	17,353.1	—	—	98	Walgreen	15,307.0
70	80	86	Supervalu	17,201.4	—	—	99	CVS	15,273.6
77	82	87	Ameritech Corp.	17,154.0	84	93	100	AlliedSignal	15,128.0

Note: Dash indicates the company was not in the top 100 for the year noted. *Source:* 1999 Fortune 500, © 1999 Time, Inc. All rights reserved. For more detailed information, visit *Fortune* on the Web, www.fortune.com/fortune500.

World's Largest Banks[1]
(in millions of U.S. dollars)

Rank	Bank	Assets	Rank	Bank	Assets
1	Bank of Tokyo-Mitsubishi Ltd., Japan	$691,920.3	29	JP Morgan & Co., Inc., New York, U.S.	$262,159.0
2	Deutsche Bank AG, Frankfurt, Ger.	580,069.0	30	BankAmerica Corp., San Francisco, U.S.	260,159.0
3	Sumitomo Bank Ltd., Osaka, Japan	483,730.4	31	Lloyds TSB Group Inc., London, U.K.	260,042.8
4	Credit Suisse Group, Zurich, Switz.	473,829.8	32	Sumitomo Trust & Banking Co. Ltd., Osaka, Japan	254,189.7
5	HSBC Holdings, Plc., London, U.K.	471,037.8			
6	Dai-Ichi Kangyo Bank Ltd., Tokyo, Japan	433,102.9	33	Credit Lyonnais, Paris, France	250,149.9
7	Sanwa Bank Ltd., Osaka, Japan	427,979.6	34	Bayerische Vereinsbank AG, Munich, Ger.	249,830.6
8	Credit Agricole Mutuel, Paris, France	419,763.2	35	Abbey National, Plc., London, U.K.	248,040.3
9	Fuji Bank Ltd., Tokyo, Japan	414,173.0	36	Compagnie Financiere de Paribas, Paris, France	245,061.1
10	ABN-AMRO Bank, N.V., Amsterdam, Neth.	412,771.9			
11	Societe Generale, Paris, France	410,842.2	37	Mitsui Trust & Banking Co., Ltd., Tokyo, Japan	241,916.0
12	Sakura Bank Ltd., Tokyo, Japan	399,491.5			
13	Union Bank of Switzerland, Zurich, Switz.	395,086.5	38	Bayerische Landesbank Girozentrale, Munich, Ger.	241,714.0
14	Norin Chunkin Bank, Tokyo, Japan	392,553.5			
15	Barclays Bank Plc., London, U.K.	385,950.3	39	Asahi Bank Ltd., Tokyo, Japan	219,939.4
16	Dresdner Bank, Frankfurt, Ger.	371,371.0	40	Halifax Plc., Leeds, U.K.	215,625.4
17	Industrial Bank of Japan Ltd., Tokyo, Japan	369,954.0	41	Rabobank Group, Utrecht, Neth.	208,739.6
			42	Deutsche Genossenschaftsbank, Frankfurt, Ger.	207,768.9
18	Chase Manhattan Corp., New York, U.S.	365,521.0			
19	Banque Nationale de Paris, France	339,648.2	43	Bayerische Hypotheken-und Wechsel- Bank AG, Munich, Ger.	203,567.0
20	Westdeutsche Landesbank Girozentrale, Duesseldorf, Ger.	335,816.2			
			44	Dexia Belgium, Brussels, Belgium	202,958.5
21	Citicorp, New York, U.S.	310,897.0	45	Bankgesellschaft Berlin AG, Berlin, Ger.	197,364.8
22	ING Bank, Amsterdam, Neth.	307,559.6	46	Long Term Credit Bank of Japan Ltd., Tokyo, Japan	188,497.4
23	NatWest Group, London, U.K.	304,941.8			
24	Swiss Bank Corp., Basel, Switz.	300,259.1	47	Royal Bank of Canada, Toronto, Can.	171,218.5
25	Commerzbank, Frankfurt, Ger.	286,946.6	48	Grupo Santander, Spain	170,927.0
26	Mitsubishi Trust & Banking Corp., Tokyo, Japan	269,524.4	49	Canadian Imperial Bank of Commerce, Toronto, Can.	166,472.4
27	NationsBank Corp., Charlotte, N.C., U.S.	264,562.0	50	Yasuda Trust & Banking Co., Ltd., Tokyo, Japan	165,784.2
28	Tokai Bank Ltd., Nagoya, Japan	262,423.7			

1. Based on total assets held on December 31, 1997. *Source: American Banker,* August 6, 1998. Reprinted with permission. Copyright © American Banker/Bond Buyer.

New Business Concerns and Business Failures

Incorporations and failures	1997	1996	1995	1994	1993	1992	1991	1990	1985	1980
New incorporations (1,000)	n.a.	n.a.	768	741	707	667	629	647	664	534
Failures, number (1,000)	83.4	71.9	71.1	71.6	86.1	97.1	88.1	60.7	57.1	11.7
Failure rate per 10,000 concerns	88	80	82	86	96	110	107	74	115	42

NOTE: Data are most recent available. *Sources:* U.S. Bureau of Economic Analysis and Dun & Bradstreet Corporation. From *Statistical Abstract of the United States 1998.* Web: www.census.gov/stat_abstract.

Estimated Annual Retail and Wholesale Sales by Kind of Business
(in millions of dollars)

Kind of business	1997	1995	Kind of business	1997	1995
Retail sales, total	$2,566,209	$2,329,310	Metals and minerals except	$107,887	$100,514
Building materials stores	116,106	98,191	petroleum		
Automotive dealers	625,682	556,708	Electrical goods	201,156	169,776
Furniture, home furnishings, and	146,679	130,348	Hardware, plumbing, and heating	75,970	67,622
equipment stores			equipment		
General merchandise stores	331,496	297,962	Machinery, equipment, and	206,441	182,748
Food stores	429,805	407,392	supplies		
Gasoline service stations	158,693	149,555	Miscellaneous durable goods	135,172	143,334
Apparel and accessory stores	117,826	110,936	Nondurable goods, total	1,188,796	1,086,535
Eating and drinking places	236,159	222,081	Paper and paper products	84,813	81,976
Drug and proprietary stores	98,182	84,705	Drugs, drug proprietaries, and	113,641	95,039
Liquor stores	23,964	21,700	druggists' sundries		
Merchant wholesale sales, total	2,500,109	2,265,732	Apparel, piece goods, and notions	82,805	70,583
Durable goods, total	1,311,313	1,179,197	Groceries and related products	327,538	304,695
Motor vehicles and automotive	216,561	202,556	Farm-product raw materials	125,302	113,691
parts and supplies			Chemical and allied products	55,673	47,774
Furniture and home furnishings	40,929	40,861	Petroleum and petroleum	166,475	150,560
Lumber and other construction	90,161	77,139	products		
materials			Beer, wine, and distilled alcoholic	54,955	54,060
Professional and commercial	237,036	194,647	beverages		
equipment and supplies			Miscellaneous nondurable goods	177,594	168,157

Source: U.S. Bureau of the Census. Web: www.census.gov.

Leading Advertising Agencies
(ranked by revenues in thousands of dollars)

Rank 1998	Rank 1997	Agency	1998 revenues	Percent change	1998 billings	Percent change
1	1	McCann-Erickson World Group	$1,950,944	13.0%	$16,370,370	22.9%
2	3	BBDO Worldwide	1,868,314	11.5	14,706,635	14.0
3	2	DDB Needham Worldwide	1,780,101	11.0	13,956,250	11.9
4	5	J. Walter Thompson	1,233,000	5.2	8,458,000	5.6
5	4	Young & Rubicam	1,209,609	10.9	11,848,076	15.7
6	9	Euro RSCG Worldwide	1,151,624	11.4	9,483,353	21.6
7	6	Ogilvy & Mather Worldwide	1,118,000	8.4	9,748,000	11.8
8	7	Ammirati Puris Lintas Worldwide	1,113,871	8.4	8,357,042	9.4
9	8	Grey Advertising	1,002,300	5.0	6,685,500[1]	5.0
10	10	Leo Burnett Co.	949,800	7.2	6,810,000	7.1
11	13	TBWA	896,953	12.0	6,301,774	12.3
12	12	D'Arcy Masius Benton & Bowles	616,700	1.5	5,794,318	0.2
13	11	Foote, Cone & Belding	576,000[2]	2.9	5,905,532	2.9
14	14	The Lowe Group	553,651	10.4	4,007,212	12.6
15	16	Saatchi & Saatchi	516,000[2]	5.9	n.a.	n.a.

NOTE: n.a. = not available. 1. Capitalized figure. 2. Adweek Estimate. Source: Adweek, Top U.S.-Based Agency Networks, April 19, 1999, edition. © 1999 Adweek. Used with permission of Adweek.

Passenger Car Production by Make

Companies and makes	1997	1995	1990	1985	1980	1975	1970
American Motors Corp.	—	—	—	109,919	164,725	323,704	276,127
Chrysler Corp.							
Plymouth	155,563	129,571	212,354	369,487	293,342	443,550	699,031
Dodge	241,058	331,253	361,769	482,388	263,169	354,482	405,699
Chrysler	44,096	121,022	136,339	414,193	82,463	102,940	158,614
Imperial	—	—	16,280	—	—	1,930	10,111
Total	**440,717**	**576,846**	**726,742**	**1,266,068**	**638,974**	**902,902**	**1,273,455**
Ford Motor Corp.							
Ford	913,440	1,012,818	933,466	1,098,627	929,627	1,301,414	1,647,918
Mercury	229,866	225,308	221,436	374,446	324,528	405,104	310,463
Lincoln	146,482	157,584	222,449	163,077	52,793	101,520	58,771
Total	**1,289,788**	**1,395,710**	**1,377,351**	**1,636,150**	**1,306,948**	**1,808,038**	**2,017,152**
General Motors Corp.							
Chevrolet	650,820	665,955	1,025,379	1,691,254	1,737,336	1,687,091	1,504,614
Pontiac	600,506	574,455	649,255	702,617	556,429	523,469	422,212
Oldsmobile	277,086	391,216	418,742	1,168,982	783,225	654,342	439,632
Buick	287,655	393,879	405,123	1,001,461	783,575	535,820	459,931

Companies and makes	1997	1995	1990	1985	1980	1975	1970
Cadillac	169,912	186,113	252,540	322,765	203,991	278,404	152,859
Saturn	271,612	301,540	4,245	—	—	—	—
Toyota/Cavalier	12,033	1,978	—	—	—	—	—
Total	**2,269,624**	**2,515,136**	**2,755,284**	**4,887,079**	**4,064,556**	**3,679,126**	**2,979,248**
Volkswagen of America	—	—	—	96,458	197,106	—	—
Honda	648,268	552,995	435,437	238,159	145,337	—	—
Nissan	279,510	333,234	95,844	43,810	—	—	—
Toyota	554,110	516,878	321,523	—	—	—	—
Mitsubishi[1]	184,675	218,161	148,379	—	—	—	—
Auto Alliance[2]	100,116	148,932	184,428	—	—	—	—
Subaru Legacy	102,180	80,669	32,461	—	—	—	—
BMW	58,293	11,872	—	—	—	—	—
Industry total [3]	**5,927,281**	**6,350,433**	**6,077,449**	**8,184,821**	**6,375,506**	**6,716,951**	**6,550,128**

1. Produces Mitsubishi and Chrysler/Dodge/Eagle vehicles. 2. Formerly listed as Mazda; includes Mazda MX-6 and 626 and Ford Probe. 3. Industry total may not be the sum of makes and companies listed due to timing of company reports. *Source:* American Automobile Manufacturers Association.

Life Insurance in Force
(in millions of dollars)

As of Dec. 31	Ordinary	Group	Industrial	Credit	Total
1900	$ 6,124	—	$ 1,449	—	$ 7,573
1915	16,650	$ 100	4,279	—	21,029
1930	78,576	9,801	17,963	$ 73	106,413
1945	101,550	22,172	27,675	365	151,762
1950	149,116	47,793	33,415	3,844	234,168
1955	216,812	101,345	39,682	14,493	372,332
1960	341,881	175,903	39,563	29,101	586,448
1965	499,638	308,078	39,818	53,020	900,554
1970	734,730	551,357	38,644	77,392	1,402,123
1975	1,083,421	904,695	39,423	112,032	2,139,571
1980	1,760,474	1,579,355	35,994	165,215	3,541,038
1985	3,247,289	2,561,595	28,250	215,973	6,053,107
1990	5,366,982	3,753,506	24,071	248,038	9,392,597
1995	6,872,252	4,604,856	18,134	201,083	11,696,325
1998	8,505,894	5,735,273	17,365	212,917	14,471,449

Source: American Council of Life Insurance.

Tonnage Handled by Principal U.S. Ports
Top 50 Ports Ranked by Total Tons

1997 rank	1996 rank	Port	1997 tonnage	1997 rank	1996 rank	Port	1997 tonnage
1	1	Port of South Louisiana	183,628,353	26	29	Freeport, Tex.	26,280,731
2	2	Houston, Tex.	166,456,278	27	29	Huntington, W. Va.	25,175,459
3	3	New York, N.Y. & N.J.	135,266,431	28	25	Chicago, Ill.	24,867,996
4	4	New Orleans, La.	89,441,772	29	27	Paulsboro, N.J.	24,391,944
5	6	Corpus Christi, Tex.	86,843,760	30	31	Richmond, Calif.	21,705,683
6	5	Baton Rouge, La.	84,023,102	31	47	Marcus Hook, Pa.	21,520,644
7	7	Valdez, Alaska	73,647,151	32	33	Boston, Mass.	20,892,983
8	8	Port of Plaquemines, La.	63,607,222	33	25	Newport News, Va.	20,755,282
9	9	Long Beach, Calif.	57,255,301	34	32	Tacoma, Wash.	20,683,326
10	10	Texas City, Tex.	56,645,675	35	34	Port Everglades, Fla.	19,924,784
11	13	Tampa, Fla.	55,333,607	36	39	Jacksonville, Fla.	18,186,104
12	12	Pittsburgh, Pa.	51,662,378	37	34	Detroit, Mich.	18,135,326
13	15	Lake Charles, La.	51,278,579	38	40	Cleveland, Ohio	18,113,321
14	12	Mobile, Ala.	49,120,007	39	34	Memphis, Tenn.	18,015,173
15	21	Beaumont, Tex.	48,665,380	40	36	Savannah, Ga.	17,929,269
16	14	Norfolk Harbor, Va.	46,322,012	41	51	Charleston, S.C.	17,874,161
17	18	Philadelphia, Pa.	44,967,869	42	38	Indiana Harbor, Ind.	16,523,799
18	19	Duluth-Superior, Minn./Wis.	41,928,885	43	42	Portland, Maine	16,333,742
19	16	Los Angeles, Calif.	41,774,252	44	41	Lorain, Ohio	15,954,569
20	17	Baltimore, Md.	40,028,849	45	45	Toledo, Ohio	14,421,587
21	20	Port Arthur, Tex.	37,318,229	46	43	San Juan, P.R.	14,067,151
22	22	St. Louis, Mo./Ill.	31,287,584	47	41	Anacortes, Wash.	13,903,514
23	24	Pascagoula, Miss.	31,270,055	48	52	Two Harbors, Minn.	13,507,844
24	23	Portland, Ore.	29,560,776	49	46	Cincinnati, Ohio	12,878,606
25	30	Seattle, Wash.	26,564,230	50	48	Honolulu, Hawaii	12,703,903

Source: U.S. Department of the Army, Corps of Engineers.

Stock Exchanges

The recent announcement that the Nasdaq stock exchange is expanding its trading hours shows just how much stock trading has changed in recent years. By making it possible for trades to execute as late as 9:00 p.m., the exchange hopes to capitalize on the trend of do-it-yourself traders who prefer to transact their own stock trades rather than go through brokers. It's also a step closer to the day when investors can trade at any time, day or night, since there's always bound to be an exchange open, or about to open, somewhere in the world.

The move toward expanded hours is also another way in which the Nasdaq seeks to differentiate itself from the more tradition-bound, and venerable, New York Stock Exchange (NYSE). Analysts often refer to the Nasdaq as "technology-laden" and occasionally as the "virtual stock market" since many of the companies listed on the Nasdaq exchange are high-tech firms, including Microsoft and Intel, and unlike the NYSE, the Nasdaq has no physical trading floor, conducting its business through a vast network of supercomputers.

One of the reasons that the Nasdaq seems to attract high-tech companies is that its virtual trading

floor appeals to the technically savvy. Another is that many high-tech firms are startups and simply lack the financial wherewithal to be listed on the NYSE. Because of the more stringent thresholds for NYSE listing, the companies that have what it takes to be listed tend to be more established, or blue-chip companies. They tend to have been around for decades, to be large and/or diversified enough to weather market fluctuations, and they tend to pay dividends to stockholders, making them preferable to conservative investors who expect predictable earnings reports and yearly dividends.

Nasdaq firms are typically newer, and many, particularly Internet companies like Amazon.com, have never turned a profit. But investors buy up their stocks believing that the inherent value of the firm will increase over time as its market potential is realized. Stocks on Nasdaq are much more volatile than those on NYSE, and large price swings are commonplace. Few firms listed on Nasdaq pay dividends, preferring to pour earnings back into the company to fund new initiatives.

Here is a summary of benchmarks comparing NYSE and Nasdaq.

NYSE vs. Nasdaq

Benchmark	NYSE	Nasdaq	Benchmark	NYSE	Nasdaq
Listing Require-ments			*or*		
			Shareholders		400
Shareholders	2,200		Net tangible assets		$18,000,000
Avg. monthly trading volume	100,000		Operating history		2 years
			Other		
or			Initial public offerings, 1998	73	287
Shareholders	500	400			
Avg. monthly trading volume	1,000,000	*no requirement*	Share volume, 1998	202,040,229,000	169,513,526,000
Net tangible assets	$40,000,000	$6,000,000	Number of companies listed	3,114	5,068
Pretax income[1]	$2,500,000	$1,000,000	Average price per share, Dec. 1998	$41.84	$31.30
Market value of public float	$40,000,000	$8,000,000			

1. NYSE requires that company has had pretax income of $2 million for each of two preceding years and $2.5 million in the most recent year, while Nasdaq requires that the company has had $1 million of pretax income in the most recent fiscal year *or* in two of the last three fiscal years. Alternatively, the NYSE may allow a company with an aggregate pretax income for three years of $6.5 million to be listed, provided the most recent year's pretax income is at least $4.5 million and all three most recent years are profitable.

Top Stocks by Market Value

Rank 1998	Company name	Shares outstanding (millions)	Market value (millions)	Rank 1998	Company name	Shares outstanding (millions)	Market value (millions)
1	General Electric Co.	3,714	$379,045	15	Johnson & Johnson	1,535	$128,733
2	Microsoft Corp.	2,500	345,825	16	Schering-Plough Corp.	2,030	112,131
3	Coca-Cola Co.	3,455	231,052	17	American International Group, Inc.	1,139	110,021
4	Merck & Co., Inc.	1,484	219,172				
5	Exxon Corp.	2,983	218,129	18	SBC Communications Inc.	1,983	106,342
6	Intel Corp.	3,315	197,881	19	BankAmerica Corp.	1,749	105,177
7	Wal-Mart Stores, Inc.	2,300	187,308	20	Berkshire Hathaway Inc.	1,448	101,326
8	Int'l Business Machines	980	181,090	21	Eli Lilly and Co.	1,123	99,816
9	Pfizer Inc.	1,379	173,019	22	Dell Computer Corp.	2,543	93,112
10	Philip Morris Co. Inc.	2,806	150,119	23	Home Depot Inc.	1,511	92,450
11	Cisco Systems Inc.	1,563	146,554	24	Fannie Mae	1,129	83,553
12	Bristol-Myers Squibb Co.	1,093	146,204	25	Bell Atlantic Corp.	1,576	83,541
13	AT&T Corp.	1,818	136,825	26	American Home Products	1,422	80,076
14	MCI WorldCom, Inc.	1,840	131,548	27	Mobil Corp.	897	78,140

Rank 1998	Company name	Shares outstanding (millions)	Market value (millions)	Rank 1998	Company name	Shares outstanding (millions)	Market value (millions)
28	Abbott Laboratories	1,544	$75,661	40	Procter & Gamble Co.	694	$63,362
29	Ameritech Corp.	1,177	74,602	41	Walt Disney Co.	2,078	62,349
30	America Online, Inc.	458	73,257	42	E.I. du Pont de Nemours and Co.	1,147	60,854
31	Warner-Lambert Co.	961	72,281				
32	PepsiCo, Inc.	1,726	70,665	43	Bank One Corp.	1,181	60,317
33	Compaq Computer Corp.	1,681	70,516	44	First Union Corp.	990	60,227
34	Hewlett-Packard Co.	1,029	70,323	45	Chase Manhattan Corp.	881	59,974
35	Lucent Technologies Inc.	637	70,033	46	Ford Motor Co.	1,020	59,871
36	Time Warner, Inc.	1,096	68,011	47	Chevron Corp.	712	59,092
37	Wells Fargo & Co.	1,682	67,167	48	Citigroup Inc.	1,144	56,612
38	Gillette Co.	1,356	65,524	49	General Motors Corp.	757	54,147
39	GTE Corp.	988	64,231	50	McDonald's Corp.	677	51,841

NOTE: Based on closing prices on December 31, 1998. *Source:* New York Stock Exchange *1998 Fact Book*; Nasdaq-Amex Market Group; and SEC filings.

Most Active Stocks on NYSE

Rank 1998	1997	Company name	Share volume (in thousands)	Rank 1998	1997	Company name	Share volume (in thousands)
1	1	Compaq Computer Corp.	2,868,400	26	—	Merrill Lynch & Co.	657,900
2	2	Philip Morris Co. Inc.	1,457,400	27	28	Texas Instruments	642,500
3	—	Cendant Corp.	1,436,100	28	19	Ford Motor Co.	637,600
4	42	Lucent Technologies Inc.	1,167,100	29	—	Gillette Co.	635,100
5	3	AT&T Corp.	1,165,700	30	36	E.I. du Pont de Nemours and Co.	625,300
6	—	America Online	1,159,200				
7	7	General Electric Co.	1,031,800	31	12	Merck & Co., Inc.	619,100
8	4	Micron Technology Inc.	911,000	32	22	CBS Corporation	616,700
9	6	Int'l Business Machines	905,900	33	—	Halliburton Co.	609,900
10	15	Boeing Co.	866,500	34	16	Motorola Inc.	598,800
11	5	PepsiCo, Inc.	852,100	35	—	EMC Corporation	596,600
12	38	Travelers Group Inc.	842,200	36	—	Citigroup Inc.	585,900
13	29	Pfizer Inc.	834,440	37	—	Home Depot Inc.	578,400
14	11	Telecomm Brasil Telebras	828,800	38	—	Amoco Corp.	576,800
15	20	Chase Manhattan Corp. (New)	793,200	39	—	Computer Associates Int'l	564,900
				40	—	Monsanto	564,600
16	—	Schlumberger Ltd.	782,100	41	31	Citicorp	564,500
17	49	BankAmerica Corp.	778,600	42	21	Bay Networks	561,300
18	17	Exxon Corp.	771,900	43	24	Fannie Mae	560,100
19	18	Chrysler	758,600	44	—	SBC Communications Inc.	559,600
20	—	Disney (Walt) & Co.	744,400	45	25	General Motors Corp.	544,200
21	8	Coca-Cola Co.	742,600	46	32	K Mart Corp.	542,000
22	14	Hewlett-Packard Co.	737,500	47	13	Seagate Technology	530,700
23	9	Wal-Mart Stores, Inc.	692,200	48	—	First Union Corp.	528,000
24	—	American Home Products	671,500	49	—	Royal Dutch Petroleum	517,300
25	—	Eli Lilly and Co.	670,900	50	23	Johnson & Johnson	506,700

NOTES: As of December 31, 1998. In case of stock splits, volume in old and new issues was combined. *Source:* New York Stock Exchange *1998 Fact Book*.

Dow for Dummies

Five Fundamental Facts about the Dow Jones Industrial Average

The Index Is Not Truly Industrial

Though its name would lead you to believe it is composed of only industrial companies, in fact the DJIA contains stocks across many "industries," not all of which are "industrial."

The industries represented include financial, food, technology, retail, heavy equipment, oil, chemical, pharmaceutical, consumer goods, and entertainment. Dow Jones also collects and reports data for two other sectors of the economy in its Transportation and Utilities indices.

The DJIA Represents Only 30 Stocks

To be chosen for inclusion in the index, a stock must be a leader in its industry and must be widely held by both individual and institutional investors (i.e., pension plans, mutual funds, etc.). Together, the 30 stocks in the average represent about 20% of the market value of all U.S. stocks, so although the DJIA is not the whole stock market, it is certainly representative of the stock market as a whole.

The DJIA Is Not Really an "Average"

A simple average is calculated by adding up a value for a number of items, then dividing by the number of items. The Dow reflects the value of stock prices, but a simple average cannot accurately reflect the value of stock prices.

Here's why. When stocks become pricey, companies routinely announce stock splits to make their stocks more appealing to individual investors.

For example, a company may have 100 shares outstanding priced at $100 per share, for a market value of $10,000. If the firm announces a 2-for-1 split, the price is cut in half, and the number of shares is doubled, so there would be 200 shares outstanding, priced at $50 per share. The market value is still $10,000, but the price point is now more attractive to smaller investors.

To take into account the changes in price associated with stock splits, the Dow Jones Industrial "Average" is adjusted to account for any stock splits in each of the included companies.

The Following 30 Companies Currently Comprise the Dow Industrials:

- AlliedSignal Inc.
- Aluminum Co. of America
- American Express Co.
- AT & T Corp.
- Boeing Co.
- Caterpillar Inc.
- Chevron Corp.
- Coca-Cola Co.
- DuPont Co.
- Eastman Kodak Co.
- Exxon Corp.
- General Electric Co.
- General Motors Corp.
- Goodyear Tire & Rubber Co.
- Hewlett-Packard Co.
- International Business Machines Corp.
- International Paper Co.
- J.P. Morgan & Co.
- Johnson & Johnson
- McDonald's Corp.
- Merck & Co.
- Minnesota Mining & Manufacturing Co.
- Philip Morris Cos.
- Procter & Gamble Co.
- Sears, Roebuck & Co.
- Travelers Group Inc.
- Union Carbide Corp.
- United Technologies Corp.
- Wal-Mart Stores Inc.
- Walt Disney Co.

Who Is Dow Jones?

Charles Dow and Edward Jones are two-thirds of the team that founded Dow Jones & Company in 1882. Charles Bergstresser was the "& Company," but by 1889 he was joined by 47 others as the company grew. They specialized in newsletters (the precursor to *The Wall Street Journal*) focusing on financial news. When Dow died in 1902, Clarence Barron, originally hired as a correspondent, purchased a controlling interest in the firm.

Dow Milestones

Date	Milestone	Close	Date	Milestone	Close
Nov. 14, 1972	1000	1003.16	Mar. 16, 1998	8700	8718.85
Dec. 11, 1985	1500	1511.70	Mar. 19, 1998	8800	8803.05
Jan. 8, 1987	2000	2002.25	Mar. 20, 1998	8900	8906.43
July 17, 1987	2500	2510.04	April 6, 1998	9000	9033.23
April 17, 1991	3000	3004.46	April 14, 1998	9100	9110.02
May 19, 1993	3500	3500.03	May 13, 1998	9200	9211.84
Feb. 23, 1995	4000	4003.33	July 16, 1998	9300	9328.19
June 16, 1995	4500	4510.79	Jan. 6, 1999	9400	9544.97
Nov. 21, 1995	5000	5023.55	Jan. 6, 1999	9500	9544.97
Feb. 8, 1996	5500	5539.45	Jan. 8, 1999	9600	9643.32
Oct. 14, 1996	6000	6010.00	Mar. 8, 1999	9700	9736.08
Nov. 25, 1996	6500	6547.79	Mar. 11, 1999	9800	9897.44
Feb. 13, 1997	7000	7022.44	Mar. 15, 1999	9900	9958.77
May 5, 1997	7100	7214.49	Mar. 29, 1999	10000	10006.78
May 5, 1997	7200	7214.49	Apr. 8, 1999	10100	10197.70
May 15, 1997	7300	7333.55	Apr. 12, 1999	10200	10339.51
June 6, 1997	7400	7435.78	Apr. 12, 1999	10300	10339.51
June 10, 1997	7500	7539.27	Apr. 14, 1999	10400	10411.66
June 12, 1997	7600	7711.47	Apr. 21, 1999	10500	10581.42
June 12, 1997	7700	7711.47	Apr. 22, 1999	10600	10727.18
July 3, 1997	7800	7895.81	Apr. 22, 1999	10700	10727.18
July 8, 1997	7900	7962.31	Apr. 27, 1999	10800	10831.71
July 16, 1997	8000	8038.88	May 3, 1999	10900	11014.69
July 24, 1997	8100	8116.93	May 3, 1999	11000	11014.69
July 30, 1997	8200	8254.89	May 13, 1999	11100	11107.19
Feb. 11, 1998	8300	8314.55	July 12, 1999	11200	11200.98
Feb. 18, 1998	8400	8451.06	Aug. 25,1999	11300	11326.04
Feb. 27, 1998	8500	8545.72			
Mar. 10, 1998	8600	8643.12			

Stock Ownership by Age and Income, 1989–1995

Age of family head and family income (constant 1995 dollars)	Families having direct or indirect stock holdings (percent)			Median value among families with holdings (thousands of constant 1995 dollars)			Stock holdings' share of group's financial assets (percent)		
	1989	1992	1995	1989	1992	1995	1989	1992	1995
All families	**31.6%**	**36.6%**	**40.3%**	**$10.4**	**$11.4**	**$14.5**	**28.6%**	**34.1%**	**41.5%**
Under 35 years old	22.3	28.4	36.7	3.7	3.8	5.1	20.4	25.2	31.6
35 to 44 years old	38.9	42.5	46.4	6.3	8.1	10.0	30.1	31.4	41.5
45 to 54 years old	41.8	46.2	48.9	16.1	16.3	25.6	36.2	41.1	44.5
55 to 64 years old	36.1	45.3	40.0	22.6	27.1	30.0	28.5	38.3	47.0
65 to 74 years old	26.7	30.0	34.2	24.9	17.9	34.0	26.4	31.6	36.2
75 years old and over	25.9	25.6	27.8	30.7	27.1	20.0	25.0	25.5	39.8
Less than $10,000	3.3	6.8	6.2	35.0	5.9	2.9	12.1	15.3	13.6
$10,000 to $24,999	13.0	18.7	23.2	7.4	4.3	6.0	12.0	15.3	28.1
$25,000 to $49,999	32.3	40.8	47.3	5.5	7.6	9.0	18.3	24.4	32.1
$50,000 to $99,999	52.4	63.4	67.3	10.4	15.2	23.4	23.5	34.5	43.2
$100,000 and more	81.8	78.5	81.1	55.2	75.4	97.7	36.6	40.7	47.3

NOTES: Constant dollar figures are based on consumer price index data published by U.S. Bureau of Labor Statistics. Families include one-person units. *Source: Statistical Abstract of the United States 1998.* Based on information from the Board of Governors of the Federal Reserve System, *Federal Reserve Bulletin*, January 1997 and unpublished revisions.

40 Richest Americans of All Time

According to the October 1998 issue of *American Heritage* magazine, published by Forbes Inc., the following table represents the forty wealthiest Americans of all time.

Name	Dates	Source of wealth	Original value of wealth	Today's value of wealth[1]
1. John D. Rockefeller	1839–1937	oil	$900 million	$189.6 billion
2. Andrew Carnegie	1835–1919	steel	$250 million	$100.5 billion
3. Cornelius Vanderbilt	1794–1877	shipping, railroads	$105 million	$95.9 billion
4. John Jacob Astor	1763–1848	real estate, fur trade	$20 million	$78 billion
5. William H. Gates III	1955–	software	$61.7 billion	$61.7 billion
6. Stephen Girard	1750–1831	shipping, real estate	$7.5 million	$55.6 billion
7. A.T. Stewart	1803–1876	retail, real estate	$50 million	$46.9 billion
8. Frederick Weyerhaeuser	1834–1914	lumber	$200 million	$43.2 billion
9. Jay Gould	1836–1892	railroads	$72 million	$42.1 billion
10. Marshall Field	1834–1906	department stores	$140 million	$40.7 billion
11. Sam Walton	1918–1992	retail	$28 billion	$37.4 billion
12. Henry Ford	1863–1947	automobiles	$1 billion	$36.1 billion
13. Warren Buffett	1930–	investing	$34.2 billion	$34.2 billion
14. Andrew W. Mellon	1855–1937	banking	$350 million	$32.3 billion
15. Richard B. Mellon	1858–1933	banking	$350 million	$32.3 billion
16. James G. Fair	1831–1894	mining	$45 million	$29.8 billion
17. William Weightman	1813–1904	chemicals	$80 million	$29.2 billion
18. Moses Taylor	1806–1882	banking	$40 million	$29.2 billion
19. Russell Sage	1816–1906	finance	$100 million	$29.1 billion
20. John Blair	1802–1899	railroads	$60 million	$28.9 billion
21. Cyrus Curtis	1850–1933	publishing	$174 million	$26.1 billion
22. Paul G. Allen	1953–	software	$25.4 billion	$25.4 billion
23. John Pierpont Morgan	1837–1913	finance	$119 million	$25 billion
24. Edward Henry Harriman	1848–1909	railroads	$100 million	$25 billion
25. Henry Huddleston Rogers	1840–1909	oil	$100 million	$25 billion
26. Oliver Hazard Payne	1839–1917	oil	$178 million	$24.6 billion
27. Henry Clay Frick	1849–1919	steel	$225 million	$22.4 billion
28. Collis Potter Huntington	1821–1900	railroads	$50 million	$22.3 billion
29. Peter A. Widener	1834–1915	streetcars	$100 million	$20.9 billion
30. Nicholas Longworth	1782–1863	real estate	$15 million	$20.3 billion
31. Philip Danforth Armour	1832–1901	meatpacking	$50 million	$20.2 billion
32. James C. Flood	1826–1889	mining	$30 million	$20 billion
33. Mark Hopkins	1813–1878	railroads	$20 million	$20 billion
34. Edward Clark	1811–1882	sewing machines	$25 million	$18.2 billion
35. Leland Stanford	1824–1893	railroads	$30 million	$18.1 billion
36. Hetty Green	1834–1916	investing	$100 million	$17.3 billion
37. James J. Hill	1838–1916	railroads	$100 million	$17.3 billion
38. William Rockefeller	1841–1922	oil	$150 million	$16.9 billion
39. Elias Hasket Derby	1739–1799	shipping	$800,000	$16.2 billion
40. Claus Spreckels	1828–1908	sugar	$50 million	$15.1 billion

1. The conversions were made using a formula comparing the original value of wealth to the size of the U.S. economy at the time. *Source: American Heritage* magazine, published by Forbes Inc. Web: www.americanheritage.com/98/oct/.

Women- and Minority-Owned Firms, 1987 and 1992

	Firms							
	Women-owned		Black-owned		Hispanic-owned		American Indian-and Asian-owned[1]	
Geographic Area	1992	1987	1992	1987	1992	1987	1992	1987
United States	**5,888,883**	**4,114,787**	**620,912**	**424,165**	**771,708**	**422,373**	**606,426**	**376,711**
Alabama	71,466	48,018	14,707	10,085	1,029	397	1,777	1,007
Alaska	19,380	13,976	739	507	766	502	3,916	5,034
Arizona	93,300	60,567	2,936	1,811	17,835	9,845	5,852	3,398
Arkansas	50,440	35,469	5,738	4,392	701	324	1,214	658
California	801,487	559,821	68,968	47,728	249,717	132,212	232,672	147,633
Colorado	121,659	89,411	4,372	2,871	13,817	9,516	5,788	3,543
Connecticut	79,931	60,924	5,714	4,061	4,502	2,235	3,485	2,051
Delaware	14,904	9,727	2,060	1,399	497	184	809	479
District of Columbia	14,599	10,987	10,111	8,275	1,452	762	1,393	807
Florida	352,048	221,361	40,371	25,527	118,208	64,413	17,499	8,902
Georgia	143,045	88,050	38,264	21,283	5,501	1,931	8,961	4,221
Hawaii	29,743	21,696	717	399	3,192	1,226	38,392	31,406
Idaho	29,946	18,973	152	94	1,865	974	759	513
Illinois	250,613	177,057	28,433	19,011	18,368	9,636	21,743	14,872
Indiana	125,411	89,949	8,349	5,867	2,454	1,427	3,193	1,808
Iowa	71,040	53,592	1,106	703	859	475	1,011	617
Kansas	66,429	53,505	3,078	2,323	2,396	1,541	1,842	1,366
Kentucky	74,280	53,454	5,097	3,738	752	359	1,614	899
Louisiana	76,849	55,852	20,312	15,331	4,983	2,697	4,826	2,808
Maine	35,260	23,922	235	131	427	139	483	233
Maryland	121,777	81,891	35,758	21,678	7,289	2,931	13,697	7,954
Massachusetts	147,572	111,376	7,225	4,761	6,914	2,636	7,009	3,916
Michigan	193,820	133,958	19,695	13,708	5,036	2,654	7,409	4,729
Minnesota	124,143	88,137	2,785	1,448	1,583	751	3,168	2,024
Mississippi	40,879	28,976	14,067	9,667	660	308	1,765	1,178
Missouri	117,885	87,658	9,973	7,832	2,216	1,247	3,451	2,193
Montana	25,310	17,747	113	77	568	304	845	612
Nebraska	43,637	32,285	1,350	863	1,147	619	670	451
Nevada	32,430	18,831	1,736	1,002	3,900	1,767	2,769	1,395
New Hampshire	31,492	22,713	326	229	487	244	666	333
New Jersey	164,798	117,373	20,137	14,556	22,198	12,094	23,116	12,665
New Mexico	40,636	25,397	925	587	21,586	14,299	4,608	2,155
New York	395,944	284,912	51,312	36,289	50,601	28,254	63,053	36,257
North Carolina	142,516	93,532	29,221	19,487	2,802	918	6,155	3,827
North Dakota	15,355	12,689	117	57	116	88	385	329
Ohio	224,693	154,084	22,690	15,983	4,289	1,989	7,146	4,011
Oklahoma	82,894	63,690	4,621	3,461	2,854	1,516	5,627	3,751
Oregon	87,970	58,941	1,447	848	3,538	1,598	5,414	3,340
Pennsylvania	227,500	167,362	15,917	11,728	5,186	2,650	12,053	7,189
Rhode Island	21,353	14,517	857	489	1,297	426	987	472
South Carolina	64,812	42,604	18,343	12,815	1,057	393	1,877	965
South Dakota	18,215	13,374	111	63	239	109	555	375
Tennessee	101,134	67,448	14,920	10,423	1,602	554	3,026	1,664
Texas	414,179	298,138	50,008	35,725	155,909	94,754	38,763	22,682
Utah	45,626	29,810	354	202	2,375	1,300	1,746	1,239
Vermont	21,033	13,802	139	98	351	118	274	111
Virginia	138,494	94,416	26,100	18,781	7,654	2,716	13,752	8,163
Washington	136,337	90,285	4,575	2,583	6,093	2,686	15,648	8,241
West Virginia	30,644	22,549	1,093	727	313	177	712	551
Wisconsin	99,357	69,185	3,446	2,381	1,762	894	2,486	1,451
Wyoming	14,617	10,796	97	81	766	584	362	233

1. Includes Alaska Native and Pacific Islander-owned. *Source:* U.S. Bureau of the Census. *State and Metropolitan Area Data Book 1997–1998.*

The articles and opinions in this section are for general information only and are not intended to provide specific advice or recommendations for any individual.

Mutual Fund Meltdown

There are about 600 mutual fund families. Most of them can't beat the market. So why do we need them?

By DANIEL EISENBERG TIME

What's the point of paying a professional to manage your money when you can do just as good a job, if not better, on your own? That was the question Hillsboro, Ore., computer consultant Larry Taylor, 40, and his friends asked themselves three years ago. Sick of sitting on the sidelines of a raging bull market, watching individual stocks skyrocket as their mutual funds crawled along, Taylor's crew decided to take matters into their own hands. Pooling assets, they chose a diversified portfolio of tech, pharmaceutical, and manufacturing stocks and have enjoyed 30% annual returns ever since. "We got tired of seeing fund managers getting rich and fees getting paid," says Taylor. "Mutual funds are for people who want to put their money into the market and just forget about it."

Competition from E-Traders

But with everyone from bellhops to biologists following every blip in the Dow on cable-TV channels and financial Web sites, passive investing is starting to become passé. "Everybody's an expert," grumbles a high-ranking executive at one fund company—a reference to the growing legion of e-traders who are sucking money from money managers at a rate that is starting to test their nerves. Sure, the $5.9 trillion fund industry is still chugging along quite nicely. But after a decade of explosive growth, it seems poised for a shakeout, as too many stock funds (about 3,500 at last count) scramble for a slowing money supply.

In the first four months of 1999, $52 billion in net new money flowed into stock funds—down a third from 1998's record levels. Moreover, as fund investors chase short-term performance above all, only a select group of the top fund families, with brand names like Vanguard, Janus, Fidelity, Putnam, and Alliance, are capturing the bulk of that new cash— and much of it is "automatic" in the form of 401(k) plans. That leaves hundreds of smaller players to fight for the scraps, according to Financial Research Corp. "There's a lot more risk now," says Jack Brennan, chairman of fund giant Vanguard, based in Valley Forge, Pa. "People may be looking for bigger, more seasoned names with a broader array of products. Or the investor may be making a bit of a market call, taking some risk off the table."

The thinness of the market—most of the gains in 1999 can be traced to relatively few stocks—has been tailor-made for the e-trade crowd, who pile into favored stocks at light-speed. It's been a hot money, risky environment, and these investors have apparently lost respect for the traditional, research-oriented investing that the pros have to offer.

Sluggish Performance

Who can blame them, considering the sorry record of most fund managers? With less than 20% of active managers outperforming the market, it is understandable that in 1998, for the first time ever, asset growth in individual stocks outpaced that of funds at discount broker and fund supermarket Charles Schwab. Or that No. 1 Fidelity has been stepping up promotion of its brokerage services, as more customers have looked to open hybrid portfolios made up of stocks and funds. "This industry has grown so rapidly that there is a shortage of good managers," says Bridget Macaskill, CEO of Oppenheimer Funds. "But mutual funds are fundamentally a good tool for small investors."

The fund industry is praying that the online trading boom and focus on just a few Internet stocks is a short-term phenomenon, the sign of a cyclical market that has got out of hand, rather than a fundamental, long-term shift. "It's based on a false sense of empowerment," claims funds watcher Avi Nachmany of Strategic Insight. Once the narrow bull market calms down, or broadens to include harder-to-choose value and small-cap stocks, Nachmany and others argue, investors will rush back to the relative safety of a diversified mutual fund. "Investors have abandoned the risk side of the equation, but it's not sustainable," says Greg Johnson, president of Franklin Templeton Distributors, which in 1999 saw investors flee its faltering value and international funds. "There are more than 10 good ideas for investing."

Eliminating the Middleman

Unfortunately for the industry, one of the most popular ideas, at least for now, is to have practically no manager at all. Nearly one out of every five new investment dollars is now going into low-cost index funds, which automatically mirror the performance of benchmarks like the Standard & Poor's 500. In 1999 billions flooded into Vanguard, the behemoth that pioneered the practice. Says John Rekenthaler of funds researcher Morningstar, "Indexing is an ongoing challenge that most of the competition is not facing up to."

It's no surprise, then, that much of the competition isn't faring too well either. Close to half the 600 or so mutual fund families experienced net withdrawals in the first quarter of 1999, and floundering funds were merged out of existence at a record pace in 1998, according to Lipper Inc. Once-high-flying firms such as Stein Roe, Pilgrim Baxter, and Berger Associates are reassigning dud managers and hustling to attract new money. Says Stephen Cone, president of customer marketing at Fidelity Investments, "We're not going to see the phenomenal growth of the past, and that may be an alarm bell for smaller firms. Their jobs have got much harder."

Survival of the Fittest

They may soon have no jobs at all. Some observers think that within a decade, more than half the 600 fund companies could disappear, as outfits with less than $50 billion in assets become ripe for the picking. With the big boys dominating the highly profitable institutional side of the business—401(k)s and other retirement plans—and much of the growth now coming from market appreciation, it will be hard for a second-tier player to shine.

Certainly, some of the smaller outfits will make it—there's always room for niche players, as the rise in focused Internet funds proves—but it is likely that the business will never again have the same kind of lock on the retail investor. Jokes veteran portfolio manager Martin Whitman of the Third Avenue Value Fund: "You haven't seen a more speculative, irrational market in years. The inmates are running the asylum." The industry just hopes that, sooner or later, it can get them back in line. □

A Nation of Stock Keepers

Online trading is quick, cheap, and growing fast. But this kind of convenience can be dangerous

By JOHN GREENWALD TIME

It's as voyeuristic as Internet sex sites, more addictive than video games, and a lot easier to play—and you can win big money! It's online investing, one of the hottest destinations in cyberspace. Ask Ardavan Arianpour of San Diego, Calif., who recently turned $1,000 into $5,000 through point-and-click trading. Arianpour is his own broker, trading as often as he likes and poring over online news, quotes, and stock charts. "I just love researching and making money," says Arianpour, who has been piling up profits for retirement. That's still a long way off, though, because he is only 18.

Electronic Fortune Hunting

The high school senior is one of millions of Americans who have hitched their computers to the tireless bull market. Once the preserve of a few computer-literate plungers, online trading could account for nearly 30% of the projected 227 million securities transactions at retail houses in 1998, according to Piper Jaffray, a Minneapolis, Minn., investment firm. "It's been on fire," Bill Burnham, a senior analyst at Piper Jaffray, says of online trading. "Hands down, it's the most successful area of consumer-based electronic commerce."

The allure of do-it-yourself trading is transforming both Wall Street and Main Street. Traditional brokerages, whose lock on vital information made them the market's gatekeepers, are changing their approach, and their fees. Meanwhile, a frenzied mob of e-traders has linked itself to a rapidly growing number of Web trading sites. In 1999, there were over 60 e-brokers, more than twice the number of the year before. Many are electronic branches of such giants as Charles Schwab and Fidelity Investments, but others, like E*Trade and Datek Online, dwell mainly in cyberspace. The e-brokerages themselves have been turbulent stocks. Shares of E*Trade soared in 1998 from $11 to $47, for example. Perhaps the biggest milestone in online investing came when Merrill Lynch announced it was starting up an Internet service in July 1999; the nation's largest traditional brokerage firm had long derided e-trading as a passing fad.

Do-It-Yourself Trading

Buying and selling securities have never been cheaper. Price wars in 1998 slashed the average commission at the 10 largest e-firms from $34.65 to $15.95 a trade. (A trade now costs more than $50 at standard off-line discounters and at least twice as much at full-service firms.) Aggressive discounters on the Internet charge less than $10, and cutthroats such as Web Street Securities charge nothing—that's zilch—to handle trades of more than 1,000 shares of NASDAQ stocks. This rock-bottom pricing reflects the lower costs of e-trading—look, Ma, no broker!—and the fact that firms can glean revenue from noncommission sources like the interest on margin accounts.

This business has lots more room for growth. Commissions from electronic trading nearly tripled to $700 million in 1997, and Forrester Research, which tracks the online industry, expects that the number of accounts will mushroom by 2002 to more than 18 million. In 1999 there were upwards of 8.4 million active Internet users with portfolios in excess of $100,000, according to @plan, a Connecticut market research firm. "There are huge numbers of people on the Internet with sizable portfolios who aren't yet shopping for stocks and mutual funds online," says Mark Wright, @plan's CEO. As a result, notes Eugene Ludwig, former U.S. Comptroller of the Currency, the projected growth curve for online trading "looks like a ski slope."

But there are plenty of risks for investors in this brave new e-world. So-called boiler-room operators who tout highly speculative or fraudulent stocks in order to unload them at a profit—"pump and dump" in the parlance—can reach vast audiences through chat rooms and bulletin boards. The Securities and Exchange Commission has been flashing red lights, bringing—and winning—40 complaints alleging scams against stock promoters since 1996. (The rule here: if it sounds like too much of a good deal, it probably is. The agency has a cyberspace alert on its Web site: www.sec.gov.)

Internet Pitfalls

Clients of e-brokers have run afoul of computer glitches that delay the execution of trades for minutes or hours—while prices shift. Such problems caused anguish in Oct. 1997 when jammed lines kept e-traders from bailing out as the market plunged 554 points.

But the biggest hazard of e-trading is trading. The ability to buy and sell stock instantly should not be confused with the word investing. Hooked hackers often trade many times a day in the hope of profiting from fractional changes in the price of a stock—a risky practice called "day trading" that can swell commissions while shrinking portfolios. "The easier it becomes to trade, the greater the danger that you'll trade too much or make poor decisions," Burnham says.

Frequent traders can also miss out on juicy profits, as Ron Garrett, who buys and sells stock while shaving, has painfully discovered. Garrett, professor of engineering at Grand Valley State University in Michigan, bought computer maker Unisys for $5 a share some time ago, only to dump it a few months later when it failed to show a quick gain. "If I didn't have easy access [to trading] maybe I wouldn't have jumped so fast," Garrett says of his sale of Unisys, which jumped to $23 a share after he sold it.

Feverish Competition

To attract and hold such customers, electronic brokers are feverishly building one-stop-shopping sites that offer everything from instant trading to tons of news and data about stocks and mutual funds. Want to check the long-term price performance of General Squid or compare it with Amalgamated Squid? Most Web sites include hot links to resources such as Big Charts (www.bigcharts.com) or StockTools (www.stocktools.com) that promptly plot the lines. Wall Street City (www.wallstreetcity.com) lets e-traders rank stocks by price-earnings ratios and popularity with big investors, among other criteria.

As in many businesses, acquiring customers is expensive, so holding on to them is vital. Ameritrade spent $25 million to add 50,000 new accounts in the fourth quarter of 1998, bringing its total to more than 200,000. That's $500 for each new account, well above the $300 that brokers usually spend to acquire new clients. Such hefty expenditures contributed to Ameritrade's loss of $11.5 million in the first half of 1999.

The market leader has been Charles Schwab, which commands nearly a third of the online trade business—or 1.5 million accounts—despite a $29.95 commission, which is three times higher than the deep discounts some others charge. Schwab's secret has been to knock down the wall between its online business and its 5 million regular account holders, giving everyone access to the entire range of products and services available at the firm. These include round-the-clock, dial-up brokers and technical support, and a financial supermarket that offers 1,500 different mutual funds.

Meanwhile, Schwab's rivals are rolling out some fancy features of their own. E*Trade, which has more than 400,000 accounts with $10.2 billion in assets, acquired OptionsLink in 1998, an electronic service that helps companies manage employee stock-option plans. Datek offers free real-time stock quotes—a service that most brokers charge for—and promises to execute trades within one minute or refund the commission. That has helped make three-year-old Datek, which has more than 80,000 active accounts, the fastest growing e-broker, measured by daily transactions.

E-Trading Revolution

The explosive growth of online investing has made personal finance the most popular channel on America Online—easily surpassing news, sports, and entertainment. AOL, which provides links to nine online brokers, says more than 5 million subscribers pull up 80 million stock quotes a day and generate some 13 million financial graphs a month.

This ceaseless demand for information has given rise to lucrative alliances between online brokers and data providers. In one such deal, Datek signed a $1.5 million agreement in January 1999 to sponsor the stock market ticker on TheStreet.com (www.thestreet.com), an electronic magazine filled with news and analysis of stocks and market trends. For its money, Datek gets a button on the site of TheStreet that brings viewers to the broker's home page.

For all their popularity, online firms are unlikely to drive full-service brokers into investment history. "There are always going to be people who don't have either the time or the confidence to manage their portfolios," says Burnham of Piper Jaffray. And with competition growing fiercer, he foresees a shakeout in which the largest e-brokers gobble up smaller ones, leaving investors with fewer online options. But with commissions having fallen to nothing and formerly hard-to-get information readily available, the future of investing is already predictable. E-trading is yet another example of the great leveling power of the Web. □

Tips for Online Investing

What you need to know about trading in fast-moving markets

Source: Securities and Exchange Commission

Every day, more and more Americans are investing in the stock market and many of them are doing so through the Internet. Online brokerages account for approximately 25% of all retail stock trades, and the number of online brokerage accounts is expected to exceed 10 million by the end of 1999.

The price of some stocks, especially recent "hot" IPOs and high tech stocks, can soar and drop suddenly. In these fast markets, when many investors want to trade at the same time and prices change quickly, delays can develop across the board. Executions and confirmations slow down, while reports of prices lag behind actual prices. In these markets, investors can suffer unexpected losses very quickly.

Investors trading over the Internet, who are used to instant access to their accounts and near instantaneous executions of their trades, especially need to understand how they can protect themselves in fast-moving markets.

You can limit your losses in fast-moving markets if you:

- know what you are buying and the risks of your investments and;
- know how trading changes during fast markets and take additional steps to guard against the typical problems investors face in these markets.

Trading is quick, investing takes time

With a click of the mouse, you can buy and sell stocks from more than 100 online brokers offering executions as low as $5 per transaction. Although online trading saves investors time and money, it does not take the homework out of making investment decisions. You may be able to make a trade in a nanosecond, but making wise investment decisions takes time. Before you trade, know why you are buying or selling, and the risk of your investment.

Set price limits

To avoid buying or selling a stock at a price higher or lower than you wanted, you need to place a limit order rather than a market order. A limit order is an order to buy or sell a security at a specific price. A buy limit order can only be executed at the limit price or lower, and a sell limit order can only be executed at the limit price or higher. When you place a market order, you can't control the price at which your order will be filled.

For example, if you want to buy a stock of a "hot" IPO that was initially offered at $9, but don't want to end up paying more than $20 for the stock, you can place a limit order to buy the stock at any price up to $20. By entering a limit order rather than a marker order, you will not be caught buying the stock at $90 and then suffering immediate losses as the stock drops later in the day or in the weeks ahead.

Remember that your limit order may never be executed because the market price may quickly surpass your limit before your order can be filled. But by using a limit order you also protect yourself from buying the stock at too high a price.

What if you can't access your account?

Most online trading firms offer alternatives for placing trades. These alternatives may include touch-tone telephone trades, faxing your order, or doing it the low-tech way—talking to a broker over the phone. Make sure you know whether using these different options may increase your costs. And remember, if you experience delays getting online, you may experience similar delays when you turn to one of these alternatives.

Don't assume your order didn't go through

Some investors have mistakenly assumed that their orders have not been executed and place another order. They end up owning either twice as much stock as they could afford or wanted, or with sell orders, selling a stock they do not own. Talk with your firm about how you should handle a situation where you are unsure if your original order was executed.

Make sure your cancel order worked

When you cancel an online trade, it is important to make sure that your original transaction was not executed. Although you may receive an electronic receipt for the cancellation, don't assume that it means the trade was canceled. Orders can only be canceled if they have not been executed. Ask your firm about how you should check to see if a cancellation order actually worked.

A word about margin trades

Now is the time to reread your margin agreement and pay attention to the fine print. If your account has fallen below the firm's maintenance margin requirement, your broker has the legal right to sell your securities at any time without consulting you first. Some investors have been rudely surprised that "margin calls" are a courtesy, not a requirement. Brokers are not required to make margin calls to their customers.

Even when your broker offers you time to put more cash or securities into your account to meet a margin call, the broker can act without waiting for you to meet the call. In a rapidly declining market, your broker can sell your entire margin account at a substantial loss to you, because the securities in the account have declined in value.

There is no time limit to make a trade

There are no Securities and Exchange Commission regulations that require a trade to be executed within a set period of time. But if firms advertise their speed of execution, they must not exaggerate or fail to tell investors about the possibility of significant delays.

If you have a complaint

Act promptly. By law, you only have a limited time to take legal action. Follow these steps to solve your problem:

1. Talk to your broker or online firm and ask for an explanation. Take notes of the answers you receive.
2. If you are dissatisfied with the response and believe you have been treated unfairly, ask to talk with the broker's branch manager. In the case of an online firm, go directly to step number three.

3. If you are still dissatisfied, write to the compliance department at the firm's main office. Explain your problem clearly, and tell the firm how you want it resolved. Ask the compliance office to respond to you in writing within 30 days.

4. If you're still dissatisfied, then send a letter of complaint to the National Association of Securities Dealers, your state securities administrator, or to the Office of Investor Education and Assistance at the SEC along with copies of the letters you've already sent to the firm. □

The Nitty-Gritty of Mortgage Shopping

Source: The Federal Interagency Task Force on Fair Lending

A mortgage—whether it's a home purchase, a refinancing, or a home equity loan—is a product, just like a car, so the price and terms may be negotiable. You'll want to compare all the costs involved in obtaining a mortgage so that you can negotiate for the best deal. Different lenders may quote you different prices, so you should contact several lenders to make sure that you are getting the best price. You can also get a home loan through a mortgage broker. Brokers arrange transactions rather than lending money directly; in other words, they find a lender for you. Brokers are not obligated to find the best deal for you unless they have contracted with you to act as your agent. Consequently, you should consider contacting more than one broker just as you should do with banks and thrift institutions.

Whether you are dealing with a lender or a broker may not always be clear. Some financial institutions operate as both lenders and brokers. And most brokers' advertisements do not use the word "broker." Therefore, be sure to ask whether a broker is involved. This information is important because brokers are usually paid a fee for their services that may be separate from and in addition to the lender's origination or other fees.

A broker's compensation may be in the form of "points" at closing or as an add-on to your interest rate, or both. You should ask each broker you work with how he or she will be compensated so that you can compare the different fees. Be prepared to negotiate with the brokers as well as the lenders.

Cost Information You Need

Know how much of a down payment you can afford, and find out all the costs involved in the loan. Knowing just the amount of the monthly payment or the interest rate is not enough. Ask for information about the same loan amount, loan term, and type of loan so that you can compare the information.

Rates. Ask each lender and broker for a list of its current mortgage interest rates and whether the rates being quoted are the lowest for that day or week. Ask whether the rate is fixed or adjustable. Keep in mind that when interest rates for adjustable-rate loans go up, generally so does the monthly payment. If the rate quoted is for an adjustable-rate loan, ask how your rate and loan payment will vary, including whether your loan payment will be reduced when rates go down.

Ask about the loan's annual percentage rate (APR). The APR takes into account not only the interest rate but also points, broker fees, and certain other credit charges that you may be required to pay, expressed as a yearly rate.

Points. Points are fees paid to the lender or broker for the loan and are often linked to the interest rate; usually the more points you pay, the lower the rate. Check your local newspaper for information about rates and points currently being offered. Also ask for points to be quoted to you as a dollar amount—rather than just as the number of points—so that you will actually know how much you will have to pay.

Fees. A home loan often involves many fees, such as loan origination or underwriting fees, broker fees, and transaction, settlement, and closing costs. Every lender or broker should be able to give you an estimate of its fees. Many of these fees are negotiable. Some fees are paid when you apply for a loan (such as application and appraisal fees), and others are paid at closing. In some cases, you can borrow the money needed to pay these fees, but doing so will increase your loan amount and total costs. "No cost" loans are sometimes available, but they usually involve higher rates.

Inquire as to what each fee includes. Several items may be lumped into one fee. Ask for an explanation of any fee you do not understand.

Down Payments and Mortgage Insurance

Some lenders require 20 percent of the home's purchase price as a down payment. However, many lenders now offer loans that require less than 20 percent down—sometimes as little as five percent on conventional loans. If a 20 percent down payment is not made, lenders usually require the home buyer to purchase private mortgage insurance (PMI) to protect the lender in case the home buyer fails to pay. When government-assisted programs such as FHA (Federal Housing Administration), VA (Veterans Administration), or Rural Development Services are available, the down payment requirements may be substantially smaller.

Ask about the lender's requirements for a down payment, including what you need to do to verify that funds for your down payment are available. Ask your lender about special programs it may offer. If PMI is required for your loan, find out how much your monthly payment will be including the PMI premium. Ask how long you will be required to carry this insurance.

Negotiate the Best Deal

On any given day, lenders and brokers may offer different prices for the same loan terms to different consumers, even if those consumers have the same loan qualifications. The most likely reason for this difference in price is that loan officers and brokers are often allowed to keep some or all of this difference as extra compensation. Generally, the difference between the lowest available price for a loan product and any higher price that the borrower agrees to pay is an overage. When overages occur, they are built into the prices quoted to consumers. They can occur in both fixed and variable-rate loans and can be in the form of points, fees, or the interest rate. Whether quoted to you by a loan officer or a broker, the price of any loan may contain overages.

Have the lender or broker write down all the costs associated with the loan. Then ask if the lender or broker will waive or reduce one or more of its fees or agree to a lower rate or fewer points. You'll want to make sure that the lender or the broker is not agreeing to lower one fee while raising another or to lower the rate while raising points. There's no harm in asking the lender or broker for better terms than the ones originally quoted.

Once you are satisfied with the terms you have negotiated, you may want to obtain a written lock-in from the lender or broker. The lock-in should include the rate that you have agreed upon, the period the lock-in lasts, and the number of points to be paid. A fee may be charged for locking in the loan rate. This fee may be refundable at closing. Lock-ins can protect you from rate increases while your loan is being processed; if rates fall, however, you could end up with a less favorable rate. Should that happen, try to negotiate a compromise with the lender or broker.   □

Mortgage Qualifications for Buying a Home

Source: Fannie Mae

Your History

Your job history is important and it will be a major factor in whether you qualify for a loan. If you have been working continuously for two years or more, you are considered to have steady employment. However, you do not have to have held the same job for two years in order to be approved for a loan. Job moves that result in equal or more pay and continue to use proven skills are a plus for you. If there are good reasons why you haven't worked continuously for the last two years, you can explain these reasons to the mortgage lender.

How you paid your bills in the past also gives a lender some indication of how you can be expected to pay them in the future. You will be asked to list all your debts, the amount of your monthly payments, and the number of months or years left to pay on the debts. Your lender will order a credit report to verify the information that you give.

Payment Options

When you buy a home, you need money for a down payment and closing costs. The amount of the down payment may vary, but generally you must make a down payment that equals at least 5% of the purchase price. Closing costs can be expensive, depending upon where you live.

The mortgage lender will want proof that you have saved the funds that you will use for a down payment and part or all of the closing costs. If the funds are in a savings account, the lender will ask the financial institution to verify the amount and the length of time that the funds have been in your account. The lender wants to make sure that you are not borrowing all the money you will use for the down payment and closing costs.

The amount of your monthly payment depends upon the amount you borrow, the interest rate, and the repayment period or "term." The shorter the term, the higher your monthly payment. For that reason, most home buyers repay their mortgage over the longest term possible, usually 30 years.

Housing Expense Guidelines

When you first approach a lender about financing your mortgage, it will use the following two commonly accepted guidelines to help determine your ability to make mortgage payments:

1. Your monthly housing costs (including mortgage payments, property taxes, homeowner and mortgage insurance, and homeowner's fees) should total no more than 28% of your monthly gross (before taxes) income. In addition to your regular pay, your income can include funds you receive from overtime work, a part-time job, or a second job; retirement, VA, and Social Security benefits; disability, welfare, and unemployment benefits; alimony; and child support.

2. Your monthly housing costs plus other long-term debts such as payments on car loans, student loans, or other installment debt (debts with more than ten months left to repay) should total no more than 36% of your monthly gross income. Depending upon your household income, you may be eligible for special assistance programs. These programs may make it easier for you to get a larger mortgage loan than you normally would be able to, using the above qualifying rules.

Financial Web Sites

FinanceNet www.financenet.gov
American Association of Individual Investors
  www.aaii.org
Mutual Funds Homepage www.fundsinteractive.com
Foreign Exchange Rates
  www.cnnfn.com/markets/currencies.html
U.S. Securities and Exchange Commission
  www.sec.gov
Federal Deposit Insurance Corporation
  www.fdic.gov
FannieMae www.fanniemae.com
United States Treasury www.ustreas.gov
U.S. Savings Bonds www.savingsbonds.gov
Debt Counselors of America www.dca.org
Pension and Welfare Benefits Administration
  www.dol.gov/dol/pwba
MetLife Online (Annuities, etc.) www.lifeadvice.com
American Express (financial information)
  www.americanexpress.com
American Consumer Credit Counseling
  www.consumercredit.com
New York Stock Exchange www.nyse.com
American Stock Exchange www.amex.com
NASDAQ www.nasdaq.com
Chicago Mercantile Exchange www.cme.com
Institute of Certified Financial Planners
  www.cfp.org

How Large a Mortgage Do You Qualify For?

This chart can help you find out how large a mortgage you might qualify for based on your annual income and the interest rate currently being quoted for 30-year fixed-rate mortgages. Rather than using the normal 28% ratio, this chart uses a 25% ratio and assumes that the amount you need to set aside to pay for taxes and insurance would amount to approximately the 3% difference. This simplified approach should give you a fairly accurate answer.

Interest rates	Annual income					
	$15,000	**$20,000**	**$25,000**	**$30,000**	**$35,000**	**$40,000**
6.5%	$49,400	$65,900	$82,400	$98,800	$115,300	$131,800
7.0	47,000	62,600	78,300	93,900	109,600	125,300
7.5	44,600	59,600	74,500	89,400	104,300	119,200
8.0	45,000	56,700	70,900	85,100	99,300	113,500
8.5	40,600	54,100	67,700	81,200	94,800	108,300
9.0	38,800	51,700	64,700	77,700	90,600	103,500
9.5	37,200	49,500	61,900	74,300	86,700	99,100
10.0	35,600	47,400	59,300	71,200	83,000	94,900
10.5	34,200	45,500	56,900	68,300	79,700	91,100
	$45,000	**$50,000**	**$55,000**	**$60,000**	**$65,000**	**$70,000**
6.5%	$148,300	$164,800	$181,300	$197,700	$214,200	$230,000
7.0	140,900	156,600	172,300	187,900	203,600	219,200
7.5	134,100	149,000	163,900	178,800	193,700	208,600
8.0	127,700	141,900	156,100	170,300	184,500	198,700
8.5	121,900	135,400	149,000	162,500	176,100	189,600
9.0	116,500	129,400	142,400	155,300	168,200	181,200
9.5	111,400	123,800	136,200	148,600	161,000	173,400
10.0	106,800	118,600	130,500	142,400	154,300	166,100
10.5	102,400	113,800	125,200	136,600	148,000	159,400

Source: Fannie Mae.

Calculate Your Mortgage Payment

Use this chart to calculate how much your monthly mortgage payment might be, based on a 30-year term. Let's suppose that you want to purchase a house that costs $50,000. If you make a $5,000 down payment, you would need a $45,000 mortgage. As you can see on the chart, the monthly payment on a $45,000 mortgage at 8% interest is $330. The $330 monthly payment only covers the principal, or a portion of the amount you borrowed, and interest on the mortgage loan. There are other expenses that will be added to your monthly payment. These include taxes and homeowner's insurance. If your down payment is less than 20%, you may need to pay private mortgage insurance. These costs vary depending upon where you live and the cost of your home, but they can add a hundred dollars or more to your monthly payment. In addition, if you are thinking about buying a unit in a condo or cooperative building, or a house in a planned unit development, you may also need to pay monthly homeowner's fees to cover maintenance expenses or special assessments related to the common areas.

Loan amount	Interest rates								
	6.5%	**7%**	**7.5%**	**8%**	**8.5%**	**9%**	**9.5%**	**10%**	**10.5%**
$20,000	$126	$133	$140	$147	$154	$161	$168	$176	$183
25,000	158	166	175	183	192	201	210	219	229
30,000	190	200	210	220	231	241	252	263	274
35,000	221	233	245	257	269	282	294	307	320
40,000	253	266	280	294	308	322	336	351	366
45,000	284	299	315	330	346	362	378	395	412
50,000	316	333	350	367	384	402	420	439	457
55,000	348	366	385	404	423	443	462	483	503
60,000	380	399	420	440	461	483	505	527	549
65,000	411	432	454	477	500	523	547	570	595
70,000	442	466	489	514	538	563	589	614	640
75,000	474	499	524	550	577	603	631	658	686
80,000	506	532	559	587	615	644	673	702	732
85,000	537	566	594	624	654	684	715	746	778
90,000	569	599	629	660	692	724	757	790	823
95,000	600	632	664	697	730	764	799	834	869
100,000	632	665	699	734	769	805	841	878	915

Source: Fannie Mae.

How to Measure the Shrinking Value of the Dollar

Source: Martin Lefkowitz, Economlst, U.S. Chamber of Commerce

How to use this table. This table provides a method for translating dollar values from the past 52 years into 1998 dollars. For example: What weekly salary would you need to earn in 1998 to equal the purchasing power of a weekly salary of $100 in 1970? Take the 1970 multiplier, 4.20, times $100 and you would need to earn $420 a week in 1998 to achieve the same salary.

Year	Value of dollar in 1998 dollars	Year	Value of dollar in 1998 dollars	Year	Value of dollar in 1998 dollars
1946	$8.36	1964	$5.26	1982	$1.69
1947	7.00	1965	5.17	1983	1.64
1948	6.76	1966	5.03	1984	1.57
1949	6.85	1967	4.88	1985	1.51
1950	6.76	1968	4.68	1986	1.49
1951	6.27	1969	4.44	1987	1.43
1952	6.15	1970	4.20	1988	1.38
1953	6.10	1971	4.02	1989	1.31
1954	6.06	1972	3.90	1990	1.25
1955	6.08	1973	3.67	1991	1.20
1956	5.99	1974	3.31	1992	1.16
1957	5.80	1975	3.03	1993	1.13
1958	5.64	1976	2.86	1994	1.10
1959	5.60	1977	2.69	1995	1.07
1960	5.51	1978	2.50	1996	1.04
1961	5.45	1979	2.25	1997	1.02
1962	5.40	1980	1.98	1998	1.00
1963	5.33	1981	1.79		

New Easy Savings Bond Plan

The U.S. Treasury created the simplest, most hassle-free way to buy popular Series EE or inflation-indexed I savings bonds at regularly scheduled intervals. The money is automatically deducted from your checking or savings accounts providing your financial institution permits electronic debits from the account you wish to use. Called the "Easy Saver," you select the amount, how the bonds are made out, and when you want your bond issued. Check with you financial institution to enroll in the new service or for more information, call toll-free, 877-811-7283, or check the Savings Bond Web site at www.savingsbonds.gov.

Series EE Bonds. The Series EE savings bond is a security that accrues interest (increases in value) until it is cashed or reaches final maturity in 30 years. The "double E" is the successor to the Series E bond (also an accrual bond) that was issued from May 1941 through June 1980. EE bonds will continue to increase in value as long as you hold them for 30 years. Depending on the interest rate and how long you keep the bond, its value can be greater than its face value.

The purchase of an EE bond is one-half the denomination (also known as the face amount). There are eight denominations available: $50, $75, $100, $200, $500, $1,000, and $5,000. You are limited to buy up to $30,000 (face amount) per person in a calendar year.

Interest is calculated as 90% of 6-month averages of 5-year Treasury Securities yields. The interest rate for series EE bonds in July 1999 was 4.31%.

I-Bonds. They became available Sept. 1, 1998, are sold at face value, and grow with inflation-indexed earnings for up to 30 years. They are issued at face value (a $100 bond costs $100). Denominations offered are: $50, $75, $100, $200, $500, $1,000, $5,000, and $10,000. You are limited to buy up to $30,000 (face amount) per person in a calendar year.

Interest is calculated as an earning of a fixed rate of return and a semiannual inflation rate based on the CPI-U. The interest rate for I-Bonds in July 1999 was 5.05%, over and above the inflation rate.

Have Your Savings Bonds Stopped Earning Interest?

Savings bonds earn interest for different lengths of time depending on the series of the bond and, in some cases, when the bond was issued. It's important to periodically check your bonds to make sure that they are still earning interest. This is especially true for Series E, EE, I, and savings notes since (unlike the H and HH series) you don't receive regular interest payments from the Treasury. Use the table below to determine how long your bonds will earn interest and promptly cash in or exchange any bonds that have stopped earning interest.

Series	Date of issue	Years bonds earn interest
E	May 1941–Nov. 1965	40 years
	Dec. 1965–June 1980	30 years
H	June 1952–Jan. 1957	29 years, 8 mo.
	Feb. 1957–Dec. 1979	30 years
Savings notes	All issues	30 years
EE	All issues	30 years
HH	All issues	20 years

Source: U.S. Treasury Department.

The Cyberspace Auction Block

Buyers, sellers—and investors—are flocking to online auctions

By DANIEL EISENBERG TIME

When you're worth $10 billion, you can afford to collect Gulfstreams, Ferraris, and yachts. But Jeff Bezos, the founder of e-tailing dynamo Amazon.com, had his sights set a little lower. Like millions of Internet surfers searching for their favorite obscure trinkets, Bezos joined an online auction, bidding for a pack of 1977 Star Wars trading cards. Alas, the buying force was not with him. He dropped out when the price got too high.

Bezos may have lost that battle, but he is determined to win the e-commerce war. In April 1999, Amazon.com launched its own electronic flea market to appeal to the millions of online hagglers who passionately bid for everything from stereos and cruises to a Coke bottling plant and the historic town of Johnsonville, Conn. Bezos's is just the latest firm to recognize the Web as the perfect medium to match buyers and sellers in a capitalist free-for-all: Net portal Yahoo rolled out an auction site in Fall 1998, and America Online has struck a partnership with industry leader eBay.

Meanwhile, Priceline.com, a patented e-commerce service that lets you name your price for airline tickets, hotel rooms, cars, and home mortgages and then goes out to find sellers willing to match it, went public in 1998, and Wall Street treated the company like a rare gemstone. At its peak in April 1999, Priceline.com's value had jumped to around $11 billion by April 1999, worth more than a few major airlines combined.

Cloning eBay

With its own auction launch, Amazon continued its mutation from bookseller to e-tailer nonpareil. The auction area is carrying tens of thousands of items, including a signed copy of Hemingway's *A Farewell to Arms*—Amazon will, of course, be strong in rare books. "Our vision is to build a place to find and discover anything our customers might want to buy . . . [including] car parts and spark plugs," says Bezos, whose firm's ever inflating stock price jumped an additional 15% on the news. Says Larry Schwartz, president of rival Auction Universe: "It's kind of frightening—they cloned eBay."

Can you really blame them? Each month, some 6 million visitors flock to eBay's sprawling virtual tag sale, according to research firm Media Metrix, right behind Amazon's 8 million. A third of those browsers regularly bid on or sell a selection of nearly 2 million items, including computers, Ginsu knives, baseball cards, and model trains, generating about $300 million in total transactions during the fourth quarter of fiscal 1998. "There's a constant trade show going on," says Steve Karas, of New York, who auctions sports cards on the site. By taking a 1.25%-to-5% cut on each of those exchanges, eBay is one of the few Net start-ups to turn a profit—albeit a small one—on sales of $47 million in 1998. Since eBay acts as an intermediary with little or no overhead to cover, "consumer-to-consumer auctions can be like printing money," says Marc Johnson, senior analyst at Jupiter Communications.

Caveat Emptor

The Net has, once again, redefined an industry, in this case the highly fragmented market for antiques, collectibles, and secondhand goods. From experienced antique dealers to homemakers and senior citizens raiding their attics, a new class of grassroots merchants is setting up shop. "It's becoming a way of life," maintains Steve Westly, vice president of marketing at eBay, who himself has amassed a collection of 3,000 toy soldiers. "People love the thrill of the hunt."

There are, however, a small group of parasites, including a Florida eBay user who was recently ordered to pay $23,000 in restitution, who continue to plague this electronic marketplace. Two-thirds of all Internet fraud complaints last year were directed at auction sites, according to the National Consumers' League. And antique dealers, who quickly adapted to e-auctions, find themselves dealing with amateurs who wouldn't know Caravaggio from formaggio. Peter Woolman, a British antiques dealer in Delray Beach, Fla., is one such frustrated buyer. "It's full of fakes," he complains. He recently flew to Texas to pick up a pair of bronze and ivory statues for which he bid $26,000, only to discover at a glance that they were knockoffs. "The sellers said they didn't know much about what they were selling . . . All I can say is, it's better odds in a Las Vegas casino."

To help improve those odds, eBay, Auction Universe, and Amazon.com all offer some type of insurance and recommend that people use escrow services. Industry pioneer Onsale.com, which conducts only business-to-consumer auctions, guarantees its products.

Tricks of the Trade

There are tricks of the trade too. Savvy bidders know how to swoop in to bag their quarry during the last few seconds of an auction (which can last hours, days, or weeks). And certain merchants collude to drive up prices artificially. For the most part, overpaying at these electronic garage sales is the consequence of being too enthusiastic—just as it is with the old-fashioned kind. Caught up in the competitive frenzy of an auction, many people don't know when to fold their cards. Says Tim Brady, vice president of production at Yahoo: "Anybody who's the least bit competitive hates to be outbid." And that's why sellers, and investors, love it so much.□

The Top Five Consumer Credit Scams

They can drain your finances, destroy your good reputation, and even get you jailed

Source: Federal Trade Commission.

Credit repair. Credit-repair companies run advertisements in newspapers, radio, TV, and the Internet, offering consumers assistance, for a price, to clean up their credit histories. The Federal Trade Commission (FTC) warns that many of the claims these companies make—that they can remove judgments, liens, and other unfavorable information from credit records, are false. They cannot legally remove accurate negative information from a credit report and any legitimate help they can offer can be pursued by consumers themselves, at little or no cost.

Advance-fee loans. The lenders appeal to consumers who, based on their credit history, can't get a loan. The scammers falsely promise that for an advance payment, even consumers with bad credit histories can get a loan. Some of these lenders make money through the 900 numbers that charge consumers who call to find out about the loans. Others simply charge consumers a fee for a loan that is never delivered.

Home equity. Unscrupulous lenders target consumers who have good credit, but have a bad cash flow. They offer credit based not on income or the ability to repay, but on the equity of the home. Exploitative lenders may take advantage of the borrower by abusive practices such as "loan flipping" by repeatedly talking the borrower into refinancing the loan, which adds to the cost of the debt. If you don't have enough income to make the monthly payments, you will probably lose your home, as many consumers do through these schemes.

Identity theft. This crime occurs when con artists steal credit card numbers, social security numbers, mother's maiden names, or other personally-identifying information without one's knowledge, to tap into the good credit histories of consumers. They then set up new credit accounts, charge purchases to existing accounts, or drain bank accounts. Frequently, consumers don't know that their credit identities have been stolen until they get bills for credit card accounts that they never opened, see charges on their bills that they didn't know anything about, or discover that their bank accounts have been fraudulently accessed.

Congress passed the Identity Theft and Assumption Deterrence Act of 1998, which makes it a federal crime to knowingly transfer or use another person's means of identification to commit any unlawful activity.

File segregation. This is a relatively new scam that could get you fined or sentenced to jail time if you use it. It is an illegal scheme used by credit-repair companies to encourage consumers with unfavorable credit histories to obtain new taxpayer identification or employer identification numbers from the Internal Revenue Service under false pretenses and use them to hide their true credit identities from creditors. For a fee, the companies promise advice on how to go about segregating their credit files. File segregation is illegal and consumers who employ it are committing a felony.

If you have a problem with any of the scams described here, contact your local consumer protection agency, state attorney general, or Better Business Bureau. You can file a complaint with the Federal Trade Commission by phoning the Consumer Response Center: Toll-free, 877-FTC-HELP (382-4357); or writing to: Consumer Response Center, Federal Trade Commission, 600 Pennsylvania Ave., N.W., Washington, DC 20580; or you may use the FTC email complaint form at www.ftc.gov.

Consumers Benefit from the "Lemon Awards"

On January 14, 1999, consumer, health, and environmental organizations from across the U.S. gathered in Washington, D.C., for the 14th annual Harlan Page Hubbard Lemon Awards. The awards are a dubious distinction, "honoring" the "most misleading, unfair, and irresponsible" ad campaigns from the past year. They are named for the 19th-century advertising executive who first brought the practice of deceptive advertising to the national level. While the awards are given out in good fun, sponsors hope to raise consumer awareness of deceptive advertising and curb advertisers from using such practices. Here are this year's winners:

- **"10–10–321"** long distance service for claiming that consumers can "save up to 50%." MCI, the owner of Telecom USA, which operates the "dial around" service, actually offers long distance rate plans that for many consumers are cheaper than "10–10–321."
- **Quaker Oatmeal** for cholesterol-reduction claims based on a study in which participants also made lifestyle changes including exercising more, eating more fruits and vegetables, and quitting smoking.
- **Saturn,** a division of General Motors, for promoting its new 3-door coupe as convenient for families. The third door is on the road (as opposed to the curb) side of the car, making it dangerous for children to use, and the commercial shows "mom" driving away before her child has buckled up.
- **US Airways** for ads touting the benefits of its frequent flyer program even though the company reserves one of the smallest percentages of seats for frequent flyers among all major airlines and within the last three years has slashed by 40% the percentage of available seats.
- **Miller Brewing Company** for ads that show people playing with a pet dog and proclaim that Miller Lite is "Man's Other Best Friend."
- **Brown and Williamson Tobacco Company** for its "B-Kool" ad campaign, which is targeted to so-called "down scale males" and "virile females."
- **The American General Financial Group** for running ads urging consumers to "trust" the company with their "livelihood" and financial "future" shortly before the company settled a class-action lawsuit requiring it to pay $250 million to more than 30% of its 12 million customers whom it was accused of defrauding.

- **First USA Visa** for a deceptive credit card offer that misleadingly states how much money one can save by transferring outstanding credit card balances from other banks. The direct mail ad omits the costs of transaction fees when calculating the purported savings and some consumers could actually lose money by transferring outstanding balances.
- **Ginsana** energy supplements for ads that claim that ginseng in Ginsana provides energy. Numer-

ous published scientific studies—two specifically on Ginsana—refute that contention.
- **Nuclear Energy Institute** for ads claiming that nuclear power is "safe," can provide electricity "without polluting the environment," and has been "proven economical." The ads were found by the National Advertising Division of the Council of Better Business Bureaus to be "inaccurate."

Consumer Information Catalog

Source: U.S. Office of Consumer Affairs.

The *Consumer Information Catalog* lists approximately 200 free or low-cost federal booklets with helpful information for consumers. Topics include careers and education, cars, childcare, the environment, federal benefits, financial planning, food and nutrition, health, housing, small businesses, and more. This free catalog is published quarterly by the Consumer Information Center of the U.S. General Services Administration. Single copies of the cata-

log only may be ordered by sending your name and address to *Catalog*, Consumer Information Center, Pueblo, CO 81009, or on the Internet at www.pueblo.gsa.gov, or by calling 719-948-4000.

Nonprofit groups that can distribute 25 copies or more each quarter may automatically receive copies by writing for a bulk mail card.

Copyrights

Source: Copyright Office, Washington, D.C.

Copyright is a form of protection provided by the laws of the United States to the creators of "original works of authorship," including literary, dramatic, musical, artistic, and certain other intellectual works. This protection is available to both published and unpublished works. The Copyright Act generally gives the owner of copyright the exclusive right to do and to authorize others to do the following:

- to reproduce the copyrighted work;
- to prepare derivative works based upon the copyrighted work;
- to distribute copies or phonorecords of the copyrighted work to the public by sale or other transfer of ownership, or by rental, lease, or lending;
- to perform the copyrighted work publicly;
- to display the copyrighted work publicly; and
- in the case of sound recordings, to perform the work publicly by means of a digital audio transmission.

It is illegal for anyone to violate these rights. However, they are limited by the doctrine of "fair use," or by a "compulsory license" under which certain limited uses of copyrighted works are permitted in exchange for payment. For further information about the limitations of any of these rights, consult the Copyright Law or write to the Copyright Office.

Copyright protection exists from the time the work is created in fixed form. The copyright in the work of authorship immediately becomes the property of the author who created it. Only the property of the author, or those deriving their rights through the author, can rightfully claim copyright.

In the case of works made for hire, the employer and not the employee is considered the author.

The authors of a joint work are co-owners of the copyright in the work, unless there is an agreement to the contrary.

Copyright in each separate contribution to a periodical or other collective work is distinct from

copyright in the collective work as a whole and vests initially with the author of the contribution.

Two General Principles:

- Mere ownership of a book, manuscript, painting, or any other copy or phonorecord does not give the possessor the copyright. The law provides that transfer of ownership of any material object that embodies a protected work does not of itself convey any rights in the copyright.
- Minors may claim copyright, but state laws may regulate the business dealings involving copyrights owned by minors. For information on relevant state laws, consult an attorney.

Copyright is secured automatically when the work is created, and a work is "created" when it is fixed in a copy or phonorecord for the first time. "Copies" are material objects from which a work can be read or visually perceived, such as books, manuscripts, sheet music, film, videotape, or microfilm. "Phonorecords" are material objects embodying fixations of sounds (excluding, by statutory definition, motion picture soundtracks), such as cassette tapes, CDs, or LPs. Thus, for example, a song (the "work") can be fixed in sheet music ("copies") or in phonograph disks ("phonorecords"), or both. Only the author, or those deriving their rights through the author, can rightfully claim copyright.

If a work is prepared over a period of time, the part of the work that is fixed on a particular date constitutes the created work as of that date.

Copyright protection is available for all unpublished works, regardless of the nationality or domicile of the author. Published works are eligible for copyright protection in the United States if any one of the several conditions regarding the nationality of the authors or place of publication is met. Check with the Copyright Office for details.

Consumer Web Sites

Consumer Information Center: www.pueblo.gsa.gov
Consumer World: www.consumerworld.org
National Fraud Information Center: www.fraud.org
Federal Trade Commission: www.ftc.gov
Consumer Product Safety Commission:
www.cpsc.gov
U.S. Dept. of Transportation:
www.dot.gov/safety.htm
American Council on Consumer Interests:
riker.ps.missouri.edu/dh/acci
Consumer Alert: www.consumeralert.org
U.S. Copyright Office: www.loc.gov/copyright
Better Business Bureau: www.bbb.org
U.S. Dept. of Justice: www.usdoj.gov
Federal Consumer Information: www.consumer.gov
Consumers Union: www.consumersunion.org

What Works Are Protected

Copyright protects "original works of authorship" that are fixed in a tangible form of expression. The fixation need not be directly perceptible so long as it may be communicated with the aid of a machine or device. Categories include:

• literary works;
• musical works, including any accompanying words;
• dramatic works, including any accompanying music;
• pantomimes and choreographic works;
• pictorial, graphic, and sculptural works;
• motion pictures and other audiovisual works;
• sound recordings; and
• architectural works.

These categories should be viewed quite broadly. For example, computer programs and most "compilations" are registrable as "literary works." Maps and architectural plans are registrable as "pictorial, graphic, and sculptural works."

Several categories of material are generally not eligible for federal copyright protection. These include among others:

• works that have not been fixed in a tangible form of expression. For example, choreographic works that have not been notated or recorded, or improvisational speeches or performances that have not been written or recorded;
• titles, names, short phrases, and slogans; familiar symbols or designs; mere variations of typographic ornamentation, lettering, or coloring; mere listings of ingredients or contents;
• ideas, procedures, methods, systems, processes, concepts, principles, discoveries, or devices, as distinguished from a description, explanation, or illustration;
• works consisting entirely of information that is common property and containing no original authorship. For example, standard calendars, height and weight charts, tape measures and rulers, and lists or tables taken from public documents or other common sources.

Notice of Copyright

The use of a copyright notice is no longer required under U.S. law, although it is often beneficial. Because prior law did contain such a requirement, however, the use of notice is still relevant to the copyright status of older works. Use of the notice may be important because it informs the public that the work is protected by copyright, identifies the copyright owners, and shows the year of first publication.

Furthermore, in the event that a work is infringed, if a proper notice of copyright appears on the published copy or copies to which a defendant in a copyright infringement suit had access, then no weight shall be given to such a defendant's interposition of a defense based on innocent infringement in mitigation of actual or statutory damages, except as provided in section 504(c)(2) of the Copyright Code. Innocent infringement occurs when the infringer did not realize that the work was protected.

The use of the copyright notice is the responsibility of the copyright owner and does not require advance permission from, or registration with, the Copyright Office.

Form of Notice for Visually Perceptible Copies

The notice for visually perceptible copies should contain all of the following three elements:

1. the symbol © (the letter C in a circle), or the word "Copyright," or the abbreviation "Copr.";
2. the year of first publication of the work; and
3. the name of the owner of copyright in the work, or an abbreviation by which the name can be recognized, or a generally known alternative designation of the owner.

Example: © 2000 John Doe

Form of Notice for Sound Recordings

The copyright notice for phonorecords of sound recordings should contain the following three elements:

1. the symbol ℗ (the letter P in a circle);
2. the year of first publication of the sound recording; and
3. the name of the owner of copyright in the sound recording, or an abbreviation by which the name can be recognized, or a generally known alternative designation of the owner. If the producer of the sound recording is named on the phonorecord labels or containers, and if no other name appears in conjunction with the notice, the producer's name shall be considered a part of the notice.

Example: ℗ 2000 A.B.C., Inc.

NOTE: Since questions may arise from the use of variant forms of the notice, any form of the notice other than those given here should not be used without first seeking legal advice.

Position of Notice

The notice should be positioned so as to "give reasonable notice of the claim of copyright." The Copyright Office has issued regulations concerning the form and position of the copyright notice. For more information, contact them directly.

Publications Incorporating United States Government Works

Works by the U.S. Government are not eligible for copyright protection. However, copies of work published before March 1, 1989, that consist primarily of one or more works of the U.S. Government should have a notice and the identifying statement. Example:

© 2000 Jane Brown. Copyright claimed in Chapters 7–10, exclusive of U.S. Government maps.

Unpublished Works

The author or other owner of copyright may wish to place a copyright notice on any unpublished copies or phonorecords that leave his or her control. An appropriate notice for an unpublished work is "Unpublished work © 2000 Jane Doe."

Copyright Protection Endurance

Works Originally Created On or After Jan. 1, 1978

A work that is created on or after Jan. 1, 1978, is automatically protected from the moment of its creation, and is ordinarily given a term of the author's life, plus an additional 70 years after the author's death. In the case of a joint work prepared by two or more authors who did not work for hire, the term lasts for 70 years after the last surviving author's death. For works made for hire, and for anonymous and pseudonymous works (unless the author's identity is revealed in Copyright Office records), the duration of copyright will be 95 years from publication or 120 years from creation, whichever is shorter.

Works Originally Created Before Jan. 1, 1978

Works that were created but not published or registered for copyright before Jan. 1, 1978, have been automatically brought under the statute and are now given federal copyright protection. The duration of copyright in these works will generally be computed in the same way as for works created on or after Jan. 1, 1978: the life-plus-70 or 95/120-year terms will apply to them as well. The law provides that in no case will the term of copyright for works in this category expire before Dec. 31, 2002, and for works published on or before Dec. 31, 2002, the term of copyright will not expire before Dec. 31, 2047. Works that were created and published or registered before Jan. 1, 1978, generally enjoy a copyright term of 75 years from the date of publication or registration. Check with the Copyright Office for details.

International Copyright Protection

There is no "international copyright" that will automatically protect an author's work throughout the entire world. Protection against unauthorized use in a particular country depends basically on the national laws of that country. However, most countries do offer protection to foreign works under certain conditions, and these conditions have been greatly simplified by international copyright treaties and conventions.

For a list of countries that maintain copyright relations with the United States, request Circular 38a from the Copyright Office.

Copyright Registration

Copyright registration makes a public record of the basic facts of a particular copyright. Even though registration is not a requirement for protection, the copyright law provides several incentives to encourage copyright owners to register. They include the following:

• Registration establishes a public record of the copyright claim;

• Before an infringement suit may be filed in court, registration is necessary for works of U.S. origin;

• If made before or within five years of publication, registration will establish *prima facie* evidence in court of the validity of the copyright and of the facts stated in the certificate;

• If registration is made within three months after publication of the work or prior to an infringement of the work, statutory damages, and attorney's fees will be available to the copyright owner in court actions. Otherwise, only an award of actual damages and profits is available to the copyright owner; and

• Copyright registration allows the owner of the copyright to record the registration with the U.S. Customs Service for protection against the importation of infringing copies.

Registration may be made at any time within the life of the copyright. When a work has been registered in unpublished form, it is not necessary to make another registration when the work becomes published (although the copyright owner may register the published edition, if desired).

To register a work, send the following three elements in the same envelope or package to the Registrar of Copyrights, Copyright Office, Library of Congress, 101 Independence Ave., S.E., Washington, D.C. 20559-6000:

1. a properly completed application form;

2. a nonrefundable filing fee of $30 for each application; and

3. a nonreturnable deposit of the work that is being registered. The deposit requirements vary in particular situations. Contact the Copyright Office for current information on fees and special requirements.

A copyright registration is effective on the date the Copyright Office receives all of the required elements in acceptable form, regardless of how long it takes to process the application and mail the certificate of registration. The time the Copyright Office requires to process an application varies, depending on the amount of material the office is receiving. If you apply for copyright registration, you will not receive an acknowledgment that your application has been received, but you can expect a certificate of registration indicating that the work has been registered, or if the application cannot be accepted, a letter explaining why it has been rejected.

Requests to have certificates sent by Federal Express or another mail service cannot be honored. If you want to know the date that the Copyright Office receives your material, send it by registered or certified mail and request a return receipt.

For More Information

Information on registration and application forms may be obtained free of charge by writing or calling the Copyright Office. Address inquiries to the Copyright Office, Publications Section, LM-455, Library of Congress, 101 Independence Ave., S.E., Washington, D.C. 20559-6000. To speak with an information specialist, call 202-707-3000 (TTY: 202-707-6737) between 8:30 a.m. and 5:00 p.m., Eastern Time, Monday to Friday, except federal holidays. Recorded information is available 24 hours a day.

Copyright information, including the most frequently requested circulars, is available on the Web at www.loc.gov/copyright.

Trademarks

Source: Department of Commerce, Patent and Trademark Office.

A trademark may be defined as a word, letter, device, or symbol, as well as any combination of these, that is used in connection with merchandise and that points distinctly to the origin of the goods.

Certificates of registration of trademarks are issued under the seal of the Patent and Trademark Office and may be registered by the owner if he or she is engaged in interstate or foreign commerce. Federal jurisdiction over trademarks arises under the commerce clause of the Constitution. Effective November 16, 1989, applications to register may also be based on a "bona fide intention to use the mark in commerce." Trademarks may be registered by foreign owners who comply with our law, as well as by citizens of foreign countries with which the U.S. has treaties relating to trademarks. American citizens may register trademarks in foreign countries by complying with the laws of those countries. The right to registration and protection of trademarks in many foreign countries is guaranteed by treaties.

General jurisdiction in trademark cases involving Federal Registrations is given to Federal courts. Adverse decisions of examiners on applications for registration are appealable to the Trademark Trial and Appeal Board, whose affirmances and decisions in *inter partes* proceedings are subject to court review. Before adopting a trademark, a person should make a search of prior marks to avoid unwittingly infringing upon them.

The duration of a trademark registration is 10 years, but it may be renewed indefinitely for 10-year periods, provided the trademark is still in use at the time of expiration.

The application fee is $245 per class.

Patents

Source: Department of Commerce, Patent and Trademark Office.

A patent, in the most general sense, is a document issued by a government, conferring some special right or privilege. The term is now restricted mainly to patents for inventions, and occasionally, land patents.

The grant of a patent for an invention gives the inventor the privilege, for a limited period of time, of excluding others from making, using, or selling a certain article.

In the U.S., the law provides that a patent may be granted, for a term of 20 years from the date of application, to any person who has invented or discovered any new and useful art, machine, manufacture, or composition of matter, as well as any new and useful improvements thereof. A patent may also be granted to a person who has invented or discovered and asexually reproduced a new and distinct variety of plant (other than a tuber-propagated one) or has invented a new, original, and ornamental design for an article of manufacture, for a term of 20 years and 14 years, respectively.

A patent is granted only upon receipt of a complete, regularly filed application and the appropriate fees, and upon determination that the invention is new, useful, and, in view of the prior art, unobvious to one skilled in the art. The disclosure must be of such nature as to enable others to reproduce the invention.

A complete application, which must be addressed to the Commissioner of Patents and Trademarks, Washington, D.C. 20231, consists of a specification with one or more claims; oath or declaration; drawing (whenever the nature of the case admits of it); and a basic filing fee of $380. The filing fee is not returned to the applicant if the patent is refused. If the patent is allowed, another fee of $660 is required before the patent is issued. The fee for design patent application is $155; the issue fee is $215. The fee for a plant patent application is $240; the issue fee is $290. Maintenance fees are required on utility patents at stipulated intervals. Phone 1-800-786-9199 for the latest fees.

Applications are ordinarily considered in the order in which they are received. Patents are not granted for printed matter, for methods of doing business, or for devices for which claims contrary to natural laws are made. Applications for a perpetual-motion machine have been made from time to time, but until a working model is presented that actually fulfills the claim, no patent will be issued.

NOTE: Fees are subject to change in October of each year.

Beware of Illegal Patent Services

It is illegal under patent law (35 USC 33) for anyone to hold himself out as qualified to prepare and prosecute patent applications unless he is registered with the Patent Office. Also, Patent Office regulations forbid registered practitioners advertising for patent business. Some inventors, unaware of this, enter into binding contracts with persons and firms that advertise their assistance in making patent searches and preparing drawings, specifications, and patent applications, only to discover much later that their applications require the services of fully qualified agents or attorneys.

National Consumer Organizations

NOTE: For other organizations, *see* Societies & Associations, pp. 606–615.

Alliance Against Fraud In Telemarketing (AAFT), c/o National Consumers League, 1701 K St., N.W., Ste. 1200, Washington, DC 20006; 202-835-3323; 202-835-0747 (fax).

The Alliance, coordinated by the National Consumers League, is an international coalition of public interest groups, trade associations, labor unions, businesses, law enforcement agencies, consumer reporters, and consumer protection agencies. AAFT members promote cooperative educational efforts to warn consumers of the threat of telemarketing fraud and to provide information on how consumers can protect themselves.

American Association of Retired Persons (AARP), Consumer Affairs Section, 601 E St., N.W., Washington, DC 20049; 800-424-3410; 202-434-6466 (fax).

AARP's Consumer Affairs Section advocates on behalf of mid-life and older consumers, develops and distributes consumer information, and educates the private sector about the specific needs of older consumers. It offers programs and materials on housing, insurance, funeral practices, eligibility for public benefits, financial security, transportation, and consumer protection issues, with special focus on the needs and problems of older consumers.

American Council on Consumer Interests (ACCI), 240 Stanley Hall, University of Missouri, Columbia, MO 65211–0001; 573-882-3817; 573-884-6571 (fax); email: acci@showme.missouri.edu.
Contact: Anita B. Metzen, Executive Director.

Serving the professional needs of consumer educators, researchers, and policymakers, ACCI publications and educational programs foster the production, synthesis, and dissemination of information in the consumer interest.

American Council on Science and Health (ACSH), 1995 Broadway, 2nd Fl., New York, NY 10023-5860; 212-362-7044; 212-362-4919 (fax).

A nonprofit public education group, ACSH's goal is to provide up-to-date, sound information on the relationship between people's health and chemicals, foods, lifestyles, and the environment. Booklets and special reports on a variety of topics are available, as is a quarterly magazine, *Priorities.*

American Savings Education Council, 2121 K Street, N.W., Suite 600, Washington, DC 20037; 202-659-0670; email: asecinfo@asec.org; Web: www.asec.org.

The Council is a coalition of private and public sector institutions that undertakes initiatives to raise public awareness about what is needed to ensure long-term personal financial independence.

Better Business Bureau *See* Council of Better Business Bureaus, Inc. (CBBB)

Center for Auto Safety (CAS), 1825 Connecticut Ave., N.W., Ste. 3301, Washington, DC 20009; 202-328-7700.

CAS advocates on behalf of consumers in auto safety and quality, fuel efficiency, emissions, and related issues. For advice on specific problems, consumers should write to CAS, including a brief statement of the problem or question; year, make, and model of the vehicle; and a stamped self-addressed envelope.

Center for Science in the Public Interest (CSPI), 1875 Connecticut Ave., N.W., Ste. 300, Washington, DC 20009; 202-332-9110; 202-265-4954 (fax).

A nonprofit, membership organization, CSPI conducts research, education, and advocacy on nutrition, health, food safety, and related issues, and publishes the monthly *Nutrition Action Healthletter* as well as other consumer materials.

Citizen Action, 1730 Rhode Island Ave., N.W., Ste. 403, Washington, DC 20036; 202-775-1580; 202-296-4054 (fax).

Citizen Action works on behalf of its 3 million members and 32 state organizations on health care reform, environment, and energy issues.

Coalition Against Insurance Fraud, 1010 Vermont Ave., N.W., Suite 817, Washington DC; 202-393-7330; Web: www.insurancefraud.org.

An independent, nonprofit organization of consumers, government agencies, and insurers dedicated to combating all forms of insurance fraud through public information and advocacy.

Congress of Consumer Organizations (COCO), P.O. Box 158, Newton Centre, MA 02159; 617-552-8184; 617-552-2380 (fax); Web: www.essential.org.

COCO publishes a monthly newsletter, the *COCO INTERCOM,* on a broad range of consumer issues.

Congress Watch, 215 Pennsylvania Ave., S.E., Washington, DC 20003; 202-546-4996; 202-547-7392 (fax).

An arm of Public Citizen, Congress Watch works for consumer-related legislation, regulation, and policies in such areas as trade, health and safety, and campaign financing, and has publications available on the issues with which it deals.

Consumer Action (CA), 116 New Montgomery, Ste. 233, San Francisco, CA 94105; 415-777-9635 (consumer hotline, 10 a.m.–2 p.m., PST); 415-777-9456 (voice/ttd); 415-777-5267 (fax).

An education and advocacy organization specializing in credit, finance, and telecommunications issues, Consumer Action offers a multilingual consumer complaint hotline, free information on its surveys of banks and long-distance telephone companies, and consumer education materials in as many as eight languages.

Consumer Alert, 1001 Connecticut Ave., N.W., Ste. 1128, Washington, DC 20036; 202-467-5809; 202-467-5814 (fax); Web: www.consumeralert.org.

Consumer Alert is a nonprofit, membership organization whose mission is to inform the public about the consumer benefits of competitive enterprise, advancing competition as the best regulator of business. A bimonthly newsletter and other materials are available.

Consumer Federation of America (CFA), 1424 16th St., N.W., Ste. 604, Washington, DC 20036; 202-387-6121; 202-265-7989 (fax).

Made up of more than 240 organizations representing 50 million consumers, CFA is a consumer advocacy and education organization. Issues on which it currently represents consumer interests before Congress and federal regulatory agencies include telephone service, insurance and financial services, product safety, indoor air pollution, health care, product liability, and utility rates. It develops and distributes studies of various consumer issues, as well as consumer guides in book and pamphlet form. In addition, CFA publishes several newsletters.

Consumers for World Trade (CWT), 2000 L St., N.W., Ste. 200, Washington, DC 20036; 202-785-4835; 202-416-1734 (fax).

A nonprofit organization, CWT supports trade expansion and liberalization to promote economic growth and increase consumer choice and price competition in the marketplace. Various publications are available.

Consumers Union of U.S., Inc. (CU), 101 Truman Ave., Yonkers, NY 10703-1057; 914-378-2000; 914-378-2928 (fax). Available online via CompuServe.

A nonprofit, independent organization, CU researches and tests consumer goods and services and disseminates the results in its monthly magazine, *Consumer Reports,* as well as other publications and media.

Council of Better Business Bureaus, Inc. (CBBB), 4200 Wilson Blvd., Suite 800, Arlington, VA 22203–1804; 703-276-0100; 703-525-8277 (fax); Web: www.bbb.org.

Sponsored by national companies, the Council of Better Business Bureaus provides coordination and leadership to the 163 Better Business Bureaus (BBBs) in the U.S., and offers a national advertising review program, dispute resolution services, an advisory service that reports on national charities, consumer information services, and voluntary industry guidelines for advertising and selling products and services.

Families USA Foundation, 1334 G St., N.W., Washington, DC 20005; 202-628-3030; 202-347-2417 (fax); email: info@familiesusa.org.

A national, nonprofit membership organization, Families USA works to educate and mobilize consumers on health care issues. Families USA supports two grassroots advocacy networks: a.s.a.p., a network of health- and long-term care reform activists; and HealthLink USA, a nationwide health reform computer network for public interest groups. The organization also develops and distributes reports and other materials on health- and long-term care issues.

Health Research Group (HRG), 1600 20th St., N.W., Washington, DC 20009; 202-885-1000.

A division of Public Citizen, HRG works for protection against unsafe foods, drugs, medical devices, and workplaces, and advocates for greater consumer control over personal health decisions. A monthly *Health Letter* and other publications are available.

Insurance Information Institute, 110 William Street, New York, NY 10038; 212-669-9200; 212-791-1087 (fax); Web: www.iii.org.

A nonprofit, educational, and communications organization dedicated to helping consumers find high-quality, reasonably priced insurance services.

National Association of Consumer Agency Administrators (NACAA), 1010 Vermont Ave., N.W., Ste. 514, Washington, DC 20005; 202-347-7395; 202-347-2563 (fax).

An association of the administrators of local, state, and federal government consumer protection agencies, NACAA provides training programs, public policy studies, and conferences, professional publications, and other member services.

National Association of State Utility Consumer Advocates (NASUCA), 1133 15th St., N.W., Ste. 550, Washington, DC 20005; 202-727-3908; 202-727-3911 (fax); email: nacaa@essential.org.

A national organization of 41 utility ratepayer advocate offices in 38 states and the District of Columbia, NASUCA members represent millions of consumers served by investor-owned gas, telephone, electric, and water companies before Congress, state regulatory commissions, the courts, the Federal Energy Regulatory Commission, and the Federal Communications Commission.

National Coalition for Consumer Education (NCCE), 295 Main St., Ste. 200, Madison, NJ 07940; 201-377-8987; 201-377-4828 (fax).

The coalition brings together people and resources from government, business, education, consumer organizations, and the media to educate consumers about such important issues as financial management, health and safety, and the environment. The coalition develops and provides educational materials and resources to consumer educators, but does not handle requests from individuals.

National Consumers League (NCL), 1701 K St., N.W., Ste. 1201, Washington, DC 20006; 202-835-3323; 202-835-0747 (fax).

Founded in 1899, NCL is America's pioneer consumer advocacy organization. The league is a nonprofit, membership organization working for consumer health and safety protection and fairness in the marketplace and workplace. Current principal issue areas include consumer fraud, food and drug safety, fair labor standards, child labor, health care, the environment, financial services, and telecommunications. The league develops and distributes consumer education materials and newsletters.

National Foundation for Consumer Credit, Inc. (NFCC), 8611 2nd Ave., Ste. 100, Silver Spring, MD 20910; 301-589-5600 or 800-388-2227; 301-495-5623 (fax).

A membership organization for nonprofit community organizations that are often called Consumer Credit Counseling Service agencies and are in more than 1,100 locations in the United States and Canada. The agencies educate and counsel individuals and families on credit issues. Consumers are taught to budget and use credit wisely and may receive help in resolving their credit problems. The 800 number provides the location of the nearest agency.

National Fraud Information Center (NFIC), P.O. Box 65868, Washington, DC 20035; 800-876-7060 (TDD available); 202-835-0767 (fax); Web: www.fraud.org.

A project of the National Consumers League, the center's toll-free hotline assists consumers with information to help them avoid becoming victims of fraud, refers them to appropriate law enforcement agencies and professional associations, and assists them in filing complaints. The center also provides professionals involved in consumer fraud prevention and enforcement with telecommunications systems and data links to improve fraud regulation, prevention, and law enforcement.

National Institute for Consumer Education (NICE), 559 Gary M. Owen Bldg., 300 W. Michigan Ave., Ypsilanti, MI 48197; 734-487-2292; 734-487-7153 (fax).

A consumer education resource and professional development center for K–12 classroom teachers and business, government, labor, and community educators, NICE conducts training programs, develops teaching guides and resource lists, and manages a national clearinghouse of consumer education materials, including videos, software programs, textbooks, and curriculum guides.

National Senior Citizens Law Center, 1101 14th St. N.W., Suite 400, Washington, DC 20005; 202-289-6976; 202-289-7224 (fax); email: nsclc@nsclc.org; Web: www.nsclc.org.

The National Senior Citizens Law Center (NSCLC) was established in 1972 to help older Americans live their lives in dignity and freedom from poverty, through legal work in support of elderly poor clients, client groups, and Elder Law attorneys. NSCLC attorneys are knowledgeable in a broad range of legal issues and practice areas that affect the security and welfare of older persons of limited income.

Public Citizen, Inc., 1600 20th St., N.W., Washington, DC 20009; 202-885-1000.

A national, nonprofit membership organization representing consumer interests through lobbying, litigation, research, and publications, Public Citizen represents consumer interests in Congress, the courts, government agencies, and the media. Primary current areas of interest include product liability, health care delivery, safe medical devices and medications, open and ethical government, and safe and sustainable energy use.

Public Voice for Food and Health Policy, 1012 14th St., N.W., Washington, DC 20005; 202-347-6200; 202-347-6261 (fax); email: pvoice@ix.netcom.com.

A national research, education, and advocacy organization, Public Voice works for food, health, and agriculture policies and practices that will protect the environment and improve the safety and affordability of the food supply. Public Voice develops and distributes consumer information materials on pesticide reduction, nutrition labeling, and seafood safety. The organization recently merged with Consumer Federation of America.

Society of Consumer Affairs Professionals in Business (SOCAP), 801 N. Fairfax St., Ste. 404, Alexandria, VA 22314; 703-519-3700; 703-549-4886 (fax).

An international professional organization, SOCAP provides training, conferences, and publications to encourage and maintain the integrity of businesses in transactions with consumers; to encourage and promote effective communication and understanding among businesses, government, and consumers; and to define and advance the consumer affairs profession.

U.S. Public Interest Research Group (U.S. PIRG), 218 D St., S.E., Washington, DC 20003; 202-546-9707; email: pirg@pirg.org; Web: www.pirg.org.

This is the national lobbying office for the 33 state PIRGs, which are consumer/environmental advocacy groups that lobby and publish reports on issues including credit bureau errors; bank fees and services; toy, ATV, and product safety; toxic chemicals in art supplies and other consumer products; and recycling, over-packaging, and green consumerism. U.S. PIRG does not handle individual consumer complaints directly, but measures complaint levels to gauge the need for remedial legislation.

A Get-Tough Policy That Failed

Mandatory sentencing was once America's law-and-order panacea.
Here's why the three-strikes law isn't working

By JOHN CLOUD TIME

Remember Polly Klaas? She was the 12-year-old Petaluma, Calif., girl whisked from a slumber party in 1993 and found murdered two months later. Her father, Marc, horrified to learn that her killer was on parole and had attacked children in the past, called for laws making parole less common. He joined others to back a "three strikes and you're out" law—no parole, ever, for those convicted of three felonies. Klaas went on TV, got in the papers, met the President—all within weeks after his body was found.

Then he studied how the three-strikes law would actually work, noticing that a nonviolent crime—burglary, for instance—could count as a third strike. "That meant you could get life for breaking into someone's garage and stealing a stereo," he says. "I've had my stereo stolen, and I've had my daughter stolen. I believe I know the difference."

Klaas began speaking against three strikes. But his daughter had already become a symbol for the crackdown on crime, and California's legislature passed the three-strikes law. It now seems politically untouchable, despite horror stories like the one about a Los Angeles 27-year-old who got 25 years to life for stealing pizza.

Throwing Away the Key

In 1998 two state senators tried to limit the measure to violent crimes, but the bill didn't make it out of committee. Governor Pete Wilson vetoed a bill simply to study the effects of the law. Wilson probably knew what the study would conclude: while three-strikes laws sound great to the public, they aren't working. A growing number of states and private groups have scrutinized these and other "mandatory-minimum laws," the generic name for statutes forcing judges to impose designated terms. The studies are finding that the laws cost enormous amounts of money, largely to lock up such nonviolent folks as teenage drug couriers, dope-starved addicts, and hapless offenders like the Iowa man who got 10 years for stealing $30 worth of steaks from a grocery store and then struggling with a store clerk who tackled him (struggling made it a felony).

How much are we spending? Put it this way: mandatory minimums are the reason so many prisons are booming in otherwise impoverished rural counties across America. The U.S. inmate population has more than doubled (to nearly 2 million) since the mid-'80s, when mandatory sentencing became the hot new intoxicant for politicians. New York (the first state to enact mandatory minimums) has sloshed $600 million into prison construction since 1988; not coincidentally, in the same period it has sliced $700 million from higher education.

Americans will have to spend even more in the future to house and treat all the aging inmates. California has already filled its 114,000 prison beds, and double-bunks 46,000 additional inmates.

Locking Up the Wrong People

More important, mandatory minimums for nonviolent (and arguably victimless) drug crimes insult justice. Most mandatory sentences were designed as weapons in the drug war, with an awful consequence: we now live in a country where it's common to get a longer sentence for selling a neighbor a joint than for, say, sexually abusing her. (According to a 1997 federal report, those convicted of drug trafficking have served an average of almost seven years, nearly a year longer than those convicted of sexual abuse.) Several new books, including Michael Massing's *The Fix*, point out that the tough-on-drugs policies of the past 15 years haven't had much impact on the heart of the drug problem, abuse by long-term urban addicts. Even the usually hard-line drug czar Barry McCaffrey has written that "we can't incarcerate our way out of the drug problem." He has urged Congress to reduce mandatory minimums for crack, which are currently 100 times as heavy as those for powdered coke and impact most on minority youth.

This injustice is most palpable on city streets. In places like New York there are more black and Hispanic kids in prison than in college. That injustice may have played a role in the fate of Derrick Smith, a New York City youth who, in October 1998, faced a sentence of 15 years to life for selling crack. At the sentence hearing a distraught Smith told the judge, "I'm only 19. This is terrible." He then hurled himself out of a courtroom window and fell 16 stories to his death. "He didn't kill anyone; he didn't rob anyone," says his mother. "This happened because we are black and poor."

Neither Just nor Effective

Worst of all, mandatory minimums have done little to solve the problems for which they were crafted. Casual drug use has declined since the 1970s, but the size of the addict population has remained stable. And even conservative criminologists concede that demographics (i.e., fewer young men) and better policing are more responsible for the dropping crime rate than criminals' fear of mandatory minimums. John DiIulio Jr., the Princeton professor who wrote a 1994 defense of mandatory sentencing for the *Wall Street Journal* with the charming headline LET 'EM ROT, now opposes mandatory minimums for drug crimes. He points out that more and more young, nonviolent, first-time offenders are being incarcerated—"and they won't find suitable role models in prison."

Common Sense Is Dawning

The good news is that a consensus is emerging among judges (including Reagan-appointee Chief Justice William Rehnquist), law enforcers, and crime experts—among them many conservatives who once supported the laws—that mandatory minimums are foolish. In January 1999, the Supreme Court declined to hear a case challenging the California three-strikes law, but four Justices expressed concern about the law's effect and seemed to invite other challenges. A few brave politicians have gingerly suggested that the laws may be something we should rethink. Some states are starting to backtrack on tough sentencing laws:

MICHIGAN: In February 1998, former Republican Governor William Milliken called the "650 Lifer Law" his biggest mistake. The 1978 law mandated a life-without-parole term for possession with intent to deliver at least 650 g (about 1.4 lbs.) of heroin or cocaine. But though the law was intended to net big fish, few major dealers got hit. In fact, 86% of the "650 lifers" had never done time; 70% were poor. "A lot of them were young people who made very stupid mistakes but shouldn't have to pay for it for the rest of their lives," says state representative Barbara Dobb, the Republican who began a reform effort. In August 1998, G.O.P. Governor John Engler signed a law allowing 650 lifers to be paroled after 15 years.

UTAH: In March 1995, Republican senate president Lane Beattie, concerned about the excesses of mandatory minimums, introduced a bill to eliminate them in certain cases. Worried about the political fallout, he did so near midnight on the last day of the legislative session. The bill passed quietly, without debate, but victims' groups noticed. Though a public outcry followed, the G.O.P. Governor said he agreed with the bill and refused to veto it.

GEORGIA: In the final minutes of the 1996 legislative session, state lawmakers nixed mandatory life sentences for second-time drug offenders. State statistics showed that four-fifths of those serving life had hawked less than $50 in narcotics. Even state prosecutors backed the change.

NEW YORK: John Dunne, a former Republican legislator who helped devise the Rockefeller Drug Laws, the mandatory-sentencing legislation promulgated in the 1970s by Governor Nelson Rockefeller, is lobbying to end them. "This was a good idea 25 years ago, but the sad experience is that it has not had an effect," says Dunne, who also served in the Bush Administration. "Behind closed doors, virtually everyone will say these drug laws are not working, but they cannot say that publicly."

Certainly no one in Washington is saying it publicly. The House Judiciary Committee didn't even hold hearings on the bill that created the current minimums, which coasted to victory just in time for the 1986 midterm elections. In 1998 Congress and President Clinton added a new mandatory minimum to the books: five years for 5 g of crystal meth, the crack of the '90s. Mandatory minimums remain political beasts, and it would probably take Nixon-goes-to-China leadership from a Republican to turn public opinion against them. Either that or more Jean Valjeans serving 10-year sentences for stealing steaks. □

State Prison Inmates, by Most Serious Offense, 1996[1]

Most Serious Offense	Number of Prisoners	Percent
Total	326,547	100.0%
Violent offenses	96,300	29.5
Murder[2]	9,200	2.8
Negligent manslaughter	3,600	1.1
Sexual assault[3]	19,700	6.0
Robbery	29,700	9.1
Aggravated assault	28,400	8.7
Other violent	5,700	1.8
Property offenses	94,800	29.0%
Burglary	39,000	12.0
Larceny/theft	24,400	7.5
Motor vehicle theft	6,800	2.1
Fraud	13,200	4.1
Other property	11,400	3.3
Drug offenses	98,700	30.2%
Public-order offenses	34,600	10.6%
Other	2,100	0.7%

NOTE: Data may not sum to total due to rounding. 1. Includes only those with sentences of more than one year. 2. Includes nonnegligent manslaughter. 3. Includes rape and other sexual assault. *Source:* National Corrections Reporting Program, Bureau of Justice Statistics.

Federal Prison Inmates, by Most Serious Offense, 1996

Most Serious Offense	Number of Prisoners	Percent
Total	92,672	100.0%
Violent offenses	11,523	12.6%
Homicide[1]	1,084	1.2
Assault	645	0.7
Robbery	8,334	9.1
Other Violent[2]	1,460	1.6
Property offenses	7,781	8.5%
Burglary	181	0.2
Fraud[3]	5,807	6.3
Larceny/theft	1,793	2.0
Drug offenses	55,194	60.2%
Public-order offenses	17,227	18.8%
Immigration	4,476	4.9
Weapons	7,480	8.2
Escape/court	325	0.4
Other public-order	4,946	5.4

1. Includes murder, nonnegligent manslaughter, and negligent manslaughter. 2. Includes kidnapping, rape, and other sexual assault, threats against the President, and other offenses. 3. Includes embezzlement, counterfeiting, forgery, bankruptcy, and fraud (excluding tax fraud but including securities fraud). *Source:* BJS Federal justice database.

Total Arrests Age 18 and Under: 1997

	Number of arrests	Percent distribution		Number of arrests	Percent distribution
Total, all ages	10,544,624	100.0%	16	462,963	4.4%
Total, under 18	1,969,407	18.7	15	381,821	3.6
Total, under 15	634,013	6.0	13–14	457,809	4.3
18	517,177	4.9	10–12	146,420	1.4
17	490,610	4.7	Under 10	29,784	0.3

NOTE: Because of rounding, the percentages may not add up to total. Source: Department of Justice, Federal Bureau of Investigation, Uniform Crime Reports for the United States, 1997.

Lessons in Violence

A Timeline of Recent School Shootings

Feb. 2, 1996
Moses Lake, Wash. 2 students and 1 teacher killed, 1 other wounded when 14-year-old Barry Loukaitis opened fire on his algebra class.

Feb. 19, 1997
Bethel, Alaska Principal and 1 student killed, 2 others wounded by Evan Ramsey, 16, at his high school.

Oct. 1, 1997
Pearl, Miss. 2 students killed and 7 wounded by a 16-year-old who was also accused of killing his mother. He and several friends thought to be in on the plot were said to be outcasts who worshipped Satan.

Dec. 1, 1997
West Paducah, Ky. 3 students killed, 5 wounded by a 14-year-old boy as they participated in a prayer circle at Heath High School.

Dec. 15, 1997
Stamps, Ark. 2 students wounded. Colt Todd, 14, was hiding in the woods when he shot the students as they stood in the parking lot.

March 24, 1998
Jonesboro, Ark. 4 students and 1 teacher killed, 10 others wounded outside as Westside Middle School emptied during a false fire alarm. Mitchell Johnson, 13, and Andrew Golden, 11, shot at their classmates and teachers from the woods.

April 24, 1998
Edinboro, Pa. 1 teacher killed, 2 students wounded at a dance at James W. Parker Middle School. A 14-year-old boy was charged.

May 19, 1998
Fayetteville, Tenn. 1 student killed in the parking lot at Lincoln County High School three days before he was to graduate. The victim was dating the ex-girlfriend of his killer, 18-year-old honor student Jacob Davis.

May 21, 1998
Springfield, Ore. 2 students killed, 22 others wounded in the cafeteria at Thurston High School by 15-year-old Kip Kinkel. Kinkel had been arrested and released to his parents a day earlier, after it was discovered that he had a gun at school. His parents were later found dead at home.

June 15, 1998
Richmond, Va. 1 teacher and 1 guidance counselor wounded by a 14-year-old boy in the hallway of a Richmond high school.

April 20, 1999
Littleton, Colo. 14 students (including killers) and 1 teacher killed, 23 others wounded at Columbine High School in the nation's deadliest school shooting. Eric Harris, 18, and Dylan Klebold, 17, had plotted for a year to kill at least 500 and blow up their school. At the end of their hour-long rampage, they turned their guns on themselves.

April 28, 1999
Taber, Alberta, Canada 1 student killed, 1 wounded at W. R. Myers High School in first fatal high school shooting in Canada in 20 years. The suspect, a 14-year-old boy, had been unhappy at Myers and dropped out in order to begin home schooling.

May 20, 1999
Conyers, Ga. 6 students injured at Heritage High School by a 15-year-old boy who was reportedly depressed after breaking up with his girlfriend.

Committing Murder: By Type of Weapon and Age Group, 1997

Among murderers, those 20 and under were more likely to use a firearm than adults—about three-quarters of the homicides committed by offenders under 21 involved firearms.

	Age of offender			
Type of weapon	17 years and under	18–20 years	21 years and older	Total
Gun	74.6%	74.0%	61.0%	65.5%
Other weapon	23.3	23.8	35.1	31.2
Unknown weapon	2.1	2.2	3.9	3.3
Total no. of homicide offenders	1,487	2,420	7,723	11,630

Source: FBI Uniform Crime Reports, Supplemental Homicide Reports, 1997, special tabulation prepared by Northeastern University, Boston, Mass.

Crime Declined for the Seventh Straight Year

According to the Justice Department, both violent crimes (murder, rape, robbery, and aggravated assault) and property offenses (burglary, larceny-theft, car theft, and arson) dropped 7% in 1998. For the past seven years crime has steadily decreased—making this period the longest uninterrupted drop in crime since the 1950s. The 7% drop in 1998 was the greatest annual decrease since the decline began in 1992.

The drop in the homicide rate has been particularly dramatic. The rate had doubled in the mid-

1960s to late 1970s, and peaked in 1980 at a rate of 10.2 per 100,000 population. But by 1998 it had plunged to its lowest rate since 1968. And for the first time ever, New York City was not the murder capital of America—that distinction had been passed on to Chicago. In 1998, there were 633 murders in New York compared to 694 in Chicago. Only larceny, which includes pickpocketing and shoplifting, had not shown a decrease.

Crime Index Trends by Geographic Region
(Preliminary 1998 figures)

Region	Crime index total	Violent crime	Property crime	Murder	Forcible rape	Robbery	Aggravated assault	Burglary	Larceny-theft	Motor vehicle theft	Arson
Total	−7	−7	−7	−8	−5	−11	−5	−7	−6	−10	−7
Northeast	−8	−7	−8	−11	−6	−12	−4	−11	−7	−14	−12
Midwest	−4	−4	−4	−5	−3	−8	−2	−4	−4	−8	−9
South	−6	−7	−6	−7	−6	−12	−5	−5	−6	−8	−5
West	−8	−9	−8	−11	−4	−13	−7	−9	−7	−11	−6

Source: FBI, Uniform Crime Reports, preliminary 1998 figures.

Homicide Rate (per 100,000), 1950–1998

Year	Homicide rate	Year	Homicide rate	Year	Homicide rate	Year	Homicide rate	Year	Homicide rate
1950	4.6	1960	5.1	1970	7.9	1980	10.2	1990	9.4
1951	4.4	1961	4.8	1971	8.6	1981	9.8	1991	9.8
1952	4.6	1962	4.6	1972	9.0	1982	9.1	1992	9.3
1953	4.5	1963	4.6	1973	9.4	1983	8.3	1993	9.5
1954	4.2	1964	4.9	1974	9.8	1984	7.9	1994	9.0
1955	4.1	1965	5.1	1975	9.6	1985	7.9	1995	8.2
1956	4.1	1966	5.6	1976	8.8	1986	8.6	1996	7.4
1957	4.0	1967	6.2	1977	8.8	1987	8.3	1997	6.8
1958	4.8	1968	6.9	1978	9.0	1988	8.4	1998*	6.2
1959	4.9	1969	7.3	1979	9.7	1989	8.7		

*Preliminary 1998 figures. Source: FBI, Uniform Crime Reports.

Arrests by Race, 1997

	Percent distribution[1]					Percent distribution[1]			
Offense charged	White	Black	American Indian or Alaskan Native	Asian or Pacific Islander	Offense charged	White	Black	American Indian or Alaskan Native	Asian or Pacific Islander
Total	67.1%	30.4%	1.3%	1.2%	Sex offenses, except forcible rape and prostitution	74.0%	23.6%	1.2%	1.2%
Murder[2]	41.9	56.4	.7	1.0					
Forcible rape	58.2	39.7	1.1	1.0					
Robbery	41.2	57.1	.6	1.2	Drug abuse violation	62.0	36.8	.5	.7
Aggravated assault	61.2	36.6	1.0	1.1	Gambling	28.9	67.1	.5	3.5
Burglary	68.0	29.6	1.0	1.3	Offenses against family and children	66.0	31.1	1.0	1.9
Larceny-theft	64.7	32.4	1.2	1.7					
Motor vehicle theft	58.1	39.0	1.1	1.8	Driving under the influence	86.3	10.9	1.5	1.3
Arson	73.2	24.9	.8	1.1					
Other assaults	62.6	35.1	1.3	1.0	Liquor laws	83.5	12.5	3.1	.9
Forgery and counterfeiting	66.0	32.2	.6	1.2	Drunkenness	80.3	16.9	2.3	.4
Fraud	68.1	30.7	.5	.7	Disorderly conduct	62.1	35.9	1.4	.7
Embezzlement	63.2	34.8	.5	1.5	Vagrancy	51.5	46.3	1.9	.3
Stolen property—buying, receiving, possessing	56.9	41.1	.8	1.1	All other offenses except traffic	63.0	34.6	1.2	1.2
Vandalism	73.0	24.7	1.3	1.0	Suspicion	64.0	33.9	1.5	.6
Weapons—carrying, possessing, etc.	58.7	39.6	.7	1.0	Curfew and loitering law violations	74.8	22.6	1.3	1.3
Prostitution and commercialized vice	57.9	40.4	.5	1.2	Runaways	77.2	18.1	1.1	3.6

1. Because of rounding, the percentages may not add up to total. 2. Includes nonnegligent manslaughter. Source: Uniform Crime Reports, 1997.

Crime Rates for Selected Large Cities: 1996

(Offenses known to the police per 100,000 population.)

City ranked by population size, 1995[1]	Crime index, total	Violent crime				Property crime	
		Murder	Forcible rape	Robbery	Aggravated assault	Burglary	Larceny-theft
New York, N.Y.	5,212.2	13.4	31.8	676.7	622.3	834.8	2,210.6
Los Angeles, Calif.	6,725.2	20.3	41.8	720.1	1,014.2	1,025.3	2,717.7
Chicago, Ill.[2]	n.a.	28.6	n.a.	975.3	1,347.0	1,469.6	4,338.7
Houston, Tex.	7,636.5	14.7	56.5	467.0	728.9	1,433.4	3,672.4
Philadelphia, Pa.	6,920.0	27.1	46.1	1,013.1	442.6	1,060.2	2,817.6
San Diego, Calif.	5,270.0	6.8	31.5	256.6	573.7	736.8	2,712.2
Phoenix, Ariz.	9,541.1	16.3	40.4	329.6	537.5	1,716.0	5,313.7
Dallas, Tex.	9,466.6	20.5	69.8	577.2	867.5	1,693.4	4,621.8
San Antonio, Tex.	8,586.6	11.5	62.4	230.1	160.3	1,339.7	5,921.6
Detroit, Mich.	11,991.2	42.7	111.6	948.2	1,216.0	2,144.2	4,109.9
Honolulu, Hawaii	6,840.1	3.1	25.3	161.8	122.8	1,028.0	4,773.7
San Jose, Calif.	6,849.8	19.4	57.1	439.1	496.0	1,402.1	3,482.7
Las Vegas, Nev.	4,129.1	4.8	41.1	132.2	553.5	566.0	2,383.6
San Francisco, Calif.	7,594.9	11.0	40.0	743.4	532.4	950.0	4,168.7
Baltimore, Md.	12,001.2	45.8	89.5	1,450.6	1,136.9	2,066.0	5,656.0
Jacksonville, Fla.	8,623.5	12.3	98.6	404.4	899.1	1,907.8	4,613.8
Columbus, Ohio	9,539.8	13.9	89.2	518.2	349.5	2,032.3	5,348.1
Memphis, Tenn.	11,127.0	25.5	124.9	945.2	889.0	2,633.5	4,247.5
Milwaukee, Wisc.	7,912.6	20.7	44.8	534.7	352.4	1,215.4	4,137.5
El Paso, Tex.	7,485.5	5.0	40.6	198.2	608.3	653.8	5,256.5
Washington, D.C.	11,889.0	73.1	47.9	1,186.7	1,162.1	1,809.9	5,772.2
Boston, Mass.	8,092.2	10.7	74.9	628.0	943.1	914.4	3,843.1
Charlotte, N.C.	9,659.1	12.8	55.2	468.2	1,072.8	1,845.8	5,450.4
Seattle, Wash.	10,310.8	6.9	48.4	363.8	422.9	1,455.7	6,835.4
Austin, Tex.	7,865.9	7.4	50.2	256.0	397.2	1,409.3	5,058.2
Nashville-Davidson, Tenn.	11,218.9	16.8	91.9	549.0	1,232.9	1,514.0	6,262.5
Denver, Colo.	6,647.1	12.4	69.3	257.1	403.5	1,508.6	3,345.3
Cleveland, Ohio	7,541.4	20.8	129.6	818.9	569.1	1,553.9	2,709.6
New Orleans, La.	11,042.2	71.9	79.9	1,167.3	937.9	2,038.5	4,663.9
Oklahoma City, Okla.	12,158.5	14.3	101.6	314.7	699.7	2,276.3	7,656.4
Fort Worth, Tex.	8,272.6	14.5	67.8	359.8	617.8	1,683.6	4,568.0
Portland, Ore.	10,751.3	10.9	85.9	439.6	1,138.0	1,526.4	6,160.0
Tucson, Ariz.	9,819.3	9.7	59.7	272.7	758.5	1,420.5	6,024.7
Kansas City, Mo.	11,661.8	23.2	91.9	642.4	1,223.7	1,995.0	6,271.0
Long Beach, Calif.	5,978.8	21.6	35.9	552.5	542.0	1,137.0	2,652.4
Virginia Beach, Va.	4,733.2	4.5	28.9	103.4	107.5	696.4	3,566.7
Albuquerque, N.M.	11,307.5	16.4	87.9	468.2	896.1	2,117.7	6,083.6
Atlanta, Ga.	17,070.2	47.4	94.9	1,163.1	2,010.5	2,534.6	8,981.3
Fresno, Calif.	10,633.1	17.6	55.1	532.3	787.9	1,751.8	5,147.3
Miami, Fla.	13,745.8	32.2	52.2	1,334.9	1,695.2	2,546.7	6,086.4
Tulsa, Okla.	7,207.3	8.2	80.0	228.5	849.1	1,614.3	3,303.1
Sacramento, Calif.	8,906.3	11.3	40.6	494.1	431.3	1,884.6	4,440.5
St. Louis, Mo.	15,128.8	44.4	71.9	1,092.4	1,519.1	2,643.3	7,814.1
Oakland, Calif.	10,526.5	25.0	86.5	973.3	1,110.1	1,627.9	5,341.5
Cincinnati, Ohio	7,616.7	8.9	87.4	492.2	499.4	1,577.7	4,445.7
Minneapolis, Minn.	11,290.5	23.0	142.7	896.6	820.5	2,123.4	5,721.9
Pittsburgh, Pa.	5,296.0	13.3	58.1	441.7	290.7	860.6	2,838.5
Omaha, Neb.	7,683.5	7.7	59.0	223.0	1,062.7	1,013.1	4,278.0
Mesa, Ariz.	7,551.0	5.3	32.3	148.5	535.5	1,139.3	4,571.9
Colorado Springs, Colo.	6,199.9	3.6	71.9	136.8	269.5	998.1	4,304.3
Toledo, Ohio	8,468.0	9.2	85.3	399.6	317.6	1,724.2	4,996.1
Buffalo, N.Y.	8,506.0	19.2	86.8	837.7	503.1	2,010.6	3,612.0
Wichita, Kans.	7,956.7	7.7	72.6	263.2	415.1	1,660.7	4,776.4
Arlington, Tex.	7,136.5	5.7	52.2	206.9	564.9	1,136.9	4,408.4
Santa Ana, Calif.	4,479.5	15.6	21.0	399.4	320.4	617.7	2,204.0
Tampa, Fla.	14,549.5	14.6	89.6	906.4	1,938.1	2,502.1	7,054.3
Anaheim, Calif.	5,126.8	4.9	28.3	341.8	348.8	942.9	2,638.5
Corpus Christi, Tex.	10,628.3	6.3	96.3	169.2	781.8	1,316.2	7,676.7
Louisville, Ky.	7,661.0	23.0	47.7	660.1	502.4	1,759.5	3,454.9
Birmingham, Ala.	10,759.1	41.5	84.1	675.3	821.5	2,194.6	5,614.2
St. Paul, Minn.	7,745.8	9.7	87.5	327.4	487.1	1,544.0	4,303.9
Newark, N.J.	13,148.5	35.1	68.3	1,610.9	1,630.7	2,287.4	4,464.5
Aurora, Colo.	6,096.1	4.2	73.6	213.2	330.3	987.5	3,954.0

1. Crime data were not available for Indianapolis, Ind. 2. The rates for forcible rape, violent crime, and crime index are not shown because the forcible rape figures were not in accordance with national Uniform Crime Reporting guidelines. *Source:* U.S. Federal Bureau of Investigation, *Crime in the United States,* annual.

Crime Index by State, 1997

State	Crime index total Number	Rate per 100,000	Violent crime	Property crime	Murder[1]
Ala.	211,188	4,889.7	24,379	186,809	426
Alaska	32,110	5,272.6	4,270	27,840	54
Ariz.	327,734	7,195.0	28,411	299,323	375
Ark.	119,052	4,718.7	13,293	105,759	250
Calif.	1,569,949	4,865.3	257,582	1,312,367	2,579
Colo.	181,041	4,650.4	14,139	166,902	157
Conn.	130,286	3,984.3	12,781	117,505	124
Del.	37,612	5,138.3	4,962	32,650	18
D.C.	52,049	9,839.1	10,708	41,341	301
Fla.	1,065,609	7,271.8	149,996	915,613	1,012
Ga.	433,563	5,791.7	45,408	388,155	563
Hawaii	71,492	6,022.9	3,299	68,193	47
Idaho	47,495	3,925.2	3,107	44,388	39
Ill.[2]	611,589	5,141.1	102,476	509,113	1,096
Ind.	261,902	4,446.3	30,179	231,723	430
Iowa	108,827	3,815.8	8,841	99,986	52
Kans.[2]	118,422	4,563.5	10,619	107,803	155
Ky.[2]	122,205	3,127.0	12,386	109,819	228
La.	280,671	6,449.2	37,248	243,423	682
Maine	38,896	3,131.7	1,500	37,396	25
Md.	287,969	5,653.1	43,127	244,842	502
Mass.	224,848	3,675.2	39,411	185,437	119
Mich.	480,579	4,916.9	57,663	422,916	759
Minn.	206,833	4,413.8	15,827	191,006	129
Miss.	126,452	4,630.2	12,808	113,644	358
Mo.	260,081	4,814.5	31,192	228,889	426
Mont.[2]	38,753	4,408.8	1,161	37,592	42
Nebr.	70,982	4,238.8	7,265	63,717	50
Nev.	101,702	6,064.5	13,395	88,307	187
N.H.[2]	30,963	2,639.6	1,328	29,635	16
N.J.	326,711	4,057.0	39,673	287,038	337
N.M.	119,483	6,906.5	14,762	104,721	134
N.Y.	709,328	3,910.9	124,890	584,438	1,093
N.C.	407,743	5,491.5	45,071	362,672	614
N.D.	17,380	2,711.4	559	16,821	6
Ohio	505,005	4,514.6	48,706	456,299	523
Okla.	182,258	5,494.7	18,560	163,698	229
Ore.	203,328	6,269.8	14,412	188,916	95
Pa.	412,463	3,431.5	53,140	359,323	705
P.R.	94,875	n.a.	19,595	75,280	723
R.I.	36,069	3,654.4	3,292	32,777	25
S.C.	230,637	6,134.0	37,235	193,402	314
S.D.	23,948	3,245.0	1,457	22,491	10
Tenn.	295,873	5,511.8	42,389	253,484	511
Tex.	1,065,357	5,480.5	117,126	948,231	1,327
Utah	123,447	5,995.5	6,878	116,569	50
Vt.[2]	16,658	2,828.2	705	15,953	9
Va.	261,022	3,876.2	23,249	237,773	488
Wash.	332,466	5,926.3	24,724	307,742	241
W.Va.	44,839	2,469.1	3,971	40,868	75
Wisc.	190,133	3,677.6	13,988	176,145	205
Wyo.	20,068	4,180.8	1,225	18,843	17
U.S. total	13,175,070	4,922.7	1,634,773	11,540,297	18,209

NOTE: The Crime Index is composed of the violent and property crime categories. Violent crimes are murder, forcible rape, robbery, and aggravated assault. Property crimes are burglary, larceny-theft, and auto-theft. Data are not included for the property crime of arson. 1. Includes nonnegligent manslaughter 2. Complete data were not available for the states of Illinois, Kansas, Kentucky, Montana, New Hampshire, and Vermont; therefore it was necessary that their crime counts be estimated. *Source: F.B.I. Uniform Crime Reports for the United States, 1997.*

Summary of Hate Crime Statistics, 1997

	Number of incidents	Number of offenses	Number of victims	Number of known offenders
Single-bias incidents				
Race:	**4,710**	**5,898**	**6,084**	**5,444**
Anti-white	993	1,267	1,293	1,520
Anti-black	3,120	3,838	3,951	3,301
Anti-American Indian/Alaskan Native	36	44	46	45
Anti-Asian/Pacific Islander	347	437	466	351
Anti-multi-racial group	214	312	328	227
Ethnicity/national origin:	**836**	**1,083**	**1,132**	**906**
Anti-Hispanic	491	636	649	614
Anti-other ethnicity/national origin	345	447	483	292
Religion:	**1,385**	**1,483**	**1,586**	**792**
Anti-Jewish	1,087	1,159	1,247	598
Anti-Catholic	31	32	32	16
Anti-Protestant	53	59	61	19
Anti-Islamic	28	31	32	22
Anti-other religious group	159	173	184	120
Anti-multi-religious group	24	26	27	11
Anti-atheism/agnosticism/etc.	3	3	3	6
Sexual orientation:	**1,102**	**1,375**	**1,401**	**1,315**
Anti-male homosexual	760	912	927	1,032
Anti-female homosexual	188	229	236	158
Anti-homosexual	133	210	214	103
Anti-heterosexual	12	14	14	14
Anti-bisexual	9	10	10	8
Multiple-bias incidents	**4**	**10**	**40**	**3**
Total	**8,049**	**9,861**	**10,255**	**8,474**

Source: U.S. Department of Justice, *Uniform Crime Reports.*

Law Enforcement Officers Killed or Assaulted[1]

	1996	1995	1994	1993	1992	1991	1990	1989	1988	1980
Total officers killed	100	130	133	129	129	122	132	144	151	164
Officers assaulted										
Firearm	1,887	2,277	3,168	4,002	4,455	3,532	3,662	3,154	2,759	3,295
Knife or cutting instrument	871	1,325	1,513	1,574	2,095	1,493	1,641	1,379	1,367	1,653
Other dangerous weapon	5,084	6,299	7,210	7,551	8,604	7,014	7,390	5,778	5,573	5,415
Hands, fists, feet, etc.	38,853	46,634	53,021	53,848	66,098	50,813	59,101	51,861	49,053	47,484
Total assaulted	**46,695**	**56,535**	**64,912**	**66,975**	**81,252**	**62,852**	**71,794**	**62,172**	**58,752**	**57,847**

1. Covers officers killed feloniously and accidentally in line of duty; Includes federal officers. 1988 excludes Florida and Kentucky. NOTE: Data are latest available. Source: Statistical Abstract of the United States, 1998.

Federal Prosecutions of Public Corruption

Prosecution status	1996	1995	1994	1993	1992	1991	1990	1989	1985	1980
Total: Indicted	952	1,051	1,165	1,371	1,189	1,452	1,176	1,348	1,157	727
Convicted	878	878	969	1,362	1,081	1,194	1,084	1,149	997	602
Federal officials: Indicted	440	527	571	627	624	803	615	695	563	123
Convicted	450	438	488	595	532	665	583	610	470	131
State officials: Indicted	66	61	99	113	84	115	96	71	79	72
Convicted	55	61	97	133	92	77	79	54	66	51
Local officials: Indicted	232	236	248	309	232	242	257	269	248	247
Convicted	190	191	202	272	211	180	225	201	221	168

NOTE: Figures are latest available. Source: U.S. Department of Justice, Report to Congress on the Activities and Operations of the Public Integrity Section, annual, from Statistical Abstract of the United States 1998.

Methods of Execution

State	Minimum age	Method
Alabama	16	Electrocution
Alaska	—	No death penalty
Arizona[1]	none	Lethal Injection or gas
Arkansas[2]	14	Lethal injection or electrocution
California	18	Lethal gas or injection
Colorado	18	Lethal injection
Connecticut	18	Lethal injection
Delaware[3]	16	Lethal injection or hanging
D.C.	—	No death penalty
Florida	16	Electrocution
Georgia	17	Electrocution
Hawaii	—	No death penalty
Idaho	none	Lethal injection or firing squad
Illinois	18	Lethal injection
Indiana	16	Lethal injection
Iowa	—	No death penalty
Kansas	18	Lethal injection
Kentucky	16	Electrocution
Louisiana	none	Lethal injection
Maine	—	No death penalty
Maryland[4]	18	Lethal injection or gas
Massachusetts	—	No death penalty
Michigan	—	No death penalty
Minnesota	—	No death penalty
Mississippi[5]	16	Lethal injection or gas
Missouri	16	Lethal injection or gas
Montana	none	Lethal injection
Nebraska	18	Electrocution
Nevada	16	Lethal injection
New Hampshire[6]	17	Lethal injection or hanging

State	Minimum age	Method
New Jersey	18	Lethal injection
New Mexico	18	Lethal injection
New York	18	Lethal injection
North Carolina	17	Lethal gas or injection
North Dakota	—	No death penalty
Ohio	18	Electrocution or lethal injection
Oklahoma[7]	16	Lethal injection, electrocution, or firing squad
Oregon	18	Lethal Injection
Pennsylvania	none	Lethal injection
Rhode Island	—	No death penalty
South Carolina	none	Electrocution or lethal injection
South Dakota	none	Lethal injection
Tennessee	18	Electrocution
Texas	17	Lethal injection
Utah	none	Firing squad or lethal injection
Vermont	—	No death penalty
Virginia	14	Electrocution or lethal injection
Washington	18	Hanging or lethal injection
West Virginia	—	No death penalty
Wisconsin	—	No death penalty
Wyoming[8]	16	Lethal injection or gas
U.S. (Fed. Govt.)[9]	18	Lethal injection
American Samoa	—	No death penalty
Guam	—	No death penalty
Puerto Rico	—	No death penalty
Virgin Islands	—	No death penalty

1. Arizona authorizes lethal injection for persons sentenced after 11/15/92; those sentenced before that date may select lethal injection or lethal gas. 2. Arkansas authorizes lethal injection for persons committing a capital offense after 7/4/83; those who committed the offense before that date may select lethal injection or electrocution. 3. Delaware authorizes lethal injection for those whose capital offense occurred after 6/13/86; those who committed the offense before that date may select lethal injection or hanging. 4. Maryland authorizes lethal injection for all inmates, as of 3/25/94. One inmate, convicted prior to that date, has selected lethal gas for method of execution. 5. Mississippi authorizes lethal injection for those convicted after 7/1/84 and lethal gas for those convicted earlier. 6. New Hampshire authorizes hanging only if lethal injection cannot be given. 7. Oklahoma authorizes electrocution if lethal injection is ever held to be unconstitutional and firing squad if both lethal injection and electrocution are held unconstitutional. 8. Wyoming authorizes lethal gas if lethal injection is ever held to be unconstitutional. 9. The method of execution of Federal prisoners is lethal injection, pursuant to 28 CFR, Part 26. For offenses under the Violent Crime Control and Law Enforcement Act of 1994, the method is that of the state in which the conviction took place, pursuant to 18 USC 3596. Source: Capital Punishment, 1997.

Number of Persons Executed,[1] by Jurisdiction, 1930–1997

State	Number executed since 1930	1977[2]	State	Number executed since 1930	1977[2]
Texas	441	144	Arizona	46	8
Georgia	388	22	Indiana	46	5
New York	329	—	District of Columbia	40	—
California	296	4	West Virginia	40	—
North Carolina	271	8	Nevada	35	6
Florida	209	39	Federal system	33	—
South Carolina	175	13	Massachusetts	27	—
Ohio	172	—	Connecticut	21	—
Mississippi	158	4	Oregon	21	2
Louisiana	157	24	Delaware	20	8
Pennsylvania	154	2	Iowa	18	—
Alabama	151	16	Utah	18	5
Virginia	138	46	Kansas	15	—
Arkansas	134	16	New Mexico	8	—
Kentucky	104	1	Wyoming	8	1
Illinois	100	10	Montana	7	1
Tennessee	93	—	Nebraska	7	3
Missouri	91	29	Idaho	4	1
New Jersey	74	—	Vermont	4	—
Maryland	70	2	New Hampshire	1	—
Oklahoma	69	9	South Dakota	1	—
Washington	49	2	U.S. total	4,291	432
Colorado	48	1			

1. Executed under civil authority; military authorities carried out an additional 160 executions, 1930–97. 2. In 1972 the Supreme Court ruled that capital punishment, as it was then administered, was "cruel and unusual" and therefore unconstitutional. On July 1, 1976, however, the Court overturned the ruling by a 7–2 decision, and capital punishment was reinstated. *Source: Capital Punishment, 1997.*

Women on Death Row
(as of 12/31/97)

State	Total	White	Black	State	Total	White	Black
California	8	6	2	Illinois	2	0	2
Texas	7	5	2	Arizona	1	1	0
Florida	6	4	2	Idaho	1	1	0
Pennsylvania	4	1	3	Mississippi	1	1	0
North Carolina	3	3	0	Missouri	1	1	0
Alabama	3	2	1	New Jersey	1	1	0
Oklahoma	3	2	1	Nevada	1	0	1
Tennessee	2	2	0	Total	44	30	14

Source: Capital Punishment, 1997.

Characteristics of Prisoners under Sentence of Death[1]

Characteristic	1980	1990	1996	Characteristic	1980	1990	1996
White	418	1,368	1,820	Marital status:			
Black and other	270	978	1,399	Never married	268	998	1,498
Under 20 years	11	8	16	Married	229	632	731
20 to 24 years	173	168	281	Divorced[1]	217	726	990
25 to 34 years	334	1,110	1,076	Time elapsed since sentencing:			
35 to 54 years	186	1,006	1,707	Less than 12 months	185	231	285
55 years and over	10	64	139	12 to 47 months	389	753	815
Years of schooling completed:				48 to 71 months	102	438	447
7 years or less	68	178	196	72 months and over	38	934	1,672
8 years	74	186	199	Legal status at arrest:			
9 to 11 years	204	775	1,026	Not under sentence	384	1,345	1,863
12 years	162	729	1,034	Parole or probation[2]	115	578	892
More than 12 years	43	209	280	Prison or escaped	45	128	111
Unknown	163	279	484	Unknown	170	305	353
				Total	688	2,346	3,219

1. Includes widows, widowers, and unknown. 2. Includes persons on mandatory conditional release, work release, leave, AWOL, or bail. Excludes prisoners under sentence of death confined in local correctional systems pending appeal or who had not been committed to prison. *Source:* U.S. Bureau of Justice Statistics, *Capital Punishment,* annual, from *Statistical Abstract of the United States, 1998.*

Driving Laws, 1999

Currently all states have child safety seat laws and enforce a drinking age of 21. Mandatory belt-use laws are in effect in 49 states plus D.C. Laws regulating breath-alcohol ignition interlock devices are currently in effect in 33 states. A national speed limit of 55 mph was imposed in 1974, and in 1987 it was modified to allow 65-mile-per-hour speeds on some rural freeways. The federal law was entirely repealed in 1995, giving states the right to set their own limits. In 1999, the maximum daylight speed limit on interstates is 65 mph or greater in 49 states—Hawaii is the exception. Montana, which had been the only state with no speed limit—asking only that its drivers use "reasonable and proper judgment"—imposed a 75-mile-an-hour limit in 1999. After the repeal of the national limit, driving fatalities were expected to increase. They in fact declined between 1995 and 1998 by 11%, and are now at an all-time low.

State	Age for driver's license[1]	License revocation for alcohol offenses since	Blood alcohol concentration limit[2]	Alcohol ignition interlock device[3]	Mandatory belt-use law seating positions	Motorcycle helmet law[5]	Maximum allowable speed limit 1995[6]	Maximum allowable speed limit 1999
Alabama	16	1996	0.08	no	front	yes	65	70
Alaska	16	1983	0.10	yes	all	18	—	65
Arizona	18	1992	0.10	no	front	18	55	75
Arkansas	16	1995	0.10	yes	front	21	65	70
California	18	1989	0.08	yes	all	yes	55	70
Colorado	21	1983	0.10	yes	front	no	65	75
Connecticut	16	1990	0.10	no	front	18	55	65
Delaware	18	yes	0.10	yes	front	19	—	65
D.C.	18	yes	0.10	no	all	yes	—	—
Florida	16	1990	0.08	yes	front	yes	65	70
Georgia	16	1995	0.10	yes	front[4]	yes	55	70
Hawaii	18	1990	0.08	no	front	18	—	55
Idaho	17	1994	0.08	yes	front	18	65	75
Illinois	18	1986	0.08	yes	front	no	65	65
Indiana	18	yes	0.10	yes	front	18	65	65
Iowa	18	1963	0.10	yes	front	no	55	65
Kansas	16	1988	0.08	yes	front	18	65	70
Kentucky	18	no	0.10	no	all	yes	65	65
Louisiana	15	1984	0.10	yes	front[4]	yes	65	70
Maine	17	1984	0.08	yes	all	15	65	65
Maryland	18	1989	0.10	yes	front[4]	yes	55	65
Massachusetts	17	no	0.08	no	all	yes	55	65
Michigan	18	no	0.10	yes	front[4]	yes	55	70
Minnesota	18	1976	0.10	no	front[4]	18	65	70
Mississippi	16	1983	0.10	no	front	yes	65	70
Missouri	16	1987	0.10	yes	front[4]	yes	70	70
Montana	18	no	0.10	yes	all	18	65	75
Nebraska	16	1993	0.10	yes	front	yes	65	75
Nevada	16	1983	0.10	yes	all	yes	55	75
New Hampshire	18	1994	0.08	no	—	18	65	65
New Jersey	17	no	0.10	no	front	yes	—	65
New Mexico	16	1984	0.08	no	front[4]	18	65	75
New York	17	1994	0.10	yes	front[4]	yes	55	65
North Carolina	18	1983	0.08	yes	front	yers	55	70
North Dakota	16	1983	0.10	no	front	18	65	70
Ohio	18	1993	0.10	yes	front	18	65	65
Oklahoma	16	1983	0.10	yes	front	18	65	75
Oregon	16	1983	0.08	yes	all	yes	65	65
Pennsylvania	16	no	0.10	no	front	yes	55	65
Rhode Island	18	no	0.10	yes	all	7	55	65
South Carolina	16	no	0.10	no	front	21	65	65
South Dakota	16	no	0.10	no	front	18	65	75
Tennessee	16	no	0.10	yes	front[4]	yes	65	70
Texas	18	1995	0.10	yes	front	yes	65	70
Utah	16	1983	0.08	yes	front	18	55	75
Vermont	18	1969	0.08	no	all	yes	65	65
Virginia	18	1995	0.08	yes	front	yes	65	65
Washington	16	1994	0.10	yes	all	yes	55	70
West Virginia	18	1981	0.10	yes	front	yes	65	70
Wisconsin	18	1988	0.10	yes	front	18	65	65
Wyoming	16	1973	0.10	no	front	18	65	75

NOTES: A driver's license is required in every state. All states have an *implied consent* Chemical Test Law for alcohol. 1. Refers to age for regular driver's license, not learner's permit. 2. Blood alcohol concentration that constitutes the threshold of legal intoxication. 3. Legislation for instruments designed to prevent drivers from starting their cars when breath alcohol content is at or above a set point. 4. Required for certain ages at all seating positions. 5. Presence of law, or age below which riders are required to wear helmet. 6. In 1995, Congress repealed the national 55-miles-per-hour speed limit. 7. Operators under 21 for first year; passengers. *Sources:* National Safety Council, National Motorists Organization.

The Test of Their Lives

As state grade school exams spread, some ask: Are the stakes too high?

By **JODIE MORSE** TIME

For Lajoi Moore, the past year has been all about The Test. She started preparing in the summer of 1998 with a six-week Kaplan test-prep course, in which she took mock exams and brushed up on test-taking strategies. Since then, she has dedicated part of each afternoon—and nearly all her Christmas vacation—to writing practice essays and memorizing 150 vocabulary words on flash cards. In the final days before the test, she stepped up her studying regimen, cramming sometimes until after midnight. And when the big day arrived in February 1999, Lajoi took a lucky rabbit's foot to the test along with her No. 2 pencils. "If I don't do well, it would just be frightening to me," she says. "I won't be able to get into college."

It's a little early for that kind of worry. Lajoi is only 10, and the test she was fretting about is the FCAT, or Florida Comprehensive Assessment Test, given to the state's fourth-, fifth-, eighth-, and 10th-graders in February 1999. While poor FCAT scores won't keep her out of college just yet, they could hold Lajoi back from fifth grade.

Nationwide Examination

Florida students aren't the only ones sweating new standardized tests these days. With President Clinton's proposal for national reading and math tests shelved by Congress, states are rushing to roll out tests of their own. Since 1997, some 20 states have unveiled custom-made exams intended to hold students (and their schools) to higher educational standards. What's more, unlike the old-style multiple-choice exams, in which lucky guesses often padded scores, tests in more and more states now include subjective "performance questions" that ask students to craft essays and show their work on math problems. What's at stake in these new breeds of tests can be everything from a school's accreditation to teachers' bonuses to a student's high school diploma.

The high stakes, educators hope, will translate into high scores. That has apparently been the case in Texas, which has long used its Texas Assessment of Academic Skills to tag schools that are low performers. In 1994, just over half the state's students passed all the components of the TAAS; in 1998 more than three-quarters did.

In many states, the tests have sparked worry about the number of students who aren't measuring up. Virginia's board of education disclosed in January 1999 that nearly 98% of the state's schools failed to meet suggested accreditation minimums on the new Standards of Learning test, though many educators claim the test was unfair because it was not geared specifically to school curriculums. In Massachusetts, which introduced its exam in the spring of 1998, more than 80% of fourth-graders got a failing score

or a "needs improvement" in English; half of all 10th-graders failed the math portion of the test. Governor Paul Cellucci calls the performance "unacceptable." Maybe so, but it's not surprising, says Harvard lecturer S. Paul Reville. "We were having difficulty reaching lower standards, and now we've raised the bar by a factor of 25% to 30%."

Assessing the Tests

Has the bar been raised too high? Some teachers and parents complain that the tests are too exhaustive—and exhausting—for young students. The Massachusetts test clocked in at 16 hours, spread over several weeks. More worrisome is how a 10-year-old will react if his or her result is branded with a scarlet F. Says Harvard's Reville: "An overload of negative feedback runs the risk that students are going to shut down and not make an effort in the future."

This could be especially true of disadvantaged students, who routinely score much lower on these tests. "If you give me the income tax returns of all the students being tested," says Kitty Kelly Epstein, who teaches education at California's Holy Names College, "I could predict how they would score and save millions of dollars." Well-off New York City parents hire tutors to give their kids a leg up, while poorer students depend on the goodwill of teachers generous enough to tutor them after school.

Shifting the Syllabus

Many teachers rave about the high-stakes exams, claiming that they have galvanized students. But other teachers find themselves forsaking important lessons simply to "teach for the test." Even in North Carolina, whose soaring scores earned accolades in Clinton's 1999 State of the Union address, some teachers tailor over 80% of their lessons to the test, according to a University of North Carolina survey. "Teachers must go way beyond textbook instruction," says Felicita Santiago, principal of a Brooklyn public elementary school where teachers came in an hour early to help kids get ready for the exam. "Preparing for the test is a whole shift in methods of instruction."

Another problem is the piecemeal way in which these tests are developed, with no attempt to coordinate them nationally. In January 1999 Achieve Inc., a bipartisan resource center on standards, was host to a conference in Washington, where representatives from 20 states pledged to work toward a shared national standard by offering uniform exam questions. In the meantime, students like Lajoi probably have less to worry about than the people in charge of teaching them. The Maryland board of education has just targeted three elementary schools in Prince George's County for state takeover because of poor test results. And the county's school board voted not to renew the contract of its superintendent. □

Science and Mathematics Performance around the World

Eighth grade science

Country	Difference in points from international average
Significantly higher than international average	
Czech Republic	59
Netherlands	45
Slovenia	45
Austria	43
Hungary	39
Australia	30
Russian Federation	23
Sweden	20
United States	20
Germany	16
Canada	16
Norway	12
Not significantly different from international average	
New Zealand	11
Switzerland	7
Significantly lower than international average	
France	−17
Iceland	−21
Denmark	−37
Lithuania	−38
Cyprus	−52
South Africa	−189
International average score (average of all country means)	515

Final year of secondary school science

Country	Difference in points from international average
Significantly higher than international average	
Sweden	59
Netherlands	58
Iceland	49
Norway	44
Canada	32
New Zealand	29
Switzerland	23
Austria	20
Not significantly different from international average	
Australia	27
Slovenia	17
Denmark	9
Germany	−3
France	−13
Czech Republic	−13
Significantly lower than international average	
Russian Federation	−19
United States	−20
Hungary	−29
Lithuania	−39
Cyprus	−52
South Africa	−151
International average score (average of all country means)	500

Eighth grade mathematics

Country	Difference in points from international average
Significantly higher than international average	
Czech Republic	53
Switzerland	35
Netherlands	30
Slovenia	30
Austria	29
France	27
Hungary	27
Russian Federation	25
Australia	19
Canada	17
Not significantly different from international average	
Sweden	8
Germany	−1
New Zealand	−3
Denmark	−8
United States	−11
Significantly lower than international average	
Norway	−7
Iceland	−24
Lithuania	−33
Cyprus	−37
South Africa	−157
International average score (average of all country means)	511

Final year of secondary school mathematics

Country	Difference in points from international average
Significantly higher than international average	
Netherlands	60
Sweden	52
Denmark	47
Switzerland	40
Iceland	34
Norway	28
France	23
New Zealand	22
Canada	19
Austria	18
Not significantly different from international average	
Australia	22
Slovenia	12
Germany	−5
Czech Republic	−34
Significantly lower than international average	
Hungary	−17
Russian Federation	−29
Lithuania	−31
United States	−39
Cyprus	−54
South Africa	−144
International average score (average of all country means)	500

NOTES: Because results are rounded to the nearest whole number, some totals may appear inconsistent. Countries shown in italics did not satisfy one or more guidelines for sample participation rates or student sampling procedures. Because of differing margins of error, some countries may be ranked higher than others even though they have lower average scores. Tables include countries that participated in TIMSS testing at both eighth grade and final year of secondary school. *Source:* National Center for Education Statistics, Dept. of Education, Third International Mathematics and Science Study (TIMSS), conducted in 1996.

Percent of Population Enrolled in School[1], 1997

Age	Total	White, non-Hispanic	Black, non-Hispanic	Hispanic origin	Male	Female
Total, 3 to 34 years	55.6%	55.6%	58.6%	50.8%	55.8%	55.4%
3 and 4 years	52.6	54.9	60.0	36.6	51.9	53.2
5 and 6 years	96.5	96.9	95.7	96.6	96.7	96.4
7 to 9 years	98.8	98.9	99.2	98.6	98.6	99.1
10 to 13 years	99.3	99.2	99.4	99.6	99.4	99.3
14 and 15 years	98.9	98.9	99.2	98.4	99.1	98.7
16 and 17 years	94.3	95.1	93.5	91.1	94.2	94.4
18 and 19 years	61.5	64.0	57.8	49.4	60.5	62.4
20 and 21 years	45.9	49.9	36.0	28.9	44.4	47.4
22 to 24 years	26.4	27.8	25.7	16.4	25.4	27.4
25 to 29 years	11.8	12.2	10.6	7.3	11.7	11.9
30 to 34 years	5.7	5.6	6.5	3.7	4.7	6.6

NOTES: Data are based upon sample surveys of the civilian noninstitutional population. 1. Includes enrollment in any type of graded public, parochial, or other private schools. Includes nursery schools, kindergartens, elementary schools, high schools, colleges, universities, and professional schools. Attendance may be on either a full-time or part-time basis and during the day or night. Enrollments in "special" schools, such as trade schools, business colleges, or correspondence schools, are not included. *Source:* U.S. Dept. of Commerce, Bureau of the Census.

Students with Disabilities

In 1995–1996, 5.6 million children (ages 0 to 21), or about 12% of public school children, were enrolled in special education programs. The number of students participating in federal programs for children with disabilities has increased at a faster rate than total public school enrollment. Between 1977 and 1995, the number of students involved in federal programs for children with disabilities increased 47%, while total public school enrollment decreased by 2%. Most students enrolled in special education programs have specific learning disabilities or language impairments, or have serious emotional disturbances.

Type of disability	Percent of All Students Served by Federally Supported Programs for Students with Disabilities[1]			
	1976–77	1980–81	1990–91	1995–96
All disabilities	8.33%	10.13%	11.55%	12.43%
Specific learning disabilities	1.80	3.58	5.17	5.75
Speech or language impairments	2.94	2.86	2.39	2.28
Mental retardation	2.16	2.03	1.30	1.27
Serious emotional disturbance	0.64	0.85	0.95	0.98
Hearing impairments	0.20	0.19	0.14	0.15
Orthopedic impairments	0.20	0.14	0.12	0.14
Other health impairments	0.32	0.24	0.13	0.30
Visual impairments	0.09	0.08	0.06	0.06
Multiple disabilities	—	0.17	0.23	0.21
Deaf–blindness	—	0.01	(2)	(2)
Autism and others	—	—	—	0.09
Preschool disabled[3]	(3)	(3)	1.07	1.21

NOTES: Counts are based on reports from the 50 states and District of Columbia. Increases since 1987–1988 are due in part to legislation enacted in fall 1986, which mandates public school special education services of all handicapped children ages 3 through 5. Because of rounding, details may not add to totals. 1. Based on the enrollment in public schools, kindergarten through 12th grade, including a relatively small number of prekindergarten students. Includes students ages 0 to 21. 2. Less than .005%. 3. Prior to 1987–1988, these students were included in the counts by handicapping condition. Beginning in 1987–1988, states were no longer required to report preschool handicapped students (0–5 years) by handicapping condition. *Source:* National Center for Education Statistics, U.S. Dept. of Education, *Digest of Education Statistics, 1997.*

Public Schools with Access to the Internet, 1994–1998

School characteristic	Percent of schools with Internet access					School characteristic	Percent of schools with Internet access				
	1994	1995	1996	1997	1998		1994	1995	1996	1997	1998
Total	35%	50%	65%	78%	89%	Percent minority enrollment:					
Instructional level[1]:						Less than 6 percent	38%	52%	65%	84%	91%
Elementary	30	46	61	75	88	6 to 20 percent	38	58	72	87	93
Secondary	49	65	77	89	94	21 to 49 percent	38	54	65	73	91
Size of enrollment:						50 percent or more	27	40	56	63	82
Less than 300	30	39	57	75	87						
300 to 999	35	52	66	78	89						
1,000 or more	58	69	80	89	95						

NOTES: Excludes special education, vocational education, and alternative based on sample and subject to sampling error. 1. Data for combined schools are included in the totals and in analyses by other school characteristics but are not shown separately. *Source:* U.S. National Center for Education Statistics, "Advanced Telecommunications in U.S. Public Elementary and Secondary Schools, Fall 1999."

Percent of High School Dropouts by Sex, 1960–1997

Year	Total	Male	Female
1960	27.2%	27.8%	26.7%
1970	15.0	14.2	15.7
1980	14.1	15.1	13.1
1985	12.6	13.4	11.8
1990	12.1	12.3	11.8
1992	11.0	11.3	10.7
1993	11.0	11.2	10.9
1994	11.4	12.3	10.6
1995	12.0	12.2	11.7
1996	11.1	11.4	10.9
1997	11.0	11.9	10.1

Percent of High School Dropouts by Race/Ethnicity, 1960–1997

Year	White	Black	Hispanic
1960	n.a	n.a	n.a
1970	13.2%	27.9%	n.a.
1980	11.4	19.1	35.2%
1985	10.4	15.2	27.6
1990	9.0	13.2	32.4
1992	7.7	13.7	29.4
1993	7.9	13.6	27.5
1994	7.7	12.6	30.0
1995	8.6	12.1	30.0
1996	7.3	13.0	29.4
1997	7.6	13.4	25.3

NOTE: n.a. = not available. Data apply to persons ages 16–24. Source: U.S. Dept. of Education, National Center for Education Statistics, Digest of Education Statistics, 1998.

Drugs and Violence on School Property, 1995

Type of violence or drug-related behavior	1997				Type of violence or drug-related behavior	1997			
	Total	White	Black	Hispanic		Total	White	Black	Hispanic
Carried a weapon[1,2]	8.5%	7.8%	9.2%	10.4%	Cigarette use[1]	14.6%	15.8%	8.8%	11.9%
Male	12.5	12.3	10.7	15.6	Male	15.9	16.5	12.4	15.3
Female	3.7	2.1	7.8	4.3	Female	13.0	14.9	5.5	7.7
Threatened or injured with a weapon[3]	7.4	6.2	9.9	9.0	Smokeless tobacco use[4]	5.1	6.5	1.4	3.3
Male	10.2	8.2	14.0	12.7	Male	9.0	11.3	2.5	5.8
Female	4.0	3.7	5.8	4.6	Female	0.4	0.4	0.4	0.3
In a physical fight[3]	14.8	13.3	20.7	19.0	Alcohol use[1]	5.6	4.8	5.6	8.2
Male	20.0	19.1	24.6	24.7	Male	7.2	6.3	7.3	8.7
Female	8.6	5.9	17.0	12.3	Female	3.6	2.9	4.0	7.6
Property stolen or deliberately damaged[3]	32.9	32.6	34.0	32.1	Marijuana use[1]	7.0	5.8	9.1	10.4
Male	36.1	35.7	37.5	33.4	Male	9.0	7.3	13.0	14.1
Female	29.0	28.6	30.6	30.6	Female	4.6	3.9	5.4	5.9
					Offered, sold, or given an illegal drug[3]	31.7	31.0	25.4	41.1
					Male	37.4	36.1	34.6	46.8
					Female	24.7	24.5	16.7	34.4

NOTES: For American students grades 9–12. 1. On one or more of the 30 days preceding the survey. 2. Such as a gun, knife, or club. 3. One or more times during the 12 months preceding the survey. 4. Used chewing tobacco or snuff during the 30 days preceding the survey. Source: U.S. Dept. of Education, National Center for Education Statistics, Digest of Education Statistics 1997.

Educational Attainment by Race and Hispanic Origin, 1960–1997

(percent of persons 25 years and over who completed at least four years of college)

Year	Total[1]	White	Black	Asian and Pacific Islander	Hispanic[2]			
					Total[3]	Mexican	Puerto Rican	Cuban
Completed 4 years of college or more								
1960	7.7%	8.1%	3.1%	n.a.	n.a.	n.a.	n.a.	n.a.
1965	9.4	9.9	4.7	n.a.	n.a.	n.a.	n.a.	n.a.
1970	10.7	11.3	4.4	n.a.	4.5%	2.5%	2.2%	11.1%
1975	13.9	14.5	6.4	n.a.	n.a.	n.a.	n.a.	n.a.
1980	16.2	17.1	8.4	n.a.	7.6	4.9	5.6	16.2
1985	19.4	20.0	11.1	n.a.	8.5	5.5	7.0	13.7
1990	21.3	22.0	11.3	39.9%	9.2	5.4	9.7	20.2
1994[4]	22.2	22.9	12.9	41.2	9.1	6.3	9.7	16.2
1995[4]	23.0	24.0	13.2	n.a.	9.3	6.5	10.7	19.4
1996[4]	23.6	24.3	13.6	41.7	9.3	6.5	11.0	18.8
1997[4]	23.9	24.6	13.3	42.2	10.3	7.5	10.7	19.7

NOTES: n.a. = not available. 1960, 1970, and 1980 as of April 1 and based on sample data from the censuses of population. Other years as of March and based on the Current Population Survey. 1. Includes other races, not shown separately. 2. Persons of Hispanic origin may be of any race. 3. Includes persons of other Hispanic origin, not shown separately. 4. Beginning 1994, persons who were high school graduates and those with a BA degree or higher. Source: U.S. Bureau of the Census, U.S. Census of Population, U.S. Summary, PC80-1-C1 and Current Population Reports P20-455, P20-459, P20-462, P20-465RV, P20-489, P20-493, P20-505; and unpublished data.

International Ranks in Educational Attainment, 1995
(percent who completed secondary and higher education)

Country	Secondary education[1]	Higher education	Country	Secondary education[1]	Higher education
Canada	83.9%	19.5%	Japan[2]	90.6%	22.9%
France	85.5	14.0	United Kingdom	86.1	14.8
Germany	88.9	12.5	**United States**	**87.1**	**25.0**
Italy	49.1	8.2			

NOTES: Data applies to population ages 25–34 living in large industrialized countries. 1. Includes individuals who have completed at least secondary education. 2. Data are for 1989. Source: National Center for Education Statistics, U.S. Department of Education, The Condition of Education, 1998, Indicator 23, page 52.

Educational Attainment by Sex, 1910–1997
(percent of population ages 25 and older)

	Both Sexes			Male			Female		
Year	Less than 5 years of elementary school	High school completion or higher[1]	4 or more years of college[2]	Less than 5 years of elementary school	High school completion or higher	4 or more years of college	Less than 5 years of elementary school	High school completion or higher	4 or more years of college
1910[3]	23.8%	13.5%	2.7%	n.a.	n.a.	n.a.	n.a.	n.a.	n.a.
1920[3]	22.0	16.4	3.3	n.a.	n.a.	n.a.	n.a.	n.a.	n.a.
1930[3]	17.5	19.1	3.9	n.a.	n.a.	n.a.	n.a.	n.a.	n.a.
April 1940	13.7	24.5	4.6	15.1%	22.7%	5.5%	12.4%	26.3%	3.8%
April 1950	11.1	34.3	6.2	12.2	32.6	7.3	10.0	36.0	5.2
April 1960	8.3	41.1	7.7	9.4	39.5	9.7	7.4	42.5	5.8
March 1970	5.3	55.2	11.0	5.9	55.0	14.1	4.7	55.4	8.2
March 1980	3.4	68.6	17.0	3.6	69.2	20.9	3.2	68.1	13.6
March 1985	2.7	73.9	19.4	n.a.	n.a.	n.a.	n.a.	n.a.	n.a.
March 1990	2.5	77.6	21.3	2.7	77.7	24.4	2.2	77.5	18.4
March 1994	1.9	80.9	22.2	2.1	81.1	25.1	1.7	80.8	19.6
March 1995	1.9	81.7	23.0	2.0	81.7	26.0	1.7	81.6	20.2
March 1996	1.8	81.7	23.6	1.9	81.9	26.0	1.7	81.6	21.4
March 1997	1.7	82.1	23.9	1.8	82.0	26.2	1.6	82.2	21.7

NOTES: n.a. = not available. Data for 1980 and subsequent years are for the noninstitutional population. 1. Data for years prior to 1993 include all persons with at least 4 years of high school. 2. Data for 1993 and later years are for persons with a bachelor's degree or higher. 3. Estimates based on Bureau of the Census retrojection of 1940 Census data on education by age. Source: Dept. of Education. Based on data from the U.S. Department of Commerce, Bureau of the Census, U.S. Census of Population, 1960, Vol. 1, part 1; Current Population Reports, Series P-20 and unpublished data; and 1960 Census Monograph, "Education of the American Population," by John K. Folger and Charles B. Nam.

Median Annual Income by Level of Education, 1989–1997

Sex and year	Total	Less than 9th grade	9th to 12th grade, no diploma[1]	High school graduate[2]	Some college, no degree[3]	Associate degree[4]	Bachelor's degree or higher[5]
Men							
1989	$30,465	$17,555	$21,065	$26,609	$31,308	n.a.	$41,892
1990	30,733	17,394	20,902	26,653	31,734	n.a.	42,671
1991	31,613	17,623	21,402	26,779	31,663	$33,817	45,138
1992	32,057	17,294	21,274	27,280	32,103	33,433	45,802
1993	32,359	16,863	21,752	27,370	32,077	33,690	47,740
1994	33,440	17,532	22,048	28,037	32,279	35,794	49,228
1995	34,551	18,354	22,185	29,510	33,883	35,201	50,481
1996	35,622	17,962	22,717	30,709	34,845	37,131	51,436
1997	36,678	19,291	24,726	31,215	35,945	38,022	53,450
Women							
1989	$20,570	$12,188	$13,923	$17,528	$21,631	n.a.	$28,799
1990	21,372	12,251	14,429	18,319	22,227	n.a.	30,377
1991	22,043	12,066	14,455	18,836	22,143	$25,000	31,310
1992	23,139	12,958	14,559	19,427	23,157	25,624	32,304
1993	23,629	12,415	15,386	19,963	23,056	25,883	34,307
1994	24,399	12,430	15,133	20,373	23,514	25,940	35,378
1995	24,875	13,577	15,825	20,463	23,997	27,311	35,259
1996	25,808	14,414	16,953	21,175	25,167	28,083	36,461
1997	26,974	14,161	16,697	22,067	26,335	28,812	38,038

NOTES: n.a. = not available or not applicable. Applies to Americans working year-round, full-time. Data for 1982 and later years are based on 1990 census counts. Due to rounding, numbers may not add to totals. Data in current dollars. 1. Includes 1 to 3 years of high school for 1989 and 1990. 2. Includes 4 years of high school for 1989 and 1990, and equivalency certificates for the other years. 3. Includes 1 to 3 years of college and associate degrees for 1989 and 1990. 4. Not reported separately for 1989 and 1990. 5. Includes 4 or more years of college for 1989 and 1990. Source: U.S. Department of Commerce, Bureau of the Census, Current Population Reports.

College and University Endowments, 1996–1997

Top 50, in millions of dollars

Institution	Endowment[1]	Institution	Endowment[1]	Institution	Endowment[1]
Harvard Univ.	$11,161.8	Dartmouth Col.	$1,277.8	Univ. of N.C.–Chapel	$719.9
Yale Univ.	5,794.1	Duke Univ.	1,190.5	Hill	
Princeton Univ.	5,099.7	Case Western	1,158.0	Wellesley Col.	691.1
Stanford Univ.	4,667.0	Reserve Univ.		Smith Col.	683.4
Columbia Univ.	3,038.9	Johns Hopkins Univ.	1,156.6	Washington and Lee	680.2
Massachusetts Inst.	3,023.6	Univ. of Minnesota	1,126.8	Univ.	
of Tech.		California Inst. of	1,027.0	Boston Col.	676.9
Washington Univ.	2,844.7	Tech.		Texas Christian Univ.	675.5
Texas A&M Univ.	2,629.0	Univ. of Texas–Austin	1,020.7	Univ. of Richmond	672.0
Univ. of Pennsylvania	2,535.3	Brown Univ.	965.2	Williams Col.	663.6
Northwestern Univ.	2,447.7	Univ. of Virginia	961.6	Univ. of Delaware	662.8
William Marsh Rice	2,300.0	Univ. of Rochester	942.5	Baylor Col. of Medi-	659.0
Univ.		Univ. of Calif.–Los	890.8	cine	
Cornell Univ.	2,155.9	Angeles		Southern Methodist	645.5
Univ. of Michigan	2,045.2	New York Univ.	878.4	Univ.	
Univ. of Chicago	2,031.0	Purdue Univ.	870.4	Univ. of Wisconsin–	636.4
Univ. of Notre Dame	1,515.2	Rockefeller Univ.	803.1	Madison	
Mayo Foundation	1,430.9	Georgia Inst. of Tech.	775.4	Univ. of Kansas	620.4
Univ. of Calif.–	1,361.3	Ohio State Univ.	767.7	Univ. of Pittsburgh	614.7
Berkeley		Grinnell Col.	754.6		
Vanderbilt Univ.	1,311.9	Swarthmore Col.	748.2		

NOTES: List includes only institutions that participated in the 1996–1997 Voluntary Support of Education Survey. State systems that submitted combined endowments above the current cut-off are not included. 1. Endowment is market value at fiscal year-end 1997. *Source:* Survey of Voluntary Support of Education 1997. Council for Aid to Education, N.Y.

Top 50 Colleges for Black Students

Based on responses from more than 1,000 African-American professionals in higher education, *Black Enterprise* magazine has ranked the top 50 colleges and universities where African-American students are most likely to succeed. The ranking considers factors such as black population (at least 1.5%), academic strengths, social environment, and graduation rates. (Web: www.blackenterprise.com)

			1996–1997	
Ranking	Name, location	Internet address	Student population	(% black)
1	Spelman College, Atlanta, Ga.	www.spelman.edu	1,961	95%
2	Morehouse College, Atlanta, Ga.	www.morehouse.edu	2,889	99
3	Florida A&M University, Tallahassee, Fla.	www.famu.edu	10,306	88
4	Clark Atlanta University, Atlanta, Ga.	www.cau.edu	5,311	96
5	Howard University, Washington, D.C.	www.howard.edu	10,332	91
6	Xavier University, New Orleans, La.	www.xula.edu	3,463	90
7	Hampton University, Hampton, Va.	www.hamptonu.edu	6,035	84
8	Tuskegee University, Tuskegee, Ala.	www.tusk.edu	3,100	92
9	North Carolina A&T Univ., Greensboro, N.C.	www.ncat.edu	7,947	87
10	Stanford University, Palo Alto, Calif.	www.stanford.edu	16,003	5
11	Georgetown University, Washington, D.C.	www.georgetown.edu	12,618	6
12	Oberlin College, Oberlin, Ohio	www.oberlin.edu	2,892	8
13	Swarthmore College, Swarthmore, Pa.	www.swarthmore.edu	1,353	6
14	Vassar College, Poughkeepsie, N.Y.	www.vassar.edu	2,346	6
15	Columbia University, New York, N.Y.	www.columbia.edu	19,302	6
16	Emory University, Atlanta, Ga.	www.emory.edu	11,308	12
17	Amherst College, Amherst, Mass.	www.amherst.edu	1,623	7
18	Johnson C. Smith University, Charlotte, N.C.	www.jcsu.edu	1,398	99
19	University of North Carolina, Chapel Hill, N.C.	www.unc.edu	24,439	9
20	Duke University, Durham, N.C.	www.duke.edu	11,512	7
21	Morgan State University, Baltimore, Md.	www.morgan.edu	6,016	94
22	Wesleyan University, Middletown, Conn.	www.wesleyan.edu	3,244	7
23	Fisk University, Nashville, Tenn.	www.fisk.edu	879	99
24	Tennessee State University, Nashville, Tenn.	www.tnstate.edu	8,464	65
25	Bryn Mawr College, Bryn Mawr, Pa.	www.brynmawr.edu	1,821	5
26	Florida State University, Tallahassee, Fla.	www.fsu.edu	30,155	10
27	Bethune-Cookman College, Daytona Beach, Fla.	www.bethune.cookman.edu	2,402	93
28	Harvard University, Cambridge, Mass.	www.harvard.edu	24,687	6
29	Johns Hopkins University, Baltimore, Md.	www.jhu.edu	15,765	7
30	Univ. of Southern California, Los Angeles, Calif.	www.usc.edu	27,971	6
31	North Carolina Central Univ., Durham, N.C.	www.nccu.edu	5,555	83
32	Morris Brown College, Atlanta, Ga.	www.morrisbrown.edu	2,065	96
33	Southern University, New Orleans, La.	www.subr.edu	10,359	93

Ranking	Name, location	Internet address	1996–1997 Student population	(% black)
34	University of Pennsylvania, Philadelphia, Pa.	www.upenn.edu	22,148	6%
35	Williams College, Williamstown, Mass.	www.williams.edu	2,055	6
36	George Washington University, Washington, D.C.	www.gwu.edu	19,670	8
37	Dillard University, New Orleans, La.	www.dillard.edu	1,562	98
38	Jackson State University, Jackson, Miss.	www.jsums.edu	6,313	94
39	Grambling State University, Grambling, La.	www.gram.edu	6,800	95
40	Wellesley College, Wellesley, Mass.	www.wellesley.edu	2,257	6
41	Yale University, New Haven, Conn.	www.yale.edu	10,893	6
42	Univ. of California Los Angeles, Los Angeles, Calif.	www.ucla.edu	34,713	6
43	New York University, New York, N.Y.	www.nyu.edu	35,835	7
44	Smith College, Northampton, Mass.	www.smith.edu	3,189	4
45	Mass. Institute of Technology, Cambridge, Mass.	www.mit.edu	9,960	4
46	Mount Holyoke College, South Hadley, Mass.	www.mtholyoke.edu	1,896	4
47	Lincoln University, Lincoln University, Pa.	www.lincoln.edu	1,553	92
48	South Carolina State University, Orangeburg, S.C.	www.scsu.edu	4,993	92
49	Alabama A&M University, Normal, Ala.	www.aamu.edu	5,400	76
50	Cornell University, Ithaca, N.Y.	www.cornell.edu	11,865	4

Accredited U.S. Senior Colleges and Universities

Source: The information below comes to us from *The Princeton Review's Complete Book of Accredited Colleges, 2000 Edition.*

Schools are listed alphabetically within each state and are accredited four-year institutions offering at least a Bachelor's degree. Tuition, room, and board listed are average annual figures (including fees) subject to fluctuation, usually covering two semesters, two out of three trimesters, or three out of four quarters, depending on the school calendar. Note that some schools include room and board expenses within the tuition figures rather than reporting them separately. List includes only schools for which data was provided. For further information, write to the registrar of the school concerned.

(Pr) = private; (Pu) = public.

Institution name; city, state (control)	Students	Percent Accepted	Women	Tuition In-state	Out-of-state	Room and board
ALABAMA						
Alabama A&M University; Normal, Ala. (Pu)	3,903	66%	43%			
Alabama State University; Montgomery, Ala. (Pu)	4,682		55		$ 3,600	$4,820
Athens State University; Athens, Ala. (Pu)	1,271			$ 1,656	$ 3,312	$4,800
Auburn University; Auburn, Ala. (Pu)	18,538	92	48	$ 2,760	$ 8,280	
Auburn University-Montgomery; Montgomery, Ala. (Pu)	5,645			$ 2,289	$ 6,867	
Birmingham-Southern College; Birmingham, Ala. (Pr)	1,447	96	59	$14,450	$14,450	$5,365
Faulkner University; Montgomery, Ala. (Pr)	1,892	75	60	$ 7,185	$ 7,185	$3,500
Huntingdon College; Montgomery, Ala. (Pr)	699	74	62	$10,500	$10,500	$5,200
Jacksonville State University; Jacksonville, Ala. (Pu)	6,477		55	$ 2,040	$ 4,080	$2,870
Judson College; Marion, Ala. (Pr)	322	81	97	$ 7,100	$ 7,100	$4,430
Samford University; Birmingham, Ala. (Pr)	2,894	92	61	$10,300	$10,300	$4,560
Spring Hill College; Mobile, Ala. (Pr)	1,131	90	58	$14,390	$14,390	$5,520
Talladega College; Talladega, Ala. (Pr)	642			$ 5,666	$ 5,666	$2,964
Troy State University at Montgomery; Montgomery, Ala. (Pu)	2,896		65	$ 1,980	$ 3,960	
Troy State University at Troy; Troy, Ala. (Pu)	5,194	76	61	$ 2,660	$ 5,320	$3,854
Tuskegee University; Tuskegee, Ala. (Pr)	2,708	90	60	$ 9,500	$ 9,500	$4,900
University of Alabama-Birmingham; Birmingham, Ala. (Pu)	10,433	87	57	$ 2,610	$ 5,220	$7,875
University of Alabama-Huntsville; Huntsville, Ala. (Pu)	5,639	95	50			
University of Alabama-Tuscaloosa; Tuscaloosa, Ala. (Pu)	14,403	94	52	$ 2,684	$ 7,216	$3,810
University of Mobile; Mobile, Ala. (Pr)	1,707	89	60			
University of Montevallo; Montevallo, Ala. (Pu)	2,678	83	68	$ 3,040	$ 6,080	
University of North Alabama; Florence, Ala. (Pu)	5,090		58		$ 4,272	$3,672
University of South Alabama; Mobile, Ala. (Pu)	9,360	94	57	$ 2,475	$ 4,950	$2,883
University of West Alabama; Livingston, Ala. (Pu)	1,838			$ 2,280	$ 4,560	$2,460
ALASKA						
Alaska Pacific University; Anchorage, Alaska (Pr)	389		56	$11,950	$11,950	$5,000
Sheldon Jackson College; Sitka, Alaska (Pr)	275	50	59	$ 6,850	$ 6,850	$5,150
University of Alaska-Anchorage; Anchorage, Alaska (Pu)	14,475		62	$ 2,016	$ 3,006	$5,480
University of Alaska-Fairbanks; Fairbanks, Alaska (Pu)	6,225	82	58	$ 2,190	$ 6,810	$4,150
University of Alaska-Southeast; Juneau, Alaska (Pu)	2,782			$ 2,168	$ 6,428	$7,650

Institution name; city, state (control)	Students	Percent Accepted	Percent Women	Tuition In-state	Tuition Out-of-state	Room and board
ARIZONA						
Arizona State University; Tempe, Ariz. (Pu)	33,268		52%	$ 2,088	$ 9,040	$4,825
Arizona State University East; Tempe, Ariz. (Pu)	804		30	$ 2,188	$ 9,340	$5,010
Arizona State University West; Phoenix, Ariz. (Pu)	3,608	92%	69	$ 2,088	$ 9,040	
DeVry Institute of Technology; Phoenix, Ariz. (Pr)	3,747		22			
Embry-Riddle Aeronautical University; Prescott, Ariz. (Pr)	1,526	85	17	$10,100	$10,100	$2,260
Grand Canyon University; Phoenix, Ariz. (Pr)	1,594	76	66	$ 7,680	$ 7,680	$4,246
Northern Arizona University; Flagstaff, Ariz. (Pu)	13,906	83	57	$ 2,124	$ 8,004	$4,240
Prescott College; Prescott, Ariz. (Pr)	718		62	$11,500	$11,500	$4,706
University of Arizona; Tucson, Ariz. (Pu)	26,157	82	52	$ 2,158	$ 9,110	$5,042
ARKANSAS						
Arkansas State University; Jonesboro, Ark. (Pu)	9,273	81	57	$ 2,184	$ 5,592	$2,990
Arkansas Tech University; Russellville, Ark. (Pu)	4,202		52	$ 2,196	$ 4,356	$3,138
Central Baptist College; Conway, Ark. (Pr)	335		45	$ 5,424	$ 5,424	$3,634
Harding University; Searcy, Ark. (Pr)	3,579	80	56	$ 7,795	$ 7,795	$4,295
Henderson State University; Arkadelphia, Ark. (Pu)	3,263	93	58	$ 2,136	$ 4,272	$2,936
Hendrix College; Conway, Ark. (Pr)	1,047	83	55	$11,440	$11,440	$4,415
John Brown University; Siloam Springs, Ark. (Pr)	1,393	54	54	$ 9,482	$ 9,482	$4,478
Lyon College; Batesville, Ark. (Pr)	462	84	57	$10,272	$10,272	$4,713
Ouachita Baptist University; Arkadelphia, Ark. (Pr)	1,536	80	54	$ 8,410	$ 8,410	$3,100
Philander Smith College; Little Rock, Ark. (Pr)	918	55	64	$ 3,360	$ 3,360	$2,746
Southern Arkansas University-Magnolia; Magnolia, Ark. (Pu)	2,469		56	$ 1,992	$ 3,048	$2,690
University of Arkansas-Fayetteville; Fayetteville, Ark. (Pu)	12,003	88	48			
University of Arkansas-Little Rock; Little Rock, Ark. (Pu)	8,559			$ 1,131	$ 2,916	$2,435
University of Arkansas-Monticello; Monticello, Ark. (Pu)	2,200			$ 2,040	$ 4,248	$2,930
University of Arkansas-Pine Bluff; Pine Bluff, Ark. (Pu)	3,425			$ 1,680	$ 3,888	$3,470
University of Central Arkansas; Conway, Ark. (Pu)	7,914	75	61	$ 1,494	$ 2,742	$2,920
University of the Ozarks; Clarksville, Ark. (Pr)	573			$ 7,750	$ 7,750	$3,750
Williams Baptist College; Walnut Ridge, Ark. (Pr)	686	78	54	$ 6,000	$ 6,000	$3,200
CALIFORNIA						
Academy of Art College; San Francisco, Calif. (Pr)	4,311	65	41	$10,800	$10,800	
Art Center College of Design; Pasadena, Calif. (Pr)	1,308	64	38			
Art Institutes International at San Francisco; San Francisco, Calif. (Pr)	79	100	51			$5,060
Azusa Pacific University; Azusa, Calif. (Pr)	2,795	83	62	$14,290	$14,290	$4,690
Biola University; La Mirada, Calif. (Pr)	2,391	83	63	$15,914	$15,914	$5,139
Bishop's University; Quebec, Calif. (Pu)	2,333	81	55		$ 3,400	$5,400
Brooks Institute of Photography; Santa Barbara, Calif. (Pr)	302		32	$15,000	$15,000	
California Baptist College; Riverside, Calif. (Pr)	1,690	93	59	$ 9,308	$ 9,308	$4,848
California College of Arts and Crafts; San Francisco, Calif. (Pr)	1,065	68	61	$18,188	$18,188	$5,858
California Institute of Technology; Pasadena, Calif. (Pr)	901	18	28	$19,260	$19,260	$6,000
California Institute of the Arts; Valencia, Calif. (Pr)	777	43	45	$18,950	$18,950	$5,500
California Lutheran University; Thousand Oaks, Calif. (Pr)	1,751	78	55	$16,020	$16,020	$6,240
California Maritime Academy of California State University; Vallejo, Calif. (Pu)	389	70	12	$ 1,506	$ 7,380	$5,801
California Polytechnic State University-San Luis Obispo; San Luis Obispo, Calif. (Pu)	15,348	38	43	$ 1,506	$ 5,409	$5,355
California State Polytechnic University-Pomona; Pomona, Calif. (Pu)	15,351	65	43		$ 8,964	$5,477
California State University-Bakersfield; Bakersfield, Calif. (Pu)	4,309		62	$ 1,506	$ 7,380	$5,801
California State University-Chico; Chico, Calif. (Pu)	12,506	80	53	$14,143	$14,143	
California State University-Dominguez Hills; Carson, Calif. (Pu)	8,323	74	67	$ 1,506	$ 7,380	$5,801
California State University-Fresno; Fresno, Calif. (Pu)	14,518	66	55	$ 1,754	$ 9,134	$5,659
California State University-Fullerton; Fullerton, Calif. (Pu)	21,279	73	57		$ 7,380	$3,747
California State University-Hayward; Hayward, Calif. (Pu)	9,626	84	64	$ 1,506	$ 8,886	
California State University-Long Beach; Long Beach, Calif. (Pu)	21,094			$ 1,506	$ 7,380	$5,801
California State University-Los Angeles; Los Angeles, Calif. (Pu)	13,935		60	$ 1,506	$ 7,380	$5,801
California State University-Northridge; Northridge, Calif. (Pu)	20,955	78	57	$ 1,506	$ 7,874	$5,801
California State University-Sacramento; Sacramento, Calif. (Pu)	18,713	65		$ 1,506	$ 7,380	$5,801
California State University-San Bernardino; San Bernardino, Calif. (Pu)	11,007			$ 1,506	$ 7,380	$5,801
California State University-San Marcos; San Marcos, Calif. (Pu)	4,103	65	65		$ 7,616	
California State University-Stanislaus; Turlock, Calif. (Pu)	4,992	72	63	$ 1,877	$ 9,257	$6,291
Chapman University; Orange, Calif. (Pr)	2,489	56	57	$19,926	$19,926	
Christian Heritage College; El Cajon, Calif. (Pr)	617		60	$10,240	$10,240	$4,500
Claremont McKenna College; Claremont, Calif. (Pr)	1,024	28	44	$20,600	$20,600	$7,060
Cogswell Polytechnical College; Sunnyvale, Calif. (Pr)	500	85	13	$ 7,800	$ 7,800	
College of Notre Dame; Belmont, Calif. (Pr)	813		65	$14,976	$14,976	$6,400
Concordia University-Irvine; Irvine, Calif. (Pr)	982	77	65	$13,600	$13,600	$5,480
DeVry Institute of Technology-Long Beach; Long Beach, Calif. (Pr)	2,398		27			
DeVry Institute of Technology-Pomona; Pomona, Calif. (Pr)	3,562		25			
Dominican College of San Rafael; San Rafael, Calif. (Pr)	957		82	$16,512	$16,512	$8,036

Institution name; city, state (control)	Students	Percent Accepted	Percent Women	Tuition In-state	Tuition Out-of-state	Room and board
Fresno Pacific University; Fresno, Calif. (Pr)	816			$12,480	$12,480	$ 4,950
Golden Gate University; San Fransisco, Calif. (Pr)	1,407	83%	57%	$ 8,592	$ 8,592	
Harvey Mudd College; Claremont, Calif. (Pr)	667	43	24	$20,754	$20,754	$ 7,502
Holy Names College; Oakland, Calif. (Pr)	400		81	$14,300	$14,300	$ 6,400
Humboldt State University; Arcata, Calif. (Pu)	6,534	78	52	$ 1,918	$ 5,904	$ 5,932
Humphreys College; Stockton, Calif. (Pr)	363	81	84	$ 6,552	$ 6,552	$ 3,441
John F. Kennedy University; Orinda, Calif. (Pr)	318		75	$ 7,380	$ 7,380	
LaSierra University; Riverside, Calif. (Pr)	1,169		54			
Life Bible College; San Dimas, Calif. (Pr)	495	62	53	$ 4,950	$ 4,950	$ 3,000
Loma Linda University; Loma Linda, Calif. (Pr)	1,255			$13,650	$13,650	$ 1,890
Loyola Marymount University; Los Angeles, Calif. (Pr)	4,486		58	$17,932	$17,932	
Master's College; Santa Clarita, Calif. (Pr)	969	82	51	$13,200	$13,200	$ 5,400
Menlo College; Atherton, Calif. (Pr)	534	93	38	$15,980	$15,980	$ 6,800
Mills College; Oakland, Calif. (Pr)	746	77	100	$17,250	$17,250	$ 7,296
Monterey Institute of International Studies; Monterey, Calif. (Pr)	22			$18,750	$18,750	
Mount Saint Mary's College; Los Angeles, Calif. (Pr)	1,687	78	93	$15,452	$15,452	$ 6,300
National University; La Jolla, Calif. (Pr)	4,481		54	$ 7,830	$ 7,830	
New College of California; San Francisco, Calif. (Pr)	1,402		57	$ 8,200	$ 8,200	
Occidental College; Los Angeles, Calif. (Pr)	1,554	77	57	$22,709	$22,709	$ 6,551
Otis College of Art & Design; Los Angeles, Calif. (Pr)	763	73	59	$17,950	$17,950	
Pacific Oaks College; Pasadena, Calif. (Pr)	247		94	$12,000	$12,000	$ 0
Pacific Union College; Angwin, Calif. (Pr)	1,554	68	55	$14,475	$14,475	$ 4,425
Pepperdine University; Malibu, Calif. (Pr)	3,256	46	59			$ 6,840
Pitzer College; Claremont, Calif. (Pr)	880	64	60	$20,880	$20,880	$ 6,214
Point Loma Nazarene University; San Diego, Calif. (Pr)	2,312	88	61	$12,210	$12,210	$ 5,220
Pomona College; Claremont, Calif. (Pr)	1,605	32	48	$21,420	$21,420	$ 8,270
Saint Mary's College; Moraga, Calif. (Pr)	3,234	83	61	$17,340	$17,340	$ 7,370
Samuel Merritt College; Oakland, Calif. (Pr)	286	63	88	$14,560	$14,560	$ 3,330
San Diego State University; San Diego, Calif. (Pu)	25,773	77	56	$ 1,506	$ 8,886	$ 7,110
San Francisco Art Institute; San Francisco, Calif. (Pr)	522	65	52	$18,400	$18,400	$ 6,300
San Francisco Conservatory of Music; San Francisco, Calif. (Pr)	158		52	$18,400	$18,400	
San Francisco State University; San Francisco, Calif. (Pu)	21,044	69	59	$ 1,904	$ 7,802	$ 6,720
San Jose State University; San Jose, Calif. (Pu)	20,681	75	52		$ 7,843	$ 6,248
Santa Clara University; Santa Clara, Calif. (Pr)	4,332	68	54	$18,786	$18,786	$ 7,644
Scripps College; Claremont, Calif. (Pr)	782	78	100	$20,599	$20,599	$ 8,111
Simpson College and Graduate School; Redding, Calif. (Pr)	955	72	65	$ 8,200	$ 8,200	$ 4,100
Sonoma State University; Rohnert Park, Calif. (Pu)	5,856	80	65	$ 1,027	$ 9,432	$ 6,049
Stanford University; Stanford, Calif. (Pr)	7,094	13	51	$23,058	$23,058	$ 7,881
Thomas Aquinas College; Santa Paula, Calif. (Pr)	246	61	40	$14,900	$14,900	$ 4,300
United States International University; San Diego, Calif. (Pr)	401	59	54	$12,015	$12,015	$ 5,040
University of California-Berkeley; Berkeley, Calif. (Pu)	22,261	28	50		$ 9,384	$ 8,122
University of California-Davis; Davis, Calif. (Pu)	19,403	66	55		$13,596	$ 5,946
University of California-Irvine; Irvine, Calif. (Pu)	14,400	63	53		$ 9,384	$ 5,233
University of California-Los Angeles; Los Angeles, Calif. (Pu)	24,103	33	54			$ 7,285
University of California-Riverside; Riverside, Calif. (Pu)	9,130	80	53	$ 4,000	$ 9,390	$ 6,579
University of California-San Diego; La Jolla, Calif. (Pu)	15,837	48	49	$ 4,027	$13,545	$ 6,864
University of California-Santa Barbara; Santa Barbara, Calif. (Pu)		61	55	$ 865	$ 6,785	$14,633
University of California-Santa Cruz; Santa Cruz, Calif. (Pu)	9,960	79	59	$ 4,359	$13,933	$ 6,900
University of Judaism; Bel Air, Calif. (Pr)	105	83	62	$13,910	$13,910	$ 7,290
University of La Verne; La Verne, Calif. (Pr)	2,953			$15,500	$15,500	$ 4,820
University of Redlands; Redlands, Calif. (Pr)	1,511	84	55	$19,490	$19,490	$ 7,368
University of San Diego; San Diego, Calif. (Pr)	2,537	63	57	$17,780	$17,780	$ 7,920
University of San Francisco; San Francisco, Calif. (Pr)	4,690	77	62	$17,710	$17,710	$ 7,838
University of Southern California; Los Angeles, Calif. (Pr)	15,552	45	49	$20,962	$20,962	$ 6,834
University of the Pacific; Stockton, Calif. (Pr)	2,805	83	57	$19,570	$19,570	$ 6,792
Vanguard University of Southern California; Costa Mesa, Calif. (Pr)	1,181	90	60	$12,560	$12,560	$ 5,060
Westmont College; Santa Barbara, Calif. (Pr)	1,316	78	62	$19,188	$19,188	$ 6,668
Whittier College; Whittier, Calif. (Pr)	1,301			$18,622	$18,622	$ 5,813
Woodbury University; Burbank, Calif. (Pr)	974	83	55	$15,800	$15,800	$ 5,728
COLORADO						
Adams State College; Alamosa, Colo. (Pu)	2,025	85	58		$ 5,748	$ 5,320
Colorado Christian University; Lakewood, Colo. (Pr)	1,750	82	56	$ 9,960	$ 9,960	$ 5,160
Colorado College; Colorado Springs, Colo. (Pr)	1,968	45	54	$21,822	$21,822	$ 5,568
Colorado Institute of Art; Denver, Colo. (Pr)	1,750	65	42			$ 9,420
Colorado School of Mines; Golden, Colo. (Pu)	2,429	77	24	$ 4,616	$14,716	$ 4,920
Colorado State University; Fort Collins, Colo. (Pu)	18,640	76	52	$ 2,933	$10,155	$ 4,878
Colorado Technical University; Colorado Springs, Colo. (Pr)	1,232	83	8			
Fort Lewis College; Durango, Colo. (Pu)	4,314	88	48	$ 1,676	$ 8,128	$ 4,514
Mesa State College; Grand Junction, Colo. (Pu)	4,926	94	56	$ 1,576	$ 5,966	$ 5,048

Institution name; city, state (control)	Students	Percent Accepted	Percent Women	Tuition In-state	Tuition Out-of-state	Room and board
Metropolitan State College of Denver; Denver, Colo. (Pu)	17,624			$ 1,976	$ 7,062	
Regis University; Denver, Colo. (Pr)	1,103	89%	56%	$15,600	$15,600	$6,200
Teikyo Loretto Heights University; Denver, Colo. (Pr)				$13,600	$13,600	$5,400
United States Air Force Academy; Colo. Springs, Colo. (Pu)	4,107	12	16	$ 0	$ 0	$ 0
University of Colorado-Boulder; Boulder, Colo. (Pu)	20,595	85	48	$ 2,386	$14,868	$4,908
University of Colorado-Colorado Springs; Colo. Springs, Colo. (Pu)	4,776	80	59		$ 9,004	$5,500
University of Colorado-Denver; Denver, Colo. (Pu)	7,920	75	54	$ 1,970	$10,416	
University of Denver; Denver, Colo. (Pr)	3,648	84	58	$18,936	$18,936	$6,234
University of Northern Colorado; Greeley, Colo. (Pu)	9,953	82	59	$ 1,967	$ 8,997	$4,570
University of Southern Colorado; Pueblo, Colo. (Pu)	5,082	83	57	$ 1,810	$ 8,434	$4,661
Western State College of Colorado; Gunnison, Colo. (Pu)	2,432	89	40	$ 1,480	$ 6,860	$4,744
CONNECTICUT						
Albertus Magnus College; New Haven, Conn. (Pr)	1,416	93	68	$13,500	$13,500	$6,324
Central Connecticut State University; New Britain, Conn. (Pu)	9,153	72	51	$ 2,062	$ 6,674	$5,446
Charter Oak State College; New Britain, Conn. (Pu)	1,348		50	$ 430	$ 628	
Connecticut College; New London, Conn. (Pr)	1,719	41	57			
Eastern Connecticut State University; Willimantic, Conn. (Pu)	4,335	81	57	$ 2,062	$ 6,674	$5,048
Fairfield University; Fairfield, Conn. (Pr)	4,281	66	52	$18,800	$18,800	$7,234
Mitchell College; New London, Conn. (Pr)	640		49	$14,100	$14,100	$6,740
Quinnipiac College; Hamden, Conn. (Pr)	4,197	62	66	$16,120	$16,120	$7,790
Sacred Heart University; Fairfield, Conn. (Pr)	4,000	83	62	$14,530	$14,530	$7,146
Saint Joseph College; West Hartford, Conn. (Pr)	1,185	68	97	$15,900	$15,900	$6,610
Southern Connecticut State University; New Haven, Conn. (Pu)	7,445	70	58		$ 6,874	$5,934
Teikyo Post University; Waterbury, Conn. (Pr)	1,340	66	65	$13,125	$13,125	$5,900
Trinity College; Hartford, Conn. (Pr)	2,088	44	50	$22,810	$22,810	$6,630
United States Coast Guard Academy; New London, Conn. (Pu)	795	7	29			
University of Bridgeport; Bridgeport, Conn. (Pr)	1,214		51	$13,400	$13,400	$6,810
University of Connecticut; Storrs, Conn. (Pu)	11,715	73	52		$12,676	$5,544
University of Hartford; West Hartford, Conn. (Pr)	5,230	81	52	$17,910	$17,910	$7,538
University of New Haven; West Haven, Conn. (Pr)	2,880		38	$14,250	$14,250	$6,500
Wesleyan University; Middletown, Conn. (Pr)	2,750	32	51	$24,330	$24,330	$6,510
Western Connecticut State University; Danbury, Conn. (Pu)	4,411	68	54		$ 6,674	$5,034
Yale University; New Haven, Conn. (Pr)	5,440	18	50	$24,500	$24,500	$7,440
DELAWARE						
Delaware State University; Dover, Del. (Pu)	3,057	44	57	$ 7,672	$11,332	$4,522
Goldey-Beacom College; Wilmington, Del. (Pr)	894	77	48	$ 7,200	$ 7,200	$3,290
University of Delaware; Newark, Del. (Pu)	15,443	67	58	$ 9,668	$17,668	
Wilmington College; New Castle, Del. (Pr)	583			$ 4,752	$ 4,752	
DISTRICT OF COLUMBIA						
American University; Washington, D.C. (Pr)	5,494	75	60	$20,118	$20,118	$7,982
Catholic University of America; Washington, D.C. (Pr)	2,412	86	55	$17,325	$17,325	$7,360
Corcoran School of Art; Washington, D.C. (Pr)	312	69	63	$14,140	$14,140	
Gallaudet University; Washington, D.C. (Pr)	1,258	74	53	$ 6,424	$ 6,424	$6,922
George Washington University; Washington, D.C. (Pr)	8,154	49	54	$22,340	$22,340	$8,210
Georgetown University; Washington, D.C. (Pr)	6,272	24	54	$23,088	$23,088	$8,693
Howard University; Washington, D.C. (Pr)	4,285			$ 8,750	$ 8,750	$5,250
Mount Vernon College; Washington, D.C. (Pr)	341					$7,730
Southeastern University; Washington, D.C. (Pr)	806	64		$ 6,660	$ 6,660	
Strayer University; Washington, D.C. (Pr)	9,111		56	$ 8,100	$ 8,100	
Trinity College; Washington, D.C. (Pr)	1,096	68	100	$13,470	$13,470	$6,310
University of the District of Columbia; Washington, D.C. (Pu)	10,004			$ 2,360	$ 5,660	
FLORIDA						
Barry University; Miami Shores, Fla. (Pr)	5,086	41	66			$6,220
Bethune-Cookman College; Daytona Beach, Fla. (Pr)	2,481	74	57	$ 8,450	$ 8,450	$5,400
Eckerd College; St. Petersburg, Fla. (Pr)	1,504	76	57	$18,025	$18,025	$4,960
Embry-Riddle Aeronautical University; Daytona Beach, Fla. (Pr)	4,445	82	14	$10,100	$10,100	$5,234
Flagler College; St. Augustine, Fla. (Pr)	1,669	30	64	$ 5,950	$ 5,950	$3,680
Florida A&M University; Tallahassee, Fla. (Pu)	10,492		57	$ 2,133	$ 8,789	$3,690
Florida A&M University/Florida State University; Tallahassee, Fla. (Pu)	9,765	81	56	$ 1,585	$ 6,318	$3,360
Florida Atlantic University; Boca Raton, Fla. (Pu)	16,017	75	61	$ 1,695	$ 7,020	$4,774
Florida Baptist Theological College; Graceville, Fla. (Pr)	502	93	30	$ 3,760	$ 3,760	$3,150
Florida Gulf Coast University; Ft. Myers, Fla. (Pu)	2,362	68	67	$ 1,492	$ 6,816	$3,058
Florida Institute of Technology; Melbourne, Fla. (Pr)	1,943	87	31	$17,300	$17,300	$5,270
Florida International University; Miami, Fla. (Pu)	24,870	67	56	$ 2,198	$ 8,863	$9,056
Florida Memorial College; Miami, Fla. (Pr)	1,488			$ 5,420	$ 5,420	$2,428
Florida Southern College; Lakeland, Fla. (Pr)	1,780	77	60	$11,114	$11,114	$5,600
Florida State University; Tallahassee, Fla. (Pu)	24,699	75	55	$ 1,697	$ 8,685	$4,951
International Academy of Merchandising & Design, Inc.; Tampa, Fla. (Pr)	696	95	70			
Jacksonville University; Jacksonville, Fla. (Pr)	1,857	66	52	$14,390	$14,390	$5,210

Institution name; city, state (control)	Students	Percent Accepted	Percent Women	Tuition In-state	Tuition Out-of-state	Room and board
Lynn University; Boca Raton, Fla. (Pr)	1,633	80%	54%	$17,300	$17,300	$6,550
New College of the University of South Florida; Sarasota, Fla. (Pu)	618	68	59	$ 2,525	$10,910	$4,663
Nova Southeastern University; Ft. Lauderdale, Fla. (Pr)	4,153	74	70	$11,600	$11,600	$6,200
Palm Beach Atlantic College; West Palm Beach, Fla. (Pr)	1,543			$10,500	$10,500	$4,700
Ringling School of Art & Design; Sarasota, Fla. (Pr)	853	48	39	$14,450	$14,450	$7,000
Rollins College; Winter Park, Fla. (Pr)	1,485	73	61	$21,250	$21,250	$6,700
Saint Leo University; Saint Leo, Fla. (Pr)	1,464	83	60	$11,450	$11,450	$6,050
Saint Thomas University; Miami, Fla. (Pr)	2,326					$4,000
Southeastern College of Assemblies of God; Lakeland, Fla. (Pr)	1,078	83	49	$ 4,650	$ 4,650	$3,382
Stetson University; DeLand, Fla. (Pr)	1,987		57	$15,850	$15,850	$5,730
University of Central Florida; Orlando, Fla. (Pu)	25,151		55	$ 2,025	$ 7,940	$3,610
University of Florida; Gainesville, Fla. (Pu)	31,477		51	$ 1,926	$ 7,843	
University of Miami; Coral Gables, Fla. (Pr)	8,391	59	54	$20,960	$20,960	$7,782
University of North Florida; Jacksonville, Fla. (Pu)	9,831	84	59			
University of South Florida; Tampa, Fla. (Pu)	25,565	68	58	$ 2,183	$ 8,838	$4,734
University of Tampa; Tampa, Fla. (Pr)	2,476	93	60	$13,938	$13,938	
University of West Florida; Pensacola, Fla. (Pu)	6,329	89	58	$ 2,143	$ 8,729	
Warner Southern College; Lake Wales, Fla. (Pr)	781	63	59	$ 8,340	$ 8,340	$4,500
Webber College; Babson Park, Fla. (Pr)	446	86	49	$ 8,160	$ 8,160	$3,570
GEORGIA						
Agnes Scott College; Decatur, Ga. (Pr)	808	77	100	$15,340	$15,340	$6,440
Albany State University; Albany, Ga. (Pu)	2,771		65	$ 1,730	$ 6,950	$3,226
Armstrong Atlantic State University; Savannah, Ga. (Pu)	5,088		62	$ 2,020	$ 7,240	$6,304
Atlanta Christian College; East Point, Ga. (Pr)	352	76	52			
Atlanta College of Art; Atlanta, Ga. (Pr)	429	77	38	$13,180	$13,180	
Augusta State University; Augusta, Ga. (Pu)	4,726	77	64	$ 1,680	$ 6,141	
Berry College; Mount Berry, Ga. (Pr)	1,933	65	62	$11,550	$11,550	$5,700
Brenau University; Gainesville, Ga. (Pr)	634	73	100	$11,730	$11,730	$6,876
Brewton-Parker College; Mt. Vernon, Ga. (Pr)	1,682			$ 5,560	$ 5,560	$2,250
Clark Atlanta University; Atlanta, Ga. (Pr)	5,477		71	$10,250	$10,250	$7,142
Columbus State University; Columbus, Ga. (Pu)	4,584		62	$ 2,202	$ 6,660	$4,130
Covenant College; Lookout Mountain, Ga. (Pr)	970	78	56	$14,400	$14,400	$4,400
DeVry Institute of Technology; Decatur, Ga. (Pr)	3,000		38			
Emmanuel College; Franklin Springs, Ga. (Pr)	854	66	52	$ 7,165	$ 7,165	$3,600
Emory University; Atlanta, Ga. (Pr)	4,500		55	$21,870	$21,870	$7,100
Fort Valley State College; Fort Valley, Ga. (Pu)	2,124					$3,075
Georgia Baptist College of Nursing; Atlanta, Ga. (Pr)	327	49	98	$ 9,000	$ 9,000	
Georgia College & State University; Milledgeville, Ga. (Pu)	4,085	69	63			
Georgia Institute of Technology; Atlanta, Ga. (Pu)	12,507	75	28	$ 2,426	$ 9,704	$5,700
Georgia Southern University; Statesboro, Ga. (Pu)	12,386	77	54	$ 1,730	$ 6,950	$4,138
Georgia Southwestern College; Americus, Ga. (Pu)	2,071					$3,130
Georgia State University; Atlanta, Ga. (Pu)	16,151	53	62	$ 2,322	$ 9,288	
Kennesaw State College; Kennesaw, Ga. (Pu)	10,994			$ 1,730	$ 6,950	
Mercer University-Macon; Macon, Ga. (Pr)	4,097	80	64	$15,465	$15,465	$5,080
Morehouse College; Atlanta, Ga. (Pr)	3,148	64	0			$6,214
Morris Brown College; Atlanta, Ga. (Pr)	1,891					$4,750
North Georgia College and State University; Dahlonega, Ga. (Pu)	3,005	80	66	$ 2,192	$ 7,686	$3,542
Oglethorpe University; Atlanta, Ga. (Pr)	1,058	76	64	$16,660	$16,660	$5,140
Paine College; Augusta, Ga. (Pr)	812		68	$11,114		$3,020
Piedmont College; Demorest, Ga. (Pr)	1,025	77	65	$ 8,200	$ 8,200	$3,930
Reinhardt College; Waleska, Ga. (Pr)	1,046	78				
Savannah College of Art & Design; Savannah, Ga. (Pr)	3,345	80	42	$14,850	$14,850	$6,475
Savannah State University; Savannah, Ga. (Pu)	2,822					$3,495
Shorter College; Rome, Ga. (Pr)	1,802	83	61	$ 8,650	$ 8,650	$4,450
South College; Savannah, Ga. (Pr)	445		81			
Southern Polytechnic State University; Marietta, Ga. (Pu)	3,117	83	18		$ 7,270	$3,450
Spelman College; Atlanta, Ga. (Pr)	1,899			$ 9,250	$ 9,250	$6,560
State University of West Georgia; Carrollton, Ga. (Pu)	6,172	73	61	$ 2,158	$ 7,378	$3,596
Thomas College; Thomasville, Ga. (Pr)	721	100	66	$ 7,500	$ 7,500	$1,500
Toccoa Falls College; Toccoa Falls, Ga. (Pr)	972		46	$ 8,384	$ 8,384	$3,896
University of Georgia; Athens, Ga. (Pu)	23,506	66	55	$ 2,930	$ 9,860	$4,672
Valdosta State University; Valdosta, Ga. (Pu)	8,345	66	59		$ 6,950	$3,780
Wesleyan College; Macon, Ga. (Pr)	568	78	100	$15,450	$15,450	$6,600
West Georgia College; Carrollton, Ga. (Pu)	6,189					$3,471
HAWAII						
Brigham Young University; Laie Oahu, Hawaii (Pr)	2,294	47	62	$ 2,665	$ 2,665	$4,900
Chaminade University of Honolulu; Honolulu, Hawaii (Pr)	2,034	83	51	$11,180	$11,180	$6,640
Hawaii Pacific University; Honolulu, Hawaii (Pr)	7,429	75	51	$ 8,460	$ 8,460	$8,120
University of Hawaii-Hilo; Hilo, Hawaii (Pu)	2,723			$ 1,344	$ 6,960	$3,400
University of Hawaii-Manoa; Honolulu, Hawaii (Pu)	11,785	67	54	$ 3,024	$ 9,504	$5,297

Institution name; city, state (control)	Students	Percent Accepted	Percent Women	Tuition In-state	Tuition Out-of-state	Room and board
IDAHO						
Albertson College; Caldwell, Idaho (Pr)	671	87%	53%	$15,600	$15,600	$4,050
Boise State University; Boise, Idaho (Pu)	13,287	87	57	$ 2,294	$ 8,174	$3,370
Idaho State University; Pocatello, Idaho (Pu)	10,230	88	55		$ 6,240	$3,730
Lewis-Clark State College; Lewiston, Idaho (Pu)	3,073	83	59	$ 2,044	$ 7,316	$3,586
Northwest Nazarene College; Nampa, Idaho (Pr)	1,116	46	57	$12,141	$12,141	$3,519
University of Idaho; Moscow, Idaho (Pu)	7,829		45	$ 2,348	$ 6,000	$3,977
ILLINOIS						
Northwestern University; Evanston, Ill. (Pr)	7,646	33	53	$23,496	$23,496	$7,114
Augustana College; Rock Island, Ill. (Pr)	2,301	77	58	$16,866	$16,866	$5,037
Aurora University; Aurora, Ill. (Pr)	1,270			$11,700	$11,700	$4,491
Barat College; Lake Forest, Ill. (Pr)	813	93	74	$13,500	$13,500	$5,250
Benedictine University; Lisle, Ill. (Pr)	1,750	92	56	$13,700	$13,700	$5,230
Blackburn College; Carlinville, Ill. (Pr)	448			$ 7,795	$ 7,795	$3,240
Bradley University; Peoria, Ill. (Pr)	4,873	88	53	$13,880	$13,880	$5,300
Chicago State University; Chicago, Ill. (Pu)	7,237			$ 2,496	$ 7,002	$5,825
Columbia College; Chicago, Ill. (Pr)	8,273		49	$ 9,544	$ 9,544	$4,750
Concordia University-River Forest; River Forest, Ill. (Pr)	1,273	82	66	$12,800	$12,800	$5,266
DePaul University; Chicago, Ill. (Pr)	11,186		60	$14,670	$14,670	$6,198
DeVry Institute of Technology; Chicago, Ill. (Pr)	3,819		31			
Dominican University; River Forest, Ill. (Pr)	1,049	83	69	$14,160	$14,160	$4,880
Eastern Illinois University; Charleston, Ill. (Pu)	10,174	71	58	$ 2,254	$ 6,762	$3,932
Elmhurst College; Elmhurst, Ill. (Pr)	2,842	72	65	$12,770	$12,770	$5,104
Eureka College; Eureka, Ill. (Pr)	502			$14,540	$14,540	$4,400
Greenville College; Greenville, Ill. (Pr)	1,053	71	57	$12,576	$12,576	$4,850
Illinois College; Jacksonville, Ill. (Pr)	883	81	57	$10,200	$10,200	$4,500
Illinois Institute of Technology; Chicago, Ill. (Pr)	1,848	61	22	$17,000	$17,000	$5,090
Illinois State University; Normal, Ill. (Pu)	17,518	77	57	$ 3,128	$ 9,383	$4,116
Illinois Wesleyan University; Bloomington, Ill. (Pr)	2,022	59	55	$19,244	$19,244	$4,980
Judson College; Elgin, Ill. (Pr)	975		57	$12,580	$12,580	$5,060
Kendall College; Evanston, Ill. (Pr)	497					$4,998
Knox College; Galesburg, Ill. (Pr)	1,194	75	55	$19,608	$19,608	$5,280
Lake Forest College; Lake Forest, Ill. (Pr)	1,193	79	57	$20,240	$20,240	$4,820
Lewis University; Romeoville, Ill. (Pr)	3,103	74	55	$13,664	$13,664	$5,730
Loyola University of Chicago; Chicago, Ill. (Pr)	7,669			$16,074	$16,074	$7,000
MacMurray College; Jacksonville, Ill. (Pr)	635	81	55	$12,300	$12,300	$4,430
McKendree College; Lebanon, Ill. (Pr)	1,883	72	60	$10,500	$10,500	$4,170
Millikin University; Decatur, Ill. (Pr)	2,173	80	58	$14,758	$14,758	$5,271
Monmouth College; Monmouth, Ill. (Pr)	1,077	81	56	$15,720	$15,720	$4,410
National College of Chiropractic; Lombard, Ill. (Pr)	850			$16,800	$16,800	
National-Louis University; Evanston, Ill. (Pr)	3,586	100	72	$13,095	$13,095	$6,884
North Central College; Naperville, Ill. (Pr)	2,600	76	57	$14,520	$14,520	$5,250
North Park University; Chicago, Ill. (Pr)	1,620	39	61	$15,420	$15,420	$5,030
Northeastern Illinois University; Chicago, Ill. (Pu)	7,892		61	$ 2,789	$ 7,157	
Northern Illinois University; DeKalb, Ill. (Pu)	16,341	72	54	$ 4,347		$5,010
Olivet Nazarene University; Kankakee, Ill. (Pr)	1,700			$11,178	$11,178	$4,696
Parks College of Saint Louis University; Cahokia, Ill. (Pr)	803					$5,110
Principia College; Elsah, Ill. (Pr)	584	92	54	$14,988	$14,988	$5,784
Quincy University; Quincy, Ill. (Pr)	1,014	73	7	$13,450	$13,450	$4,370
Robert Morris College; Chicago, Ill. (Pr)	3,728	63	72			
Rockford College; Rockford, Ill. (Pr)	1,043	41	69	$14,750	$14,750	$4,900
Roosevelt University; Chicago, Ill. (Pr)	4,180		61	$10,930	$10,930	
Saint Anthony College of Nursing; Rockford, Ill. (Pr)	86		93	$10,880	$10,880	
Saint Francis Medical Center of Nursing; Peoria, Ill. (Pr)	151		92	$ 8,448	$ 8,448	
Saint Xavier University; Chicago, Ill. (Pr)	2,338	99	80	$13,050	$13,050	$5,340
School of the Art Institute of Chicago; Chicago, Ill. (Pr)	1,725	78	62			$3,225
Southern Illinois University-Carbondale; Carbondale, Ill. (Pu)	17,939	74	43	$ 2,781	$ 8,343	$3,777
Southern Illinois University-Edwardsville; Edwardsville, Ill. (Pu)	9,044	86	59	$ 2,143	$ 4,286	$4,288
Trinity Christian College; Palos Heights, Ill. (Pr)	630	87	63	$12,750	$12,750	$5,060
Trinity International University; Deerfield, Ill. (Pr)	945	72	52	$12,840	$12,840	$4,800
University of Chicago; Chicago, Ill. (Pr)	3,809	61	48	$23,820	$23,820	$7,835
University of Illinois at Chicago; Chicago, Ill. (Pu)	16,347	63	55	$ 3,138	$ 9,414	$5,856
University of Illinois at Urbana-Champaign; Urbana, Ill. (Pu)	27,452	71	47	$ 4,746	$21,240	$8,270
University of St. Francis; Joliet, Ill. (Pr)	3,153	84	84	$11,670	$11,670	$4,740
Vandercook College of Music; Chicago, Ill. (Pr)	62			$10,000	$10,000	$5,100
West Suburban College of Nursing; Oak Park, Ill. (Pr)	141					$4,623
Western Illinois University; Macomb, Ill. (Pu)	10,192	69	51	$ 5,460	$ 5,460	$4,292
Wheaton College; Wheaton, Ill. (Pr)	2,340	56	52	$14,930	$14,930	$5,080
INDIANA						
Anderson University; Anderson, Ind. (Pr)	1,977	82	60	$13,740	$13,740	$4,540
Ball State University; Muncie, Ind. (Pu)	16,486	81	53	$ 1,727	$ 4,658	$4,520
Bethel College; Mishawaka, Ind. (Pr)	1,553	84	67	$11,850	$11,850	$4,000

Institution name; city, state (control)	Students	Percent Accepted	Women	Tuition In-state	Out-of-state	Room and board
Butler University; Indianappolis, Ind. (Pr)	3,284	87%	62%	$17,180	$17,180	$5,850
DePauw University; Greencastle, Ind. (Pr)	2,250	76	56	$18,530	$18,530	$6,080
Earlham College; Richmond, Ind. (Pr)	1,075	82	54	$19,334	$19,334	$4,674
Franklin College of Indiana; Franklin, Ind. (Pr)	959	81	50	$12,210	$12,210	
Goshen College; Goshen, Ind. (Pr)	1,045	98	57	$12,320	$12,320	$4,340
Grace College and Seminary; Winona Lake, Ind. (Pr)	765	85	53	$10,500	$10,500	$4,600
Hanover College; Hanover, Ind. (Pr)	1,087	86	53	$10,700	$10,700	$4,655
Huntington College; Huntington, Ind. (Pr)	855	89	60	$12,250	$12,250	$4,770
Indiana Institute of Technology; Fort Wayne, Ind. (Pr)	1,645		51	$12,300	$12,300	$4,564
Indiana State University; Terre Haute, Ind. (Pu)	9,343	87	52	$ 3,324	$ 8,252	$4,142
Indiana University-Bloomington; Bloomington, Ind. (Pu)	25,451		54	$ 4,244	$12,900	$5,492
Indiana University-Purdue Univ. Fort Wayne; Fort Wayne, Ind. (Pu)	9,815	98	56	$ 3,213	$ 7,361	
Indiana University-South Bend; South Bend, Ind. (Pu)	6,102			$ 2,985	$ 7,784	
Indiana Wesleyan University; Marion, Ind. (Pr)	1,947					$4,158
Manchester College; North Manchester, Ind. (Pr)	1,024	84	52	$13,930	$13,930	$5,110
Marian College; Indianapolis, Ind. (Pr)	1,352			$12,458	$12,458	$4,422
Oakland City University; Oakland City, Ind. (Pr)	1,016					$3,146
Purdue University-Calumet; Hammond, Ind. (Pu)	8,350		55	$ 2,262	$ 5,688	
Purdue University-West Lafayette; West Lafayette, Ind. (Pu)	30,159	87	43	$ 3,500	$11,720	$5,260
Rose-Hulman Institute of Technology; Terre Haute, Ind. (Pr)	1,590	74	18	$18,567	$18,567	$5,475
Saint Joseph's College; Rensselaer, Ind. (Pr)	1,355	81	100	$14,070	$14,070	$5,080
Saint Mary-of-the-Woods College; Saint Mary-of-the-Woods, Ind. (Pr)	1,260	82		$13,160	$13,160	$5,000
Saint Mary's College; Notre Dame, Ind. (Pr)	1,355	85	100	$16,184	$16,184	$5,632
Taylor University; Upland, Ind. (Pr)	1,880	66	53	$14,900	$14,900	$4,630
Taylor University-Fort Wayne Campus; Fort Wayne, Ind. (Pr)	410		57	$12,550	$12,550	$4,230
Tri-State University; Angola, Ind. (Pr)	1,081		28	$12,700	$12,700	$4,950
University of Evansville; Evansville, Ind. (Pr)	3,085			$14,400	$14,400	$4,560
University of Indianapolis; Indianapolis, Ind. (Pr)	2,715	87	66	$14,000	$14,000	$5,000
University of Notre Dame; Notre Dame, Ind. (Pr)	7,875	42	45	$22,200	$22,200	$5,750
University of Saint Francis; Fort Wayne, Ind. (Pr)	794	82	65	$10,310	$10,310	$4,270
University of Southern Indiana; Evansville, Ind. (Pu)	7,935		61	$ 2,720	$ 6,673	
Valparaiso University; Valparaiso, Ind. (Pr)	2,990	80	54	$16,280	$16,280	$4,360
Wabash College; Crawfordsville, Ind. (Pr)	789	73	0	$15,400	$15,400	$4,780
IOWA						
Allen College; Waterloo, Iowa (Pr)	233		93	$ 7,620	$ 7,620	
Briar Cliff College; Sioux City, Iowa (Pr)	1,001	82	65	$12,690	$12,690	$4,071
Buena Vista University; Storm Lake, Iowa (Pr)	2,651	90	61	$15,292	$15,292	$4,507
Central College; Pella, Iowa (Pr)	1,208	66	56	$14,070	$14,070	$4,944
Clarke College; Dubuque, Iowa (Pr)	1,126	85	69	$13,196	$13,196	$5,220
Coe College; Cedar Rapids, Iowa (Pr)	1,213	82	53	$17,390	$17,390	$5,020
Cornell College; Mount Vernon, Iowa (Pr)	1,024	83	57	$18,835	$18,835	$5,140
Dordt College; Sioux Center, Iowa (Pr)	1,301	93	50	$14,480	$14,480	$3,030
Drake University; Des Moines, Iowa (Pr)	3,474	92	61	$16,480	$16,480	$4,870
Graceland College; Lamoni, Iowa (Pr)	4,068	67	81	$11,700	$11,700	$3,830
Grand View College; Des Moines, Iowa (Pr)	1,433	85	65	$11,340	$11,340	$3,775
Grinnell College; Grinnell, Iowa (Pr)	1,345	58	57	$18,990	$18,990	$5,600
Iowa State University; Ames, Iowa (Pu)	21,035	91	44	$ 2,786	$ 9,346	$3,958
Iowa Wesleyan College; Mt. Pleasant, Iowa (Pr)	828	89	66	$12,700	$12,700	$4,250
Loras College; Dubuque, Iowa (Pr)	1,736					$4,775
Luther College; Decorah, Iowa (Pr)	2,472	90	60	$17,290	$17,290	$3,810
Marycrest International University; Davenport, Iowa (Pr)	905					$4,128
Morningside College; Sioux City, Iowa (Pr)	1,178					$4,258
Mount Mercy College; Cedar Rapids, Iowa (Pr)	1,257	91	69	$13,190	$13,190	$4,370
Mount Saint Clare College; Clinton, Iowa (Pr)	567	51	58	$12,580	$12,580	$4,450
Northwestern College; Orange City, Iowa (Pr)	1,190	95	58	$12,100	$12,100	$3,400
Saint Ambrose University; Davenport, Iowa (Pr)	1,960	85	60	$12,850	$12,850	$4,810
Simpson College; Indianola, Iowa (Pr)	1,992	80	55	$13,620	$13,620	$4,570
University of Dubuque; Dubuque, Iowa (Pr)	672			$12,640	$12,640	$4,340
University of Iowa; Iowa City, Iowa (Pu)	19,337	84	55	$ 2,786	$10,228	$4,370
University of Northern Iowa; Cedar Falls, Iowa (Pu)	11,858	84	57	$ 2,786	$ 7,546	$3,926
Upper Iowa University; Fayette, Iowa (Pr)	4,239	69	56	$10,240	$10,240	$3,958
Wartburg College; Waverly, Iowa (Pr)	1,541	85	58	$14,740	$14,740	$4,250
William Penn College; Oskaloosa, Iowa (Pr)	1,096	88	50	$11,924	$11,924	$4,140
KANSAS						
Baker University; Baldwin City, Kans. (Pr)	1,424			$11,300	$11,300	$4,650
Barclay College; Haviland, Kans. (Pr)	117	92	51			
Benedictine College; Atchison, Kans. (Pr)	1,245	87	56			
Bethany College; Lindsborg, Kans. (Pr)	590	33	47	$11,575	$11,575	$3,579
Bethel College; North Newton, Kans. (Pr)	618	73	56	$11,350	$11,350	$4,520
Emporia State University; Emporia, Kans. (Pu)	4,129	100	60	$ 1,982	$ 6,346	$3,560

Institution name; city, state (control)	Students	Percent Accepted	Percent Women	Tuition In-state	Tuition Out-of-state	Room and board
Fort Hays State University; Hays, Kans. (Pu)	4,346			$ 2,061	$ 6,530	$3,600
Friends University; Wichita, Kans. (Pr)	2,389	85%		$11,050	$11,050	$3,420
Kansas State University; Manhattan, Kans. (Pu)	17,532	69	47%	$ 2,042	$ 8,490	$3,780
Kansas Wesleyan University; Salina, Kans. (Pr)	684	70	60	$11,000	$11,000	$4,000
McPherson College; McPherson, Kans. (Pr)	507	78	46	$10,800	$10,800	$4,666
Mid America Nazarene University; Olathe, Kans. (Pr)	1,266					$4,496
Newman University; Wichita, Kans. (Pr)	1,489	84	64	$ 9,000	$ 9,000	
Ottawa University; Ottawa, Kans. (Pr)	521	62	43	$ 9,560	$ 9,560	$3,620
Pittsburg State University; Pittsburg, Kans. (Pu)	5,115		47	$ 2,100	$ 6,464	$3,544
Saint Mary College; Leavenworth, Kans. (Pr)	839					$4,300
Southwestern College; Winfield, Kans. (Pr)	810	96	51	$10,600	$10,600	$4,170
Sterling College; Sterling, Kans. (Pr)	457	70	47	$10,076	$10,076	$3,884
Tabor College; Hillsboro, Kans. (Pr)	510		46	$11,000	$11,000	$4,180
University of Kansas; Lawrence, Kans. (Pu)	19,183		52	$ 2,090	$ 8,693	$3,941
Washburn University; Topeka, Kans. (Pu)	4,829	100	60			$3,950
Wichita State University; Wichita, Kans. (Pu)	10,536		55	$ 1,900	$ 8,202	$3,945
KENTUCKY						
Alice Lloyd College; Pippa Passes, Ky. (Pr)	501	51	50	$ 6,360	$ 6,360	$2,680
Asbury College; Wilmore, Ky. (Pr)	1,286	97	57	$12,810	$12,810	$3,460
Bellarmine College; Louisville, Ky. (Pr)	2,444	91	63	$12,480	$12,480	$3,940
Berea College; Berea, Ky. (Pr)	1,517	35	59			$3,686
Brescia University; Owensboro, Ky. (Pr)	676	83	67	$ 8,990	$ 8,990	$4,008
Campbellsville University; Campbellsville, Ky. (Pr)	1,592	76	59	$ 8,000	$ 8,000	$3,990
Centre College; Danville, Ky. (Pr)	1,052	86	50	$20,350	$20,350	$5,300
Cumberland College; Williamsburg, Ky. (Pr)	1,596		55	$ 8,798	$ 8,798	$3,976
Eastern Kentucky University; Richmond, Ky. (Pu)	13,478	95	57	$ 2,190	$ 6,030	$3,396
Georgetown College; Georgetown, Ky. (Pu)	1,356	93	57			$4,400
Kentucky Christian College; Grayson, Ky. (Pr)	561	85	54	$ 6,496	$ 6,496	$3,774
Kentucky State University; Frankfort, Ky. (Pu)	2,204		59	$ 1,920	$ 5,760	$3,276
Kentucky Wesleyan College; Owensboro, Ky. (Pr)	721	82	59	$ 9,480	$ 9,480	$4,630
Lindsey Wilson College; Columbia, Ky. (Pr)	1,006					$4,230
Midway College; Midway, Ky. (Pr)	974		90	$ 9,062	$ 9,062	$4,600
Morehead State University; Morehead, Ky. (Pu)	6,734	89	59	$ 0	$13,470	$6,310
Murray State University; Murray, Ky. (Pu)	7,120			$ 2,300	$ 6,140	$3,540
Northern Kentucky University; Highland Heig, Ky. (Pu)	10,602	100	59	$ 2,120	$ 5,720	$3,439
Pikeville College; Pikeville, Ky. (Pr)	735	100	69	$ 7,500	$ 7,500	$3,175
Spalding University; Louisville, Ky. (Pr)	1,128	85	81	$10,300	$10,300	$2,790
Thomas More College; Crestiew Hill, Ky. (Pr)	1,417		54	$11,578	$11,578	$4,500
Transylvania University; Lexington, Ky. (Pr)	1,073	89	57	$14,070	$14,070	$5,370
Union College; Barbourville, Ky. (Pr)	697	94	49	$10,590	$10,590	$3,450
University of Kentucky; Lexington, Ky. (Pu)	17,155		52	$ 2,680	$ 8,040	$3,470
University of Louisville; Louisville, Ky. (Pu)	14,548	89	53	$ 2,400	$ 7,200	$4,982
Western Kentucky University; Bowling Green, Ky. (Pu)	12,697	87	57	$ 2,390	$ 6,430	$3,006
LOUISIANA						
Centenary College of Louisiana; Shreveport, La. (Pr)	852	86	59	$13,200	$13,200	$4,210
Dillard University; New Orleans, La. (Pr)	1,584			$ 8,500	$ 8,500	$4,464
Grambling State University; Grambling, La. (Pu)	6,828			$ 2,208	$ 7,358	$2,636
Louisiana College; Pineville, La. (Pr)	1,003			$ 6,210	$ 6,210	$3,112
Louisiana State University-Baton Rouge; Baton Rouge, La. (Pu)	24,760	81	53	$ 2,301	$ 6,202	$3,910
Louisiana State University-Shreveport; Shreveport, La. (Pu)	3,354			$ 1,950	$ 5,290	$1,827
Louisiana Tech University; Ruston, La. (Pu)	8,291	99	49	$ 2,532	$ 5,847	$2,850
Loyola University New Orleans; New Orleans, La. (Pr)	3,298	88	62	$14,140	$14,140	$6,237
McNeese State University; Lake Charles, La. (Pu)	7,045	99	58	$ 2,006	$ 6,446	$2,310
Nicholls State University; Thibodaux, La. (Pu)	6,619		61	$ 3,290	$ 5,917	$2,850
Northeast Louisiana University; Monroe, La. (Pu)	9,800	92	60		$ 2,400	$3,380
Northwestern State University of Louisiana; Natchitoches, La. (Pu)	7,640	95	66	$ 2,147	$ 6,437	$2,416
Our Lady of Holy Cross College; New Orleans, La. (Pr)	1,192	78	77	$ 4,810	$ 4,810	
Southeastern Louisiana University; Hammond, La. (Pu)	13,581	90	61	$ 2,150	$ 6,446	$2,400
Southern University and Agricultural and Mechanical College; Shreveport, La. (Pu)	1,345	100	69	$ 1,104	$ 2,394	
Southern University-Baton Rouge; Baton Rouge, La. (Pu)	7,976			$ 2,065	$ 5,852	$3,228
Tulane University; New Orleans, La. (Pr)	6,801	79	52	$22,590	$22,590	$6,700
University of New Orleans; New Orleans, La. (Pu)	11,638	84	56	$ 2,362	$ 7,888	$3,150
University of Southwestern Louisiana; Lafayette, La. (Pu)	15,530	97	57	$ 2,009	$ 7,241	$2,592
Xavier University of Louisiana; New Orleans, La. (Pr)	3,145	91	71	$ 8,500	$ 8,500	$4,900
MAINE						
Bates College; Lewiston, Maine (Pr)	1,713	38	52			
Bowdoin College; Brunswick, Maine (Pr)	1,583	31	50	$23,395	$23,395	$6,285
Colby College; Waterville, Maine (Pr)	1,802	34	53			
College of the Atlantic; Bar Harbor, Maine (Pr)	283	55	66	$19,248	$19,248	$5,220
Husson College; Bangor, Maine (Pr)	979	82	61	$ 9,210	$ 9,210	$4,990

Institution name; city, state (control)	Students	Percent Accepted	Percent Women	Tuition In-state	Tuition Out-of-state	Room and board
Maine College of Art; Portland, Maine (Pr)	315	73%	59%	$16,530	$16,530	$7,042
Saint Joseph's College; Windham, Maine (Pr)	1,172		76	$11,900	$11,900	$5,770
Thomas College; Waterville, Maine (Pr)	703	97	61	$11,450	$11,450	$5,175
Unity College; Unity, Maine (Pr)	509	90	28	$11,740	$11,740	$5,200
University of Maine-Augusta; Augusta, Maine (Pu)	5,130	63	74			
University of Maine-Farmington; Farmington, Maine (Pu)	2,396	75	68		$ 8,280	$4,500
University of Maine-Fort Kent; Fort Kent, Maine (Pu)	827		65	$ 3,030	$ 7,410	$3,910
University of Maine-Machias; Machias, Maine (Pu)	889		65	$ 3,030	$ 7,410	$4,185
University of Maine-Orono; Orono, Maine (Pu)	7,109	80	49	$ 3,990	$11,250	$5,256
University of Maine-Presque Isle; Presque Isle, Maine (Pu)	1,344	85	60	$ 3,210	$ 7,410	$3,970
University of New England; Biddeford, Maine (Pr)	1,419	81	76	$14,990	$14,990	$6,050
University of Southern Maine; Gorham, Maine (Pu)	8,463	79	60	$ 3,540	$ 9,810	$4,987
Wesley College; Florence, Maine (Pr)	81		41	$ 2,500	$ 2,500	$2,150
MARYLAND						
Baltimore Hebrew University; Baltimore, Md. (Pr)	204	100	68	$ 5,035	$ 5,035	
Bowie State University; Bowie, Md. (Pu)	2,960			$ 3,357	$ 7,792	$4,427
Capitol College; Laurel, Md. (Pr)	695	96	21	$10,542	$10,542	
College of Notre Dame of Maryland; Baltimore, Md. (Pr)	2,270	75	93	$14,680	$14,680	$6,330
Columbia Union College; Tacoma Park, Md. (Pr)	1,172					$4,150
Coppin State College; Baltimore, Md. (Pu)	2,931			$ 3,012	$ 7,392	$4,884
Frostburg State University; Frostburg, Md. (Pu)	4,351	80	53	$ 3,216	$ 7,916	$4,956
Goucher College; Baltimore, Md. (Pr)	1,137	79	73	$20,200	$20,200	$7,380
Hood College; Fredrick, Md. (Pr)	1,022	77	88	$16,700	$16,700	$3,700
Johns Hopkins University; Baltimore, Md. (Pr)	3,743	41	41	$23,660	$23,660	$7,870
Loyola College; Baltimore, Md. (Pr)	3,255	67	56	$17,440	$17,440	$8,730
Maryland Institute, College of Art; Baltimore, Md. (Pr)	1,060	49	54	$18,460	$18,460	$5,840
Morgan State University; Baltimore, Md. (Pu)	5,356			$ 1,853	$ 4,405	$5,296
Mount Saint Mary's College; Emmitsburg, Md. (Pr)	1,334	83	55	$16,520	$16,520	$6,650
Salisbury State University; Salisbury, Md. (Pu)	5,534	60	57	$ 2,856	$ 7,066	$5,390
St. John's College; Annapolis, Md. (Pr)	434	65	45	$23,290	$23,290	$6,360
St. Mary's College of Maryland; St. Marys City, Md. (Pu)	1,682	66	58	$ 6,100	$10,800	$5,970
Towson University; Towson, Md. (Pu)	13,559	69	60	$ 3,332	$ 9,514	$5,490
United States Naval Academy; Annapolis, Md. (Pu)	4,020	16	15			
University of Baltimore; Baltimore, Md. (Pu)	1,925		53	$ 1,771	$ 5,442	$ 0
University of Maryland-Baltimore County; Baltimore, Md. (Pu)	8,638	75	51	$ 4,046	$ 8,519	$5,252
University of Maryland-College Park; College Park, Md. (Pu)	24,776	64	49	$ 4,050	$10,938	$6,216
University of Maryland-Eastern Shore; Princess Anne, Md. (Pu)	2,862			$ 2,577	$ 7,219	$4,530
University of Maryland-University College; College Park, Md. (Pu)	10,436	100	56	$ 4,416	$ 5,664	
Villa Julie College; Stevenson, Md. (Pr)	2,006	79	73	$10,250	$10,250	
Washington Bible College; Lanham, Md. (Pr)	352		42	$10,140	$10,140	$4,180
Washington College; Chestertown, Md. (Pr)	1,079	84	58	$19,750	$19,750	$5,740
Western Maryland College; Westminster, Md. (Pr)	1,574	76	55	$18,650	$18,650	$5,350
MASSACHUSETTS						
American International College; Springfield, Mass. (Pr)	1,426			$11,800	$11,800	$5,692
Amherst College; Amherst, Mass. (Pr)	1,650	23	48	$24,800	$24,800	$6,560
Anna Maria College; Paxton, Mass. (Pr)	805	76	62	$12,600	$12,600	$5,950
Art Institute of Boston at Lesley; Boston, Mass. (Pr)	477	84	48	$12,500	$12,500	$7,250
Assumption College; Worcester, Mass. (Pr)	2,246	74	65	$17,320	$17,320	$6,760
Atlantic Union College; South Lancaster, Mass. (Pr)	1,193			$12,125	$12,125	$3,900
Babson College; Babson Park, Mass. (Pr)	1,685	46	37	$21,072	$21,072	$8,392
Becker College-Worcester Campus; Worcester, Mass. (Pr)	1,113	73	74	$11,490	$11,490	$5,830
Bentley College; Waltham, Mass. (Pr)	4,186	63	44	$17,730	$17,730	$8,260
Berklee College of Music; Boston, Mass. (Pr)	2,953			$14,990	$14,990	$7,890
Boston College; Chestnut Hill, Mass. (Pr)	8,925	40	53	$21,700	$21,700	
Boston Conservatory; Boston, Mass. (Pr)	350		71	$17,300	$17,300	$8,200
Boston University; Boston, Mass. (Pr)	18,270	60	57	$23,770	$23,770	$8,130
Bradford College; Haverhill, Mass. (Pr)	585	80	67	$16,830	$16,830	$7,050
Brandeis University; Waltham, Mass. (Pr)	3,141	57	57	$24,421	$24,421	$7,040
Bridgewater State College; Bridgewater, Mass. (Pu)	7,320	70	61		$ 6,450	$4,502
Clark University; Worcester, Mass. (Pr)	2,242	80	59	$22,400	$22,400	$4,150
College of the Holy Cross; Worcester, Mass. (Pr)	2,789	47	52	$22,500	$22,500	$7,320
Curry College; Milton, Mass. (Pr)	2,082	82	53	$16,500	$16,500	$6,600
Eastern Nazarene College; Quincy, Mass. (Pr)	1,508					$3,976
Elms College; Chicopee, Mass. (Pr)	836	92	91	$13,470	$13,470	$5,300
Emerson College; Boston, Mass. (Pr)	3,046	63	59	$18,112	$18,112	$8,480
Emmanuel College; Boston, Mass. (Pr)	1,290	74	90	$15,488	$15,488	
Endicott College; Beverly, Mass. (Pr)	1,261	79	70	$14,000	$14,000	$7,410
Fitchburg State College; Fitchburg, Mass. (Pu)	2,800			$ 3,296	$ 7,976	$4,410
Framingham State College; Framingham, Mass. (Pu)	4,390	64	63	$ 1,150	$ 7,050	$4,060
Gordon College; Wenham, Mass. (Pr)	1,475	81	67	$15,740	$15,740	$5,050
Hampshire College; Amherst, Mass. (Pr)	1,160	65	56	$24,984	$24,984	$6,622

Institution name; city, state (control)	Students	Percent Accepted	Percent Women	Tuition In-state	Tuition Out-of-state	Room and board
Harvard and Radcliffe Colleges; Cambridge, Mass. (Pr)	6,704	12%	46%	$21,342	$21,342	$7,514
Hellenic College; Brookline, Mass. (Pr)	64	63	36	$ 7,600	$ 7,600	$5,900
Lasell College; Newton, Mass. (Pr)	672	80	86			
Lesley College; Cambridge, Mass. (Pr)	1,366	81	87	$15,450	$15,450	$6,700
Massachusetts College of Art; Boston, Mass. (Pu)	2,211	47	63		$ 8,000	$6,400
Massachusetts College of Liberal Arts; North Adams, Mass. (Pu)	1,481	65	60	$ 1,090	$ 7,050	$5,206
Massachusetts College of Pharmacy & Allied Health; Boston, Mass. (Pr)	978	70	64	$14,900	$14,900	$7,800
Massachusetts Institute of Technology; Cambridge, Mass. (Pr)	4,372	23	41	$25,000	$25,000	$6,900
Merrimack College; North Andover, Mass. (Pr)	3,003	77	52	$15,110	$15,110	$7,230
Montserrat College of Art; Beverly, Mass. (Pr)	358	88	53	$12,550	$12,550	$3,638
Mount Holyoke College; South Hadley, Mass. (Pr)	1,885	64	100	$23,200	$23,200	$6,820
Mount Ida College; Newton, Mass. (Pr)	2,009					$8,460
New England Conservatory of Music; Boston, Mass. (Pr)	387	45	50	$18,750	$18,750	$8,600
Nichols College; Dudley, Mass. (Pr)	1,145	78	50			
Northeastern University; Boston, Mass. (Pr)	19,447	66	50	$14,830	$14,830	$5,680
Pine Manor College; Chestnut Hill, Mass. (Pr)	306	82	100	$11,440	$11,440	$7,245
Regis College; Weston, Mass. (Pr)	1,085	86	98	$16,860	$16,860	$7,870
Salem State College; Salem, Mass. (Pu)	7,336	69	62	$ 1,150	$ 6,450	$4,086
School of the Museum of Fine Arts; Boston, Mass. (Pr)	522			$ 1,800	$ 1,800	
Simmons College; Boston, Mass. (Pr)	1,211	73	100	$19,520	$19,520	$8,046
Simon's Rock College of Bard; Gt. Barrington, Mass. (Pr)	374	82	58	$20,800	$20,800	$6,410
Smith College; Northampton, Mass. (Pr)	2,655	56	100	$21,680	$21,680	$7,560
Springfield College; Springfield, Mass. (Pr)	2,046	59				
Stonehill College; Easton, Mass. (Pr)	2,658	54	59	$15,736	$15,736	$7,852
Suffolk University; Boston, Mass. (Pr)	3,247	78	57	$14,580	$14,580	$9,210
Tufts University; Medford, Mass. (Pr)	4,791	33	52	$23,106	$23,106	$7,108
University of Massachusetts-Amherst; Amherst, Mass. (Pu)	18,752	74	50	$ 1,714	$ 9,756	$4,790
University of Massachusetts-Boston; Boston, Mass. (Pu)	10,132	59	56	$ 1,908	$ 8,930	
University of Massachusetts-Dartmouth; North Dartmouth, Mass. (Pu)	5,828	72	53	$ 1,417	$ 7,845	$5,800
University of Massachusetts-Lowell; Lowell, Mass. (Pu)	9,354	74	38	$ 1,534	$ 7,871	$4,836
Wellesley College; Wellesley, Mass. (Pr)	2,287	45	100	$22,114	$22,114	$6,990
Wentworth Institute of Technology; Boston, Mass. (Pr)	3,076	48	15	$12,450	$12,450	$6,400
Western New England College; Springfield, Mass. (Pr)	3,103	76	37	$11,130	$11,130	$6,544
Westfield State College; Westfield, Mass. (Pu)	4,187		53		$ 5,440	$4,440
Wheaton College; Norton, Mass. (Pr)	1,451	72	67	$22,950	$22,950	$6,730
Wheelock College; Boston, Mass. (Pr)	735	84	96	$16,740	$16,740	$6,615
Williams College; Williamstown, Mass. (Pr)	2,028		49	$23,860	$23,860	$6,480
Worcester Polytechnic Institute; Worcester, Mass. (Pr)	2,783	78	22	$21,770	$21,770	$6,912
Worcester State College; Worcester, Mass. (Pu)	4,585	60	63	$ 1,210	$ 6,450	$4,140
MICHIGAN						
Adrian College; Adrian, Mich. (Pr)	1,049		49	$13,150	$13,150	$4,320
Albion College; Albion, Mich. (Pr)	1,490	90	55	$17,984	$17,984	$5,220
Alma College; Alma, Mich. (Pr)	1,442	83	58	$14,998	$14,998	$5,460
Andrews University; Berrien Springs, Mich. (Pr)	1,847		57	$11,685	$11,685	$3,630
Aquinas College; Grand Rapids, Mich. (Pr)	1,913	88	66	$13,366	$13,366	$4,652
Baker College of Auburn Hills; Auburn Hills, Mich. (Pr)	1,319	50	70	$ 6,950	$ 6,950	
Baker College of Jackson; Jackson, Mich. (Pr)	1,010		76	$ 6,950	$ 6,950	
Baker College of Muskegon; Muskegon, Mich. (Pr)	2,370	100	73	$ 6,950	$ 6,950	
Calvin College; Grand Rapids, Mich. (Pr)	4,073	99	56	$13,420	$13,420	$4,675
Center for Creative Studies; Detroit, Mich. (Pr)	921			$14,280	$14,280	$5,500
Central Michigan University; Mount Pleasant, Mich. (Pu)	17,290	89	58	$ 3,147	$ 8,169	$4,480
Cleary College; Howell, Mich. (Pr)	642		66	$ 7,605	$ 7,605	$ 0
Detroit College of Business; Dearborn, Mich. (Pr)	6,182	100	78	$ 9,024	$ 9,024	$ 0
Eastern Michigan University; Ypsilanti, Mich. (Pu)	17,701		59	$ 2,984	$ 9,874	$ 450
Ferris State University; Big Rapids, Mich. (Pu)	9,246	92	44	$ 3,998	$ 8,350	$4,966
Grace Bible College; Grand Rapids, Mich. (Pr)	158	43	52	$ 6,800	$ 6,800	$4,150
Grand Valley State University; Allendale, Mich. (Pu)	11,734			$ 3,362	$ 7,342	$5,000
Hillsdale College; Hillsdale, Mich. (Pr)	1,190	87	51	$13,230	$13,230	$5,650
Hope College; Holland, Mich. (Pr)	2,920	93	60	$15,934	$15,934	$5,030
Kalamazoo College; Kalamazoo, Mich. (Pr)	1,357	88	57	$19,188	$19,188	$5,787
Kendall College of Art and Design; Grand Rapids, Mich. (Pr)	527			$10,500	$10,500	
Kettering University; Flint, Mich. (Pr)	2,571	74	20	$14,640	$14,640	$3,960
Lake Superior State University; Sault Ste. Marie, Mich. (Pu)	3,332		52	$ 3,727	$ 7,320	$4,738
Lawrence Technological University; Southfield, Mich. (Pr)	3,073					$4,200
Madonna University; Livonia, Mich. (Pr)	3,307	65	78	$ 6,610	$ 6,610	$4,676
Marygrove College; Detroit, Mich. (Pr)	990		84	$10,066	$10,066	$5,200
Michigan State University; East Lansing, Mich. (Pu)	33,308		53	$ 4,223	$11,288	$4,052
Michigan Technological University; Houghton, Mich. (Pu)	5,620	97	27	$ 4,236	$10,077	$4,590
Northern Michigan University; Marquette, Mich. (Pu)	7,049	89	53		$12,035	$4,602

Institution name; city, state (control)	Students	Percent Accepted	Women	Tuition In-state	Out-of-state	Room and board
Northwood University; Midland, Mich. (Pr)	2,458	94%	46%	$11,325	$11,325	$5,208
Oakland University; Rochester, Mich. (Pu)	11,111		65	$ 3,766	$10,931	$4,555
Olivet College; Olivet, Mich. (Pr)	824			$12,762	$12,762	$4,094
Rochester College; Rochester Hills, Mich. (Pr)	467		52			
Sacred Heart Major Seminary; Detroit, Mich. (Pr)	179					$4,220
Saginaw Valley State University; University Center, Mich. (Pu)	6,658		60	$ 3,257	$ 6,681	$4,690
Saint Mary's College; Orchard Lake, Mich. (Pr)	310	70	43	$ 5,352	$ 5,352	$5,600
Siena Heights College; Adrian, Mich. (Pr)	993					$4,630
Spring Arbor College; Spring Arbor, Mich. (Pr)	1,916			$10,280	$10,280	$4,190
University of Detroit Mercy; Detroit, Mich. (Pr)	4,275		66	$13,350	$13,350	$5,380
University of Michigan-Ann Arbor; Ann Arbor, Mich. (Pu)	24,015	69	50	$ 6,070	$18,910	$5,486
University of Michigan-Dearborn; Dearborn, Mich. (Pu)	6,744		53			
University of Michigan-Flint; Flint, Mich. (Pu)	5,984			$ 3,309	$ 9,823	
Wayne State University; Detroit, Mich. (Pu)	18,518	85	61	$ 3,330	$ 7,530	
Western Michigan University; Kalamazoo, Mich. (Pu)	20,646	83	54	$ 3,228	$ 8,126	$4,591
William Tyndale College; Farmington Hi, Mich. (Pr)	640	93	51	$ 6,600	$ 6,600	$2,600
MINNESOTA						
Augsburg College; Minneapolis, Minn. (Pr)	2,732	78	62	$15,084	$15,084	$5,240
Bemidji State University; Bemidji, Minn. (Pu)	4,136	66	54	$ 3,010	$ 6,110	$3,084
Bethel College; Saint Paul, Minn. (Pr)	2,524	69	63			
Carleton College; Northfield, Minn. (Pr)	1,881	56	53	$22,470	$22,470	$4,584
College of Saint Benedict; Saint Joseph, Minn. (Pr)	1,977	91	100	$16,195	$16,195	$5,025
College of Saint Catherine; Saint Paul, Minn. (Pr)	2,342	89	99	$14,144	$14,144	$4,402
College of Saint Scholastica; Duluth, Minn. (Pr)	1,365	91	74	$15,420	$15,420	$4,760
Concordia College-Moorhead; Moorhead, Minn. (Pr)	2,969	90	63	$12,655	$12,655	$3,645
Concordia College-Saint Paul; Saint Paul, Minn. (Pr)	1,027			$12,658	$12,658	$4,726
Crown College; St. Bonifacius, Minn. (Pr)	734		65	$ 9,450	$ 9,450	$4,316
Gustavus Adolphus College; Saint Peter, Minn. (Pr)	2,528	82	56	$17,200	$17,200	$4,320
Hamline University; Saint Paul, Minn. (Pr)	1,709	85	63	$15,574	$15,574	$5,450
Macalester College; Saint Paul, Minn. (Pr)	1,791	56	57	$19,673	$19,673	$5,593
Mankato State University; Mankato, Minn. (Pu)	10,350	85	53	$ 2,582	$ 5,769	$2,965
Martin Luther College; New Ulm, Minn. (Pr)	811	89	48	$ 4,130	$ 4,130	$2,285
Minneapolis College of Art & Design; Minneapolis, Minn. (Pr)	537	74	40	$17,910	$17,910	$4,375
Moorhead State University; Moorhead, Minn. (Pu)	6,148		64		$ 5,596	$3,256
North Central Bible College; Minneapolis, Minn. (Pr)	1,041					$3,550
Northwestern College; Saint Paul, Minn. (Pr)	1,664	70	60	$13,920	$13,920	$4,173
Saint Cloud State University; Saint Cloud, Minn. (Pu)	12,416	18	54	$ 3,059	$ 5,478	$3,600
Saint John's University/College of Saint Benedict; Collegeville, Minn. (Pr)	1,738	86	2	$16,195	$16,195	$4,930
Saint Mary's University of Minnesota; Winona, Minn. (Pr)	1,746		51	$13,300	$13,300	$4,400
Saint Olaf College; Northfield, Minn. (Pr)	2,981	83	57	$18,250	$18,250	$4,320
Southwest State University; Marshall, Minn. (Pu)	2,900			$ 2,648	$ 5,965	$3,000
University of Minnesota-Duluth; Duluth, Minn. (Pu)	8,100	78	51	$ 4,029	$11,524	$4,011
University of Minnesota-Morris; Morris, Minn. (Pu)	1,959	88	60	$ 4,740	$ 9,480	$3,934
University of Minnesota-Twin Cities; Minneapolis, Minn. (Pu)	23,868	77	52	$ 4,121	$11,796	$4,494
University of Saint Thomas; Saint Paul, Minn. (Pr)	5,304	87	54	$16,128	$16,128	$5,180
Winona State University; Winona, Minn. (Pu)	6,160	69	61	$ 2,600	$ 5,800	$3,330
MISSISSIPPI						
Alcorn State University; Lorman, Miss. (Pu)	2,555			$ 2,685	$ 5,546	$2,427
Belhaven College; Jackson, Miss. (Pr)	1,284		62	$ 9,960	$ 9,960	$3,850
Delta State University; Cleveland, Miss. (Pu)	3,464		61	$ 2,596	$ 5,546	$2,600
Jackson State University; Jackson, Miss. (Pu)	5,250			$ 2,688	$ 5,546	$3,800
Millsaps College; Jackson, Miss. (Pr)	1,198	89	54	$14,190	$14,190	$6,106
Mississippi College; Clinton, Miss. (Pr)	2,396	85	57	$ 8,640	$ 8,640	$4,010
Mississippi State University; Mississippi State, Miss. (Pu)	12,708	71	44	$ 3,017	$ 6,119	$3,510
Mississippi University for Women; Columbus, Miss. (Pu)	3,180	78	81	$ 2,556	$ 5,546	$2,557
Mississippi Valley State University; Itta Bena, Miss. (Pu)	2,169					$2,490
Rust College; Holly Springs, Miss. (Pr)	852	31	58	$ 5,025	$ 5,025	$2,275
Tougaloo College; Tougaloo, Miss. (Pr)	982			$ 6,250	$ 6,250	$3,000
University of Mississippi; University, Miss. (Pu)	8,888	78	53	$ 3,053	$ 6,155	$3,360
University of Southern Mississippi; Hattiesburg, Miss. (Pu)	12,049	65	60	$ 2,870	$ 5,972	$2,965
William Carey College; Hattiesburg, Miss. (Pr)	1,524	94	66	$ 6,880	$ 6,880	$3,060
MISSOURI						
Avila College; Kansas City, Mo. (Pr)	1,061	96	71	$11,800	$11,800	$4,800
Central Methodist College; Fayette, Mo. (Pr)	1,258	88	60	$10,350	$10,350	$4,110
Central Missouri State University; Warrensburg, Mo. (Pu)	8,868	92	53	$ 2,184	$ 4,368	$3,970
College of the Ozarks; Point Lookout, Mo. (Pr)	1,488	14	55	$ 0	$ 0	$2,500
Columbia College; Columbia, Mo. (Pr)	7,958	64	57	$ 9,808	$ 9,808	$4,399
Culver-Stockton College; Canton, Mo. (Pr)	943	83	61	$10,100	$10,100	$4,570
Deaconess College of Nursing; St. Louis, Mo. (Pr)	305		93			$3,200
Drury College; Springfield, Mo. (Pr)	1,384		53	$10,150	$10,150	$4,050
Evangel College; Springfield, Mo. (Pr)	1,616	88	56	$ 8,390	$ 8,390	$3,440

Institution name; city, state (control)	Students	Percent Accepted	Percent Women	Tuition In-state	Tuition Out-of-state	Room and board
Fontbonne College; Saint Louis, Mo. (Pr)	1,307	88%	70%	$10,650	$10,650	$4,700
Hannibal-LaGrange College; Hannibal, Mo. (Pr)	1,026		60	$ 7,770	$ 7,770	$2,927
Harris-Stowe State College; Saint Louis, Mo. (Pu)	1,723			$ 1,992	$ 3,924	
Kansas City Art Institute; Kansas City, Mo. (Pr)	590	74		$16,896	$16,896	
Lincoln University; Jefferson City, Mo. (Pu)	2,959		59	$ 2,216	$ 4,432	$3,300
Lindenwood College; Saint Charles, Mo. (Pr)	2,891					$5,000
Maryville University of Saint Louis; Saint Louis, Mo. (Pr)	2,547	81	72	$12,160	$12,160	$5,400
Missouri Baptist College; Saint Louis, Mo. (Pr)	2,714	66	65	$ 9,090	$ 9,090	$4,480
Missouri Southern State College; Joplin, Mo. (Pu)	5,547	88	58	$ 2,265	$ 4,530	$3,485
Missouri Valley College; Marshall, Mo. (Pr)	1,192					$5,000
Missouri Western State College; Saint Joseph, Mo. (Pu)	5,182	100	61	$ 2,622	$ 4,830	$3,374
Northwest Missouri State University; Maryville, Mo. (Pu)	5,304		55	$ 2,723	$ 4,733	$3,890
Park College; Parkville, Mo. (Pr)	993	88	62	$ 4,770	$ 4,770	$4,790
Rockhurst College; Kansas City, Mo. (Pr)	2,074	88	54	$12,500	$12,500	$4,920
Saint Louis College of Pharmacy; Saint Louis, Mo. (Pr)	793		64	$12,000	$12,000	$5,050
Saint Louis University; Saint Louis, Mo. (Pr)	9,836	69	57	$17,230	$17,230	$5,900
Southeast Missouri State University; Cape Girardeau, Mo. (Pu)	7,443	94	60		$ 5,559	$5,187
Southwest Baptist University; Bolivar, Mo. (Pr)	2,498					$2,623
Southwest Missouri State University; Springfield, Mo. (Pu)	14,067	87	54	$ 3,030	$ 6,060	$3,700
Stephens College; Columbia, Mo. (Pr)	765	84	94	$15,067	$15,067	$5,790
Truman State University; Kirksville, Mo. (Pu)	6,085	78	58	$ 3,544	$ 6,344	$4,400
University of Missouri-Columbia; Columbia, Mo. (Pu)	17,346	80	53			
University of Missouri-Kansas City; Kansas City, Mo. (Pu)	6,108	63	58	$ 4,560	$12,476	$5,600
University of Missouri-Rolla; Rolla, Mo. (Pu)	4,059	97	25	$ 3,978	$11,892	$4,557
University of Missouri-Saint Louis; Saint Louis, Mo. (Pu)	9,623		58	$ 3,474	$ 9,429	$4,000
Washington University; Saint Louis, Mo. (Pr)	6,328	37	51	$23,400	$23,400	$7,313
Webster University; Saint Louis, Mo. (Pr)	3,263		65	$11,460	$11,460	$5,282
Westminster College; Fulton, Mo. (Pr)	654	84	41	$12,300	$12,300	$4,450
William Jewell College; Liberty, Mo. (Pr)	1,160	92	60	$13,020	$13,020	$4,010
William Woods University; Fulton, Mo. (Pr)	697	83	76	$12,900	$12,900	$5,400
MONTANA						
Carroll College; Helena, Mont. (Pr)	1,247	96	60	$11,490	$11,490	$4,540
Dawson Community College; Glendive, Mont. (Pu)	509	100	52	$ 1,442	$ 4,816	
Miles Community College; Miles City, Mont. (Pu)	568	100	62	$ 1,440	$ 4,200	$3,500
Montana State University-Billings; Billings, Mont. (Pu)	3,810		62	$ 2,816	$ 7,576	$3,240
Montana State University-Bozeman; Bozeman, Mont. (Pu)	10,466	86	45	$ 2,086	$ 7,515	$4,275
Montana State University-Northern; Havre, Mont. (Pu)	1,509					$3,700
Montana Tech of the University of Montana; Butte, Mont. (Pu)	1,708	71	41	$ 2,705	$ 7,783	$3,900
Rocky Mountain College; Billings, Mont. (Pr)	775	91	58	$11,568	$11,568	$4,061
University of Montana College of Technology; Missoula, Mont. (Pu)	10,501	85	53	$ 2,365	$ 5,085	$4,000
University of Great Falls; Great Falls, Mont. (Pr)	958	100	69	$10,870	$10,870	$ 0
University of Montana-Missoula; Missoula, Mont. (Pu)	10,501	84	53	$ 2,776	$ 7,676	$4,150
Western Montana College; Dillon, Mont. (Pu)	1,053	95	55	$ 1,979	$ 6,581	$3,800
NEBRASKA						
Bellevue University; Bellevue, Nebr. (Pr)	2,450		48	$ 3,870	$ 3,870	
Chadron State College; Chadron, Nebr. (Pu)	2,443	100	58	$ 1,785	$ 3,570	$3,250
Clarkson College; Omaha, Nebr. (Pr)	380		89	$ 6,528	$ 6,528	
College of Saint Mary; Omaha, Nebr. (Pr)	1,035	77	94	$12,428	$12,428	$4,598
Concordia College; Seward, Nebr. (Pr)	1,087		57	$11,310	$11,310	$3,786
Creighton University; Omaha, Nebr. (Pr)	3,917	89	59	$12,858	$12,858	$5,190
Dana College; Blair, Nebr. (Pr)	594	90	54	$11,130	$11,130	$3,880
Doane College; Crete, Nebr. (Pr)	1,561	90	55	$11,530	$11,530	
Hastings College; Hastings, Nebr. (Pr)	1,110	87	54	$11,916	$11,916	$3,986
Midland Lutheran College; Fremont, Nebr. (Pr)	1,033	93	58	$12,800	$12,800	$3,450
Nebraska Christian College; Norfolk, Nebr. (Pr)	152	70	49	$ 4,500	$ 4,500	$2,960
Nebraska Methodist College of Nursing and Allied Health; Omaha, Nebr. (Pr)	415	100	92	$ 8,160	$ 8,160	
Nebraska Wesleyan University; Lincoln, Nebr. (Pr)	1,741	96	59	$12,584	$12,584	$3,890
Peru State College; Peru, Nebr. (Pu)	1,618	88	52	$ 2,085	$ 2,085	$3,060
University of Nebraska-Kearney; Kearney, Nebr. (Pu)	5,886		56	$ 2,101	$ 3,765	$3,150
University of Nebraska-Lincoln; Lincoln, Nebr. (Pu)	17,980	82	47	$ 2,483	$ 6,750	$3,865
University of Nebraska-Omaha; Omaha, Nebr. (Pu)	12,078			$ 2,627	$ 5,646	
Wayne State College; Wayne, Nebr. (Pu)	3,201	100	56	$ 2,090	$ 3,823	
NEVADA						
Deep Springs College; Dyer, Nev. (Pr)	26	11	0	$ 0	$ 0	
University of Nevada-Las Vegas; Las Vegas, Nev. (Pr)	14,931	81	54		$ 8,492	$5,502
University of Nevada-Reno; Reno, Nev. (Pu)	9,150			$ 1,920	$ 7,020	$5,200
NEW HAMPSHIRE						
Colby-Sawyer College; New London, N.H. (Pr)	786	81	66	$18,060	$18,060	$6,890
Daniel Webster College; Nashua, N.H. (Pr)	536			$14,280	$14,280	$5,662
Dartmouth College; Hanover, N.H. (Pr)	4,023	21	49	$24,624	$24,624	$7,209

Institution name; city, state (control)	Students	Percent Accepted	Women	Tuition In-state	Out-of-state	Room and board
Franklin Pierce College; Rindge, N.H. (Pr)	1,495	74%	50%	$17,250	$17,250	$6,050
Keene State College; Keene, N.H. (Pu)	4,187	77	56	$ 3,240	$ 8,740	$4,660
New England College; Henniker, N.H. (Pr)	762	90	55	$17,674	$17,674	$6,214
New Hampshire College; Manchester, N.H. (Pr)	1,394		54	$13,800	$13,800	$6,256
Notre Dame College; Manchester, N.H. (Pr)	732		76	$14,098	$14,098	$5,713
Plymouth State College; Plymouth, N.H. (Pu)	3,513	81	48	$ 3,620	$ 8,920	$4,706
Rivier College; Nashua, N.H. (Pr)	1,622	83	80	$13,950	$13,950	$5,690
Saint Anselm College; Manchester, N.H. (Pr)	2,064	68	56	$17,300	$17,300	$6,520
Thomas More College of Liberal Arts; Merrimack, N.H. (Pr)	62	100	42	$ 9,600	$ 9,600	$7,400
University of New Hampshire; Durham, N.H. (Pu)	10,765	78	58	$ 6,555	$14,340	$4,798
NEW JERSEY						
Bloomfield College; Bloomfield, N.J. (Pr)	1,958	60	71			
Caldwell College; Caldwell, N.J. (Pr)	1,768	70	66	$11,600	$11,600	$5,600
Centenary College; Hackettstown, N.J. (Pr)	926	85	75	$13,800	$13,800	$6,150
College of New Jersey; Ewing, N.J. (Pu)	5,853	56	60	$ 4,168	$ 7,278	$6,161
College of Saint Elizabeth; Morristown, N.J. (Pr)	1,353	86	92	$13,500	$13,500	$6,440
Drew University; Madison, N.J. (Pr)	1,526	74	59	$21,702	$21,702	$6,372
Fairleigh Dickinson University-Teaneck Campus; Teaneck, N.J. (Pr)	2,077	64	55	$13,996	$13,996	
Felician College; Lodi, N.J. (Pr)	978					$6,028
Georgian Court College; Lakewood, N.J. (Pr)	1,521	91	91	$12,134	$12,134	$4,000
Kean University; Union, N.J. (Pu)	9,510		64	$ 3,213	$ 4,829	$5,316
Monmouth University; West Long Branch, N.J. (Pr)	5,300			$14,520	$14,520	$6,448
Montclair State University; Upper Montclair, N.J. (Pu)	9,203	41	61	$ 3,204	$ 4,946	$5,802
New Jersey City University; Jersey City, N.J. (Pu)	6,412	49	61	$ 2,880	$ 4,898	$5,000
New Jersey Institute of Technology; Newark, N.J. (Pu)	5,178	55	21	$ 5,250	$ 9,594	$6,595
Princeton University; Princeton, N.J. (Pr)	4,624	13	47	$24,630	$24,630	$6,969
Ramapo College of New Jersey; Mahwah, N.J. (Pu)	4,658	47	57			
Richard Stockton College of New Jersey; Pomona, N.J. (Pu)	5,895	50	56	$ 3,280	$ 5,312	$5,418
Rider University; Lawrenceville, N.J. (Pr)	4,146	84	59	$16,520	$16,520	$6,510
Rowan University; Glassboro, N.J. (Pu)	8,173	49	57	$ 3,420	$ 6,840	$5,592
Rutgers University-Camden College of Arts & Sciences; Camden, N.J. (Pu)		65	59	$ 5,602	$10,326	$5,322
Rutgers University-Camden Region; Camden, N.J. (Pu)	3,455	65	58	$ 5,602	$10,326	$5,322
Rutgers University-College of Engineering; Piscataway, N.J. (Pu)	2,192	68	23	$ 5,286	$10,754	
Rutgers University-College of Nursing; Newark, N.J. (Pu)	440	28	91	$ 4,562	$ 9,286	$6,115
Rutgers University-College of Pharmacy; New Brunswick, N.J. (Pu)	860	42	62	$ 5,286	$10,754	
Rutgers University-Cook College; Piscataway, N.J. (Pu)	3,248	63	50	$ 5,286	$10,754	
Rutgers University-Douglass College; Piscataway, N.J. (Pu)	3,064	69	100	$ 4,562	$ 9,286	$6,115
Rutgers University-Livingston College; Piscataway, N.J. (Pu)	3,160	60	39	$ 4,562	$ 9,286	$6,115
Rutgers University-Mason Gross School of the Arts; Piscataway, N.J. (Pu)	570	25	56	$ 4,262	$ 8,676	$5,314
Rutgers University-New Brunswick Region; Piscataway, N.J. (Pu)	27,086	63	53	$ 4,732	$ 9,626	$5,314
Rutgers University-Newark College of Arts & Sciences; Newark, N.J. (Pu)	3,615	58	55	$ 4,562	$ 9,286	$6,115
Rutgers University-Newark Region; Newark, N.J. (Pu)	5,750	56	58	$ 4,262	$ 8,676	$5,314
Rutgers University-Rutgers College; Piscataway, N.J. (Pu)	10,737	49	51	$ 4,562	$ 9,286	$6,115
Saint Peter's College; Jersey City, N.J. (Pr)	3,211	79	57	$14,100	$14,100	$5,060
Seton Hall University; South Orange, N.J. (Pr)	5,718	82	54	$13,830	$13,830	$7,230
Stevens Institute of Technology; Hoboken, N.J. (Pr)	1,533	67	22	$20,890	$20,890	$7,280
Thomas Edison State College; Trenton, N.J. (Pu)	8,399		44	$ 2,200	$ 3,150	
William Paterson University; Wayne, N.J. (Pu)	8,071	56	58	$ 4,150	$ 6,580	$5,320
NEW MEXICO						
College of Santa Fe; Santa Fe, N.M. (Pr)	1,316	84	63	$15,000	$15,000	$4,892
College of the Southwest; Hobbs, N.M. (Pr)	579	83	74	$ 0	$ 0	$3,414
Eastern New Mexico University; Portales, N.M. (Pu)	3,029		60	$ 1,752	$ 6,510	$3,104
New Mexico Highlands University; Las Vegas, N.M. (Pu)	2,054			$ 1,782	$ 7,122	$2,171
New Mexico Institute of Mining & Technology; Socorro, N.M. (Pu)	1,156	69	37	$ 1,524	$ 6,286	$3,584
New Mexico State University; Las Cruces, N.M. (Pu)	12,621	69	53	$ 2,502	$ 8,166	$3,426
Saint John's College; Santa Fe, N.M. (Pr)	423	86	45	$20,500	$20,500	$6,200
University of New Mexico; Albuquerque, N.M. (Pu)	16,295	91	58	$ 2,242	$ 8,461	$4,300
NEW YORK						
Adelphi University; Garden City, N.Y. (Pr)	2,774	78	67	$14,000	$14,000	$6,850
Albany College of Pharmacy; Albany, N.Y. (Pr)	652	77	58	$11,250	$11,250	
Alfred University; Alfred, N.Y. (Pr)	2,027		50	$18,498	$18,498	$6,790
Audrey Cohen College; New York, N.Y. (Pr)	1,019	76	78	$ 4,960	$ 4,960	$ 0
Bard College; Annandale-on-Hudson, N.Y. (Pr)	1,248	49	58	$22,570	$22,570	$7,016
Barnard College; New York, N.Y. (Pr)	2,270	36	100	$21,410	$21,410	$9,084
Canisius College; Buffalo, N.Y. (Pr)	3,502	87	49	$15,160	$15,160	$6,340

Institution name; city, state (control)	Students	Percent Accepted	Women	Tuition In-state	Out-of-state	Room and board
City University of New York-Baruch College; New York, N.Y. (Pu)	12,386	19%	56%	$ 3,330	$ 6,930	
City University of New York-Brooklyn College; Brooklyn, N.Y. (Pu)	10,417	70	61	$ 3,200	$ 6,800	
City University of New York-City College; New York, N.Y. (Pu)	8,930		52	$ 3,200	$ 6,800	
City University of New York-College of Staten Island; Staten Island, N.Y. (Pu)	10,607		58	$ 3,200	$ 6,800	
City University of New York-Hunter College; New York, N.Y. (Pu)	15,251	42	70	$ 3,200	$ 6,800	$ 1,840
City University of New York-John Jay College of Criminal Justice; New York, N.Y. (Pu)	9,772			$ 2,450	$ 5,050	
City University of New York-Lehman College; Bronx, N.Y. (Pu)	7,698			$ 3,200	$ 6,800	
City University of New York-Medgar Evers College; New York, N.Y. (Pu)	5,401			$ 3,200	$ 6,800	
City University of New York-Queens College; Flushing, N.Y. (Pu)	12,020	52	63	$ 3,200	$ 6,800	
City University of New York-York College; Jamaica, N.Y. (Pu)	6,869			$ 3,200	$ 6,800	
Clarkson University; Potsdam, N.Y. (Pr)	2,457	84	25	$19,825	$19,825	$ 7,484
Colgate University; Hamilton, N.Y. (Pr)	2,769	43	51	$24,575	$24,575	$ 6,330
College of Aeronautics; Flushing, N.Y. (Pr)	1,272	91	6	$ 8,550	$ 8,550	$ 4,280
College of Mount Saint Vincent; Riverdale, N.Y. (Pr)	1,359	72	79	$14,200	$14,200	$ 6,750
College of New Rochelle; New Rochelle, N.Y. (Pr)	732	64	99	$11,300	$11,300	$ 5,850
College of Saint Rose; Albany, N.Y. (Pr)	2,690	78	71	$12,434	$12,434	$ 6,358
Columbia University; New York, N.Y. (Pr)	7,530	14	50	$23,244	$23,244	$ 7,492
Concordia College; Bronxville, N.Y. (Pr)	599	82	60	$12,590	$12,590	$ 5,750
Cooper Union; New York, N.Y. (Pr)	902	13	35	$ 8,300	$ 8,300	$10,000
Cornell University; Ithaca, N.Y. (Pr)	13,442	34	47	$18,854	$18,854	$ 0
Daemen College; Amherst, N.Y. (Pr)	1,796	73	73	$11,100	$11,100	$ 5,800
Dominican College of Blauvelt; Orangeburg, N.Y. (Pr)	1,679	72	75			
Dowling College; Oakdale, N.Y. (Pr)	3,375	93	58	$11,940	$11,940	$ 5,705
D'Youville College; Buffalo, N.Y. (Pr)	1,221		74	$ 9,840	$ 9,840	$ 4,760
Eastman School of Music; Rochester, N.Y. (Pr)	503	29	55	$20,320	$20,320	$ 7,512
Elmira College; Elmira, N.Y. (Pr)	1,625	73	68	$20,930	$20,930	$ 7,080
Eugene Lang College; New York, N.Y. (Pr)	463	60	69	$19,620	$19,620	$ 8,857
Five Towns College; Dix Hills, N.Y. (Pr)	724		25			
Fordham University; New York, N.Y. (Pr)	6,358	65	59	$18,295	$18,295	$ 7,810
Hamilton College; Clinton, N.Y. (Pr)	1,733	40	50	$25,000	$25,000	$ 6,200
Hartwick College; Oneonta, N.Y. (Pr)	1,488	90	53	$23,745	$23,745	
Hilbert College; Hamburg, N.Y. (Pr)	853	89	66			
Hobart and William Smith Colleges; Geneva, N.Y. (Pr)	1,843	75	53	$23,865	$23,865	$ 6,882
Hofstra University; Hempstead, N.Y. (Pr)	8,915		53	$13,238	$13,238	$ 6,880
Houghton College; Houghton, N.Y. (Pr)	1,355	86	64	$14,590	$14,590	$ 5,160
Iona College; New Rochelle, N.Y. (Pr)	3,482	77	53	$14,000	$14,000	$ 7,950
Ithaca College; Ithaca, N.Y. (Pr)	5,641	70	56	$18,410	$18,410	$ 7,956
Jewish Theological Seminary of America; New York, N.Y. (Pr)	435		55	$ 8,320	$ 8,320	$ 6,450
Juilliard School; New York, N.Y. (Pr)	465	8	51	$14,400	$14,400	$ 8,100
Keuka College; Keuka Park, N.Y. (Pr)	849	44	77			
Laboratory Institute of Merchandising; New York, N.Y. (Pr)	232	82		$12,300	$12,300	
Le Moyne College; Syracuse, N.Y. (Pr)	2,350	87	60	$14,580	$14,580	$ 6,320
Long Island University-Brooklyn; Brooklyn, N.Y. (Pr)	4,193					$ 7,620
Long Island University-C.W. Post; Brookville, N.Y. (Pr)	5,748	85	57			
Long Island University-Southampton; Southhampton, N.Y. (Pr)	1,273					$ 6,850
Manhattan College; Riverdale, N.Y. (Pr)	2,536	81	45	$ 7,200	$ 7,200	$ 7,250
Manhattan School of Music; New York, N.Y. (Pr)	400	40	47	$18,200	$18,200	
Manhattanville College; Purchase, N.Y. (Pr)	1,312	67	68	$17,430	$17,430	$ 8,000
Mannes College of Music; New York, N.Y. (Pr)	106					$ 6,000
Marist College; Poughkeepsie, N.Y. (Pr)	4,107	54	56	$14,394	$14,394	$ 7,542
Marymount College; Tarrytown, N.Y. (Pr)	842	83	95			
Marymount Manhattan College; New York, N.Y. (Pr)	2,319	69	81	$12,500	$12,500	
Medaille College; Buffalo, N.Y. (Pr)	1,104		70	$11,450	$11,450	$ 5,300
Mercy College; Dobbs Ferry, N.Y. (Pr)	5,868			$ 7,800	$ 7,800	$ 6,500
Molloy College; Rockville Centre, N.Y. (Pr)	1,980		80	$10,600	$10,600	
Mount Saint Mary College; Newburgh, N.Y. (Pr)	1,647	83	68	$ 9,870	$ 9,870	$ 5,650
Nazareth College of Rochester; Rochester, N.Y. (Pr)	1,822	78	75			
New York Institute of Technology; Old Westbury, N.Y. (Pr)	5,710	82	36	$11,900	$11,900	$ 6,510
New York School of Interior Design; New York, N.Y. (Pr)	692		91	$15,200	$15,200	
New York University; New York, N.Y. (Pr)	17,673	35	58	$23,456	$23,456	$ 8,676
Niagara County Community College; Sanborn, N.Y. (Pu)	4,828	100	58			
Niagara University; Niagara Univ., N.Y. (Pr)	2,322	84	61	$13,400	$13,400	$ 6,330
Nyack College; Nyack, N.Y. (Pr)	1,293	72	59	$11,440	$11,440	$ 5,600
Pace University; New York, N.Y. (Pr)	9,042	76	60	$19,570	$19,570	$ 6,350
Parsons School of Design; New York, N.Y. (Pr)	2,422	46	73	$20,240	$20,240	$ 8,857
Polytechnic University-Brooklyn; Brooklyn, N.Y. (Pr)	1,709	65	18	$20,312	$20,312	$ 4,600

Institution name; city, state (control)	Students	Percent Accepted	Percent Women	Tuition In-state	Tuition Out-of-state	Room and board
Pratt Institute; Brooklyn, N.Y. (Pr)	2,495	74%	47%	$18,612	$18,612	$7,762
Rensselaer Polytechnic Institute; Troy, N.Y. (Pr)	4,591	81	25	$22,300	$22,300	$7,692
Rochester Institute of Technology; Rochester, N.Y. (Pr)	10,626	78	35	$17,328	$17,328	$6,852
Russell Sage College; Troy, N.Y. (Pr)	1,000	95	100	$14,920	$14,920	$5,950
Saint Bonaventure University; St. Bonaventure, N.Y. (Pr)	2,209	93	51	$13,280	$13,280	$5,400
Saint Francis College; Brooklyn Heights, N.Y. (Pr)	2,448	82	61			
Saint John Fisher College; Rochester, N.Y. (Pr)	2,088	77		$13,990	$13,990	$6,000
Saint Joseph's College-Brooklyn; Brooklyn, N.Y. (Pr)	2,912	53	75	$ 8,850	$ 8,850	
Saint Joseph's College-Suffolk Campus; Patchogue, N.Y. (Pr)	2,869	78	77	$ 8,550	$ 8,550	
Saint Lawrence University; Canton, N.Y. (Pr)	1,921	71	49	$21,175	$21,175	$6,340
Saint Thomas Aquinas College; Sparkill, N.Y. (Pr)	2,038		58	$11,100	$11,100	$6,910
Sarah Lawrence College; Bronxville, N.Y. (Pr)	1,114	49	73	$24,810	$24,810	$7,991
School of Visual Arts; New York, N.Y. (Pr)	5,014	64	50			
Siena College; Loudonville, N.Y. (Pr)	2,954	71	53	$13,075	$13,075	$5,835
Skidmore College; Saratoga Springs, N.Y. (Pr)	2,184	48	61	$24,000	$24,000	$6,950
St. John's University-Jamaica & Staten Island, NY; Jamaica, N.Y. (Pr)	13,877	83	56	$12,800	$12,800	$8,550
State University of New York at Albany; Albany, N.Y. (Pu)	11,617	63	49	$ 3,400	$ 8,300	$5,472
State University of New York at Buffalo; Buffalo, N.Y. (Pu)	15,663	71	47	$ 3,400	$ 8,300	$5,804
State University of New York at Stony Brook; Stony Brook, N.Y. (Pu)	12,260	54	51	$ 3,400	$ 8,300	$6,230
State University of New York College at Brockport; Brockport, N.Y. (Pu)	6,691	62	56		$ 8,300	$5,150
State University of New York College at Cortland; Cortland, N.Y. (Pu)	5,252	58	57			
State University of New York College at Fredonia; Fredonia, N.Y. (Pu)	4,591	63	59	$ 3,400	$ 8,300	$5,400
State University of New York College at Geneseo; Geneseo, N.Y. (Pu)	5,197		66	$ 3,400	$ 8,300	$4,820
State University of New York College at New Paltz; New Paltz, N.Y. (Pu)	6,005		64	$ 3,400	$ 8,300	$4,990
State University of New York College at Old Westbury; Old Westbury, N.Y. (Pu)	3,360	88	57	$ 3,400	$ 8,300	$5,903
State University of New York College at Oneonta; Oneonta, N.Y. (Pu)	5,038	68	60		$ 8,300	$5,420
State University of New York College at Oswego; Oswego, N.Y. (Pu)	6,700	60	53	$ 3,400	$ 8,300	$2,730
State University of New York College at Potsdam; Potsdam, N.Y. (Pu)	3,511	82	59	$ 3,400	$ 8,300	$5,440
State University of New York College at Purchase; Purchase, N.Y. (Pu)	3,536	37	57	$ 3,400	$ 8,300	$5,850
State University of New York College of A&T at Cobleskill; Cobleskill, N.Y. (Pu)	2,325	79	45	$ 3,200	$ 5,000	$5,620
State University of New York College of Technology at Canton; Canton, N.Y. (Pu)	2,078	82	46	$ 3,200	$ 5,000	$5,510
State University of New York College of Technology at Delhi; Delhi, N.Y. (Pu)	1,893		45	$ 3,200		
State University of New York Empire State College; Saratoga, N.Y. (Pu)	7,213		52	$ 3,400	$ 8,300	
State University of New York-Plattsburgh; Plattsburgh, N.Y. (Pu)	5,310	69	57	$ 3,400	$ 8,300	$4,556
State University of New York-Binghamton University; Binghamton, N.Y. (Pu)	9,603	41	54	$ 3,400	$ 8,300	$5,308
State University of New York-Buffalo College; Buffalo, N.Y. (Pu)	9,421			$ 3,400	$ 8,300	$5,420
State University of New York-College of Environmental Science and Forestry; Syracuse, N.Y. (Pu)	1,171	50	37	$ 3,400	$ 8,300	$7,370
State University of New York-Health Science Center at Syracuse; Syracuse, N.Y. (Pu)	303		74		$ 8,300	$5,680
State University of New York-Institute of Technology at Utica/Rome; Utica N.Y. (Pu)			50	$ 3,949	$ 3,949	
Syracuse University; Syracuse, N.Y. (Pr)	10,491	58	53	$19,360	$19,360	$8,400
Touro College; New York, N.Y. (Pr)	6,777	74	69	$ 9,250	$ 9,250	
Union College; Schenectady, N.Y. (Pr)	2,107	48	47	$23,892	$23,892	$6,474
United States Military Academy; West Point, N.Y. (Pu)	4,087	14	14			
University of Rochester; Rochester, N.Y. (Pr)	4,452	62	49			
Utica College of Syracuse University; Utica, N.Y. (Pr)	1,973	84	65	$16,150	$16,150	$6,350
Vassar College; Poughkeepsie, N.Y. (Pr)	2,396	43	61	$22,670	$22,670	$6,620
Wagner College; Staten Island, N.Y. (Pr)	1,504	70	58	$18,000	$18,000	$6,500
Webb Institute; Glen Cove, N.Y. (Pr)	85	41	20	$ 0	$ 0	$6,250
Wells College; Aurora, N.Y. (Pr)	352	92	99	$11,850	$11,850	$5,900
Yeshiva University; New York, N.Y. (Pr)	1,990			$14,920	$14,920	$4,750
NORTH CAROLINA						
Appalachian State University; Boone, N.C. (Pu)	12,386	72	52	$ 962	$ 8,232	$3,340
Barber Scotia College; Concord, N.C. (Pr)	488	64	45	$ 7,400	$ 7,400	$3,500

Institution name; city, state (control)	Students	Percent		Tuition		Room and board
		Accepted	Women	In-state	Out-of-state	
Barton College; Wilson, N.C. (Pr)	1,271	87%	68%	$10,030	$10,030	$3,892
Belmont Abbey College; Belmont, N.C. (Pr)	873	90	56	$11,650	$11,650	$5,978
Bennett College; Greensboro, N.C. (Pr)	664	72		$ 6,400	$ 6,400	$3,525
Brevard College; Brevard, N.C. (Pr)	674	87	43	$ 9,500	$ 9,500	$4,580
Campbell University; Buies Creek, N.C. (Pr)	2,274		56	$ 9,993	$ 9,993	$3,630
Catawba College; Salisbury, N.C. (Pr)	1,230	82	51	$12,600	$12,600	$4,840
Chowan College; Murfreesboro, N.C. (Pr)	691	77	43	$11,470	$11,470	$4,600
Davidson College; Davidson, N.C. (Pr)	658	37	56	$20,658	$20,658	$6,126
Duke University; Durham, N.C. (Pr)	6,388	28	48	$23,210	$23,210	$7,088
East Carolina University; Greenville, N.C. (Pu)	14,684	78	58	$ 916	$ 8,028	$3,680
Elizabeth City State College; Elizabeth City, N.C. (Pu)	1,937	72	63	$ 1,552	$ 7,816	$4,952
Elon College; Elon College, N.C. (Pr)	3,641	61	60	$17,447	$17,447	
Fayetteville State University; Fayetteville, N.C. (Pu)	3,249	87		$ 900	$ 8,028	$3,400
Gardner-Webb University; Boiling Springs, N.C. (Pr)	2,369	87	64			
Greensboro College; Greensboro, N.C. (Pr)	982	65	55	$11,500	$11,500	$4,900
Guilford College; Greensboro, N.C. (Pr)	1,398	76	54	$15,550	$15,550	$5,610
High Point University; High Point, N.C. (Pr)	2,411			$11,120	$11,120	$5,300
Johnson C. Smith University; Charlotte, N.C. (Pr)	1,283			$ 8,126	$ 8,126	$3,846
Lees-McRae College; Banner Elk, N.C. (Pr)	462			$10,030	$10,030	$9,670
Lenoir-Rhyne College; Hickory, N.C. (Pr)	1,452	83	63	$12,310	$12,310	$4,750
Mars Hill College; Mars Hill, N.C. (Pr)	1,300					$3,800
Meredith College; Raleigh, N.C. (Pr)	2,413	84	99	$ 9,290	$ 9,290	$4,100
Methodist College; Fayetteville, N.C. (Pr)	1,851	94	44	$12,600	$12,600	$4,830
Montreat College; Montreat, N.C. (Pr)	678		56	$10,862	$10,862	$4,310
Mount Olive College; Mount Olive, N.C. (Pr)	970					$3,215
North Carolina A&T State University; Greensboro, N.C. (Pu)	6,449	34	51	$ 918	$ 8,188	$3,860
North Carolina Central University; Durham, N.C. (Pu)	4,110	18	63	$ 900	$ 8,028	$3,475
North Carolina School of the Arts; Winston-Salem, N.C. (Pu)	716	46	38	$ 1,527	$10,155	$4,462
North Carolina State University; Raleigh, N.C. (Pu)	21,674	69	41	$ 1,456	$10,622	$4,560
North Carolina Wesleyan College; Rocky Mount, N.C. (Pr)	1,700					$4,830
Queens College; Charlotte, N.C. (Pr)	1,281	74	79	$10,020	$10,020	$5,680
Saint Andrews Presbyterian College; Laurinburg, N.C. (Pr)	660	86	57	$13,515	$13,515	$5,300
Saint Augustine's College; Raleigh, N.C. (Pr)	1,598	45	58			
Salem College; Winston-Salem, N.C. (Pr)	923	88	98	$13,200	$13,200	$7,920
Shaw University; Raleigh, N.C. (Pr)	2,456	74	63	$ 6,272	$ 6,272	$4,342
University of North Carolina-Asheville; Asheville, N.C. (Pu)	3,135	67	57	$ 768	$ 7,186	$4,058
University of North Carolina-Pembroke; Pembroke, N.C. (Pu)	2,703	88	61		$ 8,664	$3,202
University of North Carolina-Chapel Hill; Chapel Hill, N.C. (Pu)	15,291	35	61	$ 1,456	$10,622	$5,010
University of North Carolina-Charlotte; Charlotte, N.C. (Pu)	14,181	77	54	$ 918	$ 8,188	$3,670
University of North Carolina-Greensboro; Greensboro, N.C. (Pu)	10,128	76	66	$ 1,036	$ 9,490	$4,044
University of North Carolina-Pembroke; Pembroke, N.C. (Pu)	2,649	86	61	$ 918	$ 8,188	$3,202
University of North Carolina-Wilmington; Wilmington, N.C. (Pu)	9,041	66	60	$ 918	$ 8,188	$4,420
Wake Forest University; Winston-Salem, N.C. (Pr)	3,877		50	$19,450	$19,450	$5,450
Warren Wilson College; Asheville, N.C. (Pr)	652	80	60	$13,600	$13,600	$4,444
Western Carolina University; Cullowhee, N.C. (Pu)	5,314	86	52	$ 918	$ 8,188	$3,050
Wingate University; Wingate, N.C. (Pr)	1,118	86	49	$11,600	$11,600	$4,300
Winston-Salem State University; Winston-Salem, N.C. (Pu)	2,865	80	67	$ 1,575	$ 7,868	
NORTH DAKOTA						
Dickinson State University; Dickinson, N.D. (Pu)	1,800	100	59	$ 2,096	$ 5,256	$2,670
Jamestown College; Jamestown, N.D. (Pr)	1,141	99	55	$ 7,150	$ 7,150	$3,200
Mayville State University; Mayville, N.D. (Pu)	740		52		$ 4,892	$2,694
Medcenter One College of Nursing; Bismarck, N.D. (Pr)	87		85	$ 2,955	$ 2,955	
Minot State University; Minot, N.D. (Pu)	2,979	97	61	$ 2,340	$ 5,754	$1,744
North Dakota State University; Fargo, N.D. (Pu)	8,677		42	$ 2,512	$ 6,456	$3,461
University of Mary; Bismarck, N.D. (Pr)	1,934	95	63	$ 7,900	$ 7,900	$3,150
University of North Dakota; Grand Forks, N.D. (Pu)	8,483	71	49	$ 2,362	$ 6,306	$3,243
Valley City State University; Valley City, N.D. (Pu)	1,081	95	55		$ 5,842	$2,694
OHIO						
Antioch College; Yellow Spring, Ohio (Pr)	595	85	66	$21,628	$21,628	$4,176
Art Academy of Cincinnati; Cincinnati, Ohio (Pr)	187			$ 9,990	$ 9,990	
Ashland University; Ashland, Ohio (Pr)	2,000	81	58	$14,275	$14,275	$5,448
Baldwin-Wallace College; Berea, Ohio (Pr)	3,950	82	61	$14,640	$14,640	$5,360
Bluffton College; Bluffton, Ohio (Pr)	981	94	56	$13,156	$13,156	$5,122
Bowling Green State University; Bowling Green, Ohio (Pu)	15,040	92	57	$ 3,870	$ 9,158	$4,392
Capital University; Columbus, Ohio (Pr)	2,856	84	63	$16,000	$16,000	$4,900
Case Western Reserve University; Cleveland, Ohio (Pr)	3,397	74	40	$19,200	$19,200	$5,470
Cedarville College; Cedarville, Ohio (Pr)	2,664	79	55	$10,608	$10,608	$4,716
Central State University; Wilberforce, Ohio (Pu)	998	42	57	$ 3,318	$ 7,293	$4,695
Cincinnati Bible College and Seminary; Cincinnati, Ohio (Pr)	637		43	$ 5,984	$ 5,984	$3,800
Cleveland Institute of Music; Cleveland, Ohio (Pr)	218	37	53	$17,875	$17,875	$5,590
Cleveland State University; Cleveland, Ohio (Pu)	11,215	79	54	$ 3,600	$ 7,200	$4,852

Institution name; city, state (control)	Students	Percent Accepted	Percent Women	Tuition In-state	Tuition Out-of-state	Room and board
College of Mount Saint Joseph; Cincinnati, Ohio (Pr)	2,129	82%	72%	$11,300	$11,300	$5,050
College of Wooster; Wooster, Ohio (Pr)	1,747	83	52	$19,940	$19,940	$5,260
Columbus College of Art and Design; Columbus, Ohio (Pr)	1,494				$13,440	$6,000
Defiance College; Defiance, Ohio (Pr)	738		55	$13,400	$13,400	
Denison University; Granville, Ohio (Pr)	2,156	76	54	$20,680	$20,680	$5,760
DeVry Institute of Technology; Columbus, Ohio (Pr)	3,276		25			
Franciscan University of Steubenville; Steubenville, Ohio (Pr)	1,611	91	60	$11,990	$11,990	$4,970
Franklin University; Columbus, Ohio (Pr)	4,005			$ 5,460	$ 5,460	
Heidelberg College; Tiffin, Ohio (Pr)	1,299	87	52	$16,422	$16,422	$5,945
Hiram College; Hiram, Ohio (Pr)	1,129	87	57	$17,010	$17,010	$5,594
John Carroll University; University Heights, Ohio (Pr)	3,599	89	52	$15,424	$15,424	$5,950
Kent State University; Kent, Ohio (Pu)	16,862		60	$ 5,014	$ 9,918	$4,530
Kenyon College; Gambier, Ohio (Pr)	1,568	73	56	$22,990	$22,990	$4,110
Lake Erie College; Painesville, Ohio (Pr)				$14,280	$14,280	$5,070
Lourdes College; Sylvania, Ohio (Pr)	1,298	84	85	$ 8,770	$ 8,770	
Malone College; Canton, Ohio (Pr)	1,894					$4,600
Marietta College; Marietta, Ohio (Pr)	1,219	93	51	$17,310	$17,310	$4,970
Miami University; Oxford, Ohio (Pu)	14,803	78	55	$ 4,766	$11,226	$5,070
Mount Union College; Alliance, Ohio (Pr)	1,407					$3,870
Mount Vernon Nazarene College; Mount Vernon, Ohio (Pr)	1,800	51	56	$10,792	$10,792	$4,041
Muskingum College; New Concord, Ohio (Pr)	1,444	82	52	$11,650	$11,650	$4,900
Notre Dame College of Ohio; South Euclid, Ohio (Pr)	580	78	98	$13,418	$13,418	$5,248
Oberlin College; Oberlin, Ohio (Pr)	2,932	54	59	$23,174	$23,174	$6,238
Ohio Dominican College; Columbus, Ohio (Pr)	1,977	75	68	$10,250	$10,250	$5,070
Ohio Northern University; Ada, Ohio (Pr)	2,359	95	49	$20,610	$20,610	$5,070
Ohio State University-Columbus; Columbus, Ohio (Pu)	36,252	79	48	$ 3,879	$11,448	$5,289
Ohio State University-Lima; Lima, Ohio (Pu)	1,166			$ 3,528	$11,097	$4,278
Ohio University-Athens; Athens, Ohio (Pu)	16,619	74	55	$ 4,530	$ 9,531	$5,076
Ohio Wesleyan University; Delaware, Ohio (Pr)	1,873	85	51	$20,940	$20,940	$6,560
Otterbein College; Westerville, Ohio (Pr)	2,389	72	63	$16,260	$16,260	$5,121
Shawnee State University; Portsmouth, Ohio (Pu)	3,438	100	64	$ 2,664	$ 5,007	$4,096
Tiffin University; Tiffin, Ohio (Pr)	1,150	23		$ 9,210	$ 9,210	$4,400
Union Institute; Cincinnati, Ohio (Pr)	782		60			
University of Akron; Akron, Ohio (Pu)	19,542	100	55	$ 3,542	$ 9,392	$4,835
University of Cincinnati; Cincinnati, Ohio (Pu)	20,656	86	48	$ 4,026	$11,532	$5,958
University of Dayton; Dayton, Ohio (Pr)	6,906	87	51	$15,020	$15,020	$4,870
University of Findlay; Findlay, Ohio (Pr)	3,155			$14,320	$14,320	$5,510
University of Rio Grande; Rio Grande, Ohio (Pr)	1,971			$ 7,593	$ 7,593	$4,612
University of Toledo; Toledo, Ohio (Pu)	16,729	95	55			
Urbana University; Urbana, Ohio (Pr)	1,113	79	49			$4,350
Walsh University; North Canton, Ohio (Pr)	1,261			$10,900	$10,900	$5,110
Wilberforce University; Wilberforce, Ohio (Pr)	775			$ 7,760	$ 7,760	$4,260
Wilmington College; Wilmington, Ohio (Pr)	1,093	81	51	$13,536	$13,536	$5,070
Wittenberg University; Springfield, Ohio (Pr)	2,088	79	58	$19,716	$19,716	$5,206
Wright State University; Dayton, Ohio (Pu)	10,992			$ 3,930	$ 7,860	$4,916
Xavier University; Cincinnati, Ohio (Pr)	3,855	89	59	$14,950	$14,950	$6,200
Youngstown State University; Youngstown, Ohio (Pu)	11,353	88	54			
OKLAHOMA						
Bartlesville Wesleyan College; Bartlesville, Okla. (Pr)	571	60	64	$ 8,200	$ 8,200	$3,800
Cameron University; Lawton, Okla. (Pu)	4,559	92	56	$ 1,910	$ 4,520	$2,720
East Central University; Ada, Okla. (Pu)	3,786			$ 1,106	$ 3,323	$2,200
Langston University; Langston, Okla. (Pu)	3,864					$2,944
Northeastern State University; Talequah, Okla. (Pu)	7,075					$2,640
Northwestern Oklahoma State University; Alva, Okla. (Pu)	1,648	100	55	$ 1,830	$ 4,340	$2,316
Oklahoma Baptist University; Shawnee, Okla. (Pr)	2,148	94	54	$ 8,300	$ 8,300	$3,400
Oklahoma Christian University of Science and Arts; Oklahoma City, Okla. (Pr)	1,593	90	47	$ 8,200	$ 8,200	$3,840
Oklahoma City University; Oklahoma City, Okla. (Pr)	2,174	83	56	$ 8,380	$ 8,380	$3,990
Oklahoma Panhandle State University; Goodwell, Okla. (Pu)	1,589					$2,330
Oklahoma State University; Stillwater, Okla. (Pu)	15,508	86	47	$ 1,800	$ 6,060	$4,536
Oral Roberts University; Tulsa, Okla. (Pr)	2,788		57	$10,160	$10,160	$4,728
Phillips University; Enid, Okla. (Pr)	525			$ 6,685	$ 6,685	$3,900
Southeastern Oklahoma State University; Durant, Okla. (Pu)	3,415	98	55	$ 1,395	$ 3,900	$2,689
Southern Nazarene University; Bethany, Okla. (Pr)	1,536					$4,028
Southwestern Oklahoma State University; Weatherford, Okla. (Pu)	4,004			$ 1,380	$ 3,735	$2,216
University of Central Oklahoma; Edmond, Okla. (Pu)	11,476	95	57	$ 1,372	$ 3,713	$2,690
University of Oklahoma; Norman, Okla. (Pu)	17,841	88	49	$ 1,748	$ 5,768	$4,314
University of Sciences and Arts of Oklahoma; Chickasha, Okla. (Pu)	1,498	73	63	$ 0	$ 3,877	$2,025
University of Tulsa; Tulsa, Okla. (Pr)	2,920	80	52	$13,400	$13,400	$4,660

Institution name; city, state (control)	Students	Percent Accepted	Women	Tuition In-state	Out-of-state	Room and board
OREGON						
Concordia University; Portland, Ore. (Pr)	887	83%	62%			$4,165
Eastern Oregon State College; LaGrande, Ore. (Pu)	2,056	50	52	$ 2,316	$ 2,316	$4,165
Eugene Bible College; Eugene, Ore. (Pr)	201	64	44	$ 5,913	$ 5,913	$3,663
George Fox University; Newberg, Ore. (Pr)	1,682	91	62	$16,600	$16,600	$5,325
Lewis & Clark College; Portland, Ore. (Pr)	1,706	67	59	$20,136	$20,136	$6,208
Linfield College; McMinnville, Ore. (Pr)	2,760	93	64	$17,590	$17,590	$5,300
Marylhurst University; Marylhurst, Ore. (Pr)	931	100	74	$ 7,812	$ 7,812	$5,700
Northwest Christian College; Eugene, Ore. (Pr)	384					$4,310
Oregon Health Sciences University; Portland, Ore. (Pu)	663		61	$ 3,436	$ 8,092	$3,804
Oregon Institute of Technology; Klamath Falls, Ore. (Pu)	2,461		44	$ 3,309	$10,083	$3,910
Oregon State University; Corvallis, Ore. (Pu)	12,194		46	$ 3,549	$11,817	$5,064
Pacific Northwest College of Art; Portland, Ore. (Pr)	280			$10,674	$10,674	$4,670
Pacific University; Forest Grove, Ore. (Pr)	1,058	88	64	$16,800	$16,800	$4,720
Portland State University; Portland, Ore. (Pu)	11,855	80	55	$ 2,694	$10,569	$6,150
Reed College; Portland, Ore. (Pr)	1,332	75	52			
Southern Oregon University; Ashland, Ore. (Pu)	4,849	66	57	$ 2,520	$ 9,183	$4,350
University of Oregon; Eugene, Ore. (Pu)	13,580	91	53	$ 2,694	$11,478	$5,100
University of Portland; Portland, Ore. (Pr)	2,250	94	56	$16,200	$16,200	$4,990
Warner Pacific College; Portland, Ore. (Pr)	594			$11,190	$11,190	$4,100
Western Baptist College; Salem, Ore. (Pr)	710	82	59	$13,350	$13,350	$4,820
Western Oregon University; Monmouth, Ore. (Pu)	3,927		60	$ 3,198	$ 4,410	$4,410
Willamette University; Salem, Ore. (Pr)	1,803	89	56	$21,000	$21,000	$5,530
PENNSYLVANIA						
Albright College; Reading, Pa. (Pr)	1,250	87	54	$18,910	$18,910	$5,780
Allegheny College; Meadville, Pa. (Pr)	1,897	82	53	$20,410	$20,410	$4,970
Allentown College of Saint Francis de Sales; Center Valley, Pa. (Pr)	1,751	76		$11,600	$11,600	$5,470
Alvernia College; Reading, Pa. (Pr)	1,284	78	65	$11,730	$11,730	$5,770
Baptist Bible College and Seminary of Pennsylvania; Clarks Summit, Pa. (Pr)	592	75	59	$ 8,128	$ 8,128	$4,714
Beaver College; Glenside, Pa. (Pr)	1,656	84	73	$16,880	$16,880	$7,310
Bloomsburg University of Pennsylvania; Bloomsburg, Pa. (Pu)	6,964	59	63	$ 3,468	$ 8,824	$3,550
Bryn Mawr College; Bryn Mawr, Pa. (Pr)	1,312	60	98	$22,730	$22,730	$8,100
Bucknell University; Lewisburg, Pa. (Pr)	3,456	50	48	$22,740	$22,740	$5,469
Cabrini College; Radnor, Pa. (Pr)	1,731	87	68	$15,250	$15,250	$7,200
California University of Pennsylvania; California, Pa. (Pu)	4,918	70		$ 3,468	$ 8,824	$4,628
Carlow College; Pittsburgh, Pa. (Pr)	2,056	81	93	$11,970	$11,970	$4,880
Carnegie Mellon University; Pittsburgh, Pa. (Pr)	5,050	42	35	$22,100	$22,100	$6,810
Cedar Crest College; Allentown, Pa. (Pr)	1,451	80	95	$16,450	$16,450	$6,215
Chatham College; Pittsburgh, Pa. (Pr)	594	86	99	$17,388	$17,388	$6,120
Chestnut Hill College; Philadelphia, Pa. (Pr)	486	80	87	$15,527	$15,527	$6,510
Cheyney University of Pennsylvania; Cheyney, Pa. (Pu)	1,075	69	54	$ 3,468	$ 8,824	$4,646
Clarion University of Pennsylvania; Clarion, Pa. (Pu)	5,436	92	61	$ 3,468	$ 5,202	$3,480
College Misericordia; Dallas, Pa. (Pr)		66	75			$6,210
Delaware Valley College; Doylestown, Pa. (Pr)	2,081	85	51	$15,745	$15,745	$6,379
Dickinson College; Carlisle, Pa. (Pr)	1,844	74	58	$23,120	$23,120	
Drexel University; Philadelphia, Pa. (Pr)	8,902	69	36	$24,280	$24,280	$7,950
Duquesne University; Pittsburgh, Pa. (Pr)	5,513	69	58	$13,628	$13,628	$6,158
East Stroudsburg University of Pennsylvania; East Stroudsburg, Pa. (Pu)	4,815	68	58	$ 3,468	$ 8,824	$3,780
Eastern College; St. Davids, Pa. (Pr)	1,744	51	65	$13,200	$13,200	$5,654
Edinboro University of Pennsylvania; Edinboro, Pa. (Pu)	6,445	83	57	$ 3,468	$ 6,936	$3,674
Elizabethtown College; Elizabethtown, Pa. (Pr)	1,730	77	67	$17,700	$17,700	$5,380
Franklin & Marshall College; Lancaster, Pa. (Pr)	1,862	54	50	$23,720	$23,720	$5,730
Gannon University; Erie, Pa. (Pr)	2,600	86	57	$13,020	$13,020	$5,500
Geneva College; Beaver Falls, Pa. (Pr)	1,763		53			$4,750
Gettysburg College; Gettysburg, Pa. (Pr)	2,123	73	52	$23,112	$23,112	$5,346
Grove City College; Grove City, Pa. (Pr)	2,323	47	49	$ 6,740	$ 6,740	$3,912
Gwynedd-Mercy College; Gwynedd Valley, Pa. (Pr)	1,407	67	80	$13,500	$13,500	$6,300
Haverford College; Haverford, Pa. (Pr)	1,147	36	53	$23,556	$23,556	$7,620
Holy Family College; Philadephia, Pa. (Pr)	1,971	85	75	$11,500	$11,500	
Immaculata College; Immaculata, Pa. (Pr)	1,975	83	83	$12,500	$12,500	$6,200
Indiana University of Pennsylvania; Indiana, Pa. (Pu)	12,193	62	56	$ 3,468	$ 8,824	$3,662
Juniata College; Huntingdon, Pa. (Pr)	1,244	83	56	$18,030	$18,030	$5,110
King's College; Wilkes-Barre, Pa. (Pr)	2,104	84	52	$15,240	$15,240	$6,620
Kutztown University; Kutztown, Pa. (Pu)	6,917	75	59	$ 4,251	$ 9,607	$3,820
Lafayette College; Easton, Pa. (Pr)	2,244	54	46	$22,844	$22,844	$7,106
Lancaster Bible College; Lancaster, Pa. (Pr)	709	84	54			$4,300
LaRoche College; Pittsburgh, Pa. (Pr)	1,274		69	$11,100	$11,100	$6,030
LaSalle University; Philadelphia, Pa. (Pr)	3,888		58	$17,260	$17,260	$6,702
Lebanon Valley College; Annville, Pa. (Pr)	1,707	76	58	$16,730	$16,730	$5,490

Institution name; city, state (control)	Students	Percent Accepted	Women	Tuition In-state	Out-of-state	Room and board
Lehigh University; Bethlehem, Pa. (Pr)	4,487	52%	40%	$23,150	$23,150	$6,630
Lincoln University; Lincoln University, Pa. (Pu)	1,576	28	57			
Lock Haven University of Pennsylvania; Lock Haven, Pa. (Pu)	3,633	78	55	$ 3,468	$ 6,824	$3,676
Lycoming College; Williamsport, Pa. (Pr)	1,475	80	57	$16,500	$16,500	$4,700
Mansfield University of Pennsylvania; Mansfield, Pa. (Pu)	2,812	81	57	$ 3,468	$ 8,824	$3,770
Marywood University; Scranton, Pa. (Pr)	1,608	83	74	$15,008	$15,008	$6,540
Mercyhurst College; Erie, Pa. (Pr)	2,671	81	56	$12,660	$12,660	$5,106
Messiah College; Grantham, Pa. (Pr)	2,697	89	62	$15,000	$15,000	$5,500
Millersville University of Pennsylvania; Millersville, Pa. (Pu)	6,540	60	58	$ 3,468	$ 8,824	$4,650
Moore College of Art & Design; Philadelphia, Pa. (Pr)	431	60	100	$15,475	$15,475	$6,000
Moravian College; Bethlehem, Pa. (Pr)	1,706	83	58	$17,570	$17,570	$5,830
Mount Aloysius College; Cresson, Pa. (Pr)	1,399	54	76	$ 9,460	$ 9,460	$4,580
Muhlenberg College; Allentown, Pa. (Pr)	2,460	65	57	$20,085	$20,085	$5,390
Neumann College; Aston, Pa. (Pr)	1,264	56	71	$13,350	$13,350	$6,500
Pennsylvania State University-Behrend College; Erie, Pa. (Pu)	3,174	86	36	$ 5,632	$11,774	$4,640
Pennsylvania State University-Harrisburg; Middletown, Pa. (Pu)	2,016		53	$ 5,632	$11,774	$4,640
Pennsylvania State University-University Park; University Park, Pa. (Pu)	34,264		46		$12,306	$4,338
Philadelphia College of Bible; Langhorne, Pa. (Pr)	1,005	98	54	$ 9,640	$ 9,640	$4,995
Philadelphia College of Textiles and Science; Philadelphia, Pa. (Pr)	2,751	81	63	$14,692	$14,692	$6,576
Point Park College; Pittsburgh, Pa. (Pr)	2,283	90	53	$11,602	$11,602	$5,252
Robert Morris College; Moon Township, Pa. (Pr)	3,947	91	50	$ 7,650	$ 7,650	$4,744
Rosemont College; Rosemont, Pa. (Pr)	878	88	90	$14,020	$14,020	$7,000
Saint Francis College; Loretto, Pa. (Pr)	1,458	84	60	$13,312	$13,312	$6,290
Saint Joseph's University; Philedelphia, Pa. (Pr)	4,153	67	56	$17,030	$17,030	$6,972
Saint Vincent College; Latrobe, Pa. (Pr)	1,155	88	51	$14,136	$14,136	$4,894
Seton Hill College; Greensburg, Pa. (Pr)	1,100	85	86	$14,500	$14,500	$5,050
Shippensburg University of Pennsylvania; Shippensburg, Pa. (Pu)	5,725	68	54	$ 3,468	$ 8,824	$4,012
Slippery Rock University of Pennsylvania; Slippery Rock, Pa. (Pu)	6,337	83	57	$ 3,618	$ 9,046	
Susquehanna University; Selinsgrove, Pa. (Pr)	1,765	79	58	$19,380	$19,380	$5,500
Swarthmore College; Swarthmore, Pa. (Pr)	1,388	19	53	$23,964	$23,964	$7,500
Temple University; Philadelphia, Pa. (Pu)	17,620	68	57			
Thiel College; Greenville, Pa. (Pr)	914	79	53	$14,216	$14,216	$5,490
University of Pennsylvania; Philadelphia, Pa. (Pr)	9,501		49	$24,230	$24,230	$7,910
University of Pittsburgh-Johnstown; Johnstown, Pa. (Pu)	3,170	85	55	$ 5,884	$12,918	$5,700
University of Pittsburgh-Bradford; Bradford, Pa. (Pu)	1,236	81	60		$13,564	$5,061
University of Pittsburgh-Greensburg; Greensburg, Pa. (Pu)	1,501	80	53	$ 5,658	$12,422	$4,130
University of Pittsburgh-Pittsburgh; Pittsburgh, Pa. (Pu)	16,798	68	53	$ 5,884	$12,918	$5,598
University of Scranton; Scranton, Pa. (Pr)	4,018	77	58	$16,620	$16,620	$7,346
University of the Arts; Philadelphia, Pa. (Pr)	1,655	58	49	$15,300	$15,300	
University of the Sciences in Philadelphia; Philadelphia, Pa. (Pr)	1,137	77	62			$6,000
Ursinus College; Collegeville, Pa. (Pr)	1,229	76	53	$19,950	$19,950	$5,970
Villanova University; Villanova, Pa. (Pr)	7,130	62	51	$20,555	$20,555	$3,040
Washington & Jefferson College; Washington, Pa. (Pr)	1,225	86	51	$18,675	$18,675	$4,750
Waynesburg College; Waynesburg, Pa. (Pr)	1,226	79	49	$10,970	$10,970	$4,430
West Chester University of Pennsylvania; West Chester, Pa. (Pu)	9,781	59	60		$ 8,824	$4,460
Westminster College; New Wilmington, Pa. (Pr)	1,447	88	62	$15,485	$15,485	$4,760
Widener University; Chester, Pa. (Pr)	3,814	87	56	$15,750	$15,750	$3,400
Wilkes University; Wilkes-Barre, Pa. (Pr)	1,963	78	51	$15,050	$15,050	$6,830
Wilson College; Chambersburgh, Pa. (Pr)	833	89	84	$13,238	$13,238	$6,152
York College of Pennsylvania; York, Pa. (Pr)	4,897	72	59	$ 6,280	$ 6,280	$4,670
PUERTO RICO						
American University of Puerto Rico; Bayamon, P.R. (Pr)	3,515	100	58	$ 394	$ 394	
Inter American University of Puerto Rico-San German; San German, P.R. (Pr)	4,894	94	57	$ 3,150	$ 3,150	$2,200
RHODE ISLAND						
Brown University; Providence, R.I. (Pr)	6,112	17	54	$23,616	$23,616	$6,898
Bryant College; Smithfield, R.I. (Pr)	2,886	79	41	$16,350	$16,350	$6,950
Johnson and Wales University-Providence; Providence, R.I. (Pr)	7,843	83	47	$12,885	$12,885	$5,829
Providence College; Providence, R.I. (Pr)	4,630	70	60	$16,980	$16,980	$7,125
Rhode Island College; Providence, R.I. (Pu)	6,873		67	$ 2,675	$ 7,600	$5,640
Rhode Island School of Design; Providence, R.I. (Pr)	8,505		60			$6,390
Roger Williams University; Bristol, R.I. (Pr)	2,100			$16,560	$16,560	$7,640
Salve Regina University; Newport, R.I. (Pr)	1,701	85	66	$16,500	$16,500	$7,500
University of Rhode Island; Kingston, R.I. (Pu)	10,483	79	56	$ 3,282	$11,286	$6,166

Institution name; city, state (control)	Students	Percent Accepted	Women	Tuition In-state	Out-of-state	Room and board
SOUTH CAROLINA						
Anderson College; Anderson, S.C. (Pr)	1,081	75%	58%	$15,820	$15,820	$ 0
Benedict College; Columbia, S.C. (Pr)	2,208	79	53	$ 7,284	$ 7,284	$4,182
Charleston Southern University; Charleston, S.C. (Pr)	2,226		59	$ 9,820	$ 9,820	$3,776
Citadel, the Military College of S.C.; Charleston, S.C. (Pu)	1,939	82	6			
Claflin College; Orangeburg, S.C. (Pr)	1,161	54	60	$ 5,538	$ 5,538	$ 0
Clemson University; Clemson, S.C. (Pu)	13,053	69	46	$ 3,154	$ 8,910	$4,044
Coastal Carolina University; Conway, S.C. (Pu)	4,428	78	57	$ 3,150	$ 8,720	$4,800
Coker College; Hartsville, S.C. (Pr)	938	72	65	$14,352	$14,352	$4,516
College of Charleston; Charleston, S.C. (Pu)	9,252	67	63	$ 3,290	$ 6,580	$3,850
Columbia College; Columbia, S.C. (Pr)	1,242	77	100	$13,200	$13,200	$4,500
Columbia International University; Columbia, S.C. (Pr)	519	76		$ 7,871	$ 7,871	$4,110
Converse College; Spartanburg, S.C. (Pr)	730					$4,080
Erskine College; Due West, S.C. (Pr)	469	91	58	$14,265	$14,265	$4,921
Francis Marion University; Florence, S.C. (Pu)	3,076	61	59	$ 3,260	$ 6,520	$3,550
Furman University; Greenville, S.C. (Pr)	2,643	67	55	$17,888	$17,888	$4,848
Lander University; Greenwood, S.C. (Pu)	2,431		64			$3,340
Limestone College; Gaffey, S.C. (Pr)	1,784	80	58	$13,900	$13,900	$ 0
Medical University of South Carolina; Charleston, S.C. (Pu)	1,048			$ 4,450	$12,974	
Morris College; Sumter, S.C. (Pr)	971	71	65	$ 5,355	$ 5,355	$2,770
Newberry College; Newberry, S.C. (Pr)	744	95	48	$13,602	$13,602	$3,960
North Greenville College; Tigerville, S.C. (Pr)	1,081		43	$ 7,200	$ 7,200	$4,280
Presbyterian College; Clinton, S.C. (Pr)	1,081	82	52	$21,596	$21,596	$5,072
South Carolina State University; Orangeburg, S.C. (Pu)	4,911					$4,100
Southern Wesleyan University; Central, S.C. (Pr)	1,269	39	59	$11,148	$11,148	$3,852
University of South Carolina Aiken; Aiken, S.C. (Pu)	3,107		65		$ 7,544	$3,890
University of South Carolina-Columbia; Columbia, S.C. (Pu)	15,907	71	55	$ 3,530	$ 9,242	$4,126
University of South Carolina-Spartanburg; Spartanburg, S.C. (Pu)	3,285	71	63	$ 2,874	$ 7,184	$3,200
Voorhees College; Denmark, S.C. (Pr)	966	81	65			$2,866
Winthrop University; Rock Hill, S.C. (Pu)	4,340		69	$ 4,126	$ 7,434	$4,022
Wofford College; Spartanburg, S.C. (Pr)	1,081	77	47			
SOUTH DAKOTA						
Augustana College; Sioux Falls, S.D. (Pr)	1,639	91	65	$13,960	$13,960	$4,058
Black Hills State University; Spearfish, S.D. (Pu)	3,446		61	$ 1,728	$ 5,496	$2,614
Dakota State University; Madison, S.D. (Pu)	1,322		51	$ 3,301	$ 7,000	
Dakota Wesleyan University; Mitchell, S.D. (Pr)	661		60	$ 9,355	$ 9,355	$3,540
Huron University; Huron, S.D. (Pr)	404			$ 8,100	$ 8,100	$3,600
Mount Marty College; Yankton, S.D. (Pr)	942	99	69	$ 9,248	$ 9,248	$4,020
National American University; Rapid City, S.D. (Pr)	771		53	$ 6,660		$3,615
Northern State University; Aberdeen, S.D. (Pu)	2,659	97	59	$ 1,868	$ 5,940	
Presentation College; Aberdeen, S.D. (Pr)	461		78	$ 6,820	$ 6,820	$3,100
South Dakota School of Mines & Technology; Rapid City, S.D. (Pu)	2,225		28	$ 1,797	$ 5,717	$2,900
South Dakota State University; Brookings, S.D. (Pu)	7,561		51		$ 5,940	$2,864
University of Sioux Falls; Sioux Falls, S.D. (Pr)	914		59	$11,500	$11,500	$3,660
University of South Dakota; Vermillion, S.D. (Pu)	5,342		57	$ 1,797	$ 5,717	$2,988
TENNESSEE						
Austin Peay State University; Clarksville, Tenn. (Pu)	6,974	57	57	$ 2,470	$ 7,296	$4,160
Belmont University; Nashville, Tenn. (Pr)	2,461	79	61	$11,300	$11,300	$5,000
Bethel College; McKenzie, Tenn. (Pr)	645	58	52	$ 7,550	$ 7,550	$4,380
Carson-Newman College; Jefferson Cit, Tenn. (Pr)	2,066	90	57	$10,960	$10,960	$3,910
Christian Brothers University; Memphis, Tenn. (Pr)	1,630	84	52	$13,140	$13,140	$4,080
Cumberland University; Lebanon, Tenn. (Pr)	966	72	52	$ 8,000	$ 8,000	$5,200
East Tennessee State University; Johnson City, Tenn. (Pu)	9,276	83	58	$ 1,816	$ 6,412	
Fisk University; Nashville, Tenn. (Pr)	759	82	72	$ 8,420	$ 8,420	$4,750
Freed-Hardeman University; Henderson, Tenn. (Pr)	1,391	71	55			$2,090
Johnson Bible College; Knoxville, Tenn. (Pr)	388					$3,200
King College; Bristol, Tenn. (Pr)	562	78	59	$10,030	$10,030	$3,850
Knoxville College; Knoxville, Tenn. (Pr)	1,177			$ 5,400	$ 5,400	$3,450
Lambuth University; Jackson, Tenn. (Pr)	966	70	56	$ 7,418	$ 7,418	$4,320
Lane College; Jackson, Tenn. (Pr)	768					$3,600
Lee University; Cleveland, Tenn. (Pr)	3,014	89	56	$ 6,118	$ 6,118	$3,840
LeMoyne-Owen College; Memphis, Tenn. (Pr)	1,121					$3,916
Lincoln Memorial University; Harrogate, Tenn. (Pr)	1,237	76	69	$ 7,800	$ 7,800	$3,300
Lipscomb University; Nashville, Tenn. (Pr)	2,447		55	$ 8,470	$ 8,470	$3,910
Martin Methodist College; Pulaski, Tenn. (Pr)						$3,400
Maryville College; Maryville, Tenn. (Pr)	944	80	56	$15,600	$15,600	$5,080
Memphis College of Art; Memphis, Tenn. (Pr)	225		48	$11,450	$11,450	$4,500
Middle Tennessee State University; Merfreesboro, Tenn. (Pu)	15,890			$ 1,906	$ 6,732	$3,030
Milligan College; Milligan College, Tenn. (Pr)	828	71	61	$11,100	$11,100	$4,000
Rhodes College; Memphis, Tenn. (Pr)	1,452	76	55	$18,038	$18,038	$5,332

Institution name; city, state (control)	Students	Percent Accepted	Percent Women	Tuition In-state	Out-of-state	Room and board
Tennessee State University; Nashville, Tenn. (Pu)	7,021	56%	62%	$ 2,308	$ 7,134	$3,060
Tennessee Technological University; Cookeville, Tenn. (Pu)	7,007			$ 2,300	$ 4,826	$3,100
Tennessee Wesleyan College; Athens, Tenn. (Pr)	2,090		61	$ 6,500	$ 6,500	$3,670
Trevecca Nazarene College; Nashville, Tenn. (Pr)	1,067	100	58	$ 9,344	$ 9,344	$4,448
Tusculum College; Greenville, Tenn. (Pr)	1,137		54	$11,800	$11,800	$3,900
Union University; Jackson, Tenn. (Pr)	1,916		61	$ 9,180	$ 9,180	$3,360
University of Memphis; Memphis, Tenn. (Pu)	15,485					$3,995
University of Tennessee-Martin; Martin, Tenn. (Pu)	5,491		58	$ 2,342	$ 7,168	$3,396
University of Tennessee-Chattanooga; Chattanooga, Tenn. (Pu)	7,323		57	$ 2,496	$ 4,200	$1,300
University of Tennessee-Knoxville; Knoxville, Tenn. (Pu)	19,070	76	50	$ 2,744	$ 7,800	$3,916
University of the South; Sewanee, Tenn. (Pr)	1,326	69	52	$18,900	$18,900	$5,230
Vanderbilt University; Nashville, Tenn. (Pr)	5,704	59	51	$21,930	$21,930	$7,738
TEXAS						
Abilene Christian University; Abilene, Tex. (Pr)	4,127	79	54	$ 9,810	$ 9,810	$4,020
Angelo State University; San Angelo, Tex. (Pu)	5,828	71	55		$12,400	$4,152
Austin College; Sherman, Tex. (Pr)	1,218	74	52	$14,450	$14,450	$5,612
Baylor University; Waco, Tex. (Pr)	11,124		57	$ 9,870	$ 9,870	$5,008
Concordia Lutheran College; Austin, Tex. (Pr)	706			$ 9,800	$ 9,800	$5,000
Dallas Baptist University; Dallas, Tex. (Pr)	2,974		61	$ 8,250	$ 8,250	$3,510
East Texas Baptist University; Marshall, Tex. (Pr)	1,192	80	59	$ 7,200	$ 7,200	$3,098
East Texas State University; Commerce, Tex. (Pu)	5,347					$3,600
Hardin-Simmons University; Abilene, Tex. (Pr)	1,980	91	53	$ 6,960	$ 6,960	$3,336
Houston Baptist University; Houston, Tex. (Pr)	1,730	20	68	$ 4,608	$ 4,608	$2,300
Howard Payne University; Brownwood, Tex. (Pr)	1,488		50			
Huston-Tillotson College; Austin, Tex. (Pr)	701					$4,253
Lamar University; Beaumont, Tex. (Pu)	9,496			$ 864	$ 5,976	$3,040
LeTourneau University; Longview, Tex. (Pr)	1,842		45	$11,124	$11,124	$5,220
Lubbock Christian University; Lubbock, Tex. (Pr)	1,278	91	59	$ 8,760	$ 8,760	$3,700
McMurry University; Abilene, Tex. (Pr)	1,366	70	47	$ 9,075	$ 9,075	$4,244
Midwestern State University; Wichita Falls, Tex. (Pu)	5,093		57	$ 0	$ 6,804	$3,534
Our Lady of the Lake University; San Antonio, Tex. (Pr)	2,421		78	$10,618	$10,618	$4,206
Paul Quinn College; Dallas, Tex. (Pr)	517					$3,450
Prairie View A&M University; Prarie View, Tex. (Pu)	4,738	77	55	$ 2,644	$ 9,124	$4,184
Rice University; Houston, Tex. (Pr)	2,807	24	47	$15,350	$15,350	$6,600
Saint Edward's University; Austin, Tex. (Pr)	2,782		58	$11,438	$11,438	$3,400
Saint Mary's University of San Antonio; San Antonio, Tex. (Pr)	2,642	86	59	$10,900	$10,900	$4,908
Sam Houston State University; Huntsville, Tex. (Pu)	11,223			$ 1,670	$ 6,898	$3,300
Schreiner College; Kerrville, Tex. (Pr)	695	76	57	$10,490	$10,490	$6,480
Southern Methodist University; Dallas, Tex. (Pr)	5,620	90	54	$15,640	$15,640	$6,579
Southwest Texas State University; San Marcos, Tex. (Pu)	18,486	76	54	$ 1,140	$ 7,620	$4,104
Southwestern Adventist University; Keene, Tex. (Pr)	1,065					$4,084
Southwestern University; Georgetown, Tex. (Pr)	1,255	72	58	$15,000	$15,000	$5,190
Stephen F. Austin State University; Nonacogdoches, Tex. (Pu)	10,116			$ 1,080	$ 7,470	$4,118
Sul Ross State University; Alpine, Tex. (Pu)	2,270		53	$ 1,080	$ 7,470	$3,480
Tarleton State University; Stephenville, Tex. (Pu)	5,551	75	52			$3,570
Texas A&M University-Galveston; Galveston, Tex. (Pu)	1,168	90	48	$ 1,275	$ 7,440	$3,653
Texas A&M University-College Station; College Station, Tex. (Pu)	35,889	86	47	$ 912	$ 6,096	$4,898
Texas A&M University-Commerce; Commerce, Tex. (Pu)	4,773	68	56	$ 2,526	$ 9,006	
Texas A&M University-Corpus Christi; Corpus Christi, Tex. (Pu)	4,690	88	60	$ 864	$ 5,976	$5,259
Texas Christian University; Fort Worth, Tex. (Pr)	6,254	77	59	$11,590	$11,590	$4,000
Texas Southern University; Houston, Tex. (Pu)	8,832			$ 2,058	$ 7,180	$4,000
Texas Tech University; Lubbock, Tex. (Pu)	20,024	74	46	$ 1,140	$ 7,620	$4,788
Texas Wesleyan University; Fort Worth, Tex. (Pr)	2,106	86	62	$ 8,000	$ 8,000	$3,850
Texas Woman's University; Denton, Tex. (Pu)	5,752			$ 2,084	$ 7,196	$3,578
Trinity University; San Antonio, Tex. (Pr)	2,264	75	52	$15,120	$15,120	$6,355
University of Central Texas; Killeen, Tex. (Pr)	1,117		57	$ 3,144	$ 3,144	$3,449
University of Dallas; Irving, Tex. (Pr)	1,157	82	58	$14,450	$14,450	$5,562
University of Houston; Houston, Tex. (Pu)	24,268	74	53	$ 912	$ 6,096	$4,513
University of Houston-Victoria Campus; Victoria, Tex. (Pu)	711		74	$ 816	$ 5,952	
University of Mary Hardin-Baylor; Belton, Tex. (Pr)	2,010			$ 6,500	$ 6,500	$4,000
University of North Texas; Denton, Tex. (Pu)	25,514	76		$ 1,928	$ 8,318	$7,876
University of Saint Thomas; Houston, Tex. (Pr)	1,597	85	66	$11,700	$11,700	$4,860
University of Texas-Austin; Austin, Tex. (Pu)	37,203	71	50	$ 2,160	$ 8,550	$4,537
University of Texas-Dallas; Richardson,, Tex. (Pu)	5,521		50	$ 2,160	$ 8,550	
University of Texas Medical Branch-Galveston; Galveston, Tex. (Pu)	690	31	75	$ 1,296	$ 8,964	
University of Texas-Arlington; Arlington, Tex. (Pu)	14,844	96	52	$ 864	$ 5,976	$1,587
University of Texas-El Paso; El Paso, Tex. (Pu)	12,852	87	53		$ 7,440	
University of Texas-Permian Basin; Odessa, Tex. (Pu)	1,219			$ 1,776	$ 8,166	$3,934
University of Texas-San Antonio; San Antonio, Tex. (Pu)	15,536	84	54	$ 2,160	$ 8,640	$5,876
University of the Incarnate Word; San Antonio, Tex. (Pr)	2,899	98	72	$11,960	$11,960	$4,870

Institution name; city, state (control)	Students	Percent Accepted	Women	Tuition In-state	Out-of-state	Room and board
Wayland Baptist University; Plainview, Tex. (Pr)	3,902	100%	44%	$ 6,120	$ 6,120	$3,314
West Texas A&M University; Canyon, Tex. (Pu)	5,316	72	54	$ 1,404	$ 6,468	$3,194
Wiley College; Marshall, Tex. (Pr)	463			$ 4,080	$ 4,080	$3,230
UTAH						
Brigham Young University; Provo, Utah (Pr)	29,565	71	53			$4,150
Southern Utah University; Cedar City, Utah (Pu)	5,383	86		$ 1,480	$ 5,586	$2,432
University of Utah; Salt Lake City, Utah (Pu)	20,344		45	$ 2,601	$ 7,998	$4,620
Utah State University; Logan, Utah (Pu)	16,507	98	53			
Weber State University; Ogden, Utah (Pu)	13,741	100	53	$ 1,560	$ 5,460	$3,605
Westminster College of Salt Lake City; Salt Lake City, Utah (Pr)	1,711	90	63	$12,456	$12,456	$4,750
VERMONT						
Bennington College; Bennington, Vt. (Pr)	401	80	70	$26,400	$26,400	
Burlington College; Burlington, Vt. (Pr)	160	91		$ 8,420	$ 8,420	
Castleton State College; Castleton, Vt. (Pu)	1,660		86	$ 3,924	$ 9,192	$5,206
Champlain College; Burlington, Vt. (Pr)	2,274	83	57	$10,485	$10,485	$7,450
College of Saint Joseph in Vermont; Rutland, Vt. (Pr)	393	97	64	$11,250	$11,250	$6,050
Goddard College; Plainfield, Vt. (Pr)	315	81	59	$15,218	$15,218	$5,288
Green Mountain College; Poultney, Vt. (Pr)	616	59	53	$17,000	$17,000	$4,150
Johnson State College; Johnson, Vt. (Pu)	1,455		53			
Lyndon State College; Lyndonville, Vt. (Pu)	1,202		47	$ 0	$ 8,760	$4,854
Marlboro College; Marlboro, Vt. (Pr)	284	71	58	$18,800	$18,800	$6,750
Middlebury College; Middlebury, Vt. (Pr)	2,273	32	51	$30,475	$30,475	
Norwich University; Northfield, Vt. (Pr)	2,214	94	40	$14,926	$14,926	$5,718
Saint Michael's College; Colchester, Vt. (Pr)	2,070	69	54	$17,500	$17,500	$7,253
Southern Vermont College; Bennington, Vt. (Pr)	604	87	63	$10,990	$10,990	$5,350
Trinity College of Vermont; Burlington, Vt. (Pr)	779	93	89	$13,620	$13,620	$6,700
University of Vermont; Burlington, Vt. (Pu)	8,813	82	55	$ 7,248	$18,120	$5,440
VIRGINIA						
Averett College; Danville, Va. (Pr)	1,506	78	60	$12,585	$12,585	$4,200
Bluefield College; Bluefield, Va. (Pr)	818	100	52	$ 8,770	$ 8,770	$4,610
Bridgewater College; Bridgewater, Va. (Pr)	1,124	90	59	$13,960	$13,960	$6,500
Christendom College; Front Royal, Va. (Pr)	240	94	51	$10,850	$10,850	$3,850
Christopher Newport University; Newport News, Va. (Pu)	4,804	71	60	$ 3,474	$ 8,424	$4,950
Clinch Valley College of the University of Virginia; Wise, Va. (Pu)	1,515	76	56	$ 2,368	$ 7,236	$4,284
College of William and Mary; Williamsburg, Va. (Pu)	5,642	45	59	$ 4,609	$16,433	$4,897
Eastern Mennonite University; Harrisonburg, Va. (Pr)	1,094	88	60	$13,480	$13,480	$4,950
Emory and Henry College; Emory, Va. (Pr)	956	72	50	$12,596	$12,596	$5,242
Ferrum College; Ferrum, Va. (Pr)	951	82	44	$10,990	$10,990	$5,000
George Mason University; Fairfax, Va. (Pu)	14,234	63	56	$ 3,756	$12,516	$5,190
Hampden-Sydney College; Hampden-Sydney, Va. (Pr)	961	81	0	$16,048	$16,048	$5,898
Hampton University; Hampton, Va. (Pr)	5,228	49	60	$ 9,038	$ 9,038	$4,422
Hollins University; Roanoke, Va. (Pr)	809	83	99	$15,600	$15,600	$6,125
James Madison University; Harrisonburg, Va. (Pu)	13,733	59	56	$ 3,932	$ 9,532	$5,182
Liberty University; Lynchburg, Va. (Pr)	5,928		49	$ 8,550	$ 8,550	$4,800
Longwood College; Farmville, Va. (Pu)	3,114	73	65			$4,360
Lynchburg College; Lynchburg, Va. (Pr)	1,652	76	64	$17,120	$17,120	$4,400
Mary Baldwin College; Staunton, Va. (Pr)	1,488	90	93	$14,475	$14,475	$7,450
Mary Washington College; Fredericksburg, Va. (Pu)	3,770		67			
Marymount University; Arlington, Va. (Pr)	1,969	78	72	$13,750	$13,750	$6,160
Norfolk State University; Norfolk, Va. (Pu)	6,734	96	62	$ 3,000	$ 6,802	$4,166
Old Dominion University; Norfolk, Va. (Pu)	12,611	80	56	$ 3,892	$10,220	$5,000
Radford University; Radford, Va. (Pu)	8,368	76	61			
Randolph-Macon College; Ashland, Va. (Pr)	1,114	78	52	$17,160	$17,160	$4,520
Randolph-Macon Woman's College; Lynchburg, Va. (Pr)	686	89	99	$16,730	$16,730	$7,010
Roanoke College; Salem, Va. (Pr)	1,733	82	59	$16,035	$16,035	$5,250
Shenandoah University; Winchester, Va. (Pr)	1,248	84	64			
Sweet Briar College; Sweet Briar, Va. (Pr)	731	91	95	$16,435	$16,435	$6,715
University of Richmond; Richmond, Va. (Pr)	2,940	44	50	$19,340	$19,340	$4,050
University of Virginia; Charlottesville, Va. (Pu)	13,369	34	54	$ 3,832	$14,780	$4,421
Virginia Commonwealth University; Richmond, Va. (Pu)	15,383	77	59	$ 4,182	$12,666	$4,624
Virginia Intermont College; Bristol, Va. (Pr)	830	56	78	$11,150	$11,150	$4,950
Virginia Military Institute; Lexington, Va. (Pu)	1,328	78	4	$ 3,655	$11,485	$4,210
Virginia State University; Petersburg, Va. (Pu)	3,369	77	58	$ 1,588	$ 7,132	$5,096
Virginia Tech; Blacksburg, Va. (Pu)	21,415	78	41	$ 2,792	$11,016	$3,780
Virginia Wesleyan College; Norfolk, Va. (Pr)	1,568			$13,400	$13,400	$5,500
Washington and Lee University; Lexington, Va. (Pr)	1,696	33	44	$16,950	$16,950	$5,350
WASHINGTON						
Central Washington University; Ellensburg, Wash. (Pu)	7,962	84	54	$ 2,753	$ 9,781	$5,122
City University; Renton, Wash. (Pr)	2,509		48	$ 1,860	$ 1,860	
Cornish College of the Arts; Seattle, Wash. (Pr)	694	77		$12,600	$12,600	
Eastern Washington University; Cheney, Wash. (Pu)	6,726	91	57	$ 2,727	$ 9,687	$4,294

Institution name; city, state (control)	Students	Percent Accepted	Percent Women	Tuition In-state	Tuition Out-of-state	Room and board
Evergreen State College; Olympia, Wash. (Pu)	3,932	89%	59%	$ 2,637	$ 9,330	$4,530
Gonzaga University; Spokane, Wash. (Pr)	2,619	87	55	$15,960	$15,960	$5,560
Lutheran Bible Institute of Seattle; Issaquah, Wash. (Pr)	132		62	$ 5,750	$ 5,750	$4,525
Northwest College; Kirkland, Wash. (Pr)	848	99	57	$ 9,672	$ 9,672	$5,030
Pacific Lutheran University; Tacoma, Wash. (Pr)	3,410	85	60	$15,680	$15,680	$4,890
Saint Martin's College; Lacey, Wash. (Pr)	1,139	91	60	$14,050	$14,050	$4,768
Seattle Pacific University; Seattle, Wash. (Pr)	2,624	92	64	$14,541	$14,541	$5,574
Seattle University; Seattle, Wash. (Pr)	3,115	86	58	$15,255	$15,255	$5,334
University of Puget Sound; Tacoma, Wash. (Pr)	2,701	76	61	$20,450	$20,450	$5,270
University of Washington; Seattle, Wash. (Pu)	25,273	66	52	$ 3,486	$11,508	$4,779
Walla Walla College; College Place, Wash. (Pr)	1,455	88	49	$13,806	$13,806	$2,946
Washington State University; Pullman, Wash. (Pu)	17,138	90	51	$ 3,396	$10,554	$4,540
Western Washington University; Bellingham, Wash. (Pu)	10,914		56	$ 2,521	$ 8,956	$4,635
Whitman College; Walla Walla, Wash. (Pr)	1,387	57	55	$20,720	$20,720	$5,900
Whitworth College; Spokane, Wash. (Pr)	1,771	88	59	$15,970	$15,970	$5,400
WEST VIRGINIA						
Alderson-Broaddus College; Philippi, W.Va. (Pr)	650		58	$13,230	$13,230	$5,100
Bethany College; Bethany, W.Va. (Pr)	730			$17,362	$17,362	$5,830
Bluefield State College; Bluefield, W.Va. (Pu)	2,405	69	57	$ 2,110	$ 5,126	
Concord College; Athens, W.Va. (Pr)	2,662	70	57			$4,018
Davis & Elkins College; Elkins, W.Va. (Pr)	658	94	56	$12,080	$12,080	$5,330
Fairmont State College; Fairmont, W.Va. (Pu)	6,712	100	56	$ 2,106	$ 4,996	$3,696
Glenville State College; Glenville, W.Va. (Pu)	2,179					$3,480
Marshall University; Huntington, W.Va. (Pu)	9,304	92	56	$ 2,348	$ 6,294	$4,576
Ohio Valley College; Parkersburg, W.Va. (Pr)	430	35	48	$ 6,620	$ 6,620	$3,620
Salem-Teikyo University; Salem, W.Va. (Pr)	163	70	42	$12,800	$12,800	$4,408
Shepherd College; Shepherdstown, W.Va. (Pu)	4,055	93	60	$ 2,228	$ 5,348	$4,139
University of Charleston; Charleston, W.Va. (Pr)	1,286	75	69	$12,800	$12,800	$4,470
West Liberty State College; West Liberty, W.Va. (Pu)	2,397	95	55	$ 2,190	$ 5,630	$3,100
West Virginia Institute of Technology; Montgomery, W.Va. (Pu)	2,496	100	40			
West Virginia State College; Institute, W.Va. (Pu)	4,530			$ 2,116	$ 5,150	$3,550
West Virginia University; Morgantown, W.Va. (Pu)	15,175	93	46	$ 2,748	$ 8,100	$4,832
West Virginia Wesleyan College; Buckhannon, W.Va. (Pr)	1,586	87	54	$16,300	$16,300	$4,250
Wheeling Jesuit University; Wheeling, W.Va. (Pr)	1,296			$14,000	$14,000	$4,980
WISCONSIN						
Alverno College; Milwaukee, Wis. (Pr)	1,982		100	$10,800	$10,800	$4,250
Beloit College; Beloit, Wis. (Pr)	1,258	70	59	$20,220	$20,220	$4,628
Cardinal Stritch College; Milwaukee, Wis. (Pr)	2,609		64	$ 5,040	$ 5,040	$3,880
Carroll College; Waukesha, Wis. (Pr)	2,444		66	$14,740	$14,740	$4,600
Carthage College; Kenosha, Wis. (Pr)	2,060	93	59	$ 0	$ 0	$4,195
Concordia University Wisconsin; Mequon, Wis. (Pr)	3,833	76	64	$12,400	$12,400	$4,200
Edgewood College; Madison, Wis. (Pr)	1,448	90	73	$10,700	$10,700	$4,254
Lakeland College; Sheboygan, Wis. (Pr)	3,160	57	62	$11,480	$11,480	$4,860
Lawrence University; Appleton, Wis. (Pr)	1,235	82	54	$20,882	$20,882	$4,697
Marian College of Fond du Lac; Fond du Lac, Wis. (Pr)	1,537		68	$11,966	$11,966	$4,400
Marquette University; Milwaukee, Wis. (Pr)	7,320	87	53	$ 5,620	$ 5,620	$5,754
Milwaukee Institute of Art and Design; Milwaukee, Wis. (Pr)	567	79	46	$14,950	$14,950	$6,458
Milwaukee School of Engineering; Milwaukee, Wis. (Pr)	2,084	81	16	$17,850	$17,850	$4,440
Mount Mary College; Milwaukee, Wis. (Pr)	1,174	83	99	$11,380	$11,380	$3,970
Mount Senario College; Ladysmith, Wis. (Pr)	1,145	72	34	$10,650	$10,650	$4,550
Northland College; Ashland, Wis. (Pr)	846	92	55	$13,610	$13,610	$4,470
Ripon College; Ripon, Wis. (Pr)	650	82	50	$18,000	$18,000	$4,400
Saint Norbert College; De Pere, Wis. (Pr)	1,925	91	59	$15,600	$15,600	$5,162
Silver Lake College; Manitowoc, Wis. (Pr)	700	48	69	$11,150	$11,150	$4,365
University of Wisconsin-Eau Claire; Eau Claire, Wis. (Pu)	10,158	77	59	$ 3,009	$ 9,291	$3,133
University of Wisconsin-Green Bay; Green Bay, Wis. (Pu)	5,460	87	64	$ 2,550	$ 9,150	$3,000
University of Wisconsin-LaCrosse; LaCrosse, Wis. (Pu)	8,636	75	57	$ 3,161	$ 9,757	$3,400
University of Wisconsin-Madison; Madison, Wis. (Pu)	27,535		51	$ 3,406	$11,586	$4,206
University of Wisconsin-Milwaukee; Milwaukee, Wis. (Pu)	17,032	84	54	$ 3,479	$11,370	$3,594
University of Wisconsin-Oshkosh; Oshkosh, Wis. (Pu)	9,295	89	58	$ 2,950	$ 9,606	$3,130
University of Wisconsin-Parkside; Kenosha, Wis. (Pu)	4,486		60	$ 2,838	$ 9,120	$3,730
University of Wisconsin-Platteville; Platteville, Wis. (Pu)	4,665			$ 2,806	$ 9,068	$3,254
University of Wisconsin-River Falls; River Falls, Wis. (Pu)	5,086		61	$ 2,797	$ 9,079	$3,274
University of Wisconsin-Stevens Point; Stevens Point, Wis. (Pu)	8,164	66	55	$ 3,130	$ 9,860	$3,524
University of Wisconsin-Stout; Menomonie, Wis. (Pu)	6,749		48	$ 2,836	$ 9,118	$3,156
University of Wisconsin-Superior; Superior, Wis. (Pu)	2,314			$ 2,768	$ 9,050	$3,296
University of Wisconsin-Whitewater; Whitewater, Wis. (Pu)	9,537	84	53	$ 3,000	$ 9,113	$2,800
Viterbo College; La Crosse, Wis. (Pr)		84	74			
Wisconsin Lutheran College; Milwaukee, Wis. (Pr)	440	93	60	$11,960	$11,960	$4,500
WYOMING						
University of Wyoming; Laramie, Wyo. (Pu)	8,597	97	52	$ 1,944	$ 7,032	$4,278

The Olympic Games

1896	Athens	1948	St. Moritz (W)	1976	Montreal (S)
1900	Paris	1948	London (S)	1980	Lake Placid (W)
1904	St. Louis	1952	Oslo (W)	1980	Moscow (S)
1906	Athens	1952	Helsinki (S)	1984	Sarajevo, Yugoslavia (W)
1908	London	1956	Cortina d'Ampezzo, Italy (W)	1984	Los Angeles (S)
1912	Stockholm	1956	Melbourne (S)	1988	Calgary, Alberta (W)
1920	Antwerp	1960	Squaw Valley, Calif. (W)	1988	Seoul, South Korea (S)
1924	Chamonix (W)	1960	Rome (S)	1992	Albertville, France (W)
1924	Paris (S)	1964	Innsbruck, Austria (W)	1992	Barcelona, Spain (S)
1928	St. Moritz (W)	1964	Tokyo (S)	1994	Lillehammer, Norway (W)
1928	Amsterdam (S)	1968	Grenoble, France (W)	1996	Atlanta, Ga. (S)
1932	Lake Placid (W)	1968	Mexico City (S)	1998	Nagano, Japan (W)
1932	Los Angeles (S)	1972	Sapporo, Japan (W)	2000	Sydney, Australia (S)
1936	Garmisch-Partenkirchen (W)	1972	Munich (S)	2002	Salt Lake City (W)
1936	Berlin (S)	1976	Innsbruck, Austria (W)	2004	Athens (S)

(W)—Site of Winter Games. (S)—Site of Summer Games

The first Olympic Games of which there is record were held in 776 B.C.E., and consisted of one event, a great foot race of about 200 yards held on a plain by the River Alpheus (now the Ruphia) just outside the little town of Olympia in Greece. It was from that date the Greeks began to keep their calendar by "Olympiads," the four-year spans between the celebrations of the famous games.

The modern Olympic Games, which started in Athens in 1896, are the result of the devotion of a French educator, Baron Pierre de Coubertin, to the idea that, since young people and athletics have gone together through the ages, education and athletics might go hand-in-hand toward a better international understanding.

The principal organization responsible for the staging of the Games is the International Olympic Committee (IOC). Other important roles are played by the National Olympic Committees in each participating country, international sports federations, and the organizing committee of the host city.

Beginning in 1994, the IOC decided to change the format of having both the Summer and Winter Games in the same year. Summer and Winter Olympics now alternate every two years. In 1994, the Winter Games were staged in Lillehammer, Norway, just two years after they'd been held in Albertville, France. The Winter Games will next be held in Salt Lake City, Utah, in 2002. The next Summer Olympics will be 2000 in Sydney, Australia.

The headquarters of the 89-member International Olympic Committee are in Lausanne, Switzerland. The president of the IOC is Juan Antonio Samaranch of Spain.

The Olympic motto is "Citius, Altius, Fortius,"—"Faster, Higher, Stronger." The Olympic symbol is five interlocking circles colored blue, yellow, black, green, and red, on a white background, representing the five continents. At least one of those colors appears in the national flag of every country.

In February, 1998, IOC President Samaranch announced that if any new sports are added to future Olympics, they must include women's events.

Winter Games: Gold Medals

FIGURE SKATING—MEN

1908	Ulrich Salchow, Sweden
1920	Gillis Grafström, Sweden
1924	Gillis Grafström, Sweden
1928	Gillis Grafström, Sweden
1932	Karl Schäfer, Austria
1936	Karl Schäfer, Austria
1948	Dick Button, United States
1952	Dick Button, United States
1956	Hayes Alan Jenkins, United States
1960	David Jenkins, United States
1964	Manfred Schnelldorfer, Germany
1968	Wolfgang Schwarz, Austria
1972	Ondrej Nepela, Czechoslovakia
1976	John Curry, Great Britain
1980	Robin Cousins, Great Britain
1984	Scott Hamilton, United States
1988	Brian Boitano, United States
1992	Viktor Petrenko, Unified Team*
1994	Alexei Urmanov, Russia
1998	Ilia Kulik, Russia

*Former Soviet Union team.

FIGURE SKATING—WOMEN

1908	Madge Syers, Britain
1920	Magda Julin-Mauroy, Sweden
1924	Herma Planck-Szabö, Austria
1928	Sonja Henie, Norway
1932	Sonja Henie, Norway
1936	Sonja Henie, Norway
1948	Barbara Ann Scott, Canada
1952	Jeanette Altwegg, Great Britain
1956	Tenley Albright, United States
1960	Carol Heiss, United States
1964	Sjoukje Dijkstra, Netherlands
1968	Peggy Fleming, United States
1972	Beatrix Schuba, Austria
1976	Dorothy Hamill, United States
1980	Anett Pötzsch, East Germany
1984	Katarina Witt, East Germany
1988	Katarina Witt, East Germany
1992	Kristi Yamaguchi, United States
1994	Oksana Baiul, Ukraine
1998	Tara Lipinski, United States

SPEED SKATING–MEN

(U.S. winners only)

500 Meters

1924	Charles Jewtraw	44.00
1932	Jack Shea	43.40
1952	Ken Henry	43.20
1964	Terry McDermott	40.10
1980	Eric Heiden	38.03

1,000 Meters

1976	Peter Mueller	1:19.32
1980	Eric Heiden	1:15.18
1994	Dan Jansen	1:12.43[1]

1,500 Meters

1932	Jack Shea	2:57.50
1980	Eric Heiden	1:55.44

5,000 Meters

1932	Irving Jaffee	9:40.80
1980	Eric Heiden	7:02.29

10,000 Meters

1932	Irving Jaffee	19:13.60
1980	Eric Heiden	14:28.13

1. World record.

SPEED SKATING–WOMEN

(U.S. winners only)

500 Meters

1972	Anne Henning	43.33
1976	Sheila Young	42.76
1988	Bonnie Blair	39.10
1992	Bonnie Blair	40.33
1994	Bonnie Blair	39.25

1,000 Meters

1992	Bonnie Blair	1:21.90
1994	Bonnie Blair	1:18.74

1,500 Meters

1972	Dianne Holum	2:20.85

SKIING, ALPINE–MEN

Downhill

1948	Henri Oreiller, France	2:55.00
1952	Zeno Colò, Italy	2:30.80
1956	Toni Sailer, Austria	2:52.20
1960	Jean Vuarnet, France	2:06.00
1964	Egon Zimmermann, Austria	2:18.16
1968	Jean-Claude Killy, France	1:59.85
1972	Bernhard Russi, Switzerland	1:51.43
1976	Franz Klammer, Austria	1:45.73
1980	Leonhard Stock, Austria	1:45.50
1984	Bill Johnson, United States	1:45.59
1988	Pirmin Zurbriggen, Switzerland	1:59.63
1992	Patrick Ortlieb, Austria	1:50.37
1994	Tommy Moe, United States	1:45.75
1998	Jean-Luc Cretier, France	1:50.11

Slalom

1948	Edi Reinalter, Switzerland	2:10.30
1952	Othmar Schneider, Austria	2:00.00
1956	Toni Sailer, Austria	3:14.70
1960	Ernst Hinterseer, Austria	2:08.90
1964	Pepi Stiegler, Austria	2:11.13
1968	Jean-Claude Killy, France	1:39.73
1972	Francisco Ochoa, Spain	1:49.27
1976	Piero Gros, Italy	2:03.29
1980	Ingemar Stenmark, Sweden	1:44.26
1984	Phil Mahre, United States	1:39.41
1988	Alberto Tomba, Italy	1:39.47
1992	Finn Christian Jagge, Norway	1:44.39
1994	Thomas Stangassinger, Austria	2:02.02
1998	Hans-Petter Buraas, Norway	1:49.31

Giant Slalom

1952	Stein Eriksen, Norway	2:25.00
1956	Toni Sailer, Austria	3:00.10
1960	Roger Staub, Switzerland	1:48.30
1964	François Bonlieu, France	1:46.71
1968	Jean-Claude Killy, France	3:29.28
1972	Gustav Thöni, Italy	3:09.62
1976	Heini Hemmi, Switzerland	3:26.97
1980	Ingemar Stenmark, Sweden	2:40.74
1984	Max Julen, Switzerland	2:41.18
1988	Alberto Tomba, Italy	2:06.37
1992	Alberto Tomba, Italy	2:06.98
1994	Markus Wasmeier, Germany	2:52.46
1998	Hermann Maier, Austria	2:38.51

Super Giant Slalom

1988	Frank Piccard, France	1:39.66
1992	Kjetil Andre Aamodt, Norway	1:13.04
1994	Markus Wasmeier, Germany	1:32.53
1998	Hermann Maier, Austria	1:34.84

Men's Combined (Downhill and Slalom)

		Points
1936	Franz Pfnür, Germany	99.25
1948	Henri Oreiller, France	3.27
1952–1984	Not held	
1988	Hubert Strolz, Austria	36.55
1992	Josef Polig, Italy	14.58
		Time
1994	Lasse Kjus, Norway	3:17.53
1998	Mario Reiter, Austria	3:08.06

SKIING, ALPINE–WOMEN

Downhill

1948	Hedy Schlunegger, Switzerland	2:28.30
1952	Trude Jochum-Beiser, Austria	1:47.10
1956	Madeleine Berthod, Switzerland	1:40.70
1960	Heidi Biebl, Germany	1:37.60
1964	Christl Haas, Austria	1:55.39
1968	Olga Pall, Austria	1:40.87
1972	Marie-Theres Nadig, Switzerland	1:36.68
1976	Rosi Mittermaier, West Germany	1:46.16
1980	Annemarie Moser-Pröll, Austria	1:37.52
1984	Michela Figini, Switzerland	1:13.36
1988	Marina Kiehl, West Germany	1:25.86
1992	Kerrin Lee-Gartner, Canada	1:52.55
1994	Katja Seizinger, Germany	1:35.93
1998	Katja Seizinger, Germany	1:28.89

Slalom

1948	Gretchen Fraser, United States	1:57.20
1952	Andrea Mead Lawrence, United States	2:10.60
1956	Renée Colliard, Switzerland	1:52.30
1960	Anne Heggtveit, Canada	1:49.60
1964	Christine Goitschel, France	1:29.86
1968	Marielle Goitschel, France	1:25.86
1972	Barbara Cochran, United States	1:31.24
1976	Rosi Mittermaier, West Germany	1:30.54
1980	Hanni Wenzel, Liechtenstein	1:25.09
1984	Paoletta Magoni, Italy	1:36.47
1988	Vreni Schneider, Switzerland	1:36.69
1992	Petra Kronberger, Austria	1:32.68
1994	Vreni Schneider, Switzerland	1:56.01
1998	Hilde Gerg, Germany	1:32.40

Giant Slalom

1952	Andrea Mead Lawrence, United States	2:06.80
1956	Ossi Reichert, Germany	1:56.50
1960	Yvonne Rügg, Switzerland	1:39.90
1964	Marielle Goitschel, France	1:52.24
1968	Nancy Greene, Canada	1:51.97
1972	Marie-Theres Nadig, Switzerland	1:29.90

1976	Kathy Kreiner, Canada	1:29.13
1980	Hanni Wenzel, Liechtenstein	2:41.66
1984	Debbie Armstrong, United States	2:20.98
1988	Vreni Schneider, Switzerland	2:06.49
1992	Pernilla Wiberg, Sweden	2:12.74
1994	Deborah Compagnoni, Italy	2:30.97
1998	Deborah Compagnoni, Italy	2:50.59

Super Giant Slalom

1988	Sigrid Wolf, Austria	1:19.03
1992	Deborah Compagnoni, Italy	1:21.22
1994	Diann Roffe-Steinrotter, United States	1:22.15
1998	Picabo Street, United States	1:18.02

Combined (Downhill and Slalom)

		Points
1936	Christl Cranz, Germany	97.06
1948	Trude Beiser, Austria	6.58
1952-84	Not held	
1988	Anita Wachter, Austria	29.25
1992	Petra Kronberger, Austria	2.55
		Time
1994	Pernilla Wiberg, Sweden	3:05.16
1998	Katja Seizinger, Germany	2:40.74

FREESTYLE SKIING—MEN

Moguls

1992 Edgar Grospiron, France
1994 Jean-Luc Brassard, Canada
1998 Jonny Moseley, United States

Aerials

1994 Andreas Schoenbaechler, Switzerland
1998 Eric Bergoust, United States

FREESTYLE SKIING—WOMEN

Moguls

1992 Donna Weinbrecht, United States
1994 Stine Lise Hattestad, Norway
1998 Tae Satoya, Japan

Aerials

1994 Lina Cherjazova, Uzbekistan
1998 Nikki Stone, United States

ICE HOCKEY

MEN			
1920	Canada	1972	U.S.S.R.
1924	Canada	1976	U.S.S.R.
1928	Canada	1980	United States
1932	Canada	1984	U.S.S.R.
1936	Great Britain	1988	U.S.S.R.
1948	Canada	1992	Unified Team*
1952	Canada	1994	Sweden
1956	U.S.S.R.	1998	Czech Republic
1960	United States	**WOMEN**	
1964	U.S.S.R.	1998	United States
1968	U.S.S.R.	*Former Soviet Union team.	

1998 Men's Championship
Czech Republic 1, Russia 0
1998 Women's Championship
United States 3, Canada 1

DISTRIBUTION OF MEDALS
1998 WINTER OLYMPIC GAMES
(Nagano, Japan)

	Gold	Silver	Bronze	Total
Germany	12	9	8	29
Norway	10	10	5	25
Russia	9	6	3	18
Austria	3	5	9	17
Canada	6	5	4	15
United States	6	3	4	13
Finland	2	4	6	12
Netherlands	5	4	2	11
Japan	5	1	4	10
Italy	2	6	2	10
France	2	1	5	8
China	0	6	2	8
Switzerland	2	2	3	7
South Korea	3	1	2	6
Czech Republic	1	1	1	3
Sweden	0	2	1	3
Belarus	0	0	2	2
Kazakhstan	0	0	2	2
Bulgaria	1	0	0	1
Denmark	0	1	0	1
Ukraine	0	1	0	1
Australia	0	0	1	1
Belgium	0	0	1	1
Britain	0	0	1	1

1998 UNITED STATES MEDALISTS

Figure Skating
Women—GOLD—Tara Lipinski, Sugarland, Texas
Women—SILVER—Michelle Kwan, Torrance, Calif.

Alpine Skiing
Women's Super Giant Slalom—GOLD—Picabo Street, Sun Valley, Idaho

Freestyle Skiing
Men's Moguls—GOLD—Jonny Moseley, Tiburon, Calif.
Men's Aerials—GOLD—Eric Bergoust, Missoula, Mont.
Women's Aerials—GOLD—Nikki Stone, Westborough, Mass.

Hockey
Women—GOLD—Sara Decosta, Tara Mounsey, Elizabeth Brown, Angela Ruggiero, Colleen Coyne, Karyn Bye, Suzanne Merz, Laurie Baker, Sandra Whyte, Allison Mleczko, Jennifer Schmidgall, Victoria Movsessian, Shelley Looney, Alana Blahoski, Kathryn King, Catherine Granato, Gretchen Ulion, Christina Bailey, Patricia Dunn, Sarah Tueting

Luge
Men's Doubles—SILVER—Chris Thorpe, Marquette, Mich. and Gordy Sheer, Croton, N.Y.
Men's Doubles—BRONZE—Mark Grimmette, Muskegon, Mich. and Brian Martin, Palo Alto, Calif.

Snowboarding
Men's Halfpipe—BRONZE—Ross Powers, South Londonderry, Vt.
Women's Halfpipe—BRONZE—Shannon Dunn, Steamboat Springs, Colo.

Speedskating
Women's 1,000 Meters—SILVER—Chris Witty, West Allis, Wis.
Women's 1,500 Meters—BRONZE—Chris Witty, West Allis, Wis.

Other 1998 Winter Olympic Games Champions

Biathlon
Men's 10-kilometer—Ole Einar Bjoerndalen, Norway
Men's 20-kilometer—Halvard Hanevold, Norway
Men's 4 × 7.5-kilometer relay—Germany
Women's 7.5-kilometer—Galina Koukleva, Russia
Women's 15-kilometer—Ekaterina Dafovska, Bulgaria
Women's 4 × 7.5-kilometer relay—Germany

Bobsledding
2-man—Canada I and Italy I
4-man—Germany II

Curling
Men—Switzerland
Women—Canada

Figure Skating
Pairs—Oksana Kazakova and Artur Dmitriev, Russia
Ice dancing—Pasha Grishuk and Yevgeny Platov, Russia

Luge
Men's singles—Georg Hackl, Germany
Men's doubles—Stefan Krausse, Jan Behrendt, Germany
Women's singles—Silke Kraushaar, Germany

Skiing, Nordic—Men
Combined team—Norway
Combined—Bjarte Engen Vik, Norway
70-meter jump—Jani Soininen, Finland
90-meter jump—Kazuyoshi Funaki, Japan
Team 120-meter jump—Japan
10-km cross country classical—Bjorn Dählie, Norway
15-km cross country free pursuit—Thomas Alsgaard, Norway
30-km cross country classical—Mika Myllylae, Finland
50-km cross country freestyle—Bjorn Dählie, Norway
4 × 10 kilometer relay—Norway

Skiing, Nordic—Women
5-kilometer classical—Larissa Lazutina, Russia
10-kilometer free pursuit—Larissa Lazutina, Russia
15-kilometer classical—Olga Danilova, Russia
30-kilometer freestyle—Yulia Tchepalova, Russia
4 × 5 kilometer relay—Russia

Snowboarding—Men
Giant slalom—Ross Rebagliati, Canada
Halfpipe—Gian Simmen, Switzerland

Snowboarding—Women
Giant slalom—Karine Ruby, France
Halfpipe—Nicola Thost, Germany

Speed Skating—Men
500m—Hiroyashu Shimizu, Japan
1,000m—Ids Postma, Netherlands
1,500m—Aadne Sondral, Norway
5,000m—Gianni Romme, Netherlands
10,000m—Gianni Romme, Netherlands

Speed Skating—Women
500m—Catriona LeMay-Doan, Canada
1,000m—Marianne Timmer, Netherlands
1,500m—Marianne Timmer, Netherlands
3,000m—Gunda Niemann-Stirnemann, Germany
5,000m—Claudia Pechstein, Germany

Speed Skating, Short Track—Men
500m—Takafumi Nishitani, Japan
1,000m—Kim Dong-sung, South Korea
5,000m relay—Canada

Speed Skating, Short Track—Women
500m—Annie Perreault, Canada
1,000m—Chun Lee-kyung, South Korea
3,000m relay—South Korea

Summer Games: Gold Medals

TRACK AND FIELD–MEN

100-Meter Dash
1896	Thomas Burke, United States	12.00
1900	Francis W. Jarvis, United States	10.80
1904	Archie Hahn, United States	11.00
1906	Archie Hahn, United States	11.20
1908	Reginald Walker, South Africa	10.80
1912	Ralph Craig, United States	10.80
1920	Charles Paddock, United States	10.80
1924	Harold Abrahams, Great Britain	10.60
1928	Percy Williams, Canada	10.80
1932	Eddie Tolan, United States	10.30
1936	Jesse Owens, United States	10.30[1]
1948	Harrison Dillard, United States	10.30
1952	Lindy Remigino, United States	10.40
1956	Bobby Morrow, United States	10.50
1960	Armin Hary, Germany	10.20
1964	Robert Hayes, United States	10.00
1968	James Hines, United States	09.90
1972	Valery Borzow, U.S.S.R.	10.14
1976	Hasely Crawford, Trinidad and Tobago	10.06
1980	Allan Wells, Britain	10.25
1984	Carl Lewis, United States	09.99
1988	Carl Lewis, United States	09.92[2]
1992	Linford Christie, Great Britain	09.96
1996	Donovan Bailey, Canada	09.84[3]

1. Wind assisted. 2. Lewis was awarded the gold medal when Ben Johnson of Canada, the original winner in 09.79s, was stripped of the medal after testing positive for steroid use. 3. World record.

200-Meter Dash
1900	John Tewksbury, United States	22.20
1904	Archie Hahn, United States	21.60
1908	Robert Kerr, Canada	22.60
1912	Ralph Craig, United States	21.70
1920	Allan Woodring, United States	22.00
1924	Jackson Scholz, United States	21.60
1928	Percy Williams, Canada	21.80
1932	Eddie Tolan, United States	21.20
1936	Jesse Owens, United States	20.70
1948	Melvin E. Patton, United States	21.10
1952	Andrew Stanfield, United States	20.70
1956	Bobby Morrow, United States	20.60
1960	Livio Berruti, Italy	20.50
1964	Henry Carr, United States	20.30
1968	Tommie Smith, United States	19.80
1972	Vallery Borzov, U.S.S.R.	20.00
1976	Don Quarrie, Jamaica	20.23
1980	Pietro Mennea, Italy	20.19
1984	Carl Lewis, United States	19.80
1988	Joe DeLoach, United States	19.75
1992	Mike Marsh, United States	20.01
1996	Michael Johnson, United States	19.32[1]

1. World record.

400-Meter Dash
1896	Thomas Burke, United States	54.20
1900	Maxwell Long, United States	49.40
1904	Harry Hillman, United States	49.20
1906	Paul Pilgrim, United States	53.20
1908	Wyndham Halswelle, Great Britain (walkover)	50.00
1912	Charles Reidpath, United States	48.20

1920	Bevil Rudd, South Africa	49.60
1924	Eric Liddell, Great Britain	47.60
1928	Ray Barbuti, United States	47.80
1932	William Carr, United States	46.20
1936	Archie Williams, United States	46.50
1948	Arthur Wint, Jamaica, B.W.I.	46.20
1952	George Rhoden, Jamaica, B.W.I.	45.90
1956	Charles Jenkins, United States	46.70
1960	Otis Davis, United States	44.90
1964	Mike Larrabee, United States	45.10
1968	Lee Evans, United States	43.80
1972	Vincent Matthews, United States	44.66
1976	Alberto Juantorena, Cuba	44.26
1980	Viktor Markin, U.S.S.R.	44.60
1984	Alonzo Babers, United States	44.27
1988	Steve Lewis, United States	43.87
1992	Quincy Watts, United States	43.50
1996	Michael Johnson, United States	43.49

800-Meter Run

1896	Edwin Flack, Australia	2:11.00
1900	Alfred Tysoe, Great Britain	2:01.40
1904	James Lightbody, United States	1:56.00
1906	Paul Pilgrim, United States	2:01.20
1908	Mel Sheppard, United states	1:52.80
1912	Ted Meredith, United States	1:51.90
1920	Albert Hill, Great Britain	1:53.40
1924	Douglas Lowe, Great Britain	1:52.40
1928	Douglas Lowe, Great Britain	1:51.80
1932	Thomas Hampson, Great Britain	1:49.80
1936	John Woodruff, United States	1:52.90
1948	Malvin Whitfield, United States	1:49.20
1952	Malvin Whitfield, United States	1:49.20
1956	Tom Courtney, United States	1:47.70
1960	Peter Snell, New Zealand	1:46.30
1964	Peter Snell, New Zealand	1:45.10
1968	Ralph Doubell, Australia	1:44.30
1972	David Wottle, United States	1:45.90
1976	Alberto Juantorena, Cuba	1:43.50
1980	Steve Ovett, Britain	1:45.40
1984	Joaquin Cruz, Brazil	1:43.00
1988	Paul Ereng, Kenya	1:43.45
1992	William Tanui, Kenya	1:43.66
1996	Vebjoern Rodal, Norway	1:42.58

1,500-Meter Run

1896	Edwin Flack, Australia	4:33.20
1900	Charles Bennett, Great Britain	4:06.00
1904	James Lightbody, United States	4:05.40
1906	James Lightbody, United States	4:12.00
1908	Mel Sheppard, United States	4:03.40
1912	Arnold Jackson, Great Britain	3:56.80
1920	Albert Hill, Great Britain	4:01.80
1924	Paavo Nurmi, Finland	3:53.60
1928	Harry Larva, Finland	3:53.20
1932	Luigi Becali, Italy	3:51.20
1936	Jack Lovelock, New Zealand	3:47.80
1948	Henri Eriksson, Sweden	3:49.80
1952	Joseph Barthel, Luxembourg	3:45.20
1956	Ron Delany, Ireland	3:41.20
1960	Herb Elliott, Australia	3:35.60
1964	Peter Snell, New Zealand	3:38.10
1968	Kipchoge Keino, Kenya	3:34.90
1972	Pekka Vasala, Finland	3:36.30
1976	John Walker, New Zealand	3:39.17
1980	Sebastian Coe, Britain	3:38.40
1984	Sebastian Coe, Britain	3:32.53
1988	Peter Rono, Kenya	3:35.96
1992	Fermin Cacho Ruiz, Spain	3:40.12
1996	Noureddine Morceli, Algeria	3:35.78

5,000-Meter Run

1912	Hannes Kolehmainen, Finland	14:36.60
1920	Joseph Guillemot, France	14:55.60
1024	Paavo Nurmi, Finland	14:31.20
1928	Willie Ritola, Finland	14:38.00
1932	Lauri Lehtinen, Finland	14:30.00
1936	Gunnar Hockert, Finland	14:22.20
1948	Gaston Reiff, Belgium	14:17.60
1952	Emil Zatopek, Czechoslovakia	14:06.60
1956	Vladimir Kuts, U.S.S.R.	13:39.60
1960	Murray Halberg, New Zealand	13:43.40
1964	Bob Schul, United States	13:48.80
1968	Mohamed Gammoudi, Tunisia	14:05.00
1972	Lasse Viren, Finland	13:26.40
1976	Lasse Viren, Finland	13:24.76
1980	Miruts Yifter, Ethiopia	13:21.00
1984	Saud Aouita, Morocco	13:05.59
1988	John Ngugi, Kenya	13:11.70
1992	Dieter Baumann, Germany	13:12.52
1996	Venuste Niyongabo, Burundi	13:07.96

10,000-Meter Run

1912	Hannes Kolehmainen, Finland	31:20.80
1920	Paavo Nurmi, Finland	31:45.80
1924	Willie Ritola, Finland	30:23.20
1928	Paavo Nurmi, Finland	30:18.80
1932	Janusz Kusocinski, Poland	30:11.40
1936	Ilmari Salminen, Finland	30:15.40
1948	Emil Zatopek, Czechoslovakia	29:59.60
1952	Emil Zatopek, Czechoslovakia	29:17.00
1956	Vladimir Kuts, U.S.S.R.	28:45.60
1960	Peter Bolotnikov, U.S.S.R.	28:32.20
1964	Billy Mills, United States	28:24.40
1968	Nartali Temu, Kenya	29:27.40
1972	Lasse Viren, Finland	27:38.40
1976	Lasse Viren, Finland	27:40.38
1980	Miruts Yifter, Ethiopia	27:42.70
1984	Alberto Cova, Italy	27:47.50
1988	Mly Brahim Boutaib, Morocco	27:21.46
1992	Khalid Skah, Morocco	27:47.70
1996	Haile Gebrselassie, Ethiopia	27:07.34

Marathon

1896	Spiridon Loues, Greece	2:58:50.00
1900	Michel Teato, France	2:59:45.00
1904	Thomas Hicks, United States	3:28:53.00
1906	William J. Sherring, Canada	2:51:23.65
1908	John J. Hayes, United States	2:55:18.40
1912	Kenneth McArthur, South Africa	2:36:54.80
1920	Hannes Kolehmainen, Finland	2:32:35.80
1924	Albin Stenroos, Finland	2:41:22.60
1928	A.B. El Quafi, France	2:32:57.00
1932	Juan Zabala, Argentina	2:31:36.00
1936	Kitei Son, Japan	2:29:19.20
1948	Delfo Cabrera, Argentina	2:34:51.60
1952	Emil Zatopek, Czechoslovakia	2:23:30.20
1956	Alain Mimoun, France	2:25:00.00
1960	Abebe Bikila, Ethiopia	2:15:16.20
1964	Abebe Bikila, Ethiopia	2:12:11.20
1968	Mamo Wold, Ethiopia	2:20:26.40
1972	Frank Shorter, United States	2:12:19.80
1976	Walter Cierpinski, East Germany	2:09:55.00
1980	Walter Cierpinski, East Germany	2:11:30.00
1984	Carlos Lopes, Portugal	2:09:21.00
1988	Gelindo Bordin, Italy	2:10:47.00
1992	Hwang Young-Cho, South Korea	2:13:23.00
1996	Josia Thugwane, South Africa	2:12:36.00

110-Meter Hurdles

1896	Thomas Curtis, United States	17.60
1900	Alvin Kraenzlein, United States	15.40
1904	Frederick Schule, United States	16.00
1906	R.G. Leavitt, United States	16.20
1908	Forrest Smithson, United States	15.00
1912	Frederick Kelly, United States	15.10
1920	Earl Thomson, Canada	14.80
1924	Daniel Kinsey, United States	15.00

1928	Sydney Atkinson, South Africa	14.80
1932	George Saling, United States	14.60
1936	Forrest Towns, United States	14.20
1948	William Porter, United States	13.90
1952	Harrison Dillard, United States	13.70
1956	Lee Calhoun, United States	13.50
1960	Lee Calhoun, United States	13.80
1964	Hayes Jones, United States	13.60
1968	Willie Davenport, United States	13.30
1972	Rodney Milburn, United States	13.24
1976	Guy Drut, France	13.30
1980	Thomas Munkett, East Germany	13.20
1984	Roger Kingdom, United States	13.20
1988	Roger Kingdom, United States	12.98
1992	Mark McCoy, Canada	13.12
1996	Allen Johnson, United States	12.95

200-Meter Hurdles

1900	Alvin Kraenzlein, United States	25.40
1904	Harry Hillman, United States	24.60

400-Meter Hurdles

1900	John Tewksbury, United States	57.60
1904	Harry Hillman, United States	53.00
1908	Charles Bacon, United States	55.00
1920	Frank Loomis, United States	54.00
1924	F. Morgan Taylor, United States	52.60
1928	Lord David Burghley, Great Britain	53.40
1932	Robert Tisdall, Ireland	51.80[1]
1936	Glenn Hardin, United States	52.40
1948	Roy Cochran, United States	51.10
1952	Charles Moore, United States	50.80
1956	Glenn Davis, United States	50.10
1960	Glenn Davis, United States	49.30
1964	Rex Cawley, United States	49.60
1968	David Hemery, Great Britain	48.10
1972	John Akii-Bua, Uganda	47.80
1976	Edwin Moses, United States	47.64
1980	Volker Beck, East Germany	48.70
1984	Edwin Moses, United States	47.75
1988	Andre Phillips, United States	47.19
1992	Kevin Young, United States	46.78
1996	Derrick Adkins, United States	47.54

1. Record not allowed.

2,500-Meter Steeplechase

1900	George Orton, United States	7:34.00
1904	James Lightbody, United States	7:39.60

3,000-Meter Steeplechase

1920	Percy Hodge, Great Britain	10:00.40
1924	Willie Ritola, Finland	09:33.60
1928	Toivo Loukola, Finland	09:21.80
1932	Volmari Iso-Hollo, Finland	10:33.40[1]
1936	Volmari Iso-Hollo, Finland	09:03.80
1948	Thure Sjoestrand, Sweden	09:04.60
1952	Horace Ashenfelter, United States	08:45.40
1956	Chris Brasher, Great Britain	08:41.20
1960	Zdzislaw Krzyskowiak, Poland	08:34.20
1964	Gaston Roelants, Belgium	08:30.80
1968	Amos Biwott, Kenya	08:51.00
1972	Kipchoge Keino, Kenya	08:23.60
1976	Anders Gardervd, Sweden	08:08.02
1980	Bronislaw Malinowski, Poland	08:09.70
1984	Julius Korir, Kenya	08:11.80
1988	Julius Karluki, Kenya	08:05.51
1992	Matthew Birir, Kenya	08:08.84
1996	Joseph Keter, Kenya	08:07.12

1. About 3,450 meters-extra lap by error.

10,000-Meter Walk

1912	George Goulding, Canada	46:28.40
1920	Ugo Frigerio, Italy	48:06.20
1924	Ugo Frigerio, Italy	47:49.00
1948	John Mikaelsson, Sweden	45:13.20
1952	John Mikaelsson, Sweden	45:02.80

20,000-Meter Walk

1956	Leonid Spirin, U.S.S.R.	1:31:27.40
1960	Vladimir Golubnichy, U.S.S.R.	1:34:07.20
1964	Ken Mathews, Great Britain	1:29:34.00
1968	Vladimir Golubnichy, U.S.S.R.	1:33:58.40
1972	Peter Frenkel, East Germany	1:26:42.40
1976	Daniel Bautista, Mexico	1:24:40.60
1980	Maurizio Damiliano, Italy	1:23:35.50
1984	Ernesto Conto, Mexico	1:23.13.00
1988	Jozef Pribilinec, Czechoslovakia	1:19:57.00
1992	Daniel Plaza, Spain	1:21:45.00
1996	Jefferson Perez, Ecuador	1:20:07.00

50,000-Meter Walk

1932	Thomas W. Green, Great Britain	4:50:10.00
1936	Harold Whitlock, Great Britain	4:30:41.10
1948	John Ljunggren, Sweden	4:41:52.00
1952	Giuseppe Dordoni, Italy	4:28:07.80
1956	Norman Read, New Zealand	4:30:42.80
1960	Donald Thompson, Great Britain	4:25:30.00
1964	Abdon Pamich, Italy	4:11:12.40
1968	Christoph Hohne, East Germany	4:20:13.60
1972	Bern Kannernberg, West Germany	3:56:11.60
1980	Hartwig Guader, East Germany	3:49:24.00
1984	Raul Gonzalez, Mexico	3:37:26.00
1988	Viacheslau Ivanenko, U.S.S.R.	3:48:29.00
1992	Andrei Perlov, Unified Team[1]	3:50:13.00
1996	Robert Korzeniowski, Poland	3:43:30.00

1. Former Soviet Union team.

400-Meter Relay (4x100)

1912	Great Britain	42.40
1920	United States	42.20
1924	United States	41.00
1928	United States	41.00
1932	United States	40.00
1936	United States	39.80
1948	United States	40.60
1952	United States	40.10
1956	United States	39.50
1960	Germany	39.50
1964	United States	39.00
1968	United States	38.20
1972	United States	38.19
1976	United States	38.33
1980	U.S.S.R.	38.26
1984	United States	37.83
1988	U.S.S.R.	38.19
1992	United States	37.40[1]
1996	Canada	37.69

1. World record.

1,600-Meter Relay (4x400)

1912	United States	3:16.60
1920	Great Britain	3:22.20
1924	United States	3:16.00
1928	United States	3:14.20
1932	United States	3:08.20
1936	Great Britain	3:09.00
1948	United States	3:10.40
1952	Jamaica, B.W.I.	3:03.90
1956	United States	3:04.80
1960	United States	3:02.20
1964	United States	3:00.70
1968	United States	2:56.10
1972	Kenya	2:59.80
1976	United States	2:58.65
1980	U.S.S.R.	3:01.10
1984	United States	2:57.91
1988	United States	2:56.16
1992	United States	2:55.74[1]
1996	United States	2:55.99

1. World record.

Team Race

		Pts
1900	Great Britain (5,000 meters)	26
1904	United States (4 miles)	27
1908	Great Britain (3 miles)	6
1912	United States (3,000 meters)	9
1920	United States (3,000 meters)	10
1924	Finland (3,000 meters)	9

Standing High Jump

1900	Ray Ewry, United States	5 ft. 5 in.
1904	Ray Ewry, United States	4 ft. 11 in.
1906	Ray Ewry, United States	5 ft. 1⅝ in.
1908	Ray Ewry, United States	5 ft. 2 in.
1912	Platt Adams, United States	5 ft. 4⅛ in.

Running High Jump

1896	Ellery Clark, United States	5 ft. 11¼ in.
1900	Irving Baxter, United States	6 ft. 2¾ in.
1904	Samuel Jones, United States	5 ft. 11 in.
1906	Con Leahy, Ireland	5 ft. 9⅞ in.
1908	Harry Porter, United States	6 ft. 3 in.
1912	Alma Richards, United States	6 ft. 4 in.
1920	Richmond Landon, United States	6 ft. 4¼ in.
1924	Harold Osborn, United States	6 ft. 5$^{15}/_{16}$ in.
1928	Robert W. King, United States	6 ft. 4⅜ in.
1932	Duncan McNaughton, Canada	6 ft. 5⅝ in.
1936	Cornelius Johnson, United States	6 ft. 7$^{15}/_{16}$ in.
1948	John Winter, Australia	6 ft. 6 in.
1952	Walter David, United States	6 ft. 8$^{15}/_{16}$ in.
1956	Charles Damas, United States	6 ft. 11¼ in.
1960	Robert Shavlakadze, U.S.S.R.	7 ft. 1 in.
1964	Valeri Brumel, U.S.S.R.	7 ft. 1¾ in.
1968	Dick Fosbury, United States	7 ft. 4¼ in.
1972	Yuri Tarmak, U.S.S.R.	7 ft. 3¾ in.
1976	Jacek Wszola, Poland	7 ft. 4½ in.
1980	Gerd Wessig, East Germany	7 ft. 8¾ in.
1984	Dietmar Mogenburg, West Germany	7 ft. 8½ in.
1988	Guennadi Avdeenko, U.S.S.R.	7 ft. ½ in.
1992	Javier Sotomayer, Cuba	7 ft. 8½ in.
1996	Charles Austin, United States	7 ft. 10 in.

Long Jump

1896	Ellery Clark, United States	20 ft. 9¾ in.
1900	Alvin Kraenzlein, United States	23 ft. 6⅞ in.
1904	Myer Prinstein, United States	24 ft. 1 in.
1906	Myer Prinstein, United States	23 ft. 7½ in.
1908	Frank Irons, United States	24 ft. 6½ in.
1912	Albert Gutterson, United States	24 ft. 11¼ in.
1920	William Petterssen, Sweden	23 ft. 5½ in.
1924	DeHart Hubbard, United States	24 ft. 5⅛ in.
1928	Edward B. Hamm, United States	25 ft. 4¾ in.
1932	Edward Gordon, United States	25 ft. ¾ in.
1936	Jesse Owens, United States	26 ft. 5$^{5}/_{16}$ in.
1948	Willie Steele, United States	25 ft. 8 in.
1952	Jerome Biffle, United States	24 ft. 10 in.
1956	Gregory Bell, United States	25 ft. 8¼ in.
1960	Ralph Boston, United States	26 ft. 7¾ in.
1964	Lynn Davies, Great Britain	26 ft. 5¾ in.
1968	Bob Beamon, United States	29 ft. 2½ in.
1972	Randy Williams, United States	27 ft. ½ in.
1976	Arnie Robinson, United States	24 ft. 7¾ in.
1980	Lutz Dombrowski, E. Germany	28 ft. ¼ in.
1984	Carl Lewis, United States	28 ft. ¼ in.
1988	Carl Lewis, United States	28 ft. 7¼ in.
1992	Carl Lewis, United States	28 ft. 5½ in.
1996	Carl Lewis, United States	27 ft. 10¾ in.

Triple Jump

1896	James B. Connolly, United States	45 ft.
1900	Myer Prinstein, United States	47 ft. 4¼ in.
1904	Myer Prinstein, United States	47 ft.
1906	P.G. O'Connor, Ireland	46 ft. 2 in.
1908	Timothy Ahearne, Great Britain	48 ft. 1¼ in.
1912	Gustaf Lindblom, Sweden	48 ft. 5⅛ in.
1920	Vilho Tuulos, Finland	47 ft. 6⅞ in.
1924	Archie Winter, Australia	50 ft. 11⅛ in.
1928	Mikio Oda, Japan	49 ft. 10$^{13}/_{16}$ in.
1932	Chuhei Nambu, Japan	51 ft. 7 in.
1936	Naoto Tajima, Japan	52 ft. 5⅞ in.
1948	Arne Ahman, Sweden	50 ft. 6¼ in.
1952	Adhemar da Silva, Brazil	53 ft. 2½ in.
1956	Adhemar da Silva, Brazil	53 ft. 7½ in.
1960	Jozef Schmidt, Poland	55 ft. 1¾ in.
1964	Jozef Schmidt, Poland	55 ft. 3¼ in.
1968	Viktor Saneyev, U.S.S.R.	57 ft. ¾ in.
1972	Viktor Saneyev, U.S.S.R.	56 ft. 11 in.
1976	Viktor Saneyev, U.S.S.R.	56 ft. 8¾ in.
1980	Jaak Uudmae, U.S.S.R.	56 ft. 11⅛ in.
1984	Al Joyner, United States	56 ft. 7½ in.
1988	Hristo Markov, Bulgaria	57 ft. 9¼ in.
1992	Mike Conley, United States	59 ft. 7½ in.
1996	Kenny Harrison, United States	59 ft. 4¼ in.

Pole Vault

1896	William Hoyt, United States	10 ft. 9¾ in.
1900	Irving Baxter, United States	10 ft. 9⅞ in.
1904	Charles Dvorak, United States	11 ft. 6 in.
1906	Fernand Gouder, France	11 ft. 6 in.
1908	Alfred Gilbert, United States, and Edward Cook, United States (tie)	12 ft. 2 in.
1912	Harry Babcock, United States	12 ft. 11½ in.
1920	Frank Foss, United States	13 ft. 5 $^{9}/_{16}$ in.
1924	Lee Barnes, United States	12 ft. 11½ in.
1928	Sabin W. Carr, United States	13 ft. 9⅜ in.
1932	William Miller, United States	14 ft. 1⅞ in.
1936	Earle Meadows, United States	14 ft. 3¼ in.
1948	Guinn Smith, United States	14 ft. ¼ in.
1952	Robert Richards, United States	14 ft. 11⅛ in.
1956	Robert Richards, United States	14 ft. 11½ in.
1960	Don Bragg, United States	15 ft. 5⅛ in.
1964	Fred Hansen, United States	16 ft. 8¾ in.
1968	Bob Seagren, United States	17 ft. 8½ in.
1972	Wolfgang Nordwig, East Germany	18 ft. ½ in.
1976	Tadeusz Slusarski, Poland	18 ft. ½ in.
1980	Wladyslaw Kozakiewics, Poland	18 ft. 11½ in.
1984	Pierre Quinon, France	18 ft. 10¼ in.
1988	Sergei Bubka, U.S.S.R.	18 ft. 4¼ in.
1992	Maxim Tarassov, Unified Team[1]	19 ft. 0¼ in.
1996	Jean Galfione, France	19 ft. 5¼ in.

1. Former Soviet Union team.

16-lb Shot-Put

1896	Robert Garrett, United States	36 ft. 9¾ in.
1900	Richard Sheldon, United States	46 ft. 3⅛ in.
1904	Ralph Rose, United States	48 ft. 7 in.
1906	Martin Sheridan, United States	40 ft. 4⅘ in.
1908	Ralph Rose, United States	46 ft. 7½ in.
1912	Pat McDonald, United States	50 ft. 4 in.
1920	Ville Porhola, Finland	48 ft. 7⅛ in.
1924	Clarence Houser, United States	49 ft. 2½ in.
1928	John Kuck, United States	52 ft. 11$^{11}/_{16}$ in.
1932	Leo Sexton, United States	52 ft. 6$^{3}/_{16}$ in.
1936	Hans Woellke, Germany	53 ft. 1¾ in.
1948	Wilbur Thompson, United States	56 ft. 2 in.
1952	Parry O'Brien, United States	57 ft. 1½ in.
1956	Parry O'Brien, United States	60 ft. 11 in.
1960	Bill Nieder, United States	64 ft. 6¾ in.
1964	Dallas Long, United States	66 ft. 8¼ in.
1968	Randy Matson, United States	67 ft. 4¾ in.
1972	Wladyslaw Komar, Poland	69 ft. 6 in.
1976	Udo Beyer, East Germany	69 ft. ¾ in.
1980	Vladmir Kiselyov, U.S.S.R.	70 ft. ½ in.
1984	Alessandro Andrei, Italy	69 ft. 9 in.
1988	Uhf Timmerman, East Germany	73 ft. 8¾ in.
1992	Michael Stulze, United States	71 ft. 2½ in.
1996	Randy Barnes, United States	70 ft. 11¼ in.

Discus Throw

1896	Robert Garrett, United States	95 ft. 7½ in.
1900	Rudolf Bauer, Hungary	118 ft. 2⅞ in.
1904	Martin Sheridan, United States	128 ft. 10½ in.
1906	Martin Sheridan, United States	136 ft. ⅓ in.
1908	Martin Sheridan, United States	134 ft. 2 in.
1912	Armas Taipale, Finland	145 ft. 9/16 in.
1920	Elmer Niklander, Finland	146 ft. 7 in.
1924	Clarence Houser, United States	151 ft. 5¼ in.
1928	Clarence Houser, United States	155 ft. 2⅘ in.
1932	John Anderson, United States	162 ft. 4⅞ in.
1936	Ken Carpenter, United States	165 ft. 7⅜ in.
1948	Adolfo Consolini, Italy	173 ft. 2 in.
1952	Simeon Iness, United States	180 ft. 6½ in.
1956	Al Oerter, United States	184 ft. 10½ in.
1960	Al Oerter, United States	194 ft. 2 in.
1964	Al Oerter, United States	200 ft. 1½ in.
1968	Al Oerter, United States	212 ft. 6 in.
1972	Ludvik Danek, Czechoslovakia	211 ft. 3 in.
1976	Mac Wilkins, United States	221 ft. 5 in.
1980	Viktor Rashchupkin, U.S.S.R.	218 ft. 8 in.
1984	Rolf Dannenberg, West Germany	218 ft. 6 in.
1988	Jurgen Schult, East Germany	225 ft. 9¼ in.
1992	Romas Ubartas, Lithuania	213 ft. 7¾ in.
1996	Lars Riedel, Germany	227 ft. 8 in.

Javelin Throw

1906	Eric Lemming, Sweden	175 ft. 6 in.
1908	Eric Lemming, Sweden	179 ft. 10½ in.
1912	Eric Lemming, Sweden	198 ft. 11¼ in.
1920	Jonni Myyra, Finland	215 ft. 9¾ in.
1924	Jonni Myyra, Finland	206 ft. 6¾ in.
1928	Eric Lundquist, Sweden	218 ft. 6⅛ in.
1932	Matti Jarvinen, Finland	238 ft. 7 in.
1936	Gerhard Stoeck, Germany	235 ft. 8 5/16 in.
1948	Kaj Rautavaara, Finland	228 ft. 10½ in.
1952	Cy Young, United States	242 ft.¾ in.
1956	Egil Danielsen, Norway	281 ft. 2¼ in.
1960	Viktor Tsibuelnko, U.S.S.R.	277 ft. 8⅜ in.
1964	Pauli Nevala, Finland	271 ft. 2¼ in.
1968	Janis Lusis, U.S.S.R.	295 ft. 7 in.
1972	Klaus Wolfermann, West Germany	296 ft. 10 in.
1976	Miklos Nemeth, Hungary	310 ft. 4 in.
1980	Dainis Kula, U.S.S.R.	299 ft. 2⅜ in.
1984	Arto Haerkoenen, Finland	284 ft. 8 in.
1988	Tapio Korjus, Finland	276 ft. 6 in.
1992	Jan Zelezny, Czechoslovakia	294 ft. 2 in.
1996	Jan Zelezny, Czech Republic	289 ft. 3 in.

16-lb Hammer Throw

1900	John Flanagan, United States	167 ft. 4 in.
1904	John Flanagan, United States	168 ft. 1 in.
1908	John Flanagan, United States	170 ft. 4¼ in.
1912	Matt McGrath, United States	179 ft. 7⅛ in.
1920	Pat Ryan, United States	173 ft. 5⅝ in.
1924	Fred Tootell, United States	174 ft. 10¼ in.
1928	Patrick O'Callaghan, Ireland	168 ft. 7½ in.
1932	Patrick O'Callaghan, Ireland	176 ft. 11⅛ in.
1936	Karl Hein, Germany	185 ft. 4 in.
1948	Imre Nemeth, Hungary	183 ft. 11½ in.
1952	Jozsef Csermak, Hungary	197 ft. 11 9/16 in.
1956	Harold Connolly, United States	207 ft. 2¾ in.
1960	Vasily Rudenkov, U.S.S.R.	220 ft. 1⅝ in.
1964	Romuald Klim, U.S.S.R.	228 ft. 9½ in.
1968	Gyula Zsivotzky, Hungary	240 ft. 8 in.
1972	Anatoly Bondarchuk, U.S.S.R.	247 ft. 8½ in.
1976	Yuri Sedykh, U.S.S.R.	254 ft. 4 in.
1980	Yuri Sedykh, U.S.S.R.	(81.80m) 268 ft. 4½ in.
1984	Juha Tiainen, Finland	256 ft. 2 in.
1988	Sergei Litvinov, U.S.S.R.	278 ft. 2½ in.
1992	Andrey Abduvaliyev, Unified Team[1]	270 ft. 9½ in.
1996	Balasz Kiss, Hungary	266 ft. 6 in.

1. Former Soviet Union team.

Decathlon

1912	Jim Thorpe, United States	—
	Hugo Wieslander, Sweden	—
1920	Helge Lovland, Norway	6,804.35 pts.
1924	Harold Osborn, United States	7,710.775 pts.
1928	Paavo Yrjola, Finland	8,053.29 pts.
1932	James Bausch, United States	8,462.23 pts.
1936	Glenn Morris, United States	7,900 pts.[1]
1948	Robert B. Mathias, United States	7,139 pts.
1952	Robert B. Mathias, United States	7,887 pts.
1956	Milton Campbell, United States	7,937 pts.
1960	Rafer Johnson, United States	8,392 pts.
1964	Willi Holdorf, Germany	7,887 pts.[1]
1968	Bill Toomey, United States	8,193 pts.
1972	Nikolai Avilov, U.S.S.R.	8,454 pts.
1976	Bruce Jenner, United States	8,618 pts.
1980	Daley Thompson, Britain	8,495 pts.
1984	Daley Thompson, Britain	8,797 pts.
1988	Christian Schenk, East Germany	8,488 pts.
1992	Robert Zmelik, Czechoslovakia	8,611 pts.
1996	Dan O'Brien, United States	8,824 pts.

1. Point system revised.

TRACK AND FIELD–WOMEN

100-Meter Dash

1928	Elizabeth Robinson, United States	12.20
1932	Stella Walsh, Poland	11.90
1936	Helen Stephens, United States	11.50
1948	Fanny Blankers-Koen, Netherlands	11.90
1952	Marjorie Jackson, Australia	11.50
1956	Betty Cuthbert, Australia	11.50
1960	Wilma Rudolph, United States	11.00
1964	Wyomia Tyus, United States	11.40
1968	Wyomia Tyus, United States	11.00
1972	Renate Stecher, East Germany	11.07
1976	Annegret Richter, West Germany	11.08
1980	Lyudmila Kondratyeva, U.S.S.R.	11.06
1984	Evelyn Ashford, United States	10.97
1988	Florence Griffith-Joyner, United States	10.54
1992	Gail Devers, United States	10.82
1996	Gail Devers, United States	10.94

200-Meter Dash

1948	Fanny Blankers-Koen, Netherlands	24.40
1952	Marjorie Jackson, Australia	23.70
1956	Betty Cuthbert, Australia	23.40
1960	Wilma Rudolph, United States	24.00
1964	Edith McGuire, United States	23.00
1968	Irena Szewinska, Poland	22.50
1972	Renate Stecher, East Germany	22.40
1976	Baerbel Eckert, East Germany	22.37
1980	Barbara Wockel, East Germany	22.03
1984	Valerie Brisco-Hooks, United States	21.81
1988	Florence Griffith-Joyner, United States	21.34
1992	Gwen Torrence, United States	21.81
1996	Marie-Jose Perec, France	22.12

400-Meter Dash

1964	Betty Cuthbert, Australia	52.00
1968	Colette Besson, France	52.00
1972	Monika Zehrt, East Germany	51.08
1976	Irena Szewinska, Poland	49.29
1980	Marita Koch, East Germany	48.88
1984	Valerie Brisco-Hooks, United States	48.83
1988	Olga Bryzguina, U.S.S.R.	48.65
1992	Marie Jose-Perec, France	48.83
1996	Marie Jose-Perec, France	48.25

800-Meter Run

1928	Lina Radke, Germany	2:16.80
1960	Ljudmila Shevcova, U.S.S.R.	2:04.30
1964	Ann Packer, Great Britain	2:01.10
1968	Madeline Manning, United States	2:00.90
1972	Hildegard Falck, West Germany	1:58.60

1976	Tatiana Kazankina, U.S.S.R.	1:54.94
1980	Nadezhda Olizarenko, U.S.S.R.	1:53.50
1984	Doina Melinte, Romania	1:57.60
1988	Sigrun Wodars, East Germany	1:56.10
1992	Ellen Van Langen, Netherlands	1:55.54
1993	Svetlana Masterkova, Russia	1:57.73

1,500-Meter Run

1972	Ludmila Bragina, U.S.S.R.	4:01.40
1976	Tatiana Kazankina, U.S.S.R.	4:05.48
1980	Tatiana Kazankina, U.S.S.R.	3:56.60
1984	Gabriella Dorio, Italy	4:03.25
1988	Paula Ivan, Romania	3:53.96
1992	Hassiba Boulmerka, Algeria	3:55.30
1996	Svetlana Masterkova, Russia	4:00.83

5,000-Meter Run

1996	Wang, Jun-Xia, China	14:59.88

10,000-Meter Run

1992	Derartu Tulu, Ethiopia	31:60.02
1996	Fernanda Ribeiro, Portugal	31:01.63

80-Meter Hurdles

1932	Mildred Didrikson, United States	11.70
1936	Trebisonda Valla, Italy	11.70
1948	Fanny Blankers-Koen, Netherlands	11.20
1952	Shirley S. de la Hunty, Australia	10.90
1956	Shirley S. de la Hunty, Australia	10.70
1960	Irina Press, U.S.S.R.	10.80
1964	Karin Balzer, Germany	10.50[1]
1968	Maureen Caird, Australia	10.30

1. Wind assisted.

100-Meter Hurdles

1972	Annelie Ehrhardt, East Germany	12.59
1976	Johanna Schaller, East Germany	12.77
1980	Vera Komisova, U.S.S.R.	12.56
1984	Benita Fitzgerald-Brown, United States	12.84
1988	Jordanka Donkova, Bulgaria	12.38
1992	Paraskevi Patoulidou, Greece	12.64
1996	Ludmila Engquist, Sweden	12.58

400-Meter Hurdles

1984	Nawai El Moutawakel, Morocco	54.61
1988	Debra Flintoff-King, Australia	53.17
1992	Sally Gunnell, Great Britain	53.23
1996	Deon Hemmings, Jamaica	52.82

400-Meter Relay

1928	Canada	48.40
1932	United States	47.00
1936	United States	46.90
1948	Netherlands	47.50
1952	United States	45.90
1956	Australia	44.50
1960	United States	44.50
1964	Poland	43.60
1968	United States	42.80
1972	West Germany	42.81
1976	East Germany	42.50
1980	East Germany	41.60
1984	United States	41.65
1988	United States	41.98
1992	United States	42.11
1996	United States	41.95

1,600-Meter Relay

1972	East Germany	3:23.00
1976	East Germany	3:19.23
1980	U.S.S.R.	3:20.20
1984	United States	3:18.29
1988	United States	3:15.18
1992	Unified Team[1]	3:20.20
1996	United States	3:20.91

1. Former Soviet Union team.

10,000-Meter Walk

1992	ChenYue-Ling, China	44:32
1996	Yelena Nikolayeva, Russia	41:49

Marathon

1984	Joan Benoit, United States	2:24:52
1988	Rose Mota, Portugal	2:25.40
1992	Valentina Yegorova, Unified Team	2:32.41
1996	Fatuma Roba, Ethiopia	2:26.05

Running High Jump

1928	Ethel Catherwood, Canada	5 ft. 3 in.
1932	Jean Shiley, United States	5 ft. 5¼ in.
1936	Ibolya Csak, Hungary	5 ft. 3 in.
1948	Alice Coachman, United States	5 ft. 6⅛ in.
1952	Ester Brand, South Africa	5 ft. 5¾ in.
1956	Mildred McDaniel, United States	5 ft. 9¼ in.
1960	Iolanda Balas, Romania	6 ft. ¾ in.
1964	Iolanda Balas, Romania	6 ft. 2¾ in.
1968	Miloslava Rezkova, Czechoslovakia	5 ft. 11¾ in.
1972	Ulrike Meyfarth, West Germany	6 ft. 3⅝ in.
1976	Rosemarie Ackerman, E. Germany	6 ft. 4 in.
1980	Sara Simeoni, Italy	6 ft. 5½ in.
1984	Ulrike Meyfarth, West Germany	6 ft. 7½ in.
1988	Louise Ritter, United States	6 ft. 8 in.
1992	Heike Henkel, Germany	6 ft. 7½ in.
1996	Stefka Kostadinova, Bulgaria	6 ft. 8¾ in.

Long Jump

1948	Olga Gyarmati, Hungary	18 ft. 8¼ in.
1952	Yvette Williams, New Zealand	20 ft. 5¾ in.
1956	Elzbieta Krzesinska, Poland	20 ft. 9¾ in.
1960	Vera Krepkina, U.S.S.R.	20 ft. 10¾ in.
1964	Mary Rand, Great Britain	22 ft. 2 in.
1968	Viorica Ciscopoleanu, Romania	22 ft. 4½ in.
1972	Heidemarie Rosendahl, West Germany	22 ft. 3 in.
1976	Angela Voigt, East Germany	22 ft. ½ in.
1980	Tatiana Kolpakova, U.S.S.R.	23 ft. 2 in.
1984	Anisoara Stanciu, Romania	22 ft. 10 in.
1988	Jackie Joyner-Kersee, United States	24 ft. 3½ in.
1992	Heike Drechsler, Germany	23 ft. 5¼ in.
1996	Chioma Ajunwa, Nigeria	23 ft. 4½ in.

Triple Jump

1996	Inessa Kravets, Ukraine	50 ft. 3½ in.

Shot-Put

1948	Micheline Ostermeyer, France	45 ft. 1½ in.
1952	Galina Zybina, U.S.S.R.	50 ft. 1½ in.
1956	Tamara Tishkyevich, U.S.S.R.	54 ft. 5 in.
1960	Tamara Press, U.S.S.R.	56 ft. 9⅞ in.
1964	Tamara Press, U.S.S.R.	59 ft. 6 in.
1968	Margitta Gummel, East Germany	64 ft. 4 in.
1972	Nadezhda Chizhova, U.S.S.R.	69 ft.
1976	Ivanka Christova, Bulgaria	69 ft. 5 in.
1980	Ilona Sluplanek, East Germany	73 ft. 6 in.
1984	Claudia Losch, West Germany	67 ft. 2¼ in.
1988	Natalya Lisovskaya, U.S.S.R.	72 ft. 11½ in.
1992	Svetlana Kriveleva, Unified Team[1]	69 ft. 1¼ in.
1996	Astrid Kumbernuss, Germany	67 ft. 5½ in.

1. Former Soviet Union team.

Discus Throw

1928	Helena Konopacka, Poland	129 ft. 11⅞ in.
1932	Lillian Copeland, United States	133 ft. 2 in.
1936	Gisela Mauermayer, Germany	156 ft. 3³⁄₁₆ in.
1948	Micheline Ostermeyer, France	137 ft. 6½ in.
1956	Olga Fikotova, Czechoslovakia	176 ft. 1½ in.
1960	Nina Ponomareva, U.S.S.R.	180 ft. 8¼ in.
1964	Tamara Press, U.S.S.R.	187 ft. 10¾ in.
1968	Lia Manoliu, Romania	191 ft. 2½ in.
1972	Faina Melnik, U.S.S.R.	218 ft. 7 in.
1976	Evelin Schlaak, East Germany	226 ft. 4 in.
1980	Evelin Jahl, East Germany	229 ft. 6½ in.
1984	Ria Stalman, Netherlands	214 ft. 5 in.
1988	Martina Hellmann, East Germany	237 ft. 2¼ in.
1992	Maritza Marten, Cuba	229 ft. 10¼ in.
1996	Ilke Wyludda, Germany	228 ft. 6½ in.

Javelin Throw

1932	Mildred Didrikson, United States	143 ft. 4 in.
1936	Tilly Fleischer, Germany	148 ft. 2¾ in.
1948	Herma Bauma, Austria	149 ft. 6 in.
1952	Dana Zatopek, Czechoslovakia	165 ft. 7 in.
1956	Inessa Janzeme, U.S.S.R.	176 ft. 8 in.
1960	Elvira Ozolina, U.S.S.R.	183 ft. 8 in.
1964	Mihaela Penes, Romania	198 ft. 7½ in.
1968	Angela Nemeth, Hungary	198 ft.
1972	Ruth Fuchs, East Germany	209 ft. 7 in.
1976	Ruth Fuchs, East Germany	216 ft. 4 in.
1980	Maria Colon, Cuba	224 ft. 5 in.
1984	Tessa Sanderson, Britain	228 ft. 2 in.
1988	Petra Felke, East Germany	245 ft.
1992	Silke Renke, Germany	224 ft. 2½ in.
1996	Heli Rantanen, Finland	222 ft. 11 in.

Pentathlon

1964	Irina Press, U.S.S.R.	5,246 pts.
1968	Ingrid Becker, West Germany	5,098 pts.
1972	Mary Peters, Britain	4,801 pts.
1976	Siegrun Siegl, East Germany	4,745 pts.
1980	Nadyeshzhda Tkachenko, U.S.S.R.	5,083 pts.
1984	Daniele Masala, Italy	5,469 pts.
1988	Jackie Joyner-Kersee, United States	7,291 pts.

Heptathlon

1992	Jackie Joyner-Kersee, United States	7,044 pts.
1996	Ghada Shouaa, Syria	6,780 pts.

SWIMMING–MEN

50-Meter Freestyle

1988	Matt Biondi, United States	22.14
1992	Alexander Popov, Unified Team[1]	21.91
1996	Alexander Popov, Russia	22.13

1. Former Soviet Union team.

100-Meter Freestyle

1896	Alfred Hajos, Hungary	1:22.20
1904	Zoltan de Halmay, Hungary	1:02.80[1]
1906	Charles Daniels, United States	1:13.00
1908	Charles Daniels, United States	1:05.60
1912	Duke P. Kahanamoku, United States	1:03.40
1920	Duke P. Kahanamoku, United States	1:01.40
1924	John Weissmuller, United States	0:59.00
1928	John Weissmuller, United States	0:58.60
1932	Yasuji Miyazaki, Japan	0:58.20
1936	Ferenc Csik, Hungary	0:57.60
1948	Walter Ris, United States	0:57.30
1952	Clarke Scholes, United States	0:57.40
1956	Jon Henricks, Australia	0:55.40
1960	John Devitt, Australia	0:55.20
1964	Don Schollander, United States	0:53.40
1968	Michael Wenden, Australia	0:52.20
1972	Mark Spitz, United States	0:51.22
1976	Jim Montgomery, United States	0:49.99
1980	Jorg Woithe, East Germany	0:50.40
1984	Rowdy Gaines, United States	0:49.80
1988	Matt Biondi, United States	0:48.63
1992	Alexander Popov, Unified Team[2]	0:49.02
1996	Alexander Popov, Russia	48.74s

1. 100 yards. 2. Former Soviet Union team.

200-Meter Freestyle

1900	Frederick Lane, Australia	2:25.20
1904	Charles Daniels, United States	2:44.20[1]
1968	Michael Wenden, Australia	1:55.20
1972	Mark Spitz, United States	1:52.78
1976	Bruce Furniss, United States	1:50.29
1980	Sergei Kopiliakov, U.S.S.R.	4:49.81
1984	Michael Gross, West Germany	1:47.44
1988	Duncan Armstrong, Australia	1:47.25
1992	Evgueni Sadovyi, Unified Team[2]	1:46.70
1996	Danyon Loader, New Zealand	1:47.63

1. 220 yards 2. Former Soviet Union team.

400-Meter Freestyle

1896	Paul Neumann, Austria	8:12.60[1]
1904	Charles Daniels, United States	6:16.20[2]
1906	Otto Sheff, Austria	6:23.80
1908	Henry Taylor, Great Britain	5:36.80
1912	George Hodgson, Canada	5:24.40
1920	Norman Ross, United States	5:26.80
1926	John Weissmuller, United States	5:04.20
1928	Albert Zorilla, Argentina	5:01.60
1932	Clarence Crabbe, United States	4:48.40
1936	Jack Medica, United States	4:44.50
1948	William Smith, United States	4:41.00
1952	Jean Boiteux, France	4:30.70
1956	Murray Rose, Australia	4:27.30
1960	Murray Rose, Australia	4:18.30
1964	Don Schollander, United States	4:12.20
1968	Mike Burton, United States	4:09.00
1972	Bradford Cooper, Australia	4:00.27[3]
1976	Brian Goodell, United States	3:51.93
1980	Vladimir Salnikov, U.S.S.R.	3:51.31
1984	George DiCarlo, United States	3:51.23
1988	Uwe Dassier, East Germany	3:46.95
1992	Evgueni Sadovyi, Unified Team	3:45.00[4]
1996	Danyon Loader, New Zealand	3:47.97

1. 500 meters. 2. 440 yards. 3. Rich DeMont, United States, won but was disqualified following day for medical reasons. 4. World record.

1,500-Meter Freestyle

1904	Emil Rausch, Germany	27:18.20[1]
1906	Henry Taylor, Great Britain	28:28.00[2]
1908	Henry Taylor, Great Britain	22:48.40
1912	George Hodgson, Canada	22:00.00
1920	Norman Ross, United States	22:23.20
1924	Andrew Charlton, Australia	20:06.60
1928	Arne Borg, Sweden	19:51.80
1932	Kusuo Kitamura, Japan	19:12.40
1936	Noboru Terada, Japan	19:13.70
1948	James McLane, United States	19:18.50
1952	Ford Konno, United States	18:30.00
1956	Murray Rose, Australia	17:58.90
1960	Jon Konrads, Australia	17:19.60
1964	Robert Windle, Australia	17:01.70
1968	Michael Burton, United States	16:38.90
1972	Michael Burton, United States	15:52.58
1976	Brian Goodell, United States	15:02.40
1980	Vladimir Salnikov, U.S.S.R.	14:58.27
1984	Michael O'Brien, United States	15:05.20
1988	Vladimir Salnikov, U.S.S.R.	15:00.40
1992	Kieren Perkins, Australia	14:43.48
1996	Kieren Perkins, Australia	14:56.40

1. One mile. 2. 1,600 meters

100-Meter Backstroke

1904	Walter Brack, Germany	1:16.80[1]
1908	Arno Bieberstein, Germany	1:24.60
1912	Harry Hebner, United States	1:21.20
1920	Warren Kealoha, United States	1:15.20
1924	Warren Kealoha, United States	1:13.20
1928	George Kojac, United States	1:08.20
1932	Masaji Kiyokawa, Japan	1:08.60
1936	Adolph Kiefer, United States	1:05.90
1948	Allen Stack, United States	1:06.40
1952	Yoshinobu Oyakawa, United States	1:05.40
1956	David Thiele, Australia	1:02.20
1960	David Thiele, Australia	1:01.90
1968	Roland Matthes, East Germany	0:58.70
1972	Roland Matthes, East Germany	0:56.58
1976	John Naber, United States	0:55.49
1980	Bengt Baron, Sweden	0:56.53
1984	Rick Carey, United States	0:55.79

1988	Daichi Suzuki, Japan	0:55.05
1992	Mark Tewksbury, Canada	0:53.98
1996	Jeff Rouse, United States	0:54.10

1. 100 yards

200-Meter Backstroke

1900	Ernst Hoppenberg, Germany	2:47.00
1964	Jed Graef, United States	2:10.30
1968	Roland Matthes, East Germany	2:09.60
1972	Roland Matthes, East Germany	2:02.82
1976	John Naber, United States	1:59.19
1980	Sandor Wladar, Hungary	2:01.93
1984	Rick Carey, United States	2:00.23
1988	Igor Polianski, U.S.S.R.	1:59.37
1992	Martin Lopez Zubero, Spain	1:58.47
1996	Brad Bridgewater, United States	1:58.54

100-Meter Breaststroke

1968	Donald McKenzie, United States	1:07.70
1972	Nobutaka Taguchi, Japan	1:04.94
1976	John Hencken, United States	1:03.11
1980	Duncan Goodhew, Britain	1:03.34
1984	Steve Lindquist, United States	1:01.65
1988	Adrian Moorhouse, Great Britain	1:02.04
1992	Nelson Diebel, United States	1:01.50
1996	Fred Deburghgraeve, Belgium	1:00.60[1]

1. World record.

200-Meter Breaststroke

1908	Frederick Holman, Great Britain	3:09.20
1912	Walter Bathe, Germany	3:01.80
1920	Haken Malmroth, Sweden	3:04.40
1924	Robert Skelton, United States	2:56.60
1928	Yoshiyuki Tsuruta, Japan	2:48.80
1932	Yoshiyuki Tsuruta, Japan	2:45.40
1936	Tetsuo Hamuro, Japan	2:41.50
1948	Joseph Verdeur, United States	2:39.30
1952	John Davies, Australia	2:34.40
1956	Masaura Furukawa, Japan	2:34.70
1960	Bill Muliken, United States	2:37.40
1964	Ian O'Brien, Australia	2:07.80
1968	Felipe Munoz, Mexico	2:28.70
1972	John Hencken, United States	2:21.55
1976	David Willkie, Britain	2:15.11
1980	Robertas Zulpa, U.S.S.R.	2:15.85
1984	Victor Davis, Canada	2:13.34
1988	Jozef Szabo, Hungary	2:13.52
1992	Mike Barrowman, United States	2:10.16
1996	Norbert Rozsa, Hungary	2:12.57

100-Meter Butterfly

1968	Douglas Russell, United States	55.90
1972	Mark Spitz, United States	54.27
1976	Matt Vogel, United States	54.35
1980	Par Arvidsson, Sweden	54.92
1984	Michael Gross, West Germany	53.08
1988	Anthony Nesty, Surinam	53.00
1992	Pablo Morales, United States	53.32
1996	Denis Pankratov, Russia	52.27[1]

1. World record.

200-Meter Butterfly

1956	Bill Yorzyk, United States	2:19.30
1960	Mike Troy, United States	2:12.80
1964	Kevin Berry, Australia	2:06.60
1968	Carl Robie, United States	2:08.70
1972	Mark Spitz, United States	2:00.70
1976	Mike Bruner, United States	1:59.23
1980	Sergei Fesenko, U.S.S.R.	1:59.76
1984	Jon Sieben, Australia	1:57.00
1988	Michael Gross, East Germany	1:56.94
1992	Mel Stewart, United States	1:56.26
1996	Denis Pankratov, Russia	1:56.51

200-Meter Individual Medley

1968	Charles Hickox, United States	2:12.00
1972	Gunnar Larsson, Sweden	2:07.17

1988	Tamas Darnyi, Hungary	2:00.17
1992	Tamas Darnyi, Hungary	2:00.76
1996	Attila Czene, Hungary	1:59.91

400-Meter Individual Medley

1964	Dick Roth, United States	4:45.40
1968	Charles Hickox, United States	4:48.40
1972	Gunnar Larsson, Sweden	4:31.98
1976	Rod Strachan, United States	4:23.68
1980	Aleksandr Sidorenko, U.S.S.R.	4:22.80
1984	Alex Baumann, Canada	4:17.41
1988	Tamas Darnyi, Hungary	4:14.75
1992	Tamas Darnyi, Hungary	4:14.23
1996	Tom Dolan, United States	4:14.90

400-Meter Freestyle Relay

1964	United States	3:32.20
1968	United States	3:31.70
1972	United States	3:26.42
1988	United States	3:16.52
1992	United States	3:16.74
1996	United States	3:15.41

800-Meter Freestyle Relay

1908	Great Britain	10:55.60
1912	Australia	10:11.20
1920	United States	10:04.40
1924	United States	09:53.40
1928	United States	09:36.20
1932	Japan	08:58.40
1936	Japan	08:51.50
1948	United States	08:46.10
1952	United States	08:31.10
1956	Australia	08:23.60
1960	United States	08:10.20
1964	United States	07:52.10
1968	United States	07:52.30
1972	United States	07:35.78
1976	United States	07:23.22
1980	U.S.S.R.	07:23.50
1984	United States	07:16.59
1988	United States	07:12.51
1992	Unified Team[1]	07:11.95
1996	United States	07:14.84

1. Former Soviet Union team.

400-Meter Medley Relay

1960	United States	4:05.40
1964	United States	3:58.40
1968	United States	3:54.90
1972	United States	3:48.16
1976	United States	3:42.22
1980	Australia	3:45.70
1984	United States	3:39.30
1988	United States	3:36.93
1992	United States	3:36.93
1996	United States	3:34.84[1]

1. World record.

Springboard Dive

		Points
1908	Albert Zuerner, Germany	85.50
1912	Paul Guenther, Germany	79.23
1920	Louis Kuehn, United States	675.00
1924	Albert White, United States	696.40
1928	Pete Desjardins, United States	185.04
1932	Michael Galitzen, United States	161.38
1936	Richard Degener, United States	163.57
1948	Bruce Harlan, United States	163.64
1952	David Browning, United States	205.59
1956	Robert Clotworthy, United States	159.56
1960	Gary Tobian, United States	170.00
1964	Ken Sitzberger, United States	159.90
1968	Bernard Wrightson, United States	170.15
1972	Vladimir Vasin, U.S.S.R.	594.09
1976	Phil Boggs, United States	619.05
1980	Alexsandr Portnov, U.S.S.R.	905.02

1984	Greg Louganis, United States	754.41
1988	Greg Louganis, United States	730.80
1992	Mark Lenzi, United States	676.53
1996	Xiong Ni, China	701.46

Platform Dive — **Points**

1904	G.E. Sheldon, United States	12.75
1906	Gottlob Walz, Germany	156.00
1908	Hialmar Johansson, Sweden	83.75
1912	Erik Adlerz, Sweden	73.94
1920	Clarence Pinkston, United States	100.67
1924	Albert White, United States	487.30
1928	Pete Desjardins, United States	98.74
1932	Harold Smith, United States	124.80
1936	Marshall Wayne, United States	113.58
1948	Samuel Lee, United States	130.05
1952	Samuel Lee, United States	156.28
1956	Joaquin Capilla, Mexico	152.44
1960	Bob Webster, United States	165.56
1964	Bob Webster, United States	148.58
1968	Klaus Dibiasi, Italy	164.18
1972	Klaus Dibiasi, Italy	504.12
1976	Klaus Dibiasi, Italy	600.51
1980	Falk Hoffman, E. Germany	835.65
1984	Greg Louganis, United States	710.91
1988	Greg Louganis, United States	638.61
1992	Sun, Shu-Wei, China	677.31
1996	Dmitri Saoutine, Russia	692.34

SWIMMING–WOMEN

50-Meter Freestyle

1988	Kristin Otto, East Germany	25.49
1992	Yang, Wen-Yi, China	24.79
1996	Amy Van Dyken, United States	24.87

100-Meter Freestyle

1912	Fanny Durack, Australia	1:22.20
1920	Ethelda Bleibtrey, United States	1:13.60
1924	Ethel Lackie, United States	1:12.40
1928	Albina Osipowich, United States	1:11.00
1932	Helene Madison, United States	1:06.80
1936	Hendrika Mastenbroek, Netherlands	1:05.90
1948	Greta Andersen, Denmark	1:06.30
1952	Katalin Szoke, Hungary	1:06.80
1956	Dawn Fraser, Australia	1:02.00
1960	Dawn Fraser, Australia	1:01.20
1964	Dawn Fraser, Australia	0:59.50
1968	Marge Jan Henne, United States	1:00.00
1972	Sandra Neilson, United States	0:58.59
1976	Kornelia Ender, East Germany	0:55.65
1980	Barbara Krause, East Germany	0:54.79
1984	Carrie Steinseifer, United States	0:55.92
1988	Kristin Otto, East Germany	0:54.93
1992	Zhuang Yong, China	0:54.64
1996	Le Jingyi, China	0:54.50

200-Meter Freestyle

1968	Debbie Meyer, United States	2:10.50
1972	Shane Gould, Australia	2:03.56
1976	Kornelia Ender, East Germany	1:59.26
1980	Barbara Krause, East Germany	1:58.33
1984	Mary Wayle, United States	1:59.23
1988	Heike Friedrich, East Germany	1:57.65
1992	Nicole Haislett, United States	1:57.90
1996	Claudia Poll, Costa Rica	1:58.16

400-Meter Freestyle

1920	Ethelda Bleibtrey, United States	4:34.00[1]
1924	Martha Norelius, United States	6:02.20
1928	Martha Norelius, United States	5:42.80
1932	Helene Madison, United States	5:28.50
1936	Hendrika Mastenbroek, Netherlands	5:26.40
1948	Ann Curtis, United States	5:17.80
1952	Valerie Gyenge, Hungary	5:12.10
1956	Lorraine Crapp, Australia	4:54.60

1960	Chris von Saltza, United States	4:50.60
1964	Ginny Duenkel, United States	4:43.30
1968	Debbie Meyer, United States	4:31.80
1972	Shane Gould, Australia	4:19.04
1976	Petra Thumer, East Germany	4:09.89
1980	Ines Diers, East Germany	4:08.76
1984	Tiffany Cohen, United States	4:07.10
1988	Janet Evans, United States	4:03.85
1992	Dagmar Hase, Germany	4:07.18
1996	Michelle Smith, Ireland	4:07.25

1. 300 meters.

800-Meter Freestyle

1968	Debbie Meyer, United States	9:24.00
1972	Keena Rothhammer, United States	8:53.68
1976	Petra Thumer, East Germany	8:37.14
1980	Michelle Ford, Australia	8:28.90
1984	Tiffany Cohen, United States	8:24.95
1988	Janet Evans, United States	8:20.20
1992	Janet Evans, Unites States	8:25.52
1996	Brooke Bennett, Unites States	8:27.89

100-Meter Backstroke

1924	Sybil Bauer, United States	1:23.20
1928	Marie Braun, Netherlands	1:22.00
1932	Eleanor Holm, United States	1:19.40
1936	Dina Senff, Netherlands	1:18.90
1948	Karen Harup, Denmark	1:14.40
1952	Joan Harrison, South Africa	1:14.30
1956	Judy Grinham, Great Britain	1:12.90
1960	Lynn Burke, United States	1:09.30
1964	Cathy Ferguson, United States	1:07.70
1968	Kaye Hall, United States	1:06.20
1972	Melissa Belote, United States	1:05.78
1976	Ulrike Richter, East Germany	1:01.83
1980	Rica Reinisch, East Germany	1:00.86
1984	Theresa Andrews, United States	1:02.55
1988	Kristin Otto, East Germany	1:00.89
1992	Krisztina Egerszegi, Hungary	1:00.68
1996	Beth Botsford, United States	1:01.19

200-Meter Backstroke

1968	Pokey Watson, United States	2:24.80
1972	Melissa Belote, United States	2:19.19
1976	Ulrike Richter, East Germany	2:13.43
1980	Rica Reinisch, East Germany	2:11.77
1984	Jolanda DeRover, Netherlands	2:12.38
1988	Krisztina Egerszegi, Hungary	2:09.29
1992	Krisztina Egerszegi, Hungary	2:07.06
1996	Krisztina Egerszegi, Hungary	2:07.83

100-Meter Breaststroke

1968	Djurdjica Bjedov, Yugoslavia	1:15.80
1972	Catherine Carr, United States	1:13.58
1976	Hannelore Anke, East Germany	1:11.16
1980	Ute Geweniger, East Germany	1:10.22
1984	Petra Van Staveren, Netherlands	1:09.88
1988	Tainia Dangalakova, Bulgaria	1:07.95
1992	Elena Roudkovskaia, Unified Team	1:08.00
1996	Penny Heyns, South Africa	1:07.73

200-Meter Breaststroke

1924	Lucy Morton, Great Britain	3:33.20
1928	Hilde Schrader, Germany	3:12.60
1932	Clare Dennis, Australia	3:06.30
1936	Hideko Maehata, Japan	3:03.60
1948	Nel van Vliet, Netherlands	2:57.20
1952	Eva Szekely, Hungary	2:51.70
1956	Ursula Happe, Germany	2:53.10
1960	Anita Lonsbrough, Great Britain	2:49.50
1964	Galina Prozumenschikova, U.S.S.R.	2:46.40
1968	Sharon Wichman, United States	2:44.40
1972	Beverly Whitfield, Australia	2:41.71
1976	Marina Koshevaia, U.S.S.R.	2:33.35
1980	Lina Kachushite, U.S.S.R.	2:29.54
1984	Anne Ottenbrite, Canada	2:30.38

1988	Silke Hoerner, East Germany	2:26.71
1992	Kyoko Iwasaki, Japan	2:26.65
1996	Penny Heyns, South Africa	2:25.41

100-Meter Butterfly

1956	Shelley Mann, United States	1:11.00
1960	Carolyn Schuler, United States	1:09.50
1964	Sharon Stouder, United States	1:04.70
1968	Lynn McClements, Australia	1:05.50
1972	Mayumi Aoki, Japan	1:03.34
1976	Kornelia Ender, East Germany	1:00.13
1980	Caren Metschuck, East Germany	1:00.42
1984	Mary Meagher, United States	0:59.26
1988	Kristin Otto, East Germany	0:59.00
1992	Qian Hong, China	0:58.62
1996	Amy Van Dyken, United States	0:59.13

200-Meter Butterfly

1968	Ada Kok, Netherlands	2:24.70
1972	Karen Moe, United States	2:15.57
1976	Andrea Pollack, East Germany	2:11.41
1980	Ines Geissler, East Germany	2:10.44
1984	Mary Meagher, United States	2:06.90
1988	Kathleen Nord, East Germany	2:09.51
1992	Summer Sanders, United States	2:06.67
1996	Susan O'Neill, Australia	2:07.76

200-Meter Individual Medley

1968	Claudia Kolb, United States	2:24.70
1972	Shane Gould, Australia	2:23.07
1984	Tracy Caulkins, United States	2:12.64
1988	Daniela Hunger, East Germany	2:12.59
1992	Lin Lee, China	2:11.55[1]
1996	Michelle Smith, Ireland	2:13.93

1. World record.

400-Meter Individual Medley

1964	Donna de Varona, United States	5:18.70
1968	Claudia Kolb, United States	5:08.50
1972	Gail Neall, Australia	5:02.97
1976	Ulrike Tauber, East Germany	4:42.77
1980	Petra Schneider, East Germany	4:36.29
1984	Tracy Caulkins, United States	4:39.21
1988	Janet Evans, United States	4:37.76
1992	Krisztina Egerszegi, Hungary	4:36.54
1996	Michelle Smith, Ireland	4:39.18

400-Meter Freestyle Relay

1912	Great Britain	5:52.80
1920	United States	5:11.60
1924	United States	4:58.80
1928	United States	4:47.60
1932	United States	4:38.00

DISTRIBUTION OF MEDALS—1996 SUMMER GAMES

Country	Gold	Silver	Bronze	Total	Country	Gold	Silver	Bronze	Total
United States	44	32	25	101	Ethiopia	2	0	1	3
Germany	20	18	27	65	Algeria	2	0	1	3
Russia	26	21	16	63	Iran	1	1	1	3
China	16	22	12	50	Slovakia	1	1	1	3
Australia	9	9	23	41	Argentina	0	2	1	3
France	15	7	15	37	Austria	0	1	2	3
Italy	13	10	12	35	Armenia	1	1	0	2
South Korea	7	15	5	27	Croatia	1	1	0	2
Cuba	9	8	8	25	Portugal	1	0	1	2
Ukraine	9	2	12	23	Thailand	1	0	1	2
Canada	3	11	8	22	Namibia	0	2	0	2
Hungary	7	4	10	21	Slovenia	0	2	0	2
Romania	4	7	9	20	Malaysia	0	1	1	2
Netherlands	4	5	10	19	Moldova	0	1	1	2
Poland	7	5	5	17	Uzbekistan	0	1	1	2
Spain	5	6	6	17	Georgia	0	0	2	2
Britain	1	8	7	16	Morocco	0	0	2	2
Bulgaria	3	7	5	15	Trinidad & Tobago	0	0	2	2
Belarus	1	6	8	15	Burundi	1	0	0	1
Brazil	3	2	10	15	Costa Rica	1	0	0	1
Japan	3	6	5	14	Ecuador	1	0	0	1
Czech Republic	4	3	4	11	Hong Kong	1	0	0	1
Kazakhstan	3	4	4	11	Syria	1	0	0	1
Greece	4	4	0	8	Azerbaijan	0	1	0	1
Sweden	2	4	2	8	Bahamas	0	1	0	1
Kenya	1	4	3	8	Latvia	0	1	0	1
Switzerland	4	3	0	7	Philippines	0	1	0	1
Norway	2	2	3	7	Taiwan	0	1	0	1
Denmark	4	1	1	6	Tonga	0	1	0	1
Turkey	4	1	1	6	Zambia	0	1	0	1
New Zealand	3	2	1	6	India	0	0	1	1
Belgium	2	2	2	6	Israel	0	0	1	1
Nigeria	2	1	3	6	Lithuania	0	0	1	1
Jamaica	1	3	2	6	Mexico	0	0	1	1
South Africa	3	1	1	5	Mongolia	0	0	1	1
North Korea	2	1	2	5	Mozambique	0	0	1	1
Ireland	3	0	1	4	Puerto Rico	0	0	1	1
Finland	1	2	1	4	Tunisia	0	0	1	1
Indonesia	1	1	2	4	Uganda	0	0	1	1
Yugoslavia	1	1	2	4					

1936	Netherlands	4:36.00
1948	United States	4:29.20
1952	Hungary	4:24.40
1956	Australia	4:17.10
1960	United States	4:08.90
1964	United States	4:03.80
1968	United States	4:02.50
1972	United States	3:55.19
1976	United States	3:44.82
1980	East Germany	3:42.71
1984	United States	3:44.43
1988	East Germany	3:40.63
1992	United States	3:39.46
1996	United States	3:39.29

800-Meter Freestyle Relay

1996	United States	7:59.87

400-Meter Medley Relay

1960	United States	4:41.10
1964	United States	4:33.90
1968	United States	4:28.30
1972	United States	4:20.75
1976	East Germany	4:07.95
1980	East Germany	4:06.67
1984	United States	4:08.34
1988	East Germany	4:03.74
1992	United States	4:02.54[1]
1996	United States	4:02.88

1. World record.

Springboard Dive — Points

1920	Aileen Riggin, United States	539.90
1924	Elizabeth Becker, United States	474.50
1928	Helen Meany, United States	78.62
1932	Georgia Coleman, United States	87.52
1936	Marjorie Gestring, United States	89.27
1948	Victoria M. Draves, United States	108.74
1952	Patricia McCormick, United States	147.30
1956	Patricia McCormick, United States	142.36
1960	Ingrid Kramer, Germany	155.81
1964	Ingrid Kramer Engel, Germany	145.00
1968	Sue Gossick, United States	150.77
1972	Micki King, United States	450.03
1976	Jennifer Chandler, United States	506.19
1980	Irina Kalinina, U.S.S.R.	725.91
1984	Sylvie Bernier, Canada	530.70
1988	Gao Min, China	580.23
1992	Gao Min, China	572.40
1996	Fu Ming-Xia, China	547.68

Platform Dive — Points

1912	Greta Johansson, Sweden	39.90
1920	Stefani Fryland, Denmark	34.60
1924	Caroline Smith, United States	166.00
1928	Elizabeth B. Pinkston, United States	31.60
1932	Dorothy Poynton, United States	40.26
1936	Dorothy Poynton Hill, United States	33.92
1948	Victoria M. Draves, United States	68.87
1952	Patricia McCormick, United States	79.37
1956	Patricia McCormick, United States	84.85
1960	Ingrid Kramer, Germany	91.28
1964	Lesley Bush, United States	99.80
1968	Milena Duchkova, Czechoslovakia	109.59
1972	Ulrika Knape, Sweden	390.00
1976	Elena Vaytsekhovskaia, U.S.S.R.	406.59
1980	Martina Jaschke, East Germany	596.25
1984	Zhou Ji-Hong, China	435.51
1988	Xu Yan-Mei, China	445.20
1992	Fu Ming-Xia, China	461.43
1996	Fu Ming-Xia, China	521.58

BASKETBALL–MEN

1904	United States	1972	U.S.S.R.
1936	United States	1976	United States
1948	United States	1980	Yugoslavia
1952	United States	1984	United States
1956	United States	1988	U.S.S.R.
1960	United States	1992	United States
1964	United States	1996	United States
1968	United States		

BASKETBALL–WOMEN

1976	U.S.S.R.	1988	United States
1980	U.S.S.R.	1992	Unified Team[1]
1984	United States	1996	United States

1. Former Soviet Union team.

BOXING

(U.S. winners only)

NOTE: U.S. boycotted Olympics in 1980.

Flyweight-112 pounds (51 kilograms)

1904	George Finnegan	1952	Nate Brooks
1920	Frank De Genaro	1976	Leo Randolph
1924	Fidel La Barba	1984	Steve McCrory

Bantamweight-119 (54 kg)

1904	O.L. Kirk	1988	Kennedy McKinney

Featherweight-126 pounds (57 kg)

1904	O.L. Kirk	1984	Meldrick Taylor
1924	Jackie Fields		

Lightweight-132 pounds (60 kg)

1904	H.J. Spanger	1976	Howard Davis
1920	Samuel Mosberg	1984	Pernell Whitaker
1968	Ronnie Harris	1992	Oscar De La Hoya

Light Welterweight-140 pounds (63.5 kg)

1952	Charles Adkins	1976	Ray Leonard
1972	Ray Seales	1984	Jerry Page

Welterweight-148 pounds (67 kg)

1904	Al Young	1984	Mark Breland
1932	Edward Flynn		

Light Middleweight-157 pounds (71 kg)

1960	Wilbert McClure	1996	David Reid
1984	Frank Tate		

Middleweight-165 pounds (75 kg)

1904	Charles Mayer	1960	Eddie Cook
1932	Carmen Barth	1976	Michael Spinks
1952	Floyd Patterson		

Light Heavyweight-179 pounds (81 kg)

1920	Edward Eagan	1960	Cassius Clay
1952	Norvel Lee	1976	Leon Spinks
1956	James Boyd	1988	Andrew Maynard

Heavyweight-201 pounds

1904	Sam Berger	1968	George Foreman
1952	Edward Sanders	1984	Henry Tilman
1956	Pete Rademacher	1988	Ray Mercer
1964	Joe Frazier		

Super Heavyweight (unlimited)

1984	Tyrell Biggs

Other 1996 Summer Olympic Games Champions

Archery
Women's individual—Kim Kyung Wook, South Korea
Women's team—South Korea
Men's individual—Justin Huish, United States
Men's team—United States

Badminton
Men's singles—Poul-Erik Hoyer-Larsen, Denmark
Men's doubles—Indonesia (Rexy Mainaky, Ricky Subagja)
Women's singles—Bang Soo-Hyun, South Korea
Women's doubles—China (Ge Fei, Gu Jun)
Mixed doubles—South Korea (Gil Young-Ahl, Kim Dong-Moon)

Baseball
Men—Cuba

Beach Volleyball
Women—Jackie Silva/Sandra Pires, Brazil
Men—Karch Kiraly/Kent Steffes, United States

Canoe-Kayak—Men
Canoe single slalom—Michal Martikan, Slovakia
Canoe slalom pairs—France
Kayak slalom singles—Oliver Fix, Germany
Canoe singles 500m—Martin Doktor, Czech Republic
Canoe singles 1,000m—Martin Doktor, Czech Republic
Canoe pairs 500m—Csaba Horvath/Gyorgy Kolonics, Hungary
Canoe pairs 1,000m—Andreas Dittmer/Gunar Kirchbach, Germany
Kayak singles 500m—Antonio Rossi, Italy
Kayak singles 1,000m—Knut Holmann, Norway
Kayak pairs 500m—Kay Bluhm/Torsten Gutsche, Germany
Kayak pairs 1,000m—Antonio Rossi/Daniele Scarpa, Italy
Kayak fours 1,000m—Germany

Kayak—Women
Single slalom—Stepnka Hilgertova, Czech Republic
500m singles—Rita Koban, Hungary
500m pairs—Agneta Andersson/Susanne Gunnarsson, Sweden
500m pairs—Germany

Cycling—Men
Individual road race—Pascal Richard, Switzerland
1 km time trial—Florian Rousseau, France
Individual pursuit—Andrea Collinelli, Italy
Individual spring—Jens Fiedler, Germany
Individual point race—Silvio Martinello, Italy
Team pursuit—France
Cross country—Bart Jan Brentjens, Netherlands
Individual time trial—Miguel Indurain, Spain

Cycling—Women
Individual road race—Jeannie Longo-Ciprelli, France
Track sprint—Felicia Ballanger, France
Individual pursuit—Antonella Bellutti, Italy
Point race—Nathalie Lancien, France
Cross country—Paola Pezzo, Italy
Individual time trial—Zulfiya Zabirova, Russia

Equestrian
Three-day team event—Australia
Individual three-day—Blyth Tait, New Zealand
Team dressage—Germany
Individual dressage—Isabell Werth, Germany
Team jumping—Germany
Show jumping—Ulrich Kirchhoff, Germany

Fencing—Men
Individual epee—Aleksandr Beketov, Russia
Individual sabre—Stanislav Pozydnakov, Russia
Individual foil—Alessandro Puccini, Italy
Team epee—Italy
Team sabre—Russia
Team foil—Russia

Fencing—Women
Individual epee—Laura Flessel, France
Individual foil—Laura Badea, Romania
Team epee—France
Team foil—Italy

Field Hockey
Women—Australia
Men—Netherlands

Gymnastics—Men
Team—Russia
All-around—Li Xiao-Shuang, China
Floor exercise—Ioannis Melissanidis, Greece
Vault—Alexei Nemov, Russia
Parallel bars—Rustram Sharipov, Ukraine
High bar—Andreas Wecker, Germany
Pommel horse—Li Dong-Hua, Switzerland
Rings—Yuri Chechi, Italy

Gymnastics—Women
Team—United States
All-around—Lilia Podkopayeva, Ukraine
Balance beam—Shannon Miller, United States
Floor exercise—Lilia Podkopayeva, Ukraine
Uneven bars—Svetlana Chorkina, Russia
Vault—Simona Amanar, Romania

Judo—Men
Extra-lightweight—Tadahiro Nomura, Japan
Half-lightweight—Udo Quellmalz, Germany
Lightweight—Kenzo Nakamura, Japan
Half-middleweight—Djamel Bouras, France
Middleweight—Jeon Ki Young, South Korea
Light-heavyweight—Pawel Nastula, Poland
Heavyweight—David Douillet, France

Judo—Women
Extra-lightweight—Sun Kye, North Korea
Half-lightweight—Marie-Claire Restoux, France
Lightweight—Driulis Gonzalez, Cuba
Half-middleweight—Yuko Emoto, Japan
Middleweight—Cho Min Sun, South Korea
Light-heavyweight—Ulla Werbrouck, Belgium
Heavyweight—Sun Fu-Ming, China

Modern Pentathlon
Individual—Aleksandr Parygin, Kazakhstan

Rhythmic Gymnastics
Team—Spain
Individual—Ekaterina Serebryanskaya, Ukraine

Rowing—Men
Coxless pairs—Great Britain
Coxless four—Australia
Single sculls—Xeno Müller, Switzerland
Double sculls—Italy
Lightweight double sculls—Switzerland
Eight—Netherlands
Quadruple sculls—Germany
Lightweight coxless four—Denmark

Rowing—Women
Coxless pairs—Australia
Single sculls—Yekaterina Khodotovich, Belarus
Double sculls—Canada
Eight—Romania
Quadruple sculls—Germany
Lightweight double sculls—Romania

Shooting—Women
10m air rifle—Renata Mauer, Poland
10m air pistol—Olga Klochneva, Russia
Double trap—Kim Rhode, United States
Rifle three position—Aleksandra Ivosev, Yugoslavia
24m sport pistol—Li Dui-Hong, China

Shooting—Men

10m air pistol—Roberto Di Donna, Italy
Trap—Michael Diamond, Australia
Air rifle—Artem Khadzhibekov, Russia
50m free pistol—Boris Kokorev, Russia
Double trap—Russell Mark, Australia
25m rapid fire pistol—Ralf Schumann, Germany
50m rifle prone—Christian Klees, Germany
Running game target—Yank Ling, China
50m free rifle 3-position—Jean-Pierre Amat, France
Skeet shooting—Ennio Falco, Italy

Soccer

Women—United States
Men—Nigeria

Softball

United States

Synchronized Swimming

Team—United States

Table Tennis

Women's singles—Deng Ya-Ping, China
Women's doubles—China (Deng Ya-Ping, Qiao Hong)
Men's singles—Liu Guo-Liang, China
Men's doubles—China (Kong Ling-Hui, Liu, Guo-Liang)

Team Handball

Women—Denmark
Men—Croatia

Tennis

Men's singles—Andre Agassi, United States
Men's doubles—Todd Woodbridge and Mark Woodforde, Australia
Women's singles—Lindsay Davenport, United States
Women's doubles—Gigi Fernandez and Mary Jo Fernandez, United States

Volleyball

Women—Cuba
Men—Netherlands

Water Polo

Spain

Weightlifting

119 lb—Halil Mutlu, Turkey
130 lb—Tang Ling-Shen, China
141 lb—Naim Suleymanoglu, Turkey
154 lb—Zhan Xu-Gang, China
161.5 lb—Pablo Lara, Cuba
183 lb—Pyrros Dias, Greece
200.5 lb—Aleksey Petrov, Russia
218 lb—Akakide Kakiashvilis, Greece
238 lb—Timur Taimazov, Ukraine
238+ lb—Andre Chemerkin, Russia

Wrestling—Greco-Roman

105.5 lb—Sim Kwon-Ho, South Korea
114.5 lb—Armen Nazaryan, Armenia
125.5 lb—Yuri Melnichenko, Kazakhstan

136.5 lb—Wlodzimierz Zwadzki, Poland
149.5 lb—Ryszard Wolny, Poland
163 lb—Feliberto Ascuy Aquilera, Cuba
180.5 lb—Hamza Yerlikiya, Turkey
198 lb—Vyacheslav Oleynyk, Ukraine
220 lb—Andrzej Wronski, Poland
286 lb—Aleksandr Karelin, Russia

Wrestling—Freestyle

105.5 lb—Kim Il, North Korea
114.5 lb—Valentin Jordanov, Bulgaria
125.5 lb—Kendall Cross, United States
136.5 lb—Tom Brands, United States
149.5 lb—Vadim Bogiev, Russia
163 lb—Bouvaisa Satiev, Russia
180.5 lb—Khadzhimurad Magomedov, Russia
198.5 lb—Rsaul Khadem, Iran
220 lb—Kurt Angle, United States
286 lb—Mahmut Demir, Turkey

Yachting

Men's Mistral—Nikolaos Kaklamanakis, Greece
Men's 470—Ukraine
Men's Finn—Mateusz Kusznierewicz, Poland
Women's Mistral—Lee Lai-Shan, Hong Kong
Women's Europe—Kristine Rough, Denmark
Women's 470—Spain
Open Laser—Robert Scheidt, Brazil
Open Tornado—Spain
Open Soling—Germany
Open Star—Brazil

Iditarod

27TH IDITAROD TRAIL SLED DOG RACE—1999

(Anchorage to Nome, Alaska, March 8–17, 1999)

The annual race stretches from Anchorage to Nome, Alaska. Begun in 1973, the course follows an old frozen river route and is named after a deserted mining town along the way. In even-numbered years, the trail follows the 1,151-mile long Northern Route, while in odd-numbered years it takes the slightly different 1,161-mile Southern Route. The Iditarod also commemorates a famous midwinter emergency mission to get medical supplies to Nome during a 1925 diphtheria epidemic. Men and women mushers compete together.

1999 Champion:

Doug Swingley of Lincoln, Mont., 45 years old, won the 27th annual Iditarod Trail Sled Dog Race on March 17, 1999. Swingley, who also won the race in 1995, reached Nome and the finish line of the 1,161-mile course in 9 days, 14 hours, 31 minutes, and 7 seconds. Swingley is the only musher from outside of Alaska to win the race. The Iditarod began March 8 in Anchorage. Swingley took home $60,000 and a new truck. Martin Buser, of Big Lake, Alaska, came in second with a time of 9 days, 23 hours, and 10 minutes.

Winning times since 1980:

1980, Joe May, 14 days-7 hours-11 minutes; 1981, Rick Swenson, 12-8-45; 1982, Rick Swenson, 16-4-40; 1983, Rick Mackey, 12-14-10; 1984, Dean Osmar, 12-15-7; 1985, Libby Riddles, 18-00-20; 1986, Susan Butcher, 11-15-6; 1987, Susan Butcher, 11-2-5; 1988, Susan Butcher, 11-11-41; 1989, Joe Runyan, 11-5-24; 1990, Susan Butcher, 11-1-34; 1991, Rick Swenson, 12-16-34; 1992, Martin Buser, 10-19-17; 1993, Jeff King, 10-15-38; 1994, Martin Buser, 10-13-2; 1995, Doug Swingley, 9-2-42; 1996, Jeff King, 9-5-43; 1997, Martin Buser, 9-8-31; 1998, Jeff King, 9-5-52; 1999, Doug Swingley, 9-14-31.

Football

The pastime of kicking around a ball goes back beyond the limits of recorded history. Ancient savage tribes played football of a primitive kind. There was a ball-kicking game played by Athenians, Spartans, and Corinthians 2500 years ago, which the Greeks called *Episkuros*. The Romans had a somewhat similar game called *Harpastum* and are supposed to have carried the game with them when they invaded the British Isles in the First Century, B.C.

Undoubtedly the game known in the United States as football traces directly to the English game of rugby, though the modifications have been many. Informal football was played on college lawns well over a century ago, and an annual freshman-sophomore series of "scrimmages" began at Yale in 1840. The first formal intercollegiate football game was the Princeton-Rutgers contest at New Brunswick, N.J. on Nov. 6, 1869, with Rutgers winning by 6 goals to 4.

In those days, games were played with 25, 20, 15, or 11 men on a side. In 1880, there was a convention at which Walter Camp of Yale persuaded the delegates to agree to a rule calling for 11 players on a side.

The first professional game was played in 1895 at Latrobe, Pa. The National Football League was founded in 1921. The All-American Conference went into action in 1946. At the end of the 1949 season the two circuits merged, retaining the name of the older league. In 1960, the American Football League began operations. In 1970, the leagues merged. The United States Football League played its first season in 1983, from March to July. It suspended spring operations after the 1985 season, and planned a 1986 move to fall, but suspended operations again.

In 1991, another effort at spring football was launched, but this time it had the backing of the National Football League. The World League of American Football debuted in March 1991 with ten teams. Three of them were in Europe. The other seven were in North America, including the Montreal Machine in Canada. With television contracts signed with ABC and USA Cable Network, the league seemed to be on sound footing from the beginning. But after just two seasons, it was suspended. The league returned in 1995, with six teams in Europe. In 1998, it was renamed the NFL Europe League.

College Football

NATIONAL COLLEGE FOOTBALL CHAMPIONS

The "National Collegiate Athletic Association Football Guide" recognizes as unofficial national champion the team selected each year by press association polls of writers and coaches.

1936	Minnesota	1951	Tennessee	1964	Alabama	1975	Oklahoma	1989	Miami
1937	Pittsburgh	1952	Mich. State	1965	Alabama and	1976	Pittsburgh	1990	Colorado and
1938	Texas Christian	1953	Maryland		Mich. State	1977	Notre Dame		Georgia Tech
1939	Texas A & M	1954	Ohio State and	1966	Notre Dame	1978	Alabama and	1991	Miami and
1940	Minnesota		UCLA	1967	So. Calif.		So. Calif.		Washington
1941	Minnesota	1955	Oklahoma	1968	Ohio State	1979	Alabama	1992	Alabama
1942	Ohio State	1956	Oklahoma	1969	Texas	1980	Georgia	1993	Florida State
1943	Notre Dame	1957	Auburn and	1970	Texas and	1981	Clemson	1994	Nebraska
1944	Army		Ohio State		Nebraska	1982	Penn State	1995	Nebraska
1945	Army	1958	Louisiana State	1971	Nebraska	1983	Miami	1996	Univ. of Florida
1946	Notre Dame	1959	Syracuse	1972	So. Calif.	1984	Brigham Young	1997	Michigan and
1947	Notre Dame	1960	Minnesota	1973	Notre Dame	1985	Oklahoma		Nebraska
1948	Michigan	1961	Alabama		and U. of Ala.	1986	Penn State	1998	Tennessee
1949	Notre Dame	1962	So. Calif.	1974	Oklahoma and	1987	Miami		
1950	Oklahoma	1963	Texas		So. Calif.	1988	Notre Dame		

RECORD OF ANNUAL MAJOR COLLEGE FOOTBALL BOWL GAMES

Rose Bowl (At Pasadena, Calif.)

1902	Michigan 49, Stanford 0	1929	Georgia Tech 8, California 7	1948	Michigan 49, So. Calif. 0
1916	Washington State 14, Brown 0	1930	So. Calif. 47, Pittsburgh 14	1949	Northwestern 20, California 14
1917	Oregon 14, Pennsylvania 0	1931	Alabama 24, Wash. State 0	1950	Ohio State 17, California 14
1918	Mare Island Marines 19, Camp Lewis 7	1932	So. Calif. 21, Tulane 12	1951	Michigan 14, California 6
		1933	So. Calif. 35, Pittsburgh 0	1952	Illinois 40, Stanford 7
1919	Great Lakes 17, Mare Island Marines 0	1934	Columbia 7, Stanford 0	1953	So. Calif. 7, Wisconsin 0
		1935	Alabama 29, Stanford 13	1954	Michigan State 28, UCLA 20
1920	Harvard 7, Oregon 6	1936	Stanford 7, So. Methodist 0	1955	Ohio State 20, So. Calif. 7
1921	California 28, Ohio State 0	1937	Pittsburgh 21, Washington 0	1956	Michigan State 17, UCLA 14
1922	Washington and Jefferson 0, California 0	1938	California 13, Alabama 0	1957	Iowa 35, Oregon State 19
		1939	So. Calif. 7, Duke 3	1958	Ohio State 10, Oregon 7
		1940	So. Calif. 14, Tennessee 0	1959	Iowa 38, California 12
		1941	Stanford 21, Nebraska 13	1960	Washington 44, Wisconsin 8
1923	So. Calif. 14, Penn State 3	1942	Oregon State 20, Duke 16[1]	1961	Washington 17, Minnesota 7
1924	Navy 14, Washington 14	1943	Georgia 9, UCLA 0	1962	Minnesota 21, UCLA 3
1925	Notre Dame 27, Stanford 10	1944	So. Calif. 29, Washington 0	1963	So. Calif. 42, Wisconsin 37
1926	Alabama 20, Washington 19	1945	So. Calif. 25, Tennessee 0	1964	Illinois 17, Washington 7
1927	Alabama 7, Stanford 7	1946	Alabama 34, So. Calif. 14	1965	Michigan 34, Oregon State 7
1928	Stanford 7, Pittsburgh 6	1947	Illinois 45, UCLA 14	1966	UCLA 14, Michigan State 12

1967	Purdue 14, So. Calif. 13	1966	Alabama 39, Nebraska 28	1961	Mississippi 14, Rice 6
1968	So. Calif. 14, Indiana 3	1967	Florida 27, Georgia Tech 12	1962	Alabama 10, Arkansas 3
1969	Ohio State 27, So. Calif. 16	1968	Oklahoma 26, Tennessee 24	1963	Mississippi 17, Arkansas 13
1970	So. Calif. 10, Michigan 3	1969	Penn State 15, Kansas 14	1964	Alabama 12, Mississippi 7
1971	Stanford 27, Ohio State 17	1970	Penn State 10, Missouri 3	1965	Louisiana State 13,
1972	Stanford 13, Michigan 12	1971	Nebraska 17, Louisiana		Syracuse 10
1973	So. Calif. 42, Ohio State 17		State 12	1966	Missouri 20, Florida 18
1974	Ohio State 42, So. Calif. 21	1972	Nebraska 38, Alabama 6	1967	Alabama 34, Nebraska 7
1975	So. Calif. 18, Ohio State 17	1973	Nebraska 40, Notre Dame 6	1968	Louisiana State 20,
1976	UCLA 23, Ohio State 10	1974	Penn State 16, Louisiana		Wyoming 13
1977	So. Calif. 14, Michigan 6		State 9	1969	Arkansas 16, Georgia 2
1978	Washington 27, Michigan 20	1975	Notre Dame 13, Alabama 11	1970	Mississippi 27, Arkansas 22
1979	So. Calif. 17, Michigan 10	1976	Oklahoma 14, Michigan 6	1971	Tennessee 34, Air Force
1980	So. Calif. 17, Ohio State 16	1977	Ohio State 27, Colorado 10		Academy 13
1981	Michigan 23, Washington 6	1978	Arkansas 31, Oklahoma 6	1972	Oklahoma 40, Auburn 22
1982	Washington 28, Iowa 0	1979	Oklahoma 31, Nebraska 24	1973	Oklahoma 14, Penn State 0
1983	UCLA 24, Michigan 14	1980	Oklahoma 24, Florida State 7	1974	Notre Dame 24, Alabama 23
1984	UCLA 45, Illinois 9	1981	Oklahoma 18, Florida State 17	1975	Nebraska 13, Florida 10
1985	So. Calif. 20, Ohio St. 17	1982	Clemson 22, Nebraska 15	1976	Alabama 13, Penn State 6
1986	UCLA 45, Iowa 28	1983	Nebraska 21, Louisiana	1977	Pittsburgh 27, Georgia 3
1987	Arizona State 22, Michigan 15		State 20	1978	Alabama 35, Ohio State 6
1988	Michigan State 20, So. Calif. 17	1984	Miami (Fla.) 31, Nebraska 30	1979	Alabama 14, Penn State 7
1989	Michigan 22, So. Calif. 14	1985	Washington 28, Oklahoma 17	1980	Alabama 24, Arkansas 9
1990	So. Calif. 17, Michigan 10	1986	Oklahoma 25, Penn State 10	1981	Georgia 17, Notre Dame 10
1991	Washington 46, Iowa 34	1987	Oklahoma 42, Arkansas 8	1982	Pittsburgh 24, Georgia 20
1992	Washington 34, Michigan 14	1988	Miami (Fla.) 20, Oklahoma 14	1983	Penn State 27, Georgia 23
1993	Michigan 38, Washington 31	1989	Miami (Fla.) 23, Nebraska 3	1984	Auburn 9, Michigan 7
1994	Wisconsin 21, UCLA 16	1990	Notre Dame 21, Colorado 6	1985	Nebraska 28, Louisiana
1995	Penn State 38, Oregon 20	1991	Colorado 10, Notre Dame 9		State 10
1996	South Carolina 41,	1992	Miami (Fla.) 22, Nebraska 0	1986	Tennessee 35, Miami (Fla.) 7
	Northwestern 32	1993	Florida State 27, Nebraska 14	1987	Nebraska 30, Louisiana
1997	Ohio State 20, Arizona State 17	1994	Florida State 18, Nebraska 16		State 15
1998	Michigan 21, Washington	1995	Nebraska 24, Miami (Fla.) 17	1988	Syracuse 16, Auburn 16 (tie)
	State 16	1996	Florida State 31, Notre	1989	Florida State 13, Auburn 7
1999	Wisconsin 38, UCLA 31		Dame 26	1990	Miami (Fla.) 33, Alabama 25
		1997	Nebraska 41, Virginia Tech 21	1991	Tennessee 23, Virginia 22
		1998	Nebraska 42, Tennessee 17	1992	Notre Dame 39, Florida 28
		1999	Florida 31, Syracuse 10	1993	Alabama 34, Miami (Fla.) 13

1. Played at Durham, N.C.

Orange Bowl (At Miami)

Sugar Bowl (At New Orleans)

1933	Miami (Fla.) 7, Manhattan 0	1935	Tulane 20, Temple 14	1994	Florida 41, West Virginia 7
1934	Duquesne 33, Miami (Fla.) 7	1936	Texas Christian 3, Louisiana	1995	Florida State 23, Florida 17
1935	Bucknell 26, Miami (Fla.) 0		State 2	1996	Virginia Tech 28, Texas 10
1936	Catholic 20, Mississippi 19	1937	Santa Clara 21, Louisiana	1997	Florida 52, Florida State 20
1937	Duquesne 13, Mississippi		State 14	1998	Florida State 31, Ohio State 14
	State 12	1938	Santa Clara 6, Louisiana	1999	Ohio State 24, Texas A & M 14
1938	Auburn 6, Michigan State 0		State 0		
1939	Tennessee 17, Oklahoma 0	1939	Texas Christian 15, Carnegie		
1940	Georgia Tech 21, Missouri 7		Tech 7	**Cotton Bowl (At Dallas)**	
1941	Mississippi State 14, George-	1940	Texas A & M 14, Tulane 13	1937	Texas Christian 16, Marquette 6
	town 7	1941	Boston College 19,	1938	Rice 28, Colorado 14
1942	Georgia 40, Texas Christian 26		Tennessee 13	1939	St. Mary's (Calif.) 20, Texas
1943	Alabama 37, Boston College 21	1942	Fordham 2, Missouri 0		Tech. 13
1944	Louisiana State 19, Texas	1943	Tennessee 14, Tulsa 7	1940	Clemson 6, Boston College 3
	A & M 14	1944	Georgia Tech 20, Tulsa 18	1941	Texas A & M 13, Fordham 12
1945	Tulsa 26, Georgia Tech 12	1945	Duke 29, Alabama 26	1942	Alabama 29, Texas A & M 21
1946	Miami (Fla.) 13, Holy Cross 6	1946	Oklahoma A & M 33, St. Mary's	1943	Texas 14, Georgia Tech 7
1947	Rice 8, Tennessee 0		(Calif.) 13	1944	Randolph Field 7, Texas 7
1948	Georgia Tech 20, Kansas 14	1947	Georgia 20, North Carolina 10	1945	Oklahoma A & M 34, Texas
1949	Texas 41, Georgia 28	1948	Texas 27, Alabama 7		Christian 0
1950	Santa Clara 21, Kentucky 13	1949	Oklahoma 14, North Carolina 6	1946	Texas 40, Missouri 27
1951	Clemson 15, Miami (Fla.) 14	1950	Oklahoma 35, Louisiana State 0	1947	Louisiana State 0, Arkansas 0
1952	Georgia Tech 17, Baylor 14	1951	Kentucky 13, Oklahoma 7	1948	So. Methodist 13, Penn
1953	Alabama 61, Syracuse 6	1952	Maryland 28, Tennessee 13		State 13
1954	Oklahoma 7, Maryland 0	1953	Georgia Tech 24, Mississippi 7	1949	So. Methodist 21, Oregon 13
1955	Duke 34, Nebraska 7	1954	Georgia Tech 42, West	1950	Rice 27, North Carolina 13
1956	Oklahoma 20, Maryland 6		Virginia 19	1951	Tennessee 20, Texas 14
1957	Colorado 27, Clemson 21	1955	Navy 21, Mississippi 0	1952	Kentucky 20, Texas Christian 7
1958	Oklahoma 48, Duke 21	1956	Georgia Tech 7, Pittsburgh 0	1953	Texas 16, Tennessee 0
1959	Oklahoma 21, Syracuse 6	1957	Baylor 13, Tennessee 7	1954	Rice 28, Alabama 6
1960	Georgia 14, Missouri 0	1958	Mississippi 39, Texas 7	1955	Georgia Tech 14, Arkansas 6
1961	Missouri 21, Navy 14	1959	Louisiana State 7, Clemson 0	1956	Mississippi 14, Texas
1962	Louisiana State 25, Colorado 7	1960	Mississippi 21, Louisiana		Christian 13
1963	Alabama 17, Oklahoma 0		State 0	1957	Texas Christian 28,
1964	Nebraska 13, Auburn 7				Syracuse 27
1965	Texas 21, Alabama 17			1958	Navy 20, Rice 7
				1959	Air Force 0, Texas Christian 0

1960	Syracuse 23, Texas 14	1993	Notre Dame 28, Texas A & M 3	1973	Auburn 24, Colorado 3
1961	Duke 7, Arkansas 6	1994	Notre Dame 24, Texas A & M 21	1974	Texas Tech 28, Tennessee 19
1962	Texas 12, Mississippi 7	1995	So. Calif. 55, Texas Tech 14	1975	Auburn 27, Texas 3
1963	Louisiana State 13, Texas 0	1996	Colorado 38, Oregon 6	1976	Maryland 13, Florida 0
1964	Texas 28, Navy 6	1997	Brigham Young 19, Kansas	1977	Notre Dame 20, Penn State 9
1965	Arkansas 10, Nebraska 7		State 15	1978	Pittsburgh 34, Clemson 3
1966	Louisiana State 14, Arkansas 7	1998	UCLA 29, Texas A & M 23	1979	Clemson 17, Ohio State 15
1967	Georgia 24, So. Methodist 9	1999	Texas 38, Mississippi State 11	1980	North Carolina 17, Michigan 15
1968	Texas A & M 20, Alabama 16			1981	Pittsburgh 37, South Carolina 9
1969	Texas 36, Tennessee 13	**Gator Bowl (At Jacksonville,**		1982	North Carolina 31, Arkansas 27
1970	Texas 21, Notre Dame 17	**Fla.)**		1983	Florida State 31, West
1971	Notre Dame 24, Texas 11	1953	Florida 14, Tulsa 13		Virginia 12
1972	Penn State 30, Texas 6	1954	Texas Tech 35, Auburn 13	1984	Florida 14, Iowa 6
1973	Texas 17, Alabama 13	1955	Auburn 33, Baylor 13	1985	Oklahoma State 21,
1974	Nebraska 19, Texas 3	1956	Vanderbilt 25, Auburn 13		South Carolina 14
1975	Penn State 41, Baylor 20	1957	Georgia Tech 21, Pittsburgh 14	1986	Florida State 34, Oklahoma
1976	Arkansas 31, Georgia 10	1958	Tennessee 3, Texas A & M 0		State 23
1977	Houston 30, Maryland 21	1959	Mississippi 7, Florida 3	1987	Clemson 27, Stanford 21
1978	Notre Dame 38, Texas 10	1960	Arkansas 14, Georgia Tech 7	1988	Louisiana State 30, South
1979	Notre Dame 35, Houston 34	1961	Florida 13, Baylor 12		Carolina 13
1980	Houston 17, Nebraska 14	1962	Penn State 30, Georgia	1989	Georgia 34, Mich. State 27
1981	Alabama 30, Baylor 2		Tech 15	1990	Clemson 27, West Virginia 7
1982	Texas 14, Alabama 12	1963	Florida 17, Penn State 7	1991	Michigan 35, Mississippi 3
1983	So. Meth. 7, Pittsburgh 3	1964	No. Carolina 35, Air Force 0	1992	Oklahoma 38, Virginia 14
1984	Georgia 10, Texas 9	1965	Florida State 36, Oklahoma 19	1993	Florida 27, No. Carolina St. 10
1985	Boston College 45, Houston 28	1966	Georgia Tech 31, Texas	1994	Alabama 24, No. Carolina 10
1986	Texas A & M 36, Auburn 16		Tech 21	1995	Tennessee 45, Virginia Tech 23
1987	Ohio State 28, Texas A & M 12	1967	Tennessee 18, Syracuse 12	1996	Syracuse 41, Clemson 0
1988	Texas A & M 35, Notre	1968	Penn State 17, Florida	1997	North Carolina 20, West
	Dame 10		State 17 (tie)		Virginia 13
1989	UCLA 17, Arkansas 3	1969	Missouri 35, Alabama 10	1998	North Carolina 42, Virginia
1990	Tennessee 31, Arkansas 27	1970	Florida 14, Tennessee 13		Tech 3
1991	Miami (Fla.) 46, Texas 3	1971	Auburn 35, Mississippi 28	1999	Georgia Tech 35, Notre
1992	Florida State 10, Texas A & M 2	1972	Georgia 7, North Carolina 3		Dame 28

RESULTS OF OTHER 1998–1999 BOWL GAMES

Alamo (Dec, 29, 1998)—Purdue 37, Kansas State 34
Aloha (Dec. 25, 1998)—Colorado 51, Oregon 43
Citrus (Jan. 1, 1999)—Michigan 45, Arkansas 31
Fiesta (Jan. 4, 1999)—Tennessee 23, Florida State 16
Holiday (Dec. 30, 1998)—Arizona 23, Nebraska 20
Humanitarian (Dec. 30, 1998)—Idaho 42, Southern
  Mississippi 35
Independence (Dec. 31, 1998)—Mississippi 35, Texas Tech 18
Insight.com (Dec. 26, 1998)—Missouri 34, West Virginia 31
Las Vegas (Dec. 19, 1998)—North Carolina 20, San Diego
  State 13

Liberty (Dec. 31, 1998)—Tulane 41, Brigham Young 27
Micron PC (Dec. 29, 1998)—Miami (Fla.) 46, North Carolina
  State 23
Motor City (Dec. 23, 1998)—Marshall 48, Louisville 29
Music City (Dec. 29, 1998)—Virginia Tech 38, Alabama 7
Oahu (Dec. 25, 1998)—Air Force 45, Washington 25
Outback (Jan. 1, 1999)—Penn State 26, Kentucky 14
Peach (Dec. 31, 1999)—Georgia 35, Virginia 33
Sun (Dec. 31, 1999)—Texas Christian 28, Southern
  California 19

HEISMAN MEMORIAL TROPHY WINNERS

The Heisman Memorial Trophy is presented annually by the Downtown Athletic Club of New York City to the nation's outstanding college football player, as determined by a poll of sportswriters and sportscasters.

1935	Jay Berwanger, Chicago	1956	Paul Hornung, Notre Dame	1978	Billy Sims, Oklahoma
1936	Larry Kelley, Yale	1957	John Crow, Texas A & M	1979	Charles White, So. Calif.
1937	Clinton Frank, Yale	1958	Pete Dawkins, Army	1980	George Rogers, South Carolina
1938	Davey O'Brien, Texas Christian	1959	Billy Cannon, Louisiana State	1981	Marcus Allen, So. Calif.
1939	Nile Kinnick, Iowa	1960	Joe Bellino, Navy	1982	Herschel Walker, Georgia
1940	Tom Harmon, Michigan	1961	Ernie Davis, Syracuse	1983	Mike Rozier, Nebraska
1941	Bruce Smith, Minnesota	1962	Terry Baker, Oregon State	1984	Doug Flutie, Boston College
1942	Frank Sinkwich, Georgia	1963	Roger Staubach, Navy	1985	Bo Jackson, Auburn
1943	Angelo Bertelli, Notre Dame	1964	John Huarte, Notre Dame	1986	Vinny Testaverde, Miami
1944	Leslie Horvath, Ohio State	1965	Mike Garrett, So. Calif.	1987	Tim Brown, Notre Dame
1945	Felix Blanchard, Army	1966	Steve Spurrier, Florida	1988	Barry Sanders, Oklahoma State
1946	Glenn Davis, Army	1967	Gary Beban, UCLA	1989	Andre Ware, Houston
1947	Johnny Lujack, Notre Dame	1968	O.J. Simpson, So. Calif.	1990	Ty Detmer, Brigham Young
1948	Doak Walker, So. Methodist	1969	Steve Owens, Oklahoma	1991	Desmond Howard, Michigan
1949	Leon Hart, Notre Dame	1970	Jim Plunkett, Stanford	1992	Gino Torretta, Miami
1950	Vic Janowicz, Ohio State	1971	Pat Sullivan, Auburn	1993	Charlie Ward, Florida State
1951	Dick Kazmaier, Princeton	1972	Johnny Rodgers, Nebraska	1994	Rashaan Salaam, Colorado
1952	Billy Vessels, Oklahoma	1973	John Cappelletti, Penn State	1995	Eddie George, Ohio State
1953	Johnny Lattner, Notre Dame	1974-75	Archie Griffin, Ohio State	1996	Danny Wuerffel, Florida
1954	Alan Ameche, Wisconsin	1976	Tony Dorsett, Pittsburgh	1997	Charles Woodson, Michigan
1955	Howard Cassady, Ohio State	1977	Earl Campbell, Texas	1998	Ricky Williams, Texas

1998 N.C.A.A. CHAMPIONSHIP PLAYOFFS

DIVISION I-AA

Quarterfinals
(Dec. 5, 1998)
Georgia Southern 52, Connecticut 30
Western Illinois 24, Florida A & M 21
Massachusetts 27, Lehigh 21
Northwestern State 31, Appalachian State 20

Semifinals
(Dec. 12, 1998)
Georgia Southern 42, Western Illinois 14
Massachusetts 41, Northwestern State 31

Championship
(Dec. 19, 1998)
Massachusetts 55, Georgia Southern 43

DIVISION II

Quarterfinals
(Nov. 28, 1998)
Slippery Rock 31, Shepherd 20
Carson-Newman 38, Fort Valley State 31 (OT)
Northwest Missouri State 42, Northern Colorado 17
Texas A & M-Kingsville 24, Central Oklahoma 21 (OT)

Semifinals
(Dec. 5, 1998)
Carson-Newman 47, Slippery Rock 21
Northwest Missouri State 49, Texas A & M-Kingsville 34

Championship
(Dec. 12, 1998)
Northwest Missouri State 24, Carson-Newman 6

DIVISION III

Quarterfinals
(Nov. 28, 1998)
Mount Union 21, Wittenberg, Ohio 19
Trinity 37, Lycoming 21
Rowan 19, Buffalo State 17
Wisconsin-Eau Claire 10, St. John's, Minn. 7

Semifinals
(Dec. 5, 1998)
Mount Union 34, Trinity 29
Rowan 22, Wisconsin-Eau Claire 19

Championship
(Dec. 12, 1998)
Mount Union 44, Rowan 24

1998 NATIONAL ASSOCIATION OF INTERCOLLEGIATE ATHLETICS CHAMPIONSHIPS

Quarterfinals
(Nov. 28, 1998)

Tri-State, Ind. 37, Georgetown, Ky. 23
Olivet Nazarene, Ill. 37, Sioux Falls, S.D. 34
Huron, S.D. 52, Southwestern, Kans. 6
Azusa Pacific 35, Central Washington 28

Semifinals
(Dec. 5, 1998)
Olivet Nazarene, Ill. 33, Tri-State, Ind. 28
Azusa Pacific 26, Huron, S.D. 24

Championship
(Dec. 19, 1998)
Azusa Pacific 17, Olivet Nazarene, Ill. 14

COLLEGE FOOTBALL HALL OF FAME

(P.O. Box 11146, South Bend, Indiana)
NOTE: Date given is player's last year of competition.

Players

Abell, Earl—Colgate, 1915
Agase, Alex—Purdue/Illinois, 1946
Agganis, Harry—Boston Univ., 1952
Albert, Frank—Stanford, 1941
Aldrich, Chas. (Ki)—Texas Christian, 1938
Aldrich, Malcolm—Yale, 1921
Alexander, Joseph—Syracuse, 1920
Alworth, Lance—Arkansas, 1961
Ameche, Alan (Horse)—Wisconsin, 1954
Amling, Warren—Ohio State, 1946
Anderson, Dick—Colorado, 1967
Anderson, Donny—Texas Tech, 1965
Anderson, H. (Hunk)—Notre Dame, 1921
Atkins, Doug—Tennessee, 1952
Babich, Bob—Miami-Ohio, 1968
Bacon, C. Everett—Wesleyan, 1912
Bagnell, Francis (Reds)—Pennsylvania, 1950
Baker, Hobart (Hobey)—Princeton, 1913
Baker, John—So. Calif., 1931
Baker, Terry—Oregon State, 1962
Ballin, Harold—Princeton, 1914
Banker, Bill—Tulane, 1929
Banonis, Vince—Detroit, 1941
Barnes, Stanley—So. Calif., 1921
Barrett, Charles—Cornell, 1915
Baston, Bert—Minnesota, 1916
Battles, Cliff—W. Va. Wesleyan, 1931
Baugh, Sammy—Texas Christian, 1936
Baughan, Maxie—Georgia Tech, 1959
Bausch, James—Kansas, 1930
Beagle, Ron—Navy, 1955
Beban, Gary—UCLA, 1967
Bechtol, Hub—Texas Tech, 1946
Beck, Ray—Georgia Tech, 1951
Beckett, John—Oregon, 1916
Bednariok, Chuck—Pennsylvania 1948
Behm, Forrest—Nebraska, 1940
Bell, Bobby—Minnesota, 1962

Bellino, Joe—Navy, 1960
Below, Marty—Wisconsin, 1923
Benbrook, A.—Michigan, 1911
Bentrim, Jeff—North Dakota State, 1986
Bertelli, A.—Notre Dame, 1943
Berry, Charlie—Lafayette, 1924
Berwanger, John (Jay)—Chicago, 1935
Bettencourt, Larry—St. Mary's, 1927
Biletnikoff, Fred—Florida State, 1964
Blanchard, Felix (Doc)—Army, 1946
Bock, Ed—Iowa State, 1938
Bomar, Lynn—Vanderbilt, 1924
Bomeisler, Doug (Bo)—Yale, 1913
Booth, Albie—Yale, 1931
Bork, George—Northern Illinois, 1963
Borries, Fred—Navy, 1934
Bosely, Bruce—West Virginia, 1955
Bosseler, Don—Miami (Fla.), 1956
Bottari, Vic—California, 1939
Boynton, Ben—Williams, 1920
Bozis, Al—Georgetown, 1941
Bradshaw, Terry—Louisiana Tech, 1969
Brewer, Charles—Harvard, 1895
Bright, John—Drake, 1951
Brodie, John—Stanford, 1956
Brooke, George—Pennsylvania, 1895
Brosky, Al—Illinois, 1952
Brown, Bob—Nebraska, 1963
Brown, George—Navy/San Diego State, 1947
Brown, Gordon—Yale, 1900
Brown, Jim—Syracuse, 1956
Brown, John, Jr.—Navy, 1913
Brown, Johnny Mack—Alabama, 1925
Brown, Raymond (Tay)—So. Calif., 1932
Browner, Ross—Notre Dame, 1977
Bruner, Teel—Centre College (Ky.), 1985
Buchanan, Buck—Grambling State, 1962
Budde, Brad—So. Calif., 1979

Bunker, Paul—Army, 1902
Burford, Chris—Stanford, 1959
Burton, Ron—Northwestern, 1956
Butkus, Dick—Illinois, 1964
Butler, Robert—Wisconsin, 1912
Cafego, George—Tennessee, 1939
Cagle, Chris—SW La./Army, 1929
Cain, John—Alabama, 1932
Cameron, Eddie—Wash. & Lee, 1924
Campbell, David C.—Harvard, 1901
Campbell, Earl—Texas, 1977
Cannon, Billy—Louisiana State, 1959
Cannon, Jack—Notre Dame, 1929
Cappelletti, John—Penn State, 1973
Carideo, Frank—Notre Dame, 1930
Caroline, J.C.—Illinois, 1954
Carney, Charles—Illinois, 1921
Carpenter, Bill—Army, 1959
Carpenter, C. Hunter—VPI, 1905
Carroll, Charles—Washington, 1928
Casanova, Tommy—Louisiana State, 1971
Casey, Edward L.—Harvard, 1919
Cassady, Howard—Ohio State, 1955
Chamberlain, Guy—Nebraska, 1915
Chapman, Sam—Cal.-Berkeley, 1938
Chappuis, Bob—Michigan, 1947
Christman, Paul—Missouri, 1940
Cichy, Joe—North Dakota State, 1970
Clark, Earl (Dutch)—Colo. College, 1929
Cleary, Paul—So. Calif., 1947
Clevenger, Zora—Indiana, 1903
Cloud, Jack—William & Mary, 1948
Cochran, Gary—Princeton, 1895
Cody, Josh—Vanderbilt, 1920
Coleman, Don—Mich. State, 1951
Conerly, Chuck—Mississippi, 1947
Connor, George—Notre Dame, 1947
Corbin, W.—Yale, 1888
Corbus, William—Stanford, 1933

Cowan, Hector—Princeton, 1889
Coy, Edward H. (Tad)—Yale, 1909
Crawford, Fred—Duke, 1933
Crow, John D.—Texas A & M, 1957
Crowley, James—Notre Dame, 1924
Csonka, Larry—Syracuse, 1967
Cutter, Slade—Navy, 1934
Czarobski, Ziggie—Notre Dame, 1947
Dale, Carroll—Virginia Tech, 1959
Dalrymple, Gerald—Tulane, 1931
Dalton, John—Navy, 1912
Daly, Charles—Harvard/Army, 1902
Daniell, Averell—Pittsburgh, 1936
Daniell, James—Ohio State, 1941
Davies, Tom—Pittsburgh, 1921
Davis, Ernest—Syracuse, 1961
Davis, Glenn—Army, 1946
Davis, Robert T.—Georgia Tech, 1947
Dawkins, Pete—Army, 1958
Delaney, Joe—Northwestern State, 1980
Deery, Tom—Widener, 1981
DeLong, Steve—Tennessee, 1964
Dement, Kenneth—SE Missouri, 1954
Den Herder, Vern—Central (Iowa), 1970
De Rogatis, Al—Duke, 1940
DesJardien, Paul—Chicago 1914
Devino, Aubrey—Iowa, 1921
DeWitt, John—Princeton, 1903
Dial, Buddy—Rice, 1958
Dicus, Chuck—Arkansas, 1970
Ditka, Mike—Pittsburgh, 1960
Dobbs, Glenn—Tulsa, 1942
Dodd, Bobby—Tennessee, 1930
Donan, Holland—Princeton, 1950
Donchess, Joseph—Pittsburgh, 1929
Dorsett, Tony—Pittsburgh, 1976
Dougherty, Nathan—Tennessee, 1909
Drahos, Nick—Cornell, 1940
Driscoll, Paddy—Northwestern, 1917
Drury, Morley—So. Calif., 1927
Dryer, Fred—San Diego State, 1968
Dudek, Joe—Plymouth State, 1985
Dudley, William (Bill)—Virginia, 1941
Duncan, Randy—Iowa, 1958
Easley, Ken—UCLA, 1980
Eckersall, Walter—Chicago, 1906
Edwards, Turk—Washington State, 1931
Edwards, William—Princeton, 1900
Eichenlaub, R.—Notre Dame, 1913
Eisenhauer, Steve—Navy, 1953
Elking, Larry—Baylor, 1964
Elliott, Chalmers—Purdue, 1944 & Mich., 1947
Elliott, Pete—Michigan, 1948
Elmendorf, Dave—Texas A & M, 1970
Evans, Ray—Kansas, 1947
Exendine, Albert—Carlisle, 1908
Falaschi, Nello—Santa Clara, 1937
Fears, Tom—Santa Clara/UCLA, 1947
Feathers, Beattie—Tennessee, 1933
Fenimore, Robert—Oklahoma State, 1947
Fenton, G.E. (Doc)—Louisiana State, 1910
Ferguson, Bob—Ohio State, 1961
Ferraro, John—So. Calif., 1944
Fesler, Wesley—Ohio State, 1930
Fincher, Bill—Georgia Tech, 1920
Fischer, Bill—Notre Dame, 1948
Fish, Hamilton—Harvard, 1909
Fisher, Robert—Harvard, 1911
Flowers, Abe—Georgia Tech, 1920
Flowers, Charlie—Mississippi, 1959
Floyd, George—Eastern Kentucky, 1981
Fortmann, Daniel—Colgate, 1935
Fralic, Bill—Pittsburgh, 1984
Francis, Sam—Nebraska, 1936
Franco, Edmund (Ed)—Fordham, 1937
Frank, Clint—Yale, 1937
Franz, Rodney—California, 1949
Frederickson, Tucker—Auburn, 1964
Friedman, Benny—Michigan, 1926
Gabriel, Roman—North Carolina St., 1961
Gain, Bob—Kentucky, 1950
Galiffa, Arnold—Army, 1949
Galimore, Willie—Florida A & M, 1956
Gallarneau, Hugh—Stanford, 1941

Garbisch, Edgar—Army, 1924
Garrett, Mike—So. Calif., 1965
Gelbert, Charles—Pennsylvania, 1896
Geyer, Forest—Oklahoma, 1915
Gibbs, Jake—Mississippi, 1960
Giel, Paul—Minnesota, 1953
Gifford, Frank—So. Calif., 1951
Gilbert, Chris—Texas, 1968
Gilbert, Walter—Auburn, 1936
Gilmer, Harry—Alabama, 1947
Gipp, George—Notre Dame, 1920
Gladchuk, Chet—Boston College, 1940
Glass, Bill—Baylor, 1956
Glover, Rich—Nebraska, 1972
Goldberg, Marshall—Pittsburgh, 1938
Goodreault, Gene—Boston College, 1940
Gordon, Walter—California, 1918
Governale, Paul—Columbia, 1942
Grabowski, Jim—Illinois, 1965
Graham, Otto—Northwestern, 1943
Gradishar, Randy—Ohio State, 1973
Grange, Harold (Red)—Illinois, 1925
Grayson, Roberty—Stanford, 1935
Green, Hugh—Pittsburgh, 1980
Green, Joe—North Texas State, 1968
Griese, Bob—Purdue, 1966
Griffin, Archie—Ohio State, 1975
Grinnell, William—Tufts, 1934
Groom, Jerry—Notre Dame, 1950
Gulick, Merel—Hobart, 1929
Guyon, Joe—Georgia Tech, 1919
Hadl, John—Kansas, 1961
Hale, Edwin—Mississippi Col., 1921
Hall, Parker—Mississippi, 1938
Ham, Jack—Penn State, 1970
Hamilton, Robert (Bones)—Stanford, 1935
Hamilton, Tom—Navy, 1925
Hannah, John—Alabama, 1972
Hanson, Vic—Syracuse, 1926
Harder, Pat—Wisconsin, 1942
Hardwick, H. (Tack)—Harvard, 1914
Hare, T. Truxton—Pennsylvania, 1900
Harley, Chick—Ohio State, 1919
Harmon, Tom—Michigan, 1940
Harpster, Howard—Carnegie Tech, 1928
Hart, Edward J. Princeton, 1911
Hart, Leon—Notre Dame, 1949
Hartman, Bill—Georgia, 1937
Hawkins, Frank—Nevada, 1980
Hazel, Homer—Rutgers, 1924
Healey, Ed—Dartmouth, 1916
Heffelfiner, W. (Pudge)—Yale, 1891
Hein, Mel—Washington State, 1930
Heinrich, Don—Washington, 1952
Hendricks, Ted—Miami, 1968
Henry, Wilbur—Wash. & Jefferson, 1919
Herschberger, Clarence—Chicago, 1899
Herwig, Robert—California, 1937
Heston, Willie—Michigan, 1904
Hickman, Herman—Tennessee, 1931
Hickok, William—Yale, 1895
Hill, Dan—Duke, 1938
Hillebrand, A.R. (Doc)—Princeton, 1900
Hinkey, Frank—Yale, 1894
Hinkle, Carl—Vanderbilt, 1937
Hinkle, Clark—Bucknell, 1932
Hirsch, Elroy—Wisconsin/Michigan, 1943
Hitchcock, James—Auburn, 1932
Hoffman, Frank—Notre Dame, 1931
Hogan, James J.—Yale, 1904
Holland, Jerome (Brud)—Cornell, 1938
Holleder, Don—Army, 1955
Hollenbeck, William—Pennsylvania, 1908
Holovak, Michael—Boston College, 1942
Holt, Pierce—Angelo State, 1980
Holub, E.J.—Texas Tech, 1960
Hornung, Paul—Notre Dame, 1956
Horrell, Edwin—California, 1924
Horvath, Les—Ohio State, 1944
Howe Arthur—Yale, 1911
Howell, Millard (Dixie)—Alabama, 1934
Hubbard, Cal—Centenary, 1926
Hubbard, John—Amherst, 1906
Hubert, Allison—Alabama, 1925
Huff, Robert Lee (Sam)—W. Va., 1955
Humble, Weldon G.—Rice, 1946

Hunley, Ricky—Arizona, 1983
Hunt, Joel—Texas A & M, 1927
Huntington, Ellery—Colgate, 1914
Hutson, Don—Alabama, 1934
Ingram, James—Navy, 1906
Isbell, Cecil—Purdue, 1937
Jablonsky, Harvey—Wash. U./Army, 1933
Jackson, Bo—Auburn, 1985
Janowicz, Vic—Ohio State, 1951
Jenkins, Darold—Missouri, 1941
Jensen, Jack—Cal.-Berkeley, 1948
Joesting, Herbert—Minnesota, 1927
Johnson, Billy—Widener, 1973
Johnson, Gary—Grambling State, 1974
Johnson, James—Carlisle, 1903
Johnson, Robert—Tennessee, 1967
Johnson, Ron—Michigan, 1968
Jones, Calvin—Iowa, 1955
Jones, Gormer—Ohio State, 1935
Jordan, Lee Roy—Alabama, 1962
Juhan, Frank—Univ. of South, 1910
Justice, Charlie—North Carolina, 1949
Kaer, Mort—So. Calif., 1926
Karras, Alex—Iowa, 1957
Kavanaugh, Kenneth—Louisiana State, 1939
Kaw, Edgar—Cornell, 1922
Kazmaier, Richard—Princeton, 1951
Keck, James—Princeton, 1921
Kelley, Larry—Yale, 1936
Kelly, William—Montana, 1926
Kenna, Ed—Syracuse, 1966
Kern, George—Boston College, 1941
Ketcham, Henry—Yale, 1913
Keyes, Leroy—Purdue, 1968
Killinger, William—Penn State, 1922
Kilmer, Billy—UCLA, 1960
Kimbrough, John—Texas A & M, 1940
Kinard, Frank—Mississippi, 1937
Kiner, Steve—Tennessee, 1969
King, Philip—Princeton, 1893
Kinnick, Nile—Iowa, 1939
Kipke, Harry—Michigan, 1923
Kirkpatrick, John Reed—Yale, 1910
Kitzmiller, John—Oregon, 1929
Koch, Barton—Baylor, 1931
Kitner, Malcolm—Texas, 1942
Kramer, Ron—Michigan, 1956
Kroll, Alex—Rutgers, 1961
Krueger, Charlie—Texas A & M, 1957
Kwalick, Ted—Penn State, 1968
Lach, Steve—Duke, 1941
Lane, Myles—Dartmouth, 1927
Lattner, Joseph J.—Notre Dame, 1953
Lauricella, Hank—Tennessee, 1952
Lautenschlaeger—Tulane, 1925
Layden, Elmer—Notre Dame, 1924
Layne, Bobby—Texas, 1947
Lea, Langdon—Princeton, 1895
LeBaron, Eddie—Univ. of Pacific, 1949
LeClair, Jim—North Dakota, 1971
Leech, James—Va. Mil. Inst., 1920
Lester, Darrell—Texas Christian, 1935
Lilly, Bob—Texas Christian, 1960
Little, Floyd—Syracuse, 1966
Lio, Augie—Georgetown, 1940
Locke, Gordon—Iowa, 1922
Lomax, Neil—Portland (Ore.) State, 1980
Long, Chuck—Iowa, 1985
Long, Mel—Toledo, 1971
Loria, Frank—Virginia Tech, 1967
Lourie, Don—Princeton, 1921
Lucas, Richard—Penn State, 1959
Luckman, Sid—Columbia, 1938
Lujack, John—Notre Dame, 1947
Lund, J.L. (Pug)—Minnesota, 1934
Lynch, Jim—Notre Dame, 1966
MacAfee, Ken—Notre Dame, 1977
Macomber, Bart—Illinois, 1915
MacLeod, Robert—Dartmouth, 1938
Maegle, Dick—Rice, 1954
Mahan, Edward W.—Harvard, 1915
Majors, John—Tennessee, 1956
Mallory, William—Yale, 1893
Mancha, Vaughn—Alabama, 1947
Mann, Gerald—So. Methodist, 1927

Wagner, Huber—Pittsburgh, 1913
Walker, Doak—So. Methodist, 1949
Walker, Herschel—Georgia, 1982
Wallace, Bill—Rice, 1935
Walsh, Adam—Notre Dame, 1924
Warburton, I. (Cotton)—So. Calif., 1934
Ward, Robert (Bob)—Maryland, 1951
Warner, William—Cornell, 1903
Washington, Ken—UCLA, 1939
Weatherall, Jim—Oklahoma, 1951
Webster, George—Mich. State, 1966
Wedemeyer, Herman J.—St. Mary's, 1947
Weekes, Harold—Columbia, 1902
Weiner, Art—North Carolina, 1949
Weir, Ed—Nebraska, 1925
Welch, Gus—Carlisle, 1914
Weller, John—Princeton, 1935
Wendell, Percy—Harvard, 1913
West, D. Belford—Colgate, 1919

Westfall, Bob—Michigan, 1941
Weyand, Alex—Army, 1915
Wharton, Charles—Pennsylvania, 1896
Wheeler, Arthur—Princeton, 1894
White, Byron (Whizzer)—Colorado, 1937
White, Charles—So. Calif., 1979
White, Danny—Arizona State, 1973
White, Ed—California-Berkeley, 1968
White, Randy—Maryland, 1974
Whitmire, Don—Alabama/Navy, 1944
Wickhorst, Frank—Navy, 1926
Widseth, Ed—Minnesota, 1936
Wildung, Richard—Minnesota, 1942
Williams, Bob—Notre Dame, 1950
Williams, James—Rice, 1949
Willis, William—Ohio State, 1945
Wilson, George—Washington, 1925
Wilson, George—Lafayette, 1928
Wilson, Harry—Penn State/Army, 1923

Wilson, Marc—Brigham Young, 1979
Wistert, Albert A.—Michigan, 1942
Wistert, Al—Michigan, 1942
Wistert, Frank (Whitey)—Michigan, 1933
Wood, Barry—Harvard, 1931
Wojciechowicz, Alex—Fordham, 1936
Wyant, Andrew—Bucknell/Chicago, 1894
Wyatt, Bowden—Tennessee, 1938
Wyckoff, Clint—Cornell, 1896
Yarr, Tom—Notre Dame, 1931
Yary, Ron—So. Calif., 1968
Yoder, Lloyd—Carnegie Tech, 1926
Young, Claude (Buddy)—Illinois, 1946
Young, Harry—Wash. & Lee, 1916
Young, Walter—Oklahoma, 1938
Youngblood, Jack—Florida, 1970
Youngblood, Jim—Tennessee, 1972
Zarnas, Gus—Ohio State, 1937

Coaches

Bill Alexander
Dr. Ed Anderson
Ike Armstrong
Earl Banks
Harry Baujan
Matty Bell
Hugo Bezdek
Dana X. Bible
Bernie Bierman
Bob Blackman
Earl (Red) Blaik
Frank Broyles
Paul "Bear" Bryant
Harold Burry
Jim Butterfield
James "Wally" Butts
Charles W. Caldwell
Walter Camp
Len Casanova
Frank Cavanaugh
Jerry Claiborne
Richard Colman
Don Coryell
Fritz Crisler
Duffy Daugherty
Bob Devaney
Dan Devine
Gil Dobie

Bobby Dodd
Michael Donohue
Vince Dooley
Gus Dorais
Bill Edwards
Charles (Rip) Engle
Don Faurot
Jake Gaither
Sid Gillman
Ernest Godfrey
Ray Graves
Andy Gustafson
Jack Harding
Edward K. Hall
Richard Harlow
Jesse Harper
Percy Haughton
Woody Hayes
John W. Heisman
R.A. (Bob) Higgins
Paul Hoernemann
Orin E. Hollingberry
Frank Howard
William Ingram
Don James
Morley Jennings
Howard Jones
L. (Biff) Jones

Thomas (Tad) Jones
Ralph (Shug) Jordan
Bob Keade
Andy Kerr
Chuck Klausing
Frank Kush
Frank Leahy
George E. Little
Lou Little
El (Slip) Madigan
Dave Maurer
Charley McClendon
Herbert McCracken
Daniel McGugin
John McKay
Allyn McKeen
DeOrmond (Tuss)
  McLaughry
John Merritt
L.R. (Dutch) Meyer
Bernie Moore
Scrappy Moore
Jack Mollenkopf
Ray Morrison
George A. Munger
Clarence Munn
Frank Murray
William Murray

Ed (Hooks) Mylin
Earle (Greasy) Neale
Jess Neely
David Nelson
Robert Neyland
Billy Nicks
Homer Norton
Frank (Buck) O'Neill
Tom Osborne
Bennie Owen
Ara Parseghian
Doyt Perry
James Phalen
Tommy Prothro
John Ralston
E.N. Robinson
William W. Roper
Darrell Royal
Ad Rutschman
Henry (Red) Sanders
George F. Sanford
Bo Schembechler
Francis A. Schmidt
Floyd (Ben)
  Schwartzwalder
Clark Shaughnessy

Buck Shaw
Edgar Sherman
Andrew L. Smith
Carl Snavely
Jim Sochor
Amos A. Stagg
Gilbert Steinke
Jock Sutherland
James Tatum
Frank W. Thomas
Lee Tressell
Thad Vann
John H. Vaught
Wallace Wade
Lynn Waldorf
Glenn (Pop) Warner
E.E. (Tad) Wieman
John W. Wilce
Bud Wilkinson
Henry L. Williams
George W. Woodruff
Warren Woodson
Bowden Wyatt
Fielding H. Yost
Jim Young
Robert Zuppke

Professional Football

NATIONAL FOOTBALL LEAGUE FINAL STANDINGS 1998

AMERICAN FOOTBALL CONFERENCE

	W	L	T	Pct	PF	PA
Eastern Division						
New York Jets[1]	12	4	0	.750	416	266
Miami Dolphins[2]	10	6	0	.625	321	265
Buffalo Bills[2]	10	6	0	.625	400	333
New England Patriots[2]	9	7	0	.563	337	329
Indianapolis Colts	3	13	0	.188	310	444
Central Division						
Jacksonville Jaguars[1]	11	5	0	.688	392	338
Tennessee Oilers	8	8	0	.500	330	320
Pittsburgh Steelers	7	9	0	.438	263	303
Baltimore Ravens	6	10	0	.375	269	335
Cincinnati Bengals	3	13	0	.188	268	452
Western Division						
Denver Broncos[1]	14	2	0	.875	501	309
Oakland Raiders	8	8	0	.500	288	356
Seattle Seahawks	8	8	0	.500	372	310
Kansas City Chiefs	7	9	0	.438	327	363
San Diego Chargers	5	11	0	.313	241	342

1. Division champion. 2. Wild card qualifier for playoffs. **Wild card:** Miami 24, Buffalo 17; Jacksonville 25, New England 10. **Division:** Denver 38, Miami 3; N.Y. Jets 34, Jacksonville 24. **Conference:** Denver 23, N.Y. Jets 10.

NATIONAL FOOTBALL CONFERENCE

	W	L	T	Pct	PF	PA
Eastern Division						
Dallas Cowboys[1]	10	6	0	.625	381	275
Arizona Cardinals[2]	9	7	0	.563	325	378
New York Giants	8	8	0	.500	287	309
Washington Redskins	6	10	0	.375	319	421
Philadelphia Eagles	3	13	0	.188	161	344
Central Division						
Minnesota Vikings[1]	15	1	0	.938	556	296
Green Bay Packers[2]	11	5	0	.688	408	319
Tampa Bay Buccaneers	8	8	0	.500	314	295
Detroit Lions	5	11	0	.313	306	378
Chicago Bears	4	12	0	.250	276	368
Western Division						
Atlanta Falcons[1]	14	2	0	.875	442	289
San Francisco 49ers[2]	12	4	0	.750	479	328
New Orleans Saints	6	10	0	.375	305	359
Carolina Panthers	4	12	0	.250	336	413
St. Louis Rams	4	12	0	.250	285	378

1. Division champion. 2. Wild card qualifier for playoffs. **Wild card:** Arizona 20, Dallas 7; San Francisco 30, Green Bay 27. **Division:** Atlanta 20, San Francisco 18; Minnesota 41, Arizona 21. **Conference:** Atlanta 30, Minnesota 27.

LEAGUE CHAMPIONSHIP—SUPER BOWL XXXIII

(January 31, 1999, Pro Player Stadium, Miami, Fla. Attendance: 74,803. Time: 3:18)

Scoring

	1st Q	2nd Q	3rd Q	4th Q	Final
Denver Broncos	7	10	0	17	**34**
Atlanta Falcons	3	3	0	13	**19**

1st: ATL—Morten Andersen 32-yd FG, 9:35. Drive: 48 yards in 10 plays. Key play: 25-yd pass interference on Ray Crockett to DEN 21. DEN—Howard Griffith 1-yd run (Jason Elam kick), 3:55. Drive: 80 yards in 10 plays. Key play: John Elway 41-yd pass to Rod Smith on 3rd-and-7 to ATL 24.
2nd: DEN—Elam 26-yd FG, 9:17. Drive: 63 yards in 11 plays. Key play: Elway 18-yd pass to Smith to ATL 27. DEN—Smith 80-yd pass from Elway (Elam kick), 4:54. Drive: 80 yards in 1 play. ATL—Andersen 28-yd FG, 2:25. Drive: 38 yards in 7 plays. Key play: Tim Dwight 42-yd kick-off return to DEN 49.
4th: DEN—Griffith 1-yd run (Elam kick), 14:56. Drive: 24 yards in 5 plays. Key play: Darrien Gordon 58-yd interception return to ATL 24. DEN—Elway 3-yd run (Elam kick), 11:20. Drive: 48 yards in 3 plays. Key play: Gordon 50-yd interception return to ATL 48. ATL—Dwight 94-yd kickoff return (Andersen kick), 11:01. DEN—Elam 37-yd FG, 7:08. Drive: 36 yards in 7 plays. Key play: Byron Chamberlain recovers onside kick at DEN 46. ATL—Terance Mathis 3-yd pass from Chris Chandler (2-pt attempt failed), 2:04. Drive: 76 yards in 16 plays. Key play: Chandler 17-yd pass to Tony Martin on 3rd-and 4 to ATL 47.

Individual Statistics
Rushing: DENVER: T. Davis 25–102, H. Griffith 4–9, D. Loville 2–8, J. Elway 3–2, R. Smith 1–1, B. Brister, 1–(-1). ATLANTA: J. Anderson 18–96, C. Chandler 4–30, T. Dwight 1–5.

Passing: DENVER: J. Elway 29–18. ATLANTA: C. Chandler 35–19.

Receiving: DENVER: R. Smith 5–152, E. McCaffrey 5–72, B. Chamberlain 3–29, T. Davis 2–50, S. Sharpe 2–26, H. Griffith 1–7. ATLANTA: T. Mathis 7–85, T. Martin 5–79, J. Anderson 3–16, R. Harris 2–21, O. J. Santiago 1–13, B. Kozlowski 1–5.

MVP: John Elway, Denver quarterback, 18–29 for 336 yds, 1 touchdown, 1 interception.

Statistics of the Game

	Denver	Atlanta
Touchdowns	4	2
Field Goals made/attempted	2/4	2/3
Time of possession	31:23	28:37
First downs	22	21
Total offense (net yards)	457	337
Plays	65	60
Average gain	7.0	5.6
Passing yards	336	206
Completions/attempts	18/29	19/35
Times intercepted	1	3
Times sacked/yards lost	0/0	2/13
Return yardage	180	228
Fumbles/lost	0/0	1/1
Penalties/yards	4/61	0/0

SUPER BOWLS I-XXXII

Game	Date	Winner	Loser	Site	Attendance
XXXIII	Jan. 31, 1999	Denver (AFC) 34	Atlanta (NFC) 19	Pro Player Stadium, Miami, Fla.	74,803
XXXII	Jan. 25, 1998	Denver (AFC) 31	Green Bay (NFC) 24	Qualcomm Stadium, San Diego, Calif.	68,912
XXXI	Jan. 26, 1997	Green Bay (NFC) 35	New England (AFC) 21	Superdome, New Orleans, La.	72,301
XXX	Jan. 28, 1996	Dallas (NFC) 27	Pittsburgh (AFC) 17	Sun Devil Stadium, Tempe, Ariz.	76,347
XXIX	Jan. 29, 1995	San Francisco (NFC) 49	San Diego (AFC) 26	Joe Robbie Stadium, Miami, Fla.	74,107
XXVIII	Jan. 30, 1994	Dallas (NFC) 30	Buffalo (AFC) 13	Georgia Dome, Atlanta, Ga.	72,817
XXVII	Jan. 31, 1993	Dallas (NFC) 52	Buffalo (AFC) 17	Rose Bowl, Pasadena, Calif.	98,374
XXVI	Jan. 26, 1992	Washington (NFC) 37	Buffalo (AFC) 24	Metrodome, Minneapolis, Minn.	63,130
XXV	Jan. 27, 1991	Giants (NFC) 20	Buffalo (AFC) 19	Tampa Stadium, Tampa, Fla.	73,813
XXIV	Jan. 28, 1990	San Francisco (NFC) 55	Denver (AFC) 10	Superdome, New Orleans	72,919
XXIII	Jan. 22, 1989	San Francisco (NFC) 20	Cincinnati (AFC) 16	Joe Robbie Stadium, Miami, Fla.	75,179
XXII	Jan. 31, 1988	Washington (NFC) 42	Denver (AFC) 10	Jack Murphy Stadium, San Diego, Calif.	73,302
XXI	Jan. 25, 1987	Giants (NFC) 39	Denver (AFC) 20	Rose Bowl, Pasadena, Calif.	101,063
XX	Jan. 26, 1986	Chicago (NFC) 46	New England (AFC) 10	Superdome, New Orleans	73,818
XIX	Jan. 20, 1985	San Francisco (NFC) 38	Miami (AFC) 16	Stanford Stadium, Palo Alto, Calif.	84,059
XVIII	Jan. 22, 1984	Los Angeles Raiders (AFC) 38	Washington (NFC) 9	Tampa Stadium, Tampa, Fla	72,920
XVII	Jan. 30, 1983	Washington (NFC) 27	Miami (AFC) 17	Rose Bowl, Pasadena, Calif.	103,667
XVI	Jan. 24, 1982	San Francisco (NFC) 26	Cincinnati (AFC) 21	Silverdome, Pontiac, Mich.	81,270
XV	Jan. 25, 1981	Oakland (AFC) 27	Philadelphia (NFC) 10	Superdome, New Orleans	75,500
XIV	Jan. 20, 1980	Pittsburgh (AFC) 31	Los Angeles (NFC) 19	Rose Bowl, Pasadena	103,985
XIII	Jan. 21, 1979	Pittsburgh (AFC) 35	Dallas (NFC) 31	Orange Bowl, Miami	79,484
XII	Jan. 15, 1978	Dallas (NFC) 27	Denver (AFC) 10	Superdome, New Orleans	75,583
XI	Jan. 9, 1977	Oakland (AFC) 32	Minnesota (NFC) 14	Rose Bowl, Pasadena	103,424
X	Jan. 18, 1976	Pittsburgh (AFC) 21	Dallas (NFC) 17	Orange Bowl, Miami	80,187
IX	Jan. 12, 1975	Pittsburgh (AFC) 16	Minnesota (NFC) 6	Tulane Stadium, New Orleans	80,997
VIII	Jan. 13, 1974	Miami (AFC) 24	Minnesota (NFC) 7	Rice Stadium, Houston	71,882
VII	Jan. 14, 1973	Miami (AFC) 14	Washington (NFC) 7	Memorial Coliseum, Los Angeles	90,182
VI	Jan. 16, 1972	Dallas (NFC) 24	Miami (AFC) 3	Tulane Stadium, New Orleans	81,591
V	Jan. 17, 1971	Baltimore (AFC) 16	Dallas (NFC) 13	Orange Bowl, Miami	79,204
IV	Jan. 11, 1970	Kansas City (AFL) 23	Minnesota (NFL) 7	Tulane Stadium, New Orleans	80,562
III	Jan. 12, 1969	New York (AFL) 16	Baltimore (NFL) 7	Orange Bowl, Miami	75,389
II	Jan. 14, 1968	Green Bay (NFL) 33	Oakland (AFL) 14	Orange Bowl, Miami	75,546
I	Jan. 15, 1967	Green Bay (NFL) 35	Kansas City (AFL) 10	Memorial Coliseum, Los Angeles	61,946

NOTE: Super Bowls I to IV were played before the American Football League and National Football League merged into the NFL, which was divided into two conferences, the NFC and AFC.

NATIONAL LEAGUE CHAMPIONS

Year	Champion	(W-L-T)	Year	Champion	(W-L-T)	Year	Champion	(W-L-T)
1921	Chicago Bears (Staley's)	(10-1-1)	1926	Frankford Yellow Jackets	(14-1-1)	1930	Green Bay Packers	(10-3-1)
1922	Canton Bulldogs	(10-0-2)	1927	New York Giants	(11-1-1)	1931	Green Bay Packers	(12-2-0)
1923	Canton Bulldogs	(11-0-1)	1928	Providence	(8-1-2)	1932	Chicago Bears	(7-1-6)
1924	Cleveland Indians	(7-1-1)		Steamrollers				
1925	Chicago Cardinals	(11-2-1)	1929	Green Bay Packers	(12-0-1)			

Year	Eastern Conference winners (W-L-T)	Western Conference winners (W-L-T)	League champion playoff results
1933	New York Giants (11-3-0)	Chicago Bears (10-2-1)	Chicago Bears 23, New York 21
1934	New York Giants (8-5-0)	Chicago Bears (13-0-0)	New York 30, Chicago Bears 13
1935	New York Giants (9-3-0)	Detroit Lions (7-3-2)	Detroit 26, New York 7
1936	Boston Redskins (7-5-0)	Green Bay Packers (10-1-1)	Green Bay 21, Boston 6
1937	Washington Redskins (8-3-0)	Chicago Bears (9-1-1)	Washington 28, Chicago Bears 21
1938	New York Giants (8-2-1)	Green Bay Packers (8-3-0)	New York 23, Green Bay 17
1939	New York Giants (9-1-1)	Green Bay Packers (9-2-0)	Green Bay 27, New York 0
1940	Washington Redskins (9-2-0)	Chicago Bears (8-3-0)	Chicago Bears 73, Washington 0
1941	New York Giants (8-3-0)	Chicago Bears (10-1-1)[2]	Chicago Bears 37, New York 9
1942	Washington Redskins (10-1-1)	Chicago Bears (11-0-0)	Washington 14, Chicago Bears 6
1943	Washington Redskins (6-3-1)[2]	Chicago Bears (8-1-1)	Chicago Bears 41, Washington 21
1944	New York Giants (8-1-1)	Green Bay Packers (8-2-0)	Green Bay 14, New York 7
1945	Washington Redskins (8-2-0)	Cleveland Rams (9-1-0)	Cleveland 15, Washington 14
1946	New York Giants (7-3-1)	Chicago Bears (8-2-1)	Chicago Bears 24, New York 14
1947	Philadelphia Eagles (8-4-0)[2]	Chicago Cardinals (9-3-0)	Chicago Cardinals 28, Philadelphia 21
1948	Philadelphia Eagles (9-2-1)	Chicago Cardinals (11-1-0)	Philadelphia 7, Chicago Cardinals 0
1949	Philadelphia Eagles (11-1-0)	Los Angeles Rams (8-2-2)	Philadelphia 14, Los Angeles 0
1950[1]	Cleveland Browns (10-2-0)[2]	Los Angeles Rams (9-3-0)[2]	Cleveland 30, Los Angeles 28
1951[1]	Cleveland Browns (11-1-0)	Los Angeles Rams (8-4-0)	Los Angeles 24, Cleveland 17
1952[1]	Cleveland Browns (8-4-0)	Detroit Lions (9-3-0)[2]	Detroit 17, Cleveland 7
1953	Cleveland Browns (11-1-0)	Detroit Lions (10-2-0)	Detroit 17, Cleveland 16
1954	Cleveland Browns (9-3-0)	Detroit Lions (9-2-1)	Cleveland 56, Detroit 10
1955	Cleveland Browns (9-2-1)	Los Angeles Rams (8-3-1)	Cleveland 38, Los Angeles 14
1956	New York Giants (8-3-1)	Chicago Bears (9-2-1)	New York 47, Chicago Bears 7
1957	Cleveland Browns (9-2-1)	Detroit Lions (8-4-0)[2]	Detroit 59, Cleveland 14
1958	New York Giants (9-3-0)[2]	Baltimore Colts (9-3-0)	Baltimore 23, New York 17[3]
1959	New York Giants (10-2-0)	Baltimore Colts (9-3-0)	Baltimore 31, New York 16
1960	Philadelphia Eagles (10-2-0)	Green Bay Packers (8-4-0)	Philadelphia 17, Green Bay 13
1961	New York Giants (10-3-1)	Green Bay Packers (11-3-0)	Green Bay 37, New York 0
1962	New York Giants (12-2-0)	Green Bay Packers (13-1-0)	Green Bay 16, New York 7
1963	New York Giants (11-3-0)	Chicago Bears (11-1-2)	Chicago 14, New York 10
1964	Cleveland Browns (10-3-1)	Baltimore Colts (12-2-0)	Cleveland 27, Baltimore 0
1965	Cleveland Browns (11-3-0)	Green Bay Packers (11-3-1)[2]	Green Bay 23, Cleveland 12
1966	Dallas Cowboys (10-3-1)	Green Bay Packers (12-2-0)	Green Bay 34, Dallas 27
1967	Dallas Cowboys (9-5-0)[2]	Green Bay Packers (9-4-1)[2]	Green Bay 21, Dallas 17
1968	Cleveland Browns (10-4-0)[2]	Baltimore Colts (13-1-0)[2]	Baltimore 34, Cleveland 0
1969	Cleveland Browns (10-3-1)[2]	Minnesota Vikings (12-2-0)[2]	Minnesota 27, Cleveland 7

1. League was divided into American and National Conferences, 1950-52 and again in 1970, when leagues merged. 2. Won divisional playoff. 3. Won at 8:15 of sudden death overtime period.

NATIONAL CONFERENCE CHAMPIONS

Year	Eastern Division	Central Division	Western Division	Champion
1970	Dallas Cowboys (10-4-0)	Minnesota Vikings (12-2-0)	San Francisco 49ers (10-3-1)	Dallas
1971	Dallas Cowboys (11-3-0)	Minnesota Vikings (11-3-0)	San Francisco 49ers (9-5-0)	Dallas
1972	Washington Redskins (11-3-0)	Green Bay Packers (10-4-0)	San Francisco 49ers (8-5-1)	Washington
1973	Dallas Cowboys (10-4-0)	Minnesota Vikings (12-2-0)	Los Angeles Rams (12-2-0)	Minnesota
1974	St. Louis Cardinals (10-4-0)	Minnesota Vikings (10-4-0)	Los Angeles Rams (10-4-0)	Minnesota
1975	St. Louis Cardinals (11-3-0)	Minnesota Vikings (12-2-0)	Los Angeles Rams (12-2-0)	Dallas
1976	Dallas Cowboys (11-3-0)	Minnesota Vikings (11-2-1)	Los Angeles Rams (10-3-1)	Minnesota
1977	Dallas Cowboys (12-2-0)	Minnesota Vikings (9-5-0)	Los Angeles Rams (10-4-0)	Dallas
1978	Dallas Cowboys (12-4-0)	Minnesota Vikings (8-7-1)	Los Angeles Rams (12-4-0)	Dallas
1979	Dallas Cowboys (11-5-0)	Tampa Bay Buccaneers (10-6-0)	Los Angeles Rams (9-7-0)	Los Angeles
1980	Philadelphia Eagles (12-4-0)	Minnesota Vikings (9-7-0)	Atlanta Falcons (12-4-0)	Philadelphia
1981	Dallas Cowboys (12-4-0)	Tampa Bay Buccaneers (9-7-0)	San Francisco 49ers (13-3-0)	San Francisco
1982*				
1983	Washington Redskins (14-2-0)	Detroit Lions (8-8-0)	San Francisco 49ers (10-6-0)	Washington
1984	Washington Redskins (11-5-0)	Chicago Bears (10-6-0)	San Francisco 49ers (15-1-0)	San Francisco
1985	Dallas Cowboys (10-6-0)	Chicago Bears (15-1-0)	Los Angeles Rams (11-5-0)	Chicago
1986	New York Giants (14-2-0)	Chicago Bears (14-2-0)	San Francisco 49ers (10-5-1)	New York
1987	Washington Redskins (11-4-0)	Chicago Bears (11-4-0)	San Francisco 49ers (13-2-0)	Washington
1988	Philadelphia Eagles (10-6-0)	Chicago Bears (12-4-0)	San Francisco 49ers (10-6-0)	San Francisco

Year	Eastern Division	Central Division	Western Division	Champion
1989	New York Giants (12-4-0)	Minnesota Vikings (10-6-0)	San Francisco 49ers (14-2-0)	San Francisco
1990	New York Giants (13-3-0)	Chicago Bears (11-5-0)	San Francisco 49ers (14-2-0)	New York
1991	Washington (14-2-0)	Detroit Lions (12-4-0)	New Orleans Saints (11-5-0)	Washington
1992	Dallas Cowboys (13-3-0)	Minnesota Vikings (11-5-0)	San Francisco 49ers (14-2-0)	Dallas
1993	Dallas Cowboys (12-4-0)	Detroit Lions (10-6-0)	San Francisco 49ers (10-6-0)	Dallas
1994	Dallas Cowboys (12-4-0)	Minnesota Vikings (10-6-0)	San Francisco 49ers (13-3-0)	San Francisco
1995	Dallas Cowboys (12-4-0)	Green Bay Packers (11-5-0)	San Francisco 49ers (11-5-0)	Dallas
1996	Dallas Cowboys (10-6-0)	Green Bay Packers (13-3-0)	Carolina Panthers (12-4-0)	Green Bay
1997	New York Giants (10-5-1)	Green Bay Packers (13-3-0)	San Francisco 49ers (13-3-0)	Green Bay
1998	Dallas Cowboys (10-6-0)	Minnesota Vikings (15-1-0)	Atlanta Falcons (14-2-0)	Atlanta

*Schedule reduced to 9 games from usual 16, with no standings kept in Eastern, Central, and Western Divisions, because of 57-day player strike. Washington Redskins won conference title and also had best regular-season record (8-1-0).

AMERICAN LEAGUE CHAMPIONS

Year	Eastern Division (W-L-T)	Western Division (W-L-T)	League champion, playoff results
1960	Houston Oilers (10-4-0)	Los Angeles Chargers (10-4-0)	Houston 24, Los Angeles 16
1961	Houston Oilers (10-3-1)	San Diego Chargers (12-2-0)	Houston 10, San Diego 3
1962	Houston Oilers (11-3-0)	Dallas Texans (11-3-0)	Dallas 20, Houston 17[1]
1963	Boston Patriots (8-6-1)[2]	San Diego Chargers (11-3-0)	San Diego 51, Boston 10
1964	Buffalo Bills (12-2-0)	San Diego Chargers (8-5-1)	Buffalo 20, San Diego 7
1965	Buffalo Bills (10-3-1)	San Diego Chargers (9-2-3)	Buffalo 23, San Diego 0
1966	Buffalo Bills (9-4-1)	Kansas City Chiefs (11-2-1)	Kansas City 31, Buffalo 7
1967	Houston Oilers (9-4-1)	Oakland Raiders (13-1-0)	Oakland 40, Houston 7
1968	New York Jets (11-3-0)	Oakland Raiders (12-2-0)[2]	New York 27, Oakland 23
1969	New York Jets (10-4-0)	Oakland Raiders (12-1-1)	Kansas City 17, Oakland 7[3]

1. Won at 2:45 of second sudden death overtime period. 2. Won divisional playoff. 3. Kansas City defeated New York, 13-6, and Oakland defeated Houston, 56-7, in interdivisional playoffs.

AMERICAN CONFERENCE CHAMPIONS

Year	Eastern Division	Central Division	Western Division	Champion
1970	Baltimore Colts (11-2-1)	Cincinnati Bengals (8-6-0)	Oakland Raiders (8-4-2)	Baltimore
1971	Miami Dolphins (10-3-1)	Cleveland Browns (9-5-0)	Kansas City Chiefs (10-3-1)	Miami
1972	Miami Dolphins (14-0-0)	Pittsburgh Steelers (11-3-0)	Oakland Raiders (10-3-1)	Miami
1973	Miami Dolphins (12-2-0)	Cincinnati Bengals (10-4-0)	Oakland Raiders (9-4-1)	Miami
1974	Miami Dolphins (11-3-0)	Pittsburgh Steelers (10-3-1)	Oakland Raiders (12-2-0)	Pittsburgh
1975	Baltimore Colts (10-4-0)	Pittsburgh Steelers (12-2-0)	Oakland Raiders (12-2-0)	Pittsburgh
1976	Baltimore Colts (11-3-0)	Pittsburgh Steelers (10-4-0)	Oakland Raiders (13-1-0)	Oakland
1977	Baltimore Colts (10-4-0)	Pittsburgh Steelers (9-5-0)	Denver Broncos (12-2-0)	Denver
1978	New England Patriots (11-5-0)	Pittsburgh Steelers (14-2-0)	Denver Broncos (10-6-0)	Pittsburgh
1979	Miami Dolphins (10-6-0)	Pittsburgh Steelers (12-4-0)	San Diego Chargers (12-4-0)	Pittsburgh
1980	Buffalo Bills (11-5-0)	Cleveland Browns (11-5-0)	San Diego Chargers (11-5-0)	Oakland
1981	Miami Dolphins (11-4-1)	Cincinnati Bengals (12-4-0)	San Diego Chargers (10-6-0)	Cincinnati
1982*	Miami Dolphins won the conference title, but the Los Angeles Raiders had best regular-season record (8-1-0).			
1983	Miami Dolphins (12-4-0)	Pittsburgh Steelers (10-6-0)	Los Angeles Raiders (12-4-0)	Los Angeles
1984	Miami Dolphins (14-2-0)	Pittsburgh Steelers (9-7-0)	Denver Broncos (13-3-0)	Miami
1985	Miami Dolphins (12-4-0)	Cleveland Browns (8-8)	Los Angeles Raiders (12-4-0)	New England
1986	New England Patriots (11-5-0)	Cleveland Browns (12-4-0)	Denver Broncos (11-5-0)	Denver
1987	Indianapolis Colts (9-6-0)	Cleveland Browns (10-5-0)	Denver Broncos (10-4-1)	Denver
1988	Buffalo Bills (12-4-0)	Cincinnati Bengals (12-4-0)	Seattle Seahawks (9-7-0)	Cincinnati
1989	Buffalo Bills (9-7-0)	Cleveland Browns (9-6-1)	Denver Broncos (11-5-0)	Denver
1990	Buffalo Bills (13-3-0)	Cincinnati Bengals (9-7-0)	Los Angeles Raiders (12-4-0)	Buffalo
1991	Buffalo Bills (13-3-0)	Houston Oilers (11-5-0)	Denver Broncos (12-4-0)	Buffalo
1992	Miami Dolphins (11-5-0)	Pittsburgh Steelers (11-5-0)	San Diego Chargers (11-5-0)	Buffalo
1993	Buffalo Bills (12-4-0)	Houston Oilers (12-4-0)	Kansas City Chiefs (11-5-0)	Buffalo
1994	Miami Dolphins (10-6-0)	Pittsburgh Steelers (12-4-0)	San Diego Chargers (11-5-0)	San Diego
1995	Buffalo Bills (10-6-0)	Pittsburgh Steelers (11-5-0)	Kansas City Chiefs (13-3-0)	Pittsburgh
1996	New England Patriots (11-5-0)	Pittsburgh Steelers (10-6-0)	Denver Broncos (13-3-0)	New England
1997	New England Patriots (10-6-0)	Pittsburgh Steelers (11-5-0)	Kansas City Chiefs (13-3-0)	Denver
1998	New York Jets (12-4-0)	Jacksonville Jaguars (11-5-0)	Denver Broncos (14-2-0)	Denver

*Schedule reduced to 9 games from usual 16, with no standings kept in Eastern, Central, and Western Divisions, because of 57-day player strike.

PRO FOOTBALL HALL OF FAME

(National Football Museum, Canton, Ohio)

Teams named are those with which player is best identified; figures in parentheses indicate number of playing seasons.

Adderley, Herb, defensive back, Packers, Cowboys (12)	1961–72
Alworth, Lance, wide receiver, Chargers, Cowboys (12)	1961–72
Atkins, Doug, defensive end, Browns, Bears, Saints (17)	1953–69
Badgro, Morris, end, N.Y. Yankees, Giants, Brooklyn Dodgers (8)	1927, 1930–36
Barney, Lem, defensive back, Lions (11)	1967–78
Battles, Cliff, back, Redskins (6)	1932–37
Baugh, Sammy, quarterback, Redskins (16)	1936–52
Bednarik, Chuck, center-linebacker, Eagles (14)	1949–62
Bell, Bert, NFL founder, Eagles and Steelers, NFL Commissioner	1946–59
Bell, Bobby, linebacker, Chiefs (12)	1963–74
Berry, Raymond, end, Colts (13)	1955–67
Bidwell, Charles W., owner, Chicago Cardinals	1933–47
Biletnikoff, Fred, wide receiver, Raiders (14)	1965–78
Blanda, George, quarterback-kicker, Bears, Oilers, Raiders (27)	1949–75
Blount, Mel, cornerback, Pittsburgh Steelers (14)	1970–83
Bradshaw, Terry, quarterback, Pittsburgh Steelers (14)	1970–83
Brown, Jim, fullback, Browns (9)	1957–65
Brown, Paul E., coach, Browns (1946–62), Bengals (1968–75)	1946–75
Brown, Roosevelt, tackle, Giants (13)	1953–65
Brown, Willie, cornerback, Broncos, Raiders (16)	1963–78
Buchanan, Buck, tackle, Chiefs (11)	1963–73
Butkus, Dick, linebacker, Bears (9)	1965–73
Campbell, Earl, running back, Oilers, Saints (8)	1978–85
Canadeo, Tony, back, Packers (11)	1941–52
Carr, Joe, NFL president (18)	1921–39
Chamberlin, Guy, end, 4 teams (9)	1919–27
Christiansen, Jack, defensive back, Lions (8)	1951–58
Clark, Earl (Dutch), quarterback, Spartans, Lions (7)	1931–38
Connor, George, tackle, linebacker, Bears (8)	1948–55
Conzelman, Jimmy, quarterback, 5 teams (10), owner, Detroit Panthers	1921–48
Creekmur, Lou, offensive tackle/guard, Lions (10)	1950–59
Csonka, Larry, back, Dolphins, Giants (11)	1968–79
Davis, Al, owner, Raiders, coach, general manager	1963–
Davis, Willie, defensive end, Packers (10)	1960–69
Dawson, Len, quarterback, Steelers, Browns, Texans, Chiefs (19)	1957–75
Dickerson, Eric, running back, Rams, Colts, Raiders, Falcons (11)	1983–93
Dierdorf, Dan, tackle/center, Cardinals (13)	1971–83
Ditka, Mike, tight end, Bears, Eagles, Cowboys (12)	1961–72
Donovan, Art, defensive tackle, Colts (12)	1950–61
Dorsett, Tony, running back, Cowboys, Broncos (12)	1977–88
Driscoll, John (Paddy), quarterback, Cards, Bears (11)	1919–29
Dudley, Bill, back, Steelers, Lions, Redskins (9)	1942–53
Edwards, Albert Glen (Turk), tackle, Redskins (9)	1932–40
Ewbank, Weeb, coach, Colts, Jets (20)	1954–73
Fears, Tom, end, Rams (9); coach, Saints	1948–56
Finks, Jim, administrator/general manager, Vikings, Bears, Saints	1964–93
Flaherty, Ray, end, Yankees, Giants (9); coach, Redskins, Yankees (14)	1928–49
Ford, Len, end, defensive end, Browns, Packers (11)	1948–58
Fouts, Dan, quarterback, Chargers (15)	1973–87
Fortmann, Daniel J., guard, Bears (8)	1936–43
Gatski, Frank, offensive lineman, Browns (12)	1946–57
George, Bill, linebacker, Bears, Rams (15)	1952–66
Gibbs, Joe, coach, Redskins (11)	1981–92
Gifford, Frank, back, Giants (12)	1952–64
Gillman, Sid, coach, Rams, Chargers, Oilers (18)	1955–70, 73–74
Graham, Otto, quarterback, Browns (10)	1946–55
Grange, Harold (Red), back, Bears, Yankees (9)	1925–34
Grant, Bud, coach, Vikings (18)	1967–85
Greene, Joe, defensive tackle, Steelers (13)	1968–81
Gregg, Forrest, tackle, Packers (15)	1956–71
Griese, Bob, quarterback, Dolphins (14)	1967–80
Groza, Lou, place-kicker, tackle, Browns (21)	1946–67
Guyon, Joe, back, 6 teams (8)	1919–27
Halas, George, NFL founder, owner and coach, Staleys and Bears, end (11)	1919–27
Ham, Jack, linebacker, Steelers (13)	1970–82
Hannah, John, guard, Patriots (13)	1973–85
Harris, Franco, running back, Steelers, Seahawks (13)	1972–84
Haynes, Mike, defensive back, Patriots, Raiders (10)	1976–85
Healey, Ed, tackle, Bears (8)	1920–27
Hein, Mel, center, Giants (15)	1931–45
Hendricks, Ted, linebacker, Colts, Packers, Raiders (15)	1969–83
Henry, Wilbur (Pete), tackle, Bulldogs, Giants (8)	1920–28
Herber, Arnie, quarterback, Packers, Giants (13)	1930–45
Hewitt, Bill, end, Bears, Eagles (9)	1932–43
Hinkle, Clarke, fullback, Packers (10)	1932–41
Hirsch, Elroy (Crazy Legs), back, end, Rams (12)	1946–57
Hornung, Paul, running back, Packers (9)	1957–62, 64–66
Houston, Ken, defensive back, Oilers, Redskins (14)	1967–80
Hubbard, R. (Cal), tackle, Giants, Packers (9)	1927–36
Huff, Sam, linebacker, Giants, Redskins (13)	1956–67, 1969
Hunt, Lamar, founder A.F.L., owner Texans, Chiefs	1959–
Hutson, Don, end, Packers (11)	1935–45
Johnson, John Henry, back, 49ers, Lions, Steelers, Oilers (13)	1954–66
Johnson, Jimmy, cornerback, 49ers (16)	1961–76
Joiner, Charlie, receiver, Oilers, Bengals, Chargers (18)	1969–86
Jones, David (Deacon), defensive end, Rams, Chargers, Redskins (14)	1961–74
Jones, Stan, defensive tackle, Bears, Redskins (13)	1954–66
Jordan, Henry, defensive tackle, Browns, Packers (13)	1957–69
Jurgensen, Sonny, quarterback, Eagles, Redskins (18)	1957–74
Kelly, Leroy, running back, Browns (10)	1964–73
Kiesling, Walt, guard, 6 teams (13)	1926–38
Kinard, Frank (Bruiser), tackle, Dodgers (9)	1938–47
Krause, Paul, safety, Redskins, Vikings (16)	1964–79
Lambeau, Earl (Curly), NFL founder, coach, end, back, Packers (11)	1919–53
Lambert, Jack, linebacker, Steelers (11)	1974–84
Landry, Tom, coach, Cowboys (29)	1960–88
Lane, Richard (Night Train), defensive back, Rams, Cardinals, Lions (14)	1952–65
Langer, Jim, center, Dolphins, Vikings (12)	1970–81
Lanier, Willie, linebacker, Chiefs (11)	1967–77
Largent, Steve, receiver, Seahawks (14)	1976–89
Lary, Yale, defensive back, punter, Lions (11)	1952–64
Laveill, Dante, end, Browns (11)	1946–56
Layne, Bobby, quarterback, Bears, Lions, Steelers (15)	1948–62
Leemans, Alphonse (Tuffy), back, Giants (8)	1936–43
Lilly, Bob, defensive tackle, Cowboys (14)	1961–74
Little, Larry, guard, Dolphins, Chargers (14)	1967–80
Lombardi, Vince, coach, Packers, Redskins (11)	1959–70
Luckman, Sid, quarterback, Bears (12)	1939–50
Lyman, Roy (Link), tackle, Bulldogs, Bears (11)	1922–34
Mack, Tom, guard, Rams (13)	1966–78
Mackey, John, tight end, Colts, Chargers (10)	1963–72
Mara, Tim, NFL founder, owner, Giants	1925–59
Mara, Wellington, NFL executive, owner, Giants	1937–
Marchetti, Gino, defensive end, Colts (14)	1952–66
Marshall, George P., NFL founder, owner, Redskins	1932–65
Matson, Ollie, back, Cardinals, Rams, Lions, Eagles (14)	1952–66
Maynard, Don, receiver, Giants, Jets, Cardinals (15)	1958–73
McAfee, George, back, Bears (8)	1940–50
McCormack, Mike, tackle, N.Y. Yankees, Cleveland Browns (10)	1951–62
McDonald, Tommy, wide receiver, Eagles, Cowboys, Rams, Falcons, Browns (12)	1957–68
McElhenny, Hugh, back, 49ers, Vikings, Giants (13)	1952–64
McNally, John (Blood), back, 7 teams (15)	1925–39
Michalske, August, guard, Yankees, Packers (11)	1926–37
Millner, Wayne, end, Redskins (7)	1936–45
Mitchell, Bobby, wide receiver, Browns, Redskins (11)	1958–68
Mix, Ron, tackle, Chargers (11)	1960–71
Moore, Lenny, back, Colts (12)	1956–67
Motley, Marion, fullback, Browns, Steelers (9)	1946–55
Munoz, Anthony, tackle, Bengals (13)	1980–92

Musso, George, guard-tackle, Bears (12)	1933–44
Nagurski, Bronko, fullback, Bears (9)	1930–43
Namath, Joe, quarterback, Jets, Rams (13)	1965–77
Neale, Earle (Greasy), coach, Eagles	1941–50
Nevers, Ernie, fullback, Chicago Cardinals (5)	1926–31
Newsome, Ozzie, tight end, Browns (13)	1978–90
Nitschke, Ray, linebackers, Packers (15)	1958–72
Noll, Chuck, coach, Steelers (23)	1969–81
Nomellini, Leo, defensive tackle, 49ers (14)	1950–63
Olsen, Merlin, defensive tackle, Rams (15)	1962–76
Otto, Jim, center, Raiders (15)	1960–74
Owen, Steve, tackle, Giants (9), coach, Giants (13)	1924–53
Page, Alan, defensive tackle, Vikings, Bears (15)	1967–81
Parker, Clarence (Ace), quarterback, Dodgers (7)	1937–46
Parker, Jim, guard, tackle, Colts (11)	1957–67
Payton, Walter, running back, Bears (13)	1977–89
Perry, Joe, fullback, 49ers, Colts (16)	1948–63
Pihos, Pete, end, Eagles (9)	1947–55
Ray, Hugh (Shorty), NFL advisor	1938–52
Reeves, Dan, owner, Rams	1941–71
Renfro, Mel, cornerback, safety, Cowboys (14)	1964–77
Riggins, John, running back, Jets, Redskins (14)	1971–84
Ringo, Jim, center, Packers (15)	1953–67
Robustelli, Andy, defensive end, Rams, Giants (14)	1951–64
Rooney, Art, NFL founder, owner, Steelers	1933–88
Rozelle, Pete, commissioner, NFL	1960–89
St. Claire, Bob, tackle, 49ers (11)	1953–63
Sayers, Gale, back, Bears (7)	1965–71
Schmidt, Joe, linebacker, Lions (13)	1953–65
Schramm, Tex, administrator, Rams, Cowboys (42)	1947–89
Selmon, Lee Roy, defensive end, Buccaneers (13)	1976–84
Shaw, Billy, guard, Bills (9)	1961–69
Shell, Art, tackle, Raiders (15)	1968–82
Shula, Don, coach, Colts, Dolphins (33)	1963–95
Simpson, O.J., back, Bills, 49ers (11)	1969–79

Singletary, Mike, linebacker, Bears (12)	1981–92
Smith, Jackie, tight end, Cardinals, Cowboys (16)	1963–78
Starr, Bart, quarterback, coach, Packers (16)	1956–71
Staubach, Roger, quarterback, Cowboys (11)	1969–79
Stautner, Ernie, defensive tackle, Steelres (14)	1950–63
Stenerud, Jan, placekicker, Chiefs, Packers, Vikings (19)	1967–85
Stephenson, Dwight, center, Dolphins (8)	1980–87
Strong, Ken, back, Giants, Yankees (14)	1929–47
Stydahar, Joe, tackle, Bears (9); coach, Rams, Cardinals (5)	1936–54
Tarkenton, Fran, quarterback, Vikings, Giants (18)	1961–78
Taylor, Charlie, wide receiver, Redskins (14)	1964–77
Taylor, Jim, fullback, Packers, Saints (10)	1958–67
Taylor, Lawrence, linebacker, Giants (13)	1981–93
Thorpe, Jim, back, 7 teams (12)	1915–28
Tittle, Y.A., quarterback, Colts, 49ers, Giants (17)	1948–64
Trafton, George, center, Bears (13)	1920–32
Trippi, Charley, back, Chicago Cardinals (9)	1947–55
Tunnell, Emlen, defensive back, Giants, Packers (14)	1948–61
Turner, Clyde (Bulldog), center, Bears (13)	1940–52
Unitas, John, quarterback, Colts (18)	1956–73
Upshaw, Gene, guard, Raiders (15)	1967–81
Van Brocklin, Norm, quarterback, Rams, Eagles (12)	1949–60
Van Buren, Steve, back, Eagles (8)	1944–51
Walker, Doak, running back, def. back, kicker, Lions (6)	1950–55
Walsh, Bill, coach, 49ers (10)	1979–88
Warfield, Paul, wide receiver, Browns, Dolphins (13)	1964–74, 76–77
Waterfield, Bob, quarterback, Rams (8)	1945–52
Webster, Mike, center, Steelers, Chiefs (17)	1974–90
Weinmeister, Arnie, tackle, N.Y. Yankees, Giants (6)	1948–53
White, Randy, defensive tackle, Cowboys (14)	1975–88
Willis, Bill, guard, Browns (8)	1946–53
Wilson, Larry, defensive back, Cardinals (13)	1960–72
Winslow, Kellen, tight end, Chargers (9)	1979–87
Wood, Willie, safety, Packers (12)	1960–71
Wojciechowicz, Alex, center, Lions, Eagles (13)	1938–50

N.F.L. INDIVIDUAL LIFETIME, SEASON, AND GAME RECORDS

(American Football League records were incorporated into NFL records after merger of the leagues) Players listed in boldface were active during the 1998 season. The NFL does not recognize records from the All-American Football Conference (AAFC) which existed from 1946 to 1949. The 49ers, Browns, and Colts merged with the NFL in 1949.

All-Time Leading Touchdown Scorers (Through 1998)

		Yrs	Rush	Rec	Ret	Total
1	**Jerry Rice**	14	10	164	1	175
2	Marcus Allen	16	123	21	1	145
3	**Emmitt Smith**	9	125	9	0	134
4	Jim Brown	9	106	20	0	126
5	Walter Payton	13	110	15	0	125
6	John Riggins	14	104	12	0	116
7	Lenny Moore	12	63	48	2	113
8	**Barry Sanders**	10	99	10	0	109
9	Don Hutson	11	3	99	3	105
10	**Cris Carter**	12	0	101	1	102
11	Steve Largent	14	1	100	0	101
12	Franco Harris	13	91	9	0	100
13	Eric Dickerson	11	90	6	0	96
14	Jim Taylor	10	83	10	0	93
15	Tony Dorsett	12	77	13	1	91
	Bobby Mitchell	11	18	65	8	91

All-Time Leading Receivers (Through 1998)

		Yrs	No	Yards	Avg	TD
1	**Jerry Rice**	14	1,139	17,612	15.5	164
2	Art Monk	16	940	12,721	13.5	68
3	Andre Reed	14	889	12,559	14.1	85
4	**Cris Carter**	12	834	10,447	12.5	101
5	Steve Largent	14	819	13,089	16.0	100
6	**Henry Ellard**	16	814	13,777	16.9	65
7	**Irving Fryar**	15	784	11,983	15.3	77
8	James Lofton	16	764	14,004	18.3	75
9	Charlie Joiner	18	750	12,146	16.2	65
10	**Michael Irvin**	11	740	11,737	15.9	62
11	Gary Clark	11	699	10,856	15.5	65
12	**Andre Rison**	10	681	9,381	13.8	78
13	**Tim Brown**	11	680	9,600	14.1	69
14	Ozzie Newsome	13	662	7,980	12.1	47
15	Charley Taylor	13	649	9,110	14.0	79

All-Time Leading Passers (Minimum 1,500 attempts. Through 1998)

		Yrs	Att	Cmp	Cmp%	Yards	Avg Gain	TD	TD%	Int	Int%	Rating
1	**Steve Young**	14	4,065	2,622	64.5	32,678	8.04	229	5.6	103	2.5	97.6
2	Joe Montana	15	5,391	3,409	63.2	40,551	7.52	273	5.1	139	2.6	92.3
3	**Brett Favre**	8	3,757	2,318	61.7	26,803	7.13	213	5.7	118	3.1	89.0
4	**Dan Marino**	16	7,989	4,763	59.6	58,913	7.37	408	5.1	235	2.9	87.3
5	**Mark Brunell**	6	1,719	1,038	60.4	12,512	7.28	72	4.2	43	2.5	86.3
6	Jim Kelly	11	4,779	2,874	60.1	35,467	7.42	237	5.0	175	3.7	84.4
7	Roger Staubach	11	2,958	1,685	57.0	22,700	7.67	153	5.2	109	3.7	83.4
8	**Troy Aikman**	10	4,011	2,479	61.8	28,346	7.07	141	3.5	115	2.9	82.8

		Yrs	Att	Cmp	Cmp%	Yards	Avg Gain	TD	TD%	Int	Int%	Rating
9	Neil Lomax	8	3,153	1,817	57.6	22,771	7.22	136	4.3	90	2.9	82.7
10	Sonny Jurgensen	18	4,262	2,433	57.1	32,224	7.56	255	6.0	189	4.4	82.6
11	Len Dawson	19	3,741	2,136	57.1	28,711	7.67	239	6.4	183	4.9	82.5
12	Ken Anderson	16	4,475	2,654	59.3	32,838	7.34	197	4.4	160	3.6	81.9
13	Bernie Kosar	12	3,365	1,994	59.3	23,301	6.92	124	3.7	87	2.6	81.8
14	Danny White	13	2,950	1,761	59.7	21,959	7.44	155	5.3	132	4.5	81.7
15	Neil O'Donnell	9	2,862	1,650	57.7	19,026	6.65	104	3.6	57	2.0	81.6

Note: The NFL does not recognize records from the All-American Football Conference (1946-49). If it did, **Otto Graham** would rank 5th (after Marino) with the following stats: 10 Yrs; 2,626 Att; 1,464 Comp; 55.8 Comp Pct; 23,584 Yards; 8.98 Avg Gain; 174 TD; 6.6 TD Pct; 135 Int; 5.1 Int Pct; and 86.6 Rating Pts.

All-Time Leading Scorers (Through 1998)

		Yrs	TD	FG	PAT	Total
1	George Blanda	26	9	335	943	2,002
2	Gary Anderson	17	0	420	585	1,845
3	Morten Andersen	17	0	401	558	1,761
4	Nick Lowery	18	0	383	562	1,711
5	Jan Stenerud	19	0	373	580	1,699
6	Norm Johnson	17	0	348	613	1,657
7	Eddie Murray	17	0	337	521	1,532
8	Pat Leahy	18	0	304	558	1,470
9	Jim Turner	16	1	304	521	1,439
10	Matt Bahr	17	0	300	522	1,422
11	Mark Moseley	16	0	300	482	1,382
12	Jim Bakken	17	0	282	534	1,380
13	Fred Cox	15	0	282	519	1,365
14	Al Del Greco	17	0	299	463	1,360
15	Lou Groza	17	1	234	641	1,349

Scoring

Most points scored, lifetime—2,002, George Blanda, Chicago Bears, 1949-58; Baltimore, 1950; Houston, 1960–66; Oakland, 1967–75 (9 tds, 943 pat, 335 fg).

Most points, season—176, Paul Hornung, Green Bay, 1960 (15 td, 41 pat, 15 fg).

Most points, game—40, Ernie Nevers, Chicago Cardinals, 1929 (6 td, 4 pat).

Most touchdowns, lifetime—175, Jerry Rice, San Francisco, 1985–98.

Most touchdowns, season—25, Emmitt Smith, Dallas, 1995.

Most points after touchdown, lifetime—943, George Blanda, Chicago Bears, 1949–58; Baltimore, 1950; Houston, 1960–66; Oakland, 1967-75.

Most points after touchdown, game—9, Pat Harder, Cardinals, 1948; Bob Waterfield, Los Angeles Rams, 1950; Charlie Gogolak, Washington, 1966.

Most field goals, lifetime—420, Gary Anderson, Pittsburgh, 1982–94; Philadelphia, 1995–96; San Francisco, 1997; Minnesota, 1998.

Most field goals, season—37, John Kasay, Carolina, 1996.

Most field goals, game—7, Jim Bakken, St. Louis, 1967; Rich Karlis, Minnesota, 1989; and Chris Boniol, Dallas, 1996.

Longest field goal—63 yards, Tom Dempsey, New Orleans, 1970; Jason Elam, Denver, 1998.

Rushing

Most yards gained, lifetime—16,726, Walter Payton, Chicago Bears, 1975–87.

Most yards gained, season—2,105, Eric Dickerson, Los Angeles, 1984.

Most yards gained, game—275, Walter Payton, Chicago Bears, 1977.

Most touchdowns, lifetime—110, Walter Payton, Chicago Bears, 1975–87.

Most touchdowns, season—25, Emmitt Smith, Dallas, 1995.

Most touchdowns, game—6, Ernie Nevers, Chicago Cardinals, 1929.

Longest run from scrimmage—99 yards, Tony Dorsett, Dallas, 1983.

All-Time Leading Rushers (Through 1998)

		Yrs	Car	Yards	Avg	TD
1	Walter Payton	13	3,838	16,726	4.4	110
2	Barry Sanders	10	3,062	15,269	5.0	99
3	Eric Dickerson	11	2,996	13,259	4.4	90
4	Tony Dorsett	12	2,936	12,739	4.3	77
5	Emmitt Smith	9	2,914	12,566	4.3	125
6	Jim Brown	9	2,359	12,312	5.2	106
7	Marcus Allen	16	3,022	12,243	4.1	123
8	Franco Harris	13	2,949	12,120	4.1	91
9	Thurman Thomas	11	2,813	11,786	4.2	65
10	John Riggins	14	2,916	11,352	3.9	104
11	O.J. Simpson	11	2,404	11,236	4.7	61
12	Ottis Anderson	14	2,562	10,273	4.0	81
13	Earl Campbell	8	2,187	9,407	4.3	74
14	Jim Taylor	10	1,941	8,597	4.4	83
15	Joe Perry	14	1,737	8,378	4.8	53

Receiving

Most pass receptions, lifetime—1,139, Jerry Rice, San Francisco, 1985–98.

Most pass receptions, season—123, Herman Moore, Detroit, 1995.

Most pass receptions, game—18, Tom Fears, Los Angeles, 1950.

Most yards gained, pass receptions, lifetime—17,612, Jerry Rice, San Francisco, 1985–98.

Most yards gained, receptions, season—1,848, Jerry Rice, San Francisco, 1995.

Most yards gained, receptions, game—336, Flipper Anderson, Los Angeles Rams, 1989.

Most touchdown receptions, lifetime—164, Jerry Rice, San Francisco, 1985–98.

Most touchdown pass receptions, season—22, Jerry Rice, San Francisco, 1987.

Most touchdown pass receptions, game—5, Bob Shaw, Chicago Cards, 1950; Kellen Winslow, San Diego, 1981; Jerry Rice, San Francisco, 1990.

Interceptions

Most pass interceptions, lifetime—81, Paul Krause, Washington, 1964-67; Minnesota, 1968–79.

Most pass interceptions, season—14, Richard (Night Train) Lane, Detroit, 1952.

Most pass interceptions, game—4, by 17 players.

Longest pass interception return—104 yards, James Willis, Philadelphia, 1996.

Kicking

Highest average punting, lifetime—45.1 yards, Sammy Baugh, Washington, 1937–52.

Longest punt return—103 yards, Robert Bailey, L.A. Rams, 1994.

Longest kick-off return—106 yards, Roy Green, St. Louis, 1979; Al Carmichael, Green Bay, 1956; Noland Smith, Kansas City, 1967.

Passing

Most touchdown passes, season—48, Dan Marino, Miami, 1984.

Most touchdown passes, game—7, Sid Luckman, Chicago Bears, 1943; Adrian Burk, Philadelphia, 1954; George Blanda, Houston, 1961; Y. A. Tittle, N.Y. Giants, 1962; Joe Kapp, Minnesota, 1969.

Longest pass completion—99 yards, Frank Filchock (to Andy Farkas), Washington, 1939; George Izo (to Bob Mitchell), Washington, 1963; Karl Sweetan (to Pat Studstill), Detroit, 1966; Sonny Jurgensen (to Gerry Allen), Washington, 1968; Jim Plunkett (to Cliff Branch) L.A. Raiders, 1983; Ron Jaworski (to Mike Quick), Philadelphia, 1985; Stan Humphries (to Tony Martin), San Diego, 1994; Brett Favre (to Robert Brooks), Green Bay, 1995.

Most passes completed, lifetime—4,763, Dan Marino, Miami, 1983–98.

Most passes completed, season—404, Warren Moon, 1991.

Most passes completed, game—45, Drew Bledsoe, New England, 1994.

Most touchdown passes, lifetime—408, Dan Marino, Miami, 1983–98.

Most yards gained, lifetime—58,913, Dan Marino, Miami, 1983–98.

Most yards gained, season—5,084, Dan Marino, Miami, 1984.

Most yards gained, game—554, Norm Van Brocklin, Los Angeles, 1951.

Sports Personalities

A name in parentheses is the original name or form of name. Localities are places of birth. Dates of birth appear as month/day/year. **Boldface** years in parentheses are dates of **(birth-death)**.

Information has been gathered from many sources, including the individuals themselves. However, the almanac cannot guarantee the accuracy of every individual item.

Aaron, Hank (Henry) (baseball); Mobile, Ala., 2/5/34
Abdul-Jabbar, Kareem (Lewis Ferdinand Alcindor, Jr.) (basketball); New York City, 4/16/47
Affleck, Francis (auto racing) **(1951–1985)**
Agassi, Andre (tennis); Las Vegas, Nev., 4/29/70
Aikman, Troy (football); Henryetta, Okla., 11/21/66
Ali, Muhammad (Cassius Clay) (boxing); Louisville, Ky., 1/18/42
Allen, Dick (Richard Anthony) (baseball); Wampum, Pa., 3/8/42
Allen, George (football) **(1918–1990)**
Allison, Bobby (Robert Arthur) (auto racing); Hueytown, Ala., 12/3/37
Allison, Davey (auto racing); Hueytown, Ala. **(1961–1993)**
Alston, Walter (baseball); Venice, Ohio **(1911–1984)**
Alworth, Lance (football); Houston, 8/3/40
Ameche, Alan (football); Houston, Tex. **(1933–1988)**
Anderson, Sparky (George) (baseball); Bridgewater, S.D., 2/22/34
Andretti, Mario (auto racing); Montona, Trieste, Italy, 2/28/40
Anthony, Earl (bowling); Kent, Wash., 4/27/38
Appling, Luke (baseball); High Point, N.C **(1907–1990)**
Arcaro, Eddie (George Edward) (jockey); Cincinnati **(1916–1997)**
Ashe, Arthur (tennis); Richmond, Va. **(1943–1993)**
Ashford, Evelyn (track & field); Shreveport, La., 4/15/57
Austin, Tracy (tennis); Rolling Hills, Calif., 12/2/62
Averill, Earl (baseball); Everett, Wash. **(1915–1983)**
Babashoff, Shirley (swimming); Whittier, Calif., 1/31/57
Baer, Max (boxing); Omaha, Neb. **(1909–1959)**
Bailey, Donovan (track); Canada, 12/16/67
Banks, Ernie (baseball); Dallas, 1/31/31
Bannister, Roger (runner); Harrow, England, 3/24/29
Barkley, Charles (basketball); Leeds, Ala., 2/20/63
Barry, Rick (Richard) (basketball); Elizabeth, N.J., 3/28/44
Bauer, Hank (Henry) (baseball); East St. Louis, Ill., 7/31/22
Baugh, Sammy (football); Temple, Tex., 3/17/14
Baylor, Elgin (basketball); Washington, D.C., 9/16/34
Beamon, Bob (long jumper); New York City, 8/2/46
Becker, Boris (tennis); Leiman, W. Germany, 11/22/67
Bee, Clair (basketball); Cleveland, Ohio **(1896–1983)**
Beliveau, Jean (hockey); Three Rivers, Quebec, Canada, 8/31/31
Belle, Albert (baseball); Shreveport, La., 8/25/66
Beman, Deane (golf); Washington, D.C., 4/22/38
Bench, Johnny (Johnny Lee) (baseball); Oklahoma City, 12/7/47
Berg, Patty (Patricia Jane) (golf); Minneapolis, 2/13/18
Berra, Yogi (Lawrence) (baseball); St. Louis, 5/12/25
Biletnikoff, Frederick (football); Erie, Pa., 2/23/43
Bing, Dave (basketball); Washington, D.C., 11/24/43
Bird, Larry (basketball); French Lick, Ind., 12/7/56
Blaik, Earl H. (football); Detroit **(1897–1989)**
Blanda, George Frederick (football); Youngwood, Pa., 9/17/27
Bledsoe, Drew (football); Walla Walla, Wash., 2/14/72
Blue, Vida (baseball); Mansfield, La., 7/28/49
Bodine, Brett (auto racing); Chemung, N.Y., 1/11/59
Bodine, Geoff (auto racing); Chemung, N.Y., 4/18/49
Boggs, Wade (baseball); Omaha, Neb., 6/15/58
Bonds, Barry (baseball); Riverside, Calif., 7/24/64
Borg, Björn (tennis); Stockholm, Sweden, 6/6/56
Boros, Julius (golf); Fairfield, Conn. **(1920–1994)**
Bossy, Mike (hockey); Montreal, 1/22/57
Boston, Ralph (long jumper); Laurel, Miss., 5/9/39
Bourque, Ray (hockey); Montreal, Que., 12/28/60

Bradley, Bill (William Warren) (basketball); Crystal City, Mo., 7/28/43
Bradley, Pat (golf); Westford, Mass., 3/24/51
Bradshaw, Terry (football); Shreveport, La., 9/2/48
Breedlove, Craig (Norman) (speed driving); Los Angeles, 3/23/38
Brett, George (baseball); Glendale, W. Va., 5/15/53
Brock, Louis Clark (baseball); El Dorado, Ark., 6/18/39
Brown, Jim (football); St. Simon Island, Ga., 2/17/36
Brumel, Valeri (high jumper); Tolbuzino, Siberia, 4/14/42
Bryant, Paul "Bear" (football); Morro Bottom, Ark. **(1913–1983)**
Bryant, Rosalyn Evette (track); Chicago, 1/7/56
Burton, Michael (swimming); Des Moines, Iowa, 7/3/47
Butkus, Dick (Richard Marvin) (football); Chicago, 12/9/42
Calipari, John (basketball); Moon, Pa., 2/10/59
Campanella, Roy (baseball); Homestead, Pa. **(1921–1993)**
Campbell, Earl (football); Tyler, Tex., 3/29/55
Canseco, Jose (baseball); Havana, Cuba, 7/2/64
Caponi, Donna Maria (golf); Detroit, 1/29/45
Cappelletti, Gino (football); Keewatin, Minn., 3/26/34
Carew, Rod (Rodney Cline) (baseball); Gatun, Panama, 10/1/45
Carlos, John (sprinter); New York City, 6/5/45
Carlton, Steven Norman (baseball); Miami, Fla., 12/22/44
Carner, Joanne Gunderson, Mrs. Don (golf); Kirkland, Wash., 3/4/39
Casals, Rosemary (tennis); San Francisco, 9/16/48
Casper, Billy (golf); San Diego, Calif., 6/24/31
Caulkins, Tracy (swimming); Winona, Minn., 1/11/63
Cauthen, Steve (jockey); Covington, Ky., 5/1/60
Chamberlain, Wilt (Wilton) (basketball); Philadelphia, 8/21/36
Chandler, A.B. (Happy) (baseball); Louisville, Ky. **(1899–1991)**
Chandler, Spud (baseball); Commerce, Ga. **(1907–1990)**
Chang, Michael (tennis); Hoboken, N.J., 2/22/72
Chapot, Frank (equestrian); Camden, N.J., 2/24/34
Chastain, Brandi (soccer); San Jose, Calif., 7/21/68
Chinaglia, Giorgio (soccer); Carrara, Italy, 1/24/47
Clarke, Bobby (Robert Earle) (hockey); Flin Flon, Manitoba, Canada, 8/13/49
Clemens, Roger (baseball); Dayton, Ohio, 8/4/62
Clemente, Roberto Walker (baseball); Carolina, Puerto Rico **(1934–1972)**
Cobb, Ty (Tyrus Raymond) (baseball); Narrows, Ga. **(1886–1961)**
Cochran, Barbara Ann (skiing); Claremont, N.H., 1/14/51
Cochran, Marilyn (skiing); Burlington, Vt., 2/7/50
Cochran, Robert (skiing); Claremont, N.H., 12/11/51
Coe, Sebastian Newbold (track); London, England, 9/29/56
Coffey, Paul (hockey); Weston, Ont., 6/1/61
Colavito, Rocky (Rocco Domenico) (baseball); New York City, 8/10/33
Coleman, Derrick (basketball); Mobile, Ala., 6/21/67
Comaneci, Nadia (gymnast); Onesti, Romania, 11/12/61
Conigliaro, Tony (baseball); Revere, Mass. **(1945–1990)**
Connors, Jimmy (James Scott) (tennis); East St. Louis, Ill., 9/2/52
Cooper, Cynthia (basketball); Chicago, Ill., 4/14/63
Cordero, Angel (jockey); Santurce, Puerto Rico, 5/8/42
Cosell, Howard (broadcaster); Winston-Salem, N.C. **(1918–1995)**
Courier, Jim (tennis); Sanford, Fla., 8/17/70
Cournoyer, Yvan Serge (hockey); Drummondville, Quebec, Canada, 11/22/43
Court, Margaret Smith (tennis); Albury, New South Wales, Australia, 7/16/42
Cousy, Bob (basketball); New York City, 8/9/28

Crabbe, Buster (swimming); Scottsdale, Ariz. **(1908–1983)**
Crenshaw, Ben (golf); Austin, Tex., 1/11/52
Cronin, Joe (baseball executive); San Francisco **(1906–1984)**
Cruyff, Johan (soccer); Amsterdam, Netherlands, 4/25/47
Csonka, Larry (Lawrence Richard) (football); Stow, Ohio, 12/25/46
Dancer, Stanley (harness racing); New Egypt, N.J., 7/25/27
Dark, Alvin (baseball); Comanche, Okla., 1/7/22
Davenport, Willie (track); Troy, Ala., 6/6/43
Dawson, Andre (baseball); Miami, Fla., 7/10/54
Dawson, Leonard Ray (football); Alliance, Ohio, 6/20/35
Dean, Dizzy (Jay Hanna) (baseball); Lucas, Ark. **(1911–1974)**
DeBusschere, Dave (basketball); Detroit, 10/16/40
De La Hoya, Oscar (boxing); East Los Angeles, Calif., 2/4/73
Delvecchio, Alex Peter (hockey); Fort William, Ontario, Canada, 12/4/31
Demaret, Jim (golf); Houston **(1910–1983)**
Dempsey, Jack (William H.) (boxing); Manassa, Colo. **(1895–1983)**
DeVicenzo, Roberto (golf); Buenos Aires, 4/14/23
Dibbs, Edward George (tennis); Brooklyn, New York, 2/23/51
Dietz, James W. (rowing); New York, N.Y., 1/12/49
DiMaggio, Joe (baseball); Martinez, Calif. **(1914–1999)**
Dionne, Marcel (hockey); Drummondville, Quebec, Canada, 8/3/51
Dorsett, Tony (football); Rochester, Pa., 4/7/54
Dryden, Kenneth (hockey); Hamilton, Ontario, Canada, 8/4/47
Drysdale, Don (baseball); Van Nuys, Calif. **(1936–1993)**
Duran, Roberto (boxing); Panama City, 6/16/51
Durocher, Leo (baseball); West Springfield, Mass. **(1906–1991)**
Durr, Francois (tennis); Algiers, Algeria, 12/25/42
Eckersley, Dennis (baseball); Oakland, Calif., 10/3/54
Elder, Lee (golf); Dallas, 7/14/34
Elway, John (football); Port Angeles, Wash., 6/28/60
Emerson, Roy (tennis); Kingsway, Australia, 11/3/36
Ender, Kornelia (swimming); Plauen, East Germany, 10/25/58
Erving, Julius ("Dr. J") (basketball); Roosevelt, N.Y., 2/22/50
Esposito, Phil (Philip Anthony) (hockey); Sault Ste. Marie, Ontario, Canada, 2/20/42
Evans, Lee (runner); Mandena, Calif., 2/25/47
Evert, Chris (Christine Marie) (tennis); Fort Lauderdale, Fla., 12/21/54
Ewbank, Weeb (football); Richmond, Ind. **(1907–1998)**
Ewing, Patrick (basketball); Kingston, Jamaica, 8/5/62
Favre, Brett (football); Gulfport, Miss., 10/10/69
Feller, Robert (Bob) (baseball); Van Meter, Iowa, 11/3/18
Feuerbach, Allan Dean (track); Preston, Iowa, 1/12/48
Finley, Charles O. (sportsman); Ensley, Ala. **(1918–1996)**
Fischer, Bobby (chess); Chicago, 3/9/43
Fitzsimmons, Bob (Robert Prometheus) (boxing); Cornwall, England **(1862–1917)**
Fleming, Peggy Gale (ice skating); San Jose, Calif., 7/27/48
Ford, Whitey (Edward) (baseball); New York City, 10/21/28
Foreman, George (boxing); Marshall, Tex., 1/10/49
Fosbury, Richard (high jumper); Portland, Ore., 3/6/47
Fox, Nellie (Jacob Nelson) (baseball); St. Thomas, Pa. **(1927–1975)**
Foxx, James Emory (baseball); Sudlersville, Md. **(1907–1967)**
Foyt, A. J. (auto racing); Houston, 1/16/35
Frazier, Joe (boxing); Beauford, S.C., 1/17/44
Frazier, Walt (basketball); Atlanta, 3/29/45
Frick, Ford C. (baseball); Wawaka, Ind. **(1894–1978)**
Furniss, Bruce (swimming); Fresno, Calif., 5/27/57
Gable, Dan (wrestling); Waterloo, Iowa, 10/25/45
Gabriel, Roman (football); Wilmington, N.C., 8/5/40
Gallagher, Michael Donald (skiing); Yonkers, N.Y., 10/3/41
Garvey, Steve (baseball); Tampa, Fla., 12/22/48
Gehrig, Lou (Henry Louis) (baseball); New York City **(1903–1941)**
Gehringer, Charlie (baseball); Fowlerville, Mich. **(1903–1993)**
Geoffrion, "Boom Boom" (Bernie) (hockey); Montreal, 2/14/31
Gerulaitis, Vitas (tennis); Brooklyn, N.Y. **(1954–1994)**
Gervin, George (basketball); Long Beach, Calif., 4/27/52
Giacomin, Ed (hockey); Sudbury, Ontario, Canada, 6/6/39
Giamatti, A. Bartlett (baseball); South Hadley, Mass. **(1938–1989)**
Gibson, Bob (baseball); Omaha, Neb., 11/9/35
Gifford, Frank (football); Santa Monica, Calif. 8/16/30
Gilbert, Rod (Rodrique) (hockey); Montreal, 7/1/41
Gilmore, Artis (basketball); Chipley, Fla., 9/21/49
Glance, Harvey (track); Phenix City, Ala., 3/28/57
Gonzalez, Pancho (tennis); Los Angeles **(1928–1995)**
Goodell, Brian Stuart (swimming); Stockton, Calif., 4/2/59
Gooden, Dwight (baseball); Tampa, Fla., 11/16/64
Goodrich, Gail (basketball); Los Angeles, 4/23/43
Goolagong, Cawley, Evonne (tennis); Griffith, Australia, 7/31/51
Gordon, Jeff (auto racing); Vallejo, Calif., 8/4/71
Gossage, "Goose" (Rich) (baseball); Colorado Springs, Colo., 4/5/51
Graf, Steffi (tennis); Mannheim, W. Germany, 6/14/69
Graham, David (golf); Windson, Australia, 5/23/46
Graham, Otto Everett (football); Waukegan, Ill., 12/6/21
Grange, Red (Harold) (football); Forksville, Pa. **(1904–1991)**
Green, Hubert (golf); Birmingham, Ala., 12/28/46
Greene, Charles E. (sprinter); Pine Bluff, Ark., 3/21/45

Greene, "Mean" (Joe) (football); Temple, Tex., 9/24/46
Gretzky, Wayne (hockey); Brantford, Ont., 1/26/61
Griese, Bob (Robert Allen) (football); Evansville, Ind., 2/3/45
Griffey, Ken, Jr. (baseball); Donora, Pa., 11/21/69
Grove, Lefty (Robert Moses) (baseball); Lonaconing, Md. **(1900–1975)**
Groza, Lou (football); Martins Ferry Ohio, 1/25/24
Guidry, Ronald Ames (baseball); Lafayette, La., 8/28/50
Gwynn, Tony (baseball); Los Angeles, Calif., 5/9/60
Halas, George (football); Chicago **(1895–1983)**
Hall, Gary (swimming); Fayetteville, N.C., 8/7/51
Hamill, Dorothy (figure skating); Chicago, 1956(?)
Hamilton, Scott (figure skating); Bowling Green, Ohio, 8/28/58
Hamm, Mia (soccer); Selma, Ala., 3/17/72
Hammond, Kathy (runner); Sacramento, Calif., 11/2/51
Hardaway, Anfernee (basketball); Memphis, Tenn., 7/18/72
Harding, Tonya (figure skating); Portland, Ore., 11/12/70
Harris, Franco (football); Ft. Dix, N.J., 3/7/50
Hartack, William, Jr. (jockey); Colver, Pa., 12/9/32
Hasek, Dominik (hockey); Pardubice, Czechoslovakia, 1/29/65
Haughton, William (harness racing); Gloversville, N.Y. **(1923–1986)**
Havlicek, John (basketball); Martins Ferry, Ohio, 4/8/40
Hayes, Elvin (basketball); Rayville, La., 11/17/45
Hayes, Woody (football); Upper Arlington, Ohio **(1913–1987)**
Heiden, Eric (speed skating); Madison, Wis., 6/14/58
Hencken, John (swimming); Culver City, Calif., 5/29/54
Henderson, Rickey (baseball); Chicago, 12/25/58
Henie, Sonja (ice skater); Oslo **(1912–1969)**
Herman, Floyd Caves (Babe) (baseball); Buffalo, N.Y. **(1903–1987)**
Hernandez, Keith (baseball); San Francisco, 10/20/53
Hershiser, Orel (baseball); Buffalo, N.Y., 9/16/58
Hickcox, Charles (swimming); Phoenix, Ariz., 2/6/47
Hines, James (sprinter); Dumas, Ark., 9/10/46
Hingis, Martina (tennis); Kosice, Slovakia, 9/30/80
Hodges, Gil (baseball); Princeton, Ind. **(1924–1972)**
Hogan, Ben (golf); Dublin, Tex. **(1912–1997)**
Holmes, Larry (boxing); Cuthert, Ga., 11/3/49
Holyfield, Evander (boxing); Atlanta, Ga., 10/19/62
Hornsby, Rogers (baseball); Winters, Tex. **(1896–1963)**
Hornung, Paul (football); Louisville, Ky., 12/23/35
Houk, Ralph (baseball); Lawrence, Kan., 8/9/19
Howard, Elston (baseball); St. Louis **(1929–1980)**
Howe, Gordon (hockey); Floral, Sask., Canada, 3/31/28
Howell, Jim Lee (football); Lonoke, Ark. **(1914–1995)**
Howser, Dick (baseball); Miami, Fla. **(1937–1987)**
Hubbell, Carl (baseball); Carthage, Mo. **(1903–1988)**
Huff, Sam (Robert Lee) (football); Morgantown, W. Va., 10/4/34
Hull, Bobby (hockey); Point Anne, Ontario, Canada, 1/3/39
Hunter, "Catfish" (Jim) (baseball); Hertford, N.C. **(1946–1999)**
Hutson, Donald (football); Pine Bluff, Ark. **(1913–1997)**
Irwin, Hale (golf); Joplin, Mo., 6/3/45
Jacobs, Helen Hull (tennis); Globe, Ariz. **(1908–1997)**
Jackson, Phil (basketball coach); Deer Lodge, Mont., 9/17/45
Jackson, Reggie (baseball); Wyncote, Pa., 5/18/46
Jagr, Jaromir (hockey); Kladno, Czechoslovakia, 2/15/72
Jeffries, James J. (boxing); Carroll, Ohio **(1875–1953)**
Jenkins, Ferguson Arthur (baseball); Chatham, Ontario, Canada, 12/13/43
Jenner, (W.) Bruce (track); Mt. Kisco, N.Y., 10/28/49
Jezek, Linda (swimming); Palo Alto, Calif., 3/10/60
Johnson, "Magic" (Earvin) (basketball); E. Lansing, Mich., 8/14/59
Johnson, Anthony (rowing); Washington, D.C., 11/16/40
Johnson, Jack (John Arthur) (boxing); Galveston, Tex. **(1876–1946)**
Johnson, Jimmy (football); Port Arthur, Tex., 8/14/43
Johnson, Michael (track); Dallas, Tex., 9/13/67
Johnson, Rafer (decathlon); Hillsboro, Tex., 8/18/35
Johnson, Randy (baseball); Walnut Creek, Calif., 9/10/63
Johnson, Wilham Julius (Judy) (baseball); Wilmington, Del. **(1899–1989)**
Jones, Cobi (soccer); Detroit, Mich., 6/16/70
Jones, Deacon (David) (football); Eatonville, Fla., 12/9/38
Jordan, Michael (basketball); Brooklyn, N.Y., 2/17/63
Joyner, Florence Griffith (sprinter); Mojave Desert, Calif. **(1959–1998)**
Joyner-Kersee, Jackie (track); East St. Louis, Ill., 3/3/62
Juantoreno, Alberto (track); Santiago, Cuba, 12/3/51
Jurgensen, Sonny (football); Wilmington, N.C., 8/23/34
Justice, Dave (baseball); Cincinnati, Ohio, 4/14/66
Kaat, Jim (baseball); Zeeland, Mich., 11/7/38
Kaline, Al (Albert) (baseball); Baltimore, 12/19/34
Keino, Kipchoge (runner); Kapchemoiyrno, Kenya, 1/17/40
Kelly, Leroy (football); Philadelphia, 5/20/42
Kelly, Red (Leonard Patrick) (hockey); Simcoe, Ontario, Canada, 7/9/27
Kerrigan, Nancy (figure skating); Woburn, Mass., 10/13/69
Killebrew, Harmon (baseball); Payette, Idaho, 6/29/36
Killy, Jean-Claude (skiing); Saint-Cloud, France, 8/30/43
Kilmer, Bill (William Orland) (football); Topeka, Kan., 9/5/39
King, Bille Jean (Bille Jean Moffitt) (tennis); Long Beach, Calif., 11/22/43

Kinsella, John (swimming); Oak Park, Ill., 8/26/52
Kluszewski, Ted (baseball); Argo, Ill. **(1924–1988)**
Kodes, Jan (tennis); Prague, 3/1/46
Kolb, Claudia (swimming); Hayward, Calif., 12/19/49
Korbut, Olga (gymnast); Grodno, Byelorussia, U.S.S.R., 5/16/55
Koufax, Sandy (Sanford) (baseball); Brooklyn, N.Y., 12/30/35
Kramer, Jack (tennis); Las Vegas, Nev., 8/1/21
Kramer, Jerry (football); Jordan, Mont., 1/23/36
Kuenn, Harvey (baseball); West Allis, Wis. **(1930–1988)**
Kuhn, Bowie Kent (baseball); Takoma Park, Md., 10/28/26
Kwan, Michelle (figure skating); Torrance, Calif., 7/7/80
Lafleur, Guy Damien (hockey); Thurson, Quebec, Canada, 8/20/51
Laird, Ronald (walker); Louisville, Ky., 5/31/35
Lalas, Alexi (soccer); Birmingham, Mich., 6/1/70
Lamonica, Daryle (football); Fresno, Calif., 7/17/41
Landis, Kenesaw Mountain (1st baseball commissioner); Millville, Ohio **(1866–1944)**
Landry, Tom (football); Mission, Tex., 9/11/24
Landy, John (runner); Australia, 4/4/30
Larrieu, Francie (track); Palo Alto, Calif., 11/28/52
La Russa, Tony (baseball); Tampa, Fla., 10/4/44
Lasorda, Tom (baseball); Norristown, Pa., 9/22/27
Laver, Rod (tennis); Rockhampton, Australia, 8/9/38
Layne, Bobby (football); Lubbock, Texas **(1927–1986)**
Leetch, Brian (hockey); Corpus Christi, Tex., 3/3/68
Lemieux, Mario (hockey); Montreal, Quebec, Canada, 10/5/65
Lendl, Ivan (tennis); Prague, 3/7/60
Leonard, Benny (Benjamin Leiner) (boxing); New York City **(1896–1947)**
Leonard, Sugar Ray (boxing); Wilmington, N.C., 5/17/56
Lewis, Carl (track); Willingboro, N.J., 7/1/61
Lindros, Eric (hockey); London, Ont., 2/28/73
Lipinski, Tara (figure skating); Philadelphia, Pa., 6/10/82
Liquori, Marty (runner); Montclair, N.J., 9/11/49
Little, Lou (football); Leominster, Mass. **(1893–1979)**
Littler, Gene (golf); La Jolla, Calif., 7/21/30
Lobo, Rebecca (basketball); Southwick, Mass., 10/6/73
Lombardi, Vince (football); Brooklyn, N.Y. **(1913–1970)**
Longden, Johnny (horse racing); Wakefield, England, 2/14/07
Lopat, Eddie (baseball); New York, N.Y. **(1918–1992)**
Lopez, Al (baseball); Tampa, Fla., 8/20/08
Lopez, Nancy (golf); Torrance, Calif., 1/6/57
Louis, Joe (Joe Louis Barrow) (boxing); Lafayette, Ala. **(1914–1981)**
Lukas, D. Wayne (horse racing); Antigo, Wis., 9/2/35
Lynn, Frederic Michael (baseball); Chicago, Ill., 2/3/52
Lynn, Janet (figure skating); Rockford, Ill., 4/6/53
Mack, Connie (Cornelius Alexander McGillicuddy) (baseball executive); East Brookfield, Mass. **(1862–1956)**
Mackey, John (football); New York City, 9/24/41
Maddux, Greg (baseball); San Angelo, Texas, 4/15/67
Mahovlich, Frank (Francis William) (hockey); Timmins, Ontario, Canada, 1/10/38
Mahre, Phil (skiing); White Pass, Wash., 5/10/57
Malone, Karl (basketball); Summerfield, La., 7/24/63
Malone, Moses (basketball); Petersburg, Va., 3/23/55
Mandlikova, Hana (tennis); Prague, Czechoslovakia, 2/62
Mann, Carol (golf); Buffalo, N.Y., 2/3/41
Manning, Madeline (runner); Cleveland, 1/11/48
Mantle, Mickey Charles (baseball); Spavinaw, Okla. **(1931–1995)**
Maravich, "Pistol Pete" (Peter) Aliquippa, Pa. **(1948–1988)**
Marble, Alice (tennis); Palm Springs, Calif. **(1913–1990)**
Marciano, Rocky (boxing); Brockton, Mass. **(1923–1969)**
Marichal, Juan (baseball); Laguna Verde, Montecristi, Dominican Republic, 10/20/37
Marino, Dan (football); Pittsburgh, Pa., 9/15/61
Maris, Roger (baseball); Hibbing, Minn. **(1934–1985)**
Martin, Billy (Alfred Manuel) (baseball); Berkeley, Calif. **(1928–1989)**
Martin, Christy (boxing); Mullers, W.Va.,
Martin, Rick (Richard Lionel) (hockey); Verdun, Quebec, Canada, 7/26/51
Mathews, Ed (Edwin) (baseball); Texarkana, Tex., 10/13/31
Mattingly, Don (baseball); Evansville, Ind., 4/20/61
Matson, Randy (shot putter); Kilgore, Tex., 3/5/45
Mays, Willie (baseball); Westfield, Ala., 5/6/31
McAdoo, Bob (basketball); Greensboro, N.C., 9/25/51
McCarthy, Joe (Joseph Vincent) (baseball); Philadelphia **(1887–1978)**
McCovey, Willie Lee (baseball); Mobile, Ala., 1/10/38
McDonald, Lanny (hockey); Hanna, Alberta, Canada, 2/16/53
McDowell, Jack (baseball); Van Nuys, Calif., 1/16/66
McEnroe, John Patrick, Jr. (tennis); Wiesbaden, Germany, 2/16/59
McGraw, John (baseball); Truxton, N.Y. **(1873–1934)**
McGwire, Mark (baseball); Pomona, Calif., 10/1/63
McLain, Dennis (baseball); Chicago, 3/24/44
McMillan, Kathy Laverne (track); Raeford, N.C., 11/7/57
Merrill, Janice (track); New London, Conn., 6/18/62
Messier, Mark (hockey); Edmonton, Alberta, Canada, 1/18/61
Meyer, Deborah (swimming); Haddonfield, N.J., 8/14/52

Meyers, Anne (basketball); San Diego, Calif., 3/26/55
Middlecoff, Cary (golf); Halls, Tenn. **(1921–1998)**
Mikita, Stan (hockey); Sokolce, Czechoslovakia, 5/20/40
Milburn, Rodney, Jr. (hurdler); Opelousas, La., 5/18/50
Miller, Cheryl (basketball); Riverside, Calif., 1/3/64
Miller, Johnny (golf); San Francisco, 4/29/47
Miller, Reggie (basketball); Riverside, Calif. 8/24/65
Montana, Joe (football); New Eagle, Pa., 6/11/56
Montgomery, Jim (swimming); Madison, Wis., 1/24/55
Moody, Helen Wills (tennis); Centerville, Calif. **(1906–1998)**
Moore, Archie (boxing); Benoit, Miss. **(1916–1998)**
Morgan, Joe Leonard (baseball); Bonham, Tex., 9/19/43
Morrall, Earl (football); Muskegon, Mich., 5/17/34
Morton, Craig L. (football); Flint, Mich., 2/5/43
Mosconi, Wilie (pocket billiards); Philadelphia **(1913–1993)**
Moses, Edwin Corley (track); Dayton, Ohio, 8/31/58
Mungo, Van Lingo (baseball); Pageland, S.C. **(1911–1985)**
Munson, Thurman (baseball); Akron, Ohio **(1947–1979)**
Murphy, Calvin (basketball); Norwalk, Conn., 5/9/48
Murray, Eddie (baseball); Los Angeles, Calif., 2/24/56
Musial, Stan (baseball); Donora, Pa., 11/21/20
Myers, Linda (archery); York, Pa., 6/19/47
Naber, John (swimming); Evanston, Ill., 1/20/56
Namath, Joe (Joseph William) (football); Beaver Falls, Pa., 5/31/43
Nastase, Ilie (tennis); Bucharest, 7/19/46
Navratilova, Martina (tennis); Prague, 10/18/56
Nehemiah, Renaldo (track); Newark, N.J., 3/24/59
Nelson, Cindy (skiing); Lutsen, Minn., 8/19/55
Newcombe, John (tennis); Sydney, Australia, 5/23/43
Niekro, Phil (baseball); Lansing, Ohio, 4/1/39
Nicklaus, Jack (golf); Columbus, Ohio, 1/21/40
Norman, Gregory (golf); Mount Isa, Australia, 2/10/55
Oerter, Al (discus thrower); New York City, 9/19/36
Olajuwon, Hakeem (basketball); Lagos, Nigeria, 1/21/63
Oldfield, Barney (racing driver); Fulton County, Ohio **(1878–1946)**
Oliva, Tony (Pedro) (baseball); Pinar Del Rio, Cuba, 7/20/40
Olsen, Merlin Jay (football); Logan, Utah, 9/15/40
O'Malley, Walter (baseball executive); New York City **(1903–1979)**
O'Neal, Shaquille (basketball); Newark, N.J., 3/6/72
Orantes, Manuel (tennis); Granada, Spain, 2/6/49
Orr, Bobby (hockey); Parry Sound, Ontario, Canada, 3/20/48
Ovett, Steve (track); Brighton, England, 10/9/55
Owens, Jesse (track); Decatur, Ala. **(1914–1980)**
Paige, Satchel (Leroy) (baseball); Mobile, Ala. **(1906–1982)**
Palmer, Arnold (golf); Latrobe, Pa., 9/10/29
Palmer, James Alvin (baseball); New York City, 10/15/45
Parcells, Bill (football coach); Englewood, N.J., 8/22/41
Parent, Bernard Marcel (hockey); Montreal, 4/3/45
Park, Brad (Douglas Bradford) (hockey); Toronto, Ontario, Canada, 7/6/48
Parseghian, Ara (football); Akron, Ohio, 5/21/23
Pasarell, Charles (tennis); San Juan, Puerto Rico, 2/12/44
Patterson, Floyd (boxing); Waco, N.C., 1/4/35
Peete, Calvin (golf); Detroit, Mich., 7/18/43
Pelé (Edson Arantes do Nascimento) (soccer); Tres Coracoes, Brazil, 10/23/40
Perry, Gaylord (baseball); Williamston, N.C., 9/15/38
Perry, Jim (baseball); Williamston, N.C., 10/30/36
Pettit, Bob (basketball); Baton Rouge, La., 12/12/32
Petty, Richard Lee (auto racing); Randleman, N.C., 7/2/37
Pincay, Laffit, Jr. (jockey); Panama City, Panama, 12/29/46
Pippen, Scottie (basketball); Trenton, N.J., 9/25/65
Plager, Barclay (ice hockey); Kirkland Lake, Ontario **(1941–1988)**
Plante, Jacques (hockey); Sahwinigan Falls, Quebec, Canada, 1/17/29
Player, Gary (golf); Johannesburg, South Africa, 11/1/35
Plunkett, Jim (football); San Jose, Calif., 12/5/47
Potvin, Denis Charles (hockey); Hull, Quebec, Canada, 10/29/53
Powell, Boog (John) (baseball); Lakeland, Fla., 8/17/41
Powell, Mike (track); Philadelphia, 11/10/63
Prefontaine, Steve Roland (runner); Coos Bay, Ore. **(1951–1975)**
Prince, Bob (baseball announcer); Pittsburgh **(1917–1985)**
Proell, Annemarie Moser (Alpine skier); Kleinarl, Austria, 3/27/53
Rafter, Patrick (tennis); Brisbane, Australia, 12/28/72
Ralston, Dennis (tennis); Bakersfield, Calif., 7/27/42
Rankin, Judy Torluemke (golf); St. Louis, Mo., 2/18/45
Raschi, Vic (baseball); West Springfield, Mass. **(1919–1988)**
Ratelle, Jean (Joseph Gilbert Yvon Jean) (hockey); St. Jean, Quebec, Canada, 10/29/53
Rawls, Betsy (Elizabeth Earle) (golf); Spartanburg, S.C., 5/4/28
Reed, Willis (basketball); Hico, La., 6/25/42
Reese, Pee Wee (Harold) (baseball); Ekron, Ky. **(1919–1999)**
Resch, Glenn "Chico" (hockey); Moose Jaw, Saskatchewan, Canada, 7/10/48
Rice, Jerry (football); Crawford, Miss., 10/13/62
Richard, Maurice (hockey); Montreal, 8/14/24
Riessen, Martin (tennis); Hinsdale, Ill., 12/4/41
Rigney, William (baseball); Alameda, Calif., 1/29/18

Rios, Marcelo (tennis); Santiago, Chile, 12/26/75
Ripken, Cal, Jr. (baseball); Havre de Grace, Md., 8/24/60
Rizzuto, Phil (baseball); New York City, 9/25/18
Robertson, Oscar (basketball); Charlotte, Tenn., 11/24/38
Robinson, Arnie (track); San Diego, Calif., 4/7/48
Robinson, Brooks (baseball); Little Rock, Ark., 5/18/37
Robinson, David (basketball); Key West, Fla., 8/6/65
Robinson, Frank (baseball); Beaumont, Tex., 8/31/35
Robinson, Jackie (baseball); Cairo, Ga. **(1919–1972)**
Robinson, Larry Clark (hockey); Marvelville, Ontario, Canada, 6/2/51
Robinson, "Sugar" Ray (boxing); Detroit **(1920–1989)**
Rockne, Knute Kenneth (football); Voss, Norway **(1888–1931)**
Rockwell, Martha (skiing); Providence, R.I., 4/26/44
Rodman, Dennis (basketball); Trenton, N.J., 5/13/61
Ronaldo (soccer); Bento Ribeiro, Brazil, 9/22/76
Rono, Harry (track); Kiptaragon, Kenya, 2/12/52
Rooney, Art (football); Pittsburgh, Pa. **(1901–1988)**
Rose, Pete (Peter Edward) (baseball); Cincinnati, 4/14/41
Rosenbloom, Maxie (boxing); New York City **(1904–1976)**
Rosewall, Ken (tennis); Sydney, Australia, 11/2/34
Rote, Kyle (football); San Antonio, 10/27/28
Roush, Edd (baseball); Oakland City, Ind. **(1893–1988)**
Rozelle, Pete (Alvin Ray) (commissioner of National Football League); South Gate, Calif. **(1926–1996)**
Rudolph, Wilma Glodean (sprinter); St. Bethlehem, Tenn. **(1940–1994)**
Russell, Bill (basketball); Monroe, La., 2/12/34
Ruth, Babe (George Herman Ruth) (baseball); Baltimore **(1895–1948)**
Rutherford, Johnny (auto racing); Fort Worth, 3/12/38
Ryan, Nolan (Lynn Nolan, Jr.) (baseball); Refugio, Tex., 1/31/47
Ryon, Luann (archery); Long Beach, Calif., 1/13/53
Ryun, Jim (runner); Wichita, Kan., 4/29/47
Salazar, Alberto (track); Havana, 8/7/58
Sampras, Pete (tennis); Washington, D.C., 8/12/71
Samuels, Howard (horse racing soccer); New York City **(1920–1984)**
Sanders, Barry (football); Wichita, Kan., 7/16/68
Sanders, Deion (baseball/football); Ft. Myers, Fla., 8/9/67
Santana, Manuel (Manuel Santana Martinez) (tennis); Chamartin, Spain, 5/10/38
Sayers, Gale (football); Wichita, Kan., 5/30/43
Schmidt, Mike (baseball); Dayton, Ohio, 9/27/49
Schoendienst, Red (Albert) (baseball); Germantown, Ill., 2/2/23
Schollander, Donald (swimming); Charlotte, N.C., 4/30/46
Scurry, Briana (soccer); Minneapolis, Minn., 9/7/71
Seagren, Bob (Robert Lloyd) (pole vaulter); Pomona, Calif., 10/17/46
Seau, Junior (football); Oceanside, Calif., 1/19/69
Seaver, Tom (baseball); Fresno, Calif., 11/17/44
Seidler, Maren (track); Brooklyn, N.Y., 6/11/62
Seles, Monica (tennis); Novi Sad, Yugoslavia, 12/2/73
Selke, Frank (ice hockey); Canada **(1893–1985)**
Sewell, Joe (baseball); Titus, Ala. **(1898–1990)**
Shepherd, Lee (auto racing) **(1945–1985)**
Shero, Fred (hockey); Camden, N.J. **(1925–1990)**
Shoemaker, Willie (jockey); Fabens, Tex., 8/19/31
Shore, Eddie (ice hockey); Saskatchewan, Canada **(1902–1985)**
Shorter, Frank (runner); Munich, Germany, 10/31/47
Shriver, Pam (tennis); Baltimore, 7/4/62
Shula, Don (Donald Francis) (football); Grand River, Ohio, 1/4/30
Silvester, Jay (discus thrower); Tremonton, Utah, 2/27/37
Simpson, O.J. (Orenthal James) (football); San Francisco, 7/9/47
Sims, Billy (football); St. Louis, 9/18/55
Smith, Bubba (Charles Aaron) (football); Orange, Tex., 2/28/45
Smith, Emmitt (football); Pensacola, Fla., 5/15/69
Smith, Ozzie (baseball); Mobile, Ala., 12/26/54
Smith, Ronnie Ray (sprinter); Los Angeles, 3/28/49
Smith, Stanley Roger (tennis); Pasadena, Calif., 12/14/46
Smith, Tommie (sprinter); Clarksville, Tex., 6/5/44
Smoke, Marcia Jones (canoeing); Oklahoma City, 7/18/41
Snead, Sam (golf); Hot Springs, Va., 5/27/12
Sneva, Tom (auto racing); Spokane, Wash., 6/1/48
Snider, Duke (Edwin) (baseball); Los Angeles, 9/19/26
Solomon, Harold (tennis); Washington, D.C., 9/17/52
Sosa, Sammy (Samuel) (baseball); San Pedro de Macoris, Dominican Republic, 11/12/68
Spahn, Warren (baseball); Buffalo, N.Y., 4/23/21
Speaker, Tristram (baseball); Hubbard City, Tex. **(1888–1958)**
Spencer, Brian (ice hockey); Fort St. James, British Columbia **(1949–1988)**
Spinks, Leon (boxing); St. Louis, 7/11/53
Spitz, Mark (swimming); Modesto, Calif., 2/10/50
Stabler, Kenneth (football); Foley, Ala., 12/25/45
Stagg, Amos Alonzo (football); West Orange, N.J. **(1862–1965)**
Stargell, Willie (Wilver Dornell) (baseball); Earlsboro, Okla., 3/6/41
Starr, Bart (football); Montgomery, Ala., 1/9/34
Staub, "Rusty" (Daniel) (baseball); New Orleans, 4/4/44
Staubach, Roger (football); Cincinnati, 2/5/42
Steinkraus, William C. (equestrian); Cleveland, 10/12/25

Stenerud, Jan (football); Fetsund, Norway, 11/26/42
Stengel, Casey (Charles Dillon) (baseball); Kansas City, Mo. **(1891–1975)**
Stenmark, Ingemar (Alpine skier); Tarnaby, Sweden, 3/18/56
Stevens, Scott (hockey); Completon, New Brunswick, 5/4/66
Stockton, Richard LaClede (tennis); New York City, 2/18/51
Stones, Dwight Edwin (track); Los Angeles, 12/6/53
Strawberry, Darryl (baseball); Los Angeles, 3/12/62
Street, Picabo (skiing); Triumph, Idaho, 4/3/71
Sullivan, John Lawrence (boxing); Boston **(1858–1918)**
Summitt, Pat (basketball); Henrietta, Tenn., 6/14/52
Sutton, Don (Donald Howard) (baseball); Clio, Ala., 4/2/45
Swann, Lynn (football); Alcoa, Tenn., 3/7/52
Swoopes, Sheryl (basketball); Brownfield, Tex., 3/25/71
Tanner, Leonard Roscoe III (tennis); Chattanooga, Tenn., 10/15/51
Tarkenton, Fran (Francis) (football); Richmond, Va., 2/3/40
Tebbetts, Birdie (George R.) (baseball); Nashua, N.H. **(1914–1999)**
Theismann, Joe (football); New Brunswick, N.J., 9/9/46
Thomas, Frank (baseball); Columbus, Ga., 5/27/68
Thomas, Isiah (basketball); Chicago, Ill., 4/30/61
Thomas, Thurman (football); Houston, Texas, 5/16/66
Thompson, David (basketball); Shelby, N.C., 7/13/54
Thorpe, Jim (James Francis) (all-around athlete); nr. Prague, Okla. **(1888–1953)**
Tilden, William Tatem II (tennis); Philadelphia **(1893–1953)**
Tittle, Y. A. (Yelberton Abraham) (football); Marshall, Tex., 10/24/26
Toomey, William (decathlon); Philadelphia, 1/10/39
Trevino, Lee (golf); Dallas, 12/1/39
Trottier, Bryan (hockey); Val Marie, Sask., Canada, 7/17/56
Tunney, Gene (James J.) (boxing); New York City **(1898–1978)**
Tyson, Mike (boxing); Brooklyn, N.Y., 6/30/66
Tyus, Wyomia (runner); Griffin, Ga., 8/29/45
Ueberroth, Peter (baseball executive); Evanston, Ill., 9/2/37
Unitas, John (football); Pittsburgh, 5/7/33
Unser, Al (auto racing); Albuquerque, N. Mex., 5/29/39
Unser, Bobby (auto racing); Albuquerque, N. Mex., 2/20/34
Valenzuela, Fernando (baseball); Sonora, Mexico, 11/1/60
Valvano, Jim (basketball); New York, N.Y. **(1946–1993)**
Van Brocklin, Norm (football); Eagle Butte, S. Dak. **(1926–1983)**
Vaughn, Mo (baseball); Norwalk, Conn., 12/15/67
Vilas, Guillermo (tennis); Mar del Plata, Argentina, 8/17/52
Viola, Frank (baseball); Hempstead, N.Y., 4/19/60
Viren, Lasse (track); Myrskyla, Finland, 7/12/49
Vitale, Dick (basketball); E. Rutherford, N.J., 6/9/39
Wade, Virginia (tennis); Bournemouth, England, 7/10/45
Wagner, Honus (John Peter Honus) (baseball); Carnegie, Pa. **(1867–1955)**
Waitz, Grete (Andersen) (running); Oslo, Norway, 10/1/53
Walcott, Jersey Joe (Arnold Cream) (boxing); Merchantville, N.J. **(1914–1994)**
Wallace, Rusty (auto racing); St. Louis, Mo., 8/14/56
Walsh, Adam (football) **(1902–1985)**
Walton, Bill (basketball); La Mesa, Calif., 11/5/52
Waterfield, Bob (football); Burbank, Calif **(1921–1983)**
Watson, Martha Rae (track); Long Beach, Calif., 8/19/46
Watson, Tom (golf); Kansas City, Mo., 9/4/49
Weaver, Earl (baseball); St. Louis, 8/14/30
Weiskopf, Tom (golf); Massillon, Ohio, 11/9/42
Weiss, George (baseball executive); New Haven, Conn. **(1895–1972)**
Weissmuller, Johnny (swimmer and actor); Windber, Pa. **(1904–1984)**
West, Jerry (basketball); Cheylan, W. Va., 5/28/38
White, Reggie (football); Chattanooga, Tenn., 12/19/61
White, Willye B. (long jumper); Money, Miss., 1/1/36
Whitworth, Kathy (golf); Monahans, Tex., 9/27/39
Wilkens, Mac Maurice (track); Eugene, Ore., 11/15/50
Wilkins, Lennie (basketball) 11/25/37
Wilkinson, Bud (football); Minneapolis **(1916–1994)**
Williams, Dick (baseball); St. Louis, 5/7/29
Williams, Serena (tennis); Saginaw, Mich., 9/26/81
Williams, Ted (baseball); San Diego, Calif., 8/30/18
Williams, Venus (tennis); Lynnwood, Calif., 6/17/80
Wills, Maury (baseball); Washington, D.C., 10/2/32
Winfield, Dave (baseball); St. Paul, Minn., 10/3/51
Wohlhuter, Richard C. (runner); Geneva, Ill., 12/23/45
Wood, "Smokey Joe" (Joseph) (baseball); Kansas City, Mo. **(1890–1985)**
Woods, Tiger (Eldrick) (golf); Long Beach, Calif., 12/30/75
Wottle, David James (runner); Canton, Ohio, 8/7/50
Wright, Mickey (Mary Kathryn) (golf); San Diego, Calif., 2/14/35
Yarborough, Cale (William Caleb) (auto racing); Timmonsville, S.C., 3/27/39
Yastrzemski, Carl (baseball); Southampton, N.Y., 8/22/39
Young, Cy (Denton True) (baseball); Gilmore, Ohio **(1867–1955)**
Young, Sheila (speed skater, bicycle racer); Detroit, 10/14/50
Young, Steve (football); Salt Lake City, Utah, 10/11/61
Zaharias, Babe Didrikson (golf); Port Arthur, Tex. **(1913–1956)**

Basketball

Basketball may be the one sport whose exact origin is definitely known. In the winter of 1891–92, Dr. James Naismith, an instructor in the Y.M.C.A. Training College (now Springfield College) at Springfield, Mass., deliberately invented the game of basketball in order to provide indoor exercise and competition for the students between the closing of the football season and the opening of the baseball season. He affixed peach baskets overhead on the walls at opposite ends of the gymnasium and organized teams to play his new game in which the purpose was to toss an association (soccer) ball into one basket and prevent the opponents from tossing the ball into the other basket. The game is fundamentally the same today, though there have been improvements in equipment and some changes in rules.

Because Dr. Naismith had eighteen available players when he invented the game, the first rule was: "There shall be nine players on each side." Later the number of players became optional, depending upon the size of the available court, but the five-player standard was adopted when the game spread over the country. United States soldiers brought basketball to Europe in World War I, and it soon became a world-wide sport.

College Basketball

NATIONAL COLLEGIATE A.A. CHAMPIONS

1938 Temple	1952 Kansas	1966 Texas Western	1986 Louisville
1939 Oregon	1953 Indiana	1967–73 UCLA	1987 Indiana
1940 Indiana & USC	1954 La Salle	1974 No. Carolina State	1988 Kansas
1941 Wisconsin	1955 San Francisco	1975 UCLA	1989 Michigan
1942 Stanford	1956 San Francisco	1976 Indiana	1990 UNLV
1943 Wyoming	1957 North Carolina	1977 Marquette	1991 Duke
1944 Utah	1958 Kentucky	1978 Kentucky	1992 Duke
1945 Oklahoma A & M	1959 California	1979 Michigan State	1993 North Carolina
1946 Oklahoma A & M	1960 Ohio State	1980 Louisville	1994 Arkansas
1947 Holy Cross	1961 Cincinnati	1981 Indiana	1995 UCLA
1948 Kentucky	1962 Cincinnati	1982 North Carolina	1996 Kentucky
1949 Kentucky	1963 Loyola (Chicago)	1983 North Carolina State	1997 Arizona
1950 C.C.N.Y.	1964 UCLA	1984 Georgetown	1998 Kentucky
1951 Kentucky	1965 UCLA	1985 Villanova	1999 Connecticut

NATIONAL INVITATION TOURNAMENT (NIT) CHAMPIONS

1938 Temple	1955 Duquesne	1971 North Carolina	1987 So. Mississippi
1939 Long Island U.	1956 Louisville	1972 Maryland	1988 Connecticut
1940 Colorado	1957 Bradley	1973 Virginia Tech	1989 St. John's (N.Y.C.)
1941 Long Island U.	1958 Xavier (Cincinnati)	1974 Purdue	1990 Vanderbilt
1942 West Virginia	1959 St. John's (N.Y.C.)	1975 Princeton	1991 Stanford
1943–44 St. John's (N.Y.C.)	1960 Bradley	1976 Kentucky	1992 Virginia
1945 DePaul	1961 Providence	1977 St. Bonaventure	1993 Minnesota
1946 Kentucky	1962 Dayton	1978 Texas	1994 Villanova
1947 Utah	1963 Providence	1979 Indiana	1995 Virginia Tech
1948 St. Louis	1964 Bradley	1980 Virginia	1996 Nebraska
1949 San Francisco	1965 St. John's (N.Y.C.)	1981 Tulsa	1997 Michigan
1950 C.C.N.Y.	1966 Brigham Young	1982 Bradley	1998 Minnesota
1951 Brigham Young	1967 So. Illinois	1983 Fresno State	1999 California
1952 La Salle	1968 Dayton	1984 Michigan	
1953 Seton Hall	1969 Temple	1985 UCLA	
1954 Holy Cross	1970 Marquette	1986 Ohio State	

N.C.A.A. DIVISION I INDIVIDUAL SCORING RECORDS

Points	Yrs	Last	Gm	Pts	Average	Yrs	Last	Pts	Avg
Pete Maravich, LSU	3	1970	83	3,667	Pete Maravich, LSU	3	1970	3,667	44.2
Freeman Williams, Port. St.	4	1978	106	3,249	Austin Carr, Notre Dame	3	1971	2,560	34.6
Lionel Simmons, La Salle	4	1990	131	3,217	Oscar Robertson, Cin.	3	1960	2,973	33.8
Alphonzo Ford, Miss. Val. St.	4	1993	109	3,165	Calvin Murphy, Niagara	3	1970	2,548	33.1
Harry Kelly, Texas Southern	4	1983	110	3,066	Dwight Lamar, SW La.	2	1973	1,862	32.7
Hersey Hawkins, Bradley	4	1988	125	3,008	Frank Selvy, Furman	3	1954	2,538	32.5
Oscar Robertson, Cincinnati	3	1960	88	2,973	Rick Mount, Purdue	3	1970	2,323	32.3
Danny Manning, Kansas	4	1988	147	2,951	Darrell Floyd, Furman	3	1956	2,281	32.1
Alfredrick Hughes, Loyola-Ill.	4	1985	120	2,914	Nick Werkman, Seton Hall	3	1964	2,273	32.0
Elvin Hayes, Houston	3	1968	93	2,884	Willie Humes, Idaho St.	2	1971	1,510	31.5

N.C.A.A. DIVISION I INDIVIDUAL REBOUND RECORDS

Before 1973

Total	Yrs	Last	Gm	No
Tom Gola, La Salle	4	1955	118	2,201
Joe Holup, G. Washington	4	1956	104	2,030
Charlie Slack, Marshall	4	1956	88	1,916
Ed Conlin, Fordham	4	1955	102	1,884
Dickie Hemric, Wake Forest	4	1955	104	1,802
Paul Silas, Creighton	3	1964	81	1,751
Art Quimby, Connecticut	4	1955	80	1,716
Jerry Harper, Alabama	4	1956	93	1,688
Jeff Cohen, Wm. & Mary	4	1961	103	1,679
Steve Hamilton, Morehead St.	4	1958	102	1,675

Since 1973

Total	Yrs	Last	Gm	No
Tim Duncan, Wake Forest	4	1997	128	1,570
Derrick Coleman, Syracuse	4	1990	143	1,537
Ralph Sampson, Virginia	4	1983	132	1,511
Pete Padgett, Nevada-Reno	4	1976	104	1,464
Lionel Simmons, La Salle	4	1990	131	1,429
Anthony Bonner, St. Louis	4	1990	133	1,424
Tyrone Hill, Xavier (Ohio)	4	1990	126	1,380
Popeye Jones, Murray St.	4	1992	123	1,374
Michael Brooks, La Salle	4	1980	114	1,372
Xavier McDaniel, Wichita St.	4	1985	117	1,359

N.C.A.A. INDIVIDUAL ASSISTS RECORDS

Total	Yrs	Last	Gm	No
Bobby Hurley, Duke	4	1993	140	1,076
Chris Corchiani, N.C. State	4	1991	124	1,038
Keith Jennings, E. Tenn. St.	4	1991	127	983
Sherman Douglas, Syracuse	4	1989	138	960
Tony Miller, Marquette	4	1995	123	956
Greg Anthony, Portland/UNLV	4	1991	138	950
Gary Payton, Oregon St.	4	1990	120	938
Orlando Smart, San Francisco	4	1994	116	902
Andre LaFleur, Northeastern	4	1987	128	894
Jim Les, Bradley	4	1986	118	884

Average	Yrs	Last	No	Avg
A. Johnson, Cameron/Southern	3	1988	838	8.91
Sam Crawford, N. Mexico St.	2	1993	592	8.84
Mark Wade, Oklahoma/UNLV	3	1987	693	8.77
Chris Corchiani, N.C. State	4	1991	1,038	8.37
Taurence Chisholm, Delaware	4	1988	877	7.97
Van Usher, Tennessee Tech	3	1992	676	7.95
Anthony Manuel, Bradley	3	1989	855	7.92
Gary Payton, Oregon St.	4	1990	938	7.82
Orlando Smart, San Francisco	4	1994	902	7.78
Tony Miller, Marquette	4	1995	956	7.77

Note: minimum 550 assists.

N.C.A.A. DIVISION I SINGLE-GAME SCORING MARKS

	Year	Pts
Kevin Bradshaw, US Int'l vs Loyola-CA	1991	72
Pete Maravich, LSU vs Alabama	1970	69
Calvin Murphy, Niagara vs Syracuse	1969	68
Jay Handlan, Wash. & Lee vs Furman	1951	66
Pete Maravich, LSU vs Tulane	1969	66
Anthony Roberts, Oral Rbts. vs N.C. A.&T.	1977	66

	Year	Pts
Anthony Roberts, Oral Rbts. vs Ore.	1977	65
Scott Haffner, Evansville vs Dayton	1989	65
Pete Maravich, LSU vs Kentucky	1970	64
Johnny Neumann, Ole Miss vs LSU	1971	63
Hersey Hawkins, Bradley vs Detroit	1988	63

MEN'S N.C.A.A. BASKETBALL CHAMPIONSHIPS—1999

Division I
First Round—East
Cincinnati 72, George Mason 48
Temple 61, Kent 54
Miami (Fla.) 75, Lafayette 54
Purdue 58, Texas 54
Tennessee 62, Delaware 52
Southwest Missouri State 43,
  Wisconsin 32
Duke 99, Florida A & M 58
Tulsa 62, College of Charleston 53
First Round—West
Iowa 77, Alabama-Birmingham 64
Arkansas 94, Siena 80
New Mexico 61, Missouri 59
Connecticut 91, UT-San Antonio 66
Gonzaga 75, Minnesota 63
Stanford 69, Alcorn State 57
Florida 75, Pennsylvania 61
Weber State 76, North Carolina 74
First Round—Midwest
Utah 80, Arkansas State 58
Miami (Ohio) 59, Washington 58
Kansas 95, Evansville 74
Kentucky 82, New Mexico State 60
UNC-Charlotte 81, Rhode Island 70
Oklahoma 61, Arizona 60
Michigan State 76, Mount
  St. Mary's 53
Mississippi 72, Villanova 70
First Round—South
Maryland 82, Valparaiso 60
Creighton 62, Louisville 58

St. John's 69, Samford 43
Indiana 108, George Washington 88
Oklahoma State 69, Syracuse 61
Auburn 80, Winthrop 41
Ohio State 72, Murray State 58
Detroit 56, UCLA 53
Second Round—East
Temple 64, Cincinnati 54
Purdue 75, Miami (Fla.) 63
Duke 97, Tulsa 56
Southwest Missouri State 81,
  Tennessee 51
Second Round—West
Connecticut 78, New Mexico 56
Iowa 82, Arkansas 72
Gonzaga 82, Stanford 74
Florida 82, Weber State 74
Second Round—Midwest
Miami (Ohio) 66, Utah 58
Kentucky 92, Kansas 88
Oklahoma 85, UNC-Charlotte 72
Michigan State 74, Mississippi 66
Second Round—South
St. John's 86, Indiana 61
Maryland 75, Creighton 63
Auburn 81, Oklahoma State 74
Ohio State 75, Detroit 44
Third Round—East
Duke 78, Southwest Missouri
  State 61
Temple 77, Purdue 55
Third Round—West

Gonzaga 73, Florida 72
Connecticut 78, Iowa 68
Third Round—Midwest
Michigan State 54, Oklahoma 46
Miami (Ohio) 43, Kentucky 58
Third Round—South
St. John's 76, Maryland 62
Ohio State 72, Auburn 64
Regional Finals
East—Duke 85, Temple 64
West—Connecticut 67, Gonzaga 62
Midwest—Michigan State 73,
  Kentucky 66
South—Ohio State 77, St. John's 74
National Semifinals
March 27, 1999, St. Petersburg, Fla.
Connecticut 64, Ohio State 58
Duke 68, Michigan State 62
National Final
March 29, 1999, St. Petersburg, Fla.
Connecticut 77, Duke 74

Division II
Semifinals
Metropolitan State 69, Truman
  State 65
Kentucky Wesleyan 87, Florida
  Southern 67
Championship
Kentucky Wesleyan 75, Metropolitan
  State 60

WOMEN'S N.C.A.A. CHAMPIONSHIPS—1999

Division I

First Round—East
Boston College 72, Ohio State 59
Tennessee 113, Appalachian
  State 54
Virginia Tech 73, St. Peter's 48
Auburn 69, Texas 61
St. Joseph's 83, Tulane 72
Duke 79, Holy Cross 51
Maine 60, Stanford 58
Old Dominion 74, Tennessee Tech 48

First Round—Mideast
Connecticut 97, St. Francis (Pa.) 46
Xavier 85, Florida International 71
Oregon 65, Cincinnati 56
Iowa State 74, Santa Clara 61
Southern Methodist 9, Toledo 76
Georgia 73, Liberty 52
Illinois 69, Louisville 67
Clemson 76, Florida A & M 45

First Round—Midwest
Kansas 64, Marquette 58
Purdue 68, Oral Roberts 48
Alabama 80, Grambling 68
North Carolina 64, Northeastern 55
Arizona 87, Florida 84
Rutgers 84, Dartmouth 70
N.C. State 76, Mississippi State 57
Texas Tech 80, Stephen F. Austin 54

First Round—West
Penn State 82, Virginia 69

Louisiana Tech 90, Central Florida 48
Notre Dame 61, St. Mary's (Cal.) 57
LSU 78, Evansville 69
Kentucky 98, Nebraska 92
UCLA 76, Wisconsin-Green Bay 69
Southwest Missouri State 72,
  UC-Santa Barbara 70
Colorado State 71, Cal State-
  Northridge 59

Second Round—East
Tennessee 89, Boston College 62
Virginia Tech 76, Auburn 61
Duke 66, St. Joseph's 60
Old Dominion 72, Maine 62

Second Round—Mideast
Connecticut 86, Xavier 84
Iowa State 85, Oregon 70
Georgia 68, Southern Methodist 55
Clemson 63, Illinois 51

Second Round—Midwest
Purdue 55, Kansas 41
North Carolina 70, Alabama 56
Rutgers 90, Arizona 47
Texas Tech 85, N.C. State 78

Second Round—West
Louisiana Tech 79, Penn State 62
LSU 74, Notre Dame 64
UCLA 87, Kentucky 63
Colorado State 86, Southwest
  Missouri State 70

Third Round—East
Duke 76, Old Dominion 63
Tennessee 68, Virginia Tech 52

Third Round—Mideast
Iowa State 64, Connecticut 58
Georgia 67, Clemson 54

Third Round—Midwest
Purdue 82, North Carolina 59
Rutgers 53, Texas Tech 42

Third Round—West
Louisiana Tech 73, LSU 52
UCLA 77, Colorado State 68

Regional Finals
East—Duke 69, Tennessee 63
Mideast—Georgia 89, Iowa State 71
Midwest—Purdue 75, Rutgers 62
West—Louisiana Tech 88, UCLA 62

National Semifinals
March 26, 1999, San Jose, Calif.
Duke 81, Georgia 69
Purdue 77, Louisiana Tech 63

National Championship
March 28, 1999, San Jose, Calif.
Purdue 62, Duke 45

Division II

Semifinals
North Dakota 87, Emporia State 81
Arkansas Tech 62, Northern
  Kentucky 57

Championship
North Dakota 80, Arkansas Tech 63

LEADING N.C.A.A. DIVISION I MEN—1998–1999

Scoring

	Gm	Pts	Avg
Alvin Young, Niagara	29	728	25.1
Ray Minlend, St. Francis-N.Y.	28	680	24.3
Wally Szczerbiak, Miami-Ohio	32	775	24.2
Brian Merriweather, Tex.-Pan Am.	27	641	23.7
Damian Woolfolk, Norfolk St.	27	635	23.5
Quincy Lewis, Minnesota	27	625	23.1
Jason Hartman, Portland St.	28	639	22.8
Lee Nailon, TCU	31	707	22.8
Maurice Evans, Wichita St.	31	632	22.6
Harold Arceneaux, Weber St.	32	713	22.3

Rebounding

	Gm	No	Avg
Ian McGinnis, Dartmouth	26	317	12.2
Todd MacCulloch, Washington	29	345	11.9
Jeff Foster, SW Texas St.	28	316	11.3
Chris Mihm, Texas	32	351	11.0
K'Zell Wesson, La Salle	28	301	10.8
Bud Eley, SE Mo. St.	29	310	10.7
Quentin Richardson, DePaul	31	327	10.5
Michael Ruffin, Tulsa	33	342	10.4
Derek Hood, Arkansas	34	349	10.3
Eric Dow, Denver	27	276	10.2

Assists

	Gm	No	Avg
Doug Gottlieb, Oklahoma St.	34	299	8.8
Chico Fletcher, Arkansas St.	30	250	8.3
Ali Ton, Davidson	25	190	7.6
Ed Cota, North Carolina	32	238	7.4
Chris Herren, Fresno St.	25	181	7.2

	Gm	No	Avg
Mateen Cleaves, Michigan St.	38	274	7.2
Prince Fowler, TCU	32	226	7.1
Devan Clark, Southern U.	28	194	6.9
Shawnta Rogers, G. Washington	29	196	6.8
Tim Hill, Harvard	26	172	6.6

LEADING N.C.A.A. DIVISION I WOMEN—1998–1999

Scoring

	Gm	Pts	Avg
Tamika Whitmore, Memphis	32	843	26.3
Jackie Stiles, SW Missouri St.	32	823	25.7
Kim Knuth, Toledo	31	788	25.4
Kristina Behnfeldt, Marshall	26	621	23.9
Jamie Cassidy, Maine	31	738	23.8
Linda Froehlich, UNLV	28	657	23.5
Becky Hammon, Colorado St.	36	824	22.9
Diana Caramonico, Pennsylvania	26	590	22.7
Chari Nordgaard, Wis.-Green Bay	29	653	22.5
Jess Zinobile, St. Francis-N.Y.	29	653	22.5

Rebounding

	Gm	No	Avg
Monica Logan, UMBC	27	364	13.5
Diana Caramonico, Pennsylvania	26	333	12.8
Malveata Johnson, North Carolina	28	353	12.6
AuBree Hamilton, Miami-Ohio	24	285	11.9
Carolyn Harvey, St. Francis-N.Y.	27	314	11.6
Kate Sanford, Charleston Southern	28	323	11.5
Kiesha Brooks, Coppin St.	26	298	11.5
Amy Herrig, Iowa	27	306	11.3
Elise James, Robert Morris	26	287	11.0
April Cromartie, Campbell	28	306	10.9

Assists

	Gm	No	Avg		Gm	No	Avg
Dalma Ivanyi, Fla. International	30	265	8.8	Helen Darling, Penn St.	30	226	7.5
Nikki Kremer, Xavier-Ohio	32	275	8.6	Brandi McCain, Florida	33	246	7.5
Lisa Witherspoon, Virginia Tech	30	246	8.2	Milena Flores, Stanford	30	219	7.3
Amy Vachon, Maine	29	234	8.1	Tasha Pointer, Rutgers	33	226	6.8
Amy Sheiron, Sam Houston St.	27	215	8.0	Kristen Pool, UNLV	28	191	6.8

OTHER TOURNAMENTS: 1998–1999

MEN
NIT—California 61, Clemson 60
NAIA Div. I—Life (Ga.) 63, Mobile (Ala.) 60
NAIA Div. II—Cornerstone (Mich.) 113, Bethel (Ind.) 109

WOMEN
NIT—Arkansas 67, Wisconsin 64
NAIA Div. I—Oklahoma City 72, Simon Fraser (B.C.) 55
NAIA Div. II—Shawnee State (Ohio) 80, St. Francis (Ind.) 65

Professional Basketball

NATIONAL BASKETBALL ASSOCIATION CHAMPIONS

The National Basketball Association was originally the Basketball Association of America. It took its current name in 1949 when it merged with the National Basketball League. The following table lists the teams with the most wins in the conference. Playoff champions may have been wild card teams.

Season	Eastern Conference (W-L)	Western Conference (W-L)	Playoff Champions
1946–47	Washington Capitols (49-11)	Chicago Stags (39-22)	Philadelphia Warriors
1947–48	Philadelphia Warriors (27-21)	St. Louis Bombers (29-19)	Baltimore Bullets
1948–49	Washington Capitols (38-22)	Rochester Royals (45-15)	Minneapolis Lakers
1949–50	Syracuse Nationals (51-13)	Indianapolis Olympians (39-25)	Minneapolis Lakers
1950–51	Philadelphia Warriors (40-26)	Minneapolis Lakers (44-24)	Rochester Royals
1951–52	Syracuse Nationals (40-26)	Rochester Royals (41-25)	Minneapolis Lakers
1952–53	New York Knickerbockers (47-23)	Minneapolis Lakers (48-22)	Minneapolis Lakers
1953–54	New York Knickerbockers (44-28)	Minneapolis Lakers (46-26)	Minneapolis Lakers
1954–55	Syracuse Nationals (43-29)	Ft. Wayne Pistons (43-29)	Syracuse Nationals
1955–56	Philadelphia Warriors (45-27)	Ft. Wayne Pistons (37-35)	Philadelphia Warriors
1956–57	Boston Celtics (44-28)	St. Louis Hawks (38-34)	Boston Celtics
1957–58	Boston Celtics (48-23)	St. Louis Hawks (41-31)	St. Louis Hawks
1958–59	Boston Celtics (52-20)	St. Louis Hawks (49-23)	Boston Celtics
1959–60	Boston Celtics (59-16)	St. Louis Hawks (46-29)	Boston Celtics
1960–61	Boston Celtics (57-22)	St. Louis Hawks (51-28)	Boston Celtics
1961–62	Boston Celtics (60-20)	Los Angeles Lakers (54-26)	Boston Celtics
1962–63	Boston Celtics (58-22)	Los Angeles Lakers (53-27)	Boston Celtics
1963–64	Boston Celtics (59-21)	San Francisco Warriors (48-32)	Boston Celtics
1964–65	Boston Celtics (62-18)	Los Angeles Lakers (49-31)	Boston Celtics
1965–66	Philadelphia 76ers (55-25)	Los Angeles Lakers (45-35)	Boston Celtics
1966–67	Philadelphia 76ers (68-13)	San Francisco Warriors (44-37)	Philadelphia 76ers
1967–68	Philadelphia 76ers (62-20)	St. Louis Hawks (56-26)	Boston Celtics
1968–69	Baltimore Bullets (57-25)	Los Angeles Lakers (55-27)	Boston Celtics
1969–70	New York Knickerbockers (60-22)	Atlanta Hawks (48-34)	New York Knicks
1970–71	Baltimore Bullets (42-40)	Milwaukee Bucks (66-16)	Milwaukee Bucks
1971–72	New York Knickerbockers (48-34)	Los Angeles Lakers (69-13)	Los Angeles Lakers
1972–73	New York Knickerbockers (57-25)	Los Angeles Lakers (60-22)	New York Knicks
1973–74	Boston Celtics (56-26)	Milwaukee Bucks (59-23)	Boston Celtics
1974–75	Washington Bullets (60-22)	Golden State Warriors (48-34)	Golden State Warriors
1975–76	Boston Celtics (54-28)	Phoenix Suns (42-40)	Boston Celtics
1976–77	Philadelphia 76ers (50-32)	Portland Trail Blazers (49-33)	Portland Trail Blazers
1977–78	Washington Bullets (44-38)	Seattle SuperSonics (47-35)	Washington Bullets
1978–79	Washington Bullets (54-28)	Seattle SuperSonics (52-30)	Seattle SuperSonics
1979–80	Philadelphia 76ers (59-23)	Los Angeles Lakers (60-22)	Los Angeles Lakers
1980–81	Boston Celtics (62-20)	Houston Rockets (40-42)	Boston Celtics
1981–82	Philadelphia 76ers (58-24)	Los Angeles Lakers (57-25)	Los Angeles Lakers
1982–83	Philadelphia 76ers (65-17)	Los Angeles Lakers (58-24)	Philadelphia 76ers
1983–84	Boston Celtics (56-26)	Los Angeles Lakers (58-24)	Boston Celtics
1984–85	Boston Celtics (63-19)	Los Angeles Lakers (62-20)	Los Angeles Lakers
1985–86	Boston Celtics (67-15)	Houston Rockets (51-31)	Boston Celtics
1986–87	Boston Celtics (59-23)	Los Angeles Lakers (65-17)	Los Angeles Lakers
1987–88	Detroit Pistons (54-28)	Los Angeles Lakers (62-20)	Los Angeles Lakers
1988–89	Detroit Pistons (63-18)	Los Angeles Lakers (57-25)	Detroit Pistons
1989–90	Detroit Pistons (59-23)	Portland Trail Blazers (59-23)	Detroit Pistons
1990–91	Chicago Bulls (61-21)	Los Angeles Lakers (58-24)	Chicago Bulls
1991–92	Chicago Bulls (67-15)	Portland Trail Blazers (57-25)	Chicago Bulls
1992–93	Chicago Bulls (57-25)	Phoenix Suns (62-20)	Chicago Bulls

Season	Eastern Conference (W-L)	Western Conference (W-L)	Playoff Champions
1993–94	New York Knicks (57-25)	Houston Rockets (58-24)	Houston Rockets
1994–95	Orlando Magic (57-25)	Houston Rockets (47-35)	Houston Rockets
1995–96	Chicago Bulls (72-10)	Seattle SuperSonics (64-18)	Chicago Bulls
1996–97	Chicago Bulls (69-13)	Utah Jazz (64-18)	Chicago Bulls
1997–98	Chicago Bulls (62-20)	Utah Jazz (62-20)	Chicago Bulls
1998–99[1]	Miami Heat (33-17)	San Antonio Spurs (37-13)	San Antonio Spurs

1. Season shortened by lockout.

INDIVIDUAL N.B.A. SCORING CHAMPIONS

Season	Player, Team	G	FG	FT	Pts	Avg
1953–54	Neil Johnston, Philadelphia Warriors	72	591	577	1,759	24.4
1954–55	Neil Johnston, Philadelphia Warriors	72	521	589	1,631	22.7
1955–56	Bob Pettit, St. Louis Hawks	72	646	557	1,849	25.7
1956–57	Paul Arizin, Philadelphia Warriors	71	613	591	1,817	25.6
1957–58	George Yardley, Detroit Pistons	72	673	655	2,001	27.8
1958–59	Bob Pettit, St. Louis Hawks	72	719	667	2,105	29.2
1959–60	Wilt Chamberlain, Philadelphia Warriors	72	1,065	577	2,707	37.6
1960–61	Wilt Chamberlain, Philadelphia Warriors	79	1,251	531	3,033	38.4
1961–62	Wilt Chamberlain, Philadelphia Warriors	80	1,597	835	4,029	50.4
1962–63	Wilt Chamberlain, San Francisco Warriors	80	1,463	660	3,586	44.8
1963–64	Wilt Chamberlain, San Francisco Warriors	80	1,204	540	2,948	36.9
1964–65	Wilt Chamberlain, San Francisco Warriors/Phila. 76ers	73	1,063	408	2,534	34.7
1965–66	Wilt Chamberlain, Philadelphia 76ers	79	1,074	501	2,649	33.5
1966–67	Rick Barry, San Francisco Warriors	78	1,011	753	2,775	35.6
1967–68	Dave Bing, Detroit Pistons	79	835	472	2,142	27.1
1968–69	Elvin Hayes, San Diego Rockets	82	930	467	2,327	28.4
1969–70	Jerry West, Los Angeles Lakers	74	831	647	2,309	31.2
1970–71	Lew Alcindor,[1] Milwaukee Bucks	82	1,063	470	2,596	31.7
1971–72	Kareem Abdul-Jabbar, Milwaukee Bucks	81	1,159	504	2,822	34.8
1972–73	Nate Archibald, Kansas City/Omaha Kings	80	1,028	663	2,719	34.0
1973–74	Bob McAdoo, Buffalo Braves	74	901	459	2,261	30.8
1974–75	Bob McAdoo, Buffalo Braves	82	1,095	641	2,831	34.5
1975–76	Bob McAdoo, Buffalo Braves	78	934	559	2,427	31.1
1976–77	Pete Maravich, New Orleans Jazz	73	886	501	2,273	31.1
1977–78	George Gervin, San Antonio Spurs	82	864	504	2,232	27.2
1978–79	George Gervin, San Antonio Spurs	80	947	471	2,365	29.6
1979–80	George Gervin, San Antonio Spurs	78	1,024	505	2,585	33.1
1980–81	Adrian Dantley, Utah Jazz	80	909	632	2,452	30.7
1981–82	George Gervin, San Antonio Spurs	79	993	555	2,551	32.3
1982–83	Alex English, Denver Nuggets	82	959	406	2,326	28.4
1983–84	Adrian Dantley, Utah Jazz	79	802	813	2,418	30.6
1984–85	Bernard King, New York Knicks	55	691	426	1,809	32.9
1985–86	Dominique Wilkins, Atlanta Hawks	78	888	527	2,366	30.3
1986–87	Michael Jordan, Chicago Bulls[2]	82	1,098	833	3,041	37.1
1987–88	Michael Jordan, Chicago Bulls[3]	82	1,069	723	2,868	35.0
1988–89	Michael Jordan, Chicago Bulls[4]	81	966	674	2,633	32.5
1989–90	Michael Jordan, Chicago Bulls[5]	82	1,034	593	2,753	33.6
1990–91	Michael Jordan, Chicago Bulls[6]	82	990	571	2,580	31.5
1991–92	Michael Jordan, Chicago Bulls[7]	80	943	491	2,404	30.1
1992–93	Michael Jordan, Chicago Bulls[8]	78	992	476	2,541	32.6
1993–94	David Robinson, San Antonio Spurs[9]	80	840	693	2,383	29.8
1994–95	Shaquille O'Neal, Orlando Magic[10]	79	930	455	2,315	29.3
1995–96	Michael Jordan, Chicago Bulls[11]	82	916	548	2,491	30.4
1996–97	Michael Jordan, Chicago Bulls[11]	82	920	480	2,431	29.6
1997–98	Michael Jordan, Chicago Bulls [12]	82	881	565	2,357	28.7
1998–99	Allen Iverson, Philadelphia 76ers [13]	48	435	356	1,284	26.8

1. (Kareem Abdul-Jabbar). 2. Also had 12 3-point field goals. 3. Also had 7 3-point field goals. 4. Also had 27 3-point field goals. 5. Also had 92 3-point field goals. 6. Also had 29 3-point field goals. 7. Attempted 27 3-point field goals. 8. Also had 81 3-point field goals. 9. Also had 10 3-point field goals. 10. O'Neal scored no 3-point field goals in 1994–1995. 11. Also had 111 3-point field goals in both 1995–96 and 1996–97. 12. Also had 30 3-point field goals. 13. Also had 58 3-point field goals.

N.B.A. MOST VALUABLE PLAYERS

1956 Bob Pettit, St. Louis
1957 Bob Cousy, Boston
1958 Bill Russell, Boston
1959 Bob Pettit, St. Louis
1960 Wilt Chamberlain, Philadelphia
1961–63 Bill Russell, Boston
1964 Oscar Robertson, Cincinnati

1965 Bill Russell, Boston
1966–68 Wilt Chamberlain, Philadelphia
1969 Wes Unseld, Baltimore
1970 Willis Reed, New York
1971–72 Lew Alcindor (Kareem Abdul-Jabbar), Milwaukee

1973 Dave Cowens, Boston
1974 Kareem Abdul-Jabbar, Milwaukee
1975 Bob McAdoo, Buffalo
1976–77 Kareem Abdul-Jabbar, L.A. Lakers
1978 Bill Walton, Portland

1979	Moses Malone, Houston	1986	Larry Bird, Boston	1994	Hakeem Olajuwon, Houston
1980	Kareem Abdul-Jabbar, L.A. Lakers	1987	Earvin Johnson, L.A. Lakers	1995	David Robinson, San Antonio
		1988	Michael Jordan, Chicago	1996	Michael Jordan, Chicago
1981	Julius Erving, Philadelphia	1989	Earvin Johnson, L.A. Lakers	1997	Karl Malone, Utah
1982	Moses Malone, Houston	1990	Earvin Johnson, L.A. Lakers	1998	Michael Jordan, Chicago
1983	Moses Malone, Philadelphia	1991	Michael Jordan, Chicago	1999	Karl Malone, Utah
1984	Larry Bird, Boston	1992	Michael Jordan, Chicago		
1985	Larry Bird, Boston	1993	Charles Barkley, Phoenix		

N.B.A. LIFETIME LEADERS
(Through 1999 season)

Free Throws

	FT	Att	Pct
Moses Malone	8,531	11,090	.769
Oscar Robertson	7,694	9,185	.838
Karl Malone[1]	7,511	10,288	.730
Jerry West	7,160	8,801	.814
Dolph Schayes	6,979	8,273	.844
Adrian Dantley	6,832	8,351	.818
Michael Jordan	6,798	8,115	.838
Kareem Abdul-Jabbar	6,712	9,304	.721
Charles Barkley[1]	6,278	8,533	.736
Bob Pettit	6,182	8,119	.761

Field Goals

	FG	Att	Pct
Kareem Abdul-Jabbar	15,837	28,307	.559
Wilt Chamberlain	12,681	23,497	.540
Elvin Hayes	10,976	24,272	.452
Michael Jordan	10,958	21,686	.505
Karl Malone[1]	10,683	20,301	.526
Alex English	10,659	21,036	.507
John Havlicek	10,513	23,930	.439
Hakeem Olajuwon[1]	10,079	19,584	.515
Dominique Wilkins[1]	9,963	21,589	.461
Robert Parish	9,614	17,914	.537

Scoring Average
Minimum of 400 games or 10,000 points.

	Gm	Pts	Avg
Michael Jordan	930	29,277	31.5
Wilt Chamberlain	1,045	31,419	30.1
Elgin Baylor	846	23,149	27.4
Shaquille O'Neal[1]	455	12,343	27.1
Jerry West	932	25,192	27.0
Bob Pettit	792	20,880	26.4
George Gervin	791	20,708	26.2
Karl Malone[1]	1,110	28,946	26.1
Oscar Robertson	1,040	26,710	25.7
Dominique Wilkins[1]	1,074	26,668	24.8

1. Active 1999 season.

Most Games Played

			Personal Fouls	
Robert Parish	1,611		Kareem Abdul-Jabbar	4,657
Kareem Abdul-Jabbar	1,560		Robert Parish	4,443
Moses Malone	1,329		Buck Williams	4,267
Buck Williams	1,307		Elvin Hayes	4,193
Elvin Hayes	1,303		James Edwards	4,042

Blocked Shots

			Steals	
Hakeem Olajuwon[1]	3,582		John Stockton[1]	2,701
Kareem Abdul-Jabbar	3,189		Maurice Cheeks	2,310
Mark Eaton	3,064		Michael Jordan	2,306
Patrick Ewing[1]	2,674		Clyde Drexler	2,207
Tree Rollins	2,542		Alvin Robertson	2,112

Rebounds

Wilt Chamberlain	23,924		Robert Parish	14,715
Bill Russell	21,620		Nate Thurmond	14,464
Kareem Abdul-Jabbar	17,440		Walt Bellamy	14,241
Elvin Hayes	16,279		Wes Unseld	13,769
Moses Malone	16,212		Buck Williams	13,017

Assists

John Stockton[1]	13,087		Maurice Cheeks	7,392
Magic Johnson	10,141		Lenny Wilkens	7,211
Oscar Robertson	9,887		Bob Cousy	6,955
Isiah Thomas	9,061		Guy Rodgers	6,917
Mark Jackson[1]	7,924		Kevin Johnson	6,687

Points

Kareem Abdul-Jabbar	38,387		Elvin Hayes	27,313
Wilt Chamberlain	31,419		Oscar Robertson	26,710
Michael Jordan	29,277		Dominique Wilkins[1]	26,668
Karl Malone[1]	28,946		John Havlicek	26,395
Moses Malone	27,409		Alex English	25,613

N.B.A. INDIVIDUAL RECORDS
(Through 1998–99 season)

Most points, game—100, Wilt Chamberlain, Philadelphia, 1962

Most points, quarter—33, George Gervin, San Antonio, 1978

Most points, half—59, Wilt Chamberlain, Philadelphia, 1962

Most free throws, game—28, Wilt Chamberlain, Philadelphia, 1962; 28, Adrian Dantley, Utah, 1984

Most free throws, quarter—14, Rick Barry, San Francisco, 1966; 14, Johnny Newman, Denver, 1998

Most free throws, half—20, Michael Jordan, Chicago, 1992

Most field goals, game—36, Wilt Chamberlain, Philadelphia, 1962

Most consecutive field goals, game—18, Wilt Chamberlain, San Francisco, 1963; Philadelphia, 1967

Most assists, game—30, Scott Skiles, Orlando vs. Denver, 1990

Most rebounds, game—55, Wilt Chamberlain, Philadelphia vs. Boston, 1960

Most 3-pt. field goals, game—11, Dennis Scott, Orlando vs. Atlanta, 1996

N.B.A. TEAM RECORDS

Most points, game—186, Detroit vs. Denver, 3 overtimes, 1983
Most points, quarter—58, Buffalo vs. Boston, 1972
Most points, half—107, Phoenix vs. Denver, 1990
Most points, overtime period—22, Detroit vs. Cleveland, 1973
Most field goals, game—74, Detroit, 1983
Most field goals, quarter—24, Phoenix, 1990
Most field goals, half—43, Phoenix, 1990
Most assists, game—53, Milwaukee, 1978
Most rebounds, game—109, Boston, 1960
Most points, both teams, game—370 (Detroit 186, Denver 184) 3 overtimes, Denver, December 13, 1983

Most points, both teams, quarter—99 (San Antonio 53, Denver 46), 1984
Most points, both teams, half—174 (Phoenix 107, Denver 67), 1990
Longest winning streak—33, L.A. Lakers, 1971–72
Longest losing streak—24, Cleveland, March–Nov. 1982
Longest winning streak at home—44, Chicago, March 1995–April 1996
Most games won, season—72, Chicago, 1995–96
Most games lost, season—73, Philadelphia, 1972–73
Highest average points per game—126.5, Denver, 1981–82

NATIONAL BASKETBALL ASSOCIATION FINAL STANDINGS: 1998–99

NOTE: The 1998–99 N.B.A. season was curtailed by a 191-day lockout which began July 1, 1998. The 50-game season began on Jan. 24, 1999.

EASTERN CONFERENCE
Atlantic Division

	W	L	Pct	GB
*Miami Heat	33	17	.660	—
xOrlando Magic	33	17	.660	—
xPhiladelphia 76ers	28	22	.560	5
xNew York Knicks	27	23	.540	6
Boston Celtics	19	31	.380	14
Washington Wizards	18	32	.360	15
New Jersey Nets	16	34	.320	17

Central Division

	W	L	Pct	GB
*Indiana Pacers	33	17	.660	—
xAtlanta Hawks	31	19	.620	2
xDetroit Pistons	29	21	.580	4
xMilwaukee Bucks	28	22	.560	5
Charlotte Hornets	26	24	.520	7
Toronto Raptors	23	27	.460	10
Cleveland Cavaliers	22	28	.440	11
Chicago Bulls	13	37	.260	20

*Division champion. xPlayoff qualifier.

WESTERN CONFERENCE
Midwest Division

	W	L	Pct	GB
*San Antonio Spurs	37	13	.740	—
xUtah Jazz	37	13	.740	—
xHouston Rockets	31	19	.620	6
xMinnesota Timberwolves	25	25	.500	12
Dallas Mavericks	19	31	.380	18
Denver Nuggets	14	36	.280	23
Vancouver Grizzlies	8	42	.160	29

Pacific Division

	W	L	Pct	GB
*Portland Trail Blazers	35	15	.700	—
xL.A. Lakers	31	19	.620	4
xSacramento Kings	27	23	.540	8
xPhoenix Suns	27	23	.540	8
Seattle SuperSonics	25	25	.500	10
Golden State Warriors	21	29	.420	14
L.A. Clippers	9	41	.180	26

N.B.A. PLAYOFFS—1999
(All caps denotes home team)

EASTERN CONFERENCE
First Round
(Best of 5)
New York defeated Miami, 3 games to 2
Indiana defeated Milwaukee, 3 games to 0
Philadelphia defeated Orlando, 3 games to 1
Atlanta defeated Detroit, 3 games to 2
Semifinals
(Best of 7)
New York defeated Atlanta, 4 games to 0
Indiana defeated Philadelphia, 4 games to 0
Conference Finals
(Best of 7)
New York defeated Indiana, 4 games to 2
  May 30—New York 93, INDIANA 90
  June 1—INDIANA 88, New York 86
  June 5—NEW YORK 92, Indiana 91
  June 7—Indiana 90, NEW YORK 78
  June 9—New York 101, INDIANA 94
  June 11—NEW YORK 90, Indiana 82

WESTERN CONFERENCE
First Round
(Best of 5)
San Antonio defeated Minnesota, 3 games to 1
Portland defeated Phoenix, 3 games to 0
Utah defeated Sacramento, 3 games to 2
L.A. Lakers defeated Houston, 3 games to 1
Semifinals
(Best of 7)
Portland defeated Utah, 4 games to 2
San Antonio defeated L.A. Lakers, 4 games to 0
Conference Finals
(Best of 7)
San Antonio defeated Portland, 4 games to 0
  May 29—SAN ANTONIO 80, Portland 76
  May 31—SAN ANTONIO 86, Portland 85
  June 4—San Antonio 85, PORTLAND 63
  June 6—San Antonio 94, PORTLAND 80

CHAMPIONSHIP
San Antonio Spurs defeated New York Knicks, 4 games to 1
Tim Duncan, San Antonio, named Finals MVP

June 16—SAN ANTONIO 89, New York 77
June 18—SAN ANTONIO 80, New York 67
June 21—NEW YORK 89, San Antonio 81

June 23—San Antonio 96, NEW YORK 89
June 25—San Antonio 78, NEW YORK 77

LEADING SCORERS: 1998–1999

Minimum of 49 games played or 1,344 points scored

	Gm	Pts	Avg
Allen Iverson, Philadelphia	48	1,284	26.8
Shaquille O'Neal, L.A. Lakers	49	1,289	26.3
Karl Malone, Utah	49	1,164	23.8
Shareef Abdur-Rahim, Vancouver	50	1,152	23.0
Keith Van Horn, New Jersey	42	916	21.8
Tim Duncan, San Antonio	50	1,084	21.7
Gary Payton, Seattle	50	1,084	21.7
Stephon Marbury, Minn./N.J.	49	1,044	21.3
Antonio McDyess, Denver	50	1,061	21.2
Grant Hill, Detroit	50	1,053	21.1
Kevin Garnett, Minnesota	47	977	20.8
Shawn Kemp, Cleveland	42	862	20.5
Michael Finley, Dallas	50	1,009	20.2
Alonzo Mourning, Miami	46	924	20.1
Kobe Bryant, L.A. Lakers	50	996	19.9

REBOUND LEADERS: 1998–1999

Minimum of 49 games played or 768 rebounds

	Gm	Reb	Avg
Chris Webber, Sacramento	42	545	13.0
Charles Barkley, Houston	42	516	12.3
Dikembe Mutombo, Atlanta	50	610	12.2
Danny Fortson, Denver	50	581	11.6
Tim Duncan, San Antonio	50	571	11.4
Alonzo Mourning, Miami	46	507	11.0
Antonio McDyess, Denver	50	537	10.7
Shaquille O'Neal, L.A. Lakers	49	525	10.7
Kevin Garnett, Minnesota	47	489	10.4
Vlade Divac, Charlotte	50	501	10.0
David Robinson, San Antonio	49	492	10.0
Brian Grant, Portland	48	470	9.8
Hakeem Olajuwon, Houston	50	478	9.6
Karl Malone, Utah	49	463	9.4
Tom Gugliotta, Phoenix	43	381	8.9

ASSISTS LEADERS: 1998–1999

Minimum of 49 games played or 384 assists

	Gm	Ast	Avg
Jason Kidd, Phoenix	50	539	10.8
Rod Strickland, Washington	44	434	9.9
Stephon Marbury, Minnesota	49	437	8.9
Gary Payton, Seattle	50	436	8.7
Terrell Brandon, Minnesota	36	309	8.6
Mark Jackson, Indiana	49	386	7.9
Brevin Knight, Cleveland	39	302	7.7
John Stockton, Utah	50	374	7.5
Avery Johnson, San Antonio	50	369	7.4
Nick Van Exel, L.A. Lakers	50	368	7.4

FIELD GOAL PERCENTAGE LEADERS: 1998–1999

Minimum of 288 field goals made

	Gm	FG	Att	Pct
Shaquille O'Neal, L.A. Lakers	49	510	885	.576
Otis Thorpe, Washington	49	240	440	.545
Hakeem Olajuwon, Houston	50	373	725	.514
Alonzo Mourning, Miami	46	324	634	.511
David Robinson, San Antonio	49	268	527	.509
Rasheed Wallace, Portland	49	242	476	.508
Bison Dele, Detroit	49	216	431	.501
Tim Duncan, San Antonio	50	418	845	.495
Danny Fortson, Denver	50	191	386	.495
Vitaly Potapenko, Boston	50	204	412	.495

FREE-THROW PERCENTAGE LEADERS: 1998–1999

Minimum of 120 free throws made

	Gm	FT	Att	Pct
Reggie Miller, Indiana	50	226	247	.915
Chauncey Billups, Denver	45	157	172	.913
Darrell Armstrong, Orlando	50	161	178	.904
Ray Allen, Milwaukee	50	176	195	.903
Hersey Hawkins, Seattle	50	119	132	.902
Jeff Hornacek, Utah	48	125	140	.893
Chris Mullin, Indiana	50	80	92	.870
Glenn Robinson, Milwaukee	47	140	161	.870
Mario Elie, San Antonio	47	103	119	.866
Eric Piatkowski, L.A. Clippers	49	88	102	.863

3-POINT FIELD GOAL PERCENT LEADERS: 1998–1999

Minimum of 82 3-point field goals made

	Gm	3FG	Att	Pct
Dell Curry, Milwaukee	42	69	145	.476
Chris Mullin, Indiana	50	73	157	.465
Hubert Davis, Dallas	50	65	144	.451
Walt Williams, Portland	48	63	144	.438
Michael Dickerson, Houston	50	71	164	.433
Dale Ellis, Seattle	48	94	217	.433
Jeff Hornacek, Utah	48	34	81	.420
Clifford Robinson, Phoenix	50	58	139	.417
George McCloud, Phoenix	48	69	166	.416
Jud Buechler, Detroit	50	61	148	.412

BLOCKED-SHOTS LEADERS: 1998–1999

Minimum of 49 games played or 96 block shots

	Gm	Blk	Avg
Alonzo Mourning, Miami	46	180	3.91
Shawn Bradley, Dallas	49	159	3.24
Theo Ratliff, Philadelphia	50	149	2.98
Dikembe Mutombo, Atlanta	50	147	2.94
Greg Ostertag, Utah	48	131	2.73
Patrick Ewing, New York	38	100	2.63
Tim Duncan, San Antonio	50	126	2.52
Hakeem Olajuwon, Houston	50	123	2.46
David Robinson, San Antonio	49	119	2.43
Antonio McDyess, Denver	50	115	2.30

STEALS LEADERS: 1998–1999

Minimum of 49 games played or 120 steals

	Gm	Stl	Avg
Kendall Gill, New Jersey	50	134	2.68
Eddie Jones, Charlotte	50	125	2.50
Allen Iverson, Philadelphia	48	110	2.29
Jason Kidd, Phoenix	50	114	2.28
Doug Christie, Toronto	50	113	2.26
Anfernee Hardaway, Orlando	50	111	2.22
Gary Payton, Seattle	50	109	2.18
Darrell Armstrong, Orlando	50	108	2.16
Eric Snow, Philadelphia	48	100	2.08
Mookie Blaylock, Atlanta	48	99	2.06

Women's Professional Basketball

WOMEN'S NATIONAL BASKETBALL ASSOCIATION—1999 SEASON

Eastern Conference

	W	L	Pct	GB	Home	Road
x-New York Liberty	18	14	.563	—	12–4	6–10
y-Charlotte Sting	15	17	.469	3	8–8	7–9
y-Detroit Shock	15	17	.469	3	7–9	8–8
Orlando Miracle	15	17	.469	3	8–8	7–9
Washington Mystics	12	20	.375	6	6–10	6–10
Cleveland Rockers	7	25	.219	11	5–15	2–14

Western Conference

	W	L	Pct	GB	Home	Road
x-Houston Comets	26	6	.813	—	15–1	11–5
y-Los Angeles Sparks	20	12	.625	6	13–3	7–9
y-Sacramento Monarchs	19	13	.594	7	11–5	8–8
Phoenix Mercury	15	17	.469	11	12–4	3–13
Minnesota Lynx	15	17	.469	11	8–8	7–9
Utah Starzz	15	17	.469	11	11–5	4–12

NOTES: x—conference champion. y—clinched playoff qualifier. GB refers to Games Behind leader.

Conference Championship Series (Best of 3)

Date	Result
Aug. 27	at Charlotte 78, New York 67
Aug. 29	at New York 74, Charlotte 70
Aug. 30	at New York 69, Charlotte 54
	New York wins series, 2–1

Date	Result
Aug. 26	at Los Angeles 75, Houston 60
Aug. 29	at Houston 83, Los Angeles 55
Aug. 30	at Houston 72, Los Angeles 62
	Houston wins series, 2–1

League Championship Series (Best of 3)
Houston wins championship, 2 games to 1

Date	Result
Sept. 2	Houston 73, at New York 60
Sept. 4	New York 68, at Houston 67
Sept. 5	at Houston 59, New York 47

WNBA ANNUAL AWARDS—1999 SEASON

Most Valuable Player: Yolanda Griffith, Sacramento
Defensive Player of the Year: Yolanda Griffith, Sacramento.
Sportsmanship Award: Suzie McConnell Serio, Cleveland

Coach of the Year: Van Chancellor, Houston
Newcomer of the Year: Yolanda Griffith, Sacramento
Rookie of the Year: Chamique Holdsclaw, Washington

1999 WNBA LEAGUE LEADERS

SCORING

	Gm	Pts	Avg
Cynthia Cooper, Houston	31	686	22.1
Yolanda Griffith, Sacramento	29	545	18.8
Sheryl Swoopes, Houston	32	585	18.3
Natalie Williams, Utah	28	504	18.0
Nikki McCray, Washington	32	561	17.5
Chamique Holdsclaw, Washington	31	525	16.9
Brandy Reed, Minnesota	25	402	16.1
Lisa Leslie, Los Angeles	32	500	15.6
Jennifer Gillom, Phoenix	32	485	15.2
Adrienne Goodson, Utah	32	476	14.9

REBOUNDING

	Gm	Reb	Avg
Yolanda Griffith, Sacramento	29	329	11.3
Natalie Williams, Utah	28	257	9.2
Chamique Holdsclaw, Washington	31	246	7.9
Lisa Leslie, Los Angeles	32	248	7.8
Taj McWilliams, Orlando	32	239	7.5
Marlies Askamp, Phoenix	30	215	7.2
Sue Wicks, New York	32	223	7.0
Vicky Bullett, Charlotte	32	219	6.8
Muriel Page, Washington	32	213	6.7
Val Whiting, Detroit	31	207	6.7

ASSISTS

	Gm	Ast	Avg
Ticha Penicheiro, Sacramento	32	226	7.1
Teresa Weatherspoon, New York	32	205	6.4
Dawn Staley, Charlotte	32	177	5.5
Cynthia Cooper, Houston	31	162	5.2
Debbie Black, Utah	32	161	5.0
Michele Timms, Phoenix	30	151	5.0

BLOCKS

	Gm	Blk	Avg
Malgorzata Dydek, Utah	32	77	2.41
Maria Stepnova, Phoenix	32	62	1.94
Yolanda Griffith, Sacramento	29	54	1.86
Lisa Leslie, Los Angeles	32	49	1.53
Sheryl Swoopes, Houston	32	46	1.44

STEALS

	Gm	Stl	Avg
Yolanda Griffith, Sacramento	29	73	2.52
Teresa Weatherspoon, New York	32	78	2.44
Debbie Black, Utah	32	77	2.41
Sheryl Swoopes, Houston	32	76	2.38
Nykesha Sales, Orlando	32	69	2.16

AMERICAN BASKETBALL LEAGUE

The American Basketball League suspended operations Dec. 22, 1998

LEAGUE CHAMPIONS

Year	Champions	Head Coach	Series	Runners-up	Head Coach
1997	Columbus Quest	Brian Agler	3-2	Richmond Rage	Lisa Boyer
1998	Columbus Quest	Brian Agler	3-2	Long Beach StingRays	Maura McHugh
1999	league folded				

Hockey

Ice hockey, by birth and upbringing a Canadian game, is an offshoot of field hockey. Some historians say that the first ice hockey game was played in Montreal in December 1879 between two teams composed almost exclusively of McGill University students, but others assert that earlier hockey games took place in Kingston, Ontario, or Halifax, Nova Scotia. In the Montreal game of 1879, there were fifteen players on a side, who used an assortment of crude sticks to keep the puck in motion. Early rules allowed nine men on a side, but the number was reduced to seven in 1886 and later to six.

The first governing body of the sport was the Amateur Hockey Association of Canada, organized in 1887. In the winter of 1894–95, a group of college students from the United States visited Canada and saw hockey played. They became enthused over the game and introduced it as a winter sport when they returned home. The first professional league was the International Hockey League, which operated in northern Michigan in 1904–06.

Until 1910, professionals and amateurs were allowed to play together on "mixed teams," but this arrangement ended with the formation of the first "big league," the National Hockey Association, in eastern Canada in 1910. The Pacific Coast League was organized in 1911 for western Canadian hockey. The league included Seattle and later other American cities. The National Hockey League replaced the National Hockey Association in 1917. Boston, in 1924, was the first American city to join that circuit. The league expanded to include western cities in 1967. The Stanley Cup was competed for by "mixed teams" from 1894 to 1910, thereafter by professionals. It was awarded to the winner of the NHL playoffs from 1926–67 and now to the league champion. The World Hockey Association was organized in October 1972 and was dissolved after the 1978–79 season when the NHL absorbed four of the teams.

Rule changes have been implemented to steer the league from its violent reputation in order to better showcase the world's most talented stars.

Hockey, once considered a cold-weather sport, has taken major strides in increasing its fan base to the southern and western part of the United States as well. In the 1995–96 season, Florida and Colorado battled in the Stanley Cup Finals, the San Jose Sharks sold out all 41 of their home games, and the second team in two years (Winnipeg) migrated from Canada to the Southwest region of the U.S. (Phoenix).

The league continues to expand as the Nashville Predators joins the league in the 1998–99 season. In 1999–2000, the Atlanta Thrashers will begin to play, and the 2000–2001 season will see the addition of the Columbus Blue Jackets and the Minnesota Wild.

STANLEY CUP WINNERS

Emblematic of World Professional Championship; N.H.L. Championship after 1967

1893 Montreal A.A.A.	1924 Montreal Canadiens	1956–60 Montreal Canadiens
1894 Montreal A.A.A.	1925 Victoria Cougars	1961 Chicago Black Hawks
1895 Montreal Victorias	1926 Montreal Maroons	1962–64 Toronto Maple Leafs
1896 (Feb.) Winnipeg Victorias	1927 Ottawa Senators	1965–66 Montreal Canadiens
1896 (Dec.) Montreal Victorias	1928 N.Y. Rangers	1967 Toronto Maple Leafs
1897–99 Montreal Victorias	1929 Boston Bruins	1968–69 Montreal Canadiens
1899–1900 Montreal Shamrocks	1930–31 Montreal Canadiens	1970 Boston Bruins
1901 Winnipeg Victorias	1932 Toronto Maple Leafs	1971 Montreal Canadiens
1902 Montreal A.A.A.	1933 N.Y. Rangers	1972 Boston Bruins
1903–05 Ottawa Silver Seven	1934 Chicago Black Hawks	1973 Montreal Canadiens
1906 Montreal Wanderers	1935 Montreal Maroons	1974–75 Philadelphia Flyers
1907 (Jan.) Kenora Thistles	1936–37 Detroit Red Wings	1976–79 Montreal Canadiens
1907 (March) Montreal Wanderers	1938 Chicago Red Hawks	1980–83 N.Y. Islanders
1908 Montreal Wanderers	1939 Boston Bruins	1984–85 Edmonton Oilers
1909 Ottawa Senators	1940 N.Y. Rangers	1986 Montreal Canadiens
1910 Montreal Wanderers	1941 Boston Bruins	1987–88 Edmonton Oilers
1911 Ottawa Senators	1942 Toronto Maple Leafs	1989 Calgary Flames
1912–13 Quebec Bulldogs	1943 Detroit Red Wings	1990 Edmonton Oilers
1914 Toronto Blueshirts	1944 Montreal Canadiens	1991–92 Pittsburgh Penguins
1915 Vancouver Millionaires	1945 Toronto Maple Leafs	1993 Montreal Canadiens
1916 Montreal Canadiens	1946 Montreal Canadiens	1994 N.Y. Rangers
1917 Seattle Metropolitans	1947–49 Toronto Maple Leafs	1995 N.J. Devils
1918 Toronto Arenas	1950 Detroit Red Wings	1996 Colorado Avalanche
1919 No champion	1951 Toronto Maple Leafs	1997–98 Detroit Red Wings
1920–21 Ottawa Senators	1952 Detroit Red Wings	1999 Dallas Stars
1922 Toronto St. Patricks	1953 Montreal Canadiens	
1923 Ottawa Senators	1954–55 Detroit Red Wings	

N.H.L. CHAMPIONS

Wales Trophy

				Eastern Division	
1939–41 Boston	1948–55 Detroit	1964 Montreal			1974 Boston
1942 New York	1956 Montreal	1965 Detroit		1968–69 Montreal	
1943 Detroit	1957 Detroit	1966 Montreal		1970 Chicago	**Eastern Conference**[1]
1944–47 Montreal	1958–62 Montreal	1967 Chicago		1971–72 Boston	
1948 Toronto	1963 Toronto			1973 Montreal	1975 Buffalo
					1976–79 Montreal

1980	Buffalo	1985	Philadelphia	1989	Montreal	1994	N.Y. Rangers	1998	Washington
1981	Montreal	1986	Montreal	1990	Boston	1995	New Jersey	1999	Buffalo
1982–84	N.Y.	1987	Philadelphia	1991–92	Pittsburgh	1996	Florida		
	Islanders	1988	Boston	1993	Montreal	1997	Philadelphia		

1. Prior to 1994 was the Wales Conference.

CAMPBELL BOWL

Western Division		**Western Conference**[2]		1986	Calgary	1993	Los Angeles
1968–70	St. Louis	1975–77	Philadelphia	1987–88	Edmonton	1994	Vancouver
1971–73	Chicago	1978–79	N.Y. Islanders	1989	Calgary	1995	Detroit
1974	Philadelphia	1980	Philadelphia	1990	Edmonton	1996	Colorado
		1981	N.Y. Islanders	1991	Minnesota	1997–98	Detroit
		1982–85	Edmonton	1992	Chicago	1999	Dallas

2. Prior to 1994 was the Campbell Conference.

NATIONAL HOCKEY LEAGUE YEARLY TROPHY WINNERS

The Hart Trophy—Most Valuable Player

1924 Frank Nighbor, Ottawa
1925 Billy Burch, Hamilton
1926 Nels Stewart, Montreal Maroons
1927 Herb Gardiner, Montreal Canadiens
1928 Howie Morenz, Montreal Canadiens
1929 Roy Worters, N.Y. Americans
1930 Nels Stewart, Montreal Maroons
1931–32 Howie Morenz, Montreal Canadiens
1933 Eddie Shore, Boston
1934 Aurel Joliat, Montreal Canadiens
1935–36 Eddie Shore, Boston
1937 Babe Siebert, Montreal Canadiens
1938 Eddie Shore, Boston
1939 Toe Blake, Montreal Canadiens
1940 Ebbie Goodfellow, Detroit
1941 Bill Cowley, Boston
1942 Tommy Anderson, N.Y. Americans
1943 Bill Cowley, Boston
1944 Babe Pratt, Toronto
1945 Elmer Lach, Montreal Canadiens
1946 Max Bentley, Chicago
1947 Maurice Richard, Montreal Canadiens
1948 Buddy O'Connor, N.Y. Rangers
1949 Sid Abel, Detroit
1950 Chuck Rayner, N.Y. Rangers
1951 Milt Schmidt, Boston
1952–53 Gordie Howe, Detroit
1954 Al Rollins, Chicago
1955 Ted Kennedy, Toronto
1956 Jean Belveau, Montreal Canadiens
1957–58 Gordie Howe, Detroit
1959 Andy Bathgate, N.Y. Rangers
1960 Gordie Howe, Detroit
1961 Bernie Geoffrion, Montreal Canadiens
1962 Jacques Plante, Montreal Canadiens
1963 Gordon Howe, Detroit
1964 Jean Beliveau, Montreal Canadiens
1965–66 Bobby Hull, Chicago
1967–68 Stan Mikita, Chicago
1969 Phil Esposito, Boston

1970–72 Bobby Orr, Boston
1973 Bobby Clarke, Philadelphia
1974 Phil Esposito, Boston
1975–76 Bobby Clarke, Philadelphia
1977–78 Guy Lafleur, Montreal
1979 Bryan Trottier, N.Y. Islanders
1980–87 Wayne Gretzky, Edmonton
1988 Mario Lemieux, Pittsburgh
1989 Wayne Gretzky, Los Angeles
1990 Mark Messier, Edmonton
1991 Brett Hull, St. Louis
1992 Mark Messier, N.Y. Rangers
1993 Mario Lemieux, Pittsburgh
1994 Sergei Fedorov, Detroit
1995 Eric Lindros, Philadelphia
1996 Mario Lemieux, Pittsburgh
1997–98 Dominik Hasek, Buffalo
1999 Jaromir Jagr, Pittsburgh

Vezina Trophy—Leading Goalkeeper

1956–60 Jacques Plante, Montreal
1961 Johnny Bower, Toronto
1962 Jacques Plante, Montreal
1963 Glenn Hall, Chicago
1964 Charlie Hodge, Montreal
1965 Terry Sawchuk—Johnny Bower, Toronto
1966 Gump Worsley—Charlie Hodge, Montreal
1967 Glen Hall—Denis Dejordy, Chicago
1968 Gump Worsley—Rogie Vachon, Montreal
1969 Glenn Hall—Jacques Plante, St. Louis
1970 Tony Esposito, Chicago
1971 Ed Giacomin—Gilles Villemure, N.Y. Rangers
1972 Tony Esposito—Gary Smith, Chicago
1973 Ken Dryden, Montreal
1974 Bernie Parent, Philadelphia and Tony Esposito, Chicago
1975 Bernie Parent, Philadelphia
1976 Ken Dryden, Montreal
1977–79 Ken Dryden—Bunny Larocque, Montreal
1980 Bob Sauve—Don Edwards, Buffalo
1981 Richard Sevigny—Denis Herron—Bunny Larocque, Montreal
1982 Billy Smith, N.Y. Islanders
1983 Pete Peeters, Boston

1984 Tom Barrasso, Buffalo
1985 Pelle Lindbergh, Philadelphia
1986 John Vanbiesbrouck, N.Y. Rangers
1987 Ron Hextall, Philadelphia
1988 Grant Fuhr, Edmonton
1989–90 Patrick Roy, Montreal
1991 Ed Belfour, Chicago
1992 Patrick Roy, Montreal
1993 Ed Belfour, Chicago
1994–95 Dominik Hasek, Buffalo
1996 Jim Carey, Washington
1997–99 Dominik Hasek, Buffalo

James Norris Trophy— Defenseman

1954 Red Kelly, Detroit
1955–58 Doug Harvey, Montreal
1959 Tom Johnson, Montreal
1960–62 Doug Harvey, Montreal, N.Y. Rangers (62)
1963–65 Pierre Pilote, Chicago
1966 Jacques Laperriere, Montreal
1967 Harry Howell, N.Y. Rangers
1968–75 Bobby Orr, Boston
1976 Denis Potvin, N.Y. Islanders
1977 Larry Robinson, Montreal
1978–79 Denis Potvin, N.Y. Islanders
1980 Larry Robinson, Montreal
1981 Randy Carlyle, Pittsburgh
1982 Doug Wilson, Chicago
1983–84 Rod Langway, Washington
1985–86 Paul Coffey, Edmonton
1987–88 Ray Bourque, Boston
1989 Chris Chelios, Montreal
1990–91 Ray Bourque, Boston
1992 Brian Leetch, N.Y. Rangers
1993 Chris Chelios, Chicago
1994 Ray Bourque, Boston
1995 Paul Coffey, Detroit
1996 Chris Chelios, Chicago
1997 Brian Leetch, N.Y. Rangers
1998 Rob Blake, Los Angeles
1999 Al MacInnis, St. Louis

Lady Byng Trophy— Sportsmanship

1960 Don McKenney, Boston
1961 Red Kelly, Toronto
1962–63 Dave Keon, Toronto
1964 Ken Wharram, Chicago
1965 Bobby Hull, Chicago
1966 Alex Delvecchio, Detroit
1967–68 Stan Mikita, Chicago
1969 Alex Delvecchio, Detroit

1970	Phil Goyette, St. Louis
1971	Johnny Bucyk, Boston
1972	Jean Ratelle, N.Y. Rangers
1973	Gilbert Perreault, Buffalo
1974	Johnny Bucyk, Boston
1975	Marcel Dionne, Detroit
1976	Jean Ratelle, N.Y. Rangers, Boston
1977	Marcel Dionne, Los Angeles
1978	Butch Goring, Los Angeles
1979	Bob MacMillan, Atlanta
1980	Wayne Gretzky, Edmonton
1981	Rick Kehoe, Pittsburgh
1982	Rick Middleton, Boston
1983–84	Mike Bossy, N.Y. Islanders
1985	Jari Kurri, Edmonton
1986	Mike Bossy, N.Y. Islanders
1987	Joey Mullen, Calgary
1988	Mats Naslund, Montreal
1989	Joey Mullen, Calgary
1990	Brett Hull, St. Louis
1991–92	Wayne Gretzky, Los Angeles
1993	Pierre Turgeon, N.Y. Islanders
1994	Wayne Gretzky, Los Angeles
1995	Ron Francis, Pittsburgh
1996–97	Paul Kariya, Anaheim
1998	Ron Francis, Pittsburgh
1999	Wayne Gretzky, N.Y. Rangers

Calder Trophy—Rookie

1962	Bobby Rousseau, Montreal
1963	Kent Douglas, Toronto
1964	Jacques Laperriere, Montreal
1965	Roger Crozier, Detroit
1966	Brit Selby, Toronto
1967	Bobby Orr, Boston
1968	Derek Sanderson, Boston
1969	Danny Grant, Minnesota
1970	Tony Esposito, Chicago
1971	Gilbert Perreault, Buffalo
1972	Ken Dryden, Montreal
1973	Steve Vickers, N.Y. Rangers
1974	Denis Potvin, N.Y. Islanders
1975	Eric Vail, Atlanta
1976	Bryan Trottier, N.Y. Islanders
1977	Willi Plett, Atlanta
1978	Mike Bossy, N.Y. Islanders
1979	Bobby Smith, Minnesota
1980	Ray Bourque, Boston
1981	Peter Stastny, Quebec
1982	Dale Hawerchuk, Winnipeg
1983	Steve Larmer, Chicago
1984	Tom Barrasso, Buffalo
1985	Mario Lemieux, Pittsburgh
1986	Gary Suter, Calgary
1987	Luc Robitaille, Los Angeles
1988	Joe Nieuwendyk, Calgary
1989	Brian Leetch, N.Y. Rangers
1990	Sergei Makarov, Calgary
1991	Ed Belfour, Chicago
1992	Pavel Bure, Vancouver
1993	Teemu Selanne, Winnipeg
1994	Martin Brodeur, N.J. Devils
1995	Peter Forsberg, Quebec
1996	Daniel Alfredsson, Ottawa

1997	Bryan Berard, N.Y. Islanders
1998	Sergei Samsonov, Boston
1999	Chris Drury, Colorado

Art Ross Trophy—Leading Scorer

1955	Bernie Geoffrion, Montreal
1956	Jean Beliveau, Montreal
1957	Gordie Howe, Detroit
1958–59	Dickie Moore, Montreal
1960	Bobby Hull, Chicago
1961	Bernie Geoffrion, Montreal
1962	Bobby Hull, Chicago
1963	Gordie Howe, Detroit
1964–65	Stan Mikita, Chicago
1966	Bobby Hull, Chicago
1967–68	Stan Mikita, Chicago
1969	Phil Esposito, Boston
1970	Bobby Orr, Boston
1971–74	Phil Esposito, Boston
1975	Bobby Orr, Boston
1976–78	Guy Lafleur, Montreal
1979	Bryan Trottier, N.Y. Islanders
1980	Marcel Dionne, Los Angeles
1981–87	Wayne Gretzky, Edmonton
1988–89	Mario Lemieux, Pittsburgh
1990–91	Wayne Gretzky, Los Angeles
1992–93	Mario Lemieux, Pittsburgh
1994	Wayne Gretzky, Los Angeles
1995	Jaromir Jagr, Pittsburgh
1996–97	Mario Lemieux, Pittsburgh
1998–99	Jaromir Jagr, Pittsburgh

STANLEY CUP PLAYOFFS—1999

NOTE: Home teams are in capitals.

EASTERN CONFERENCE

Pittsburgh Penguins defeated New Jersey Devils,
4 games to 3
Buffalo Sabres defeated Ottawa Senators,
4 games to 0
Boston Bruins defeated Carolina Hurricanes,
4 games to 2
Toronto Maple Leafs defeated Philadelphia Flyers,
4 games to 2

Semifinals

Toronto Maple Leafs defeated Pittsburgh Penguins,
4 games to 2
Buffalo Sabres defeated Boston Bruins,
4 games to 2

Finals

Buffalo Sabres defeated Toronto Maple Leafs,
4 games to 1
May 23—Buffalo 5, TORONTO 4
May 25—TORONTO 6, Buffalo 3
May 27—BUFFALO 4, Toronto 2
May 29—BUFFALO 5, Toronto 2
May 31—BUFFALO 4, Toronto 2

WESTERN CONFERENCE

Quarterfinals

Dallas Stars defeated Edmonton Oilers,
4 games to 0
Colorado Avalanche defeated San Jose Sharks,
4 games to 2
Detroit Red Wings defeated Anaheim Mighty Ducks,
4 games to 0
St. Louis Blues defeated Phoenix Coyotes,
4 games to 3

Semifinals

Dallas Stars defeated St. Louis Blues,
4 games to 2
Colorado Avalanche defeated Detroit Red Wings,
4 games to 2

Finals

Dallas Stars defeated Colorado Avalanche,
4 games to 3
May 22—Avalanche 2, DALLAS 1
May 24—DALLAS 4, Avalanche 2
May 26—Dallas 3, COLORADO 0
May 28—AVALANCHE 3, Dallas 2 (OT)
May 30—Avalanche 7, DALLAS 5
June 1—Dallas 4, COLORADO 1
June 4—DALLAS 4, Avalanche 1

STANLEY CUP CHAMPIONSHIP FINALS

Dallas Stars defeated Buffalo Sabres, 4 games to 2

June 8—Buffalo 3, DALLAS 2 (OT)
June 10—DALLAS 4, Buffalo 2
June 12—Dallas 2, BUFFALO 1

June 15—BUFFALO 2, Dallas 1
June 17—DALLAS 2, Buffalo 0
June 19—Dallas 2, BUFFALO 1 (3 OT)

Conn Smythe Trophy for most valuable player in the playoffs: Joe Nieuwendyk, Dallas

OTHER N.H.L. AWARDS—1999

Frank Selke Trophy (Top defensive forward)—Jere Lehtinen, Dallas

King Clancy Trophy (Humanitarian community involvement)—Rob Ray, Buffalo

Jack Adams Award (Coach of the Year)—Jacques Martin, Ottawa

Bill Masterson Trophy (Perseverance, sportsmanship, and dedication to hockey)—John Cullen, Tampa Bay

NATIONAL HOCKEY LEAGUE FINAL STANDINGS OF THE CLUBS: 1998–1999

EASTERN CONFERENCE

Northeast Division

	W	L	T	Pts	GF	GA
1Ottawa Senators	44	23	15	103	239	179
2Toronto Maple Leafs	45	30	7	97	268	231
2Boston Bruins	39	30	13	91	214	181
2Buffalo Sabres	37	28	17	91	207	175
Montreal Canadiens	32	39	11	75	184	209

Atlantic Division

	W	L	T	Pts	GF	GA
1New Jersey Devils	47	24	11	105	248	196
2Philadelphia Flyers	37	26	19	93	231	196
2Pittsburgh Penguins	38	30	14	90	242	225
N.Y. Rangers	33	38	11	77	217	227
N.Y. Islanders	24	48	10	58	194	244

Southeast Division

	W	L	T	Pts	GF	GA
1Carolina Hurricanes	34	30	18	86	210	202
Florida Panthers	30	34	18	78	210	228
Washington Capitals	31	45	6	68	200	218
Tampa Bay Lightning	19	54	9	47	179	292

WESTERN CONFERENCE

Central Division

	W	L	T	Pts	GF	GA
1Detroit Red Wings	43	32	7	93	245	202
2St. Louis Blues	37	32	13	87	237	209
Chicago Blackhawks	29	41	12	70	202	248
Nashville Predators	28	47	7	63	190	261

Pacific Division

	W	L	T	Pts	GF	GA
1Dallas Stars	51	19	12	114	236	168
2Phoenix Coyotes	39	31	12	90	205	197
2Anaheim Mighty Ducks	35	34	13	83	215	206
2San Jose Sharks	31	33	18	80	196	191
Los Angeles Kings	32	45	5	69	189	222

Northwest Division

	W	L	T	Pts	GF	GA
1Colorado Avalanche	44	28	10	98	239	205
2Edmonton Oilers	33	37	12	78	230	226
Calgary Flames	30	40	12	72	211	234
Vancouver Canucks	23	47	12	58	192	258

1. Division champion. 2. Playoff qualifier.

N.H.L. LEADING SCORERS: 1998–1999

	GP	G	A	Pts
Jaromir Jagr, Pittsburgh	81	44	83	127
Teemu Selanne, Anaheim	75	47	60	107
Paul Kariya, Anaheim	82	39	62	101
Peter Forsberg, Colorado	78	30	67	97
Joe Sakic, Colorado	73	41	55	96
Alexei Yashin, Ottawa	82	44	50	94
Eric Lindros, Philadelphia	71	40	53	93
Theo Fleury, Calgary–Colorado	75	40	53	93
John LeClair, Philadelphia	76	43	47	90
Pavol Demitra, St. Louis	82	37	52	89

N.H.L. CAREER SCORING LEADERS

(Through 1998–1999 season)

		Yrs	Gm	G	A	Pts
1	Wayne Gretzky	20	1,487	894	1,963	2,857
2	Gordie Howe	26	1,767	801	1,049	1,850
3	Marcel Dionne	18	1,348	731	1,040	1,771
4	Mark Messier	20	1,413	610	1,050	1,660
5	Phil Esposito	18	1,282	717	873	1,590
6	Mario Lemieux	12	745	613	881	1,494
7	Paul Coffey	19	1,322	385	1,102	1,487
8	Ron Francis	18	1,329	449	1,037	1,486
9	Steve Yzerman	16	1,178	592	891	1,483
10	Ray Bourque	20	1,453	385	1,083	1,468

Players active during 1998–99 season in **bold** type.

N.H.L. LEADING GOALTENDERS: 1998–1999

	GP	Min	GAA	Record
Ron Tugnutt, Ottawa	43	2,508	1.79	22–10–8
Dominik Hasek, Buffalo	64	3,817	1.87	30–18–14
Ed Belfour, Dallas	61	3,536	1.99	35–15–9
Byron Dafoe, Boston	68	4,001	1.99	32–23–11
Roman Turek, Dallas	26	1,382	2.08	16–3–3
Nikolai Khabibulin, Phoenix	63	3,657	2.13	32–23–7
John Vanbiesbrouck, Philadelphia	62	3,712	2.18	27–18–15
Steve Shields, San Jose	37	2,162	2.22	15–11–8
Arturs Irbe, Carolina	62	3,643	2.22	27–20–12
Mike Vernon, San Jose	49	2,831	2.27	16–22–10

N.H.L. CAREER GOALTENDING LEADERS

(Through 1998–1999 season)

		Yrs	Gm	W	L	T	Pct
1	Terry Sawchuk	21	971	447	330	172	.562
2	Jacques Plante	18	837	434	247	146	.614
3	Tony Esposito	16	886	423	306	152	.566
4	Patrick Roy	14	778	412	243	95	.613
5	Glenn Hall	18	906	407	326	163	.545
6	Grant Fuhr	18	845	398	282	112	.573
7	Andy Moog	18	713	372	209	88	.622
8	Rogie Vachon	16	795	355	291	127	.541
9	Mike Vernon	16	673	347	223	83	.595
10	Tom Barrasso	16	708	345	248	79	.572

Players active during 1998–99 season in **bold** type.

Chess

WORLD CHAMPIONS

1894–1921	Emanuel Lasker, Germany
1921–27	Jose R. Capablanca, Cuba
1927–35	Alexander A. Alekhine, U.S.S.R.
1935–37	Dr. Max Euwe, Netherlands
1937–46	Alexander A. Alekhine, U.S.S.R.[1]
1948–57	Mikhail Botvinnik, U.S.S.R.
1957–58	Vassily Smyslov, U.S.S.R.
1958–60	Mikhail Botvinnik, U.S.S.R.
1960–61	Mikhail Tal, U.S.S.R.
1961–63	Mikhail Botvinnik, U.S.S.R.
1963–68	Tigran Petrosian, U.S.S.R.
1969–71	Boris Spassky, U.S.S.R.
1972–74	Bobby Fischer, United States
1975	Bobby Fischer, United States[2]; Anatoly Karpov, U.S.S.R.
1976–85	Anatoly Karpov, U.S.S.R.[3]
1985–	Garry Kasparov, Russia[4]
1993–99	Anatoly Karpov, Russia[5]
1999–	Alexander Khalifman, Russia[5]

1. Alekhine, a French citizen, died while champion. 2. Relinquished title. 3. In 1978, Karpov defeated Viktor Korchnoi 6 games to 5. 4. PCA (Professional Chess Association) world champion after 1993. 5. FIDE (International Chess Federation) world champion.

UNITED STATES CHAMPIONS

1909–36	Frank J. Marshall, New York
1936–44	Samuel Reshevsky, New York[1]
1944–46	Arnold S. Denker, New York
1946	Samuel Reshevsky, Boston
1948	Herman Steiner, Los Angeles
1951–52	Larry Evans, New York
1954–57	Arthur Bisguier, New York
1958–61	Bobby Fischer, Brooklyn, N.Y.
1962	Larry Evans, New York
1963–67	Bobby Fischer, New York
1968	Larry Evans, New York
1969–71	Samuel Reshevsky, Spring Valley, N.Y.
1972	Robert Byrne, Ossining, N.Y.
1973	Lubomir Kavelek, Washington; John Grefe, San Francisco
1974–77	Walter Browne, Berkeley, Calif.
1978–79	Lubomir Kavalek, New York
1980	Tie, Walter Browne, Berkeley, Calif. Larry Christiansen, Modesto, Calif. Larry Evans, Reno, Nev.
1981–82[2]	Tie, Walter Browne, Berkeley, Calif. Yasser Seirawan, Seattle, Wash.
1983	Tie, Walter Browne, Berkeley, Calif. Larry Christiansen, Los Angeles, Calif., Roman Dzindzichashvili, Corona, N.Y.
1984–85	Lev Alburt, New York City
1986	Yasser Seirawan, Seattle, Wash.
1987	Tie, Nick Defirmian, San Francisco Joel Benjamin, Brooklyn, N.Y.
1988	Michael Wilder, Princeton, N.J.
1989	Tie, Stuart Rachels, Birmingham, Ala. Yasser Seirawan, Seattle, Wash. Roman Dzindzichashvili, New York, N.Y.
1990–91	Lev Alburt, New York, N.Y.
1992	Gata Kamsky, Brooklyn, N.Y. Patrick Wolff, Somerville, Mass.
1993	Tie, Alexander Shabalov, Pittsburgh, Pa. Alex Yermolinski, Edison, N.J.
1994	Boris Gulko, Fairlawn, N.J.
1995	Patrick Wolff, Somerville, Mass.
1996	Alex Yurmolinsky, Cleveland, Ohio
1997	Esther Epstein, Mass. (women) Joel Benjamin, N.Y. (men)
1998	Irina Krush, Brooklyn, N.Y. (women) Nick de Firmian, New York City (men)

1. In 1942, Isaac I. Kashdan of New York was co-champion for a while because of a tie with Reshevsky in that year's tournament. Reshevsky won the play-off. 2. Championship not contested in 1982.

Bowling

The game of bowling in the United States is an indoor development of the more ancient outdoor game that survives as lawn bowling. The outdoor game is prehistoric in origin and probably goes back to Primitive Man and round stones that were rolled at some target. It is believed that a game something like nine-pins was popular among the Dutch, Swiss, and Germans as long ago as A.D. 1200. The game was played outdoors with an alley consisting of a single plank 12 to 18 inches wide, along which a ball was rolled toward three rows of three pins each placed at the far end of the alley. When the first indoor alleys were built and how the game was modified from time to time are matters of dispute.

It is supposed that the early settlers of New Amsterdam (New York City), being Dutch, brought their two bowling games with them. About a century ago the game of nine-pins was flourishing in the United States but so corrupted by gambling on matches that it was barred by law in New York and Connecticut. Since the law specifically barred "nine-pins," it was eventually evaded by adding another pin and thus legally making it a new game.

Various organizations were formed to make rules for bowling and supervise competition in the United States but none was successful until the American Bowling Congress, organized Sept. 9, 1895, became the ruling body.

AMERICAN BOWLING CONGRESS CHAMPIONS

Year	Singles	All-events	Year	Singles	All-events
1959	Ed Lubanski	Ed Lubanski	1966	Don Chapman	John Wilcox
1960	Paul Kulbaga	Vince Lucci	1967	Frank Perry	Gary Lewis
1961	Lyle Spooner	Luke Karen	1968	Wayne Kowalski	Vince Mazzanti
1962	Andy Renaldo	Billy Young	1969	Greg Campbell	Eddie Jackson
1963	Fred Delello	Bus Owalt	1970	Jake Yoder	Mike Berlin
1964	Jim Stefanich	Les Zikes, Jr.	1971	Al Cohn	Al Cohn
1965	Ken Roeth	Tom Hathaway	1972	Bill Pointer	Mac Lowry

Year	Singles	All-events	Year	Singles	All-events
1973	Ed Thompson	Ron Woolet	1987	Terry Taylor	Ryan Schafer
1974	Gene Krause	Bob Hart	1988	Steve Hutkowski	Rick Steelsmith
1975	Jim Setser	Bobby Meadows	1989	Paul Tetreault	George Hall
1976	Mike Putzer	Jim Lindquist	1990	Bob Hochrein	Mike Neumann
1977	Frank Gadaleto	Bud Debenham	1991	Ed Deines	Tom Howery
1978	Rich Mersek	Chris Cobus	1992	Bob Youker and Gary Blatchford	Mike Tucker
1979	Rick Peters	Bob Basacchi		(tie)	
1980	Mike Eaton	Steve Fehr	1993	Dan Bock	Jeff Nimke
1981	Rob Vital	Rod Toft	1994	John Weltzien	Thomas Holt
1982	Bruce Bohm	Rich Wonders	1995	Matt Surina	Jeff Kwiatkowski
1983	Rick Kendrick	Tony Cariello	1996	Donald Scudder, Jr.	Scott Kurtz
1984	Bob Antczak and Neal Young (tie)	Bob Goike	1997	John Socha	Jeff Richgels
1985	Glen Harbison	Barry Asher	1998	John Gaines	Chris Barnes
1986	Jess Mackey	Ed Marazka	1999	Dan Winter	Thomas A. Jones

PROFESSIONAL BOWLERS ASSOCIATION

National Championship Tournament

1960	Don Carter	1970	Mike McGrath	1980	Johnny Petraglia	1990	Jim Pencak
1961	Dave Soutar	1971	Mike Lemongello	1981	Earl Anthony	1991	Mike Miller
1962	Carmen Salvino	1972	Johnny Guenther	1982	Earl Anthony	1992	Eric Forkel
1963	Billy Hardwick	1973	Earl Anthony	1983	Earl Anthony	1993	Ron Palombi
1964	Bob Strampe	1974	Earl Anthony	1984	Bob Chamberlain	1994	David Traber
1965	Dave Davis	1975	Earl Anthony	1985	Mike Aulby	1995	Scott Alexander
1966	Wayne Zahn	1976	Paul Colwell	1986	Tom Crites	1996	Butch Soper
1967	Dave Davis	1977	Tommy Hudson	1987	Randy Pedersen	1997	Rich Steelsmith
1968	Wayne Zahn	1978	Warren Nelson	1988	Brian Voss	1998	Pete Weber
1969	Mike McGrath	1979	Mike Aulby	1989	Pete Weber	1999	Tim Criss

BOWLING PROPRIETORS' ASSOCIATION OF AMERICA—MEN

United States Open[1]

1971	Mike Lemongello	1979	Joe Berardi	1987	Del Ballard	1995	Dave Husted
1972	Don Johnson	1980	Steve Martin	1988	Pete Weber	1996	Dave Husted
1973	Mike McGrath	1981	Marshall Holman	1989	Mike Aulby	1997	Not held
1974	Larry Laub	1982	Dave Husted	1990	Ron Palumbi, Jr.	1998	Walter Ray Williams, Jr.
1975	Steve Neff	1983	Gary Dickinson	1991	Pete Weber		
1976	Paul Moser	1984	Mark Roth	1992	Robert Lawrence	1999	Bob Learn, Jr.
1977	Johnny Petraglia	1985	Marshall Holman	1993	Del Ballard, Jr.		
1978	Nelson Burton, Jr.	1986	Steve Cook	1994	Justin Hromek		

1. Replaced All-Star tournament and is rolled as part of B.P.A. tour.

WOMEN'S INTERNATIONAL BOWLING CONGRESS CHAMPIONS

Year	Singles	All events	Year	Singles	All events
1959	Mae Bolt	Pat McBride	1982	Gracie Freeman	Aleta Rzepecki
1960	Marge McDaniels	Judy Roberts	1983	Aleta Rzepecki	Virginia Norton
1961	Elaine Newton	Evelyn Teal	1984	Freida Gates	Shinobu Saitoh
1962	Martha Hoffman	Flossie Argent	1985	Polly Schwarzel	Aleta Sill
1963	Dot Wilkinson	Helen Shablis	1986	Dana Stewart	Robin Romeo and Maria
1964	Jean Havlish	Jean Havlish			Lewis (tie)
1965	Doris Rudell	Donna Zimmerman	1987	Regi Junak	Leanne Barrette
1966	Gloria Bouvia	Kate Helbig	1988	Michelle Meyer-Welty	Lisa Wagner
1967	Gloria Paeth	Carol Miller	1989	Lorraine Anderson	Nancy Fehn
1968	Norma Parks	Susie Reichley	1990	Dana Miller-Mackie and	Carol Norman
1969	Joan Bender	Helen Duval		Paula Carter (tie)	
1970	Dorothy Fothergill	Dorothy Fothergill	1991	Debbie Kuhn	Debbie Kuhn
1971	Mary Scruggs	Lorrie Nichols	1992	Patty Ann	Mitsuko Tokimoto
1972	D. D. Jacobson	Mildred Martorella	1993	Karen Collurs and Kari	Bertha Blackshur and
1973	Bobby Buffaloe	Toni Calvery		Murph (tie)	Sharon Davis (tie)
1974	Shirley Garms	Judy C. Soutar	1994	Vicki Fifield	Wendy Macpherson-
1975	Barbara Leicht	Virginia Norton			Papanos
1976	Bev Shonk	Betty Morris	1995	Beth Owen	Beth Owen
1977	Akiko Yamaga	Akiko Yamaga	1996	Cindy Berlanga	Lorrie Nichols
1978	Mae Bolt	Annese Kelly	1997	Jean Schmidt	Kendra Cameron
1979	Betty Morris	Betty Morris	1998	Nellie Glandon	Liz Johnson
1980	Betty Morris	Cheryl Robinson	1999	Maggie Matheson	Marlene Walls
1981	Virginia Norton	Virginia Norton			

BOWLING PROPRIETORS' ASSOCIATION OF AMERICA—WOMEN

United States Open

1971 Paula Carter	1979 Diana Silva	1987 Carol Nurman	1995 Tish Johnson
1972 Lorrie Nichols	1980 Pat Costello (Calif.)	1988 Lisa Wagner	1996 Liz Johnson
1973 Mildred Martorella	1981 Donna Adamek	1989 Robin Romeo	1997 Not held
1974 Pat Costello (Calif.)	1982 Shinobu Saitoh	1990 Dana Miller-Mackie	1998 Aleta Sill
1975 Paula Carter	1983 Dana Miller	1991 Anne Marie Duggan	1999 Kim Adler
1976 Patty Costello (Pa.)	1984 Karen Ellingsworth	1992 Tish Johnson	
1977 Betty Morris	1985 Pat Mercatanti	1993 Dede Davidson	
1978 Donna Adamek	1986 Wendy Macpherson	1994 Aleta Sill	

WIBC QUEENS TOURNAMENT CHAMPIONS

1961 Janet Harman	1971 Mildred Martorella	1981 Katsuko Sugimoto	1991 Dede Davidson
1962 Dorothy Wilkinson	1972 Dorothy Fothergill	1982 Katsuko Sugimoto	1992 Cindy Coburn-Carroll
1963 Irene Monterosso	1973 Dorothy Fothergill	1983 Aleta Rzepecki	1993 Jan Schmidt
1964 D.D. Jacobson	1974 Judy Soutar	1984 Kazue Inahashi	1994 Anne Marie Duggan
1965 Betty Kuczynski	1975 Cindy Powell	1985 Aleta Sill	1995 Sandy Postma
1966 Judy Lee	1976 Pamela Buckner	1986 Cora Fiebig	1996 Lisa Wagner
1967 Mildred Martorella	1977 Dana Stewart	1987 Cathy Almeida	1997 Sandra-Jo Shiery-Odom
1968 Phyllis Massey	1978 Loa Boxberger	1988 Wendy Macpherson	
1969 Ann Feigel	1979 Donna Adamek	1989 Carol Gianotti	1998 Lynda Norry
1970 Mildred Martorella	1980 Donna Adamek	1990 Patty Ann	1999 Leanne Barrette

PROFESSIONAL BOWLERS ASSOCIATION CHAMPIONSHIP—1999

(Feb. 21–27, 1999, Toledo, Ohio)
Winner—Tim Criss, Bel Air, Md., defeated Dave Arnold, Gilbert, Ariz., 238–161 in title match.
3. Chris Barnes, Wichita, Kan.
4. Danny Wiseman, Baltimore, Md.
5. Lonnie Waliczek, Wichita, Kan.

AMERICAN BOWLING CONGRESS TOURNAMENT—1999

(Feb. 13–June 19, 1999, Syracuse, N.Y.)
Regular Division

Singles— Dan Winter, Rockford, Ill.	825
Doubles— Ryan J. Lever, Waterford, Wis., and Dale Traber, Cedarburg, Wis.	1,506
All Events—Thomas A. Jones, Greenville, S.C.	2,158
Team—Zawadzki Jewelers, Lackawana, N.Y.	3,336

WOMEN'S INTERNATIONAL BOWLING CONGRESS TOURNAMENT—1999

(Apr. 8–June 18, 1999, Indianapolis, Ind.)

Singles— Maggie Matheson, Chula Vista, Calif.	709
Doubles— Sherry Brumley and Betty Abrams, Garfield, Ark.	1,219
All Events— Marlene Walls, Morris, Ill.	1,831
Team— KFC All Stars, Las Cruces, N. Mex.	2,852

B.P.A.A. U.S. OPEN—1999

(July 25–Aug. 1, 1999, Milford, Conn.)
Men
  Bob Learn, Jr., Erie, Pa., defeated Jason Couch, Clermont, Fla., 231–215 in final match.
  3. Dave Arnold, Gilbert, Ariz.
Women
  Kim Adler, Las Vegas, Nev., defeated Lynda Barnes, Wichita, Kans., 213–195 in final match.
  3. Cara Honeychurch, Australia

Skiing

HISTORY OF SKIING IN THE UNITED STATES

Skis were devised for utility, to aid those who had to travel over snow. The Norwegians, Swedes, Lapps, and other inhabitants of northern lands used skis for many centuries before skiing became a sport. Emigrants from these countries brought skis to the United States with them. The first skier of record in the United States was a mailman by the name of "Snowshoe" Thompson, born and raised in Telemarken, Norway, who came to the United States and, beginning in 1850, used skis through 20 successive winters in carrying mail from Northern California to Carson Valley, Idaho.

Ski clubs sprang up over 100 years ago where there were Norwegian and Swedish settlers in Wisconsin and Minnesota and ski contests were held in that territory in 1886. On Feb. 21, 1904, at Ishpenning, Mich., a small group of skiers organized the National Ski Association. In 1961 it was renamed the United States Ski Association.

ALPINE SKIING

1999 United States Alpine Championships
(March 19–24, Park City, Utah)

Men

Downhill—1. Chad Fleischer, Vail, Colo.; 2. Daron Rahlves, Truckee, Calif.; 3. Marco Sullivan, Tahoe City, Calif.

Giant Slalom—1. Uros Pavlovcic, Slovenia; 2. Andy Martin, Warner, N.H.; 3. Thomas Vonn, Newburgh, N.Y.

Slalom—1. Sacha Gros, Vail, Colo.; 2. Drew Thorne-Thomsen, Stratton Mtn., Vt.; 3. Marco Pastore, Italy

Super G—1. Jakub Fiala, Breckenridge, Colo.; 2. Chad Fleischer, Vail, Colo.; 3. Daron Rahlves, Truckee, Calif.

Women

Downhill—1. Kirsten Clark, Raymond, Maine; 2. Caroline Lalive, Steamboat Springs, Colo.; 3. Megan Gerety, Anchorage, Alaska

Giant Slalom—1. Alex Shaffer, Park City, Utah; 2. Sarah Schleper, Vail, Colo.; 3. Marika Fave, Italy

Slalom—1. Alex Shaffer, Park City, Utah; 2. Kristina Koznick, Burnsville, Minn.; 3. Caroline Lalive, Steamboat Springs, Colo.

Super G—1. Katie Monahan, Aspen, Colo.; 2. Megan Gerety, Anchorage, Alaska; 3. Kjersti Bjorn-Roli, Anchorage, Alaska

1999 Alpine World Cup Champions

Men	Pts
Overall—Lasse Kjus, Norway	1,465
Downhill—Lasse Kjus, Norway	760
Giant Slalom—Michael von Gruenigen, Switzerland	483
Slalom—Thomas Stangassinger, Austria	566
Super G—Hermann Maier, Austria	516

Women	Pts
Overall—Alexandra Meissnitzer, Austria	1,672
Downhill—Renate Goetschl, Austria	610
Giant Slalom—Alexandra Meissnitzer, Austria	652
Slalom—Sabine Egger, Austria	425
Super G—Alexandra Meissnitzer, Austria	459

1999 Disabled Alpine World Cup Final
(Feb. 20–27, 1999, Breckenridge, Colo.)

Men

Downhill—**Sitting:** Chris Waddell, Granby, Mass.; **Standing:** Steve Bayley, New Zealand; **Blind:** Stefan Kopcik, Slovakia

Giant Slalom—**Sitting:** Karl Lotz, Germany; **Standing:** Gerd Schonfelder, Germany; **Blind:** Bobby McMullen, Redding, Calif.

Slalom—**Sitting:** Daniel Wesley, Canada; **Standing:** Gerd Schonfelder, Germany; **Blind:** Kurt Primus, Austria

Super G—**Sitting:** Chris Waddell, Granby, Mass.; **Standing:** Jacob Rife, Pocatello, Idaho; **Blind:** Bobby McMullen, Redding, Calif.

Women

Downhill—**Sitting:** Sarah Will, Vail, Colo.; **Standing:** Sarah Billmeier, Yarmouth, Maine; **Blind:** Katarina Tepla, Czech Republic

Giant Slalom—**Sitting:** Sarah Will, Vail, Colo.; **Standing:** Mary Riddell, Dove Creek, Colo.; **Blind:** Katerina Tepla, Czech Republic

Slalom—**Sitting:** Sarah Will, Vail, Colo.; **Standing:** Karolina Wisniewska, Canada; **Blind:** Gabriele Huemer, Austria

Super G—**Sitting:** Muffy Davis, Sun Valley, Idaho; **Standing:** Karolina Wisniewska, Canada; **Blind:** Katerina Tepla, Czech Republic

NORDIC SKIING/SKI JUMPING/CROSS COUNTRY

1999 U.S. Ski Jumping/Nordic Combined Championships
(Feb. 6–7, 1999, Lake Placid, N.Y.)

Men

Large Hill (K120m)—1. Alan Alborn, Anchorage, Alaska; 2. Brendan Doran, Steamboat Springs, Colo.; 3. Todd Lodwick, Steamboat Springs, Colo.

Normal Hill (K90m)—1. Todd Lodwick, Steamboat Springs, Colo.; 2. Rhys Hecox, Ishpeming, Mich.; 3. Alan Alborn, Anchorage, Alaska

Nordic Combined (90m jumping–10k race)—1. Todd Lodwick, Steamboat Springs, Colo.; 2. Matt Dayton, Breckenridge, Colo.; 3. Nathan Gerhart, Steamboat Springs, Colo.

Women

90 Meter Hill—1. Lindsey Van, Park City, Utah; 2. Liz Szotyori, Saugerties, N.Y.; 3. Veronica Myhra, Stillwater, Minn.

1999 Cross Country U.S. Nationals
(Jan. 16–24, 1999, Rumford, Maine)

Men

10k Classic—Marcus Nash
15k Freestyle Pursuit—Marcus Nash
30k Freestyle—John Bauer
50k Classic—Patrick Weaver
Sprint—Marcus Nash

Women

5k Classic—Nina Kemppel
10k Freestyle Pursuit—Nina Kemppel
15k Freestyle—Nina Kemppel
30k Classic—Nina Kemppel
Sprint—Nina Kemppel

FREESTYLE SKIING

1999 Freestyle Skiing World Championships
(March 6–14, 1999, Meiringen-Hasliberg, Switzerland)
Men
  Acro—Ian Edmondson, United States
  Moguls—Janne Lahtela, Finland
  Aerials—Eric Bergoust, United States
  Dual Moguls—Johann Gregoire, France
Women
  Acro—Natalia Razumovskaya, Russia
  Moguls—Ann Battelle, United States
  Aerials—Jacqui Cooper, Austria
  Dual Moguls—Sandra Schmitt, Germany

1999 U.S. Freestyle Championships
(March 17–25, 1999, Park City, Utah)
Men
  Acro—Steve Roxberg, Lakeville, Minn.
  Moguls—Travis Cabral, S. Lake Tahoe, Calif.
  Aerials—Joe Pack, Park City, Utah
  Dual Moguls—Ryan Riley, Steamboat Springs, Colo.
Women
  Acro—Maria Guarnieri, Mahopac, N.Y.
  Moguls—Ann Battelle, Steamboat Springs, Colo.
  Aerials—Marissa Berman, Mt. Kisco, N.Y.
  Dual Moguls—Ann Battelle, Steamboat Springs, Colo.

SNOWBOARDING

1999 World Snowboard Championships
(Jan. 10–17, 1999, Berchtesgaden, Germany)
Men
  Cross—Henrik Jansson, Sweden
  Halfpipe—Ricky Bower, United States
  Parallel Slalom—Nicolas Huet, France
  Parallel Giant Slalom—Richard Richardsson, Sweden
  Giant Slalom—Markus Ebner, Germany
Women
  Cross—Julie Pomagalski, France
  Halfpipe—Kim Stacey, United States
  Parallel Slalom—Marion Posch, Italy
  Parallel Giant Slalom—Isabelle Blanc, France
  Giant Slalom—Margerita Parini, Italy

1999 U.S. Snowboard Championships
(March 22–28, 1999, Okemo Mountain Resort, Vt.)
Men
  Cross—Ryan Neptune, Boise, Idaho
  Halfpipe—Ross Powers, South Londonderry, Vt.
  Giant Slalom—Mark Fawcett, Canada
  Slalom—Jeff Greenwood, Granby, Conn.

Women
  Cross—Amy Johnson, Bondville, Vt.
  Halfpipe—Shannon Dunn, Steamboat Springs, Colo.
  Giant Slalom—Sondra Van Ert, Ketchum, Idaho
  Slalom—Rosey Fletcher, Anchorage, Alaska

JAMES E. SULLIVAN MEMORIAL AWARD WINNERS
(Amateur Athlete of the Year Chosen in Amateur Athletic Union Poll)

1930	Robert Tyre Jones, Jr.	Golf
1931	Bernard E. Berlinger	Track and field
1932	James A. Bausch	Track and field
1933	Glenn Cunningham	Track and field
1934	William R. Bonthron	Track and field
1935	W. Lawson Little, Jr.	Golf
1936	Glenn Morris	Track and field
1937	J. Donald Budge	Tennis
1938	Donald R. Lash	Track and field
1939	Joseph W. Burk	Rowing
1940	J. Gregory Rice	Track and field
1941	Leslie MacMitchell	Track and field
1942	Cornelius Warmerdam	Track and field
1943	Gilbert L. Dodds	Track and field
1944	Ann Curtis	Swimming
1945	Felix (Doc) Blanchard	Football
1946	Y. Arnold Tucker	Football
1947	John B. Kelly, Jr.	Rowing
1948	Robert B. Mathias	Track and field
1949	Richard T. Button	Figure skating
1950	Fred Wilt	Track and field
1951	Robert E. Richards	Track and field
1952	Horace Ashenfelter	Track and field
1953	Sammy Lee	Diving
1954	Malvin Whitfield	Track and field
1955	Harrison Dillard	Track and field
1956	Patricia McCormick	Diving
1957	Bobby Jo Morrow	Track and field
1958	Glenn Davis	Track and field
1959	Parry O'Brien	Track and field
1960	Rafer Johnson	Track and field
1961	Wilma Rudolph Ward	Track and field
1962	Jim Beatty	Track and field
1963	John Pennel	Track and field
1964	Don Schollander	Swimming
1965	Bill Bradley	Basketball
1966	Jim Ryun	Track and field
1967	Randy Matson	Track and field
1968	Debbie Meyer	Swimming
1969	Bill Toomey	Decathlon
1970	John Kinsella	Swimming
1971	Mark Spitz	Swimming
1972	Frank Shorter	Marathon
1973	Bill Walton	Basketball
1974	Rick Wohlhuter	Track and field
1975	Tim Shaw	Swimming
1976	Bruce Jenner	Track and field
1977	John Naber	Swimming
1978	Tracy Caulkins	Swimming
1979	Kurt Thomas	Gymnastics
1980	Eric Heiden	Speed skating
1981	Carl Lewis	Track and field
1982	Mary Decker Tabb	Track and field
1983	Edwin Moses	Track and field
1984	Greg Louganis	Diving
1985	Joan Benoit-Samuelson	Marathon
1986	Jackie Joyner-Kersee	Heptathlon
1987	Jim Abbott	Baseball
1988	Florence Griffith-Joyner	Track and field
1989	Janet Evans	Swimming
1990	John Smith	Wrestling
1991	Mike Powell	Track and field
1992	Bonnie Blair	Speed skating
1993	Charles Ward	Football/Basketball
1994	Dan Jansen	Speed skating
1995	Bruce Baumgartner	Wrestling
1996	Michael Johnson	Track and field
1997	Peyton Manning	Football
1998	Chamique Holdsclaw	Basketball

Speed Skating

WORLD SPEED SKATING RECORDS (LONG TRACK)

Distance	Time	Skater	Place	Date
Men				
500m	34.76	Jeremy Wotherspoon, Canada	Calgary, Canada	Feb. 20, 1999
1,000m	1:08.55	Jan Bos, Netherlands	Calgary, Canada	Feb. 21, 1999
1,500m	1:46.43	Ådne Søndrål, Norway	Calgary, Canada	March 28, 1998
3,000m	3:45.23	Steven Elm, Canada	Calgary, Canada	March 19, 1999
5,000m	6:21.49	Gianni Romme, Netherlands	Calgary, Canada	March 27, 1998
10,000m	13:08.71	Gianni Romme, Netherlands	Calgary, Canada	March 29, 1998
Women				
500m	37.55	Catriona LeMay Doan, Canada	Calgary, Canada	Dec. 29, 1997
1,000m	1:14.61	Monique Garbrecht, Germany	Calgary, Canada	Feb. 21, 1999
1,500m	1:55.50	Annamarie Thomas, Netherlands	Calgary, Canada	March 20, 1999
3,000m	4:01.67	Gunda Niemann-Stirnemann, Germany	Calgary, Canada	March 27, 1998
5,000m	6:57.24	Gunda Niemann-Stirnemann, Germany	Hamar, Norway	Feb. 7, 1999

WORLD SPRINT CHAMPIONSHIPS—1999
(Feb. 20–21, 1999, Calgary, Alberta, Canada)

Men	Times	Women	Times
500m—Jeremy Wotherspoon, Canada	34.76, 34.93	500m—Catriona LeMay Doan, Canada	37.86, 37.89
1,000m—Jeremy Wotherspoon, Canada	1:08.58, 1:08.66	1.000m—Monique Garbrecht, Germany	1:14.61, 1:15.46
Overall standings:	**Points**	Overall standings:	**Points**
1. Jeremy Wotherspoon, Canada	138.310	1. Monique Garbrecht, Germany	151.605
2. Jan Bos, Netherlands	138.960	2. Catriona LeMay Doan, Canada	151.640
3. Shimizu Hiroyasu, Japan	139.895	3. Sabine Volker, Germany	151.860

WORLD CUP CHAMPIONS: 1998–1999

Men		Women	
500m	Jeremy Wotherspoon, Canada	500m	Catriona LeMay Doan, Canada
1,000m	Jeremy Wotherspoon, Canada	1,000m	Monique Garbrecht, Germany
1,500m	Ådne Søndrål, Norway	1,500m	Gunda Niemann-Stirnemann, Germany
5,000m	Bart Veldkamp, Belgium	3,000m/5,000m	Gunda Niemann-Stirnemann, Germany

WORLD SHORT TRACK CHAMPIONSHIPS—1999
(March 19–21, 1999, Sofia, Bulgaria)

Men	Time	Women	Time
500m—Jiajun Li, China	42.565	500m—Yang Yang (A), China	44.640
1,000m—Satoru Terao, Japan	1:30.913	1,000m—Yang Yang (A), China	1:37.440
1,500m—Fabio Carta, Italy	2:27.533	1,500m—Yang Yang (S), China	2:34.645
3,000m—Jiajun Li, China	5:11.544	3,000m—Yang Yang (A), China	5:48.541
Relay—China	7:07.395	Relay—China	4:23.725

Figure Skating

WORLD CHAMPIONS

Men					
1960	Alain Giletti, France	1974	Jan Hoffman, East Germany	1987	Brian Orser, Canada
1961	No competition	1975	Sergei Yolkov, U.S.S.R.	1988	Brian Boitano, United States
1962	Donald Jackson, Canada	1976	John Curry, Britain	1989–91	Kurt Browning, Canada
1963	Don McPherson, Canada	1977	Vladimir Kovalev, U.S.S.R.	1992	Viktor Petrenko, Unified Team
1964	Manfred Schnelldorfer, West Germany	1978	Charles Tickner, United States	1993	Kurt Browning, Canada
1965	Alain Calmat, France	1979	Vladimir Kovalev, U.S.S.R.	1994–95	Elvis Stojko, Canada
1966–68	Emmerich Danzer, Austria	1980	Jan Hoffman, East Germany	1996	Todd Eldredge, United States
1969–70	Tim Wood, United States	1981–84	Scott Hamilton, United States	1997	Elvis Stojko, Canada
1971–73	Ondrej Nepela, Czechoslovakia	1985	Alexandr Fadeev, U.S.S.R.	1998–99	Alexei Yagudin, Russia
		1986	Brian Boitano, United States		

Women

1956–60	Carol Heiss, United States
1961	No competition
1962–64	Sjoukje Dijkstra, Netherlands
1965	Petra Burka, Canada
1966–68	Peggy Fleming, United States
1969–70	Gabriele Seyfert, East Germany
1971–72	Beatrix Schuba, Austria
1973	Karen Magnusson, Canada
1974	Christine Errath, East Germany
1975	Dianne de Leeuw, Netherlands
1976	Dorothy Hamill, United States
1977	Linda Fratianne, United States
1978	Anett Poetzsch, East Germany
1979	Linda Fratianne, United States
1980	Anett Poetzsch, East Germany
1981	Denise Beillmann, Switzerland
1982	Elaine Zayak, United States
1983	Rosalynn Sumners, United States
1984–85	Katarina Witt, East Germany
1986	Debi Thomas, United States
1987–88	Katarina Witt, East Germany
1989	Midori Ito, Japan
1990	Jill Trenary, United States
1991–92	Kristi Yamaguchi, United States
1993	Oksana Baiul, Ukraine
1994	Yuka Sato, Japan
1995	Chen Lu, China
1996	Michelle Kwan, United States
1997	Tara Lipinski, United States
1998	Michelle Kwan, United States
1999	Maria Butyrskaya, Russia

U.S. CHAMPIONS

Men

1946–52	Richard Button
1953–56	Hayes Jenkins
1957–60	David Jenkins
1961	Bradley Lord
1962	Monty Hoyt
1963	Tommy Liz
1964	Scott Allen
1965	Gary Visconti
1966	Scott Allen
1967	Gary Visconti
1968–70	Tim Wood
1971	John M. Petkevich
1972	Ken Shelley
1973–75	Gordon McKellen
1976	Terry Kubicka
1977–80	Charles Tickner
1981–84	Scott Hamilton
1985–88	Brian Boitano
1989	Christopher Bowman
1990–91	Todd Eldredge
1992	Christopher Bowman
1993–94	Scott Davis
1995	Todd Eldredge
1996	Rudy Galindo
1997–98	Todd Eldredge
1999	Michael Weiss

Women

1943–48	Gretchen Merrill
1949–50	Yvonne Sherman
1951	Sonya Klopfer
1952–56	Tenley Albright
1957–60	Carol Heiss
1961	Laurence Owen
1962	Barbara Roles Pursley
1963	Lorraine Hanlon
1964–68	Peggy Fleming
1969–73	Janet Lynn
1974–76	Dorothy Hamill
1977–80	Linda Fratianne
1981	Elaine Zayak
1982–84	Rosalynn Sumners
1985	Tiffany Chin
1986	Debi Thomas
1987	Jill Trenary
1988	Debi Thomas
1989–90	Jill Trenary
1991	Tonya Harding
1992	Kristi Yamaguchi
1993	Nancy Kerrigan
1994	Tonya Harding
1995	Nicole Bobek
1996	Michelle Kwan
1997	Tara Lipinski
1998–99	Michelle Kwan

1999 UNITED STATES CHAMPIONSHIPS

Feb. 7–14, 1999, Salt Lake City

Men's singles
1. Michael Weiss, Fairfax, Va.
2. Trifun Zivanovic, Los Angeles, Calif.
3. Timothy Goebel, Rolling Meadows, Ill.

Women's singles
1. Michelle Kwan, Torrance, Calif.
2. Naomi Nari Nam, Irvine, Calif.
3. Angela Nikodinov, San Pedro, Calif.

Pairs
1. Danielle and Steve Hartsell, Westland, Mich.
2. Kyoko Ina, Guttenberg, N.J., and John Zimmerman, Birmingham, Ala.
3. Laura Handy and Paul Binnebose, Newark, Del.

Dance
1. Naomi Lang, Allegan, Mich., and Peter Tchernyshev, Waterford, Mich.
2. Eve Chalom, Detroit, Mich., and Mathew Gates, Baldock, England
3. Debbie Koegel, Phoenixville, Pa., and Oleg Fediukov, Brookhaven, Pa.

1999 WORLD CHAMPIONSHIPS

March 22–27, 1999, Helsinki, Finland

Men's singles
1. Alexei Yagudin, Russia
2. Evgeny Plushenko, Russia
3. Michael Weiss, United States

Women's singles
1. Maria Butyrskaya, Russia
2. Michelle Kwan, United States
3. Julia Soldatova, Russia

Pairs
1. Elena Berezhnaya and Anton Sikharulidze, Russia
2. Xue Shen and Hongbo Zhao, China
3. Dorota Zagorska and Mariusz Siudek, Poland

Dance
1. Anjelika Krylova and Oleg Ovsyannikov, Russia
2. Marina Anissina and Gwendal Peizerat, France
3. Shae-Lynn Bourne and Victor Kraatz, Canada

Swimming

WORLD RECORDS—MEN

(Through Sept. 23, 1999)

Distance	Record	Holder	Country	Date
Freestyle				
50 meters	0:21.81	Tom Jager	United States	March 24, 1990
100 meters	0:48.21	Alexander Popov	Russia	June 18, 1994
200 meters	1:46.00	Ian Thorpe	Australia	Aug. 24, 1999
400 meters	3:41.83	Ian Thorpe	Australia	Aug. 22, 1999
800 meters	7:46.00	Kieren Perkins	Australia	Aug. 24, 1994
1,500 meters	14:41.66	Kieren Perkins	Australia	Aug. 24, 1994
Backstroke				
100 meters	0:53.60	Lenny Krayzelburg	United States	Aug. 28, 1999
200 meters	1:55.87	Lenny Krayzelburg	United States	Aug. 27, 1999
Breaststroke				
100 meters	1:00.60	Fred DeBurghgraeve	Belgium	July 20, 1996
200 meters	2:10.16	Mike Barrowman	United States	July 29, 1992
Butterfly				
100 meters	0:52.15	Michael Klim	Australia	Oct. 9, 1997
200 meters	1:55.22	Denis Pankratov	Russia	June 14, 1995
Individual medley				
200 meters	1:58.16	Jani Sievinen	Finland	Sept. 11, 1994
400 meters	4:12.30	Tom Dolan	United States	Sept. 6, 1994
Medley relay				
400 meters	3:34.84	Olympic Team	United States	July 26, 1996
Freestyle relay				
400 meters	3:15.11	National Team	United States	Aug. 12, 1995
800 meters	7:08.79	National Team	Australia	Aug. 25, 1999

Approved by the International Swimming Federation (F.I.N.A.). (F.I.N.A. discontinued acceptance of records in yards in 1968). *Source:* United States Swim Team.

WORLD RECORDS—WOMEN

(Through Sept. 23, 1999)

Distance	Record	Holder	Country	Date
Freestyle				
50 meters	0:24.51	Jingyi Le	China	Sept. 11, 1994
100 meters	0:54.01	Jingyi Le	China	Sept. 5, 1994
200 meters	1:56.78	Franziska van Almsick	Germany	Sept. 6, 1994
400 meters	4:03.85	Janet Evans	United States	Sept. 22, 1988
800 meters	8:16.22	Janet Evans	United States	Aug. 20, 1989
1,500 meters	15:52.10	Janet Evans	United States	March 26, 1988
Backstroke				
100 meters	1:00.16	Cihong He	China	Sept. 10, 1994
200 meters	2:06.62	Kristina Egerszegi	Hungary	Aug. 25, 1991
Breaststroke				
50 meters	0:30.83	Penny Heyns	South Africa	Aug. 28, 1999
100 meters	1:06.52	Penny Heyns	South Africa	Aug. 29, 1999
200 meters	2:23.64	Penny Heyns	South Africa	Aug. 27, 1999
Butterfly				
100 meters	0:57.88	Jennifer Thompson	United States	Aug. 23, 1999
200 meters	2:05.96	Mary T. Meagher	United States	Aug. 13, 1981
Individual medley				
200 meters	2:09.72	Yanyan Wu	China	Oct. 17, 1997
400 meters	4:34.79	Yan Chen	China	Oct. 13, 1997
Medley relay				
400 meters	4:01.67	National Team	China	Sept. 10, 1994
Freestyle relay				
400 meters	3:37.91	National Team	China	Sept. 7, 1994
800 meters	7:55.47	National Team	East Germany	Aug. 18, 1987

Approved by the International Swimming Federation (F.I.N.A.). (F.I.N.A. discontinued acceptance of records in yards in 1968). *Source:* United States Swim Team.

AMERICAN SWIMMING RECORDS
(Through Sept. 23, 1999)

Distance	Record	Holder	Date
MEN			
Freestyle			
50 meters	0:21.81	Tom Jager	March 24, 1990
100 meters	0:48.42	Matt Biondi	Aug. 10, 1988
200 meters	1:47.72	Matt Biondi	Aug. 8, 1988
400 meters	3:48.06	Matt Cetlinski	Aug. 11, 1988
800 meters	7:52.45	Sean Killion	July 27, 1987
1,500 meters	15:01.51	George DiCarlo	June 30, 1984
Backstroke			
100 meters	0:5360	Lenny Krayzelburg	Aug. 28, 1999
200 meters	1:55.87	Lenny Krayzelburg	Aug. 27, 1999
Breaststroke			
100 meters	1:00.77	Jeremy Linn	July 20, 1996
200 meters	2:10.16	Mike Barrowman	July 29, 1992
Butterfly			
100 meters	0:52.76	Neil Walker	Aug. 12, 1997
200 meters	1:55.41	Tom Malchow	Aug. 25, 1999
Individual medley			
200 meters	2:00.11	David Wharton	Aug. 20, 1989
400 meters	4:12.30	Tom Dolan	Sept. 6, 1994
Medley relay			
400 meters	3:34.84	U.S. Olympic Team	July 26, 1996
Freestyle relay			
400 meters	3:15.11	U.S. National Team	Aug. 12, 1995
800 meters	7:12.51	U.S. National Team	Sept. 21, 1988

Distance	Record	Holder	Date
WOMEN			
Freestyle			
50 meters	0:24.87	Amy Van Dyken	July 26, 1996
100 meters	0:54.48	Jenny Thompson	March 1, 1992
200 meters	1:57.90	Nicole Haislett	July 27, 1992
400 meters	4:03.85	Janet Evans	Sept. 22, 1988
800 meters	8:16.22	Janet Evans	Aug. 20, 1989
1,500 meters	15:52.10	Janet Evans	March 26, 1988
Backstroke			
100 meters	1:00.77	Lea Maurer	Jan. 14, 1998
200 meters	2:08.60	Betsy Mitchell	June 27, 1986
Breaststroke			
100 meters	1:08.09	Amanda Beard	July 21, 1996
200 meters	2:25.35	Anita Nall	March 2, 1992
Butterfly			
100 meters	0:57.88	Jennifer Thompson	Aug. 23, 1999
200 meters	2:05.96	Mary T. Meagher	Aug. 13, 1981
Individual medley			
200 meters	2:11.91	Summer Sanders	July 30, 1992
400 meters	4:37.58	Summer Sanders	July 26, 1992
Medley relay			
400 meters	4:01.93	U.S. National Team	Jan. 16, 1998
Freestyle relay			
400 meters	3:39.29	U.S. Olympic Team	July 22, 1996
800 meters	7:57.61	U.S. National Team	Aug. 26, 1999

Source: United States Swim Team.

PAN PACIFIC CHAMPIONSHIPS
(Aug. 22–29, 1999, Sydney, Australia)
Men

50-meter freestyle—Brendon Dedekind, South Africa	0:22.06
100-meter freestyle—Michael Klim, Australia	0:48.98
200-meter freestyle—Ian Thorpe, Australia	1:46.00
400-meter freestyle—Ian Thorpe, Australia	3:41.83
1,500-meter freestyle—Grant Hackett, Australia	14:45.60
100-meter backstroke—Lenny Krayzelburg, United States	0:53.60
200-meter backstroke—Lenny Krayzelburg, United States	1:55.87
100-meter breaststroke—Simon Cowley, Australia	1:02.06
200-meter breaststroke—Simon Cowley, Australia	2:12.98
100-meter butterfly—Michael Klim, Australia	0:52.49
200-meter butterfly—Tom Malchow, United States	1:55.40
200-meter individual medley—Tom Wilkens, United States	2:01.01
400-meter individual medley—Matthew Dunn, Australia	4:16.54
400-meter freestyle relay—Australia (M. Klim, J. English, C. Fydler, I. Thorpe)	3:16.08
800-meter freestyle relay—Australia (I. Thorpe, W. Kirby, G. Hackett, M. Klim)	7:08.79
400-meter medley relay—United States (L. Krayzelburg, K. Grote, D. Wales, N. Walker)	3:36.37

Women

50-meter freestyle—Jenny Thompson, United States	0:25.51
100-meter freestyle—Jenny Thompson, United States	0:54.89
200-meter freestyle—Susan O'Neill, Australia	1:58.17
400-meter freestyle—Brooke Bennett, United States	4:08.39
800-meter freestyle—Brooke Bennett, United States	8:25.06
100-meter backstroke—Dyana Calub, Australia and Mai Kakamura, Japan (tie)	1:01.51
200-meter backstroke—Tomoko Hagiwara, Japan	2:11.36
100-meter breaststroke—Penny Heyns, South Africa	1:07.08
200-meter breaststroke—Penny Heyns, South Africa	2:23.64
100-meter butterfly—Jenny Thompson, United States	0:57.88
200-meter butterfly—Susan O'Neill, Australia	2:06.60
200-meter individual medley—Joanne Malar, Canada	2:13.63
400-meter individual medley—Joanne Malar, Canada	4:40.23
400-meter freestyle relay—United States (L. Kolbisen, R. Fox, L. Benko, J. Thompson)	3:41.86
800-meter freestyle relay—United States (L. Benko, E. Stonebraker, J. Thompson, C. Teuscher)	7:57.61
400-meter medley relay—United States (B. Bedford, M. Quann, J. Thompson, L. Kolbisen)	4:03.09

NATIONAL SWIMMING CHAMPIONSHIPS—1999
(Aug. 6–10, 1999, Minneapolis, Minn.)
Men

50-meter freestyle—Gary Hall, Jr., Paradise Valley, Ariz.	0:22.13
100-meter freestyle—Jason Lezak, Irvine, Calif.	0:49.34
200-meter freestyle—Ugur Taner, Bellevue, Wash.	1:49.19
400-meter freestyle—Chad Carvin, Laguna Hills, Calif.	3:49.68
800-meter freestyle—Ryk Neethling, South Africa	7:59.41
1,500-meter freestyle—Chad Carvin, Laguna Hills, Calif.	15:22.85
100-meter backstroke—Lenny Krayzelburg, Los Angeles, Calif.	0:54.00
200-meter backstroke—Lenny Krayzelburg, Los Angeles, Calif.	1:56.68
100-meter breaststroke—Ed Moses, Burke, Va.	1:01.21
200-meter breaststroke—Brendan Hansen, Havertown, Pa.	2:16.07
100-meter butterfly—Bryan Jones, College Station, Tex.	0:53.05
200-meter butterfly—Ugur Taner, Bellevue, Wash.	1:58.82
200-meter individual medley—Tom Wilkens, Middletown, N.J.	2:02.03
400-meter individual medley—Robert Margalis, Clearwater, Fla.	4:19.70
400-meter freestyle relay—Texas Aquatics	3:17.65
800-meter freestyle relay—Texas Aquatics	7:26.99
400-meter medley relay—Texas Aquatics	3:41.65

Women

50-meter freestyle—Amy Van Dyken, Englewood, Colo.	0:25.13
100-meter freestyle—Jenny Thompson, Dover, N.H.	0:54.66
200-meter freestyle—Jenny Thompson, Dover, N.H.	2:00.19
400-meter freestyle—Lindsay Benko, Elkhart, Ind.	4:11.31
800-meter freestyle—Cristina Teuscher, New Rochelle, N.Y.	8:38.68
1,500-meter freestyle—Brooke Bennett, Plant City, Fla.	16:14.77
100-meter backstroke—B. J. Bedford, Etna, N.H.	1:01.89
200-meter backstroke—Lindsay Benko, Elkhart, Ind.	2:12.26
100-meter breaststroke—Megan Quann, Puyallup, Wash.	1:08.70
200-meter breaststroke—Kristen Caverly, San Clemente, Calif.	2:30.11
100-meter butterfly—Jenny Thompson, Dover, N.H.	0:58.15
200-meter butterfly—Misty Hyman, Phoenix, Ariz.	2:10.14
200-meter individual medley—Kristine Quance-Julian, Northridge, Calif.	2:16.06
400-meter individual medley—Kaitlin Sanden, Lake Forest, Calif.	4:42.92
400-meter freestyle relay—Hillenbrand	3:47.53
800-meter freestyle relay—Trojan	8:13.39
400-meter medley relay—Irvine Nova	4:12.33

Boxing

Whether it be called pugilism, prize fighting, or boxing, there is no tracing "the Sweet Science" to any definite source. Tales of rivals exchanging blows for fun, fame, or money go back to earliest recorded history and classical legend. There was a mixture of boxing and wrestling called the "pancratium" in the ancient Olympic Games; in such contests rivals belabored one another with hands fortified by heavy leather wrappings that were sometimes studded with metal. More than one Olympic competitor lost his life in this brutal exercise.

There was little law or order in pugilism until Jack Broughton, one of the early champions of England, drew up a set of rules for the game in 1743. Broughton, called "the father of English box-

ing," also is credited with having invented boxing gloves. However, these gloves—or "mufflers" as they were called—were used only in teaching "the manly art of self-defense" or in training bouts. All professional championship fights were contested with bare knuckles until 1892, when John L. Sullivan lost the heavyweight championship of the world to James J. Corbett in New Orleans in a bout in which both contestants wore regulation gloves.

The Broughton Rules were superseded by the London Prize Ring Rules of 1838. In 1884 the eighth marquis of Queensberry, with the help of John G. Chambers, put forward the Queensberry Rules, a code that called for gloved contests. Amateurs took to the Queensberry Rules more quickly than the professionals did.

HISTORY OF WORLD HEAVYWEIGHT CHAMPIONSHIP FIGHTS

(Bouts in which a new champion was crowned)

Date	Where held	Winner, weight, age	Loser, weight, age	Rounds
Sept. 7, 1892	New Orleans, La.	James J. Corbett, 178 (26)	John L. Sullivan, 212 (33)	21
March 17, 1897	Carson City, Nev.	Bob Fitzsimmons, 167 (34)	James J. Corbett, 183 (30)	KO 14
June 9, 1899	Coney Island, N.Y.	James J. Jeffries, 206 (24)[1]	Bob Fitzsimmons, 167 (37)	KO 11
Feb. 23, 1906	Los Angeles	Tommy Burns, 180 (24)[2]	Marvin Hart, 188 (29)	20
Dec. 26, 1908	Sydney, Australia	Jack Johnson, 196 (30)	Tommy Burns, 176 (27)	KO 14
April 5, 1915	Havana, Cuba	Jess Willard, 230 (33)	Jack Johnson, 205½ (37)	KO 26
July 4, 1919	Toledo, Ohio	Jack Dempsey, 187 (24)	Jess Willard, 245 (37)	KO 3
Sept. 23, 1926	Philadelphia	Gene Tunney, 189 (28)[3]	Jack Dempsey, 190 (31)	10
June 12, 1930	New York	Max Schmeling, 188 (24)	Jack Sharkey, 197 (27)	WF 4
June 21, 1932	Long Island City	Jack Sharkey, 205 (29)	Max Schmeling, 188 (26)	15
June 29, 1933	Long Island City	Primo Carnera, 260½ (26)	Jack Sharkey, 201 (30)	KO 6
June 14, 1934	Long Island City	Max Baer, 209½ (25)	Primo Carnera, 263¼ (27)	KO 11
June 13, 1935	Long Island City	Jim Braddock, 193¾ (29)	Max Baer, 209½ (26)	15
June 22, 1937	Chicago	Joe Louis, 197¼ (23)	Jim Braddock, 197 (31)	KO 8
June 22, 1949	Chicago	Ezzard Charles, 181¾ (27)[4]	Joe Walcott, 195½ (35)	15
Sept. 27, 1950	New York	Ezzard Charles, 184½ (29)[5]	Joe Louis, 218 (36)	15
July 18, 1951	Pittsburgh	Joe Walcott, 194 (37)	Ezzard Charles, 182 (30)	KO 7
Sept. 23, 1952	Philadelphia	Rocky Marciano, 184 (29)[6]	Joe Walcott, 196 (38)	KO13
Nov. 30, 1956	Chicago	Floyd Patterson, 182¼ (21)	Archie Moore, 187¾ (42)	KO 5
June 26, 1959	New York	Ingemar Johansson, 196 (26)	Floyd Patterson, 182 (24)	KO 3
June 20, 1960	New York	Floyd Patterson, 190 (25)	Ingemar Johansson, 194¾ (27)	KO 5
Sept. 25, 1962	Chicago	Sonny Liston, 214 (28)	Floyd Patterson, 189 (27)	KO 1
Feb. 25, 1964	Miami Beach, Fla.	Cassius Clay (Muhammad Ali), 210 (22)[7]	Sonny Liston, 218 (30)	KO 7
March 4, 1968	New York	Joe Frazier, 204½ (24)[8]	Buster Mathis, 243½ (23)	KO 11
April 27, 1968	Oakland, Calif.	Jimmy Ellis, 197 (28)[9]	Jerry Quarry, 195 (22)	15
Feb. 16, 1970	New York	Joe Frazier, 205 (26)[10]	Jimmy Ellis, 201 (29)	KO 5
Jan. 22, 1973	Kingston, Jamaica	George Foreman, 217½ (24)	Joe Frazier, 214 (29)	KO 2
Oct. 30, 1974	Kinshasa, Zaire	Muhammad Ali, 216½ (32)	George Foreman, 220 (26)	KO 8
Feb. 15, 1978	Las Vegas, Nev.	Leon Spinks, 197 (25)	Muhammad Ali, 224½ (36)	15
June 9, 1978	Las Vegas, Nev.	Larry Holmes, 212 (28)[11]	Ken Norton, 220 (32)	15
Sept. 15, 1978	New Orleans	Muhammad Ali, 221 (36)[12]	Leon Spinks, 201 (25)	15
Oct. 20, 1979	Pretoria, S. Africa	John Tate, 240 (24)[13]	Gerrie Coetzee, 222 (24)	15
March 31, 1980	Knoxville, Tenn.	Mike Weaver, 207½ (27)	John Tate, 232 (25)	KO 15
Dec. 10, 1982	Las Vegas, Nev.	Michael Dokes, 216 (24)	Mike Weaver, 209½ (30)	KO 1
Sept. 23, 1983	Richfield, Ohio	Gerrie Coetzee, 215 (28)	Michael Dokes, 217 (25)	KO 10
March 9, 1984	Las Vegas, Nev.	Tim Witherspoon, 220½ (26)[14]	Greg Page, 239½ (25)	12
Aug. 31, 1984	Las Vegas, Nev.	Pinklon Thomas, 216 (26)	Tim Witherspoon, 217 (26)	12
Nov. 9, 1984	Las Vegas, Nev.	Larry Holmes, 221½ (35)[15]	James Smith, 227 (31)	KO 12
Dec. 1, 1984	Sun City, S. Africa	Greg Page, 236 (25)[16]	Gerry Coetzee, 217 (29)	KO 8
April 29, 1985	Buffalo, N.Y.	Tony Tubbs, 229 (26)[16]	Greg Page, 239½ (26)	15
Sept. 21,1985	Las Vegas, Nev.	Michael Spinks, 200 (29)	Larry Holmes, 221 (35)	15
Jan. 17, 1986	Atlanta, Ga.	Tim Witherspoon, 227 (28)	Tony Tubbs, 229 (27)	15
Nov. 23, 1986	Las Vegas, Nev.	Mike Tyson, 217 (20)[17]	Trevor Berbick, 220 (29)	KO 2
Dec. 12, 1986	New York, N.Y.	James Smith, 230 (33)[16]	Tim Witherspoon, 218 (29)	KO 1
March 7, 1987	Las Vegas, Nev.	Mike Tyson, 217 (20)[16]	James Smith, 230 (33)	12
Feb. 10, 1990	Tokyo	James "Buster" Douglas, 231½ (29)[18]	Mike Tyson, (220) (23)	KO 10

Date	Where held	Winner, weight, age	Loser, weight, age	Rounds
Oct. 25, 1990	Las Vegas, Nev.	Evander Holyfield, 208 (28)	James "Buster" Douglas, 246 (30)	KO 3
Nov. 13, 1992	Las Vegas, Nev.	Riddick Bowe,[19] 235 (25)	Evander Holyfield, 205 (30)	12
Nov. 6, 1993	Las Vegas, Nev.	Evander Holyfield, 217 (30)	Riddick Bowe, 246 (26)	12
April 22, 1994	Las Vegas, Nev.	Michael Moorer, 214 (26)	Evander Holyfield,[20] 214 (31)	12
Sept 24, 1994	London	Oliver McCall,[21] 228 (29)	Lennox Lewis, 238 (28)	2
Nov. 5, 1994	Las Vegas, Nev.	George Foreman,[22] 250 (45)	Michael Moorer, 222 (26)	10
April 8, 1995	Las Vegas, Nev.	Bruce Seldon,[23] 232 (28)	Tony Tucker, 238 (36)	7
Dec. 9, 1995	Stuttgart, Ger.	Frans Botha,[24] 227 (28)	Axel Schulz, 222 (27)	12
March 16, 1996	Las Vegas, Nev.	Mike Tyson,[25] 220 (29)	Frank Bruno, 247 (34)	3
June 22, 1996	Dortmund, Ger.	Michael Moorer, 222 (28)	Axel Schulz, 222 (27)	12
Sept. 7, 1996	Las Vegas, Nev.	Mike Tyson, 219 (30)	Bruce Seldon, 229 (29)	1
Nov. 9, 1996	Las Vegas, Nev.	Evander Holyfield,[23] 215 (34)	Mike Tyson, 222 (30)	11
Feb. 7, 1997	Las Vegas, Nev.	Lennox Lewis,[25] 251 (31)	Oliver McCall, 237 (30)	5
Nov. 8, 1997	Las Vegas, Nev.	Evander Holyfield,[26] 214 (35)	Michael Moorer, 223 (30)	8

1. Jeffries retired as champion in March 1905. He named Marvin Hart and Jack Root as leading contenders and agreed to referee their fight in Reno, Nev., on July 3, 1905, with the stipulation that he would term the winner the champion. Hart, 190 (28), knocked out Root, 171 (29), in the 12th round. 2. Burns claimed the title after defeating Hart. 3. Tunney retired as champion after defeating Tom Heeney on July 26, 1928. 4. After Louis announced his retirement as champion on March 1, 1949, Charles won recognition from the National Boxing Association as champion by defeating Walcott. 5. Charles gained undisputed recognition as champion by defeating Louis, who came out of retirement. 6. Retired as champion April 27, 1956. 7. The World Boxing Association (WBA) later withdrew its recognition of Clay as champion and declared the winner of a bout between Ernie Terrell and Eddie Machen would gain its version of the title. Terrell, 199 (25), won a 15-round decision from Machen, 192 (32), in Chicago on March 5, 1965. Clay, 212¼ (25) and Terrell, 212½ (27), met in Houston on Feb. 6, 1967, Clay winning a 15-round decision. 8. Winner recognized by N.Y., Mass., Maine, Ill., Tex. and Pa. to fill vacated title when Clay was stripped of championship for failing to accept U.S. Induction. 9. Bout was final of eight-man tournament to fill Clay's place and is recognized by World Boxing Association. 10. Bout settled controversy over title. 11. Holmes won World Boxing Council title after WBC had withdrawn recognition of Spinks, March 18, 1978, and awarded its title to Norton. WBC said Spinks had reneged on agreement to fight Norton. 12. Ali regained World Boxing Association championship. 13. Tate won WBA title after Ali retired and left it vacant. 14. Tim Witherspoon and Greg Page fought for the WBC heavyweight title vacated by Larry Holmes, who could not come to agreement on a deal to fight Page, the No. 1 contender. Holmes declared he would fight under the banner of the International Boxing Federation (IBF). Several dates were set and postponed for fights between Holmes and Gerry Coetzee, the WBA champ, the latest being Nov. 16, 1984. 15. First fight under banner of International Boxing Federation. 16. New WBA champion. 17. New WBC champion. 18. New undisputed champion. 19. The WBC stripped Bowe of its version of the title in December 1992 and named Lennox Lewis champion. 20. After the loss, Holyfield retired. 21. New WBC champion. Lennox Lewis had been named champion in 1992 and had won three title defenses before losing to McCall. 22. For combined WBA/IBF titles. Later WBA stripped Foreman of title for failing to fight no. 1 contender Tony Tucker. IBF also stripped Foreman on June 29, 1995. 23. New WBA champion. 24. Botha later tested positive for steroids and was stripped of the title. 25. New WBC champion. 26. New IBF champion.

OTHER WORLD BOXING TITLEHOLDERS

(Through Sept. 27, 1999)

Light Heavyweight

1903	Jack Root, George Gardner	1972–73	Bob Foster (WBA, WBC)	1984	Michael Spinks (undisputed)
1903–05	Bob Fitzsimmons	1974	John Conteh (WBA), Bob Foster (WBC)[1, 4]	1985	Michael Spinks (undisputed)[5]
1905–12	Philadelphia Jack O'Brien[1]	1975–76	Victor Galindez (WBA), John Conteh (WBC)	1986	Marvin Johnson (WBA), Dennis Andries (WBC)
1912–16	Jack Dillon	1977	Victor Galindez (WBA), John Conteh (WBC),[4] Miguel Cuello (WBC)	1987	Thomas Hearns (WBC), Virgil Hill (WBA), Bobby Czyz (IBF)
1916–20	Battling Levinsky				
1920–22	Georges Carpentier				
1923	Battling Siki	1978	Victor Galindez (WBA), Mike Rossman (WBA), Miguel Cuello (WBC), Mate Parlov (WBC), Marvin Johnson (WBC)	1988	Charles Williams (IBF), Virgil Hill (WBA), Donny LaLonde (WBC), Sugar Ray Leonard (WBC)
1923–25	Mike McTigue				
1925–26	Paul Berlenbach				
1926–27	Jack Delaney[2]				
1927	Mike McTigue	1979	Mike Rossman (WBA), Victor Galindez (WBA), Marvin Johnson (WBC), Matthew (Franklin) Saad Muhammad (WBC)	1989	Dennis Andries (WBC), Virgil Hill (WBA), Charles Williams (IBF), Jeff Harding (WBC)
1927–29	Tommy Loughran				
1930	Jimmy Slattery				
1930–34	Maxie Rosenbloom				
1934–35	Bob Olin	1980	Matthew Saad Muhammad (WBC), Marvin Johnson (WBA), Eddie (Gregory) Mustafa Muhammad (WBA)	1990	Virgil Hill (WBA), Charles Williams (IBF), Jeff Harding (WBC), Dennis Andries (WBC)
1935–39	John Henry Lewis				
1939	Melio Bettina				
1939–41	Billy Conn[2]				
1941	Anton Christoforidis (NBA)	1981	Matthew Saad Muhammad (WBC), Eddie Mustafa Muhammad (WBA), Michael Spinks (WBA), Dwight Braxton (WBC)	1991	Virgil Hill (WBA), Thomas Hearns (WBA), Dennis Andries (WBC), Charles Williams (IBF)
1941–48	Gus Lesnevich				
1948–50	Freddie Mills				
1950–52	Joey Maxim				
1952–61	Archie Moore[3]	1982	Dwight Braxton (WBC), Michael Spinks (WBA)	1992	Charles Williams (IBF), James Waring (IBF), Jeff Harding (WBC)
1961–63	Harold Johnson				
1963–65	Willie Pastrano				
1965–66	José Torres	1983	Michael Spinks (undisputed)	1993	Virgil Hill (WBA), Jeff Harding (WBC), Henry Maske (IBF)
1966–67	Dick Tiger				
1968	Dick Tiger, Bob Foster				
1969–70	Bob Foster				
1971	Vicente Rondon (WBA), Bob Foster (WBC)				

1994	Virgil Hill (WBA), Mike McCallum (WBC), Henry Maske (IBF)	1977	Carlos Monzon (WBA, WBC),[1] Rodrigo Valdez (WBA, WBC)	1919–22	Jack Britton
1995	Virgil Hill (WBA), Fabio Tiozzo (WBC), Henry Maske (IBF)	1978	Rodrigo Valdez, Hugo Corro	1922–26	Mickey Walker
				1926–27	Pete Latzo
				1927–29	Joe Dundee
		1979	Hugo Corro, Vito Antuofermo	1929–30	Jackie Fields
1996–97	Virgil Hill (WBA), Fabio Tiozzo (WBC), Henry Maske (IBF)	1980	Vito Antuofermo, Alan Minter, Marvin Hagler	1930	Young Jack Thompson
				1930–31	Tommy Freeman
1998	Roy Jones (WBA, WBC), Reggie Johnson (IBF)			1931	Young Jack Thompson
		1981	Marvin Hagler	1931–32	Lou Brouillard
1999	Roy Jones (WBA, WBC, IBF)	1982–86	Marvin Hagler (undisputed)	1932–33	Jackie Fields
				1933	Young Corbett 3rd
		1987	Marvin Hagler (undisputed), Sugar Ray Leonard (undisputed)	1933–34	Jimmy McLarnin, Barney Ross
				1934–35	Jimmy McLarnin
				1935–38	Barney Ross

1. Retired. 2. Abandoned title. 3. NBA withdrew recognition in 1961, New York Commission in 1962; recognized thereafter only by California and Europe. 4. WBC withdrew recognition. 5. Spinks relinquished title in 1985 to fight for heavyweight title.

		1988	Sumbu Kalambay (WBA), Thomas Hearns (WBC), Iran Barkley (WBC), Frank Tate (IBF), Michael Nunn (IBF), James Kinchen (NABF)	1938–40	Henry Armstrong
				1940–41	Fritzie Zivic
				1941–46	Freddie Cochrane
				1946	Marty Servo[2]
				1946–51	Ray Robinson[1]

Middleweight

1867–72	Tom Chandler			1951	Johnny Bratton (NBA)
1872–81	George Rooke	1989	Michael Nunn (IBF), Mike McCallum (WBA), Iran Barkley (WBC), Roberto Duran (WBC)	1951–54	Kid Gavilan
1881–82	Mike Donovan[1]			1954–55	Johnny Saxton
1884–91	Jack (Nonpareil) Dempsey			1955	Tony DeMarco
1891–97	Bob Fitzsimmons[2]	1990	Michael McCallum (WBA), Michael Nunn (IBF), Iran Barkley (WBC)	1955–56	Carmen Basilio
1908	Stanley Ketchel, Billy Papke			1956	Johnny Saxton
				1956–57	Carmen Basilio[1]
1908–10	Stanley Ketchel[3]	1991	Michael Nunn (IBF), James Toney (IBF), Michael McCallum (WBA)	1958	Virgil Akins
1913	Frank Klaus			1959–60	Don Jordan
1913–14	George Chip			1960–61	Benny (Kid) Paret
1914–17	Al McCoy	1992	James Toney (IBF), Julian Jackson (WBC), Reggie Johnson (WBA)	1961	Emile Griffith
1917–20	Mike O'Dowd			1961–62	Benny (Kid) Paret
1920–23	Johnny Wilson			1962–63	Emile Griffith, Luis Rodriguez
1923–26	Harry Greb	1993	Reggie Johnson (WBA), Gerald McClellan (WBA), Roy Jones (IBF)		
1926	Tiger Flowers			1963–66	Emile Griffith[1]
1926–31	Mickey Walker[2]			1966–69	Curtis Cokes
1931–41	Gorilla Jones, Ben Jeby, Marcel Thil, Lou Brouillard, Vince Dundee, Teddy Yarosz, Babe Risko, Freddy Steele, Al Hostak, Solly Kreiger, Fred Apostoli, Ceferino Garcia, Ken Overlin, Billy Soose, Tony Zale[4]	1994	Julian Jackson (WBA), Gerald McClellan (WBA), Roy Jones (IBF)	1969	Curtis Cokes, José Napoles
				1970	José Napoles, Billy Backus
		1995	Jorge Castro (WBA), Julian Jackson (WBC), Bernard Hopkins (IBF)	1971	Billy Backus, José Napoles
				1972–74	José Napoles
		1996	William Joppy (WBA), Keith Holmes (WBC), Bernard Hopkins (IBF)	1975	José Napoles (WBA, WBC),[3] Angel Espada (WBA), John Stracey (WBC)
1941–47	Tony Zale				
1947–48	Rocky Graziano	1997	Shinji Takehara (WBA), Quincy Taylor (WBC), Bernard Hopkins (IBF)	1976	Angel Espada (WBA), José Cuevas (WBA), John Stracey (WBC), Carlos Palomino
1948	Tony Zale				
1948–49	Marcel Cerdan	1998	William Joppy (WBA), Hassine Cherifi (WBC), Bernard Hopkins (IBF)	1977–78	José Cuevas (WBA), Carlos Palomino (WBC)
1949–51	Jake LaMotta				
1951–52	Ray Robinson[1]	1999	William Joppy (WBA), Keith Holmes (WBC), Bernard Hopkins (IBF)	1979	José Cuevas (WBA), Carlos Palomino (WBC), Wilfredo Benitez (WBC)
1952	Ray Robinson, Randy Turpin				
1953–55	Carl Olson				
1955–57	Ray Robinson[5]			1980	José Cuevas (WBA), Ray Leonard (WBC), Roberto Duran (WBC), Thomas Hearns (WBA)
1957	Gene Fullmer, Ray Robinson				

1. Retired. 2. Abandoned title. 3. Died. 4. National Boxing Association and New York Commission disagreed on champions. Those listed were accepted by one or the other until Zale gained world-wide recognition. 5. Ended retirement in 1954. 6. NBA withdrew recognition. 7. Recognized by New York, Massachusetts, and Europe.

1957–58	Carmen Basilio			1981	Ray Leonard (WBC), Thomas Hearns (WBA), Ray Leonard (WBC, WBA)
1958–60	Ray Robinson[6]				
1959–62	Gene Fullmer (NBA)				
1960–61	Paul Pender[7]			1982	Ray Leonard
1961–62	Terry Downes[1]			1983–85	Donald Curry (WBA), Milton McCrory (WBC)
1962	Paul Pender[1]				
1962–63	Dick Tiger	### Welterweight		1985–86	Donald Curry (undisputed)
1963–65	Joey Giardello				
1965–66	Dick Tiger	1892–94	Mysterious Billy Smith	1987	Mark Breland (WBA), Marlon Starling (WBA), Lloyd Honeyghan (IBF)
1966	Emile Griffith	1894–96	Tommy Ryan		
1967	Nino Benvenuti, Emile Griffith	1896	Kid McCoy[1]		
		1896–		1988	Marlon Starling (WBA), Tomas Molinares (WBA), Lloyd Honeyghan (WBC), Simon Brown (IBF)
1968	Emile Griffith, Nino Benvenuti	1900	Mysterious Billy Smith		
		1900	Rube Ferns		
1969	Nino Benvenuti	1900–01	Matty Matthews		
1970	Nino Benvenuti, Carlos Monzon	1901	Ruby Ferns	1989	Mark Breland (WBA), Marlon Starling (WBC), Simon Brown (IBF)
		1901–04	Joe Walcott		
1971–73	Carlos Monzon	1904	Dixie Kid[1]		
1974–75	Carlos Monzon (WBA), Rodrigo Valdez (WBC)	1904–06	Joe Walcott		
		1906–07	Honey Mellody		
1976	Carlos Monzon (WBA, WBC), Rodrigo Valdez (WBC)	1907	Mike (Twin) Sullivan[1]		
		1915–19	Ted Lewis		

1990	Mark Breland (WBA), Aaron Davis (WBA), Simon Brown (IBF), Marlon Starling (WBC), Maurice Blocker (WBC)
1991	Meldrick Taylor (WBA), Simon Brown (IBF, WBC)
1992	Meldrick Taylor (WBA), James "Buddy" McGirt (WBC), Maurice Blocker (IBF)
1993	Cristianto Espana (WBA), Pernell Whitaker (WBC), Felix Trinidad (IBF)
1994	Ike Quartey (WBA), Pernell Whitaker (WBC), Felix Trinidad (IBF)
1995	Ike Quartey (WBA), Pernell Whitaker (WBC), Felix Trinidad (IBF)
1996–97	Ike Quartey (WBA), Pernell Whitaker (WBC), Felix Trinidad (IBF)
1998	Ike Quartey (WBA), Oscar De La Hoya (WBC), Felix Trinidad (IBF)
1999	James Page (WBA), Oscar De La Hoya (WBC), Felix Trinidad (IBF, WBC)

1. Retired. 2. Abandoned title. 3. WBA withdrew recognition.

Lightweight

1869–99	Kid Lavigne
1899–	
1902	Frank Erne
1902–08	Joe Gans
1908–10	Battling Nelson
1910–12	Ad Wolgast
1912–14	Willie Ritchie
1914–17	Freddy Welsh
1917–25	Benny Leonard[1]
1925	Jimmy Goodrich
1925–26	Rocky Kansas
1926–30	Sammy Mandell
1930	Al Singer
1930–33	Tony Canzoneri
1933–35	Barney Ross[2]
1935–36	Tony Canzoneri
1936–38	Lou Ambers
1938–39	Henry Armstrong
1939–40	Lou Ambers
1940–41	Lew Jenkins
1941–42	Sammy Angott[1]
1943–47	Beau Jack (N.Y.), Bob Montgomery (N.Y.), Sammy Angott (NBA), Juan Zurita (NBA), Ike Williams (NBA)
1947–51	Ike Williams
1951–52	James Carter
1952	Lauro Salas
1952–54	James Carter
1954	Paddy DeMarco
1954–55	James Carter
1955–56	Wallace Smith
1956–62	Joe Brown
1962–65	Carlos Ortiz
1965	Ismael Laguna
1965–68	Carlos Ortiz
1968	Teo Cruz
1969	Teo Cruz, Mando Ramos
1970	Mando Ramos, Ismael Laguna, Ken Buchanan
1971	Ken Buchanan (WBA), Mando Ramos (WBC), **Pedro Carrasco (WBC)**

1972	Ken Buchanan (WBA), Roberto Duran (WBA), Pedro Carrasco (WBC), Mando Ramos (WBC), Chango Carmona (WBC), Rodolfo Gonzalez (WBC)
1973	Roberto Duran (WBA), Rodolfo Gonzalez (WBC)
1974	Roberto Duran (WBA), Rodolfo Gonzalez (WBC), Guts Ishimatsu (WBC)
1975	Roberto Duran (WBA), Guts Ishimatsu (WBC)
1976	Roberto Duran (WBA), Guts Ishimatsu (WBC), Esteban De Jesus (WBC)
1977	Roberto Duran (WBA), Esteban De Jesus (WBC)
1978	Roberto Duran (WBA, WBC)
1979	Roberto Duran,[2] Jim Watt (WBC), Ernesto Espana (WBA)
1980	Ernesto Espana (WBA), Hilmer Kenty (WBA), Jim Watt (WBC)
1981	Hilmer Kenty (WBA), Sean O'Grady (WBA), James Watt (WBC), Alexis Arguello (WBC), Arturo Frias (WBA)
1982	Arturo Frias (WBA), Ray Mancini (WBA), Alexis Arguello (WBC)
1983	Edwin Rosario (WBC), Ray Mancini (WBA)
1984	Edwin Rosario (WBC), Livingstone Bramble (WBA)
1985	Jose Luis Ramirez (WBC), Hector Camacho (WBC), Livingstone Bramble (WBA)
1986	Hector Camacho (WBC), Livingstone Bramble (WBA), Jim Paul (IBF)
1987	Edwin Rosario (WBA), Jose Luis Ramirez (WBC), Greg Haugen (IBF)
1988	Jose Luis Ramirez (WBC), Julio Cesar Chavez (WBA), Greg Haugen (IBF), Julio Cesar Chavez (WBC & WBA title unified)
1989	Pernell Whitaker (IBF, WBC), Edwin Rosario (WBA)
1990	Pernell Whitaker (IBF, WBC), Juan Nazario (WBA)
1991	Pernell Whitaker (IBF, WBA, WBC)
1992	Pernell Whitaker (IBF, WBA, WBC),[3] Joey Gamache (WBA).
1993	Dingaan Thobela (WBA), Angel Gonzalez (WBC), Freddie Pendleton (IBF)
1994	Orzubek Nazarov (WBA), Angel Gonzalez (WBC), Rafael Ruelas (IBF)
1995	Orzubek Nazarov (WBA), Angel Gonzalez (WBC), Oscar De La Hoya (IBF)
1996	Gusshie Nazarov (WBA), Jean Baptiste Mendy (WBC), Phillip Holiday (IBF)

1997	Orzubek Nazarov (WBA), Jean Baptiste Mendy (WBC), Philip Holiday (IBF)
1998	Jean Baptiste Mendy (WBA), Cesar Bazan (WBC), Shane Mosley (IBF)
1999	Stefano Zoff (WBA), Stevie Johnston (WBC), Paul Spadafora (IBF)

1. Retired. 2. Abandoned title. 3. Moving up in weight class, so resigned titles.

Featherweight

1889	Dal Hawkins[1]
1890	Billy Murphy
1892–	
1900	George Dixon
1900–01	Terry McGovern
1901	Young Corbett[1]
1901–12	Abe Attell
1912–23	Johnny Kilbane
1923	Eugene Criqui
1923–25	Johnny Dundee[1]
1925–27	Louis (Kid) Kaplan[1]
1927–28	Benny Bass
1928	Tony Canzoneri
1928–29	Andre Routis
1929–32	Battling Battalino[1]
1932	Tommy Paul (NBA), Kid Chocolate (N.Y.)
1933–36	Freddie Miller
1936–37	Petey Sarron
1937–38	Henry Armstrong[1]
1938–40	Joey Archibald
1940–41	Harry Jefra, Joey Archibald
1941–42	Chalky Wright
1942–48	Willie Pep
1948–49	Sandy Saddler[2]
1949–50	Willie Pep
1950–57	Sandy Saddler
1957–59	Kid Bassey
1959–63	Davey Moore
1963–64	Sugar Ramos
1964–67	Vicente Saldivar[2]
1968	Howard Winstone, José Legra,[3] Paul Rojas (WBA), Sho Saijo (WBA)
1969	Sho Saijo (WBA), Johnny Famechon[3]
1970	Sho Saijo (WBA), Johnny Famechon,[3] Vicente Salvidar,[3] Kuniaki Shibata[3]
1971	Sho Saijo (WBA), Antonio Gomez (WBA), Kuniaki Shibata (WBC)
1972	Antonio Gomez (WBA), Ernesto Marcel (WBA), Kuniaki Shibata (WBC), Clemente Sanchez (WBC), José Legra (WBC)
1973	Ernesto Marcel (WBA), José Legra (WBC), Eder Jofre (WBC)
1974	Ernesto Marcel (WBA),[2] Ruben Olivares (WBA), Alexis Arguello (WBA), Eder Jofre (WBC), Bobby Chacon (WBC)
1975	Alexis Arguello (WBA), Bobby Chacon (WBC), Ruben Olivares (WBC), David Kotey (WBC)
1976	Alexis Arguello (WBA),[2] David Kotey (WBC), Danny Lopez (WBC)

1977	Rafael Ortega (WBA),
	Danny Lopez (WBC)
1978	Rafael Ortega (WBA),
	Cecilio Lastra (WBA),
	Eusebio Pedroza (WBA),
	Danny Lopez (WBC)
1979	Eusebio Pedroza (WBA),
	Danny Lopez (WBC)
1980	Eusebio Pedroza (WBA),
	Danny Lopez (WBC),
	Salvador Sanchez (WBC)
1981	Eusebio Pedroza (WBA),
	Salvador Sanchez (WBC)
1982	Eusebio Pedroza (WBA),
	Salvador Sanchez (WBC)[4]
1983	Juan Laporte (WBC),
	Eusebio Pedroza (WBA)
1984	Wilfred Gomez (WBC),
	Eusebio Pedroza (WBA)
1985	Eusebio Pedroza (WBA),
	Barry McGuigan (WBA),
	Azumah Nelson (WBC)
1986	Barry McGuigan (WBA),
	Stevie Cruz (WBA),
	Azumah Nelson (WBC)
1987	Azumah Nelson (WBC),
	Antonio Esparragoza (WBA)
1988	Calvin Grove (IBF),
	Jorge Paez (IBF),
	Antonio Esparragoza (WBA),
	Jeff Fenech (WBC)
1989	Jorge Paez (IBF),
	Antonio Esparragoza (WBA),
	Jeff Fenech (WBC)
1990	Marcos Villasana (WBC),
	Antonio Esparragoza (WBA),
	Jorge Paez (IBF)
1991	Yung-Kyun Park (WBA),
	Troy Dorsey (IBF),
	Marcos Villagana (WBC)
1992	Paul Hodkinson (WBC),
	Manuel Medina (IBF),
	Yung-Kyun Park (WBA)
1993	Yung-Kyun Park (WBA),
	Goyo Vargas (WBC),
	Tom Johnson (IBF)
1994	Eloy Rojas (WBA),
	Kevin Kelley (WBC),
	Tom Johnson (IBF)
1995	Eloy Rojas (WBA),
	Alejandro Gonzalez (WBC),
	Tom Johnson (IBF)
1996	Wilfredo Vázquez (WBA),
	Luisto Espinoza (WBC),
	Tom Johnson (IBF)
1997	Elroy Rojas (WBA),
	Luisito Espinoza (WBC),
	Tom Johnson (IBF)
1998	Vacant (WBA),
	Luisito Espinoza (WBC),
	Manuel Medina (IBF)
1999	Freddie Norwood (WBA),
	Cesar Soto (WBC),
	Manuel Medina (IBF)

1. Abandoned title. 2. Retired. 3. Recognized in Europe, Mexico, and Orient. 4. Killed in auto accident.

Bantamweight

1890–92	George Dixon[1]
1894–99	Jimmy Barry[2]
1899–	
1900	Terry McGovern[1]
1901	Harry Harris[1]
1902–03	Harry Forbes
1903–04	Frankie Neil
1904	Joe Bowker[1]
1905–07	Jimmy Walsh[1]
1910–14	Johnny Coulon
1914–17	Kid Williams
1917–20	Pete Herman
1920	Joe Lynch
1920–21	Joe Lynch,
	Pete Herman,
	Johnny Buff
1922	Johnny Buff,
	Joe Lynch
1923	Joe Lynch
1924	Joe Lynch,
	Abe Goldstein, Eddie "Cannonball" Martin
1925	Eddie "Cannonball" Martin, Charlie (Phil) Rosenberg[3]
1927–28	Bud Taylor (NBA)[1]
1929–34	Al Brown
1935	Al Brown, Baltazar Sangchili
1936	Baltazar Sangchili, Tony Marino, Sixto Escobar
1937	Sixto Escobar, Harry Jeffra
1938	Harry Jeffra, Sixto Escobar
1939–40	Sixto Escobar[2]
1940–42	Lou Salica
1942–46	Manuel Ortiz
1947	Manuel Ortiz, Harold Dade
1948–50	Manuel Ortiz
1950–52	Vic Toweel
1952–54	Jimmy Carruthers[2]
1954–55	Robert Cohen
1956	Robert Cohen, Mario D'Agata, Raul Macias (NBA)
1957	Mario D'Agata, Alphonse Halimi
1958–59	Alphonse Halimi
1959–60	Jose Becerra[2]
1960–61	Alphonse Halimi[4]
1961–62	Johnny Caldwell[4]
1961–65	Eder Jofre
1965–68	Masahika "Fighting" Harada
1968	Masahika "Fighting" Harada, Lionel Rose
1969	Lionel Rose, Ruben Olivares
1970	Ruben Olivares, Chucho Castillo
1971	Chucho Castillo, Ruben Olivares
1972	Ruben Olivares, Rafael Herrera, Enrique Pinder
1973	Enrique Pinder (WBA), Romeo Anaya (WBA), Arnold Taylor (WBA), Rodolfo Martinez (WBC), Rafael Herrera
1974	Arnold Taylor (WBA), Soo Hwan Hong (WBA), Rafael Herrera (WBC), Rodolfo Martinez (WBC)
1975	Soo Hwan Hong (WBA), Alfonso Zamora (WBA), Rodolfo Martinez (WBC)

1976	Alfonso Zamora (WBA),
	Rodolfo Martinez (WBC),
	Carlos Zarate (WBC)
1977	Alfonso Zamora (WBA),
	Jorge Lujan (WBA),
	Carlos Zarate (WBC)
1978	Jorge Lujan (WBA),
	Carlos Zarate (WBC)
1979	Jorge Lujan (WBA),
	Carlos Zarate (WBC),
	Lupe Pintor (WBC)
1980	Jorge Lujan (WBA),
	Lupe Pintor (WBC),
	Julian Solis (WBA),
	Jeff Chandler (WBA)
1981	Lupe Pintor (WBC),
	Jeff Chandler (WBA)
1982	Lupe Pintor (WBC),
	Jeff Chandler (WBA)
1983	Jeff Chandler (WBA),
	Albert Dauila (WBC)
1984	Richie Sandqual (WBA),
	Albert Dauila (WBC)
1985	Richard Sandoval (WBA),
	Daniel Zaragoza (WBC),
	Miguel Lora (WBC)
1986	Richard Sandoval (WBA),
	Bernardo Pinango (WBA),
	Jeff Fenech (IBF)
1987	Bernardo Pinango (WBA),
	Takuya Muguruma (WBA),
	Miguel Lora (WBC)
1988	Wilfredo Vásquez (WBA),
	Jibaro Perez (WBC),
	Moon Sung-gil (WBA),
	Orlando Canizales (IBF)
1989	Jibaro Perez (WBC),
	Moon Sung-gil (WBA),
	Orlando Canizales (IBF),
	Kaokor Galaxy (WBA),
	Luis Espinosa (WBA)
1990	Orlando Canizales (IBF),
	Jibaro Perez (WBC),
	Luis Espinosa (WBA)
1991	Greg Richardson (WBC),
	Orlando Canizales (IBF),
	Luis Espinosa (WBA)
1992	Joichiro Tatsuyoshi (WBC),
	Victor Manuel Rabanales (WBC),
	Eddie Cook (WBA),
	Orlando Gonzales (IBF)
1993	Jorge Julio (WBA),
	Byun-Jong-il (WBC),
	Orlando Canizales (IBF)
1994	John Michael Johnson (WBA),
	Yasuei Yakushiji (WBC),
	Orlando Canizales (IBF)
1995	Daorun Chuwatang (WBA),
	Yasuei Yakushiji (WBC),
	Mbulelo Botile (IBF)
1996–97	Nana Konadu (WBA),
	Wayne McCullough (WBC),
	Mbulelo Botile (IBF)
1998	Nana Konadu (WBA),
	Joichiro Tatsuyoshi (WBC),
	Tim Austin (IBF)
1999	Paulie Ayala (WBA),
	Veeraphol Sahaprom (WBC),
	Tim Austin (IBF)

1. Abandoned title. 2. Retired. 3. Deprived of title for failing to make weight. 4. Recognized in Europe.

Horse Racing

Ancient drawings on stone and bone prove that horse racing is at least 3,000 years old, but thoroughbred racing is a modern development. Practically every thoroughbred in training today traces its registered ancestry back to one or more of three sires that arrived in England about 1728 from the Near East and became known, from the names of their owners, as the Byerly Turk, the Darley Arabian, and the Godolphin Arabian. The Jockey Club (English) was founded at Newmarket in 1750 or 1751 and became the custodian of the Stud Book as well as the court of last resort in deciding turf affairs.

Horse racing took place in this country before the Revolution, but the great lift to the breeding industry came with the importation in 1798, by Col. John Hoomes of Virginia, of Diomed, winner of the Epsom Derby of 1780. Diomed's lineal descendants included such famous stars of the American turf as American Eclipse and Lexington. From 1800 to the time of the Civil War there were race courses and breeding establishments plentifully scattered through Virginia, North Carolina, South Carolina, Tennessee, Kentucky, and Louisiana.

The oldest stake event in North America is the Queen's Plate, a Canadian fixture that was first run in the Province of Quebec in 1836. The oldest stake event in the United States is the Travers, which was first run at Saratoga in 1864. The gambling that goes with horse racing and trickery by jockeys, trainers, owners, and track officials caused attacks on the sport by reformers and a demand among horse racing enthusiasts for an honest and effective control of some kind, but nothing of lasting value to racing came of this until the formation in 1894 of the Jockey Club (American).

"TRIPLE CROWN" WINNERS IN THE UNITED STATES
(Kentucky Derby, Preakness and Belmont Stakes)

Year	Horse	Owner	Year	Horse	Owner
1919	Sir Barton	J. K. L. Ross	1946	Assault	Robert J. Kleberg
1930	Gallant Fox	William Woodward	1948	Citation	Warren Wright
1935	Omaha	William Woodward	1973	Secretariat	Meadow Stable
1937	War Admiral	Samuel D. Riddle	1977	Seattle Slew	Karen Taylor
1941	Whirlaway	Warren Wright	1978	Affirmed	Louis Wolfson
1943	Count Fleet	Mrs. John Hertz			

KENTUCKY DERBY
Churchill Downs; 3-year-olds; 1¼ miles.

Year	Winner	Jockey	Wt.	Win val.	Year	Winner	Jockey	Wt.	Win val.
1919	Sir Barton	J. Loftus	112½	$20,825	1953	Dark Star	H. Moreno	126	$90,050
1920	Paul Jones	T. Rice	126	30,375	1954	Determine	R. York	126	102,050
1921	Behave Yourself	C. Thompson	126	38,450	1955	Swaps	W. Shoemaker	126	108,400
1922	Morvich	A. Johnson	126	46,775	1956	Needles	D. Erb	126	123,450
1923	Zev	E. Sande	126	53,600	1957	Iron Liege	W. Hartack	126	107,950
1924	Black Gold	J. D. Mooney	126	52,775	1958	Tim Tam	I. Valenzuela	126	116,400
1925	Flying Ebony	E. Sande	126	52,950	1959	Tomy Lee	W. Shoemaker	126	119,650
1926	Bubbling Over	A. Johnson	126	50,075	1960	Venetian Way	W. Hartack	126	114,850
1927	Whiskery	L. McAtee	126	51,000	1961	Carry Back	J. Sellers	126	120,500
1928	Reigh Count	C. Lang	126	55,375	1962	Decidedly	W. Hartack	126	119,650
1929	Clyde Van Dusen	L. McAtee	126	53,950	1963	Chateauguay	B. Baeza	126	108,900
1930	Gallant Fox	E. Sande	126	50,725	1964	Northern Dancer	W. Hartack	126	114,300
1931	Twenty Grand	C. Kurtsinger	126	48,725	1965	Lucky Debonair	W. Shoemaker	126	112,000
1932	Burgoo King	E. James	126	52,350	1966	Kauai King	D. Brumfield	126	120,500
1933	Brokers Tip	D. Meade	126	48,925	1967	Proud Clarion	R. Ussery	126	119,700
1934	Cavalcade	M. Garner	126	28,175	1968	Forward Pass[1]	I. Valenzuela	126	122,600
1935	Omaha	W. Saunders	126	39,525	1969	Majestic Prince	W. Hartack	126	113,200
1936	Bold Venture	I. Hanford	126	37,725	1970	Dust Commander	M. Manganello	126	127,800
1937	War Admiral	C. Kurtsinger	126	52,050	1971	Canonero II	G. Avila	126	145,500
1938	Lawrin	E. Arcaro	126	47,050	1972	Riva Ridge	R. Turcotte	126	140,300
1939	Johnstown	J. Stout	126	46,350	1973	Secretariat	R. Turcotte	126	155,050
1940	Gallahadion	C. Bierman	126	60,150	1974	Cannonade	A. Cordero, Jr.	126	274,000
1941	Whirlaway	E. Arcaro	126	61,275	1975	Foolish Pleasure	J. Vasquez	126	209,600
1942	Shut Out	W. D. Wright	126	64,225	1976	Bold Forbes	A. Cordero, Jr.	126	165,200
1943	Count Fleet	J. Longden	126	60,725	1977	Seattle Slew	J. Cruguet	126	214,700
1944	Pensive	C. McCreary	126	64,675	1978	Affirmed	S. Cauthen	126	186,900
1945	Hoop Jr.	E. Arcaro	126	64,850	1979	Spectacular Bid	R. Franklin	126	228,650
1946	Assault	W. Mehrtens	126	96,400	1980	Genuine Risk	J. Vasquez	121	250,550
1947	Jet Pilot	E. Guerin	126	92,160	1981	Pleasant Colony	J. Velasquez	126	317,200
1948	Citation	E. Arcaro	126	83,400	1982	Gato del Sol	E. Delahoussaye	126	417,600
1949	Ponde	S. Brooks	126	91,600	1983	Sunny's Halo	E. Delahoussaye	126	426,000
1950	Middleground	W. Boland	126	92,650	1984	Swale	L. Pincay, Jr.	126	537,400
1951	Count Turf	C. McCreary	126	98,050	1985	Spend a Buck	A. Cordero, Jr.	126	406,800
1952	Hill Gail	E. Arcaro	126	96,300	1986	Ferdinand	W. Shoemaker	126	609,400

Year	Winner	Jockey	Wt.	Win val.	Year	Winner	Jockey	Wt.	Win val.
1987	Alysheba	C. McCarron	126	$618,600	1994	Go For Gin	C. McCarron	126	$628,800
1988	Winning Colors	G. Stevens	121	611,200	1995	Thunder Gulch	G. Stevens	126	707,400
1989	Sunday Silence	P. Valenzuela	126	574,200	1996	Grindstone	J. Bailey	126	869,800
1990	Unbridled	C. Perret	126	581,000	1997	Silver Charm	G. Stevens	126	700,000
1991	Strike the Gold	C. Antley	126	655,800	1998	Real Quiet	K. Desormeaux	126	738,800
1992	Lil E. Tee	P. Day	126	724,800	1999	Charismatic	C. Antley	126	886,200
1993	Sea Hero	J. Bailey	126	735,900					

1. Dancer's Image finished first but was disqualified after traces of drug were found in his system.

PREAKNESS STAKES
Pimlico; 3-year-olds; 1³⁄₁₆ miles.

Year	Winner	Jockey	Wt.	Win val.	Year	Winner	Jockey	Wt.	Win val.
1919	Sir Barton	J. Loftus	126	$24,500	1960	Bally Ache	R. Ussery	126	$121,000
1920	Man o' War	C. Kummer	126	(¹)	1961	Carry Back	J. Sellers	126	126,200
1921	Broomspun	F. Coltiletti	126	(¹)	1962	Greek Money	J. Rotz	126	135,800
1922	Pillory	L. Morris	126	(¹)	1963	Candy Spots	W. Shoemaker	126	127,500
1923	Vigil	B. Marinelli	126	(¹)	1964	Northern Dancer	W. Hartack	126	124,200
1924	Nellie Morse	J. Merimee	126	(¹)	1965	Tom Rolfe	R. Turcotte	126	128,100
1925	Coventry	C. Kummer	126	(¹)	1966	Kauai King	D. Brumfield	126	129,000
1926	Display	J. Maiben	126	(¹)	1967	Damascus	W. Shoemaker	126	141,500
1927	Bostonian	W. Abel	126	(¹)	1968	Forward Pass	I. Valenzuela	126	142,700
1928	Victorian	S. Workman	126	(¹)	1969	Majestic Prince	W. Hartack	126	129,500
1929	Dr. Freeland	L. Schaefer	126	(¹)	1970	Personality	E. Belmonte	126	151,300
1930	Gallant Fox	E. Sande	126	51,925	1971	Canonero II	G. Avila	126	137,400
1931	Mate	G. Ellis	126	48,225	1972	Bee Bee Bee	E. Nelson	126	135,300
1932	Burgoo King	E. James	126	50,375	1973	Secretariat	R. Turcotte	126	129,900
1933	Head Play	C. Kurtsinger	126	26,850	1974	Little Current	M. Rivera	126	156,000
1934	High Quest	R. Jones	126	25,175	1975	Master Derby	D. McHargue	126	158,100
1935	Omaha	W. Saunders	126	25,325	1976	Elocutionist	J. Lively	126	129,700
1936	Bold Venture	G. Woolf	126	27,325	1977	Seattle Slew	J. Cruguet	126	138,600
1937	War Admiral	C. Kurtsinger	126	45,600	1978	Affirmed	S. Cauthen	126	136,200
1938	Dauber	M. Peters	126	51,875	1979	Spectacular Bid	R. Franklin	126	165,300
1939	Challedon	G. Seabo	126	53,710	1980	Codex	A. Cordero	126	180,600
1940	Bimelech	F.A. Smith	126	53,230	1981	Pleasant Colony	J. Velasquez	126	270,800
1941	Whirlaway	E. Arcaro	126	49,365	1982	Aloma's Ruler	J. Kaenel	126	209,900
1942	Alsab	B. James	126	58,175	1983	Deputed	D. Miller	126	251,200
1943	Count Fleet	J. Longden	126	43,190		Testamony			
1944	Pensive	C. McCreary	126	60,075	1984	Gate Dancer	A. Cordero	126	243,600
1945	Polynesian	W.D. Wright	126	66,170	1985	Tank's Prospect	P. Day	126	423,200
1946	Assault	W. Mehrtens	126	96,620	1986	Snow Chief	A. Solis	126	411,900
1947	Faultless	D. Dodson	126	98,005	1987	Alysheba	C. McCarron	126	421,100
1948	Citation	E. Arcaro	126	91,870	1988	Risen Star	E. Delahoussaye	126	413,700
1949	Capot	T. Atkinson	126	79,985	1989	Sunday Silence	P. Valenzuela	126	438,230
1950	Hill Prince	E. Arcaro	126	56,115	1990	Summer Squall	P. Day	126	445,900
1951	Bold	E. Arcaro	126	83,110	1991	Hansel	J. Bailey	126	432,770
1952	Blue Man	C. McCreary	126	86,135	1992	Pine Bluff	C. McCarron	126	484,120
1953	Native Dancer	E. Guerin	126	65,200	1993	Prairie Bayou	M. Smith	126	471,835
1954	Hasty Road	J. Adams	126	91,600	1994	Tabasco Cat	P. Day	126	447,720
1955	Nashua	E. Arcaro	126	67,550	1995	Timber Country	P. Day	126	446,810
1956	Fabius	W. Hartack	126	84,250	1996	Louis Quatorze	P. Day	126	458,120
1957	Bold Ruler	E. Arcaro	126	65,250	1997	Silver Charm	G. Stevens	126	488,150
1958	Tim Tam	I. Valenzuela	126	97,900	1998	Real Quiet	K. Desormeaux	126	650,000
1959	Royal Orbit	W. Harmatz	126	136,200	1999	Charismatic	C. Antley	126	650,000

1. Data not available.

BELMONT STAKES
Belmont Park; 3-year-olds; 1½ miles.

Run at Jerome Park 1867 to 1890; at Morris Park 1890–94; at Belmont Park 1905–62; at Aqueduct 1963–67. Distance 1⅝ miles prior to 1874; reduced to 1½ miles, 1874; reduced to 1¼ miles, 1890; reduced to 1⅛ miles, 1893; increased to 1¼ miles, 1895; increased to 1⅜ miles, 1896; reduced to 1¼ miles in 1904; increased to 1½ miles, 1926.

Year	Winner	Jockey	Wt.	Win val.	Year	Winner	Jockey	Wt.	Win val.
1919	Sir Barton	J. Loftus	126	$11,950	1923	Zev	E. Sande	126	(¹)
1920	Man o' War	C. Kummer	126	(¹)	1924	Mad Play	E. Sande	126	(¹)
1921	Grey Lag	E. Sande	126	(¹)	1925	American Flag	A. Johnson	126	(¹)
1922	Pillory	C.H. Miller	126	(¹)	1926	Crusader	A. Johnson	126	(¹)

Year	Winner	Jockey	Wt.	Win val.	Year	Winner	Jockey	Wt.	Win val.
1927	Chance Shot	E. Sande	126	(1)	1965	Hail to All	J. Sellers	126	$104,150
1928	Vito	C. Kummer	126	(1)	1966	Amberoid	W. Boland	126	117,700
1929	Blue Larkspur	M. Garner	126	(1)	1967	Damascus	W. Shoemaker	126	104,950
1930	Gallant Fox	E. Sande	126	$66,040	1968	Stage Door Johnny	H. Gustines	126	117,700
1931	Twenty Grand	C. Kurtsinger	126	58,770					
1932	Faireno	T. Malley	126	55,120	1969	Arts and Letters	B. Baeza	126	104,050
1933	Hurryoff	M. Garner	126	49,490	1970	High Echelon	J. Rotz	126	115,000
1934	Peace Chance	W.D. Wright	126	43,410	1971	Pass Catcher	R. Blum	126	97,710
1935	Omaha	W. Saunders	126	35,480	1972	Riva Ridge	R. Turcotte	126	93,540
1936	Granville	J. Stout	126	29,800	1973	Secretariat	R. Turcotte	126	90,120
1937	War Admiral	C. Kurtsinger	126	38,020	1974	Little Current	M. Rivera	126	101,970
1938	Pasteurized	J. Stout	126	34,530	1975	Avatar	W. Shoemaker	126	116,160
1939	Johnstown	J. Stout	126	37,020	1976	Bold Forbes	A. Cordero, Jr.	126	117,000
1940	Bimelech	F.A. Smith	126	35,030	1977	Seattle Slew	J. Cruguet	126	109,080
1941	Whirlaway	E. Arcaro	126	39,770	1978	Affirmed	S. Cauthen	126	110,580
1942	Shut Out	E. Arcaro	126	44,520	1979	Coastal	R. Hernandez	126	161,400
1943	Count Fleet	J. Longden	126	35,340	1980	Temperence Hill	E. Maple	126	176,220
1944	Bounding Home	G.L. Smith	126	55,000	1981	Summing	G. Martens	126	170,580
1945	Pavot	E. Arcaro	126	56,675	1982	Conquistador Cielo	L. Pincay, Jr.	126	159,720
1946	Assault	W. Mehrtens	126	75,400					
1947	Phalanx	R. Donoso	126	78,900	1983	Caveat	L. Pincay, Jr.	126	215,100
1948	Citation	E. Arcaro	126	77,700	1984	Swale	L. Pincay, Jr.	126	310,020
1949	Capot	T. Atkinson	126	60,900	1985	Creme Fraiche	E. Maple	126	307,740
1950	Middleground	W. Boland	126	61,350	1986	Danzig Connection	C. McCarron	126	338,640
1951	Counterpoint	D. Gorman	126	82,000					
1952	One Count	E. Arcaro	126	82,400	1987	Bet Twice	C. Perret	126	329,160
1953	Native Dancer	E. Guerin	126	82,500	1988	Risen Star	E. Delahoussaye	126	303,720
1954	High Gun	E. Guerin	126	89,000	1989	Easy Goer	P. Day	126	413,520
1955	Nashua	E. Arcaro	126	83,700	1990	Go And Go	M. Kinane	126	411,600
1956	Needles	D. Erb	126	83,600	1991	Hansel	J. Bailey	126	417,480
1957	Gallant Man	W. Shoemaker	126	77,300	1992	A.P. Indy	E. Delahoussaye	126	458,880
1958	Cavan	P. Anderson	126	73,440	1993	Colonial Affair	J. Krone	126	444,450
1959	Sword Dancer	W. Shoemaker	126	93,525	1994	Tabasco Cat	P. Day	126	392,280
1960	Celtic Ash	W. Hartack	126	96,785	1995	Thunder Gulch	G.Stevens	126	415,440
1961	Sherluck	B. Baeza	126	104,900	1996	Editor's Note	R. Douglas	126	437,880
1962	Jaipur	W. Shoemaker	126	109,550	1997	Touch Gold	C. McCarron	126	432,600
1963	Chateaugay	B. Baeza	126	101,700	1998	Victory Gallop	G. Stevens	126	600,000
1964	Quadrangle	M. Ycaza	126	110,850	1999	Lemon Drop Kid	J. Santos	126	600,000

1. Data not available.

TRIPLE CROWN RACES—1999

Kentucky Derby (Churchill Downs, Louisville, Ky., May 1, 1999). Gross purse: $1,000,000. Distance: 1¼ miles. Order of finish: 1. Charismatic (Antley), mutuel returns: $64.60, $27.80, $14.40. 2. Menifee (Day), $8.40, $5.80. 3. Cat Thief (Smith), $5.80. 4. Prime Timber (Flores). 5. Excellent Meeting (Desormeaux). 6. Kimberlite Pipe (Albarado). 7. Worldly Manner (Bailey). 8. K One King (Solis). 9. Lemon Drop Kid (Santos). 10. Answer Lively (Perret). 11. General Challenge (Stevens). 12. Ecton Park (Davis). 13. Desert Hero (Nakatani). 14. Stephen Got Even (McCarron). 15. Valhol (Martinez). 16. First American (Delahoussaye). 17. Adonis (Chavez). 18. Vicar (Sellers). 19. Three Ring (Velazquez). Winner's purse: $886,200. Margin of victory: neck. Time of race: 2.03.29.

Preakness Stakes (Pimlico, Baltimore Md., May 15, 1999). Gross purse: $1,000,000. Distance: 1 ³⁄₁₆ miles. Order of finish: 1. Charismatic (Antley), mutuel returns: $18.80, $7.60, $5.80. 2. Menifee (Day), $3.60, $3.20. 3. Badge (Luzzi), $18.80. 4. Stephen Got Even (Stevens). 5. Patience Game (Nakatani). 6. Adonis (Chavez). 7. Cat Thief (Smith). 8. Kimberlite Pipe (Sellers). 9. Valhol (Prado). 10. Vicar (Albarado). Winner's purse: $650,000. Margin of victory: 1½ lengths. Time of race: 1:55⅕.

Belmont Stakes (Belmont Park, Belmont N.Y., June 5, 1999). Gross purse: $1,000,000. Distance: 1½ miles. Order of finish: 1. Lemon Drop Kid (Santos), mutuel returns: $61.50, $26.00, $10.60. 2. Vision and Verse (Castillo), $44.40, $17.00. 3. Charismatic (Antley), $3.60. 4. Best of Luck (Samyn). 5. Stephen Got Even (Sellers).

6. Patience Game (Desormeaux). 7. Silverbulletday (Bailey). 8. Menifee (Day). 9. Pineaff (LeJuene). 10. Prime Directive (Smith). 11. Teletable (Velazquez). 12. Adonis (Chavez). Winner's purse: $600,000. Margin of victory: Head. Time of race: 2:27⅘.

ECLIPSE AWARDS—1998

(Presented Feb. 16, 1999)

Horse of the Year	Skip Away
2-year-old male	Answer Lively
2-year-old female	Silverbulletday
3-year-old male	Real Quiet
3-year-old female	Banshee Breeze
Older male horse	Skip Away
Older female horse	Escena
Male turf horse	Buck's Boy
Female turf horse	Fiji
Sprinter	Reraise
Steeplechaser	Flat Top
Owner	Frank Stronach
Breeders	John and Betty Mabee
Trainer	Bob Baffert
Jockey	Gary Stevens
Apprentice jockey	Shaun Bridgmohan
Award of Merit	D. G. Van Clief, Jr.
Special Award	Oak Tree

(Based on vote by the Thoroughbred Racing Associations, the *Daily Racing Form*, and the National Turf Writers Association.)

Track and Field

WORLD RECORDS—MEN

(Through Sept. 20, 1999)

Recognized by the International Athletic Federation. The I.A.A.F. decided late in 1976 not to recognize records in yards except for the one-mile run. The I.A.A.F. also requires automatic timing for all records for races of 400 meters or less.

Event	Record	Holder	Home country	Where made	Date
Running					
100 m	0:09.79	Maurice Greene	United States	Athens, Greece	June 16, 1999
200 m	0:19.32	Michael Johnson	United States	Atlanta, Ga.	Aug. 1, 1996
400 m	0:43.18	Michael Johnson	United States	Seville, Spain	Aug. 26, 1999
800 m	1:41.11	Wilson Kipketer	Denmark	Köln, Germany	Aug. 24, 1997
1,000 m	2:12.18	Sebastian Coe	England	Oslo, Norway	July 11, 1981
1,500 m	3:26.00	Hicham El Guerrouj	Morocco	Rome, Italy	July 14, 1998
1 mile	3:43.13	Hicham El Guerrouj	Morocco	Rome, Italy	July 7, 1999
2,000 m	4:47.88	Noureddine Morceli	Algeria	Paris, France	July 3, 1995
3,000 m	7:20.67	Daniel Komen	Kenya	Rieti, Italy	Sept. 1, 1996
3,000 m steeplechase	7:55.72	Bernard Barmasai	Kenya	Köln, Germany	Aug. 24, 1997
5,000 m	12:39.36	Haile Gebrselassie	Ethiopia	Helsinki, Finland	June 13, 1998
10,000 m	26:22.75	Haile Gebrselassie	Ethiopia	Hengelo, Netherlands	June 1, 1998
20,000 m	56:55.60	Arturo Barrios	Mexico	La Fleche, France	March 30, 1991
25,000 m	1:13:55.80	Toshihiko Seko	Japan	Christchurch, N.Z.	March 22, 1981
30,000 m	1:29:18.80	Toshihiko Seko	Japan	Christchurch, N.Z.	March 22, 1981
1 hour	21,101 m	Arturo Barrios	Mexico	La Fleche, France	March 30, 1991
Marathon[1]	2:06.05	Ronaldo Da Costa	Brazil	Berlin, Germany	Sept. 20, 1998
Walking					
20,000 m	1:17:25.60	Bernardo Segura	Mexico	Bergen, Norway	May 7, 1994
30,000 m	2:01:44.10	Maurizio Damilano	Italy	Cuneo, Italy	Oct. 3, 1992
50,000 m	3:40:57.90	Thierry Toutain	France	Héricourt, France	Sept. 29, 1996
2 hours	29,572 m	Maurizio Damilano	Italy	Cuneo, Italy	Oct. 3, 1992
Hurdles					
110 m	0:12.91	Colin Jackson	Great Britain	Stuttgart, Germany	Aug. 20, 1993
400 m	0:46.78	Kevin Young	United States	Barcelona, Spain	Aug. 6, 1992
Relay races					
400 m (4 × 100)	0:37.40	National Team	United States	Barcelona, Spain	Aug. 8, 1992
	0:37.40	National Team	United States	Stuttgart, Germany	Aug. 21, 1993
800 m (4 × 200)	1:18.68	Santa Monica T.C.	United States	Walnut, Calif.	April 17, 1994
1,600 m (4 × 400)	2:54.20	National Team	United States	New York, N.Y.	July 22, 1998
3,200 m (4 × 800)	7:03.89	National Team	Britain	London	Aug. 30, 1982
Field events					
High jump	2.45 m	Javier Sotomayor	Cuba	Salamanca, Spain	July 27, 1993
Long jump	8.95 m	Mike Powell	United States	Tokyo, Japan	Aug. 30, 1991
Triple jump	18.29 m	Jonathan Edwards	Great Britain	Goteborg, Sweden	Aug. 7, 1995
Pole vault	6.14 m	Sergey Bubka	Ukraine	Sestriere, Italy	July 31, 1994
Shot-put	23.12 m	Randy Barnes	United States	Los Angeles	May 20, 1990
Discus throw	74.08 m	Jürgen Schult	East Germany	Neubrandenburg, E. Germany	June 6, 1986
Hammer throw	86.74 m	Yuriy Sedykh	U.S.S.R.	Stuttgart, Germany	Aug. 30, 1986
Javelin throw	98.48 m	Jan Zelezny	Czech Republic	Jena, Germany	May 25, 1996
Decathlon	8,994 pts.	Tomás Dvorák	Czech Republic	Prague, Czech Republic	July 4,1999

1. Not recognized by I.A.A.F. as world record, but considered to be "world best performance."

WORLD RECORDS—WOMEN

(Through Sept. 20, 1999)

Event	Record	Holder	Home country	Where made	Date
Running					
100 m	0:10.49	Florence Griffith-Joyner	United States	Indianapolis, Ind.	July 16, 1988
200 m	0:21.34	Florence Griffith-Joyner	United States	Seoul, South Korea	Sept. 29, 1988
400 m	0:47.60	Martina Koch	East Germany	Canberra, Australia	Oct. 6, 1985
800 m	1:53.28	Jarmila Kratochvilova	Czechoslovakia	Munich, W. Germany	July 26, 1983
1000 m	2:28.98	Svetlana Masterkova	Russia	Brussels, Belgium	Aug. 23, 1996
1,500 m	3:50.46	Qu Yunxia	China	Beijing, China	Sept. 11, 1993
1 mile	4:12.56	Svetlana Masterkova	Russia	Zurich, Switzerland	Aug. 14, 1996
2,000 m	5:25.36	Sonia O'Sullivan	Ireland	Edinburgh, Scotland	July 8, 1994
3,000 m	8:06.11	Wang Junxia	China	Beijing, China	Sept. 13, 1993
5,000 m	14:28.09	Jiang Bo	China	Shanghai, China	Oct. 23, 1997
10,000 m	29:31.78	Wang Junxia	China	Beijing, China	Sept. 8, 1993
20,000 m	1:06:48.80	Izumi Maki	Japan	Amagasaki, Japan	Sept. 19, 1993

Event	Record	Holder	Home country	Where made	Date
25,000 m	1:29:29.20	Karolina Szabo	Hungary	Budapest, Hungary	April 22, 1988
30,000 m	1:47:05.60	Karolina Szabo	Hungary	Budapest, Hungary	April 22, 1988
1 hour	18.340	Tegla Loroupe	Kenya	Borgholzhausen, Germany	July 8, 1999
Marathon[1]	2:20:47.0	Tegla Loroupe	Kenya	Rotterdam, The Netherlands	April 19 1999

Walking

5,000 m	20:13.26	Kerry Saxby-Junna	Australia	Hobart, Australia	Feb. 25, 1996
10,000 m	41:56.23	Nadezhda Ryashkina	Russia	Seattle, Wash.	July 24, 1990

Hurdles

100-m hurdles	0:12.21	Yordanka Donkova	Bulgaria	Stara Zagora, Bulgaria	Aug. 20, 1988
400 m	0:52.61	Kim Batten	United States	Goteborg, Sweden	Aug. 11, 1995

Relay races

400 m (4 × 100)	0:41.37	East Germany	E. Germany	Canberra, Australia	Oct. 6, 1985
800 m (4 × 200)	1:28.15	East Germany	E. Germany	Jena, E. Germany	Aug. 9, 1980
1,600 m (4 × 400)	3:15.17	U.S.S.R	U.S.S.R.	Seoul, South Korea	Oct. 1, 1988
3,200 m (4 × 800)	7:50.17	U.S.S.R.	U.S.S.R.	Moscow, U.S.S.R.	Aug. 5, 1984

Field events

High jump	2.09 m	Stefka Kostadinova	Bulgaria	Rome, Italy	Aug. 30, 1987
Pole vault	4.60 m	Emma George	Australia	Sydney, Australia	Feb. 20, 1999
	4.60 m	Stacy Dragila	United States	Seville, Spain	Aug. 8, 1999
Long jump	7.52 m	Galina Chistyakova	U.S.S.R.	Leningrad, Russia	June 11, 1988
Triple jump	15.50 m	Inessa Kravets	Ukraine	Goteborg, Sweden	Aug. 10, 1995
Shot-put	22.63 m	Natalya Lisovskaya	U.S.S.R.	Moscow, Russia	June 7, 1987
Discus throw	76.80 m	Gabriele Reinsch	East Germany	Neubrandenburg, E. Ger.	July 9, 1988
Hammer	75.97 m	Mihaela Melinte	Romania	Clermont-Ferrand, France	May 13, 1999
Javelin throw	68.19 m	Trine Solberg-Hattestad	Norway	Bergen, Norway	July 28, 1999
Heptathlon	7,291 pts	Jackie Joyner-Kersee	United States	Seoul, South Korea	Sept. 24, 1988

1. Not recognized by I.A.A.F. as world record, but considered to be "world best performance."

AMERICAN RECORDS—MEN

(Through Sept. 20, 1999)

Event	Record	Holder	Where Made	Date
Running				
100 m	0:09.79	Maurice Greene	Athens, Greece	June 16, 1999
200 m	0:19.32	Michael Johnson	Atlanta, Ga.	Aug. 1, 1996
400 m	0:43.18	Michael Johnson	Seville, Spain	Aug. 26, 1999
800 m	1:42.60	Johnny Gray	Koblenz, W. Ger.	Aug. 29, 1985
1,000 m	2:13.90	Richard Wohlhuter	Oslo, Norway	July 30, 1974
1,500 m	3:29.77	Sydney Maree	Cologne, W. Ger.	Aug. 25, 1985
1 mile	3:47.69	Steve Scott	Oslo, Norway	July 7, 1982
2,000 m	4:54.71	Steve Scott	Ingelhelm, W. Ger.	Aug. 31, 1982
3,000 m	7:31.69	Bob Kennedy	Brussels, Belgium	Aug. 23, 1996
5,000 m	12:58.21	Bob Kennedy	Zurich, Switzerland	Aug. 14, 1996
10,000 m	27:20.56	Mark Nenow	Brussels	Sept. 5, 1986
20,000 m	58:15.00	Bill Rodgers	Boston, Mass.	Aug. 9, 1977
25,000 m	1:14:11.80	Bill Rodgers	Saratoga, Cal.	Feb. 21, 1979
30,000 m	1:31:49.00	Bill Rodgers	Saratoga, Cal.	Feb. 21, 1979
1 hour	12 mi., 1,351 yds	Bill Rodgers	Boston, Mass.	Aug. 9, 1977
3,000-m steeplechase	8:09.17	Henry Marsh	Koblenz, W. Ger.	Aug. 29, 1985
Hurdles				
110 m	0:12.92	Roger Kingdom	Berlin	Aug. 16, 1989
		Allen Johnson	Brussels, Belgium	Aug. 23, 1996
400 m	0:46.78	Kevin Young	Barcelona	Aug. 6, 1992
Relay races				
400 m (4 × 100)	0:37.40	USA National Team	Stuttgart, Germany	Aug. 21, 1993
800 m (4 × 200)	1:18.68	Santa Monica T.C.	Walnut, Calif.	April 17, 1994
1,600 m (4 × 400)	2:54.20	USA National Team	New York, N.Y.	July 22, 1998
3,200 m (4 × 800)	7:06.50	Santa Monica T.C.	Walnut, Calif.	Apr. 26, 1986
Field events				
High jump	7 ft. 10½ in.	Charles Austin	Zurich	Aug. 7, 1991
Long jump	29 ft. 4½ in.	Mike Powell	Tokyo, Japan	Aug. 30, 1991
Triple jump	59 ft. 4 in.	Kenny Harrison	Atlanta, Ga.	July 27, 1996
Pole vault	19 ft. 9 in.	Jeff Hartwig	Eugene, Ore.	June 27, 1999
Shot-put	75 ft. 10¼ in.	Randy Barnes	Los Angeles	May 20, 1990
Discus throw	237 ft. 4 in.	Ben Plucknett	Stockholm, Swe.	July 7, 1981
Javelin throw	285 ft. 10 in.	Tom Pukstys	Jena	May 25, 1997
Hammer throw	270 ft. 9 in.	Lance Deal	Milan, Italy	July 9, 1996
Decathlon	8,891 pts	Dan O'Brien	Talence, France	Sept. 4–5, 1992

AMERICAN RECORDS—WOMEN
(Through Sept. 20, 1999)

Event	Record	Holder	Where Made	Date
Running				
100 m	0:10.49	Florence Griffith-Joyner	Indianapolis, Ind.	July 16, 1988
200 m	0:21.56	Florence Griffith-Joyner	Seoul, South Korea	Oct. 1, 1988
400 m	0:48.83	Valerie Brisco-Hooks	Los Angeles, Cal.	Aug. 6, 1984
800 m	1:56.40	Jearl Miles-Clark	Zürich, Switzerland	Aug. 11, 1999
1,500 m	3:57.12	Mary Decker Slaney	Stockholm, Swe.	July 26, 1983
1,000 m	2:34.8	Mary Decker Slaney	Eugene, Ore.	July 4, 1985
1 mile	4:16.71	Mary Decker Slaney	Zurich	Aug. 21, 1985
3,000 m	8:29.69	Mary Decker Slaney	Cologne	Aug. 25, 1985
5,000 m	14:52.49	Regina Jacobs	Brunswick, Maine	July 4, 1998
10,000 m	31:28.92	Francie L. Smith	Austin, Texas	April 4, 1991
Hurdles				
100 m hurdles	0:12.37	Gail Devers	Seville, Spain	Aug. 28, 1999
400 m hurdles	0:52.61	Kim Batten	Gothenburg, Sweden	Aug. 11, 1995
Relay races				
400 m (4 × 100)	41.47	U.S.A. National Team	Athens, Greece	Aug. 9, 1997
800 m (4 × 200)	1:30.20	Nike International	Philadelphia, Pa.	Apr. 26, 1997
1,600 m (4 × 400)	3:15.51	U.S. Olympic Team	Seoul, South Korea	Oct. 1, 1988
Field events				
Pole vault	15 ft. ¼ in.	Stacy Dragila	Seville, Spain	Aug. 21, 1999
High jump	6 ft. 8 in.	Louise Ritter	Austin, Tex.	July 9, 1988
Long jump	24 ft. 7 in.	Jackie Joyner-Kersee	New York, N.Y.	May 22, 1994
Triple jump	47 ft. 3½ in.	Sheila Hudson	Stockholm, Sweden	July 8, 1996
Shot-put	66 ft. 2½ in.	Ramon Pagel	San Diego, Calif.	June 25, 1988
Discus throw	230 ft. 2 in.	Dawn Ellerbe	Laramie, Wyo.	May 15, 1999
Hammer throw	210 ft. 8 in.	Dawn Ellerbe	Walnut, Calif.	April 19, 1997
Javelin throw	227 ft. 5 in.	Kate Schmidt	Furth, W. Ger.	Sept. 10, 1977
Heptathlon	7,291 pts	Jackie Joyner-Kersee	Seoul, South Korea	Sept. 23–24, 1988

HISTORY OF THE RECORD FOR THE MILE RUN

Source: USA Track & Field

Time	Athlete	Country	Year	Location
4:26.0	Walter Slade	England	1874	England
4:24.5	Walter Slade	England	1875	London
4:23.2	Walter George	England	1880	London
4:21.4	Walter George	England	1882	London
4:18.4	Walter George	England	1884	Birmingham, England
4:18.2	Fred Bacon	Scotland	1894	Edinburgh, Scotland
4:17.0	Fred Bacon	Scotland	1895	London
4:15.6	Thomas Conneff	United States	1895	Travers Island, N.Y.
4:15.4	John Paul Jones	United States	1911	Cambridge, Mass.
4:14.4	John Paul Jones	United States	1913	Cambridge, Mass.
4:12.6	Norman Taber	United States	1915	Cambridge, Mass.
4:10.4	Paavo Nurmi	Finland	1923	Stockholm
4:09.2	Jules Ladoumegue	France	1931	Paris
4:07.6	Jack Lovelock	New Zealand	1933	Princeton, N.J.
4:06.8	Glenn Cunningham	United States	1934	Princeton, N.J.
4:06.4	Sydney Wooderson	England	1937	London
4:06.2	Gundar Hägg	Sweden	1942	Goteborg, Sweden
4:06.2	Arne Andersson	Sweden	1942	Stockholm
4:04.6	Gunder Hägg	Sweden	1942	Stockholm
4:02.6	Arne Andersson	Sweden	1943	Goteborg, Sweden
4:01.6	Arne Andersson	Sweden	1944	Malmo, Sweden
4:01.4	Gunder Hägg	Sweden	1945	Malmo, Sweden
3:59.4	Roger Bannister	England	1954	Oxford, England
3:58.0	John Landy	Australia	1954	Turku, Finland
3:57.2	Derek Ibbotson	England	1957	London
3:54.5	Herb Elliott	Australia	1958	Dublin
3:54.4	Peter Snell	New Zealand	1962	Wanganui, N.Z.
3:54.1	Peter Snell	New Zealand	1964	Auckland, N.Z.
3:53.6	Michel Jazy	France	1965	Rennes, France
3:51.3	Jim Ryun	United States	1966	Berkeley, Calif.
3:51.1	Jim Ryun	United States	1967	Bakersfield, Calif.
3:51.0	Filbert Bayi	Tanzania	1975	Kingston, Jamaica
3:49.4	John Walker	New Zealand	1975	Goteborg, Sweden
3:49.0	Sebastian Coe	England	1979	Oslo
3:48.8	Steve Ovett	England	1980	Oslo
3:48.53	Sebastian Coe	England	1981	Zurich, Switzerland

Time	Athlete	Country	Year	Location
3:48.40	Steve Ovett	England	1981	Koblenz, W. Ger.
3:47.33	Sebastian Coe	England	1981	Brussels
3:46.31	Steve Cram	England	1985	Oslo
3:44.39	Noureddine Morceli	Algeria	1993	Rieti, Italy
3:43.13	Hicham El Guerrouj	Morocco	1999	Rome, Italy

TOP TEN WORLD'S FASTEST OUTDOOR MILES

Source: USA Track & Field

Time	Athlete	Country	Date	Location
3:43.13	Hicham El Guerrouj	Morocco	July 27, 1999	Rome, Italy
3:44.39	Nouraddine Morceli	Algeria	Sept. 5, 1993	Rieti, Italy
3:46.31	Steve Cram	England	July 27, 1985	Oslo
3:47.33	Sebastian Coe	England	Aug. 28, 1981	Brussels
3:47.69	Steve Scott	United States	July 7, 1982	Oslo
3:47.79	Jose Gonzalez	Spain	July 27, 1985	Oslo
3:48.40	Steve Ovett	England	Aug. 26, 1981	Koblenz, W. Ger.
3:48.53	Sebastian Coe	England	Aug. 19, 1981	Zurich
3:48.53	Steve Scott	United States	June 26, 1982	Oslo
3:48.8	Steve Ovett	England	July 1, 1980	Oslo

NOTE: Professional marks not included.

TOP TEN WORLD'S FASTEST INDOOR MILES

Source: USA Track & Field

Time	Athlete	Country	Date	Location
3:48.45	Hicham El Guerrouj	Morocco	Feb, 12, 1997	Gent, Netherlands
3:49.78	Eamonn Coghlan	Ireland	Feb. 27, 1983	East Rutherford, N.J.
3:50.6	Eamonn Coghlan	Ireland	Feb. 20, 1981	San Diego
3:50.7	Noureddine Morceli	Algeria	Feb. 20, 1993	Birmingham, England
3:50.94	Marcus O'Sullivan	Ireland	Feb. 13, 1988	East Rutherford, N.J.
3:51.2	Ray Flynn[1]	Ireland	Feb. 27, 1983	East Rutherford, N.J.
3:51.66	Marcus O'Sullivan	Ireland	Feb. 10, 1989	East Rutherford, N.J.
3:51.8	Steve Scott[1]	United States	Feb. 20, 1981	San Diego
3:52.28	Steve Scott[2]	United States	Feb. 27, 1983	East Rutherford, N.J.
3:52.30	Frank O'Mara	Ireland	Feb. 1986	New York

1. Finished second. 2. Finished third.

IAAF WORLD CHAMPIONSHIPS, 1999

(Seville, Spain, Aug. 21–29, 1999)

Men's Events

100m—Maurice Greene, United States	09.80
200m—Maurice Greene, United States	19.90
400m—Michael Johnson, United States	43.18
800m—Wilson Kipketer, Denmark	1:43.30
1,500m—Hicham El Guerrouj, Morocco	3:27.65
5,000m—Salah Hissou, Morocco	12:58.13
10,000m—Haile Gebrselassie, Ethiopia	27:57.27
Marathon—Abel Antón, Spain	2:13.36
3,000m steeplechase—Christopher Koskei, Kenya	8:11.76
110m hurdles—Colin Jackson, Great Britain	13.04
400m hurdles—Fabrizio Mori, Italy	47.72
High jump—Vyacheslav Voronin, Russia	2.37m
Pole vault—Maksim Tarasov, Russia	6.02m
Long jump—Iván Pedroso, Cuba	8.56m
Triple jump—Charles Michael Friedek, Germany	17.59m
Shot put—C. J. Hunter, United States	21.79m
Discus throw—Anthony Washington, United States	69.08m
Hammer throw—Karsten Kobs, Germany	80.24m
Javelin throw—Aki Parviainen, Finland	89.52m
4 x 100m—United States	37.59
4 x 400m—United States	2:56.45
Decathlon—Tomás Dvorák, Czech Republic	8,744 pts.

Women's Events

100m—Marion Jones, United States	10.70
200m—Inger Miller, United States	21.77
400m—Cathy Freeman, Australia	49.67
800m—Ludmila Formanová, Czech Republic	1:56.68
1,500m—Svetlana Masterkova, Russia	3:59.53
5,000m—Gabriela Szabo, Romania	14:41.82
10,000m—Gete Wami, Ethiopia	30:24.56
Marathon—Song-Ok Jong, North Korea	2:26.59
100m hurdles—Gail Devers, United States	12.37
400m hurdles—Daimi Pernia, Cuba	52.89
High jump—Inga Babakova, Ukraine	1.99m
Pole vault—Stacy Dragila, United States	4.60m
Long jump—Niurka Montalvo, Spain	7.06m
Triple jump—Paraskeví Tsiamíta, Greece	14.88m
Shot put—Astrid Kumbernuss, Germany	19.85m
Discus throw—Franka Dietzsch, Germany	68.14m
Hammer throw—Mihaela Melinte, Romania	75.20m
Javelin throw—Mirela Manjani-Tzelili, Greece	67.09m
4 x 100m—Bahamas	41.92
4 x 400m—Russia	3:21.98
Heptathlon—Eunice Barber, France	6,861 pts.

1999 USA OUTDOOR CHAMPIONSHIPS

(Eugene, Ore., June 24–27, 1999)

Men's Events

100m—Dennis Mitchell, Unattached	9.97
200m—Maurice Greene, Nike	19.93
400m—Jerome Young, Adidas	44.24
800m—Khadevis Robinson SMTC	1:45.92
1,500m—Steve Holman, Nike Inter.	3:39.21
5,000m—Adam Goucher, Team Fila	13:25.59
10,000m—Alan Culpepper, Adidas	28:22.46
110m hurdles—Mark Crear, God Speed TC	13.09
400m hurdles—Angelo Taylor, Nike	48.49
3,000m steeplechase—Pascal Dobert, Nike Inter.	8:21.48
High jump—Charles Austin, Unattached	2.28m
Pole vault—Jeff Hartwig, Nike Inter.	6.02m
Long jump—Kevin Dilworth, Adidas	8.12m
Triple jump—LaMark Carter, Nike	17.15m
Shot put—John Godina, Reebok–Bruin	22.02m
Discus throw—Anthony Washington, Team U.S. West	67.95m
Hammer throw—Lance Deal, NYAC	80.35m
Javelin throw—Tom Pukstys, Adidas	78.02m
Decathlon—Chris Huffins, Oakley	8,350 pts.
20,000m race walk—Curt Clausen, NYAC	1:23:34.00

Women's Events

100m—Inger Miller, Nike	10.96
200m—Marion Jones, Nike	22.10
400m—Maicel Malone-Wallace, New Balance	51.29
800m—Jearl Miles-Clark, Reebok	1:59.47
1,500m—Regina Jacobs, Mizuno	4:02.41
5,000m—Regina Jacobs, Mizuno	15:24.80
10,000m—Libbie Hickman, Nike	31:41.33
100m hurdles—Gail Devers, Nike	12.54
400m hurdles—Sandra Glover, Unattached	54.95
3,000m steeplechase—Elizabeth Jackson, Brigham Young Univ.	10:07.23
High jump—Tisha Waller, HSI	1.99m
Pole vault—Stacy Dragila, Reebok	4.45m
Long jump—Dawn Burrell, U.S. Army	6.96m
Triple jump—Stacey Bowers, Baylor Univ.	13.66m
Shot put—Connie Price-Smith, Indiana Invaders	18.86m
Discus throw—Seiala Sua, Reebok-Bruin	62.08m
Hammer throw—Dawn Ellerbe, NYAC	64.75m
Javelin throw—Linda Bluetrich, M-F Athletic	55.53m
Heptathlon—Sheila Burrell, Unattached	6,101 pts.
20,000m race walk—Michelle Rohl, Moving Comf.	1:33:17.00

Tennis

Lawn tennis is a comparatively modern modification of the ancient game of court tennis. Major Walter Clopton Wingfield thought that something like court tennis might be played outdoors on lawns, and in December, 1873, at Nantclwyd, Wales, he introduced his new game under the name of *Sphairistike* at a lawn party. The game was a success and spread rapidly, but the name was a total failure and almost immediately disappeared when all the players and spectators began to refer to the new game as "lawn tennis." In the early part of 1874, a young lady named Mary Ewing Outerbridge returned from Bermuda to New York, bringing with her the implements and necessary equipment of the new game, which she had obtained from a British Army supply store in Bermuda. Miss Outerbridge and friends played the first game of lawn tennis in the United States on the grounds of the Staten Island Cricket and Baseball Club in the spring of 1874.

For a few years, the new game went along in haphazard fashion until about 1880, when standard measurements for the court and standard equipment within definite limits became the rule. In 1881, the U.S. Lawn Tennis Association (whose name was changed in 1975 to U.S. Tennis Association) was formed and conducted the first national championship at Newport, R.I. The international matches for the Davis Cup began with a series between the British and United States players on the courts of the Longwood Cricket Club, Chestnut Hill, Mass., in 1900, with the home players winning.

Professional tennis, which got its start in 1926 when the French star Suzanne Lenglen was paid $50,000 for a tour, received full recognition in 1968. Staid old Wimbledon, the London home of what are considered the world championships, let the pros compete. This decision ended a long controversy over open tennis and changed the format of the competition. The United States championships were also opened to the pros and the site of the event, long held at Forest Hills, N.Y., was shifted to the National Tennis Center in Flushing Meadows, N.Y., in 1978. Pro tours for men and women became worldwide in play that continued throughout the year.

DAVIS CUP CHAMPIONSHIPS

No matches in 1901, 1910, 1915–18, and 1940–45.

1900 United States 3, British Isles 0	1911 Australasia 5, United States 0	1924 United States 5, Australasia 0
1902 United States 3, British Isles 2	1912 British Isles 3, Australasia 2	1925 United States 5, France 0
1903 British Isles 4, United States 1	1913 United States 3, British Isles 2	1926 United States 4, France 1
1904 British Isles 5, Belgium 0	1914 Australasia 3, United States 2	1927 France 3, United States 2
1905 British Isles 5, United States 0	1919 Australasia 4, British Isles 1	1928 France 4, United States 1
1906 British Isles 5, United States 0	1920 United States 5, Australasia 0	1929 France 3, United States 2
1907 Australasia 3, British Isles 2	1921 United States 5, Japan 0	1930 France 4, United States 1
1908 Australasia 3, United States 2	1922 United States 4, Australasia 1	1931 France 3, Great Britain 2
1909 Australasia 5, United States 0	1923 United States 4, Australasia 1	1932 France 3, United States 2

1933 Great Britain 3, France 2
1934 Great Britain 4, United States 1
1935 Great Britain 5, United States 0
1936 Great Britain 3, Australia 2
1937 United States 4, Great Britain 1
1938 United States 3, Australia 2
1939 Australia 3, United States 2
1946 United States 5, Australia 0
1947 United States 4, Australia 1
1948 United States 5, Australia 0
1949 United States 4, Australia 1
1950 Australia 4, United States 1
1951 Australia 3, United States 2
1952 Australia 4, United States 1
1953 Australia 3, United States 2
1954 United States 3, Australia 2
1955 Australia 5, United States 0
1956 Australia 5, United States 0
1957 Australia 3, United States 2
1958 United States 3, Australia 2
1959 Australia 3, United States 2

1960 Australia 4, Italy 1
1961 Australia 5, Italy 0
1962 Australia 5, Mexico 0
1963 United States 3, Australia 2
1964 Australia 3, United States 2
1965 Australia 4, Spain 1
1966 Australia 4, India 1
1967 Australia 4, Spain 1
1968 United States 4, Australia 1
1969 United States 5, Romania 0
1970 United States 5, West
     Germany 0
1971 United States 3, Romania 2
1972 United States 3, Romania 2
1973 Australia 5, United States 0
1974 South Africa (Default by India)
1975 Sweden 3, Czechoslovakia 2
1976 Italy 4, Chile 1
1977 Australia 3, Italy 1
1978 United States 4, Britain 1
1979 United States 5, Italy 0

1980 Czechoslovakia 3, Italy 2
1981 United States 3, Argentina 1
1982 United States 3, France 0
1983 Australia 3, Sweden 2
1984 Sweden 4, United States 1
1985 Sweden 3, West Germany 2
1986 Australia 3, Sweden 2
1987 Sweden 5, India 0
1988 West Germany 4, Sweden 1
1989 West Germany 3, Sweden 2
1990 United States 3, Australia 2
1991 France 3, United States 1
1992 United States 3, Switzerland 1
1993 Germany 4, Australia 1
1994 Sweden 4, Russia 1
1995 United States 3, Russia 1
1996 France 3, Sweden 2
1997 Sweden 5, United States 0
1998 Sweden 4, Italy 1

FEDERATION CUP CHAMPIONSHIPS

World team competition for women conducted by International Lawn Tennis Federation.

1963 United States 2, Australia 1
1964 Australia 2, United States 1
1965 Australia 2, United States 1
1966 United States 3, West Germany 0
1967 United States 2, Britain 0
1968 Australia 3, Netherlands 0
1969 United States 2, Australia 1
1970 Australia 3, West Germany 0
1971 Australia 3, Britain 0
1972 South Africa 2, Britain 1
1973 Australia 3, South Africa 0
1974 Australia 2, United States 1
1975 Czechoslovakia 3, Australia 0
1976 United States 2, Australia 1

1977 United States 2, Australia 1
1978 United States 2, Australia 1
1979 United States 3, Australia 0
1980 United States 3, Australia 0
1981 United States 3, Britain 0
1982 United States 3, West Germany 0
1983 Czechoslovakia 2, West
     Germany 1
1984 Czechoslovakia 2, Australia 1
1985 Czechoslovakia 2, United
     States 1
1986 United States 3,
     Czechoslovakia 0
1987 West Germany 2, United States 1

1988 Czechoslovakia 2, Soviet Union 1
1989 United States 3, Spain 0
1990 United States 2, Soviet Union 1
1991 Spain 2, United States 1
1992 Germany 2, Spain 1
1993 Spain 3, Australia 0
1994 Spain 3, United States 0
1995 Spain 3, United States 2
1996 United States 5, Spain 0
1997 France 4, Netherlands 1
1998 Spain 3, Switzerland 2
1999 United States 4, Russia 1

U.S. NATIONAL AND OPEN CHAMPIONS

SINGLES—MEN

NATIONAL
1881–87 Richard D. Sears
1888–89 Henry Slocum, Jr.
1890–92 Oliver S. Campbell
1893–94 Robert D. Wrenn
1895   Fred H. Hovey
1896–97 Robert D. Wrenn
1898–
1900   Malcolm Whitman
1901–02 William A. Larned
1903   Hugh L. Doherty
1904   Holcombe Ward
1905   Beals C. Wright
1906   William J. Clothier
1907–11 William A. Larned
       Maurice McLough-
1912–13 lin[1]
1914   R. N. Williams II
1915   William Johnston
1916   R. N. William II
1917–18 R. Lindley Murray[2]
1919   William Johnston

1920–25 Bill Tilden
1926–27 Jean Rene Lacoste
1928   Henri Cochet
1929   Bill Tilden
1930   John H. Doeg
1931–32 Ellsworth Vines
1933–34 Fred J. Perry
1935   Wilmer L. Allison
1936   Fred J. Perry
1937–38 Don Budge
1939   Robert L. Riggs
1940   Donald McNeill
1941   Robert L. Riggs
1942   Fred Schroeder
1943   Joseph Hunt
1944–45 Frank Parker
1946–47 Jack Kramer
1948–49 Richard Gonzales
1950   Arthur Larsen
1951–52 Frank Sedgman
1953   Tony Trabert
1954   Vic Seixas

1955   Tony Trabert
1956   Ken Rosewall
1957   Mal Anderson
1958   Ashley Cooper
1959–60 Neale Fraser
1961   Roy Emerson
1962   Rod Laver
1963   Rafael Osuna
1964   Roy Emerson
1965   Manuel Santana
1966   Fred Stolle
1967   John Newcombe
1968   Arthur Ashe
1969   Rod Laver

OPEN
1968   Arthur Ashe
1969   Rod Laver
1970   Ken Rosewall
1971   Stan Smith
1972   Ilie Nastase
1973   John Newcombe

1974   Jimmy Connors
1975   Manuel Orantes
1976   Jimmy Connors
1977   Guillermo Vilas
1978   Jimmy Connors
1979   John McEnroe
1980–81 John McEnroe
1982   Jimmy Connors
1983   Jimmy Connors
1984   John McEnroe
1985–87 Ivan Lendl
1988   Mats Wilander
1989   Boris Becker
1990   Pete Sampras
1991   Stefan Edberg
1992   Stefan Edberg
1993   Pete Sampras
1994   Andre Agassi
1995   Pete Sampras
1996   Pete Sampras
1997–98 Patrick Rafter
1999   Andre Agassi

1. Challenge Round Abandoned in 1912. 2. Patriotic Tournament in 1917.

SINGLES—WOMEN

NATIONAL			
1887 Ellen F. Hansel	1912–14 Mary K. Browne	1948–50 Margaret Osborne duPont	1975–78 Chris Evert
1888–89 Bertha Townsend	1915–18 Molla Bjurstedt	1951–53 Maureen Connolly	1979 Tracy Austin
1890 Ellen C. Roosevelt	1919 Hazel Hotchkiss Wightman	1954–55 Doris Hart	1980 Chris Evert-Lloyd
1891–92 Mabel E. Cahill	1920–22 Molla Bjurstedt Mallory	1956 Shirley Fry	1981 Tracy Austin
1893 Aline M. Terry		1957–58 Althea Gibson	1982 Chris Evert-Lloyd
1894 Helen R. Helwig	1923–25 Helen N. Wills	1959 Maria Bueno	1983–84 Martina Navratilova
1895 Juliette P. Atkinson	1926 Molla B. Mallory	1960–61 Darlene Hard	1985 Hana Mandlikova
1896 Elisabeth H. Moore	1927–29 Helen N. Wills	1962 Margaret Smith	1986–87 Martina Navratilova
1897–98 Juliette P. Atkinson	1930 Betty Nuthall	1963–64 Maria Bueno	1988 Steffi Graf
1899 Marion Jones	1931 Helen Wills Moody	1965 Margaret Smith	1989 Steffi Graf
1900 Myrtle McAteer	1932–35 Helen Jacobs	1966 Maria Bueno	1990 Grabriela Sabatini
1901 Elisabeth H. Moore	1936 Alice Marble	1967 Billie Jean King	1991 Monica Seles
1902 Marion Jones	1937 Anita Lizana	1968–69 Margaret Smith Court[1]	1992 Monica Seles
1903 Elisabeth H. Moore	1938–40 Alice Marble		1993 Steffi Graf
1904 May Sutton	1941 Sarah Palfrey Cooke	**OPEN**	1994 Arantxa Sanchez Vicario
1905 Elisabeth H. Moore		1968 Virginia Wade	
1906 Helen Homans	1942–44 Pauline Betz	1969–70 Margaret Court	1995 Steffi Graf
1907 Evelyn Sears	1945 Sarah Cooke	1971–72 Billie Jean King	1996 Steffi Graf
1908 Maud Bargar-Wallach	1946 Pauline Betz	1973 Margaret Court	1997 Martina Hingis
1909–11 Hazel V. Hotchkiss	1947 Louise Brough	1974 Billie Jean King	1998 LIndsay Davenport
			1999 Serena Williams

1. With the inaugural of the Open Tournament in 1968, the United States Lawn Tennis Association held a championship at Longwood, Chestnut Hill, Mass. which barred contract professionals in 1968 and 1969.

DOUBLES—MEN

NATIONAL		
1920 Bill Johnston–C. J. Griffin	1952 Vic Seixas–Mervyn Rose	1979 John McEnroe–Peter Fleming
1921–22 Bill Tilden–Vincent Richards	1953 Mervyn Rose–Rex Hartwig	1980 Stan Smith–Bob Lutz
1923 Bill Tilden–B. I. C. Norton	1954 Vic Seixas–Tony Trabert	1981 John McEnroe–Peter Fleming
1924 H. O. Kinsey–R. G. Kinsey	1955 Kosei Kamo–Atsushi Miyagi	1982 Kevin Curren–Steve Denton
1925–26 Vincent Richards–R. N. Williams II	1956 Lewis Hoad–Ken Rosewall	1983 John McEnroe–Peter Fleming
1927 BIll Tilden–Frank Hunter	1957 Ashley Cooper–Neale Fraser	1984 John Fitzgerald–Tomas Smid
1928 G. M. Lott, Jr.–V. Hennessy	1958 Ham Richardson–Alex Olmedo	1985 Ken Flach–Robert Seguso
1929–30 G. M. Lott, Jr.–J. H. Doeg	1959–60 Neale Fraser–Roy Emerson	1986 Andres Gomez–Slobodan Zivojinovic
1931 W. L. Allison–John Van Ryn	1961 Chuck McKinley–Dennis Ralston	1987 Stefan Edberg–Anders Jarryd
1932 E. H. Vines, Jr.–Keith Gledh	1962 Rafael Osuna–Antonio Palafox	1988 Sergio Casal–Emilio Sanchez
1933–34 G. M. Lott, Jr.–L. R. Stoefen	1963–64 Chuck McKinley–Dennis Ralston	1989 John McEnroe–Mark Woodforde
1935 W. L. Allison–John Van Ryn	1965–66 Fred Stolle–Roy Emerson	1990 Pieter Aldrich–Danie Visser
1936 Don Budge–Gene Mako	1967 John Newcombe–Tony Roche	1991 John Fitzgerald–Anders Jarryd
1937 G. von Cramm–H. Henkel	1968 Stan Smith–Bob Lutz[1]	1992 Jim Grabb–Richey Reneberg
1938 Don Budge–Gene Mako	1969 Richard Crealy–Allan Stone[1]	1993 Ken Flach–Rick Leach
1939 A. K. Quist–J. E. Bromwich		1994 Jacco Hingh–Paul Haarhuis
1940–41 Jack Kramer–F. R. Schroeder	**OPEN**	1995–96 Todd Woodbridge–Mark Woodforde
	1968 Stan Smith–Bob Lutz	1997 Yevgeny Kafelnikov–Daniel Vacek
1942 Gardnar Mulloy–Bill Talbert	1969 Fred Stolle–Ken Rosewall	1998 Sandon Stolle–Cyril Zuk
1943 Jack Kramer–Frank Parker	1970 Nikki Pilic–Fred Barthes	1999 Sebastien Lareau–Alex O'Brien
1944 Don McNeill–Bob Falkenburg	1971 John Newcombe–Roger Taylor	
1945 Gardnar Mulloy–Bill Talbert	1972 Cliff Drysdale–Roger Taylor	
1946 Gardnar Mulloy–Bill Talbert	1973 John Newcombe–Owen Davidson	
1947 Jack Kramer–Fred Schroeder	1974 Bob Lutz–Stan Smith	
1948 Gardnar Mulloy–Bill Talbert	1975 Jimmy Connors–Ilie Nastase	
1949 John Bromwich–William Sidwell	1976 Marty Riessen–Tom Okker	
1950 John Bromwich–Frank Sedgman	1977 Frew McMillan–Bob Hewitt	
1951 Frank Sedgman–Ken McGregor	1978 Bob Lutz–Stan Smith	

1. With the inaugural of the Open Tournament in 1968, the United States Lawn Tennis Association held a national championship at Longwood, Chestnut Hill, Mass. which barred contract professionals in 1968 and 1969.

DOUBLES—WOMEN

NATIONAL

1924	G. W. Wightman–Helen Wills
1925	Mary K. Browne–Helen Wills
1926	Elizabeth Ryan–Eleanor Goss
1927	L. A. Godfree–Ermyntrude Harvey
1928	Hazel Hotchkiss Wightman–Helen Wills
1929	Phoebe Watson–L. R. C. Michell
1930	Betty Nuthall–Sarah Palfrey
1931	Betty Nuthall–E. B. Wittingstall
1932	Helen Jacobs–Sarah Palfrey
1933	Betty Nuthall–Freda James
1934	Helen Jacobs–Sarah Palfrey
1935	Helen Jacobs–Sarah Palfrey Fabyan
1936	Marjorie G. Van Ryn–Carolin Babcock
1937–40	Sarah Palfrey Fabyan–Alice Marble
1941	Sarah Palfrey Cooke–Margaret Osborne
1942–47	A. Louise Brough–Margaret Osborne
1948–50	A. Louise Brough–Margaret O. duPont
1951–54	Doris Hart–Shirley Fry
1955–57	A. Louise Brough–Margaret O. duPont
1958–59	Darlene Hard–Jeanne Arth
1960	Darlene Hard–Maria Bueno
1961	Darlene Hard–Lesley Turner

1962	Darlene Hard–Maria Bueno
1963	Margaret Smith–Robyn Ebbern
1964	Karen Hantze Susman–Billie Jean Moffitt
1965	Nancy Richey–Carole Caldwell Graebner
1966	Nancy Richey–Maria Bueno
1967	Billie Jean King–Rosemary Casals
1968	Margaret Court–Maria Bueno[1]
1969	Margaret Court–Virginia Wade[1]

OPEN

1968	Maria Bueno–Margaret Court
1969	Darlene Hard–Francoise Durr
1970	Margaret Court–Judy Dalton
1971	Rosemary Casals–Judy Dalton
1972	Francoise Durr–Betty Stove
1973	Margaret Court–Virginia Wade
1974	Billie Jean King–Rosemary Casals
1975	Margaret Court–Virginia Wade
1976	Linky Boshoff–Ilana Kloss
1977	Martina Navratilova–Betty Stove
1978	Billie Jean King–Martina Navratilova

1979	Betty Stove–Wendy Turnbull
1980	Billie Jean King–Martina Navratilova
1981	Kathy Jordan–Anne Smith
1982	Rosemary Casals–Wendy Turnbull
1983–84	Martina Navratilova–Pam Shriver
1985	Claudia Khode-Kilsch–Helena Sukova
1986–87	Martina Navratilova–Pam Shriver
1988	Gigi Fernandez–Robin White
1989	Hana Mandlikova–Martina Navratilova
1990	Gigi Fernandez–Martina Navratilova
1991	Pam Shriver–Natalia Zvereva
1992	Gigi Fernandez–Natalia Zvereva
1993	Arantxa Sanchez Vicario–Helena Sukova
1994	Jana Novotna–Arantxa Sanchez Vicario
1995	Gigi Fernandez–Natasha Zvereva
1996	Gigi Fernandez–Natasha Zvereva
1997	Lindsay Davenport–Jana Novotna
1998	Martina Hingis–Jana Novotna
1999	Serena Williams–Venus Williams

1. With the inaugural of the Open Tournament in 1968, the United States Lawn Tennis Association held a national championship at Longwood, Chestnut Hill, Mass. which barred contract professionals in 1968 and 1969.

U.S. OPEN CHAMPIONS—1999
United States Open
(Flushing Meadow, N.Y., Aug. 30–Sept. 12, 1998)

Men's singles—Andre Agassi defeated Todd Martin, 6–4, 6–7 (5–7), 6–7 (2–7), 6–3, 6–2.

Women's singles—Serena Williams defeated Martina Hingis, 6–3, 7–6 (7–4).

Men's doubles—Sebastien Lareau and Alex O'Brien defeated Mahesh Bhupathi and Leander Paes, 7–6 (9–7), 6–4.

Women's doubles—Serena and Venus Williams defeated Chanda Rubin and Sandrine Testud, 4–6, 6–1, 6–4.

Mixed doubles—Ai Sugiyama and Mahesh Bhupathi defeated Kimberly Po and Donald Johnson, 6-4, 6-4.

BRITISH (WIMBLEDON) CHAMPIONS

(Amateur from inception in 1877 through 1967)

SINGLES—MEN

1908–09 Arthur Gore	1933 J. H. Crawford	1959 Alex Olmedo	1983–84 John McEnroe
1910–13 A. F. Wilding	1934–36 Fred Perry	1960 Neale Fraser	1985–86 Boris Becker
1914 N. E. Brookes	1937–38 Don Budge	1961–62 Rod Laver	1987 Pat Cash
1919 G. L. Patterson	1939 Robert L. Riggs	1963 Chuck McKinley	1988 Stefan Edberg
1920–21 Bill Tilden	1946 Yvon Petra	1964–65 Roy Emerson	1989 Boris Becker
1922 G. L. Patterson	1947 Jack Kramer	1966 Manuel Santana	1990 Stefan Edberg
1923 William Johnston	1948 R. Falkenburg	1967 John Newcombe	1991 Michael Stich
1924 Jean Borotra	1949 Fred Schroeder	1968–69 Rod Laver	1992 Andre Agassi
1925 Rene Lacoste	1950 Budge Patty	1970–71 John Newcombe	1993 Peter Sampras
1926 Jean Borotra	1951 Richard Savitt	1972 Stan Smith	1994 Pete Sampras
1927 Henri Cochet	1952 Frank Sedgman	1973 Jan Kodes	1995 Pete Sampras
1928 Rene Lacoste	1953 Vic Seixas	1974 Jimmy Connors	1996 Richard Krajicek
1929 Jean Cochet	1954 Jaroslav Drobny	1975 Arthur Ashe	1997–99 Pete Sampras
1930 Bill Tilden	1955 Tony Trabert	1976–80 Bjorn Borg	
1931 S. B. Wood	1956–57 Lewis Hoad	1981 John McEnroe	
1932 Ellsworth Vines	1958 Ashley Cooper	1982 Jimmy Connors	

SINGLES—WOMEN

1919–23	Suzanne Lenglen	1946	Pauline M. Betz	1966–67	Billie Jean King	1982–87	Martina Navratilova
1924	Kathleen McKane	1947	Margaret Osborne	1968	Billie Jean King	1988–89	Steffi Graf
1925	Suzanne Lenglen	1948–50	A. Louise Brough	1969	Ann Jones	1990	Martina Navratilova
1926	Kathleen Godfree	1951	Doris Hart	1970	Margaret Court	1991	Steffi Graf
1927–29	Helen Wills	1952–54	Maureen Connolly	1971	Evonne Goolagong	1992	Steffi Graf
1930	Helen Wills Moody	1955	A. Louise Brough	1972–73	Billie Jean King	1993	Steffi Graf
1931	Frl. C. Aussen	1956	Shirley Fry	1974	Chris Evert	1994	Conchita Martinez
1932–33	Helen Wills Moody	1957–58	Althea Gibson	1975	Billie Jean King	1995	Steffi Graf
1934	D. E. Round	1959–60	Maria Bueno	1976	Chris Evert	1996	Steffi Graf
1935	Helen Wills Moody	1961	Angela Mortimer	1977	Virginia Wade	1997	Martina Hingis
1936	Helen Jacobs	1962	Karen Susman	1978–79	Martina Navratilova	1998	Jana Novotna
1937	D. E. Round	1963	Margaret Smith	1980	Evonne Goolagong	1999	Lindsay Davenport
1938	Helen Wills Moody	1964	Maria Bueno		Cawley		
1939	Alice Marble	1965	Margaret Smith	1981	Chris Evert-Lloyd		

DOUBLES—MEN

1953	K. Rosewall–L. Hoad	1971	Rod Laver–Roy Emerson	1985	Heinz Gunthardt–Balazs
1954	R. Hartwig–M. Rose	1972	Bob Hewitt–Frew McMillan		Taroczy
1955	R. Hartwig–L. Hoad	1973	Jimmy Connors–Ilie Nastase	1986	Joakim Nystrom–Mats
1956	L. Hoad–K. Rosewall	1974	John Newcombe–Tony		Wilander
1957	Gardnar Mulloy–Budge Patty		Roche	1987	Ken Flach–Robert Seguso
1958	Sven Davidson–Ulf Schmidt	1975	Vitas Gerulaitis–Sandy	1988	Ken Flach–Robert Seguso
1959	Roy Emerson–Neale Fraser		Mayer	1989	John Fitzgerald–Anders
1960	Dennis Ralston–Rafael	1976	Brian Gottfried–Raul		Jarryd
	Osuna		Ramirez	1990	Rick Leach–Jim Pugh
1961	Roy Emerson–Neale Fraser	1977	Ross Case–Geoff Masters	1991	Anders Jarryd–John
1962	Fred Stolle–Bob Hewitt	1978	Fred McMillan–Bob Hewitt		Fitzgerald
1963	Rafael Osuna–Antonio	1979	Peter Fleming–John	1992	John McEnroe–Michael
	Palafox		McEnroe		Stich
1964	Fred Stolle–Bob Hewitt	1980	Peter McNamara–Paul	1993–97	Todd Woodbridge–Mark
1965	John Newcombe–Tony		McNamee		Woodforde
	Roche	1981	John McEnroe–Peter	1998	Jacco Eltingh–Paul Haarhuis
1966	John Newcombe–Ken		Fleming	1999	Mahesh Bhupathi–Leander
	Fletcher	1982	Paul McNamee–Peter		Paes
1967	Bob Hewitt–Frew McMillan		McNamara		
1968–70	John Newcombe–Tony	1983–84	John McEnroe–Peter		
	Roche		Fleming		

DOUBLES—WOMEN

1956	Althea Gibson–Angela	1974	Evonne Goolagong–Peggy	1989	Jana Novotna–Helena
	Buxton		Michel		Sukova
1957	Althea Gibson–Darlene Hard	1975	Ann Kiyomura–Kazuko	1990	Jana Novotna–Helena
1958	Althea Gibson–Maria Bueno		Sawamatsu		Sukova
1959	Darlene Hard–Jeanne Arth	1976	Chris Evert–Martina	1991	Pam Shriver–Natalia
1960	Darlene Hard–Maria Bueno		Navratilova		Zvereva
1961	Karen Hantze–Billie Jean	1977	Helen Cawley–JoAnne	1992	Gigi Fernandez–Natalia
	Moffitt		Russell		Zvereva
1962	Karen Hantze Susman–Billie	1978	Wendy Turnbull–Kerry Reid	1993	Gigi Fernandez–Natalia
	Jean Moffitt	1979	Billie Jean King–Martina		Zvereva
1963	Darlene Hard–Maria Bueno		Navratilova	1994	Gigi Fernandez–Natalia
1964	Margaret Smith–Les	1980	Kathy Jordan–Anne Smith		Zvereva
	Turnerley	1981	Martina Navratilova–Pam	1995	Jana Novotna–Arantxa
1965	Billie Jean Moffitt–Maria		Shriver		Sanchez Vicario
	Bueno	1982–84	Pam Shriver–Martina	1996	Martina Hingis–Helena
1966	Nancy Richey–Maria Bueno		Navratilova		Sukova
1967–68	Billie Jean King–Rosemary	1985	Kathy Jordan–Elizabeth	1997	Gigi Fernandez–Natasha
	Casals		Smylie		Zvereva
1969	Margaret Court–Judy Tegart	1986	Pam Shriver–Martina	1998	Martina Hingis–Jana
1970–71	Billie Jean King–Rosemary		Navratilova		Novotna
	Casals	1987	Claudia Khode-Kilsch–	1999	Lindsay Davenport–Corina
1972	Billie Jean King–Betty Stove		Helena Sukova		Morariu
1973	Billie Jean King–Rosemary	1988	Steffi Graf–Gabriela Sabatini		
	Casals				

OTHER 1999 CHAMPIONS

Wimbledon Open
(Wimbledon, England, June 21–July 4, 1999)

Men's singles—Pete Sampras defeated Andre Agassi, 6–3, 6–4, 7–5.
Women's singles—Lindsay Davenport defeated Steffi Graf, 6–4, 7–5.
Men's doubles—Mahesh Bhupathi and Leander Paes defeated Paul Haarhuis and Jared Palmer 6–7 (10–12), 6–3, 6–4, 7–6 (7–4).
Women's doubles—Lindsay Davenport and Corina Morariu defeated Mariaan de Swardt and Elena Tatarkova, 6–4, 6–4.
Mixed doubles—Leander Paes and Lisa Raymond defeated Jonas Bjorkman and Anna Kournikova, 6–4, 3–6, 6–3.

French Open
(Paris, May 24–June 6, 1999)

Men's singles—Andre Agassi defeated Andrei Medvedev, 1–6, 2–6, 6–4, 6–3, 6–4.
Women's singles—Steffi Graf defeated Martina Hingis, 4–6, 7–5, 6–2.
Men's doubles—Mahesh Bhupathi and Leander Paes defeated Goran Ivanisevic and Jeff Tarango, 6–2, 7–5.
Women's doubles—Venus Williams and Serena Williams defeated Martina Hingis and Anna Kournikova, 6–3, 6–7 (2–7), 8–6.
Mixed doubles—Katarina Srebotnik and Piet Norval defeated Laris Neiland and Rich Leach, 3–6, 6–3.

1999 Australian Open
(Melbourne, Australia, Jan. 18–31, 1999)

Men's singles—Yevgeny Kafelnikov defeated Thomas Enqvist, 4–6, 6–0, 6–3, 7–6 (7–1).
Women's singles—Martina Hingis defeated Amelie Mauresmo, 6–2, 6–3.
Men's doubles—Jonas Bjorkman and Patrick Rafter defeated Mahesh Bhupathi and Leander Paes, 6–3, 4–6, 6–4, 6–7 (10–12), 6–4.
Women's doubles—Martina Hingis and Anna Kournikova defeated Lindsay Davenport and Natasha Zvereva, 7–5, 6–3.
Mixed doubles—David Adams and Mariaan de Swardt defeated Max Mirnyi and Serena Williams, 6–4, 4–6, 7–6 (7–5).

MEN'S MONEY WINNERS—1999

(through Sept. 20, 1999)

1.	Andre Agassi, United States	$2,251,128
2.	Yevgeny Kafelnikov, Russia	1,488,218
3.	Pete Sampras, United States	1,401,256
4.	Gustavo Kuerten, Brazil	1,389,309
5.	Patrick Rafter, Australia	1,254,574
6.	Marcelo Rios, Chile	917,447
7.	Todd Martin, United States	901,124
8.	Tim Henman, Great Britain	886,694
9.	Richard Krajicek, The Netherlands	875,397
10.	Mark Philippoussis, Australia	840,839
11.	Nicolas Kiefer, Germany	784,918
12.	Carlos Moya, Spain	765,457
13.	Jonas Bjorkman, Sweden	714,735
14.	Tommy Haas, Germany	690,318
15.	Nicolas Lapentti, Ecuador	686,078
16.	Thomas Enqvist, Sweden	665,256
17.	Thomas Johansson, Sweden	645,037
18.	Cedric Pioline, France	626,788
19.	Felix Mantilla, Spain	604,927
20.	Leander Paes, India	603,065

WOMEN'S MONEY WINNERS—1999

(through Sept. 13, 1999)

1.	Martina Hingis, Switzerland	$1,784,180
2.	Lindsay Davenport, United States	1,305,763
3.	Steffi Graf, Germany	1,193,367
4.	Venus Williams, United States	973,082
5.	Serena Williams, United States	749,171
6.	Jana Novotna, Czech Republic	551,679
7.	Anna Kournikova, Russia	548,624
8.	Monica Seles, United States	539,180
9.	Arantxa Sanchez-Vicario, Spain	398,721
10.	Mary Pierce, France	392,592
11.	Natasha Zvereva, Belarus	345,202
12.	Amanda Coetzer, South Africa	341,870
13.	Elena Likhotseva, Russia	336,457
14.	Amelie Mauresmo, France	315,426
15.	Corina Morariu, United States	310,930
16.	Nathalie Tauziat, France	302,807
17.	Julie Halard-Decugis, France	299,695
18.	Conchita Martinez, Spain	287,292
19.	Barbara Schett, Austria	282,885
20.	Lisa Raymond, United States	258,589

Rowing

Rowing goes back so far in history that there is no possibility of tracing it to any particular aboriginal source. The oldest rowing race still on the calendar is the "Doggett's Coat and Badge" contest among professional watermen of the Thames (England) that began in 1715. The first Oxford-Cambridge race was held at Henley in 1829. Competitive rowing in the United States began with matches between boats rowed by professional oarsmen of the New York waterfront. They were oarsmen who rowed the small boats that plied as ferries from Manhattan Island to Brooklyn and return, or who rowed salesmen down the harbor to meet ships arriving from Europe. Since the first salesman to meet an incoming ship had some advantage over his rivals, there was keen competition in the bidding for fast boats and the best oarsmen. This gave rise to match races.

Amateur boat clubs sprang up in the United States between 1820 and 1830 and seven students of Yale joined together to purchase a four-oared lap-streak gig in 1843. The first Harvard-Yale race was held Aug. 3, 1852, on Lake Winnepesaukee, N.H. The first time an American college crew went abroad was in 1869 when Harvard challenged Oxford and was defeated on the Thames. There were early college rowing races on Lake Quinsigamond, near Worcester, Mass., and on Saratoga Lake, N.Y., but the Intercollegiate Rowing Association in 1895 settled on the Hudson, at Poughkeepsie, as the setting for the annual "Poughkeepsie Regatta." In 1950 the I.R.A. shifted its classic to Marietta, Ohio, and in 1952 it was moved to Syracuse, N.Y. The National Association of Amateur Oarsmen, organized in 1872, has conducted annual championship regattas since that time.

INTERCOLLEGIATE ROWING ASSOCIATION REGATTA

(Varsity Eight-Oared Shells)

Rowed at 4 miles, Poughkeepsie, N.Y., 1895–97, 1899–1916, 1925–32, 1934–41. Rowed at 3 miles, Saratoga, N.Y., 1898; Poughkeepsie, 1921–24, 1947–49; Syracuse, N.Y., 1952–1963, 1965–67. Rowed at 2,000 meters, Syracuse, N.Y., 1964 and 1968–1994. Rowed at Camden, N.J., 1995–present. Rowed at 2 miles, Ithaca, N.Y., 1920; Marietta, Ohio, 1950–51. Suspended 1917–19, 1933, 1942–46.

Year	Time	First	Second	Year	Time	First	Second
1895	21:25	Columbia	Cornell	1952	15:08.1	Navy	Princeton
1896	19:59	Cornell	Harvard	1953	15:29.6	Navy	Cornell
1897	20:47 4/5	Cornell	Columbia	1954	16:04.4	Navy[1]	Cornell
1898	15:51 1/2	Pennsylvania	Cornell	1955	15:49.9	Cornell	Pennsylvania
1899	20:04	Pennsylvania	Wisconsin	1956	16:22.4	Cornell	Navy
1900	19:44 3/5	Pennsylvania	Wisconsin	1957	15:26.6	Cornell	Pennsylvania
1901	18:53 1/5	Cornell	Columbia	1958	17:12.1	Cornell	Navy
1902	19:03 3/5	Cornell	Wisconsin	1959	18:01.7	Wisconsin	Syracuse
1903	18:57	Cornell	Georgetown	1960	15:57	California	Navy
1904	20:22 3/5	Syracuse	Cornell	1961	16:49.2	California	Cornell
1905	20:29	Cornell	Syracuse	1962	17:02.9	Cornell	Washington
1906	19:36 4/5	Cornell	Pennsylvania	1963	17:24	Cornell	Navy
1907	20:02 2/5	Cornell	Columbia	1964	6:31.1	California	Washington
1908	19:24 1/5	Syracuse	Columbia	1965	16:51.3	Navy	Cornell
1909	19:02	Cornell	Columbia	1966	16:03.4	Wisconsin	Navy
1910	20:42 1/5	Cornell	Pennsylvania	1967	16:13.9	Pennsylvania	Wisconsin
1911	20:10 4/5	Cornell	Columbia	1968	6:15.6	Pennsylvania	Washington
1912	19:31 2/5	Cornell	Wisconsin	1969	6:30.4	Pennsylvania	Dartmouth
1913	19:28 3/5	Syracuse	Cornell	1970	6:39.3	Washington	Wisconsin
1914	19:37 4/5	Columbia	Pennsylvania	1971	6:06	Cornell	Washington
1915	19:36 3/5	Cornell	Stanford	1972	6:22.6	Pennsylvania	Brown
1916	20:15 2/5	Syracuse	Cornell	1973	6:21	Wisconsin	Brown
1920	11:02 3/5	Syracuse	Cornell	1974	6:33	Wisconsin	M.I.T.
1921	14:07	Navy	California	1975	6:08.2	Wisconsin	M.I.T.
1922	13:33 3/5	Navy	Washington	1976	6:31	California	Princeton
1923	14:03 1/5	Washington	Navy	1977	6:32.4	Cornell	Pennsylvania
1924	15:02	Washington	Wisconsin	1978	6:39.5	Syracuse	Brown
1925	19:24 4/5	Navy	Washington	1979	6:26.4	Brown	Wisconsin
1926	19:28 3/5	Washington	Navy	1980	6:46	Navy	Northeastern
1927	20:57	Columbia	Washington	1981	5:57.3	Cornell	Navy
1928	18:35 4/5	California	Columbia	1982	5:57.5	Cornell	Princeton
1929	22:58	Columbia	Washington	1983	6:14.4	Brown	Navy
1930	21:42	Cornell	Syracuse	1984	5:54.7	Navy	Pennsylvania
1931	18:54 1/5	Navy	Cornell	1985	5:49.9	Princeton	Brown
1932	19:55	California	Cornell	1986	5:50.2	Brown	Pennsylvania
1934	19:44	California	Washington	1987	6:02.9	Brown	Wisconsin
1935	18:52	California	Cornell	1988	6:14.0	Northeastern	Brown
1936	19:09 3/5	Washington	California	1989	5:56.0	Penn	Wisconsin
1937	18:33 3/5	Washington	Navy	1990	5:55.5	Wisconsin	Pennsylvania
1938	18:19	Navy	California	1991	6:05.2	Northeastern	Pennsylvania
1939	18:12 3/5	California	Washington	1992	6:10.5	Dartmouth	Harvard
1940	22:42	Washington	Cornell	1993	5:59.1	Brown	Pennsylvania
1941	18:53 3/10	Washington	California	1994	5:54.4	Brown	Princeton
1947	13:59 1/5	Navy	Cornell	1995	5:31.3	Brown	Navy
1948	14:06 2/5	Washington	California	1996	5:29.6	Princeton	Washington
1949	14:42 3/5	California	Washington	1997	5:51.0	Washington	Brown
1950	8:07.5	Washington	California	1998	5:31.48	Princeton	Washington
1951	7:50.5	Wisconsin	Washington	1999	5:23.60[2]	California	Princeton

1. Disqualified. 2. New course record.

Harness Racing

Oliver Wendell Holmes, the famous Autocrat of the Breakfast Table, wrote that the running horse was a gambling toy but the trotting horse was useful and, furthermore, "horse-racing is not a republican institution; horse-trotting is." Oliver Wendell Holmes was a born-and-bred New Englander, and New England was the nursery of the harness racing sport in America. Pacers and trotters were matters of local pride and prejudice in Colonial New England, and, shortly after the Revolution, the Messenger and Justin Morgan strains produced many winners in harness racing "matches" along the turnpikes of New York, Connecticut, Rhode Island, Massachusetts, Vermont, and New Hampshire.

There was English thoroughbred blood in Messenger and Justin Morgan, and, many years later, it was blended in Rysdyk's Hambletonian, foaled in 1849. Hambletonian was not particularly fast under harness but his descendants have had almost a monopoly of prizes, titles, and records in the harness racing game. Hambletonian was purchased as a foal with its dam for a total of $124 by William Rysdyk of Goshen, N.Y., and made a modest fortune for the purchaser.

Trotters and pacers often were raced under saddle in the old days, and, in fact, the custom still survives in some places in Europe. Dexter, the great trotter that lowered the mile record from 2:19 ¾ to 2:17 ¼ in 1867, was said to handle just as well under saddle as when pulling a sulky. But as sulkies were lightened in weight and improved in design, trotting under saddle became less common and finally faded out in this country.

HISTORY OF TRADITIONAL HARNESS RACING STAKES

THE HAMBLETONIAN

Year	Winner	Driver	Best time	Total purse
1967	Speedy Streak	Del Cameron	2:00	$122,650
1968	Nevele Pride	Stanley Dancer	1:59 ⅖	116,190
1969	Lindy's Pride	Howard Beissinger	1:57 ⅗	124,910
1970	Timothy T.	John Simpson, Jr.	1:58 ⅖[1]	143,630
1971	Speedy Crown	Howard Beissinger	1:57 ⅖	129,770
1972	Super Bowl	Stanley Dancer	1:56 ⅖	119,090
1973	Flirth	Ralph Baldwin	1:57 ⅕	144,710
1974	Christopher T	Billy Haughton	1:58 ⅗	160,150
1975	Bonefish	Stanley Dancer	1:59[2]	232,192
1976	Steve Lobell	Billy Haughton	1:56 ⅖	263,524
1977	Green Speed	Billy Haughton	1:55 ⅗	284,131
1978	Speedy Somolli	Howard Beissinger	1:55[3]	241,280
1979	Legend Hanover	George Sholty	1:56 ⅕	300,000
1980	Burgomeister	Billy Haughton	1:56 ⅗	293,570
1981	Shiaway St. Pat	Ray Remmen	2:01 ⅕[4]	838,000
1982	Speed Bowl	Tommy Haughton	1:56 ⅘	875,750
1983	Duenna	Stanley Dancer	1:57 ⅖	1,000,000
1984	Historic Free	Ben Webster	1:56 ⅖	1,219,000
1985	Prakas	Bill O'Donnell	1:54 ⅗	1,272,000
1986	Nuclear Kosmos	Ulf Thoresen	1:56	1,172,082
1987	Mack Lobell	John Campbell	1:53 ⅗	1,046,300
1988	Armbro Goal	John Campbell	1:54 ⅗	1,156,800
1989	Park Avenue Joe	Ron Wayples	1:55 ⅗	1,131,000
1990	Embassy Lobell	Michel Lachance	1:56 ⅕	1,346,000
1991	Giant Victory	Jack Moiseyev	1:54 ⅘	1,238,000
1992	Alf Palema	Mickey McNichol	1:56 ⅗	1,288,000
1993	American Winner	Ron Pierce	1:53 ⅕	1,200,000
1994	Victory Dream	Michel Lachance	1:53 ⅘	1,200,000
1995	Tagliabue	John Campbell	1:54 ⅗	1,200,000
1996	Continentalvictory	Michel La Chance	1:52 ⅘	1,200,000
1997	Malabar Man	Malvern Burroughs	1:55	1,000,000
1998	Muscles Yankee	John Campbell	1:52 ⅖	1,000,000
1999	Self Possessed	Mike La Chance	1:51 ⅗	1,000,000

Three-year-old trotters. One mile. Guy McKinney won first race at Syracuse in 1926; held at Goshen, N.Y., 1930–1942, 1944–1956; at Yonkers, N.Y., 1943; at Du Quoin, Ill., 1957–1980. Since 1981, the race has been held at The Meadowlands in East Rutherford, N.J. 1. By Formal Notice. 2. By Yankee Bambino. 3. By Speedy Somolli and Florida Pro. 4. By Super Juan.

LITTLE BROWN JUG

Year	Winner	Driver	Best time	Total purse
1967	Best of All	Jim Hackett	1:59[1]	$84,778
1968	Rum Customer	Billy Haughton	1:59 ⅗	104,226
1969	Laverne Hanover	Billy Haughton	2:00 ⅖	109,731
1970	Most Happy Fella	Stanley Dancer	1:57 ⅕	100,110
1971	Nansemond	Herve Filion	1:57 ⅖	102,994
1972	Strike Out	Keith Waples	1:56 ⅗	104,916
1973	Melvin's Woe	Joe O'Brien	1:57 ⅗	120,000
1974	Ambro Omaha	Billy Haughton	1:57	132,630
1975	Seatrain	Ben Webster	1:57[2]	147,813
1976	Keystone Ore	Stanley Dancer	1:56 ⅘[3]	153,799
1977	Governor Skipper	John Chapman	1:56 ⅕	150,000
1978	Happy Escort	William Popfinger	1:55 ⅖[4]	186,760
1979	Hot Hitter	Herve Filion	1:55 ⅗	226,455
1980	Niatross	Clint Galbraith	1:54 ⅘	207,361
1981	Fan Hanover	Glen Garnsey	1:56[5]	243,799
1982	Merger	John Campbell	1:56 ⅗	328,900

Year	Winner	Driver	Best time	Total purse
1983	Ralph Hanover	Ron Waples	1:55 ⅗	358,800
1984	Colt 46	Norman Boring	1:53 ⅗	366,717
1985	Nihilator	Bill O'Donnell	1:52 ⅕	350,730
1986	Barberry Spur	Bill O'Donnell	1:52 ⅘	407,684
1987	Jaguar Spur	Richard Stillings	1:55 ⅗	412,330
1988	B.J. Scoot	Michel Lachance	1:52 ⅗	486,050
1989	Goalie Jeff	Michel Lachance	1:54 ⅕	500,200
1990	Beach Towel	Ray Remmen	1:53 ⅗	253,049
1991	Precious Bunny	Jack Moiseyev	1:54 ⅕	575,150
1992	Fake Left	Ron Waples	1:54 ⅖	556,210
1993	Life Sign	John Campbell	1:52	465,500
1994	Magical Mike	Michel LaChance	1:52 ⅗	512,830
1995	Nick's Fantasy	John Campbell	1:51 ⅖	543,670
1996	Armbro Operative	Michel La Chance	1:52 ⅗	542,220
1997	Western Dreamer	Michel La Chance	1:51 ⅕	605,210
1998	Shady Character	Ron Pierce	1:52 ⅗	566,630
1999	Blissfull Hall	Ron Pierce	1:55 ⅗	543,980

Three-year-old pacers. One Mile. Raced at Delaware County Fair Grounds, Delaware, Ohio. 1. By Nardin's Byrd. 2. By Albert's Star. 3. By Armbro Ranger. 4. By Falcon Almahurst. 5. By Seahawk Hanover.

HARNESS HORSE OF THE YEAR

1959	Bye Bye Byrd, Pacer	1976	Keystone Ore, Pacer	1990	Beach Towell
1960–61	Adios Butler, Pacer	1977	Green Speed, Trotter	1991	Precious Bunny
1962	Su Mac Lad, Trotter	1978	Abercrombie, Pacer	1992	Artsplace
1963	Speedy Scot, Trotter	1979–80	Niatross, Pacer	1993	Staying Together
1964–66	Bret Hanover, Pacer	1981	Fan Hanover, Pacer	1994	Cam's Card Shark
1967–69	Nevele Pride, Trotter	1982–83	Cam Fella, Pacer	1995	CR Kay Suzie
1970	Fresh Yankee, Trotter	1984	Fancy Crown, Trotter	1996	Continentalvictory
1971–72	Albatross, Pacer	1985	Nihilator, Trotter	1997	Malabar Man
1973	Sir Dalrae, Pacer	1986	Forrest Skipper	1998	Moni Maker
1974	Delmonica Hanover, Trotter	1987–88	Mack Lobell		
1975	Savoir, Trotter	1989	Matt's Scooter		

Chosen in poll conducted by United States Trotting Association in conjunction with the U.S. Harness Writers Assn.

Golf

It may be that golf originated in Holland—historians believe it did—but certainly Scotland fostered the game and is famous for it. In fact, in 1457 the Scottish Parliament, disturbed because football and golf had lured young Scots from the more soldierly exercise of archery, passed an ordinance that "futeball and golf be utterly cryit doun and nocht usit." James I and Charles I of the royal line of Stuarts were golf enthusiasts, whereby the game came to be known as "the royal and ancient game of golf."

The golf balls used in the early games were leather-covered and stuffed with feathers. Clubs of all kinds were fashioned by hand to suit individual players. The great step in spreading the game came with the change from the feather ball to the gutta-percha ball about 1850. In 1860, formal competition began with the establishment of an annual tournament for the British Open championship. There are records of "golf clubs" in the United States as far back as colonial days but no proof of actual play before John Reid and some friends laid out six holes on the Reid lawn in Yonkers, N.Y., in 1888 and played there with golf balls and clubs brought over from Scotland by Robert Lockhart. This group then formed the St. Andrews Golf Club of Yonkers, and golf was established in this country.

However, it remained a rather sedate and almost aristocratic pastime until a 20-year-old ex-caddy, Francis Ouimet of Boston, defeated two great British professionals, Harry Vardon and Ted Ray, in the United States Open championship at Brookline, Mass., in 1913. This feat put the game and Francis Ouimet on the front pages of the newspapers and stirred a wave of enthusiasm for the sport. The greatest feat so far in golf history is that of Robert Tyre Jones, Jr., of Atlanta, who won the British Open, the British Amateur, the U.S. Open, and the U.S. Amateur titles in one year, 1930.

THE MASTERS TOURNAMENT WINNERS

Augusta National Golf Club, Augusta, Ga.

Year	Winner	Score	Year	Winner	Score	Year	Winner	Score
1934	Horton Smith	284	1939	Ralph Guldahl	279	1946	Herman Keiser	282
1935	Gene Sarazen[1]	282	1940	Jimmy Demaret	280	1947	Jimmy Demaret	281
1936	Horton Smith	285	1941	Craig Wood	280	1948	Claude Harmon	279
1937	Byron Nelson	283	1942	Byron Nelson[1]	280	1949	Sam Snead	282
1938	Henry Picard	285	1943–45	No Tournaments		1950	Jimmy Demaret	283

Year	Winner	Score	Year	Winner	Score	Year	Winner	Score
1951	Ben Hogan	280	1968	Bob Goalby	277	1985	Bernhard Langer	282
1952	Sam Snead	286	1969	George Archer	281	1986	Jack Nicklaus	279
1953	Ben Hogan	274	1970	Billy Casper[1]	279	1987	Larry Mize[1]	285
1954	Sam Snead[1]	289	1971	Charles Coody	279	1988	Sandy Lyle	281
1955	Cary Middlecoff	279	1972	Jack Nicklaus	286	1989	Nick Faldo[1]	283
1956	Jack Burke	289	1973	Tommy Aaron	283	1990	Nick Faldo	278
1957	Doug Ford	283	1974	Gary Player	278	1991	Ian Woosnam	277
1958	Arnold Palmer	284	1975	Jack Nicklaus	276	1992	Fred Couples	275
1959	Art Wall, Jr.	284	1976	Ray Floyd	271	1993	Bernard Langer	277
1960	Arnold Palmer	282	1977	Tom Watson	276	1994	Jose Maria Olazabal	279
1961	Gary Player	280	1978	Gary Player	277	1995	Ben Crenshaw	274
1962	Arnold Palmer[1]	280	1979	Fuzzy Zoeller[1]	280	1996	Nick Faldo	276
1963	Jack Nicklaus	286	1980	Severiano Ballesteros	275	1997	Tiger Woods	270
1964	Arnold Palmer	276	1981	Tom Watson	280	1998	Mark O'Meara	279
1965	Jack Nicklaus	271	1982	Craig Stadler[1]	284	1999	Jose Maria Olazabal	280
1966	Jack Nicklaus[1]	288	1983	Severiano Ballesteros	280			
1967	Gay Brewer, Jr.	280	1984	Ben Crenshaw	277			

1. Winner in playoff.

U.S. OPEN CHAMPIONS

Year	Winner	Score	Where played	Year	Winner	Score	Where played
1895	Horace Rawlins	173	Newport	1946	Lloyd Mangrum[1]	284	Canterbury
1896	James Foulis	152	Shinnecock Hills	1947	Lew Worsham[1]	282	St. Louis
1897	Joe Lloyd	162	Chicago	1948	Ben Hogan	276	Riviera
1898[3]	Fred Herd	328	Myopia	1949	Cary Middlecoff	286	Medinah
1899	Willie Smith	315	Baltimore	1950	Ben Hogan[1]	287	Merion
1900	Harry Vardon	313	Chicago	1951	Ben Hogan	287	Oakland Hills
1901	Willie Anderson[1]	331	Myopia	1952	Julius Boros	281	Northwood
1902	Laurie Auchterlonie	307	Garden City	1953	Ben Hogan	283	Oakmont
1903	Willie Anderson[1]	307	Baltusrol	1954	Ed Furgol	284	Baltusrol
1904	Willie Anderson	303	Glen View	1955	Jack Fleck[1]	287	Olympic
1905	Willie Anderson	314	Myopia	1956	Cary Middlecoff	281	Oak Hill
1906	Alex Smith	295	Onwentsia	1957	Dick Mayer[1]	298	Inverness
1907	Alex Ross	302	Philadelphia	1958	Tommy Bolt	283	Southern Hills
1908	Fred McLeod[1]	322	Myopia	1959	Bill Casper, Jr.	282	Winged Foot
1909	George Sargent	290	Englewood	1960	Arnold Palmer	280	Cherry Hills
1910	Alex Smith[1]	298	Philadelphia	1961	Gene Littler	281	Oakland Hills
1911	John McDermott[1]	307	Chicago	1962	Jack Nicklaus[1]	283	Oakmont
1912	John McDermott	294	Buffalo	1963	Julius Boros[1]	293	Country Club
1913	Francis Ouimet[1] [2]	304	Brookline	1964	Ken Venturi	278	Congressional
1914	Walter Hagen	290	Midlothian	1965	Gary Player[1]	282	Bellerive
1915	Jerome D. Travers[2]	297	Baltusrol	1966	Bill Casper[1]	278	Olympic
1916	Charles Evans, Jr.[2]	286	Minikahda	1967	Jack Nicklaus	275	Baltusrol
1917–18	No tournaments[4]			1968	Lee Trevino	275	Oak Hill
1919	Walter Hagen[2]	301	Brae Burn	1969	Orville Moody	281	Champions G. C.
1920	Edward Ray	295	Inverness				
1921	Jim Barnes	289	Columbia	1970	Tony Jacklin	281	Hazeltine
1922	Gene Sarazen	288	Skokie	1971	Lee Trevino[1]	280	Merion
1923	R. T. Jones, Jr.[1] [2]	296	Inwood	1972	Jack Nicklaus	290	Pebble Beach
1924	Cyril Walker	297	Oakland Hills	1973	Johnny Miller	279	Oakmont
1925	Willie Macfarlane[1]	291	Worcester	1974	Hale Irwin	287	Winged Foot
1926	R. T. Jones, Jr.[2]	293	Scioto	1975	Lou Graham[1]	287	Medinah
1927	Tommy Armour[1]	301	Oakmont	1976	Jerry Pate	277	Atlanta A.C.
1928	Johnny Farrell[1]	294	Olympia Fields	1977	Hubert Green	278	Southern Hills
1929	R. T. Jones, Jr.[1] [2]	294	Winged Foot	1978	Andy North	285	Cherry Hills
1930	R. T. Jones, Jr.[2]	287	Interlachen	1979	Hale Irwin	284	Inverness
1931	Billy Burke[1]	292	Inverness	1980	Jack Nicklaus	272	Baltusrol
1932	Gene Sarazen	286	Fresh Meadow	1981	David Graham	273	Merion
1933	John Goodman[2]	287	North Shore	1982	Tom Watson	282	Pebble Beach
1934	Olin Dutra	293	Merion	1983	Larry Nelson	280	Oakmont
1935	Sam Parks, Jr.	299	Oakmont	1984	Fuzzy Zoeller[1]	276	Winged Foot
1936	Tony Manero	282	Baltusrol	1985	Andy North	279	Oakland Hills
1937	Ralph Guldahl	281	Oakland Hills	1986	Ray Floyd	279	Shinnecock Hills
1938	Ralph Guldahl	284	Cherry Hills	1987	Scott Simpson	277	Olympic Golf Club
1939	Byron Nelson[1]	284	Philadelphia				
1940	Lawson Little[1]	287	Canterbury	1988	Curtis Strange[1]	278	The Country Club
1941	Craig Wood	284	Colonial				
1942–45	No tournaments[5]			1989	Curtis Strange	278	Oak Hill Country Club

Year	Winner	Score	Where played	Year	Winner	Score	Where played
1990	Hale Irwin[1]	280	Medinah C.C.	1996	Steve Jones	278	Oakland Hills
1991	Payne Stewart[1]	282	Hazeltine	1997	Ernie Els	276	Congressional C.C.
1992	Tom Kite	285	Pebble Beach				
1993	Lee Janzen	272	Baltusrol	1998	Lee Janzen	280	Olympic Country Club
1994	Ernie Els	279	Oakmont				
1995	Corey Pavin	280	Shinnecock Hills	1999	Payne Stewart	279	Pinehurst

1. Winner in playoff. 2. Amateur. 3. In 1898, competition was extended to 72 holes. 4. In 1917, Jock Hutchison, with a 292, won an Open Patriotic Tournament for the benefit of the American Red Cross at Whitemarsh Valley Country Club. 5. In 1942, Ben Hogan, with a 271 won a Hale American National Open Tournament for the benefit of the Navy Relief Society and USO at Ridgemoor Country Club.

U.S. AMATEUR CHAMPIONS

1895	Charles B. Macdonald	1924–25	R. T. Jones, Jr.	1954	Arnold Palmer	1978	John Cook
		1926	George Von Elm	1955–56	Harvie Ward	1979	Mark O'Meara
1896–97	H. J. Whigham	1927–28	R. T. Jones, Jr.	1957	Hillman Robbins	1980	Hal Sutton
1898	Findlay S. Douglas	1929	H. R. Johnston	1958	Charles Coe	1981	Nathaniel Crosby
1899	H. M. Harriman	1930	R. T. Jones, Jr.	1959	Jack Nicklaus	1982	Jay Sigel
1900–01	Walter J. Travis	1931	Francis Ouimet	1960	Deane Beman	1983	Jay Sigel
1902	Louis N. James	1932	Ross Somerville	1961	Jack Nicklaus	1984	Scott Verplank
1903	Walter J. Travis	1933	G. T. Dunlap, Jr.	1962	Labron Harris, Jr.	1985	Sam Randolph
1904–05	H. Chandler Egan	1934–35	Lawson Little	1963	Deane Beman	1986	Buddy Alexander
1906	Eben M. Byers	1936	John W. Fischer	1964	Bill Campbell	1987	Bill Mayfair
1907–08	Jerome D. Travers	1937	John Goodman	1965[2]	Robert Murphy, Jr.	1988	Eric Meeks
1909	Robert A. Gardner	1938	Willie Turnesa	1966	Gary Cowan[1]	1989	Chris Patton
1910	W. C. Fownes, Jr.	1939	Marvin H. Ward	1967	Bob Dickson	1990	Phil Mickelson
1911	Harold H. Hilton	1940	R. D. Chapman	1968	Bruce Fleisher	1991	Mitch Voges
1912–13	Jerome D. Travers	1941	Marvin H. Ward	1969	Steven Melnyk	1992	Justin Leonard
1914	Francis Ouimet	1946	Ted Bishop	1970	Lanny Wadkins	1993	John Harris
1915	Robert A. Gardner	1947	Robert Riegel	1971	Gary Cowan	1994	Tiger Woods
1916	Charles Evans, Jr.	1948	Willie Turnesa	1972	Vinny Giles 3d	1995	Tiger Woods
1919	S. D. Herron	1949	Charles Coe	1973[3]	Craig Stadler	1996	Tiger Woods
1920	Charles Evans, Jr.	1950	Sam Urzetta	1974	Jerry Pate	1997	Matthew Kuchar
1921	Jesse P. Guilford	1951	Billy Maxwell	1975	Fred Ridley	1998	Hank Kuehne
1922	Jess W. Sweetser	1952	Jack Westland	1976	Bill Sander	1999	David Gossett
1923	Max R. Marston	1953	Gene Littler	1977	John Fought		

1. Winner in playoff. 2. Tourney switched to medal play through 1972. 3. Return to match play.

U.S. P.G.A. CHAMPIONS

1916	Jim Barnes	1944	Bob Hamilton	1963	Jack Nicklaus	1982	Ray Floyd
1919	Jim Barnes	1945	Byron Nelson	1964	Bobby Nichols	1983	Hal Sutton
1920	Jock Hutchison	1946	Ben Hogan	1965	Dave Marr	1984	Lee Trevino
1921	Walter Hagen	1947	Jim Ferrier	1966	Al Geiberger	1985	Hubert Green
1922–23	Gene Sarazen	1948	Ben Hogan	1967	Don January[1]	1986	Bob Tway
1924–27	Walter Hagen	1949	Sam Snead	1968	Julius Boros	1987	Larry Nelson
1928–29	Leo Diegel	1950	Chandler Harper	1969	Ray Floyd	1988	Jeff Sluman
1930	Tommy Armour	1951	Sam Snead	1970	Dave Stockton	1989	Payne Stewart
1931	Tom Creavy	1952	Jim Turnesa	1971	Jack Nicklaus	1990	Wayne Grady
1932	Olin Dutra	1953	Walter Burkemo	1972	Gary Player	1991	John Daly
1933	Gene Sarazen	1954	Chick Harbert	1973	Jack Nicklaus	1992	Nick Price
1934	Paul Runyan	1955	Doug Ford	1974	Lee Trevino	1993	Paul Azinger[1]
1935	Johnny Revolta	1956	Jack Burke, Jr.	1975	Jack Nicklaus	1994	Nick Price
1936–37	Denny Shute	1957	Lionel Hebert	1976	Dave Stockton	1995	Steve Elkington
1938	Paul Runyan	1958[2]	Dow Finsterwald	1977	Lanny Wadkins[1]	1996	Mark Brooks[1]
1939	Henry Picard	1959	Bob Rosburg	1978	John Mahaffey	1997	Davis Love III
1940	Byron Nelson	1960	Jay Hebert	1979	David Graham[1]	1998	Vijay Singh
1941	Victor Ghezzi	1961	Jerry Barber[1]	1980	Jack Nicklaus	1999	Tiger Woods
1942	Sam Snead	1962	Gary Player	1981	Larry Nelson		

1. Winner in playoff. 2. Switched to medal play.

U.S. WOMEN'S AMATEUR CHAMPIONS

1916	Alexa Stirling	1923	Edith Cummings	1926	Helen Stetson	1932–34	Virginia Van Wie
1919–20	Alexa Stirling	1924	Dorothy Campbell Hurd	1927	Mrs. M. B. Horn	1935	Glenna Collett Vare
1921	Marion Hollins			1928–30	Glenna Collett	1936	Pamela Barton
1922	Glenna Collett	1925	Glenna Collett	1931	Helen Hicks	1937	Mrs. J. A. Page, Jr.

Year	Winner	Year	Winner	Year	Winner	Year	Winner
1938	Patty Berg	1958	Anne Quast	1973	Carol Semple	1988	Pearl Sinn
1939–40	Betty Jameson	1959	Barbara McIntire	1974	Cynthia Hill	1989	Vicki Goetze
1941	Mrs. Frank Newell	1960	JoAnne Gunderson	1975	Beth Daniel	1990	Pat Hurst
1946	Mildred Zaharias	1961	Anne Quast Decker	1976	Donna Horton	1991	Amy Fruhwirth
1947	Louise Suggs	1962	JoAnne Gunderson	1977	Beth Daniel	1992	Vicki Goetze
1948	Grace Lenczyk	1963	Anne Quast Welts	1978	Cathy Sherk	1993	Jill McGill
1949	Mrs. D. G. Porter	1964	Barbara McIntire	1979	Carolyn Hill	1994	Wendy Ward
1950	Beverly Hanson	1965	Jean Ashley	1980	Juli Inkster	1995	Kelli Kuehne
1951	Dorothy Kirby	1966	JoAnne Gunderson	1981	Juli Inkster	1996	Kelli Kuehne
1952	Jacqueline Pung	1967	Lou Dill	1982	Juli Inkster	1997	Silvia Cavalleri
1953	Mary Lena Faulk	1968	JoAnne G. Carner	1983	Joanne Pacillo	1998	Grace Park
1954	Barbara Romack	1969	Catherine LaCoste	1984	Deb Richard	1999	Dorothy Delasin
1955	Patricia Lesser	1970	Martha Wilkinson	1985	Michiko Hattori		
1956	Marlene Stewart	1971	Laura Baugh	1986	Kay Cockerill		
1957	JoAnne Gunderson	1972	Mary Ann Budke	1987	Kay Cockerill		

U.S. WOMEN'S OPEN CHAMPIONS

Year	Winner	Score	Year	Winner	Score	Year	Winner	Score
1946	Patty Berg (match play)	—	1964	Mickey Wright[1]	290	1983	Jan Stephenson	290
			1965	Carol Mann	290	1984	Hollis Stacy	290
1947	Betty Jameson	295	1966	Sandra Spuzich	297	1985	Kathy Baker	280
1948	Mildred D. Zaharias	300	1967	Catherine LaCoste[2]	294	1986	Jane Geddes[1]	287
1949	Louise Suggs	291	1968	Susie Berning	289	1987	Laura Davies[1]	285
1950	Mildred D. Zaharias	291	1969	Donna Caponi	294	1988	Liselotte Neumann	277
1951	Betsy Rawls	293	1970	Donna Caponi	287	1989	Betsy King	278
1952	Louise Suggs	284	1971	JoAnne Carner	288	1990	Betsy King	284
1953	Betsy Rawls[1]	302	1972	Susie Berning	299	1991	Meg Mallon	283
1954	Mildred D. Zaharias	291	1973	Susie Berning	290	1992	Patty Sheehan	280
1955	Fay Crocker	299	1974	Sandra Haynie	295	1993	Lauri Merten	280
1956	Katherine Cornelius[1]	302	1975	Sandra Palmer	295	1994	Patty Sheehan	277
1957	Betsy Rawls	299	1976	JoAnne Carner[1]	292	1995	Annika Sorenstam	278
1958	Mickey Wright	290	1977	Hollis Stacy	292	1996	Annika Sorenstam	272
1959	Mickey Wright	287	1978	Hollis Stacy	289	1997	Alison Nicholas	274
1960	Betsy Rawls	291	1979	Jerilyn Britz	284	1998	Se Ri Pak	290
1961	Mickey Wright	293	1980	Amy Alcott	280	1999	Juli Inkster	272
1962	Murle Lindstrom	301	1981	Pat Bradley	279			
1963	Mary Mills	289	1982	Janet Alex	283			

1. Winner in playoff. 2. Amateur.

BRITISH OPEN CHAMPIONS

(First tournament, held in 1860, was won by Willie Park, Sr.)

Year	Winner	Score	Year	Winner	Score	Year	Winner	Score
1920	George Duncan	303	1951	Max Faulkner	285	1976	Johnny Miller	279
1921	Jock Hutchison[1]	296	1952	Bobby Locke	287	1977	Tom Watson	268
1922	Walter Hagen	300	1953	Ben Hogan	282	1978	Jack Nicklaus	281
1923	A. G. Havers	295	1954	Peter Thomson	283	1979	Severiano Ballesteros	283
1924	Walter Hagen	301	1955	Peter Thomson	281	1980	Tom Watson	271
1925	Jim Barnes	300	1956	Peter Thomson	286	1981	Bill Rogers	276
1926	R. T. Jones, Jr.	291	1957	Bobby Locke	279	1982	Tom Watson	284
1927	R. T. Jones, Jr.	285	1958	Peter Thomson[1]	278	1983	Tom Watson	275
1928	Walter Hagen	292	1959	Gary Player	284	1984	Severiano Ballesteros	276
1929	Walter Hagen	292	1960	Kel Nagle	278	1985	Sandy Lyle	282
1930	R. T. Jones, Jr.	291	1961	Arnold Palmer	284	1986	Greg Norman	280
1931	Tommy Armour	296	1962	Arnold Palmer	276	1987	Nick Faldo	279
1932	Gene Sarazen	283	1963	Bob Charles[1]	277	1988	Seve Ballesteros	273
1933	Denny Shute1	292	1964	Tony Lema	279	1989	Mark Calcavecchia	275
1934	Henry Cotton	283	1965	Peter Thomson	285	1990	Nick Faldo	270
1935	A. Perry	283	1966	Jack Nicklaus	282	1991	Ian Baker-Finch	272
1936	A. H. Padgham	287	1967	Roberto de Vicenzo	278	1992	Nick Faldo	272
1937	Henry Cotton	290	1968	Gary Player	289	1993	Greg Norman	267
1938	R. A. Whitcombe	295	1969	Tony Jacklin	280	1994	Nick Price	268
1939	R. Burton	290	1970	Jack Nicklaus[1]	283	1995	John Daly	282
1940	Sam Snead	290	1971	Lee Trevino	278	1996	Tom Lehman	271
1947	Fred Daly	294	1972	Lee Trevino	278	1997	Justin Leonard	272
1948	Henry Cotton	283	1973	Tom Weiskopf	276	1998	Mark O'Meara	280
1949	Bobby Locke[1]	283	1974	Gary Player	282	1999	Paul Lawrie	290
1950	Bobby Locke	279	1975	Tom Watson[1]	279			

OTHER 1999 PGA TOUR WINNERS

(Through Sept. 24, 1999)

Mercedes Championships—David Duval	$468,000
Bob Hope Classic—David Duval	540,000
Phoenix Open—Rocco Mediate	540,000
Pebble Beach National Pro-Am—Payne Stewart	504,000
Buick Invitational—Tiger Woods	486,000
Nissan Open—Ernie Els	504,000
Tucson Open—Gabriel Hjertstedt	495,000
Match Play Championship—Jeff Maggert	1,000,000
Doral-Ryder Open—Steve Elkington	540,000
Honda Classic—Vijay Singh	468,000
Bay Hill Invitational—Tim Herron	486,000
The Players Championship—David Duval	900,000
BellSouth Classic—David Duval	450,000
Byron Nelson Classic—Loren Roberts	540,000
The Colonial—Olin Browne	504,000
The Memorial—Tiger Woods	459,000
Buick Open—Tom Pernice, Jr.	432,000
World Golf Championships NEC Invitational— Tiger Woods	1,000,000
Reno-Tahoe Open—Notah Begay	495,000
Canadian Open—Hal Sutton	450,000

OTHER 1999 LPGA TOUR WINNERS

(Through Sept. 24, 1999)

Naples LPGA Memorial—Meg Mallon	$112,500
Australian Ladies Masters—Karrie Webb	112,500
Standard Register PING—Karrie Webb	127,500
Nabisco Dinah Shore—Dottie Pepper	150,000
Chick-Fil-A Championship—Rachel Hetherington	120,000
Titleholders Championship—Karrie Webb	135,000
Sara Lee Classic—Meg Mallon	112,500
Philips Invitational—Akiko Fukushima	120,000
Corning Classic—Kelli Kuehne	112,500
Rochester International—Karrie Webb	150,000
ShopRite LPGA Classic—Se Ri Pak	150,000
LPGA Championship—Juli Inkster	210,000
Jamie Farr Classic—Se Ri Pak	135,000
Michelob Light Classic—Annika Sorenstam	120,000
Big Apple Classic—Sherri Steinhauer	127,500
Giant Eagle Classic—Jackie Gallagher-Smith	150,000
du Maurier Classic—Karrie Webb	180,000
areaWEB.COM Challenge—Mardi Lunn	120,000
Women's British Open—Sherri Steinhauer	160,000
Rail Classic—Mi Hyun Kim	116,250
World Championship of Golf—Se Ri Pak	150,000

Auto Racing

INDIANAPOLIS 500

Year	Winner	Car	Time	mph	Second place
1911	Ray Harroun	Marmon	6:42:08.000	74.590	Ralph Mulford
1912	Joe Dawson	National	6:21:06.000	78.720	Teddy Tetzloff
1913	Jules Goux	Peugeot	6:35:05.000	75.930	Spencer Wishart
1914	René Thomas	Delage	6:03:45.000	82.470	Arthur Duray
1915	Ralph DePalma	Mercedes	5:33:55.510	89.840	Dario Resta
1916[1]	Dario Resta	Peugeot	3:34:17.000	84.000	Wilbur D'Alene
1919	Howard Wilcox	Peugeot	5:40:42.870	88.050	Eddie Hearne
1920	Gaston Chevrolet	Monroe	5:38:32.000	88.620	René Thomas
1921	Tommy Milton	Frontenac	5:34:44.650	89.620	Roscoe Sarles
1922	Jimmy Murphy	Murphy Special	5:17:30.790	94.480	Harry Hartz
1923	Tommy Milton	H. C. S. Special	5:29.50.170	90.950	Harry Hartz
1924	L. L. Corum-Joe Boyer	Dusenberg Special	5:05:23.510	98.230	Earl Cooper
1925	Peter DePaolo	Dusenberg Special	4:56:39.450	101.130	Dave Lewis
1926[2]	Frank Lockhart	Miller Special	4:10:14.950	95.904	Harry Hartz
1927	George Souders	Dusenberg Special	5:07:33.080	97.540	Earl DeVore
1928	Louis Meyer	Miller Special	5:01:33.750	99.480	Lou Moore
1929	Ray Keech	Simplex Special	5:07:25.420	97.580	Louis Meyer
1930	Billy Arnold	Miller-Hartz Special	4:58:39.720	100.448	Shorty Cantlon
1931	Louis Schneider	Bowes Special	5:10:27.930	96.629	Fred Frame
1932	Fred Frame	Miller-Hartz Special	4:48:03.790	104.144	Howard Wilcox
1933	Louis Meyer	Tydol Special	4:48:00.750	104.162	Wilbur Shaw
1934	Bill Cummings	Boyle Products Special	4:46:05.200	104.863	Mauri Rose
1935	Kelly Petillo	Gilmore Special	4:42:22.710	106.240	Wilbur Shaw
1936	Louis Meyer	Ring Free Special	4:35:03.390	109.069	Ted Horn
1937	Wilbur Shaw	Shaw-Gilmore Special	4:24:07.800	113.580	Ralph Hepburn
1938	Floyd Roberts	Burd Piston Ring Special	4:15:58.400	117.200	Wilbur Shaw
1939	Wilbur Shaw	Boyle Special	4:20:47.390	115.035	Jimmy Snyder
1940	Wilbur Shaw	Boyle Special	4:22:31.170	114.277	Rex Mays
1941	Floyd Davis-Mauri Rose	Noc-Out Hose Clamp Special	4:20:36.240	115.117	Rex Mays
1946	George Robson	Thorne Engineering Special	4:21:26.710	114.820	Jimmy Jackson
1947	Mauri Rose	Blue Crown Special	4:17:52.170	116.338	Bill Holland
1948	Mauri Rose	Blue Crown Special	4:10:23.330	119.814	Bill Holland
1949	Bill Holland	Blue Crown Special	4:07:15.970	121.327	Johnny Parsons
1950[3]	Johnnie Parsons	Wynn's Friction Proof Special	2:46:55.970	124.002	Bill Holland
1951	Lee Wallard	Belanger Special	3:57:38.050	126.244	Mike Nazaruk
1952	Troy Ruttman	Agajanian Special	3:52:41.880	128.922	Jim Rathmann

Year	Winner	Car	Time	mph	Second place
1953	Bill Vukovich	Fuel Injection Special	3:53:01.690	128.740	Art Cross
1954	Bill Vukovich	Fuel Injection Special	3:49:17.270	130.840	Jim Bryan
1955	Bob Sweikert	John Zink Special	3:53:59.13	128.209	Tony Bettenhausen
1956	Pat Flaherty	John Zink Special	3:53:28.840	128.490	Sam Hanks
1957	Sam Hanks	Belond Exhaust Special	3:41:14.250	135.601	Jim Rathmann
1958	Jimmy Bryan	Belond A-P Special	3:44:13.800	133.791	George Amick
1959	Rodger Ward	Leader Card 500 Roadster	3:40:49.200	135.857	Jim Rathmann
1960	Jim Rathmann	Ken-Paul Special	3:36:11.360	138.767	Rodger Ward
1961	A. J. Foyt	Bowes Special	3:35:37.490	139.130	Eddie Sachs
1962	Rodger Ward	Leader Card Special	3:33:50.330	140.293	Len Sutton
1963	Parnelli Jones	Agajanian Special	3:29:35.400	143.137	Jim Clark
1964	A. J. Foyt	Sheraton-Thompson Spl.	3:23:35.830	147.350	Rodger Ward
1965	Jim Clark	Lotus-Ford	3:19:05.340	150.686	Parnelli Jones
1966	Graham Hill	Red Ball Lola-Ford	3:27:52.530	144.317	Jim Clark
1967[4]	A. J. Foyt	Sheraton-Thompson Coyote-Ford	3:18:24.220	151.207	Al Unser
1968	Bobby Unser	Rislone Eagle-Offenhauser	3:16:13.760	152.882	Dan Gurney
1969	Mario Andretti	STP Hawk-Ford	3:11:14.710	156.867	Dan Gurney
1970	Al Unser	Johnny Lightning P. J. Colt-Ford	3:12:37.040	155.749	Mark Donohue
1971	Al Unser	Johnny Lightning P. J. Colt-Ford	3:10:11.560	157.735	Peter Revson
1972	Mark Donohue	Sunoco McLaren-Offenhauser	3:04:05.540	162.962	Al Unser
1973[5]	Gordon Johncock	STP Eagle-Offenhauser	2:05:26.590	159.036	Bill Vukovich, Jr.
1974	Johnny Rutherford	McLaren-Offenhauser	3:09:10.060	158.589	Bobby Unser
1975[6]	Bobby Unser	Jorgensen Eagle-Offenhauser	2:54:55.080	149.213	Johnny Rutherford
1976[7]	Johnny Rutherford	Hy-gain McLaren-Offenhauser	1:42:52.480	148.725	A. J. Foyt
1977	A. J. Foyt	Gilmore Coyote-Foyt	3:05:57.160	161.331	Tom Sneva
1978	Al Unser	1st Nat'l City Lola-Cosworth	3:05:54.990	161.363	Tom Sneva
1979	Rick Mears	Gould Penske-Cosworth	3:08:27.970	158.899	A. J. Foyt
1980	Johnny Rutherford	Pennzoil Chaparral-Cosworth	3:29:59.560	142.862	Tom Sneva
1981[8]	Bobby Unser	Norton Penske-Cosworth	3:35:41.780	139.029	Mario Andretti
1982	Gordon Johncock	STP Wildcat-Cosworth	3:05:09.140	162.029	Rick Mears
1983	Tom Sneva	Texaco Star March-Cosworth	3:05:03.060	162.117	Al Unser
1984	Rick Mears	Pennzoil March-Cosworth	3:03:21.000	162.962	Roberto Guerrero
1985	Danny Sullivan	Miller March-Cosworth	3:16:06.069	152.982	Mario Andretti
1986	Bobby Rahal	Budweiser March-Cosworth	2:55:43.480	170.722	Kevin Cogan
1987	Al Unser, Sr.	Cummins March-Cosworth	3:04:59.147	162.175	Roberto Guerrero
1988	Rick Mears	Pennzoil Penske P.C.17-Chevrolet	3:27:10.204	144.809	Emerson Fittipaldi
1989	Emerson Fittipaldi	Marlboro Penske-Cosworth	2:59:01.040	167.581	Al Unser, Jr.
1990	Arie Luyendyk	Domino's Pizza Lola-Cosworth	2:41:18.248	185.987	Bobby Rahal
1991	Rick Mears	Marlboro Penske-Cosworth	2:50:01.018	176.460	Michael Andretti
1992	Al Unser, Jr.	Valvoline-Chevrolet	3:43.05.148	134.477	Scott Goodyear
1993	Emerson Fittipaldi	Penske-Chevrolet	3:10:49.860	157.207	Arie Luyendyk
1994	Al Unser, Jr.	Penske-Mercedes	3:06:29.006	160.872	Jacques Villeneuve
1995	Jacques Villeneuve	Reynard-Ford	3:15:17.561	156.616	Christian Fittipaldi
1996	Buddy Lazier	Reynard-Ford	3:22:45.753	147.956	Davy Jones
1997	Arie Luyendyk	G Force-Aurora	3:25:43.388	145.827	Scott Goodyear
1998	Eddie Cheever	Dallara-Aurora	3:26:40.524	145.155	Buddy Lazier
1999	Kenny Brack	Dallara-Aurora-Goodyear	3:15:51.182	153.176	Jeff Ward

1. 300 miles. 2. Race ended at 400 miles because of rain. 3. Race ended at 345 miles because of rain. 4. Race, postponed after 18 laps because of rain on May 30, was finished on May 31. 5. Race postponed May 28 and 29 was cut to 332.5 miles because of rain, May 30. 6. Race ended at 435 miles because of rain. 7. Race ended at 255 miles because of rain. 8. Andretti was awarded the victory the day after the race after Bobby Unser, whose car finished first, was penalized one lap and dropped from first place to second for passing other cars illegally under a yellow caution flag. Unser appealed the decision to the U.S. Auto Club and was upheld. A panel ruled the penalty was too severe and instead fined Unser $40,000, but restored the victory to him.

U.S. 500

The U.S. 500 was started in 1996 by IndyCar, after Indianapolis 500 race officials joined forces with IndyCar's upstart rivals the Indy Racing League. A disagreement over the number of auto-matic qualifiers that would be given to IRL drivers spurred IndyCar to stage a Memorial Day race of its own to go head-to-head with the Indy 500. In 1998 the race was held on July 26.

Year	Winner	Car	Time	mph	Second place
1996	Jimmy Vasser	Reynard-Honda	3:11:48.000	156.403	Mauricio Gugelmin
1997	Alex Zanardi	Reynard-Honda	2:59:35.580	167.044	Mark Blundell
1998	Greg Moore	Reynard-Mercedes	3:00:48.785	165.913	Jimmy Vasser
1999	Tony Kanaan	Honda Reynard	2:41:12.362	186.097	Juan Montoya

NATIONAL ASSOCIATION FOR STOCK CAR AUTO RACING
WINSTON CUP CHAMPIONS

1949	Red Byron	1962–63	Joe Weatherly	1979	Richard Petty	1990	Dale Earnhardt
1950	Bill Rexford	1964	Richard Petty	1980	Dale Earnhardt	1991	Dale Earnhardt
1951	Herb Thomas	1965	Ned Jarrett	1981	Darrell Waltrip	1992	Alan Kulwicki
1952	Tim Flock	1966	David Pearson	1982	Darrell Waltrip	1993	Dale Earnhardt
1953	Herb Thomas	1967	Richard Petty	1983	Bobby Allison	1994	Dale Earnhardt
1954	Lee Petty	1968–69	David Pearson	1984	Terry Labonte	1995	Jeff Gordon
1955	Tim Flock	1970	Bobby Isaac	1985	Darrell Waltrip	1996	Terry Labonte
1956–57	Buck Baker	1971–72	Richard Petty	1986	Dale Earnhardt	1997–98	Jeff Gordon
1958–59	Lee Petty	1973	Benny Parsons	1987	Dale Earnhardt	1999[1]	Dale Jarrett
1960	Rex White	1974–75	Richard Petty	1988	Bill Elliott		
1961	Ned Jarrett	1976–78	Cale Yarborough	1989	Rusty Wallace		

1. As of Sept. 19, 1999.

INDYCAR NATIONAL CHAMPIONS

1910	Ray Harroun	1931	Louis Schneider	1958	Tony Betten-hausen	1980	Johnny Ruther-ford
1911	Ralph Mulford	1932	Bob Carey				
1912	Ralph DePalma	1933	Louis Meyer	1959	Rodger Ward	1981–82	Rick Mears
1913	Earl Cooper	1934	Bill Cummings	1960–61	A. J. Foyt	1983	Al Unser
1914	Ralph DePalma	1935	Kelly Petillo	1962	Rodger Ward	1984	Mario Andretti
1915	Earl Cooper	1936	Mauri Rose	1963–64	A. J. Foyt	1985	Al Unser
1916	Dario Resta	1937	Wilbur Shaw	1965–66	Mario Andretti	1986–87	Bobby Rahal
1917	Earl Cooper	1938	Floyd Roberts	1967	A. J. Foyt	1988	Danny Sullivan
1918	Ralph Mulford	1939	Wilbur Shaw	1968	Bobby Unser	1989	Emerson Fitti-paldi
1919	Howard Wilcox	1940–41	Rex Mays	1969	Mario Andretti		
1920	Gaston Chevrolet	1946–48	Ted Horn	1970	Al Unser	1990	Al Unser, Jr.
1921	Tommy Milton	1949	Johnnie Parsons	1971–72	Joe Leonard	1991	Michael Andretti
1922	James Murphy	1950	Henry Banks	1973	Roger McCluskey	1992	Bobby Rahal
1923	Eddie Hearne	1951	Tony Betten-hausen	1974	Bobby Unser	1993	Nigel Mansell
1924	James Murphy			1975	A. J. Foyt	1994	Al Unser, Jr.
1925	Peter DePaolo	1952	Chuck Stevenson	1976	Gordon Johncock	1995	Jacques Ville-neuve
1926	Harry Hartz	1953	Sam Hanks	1977–78	Tom Sneva		
1927	Peter DePaolo	1954	Jimmy Bryan	1979	Rick Mears (CART), A.J. Foyt (USAC)[1]	1996	Jimmy Vasser
1928–29	Louis Meyer	1955	Bob Sweikert			1997–98	Alessandro Zanardi
1930	Billy Arnold	1956–57	Jimmy Bryan				

1. Two separate series were held in 1979. NOTE: There have been three sanctioning bodies for the series: the Automobile Association of America (1909–1955), the U.S. Auto Club (1956–1979), and the Championship Auto Racing Team (CART), 1979–present.

1999 INDY RACING LEAGUE LEADING POINT WINNERS
(after 9 of 11 races, Aug. 29, 1999)

Driver	Pts	Driver	Pts	Driver	Pts
1. Greg Ray	246	8. Jeff Ward	177	15. Scott Harrington	121
2. Scott Goodyear	202	9. Eddie Cheever, Jr.	177	16. Robby McGehee	110
3. Kenny Brack	199	10. Mark Dismore	176	17. Eliseo Salazar	106
4. Buddy Lazier	185	11. Billy Boat	174	18. John Hollansworth, Jr.	105
5. Davey Hamilton	180	12. Sam Schmidt	172	19. Tyce Carlson	100
6. Robby Unser	179	13. Buzz Calkins	147	20. Donnie Beechler	99
7. Scott Sharp	177	14. Stephan Gregoire	123	21. Raul Boesel	98

1999 NASCAR LEADING POINT WINNERS
(as of Sept. 19, 1999)

Driver	Pts	Winnings	Driver	Pts	Winnings
1. Dale Jarrett	3,972	$2,991,369	11. Mike Skinner	2,932	1,759,761
2. Bobby Labonte	3,718	2,642,406	12. Jeremy Mayfield	2,781	1,537,274
3. Mark Martin	3,700	2,112,376	13. Ken Schrader	2,731	1,465,404
4. Tony Stewart	3,683	1,844,146	14. Bobby Hamilton	2,728	1,452,824
5. Jeff Burton	3,576	4,588,856	15. Sterling Marlin	2,663	1,331,061
6. Jeff Gordon	3,554	4,646,111	16. John Andretti	2,659	1,456,541
7. Dale Earnhardt	3,415	2,210,809	17. Wally Dallenbach	2,609	1,275,193
8. Rusty Wallace	3,163	1,735,244	18. Jimmy Spencer	2,549	1,302,553
9. Terry Labonte	2,966	1,945,626	19. Bill Elliott	2,536	1,255,671
10. Ward Burton	2,933	1,646,809	20. Kenny Irwin	2,532	1,645,306

WORLD GRAND PRIX DRIVER CHAMPIONS

1950 Giuseppe Farina, Italy, Alfa Romeo	1975 Niki Lauda, Austria, Ferrari
1951 Juan Fangio, Argentina, Alfa Romeo	1976 James Hunt, Britain, McLaren-Ford
1952 Alberto Ascari, Italy, Ferrari	1977 Niki Lauda, Austria, Ferrari
1953 Alberto Ascari, Italy, Ferrari	1978 Mario Andretti, United States, Lotus
1954 Juan Fangio, Argentina, Maserati, Mercedes-Benz	1979 Jody Scheckter, South Africa, Ferrari
1955 Juan Fangio, Argentina, Mercedes-Benz	1980 Alan Jones, Australia, Williams-Ford
1956 Juan Fangio, Argentina, Lancia-Ferrari	1981 Nelson Piquet, Brazil, Brabham-Ford
1957 Juan Fangio, Argentina, Masserati	1982 Keke Rosberg, Finland, Williams-Ford
1958 Mike Hawthorn, England, Ferrari	1983 Nelson Piquet, Brazil. Brabham-BMW
1959 Jack Brabham, Australia, Cooper	1984 Nikki Lauda, Austria, McLaren-Porsche
1960 Jack Brabham, Australia, Cooper	1985 Alain Prost, France, McLaren-Porsche
1961 Phil Hill, United States, Ferrari	1986 Alain Prost, France, McLaren-Porsche
1962 Graham Hill, England, BRM	1987 Nelson Piquet, Brazil, Williams-Honda
1963 Jim Clark, Scotland, Lotus-Ford	1988 Aryton Senna, Brazil, McLaren-Honda
1964 John Surtees, England, Ferrari	1989 Alain Prost, France, McLaren-Honda
1965 Jim Clark, Scotland, Lotus-Ford	1990 Ayrton Senna, Brazil, McLaren-Honda
1966 Jack Brabham, Australia, Brabham-Repco	1991 Aryton Senna, Brazil, McLaren-Honda
1967 Denis Hulme, New Zealand, Brabham-Repco	1992 Nigel Mansell, Britain, Williams-Renault
1968 Graham Hill, England, Lotus-Ford	1993 Alain Prost, France, Williams-Renault
1969 Jackie Stewart, Scotland, Matra-Ford	1994 Michael Schumacher, Germany, Benetton
1970 Jochen Rindt, Austria, Lotus-Ford	1995 Michael Schumacher, Germany, Benetton Renault
1971 Jackie Stewart, Scotland, Tyrrell-Ford	1996 Damon Hill, Britain, Williams
1972 Emerson Fittipaldi, Brazil, Lotus-Ford	1997 Jacques Villeneuve, Canada, Williams-Renault
1973 Jackie Stewart, Scotland, Tyrrell-Ford	1998 Mika Hakkinen, Finland, McLaren-Mercedes
1974 Emerson Fittipaldi, Brazil, McLaren-Ford	1999[1] Mika Hakkinen, Finland, McLaren-Mercedes

1. As of Sept. 24, 1999.

Yachting

AMERICA'S CUP RECORD

First race in 1851 around Isle of Wight, Cowes, England. First defense and all others through 1920 held 30 miles off New York Bay. Races since 1930 held 30 miles off Newport, R.I. Conducted as one race only in 1851 and 1870; best four-of-seven basis, 1871; best two-of-three, 1876–1887; best three-of-five, 1893–1901; best four-of-seven, since 1930. Figures in parentheses indicate number of races won.

Year Winner and owner	Loser and owner
1851 AMERICA (1), John C. Stevens, U.S.	AURORA, T. Le Marchant, England[1]
1870 MAGIC (1), Franklin Osgood, U.S.	CAMBRIA, James Ashbury, England[2]
1871 COLUMBIA (2), Franklin Osgood, U.S.[3]	LIVONIA (1), James Ashbury, England
SAPPHO (2), William P. Douglas, U.S.	
1876 MADELEINE (2), John S. Dickerson, U.S.	COUNTESS OF DUFFERIN, Chas. Gifford, Canada
1881 MISCHIEF (2), J. R. Busk, U.S.	ATALANTA, Alexander Cuthbert, Canada
1885 PURITAN (2), J. M. Forbes-Gen. Charles Paine, U.S.	GENESTA, Sir Richard Sutton, England
1886 MAYFLOWER (2), Gen. Charles Paine, U.S.	GALATEA, Lt. William Henn, England
1887 VOLUNTEER (2), Gen. Charles Paine, U.S.	THISTLE, James Bell et al., Scotland
1893 VIGILANT (3), C. Oliver Iselin et al., U.S.	VALKYRIE II, Lord Dunraven, England
1895 DEFENDER (3), C. O. Iselin–W. K. Vanderbilt–E. D. Morgan, U.S.	VALKYRIE III,
	Lord Dunraven–Lord Lonsdale–Lord Wolverton, England
1899 COLUMBIA (3), J. P. Morgan–C. O. Iselin, U.S.	SHAMROCK I, Sir Thomas Lipton, Ireland
1901 COLUMBIA (3), Edwin D. Morgan, U.S.	SHAMROCK II, Sir Thomas Lipton, Ireland
1903 RELIANCE (3), Cornelius Vanderbilt et al., U.S.	SHAMROCK III, Sir Thomas Lipton, Ireland
1920 RESOLUTE (3), Henry Walters et al., U.S.	SHAMROCK IV (2), Sir Thomas Lipton, Ireland
1930 ENTERPRISE (4), Harold S. Vanderbilt et al., U.S.	SHAMROCK V, Sir Thomas Lipton, Ireland
1934 RAINBOW (4), Harold S. Vanderbilt, U.S.	ENDEAVOUR (2), T. O. M. Sopwith, England
1937 RANGER (4), Harold S. Vanderbilt, U.S.	ENDEAVOUR II, T. O. M. Sopwith, England
1958 COLUMBIA (4), Henry Sears et al., U.S.	SCEPTRE, Hugh Goodson et al., England
1962 WEATHERLY (4), Henry D. Mercer et al., U.S.	GRETEL (1), Sir Frank Packer et al., Australia
1964 CONSTELLATION (4), New York Y.C. Syndicate, U.S.	SOVEREIGN (0), J. Anthony Bowden, England
1967 INTREPID (4), New York Y.C. Syndicate, U.S.	DAME PATTIE (0), Sydney (Aust.) Syndicate
1970 INTREPID (4), New York Y.C. Syndicate, U.S.	GRETEL II (1), Sydney (Aust.) Syndicate
1974 COURAGEOUS (4), New York, N.Y. Syndicate, U.S.	SOUTHERN CROSS (0), Sydney (Aust.) Syndicate

Year	Winner and owner	Loser and owner
1977	COURAGEOUS (4), New York, N.Y. Syndicate, U.S.	AUSTRALIA (0), Sun City (Aust.) Syndicate
1980	FREEDOM (4), New York, N.Y. Syndicate, U.S.	AUSTRALIA (1), Alan Bond et al, Australia
1983	AUSTRALIA II (4), Alan Bond et al., Australia	LIBERTY, (3) New York, N.Y. Syndicate, U.S.
1987	STARS & STRIPES (4), Dennis Conner et al., United States	KOOKABURRA III (0), Iain Murray et al., Australia
1984[4]	STARS & STRIPES, Dennis Conner, et al., United States	NEW ZEALAND, Michael Fay, et al., New Zealand
1992	AMERICA 3, Bill Koch, et al., United States	IL MORO DI VENEZIA, Paul Cayard, et al., Italy
1995	BLACK MAGIC, Peter Blake, et al., New Zealand	YOUNG AMERICA, Dennis Conner, et al., United States

1. Fourteen British yachts started against America; Aurora finished second. 2. Cambria sailed against 23 U.S. yachts and finished tenth. 3. Columbia was disabled in the third race, after winning the first two; Sappho substituted and won the fourth and fifth. 4. Shortly after Dennis Conner and his 60-foot, twin-hulled catamaran easily defeated the challenge of the New Zealand, a 133-foot, single-hulled yacht in the waters off San Diego in early September 1988, a New York State Supreme Court judge ruled that the Americans did not live up to the America's Cup Deed of Gift, which means competing boats must be similar. The judge ruled that the Americans had an unfair advantage over the monohulled ship, and awarded the Cup to New Zealand. However, an Appeal awarded the Cup to the United States.

Rodeo

PROFESSIONAL RODEO COWBOY ASSOCIATION, ALL AROUND COWBOY

1953	Bill Linderman	1963–65	Dean Oliver	1976–79	Tom Ferguson	1988	Dave Appleton
1954	Buck Rutherford	1966–70	Larry Mahan	1980	Paul Tierney	1989–94	Ty Murray
1955	Casey Tibbs	1971–72	Phil Lyne	1981	Jimmie Cooper	1995–96	Joe Beaver
1956–59	Jim Shoulders	1973	Larry Mahan	1982	Chris Lybbert	1997	Dan Mortensen
1960	Harry Tompkins	1974	Tom Ferguson	1983	Roy Cooper	1998	Ty Murray
1961	Benny Reynolds	1975	Leo Camarillo and	1984	Dee Pickett	1999[1]	Fred Whitfield
1962	Tom Nesmith		Tom Ferguson	1985–87	Lewis Field		

1. Unofficial standing as of Sept. 21, 1999.

Marathons

BOSTON MARATHON

(April 19, 1999)

Men	Time	Women	Time
1. Joseph Chebet, Kenya	2:09:52	1. Fatuma Roba, Ethiopia	2:23:25
2. Silvio Guerra, Ecuador	2:10:19	2. Franziska Rochat-Moser, Switzerland	2:25:51
3. Frank Pooe, South Africa	2:11:37	3. Yuko Arimori, Japan	2:26:39
4. Abner Chipu, South Africa	2:12:46	4. Colleen De Reuck, South Africa	2:27:54
5. John Kagwe, Kenya	2:13:58	5. Martha Tenorio, Ecuador	2:27:58
Wheelchair—Franz Nietlispach, Switzerland	1:21:36	Wheelchair—Louise Sauvage, Australia	1:42:23

OTHER 1998–99 MARATHONS

Los Angeles (March 14, 1999)

Men	Time
Simon Bor, Kenya	2:09:25
Wheelchair—Saul Mendoza, Snellville, Ga.	1:28:43
Women	
Irina Bogacheva, Kyrgyzstan	2:30:32
Wheelchair—Deanna Sodoma, Escondido, Calif.	2:03:44

London (April 16, 1999)

Men	Time
Abdelkader el Mouaziz, Morocco	2:07:57
Wheelchair—Heinz Frei, Switzerland	1:35:27
Women	
Joyce Chepchumba, Kenya	2:23:22
Wheelchair—Monica Wetterstorm, Sweden	1:57:38

Paris (April 4, 1999)

Men	Time
Julius Ruto, Kenya	2:08:10
Women	
Cristina Costea, Romania	2:26:11

New York City (Nov. 1, 1998)

Men	Time
John Kagwe, Kenya	2:08:45
Wheelchair—Miguel Such, Pennsylvania	1:47:03
Women	
Franca Fiacconi, Italy	2:25:17
Wheelchair—Nadia Zibani, Algeria	3:52:48

Curling

UNITED STATES CHAMPIONSHIPS—1999

	Site	Winner's Home Club	Skip
Men's	Duluth, Minn.	Wisconsin 2 (Superior, Wis.)	Tim Somerville
Women's	Duluth, Minn.	Team USA (Madison, Wis.)	Patti Lank
Junior Men's	Waupaca, Wis.	Nebraska (Omaha, Neb.)	Andy Roza
Junior Women's	Waupaca, Wis.	Minnesota 2 (Bemidji, Minn.)	Hope Schmitt

WORLD CHAMPIONSHIPS—1999

	Site	Winner's Country	Skip
Men's	St. John, New Brunswick, Canada	Scotland	Hammy McMillan
Women's	St. John, New Brunswick, Canada	Sweden	Elisabet Gustafson
Junior Men's	Östersund, Sweden	Canada	John Morris
Junior Women's	Östersund, Sweden	Switzerland	Silvana Tirinzoni

Little League

LITTLE LEAGUE WORLD SERIES CHAMPIONS

Year	Champion	Runner-up	Score	Year	Champion	Runner-up	Score
1947	Williamsport, Pa.	Lock Haven, Pa.	16–7	1975	Lakewood, N.J.	Tampa, Fla.	4–3
1948	Lock Haven, Pa.	St. Petersburg, Fla.	6–5	1976	Tokyo, Japan	Campbell, Calif.	10–3
1949	Hammontown, N.J.	Pensacola, Fla.	5–0	1977	Kao Hsiung, Taiwan	El Cajon, Calif.	7–2
1950	Houston, Tex.	Bridgeport, Conn.	2–1	1978	Pin-Tung, Taiwan	Danville, Calif.	11–1
1951	Stamford, Conn.	Austin, Tex.	3–0	1979	Hsien, Taiwan	Campbell, Calif.	2–1
1952	Norwalk, Conn.	Monongahela, Pa.	4–3	1980	Hua Lian, Taiwan	Tampa, Fla.	4–3
1953	Birmingham, Ala.	Schenectady, N.Y.	1–0	1981	Tai-Chung, Taiwan	Tampa, Fla.	4–2
1954	Schenectady, N.Y.	Colton, Calif.	7–5	1982	Kirkland, Wash.	Hsien, Taiwan	6–0
1955	Morrisville, Pa.	Merchantville, N.J.	4–3	1983	Marietta, Ga.	Barahona, D. Rep.	3–1
1956	Roswell, N.M.	Merchantville, N.J.	3–1	1984	Seoul, S. Korea	Altamonte Springs, Fla.	6–2
1957	Monterrey, Mex.	LaMesa, Calif.	4–0	1985	Seoul, S. Korea	Mexicali, Mex.	7–1
1958	Monterrey, Mex.	Kankakee, Ill.	10–1	1986	Tianan Park, Taiwan	Tucson, Ariz.	12–0
1959	Hamtramck, Mich.	Auburn, Calif.	12–0	1987	Hua Lian, Taiwan	Irvine, Calif.	21–1
1960	Levittown, Pa.	Ft. Worth, Tex.	5–0	1988	Tai-Chung, Taiwan	Pearl City, Haw.	10–0
1961	El Cajon, Calif.	El Campo, Tex.	4–2	1989	Trumbull, Conn.	Kaohsiung, Taiwan	5–2
1962	San Jose, Calif.	Kankakee, Ill.	3–0	1990	Taipei, Taiwan	Shippensburg, Pa.	9–0
1963	Granada Hills, Calif.	Stratford, Conn.	2–1	1991	Tai-Chung, Taiwan	San Ramon Valley, Calif.	11–0
1964	Staten Island, N.Y.	Monterrey, Mex.	4–0				
1965	Windsor Locks, Conn.	Stoney Creek, Can.	3–1	1992*	Long Beach, Calif.	Zamboanga, Phil.	6–0
1966	Houston, Tex.	W. New York, N.J.	8–2	1993	Long Beach, Calif.	David Chiriqui, Pan.	3–2
1967	West Tokyo, Japan	Chicago, Ill.	4–1	1994	Maracaibo, Venezuela	Northridge, Calif.	4–3
1968	Osaka, Japan	Richmond, Va.	1–0	1995	Tainan, Taiwan	Spring, Texas	17–3
1969	Taipei, Taiwan	Santa Clara, Calif.	5–0	1996	Kao-Hsuing City, Taipei	Cranston, R.I.	13–3
1970	Wayne, N.J.	Campbell, Calif.	2–0	1997	Guadalupe, Mexico	South Mission Viejo, Calif.	5–4
1971	Tainan, Taiwan	Gary, Ind.	12–3				
1972	Taipei, Taiwan	Hammond, Ind.	6–0	1998	Toms River, N.J.	Kashima, Japan	12–9
1973	Tainan City, Taiwan	Tucson, Ariz.	12–0	1999	Hirakata, Osaka, Japan	Phenix City, Ala.	5–0
1974	Kao Hsiung, Taiwan	El Cajon, Calif.	7–2				

* Long Beach declared a 6–0 winner after the international tournament committee determined that Zamboanga City had used players that were not within its city limits.

Bicycling

TOUR DE FRANCE–1999
(July 3–25, 1999)

The winner of the 2,287-mile race, American Lance Armstrong, 27, was diagnosed with testicular cancer less than three years before his 1999 victory. He is the second American to win the Tour de France.

	Team	Behind			Team	Behind
1. Lance Armstrong, United States	U.S. Postal	—	6.	Abraham Olano, Spain	Once	16:47
2. Alex Zuelle, Switzerland	Banesto	7:37	7.	Daniele Nardello, Italy	Mapei	17:02
3. Fernando Escartin, Spain	Kelme	10:26	8.	Richard Virenque, France	Polti	17:28
4. Laurent Dufaux, Switzerland	Saeco	14:43	9.	Wladimir Belli, Italy	Festina	17:37
5. Angel Casero, Spain	Vitalicio Seguros	15:11	10.	Andrea Peron, Italy	Once	23:10

Baseball

The popular tradition that baseball was invented by Abner Doubleday at Cooperstown, N.Y., in 1839 has been enshrined in the Hall of Fame and National Museum of Baseball erected in that town, but research has proved that a game called "Base Ball" was played in this country and England before 1839. The first team baseball as we know it was played at the Elysian Fields, Hoboken, N.J., on June 19, 1846, between the Knickerbockers and the New York Nine. The next fifty years saw a gradual growth of baseball and an improvement of equipment and playing skill.

Historians have it that the first pitcher to throw a curve was William A. (Candy) Cummings in 1867. The Cincinnati Red Stockings were the first all-professional team, and in 1869 they played 64 games without a loss. The standard ball of the same size and weight, still the rule, was adopted in 1872. The first catcher's mask was worn in 1875. The National League was organized in 1876. The first chest protector was worn in 1885. The three-strike rule was put on the books in 1887, and the four-ball ticket to first base was instituted in 1889. The pitching distance was lengthened to 60 feet 6 inches in 1893, and the rules have been modified only slightly since that time.

The American League, under the vigorous leadership of B. B. Johnson, became a major league in 1901. Judge Kenesaw Mountain Landis, by action of the two major leagues, became Commissioner of Baseball in 1921.

MAJOR LEAGUE ALL-STAR GAME

Year	Date	Winning league and manager	Runs	Losing league and manager	Runs	Winning pitcher	Losing pitcher	Site	Paid attendance
1933	July 6	A.L. (Mack)	4	N.L. (McGraw)	2	Gomez	Hallahan	Chicago A.L.	47,595
1934	July 10	A.L. (Cronin)	9	N.L. (Terry)	7	Harder	Mungo	New York N.L.	48,363
1935	July 8	A.L. (Cochrane)	4	N.L. (Frisch)	1	Gomez	Walker	Cleveland A.L.	69,831
1936	July 7	N.L. (Grimm)	4	A.L. (McCarthy)	3	J. Dean	Grove	Boston N.L.	25,556
1937	July 7	A.L. (McCarthy)	8	N.L. (Terry)	3	Gomez	J. Dean	Washington A.L.	31,391
1938	July 6	N.L. (Terry)	4	A.L. (McCarthy)	1	Vander Meer	Gomez	Cincinnati N.L.	27,067
1939	July 11	A.L. (McCarthy)	3	N.L. (Hartnett)	1	Bridges	Lee	New York A.L.	62,892
1940	July 9	N.L. (McKechnie)	4	A.L. (Cronin)	0	Derringer	Ruffing	St. Louis N.L.	32,373
1941	July 8	A.L. (Baker)	7	N.L. (McKechnie)	5	E. Smith	Passeau	Detroit A.L.	54,674
1942	July 6	A.L. (McCarthy)	3	N.L. (Durocher)	1	Chandler	Cooper	New York N.L.	34,178
1943	July 13	A.L. (McCarthy)	5	N.L. (Southworth)	3	Leonard	Cooper	Philadelphia A.L.	31,938
1944	July 11	N.L. (Southworth)	7	A.L. (McCarthy)	1	Raffensberger	Hughson	Pittsburgh N.L.	29,589
1946	July 9	A.L. (O'Neill)	12	N.L. (Grimm)	0	Feller	Passeau	Boston A.L.	34,906
1947	July 8	A.L. (Cronin)	2	N.L. (Dyer)	1	Shea	Sain	Chicago N.L.	41,123
1948	July 13	A.L. (Harris)	5	N.L. (Durocher)	2	Raschi	Schmitz	St. Louis A.L.	34,009
1949	July 12	A.L. (Boudreau)	11	N.L. (Southworth)	7	Trucks	Newcombe	Brooklyn N.L.	32,577
1950	July 11	N.L. (Shotton)	4	A.L. (Stengel)	3[1]	Blackwell	Gray	Chicago A.L.	46,127
1951	July 10	N.L. (Sawyer)	8	A.L. (Stengel)	3	Maglie	Lopat	Detroit A.L.	52,075
1952	July 8	N.L. (Durocher)	3	A.L. (Stengel)	2[2]	Rush	Lemon	Philadelphia N.L.	32,785
1953	July 14	N.L. (Dressen)	5	A.L. (Stengel)	1	Spahn	Reynolds	Cincinnati N.L.	30,846
1954	July 13	A.L. (Stengel)	11	N.L. (Alston)	9	Stone	Conley	Cleveland A.L.	68,751
1955	July 12	N.L. (Durocher)	6	A.L. (Lopez)	5[3]	Conley	Sullivan	Milwaukee N.L.	45,643
1956	July 10	N.L. (Alston)	7	A.L. (Stengel)	3	Friend	Pierce	Washington A.L.	28,843
1957	July 9	A.L. (Stengel)	6	N.L. (Alston)	5	Bunning	Simmons	St. Louis N.L.	30,693
1958	July 8	A.L. (Stengel)	4	N.L. (Haney)	3	Wynn	Friend	Baltimore A.L.	48,829
1959[4]	July 7	N.L. (Haney)	5	A.L. (Stengel)	4	Antonelli	Ford	Pittsburgh N.L.	35,277
	Aug. 3	A.L. (Stengel)	5	N.L. (Haney)	3	Walker	Drysdale	Los Angeles N.L.	55,105
1960[4]	July 11	N.L. (Alston)	5	A.L. (Lopez)	3	Friend	Monbouquette	Kansas City A.L.	30,619
	July 13	N.L. (Alston)	6	A.L. (Lopez)	0	Law	Ford	New York A.L.	38,362
1961[4]	July 11	N.L. (Murtaugh)	5	A.L. (Richards)	4[5]	Miller	Wilhelm	San Francisco N.L.	44,115
	July 31	N.L (Murtaugh)	1	A.L. (Richards)	1[6]	—	—	Boston A.L.	31,851
1962[4]	July 10	N.L. (Hutchinson)	3	A.L. (Houk)	1	Marichal	Pascual	Washington A.L.	45,480
	July 30	A.L. (Houk)	9	N.L. (Hutchinson)	4	Herbert	Mahaffey	Chicago N.L.	38,359
1963	July 9	N.L. (Dark)	5	A.L. (Houk)	3	Jackson	Bunning	Cleveland A.L.	44,160
1964	July 7	N.L. (Alston)	7	A.L. (Lopez)	4	Marichal	Radatz	New York N.L.	50,850
1965	July 13	N.L. (March)	6	A.L. (Lopez)	5	Koufax	McDowell	Minnesota A.L.	46,706
1966	July 12	N.L. (Alston)	2	A.L. (Mele)	1[5]	Perry	Rickert	St. Louis N.L.	49,926
1967	July 11	N.L. (Alston)	2	A.L. (Bauer)	1[7]	Drysdale	Hunter	Anaheim A.L.	46,309
1968	July 9	N.L. (Schoendienst)	1	A.L. (Williams)	0	Drysdale	Tiant	Houston N.L.	48,321
1969	July 23	N.L. (Schoendienst)	9	A.L. (M. Smith)	3	Carlton	Stottlemyre	Washington A.L.	45,259
1970	July 14	N.L. (Hodges)	5	A.L. (Weaver)	4	Osteen	Wright	Cincinnati N.L.	51,838
1971	July 13	A.L. (Weaver)	6	N.L. (Anderson)	4	Blue	Ellis	Detroit A.L.	53,559
1972	July 25	N.L. (Murtaugh)	4	A.L. (Weaver)	3[5]	McGraw	McNally	Atlanta N.L.	53,107
1973	July 24	N.L. (Anderson)	7	A.L. (Williams)	1	Wise	Blyleven	Kansas City A.L.	40,849
1974	July 23	N.L. (Berra)	7	A.L. (Williams)	2	Brett	Tiant	Pittsburgh N.L.	50,706
1975	July 15	N.L. (Alston)	6	A.L. (Dark)	3	Matlack	Hunter	Milwaukee A.L.	51,540
1976	July 13	N.L. (Anderson)	7	A.L. (D. Johnson)	1	R. Jones	Fidrych	Philadelphia N.L.	63,974
1977	July 19	N.L. (Anderson)	7	A.L. (Martin)	5	Sutton	Palmer	New York A.L.	56,683

Year	Date	Winning league and manager	Runs	Losing league and manager	Runs	Winning pitcher	Losing pitcher	Site	Paid attendance
1978	July 11	N.L. (Lasorda)	7	A.L. (Martin)	3	Sutter	Gossage	San Diego N.L.	51,549
1979	July 17	N.L. (Lasorda)	7	A.L. (Lemon)	6	Sutter	Kern	Seattle A.L.	58,905
1980	July 8	N.L. (Tanner)	4	A.L. (Weaver)	2	Reuss	John	Los Angeles N.L.	56,088
1981[8]	Aug. 9	N.L. (Green)	5	A.L. (Frey)	4	Blue	Fingers	Cleveland A.L.	72,086
1982	July 13	N.L. (Lasorda)	4	A.L. (Martin)	1	Rogers	Eckersley	Montreal N.L.	59,057
1983	July 6	A.L. (Kuenn)	13	N.L. (Herzog)	3	Steib	Soto	Chicago A.L.	43,801
1984	July 11	N.L. (Owens)	3	A.L. (Altobelli)	1	Leg	Steib	San Francisco, N.L.	57,756
1985	July 16	N.L. (Williams)	6	A.L. (Anderson)	1	Hoyt	Morris	Minneapolis, A.L.	54,960
1986	July 15	A.L. (Howser)	3	N.L. (Herzog)	2	Clemens	Gooden	Houston, N.L.	45,774
1987	July 14	N.L. (Johnson)	2	A.L. (McNamara)	0	Smith	Howell	Oakland, A.L.	49,671
1988	July 12	A.L. (Kelly)	2	N.L. (Herzog)	1	Viola	Gooden	Cincinnati, N.L.	55,837
1989	July 11	A.L. (LaRussa)	5	N.L. (Lasorda)	3	Ryan	Smoltz	California, A.L.	64,036
1990	July 10	A.L. (LaRussa)	2	N.L. (Craig)	0	Saberhagen	Brantley	Chicago, N.L.	39,071
1991	July 9	A.L. (LaRussa)	4	N.L. (Piniella)	2	Key	Martinez	Toronto, A.L.	52,383
1992	July 14	A.L. (Kelly)	13	N.L. (Cox)	6	Brown	Glavine	San Diego, N.L.	59,372
1993	July 13	A.L. (Gaston)	9	N.L. (Cox)	3	McDowell	Burkett	Baltimore, A.L.	48,147
1994	July 12	N.L. (Fregosi)	8	A.L. (Gaston)	7	Jones	Bere	Pittsburgh, N.L.	59,568
1995	July 11	N.L. (Alou)	3	A.L. (Showalter)	2	Slocumb	Rogers	Texas, A.L.	50,920
1996	July 9	N.L. (Cox)	6	A.L. (Hargrove)	0	Smoltz	Nagy	Philadelphia, N.L.	62,670
1997	July 8	A.L. (Torre)	3	N.L. (Cox)	1	Johnson	Maddux	Cleveland, A.L.	44,916
1998	July 7	A.L. (Hargrove)	13	N.L. (Leyland)	3	Colon	Urbina	Denver, N.L.	51,267
1999	July 13	A.L. (Torre)	4	N.L. (Bochy)	1	P. Martinez	Schilling	Boston, A.L.	34,187

1. Fourteen innings. 2. Five innings, rain. 3. Twelve innings. 4. Two games. 5. Ten innings. 6. Called because of rain after nine innings. 7. Fifteen innings. 8. Game was originally scheduled for July 14, but was put off because of players' strike. NOTE: No game in 1945.

NATIONAL BASEBALL HALL OF FAME
Cooperstown, N.Y.

Fielders

Member	Active years	Member	Active years	Member	Active years
Aaron, Henry (Hank)	1954–1976	Dandridge, Ray[1]	1933–1953	Killebrew, Harmon	1954–1975
Anson, Adrian (Cap)	1876–1897	Davis, George	1890–1909	Kiner, Ralph	1946–1955
Aparicio, Luis	1956–1973	Delahanty, Edward	1888–1903	Klein, Charles H. (Chuck)	1928–1944
Appling, Lucius (Luke)	1930–1950	Dickey, William	1928–1946	Lajoie, Napoleon	1896–1916
Ashburn, Richie	1948–1962	Dihigo, Martin[1]	1923–1945	Lazzeri, Tony	1926–1939
Averill, H. Earl	1929–1941	DiMaggio, Joseph	1936–1951	Leonard, Walter (Buck)[1]	1933–1955
Baker, J. Frank (Home Run)	1908–1922	Doby, Larry	1947–1959	Lindstrom, Frederick	1924–1936
		Doerr, Bobby	1937–1951	Lloyd, John Henry[1]	1905–1931
Bancroft, David	1915–1930	Duffy, Hugh	1888–1906	Lombardi, Ernie	1932–1947
Banks, Ernest	1953–1971	Ewing, William	1880–1897	Mantle, Mickey	1951–1968
Beckley, Jacob	1888–1907	Eyers, John	1902–1919	Manush, Henry (Heinie)	1923–1939
Bell, James (Cool Papa)[1]	1920–1947	Ferrell, Rick	1929–1947	Maranville, Walter (Rabbit)	1912–1935
Bench, John	1967–1983	Flick, Elmer	1898–1910	Matthews, Edwin	1952–1968
Berra, Lawrence (Yogi)	1946–1965	Fox, Nellie	1947–1965	Mays, Willie	1951–1973
Bottomley, James	1922–1937	Foxx, James	1925–1945	McCarthy, Thomas	1884–1896
Boudreau, Louis	1938–1952	Frisch, Frank	1919–1937	McGraw, John J.	1891–1906
Bresnahan, Roger	1897–1915	Gehrig, H. Louis (Lou)	1923–1939	McCovey, Willie	1959–1980
Brett, George	1973–1993	Gehringer, Charles	1924–1942	Medwick, Joseph (Ducky)	1932–1948
Brock, Lou	1961–1980	Gibson, Josh[1]	1929–1946	Mize, John (The Big Cat)	1936–1953
Brouthers, Dennis	1879–1896	Goslin, Leon (Goose)	1921–1938	Morgan, Joe	1963–1984
Burkett, Jesse	1890–1905	Greenberg, Henry (Hank)	1933–1947	Musial, Stanley	1941–1963
Campanella, Roy	1948–1957	Hafey, Charles (Chick)	1924–1937	O'Rourke, James	1876–1894
Carew, Rod	1967–1985	Hamilton, William	1888–1901	Ott, Melvin	1926–1947
Carey, Max	1910–1929	Hartnett, Charles (Gabby)	1922–1941	Reese, Harold (Pee Wee)	1940–1958
Cepeda, Orlando	1958–1974	Heilmann, Harry	1914–1932	Rice, Edgar (Sam)	1915–1934
Chance, Frank	1898–1914	Herman, William	1931–1947	Rizzuto, Phil	1941–1956
Charleston, Oscar[1]	1915–1954	Hooper, Harry	1909–1925	Robinson, Brooks	1955–1977
Clarke, Fred	1894–1915	Hornsby, Rogers	1915–1937	Robinson, Frank	1956–1976
Clemente, Roberto	1955–1972	Irvin, Monford (Monte)[1]	1939–1956	Robinson, Jack	1947–1956
Cobb, Tyrus	1905–1928	Jackson, Reggie	1967–1987	Robinson, Wilbert	1886–1902
Cochrane, Gordon (Mickey)	1925–1937	Jackson, Travis	1922–1936	Roush, Edd	1913–1931
		Jennings, Hugh	1891–1918	Ruth, Babe	1914–1935
Collins, Edward	1906–1930	Johnson, William (Judy)[1]	1921–1937	Schalk, Raymond	1912–1929
Collins, James	1895–1908	Kaline, Albert W.	1953–1974	Schoendienst, Red	1945–1963
Comiskey, Charles	1882–1894	Keeler, William (Wee Willie)	1892–1910	Schmidt, Mike	1973–1989
Combs, Earle	1924–1935			Sewell, Joseph	1920–1933
Connor, Roger	1880–1897	Kell, George	1943–1957	Simmons, Al	1924–1944
Crawford, Samuel	1899–1917	Kelley, Joseph	1891–1908	Sisler, George	1915–1930
Cronin, Joseph	1926–1945	Kelly, George	1915–1932	Slaughter, Enos	1938–1959
Cuyler, Hazen (Kiki)	1921–1938	Kelly, Michael (King)	1878–1893	Snider, Edwin D. (Duke)	1947–1964

Member	Active years	Member	Active years	Member	Active years
Speaker, Tristram	1907–1928	Wagner, John (Honus)	1897–1917	Williams, Billy	1959–1976
Stargell, Willie	1962–1982	Wallace, Roderick (Bobby)	1894–1918	Williams, Theodore	1939–1960
Terry, William	1923–1936	Waner, Lloyd	1927–1945	Wilson, Lewis R. (Hack)	1923–1934
Thompson, Samuel	1885–1906	Waner, Paul	1926–1945	Yastrzemski, Carl	1961–1983
Tinker, Joseph	1902–1916	Ward, John (Monte)	1878–1894	Youngs, Ross (Pep)	1917–1926
Traynor, Harold (Pie)	1920–1937	Wells, Willie	1924–1949	Yount, Robin	1974–1993
Vaughan, Arky	1932–1948	Wheat, Zachariah	1909–1927		

1. Negro League player selected by special committee.

Pitchers

Alexander, Grover	1911–1930	Grove, Robert (Lefty)	1925–1941	Perry, Gaylord	1962–1983
Bender, Charles (Chief)	1903–1925	Haines, Jesse	1918–1937	Plank, Edward	1901–1917
Brown, Mordecai (3-Finger)	1903–1916	Hoyt, Waite	1918–1938	Radbourn, Charles (Hoss)	1880–1891
Bunning, Jim	1955–1971	Hubbell, Carl	1928–1943	Rixey, Eppa	1912–1933
Carlton, Steve	1965–1988	Hunter, Jim (Catfish)	1965–1979	Roberts, Robert (Robin)	1948–1966
Chesbro, John	1899–1909	Jenkins, Ferguson	1965–1983	Rogan, Wilber	1920–1938
Clarkson, John	1882–1894	Johnson, Walter	1907–1927	Ruffing, Charles (Red)	1924–1947
Coveleski, Stanley	1912–1928	Joss, Adrian	1902–1910	Rusie, Amos	1889–1901
Day, Leon[1]	1935–1955	Keefe, Timothy	1880–1893	Ryan, Jr., Nolan	1966–1973
Dean, Jerome (Dizzy)	1930–1947	Koufax, Sanford (Sandy)	1955–1966	Seaver, Tom	1967–1986
Drysdale, Don	1956–1969	Lemon, Robert	1946–1958	Spahn, Warren	1942–1965
Faber, Urban (Red)	1914–1933	Lyons, Theodore	1923–1946	Sutton, Don	1966–1988
Feller, Robert	1936–1966	Marichal, Juan	1960–1975	Vance, Arthur (Dazzy)	1915–1935
Fingers, Rollie	1968–1985	Marquard, Richard (Rube)	1908–1924	Waddell, Rube	1897–1910
Ford, Edward (Whitey)	1950–1967	Mathewson, Christopher	1900–1916	Walsh, Edward	1904–1917
Foster, Andrew (Rube)	1897–1926	McGinnity, Joseph	1899–1908	Welch, Michael (Mickey)	1880–1892
Foster, Bill	1923–1937	Newhouser, Hal	1939–1955	Wilhelm, Hoyt	1952–1972
Galvin, James (Pud)	1876–1892	Nichols, Charles (Kid)	1890–1906	Williams, Joseph	1910–1932
Gibson, Bob	1959–1975	Niekro, Phil	1959–1987	Willis, Vic	1898–1910
Gomez, Vernon (Lefty)	1930–1943	Paige, Leroy (Satchel)[1]	1926–1965	Wynn, Early	1939–1963
Griffith, Clark	1891–1914	Palmer, Jim	1965–1984	Young, Denton (Cy)	1890–1911
Grimes, Burleigh	1916–1934	Pennock, Herbert	1912–1934		

1. Negro League player selected by special committee.

Officials and Others

Alston, Walter[1]	Cummings, William A.[5]	Hulbert, William[2]	McKechnie, William B.[1]
Barlick, Al[4]	Durocher, Leo[1]	Johnson, B. Bancroft[2]	Rickey, W. Branch[1] [2]
Barrow, Edward[1] [2]	Evans, William G.[4] [2]	Klem, William[4]	Selee, Frank G.[1]
Bulkeley, Morgan G.[2]	Foster, Rube[2]	Landis, Kenesaw M.[6]	Spalding, Albert G.[4]
Cartwright, Alexander[2]	Frick, Ford C.[6] [2]	Lasorda, Tommy[1]	Stengel, Charles D.[7]
Chadwick, Henry[3]	Giles, Warren C.[2]	Lopez, Alfonso R.[7]	Veeck, Bill[2]
Chandler, A.B.[6]	Hanlon, Ned[2]	Mack, Connie[1] [2]	Weaver, Earl[1]
Chylak, Jr., Nestor[4]	Harridge, William[2]	MacPhail, Jr., Lee[2]	Weiss, George M.[2]
Comiskey, Charles[1]	Harris, Stanley R.[7]	MacPhail, Leland S.[2]	Wright, George[5]
Conlan, John[2]	Hubbard, R. Calvin[4]	McCarthy, Joseph V.[1]	Wright, Harry[5] [1]
Connolly, Thomas[4]	Huggins, Miller J.[1]	McGowan, Bill[4]	Yawkey, Thomas[2]

1. Manager. 2. Executive. 3. Writer-statistician. 4. Umpire. 5. Early player. 6. Commissioner. 7. Player-manager.

BASEBALL'S PERFECTLY PITCHED GAMES[1]
(no opposing runner reached base)

Lee Richmond—Worcester vs. Cleveland (N.L.) June 12, 1880 (1–0)

John M. Ward—Providence vs. Buffalo (N.L.) June 17, 1880 (5–0)

Cy Young—Boston vs. Philadelphia (A.L.) May 5, 1904 (3–0)

Addie Joss—Cleveland vs. Chicago (A.L.) Oct. 2, 1908 (1–0)

Ernest Shore[2]—Boston vs. Washington (A.L.) June 23, 1917 (4–0)

Charles Robertson—Chicago vs. Detroit (A.L.) April 30, 1922 (2–0)

Don Larsen[3]—New York (A.L.) vs. Brooklyn (N.L.) Oct. 8, 1956 (2–0)

Jim Bunning—Philadelphia vs. New York (N.L.) June 21, 1964 (6–0)

Sandy Koufax—Los Angeles vs. Chicago (N.L.) Sept. 9, 1965 (1–0)

Jim Hunter—Oakland vs. Minnesota (A.L.) May 8, 1968 (4–0)

Len Barker—Cleveland vs. Toronto (A.L.) May 15, 1981 (3–0)

Mike Witt—California vs. Texas (A.L.) Sept. 30, 1984 (1–0)

Tom Browning—Cincinnati vs. Los Angeles (N.L.) Sept. 16, 1988 (1–0)

Dennis Martinez—Montreal vs. Los Angeles (N.L.) July 28, 1991 (2–0)

Kenny Rogers—Texas vs. California (A.L.) July 28, 1994 (4–0)

David Wells—New York vs. Minnesota (A.L.) May 17, 1998 (4–0)

David Cone[4]—New York (A.L.) vs. Montreal (N.L.) July 18, 1999 (6–0)

1. Harvey Haddix, of Pittsburgh, pitched 12 perfect innings against Milwaukee (N.L.), May 26, 1959 but lost game in 13th on error and hit. 2. Shore, relief pitcher for Babe Ruth who walked first batter before being ejected by umpire, retired 26 batters who faced him and baserunner was out stealing. 3. World Series. 4. Interleague game.

LIFETIME BATTING, PITCHING, AND BASE-RUNNING RECORDS

(Records Through 1999)

Hits (3,000+)

Pete Rose	4,256
Ty Cobb	4,191
Henry Aaron	3,771
Stan Musial	3,630
Tris Speaker	3,515
Honus Wagner	3,430
Carl Yastrzemski	3,419
Paul Molitor	3,319
Eddie Collins	3,313
Willie Mays	3,283
Eddie Murray	3,255
Nap Lajoie	3,251
George Brett	3,154
Paul Waner	3,152
Robin Yount	3,142
Dave Winfield	3,110
Tony Gwynn	3,067
Rod Carew	3,053
Cap Anson	3,041
Lou Brock	3,023
Wade Boggs	3,010
Al Kaline	3,007
Roberto Clemente	3,000

Earned Run Average (Minimum 1,500 innings pitched)

Ed Walsh	1.82
Addie Joss	1.88
Mordecai Brown	2.06
John Ward	2.10
Christy Mathewson	2.13
Rube Waddell	2.16
Walter Johnson	2.17
Orval Overall	2.23
Tommy Bond	2.25
Ed Reulbach	2.28
Will White	2.28
Jim Scott	2.30
Ed Plank	2.35
Larry Corcoran	2.36
Ed Cicotte	2.38
Ed Killian	2.38
George McQuillan	2.38
Doc White	2.38
Nap Rucker	2.42
Terry Larkin	2.43
Jim McCormick	2.43
Jeff Tesreau	2.43

Runs Scored

Ty Cobb	2,246
Hank Aaron	2,174
Babe Ruth	2,174
Pete Rose	2,165
Rickey Henderson	2,103
Willie Mays	2,062
Cap Anson	1,996
Stan Musial	1,949
Lou Gehrig	1,888
Tris Speaker	1,882
Mel Ott	1,859
Frank Robinson	1,829
Eddie Collins	1,821
Carl Yastrzemski	1,816
Ted Williams	1,798
Paul Molitor	1,780
Charlie Gehringer	1,774
Jimmie Foxx	1,751
Honus Wagner	1,736
Jim O'Rourke	1,729
Willie Keeler	1,727
Jesse Burkett	1,720
Cap Anson	1,719
Billy Hamilton	1,690
Bid McPhee	1,678
Mickey Mantle	1,677
Dave Winfield	1,669
Joe Morgan	1,650

Strikeouts, Pitching

Nolan Ryan	5,714
Steve Carlton	4,136
Bert Blyleven	3,701
Tom Seaver	3,640
Don Sutton	3,574
Gaylord Perry	3,534
Walter Johnson	3,509
Phil Niekro	3,342
Roger Clemens	3,316
Ferguson Jenkins	3,192
Bob Gibson	3,117
Jim Bunning	2,855
Mickey Lolich	2,832
Cy Young	2,803
Frank Tanana	2,773
Warren Spahn	2,583
Bob Feller	2,581
Tim Keefe	2,560
Jerry Koosman	2,556
Christy Mathewson	2,502

Home Runs (350+)

Hank Aaron	755
Babe Ruth	714
Willie Mays	660
Frank Robinson	586
Harmon Killebrew	573
Reggie Jackson	563
Mike Schmidt	548
Mickey Mantle	536
Jimmie Foxx	534
Mark McGwire	522
Willie McCovey	521
Ted Williams	521
Eddie Mathews	512
Ernie Banks	512
Mel Ott	511
Eddie Murray	504
Lou Gehrig	493
Stan Musial	475
Willie Stargell	475
Dave Winfield	465
Carl Yastrzemski	452
Barry Bonds	445
Dave Kingman	442
Andre Dawson	438
Jose Canseco	431
Billy Williams	426
Darrell Evans	414
Duke Snider	407
Cal Ripken, Jr.	402
Al Kaline	399
Dale Murphy	398
Ken Griffey, Jr.	398
Joe Carter	396
Graig Nettles	390
Fred McGriff	390
Johnny Bench	389
Dwight Evans	385
Cal Ripken	384
Frank Howard	382
Jim Rice	382
Tony Perez	379
Orlando Cepeda	379
Norm Cash	377
Carlton Fisk	376
Rocky Colavito	374
Harold Baines	373
Gil Hodges	370
Ralph Kiner	369
Joe DiMaggio	361
Gary Gaetti	360
Johnny Mize	359
Yogi Berra	358
Lee May	354

Shutouts

Walter Johnson	110
Grover Alexander	90
Christy Mathewson	79
Cy Young	76
Ed Plank	69
Warren Spahn	63
Nolan Ryan	61
Tom Seaver	61
Bert Blyleven	60
Don Sutton	58
Pud Galvin	57
Ed Walsh	57
Bob Gibson	56
Mordecai Brown	55
Steve Carlton	55
Jim Palmer	53
Gaylord Perry	53
Juan Marichal	52

Strikeouts, Batting

Reggie Jackson	2,597
Willie Stargell	1,936
Mike Schmidt	1,883
Tony Perez	1,867
Dave Kingman	1,816
Jose Canseco	1,765
Bobby Bonds	1,757
Dale Murphy	1,748
Lou Brock	1,730
Mickey Mantle	1,710
Harmon Killebrew	1,699
Dwight Evans	1,697
Chili Davis	1,698
Dave Winfield	1,686
Andres Galarraga	1,615
Gary Gaetti	1,599
Lee May	1,570
Dick Allen	1,556
Willie McCovey	1,550
Dave Parker	1,537
Frank Robinson	1,532
Lance Parrish	1,527
Willie Mays	1,526

Walks

Babe Ruth	2,056
Ted Williams	2,019
Rickey Henderson	1,972
Joe Morgan	1,865
Carl Yastrzemski	1,845
Mickey Mantle	1,733
Mel Ott	1,708
Eddie Yost	1,614
Darrell Evans	1,605
Stan Musial	1,599
Pete Rose	1,566
Harmon Killebrew	1,559
Lou Gehrig	1,508
Mike Schmidt	1,507
Eddie Collins	1,499
Willie Mays	1,464
Jimmie Foxx	1,452
Eddie Mathews	1,444
Frank Robinson	1,420
Hank Aaron	1,402

RECORD OF WORLD SERIES GAMES
(Through 1998)

Figures in parentheses for winning pitchers (WP) and losing pitchers (LP) indicate the game number in the series.

1903—Boston A.L. 5 (Jimmy Collins); Pittsburgh N.L. 3 (Fred Clarke). WP—Bos.: Dinneen (2, 6, 8), Young (5, 7); Pitts.: Phillippe (1, 3, 4). LP—Bos.: Young (1), Hughes (3), Dinneen (4); Pitts.: Leever (2, 6), Kennedy (5), Phillippe (7, 8).

1904—No series.

1905—New York N.L. 4 (John J. McGraw); Philadelphia A.L. 1 (Connie Mack). WP—N.Y.: Mathewson (1, 3, 5); McGinnity (4); Phila.: Bender (2). LP—N.Y.: McGinnity (2); Phila.: Plank (1, 4), Coakley (3), Bender (5).

1906—Chicago A.L. 4 (Fielder Jones); Chicago N.L. 2 (Frank Chance). WP—Chi.: A.L.: Altrock (1), Walsh (3, 5), White (6); Chi.: N.L.: Reulbach (2), Brown (4). LP—Chi. A.L.: White (2), Altrock. (4); Chi.: N.L.: Brown (1, 6), Pfeister (3, 5).

1907—Chicago N.L. 4 (Frank Chance); Detroit A.L. 0 (Hugh Jennings). First game tied 3–3, 12 innings. WP—Pfeister (2), Reulbach (3), Overall (4), Brown (5). LP—Mullin (2, 5), Siever (3), Donovan (4).

1908—Chicago N.L. 4 (Frank Chance); Detroit A.L. 1 (Hugh Jennings). WP—Chi.: Brown (1, 4), Overall (2, 5); Det.: Mullin (3). LP—Chi.: Pfeister (3); Det.: Summers (1, 4), Donovan (2, 5).

1909—Pittsburgh N.L. 4 (Fred Clarke); Detroit A.L. 3 (Hugh Jennings). WP—Pitts.: Adams (1, 5, 7), Maddox (3); Det.: Donovan (2), Mullin (4, 6). LP—Pitts.: Camnitz (2), Leifield (4), Willis (6); Det.: Mullin (1), Summers (3, 5), Donovan (7).

1910—Philadelphia A.L. 4 (Connie Mack); Chicago N.L. 1 (Frank Chance). WP—Phila.: Bender (1), Coombs (2, 3, 5); Chi.: Brown (4). LP—Phila.: Bender (4); Chi.: Overall (1), Brown (2), McIntyre (3).

1911—Philadelphia A.L. 4 (Connie Mack); New York N.L. 2 (John J. McGraw). WP—Phila.: Plank (2), Coombs (3), Bender (4, 6); N.Y.: Mathewson (1), Crandall (5). LP—Phila.: Bender (1), Plank (5); N.Y.: Marquard (2), Mathewson (3, 4), Ames (6).

1912—Boston A.L. 4 (J. Garland Stahl); New York N.L. 3 (John J. McGraw). Second game tied, 6–6, 11 innings. WP—Bos.: Wood (1, 4, 8), Bedient (5); N.Y.: Marquard (3, 6), Tesreau (7). LP—Bos.: O'Brien (3, 6), Wood (7); N.Y.: Tesreau (1, 4), Mathewson (5, 8).

1913—Philadelphia A.L. 4 (Connie Mack); New York N.L. 1 (John J. McGraw). WP—Phila.: Bender (1, 4), Bush (3), Plank (5); N.Y.: Mathewson (2); LP—Phila.: Plank (2); N.Y.: Marquard (1), Tesreau (3), Demaree (4), Mathewson (5).

1914—Boston N.L. 4 (George Stallings); Philadelphia A.L. 0 (Connie Mack). WP—Rudolph (1, 4), James (2, 3). LP—Bender (1), Plank (2), Bush (3), Shawkey (4).

1915—Boston A.L. 4 (Bill Carrigan); Philadelphia N.L. 1 (Pat Moran). WP—Bos.: Foster (2, 5), Leonard (1), Shore (4); Phila.: Alexander (1). LP—Bos.: Shore (1); Phila.: Mayer (2), Alexander (3), Chalmers (4), Rixey (5).

1916—Boston A.L. 4 (Bill Carrigan); Brooklyn N.L. 1 (Wilbert Robinson). WP—Bos.: Shore (1, 5), Ruth (2), Leonard (4); Bklyn.: Coombs (3). LP—Bos.: Mays (3); Bklyn.: Marquard (1, 4), Smith (5), Pfeffer (5).

1917—Chicago A.L. 4 (Clarence Rowland); New York N.L. 2 (John J. McGraw). WP—Chi.: Cicotte (1), Faber (2, 5, 6); N.Y.: Benton (3), Schupp (4), LP—Chi.: Cicotte (5), Faber (4); N.Y.: Sallee (1, 5), Anderson (2), Benton (6).

1918—Boston A.L. 4 (Ed Barrow); Chicago N.L. 2 (Fred Mitchell). WP—Bos.: Ruth (1, 4), Mays (3, 6); Chi.: Tyler (2), Vaughn (5). LP—Bos.: Bush (2), Jones (5); Chi.: Vaughn (1, 3), Douglas (4), Tyler (6).

1919—Cincinnati N.L. 5 (Pat Moran); Chicago A.L. 3 (William Gleason). WP—Cin.: Ruether (1), Sallee (2), Ring

(4), Eller (5, 8); Chi.: Kerr (3, 6), Cicotte (7). LP—Cin.: Fisher (3), Ring (6), Sallee (7); Chi.: Cicotte (1, 4), Williams (2, 5, 8).

1920—Cleveland A.L. 5 (Tris Speaker); Brooklyn N.L. 2 (Wilbert Robinson). WP—Cleve.: Coveleski (1, 4, 7), Bagby (6), Mails (6); Bklyn.: Grimes (2), Smith (3). LP—Cleve.: Bagby (2), Caldwell (3). Bklyn.: Marquard (1), Cadore (4), Grimes (5, 7), Smith (6).

1921—New York N.L. 5 (John J. McGraw); New York A.L. 3 (Miller Huggins). WP—N.Y. N.L.: Barnes (3, 6), Douglas (4, 7), Nehf (8); N.Y. A.L.: Mays (1), Hoyt (2, 5). LP—N.Y. N.L.: Nehf (2, 5), Douglas (1). N.Y. A.L.: Quinn (3), Mays (4, 7), Shawkey (6), Hoyt (8).

1922—New York N.L. 4 (John J. McGraw); New York A.L. 0 (Miller Huggins). Second game tied 3–3, 10 innings. WP—Ryan (1), Scott (3), McQuillan (4), Nehf (5); LP—Bush (1, 5), Hoyt (3), Mays (4).

1923—New York A.L. 4 (Miller Huggins); New York N.L. 2 (John J. McGraw). WP—N.Y. A.L.: Pennock (2, 6), Shawkey (4), Bush (5); N.Y. N.L.: Ryan (1), Nehf (3). LP—N.Y. A.L.: Bush (1), Jones (3); N.Y. N.L.: McQuillan (2), Scott (4), Bentley (5), Nehf (6).

1924—Washington A.L. 4 (Bucky Harris); New York N.L. 3 (John J. McGraw). WP—Wash.: Zachary (2, 6), Mogridge (4), Johnson (7); N.Y.: Nehf (1), McQuillan (3), Bentley (5). LP—Wash.: Johnson (1, 5), Marberry (3); N.Y.: Bentley (2, 7), Barnes (4), Nehf (6).

1925—Pittsburgh N.L. 4 (Bill McKechnie); Washington A.L. 3 (Bucky Harris). WP—Pitts.: Aldridge (2, 5), Kremer (6, 7); Wash.: Johnson (1, 4), Ferguson (3). LP—Pitts.: Meadows (1), Kremer (3), Yde (4); Wash.: Coveleski (2, 5), Ferguson (6), Johnson (7).

1926—St. Louis N.L. 4 (Rogers Hornsby); New York A.L. 3 (Miller Huggins). WP—St. L.: Alexander (2, 6), Haines (3, 7); N.Y.: Pennock (1, 5), Hoyt (4). LP—St. L.: Sherdel (1, 5), Reinhart (4); N.Y.: Shocker (2), Ruether (3), Shawkey (6), Hoyt (7).

1927—New York A.L. 4 (Miller Huggins); Pittsburgh N.L. 0 (Donie Bush). WP—Hoyt (1), Pipgras (2), Pennock (3), Moore (4). LP—Kremer (1), Aldridge (2), Meadows (3), Miljus (4).

1928—New York A.L. 4 (Miller Huggins); St. Louis N.L. 0 (Bill McKechnie). WP—Hoyt (1, 4), Pipgras (2), Zachary (3). LP—Sherdel (1, 4), Alexander (2), Haines (3).

1929—Philadelphia A.L. 4 (Connie Mack); Chicago N.L. 1 (Joe McCarthy). WP—Phila.: Ehmke (1), Earnshaw (2), Rommel (4), Walberg (5); Chi.: Bush (3). LP—Phila.: Earnshaw (3) Chi.: Root (1), Malone (2, 5), Blake (4).

1930—Philadelphia A.L. 4 (Connie Mack); St. Louis N.L. 2 (Gabby Street). WP—Phila.: Grove (1, 5), Earnshaw (2, 6); St. L.: Hallahan (3), Haines (4). LP—Phila.: Walberg (3), Grove (4); St. L.: Grimes (1, 5), Rhem (2), Hallahan (6).

1931—St. Louis N.L. 4 (Gabby Street); Philadelphia A.L. 3 (Connie Mack). WP—St. L.: Hallahan (2, 5), Grimes (3, 7); Phila.: Grove (1, 6), Earnshaw (4). LP—St. L.: Derringer (1, 6), Johnson (4); Phila.: Earnshaw (2, 7), Grove (3), Hoyt (5).

1932—New York A.L. (Joe McCarthy); Chicago N.L. 0 (Charles Grimm). WP—Ruffing (1), Gomez (2), Pipgras (3), Moore (4). LP—Bush (1), Warneke (2), Root (3), May (4).

1933—New York N.L. 4 (Bill Terry); Washington A.L. 1 (Joe Cronin.). WP—N.Y.: Hubbell (1, 4), Schumacher (2), Luque (5); Wash.: Whitehill (3). LP—N.Y.: Fitzsimmons (3); Wash.: Stewart (1), Crowder (2), Weaver (4), Russell (5).

1934—St. Louis N.L. 4 (Frank Frisch); Detroit A.L. 3 (Mickey Cochrane). WP—St. L.: J. Dean (1, 7), P. Dean (3, 6); Det.: Rowe (2), Auker (4), Bridges (5). LP—St. L.: W. Walker (2, 4), J. Dean (5); Det.: Crowder (1), Bridges (3), Rowe (6), Auker (7).

1935—Detroit A.L. 4 (Mickey Cochrane); Chicago N.L. 2 (Charles Grimm). WP—Det.: Bridges (2, 6), Rowe (3), Crowder (4); Chi.: Warneke (1, 5); LP—Det.: Rowe (1, 5), Chi.: Root (2), French (3, 6), Carleton (4).

1936—New York A.L. 4 (Joe McCarthy); New York N.L. 2 (Bill Terry). WP—N.Y. A.L.: Gomez (2, 6), Hadley (3), Pearson (4); N.Y. N.L.: Hubbell (1), Schumacher (5); LP—N.Y. A.L.: Ruffing (1), Malone (5); N.Y. N.L.: Schumacher (2), Fitzsimmons (3, 6), Hubbell (4).

1937—New York A.L. 4 (Joe McCarthy); New York N.L. 1 (Bill Terry). WP—N.Y. A.L.: Gomez (1, 5), Ruffing (2), Pearson (3); N.Y. N.L.: Hubbell (4). LP—N.Y. A.L.: Hadley (4); N.Y. N.L.: Hubbell (1), Melton (2, 5), Schumacher (3).

1938—New York A.L. 4 (Joe McCarthy); Chicago N.L. 0 (Gabby Hartnett). WP—Ruffing (1, 4), Gomez (2), Pearson (3) LP—Lee (1, 4), Dean (2), Bryant (3).

1939—New York A.L. 4 (Joe McCarthy); Cincinnati N.L. 0 (Bill McKechnie). WP—Ruffing (1), Pearson (2), Hadley (3), Murphy (4). LP—Derringer (1), Walters (2), Thompson (3).

1940—Cincinnati N.L. 4 (Bill McKechnie); Detroit A.L. 3 (Del Baker). WP—Cin.: Walters (2, 6), Derringer (4, 7); Det.: Newsom (1, 5), Bridges (3). LP—Cin.: Derringer (1), Turner (4), Thompson (5); Det.: Rowe (2, 6), Trout (4), Newsom (7).

1941—New York A.L. 4 (Joe McCarthy); Brooklyn N.L. 1 (Leo Durocher). WP—N.Y.: Ruffing (1), Russo (3), Murphy (4), Bonham (5); Bklyn: Wyatt (2). LP—N.Y.: Chandler (2); Bklyn: Davis (1), Casey (3, 4), Wyatt (5).

1942—St. Louis N.L. 4 (Billy Southworth); New York A.L. 1 (Joe McCarthy). WP—St. L.: Beazley (2, 5), White (3), Lanier (4); N.Y.: Ruffing (1). LP—St. L.: Cooper (1); N.Y.: Bonham (2), Chandler (3), Donald (4), Ruffing (5).

1943—New York A.L. 4 (Joe McCarthy); St. Louis N.L. 1 (Billy Southworth). WP—N.Y.: Chandler (1, 5), Borowy (3), Russo (4); St. L.: Cooper (2). LP—N.Y.: Bonham (2); St. L.: Lanier (1), Brazle (3), Brecheen (4), Cooper (5).

1944—St. Louis N.L. 4 (Billy Southworth); St. Louis A.L. 2 (Luke Sewell). WP—St. L. N.L.: Donnelly (2), Brecheen (4), Cooper (6), Lanier (6); St. L. A.L.: Galehouse (1), Kramer (3). LP—St. L. N.L.: Cooper (1), Wilks (3); St. L. A.L.: Muncrief (2), Jakucki (4), Galehouse (5), Potter (6).

1945—Detroit A.L. 4 (Steve O'Neill); Chicago N.L. 3 (Charles Grimm). WP—Det.: Trucks (2), Trout (4), Newhouser (5, 7); Chi.: Borowy (1, 6), Passeau (3) LP—Det.: Newhouser (1), Overmire (3), Trout (6); Chi.: Wyse (2), Prim (4), Borowy (5, 7).

1946—St. Louis N.L. 4 (Eddie Dyer); Boston A.L. 3 (Joe Cronin). WP—St. L.: Brecheen (2, 6, 7), Munger (4); Bos.: Johnson (1), Ferriss (3), Dobson (5). LP—St. L.: Pollet (1), Dickson (3), Brazle (5); Bos.: Harris (2, 6), Hughson (4), Klinger (7).

1947—New York A.L. 4 (Bucky Harris); Brooklyn N.L. 3 (Burt Shotton). WP—N.Y.: Shea (1, 5), Reynolds (2), Page (7); Bklyn.: Casey (3, 4), Branca (6). LP—N.Y.: Newsom (3), Bevens (4), Page (6); Bklyn.: Branca (1), Lombardi (2), Barney (5), Gregg (7).

1948—Cleveland A.L. 4 (Lou Boudreau); Boston N.L. 2 (Billy Southworth). WP—Cleve.: Lemon (2, 6), Bearden (3), Gromek (4); Bos.: Sain (1), Spahn (5). LP—Cleve.: Feller (1, 5); Bos.: Spahn (2), Bickford (3), Sain (4), Voiselle (6).

1949—New York A.L. 4 (Casey Stengel); Brooklyn N.L. 1 (Burt Shotton). WP—N.Y.: Reynolds (1), Page (3), Lopat (4), Raschi (5); Bklyn.: Roe (2). LP—N.Y.: Raschi (2); Bklyn.: Newcombe (1, 4), Branca (3), Barney (5).

1950—New York A.L. 4 (Casey Stengel); Philadelphia N.L. 0 (Eddie Sawyer). WP—Raschi (1), Reynolds (2), Ferrick (3), Ford (4). LP—Konstanty (1), Roberts (2), Meyer (3), Miller (4).

1951—New York A.L. 4 (Casey Stengel); New York N.L. 2 (Leo Durocher). WP—N.Y. A.L.: Lopat (2, 5), Reynolds (4), Raschi (6); N.Y. N.L.: Koslo (1), Hearn (3). LP—N.Y. A.L.: Reynolds (1), Raschi (6); N.Y. N.L.: Jansen (2, 5), Maglie (4), Koslo (6).

1952—New York A.L. 4 (Casey Stengel); Brooklyn N.L. 3 (Chuck Dressen). WP—N.Y.: Raschi (2, 6), Reynolds (4, 7); Bklyn.: Black (1), Roe (3), Erskine (5). LP—N.Y.: Reynolds (1), Lopat (3), Sain (5); Bklyn.: Erskine (2), Black (4, 7), Loes (6).

1953—New York A.L. 4 (Casey Stengel); Brooklyn N.L. 2 (Chuck Dressen). WP—N.Y.: Sain (1), Lopat (2), McDonald (5), Reynolds (6); Bklyn.: Erskine (3), Loes (4). LP—N.Y.: Raschi (3), Ford (4); Bklyn.: Labine (1, 6), Roe (2), Podres (5).

1954—New York N.L. 4 (Leo Durocher); Cleveland A.L. 0 (Al Lopez). WP—Grissom (1), Antonelli (2), Gomez (3), Liddle (4). LP—Lemon (1, 4), Wynn (2), Garcia (3).

1955—Brooklyn N.L. 4 (Walter Alston); New York A.L. 3 (Casey Stengel). WP—Bklyn.: Podres (3, 7), Labine (4), Craig (5); N.Y.: Ford (1, 6), Byrne (2). LP—Bklyn.: Newcombe (1), Loes (2), Spooner (6); N.Y.: Turley (3), Larsen (4), Grim (5), Byrne (7).

1956—New York A.L. 4 (Casey Stengel); Brooklyn N.L. 3 (Walter Alston). WP—N.Y.: Ford (3), Sturdivant (4), Larsen (5), Kucks (7); Bklyn.: Maglie (1), Bessent (2), Labine (6). LP—N.Y.: Ford (1), Morgan (2), Turley (6); Bklyn.: Craig (3), Erskine (4), Maglie (5), Newcombe (7).

1957—Milwaukee N.L. 4 (Fred Haney); New York A.L. 3 (Casey Stengel). WP—Mil.: Burdette (2, 5, 7), Spahn (4); N.Y.: Ford (1), Larsen (3), Turley (6). LP—Mil.: Spahn (1), Buhl (3), Johnson (6); N.Y.: Shantz (2), Grim (4), Ford (5), Larsen (7).

1958—New York A.L. 4 (Casey Stengel); Milwaukee N.L. 3 (Fred Haney). WP—N.Y.: Larsen (3), Turley (5, 7), Duren (6); Mil.: Spahn (1, 4), Burdette (2). LP—N.Y.: Duren (1), Turley (2), Ford (4); Mil.: Rush (3), Burdette (5, 7), Spahn (6).

1959—Los Angeles N.L. 4 (Walter Alston); Chicago A.L. 2 (Al Lopez). WP—L.A.: Podres (2), Drysdale (3), Sherry (4, 6); Chi.: Wynn (1), Shaw (5). LP—L.A.: Craig (1), Koufax (5); Chi.: Shaw (2), Donovan (3), Staley (4), Wynn (6).

1960—Pittsburgh N.L. 4 (Danny Murtaugh); New York A.L. 3 (Casey Stengel). WP—Pitts.: Law (1, 4), Haddix (5, 7); N.Y.: Turley (2), Ford (3, 6). LP—Pitts.: Friend (2, 6), Mizell (3); N.Y.: Ditmar (1, 5), Terry (4, 7).

1961—New York A.L. 4 (Ralph Houk); Cincinnati N.L. 1 (Fred Hutchinson). WP—N.Y.: Ford (1, 4), Arroyo (3), Daley (5); Cin.: Jay (2). LP—N.Y.: Terry (2); Cin.: O'Toole (1, 4), Purkey (3), Jay (5).

1962—New York A.L. 4 (Ralph Houk); San Francisco N.L. 3 (Al Dark). WP—N.Y.: Ford (1), Stafford (3), Terry (5, 7); S.F. Sanford (2), Larsen (4), Pierce (6). LP—N.Y.: Terry (2), Coates (4), Ford (6); S.F.: O'Dell (1), Pierce (3), Sanford (5, 7).

1963—Los Angeles N.L. 4 (Walter Alston); New York A.L. 0 (Ralph Houk). WP—Koufax (1, 4), Podres (2), Drysdale (3). LP—Ford (1, 4), Downing (2), Bouton (3).

1964—St. Louis N.L. 4 (Johnny Keane); New York A.L. 3 (Yogi Berra). WP—St. L.: Sadecki (1), Craig (4), Gibson (5, 7); N.Y.: Stottlemyre (2), Bouton (3, 6). LP—St. L.: Gibson (2), Schultz (3), Simmons (6); N.Y.: Ford (1), Downing (4), Mikkelsen (5), Stottlemyre (7).

1965—Los Angeles N.L. 4 (Walter Alston); Minnesota A.L. 3 (Sam Mele). WP—L.A.: Osteen (3), Drysdale (5, 7); Minn.: Grant (1, 6), Kaat (2) LP—L.A.: Drysdale (1), Koufax (2), Osteen (6); Minn.: Pascual (3), Grant (4), Kaat (5, 7).

1966—Baltimore A.L. 4 (Hank Bauer); Los Angeles N.L. 0 (Walter Alston). WP—Drabowsky (1), Palmer (2), Bunker (3), McNally (4). LP—Drysdale (1, 4), Koufax (2), Osteen (3).

1967—St. Louis N.L. 4 (Red Schoendienst); Boston A.L. 3 (Dick Williams). WP—St. L.: Gibson (1, 4, 7), Briles (3); Bos.: Lonborg (2, 5), Wyatt (6). LP—St. L.: Hughes (2), Carlton (3), Lamabe (6); Bos.: Santiago (1, 4), Bell (3), Lonborg (7).

1968—Detroit A.L. 4 (Mayo Smith); St. Louis N.L. 3 (Red Schoendienst). WP—Det.: Lolich (2, 5, 7), McLain (6); St. L.: Gibson (1, 4), Washburn (3), LP—Det.: McLain (1, 4), Wilson (3); St. L.: Briles (2), Hoerner (5), Washburn (6), Gibson (7).

1969—New York N.L. 4 (Gil Hodges); Baltimore A.L. 1 (Earl Weaver). WP—N.Y.: Koosman (2, 5), Gentry (3), Seaver (4); Balt.: Cuellar (1). LP—N.Y.: Seaver (1); Balt.: McNally (2), Palmer (3), Hall (4), Watt (5).

1970—Baltimore A.L. 4 (Earl Weaver); Cincinnati N.L. 1 (Sparky Anderson) 1. WP—Balt.: Palmer (1), Phoebus (2), McNally (3), Cuellar (5); Cin.: Carroll (4). LP—Cin.: Nolan (1), Wilcox (2), Cloninger (3), Merritt (5); Balt.: Watt (4).

1971—Pittsburgh N.L. 4 (Danny Murtaugh); Baltimore A.L. 3 (Earl Weaver). WP—Pitts.: Blass (3, 7), Kison (4), Briles (5); Balt.: McNally (1, 6), Palmer (2). LP—Pitts.: Ellis (1), R. Johnson (2), Miller (6); Balt.: Cuellar (3, 7), Watt (4) McNally (5).

1972—Oakland A.L. 4 (Dick Williams); Cincinnati N.L. (Sparky Anderson) 3. WP—Oakland: Holtzman (1), Hunter (2, 7), Fingers (4); Cincinnati: Billingham (3), Grimsley (5, 6). LP—Oakland: Odom (3), Fingers (5), Blue (6); Cincinnati: Nolan (1), Grimsley (2), Carroll (4), Borbon (7).

1973—Oakland A.L. 4 (Dick Williams); New York N.L. 3 (Yogi Berra). WP—Oakland: Holtzman (1, 7), Lindblad (3), Hunter (6). New York: McGraw (2), Matlack (4), Koosman (5). LP—Oakland: Fingers (4), Holtzman (4), Blue (5). New York: Matlack (1, 7) Parker (3), Seaver (6).

1974—Oakland A.L. 4 (Al Dark); Los Angeles N.L. 1 (Walter Alston). WP—Oakland: Fingers (1), Hunter (3), Holtzman (4), Odom (5). Los Angeles: Sutton (2). LP—Oakland: Blue (2), Los Angeles: Messersmith (1, 4), Downing (3), Marshall (5).

1975—Cincinnati N.L. 4 (Sparky Anderson); Boston A.L. 3 (Darrell Johnson). WP—Cincinnati: Eastwick (2, 3), Gullett (5), Carroll (7); Boston: Tiant (1, 4), Wise (6). LP—Cincinnati: Gullett (1), Norman (4), Darcy (6); Boston: Drago (2), Willoughby (3), Cleveland (5), Burton (7).

1976—Cincinnati N.L. 4 (Sparky Anderson); New York A.L. 0 (Billy Martin). WP—Gullett (1), Billingham (2), Zachry (3), Nolan (4). LP—Alexander (1), Hunter (2), Ellis (3), Figueroa (4).

1977—New York A.L. 4 (Billy Martin); Los Angeles N.L. 2 (Tom Lasorda). WP—New York: Lyle (1), Torrez (3, 6), Guidry (4); Los Angeles: Hooton (2), Sutton (5). LP—New York: Hunter (2), Gullett (5); Los Angeles: Rhoden (1), John (3), Rau (4), Hooton (6).

1978—New York A.L. 4 (Bob Lemon), Los Angeles N.L. 2 (Tom Lasorda). WP—New York: Guidry (3), Gossage (4); Beattie (5), Hunter (6); Los Angeles: John (1), Hooton (2). LP—New York: Figueroa (1), Hunter (2); Los Angeles: Sutton (3, 6), Welch (4), Hooton (5).

1979—Pittsburgh N.L. 4 (Chuck Tanner), Baltimore A.L. 3 (Earl Weaver); WP—Pittsburgh: D. Robinson (2), Blyleven (5), Candelaria (6), Jackson (7); Baltimore: Flanagan (1), McGregor (3), Stoddard (4). LP—Pittsburgh: Kison (1), Candelaria (3), Tekulve (4); Baltimore: Stanhouse (2), Flanagan (5), Palmer (6), McGregor (7).

1980—Philadelphia N.L. 4 (Dallas Green), Kansas City A.L. 2 (Jim Frey). WP—Philadelphia: Walk (1), Carlton (2), McGraw (5), Carlton (6); Kansas City: Quisenberry (3), Leonard (4). LP—Philadelphia: McGraw (3), Christenson (4); Kansas City: Leonard (1), Quisenberry (2), Quisenberry (5), Gale (6).

1981—Los Angeles N.L. 4 (Tom Lasorda), New York A.L. 2 (Bob Lemon); WP—Los Angeles: Valenzuela (3), Howe (4), Reuss (5), Hooton (6); New York: Guidry (1), John (2). LP—Los Angeles: Reuss (1), Hooton (2); New York: Frazier (3), Frazier (4), Guidry (5), Frazier (6).

1982—St. Louis N.L. 4 (Whitey Herzog), Milwaukee A.L. 3 (Harvey Kuenn); WP—St. Louis: Sutter (2), Andujar (3), Stuper (6), Andujar (7). Milwaukee: Caldwell (1), Slaton (4), Caldwell (5). LP—St. Louis: Forsch (1), Bair (4), Forsch (5). Milwaukee: McClure (2), Vuckovich (3), Sutton (6), McClure (7).

1983—Baltimore A.L. 4 (Joe Altobelli), Philadelphia N.L. 1 (Paul Owens); WP—Baltimore: Boddicker (2), Palmer (3), Davis (4), McGregor (5). Philadelphia: Denny (1).

1984—Detroit A.L. 4 (Sparky Anderson), San Diego N.L. 1 (Dick Williams); WP—Det.: Morris (1,4), Wilcox (3), Lopez (5); San Diego: Hawkins (2). LP—Det.: Petry (2), San Diego: Thurmond (1), Lollar (3), Show (4), Hawkins (5).

1985—Kansas City A.L. 4 (Dick Howser), St. Louis N.L. 3 (Whitey Herzog); WP—KC: Saberhagen (3,7) Quisenberry (6), Jackson (5). St. Louis: Tudor (1,4) Dayley (2). LP—KC: Jackson (1), Leibrandt (2), Black (4); St. Louis: Andujar (3), Forsch (5), Worrell (6), Tudor (7).

1986—New York N.L. 4 (Dave Johnson); Boston A.L. (John McNamara) 3 WP—N.Y.—Ojeda (3), Darling (4), Aguilera (6), McDowell (7), Bos: Hurst (1), (5), Crawford (2). LP—N.Y. Darling (1), Gooden (2, 5).

1987—Minnesota, A.L. 4 (Tom Kelly); St. Louis N.L. (Whitey Herzog) 3. WP—Minn. Viola (1, 7), Blyleven (2), Schatzeder (6), St. Louis: Tudor (3), Forsch (4), Cox (5). LP—Minn. Berenguer (3), Viola (4), Blyleven (5); St. Louis: Magrane (1), Cox (2, 7), Tudor (6).

1988—Los Angeles N.L. 4 (Tommy Lasorda); Oakland A.L. (Tony LaRussa) 1. WP—Los Angeles: Hershiser (2, 5), Pena (1), Belcher (4); Oakland: Honeycutt (3). LP—Los Angeles: Howell (3); Oakland: Davis (2, 5), Eckersley (1), Stewart (4).

1989—Oakland, A.L. 4 (Tony LaRussa); San Francisco N.L. 0 (Roger Craig). WP—Oakland: Dave Stewart (1, 3), Mike Moore (2, 4). LP—San Francisco: Scott Garrelts (1, 3), Don Robinson (2), Rick Reuschel (2).

1990—Cincinnati N.L. 4 (Lou Piniella); Oakland A.L. 0 (Tony LaRussa). WP—Cincinnati: Jose Rijo (1, 4), Rob Dibble (2), Tom Browning (3). LP—Oakland: Dave Stewart (1, 4), Dennis Eckersley (2), Mike Moore (3).

1991—Minnesota, A.L. 4 (Tom Kelly); Atlanta, N.L. 3 (Bobby Cox). WP—Minnesota: Morris (1,7), Tapani (2), Aguilera (6). Atlanta: Clancy (3), Stanton (4), Glavine (5). LP—Minnesota: Aguilera (3), Gurhtie (4), Tapani (5). Atlanta: Leibrandt (1, 6), Glavine (2), Pena (7).

1992—Toronto, A.L. 4 (Cito Gaston); Atlanta, N.L. 2 (Bobby Cox). WP—Toronto: Ward (2, 3), Key (4, 6). Atlanta: Glavine (1), Smoltz (5). LP—Toronto: Morris (1, 5). Atlanta: Leibrandt (6), Reardon (2), Avery (3), Glavine (4).

1993—Toronto, A.L. 4 (Cito Gaston); Philadelphia, N.L. 2 (Jim Fregosi). WP—Toronto: Leiter (1), Hentgen (3), Castillo (4), Ward (6). Philadelphia: Mullholland (2), Schilling (5). LP—Toronto: Stewart (2), Guzman (5). Philadelphia: Schilling (1), Jackson (3), Williams (4, 6).

1994—World Series cancelled due to players' strike.

1995—Atlanta, N.L. 4 (Bobby Cox); Cleveland, A.L. 2 (Mike Hargrove). WP—Atlanta: Maddux (1), Glavine (2,6), Avery (4). Cleveland: Mesa (3), Hershiser (5). LP—Atlanta: Pena (3), Maddux (5). Cleveland: Hershiser (1), Martinez (2), Hill (4), Poole (6).

1996—New York, A.L. 4 (Joe Torre); Atlanta, N.L. 2 (Bobby Cox). WP—New York: Cone (3), Lloyd (4), Pettitte (5), Key (6). Atlanta: Smoltz (3), Maddux (2). LP—New York: Pettitte (1), Key (2). Atlanta: Glavine (3), Avery (4), Smoltz (5), Maddux (6).

1997—Florida, N.L. 4 (Jim Leyland); Cleveland, A.L. 3 (Mike Hargrove). WP—Florida: Hernandez (1, 5), Cook (3), Powell (7). Cleveland: Ogea (2, 6), Wright (4). LP—Florida: Brown (2, 6), Saunders (4). Cleveland: Hershiser (1, 5), Plunk (3), Nagy (7).

1998—New York, A.L. 4 (Joe Torre); San Diego, N.L. 0 (Bruce Bochy). WP—New York: Wells (1), Hernandez (2), Mendoza (3), Pettitte (4). LP—San Diego: Wall (1), Ashby (2), Hoffman (3), Brown (4).

WORLD SERIES CLUB STANDINGS

(Through 1998)

	Series	Won	Lost	Pct.		Series	Won	Lost	Pct.
Toronto (A)	2	2	0	1.000	Detroit (A)	9	4	5	.444
Florida (N)	1	1	0	1.000	Cleveland (A)	5	2	3	.400
Pittsburgh (N)	7	5	2	.714	New York (N-Giants)	14	5	9	.357
New York (A)	35	24	11	.686	Washington (A)	3	1	2	.333
Oakland (A)	6	4	2	.667	Atlanta (N)	4	1	3	.250
Minnesota (A)	3	2	1	.667	Philadelphia (N)	5	1	4	.200
New York (N-Mets)	3	2	1	.667	Chicago (N)	10	2	8	.200
Philadelphia (A)	8	5	3	.625	Brooklyn (N)	9	1	8	.111
St. Louis (N)	15	9	6	.600	St. Louis (A)	1	0	1	.000
Boston (A)	9	5	4	.556	San Francisco (N)	2	0	2	.000
Los Angeles (N)	9	5	4	.556	Milwaukee (A)	1	0	1	.000
Cincinnati (N)	9	5	4	.556	San Diego (N)	2	0	2	.000
Milwaukee (N)	2	1	1	.500					
Boston (N)	2	1	1	.500	**Recapitulation**				
Chicago (A)	4	2	2	.500					
Baltimore (A)	6	3	3	.500					**Won**
Kansas City (A)	2	1	1	.500	American League				54
					National League				38

LIFETIME WORLD SERIES RECORDS

(Through 1998)

Most hits—71, Yogi Berra, New York A.L., 1947, 1949–53, 1955–58, 1960–63.

Most runs—42, Mickey Mantle, New York A.L., 1951–53, 1955–58, 1960–64.

Most runs batted in—40, Mickey Mantle, New York A.L., 1951–53, 1955–58, 1960–64.

Most home runs—18, Mickey Mantle, New York A.L., 1951–53, 1955–58, 1960–64.

Most bases on balls—43, Mickey Mantle, New York A.L., 1951–53, 1955–58, 1960–64.

Most strikeouts—54, Mickey Mantle, New York A.L., 1951–53, 1955–58, 1960–64.

Most stolen bases—14, Eddie Collins, Philadelphia A.L. 1910–11, 13–14; Chicago A.L., 1917, 1919. Lou Brock, St. Louis N.L., 1964, 67–68.

Most victories, pitcher—10, Whitey Ford, New York A.L., 1950, 1953, 1955–58, 1960–64.

Most times member of winning team—10, Yogi Berra, New York A.L., 1947, 1949–53, 1956, 1958, 1961–62.

Most victories, no defeats—6, Vernon Gomez, New York A.L., 1932, 1936(2), 1937(2), 1938.

Most shutouts—4, Christy Mathewson, New York N.L., 1905 (3), 1913.

Most innings pitched—146, Whitey Ford, New York A.L., 1950, 1953, 1955–58, 1960–1964

Most consecutive scoreless innings—33⅔, Whitey Ford, New York A.L., 1960 (18), 1961 (14), 1962 (1⅔).

Most strikeouts by pitcher—94, Whitey Ford, New York A.L., 1950, 1953, 1955–58, 1960–64.

SINGLE GAME AND SINGLE SERIES RECORDS

(Through 1998)

Most hits game—5, Paul Molitor, Milwaukee A.L., first game vs. St. Louis, N.L., 1982.

Most 4-hit games, series—2, Robin Yount, Milwaukee A.L., first and fifth games vs. St. Louis N.L., 1982.

Most hits inning—2, held by many players.

Most hits series—13 (7 games) Bobby Richardson, New York A.L., 1964; Lou Brock, St. Louis N.L., 1968; Marty Barrett, Boston A.L., 1986.

Most home runs, series—5 (6 games) Reggie Jackson, New York A.L., 1977; 4 (7 games) Babe Ruth, New York A.L., 1926; Duke Snider, Brooklyn N.L., 1952, 1955; Hank Bauer, New York A.L., 1958; Gene Tenace, Oakland A.L., 1972; 4 (4 games) Lou Gehrig, New York A.L., 1928; 4 (6 games) Willie Aikens, Kansas City A.L., 1980.

Most home runs, game—3, Babe Ruth, New York A.L., 1926 and 1928; Reggie Jackson, New York A.L., 1977.

Most strikeouts, series—12 (6 games) Willie Wilson, Kansas City A.L., 1980; 11 (7 games) Ed Mathews, Milwaukee N.L., 1958; Wayne Garrett, New York N.L., 1973; 9 (5 games) Carmelo Martinez, San Diego, N.L., 1984; Duke Snider, Brooklyn N.L., 1949; 7 (4 games) Bob Muesel, New York A.L., 1927.

Most stolen bases, game—3, Honus Wagner, Pittsburgh N.L., 1909; Willie Davis, Los Angeles N.L., 1965; Lou Brock, St. Louis N.L., 1967 and 1968.

Most strikeouts by pitcher, game—17, Bob Gibson, St. Louis N.L. 1968.

Most strikeouts by pitcher in succession—6, Horace Eller, Cincinnati N.L., 1919; Moe Drabowsky, Baltimore A.L., 1966.

Most strikeouts by pitcher, series—35 (7 games) Bob Gibson, St. Louis N.L., 1968; 23 (4 games) Sandy Koufax, Los Angeles, 1963; 20 (6 games) Chief Bender, Philadelphia A.L., 1911; 18 (5 games) Christy Mathewson, New York N.L., 1905.

Most bases on balls, series—11 (7 games) Babe Ruth, New York A.L., 1926; Gene Tenace, Oakland A.L., 1973; 9 (6 games) Willie Randolph, New York A.L., 1981; 7 (5 games) James Sheckard, Chicago N.L., 1910; Mickey Cochrane, Philadelphia A.L., 1929; Joe Gordon, New York A.L., 1941; 7 (4 games) Hank Thompson, New York N.L., 1954.

Most consecutive scoreless innings one series—27, Christy Mathewson, New York N.L., 1905.

AMERICAN LEAGUE HOME RUN CHAMPIONS

Year	Player, team	No.	Year	Player, team	No.	Year	Player, team	No.
1901	Nap Lajoie, Phila.	13	1935	Jimmy Foxx, Phila., and	36	1969	Harmon Killebrew, Minn.	49
1902	Ralph Seybold, Phila.	16		Hank Greenberg, Det.		1970	Frank Howard, Wash.	44
1903	Buck Freeman, Bost.	13	1936	Lou Gehrig, N.Y.	49	1971	Bill Melton, Chicago	33
1904	Harry Davis, Phila.	10	1937	Joe DiMaggio, N.Y.	46	1972	Dick Allen, Chicago	37
1905	Harry Davis, Phila.	8	1938	Hank Greenberg, Det.	58	1973	Reggie Jackson, Oak.	32
1906	Harry Davis, Phila.	12	1939	Jimmy Foxx, Bost.	35	1974	Dick Allen, Chicago	32
1907	Harry Davis, Phila.	8	1940	Hank Greenberg, Det.	41	1975	Reggie Jackson, Oak., and	36
1908	Sam Crawford, Det.	7	1941	Ted Williams, Bost.	37		George Scott, Mil.	
1909	Ty Cobb, Det.	9	1942	Ted Williams, Bost.	36	1976	Graig Nettles, N.Y.	32
1910	J. Garland Stahl, Bost.	10	1943	Rudy York, Det.	34	1977	Jim Rice, Boston	39
1911	Franklin Baker, Phila.	9	1944	Nick Etten, N.Y.	22	1978	Jim Rice, Boston	46
1912	Franklin Baker, Phila.	10	1945	Vern Stephens, St. L.	24	1979	Gorman Thomas, Milwaukee	45
1913	Franklin Baker, Phila.	12	1946	Hank Greenberg, Det.	44	1980	Reggie Jackson, N.Y., and	41
1914	Franklin Baker, Phila., and	8	1947	Ted Williams, Bost.	32		Ben Oglivie, Mil.	
	Sam Crawford, Det.		1948	Joe DiMaggio, N.Y.	39	1981[1]	Tony Armas, Oak.,	22
1915	Robert Roth, Chi.-Cleve.	7	1949	Ted Williams, Bost.	43		Dwight Evans, Bost.,	
1916	Wally Pipp, N.Y.	12	1950	Al Rosen, Cleve.	37		Bobby Grich, Calif., and	
1917	Wally Pipp, N.Y.	9	1951	Gus Zernial, Chi.-Phila.	33		Eddie Murray, Balt. (tie)	
1918	Babe Ruth, Bost., and	11	1952	Larry Doby, Cleve.	32	1982	Gorman Thomas, Mil., and	39
	Clarence Walker, Phila.		1953	Al Rosen, Cleve.	43		Reggie Jackson, Calif.	
1919	Babe Ruth, Bost.	29	1954	Larry Doby, Cleve.	32	1983	Jim Rice, Boston	39
1920	Babe Ruth, N.Y.	54	1955	Mickey Mantle, N.Y.	37	1984	Tony Armas, Boston	43
1921	Babe Ruth, N.Y.	59	1956	Mickey Mantle, N.Y.	52	1985	Darrell Evans, Detroit	40
1922	Ken Williams, St. L.	39	1957	Roy Sievers, Wash.	42	1986	Jesse Barfield, Toronto	40
1923	Babe Ruth, N.Y.	41	1958	Mickey Mantle, N.Y.	42	1987	Mark McGwire, Oakland	49
1924	Babe Ruth, N.Y.	46	1959	Rocky Colavito, Cleve., and	42	1988	Jose Canseco, Oakland	42
1925	Bob Meusel, N.Y.	33		Harmon Killebrew, Wash.		1989	Fred McGriff, Toronto	36
1926	Babe Ruth, N.Y.	47	1960	Mickey Mantle, N.Y.	40	1990	Cecil Fielder, Detroit	51
1927	Babe Ruth, N.Y.	60	1961	Roger Maris, N.Y.	61	1991	Jose Canseco, Oakland and	44
1928	Babe Ruth, N.Y.	54	1962	Harmon Killebrew, Minn.	48		Cecil Fielder, Detroit (tie)	
1929	Babe Ruth, N.Y.	46	1963	Harmon Killebrew, Minn.	45	1992	Juan Gonzalez, Texas	43
1930	Babe Ruth, N.Y.	49	1964	Harmon Killebrew, Minn.	49	1993	Juan Gonzalez, Texas	46
1931	Lou Gehrig, N.Y., and	46	1965	Tony Conigliaro, Bost.	32	1994[2]	Ken Griffey, Jr., Seattle	40
	Babe Ruth, N.Y.		1966	Frank Robinson, Balt.	49	1995	Albert Belle, Cleveland	50
1932	Jimmy Foxx, Phila.	58	1967	Carl Yastrzemski, Bost., and	44	1996	Mark McGwire, Oakland	52
1933	Jimmy Foxx, Phila.	48		Harmon Killebrew, Minn.		1997	Ken Griffey, Jr., Seattle	56
1934	Lou Gehrig, N.Y.	49	1968	Frank Howard, Wash.	44	1998	Ken Griffey, Jr., Seattle	56
						1999	Ken Griffey, Jr., Seattle	48

1. Split season because of players' strike. 2. Season ended on August 12 because of a players' strike.

AMERICAN LEAGUE BATTING CHAMPIONS

Year	Player, team	Avg	Year	Player, team	Avg	Year	Player, team	Avg
1901	Nap Lajoie, Phila.	.422	1928	Goose Goslin, Wash.	.379	1955	Al Kaline, Det.	.340
1902	Ed Delahanty, Wash.	.376	1929	Lew Fonseca, Cleve.	.369	1956	Mickey Mantle, N.Y.	.353
1903	Nap Lajoie, Cleve.	.355	1930	Al Simmons, Phila.	.381	1957	Ted Williams, Bost.	.388
1904	Nap Lajoie, Cleve.	.381	1931	Al Simmons, Phila.	.390	1958	Ted Williams, Bost.	.328
1905	Elmer Flick, Cleve.	.306	1932	Dale Alexander, Det.-Bost.	.367	1959	Harvey Kuenn, Det.	.353
1906	George Stone, St. L.	.358	1933	Jimmy Foxx, Phila.	.356	1960	Pete Runnels, Bost.	.320
1907	Ty Cobb, Det.	.350	1934	Lou Gehrig, N.Y.	.363	1961	Norman Cash, Det.	.361
1908	Ty Cobb, Det.	.324	1935	Buddy Myer, Wash.	.349	1962	Pete Runnels, Bost.	.326
1909	Ty Cobb, Det.	.377	1936	Luke Appling, Chi.	.388	1963	Carl Yastrzemski, Bost.	.321
1910	Ty Cobb, Det.	.385	1937	Charley Gehringer, Det.	.371	1964	Tony Oliva, Minn.	.323
1911	Ty Cobb, Det.	.420	1938	Jimmy Foxx, Bost.	.349	1965	Tony Oliva, Minn.	.321
1912	Ty Cobb, Det.	.410	1939	Joe DiMaggio, N.Y.	.381	1966	Frank Robinson, Balt.	.316
1913	Ty Cobb, Det.	.390	1940	Joe DiMaggio, N.Y.	.352	1967	Carl Yastrzemski, Bost.	.326
1914	Ty Cobb, Det.	.368	1941	Ted Williams, Bost.	.406	1968	Carl Yastrzemski, Bost.	.301
1915	Ty Cobb, Det.	.369	1942	Ted Williams, Bost.	.356	1969	Rod Carew, Minn.	.332
1916	Tris Speaker, Cleve.	.386	1943	Luke Appling, Chi.	.328	1970	Alex Johnson, Calif.	.329
1917	Ty Cobb, Det.	.383	1944	Lou Boudreau, Cleve.	.327	1971	Tony Oliva, Minn.	.337
1918	Ty Cobb, Det.	.382	1945	George Stirnweiss, N.Y.	.309	1972	Rod Carew, Minn.	.318
1919	Ty Cobb, Det.	.384	1946	Mickey Vernon, Wash.	.353	1973	Rod Carew, Minn.	.350
1920	George Sisler, St. L.	.407	1947	Ted Williams, Bost.	.343	1974	Rod Carew, Minn.	.364
1921	Harry Heilmann, Det.	.394	1948	Ted Williams, Bost.	.369	1975	Rod Carew, Minn.	.359
1922	George Sisler, St. L.	.420	1949	George Kell, Det.	.343	1976	George Brett, Kansas City	.333
1923	Harry Heilmann, Det.	.403	1950	Billy Goodman, Bost.	.354	1977	Rod Carew, Minn.	.388
1924	Babe Ruth, N.Y.	.378	1951	Ferris Fain, Phila.	.344	1978	Rod Carew, Minn.	.333
1925	Harry Heilmann, Det.	.393	1952	Ferris Fain, Phila.	.327	1979	Fred Lynn, Boston	.333
1926	Heinie Manush, Det.	.378	1953	Mickey Vernon, Wash.	.337	1980	George Brett, Kansas City	.390
1927	Harry Heilmann, Det.	.398	1954	Bobby Avila, Cleve.	.341	1981[1]	Carney Lansford, Bost.	.336

Year	Player, team	Avg	Year	Player, team	Avg	Year	Player, team	Avg
1982	Willie Wilson, Kansas City	.332	1988	Wade Boggs, Boston	.366	1994[2]	Paul O'Neill, New York	.359
1983	Wade Boggs, Boston	.361	1989	Kirby Puckett, Minnesota	.339	1995	Edgar Martinez, Seattle	.356
1984	Don Mattingly, New York	.343	1990	George Brett, Kansas City	.328	1996	Alex Rodriguez, Seattle	.358
1985	Wade Boggs, Boston	.368	1991	Julio Franco, Texas	.341	1997	Frank Thomas, Chicago	.347
1986	Wade Boggs, Boston	.357	1992	Edgar Martinez, Seattle	.343	1998	Bernie Williams, New York	.339
1987	Wade Boggs, Boston	.363	1993	John Olerud, Toronto	.363	1999	Nomar Garciaparra, Boston	.357

1. Split season because of players' strike. 2. Season ended on August 12 because of a players' strike.

NATIONAL LEAGUE HOME RUN CHAMPIONS

Year	Player, team	No.	Year	Player, team	No.	Year	Player, team	No.
1876	George Hall, Phila. Athletics	5	1917	Davis Robertson, N.Y., and	12	1957	Henry Aaron, Mil.	44
1877	George Shaffer, Louisville	3		Cliff Cravath, Phila.		1958	Ernie Banks, Chi.	47
1878	Paul Hines, Providence	4	1918	Cliff Cravath, Phila.	8	1959	Ed Mathews, Mil.	46
1879	Charles Jones, Bost.	9	1919	Cliff Cravath, Phila.	12	1960	Ernie Banks, Chi.	41
1880	James O'Rourke, Bost., and	6	1920	Cy Williams, Phila.	15	1961	Orlando Cepeda, San Fran.	46
	Harry Stovey, Worcester		1921	George Kelly, N.Y.	23	1962	Willie Mays, San Fran.	49
1881	Dan Brouthers, Buffalo	8	1922	Rogers Hornsby, St. L.	42	1963	Henry Aaron, Mil., and	44
1882	George Wood, Det.	7	1923	Cy Williams, Phila.	41		Willie McCovey, San Fran.	
1883	William Ewing, N.Y.	10	1924	Jacques Fournier, Bkln.	27	1964	Willie Mays, San Fran.	47
1884	Ed Williamson, Chi.	27	1925	Rogers Hornsby, St. L.	39	1965	Willie Mays, San Fran.	52
1885	Abner Dalrymple, Chi.	11	1926	Hack Wilson, Chi.	21	1966	Henry Aaron, Atlanta	44
1886	Arthur Richardson, Det.	11	1927	Hack Wilson, Chi., and	30	1967	Henry Aaron, Atlanta	39
1887	Roger Connor, N.Y., and	17		Cy Williams, Phila.		1968	Willie McCovey, San Fran.	36
	Wm. O'Brien, Wash.		1928	Hack Wilson, Chi., and	31	1969	Willie McCovey, San Fran.	45
1888	Roger Connor, N.Y.	14		Jim Bottomley, St. L.		1970	Johnny Bench, Cin.	45
1889	Sam Thompson, Phila.	20	1929	Chuck Klein, Phila.	43	1971	Willie Stargell, Pitts.	48
1890	Tom Burns, Bklyn, and	13	1930	Hack Wilson, Chi.	56	1972	Johnny Bench, Cin.	40
	Mike Tiernan, N.Y.		1931	Chuck Klein, Phila.	31	1973	Willie Stargell, Pitts.	44
1891	Harry Stovey, Bost., and	16	1932	Chuck Klein, Phila., and	38	1974	Mike Schmidt, Phila.	36
	Mike Tiernan, N.Y.			Mel Ott, N.Y.		1975	Mike Schmidt, Phila.	38
1892	Jim Holliday, Cin.	13	1933	Chuck Klein, Phila.	28	1976	Mike Schmidt, Phila.	38
1893	Ed Delahanty, Phila.	19	1934	Mel Ott, N.Y., and	35	1977	George Foster, Cin.	52
1894	Hugh Duffy, Bost., and	18		Rip Collins, St. L.		1978	George Foster, Cin.	40
	Robert Lowe, Bost.		1935	Wally Berger, Bost.	34	1979	Dave Kingman, Chicago	48
1895	Bill Joyce, Wash.	17	1936	Mel Ott, N.Y.	33	1980	Mike Schmidt, Phila.	48
1896	Ed Delahanty, Phila., and	13	1937	Mel Ott, N.Y., and	31	1981[1]	Mike Schmidt, Phila.	31
	Sam Thompson, Phila.			Joe Medwick, St. L.		1982	Dave Kingman, N.Y.	37
1897	Nap Lajoie, Phila.	10	1938	Mel Ott, N.Y.	36	1983	Mike Schmidt, Phila.	40
1898	James Colins, Bost.	14	1939	John Mize, St. L.	28	1984	Mike Schmidt, Phila. and	36
1899	John Freeman, Wash.	25	1940	John Mize, St. L.	43		Dale Murphy, Atlanta	
1900	Herman Long, Bost.	12	1941	Dolph Camilli, Bklyn.	34	1985	Dale Murphy, Atlanta	37
1901	Sam Crawford, Con.	16	1942	Mel Ott, N.Y.	30	1986	Mike Schmidt, Phila.	37
1902	Tom Leach, Pitts.	6	1943	Bill Nicholson, Chi.	29	1987	Andre Dawson, Chicago	49
1903	James Sheckard, Bklyn.	9	1944	Bill Nicholson, Chi.	33	1988	Darryl Strawberry, N.Y.	39
1904	Harry Lumley, Bklyn.	9	1945	Tommy Holmes, Bost.	28	1989	Kevin Mitchell, San Fran-	47
1905	Fred Odwell, Cin.	9	1946	Ralph Kiner, Pitts.	23		cisco	
1906	Tim Jordan, Bklyn	12	1947	Ralph Kiner, Pitts., and	51	1990	Ryne Sandberg, Chicago	40
1907	David Brain, Bost.	10		John Mize, N.Y.		1991	Howard Johnson, N.Y.	38
1908	Tim Jordan, Bklyn.	12	1948	Ralph Kiner, Pitts., and	40	1992	Fred McGriff, San Diego	35
1909	John Murray, N.Y.	7		John Mize, N.Y.		1993	Barry Bonds, San Francisco	46
1910	Fred Beck, Bost., and	10	1949	Ralph Kiner, Pitts.	54	1994[2]	Matt Williams, San Francisco	43
	Frank Schulte, Chi.		1950	Ralph Kiner, Pitts.	47	1995	Dante Bichette, Colorado	40
1911	Frank Schulte, Chi.	21	1951	Ralph Kiner, Pitts.	42	1996	Andreas Galarraga, Colo-	40
1912	Henry Zimmerman, Chi.	14	1952	Ralph Kiner, Pitts., and	37		rado	
1913	Cliff Cravath, Phila.	19		Hank Sauer, Chi.		1997	Larry Walker, Colorado	49
1914	Cliff Cravath, Phila.	19	1953	Ed Mathews, Mil.	47	1998	Mark McGwire, St. Louis	70
1915	Cliff Cravath, Phila.	24	1954	Ted Kluszewski, Cin.	49	1999	Mark McGwire, St. Louis	65
1916	Davis Robertson, N.Y., and	12	1955	Willie Mays, N.Y.	51			
	Fred Williams, Chi.		1956	Duke Snider, Bklyn.	43			

1. Split season because of players' strike. 2. Season ended on August 12 because of a players' strike.

NATIONAL LEAGUE BATTING CHAMPIONS

Year	Player, team	Avg	Year	Player, team	Avg	Year	Player, team	Avg
1876	Roscoe Barnes, Chicago	.404	1881	Cap Anson, Chicago	.399	1886	King Kelly, Chicago	.388
1877	Jim White, Boston	.385	1882	Dan Brouthers, Buffalo	.367	1887	Cap Anson, Chicago	.421
1878	Abner Dalrymple, Mil.	.356	1883	Dan Brouthers, Buffalo	.371	1888	Cap Anson, Chicago	.343
1879	Cap Anson, Chicago	.407	1884	James O'Rourke, Buffalo	.350	1889	Dan Brouthers, Boston	.373
1880	George Gore, Chicago	.365	1885	Roger Connor, N. Y.	.371	1890	John Glasscock, N. Y.	.336

Year	Player, team	Avg	Year	Player, team	Avg	Year	Player, team	Avg
1891	William Hamilton, Phila.	.338	1927	Paul Waner; Pittsburgh	.380	1964	Roberto Clemente, Pitts.	.339
1892	Dan Brouthers, Bklyn., and	.335	1928	Rogers Hornsby, Boston	.387	1965	Roberto Clemente, Pitts.	.329
	Clarence Childs, Cleve.		1929	Lefty O'Doul, Phila.	.398	1966	Matty Alou, Pittsburgh	.342
1893	Hugh Duffy, Boston	.378	1930	Bill Terry, N.Y.	.401	1967	Roberto Clemente, Pitts.	.357
1894	Hugh Duffy, Boston	.438	1931	Chick Hafey, St. Louis	.349	1968	Pete Rose, Cincinnati	.335
1895	Jesse Burkett, Cleveland	.423	1932	Lefty O'Doul, Brooklyn	.368	1969	Pete Rose, Cincinnati	.348
1896	Jesse Burkett, Cleveland	.410	1933	Chuck Klein, Phila.	.368	1970	Rico Carty, Atlanta	.366
1897	Willie Keeler, Baltimore	.432	1934	Paul Waner, Pittsburgh	.362	1971	Joe Torre, St. Louis	.363
1898	Willie Keeler, Baltimore	.379	1935	Arky Vaughan, Pittsburgh	.385	1972	Billy Williams, Chicago	.333
1899	Ed Delahanty, Phila.	.408	1936	Paul Waner, Pittsburgh	.373	1973	Pete Rose, Cincinnati	.338
1900	Honus Wagner, Pittsburgh	.381	1937	Joe Medwick, St. Louis	.374	1974	Ralph Garr, Atlanta	.353
1901	Jesse Burkett, St. Louis	.382	1938	Ernie Lombardi, Cin.	.342	1975	Bill Madlock, Chicago	.354
1902	Clarence Beaumont, Pitts.	.357	1939	John Mize, St. Louis	.349	1976	Bill Madlock, Chicago	.339
1903	Honus Wagner, Pittsburgh	.355	1940	Debs Garms, Pittsburgh	.355	1977	Dave Parker, Pittsburgh	.338
1904	Honus Wagner, Pittsburgh	.349	1941	Pete Reiser, Brooklyn	.343	1978	Dave Parker, Pittsburgh	.334
1905	Cy Seymour, Cincinnati	.377	1942	Ernie Lombardi, Boston	.330	1979	Keith Hernandez, St. Louis	.344
1906	Honus Wagner, Pittsburgh	.339	1943	Stan Musial, St. Louis	.357	1980	Bill Buckner, Chicago	.324
1907	Honus Wagner, Pittsburgh	.350	1944	Dixie Walker, Brooklyn	.357	1981[1]	Bill Madlock, Pittsburgh	.341
1908	Honus Wagner, Pittsburgh	.354	1945	Phil Cavarretta, Chicago	.355	1982	Al Oliver, Montreal	.331
1909	Honus Wagner, Pittsburgh	.339	1946	Stan Musial, St. Louis	.365	1983	Bill Madlock, Pittsburgh	.323
1910	Sherwood Magee, Phila.	.331	1947	Harry Walker, St. L.-Phila.	.363	1984	Tony Gwynn, San Diego	.351
1911	Honus Wagner, Pittsburgh	.334	1948	Stan Musial, St. Louis	.376	1985	Willie McGee, St. Louis	.353
1912	Henry Zimmerman, Chicago	.372	1949	Jackie Robinson, Brooklyn	.342	1986	Tim Raines, Montreal	.334
1913	Jake Daubert, Brooklyn	.350	1950	Stan Musial, St. Louis	.346	1987	Tony Gwynn, San Diego	.370
1914	Jake Daubert, Brooklyn	.329	1951	Stan Musial, St. Louis	.355	1988	Tony Gwynn, San Diego	.313
1915	Larry Doyle, New York	.320	1952	Stan Musial, St. Louis	.336	1989	Tony Gwynn, San Diego	.336
1916	Hal Chase, Cincinnati	.339	1953	Carl Furillo, Brooklyn	.344	1990	Willie McGee, St. Louis	.335
1917	Edd Roush, Cincinnati	.341	1954	Willie Mays, N. Y.	.345	1991	Terry Pendleton, Atlanta	.319
1918	Zack Wheat, Brooklyn	.335	1955	Richie Ashburn, Phila.	.338	1992	Gary Sheffield, San Diego	.330
1919	Edd Roush, Cincinnati	.321	1956	Henry Aaron, Mil.	.328	1993	Andres Galarraga, Colorado	.370
1920	Rogers Hornsby, St. Louis	.370	1957	Stan Musial, St. Louis	.351	1994[2]	Tony Gwynn, San Diego	.394
1921	Rogers Hornsby, St. Louis	.397	1958	Richie Ashburn, Phila.	.350	1995	Tony Gwynn, San Diego	.368
1922	Rogers Hornsby, St. Louis	.401	1959	Henry Aaron, Mil.	.355	1996	Ellis Burks, Colorado	.344
1923	Rogers Hornsby, St. Louis	.384	1960	Dick Groat, Pittsburgh	.325	1997	Tony Gwynn, San Diego	.372
1924	Rogers Hornsby, St. Louis	.424	1961	Roberto Clemente, Pitts.	.351	1998	Larry Walker, Colorado	.363
1925	Rogers Hornsby, St. Louis	.403	1962	Tommy Davis, L. A.	.346	1999	Larry Walker, Colorado	.379
1926	Gene Hargrave, Cincinnati	.353	1963	Tommy Davis, L. A.	.326			

1. Split season because of players' strike. 2. Season ended on August 12 because of a players' strike.

AMERICAN LEAGUE PENNANT WINNERS

Year	Club	Manager	Won	Lost	Pct	Year	Club	Manager	Won	Lost	Pct
1901	Chicago	Clark C. Griffith	83	53	.610	1928[1]	New York	Miller J. Huggins	101	53	.656
1902	Philadelphia	Connie Mack	83	53	.610	1929[1]	Philadelphia	Connie Mack	104	46	.693
1903[1]	Boston	Jimmy Collins	91	47	.659	1930[1]	Philadelphia	Connie Mack	102	52	.662
1904[2]	Boston	Jimmy Collins	95	59	.617	1931	Philadelphia	Connie Mack	107	45	.704
1905	Philadelphia	Connie Mack	92	56	.622	1932[1]	New York	Joseph V. McCarthy	107	47	.695
1906[1]	Chicago	Fielder A. Jones	93	58	.616	1933	Washington	Joseph E. Cronin	99	53	.651
1907	Detroit	Hugh A. Jennings	92	58	.613	1934	Detroit	Gordon Cochrane	101	53	.656
1908	Detroit	Hugh A. Jennings	90	63	.588	1935[1]	Detroit	Gordon Cochrane	93	58	.616
1909	Detroit	Hugh A. Jennings	98	54	.645	1936[1]	New York	Joseph V. McCarthy	102	51	.667
1910[1]	Philadelphia	Connie Mack	102	48	.680	1937[1]	New York	Joseph V. McCarthy	102	52	.662
1911[1]	Philadelphia	Connie Mack	101	50	.669	1938[1]	New York	Joseph V. McCarthy	99	53	.651
1912[1]	Boston	J. Garland Stahl	105	47	.691	1939[1]	New York	Joseph V. McCarthy	106	45	.702
1913[1]	Philadelphia	Connie Mack	96	57	.627	1940	Detroit	Delmar D. Baker	90	64	.584
1914	Philadelphia	Connie Mack	99	53	.651	1941[1]	New York	Joseph V. McCarthy	101	53	.656
1915[1]	Boston	William F. Carrigan	101	50	.669	1942	New York	Joseph V. McCarthy	103	51	.669
1916[1]	Boston	William F. Carrigan	91	63	.591	1943[1]	New York	Joseph V. McCarthy	98	56	.636
1917[1]	Chicago	Clarence H. Rowland	100	54	.649	1944	St. Louis	Luke Sewell	89	65	.578
1918[1]	Boston	Ed Barrow	75	51	.595	1945[1]	Detroit	Steve O'Neill	88	65	.575
1919	Chicago	William Gleason	88	52	.629	1946	Boston	Joseph E. Cronin	104	50	.675
1920[1]	Cleveland	Tris Speaker	98	56	.636	1947[1]	New York	Stanley R. Harris	97	57	.630
1921	New York	Miller J. Huggins	98	55	.641	1948[1]	Cleveland	Lou Boudreau	97	58	.626
1922	New York	Miller J. Huggins	94	60	.610	1949[1]	New York	Casey Stengel	97	57	.630
1923[1]	New York	Miller J. Huggins	98	54	.645	1950[1]	New York	Casey Stengel	98	56	.636
1924[1]	Washington	Stanley R. Harris	92	62	.597	1951[1]	New York	Casey Stengel	98	56	.636
1925	Washington	Stanley R. Harris	96	55	.636	1952[1]	New York	Casey Stengel	95	59	.617
1926	New York	Miller J. Huggins	91	63	.591	1953[1]	New York	Casey Stengel	99	52	.656
1927[1]	New York	Miller J. Huggins	110	44	.714	1954	Cleveland	Al Lopez	111	43	.721

Year	Club	Manager	Won	Lost	Pct	Year	Club	Manager	Won	Lost	Pct
1955	New York	Casey Stengel	96	58	.623	1979	Baltimore[8]	Earl Weaver	102	57	.642
1956[1]	New York	Casey Stengel	97	57	.630	1980	Kansas City[9]	Jim Frey	97	65	.599
1957	New York	Casey Stengel	98	56	.636	1981	New York[10]	Gene Michael-Bob Lemon	59	48	.551*
1958[1]	New York	Casey Stengel	92	62	.597						
1959	Chicago	Al Lopez	94	60	.610	1982	Milwaukee[11]	Harvey Kuenn	95	67	.586
1960	New York	Casey Stengel	97	57	.630	1983[1]	Baltimore[12]	Joe Altobelli	98	64	.605
1961[1]	New York	Ralph Houk	109	53	.673	1984	Detroit[13]	Sparky Anderson	104	58	.642
1962[1]	New York	Ralph Houk	96	66	.593	1985[1]	Kansas City[14]	Dick Howser	91	71	.562
1963	New York	Ralph Houk	104	57	.646	1986	Boston[11]	John McNamara	95	66	.590
1964	New York	Yogi Berra	99	63	.611	1987	Minnesota[15]	Tom Kelly	85	77	.525
1965	Minnesota	Sam Mele	102	60	.630	1988	Oakland[16]	Tony LaRussa	104	58	.642
1966[1]	Baltimore	Hank Bauer	97	53	.606	1989	Oakland[17]	Tony LaRussa	99	63	.611
1967	Boston	Dick Williams	92	70	.568	1990	Oakland[18]	Tony LaRussa	103	59	.636
1968[1]	Detroit	Mayo Smith	103	59	.636	1991	Minnesota[19]	Tom Kelly	95	67	.586
1969	Baltimore[3]	Earl Weaver	109	53	.673	1992	Toronto[10]	Cito Gaston	96	66	.593
1970[1]	Baltimore[3]	Earl Weaver	108	54	.667	1993	Toronto[12]	Cito Gaston	95	67	.586
1971	Baltimore[4]	Earl Weaver	101	57	.639	1994	Strike ended season Aug. 11. No playoffs, no pennant winner.				
1972[1]	Oakland[5]	Dick Williams	93	62	.600						
1973[1]	Oakland[6]	Dick Williams	94	68	.580	1995	Cleveland[20]	Mike Hargrove	100	44	.694
1974[1]	Oakland[6]	Alvin Dark	90	72	.556	1996	New York[21]	Joe Torre	92	70	.568
1975	Boston[4]	Darrell Johnson	95	65	.594	1997	Cleveland[6]	Mike Hargrove	86	75	.534
1976	New York[7]	Billy Martin	97	62	.610	1998	New York[22]	Joe Torre	114	48	.704
1977[1]	New York[7]	Billy Martin	100	62	.617	1999	New York[23]	Joe Torre	98	64	.605
1978[1]	New York[7]	Billy Martin and Bob Lemon	100	63	.613						

* Split season because of players' strike. 1. World Series winner. 2. No World Series. 3. Defeated Minnesota, Western Division winner, in playoff. 4. Defeated Oakland, Western Division Leader, in playoff. 5. Defeated Detroit, Eastern Division winner, inplayoff. 6. Defeated Baltimore, Eastern Division winner, in playoff. 7. Defeated Kansas City, Western Division winner, in playoff. 8. Defeated California, Western Division winner, in playoff. 9. Defeated New York, Eastern Division winner, in playoff. 10. Defeated Oakland, Western Division winner, in playoff. 11. Defeated California, Western Division winner, in playoff. 12. Defeated Chicago, Western Division winner, in playoff. 13. Defeated Kansas City, Western Division winner, in playoff. 14. Defeated Toronto, Eastern Division winner, in playoff. 15. Defeated Detroit, Eastern winner, in playoff. 16. Defeated Boston, Eastern division winner, in playoffs. 17. Defeated Toronto, Eastern Division winner, in playoffs. 18. Defeated Boston, Eastern Division winner, in playoffs. 19. Defeated Toronto, Eastern Division winner, in playoffs. 20. Defeated Seattle Mariners, Western Division winner, in playoffs. 21. Defeated Baltimore Orioles, Eastern Division wild-card team, in playoffs. 22. Defeated Cleveland Indians, Central Division winner, in playoffs. 23. Defeated Boston Red Sox, Eastern Division wild-card team, in playoffs.

NATIONAL LEAGUE PENNANT WINNERS

Year	Club	Manager	Won	Lost	Pct	Year	Club	Manager	Won	Lost	Pct
1876	Chicago	Albert G. Spalding	52	14	.788	1906	Chicago	Frank L. Chance	116	36	.763
1877	Boston	Harry Wright	31	17	.646	1907	Chicago[1]	Frank L. Chance	107	45	.704
1878	Boston	Harry Wright	41	19	.683	1908	Chicago[1]	Frank L. Chance	99	55	.643
1879	Providence	George Wright	55	23	.705	1909	Pittsburgh[1]	Fred C. Clarke	110	42	.724
1880	Chicago	Adrian C. Anson	67	17	.798	1910	Chicago	Frank L. Chance	104	50	.675
1881	Chicago	Adrian C. Anson	56	28	.667	1911	New York	John J. McGraw	99	54	.647
1882	Chicago	Adrian C. Anson	55	29	.655	1912	New York	John J. McGraw	103	48	.682
1883	Boston	John F. Morrill	63	35	.643	1913	New York	John J. McGraw	101	51	.664
1884	Providence	Frank C. Bancroft	84	28	.750	1914	Boston[1]	George T. Stallings	94	59	.614
1885	Chicago	Adrian C. Anson	87	25	.777	1915	Philadelphia	Patrick J. Moran	90	62	.592
1886	Chicago	Adrian C. Anson	90	34	.726	1916	Brooklyn	Wilbert Robinson	94	60	.610
1887	Detroit	W. H. Watkins	79	45	.637	1917	New York	John J. McGraw	98	56	.636
1888	New York	James J. Mutrie	84	47	.641	1918	Chicago	Fred L. Mitchell	84	45	.651
1889	New York	James J. Mutrie	83	43	.659	1919	Cincinnati[1]	Patrick J. Moran	96	44	.686
1890	Brooklyn	Wm. H. McGunnigle	86	43	.667	1920	Brooklyn	Wilbert Robinson	93	61	.604
1891	Boston	Frank G. Selee	87	51	.630	1921	New York[1]	John J. McGraw	94	59	.614
1892	Boston	Frank G. Selee	102	48	.680	1922	New York[1]	John J. McGraw	93	61	.604
1893	Boston	Frank G. Selee	86	44	.662	1923	New York	John J. McGraw	95	58	.621
1894	Baltimore	Edward H. Hanlon	89	39	.695	1924	New York	John J. McGraw	93	60	.608
1895	Baltimore	Edward H. Hanlon	87	43	.669	1925	Pittsburgh[1]	Wm. B. McKechnie	95	58	.621
1896	Baltimore	Edward H. Hanlon	90	39	.698	1926	St. Louis[1]	Rogers Hornsby	89	65	.578
1897	Boston	Frank G. Selee	93	39	.705	1927	Pittsburgh	Donie Bush	94	60	.610
1898	Boston	Frank G. Selee	102	47	.685	1928	St. Louis	Wm. B. McKechnie	95	59	.617
1899	Brooklyn	Edward H. Hanlon	88	42	.677	1929	Chicago	Joseph V. McCarthy	98	54	.645
1900	Brooklyn	Edward H. Hanlon	82	54	.603	1930	St. Louis	Gabby Street	92	62	.597
1901	Pittsburgh	Fred C. Clarke	90	49	.647	1931	St. Louis[1]	Gabby Street	101	53	.656
1902	Pittsburgh	Fred C. Clarke	103	36	.741	1932	Chicago	Charles J. Grimm	90	64	.584
1903	Pittsburgh	Fred C. Clarke	91	49	.650	1933	New York[1]	William H. Terry	91	61	.599
1904	New York[2]	John J. McGraw	106	47	.693	1934	St. Louis[1]	Frank F. Frisch	95	58	.621
1905	New York[1]	John J. McGraw	105	48	.686	1935	Chicago	Charles J. Grimm	100	54	.649

Year	Club	Manager	Won	Lost	Pct	Year	Club	Manager	Won	Lost	Pct
1936	New York	William H. Terry	92	62	.597	1969	New York[1] [3]	Gil Hodges	100	62	.617
1937	New York	William H. Terry	95	57	.625	1970	Cincinnati[4]	Sparky Anderson	102	60	.630
1938	Chicago	Gabby Hartnett	89	63	.586	1971	Pittsburgh[1] [5]	Danny Murtaugh	97	65	.599
1939	Cincinnati	Wm. B. McKechnie	97	57	.630	1972	Cincinnati[4]	Sparky Anderson	95	59	.617
1940	Cincinnati[1]	Wm. B. McKechnie	100	53	.654	1973	New York[6]	Yogi Berra	82	79	.509
1941	Brooklyn	Leo E. Durocher	100	54	.649	1974	Los Angeles[4]	Walter Alston	102	60	.630
1942	St. Louis[1]	Wm. H. Southworth	106	48	.688	1975	Cincinnati[1] [4]	Sparky Anderson	108	54	.667
1943	St. Louis	Wm. H. Southworth	105	49	.682	1976	Cincinnati[7] [1]	Sparky Anderson	102	60	.630
1944	St. Louis[1]	Wm. H. Southworth	105	49	.682	1977	Los Angeles[7]	Tom Lasorda	98	64	.605
1945	Chicago	Charles J. Grimm	98	56	.636	1978	Los Angeles[7]	Tom Lasorda	95	67	.586
1946	St. Louis[1]	Edwin H. Dyer	98	58	.628	1979[1]	Pittsburgh[6]	Chuck Tanner	98	64	.605
1947	Brooklyn	Burton E. Shotton	94	60	.610	1980[1]	Philadelphia[8]	Dallas Green	91	71	.562
1948	Boston	Wm. H. Southworth	91	62	.595	1981	Los Angeles[1] [9]	Tom Lasorda	63	47	.573*
1949	Brooklyn	Burton E. Shotton	97	57	.630	1982[1]	St. Louis[3]	Whitey Herzog	92	70	.568
1950	Philadelphia	Edwin M. Sawyer	91	63	.591	1983	Philadelphia[11]	Paul Owens	90	72	.556
1951	New York	Leo E. Durocher	98	59	.624	1984	San Diego[12]	Dick Williams	92	70	.568
1952	Brooklyn	Charles W. Dressen	96	57	.630	1985	St. Louis[11]	Whitey Herzog	101	61	.623
1953	Brooklyn	Charles W. Dressen	105	49	.682	1986	New York[8]	Dave Johnson	108	54	.667
1954	New York[1]	Leo E. Durocher	97	57	.630	1987	St. Louis[5]	Whitey Herzog	95	67	.586
1955	Brooklyn[1]	Walter Alston	98	55	.641	1988	Los Angeles[10]	Tom Lasorda	94	67	.584
1956	Brooklyn	Walter Alston	93	61	.604	1989	San Fran-cisco[12]	Roger Craig	92	70	.568
1957	Milwaukee[1]	Fred Haney	95	59	.617						
1958	Milwaukee	Fred Haney	92	62	.597	1990	Cincinnati[4]	Lou Piniella	91	71	.562
1959	Los Angeles[1]	Walter Alston	88	68	.564	1991	Atlanta[4]	Bobby Cox	94	68	.580
1960	Pittsburgh[1]	Danny Murtaugh	95	59	.617	1992	Atlanta[4]	Bobby Cox	98	64	.605
1961	Cincinnati	Fred Hutchinson	93	61	.604	1993	Philadelphia[3]	Jim Fregosi	97	65	.599
1962	San Francisco	Alvin Dark	103	62	.624	1994	Strike ended season Aug. 11. No playoffs, no pennant winner.				
1963	Los Angeles[1]	Walter Alston	99	63	.611						
1964	St. Louis[1]	Johnny Keane	93	69	.574	1995	Atlanta[13]	Bobby Cox	90	54	.625
1965	Los Angeles[1]	Walter Alston	97	65	.599	1996	Atlanta[14]	Bobby Cox	96	66	.593
1966	Los Angeles	Walter Alston	95	67	.586	1997	Florida[15]	Jim Leyland	92	70	.568
1967	St. Louis[1]	Red Schoendienst	101	60	.627	1998	San Diego[16]	Bruce Bochy	98	64	.605
1968	St. Louis	Red Schoendienst	97	65	.599	1999	Atlanta[17]	Bobby Cox	103	59	.636

* Split season because of players' strike. 1. World Series winner. 2. No World Series. 3. Defeated Atlanta, Western Division winner, in playoff. 4. Defeated Pittsburgh, Eastern Division winner, in playoff. 5. Defeated San Francisco, Western Division winner, in playoff. 6. Defeated Cincinnati, Western Division winner, in playoff. 7. Defeated Philadelphia, Eastern Division winner, in playoff. 8. Defeated Houston, Western Division winner, in playoff. 9. Defeated Montreal, Eastern Division winner, in playoff. 10. Defeated New York, Eastern Division winner, in playoff. 11. Defeated Los Angeles, Western Division winner, in playoff. 12. Defeated Chicago, Eastern Division champion, in playoff. 13. Defeated Cincinnati, Central Division winner, in playoff. 14. Defeated St. Louis, Central Division winner, in playoff. 15. Eastern Division wildcard Florida defeated Atlanta, Eastern Division winner, in playoff. 16. Defeated Atlanta, Eastern Division winner, in playoff. 17. Defeated New York, Eastern Division wild card team, in playoff.

MOST VALUABLE PLAYERS
(Baseball Writers Association selections)

American League

1931	Lefty Grove, Philadelphia	1959	Nellie Fox, Chicago	1984	Willie Hernandez, Detroit
1932–33	Jimmy Foxx, Philadelphia	1960–61	Roger Maris, New York	1985	Don Mattingly, New York
1934	Mickey Cochrane, Detroit	1962	Mickey Mantle, New York	1986	Roger Clemens, Boston
1935	Hank Greenberg, Detroit	1963	Elston Howard, New York	1987	George Bell, Toronto
1936	Lou Gehrig, New York	1964	Brooks Robinson, Baltimore	1988	Jose Canseco, Oakland
1937	Charlie Gehringer, Detroit	1965	Zoilo Versalles, Minnesota	1989	Robin Yount, Milwaukee
1938	Jimmy Foxx, Boston	1966	Frank Robinson, Baltimore	1990	Rickey Henderson, Oakland
1939	Joe DiMaggio, New York	1967	Carl Yastrzemski, Boston	1991	Cal Ripken, Jr., Baltimore
1940	Hank Greenberg, Detroit	1968	Dennis McLain, Detroit	1992	Dennis Eckersley, Oakland
1941	Joe DiMaggio, New York	1969	Harmon Killebrew, Minnesota	1993	Frank Thomas, Chicago
1942	Joe Gordon, New York	1970	John (Boog) Powell, Baltimore	1994	Frank Thomas, Chicago
1943	Spurgeon Chandler, New York	1971	Vida Blue, Oakland	1995	Mo Vaughn, Boston
1944–45	Hal Newhouser, Detroit	1972	Dick Allen, Chicago	1996	Juan Gonzalez, Texas
1946	Ted Williams, Boston	1973	Reggie Jackson, Oakland	1997	Ken Griffey, Jr., Seattle
1947	Joe DiMaggio, New York	1974	Jeff Burroughs, Texas	1998	Juan Gonzalez, Texas
1948	Lou Boudreau, Cleveland	1975	Fred Lynn, Boston		
1949	Ted Williams, Boston	1976	Thurman Munson, New York	**National League**	
1950	Phil Rizzuto, New York	1977	Rod Carew, Minnesota	1931	Frank Frisch, St. Louis
1951	Yogi Berra, New York	1978	Jim Rice, Boston	1932	Chuck Klein, Philadelphia
1952	Bobby Shantz, Philadelphia	1979	Don Baylor, California	1933	Carl Hubbell, New York
1953	Al Rosen, Cleveland	1980	George Brett, Kansas City	1934	Dizzy Dean, St. Louis
1954–55	Yogi Berra, New York	1981	Rollie Fingers, Milwaukee	1935	Gabby Hartnett, Chicago
1956–57	Mickey Mantle, New York	1982	Robin Yount, Milwaukee	1936	Carl Hubbell, New York
1958	Jackie Jensen, Boston	1983	Cal Ripken, Jr., Baltimore	1937	Joe Medwick, St. Louis

1938	Ernie Lombardi, Cincinnati	1958–59	Ernie Banks, Chicago	1979	Keith Hernandez, St. Louis
1939	Bucky Walters, Cincinnati	1960	Dick Groat, Pittsburgh	1980	Mike Schmidt, Philadelphia
1940	Frank McCormick, Cincinnati	1961	Frank Robinson, Cincinnati	1981	Mike Schmidt, Philadelphia
1941	Dolph Camilli, Brooklyn	1962	Maury Wills, Los Angeles	1982	Dale Murphy, Atlanta
1942	Mort Cooper, St. Louis	1963	Sandy Koufax, Los Angeles	1983	Dale Murphy, Atlanta
1943	Stan Musial, St. Louis	1964	Ken Boyer, St. Louis	1984	Ryne Sandberg, Chicago
1944	Marty Marion, St. Louis	1965	Willie Mays, San Francisco	1985	Willie McGee, St. Louis
1945	Phil Cavarretta, Chicago	1966	Roberto Clemente, Pittsburgh	1986	Mike Schmidt, Philadelphia
1946	Stan Musial, St. Louis	1967	Orlando Cepeda, St. Louis	1987	Andre Dawson, Chicago
1947	Bob Elliott, Boston	1968	Bob Gibson, St. Louis	1988	Kirk Gibson, Los Angeles
1948	Stan Musial, St. Louis	1969	Willie McCovey, San Francisco	1989	Kevin Mitchell, San Francisco
1949	Jackie Robinson, Brooklyn	1970	Johnny Bench, Cincinnati	1990	Barry Bonds, Pittsburgh
1950	Jim Konstanty, Philadelphia	1971	Joe Torre, St. Louis	1991	Terry Pendleton, Atlanta
1951	Roy Campanella, Brooklyn	1972	Johnny Bench, Cincinnati	1992	Barry Bonds, Pittsburgh
1952	Hank Sauer, Chicago	1973	Pete Rose, Cincinnati	1993	Barry Bonds, San Francisco
1953	Roy Campanella, Brooklyn	1974	Steve Garvey, Los Angeles	1994	Jeff Bagwell, Houston
1954	Willie Mays, New York	1975–76	Joe Morgan, Cincinnati	1995	Barry Larkin, Cincinnati
1955	Roy Campanella, Brooklyn	1977	George Foster, Cincinnati	1996	Ken Caminiti, San Diego
1956	Don Newcombe, Brooklyn	1978	Dave Parker, Pittsburgh	1997	Larry Walker, Colorado
1957	Henry Aaron, Milwaukee	1979	Willie Stargell, Pittsburgh	1998	Sammy Sosa, Chicago

CY YOUNG AWARD

1956	Don Newcombe, Brooklyn N.L.	1974	Catfish Hunter, Oakland A.L.; Mike Marshall, Los Angeles N.L.	1987	Roger Clemens, Boston, A.L.; Steve Bedrosian, Philadelphia, N.L.
1957	Warren Spahn, Milwaukee N.L.	1975	Jim Palmer, Baltimore A.L.; Tom Seaver, New York N.L.	1988	Frank Viola, Minnesota, A.L.; Orel Hershiser, Los Angeles, N.L.
1958	Bob Turley, New York A.L.				
1959	Early Wynn, Chicago A.L.	1976	Jim Palmer, Baltimore A.L.; Randy Jones, San Diego N.L.		
1960	Vernon Law, Pittsburgh, N.L			1989	Bret Saberhagen, Kansas, A.L.; Mark Davis, San Diego, N.L.
1961	Whitey Ford, New York A.L.	1977	Sparky Lyle, N.Y., A.L.; Steve Carlton, Philadelphia N.L.		
1962	Don Drysdale, Los Angeles N.L.			1990	Bob Welch, Oakland, A.L.; Doug Drabek, Pittsburgh, N.L.
1963	Sandy Koufax, Los Angeles N.L.	1978	Ron Guidry, N.Y., A.L.; Gaylord Perry, San Diego N.L.		
1964	Dean Chance, Los Angeles A.L.	1979	Mike Flanagan, Baltimore, A.L.; Bruce Sutter, Chicago, N.L.	1991	Roger Clemens, Boston, A.L.; Tom Glavine, Atlanta, N.L.
1965	Sandy Koufax, Los Angeles N.L.				
1966	Sandy Koufax, Los Angeles N.L.	1980	Steve Stone, Baltimore, A.L.; Steve Carlton, Philadelphia, N.L.	1992	Dennis Eckersley, Oakland, A.L.; Greg Maddux, Atlant, N.L.
1967	Jim Lonborg, Boston A.L.; Mike McCormick, San Francisco N.L.	1981	Rollie Fingers, Milwaukee, A.L.; Fernando Valenzuela, Los Angeles, N.L.	1993	Jack McDowell, Chicago, A.L.; Greg Maddux, Atalanta, N.L.
1968	Dennis McLain, Detroit A.L.; Bob Gibson, St. Louis N.L.	1982	Pete Vuckovich, Milwaukee, A.L.; Steve Carlton, Philadelphia, N.L.	1994	David Cone, Kansas, A.L.; Greg Maddux, Atlanta, N.L.
1969	Mike Cuellar, Baltimore A.L. and Dennis McLain, Detroit A.L. (tied); Tom Seaver, N.Y. N.L.	1983	LaMarr Hoyt, Chicago, A.L.; John Denny, Philadelphia, N.L.	1995	Randy Johnson, Seattle, A.L.; Greg Maddux, Atlanta, N.L.
1970	Jim Perry, Minnesota A.L.; Bob Gibson, St. Louis N.L.	1984	Willie Hernandez, Detroit, A.L.; Rick Sutcliffe, Chicago, N.L.	1996	Pat Hentgen, Toronto, A.L.; John Smoltz, Atlanta, N.L.
1971	Vida Blue, Oakland A.L.; Ferguson Jenkins, Chicago N.L.	1985	Bret Saberhagen, A.L.; Dwight Gooden, N.L.	1997	Roger Clemens, Toronto, A.L.; Pedro Martinez, Montreal, N.L.
1972	Gaylord Perry, Cleveland A.L.; Steve Carlton, Phila. N.L.	1986	Roger Clemens, Boston, A.L.; Mike Scott, Houston, N.L.	1998	Roger Clemens, Toronto, A.L.; Tom Glavine, Atlanta, N.L.
1973	Jim Palmer, Baltimore A.L.; Tom Seaver, New York N.L.				

MAJOR LEAGUE ALL-TIME PITCHING RECORDS

(Through 1999)

Most Games Won—511, Cy Young, Cleveland N.L., 1890–98, St. Louis N.L., 1899–1900, Boston A.L., 1901–08, Cleveland A.L., 1909–11, Boston N.L., 1911.

Most Games Won, Season—59, Hoss Radbourne, Providence N.L., 1884. (Since 1900—41, Jack Chesbro, New York A.L., 1904.)

Most Consecutive Games Won—24, Carl Hubbell, New York N.L., 1936 (16) and 1937 (8).

Most Consecutive Games Won, Season—19, Tim Keefe, New York N.L., 1888; Rube Marquard, New York N.L., 1912.

Most Years Won 20 or More Games—16, Cy Young, Cleveland N.L., 1891–98, St. Louis N.L., 1899–1900, Boston A.L., 1901–04, 1907–08.

Most Shutouts—113, Walter Johnson, Wash. A.L., 1907–27.

Most Shutouts, Season—16, Grover Alexander, Philadelphia N.L., 1916.

Most Consecutive Shutouts—6, Don Drysdale, Los Angeles, N.L., 1968.

Most Consecutive Scoreless Innings—59, Orel Hershiser, Los Angeles Dodgers, 1988.

Most Strikeouts—5,714, Nolan Ryan, New York N.L., California A.L., Houston N.L., 1968–1988 Texas, 1989–93.

Most Strikeouts, Season—513, Matthew Kilroy, Baltimore A.A., 1886. (Since 1900—383, Nolan Ryan, California, A.L., 1973.)

Most Strikeouts, Game—21, Tom Cheney, Washington A.L., 1962, 16 innings. Nine innings: 20, Roger Clemens, Boston, A.L., 1986; Kerry Wood, Chicago, N.L., 1998.
Most Consecutive Strikeouts—10, Tom Seaver, New York N.L. vs. San Diego, April 22, 1970.

Most Games, Season—106, Mike Marshall, Los Angeles, N.L., 1974.
Most Complete Games, Season—75, William White, Cincinnati N.L., 1879. (Since 1900—48, Jack Chesbro, New York A.L., 1904.)

MAJOR LEAGUE LIFETIME RECORDS
(Through 1999)

Wins
*Indicates left-handed pitcher.

		Yrs	GS	W	L
1	Cy Young	22	815	511	316
2	Walter Johnson	21	666	417	279
3	Christy Mathewson	17	551	373	188
	Grover Alexander	20	598	373	208
5	Warren Spahn*	21	665	363	245
6	Kid Nichols	15	561	361	208
	Pud Galvin	14	682	361	308
8	Tim Keefe	14	594	342	225
9	Steve Carlton*	24	709	329	244
10	Eddie Plank*	17	527	327	193
11	John Clarkson	12	518	326	177
12	Don Sutton	23	756	324	256
	Nolan Ryan	27	773	324	292
14	Phil Niekro	24	716	318	274
15	Gaylord Perry	22	690	314	265
16	Old Hoss Radbourn	12	503	311	194
	Tom Seaver	20	647	311	205
18	Mickey Welch	13	549	308	209
19	Lefty Grove*	17	456	300	141
	Early Wynn	23	612	300	244
21	Tommy John*	26	700	288	231
22	Bert Blyleven	22	685	287	250
23	Robin Roberts	19	609	286	245
24	Tony Mullane	13	505	285	220
25	Ferguson Jenkins	19	594	284	226

Pitchers Active in 1999

		Yrs	GS	W	L
1	Roger Clemens	16	480	247	134
2	Greg Maddux	14	432	221	126
3	Orel Hershiser	17	460	203	145
4	Dwight Gooden	15	396	188	107
5	Tom Glavine*	13	399	187	116
6	David Cone	14	361	180	102
7	Mark Langston*	16	428	179	158
8	Bret Saberhagen	15	368	166	115
9	Chuck Finley*	14	379	165	140
10	Randy Johnson*	12	322	160	88

Leading Batters, by Batting Average
*Indicates left-handed hitter.
Boldface indicates player active in 1999.

		Yrs	AB	H	Avg
1	Ty Cobb*	24	11,429	4191	.367
2	Rogers Hornsby	23	8,137	2930	.358
3	Joe Jackson*	13	4,981	1774	.356
4	Ed Delahanty	16	7,509	2597	.346
5	Tris Speaker*	22	10,197	3514	.345
6	Ted Williams*	19	7,706	2654	.344
7	Billy Hamilton*	14	6,284	2163	.344
8	Willie Keeler*	19	8,585	2947	.343
9	Dan Brouthers*	19	6,711	2296	.342
10	Babe Ruth*	22	8,399	2873	.342
11	Harry Heilmann	17	7,787	2660	.342
12	Pete Browning	13	4,820	1646	.341
13	Bill Terry*	14	6,428	2193	.341
14	George Sisler*	15	8,267	2812	.340
15	Lou Gehrig*	17	8,001	2721	.340
16	Jesse Burkett*	16	8,413	2853	.339
17	**Tony Gwynn***	18	9,059	3067	.339
18	Nap Lajoie	21	9,592	3244	.338
19	Riggs Stephenson	14	4,508	1515	.336
20	Al Simmons	20	8,761	2927	.334
21	Paul Waner*	20	9,459	3152	.333
22	Eddie Collins*	25	9,951	3313	.333
23	Stan Musial*	22	10,972	3630	.331
24	Sam Thompson*	14	6,005	1986	.331
25	Heinie Manush*	17	7,654	2524	.330

Players Active in 1999

		Yrs	AB	H	Avg
1	Tony Gwynn*	18	9,059	3067	.339
2	Mike Piazza	8	3,653	1200	.328
3	Wade Boggs*	18	9,180	3010	.328
4	Frank Thomas	10	4,892	1564	.320
5	Edgar Martinez	13	4,876	1558	.320
6	Larry Walker*	11	4,592	1431	.312
7	Mark Grace*	12	6,646	2058	.310
8	Kenny Lofton*	9	4,379	1356	.310
9	Manny Ramirez	7	3,031	932	.307
10	Hal Morris*	12	3,829	1169	.305

MAJOR LEAGUE INDIVIDUAL ALL-TIME RECORDS
(Through 1999)

Highest Batting Average, Season—.442, James O'Neill, St. Louis, A.A., 1887; .438, Hugh Duffy, Boston, N.L., 1894 (Since 1900—.424, Rogers Hornsby, St. Louis, N.L., 1924; .422, Nap Lajoie, Phil., A.L., 1901)
Most Times at Bat—14,053, Pete Rose, Cincinnati, N.L., 1963–78; Philadelphia, N.L., 1979–83; Montreal, N.L., 1984; Cincinnati, N.L., 1984–86.
Most Years Batted .300 or Better—23, Ty Cobb, Detroit A.L., 1906–26, Philadelphia A.L., 1927–28.
Most Hits—4,256, Pete Rose, Cincinnati 1963–79, Philadelphia 1980–83, Montreal 1984, Cincinnati 1984–86.
Most Hits, Season—257, George Sisler, St. Louis A.L., 1920.

Most Hits, Game (9 innings)—7, Wilbert Robinson, Baltimore N.L., 6 singles, 1 double, 1892. Rennie Stennett, Pittsburgh N.L., 4 singles, 2 doubles, 1 triple, 1975.
Most Hits, Game (extra innings)—9, John Burnett, Cleveland A.L., 18 innings, 7 singles, 2 doubles, 1932.
Most Hits in Succession—12, Mike Higgins, Boston A.L., in four games, 1938; Walt Dropo, Detroit A.L., in three games, 1952.
Most Consecutive Games Batted Safely—56, Joe DiMaggio, New York A.L., 1941.
Most Runs—2,245, Ty Cobb, Detroit A.L., 1905–26, Philadelphia A.L., 1927–28.

Most Runs, Season—196, William Hamilton, Philadelphia N.L., 1894. (Since 1900—177, Babe Ruth, New York A.L., 1921.)

Most Runs, Game—7, Guy Hecker, Louisville A.A., 1886. (Since 1900—6, by Mel Ott, New York N.L., 1934, 1944; Johnny Pesky, Boston A.L., 1946; Frank Torre, Milwaukee N.L., 1957.)

Most Runs Batted in—2,297, Henry Aaron, Milwaukee N.L., 1954–1965; Atlanta N.L., 1966–74; Milwaukee A.L., 1975–76.

Most Runs Batted in, Season—191, Hack Wilson, Chicago N.L., 1930.

Most Runs Batted In, Game—12, Jim Bottomley, St. Louis N.L., 1924, and Mark Whiten, St. Louis N.L., 1993.

Most Home Runs—755, Henry Aaron, Milwaukee N.L., 1954–1965; Atlanta N.L., 1966–74; Milwaukee A.L., 1975–76.

Most Home Runs, Season—162-game season: 70, Mark McGwire, St. Louis N.L., 1998; 66, Sammy Sosa, Chicago N.L., 1998; 65, Mark McGwire, St. Louis N.L., 1999; 63, Sammy Sosa, Chicago N.L., 1999; 61, Roger Maris, New York A.L., 1961; 154-game season: 60, Babe Ruth, New York A.L., 1927

Most Home Runs with Bases Filled—23, Lou Gehrig, New York A.L., 1927–39.

Most 2-Base Hits—793, Tris Speaker, Boston A.L., 1907–15, Cleveland A.L., 1916–26, Washington A.L., 1927, Philadelphia A.L., 1928.

Most 2-Base Hits, Season—67, Earl Webb, Boston A.L., 1931.

Most 2-base Hits, Game—4, by many.

Most 3-Base Hits—312, Sam Crawford, Cincinnati N.L., 1899–1902, Detroit A.L., 1903–17.

Most 3-Base Hits, Season—36, Owen Wilson, Pittsburgh N.L., 1912.

Most 3-Base Hits, Game—4, George Strief, Philadelphia A.A., 1885; William Joyce, New York N.L., 1897. (Since 1900—3, by many.)

Most Games Played—3,562, Pete Rose, Cincinnati N.L., Philadelphia N.L., Montreal N.L., 1964–86.

Most Consecutive Games Played—2,632, Cal Ripken, Jr., Baltimore Orioles, A.L., 1981–

Most Bases on Balls—2,062, Babe Ruth, Boston A.L., 1914–19; New York A.L., 1920–34, Boston N.L., 1935.

Most Bases on Balls, Season—170, Babe Ruth, New York A.L., 1923.

Most Bases on Balls, Game—6, Jimmy Foxx, Boston A.L., 1938.

Most Strikeouts, Season—189, Bobby Bonds, San Francisco N.L., 1970.

Most Strikeouts, Game (9 innings)—5, by many.

Most Strikeouts, Game (extra innings)—6, Carl Weilman, St. Louis A.L., 15 innings, 1913; Don Hoak, Chicago N.L., 17 innings, 1956; Fred Reichardt, California A.L., 17, innings, 1966; Billy Cowan, California A.L., 20, 1971; Cecil Cooper, Boston A.L., 15, 1974.

Most Pinch-hits, Lifetime—150, Manny Mota, S.F., 1962; Pitt., 1963–68; Montreal, 1969; L.A., 1969–80, N.L.

Most Pinch-hits, Season—28, John Vander Wal, Colorado N.L., 1995.

Most Consecutive Pinch-hits—9, Dave Philley, Phil., N.L., 1958 (8), 1959 (1).

Most Pinch-hit Home Runs, Lifetime—20, Cliff Johnson, Houston N.L., 1972–77; New York A.L., 1977–79; Cleveland A.L., 1979–80; Chicago N.L., 1980; Oakland A.L., 1981–82; Toronto A.L., 1983–84, 1985–86; Texas A.L., 1985.

Most Pinch-hit Home Runs, Season—6, Johnny Frederick, Brooklyn, N.L., 1932.

Most Stolen Bases, Lifetime—1,334 Rickey Henderson, 1979–84 Oakland, 1985–89 New York (A.L.), 1989–93 Oakland, 1993 Toronto, 1994–95 Oakland, 1996 San Diego, 1997 Anaheim, 1998 Oakland.

Most Stolen Bases, Season—156, Harry Stovey, Phil., A.A., 1888. Since 1900: 130, Rickey Henderson, Oak., A.L., 1982; 118, Lou Brock, St. Louis, N.L., 1974.

Most Stolen Bases, Game—7, George Gore, Chicago N.L. 1881; William Hamilton, Philadelphia N.L. 1894. (Since 1900—6, Eddie Collins, Philadelphia A.L., 1912.) and Otis Nixon, Atlanta N.L., 1991.

Most Time Stealing Home, Lifetime—50, Ty Cobb, Detroit-Phil. A.L., 1905–28.

ROOKIE OF THE YEAR
(Baseball Writers Association selections)

American League

1949 Roy Sievers, St. Louis	1966 Tommy Agee, Chicago	1982 Cal Ripken, Jr., Baltimore
1950 Walt Dropo, Boston	1967 Rod Carew, Minnesota	1983 Ron Kittle, Chicago
1951 Gil McDougald, New York	1968 Stan Bahnsen, New York	1984 Alvin Davis, Seattle
1952 Harry Byrd, Philadelphia	1969 Lou Piniella, Kansas City	1985 Ozzie Guillen, Chicago
1953 Harvey Kuenn, Detroit	1970 Thurman Munson, New York	1986 Jose Canseco, Oakland
1954 Bob Grim, New York	1971 Chris Chambliss, Cleveland	1987 Mark McGwire, Oakland
1955 Herb Score, Cleveland	1972 Carlton Fisk, Boston	1988 Walter Weiss, Oakland
1956 Luis Aparicio, Chicago	1973 Alonzo Bumbry, Baltimore	1989 Gregg Olson, Baltimore
1957 Tony Kubek, New York	1974 Mike Hargrove, Texas	1990 Sandy Alomar Jr., Cleveland
1958 Albie Pearson, Washington	1975 Fred Lynn, Boston	1991 Chuck Knoblauch, Minnesota
1959 Bob Allison, Washington	1976 Mark Fidrych, Detroit	1992 Pat Listach, Milwaukee
1960 Ron Hansen, Baltimore	1977 Eddie Murray, Baltimore	1993 Tim Salmon, California
1961 Don Schwall, Boston	1978 Lou Whitaker, Detroit	1994 Bob Hamelin, Kansas City
1962 Tom Tresh, New York	1979 Alfredo Griffin, Toronto	1995 Marty Cordova, Minnesota
1963 Gary Peters, Chicago	1979 John Castino, Minnesota	1996 Derek Jeter, New York
1964 Tony Oliva, Minnesota	1980 Joe Charboneau, Cleveland	1997 Nomar Garciaparra, Boston
1965 Curt Blefary, Baltimore	1981 Dave Righetti, New York	1998 Ben Grieve, Oakland

National League

1949 Don Newcombe, Brooklyn	1952 Joe Black, Brooklyn	1955 Bill Virdon, St. Louis
1950 Sam Jethroe, Boston	1953 Jim Gilliam, Brooklyn	1956 Frank Robinson, Cincinnati
1951 Willie Mays, New York	1954 Wally Moon, St. Louis	1957 Jack Sanford, Philadelphia

1958	Orlando Cepeda, San Francisco	1972	Jon Matlack, New York	1985 Vince Coleman, St. Louis
1959	Willie McCovey, San Francisco	1973	Gary Matthews, San Francisco	1986 Todd Worrell, St. Louis
1960	Frank Howard, Los Angeles	1974	Bake McBride, St. Louis	1987 Benito Santiago, San Diego
1961	Billy Williams, Chicago	1975	John Montefusco, San Francisco	1988 Chris Sabo, Cincinnati
1962	Ken Hubbs, Chicago	1976	Pat Zachry, Cincinnati	1989 Jerome Walton, Chicago
1963	Pete Rose, Cincinnati	1976	Bruce Metzger, San Diego	1990 Dave Justice, Atlanta
1964	Richie Allen, Philadelphia	1977	Andre Dawson, Montreal	1991 Jeff Baguell, Houston
1965	Jim Lefebvre, Los Angeles	1978	Bob Horner, Atlanta	1992 Eric Karros, Los Angeles
1966	Tommy Helms, Cincinnati	1979	Rick Sutcliffe, Los Angeles	1993 Mike Piazza, Los Angeles
1967	Tom Seaver, New York	1980	Steve Howe, Los Angeles	1994 Raul Mondesi, Los Angeles
1968	Johnny Bench, Cincinnati	1981	Fernando Valenzuela, Los Angeles	1995 Hideo Nomo, Los Angeles
1969	Ted Sizemore, Los Angeles	1982	Steve Sax, Los Angeles	1996 Todd Hollandsworth, Los Angeles
1970	Carl Morton, Montreal	1983	Darryl Strawberry, New York	1997 Scott Rolen, Philadelphia
1971	Earl Williams, Atlanta	1984	Dwight Gooden, New York	1998 Kerry Wood, Chicago

MOST HOME RUNS IN ONE SEASON

(45 or More)

HR	Player/Team	Year	HR	Player/Team	Year
70	Mark McGwire, St. Louis (N.L.)	1998	48	Jimmy Foxx, Philadelphia (A.L.)	1933
66	Sammy Sosa, Chicago (N.L.)	1998	48	Harmon Killebrew, Minnesota (A.L.)	1962
65	Mark McGwire, St. Louis (N.L.)	1999	48	Frank Howard, Washington (A.L.)	1969
63	Sammy Sosa, Chicago (N.L.)	1999	48	Willie Stargell, Pittsburgh (N.L.)	1971
61	Roger Maris, New York (A.L.)	1961	48	Dave Kingman, Chicago (N.L.)	1979
60	Babe Ruth, New York (A.L.)	1927	48	Mike Schmidt, Philadelphia (N.L.)	1980
59	Babe Ruth, New York (A.L.)	1921	48	Albert Belle, Cleveland (A.L.)	1996
58	Jimmy Foxx, Philadelphia (A.L.)	1932	48	Ken Griffey, Jr., Seattle (A.L.)	1999
58	Hank Greenberg, Detroit (A.L.)	1938	47	Babe Ruth, New York (A.L.)	1926
58	Mark McGwire, Oakland (A.L.), St. Louis (N.L.)	1997	47	Ralph Kiner, Pittsburgh (N.L.)	1950
56	Hack Wilson, Chicago (N.L.)	1930	47	Ed Mathews, Milwaukee (N.L.)	1953
56	Ken Griffey, Jr., Seattle (A.L.)	1997	47	Ernie Banks, Chicago (N.L.)	1958
56	Ken Griffey, Jr., Seattle (A.L.)	1998	47	Willie Mays, San Francisco (N.L.)	1964
54	Babe Ruth, New York (A.L.)	1920	47	Henry Aaron, Atlanta (N.L.)	1971
54	Babe Ruth, New York (A.L.)	1928	47	Reggie Jackson, Oakland (A.L.)	1969
54	Ralph Kiner, Pittsburgh (N.L.)	1949	47	George Bell, Toronto (A.L.)	1987
54	Mickey Mantle, New York (A.L.)	1961	47	Kevin Mitchell, San Francisco (N.L.)	1989
52	Mickey Mantle, New York (A.L.)	1956	47	Andres Galarraga, Colorado (N.L.)	1996
52	Willie Mays, San Francisco (N.L.)	1965	47	Juan Gonzalez, Texas (A.L.)	1996
52	George Foster, Cincinnati (N.L.)	1977	47	Rafael Palmeiro, Texas (A.L.)	1999
52	Mark McGwire, Oakland (A.L.)	1996	46	Babe Ruth, New York (A.L.)	1924
51	Ralph Kiner, Pittsburgh (N.L.)	1947	46	Babe Ruth, New York, (A.L.)	1929
51	John Mize, New York (N.L.)	1947	46	Babe Ruth, New York (A.L.)	1931
51	Willie Mays, New York (N.L.)	1955	46	Lou Gehrig, New York (A.L.)	1931
51	Cecil Fielder (A.L.)	1990	46	Joe DiMaggio, New York (A.L.)	1937
50	Jimmy Foxx, Boston (A.L.)	1938	46	Ed Mathews, Milwaukee (N.L.)	1959
50	Albert Belle, Cleveland (A.L.)	1995	46	Orlando Cepeda, San Francisco (N.L.)	1961
50	Brady Anderson, Baltimore (A.L.)	1996	46	Jim Rice, Boston (A.L.)	1978
50	Greg Vaughn, San Diego (N.L.)	1998	46	Juan Gonzalez, Texas (A.L.)	1993
49	Babe Ruth, New York (A.L.)	1930	46	Barry Bonds, San Francisco (N.L.)	1993
49	Lou Gehrig, New York (A.L.)	1934	46	Jose Canseco, Toronto (A.L.)	1998
49	Lou Gehrig, New York (A.L.)	1936	46	Vinnie Castilla, Colorado (N.L.)	1998
49	Ted Kluszewski, Cincinnati (N.L.)	1954	45	Harmon Killebrew, Minnesota (A.L.)	1963
49	Willie Mays, San Francisco (N.L.)	1962	45	Willie McCovey, San Francisco (N.L.)	1969
49	Harmon Killebrew, Minnesota (A.L.)	1964	45	Johnny Bench, Cincinnati (N.L.)	1970
49	Frank Robinson, Baltimore (A.L.)	1966	45	Gorman Thomas, Milwaukee (A.L.)	1979
49	Harmon Killebrew, Minnesota (A.L.)	1969	45	Henry Aaron, Milwaukee (N.L.)	1962
49	Mark McGwire, Oakland (A.L.)	1987	45	Ken Griffey, Jr., Seattle (A.L.)	1993
49	Andre Dawson, Chicago (N.L.)	1987	45	Juan Gonzalez, Texas (A.L.)	1998
49	Ken Griffey, Jr., Seattle (A.L.)	1996	45	Manny Ramirez, Cleveland (A.L.)	1998
49	Larry Walker, Colorado (N.L.)	1997	45	Chipper Jones, Atlanta (N.L.)	1999
49	Albert Belle, Chicago (A.L.)	1998	45	Greg Vaughn, Cincinnati (N.L.)	1999

MAJOR LEAGUE BASEBALL—1999

AMERICAN LEAGUE FINAL STANDINGS

EASTERN DIVISION

Team	W	L	Pct	GB
New York Yankees	98	64	.605	—
Boston Red Sox	94	68	.580	4
Toronto Blue Jays	84	78	.519	14
Baltimore Orioles	78	84	.481	20
Tampa Bay Devil Rays	69	93	.426	29

CENTRAL DIVISION

Team	W	L	Pct	GB
Cleveland Indians	97	65	.599	—
Chicago White Sox	75	86	.466	21½
Detroit Tigers	69	92	.429	27½
Kansas City Royals	64	97	.398	32½
Minnesota Twins	63	97	.394	33

WESTERN DIVISION

Team	W	L	Pct	GB
Texas Rangers	95	67	.586	—
Oakland Athletics	87	75	.537	8
Seattle Mariners	79	83	.488	16
Anaheim Angels	70	92	.432	25

AMERICAN LEAGUE LEADERS: 1999

Batting—Nomar Garciaparra, Boston	.357
Home runs—Ken Griffey, Jr., Seattle	48
Runs batted in—Manny Ramirez, Cleveland	165
Stolen bases—Brian L. Hunter, Seattle	44
Slugging percentage—Manny Ramirez	.663
Runs scored—Roberto Alomar, Cleveland	138
Walks—Jim Thome, Cleveland	127
Doubles—Shawn Green, Toronto	45
Triples—Jose Offerman, Boston	11
Hits—Derek Jeter, New York	219

A.L. Pitching

Wins—Pedro Martinez, Boston	23
Earned run average—Pedro Martinez, Boston	2.07
Saves—Mariano Rivera, New York	45
Innings pitched—David Wells, Toronto	231.2
Strikeouts—Pedro Martinez, Boston	313
Complete games—David Wells, Toronto	7
Shutouts—Scott Erickson, Baltimore	3

American League Division Series

New York Yankees defeat Texas Rangers, 3 games to 0
Oct. 5—NEW YORK 8, Texas 0
Oct. 7—NEW YORK 3, Texas 1
Oct. 9—New York 3, TEXAS 0

Boston Red Sox defeat Cleveland Indians, 3 games to 2
Oct. 6—CLEVELAND 3, Boston 2
Oct. 7—CLEVELAND 11, Boston 1
Oct. 9—BOSTON 9, Cleveland 3
Oct. 10—BOSTON 23, Cleveland 7
Oct. 11—Boston 12, CLEVELAND 8
(HOME TEAM IN CAPS.)

NATIONAL LEAGUE FINAL STANDINGS

EASTERN DIVISION

Team	W	L	Pct	GB
Atlanta Braves	103	59	.636	—
New York Mets	97	66	.595	6½
Philadelphia Phillies	77	85	.475	26
Montreal Expos	68	94	.420	35
Florida Marlins	64	98	.395	39

CENTRAL DIVISION

Team	W	L	Pct	GB
Houston Astros	97	65	.599	—
Cincinnati Reds	96	67	.589	1½
Pittsburgh Pirates	78	83	.484	18½
St. Louis Cardinals	75	86	.466	21½
Milwaukee Brewers	74	87	.460	22½
Chicago Cubs	67	95	.414	30

WESTERN DIVISION

Team	W	L	Pct	GB
Arizona Diamondbacks	100	62	.617	—
San Francisco Giants	86	76	.531	14
Los Angeles Dodgers	77	85	.475	23
San Diego Padres	74	88	.457	26
Colorado Rockies	72	90	.444	28

NATIONAL LEAGUE LEADERS: 1999

Batting—Larry Walker, Colorado	.379
Home runs—Mark McGwire, St. Louis	65
Runs batted in—Mark McGwire, St. Louis	147
Stolen bases—Tony Womack, Arizona	72
Slugging percentage—Larry Walker, Colorado	.710
Runs scored—Jeff Bagwell, Houston	143
Walks—Jeff Bagwell, Houston	149
Doubles—Craig Biggio, Houston	56
Triples—Neifi Perez,. Colorado	11
Hits—Luis Gonzalez, Arizona	206

N.L. Pitching

Wins—Mike Hampton, Houston	22
Earned run average—Randy Johnson, Arizona	2.48
Saves—Ugueth Urbina, Montreal	41
Innings pitched—Randy Johnson, Arizona	271.2
Strikeouts—Randy Johnson, Arizona	364
Complete games—Randy Johnson, Arizona	12
Shutouts—Andy Ashby, San Diego	3

National League Division Series

Atlanta Braves defeat Houston Astros, 3 games to 1
Oct. 5—Houston 6, ATLANTA 1
Oct. 6—ATLANTA 5, Houston 1
Oct. 8—Atlanta 5, HOUSTON 3
Oct. 9—Atlanta 7, HOUSTON 5

New York Mets defeat Arizona Diamondbacks, 3 games to 1
Oct. 5—New York 8, ARIZONA 4
Oct. 6—ARIZONA 7, New York 1
Oct. 8—NEW YORK 9, Arizona 2
Oct. 9—NEW YORK 4, Arizona 3
(HOME TEAM IN CAPS.)

AMERICAN LEAGUE AVERAGES: 1999

Team Batting

	Avg	AB	R	H	HR	RBI		Avg	AB	R	H	HR	RBI
Texas	.293	5,651	945	1,653	230	897	Chicago	.277	5,644	777	1,563	162	742
Cleveland	.289	5,634	1,009	1,629	209	960	Tampa Bay	.274	5,586	772	1,531	145	728
New York	.282	5,568	900	1,568	193	855	Seattle	.269	5,572	859	1,499	244	825
Kansas City	.282	5,624	856	1,584	151	800	Minnesota	.264	5,495	686	1,450	105	643
Toronto	.280	5,642	883	1,580	212	856	Detroit	.261	5,481	747	1,433	212	704
Baltimore	.279	5,637	851	1,572	203	804	Oakland	.259	5,519	893	1,430	235	845
Boston	.278	5,579	836	1,551	176	808	Anaheim	.256	5,494	711	1,404	158	673

Individual Batting
(Based on 300 plate appearances.)

	Avg	AB	R	H	HR	RBI
Nomar Garciaparra, Boston	.357	532	103	190	27	104
Derek Jeter, New York	.349	627	134	219	24	102
Bernie Williams, New York	.342	591	116	202	25	115
Cal Ripken, Jr., Baltimore	.340	332	51	113	18	57
Edgar Martinez, Seattle	.337	502	86	169	24	86
Omar Vizquel, Cleveland	.333	574	112	191	5	66
Manny Ramirez, Cleveland	.333	522	131	174	44	165
Ivan Rodriguez, Texas	.332	600	116	199	35	113
Tony Fernandez, Toronto	.328	485	73	159	6	75
Juan Gonzalez, Texas	.326	562	114	183	39	128
Rafael Palmeiro, Texas	.324	565	96	183	47	148
Luis Polonia, Detroit	.324	333	46	108	10	32
Roberto Alomar, Clevelans	.323	563	138	182	24	120
Mike Sweeney, Kansas City	.322	575	101	185	22	102
Homer Bush, Toronto	.320	485	69	155	5	55
Randy Velarde, Oakland	.317	631	105	200	16	76
Jason Giambi, Oakland	.315	575	115	181	33	123
Joe Randa, Kansas City	.314	628	92	197	16	84
Harold Baines, Cleveland	.312	430	62	134	25	103
Corey Koskie, Minnesota	.310	342	42	106	11	58
Fred McGriff, Tampa Bay	.310	529	75	164	32	104

Individual Pitching
(Based on 10 decisions.)

	W	L	ERA	IP	H	BB	SO
Pedro Martinez, Boston	23	4	2.07	213.1	160	37	313
Bartolo Colon, Cleveland	18	5	3.95	205.0	185	76	161
Mike Mussina, Baltimore	18	7	3.50	203.1	207	52	172
Aaron Sele, Texas	18	9	4.79	205.0	244	70	186
David Wells, Toronto	17	10	4.82	231.2	246	62	169
Charles Nagy, Cleveland	17	11	4.95	202.0	238	59	126

	W	L	ERA	IP	H	BB	SO
Orlando Hernandez, New York	17	9	4.12	214.1	187	87	157
Freddy An. Garcia, Seattle	17	8	4.07	201.1	205	90	170
Kevin Appier, Oakland	16	14	5.17	209.0	230	84	131
Omar Olivares, Oakland	15	11	4.16	205.2	217	81	85
Dave Burba, Cleveland	15	9	4.25	220.0	211	96	174
Scott Erickson, Baltimore	15	12	4.81	230.1	244	99	106
Andy Pettitte, New York	14	11	4.70	191.2	216	89	121
Roger Clemens, New York	14	10	4.60	187.2	185	90	163
Kelvim Escobar, Toronto	14	11	5.69	174.0	203	81	129
Jamie Moyer, Seattle	14	8	3.87	228.0	235	48	137
Dave Micki, Detroit	14	13	4.61	199.0	219	72	120
Mike Morgan, Texas	13	10	6.24	140.0	184	48	61
Gil Heredia, Oakland	13	8	4.81	200.1	228	34	117
Rick Helling, Texas	13	11	4.84	219.1	228	85	131

Team Pitching

	W	L	ERA	SV	SO	R	IP
New York	98	64	4.13	50	10	731	1,439.2
Cleveland	97	65	4.89	46	6	860	1,450.1
Texas	95	67	5.07	47	9	859	1,436.1
Boston	94	68	4.00	50	12	718	1,436.2
Oakland	87	75	4.69	48	5	846	1,438.1
Toronto	84	78	4.92	39	9	862	1,439.0
Seattle	79	83	5.24	40	6	905	1,433.2
Baltimore	78	84	4.77	33	11	815	1,435.0
Chicago	75	86	4.92	39	3	870	1,438.1
Anaheim	70	92	4.79	37	7	826	1,431.1
Detroit	69	92	5.17	33	6	882	1,421.0
Tampa Bay	69	93	5.06	45	5	913	1,433.0
Kansas City	64	97	5.35	29	3	921	1,420.2
Minnesota	63	97	5.00	34	8	845	1,423.1

NATIONAL LEAGUE AVERAGES: 1999

Team Batting

	Avg	AB	R	H	HR	RBI
Colorado	.288	5,717	906	1,644	223	863
New York	.279	5,572	853	1,553	181	814
Arizona	.277	5,658	908	1,566	216	865
Philadelphia	.275	5,598	841	1,539	161	797
Milwaukee	.273	5,582	815	1,524	165	777
Cincinnati	.272	5,649	865	1,536	209	820
San Francisco	.271	5,563	872	1,507	188	828
Houston	.267	5,485	823	1,463	168	784
Los Angeles	.266	5,567	793	1,480	187	761
Atlanta	.266	5,569	840	1,481	197	791
Montreal	.265	5,559	718	1,473	163	680
Florida	.263	5,578	691	1,465	128	655
St. Louis	.262	5,570	809	1,461	194	763
Pittsburgh	.259	5,468	775	1,417	171	735
Chicago	.257	5,482	747	1,411	189	717
San Diego	.252	5,394	710	1,360	153	671

Individual Batting
(Based on 300 plate appearances.)

	Avg	AB	R	H	HR	RBI
Larry Walker, Colorado	.379	438	108	166	37	115
Tony Gwynn, San Diego	.338	411	59	139	10	62
Luis Gonzalez, Arizona	.336	614	112	206	26	111
Bobby Abreu, Philadelphia	.335	546	118	183	20	93
Sean Casey, Cincinnati	.332	594	103	197	25	99
Jeff Cirillo, Milwaukee	.326	607	98	198	15	88
Mark Grudzielanek, Los Angeles	.326	488	72	159	7	46
Carl Everett, Houston	.325	464	86	151	25	108
Doug Glanville, Philadelphia	.325	628	101	204	11	73
Todd Helton, Colorado	.320	578	114	185	35	113
Chipper Jones, Atlanta	.319	567	116	181	45	110

	Avg	AB	R	H	HR	RBI
Vladimir Guerrero, Montreal	.316	610	102	193	42	131
Brian Giles, Pittsburgh	.315	521	109	164	39	115
Rickey Henderson, New York	.315	438	89	138	12	42
Darryl Hamilton, New York	.315	505	82	159	9	45
Roger Cedeno, New York	.313	453	90	142	4	36
Geoff Jenkins, Milwaukee	.313	447	70	140	21	82
Rondell White, Montreal	.312	539	83	168	22	64
Eddie Taubensee, Cincinnati	.311	424	58	132	21	87

Individual Pitching
(Based on 10 decisions.)

	W	L	ERA	IP	H	BB	SO
Mike Hampton, Houston	22	4	2.90	239.0	206	101	177
Jose Lima, Houston	21	10	3.58	246.1	256	44	187
Greg Maddux, Atlanta	19	9	3.57	219.1	258	37	136
Kevin Brown, Los Angeles	18	9	3.00	252.1	210	59	221
Kevin Millwood, Atlanta	18	7	2.68	228.0	168	59	205
Russ Ortiz, San Francisco	18	9	3.81	207.2	189	125	164
Kent Bottenfield, St. Louis	18	7	3.97	190.1	197	89	124
Randy Johnson, Arizona	17	9	2.48	271.2	207	70	364
Pedro Astacio, Colorado	17	11	5.04	232.0	258	75	210
Shane Reynolds, Houston	16	14	3.85	231.2	250	37	197
Pete Harnisch, Cincinnati	16	10	3.68	198.1	190	57	120
Omar Daal, Arizona	16	9	3.65	214.2	188	79	148
Paul Byrd, Philadelphia	15	11	4.60	199.2	205	70	106
Kirk Rueter, San Francisco	15	10	5.41	184.2	219	55	94
Curt Schilling, Philadelphia	15	6	3.54	180.1	159	44	152
Todd Ritchie, Pittsburgh	15	9	3.49	172.2	169	54	107
Andy Ashby, San Diego	14	10	3.80	206.0	204	54	132
Tom Glavine, Atlanta	14	11	4.12	234.0	259	83	138
Chan Ho Park, Los Angeles	13	11	5.23	194.1	208	100	174
Darren Dreifort, Los Angeles	13	13	4.79	178.2	177	76	140

Team Pitching

	W	L	ERA	SV	SO	R	IP		W	L	ERA	SV	SO	R	IP
Atlanta	103	59	3.63	45	9	661	1,471.0	Philadelphia	77	85	4.92	32	6	846	1,438.1
Arizona	100	62	3.77	42	9	676	1,467.1	St. Louis	75	86	4.74	38	3	838	1,445.1
New York	97	66	4.27	49	7	711	1,456.2	Milwaukee	74	87	5.07	40	5	886	1,442.2
Houston	97	65	3.83	48	8	675	1,458.2	San Diego	74	88	4.47	43	6	781	1,420.1
Cincinnati	96	67	3.98	55	11	711	1,462.0	Colorado	72	90	6.01	33	2	1,028	1,429.0
San Francisco	86	76	4.71	42	3	831	1,456.1	Montreal	68	94	4.69	44	4	853	1,434.1
Pittsburgh	78	83	4.33	34	3	782	1,433.1	Chicago	67	95	5.27	32	6	920	1,430.2
Los Angeles	77	85	4.45	37	6	787	1,453.0	Florida	64	98	4.90	33	5	852	1,435.2

AMERICAN LEAGUE CHAMPIONSHIP SERIES—1999
New York Yankees win series, 4 games to 1

1st Game, at New York, Oct. 13, 1999

				R	H	E
Boston	210	000	000	0	3	8	3
New York	020	000	100	1	4	10	1

Pitchers—Boston: Mercker, Garces, Lowe, Cormier, Beck. New York: Hernandez, Rivera. Winner: Rivera. Loser: Beck. Attendance: 57,181.

2nd Game, at New York, Oct. 14, 1999

				R	H	E
Boston	000	020	000	—	2	10	0
New York	000	100	20x	—	3	7	0

Pitchers—Boston: R. Martinez, Gordon, Cormier. New York: Cone, Stanton, Nelson, Watson, Mendoza, Rivera. Winner: Cone. Loser: R. Martinez. Save: Rivera. Attendance: 57,180.

3rd Game, at Boston, Oct. 16, 1999

				R	H	E
New York	000	000	010	—	1	3	3
Boston	222	021	40x	—	13	21	1

Pitchers—New York: Clemens, Irabu, Stanton, Watson. Boston: P. Martinez, Gordon, Rapp. Winner: P. Martinez. Loser: Clemens. Attendance: 33,190.

4th Game, at Boston, Oct. 17, 1999

				R	H	E
New York	010	200	006	—	9	11	0
Boston	011	000	000	—	2	10	4

Pitchers—New York: Pettitte, Rivera. Boston: Saberhagen, Lowe, Cormier, Garces, Beck. Winner: Pettitte. Loser: Saberhagen. Attendance: 33,586.

5th Game, at Boston, Oct. 18, 1999

				R	H	E
New York	200	000	202	—	6	11	1
Boston	000	000	010	—	1	5	2

Pitchers—New York: Hernandez, Stanton, Nelson, Watson, Mendoza. Boston: Mercker, Lowe, Cormier, Gordon. Winner: Hernandez. Loser: Mercker. Save: Mendoza. Attendance: 33,589.

Series MVP—Orlando Hernandez

NATIONAL LEAGUE CHAMPIONSHIP SERIES—1999
Atlanta Braves win series, 4 games to 2

1st Game, at Atlanta, Oct. 12, 1999

				R	H	E
New York	000	100	001	—	2	6	2
Atlanta	100	011	01x	—	4	8	2

Pitchers—New York: Yoshii, Mahomes, Cook, Wendell. Atlanta: Maddux, Remlinger, Rocker. Winner: Maddux. Loser: Yoshii. Save: Rocker. Attendance: 44,172.

2nd Game, at Atlanta, Oct. 13, 1999

				R	H	E
New York	010	010	010	—	3	5	1
Atlanta	000	004	00x	—	4	9	1

Pitchers—New York: Rogers, Wendell, Benitez. Atlanta: Millwood, Rocker, Smoltz. Winner: Millwood. Loser: Rogers. Save: Smoltz. Attendance: 44,624.

3rd Game, at New York, Oct. 15, 1999

				R	H	E
Atlanta	100	000	000	—	1	3	1
New York	000	000	000	—	0	7	2

Pitchers—Atlanta: Glavine, Remlinger, Rocker. New York: Leiter, Franco, Benitez. Winner: Glavine. Loser: Leiter. Save: Rocker. Attendance: 55,911.

4th Game, at New York, Oct. 16, 1999

				R	H	E
Atlanta	000	000	020	—	2	3	0
New York	000	001	02x	—	3	5	0

Pitchers—Atlanta: Smoltz, Remlinger, Rocker. New York: Reed, Wendell, Benitez. Winner: Wendell. Loser: Remlinger. Save: Benitez. Attendance: 55,872.

5th Game, at New York, Oct. 17, 1999

						R	H	E
Atlanta	000	200	000	000	001	3	13	2
New York	200	000	000	000	002	4	11	1

Pitchers—Atlanta: Maddux, Mulholland, Remlinger, Springer, Rocker, McGlinchy. New York: Yoshii, Hershiser, Wendell, Cook, Mahomes, Franco, Benitez, Rogers, Dotel. Winner: Dotel. Loser: McGlinchy. Attendance: 55,723.

6th Game, at Atlanta, Oct. 19, 1999

					R	H	E
New York	000	003	410	10	9	15	2
Atlanta	500	002	010	11	10	10	1

Pitchers—New York: Leiter, Mahomes, Wendell, Cook, Hershiser, Franco, Benitez, Rogers. Atlanta: Millwood, Mulholland, Smoltz, Remlinger, Rocker, Springer. Winner: Springer. Loser: Rogers. Attendance: 52,335.

Series MVP—Eddie Perez

WORLD SERIES—1999

New York Yankees win series, 4 games to 0

1st Game—Atlanta, Oct. 23
New York 4, Atlanta 1

NEW YORK (A.L.)	AB	R	H	RBI		ATLANTA (N.L.)	AB	R	H	RBI
Knoblauch 2b	4	1	0	0		G. Williams lf	4	0	0	0
Jeter ss	4	1	2	1		Boone 2b	4	0	1	0
O'Neill rf	4	0	1	2		C. Jones 3b	2	1	1	1
B. Williams cf	2	0	0	0		Jordan rf	4	0	0	0
Martinez 1b	3	0	0	0		Klesko 1b	3	0	0	0
Posada c	4	0	0	0		Hunter 1b	0	0	0	0
Ledee lf	3	0	0	0		Myers ph	1	0	0	0
Leyritz ph	0	0	0	1		A. Jones cf	2	0	0	0
Nelson p	0	0	0	0		Perez c	2	0	0	0
Stanton p	0	0	0	0		Weiss ss	2	0	0	0
Rivera p	0	0	0	0		Guillen ph	0	0	0	0
Brosius 3b	4	1	3	0		Hernandez	1	0	0	0
O. Hernandez p	1	0	0	0		ph-ss				
Strawberry ph	0	0	0	0		Maddux p	2	0	0	0
Curtis pr-lf	1	1	0	0		Rocker p	0	0	0	0
						Battle ph	0	0	0	0
						Lockhart ph	1	0	0	0
						Remlinger p	0	0	0	0
Totals	**30**	**4**	**6**	**4**		**Totals**	**28**	**1**	**2**	**1**

				R	H	E
New York	000	000	040	— 4	6	0
Atlanta	000	100	000	— 1	2	2

E—Atlanta: Hunter 2. LOB—New York 7, Atlanta 4. HR—Atlanta: C. Jones (off O. Hernandez). SB—Jeter, B. Williams. CS—Jeter, C. Jones. S—O. Hernandez, Knoblauch. GIDP—New York: Posada. DP—Atlanta: 1 (Boone, Weiss, and Klesko).

New York	IP	H	R	ER	BB	SO	HR	ERA
O. Hernandez (W, 1-0)	7	1	1	1	2	10	1	1.29
Nelson	⅓	0	0	0	1	1	0	0.00
Stanton	⅓	0	0	0	1	1	0	0.00
Rivera (S, 1)	1⅓	1	0	0	1	1	0	0.00
Atlanta								
Maddux (L, 0-1)	7	5	4	2	3	5	0	2.57
Rocker	1	1	0	0	2	3	0	0.00
Remlinger	1	0	0	0	1	0	0	0.00

IBB—off Rocker (B. Williams). Umpires—Home: Marsh, 1B: Roe, 2B: Rippley, 3B: Cousins, LF: Layne, RF: Joyce. T—2:57. Att.—51,342.

2nd Game—Atlanta, Oct. 24
New York 7, Atlanta 2

NEW YORK (A.L.)	AB	R	H	RBI		ATLANTA (N.L.)	AB	R	H	RBI
Knoblauch 2b	4	1	2	1		G. Williams lf	4	0	0	0
Jeter ss	5	2	2	0		Guillen ss	4	0	0	0
O'Neill rf	4	0	1	1		C. Jones 3b	3	1	1	0
B. Williams cf	4	1	3	0		Jordan rf	3	0	0	0
Martinez 1b	5	2	2	2		Klesko 1b	4	0	0	0
Ledee lf	4	0	2	1		Lockhart 2b	2	1	0	0
Brosius 3b	5	1	2	1		Myers c	3	0	2	1
Girardi c	4	0	0	0		A. Jones cf	3	0	0	0
Cone p	4	0	0	0		McGlinchy p	0	0	0	0
Mendoza p	1	0	0	0		Boone ph	1	0	1	1
Nelson p	0	0	0	0		Millwood p	0	0	0	0
						Mulholland p	0	0	0	0
						Fabregas ph	1	0	0	0
						Springer p	0	0	0	0
						Nixon cf	2	0	1	0
Totals	**40**	**7**	**14**	**6**		**Totals**	**30**	**2**	**5**	**2**

				R	H	E
New York	302	110	000	— 7	14	1
Atlanta	000	000	002	— 2	5	1

E—New York: Cone. Atlanta: Guillen LOB—New York 11, Atlanta 7. 2B—New York: Ledee, Jeter, Brosius. Atlanta: Boone. SB—Knoblauch. S—Girardi. GIDP: New York: B. Williams. Atlanta: Guillen, A Jones, G. Williams. DP—New York: 3 (Jeter and Martinez), (Brosius, Knoblauch, and Martinez), (Knoblauch, Jeter, and Martinez). Atlanta: 1 (Guillen and Klesko).

New York	IP	H	R	ER	BB	SO	HR	ERA
Cone (W, 1-0)	7	1	0	0	5	4	0	0.00
Mendoza	1⅔	3	2	2	1	0	0	10.80
Nelson	⅓	1	0	0	0	0	0	0.00
Atlanta								
Millwood (L, 0-1)	2	8	5	4	2	2	0	18.00
Mulholland	3	3	2	1	1	3	0	6.00
Springer	2	1	0	0	1	0	0	0.00
McGlinchy	2	2	0	0	1	2	0	0.00

IBB—off Mulholland (B. Williams). Umpires—Home: Roe, 1B: Rippley, 2B: Cousins, 3B: Davis, LF: Joyce, RF: Marsh. T—3:14. Att.—51,226.

3rd Game—New York, Oct. 26
New York 6, Atlanta 5

ATLANTA (N.L.)	AB	R	H	RBI		NEW YORK (A.L.)	AB	R	H	RBI
G. Williams lf	5	2	2	0		Knoblauch 2b	4	2	2	2
Boone 2b	5	1	4	1		Jeter ss	4	0	1	0
Nixon pr	0	0	0	0		O'Neill rf	4	0	1	1
Lockhart 2b	0	0	0	0		B. Williams cf	4	0	0	0
C. Jones 3b	4	0	1	1		Davis dh	4	0	0	0
Jordan rf	3	1	1	1		Martinez 1b	4	1	1	1
A. Jones cf	5	1	0	0		Brosius 3b	4	0	0	0
J. Hernandez dh	4	0	1	2		Curtis lf	4	2	2	2
Guillen ph	1	0	0	0		Girardi c	3	1	2	0
Perez c	4	0	1	0						
Kleskho ph	1	0	1	0						
Hunter 1b	4	0	1	0						
Myers ph	1	0	0	0						
Weiss ss	4	0	1	0						
Totals	**41**	**5**	**14**	**5**		**Totals**	**35**	**6**	**9**	**6**

				R	H	E
Atlanta	103	100	000	0	5	14	1
New York	100	010	120	1	6	9	0

E—Atlanta: Jordan. LOB—Atlanta 9, New York 3. 2B—Atlanta: Boone, J. Hernandez. New York: Knoblauch. 3B—Atlanta: G. Williams. HR—New York: Curtis 2, Martinez 1, Knoblauch 1. SB—J. Hernandez. CS—Boone, Nixon. GIDP—Atlanta: Jordan. New York: O'Neill. DP—Atlanta 2 (Hunter), (Hunter, Weiss, and Boone). New York: 1 (Jeter and Martinez).

Atlanta	IP	H	R	ER	BB	SO	HR	ERA
Glavine	7	7	5	4	0	3	3	5.14
Rocker	2	1	0	0	1	0	0	0.00
Remlinger (L, 0-1)	0	1	1	1	0	1	1	9.00
New York								
Pettitte	3⅔	10	5	5	1	1	0	12.27
Grimsley	2⅓	2	0	0	2	0	0	0.00
Nelson	1	0	0	0	0	2	0	0.00
Rivera (W, 1-0)	2	2	0	0	0	2	0	0.00

WP—Pettitte. Umpires—Home: Rippley, 1B: Cousins, 2B: Davis, 3B: Joyce, LF: Marsh, RF: Roe. T—3:16. Att.—56,794.

4th Game—New York, Oct. 27
New York 4, Atlanta 1

LOB—Atlanta 5, New York 7. 2B—New York: Posada. HR—New York: Leyritz. SB—New York: Jeter 2. GIDP—Atlanta: Perez. DP—New York: 1 (Brosius, Knoblauch, and Martinez).

ATLANTA (N.L.)	AB	R	H	RBI
G. Williams lf	4	0	1	0
Boone 2b	3	0	1	1
C. Jones 3b	4	0	0	0
Jordan rf	3	0	0	0
Klesko 1b	4	0	1	0
Lockhart dh	4	0	1	0
Perez c	2	0	0	0
Myers ph	1	0	0	0
A. Jones cf	3	0	0	0
Weiss ss	3	1	1	0
Totals	31	1	5	1

NEW YORK (A.L.)	AB	R	H	RBI
Knoblauch 2b	4	1	1	0
Sojo 2b	0	0	0	0
Jeter ss	4	1	1	0
O'Neill rf	3	0	0	0
B. Williams cf	3	1	0	0
Martinez 1b	3	0	1	2
Strawberry dh	3	0	1	0
Leyritz ph	1	1	1	1
Posada c	4	0	2	1
Ledee lf	3	0	0	0
Curtis ph	1	0	0	0
Brosius 3b	3	0	1	0
Totals	32	4	8	4

Atlanta	IP	H	R	ER	BB	SO	HR	ERA
Smoltz (L, 0-1)	7	6	3	3	3	11	0	3.86
Mulholland	⅔	2	1	1	0	0	1	7.36
Springer	⅓	0	0	0	0	0	0	0.00
New York								
Clemens (W, 1-0)	7⅔	4	1	1	2	4	0	1.17
Nelson	0	1	0	0	0	0	0	0.00
Rivera (S, 2)	1⅓	0	0	0	0	0	0	0.00

IBB: off Smoltz (Williams). Umpires—Home: Cousins, 1B: Davis, 2B: Joyce, 3B: Marsh, LF: Roe, RF: Rippley. T—2:58. Att—56,752.

				R	H	E
Atlanta	000	000	010 —	1	5	0
New York	003	000	01x —	4	8	0

Series MVP—Mariano Rivera.

BEFORE THE WORLD SERIES
The N.L.–American Assn. Series, 1882–90

When the National League met the American League for the first time in the 1903 World Series, it was not the N.L.'s first venture into post-season play. From 1882–90, the N.L. pennant winner engaged in a championship series with the champion of the American Association. The Nationals won four of the eight series, lost once, and tied three times.

Year	Champion	Loser	Series	Year	Champion	Loser	Series
1882	Chicago (N.L.) & Cincinnati (A.A.)	—	1–1	1887	Detroit (N.L.)	St. Louis (A.A.)	10–5
1883	No series			1888	New York (N.L.)	St. Louis (A.A.)	6–4
1884	Providence (N.L.)	New York (A.A.)	3–0	1889	New York (N.L.)	Brooklyn (A.A.)	6–3
1885	Chicago (N.L.) & St. Louis (A.A.)	—	3–3–1	1890	Brooklyn (N.L.) & Louisville (A.A.)	—	3–3–1
1886	St. Louis (A.A.)	Chicago (N.L.)	4–2				

Early N.L. and A.L. Pennant Winners

The National League had been around 27 years before the 1903 World Series. The A.L., however, was only in its third season when the two leagues met. The following lists account for the pennant winners in those pre-World Series years and in 1904 when the N.L. champion New York Giants refused to play Boston.

N.L. Pennant Winners, 1876–1902, '04

Year	Winner	Manager	Year	Winner	Manager	Year	Winner	Manager
1876	Chicago	Al Spalding	1886	Chicago	Cap Anson	1896	Baltimore	Ned Hanlon
1877	Boston	Harry Wright	1887	Detroit	Bill Watkins	1897	Boston	Frank Selee
1878	Boston	Harry Wright	1888	New York	Jim Mutrie	1898	Boston	Frank Selee
1879	Providence	George Wright	1889	New York	Jim Mutrie	1899	Brooklyn	Ned Hanlon
1880	Chicago	Cap Anson	1890	Brooklyn	Bill McGunnigle	1900	Brooklyn	Ned Hanlon
1881	Chicago	Cap Anson	1891	Boston	Frank Selee	1901	Pittsburgh	Fred Clarke
1882	Chicago	Cap Anson	1892	Boston	Frank Selee	1902	Pittsburgh	Fred Clarke
1883	Boston	John Morrill	1893	Boston	Frank Selee	1904	New York	John McGraw
1884	Providence	Frank Bancroft	1894	Baltimore	Ned Hanlon			
1885	Chicago	Cap Anson	1895	Baltimore	Ned Hanlon			

A.L. Pennant Winners, 1901–02, '04

Year	Winner	Manager	Year	Winner	Manager	Year	Winner	Manager
1901	Chicago	Clark Griffith	1902	Philadelphia	Connie Mack	1904	Boston	Jimmy Collins

THE HANK AARON AWARD

In 1999 Major League Baseball instituted the Hank Aaron Award for the best hitters in the National and American Leagues. The award goes to the batter who has the highest total of runs batted in, home runs, and hits combined.

The first winners were **Sammy Sosa** of the Chicago Cubs and **Manny Ramirez** of the Cleveland Indians. Sosa led the National League with 141 RBIs, 63 home runs, and 180 hits. Ramirez's American League winning stats were 165 runs batted in, 44 home runs, and 174 hits.

Extreme Sports

1999 SUMMER EXTREME GAMES
(San Francisco, Calif., June 25–July 3, 1999)

MEN

Skysurfing: Eric Fradet

Sport climbing: Aaron Shamy (speed), Chris Sharma (bouldering)

Snowboarding big air: Peter Line

Bicycle stunt: Dave Mirra (street), Dave Mirra (halfpipe), Trevor Meyer (flatland), T. J. Lavin (dirt jump)

Street luge: Dennis Derammelaere (dual downhill), David Rogers (super mass)

Skateboarding: Bucky Lasek (vert), Tony Hawk and Andy Macdonald (vert doubles), Chris Senn (street)

Freestyle motocross: Travis Pastrana

Wakeboarding: Parks Bonifay

Aggressive in-line: Nicky Adams (street), Eito Yasutoko (vert), Taig Khris, Javier Bujanda, and Sven Boekhorst (vert triples)

WOMEN

Sport climbing: Renata Piszczek (speed), Stephanie Bodet (bouldering)

Snowboarding big air: Barrett Christy

Wakeboarding: Meaghan Major

Aggressive in-line: Sayaka Yabe (street), Ayumi Kawasaki (vert)

Watersports: Andrea Gaytan (wakeboard)

Soccer

The early history of the sport is uncertain. A form of the game in which a leather ball was dribbled was played in China as early as the 4th century B.C.E. The Romans played a variation of soccer which eventually spread throughout Europe. British schools and universities played soccer (known as football) during the 1800s, however, each school used different sets of rules and the number of players varied. This difficulty was corrected on Oct. 26, 1863, when the Football Association (FA) was formed in London for the purpose of unifying the rules of the game.

The Federation of International Football Associations (FIFA) was created in 1913 as a world governing body to coordinate all of the national associations in the world. The FIFA held the first World Cup Championship tournament in 1930 in Montevideo, Uruguay. Today, soccer is the world's most popular sport. The first FIFA Women's World Cup was held in 1991 with the United States winning the title.

WORLD CUP
(W) indicates Women's World Cup

1930	Uruguay	1954	West Germany	1978	Argentina	1995 Norway (W)
1934	Italy	1958	Brazil	1982	Italy	1998 France
1938	Italy	1962	Brazil	1986	Argentina	1999 United States (W)
1942	No competition	1966	England	1990	West Germany	
1946	No competition	1970	Brazil	1991	United States (W)	
1950	Uruguay	1974	West Germany	1994	Brazil	

WOMEN'S WORLD CUP—1999

FINAL GROUP STANDINGS

	W	L	T	Pts	GF	GA
Group A						
x-USA	3	0	0	9	13	1
x-Nigeria	2	1	0	6	5	8
Korea DPR	1	2	0	3	4	6
Denmark	0	3	0	0	1	8
Group B						
x-Brazil	2	0	1	7	12	4
x-Germany	1	0	2	5	10	4
Italy	1	1	1	4	3	3
Mexico	0	3	0	0	1	15
Group C						
x-Norway	3	0	0	9	13	2
x-Russia	2	1	0	6	10	3
Canada	0	2	1	1	3	12
Japan	0	2	1	1	1	10
Group D						
x-China	3	0	0	9	12	2
x-Sweden	2	1	0	6	6	3
Australia	0	2	1	1	3	7
Ghana	0	2	1	1	1	10

x-Advance to next round.

QUARTERFINALS
Norway 3, Sweden 1
China 2, Russia 0
United States 3, Germany 2
Brazil 4, Nigeria 3
  (Brazil won in sudden-death "golden goal" overtime)

SEMIFINALS
United States 2, Brazil 0
China 5, Norway 0

THIRD PLACE
Brazil 0, Norway 0 (Brazil won 5–4 on penalty kicks)

CHAMPIONSHIP
United States 0, China 0 (The United States won 5–4 on penalty kicks)

WORLD CUP—1998

QUARTERFINALS
Denmark 2, Brazil 3
Argentina 1, Netherlands 2
France 0, Italy 0 (France won 4–3 in shootout)
Croatia 3, Germany 0
SEMIFINALS
Netherlands 1, Brazil 1 (Brazil won 4–2 in shootout)
Croatia 1, France 2

THIRD PLACE
Croatia 2, Netherlands 1

CHAMPIONSHIP
France 3, Brazil 0

WORLD CUP

All-Time Top 10

		Points	Matches	Record (W–T–L)	GF	GA			Points	Matches	Record (W–T–L)	GF	GA
1.	Brazil	120	80	53–14–13	173	78	6.	France	48	41	21–6–14	86	58
2.	West Germany	107	78	45–17–16	162	103	7.	Spain	42	40	16–10–14	61	48
3.	Italy	92	66	38–16–12	105	62	8.	Yugoslavia	40	37	16–8–13	60	46
4.	Argentina	68	57	29–10–18	100	69	9.	Uruguay	38	37	15–8–14	61	52
5.	England	53	45	20–13–12	62	42	10.	U.S.S.R./ Russia	38	34	16–6–12	60	40

MAJOR LEAGUE SOCCER 1999 FINAL STANDINGS

Conference champions (*) and playoff qualifiers (+) are noted. SOW refers to shootout wins. Teams receive three points for a win but just one point for a shootout win. The GF and GA columns refer to Goals For and Goals Against in regulation play. The 1999 MLS Cup game was held after the almanac went to press.

EASTERN CONFERENCE

	Team	W	L	Pts	GF	GA	SOW
*	D.C. United	23	9	57	65	43	6
+	Columbus Crew	19	13	45	48	39	6
+	Tampa Bay Mutiny	14	18	32	51	50	5
+	Miami Fusion	13	19	29	42	59	5
	N.E. Revolution	12	20	26	38	53	5
	N.Y./N.J. MetroStars	7	25	15	32	64	3

*Conference champions. +Playoff qualifiers.

WESTERN CONFERENCE

	Team	W	L	Pts	GF	GA	SOW
*	Los Angeles Galaxy	20	12	54	49	29	3
+	Dallas Burn	19	13	51	54	35	3
+	Chicago Fire	18	14	48	51	36	3
+	Colorado Rapids	20	12	48	38	39	6
	San Jose Clash	19	13	37	48	49	10
	Kansas City Wizards	8	24	20	33	53	2

*Conference champions. +Playoff qualifiers.

1999 REGULAR SEASON

LEADING SCORERS

	Gm	G	A	Pts
Jason Kreis, Dallas	32	18	15	51
Roy Lassiter, D.C.	30	18	11	47
Ronald Cerritos, San Jose	31	15	9	39
Stern John, Columbus	28	18	2	38
Joe-Max Moore, New England	29	15	8	38
Ante Razov, Chicago	30	14	7	35
Jaime Moreno, D.C.	25	10	13	33
Raul Diaz Arce, Tampa Bay	31	13	7	33
Musa Shannon, Tampa Bay	27	12	5	29
Jeff Cunningham, Columbus	28	12	5	29

LEADING GOALKEEPERS

	Gm	Min	Shots	Svs	W–L
Kevin Hartman, Los Angeles	32	2,870	150	118	20–12
M. Hahnemann, Colorado	13	1,170	85	68	10–3
Matt Jordon, Dallas	29	2,584	172	133	17–11
Zach Thornton, Chicago	30	2,633	137	99	17–12
Mark Dougherty, Columbus	31	2,745	152	106	18–12
Ian Feuer, Colorado	19	1,696	99	70	10–9
Scott Garlick, Tampa Bay	28	2,471	193	152	14–13
Joe Cannon, San Jose	24	2,160	129	95	14–10
Tom Presthus, D.C.	26	2,227	129	88	16–8
Chris Snitko, Kansas City	16	1,395	95	66	4–10

GOAL-SCORING

	Gm	No
Stern John, Columbus	28	18
Roy Lassiter, D.C.	30	18
Jason Kreis, Dallas	32	18
Joe-Max Moore, New England	29	15
Ronald Cerritos, San Jose	31	15
Ante Razov, Chicago	30	14
Raul Diaz Arce, Tampa Bay	31	13
Musa Shannon, Tampa Bay	27	12
Jeff Cunningham, Columbus	28	12

SHOTS

	Gm	No
Jason Kreis, Dallas	32	114
Stern John, Columbus	28	104
Preki, Kansas City	30	97
Mauricio Ramos, Tampa Bay	30	95
Ante Razov, Chicago	30	90

ASSISTS

	Gm	No
Steve Ralston, Tampa Bay	32	18
Marco Etcheverry, D.C.	22	17
Mauricio Cienfuegos, Los Angeles	30	17
Carlos Valderrama, Tampa Bay	31	15
Jason Kreis, Dallas	32	15
Eddie Lewis, San Jose	29	14

SHOTS ON GOAL

	Gm	No
Jason Kreis, Dallas	32	57
Ante Razov, Chicago	30	49
Joe-Max Moore, New England	29	47
Roy Lassiter, D.C.	30	47
Stern John, Columbus	28	45
Ronald Cerritos, San Jose	31	45

History of the Income Tax in the United States

Source: Ernst & Young LLP

The nation had few taxes in its early history. From 1791 to 1802, the United States Government was supported by internal taxes on distilled spirits, carriages, refined sugar, tobacco and snuff, property sold at auction, corporate bonds, and slaves. The high cost of the War of 1812 brought about the nation's first sales taxes on gold, silverware, jewelry, and watches. In 1817, however, Congress did away with all internal taxes, relying on tariffs on imported goods to provide sufficient funds for running the Government.

In 1862, in order to support the Civil War effort, Congress enacted the nation's first income tax law. It was a forerunner of our modern income tax in that it was based on the principles of graduated, or progressive, taxation and of withholding income at the source. During the Civil War, a person earning from $600 to $10,000 per year paid tax at the rate of 3%. Those with incomes of more than $10,000 paid taxes at a higher rate. Additional sales and excise taxes were added, and an "inheritance" tax also made its debut. In 1866, internal revenue collections reached their highest point in the nation's 90-year history—more than $310 million, an amount not reached again until 1911.

The Act of 1862 established the office of Commissioner of Internal Revenue. The Commissioner was given the power to assess, levy, and collect taxes, and the right to enforce the tax laws through seizure of property and income and through prosecution. His powers and authority remain very much the same today.

In 1868, Congress again focused its taxation efforts on tobacco and distilled spirits and eliminated the income tax in 1872. It had a short-lived revival in 1894 and 1895. In the latter year, the U.S. Supreme Court decided that the income tax was unconstitutional because it was not apportioned among the states in conformity with the Constitution.

In 1913, the 16th Amendment to the Constitution made the income tax a permanent fixture in the U.S. tax system. The amendment gave Congress legal authority to tax income and resulted in a revenue law that taxed incomes of both individuals and corporations. In fiscal year 1918, annual internal revenue collections for the first time passed the billion-dollar mark, rising to $5.4 billion by 1920. With the advent of World War II, employment increased, as did tax collections—to $7.3 billion. The withholding tax on wages was introduced in 1943 and was instrumental in increasing the number of taxpayers to 60 million and tax collections to $43 billion by 1945.

In 1981, Congress enacted the largest tax cut in U.S. history, approximately $750 billion over six years. The tax reduction, however, was partially offset by two tax acts, in 1982 and 1984, which attempted to raise approximately $265 billion.

On Oct. 22, 1986, President Reagan signed into law The Tax Reform Act of 1986, one of the most far-reaching reforms of the United States tax system since the adoption of the income tax. In an attempt to remain revenue neutral, the Act called for a $120 billion increase in business taxation and a corresponding decrease in individual taxation over a five-year period.

Following what seemed to be a yearly tradition of new tax acts which began in 1986, the Revenue Reconciliation Act of 1990 was signed into law on November 5, 1990. As with the '87, '88, and '89 acts, the 1990 act, while providing a number of substantive provisions, was small in comparison with the 1986 act. The emphasis of the 1990 act was increased taxes on the wealthy.

On August 10, 1993, President Clinton signed the Revenue Reconciliation Act of 1993 into law. The Act's purpose was to reduce by approximately $496 billion the Federal deficit that would otherwise accumulate in fiscal years 1994 through 1998. Approximately $241 billion of the deficit reduction will be accomplished through tax increases.

On August 5, 1997, President Clinton signed the Taxpayer Relief Act of 1997. The Act included $152 billion in tax cuts. The bill includes a cut in capital gains tax for individuals, a $500 per child tax credit, estate tax relief, tax incentives for education and a host of revenue-raising and tax-simplification provisions.

Internal Revenue Service

The Internal Revenue Service (IRS), a bureau of the U.S. Treasury Department, is the federal agency charged with the administration of the tax laws passed by Congress. The IRS functions through a national office in Washington, 4 regional offices, 63 district offices, and 10 service centers.

Operations involving most taxpayers are carried out in the district offices and service centers. District offices are organized into Resources Management, Examination, Collection, Taxpayer Service, Employee Plans and Exempt Organizations, and Criminal Investigation. All tax returns are filed with the service centers, where the IRS computer operations are located.

IRS service centers are processing an ever increasing number of returns and documents. Prior to 1987, all tax return processing was performed by hand. This process was time consuming and costly. In an attempt to improve the speed and efficiency of the manual processing procedure, the IRS began testing an electronic return filing system beginning with the filing of 1985 returns.

Internal Revenue Service

	1996	1995	1994	1993	1992	1970
U.S. population (in thousands)	266,109	263,730	261,698	259,015	256,219	204,878
Number of IRS employees	102,082	112,023	110,665	113,352	116,673	68,683
Cost to govt. of collecting $100 in taxes	$0.49	$0.55	$0.58	$0.60	$0.58	$0.45
Tax per capita	$5,586.00	$5,216.44	$4,878.00	$4,543.33	$4,374.38	$955.31
Collections by principal sources (in thousands of dollars)						
Total IRS collections	$1,486,546,674	$1,375,731,835	$1,276,466,776	$1,176,685,625	$1,120,799,558	$195,722,096
Income and profits taxes						
Individual	$745,313,276	$675,779,337	$619,819,153	$585,774,159	$557,723,156	$103,651,585
Corporation	$189,054,791	$174,422,173	$154,204,684	$131,547,509	$117,950,796	$35,036,983
Employment taxes	$492,365,178	$465,405,305	$443,831,352	$411,510,516	$400,080,904	$37,449,188
Estate and gift taxes	$17,591,817	$15,144,394	$15,606,793	$12,890,965	$11,479,116	$3,680,076
Alcohol taxes	(1)	(1)	(1)	(1)	(1)	$4,746,382
Tobacco taxes	(1)	(1)	(1)	(1)	(1)	$2,094,212
Manufacturers' excise taxes	(2)	(2)	(2)	(2)	(2)	6,683,061
All other taxes	$42,221,611	$44,980,627	$43,004,794	$34,962,476	$33,565,587	$2,380,609

NOTE: For fiscal year ending September 30th. 1. Alcohol and tobacco tax collections are now collected and reported by the Bureau of Alcohol, Tobacco, and Firearms. 2. Manufacturers' excise taxes are included in the "All other taxes" amount. Source: IRS 1996 Annual Report.

The two most significant results of the test were that refunds for the electronically filed returns were issued more quickly and the tax processing error rate was significantly lower when compared to paper returns. Electronic filing of individual income tax returns with refunds became an operational program in selected areas for the 1987 processing year. In 1994 13,510,000 individual returns were filed electronically, compared to 11,143,000 in 1995, and 14,977,123 in 1996.

Auditing Tax Returns

Most taxpayers' contacts with the IRS arise through the auditing of their tax returns. The Service has been empowered by Congress to inquire about all persons who may be liable for any tax and to obtain for review the books and/or records pertinent to those taxpayers' returns. A wide-ranging audit operation is carried out in the 63 district offices by 16,078 revenue agents and 2,831 tax auditors.

The primary method used by the IRS in selecting returns for audits is a computer program that measures the probability of tax error in each return. The higher the score, the greater the tax change potential. Other returns are selected for examination on the basis of claims for refund, multi-year audits, related return audits, and other audits initiated by the IRS as a result of informants' information, special compliance programs, and the information

document matching program. In 1996, the IRS recommended additional tax and penalties on 1,941,546 individual returns, totaling $7.6 billion.

The Appeals Process

The IRS attempts to resolve tax disputes through an administrative appeals system. Taxpayers who, after audit of their tax returns, disagree with a proposed change in their tax liabilities are entitled to an independent review of their cases. Taxpayers are able to seek an immediate, informal appeal with the Appeals Office. If, however, the dispute arises from a field audit and the amount in question exceeds $10,000, a taxpayer must submit a written protest. Alternatively, the taxpayer can wait for the examiner's report and then request consideration by the Appeals Office and file a protest if necessary. Taxpayers may represent themselves or be represented by an attorney, accountant, or any other advisor authorized to practice before the IRS. Taxpayers can forego their right to the above process and await receipt of a deficiency notice. At this juncture, taxpayers can either (1) not pay the deficiency and petition the Tax Court by a required deadline or (2) pay the deficiency and file a claim for refund with the District Director's office. If the claim is not allowed, a suit for refund may be brought either in the District Court or the Claims Court within a specified period.

Federal Income Tax Comparisons
Taxes at Selected Rate Brackets After Standard Deductions and Personal Exemptions[1]

Adjusted gross income	Single return listing no dependents					Joint return listing two dependents				
	1998	1997	1996	1995	1975	1998	1997	1996	1995	1975
$10,000	$ 457	$ 493	$ 518	$ 540	$ 1,506	$ −5,200	$ −3,500	$ −3,556	$−3,110[2]	$ 829
20,000	1,958	1,980	2,018	2,040	4,153	720	975	−1,324	−773	2,860
30,000	3,458	3,480	3,518	3,573	8,018	2,200	2,475	1,965	2,018	5,804
40,000	5,595	6,092	6,246	6,373	12,765	3,720	3,975	3,465	3,518	9,668
50,000	6,549	8,892	9,046	9,173	18,360	6,449	5,475	4,965	5,018	14,260

1. For comparison purposes, tax rate schedules were used. 2. Refund based on a basic earned income credit for families with dependent children.

Federal Individual Income Tax

Tax Brackets—1998 Taxable Income

Joint return	Single taxpayer	Rate
$0–$42,350	$0–$25,350	15.0%
42,350–102,300	25,350–61,400	28.0%
102,300–155,950	61,400–128,100	31.0%[2]
155,950–278,450	128,100–278,450	36.0%[2]
278,450 and up[1]	278,450 and up[1]	39.6%[2]

1. The deduction for personal exemptions is phased out as the taxpayer's gross income exceeds $186,800 for a joint return and $124,500 for single taxpayers. 2. The tax rate is effectively increased because total otherwise allowable itemized deductions are reduced by 3% of the taxpayer's adjusted gross income in excess of $124,500.

The Federal individual income tax is levied on the worldwide income of U.S. citizens and resident aliens and on certain types of U.S. source income of non-residents. For a non-itemizer, "tax table income" is adjusted gross income less $2,700 for each personal exemption and the standard deduction. If a taxpayer itemizes, tax table income is adjusted gross income minus total itemized deductions and personal exemptions. In addition, individuals may also be subject to the alternative minimum tax.

Who Must File a Return[1]

You must file a return if you are:	and your gross income is at least:
Single (legally separated, divorced, or married living apart from spouse with dependent child)	$6,950
Head of household	$8,950
Married, filing jointly, living together at end of year (or at date of death of spouse)	$12,500
Married, filing separate return, or married but not living together at end of year over age 65	$2,700

1. In 1997.

Adjusted Gross Income

Gross income consists of wages and salaries, unemployment compensation, tips and gratuities, interest, dividends, annuities, rents and royalties, up to 85% of Social Security benefits if the recipient's income exceeds a base amount, and certain other types of income. Among the items excluded from gross income, and thus not subject to tax, are public assistance benefits and interest on exempt securities (mostly state and local bonds).

Adjusted gross income is determined by subtracting from gross income: alimony paid, penalties on early withdrawal of savings, payments to an I.R.A. (reduced proportionally based upon adjusted gross income levels if taxpayer is an active participant in an employer maintained retirement plan), payments to a Keogh retirement plan, and self-employed health insurance payments and moving expenses.

Itemized Deductions

Taxpayers may itemize deductions or take the standard deduction. The standard deduction amounts for 1998 are as follows: Married filing jointly and surviving spouses, $7,100; Heads of household, $6,250; Single, $4,250; and Married filing separate returns, $3,550. Taxpayers who are age 65 or over or are blind are entitled to an additional standard deduction of $1,000 for single taxpayers and $800 for a married taxpayer.

In itemizing deductions, the following are major items that may be deducted in 1998: state and local income and property taxes, charitable contributions, employee moving expenses, medical expenses (exceeding 7.5% of adjusted gross income), casualty losses (only the amount over the $100 floor which exceeds 10% of adjusted gross income), mortgage interest, and miscellaneous deductions (deductible only to the extent by which cumulatively they exceed 2% of adjusted gross income).

Personal Exemptions

Personal exemptions are available to the taxpayer for himself, his spouse, and his dependents. The 1998 amount is $2,700 for each individual. No exemption is allowed to a taxpayer who can be claimed as a dependent on another taxpayer's return.

Credits

Taxpayers can reduce their income tax liability by claiming the benefit of certain tax credits. Each dollar of tax credit offsets a dollar of tax liability. The following are a few of the available tax credits.

Certain low-income households may claim an Earned Income Credit. The maximum Earned Income Credit is $341 for taxpayers with no qualifying children, $2,271 for taxpayers with one qualifying child and $3,756 for taxpayers with two or more qualifying children. This maximum credit will be reduced if earned income or adjusted gross income exceeds $12,260, or $5,570 for taxpayers with no qualifying children. For families with one qualifying child, the credit will be zero if earned income or adjusted gross income exceeds $26,473; for families with two or more qualifying children, the credit will be zero if income exceeds $30,095, and for families with no qualifying children, the credit will be zero if income exceeds $10,030. The earned income credit is a refundable credit.

A credit for Child and Dependent Care Expenses is available for amounts paid to care for a child or other dependent so that the taxpayer can work. The credit is between 20% and 30% (depending on adjusted gross income) of up to $2,400 of employment-related expenses for one qualifying child or dependent and up to $4,800 of expenses for two or more qualifying individuals.

The elderly and those under 65 who are retired under total disability may be entitled to a credit of up to $750 (if single) or $1,125 (if married and filing jointly). No credit is available if the taxpayer is single and has adjusted gross income of $17,500 or more. Similarly, the credit is unavailable to a married couple filing jointly if their adjusted gross income exceeds $25,000.

Effective for tax years beginning after December 1, 1997, taxpayers who have qualifying children for whom the taxpayer may claim a dependency exemption and who is less than 17 years old as of the close of the tax year are entitled to the child tax credit. The amount of the credit for 1998 is $400. The child credit begins to phase out when AGI reaches $110,000 for joint filers and $75,000 for singles. Taxpayers who have three or more qualifying children may also be entitled to an additional credit.

State Taxes on Individuals

(as of July 1, 1999)

State	Sales/use tax (percent)[1]	Income tax (percent)[2]	State	Sales/use tax (percent)[1]	Income tax (percent)[2]
Alabama	4.0	2.0 – 5.0	Nebraska	5.0	2.62 – 6.99
Alaska	none	none	Nevada	6.5	none
Arizona	5.0	2.87 – 5.04	New Hampshire	none	(3)
Arkansas	4.625	1.0 – 7.0	New Jersey	6.0	1.4 – 6.37
California	6.0	1.0 – 9.3	New Mexico	5.0	1.7 – 8.5
Colorado	3.0	5.0	New York	4.0	4.0 – 6.85
Connecticut	6.0	3.0 – 4.5	North Carolina	4.0	6.0 – 7.75
Delaware	none	2.6 – 6.4	North Dakota	5.0	2.67 – 12.0
Florida	6.0	none	Ohio	5.0	0.673 – 6.799
Georgia	4.0	1.0 – 6.0	Oklahoma	4.5	0.5 – 6.75
Hawaii	4.0	1.6 – 8.75	Oregon	none	5.0 – 9.0
Idaho	5.0	2.0 – 8.2	Pennsylvania	6.0	2.8
Illinois	6.25	3.0	Rhode Island	7.0	26.5[4]
Indiana	5.0	3.4	South Carolina	5.0	2.5 – 6.75
Iowa	5.0	0.36 – 8.98	South Dakota	4.0	none
Kansas	4.9	4.1 – 6.45	Tennessee	6.0	(3)
Kentucky	6.0	2.0 – 6.0	Texas	6.25	none
Louisiana	4.0	2.0 – 6.0	Utah	4.75	2.3 – 7.0
Maine	5.5	2.0 – 8.5	Vermont	5.0	25[4]
Maryland	5.0	2.0 – 4.85	Virginia	3.5	2.0 – 5.75
Massachusetts	5.0	5.95	Washington	6.5	none
Michigan	6.0	4.4	West Virginia	6.0	3.0 – 6.5
Minnesota	6.5	6.0 – 8.5	Wisconsin	5.0	4.77 – 6.77
Mississippi	7.0	3.0 – 5.0	Wyoming	4.0	none
Missouri	4.225	1.5 – 6.0	Washington, D.C.	5.75	6.0 – 9.5
Montana	none	2.0 – 11.0			

1. Local and county taxes, if any, are additional. 2. Tax rate for individuals; unless otherwise noted, range denotes progressive structure; higher income pays higher rate. 3. Income tax limited to dividends and interest income only. 4. Percent of federal tax liability (e.g., if you owe the IRS $2,000 for the year, you owe the State of Vermont 25% of that, or $500). *Source:* The Federation of Tax Administrators.

Federal Corporation Taxes

Corporations are taxed under a graduated tax rate structure. If a corporation has taxable income in excess of $100,000, the amount of tax shall be increased by the lesser of five percent of such excess or $11,750. When a corporation has taxable income in excess of $15,000,000 the amount of tax shall be increased by an additional amount equal to the lesser of three percent of such excess or $100,000.

If the corporation qualifies, it may elect to be an S corporation. If it makes this election, the corporation will not (with certain exceptions) pay corporate tax on its income. Its income is instead passed through and taxed to its shareholders. There are several requirements a corporation must meet to qualify as an S corporation, including having 75 or fewer shareholders and having only one class of stock.

Tax Brackets—1998

Taxable income	Tax rate
$0–$50,000	15%
$50,001–$75,000	25%
$75,001–$100,000	34%
$100,001–$335,000	39%
$335,001–$10,000,000	34%
$10m–$15m	35%
$15m–$18.3m	38%
$18.3m and up	35%

State Corporation Income and Franchise Taxes

All states except Texas, Nevada, South Dakota, Washington, and Wyoming impose a tax on corporation net income. The majority of states impose the tax at flat rates ranging from 2.3% to approximately 10.75%. Several states have adopted a graduated basis of rates for corporations.

Nearly all states follow the federal law in defining net income. However, many states provide for varying exclusions and adjustments.

A state is empowered to tax all of the net income of its domestic corporations. With regard to non-resident corporations, however, it may only tax the net income on business carried on within its boundaries. Corporations are, therefore, required to apportion their incomes among the states where they do business, and pay a tax to each of these states. Nearly all states provide an apportionment to their domestic corporations, too, in order that they not be unduly burdened. Several states tax unincorporated businesses separately.

Federal Estate and Gift Taxes

A Federal Estate Tax Return must generally be filed for the estate of every U.S. citizen or resident whose gross estate, adjusted taxable gifts, and specific exemption exceed $625,000. An estate tax return must also generally be filed for the estate of a non-resident who died during 1998 if the value of his gross estate in the U.S. is more than $60,000 at the date of death. The estate tax return is due 9 months after the date of death of the decedent, but a 6-month extension of time to file may be obtained for good reason.

Under the unified federal estate and gift tax structure, individuals who made taxable gifts during the calendar year are required to file a gift tax return by April 15 of the following year.

A unified credit of $202,050 is available to offset both estate and gift taxes. Any part of the credit used to offset gift taxes is not available to offset estate taxes. As a result, although they are still taxable as gifts, lifetime taxable transfers no longer cushion the impact of progressive estate tax rates. Lifetime transfers and transfers made at death are combined for estate tax rate purposes.

Gift taxes are computed by applying the uniform rate schedule to lifetime taxable transfers (after deducting the unified credit) and subtracting the taxes payable for prior taxable periods. In general, estate taxes are computed by applying the uniform rate schedule to cumulative transfers and subtracting the gift taxes paid. An appropriate adjustment is made for taxes on lifetime transfers—such as certain gifts within three years of death—in a decedent's estate.

Among the deductions allowed in computing the amount of the estate subject to tax are funeral expenditures, administrative costs, claims and bequests to religious, charitable, and fraternal organizations or government welfare agencies, and state inheritance taxes. For transfers made after 1981 during life or death, there is an unlimited marital deduction.

An annual gift tax exclusion is provided that permits tax-free gifts to each donee of $10,000 for each year. A husband and wife who agree to treat gifts to third persons as joint gifts can exclude up to $20,000 a year to each donee. An unlimited exclusion for medical expenses and school tuition both paid directly to the institution for the benefit of any donee is also available in addition to the annual gift tax exclusion.

Federal Taxes Collected and Spent, by State

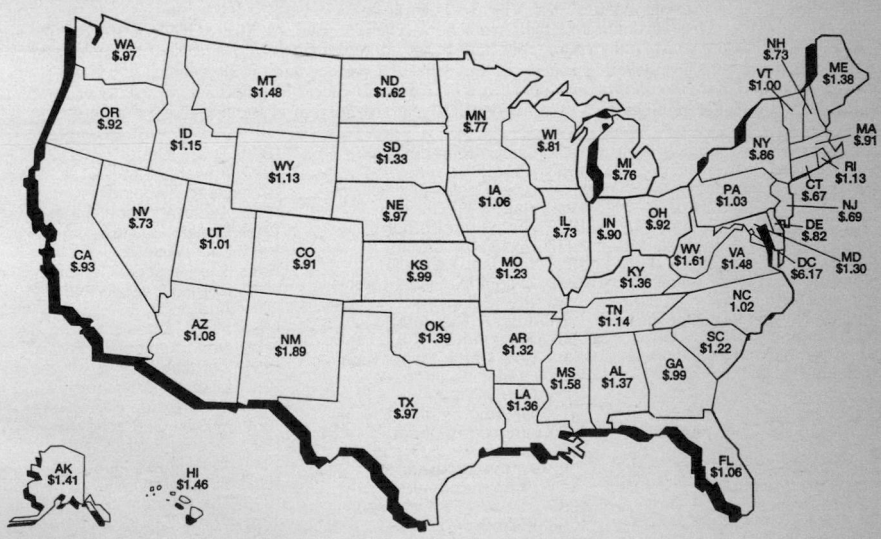

Federal Expenditures for Every Dollar of Taxes Sent to Washington
FY 1997

Source: Tax Foundation.

The Man of the Year

How "Lucky Lindy"—and a slow week for news— gave birth to a memorable annual tradition

The founders of TIME Magazine, Henry Luce and Briton Haddon, were strong believers in the idea that history is shaped by the deeds of extraordinary men and women. This thesis, most memorably advanced by the British writer Thomas Carlyle, was well-suited to the American vision of the two Yale graduates since it ran counter to the assertions of Karl Marx and others that history is the residue of impersonal economic and social forces.

TIME's insistence on the primacy of the individual found its most memorable form in the magazine's annual designation of a Man or Woman of the Year—the person whose actions had most affected the course of the news within the last twelve months. But the magazine's signature annual tribute was not the result of high-level philosophizing; rather, it was driven by something far more important to journalists—a deadline.

The year was 1927; it was the last week in December. During the holiday season, the normal flow of public events had temporarily ebbed to a trickle. Looking to 1928, the editors at TIME were having trouble finding a newsworthy cover subject for the first issue of the new year. At the same time, they realized that they had passed up several opportunities during the year to put aviator Charles Lindbergh on its cover. Since his nonstop flight from New York to Paris in late May, the young pilot had been idolized—yet he had never appeared on the magazine's cover. So the editors came up with a new concept: instead of highlighting a personality of the week, it was decided that the cover for January 2, 1928, would feature Lindbergh, and that beneath his likeness would be the words "Man of the Year."

A year later, the cover for TIME's first issue of 1929 revealed that its editors had named car magnate Walter P. Chrysler as Man of the Year for 1928—and it was obvious that an annual tradition had been born. By the mid-1930s, TIME readers were happily forwarding their suggestions for the Man of the Year to the editors as early as October.

The term "Man of the Year"—redolent of countless Chamber of Commerce dinners—suggests to many people that it is awarded as an accolade. It is not. Rather, it designates the person who, in the editors' opinion, has most affected the course of history in the past twelve months—for good or for ill.

In 1938, for instance, Adolf Hitler completed his Anschluss of Austria and brokered the tragic agreement at Munich that put Czechoslovakia into his hands. However reluctantly, the editors concluded that Hitler's actions had most affected history's course, and he became the 1938 Man of the Year. Similarly, in 1979, Ayatullah Khomeini was named Man of the Year, even while he held Americans hostage in Tehran. TIME received more than 14,000 letters complaining about the choice; many readers wrote to cancel their subscription.

After 75 years, the Man of the Year has become an institution: whereas in one sense it is a sort of intellectual parlor game, it also challenges TIME's editors and readers to reflect on the events of the past year critically, dispassionately, and rigorously. ◻

1927 Charles Lindbergh	1952 Queen Elizabeth II	1976 Jimmy Carter
1928 Walter P. Chrysler	1953 Konrad Adenauer	1977 Anwar Sadat
1929 Owen D. Young	1954 John Foster Dulles	1978 Deng Xiaoping
1930 Mahatma Gandhi	1955 Harlow H. Curtice	1979 Ayatullah Khomeini
1931 Pierre Laval	1956 Hungarian Patriot	1980 Ronald Reagan
1932 Franklin D. Roosevelt	1957 Nikita Khrushchev	1981 Lech Walesa
1933 Hugh S. Johnson	1958 Charles DeGaulle	1982 The Personal Computer
1934 Franklin D. Roosevelt	1959 Dwight D. Eisenhower	1983 Ronald Reagan and Yuri
1935 Haile Selassie	1960 U.S. Scientists	Andropov
1936 Wallis Warfield Simpson	1961 John F. Kennedy	1984 Peter Ueberroth
1937 Gen. and Mrs. Chiang	1962 Pope John XXIII	1985 Deng Xiaoping
Kai-shek	1963 Rev. Martin Luther King, Jr.	1986 Corazon Aquino
1938 Adolf Hitler	1964 Lyndon B. Johnson	1987 Mikhail Gorbachev
1939 Joseph Stalin	1965 Gen. William	1988 Endangered Earth
1940 Winston Churchill	Westmoreland	1989 Mikhail Gorbachev
1941 Franklin D. Roosevelt	1966 Americans under 25	1990 George Bush
1942 Joseph Stalin	1967 Lyndon B. Johnson	1991 Ted Turner
1943 Gen. George C. Marshall	1968 Astronauts Anders,	1992 Bill Clinton
1944 Gen. Dwight D.	Borman, Lovell	1993 The Peacemakers: Rabin,
Eisenhower	1969 The Middle Americans	Arafat, Mandela, De Klerk
1945 Harry S. Truman	1970 Willy Brandt	1994 Pope John Paul II
1946 James F. Byrnes	1971 Richard M. Nixon	1995 Newt Gingrich
1947 Gen. George C. Marshall	1972 Richard M. Nixon and	1996 Dr. David Ho
1948 Harry S. Truman	Henry Kissinger	1997 Andrew Grove
1949 Winston Churchill	1973 Judge John J. Sirica	1998 Bill Clinton and
1950 G.I. Joe	1974 King Faisal	Kenneth Starr
1951 Mohammed Mossadegh	1975 American Women	

The TIME 100

The most influential individuals of the 20th century

As the century neared its end, TIME's editors compiled a list of the 100 individuals who most influenced the course of 20th century history, for good or ill. TIME asked 100 noted authorities—including a number of the magazine's own critics—to write profiles of the selected individuals. In late December 1999, the TIME 100 series will culminate with the naming of TIME's Person of the Century.

Leaders & Revolutionaries

Theodore Roosevelt (1858–1919) Energetic polymath
"In his protean variety, his febrile energy, his incessant self-celebration, the great 'Teddy' represents 20th century dynamism." —Biographer Edmund Morris

Vladimir I. Lenin (1870–1924) Prophet of revolution
"Lenin was the initiator of the central drama—the tragedy—of our era, the rise of totalitarian states." —*New Yorker* editor David Remnick

Margaret Sanger (1879–1966) Crusader for birth control
"She taught us, first, to look at the world as if women mattered." —Feminist editor Gloria Steinem

Theodore Roosevelt

Franklin D. Roosevelt (1882–1945) Architect of the New Deal
"F.D.R. was loved because, though patrician by birth and style, he believed in and fought for plain people." —Historian Arthur Schlesinger Jr.

Adolf Hitler (1889–1945) Avatar of fascism
"The savior admired by his own even as he dragged them into his madness, the Satan and exterminating angel feared and hated by all others, Hitler led his people to a shameful defeat." —Nobel laureate Elie Wiesel

Winston Churchill (1874–1965) Master statesman
"Churchill was uniquely stirred by the challenge of war and found his fulfillment in leading the democracies to victory." —Military historian John Keegan

Eleanor Roosevelt (1884–1962) Crusader for social justice
"She was the first woman to speak in front of a national convention, to write a syndicated column, to earn money as a lecturer, to be a radio commentator, and to hold regular press conferences."—Historian Doris Kearns Goodwin

Margaret Sanger

Mohandas Gandhi (1869–1948) India's liberator
"The harshest truth is that Gandhi is increasingly irrelevant in the country whose 'little father'—Bapu—he was." —Novelist Salman Rushdie

David Ben-Gurion (1886–1973) Founder of Israel
"Ben-Gurion's iron-will leadership during Israel's early years turned him from 'first among equals' in the Zionist leadership into a modern-day King David." —Novelist Amos Oz

Eleanor Roosevelt

Mao Zedong (1893–1976) Founder of Communist China
"A curious mixture of jocularity and cruelty, of utopian visions and blinkered perceptions, lay at the heart of his character." —China scholar Jonathan D. Spence

Ho Chi Minh (1890–1969) Communist guerrilla
"He cultivated the image of a humble, benign 'Uncle Ho.' But he was a seasoned revolutionary and passionate nationalist obsessed by a single goal: independence for his country." —Author Stanley Karnow

Martin Luther King, Jr. (1929–1968) Civil rights leader
"For all King did to free blacks from the yoke of segregation, whites may owe him the greatest debt, for liberating them from America's burden of hypocrisy about race." —TIME columnist Jack E. White

David Ben-Gurion

Ayatollah Khomeini (1900–1989) Prophet of Islam
"His well-advertised piety complemented a prodigious skill in grasping and shaping Iran's complex politics." —Middle East scholar Milton Viorst

Margaret Thatcher (1925–) Champion of free markets
"The triumph of capitalism, the collapse of Soviet imperialism, the downsizing of the state—she played a part in all those transformations." —Historian Paul Johnson

John Paul II (1920–) Pilgrim pope
"The most radiant face on the public scene, a presence so commanding as to have arrested a generation of humankind." —Writer William F. Buckley

Ho Chi Minh

Ronald Reagan (1911–) Champion of conservativism

"Under his leadership, a conflict that had absorbed a half-century of Western blood and treasure was ended—and the good guys finally won."
—Speechwriter Peggy Noonan

Lech Walesa (1943–) Founder of Solidarity

"It is one of history's great ironies that the nearest thing we have ever seen to a genuine workers' revolution was directed against a so-called workers' state."
—Historian Timothy Garton Ash

Lech Walesa

Mikhail Gorbachev (1931–) Communist reformer

"He attempted simultaneously to contain and transform the country, to destroy and reconstruct, right on the spot." —Novelist Tatyana Tolstoya

Nelson Mandela (1918–) Victor over apartheid

"Mandela proves by his own example that faith, hope, and charity are qualities attainable by humanity as a whole." —Professor and writer André Brink

The Unknown Rebel: Hero of Tiananmen Square

"The man who stood before the column of tanks near Tiananmen Square in 1989 reminded us that the conviction of the young can generate a courage that their elders sometimes lack." —Writer Pico Iyer

"Unknown Rebel"

Heroes & Icons

Billy Graham (1918–) America's spiritual counselor

"He is an icon essential to a country in which, for two centuries now, religion has been not the opiate but the poetry of the people."
—Yale scholar and author Harold Bloom

Bill W. (Wilson) (1895–1971) Alcoholics Anonymous founder

"Wilson believed the key to sobriety was a change of heart . . . a restitution for harm done, a call to service and a surrender to some personal God."
—Author Susan Cheever

Billy Graham

The Kennedys: Legendary political family

"They . . . [became legends] through cold calculation and their immense wealth but also because of honorable service to the nation, their reckless exuberance and glamour—and family tragedy without measure." —TIME White House columnist Hugh Sidey

Helen Keller (1880–1968) Voice of the disabled

"She proved how language could liberate the blind and the deaf."
—Jazz singer Diane Schuur

Helen Keller

Rosa Parks (1913–) Civil rights pioneer

"She inspires . . . the hope that all of us could be that brave, that serenely human, when crunch time comes." —Former U.S. poet laureate Rita Dove

Emmeline Pankhurst (1858–1928) Suffragist

"Mrs. Pankhurst was born a Victorian Englishwoman, but she shaped an idea of women for our time; she shook society into a new patttern from which there could be no going back." —Writer Marina Warner

Harvey Milk (1930–1978) Gay rights pioneer

"Milk suspected emotional trauma was gays' worst foe—particularly for those in the closet, who probably still constitute a majority of the gay world."
—TIME writer John Cloud

Harvey Milk

Andrei Sakharov (1921–1989) Dissident physicist

"Sakharov believed that science was a force for rationality and, from there, democracy." —Chinese astrophysicist and democracy advocate Fang Lizhi

Diana, Princess of Wales (1961–1997) Uncommon royal

"She became the patron saint of victims, the sick, the discriminated against, the homeless. Women in unhappy marriages identified with her; so did outsiders of one kind or another, ethnic, sexual or social." —Writer Ian Buruma

Charles Lindbergh (1902–1974) Aviation pioneer

"He never talked to me about the past . . . He did talk a great deal about the urgent need for balance between technological advancement and environmental preservation." —Daughter Reeve Lindbergh

Andrei Sakharov

The American G.I.: Fighters for freedom

"They were truly a 'people's army,' going forth on a crusade to save democracy and freedom." —Former chairman of the Joint Chiefs of Staff Colin Powell

Anne Frank (1929–1945) Voice for human dignity

"She was not simply born blessed with generosity; she struggled toward it by way

of self-doubt, impatience, rage, ennui—all things that test the value of a mind."
—TIME essayist Roger Rosenblatt

Mother Teresa (1910–1997) Exemplar of charity
"In her care of the terminally ill and destitute . . . she wasn't interested in prolonging their life. What she railed against was the squalor and loneliness of their last hours." —Novelist Bharati Mukherjee

Muhammad Ali (1942–) "The greatest"
"Oscar Wilde once suggested that you kill the thing you love. In Ali's case, it was the reverse: what he loved, in a sense, killed him."
—Author and editor George Plimpton

Jackie Robinson

Jackie Robinson (1919–1972) Athlete, civil rights pioneer
"Jackie had the strength to sacrifice his pride for his people's. It was an incredible act of selflessness that brought the races closer together than ever before."
—Baseball great Henry Aaron

Pelé (1940–) Soccer's ambassador
"Pelé scored goals with an infectious joy that caused even the teams over which he triumphed to share in his pleasure." —Former Secretary of State Henry Kissinger

Bruce Lee (1940–1973) Embodiment of fitness
"He is the patron saint of the cult of the body . . . If only we submit to the right combinations of exercise, diet, meditation, and weight training, we can sculpt ourselves into demigods." —TIME columnist Joel Stein

Pelé

Edmund Hillary & Tenzing Norgay: Conquerors of Everest
"The two of them rose above celebrity to stand up for the unluckier third of humanity, who generally cannot spare the time or energy, let alone the money, to mess around in mountains." —Travel writer Jan Morris

Marilyn Monroe (1926–1962) Sex symbol
"Marilyn may represent some unique alchemy of sex, talent, and Technicolor. She is pure movies." —Playwright Paul Rudnick

Great Minds of the Century

Sigmund Freud (1856–1939) Explorer of the unconscious
"For good or ill, Sigmund Freud, more than any other explorer of the psyche, has shaped the mind of the 20th century." —Yale historian Peter Gay

The Wright Brothers

The Wright Brothers: Pioneers of manned flight
"Their invention effectively became the World Wide Web of that era, bringing people, languages, ideas and values together." —Microsoft founder Bill Gates

Albert Einstein (1879–1955) Redefiner of time and space
"In this busy century, dominated like no other by science—and exalting the ideal of pure intelligence—he stands alone as our emblem of intellectual power."
—Science writer and biographer James Glieck

Robert Goddard

Leo Baekeland (1863–1944) Inventor of plastic
"In 1909 Baekeland unveiled the world's first fully synthetic plastic . . . it was 20th century alchemy." —PBS science correspondent Ivan Amato

Ludwig Wittgenstein (1889–1951) Pioneering philosopher
"He showed us new ways of being suspicious of our own convictions when confronting the mysteries of the mind." —Philosopher Daniel Dennett

Philo Farnsworth (1906–1971) Father of television
"He conceived the idea of electronic television . . . while he was tilling a potato field back and forth with a horse-drawn harrow." —Media scholar Neil Postman

John Maynard Keynes

Robert Goddard (1882–1945) Rocket scientist
"When a German scientist was asked about the origin of the V-2, he was said to have responded: 'Why don't you ask your own Dr. Goddard? He knows better than any of us.'" —TIME science writer Jeffrey Kluger

John Maynard Keynes (1883–1946) Revolutionary economist
"[Keynes] transformed the dismal science into a revolutionary engine of social progress." —Former U.S. secretary of labor Robert B. Reich

Jonas Salk (1914–1995) Developer of polio vaccine
"Salk's career stands out in at least two respects: the sheer speed with which he outraced all the tortoises in the field and the honors he did not receive for doing so." —Novelist Wilfred Sheed

Jonas Salk

Jean Piaget (1896–1980) Explorer of learning
"Piaget began to suspect that behind the cute and seemingly illogical utterances of children were thought processes that had their own special logic." —M.I.T. professor Seymour Papert

James Watson

Francis Crick

Rachel Carson

Tim Berners-Lee

Louis B. Mayer

David Sarnoff

Kurt Gödel (1906–1978) Liberator of mathematics
"His famous 'incompleteness theorem' proved that nearly a century of effort by the world's greatest mathematicians was doomed to failure."
—Science writer Douglas Hofstadter

Alan Turing (1912–1954) Computer pioneer
"Everyone who taps at a keyboard and opens a spreadsheet or a word-processing program is working on an incarnation of a Turing machine."
—TIME writer Paul Gray

Enrico Fermi (1901–1954) Father of atomic power
"His theory of beta decay introduced the last of the four basic forces known in nature; he also invented and designed the first man-made nuclear reactor."
—Science writer Richard Rhodes

William Shockley (1910–1989) Father of the transistor
"Shockley's invention [of the transistor with two subordinates] created a new industry, one that underlies all of modern electronics." —Intel co-founder Gordon Moore

Edwin Hubble (1889–1953) Magellan of astronomers
"Hubble did nothing less than invent the idea of the universe and then provide the first evidence for the Big Bang theory." —TIME science writer Michael D. Lemonick

James Watson & Francis Crick: Describers of the double helix
"The structure they figured out—a 'double helix' that can 'unzip' to make copies of itself—confirmed suspicions that DNA carries life's hereditary information."
—Science writer Robert Wright

Rachel Carson (1907–1964) Advocate for the environment
"Carson was not a born crusader but an intelligent and dedicated woman who rose heroically to the occasion." —Novelist Peter Matthiessen

The Leakey Family: Groundbreaking anthropologists
"Louis Leakey became the patriarch of a family that dominated anthropology as no family has dominated a scientific field before or since."
—"Lucy" finder Donald C. Johanson

Tim Berners-Lee (1955–) Weaver of the World Wide Web
"The World Wide Web is Berners-Lee's alone. He designed it. He loosed it on the world. And he more than anyone else has fought to keep it open, nonproprietary, and free." —TIME writer Joshua Quittner

Builders & Titans

Henry Ford (1863–1947) Automobile visionary
"His vision would help create a middle class in the U.S., one marked by urbanization, rising wages and some free time in which to spend them."
—Former auto executive Lee Iacocca

Louis B. Mayer (1885–1957) Hollywood mogul
"This self-inflated, ruthless, and cloyingly sentimental monarch . . . left a legacy of clasic, inimitable films that defined America's aspirations, if not its realities."
—Novelist Budd Schulberg

David Sarnoff (1891–1971) Radio and TV visionary
"Not only was he instrumental in creating both radio and television as we know them, he was also nearly clairvoyant in seeing how each medium would develop."
—TV producers Marcy Carsey and Tom Werner

A. P. Giannini (1870–1949) Banking pioneer
"His great vision was that a bank doing business in all parts of a state or the nation would be less vulnerable to any one region's difficulties."
—TIME columnist Daniel Kadlec

Charles Merrill (1885–1956) Investment pioneer
"Merrill was the first person to openly advocate that the stock market should not just be a plaything for Wall Street insiders but should also be an avenue for the broad mass of Americans." —Fortune editor Joseph Nocera

Willis Carrier (1876–1950) Father of air-conditioning
"Slapped down by the Great Depression, he fought back to build a concern that to this good day is the world's leading maker of air-conditioning, heating, and ventilation systems." —Newspaper columnist Molly Ivins

Stephen Bechtel (1900–1989) Master builder
"Bechtel was a visionary whose imagination was fired by grandiose projects—the more seemingly impossible the better." —TIME writer George J. Church

Walt Disney (1901–1966) Multimedia fantasist
"He created Mickey Mouse and produced the first full-length animated movie. He invented the theme park and originated the modern multimedia corporation."
—TIME film critic Richard Schickel

Lucky Luciano (1897–1962) Criminal mastermind
"His story was Horatio Alger with a gun, an ice pick, and a dark vision of Big Business." —Crime writer Edna Buchanan

Juan Trippe (1899–1981) Airline pioneer
"Before anyone else, he believed in airline travel as something to be enjoyed by ordinary mortals, not just a globe-trotting élite."
—Virgin Atlantic founder Richard Branson

Walt Disney

William Levitt (1907–1994) Father of the suburb
"Levittown, New York, is a town that is as much an achievement of its cultural moment as Venice or Jerusalem." —TIME writer Richard Lacayo

Walter Reuther (1907–1970) Union leader
"While he arrived on the national scene with blood on his face, he would evolve into one of labor's most dynamic and innovative leaders, as well as a humanitarian." —Labor leader Irving Bluestone

Leo Burnett (1891–1971) Visionary adman
"Leo Burnett, the jowly genius of the heartland subconscious, is the man most responsible for the blizzard of visual imagery that assaults us today."
—Media scholar Stuart Ewen

Estée Lauder

Thomas Watson Jr. (1914–1993) Computer builder
"He boldly took IBM—and the world—into the computer age."
—TIME writer John Greenwald

Ray Kroc (1902–1984) Fast-food pioneer
"Instead of structured, ritualistic codes and routine, he gave people a simple, casual and identifiable restaurant with friendly service, low prices, no waiting, and no reservations." —Chef and author Jacques Pepin

Estée Lauder (1910–1982) Cosmetics queen
"She utilized a personal selling approach that proved as potent as the promise of her skin regimens and perfumes." —Fashion editor Grace Mirabella

Sam Walton

Pete Rozelle (1926–1996) Sports czar
"He was an iron-willed business tycoon who created the business model for all of professional sports." — Financial writer Michael Lewis

Akio Morita (1921–1999) Electronics pioneer
"Sony's product design, production and marketing helped change the image of MADE IN JAPAN from cheap imitations to superior quality."
—Executive and author Kenichi Ohmae

Sam Walton (1918–1992) Retail visionary
"He didn't merely alter the way much of America shopped; he instigated the shift of power from manufacturer to consumer." —Fortune editor John Huey

Bill Gates

Bill Gates (1955–) Software tycoon
"He is Microsoft's chief and cofounder, he is the world's richest man, and his career delivers this message: It can be wiser to follow than to lead."
—Yale professor David Gelernter

Artists & Entertainers

Coco Chanel

Pablo Picasso (1881–1973) Protean artist
"He is the very prototype of of the modern artist as public figure, the Minotaur in a canvas-and-paper labyrinth of his own construction."
—TIME art critic Robert Hughes

Le Corbusier (1887–1965) Architect of the industrial age
"Irascible, caustic, Calvinistic, 'Corbu' was modern architecture's conscience."
—Architect and writer Witold Rybczynski

Coco Chanel (1883–1971) Innovative fashion designer
"She mixed up the vocabulary of male and female clothes and created fashion that offered the wearer a feeling of hidden luxury rather than ostentation."
—Fashion editor Ingrid Sischy

James Joyce

James Joyce (1882–1941) Protean writer
"Its multiple narrative voices and extravagant wordplay made *Ulysses* a virtual thesaurus of styles for writers wrestling with the problem of rendering contemporary life." —TIME book critic Paul Gray

T. S. Eliot

Marlon Brando

Igor Stravinsky

Aretha Franklin

Bob Dylan

Oprah Winfrey

T. S. Eliot (1888–1965) Poet of the modern age
"*The Waste Land* went off like a bomb in a genteel drawing-room, as he had intended it to." —Harvard professor Helen Vendler

Charlie Chaplin (1889–1977) Comedian and film pioneer
"He was the first, and to date the last, person to control every aspect of the film-making process—founding his own studio and producing, casting, directing, writing, scoring, and editing the movies he starred in." —Writer Ann Douglas

Steven Spielberg (1947–) Blockbuster film director
"Spielberg has a direct line to our unconscious; when his movies work, they work on every level that a film can reach." —Film critic Roger Ebert

Marlon Brando (1924–) Iconic actor
"No figure of his influence has so precariously balanced a handful of unforgettable achievements against a brimming barrelful of embarrassments." —TIME film critic Richard Schickel

Igor Stravinsky (1882–1971) Modernist composer
"Over the years, he experimented with virtually every technique of 20th century music: tonal, polytonal, and 12-tone serialism. His own musical voice always prevailed." —Composer Philip Glass

The Beatles: Pop music innovators
"Their overflowing gifts for songcraft, harmony, and instrumental excitement, their buoyant spirits, their bottomless charm, their irrepressible wit, made them appear almost otherworldly." —MTV news anchor Kurt Loder

Aretha Franklin (1942–) Soul singer
"From the moment she sang 'Respect,' she helped convert American pop from a patriarchal monologue into a coed dialogue." —TIME music critic Chrisopher John Farley

Bob Dylan (1941–) Folk-rock sodbuster
"In two years, he turned folk music inside out, then subsumed it inside raucous, unyielding, cataclysmic rock 'n' roll." —TIME music critic Jay Cocks

Louis Armstrong (1901–1971) Jazz pioneer
"He supplied revolutionary language that took on such pervasiveness that it became commonplace, like the light bulb, the airplane, the telephone." —Essayist Stanley Crouch

Frank Sinatra (1915–1998) Pop singer
"Beyond his technical prowess as a jazz-influenced pop singer is the sheer force of conviction, feeling, the weight of personal history in his voice." —TIME writer Bruce Handy

Rodgers & Hammerstein: Broadway musical innovators
"*Oklahoma!* —a revolutionary, naturalistic musical—changed the mainstream of the genre forever." —Composer Andrew Lloyd Webber

Lucille Ball (1911–1989) Doyenne of TV comedy
"Ball's dizzy redhead with the elastic face and saucer eyes was the model for scores of comic TV females to follow. She and her show, moreover, helped define a still nascent medium." —TIME TV critic Richard Zoglin

Jim Henson (1936–1990) Muppetmaster
"Through his work, he helped sustain the qualities of fancifulness, warmth and consideration that have been so threatened by our coarse, cynical age." —TIME writer James Collins

Oprah Winfrey (1954–) Television personality
"She stands as a beacon, not only in the worlds of media and entertainment, but also in the larger realm of public discourse." —Professor and author Deborah Tannen

Martha Graham (1894–1991) Innovative choreographer
"If Graham ever gave birth, one critic quipped, it would be to a cube; instead, she became the mother of American dance." —Dance critic Terry Teachout

Bart Simpson (1987–) Subversive animated being
"He is a complex weave of grace, attitude, and personality, deplorable and adorable, a very '90s slacker who embodies a century of popular culture and is one of the richest characters in it." —TIME film critic Richard Corliss

People in the News, 1999

King Abdullah II, 37, became the fourth ruler of the Hashemite Kingdom of Jordan in February, succeeding his father, **King Hussein,** who died after losing an 8-month battle with cancer. Abdullah, the former commander of the Jordanian Special Forces, was surprised—as was the world—when King Hussein, only days before his death, declared Abdullah crown prince. King Hussein's younger brother, **Prince Hassan,** had been crown prince since 1965.

Andre Agassi, 29, professional tennis player, made the comeback of his life in June when he won the French Open. The win made him the first American in 61 years to win all four majors. He went on to garner the U.S. Open in September. In 1997, the same year he married actress **Brooke Shields,** Agassi's ranking dropped to 141. The couple separated in early 1999.

Lance Armstrong, 27, won the 86th Tour de France in July, only three years after being diagnosed with aggressive testicular cancer, which spread to the Texas native's abdomen, lungs, and brain.

Capt. Richard J. Ashby, 32, Marine pilot, was cleared in March of manslaughter charges stemming from the 1998 accident in which the jet he was flying severed ski gondola cables, killing 20 at an Italian resort. Ashby and his navigator, **Capt. Joseph Schweitzer,** 31, were later discharged after being found guilty of obstruction of justice for destroying evidence.

Ehud Barak, 57, Israeli politician, was elected prime minister of Israel in a landslide victory in May over incumbent **Benjamin Netanyahu.** Barak immediately restarted talks with Palestinian leader **Yasir Arafat** and vowed to have solid Mideast peace plans in place by October 2000.

Mark O. Barton, 44, day trader, killed nine people in a July shooting rampage in Atlanta, before turning a gun on himself. Barton is suspected of murdering his wife and two children in Stockbridge, Ga., days before the Atlanta massacre. He was also a suspect in the 1993 beating death of his first wife and her mother.

Warren Beatty, 62, actor and director, toyed with running for president as a liberal Democrat. Beatty said he was most concerned about campaign finance reform and criticized other presidential hopefuls for not thoughtfully addressing the issues.

Roberto Benigni, 47, larger-than-life Italian actor, director, and writer, won the hearts of millions with his emotional, acrobatic reaction to winning Best Actor and Best Foreign-Language Film honors at the 1998 Academy Awards in March for *Life Is Beautiful.*

Bill Bradley, 56, former senator from New Jersey, was the only Democrat to challenge **Al Gore, Jr.,** for the party's presidential nomination. Until the fall, Gore had all but ignored Bradley's campaign, but as Bradley gained public support and an endorsement by **Sen. Daniel Patrick Moynihan** of N.Y., Gore revamped his campaign.

Patrick J. Buchanan, 61, columnist, television commentator, and politician, bolted from the Republican Party to seek the presidential nomination as a Reform candidate. He was widely criticized for the controversial views he outlined in *A Republic, Not an Empire.* In it he said Nazi Germany posed "no physical threat to the United States after 1940."

George W. Bush, 53, governor of Texas, emerged as the front-runner in a crowded field of Republican presidential hopefuls. In his first four months of fund-raising, he amassed an astounding $37 million. His early platform stressed "compassionate conservatism," though his definition of the slogan was intentionally vague.

Charlotte Church, 13, Welsh soprano, took the world by storm with the release of her appropriately titled debut album, *Voice of an Angel.* She has performed for Queen Elizabeth, Pope John Paul II, and **President Clinton.** Though she's considered a budding opera diva, Church said she would love to share a microphone with **Sean "Puffy" Combs.**

Gen. Wesley Clark, 54, NATO's supreme commander, organized the 19-nation force in the 11-week air war against Yugoslavia in the spring and was instrumental in forging a peace agreement with Yugoslav president **Slobodan Milosevic.** In July, the Clinton administration announced that Clark would be removed from office three months early so that **Joseph Ralston,** vice chairman of the Joint Chiefs of Staff, could assume the position.

Hillary Rodham Clinton, 52, first lady, launched an exploratory committee in July to consider a run for the U.S. Senate. If she follows through, Clinton will become the first lady to run for public office. She faces a stiff challenge from New York City mayor **Rudolph Giuliani.** While she'll have no problem with name recognition, Clinton will have to face down the carpetbagger issue. The Illinois native and former Arkansas resident has never lived in New York.

Col. Eileen Marie Collins, 42, decorated Air Force pilot, became the first woman to command a space shuttle mission when *Columbia* was launched into orbit in July. She had participated in two earlier shuttle missions, both to Russian space station *Mir.*

Robert A. Daly, 62, and **Terry Semel,** 55, cochairmen of Warner Bros., resigned in July from the entertainment empire. The pair, who have been partners at Warners for almost 20 years, plan to form a new company. In addition to the movie and music divisions, Daly and Semel headed the television division, which includes the WB network.

Amadou Diallo, 22, West African immigrant, was shot 19 times in February in the vestibule of his Bronx apartment by four plainclothes police officers. Diallo, a street peddler, was unarmed. The officers, **Sean Carroll, Edward McMellon, Kenneth Boss,** and **Richard Murphy,** were all indicted on two counts of second-degree murder. They all pleaded guilty and were freed on bail.

Elizabeth Dole, 63, former president of the American Red Cross, began campaigning for the Republican presidential nomination in May. No stranger to the campaign trail, she stumped for her husband, former Senate leader **Bob Dole,** in his unsuccessful runs for the White House in 1980, 1988, and 1996. Despite a promising start, she failed to match the small fortune raised by competitor **George W. Bush.** Dole announced in October that she was stepping out of the race due to insufficient funds.

Carleton "Carly" Fiorina, 44, high-tech executive, was named president and chief executive officer of Hewlett-Packard Co. in July. At a press conference Fiorina said, "I hope that we are at a point that everyone has figured out that there is not a glass ceiling."

Martin R. Frankel, 45, fugitive financier, allegedly bilked insurance companies of more than $200 million, pulling off the biggest insurance scam in the country's history. With investigators closing in on him in June, Frankel bought millions of dollars worth of diamonds, wired money to accounts all over the world, torched any remaining paper trail, and fled the country. He was captured in Germany in September.

Buford O. Furrow, 37, white supremacist, opened fire in August at a Los Angeles Jewish community center, injuring five people, and an hour later killed Filipino-American letter carrier **Joseph Ileto,** 39. The next day, Furrow took a 275-mile cab ride to Las Vegas, where he turned himself in. He told authorities he was "concerned about the decline of the white race and wanted to send a message to America by killing Jews."

Sonia Gandhi, 52, Indian politician, resigned in May from her post as president of India's Congress Party after fellow party leaders contested her candidacy as prime minister because she is not a native Indian. A week later, after an outpouring of support from her followers, the Italian-born Gandhi withdrew her resignation. She is the wife of slain prime minister, **Rajiv Gandhi,** and the daughter-in-law of former prime minister **Indira Gandhi,** who was assassinated in 1984.

Bill Gates, 44, Microsoft chairman, in September pledged $1 billion to send about 1,000 minorities to college. The scholarships will be distributed over the next 20 years to black, Hispanic, Native American, and Asian students who plan to pursue degrees in engineering, math, science, and education.

Al Gore, Jr., 51, vice president, announced his candidacy for president in June. While his pronouncement was not much of a surprise, many were taken aback by Gore's repeated attacks on **President Clinton's** character, apparently attempts to distance himself from the scandalous president. He also tried to perk up his lackluster speaking style, though only the volume of his voice was affected.

Steffi Graf, 30, professional tennis player, retired from the court in August after 17 years as a pro. She was ranked third in the world at the time of her retirement, but had held the top spot for 377 weeks, longer than any other player—man or woman.

José Gusmão, 53, East Timorese guerrilla leader, was widely expected to lead the newly independent East Timor through its uneasy period of transition. He is seen as a conciliator who can work with both East Timorese and the Indonesian government, which watched idly as militias launched a campaign of terror on the tiny territory after it voted in August to separate from Indonesia. He has been fighting for independence since the 1970s, since Indonesia annexed East Timor after the Portuguese withdrawal. He was jailed in 1992 and released in September by **B. J. Habibie,** then president of Indonesia. Many acknowledge that Gusmão should have shared the 1996 Nobel Peace Prize with **José Ramos-Horta** and **Bishop Carlos Ximenes Belo.**

Eric Harris, 18, and **Dylan Klebold,** 17, high school students, went on a shooting rampage on April 20 at Littleton, Colorado's Columbine High School, killing 12 students and 1 teacher before turning guns on themselves. The pair, who were members of the school's "trenchcoat mafia," had been planning the attack for a year and were armed with sawed-off shotguns, a semiautomatic rifle, and homemade bombs. They targeted athletes and minorities. The tragedy led to soul-searching in Washington, with politicians blaming everything from Ritalin to the entertainment industry to day care for the deadly spate of school violence.

J. Dennis Hastert, 57, congressman, was chosen Speaker of the House in January by members of the 106th Congress. The Republican from Illinois called for bipartisan cooperation. Hastert was tapped after Speaker-designate **Bob Livingston** resigned from the House in December 1998 and confessed that he'd had several extramarital affairs. Livingston's admission was prompted by *Hustler* publisher **Larry Flynt,** who said he knew of four instances of Livingston's infidelity. In October 1998, Flynt proclaimed that he would pay $1 million to any woman who could prove she had a fling with a member of Congress.

Russell Henderson, 21, drew two consecutive life sentences after pleading guilty in April in a Wyoming court to the 1998 kidnapping and murder of **Matthew Shepard,** a 21-year-old gay college student. The trial of Henderson's suspected accomplice, **Aaron McKinney,** 21, was set to begin in the fall.

Lauryn Hill, 24, versatile singer and record producer, fused rap, soul, reggae, and R&B on her chart-topping, Grammy-winning solo debut *The Miseducation of Lauryn Hill.* In February, she walked away with five Grammys, including Album of the Year and Best New Artist, the most trophies ever won by a woman. She also won four 1999 MTV Music Video Awards. Hill recorded the album while on hiatus from the hip-hop band The Fugees.

Richard C. Holbrooke, 58, diplomat, was finally confirmed as chief American diplomat to the United Nations by the Senate in August, ending a 14-month-long nomination process that languished amid partisan bickering and political maneuvering. Holbrooke, the former ambassador to Germany, engineered the 1995 Dayton agreement that brought peace to war-torn Bosnia.

Michael Jordan, 36, professional basketball player, announced his retirement from the NBA—again—in January. (He also retired in 1993, only to return to the game in 1995, after a brief stint with the Chicago White Sox's minor league team.) In his 13 seasons with the NBA, Jordan led the Bulls to six championships and was league MVP five times.

Jeffrey Katzenberg, 49, entertainment executive, settled a breach-of-contract suit in June with his former boss at Disney, **Michael Eisner,** 57, for a reported $250 million. Katzenberg claimed Disney owed him an incentive bonus of at least $250 million—2 percent of the profits from movies produced during his tenure with the company. Katzenberg's hits include *The Lion King* and *Pretty Woman.* Disney said he forfeited his bonus when he left the company before his contract expired.

Elia Kazan, 89, director, won a controversial Lifetime Achievement Award at the 71st Annual Academy Awards in March. While no one denied Kazan's contribution to film, many in the industry were outraged that the Academy chose to honor the man who, in 1952 before the House Committee on Un-American Activities, ratted on eight of his friends who, with him, had been members of the American Communist Party in the 1930s. His films include *On the Waterfront, East of Eden,* and *A Streetcar Named Desire.*

Jack Kevorkian, 71, physician, made the leap from assisted-suicide doctor to murderer when he administered a lethal injection to Lou Gehrig's disease patient **Thomas Youk**. Kevorkian had the 1998 event videotaped and CBS broadcast it on *60 Minutes*. He was convicted of second-degree murder and was sentenced to 10 to 25 years in prison in April. "Doctor Death" has helped more than 130 people kill themselves and has been charged with doctor-assisted suicide four times. He was acquitted three times; the fourth trial ended in a mistrial.

John William King, 24, and **Lawrence Russell Brewer**, 32, white supremacists, were convicted and sentenced to death by Texas juries for their involvement in the 1998 dragging death of **James Byrd, Jr.**, 49, their black victim. The third defendant, **Shawn Allen Berry**, 24, still faces trial.

Lee Teng-hui, 76, president of Taiwan, nearly set off an international crisis in July when he announced that he considers Taiwan a state that would bargain with China only on a "state-to-state" basis. Beijing and Taipei hammered out an agreement in 1993 that said each country had its own government but each was part of "one China."

Wen Ho Lee, 59, Taiwan-born American scientist, was fired from his job at Los Alamos National Laboratory in March for allegedly passing on classified information on the W-88 nuclear warhead technology to China. Lee allegedly leaked the documents by moving them electronically onto an unsecured computer network. Lee broke his silence in his August appearance on *60 Minutes,* when he denied any wrongdoing. He has not been indicted.

Rev. Henry Lyons, 57, president of the National Baptist Convention USA, was convicted by a St. Petersburg, Florida, jury of racketeering and grand theft in February. The animated preacher siphoned off millions from the church to buy a luxury villa, a Mercedes, and a diamond ring for his mistress.

Ricky Martin, 27, Latino pop singer, burst onto the music scene in the U.S. after his hip-shaking performance at the February Grammy Awards. His self-titled English-language debut album hit stores in May and immediately shot up the charts. The single "Livin' la Vida Loca" sent millions of women swooning. Martin was a member of **Menudo**, the Puerto Rican boy band. He also did a stint on *General Hospital.*

Joyce Maynard, 45, writer and self-promoter, auctioned off the love letters reclusive author **J. D. Salinger** wrote her during their 9-month affair that began in 1972, when Maynard was a student at Yale. She earned $56,500 in the June auction, managed by Sotheby's. She said she plans to use the money for her children's college tuition.

Thabo Mbeki, 57, South African politician, was elected president in June, succeeding **Nelson Mandela**. Mbeki eased into his new role, having already assumed many of Mandela's governing responsibilities shortly after Mandela won South Africa's first democratic election in 1994.

John McCain, 62, senator from Arizona, launched a campaign for the Republican presidential nomination. Though he presented himself as an outsider, McCain has served 17 years in the Senate. He is, however, somewhat of a maverick in his party. He cosponsored a campaign-finance reform bill that most fellow Republican congressmen were loathe to even discuss, and he steered clear of the Iowa straw poll, which essentially put votes up for sale. McCain endured 5 1/2 harrowing years as a prisoner of war in Vietnam.

Slobodan Milosevic, 57, president of Yugoslavia, balked at repeated warnings from NATO to withdraw Yugoslav troops and weapons from Albanian-dominated Kosovo, which had been fighting for full independence from Serbia. NATO-led air strikes began in late March and continued through early June, until Milosevic finally relented and withdrew his troops. Reports of atrocities against Albanian civilians were widespread, and in May the United Nations International War Crimes Tribunal formally indicted Milosevic and four other Yugoslav officials for crimes against humanity. They were accused of deporting 740,000 ethnic Albanians from Kosovo in 1999 and murdering more than 340 identified victims.

Seti Mohammed, 36, became **King Mohammed IV** in July, succeeding his father, **King Hassan II**, who ruled Morocco for 38 years until his death at age 70. Prior to ascending to the throne, King Mohammed was a four-star general in the Royal Armed Forces.

Edmund Morris, 59, Pulitzer Prize-winning biographer, wove together fact and fiction and inserted himself as a character in his authorized biography of **Ronald Reagan**, *Dutch: A Memoir of Ronald Reagan*. Morris claimed that despite unprecedented access to the president, he never got to know the real Reagan.

Daniel Myrick, 35, and **Eduardo Sanchez**, 30, filmmakers, directed and wrote the most profitable film of all time, *The Blair Witch Project*. The film cost $35,000 to make and has grossed more than $120 million. The success of the film is widely credited to an innovative—and ingenious—marketing plan, which included a Web site that blurred the line between fact and fiction, a recurring special on the Sci Fi Channel, and unprecedented word-of-mouth buzz.

Olusegun Obasanjo, 62, retired general, was elected president of Nigeria in February, becoming the first civilian ruler in 15 years for Africa's most populous nation. His victory was overshadowed by allegations of fraud and ballot-box tampering.

Abdullah Ocalan, 50, Kurdish rebel leader, was sentenced to death in June after being found guilty of treason in a Turkish court. The leader of the Kurdistan Workers Party has waged a 15-year guerrilla war against the Turkish government, claiming Turkey has suppressed the Kurdish language and culture. Ocalan shocked many observers during his trial when he acknowledged that his group killed thousands, and he said he would devote his life to "bringing Turks and Kurds together" if he was spared the death penalty.

Chris Ofili, 31, British artist, received hordes of free publicity when his collage, *The Holy Virgin Mary*, which featured a black Virgin Mary with elephant feces on one breast and cutouts from pornographic magazines glued in the background, was part of the Brooklyn Museum of Art's October exhibit, "Sensation: Young British Artists from the Saatchi Collection." New York City mayor **Rudolph Giuliani** announced the city would withdraw its funding of the museum and evict it from its space, which is leased from the city, unless the museum canceled the exhibit. The museum then filed a lawsuit saying the mayor was violating its First Amendment rights.

Gwyneth Paltrow, 27, actress, won praise and a truckload of awards, including a Best Actress Oscar, for her nuanced performance in *Shakespeare in Love*. Formerly best known as **Brad Pitt**'s girlfriend, Paltrow has achieved superstar status in her own right, with fully realized turns in such films as *Sliding Doors* and *Emma*.

Richie Phillips, 58, lawyer and combative union leader, seriously misjudged Major League Baseball when he urged umpires in July to collectively resign unless the league agreed to sign a new contract (before the old one expired) that would give them higher salaries, more vacation time, and more respect. The contentious plan divided the union, and the league called his bluff and fired more than 20 umpires.

Rafael Reséndez-Ramirez, 39, Mexican fugitive, evaded authorities for weeks by hopping freight trains but surrendered in July after his sister called a Texas Ranger and negotiated terms of his arrest. Authorities believe he killed eight people since August 1997 and may have been responsible for several other murders.

Sophie Rhys-Jones, 34, British public relations executive, became the newest member of England's royal family when she married **Prince Edward,** 35, **Queen Elizabeth**'s youngest son, in June.

Ibrahim Rugova, 55, Albanian leader of the Democratic League of Kosovo, was once considered the leader of Kosovo Albanians but lost power during the war in Yugoslavia. He fled to Italy six weeks into the fighting, essentially passing the torch to the Kosovo Liberation Army and its 29-year-old leader, **Hashim Thaci.**

Benjamin N. Smith, 21, white supremacist, went on a shooting spree over the Fourth of July weekend, targeting minorities in Bloomington, Ind., and Chicago. He shot and killed **Ricky Byrdsong,** 43, an African-American former basketball coach at Northwestern University, and **Won Joon Yoon,** 26, a Korean-American graduate student, and wounded nine others before killing himself.

David L. Smith, 30, computer programmer, was arrested in April for launching Melissa, the computer virus that wreaked havoc with email systems nationwide in March. Smith was charged with interfering with public communication and theft of computer services.

T. J. Solomon, 15, high school student, went on a shooting rampage in May at Conyers, Georgia's Heritage High, wounding several students before tearfully surrendering to an assistant principal.

Brittany Spears, 17, teen pop sensation, burst onto the music scene with the release of her vaguely promiscuous single, ". . . Baby One More Time." Early in her career, Spears appeared on *The Mickey Mouse Club* and in several television commercials and stage productions.

Jerry Springer, 55, talk-show host, briefly toyed with running for a seat in the U.S. Senate. While Springer is best known for his raunchy talk show, he once had a career in politics, having served as a Cincinnati city councilor and mayor of Cincinnati in the 1970s.

Cary Stayner, 37, motel handyman, confessed to the July killing of a 26-year-old Yosemite National Park naturalist, **Joie Ruth Armstrong,** and the February massacre of three sight-seers, **Carole Sund,** 42; her daughter, **Juli Sund,** 15; and **Silvina Pelosso,** a 16-year-old foreign-exchange student from Argentina. All four murders occurred in or near Yosemite. Stayner was charged with the murder of Armstrong, while authorities continue to investigate the other deaths. Stayner said he fantasized about killing women and was driven to murder by voices in his head.

Alexandra Stevenson, 18, professional tennis player, shocked the tennis world when she became the first qualifying player to advance to the semifinals at Wimbledon. But the real surprise came when basketball hall-of-famer **Julius Erving** acknowledged that he is Stevenson's father. Stevenson's mother, freelance sports journalist **Samantha Stevenson** raised her daughter alone, with financial support from Erving.

John Thompson, 57, venerated longtime Georgetown University basketball coach, resigned in January for personal reasons. Under Thompson's 27-year tutelage, Georgetown's Hoyas spawned **Patrick Ewing,** reached the NCAA tournament 20 times, and won a national championship.

Tinky Winky, purple Teletubby, was outted in February by **Rev. Jerry Falwell,** who deduced that Tinky Winky is gay because he's purple, carries a purse, and has a triangle on his head.

U.S. Women's Soccer Team won the World Cup in July in a 5–4 win on penalty kicks over China. More than 90,000 fans packed the Rose Bowl for the final game. Though all eyes were on **Mia Hamm,** who's considered the world's best female soccer player and has scored more goals in international soccer history than any other female or male player, **Brandi Chastain** and **Michelle Akers** proved indefatigable players. More people attended and tuned into the matches than any other women's sports event in history.

Jesse Ventura, 48, governor of Minnesota who was formerly known as boa-wearing professional wrestler "the Body," gained political credibility as the Reform Party's highest-ranking elected official. Though Minnesotans think he's doing a fine job as governor, they don't consider him a role model. He got himself in trouble when he called organized religion a "sham and a crutch for weak-minded people" in the November issue of *Playboy*.

Justin A. Volpe, 27, New York City police officer, admitted in court in May that he tortured and meant to humiliate Haitian immigrant **Abner Louima** when he rammed a broom handle into the man's rectum and then stuck the feces-stained pole in his face in a 1997 assault in the restroom of Brooklyn's 70th Precinct station. Facing almost certain conviction, Volpe made the admission before the jury began deliberating in hope of a more lenient sentence. He faces life in prison. Volpe did not implicate the four other officers who were on trial with him. Officer **Charles Schwarz,** 33, was convicted of violating Louima's civil rights. Officer **Thomas Wiese,** 35, Officer **Thomas Bruder,** 33, and Sgt. **Michael Bellomo,** 37, who were all charged with beating Louima, were acquitted.

Ty Warner, 59?, toy executive, shocked millions of children and parents when he announced on his Web site in August that he plans to retire all Beanie Babies on Dec. 31, 1999. No one was quite sure if the move was a marketing ploy to drive up prices or if the King of Plush was ready to move on to another craze.

Venus Williams, 19, and **Serena Williams,** 18, professional tennis players, made history when they met in the finals of Florida's Lipton Championships in March, the first time in 115 years that sisters faced off in the finals and the first such pairing of African Americans. Serena went on to win the U.S. Open in September, beating rival **Martina Hingis**.

Boris Yeltsin, 68, Russian president, fired Prime Minister **Sergei Stepashin,** 47, and the entire cabinet in August. It was the fourth time in 17 months that Yeltsin had ousted Russia's government. He named **Vladimir Putin,** the head of the Federal Security Service, as prime minister. Stepashin had been in office since May, when he replaced **Yevgeny M. Primakov,** who held the position for only eight months and had allegedly been plotting a Communist resurgence.

1999 Deaths

(through Oct. 15, 1999)

Alice Adams, 72: skilled novelist and short-story writer. Adams, who wrote perceptively about the lives of women, authored ten novels and five collections of short stories, and was a frequent contributor to the *New Yorker.* May 27, 1999.

Martin Agronsky, 84: long-time news media figure. He began his career in newspaper journalism, transitioned to radio, and finally landed on TV, where he was a political correspondent and commentator of his own syndicated program between 1943 and 1988. July 25, 1999.

Avery C. Alexander, 88: Baptist minister, former state representative, and longtime civil-rights activist from New Orleans. His devotion to the fight against discrimination led to countless arrests at demonstrations between 1937 and 1990. March 5, 1999.

Luis Argana, 66: Vice President of Paraguay. He was killed by several gunmen who sprayed his Jeep with bullets and a grenade as it rode through a street in Asuncion, the capital. Supporters of Argana, the leader of an effort to oust President Raul Cubas, blamed Cubas for the killing. March 23, 1999.

Michael Aris, 53: husband of 1991 Nobel Peace Prize winner Aung San Suu Kyi, the leading dissident of Myanmar, formerly Burma. Myanmar's military junta refused to allow Aris, who was dying from cancer, to visit his wife, whom he had not seen since 1995. Fearful the junta would bar her return, she chose not to leave her country. March 27, 1999.

Abdel-Latif Baghdadi, 81: charismatic Egyptian political leader who helped Gamal Abdel Nasser overthrow King Farouk in 1952 and later served in key government posts under Nasser. Jan. 8, 1999.

Leon Barzin, 98: famous conductor who headed the National Orchestra Association for 36 years. He was also the musical head of the New York City Ballet in the 1940s and '50s. April 29, 1999.

Vere Bird, 89: Antiguan who became powerful during the island's colonial period and went on to lead his country after it gained independence from Britain in 1981. The former prime minister, who was succeeded by his oldest son, Vere Bird, Jr., after retiring in 1994, began a political dynasty that was notoriously corrupt. June 28, 1999.

Harry Blackmun, 90: former U.S. Supreme Court Justice who galvanized a fiery national political debate by writing the landmark 1973 opinion for *Roe* v. *Wade,* which legalized abortion. Although appointed by Richard Nixon in the hopes of moving the court in a more conservative direction, Blackmun left a largely liberal legacy. March 4, 1999.

Dirk Bogarde (Derek van den Bogaerde), 78: British actor who transcended matinee-idol looks with darkly serious roles. He will be best remembered for *Victim* (1961), a tale of homosexual blackmail, and his acclaimed performance in the film version of *Death in Venice* (1971). May 8, 1999.

BoxCar Willie (Lecil Martin), 67: country singer who was the son of a railroad man and grew up alongside a train track. In the 1960s he spotted a hobo who reminded him of Willie Nelson and was moved to write the song "BoxCar Willie." He later adopted the hobo persona of stubble and a crumpled hat. April 12, 1999.

Marion Zimmer Bradley 69: prolific sci-fi and gothic novelist. Bradley's imaginative fiction, including the Darkover series and the bestseller *The Mists of Avalon* (1984), earned her a loyal following and a Locus Award. Sept. 25, 1999.

Charles Brown, 76: blues singer and pianist whose smooth, sophisticated style influenced the development of lounge blues. Brown was a member of Johnny Moore and the Three Blazers, who sang the hit "Merry Christmas." Jan. 21, 1999.

Dennis Brown, 42: Jamaican reggae singer who established his popularity in the 1970s at the age of 12. The "Crown Prince of Reggae" earned a Grammy nomination in 1995 for his album *Light My Fire.* July 1, 1999.

George E. Brown Jr., 79: oldest member of the House of Representatives. The senior Democrat on the House Science Committee, Rep. Brown had a fascination with science and space exploration. He was serving his 18th term in Congress for California's 42nd District. July 16, 1999.

Vanessa Brown, 71: actress and writer who began her career in the Broadway show *Watch on the Rhine* at the age of 13. She went on to act in several films and television shows, and still later found success as a playwright, novelist, and journalist. May 21, 1999.

Jaki Byard, 76: versatile pianist, saxophonist, and educator whose talent was demonstrated in his mastery of many styles of jazz. Feb. 11, 1999.

Rory Calhoun (Francis Durgin), 76: rugged film and TV heartthrob. While horseback riding in the Hollywood Hills in 1943, Calhoun, then a laborer, was approached by Alan Ladd, who suggested a career in show business. Calhoun was best known for his roles in westerns and on the late '50s CBS drama *The Texan.* April 28, 1999.

Harry Callahan, 86: innovative photographer who celebrated the ordinary. The self-effacing Midwesterner took to shooting city streets, clouds, pedestrians and, most memorably, his wife Eleanor. Influenced by Ansel Adams and Alfred Stieglitz, Callahan infused his images with stark lines and contrasts. March 15, 1999.

Anita Carter (Ina Anita Carter), 66: musician who began singing professionally at an early age with her parents, sisters, and other relatives as the influential country group, the Carter Family. She went on to record a number of albums and singles, including "I Got You," a duet with Waylon Jennings. July 29, 1999.

Peggy Cass (Mary Margaret Cass), 74: Tony Award-winning actress and comedian best known for her roles in the Broadway and film productions of *Auntie Mame.* March 8, 1999.

Leo Castelli, 91: influential dealer who championed contemporary art. Castelli helped bring American painters Jasper Johns, Roy Lichtenstein, and others international acclaim. Aug. 21, 1999.

Wilton Norman ("Wilt") Chamberlain, 63: one of the century's most recognized athletes. A dominant basketball center, Wilt the Stilt was best remembered for scoring 100 points in a game (on March 2, 1962). Oct. 12, 1999.

Iron Eyes Cody, 94: Cree-Cherokee actor and activist who appeared in 100 films. Cody achieved celebrity with a role in a 1971 public-service spot for Keep America Beautiful. As the American Indian who sheds a tear at the sight of a landscape littered with garbage and polluted by smoke, Cody brought the nonprofit group unprecedented attention and support. Jan. 5, 1999.

Charles ("Pete") Conrad, 69: third man to walk on the moon. Conrad was one of the more colorful astronauts. Setting foot on the lunar surface he said, "Whoopee! That may have been one small [step] for Neil, but it's a long one for me!" July 8, 1999.

Charles Crichton, 89: British film director of *The Lavender Hill Mob,* among other comedies of the '40s and '50s. Most recently, Crichton was nominated for an Oscar for the farcical 1988 John Cleese blockbuster, *A Fish Called Wanda,* his first feature film in nearly 25 years. Sept. 14, 1999.

Jill Dando, 37: high-profile British television journalist who hosted a popular travel show and presented the news for the BBC. Dando's shocking murder may have been linked to the monthly real-life crime show she also hosted. April 26, 1999.

Eddie Dean (Edgar Dean Glosup), 91: one of the most popular singing cowboys in the 1940s, he appeared in more than 30 films. His remarkable singing voice earned him the moniker "the golden-throated cowboy." March 4, 1999.

Sarah ("Sadie") Delany, 109: pioneer educator and co-author, with her late sister Bessie, of the best-seller turned Broadway hit *Having Our Say: The Delany Sisters' First 100 Years.* The daughter of a slave, she earned her master's degree in education at Columbia and became the first black woman to teach home economics in New York City's public schools. Jan. 25, 1999.

Joe DiMaggio, 84: unequaled New York Yankees center fielder whose skill, chivalrous professionalism, and marriage to Marilyn Monroe cemented his status as an American icon and one of the most revered sports figures in U.S. history. Over 13 seasons, the Yankee Clipper compiled a sparkling .325 batting average. In 1941, he hammered out hits in a record 56 consecutive games. March 8, 1999.

Andre Dubus, 62: short-story craftsman and novelist. In 1986 Dubus was struck by a car, leaving him wheelchair-bound. He subsequently produced some of his finest stories, notably in the 1996 book *Dancing After Hours.* Feb. 24, 1999.

Virginia Foster Durr, 95: inspirational white civil-rights activist who helped put an end to racist poll taxes and, with her husband (civil-rights lawyer and activist Clifford Durr), posted bail for Rosa Parks after the famous 1955 bus incident. Feb. 24, 1999.

Ben Edwards, 82: prolific set designer whose career included work on scores of Broadway productions, TV shows, and movies. He was honored with a Lifetime Achievement Award at the 1998 Tony Awards. Feb. 12, 1999.

John Ehrlichman, 73: pugnacious Nixon domestic-affairs adviser and leak plugger who was imprisoned for his role in Watergate. Disbarred for his crimes, Ehrlichman later wrote novels, worked at an engineering firm, and often insisted the scandal was overblown. Feb. 14, 1999.

Gertrude B. Elion, 81: pioneer in drug research who shared the Nobel Prize for Physiology or Medicine in 1988. Elion developed drugs for many conditions, including leukemia, malaria, and AIDS. Feb. 21, 1999.

Carl Elliott, 85: courageous former U.S. congressman from Alabama. His support for federal initiatives in education, health, and civil rights cost him his career after eight terms in the House, as support for states' rights grew in Alabama. Jan. 9, 1999.

Clifton Fadiman, 95: impassioned essayist and critic dedicated to making intellectual works accessible. Fadiman judged Book-of-the-Month Club selections for 50 years, moderated the '30s and '40s radio show *Information Please,* and edited more than 20 anthologies. June 20, 1999.

James Farmer, 79: courageous Gandhian who along with Martin Luther King Jr., Whitney Young, and Roy Wilkins was one of the four great architects of the U.S. civil rights movement. July 9, 1999.

Lowell Fulson, 77: prominent blues and rhythm-and-blues hall-of-famer who recorded several hits from the '40s into the '60s. The tireless musician continued to tour and record into the '90s. March 6, 1999.

Allen Funt, 84: creator of *Candid Camera.* Funt started the hit show on the radio after experimenting with concealed microphones in the Army during World War II. *Candid Camera* aired on TV, on and off, from 1948 to 1990. Sept. 5, 1999.

W. Arthur Garrity, Jr. 79: the federal judge who in 1974 triggered riots and "white flight" by ordering the desegregation, by student busing, of Boston schools. Sept. 17, 1999.

Raisa Gorbachev, 67: glamorous wife of former Soviet Union President Mikhail Gorbachev. Born into a railworker's family, she studied philosophy at Moscow University before marrying the future leader of the U.S.S.R. in 1954. Sept. 20, 1999.

Meg Greenfield, 68: 20-year editor of the *Washington Post* editorial page. She was noted in the nation's capital and beyond for her sharp analysis of a generation of policy makers, which won her a 1978 Pulitzer Prize. May 13, 1999.

Ernest Gross, 92: influential American diplomat and lawyer. Gross held key positions in the State Department and the U.N. during the Cold War and took significant actions against genocide and South African apartheid. May 2, 1999.

Jerzy Grotowski, 65: innovative Polish director who had an important influence on the development of modern theater. Jan. 14, 1999.

Henry ("Huntz") Hall, 78: pop-eyed, baseball cap-sporting comedic actor and member of Hollywood's renowned gang of street toughs, the Dead End Kids (a.k.a. East Side Kids and Bowery Boys). Hall played the same character in more than 80 of his 120 films. Jan. 30, 1999.

Clarence L. Harris, 94: lunch manager who in 1960 let four black students remain at Woolworth's whites-only counter. Harris did not serve the protesters, but his insistence that police not be called helped energize the sit-in, which after six months succeeded in integrating the counter. The action sparked similar tests across the South. July 12, 1999.

Hassan II (Moulay Hassan), 70: king of Morocco for 38 years with an uncanny survival instinct. The ever-diplomatic, pro-Western Hassan helped facilitate a number of key Middle East negotiations. July 23, 1999.

Al Hirt (Alois Maxwell Hirt), 76: corpulent pop and jazz trumpeter also known as "Jumbo" and "the Round Mound of Sound." During a five-decade career, he toured with Big Bands led by Benny Goodman and Tommy Dorsey, recorded more than 50 albums, and won a Grammy. April 27, 1999.

Basil Cardinal Hume, 76: leader of the Roman Catholic Church in England and Wales. Hume, appointed by Pope Paul VI in 1976, was entrenched in tradition, yet had a modern sensibility that irked his critics. June 17, 1999.

Jim ("Catfish") Hunter, 53: Hall of Fame pitcher. During his 15-year career with the Oakland A's and the New York Yankees, Hunter won five World Series, pitched a perfect game, won a Cy Young Award, and became the first multimillion-dollar player when he declared free agency in 1974. Sept. 9, 1999.

Hussein I (King of Jordan), 63: widely admired ruler of Jordan for more than four decades who made peace in the volatile Middle East a priority. One of his last accomplishments was helping to finalize the Wye Peace Accord between Israel and the Palestine Liberation Organization in Oct. 1998. Feb. 7, 1999.

Frank M. Johnson, Jr., 80: uncompromising federal judge from Alabama whose rulings helped desegregate many of Montgomery's public facilities and cleared the way for Martin Luther King Jr. and thousands of supporters to march from Selma to Montgomery in 1965. A Republican appointee, Johnson always insisted he was simply upholding "the supremacy of the law." July 23, 1999.

Henry Jones, 86: Tony-winning character actor seen by millions in his 350 TV shows, more than 50 movies, and dozens of theater productions. Among his most notable performances was a monologue in Alfred Hitchcock's *Vertigo* (1958). May 17, 1999.

Sheik Isa bin Salman al-Khalifa, 65: leader of Bahrain since 1961 and an important Persian Gulf ally to Western nations. In recent years the emir, a Sunni Muslim, struggled to calm unrest from Bahrain's Shiite majority. March 7, 1999.

Garson Kanin, 86: playwright and director whose *Born Yesterday* (1946 on stage, 1950 in film) is considered a comedy classic. With his wife, the actress Ruth Gordon, Kanin wrote the scripts for several of the more celebrated movie pairings of Spencer Tracy and Katharine Hepburn, including *Adam's Rib* (1949). March 13, 1999.

Karekin I (Neshan Sarkissian), 66: spiritual leader who, under the title Supreme Patriarch and Catholicos of All Armenians, led Armenian Orthodox Christians worldwide. He was the 131st leader of the ancient church that extends back as far as A.D. 301. June 29, 1999.

DeForest Kelley, 79: actor best known for his role as the humane Dr. Leonard ("Bones") McCoy on *Star Trek*'s U.S.S. Enterprise. On the cult hit TV series and in six film versions, Dr. McCoy battled Leonard Nimoy's hyperlogical Mr. Spock, whose emotional pulselessness McCoy disdained. June 11, 1999.

Henry W. Kendall, 72: Nobel-winning physicist who helped discover that protons and neutrons, formerly thought to be the basic building blocks of matter, are made up of quarks. Firmly against the development of nuclear weapons, he co-founded the Union of Concerned Scientists in 1969. Feb. 15, 1999.

Carolyn Bessette Kennedy, 33: press-shy fashion publicist who was thrown into the media spotlight when she married John F. Kennedy, Jr., in 1996. She managed to maintain a certain degree of privacy in spite of her husband's fame, but their tragic death in a plane crash attracted enormous worldwide attention. July 16, 1999.

John Fitzgerald Kennedy, Jr., 38: charismatic magazine editor and former lawyer who, born just three weeks after his father's election to the presidency, grew up in the spotlight and never escaped it. Admired for his enthusiasm, his charity, and his photogenic good looks, Kennedy was mourned by thousands worldwide after his tragic death when the plane he was piloting crashed near Martha's Vineyard, Mass. July 16, 1999.

Richard Kiley, 76: acclaimed actor who was best known for his Broadway portrayal of Don Quixote in *Man of La Mancha*, a role that won him a Tony Award. He also won Emmy Awards for his roles in the miniseries *The Thorn Birds* (1983) and the drama series *A Year in the Life* (1988). March 5, 1999.

(Joseph) Lane Kirkland, 77: president of the AFL–CIO from 1979 to 1995. As head of the federation, Kirkland fought to sustain the unions' waning power. Aug. 14, 1999.

Stanley Kubrick, 70: influential director whose list of credits includes such disturbing but popular films as *2001: A Space Odyssey* (1968), *A Clockwork Orange* (1971), *Dr. Strangelove* (1964), and *The Shining* (1980). March 7, 1999.

Wassily Leontief, 93: economist who won the Nobel Prize in 1973 for his production analyses showing how changes in one sector of the economy can affect others. Feb. 5, 1999.

Lucille Lortell, 98: patron of noncommercial theater. Lortel was dedicated to providing creative havens for innovative artists. April 4, 1999.

Alex Lowe 40: perhaps the greatest American mountaineer in recent years. Lowe climbed the nose of El Capitan in 10 hrs. and made the first solo ascent of the north face of Wyoming's Grand Teton. He conquered Everest twice. Lowe died in a massive avalanche on Tibet's Shisha Pangma, the world's 14th highest peak. Oct. 5, 1999.

Ibrahim Bare Mainassara, 49: President of Niger. He died in a spray of gunfire, reportedly from his bodyguards, at the Diori-Hamani airport. The shooting came at the end of a frenzied week in which Mainassara's opposition accused him of fixing an election. Niger's Prime Minister said he died in an "unfortunate accident." April 9, 1999.

Victor Mature, 86: handsome actor known for his barrel chest—and roles in epics like *Samson and Delilah* and *The Robe*. "Mr. Beautiful" got his big break in 1940, after a brief appearance in *The Housekeeper's Daughter* generated 20,000 fan letters. Aug. 5, 1999.

Paul Mellon, 91: assiduous cultural benefactor and environmentalist. The only son of famed financier Andrew Mellon, he established such treasures as the Yale Center for British Art and the Cape Hatteras National Seashore. For decades, he helped run Washington's National Gallery of Art, which he founded in partnership with his father. Feb. 1, 1999.

Yehudi Menuhin, 83: icon of 20th century music and world-renowned humanitarian. The gifted violinist, who first performed at age seven, was endlessly open-minded and was consumed with using his music to promote world peace. March 12, 1999.

Naomi Mitchison, 101: outspoken British author known as an early feminist and free-thinker. Mitchison wrote more than 70 novels, biographies, and books of poetry. Jan. 11, 1999.

Brian Moore, 77: Belfast-born author. In his 20 novels, Moore used sparse prose to tackle giant themes including faith, morality, and the bigotry of denizens of his native city. Moore amazed critics with his empathically crafted female characters, particularly in his first novel, *The Lonely Passion of Judith Hearne* (1988). Jan. 11, 1999.

Akio Morita 78: Japanese Sony co-founder who was a major influence in the globalization of business. The imaginative marketing wizard was responsible for inventing the Walkman and making Sony a top brand name in America. Oct. 3, 1999.

Willie Morris, 64: American writer and former *Harper's* magazine editor whose mellifluous prose captured the homey small-town rhythms and jarring racist quirks of his beloved Mississippi Delta. Aug. 2, 1999.

Iris Murdoch, 79: erudite and macabre British writer, philosopher, and Booker Prize winner. In her 26 novels, including *A Severed Head* and *An Accidental Man*, Murdoch described in intricate detail middle-class characters in the throes of what she called "erotic mysteries and deep, dark struggles between good and evil." Feb. 8, 1999.

Kathryn Murray, 92: dance-studio executive and early television personality who hosted *The Arthur Murray Party* with her late husband in the 1950s. The comedic show helped spread interest in ballroom dancing. Aug. 6, 1999.

Anthony Newley, 67: showman. He co-wrote, directed, and starred in the 1962 hit musical *Stop the World—I Want to Get Off* and helped write the *Goldfinger* theme and the score for *Willy Wonka & the Chocolate Factory*. Newley was married three times, once to actress Joan Collins. April 14, 1999.

Joshua Nkomo, 82: Father of Zimbabwe. Nkomo spent years fighting Britain and later white Rhodesia for independence. Despite Nkomo's leadership, his erstwhile ally Robert Mugabe became prime minister in 1980. A subsequent split led to bloody clashes that ended with a 1987 peace accord and Nkomo's appointment to a powerless vice-presidential post. July 1, 1999.

Julius Nyerere, 77: symbol of the African independence movement who served as Tanzania's first president after leading the country to independence from Britain in 1961. After voluntarily stepping down from his post in 1985, Nyerere continued to work toward an end to the civil war in Burundi and the widespread violence plaguing central and southern Africa over the past decade. Oct. 14, 1999.

Mark O'Brien, 49: author and poet. O'Brien, the subject of the Academy Award-winning documentary *Breathing Lessons*, wrote by typing with a stick in his mouth. He lived in a 650-lb. iron lung most of his life. July 3, 1999.

Col. George Papadopoulos, 80: Greek dictator. In 1967 Papadopoulos helped overthrow King Constantine and was installed as prime minister. His junta tortured and killed opponents and banned such Western styles as long hair on men and miniskirts for women. Overthrown in 1973, Papadopoulos was sentenced to life in prison for treason. June 27, 1999.

Jennifer Paterson, 71: plump TV chef who co-starred in the humorous, high-cholesterol British cooking series *Two Fat Ladies*. Along with co-host Clarissa Dickson Wright, Paterson toured the English countryside exchanging recipes that would horrify the health-conscious. Aug. 10, 1999.

Kim Perrot, 32: popular point guard who led the Houston Comets to two WNBA championships. Described as the heart and soul of the team, Perrot gave effusive motivational talks, often to kids, throughout her fight with lung cancer. Aug. 19, 1999.

Michel Petrucciani, 36: acclaimed French pianist whose aggressively romantic style of jazz earned him international popularity. Jan. 6, 1999.

Dana Plato, 34: child star of the sitcom *Diff'rent Strokes*. She died of an apparent drug overdose at the home of her fiance's parents. Plato and her onscreen siblings Gary Coleman and Todd Bridges have all had run-ins with the law since the hit series was canceled in 1986. May 8, 1999.

J. F. Powers (James Farl Powers), 81: National Book Award-winning author for *Morte d'Urban*, his first

novel. Powers never reached a wide audience, but his tales of the lives of Roman Catholic priests were storytelling gems. June 12, 1999.

Jay Pritzker, 76: billionaire philanthropist and founder of the Hyatt hotel chain. In 1979 he established the Pritzker Architecture Prize, which is now considered the most prestigious honor in the field. Jan. 23, 1999.

Mario Puzo, 78: author who penned *The Godfather*, a bestseller that would later be made into one of the most popular movies of all time. He also wrote the follow-up novels in the *Godfather* trilogy and several other books and screenplays. Puzo denied having any ties to the Mafia scene about which he so convincingly wrote. July 2, 1999.

José Quintero, 74: Panamanian-born Tony Award-winning theater director who helped spark the off-Broadway movement. Quintero was best known for his devotion to the dramas of Eugene O'Neill, having directed more than a dozen of the playwright's works. Feb. 26, 1999.

Harold Henry ("Pee Wee") Reese, 81: Hall of Fame baseball shortstop and captain of the Brooklyn Dodgers in 1947, when Jackie Robinson joined the team and began the historic racial integration of the sport. Reese's very public camaraderie with Robinson was crucial in dissipating the ugliness that greeted the rookie. Reese led the Dodgers to seven National League pennants and, in 1955, to Brooklyn's only world championship. Aug. 14, 1999.

Cal Ripken Sr., 63: sharp-tongued veteran baseball manager and the only coach to have managed two of his sons, Cal Jr. and Billy, on the same team. Ripken spent 36 years with the Baltimore Orioles in both the minor and major leagues. March 25, 1999.

Joaquin Rodrigo, 97: celebrated Spanish composer who, blinded at the age of three, learned to play piano and violin using Braille. Among his most famous works is the "Concierto de Aranjuez" (1939), written for the guitar. July 6, 1999.

Charles ("Buddy") Rogers, 94: dashing star of *Wings* (1927), the first film to win an Oscar. He was a versatile actor and musician who was also known for his 42-year marriage to "America's Sweetheart," Mary Pickford, who died in 1979. April 21, 1999.

Ruth Roman, 75: actress who combined good-girl wholesomeness with bad-girl edge. She starred in more than 30 films, including *Champion* (1949), *Strangers on a Train* (1951), and *Colt .45* (1950). Sept. 9, 1999.

Martha Rountree, 87: pioneering journalist who co-created NBC's *Meet the Press*, TV's longest-running program, in 1947. Before founding *MTP* (and becoming its first moderator), Rountree started radio's first panel show, *Leave It to the Girls*. Aug. 23, 1999.

Jaime Sabines, 72: Mexican poet who was considered one of the best in the Spanish language. A master of imagery, his several awards included the Chiapas Prize (1959) and the National Letters (1983). He also served as a congressman from 1976 to 1979 and in 1988. March 19, 1999.

Gene Sarazen, 97: golfer and inventor of the sand wedge. Nicknamed the "Squire" for his diminutive size and enormous panache, Sarazen won two major championships before turning 21. May 13, 1999.

Bidu Sayao, 94: accomplished opera diva whose enchanting voice won her international acclaim. Originally from Brazil, the soprano obtained American citizenship in 1959. March 12, 1999.

Arthur Schawlow, 77: Nobel-winning physicist who collaborated with Dr. Charles H. Townes in the development of Light Amplification by Stimulated

Emission of Radiation, now commonly known as "laser." Though it is disputed who was the first to invent lasers, Schawlow's contributions as a pioneer in laser development were unquestionably significant. April 28, 1999.

George C(ampbell) Scott, 71: commanding and prickly actor. Scott was best known for his iconic title role in *Patton*, for which he won—but refused to accept—a 1970 Oscar as best actor. Other standouts in a prolific career include a definitive Willy Loman in a Broadway production of *Death of a Salesman* and the trigger-happy General Buck Turgidson in Stanley Kubrick's *Dr. Strangelove*. Sept. 22, 1999.

Glenn Seaborg, 86: former chairman of the Atomic Energy Commission and Nobel prizewinner. He led the research team that discovered plutonium and was the first living person to have an element, seaborgium, named for him. After helping build the Bomb on the Manhattan Project, Seaborg championed the peaceful use of atomic energy. Feb. 25, 1999.

Robert Shaw, 82: longtime music director of the Atlanta Symphony and dean of American choral conducting. In 1948 Shaw founded the popular, internationally traveled Robert Shaw Chorale. Jan. 25, 1999.

Bobby Sheehan 31: bassist for the Grammy-winning blues-rock band Blues Traveler. The band, originally formed in 1987, helped spawn a newfound interest in the jam band scene in the 1990s. Aug. 20, 1999.

Jean Shepherd 78: radio personality whose popularity carried over to movies, TV, the stage, and the literary world. A gifted storyteller who appealed to a wide audience, one of Sheperd's most familiar creations was the classic 1983 film *A Christmas Story*. Oct. 16, 1999.

Sylvia Sidney (Sophia Kosow), 88: iconic actress from Hollywood's golden era whose career, spanning seven decades, saw her graduate from a specialty in victim roles to tough-talking, chain-smoking senior citizen. After a hiatus of 17 years, she returned to the movies in 1973 and was nominated for a supporting Oscar for *Summer Wishes, Winter Dreams*. Sidney won a Golden Globe for her part in the 1985 TV movie *An Early Frost*. July 1, 1999.

Shel Silverstein, 66: children's author, playwright, Playboy cartoonist, and Oscar-nominated songwriter. Silverstein was best known for writing and illustrating several charmingly mischievous books of poetry for children (*Where the Sidewalk Ends, A Light in the Attic*)—a career he never intended, even though he sold 14 million books. May 10, 1999.

Gene Siskel (Eugene Kal Siskel), 53: movie critic who, with Roger Ebert, formed the incompatible but entertaining duo of reviewers whose "two thumbs-up" was among the most coveted symbols of approval in Hollywood. Their onscreen skirmishes were first aired on the hugely popular *Sneak Previews* on PBS. Feb. 20, 1999.

Dusty Springfield (Mary Isabel Catherine Bernadette O'Brien), 59: soulful British pop songstress. Springfield hit the top of the charts in 1966 with "You Don't Have to Say You Love Me" and relished a comeback with the 1994 *Pulp Fiction* soundtrack inclusion of her sultry "Son of Preacher Man." She was to be inducted into the Rock and Roll Hall of Fame eleven days after her death. March 2, 1999.

Paco Stanley (Francisco Stanley), 56: popular, comedic Mexican entertainer who was gunned down while in his car. His morning TV show combined the talk and variety formats, starting off the day for many Mexicans with laughter. June 7, 1999.

Saul Steinberg, 84: artist and cartoonist whose work appeared in *The New Yorker* for more than half a century. He was noted for elevating comic illustration to the level of fine art. May 12, 1999.

Willi Stoph, 84: two-time prime minister of East Germany. He held office during the reconciliation between East and West Germany, stepping down days before the fall of the Berlin Wall in 1989. April 13, 1999.

Susan Strasberg, 60: actress and buddy of Marilyn Monroe. The daughter of acting teacher Lee Strasberg, she debuted on Broadway in 1955 as Anne Frank and appeared in two dozen films, including *Stage Struck* and *Picnic*. Jan. 21, 1999.

David Strickland, 28: film and TV actor who played a music critic on the NBC sitcom *Suddenly Susan*. Strickland, who was found in a motel room after an apparent suicide, was due to appear in court the week before his death as part of his probation for a 1998 cocaine-possession arrest. March 22, 1999.

Su Shueh-lin, 104: distinguished Chinese writer who published more than 50 works, including essay collections, poetry, novels, and literary criticism. Her ardent support for free expression and other democratic principles influenced many leaders and political reformers. April 21, 1999.

Roderick Thorp, 62: popular crime novelist and former detective who wrote the bestsellers *The Detective* (1966) and *Nothing Lasts Forever* (1979). April 28, 1999.

Mel Torme, 73: consummate vocalist known, to his dismay, as the Velvet Fog. Torme began performing at age four; his voice's preternatural lushness was due in part to a small second growth of tonsil after a tonsillectomy. His artistry, however, was earned, and appreciated by fans from many generations. June 5, 1999.

Gonzalo Torrente Ballester, 88: Spanish novelist whose talent for interweaving realism and fantasy earned him the 1985 Cervantes Prize for Literature as well as his reputation as an important literary figure. Jan. 27, 1999.

Otumfuo Nana Opoku Ware II, 79: venerable spiritual and cultural leader of the Ashanti people of Ghana. A London-trained lawyer, the Asantehene became the 15th king of the Ashanti in July 1970. Feb. 25, 1999.

Señor Wences (Wenceslao Moreno), 103: ventriloquist who created impish dummies out of his thumb and forefinger. On the '50s and '60s variety shows of Ed Sullivan, Milton Berle, and Sid Caesar, among others, he delighted audiences with sweetly silly exchanges. April 20, 1999.

Norman Wexler, 73: Harvard-educated screenwriter known for his astute portrayals of street-smart characters. Wexler wrote *Saturday Night Fever* (1977) and co-wrote *Serpico* (1973), for which he was nominated for an Oscar. Aug. 23, 1999.

William H. Whyte, 81: optimistic social thinker and urban planner whose opus on corporate America, *The Organization Man* (1956), warned against conformity and its accompanying spiritlessness. Jan. 12, 1999.

Joe Williams (Joseph Goreed), 80: jazz icon who sang with the Count Basie Orchestra. During his five-decade career, Williams appeared on *The Cosby Show* as Grandpa Al. March 29, 1999.

John Minor Wisdom, 93: pioneering civil rights judge and an architect of the New South, whose opinions helped end segregation. May 15, 1999.

PEOPLE IN THE
NEWS AND
DEATHS

SPORTS

BUSINESS,
ECONOMY, AND
PERSONAL
FINANCE

U.S. CITIES,
STATES, AND
STATISTICS

AWARDS,
ENTERTAINMENT,
AND CULTURE

PEOPLE

CROSSWORD
PUZZLE GUIDE

ENVIRONMENT,
WEATHER,
AND CLIMATE

SCIENCE,
INVENTIONS, AND
COMPUTERS

THE YEAR
IN PICTURES,
FLAGS, AND MAPS

See first page of book for additional tabs.